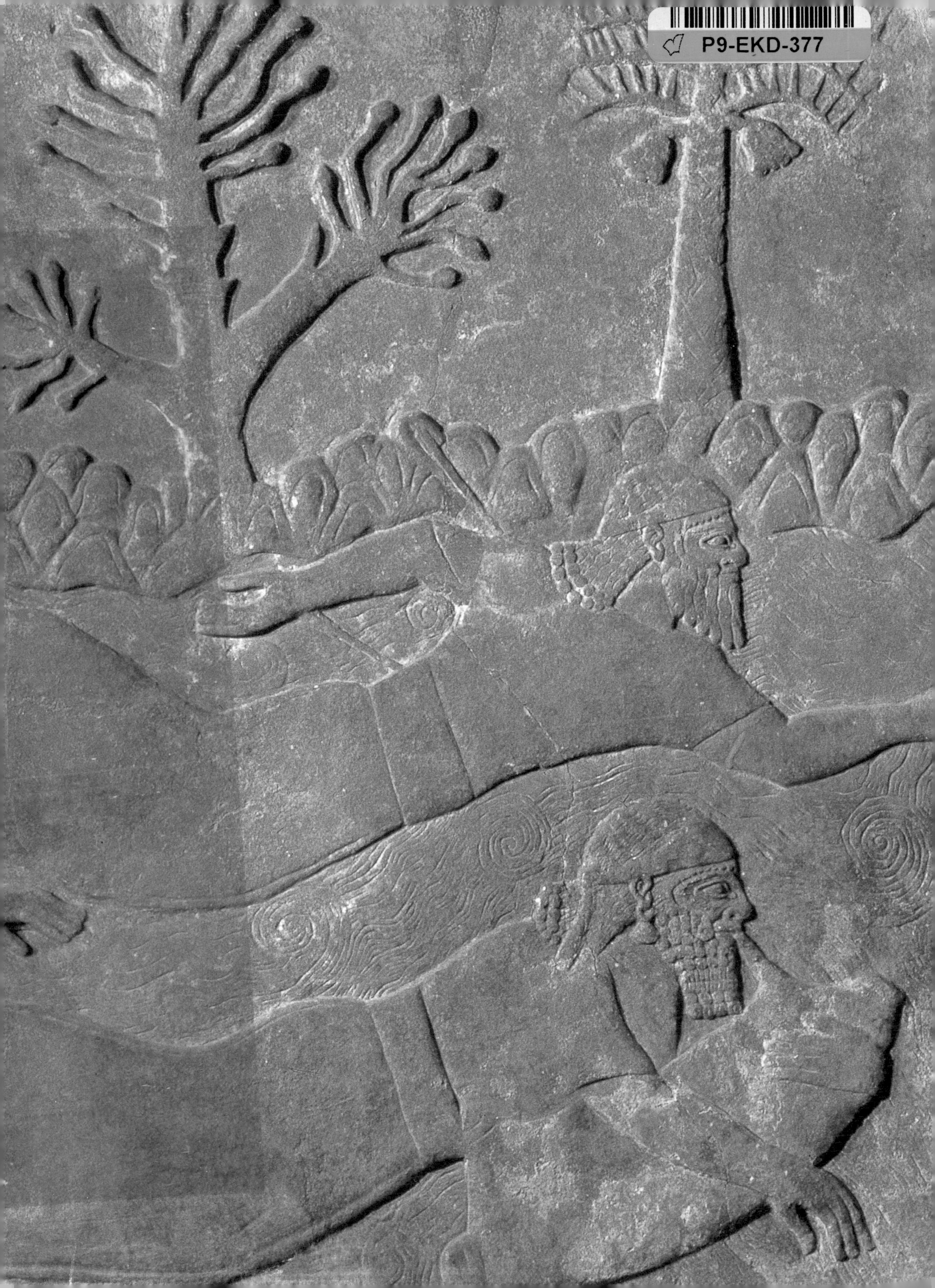
P9-EKD-377

OCT 2001

History *of* Art

SIXTH EDITION

History of Art

SIXTH EDITION

H. W. Janson
Anthony F. Janson
University of North Carolina, Wilmington

PRENTICE-HALL, INC., AND
HARRY N. ABRAMS, INC., PUBLISHERS

PROPERTY OF
ANAHEIM PUBLIC LIBRARY
500 WEST BROADWAY
ANAHEIM, CALIFORNIA 92805
EUCLID

PROJECT MANAGER: Katherine Rangoon Doyle
EDITORS: Katherine Rangoon Doyle and Elaine M. Stainton
EDITORIAL ASSISTANTS: Erin Barnett and Holly Jennings
PHOTO EDITOR: Barbara Lyons
ART DIRECTOR: Beth Tondreau
DESIGN: BTDNYC. Designers: Beth Tondreau, Daniel Rodney, Adrian Kitzinger, and Mia Risberg
MAPS: Adrian Kitzinger
INDEXING: Peter and Erica Rooney

Library of Congress Cataloging-in-Publication Data

Janson, H. W. (Horst Woldemar), 1913–82
History of art / H. W. Janson and Anthony F. Janson.– 6th ed.
p. cm.
Includes bibliographical references and index.
ISBN 0-8109-3446-9 (Abrams) – ISBN 0-13-019732-7 (PH) –
ISBN 0-13-019729-7 (PH : pbk. : v. 1) – ISBN 0-13-019731-9 (PH : pbk. : v. 2)
ISBN 0-8109-4159-7 (book club:jkt.) – ISBN 0-8109-2986-4 (book club:pbk.)
1. Art–History. I. Janson, Anthony F. II. Title.

N5300 .J3 2000
709–dc21 00-21587

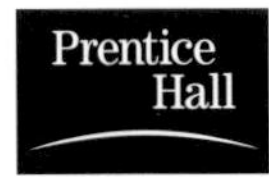

Prentice-Hall, Inc.
A Division of Pearson Education
Upper Saddle River, New Jersey 07458
Send inquiries to:
Marketing Manager
Humanities & Social Sciences, Prentice-Hall, Inc.
One Lake Street
Upper Saddle River, N.J. 07458
http://www.prenhall.com

Copyright © 1991, 1995, 1997, 2001 Harry N. Abrams, Inc.

Published in 2001 by Harry N. Abrams, Incorporated, New York

All rights reserved. No part of the contents of this book may be reproduced
in any form or by any means without the written permission of the publisher.

Printed and bound in Japan

NOTE ON THE PICTURE CAPTIONS: Each illustration is placed as close as possible to its first discussion in the text. Measurements are given throughout, except for objects that are inherently large: architecture, architectural sculpture, interiors, and wall paintings. Height precedes width. A probable measuring error of more than one percent is indicated by "approx." Titles of works are those designated by the institutions owning the works, where applicable, or by custom. Dates are based on documentary evidence, unless preceded by "c."

The birth, death, and ruling dates of individuals, when contained within parentheses, are abbreviated throughout the text as follows: b. = born; d. = died; r. = ruled; fl. = flourished.

First Edition 1962, revised and enlarged, 1969
Second Edition 1977
Third Edition 1986
Fourth Edition 1991
Fifth Edition 1995, revised 1997
Sixth Edition 2001

ENDPAPER IMAGE: *Fugitives Crossing River*, from the Northwest Palace of Ashurnasirpal II, Nimrud (Calah), Iraq. c. 883–859 B.C. Alabaster relief, height c. 39" (98 cm). The British Museum, London. Figure 3-19
PAGES 14–15: detail from the *Standard of Ur*. c. 2600 B.C. Wood inlaid with shell, limestone and lapis lazuli, height 8" (20.3 cm). The British Museum, London. Figure 3-10

Contents

[ALL SIDEBARS ARE IN SMALL ITALICS]

Preface and Acknowledgments to the First Edition

The title of this book has a dual meaning: it refers both to the events that *make* the history of art and to the scholarly discipline that deals with these events. Perhaps it is just as well that the record and its interpretation are thus designated by the same term. For the two cannot be separated, try as we may. There are no "plain facts" in the history of art—or in the history of anything else for that matter, only degrees of plausibility. Every statement, no matter how fully documented, is subject to doubt and remains a "fact" only so long as nobody questions it. To doubt what has been taken for granted, and to find a more plausible interpretation of the evidence, is every scholar's task. Nevertheless, there is always a large body of "facts" in any field of study; they are the sleeping dogs whose very inertness makes them landmarks on the scholarly terrain. Fortunately, only a minority of them can be aroused at the same time, otherwise we should lose our bearings; yet all are kept under surveillance to see which ones might be stirred into wakefulness and locomotion. It is these "facts" that fascinate the scholar. I believe they will also interest the general reader. In a survey such as this, the sleeping dogs are indispensable, but I have tried to emphasize that their condition is temporary and to give the reader a fairly close look at some of the wakeful ones.

I am under no illusion that my account is adequate in every respect. The history of art is too vast a field for anyone to encompass all of it with equal competence. If the shortcomings of my book remain within tolerable limits, this is due to the many friends and colleagues who have permitted me to tax their kindness with inquiries, requests for favors, or discussions of doubtful points. I am particularly indebted to Bernard Bothmer, Richard Ettinghausen, M. S. İpşiroğlu, Richard Krautheimer, Max Loehr, Wolfgang Lotz, Alexander Marshack, and Meyer Schapiro, who reviewed various aspects of the book and generously helped in securing photographic material. I must also record my gratitude to the American Academy in Rome, which made it possible for me, as art historian in residence during the spring of 1960, to write the chapters on ancient art under ideal conditions, and to the Academy's indefatigable librarian, Nina Langobardi. Irene Gordon, Celia Butler, and Patricia Egan have improved the book in countless ways. Patricia Egan also deserves the chief credit for the reading list. I should like, finally, to acknowledge the admirable skill and patience of Philip Grushkin, who is responsible for the design and layout of the volume; my thanks go to him and to Adrienne Onderdonk, his assistant.

H. W. J.
1962

Preface and Acknowledgments to the Sixth Edition

The previous edition of this book saw a major revision of art before the High Renaissance as a sequel to the sweeping overhaul of art after 1520. The present edition focuses on changes to ancient art that could not be completed last time due to time constraints. The history of Western architecture has also been extensively rewritten. French Romantic painting has been reconsidered, as has French Realism and Impressionism to a lesser extent. In several instances, I have included recent interpretations in preference, or as alternatives, to the standard ones, even though they are controversial. I did so in order to introduce the reader to the kind of scholarly debate that makes up the discipline of art history, which is by no means as monolithic as a survey book would suggest. Finally, the entire book has been edited anew to modernize the language and to make it more readable without, however, dumbing it down.

It would seem fitting to reassess contemporary art as we enter the new millennium. No matter that the date is a miscalculation. (Jesus was born at least several years earlier than previously thought.) It is still a momentous occasion, if only to allow people to take stock. Yet I have refrained from doing so. Art criticism reminds me of nothing so much as the six blind men trying to describe an elephant. Even if the men could see they probably wouldn't be much more successful because they would be too close to see the entire elephant. It is a commonplace that the art of today can't be properly assessed because we don't have the benefit of historical perspective. Historians, by contrast, can't capture the flavor of periods they never lived in and thus cannot truly understand because of their lack of direct experience. I have tried to include most of the notable artists on the scene today. I would be the first to admit, however, that the selection is both limited as a matter of necessity and biased as a matter of choice. I am acutely aware that my account omits much of what has been called avant-garde in the past quarter-century. I have instead chosen artists who in my opinion still have that magical ability to appeal to the viewer's deepest understanding.

Nearly every statement in this book requires a great deal of inquiry before I am reasonably satisfied with the state of knowledge, but the material can be difficult to obtain. I am indebted to many people for their help and advice. Pamela Scott generously shared her material on French Enlightenment architecture. Melissa Sprague reminded me once again of Delacroix's importance as an illustrator. David Jeffrey provided fresh insights into the relation between Erasmus and St. Jerome. Joseph Jacobs pointed out the work of Pepón Osorio. Erin Barnett made helpful suggestions regarding postmodern theory. As always, Mary Ellen Soles acted as a valued adviser on antiquities.

This edition is dedicated to my lifelong friends Michael and Nancy van Itallie, whose generosity enabled me to undertake additional research at a critical stage in the preparation of this edition. Their sympathy and understanding were as important to me as their help. No writer ever had truer supporters.

A. F. J.

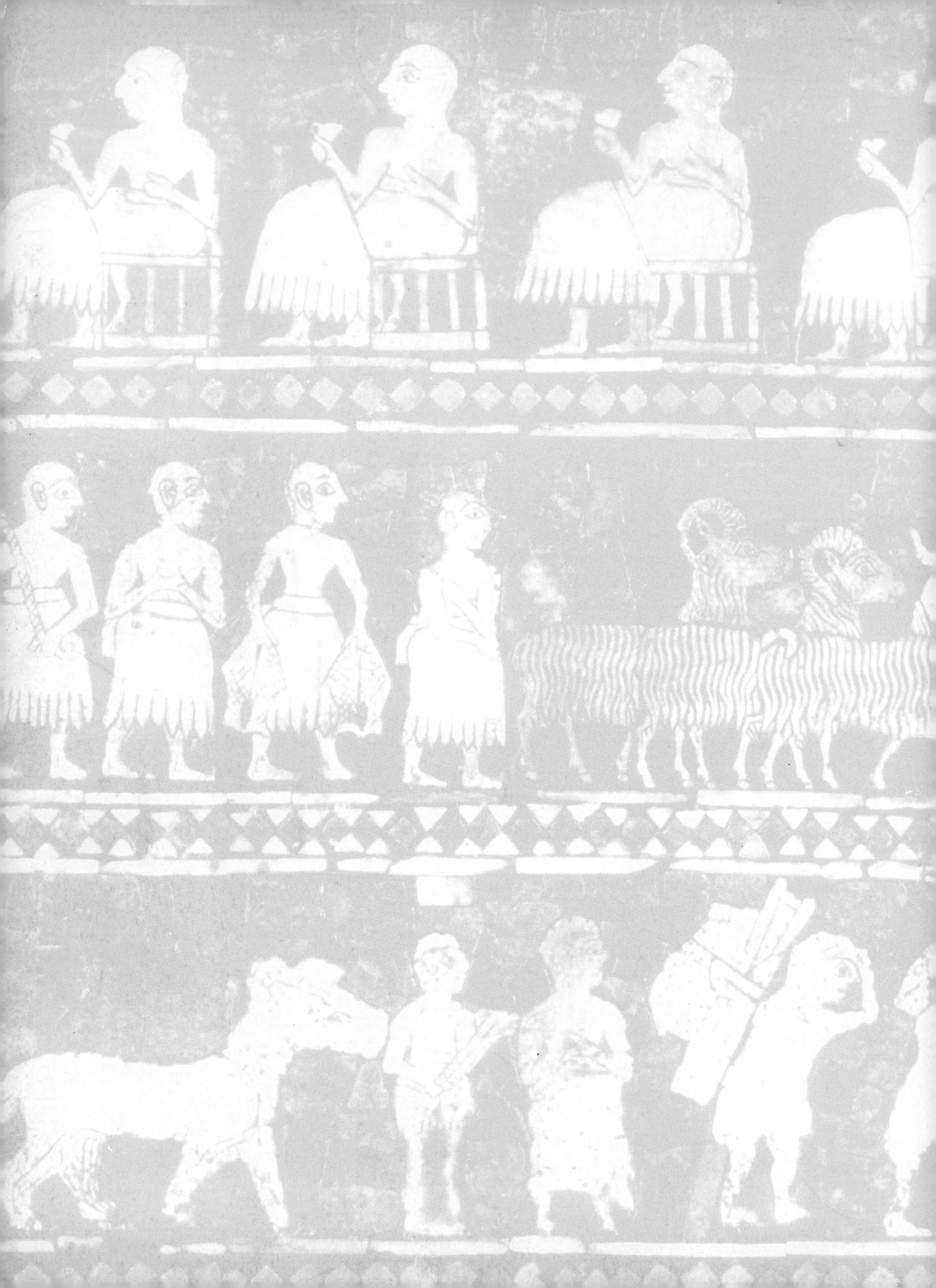

History *of* Art

Introduction

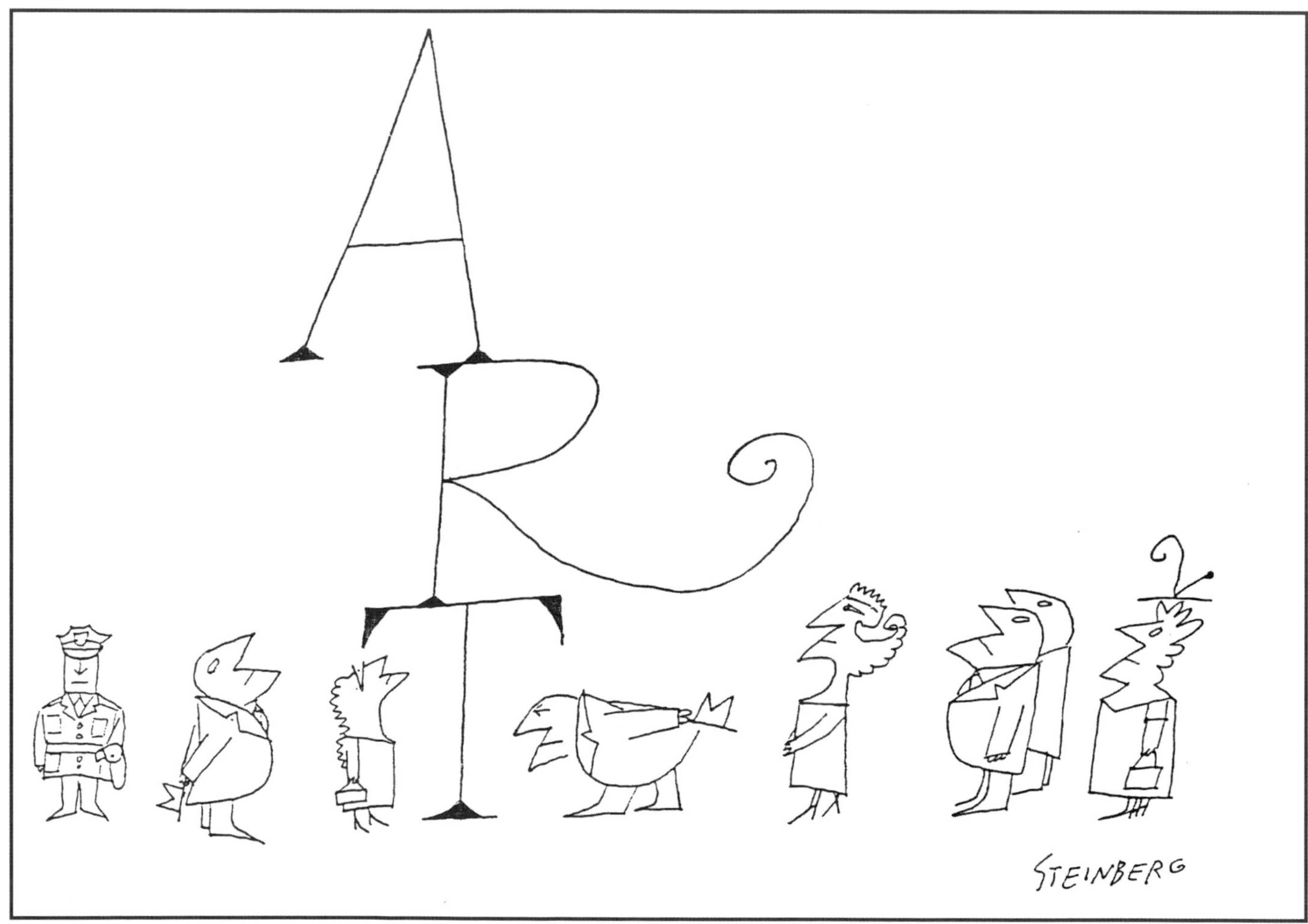

© Saul Steinberg, 1960. Reprinted by permission of the Estate of Saul Steinberg/Artists Rights Society (ARS), New York. Originally published in *The New Yorker*

ART AND THE ARTIST

What is art? Few questions have given rise to so many different answers. The problem, as we see in the above cartoon, is that art is an object and a word. Both vary widely in different times and places and in different cultures. In the past hundred years they have changed so much that all the old definitions and even the categories of art are obsolete. The reason is not hard to find: more change occurred in the twentieth century than in any other period in history. The modern era has been both exhilarating and disturbing. It opened up new horizons that greatly expanded life's possibilities, but at the same time it challenged our most cherished beliefs. Art as we know it is a direct outgrowth of the industrialized world, with its advanced technology, global economy, large middle class yet highly fragmented society, and democratic institutions. Under such unique conditions it is impossible to come up with a universally valid definition of art. We must therefore leave this task to philosophers and aestheticians.

Nevertheless, there is still a good deal that can be said. Looking again at our cartoon, we see that art is not just any kind of object. It is an *aesthetic object*. Art is meant to be looked at and appreciated for its own sake. Its special qualities set art apart, so that it is often placed away from everyday life—in museums, caves, or churches—though much of it was made to be lived with. What does *aesthetic* mean? It is defined as "that which concerns the beautiful." Of course, not all art is beautiful to each person's eyes, but it is still art. No matter how unsatisfactory, the term will have to do for lack of a better one.

Aesthetics is a branch of philosophy that has occupied thinkers from Plato to the present day. Like all philosophical matters, it is subject to debate. During the last hundred years, aesthetics has also become a field of psychology, which has come to equally little agreement. Why is this so? On the one hand, people the world over make many the same basic judgments. Our brains and nervous systems are the same because, according to recent theory, every human being is descended from one woman who lived in Africa a quarter-million years ago. On the other hand, taste is a product of culture, which is so varied that it is impossible to judge art by any one set of standards. It seems, therefore, that we cannot establish absolute standards for judging art. Instead, we must view works of art in the context of the culture in which they were created, whether past or present. How indeed could it be otherwise, so long as art is still being created all around us, opening our eyes almost daily to new experiences and forcing us to adjust our thinking?

Imagination

We all dream. That is imagination at work. To imagine means to make an image—a picture—in our minds. Human beings are not the only creatures who have imagination. Animals also dream. However, humans are the only creatures who can tell one another about imagination in words, pictures, or music. No other animal has ever been observed to draw a recognizable image spontaneously in the wild. In fact, their only images have been produced under carefully controlled laboratory conditions that tell us more about the experimenter than they do about art. There can be little doubt, though, that humans have the ability to create art. By the age of five every normal child has drawn a moon pie-face. This ability is one of our most distinctive features.

Imagination is a mysterious gift. It can be viewed as the link between the conscious and the subconscious, where most of our brain activity takes place. It is the glue that holds our personality, intellect, and spirituality together. Because it responds to all three, it acts in ways that are determined by the mind. Imagination is important, as it allows us to conceive of all kinds of possibilities in the future and to understand the past in a way that has real survival value. It therefore is an essential part of our makeup. In contrast, the ability to make art must have been acquired relatively recently in the course of human evolution. Human beings have been walking the earth for nearly 4.5 million years, although our own species (*homo sapiens*) is much younger than that. By comparison, the oldest known prehistoric art was made only about 35,000 years ago, but it was undoubtedly the culmination of a long process of development that we cannot trace because the record of the earliest art is lost.

Who were the first artists? In all likelihood, they were shamans. Like the legendary Greek poet Orpheus, who sang his words while playing the lyre, they were believed to have divine powers of inspiration and to be able to enter the underworld of the subconscious in a deathlike trance—but unlike ordinary mortals, they could then return to the realm of the living. With this unique ability to penetrate the unknown and express it through art, the artist-shaman gained control over the forces hidden in human beings and nature. Even today artists are magicians whose work can mystify and move us—an embarrassing fact to civilized people, who do not like to give up their veneer of rational control.

Creativity

The making of a work of art is much like the story of Creation told in the Bible. However, this divine ability was not fully realized until Michelangelo described the creative experience as "liberating the figure from the marble that imprisons it." Perhaps that is why the concept of creativity was once reserved for God, as only he could give material form to an idea. In human terms, the metaphor of birth comes closer to the truth than the notion of a transfer or projection of an image from the artist's mind. The making of a work of art is both joyous and painful, full of surprises, and in no sense mechanical. Moreover, artists themselves tend to look upon their creations as living things. This magical aspect of art was given charming expression by the Roman poet Ovid in his *Metamorphoses*. He tells the story of Pygmalion, who carved such a beautiful statue of the nymph Galatea that he fell in love with it and prayed to Venus, the goddess of love, to bring it to life. Fortunately for him, his wish was granted. (The tale is familiar to us as the basis for the musical *My Fair Lady*.) We can readily understand the tale when it comes to realistic sculpture. But would the artist feel the same way today, when abstract art is the norm? Strange though it may seem, the answer is "Yes," as the cartoon on this page suggests. The reason is that a work represents the artist's highest aspirations and deepest understanding, no matter what form it takes.

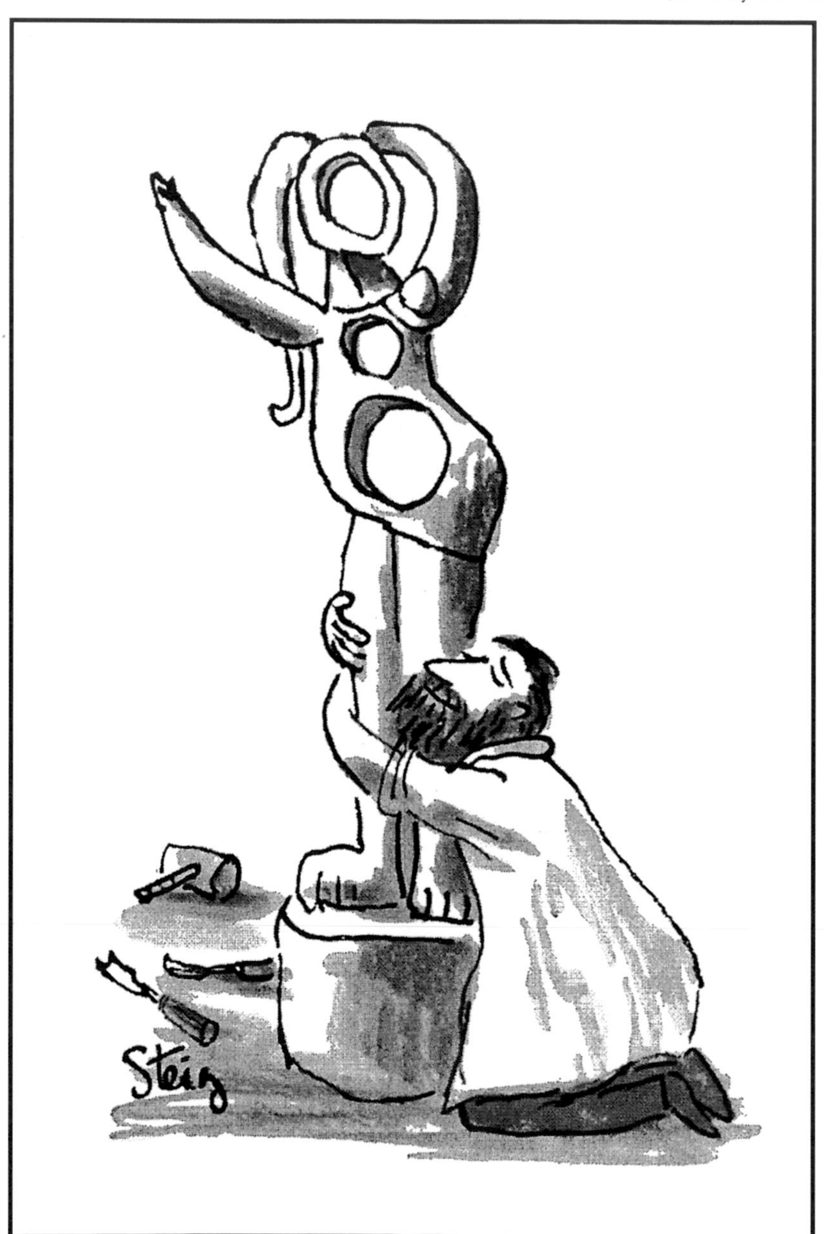

© The New Yorker Collection 1964 William Steig from cartoonbank.com. All Rights Reserved

The creation of a work of art has little in common with what we usually mean by "making." It is a strange and risky business in which the makers never quite know what they are making until they have actually made it. To put it another way, making art is like a game of hide-and-seek in which the seekers are not sure what they are looking for until they have found it. In some cases, it is the bold "finding" that impresses us most; in others, it is the strenuous "seeking." For the non-artist, it is hard to believe that this uncertainty, this need to take a chance, is the essence of the artist's work. Whereas artisans generally attempt what they know to be possible, artists are driven to attempt the impossible—or at least the improbable or seemingly unimaginable. What defines art, then, is not any difference in materials or techniques from the applied arts. Rather, art is defined by the artist's willingness to take risks in the quest for bold, new ideas.

What sets great artists apart from others is not simply the desire to *seek* but the mysterious ability to *find*. This talent is often called a "gift," implying that it is a sort of present from some higher power. It is also described as "genius," a term that originally meant that a higher power—a kind of "good demon"—inhabits and acts through the artist. When creativity is at its height, artists speak of being inspired by the muses that were believed to govern the liberal arts in antiquity. And when the well runs dry, they feel as if the muse has abandoned them.

Inspiration is sometimes experienced as a sudden leap of the imagination, but only rarely does a new idea emerge full-blown like the Greek goddess Athena from the head of Zeus, her father. Instead, it is usually preceded by a long period in which all the hard work is done without finding the solution to the problem. At the critical point, the imagination makes connections between seemingly unrelated parts. Ordinarily, artists work with materials that have little or no shape of their own. The creative process then consists of a long series of smaller leaps of the imagination and the artist's attempts to give them form by shaping the material.

One of the attributes that distinguishes great artists is their great mastery of technique, which enables them to give their ideas full expression in visible form. Their superior ability is recognized by other artists, who admire their work and seek to emulate it. This is not to say that facility alone is all that is needed. Far from it! The academic painters and sculptors of the nineteenth century were among the most proficient artists in history—as well as the dullest. Clearly, the making of a work of art should not be confused with manual skill or craftsmanship. Some works of art may demand a great deal of technical skill; others do not. And even the most painstaking piece of craft does not deserve to be called a work of art unless it involves a leap of the imagination.

Nor should talent be confused with aptitude. Aptitude is what the artisan needs. It means a better-than-average knack for doing something. An aptitude is fairly constant and specific. It can be measured with some success by means of tests that permit us to predict future performance. Creative talent, on the other hand, is utterly unpredictable. It can be spotted only on the basis of *past* performance. Even past performance is not enough to ensure that a given artist will continue to produce on the same level. Some artists reach a creative peak early in their careers and then "go dry," while others, after a slow start, may do astonishingly original work in middle age or even later.

Originality and Tradition

Originality is what distinguishes art from craft. It is the yardstick of artistic greatness or importance. Unfortunately, it is also very hard to define. The usual synonyms—uniqueness, novelty, freshness—do not help us very much. Unless a work is a copy, the problem comes not in deciding whether it is original but in saying exactly *how* original it is. In addition, every work of art has its own place in tradition. Without tradition—the word means "that which has been handed down to us"—no originality would be possible. Tradition provides the platform from which artists make their leap of the imagination. The place where they land becomes the point of departure for further leaps. Tradition also serves as the meeting ground of art and craft. What the art student or apprentice learns are skills and techniques: ways of drawing, painting, carving, designing—established ways of *seeing*.

For us, too, tradition is essential. Whether we are aware of it or not, tradition is the framework within which we form our opinions of works of art and assess their originality. This is especially true of masterpieces, the standards by which we measure other works of art. A masterpiece is a work that can bear close scrutiny and withstand the test of time. Such judgments are always subject to revision, however. In fact, tastes have varied greatly over time. Works that were once thought of as cornerstones of tradition have been discarded, while others that were ignored or even despised are now seen as important. Thus the "canon," or core body, of Western art is not static and unchanging but is constantly shifting. Although it is fashionable to attack the idea of a canon, some works really are better than others, whether we wish to acknowledge it or not.

Meaning and Style

Why do people create art? Surely one reason is the urge to adorn themselves and decorate the world around them. Both are part of a larger desire, not merely to remake the world in their image but to recast themselves and their environment in ideal form. Art is, however, much more than decoration. Like science and religion, it fulfills the urge of human beings to understand themselves and the universe. This function makes art especially important and worthy of our attention. Art allows us to communicate our understanding in ways that cannot be expressed otherwise. In art, as in language, people invent symbols that convey complex thoughts in new ways. We must think of art not in terms of prose but of poetry, which is free to rearrange words and syntax in order to convey new, often multiple, meanings and moods. A work of art likewise suggests much more than it states. And as with poetry, the value of art lies equally in what it says and how it says it. But what is art trying to say? Artists often provide no clear explanation, since the work itself is the statement. If they could say what they mean in words, they would be writers instead.

Nevertheless, art is full of meaning, even if its content is slender or obscure at times. What do we mean by content? The word refers not only to a work's subject and literal meaning (its iconography) but to its appearance as well, for the visual elements are themselves filled with significance. Hence the content of art is inseparable from its formal qualities, that is, its style. For that reason, understanding a work of art begins with a sensitive appreciation of its surface. (In fact, art can be enjoyed for its purely visual appeal.) The word *style* is derived from *stilus,* the writing tool of the ancient Romans. Originally, it referred to distinctive ways of writing—the shape of the letters as well as the choice of words. Today it refers to the distinctive way in which a thing is done. In the visual arts, style means the specific way in which the forms that make up any given work of art are chosen and fitted together. To art historians the study of styles is of great importance. Not only does it enable them to find out, through careful analysis and comparison, when, where, and by whom something was produced, it also leads them to understand the artist's intention as expressed in the way it looks. This intention depends on both the artist's personality and the context of time and place. Thus art historians often speak of "period styles."

Art, like language, requires that we learn the style and outlook of a country, period, and artist if it is to be understood properly. Style need only be appropriate to the *intent* of the work. This idea is not always easy to accept. Westerners are used to a tradition of naturalism, in which art imitates nature as closely as possible. But accurate reproduction of visual phenomena, called illusionism, is just one means of expressing an artist's understanding of reality. Truth, it seems, is indeed relative. It is a matter not simply of what our eyes tell us but also of the concepts through which our perceptions are filtered. An image is a separate and self-contained reality that has its own ends and responds to its own rules as determined by the artist's creativity. Even the most convincing illusion is the product of the artist's imagination and understanding, so that we must always ask why this subject was chosen and expressed in this way rather than in some other way.

Self-Expression and Audience

The birth of a work of art is a very private experience, so much so that many artists can work only when they are alone and refuse to show their unfinished works to anyone. Yet for the birth to be successful, the work must be shared with the public. Artists do not create art just to satisfy themselves. They want their work validated by others. In fact, the creative process is not completed until the work has found an audience. In the end, works of art exist in order to be liked rather than to be debated. This paradox can be resolved once we understand what artists mean by "public." They are concerned not with *the* public at large but with their particular public, their audience. What matters to them is quality rather than wide approval. This audience is a limited and special one. Its members may be other artists as well as patrons, friends, critics, and interested viewers. What they all have in common is an informed love of works of art—an attitude at once discriminating and enthusiastic that lends particular weight to their judgments. They are, in a word, experts, people whose authority rests on experience and knowledge (see the cartoon on this page).

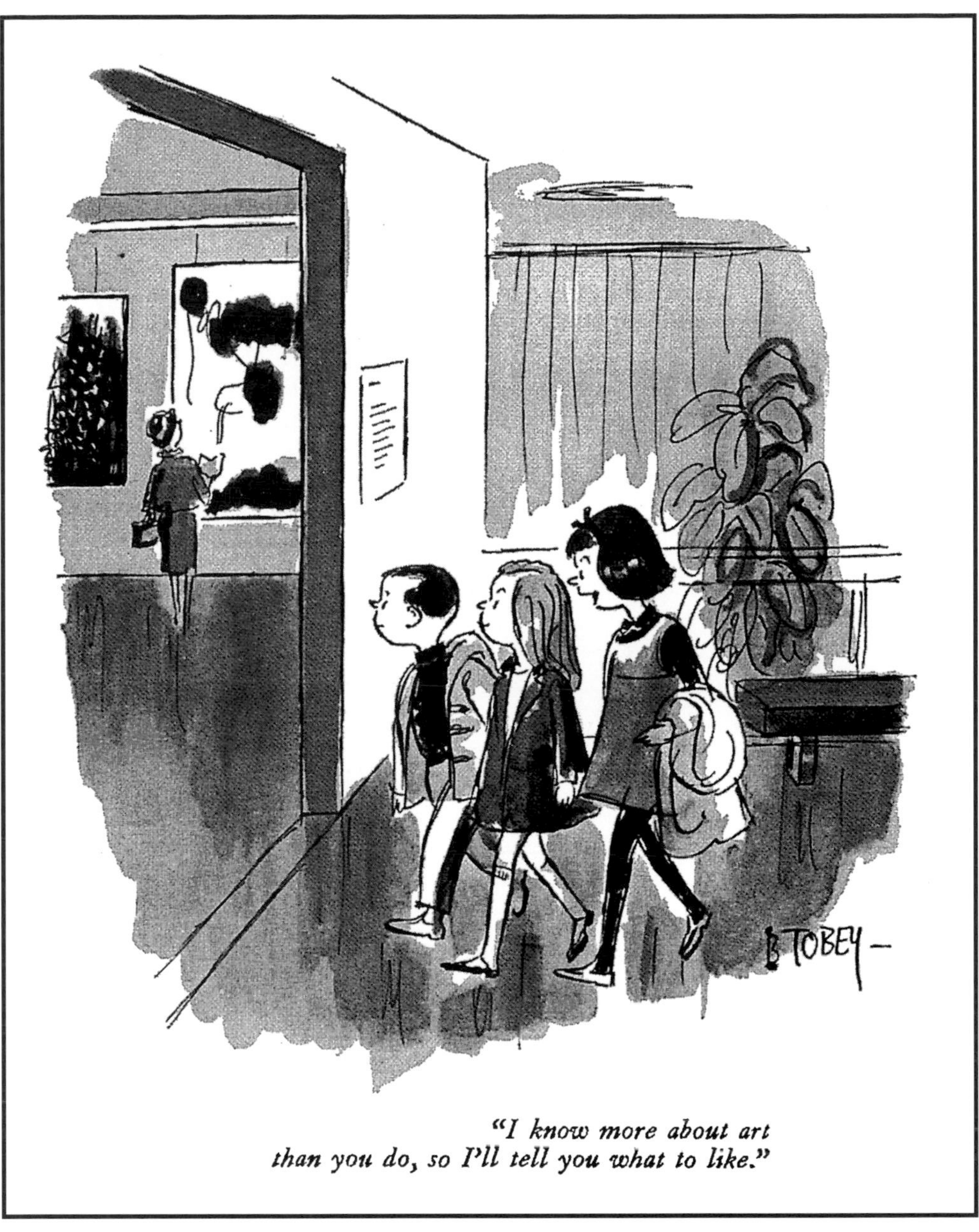

"*I know more about art than you do, so I'll tell you what to like.*"

© The New Yorker Collection 1966 Barney Tobey from cartoonbank.com. All Rights Reserved

Tastes

The road to expertise in art is open to anyone who wants to take it. All that is required is an open mind and a capacity to absorb new experiences. The biggest roadblock is the old saying, "I don't know much about art, but I know what I like." When they say, "I know what I like," people really mean, "I like what I know (and I am uncomfortable with whatever is unfamiliar)." Such likes are not products of personal choice; they are imposed by habit and culture. Art is part of the fabric of our daily life; we see it all the time, even if only in the form of magazine covers, advertising posters, war memorials, television, and the buildings where we live, work, and worship. Much of this art, to be sure, is pretty shoddy, representing the common denominator of popular taste. Still, it is art of a sort, and since it is the only art most people experience, it molds their ideas about art in general. When faced with unfamiliar art, they often ask, "Why is that art?" when what they really mean is, "Why is that good art?" Deciding what is art and rating a work of art are two separate problems. Even if there were a tried-and-true way of distinguishing art from non-art, it would not necessarily help in measuring quality. Even so, people tend to combine these two problems into one.

But isn't the average person's opinion just as valid as an expert's? This notion has strong appeal in a democratic society. Let's see if it holds up to closer scrutiny. Take any subject in which you have some expertise. It might be sports, cars, carpentry, fashion, pop music. If I happen to be ignorant in the same area, is my judgment really as good as yours? Of course not! The expert always has the edge. As you also know from your own experience, having expertise in a subject greatly increases your enjoyment. The same is true of art. As their understanding grows, most people find themselves liking many more things than they had thought possible. They gradually acquire the courage of their own convictions, until they are able to say, with some justice, that they know what they like.

LOOKING AT ART

How we experience art has changed greatly over the course of history. To view art, most people go to museums. Museums, however, are a relatively recent invention. Although the Akropolis in Athens included a *pinakotheke,* or painting gallery, the idea of a museum ("home of the muses") where the public can go for inspiration arose only in the early nineteenth century. Before then, most people could see art only in churches. Except in seventeenth-century Holland, only wealthy collectors, most often members of the aristocracy, could afford to own art. Today museums have become temples where anyone can worship at the altar of art. Of course, most works of art were not created for such a setting. The art in museums is not the only kind worth looking at. On the contrary, it should provide the point of departure for exploring other forms of art.

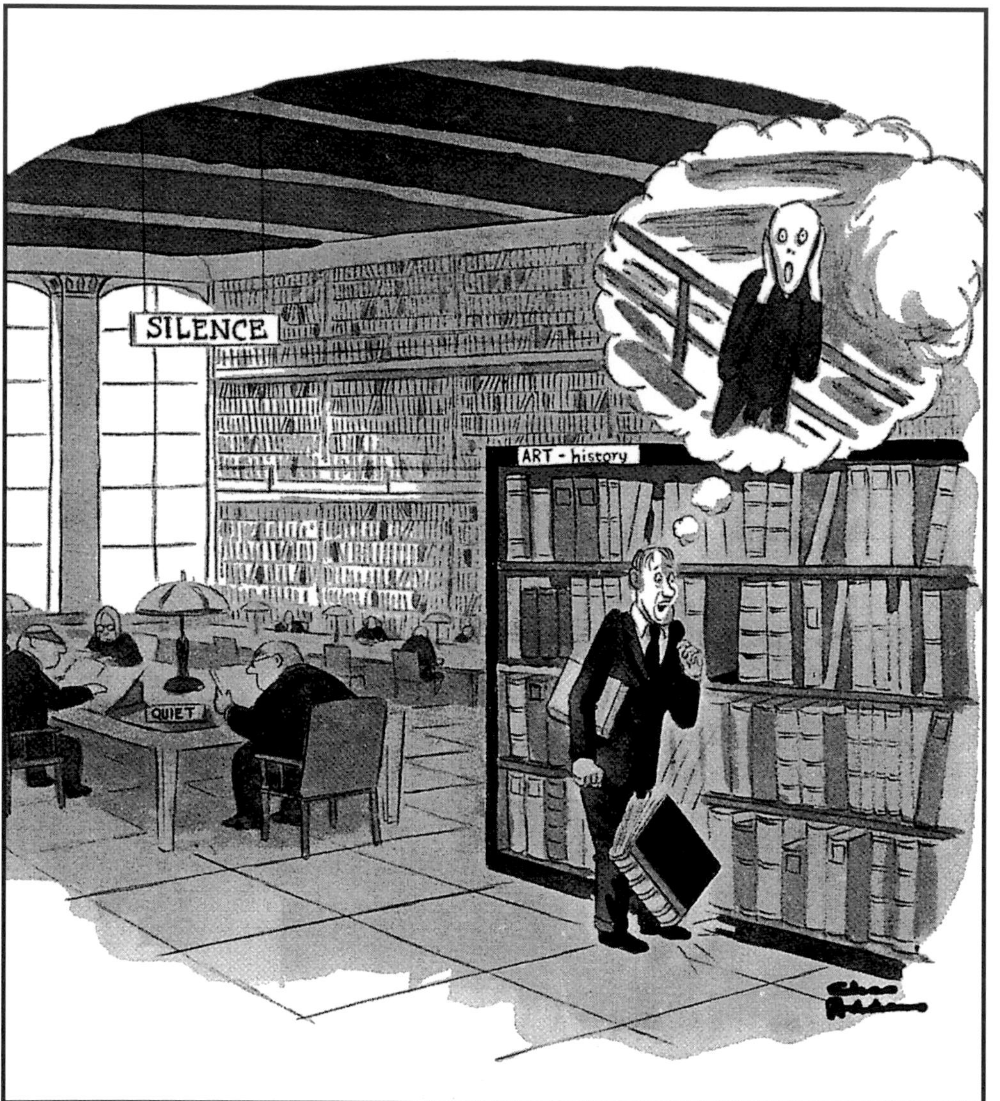

© The New Yorker Collection 1983 Charles Addams from cartoonbank.com. All Rights Reserved

Books like this one can serve as a guide to art, but no text or reproduction can substitute for viewing original works, even in an era when the written word has higher status than artists and their works. To those who love art, few pursuits are more pleasurable. A major benefit is being able to understand cartoons about art, since their humor is not obvious to everyone. Finding the cartoon on this page amusing requires knowing the painting entitled *The Scream* by Edvard Munch (see fig. 23-21). Learning to look at art is not an easy task, however, for art has become commonplace. We live in a sea of images that convey the culture and learning of modern civilization. Fueled by the mass media, this "visual background noise" has become so much a part of our daily lives that we take it for granted. In the process, we have become desensitized to art as well. Anyone can buy cheap paintings and reproductions to decorate a room, where they often hang unnoticed, perhaps deservedly so. It is small wonder that we look at the art in museums with equal casualness. We pass quickly from one object to another, sampling them like dishes in a cafeteria line. We may pause briefly before a famous masterpiece that we have been told we are supposed to admire. But we are likely to ignore the equally beautiful and important works around it (see the cartoon on page 21). We will have *seen* the art but not really *looked* at it.

Looking at great art is not an easy task, for art rarely reveals its secrets at first glance. While the experience of a work can be electrifying, we sometimes do not realize its impact until it has had time to filter through our imagination. It even happens that something which at first repelled or confused us emerges many years later as one of the most important artistic events of our lives. If we are going to get the most out of art, we will have to learn how to look and think for ourselves in an intelligent way, which is perhaps the hardest task of all. After all, we will not always have someone at our side to help us. In the end, the confrontation of viewer and art remains as solitary an act as making it.

Art represents the play between artists' imaginations and their surroundings. It also provides a personal record of life as it has been experienced by people at very different times and places. Because so much goes into art, it makes many of the same demands on us that it did on the person who created it. For that reason, we must be able to respond to a work on many levels. To understand it therefore requires a knowledge of both art history and life. The two go hand in hand. The more one knows about one, the more one can appreciate the other.

What people get out of art varies greatly from person to person. We each have different talents. Just as some people have a special ability in athletics or a knack for fixing things, others have a bent for spirituality or philosophy, or they may possess a historical imagination or a playful mind. Moreover, we each have different backgrounds and experiences. Thus we bring different skills to bear on looking at art, just as artists do in making it. Variety is indeed the spice of life. The world would be a dull place if everyone had the same views and backgrounds. Fortunately, there is room for almost limitless diversity. At the same time, there are broad common denominators, including culture and tradition, that bind us together just as much as human nature itself does.

APPROACHES TO ART HISTORY

The art historical approach of this book is often labeled *formalistic* insofar as it is concerned with the evolution of style. Thus it is akin to connoisseurship, although this should not be taken to mean the visual analysis of aesthetic qualities. It also draws on *iconography,* that is, the meaning of a work of art, and what Erwin Panofsky called *iconology,* its cultural context. This book takes a *classical* approach to art history as defined by three generations of mainly German-born scholars—including H. W. Janson, a student of Panofsky. It is well suited to introducing beginners to art history by providing the framework for how to look at and respond to art in museums and galleries—something both authors have greatly enjoyed throughout their lives. In nearly every case, the works illustrated here (or very similar ones) have been seen by one or both authors to be certain that they are indeed worthy of inclusion. In some cases we have changed our minds, especially when it comes to recent art that has not had the benefit of time to gain the historical perspective needed for a full appraisal.

Readers should be aware that there are other approaches. The oldest is Marxism, which views art in terms of the social and political conditions determined by the prevailing economic system. Marxist analysis has been especially useful in treating art since the Industrial Revolution, which created the conditions that were analyzed by Karl Marx in the mid-nineteenth century. It remains to be seen what will become of Marxist art history in the wake of the collapse of Communism in Russia and Eastern Europe.

Psychology, too, has added many insights into the meaning works of art have for their creators, particularly when that meaning is hidden even from the artists themselves. The more extreme attempts to psychoanalyze Leonardo and Michelangelo, for instance, have caused some scholars to distrust this method. But some works, such as Fuseli's *The Nightmare* (whose meaning was analyzed by H. W. Janson in a pioneering article), cannot be understood without it. Here is another case in point: at my editor's suggestion, I have traced the theme of a woman holding a mirror from the sixteenth century to modern times, using works by Hans Baldung Grien, Simon Vouet, François Boucher, Pablo Picasso, Erich Heckel, and Cindy Sherman as examples. The meaning of this fascinating image is enriched by knowing that it represents the anima, one of the psychological archetypes defined by Freud's former disciple Carl Jung, which personifies the feminine tendencies in the male psyche and acts as a guide to the inner realm. This discovery opens up a field of analysis that I invite readers to explore on their own.

Three new approaches—feminism, multiculturalism, and deconstruction—are perhaps the most radical of all. Feminism reexamines art history from the point of view of gender. Depictions of the woman with a mirror call for a feminist treatment, which yields a very different understanding of their hidden meaning, as readers may discover by questioning these works themselves. Because this approach is embedded in current gender politics, there is a risk that a major shift in social outlook might call some of feminism's conclusions into question. In principle, however, feminist theory can be applied to all of art history. It certainly forces us to reconsider what is "good" art. After all, when this book first appeared, not a single woman artist was included—nor was one to be found in any other art history survey. Today such omissions seem nothing short of astonishing.

Feminism is related to the larger shift toward multiculturalism, which addresses the gap in our understanding of the art of nontraditional and non-Western cultures. Why should we not include artists who express very different sensibilities from that of the European and American mainstream? Indeed, there is no reason whatsoever not to. However, this book is limited to Western art for both practical and philosophical reasons. I have chosen instead to focus on the contribution of African-American art. In the process, however, I have taken a stand about what art is most important that not all readers will agree with, since it favors universalism over ethnocentrism. In part, this reflects my own views on the stereotyping ethnocentrism fosters on both sides of the racial fence. In my opinion, such an approach is doomed as a cultural dead end, although I cannot deny that art with a racial "edge" has a legitimate place. Feminism and multiculturalism have both attacked the "canon" of masterpieces in this and similar books as embodying male chauvinism and colonialist attitudes. Readers should judge the issue for themselves. I would only point out that one must walk before one can run.

Because they are so central to postmodern thought, semiotics and deconstruction are briefly summarized toward the end of the book. I am sympathetic to semiotics, which I first became interested in more than 20 years ago, although I find Noam Chomsky's theory of linguistics more satisfying. Deconstruction has likewise made art historians consider meaning in new ways that have breathed fresh life into the field. Nevertheless, I know from classroom experience that it is nearly impossible for beginning art history students to understand semiotics. Deconstruction is even more taxing. What began as a feud between two schools of French semiologists has spread to art history, where it pits older, mostly German-trained scholars against a younger generation. And perhaps that is the point. People are constantly reinventing art history in their image. But if art history reflects our times, the reader may wonder how it can have any claim to objectivity and, hence, validity. In fact, people's understanding of history has always changed with the times. How could it be otherwise? It seems almost necessary for each generation to reinvent history so that we may understand both the past and the present. Yet the danger is that ideology, regardless of its noble intent, will undermine the search for truth, no matter how relative truth may be. Such a thing happened during the 1930s, when scholarship was made to serve the political ends of dictatorships—which led Panofsky and Janson to leave Germany.

Neither author is an ideologue. Both are humanists who believe that the study of humane letters is enjoyable and enriching. Such a view requires that scholarly discourse be temperate, although it is rarely dispassionate. I would encourage the reader to examine all forms of art history with an open mind. One cannot view something as rich and complex as art from a single perspective any more than it is possible to see a diamond from a single vantage point. Each approach can add to our understanding. To be sure, a plea for tolerance may seem outdated at a time when art history, like all fields, has become so contentious. In this regard, scholarship reflects the rapid political change, social unrest, ideological dogmatism, and religious fanaticism that characterize postindustrial society and the new world order that is emerging in its wake. Let all ideas meet the test of the marketplace of ideas, where they can be discussed openly and fairly. Let us also allow everyone to tend his own intellectual garden in peace. Some may have a larger plot than others, but even the biggest of them is rather small in the scheme of things, as H. W. Janson, among the most famous art historians of his time, came to understand.

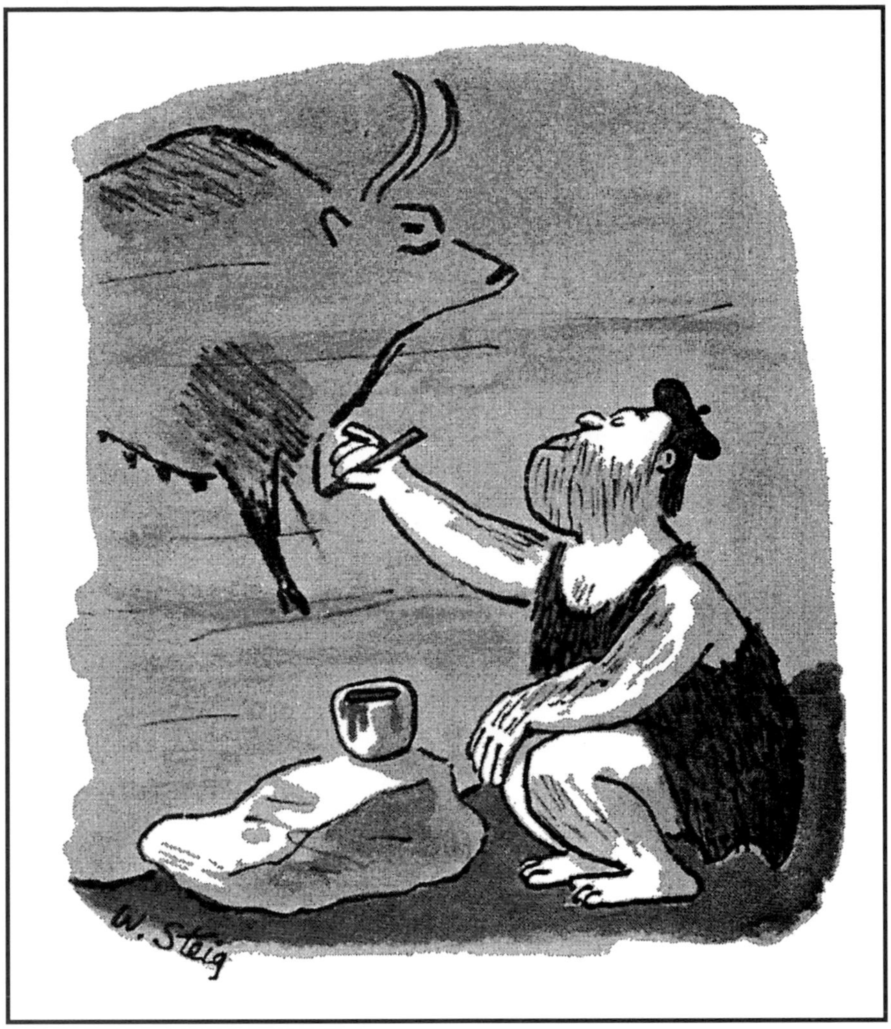

© The New Yorker Collection 1954 William Steig from cartoonbank.com. All Rights Reserved

Both authors have given a great deal of thought to this book, which is written in the authoritative tones that intellectuals habitually adopt as their public voice. It is difficult, of course, to resist the temptation to pontificate—to hand down the "canon" as if it were immutable law. Yet, if the truth be told, the experience of surveying such a broad field as art history provides a lesson in humility. One becomes only too aware of the painful omissions and how little one knows about any given subject in this age of increasing specialization. If it requires the egotism of the gods to undertake such a project in the first place, in the end one sees it clearly for what it is: an act of hubris. It also requires a faith in the power of reason to produce such a synthesis, something that is in short supply these days.

PART ONE

The Ancient World

Art history is more than a stream of art objects created over time. It is closely tied to history itself, that is, the recorded evidence of human events. We must therefore consider the *concept* of history. History, we are often told, began with the invention of writing by the "historic" civilizations of Mesopotamia and Egypt some 5,000 years ago. Without writing, the growth we have known would have been impossible. However, the development of writing seems to have taken place over a period of several hundred years—roughly between 3300 and 3000 B.C., with Mesopotamia in the lead—after the new societies were past their first stage. Thus "history" was well under way by the time writing could be used to record events.

The invention of writing serves as a landmark, for the lack of written records is one of the key differences between prehistoric and historic societies. But as soon as we ask why this is so, we face some intriguing problems. First of all, how valid is the distinction between "prehistoric" and "historic"? Does it merely reflect a difference in our *knowledge* of the past? (Thanks to the invention of writing, we know a great deal more about history than about prehistory.) Or was there a real change in the way things happened, and in the kinds of things that happened, after "history" began? Obviously, prehistory was far from uneventful. Yet the events of this period, decisive though they were, seem slow-paced and gradual when measured against the events of the last 5,000 years. The beginning of "history," then, means a sudden increase in the speed of events, a shift from low gear to high gear, as it were. It also means a change in the *kinds* of events. Historic societies literally make history. They not only bring forth "great individuals and great deeds" (one definition of history) by demanding human effort on a large scale, but they make these achievements *memorable*. And for an event to be memorable, it must be more than "worth remembering." It must also occur quickly enough to be grasped by human memory, not spread over many centuries. Taken together, memorable events have caused the ever-quickening pace of change during the past five millennia, which begin with what we call the ancient world.

This period was preceded by a vast prehistoric era of which we know almost nothing until the last Ice Age in Europe, which lasted from about 40,000 to 8000 B.C. (There had been at least three previous ice ages, alternating with periods of subtropical warmth, at intervals of about 25,000 years.) At that time, the climate between the Alps and Scandinavia resembled that of present-day Siberia or Alaska. Huge herds of reindeer and other large herbivores roamed the plains and valleys, preyed upon by the ancestors of today's lions and tigers, as well as by our own ancestors. These people liked to live in caves or in the shelter of overhanging rocks. Many such sites have been found, mostly in Spain and in southern France. This phase of prehistory is known as the Old Stone Age, or Paleolithic era, because tools were made only from stone. Adapted almost perfectly to the special conditions of the receding Ice Age, it was a way of life that could not survive beyond then.

The Old Stone Age came to a close with what is termed the Neolithic Revolution, which ushered in the New Stone Age. And a revolution it was indeed, even though it was a period of transition that extended over several thousand years during the Mesolithic Age. It first occurred in the Fertile Crescent of the Near East (an area covering what is now Turkey, Iraq, Iran, Jordan, Israel, Lebanon, and Syria) sometime about 12,000–8000 B.C., with the first successful attempts to domesticate animals and food grains. The Neolithic came later to Europe but then spread much more rapidly.

The cultivation of regular food sources was one of the most decisive achievements in human history. People in Paleolithic societies had led the unsettled life of the hunter and food gatherer, reaping wherever nature sowed. They were at the mercy of forces that they could neither understand nor control. But having learned how to ensure a food supply through their own efforts, they settled down in permanent villages. A new discipline and order entered their lives. There is, then, a very basic difference between the Neolithic and the Paleolithic, despite the fact that at first both still depended on stone for tools and weapons. The new mode of life brought forth a number of new crafts and inventions long before the appearance of metals. Among them were pottery, weaving, and spinning, as well as basic methods of construction in wood, brick, and stone. These changes must have been accompanied by a profound shift in people's view of themselves and the world. When metallurgy in the form of copper finally appeared in southeast Europe around 4500 B.C. at the beginning of the so-called Eneolithic era, it was as a direct outgrowth of the technology gained from pottery. As such, it did not in itself constitute a major advance; nor, surprisingly enough, did it have an immediate impact.

The Neolithic Revolution placed us on a level at which we might well have remained indefinitely. The forces of nature would never again challenge men and women as they had Paleolithic peoples. In a few places, however, the balance between humans and nature was upset by a new threat, one posed not by nature but by people themselves. Evidence of that threat can be seen in the earliest Neolithic fortifications, built almost 9,000 years ago in the Near East. What was the source of the human conflict that made these defenses necessary? Competition for grazing land among groups of herders or for arable soil among farming communities? The basic cause, we suspect, was that the Neolithic Revolution had been too successful. It had allowed population groups to grow beyond the available food supply. This situation might have been resolved in a number of ways. Constant warfare could have reduced the population. Or the people could have united in larger and more disciplined social units for the sake of group efforts—such as the building of fortifications—that no loosely organized society could achieve on its own.

We do not know the outcome of the struggle in the region. (Future excavations may tell us how far the urbanizing process extended.) But about 3,000 years later, similar conflicts, on a larger scale, arose in the Nile Valley and again in the plains of the Tigris and Euphrates rivers. The pressures that forced the people in these regions to abandon Neolithic village life may well have been the same. These conflicts created enough pressure to produce the first civilizations (the word "civilization" derives from the Latin term for city, *civilis*), new societies organized into much larger units—cities and city-states—that were far more complex and efficient than had ever existed before. First in Mesopotamia and Egypt, somewhat later in neighboring areas, and in the Indus Valley and along the Yellow River in China, people would henceforth live in a more dynamic world. Their capacity to survive would be challenged not by the forces of nature but by human forces—by tensions and conflicts arising either within society or as the result of competition between societies. Efforts to cope with these human forces have proved to be a far greater challenge than the earlier struggle with nature. The problems and pressures faced by historic societies thus are very different from those faced by peoples in the Paleolithic or Neolithic eras.

These momentous changes also spurred the development of new technologies in what we term the Bronze Age and the Iron Age, which, like the Neolithic, are stages, not distinct eras. People first began to cast bronze, an alloy of copper and tin, in the Middle East around 3500 B.C., at the same time that the earliest cities arose in Egypt and Mesopotamia. The smelting and forging of iron were invented about 2000–1500 B.C. by the Hittites, an Indo-European–speaking people who settled in Cappadocia (today's east-central Turkey), a high plateau with abundant copper and iron ore. Indeed, it was the competition for mineral resources that helped create the conflicts that beset civilizations everywhere.

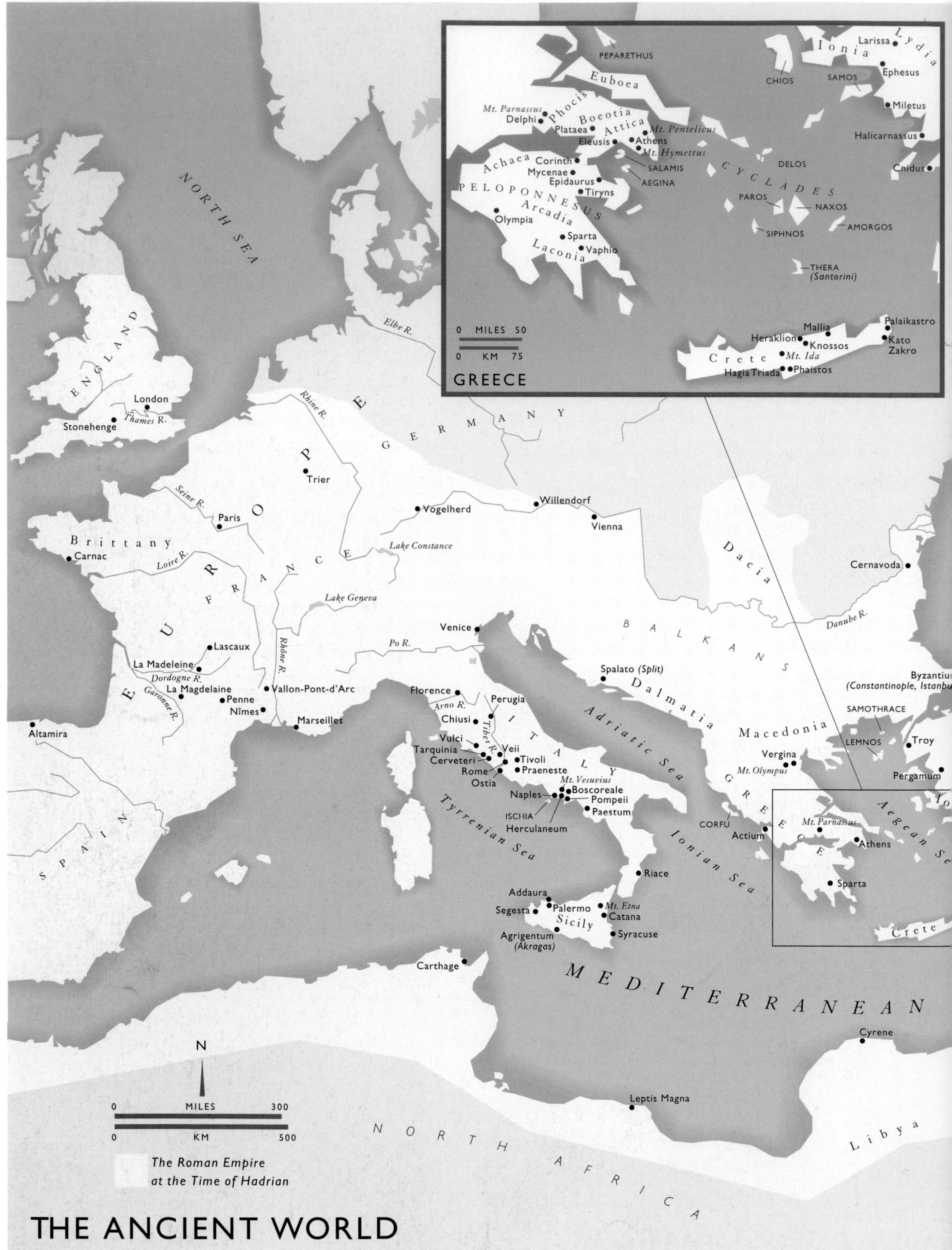

THE ANCIENT WORLD

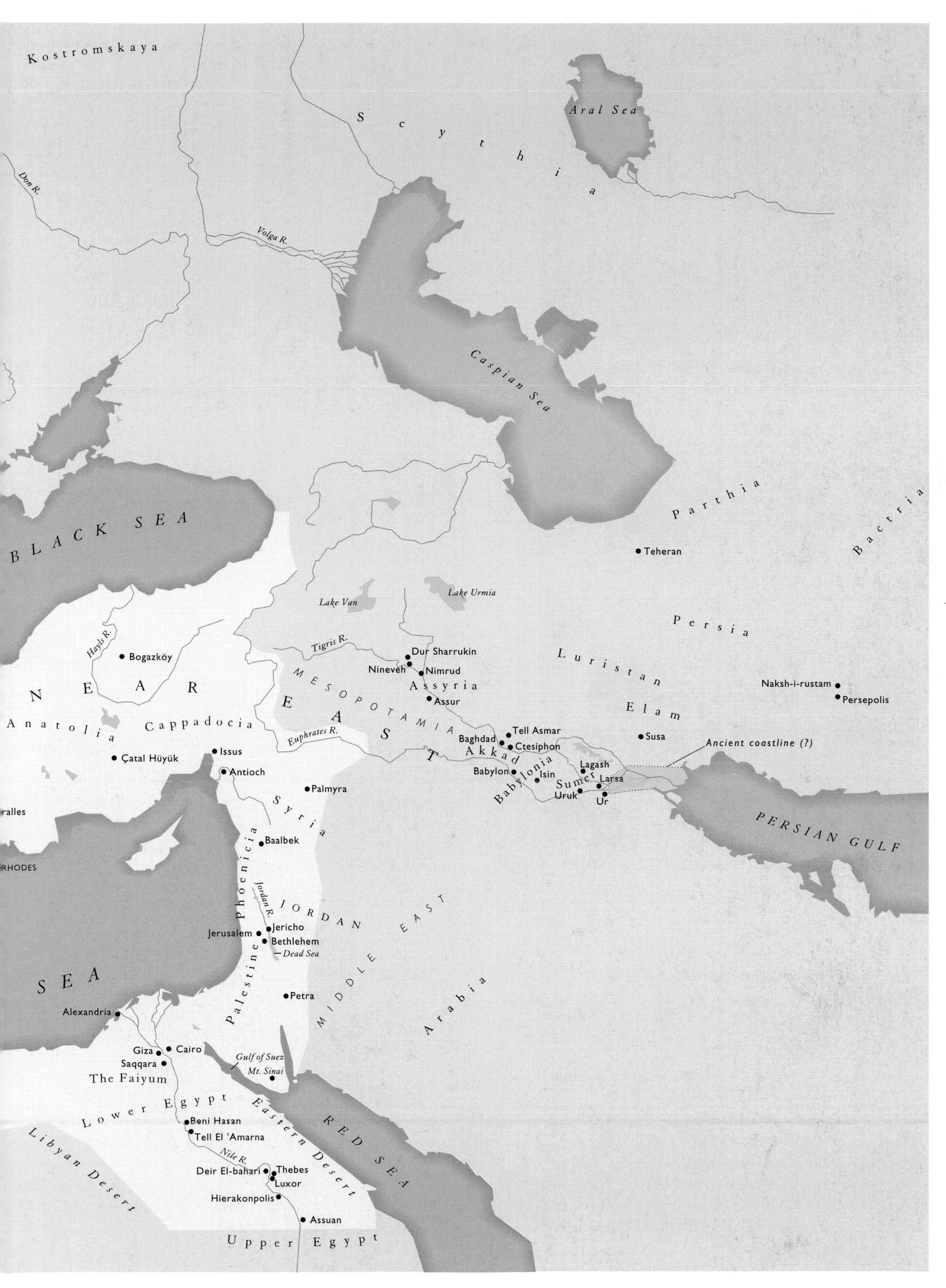
Kostromskaya
Scythia
Aral Sea
Don R.
Volga R.
Caspian Sea
Parthia
Bactria
BLACK SEA
Teheran
Lake Van
Lake Urmia
Persia
Hayls R.
Tigris R.
Dur Sharrukin
Nineveh
Nimrud
Luristan
Bogazköy
MESOPOTAMIA
Assyria
Naksh-i-rustam
Persepolis
NEAR
EAST
Assur
Elam
Anatolia
Cappadocia
Euphrates R.
Baghdad
Tell Asmar
Ctesiphon
Susa
Ancient coastline (?)
Çatal Hüyük
Issus
Akkad
Antioch
Babylon
Isin
Lagash
Palmyra
Babylonia
Sumer
Larsa
Uruk
Ur
ralles
Syria
PERSIAN GULF
Baalbek
RHODES
Phoenicia
Jordan R.
JORDAN
MIDDLE EAST
Jericho
Jerusalem
Bethlehem
Dead Sea
SEA
Palestine
Petra
Arabia
Alexandria
Giza
Cairo
Saqqara
Gulf of Suez
Mt. Sinai
The Faiyum
Lower Egypt
Eastern Desert
Beni Hasan
RED SEA
Libyan Desert
Tell El 'Amarna
Nile R.
Deir El-bahari
Thebes
Luxor
Hierakonpolis
Assuan
Upper Egypt

CHAPTER ONE

Prehistoric Art

THE OLD STONE AGE

When did human beings start creating works of art? What prompted them to do so? What did these works of art look like? Every history of art must begin with these questions—and with the admission that we cannot answer them. Our earliest known ancestors began to walk on two feet about four million years ago, but we do not know how they used their hands. Not until more than two million years later do we meet the earliest evidence of toolmaking. Humans must have been using tools all along, however. After all, apes will pick up a stick to knock down a banana or a stone to throw at an enemy. The making of tools is a more complex matter. It demands the ability to think of sticks or stones as "fruit knockers" or "bone crackers," not only when they are needed for such purposes but at other times as well.

Once humans were able to do this, they gradually found that some sticks or stones had a handier shape than others. They put these aside for future use. They chose certain sticks or stones as tools because they had begun to connect form and function. The sticks, of course, have not survived, but a few of the stones have. They are large pebbles or chunks of rock that show the marks of repeated use for the same task, whatever that may have been. The next step was to try chipping away at these stones in order to improve their shape. This is the first craft of which we have evidence. With it we enter a phase of human development known as the Paleolithic, or Old Stone Age, which lasted from about 40,000 to 10,000 B.C.

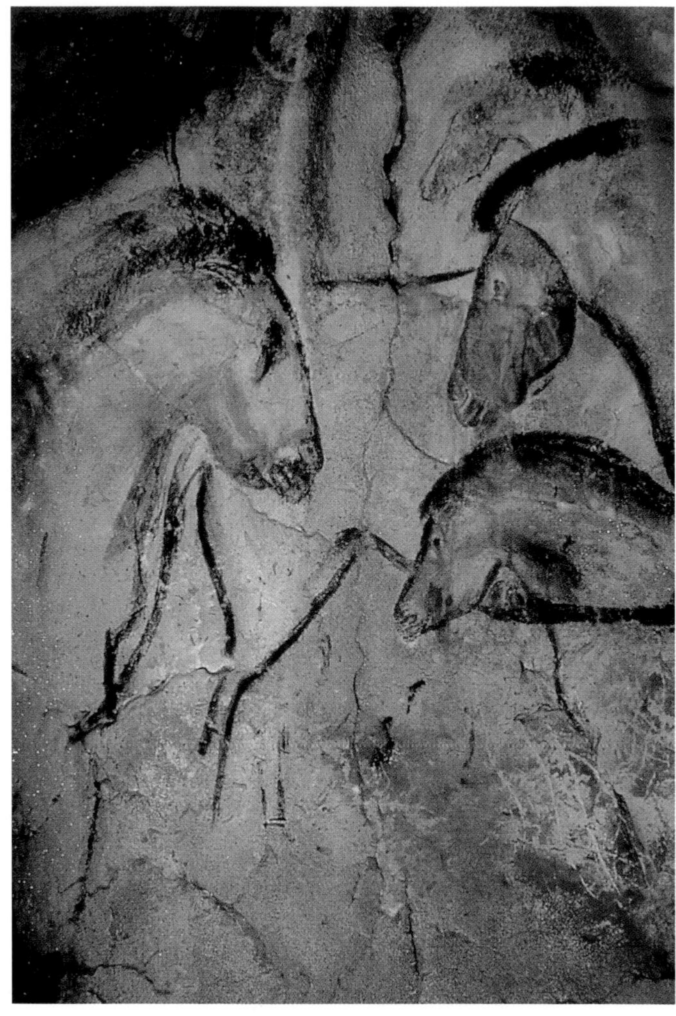

1-1. *Horses.* Cave painting. c. 28,000 B.C. Chauvet cave, Vallon-pont-d'Arc, Ardèche gorge, France

Cave Art

CHAUVET. The most striking works of Paleolithic art are the images of animals incised, painted, or sculptured on the rock surfaces of caves. In the recently discovered Chauvet cave in southeastern France, we meet the earliest paintings known to us, dating from more than 30,000 years ago. Ferocious lions, panthers, rhinoceroses, bears, reindeer, and mammoths are depicted with extraordinary vividness, along with bulls, horses, birds, and occasionally humans. These paintings already show an assurance and refinement far removed from any humble beginnings. What a vivid, lifelike image is the depiction of horses seen in figure 1-1! We are amazed not only by the keen observation and the strong outlines but also by the power and expressiveness of these creatures. It is highly unlikely that images such as this came into being in a single, sudden burst. We must assume that they were preceded by thousands of years of development about which we know nothing at all.

ALTAMIRA AND LASCAUX. On the basis of differences among the tools and other remains found there, scholars have divided up later "cavemen" into several groups, each named after a specific site. Among these, the so-called Aurignacians and Magdalenians stand out for the gifted artists they produced and for the important role art must have played in their lives. Besides Chauvet, the major sites are at Altamira, in northern Spain (fig. 1-2), and Lascaux, in the Dordogne region of France (fig. 1-3). At Lascaux, as at Chauvet, bison, deer, horses, and cattle race across walls and ceiling. Some of them are outlined in black, others filled in with bright earth colors, but all show the same uncanny sense of life. The style in both caves is essentially the same despite a gap of thousands of years—evidence of the stability of Paleolithic culture. Gone, however, are the fiercest beasts.

How did this amazing art survive intact over so many thousands of years? The question can be answered easily enough. The pictures never appear near the mouth of a cave, where they would be open to easy view and destruction. They are found only in dark

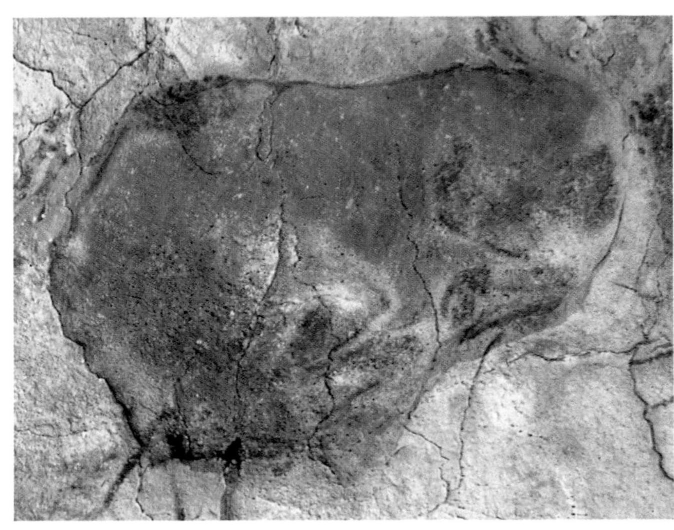

1-2. *Wounded Bison.* Cave painting. c. 15,000–10,000 B.C. Altamira, Spain

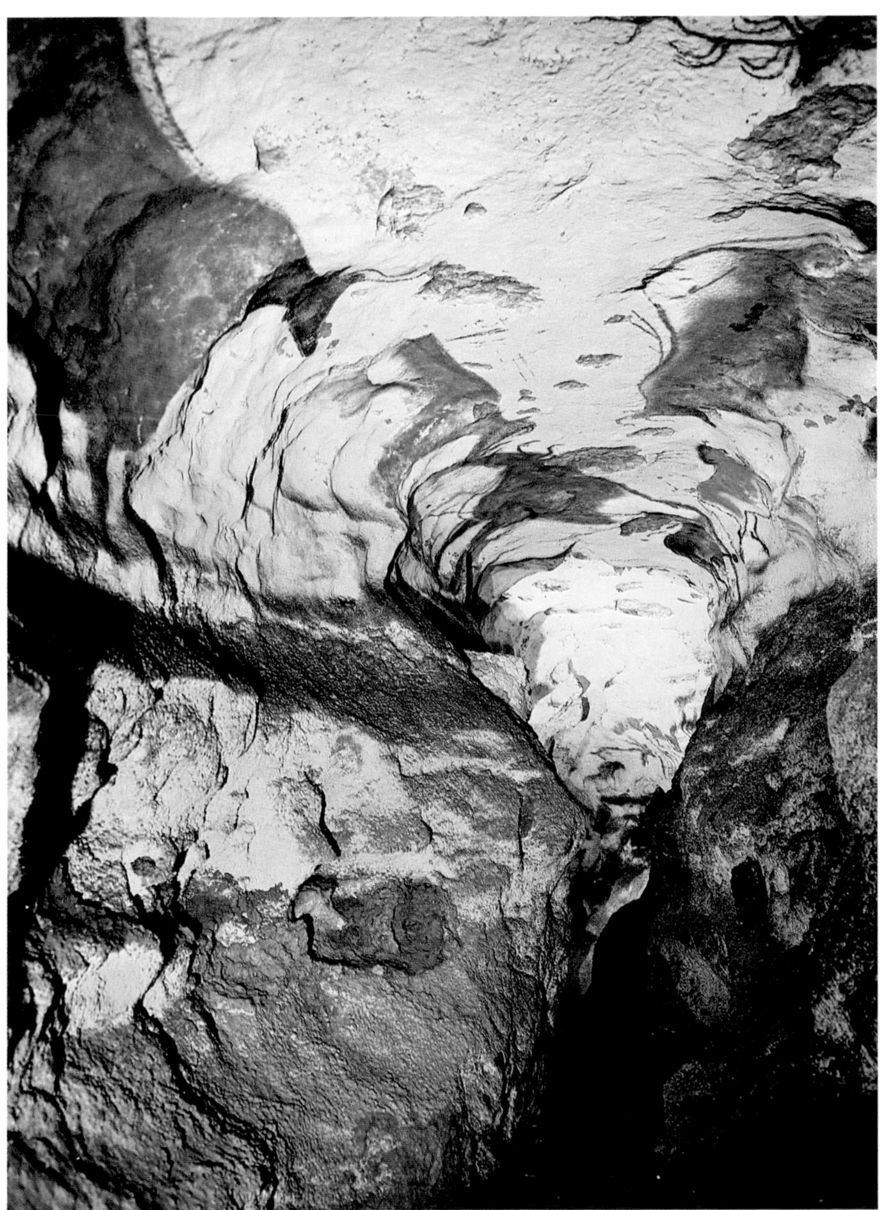

1-3. Axial Gallery, Lascaux. 15,000–10,000 B.C. (Montignac, Dordogne), France

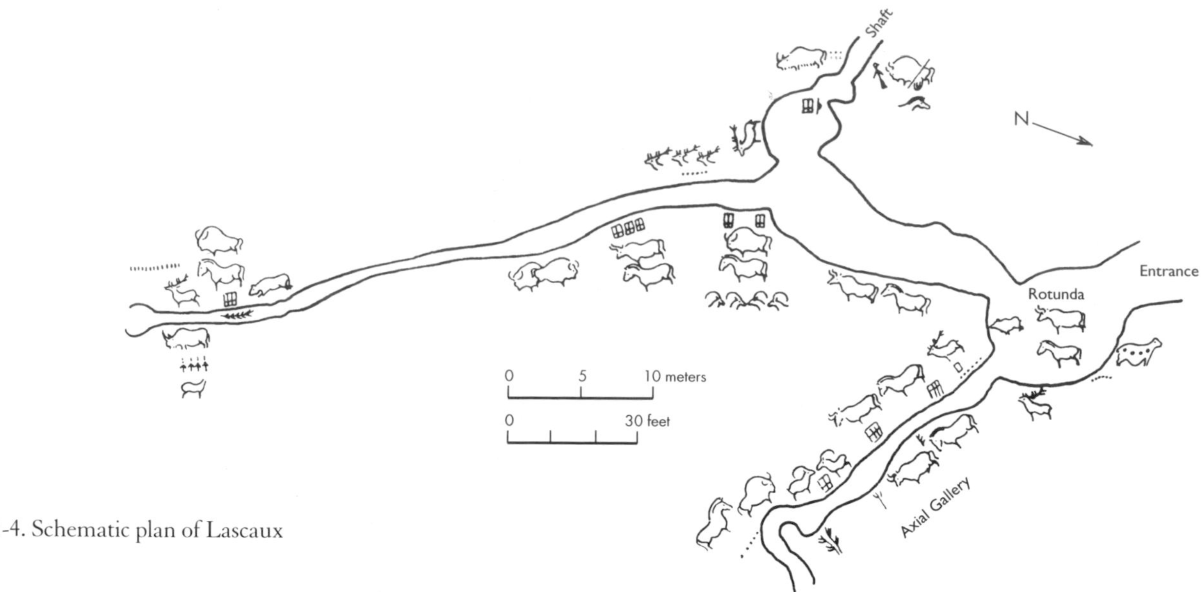

1-4. Schematic plan of Lascaux

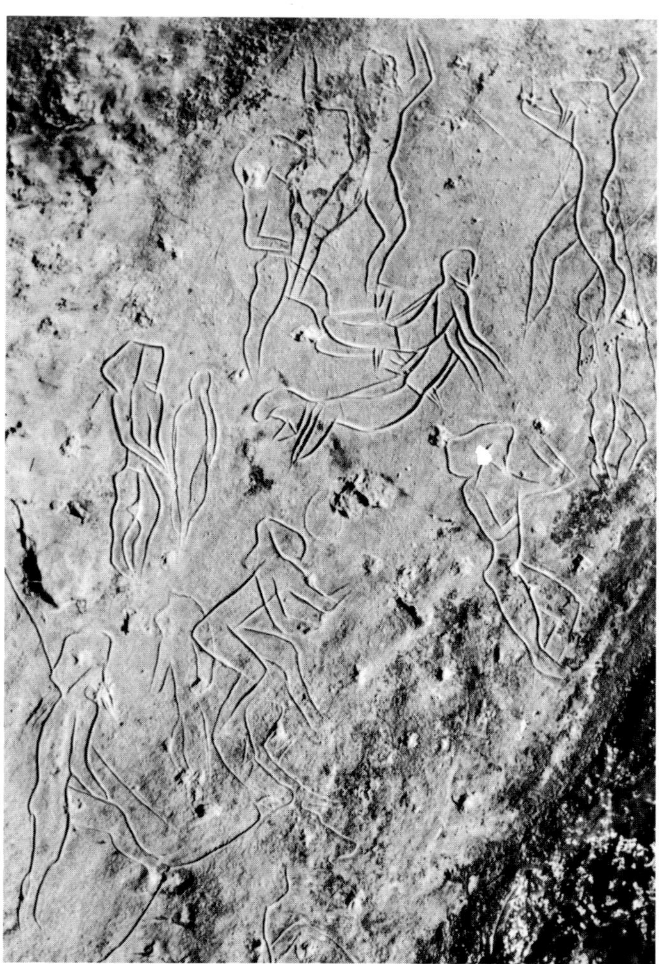
1-5. *Ritual Dance (?)*. Rock engraving. c. 10,000 B.C. Height of figures approx. 10" (25.4 cm). Cave of Addaura, Monte Pellegrino (Palermo), Sicily

recesses, as far from the entrance as possible (fig. 1-4). Some can be reached only by crawling on hands and knees. Often the path is so intricate that one would soon be lost without an expert guide. In fact, the cave at Lascaux was discovered by chance in 1940 by some boys whose dog had fallen into a hole that led to the underground chamber.

What purpose did these images serve? Hidden away as they are, in order to protect them from intruders, they must have been viewed as much more than decoration. There can be little doubt that they were made as part of a ritual. But of what kind? The standard explanation is that they are a form of hunting magic. According to this theory, in "killing" the image of an animal, people of the Old Stone Age thought they had killed its vital spirit. This later evolved into fertility magic, carried out deep in the bowels of the earth. But how are we to account for the presence at Chauvet of lions and other fierce beasts that we know were not hunted? Perhaps at first, cavemen took on the identity of lions and bears to aid in the hunt. Although it cannot be disproved, this proposal is not completely satisfying. Besides being speculative, it fails to explain many curious features of cave art.

There is a growing consensus that cave paintings must embody a very early form of religion. If so, the creatures found in them have a spiritual meaning that makes them the distant ancestors of the animal divinities and their half-human, half-animal cousins we shall meet throughout the Near East and the Aegean. Indeed, how else are we to account for them? Moreover, such a proposal accords with the belief that nature is filled with spirits. Known as animism, this belief was found the world over in the ethnographic societies that survived intact until recently.

The existence of cave rituals dealing with both human and animal fertility seems to be confirmed by a group of Paleolithic drawings found in the 1950s on the walls of the cave of Addaura, near Palermo in Sicily (fig. 1-5). These images, incised into the rock with quick and sure lines, show human figures in dancelike movements, along with some animals; as at Lascaux, we again find several layers of images superimposed on one another. Here, then, we seem to be on the verge of the fusion of human and animal identity found in the earliest historical religions of Egypt and Mesopotamia.

Cave art is also important as the earliest evidence of a long tradition found in civilizations everywhere: the urge to decorate walls and ceilings with painted and carved images that have a spiritual meaning. Because they were not constructed, caves such as Lascaux do not qualify as architecture (see below). Yet they served the same function as a church or temple. In that sense, they are the precursors of the religious architecture we shall meet throughout this book.

POSSIBLE ORIGINS. Some of the cave pictures may even provide a clue to their origin. In many cases the shape of an animal seems to have been suggested by the natural formation of the rock, its body coinciding with a bump, or its contour following a vein or crack. We all know how our imagination sometimes makes us see many sorts of images in clouds or blots. Perhaps at first the Stone Age artist merely reinforced the outlines of such images with a charred stick. It is tempting to think that those who were very good at finding such images were given a special status as artist-shamans. With this status, they could perfect their image-hunting until they learned how to make images with little or no help from chance formations.

Carved and Painted Objects

Apart from large-scale cave art, the people of the Upper Paleolithic also produced small, hand-sized drawings and carvings in bone, horn, or stone, skillfully cut with flint tools. The earliest of these found so far are small figures of mammoth ivory, made 30,000 years ago, which came from a cave in southwestern Germany. Even they, however, are so refined that they, too, must have been preceded by thousands of years of development. The graceful, harmonious curves of a running horse (fig. 1-6) could hardly be improved upon by a more recent sculptor. Many years of handling have worn down some details. (The two converging lines on the shoulder, indicating a dart or wound, were not part of the original design.)

Some of these carvings suggest that the objects may have stemmed from the perception of a chance resemblance. Earlier Stone Age people were content to collect pebbles in whose natural shape they saw something that made them special. Echoes of this approach can sometimes be felt in later pieces. The so-called *"Venus" of Willendorf* (fig. 1-7), one of many such female figurines, has a bulbous roundness of form that recalls an egg-shaped "sacred pebble." Her navel, the central point of the design, is a natural cavity in the stone. Such carvings are often thought to be fertility figures, based on the spiritual beliefs of "preliterate" societies of modern times. Although the idea is tempting, we cannot be sure that such beliefs existed in the Old Stone Age. Likewise, the masterful *Bison* in figure 1-8 owes its expressive outline in part to the contours of the palm-shaped piece of reindeer horn from which it was carved. It is a worthy companion to the splendid beasts at Altamira, Lascaux, and Chauvet.

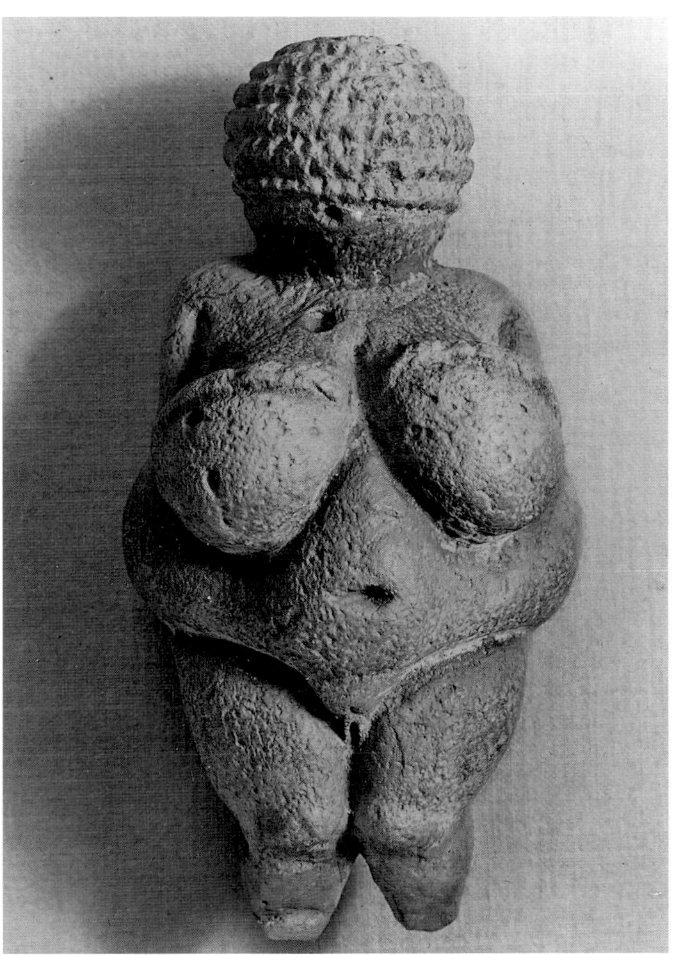

1-7. *"Venus" of Willendorf.* c. 25,000–20,000 B.C. Limestone, height $4\frac{3}{8}$" (11.1 cm); shown actual size. Naturhistorisches Museum, Vienna

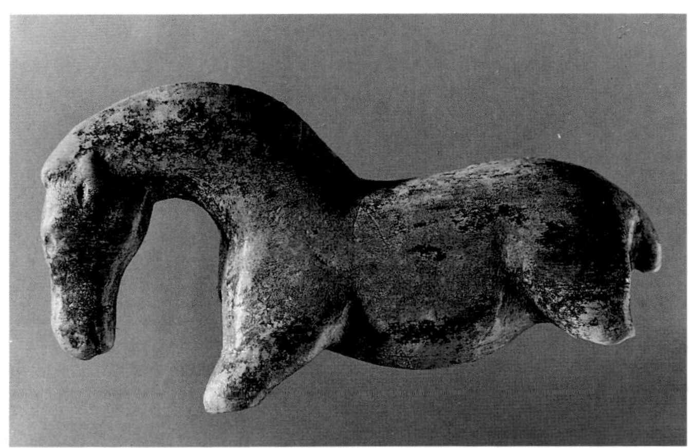

1-6. *Horse,* from Vogelherd cave. c. 28,000 B.C. Mammoth ivory, length $2\frac{1}{2}$" (6.4 cm). Private collection

PHOTOGRAPH COPYRIGHT ALEXANDER MARSHACK

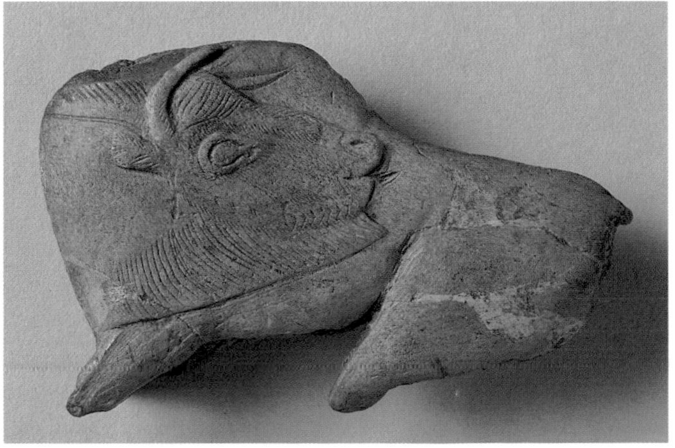

1-8. *Bison,* from La Madeleine near Les Eyzies (Dordogne). c. 15,000–10,000 B.C. Reindeer horn, length 4" (10.1 cm). Musée des Antiquités Nationales, St.-Germain-en-Laye, France

THE NEW STONE AGE

The art of the Old Stone Age in Europe as we know it today marks the highest achievement of a way of life that began to decline soon afterward. Well suited to the conditions of the receding Ice Age, that way of life could not survive beyond then. Unfortunately, the tangible remains of Neolithic settlements tell us very little about the spiritual life of the New Stone Age. Those remains, uncovered by excavation, include stone tools of ever greater technical refinement and beauty of shape. Also present are a great variety of clay vessels covered with abstract patterns. But none of these items can be compared to the painting and sculpture of the Paleolithic. The shift from hunting to husbandry must nonetheless have been accompanied by profound changes in the people's view of themselves and the world. These changes must have been reflected in their art. There may be a vast chapter in the development of art that is largely lost because Neolithic artists worked in wood or other impermanent materials. Only a few new sites have been discovered by archaeologists in recent years, and they have yielded little new evidence as yet. Perhaps future excavations will help fill the gap.

JERICHO. Prehistoric Jericho (now in the West Bank territory), the most extensively excavated site thus far, has yielded some tantalizing discoveries. These include a group of impressive sculptured heads dating from about 7000 B.C. (fig. 1-9). They are actual human skulls whose faces have been "reconstituted" in tinted plaster, with pieces of seashell for the eyes. The subtlety and precision of the modeling, the gradation of planes and ridges, and the feeling for the relationship of flesh and bone are remarkable, quite apart from the early date. The features, moreover, do not conform to a single type; each has a strongly individual cast. Mysterious as they are, these Neolithic heads point to Mesopotamian art (compare fig. 3-5). They are the first sign of a type of portraiture that will continue until the collapse of the Roman Empire.

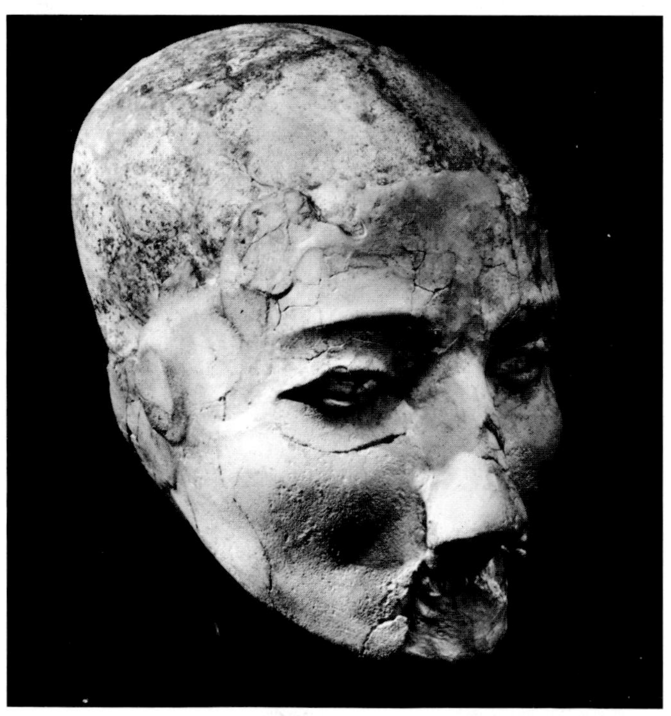

1-9. Neolithic plastered skull, from Jericho. c. 7000 B.C. Lifesize. Archaeological Museum, Amman, Jordan

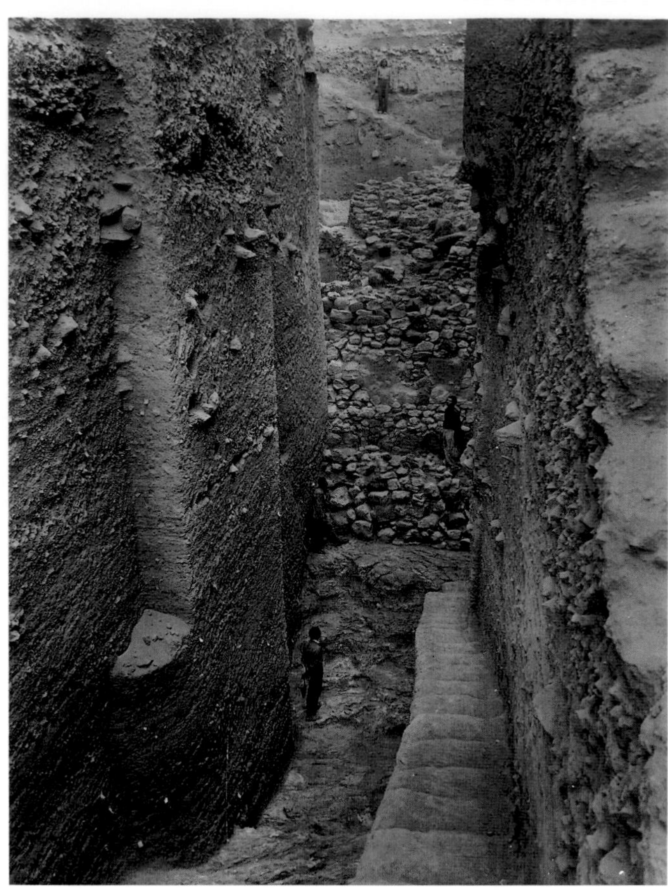

1-10. Early Neolithic wall and tower, Jericho, Jordan. c. 7000 B.C.

Unlike Paleolithic art, which had grown from the perception of chance images, the Jericho heads are not intended to "create" life but to perpetuate it beyond death by replacing the flesh with a more enduring substance. From the circumstances in which they were found, we gather that these heads were displayed above ground while the rest of the body was buried beneath the floor of the house. We can presume that they belonged to honored ancestors whose beneficent presence was thus ensured. Paleolithic societies, too, had buried their dead, but we do not know what ideas they associated with the grave. Was death merely a return to the womb of mother earth, or did they have some conception of the beyond?

The Jericho heads suggest that some peoples of the Neolithic era believed in a spirit or soul, located in the head, that could survive the death of the body. Thus it could affect the fortunes of later generations and had to be appeased or controlled. The preserved heads apparently were "spirit traps" designed to keep the spirit in its original dwelling place. They express the sense of tradition, of family or clan continuity, that sets off the settled life of the village from the roving existence of the hunting group. And Neolithic Jericho was a well-settled community. It was a fortified town protected by walls and towers of rough masonry to safeguard the spring that gave life in this arid region (fig. 1-10). Stone, being scarce, was used only for foundations of houses, which were made of baked mud brick with neat plaster floors. Surprisingly, the people of Jericho had no pottery. The technique of baking clay in a kiln, which requires large amounts of wood, was not invented until several millennia later.

ÇATAL HÜYÜK. Excavations at Çatal Hüyük in Anatolia (modern Turkey) brought to light another Neolithic town, roughly a thousand years younger than Jericho. Its residents traded in obsidian (a volcanic glass used for cutting) and ores, making it a center of metalworking. The people lived in houses built of mud bricks and timber, clustered around open courtyards. Since there were no streets, the houses had no front doors, only doors facing onto the courtyards. People apparently entered through a hole in the roof that doubled as a smoke hole.

Only a small, mostly residential, portion of the site was uncovered during the initial phase in the 1950s and '60s. The results of more recent work suggest that most religious activity took place in individual homes, each of which seems to have had its own altar. The settlement did include a number of religious shrines, the oldest found so far. On their plaster-covered walls we find the earliest paintings on a man-made surface. Animal hunts, with small running figures surrounding huge bulls or stags (fig. 1-11), remind us of cave paintings. This similarity is a sign that the Neolithic Revolution must have been a recent event at the time, but the balance has already shifted: these hunts appear to be rituals honoring the deity to whom the bull and stag were sacred. They thus continue the transformation of animals into gods that began in the Old Stone Age.

Compared to the animals of the cave paintings, those at Çatal Hüyük are simple and static; here it is the hunters who are in motion. Animals associated with female deities appear even more rigid. A pair of leopards forms the sides of the throne of a fertility goddess (fig. 1-12). The most surprising of the wall paintings at Çatal Hüyük is a view of the town itself, with the twin cones of an erupting volcano above it (fig. 1-13). The densely packed houses are seen from above, while the mountain is shown in profile, its slope covered with dots representing blobs of lava. Such a volcano can still be seen from Çatal Hüyük. Its eruption must have terrified the people of the town. How could they have viewed it as anything but

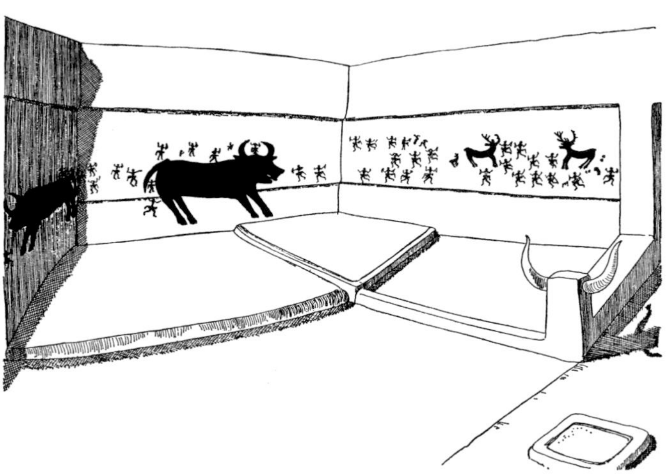

1-11. *Animal Hunt.* Restoration of Main Room, Shrine A.III.1, Çatal Hüyük (after Mellaart). c. 6000 B.C. 27 x 65" (68.5 x 165 cm)

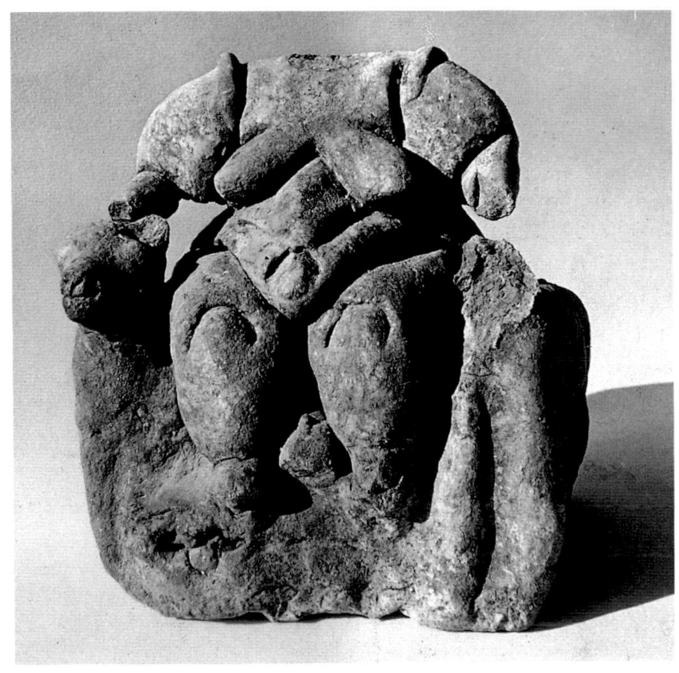

1-12. *Fertility Goddess,* from Shrine A.II.1, Çatal Hüyük. c. 6000 B.C. Baked clay, height 8" (20.3 cm). Archaeological Museum, Ankara, Turkey

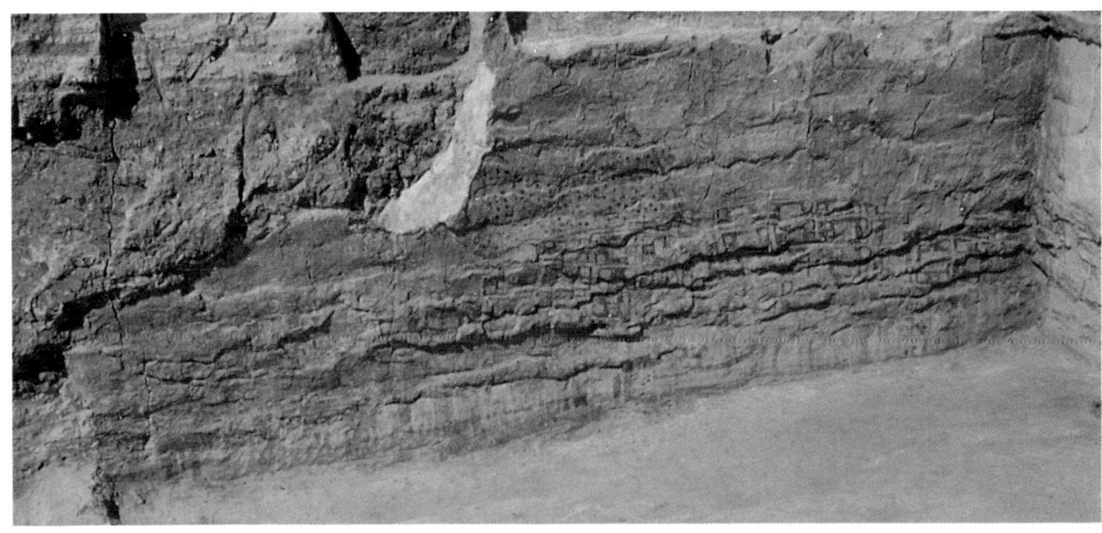

1-13. *View of Town and Volcano.* Wall painting, Shrine VII.14, Çatal Hüyük. c. 6000 B.C.

the manifestation of a deity's power? Nothing less could have brought forth this image, halfway between a map and a landscape.

Neolithic Europe

The Near East became the cradle of civilization: to be civilized, after all, means to live as a citizen, a town dweller. About 5000 B.C. Near Eastern influences began to spread to Europe. This development can be traced through clay pottery, which is breakable but durable, so that it has survived in large numbers of fragments, known as shards. These can often be pieced together to reconstruct entire pots. Fired pottery and figurines had already appeared during that transition between the last ice age and the Neolithic known as the Mesolithic era. Because the remains are so sparse, it is unclear whether pottery making at first arose independently in several places or was transmitted through direct contact. Over time, the patterns of distribution become clearer, with different forms that make it possible to chart successive changes in culture.

Painted pottery notable for its ambitious size and sophisticated decoration seems to have appeared first in Mesopotamia during the sixth millennium B.C. From there it was diffused to Egypt to the southwest, as well as across the Fertile Crescent to Anatolia in Turkey. Later it reached the northern shore of the Mediterranean and continued in a great arc around the Balkans in southeastern Europe, from which the finest examples come. The decorations on the pots in figure 1-14 from Ukraine have a skill and liveliness that are unmatched before Minoan Kamares ware (see fig. 4-11). Soon, high-quality pottery was being made throughout western Europe as well, from central Germany to France and as far north as Denmark, where it took on a distinctive character: many of the shapes and patterns are derived from basket weaving.

The earliest baked clay figurines of fertility goddesses from the Balkans, also dating about 5000 B.C., have their closest relatives in Asia Minor (compare fig. 1-12); but one of around 2,000 years later (fig. 1-15) has, despite the massive legs, an almost girlish figure,

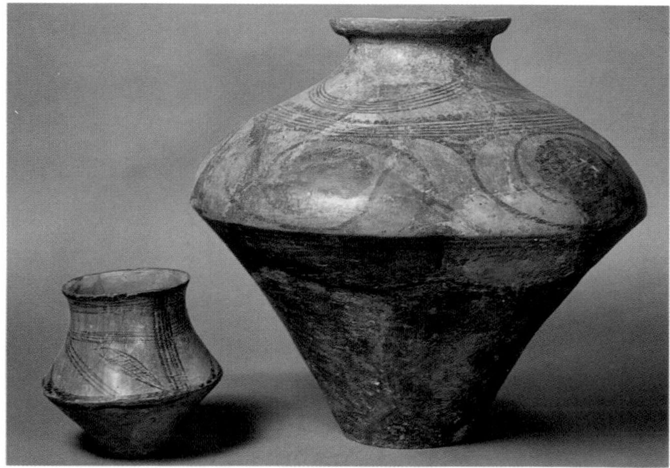

1-14. Biconical vessels of the Tripole group, Ukraine. c. 3000 B.C. Red burnished ware, dimensions of left vessel 5¼ x 5⁹⁄₁₆" (13.1 x 14.1 cm); dimensions of right vessel 13⅛ x 14½" (33.5 x 37 cm). Ashmolean Museum, Oxford

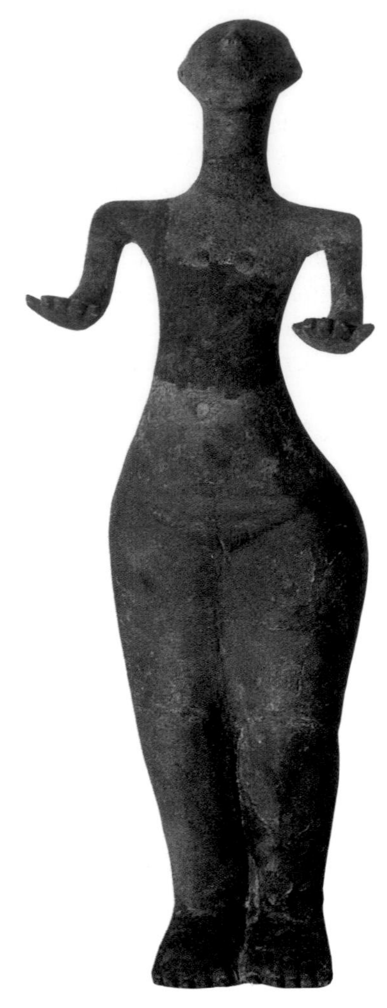

1-15. *Woman,* from Hluboké Masuvky, Moravia, Czechoslovakia. c. 3000 B.C. Clay, height 13" (33 cm). Vildomec collection, Brno

which lends her a surprisingly modern appearance. With arms and head raised in a gesture of worship, she radiates an immediate and very human charm that is as irresistible today as it must have been when our statuette was made.

Bronze Age Europe

DOLMENS AND CROMLECHS. Long after the introduction of bronze around the middle of the third millennium B.C., a sparse population continued to lead the simple tribal life of small village communities in central and northern Europe. Hence there is no clear distinction from the Neolithic. Neolithic and Bronze Age Europe never reached the level of social organization that produced the masonry construction of Jericho or the urban community of Çatal Hüyük, although rough stone fortifications have been discovered at Early Bronze Age sites in the Carpathian Mountains. Instead we find monumental stone structures of a different kind in France, Scandinavia, and then England. These structures are termed *megalithic* because they are made of huge blocks or boulders used either singly or placed upon each other without mortar. Even today these monuments, built about 4500–1500 B.C., have a superhuman air about them, as if they were the work of a race of giants.

The simplest are menhirs: upright slabs that served as grave markers. Sometimes they were arranged in rows, as at Carnac, France. Carnac features another type as well, known as dolmens.

Originally underground, these are tombs resembling "houses of the dead." The walls are upright stones, and the roof is a single giant slab (fig. 1-16). Finally, there are the so-called cromlechs, found only in the British Isles, which were the settings of religious rites. The huge effort required to construct them could be compelled only by religious faith—a faith that almost literally demanded the moving of mountains.

The last and most famous of these is Stonehenge in southern England (figs. 1-17, 1-18, and 1-19). What we see today is the result of several distinct building campaigns, beginning in the New Stone Age and continuing into the Early Bronze Age. During the first phase, which we know from carbon-14 dating corresponds roughly to 3500–2900 B.C., a nearly continuous circle (henge) was dug into the chalk ground. A silted ditch was added around 3300–2140 B.C., as was the avenue down to the Avon River sometime from 2580–1890 B.C. The sandstone (sarsen) circle of evenly spaced trilithons, consisting of uprights (posts) and horizontal slabs (lintels), was erected during the early Bronze Age Wessex culture, between 2850 and 2200 B.C. (fig. 1-17). These immense stones were evidently dragged from Marlborough Downs some 20 miles away—a feat as awesome as raising them. But whether the inner bluestone circle and horseshoe, which date from several hundred years later (2480–1940 B.C.), were deposited by glaciers or carried by carts and rafts from the Preseli Mountains in Wales some 200 miles to the west is far from clear. During the final phase, 2030–1520 B.C., this arrangement was echoed in two similarly

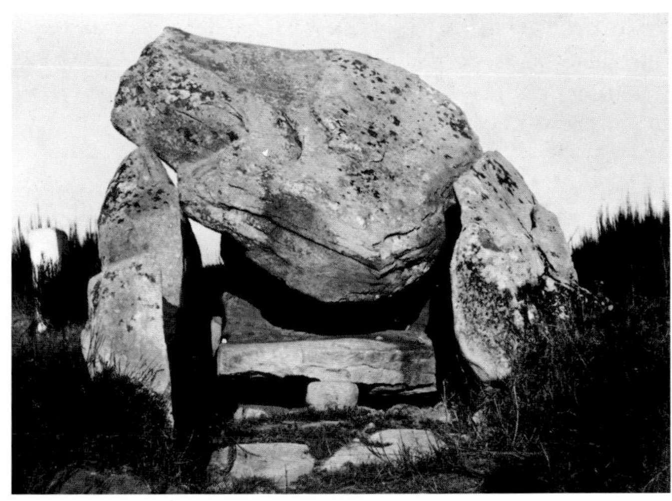

1-16. Dolmen, Carnac (Brittany), France. c. 1500 B.C.

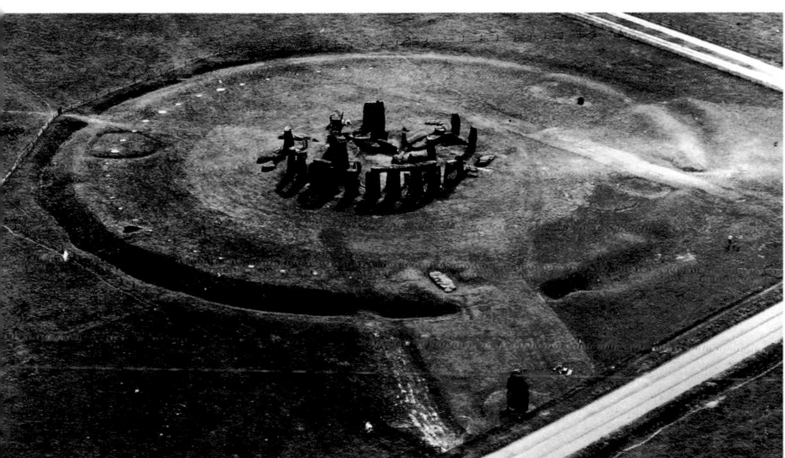

1-17. Stonehenge (aerial view), Salisbury Plain (Wiltshire), England. c. 2000 B.C. Diameter of circle 97' (29.6 m)

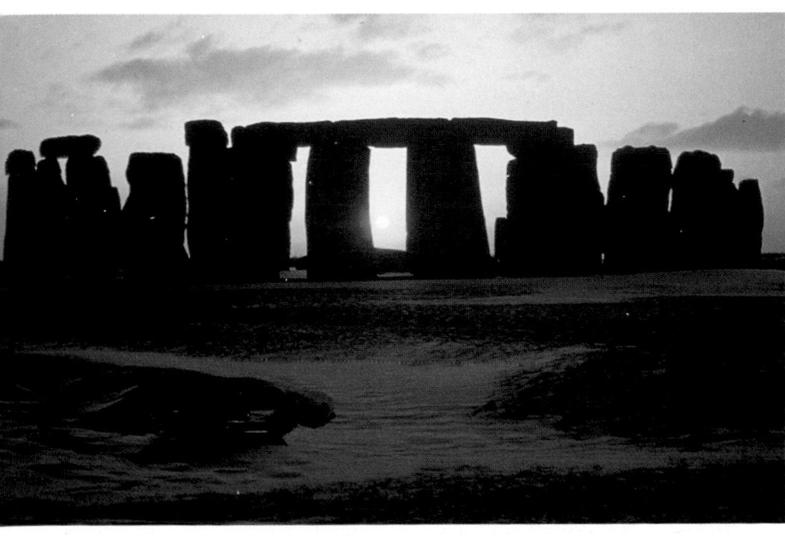

1-18. Stonehenge at sunset

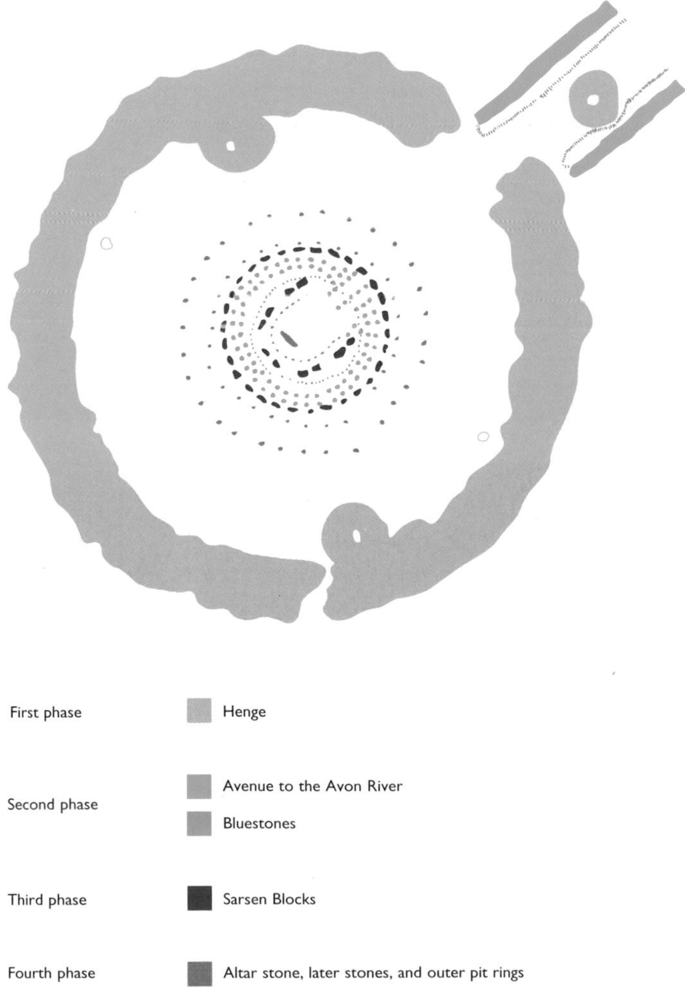

1-19. Diagram of original arrangement of stones at Stonehenge (after an original drawing by Richard Tobias)

marked circles and a smaller horseshoe that enclose an altarlike stone at the center.

The more important issue is why Stonehenge was built in the first place. The widely held belief that the so-called Heel Stone was positioned so that the sun would rise directly above it on the day of the summer solstice (when the sun is farthest from the equator) has long been known to be incorrect. It appears that Stonehenge was originally aligned with the major and minor northern moonrises. Only later did the structure become oriented toward the sun when the Heel Stone and fallen "Slaughter Stone," along with other stones, were rearranged with the axis of the causeway in the direction of the midsummer sunrise. As our illustration suggests (see fig. 1-18), Stonehenge probably served a sun-worshiping ritual that must have been related to a larger cosmology.

Each of these building phases was linked to broader changes during the Neolithic and Bronze Age. Burial mounds, called barrows, and henges as early as 3500 B.C. have been found in Scandinavia and northern Britain as part of the changeover to a settled agrarian way of life; their persistence until about 2000 B.C. testifies to a relatively stable Neolithic culture. By contrast, the people who created the Wessex culture probably crossed the English Channel from Brittany in northwest France, where megalithic horseshoes constructed along astronomical axes are far more common than in England. They brought with them Bronze Age technologies and ideas that must have seemed revolutionary to the local population they encountered, who initially put up a stiff resistance. At Stonehenge and elsewhere in southern England, these newcomers imposed their own traditions on established practices. In addition to erecting even larger cromlechs, they buried their leaders in barrows lined with boulders rather than timber, making, in effect, underground dolmens. Some of these tombs even have a rudimentary form of vaulting known as corbeling, which is also found in Mycenaean "beehive" tombs (see fig. 4-14) and Etruscan tumulus tombs (see page 150). Stonehenge was eventually abandoned around 1100 B.C. as part of another change that occurred during the late Bronze Age: the preference for cremation over burials for the dead.

By definition, menhirs and dolmens are monuments: not only are they large, but they commemorate the dead. Whether they and cromlechs should be termed architecture is likewise a matter of definition. We tend to think of architecture in terms of enclosed interiors, but we also have landscape architects who design gardens, parks, and playgrounds. And open-air theaters or sports stadiums are likewise thought of as architecture. To the ancient Greeks, who coined the term, "archi-tecture" meant something higher than "tecture" ("construction" or "building"), much as an archbishop ranks above a bishop. Architecture differed from practical, everyday building in scale, order, permanence, or purpose. A Greek would have viewed Carnac and Stonehenge as architecture, since those structures rearranged nature to serve as settings for human activities and to express shared beliefs. We, too, will be able to accept them as architecture once we understand that it is not necessary to enclose space in order to define it. If architecture is "the art of shaping space to human needs and aspirations," then Carnac and Stonehenge more than meet the test.

Neolithic America

The "earth art" of the prehistoric Indians of North America, the so-called Mound Builders, may be compared to the megalithic monuments of Europe in terms of the effort involved. The term is misleading since these mounds vary greatly in shape and purpose as well as in date, ranging from about 2000 B.C. to the time of the Europeans' arrival in the late fifteenth century. Of particular interest are the "effigy mounds" in the shape of animals, which presumably must have been the totems of the tribes that produced them. The most spectacular is the Great Serpent Mound (fig. 1-20), a snake some 1,400 feet long that slithers along the crest of a ridge by a small river in southern Ohio. The huge head, its center marked by a heap of stones that may once have been an altar, occupies the highest point. It appears that the natural formation of the terrain inspired this extraordinary work of landscape architecture, as mysterious and moving in its way as Stonehenge.

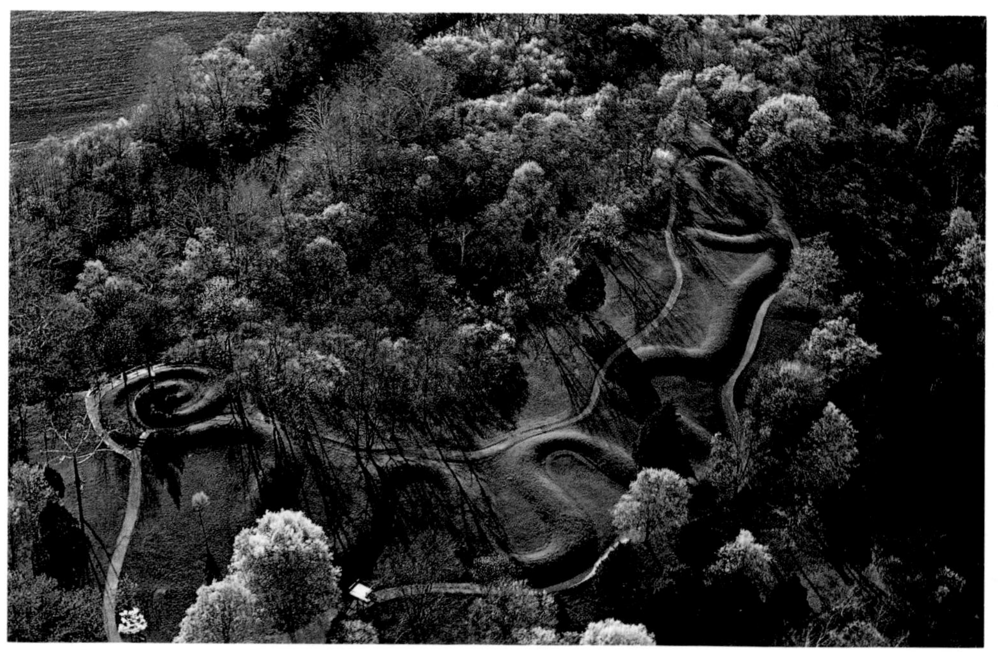

1-20. Great Serpent Mound, Adams County, Ohio. c. 1070 A.D. Length 1,400' (426.7 m)

© TONY LINCK, FORT LEE, NEW JERSEY

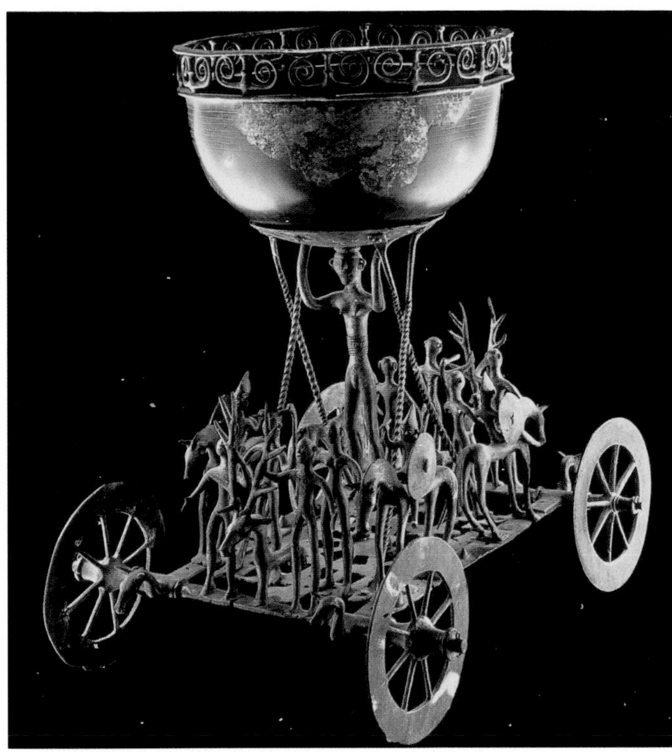

1-21. Cult Wagon, from Strettweg, Austria. 7th century B.C. Bronze, height 13⅛" (33.3 cm); length 17½" (44.5 cm). Steiermarkisches Landesmuseum Joanneum, Graz

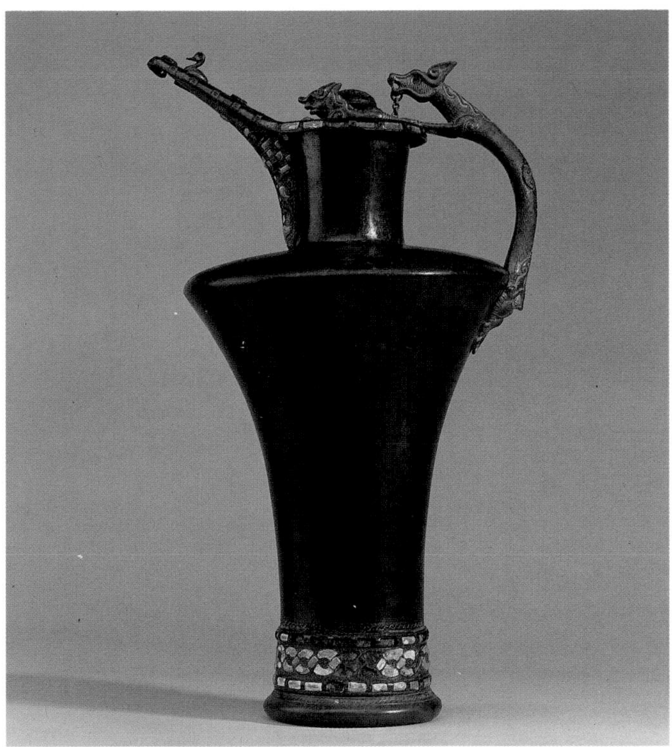

1-22. Flagon from Basse-Yutz, Lorraine. 5th century B.C. Bronze, coral, enamel. Height 15" (39.6 cm). The British Museum, London

Iron Age Europe

HALLSTATT CULTURE. The introduction of iron during the eighth century B.C. had little immediate impact on the way of life in central and northern Europe. More important was the growth of trade with Greece and Italy, which had begun to emerge into the light of history. An excellent example of the art that prevailed during the seventh century B.C. is a bronze cult wagon from Strettweg, Austria, not far from the burial ground at Hallstatt that gave its name to the culture of the early Iron Age in central Europe (fig. 1-21). The Hallstatt Geometric includes a curious mixture of styles. The nude warriors recall the stick figures in wood and bronze, as well as rock carving, found throughout the north. But the female deity with a large, shallow dish on her head is very close to early Geometric Greek bronzes. So is the cart itself, though it is of a type unique to Hallstatt culture. The influence of Western Greek colonies in Italy and from Etruria can also be seen in this and other Hallstatt bronzes. That influence is not surprising, given the growing commerce and the likely route over which the Bronze Age was carried. These sources do not, however, explain the meaning of the ritual. The scene has been described variously as a hunt, a sacrifice, or a celebration of the harvest, but there is no solid evidence to support any of these proposals. Whatever its purpose, the Strettweg cult wagon remains the most tantalizing evidence we have of the early Iron Age culture in Europe.

LA TÈNE CULTURE. Hallstatt culture was followed in the mid-fifth century B.C. by La Tène culture, named for the underwater site on Lake Neuchâtel in Switzerland where it was first unearthed. La Tène is synonymous with the art of the Celts. Hallstatt culture is sometimes identified with them as well, for the two occurred in adjacent areas, and eventually overlapped. However, it is best to treat Hallstatt as a precursor of La Tène. The Celts had settled in southwest Germany and eastern France (the area later known as Gaul by the Romans) during the second millennium B.C. They expanded across much of Europe and into Asia Minor, where they fought the Greeks (see page 143). Pressed by neighboring Germanic peoples, who had come from the Baltic region, they crossed the English Channel in the fourth century B.C. and colonized Britain and Ireland. At the beginning of the century, they invaded Italy and even conquered Rome. They were not fully put down until Julius Caesar defeated Vercingetorix in 46 B.C.

La Tène thus represents the Celts at the height of their culture, when they enjoyed considerable power and wealth from their far-flung trade. Like Hallstatt art, Celtic art is a mixture of elements. The best examples, such as one of a pair of fifth-century B.C. bronze flagons from Basse-Yutz in the Lorraine region of France (fig. 1-22), are very sophisticated indeed. Our flagon adapts an Etruscan shape that had previously been imported as a luxury item and adds lid and spout decorated with Hallstatt motifs. The animal-style handle, while similar to Scythian and Persian motifs (see pages 75–76), was probably derived from the Greeks, who became the leading gold- and silversmiths in the sixth century B.C. The intricate inlay of red enamel and coral, imported from the Mediterranean, is characteristic of Celtic art in its abstract patterns. Yet we have no sense of eclecticism, thanks to the masterful integration of elements and superb workmanship. It is ironic that La Tène culture flourished as a result of contact with the civilizations of the Near East and Mediterranean, while northern Europe remained "prehistoric" until a few hundred years before the birth of Jesus.

CHAPTER TWO

Egyptian Art

Egyptian civilization has long been considered the most rigid and conservative ever. Plato said that Egyptian art had not changed in 10,000 years. Perhaps "enduring" and "continuous" are better terms for it, although at first glance all Egyptian art between 3000 and 500 B.C. does have a certain sameness. The basic pattern of Egyptian institutions, beliefs, and artistic ideas was formed during the first few centuries of that vast span of time and was maintained until the end. Over the years, however, this pattern went through ever more severe crises that threatened its ability to survive. Had it been as inflexible as supposed, Egyptian civilization would have collapsed long before it finally did. Egyptian art alternates between conservatism and innovation but is rarely static. Moreover, some of its great achievements had a decisive influence on Greek and Roman art; thus we still feel ourselves linked to the Egypt of 5,000 years ago by a continuous tradition.

THE OLD KINGDOM

DYNASTIES. The history of Egypt is divided into dynasties of rulers in agreement with ancient Egyptian practice. It begins with the First Dynasty shortly after 3000 B.C. (The dates of the earliest rulers are difficult to translate exactly into our calendar; the dating system used in this book is that of French Egyptologist Nicolas Grimal.) The transition from prehistory to the First Dynasty is called the predynastic period. The next major period, known as the Old Kingdom, lasted from about 2700 B.C. until about 2190 B.C., the end of the Sixth Dynasty. This method of counting historic time by dynasties conveys both the strong Egyptian sense of continuity and the prime importance of the pharaoh (king), who was not only the supreme ruler but also a god. The pharaoh transcended all people, for his kingship was not a privilege derived from a superhuman source but was absolute, divine. This belief was the key feature of Egyptian civilization and largely shaped the character of Egyptian art. We do not know exactly the steps by which the early pharaohs established their claim to divinity, but we know their historic achievements. They molded the Nile Valley from the first cataract at Assuan to the Nile Delta into a single state and increased its fertility by regulating the river waters through dams and canals.

TOMBS AND RELIGION. Of these vast public works nothing remains today, and very little has survived of ancient Egyptian palaces and cities. Our knowledge of Egyptian civilization rests almost entirely on tombs and their contents. This is no accident, since these tombs were built to last forever. Yet we must not make the mistake of concluding that the Egyptians viewed life on this earth mainly as a road to the grave. Their cult of the dead is a link with the Neolithic past, but the meaning they gave it was new. The dark fear of the spirits of the dead that dominates primitive ancestor cults seems to be absent. Instead, the Egyptian attitude was that people must provide for their own happy afterlives. They equipped their tombs as replicas of their daily environment for their spirits (*kas*) to enjoy in order to make sure that the *ka* had both a home and a body to dwell in (their own mummified corpse or, if that should be destroyed, a statue of themselves).

There is a blurring of the line between life and death in this practice, which was perhaps the main impulse behind these mock households. People who knew that after death their *kas* would enjoy the same pleasures they did, and who had provided these pleasures in advance, could look forward to active and happy lives without being haunted by fear of the great unknown. In a sense, the Egyptian tomb was an investment in peace of mind. Such, at least, is the impression one gains of Old Kingdom tombs. Later, this concept of death was altered by a tendency to subdivide the spirit or soul into two or more separate identities and by the introduction of the weighing of souls [see Primary Sources, no. 1, page 192]. Only then do we find expressions of the fear of death.

Egyptian Style and the Palette of King Narmer

During the predynastic period, Egypt was still learning the use of bronze tools. The country, we may assume, was governed by local rulers who barely outranked tribal chiefs. From these territories emerged two rival kingdoms: Upper Egypt, to the south, and Lower Egypt near the Nile Delta, which empties into the Mediterranean. Judging from pottery made in the fourth millennium B.C.,

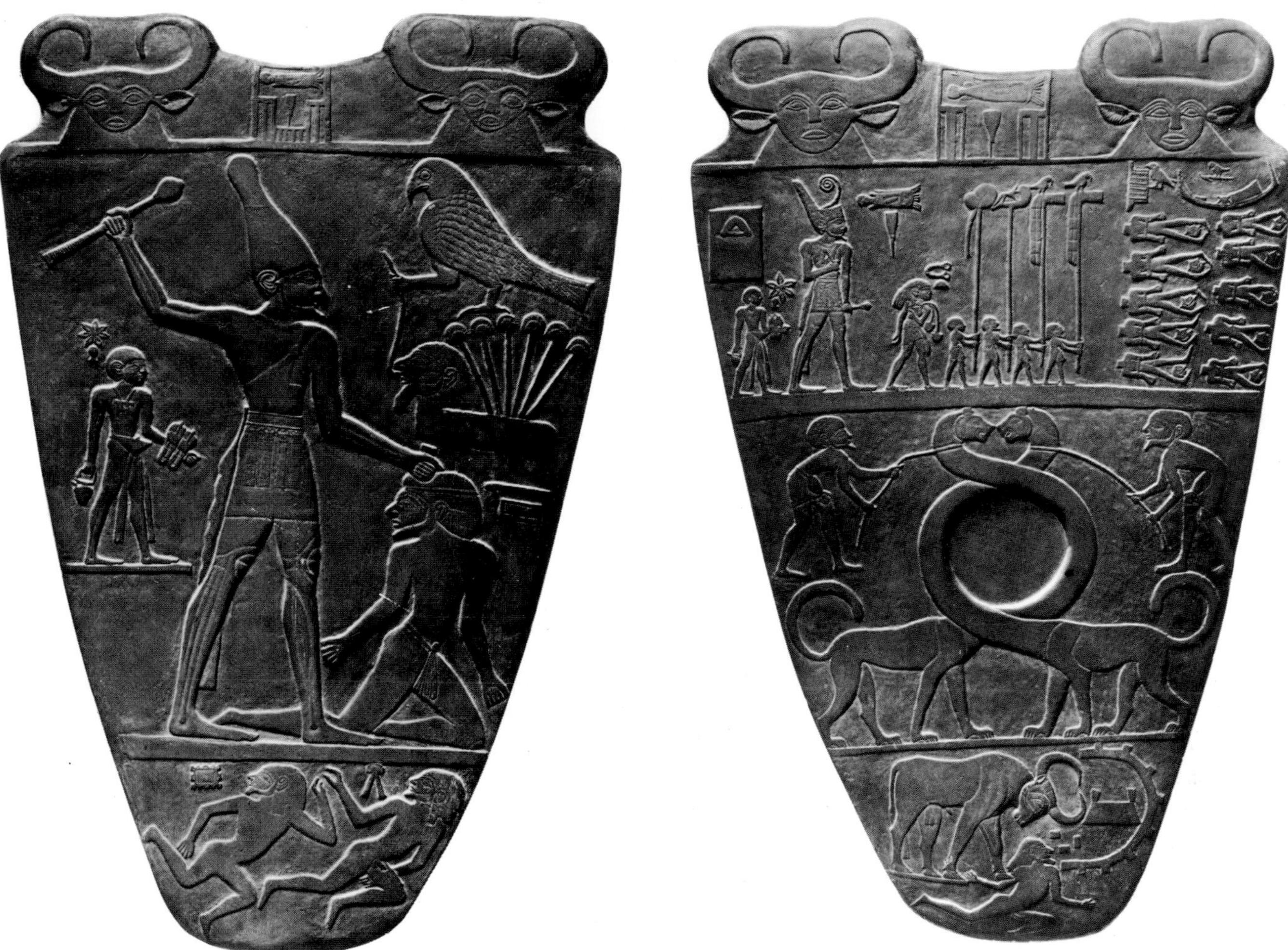

2-1, 2-2. *Palette of King Narmer* (both sides), from Hierakonpolis. c. 3150–3125 B.C. Slate, height 25" (63.5 cm). Egyptian Museum, Cairo

Upper Egypt, with its capital at Naqada near Thebes, was more advanced at first. The struggle between them ended when the Upper Egyptian kings conquered Lower Egypt and combined the two realms.

One of these kings was Narmer, who appears on the ceremonial slate palette in figures 2-1 and 2-2. This palette probably celebrates a victory over Lower Egypt, though the precise meaning is a matter of dispute. (Note the different crowns worn by the king.) In many ways, the Narmer palette can be claimed as the oldest historic work of art we know. Not only is it the earliest surviving image of a historic personage identified by name but its character is no longer primitive. In fact, it already shows most of the features of late Egyptian art. The Narmer palette evidently celebrates a victory over Lower Egypt, but its meaning is largely ceremonial. Egypt had already been unified under earlier kings, so that the traditional identification of Narmer with King Menes, the founder of the First Dynasty, is unlikely.

Let us first "read" the scenes on both sides. (The fact that we are able to do so is another sign that we have left prehistoric art behind.) The meaning of these reliefs is made explicit by hieroglyphic labels. (*Hieroglyph* means sacred pictorial writing.) This system of writing was of very recent origin. The earliest examples we know of, which were found in the tomb of King Scorpion some 300 miles south of Cairo, date from about 3300–3200 B.C. The meaning is also made clear by symbols that convey precise messages and—most important—through the rational orderliness of the design. In figure 2-1 Narmer, seen wearing the white crown of Upper Egypt, has seized a fallen enemy by the hair and is about to slay him with his mace. Two more defeated enemies are placed in the bottom compartment. (The small rectangular shape next to the man on the left stands for a fortified town or citadel.) Facing the king in the upper right we see a complex bit of picture writing: a falcon standing above a clump of papyrus plants holds a tether attached to a human head that "grows" from the same soil as the plants. This image repeats the main scene on a symbolic level. The head and papyrus plant stand for Lower Egypt, while the victorious falcon is Horus, the local god of Upper Egypt. Horus and Narmer are the same; a god triumphs over human foes. Hence, Narmer's gesture must not be seen as representing a real fight. The enemy is helpless from the start, and the slaying is a ritual rather than a physical act. We know it is ritual because Narmer has taken off his sandals (the court official behind him carries them in his right hand), a sign that he is standing on holy ground. (The same notion recurs in the Old Testament, apparently as the result of Egyptian influence, when the Lord commands Moses to remove his shoes before he appears to him in the burning bush.)

On the other side of the palette (see fig. 2-2), the king again appears barefoot, wearing now the red crown of Lower Egypt and followed by the sandal carrier. He walks behind a group of standard-bearers to inspect the beheaded bodies of prisoners. The bottom compartment depicts the victory on a symbolic level. The pharaoh is represented as a strong bull trampling an enemy and knocking down a citadel. (A bull's tail hanging down from his belt is shown in both images of Narmer; it became part of the pharaoh's ceremonial garb for the next 3,000 years.) Only the center section does not convey a clear meaning. The intertwined snake-necked lions and their two attendants have no identifying features. However, similar beasts are found in "protoliterate" Mesopotamian cylinder seals of about 3300–3200 B.C., an art form that was soon adopted in Egypt as well (see Chapter Three). There they combine the lioness attribute of the mother goddess with the copulating snakes that signify the god of fecundity. They thus form a fertility symbol that unites the female and male principles in nature. Perhaps they refer to the union of Upper and Lower Egypt. Whatever their meaning on Narmer's palette, their presence is evidence of contact between the two civilizations at an early and critical stage of their development. In any case, they do not reappear in Egyptian art.

THE LOGIC OF EGYPTIAN STYLE. The Narmer palette has a clear inner logic that is readily apparent. What strikes us first is its strong sense of order. The surface is divided into horizontal bands, or registers. Each figure stands on a line, or strip, denoting the ground. The only exceptions are the attendants of the long-necked beasts, whose role seems mainly ornamental; the hieroglyphic signs, which belong to a different level of reality; and the dead enemies, which are seen from above, instead of from the side. The modern way of depicting a scene as it would appear to a single viewer at a single moment is as alien to Egyptian artists as it was to those of the Neolithic era. They strive for clarity, not illusion, and therefore pick the most characteristic view in each case.

But they impose a strict rule on themselves. When the angle of vision changes, it must be by 90 degrees, as if sighting along the edges of a cube. Hence, only three views are possible: full face, strict profile, and vertically from above. Any other position is embarrassing. (Note the rubberlike figures of the fallen enemies at the bottom of figure 2-1.) Moreover, the standing human figure does not have a single main profile. Instead, it has two different profiles, which must be combined for the sake of clarity. The method of doing this (which was to survive unchanged for 2,500 years) is shown in the large figure of Narmer in figure 2-1: eye and shoulders in frontal view, head and legs in profile. This formula was worked out so as to show the pharaoh (and all those who move in the aura of his divinity) in the most complete way possible. And since the scenes depict solemn and, as it were, timeless rituals, our artist did not have to concern himself with the fact that this method of depicting the human body made movement or action almost impossible. In fact, the frozen quality of the image seems well suited to the divine nature of the pharaoh. Mere mortals act; he simply is.

Whenever any movement requiring some sort of effort or strain must be depicted, the Egyptian artist abandons the combined view, for such activities are always performed by underlings whose dignity does not have to be preserved. Thus in our palette the two animal trainers and the four men carrying standards are shown in strict profile, except for the eyes. The composite view seems to have been created specifically by artists working for the royal court to convey the majesty of the divine king. It never lost its sacred flavor, even in later times, when it had to serve other purposes as well.

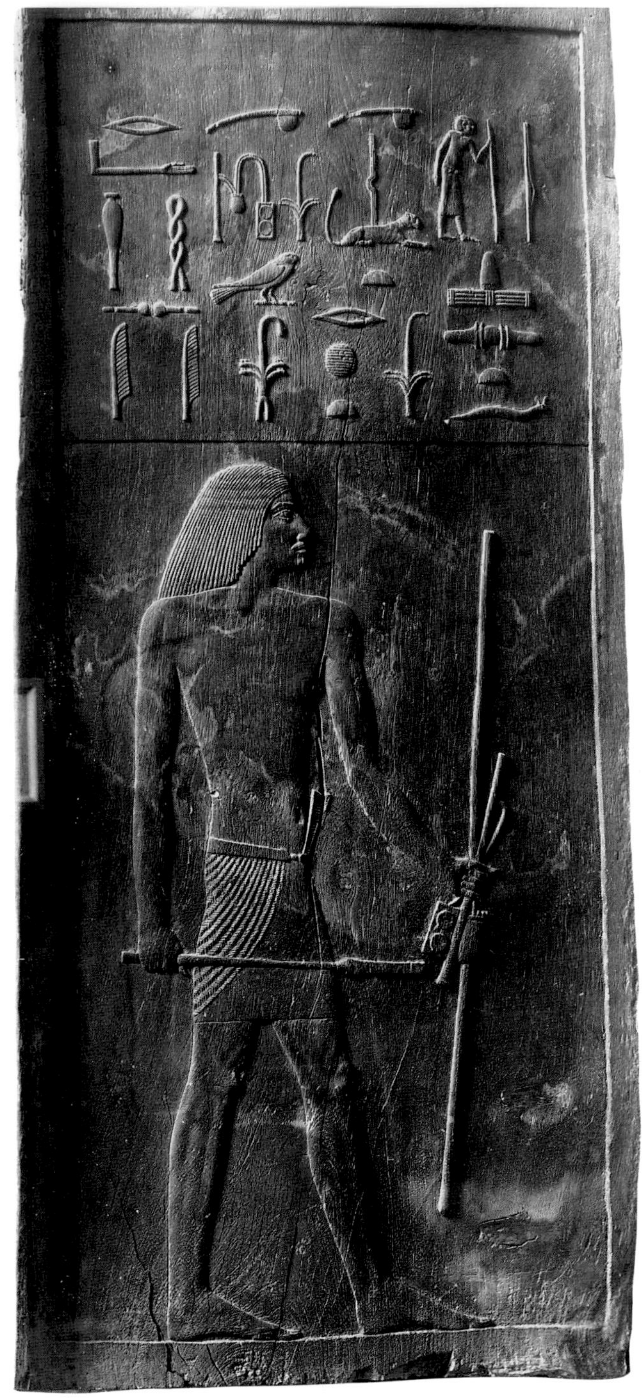

2-3. *Portrait Panel of Hesy-ra,* from Saqqara. c. 2660 B.C. Wood, height 45" (114.3 cm). Egyptian Museum, Cairo

Third Dynasty

The beauty of the style we saw in the Narmer palette did not develop fully until about five centuries later, during the Third Dynasty, and especially under the reign of King Djoser, its greatest figure. From the Tomb of Hesy-ra, one of Djoser's high officials, comes the masterly wooden relief (fig. 2-3) showing the deceased with the emblems of his rank, including writing materials, since the position of scribe was highly honored. The view of the figure matches that of Narmer on the palette, but the proportions are far more balanced and harmonious. The carving of the physical details shows keen observation as well as great delicacy of touch.

TOMBS. When we speak of the Egyptians' attitude toward death and afterlife, we do not mean that of the average Egyptian. We are referring to the outlook of the small aristocratic caste clustered around the royal court. The tombs of this class of high officials, who were often relatives of the royal family, are usually found near the pharaohs'. Their shape and contents reflect, or are related to, the tombs of the kings. We still have a great deal to learn about the origin and significance of Egyptian tombs, but the concept of afterlife we find in the so-called private tombs initially seems to have applied only to the privileged few because of their association with the pharaohs. Ordinary mortals could only look forward to a shadowy afterlife in the underground realm of the dead. As early as the Fourth Dynasty, wealthy individuals built tombs in imitation of royal examples, complete with paintings and reliefs, cut into the bedrock near Giza.

MASTABAS. The standard form of these tombs was the mastaba (the word comes from the Arabic for "bench" because of their shape), a squarish mound faced with brick or stone. The mastaba was built above the burial chamber, which was deep underground and linked to the mound by a shaft (figs. 2-4 and 2-5). Inside is a chapel for offerings to the *ka* and a secret cubicle for the statue of the deceased. Royal mastabas became quite large as early as the First Dynasty, and their exteriors sometimes resembled that of a royal palace. During the Third Dynasty, they developed into step pyramids. The best known (and probably the first) is that of King Djoser (fig. 2-6), which was built over a traditional mastaba in a series of expanding layers (see figs. 2-5 and 2-7). The pyramid itself, unlike later ones, is a solid structure with underground burial chambers. Its function was not so much funereal as memorial and religious. It declares the pharaoh's supreme power and divine status. The height and shape suggest Mesopotamian ziggurats (see fig. 3-4). The step pyramid, too, was perhaps intended to bridge the gap with the heavens by serving as the "stairway" and "jumping-off" point for Djoser to ascend to the heavens and fulfill his cosmological role as a god.

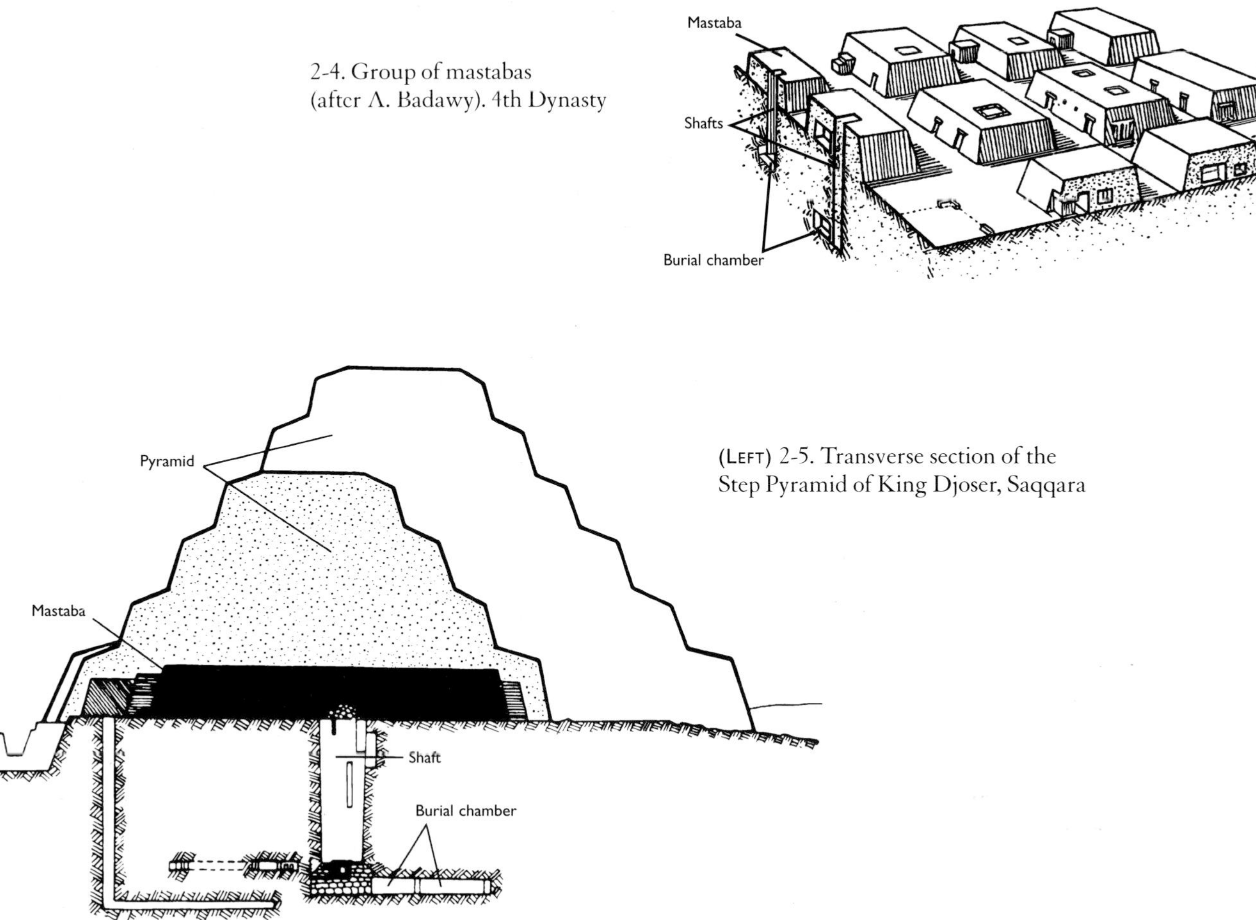

2-4. Group of mastabas (after A. Badawy). 4th Dynasty

(LEFT) 2-5. Transverse section of the Step Pyramid of King Djoser, Saqqara

2-6. Imhotep. Step Pyramid of King Djoser, Saqqara. 3rd Dynasty. c. 2681–2662 B.C.

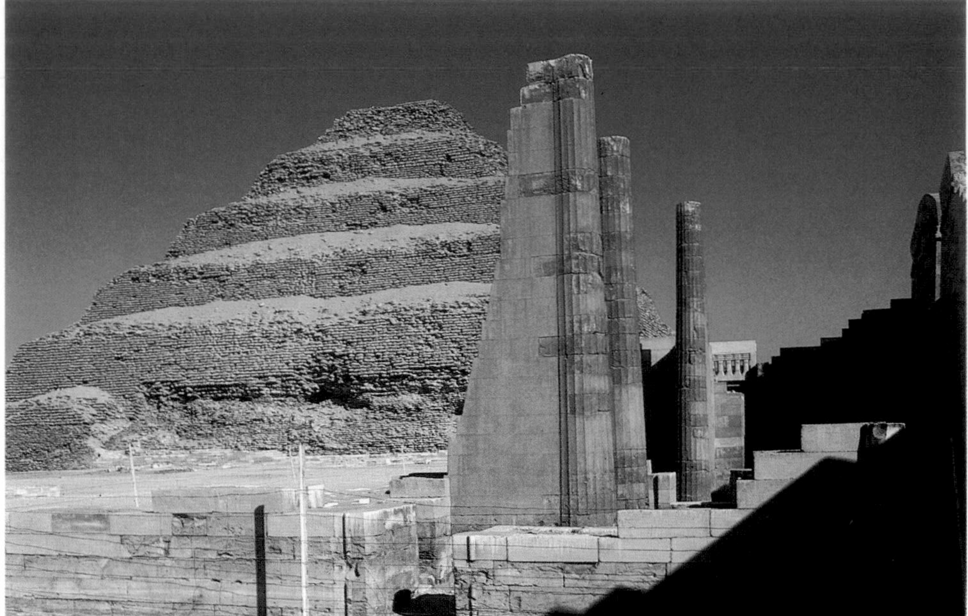

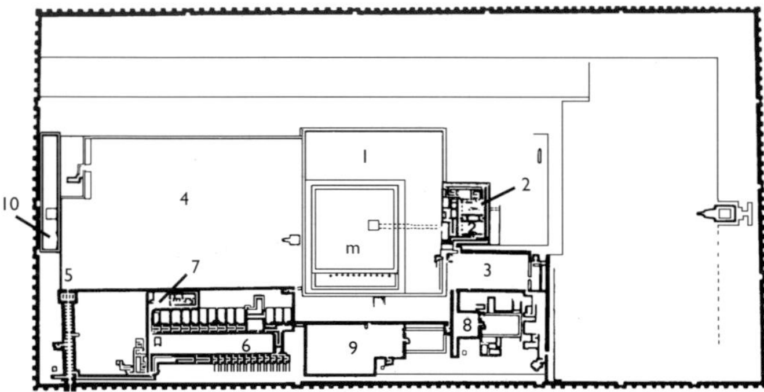

2-7. Plan of the funerary district of King Djoser, Saqqara (M. Hirmer after J. P. Lauer)

1) pyramid (m=mastaba); 2) funerary temple; 3, 4, 6) courts; 5) entrance hall; 7) small temple; 8) court of North Palace; 9) court of South Palace; 10) southern tomb

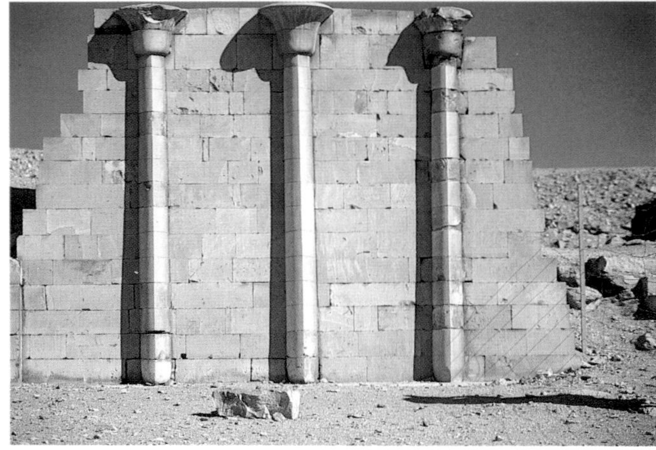

2-8. Papyrus-shaped half-columns, North Palace, funerary district of King Djoser, Saqqara

FUNERARY DISTRICTS. The modern imagination, enamored of "the silence of the pyramids," is apt to create a false picture of these monuments. They were not isolated structures in the middle of the desert but were part of vast funerary districts, with temples and other buildings where religious rites were held during the pharaoh's lifetime as well as after. The earliest is the funerary district around the Step Pyramid of Djoser (fig. 2-7). It is also the first built entirely of stone, which had been used sparingly before that time. Enough of it has survived for us to see why its creator, Imhotep, came to be revered as the founder of Egyptian culture. He was both vizier (overseer) to the king and high priest of Ra. Imhotep is the first architect whose name has been recorded in history, and deservedly so. He is also the first in a long line of Egyptian architects who are known to us. His achievement is impressive not only for its scale but also for its unity, which embodies the concept of the pharaoh to perfection. The funerary district proclaims Djoser king of both Upper and Lower Egypt. There are two of everything, including a north and a south palace. Also, for the first time, there is a second tomb (no. 10 on the plan in fig. 2-7), which traditionally had been located at Abydos halfway up the Nile. The large court (no. 4) to the south of the pyramid was used for ritual purposes during the pharaoh's coronation and was intended for its reenactment as part of the Sed festival to celebrate his jubilee 30 years later. (Djoser's reign lasted only 19 years.) Imhotep must have had remarkable intellect as well as outstanding ability—he was renowned as an astronomer and was later deified as a healer. In this regard he set a precedent for the great architects who followed in his footsteps. Even today architects address the important ideas and issues of their time.

COLUMNS. Egyptian architecture had begun with structures made of mud bricks, wood, reeds, and other light materials. Imhotep used cut-stone masonry, but his architectural forms reflected shapes or devices developed for less durable materials.

Thus we find several kinds of columns—always engaged (set into the wall) rather than freestanding—that echo the bundles of reeds or wooden supports that used to be set into mud-brick walls in order to strengthen them. But the very fact that they no longer had their original function made it possible for Imhotep and his fellow architects to make them serve a new, expressive purpose. The idea that architectural forms can express anything may seem hard to grasp at first. We tend to assume that unless these forms have a clear-cut structural role, such as supporting or enclosing, they are mere decoration. But the slender, tapered, fluted columns in figure 2-6, or the papyrus-shaped half-columns in figure 2-8 do not simply decorate the walls to which they are attached. They interpret them and give them life. Their proportions, the feeling of strength and resilience they convey, their spacing, the degree to which they project—all share in this task.

We shall learn more about their expressive role when we discuss Greek architecture, which took over the Egyptian stone column and developed it further. For the time being, let us note another factor that may enter into their design: announcing the symbolic purpose of the building. The papyrus-shaped half-columns in figure 2-8 are linked with Lower Egypt (compare the papyrus plants in fig. 2-1); hence they appear in the North Palace of Djoser's funerary district. The South Palace has columns of a different shape, which is linked with Upper Egypt.

Fourth Dynasty

THE PYRAMIDS OF GIZA. Djoser's successors soon adapted the step pyramid to the smooth-sided shape that is familiar to us, though the process took several generations. The first to do so was Sneferu, the founder of the Fourth Dynasty. He built three pyramids, of which the most important is the so-called "Red" or "Bent" Pyramid at Dahshur, where he was probably buried. (The two earlier step pyramids were later remodeled.) The development of the pyramid reaches its climax during the Fourth Dynasty in the three great pyramids at Giza (figs. 2-9 and 2-10), the earliest and largest of which was built by Sneferu's son, Khufu. They originally had an outer casing of carefully dressed stone, which has disappeared except near the top of the Pyramid of Khafre. The top of each was also covered with a thin layer of gold. The pyramid evidently was identified with the pharaoh's "father," the sun-god Ra, and perhaps served as the final resting place of the sun. The three differ slightly from each other in scale, as well as in some details, but the basic features are shown in the section of Khufu's pyramid (fig. 2-11). The burial chamber is near the center of the structure rather than below ground, as in the Step Pyramid of Djoser. This placement was a vain attempt to safeguard the chamber from robbers.

According to a recent theory, the three pyramids are arranged in the same formation as the stars in the constellation Orion, which was identified with the god Osiris. The mythical founder of Egypt, Osiris was associated first with the Nile and later with the underworld as the god of fertility, death, and resurrection. In ancient tradition, he was murdered and dismembered by his brother Seth, who sealed him in a casket that was cast into the Nile. Seth then scattered his remains after the casket was retrieved by Osiris' consort, Isis. She eventually recovered his parts and reassembled them into the first mummy, from which she conceived her son, Horus. Horus avenged his father's death by besting Seth in a series of contests lasting 80 years. As a result, Osiris became lord of the underworld, Horus the ruler of the living, and Seth the god of chaos and evil who governed the deserts.

One of the so-called "air shafts" in the king's chamber of the

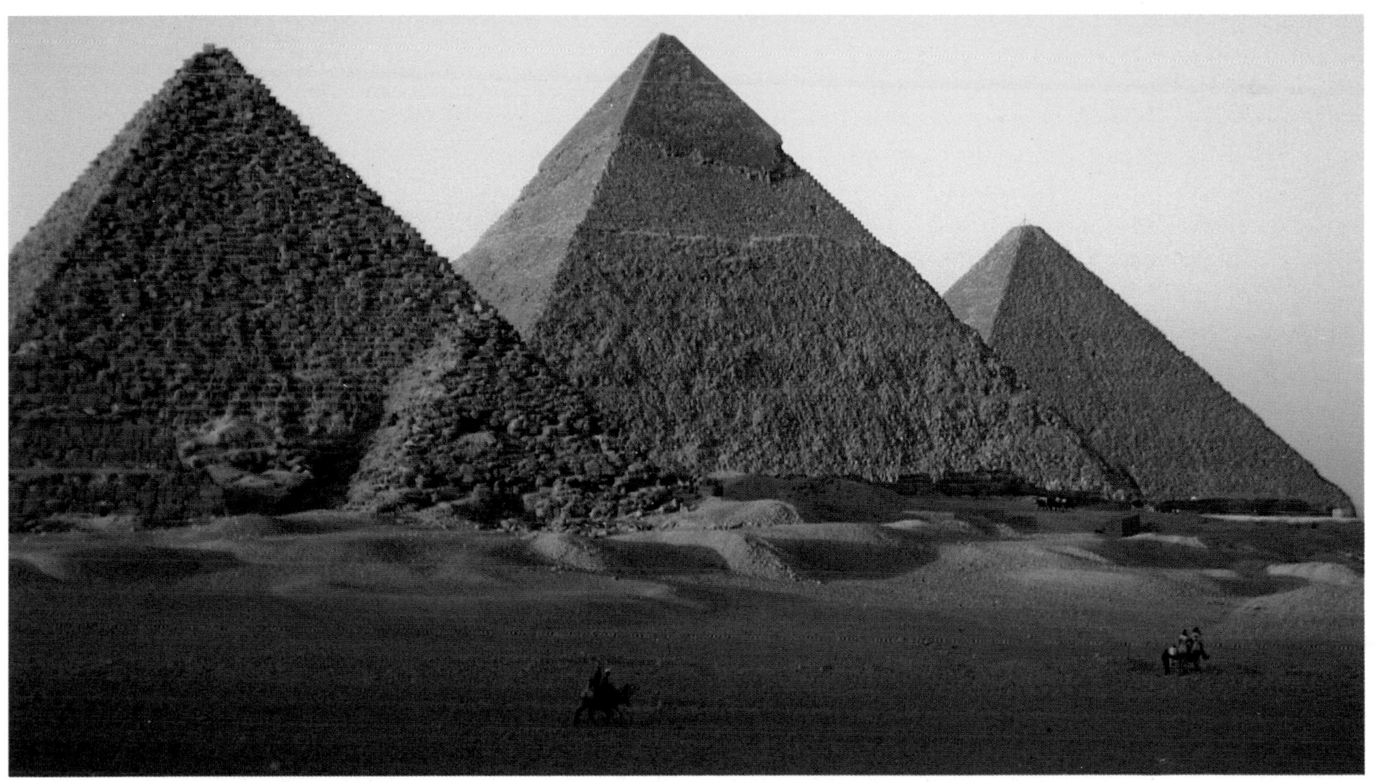

2-9. The Pyramids of Menkaure (c. 2533–2515 B.C.), Khafre (c. 2570–2544 B.C.), and Khufu (c. 2601–2528 B.C.), Giza

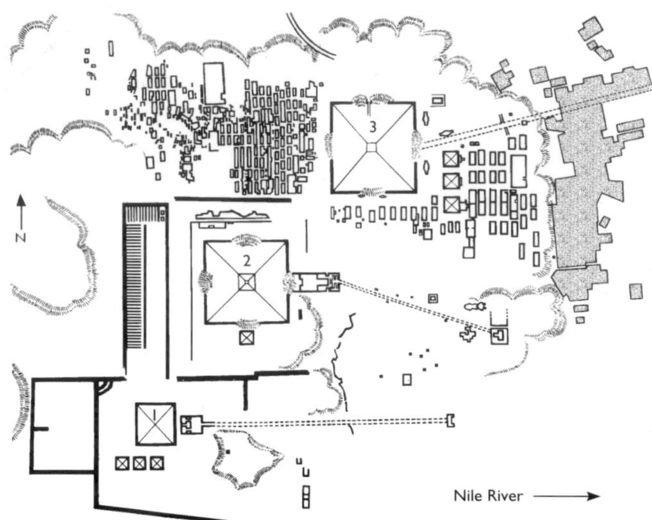

2-10. Plan of the pyramids at Giza: 1) Menkaure; 2) Khafre; 3) Khufu

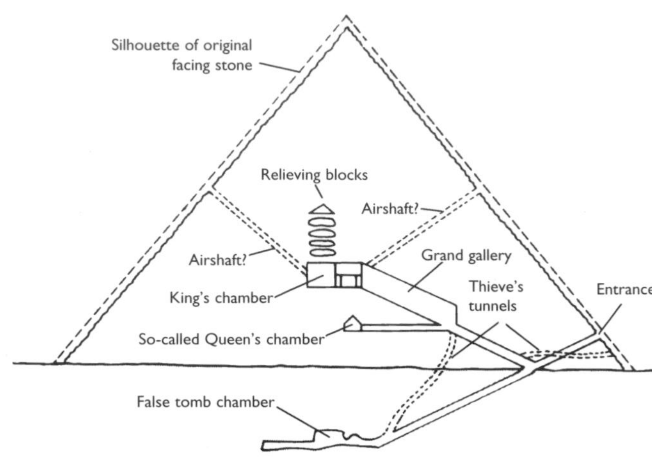

2-11. North–south section of Pyramid of Khufu (after L. Borchardt)

Pyramid of Khufu pointed to the polar stars in the north, which are always visible; in ancient times the other lined up with Orion when it was visible in the southern sky after an absence of some two months. The shaft thus served as a kind of "escape hatch" that allowed the pharaoh to take his place as a star in the cosmos. Another hidden shaft in the queen's chamber was aligned with the star of Isis (Sirius). It seems to have been used in the ritual of fertilization and rebirth described in the Egyptian Book of the Dead. The proposal, though controversial, is tantalizing, for it helps to explain many puzzling features of the pyramids in light of The Pyramid Texts of the two dynasties that followed. [See Primary Sources, no. 1, page 192.]

Clustered about the three great pyramids are several smaller ones and a large number of mastabas for members of the royal family and high officials. The unified funerary district of Djoser has given way to a simpler arrangement. Adjoining each of the great pyramids to the east is a mortuary temple, where the pharaoh's body was brought for embalming and last rites. From there a causeway leads to a second temple at a lower level, in the Nile Valley, about a third of a mile away. This arrangement represents the final step in the evolution of kingship in Egypt. It links the pharaoh to the eternal cosmic order by connecting him, in both physical and ritual terms, to the Nile River, whose annual cycles give life and dictate its rhythm in Egypt to this very day.

The pyramids of Giza mark the high point of pharaonic power. After the end of the Fourth Dynasty, less than two centuries later, pyramids on such a scale were never attempted again in the Old Kingdom, although more modest ones continued to be built. The world has always marveled at the sheer size of the great pyramids as well as at the technical accomplishment they represent. To design and build them required both considerable skill and a grasp of geometry. Egyptian mathematics seems to have been based on practical problem-solving rather than abstract numbers. Despite this limitation, which precluded the development of formulas that underlie higher mathematics, it was possible to calculate the volume of a pyramid, for example, by using a complex sequence of steps to arrive at the correct answer. The ingenious methods used to construct the pyramids are even more remarkable given the simple tools and measuring devices. Much of the work was done with stone tools, such as chisels and axes, though metal ones were also used.

The pyramids have come to be seen as symbols of slave labor, with thousands of men forced by cruel masters to work at their construction. Such a picture may not be entirely just. Records show that much of the labor was paid for, and that shelter, clothing, and food (part of it in mead, a form of beer) were often furnished. It may be closer to the truth to view these monuments as vast public works that provided a livelihood for a good part of the population. At the same time, criminals, prisoners of war, and others were forced to work on the pyramids. Even under the best conditions the labor was hard and dangerous.

THE GREAT SPHINX. Next to the valley temple of the Pyramid of Khafre stands the Great Sphinx, which was carved from the live rock (fig. 2-12). (Sphinx is an ancient Greek word for "strangler"; it was probably derived from the Egyptian *shesep ankh,* meaning "living image.") It is an even more impressive symbol of divine kingship than the pyramids themselves. The royal head rising from the body of the lion reaches a height of 65 feet. Damage inflicted during Islamic times has obscured the details of the face, and parts of the topmost section of the head are missing. Despite its location the Great Sphinx bears, in all probability, the features not of Khafre but of Khufu. The statue can be regarded as a colossal guardian figure in the guise of the lion-god Ruty. (Lions became associated with the pharaoh, perhaps through hunting, as early as the predynastic period, when they were still plentiful. The sphinx in its original form was a griffin and destroyer of the enemy.) Its awesome majesty is such that the Great Sphinx could also be considered an image of the sun-god a thousand years later, when the lion became the personification of Ra (see page 56). It acquired this connection through its nearness to the temple of the solar deity Harmakhis, which lies just before it.

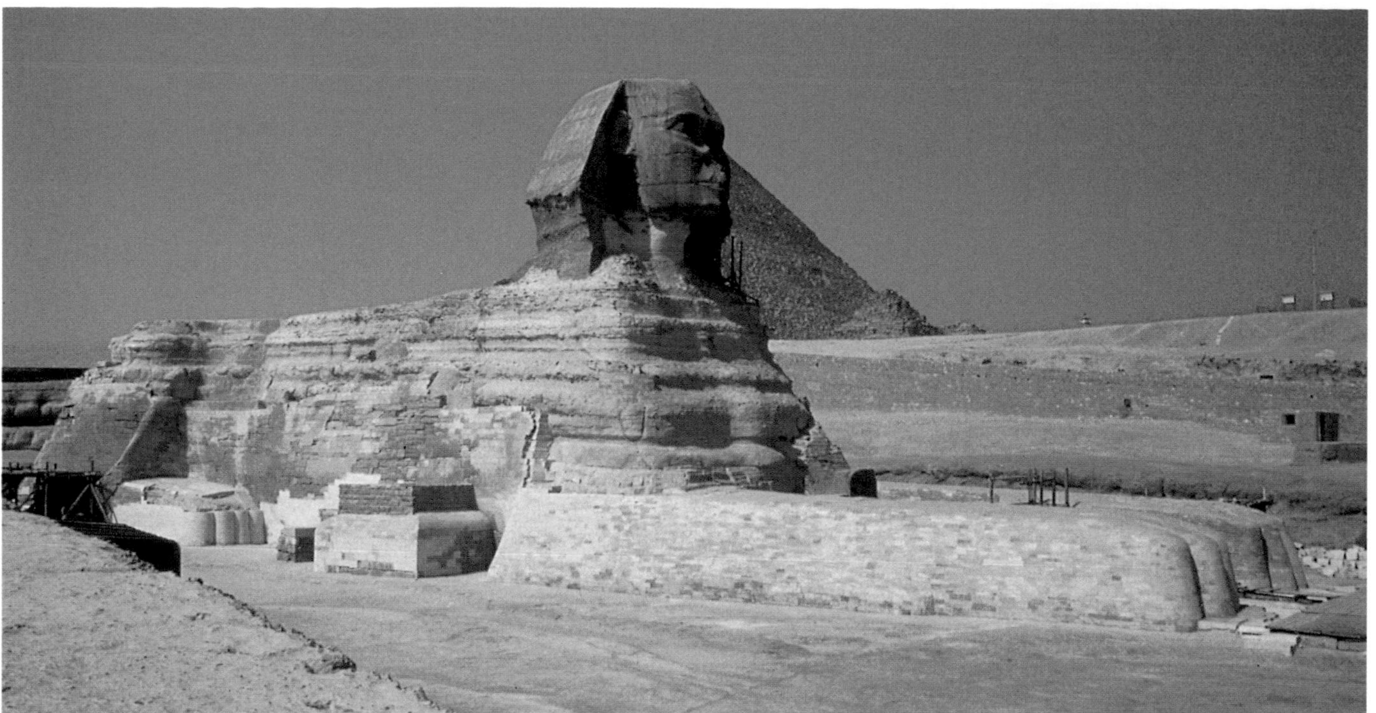

2-12. The Great Sphinx, Giza. c. 2570–2544 B.C. Sandstone, height 65' (19.8 m)

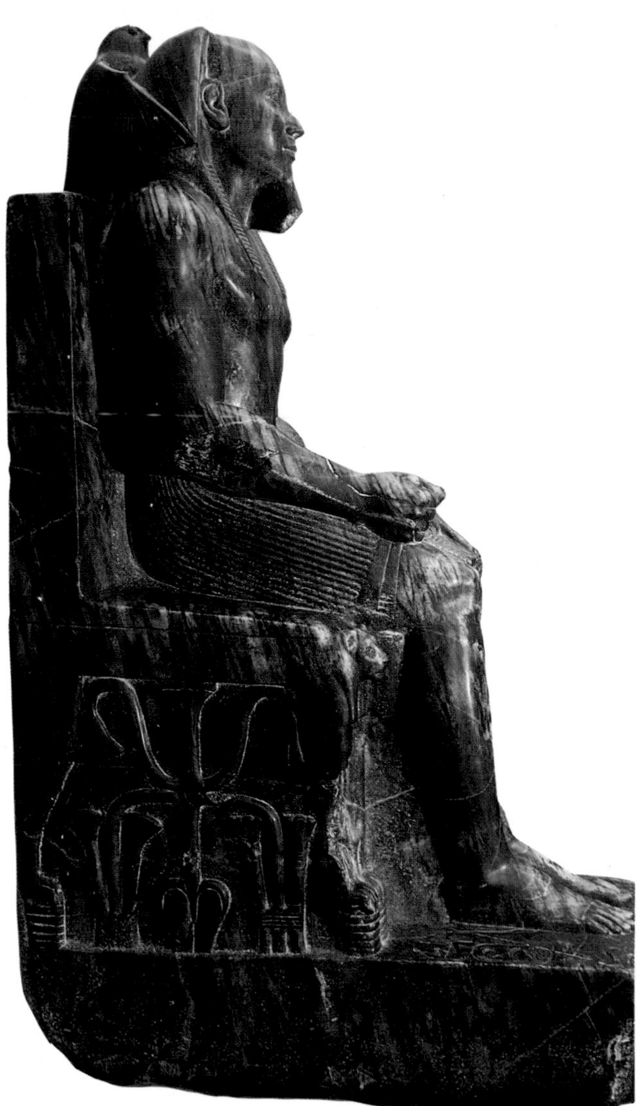

2-13. *Khafre,* from Giza. c. 2500 B.C. Diorite, height 66" (167.7 cm). Egyptian Museum, Cairo

PORTRAITURE. Apart from great works of architecture, the chief glories of Egyptian art are the portrait statues found in funerary temples and tombs. One of the finest is of Khafre, which came from the valley temple of his pyramid (fig. 2-13). Carved of diorite, an extremely hard stone, it shows the king enthroned, with the falcon of the god Horus enfolding the back of the head with its wings. (The pharaoh was often equated with Horus as the son of Osiris and Isis; the association, in different form, is also seen in the Narmer palette; see fig. 2-1.)

Here the "cubic" view of the human form appears in full force. After marking the faces of the block with a grid, the sculptor drew the front, top, and side views of the statue, then worked inward until these views met. This approach encouraged the development of the systematic proportions used in representing the pharaoh. In fact, the canon of forms can be readily deduced, so standardized did it become, though it varied somewhat over time. The grid system and carving techniques used in Egyptian sculpture were not very different from those of the pyramids at Giza. The result is a figure almost overwhelming in its firmness and immobility. Truly it is a fitting vessel for the spirit! The body, at once powerful yet idealized, is completely impersonal. Only the face suggests some individual traits, as will be seen if we compare it with that of Menkaure (fig. 2-14), Khafre's successor and the builder of the third and smallest pyramid at Giza.

Menkaure and his queen, Khamerernebty, are standing. Both have the left foot forward, yet there is no hint of forward movement. These are idealized portraits; a similar but much smaller group, showing Menkaure between two goddesses, hardly differs in appearance. Since the figures are about the same height, they allow us to compare male and female beauty as interpreted by one of the finest Old Kingdom sculptors. The artist knew not only how to contrast the structure of the two bodies but also how to emphasize the soft, swelling forms of the queen through her close-fitting gown.

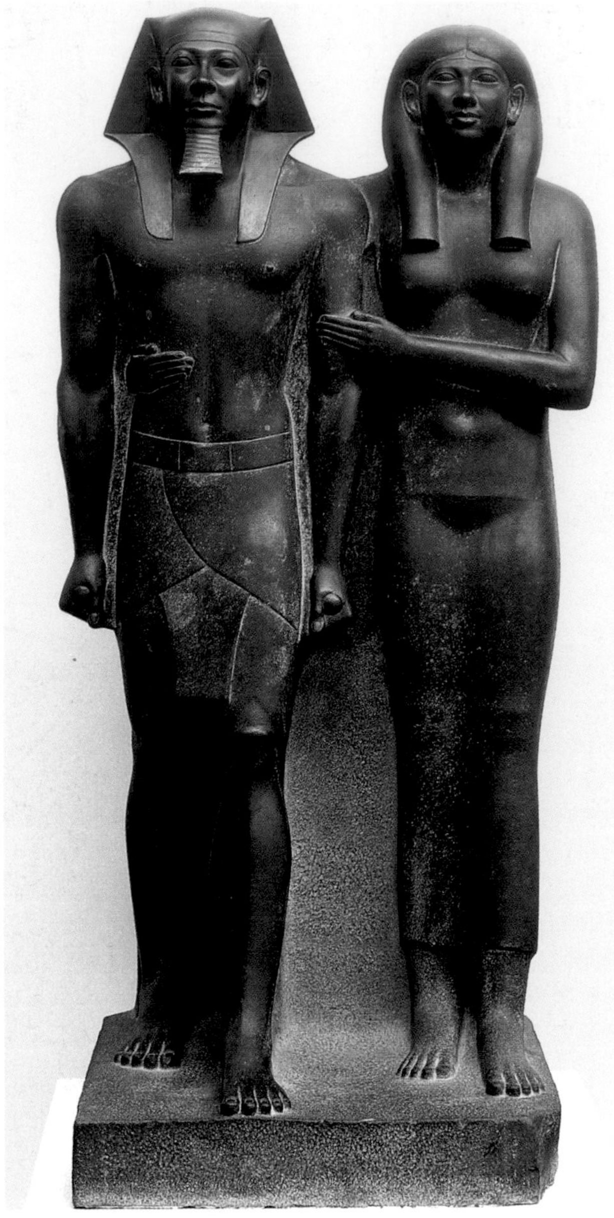

2-14. *Menkaure and His Wife, Queen Khamerernebty,* from Giza. c. 2515 B.C. Slate, height 54½" (138.4 cm). Museum of Fine Arts, Boston. Harvard–Museum of Fine Arts Expedition

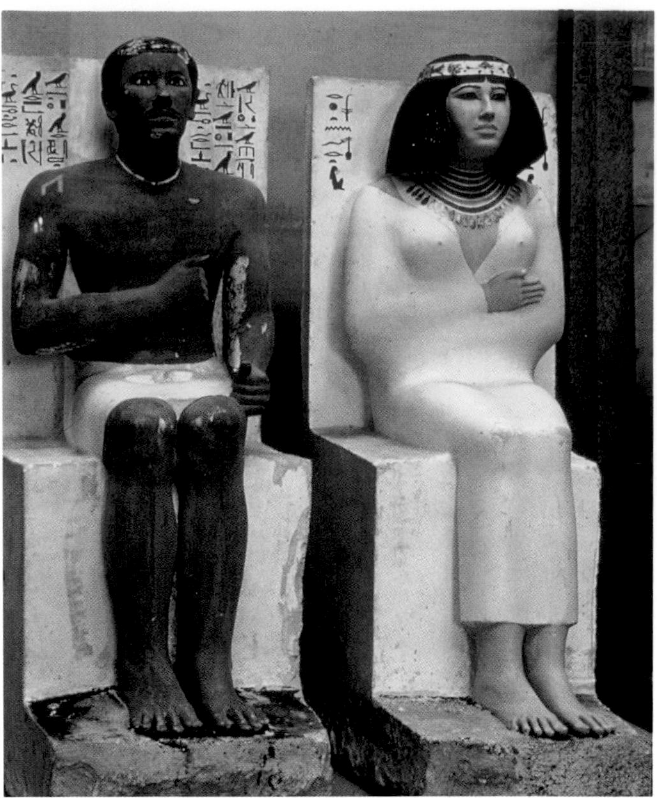

2-15. *Prince Rahotep and His Wife, Nofret.* c. 2580 B.C. Painted limestone, height 47¼" (120 cm). Egyptian Museum, Cairo

The sculptor who carved the statues of Prince Rahotep and his wife, Nofret (fig. 2-15), was less subtle. They owe their lifelike appearance to their vivid coloring. (Other such statues must also have been painted in this way, but the coloring has survived intact in only a few instances.) The darker body color of the prince is the standard for males in Egyptian art. The eyes have been inlaid with shining quartz to make them look as alive as possible, and the portrait quality of the faces is striking.

Standing and seated figures are the basic forms of Egyptian large-scale sculpture in the round. At the end of the Fourth Dynasty, a third pose was added, as symmetrical and immobile as the first two: that of the scribe sitting cross-legged on the ground. The finest of these scribes dates from the beginning of the Fifth Dynasty (fig. 2-16). The name of the sitter (in whose tomb at Saqqara the statue was found) is unknown, but we must not think of him as a secretary waiting to take dictation. Rather, he was a high court official, a "master of sacred—and secret—letters." The solid, incisive treatment of form bespeaks the dignity of his station, which at first seems to have been restricted to the sons of pharaohs. Our example stands out for the vividly alert expression of the face and for the individual handling of the torso, which records the somewhat flabby body of a man past middle age.

Another invention of Old Kingdom art was the portrait bust. This type of sculpture is so familiar that we tend to take it for granted; yet its origin is puzzling. Was it simply a cheap substitute for a full-length figure? Or did it have a purpose of its own, perhaps as a remote echo of the Neolithic custom of keeping the head of the deceased separate from the rest of his body (see page 36)? Be that as it may, the earliest of these busts (fig. 2-17) is also the finest. Indeed, it is one of the great portraits of all time. In this noble head, we find a memorable image of the sitter's character. With remarkable skill the artist has rendered the subtle distinction between the solid shape of the skull and its soft, flexible covering of flesh, aided by the well-preserved color.

TOMB DECORATION. Before we leave the Old Kingdom, let us look at some scenes of daily life from nonroyal tombs, such as that of the architectural overseer Ti at Saqqara. The hippopota-

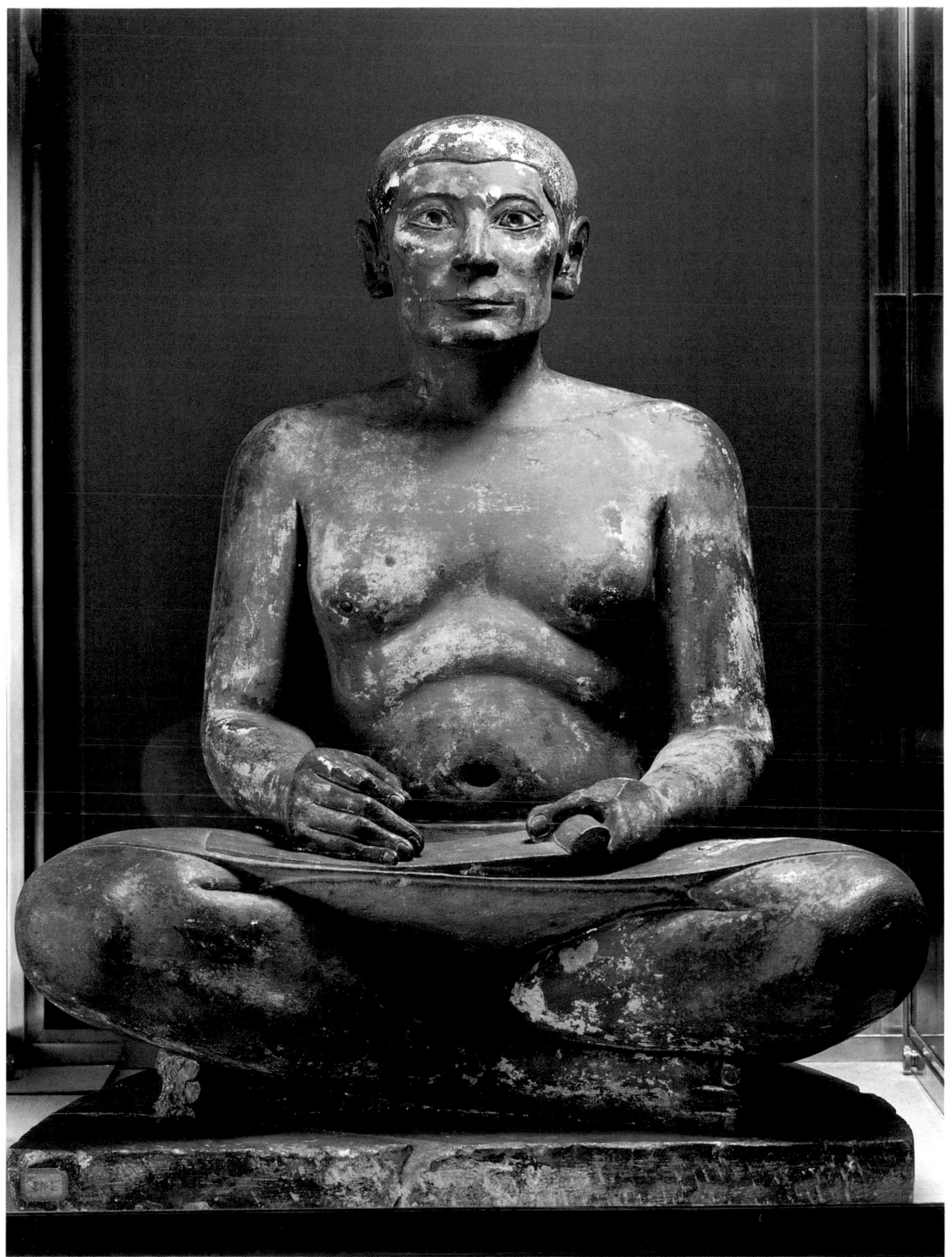

2-16. *Seated Scribe,* from Saqqara. c. 2400 B.C. Limestone, height 21" (53.3 cm). Musée du Louvre, Paris

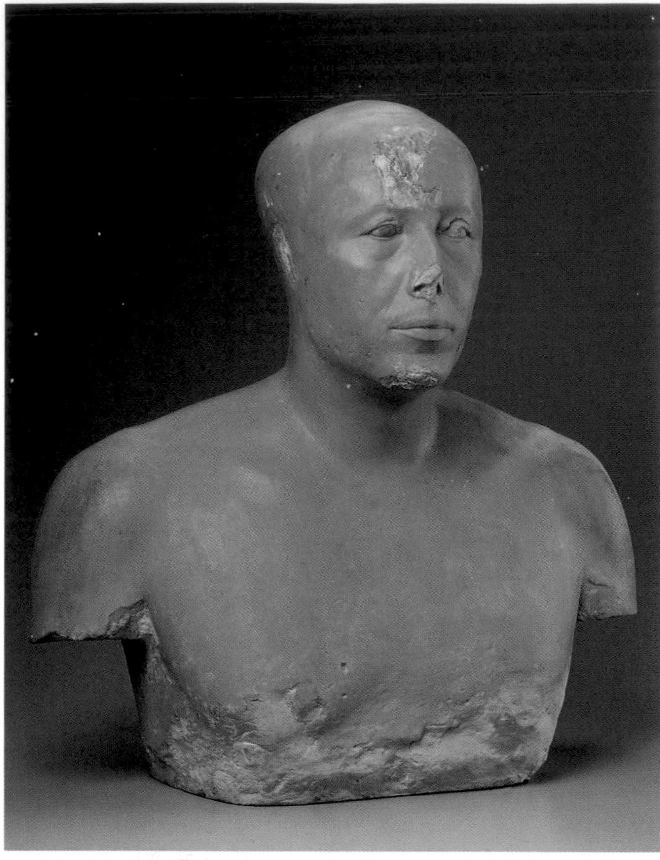

2-17. *Bust of Vizier Ankh-haf,* from Giza. c. 2520 B.C. Limestone, partially molded in plaster, height 21" (53.3 cm). Museum of Fine Arts, Boston. Harvard–Museum of Fine Arts Expedition

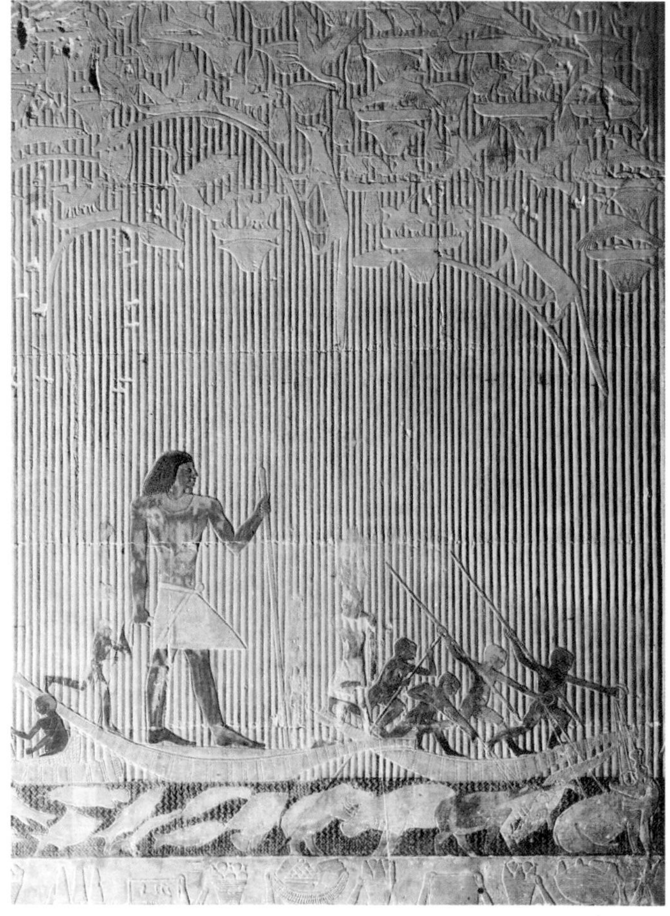

2-18. *Ti Watching a Hippopotamus Hunt.* c. 2510–2460 B.C. Painted limestone relief, height approx. 45" (114.3 cm). Tomb of Ti, Saqqara

mus hunt in figure 2-18 is of special interest because of its landscape setting. The background is a papyrus thicket. The stems form a regular design that erupts in the top zone into an agitated scene of nesting birds menaced by small predators. The water in the bottom zone, marked by a zigzag pattern, is equally crowded with struggling hippopotamuses and fish. All these, as well as the hunters in the first boat, are carefully observed and full of action. Only Ti himself, standing in the second boat, is immobile, as if he belonged to a different world. His pose is that of the funerary portrait reliefs and statues (compare fig. 2-3). He towers above the other men, since he is more important than they.

Ti's size also lifts him out of the context of the hunt. He does not direct it; he simply observes. His passive role is typical of representations of the deceased in all such scenes from the Old Kingdom. It seems to be a way of conveying that the body is dead but the spirit is alive and aware of the pleasures of this world, though the man can no longer take part in them directly. We should also note that these scenes do not depict the dead man's favorite pastimes. If they did, he would be looking back, and such nostalgia is alien to the spirit of Old Kingdom tombs. It has been shown, in fact, that these scenes form a seasonal cycle. They are a sort of calendar of human activities for the spirit of the deceased to watch year in and year out. The hunt may have symbolic meaning as well. The hippopotamus was often viewed as an animal of evil and chaos that destroyed crops and thus as the embodiment of Seth. In turn, the deceased may be likened to Osiris, god of the Nile and of death and resurrection. Moreover, the papyrus thicket was where Isis hid Horus to protect him from Seth, so that it was seen as a place of rebirth, much like the tomb itself.

For the artist, these scenes, which combine sculpture and painting, offered a chance to widen his powers of observation. We often find astounding bits of realism in the description of plant and animal life. Note, for example, the hippopotamus in the lower right-hand corner turning its head in fear and anger to face its attackers. Such a sympathetic portrayal is as delightful as it is unexpected in Old Kingdom art. It will be some time before we find anything similar in the human realm. Even more remarkable is the variety of poses among the hunters, which break the rules observed in the figure of Ti. Eventually we shall even see the deceased abandoning his passive, timeless stance to participate in scenes of daily life (see fig. 2-27).

THE MIDDLE KINGDOM

After the collapse of centralized pharaonic power at the end of the Sixth Dynasty, Egypt entered a period of political disturbances and ill fortune that was to last almost 700 years. During most of this time, power was in the hands of local or regional overlords, who revived the old rivalry of Upper and Lower Egypt. Many dynasties followed one another in rapid succession. Only two, the Eleventh and Twelfth, which make up the Middle Kingdom (2040–1674 B.C.), are worthy of note. During this period a series of able rulers managed to reassert themselves against the provincial nobility. However, soon after the close of the Twelfth Dynasty the weakened country was taken over by the Hyksos (the term essentially meant "foreign ruler"), a group of western Asiatic peoples of somewhat mysterious origin who had evidently been living in Egypt for some time. They seized the Nile Delta area and ruled it for 150 years until their defeat by King Ahmose of Thebes about 1552 B.C.

ARCHITECTURE. The unsettled times gave rise to a great deal of experimentation in Egyptian art, even though it continued to look back to the Old Kingdom. The most spectacular example was the funerary monument at Deir el Bahri of Mentuhotep II, the king who reunited Egypt around 2052 B.C. and began the Eleventh Dynasty (see fig. 2-25, left). Now in ruins, it was a terraced structure that extended into the living rock. It was topped off with a pyramid or, more likely, a mastaba. As such, it was a brilliant mixture of traditional elements with new ones introduced by Mentuhotep's Middle Kingdom predecessors.

PORTRAITURE. The spell of divine kingship, having once been broken, never regained its old effectiveness. The authority of the Middle Kingdom pharaohs tended to be personal rather than institutional. Egyptian sculptors faced the challenge of imposing a sense of individuality on established forms, and they managed to do so with great inventiveness. The unquiet spirit of the Middle Kingdom is reflected in royal portraits such as the one in figure 2-19 of Sesostris III. There is a real sense of shock on first seeing this strangely modern face. The serene assurance of the Old Kingdom has given way to a troubled expression that testifies to the difficulty of holding power as an act of supreme will. (Sesostris III nevertheless ranks with Mentuhotep II as one of the great pharaohs of the Middle Kingdom.) At first glance the link with tradition seems to have been broken entirely. Lacking its royal trappings, our fragment displays a physical and psychological realism that bespeaks a new level of self-awareness. Here is another enduring achievement of Egyptian art that was destined to live on in Roman portraiture.

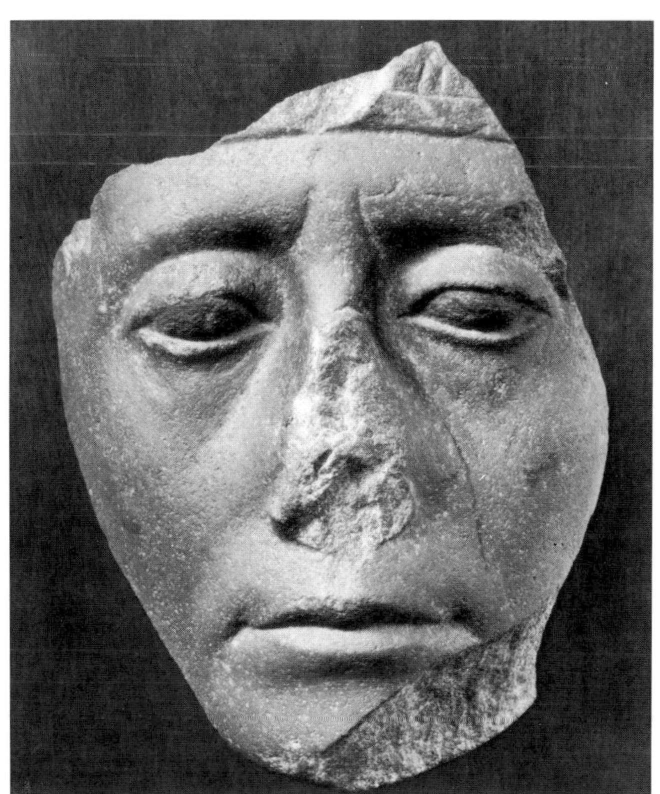

2-19. *Portrait of Sesostris III* (fragment). c. 1850 B.C. Quartzite, height 6 ½" (16.5 cm). The Metropolitan Museum of Art, New York

CARNARVON COLLECTION, GIFT OF EDWARD S. HARKNESS, 1926

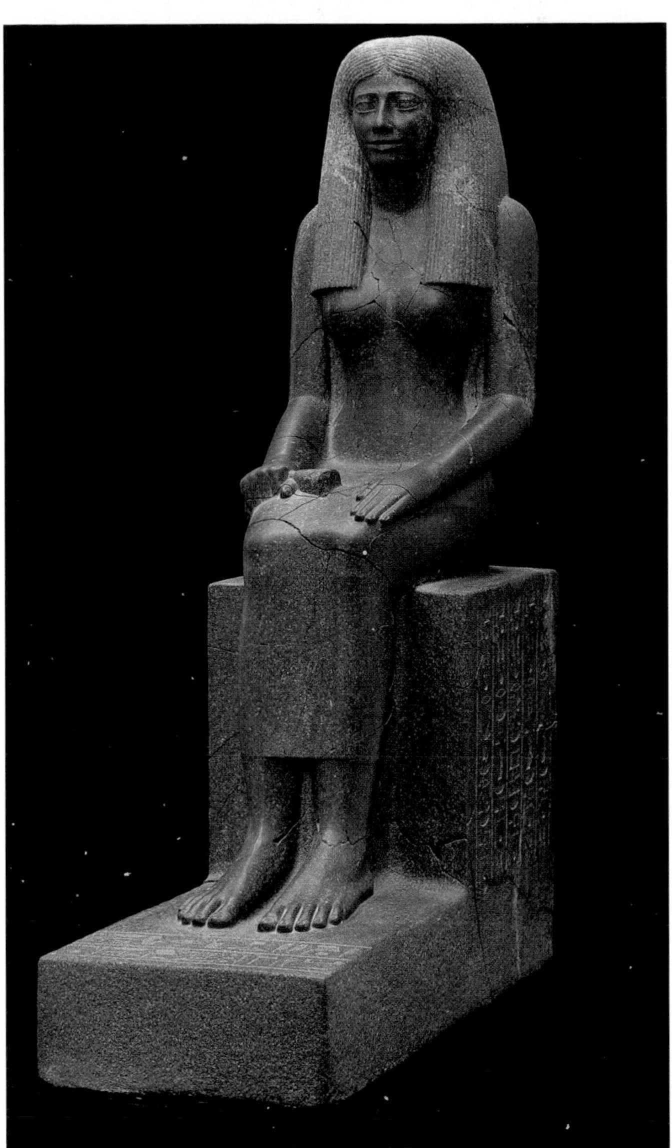

2-20. *Statue of the Lady Sennuwy.* c. 1920 B.C. Granite, height 67 ¾" (172 cm), depth 45 ⅞" (116.5 cm). Museum of Fine Arts, Boston

Middle Kingdom sculpture ranges from colossal statues to smaller figures of the utmost delicacy and precision. The finest of the latter is a portrait of Lady Sennuwy, the wife of Prince Hepzefa, provincial governor of Assiut, though the statue was found at Kerma in Upper Nubia (fig. 2-20). She reminds us of Queen Khamerernebty in figure 2-14, but her features have a refinement and the figure a youthful slenderness unknown in earlier Egyptian art. The same elegance is found in Middle Kingdom literature, which achieved classic status. So did the style announced in the statue of Lady Sennuwy, which probably originated in Thebes and remained influential well into the New Kingdom.

PAINTING AND RELIEF. A relaxation of the rules can also be seen in Middle Kingdom painting and relief, which often departs from convention. This loosening is most evident in the decoration of the tombs of local princes at Beni Hasan. Because they were carved into the living rock, these tombs have survived

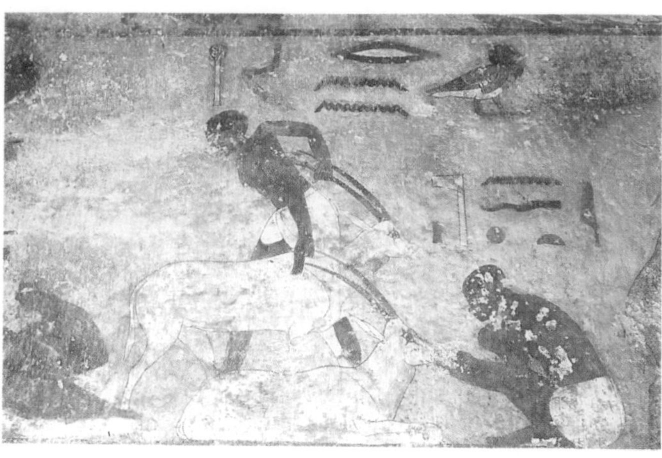

2-21. *Feeding the Oryxes*. c. 1928–1895 B.C. Detail of a wall painting. Tomb of Khnum-hotep, Beni Hasan

better than most Middle Kingdom monuments. The mural *Feeding the Oryxes* (fig. 2-21) comes from one of these tombs, that of Khnum-hotep. (As the prince's emblem, the oryx antelope seems to have been a sort of honored pet in his household.) According to the standards of Old Kingdom art, all the figures ought to share the same ground-line. If not, the second oryx and its attendant ought to be placed above the first (a system known as vertical recession). Instead, the painter employs a secondary ground-line only slightly higher than the primary one. As a result the two groups are related in a way similar to normal appearances. This interest in spatial effects can also be seen in the awkward but bold foreshortening of the shoulders of the two attendants. If we cover up the hieroglyphic signs, which emphasize the flatness of the wall, we can "read" the depth with surprising ease.

THE NEW KINGDOM

The 500 years after the Hyksos were expelled, which make up the Eighteenth, Nineteenth, and Twentieth dynasties, represent the third and final flowering of Egypt. Once again united under strong kings, the country extended its frontiers far to the east, into Palestine and Syria; hence this period is also known as the Empire.

New Kingdom art covers a wide range of styles and quality. We find rigid conservatism and brilliant inventiveness, massive ostentation and delicate refinement. These different strands are interwoven into fabric so complex that, as with the art of Imperial Rome 1,500 years later, it is difficult to come up with a representative sampling that conveys its flavor and variety.

EIGHTEENTH DYNASTY

Wall Paintings and Reliefs

Perhaps not surprisingly, New Kingdom artists at first turned to the style of the Middle Kingdom. The result was a traditionalism that was more flexible than may at first appear. It is seen at its best in a low relief (fig. 2-22) from the tomb of Ramose at the new capital, Thebes. The relief was done at the end of the reign of Amenhotep III, whom Ramose served as vizier before moving to Tell el'Amarna under Akhenaten (see below). (As a result, the tomb, lavishly decorated with paintings and reliefs, remained unfinished.) Our detail has a subtlety that was never surpassed. Here beauty has become an end in itself. To a striking degree, the artist succeeds in the quest for a more refined vocabulary, which soon took the place of the heroic forms of the Old Kingdom.

The experimental spirit of Middle Kingdom wall painting was revived intact during the New Kingdom. In the Theban tomb of Nebamun, it blossoms into a fascination with nature (fig. 2-23). Such gardens were a feature of wealthy homes during the New Kingdom. Besides providing a home for fish and fowl, the pool had sacred overtones, thanks to the life-giving power of water. (A nearly identical garden with Osiris and Maat is often depicted in The Book of the Dead; see below.) The scene has a freshness and attention to detail that are unequaled in Egyptian art (compare

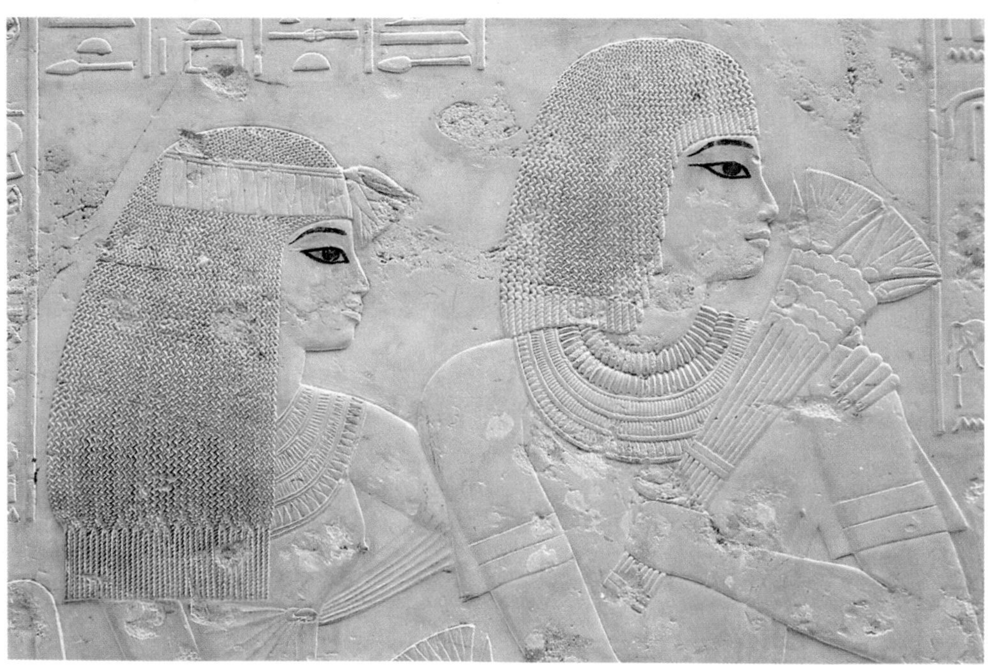

2-22. *Mai and His Wife, Urel*. Detail of a limestone relief. c. 1375 B.C. Tomb of Ramose, Thebes

2-23. *A Pond in a Garden.* Fragment of a wall painting, from the Tomb of Nebamun, Thebes. c. 1400 B.C. The British Museum, London

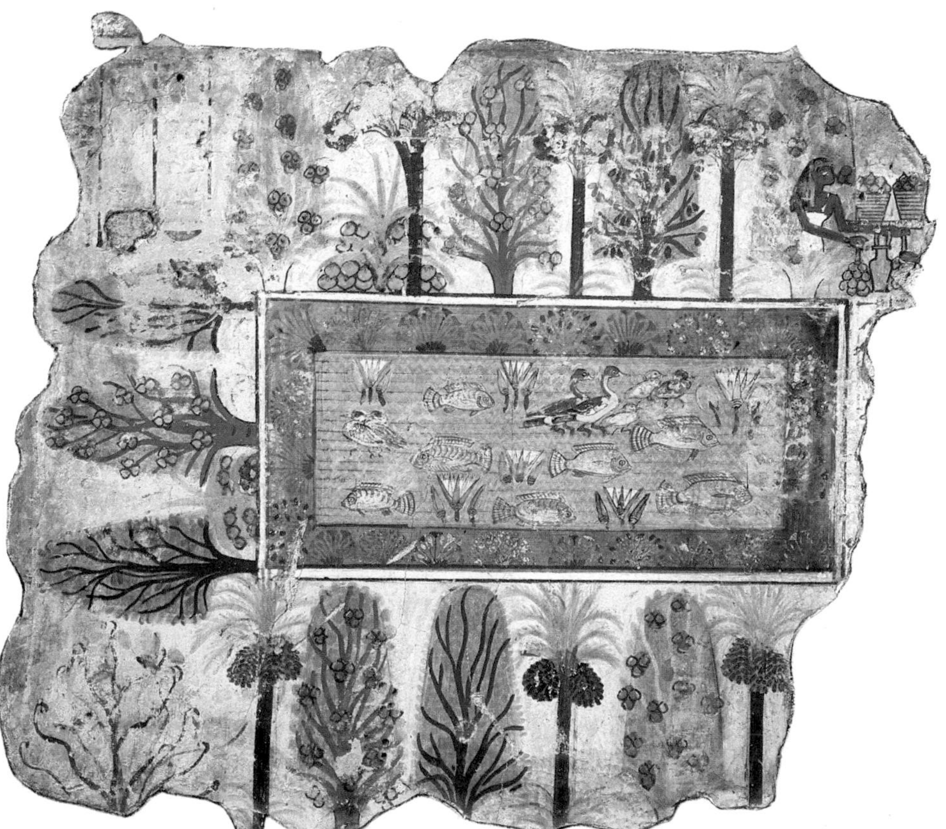

2-24. *Musicians and Dancers,* fragment of a wall painting from the Tomb of Nebamun, Thebes. 1350 B.C. Height 24" (61 cm). The British Museum, London

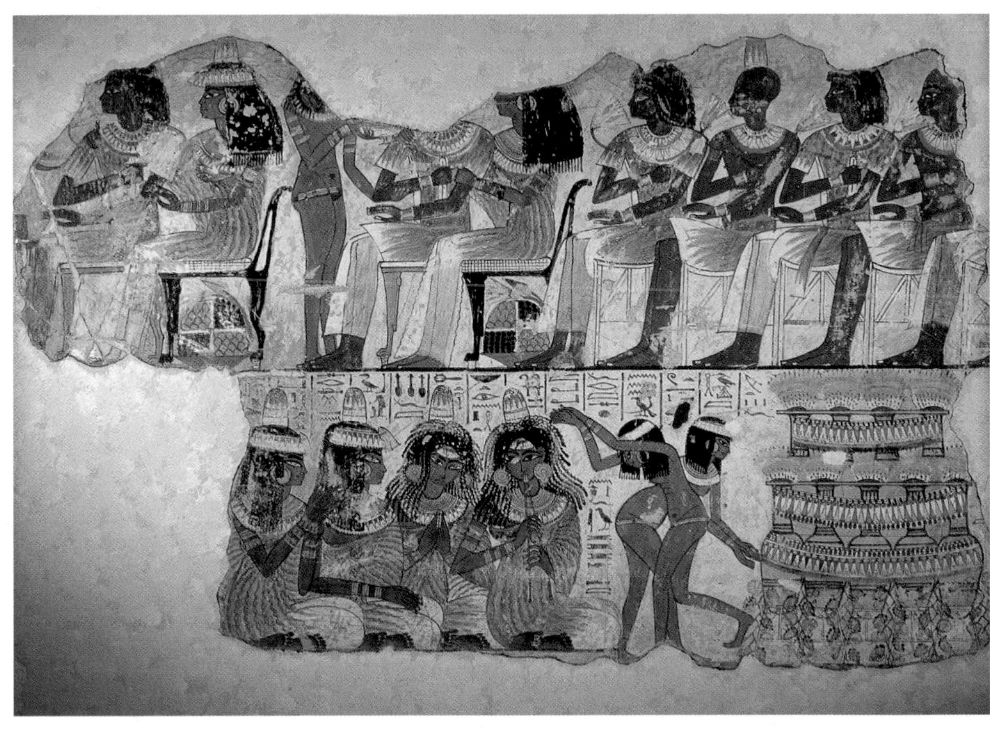

fig. 2-21). The artist was surely aware of Minoan wall painting, which shares these very qualities (see Chapter Four).

Aegean art must also have influenced how the movement of animals was shown in Egyptian art around the same time. This theory is supported by the discovery at Tell el-Daba of Minoan-style fresco remnants (including a bull-jumping scene; compare fig. 4-10) painted toward the beginning of the Eighteenth Dynasty. Strangely enough, they may well have been done by an Egyptian artist who had visited Crete. Yet the influence can hardly have been one-sided. Egypt had a rich landscape tradition reaching back to the Old Kingdom that had always provided opportunities to break the rules (compare fig. 2-18).

Happily, the two facets of New Kingdom art were not mutually exclusive. Innovation and beauty are united in a banquet scene from the same tomb that gives us a tantalizing glimpse of Egyptian dance and music (fig. 2-24). If only we knew what it sounded like! Pictures such as this provided the *ka* with all the earthly pleasures in the afterlife. The artist depicts the rapt inspiration of the musicians and the graceful movements of the dancing girls, while enriching the surface with lavish decoration. For all its gaiety, our detail probably represents the annual funerary "feast of the valley," when the god Amun would cross the Nile from Karnak to visit the tombs on the west bank and bless the deceased.

Architecture

THE TEMPLE OF HATSHEPSUT. The climactic period of the New Kingdom extended from about 1500 B.C. to the end of the reign of Ramesses III in 1145 B.C. During this era tremendous architectural projects were carried out, centering on the region of Thebes. The return of prosperity and stability was first marked by the revival of Middle Kingdom architectural forms to signify royal power.

Among the architectural undertakings that have survived from the early years of the New Kingdom, the outstanding one is the Funerary Temple of Queen Hatshepsut (fig. 2-25). Built by her vizier Senenmut about 1478–1458 B.C. against the rocky cliffs of Deir el-Bahri, it imitates Mentuhotep II's funerary temple of more than 500 years earlier (seen to the left in fig. 2-25). It is, however, very much larger. (A third temple, built somewhat later by her nephew, Tuthmosis III, was sandwiched between them but is in such ruins that it was not unearthed until 1961.) The worshiper is led toward the holy of holies—a small chamber driven deep into the rock—through three large courts on ascending levels, which are linked by ramps among long colonnades. Together they form a processional road similar to those at Giza, but with the mountain instead of a pyramid at the end. The ramps and colonnades echo the shape of the cliff. This magnificent union of architecture and nature makes Hatshepsut's temple the rival of any of the Old Kingdom monuments.

The temple complex (fig. 2-26) was dedicated to Amun and several other deities. During the New Kingdom, divine kingship was asserted by claiming the god Amun as the father of the reigning monarch. By fusing his identity with that of the sun-god Ra, Amun became the supreme deity, ruling the lesser gods much as the pharaoh dominated the provincial nobility.

Akhenaten

Over time the priests of Amun grew into a caste of such wealth and power that they posed a threat to royal authority. The pharaoh could maintain his position only with their consent. Amenhotep IV, the most remarkable figure of the Eighteenth Dynasty, tried to defeat them by proclaiming his faith in a single god, the sun disk Aten. He changed his name to Akhenaten ("Effective for the Aten"), closed the Amun temples, and moved the capital to central Egypt, near the modern Tell el'Amarna. However, his attempt to place himself at the head of a new faith did not outlast his reign (1348–1336/5 B.C.).

Of the great projects built by Akhenaten hardly anything remains above ground. He must have been a revolutionary not only in his religious beliefs but in his artistic tastes as well. Through his choice of masters, he fostered a new style. Known as the Amarna style, it can be seen at its best in a sunken relief portrait of Akhenaten and his family (fig. 2-27). The intimate domes-

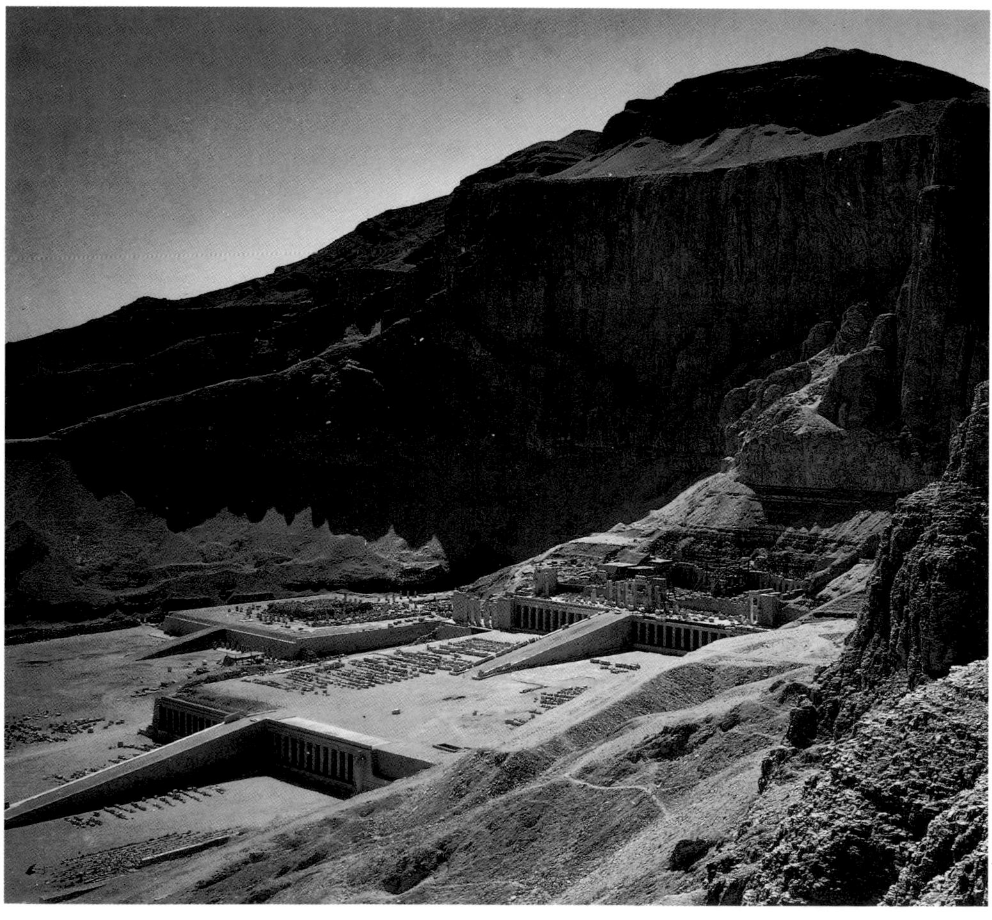

2-25. Temple of Queen Hatshepsut, Deir el-Bahri. c. 1478–1458 B.C.

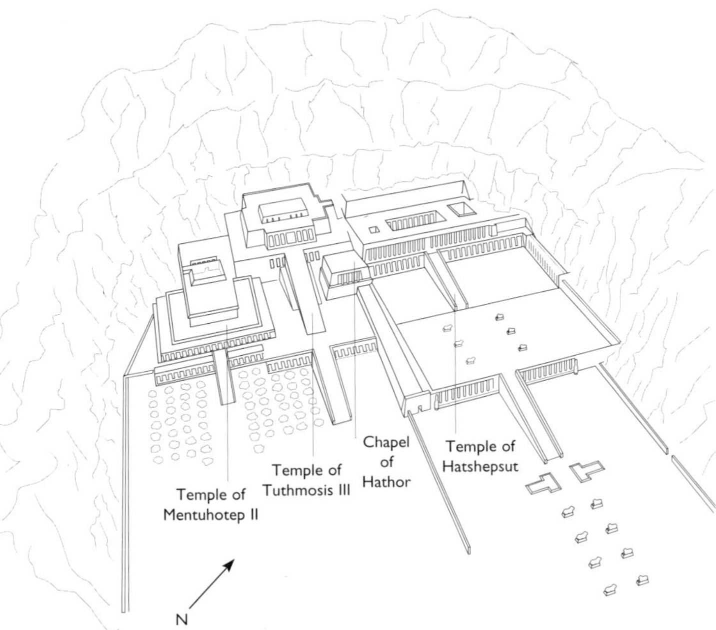

2-26. Reconstruction of temples, Deir el-Bahri, with temples of Mentuhotep II, Tuthmosis III, and Queen Hatshepsut (after a drawing by Andrea Mazzei/Archivio White Star, Vercelli, Italy)

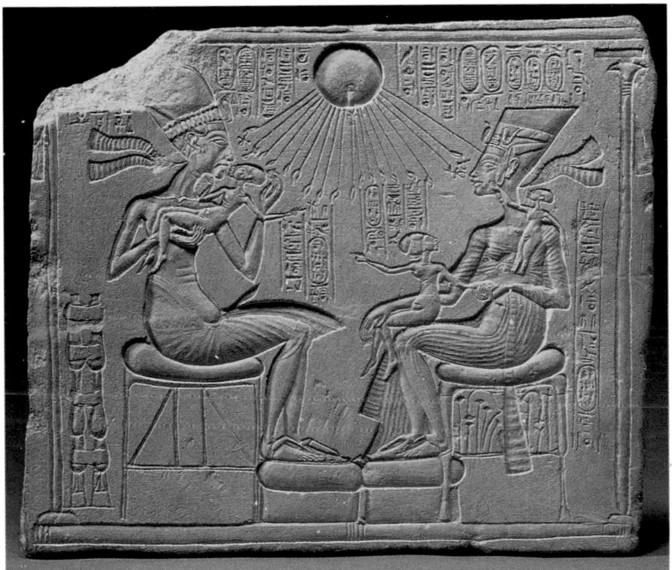

2-27. *Akhenaten and His Family.* c. 1355 B.C. Limestone, 12¾ x 15¼" (31.1 x 38.7 cm). Staatliche Museen zu Berlin, Preussischer Kulturbesitz, Ägyptisches Museum

tic scene suggests that the relief was meant to serve as a shrine in a private household. The life-giving rays of the sun help to unify the composition and identify the royal couple as the living counterparts of Aten. Despite their very human qualities, their divine status is proclaimed by the new ideal, with its oddly haggard features and overemphatic outlines. That this was a conscious choice, not merely an exaggeration of their anatomy, can be seen in the way the features of Akhenaten's queen, Nefertiti, have been subtly altered to resemble his (compare fig. 2-28). The same must be true of the egg-shaped skulls of the three princesses, one of them still an infant. They express the theme of life and creativity and are not simply a genetic oddity. The seemingly playful gestures, so appealing to modern eyes, are intended to ward off evil spirits and protect the household from harm. The informal, tender poses nonetheless defy all conventions of pharaonic dignity and bespeak a new view of humanity.

The contrast with the past becomes strikingly clear if we compare the Amarna relief with the detail from the Tomb of Ramose (see fig. 2-22), which is only slightly earlier in date. The subtlety of the carving, the precision of the lines, and the refinement of the forms in the latter make the treatment of Akhenaten seem, at first glance, like a brutal caricature. In actual fact, the royal family scene is equally skillful in its execution. The sculptor separates the complex overlapping planes with surprising ease. What distinguishes this style is not greater realism so much as a new sense of form that seeks to unfreeze the traditional immobility of Egyptian art. Not only the contours but the shapes, too, seem more pliable, nearly antigeometric.

Despite its unique qualities, the Amarna revolution was partly an outgrowth of developments earlier in the Eighteenth Dynasty. The process was already highly evolved under Akhenaten's father, Amenhotep III. Indeed, the new ideal can already be seen emerging in certain portraits of Hatshepsut. The famous bust of Nefertiti (fig. 2-28), the greatest masterpiece of the "Akhenaten style," does not abandon the style found in the Ramose relief. Rather, it relaxes the forms for the sake of a more elegant effect, reminding us that her name means "the beautiful one is come." Its perfection comes from a command of geometry that is at once precise—the face is completely symmetrical—and

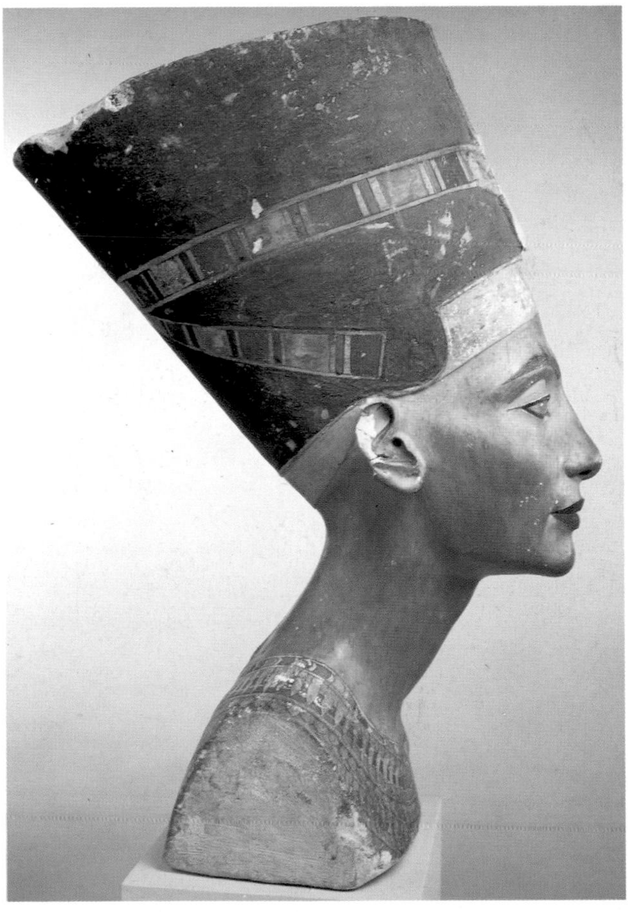

2-28. *Queen Nefertiti.* c. 1348–1336/5 B.C. Limestone, height 19" (48.3 cm). Staatliche Museen zu Berlin, Preussischer Kulturbesitz, Ägyptisches Museum

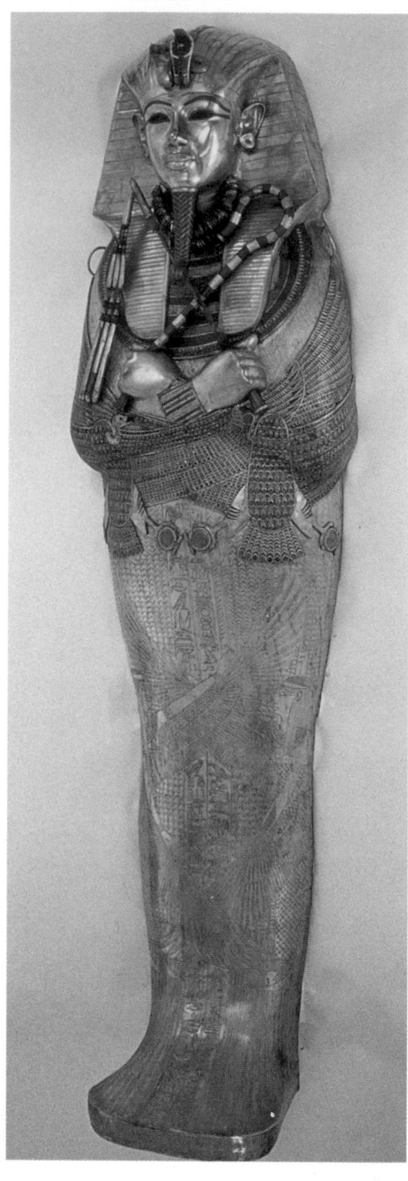

2-29. Cover of the coffin of Tutankhamen. 18th Dynasty. Gold, height 72" (182.9 cm). Egyptian Museum, Cairo

PHOTO: LEE BOLTIN PICTURE LIBRARY, HASTINGS-ON-HUDSON, NY

wonderfully subtle. Strangely enough, the bust remained unfinished (the left eye lacks the inlay of the right). It was left behind with a nearly identical head in the workshop of the royal sculptor Thutmose when he moved from Amarna to Memphis after Akhenaten's death.

Thutmose, like Imhotep before him, must have been a great genius—he was the "king's favorite and master of the works"—one who could give visible form to the pharaoh's ideas. He is not the first Egyptian artist known to us by name—but he is the first we can identify with a personal style. Thutmose was the last of several sculptors in succession who were mainly responsible for the Amarna style. This union of a powerful patron and a sympathetic artist is rare. We shall not see it again until Periklean Greece (see page 116).

Tutankhamen

Akhenaten's successor, Smenkhkara, died soon after becoming pharaoh. The throne then passed to Tutankhamen, then only about nine or ten years old. Tutankhamen, who was probably also Akhenaten's nephew and married to his daughter Ankhesenpaaten, died at the age of 18, perhaps of consumption (tuberculosis). (There is no solid evidence to support the popular conspiracy theories.) He owes his fame entirely to the fact that his is the only pharaonic tomb that has been found in our times with most of its contents intact. The immense value of the contents (Tutankhamen's gold coffin alone weighs 250 pounds) makes it easy to understand why grave robbing has been practiced in Egypt ever since the Old Kingdom. To us, the exquisite workmanship of the coffin cover (fig. 2-29), with the rich play of colored inlays against the polished gold surfaces, is even more impressive.

The old religion was restored by Tutankhamen and his short-lived successor, the aged Ay, who seems to have served as his vizier and married his widow to preserve the throne. The process was completed under Horemheb, who had been head of the army under Tutankhamen and became the last king of the Eighteenth Dynasty. He set out to erase all traces of the Amarna revolution, but its effects could be felt in Egyptian art for some time to come. Thus the scene of workmen struggling with a heavy beam (fig. 2-30), from a battle scene in Horemheb's own tomb at Saqqara, shows a freedom and an expressiveness that would have been unthinkable in earlier times.

Papyrus Scrolls

Since the First Dynasty, if not before, books in the form of scrolls had been made of papyrus plants, which grow in large numbers in the marshes of the Nile Delta. Such scrolls came to be used throughout the Mediterranean. (The modern book, or codex, was not invented until Roman times; see page 224.) Perhaps the most important of these texts was The Book of the Dead, which began to appear shortly before the New Kingdom. This collection of more than 200 incantations was usually placed inside the coffin or included in the mummy bandaging itself. During this period we may say that the afterlife was democratized. No longer was it the sole right of the pharaoh and his court. Now everyone was entitled to it, with the protection of the right spells. What is new to The Book of the Dead is the emphasis on morality, which culminates in Chapter 125 with the weighing of the soul and judgment of the dead by Osiris. [See Primary Sources, no. 1, page 192.] Even more remarkable is that this scene was often depicted, making it among the earliest examples of true book illustration we know of. Moreover, it was copied in wall paintings, thus creating a link between the two mediums that persisted in Early Christian art.

Let us look closely at this chapter as seen in The Book of the Dead of Hunefer, one of the finest examples that has come down to us (fig. 2-31). It conforms to a well-defined type that must have been passed from one workshop to another. The style, though derived from traditional tomb painting, has been adapted to the format of the scroll through a process known as continuous narration. At the left, Hunefer is led into the Hall of the Two Truths by Anubis, the jackal-faced guardian of the underworld. Anubis then weighs the heart of the dead against the ostrich feather of Maat, whose head appears on the top of the scales. Maat, the goddess of truth and justice, symbolized the divine order and governed ethical behavior; hence, her feather was an emblem of law. The results are recorded by the ibis-headed scribe Thoth, who was sometimes shown in the guise of a baboon. Looking on with keen

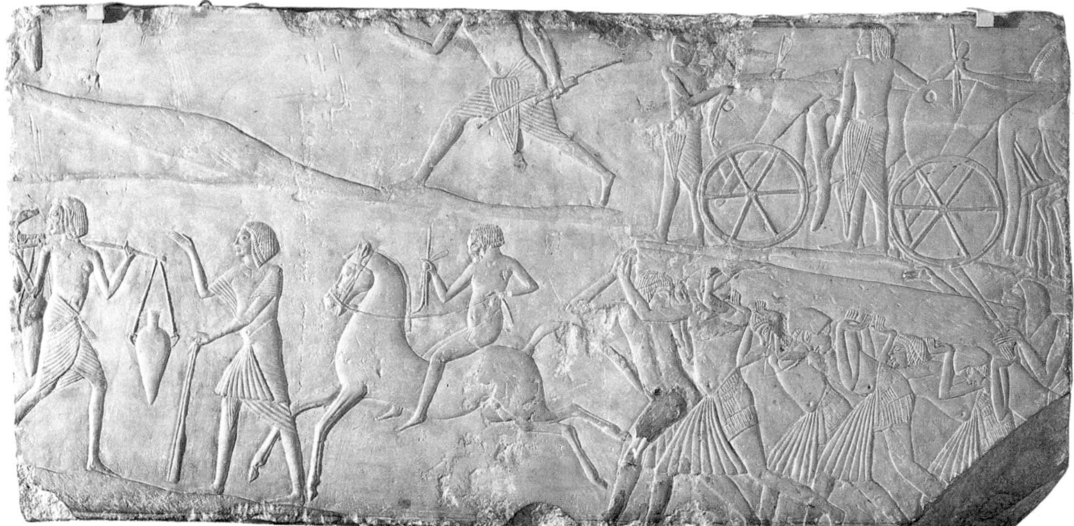

2-30. *Workmen Carrying a Beam.* Detail of a relief, from the Tomb of Horemheb, Saqqara. c. 1325 B.C. Museo Civico, Bologna

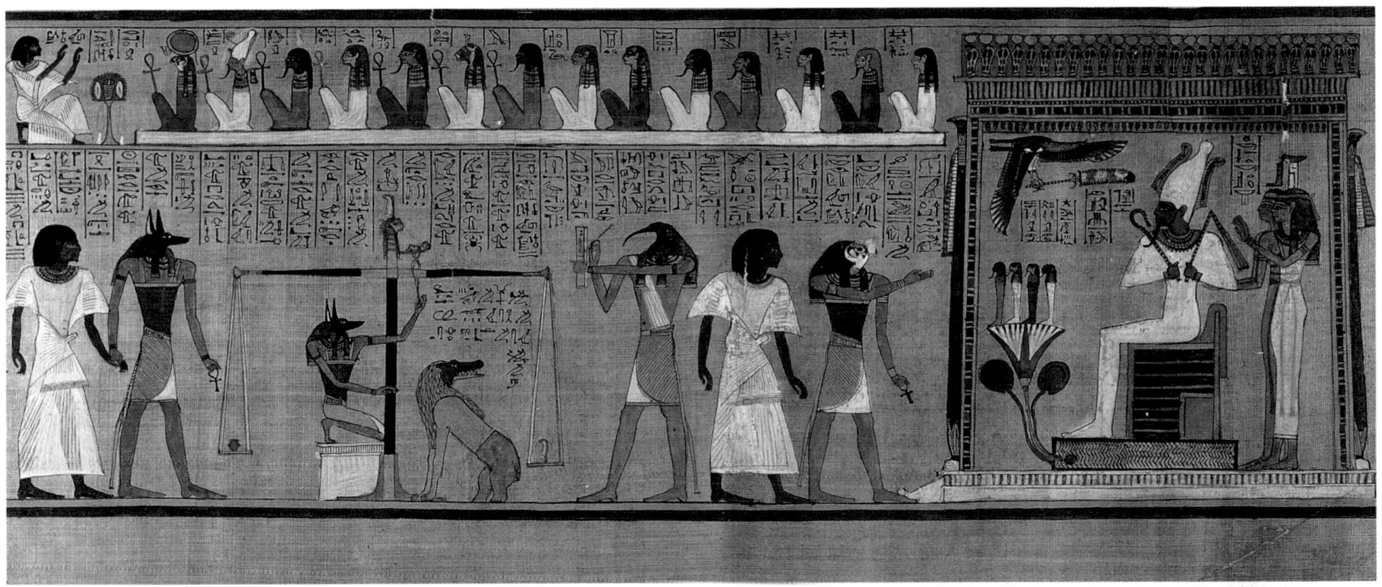

(BELOW) 2-31. *The Weighing of the Heart and Judgment of Osiris,* from The Book of the Dead of Hunefer. 1285 B.C. Painted papyrus, height 15⅝" (39.5 cm). The British Museum, London

interest is Ammut, the devourer of those whose evil deeds made them unworthy of an afterlife. She has the head of a crocodile, the body and legs of a lion, and the hindquarters of a hippopotamus—all ferocious beasts.

The deceased had to swear to each of the deities seen overhead that he had not sinned. Having been declared "true of voice," he is presented by Horus to his father, Osiris, shown here with Isis and her sister Nephthys, mother of Anubis and protector of the dead. In front of the throne are the four sons of Horus standing on a white lotus blossom, symbol of rebirth. Also known as the four gods of the cardinal points, they protected the internal organs that were removed as part of the embalming process and placed in canopic jars. Above, a symbol of Horus (identified by his sacred *udjat* eye, which restored Osiris to health) bears an ostrich feather representing the presumably favorable judgment of Maat. It is a strange realm indeed, at least to modern eyes. Yet once we know how to read the scene, we recognize in it the antecedents, thematic and moral, of the Last Judgment, with its weighing of souls, which was to become one of the great subjects of medieval Christian art (compare fig. 10-24).

Later Architecture

THE TEMPLE AT LUXOR. The rulers of the New Kingdom devoted an ever greater share of their architectural energies to huge temples of Amun. The cult's center was Thebes, which included Karnak and Luxor on the east bank of the Nile and Deir-el-Bahri on the west bank. Beyond lay the Valley of the Kings to the north and the Valley of the Queens to the south. Vast temple complexes at Karnak and Luxor were begun during the Middle Kingdom and greatly enlarged more than a century later during the Nineteenth Dynasty.

At Luxor, Amenhotep III replaced an earlier temple with a huge new one. It was completed by Rameses II, the greatest of the New Kingdom pharaohs, who built on an unprecedented scale. Its plan is typical of later Egyptian temples. The facade consists of two massive walls, with sloping sides, that form the entrance. This unit, which is known as the gateway or pylon (fig. 2-32, far left, and fig. 2-33), leads to the court (fig. 2-34, A). (The court is in the shape of a parallelogram because Ramesses II changed its axis to conform with the direction of the Nile.) We then enter a pillared

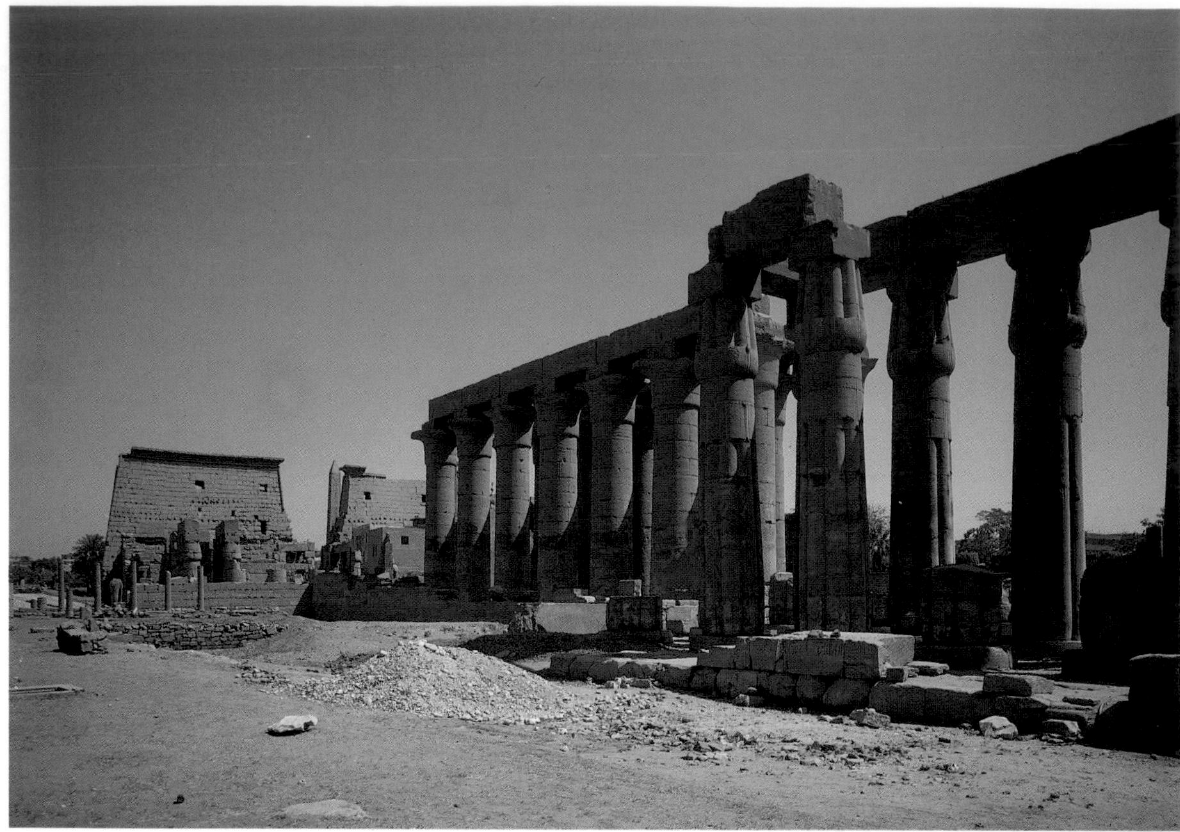

2-32. Court and pylon of Ramesses II (c. 1279–1212 B.C.) and colonnade and court of Amenhotep III (c. 1350 B.C.), temple complex of Amun-Mut-Khonsu, Luxor

hall, which brings us to the second court (fig. 2-34, B and C; fig. 2-32, center and right). On its far side we find another pillared hall. Beyond it is the temple itself, a series of symmetrically arranged halls and chapels. They shield the holy of holies, a square room with four columns containing a colossal statue of Amun (fig. 2-34, extreme right). The temple was regarded as the actual house of the god. The cult statue, as his manifestation, was bathed, anointed, clothed, and fed by priests in elaborate daily rituals.

The temple complex was enclosed by high walls that shut off the outside world. Except for the monumental pylon (see fig. 2-33), such a structure is designed to be seen from within. Ordinary worshipers were confined to the courts and could but marvel at the forest of columns that screened the sanctuary (known as a hypostyle hall for its many columns). The columns had to be closely spaced, for they supported the stone lintels of the ceiling, which were necessarily short to keep them from breaking under their own weight. Yet the architect has exploited this condition by making the columns far heavier than they need be. The viewer feels almost crushed by their sheer mass. The result is impressive, but it is also rather coarse when measured against earlier masterpieces of Egyptian architecture. We need only compare the papyrus-shaped columns of the colonnade of Amenhotep III with their ancestors in Djoser's North Palace (see fig. 2-8) to see how little of the genius of Imhotep has survived at Luxor. The decline is even more apparent in the massive statues that flank the pylon of Ramesses II (see fig. 2-33). Although skillfully carved, they are a far cry from the alert, muscular figure of Khafre (see fig. 2-13) from which they descend.

The most interesting sculptural works at the temples at Luxor, Karnak, and elsewhere are the reliefs of hunting and combat.

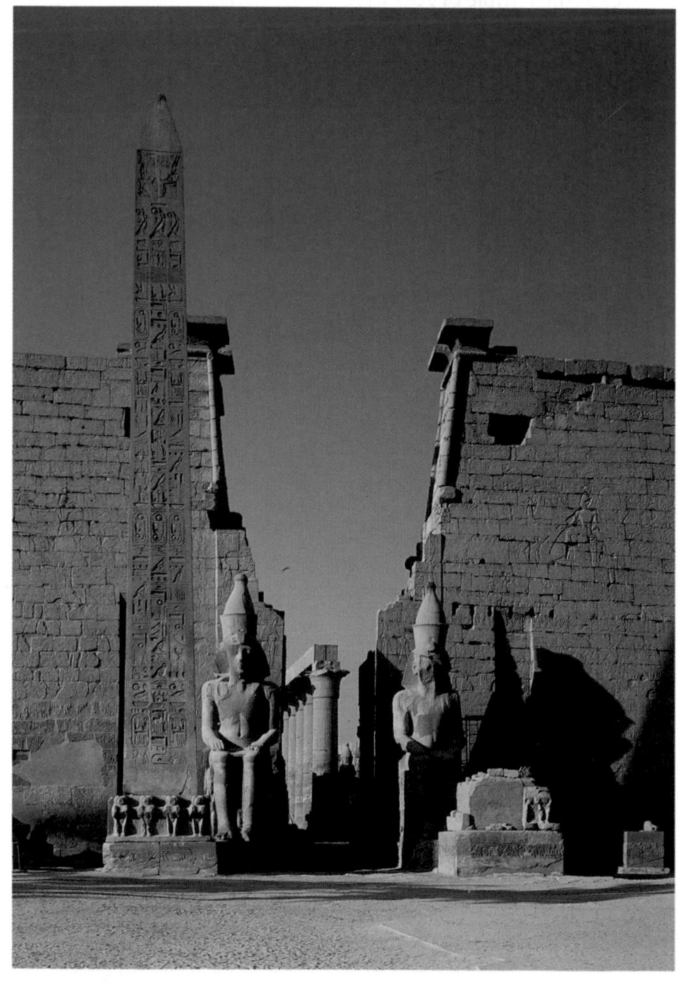

2-33. Pylon and court of Ramesses II, Temple of Amun, Luxor. c. 1279–1212 B.C.

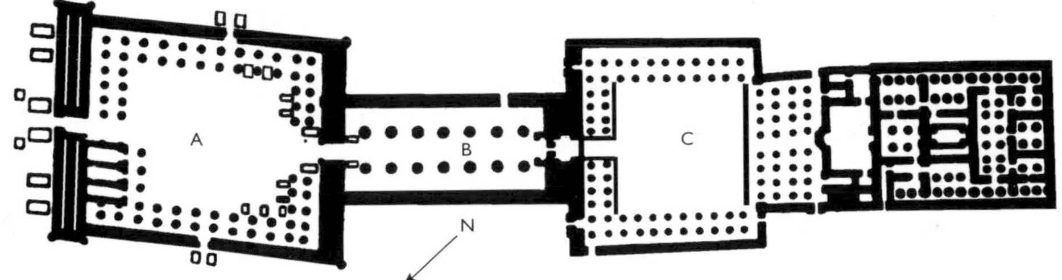

2-34. Plan of the Temple of Amun, Luxor (after N. de Garis Davies)

These subjects were intended to glorify the pharaoh by showing him defeating age-old enemies; even hunting, based on ancient ritual, was primarily of symbolic significance. Both kinds of scenes represent him as the protector of his people by equating his prowess in hunting with his courage in battle, and often there is little difference between them. Such scenes had been common since the late years of the Old Kingdom and were revived in the early Eighteenth Dynasty, when they were standardized. There is an even older custom stretching back to the Fourth Dynasty of reliefs that document actual military campaigns. During the Old Kingdom these most often show sacks of Asiatic cities. It was the Middle Kingdom pharaohs Mentuhotep II and especially Amenhotep III who initiated the custom of recording battles on a monumental scale and in great detail. The scenes in figure 2-35 (below) and sacking the Hittite city of Kadesh on the Orontes River (above) in the temple of Amun at Karnak combine aspects of both traditions. Following convention, the king and his horse-drawn chariot remain frozen against a background filled with hieroglyphs and soldiers, who are much smaller in scale in order to glorify his role. Victory seems ensured by the pharaoh's might and the ruthless efficiency of his forces, although neither battle was, in fact, decisive. Despite the frantic activity, the carving seems strangely uninspired. Only in certain details, such as the hapless prisoners in another scene, do we still find echoes of the Amarna style as seen in Horemheb's tomb (compare fig. 2-30). In any event, the precedent established by Egyptian artists was eventually taken up by the Assyrians, who were just beginning to assert their power, and later by the Romans, who were to conquer the entire region.

As an expression of pharaonic power the temples at Luxor and Karnak are without equal—perhaps justifiably, for the Ramesside period, as the Ninteenth and Twentieth dynasties are known, represents the height of Egyptian power. Nevertheless, the artistic degeneration portends the decline of Egypt itself. About 1076 B.C., barely 125 years after the temple was enlarged by Ramesses II, the country began a long period of decay. The priests gained more and more power, until the cult of Amun took control during the Twenty-first Dynasty. Egyptian civilization ended in a welter of esoteric religious doctrines.

The last phase of ancient Egypt belongs to the Greeks and the Romans. The country was conquered in 323 B.C. by Alexander the Great, who founded the city of Alexandria before his death later that year. His general, Ptolemy, became king, beginning a dynasty that lasted until Cleopatra's son by the Roman emperor Julius Caesar, Ptolemy XIV, was put to death by Augustus in 30 B.C. Although Alexandria became the leading center of learning in the Graeco-Roman world, it was not until the Christian era that Egyptian art flourished briefly once again in the encaustic portraits on Coptic mummy cases (see fig. 7-55).

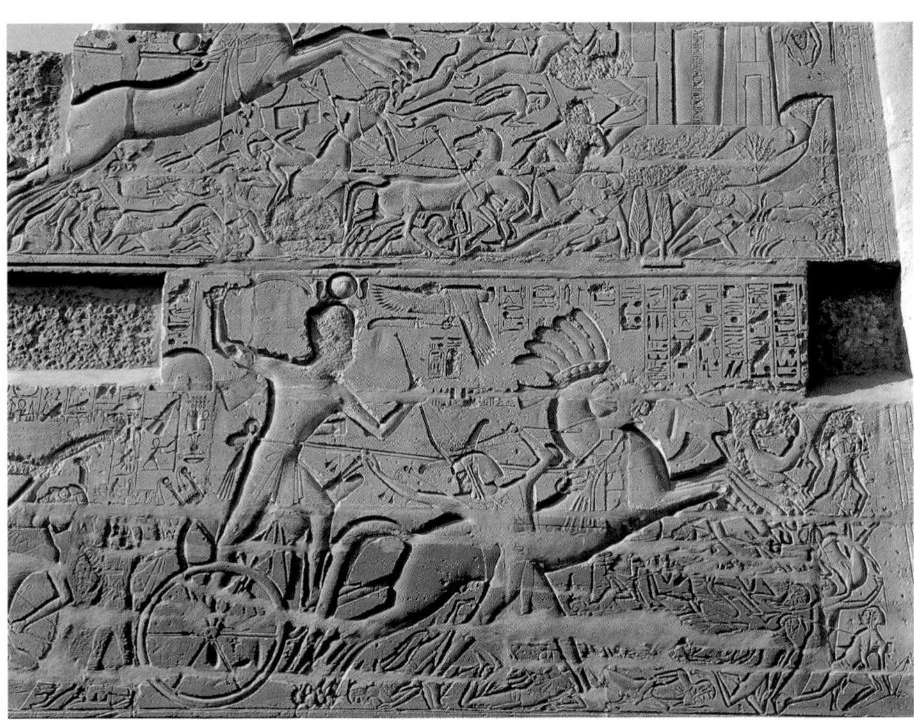

2-35. *Sety I's Campaigns* from the Temple of Amun at Karnak, Thebes (exterior wall, north side of hypostyle). c. 1280 B.C. Sandstone, sunk relief

CHAPTER THREE

Ancient Near Eastern Art

SUMERIAN ART

It is an astonishing fact that human civilization emerged in two places at about the same time. Between 3500 and 3000 B.C., when Egypt was being united under pharaonic rule, another great civilization arose in Mesopotamia, the "land between the rivers." Indeed, the latter may well claim to have developed first. And for close to 3,000 years the two regions retained their distinct features, even though they had contact with each other from the start and their destinies were interwoven in many ways. The pressures that forced the people of both regions to abandon Neolithic village life may well have been the same (see fig. 1-10).

Today Mesopotamia is a largely arid plain, but there is written evidence that at the dawn of civilization it was covered with lush vegetation. However, the valley of the Tigris and Euphrates rivers, unlike that of the Nile, is not a narrow fertile strip protected by deserts on either side. It is a wide, shallow trough crisscrossed by the two rivers and their tributaries. With few natural defenses, it is easily entered from any direction.

Thus the facts of geography tended to discourage the idea of uniting the entire area under a single head. Rulers who had this ambition did not appear, so far as we know, until about a thousand years after the beginning of Mesopotamian civilization, and they succeeded in carrying it out only for brief periods and at the cost of almost continuous warfare. As a result, the history of ancient Mesopotamia has no underlying theme of the sort that divine kingship provides for Egypt. It is a mix of local rivalries, foreign incursions, and the sudden upsurge and collapse of military power. Against this background, the continuity of the region's cultural traditions is remarkable. This common heritage was largely created by the founders of Mesopotamian civilization, whom we call Sumerians after the region of Sumer in which they lived, near the confluence of the Tigris and Euphrates rivers.

The origin of the Sumerians is obscure. Their language is not related to any other known tongue. Sometime before 4000 B.C., they came to southern Mesopotamia from Iran. There, within the next thousand years, they founded a number of city-states. They also developed a distinctive form of writing in cuneiform (wedge-shaped) characters on clay tablets. This phase, which corresponds to the predynastic period in Egypt, is called "protoliterate"; it leads to the early dynastic period, from about 3000 to 2340 B.C.

ARCHAEOLOGICAL CONDITIONS. The first evidence of Bronze Age culture is seen in Sumer about 4000 B.C. Unfortunately, the tangible remains of Sumerian civilization are scanty compared to those of ancient Egypt. Because there was no stone for building, the Sumerians used mud brick and wood, so that almost nothing is left of their structures but the foundations. Nor did they share the Egyptians' concern with the afterlife, though some rich tombs from the early dynastic period, in the shape of vaulted chambers below ground, have been found in the city of Ur. Our knowledge of Sumerian civilization thus depends largely on chance fragments brought to light by excavation; among these are vast numbers of inscribed clay tablets. Yet we have learned enough to form a general picture of this inventive and disciplined people.

RELIGION. Each Sumerian city-state had its own local god, who was regarded as its "king" and owner. It also had a human ruler—the steward of the "king"—who led the people in serving the deity; in effect, he was a priest-king. The local god, in return, was expected to speak for the people of the city-state among the other gods who controlled the forces of nature, such as wind and weather, water, fertility, and the heavenly bodies. The idea of divine ownership was not a pious fiction. The god was believed to own not only the territory of the city-state but also the labor of the population and its products. All these were subject to his commands, which were transmitted to the people by his human steward, the ruler. The result was a system that has been dubbed "theocratic socialism," a planned society administered from the temple. The temple controlled the pooling of labor and resources for communal projects such as the building of dikes or irrigation ditches, and it collected and distributed much of the harvest. All this required detailed written records. Hence it is no surprise that early Sumerian texts deal largely with economic and administrative rather than religious matters (although writing was a priestly privilege).

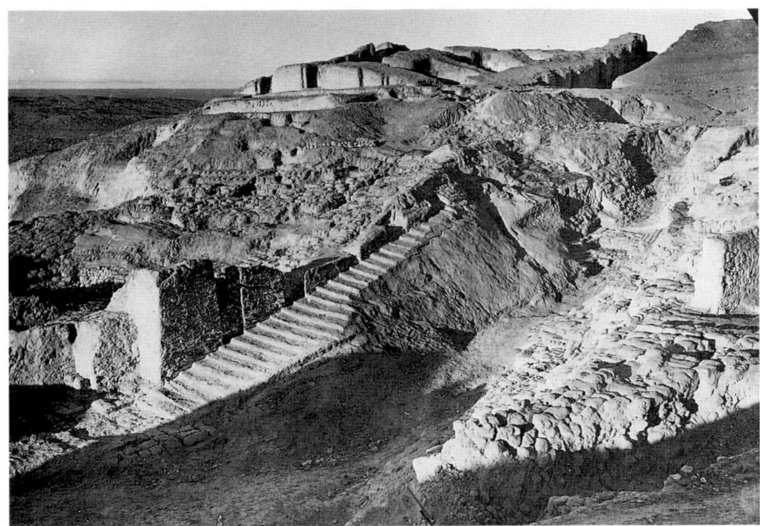

3-1. Remains of the "White Temple" on its ziggurat, Uruk (Warka), Iraq. c. 3500–3000 B.C.

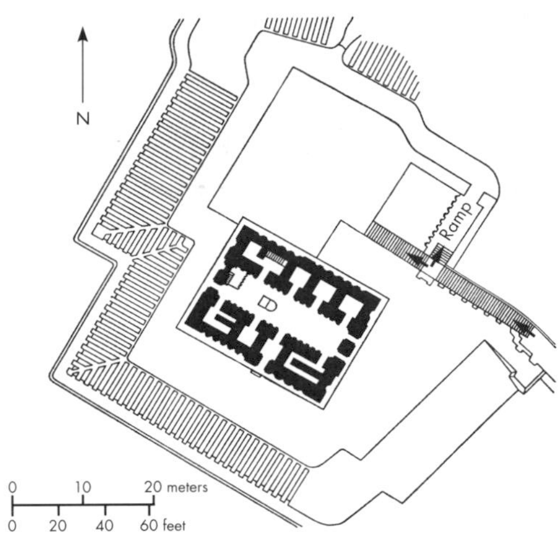

3-2. Plan of the "White Temple" on its ziggurat (after H. Frankfort)

ARCHITECTURE. The role of the temple as the center of both spiritual and physical life can be seen in the layout of Sumerian cities. The houses were clustered about a sacred area that was a vast architectural complex containing not only shrines but workshops, storehouses, and scribes' quarters as well. In their midst, on a raised platform, stood the temple of the local god. Perhaps reflecting the Sumerians' origin in the mountains to the north, these platforms soon reached the height of true mountains. They can be compared to the pyramids of Egypt in the immense effort required to build them and in their effect as landmarks that tower above the plain. They are known as ziggurats.

The most famous of them, the biblical Tower of Babel, has been destroyed, but a much earlier example, built shortly before 3000 B.C. (and thus several centuries older than the first of the pyramids), survives at Warka, the site of the Sumerian city of Uruk (called Erech in the Bible). The 40-foot-high mound has sloping sides reinforced by brick masonry. Stairs and ramps lead up to the platform on which stands the sanctuary, called the "White Temple" because of its whitewashed brick exterior (figs. 3-1 and 3-2). Its heavy walls, with regularly spaced projections and recesses, are well enough preserved to suggest the original appearance of the structure. The main room, or cella (fig. 3-3), where sacrifices were made before the statue of the god, is a narrow hall that runs the length of the temple and is flanked by smaller chambers. Its main entrance is on the southwest side, rather than on the side facing the stairs or on one of the narrow sides of the temple, as one might expect. To understand why this is the case, we must view the ziggurat and temple as a whole. The entire complex is planned in such a way that the worshiper, starting at the bottom of the stairs on the east side, is forced to go around as many corners as possible before reaching the cella. In other words, the path is a sort of angular spiral.

This "bent-axis approach" is a basic feature of Mesopotamian religious architecture, in contrast to the straight, single axis of Egyptian temples (see fig. 2-34). During the following 2,500 years, it was elaborated into ever taller ziggurats rising in multiple stages. These were generally erected by the priest–king in his role as royal builder. The one built by King Urnammu at Ur about 2100 B.C. and dedicated to the moon-god Nanna had three levels (fig. 3-4). Little is left of the upper two stages, but the bottom one, some 50 feet high, has survived fairly well, and its facing of brick has been restored. What was the inspiration behind these structures? Certainly not the kind of pride attributed to the builders of the Tower of Babel in the Old Testament. Rather, they reflect the belief that mountaintops are the dwelling places of the gods. (We need only think of the Mount Olympus of the Greeks.) The Sumerians felt they could provide a fitting home for a god only by creating their own artificial mountains.

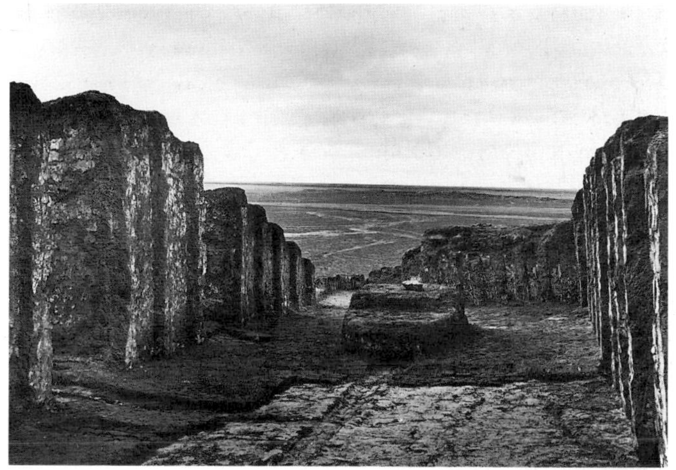

3-3. Interior of the cella of the "White Temple"

STONE SCULPTURE. The image of the god to whom the "White Temple" was dedicated—probably Anu, the god of the sky—is lost. But a splendid female head from the same period at Uruk (Warka) may have belonged to another cult statue, perhaps

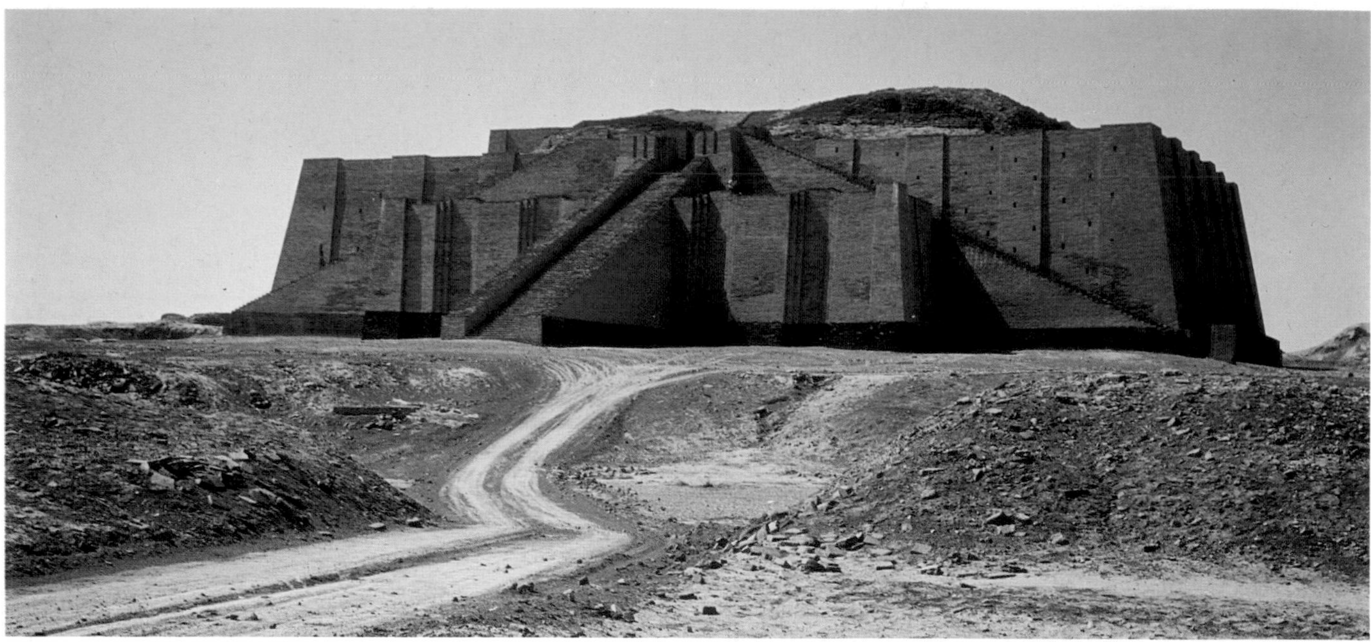

3-4. Ziggurat of King Urnammu, Ur (El Muqeiyar), Iraq. c. 2100 B.C.

of the mother goddess (fig. 3-5). It is carved from limestone, and the hair, eyes, and eyebrows were inlaid with colored materials. The rest of the figure, which must have been close to lifesize, was probably of wood. This head is on a par with the finest works of Egyptian Old Kingdom sculpture. The softly swelling cheeks and the delicate curves of the lips, combined with the steady gaze of the huge eyes, create a balance of sensuousness and severity that seems worthy of any goddess.

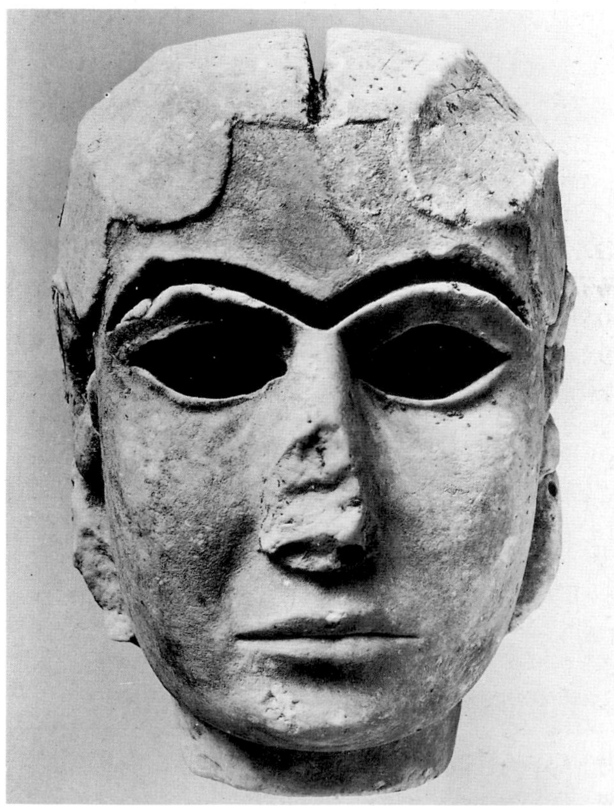

3-5. *Female Head,* from Uruk (Warka). c. 3500–3000 B.C. Limestone, height 8" (20.3 cm). Iraq Museum, Baghdad

It was the geometric and expressive aspects of the Uruk head, rather than the realistic ones, that survived in the stone sculpture of the early dynastic period. They can be seen in a group of figures from Tell Asmar (fig. 3-6) that were carved about five centuries later than the head. Although the two tallest figures have been thought to represent Abu, the god of vegetation, and a mother goddess, it is likely that all are votive statues of priests and worshipers. Despite the difference in size, all but the kneeling figure to the lower right have the same pose of humble worship. The enormous eyes convey a sense of awe that is wholly appropriate to the often-terrifying gods they worshiped. Their stare is emphasized by colored inlays, which are still in place. The entire group must have stood in the cella of the Abu temple, the priests and worshipers communicating with the god through their eyes.

"Representation" here had a very direct meaning: the gods were believed to be present in their images, and the statues of the worshipers served as stand-ins for the persons they portrayed, offering prayers or transmitting messages to the god. Yet none of them shows any attempt to achieve a real likeness. The bodies as well as the faces are highly simplified so as not to distract attention from the eyes, "the windows of the soul." If the Egyptian sculptor's sense of form was based on the cube, that of the Sumerian was derived from the cone and cylinder. Arms and legs have the roundness of pipes, and the long skirts are as smoothly curved as if they had been turned on a lathe. This preference for round forms may have stemmed in part from the shape of the blocks supplied from afar. But it appears even in later times, when Mesopotamian sculpture had gained a far richer repertory of shapes.

ASSEMBLED SCULPTURE. The simplification of the Tell Asmar statues is characteristic of the carver, who works by cutting forms out of a solid block. A far more realistic style is found in Sumerian sculpture that was made by addition rather than subtraction. (That is, it is either modeled in soft materials for casting in bronze or put together from varied substances such as wood,

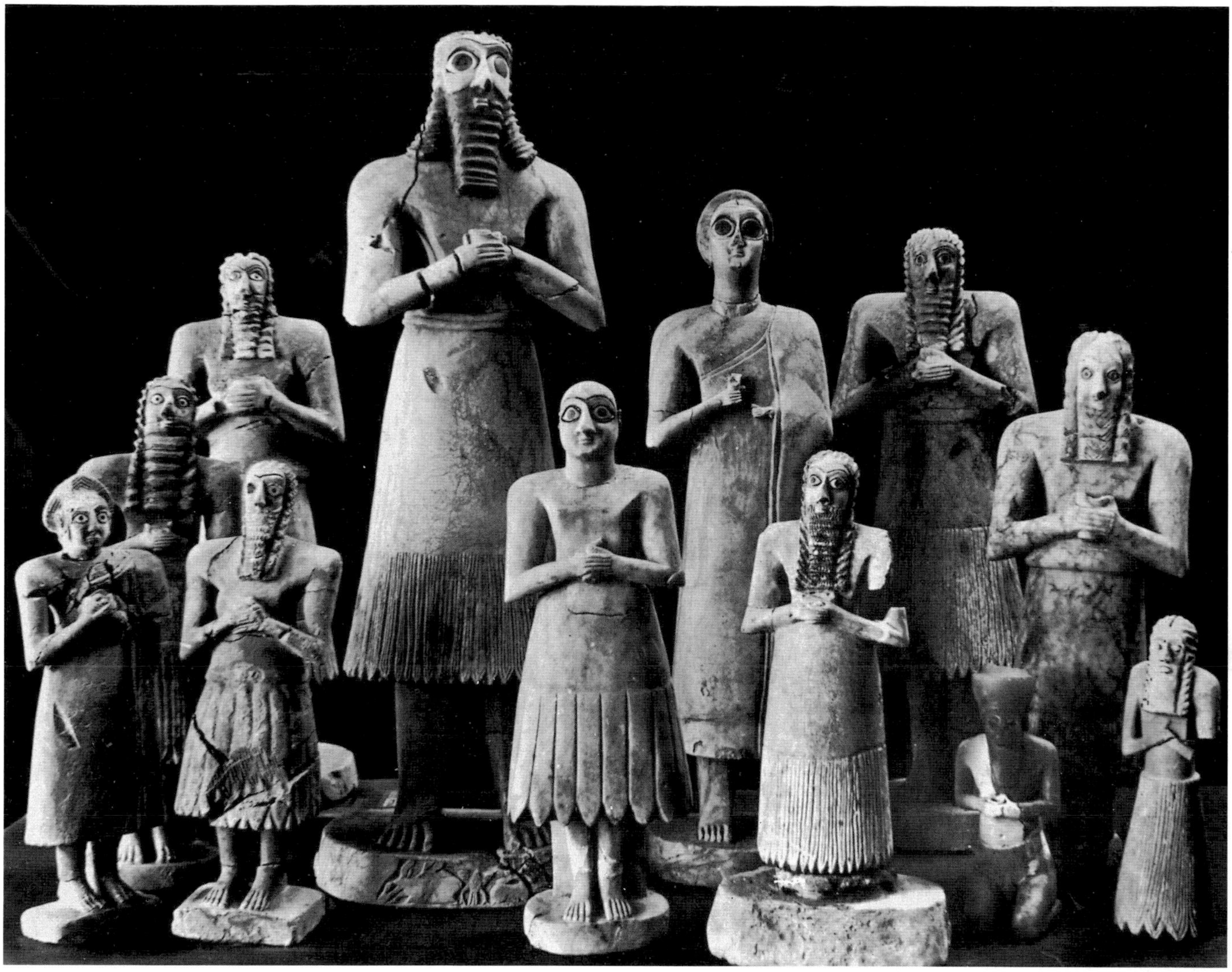

3-6. Statues, from the Abu Temple, Tell Asmar, Iraq. c. 2700–2500 B.C. Limestone, alabaster, and gypsum, height of tallest figure approx. 30" (76.3 cm). Iraq Museum, Baghdad, and The Oriental Institute Museum of The University of Chicago

gold leaf, and lapis lazuli.) Some pieces of the latter kind, roughly contemporary with the Tell Asmar figures, have been found in the tombs at Ur mentioned earlier. They include the fascinating object shown in figure 3-7, an offering stand in the shape of a ram rearing up against a flowering tree. The marvelously alive animal has an almost demonic expression as it gazes from between the branches of the symbolic tree. And well it might, for it is sacred to the god Tammuz and thus embodies the male principle in nature. Even more striking is the copper relief of the storm god Imdugud in the guise of a lion-headed eagle between two heraldically arranged stags (fig. 3-8). In this relief, which probably came from a lintel over a doorway, the awesome power of Mesopotamian gods and goddesses becomes terrifyingly clear.

Such an association of animals with deities is a carry-over from prehistoric times (see pages 34–35). We find it not only in Mesopotamia but in Egypt as well (see the falcon of Horus in fig.

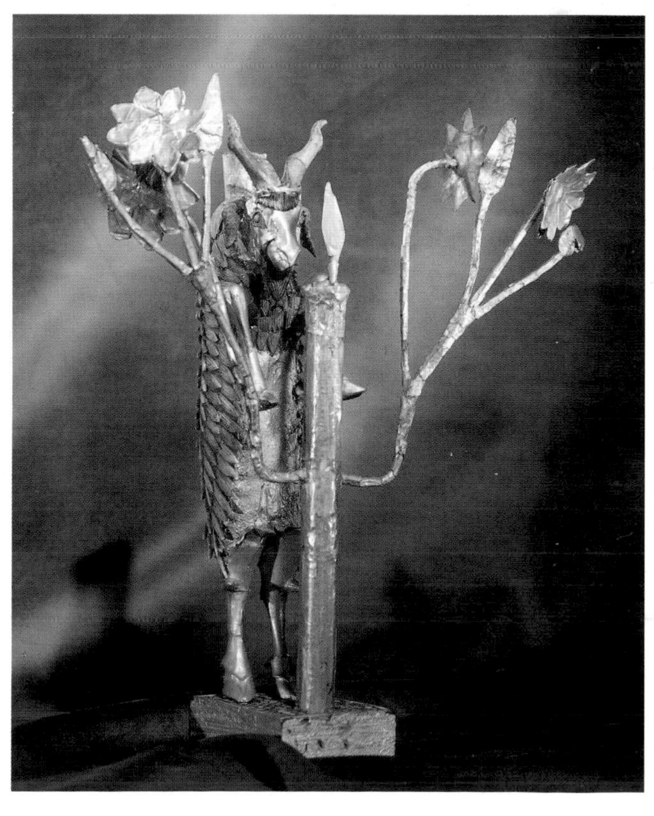

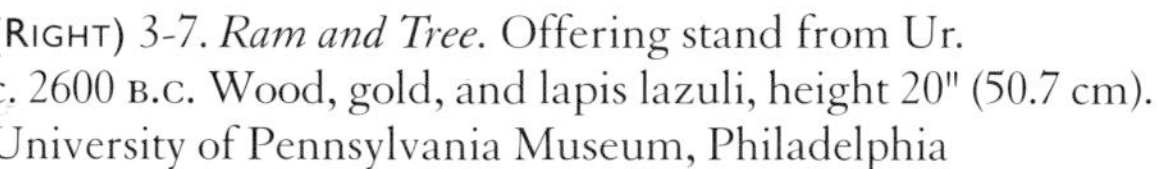

(RIGHT) 3-7. *Ram and Tree.* Offering stand from Ur. c. 2600 B.C. Wood, gold, and lapis lazuli, height 20" (50.7 cm). University of Pennsylvania Museum, Philadelphia

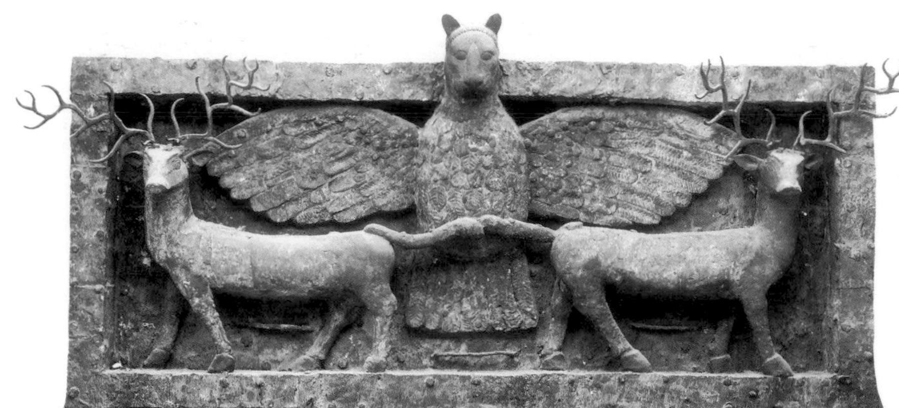

3-8. *Imdugud and Two Stags.* c. 2500 B.C. Copper over wood, 3'6⅛" x 7'10" (1 x 2.3 m). The British Museum, London

2-1). What distinguishes the sacred animals of the Sumerians is the active part they play in mythology. Much of this lore has not come down to us in written form, but we catch glimpses of it in pictorial representations such as those on an inlaid panel from a harp (fig. 3-9) that was recovered together with the offering stand at Ur. The hero embracing two human-headed bulls in the top compartment was such a popular subject that its design has become a rigidly symmetrical, decorative formula. The other sections, however, show animals performing human tasks in surprisingly lively fashion. The wolf and the lion carry food and drink to an unseen banquet, while the ass, bear, and deer provide music. (The bull-headed harp is the same type as the instrument to which our panel was attached.) At the bottom, a scorpion-man and a goat carry objects that they have taken from a large vessel.

The artist who created these scenes was far less constrained by rules than the Egyptian. Even though the figures are placed on ground-lines, there is no fear of overlapping forms or foreshortened shoulders. However, we must be careful not to mistake the intent. What strikes us as delightfully humorous was most likely meant to be viewed seriously. If only we knew the context! The animals, which probably descend from tribal totems or worshipers wearing masks, presumably represent deities engaged in familiar human activities. Yet we may view them as the earliest known ancestors of the animal fable that flourished in the West from Aesop to La Fontaine. The ass with the harp and the hero between two animals survived as fixed images; we meet them again almost 4,000 years later in medieval sculpture.

The royal *Standard of Ur,* which celebrates an important military victory, further attests to the Sumerian artist's skill at inlaywork (fig. 3-10). The side depicting "war" records the conquest itself in fascinating detail, including costume elements and a row of chariots pulled by wild asses known as onagers, with a driver and spearman in each chariot. The "peace" side shows officials celebrating as animals are brought in for the feast, while on the bottom register onagers and other booty are being brought back. The triangular end panels also had animal scenes. The figures have the same squat proportions and rounded forms as the statues from Tell Asmar. Here the artist combines profile and frontal views in the manner familiar to us from Egyptian art, which became the convention in Mesopotamia as well.

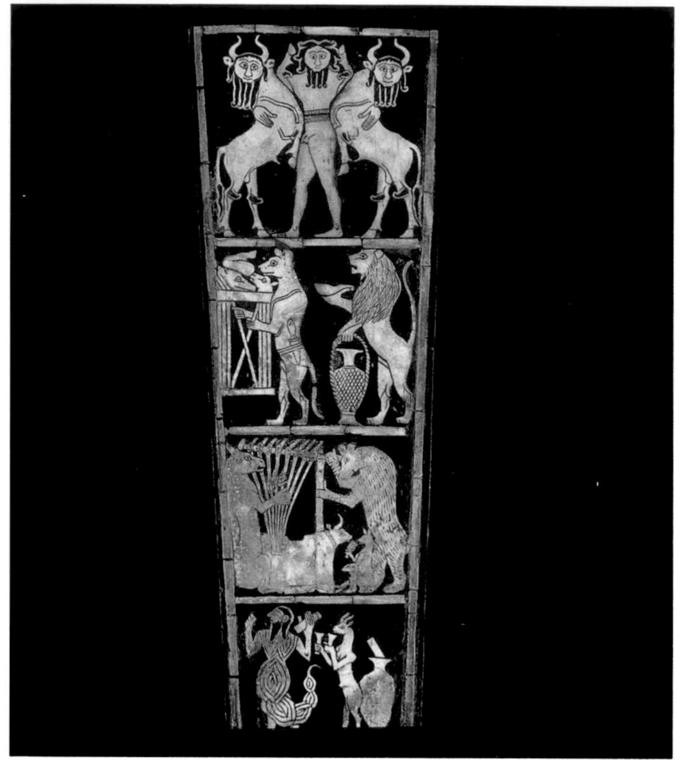

3-9. Inlay panel from the soundbox of a lyre, from Ur. c. 2600 B.C. Shell and bitumen, 12¼ x 4½" (31.1 x 11.3 cm). University of Pennsylvania Museum, Philadelphia

CYLINDER SEALS. An art form distinctive to Mesopotamia was the cylinder seal. These seals, which have survived in vast numbers, were used to seal jars and secure storerooms with the same clay found in writing tablets. Many are not of high quality, reflecting their administrative purpose, but the finest are very beautiful. Our example (fig. 3-11) shows the feeding of the temple herd, which will soon be sacrificed. Both were important functions of the priest-king (identified by his distinctive costume and hat) as shepherd of his people. The stone is carved with great skill. What a wealth of detail has been included in this relief only a few inches high! The artist shows a real feel for nature. We can readily imagine the hilly landscape and rams straining to eat the rosette-shaped leaves of the tree that seems to blossom from the priest-king himself. In effect, he becomes Tammuz, the shepherd-god of fertility who was identified particularly with the ram (see fig. 3-7). Cylinder seals such as this provide us with information that is often missing from the written records. They include many gods and heroes whose identities are not otherwise known. From this evidence it is clear that a great deal is missing from our knowledge of Mesopotamian life and culture.

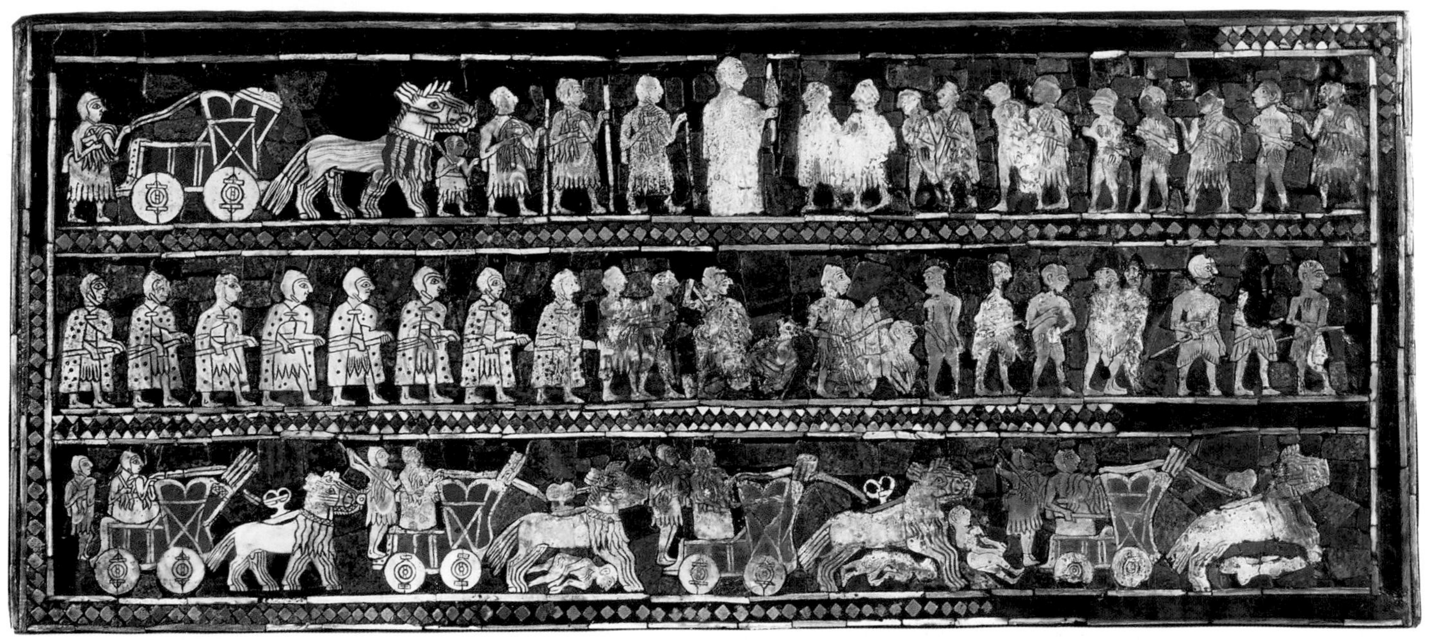

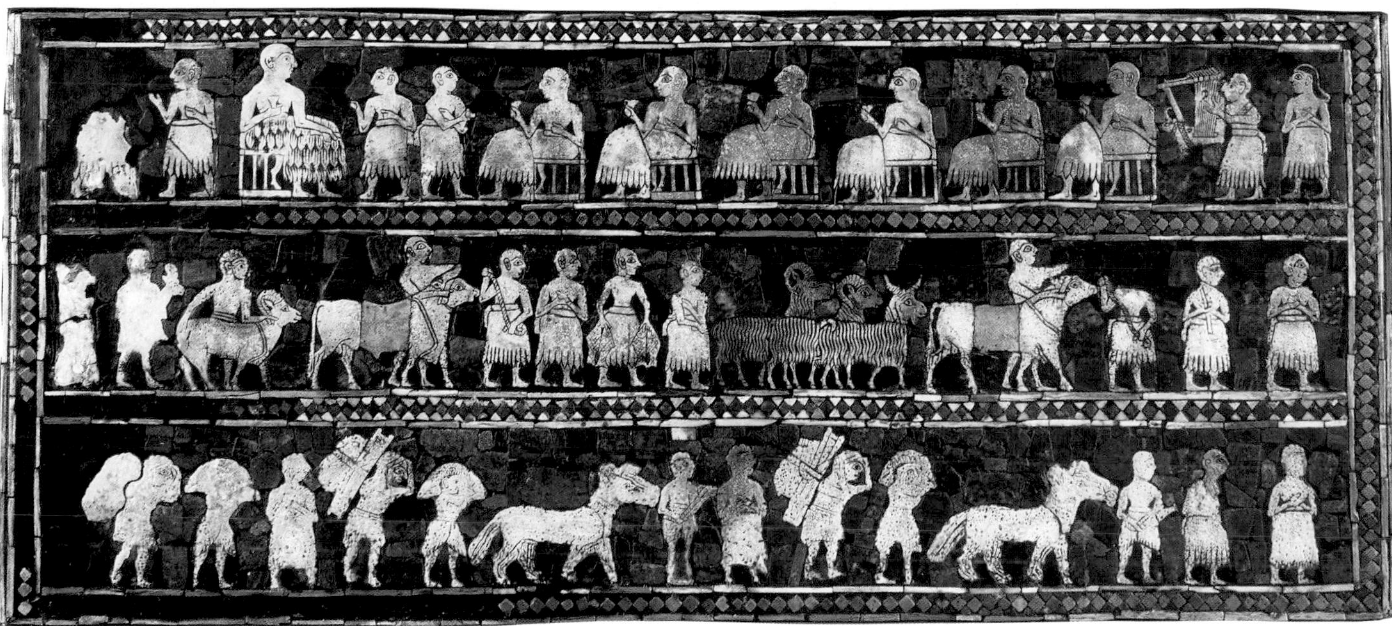

3-10. *Standard of Ur,* front and back sides. c. 2600 B.C. Wood inlaid with shell, limestone, and lapis lazuli, height 8" (20.3 cm). The British Museum, London

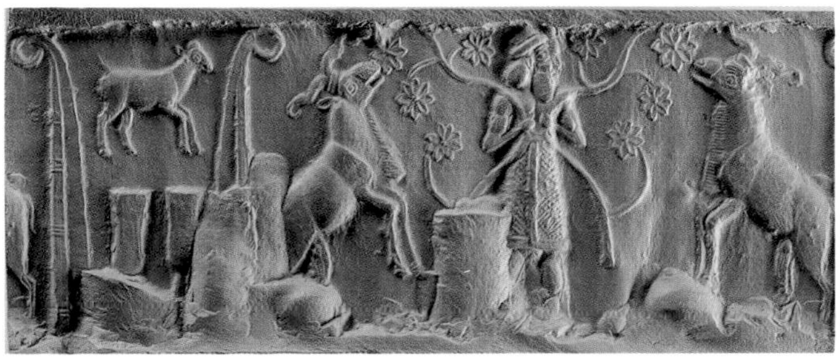

3-11. *Priest-King Feeding Sacred Sheep,* from vicinity of Uruk (Warka). c. 3300 B.C. Marble cylinder seal, height 2⅛" (5.4 cm); diameter 1¾" (4.5 cm). Staatliche Museen zu Berlin, Preussischer Kulturbesitz, Vorderasiatisches Museum

Akkadian Art

Toward the end of the early dynastic period, the theocratic socialism of the Sumerian city-states began to decay. The local "stewards of the god" had in practice become ruling kings. The more ambitious tried to enlarge their domain by conquering their neighbors. At the same time, the Semitic-speaking inhabitants of northern Mesopotamia drifted south in ever-larger waves, until they outnumbered the Sumerian peoples in many places. These newer arrivals had adopted many features of Sumerian civilization but were less bound to the tradition of the city-state. So it is perhaps not surprising that Sargon of Akkad (his name means "true king") and his successors (2340–2180 B.C.) were the first Mesopotamian rulers who openly called themselves kings and proclaimed their ambition to rule the entire earth.

Sargon united the Sumerian and Akkadian gods and goddesses in a new pantheon. His goal was to unite the country and break down the traditional link between cities and their local gods. Under the Akkadians, Sumerian art faced a new task: glorifying the monarch. The most impressive work of this kind that has survived is a magnificent portrait head in bronze from Nineveh (fig. 3-12). Despite the gouged-out eyes (once inlaid with precious materials), it remains both majestic and moving. Equally admirable is the richness of the surfaces framing the face. The plaited hair and the finely curled strands of the beard are shaped with incredible precision, yet they do not lose their organic character and become mere ornament. The complex technique of casting and chasing has been handled with an assurance that bespeaks true mastery. Indeed, this head can hold its own among the greatest works of any period.

THE STELE OF NARAM-SIN. Sargon's grandson, Naram-Sin, had himself and his victorious army immortalized in relief on a large stele (fig. 3-13)—an upright stone slab used as a marker. The stele owes its survival to the fact that it was later carried off as booty to Susa, where it was found by modern archaeologists. There are no ground-lines here. We see the king's forces advancing among the trees on a mountainside. Above them, Naram-Sin stands triumphant, as the defeated enemy soldiers plead for mercy. He is as vigorous as his men, but his size and isolated position give him superhuman status. Moreover, he wears the horned crown hitherto reserved for the gods. There is nothing above him except the mountaintop and the celestial bodies, his "good stars."

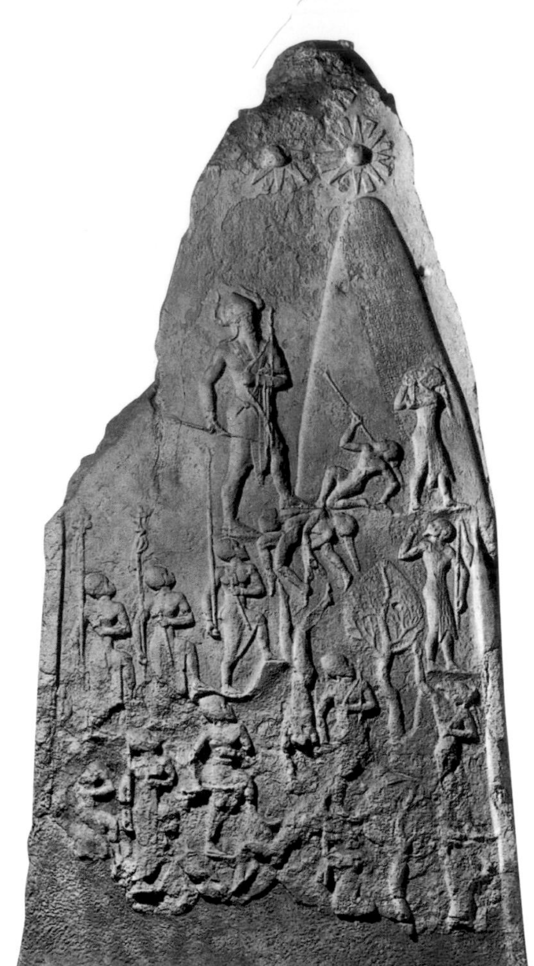

3-13. *Victory Stele of Naram-Sin.* c. 2300–2200 B.C. Stone, height 6'6" (2 m). Musée du Louvre, Paris

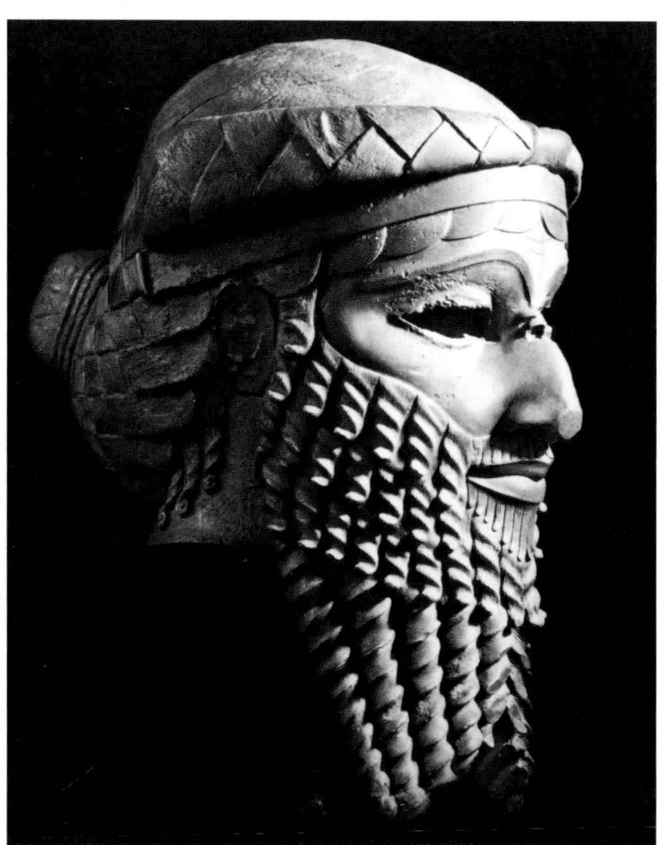

3-12. *Head of an Akkadian Ruler,* from Nineveh (Kuyunjik), Iraq. c. 2300–2200 B.C. Bronze, height 12" (30.7 cm). Iraq Museum, Baghdad

Ur

The rule of the Akkadian kings came to an end when tribesmen from the northeast descended into the Mesopotamian plain and gained control of it for more than half a century. They were driven out in 2125 B.C. by the kings of Ur, who reestablished a united realm that was to last a hundred years.

GUDEA. During the period of foreign dominance, Lagash (the modern Telloh), one of the lesser Sumerian city-states, managed to remain independent. Its ruler, Gudea, who lived at about the same time as Urnammu, took care to reserve the title of king for the city-god, Ningirsu, whose cult he promoted by an ambitious rebuilding of his temple. [See Primary Sources, no. 2, pages 192–93.] Nothing remains of the temple, but Gudea also had numerous statues of himself placed in the shrines of Lagash. (Some 20 examples, all of the same general type, have been found so far.) However devoted he was to the Sumerian city-state, Gudea seems to have inherited the sense of personal importance that we saw in the Akkadian kings, though he prided himself on his relations with the gods rather than on secular power.

The statue of Gudea in figure 3-14 tells us much about how he viewed himself. It was dedicated to Geshtinanna, the goddess of poetry and interpreter of dreams, for it was in a dream that Ningirsu ordered Gudea to build a temple when the Tigris failed to rise. The king played an active role in the building of the ziggurat. He not only laid out the temple according to the design

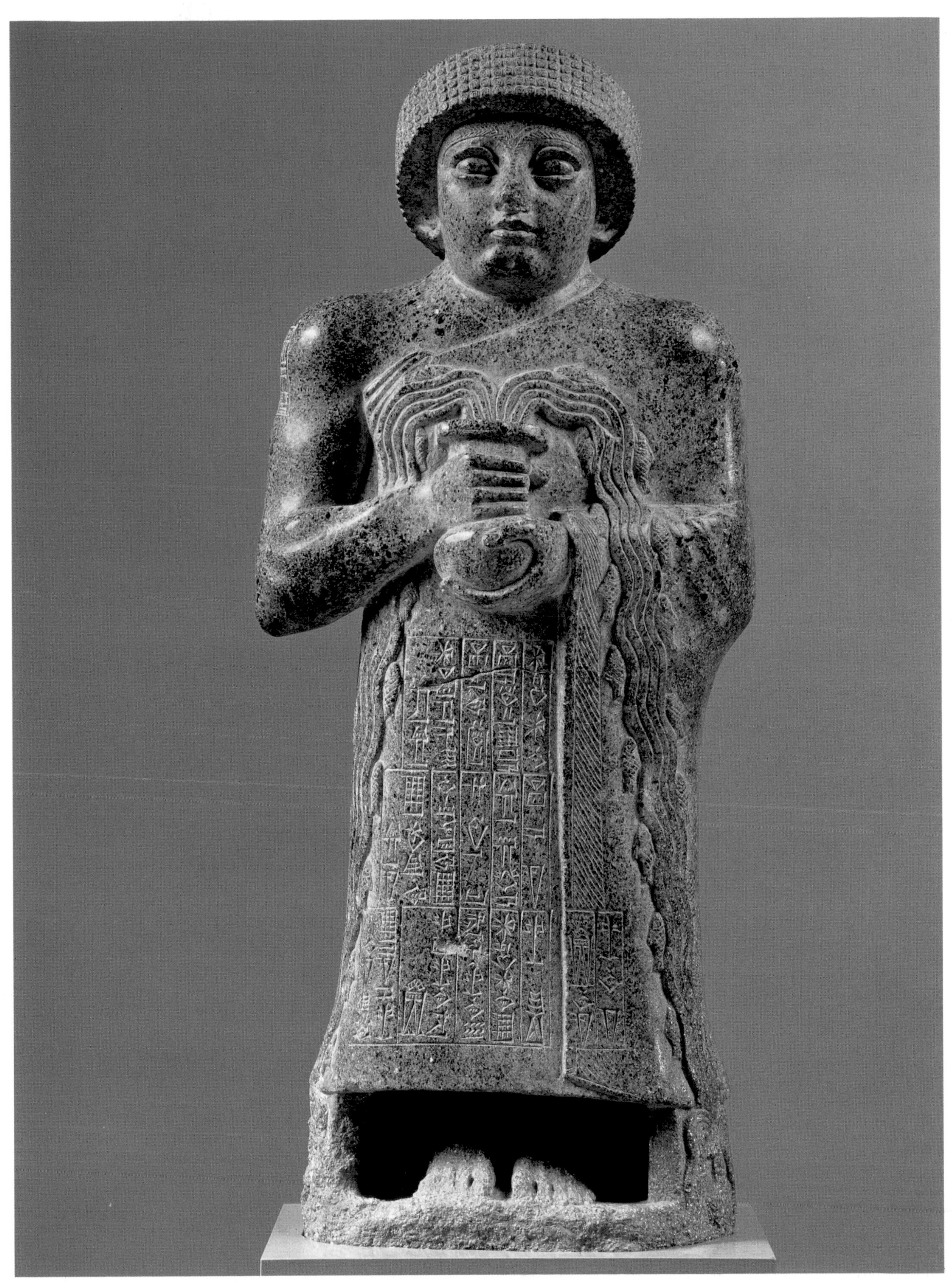

3-14. *Gudea,* from Lagash (Telloh), Iraq. c. 2120 B.C. Diorite, height 29" (73.7 cm). Musée du Louvre, Paris

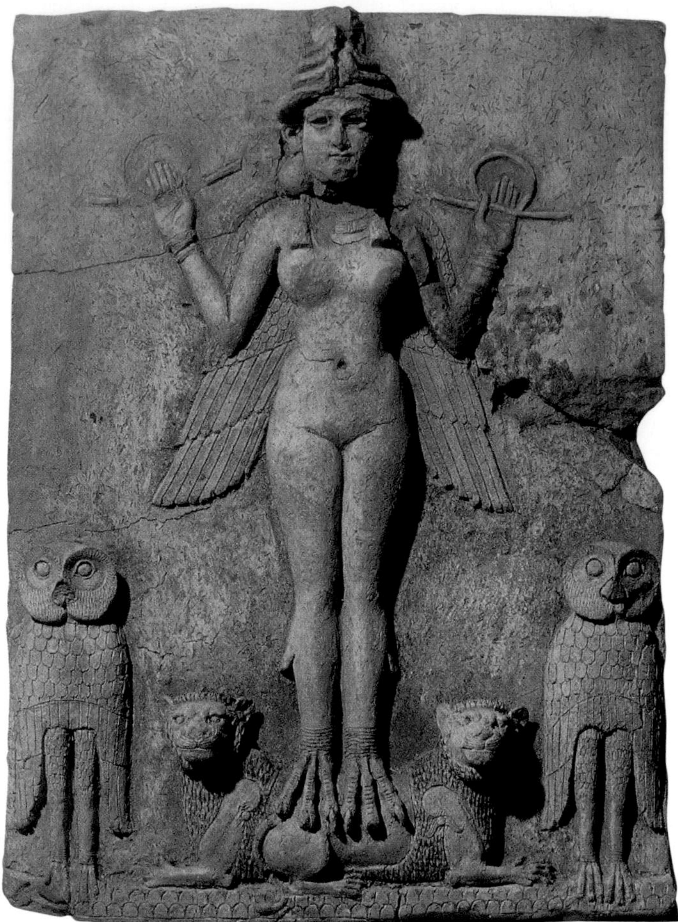

3-15. *Inanna-Ishtar*. c. 2025–1763 B.C. Terra-cotta, height approx. 20" (50.8 cm). Collection Goro Sakamoto, Kyoto, Japan

revealed to him by Enki, the god of building, but also helped make and carry the mud bricks. (A second statue shows him seated with the ground plan on his lap.) The process had to be followed scrupulously to ensure the sanctity of the ziggurat, or else the god would be displeased. We can be sure that Gudea's effort was rewarded, as the statue was an offering to the goddess for her role in helping to end the drought. He is holding a vase from which flow two streams of life-giving water that represent the Tigris and Euphrates rivers. This attribute, which was reserved for water goddesses and female votive figures, may also allude to the king's role in providing irrigation canals and attests to his beneficent rule.

The stone has been worked to a high finish that invites a play of light upon the features. The head appears much less individualized when compared with that of the Akkadian ruler, yet its fleshy roundness is far removed from the geometric simplicity of the Tell Asmar statues. The figure conforms to the same general type as other statues of Gudea. For the first time in Mesopotamian art, we may speak of a canon of forms. (*Canon* means rule; see page 125, Music in Ancient Greece.) Such consistency was probably inspired by Egyptian sculpture, which was based on set proportions. Moreover, the statues are carved of diorite, the hard stone favored by the Egyptians, and are far more ambitious than those from Tell Asmar. The figure nevertheless contrasts with Egyptian statues such as those in figures 2-13 and 2-15. The Sumerian carver has rounded off all the corners to stress the cylindrical quality of the forms. Equally characteristic is the muscular tension in Gudea's bare arm and shoulder, compared with the passive, relaxed limbs of Egyptian sculpture.

Babylonian Art

The third millennium B.C. was a time of turmoil in Mesopotamia. The ethnic clash that brought the Hyksos to Egypt had an even more disruptive effect on the valley of the Tigris and Euphrates. There the invasion of the Elamites from the east and the Amorites from the northwest gave rise to the rival city-states of Isin and Larsa after 2025 B.C. As we might expect, the art and architecture that have come down to us from this period are modest. Sculpture consists for the most part of small terracotta reliefs.

Among them is a cult statue of remarkable quality (fig. 3-15). The sculpture is modeled so deeply as to be nearly in the round, lending it a monumentality that belies the modest size. Who can this winged creature with taloned feet be? She is Inanna-Ishtar, whose emblem is the lion. One of the most widely worshiped of all Mesopotamian deities, she unites the Sumerian goddess of fertility with the winged Semitic goddess of war and hunting. The four-horned headdress is a sign of divinity. The figure's voluptuous nudity is characteristic of Ishtar in her guise as the goddess of love, identified with the planet Venus. Missing, however, are Ishtar's key attributes: weapons in her hands and sprouting from her shoulders. Instead, she bears in each hand the rod and ring of kingship, which she brought with her in her descent into the underworld for the return of her consort, Tammuz.

The myth of Ishtar's descent into the underworld is a model of female self-discovery and empowerment. The goddess of death strips her of all her clothing, which eventually is returned to her, and she emerges transformed. Ishtar thus is also a goddess of death and resurrection. This aspect is denoted by the owl, which also establishes her as Kilili, the forerunner of the Assyrian storm goddess Lilitu and the Semitic demon Lilith. Such a mingling of identities is typical of Sumerian religion after Sargon united the ancient deities in a new pantheon. Yet the image, not seen before in Mesopotamian art, remains unique, for it is never found again.

Central power by native rulers prevailed only from about 1760 to 1600 B.C., when Babylon assumed the role formerly played by Akkad and Ur. Hammurabi (c. 1792–1750 B.C.), the founder of the Babylonian dynasty, is by far the greatest figure of the age. Combining military prowess with a deep respect for Sumerian tradition, he saw himself as "the favorite shepherd" of the sun-god Shamash, whose mission was "to cause justice to prevail in the land." Under him and his successors, Babylon became the cultural center of Sumer. The city was to retain this prestige for more than a thousand years after its political power had waned.

THE CODE OF HAMMURABI. Hammurabi's greatest achievement is his law code. Justly famous as one of the earliest uniform written bodies of law, it is amazingly rational and humane. This code was engraved on a tall diorite stele whose top shows Hammurabi confronting the sun-god (fig. 3-16). (Note the rays coming from his shoulders.) The god holds the ring and rod

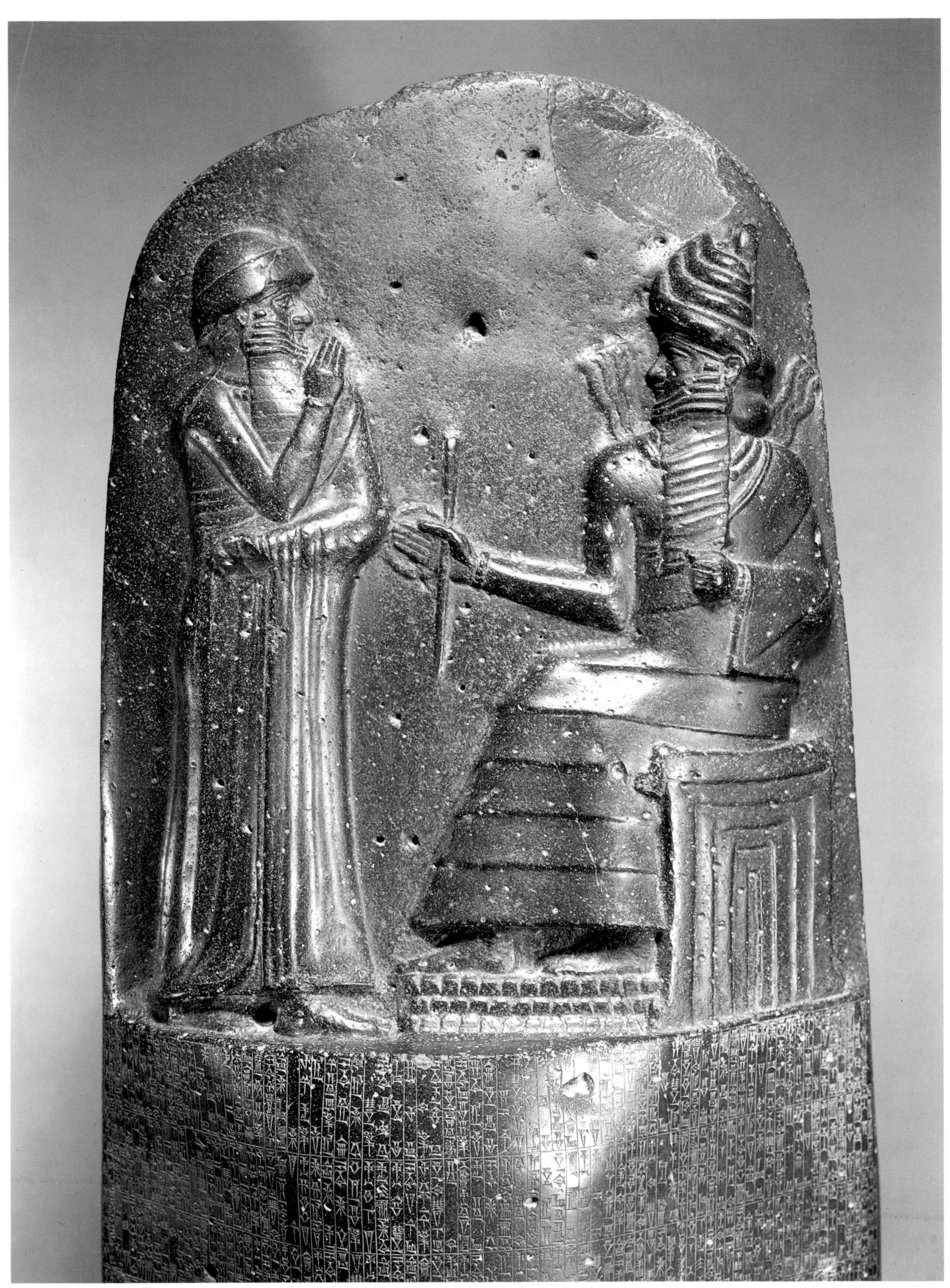

3-16. Upper part of stele inscribed with the Law Code of Hammurabi. c. 1760 B.C.
Diorite, height of stele approx. 7' (2.1 m); height of relief 28" (71 cm). Musée du Louvre, Paris

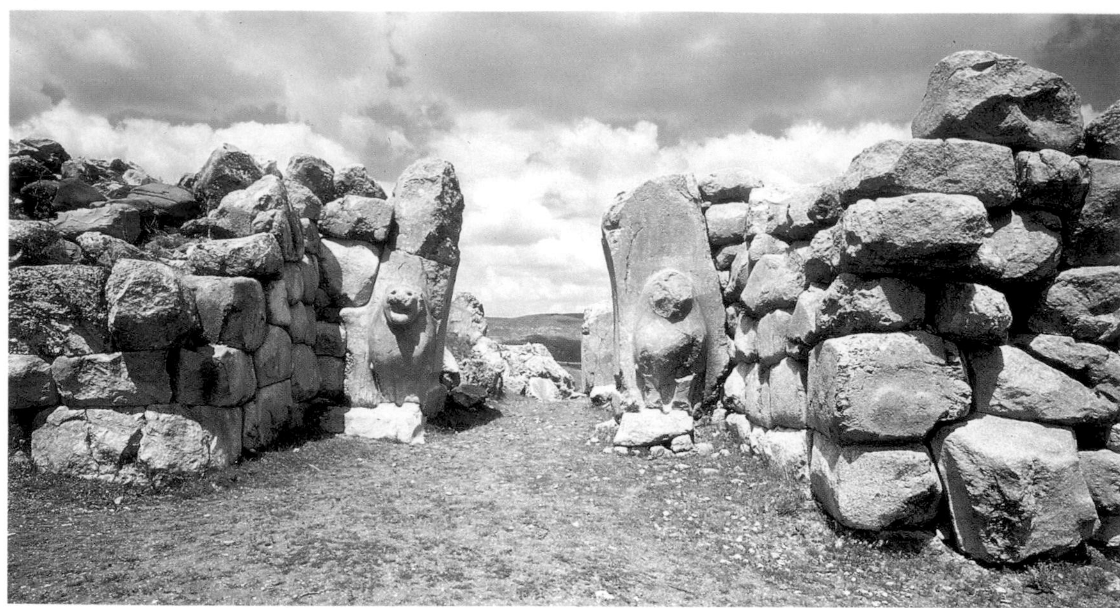

3-17. The Lion Gate, Bogazköy, Anatolia, Turkey. c. 1400 B.C.

of kingship, which here stand for justice as well. The ruler's right arm is raised almost in a speaking gesture, as if he were reporting his work to the divine king. The image conforms to a type of "introduction scene" found on cylinder seals: an individual, his hand raised in prayer, is led by a goddess before a seated deity who bestows his blessing or, if it is an enthroned king, his office. He is, then, a supplicant. But in this case he appears without the benefit—or need—of a divine intercessor. Hence, their relationship is unusually direct. Although this scene was carved four centuries after the Gudea statues, it is closely related to them in both style and technique. In fact, the relief here is so high that the two figures almost give the impression of statues sliced in half when we compare them with the pictorial treatment of the Naram-Sin stele (see fig. 3-13). As a result, the sculptor has been able to render the eyes in the round, so that Hammurabi and Shamash gaze at each other with an immediacy that is unique in works of this kind. They make us recall the statues from Tell Asmar (see fig. 3-6), whose enormous eyes indicate an attempt to establish the same rapport between humans and god in an earlier phase of Sumerian civilization.

THE HITTITES. Babylon was overthrown in 1595 B.C. by the Hittites, an Indo-European tribe that had probably entered Turkey from south Russia in the late third millennium B.C. and settled on the rocky plateau of Anatolia. Their capital, Yazilikaya, near Khattusha (the present-day Turkish village of Bogazköy), was protected by fortifications built of large, roughly cut stones. Flanking the gates were lions and other guardian figures protruding from the blocks that formed the jambs of the doorway (fig. 3-17). The Hittite Empire reached its height between 1400 and 1200 B.C., extending over most of Turkey and Syria. Its greatest king, Suppiluliuma, was in contact with the Egyptian pharaohs Akhenaten and Tutankhamen (see pages 56–58). About 1360 B.C., the Hittites attacked the Mitannians, a people of Hurrian stock who had entered eastern Turkey around the same time as the Hittites. The Mitannians had formed a kingdom in the northern parts of Syria and northern Mesopotamia, including Assur. They were allies of the Egyptians, who could send no effective aid because of the internal crisis provoked by the religious reforms of Akhenaten. The Mitannians were hence defeated.

THE KASSITES. Meanwhile, Babylon was taken over by the Kassites from the northwest, who traded with the Amarna pharaohs during the mid-fourteenth century B.C. They in turn were toppled by the Elamite king Shutruk-Nahhunte I around 1157 B.C., about the time that the Medes and Persians began entering western Iran. However, a second Isid dynasty quickly seized power. Their typical art form was the *kudurru,* a kind of boundary stone set up in temples to record land grants. The finest depicts King Marduk-nadin-akhe (d. 1082 B.C.), the grandson of Nebuchadnezzar I, known as "the avenger of his people" (fig. 3-18). It

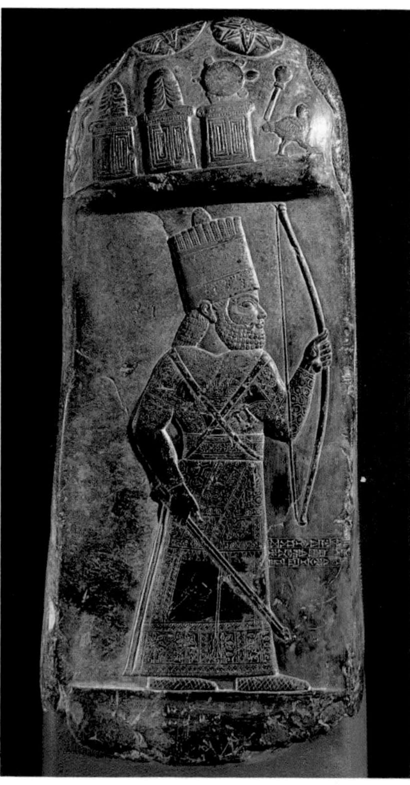

3-18. *Kudurru (Boundary Stone) of Marduk-nadin-akhe.* 1099–1082 B.C. Black limestone, height 24" (61 cm). The British Museum, London

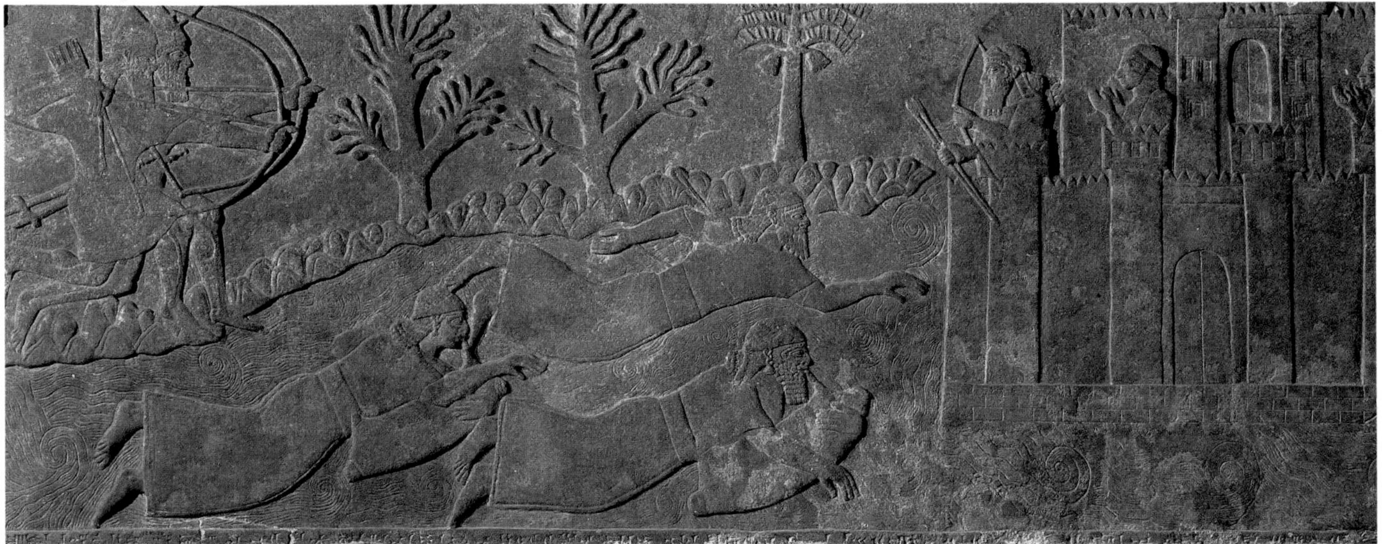

3-19. *Fugitives Crossing River,* from the Northwest Palace of Ashurnasirpal II, Nimrud (Calah), Iraq. c. 883–859 B.C. Alabaster relief, height c. 39" (98 cm). The British Museum, London

has been argued that there is no such thing as true Kassite style, but despite the apparent debt to the statue of Gudea and the Law Code of Hammurabi (see figs. 3-14 and 3-16), the slab is important. It established a revised canon of forms and new standard of skill that were to prevail with very little change in the reliefs of the Assyrians, who conquered southern Mesopotamia soon thereafter.

ASSYRIAN ART

With the defeat of the Mitannians by the Hittites, the city-state of Assur on the upper course of the Tigris regained its independence. Under a series of able rulers, beginning with Ashur-buballit (r. 1363-1328? B.C.), who also had contact with the Amarna kings, the Assyrian Empire gradually expanded. In time it covered not only Mesopotamia proper but the surrounding regions as well. At the height of its power, from about 1000 to 612 B.C., it stretched from the Sinai peninsula to Armenia. Even Lower Egypt was successfully invaded about 670 B.C.

Palaces and Their Decoration

The Assyrians, it has been said, were to the Sumerians what the Romans were to the Greeks. Assyrian civilization drew on the achievements of the south but adapted them to fit its own distinct character. The temples and ziggurats they built were adapted from Sumerian models, while the palaces of Assyrian kings grew to unprecedented size and magnificence.

NIMRUD. Although the Assyrians, like the Sumerians, built in brick, they liked to line gateways and the lower walls of interiors with slabs of limestone (which was easier to obtain in northern Mesopotamia). These panels were decorated with long series of reliefs illustrating the conquests of the royal armies. Every campaign is shown in detail, with inscriptions giving further data. The Assyrian forces always seem to be on the march, meeting the enemy at every frontier of the empire, destroying his strong points, and carrying away booty and prisoners. There is neither drama nor heroism in these scenes—the outcome is never in doubt—and they are often repetitious. Yet they are filled with fascinating vignettes. Our detail, from the Palace of Ashurnasirpal II (d. 859 B.C.) at Nimrud (Calah), shows the enemy fleeing an advance party (fig. 3-19). They swim on inflatable animal skins across a river toward their fortified city, while the king and two women look on in horror. As the earliest large-scale efforts at narrative in Mesopotamian art, they represent an achievement of great importance. Earlier Sumerian art did not describe the progress of specific events in time and space; even the scene on the stele of Naram-Sin is symbolic rather than historic. Assyrian artists may have been aware of Middle and New Kingdom Egyptian reliefs, which depicted military campaigns in considerable detail beginning with the tomb of Horemheb (see fig. 2-30). The battle scenes from Nimrud are similar to those carved in the reigns of Sety I and Ramesses II during the Ramesside period (compare fig. 2-35). Yet the Assyrian sculptor had to develop new techniques to cope with the demands of pictorial storytelling. While the results can hardly be called beautiful, they achieve their main purpose: to be clearly readable.

LION HUNTS. The mass of detail in the reliefs of military campaigns often leaves little room for glorifying the king. This purpose is served by another frequent subject, the royal lion hunts. As in Egypt, their source, they were more like ritual combats than actual hunts: the animals were released from cages into a square formed by troops with shields. (At a much earlier time, lion hunting had been an important duty of Mesopotamian rulers as the "shepherds" of the communal flocks.) Here the Assyrian sculptor rises to his greatest heights. In figure 3-20, the lion attacking the royal chariot from the rear is clearly the hero of the scene. Of magnificent strength and courage, the wounded animal seems to embody all the dramatic emotion that we miss in the pictorial accounts of war. The dying lion on the right is equally impressive in its agony. Despite the debt to Egypt, how differently the Assyr-

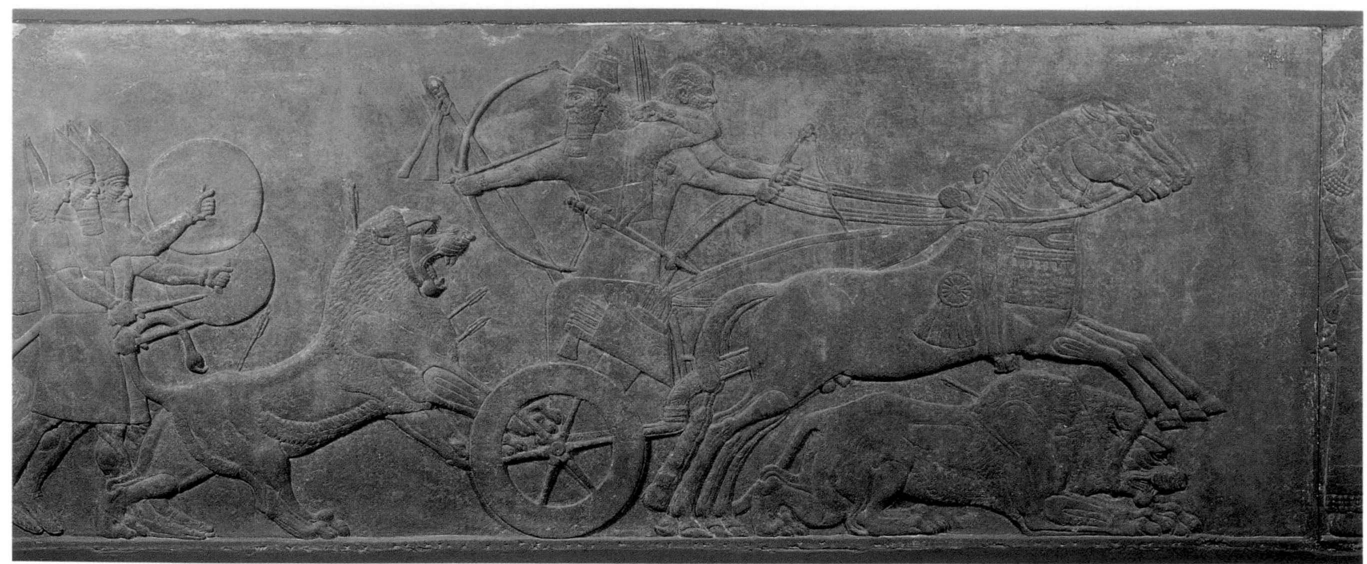

3-20. *Ashurnasirpal II Killing Lions,* from the Palace of Ashurnasirpal II, Nimrud (Calah), Iraq. c. 850 B.C. Limestone, 3'3" x 8'4" (1 x 2.5 m). The British Museum, London

ian had interpreted the same subject! We need only compare the horses: the Assyrian ones are less graceful but more energetic as they flee, ears folded back in fear, from the lion. The figures, it is clear, are descendants of King Marduk-nadin-akhe on the Kassite boundary marker in figure 3-18.

DUR SHARRUKIN. The same impression of royal power was reinforced at the entrance to another of these palaces, that of Sargon II (d. 705 B.C.) at Dur Sharrukin (the modern Khorsabad). This palace was surrounded by a citadel with turreted walls that shut it off from the rest of the town. Figure 3-21 shows one of the two gates of the citadel during excavation. The two guardian figures (called Lamassus) are an odd mixture of relief and sculpture in the round: each has a fifth leg so that it will seem complete from the side. They must have been inspired by Hittite examples such as the Lion Gate at Bogazköy (see fig. 3-17). Awesome in size and appearance, the gates were meant to impress visitors with the authority and majesty of the king.

Neo-Babylonian Art

The Assyrian Empire came to an end in 612 B.C., when Nineveh fell to the Medes and Scythians from the east. At that time the commander of the Assyrian army in southern Mesopotamia made himself king of Babylon. Under him and his successors the ancient city had a final brief flowering between 612 and 539 B.C., before it

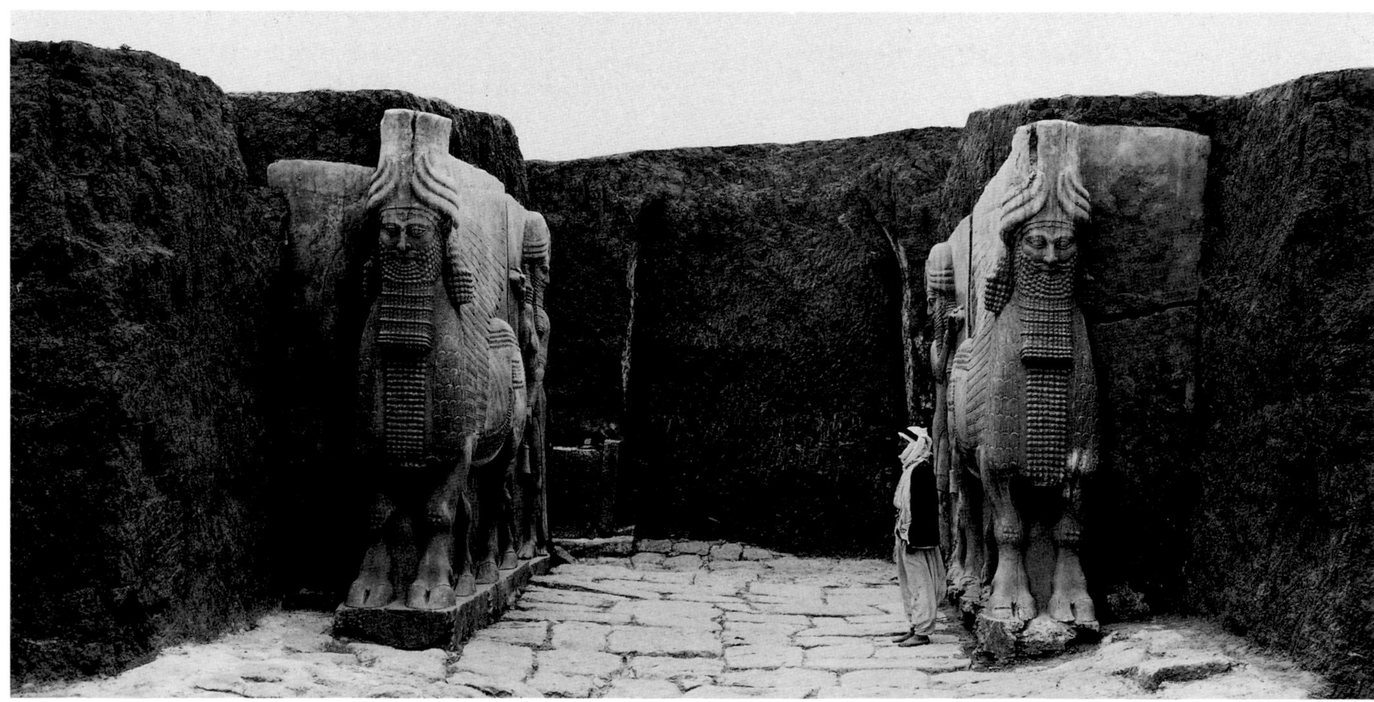

3-21. Gate of the Citadel of Sargon II, Dur Sharrukin (Khorsabad), Iraq (during excavation). 742–706 B.C.

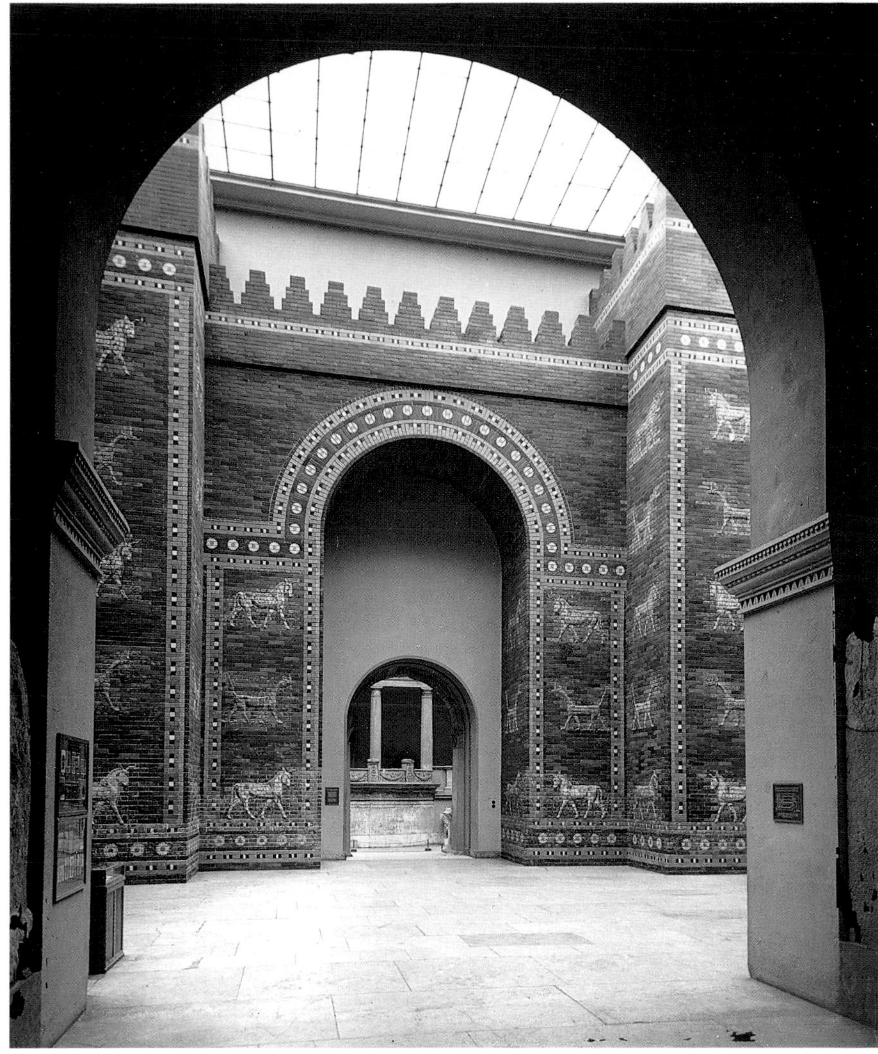

3-22. Ishtar Gate (restored), from Babylon, Iraq. c. 575 B.C. Glazed brick. Staatliche Museen zu Berlin, Preussischer Kulturbesitz, Vorderasiatisches Museum

was conquered by the Persians. The best known of these Neo-Babylonian rulers was Nebuchadnezzar II (d. 562 B.C.), the builder of the Tower of Babel. That famous structure was only one part of a large complex comparable to the Citadel of Sargon II at Dur Sharrukin.

Whereas the Assyrians had used carved stone slabs, the Neo-Babylonians (who were farther removed from the sources of such slabs) substituted baked and glazed brick. This technique, too, had been developed in Assyria. Now, however, it was used on a far greater scale, both for surface ornament and for reliefs. Its distinctive effect becomes evident if we compare the gate of Sargon's citadel (see fig. 3-21) with the Ishtar Gate of Nebuchadnezzar's sacred precinct in Babylon, which has been rebuilt from the thousands of glazed bricks that covered its surface (fig. 3-22). The procession of bulls, dragons, and other animals has a stately grace that is far removed from the ponderous guardian monsters of the Assyrians. Here again we sense the special genius of Mesopotamian art for the portrayal of animals.

PERSIAN ART

Persia, the mountain-fringed high plateau to the east of Mesopotamia, takes its name from the people who occupied Babylon in 539 B.C. Today the country is called Iran, its older and more suitable name. (The Persians were latecomers who arrived on the scene only a few centuries before they began their conquests.) Iran has been inhabited since prehistoric times and seems to have been a gateway for migratory tribes from the Asiatic steppes to the north as well as from India to the east. The new arrivals would settle down for a while, dominating or mingling with the local population, until the next wave of emigrants forced them to move on—to Mesopotamia, Asia Minor (roughly, Asian Turkey), or southern Russia.

Not much is known about these movements; the information we have is vague and uncertain. Since nomadic tribes leave no permanent structures or records, we can trace their wanderings only by careful study of the articles they buried with their dead. Such objects, of wood, bone, or metal, are a distinct kind of portable art that we call the nomad's gear. They include weapons, bridles, buckles, fibulas and other articles of adornment, cups, bowls, and the like. They have been found over a vast area, from Siberia to central Europe, from Iran to Scandinavia. They have in common not only their ornamental design but also a set of forms known as the "animal style." This style's main feature, as the name suggests, is the use of animal motifs in abstract and imaginative ways.

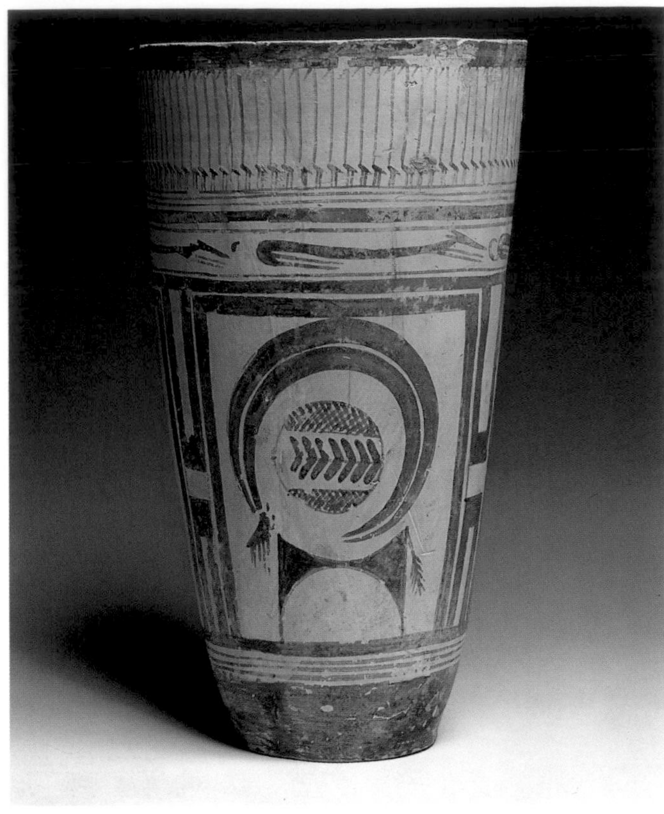

3-23. Painted beaker, from Susa. c. 5000–4000 B.C. Height 11 1/4" (28.3 cm). Musée du Louvre, Paris

3-24. Fragment of a belt, probably from Ziwiye. 7th century B.C. Gold sheet, width 6 1/2" (16.5 cm). The British Museum, London

THE ANIMAL STYLE. One of the sources of this animal style appears to be ancient Iran. We find its earliest ancestors on the prehistoric painted pottery of western Iran. An example is the beaker in figure 3-23, which shows an ibex (mountain goat) reduced to a few sweeping curves, so that the body becomes an appendage of the horns. The racing hounds above the ibex are little more than horizontal streaks. When we look closely, we see that the striations below the rim are long-necked birds. In Sumer this style soon gave way to an interest in the organic unity of animal bodies (see figs. 3-7 and 3-9), but in Iran it survived despite the strong influence of Mesopotamia.

Several thousand years later, in the tenth to seventh centuries B.C., the style reappears in western Iran, though the exact origin and date of most objects are by no means certain. The remains of a seventh-century B.C. gold belt, probably from Ziwiye in the northwestern part of the country, which was ruled by the Manneans, is an example (fig. 3-24). Here the animal style is at its finest—and most puzzling. The kneeling ibex is a descendant of the one on the vase from Susa. But what are we to make of the other creatures? The stag, which is not native to the region, is a motif from the steppes of central Asia that was transported by the Scythians. The alternating rows of ibexes and stags are enclosed in a pattern of abstract lion heads; this pattern was native to Urartu (the biblical Ararat) in eastern Turkey, which was conquered by Sargon II of Assyria in 714 B.C. Similar belts of bronze have also been found in Urartian tombs.

The Scythians belonged to a group of nomadic Indo-European tribes, including the Medes and the Persians, that began to filter into Iran soon after 1000 B.C. (An alliance of Medes and

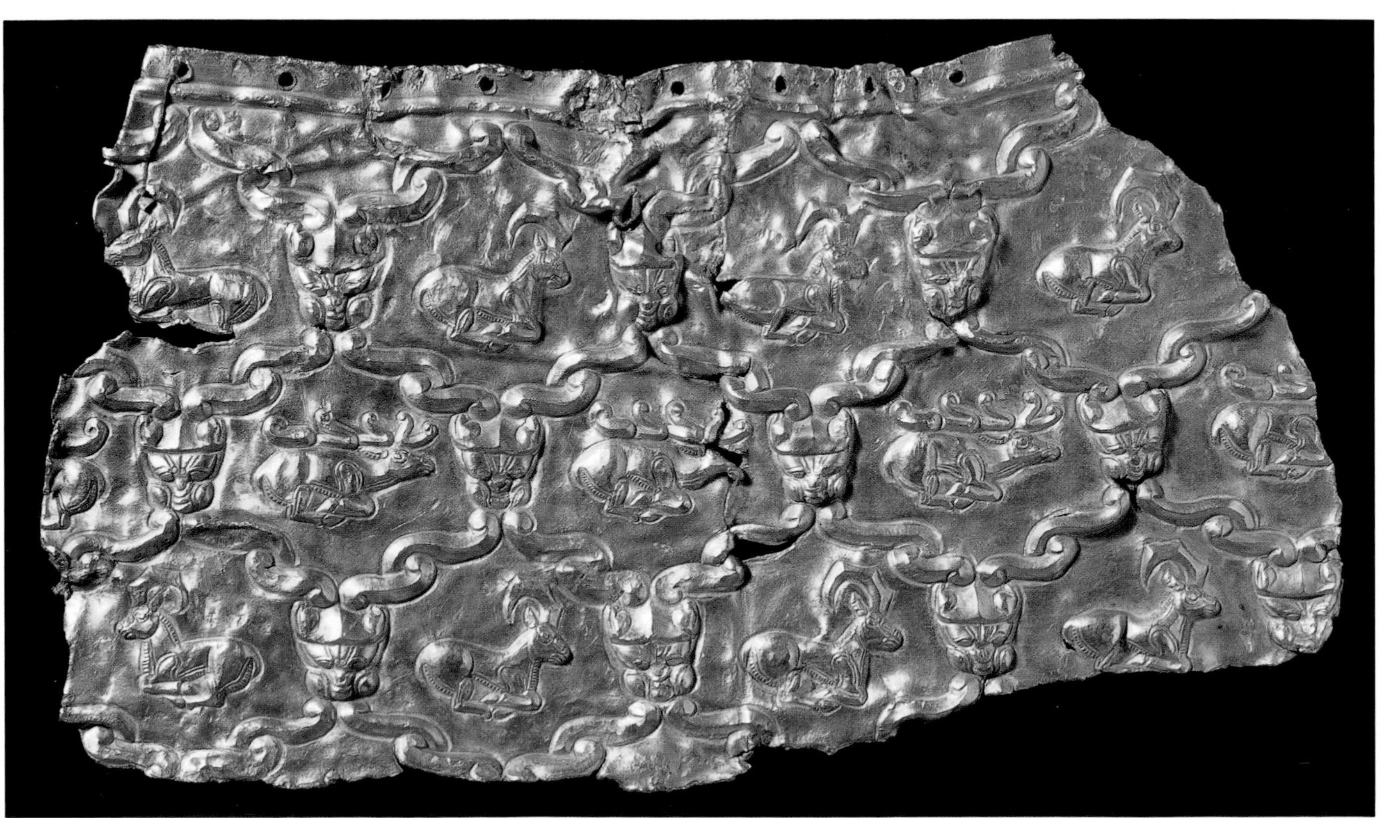

Scythians, it will be recalled, crushed Nineveh in 612 B.C.) The animal style of the Scythians merged with that of the Luristan region in western Iran during the late eighth century B.C. These peoples, however, were makers of bronze. Although goldsmithing was of ancient origin and widely diffused (see figs. 3-7 and 4-16–4-18), it was probably the Phoenicians who translated the animal style into gold: a pectoral (breastplate) from the same hoard as figure 3-24 depicts Phoenician deities in a similar fashion. These seafaring traders, originally from Canaan, began ranging throughout the Mediterranean sea after the fall of Mycenae around 1200 B.C. The seventh century B.C. was a time of intense contact between east and west. The cultural exchange gave rise to the Orientalizing style in Greece (see pages 98–100), which in turn contributed new motifs to the Near East. The Phoenicians played a key role in this process. They were superb metalworkers, especially of gold, who made use of motifs derived from their travels. Around 800 B.C. they settled on nearby Cyprus, which soon became a center of silver- and goldsmithing and was equally open to diverse influences. Whether Phoenician (as seems likely) or Cypriot, the artist who created our gold belt has brought together the elements of the animal style into a masterful design and fashioned it with impressive skill.

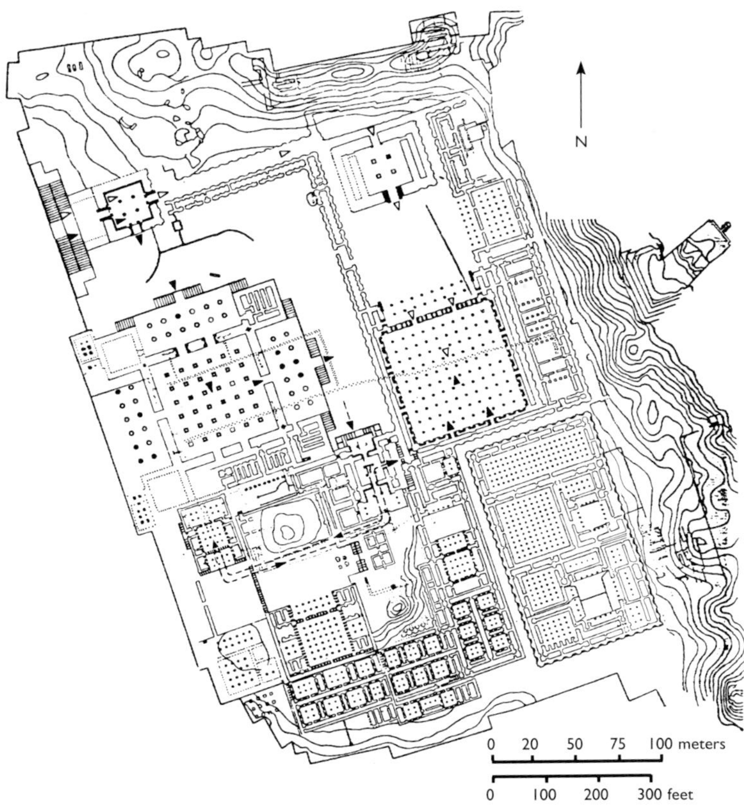

3-25. Plan of the Palace of Darius and Xerxes, Persepolis. 518–460 B.C. Solid triangles show the processional route taken by Persian and Mede notables; open triangles indicate the way taken by heads of delegations and their suites

Achaemenid Art

The Near East long remained a vast melting pot. During the middle of the sixth century B.C., however, the entire region came under the sway of the Persians. After overthrowing Astyages, king of the Medes, Cyrus the Great (c. 600–529 B.C.) conquered Babylon in 539 B.C. Along with the title king of Babylon, he assumed ambitions of the Assyrian rulers. The empire he founded continued to expand under his successors. Egypt as well as Asia Minor fell to them, while Greece escaped by a narrow margin. At its height, under Darius I (c. 550–486 B.C.) and his son Xerxes (519–465 B.C.), the Persian Empire was far larger than the Egyptian and Assyrian empires combined. This huge domain endured for two centuries, and during most of its life it was ruled both efficiently and humanely. For an obscure tribe of nomads to have achieved all this is little short of a miracle. Within a single generation, the Persians not only learned how to administer an empire but also developed a highly original monumental art to express the grandeur of their rule. Despite their genius for adaptation, the Persians retained their religious beliefs, which were drawn from the prophecies of Zoroaster. This faith was based on the dualism of Good and Evil, embodied in Ahuramazda (Light) and Ahriman (Darkness). Since the cult of Ahuramazda centered on fire altars in the open air, the Persians had no religious architecture. Their palaces, on the other hand, were huge and impressive.

PERSEPOLIS. The most ambitious palace, at Persepolis, was begun by Darius I in 518 B.C. Its layout as shown in figure 3-25—a great number of rooms, halls, and courts on a raised platform—recalls the palaces of Assyria (see fig. 3-21). Assyrian traditions are the strongest element throughout. Yet they do not determine the character of the building, for they have been combined with influences from every corner of the empire to create a new, uniquely Persian style.

At Persepolis columns are used on a grand scale. The Audience Hall of Darius and Xerxes, a room 250 feet square, had a wooden ceiling supported by 36 columns 40 feet tall, a few of which are still standing (fig. 3-26). Such a massing of columns suggests Egyptian architecture (compare fig. 2-32), and Egyptian influence can indeed be seen in the ornamental detail of the bases and capitals. However, the slender, fluted shaft of the Persepolis columns is derived from the Ionian Greeks in Asia Minor, who are known to have sent artists to the Persian court.

The columns are crowned by a strange "cradle" for the beams of the ceiling (fig. 3-27). Composed of the front parts of two bulls or similar creatures, it has no precedent. While the animals themselves are of Assyrian origin, the way they are combined suggests a greatly enlarged version of the animal style from western Iran. This seems to be the only instance of Persian architects drawing upon their artistic heritage of nomad's gear.

The double stairway leading up to the Audience Hall is decorated with long rows of marching figures in low relief (see fig. 3-26). Their repetitive, ceremonial character, which stresses their subservience to the architectural setting, is typical of Persian

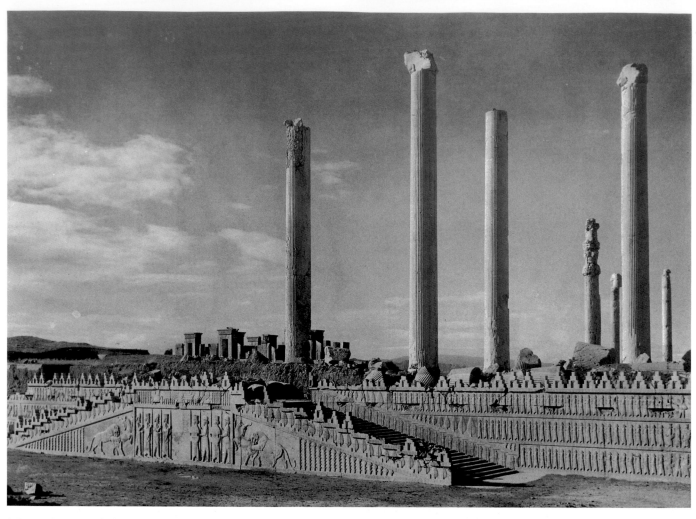

3-26. Audience Hall of Darius and Xerxes, Persepolis, Iran. c. 500 B.C.

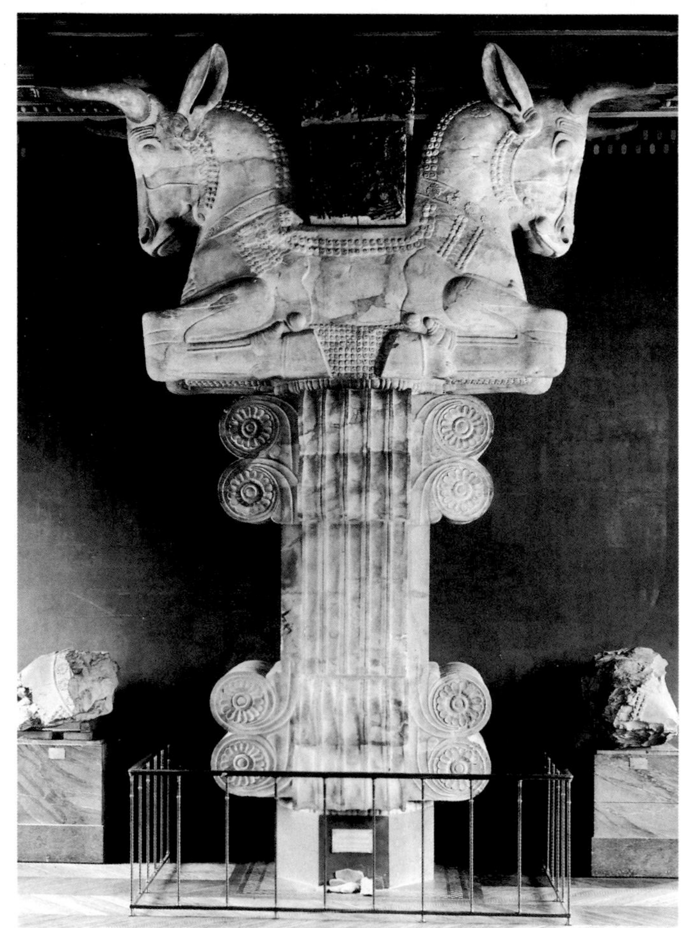

(RIGHT) 3-27. Bull capital, from Persepolis. c. 500 B.C. Musée du Louvre, Paris

sculpture. We find it even in scenes of special importance, such as *Darius and Xerxes Giving Audience* (fig. 3-28). Here the expressive energy and narrative skill of Assyrian relief have been rejected in favor of formal grandeur.

PERSIAN STYLE. At first glance, the style of these Persian carvings seems to be a softer and more refined echo of the Mesopotamian tradition. Even so, we find that the Assyrian-Babylonian heritage has been enriched in one important way. There is no precedent in Near Eastern sculpture for the layers of pleated folds such as we see in the *Darius and Xerxes* relief. Another surprising effect is the way the arms and shoulders of these figures press through the fabric. These innovations stem from the Ionian Greeks, who had created them in the course of the sixth century B.C.

Persian art under the Achaemenids, then, is a remarkable marriage of many diverse elements. Yet it lacked a capacity for growth. The style developed under Darius I about 500 B.C. continued without major change until the end of the empire. The Persians, it seems, were preoccupied with decorative effects regardless of scale, a carryover from their nomadic past. There is no real difference between the bull capital (see fig. 3-27) and the

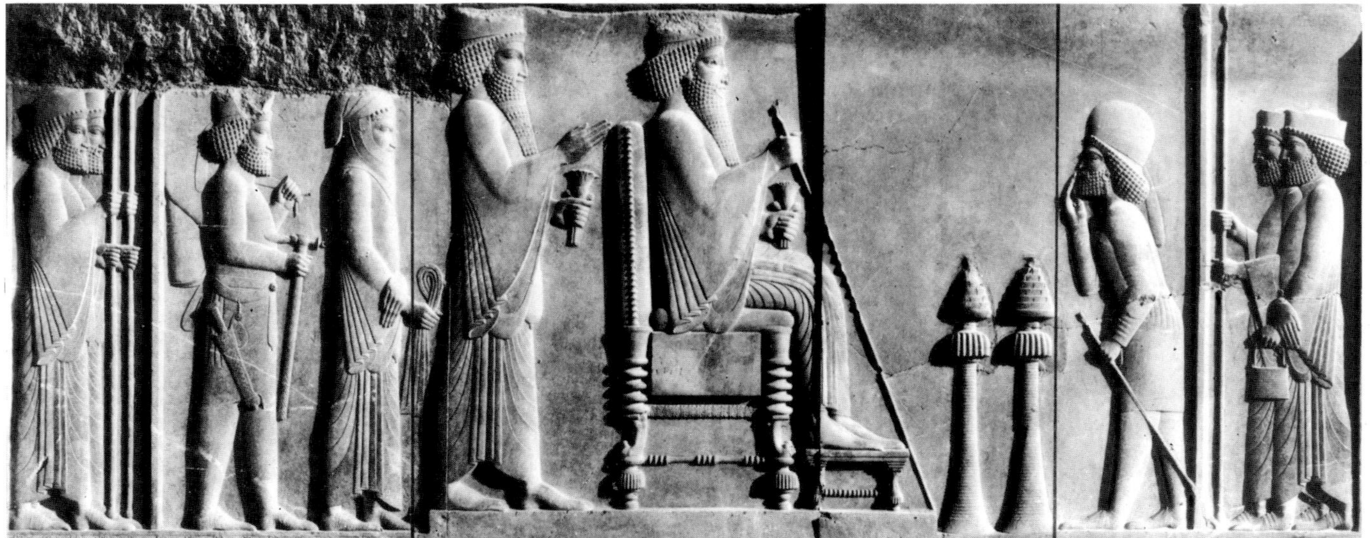

3-28. *Darius and Xerxes Giving Audience*. c. 490 B.C. Limestone, height 8'4" (2.5 m). Archaeological Museum, Tehran

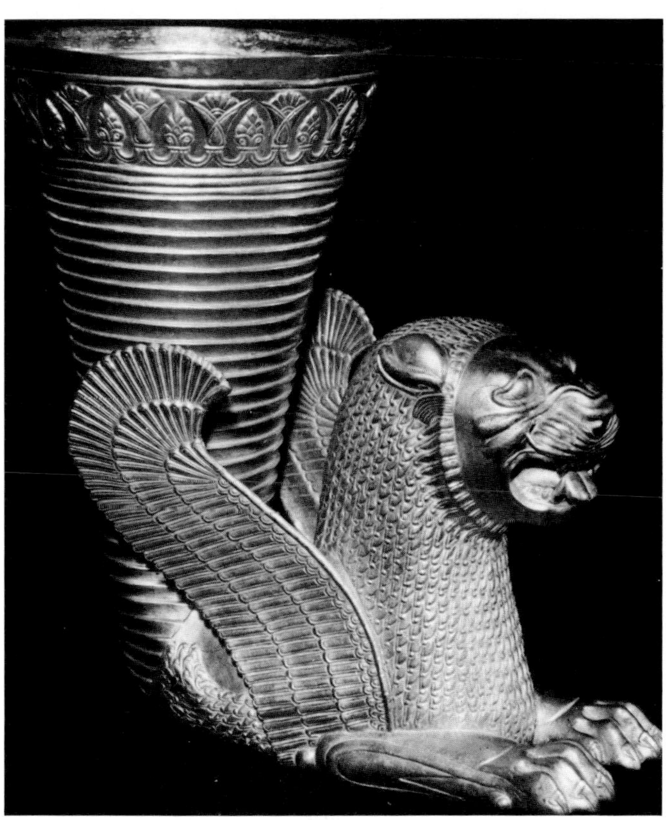

3-29. Gold rhyton. Achaemenid. 5th–3rd centuries B.C. Archaeological Museum, Tehran

rhyton in figure 3-29, which maintains the animal style in the senmurv, a mythical creature with the body of a lion sprouting a griffin's wings and a peacock's tail that is transformed almost miraculously into the body of the drinking cup. The ferocious beast, descended from the animals of Assyrian reliefs (see fig. 3-20), has been tamed, thanks to the small scale and fine goldsmith's work, which reveals a debt to the belt in figure 3-24. The tradition of portable art in Achaemenid Persia, unlike that of monumental architecture and sculpture, somehow managed to survive the more than 500 years during which the Persian Empire was under Greek and Roman domination. It would flower once more when Persia regained its independence under the Sassanians.

Sassanian Art

The Achaemenids were toppled by Alexander the Great (356–323 B.C.) in 331 B.C. After his death eight years later, his realm was divided among his generals. Seleucis (r. 312–281 B.C.) received much of the Near East except Egypt, which was given to Ptolemy (d. 284 B.C.). The Seleucids were succeeded by the Parthians, who gained control over the region in 238 B.C. The Parthians were fierce fighters who fended off the Romans until the time of Trajan in the second century A.D. Although their power later declined, it was not until 224 A.D. that Artabanus V, the last Parthian king, was overthrown by one of his governors, Ardashir (d. 240 A.D.). Ardashir founded the Sassanian dynasty, which endured until it fell to the Arabs in 651 A.D. Throughout the Parthian and Sassanian eras, Mesopotamia was part of the Greek and Roman world, though it retained aspects of its ancient culture.

The greatest Sassanian ruler, Shapur I (d. 272 A.D.), was as ambitious as Darius had been. At Naksh-i-Rustam, the burial place of the Achaemenid kings not far from Persepolis, he commemorated his victory over two Roman emperors in an immense relief hewn into the rock (fig. 3-30). The source of this scene is a well-known subject in Roman sculpture, except that here the emperors, rather than the barbarians, have been defeated. The style, too, is Roman (compare fig. 7-36), but the flattening of the volumes and the ornamental treatment of the draperies indicate a revival of Persian qualities. The way the two elements are held in balance is what makes the relief so impressive. A blending of Roman and Near Eastern elements can also be seen in the later palace at Ctesiphon, near Babylon, with its huge brick-vaulted audience hall (fig. 3-31). The blind arcades of the facade, strikingly Roman in flavor (compare fig. 7-11), again emphasize decorative surface pattern.

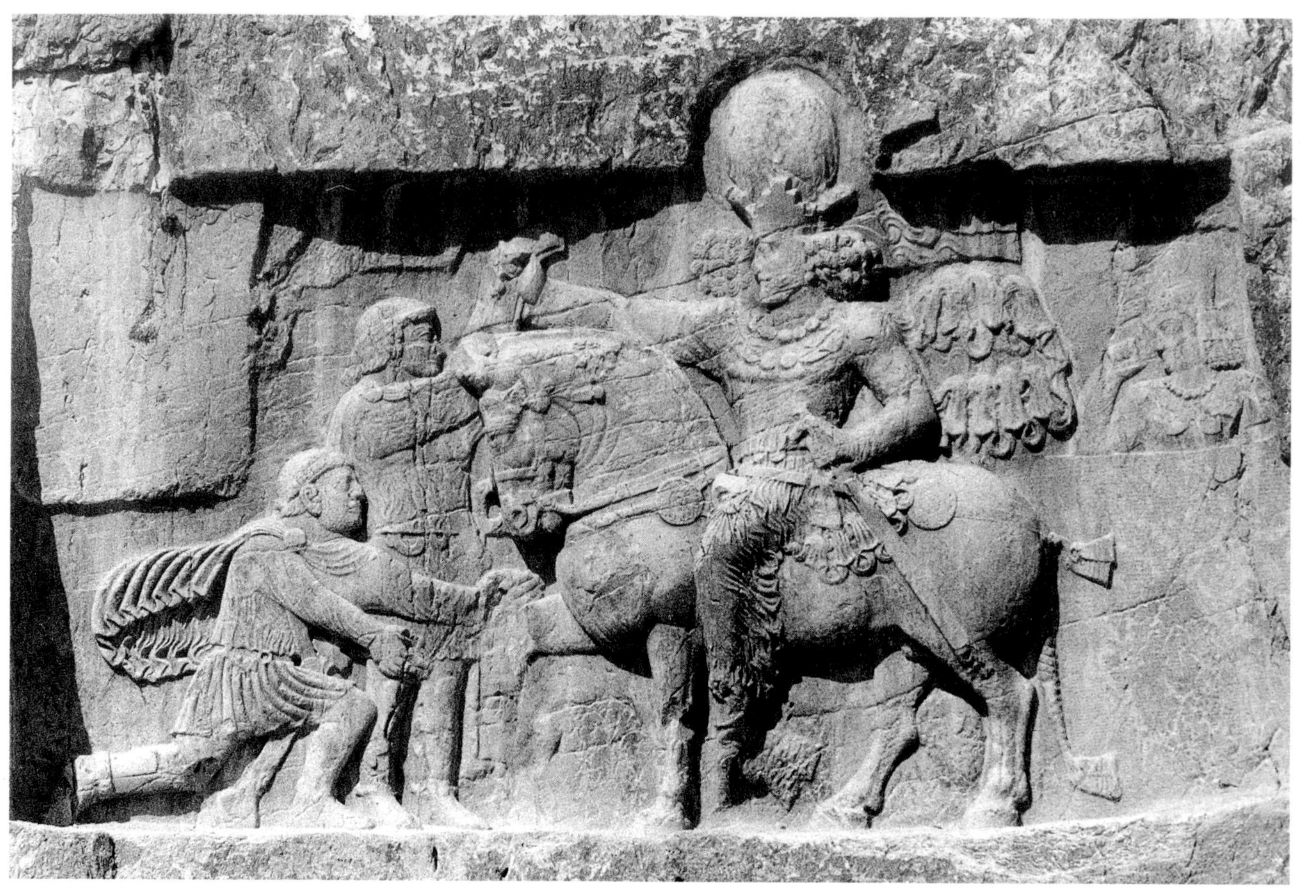

3-30. *Shapur I Triumphing Over the Emperors Philippus the Arab and Valerian*. 260–72 A.D. Naksh-i-Rustam (near Persepolis), Iran

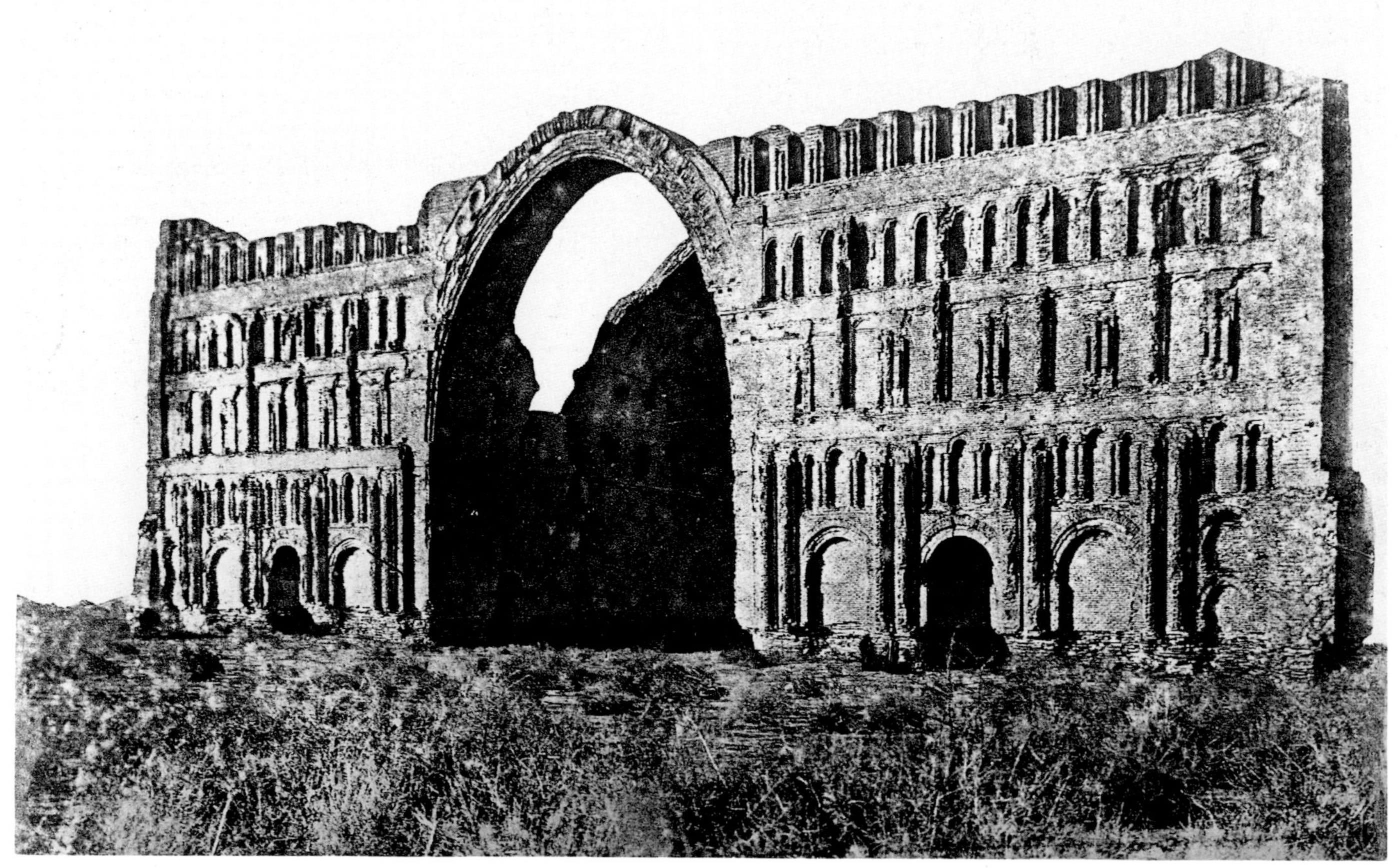

3-31. Palace of Shapur I, Ctesiphon, Iraq. 242–72 A.D.

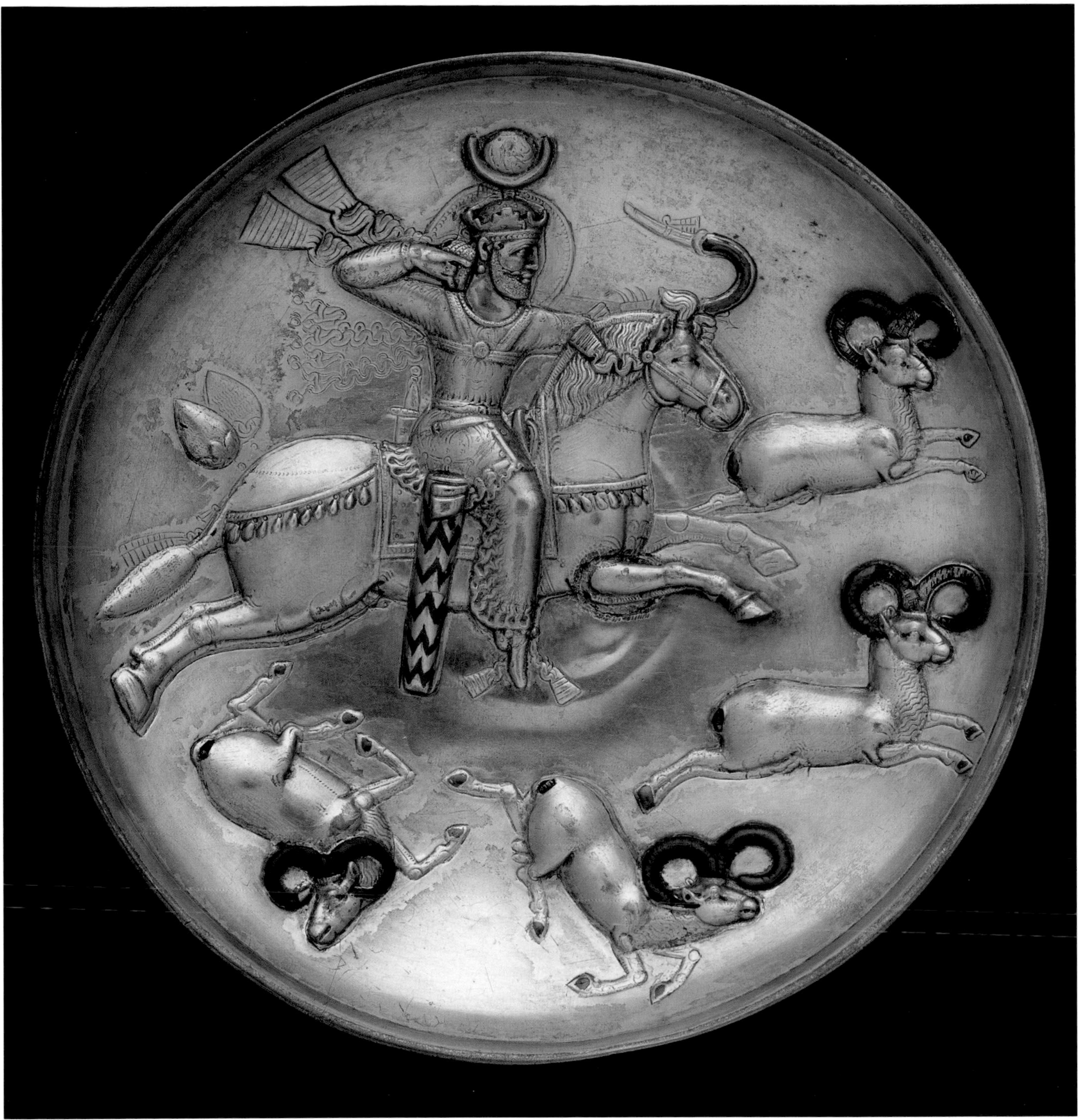

3-32. *King Peroz I* (457–483) *Hunting Gazelles.* Late 5th century A.D. Silver-gilt, engraved, embossed, and inlaid with niello, diameter 8 ⅝" (21.9 cm). The Metropolitan Museum of Art, New York

FLETCHER FUND, 1934 (34.33)

Monumental art under Sassanian rule proved as incapable of further evolution as it had under the Achaemenids. Metalwork and textiles, on the other hand, continued to flourish. The chief glory of Sassanian art is its silver bowls, such as the one in figure 3-32. Turned on a lathe and gilt with mercury highlights, it is a marvel of craftsmanship. In this miniaturized form, a rich tradition lives on. The subject, King Peroz hunting gazelles, is the descendant of Assyrian royal hunts. It also reaches back to Egyptian art, but with overtones of the animal style (compare figs. 2-18, 3-20, and 3-24). In typical Sassanian fashion, a strong Roman element has been added to this blend of Near Eastern motifs: the rider is related to *Hadrian Hunting a Boar* (see fig. 7-47, left), which has its roots in Greek Classical art (compare fig. 5-54). Finally, the style remains Phoenician in flavor.

Much Sassanian ware was exported both to Constantinople and to the Christian West, where it had a strong effect on the art of the Middle Ages. And since its manufacture was resumed after the Sassanian realm fell to the Arabs in the mid-seventh century, it served as a source of design motifs for Islamic art as well.

CHAPTER FOUR

Aegean Art

If we sail from the Nile Delta northwestward across the Mediterranean, our first glimpse of Europe will be the eastern tip of Crete. Beyond it we find a scattered group of small islands, the Cyclades. A little farther on is the mainland of Greece, facing the coast of Asia Minor across the Aegean Sea. To archaeologists, "Aegean" is not just a geographic term. They use it to refer to the civilizations that flourished in this area during the third and second millennia B.C., before the development of Greek civilization proper. There were three closely related yet distinct cultures: Minoan (after the legendary King Minos) on the isle of Crete; Cycladic, on the small islands north of Crete; and Helladic, on the Greek mainland, which includes Mycenaean civilization. Each has in turn been divided into three phases—Early, Middle, and Late—that correspond, very roughly, to the Old, Middle, and New Kingdoms in Egypt. Their greatest artistic achievements date from the latter part of the Middle phase and from the Late phase.

Aegean civilization was long known only from Homer's account of the Trojan War in the *Iliad* and the *Odyssey,* as well as from Greek legends centering on Crete. The earliest excavations (by Heinrich Schliemann during the 1870s in Asia Minor and Greece and by Sir Arthur Evans in Crete shortly before 1900) were undertaken to find out whether these tales had a factual basis. Since then, a great deal of fascinating material has been brought to light—far more than written sources would lead us to expect. But even now, due to a lack of written records, our knowledge of Aegean civilization is much more limited than our knowledge of Egypt or the ancient Near East.

MINOAN SCRIPT AND LINEAR B. In Crete a system of writing was developed about 2000 B.C. A late form of this Minoan script, called Linear B, which was in use about six centuries later both in Crete and on the Greek mainland, was deciphered in the early 1950s. The language of Linear B is Greek, yet this apparently was not the language for which Minoan script was used before the fifteenth century B.C. Hence, being able to read Linear B does not help us to understand earlier Minoan inscriptions. Moreover, most Linear B texts are inventories and records; they do reveal something about the history, religion, and political organization of the people who wrote them, but we still have little of the background knowledge required for an understanding of Aegean art.

Although the forms of Aegean art are linked to Egypt and the Near East on the one hand and to later Greek art on the other, they are no mere transition between these worlds. They have a haunting beauty of their own that belongs to neither. Among the many remarkable qualities of Aegean art are its freshness and spontaneity, which make us forget how little we know of its meaning.

CYCLADIC ART

After about 2800 B.C. the people of the Cycladic Islands often buried their dead with impressive marble sculptures. Almost all of these are of a nude female figure with arms folded across the chest (fig. 4-1). They also share a distinctive form, which at first glance recalls the angular, abstract qualities of Paleolithic and Neolithic sculpture. Generally they have a flat, wedge-shaped body; strong, columnar neck; tilted, oval shield of the face; and long, ridgelike nose. (Other features were painted in.) Within this narrowly defined and stable type, however, the Cycladic figures show wide variations in scale and form that lend them a surprising individuality. The best of these figures, such as that in figure 4-1, represent a late, highly developed phase around 2500–2400 B.C.

Our example has a disciplined refinement utterly beyond the range of Paleolithic or Neolithic art. The longer we study this piece, the more we become aware of its elegance and sophistication. What an extraordinary feeling for the organic structure of the body is shown in the delicate curves of the outline and in the hints of convexity at the knees and abdomen! Even if we discount its deceptively modern look, the figure is unlike anything we have seen before. There is no lack of earlier female figures, but almost all of them are descended from the heavy-bodied type of the Old Stone Age (see fig. 1-7). In fact, the earliest Cycladic figurines, too, were of that kind.

We do not know what led Cycladic sculptors to adopt the "girlish" ideal of figure 4-1. The transformation may have been related to a change in religious beliefs and practices. Perhaps there

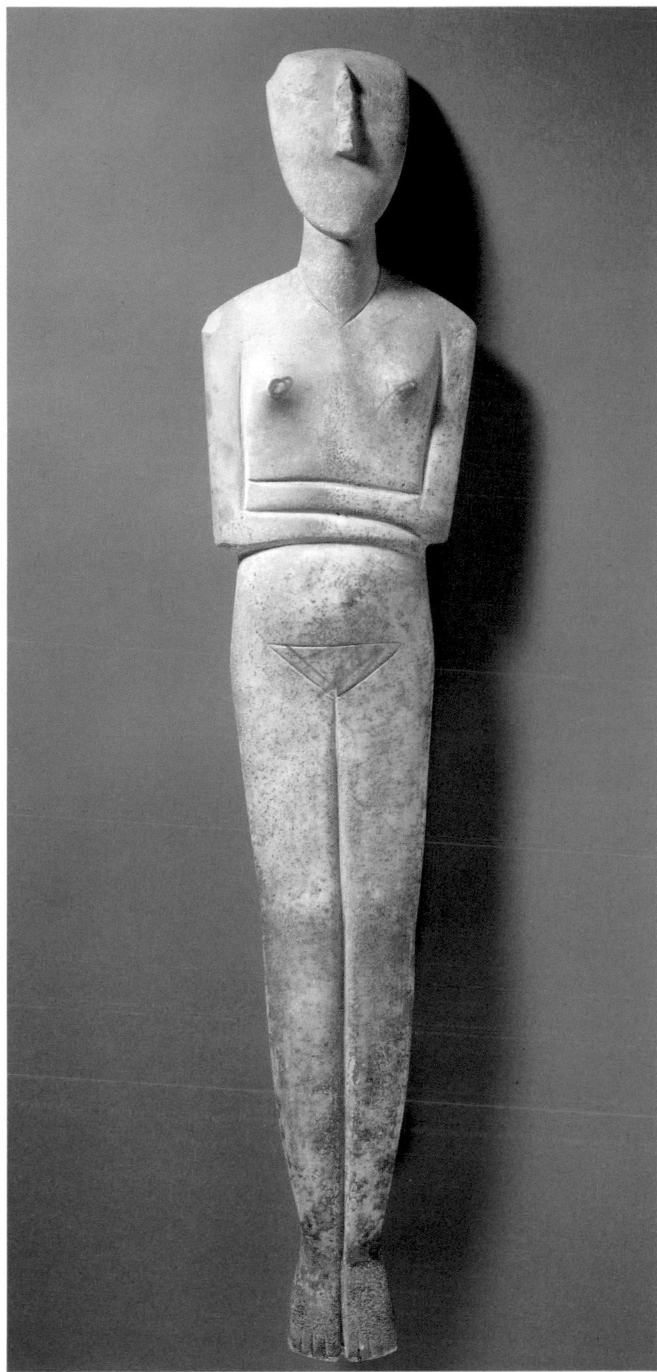

4-1. *Figure,* from Amorgos, Cyclades. c. 2500 B.C. Marble, height 30" (76.3 cm). Ashmolean Museum, Oxford, England

was a shift *away* from the mother and fertility goddess known to us from Asia Minor and the ancient Near East, whose ancestry reaches back to the Old Stone Age. The largest figures were probably cult statues to a female divinity who may have been identified with the sun in the great cycle of life and death. The smaller ones might have been displayed in houschold shrines or even used as votive offerings. Although their meaning is far from clear, their purpose was not simply funereal. Rather, they were important objects that were included in graves with others from everyday life. There they served as either presents for the deity or provisions for the afterlife. Rarely were they freestanding. Most have been found in a reclining position, but they may also have been propped upright during normal use.

Be that as it may, the Cycladic sculptors of the third millennium B.C. produced the oldest large-scale figures of the female nude we know. In fact, for many hundreds of years they were the only ones to do so. In Greek art, we find very few nude female statues until the middle of the fourth century B.C., when Praxiteles and others began to create cult images of the nude Aphrodite (see fig. 5-67). It can hardly be by chance that the most famous of these Venuses were made for sanctuaries on the Aegean Islands or the coast of Asia Minor, the region where the Cycladic idols had flourished.

A second group of figures, evidently produced at a slightly later date by a single workshop and distributed throughout the Aegean, represents musicians playing harps and double flutes—instruments that were used by the Greeks as well (see page 125). The example in figure 4-2 probably shows a bard singing his legend. A highly complex work for its time, it was carved by a gifted artist who makes us feel the poet's visionary rapture through the rounded forms and tilt of the head.

MINOAN ART

Minoan civilization is by far the richest, as well as the strangest, of the Aegean world. What sets it apart, not only from Egypt and the Near East but also from the Classical civilization of Greece, is its lack of continuity. The different phases appear and disappear so abruptly that they must have been caused by sudden violent

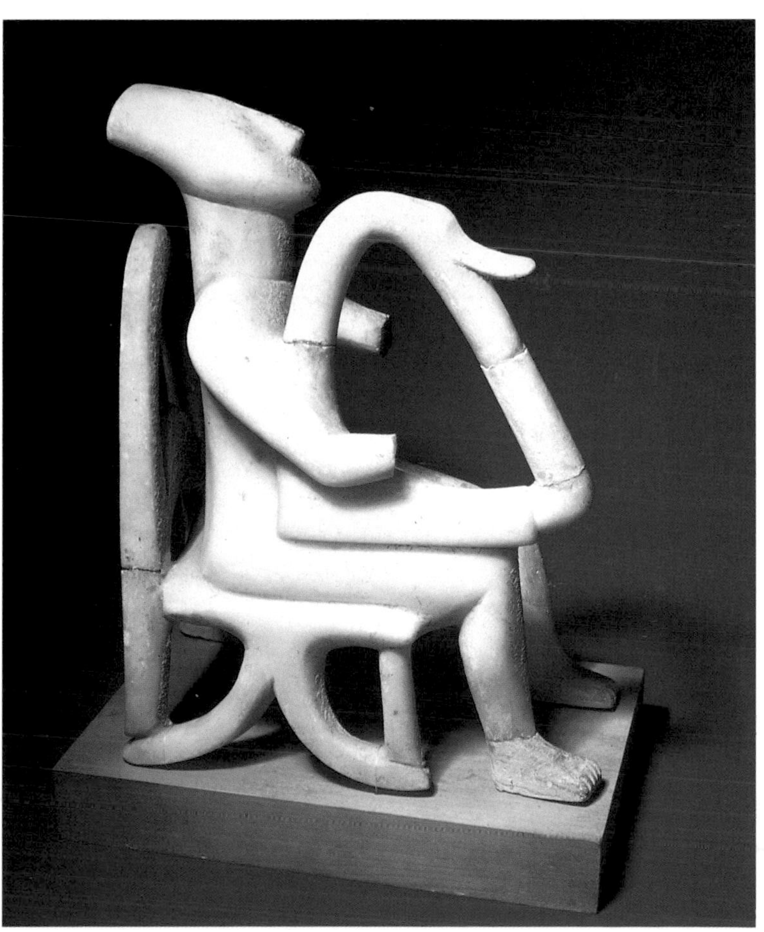

4-2. *Harpist,* so-called Orpheus, from Amorgos, Cyclades. Latter part of the 3rd millennium B.C. Marble statuette, height 8½" (21.5 cm). National Archaeological Museum, Athens

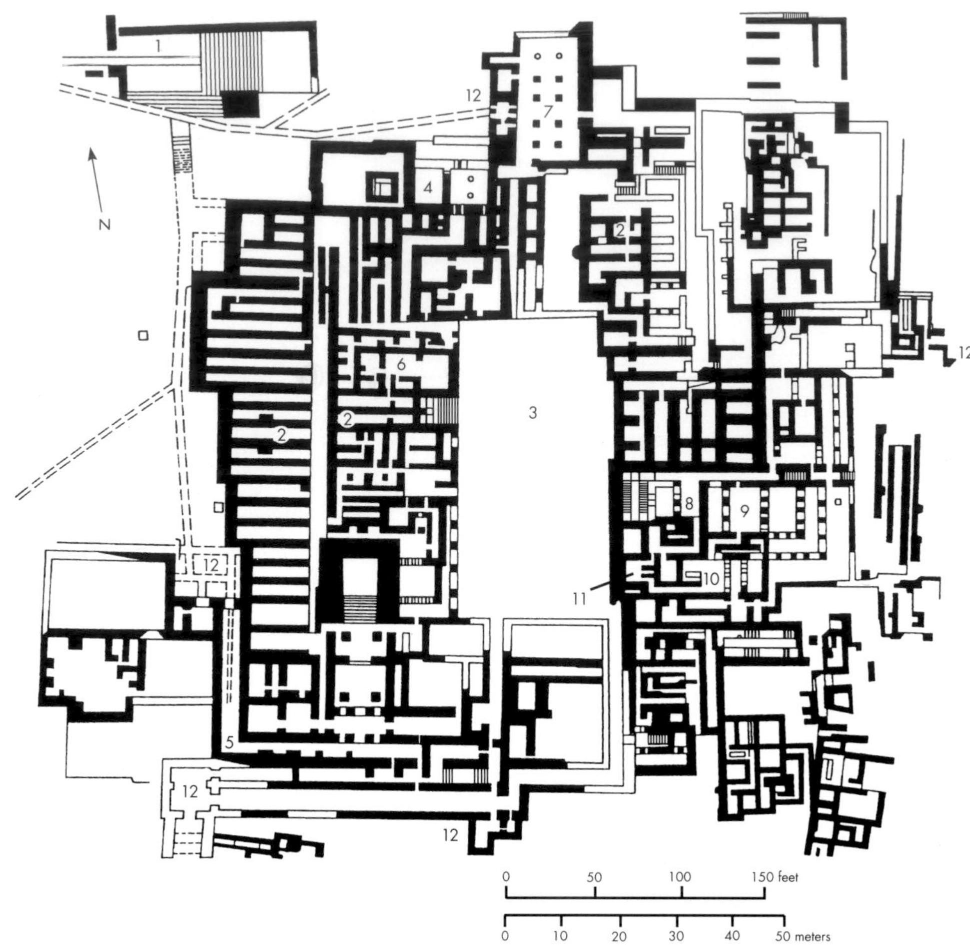

4-3. Plan of the Palace of Minos, Knossos, Crete. The palace is organized in two wings, to the east and west of a central court, and is on several levels:

1) stairway and theater area
2) storerooms
3) central court
4) antechamber
5) corridor of the procession
6) throne room
7) north pillar hall
8) hall of the colonnade
9) hall of the double axes
10) queen's megaron
11) queen's bath
12) entrances and atriums

changes affecting the entire island. They appear to be due to archaeological accidents as well as historical forces. Yet Minoan art, which is gay, even playful, and full of rhythmic motion, conveys no hint of such threats.

Architecture

The first of these abrupt shifts occurred about 2000 B.C. Until that time, during the thousand years of the Early Minoan era, the Cretans had not advanced much beyond the Neolithic level of village life, although they do seem to have engaged in some trade that brought them contact with Egypt. Then they created not only their own system of writing but an urban civilization as well, centering on several great palaces. At least three palaces were built in short order at Knossos, Phaistos, and Mallia. Little is left of this sudden spurt of large-scale building. The three early palaces were all destroyed at the same time, about 1700 B.C., apparently by an earthquake. After a short interval, new and even larger structures were built on the same sites, only to be demolished by another earthquake about 1450 B.C. After that, Phaistos and Mallia were abandoned, but the palace at Knossos was occupied by the Mycenaeans, who took over the island almost immediately.

Minoan civilization therefore has a complex chronology. Archaeologists divide the time span that concerns us into two periods: the Old Palace period, comprising Middle Minoan I and Middle Minoan II, which together lasted from 2000 B.C. until about

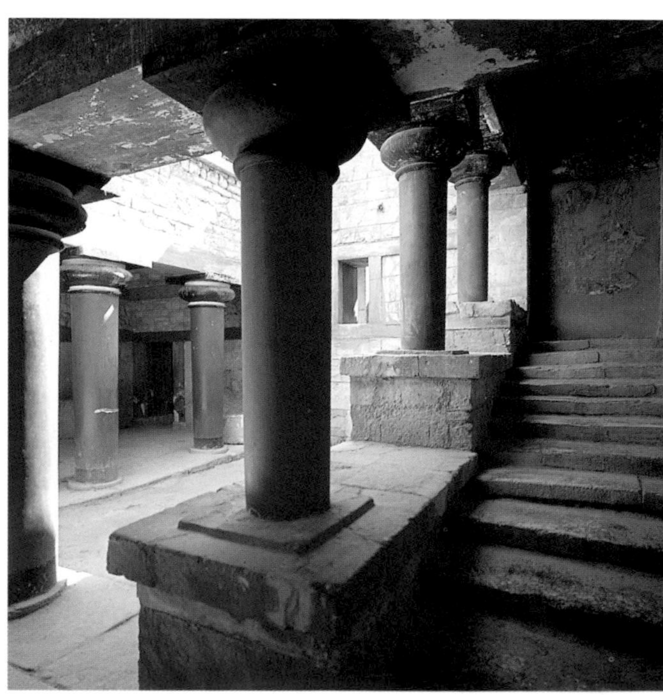

4-4. Staircase, east wing, Palace of Minos, Knossos, Crete. c. 1500 B.C.

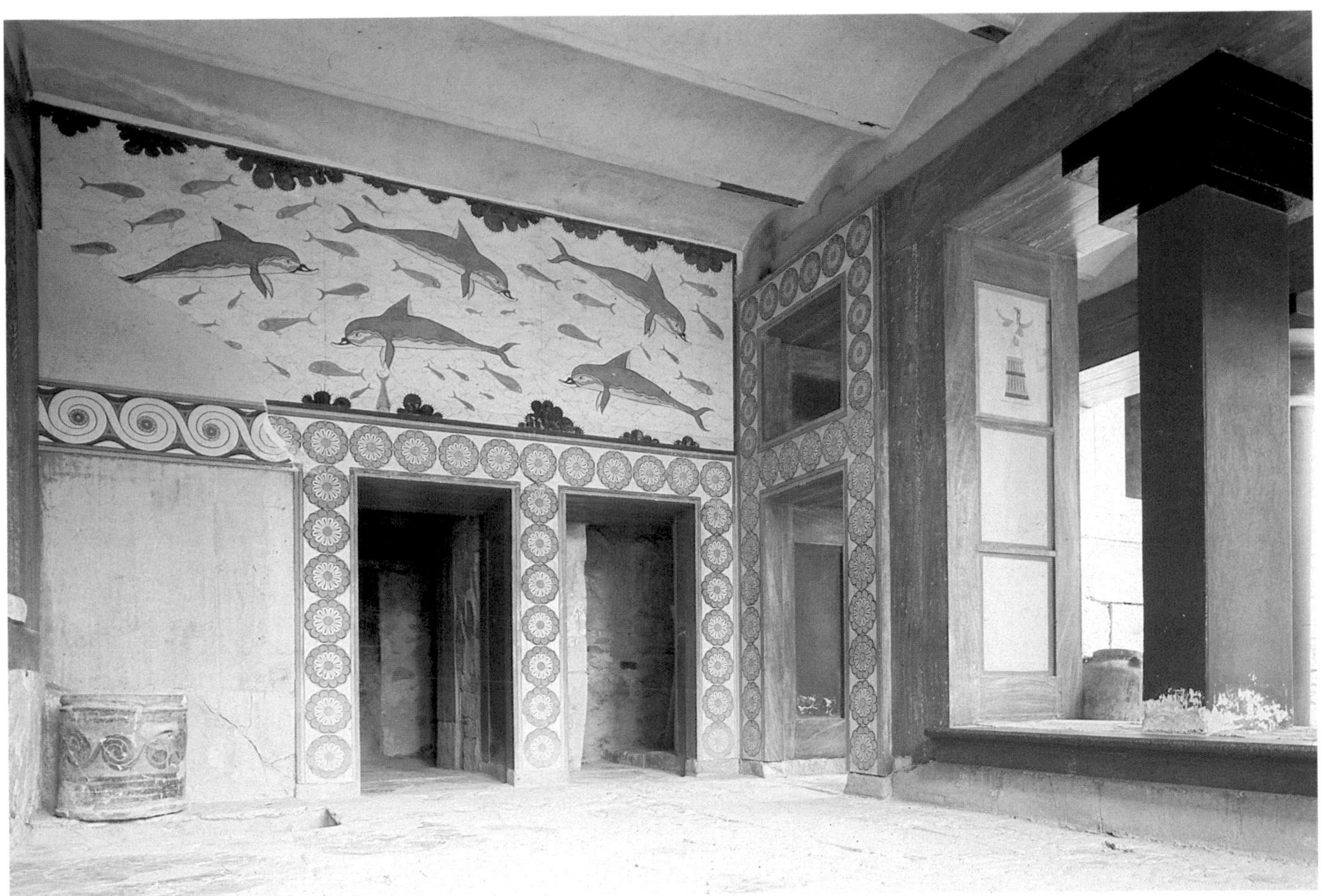

4-5. The Queen's Megaron, Palace of Minos, Knossos, Crete. c. 1700–1300 B.C.

1700 B.C.; and the New Palace period, including Middle Minoan III, Late Minoan IA, and Late Minoan IB, which ended around 1450 B.C. (The dates of these internal divisions, which are constantly being debated, need not concern us here.) The eruption of the volcano on the island of Thera (Santorini) occurred during the New Palace period, at the end of Late Minoan IA. It did little damage to Crete, however, and ushered in the Late Minoan IB stage, which marked the peak of Minoan civilization. For our purposes, we need only remember that the Old Palace period coincides very roughly with the Middle Kingdom and the New Palace period with the onset of the New Kingdom in Egypt.

The "new" palaces are our main source of information about Minoan architecture. The one at Knossos, called the Palace of Minos, was the most ambitious, covering a large area and containing so many rooms that it survived in Greek legend as the labyrinth of the Minotaur (fig. 4-3). It has been carefully excavated and partly restored. There was no striving for a unified effect, and the exterior was modest compared with Assyrian or Persian palaces (see fig. 3-26). The individual units are rather small and the ceilings low (figs. 4-4 and 4-5), so that even those parts of the structure that were several stories high could not have seemed very tall. Nevertheless, the many porticoes, staircases, and air shafts must have given the palace an open, airy look. Some of the interiors, with their richly decorated walls, still retain their elegant appearance. The masonry construction is excellent, but the columns were always of wood. Although none has survived (those in fig. 4-4 are reconstructions), their form is known from paintings and sculptures. They had a smooth shaft tapering downward and were topped by a wide, cushion-shaped capital. About the origins of this type of column (which in some contexts could also serve as a religious symbol), or about its possible links with Egyptian architecture, we can say nothing at all.

Who were the rulers who built these palaces? We do not know their names or deeds, except for the legendary Minos, but the archaeological evidence suggests that they were not warriors. No fortifications have been found anywhere in Minoan Crete, and military subjects are almost unknown in Minoan art. Nor is there any hint that they were sacred kings like those of Egypt or Mesopotamia, although they may have presided at religious festivals, and their palaces certainly were centers of religious life. However, the only parts that can be identified as places of worship are small chapels, which suggests that religious ceremonies took place out of doors, or at outlying shrines. The many storerooms, workshops, and "offices" at Knossos show that the palace was not only a royal residence but a center of administration and commerce. Shipping and trade were a major part of Minoan economic life, to judge from elaborate harbor constructions and from Cretan export articles found in Egypt and elsewhere. Perhaps, then, the king should be viewed as the head of a merchant aristocracy. Just how much power he had and how far it extended are still unclear.

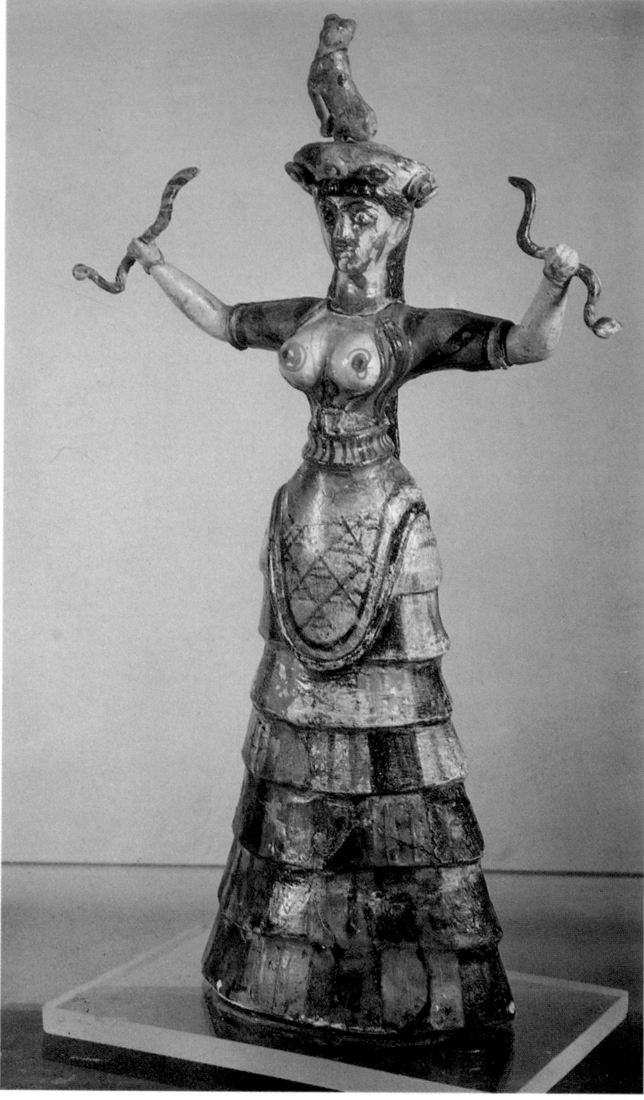

4-6. *"Snake Goddess."* c. 1650 B.C. Faience, height 11⅝" (29.5 cm). Archaeological Museum, Heraklion, Crete

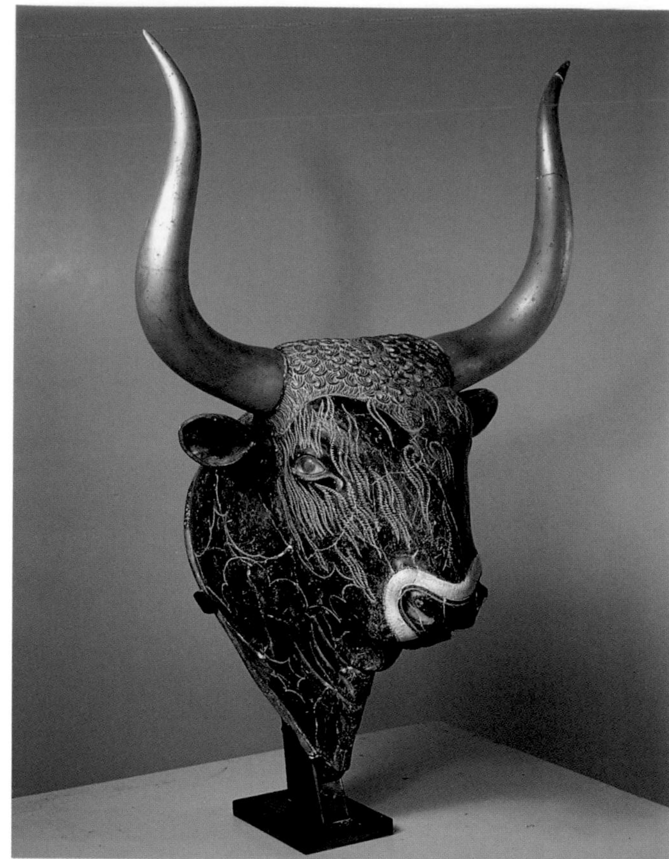

4-7. Rhyton in the shape of a bull's head, from Knossos. c. 1500–1450 B.C. Serpentine, crystal, and shell inlay (horns restored), height 8⅛" (20.6 cm). Archaeological Museum, Heraklion, Crete

Sculpture

The religious life of Minoan Crete is even harder to define than the political or social order. It centered on certain sacred places, such as caves or groves. Its chief deity (or deities?) was female, akin to the mother and fertility goddesses we have met before. Since the Minoans had no temples, we are not surprised to find that they lacked large cult statues. But even on a small scale there are few religious subjects in Minoan art, and their significance is not known. Two statuettes of about 1650 B.C. from Knossos must represent the goddess, although the costume gives her a "fashionable" air (compare fig. 4-8). One of them (fig. 4-6) shows her with three long snakes wound around her arms, body, and headdress. Snakes are associated with earth deities and male fertility in many ancient religions, and the statuette's bare breasts suggest fecundity. The style hints at a foreign source: the voluptuous bosom, the conical shape of the figure, and the large eyes and arched eyebrows suggest a remote and indirect kinship—indirect, perhaps through Asia Minor—with Mesopotamian art (compare fig. 3-15).

Minoan civilization also featured a cult centering on bulls (see below). One of them is shown tamed on a splendid rhyton, or drinking horn (fig. 4-7), that may have been a ritual vessel. (It was filled from a hole in the neck, while another hole below the mouth served as a spout.) Carved from serpentine stone, with painted crystal eyes, a shell-inlay muzzle, and incised lines to indicate its shaggy fur, it creates an astonishingly lifelike impression despite its small size. (The horns are restored.) Not since the offering stand from Ur (see fig. 3-7) have we seen such a magnificent beast in the round. Can it be that the Minoans learned how to carve from the artistic descendants of Mesopotamians more than a thousand years earlier?

Paintings, Pottery, and Reliefs

After the earlier palaces were destroyed, there was an explosive increase in wealth and a remarkable outpouring of creative energy that produced most of what we have in Minoan architecture, sculpture, and painting. The most surprising aspect of this sudden flowering, however, is its painting. Unfortunately, the murals that covered the walls of the new palaces have survived mainly in fragments; we rarely have a complete composition, let alone the design of an entire wall.

The settlement at Akrotiri on the island of Thera has been extensively excavated and a large number of frescoes recovered, the earliest Minoan examples we have. Belonging to the Late Minoan IA period (1670–1620 B.C.), they vary greatly in subject and style. Of these, the most remarkable is the scene of a young woman offering crocuses (the source of saffron) to a snake goddess. Nicknamed

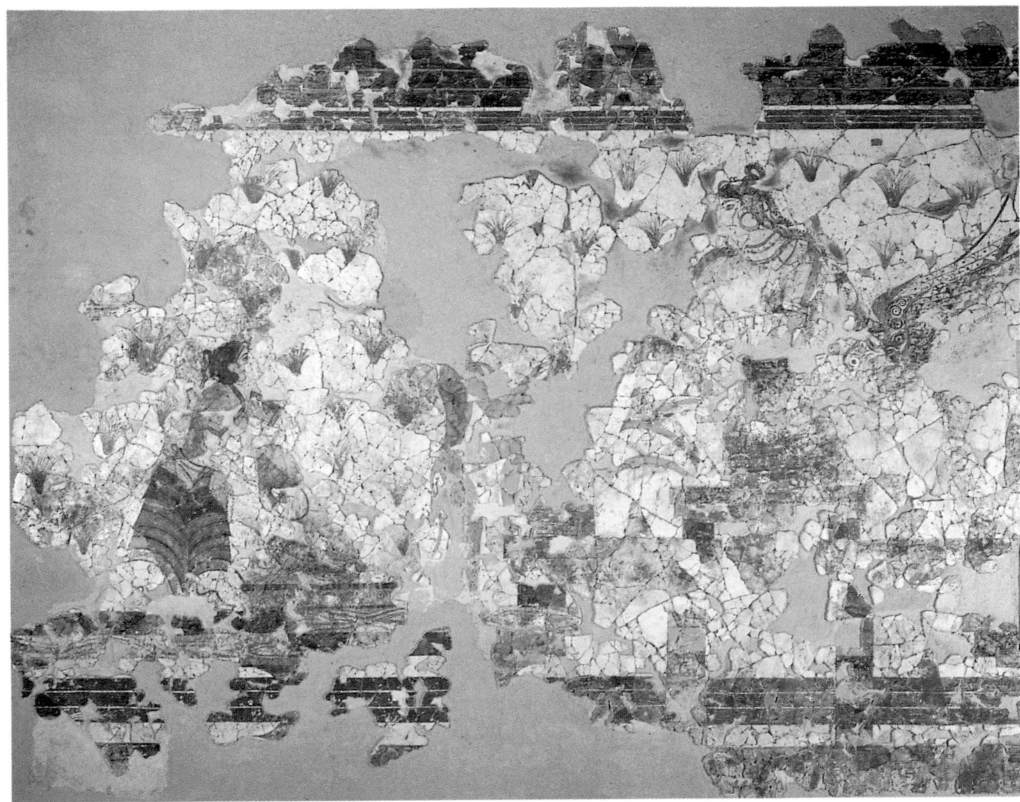

4-8. *Crocus Girl* (left) and *"The Mistress of the Animals"* (right). Mural fragments from Akrotiri, Thera (Santorini). c. 1670–1620 B.C. National Archaeological Museum, Athens

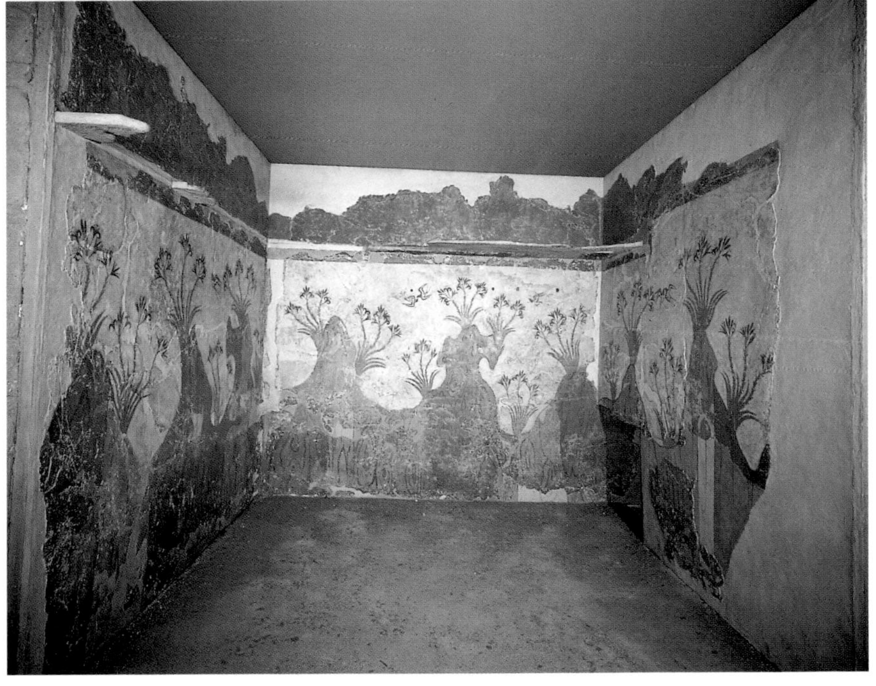

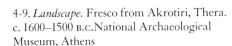

4-9. *Landscape.* Fresco from Akrotiri, Thera. c. 1600–1500 B.C.National Archaeological Museum, Athens

"The Mistress of the Animals," the deity is seated on an altar with an oil jar (fig. 4-8). What an astonishing achievement it is, despite its fragmentary state and the artist's occasional problems with anatomy. We would recognize the goddess' special status even if she were not seated on the thronelike altar, with a snake in her hair (which makes her a forerunner of Medusa; see page 98) and a griffin behind her. The contrast between her awesomeness and the girlish charm of the crocus bearer is striking.

The flat forms, silhouetted against the landscape, recall Egyptian painting, and the treatment of the plants also suggests Egyptian art. While Minoan wall painting may owe its origin to Egyptian influence, it betrays an attitude very different from that of the Egyptians. To the Minoans, nature was an enchanted realm on which they focused from the very beginning. Egyptian painters could explore nature only by relaxing the conventions of their art. The frescoes at Akrotiri include the first pure landscape paintings we know of. Not even the most adventurous Egyptian artist of the Middle Kingdom would have devoted an entire composition to the out-of-doors. (Figure 2-23, after all, is not only later but also a fragment of a much larger mural whose content we can only guess at.) Our example (fig. 4-9) evokes the dunes along the coast of Thera, but the artist has given the scene a liveliness and beauty that

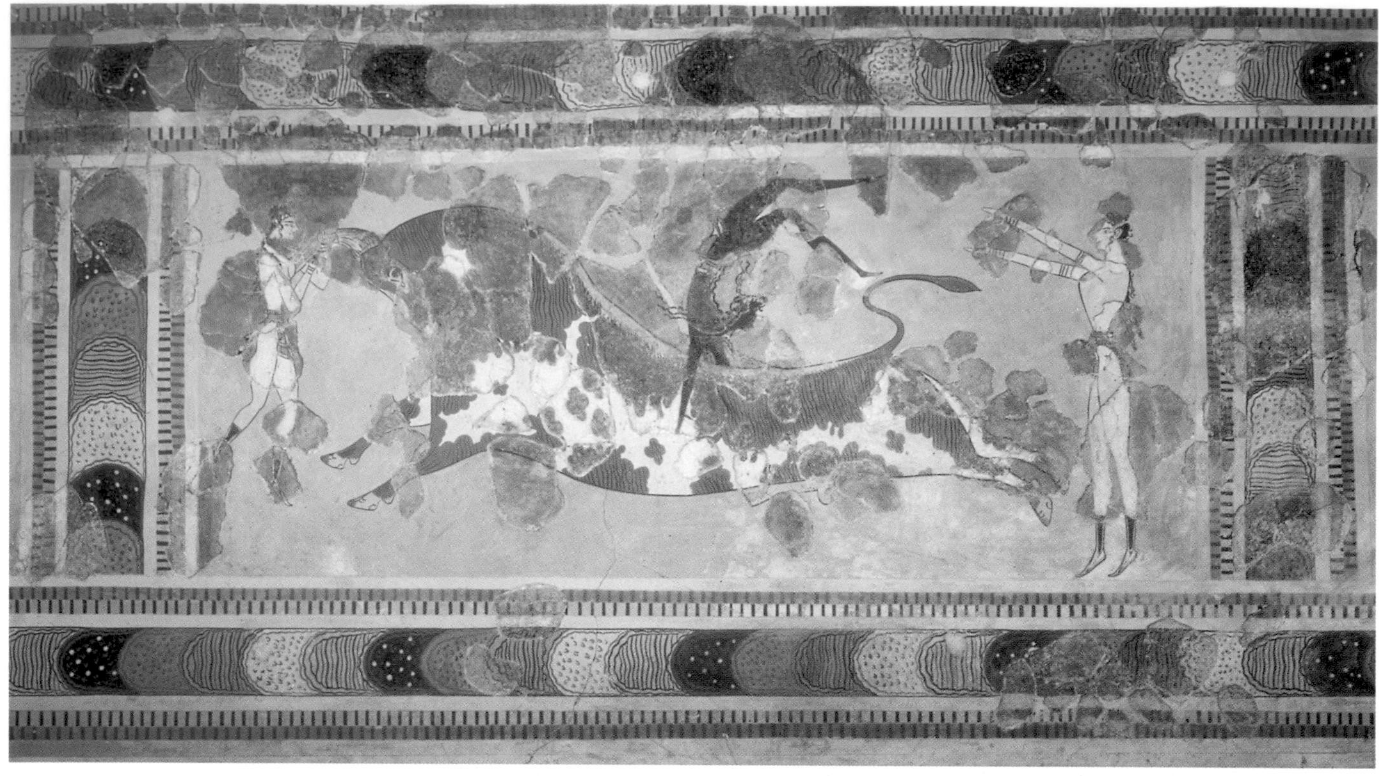

4-10. *"The Toreador Fresco."* c. 1500 B.C. Height including upper border approx. 24½" (62.3 cm). Archaeological Museum, Heraklion, Crete

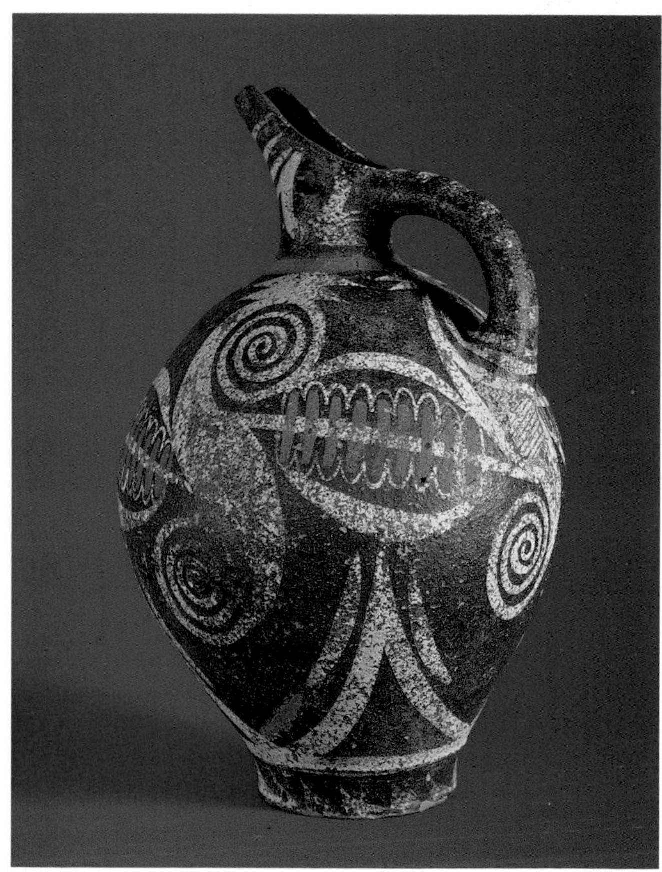

4-11. Beaked jug (Kamares style), from Phaistos. c. 1800 B.C. Height 10⅝" (27 cm). Archaeological Museum, Heraklion, Crete

bespeak the same sense of wonder we found in the encounter between mortal and goddess in figure 4-8.

Marine life (as seen in the fish and dolphin fresco in fig. 4-5) was a favorite subject of Minoan painting after 1600 B.C. Indeed, a marine feeling seems to pervade Minoan art. Instead of permanence and stability we find a passion for rhythmic movement, and the forms themselves have an oddly weightless quality. They seem to float, or sway, in a world without gravity. It is as if the scenes took place underwater, even though a great many of them show animals, birds, and plants, as well as sea life. We sense this even in *"The Toreador Fresco,"* the most dynamic Minoan mural recovered so far (fig. 4-10). (The darker patches are the original fragments on which the restoration is based.) The conventional title should not mislead us. What we see here is not a bullfight but a ritual game in which the performers vault over the back of the animal. Two of the slim-waisted athletes are girls, distinguished (as in Egyptian art) mainly by their lighter skin color.

The bull was a sacred animal to the Minoans, and bull-vaulting played an important role in their religious life. There are echoes of such scenes in the Greek legend of the youths and maidens sacrificed to the minotaur, a half-animal, half-human creature. The three figures probably show different phases of the same action. But if we try to "read" the fresco as a description of what went on during these performances, we find it strangely ambiguous. This does not mean that the Minoan artist was unskilled. It would be absurd to find fault for failing to achieve what was never intended in the first place. Fluid, effortless movement clearly was more

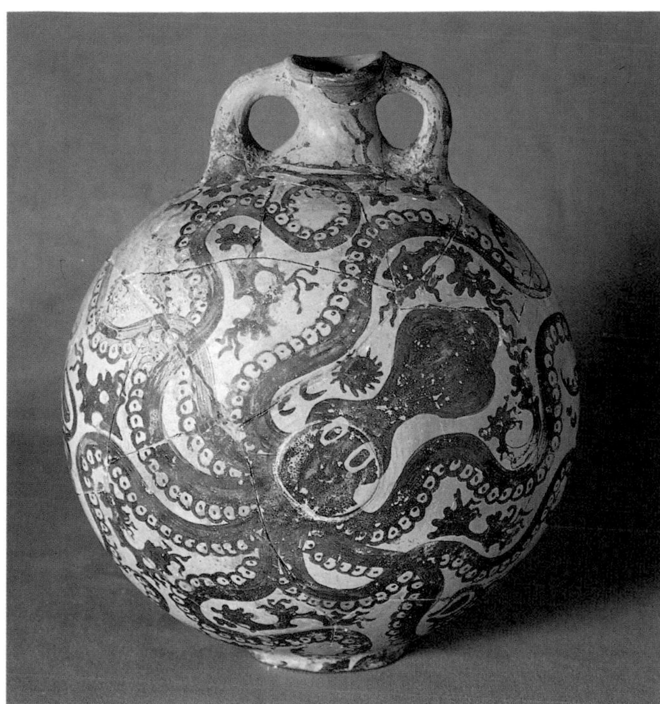

4-12. *"Octopus Vase,"* from Palaikastro, Crete. c. 1500 B.C. Height 11" (28 cm). Archaeological Museum, Heraklion, Crete

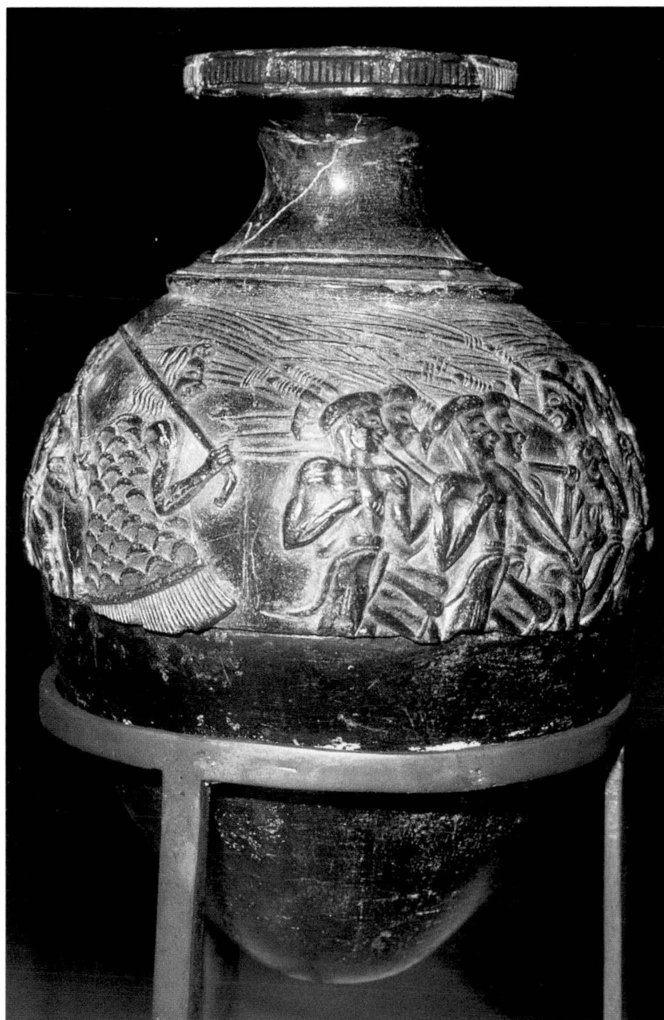

4-13. *Harvester Vase,* from Hagia Triada. c. 1550–1500 B.C. Stone/Steatite. Archaeological Museum, Heraklion, Crete

important than precision or drama. The painting, as it were, idealizes the ritual. It stresses its harmonious, playful aspect to the point that the performers behave like dolphins frolicking in the sea.

The floating world of Minoan wall painting was an imaginative creation so rich and original that its influence can be felt throughout Minoan art during the era of the new palaces. At the time of the earlier palaces, between 2000 and 1700 B.C., Crete had developed a type of pottery (known as Kamares ware after the center where it was discovered) that was famous for its technical perfection and its dynamic, swirling ornament, consisting of organic abstractions filled with life (fig. 4-11). This in no way prepares us for the new designs drawn from plant and animal life. Some vessels are covered with fish, shells, and octopuses, as if the sea itself had been caught within them (fig. 4-12).

Monumental sculpture, had there been any, might have retained its independence. The Minoan sculptor was confined to small-scale works, however, and these are often closely akin to the style of the murals. The vivid relief on the so-called *Harvester Vase* (fig. 4-13; the lower part is lost) depicts a procession of slim, muscular men, nude to the waist, carrying long-handled tools that look like a combination of scythe and rake. A harvest festival? Probably, although here again the lively rhythm of the composition takes precedence over descriptive clarity. Our view of the scene includes three singers led by a fourth who is swinging a sistrum (a rattle of Egyptian origin). They are bellowing with all their might, especially the "choirmaster," whose chest is so distended that the ribs press through the skin. What makes the relief so remarkable—in fact, unique—is its emphasis on physical strain, its energetic, raucous gaiety. How many works of this sort did Minoan artists produce? Only once have we met anything at all like it: in the relief of workmen carrying a beam (see fig. 2-30), carved almost two centuries later in the Akhenaten style (see pages 56–57). Could pieces like the *Harvester Vase* have stimulated Egyptian artists during that brief but important period?

MYCENAEAN ART

During Late Helladic times (c. 1400–1100 B.C.), there were a number of settlements along the southeastern shores of the Greek mainland that corresponded in many ways to those of Minoan Crete. They, too, were grouped around palaces. Their inhabitants have come to be called Mycenaeans, after Mycenae, the most important of these sites. Since the works of art unearthed there often showed a strikingly Minoan character, the Mycenaeans were at first thought to have come from Crete. It is now agreed, however, that they were the descendants of the earliest Greek clans that had entered the country soon after 2000 B.C.

Tombs and Their Contents

For some 400 years, these people had led a pastoral life in their new homeland. Their modest tombs contained only simple pottery and a few bronze weapons. Toward 1600 B.C., however, they suddenly began to bury their dead in deep shaft graves. A little later, burials were in conical stone chambers, known as beehive tombs. This trend reached its height toward 1300 B.C. in structures such as the

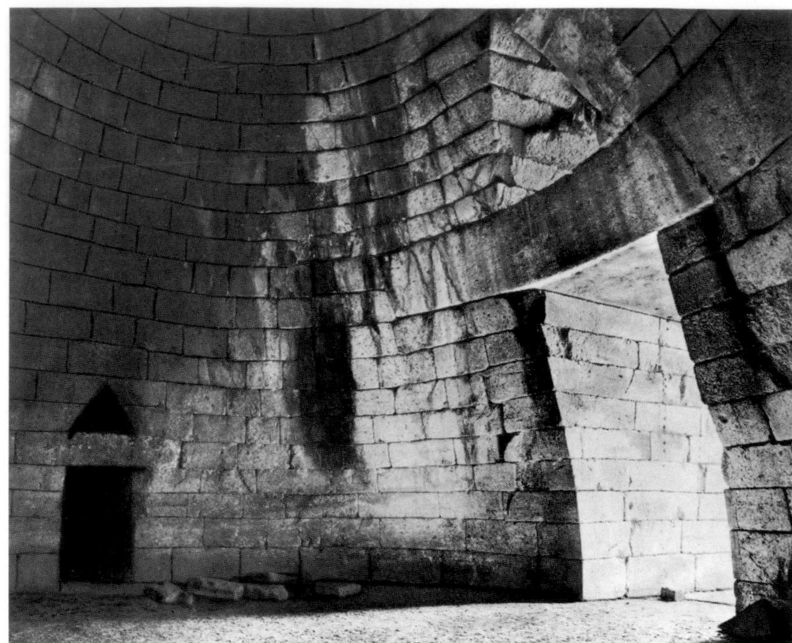

(LEFT) 4-14. Interior, Treasury of Atreus, Mycenae, Greece. c. 1300–1250 B.C.

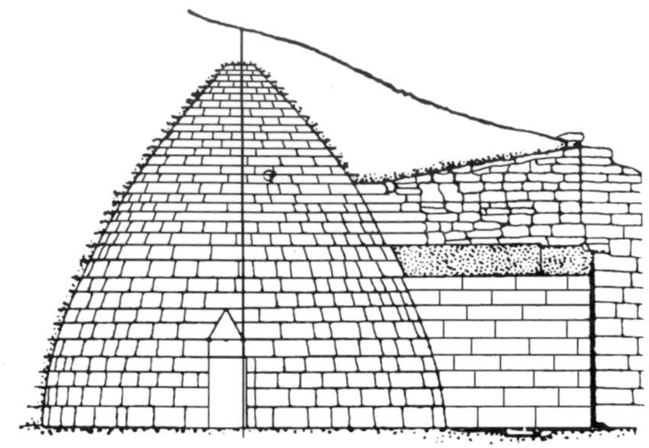

4-15. Section, Treasury of Atreus

one shown in figures 4-14 and 4-15. These tombs were built of concentric layers of precisely cut stone blocks that taper inward toward the highest point. (This method of spanning space is called corbeling.) Its discoverer thought it far too ambitious for a tomb and gave it the misleading name Treasury of Atreus. Burial places as elaborate as this can be matched only in Egypt during the same period.

The Treasury of Atreus had been robbed of its contents long ago, but other Mycenaean tombs were found intact. Their contents caused even greater surprise: beside the royal dead were placed masks of gold or silver, presumably to cover their faces. If so, these masks were similar in purpose (if not in style) to those found in pharaonic tombs of the Middle and New Kingdoms (compare fig. 2-29). There was also considerable personal equipment, such as drinking vessels, jewelry, and weapons. Many of these pieces were of gold and exquisite in workmanship. Some, such as the gold vessel in the shape of a lion's head (fig. 4-16), show a bold style of smooth planes bounded by sharp ridges, which suggests contact with the Near East. Others are so Minoan in flavor that they might be imports from Crete.

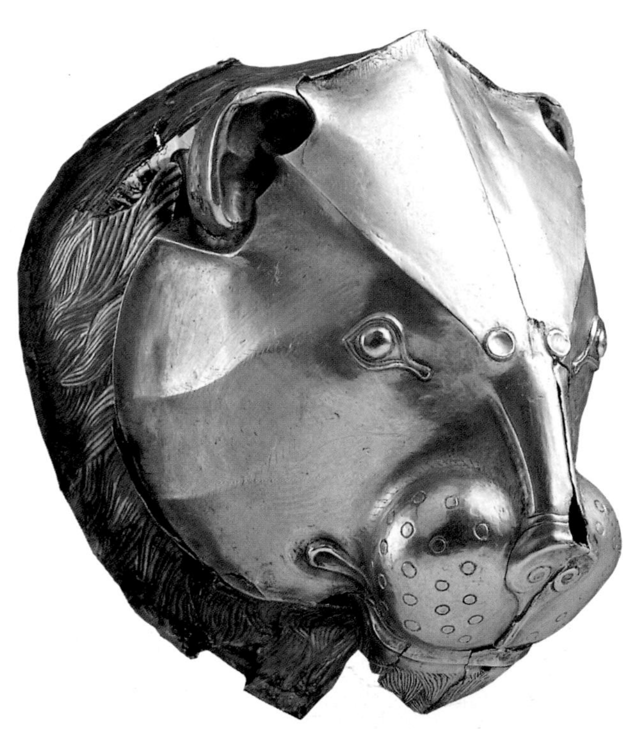

4-16. Rhyton in the shape of a lion's head, from a shaft grave at Mycenae. c. 1550 B.C. Gold, height 8" (20.3 cm). National Archaeological Museum, Athens

The problem "Minoan or Mycenaean" is central to two gold cups from a Mycenaean tomb at Vaphio (figs. 4-17 and 4-18). They were probably made about 1500 B.C., a few decades after the lion vessel. But where, for whom, and by whom? The issue is not as idle as it may seem, for it tests our ability to distinguish between the two neighboring cultures. It also forces us to consider every aspect of the cups. Do we find anything in their style or content that is un-Minoan? On the one hand, we note the similarity of the human figures to those on the *Harvester Vase* and that of the bulls to the animal in *"The Toreador Fresco."* To be sure, the men on the *Vaphio Cups* are not engaged in the Cretan bull-vaulting game but in catching the animals on the range. However, this subject also occurs in Minoan art. On the other hand, we cannot overlook the fact that the design on the cups does not quite match the rhythmic movement of Minoan compositions and that the bulls, for all their power, have the look of cattle rather than of sacred animals. It nevertheless seems, on balance, that the cups are by a Minoan artist working for Mycenaean patrons.

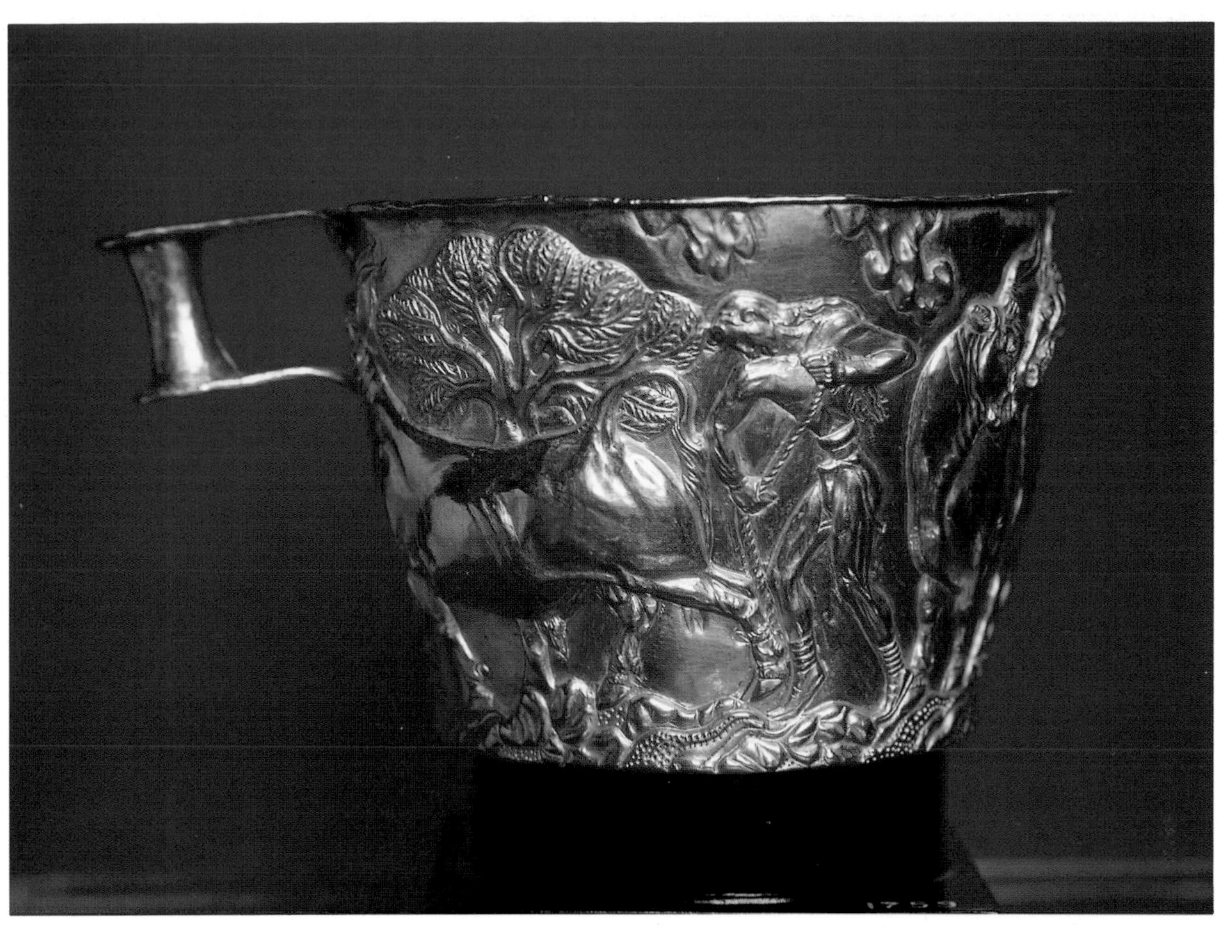

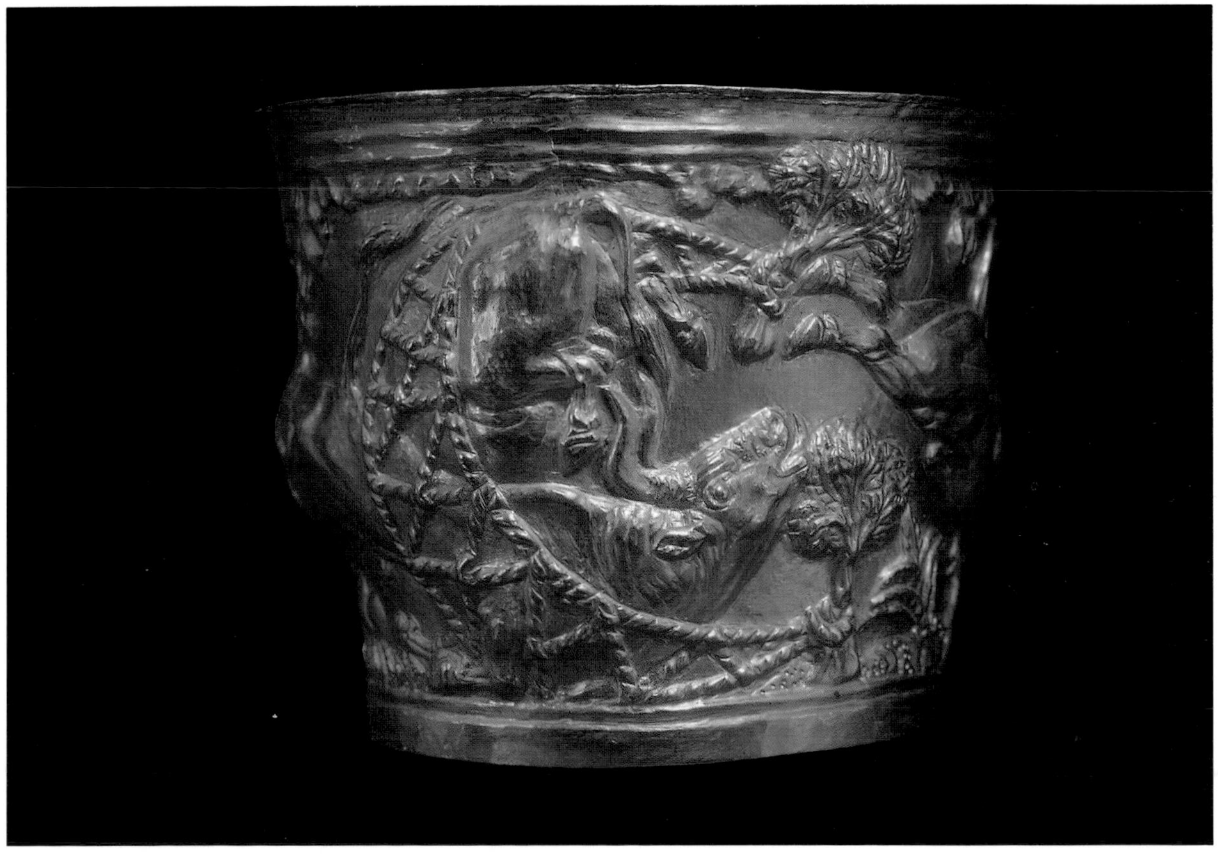

4-17, 4-18. *Vaphio Cups.* c. 1500 B.C. Gold, heights 3"; 3 ½" (7.5; 9 cm). Shown actual size.
National Archaeological Museum, Athens

MYCENAE, CRETE, AND EGYPT. In the sixteenth century B.C., Mycenae presents a strange picture. What appears to be an Egyptian influence on burial customs is combined with a strong artistic influence from Crete and with great wealth, as expressed in the lavish use of gold. We need a theory that involves the Mycenaeans with Crete as well as Egypt about a century before the new palaces were destroyed. Such a theory—fascinating though hard to confirm in detail—runs as follows: between 1700 and 1580 B.C., the Egyptians were trying to rid themselves of the Hyksos, who had seized the Nile Delta (see pages 52–53). For this they gained the aid of warriors from Mycenae, who returned home laden with gold (of which Egypt had an ample supply) and impressed with Egyptian funerary customs. The Minoans, not military but famous as sailors, ferried the Mycenaeans back and forth, so that they, too, had closer contact with Egypt. This hypothesis may help to explain their sudden prosperity toward 1600 B.C. It may also account for the rapid development of naturalistic wall painting (see also page 55). In any event, the close relations between Crete and Mycenae, once established, were to last a long time.

Architecture

The great monuments of Mycenaean architecture were all built between 1400 B.C., when Linear B script began to appear, and 1200 B.C. Apart from such details as decorative motifs or the shape of the columns, Mycenaean architecture owes little to the Minoan tradition. The palaces were hilltop fortresses surrounded by defensive walls of huge stone blocks. This type of construction, unknown in Crete, was similar to the Hittite fortifications at Bogazköy (see fig. 3-17). The Lioness Gate at Mycenae (fig. 4-19) is the most impressive remnant of these massive ramparts, which inspired such awe in the Greeks of later times that they were regarded as the work of the Cyclopes, a mythical race of one-eyed giants. Even the Treasury of Atreus, although built of smaller and more precisely shaped blocks, has a Cyclopean lintel (see fig. 4-14).

The stone relief over the doorway of the Lioness Gate also departs from the Minoan tradition. The two lionesses flanking a symbolic Minoan column have the same grim, heraldic majesty as the golden lion's head in figure 4-16. Their function as guardians,

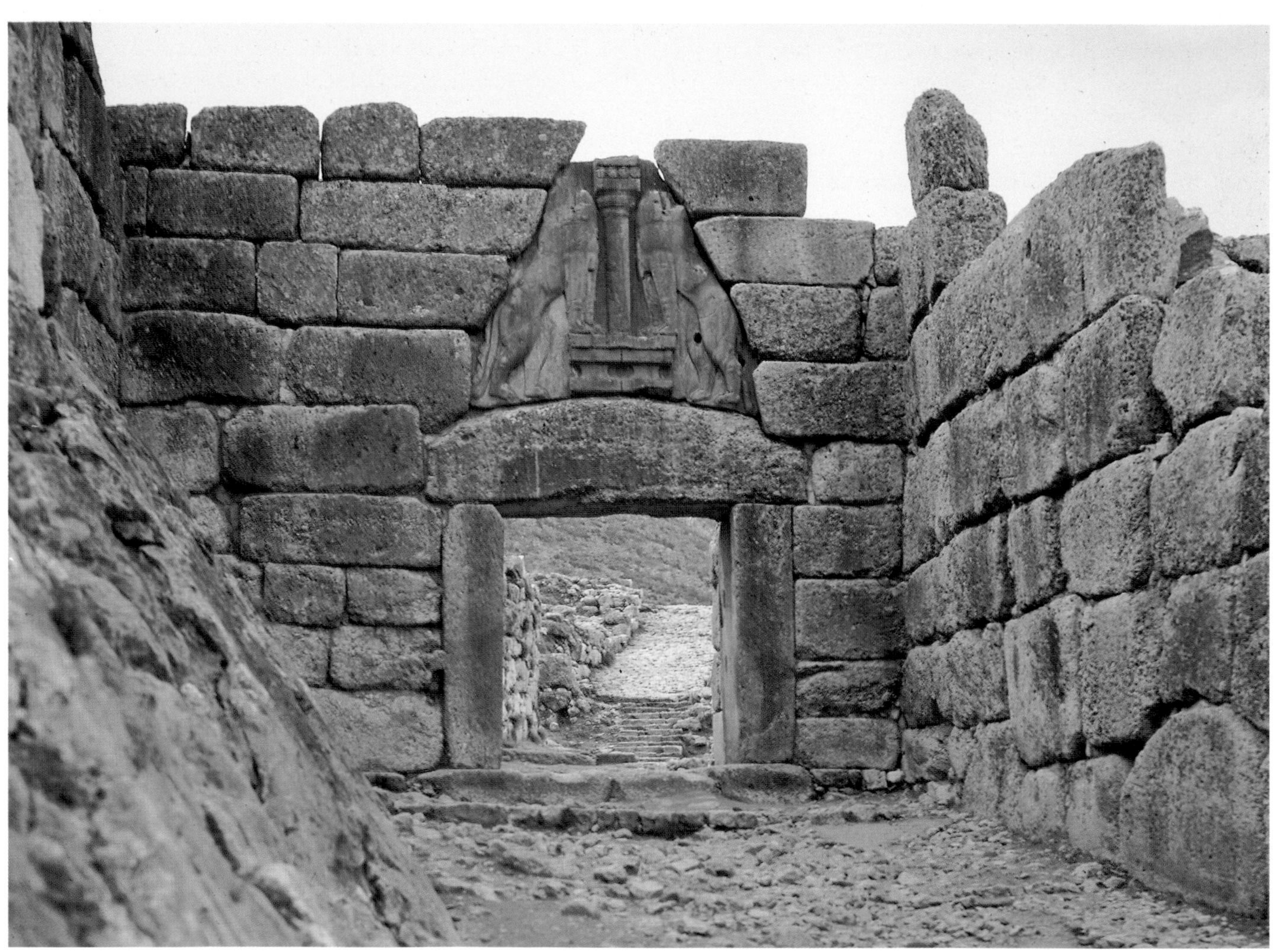

4-19. The Lioness Gate, Mycenae, Greece. 1250 B.C.

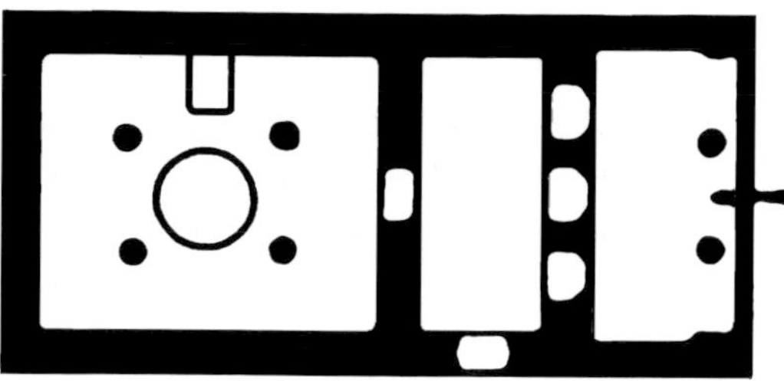

4-20. Plan of a Mycenaean megaron

their tense, muscular bodies, and their symmetrical design again suggest an influence from the Near East. We may at this point recall the Trojan War, which brought the Mycenaeans to Asia Minor soon after 1200 B.C. It seems likely, however, that the Mycenaeans began to cross the Aegean, for trade or war, much earlier than that.

The center of the Mycenaean palace was the audience hall, called the megaron. Only its plan is known for certain: a large rectangular room with a round hearth in the middle and four columns to support the roof beams (fig. 4-20). It was entered through a deep porch with two columns and an antechamber. This design is an enlarged version of the simple houses of earlier generations; its ancestry can be traced back to Troy as early as 3000 B.C. There may have been a rich decorative scheme of wall paintings and ornamental carvings to stress its dignity as the king's abode.

Sculpture

As in Crete, Mycenaean religious architecture was confined to modest structures with cult statues set apart from the palaces, which also included small shrines. A wide variety of gods were worshiped in them, although their identity is sometimes a matter of dispute. Mycenaean religion included not only Minoan elements but also influences from Asia Minor, as well as deities of Greek origin. Among these were a number of the later Olympian gods, such as Poseidon. But gods have an odd way of merging or exchanging their identities, so that the religious images in Mycenaean art are hard to interpret.

What, for instance, are we to make of the exquisite little ivory group (fig. 4-21) found at Mycenae in 1939? The style of the piece—its curved shapes and flexible movements—echoes Minoan art, though the carving has an unmistakably Near Eastern air (compare figs. 3-5 and 3-16). The subject, however, is strange. Two kneeling women, closely united, tend a single child. But whose is he? The natural interpretation would be to regard the now-headless figure as the mother, since the child clings to her arm and turns toward her. The second woman, whose left hand rests on the other's shoulder, would then be the grandmother. Such three-generation family groups are a well-known subject in Christian art, in which we often find St. Anne, the Virgin Mary, and the Infant Christ combined in similar fashion.

The memory of these later works colors our view of the Mycenaean ivory. Yet we search in vain for a subject in ancient religion that fits our reading of the group. On the other hand, there is a widespread myth about a divine child who is abandoned by his mother and reared by nymphs, goddesses, or even animals. His name varies from place to place and includes Bacchus and Jupiter. Thus in all likelihood our ivory shows a motherless child god with his nurses. The real mystery, however, lies deeper: in the tender play of gestures, the intimate human feeling, that binds the three figures together. Nowhere in ancient art before the Greeks do we find gods—or people, with only one exception (see fig. 2-27)—expressing affection with such warmth and eloquence.

Something quite new is reflected here, a familiar view of divine beings that makes the Minoan snake goddess (see fig. 4-6) seem even more awesome and remote. Was this change of attitude, and the ability to express it in art, a Mycenaean achievement? Or did they inherit it from the Minoans? Whatever the case, our ivory group opens up a realm of experience that was to be explored by Greek artists.

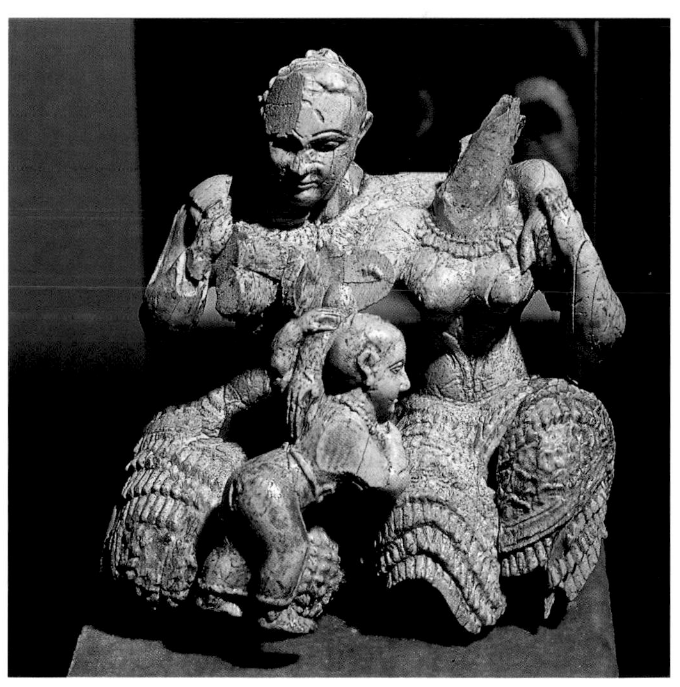

4-21. *Three Deities,* from Mycenae. c. 1500–1400 B.C. Ivory, height 3" (7.5 cm). National Archaeological Museum, Athens

CHAPTER FIVE

Greek Art

To people of European heritage, the works of art discussed so far seem like fascinating strangers because of the vast gaps in time and culture from our own. Greek architecture, sculpture, and painting, by contrast, are more like relatives, older members of a family that are immediately recognizable. A Greek temple reminds us at a glance of the bank around the corner, a Greek statue brings to mind countless other statues that we have seen somewhere, and a Greek coin makes us want to reach for the small change in our own pockets. But the tradition linking us with the ancient Greeks can be a handicap as well as an advantage in looking at Greek art. Sometimes the contribution of original works is obscured by our familiarity with later imitations. However, we shall find that Greek art owes a great deal to its predecessors, so that we may consider them, too, among the direct ancestors of Western civilization.

Another complication in the study of Greek art arises from the fact that we have three separate, and sometimes conflicting, sources of information on the subject. There are, first of all, the monuments themselves, a reliable but often inadequate source. Then we have Roman copies that tell us something about important works that would otherwise be lost to us entirely. These copies, however, pose a problem. Some are of such high quality that we cannot be sure that they really are copies. Others make us wonder how closely they follow their model—especially if we have several copies, all slightly different, of the same lost original.

Finally, there are the literary sources. The Greeks were the first people in history to write at length about their own artists, and their accounts were eagerly collected by the Romans, who handed them down to us. From them we learn what the Greeks themselves considered their most important achievements in architecture, sculpture, and painting. This written testimony has helped us to identify some celebrated artists and monuments, but much of it deals with works of which no visible trace remains today, while other works, which do survive and which strike us as among the greatest masterpieces of their time, are not mentioned at all. To reconcile the literary evidence with that of the copies and the original works, and to weave these strands into a coherent picture of the development of Greek art, is a difficult task, despite the enormous amount of work that has been done since the beginnings of archaeological scholarship some 250 years ago.

Who were the Greeks? We have met some of them before, such as the Mycenaeans, who came to Greece about 2000 B.C. Other Greek-speaking tribes entered the peninsula from the north toward 1100 B.C. These newcomers absorbed the Mycenaeans and gradually spread to the Aegean Islands and Asia Minor. During the following centuries they created what we now call Greek civilization. We do not know how many separate tribal units there were at first, but three main groups, who settled mainland Greece, the coast of Asia Minor, and the Aegean Islands, stand out. They are the Aeolians, who took over the north; the Dorians, who inhabited the south, including the Cycladic islands; and the Ionians, who colonized Attica, Euboea, most of the Aegean Islands, and the central coast of nearby Asia Minor. In the eighth century B.C., the Greeks also spread westward, founding important settlements in Sicily and southern Italy.

Despite a strong sense of kinship based on language and common beliefs, expressed in such traditions as the four great Panhellenic (all-Greek) festivals, the Greeks remained divided into small city-states. The pattern may be an echo of age-old tribal loyalties, an inheritance from the Mycenaeans, or a response to the geography of Greece, whose mountain ranges, narrow valleys, and jagged coastline would have made political unification difficult. Perhaps all of these factors worked together. In any event, the intense rivalry of these states undoubtedly spurred the growth of ideas and institutions.

Our own thinking about government uses many terms of Greek origin that reflect the evolution of the city-state. They include monarchy, aristocracy, tyranny, democracy, and, most important, politics (derived from *polites,* the citizen of the *polis,* or city-state). In the end, however, the Greeks paid dearly for their inability to broaden the concept of the state beyond the local limits of the *polis.* They engaged in constant warfare involving shifting alliances and banded together only when threatened with their common enemy, the Persians. The latter first invaded Greece in 490 B.C. under Darius I, only to be repulsed at the Battle of Marathon by a much smaller contingent of Athenians. They invaded again ten years later under Darius' son, Xerxes I, who was defeated in a series of famous battles at Thermopylae, Salamis, and Plataea in 480–479 B.C. After less than a half-century of peace, Athens and Sparta resumed their rivalry in the Peloponnesian War (431–404 B.C.), which ruined Athens and left Greece so weak that it was easily defeated by Philip II of Macedonia and his son, Alexander the Great, in the late fourth century B.C.

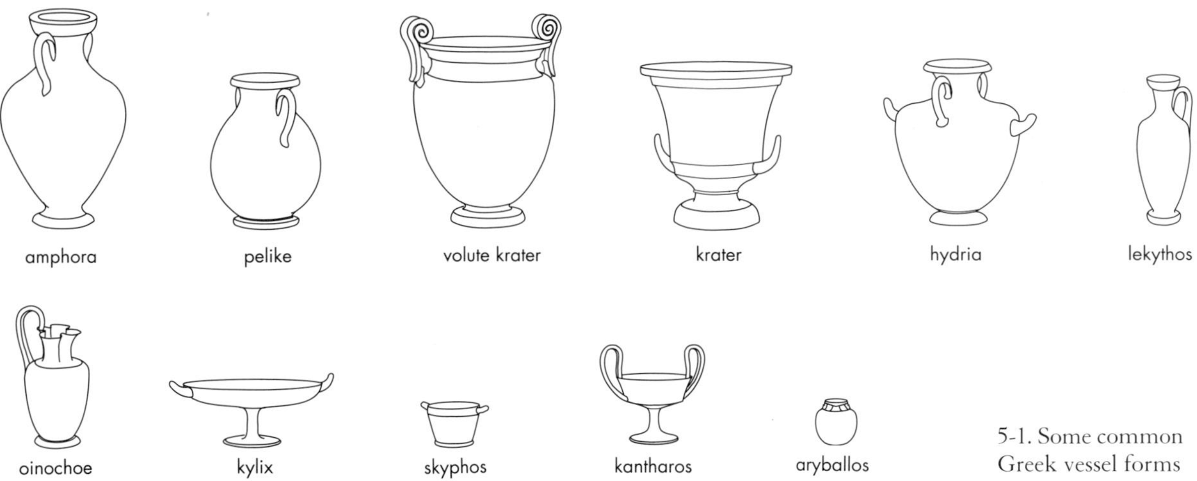

5-1. Some common Greek vessel forms

THE GEOMETRIC STYLE

The formative phase of Greek civilization covers about 400 years, from about 1100 to 700 B.C. We know very little about the first three centuries of this period, but after about 800 B.C. the Greeks rapidly emerged into the full light of history. The earliest specific dates that have come down to us are from that time. The main ones are the founding of the Olympic Games in 776 B.C., the starting point of Greek chronology, as well as slightly later dates for the founding of various cities. Also during that time the oldest Greek style in the fine arts, the so-called Geometric, developed. We know it only from painted pottery and small-scale sculpture. (Monumental architecture and sculpture in stone did not appear until the seventh century B.C.) The two forms are closely related. The pottery was often adorned with the same kinds of figures found in sculpture, which was made of clay or bronze. These early bronzes leave little doubt that the Greeks learned the technique of casting from the Mycenaeans.

Greek potters soon developed a considerable variety of shapes. (The basic ones are shown in fig. 5-1.) Chief among them was the *amphora,* a two-handled vase for storing wine or oil. Variants were the *pelike* and the *stamnos,* used for wine or water; these could also be poured from a type of jar known as an *oinochoe.* The principal vessel for water was the *hydria.* Wine was heavily diluted with water in a *krater,* which came in assorted shapes. This mixture was drunk from a shallow cup, the *kylix;* a deeper one called a *kantharos;* or the bowl-shaped *skyphos.* The main oil bottles were the *lekythos,* often used for sepulchral offerings, and the tiny *aryballos.* Each type was well adapted to its function, which was reflected in its form. As a result, each shape presented unique challenges to a painter, and some became specialists at decorating certain types of vases. However, the larger pots generally attracted the best artists because they provided more generous fields to work on. Since both the making and the decorating of vases were complex processes, these were usually separate professions, but the finest painters were sometimes potters as well.

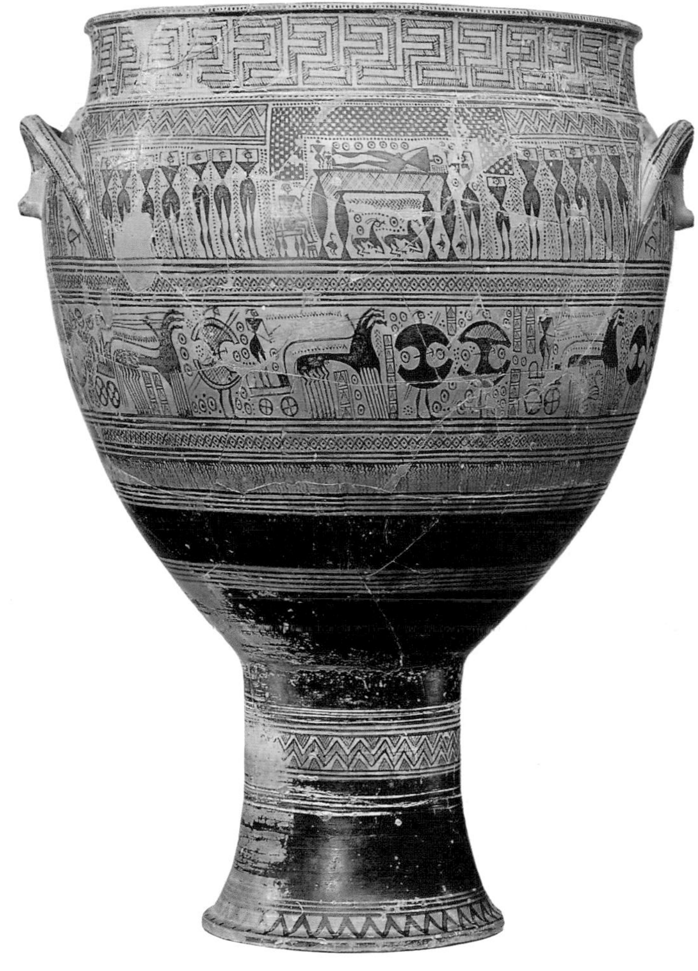
5-2. *Dipylon Vase.* 8th century B.C. Height 40 ½" (102.9 cm). The Metropolitan Museum of Art, New York.
ROGERS FUND, 1914

THE DIPYLON VASE. At first the pottery was decorated only with abstract designs: triangles, checkers, concentric circles. Toward 800 B.C. human and animal figures began to appear within the geometric framework. In the most mature examples these figures formed elaborate scenes. Our example (fig. 5-2), from the Dipylon cemetery near the double gate at the northwestern corner of Athens, belongs to a group of very large vases that served as grave monuments. Its bottom has holes through which liquid offerings could filter down to the dead below. On the body of the vase we see the deceased lying in state, flanked by figures with their arms raised in a gesture of mourning. Below is a funeral procession of chariots and warriors on foot.

The most remarkable thing about this vase is that it does not refer to an afterlife. Its purpose is to commemorate the deceased. Here lies a worthy man, it tells us, who was mourned by many and had a splendid funeral. Did the Greeks, then, have no concept of a hereafter? They did, but to them the realm of the dead was a colorless, ill-defined region where the souls, or "shades," led a feeble and passive existence without making any demands upon the living. When the warrior Odysseos conjures up the shade of Achilles in Homer's *Odyssey,* all the dead hero can do is mourn his own death: "Speak not conciliatorily of death, Odysseos. I'd rather serve on earth the poorest man . . . than lord it over all the wasted dead." Although the Greeks marked and tended their graves, and even poured liquid offerings over them, they did so in a spirit of pious remembrance, rather than to satisfy the needs of the deceased. Clearly, they had refused to adopt the elaborate burial customs of the Mycenaeans (see pages 89–90). Nor is the Geometric style an outgrowth of the Mycenaean tradition. It is a fresh, in some ways primitive, start. Yet it also owes a great deal to Near Eastern art: the repertory of forms can be traced back to prehistoric Mesopotamian pottery, though how they survived to be transmitted to the Greeks is not known.

Given the limited number of shapes, the artist who painted our vase has achieved a highly varied effect. The width, density, and spacing of the bands are subtly related to the structure of the vessel. His interest in representation is limited, however. The figures or groups, repeated at regular intervals, are little more than another kind of ornament. They form part of the same overall texture, so that their size varies according to the area to be filled. Organic and geometric elements still coexist in the same field, and often it is hard to distinguish between them. Lozenges indicate legs, whether of a man, a chair, or a bier. Circles with dots may or may not be human heads. The chevrons, boxed triangles, and so on between the figures may be decorative or descriptive—we cannot tell.

Geometric pottery has been found not only in Greece but in Italy and the Near East as well. This wide distribution is a clear sign that Greek traders were established throughout the eastern Mediterranean in the eighth century B.C. What is more, they had already adapted the Phoenician alphabet to their own use, as we know from inscriptions on these same vases. The greatest Greek achievements of this era, however, are the two Homeric epics, the *Iliad* and the *Odyssey.* The scenes on Geometric vases barely hint at the narrative power of these poems. If our knowledge of eighth-century Greece were based on the visual arts alone, we would inevitably think of it as a far simpler and more provincial society than the literary evidence suggests.

There is a paradox here. Perhaps at this time Greek civilization was so language-minded that painting and sculpture played a less important role than they would in later centuries. In that event, the Geometric style may have been something of an anachronism, a conservative tradition about to burst at the seams. Representation and narrative demand greater scope than the style could provide. The dam finally burst toward 725 B.C., when Greek art entered another phase, which we call the Orientalizing style, and new forms came flooding in.

THE ORIENTALIZING STYLE

As its name implies, the new style reflects influences from Egypt and the Near East, spurred by increasing trade with these regions. Between about 725 and 650 B.C. Greek art absorbed a host of Oriental motifs and ideas and was profoundly transformed in the process. It would be difficult to overestimate the impact of these influences. Whereas earlier Greek art is Aegean in flavor, the Orientalizing phase has a new monumentality and variety. Its wild exuberance reflects the efforts of painters and sculptors to master the new forms that came in waves, like immigrants from afar. The later development of Greek art is unthinkable without this vital period of experimentation.

Some of the subjects and motifs that we think of as typically Greek were, in fact, derived from Mesopotamia and Egypt, where they had a long history reaching back to the dawn of Near Eastern civilization. Another major source was Syrian art of the previous 150 years, when the region was ruled by the Aramaeans; the result was a crude but vigorous blend of Hittite and Assyrian art. The Greeks were active at the north Syrian port of Al Mina, at the mouth of the Orontes River. So were the Etruscans and Phoenicians, who also played an intermediary role as both artists and

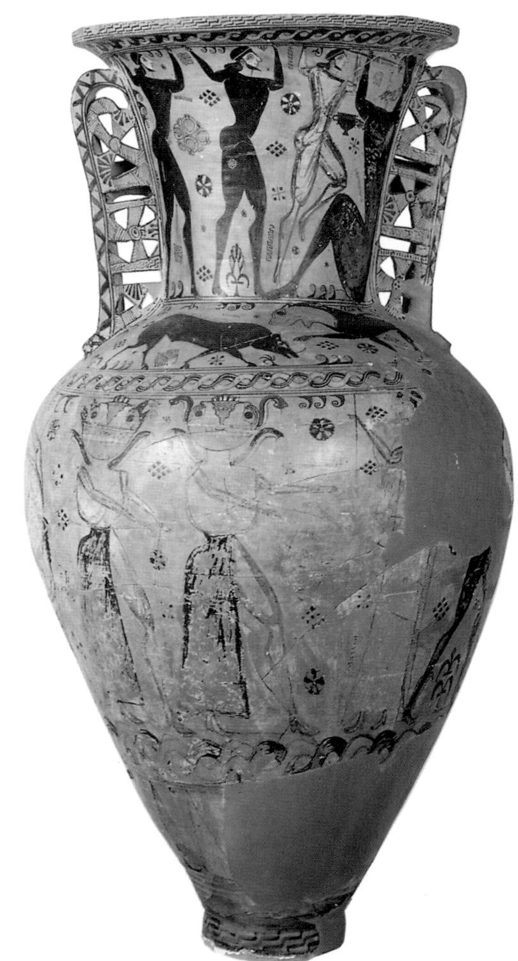

5-3. *The Blinding of Polyphemus and Gorgons,* on a Proto-Attic amphora. c. 675–650 B.C. Height 56" (142.3 cm). Archaeological Museum, Eleusis, Greece

THE GREEK GODS AND GODDESSES

All early civilizations and preliterate cultures had creation myths to explain the origin of the universe and humanity's place in it. Over time, these myths evolved into complex cycles that represent a comprehensive attempt to understand the world. The Greek stories of the gods and heroes—the myths and legends—were the result of combining local Doric and Ionic deities and folktales with the pantheon of Olympian gods. These tales had been brought to Greece from the ancient Near East through successive waves of immigration. The gods and goddesses, though immortal, were very human in behavior. They quarreled, and had children with each other's spouses and often with mortals as well. They were sometimes threatened and even overthrown by their own children. The principal Greek gods and goddesses, with their Roman counterparts in parentheses, are given below.

Zeus (Jupiter), god of sky and weather, was the king of the Olympian deities. His parents were Kronos and Rhea. It had been prophesied that one of Kronos' children would overthrow him, and he had thus taken the precaution of eating his children as soon as they were born. After Zeus' birth, Rhea hid him so that he would not suffer the same fate as his siblings. Zeus later tricked Kronos into disgorging his other children, who then overthrew their father with the help of the earth goddess, Gaea. Gaea was both the mother and wife of the sky god Uranus and the wife of Pontus, god of the sea. She was also the mother of the Cyclopes, who forged the weapons of the Olympians, as well as the Titans and Hundred-Handed Ones. The descendants of the Titans included Atlas (who was credited with holding up the earth), Hecate (an underworld goddess), Selene (goddess of the moon), Helios (a god of the sun), and Prometheus (a demigod, who gave humanity the gift of fire and was severely punished for doing so). After the defeat of Kronos, Zeus divided the universe by lot with his brothers Poseidon (Neptune), who ruled the sea, and Hades (Pluto), who became lord of the underworld.

Zeus fathered Ares (Mars, the god of war), Hephaestus (Vulcan, the god of armor and the forge), and Hebe (the goddess of youth) with his queen, Hera (Juno), goddess of marriage and fruitfulness, who was both his wife and sister. He also had numerous children through his love affairs with other goddesses and with mortal women. Chief among his children was Athena (Minerva), goddess of war. She was born of the liaison between Metis and Zeus, who swallowed her alive because, like his own father, he was told he would be toppled by one of his offspring. Athena later emerged fully armed from the head of Zeus. Although a female counterpart to the war god Ares, Athena was also the goddess of peace, a protector of heroes, a patron of arts and crafts (especially spinning and weaving) and, later, of wisdom. She became the patron goddess of Athens, an honor she won in a contest with Poseidon. Her gift to the city was an olive tree, which she caused to sprout on the Akropolis. Poseidon had offered a useless saltwater spring.

Zeus sired other goddesses, among them Aphrodite (Venus), the goddess of love, beauty, and fertility. She became the wife of Hephaestus and a lover of Ares, by whom she bore Harmonia, Eros, and Anteros. Aphrodite was also the mother of Hermaphroditus (with Hermes), Priapus (with Dionysos), and Aeneas (with the Trojan prince Anchises). Artemis (Diana), who with her twin brother Apollo was born of Leto and Zeus, was the virgin goddess of the hunt. She was also sometimes considered a moon goddess with Selene and Hecate.

Zeus begat other major gods as well. Hermes (Mercury), son of Maia, was the messenger of the gods, conductor of souls to Hades, and the god of travelers and commerce. He was sometimes credited with inventing the lyre and the shepherd's flute. The main god of civilization (including art, music, poetry, law, and philosophy) was the sun-god Apollo (Helios), who was also the god of prophecy and medicine, flocks and herds. Apollo was opposite in temperament to Dionysos (Bacchus), the son of Zeus and of either Persephone (Proserpina), queen of the underworld, or the moon goddess Semele. Dionysos was raised on Mount Nysa, where he invented wine making. His followers, the half-man, half-goat satyrs (the oldest of whom was Silenus, the tutor of Dionysos) and their female companions, the nymphs and humans known as maenads (bacchantes), were given to orgiastic excess. However, there was a temperate side to Dionysos. As the god of fertility, he was also the god of vegetation, as well as the god of peace, hospitality, and the civilized arts.

traders (see page 151). It was the merging of these influences with Aegean tendencies and the distinctive Greek cast of mind that soon gave rise to what we think of as Greek art proper.

THE ELEUSIS AMPHORA. The change becomes evident if we compare the large amphora from Eleusis (fig. 5-3) with the *Dipylon Vase* of a hundred years earlier (see fig. 5-2). Geometric ornament has not disappeared from this vase altogether, but now it is confined to the foot, handles, and lip. New, curvilinear motifs—such as spirals, interlacing bands, palmettes, and rosettes—appear everywhere. On the shoulder of the vessel is a frieze of fighting animals, derived from Near Eastern art. The major areas, however, are given over to narrative, which now dominates the vase.

The Greek myths and legends (see box above) were a vast source of subjects for narrative painting. These tales, many of which can be traced back to the Akkadians (see pages 68–69), were the result of mixing local Doric and Ionic gods and heroes into the pantheon of Olympian gods and Homeric sagas. They also represent a comprehensive attempt to understand the world. The

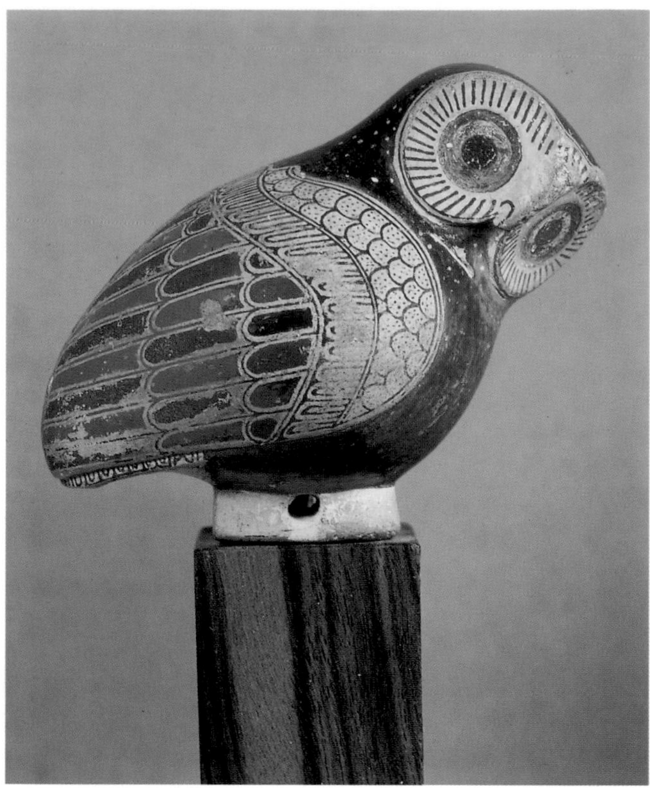

5-4. Proto-Corinthian perfume vase. c. 650 B.C. Height 2" (5 cm). Musée du Louvre, Paris

Greek interest in heroes and deities helps to explain the appeal of Oriental lions and monsters to the Greek imagination. These terrifying creatures embodied the unknown forces faced by the hero. This fascination can be seen on the Eleusis amphora. The figures have gained so much in size and descriptive precision that the decorative patterns scattered among them can no longer interfere with their actions. Ornament of any sort now belongs to a separate and lesser realm clearly distinguished from that of representation.

The neck of the Eleusis amphora shows the blinding of the giant one-eyed cyclops Polyphemos, a son of Poseidon, by Odysseos and his companions, whom Polyphemos had imprisoned. The story, recounted in the *Odyssey* but undoubtedly known from other retellings, is portrayed with memorable directness and dramatic force. If these men lack the beauty we expect of epic heroes in later art, their movements have an expressive vigor that makes them seem thoroughly alive. The slaying of another monstrous creature is shown on the body of the vase, which has been so badly damaged that only two figures have survived intact. They are Gorgons, the sisters of the snake-haired Medusa whom Perseus (partly seen running away to the right) killed with the aid of the gods. Even here we notice an interest in the articulation of the body that goes far beyond the limits of the Geometric style.

The Eleusis vase belongs to a group of ceramics called Proto-Attic. They are the ancestors of the great tradition of vase painting that was soon to develop in Attica, the region around Athens. A second family of Orientalizing vases is known as Proto-Corinthian, since it points toward the later pottery of Corinth. These vases, noted for their spirited animal motifs, show close links with the Near East. Some of them, such as the perfume vase in figure 5-4, are shaped like animals. The enchanting little owl, streamlined to fit the palm of a lady's hand and yet so animated in pose and expression, helps us to understand why Greek pottery came to be in demand throughout the Mediterranean world.

ARCHAIC VASE PAINTING

The Orientalizing phase of Greek art was a period of transition, in contrast to the stable Geometric style. Once the new elements from the East had been assimilated, another style emerged, as well defined as the Geometric but much greater in range: the Archaic, which lasted from the later seventh century to about 480 B.C., the time of the famous Greek victories over the Persians at Salamis and Plataea. During the Archaic period, we see the unfolding of the artistic genius of Greece, not only in vase painting but also in architecture and sculpture. While Archaic art lacks the balance and the sense of perfection of the Classical style of the later fifth century, it has such freshness that many people consider it the most vital phase in the development of Greek art.

Greek architecture and sculpture on a large scale must have begun to develop long before the mid-seventh century. Until that time, however, both were mainly of wood, and nothing of them has survived except the foundations of a few buildings. The desire to build and sculpt in stone, for the sake of permanence, was the most important new idea that entered Greece during the Orientalizing period. Moreover, the revolution in material and technique must have brought about decisive changes of style as well, so that we cannot safely reconstruct the appearance of the lost wooden temples or statues on the basis of later works. In vase painting, on the other hand, there was no such break in continuity. It thus seems best to deal with Archaic vases before we turn to the sculpture and architecture of the period.

The significance of Archaic vase painting is in some ways completely unique. Decorated pottery, however great its value to archaeologists, rarely enters the mainstream of the history of art. We think of it, in general, as a craft or industry. This remains true even of Minoan vases, despite their exceptional beauty and technical refinement, and the same may be said of most of Greek pottery. Yet if we study such pieces as the *Dipylon Vase* or the amphora from Eleusis, they are impressive not only by virtue of their sheer size but for their narrative paintings, and we cannot escape the feeling that they are among the most ambitious works of art of their day.

There is no way to prove this, of course—far too much has been lost—but it is clear that these objects are highly individual. They are not routine ware produced in quantity according to set patterns. Archaic vases are generally a good deal smaller than their predecessors, since pottery vessels no longer served as grave monuments (which were now made of stone). Their painted decoration, however, shows a far greater emphasis on pictorial subjects (see fig. 5-6). Scenes from mythology, legend, and everyday life appear in endless variety, and the artistic level is often very high, especially among Athenian vases.

After the middle of the sixth century, many of the finest vases bear the signatures of the artists who made them. This shows not only that potters, as well as painters, took pride in their work but also that they could become famous for their personal style. To us, such signatures do not mean much in and of themselves. They are no more than useful labels unless we know enough of an artist's work to gain some insight into his personality. Remarkably enough, that is possible with a good many Archaic vase painters. Some of them have so distinctive a style that their artistic "handwriting" can be recognized even without a signature. In a few cases we are lucky enough to have dozens (in one instance, more than 200) of vases by the same hand, so that we can trace one master's development over a considerable period. Archaic vase painting thus introduces us to the first clearly defined personalities in the history of art. (Signatures occur in Archaic sculpture and architecture as well, but they have not helped us to identify the personalities of individual masters.)

Archaic Greek painting was, of course, not confined to vases. There were murals and panels, too. Although almost nothing has survived of them, we can form some idea of what they might have looked like from the wall paintings in Etruscan tombs of the same period (see figs. 6-3 and 6-4). How were these large-scale works related to the vase pictures? We do not know, but one thing seems certain: all Archaic painting was essentially drawing filled in with solid, flat color. Murals therefore could not have looked very different from vase pictures.

According to the literary sources, Greek wall painting did not come into its own until about 475–450 B.C., after the Persian wars. During this period artists gradually discovered how to model figures and objects and how to create a sense of spatial depth. [See Primary Sources, no. 3, page 193.] From that time on, vase painting became a lesser art, since depth and modeling were beyond its limited technical means; by the end of the fifth century its decline was obvious. Thus the great age of vase painting was the Archaic era. Until about 475 B.C., the best vase painters enjoyed as much prestige as other artists. Whether or not their work directly reflects the lost wall paintings, it deserves to be viewed as a major achievement.

THE BLACK-FIGURED STYLE. The difference between Orientalizing and Archaic vase painting is one of artistic discipline. In the amphora from Eleusis (see fig. 5-3), the figures are shown partly as solid silhouettes, partly in outline, or as a combination of both. Toward the end of the seventh century, Attic vase painters adopted the "black-figured" style, in which the entire design is silhouetted in black against the reddish clay. Internal details are scratched in with a needle, and white and purple may be added on top of the black to make certain areas stand out. The virtues of this technique, which favors a decorative, two-dimensional effect, are apparent in figure 5-5, a kylix (drinking cup) by Exekias of about 540 B.C. The slender, sharp-edged forms have a lacelike delicacy, yet also resilience and strength, so that the design adapts itself to the circular surface without becoming mere ornament. Dionysos reclines in his boat (the sail was once entirely white), which moves with the same ease as the dolphins, whose lithe forms are balanced by the heavy clusters of grapes.

But why is he at sea? According to a Homeric hymn, the god of wine had once been abducted by Etruscan pirates. He thereupon caused vines to grow all over the ship and frightened his captors until they jumped overboard and were turned into dolphins. We see him on his return journey—an event to be gratefully recalled by every Greek drinker—accompanied by seven dolphins and seven bunches of grapes for good luck.

While the spare elegance of Exekias retains something of the spirit of Geometric pottery, the work of the slightly younger Psiax is the direct outgrowth of the forceful Orientalizing style. Herakles killing the Nemean lion (fig. 5-6), the first of his 12 labors (see box on page 101), reminds us of the hero on the soundbox of the harp from Ur (see fig. 3-9). Both show a man facing unknown forces in the form of terrifying creatures. The lion also serves to underscore the hero's might and courage against demonic forces. The scene on Psiax's amphora is all grimness and violence. The two heavy bodies are locked in combat, so that they almost grow together into a single unit. Lines and colors have been added with utmost economy in order to avoid breaking up the massive expanse of black. Yet both figures show such a wealth of knowledge of anatomy and skillful foreshortening that they give an illusion of existing in the round. (Note the way the abdomen and shoulders of Herakles are rendered.) Only in such details as the eye of Herakles do we still find the traditional combination of front and profile views.

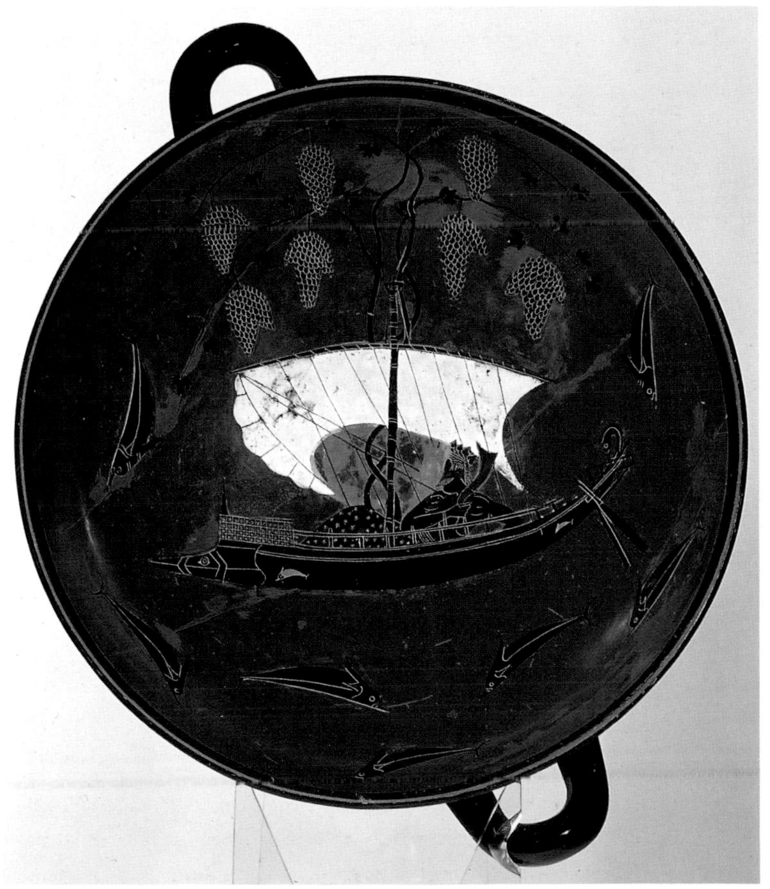

5-5. Exekias. *Dionysos in a Boat.* Interior of an Attic black-figured kylix. c. 540 B.C. Diameter 12" (30.5 cm). Staatliche Antikensammlungen, Munich

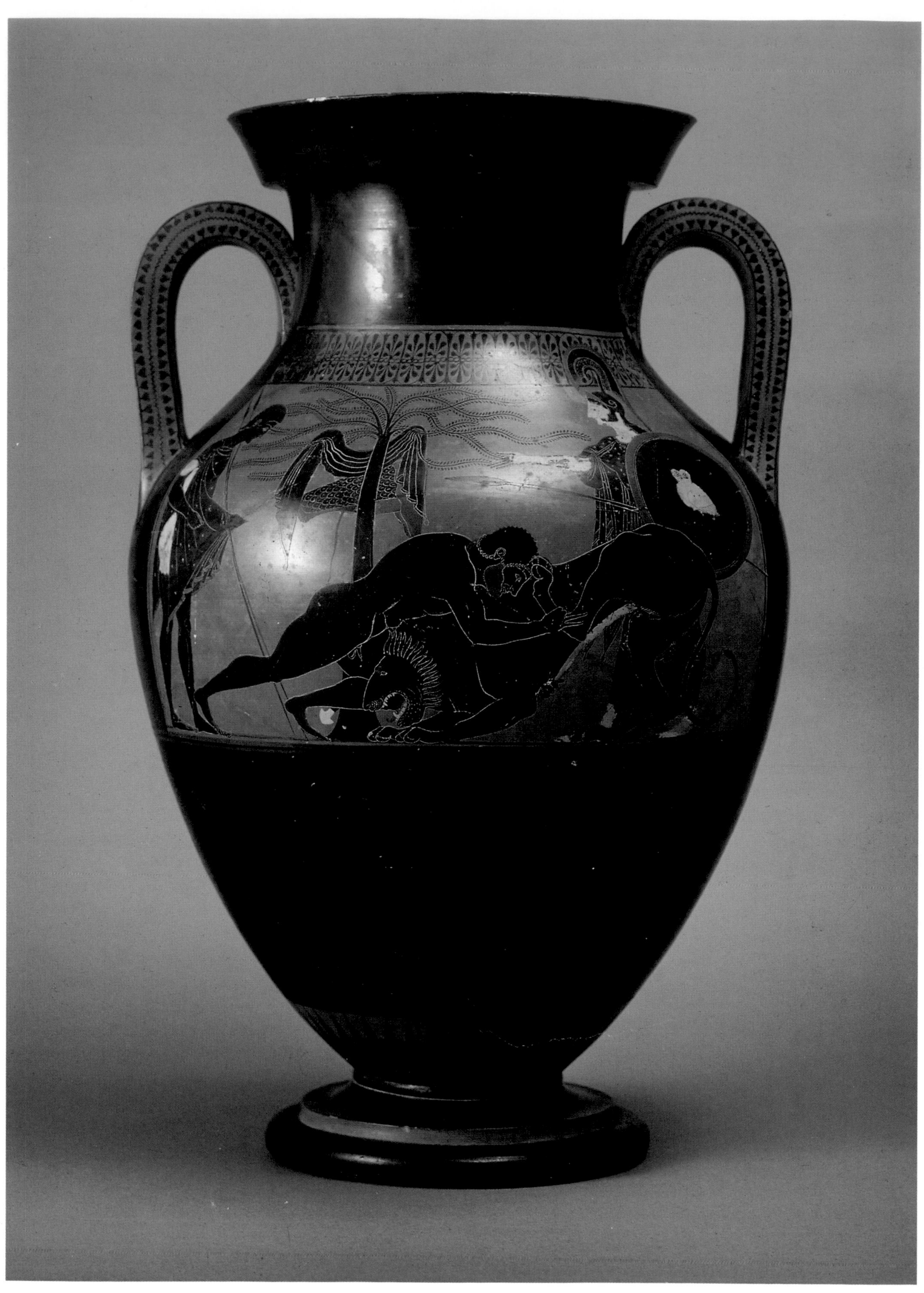

5-6. Psiax. *Herakles Strangling the Nemean Lion,* on an Attic black-figured amphora from Vulci, Italy. c. 525 B.C. Height 19 ½" (49.5 cm). Museo Civico dell'Età Cristiana, Brescia

THE HERO IN GREEK LEGEND

The early Greeks interpreted the meaning of events in terms of fate and human character rather than as accidents of history, in which they had little interest before about 500 B.C. The main focus in the writings of Greek authors was on explaining why the legendary heroes of the past seemed incomparably greater than people of their own day. Some of these heroes were historical figures, but all were believed to be descendants of the gods, who often had children with mortals. Such a lineage helped to explain the hero's extraordinary power. This power (called *arete* by the Greeks) could, in excess, lead to overweening pride (*hubris*) and to moral error (*hamartia*). The tragic results of hamartia were the subject of many Greek plays, especially those by Sophocles. The Greek ideal became moderation in all things, personified by Apollo, the god of art and civilization. Arete came to be identified over time with personal and civic virtues, such as modesty and piety.

The greatest of all Greek heroes was Herakles (Hercules to the Romans). The son of Zeus and the princess Alkmene, he became the only mortal ever to ascend to Mount Olympus upon his death. His greatest exploits were the 12 labors. Undertaken over 12 years at the command of King Eurystheus in Tiryns, they were acts of atonement for killing his wife and children after he was driven mad by Hera (the wife of Zeus) for his excesses.

THE RED-FIGURED STYLE. Psiax must have felt that the silhouettelike black-figured technique made foreshortening unduly difficult, for in some of his vases he tried the reverse procedure, leaving the figures red and filling in the background. This red-figured technique gradually replaced the older method toward 500 B.C. Its advantages can be seen in figure 5-7, a krater of about 510 B.C. by Euphronios showing Herakles wrestling the giant Antaios. The details have been applied by squeezing a bladder rather like a pastry tube, or freely drawn with the brush, rather than incised. As a result, the picture depends far less on the profile view than before. Instead, the artist uses the internal lines to show boldly foreshortened and overlapping limbs, precise details of costume (note the pleated dresses of the three women), and intense facial expressions. He is so fascinated by these new effects that he has made the figures as large as possible. They almost seem to burst from the field of the vase!

A similar striving for monumental effect, but with more harmonious results, may be seen in the *Eos and Memnon* by Douris (fig. 5-8), one of the masterpieces of late Archaic vase painting. It shows the goddess of dawn holding the body of her son, who had been killed and stripped of his armor by Achilles. In this moving evocation of grief, Greek art touches a mood prophetic of the Christian *Pietà* (see fig. 11-54). Notable, too, is the expressive freedom of the draftsmanship: the lines are as flexible as if they had been drawn with a pen. Douris knows how to trace the contours of limbs beneath the drapery and how to contrast vigorous outlines with more delicate secondary strokes, such as those indicating the anatomical details of Memnon's body. This vase is also of interest for its inscription, which includes the signatures of both painter and potter, as well as a dedication typical of Greek vases: "Hermogenes is beautiful."

THE SYMPOSIUM. The four vases we have just discussed are all associated with wine: the amphora for storing it, the krater for mixing it, and the kylix for drinking it. Obviously they were not meant for everyday use (undecorated vases served that purpose).

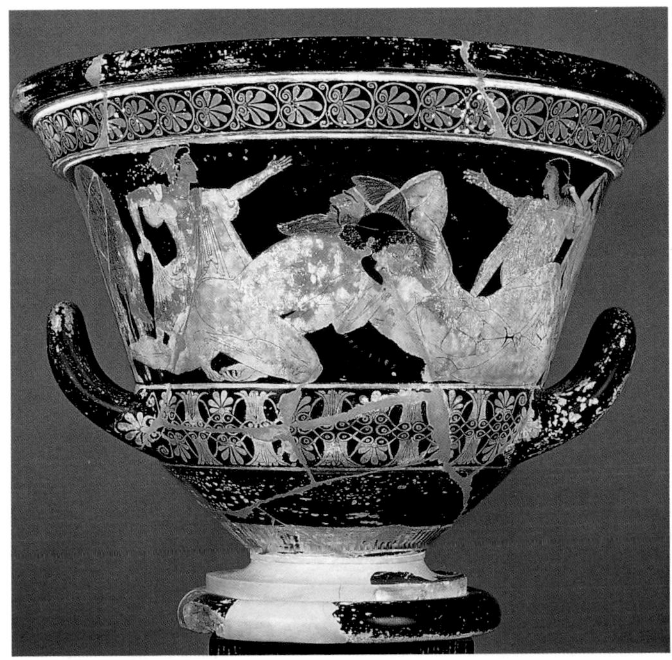

5-7. Euphronios. *Herakles Wrestling Antaios,* on an Attic red-figured krater. c. 510 B.C. Height 19" (48 cm). Musée du Louvre, Paris

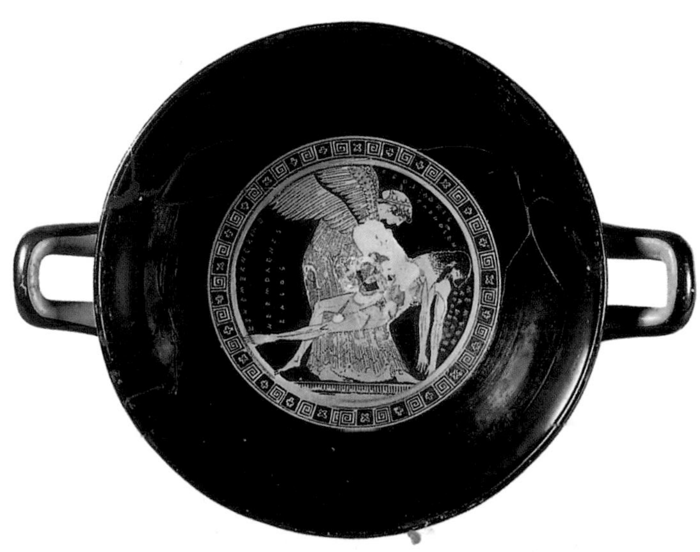

5-8. Douris. *Eos and Memnon.* Interior of an Attic red-figured kylix. c. 490–480 B.C. Diameter 10½" (26.7 cm). Musée du Louvre, Paris

THEATER IN ANCIENT GREECE

Greek theater combined words, music, and dance, reflecting its origin in revels which began to be held four times yearly in honor of the wine god Dionysos during the ninth century B.C. The hymns in praise of Dionysos, called *dithyrambs,* that were sung at these theatrical presentations continued to be improvised until the early sixth century B.C., when they began to be set down in literary form by Arion of Corinth (c. 625–585 B.C.), the city that also claimed to have invented comedy. The main development of Greek theater began in 534 B.C., the year Athens reorganized the Dionysian festival and held the first drama contest, which was won by Thespis, who added spoken texts to what had previously been sung. (Thespis, who was also the first actor, is honored with the use of the term *thespian* to denote actors and actresses.) Unfortunately, out of the more than 1,000 plays that are recorded, we have only 31, composed by four writers in Athens during the fifth century B.C. Each of these authors had a distinct literary personality. Aeschylus (c. 523–456) was the most philosophical; Sophocles (c. 496–406) the most psychologically penetrating; Euripides (c. 480–406) the most modern and gripping; while Aristophanes (c. 448–c. 388 B.C.) reigned supreme in comedy. Despite their great differences, all relied on past myths and history, which they freely altered.

Initially the author was also the principal actor, but this practice became unnecessary, as well as undesirable, after Aeschylus introduced a second actor, to which Sophocles added a third. In addition to writing and directing his play, each author was generally responsible for composing his own music, training the actors and chorus, and devising his own choreography for the annual contests. Even though the number of festivals was increased over time, acting never became a full-time profession, and the chorus was always made up solely of amateurs, who underwent a rigorous training. Despite the fragmentary remains, we know that substantial portions of Greek tragedies were set to music. (*Tragedy* originally meant "goat song" in ancient Greek.) Thus the Greek chorus intoned its lines to musical accompaniment while moving in intricate patterns on the stage. Tragedians could be innovators in music as well as drama. Sophocles introduced new musical modes and Euripides promoted chromaticism. Nevertheless, drama generally followed the lead of the dithyrambists and kitharodes (kithara players) in musical matters. For example, Agathon, who won his first tragedy contest in 416 B.C., was an unabashed modernist noted for his sensuous and intricate melodies.

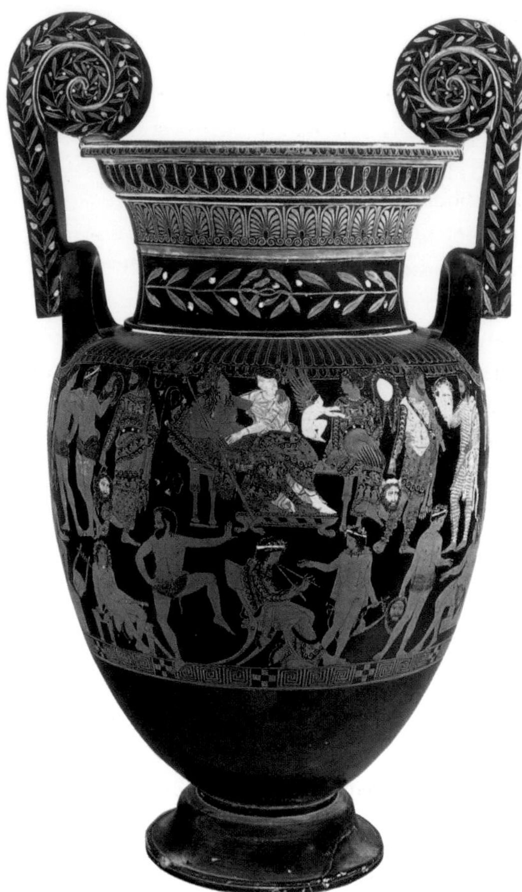

The Prononomos Painter. *Dionysos and Ariadne Amidst Players and Characters of the Theater.* End of 5th century B.C. Volute krater. National Museum, Naples

Our understanding of Greek tragedy is largely based on Aristotle's *Poetics.* This book was derived from lectures he gave around 335 B.C. at the Lyceum, the sacred grove of Apollo Lyceius near Athens where he established his school. With his inquisitive mind, everything became the subject of systematic philosophical thought. Aristotle's argument proceeds from the belief that tragedy is the highest form of drama and that *Oedipus Rex* by Sophocles is its greatest representative. His theory is based on the complex idea of imitation. By this he means "not of men

Decorated vases were reserved for important occasions, the most important of which was the symposium (*symposion*), an exclusive drinking party for men. The participants reclined on couches around the edges of a room; in the middle was a large mixing bowl, overseen by a master of ceremonies, who filled the drinkers' cups. Music, poetry, storytelling, and word games accompanied the festivities. The event often ended in sexual liaisons, both homo- and heteroerotic, which are frequently depicted on drinking cups. There was also a serious side to symposia, as described by Plato and Xenophon, which centered on debates about politics, ethics, and morality.

THE CHANGING GREEK WORLDVIEW. Greek vases we have looked at show a gradual change in attitude toward myth and legend. Let us examine the evolution more closely. The Eleusis ampora (see fig. 5-3) presents a witty play on vision. Perseus flees the Gorgons after slaying Medusa, whose hideous faces can turn anyone who looks at her to stone, while Odysseos deprives the cyclops but of life, an action," which is conveyed by plot, words, song, costumes, and scenery. Plot is the very soul of tragedy, for through it is revealed the moral quality (*ethos*) of the main character. In "complex" dramas, the hero achieves a new understanding (*peripety*) as the result of a reversal in fortune that is brought about by an error in moral judgment (*hamartia*) rather than evil intent. To be successful, the plot must have unity of action and preferably take place within one day, though not necessarily in the same place, as later theorists demanded. The concept of overweening pride (*hubris*) credited to Aristotle is nowhere to be found in the *Poetics,* and the importance of emotional release (*katharsis*) has been overstated mainly because of Sigmund Freud, the founder of early-twentieth-century psychiatry.

Comedy was represented by the bawdy satyr play, the distant ancestor of modern burlesque theater, which seemingly was invented by Pratinas in the late sixth century B.C. The only surviving examples are Euripides' *Cyclops* and a fragment from Sophocles' *The Trackers,* both parodies of tragic dramas. Entirely different in character and perhaps origin are the comic plays of Aristophanes, which are commentaries on the contemporary scene. Be it society, politics, war, or literature, no subject was too sacred for his irreverent satire. His favorite targets were philosophers and his fellow dramatists. Nothing of later Greek comedy remains, but we know from other documents that it centered on the daily life of the middle class.

The visual arts contributed surprisingly little to Greek theater, which made sparse use of scenery. (The term derives from *skena,* the hut where actors changed their costumes.) Scene painting probably began around the middle of the fifth century B.C. and is variously credited to Aeschylus or Sophocles. According to the first century B.C. Roman architect and historian Vitruvius, scene painting consisted of architectural designs on a flat surface. It also made use of *pinakes* (painted panels) and *periaktoi* (triangular prisms) that were rotated. However, Vitruvius looked on the Classical past through distinctly Roman eyes, as did the poet Horace, who wrote about Greek tragedy and comedy. In all likelihood, scenery was very simple and changes minimal. Indeed, the advances sometimes attributed to Greek scenographers, especially in illusionism, appear to have been much later developments made in Roman times not long before Vitruvius himself.

of his sight. The artist, in turn, gives us a "sharp-eyed" portrayal of these fascinating figures, who belong to another realm. Exekias (see fig. 5-5) brings the human into more intimate, but no less whimsical, contact with the divine, as Dionysos sails the watery mix of wine in the cup held by the drinker. In Psiax's amphora (see fig. 5-6), the realm of legend still remains at one remove from the human. The combat emphasizes Herakles' might in overcoming the fearsome lion. The outcome is never in doubt, as can be seen from the composition and from the gesture of Athena, goddess of heroes.

The decisive shift comes in red-figure vase painting. It is as if the heightened naturalism made possible by the new technique allowed the artist to explore a new world of feeling as well. Euphronios takes care to show even subtle differences in appearance between Herakles and Antaios (see fig. 5-7) in order to make clear the distinction in their character, which the Greeks called *ethos* (see box on this page). Whereas Psiax's lion roars in rage, Euphronios makes us feel the suffering, not just the pain, of the shaggy Antaios, who clearly will lose out to the neatly coiffed Herakles. He also depicts the fear of the mortal women on either side, who support the combatants but cannot protect them. Thus for the first time we see sympathy for the vanquished as victim.

The circle of myth, legend, and human experience is closed in the cup with Eos and Memnon (see fig. 5-8). Memnon was defeated by Achilles after their mothers sought the help of Jupiter, who weighed their souls on a scale that tipped against Memnon. Douris renders the tragedy of death with unforgettable tenderness. He invites the drinker to think about the meaning of this poignant image and question the role of the hero and the gods who intervene in fate. Was Achilles' soul really greater than Memnon's, especially since they were otherwise evenly matched? How is individual worth measured? Can Memnon's death be justified against the grief of a mother's loss? This altered conception is not confined to vase painting. It is part of a more complex understanding of life found in Greek philosophy, literature, and theater—changes that must have been discussed in symposia as well. We shall meet this new view again in architectural sculpture (compare figs. 5-16, 5-20, and 5-22). The latter, however, belongs for the most part to religious buildings that also served as civic monuments, so that its content was often determined by historical events and hence is less personal than vase painting.

ARCHAIC SCULPTURE

The new motifs that distinguish the Orientalizing style from the Geometric—fighting animals, winged monsters, scenes of combat—had reached Greece mainly through the importation of ivory carvings and metalwork from Phoenicia or Syria. Those pieces reflected Mesopotamian as well as Egyptian influences. Since such objects have been found on Greek soil, we can regard this channel of transmission as well established. They do not help us, however, to explain the rise of monumental architecture and sculpture in stone about 650 B.C., which must have been based on knowledge of Egyptian works that could be studied only on the spot. We know that small colonies of Greeks existed in Egypt at the time. But why, we wonder, did the Greeks suddenly develop a taste for monumental art, and how did their artists master stone carving so quickly? All the Greek sculpture we know from the Geometric period consists of simple clay or bronze figurines of animals and warriors only a few inches in size. The mystery may never be cleared up, for the oldest surviving Greek stone sculpture and architecture show that the Egyptian tradition had already been absorbed and Hellenized, though the link with Egypt is still clearly visible.

Kouros and Kore

Let us consider two very early Greek statues, a small female figure of about 650 B.C. (fig. 5-9) and a lifesize nude youth of about 600 B.C. (fig. 5-10). If we compare them with their Egyptian predecessors (see fig. 2-14), the similarities are striking. We note the block-conscious, cubic character of all four statues, the slim, broad-shouldered silhouette of the male figures, the position of their arms, their clenched fists, the way they stand with the left leg forward, and the emphatic rendering of the kneecaps. The wiglike treatment of the hair, the close-fitting garment of the female figures, and their raised arms are also much alike. Judged by Egyptian standards, the Archaic statues seem somewhat primitive: rigid, oversimplified, awkward, less close to nature. Whereas the Egyptian sculptor allows the legs and hips of the female figure to press through the skirt, the Greek shows a solid mass from which only the toes protrude.

But the Greek statues have virtues that cannot be measured in Egyptian terms. First of all, they are truly freestanding. In fact, they are the earliest large stone images of the human form in the

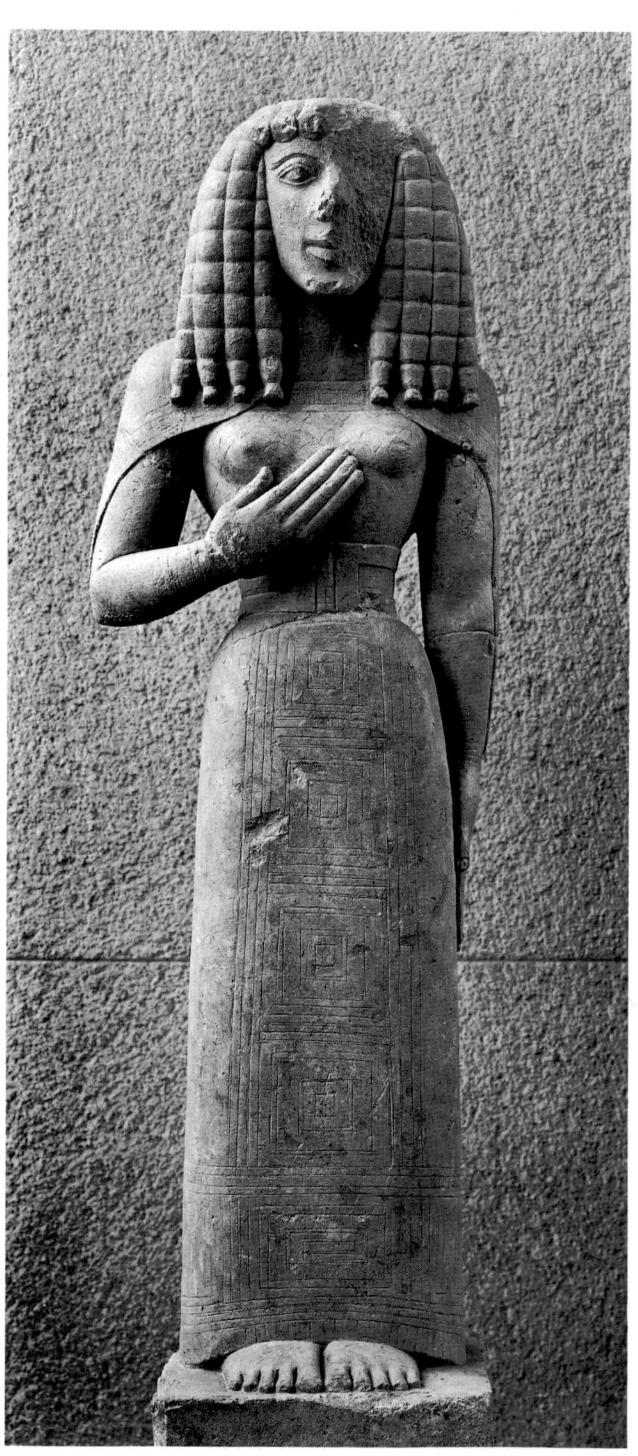

5-9. *Female Figure (Kore)*. c. 650 B.C. Limestone, height 24½" (62.3 cm). Musée du Louvre, Paris

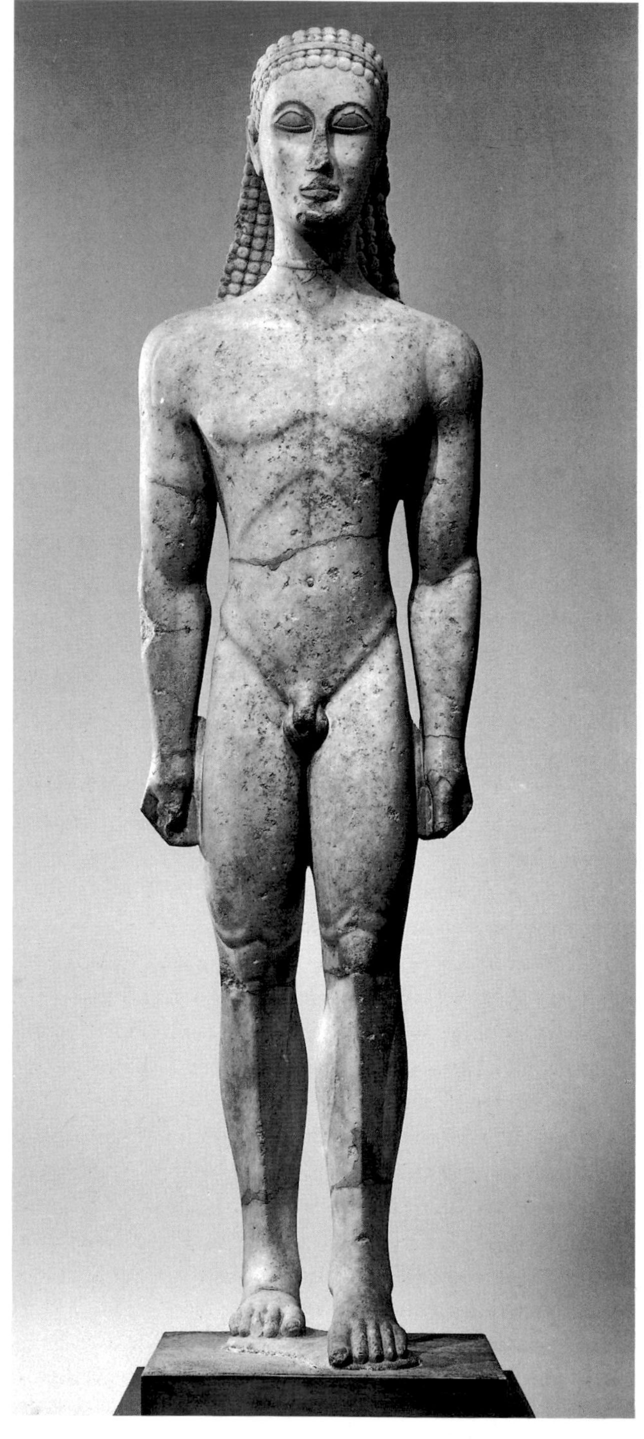

5-10. *Standing Youth (Kouros)*. c. 600 B.C. Marble, height 6'1½" (1.88 m). The Metropolitan Museum of Art, New York. FLETCHER FUND, 1932

entire history of art of which this can be said. Egyptian carvers had never freed such figures completely from the stone. They remain immersed in it, so that the empty spaces between the forms are always partly filled. There are never any holes in Egyptian stone figures. The Greek sculptor, in contrast, does not mind holes in the least. The arms are separated from the torso and the legs from each other (unless they are encased in a skirt), and the carver goes to great lengths to cut away all the rest of the stone. (The only exceptions are the tiny bridges between the fists and the thighs of the nude youth.) Apparently the Greeks felt that a statue must consist only of stone that has representational meaning within an organic whole. The stone must be transformed; it cannot be allowed to remain inert or neutral.

This is not a question of technique but of artistic intention. The liberation of our two figures gives them a spirit quite different from that of Egyptian statues. While the latter seem becalmed by a spell that has released them from every strain for all time, the Greek images are tense and full of hidden life. The direct stare of their huge eyes offers the most telling contrast to the gentle, faraway gaze of the Egyptian figures.

Whom do they represent? We call a female statue of this type a *Kore* (Maiden), a male one a *Kouros* (Youth), terms that gloss over the difficulty of identifying them further. The Kouros is always nude while the Kore is clothed. (In art, as in life, public nudity was acceptable for males, but not for females.) Both types were produced in large numbers throughout the Archaic era, and their general outlines remained constant. Some are inscribed with the names of artists ("So-and-so made me") or with dedications to various deities. These, then, were votive offerings. But in most cases we do not know whether they represent the donor, the deity, or a divinely favored person such as a victor in athletic games. Others were placed on graves, yet they represent the deceased only in a broad (and completely impersonal) sense. This lack of differentiation seems to be part of the essential character of these figures. They are neither gods nor mortals but something in between, an ideal of physical perfection and vitality shared by mortal and immortal alike.

The artistic treatment of the Kouros and the Kore shows the same dynamic we have traced in Archaic vase painting. The pace of this development is clear if we compare the Kouros of figure 5-10 with one that was carved some 75 years later (fig. 5-11). An inscription on its base identifies the latter as the funerary statue of Kroisos, who had died a hero's death in battle. Like all such figures, it was painted. (Traces of color can still be seen in the hair and the pupils of the eyes.) Instead of the sharp planes of the older statue, we now find swelling curves. The body shows greater awareness of massive volumes, but also a new elasticity. Anatomical details are rendered more functionally than before. The style of the *Kroisos* thus corresponds to that of Psiax's *Herakles* (see fig. 5-6). Here we witness the transition from black-figured to red-figured in sculptural terms.

There are numerous statues from the middle years of the sixth century marking previous way stations along the same road. The magnificent *Calf-Bearer* of about 570 B.C. (fig. 5-12) is a votive figure that represents the donor, Rhonbos, with the sacrificial animal he is offering to Athena. Needless to say, it is not a portrait, any

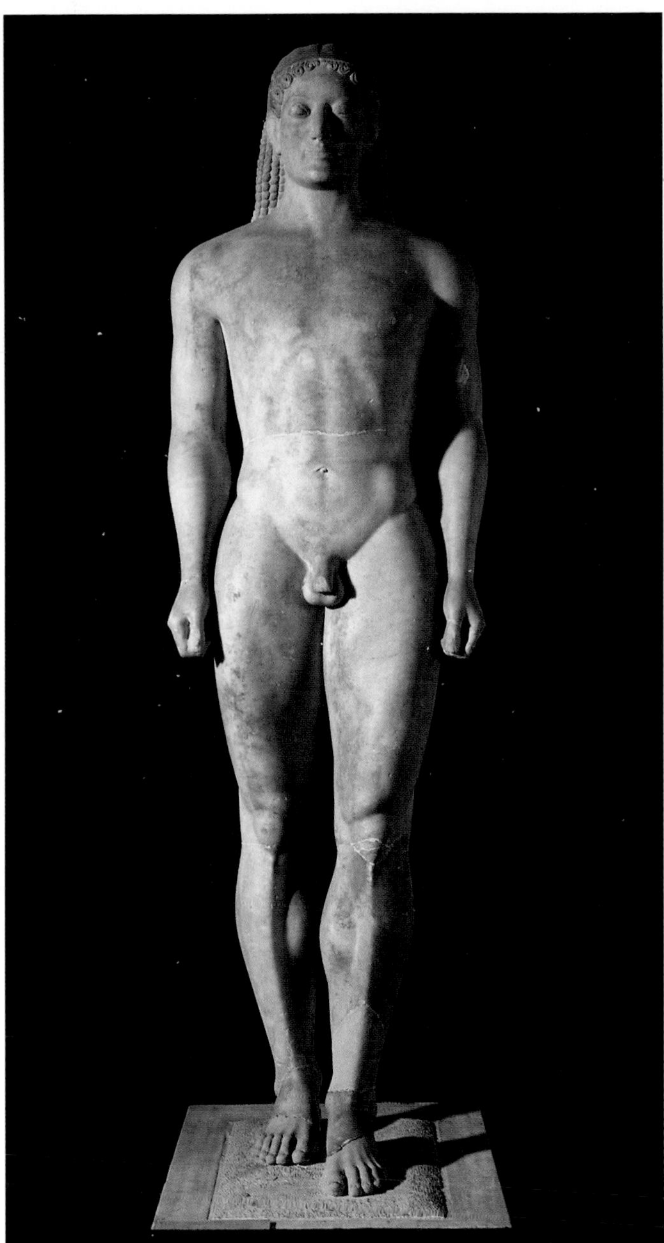

5-11. *Kroisos (Kouros from Anavysos)*. c. 525 B.C. Marble, height 6'4" (1.9 m). National Archaeological Museum, Athens

more than the *Kroisos* is, but it shows a type; the beard indicates a man of mature years. The *Calf-Bearer* originally stood in the conventional Kouros pose, and its body conforms to the Kouros ideal of physical perfection. Its vigorous, compact forms are emphasized, rather than obscured, by the thin cloak, which fits them like a second skin, detaching itself only at the elbows. The face, framed by the soft curve of the animal, no longer has the masklike quality of the early Kouros. The features have, as it were, caught up with the rest of the body in that they, too, are expressive of life: the lips are drawn up in a smile. We must be careful not to impute any psychological meaning to this "Archaic smile," for the same radiant expression occurs throughout sixth-century Greek sculpture, even on the face of the dead hero Kroisos. Only after 500 B.C. does it gradually fade out.

The Kore type is somewhat more variable than that of the Kouros, although it follows the same pattern of development. A

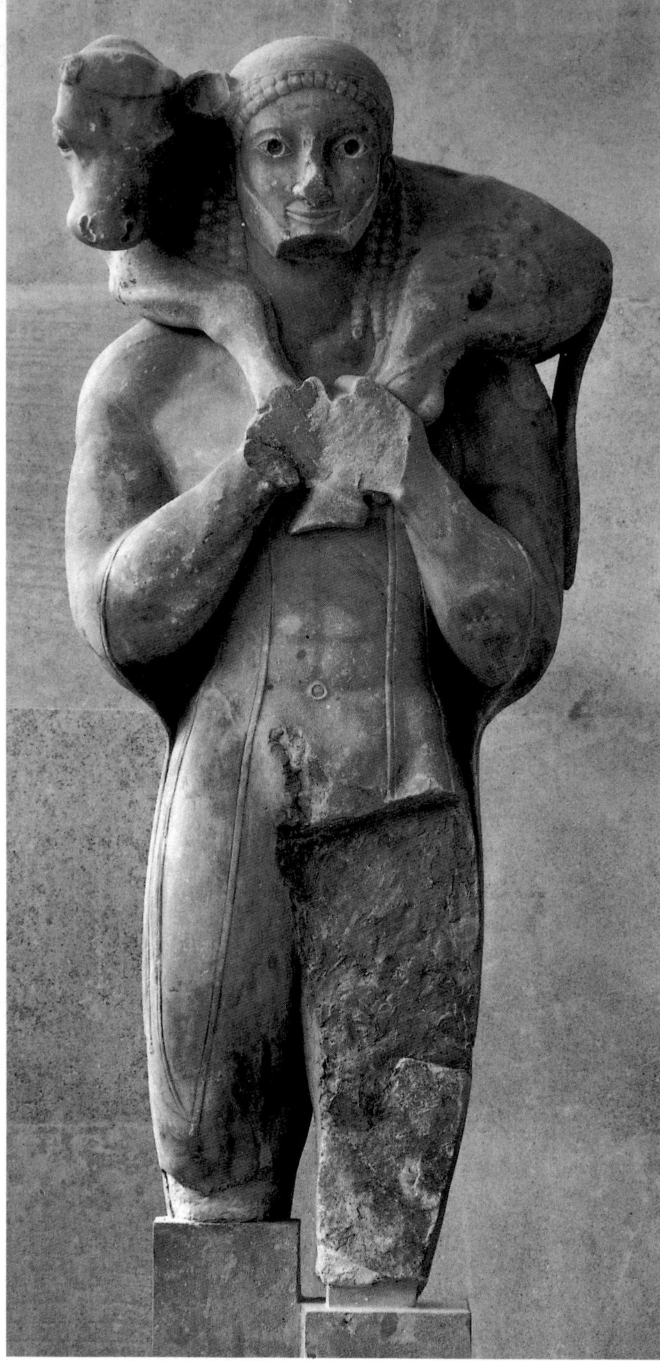

5-12. *Calf-Bearer.* c. 570 B.C. Marble, height of entire statue 65" (165 cm). Akropolis Museum, Athens

clothed figure by definition, it poses the problem of how to relate body and drapery. It is also likely to reflect changing habits or local styles of dress. Thus the statue in figure 5-13, carved about the same time as the *Calf-Bearer,* does not represent a more evolved stage of the Kore in figure 5-9. Rather, it reveals an alternative approach to the same basic task. This Kore was found in the Temple of Hera on the island of Samos. She may well have been an image of the goddess because of her size as well as her dignity. Whereas the earlier Kore echoes the planes of a rectangular slab, the *"Hera"* seems like a column come to life. Instead of clear-cut accents, such as the nipped-in waist in figure 5-9, we find a smooth flow of lines uniting limbs and body. Yet the majestic effect of the statue depends not so much on its abstraction as on the way the form blossoms into the swelling softness of a living body. The upward sweep of the lower third of the figure gradually divides to reveal several layers of garments, and its pace is slowed further (but never fully stopped) as it meets the protruding shapes of arms, hips, and torso. In the end, the drapery, so architectonic up to the knee region, turns into a second skin of the kind we have seen in the *Calf-Bearer.*

The Kore of figure 5-14, in contrast, seems a direct descendant of our first Kore, even though she was carved a full century later. She, too, is blocklike rather than columnar, with a strongly accented waist. The simplicity of her garments is new, however. The heavy cloth of the peplos forms a distinct layer over the body, covering but not hiding the rounded shapes beneath. The left hand, which extended forward to offer a votive gift, must have given the statue a spatial quality quite beyond the two earlier Kore figures we have discussed. Equally new is the more organic treatment of the hair, which falls over the shoulders in soft, curly strands, in contrast to the rigid wig in figure 5-9. Most noteworthy of all is the full, round face with its enchantingly gay expression—a gentler, more natural smile than any we have seen so far. Here, as in the *Kroisos,* we sense the approaching red-figured phase of Archaic art.

Our final Kore (fig. 5-15), from about a decade later, has none of the severity of figure 5-14, though both were found on the Akropolis of Athens. In many ways she seems more like the *"Hera"* from Samos. In fact, she probably came from Chios, another island of Ionian Greece. The grandeur of the *"Hera,"* though, has given way to a refined grace. The layers of the garment (the light Ionian chiton) still loop around the body in soft curves, but the play of richly differentiated folds, pleats, and textures has almost become an end in itself. Color must have played an important role in such works, and we are fortunate that so much of it survives in this example.

Architectural Sculpture

When the Greeks began to build temples in stone, they fell heir to the age-old tradition of architectural sculpture. The Egyptians had been covering walls and columns with reliefs since the Old Kingdom, but these carvings were so shallow (for example, see figs. 2-18 and 2-30) that they did not break the continuity of the surface and had no weight or volume of their own. Thus they were related to their architectural setting only in the same limited sense as wall paintings (with which they were, in practice, interchangeable). This is also true of the reliefs on Assyrian, Babylonian, and Persian buildings (for example, see figs. 3-20 and 3-28). In the Near East, however, there was another kind of architectural sculpture, which seems to have begun with the Hittites: the guardian monsters protruding from the blocks that framed the gateways of fortresses or palaces (see figs. 3-17 and 3-21). This tradition must have inspired, perhaps indirectly, the carving over the Lioness Gate at Mycenae (see fig. 4-19).

We must nevertheless note one important feature that distinguishes the Mycenaean guardian figures from their predecessors. Although they are carved in high relief on a huge slab, this slab is thin and light compared to the enormous Cyclopean blocks

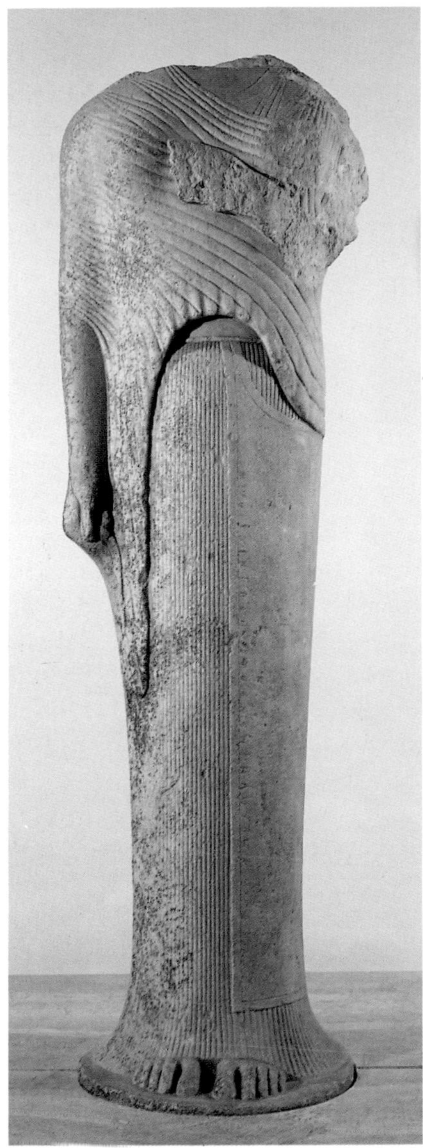

5-13. *"Hera,"* from Samos. c. 570–560 B.C. Marble, height 6'4" (1.9 m). Musée du Louvre, Paris

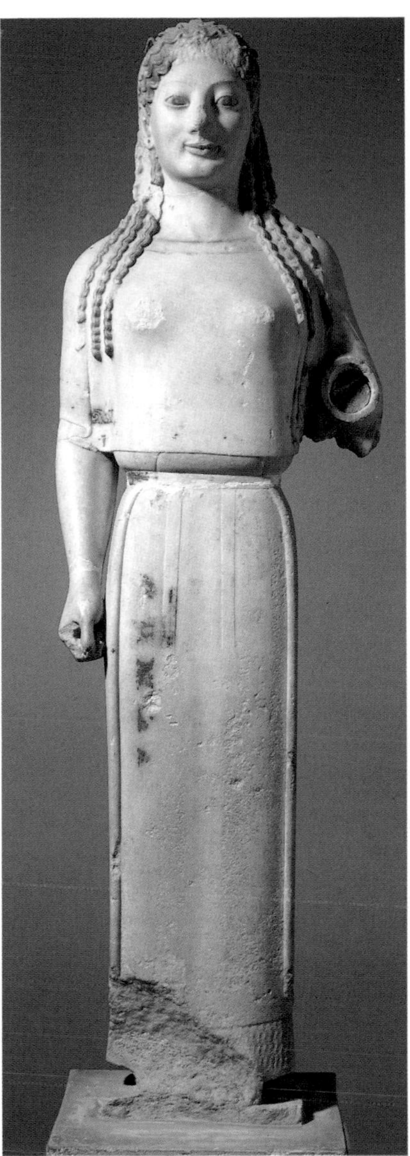

5-14. *Kore in Dorian Peplos.* c. 530 B.C. Marble, height 48" (122 cm). Akropolis Museum, Athens

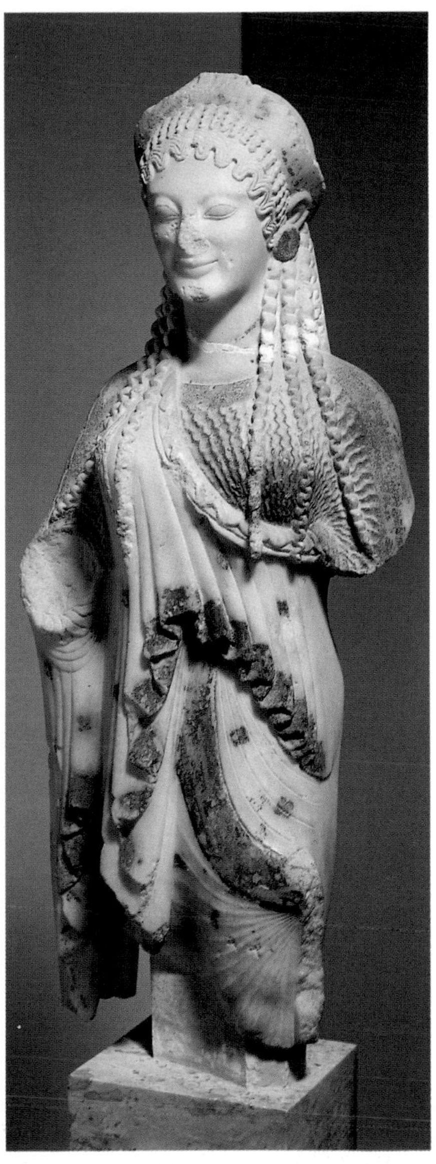

5-15. *Kore,* from Chios (?). c. 520 B.C. Marble, height 21⅞" (55.3 cm). Akropolis Museum, Athens

around it. In building the gate, the Mycenaean architect left an empty triangular space above the lintel, for fear that the weight of the wall above would crush it. That space was then filled with the lightweight relief panel. Here we have a new kind of architectural sculpture: a work integrated with the structure yet also a separate entity rather than a modified wall surface or block.

THE TEMPLE OF ARTEMIS, CORFU. That the Lioness Gate relief is the direct ancestor of Greek architectural sculpture is clear when we compare it with the facade of the early Archaic Temple of Artemis on the island of Corfu, erected soon after 600 B.C. (figs. 5-16 and 5-17). Here again the sculpture is confined to a zone framed by structural members: the triangle between the horizontal ceiling and the sloping sides of the roof. This area, called the pediment, need not be filled in at all except to protect the wooden rafters behind it against moisture. It demands not a wall but merely a thin screen. And it is against this screen that the pedimental sculpture is displayed.

Technically, these carvings are in high relief, like the guardian lionesses at Mycenae. However, the bodies are strongly undercut so that they are nearly detached from the background. Even at this early stage, the sculptor wanted the figures to be independent of their architectural setting. The head of the central figure actually overlaps the frame. Who is this frightening creature? Not Artemis, surely, athough the temple was dedicated to that goddess. As a matter of fact, we have met her before: she is a Gorgon, a descendant of those on the Eleusis amphora (see fig. 5-3). (A trio of nearly identical figures appears on a black-figure amphora of about the same time.) Her purpose here, and that of the two huge lions, was to ward off evil from the temple and the sacred image of the goddess within. (The other pediment, of which only small fragments survive, had a similar figure.) She might be defined, therefore, as a monumental and still rather frightening hex sign. On her face, the Archaic smile appears as a hideous grin. And to emphasize how alive and real she is, she is shown running, or rather flying, in a pinwheel stance that conveys movement without locomotion.

The heraldic arrangement of the Gorgon and the two animals reflects an Oriental scheme that we know not only from the

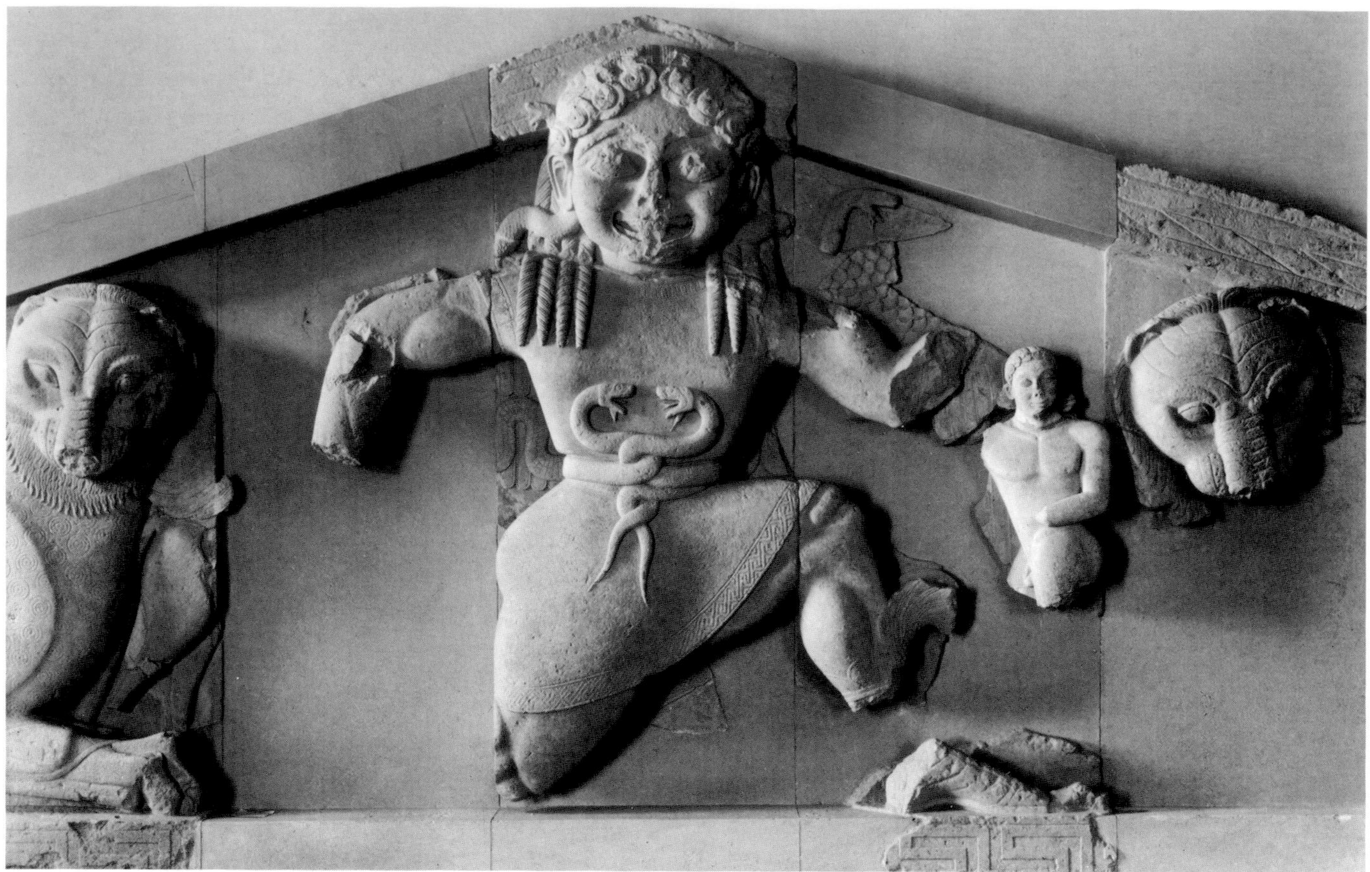

5-16. Central portion of the west pediment of the Temple of Artemis at Corfu, Greece. c. 600–580 B.C. Limestone, height 9'2" (2.8 m). Archaeological Museum, Corfu, Greece

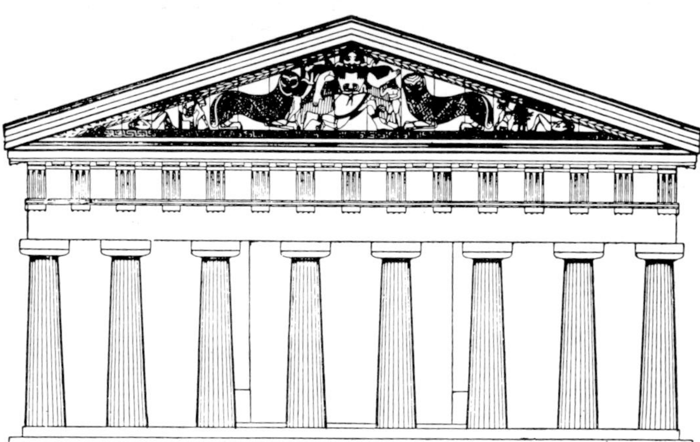

5-17. Reconstruction drawing of the west front of the Temple of Artemis at Corfu (after Rodenwaldt)

Lioness Gate at Mycenae but from many earlier examples as well (see fig. 3-9, top). Because of its ornamental character, it fits the shape of the pediment perfectly. Yet the sculptor was not content with this decorative scheme. The pediment must contain narrative scenes. Therefore a number of smaller figures were added in the spaces left between or behind the main group. On either side are Medusa's children, Pegasus and Chrysaor, who will be born when Perseus decapitates her; the corners may have depicted Zeus and Poseidon battling Titans. The design of the pediment thus shows two conflicting purposes in uneasy balance. As we might expect, narrative will soon win out over heraldry.

It is a striking feature of Greek temples and other religious buildings that they were designed with sculpture in mind almost as soon as they began to be built of stone (see page 112). Indeed, early Greek architects such as Theodoros of Samos were often sculptors. Thus to a Greek, a temple would have seemed "undressed" without sculpture, which was usually designed at the same time as the structure itself. Architecture and sculpture became so closely linked that Greek architecture is highly sculptural and has the same organic quality as the figures that populate it. The sculpture, in turn, plays an important role in helping to articulate the structure and bring it to life.

Aside from the pediment, however, there were not many places that the Greeks deemed suitable for architectural sculpture. They might put freestanding figures (often of terra-cotta) above the ends and the center of the pediment to break the severity of its outline. And they often placed reliefs in the zone just below the pediment. In Doric temples such as that at Corfu (see fig. 5-17), this "frieze" consists of triglyphs (blocks with three vertical markings) alternating with metopes. The latter originally were empty spaces between the ends of the ceiling beams; hence they, like the pediment, could be filled with sculpture. In Ionic architecture, the triglyphs were omitted, and the frieze became what the term usually conveys to us, a continuous band of painted or sculptured decoration. The Ionians would also sometimes support the roof of a porch with female statues instead of columns. This is not very surprising in view of the columnar quality of the *"Hera"* from Samos (see fig. 5-13).

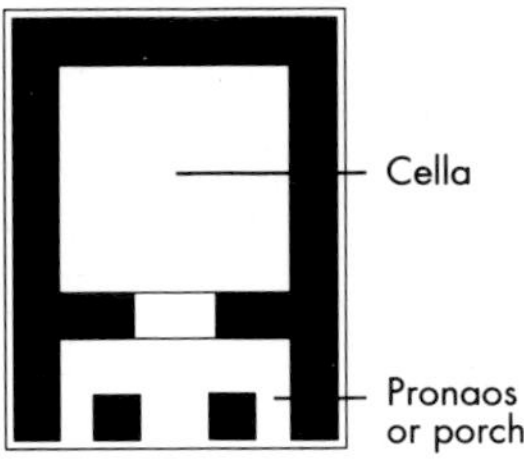

(Above) 5-18. Plan of the Treasury of the Siphnians

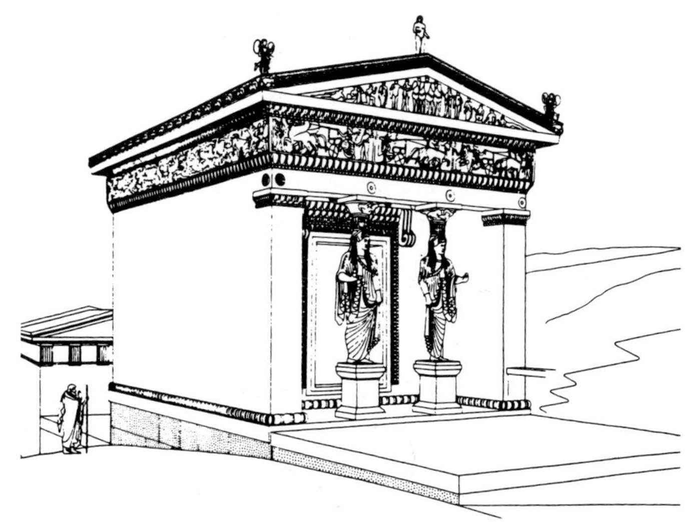

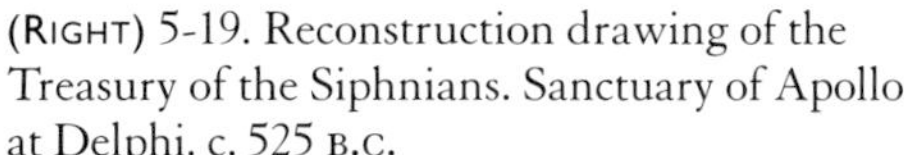
(Right) 5-19. Reconstruction drawing of the Treasury of the Siphnians. Sanctuary of Apollo at Delphi. c. 525 B.C.

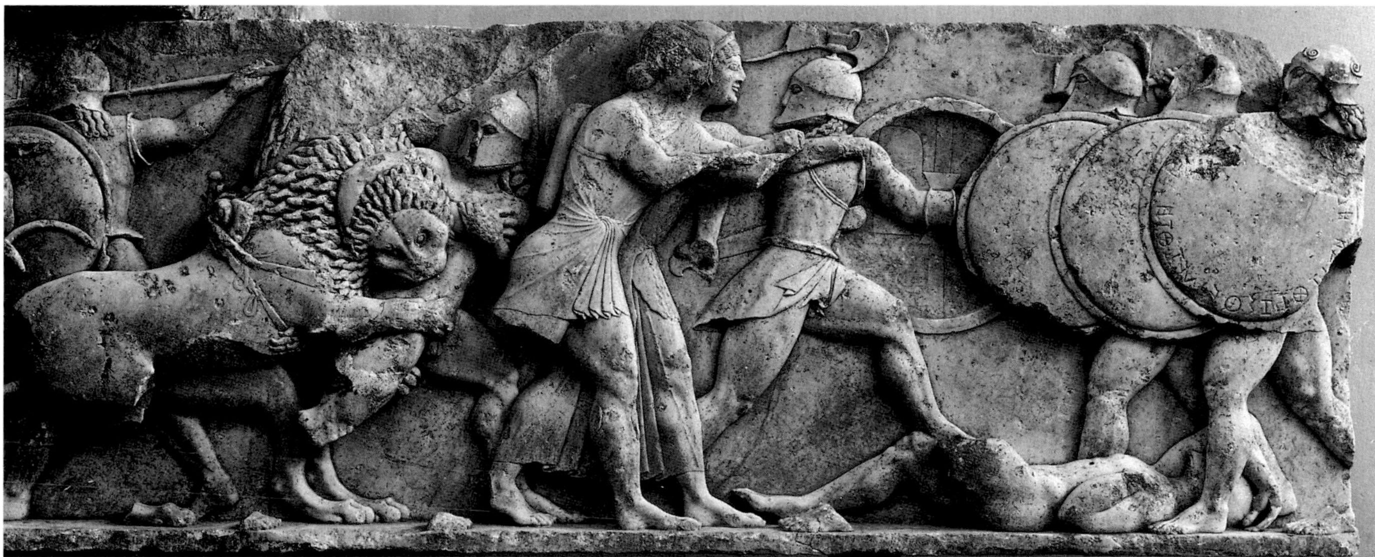

5-20. *Battle of the Gods and Giants,* from the north frieze of the Treasury of the Siphnians. c. 530 B.C. Marble, height 26" (66 cm). Archaeological Museum, Delphi

THE SIPHNIAN TREASURY, DELPHI. All these possibilities are combined in the Treasury (a miniature temple for storing votive gifts) built at Delphi shortly before 525 B.C. by the people of the Ionian island of Siphnos. Although the building no longer stands, we can get an idea of its appearance from the reconstruction in figures 5-18 and 5-19. Its chief feature was two female caryatids, or column-figures, supporting the architrave. It appears that such figures were first used by the Syrians at Tell-Halaf some 300 years earlier, yet we know of no intervening examples. Hence, their presence here must be considered as novel.

The most impressive part of the Treasury's sculptural decor is the splendid frieze. The detail shown here (fig. 5-20) depicts part of the battle of the Greek gods against the giants. At the far left, two lions (who pull the chariot of the mother goddess Cybele) are tearing apart an anguished giant. In front of them, Apollo and Artemis advance together, shooting their arrows. A dead giant, stripped of his armor, lies at their feet, while three others enter from the right.

The high relief, with its deep undercutting, recalls the Corfu pediment, but the Siphnian sculptor has taken full advantage of the spatial possibilities offered by this technique. The ledge at the bottom of the frieze is used as a stage on which he can place his figures in depth. The arms and legs of those nearest the viewer are carved in the round. In the second and third layers, the forms become shallower, yet even those farthest from us do not merge with the background. The result is a condensed but convincing space that permits a dramatic relationship between the figures such as we have never seen before in narrative reliefs. Compared with older examples (such as fig. 4-17), Archaic art has conquered a new dimension here, not only in the physical but also in the expressive sense.

THE TEMPLE OF APHAIA, AEGINA. Meanwhile, in pedimental sculpture, relief has been abandoned altogether. Instead, we find statues placed side by side in dramatic sequences designed to fit the triangular frame. The most ambitious groups of this kind were the pediments of the Temple of Aphaia at Aegina. The original east pediment was evidently destroyed by the Persians when they took the island in 490 B.C. The present one (fig. 5-21) was commissioned after their defeat at the battle of Salamis in 480 B.C.

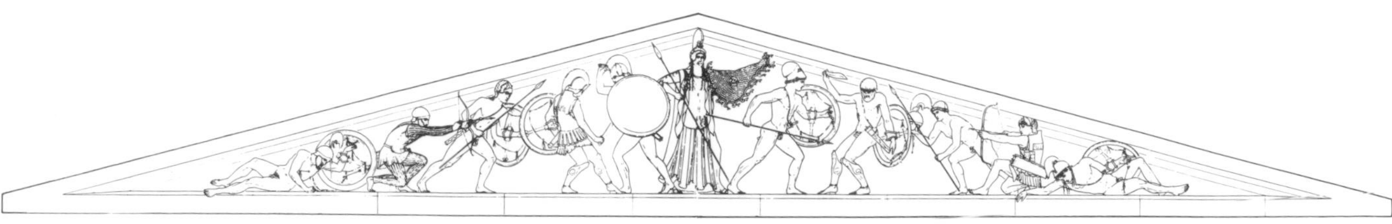

5-21. Reconstruction drawing of the east pediment of the Temple of Aphaia, Aegina (after Ohly)

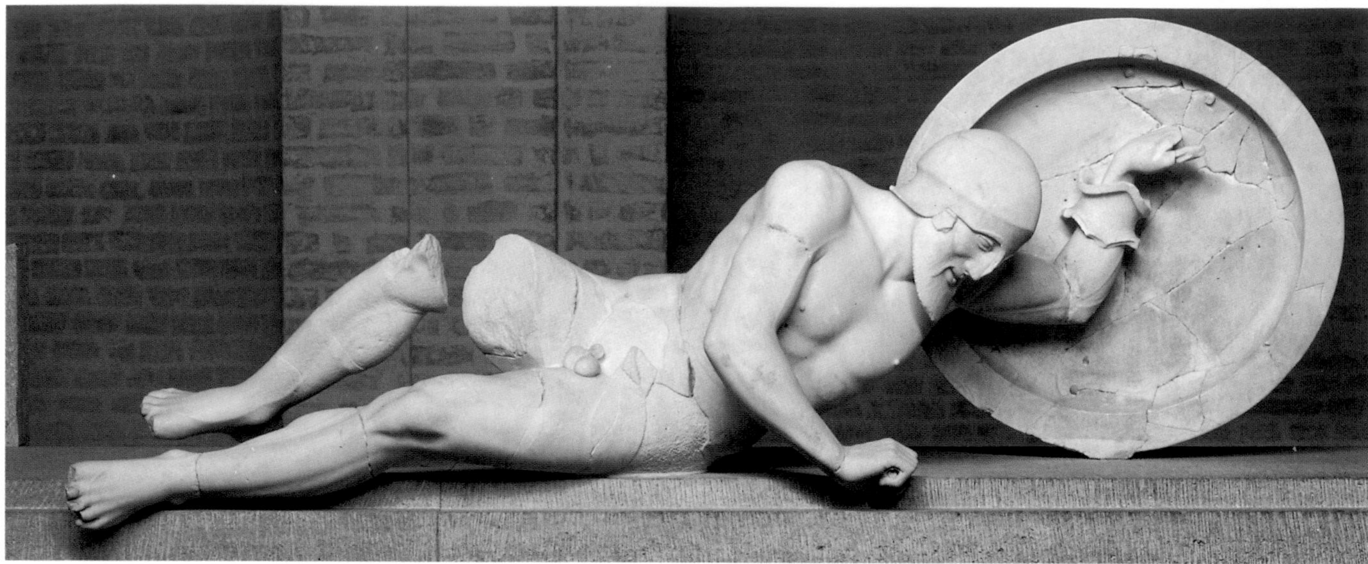

5-22. *Dying Warrior,* from the east pediment of the Temple of Aphaia, Aegina. c. 480 B.C. Marble, length 6' (1.83 m). Staatliche Antikensammlungen und Glyptothek, Munich

It shows the first sack of Troy by Herakles, who had completed his 12 labors, and Telamon, king of Salamis, who had fled Aegina after he and Peleus killed their half brother. The west pediment, which dates from about 510 to 500 B.C., depicts the second siege of Troy (recounted in the *Iliad*) by Agamemnon, who was related to Herakles by descent from King Pelops (see below), and Ajax, Telamon's son. The pairing of the subjects attests to the important role played by the heroes of Aegina in both battles—and, by extension, at Salamis, where their navy helped win the day. This elevation of the historical cycle to a universal plane through allegory was typical of the Greek mentality.

The east pediment brings us to the final stage in the evolution of Archaic sculpture. The figures were found in pieces on the ground. Although the exact arrangement has been a matter of much debate, the relative position of each within the pediment can be determined with reasonable accuracy, since their height (but not their scale) varies with the sloping sides of the triangle (see fig. 5-21). The center is accented by the standing goddess Athena, who presides over the battle between Greeks and Trojans that rages to either side of her.

The symmetrical arrangement of the poses on the two halves of the pediment creates a balanced design. Yet it also forces us to see the statues as elements in an ornamental pattern and thus robs them of their individuality to some extent. They speak most strongly to us when viewed one by one. Among the most impressive are the fallen warrior from the left-hand corner (fig. 5-22) and the kneeling *Herakles,* who once held a bronze bow, from the right-hand half (fig. 5-23). Both are lean, muscular figures whose bodies seem mar-

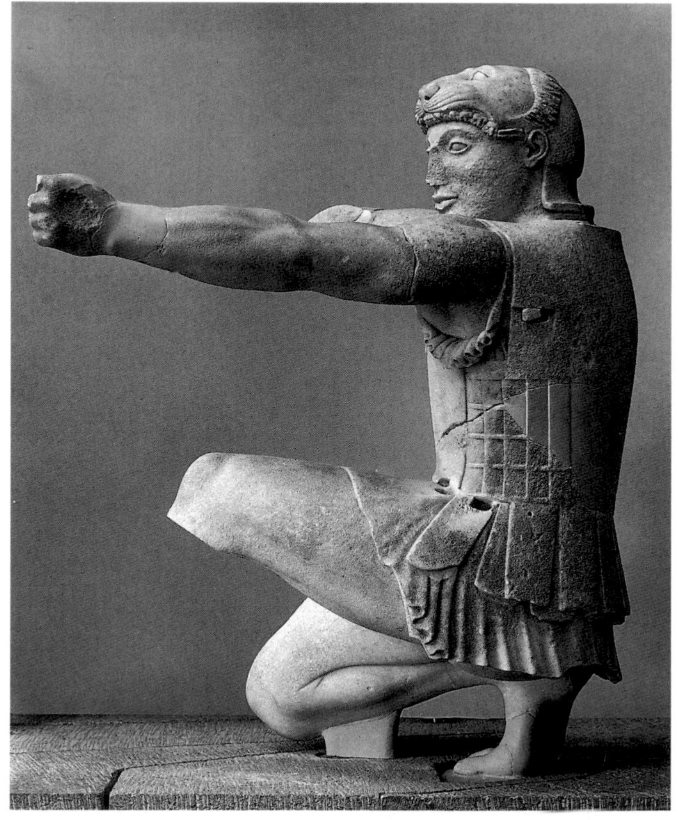

5-23. *Herakles,* from the east pediment of the Temple of Aphaia, Aegina. c. 480 B.C. Marble, height 31" (78.7 cm). Staatliche Antikensammlungen und Glyptothek, Munich

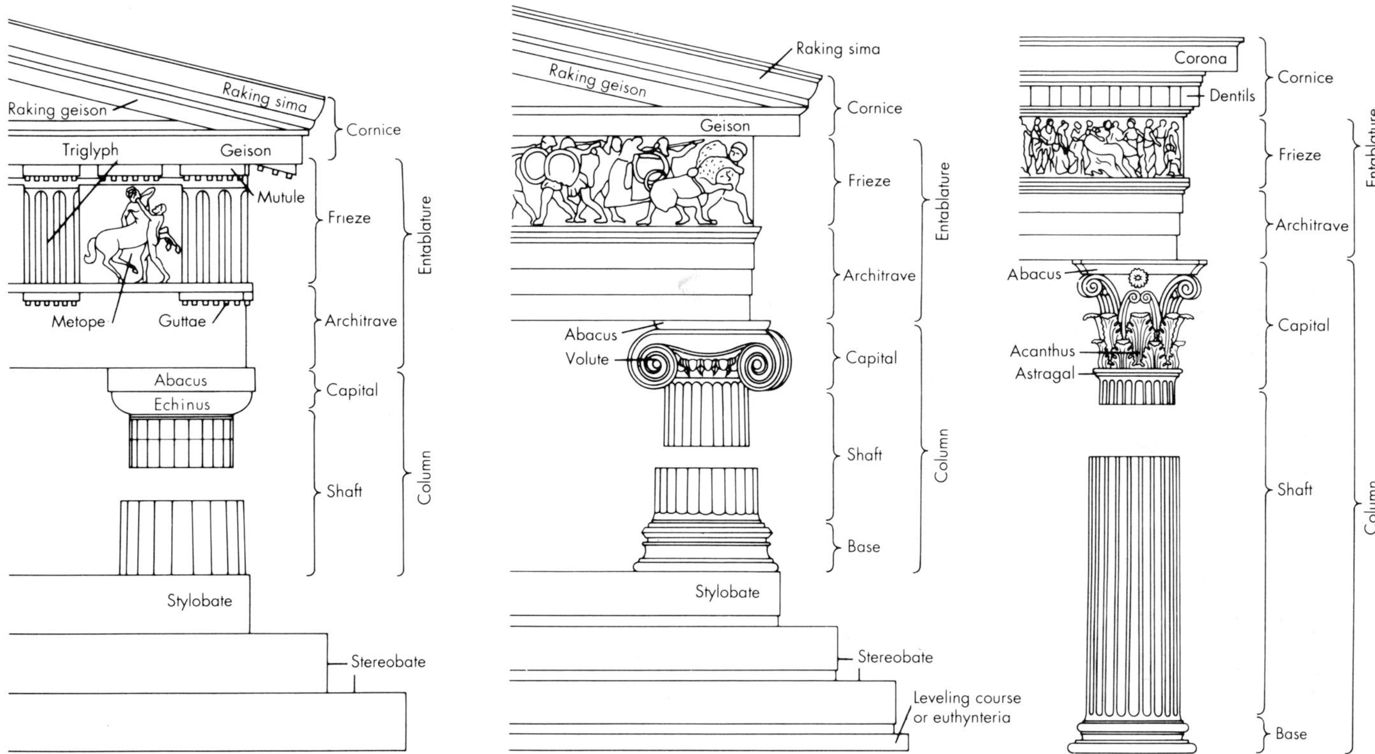

5-24. Doric, Ionic, and Corinthian orders

velously functional and organic. That in itself, however, does not explain their great beauty, much as we may admire the artist's command of the human form in action. What really moves us is their nobility of spirit, whether in the agony of dying or in the act of killing. These men, we sense, are suffering—or carrying out—what fate has decreed, and they are doing so with tremendous dignity and resolve. This spirit is conveyed to us in the very feel of the magnificently firm shapes of which they are composed.

ARCHITECTURE

Orders and Plans

Since Roman times, the Greek achievement in architecture has been identified with the three Classical orders: Doric, Ionic, and Corinthian. [See Primary Sources, no. 4, page 195.] Actually, there are only two; the Corinthian is a variant of the Ionic. (The dentils, or toothlike blocks, are sometimes found in the Doric and Ionic orders as well.) The Doric, so named because its home is a region of the Greek mainland, may well be the basic order. It is older and more sharply defined than the Ionic, which developed on the Aegean Islands and the coast of Asia Minor.

What do we mean by an architectural "order"? By common agreement, the term is used only for Greek architecture (and its descendants); and rightly so, for none of the other architectural systems known to us produced anything like it. Perhaps the simplest way to make this point is to note that there is no such thing as "the Egyptian temple" or "the Gothic church." The individual buildings, however much they may have in common, are so varied that we cannot say that they represent a type. But "the Doric temple" is a real entity that forms in our minds as we study the monuments themselves. We must be careful, of course, not to think of this abstraction as an ideal that permits us to measure the degree of perfection of any given Doric temple. It simply means that the elements of which a Doric temple is composed are extraordinarily constant in number, in kind, and in their relation to one another. As a result, Doric temples all belong to the same easily recognized family, just as Kouros statues do. And like Kouros statues, the Doric temples show an internal consistency that gives them a unique quality of organic unity. Nor is the similarity a coincidence. According to the Roman architect Vitruvius, no doubt basing himself on Greek sources, "Without symmetry and proportion there can be no principles in the design of any temple; that is, if there is no precise relation between its members, as in the case of a well-shaped man."

THE DORIC ORDER. The term *Doric order* refers to the standard parts—and their sequence—that constitute the exterior of any Doric temple. The order's general outlines are already familiar to us from the facade of the Temple of Artemis at Corfu (see fig. 5-17). The diagram in figure 5-24 shows it in detail, along with the names of all its parts. To the nonspecialist, the detailed terminology of Greek architecture may seem something of a nuisance. Yet many of these terms have become part of our general architectural vocabulary. They remind us that analytical thinking, in architecture as in countless other fields, began with the Greeks. Let us first look at the three main divisions: the stepped platform (consisting of the stylobate and stereobate), the columns, and the entablature (which includes all the horizontal components that rest on the columns). The Doric column consists of the shaft, marked by 20 shallow vertical grooves known as flutes, and the capital, which is made up of the flaring, cushionlike echinus and a square tablet called the abacus. These bear a strict ratio to each other, though the proportions became taller over time. The entablature is the most complex of the three major units. It is subdivided into the architrave (a series of stone blocks directly supported by the columns); the frieze, with its triglyphs and metopes; and the projecting cornice, or geison, which may include a gutter (sima). The entablature in turn supports the triangular pediment and the roof elements (the raking geison and raking sima).

The entire structure is built of stone blocks fitted together without mortar. Naturally, the blocks had to be shaped with great precision to achieve smooth joints. Where necessary, they were fastened together with metal dowels or clamps. Columns, with very rare exceptions, were composed of sections, called drums (clearly visible in fig. 5-26). The roof was made of terra-cotta tiles supported by wooden rafters, and wooden beams were used for the ceiling, so that the threat of fire was constant.

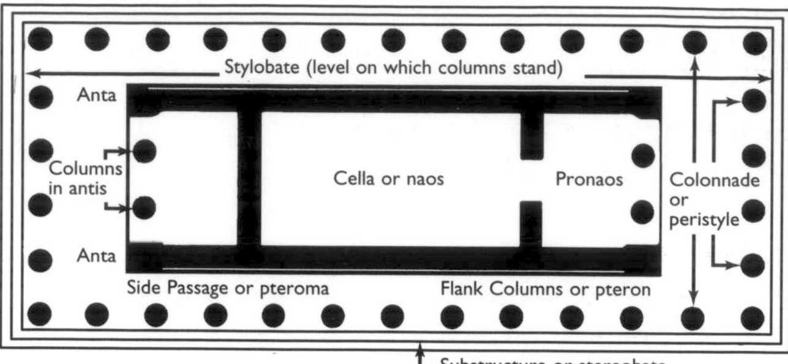

5-25. Ground plan of a typical Greek peripteral temple (after Grinnell)

TEMPLE PLANS. The plans of Greek temples are not directly linked to the orders (which, as we have seen, concern only the elevation), but may vary according to the size of the building or regional preferences. However, their basic features are so much alike that it is useful to study them from a "typical" plan (fig. 5-25). The nucleus is the cella or naos (the room in which the image of the deity was placed) and the porch (pronaos), with its two columns flanked by pilasters (antae). The Siphnian Treasury exemplifies this basic plan (see fig. 5-18). Often we find a second porch added behind the cella, to make the design more symmetrical. In the larger temples, the central unit of cella and porches is surrounded by a colonnade called the peristyle. The peristyle consists of six to eight columns at front and back, and usually 12 to 14 along the sides (the corner columns are counted twice); the structure is then known as peripteral. The very largest temples of Ionian Greece may even have a double colonnade. In most Greek temples the entrance faces east, toward the rising sun. This orientation reaches back to Stonehenge (see fig. 1-18) and is continued in Christian basilicas (see pages 214–15), which also face east but were entered from the west.

Doric Temples

How did the Doric order originate? What factors shaped it? These questions have occupied archaeologists for many years, but even now they can be answered only in part, for we have hardly any remains from the time when the system was being formed. The earliest stone temples were probably built north of Mycenae near Corinth, the leading cultural center of Greece during the late seventh century B.C. From there the idea spread across the isthmus that connects the Peloponnesus to the mainland and up the coast to Delphi and Corfu, then rapidly throughout the Hellenic world. The importance of this architectural revolution can be seen in the fact that soon thereafter the first Greek architects become known to us by name. Nor is it a coincidence that they began to write treatises on architecture—the first we know of. The oldest temples that have come down to us, such as that of Artemis at Corfu (see fig. 5-17), show that the main features of the Doric order were already well established soon after 600 B.C. But how they developed, individually and in combination, and why they coalesced into a system so quickly, remain a puzzle to which we have few reliable clues.

The early Greek builders in stone seem to have drawn upon three sources of inspiration: Egypt, Mycenae, and pre-Archaic Greek architecture in wood and mud brick. Of the three, Mycenae is the most tangible, although probably not the most important. The central unit of the Greek temple, the cella and porch, is clearly derived from the megaron (see fig. 4-20), either through tradition or by way of revival. There is something oddly symbolic about the fact that the Mycenaean royal hall should have been converted into the dwelling place of the Greek gods. The entire Mycenaean era had become part of Greek mythology, as attested to by the Homeric epics, and the walls of the Mycenaean fortresses were thought to be the work of mythical giants, the Cyclopes. The awe the Greeks felt toward these remains also helps us to understand the link between the Lioness Gate relief at Mycenae and the sculptured pediments on Doric temples. Finally, the flaring, cushionlike capital of the Minoan-Mycenaean column is much closer to the Doric echinus and abacus than is any Egyptian capital. The shaft of the Doric column, on the other hand, tapers upward, not downward, as does the Minoan-Mycenaean column, and this points to Egyptian influence.

Perhaps we will recall with some surprise the fluted columns (or rather half-columns) in the funerary district of Djoser at Saqqara (see fig. 2-6). They look like the Doric shaft, but they are more than 2,000 years earlier. Moreover, the very notion that temples ought to be built of stone, and that they should have large numbers of columns, must have come from Egypt. It is true, of course, that the Egyptian temple is designed to be seen from the inside, while the Greek temple is arranged so that the exterior matters most. (People were allowed to see the cult statue in the dimly lit cella, but most religious rites took place at altars set up outdoors, with the temple facade as a backdrop.) A peripteral temple might be viewed as the columned court of an Egyptian sanctuary turned inside out. The Greeks must have gained many of their stonecutting and masonry techniques from the Egyptians. Also from Egypt came their knowledge of architectural ornament and the geometry needed to lay out temples and to fit the parts together. Yet we cannot say just how they went about all this, or exactly what they took over, technically and artistically, although there can be little doubt that they owed more to the Egyptians than to the Minoans or the Mycenaeans.

DOES FORM FOLLOW FUNCTION? The problem of origins becomes acute when we consider a third factor: to what extent can the Doric order be seen as a reflection of wooden structures? Those historians of architecture who believe that form follows function—that an architectural form will always reflect its purpose—have pursued this approach at length, especially in trying to explain the details of the entablature. Up to a point, their arguments are convincing. It seems plausible that at one time the triglyphs did mask the ends of wooden beams. It also makes sense that the droplike shapes below, called guttae (see fig. 5-24), are the descendants of wooden pegs. It is more difficult to see the odd vertical subdivisions of the triglyphs as an echo of three half-round logs. And when we come to the flutings of the column, our doubts continue to rise. Were they really developed from adz marks on a tree trunk, or did the Greeks take them over ready-made from the "proto-Doric" stone columns of Egypt?

As a further test of the functional theory, we would have to ask how the Egyptians came to put flutes in their columns. They, too, had to translate architectural forms from impermanent materials into stone. Perhaps it was they who turned adz marks into flutes? But the predynastic Egyptians had so little timber that they seem to have used it only for ceilings. The rest of their buildings were made of mud brick, strengthened by bundles of reeds. And since the proto-Doric columns at Saqqara are not freestanding but are attached to walls, their flutings might be an abstract imitation of bundles of reeds. (There are also columns at Saqqara with convex rather than concave flutes that come much closer to the notion of a bundle of thin staves.) On the other hand, the Egyptians may have developed the habit of fluting without reference to any earlier building techniques. Perhaps they used it to disguise the horizontal joints between the drums and to stress the continuity of the shaft. Even the Greeks did not flute the shafts of their columns drum by drum but waited until the entire column was assembled and in position. Be that as it may, fluting certainly enhances the expressive character of the column. A fluted shaft looks stronger, more energetic and resilient, than a smooth one. This expressive quality, rather than how the habit began, surely accounts for its persistence.

Why did we enter into an argument that seems inconclusive? Mainly in order to suggest the complexity, as well as the limitations, of the technological approach to problems of architectural form. The question of how far stylistic features can be explained in terms of function will face us again and again. Obviously, the history of architecture cannot be fully understood if we view it only as an evolution of style and do not consider the purposes of building or its technical aspects. But we must likewise be prepared to accept the aesthetic impulse in its own right. At the very start, Doric architects certainly imitated in stone some features of wooden temples, if only because these features were deemed necessary in order to identify a building as a temple. Thus the triglyphs were derived from the ends of ceiling beams decorated with three grooves and secured with wooden pegs. The shape of these pegs is echoed in the guttae. Metopes evolved out of the boards that filled in the gaps between the triglyphs to guard against the weather. Likewise, mutules (flat projecting blocks) reflect the rafter ends of wooden roofs. When Greek architects made them part of the Doric order, however, they did not do so from mere force of habit. The wooden forms had by now been so thoroughly transformed that they were an organic part of the stone structure.

TEMPLES AT PAESTUM. We must confront the problem of function once more when we look at the best-preserved sixth-century Doric temple, the Temple of Hera I (the so-called "Basilica") at Paestum in southern Italy (fig. 5-27, left; fig. 5-26), in relation to its neighbor, the Temple of Hera II (fig. 5-27, right), built almost a century later. (The latter was previously thought to be a Temple of Poseidon because Paestum was once named for the Greek god of the sea.) Both are Doric, but there are striking differences in their proportions. The Temple of Hera I seems low and sprawling—and not just because so much of the entablature is missing—while the Temple of Hera II looks tall and compact. Even the columns are different. Those of the older temple taper much more and their capitals are larger and more flaring. Why the difference?

The peculiar shape of the columns of the Temple of Hera I (peculiar, that is, compared to fifth-century Doric) has been

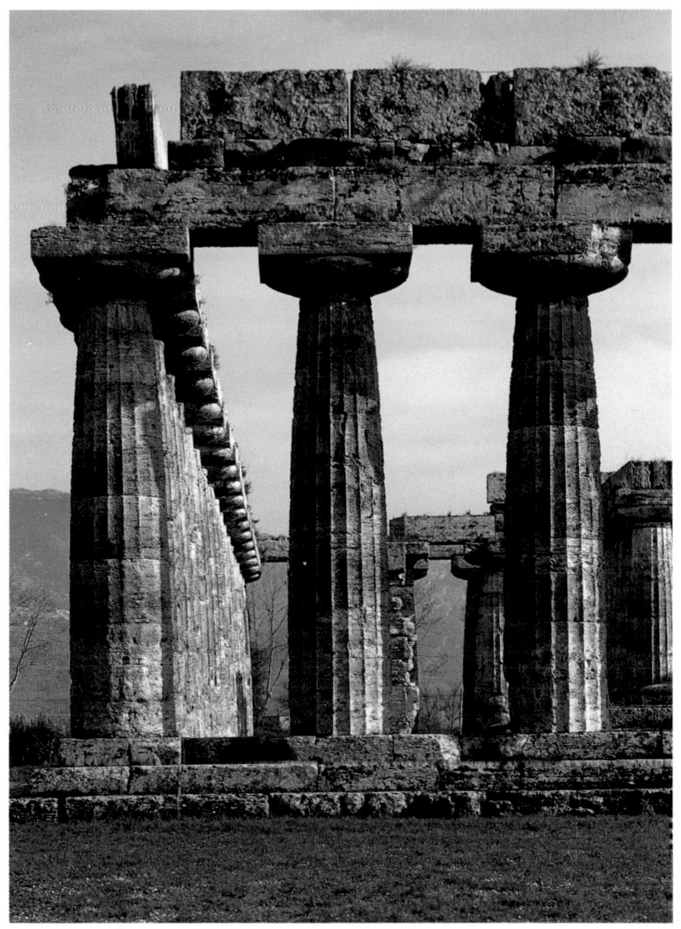

5-26. Corner of the Temple of Hera I, Paestum. c. 550 B.C.

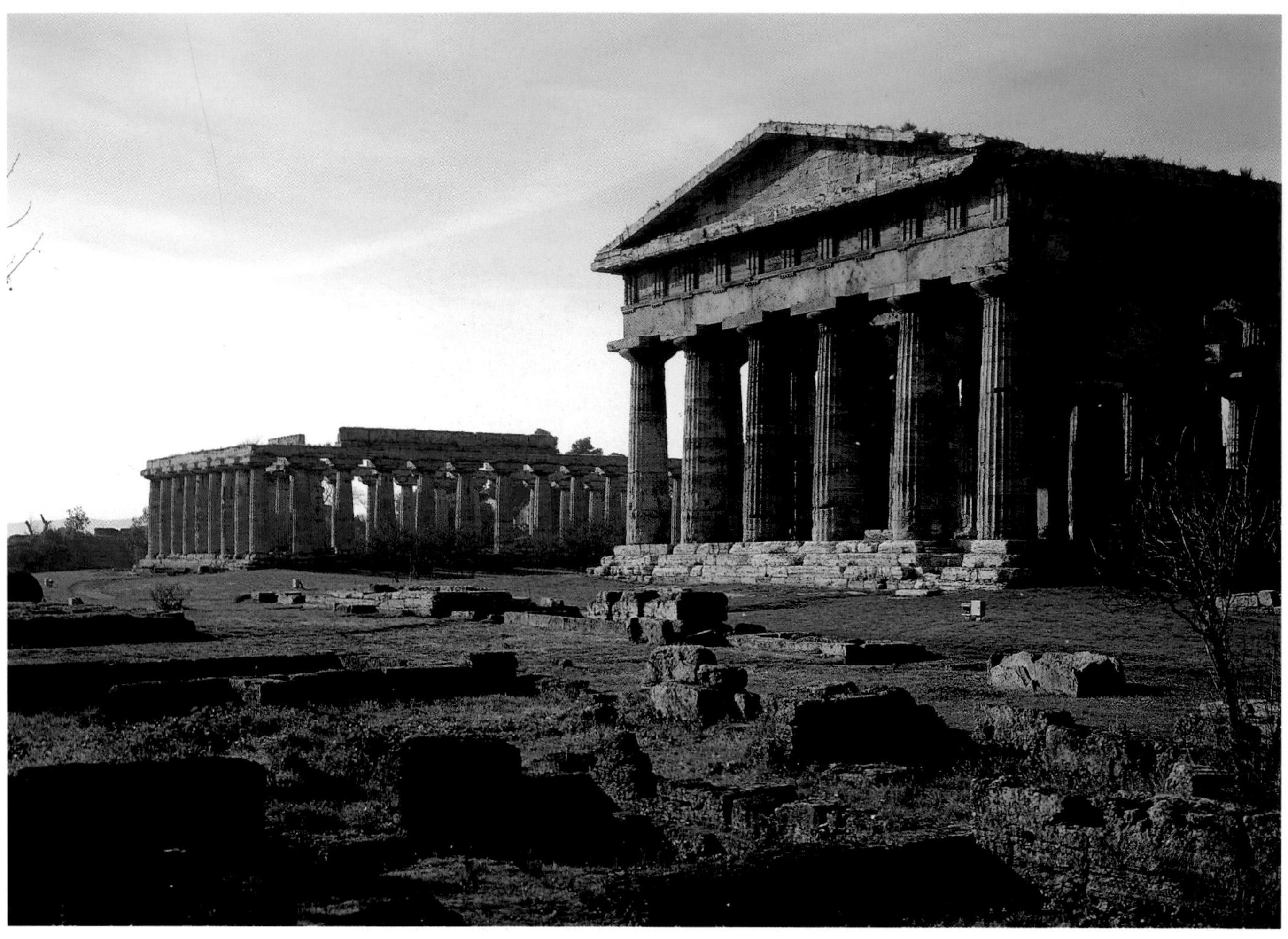

5-27. The Temple of Hera I ("Basilica"), c. 550 B.C., and the Temple of Hera II ("Temple of Poseidon"), c. 460 B.C. Paestum, Italy

explained as being due to overcompensation. The architect was not yet fully familiar with the properties of stone as compared with wood. He therefore exaggerated the taper of the shaft for greater stability and enlarged the capitals so as to narrow the gaps to be spanned by the blocks of the architrave. Maybe so, but if we view this explanation as adequate to account for the design of these Archaic columns, do we not judge them by the standards of a later age? To label them primitive or awkward would be to disregard their expressive effect.

The columns of the Temple of Hera I seem to be more burdened by their load than those of the Temple of Hera II. Hence, the contrast between the supporting and supported members is dramatized rather than balanced, as it is in the later building. Various factors contribute to this impression. Not only is the echinus of the Temple of Hera I's capitals larger than that of the capitals in the Temple of Hera II but it also seems more elastic and hence more distended by the weight it carries, almost as if it were made of rubber. And the shafts show not only a more pronounced taper but also a particularly strong bulge or curve along the line of taper. As a result, they, too, convey a sense of elasticity and compression compared with the rigidly geometric blocks of the entablature. This curve, called entasis, is a basic feature of the Doric column. Although it may be very slight, it gives the shaft a muscular quality unknown in Egyptian or Minoan-Mycenaean columns.

The Temple of Hera II (fig. 5-28; and see fig. 5-27, right) is among the best preserved of all Doric sanctuaries. Of special interest are the interior supports of the cella ceiling (see fig. 5-28). The two rows of columns each support a smaller set of columns in a way that makes the tapering seem continuous despite the architrave in between. Such a two-story interior became a practical necessity in the larger Doric temples. It is first found at the Temple of Aphaia at Aegina around the beginning of the fifth century. That temple is shown here in a reconstruction drawing in figure 5-29, which shows the structural system in detail.

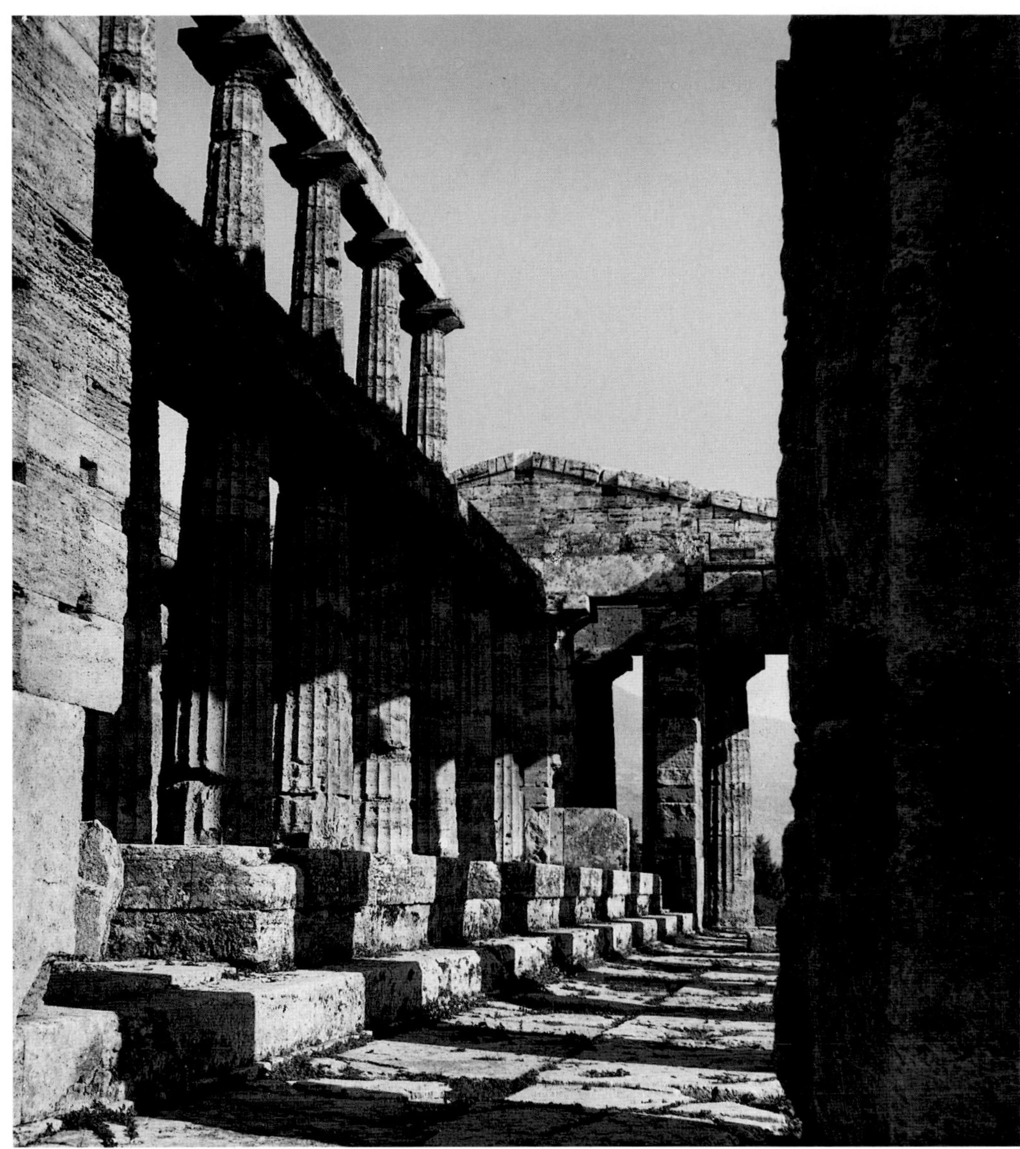

5-28. Interior, Temple of Hera II, Paestum. c. 500 B.C.

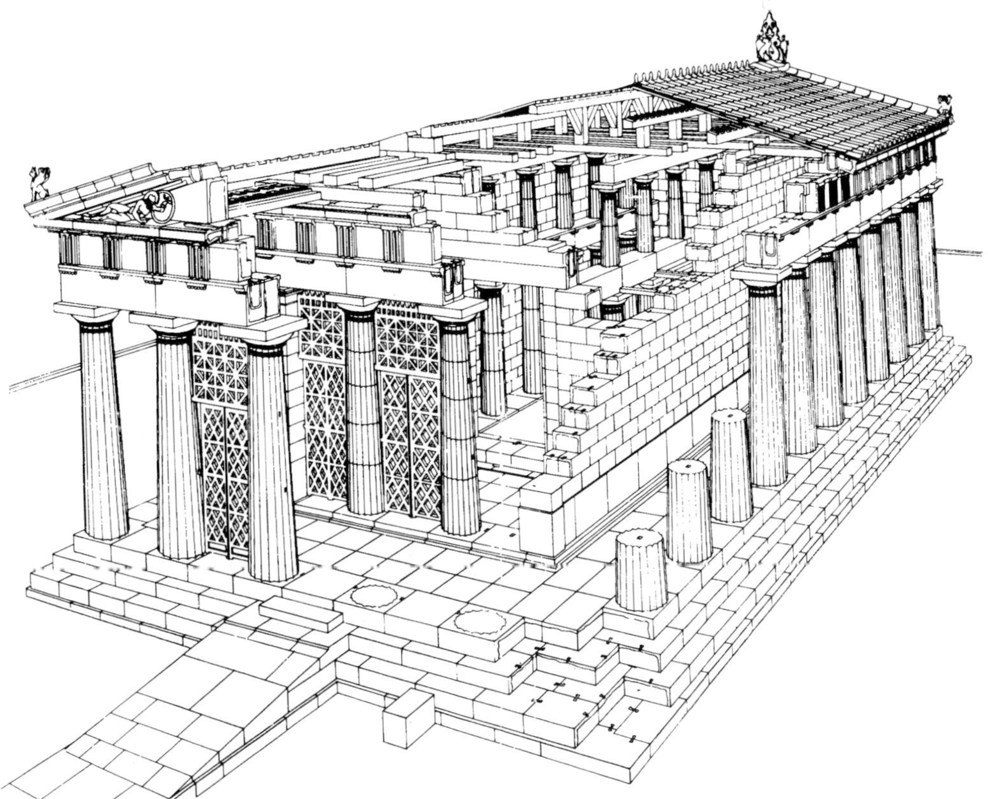

5-29. Sectional view (restored) of the Temple of Aphaia, Aegina

ATHENS, PERIKLES, AND THE PARTHENON. In 480 B.C., shortly before their defeat by the Greeks, the Persians destroyed the temple and statues on the Akropolis (literally, highest part of the city), the sacred hill above Athens, which had been a fortified site since Mycenaean times. (For modern archaeologists, this disaster has turned out to be a blessing in disguise, since the debris from the sack, which was later used as fill, yielded many fine Archaic pieces, such as those in figures 5-12, 5-14, and 5-15, which would not have survived otherwise.) The rebuilding of the Akropolis under the leadership of Perikles during the later fifth century was the most ambitious enterprise in the history of Greek architecture. [See Primary Sources, no. 5, page 196.] This achievement is all the more surprising in light of the fact that, by today's standards, Athens was only a modest city, with no more than about 50,000 inhabitants even at the height of its power. The Akropolis nevertheless represents the artistic climax of Greek art. Individually and collectively, these structures exemplify the Classical phase of Greek art in full maturity. The inspiration for such a complex can only have come from Egypt. So must Perikles' idea of treating it as a vast public works project, for which he spared no expense.

The greatest temple, and the only one to be completed before the Peloponnesian War, is the Parthenon (figs. 5-30 and 5-31). It was dedicated to the virgin goddess Athena, the patron deity in whose honor Athens was named. Built of marble on the most prominent site along the southern flank of the Akropolis, it dominates the city and the surrounding countryside, a brilliant landmark against the backdrop of mountains to the north. The architects Iktinos, Kallikrates, and Karpion built it between 448 and 432 B.C., an amazingly brief span of time for a project of this size.

The history of the Parthenon is as unusual as its artistic significance. It is the only sanctuary we know that has served four different faiths in succession. In Christian times, the Virgin Mary took the place of Athena: the Parthenon became first a Byzantine church, then a Catholic cathedral. Finally, under the Turks, it was a mosque. It has been a ruin since 1687, when gunpowder the Turks had stored in the cella exploded during a siege.

To meet the huge expense of building the largest and most lavish temple on the Greek mainland, Perikles used funds that had been collected from states allied with Athens for mutual defense against the Persians. He may have felt that the danger was no longer real and that Athens, the chief victim and victor of the Persian wars in 480–479 B.C., was justified in using the money to rebuild what the Persians had destroyed. His act weakened Athens' position, however, and contributed to the disastrous outcome of the Peloponnesian War. (Thucydides, who wrote a history of the war, reproached him for adorning the city "like a harlot with precious stones, statues, and temples costing a thousand talents.")

The Parthenon is unconventional in plan (see fig. 5-32). The cella is unusually wide and somewhat shorter than in other temples, so as to accommodate the large cult statue of Athena Parthenos (Athena the Virgin) by Pheidias as well as a second room

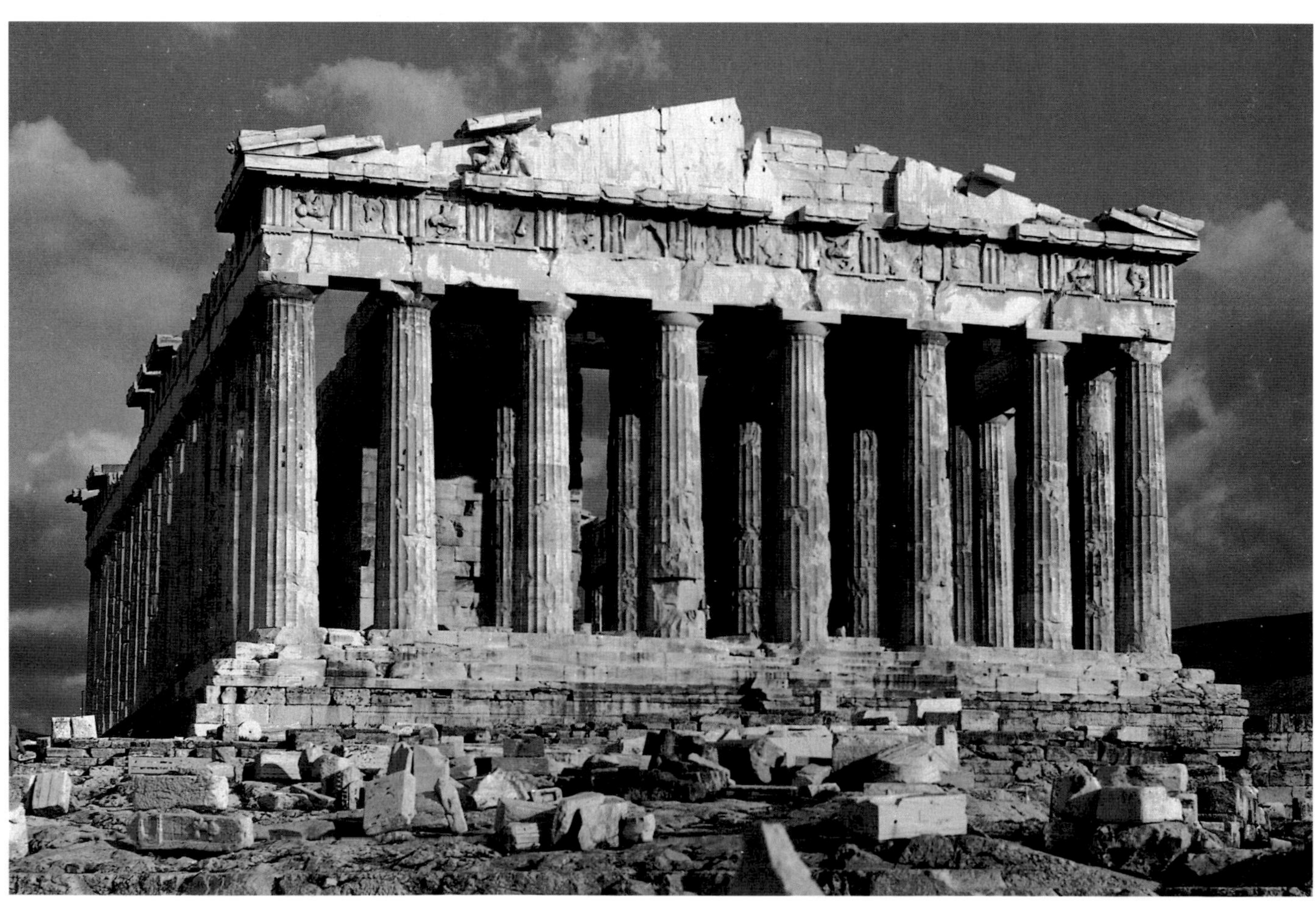

5-30. Iktinos, Kallikrates, and Karpion. The Parthenon (view from the west), Akropolis, Athens. 448–432 B.C.

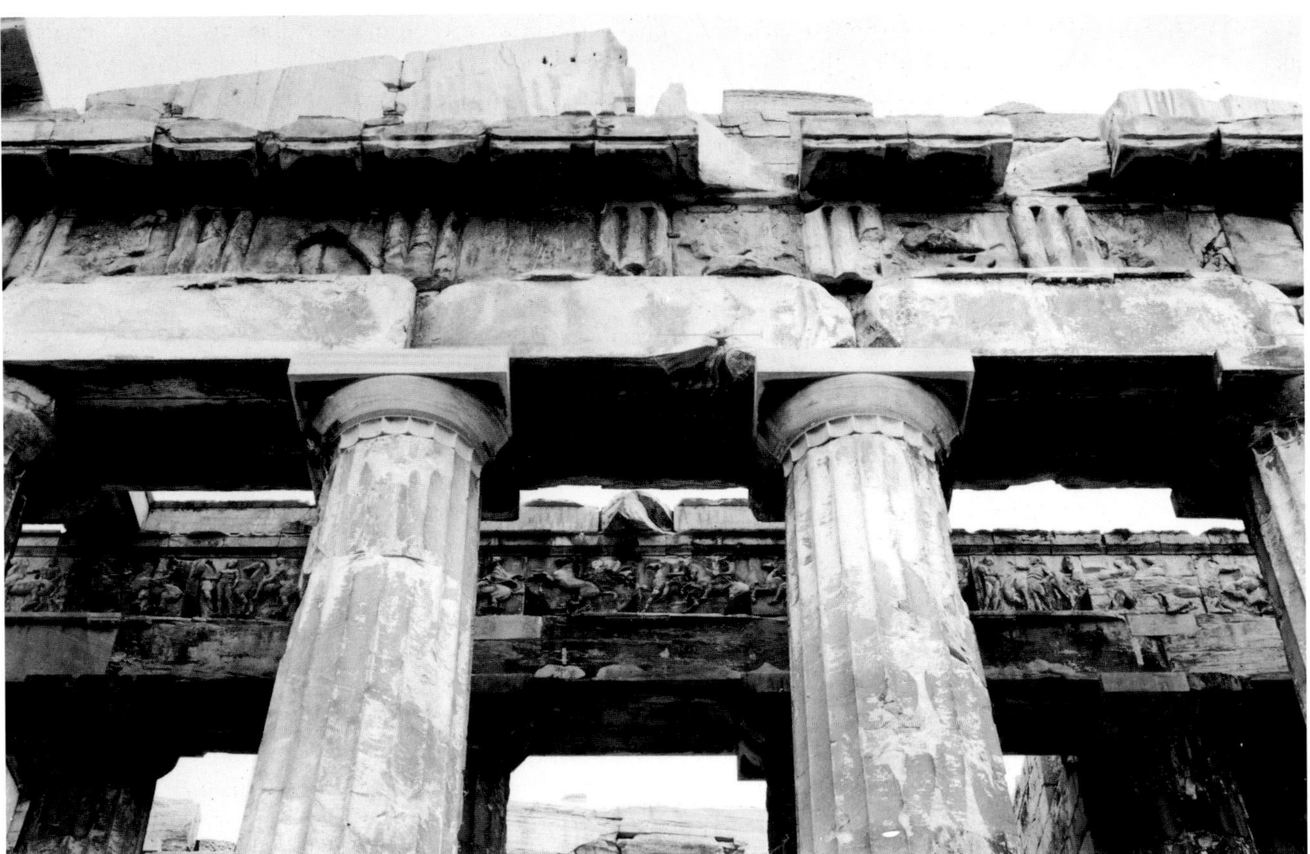

5-31. Frieze above the western entrance of the cella of the Parthenon

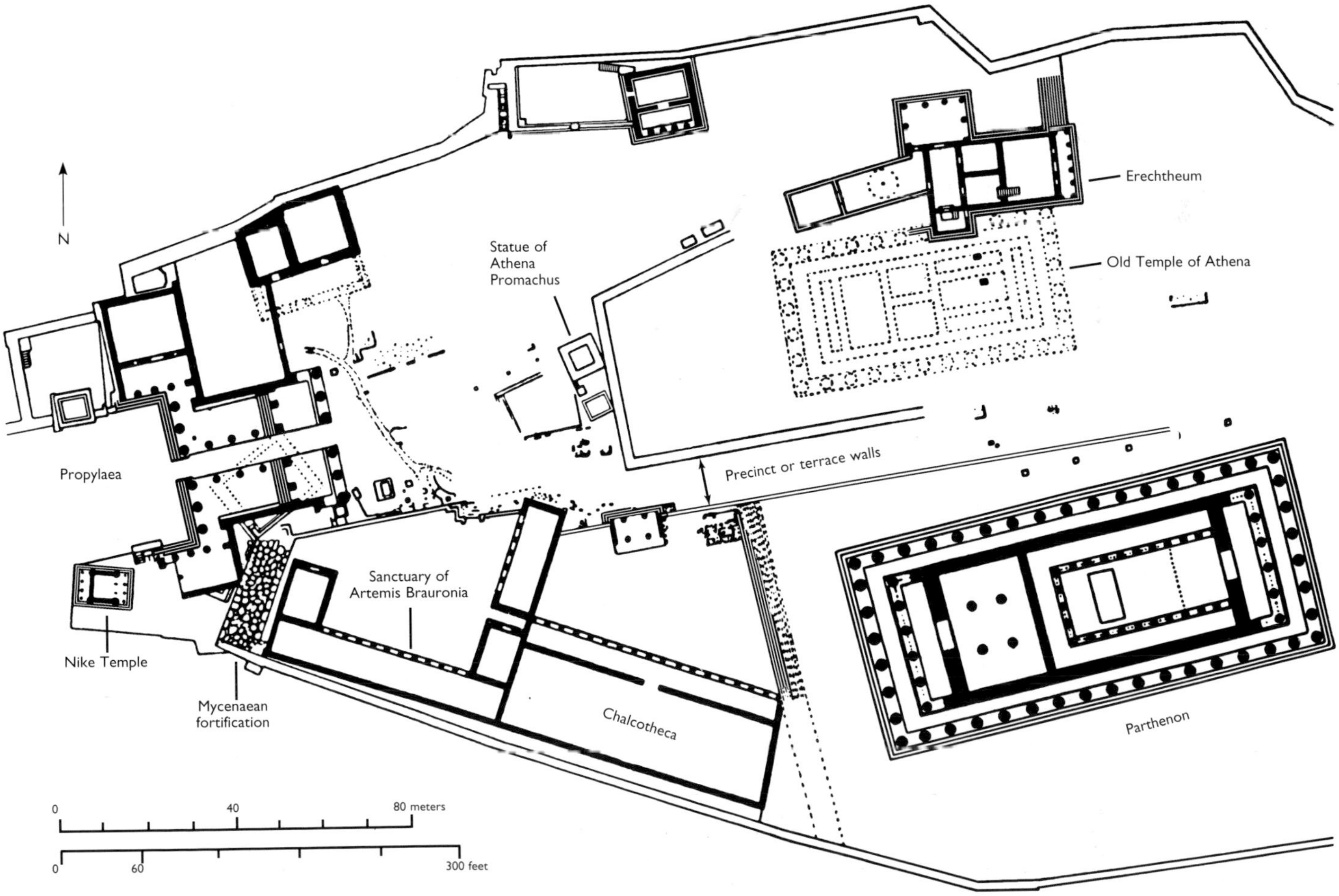

N
Statue of Athena Promachus
Erechtheum
Old Temple of Athena
Propylaea
Precinct or terrace walls
Sanctuary of Artemis Brauronia
Nike Temple
Mycenaean fortification
Chalcotheca
Parthenon
0 40 80 meters
0 60 300 feet

5-32. Plan of the Akropolis at Athens in 400 B.C. (after A. W. Lawrence)

behind it. The pronaos and its counterpart at the western end have almost disappeared. However, there is an extra row of columns in front of each entrance. The architrave above these columns is more Ionic than Doric, since it has no triglyphs and metopes but a continuous frieze that encircles the cella (see fig. 5-31).

As the perfect embodiment of Classical Doric architecture, the Parthenon makes an instructive contrast with the Temple of Hera II at Paestum (see fig. 5-27). Despite its greater size, it seems far less massive. Instead, it creates an impression of festive, balanced grace within the austere scheme of the Doric order. This effect has been achieved by lightening and readjusting the proportions. The entablature is lower in relation to its width and to the height of the columns, and the cornice projects less. The proportions were determined by the fact that, as a matter of convenience as well as economic necessity, the architects reused numerous column drums from the unfinished first Parthenon, which was burned by the Persians. The columns themselves are much more slender, and their tapering and entasis less pronounced; the capitals are smaller and less flaring; yet the spacing of the columns is wider. We might say that the load carried by the columns has decreased, and as a result the supports can fulfill their task with a new sense of ease.

THE PARTHENON'S REFINEMENTS. The Parthenon features these and a number of other so-called "refinements"—intentional departures from the strict regularity of its design. For example, the stepped platform and the entablature are not absolutely straight but slightly curved, so that the center is a bit higher than the ends. Similarly, the columns lean inward; the space between the corner column and its neighbors is smaller than the standard interval used in the colonnade as a whole; and every capital of the colonnade is slightly distorted to fit the curving architrave.

A great deal has been written about these deviations from mechanical exactitude. That they are planned rather than accidental is beyond doubt, but why did the architects go to the trouble of carrying them through, since they are not necessary? They used to be thought of as optical corrections designed to produce the illusion of absolutely straight horizontals and verticals. However, this functional explanation does not work. If it did, we would not be able to perceive the deviations except by careful measurement. Yet the fact is that, though unobtrusive, they are visible to the naked eye, even in photographs such as our figure 5-30. Moreover, in temples that do not have these refinements, the columns do not appear to be leaning outward, nor do the horizontal lines look "dished." Plainly, then, these intentional departures from strict geometric regularity were built into the Parthenon for aesthetic reasons: they were thought to add to its beauty and were meant to be noticed. They do contribute, in ways that are hard to define, to the harmonious quality of the structure. These adjustments give us visual reassurance that the points of greatest stress are supported and that they are provided with a counterstress as well.

Even this explanation does not fully account for the Parthenon's remarkable persuasiveness, which has never been surpassed. The Roman architect Vitruvius records that Iktinos based his design on carefully thought out proportions. The ratio of spacing between the columns to their lower diameter (9:4) was used throughout the building. This proportion was slightly greater than the multiples of two used by Libon of Elis in the Temple of Zeus at Olympia, the first Greek temple we know of to make such a systematic use of ratios. But accurate measurements show that the system of the Parthenon is far from simple. There are many subtle adjustments, which give the temple an organic quality. In this respect the Parthenon's design closely parallels the principles of Classical sculpture (see pages 123–24). Indeed, with its sculpture in place, the Parthenon must have seemed animated with the same inner life as the pediment figures, for example the *Three Goddesses* (see fig. 5-52).

THE PROPYLAEA. Soon after the completion of the Parthenon, Perikles commissioned another costly project. This was the monumental entry gate at the western end of the Akropolis, called the Propylaea (see plan, fig. 5-32). It was begun in 437 B.C. under the architect Mnesikles, who completed the main part in five years; the remainder had to be abandoned because of the Peloponnesian War. Again, the entire structure was built of marble and included refinements like those of the Parthenon. It is fascinating to see how the elements of a Doric temple have been adapted to a totally different task on an irregular and steeply rising site. Mnesikles' design not only fits the difficult terrain but transforms it from a rough passage among rocks into a splendid entrance to the sacred precinct.

Of the two porches (or facades) at either end, only the eastern one is in fair condition today (fig. 5-33). It resembles a Classical Doric temple front, except for the wide opening between the third and fourth columns. The western porch was flanked by two wings (fig. 5-34). The larger one to the north included a picture gallery (*pinakotheke*), the first known instance of a room especially designed for the display of paintings. Along the central roadway that passes through the Propylaea, we find two rows of columns that are Ionic rather than Doric. Apparently, at that time, the trend in Athenian architecture was toward using Ionic elements inside Doric structures. (We recall the sculptured frieze of the Parthenon cella.)

Ionic Temples

Athens, with its strong Aegean orientation, had been open to the eastern Greek style of building from the mid-fifth century on. In fact, the finest surviving examples of the Ionic order are on the Akropolis. Not much is known about the previous history of the order, which first appears about a half-century after the Doric. Of the huge Ionic temples that were erected in Archaic times—the Temple of Hera built around 575 B.C. by Theodoros of Samos, according to Vitruvius, and the Temple of Artemis at Ephesus, designed some 15 years later by Chersiphon and his son Metagenes—little has survived except the plans. These are the earliest dipteral (double-colonnaded) temples we know of. The Ionic style seems to have been fairly fluid, however, with strong links to the Near East (see figs. 3-26 and 3-27). It did not become an order in the strict sense until the Classical period. Even then it remained more flexible than the Doric order. Its most striking features are the continuous frieze, which lacks the alternating triglyphs and

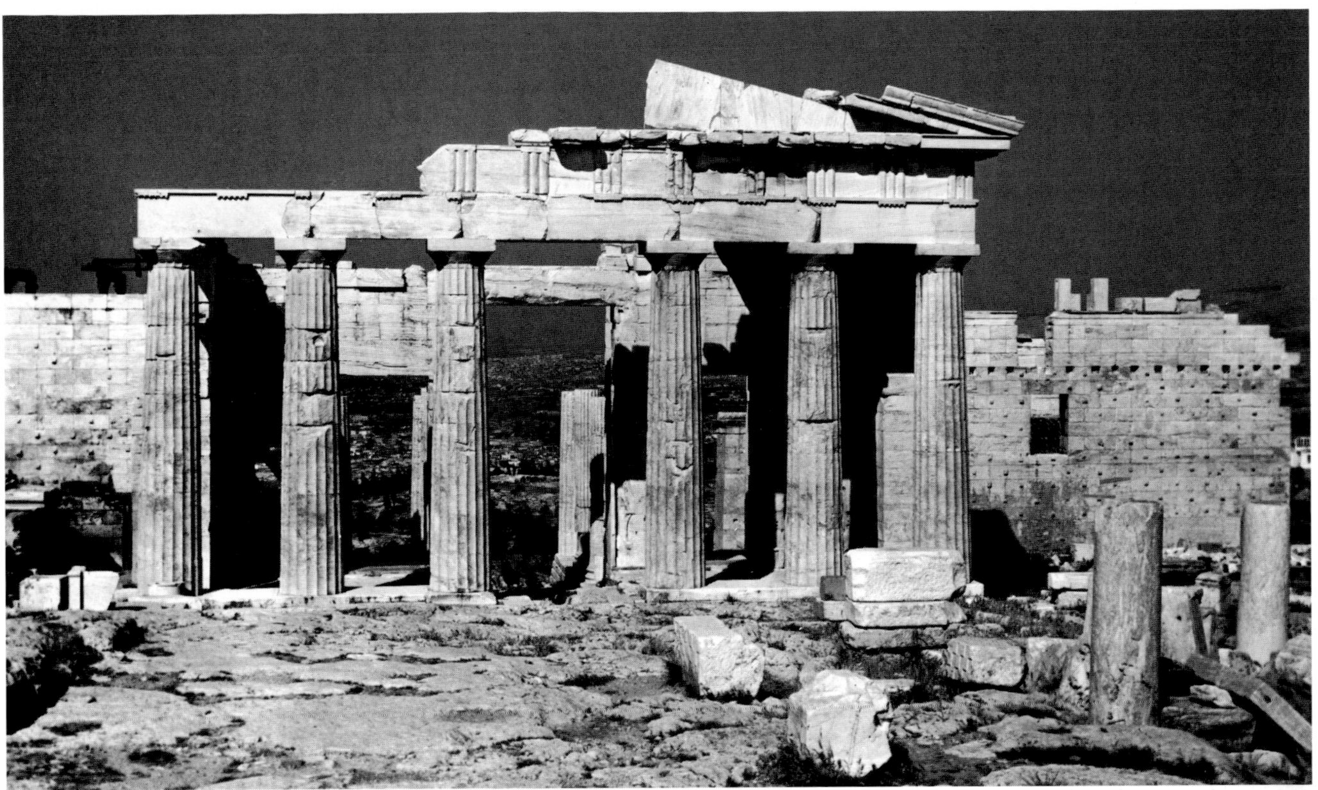

5-33. Mnesikles. The Propylaea (view from the east), Akropolis, Athens. 437–432 B.C.

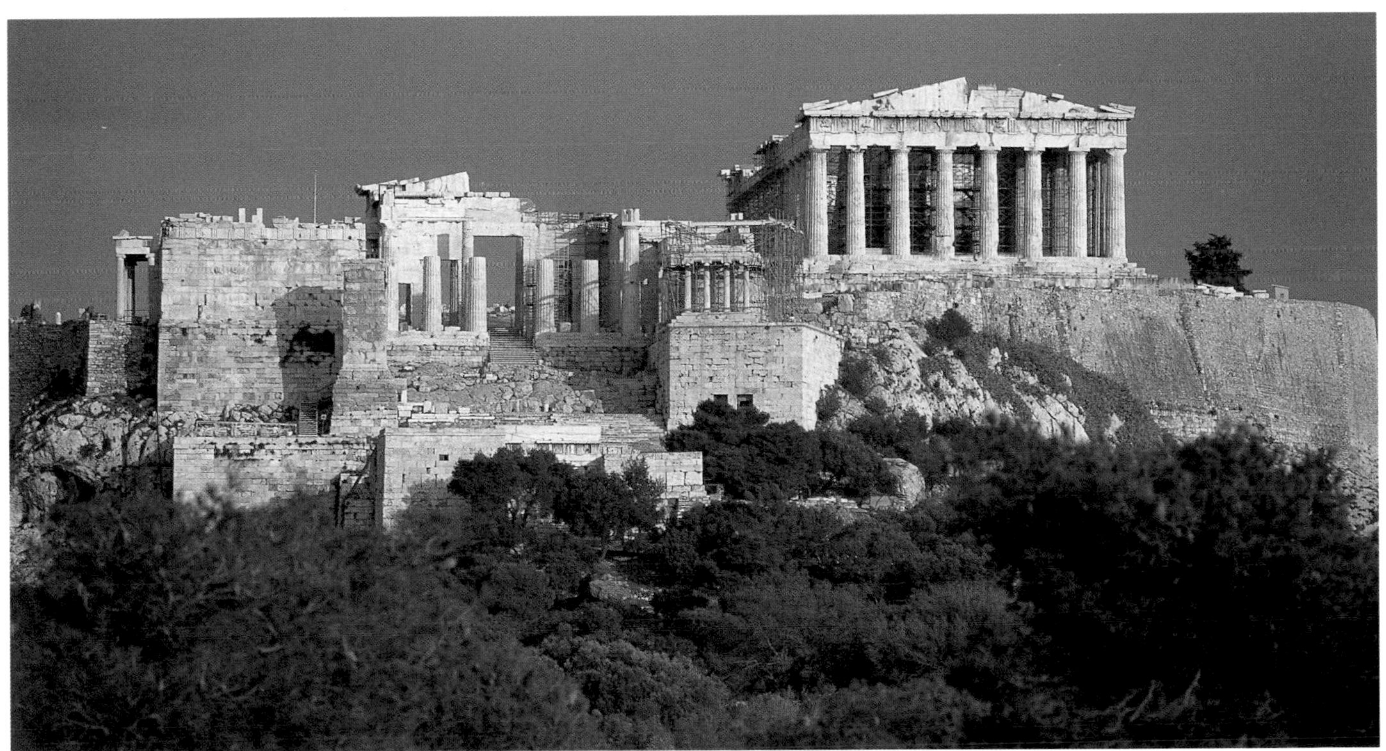

5-34. The Propylaea, 437–432 B.C.; Temple of Athena Nike, 427–424 B.C., Akropolis (view from the west), Athens

metopes of the Doric order, and the Ionic column, which differs from the Doric not only in body but also in spirit (see fig. 5-24). The Ionic column rests on an ornate base of its own, perhaps used at first to protect the bottom from rain. The shaft is more slender, and there is less tapering and entasis. The capital shows a large double scroll, or volute, below the abacus, which projects strongly beyond the width of the shaft.

When we turn from the diagram to an actual building, it becomes clear that these details add up to an entity very distinct from the Doric column. How shall we define it? The Ionic col-

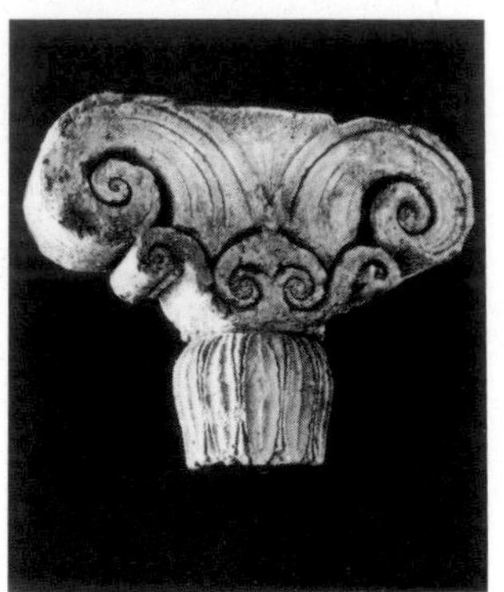

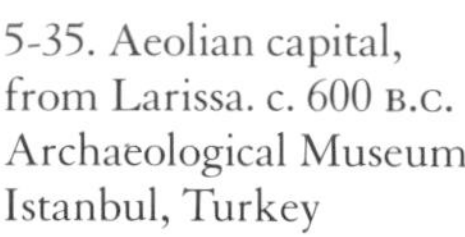

5-35. Aeolian capital, from Larissa. c. 600 B.C. Archaeological Museum, Istanbul, Turkey

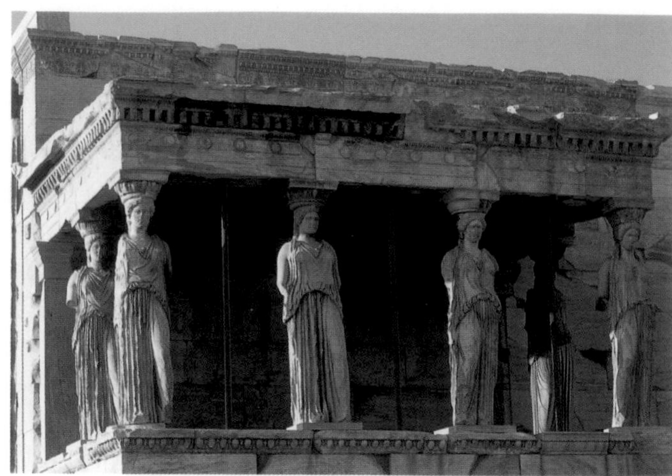

5-36. Porch of the Maidens, the Erechtheum, Akropolis, Athens. 421–405 B.C.

umn is lighter and more graceful. It lacks the muscular quality of its mainland cousin. Instead, it evokes a growing plant, something like a formalized palm tree. This vegetal analogy is not sheer fancy, for we have early ancestors, or relatives, of the Ionic capital that bear it out (fig. 5-35). If we were to pursue these plantlike columns back to their point of origin, we would find ourselves at Saqqara. There we see not only "proto-Doric" supports but also the papyrus half-columns of figure 2-8, with their flaring capitals. It may well be that the form of the Ionic column, too, had its source in Egypt. But instead of reaching Greece by sea, as we suppose the proto-Doric column did, it traveled a slow and tortuous path by land through Syria and Asia Minor.

In pre-Classical times, the only Ionic structures on the Greek mainland had been the small treasuries built by eastern Greek states at Delphi in their regional styles (see fig. 5-19). Hence when Athenian architects first used the Ionic order, about 450 B.C., they thought of it as suitable only for small temples with simple plans. Such a building is the little Temple of Athena Nike on the southern flank of the Propylaea (fig. 5-34), which was probably built between 427 and 424 B.C. from a design prepared 20 years earlier by Kallikrates.

THE ERECHTHEUM. The Erechtheum (see fig. 5-32) is larger and more complex. Located on the northern edge of the Akropolis, opposite the Parthenon, it was built between 421 and 405 B.C., probably by Mnesikles. Like the Propylaea, it is well adapted to an irregular, sloping site. The area had various associations with the mythical founding of Athens, so that the Erechtheum served several religious functions at once. Apparently there were four rooms, as well as a basement on the western side, although their exact purpose is disputed. One held a statue of Erechtheus, a legendary king of Athens, who promoted the worship of Athena and for whom the building is named. The Erechtheum may have covered the spot where the contest between Athena and Poseidon, depicted on the east pediment of the Parthenon, was believed to have taken place (see box page 97). In addition to the olive tree given by Athena, it included the saltwater pool that sprang up where Poseidon threw his trident. The eastern room was dedicated to Athena Polias (Athena the City Goddess) and contained the old statue that had been replaced by Pheidias, while the western room was dedicated to Poseidon.

Instead of a west facade, the Erechtheum has two porches attached to its flanks: a very large one facing north, which was the main entrance, and a small one toward the Parthenon. The latter is the famous Porch of the Maidens (fig. 5-36). Its roof is held up by six female figures (caryatids) on a high parapet, instead of columns (compare fig. 5-19). Here the exquisite refinement of the Ionic order conveys what Vitruvius might have called a "feminine" quality, compared with the "masculinity" of the Parthenon. [See Primary Sources, no. 4, pages 195–96.] Apart from the caryatids, sculptural decoration on the Erechtheum was confined to the frieze, of which very little survives. The pediments remained bare, perhaps for lack of funds at the end of the Peloponnesian War. However, the carving on the bases and capitals of the columns, and on the frames of doorways and windows, is extraordinarily delicate and rich. Its cost, according to the accounts inscribed on the building, was higher than that of figure sculpture.

THE CORINTHIAN CAPITAL. Such emphasis on ornament became characteristic of Greek architecture from the late fifth century on, when the Doric increasingly lost favor to the Ionic. It was at this time, too, that the Corinthian capital was invented (by the metalworker Kallimachos, according to Vitruvius). The Corinthian capital was an elaborate substitute for the Ionic. (For a comparison of Doric, Ionic, and Corinthian capitals, see fig. 5-24.) Its shape is that of an inverted bell covered with the curly shoots and leaves of the acanthus plant, which seem to sprout from the top of the column shaft (fig. 5-37). At first, Corinthian capitals were used only for interiors in temples at Bassae and Delphi. Not until the fourth century do we find them replacing Ionic capitals on the exterior.

The earliest known instance of a Corinthian capital on a facade is the tholos (a circular building with a conical roof) built around 375 B.C. at Delphi by Theodoros of Phocaea, whose book helped to popularize both. The spirited example in figure 5-37 comes from the slightly later tholos at Epidauros by Polykleitos the Younger, who is sometimes credited with having brought the Corinthian capital to maturity. The only intact specimen is the Monument of Lysikrates in Athens (fig. 5-38), built soon after 334 B.C. The round structure, resting on a tall base, is not really a building in the full sense of the term—the interior, though hollow, has no entrance—but an elaborate support for a tripod won by Lysikrates in a choral contest at the Athenian theater (see box page 102). The columns here are engaged rather than freestanding, to make the monument more compact. Soon after, the Corinthian capital came to be used on the exteriors of large buildings as well, and in Roman times it was the standard capital for almost any purpose.

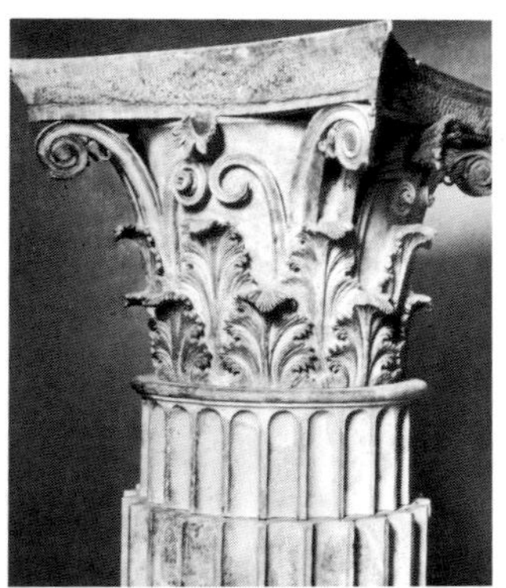

5-37. Corinthian capital, from the Tholos at Epidauros. c. 350 B.C. Museum, Epidauros, Greece

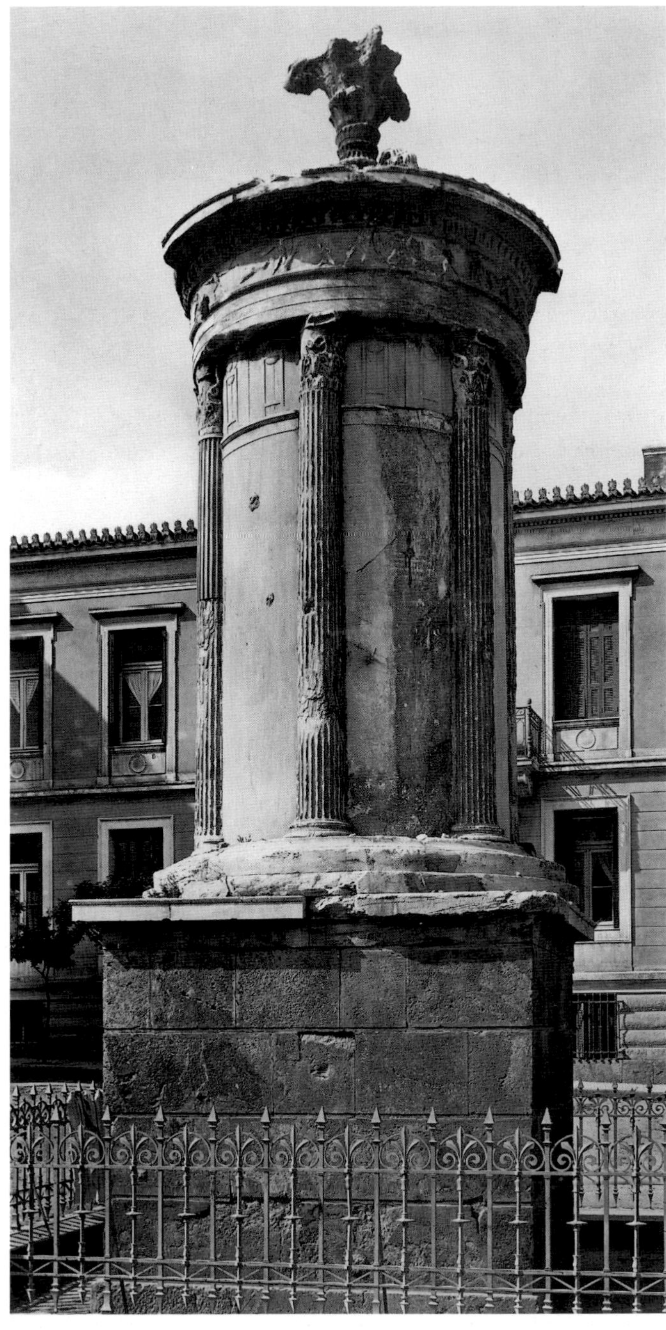

5-38. Monument of Lysikrates, Athens, c. 334 B.C.

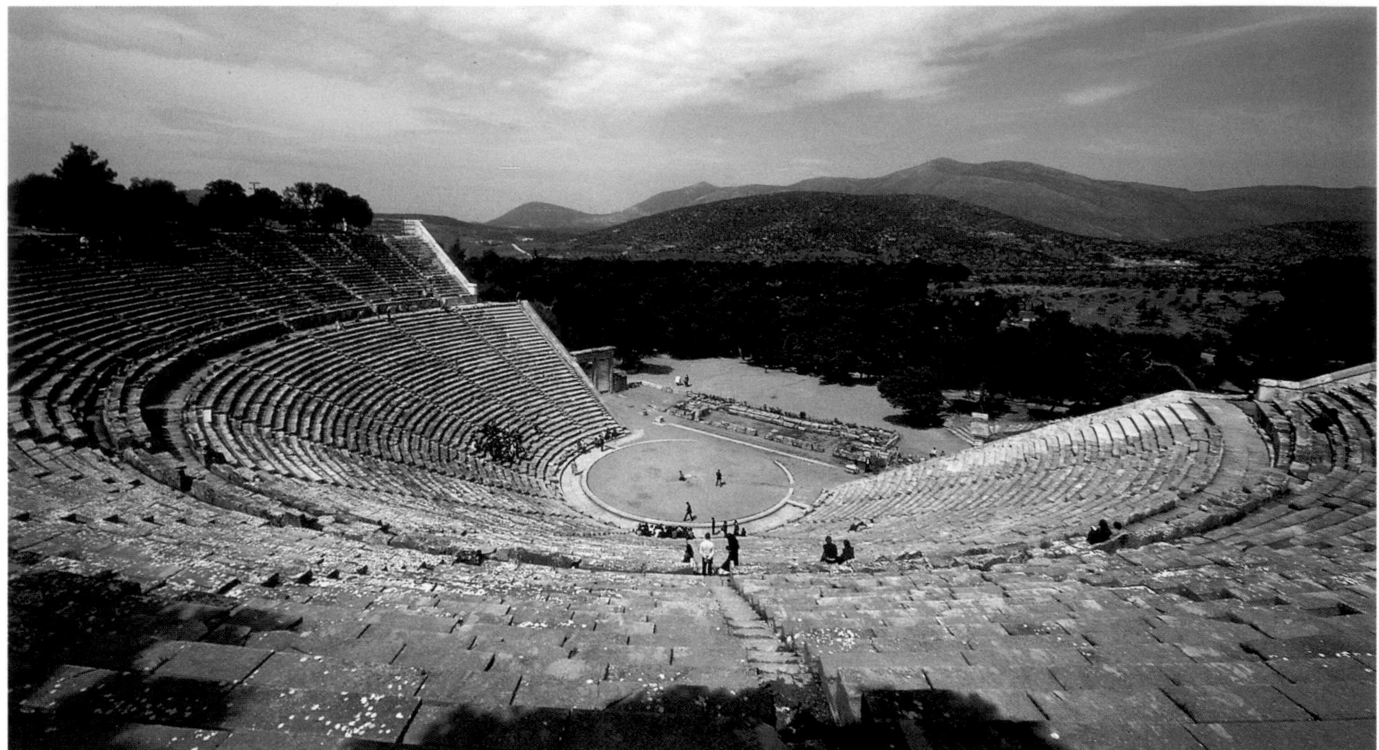

5-39. Theater, Epidauros. c. 350 B.C.

TOWN PLANNING AND THEATERS. Temples, of course, were not the only structures erected by the Greeks. The stoa was a colonnaded hall with a covered portico (porch). Such structures lined the agora (marketplace), the center of civic and commercial life. It was here that the ecclesia (general assembly of citizens) met. Other important buildings were the boueleuterion, where meetings of the town council (Boule) were held; and the prytaneion, where the 50 members of the presiding council (Prytany) sat. Yet in both technical and aesthetic terms, the architectural vocabulary remained that of the late-fifth-century temples. It was around the middle of the century that town planning on a rectangular grid pattern, which had been introduced as early as the eighth century B.C., took on new importance. According to Aristotle, Hippodamos of Miletos used such a grid to lay out his hometown in 466 B.C. and the port city of Piraeus near Athens soon thereafter.

During the three centuries between the end of the Peloponnesian War and the Roman conquest, Greek architecture showed little further development on the mainland. It is in the Greek cities of Asia Minor and the nearby Aegean islands of Rhodes and Kos where most building activity occurred. Even before the time of Alexander the Great, we see structures of a new kind. Often these reveal Oriental influence, as in the huge Tomb of Mausolos at Halikarnassos (see figs. 5-63 and 5-65) and the Great Pergamon Altar (see figs. 5-72, 5-73, and 5-74). But the main tendency was to make buildings, including private houses, larger and more ornate than before. There was also a trend to combine structures to create ever more elaborate complexes, which were as theatrical as the sculpture of the period. Such compounds served new commercial, educational, and athletic functions. An important addition was the

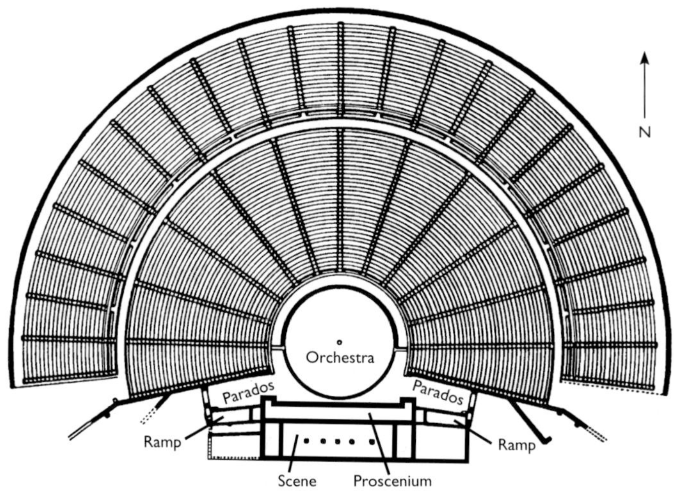

5-40. Plan of the Theater, Epidauros (after Picard-Cambridge)

gymnasium, the forerunner of today's schools of higher education. It was made up of a series of stoas around a central courtyard, and might include lecture rooms, a wrestling school (palaestra), and even a covered running track (xystos). The largest religious precincts were the forerunners of the Roman Sanctuary of Fortuna Primigenia at Praeneste (see fig. 7-7).

The basic forms of Greek architecture increased in only one respect: the open-air theater took on a regular shape. Before the mid-fourth century, the auditorium had been a natural slope, preferably curved, equipped with stone benches. Now the hillside was covered with concentric rows of seats, with staircase-aisles at regular intervals, as at Epidauros (figs. 5-39 and 5-40). In the center was the orchestra, where most of the action took place.

THE CONTRIBUTION OF GREEK ARCHITECTURE. The greatest achievement of Greek architecture was much more than just beautiful buildings. Greek temples are governed by a structural logic that makes them look stable because of the precise arrangement of their parts. The Greeks tried to regulate their temples in accordance with the harmony of nature by constructing them of measured units whose proportions were in perfect agreement. ("Perfect" was as important an idea to the Greeks as "forever" was to the Egyptians.) Now architects could create organic unities, not by copying nature, not by divine inspiration, but by design. Thus their temples seem to be almost alive. They achieved this triumph chiefly by expressing the structural forces active in buildings, known as architectonics. In the Classical period, expressions of force and counterforce in both Doric and Ionic temples were proportioned so exactly that they produced the effect of a perfect balance and a perfect harmony. This is the real reason why, for so many centuries, the orders have been considered the only true basis for beautiful architecture. They are so perfect that they could not be surpassed, only equaled.

LIMITATIONS OF GREEK ARCHITECTURE. How are we to account for the fact that Greek architecture did not grow much beyond the stage it had reached at the time of the Peloponnesian War? After all, neither intellectual life nor the work of sculptors and painters show any tendency toward staleness during the last 300 years of Greek civilization. Are we perhaps misjudging the architecture of the Greeks after 400 B.C.? Or were there inherent limitations that prevented Greek architecture from continuing the pace of development it had maintained in Archaic and Classical times? A number of such limitations come to mind: the concern with exteriors at the expense of interior space, the focus on temples of one particular type, and the lack of interest in any structural system more advanced than the post-and-lintel (uprights supporting horizontal beams). Until the late fifth century, these had all been advantages. Without them, the great works of the Periklean age would have been unthinkable. But the possibilities of the Doric temple were nearly exhausted by then, as can be seen in the attention given to expensive refinements.

What Greek architecture needed after the Peloponnesian War was a revival of the experimental spirit of the seventh century that would create an interest in new building materials, vaulting, and interior space. What prevented the breakthrough? Could it have been the architectural orders or, rather, the cast of mind that produced them? One suspects that it was the very coherence and rigidity of these orders that made it impossible for Greek architects to break from them. What had been their great strength in earlier days became a tyranny. It remained for later ages to adapt the Greek orders to brick and concrete, arches and vaults. Such adaptation required violating the original character of the orders—something the Greeks, it seems, were unable to do.

CLASSICAL SCULPTURE

THE KRITIOS BOY. Among the statues excavated from the debris the Persians had left behind after sacking the Akropolis in 480 B.C., there is one Kouros (fig. 5-41) that stands apart. It must have been carved shortly before that fateful event. This remarkable work, which some have attributed to the Athenian sculptor Kritios and which therefore has come to be known as the *Kritios Boy,* differs in subtle but important ways from the Archaic Kouros figures we discussed above (see figs. 5-10 and 5-11): it is the first statue we know that *stands* in the full sense of the word. Of course, the earlier figures also stand, but only in the sense that they are in an upright position and are not reclining, sitting, kneeling, or running. Their stance is really an arrested walk, with the weight of the body resting evenly on both legs. Thus early Greek statues have almost a military air, as if they were standing at attention.

The *Kritios Boy,* too, has one leg placed forward, yet we never doubt that he is standing still. Just as in military drill, this is simply a matter of allowing the weight of the body to shift. When we compare the left and right half of his body, we find that the symmetry of the Archaic Kouros has given way to a calculated nonsymmetry. The knee of the forward leg is lower than the other, the right hip is thrust down and inward, and the left hip is up and outward. If we trace the axis of the body, we see that it is not a straight vertical line but an S-curve (or, to be exact, a reversed S-curve). Taken together, all these small departures from symmetry tell us that the weight of the body rests mainly on the left leg and that the right leg plays the role of a prop to make sure that the body keeps its balance.

CONTRAPPOSTO. The *Kritios Boy,* then, not only stands, he stands at ease. The artist has masterfully observed the balanced nonsymmetry of this relaxed natural stance. To describe it, we use the Italian word *contrapposto* (counterpoise). The leg that carries the main weight is called the engaged leg; the other, the free leg. These terms are a useful shorthand, for from now on we shall often mention contrapposto. It was a very basic discovery. Only by learning how to represent the body at rest could the sculptor gain the freedom to show it in motion. But is there not plenty of motion in Archaic art? There is indeed (see figs. 5-16, 5-20, 5-22, and 5-23), but it is somewhat mechanical. We read it from the poses without really feeling it.

In the *Kritios Boy,* on the other hand, we sense not only a new repose but also an animation that evokes our experience of our own body. The use of contrapposto brings about all kinds of subtle curvatures: the bending of the free knee results in a slight swiveling of the pelvis, a compensating curvature of the spine, and an adjusting tilt of the shoulders. Like the refined details of the Parthenon, these adjustments have nothing to do with the statue's ability to stand erect. Rather, they serve to enhance its lifelike impression. In repose, it will still seem able to move; in motion, it will seem able to maintain its stability. The entire figure seems so alive that the Archaic smile, the "sign of life," is no longer needed. It has given way to a serious expression characteristic of the early phase of Classical sculpture (or, as it is often called, the Severe style). Once the Greek statue was free to move, as it were, it became free to think, not merely to act. The two—movement and thought—are inseparable aspects of Greek classicism.

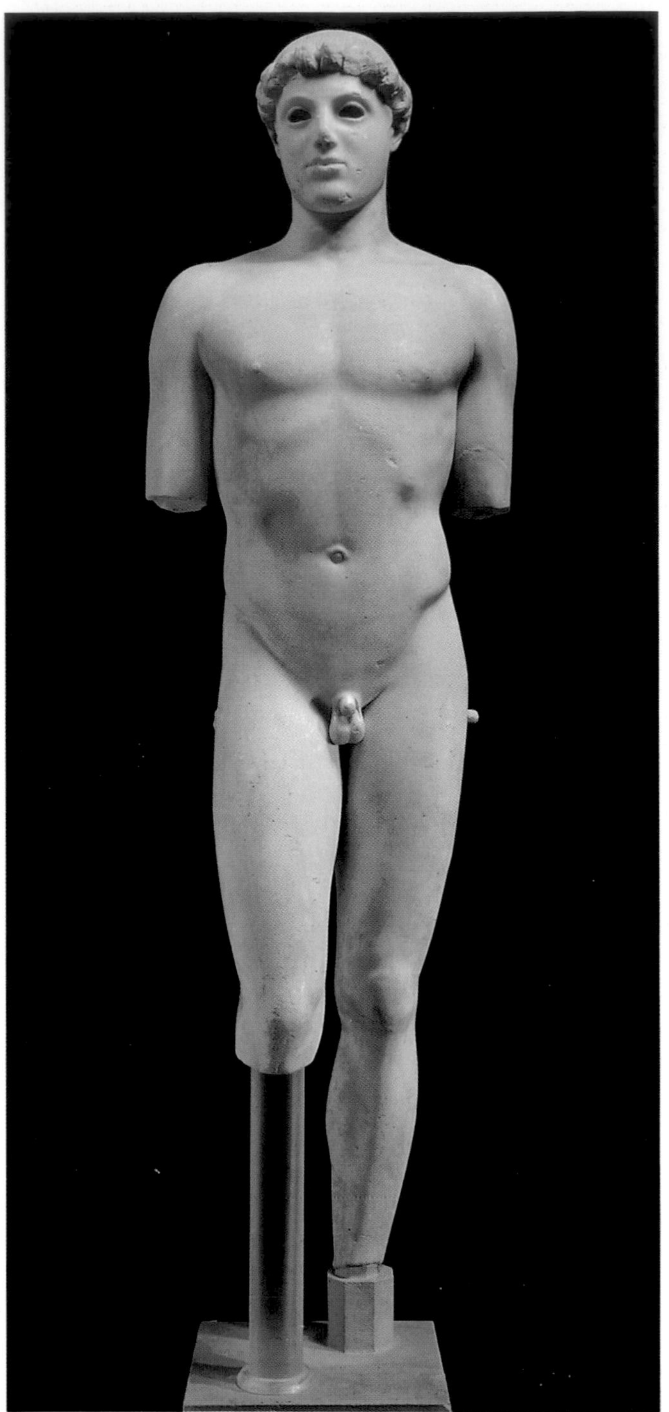

5-41. *Standing Youth (Kritios Boy).* c. 480 B.C.
Marble, height 46" (116.7 cm). Akropolis Museum, Athens

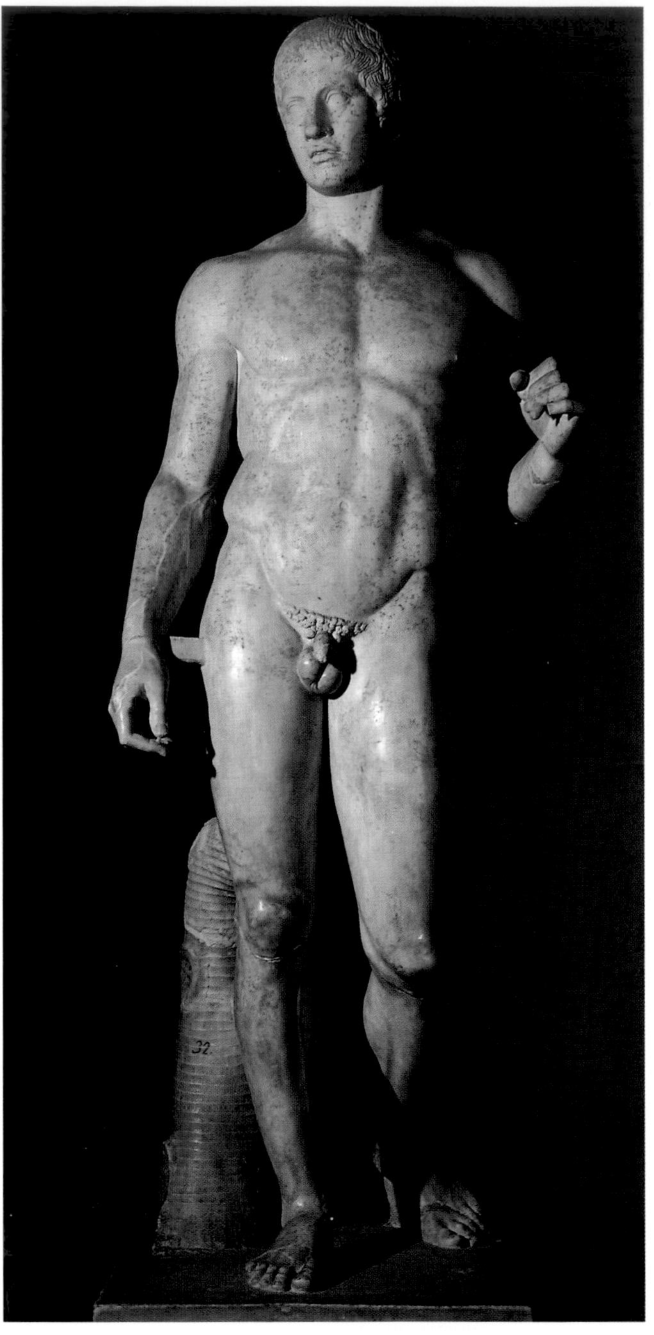

5-42. *Doryphoros (Spear Bearer).* Roman copy after an original of c. 450–440 B.C. by Polykleitos.
Marble, height 6'6" (2 m). Museo Archeologico Nazionale, Naples

POLYKLEITOS. The articulation of the body that appears in the *Kritios Boy* reached its full development within half a century in the mature Classical style of the Periklean era. The most famous Kouros statue of that time, the *Doryphoros (Spear Bearer)* by Polykleitos (fig. 5-42), is known to us only through Roman copies, which must convey little of the beauty of the original. Still, it is instructive to compare this work with the *Kritios Boy.* Everything is a harmony of complementary opposites. The contrapposto is now much more emphatic. The differentiation between the halves of the body can be seen in every muscle. The turn of the head, barely hinted at in the *Kritios Boy,* is pronounced. The "working" left arm is balanced by the "engaged" right leg in the forward position, and the relaxed right arm by the "free" left leg. This studied poise, the precise anatomical details, and above all the harmonious proportions of the figure made the *Doryphoros* renowned as the embodiment of the Classical ideal of beauty. The ideal here must be understood in a dual sense: as a perfect model and as a prototype. According to one ancient writer, it was known simply as the Canon (rule, measure). [See Primary Sources, no. 3, pages 194–95.]

The *Doryphoros* was more than an exercise in abstract geometry. It embodied not only *symmetria* (structure, proportion) but also *rhythmos* (composition, movement). Both were basic aspects of

MUSIC IN ANCIENT GREECE

Although the earliest surviving remnants of Greek culture can be traced back to the eighth century B.C., they must have been preceded by at least 400 years of development now lost to us. In the eighth century we find the earliest works of Greek sculpture, painting, and architecture, however primitive they may be; the beginnings of Greek philosophy at Miletos; and, above all, the creation of two epic poems, the *Iliad* and the *Odyssey* (which probably treat an actual war of about 1200 B.C.), out of preexisting material. Homer, to whom these poems are attributed, lived in Asia Minor and sang his poetry while playing a lyre. This unity of words and music was to be a constant feature of Greek poetry and theater. It was embodied by the legendary bard Orpheus, whose music, it was said, could move even animals and stones.

Early Greek music as sung by the bards was of a very rudimentary sort called *stithic*. Melodies consisted of only three or four notes sung repetitively in lines of simple rhythm and unchanging length. There was also a strophic form that could be closed (small, using a few basic meters, and clear in structure) or open (larger, more complex, with no fixed meter). Early Greek vocal music was accompanied by lyres having only a few strings ("lyric" poetry was sung to a lyre) or a primitive form of the aulos, an oboelike reed instrument that was always played in pairs. The harp, an import from Lydia and Ionia in Asia Minor, was preferred by the poetess Sappho of Lesbos (early sixth century B.C.) and remained chiefly an instrument for women.

We owe much of what we know about Greek harmonics to the Roman writer Vitruvius. Because it involved only four notes, early Greek music was organized in tetrachords. At first, it was governed by the "enharmonic" (in tune) genus. By the fifth century B.C., a second genus, chromaticism, began to gain favor because it was easier to play. Chromaticism virtually displaced the enharmonic genus toward the end of the fourth century B.C. Even easier was the diatonic genus, which was used for most late Greek music, and has been for the vast majority of Western music since then. Two successive tetrachords were joined by a common note to form a seven-note scale, which gave rise to the standard seven-string kithara (lyre). Not until the early seventh century B.C. was the scale extended to the modern octave by Terpander.

These scales, with their varying intervals, were the basis of the so-called modes. Although the notes can be reconstructed readily enough, individual modes were associated with certain rhythms, meters, and melodies. Each had a distinctive character (*ethos*) that can only be guessed at. All that remains of Greek music is some 51, mostly late, fragments supplemented by a small but crucial body of theory. There were five standard modes. The Dorian mode was used for invocations, lamentations, tragedy, and choral songs. The Phrygian mode, introduced into Athens by Sophocles, could be cheerful and pious, according to the philosopher Plato (427?–347 B.C.), or wildly emotional (orgiastic) according to his pupil Aristotle (384–322 B.C.). The Lydian mode was a soft ("slack") mode used by the poet Anacreon (c. 570–c. 485 B.C.) at symposia that perhaps arose from the aulos airs composed by Olympus in the late eighth century B.C. The Mixolydian was a highly emotional mode used by Sappho and was deemed especially suitable for laments, which was the main tragic mode with the Dorian before the time of Sophocles. The Ionian was a soft mode that was derived from Asiatic laments and was therefore also appropriate for tragedy. All other modes were probably derived from these five. Their names attest to the fact that Greece was a vast melting pot both musically and ethnically. In fact, there were rival musical centers throughout Greece. Sparta and Lesbos were the leaders throughout the seventh century B.C. They were succeeded by Argos during the sixth century B.C. Around 450 B.C. Syracuse emerged as the capital of Greek music, though Thebes continued to reign supreme on the aulos.

The modes could be varied through modulations of genus, scale, key, and ethos. The growing complexity of music was spurred by the rise of instrumental music independent of singing. It began in Phrygia in the late eighth century B.C. with the first aulos player (*aulete*), variously considered to be Olympus or Hyagnis (Agnis). A piper's contest (*agones*) was held during the Phrygian games in 586 B.C., which was won by Sakada of Argos. The first kithara contest was added to the Phrygian games 28 years later. No longer tied to words, instrumental music was free to develop ever more novel, complex forms. It also underwent a change in character toward the ecstatic, serpentine music still found in the Near East today. By the mid-fifth century B.C., the emphasis was on virtuosity, which inevitably influenced vocal music as well. For example, Pindar (518?–c. 438 B.C.), the great composer of odes (music meant to be sung by a chorus), emphasized the intricacy and variety of his music. This trend reached its zenith in the late fifth century B.C. under Melanippides of Melos, a composer who created a more expressive singing style shaped to the words. *The Persians,* by his contemporary, Timotheus the Milesian, strikingly anticipated *The Battle of Issos* (see fig. 5-60) in its representation of the sounds and color of combat. These innovations, however, met with stiff resistance from conservatives, who lamented the loss of simplicity and dignity in favor of corrupt styles catering to popular taste.

(box continues on following page)

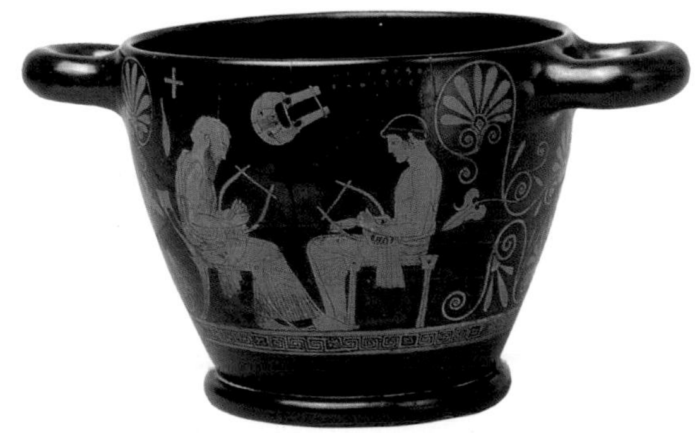

The Pistoxenos Painter. *Linos and Iphikles at Music Lesson.* c. 470 B.C. Attic red-figure drinking cup (*skyphos*). Staatliches Museum, Schwerin

MUSIC IN ANCIENT GREECE *(continued from preceding page)*

It became essential to unify the scales after the invention in the sixth century B.C. of sophisticated lyres and auloi that could change modes without retuning. The first consistent system was devised in the fourth century B.C. by Aristoxenus of Tarentum, a pupil of Aristotle, on whom Vitruvius based his account of Greek music. His 13-note scale was eventually superseded by a 15-note "perfect system," although Ptolemy tried to reduce the number back to seven in the second century B.C. Surprisingly, the great age of Greek music was soon over. By the early fourth century, composers were replaced by star performers, who relied for the most part on the music of the past.

Music was of great importance in ancient Greece. The word *music* derives from *muse,* the personification and inspiration of the nine branches of art and learning. Thus an educated person was a "musical" person. Music was closely linked to art through philosophy. The mathematician and philosopher Pythagoras (c. 582–c. 507 B.C.) believed that the universe was governed by numbers. He is generally credited with discovering that an octave is exactly half the length of the next lower one on a chord stretched over a graduated rule (*kanon*). (However, it may have actually been the work of the fifth-century theorist Simos.) Also during the sixth century, Epigonos used a zither divided into quarter tones to determine the relationships between the modal scales. From then on, Greek aesthetics as a branch of philosophy was founded on the belief in harmonious proportion. Nevertheless, musical theory for the most part continued to be based on tonal intervals, which do not bear a simple mathematical relationship to each other. The importance of ratio was acknowledged by the great philosopher Plato, for whom the music of the spheres was made by eight Sirens representing the eight notes of the standard diatonic scale.

During the fifth century B.C., Greek sculptors sought to infuse their work with inner life by investing it with *rhythmos* (composition, movement) and *symmetria* (structure, proportion), terms taken from music and dance with strong philosophical connotations. Moreover, beauty itself was regarded as having inherent ethical associations and educative functions by Plato and his successor, Aristotle, who became the teacher of Alexander the Great. This concept, too, was rooted in music. It was first voiced in the 440s by Damon, Perikles' teacher, who spelled out a comprehensive theory of modes according to their expressive effect and impact on character. Damon warned against revolutions in music as bad for society. This idea was taken up as well by Plato, who had studied music under Damon's pupil Dracon. While it was challenged by the Epicurean philosophers in particular, the concept of musical ethos reached its height with Ptolemy, whose system of cosmic proportions was founded on his belief in the "tuning" of the soul.

Greek aesthetics, derived from music and dance (see box on pages 125–26). A faith in ratio can be found throughout Greek philosophy beginning with the Pythagoreans, who believed that the harmony of the universe, like musical harmony, could be expressed in mathematical terms. The Greeks were not the first to explore proportions, of course; the Egyptians had done so earlier. But the Greeks were more systematic in their study, thanks to their passion for abstract numbers, which enabled them to devise the algebraic formulas required for solving complex problems. This method was beyond the grasp of the Egyptians, who remained wedded to a practical approach (see pages 46–47). Thus the Greeks easily solved problems that posed great difficulty for Egyptian mathematicians. There is considerable evidence that East Greeks living in Anatolia, along the coast of modern-day Turkey, gained their theoretical bent from Mesopotamia. In fact, Pythagoras' theorem $a^2 + b^2 = c^2$ had been solved a thousand years earlier, around the time of Hammurabi. Once they had acquired this taste for mathematics, the Greeks never lost it. Plato, too, made numbers the basis of his doctrine of ideal forms and acknowledged that the concept of beauty was commonly based on proportion, though he seems to have had little use for art. [See Primary Sources, no. 6, pages 196–97.]

Polykleitos' faith in numbers also had a moral dimension often found in Classical Greek philosophy, notably that of Plato. Contemplation of harmonious proportions was equated with contemplation of the good. To the Greeks, pose and expression reflected character and feeling, which revealed the inner person and, with it, *arete* (excellence or virtue). Thus the lowered gaze of the *Doryphoros* may be seen as denoting modesty, a chief virtue to the Classical Greeks. Rather than being opposed to naturalism, this moral dimension was linked to a more careful treatment of form that makes the human figure appear more lively as well as more real. Classical Greek sculpture appeals to both the mind and the eye, so that human and divine beauty become one. No wonder that figures of victorious athletes have sometimes been mistaken for gods!

We can get some idea of what the *Doryphoros* might have looked like in its original bronze form from a pair of figures that created a sensation when they were found in the sea near Riace, Italy, in 1972 (figs. 5-43 and 5-44). They owe their importance to their fine workmanship and the extreme rarity of intact monumental bronze statues from ancient Greece. Miraculously, these statues still have their ivory and glass-paste eyes, bronze eyelashes, and copper lips. Combined with the detailed anatomy, they create an astonishingly lifelike presence. The pair challenges our understanding of Greek sculpture in many ways. What or whom do these statues represent? When and where were they made? What purpose did they serve? We do not yet have the answers to these questions. The stylistic and technical evidence suggests that they were made around the same time as the *Doryphoros.* Although they have sometimes been dated slightly earlier, our sculptor may well have been an older artist who was used to working in the Severe style and had not fully adapted to the new Classicism. (Compare the heads to that of *Zeus* in fig. 5-48.)

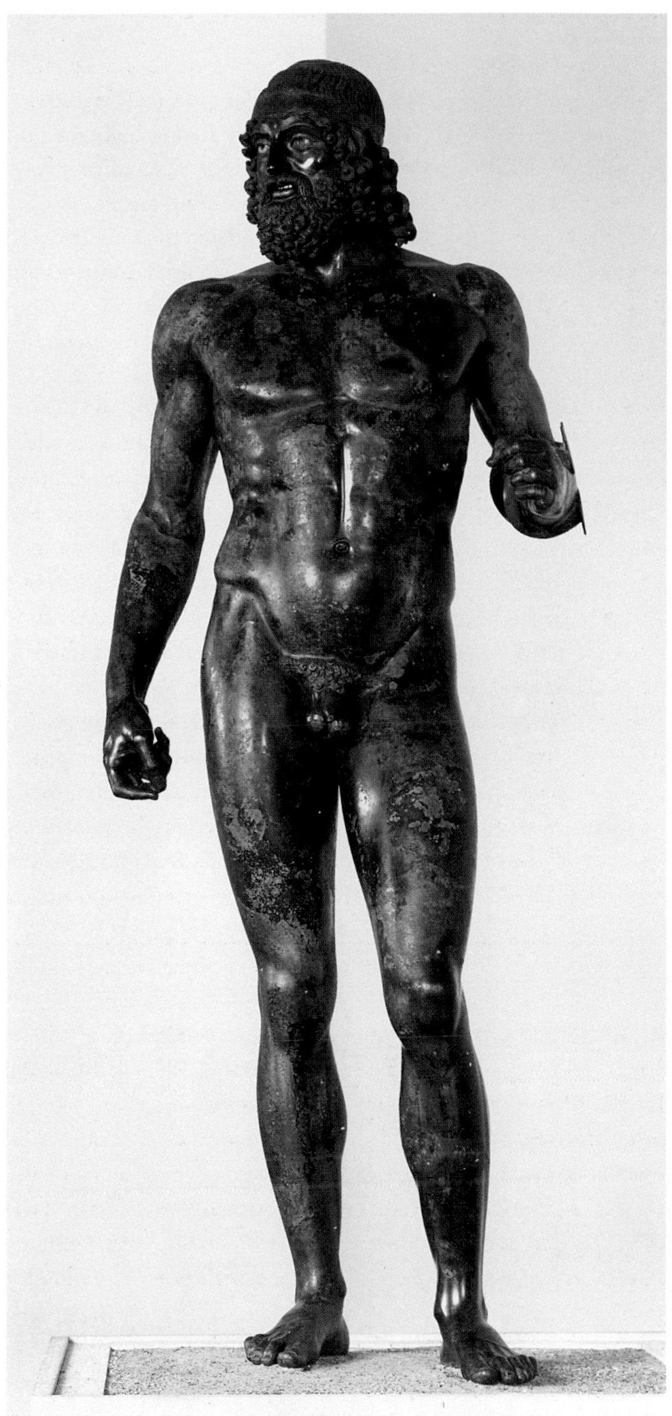

5-43. *Riace Warrior A,* found in the sea off Riace, Italy. c. 450 B.C. Bronze, height 6'8" (2.03 m). Museo Archeologico, Reggio Calabria, Italy

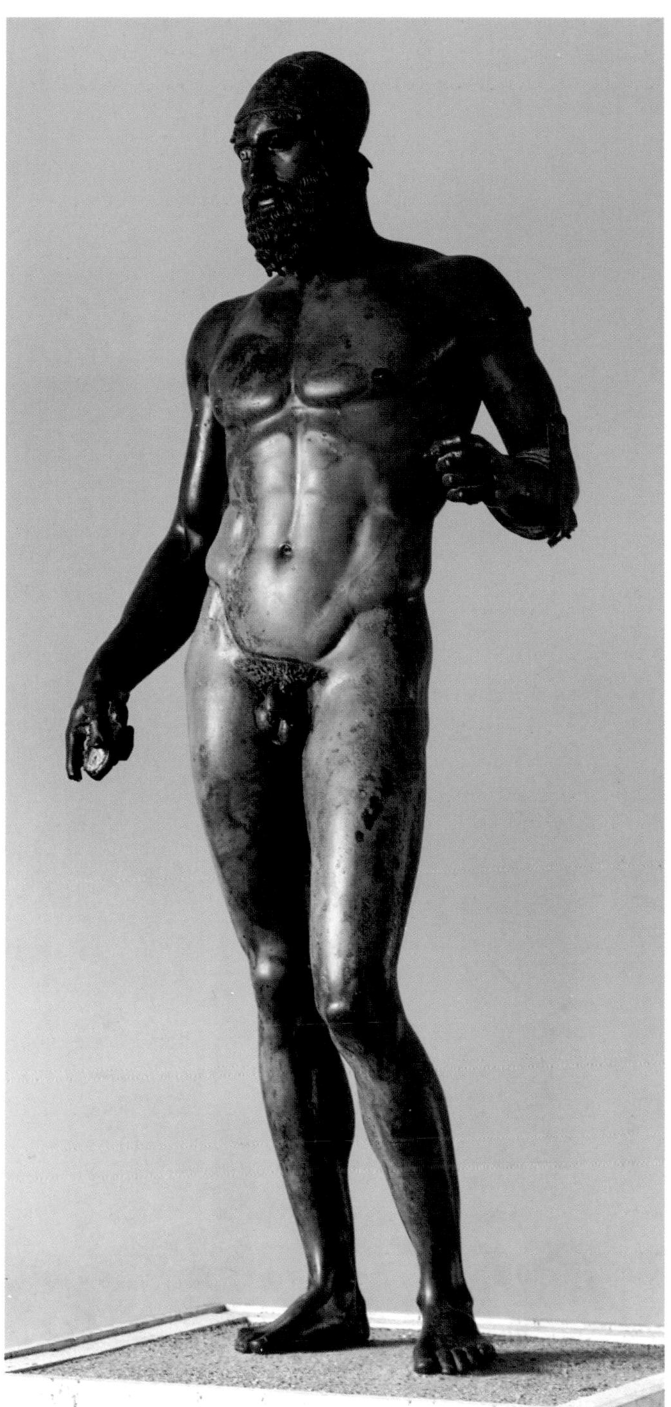

5-44. *Riace Warrior B,* found in the sea off Riace. c. 450 B.C. Bronze, height 6'8" (2.03 m). Museo Archeologico, Reggio Calabria, Italy

A clue is provided by the statue in figure 5-44, which belongs to a widespread type. (In contrast, the first figure does not conform to any known model.) He is, it seems, a warrior rather than an athlete, in contrast to the *Doryphoros.* The extraordinary realism of the heads, so out of keeping with the idealization characteristic of Greek art, has yet to be explained. Were they meant to honor two heroes? It is tempting to think so. If that is the case, why were their names not recorded by ancient historians? Moreover, portraits are unknown from this time. Perhaps, then, their features were varied to distinguish them from other members of a larger group, although freestanding groups of more than two figures are not recorded before the Late Classical era.

Conceptually, these figures are not altogether satisfying. The contrast between the individuality of the faces and the generalized treatment of the bodies is both fascinating and disturbing. Were there similar statues that we do not know of simply because they have not survived? Our view of Greek sculpture may be as distorted by the incomplete record as was that of the poet Goethe, who could not reconcile the Aegina statues with his understanding of Greek art.

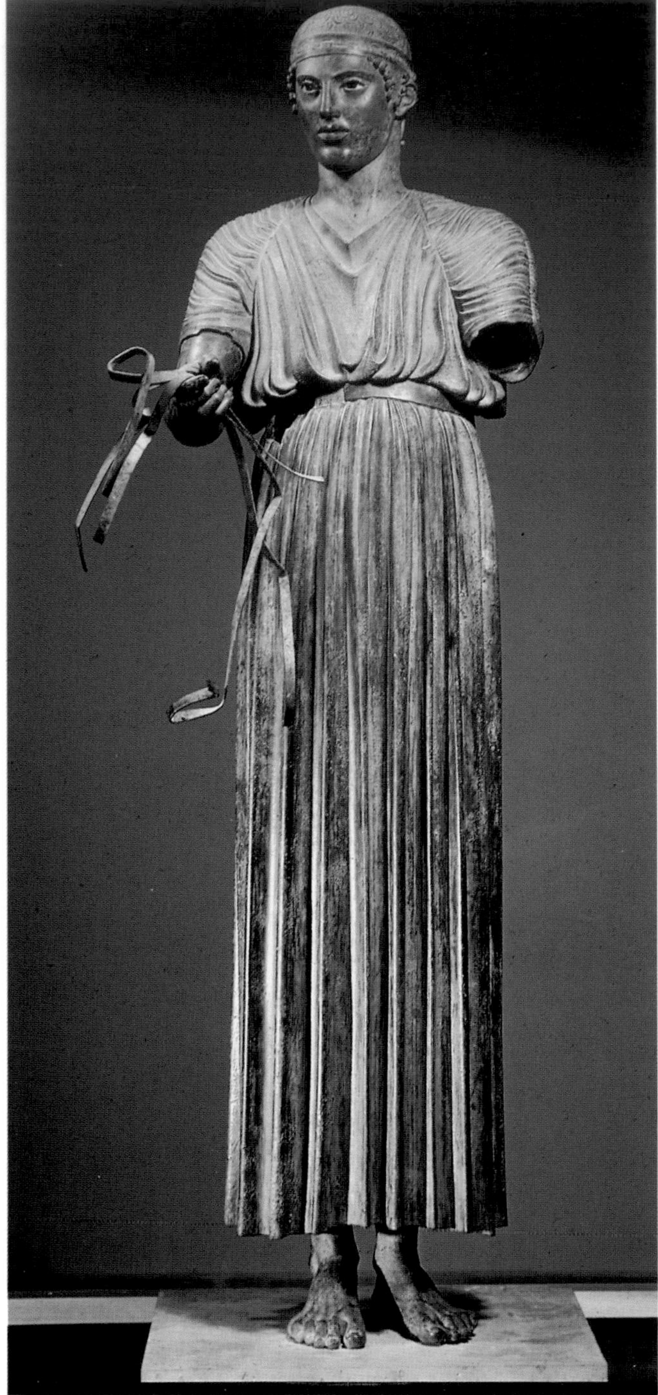

5-45. *Charioteer,* from the Sanctuary of Apollo at Delphi. c. 470 B.C. Bronze, height 71" (180 cm). Archaeological Museum, Delphi

THE SEVERE STYLE. The *Charioteer* from Delphi (fig. 5-45), one of the earliest surviving large bronze statues in Greek art, shows why Greek sculpture done between about 480 and 450 B.C. is said to be in the Severe style. It must have been made about a decade later than the *Kritios Boy* as a votive offering after a race: the young victor originally stood on a chariot drawn by four horses. Despite the long, heavy garment, there is a hint of contrapposto in the body. The feet are differentiated so as to show that the left leg is the engaged one, and the shoulders and head turn slightly to the right. The garment is severely simple, yet compared with Archaic drapery the folds seem softer and more pliable. We feel (probably for the first time in the history of sculpture) that they reflect the behavior of real cloth.

Not only the body but the drapery, too, reveals a new understanding of functional relationships. Every fold is shaped by the forces that act upon it: the pull of gravity, the shape of the body, and the belts or straps that constrict its flow. The face has the pensive look we saw in the *Kritios Boy,* but the colored inlay of the eyes and the slightly parted lips give it a more animated expression. The entire figure conveys the solemnity of the event it commemorates, for chariot races and similar contests were competitions for divine favor, not mere sporting events in the modern sense.

THE TEMPLE OF ZEUS, OLYMPIA. The greatest sculptural ensemble of the Severe style is the pair of pediments of the Temple of Zeus at Olympia. They were carved about 460 B.C., perhaps by Ageladas of Argos, and have been reassembled in the local museum. The temple was paid for with booty from the victory of Elis over its neighbor Pisa in 470 B.C. (see also page 116; discussion of temple under Parthenon), which is reflected in the east pediment. The subject is Pelops' triumph over Oinomaos, the king of Pisa, in a chariot race for which the prize was the hand of the latter's daughter, Hippodamia. Pelops (for whom the Peloponnesus is named) held a position of special importance, for he was thought to have founded the games at Olympia. But because he won by trickery, he and his descendants, which included Herakles and Agamemnon, were cursed. Hence, his example also served as a warning to contestants as they paraded past the temple.

In the west pediment, the more mature of the two, we see the victory of the Lapiths over the Centaurs. Centaurs were the offspring of Ixion, king of the Lapiths, and a phantom of Hera, whom he tried to seduce while in Olympos. (Zeus had brought him there to be purified for having murdered his father-in-law in order to avoid paying for his bride.) In punishment for his impiety, Ixion was chained forever to a fiery wheel in Tartarus. Since they were the half brothers of the Lapiths, the Centaurs were invited to the wedding of the Lapith king Peirithoös and Hippodamia (no relation to her namesake on the other pediment). Because they were half-animals, the centaurs became drunk and got into a brawl with the Lapiths, who subdued them with the aid of Peirithoös' friend Theseus.

The action takes place under the aegis of Apollo, who stands at the center (fig. 5-46). His commanding figure is part of the drama and yet above it. The outstretched right arm and the strong turn of the head show his active role. He wills the victory but, as befits a god, does not physically help to achieve it. Still, there is a tenseness in this powerful body that makes its outward calm even more impressive. The forms themselves are massive and simple, with soft contours and undulating surfaces. In the group of the Centaur king, Eurytion, who has seized Hippodamia, we see another achievement of the Severe style. The passionate struggle is expressed not only through action and gesture but through the emotions mirrored in the face of the Centaur, whose pain and desperate effort contrast vividly with the stoic calm on the face of the woman.

The pediment makes a clear moral distinction in the contrast between the bestial Centaurs and the humans, who share Apollo's nobility. Thus it is Apollo, as the god of music and poetry, who is

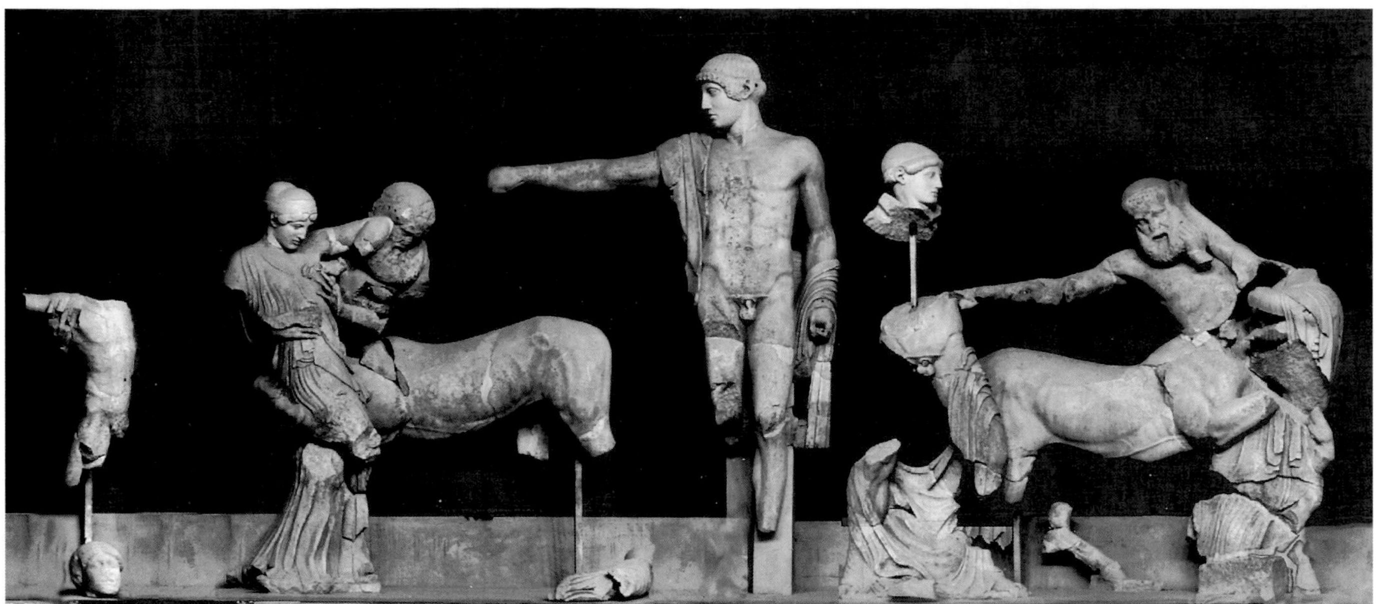

5-46. Photographic reconstruction (partial) of the *Battle of the Lapiths and Centaurs,* from the west pediment of the Temple of Zeus at Olympia. c. 460 B.C. Marble, slightly over-lifesize. Archaeological Museum, Olympia

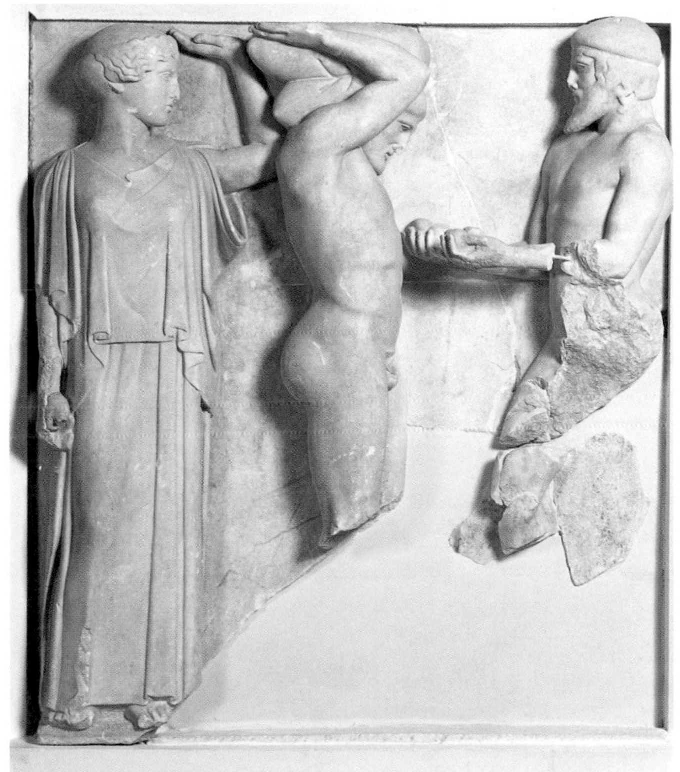

5-47. *Atlas Bringing Herakles the Apples of the Hesperides.* c. 456 B.C. Marble, height 63" (160 cm). Archaeological Museum, Olympia

the real hero, since he ensures the triumph of civilization. In general, the pediment stands for the victory of humanity's rational and moral sides over its animal nature. The pediment thus celebrates the triumph of Greek civilization over barbarianism as a whole and the victory over the Persians in particular. It may also have served as a gentle reminder to visitors at the Olympic Games to behave in a dignified manner.

Equally important are the metopes depicting the labors of Herakles, Pelops' great-grandson, who according to legend laid out the stadium at Olympia. Narrative scenes had been a feature of metopes since the early sixth century B.C., but it was not until a hundred years later that they began to outgrow their crude beginnings. At Olympia the pictorial and dramatic possibilities are fully exploited for the first time. Our example, which was featured prominently over the entrance on the east side of the temple, shows Atlas returning with the apples of the Hesperides (fig. 5-47). During Atlas' absence, Herakles has held the celestial globe on his shoulders with the seemingly effortless support of Athena. He looks on almost in astonishment as he tries to think of a way to trick Atlas into giving up the apples. In contrast to the grim combats featured in Archaic Greek art (see figs. 5-6, 5-7), Herakles takes on the more thoughtful air that is basic to the Classical spirit. The scene is depicted with a wonderful economy of pose and expression that further serves to enhance the hero's stature. The carving is no less beautiful than on the pediment and participates fully in the development of the Severe style.

MOVEMENT IN STATUES. To return to the pediment itself, no Archaic artist would have known how to combine the figures of Hippodamia and the Centaur into a group so compact, so full of interlocking movements. Strenuous action, of course, had already appeared in pedimental sculpture of the late Archaic period (see figs. 5-22 and 5-23). However, such figures, although technically carved in the round, are not freestanding. Rather, they are a kind of super-relief, since they are designed to be seen against a background and from one direction only. To infuse the same freedom of movement into genuinely freestanding statues was a far greater challenge. Not only did it run counter to an age-old tradition that denied mobility to these figures, but unfreezing them had to be done in such a way that their all-around balance and self-sufficiency would be preserved. The problem could not really be tackled until the concept of contrapposto was established. Once this was done, the solution no longer presented serious difficulties.

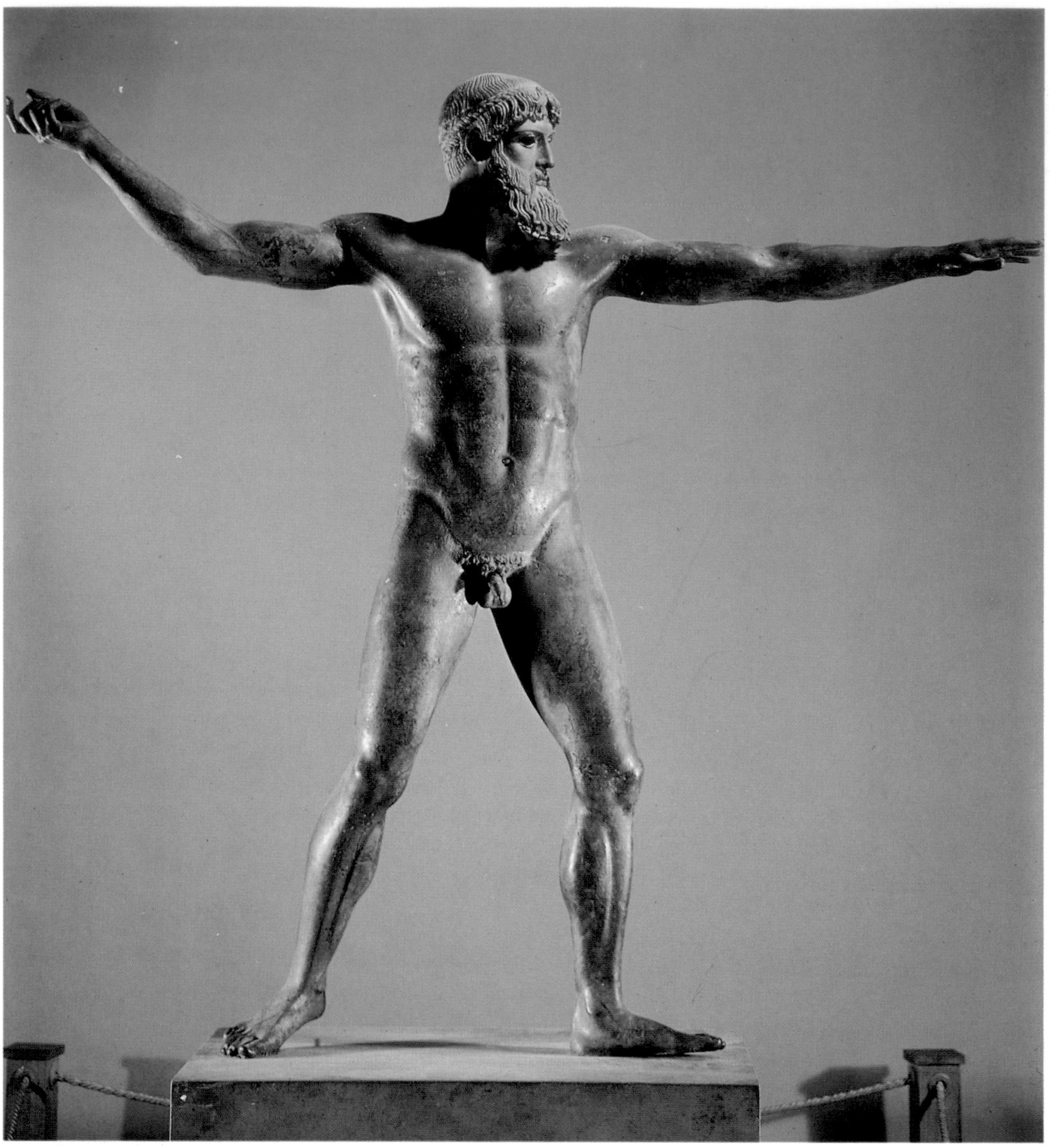

5-48. *Zeus*. c. 460–450 B.C. Bronze, height 6'10" (2.08 m). National Archaeological Museum, Athens

Large, freestanding statues in motion are the most important achievement of the Severe style. The finest figure of this kind was recovered from the sea near the coast of Greece (fig. 5-48): a magnificent nude bronze, almost seven feet tall, of Zeus throwing a thunderbolt. Here, stability in the midst of action becomes outright grandeur. The pose is that of an athlete, yet it is not so much the arrested phase of a continuous succession of movements as an awe-inspiring gesture that reveals the power of the god. Hurling a weapon thus becomes a divine attribute here, rather than a specific act aimed at a particular adversary.

Some years after the *Zeus,* about 450 B.C., Myron created his bronze statue of the *Diskobolos (Discus Thrower),* which became as famous as the *Doryphoros.* Like the latter, it is known to us only from Roman copies (fig. 5-49). [See Primary Sources, no. 3, pages 194–95.] Here the problem of how to condense a sequence of movements into a single pose without freezing it is a much more complex one. It involves a violent twist of the torso in order to bring the arms into the same plane as the action of the legs. The pose conveys the essence of the action by presenting the coiled figure in perfect balance. (The copy makes the design seem harsher and less poised than it must have been in the original.)

THE CLASSICAL STYLE. The *Diskobolos* brings us to the second half of the century, the era of the mature Classical style. The conquest of movement in a freestanding statue had a liberating effect on pedimental sculpture, which gained a new fluidity and balance. The *Dying Niobid* (fig. 5-50), a work of the 440s B.C., is so three-dimensional that we hardly suspect she was carved for the pediment of a Doric temple. According to legend, Niobe had humiliated the mother of Apollo and Artemis by boasting of her own seven sons and seven daughters. In revenge, the two gods killed all of Niobe's children. Our *Niobid* ("child of Niobe") has been shot in the back while running. Her strength broken, she sinks to the ground while trying to extract the fatal arrow. The violent movement of her arms has made her garment slip off. Her nudity is thus a dramatic device, rather than a necessary part of the story.

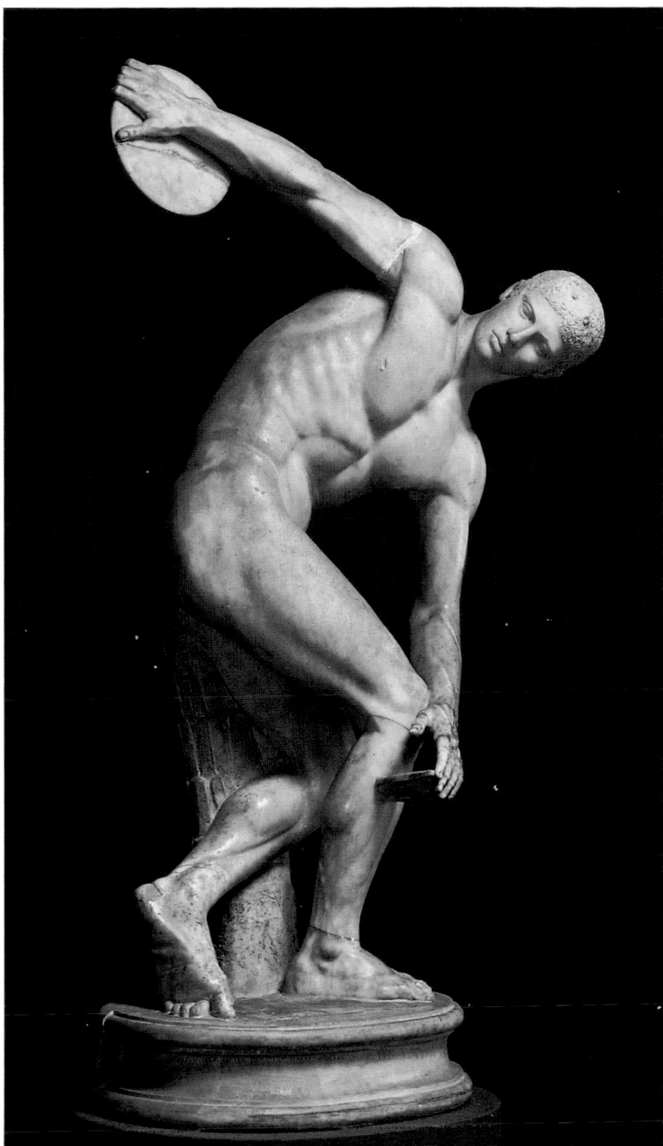

5-49. *Diskobolos (Discus Thrower).*
Roman marble copy after a bronze original of c. 450 B.C.
by Myron. Lifesize. Museo delle Terme, Rome

The *Niobid* is the earliest known large female nude in Greek art. The artist's main goal was to display a beautiful female body in the kind of strenuous action that previously had been reserved for the male nude. Still, we must not misread the intent. It was not a detached interest in the physical aspect of the event alone but the desire to unite motion and emotion and thus to make the beholder experience the suffering of this victim of a cruel fate. In the *Niobid,* human feeling is for the first time expressed as eloquently in the features as in the rest of the figure.

A brief glance at the wounded warrior from Aegina (see fig. 5-22) will show us how differently the agony of death had been conceived only half a century before. What separates the *Niobid* from the world of Archaic art is summed up in the Greek word *pathos.* Pathos means suffering, but particularly suffering conveyed with nobility and restraint, so that it touches rather than horrifies us. Late Archaic art may approach it now and then, as in the Eos and Memnon group (see fig. 5-8). Yet the full force of pathos can be felt only in Classical works such as the *Niobid.*

To measure the astonishing development of Greek sculpture in less than two centuries, let us compare the *Niobid* with the Gorgon from Corfu (see fig. 5-16). In doing so, we realize that these two works, worlds apart as they may be, do in fact belong to the same artistic tradition. The *Niobid,* too, shows the pinwheel stance, even though its meaning is vastly different. Once we recognize the ancient origin of her pose, we understand why the *Niobid,* despite her suffering, remains so monumentally self-contained.

THE PARTHENON. The largest, as well as the greatest, group of Classical sculptures that has come down to us consists of the remains of the marble decoration of the Parthenon. Unfortunately, many of these works are in battered and fragmentary condition. Much of the sculpture was removed between 1801 and 1803 by Lord Elgin; the Elgin Marbles are today housed in the British Museum. The centers of both pediments are gone, and of the figures in the corners only those from the east pediment are well enough preserved to convey something of the quality of the whole. They represent various deities, most in sitting or reclining poses, witnessing the birth of Athena from the head of Zeus (figs. 5-51

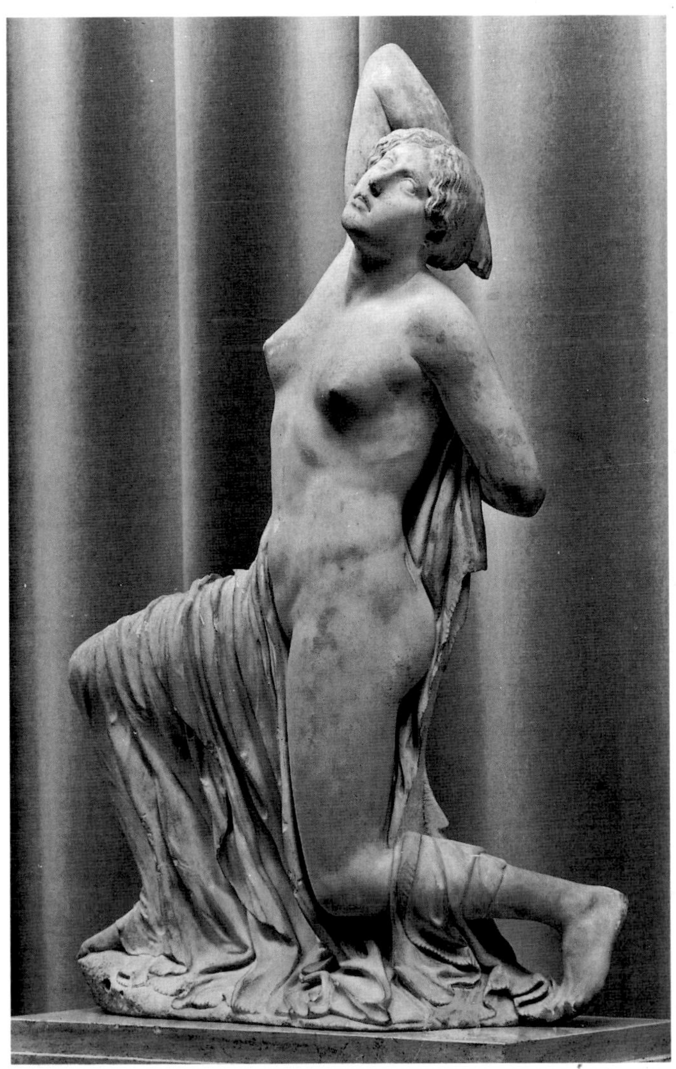

5-50. *Dying Niobid.* c. 450–440 B.C.
Marble, height 59" (150 cm). Museo delle Terme, Rome

(RIGHT) 5-51. *Dionysos,* from the east pediment of the Parthenon. c. 438–432 B.C. Marble, over-lifesize. The British Museum, London

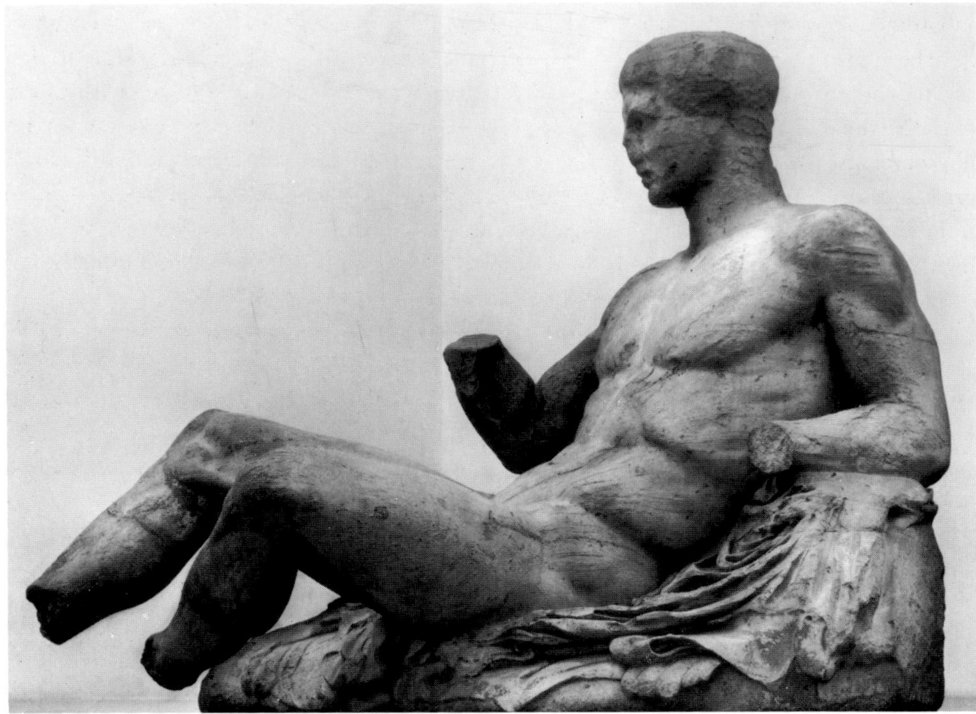

(BELOW) 5-52. *Three Goddesses,* from the east pediment of the Parthenon. c. 438–432 B.C. Marble, over-lifesize. The British Museum, London

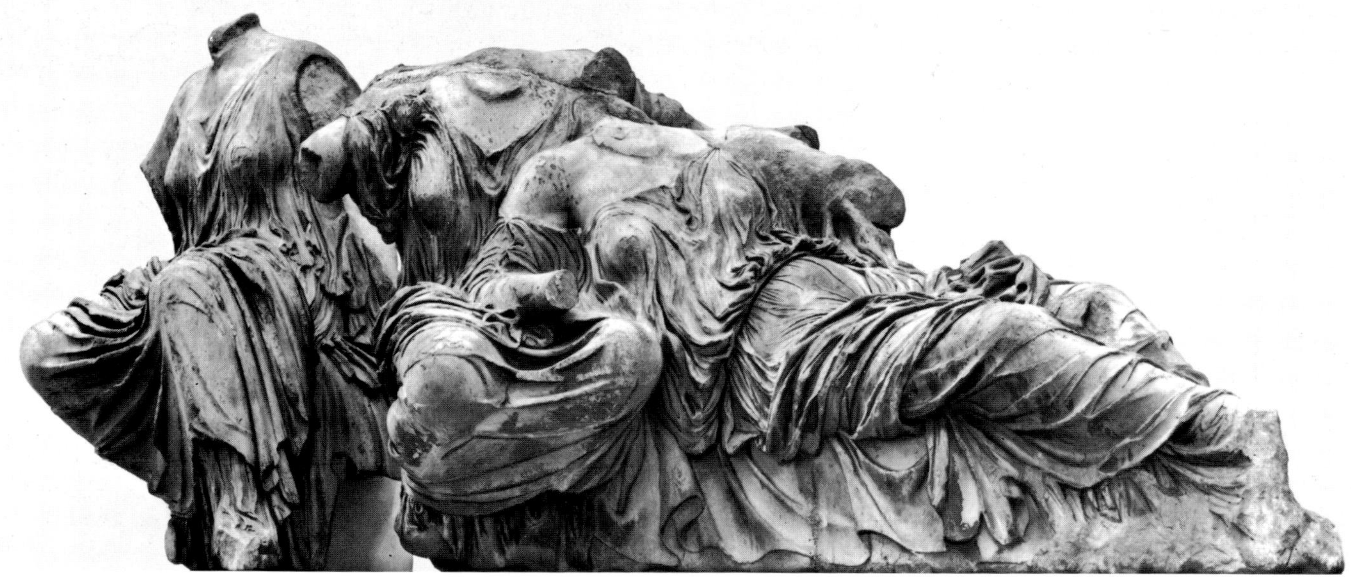

and 5-52). (The west pediment portrayed the struggle of Athena and Poseidon for Athens.)

Here, even more than in the case of the *Dying Niobid,* we marvel at the ease of movement of these statues, even in repose. There is neither violence nor pathos in them, indeed, no specific action of any kind, only a deeply felt poetry of being. We find it equally in the relaxed masculine body of Dionysos and in the soft fullness of the three goddesses, enveloped in thin drapery that seems to share the qualities of a liquid substance as it flows around the forms underneath. Though all are seated or half-reclining, the turning of the bodies under the folds of their costumes makes them seem anything but static. Indeed, the "wet" drapery unites them in one continuous action, so that they seem to be in the process of arising.

The figures are so freely conceived in depth that they create their own space. It is hard to imagine them "shelved" upon the pediment. Evidently the great master who achieved such lifelike figures also found this idea incongruous, for the composition as a whole (fig. 5-53) treats the triangular field as a purely physical limit. For example, two horses' heads are placed in the sharp angles at the corners, at the feet of Dionysos and the reclining goddesses. They represent the chariots of the sun and the moon—one emerging into the pedimental space and the other dipping below it. But visually the heads are merely two fragments cut off by the frame. Clearly, we are approaching a time when the pediment will no longer be the focal point of Greek architectural sculpture. In fact, the sculptural decoration of later buildings tends to be placed in areas where it would seem less boxed in, as well as more visible.

The frieze of the Parthenon, a continuous band 525 feet in length (see fig. 5-31), is of the same high quality as the pedimental sculptures. In a somewhat different way it, too, suffered from its subordination to its setting. Placed just below the ceiling, it must have been poorly lit and difficult to see. The depth of the carving and the concept of relief are not radically different from the frieze of the Siphnian Treasury (see figs. 5-19 and 5-20). However, the illusion of space and of rounded form is now achieved with the greatest ease. The most noteworthy aspect of the Parthenon frieze is the rhythmic grace of the design, especially the spirited movement of the groups of horsemen (fig. 5-54).

The frieze is widely believed to depict a Panathenaic procession. Such events were held annually, with a greater one every four years, to honor Athena in the presence of the other Olympic gods. Although the figures and their groupings are typical of the participants in these processions, the account is an idealized one, unified thematically rather than in time and place. In addition, it has been argued that this is a "heroicized" representation that honors the 192 Athenians slain at the Battle of Marathon. This argument is based on the grounds that the frieze originally had a like number of equestrian figures, although it cannot be proven. Their sacrifice was honored by the original Parthenon, which was begun soon after the battle but was burned by the Persians in 480 B.C. The battle was the subject of a famous painting by Polygnotos of Thasos in the Athenian stoa (see page 122), as well as one in the pinakotheke at the entrance to the Akropolis itself (see fig. 5-34).

The most problematic aspect of the relief is the detail in figure 5-55. According to one recent theory, this scene depicts not the folding of the new peplos for the Archaic statue of Athena but the sacrifice by King Erechtheus of his three daughters. Their death was demanded by the oracle at Delphi, in order to save Athens from its enemies, though Erechtheus himself was to perish during his victory over Eumolpos, the son of Poseidon. The subject would have been especially significant to the city following its victory over the Persians, who had desecrated the old Temple of Athena.

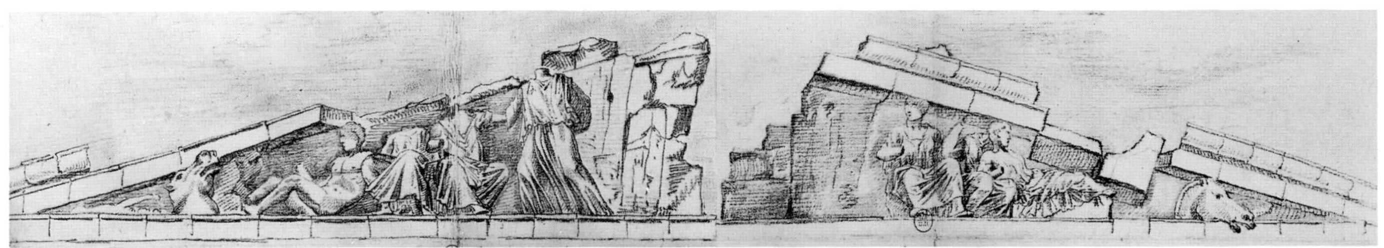

5-53. Jacques Carrey. Drawings of the east pediment of the Parthenon. 1674. Bibliothèque Nationale, Paris

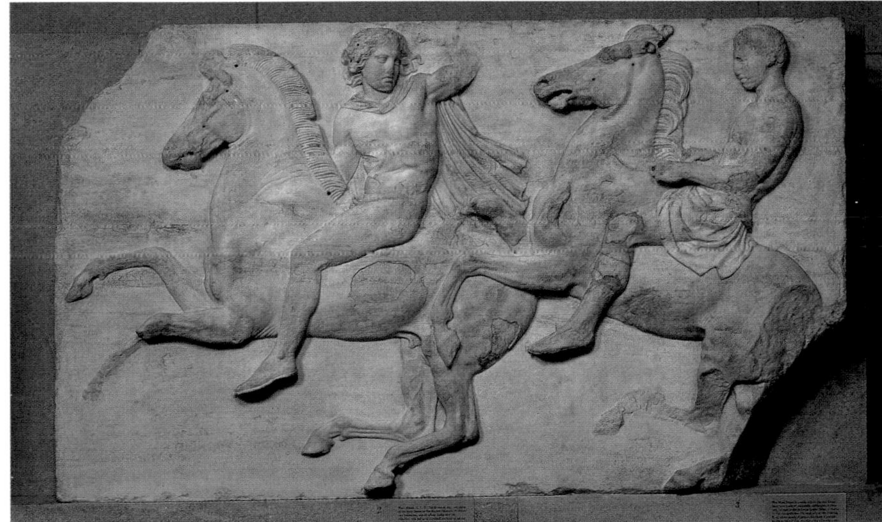

5-54. *Horsemen,* from the west frieze of the Parthenon. c. 488–32 B.C. Marble, height 43" (109.3 cm). The British Museum, London

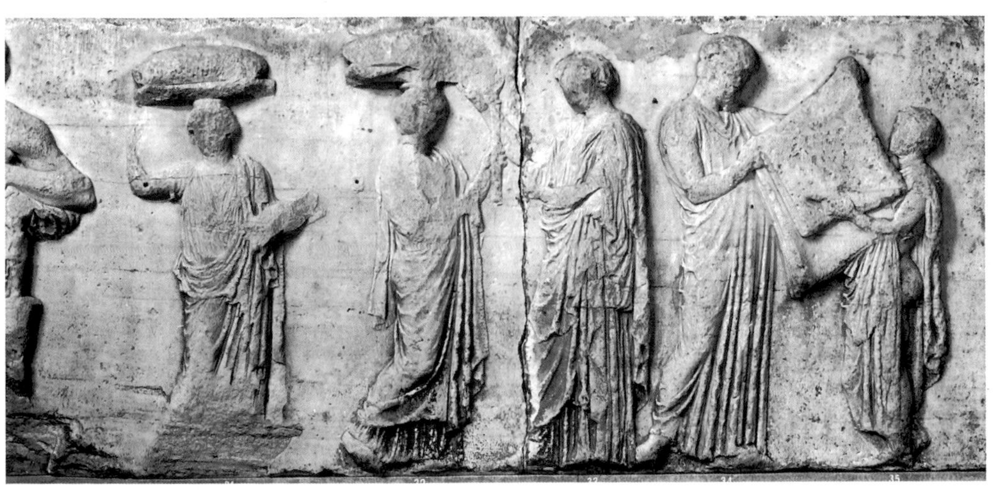

5-55. *The Sacrifice of King Erechtheus' Daughters,* from the east frieze of the Parthenon. c. 440 B.C. Marble, height 43" (109.3 cm). The British Museum, London

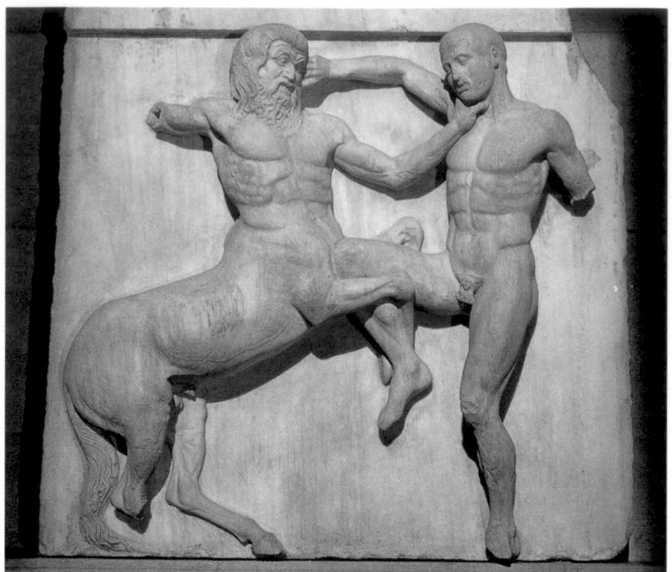

5-56. *Lapith and Centaur,* metope from the south side of the Parthenon. c. 440 B.C. Marble, height 56" (142.2 cm). The British Museum, London

This theory, which is highly controversial, hinges in part on whether the younger figure to the right is indeed a girl instead of a boy, as some have suggested. Yet it has the advantage of integrating the frieze into the rest of the design of the Parthenon, and the Akropolis as a whole. Each of these three options is tempting, yet none accounts for every element. It is even possible that all three played a role. The issue, which may never be fully resolved, is typical of the problems that confront scholars in even the most familiar monuments.

The metopes, which date from the 440s B.C., are very different from the rest of the sculpture on the Parthenon because they show violent action. We have met two of the subjects before: the combat of the gods and giants and the battle of Lapiths and Centaurs (see figs. 5-20 and 5-46). It is the other two subjects that provide the key to their meaning. They are the Sack of Troy by the Greeks, and Greeks fighting Amazons, who, according to legend, had once desecrated the Akropolis. The entire cycle forms an allegory of the Athenian victory over the Persians, who likewise had destroyed the Akropolis. But rather than presenting the war as historical fact, the Greek artist cloaked it in the guise of myth and legend in order to explain the outcome, as if it had been preordained.

The metopes vary in quality and do not form a fully coherent program. However, the best of them, such as our scene of a Lapith fighting a Centaur (fig. 5-56), have a dramatic force that is still grounded in the pediment at Olympia of almost 20 years earlier (see fig. 5-46). The sculptor has been remarkably successful in overcoming the obstacles presented by the metope. Because it was placed high above the ground, where it could barely be seen, the figures fill as much of the field as possible and are carved deeply so as to appear nearly in the round. Although the action seems somewhat forced in both pose and expression, it has been beautifully choreographed for maximum clarity and impact.

PHEIDIAS. These sculptures have long been associated with the name of Pheidias who, according to Plutarch, was the chief overseer of all the artistic projects sponsored by Perikles. [See Primary Sources, no. 5, page 196.] According to ancient writers, Pheidias was famous for a huge ivory-and-gold statue of Athena that he made for the cella of the Parthenon. He was also celebrated for a colossal figure of Zeus in the same technique for the temple of that god in Olympia, and for an equally large bronze statue of Athena that stood on the Akropolis facing the Propylaea. None of these works survives, and small-scale copies made in later times cannot convey the artist's style. It is hard to imagine that immense cult images of this sort, burdened with the demands of a difficult technique, shared the vitality of the Elgin Marbles. The admiration they aroused may have been due to their size, the cost of the materials, and the aura of religious awe surrounding them. We therefore know very little about Pheidias' personality. He may have been simply a very able supervisor, but more likely he was a great genius, comparable to Imhotep (see page 46), who could give powerful expression to the ideas of his patron, Perikles.

The term "Pheidian style" used to describe the Parthenon sculptures is little more than a label; undoubtedly, a large number of masters were involved, since the frieze and the two pediments were executed in less than ten years (c. 440–432 B.C.). But while the label is not entirely accurate, it is convenient. The Pheidian ideal was not merely artistic but extended to life itself: it denotes a distinctive attitude in which the gods are aware of, yet aloof from,

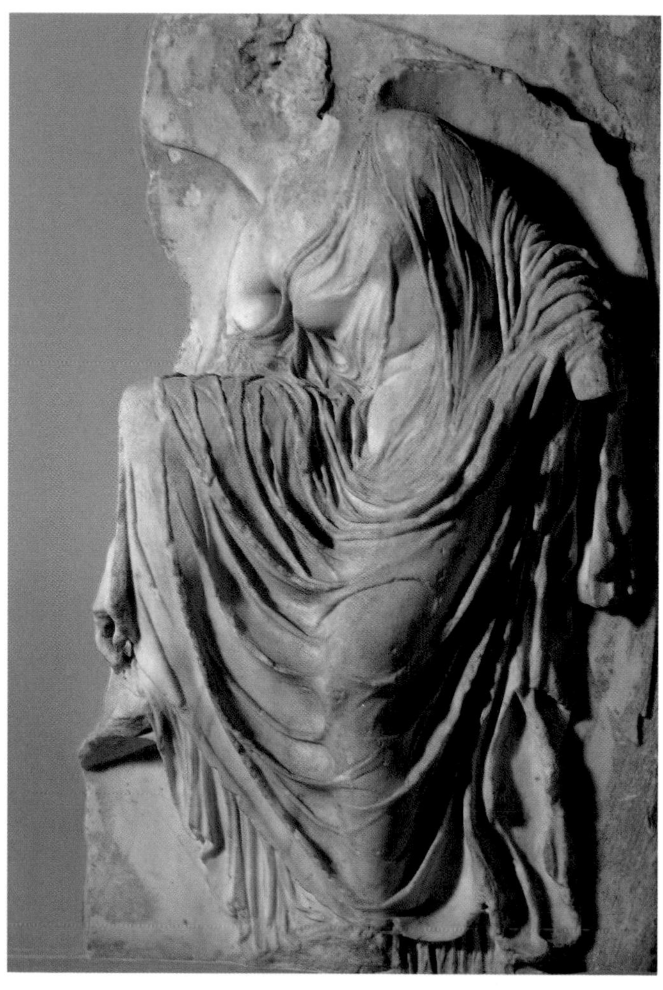

5-57. *Nike,* from the balustrade of the Temple of Athena Nike. c. 410–407 B.C. Marble, height 42" (106.7 cm). Akropolis Museum, Athens

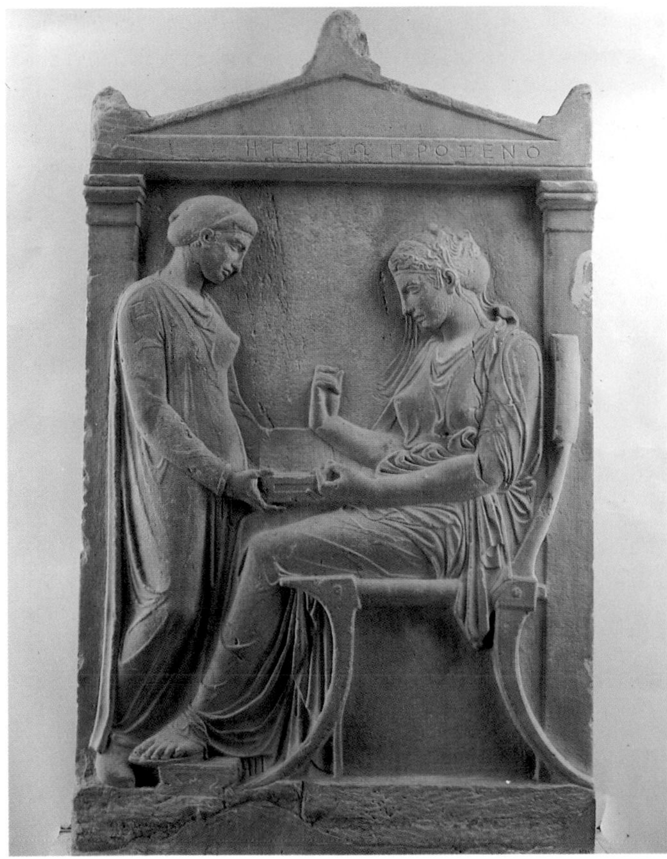

5-58. *Grave Stele of Hegeso.* c. 410–400 B.C. Marble, height 59" (150 cm). National Archaeological Museum, Athens

human affairs as they fulfill their cosmic roles. This outlook came to be widely shared among Greek philosophers, especially in the fourth century B.C.

It is hardly surprising that the Pheidian style should have dominated Athenian sculpture until the end of the fifth century and beyond, even though large-scale sculptural enterprises gradually came to a halt because of the Peloponnesian War. The last of these projects was the balustrade built around the small Temple of Athena Nike about 410–407 B.C. Like the Parthenon frieze, it shows a festive procession, but the participants are winged personifications of victory (*Nike* means victory) rather than citizens of Athens. One Nike (fig. 5-57) is taking off her sandals, in conformity with an age-old tradition, indicating that she is about to step on holy ground (see page 43). Her wings—one open, the other closed—help her keep her balance, so that she performs this normally awkward act with consummate elegance and ease. Her figure is more strongly detached from the relief ground than are those on the Parthenon frieze, and her garments, with their deeply cut folds, cling to her body. We have seen an earlier phase of this "wet" drapery in the *Three Goddesses* of the Parthenon (see fig. 5-52).

Also "Pheidian," and also from the last years of the century, is the beautiful *Grave Stele of Hegeso* (fig. 5-58). Memorials of this kind were produced in large numbers by Athenian sculptors, and their export must have helped to spread the Pheidian style throughout the Greek world. Few of them, however, can match the harmonious design and the gentle melancholy of our example. The deceased is represented in a simple domestic scene that was a standard subject for sculptured and painted memorials of young women. She has picked a necklace from the box held by the girl servant and seems to be contemplating it as if it were a keepsake. The delicacy of the carving can be seen especially well in the forms farthest removed from the viewer, such as the servant's left arm supporting the lid of the jewel box, or the veil behind Hegeso's right shoulder. Here the relief merges with the background, so that the ground appears more like empty space than a solid surface. This novel effect was probably inspired by paintings. Indeed, the subject is similar to those found on white-ground *lekythoi* (oil jugs) of the same period (see fig. 5-61).

CLASSICAL PAINTING

Written sources tell us a great deal about how Classical painting evolved, but rarely in enough detail for us to know what it looked like. The great age of Greek painting began in the Early Classical period with Polygnotos of Thasos and his collaborator, Mikon of Athens, who were sculptors as well. Polygnotos was the first artist to place figures at various heights in a landscape setting and to depict women in transparent drapery. But, above all, he introduced the "representation of emotion and character [and the] use of patterns of composition," which became as central to Classical painting as it was to sculpture. A major advance came a hundred years later with the invention of shading by Apollodoros of Athens.

Painting reached its peak in the fourth century B.C., when it was recognized as one of the liberal arts. During this period, numerous rival schools emerged as panel painting replaced wall

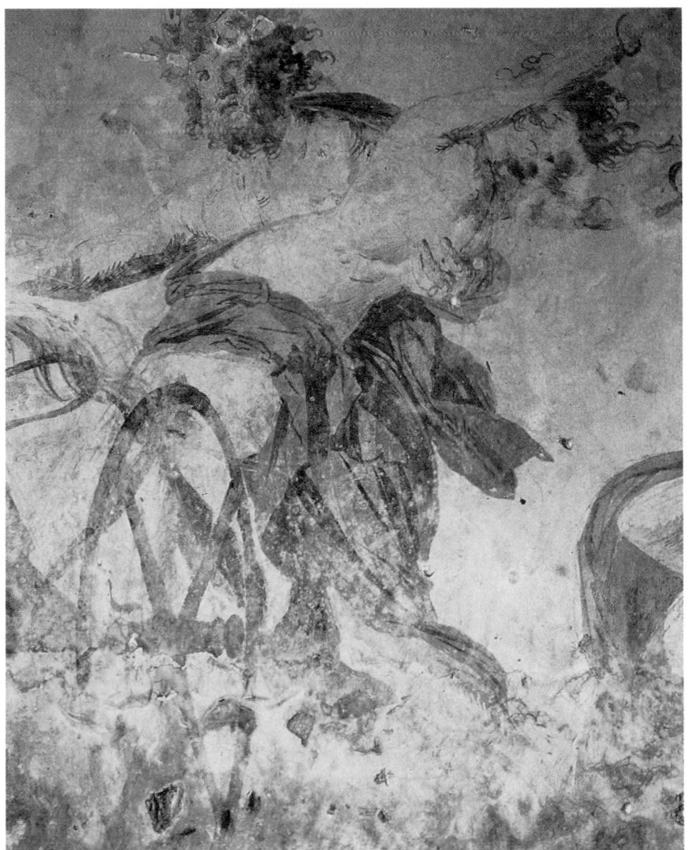

5-59. *The Abduction of Proserpine.* Detail of a wall painting in Tomb I, Vergina, Macedonia. c. 340–330 B.C.

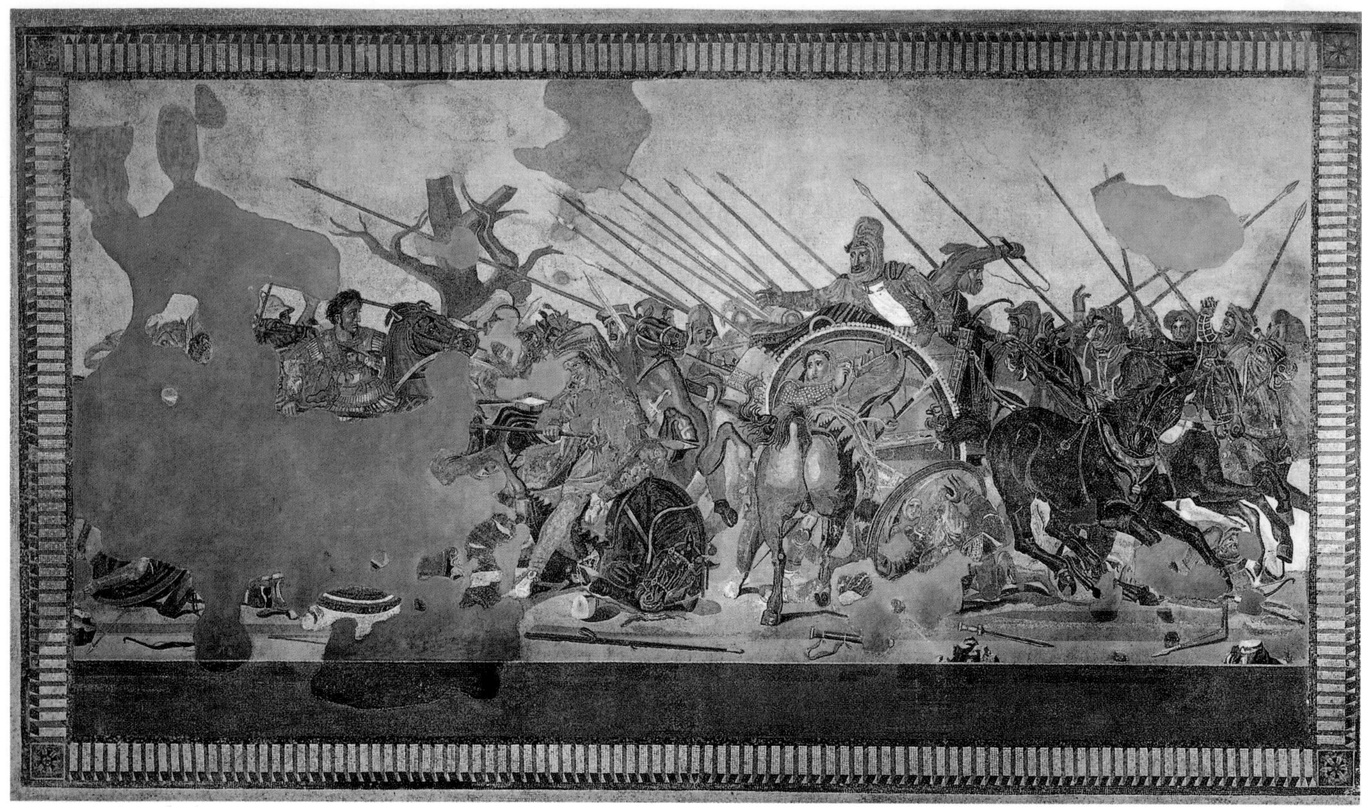

5-60. *The Battle of Issos* or *Battle of Alexander and the Persians*. Mosaic copy from Pompeii of a Hellenistic painting of c. 315 B.C. 8'11" x 16'9½" (2.7 x 5.1 m). Museo Archeologico Nazionale, Naples

painting. Among the leading artists mentioned by the Roman writer Pliny the Elder are Zeuxis of Herakleia, a master of texture, and Parrhasios of Ephesos, who "first gave proportion to painting . . . and was supreme in painting contour lines, which is the most subtle aspect of painting." Pliny also mentions Apelles of Kos, Alexander the Great's favorite artist and the most famous painter of his day, celebrated for his grace; and Nikomachos of Athens, renowned for his rapid brush. [See Primary Sources, no. 3, page 193.]

We get a tantalizing glimpse of Classical painting in *The Abduction of Proserpine* (fig. 5-59). This painting comes from one of several Macedonian tombs, including that of Phillip II, at Vergina, of about 340–330 B.C. Discovered only in 1976, these tombs are of great importance for containing the only Greek wall paintings to come to light. The subject is appropriate to the funereal setting. Proserpine, goddess of vegetation, was abducted by Hades, ruler of the underworld, to be his queen. Thanks to Zeus' intervention, however, she was allowed to return to earth for six months of every year. The painting may well be based on a famous work by Nikomachos of Athens. The forceful expressiveness more than makes up for any technical deficiencies of the artist, who clearly was not of the first rank: the scene has a magnificent sweep that captures the frenzy of the moment. The technique reflects the main tradition of Greek painting, which gave primacy to line, although there was also a competing tendency that emphasized color.

We can get some further idea of what Greek wall painting looked like from Roman copies and imitations, although their relation is problematic (see pages 187–91). According to Pliny, at the end of the fourth century Philoxenos of Eretria painted the victory of Alexander the Great over Darius III at Issos. The same subject—or another battle of Alexander's war against the Persians—is shown in an exceptionally large and technically skilled floor mosaic from a Pompeian house of about 100 B.C. (fig. 5-60). This mosaic depicts Darius and the fleeing Persians on the right and, in the badly damaged left-hand portion, the figure of Alexander.

While there is no special reason to link this mosaic with Pliny's account (several others are recorded), we can hardly doubt that it is an excellent copy of a Hellenistic painting from the late fourth century B.C. The picture follows the four-color scheme (yellow, red, black, and white) that is known to have been widely used at that time. [See Primary Sources, no. 3, page 193.] The crowding, the air of frantic excitement, the powerfully modeled and foreshortened forms, and the precise shadows make the scene far more complicated and dramatic than any other work of Greek art from the period. And for the first time it shows something that actually happened, without the symbolic overtones of the *Battle of the Lapiths and Centaurs* (see figs. 5-6 and 5-46). In character and even in appearance, it is close to Roman reliefs commemorating specific historic events (see figs. 7-35–7-37). Yet there can be little doubt that the mosaic was created by a Greek, as this technique originated in Hellenistic times and remained a specialty of Greek artists to the end.

According to literary sources, Greek painters of the Classical period made a breakthrough in mastering illusionistic space. [See

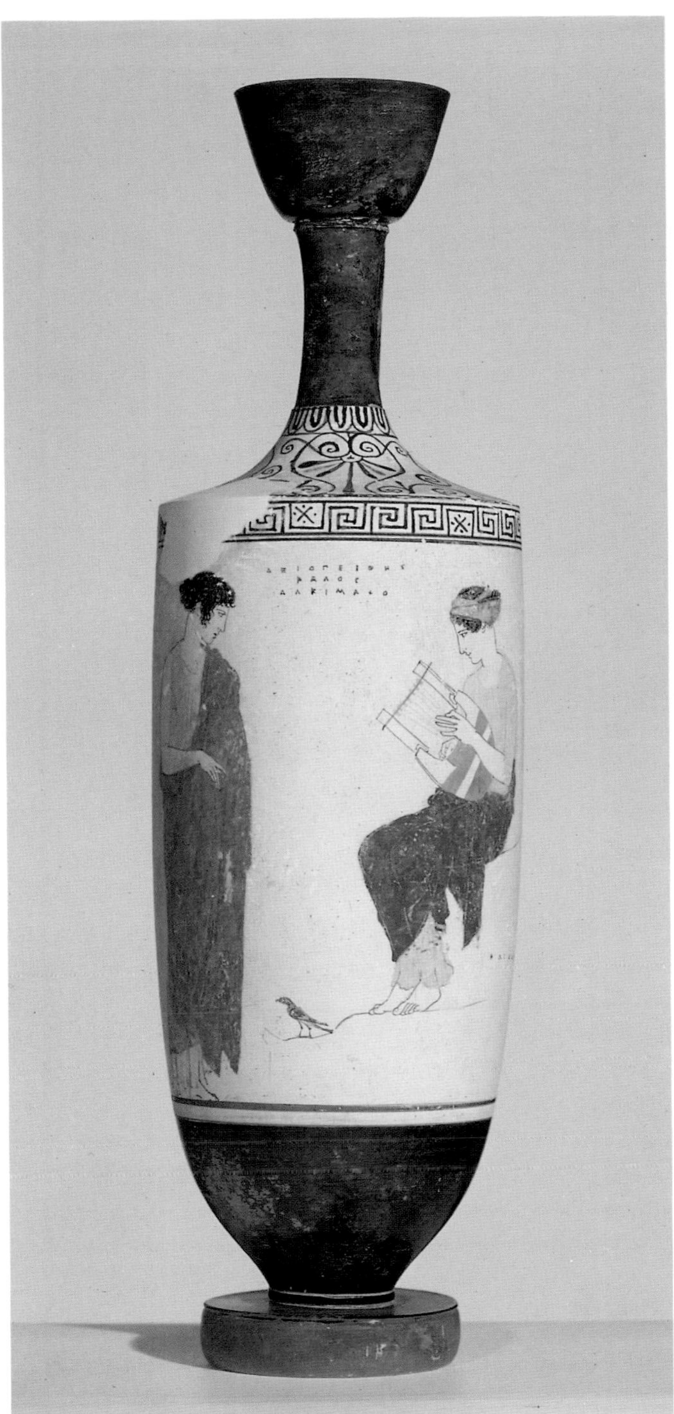

5-61. The Achilles Painter. *Muse and Maiden,* on an Attic white-ground lekythos. c. 440–430 B.C. Height 16" (40.7 cm). Staatliche Antikensammlungen, Munich

Primary Sources, no. 3, page 193, and no. 6, pages 196–97.] This claim is supported in part by murals found in Macedonia. By its very nature, vase painting was limited in its ability to make use of the new concept of pictorial space. Still, there are some exceptions to this rule. We find them mostly in the lekythoi (oil jugs) used as funerary offerings. These had a white coating on which painters could draw as freely and with the same spatial effect as if they were using pen and paper. The white ground is treated as empty space from which the forms seem to emerge—if the draftsman knows how to achieve this effect.

Only a few lekythos painters were able to create this illusion. Foremost among them is the unknown artist, nicknamed the Achilles Painter, who drew the woman in figure 5-61. Although some 25 years older than the Hegeso stele, this vase shows a similar scene. There is the same mood of "Pheidian" reverie, as a woman (perhaps a poetess seeking inspiration) listens to the muse playing her lyre on Mount Helikon, accompanied by a nightingale. Our chief interest, however, is in the masterly draftsmanship. With a few lines, sure, fresh, and fluid, the artist not only creates a three-dimensional figure but reveals the body beneath the drapery as well. What persuades us that these shapes exist in depth rather than merely on the surface of the vase? First of all, the use of foreshortening. But the "internal dynamics" of the lines are equally important. Their swelling and fading make some contours stand out while others merge with one another or disappear into the white ground. The effect is completed by the color, which is unusually elaborate for a lekythos: vermilion for the himations and the muse's head scarf, ocher for her chiton. The artist has made skillful use of the white ground to enliven the "empty" space by adding an inscription: "Axiopeithes, the son of Alkimachos, is beautiful."

In view of its artistic advantages, we might expect wider use of the white-ground technique. Such, however, was not the case. Instead, from the mid-fifth century on, the impact of monumental painting gradually transformed vase painting as a whole into a satellite art. Vase painters tried to reproduce large-scale compositions in a kind of shorthand dictated by their limited technique. The result, more often than not, was spotty and overcrowded.

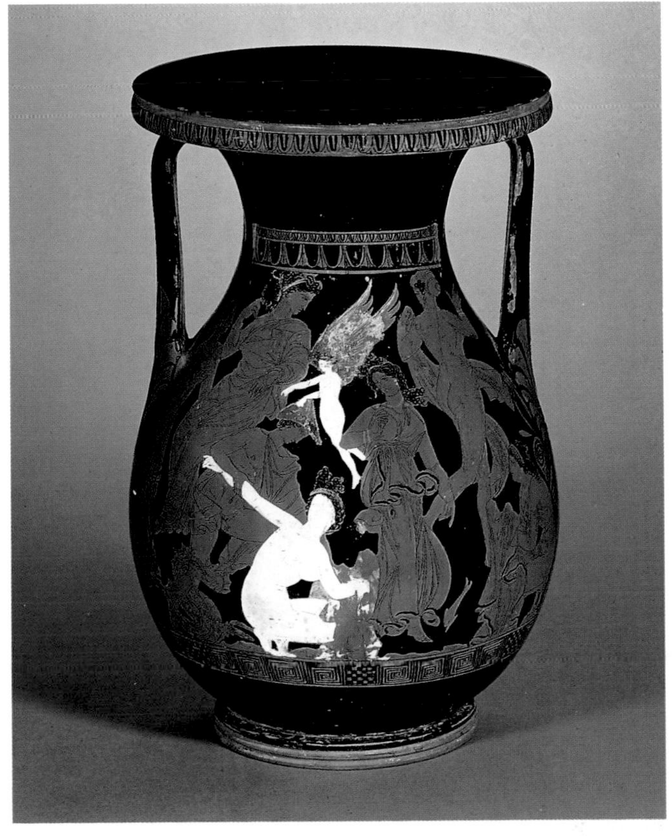

5-62. The Marsyas Painter. *Peleus and Thetis,* on a Kerch-style pelike. c. 340 B.C. Height 16 3/4" (42.5 cm). The British Museum, London

Even the finest examples suffer from this defect, as we can see in figure 5-62. This vase was produced near the end of the Classical period by an Athenian master known as the Marsyas Painter. It shows Thetis, who is about to bathe in the sea, being abducted by Peleus as two of her maids flee in panic. The main figures are placed on a firm ground-line, with a bit of wavy water to suggest the spatial setting. The others, intended to be farther away, seem to be suspended in midair. Although the turning poses also try to create the illusion of space, the effect remains flat and silhouette-like because of the black background.

In an attempt to enlarge the color range, the body of Thetis has been painted white, as has that of Eros crowning Peleus. (Thetis' dress has been filled in with green as well.) However, the medium does not permit shading or modeling. Our artist must therefore rely on the network of lines to hold the scene together and create maximum excitement. And, being a good draftsman, he almost succeeds. Still, it is a success at second hand, for the composition must have been inspired by a mural or panel picture. The Marsyas Painter is, as it were, fighting for a lost cause. In effect, we have reached the end of Greek vase painting, which disappeared altogether by the end of the century.

5-63. Reconstruction drawing of the Mausoleum at Halikarnassos. 359–351 B.C.

FOURTH-CENTURY SCULPTURE

This Athenian style, so harmonious in both feeling and form, did not long survive the defeat of Athens by Sparta in the Peloponnesian War. Building and sculpture continued in the same tradition for another three centuries, but without the subtleties of the Classical age. Unfortunately, there is no single word, like Archaic or Classical, that we can use to designate this third and final phase in the development of Greek art, which lasted from about 400 to the first century B.C. The 75-year span between the end of the Peloponnesian War and the rise of Alexander the Great used to be called "Late Classical." The remaining two centuries and a half were labeled "Hellenistic," a term that was meant to convey the spread of Greek civilization southeastward to Asia Minor and Mesopotamia, Egypt, and the borders of India. It was natural to expect that the conquests of Alexander between 333 and 323 B.C. would bring about an artistic revolution. However, the history of style is not always in tune with political history. Although the center of Greek thought shifted to Alexandria, the city founded by Alexander in Egypt shortly before his death, there was no decisive break in the tradition of Greek art at the end of the fourth century. The art of the Hellenistic era is the direct outgrowth of developments that occurred, not at the time of Alexander, but during the preceding 50 years.

Here, then, is our dilemma: "Hellenistic" is a concept so closely linked with the political and cultural effects of Alexander's conquests that we cannot extend it backward to the early fourth century. This is so even though there is wide agreement that the art of the years 400 to 325 B.C. can be understood far better if we view it as pre-Hellenistic rather than as Late Classical. But until the right word is found and becomes widely accepted, we shall have to make do with the existing terms, always keeping in mind the continuity of the third phase that we are about to examine.

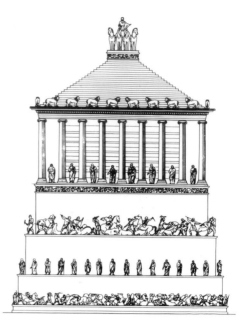

THE MAUSOLEUM AT HALIKARNASSOS. The contrast between Classical and pre-Hellenistic is readily seen in the only project of the fourth century that equals the Parthenon in size and ambition. It is not a temple but a huge tomb—so huge, in fact, that its name, Mausoleum, has come to be used for all oversized funerary monuments. Designed by Pytheos of Priene, it was built at Halikarnassos in Asia Minor just before and after 360 B.C. by Mausolos, satrap of the Persians, and his widow, Artemisia. The structure itself has been destroyed, but its dimensions and appearance can be reconstructed on the basis of ancient descriptions and the remaining fragments, which include a good deal of sculpture. [See Primary Sources, no. 3, pages 194–95.]

The drawing in figure 5-63 is not exact. We know, however, that the building rose in three stages to a height of about 160 feet. A tall rectangular base 117 feet wide and 82 feet deep supported a colonnade of Ionic columns 40 feet tall. Above this rose a pyramid crowned by an enormous quadriga (four-horse chariot) with statues of Mausolos and Artemisia. The sculpture included two friezes showing Greeks battling Persians and Greeks fighting Amazons, each as long as the Parthenon frieze. Between them was a row of Greek and Persian figures. Along the colonnade were 36 large statues of Mausolos' family, and on the roof was a row of carved guardian lions.

The commemorative character of the monument, based on the idea of life as a glorious struggle or chariot race, is entirely Greek. Yet we immediately notice the un-Greek way in which it has been carried out. The vast size of the tomb and the pyramid form are derived from Egypt. They imply an exaltation of the ruler far beyond ordinary human status. His kinship with the gods may also have been hinted at. Apparently Mausolos took the view of himself as a divinely ordained sovereign from the Persians, who in turn had inherited it from the Assyrians and Egyptians. Howev-

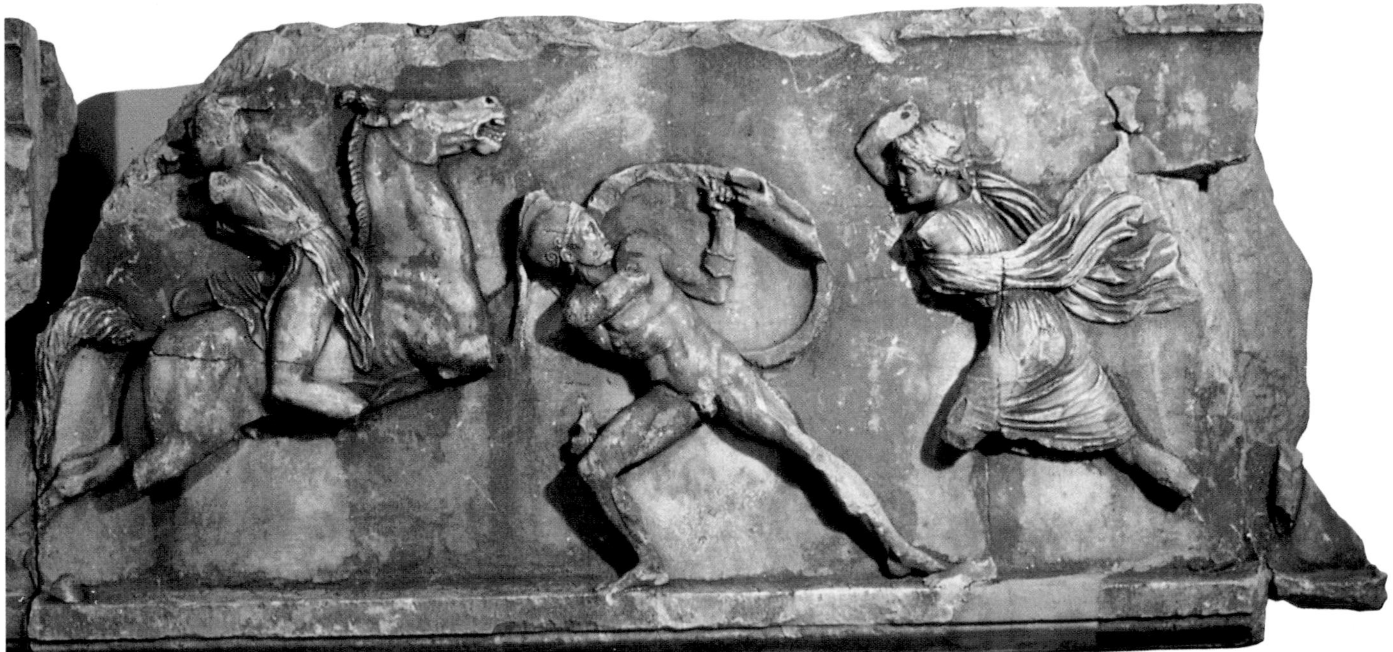

5-64. Skopas (?). *Battle of the Greeks and Amazons,* from the east frieze of the Mausoleum, Halikarnassos. 359–351 B.C. Marble, height 35" (89 cm). The British Museum, London

er, he seems to have wanted to glorify his personality as much as his office. The structure must have struck his contemporaries as impressive and monstrous at the same time, with its multiple friezes and a pyramid instead of pediments above the colonnade.

SKOPAS. According to Pliny, the sculpture on each of the four sides of the monument was done by a different master, chosen from among the best of the time. Bryaxis did the north side, Timotheos the south, Leochares the west, and Skopas, the most famous, the main one on the east. [See Primary Sources, no. 3, pages 194–95.] Skopas' style has been recognized in some parts of the Amazon frieze, such as the portion in figure 5-64. The Parthenon tradition can still be felt here, but there is also an un-Classical violence, physical as well as emotional, that is conveyed through strained movements and passionate expressions. (Deep-set eyes are a hallmark of Skopas' style.) As a result, we no longer find the rhythmic flow of the Parthenon frieze. Continuity and harmony have been sacrificed so that each figure may have greater scope for sweeping, impulsive gestures.

Clearly, if we are to do justice to this explosive, energetic style we must not judge it by Classical standards. What the composition lacks in unity, it more than makes up for in boldness (note, for instance, the Amazon seated backward on her horse) and heightened expressiveness. In a sense, Skopas turned backward as well—to the scenes of violent action that were popular in the Archaic period, such as the Siphnian *Battle of the Gods and Giants* (see fig. 5-20). But he clearly also learned from the example of the Parthenon metopes (see fig. 5-56).

The "pre-Hellenistic" flavor is even more pronounced in one of the statues from the colonnade, sometimes presumed to portray Mausolos himself (fig. 5-65). The figure must be the work of a man younger than Skopas and even less tied to Classical standards, probably Bryaxis, the master of the north side. Through Roman

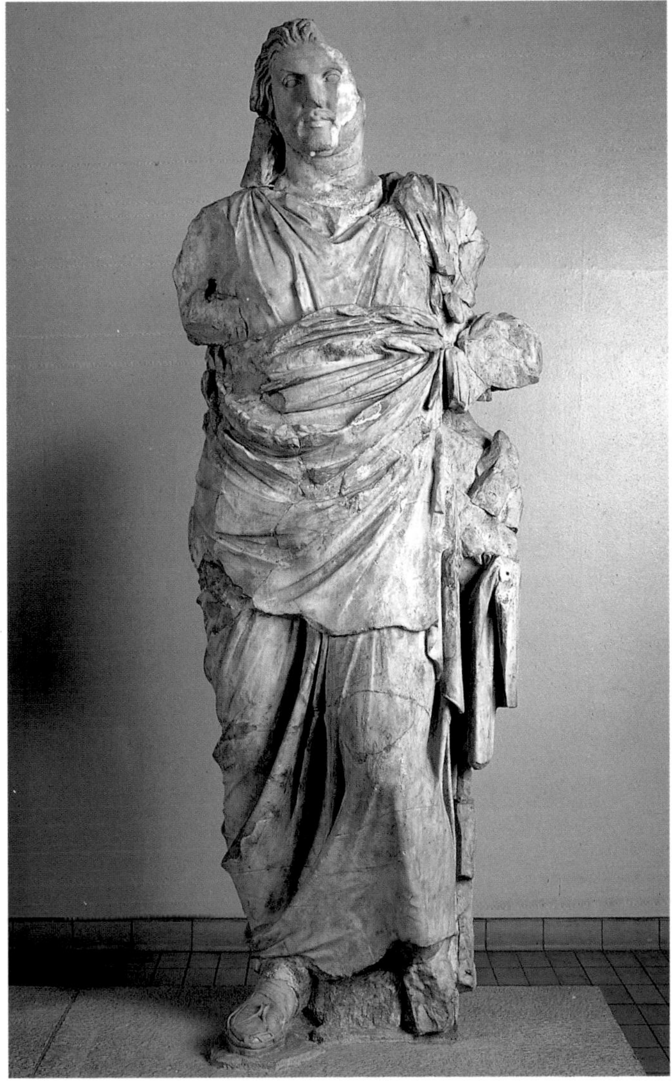

5-65. *"Mausolos,"* from the Mausoleum at Halikarnassos. c. 360 B.C. Marble, height 9'10" (3.1 m). The British Museum, London

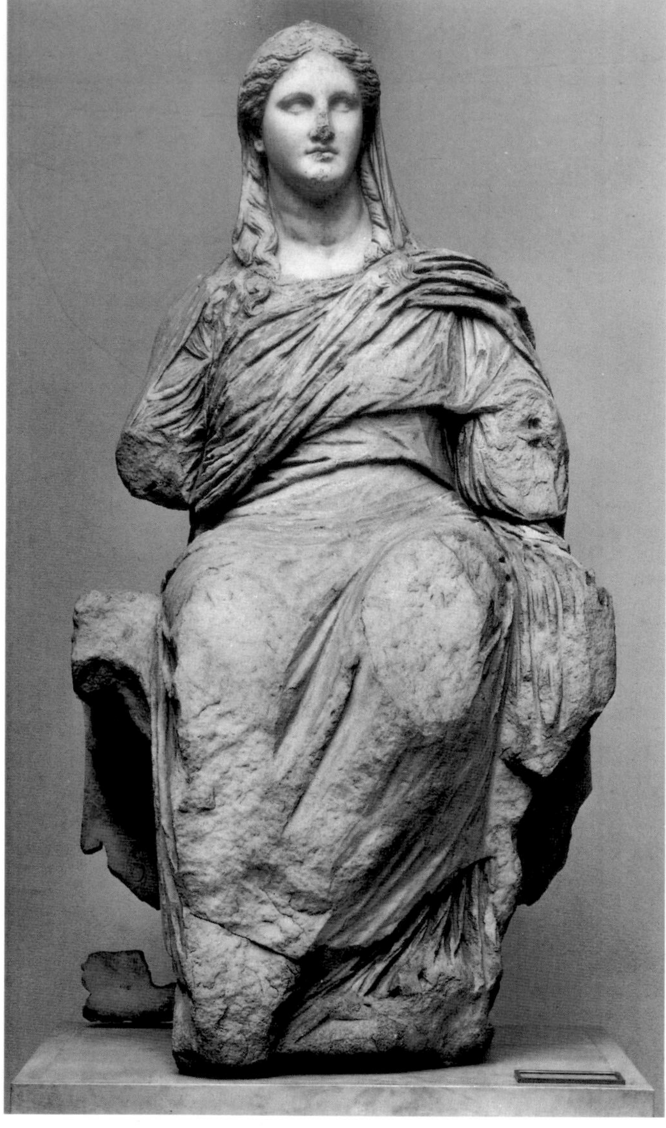

5-66. *Demeter,* from Knidos. c. 330 B.C. Marble, height 60" (152.3 cm). The British Museum, London

copies, we know of some Greek portraits of Classical times, but they seem to represent types rather than individuals. Such is probably the case here. The figure is a distinctly non-Greek sort; not until Hellenistic times would individual likenesses become important. Still, the head has a surprisingly personal character, with its heavy jaws and small, sensuous mouth—features later found in the Hellenistic portrait head from Delos (see fig. 5-77). The thick neck and fleshy body seem equally individual. The massiveness of the forms is emphasized by the stiff-textured drapery, which might be said to encase, rather than merely clothe, the body. The great volumes of folds across the abdomen and below the left arm seem designed for picturesque effect more than for functional clarity.

THE DEMETER OF KNIDOS. Some of the features of the Mausoleum sculpture recur in other important works of the period. Foremost among these is the seated figure of the goddess Demeter from her temple at Knidos (fig. 5-66). Here again the drapery, though more finely textured, has an impressive volume of its own. Motifs such as the S-curve of folds across the chest form a counterpoint to the shape of the body beneath. The deep-set eyes gaze into the distance with an intensity that suggests the influence of Skopas. The modeling of the head, on the other hand, has a softness that points to a different source: Praxiteles, the master of feminine grace and sensuous rendering of flesh.

PRAXITELES. The *Demeter* is probably only slightly later than Praxiteles' most famous statue, an *Aphrodite* of about 340–330 B.C. (fig. 5-67). This work was purchased by the island of Knidos, while a clothed version was acquired, so Pliny tells us, by the people of Kos. [See Primary Sources, no. 3, pages 194–95.] Hence the sculptor who carved the *Demeter* would have had no trouble giving his own work some Praxitelean qualities. Unlike many freestanding Classical Greek sculptures, the *Knidian Aphrodite* was

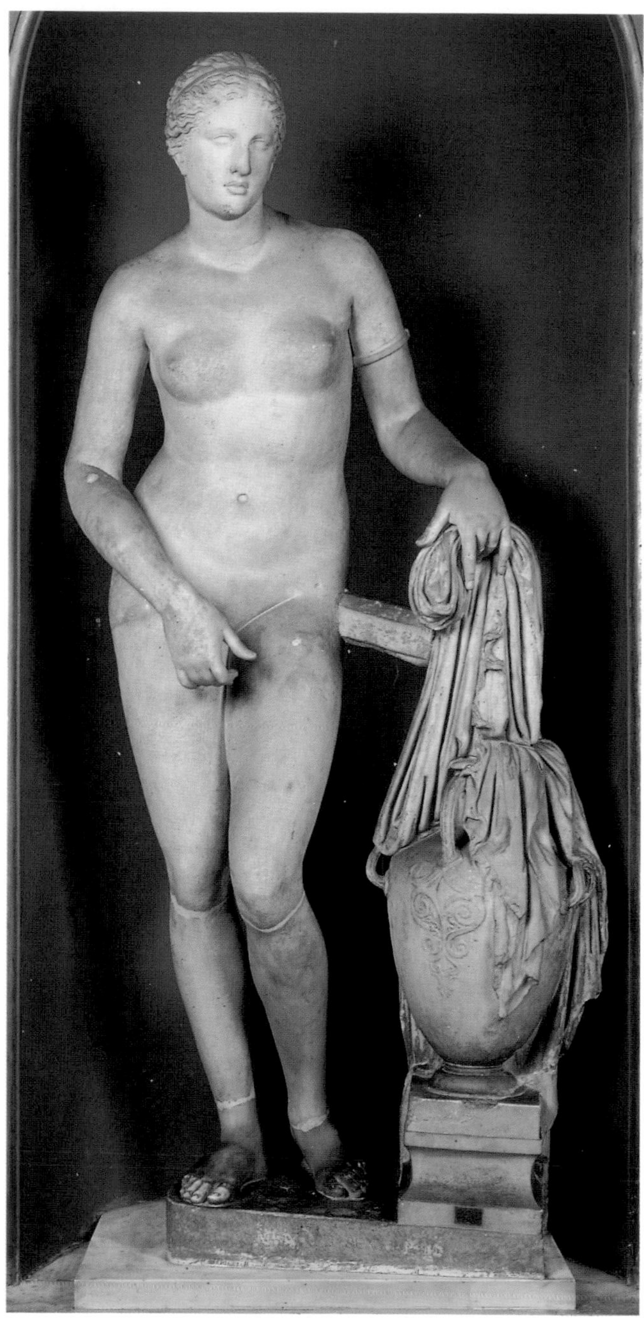

5-67. *Knidian Aphrodite.* Roman copy after an original of c. 340–330 B.C., by Praxiteles. Marble, height 6'8" (2 m). Musei Vaticani, Museo Pio Clementino, Gabinetto delle Maschere, Città del Vaticano, Rome

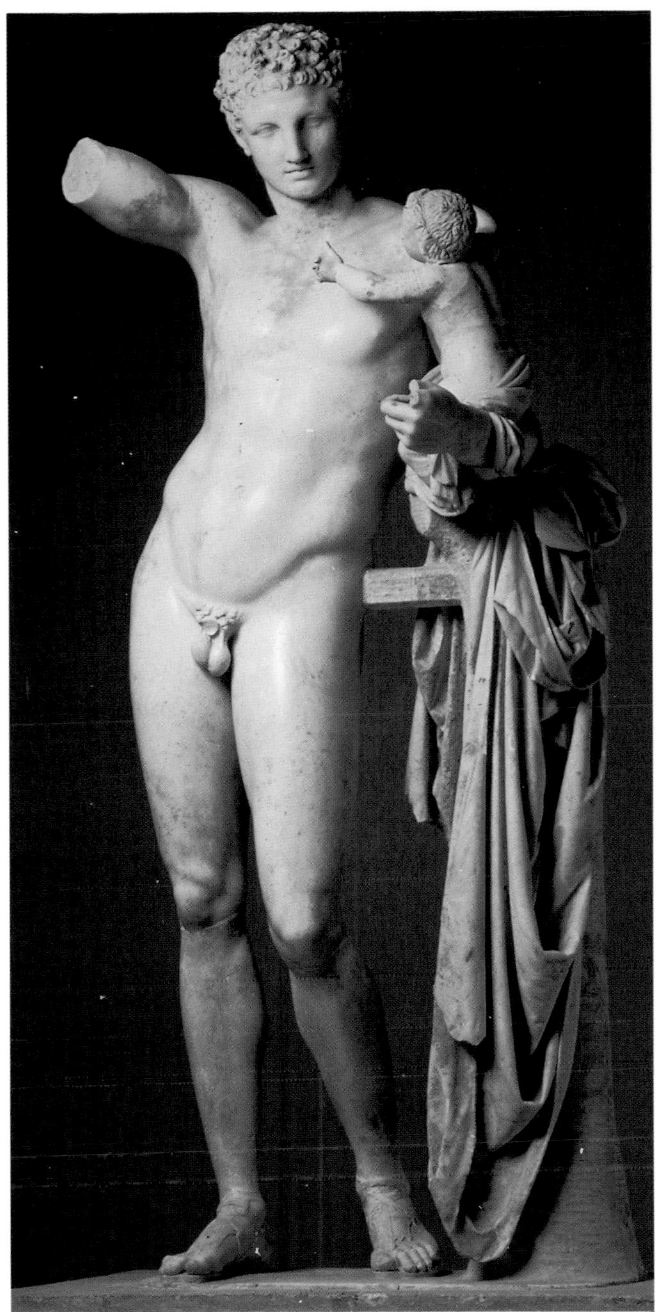

5-68. *Hermes.* Roman copy after an original of c. 320–310 B.C., by Praxiteles. Marble, height 7'1" (2.16 m). Archaeological Museum, Olympia

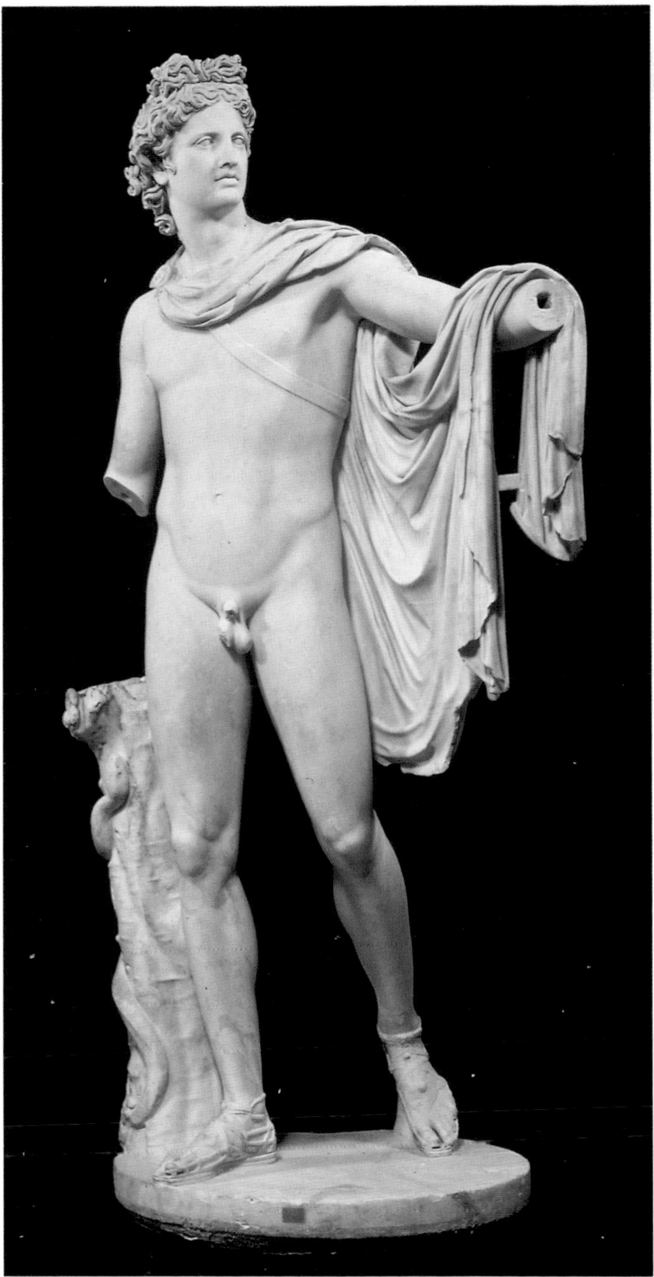

5-69. *Apollo Belvedere.* Roman marble copy, probably of a Greek original of the late 4th century B.C. Height 7'4" (2.3 m). Musei Vaticani, Museo Pio Clementino, Cortile Ottagono, Città del Vaticano, Rome

done in marble, which Praxiteles came to prefer over bronze early in his career. She achieved such fame that she is often referred to in ancient literature as a synonym for perfection. (According to one account, Alexander the Great's mistress, Phryne, posed for the statue.) She was to have countless descendants in Hellenistic and Roman art. To what extent her fame was based on her beauty is difficult to say, for the statue is known to us only through Roman copies that can be no more than pale reflections of the original. Her reputation rested at least as much on the fact that she was (so far as we know) the first completely nude monumental cult statue of a goddess in Greek art. She was placed in an open-air shrine in such a way that the viewer "discovered" her in the midst of bathing; yet through her pose and expression she maintains a chaste modesty so as to disarm any critic.

A more faithful example of Praxitelean beauty is the group of Hermes with the infant Bacchus (fig. 5-68). Pausanias mentions seeing such a statue by Praxiteles at the Temple of Hera at Olympia, where this marble was found in 1877. It is of such high quality that it was long regarded as a late work by Praxiteles. Now, however, most scholars believe it to be a very fine Greek copy of the first century B.C. because of the strut support and unfinished back. The dispute does not matter for us, except perhaps in one respect: it emphasizes the fact that we do not have a single undisputed original work by any of the famous sculptors of Greece. Still, the *Hermes* is the most Praxitelean statue we know. The sensuousness, the lithe proportions, the curve of the torso, the play of gentle curves, the sense of complete relaxation (enhanced by the use of an outside support for the figure to lean against) all agree with the character of the *Knidian Aphrodite.* We also find many refinements here that are usually lost in a copy. These include the caressing treatment of the marble, the faint smile, and the soft, "veiled" modeling of the features. Even the hair, left rough for contrast, shares the silky feel of the rest of the work. Here, for the first time, is an attempt to give a statue a less stony look by creating the illusion of a surrounding atmosphere.

THE APOLLO BELVEDERE. The same qualities recur in many other statues, all of them Roman copies of Greek works in a more or less Praxitelean vein. The best known is the *Apollo Belvedere* (fig. 5-69), sometimes attributed to Leochares. This work was very popular during the eighteenth and nineteenth centuries. The antiquarian Johann Winckelmann, Goethe, and other leaders of the Greek Revival saw it as the perfect exemplar of Classical beauty. Plaster casts or copies of it were found in all museums, art academies, and liberal arts colleges. Generations of students grew up with the belief that it embodied the Greek spirit. This enthusiasm tells us a good deal, not about the qualities of the *Apollo Belvedere* but about the character of the Greek Revival. Our own time takes a less enthusiastic view of the statue.

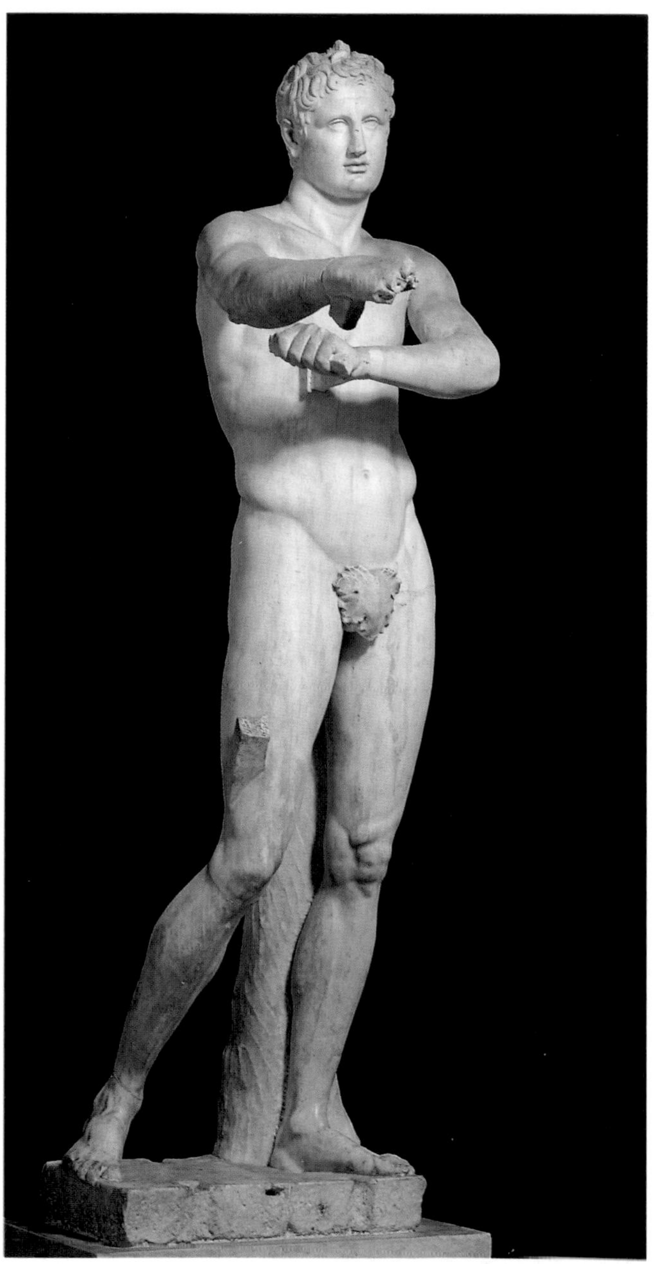

5-70. *Apoxyomenos (Scraper).* Roman marble copy, probably after a bronze original of c. 330 B.C. by Lysippos. Height 6'9" (2.1 m). Musei Vaticani, Museo Pio Clementino, Gabinetto dell'Apoxyomenos, Città del Vaticano, Rome

LYSIPPOS. Besides Skopas and Praxiteles, there is another great name in pre-Hellenistic sculpture: Lysippos. This sculptor's career may have begun as early as about 370 B.C. and continued to the end of the century. The main features of his style, however, are more difficult to grasp than those of his two famous contemporaries because of the contradictory evidence of Roman copies. Ancient authors praised him for replacing the canon of Polykleitos with a new set of proportions that produced a more slender body and a smaller head. [See Primary Sources, no. 3, page 194.] He was famous, too, for his realism: he is said to have had no master other than nature. But these statements describe little more than a general trend toward the end of the fourth century. Certainly the proportions of Praxiteles' statues are "Lysippic" rather than "Polykleitan." Nor could Lysippos have been the only artist of his time to conquer new aspects of reality.

Even in the case of the *Apoxyomenos* (fig. 5-70), the statue most often linked with his name, the evidence is far from conclusive. It shows a young athlete cleaning himself with a scraper, a frequent motif in Greek art from Classical times on. Unlike all other versions, here the arms are extended in front of the body. This bold thrust into space, although it obstructs the view of the torso, is a major feat, whether or not we credit it to Lysippos. It endows the figure with a new capacity for three-dimensional movement. A similar freedom is suggested by the diagonal line of the free leg. Even the unruly hair reflects the new trend toward spontaneity.

HELLENISTIC SCULPTURE

We have no direct evidence of the artistic projects sponsored by Alexander the Great, such as the many portraits of him by Lysippos. In fact, we know very little about the development of Greek sculpture during the first hundred years of the Hellenistic era. Even after that, we have few fixed points of reference. Only a small fraction of the many works that have survived can be firmly identified as to date and place of origin. Moreover, Greek sculpture was now being produced throughout such a vast territory that the interplay of local and international currents must have formed a complex pattern, of which we can trace only some isolated strands.

Hellenistic sculpture is nevertheless quite different from that of the Classical era. It has a more pronounced realism and expressiveness, as well as a greater variety of drapery and pose, which is often marked by extreme torsion. This willingness to experiment should be seen as a valid, even necessary, attempt to extend the subject matter and dynamic range of Greek art in accordance with a new outlook.

THE DYING TRUMPETER. This new, more human conception can be seen in the bronze groups dedicated by Attalos I of Pergamon (a city in northwestern Asia Minor) between about 240

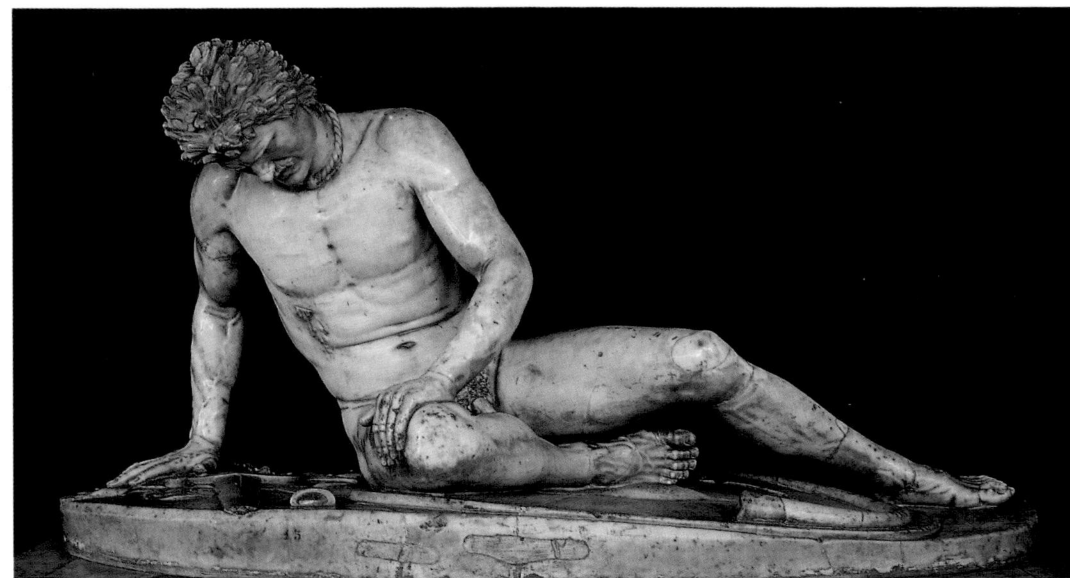

5-71. Epigonos of Pergamon (?). *Dying Trumpeter.* Roman copy after a bronze original of c. 230–220 B.C. Marble, lifesize. Museo Capitolino, Rome

and 200 B.C. These works celebrated his victories over the Celts, who repeatedly raided the Greek states from Galatia, the area around present-day Ankara, until Attalos forced them to settle down. The bronze statues were copied in marble for the Romans, for whom they may have had an appeal because of their own troubles with Celtic tribes in northwestern Europe. A number of these copies have survived. Among them is the famous *Dying Trumpeter* (fig. 5-71), which presumably replicates a statue by Epigonos of Pergamon mentioned in Pliny's *Natural History.*

The sculptor must have known the Celts well, for the ethnic type is carefully rendered in the facial structure and in the bristly shock of hair. The torque around the neck is another Celtic feature. Otherwise, the *Trumpeter* shares the heroic nudity of Greek warriors, such as those on the Aegina pediments (see fig. 5-22). Although his agony seems much more realistic in comparison, it still has a great deal of dignity and pathos. Clearly, the Celts were considered worthy foes. "They knew how to die, barbarians though they were" is the idea conveyed by the statue. Yet we also sense something else, an animal quality that had never before been part of Greek images of men. Death, as we witness it here, is a very concrete physical process. No longer able to move his legs, the *Trumpeter* puts all his waning strength into his arms, as if to prevent a tremendous invisible weight from crushing him against the ground.

THE PERGAMON ALTAR. Some four decades later, we find a second sculptural style flourishing at Pergamon. About 180 B.C.,

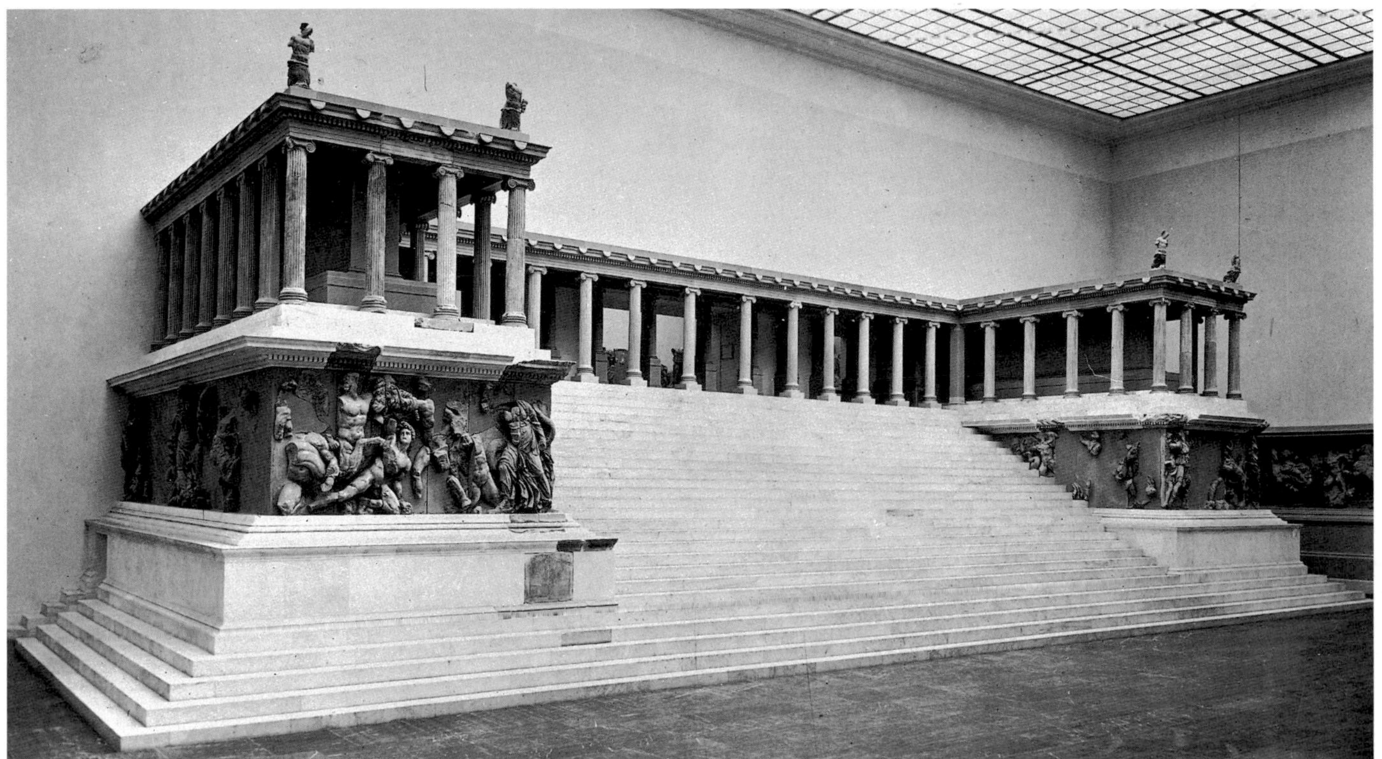

5-72. The west front of the Great Pergamon Altar (restored). Staatliche Museen zu Berlin, Preussischer Kulturbesitz, Antikensammlung

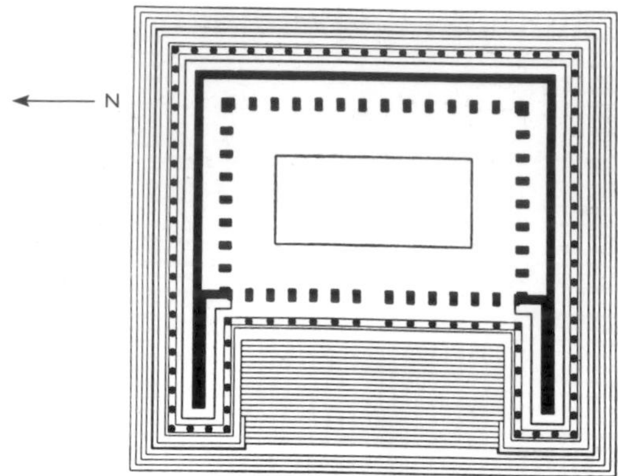

5-73. Plan of the Great Pergamon Altar (after J. Schrammen)

Eumenes II, the son and successor of Attalos I, had an enormous altar built on a hill above the city to commemorate the victory of Rome and her allies over Antiochos the Great of Syria eight years before (a victory that had given him much of the Seleucid Empire). A large part of the sculptural decoration has been recovered, and the entire west front of the monument, with the great flight of stairs leading to its entrance, has been reconstructed in Berlin (fig. 5-72). It is an impressive structure indeed. The altar itself is at the center of a rectangular court surrounded by an Ionic colonnade, which rises on a tall base about 100 feet square (fig. 5-73). Altar structures of such great size seem to have been an Ionian tradition since Archaic times, but the Pergamon Altar is the most elaborate of all. It is also the only one of which considerable portions have survived. Its boldest feature is the frieze covering the base, which is 400 feet long and more than 7 feet tall. The huge figures, cut so deep that they seem almost detached from the background, have the scale and weight of pedimental statues, but they have been freed from the confining triangular frame and placed in a frieze. This unique blend of two traditions brings the development of Greek architectural sculpture to a thundering climax (fig. 5-74).

The carving of the frieze, though not very subtle, has tremendous dramatic force. The muscular bodies rush at each other, and the high relief creates strong accents of light and dark. The beating wings and windblown garments are almost overwhelming in their dynamism. A writhing movement pervades the entire design, down to the last lock of hair, linking the figures in a single continuous rhythm. This sense of unity restrains the violence of the struggle and keeps it—but just barely—from exploding its architectural frame. Indeed, the action spills out onto the stairs, where several figures are locked in combat.

The subject, the battle of the gods and giants, is a traditional one for Ionic friezes. (We saw it before on the Siphnian Treasury, fig. 5-20.) At Pergamon, however, it has a novel significance. It promotes Pergamon as a new Athens—the patron goddess of both cities was Athena, who has a prominent place in the great frieze. Moreover, it almost surely incorporates a cosmological program, whose meaning, however, is disputed. Finally, the victory of the gods is meant to symbolize Eumenes' own victories. Such translations of history into mythology had been common in Greek art for a long time (see page 134). But to place Eumenes in analogy with the gods themselves implies an exaltation of the ruler that is Oriental rather than Greek. The analogy was reinforced by a second

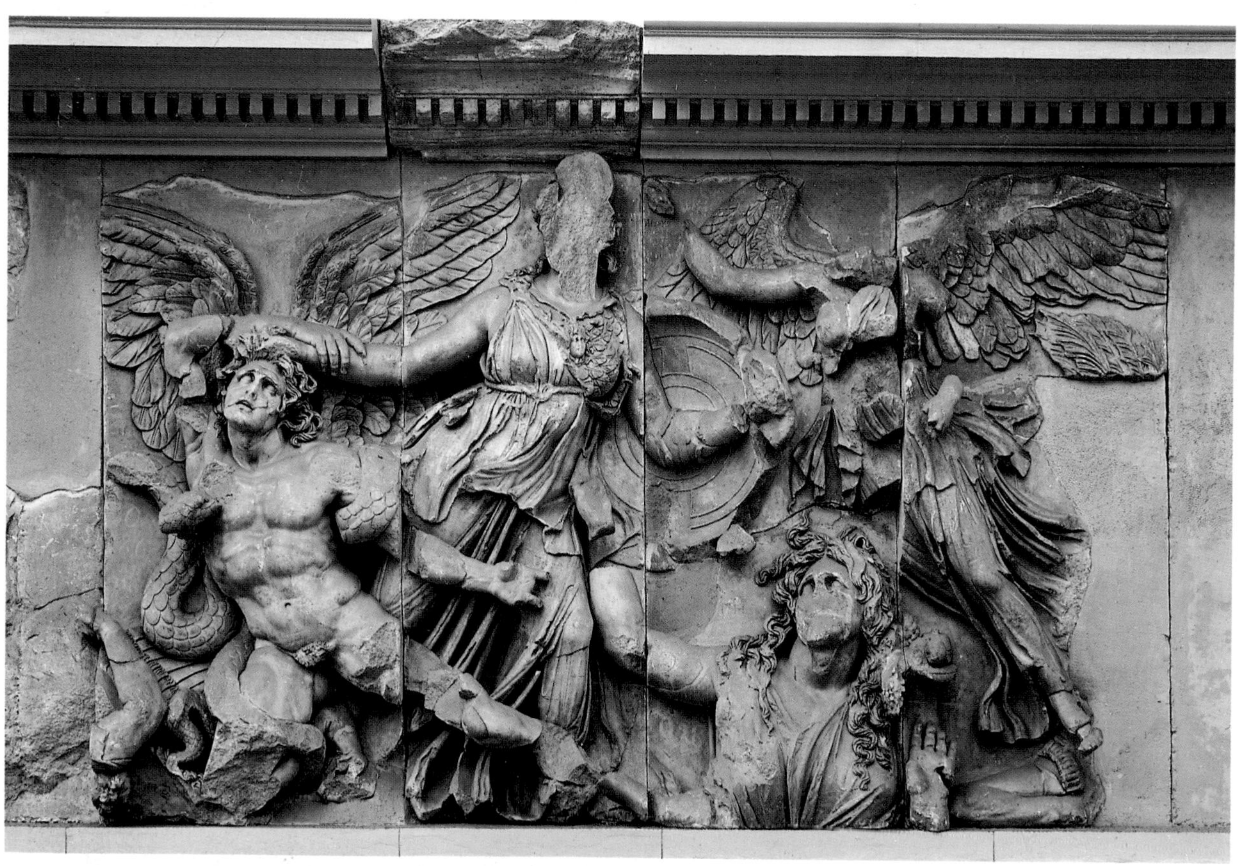

5-74. *Athena and Alkyoneus,* from the east side of the Great Frieze of the Great Pergamon Altar. c. 166–156 B.C. Marble, height 7'6" (2.29 m). Staatliche Museen zu Berlin, Preussischer Kulturbesitz, Antikensammlung

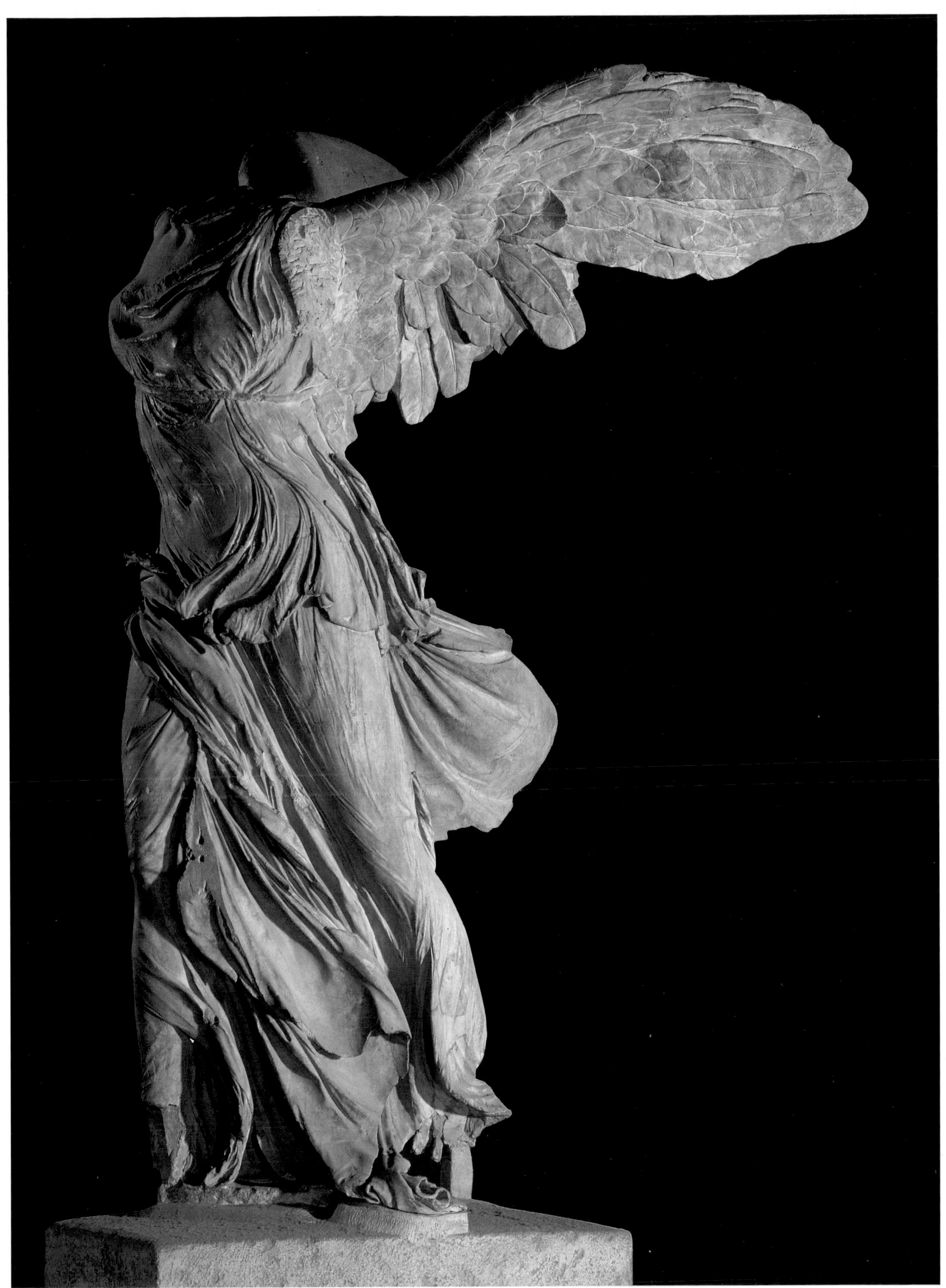

5-75. Pythokritos of Rhodes (?). *Nike of Samothrace.* c. 200–190 B.C. Marble, height 8' (2.4 m). Musée du Louvre, Paris

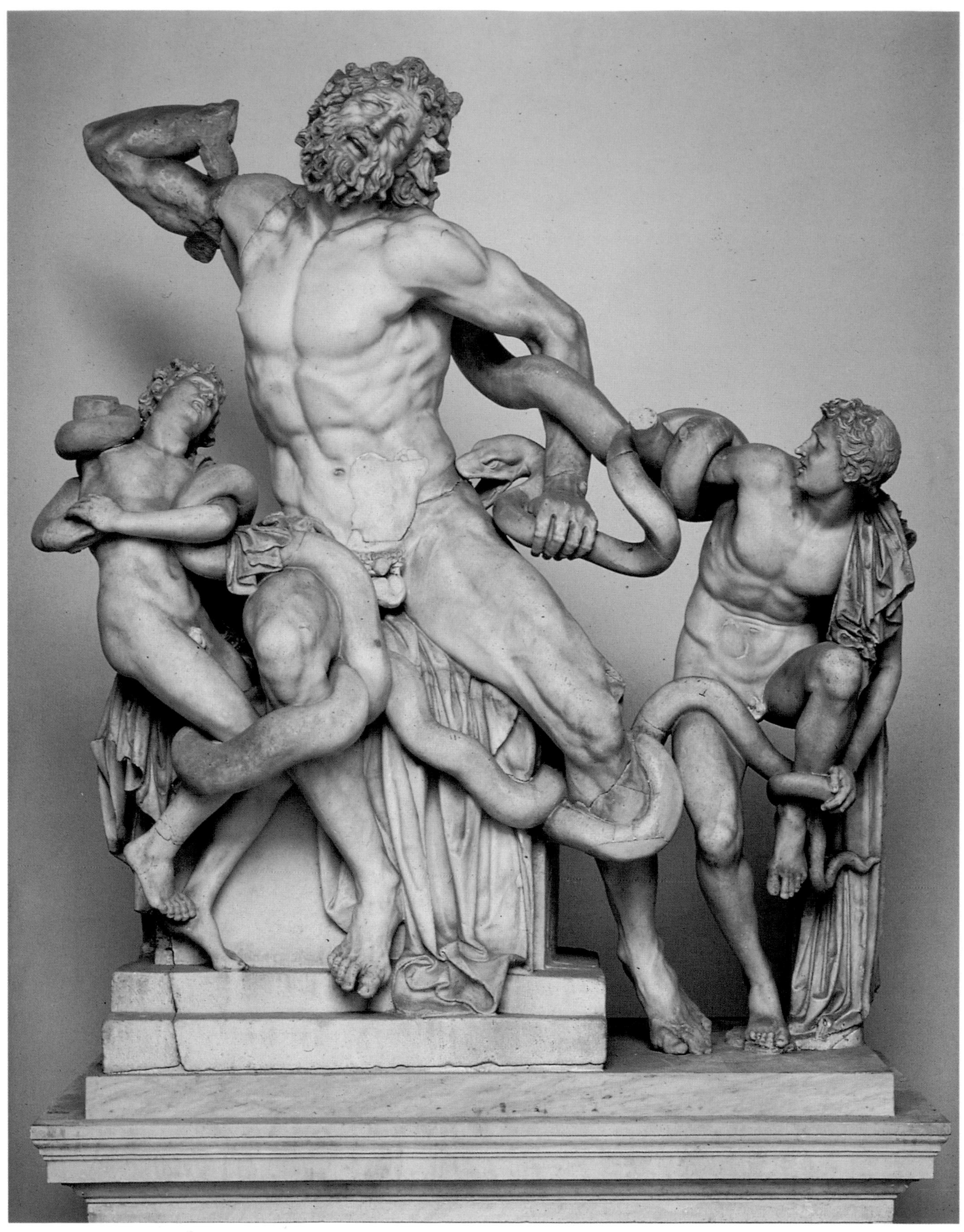

5-76. *The Laocoön Group.* Perhaps by Agesander, Athenodoros, and Polydoros of Rhodes (present state, former restorations removed). 1st century B.C. Marble, height 7' (2.1 m). Musei Vaticani, Museo Pio Clementino, Cortile Ottagono, Città del Vaticano, Rome frieze, entirely different in character, along the interior wall of the altar, which depicted the life of Telephos, the legendary founder of Pergamon and the son of Herakles, who was born of Zeus. After the time of Mausolos (who may have been the first to introduce it on Greek soil), the idea of divine kingship had been adopted by Alexander the Great and the lesser sovereigns who divided his realm, including the rulers of Pergamon. It later became central to Imperial Rome from Augustus onward (see pages 171–72).

NIKE OF SAMOTHRACE. Equally dramatic is another victory monument of the early second century B.C., the *Nike of Samothrace* (fig. 5-75). This sculpture may commemorate the naval victory of Eudamos of Rhodes over Antiochos the Great in 190 B.C. The style is Rhodian, and the statue may well have been carved by the island's leading sculptor, Pythokritos. The goddess has just descended to the prow of a ship. Her great wings spread wide, she is still partly airborne by the powerful head wind against which she advances. The invisible force of onrushing air here becomes a tangible reality. It not only balances the forward movement of the figure but also shapes every fold of the wonderfully animated drapery. As a result, there is an active relationship between the statue and the space around it, such as we have never seen before. By comparison, all earlier examples of active drapery seem inert. This is true even of the three goddesses from the Parthenon (see fig. 5-52), whose wet drapery responds not to the atmosphere around it but to an inner impulse that is independent of motion. Nor shall we see its like again for a long time to come. The *Nike of Samothrace* deserves her fame as the greatest masterpiece of Hellenistic sculpture.

LAOCOÖN. Until the *Nike* was discovered more than 100 years ago, the most admired work of Hellenistic sculpture had been a group showing the death of Laocoön and his two sons (fig. 5-76). [See Primary Sources, no. 8, page 197.] Found in Rome in 1506, it made a tremendous impression on Michelangelo and many others. The history of its fame is like that of the *Apollo Belvedere.* The two were treated as complementary: the *Apollo* exemplified harmonious beauty and the *Laocoön* sublime tragedy. (Laocoön was the priest who was punished by the gods for telling the Trojans not to admit the Greeks' wooden horse into the city. His warning went unheeded, which led to the Trojans' defeat.) Today we tend to find the pathos of the group somewhat calculated, and its surface finish strikes us merely as a display of virtuoso technique.

In style, including the relieflike spread of the three figures, it clearly descends from the Pergamon frieze. Here, though, the dynamism has become rather self-conscious. The *Laocoön* was long thought to be a Greek original and was identified with a group by Agesander, Athenodoros, and Polydoros of Rhodes that the Roman writer Pliny mentions as being in the palace of the emperor Titus. [See Primary Sources, no. 3, pages 194–195.] We now know that these sculptors were skilled copyists who were active just before or after the birth of Jesus. The subject must have held a special meaning for the Romans. Laocoön's fate forewarned Aeneas of the fall of Troy, prompting him to flee in time. Since Aeneas was believed to have come to Italy and to have been the ancestor of Romulus and Remus, the death of Laocoön could be viewed as the first link in a chain of events that ultimately led to the founding of Rome.

PORTRAITS. Individual likenesses were unknown in Classical art, which sought a timeless ideal. [See Primary Sources, no. 7, page 197.] Portraiture first arose as a major branch of Greek sculpture in the mid-fourth century; it continued to flourish in Hellenistic times. Its achievements, however, are known to us only indirectly, for the most part through Roman copies. One of the few originals is a vivid bronze head from Delos, a work of the early first century B.C. (fig. 5-77). It was not made as a bust. Rather, in accordance with Greek custom, it was part of a full-length statue. The man's identity is not known, but whoever he was, his likeness has been fused with a distinctive Hellenistic type (compare the face of Alkyoneus in figure 5-74). The result is an intensely private view of the subject that captures the character of the age.

The distant stare of the *"Mausolos"* (see fig. 5-65) has been replaced by a troubled look. The fluid modeling of the somewhat flabby features, the uncertain mouth, and the unhappy eyes under furrowed brows reveal an individual beset by doubts and worries—a very human, unheroic personality. There are echoes of pathos in these features, but it is a pathos translated into psychological terms. People who felt such inner turmoil had certainly existed earlier in the Greek world, just as they do today. Yet it is significant that their complex character could be conveyed in art

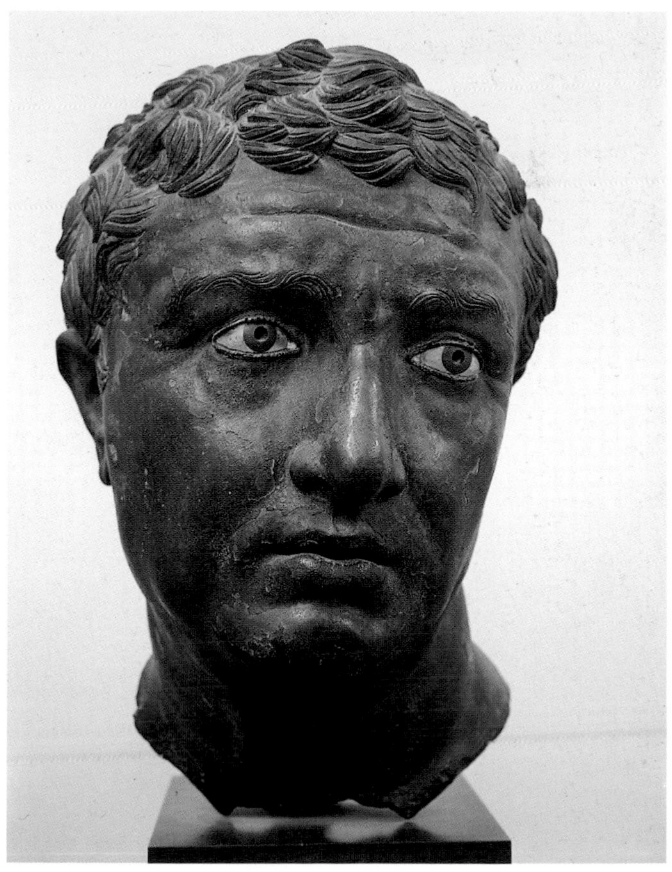

5-77. *Portrait Head,* from Delos. c. 80 B.C. Bronze, height 12¾" (32.4 cm). National Archaeological Museum, Athens

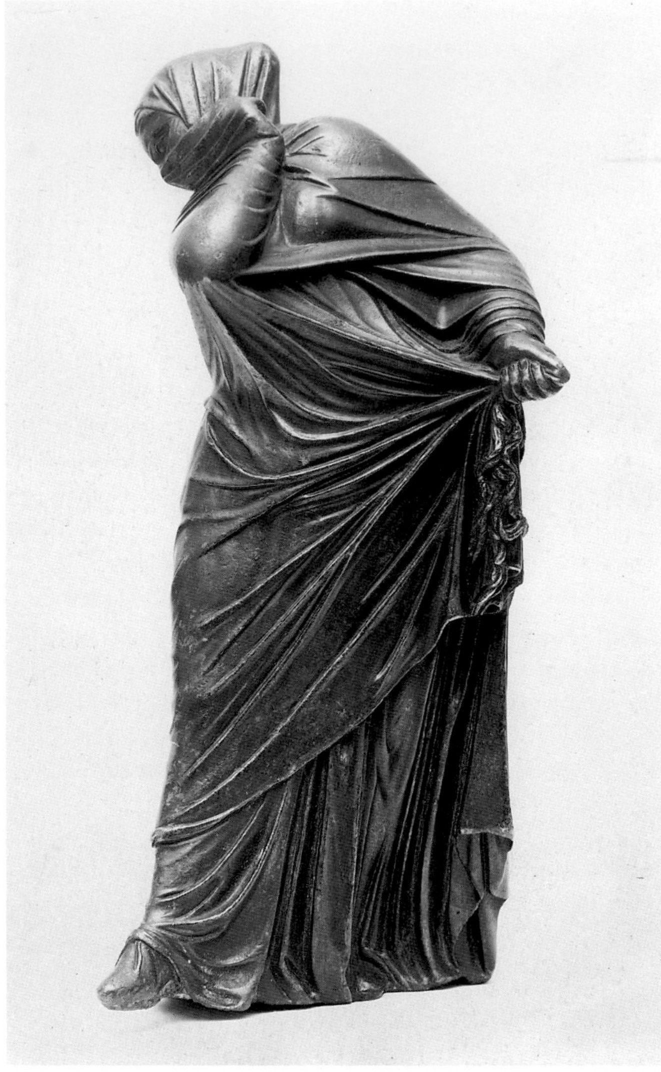

5-78. *Veiled Dancer.* c. 200 B.C.? Bronze statuette, height $8\frac{1}{8}$" (20.6 cm). The Metropolitan Museum of Art, New York
BEQUEST OF WALTER C. BAKER, 1971

only when Greek independence was about to come to an end, culturally as well as politically.

STATUETTES. Before we leave Hellenistic sculpture, we must look briefly at another aspect of it, represented by the enchanting bronze statuette of a veiled dancer (fig. 5-78). She introduces us to the wide variety of small-scale works produced for private ownership. These works form a special category, often called Tanagra figures after the site where many have been found. Such pieces were collected in much the same way as painted vases had been in earlier times. Like vase paintings, they show a range of subject matter far broader than that of monumental sculpture. Besides the familiar mythological themes, we find many everyday subjects: beggars, street entertainers, peasants, young ladies of fashion. The grotesque, the humorous, the picturesque—rarely found in Greek monumental art—are highly visible here. Most of these figurines are routine pieces that were mass-produced in clay or bronze. But at their best, they have a freedom that is rarely matched on a larger scale. The bold spiral twist of the veiled dancer, reinforced in the diagonal folds of the drapery, creates a variety of interesting views that practically force the viewer to turn the statuette in his hands. No less remarkable is the interplay of concave and convex forms, the contrast between the compact silhouette of the figure and the mobility of the body within.

COINS

We rarely think of coins as works of art, and the majority of them are not. The study of coins, known as numismatics, offers many rewards, but visual delight is often the least of these. If many Greek coins are exceptions to this rule, it is not simply because they are the earliest. (The idea of stamping metal pellets of standard weight with an identifying design originated in Ionian Greece sometime before 600 B.C.) After all, the first postage stamps were not more works of art than stamps are today. The reason, rather, is the individualism of Greek political life. Every city-state had its own coinage, with its own emblem, and the designs were changed often so as to take account of treaties, victories, or other occasions for local pride. As a result, the number of coins struck at any one time was relatively small, while the number of coinages was large.

The constant demand for new designs produced highly skilled specialists who took such pride in their work that they sometimes signed it. Greek coins thus are not only a valuable source of historical knowledge but an authentic expression of the changing Greek sense of form. They illustrate the development of Greek sculpture from the sixth to the second century B.C. as faithfully as the larger works we have discussed. And since they form a continuous series, with the place and date of almost every item well established, they reflect this development more fully in some respects than do the works of monumental art.

Some of the finest coins of Archaic and Classical Greece were produced not by the most powerful states such as Athens, Corinth, or Sparta, but by the lesser ones. Our first example (fig. 5-79), from the Aegean island of Peparethus, reflects the origin of coinage: a square die embedded in a rather shapeless pellet, like an impression in sealing wax. The winged god, whose pinwheel stance is so perfectly adapted to the frame, is a summary-in-miniature of Archaic art, down to the smile (see fig. 5-16). On the coin from Naxos in Sicily (fig. 5-80), almost half a century later, the die fills the entire area of the coin. The surprisingly monumental figure shows the articulation and organic vitality of the Severe style (compare fig. 5-46). Our third coin (fig. 5-81) was struck in the Sicilian town of Catana toward the end of the Peloponnesian War. It is signed with the name of its maker, Herakleidas, and it deserves to be, for it is one of the true masterpieces of Greek coinage. Who would have thought it possible to give such plasticity to a full-face view of a head in low relief? This radiant image of Apollo has the swelling roundness of the mature Classical style. Its grandeur completely transcends the limitations of the tiny scale of a coin.

From the time of Alexander the Great onward, coins began to show profile portraits of rulers. At first the successors of Alexander put his features on their coins to stress their link with him. Such a piece is shown in figure 5-82. Alexander displays the horns

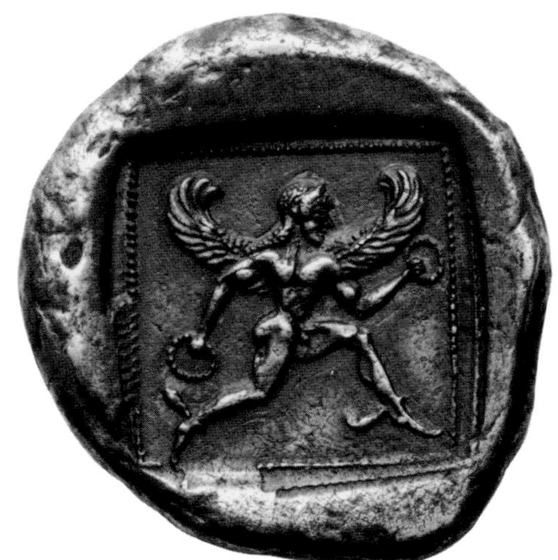

5-79. *Winged God.* Silver coin from Peparethus. c. 500 B.C. Diameter 1½" (3.7 cm). The British Museum, London

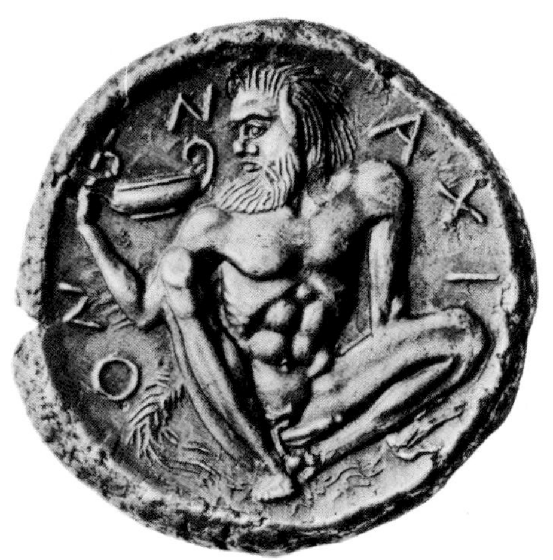

5-80. *Silenus.* Silver coin from Naxos. c. 460 B.C. Diameter 1¼" (3.3 cm). The British Museum, London

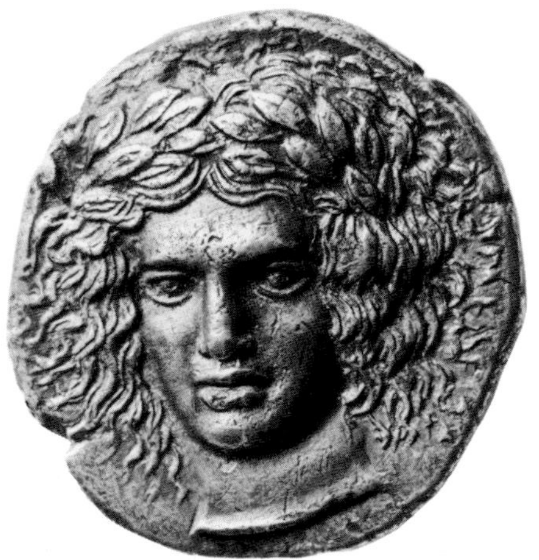

5-81. *Apollo.* Silver coin from Catana. c. 415–400 B.C. Diameter 1⅛" (3 cm). The British Museum, London

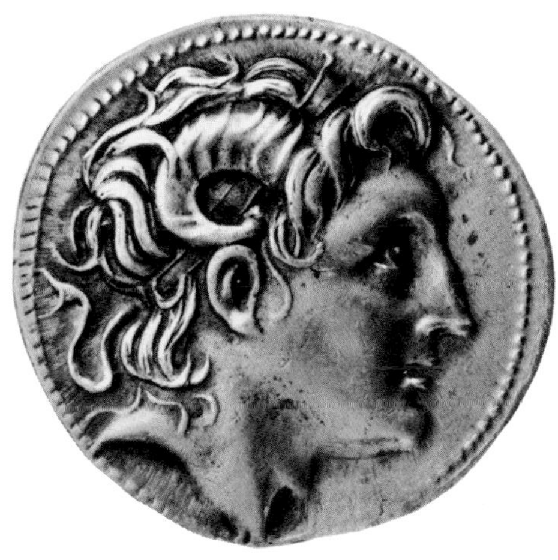

5-82. *Alexander the Great with Amun Horns.* Four-drachma silver coin issued by Lysimachos. c. 297–281 B.C. Diameter 1⅛" (3 cm)

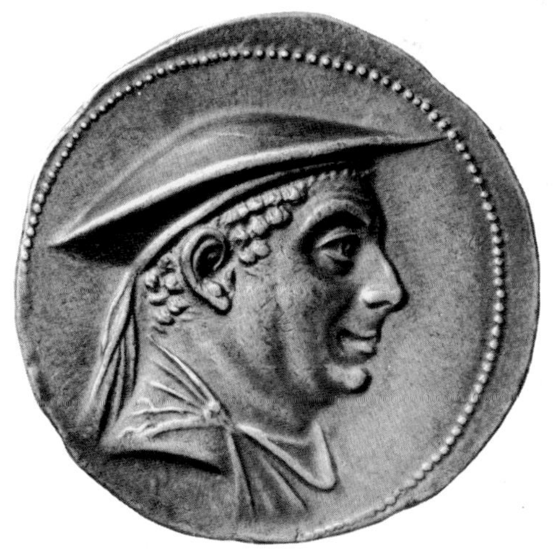

5-83. *Antimachos of Bactria.* Silver coin. c. 185 B.C. Diameter 1¼" (3.3 cm). The British Museum, London

that identify him with the ram-headed Egyptian god Amun. His "inspired" expression, conveyed by the half-open mouth and the upward-looking eyes, is characteristic of the emotionalism of Hellenistic art, as are the fluid modeling of the features and the agitated, snakelike hair. As a likeness, this head can have only a slight relation to the way Alexander actually looked. Yet this idealized image of the deified conqueror projects the flavor of the new era more eloquently than do the large-scale portraits of Alexander.

Once the Hellenistic rulers started putting themselves on their coins, the likenesses became more individual. Perhaps the most astonishing of these (fig. 5-83) is the head of Antimachos of Bactria (present-day Afghanistan), which stands at the opposite end of the scale from the Alexander-Amun. Its mobile features show a man of sharp intelligence and wit, a bit skeptical perhaps about himself and others and, in any event, without any desire for self-glorification. This penetratingly human portrait seems to point the way to the bronze head from Delos (see fig. 5-77) a hundred years later. It has no counterpart in the monumental sculpture of its own time and thus helps to fill an important gap in our knowledge of Hellenistic portraiture.

CHAPTER SIX

Etruscan Art

The Italian peninsula did not emerge into the light of history until fairly late. The Bronze Age, which dawned first in Mesopotamia about 4000 B.C., came to an end in the Italian peninsula only around 1000 B.C. At that time the Villanovans established an early Iron Age culture near Bologna that had strong ties to central Europe. They were succeeded by the Etruscans in the eighth century B.C., at about the time the Greeks first began to settle along the southern shores of Italy and in Sicily. Interestingly, the Classical Greek historian Herodotus believed that the Etruscans (*Tyrrhenoi* to the Greeks) had left their homeland of Lydia in Asia Minor about 1200 B.C. According to him, they had settled in the area between Florence and Rome, called Rasenna by the Etruscans and Etruria by the Romans, and now known as Tuscany.

Herodotus' claim was already disputed in Roman times by the Greek historian Dionysius of Halicarnassus. It is likely that the Etruscans were actually descended through the Villanovans from the Bronze Age peoples who had occupied central Italy since about 3000 B.C.

In any case, the Etruscans had strong cultural links with Asia Minor and the ancient Near East. Yet they also show many traits that are not found anywhere else. The sudden flowering of Etruscan civilization resulted in large part from the influx of Greek culture. For example, the Etruscans borrowed their alphabet from the Greeks toward the end of the eighth century. Nevertheless, their language is unlike any other. The only Etruscan writings that have come down to us are brief funerary inscriptions and a few somewhat longer texts relating to religious ritual. However, Roman authors, notably the emperor Claudius, tell us that a rich Etruscan literature once existed. In fact, we would know almost nothing about the Etruscans at first hand were it not for their tombs. They were not disturbed when the Romans destroyed or rebuilt Etruscan cities, and as a result they have survived intact until modern times.

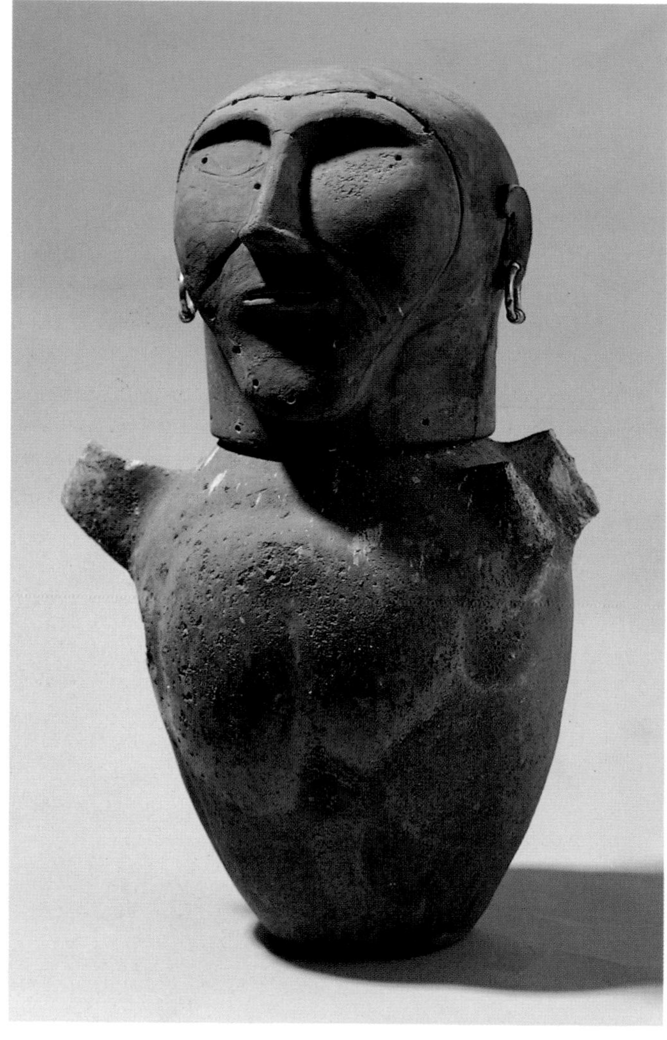

6-1. Human-headed cinerary urn. c. 675–650 B.C.
Terra-cotta, height 25½" (64.7 cm). Museo Etrusco, Chiusi, Italy

Italian Bronze Age burials, like those elsewhere in prehistoric Europe, were modest. The remains of the deceased, contained in a pottery vessel or urn, were placed in a simple pit along with the equipment they required in an afterlife: weapons for men, jewelry and household tools for women. In Mycenaean Greece, this primitive cult of the dead became more elaborate under Egyptian influence, as shown by the monumental beehive tombs. Something very similar happened eight centuries later in Tuscany during the Orientalizing phase of Etruscan art, which lasted from roughly 750

B.C. to 575 B.C. Toward 700 B.C., Etruscan tombs began to imitate, in stone, the interiors of dwellings, covered by great conical mounds of earth. These tumulus tombs could be roofed by vaults or corbeled domes built of horizontal, overlapping courses of stone blocks, as was the Treasury of Atreus at Mycenae (see fig. 4-14).

At the same time, the pottery urns gradually took on human shape. The lid grew into the head of the deceased, and body markings appeared on the vessel itself (fig. 6-1). Sometimes the urn was placed on a sort of throne to indicate high rank. The style, primitive though it may be, has much in common with that of north Syrian sculpture of the ninth century B.C. at Tell Halaf. It was in Syria, too, that the funerary meal, a frequent theme in Etruscan art, most likely originated. Like the Greeks, Etruscan sailors made Al Mina a port of call.

Alongside the modest beginnings of funerary sculpture, we find sudden evidence of great wealth in the form of goldsmiths' work. These objects were probably made by the Phoenicians, with whom the Etruscans forged trade agreements and peace treaties. They were decorated with motifs like those on the Orientalizing Greek vases of the same period (see fig. 5-4). Also found in the tombs were precious objects imported from the ancient Near East.

In the seventh and sixth centuries B.C. the Etruscans reached the height of their power. Their cities rivaled those of the Greeks; their fleet dominated the western Mediterranean and protected a vast commercial empire that competed with the Greeks and Phoenicians; and their territory extended as far as Naples in the south and the lower Po Valley in the north. But the Etruscans, like the Greeks, never formed a unified nation. They were no more than a loose federation of individual city-states given to quarreling among themselves and were slow to unite against a common enemy. The Etruscan fleet was defeated by the navy of its archrival, Syracuse, in 474 B.C. And during the later fifth and fourth centuries B.C., one Etruscan city after another fell to the Romans. By 270 B.C., all of them had lost their independence, although many continued to prosper, if we are to judge by the richness of their tombs during the period of political decline.

Tombs and Their Decoration

The flowering of Etruscan civilization coincides with the Archaic age in Greece. During this period, especially near the end of the sixth and early in the fifth century B.C., Etruscan art showed its greatest vigor. Greek Archaic influence had displaced the Orientalizing tendencies (many of the finest Greek vases have been found in Etruscan tombs of that time) but Etruscan artists did not simply imitate their Hellenic models. Working in a very different cultural setting, they retained their own clear-cut identity.

One might expect the Etruscan cult of the dead to have waned under Greek influence. On the contrary, tombs and equipment grew more elaborate as the skills of the sculptor and painter increased. The deceased could now be shown full-length, reclining on the lids of sarcophagi shaped like couches, as if they were participants in a festive repast similar to the Greek symposium. The Etruscans, however, made such feasts into family affairs instead of restricting them to men. (When women do appear in Greek banquet scenes, it is on red-figured pots with amorous subjects.) The example in figure 6-2 shows a husband and wife side by side, an Archaic smile on their lips, so that they seem gay and majestic at the same time. His right hand may have held an egg, his left a drinking cup; hers perhaps held a perfume vase and a piece of fruit. The entire work is of terra-cotta and was once painted in bright colors. The rounded forms reveal the Etruscan sculptor's preference for modeling in soft materials, in contrast to the Greek love of stone carving. There is less formal discipline here but an extraordinary directness and vivacity that are characteristic of Etruscan art.

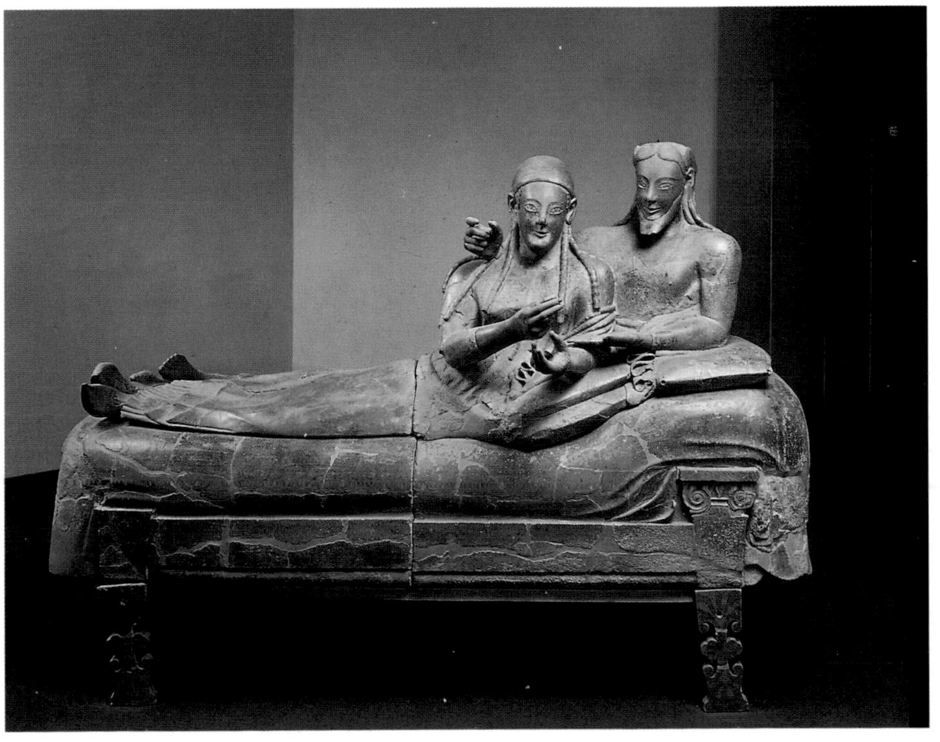

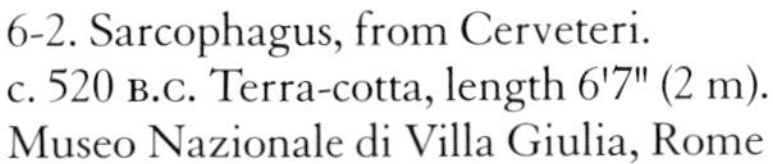

6-2. Sarcophagus, from Cerveteri. c. 520 B.C. Terra-cotta, length 6'7" (2 m). Museo Nazionale di Villa Giulia, Rome

EARLY FUNERARY BELIEFS. We do not know precisely what ideas the Archaic Etruscans held about the afterlife. Effigies such as our reclining couple, which for the first time in history show the deceased as alive and enjoying themselves, suggest that they regarded the tomb as a home not only for the body but also for the soul. (In contrast, the Egyptians thought that the soul roamed freely; their funerary sculpture therefore was "inanimate.") How else are we to understand the purpose of the wonderfully rich array of murals in these tombs? Since nothing of the sort has survived in Greek territory, they are uniquely important not only as an Etruscan achievement but also as a possible reflection of Greek wall painting.

THE TOMB OF HUNTING AND FISHING. Perhaps the most remarkable murals are found in the Tomb of Hunting and Fishing at Tarquinia of about 520 B.C. Figure 6-3 shows a marine panorama at one end of the low chamber. In this vast expanse of water and sky, the fishermen seem to play only an incidental part. Exekias' *Dionysos in a Boat* (see fig. 5-5) is the closest Greek counterpart to our scene. (In the myth, the dolphins were Etruscan sailors!) The differences, however, are as revealing as the similarities. One wonders if any Greek Archaic artist knew how to place human figures in a natural setting as effectively as the Etruscan painter did. Could the mural have been inspired by Egyptian scenes of hunting in the marshes, such as the one in figure 2-18? They seem the most likely precedent for our subject. If so, the Etruscan artist has brought the scene to life, just as the reclining couple in figure 6-2 has been brought to life compared with Egyptian funerary statues.

The free, rhythmic movement of birds and dolphins also reminds us of Minoan painting of a thousand years earlier (see fig. 4-5). So far as we know, the Minoans were the only people to paint murals devoted solely to landscape before the Etruscans. How are we to account for this apparent debt to Egyptian and Minoan art of so many centuries earlier amid the obvious Greek influences? Perhaps the contact came through the Etruscan navy, which roamed throughout the Mediterranean, including Egypt—where, we recall, Minoan-style frescoes could also be seen (see page 52). The mystery may never be cleared up, however.

Despite the air of enchantment, the scene is not without its ominous overtones. The giant hunter with a slingshot from whom the birds flee in all directions is very likely a demon of death, closely related to another masked demon named Phersu who appears in other Etruscan murals. This dualism also is continued in the

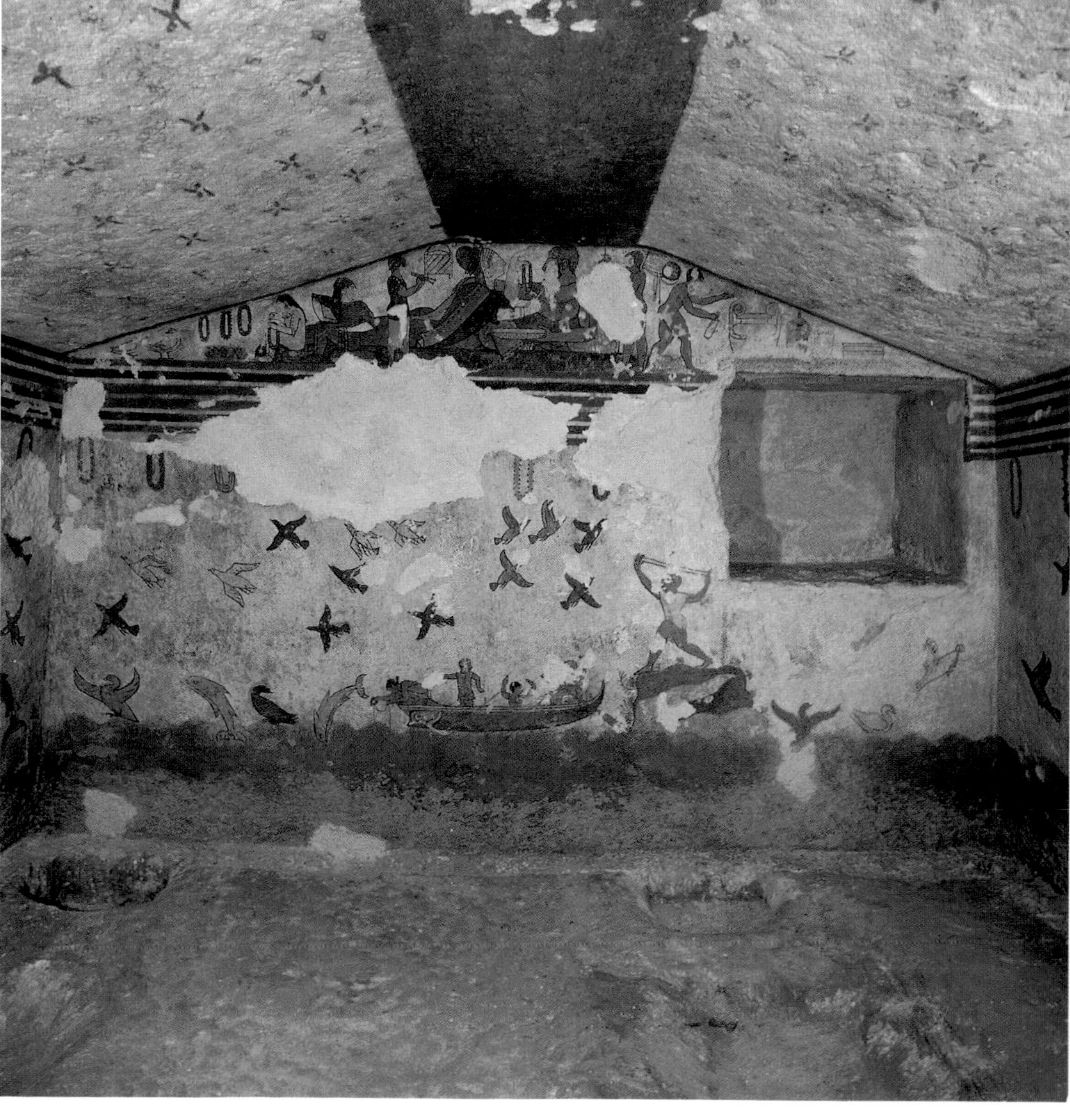

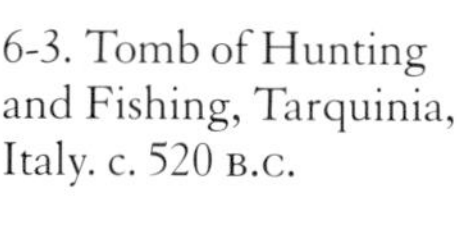

6-3. Tomb of Hunting and Fishing, Tarquinia, Italy. c. 520 B.C.

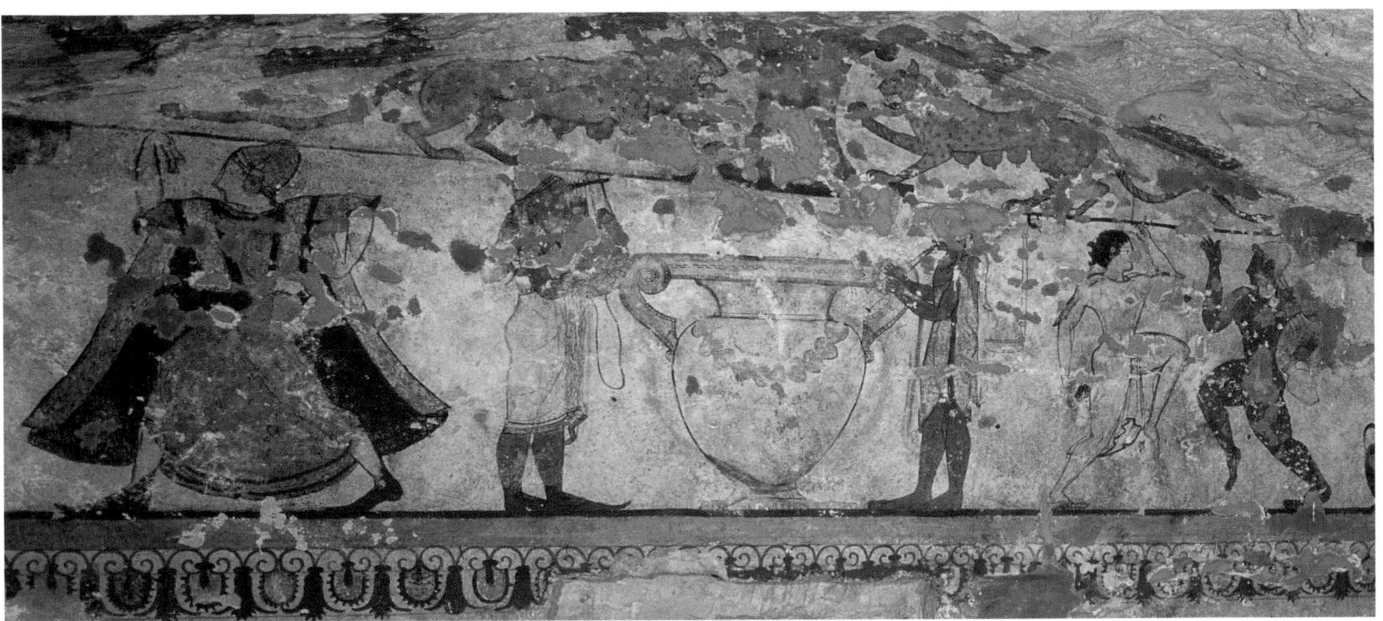

6-4. *Musicians and Two Dancers.* Detail of a wall painting. c. 470–460 B.C. Tomb of the Lionesses, Tarquinia, Italy

niche above: we see a couple enjoying themselves on a couch, flanked by a musician and servants. One of the servants is drawing wine from a large mixing bowl, or krater (see fig. 5-1), while another is making wreaths. From the Greeks, the Etruscans adopted the cult of Dionysos, whom they called Fufluns or Pachies (from Bacchos [Latin, Bacchus], his other Greek name; see page 97). Besides being the god of wine, he was the god of vegetation and hence, death and resurrection, like Osiris. (By contrast, paintings of the final supper, found at the entrances to Egyptian tombs, show only the deceased seated at a table.) Thus the painting has a funereal content whose full meaning escapes us. In this context, for example, the couple may be seen as counterparts to Bacchus and Ariadne (known as Ariatha to the Etruscans). These two figures recline in eternal love on the pediment of a late Etruscan temple, where they serve as symbols of regeneration. In any case, the mural's purpose is essentially commemorative, ushering the deceased into the next life.

THE TOMB OF THE LIONESSES. The importance of Dionysos can be seen in other tombs as well. A somewhat later example from another tomb in Tarquinia (fig. 6-4) shows a pair of ecstatic dancers beside an immense krater. The passionate energy of their movements again strikes us as uniquely Etruscan rather than Greek in spirit. Of particular interest is the transparent garment of the woman, which lets the body shine through. In Greece, this treatment appears only a few years earlier, during the final phase of Archaic vase painting. The contrasting body color of the two figures continues a practice that was begun by the Egyptians more than 2,000 years before (see fig. 2-15) and was carried on by the Greeks. The dancers are descended from Greek depictions of satyrs and maenads, thereby establishing a link to the cult of Dionysos. And, as we have seen, the Minoan-looking dolphins also had Dionysian associations.

Yet the meaning of the mural as a whole remains obscure. What are we to make of the lactating lioness? (Her heraldic mirror image does not appear in the figure.) She is kin to ancient Sumerian depictions of the mother goddess in leonine form. These and other images from the Near East first appeared in the Orientalizing style. Lions were also linked to Dionysos. Here the lioness is evidently seen in her dual guise as a giver of life and dispenser of death, thus suggesting regeneration in a life beyond. The motif reappears in a later Etruscan funerary relief, executed in a curiously Syrian manner, of a lioness nursing a youth. This lioness may be a forerunner of the she-wolf that, according to legend, suckled Romulus and Remus (see below).

LATER FUNERARY BELIEFS. During the fifth century B.C., the Etruscan view of the hereafter must have become a good deal more complex and less festive. We notice the change immediately if we compare the group in figure 6-5, a cinerary container carved of soft local stone soon after 400 B.C., with its predecessor in figure 6-2. The woman now sits at the foot of the couch, but she is not the wife of the young man. Her wings show that she is the demon of death, and the scroll in her left hand records the fate of the deceased.

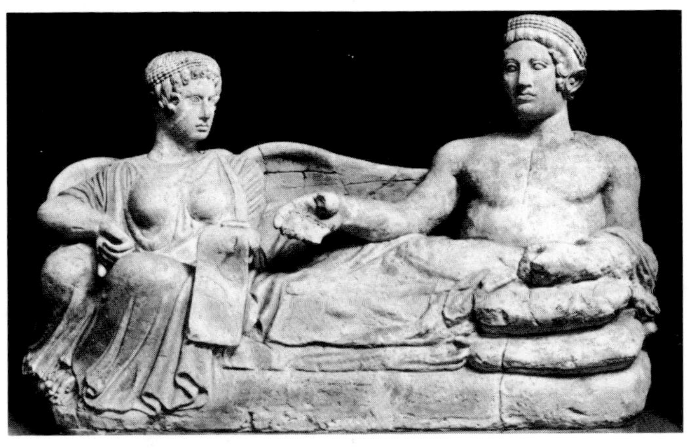

6-5. *Youth and Demon of Death.* Cinerary container. Early 4th century B.C. Stone (*pietra fetida*), length 47" (119.4 cm). Museo Archeologico Nazionale, Florence

The young man is pointing to it as if to say, "Behold, my time has come." The thoughtful, melancholy air of the two figures may be due, to some extent, to the influence of Classical Greek art, which pervades the style of our group (compare fig. 5-58). A new mood of uncertainty and regret is felt. Human destiny is in the hands of inexorable supernatural forces, and death is now the great divide rather than a continuation, albeit on a different plane, of life on earth.

In later tombs, the demons of death gain an even more fearful aspect. Other, more terrifying demons enter the scene. Often they are shown battling against benevolent spirits for possession of the soul of the deceased—a prefiguration of the Last Judgment in medieval art (see fig. 10-24). One of these demons appears in the center of figure 6-6, a tomb of the third century B.C. at Cerveteri, richly decorated with stucco reliefs rather than paintings. The entire chamber, cut into the live rock, imitates the interior of a house, including the beams of the roof. The sturdy pilasters (note the capitals, which recall the Aeolian type from Asia Minor in fig. 5-35), as well as the wall surfaces between the niches, are covered with exact reproductions of weapons, armor, household implements, small domestic animals, and busts of the deceased. In such a setting, the snake-legged demon and his three-headed hound (whom we recognize as Cerberus, the guardian of hell) seem particularly disquieting.

Temples and Their Decoration

Only the stone foundations of Etruscan temples have survived, since the buildings themselves were built of wood. Apparently the Etruscans, though they were masters of masonry construction for other purposes, rejected the use of stone in temple architecture for religious reasons. The design of their sanctuaries bears a general resemblance to the simpler Greek temples (fig. 6-7). But they also have several distinctive features, some of which were later employed by the Romans. The entire structure rests on a tall base, or podium, that is no wider than the cella and has steps only on the south side. The steps lead to a deep porch, supported by two rows of four columns each, and to the cella beyond. Because Etruscan religion was dominated by a triad of gods, the predecessors of the Roman Juno, Jupiter, and Minerva, the cella is generally subdivided into three compartments. The shape of Etruscan temples, then, must have been squat and squarish compared to the graceful lines of Greek sanctuaries and was more closely linked with domestic architecture. Needless to say, it provided no place for stone sculpture. The decoration usually consisted of terra-cotta plaques covering the architrave and the edges of the roof. Only after 400 B.C. do we occasionally find large-scale terra-cotta groups designed to fill the pediment above the porch.

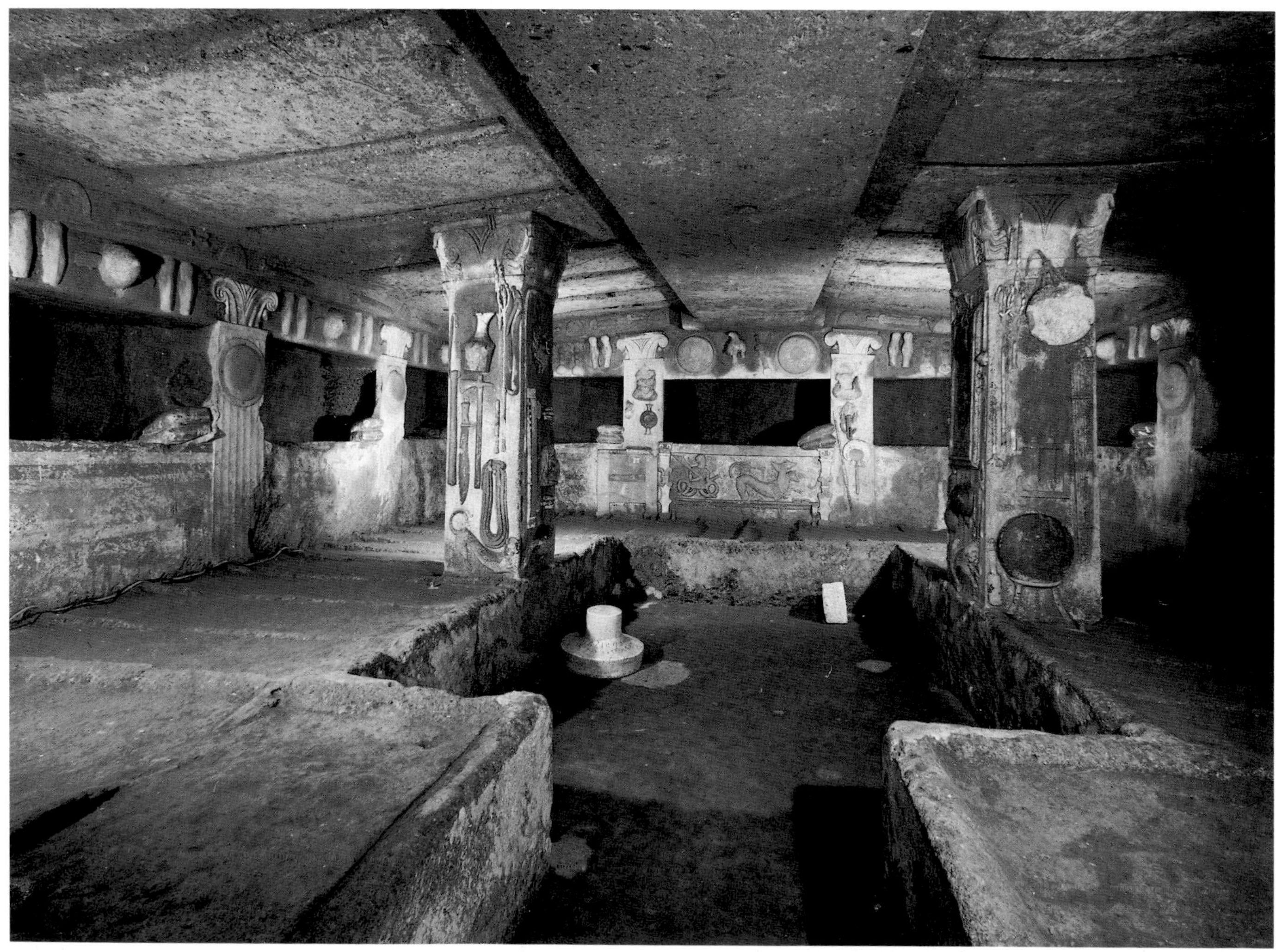

6-6. Burial chamber. Tomb of the Reliefs, Cerveteri, Italy. 3rd century B.C.

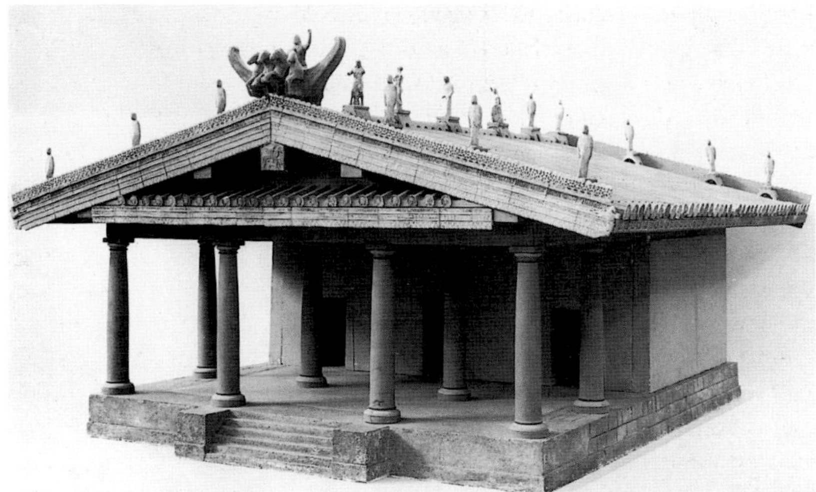

6-7. Reconstruction of an Etruscan temple. Museo delle Antichità Etrusche e Italiche, Rome

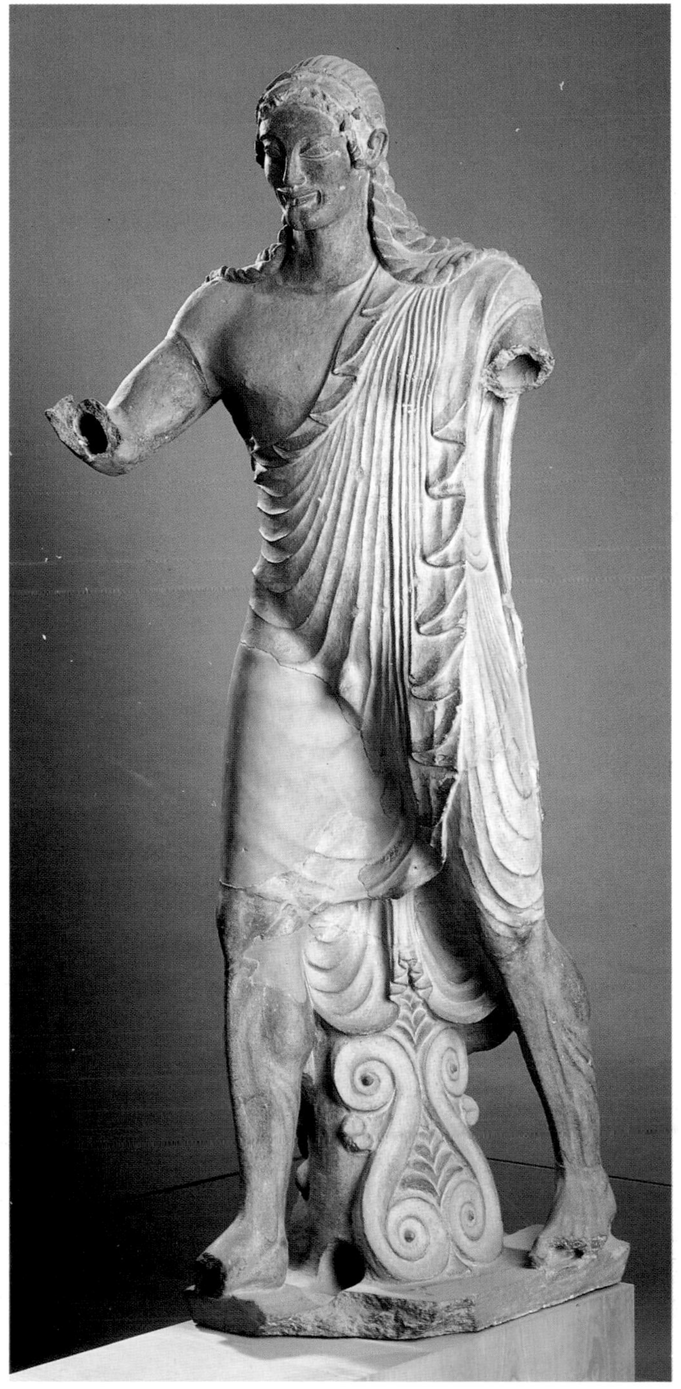

(RIGHT) 6-8. *Apollo,* from Veii. c. 510 B.C. Terra-cotta, height 69" (175.3 cm). Museo Nazionale di Villa Giulia, Rome

VEII. We know, however, of one earlier attempt—and an astonishingly bold one—to find a place for monumental sculpture on the exterior of an Etruscan temple. The so-called Temple of Apollo at Veii, not very far north of Rome, was a structure of standard type in every other way. However, it had four lifesize terra-cotta statues on the ridge of its roof (seen also in the reconstruction model, fig. 6-7). They formed a dramatic group of the sort we might expect in Greek pedimental sculpture: the contest of Hercules and Apollo for the sacred hind (female deer), in the presence of other deities. The best preserved of these figures is the *Apollo* (fig. 6-8), acknowledged to be the masterpiece of Etruscan Archaic sculpture. His massive body, revealed beneath the ornamental striations of the drapery; the sinewy, muscular legs; the hurried, purposeful stride—all these possess an expressive force that has no counterpart in freestanding Greek statues of the same date.

That Veii was indeed a sculptural center at the end of the sixth century B.C. seems to be confirmed by the Roman tradition that the last of the Etruscan rulers of the city called on a master from Veii to make the terra-cotta image of Jupiter for the temple on the Capitoline Hill. This image has been lost, but an even more famous one is still in existence (fig. 6-9). According to a myth promulgated by Vergil, Livy, and others during the time of Augustus to legitimize his reign, Rome was founded in 753 B.C. by Romulus and Remus. These two brothers, descendants of refugees from Troy in Asia Minor (see page 150), were said to have been nourished by a she-wolf after being abandoned. [See Primary Sources, no. 9, page 198.] (The two babes beneath the wolf were added during the Renaissance.) The early history of the statue is obscure, and some scholars have even suspected it of being a medieval work. Nevertheless, it is almost surely an Etruscan Archaic original, for the wonderful ferocity of expression and the latent physical power of the body and legs have the same awesome quality that we sense in the *Apollo* from Veii. Furthermore, the she-wolf has strong links with Etruscan mythology, in which wolves seem to have played an important part from very early times.

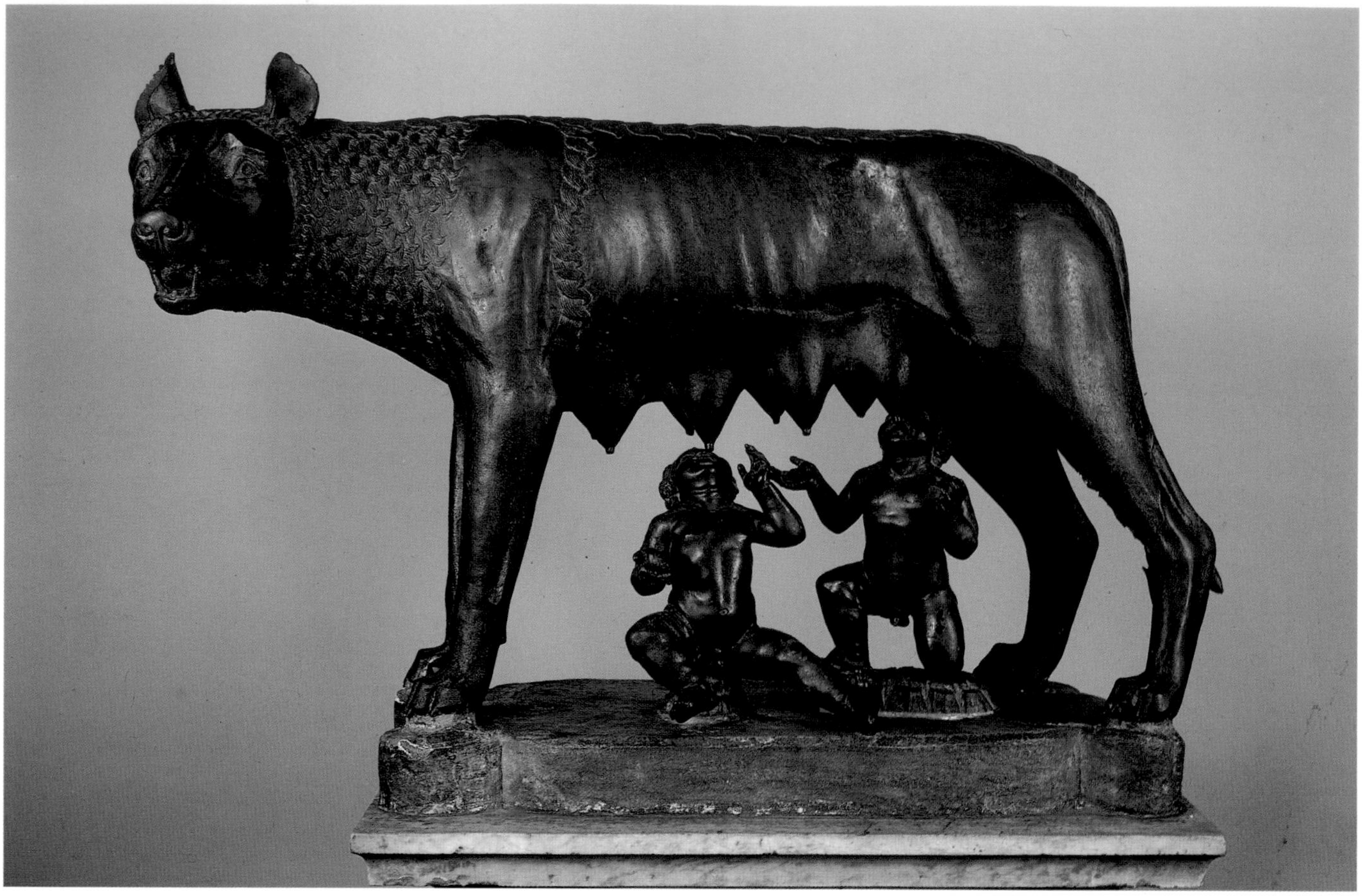

6-9. *She-Wolf.* c. 500 B.C. Bronze, height 33½" (85 cm). Museo Capitolino, Rome

Portraiture and Metalwork

The Etruscan concern with images of the deceased might lead us to expect an early interest in portraiture. Yet the features of funerary images such as those in figures 6-2 and 6-5 are impersonal. Only toward 300 B.C., under the influence of Greek portraiture, did individual likenesses begin to appear in Etruscan sculpture. The finest of them are not funerary portraits, which tend to be rather crude and perfunctory, but the heads of bronze statues. *Portrait of a Boy* (fig. 6-10) is a masterpiece of its kind. The firmness of modeling lends a special poignancy to the sensitive mouth and the gentle, melancholy eyes.

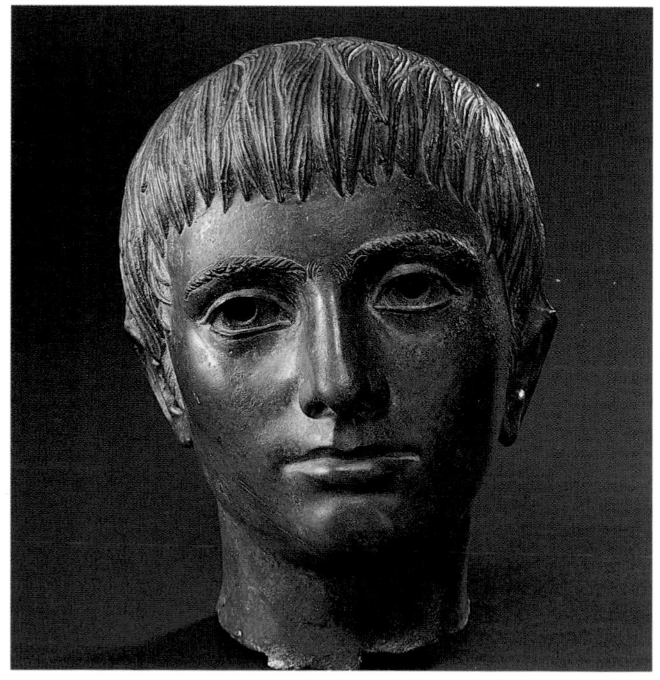

6-10. *Portrait of a Boy.* Early 3rd century B.C. Bronze, height 9" (23 cm). Museo Archeologico Nazionale, Florence

No less impressive is the high quality of the casting and finishing, which bears out the ancient Etruscans' fame as master craftsmen in metal. This ability was of long standing, for the wealth of Etruria was founded on the exploitation of copper and iron deposits. From the sixth century B.C. on, they produced large numbers of bronze statuettes, mirrors, and such, both for export and for domestic use. The backs of mirrors were often engraved with scenes taken from Etruscan versions of Greek myths devoted to the loves of the gods. Such amorous subjects were entirely appropriate to an object used for self-admiration. (We recall the myth of Narcissus, the beautiful youth who fell in love with his reflection in a pool.) The design on the back of a mirror done soon after 400 B.C.

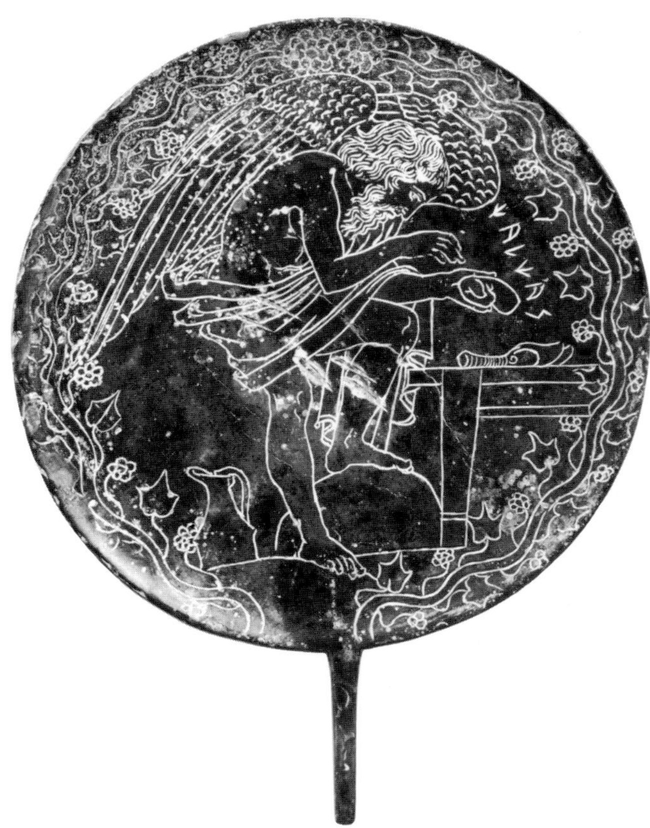

6-11. Engraved back of a mirror. c. 400 B.C. Bronze, diameter 6" (15.3 cm). Musei Vaticani, Museo Gregoriano Etrusco, Città del Vaticano, Rome

(fig. 6-11) shows another aspect of mirrors. Within an undulating wreath of vines, we see a winged old man, identified as the seer Chalchas, examining a roundish object. The draftsmanship is so beautifully balanced and assured that we are tempted to assume that Classical Greek art was the direct source of inspiration.

DIVINATION. So far as the style of our piece is concerned, this may well be the case, but the subject is uniquely Etruscan, for the winged genius is gazing at the liver of a sacrificial animal. We are witnessing a practice that loomed as large in the lives of the Etruscans as the care of the dead: the search for omens or portents. The Etruscans believed that the will of the gods was expressed through signs in the natural world, such as thunderstorms or the flight of birds. By reading these signs, people could find out whether the gods approved or disapproved of their acts. The priests who knew the secret language of these signs enjoyed great prestige. Even the Romans consulted them before any major public or private event. Divination (as the Romans called the art of interpreting omens) can be traced back to ancient Mesopotamia, and the practice was not unknown in Greece, but the Etruscans carried it further. They put special trust in the livers of sacrificial animals—on which, they thought, the gods had inscribed the hoped-for message. In fact, they viewed the liver as a sort of microcosm, divided into regions that corresponded to the regions of the sky. Mirrors, too, were valued for their ability to reveal the future, which is why this scene is represented here.

Arcane and irrational as they were, these practices became part of our cultural heritage. True, we no longer try to tell the future by watching the flight of birds or by examining animal livers, but tea leaves and horoscopes are still prophetic to many people. And we speak of auspicious events or events that indicate a favorable future, unaware that "auspicious" originally referred to a favorable flight of birds. Perhaps we do not believe very seriously that four-leaf clovers bring good luck and black cats or broken mirrors bad luck, yet a surprising number of us admit to being superstitious.

The Architecture of Cities

According to Roman writers, the Etruscans were masters of architectural engineering and of town planning and surveying. There is little doubt that the Romans learned a good deal from them. But it is difficult to say how much the Etruscans contributed to Roman architecture, since very little Etruscan or early Roman architecture remains standing above ground. Roman temples certainly retained many Etruscan features. The atrium, the central hall of the Roman house (see fig. 7-21), also originated in Etruria. In town planning and surveying, too, the Etruscans have a good claim to priority over the Greeks.

The original homeland of the Etruscans, Tuscany, was too hilly for geometric town schemes. However, when they colonized the flatlands south of Rome in the sixth century B.C., they laid out their newly founded cities as a network of streets centering on the intersection of two main thoroughfares, the *cardo* (which ran north and south) and the *decumanus* (which ran east and west). The four quarters thus obtained could be further subdivided or expanded, according to need. This system, which the Romans adopted for the new cities they were to found throughout Italy, western Europe, and North Africa, may have been derived from the plan of Etruscan military camps. Yet it also seems to reflect the religious beliefs that made the Etruscans divide the sky into regions according to the points of the compass and place their temples along a north-south axis. The Etruscans must also have taught the Romans how to build fortifications, bridges, drainage systems, and aqueducts, but hardly anything remains of these works.

CHAPTER SEVEN

Roman Art

Among the civilizations of the ancient world, that of the Romans is far more accessible to us than any other. We know a great deal about its history: its growth from city-state to empire; its military and political struggles; its changing social structure; the development of its institutions; and the lives of its leading figures. Nor is this a matter of chance. The Romans themselves seem to have wanted it that way. They left a vast literary legacy, from poetry and philosophy to inscriptions recording everyday events. They also built vast numbers of monuments throughout their empire, from England to the Persian Gulf, from Spain to Romania. And yet there are few questions more difficult to answer than "What is Roman art?" The Roman genius, so visible elsewhere, becomes oddly elusive when we ask whether there was a characteristic Roman style in the fine arts.

Why is this so? The most obvious reason is the Romans' admiration for Greek art. They imported Archaic, Classical, and Hellenistic originals by the thousands and had them copied in even greater numbers. In addition, their own works were clearly based on Greek sources, and many of their artists, from Republican times (510–27 B.C.) to the end of the Empire (27 B.C.–A.D. 395), were of Greek origin. Moreover, Roman authors show little concern with the art of their own time. They tell us a good deal about the development of Greek art as described in Greek writings on the subject, and they also discuss Roman art during the early days of the Republic, of which not a trace survives today. But they rarely speak of works done in their own time. While anecdotes or artists' names may be mentioned in other contexts, the Romans never developed a rich literature on the history and theory of art such as had existed among the Greeks. The sole exception is Vitruvius, whose treatise on architecture is of great importance for later eras. Nor do we hear of more than a handful of Roman artists who were famous, though the greatest Greek artists—Polykleitos, Pheidias, Praxiteles, Lysippos (Polyclitus, Phidias, Praxiteles, and Lysippus in Latin)—were praised as highly as ever.

One might be tempted to conclude, therefore, that the Romans viewed the art of their time as being in decline compared with that of the Greek past. This was also the prevalent attitude among scholars until not very long ago. Roman art, they claimed, is Greek art in its final phase—Greek art under Roman rule. Hence there is no such thing as Roman style, only Roman subject matter. Yet the fact remains that, as a whole, Roman art looks distinctly different from Greek art. Otherwise the "problem" would not have arisen. If we insist on judging this difference by Greek standards, it will appear as a process of decay. If, on the other hand, we interpret it as expressing different intentions, we are likely to see it in a more positive light.

Rome, after all, was not simply an outgrowth of Greece. It was ruled by Etruscan kings for about a century, until 510 B.C., when the Republic was established. It was Etruscan kings who threw the first defensive wall around the seven hills, drained the swampy plain of the Forum, and built the original temple on the Capitoline Hill, thus making a city out of what had been little more than a group of villages consisting of rude huts. Equally important, they provided Rome with its early institutions and introduced the latest techniques of warfare, thereby establishing the foundations for its future greatness. These Etruscan influences, as well as native traditions, made Roman civilization quite distinct from that of the Greeks. (See also page 189; Roman music and theater.)

Once we acknowledge that art under the Romans had un-Greek aspects, we cannot say that they belong to the final phase of Greek art, no matter how many artists of Greek origin we may find in Roman records. Actually, the Greek names of these men do not mean much. Most of the artists, it seems, were fully Romanized. In any event, most Roman works of art are unsigned, and their makers, for all we know, may have come from any part of the far-flung Roman domain.

In the Roman Empire, national or regional traits were absorbed into the pattern set by the capital, the city of Rome. From the very start Roman society proved astonishingly tolerant of non-Roman traditions. It was able to make room for them all, so long as they did not threaten the security of the state. The populations of newly conquered provinces were not forced to change their ways but, rather, were put into a fairly low-temperature melting pot. Law and order, and respect for the symbols of Roman rule, were imposed on them. At the same time, however, their gods and sages were hospitably received in the capital, and eventually they themselves would be given the rights of citizenship. Roman civilization and Roman art thus acquired not only the Greek heritage but, to a lesser extent, that of the Etruscans, and of Egypt and the Near East as well.

All this made for a complex and open society that was uniform and diverse at the same time. The sanctuary of Mithras accidentally unearthed in the center of London offers a striking illustration of the cosmopolitan character of Roman society. The god is Persian in origin (see fig. 8-1), but he had long since become a Roman "citizen." His sanctuary, now thoroughly Roman in form, resembles hundreds of others throughout the Empire.

Under such conditions, we cannot expect Roman art to show a consistent style such as we found in Egypt, or the clear-cut evolution that distinguishes the art of Greece. To the extent that we understand it today, its development consists of a set of tendencies that may exist side by side, even within a single monument, none of which is dominant. The "Roman-ness" of Roman art must be found in this complex pattern, rather than in a single, consistent quality of form—and that is precisely its strength.

ARCHITECTURE

While the originality of Roman sculpture and painting has been questioned, there is no such doubt about Roman architecture, which is a creative feat of extraordinary magnitude. From the very start, its growth reflected a distinct Roman way of public and private life. Greek models, though much admired, could not accommodate the sheer numbers of people in large public buildings required by the Empire. And when it came to supplying citizens with everything they needed, from water to entertainment on a grand scale, new forms had to be invented, and cheaper materials and quicker methods had to be used.

We cannot imagine the growth of Rome without the arch and the vaulting systems derived from it: the barrel vault, a half-cylinder; the groin vault (two barrel vaults that intersect at right angles); and the dome (see figs. 7-1 and 8-33). True arches are constructed of wedge-shaped blocks, called voussoirs, each pointing toward the center of the semicircular opening. Such an arch is strong and self-sustaining, in contrast to the "false" arch made up of horizontal courses of masonry or brickwork (like the opening above the lintel of the Lioness Gate at Mycenae, fig. 4-19). The true arch—and its extension, the barrel vault—had been discovered in Egypt as early as about 2700 B.C. But the Egyptians had used it mainly in underground tombs and in utilitarian buildings, never in temples. Apparently they did not think it was suited to monumental architecture. In Mesopotamia the true arch was used for city gates and perhaps elsewhere as well, but to what extent we cannot determine for lack of preserved examples. The Greeks knew the principle of the true arch from the fifth century on, but they confined its use to underground structures or simple gateways and refused to combine it with the architectural orders.

No less vital to Roman architecture was concrete, a mixture of mortar and gravel with rubble (small pieces of building stone and brick). Concrete construction had been invented in the Near East more than a thousand years earlier, but the Romans made it their chief building technique. The advantages of concrete are obvious: it is strong, cheap, and flexible. Concrete made possible the vast architectural works that are the chief reminders of "the grandeur that was Rome." The Romans knew how to hide the unattractive concrete surface by adding a facing of brick, stone, or marble, or by covering it with smooth plaster. Today this decorative skin has disappeared from most Roman buildings, thus leaving the concrete core exposed and depriving these ruins of the appeal that those of Greece have for us.

Republican Religious Architecture

THE "TEMPLE OF FORTUNA VIRILIS." Any elements borrowed from the Etruscans or Greeks were soon marked with an unmistakable Roman stamp. These links with the past are strongest in the temple types developed during the Republican period (510–60 B.C.), the heroic age of Roman expansion. The delightful small "Temple of Fortuna Virilis" is the oldest well-preserved example of its kind (fig. 7-2). (The name is sheer fancy, for it seems to have been dedicated to the Roman god of harbors, Portunus.) Built in Rome during the last years of the second century B.C., it suggests, in the elegant proportions of its Ionic columns and entablature, the wave of Greek influence following the

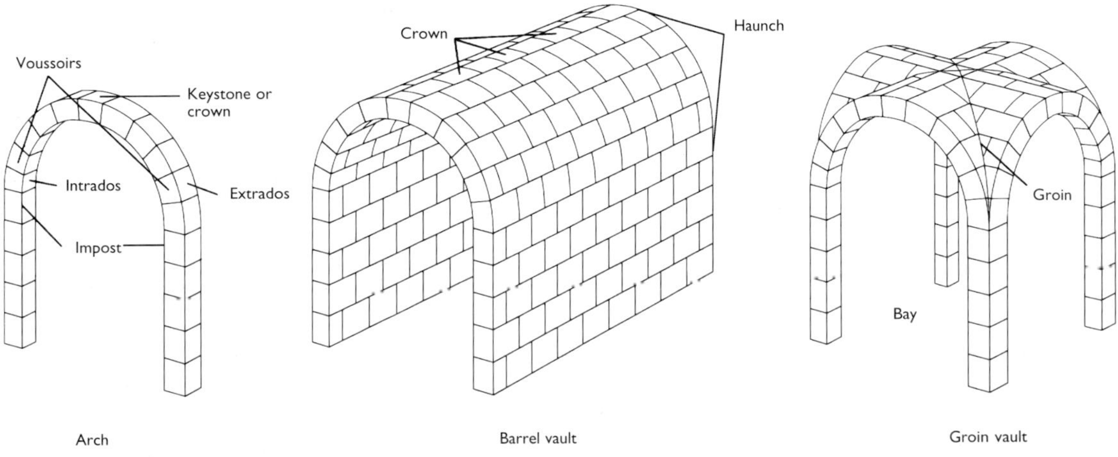

7-1. Arch, barrel vault, and groin vault

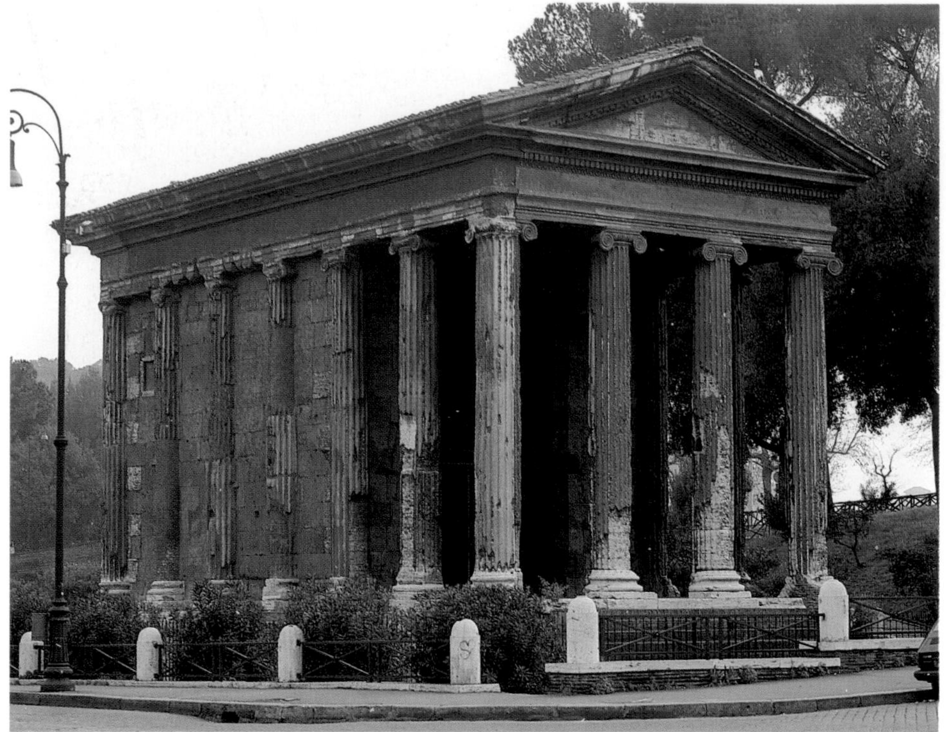

7-2. "Temple of Fortuna Virilis," Rome. Late 2nd century B.C.

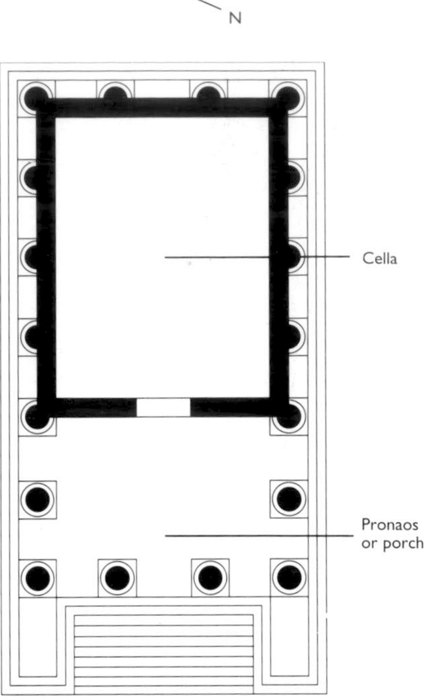

7-3. Plan of the "Temple of Fortuna Virilis"

Roman conquest of Greece in 146 B.C. Yet it is not simply a copy of a Greek temple, for we recognize a number of Etruscan elements: the high podium, the deep porch, and the wide cella, which engages the columns of the peristyle. However, the cella is no longer subdivided into three compartments as it had been under the Etruscans; it now encloses a single unified space (fig. 7-3).

The Romans needed spacious temple interiors, since they used them not only for the image of the god but also for the display of trophies (statues, weapons, etc.) brought back by their armies. The "Temple of Fortuna Virilis" thus represents a new type of temple designed for Roman needs, not a haphazard cross of Etruscan and Greek elements. It was to have a long life. Numerous examples of it, usually large and with Corinthian columns, can be found as late as the second century A.D., both in Italy and in the provincial capitals of the Empire.

THE TEMPLE OF THE SIBYL. Another type of Republican temple is seen in the so-called "Temple of the Sibyl" at Tivoli (figs. 7-4 and 7-5), built a few decades later than the "Temple of Fortuna Virilis." It, too, merges two traditions. Its original ancestor was a structure in the center of Rome in which the sacred flame of the city was kept. This building at first had the shape of the traditional round peasant huts in the Roman countryside. Later it was redesigned in stone, under the influence of Greek structures of the tholos type (see pages 120–21), and thus became the model for the round temples of late Republican times. Here again we find the high podium, with steps only at the entrance, and a Greek-inspired exterior. As we look closely at the cella, we note that while the door and window frames are of cut stone, the wall is built in concrete, which can be seen now that the marble facing that once disguised it is gone.

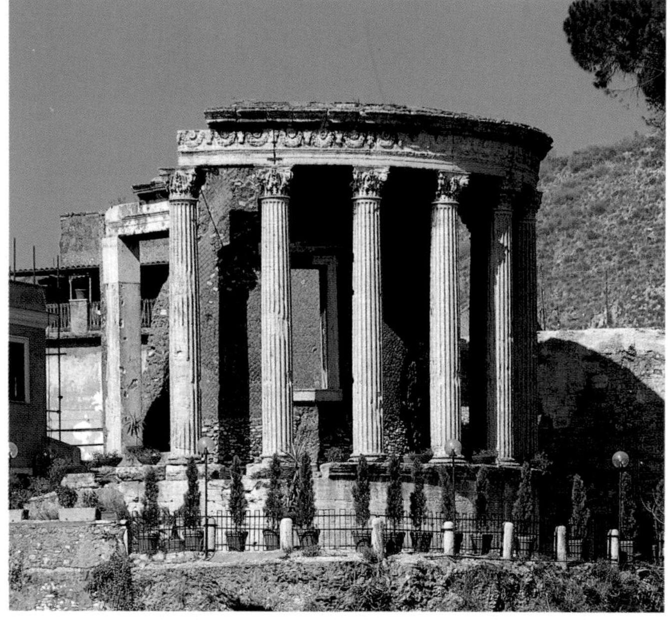

7-4. "Temple of the Sibyl," Tivoli. Early 1st century B.C.

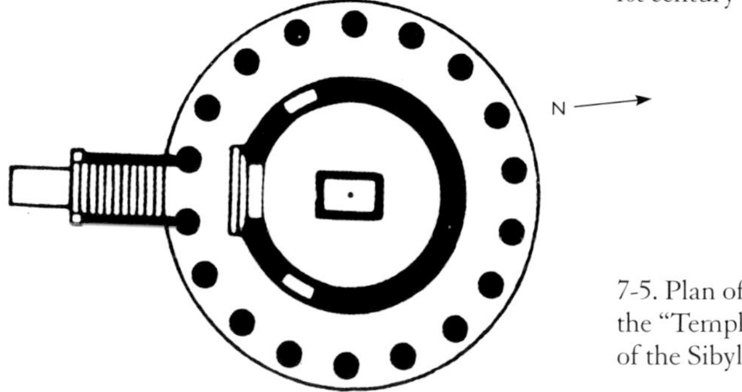

7-5. Plan of the "Temple of the Sibyl"

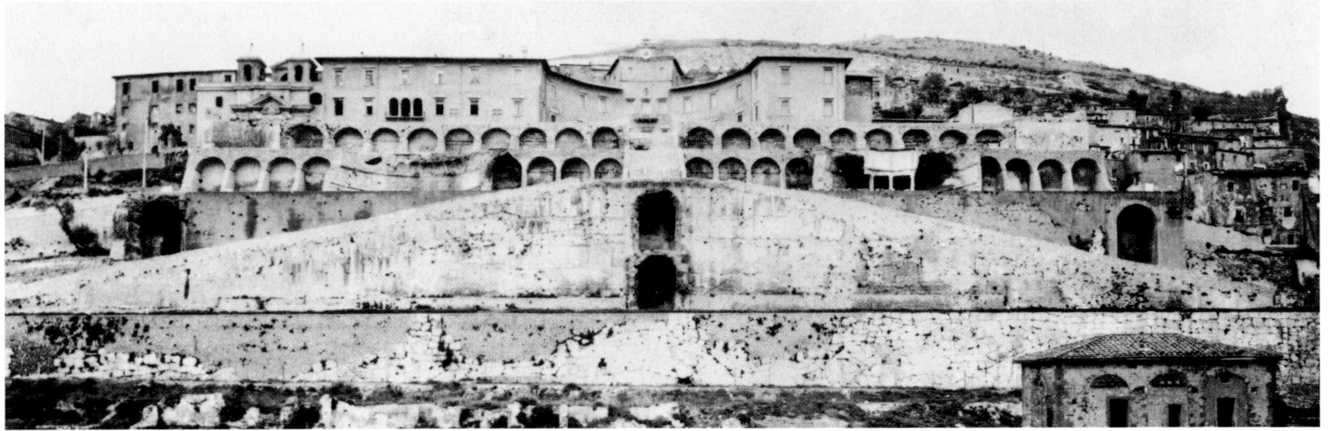

7-6. Sanctuary of Fortuna Primigenia, Praeneste (Palestrina). Early 1st century B.C.

THE SANCTUARY OF FORTUNA PRIMIGENIA. Roman buildings characteristically speak to us through their massive size and boldness of conception. The oldest monument in which these qualities are fully in evidence is the Sanctuary of Fortuna Primigenia at Palestrina, in the foothills of the Apennines east of Rome (fig. 7-6). Here, in what was once an important Etruscan stronghold, a strange cult had been established since early times, dedicated to Fortuna (Fate) as a mother deity, and combined with a famous oracle. The Roman sanctuary dates from the early first century B.C. Its size and shape were almost completely hidden by the medieval town that had been built over it. In 1944, however, a bombing attack destroyed most of the later houses and revealed the ancient temple precinct.

The site originally had a series of ramps leading up to a broad colonnaded terrace. At the top of the entire structure was a great colonnaded court (fig. 7-7). (The semicircular structure is of a much later date.) The first terrace was marked by semicircular recesses, the second by arched openings framed by engaged columns and architraves. The openings were covered by barrel vaults, another typical feature of Roman architecture. Except for one niche with the columns and entablature on the lower terrace, all the surfaces now visible are of concrete, like the cella of the round temple at Tivoli. Indeed, it is hard to imagine how such a huge complex could have been constructed otherwise.

What makes the sanctuary at Palestrina so imposing, however, is not merely its scale but the superb way it fits the site. An entire hillside, comparable to the Akropolis of Athens in its commanding position, has been transformed. The architectural forms seem to grow out of the rock, as if human beings had simply completed a design laid out by nature itself. Such a molding of open spaces had never been possible, or even desired, in the Classical Greek world. The only comparable projects are found in Egypt (see the Temple of Queen Hatshepsut, fig. 2-25). Nor did it express the spirit of the Roman Republic. Significantly the Palestrina sanctuary dates from the time of Sulla, whose dictatorship (82–79 B.C.) marked the transition from Republican government to the one-man rule of Julius Caesar and the emperors who followed him. Since Sulla had won a great victory against his enemies in the civil war at Palestrina, it is tempting to assume that he personally ordered the complex built, both as an offering to Fortuna and as a monument to his own fame.

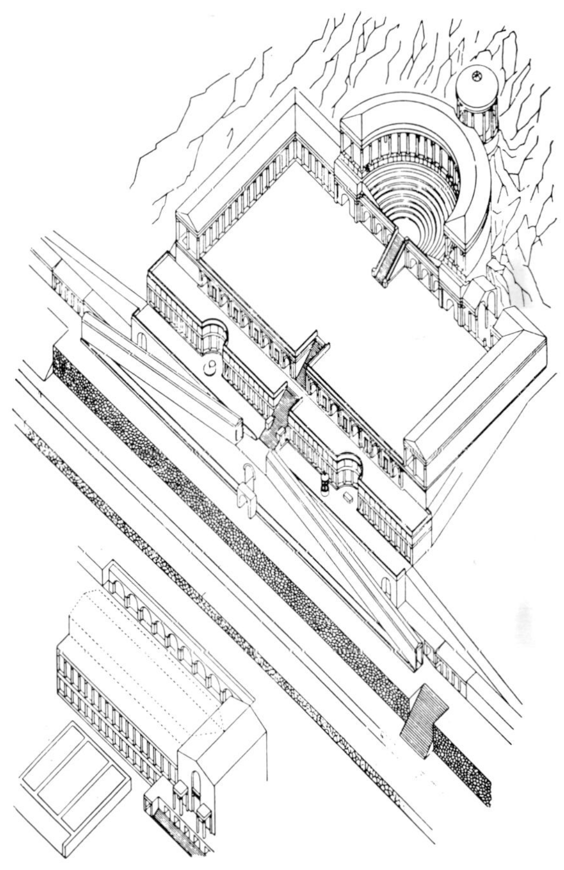

7-7. Axonometric reconstruction of the Sanctuary of Fortuna Primigenia, Praeneste

FORUMS. Perhaps inspired by the Palestrina sanctuary, Julius Caesar sponsored a project on a similar scale in Rome itself: the Forum Julium. Done near the end of Caesar's life, it was a great architecturally framed square adjoining the Temple of Venus Genetrix, the mythical ancestress of Caesar's family. Here the merging of religious cult and personal glory is even more overt. The Forum of Caesar set the pattern for all the later Imperial forums, which were linked to it by a common major axis to form the most magnificent architectural sight of the Roman world (fig. 7-8). Unfortunately, nothing is left of the forums today but a field of ruins that conveys little of their original splendor.

Republican Secular Architecture

The arch and vault, as we saw at Palestrina, were an essential part of Roman monumental architecture. They also formed the basis of construction projects such as sewers, bridges, and aqueducts, which were designed for efficiency rather than beauty. The first structures of this kind were built in Rome as early as the end of the fourth century B.C., but only traces of them survive today. There are, however, many others of later date throughout the Empire. An example is the well-preserved aqueduct at Nîmes in southern France known as the Pont du Gard (fig. 7-9). Its rugged, clean

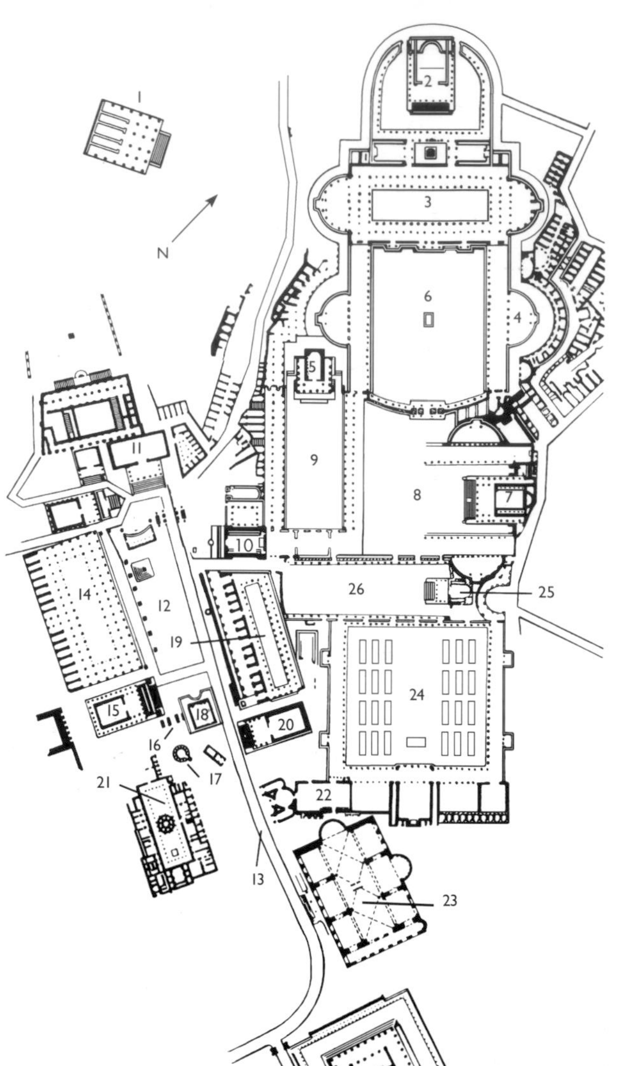

(LEFT) 7-8. Plan of the Forums, Rome:

1) Temple of Capitoline Jupiter; 2) Temple of Trajan; 3) Basilica Ulpia; 4) Market of Trajan; 5) Temple of Venus Genetrix; 6) Forum of Trajan; 7) Temple of Mars Ultor; 8) Forum of Augustus; 9) Forum of Julius Caesar; 10) Senate Chamber; 11) Temple of Concord; 12) Roman Forum; 13) Sacred Way; 14) Basilica Julia; 15) Temple of Castor and Pollux; 16) Arch of Augustus; 17) Temple of Vesta; 18) Temple of Julius Caesar; 19) Basilica Aemilia; 20) Temple of Antoninus and Faustina; 21) House of the Vestal Virgins; 22) Temple of Romulus; 23) Basilica of Maxentius and Constantine; 24) Forum of Vespasian; 25) Temple of Minerva; 26) Forum of Nerva

(BELOW) 7-9. Pont du Gard, Nîmes, France. Early 1st century A.D.

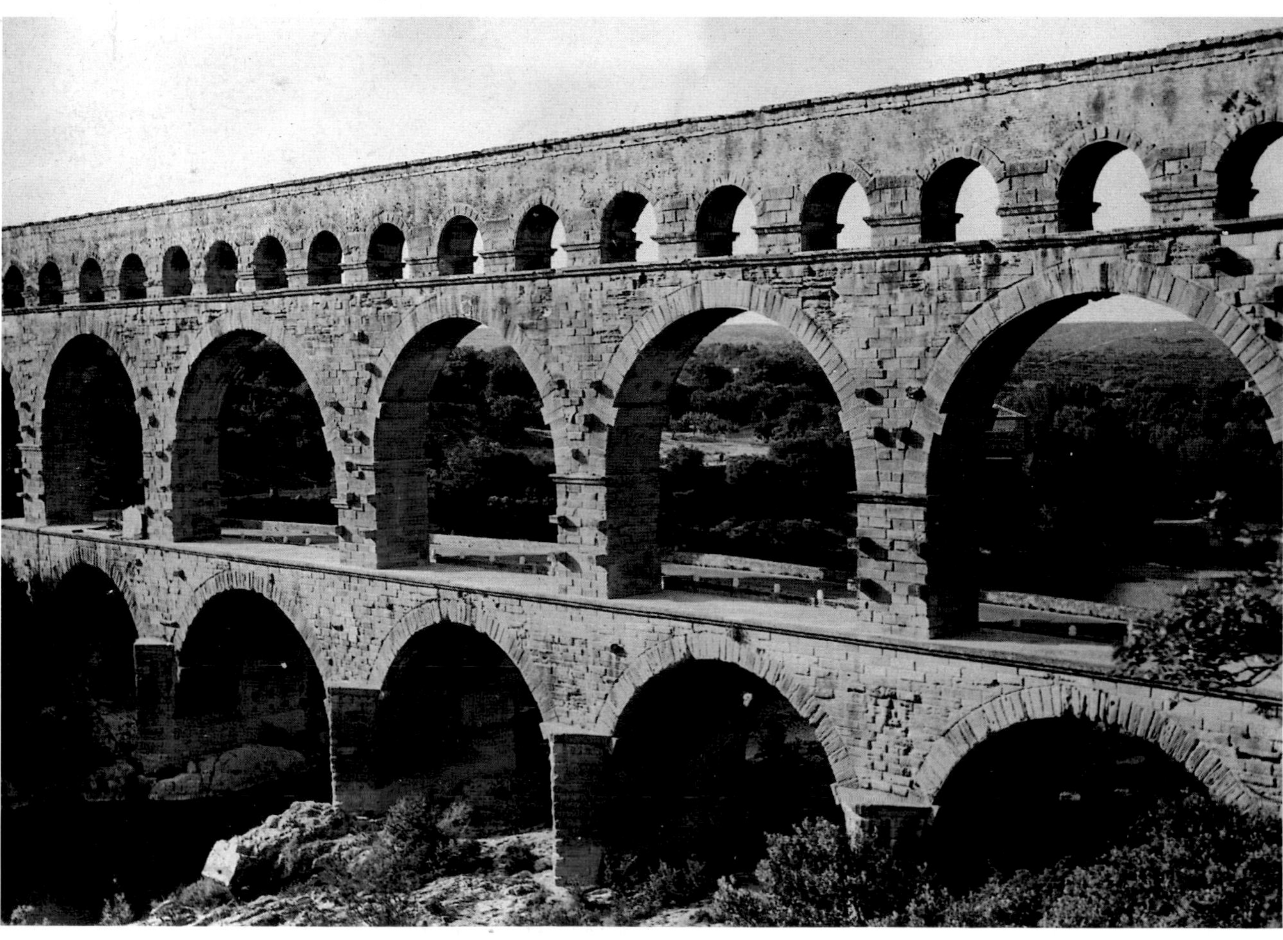

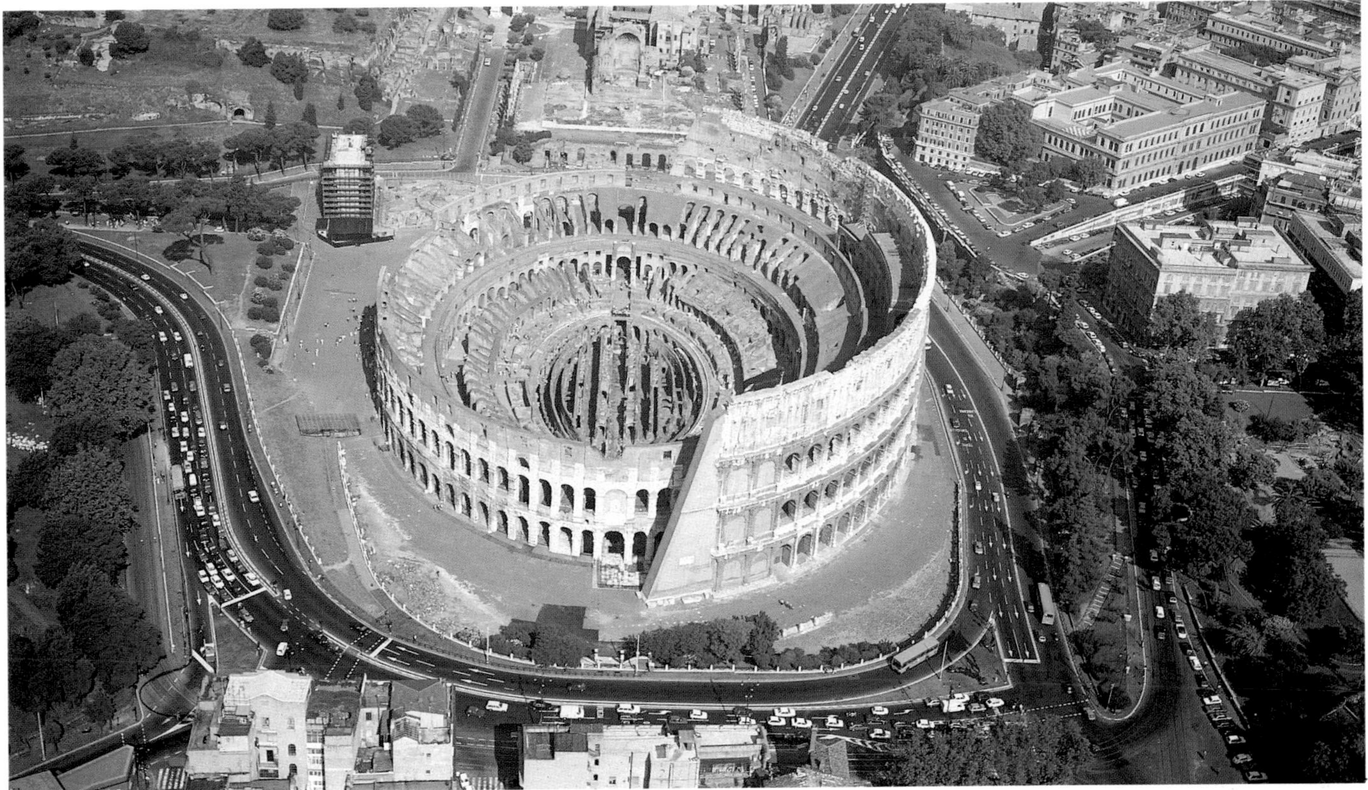

7-10. The Colosseum (aerial view), Rome. 72–80 A.D.

lines spanning the wide valley are a tribute not only to the high caliber of Roman engineering but also to the sense of order and permanence that inspired these efforts. It is these qualities, one may argue, that underlie all Roman architecture and define its unique character.

THE COLOSSEUM. They impress us again in the Colosseum, the huge amphitheater for gladiatorial games in the center of Rome (figs. 7-10 and 7-11). Completed in 80 A.D., it is, in terms of sheer mass, one of the largest single buildings anywhere: it could hold more than 50,000 spectators. The concrete core, with its miles of stairways and barrel- and groin-vaulted corridors, is an outstanding feat of engineering whose purpose was to ensure the smooth flow of traffic to and from the arena. It utilizes both the familiar barrel vault and a more complex form, the groin vault (see fig. 7-1). The exterior, dignified and monumental, reflects the interior articulation of the structure, but clothes and accentuates it in cut stone. There is a fine balance between vertical and horizontal elements in the framework of engaged columns and entablatures that contains the endless series of arches. The three Classical orders are superimposed according to their "weight": Doric, the oldest and most severe, on the ground floor, followed by Ionic and Corinthian. The lightening of the proportions, however, is barely noticeable, for the Roman versions of the orders are almost alike. Structurally they have become ghosts, yet they still serve an aesthetic function. It is through them that this enormous facade is related to the human scale.

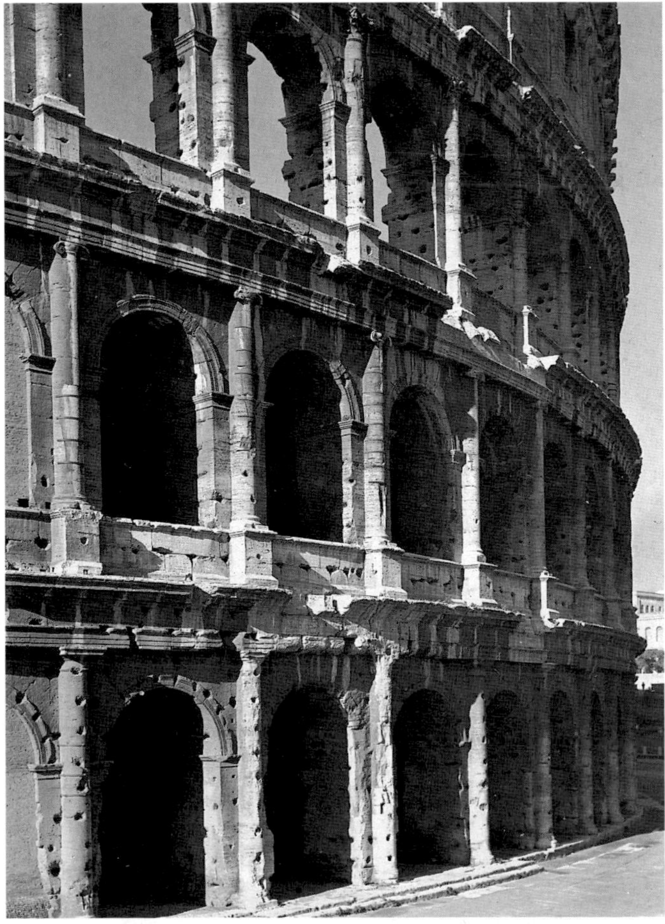

7-11. View of the outer wall of the Colosseum

Imperial Religious Architecture

Arches, vaults, and concrete permitted the Romans to create huge uninterrupted interior spaces for the first time in the history of architecture. The potential of all three was explored especially in building the great baths, or *thermae,* which were major centers of social life in Imperial Rome. The experience gained there could then be applied to more traditional types of buildings, sometimes with revolutionary results.

THE PANTHEON. Perhaps the most striking example of this process is the famous Pantheon in Rome, a very large round temple of the early second century A.D. whose interior is one of the best preserved, as well as the most impressive, of any Roman structure (figs. 7-12, 7-13, 7-14, and 7-15). There had been round temples long before this time, but their shape, as seen in the "Temple of the Sibyl" (see figs. 7-4 and 7-5), is so different from that of the Pantheon that the latter could not have been derived from them. On the outside, the cella of the Pantheon appears as a plain cylindrical drum, surmounted by a gently curved dome. The entrance is emphasized by a deep porch of the kind familiar to us from Roman temples of the "Fortuna Virilis" type (see figs. 7-2 and 7-3). (The inscription refers to Marcus Agrippa, who built the first temple on the site toward the end of the first century B.C.)

The junction of these two elements seems rather abrupt, but we no longer see the building raised high on a podium as it was meant to be seen. Today the level of the surrounding streets is a good deal higher than it was in antiquity. As a result, the steps leading up to the porch are now submerged. Moreover, the porch was part of a rectangular, colonnaded forecourt, which must have had the effect of detaching it from the rotunda. So far as the cella is concerned, therefore, the architect seems to have discounted the effect of the exterior and put all the emphasis on the great domed space that opens before us as we step through the entrance.

The heavy plainness of the exterior wall suggests that the architects did not have an easy time with the problem of supporting the huge dome. Nothing on the outside, however, gives any hint of the interior. Indeed, its airiness and elegance are utterly different from what the severe exterior would lead us to expect. The impact of the interior, awe-inspiring and harmonious at the same time, is impossible to convey in photographs. Even the painting in figure 7-12 fails to do it justice.

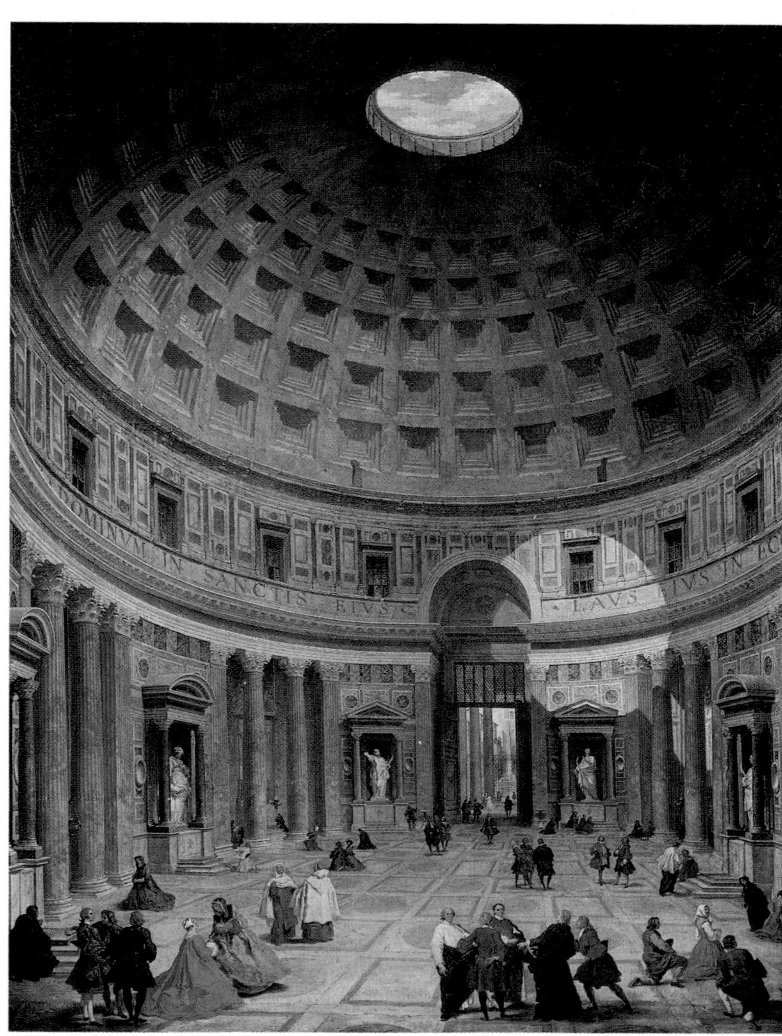

7-12. Giovanni Paolo Panini. *The Interior of the Pantheon.* c. 1740. Oil on canvas, 50½" x 39" (128.3 x 99.1 cm). National Gallery of Art, Washington, D.C. Samuel H. Kress Collection

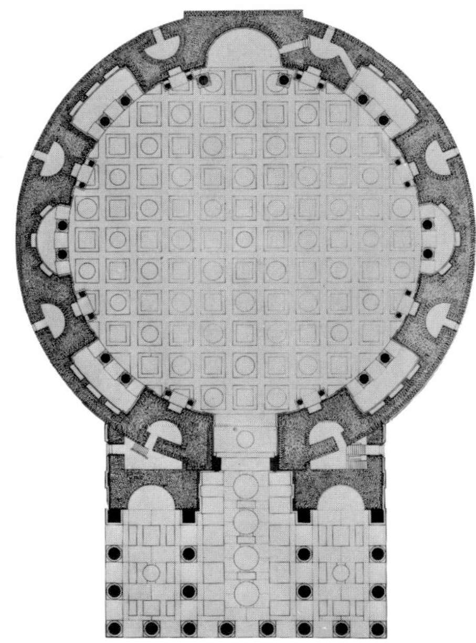

7-13. Plan of the Pantheon

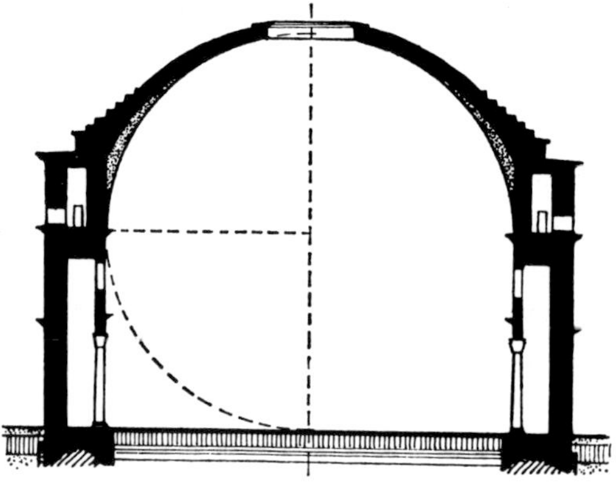

7-14. Transverse section of the Pantheon

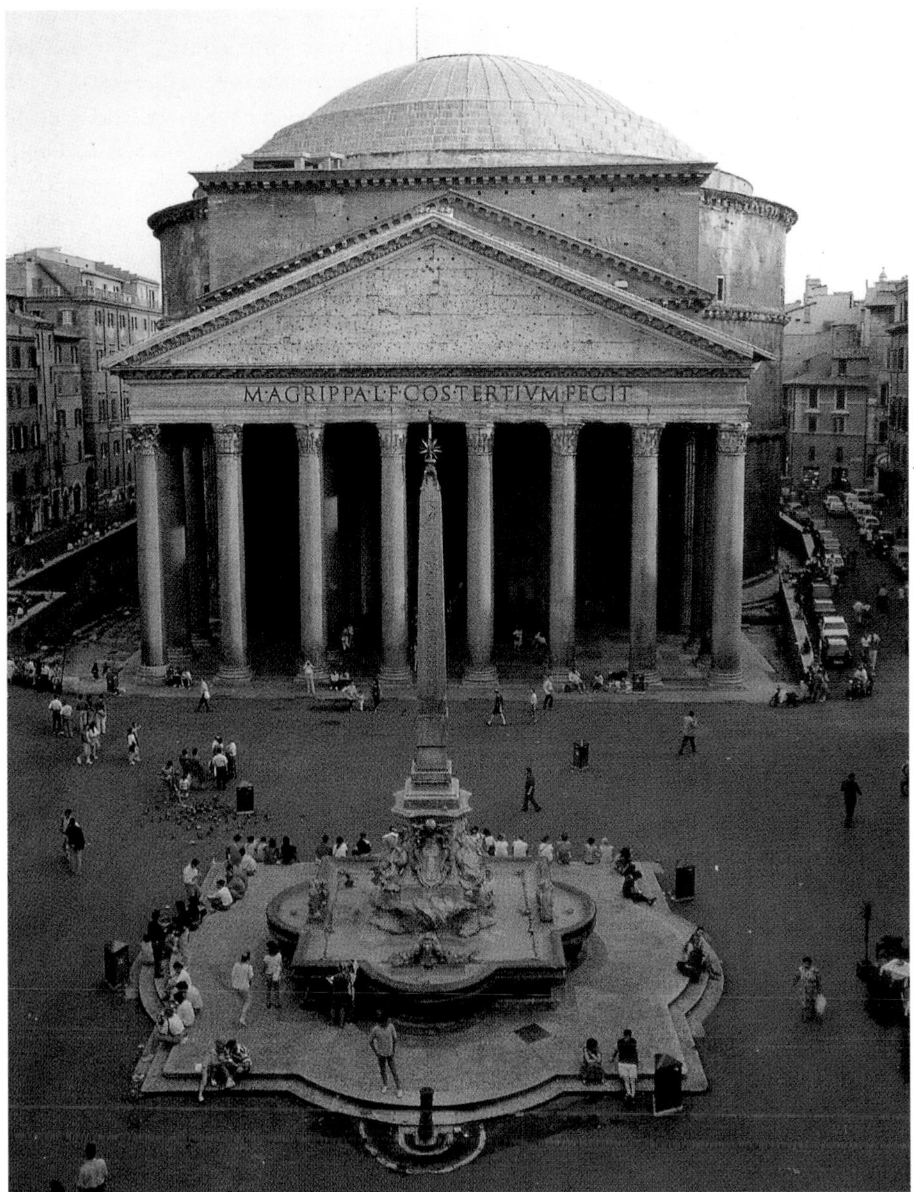

7-15. The Pantheon, Rome. 118–25 A.D.

The dome is a true hemisphere of ingenious design. The interlocking ribs form a structural cage that permits the use of relatively lightweight coffers arranged in five rings. The circular opening in its center (called the oculus, or eye) admits an ample and even flow of light. The height from the floor to the oculus is 143 feet, which is also the diameter of the dome's base and the interior (see fig. 7-14). The dome and drum are likewise of equal heights, so that all the proportions are in exact balance. This balance could not be achieved on the exterior because the outward thrust of the dome had to be contained by making its base much heavier than the top. (The thickness of the dome increases downward from 6 feet to 20 feet.)

The weight of the dome does not rest uniformly on the drum but is concentrated on the eight wide "pillars" (see fig. 7-13). Between them, niches are hollowed out of the massive concrete, and although they are closed in back, the screen of columns gives them the effect of openings that lead to adjoining rooms. This sense of open space behind the supports helps to prevent us from feeling imprisoned inside the Pantheon. It also makes us feel that the walls are less thick and the dome much lighter than they actually are. The columns, the colored marble paneling of the wall surfaces, and the floor remain largely as they were in Roman times. Originally, however, the coffers were gilded.

As its name suggests, the Pantheon was dedicated to all the gods or, more precisely, to the seven planetary gods. (There are seven niches. The sculpture that fills them in our illustration dates from the Baroque era.) It seems reasonable, therefore, to assume that the golden dome had a symbolic meaning—that it represented the Dome of Heaven. Yet this solemn and splendid structure grew from rather humble beginnings. Vitruvius, writing more than a century earlier, describes the domed steam chamber of a bath that foreshadows (on a much smaller scale) the basic features of the Pantheon: a hemispherical dome, a proportional relationship of height and width, and the circular opening in the center. (The opening could be closed by a bronze shutter on chains to adjust the temperature of the steam room.)

BASILICAS. The Basilica of Constantine is an even more direct example of how thermae were transformed in new types of buildings. Actually begun by Constantine's predecessor, Maxentius, it was built in the early fourth century A.D. Unlike other basilicas, which we will discuss below, the Basilica of Constantine derives its shape from the main halls of the public baths built by two earlier emperors, Caracalla and Diocletian. The scale is even grander, however. It must have been the largest roofed interior in all of Rome. Today only the north aisle, consisting of three huge barrel-vaulted compartments, is still standing (fig. 7-16). The center tract,

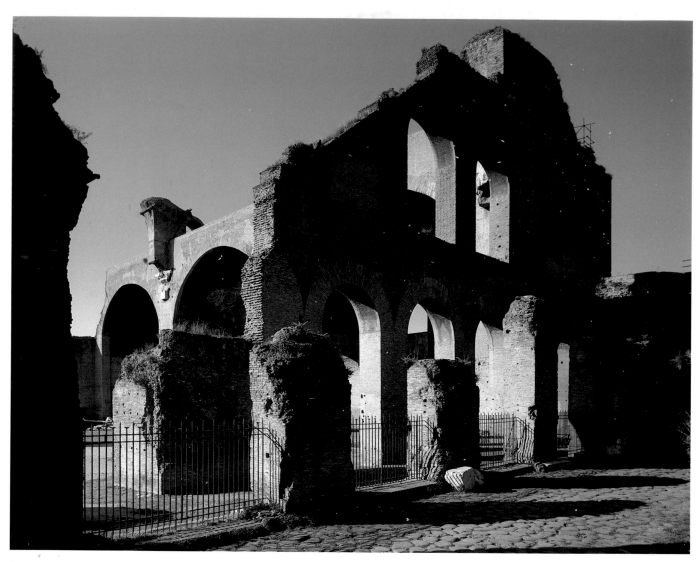

7-16. The Basilica of Constantine, Rome. c. 307–20 A.D.

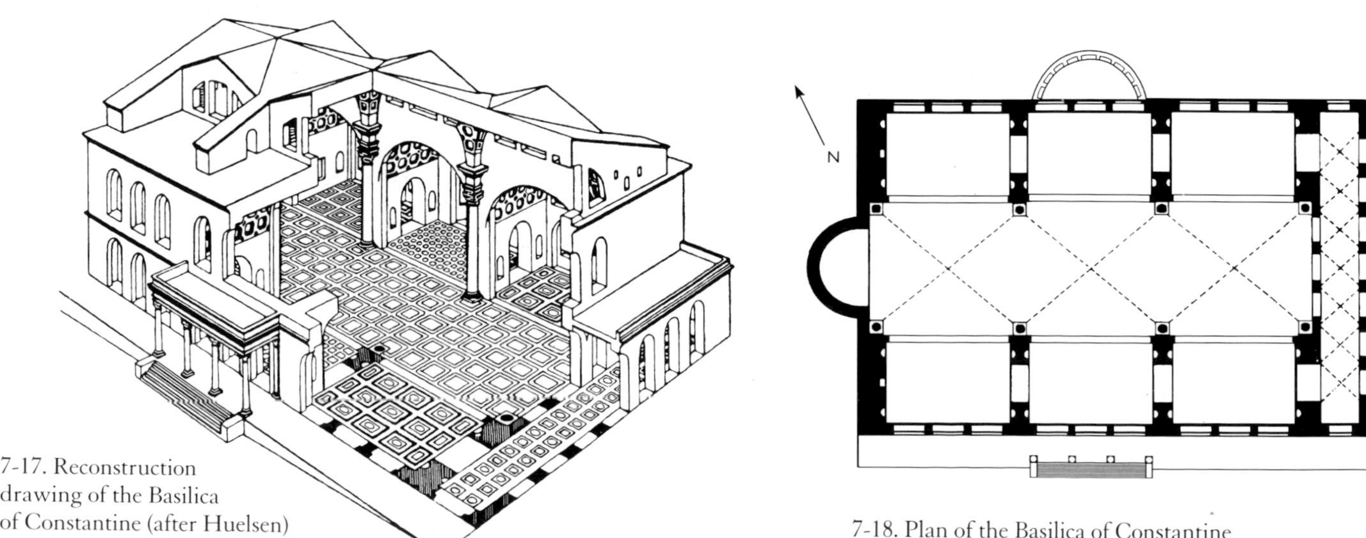

7-17. Reconstruction drawing of the Basilica of Constantine (after Huelsen)

7-18. Plan of the Basilica of Constantine

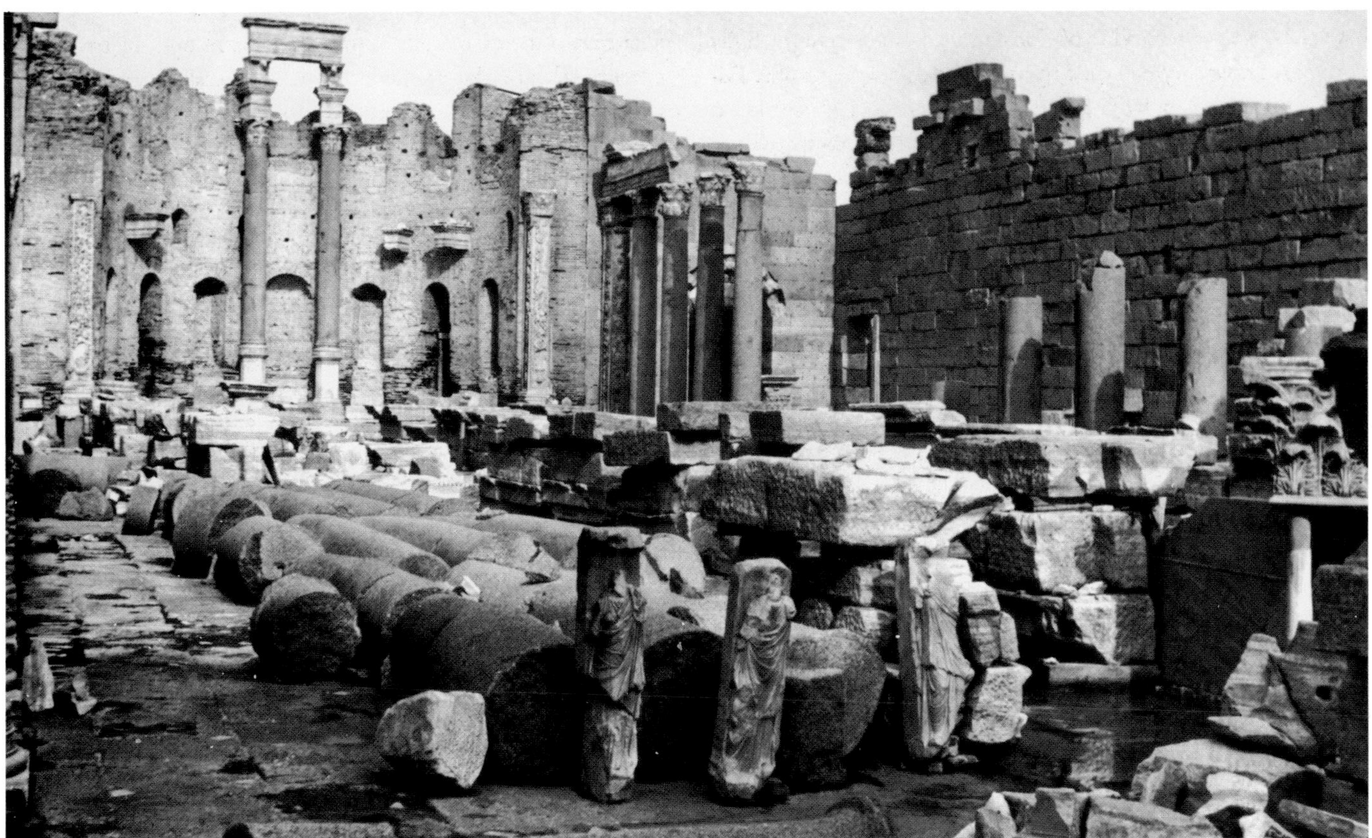

7-19. Basilica, Leptis Magna, Libya. Early 3rd century A.D.

or nave, was covered by three groin vaults (figs. 7-17 and 7-18) and rose a good deal higher. Since a groin vault, like a canopy, has its weight and thrust concentrated at the four corners (see fig. 7-1), the upper walls of the nave could be pierced by large windows (called the clerestory). As a result, the interior of the basilica must have had a light and airy quality despite its enormous size. We meet its echoes in many later buildings, from churches to railway stations.

The Basilica of Constantine was entered through a vestibule, or narthex, at the east end. At the opposite end was a semicircular niche, called an apse, where the colossal statue of Constantine was found (see fig. 7-45). Perhaps to make room for his cult statue, Constantine modified the building by adding a second entrance to the south and a second apse opposite it where he could sit as emperor.

Basilicas, long halls used for civic purposes, had first been developed in Hellenistic Greece toward the end of the third century B.C. (In ancient Greek, "basilica" meant "royal house," from *basileus,* "king.") They never conformed to a single type but varied from region to region. Roman basilicas, whose origins can be traced back to 184 B.C., eventually became a standard feature of every major town. One of their chief functions was to provide a dignified setting for the courts of law that dispensed justice in the name of the emperor. According to Vitruvius, their placement and proportions followed set principles. [See Primary Sources, no. 4, page 195.]

Rome itself had a number of basilicas, but very little remains of them today. Those in the provinces have fared somewhat better. The outstanding one at Leptis Magna in North Africa (figs. 7-

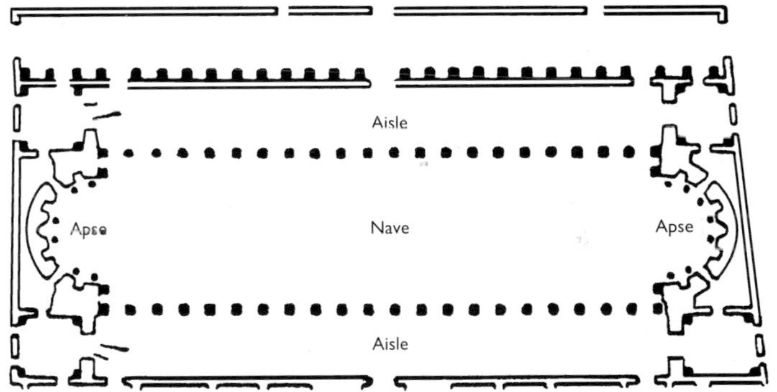

7-20. Plan of the Basilica, Leptis Magna

19 and 7-20) has most of the features of the Imperial type. The long nave, with its two-story colonnade, terminates in a semicircular apse at either end. Its walls rest on colonnades to provide access to the side aisles, which are lower than the nave to permit clerestory windows in the upper part of the nave wall.

These basilicas had wooden ceilings instead of masonry vaults for reasons of convenience and tradition rather than necessity. Thus they were often destroyed by fire. The one at Leptis Magna, ruined though it is, is one of the best-preserved examples. The Basilica of Constantine in Rome was a daring attempt to create a new, vaulted type, but it seems to have met with little public favor. Perhaps people felt that it lacked dignity because of its resemblance to the public baths. Whatever the reason, the Christian basilicas of the fourth century were modeled on the older, wooden-roofed type (see fig. 8-6). Not until 700 years later did vaulted basilican churches become common in western Europe.

Imperial Domestic Architecture

One of the delights in studying Roman architecture is that it includes not only great public buildings but also a wide variety of dwellings, from Imperial palaces to the homes of the urban poor. If we disregard these two extremes, we are left with two basic house types that account for most of the domestic architecture that has survived. The *domus* is a single-family house based on ancient Italic tradition. Its distinctive feature is the atrium, a square or oblong central hall lit by an opening in the roof, around which the other rooms are grouped. In Etruscan times, it had been a rural dwelling, but the Romans "citified" it to create the typical home of the well-to-do, discussed at length by Vitruvius. [See Primary Sources, no. 4, pages 195–96.]

Many examples of the domus have come to light at Herculaneum and Pompeii, the two towns that were buried under volcanic ash during an eruption of Mount Vesuvius in 79 A.D. As we enter the House of the Silver Wedding at Pompeii (which received its nickname when the king and queen of Italy visited the site during their silver anniversary in 1893), we see the view in figure 7-21, taken from the vestibule, along the main axis of the domus. Here the atrium has become a room of impressive size. The four Corinthian columns at the corners of the opening in the roof give it the quality of an enclosed court. There is a shallow basin in the center to catch the rainwater (the roof slants inward). The atrium was the traditional place for keeping portraits of ancestors. At its far end, to the right, we see a recess for storing family records (the *tablinum*). Beyond it is the garden, surrounded by a colonnade (the *peristyle*). In addition to the rooms around the atrium, there may be rooms attached to the back of the house. The domus is shut off from the street by windowless walls. Obviously, privacy and self-sufficiency were more important to the wealthy Roman. Yet the domus was also a public space shared with favored guests, who were entertained amid sumptuous decorations—stucco, wall paintings, and mosaics—that testified to the family's wealth, status, and good taste.

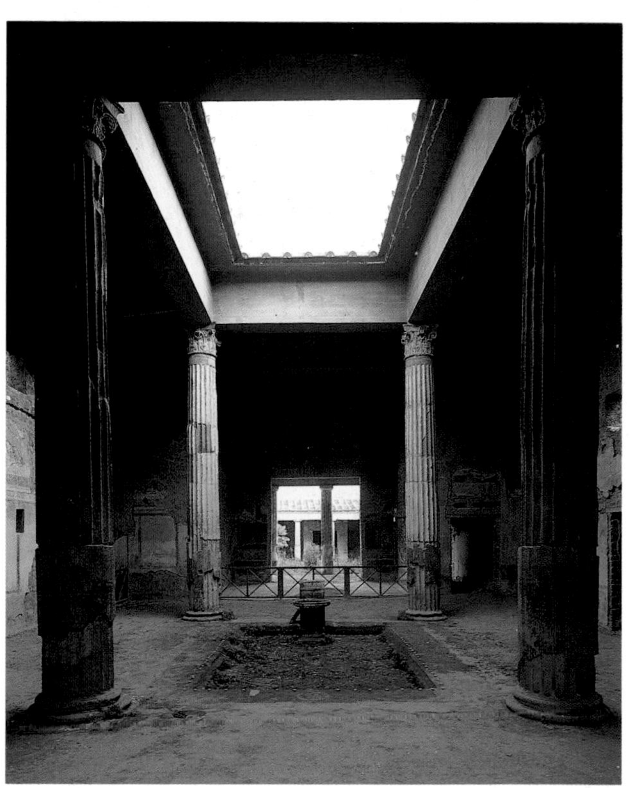

7-21. Atrium, House of the Silver Wedding, Pompeii. Early 1st century A.D.

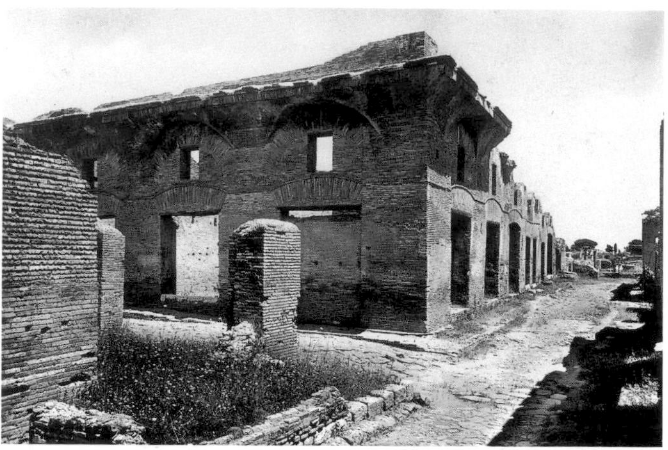

7-22. Insula of the House of Diana, Ostia. c. 150 A.D.

Less elegant than the domus, and urban from the start, is the *insula,* or city block, which we find mainly in Rome itself and in Ostia, the ancient port of Rome near the mouth of the Tiber. The insula has many features of the modern apartment house. It is a good-sized concrete-and-brick building (or a chain of such buildings) around a small central court. On the ground floor are shops and taverns open to the street; above it are living quarters for numerous families. Some insulae had as many as five stories, with balconies above the second floor (fig. 7-22). The daily life of the artisans and shopkeepers who lived in them was oriented toward the street, as it still is to a large extent in modern Italy. The privacy of the domus was reserved for the few who could afford it.

Late Roman Architecture

In discussing the new forms of construction, we have noted the Romans' allegiance to the Classical Greek orders. While they no longer relied on them in the structural sense, they remained faithful to their spirit by continuing to use the post-and-lintel system as an organizing principle. Column, architrave, and pediment might be merely superimposed on a vaulted brick-and-concrete core, but their shapes, as well as their relationships to one another, were still determined by the original orders.

This orthodox attitude toward the architectural vocabulary of the Greeks prevailed from the Roman conquest of Greece until the end of the first century A.D. After that, we find growing evidence of a contrary trend: a taste for imaginative transformations of the Greek vocabulary. Just when and where this tendency began is still a matter of dispute. There is some evidence that it may go back to late Hellenistic times in the Near East, since it certainly was most pronounced in the Asiatic and African provinces of the Empire. A characteristic example is the Market Gate from Miletus of about 160 A.D. (rebuilt in the state museums in Berlin; fig. 7-23). One might refer to it as display architecture in terms of

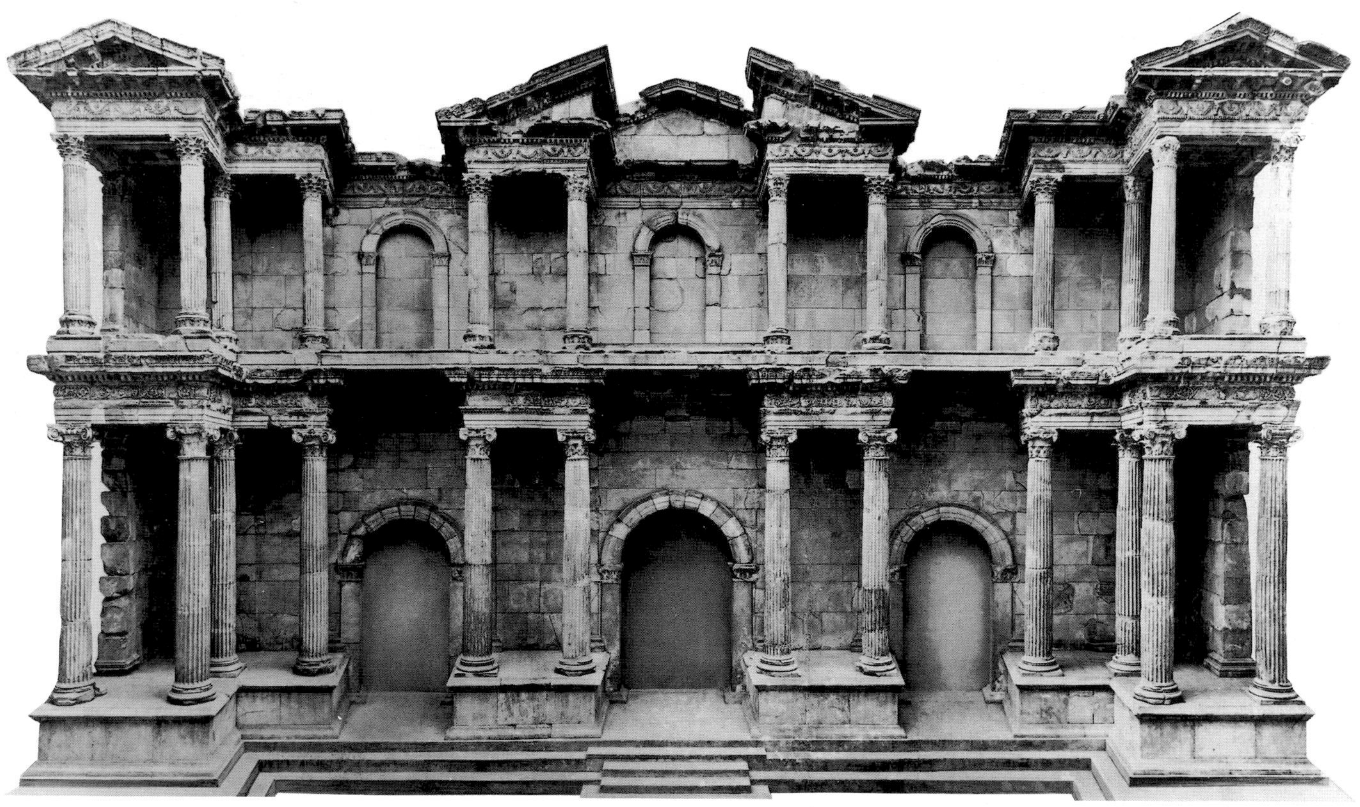

7-23. Market Gate from Miletus (restored). c. 160 A.D. Staatliche Museen zu Berlin, Preussischer Kulturbesitz, Antikensammlung

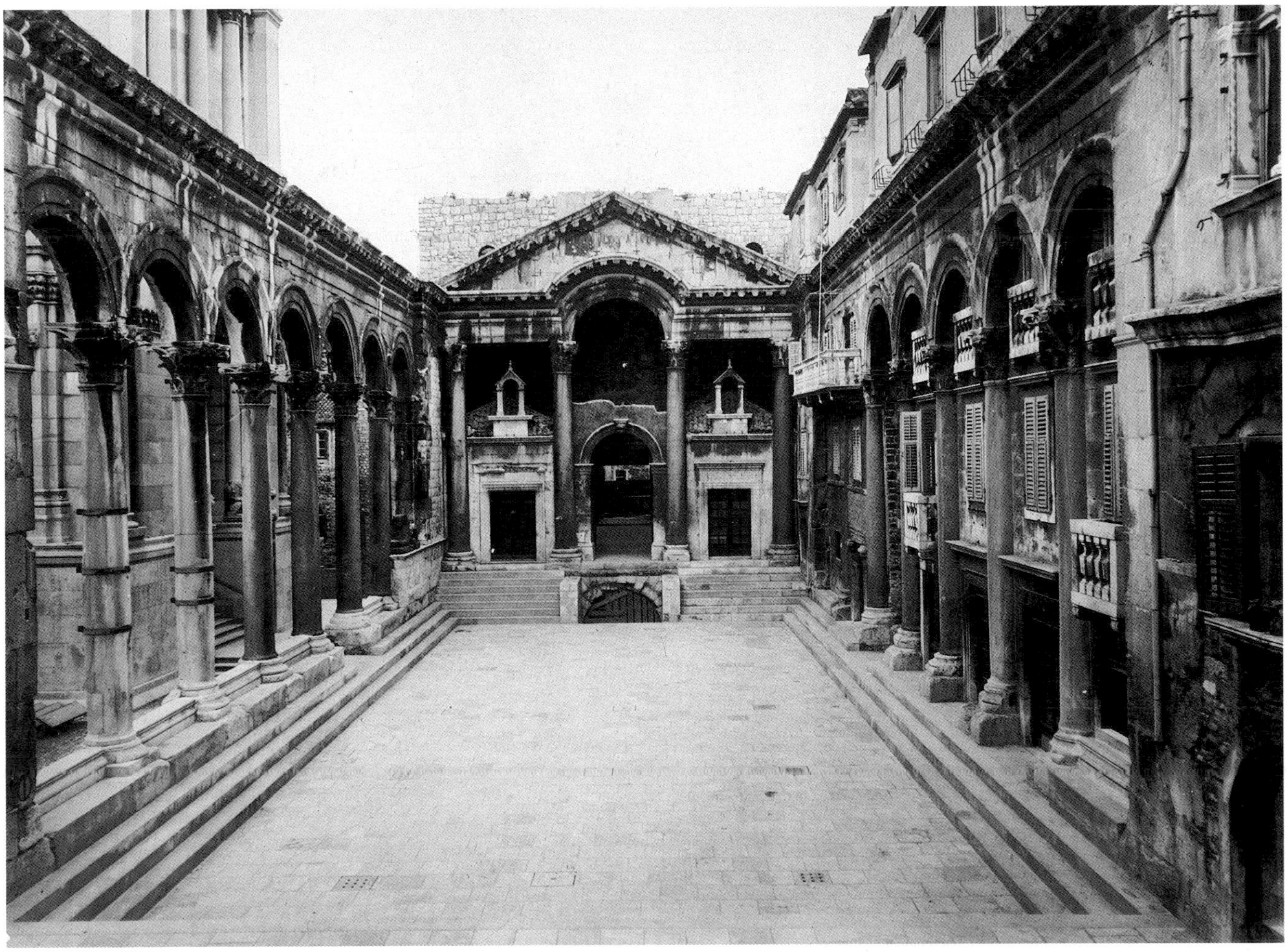

7-24. Peristyle, Palace of Diocletian, Spalato (Split), Croatia. c. 300 A.D.

both its effect and its ancestry. The facade, with its alternating recesses and projections, is derived from the architectural stage backgrounds of the Roman theater. The continuous in-and-out rhythm even appears in the pediment above the central doorway, breaking it into three parts.

By the late third century, ideas such as these had become so well established that the traditional grammar of the Greek orders was dissolving everywhere. At the end of the peristyle in the Palace of Diocletian (fig. 7-24) at Spalato (Split), the architrave between the two center columns is curved to create a novel effect by echoing the arch of the doorway below. On either side we see an even more revolutionary device: a series of arches resting directly on columns. A few arcades of this sort can be found earlier, but it was only now, on the eve of the victory of Christianity, that the marriage of arch and column was fully accepted. This union, indispensable to the future development of architecture, seems so natural to us that we can hardly understand why it was ever opposed.

SCULPTURE

The dispute over the question "Is there such a thing as a Roman style?" has centered largely on sculpture, and for good reason. Even if we discount the importing and copying of Greek originals, the reputation of the Romans as imitators seems to be borne out by large numbers of works that are probably based on Greek models. While the Roman demand for sculpture was tremendous, much of it may be attributed to a taste for antiquities and for sumptuous interior decoration. There are thus whole categories of sculpture produced under Roman auspices that deserve to be classified as "deactivated" echoes of Greek creations, emptied of their former meaning and reduced to the status of highly refined works of craftsmanship. At times this attitude extended to Egyptian sculpture as well and even created a vogue for pseudo-Egyptian statuary. On the other hand, there can be no doubt that some kinds of sculpture had important functions in ancient Rome. These works represent the living sculptural tradition, as opposed to the antiquarian-decorative trend. We shall concern ourselves here mainly with two aspects of Roman sculpture that are rooted in Roman society: portraiture and narrative relief.

Republican Sculpture

We know from literary accounts that from early Republican times on, great political or military leaders were honored by having their statues put on public display. This custom was to continue until the end of the Empire a thousand years later. It may have been derived from the Greek custom of placing votive statues of athletic victors and other important individuals in the precincts of such sanctuaries as Delphi and Olympia (see fig. 5-45). Unfortunately, the first 400 years of this Roman tradition are a closed book. Not a single Roman portrait has come to light that can be securely dated before the first century B.C. How were those early statues related to Etruscan or Greek sculpture? Did they have any specifically Roman qualities? Were they individual likenesses, or were their subjects identified only by pose, costume, attributes, and inscriptions?

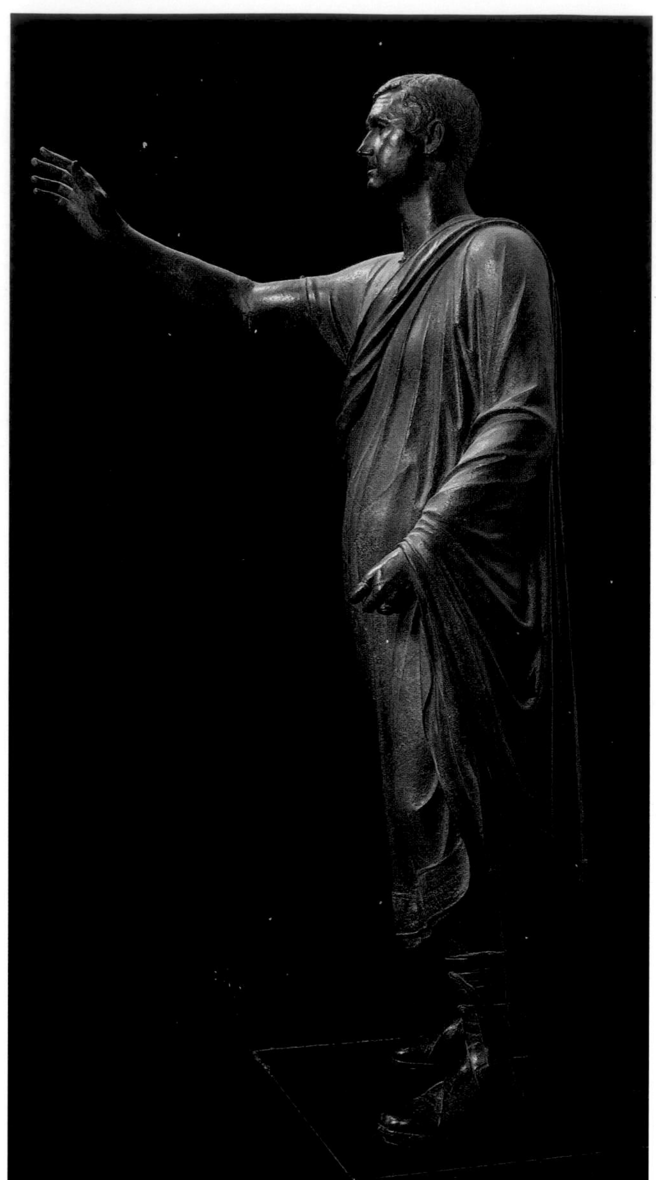

7-25. *Aulus Metellus (L'Arringatore).*
Early 1st century B.C. Bronze, height 71" (280 cm).
Museo Archeologico Nazionale, Florence

L'ARRINGATORE. Our sole clue is the lifesize bronze sculpture of an orator called *L'Arringatore* (fig. 7-25). It was once assigned to the second century B.C. but now is generally placed in the early years of the first. The statue comes from southern Etruscan territory and bears an Etruscan inscription that includes the name Aule Metele (Aulus Metellus in Latin), presumably the name of the person it represents. He must have been a Roman, or at least an official appointed by the Romans. The workmanship is evidently Etruscan, as indicated by the inscription. But the gesture, which denotes both address and salutation, recurs in hundreds of Roman statues of the same sort. The costume, an early kind of toga, is Roman. One suspects, therefore, that our sculptor tried to conform to an established Roman type of portrait statue, not only in these features but in style as well. We see very little of the Hellenistic flavor of the later Etruscan tradition. What makes the figure remarkable is its serious, factual quality, down to the neatly tied shoelaces.

PORTRAITS. It appears that a clearly Roman portrait style was not achieved until the time of Sulla, when Roman architecture, too, came of age (see pages 160–62). It arose from a very ancient custom. [See Primary Sources, no. 10, page 198.] Upon the death of the male head of the family, a wax image was made of his face, which was then preserved in a special shrine or family altar. At funerals, these ancestral images were carried in the procession. The patrician (noble) families of Rome clung tenaciously to this kind of ancestor worship well into Imperial times. The desire to have these perishable wax likenesses reproduced in marble may have come about because the patricians, feeling that their traditional position of leadership was threatened, wanted to make a greater public display of their ancestors in order to stress their ancient lineage.

Such display is certainly the purpose of the statue in figure 7-26. It shows an unknown Roman holding two busts of his ancestors, presumably his father and grandfather. The impressive heads of the two ancestors are copies of the lost originals. (Differences in style and in the shape of the bust indicate that the original of the head on the left is about 30 years older than that of the one on the right.) The somber face and grave demeanor of this dutiful Roman are strangely affecting and indeed seem to project a spirit of patriarchal dignity that was probably not present in the original wax portraits. Thus the process of translating ancestor portraits into marble not only made the images permanent but monumentalized them in the spiritual sense as well.

What mattered, however, was the face itself, not the style of the artist who recorded it. For that reason, these portraits have a serious, prosaic quality. The term "uninspired" suggests itself—not as a criticism but as a way to describe the attitude of the Roman artist in contrast to that of Greek or even Etruscan portraitists. That seriousness was a positive value becomes clear when we compare the right-hand ancestral head in our group with the Hellenistic portrait from Delos in figure 5-77. It would be hard to imagine a greater contrast. Both are persuasive likenesses, yet they seem worlds apart. Whereas the Hellenistic head impresses us with its grasp of the sitter's psychology, the Roman bust may strike us at first glance as no more than a detailed record of the face's topography, in which the sitter's character appears only incidentally. And yet this is not really the case. The features are true to life, no doubt, but the carver has emphasized them selectively to bring out a specifically Roman personality: stern, rugged, devoted to duty. It is a father image of frightening authority, and the facial details are like individual biographical data that distinguish it from others.

Imperial Sculpture

PORTRAITS. As we approach the reign of the emperor Augustus (27 B.C.–14 A.D.), we find a new trend in Roman portraiture, which reaches its climax in the images of Augustus himself. At first glance, we may not be certain whether his statue from Primaporta (fig. 7-27) represents a god or a human being. This doubt is appropriate, for the figure is meant to be both. Here we meet a concept that is familiar to us from Egypt and the ancient Near East: that of the divine ruler. It had entered the Greek world in the fourth century B.C. (see fig. 5-65). Alexander the Great adopted it, as did his successors, who modeled themselves after him. They, in turn, transmitted it to Julius Caesar and the Roman emperors, who at first encouraged the worship of themselves only in the eastern provinces, where belief in a divine ruler was a tradition.

The idea of giving the emperor divine stature, thus enhancing his authority, soon became official policy. While Augustus did not carry it as far as later emperors, the *Primaporta* statue clearly shows

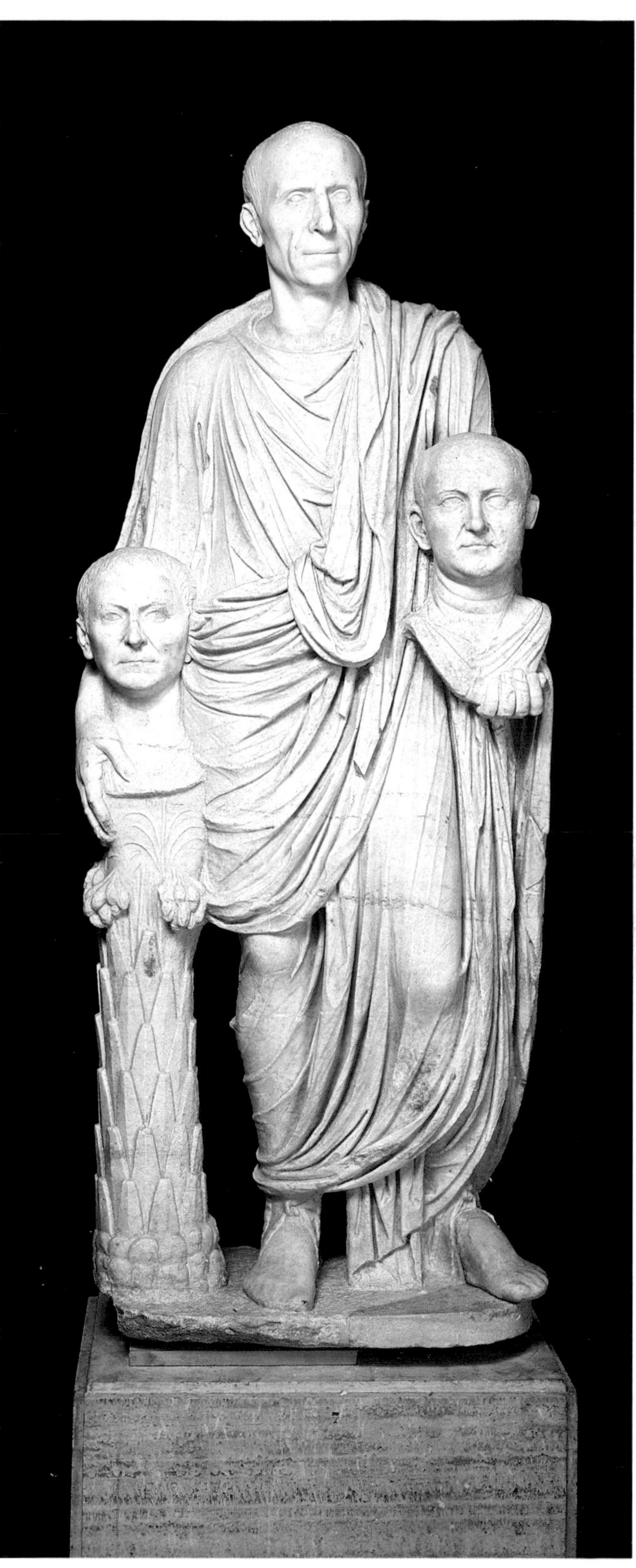

7-26. *A Roman Patrician with Busts of His Ancestors.* Late 1st century B.C. Marble, lifesize. Museo Capitolino, Rome

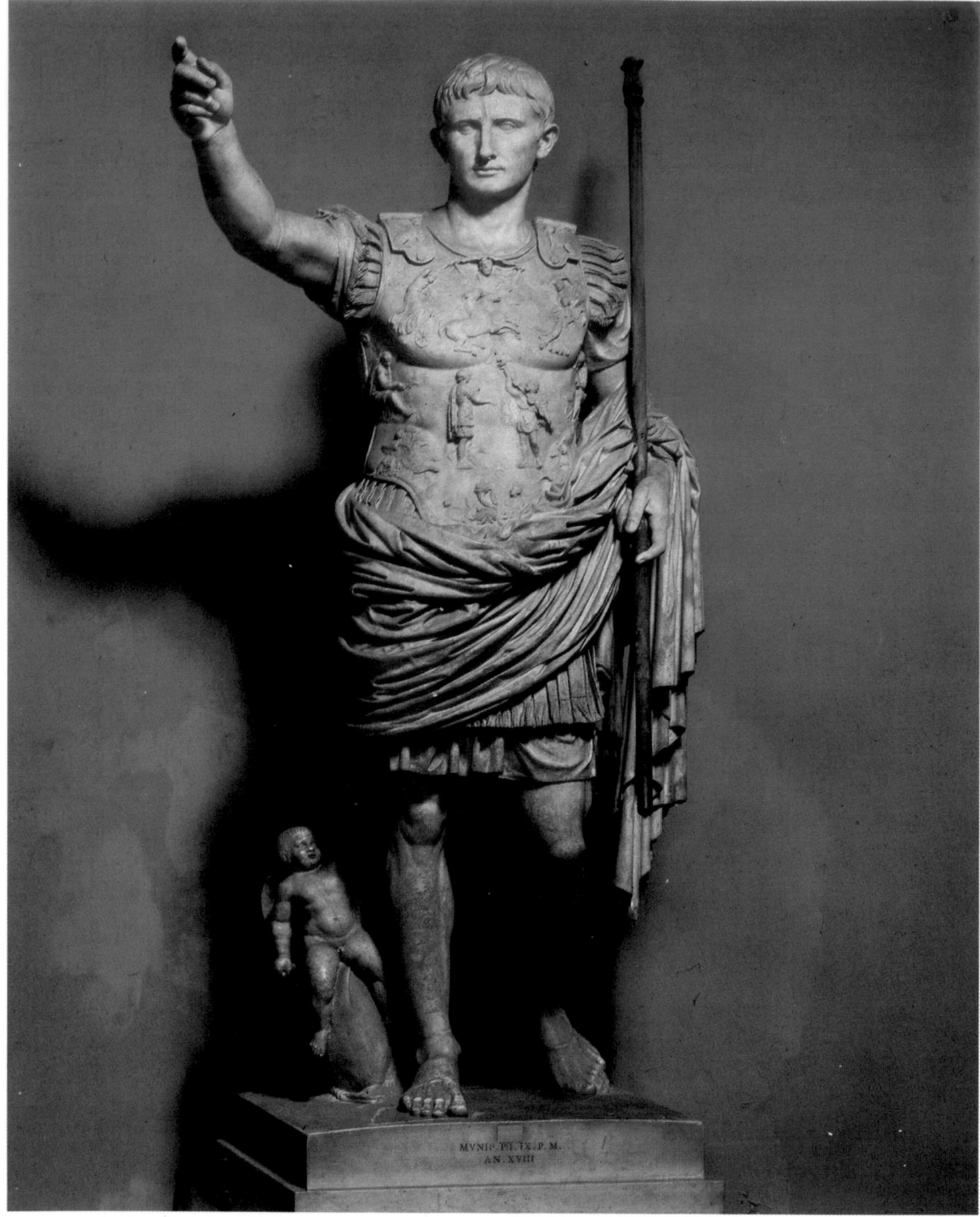

7-27. *Augustus of Primaporta.* Roman copy c. 20 A.D. of a Roman original of c. 15 B.C. Marble, height 6'8" (2 m). Musei Vaticani, Braccio Nuovo, Rome

him enveloped in an air of divinity. (He also was the chief priest of the state religion; see fig. 7-32.) The idealized body is clearly derived from the *Doryphoros* of Polykleitos (see fig. 5-42), while the Cupid at his feet suggests the infant Bacchus in Praxiteles' *Hermes* (see fig. 5-68). However, the statue has an unmistakably Roman flavor. The emperor's gesture is familiar from *Aulus Metellus* (see fig. 7-25). The head is idealized, or better yet "Hellenized." Small details are omitted, and the focus on the eyes creates something like the "inspired" look we find in portraits of Alexander the Great (compare fig. 5-82). Even so, the face is a definite likeness, idealized yet clearly individual, as we know from many other portraits of Augustus. All Romans would have recognized it, for they knew it from coins and countless other representations. In fact, the emperor's image soon came to play the symbolic role of a national flag.

Although it was found in the villa of Augustus' wife, Livia, the *Primaporta* statue may be a later copy of a lost original. The bare feet indicate that he has been deified, so that the sculpture was probably made after his death. (It should be noted, however, that Hadrian had a statue erected of himself as a nude god while he was still alive.) Myth and reality are blended in order to glorify the emperor. The little Cupid on a dolphin serves both to support the heavy marble figure and to remind viewers of the claim that the Julian family was descended from Venus. (He has also been seen as representing Gaius Caesar, Augustus' nephew and designated successor who died early in life, though this proposal seems unlikely.)

The costume's surface texture conveys the actual touch of cloth, metal, and leather. The breastplate (fig. 7-28) illustrates Augustus' victory over the Parthians in 39–38 B.C., which avenged

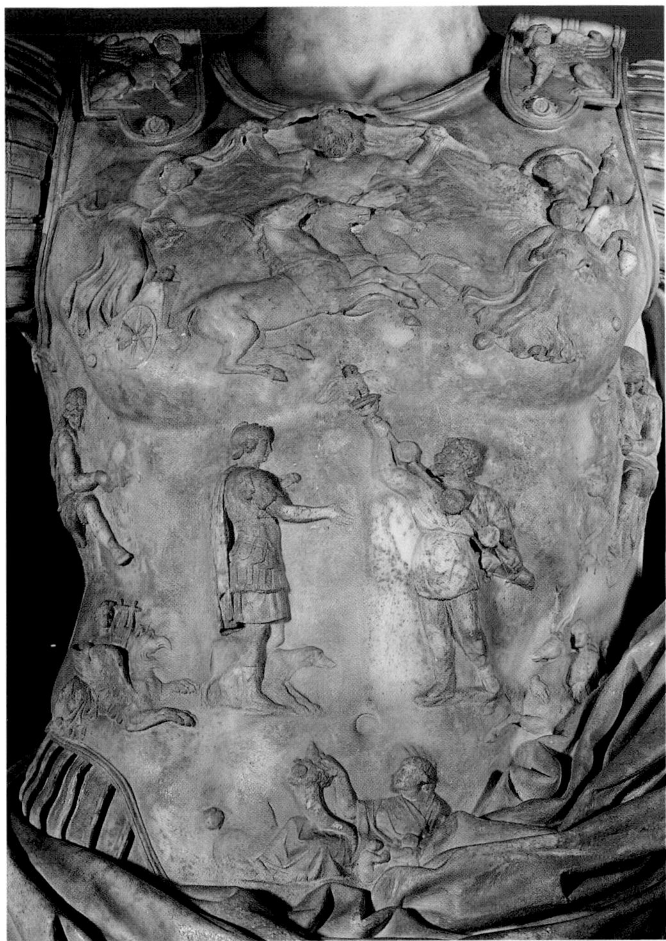

7-28. *Augustus of Primaporta.* Detail of breastplate

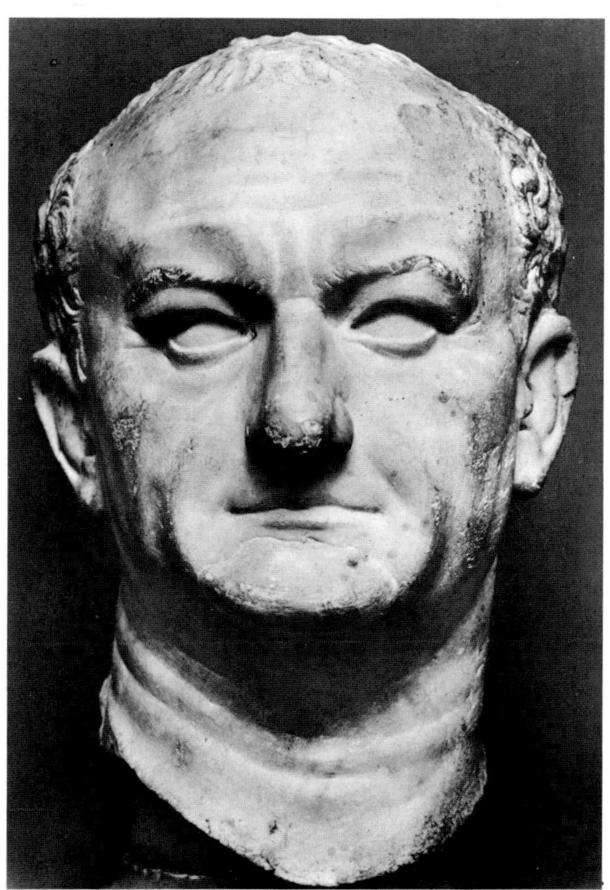

7-29. *Vespasian.* c. 75 A.D. Marble, lifesize, with damaged chin repaired. Museo delle Terme, Rome

a Roman defeat at their hands nearly 15 years earlier. Characteristically, however, the event is shown as an allegory. The presence of gods and goddesses raises it to cosmic significance, while the symbolic aspects of the work proclaim that this triumph, which Augustus viewed as pivotal, began an era of peace and plenty. Representing their respective armies, a Parthian returns a captured military standard to a Roman. Are they personifications, as seems likely, or are they historical figures—Phraates IV and either Augustus himself or his stepson and successor Tiberius? (According to the historian Suetonius, Tiberius was Augustus' intermediary and would have benefited from this bit of visual propaganda.) The issue may never be resolved.

If we regard the Republican ancestral images and the Greek-inspired *Augustus of Primaporta* as two extremes, we can find almost any kind of mixture of the two. Vast numbers of portraits were made, and the diversity of types and styles mirrors the ever more complex nature of Roman society. The head of the emperor Vespasian (fig. 7-29), of about 75 A.D., is a case in point. He was the first of the Flavian emperors, which included his sons Titus (see below) and Domitian. A military man, he assumed the throne after the infamous emperor Nero was overthrown in 68 A.D. Vespasian must have been skeptical about the idea of emperor worship: When he was dying, he is reported to have said, "Alas, it seems I am about to become a god." His humble origin and simple tastes may be reflected in the Republican flavor of his portrait.

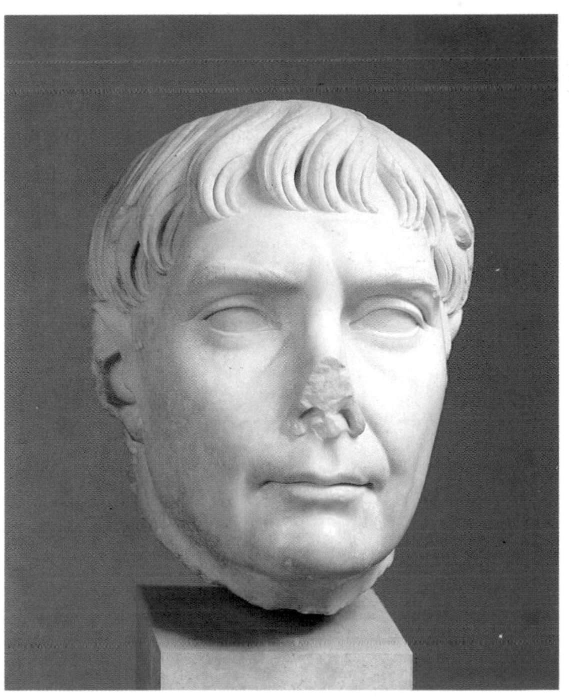

7-30. *Trajan.* c. 100 A.D. Marble, lifesize. Museum, Ostia

The soft, veiled quality of the carving, on the other hand, with its emphasis on texture, is so Greek that it recalls the technique of Praxiteles and his school (compare fig. 5-68). More classical still is the wonderful head of Trajan (fig. 7-30). Its rounded forms recall the *Augustus of Primaporta* (see fig. 7-27), as does the commanding look of the eyes under strongly projecting brows. The face, however, has an emotional intensity that is difficult to define—a kind of Greek pathos translated into Roman nobility (compare fig. 5-77).

NARRATIVE RELIEF. Imperial art was not confined to portraiture. The emperors also commemorated their achievements in reliefs on monumental altars, triumphal arches, and columns. Similar scenes are familiar to us from the ancient Near East (see figs. 3-13 and 3-28) but not from Greece. Historical events—that is, events which occurred only once, at a specific time and place—had not been shown in Classical Greek sculpture. If a victory over the Persians was to be commemorated, it would be portrayed as a mythical event outside any space-time context: a combat of Lapiths and Centaurs or Greeks and Amazons (see figs. 5-56 and 5-64). This attitude persisted in Hellenistic times, although not quite as absolutely. When the kings of Pergamon (Pergamum in Latin) celebrated their victories over the Celts, the latter were represented faithfully (see fig. 5-71), but in typical poses of defeat rather than in the framework of a particular battle.

Greek painters, on the other hand, had depicted historical subjects such as the Battle of Salamis as early as the mid-fifth century, although we do not know how specific these pictures were in detail. As we have seen, the mosaic from Pompeii showing the Battle of Issos (see fig. 5-60) probably reflects a famous Hellenistic painting of about 315 B.C. depicting the defeat of the Persian king Darius by Alexander the Great. In Rome, too, historic events had been portrayed from the third century B.C. on. A victorious military leader would have his deeds painted on panels that were carried in his triumphal procession or shown in public places. These pictures seem to have had the fleeting nature of posters advertising the hero's achievements; none have survived. Sometime during the late years of the Republic, such images began to take on a more monumental and permanent form. They were no longer painted, but carved and attached to structures intended to last indefinitely. They proved a ready tool for glorifying Imperial rule, and the emperors used them on a large scale.

THE ARA PACIS. Augustus preferred to be represented as the "Prince of Peace" rather than as the all-conquering military hero. The most important of his monuments was the Ara Pacis (Altar of Peace), voted by the Roman Senate in 13 B.C. and completed four years later, which can be identified with the richly carved Augustan altar that bears this name today. The entire structure (fig. 7-31) recalls the Pergamon Altar, though on a much smaller scale (compare figs. 5-72 and 5-74). On the wall that screens the altar itself, a monumental frieze depicts allegorical and legendary scenes, as well as a procession led by the emperor himself.

Here the "Hellenic" style we noted in the *Augustus of Primaporta* reaches its fullest expression. Yet if we compare the Ara Pacis frieze (fig. 7-32) with that of the Parthenon (figs. 5-31 and 7-33), we see how different they really are, despite the many surface similarities. The Parthenon frieze belongs to an ideal, timeless world. It depicts a procession that took place in the remote past, beyond living memory. What holds it together is the formal rhythm of the ritual itself, not its variable details. On the Ara Pacis, in contrast, we see a procession that celebrates a recent event—probably the founding of the altar in 13 B.C. It has been idealized so as to evoke the solemn air that surrounds the Parthenon procession, yet it is filled with the concrete details of a remembered event. The participants, at least those that belong to the Imperial family, are meant to be portraits, though all are idealized. To the left is Augustus, wearing a shroud as Pontifex Maximus, the chief priest of the state religion; and toward the center are his wife, Livia, and his son-in-law, Agrippa, who served as his chief adviser. The children, dressed in miniature togas, are too young to grasp the significance of the occasion: the little boy in the center is tugging at the mantle of the young man in front of him, while the somewhat older child to his left seems to be telling him to behave. The Roman artist also shows more concern with spatial depth than Classical Greek artists. The softening of the background, which we first saw in the much earlier *Grave Stele of Hegeso* (see fig. 5-58), has been carried so far that the figures farthest away seem partly immersed in the stone. Note, for example, the woman on the left, whose face appears behind the shoulder of the young mother in front of her.

The same interest in space appears even more strongly in the allegorical panel in figure 7-34, showing Mother Earth flanked by two personifications of winds. She not only embodies human, animal, and plant fertility but also serves as a symbol of Augustus' reign that reflects a time of peace and plenty. Here the figures are placed in a landscape setting of rocks, water, and vegetation. The blank background clearly stands for the empty sky. Whether this treatment of space is a Hellenistic or Roman invention is a matter of dispute. There can be no question, however, about the Hel-

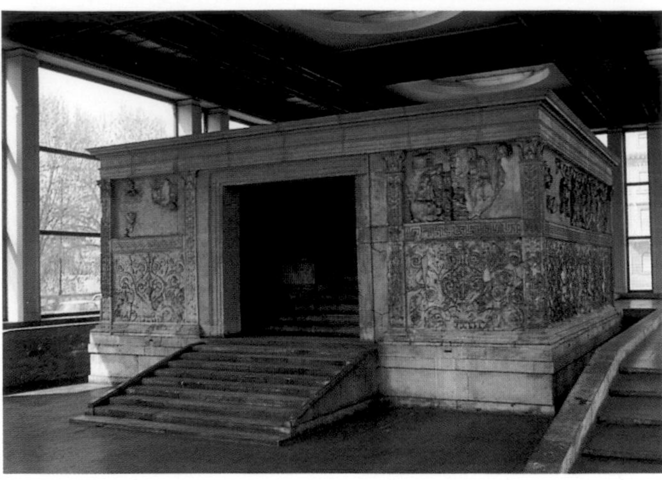

7-31. Ara Pacis. c. 13–9 B.C. Marble, width of altar approx. 35' (10.7 m). Museum of the Ara Pacis, Rome

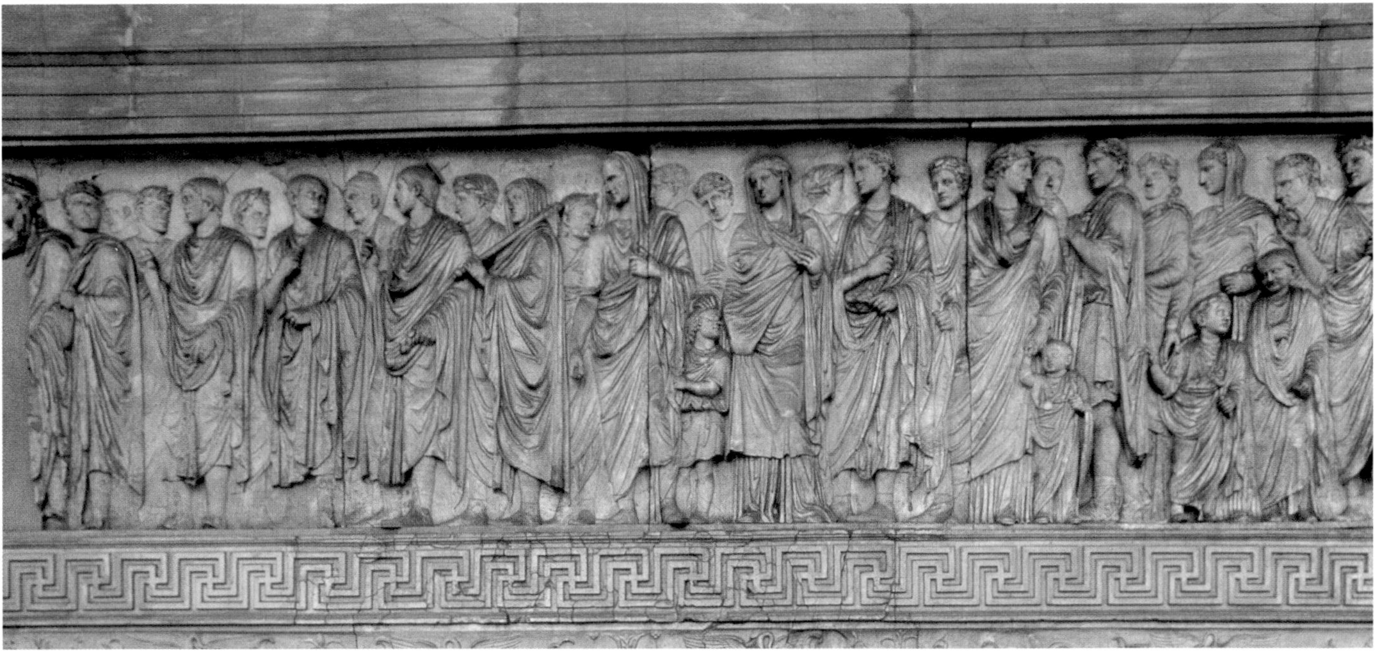

7-32. *Imperial Procession,* a portion of the frieze of the Ara Pacis. 13–9 B.C. Marble, height 63" (1.6 m)

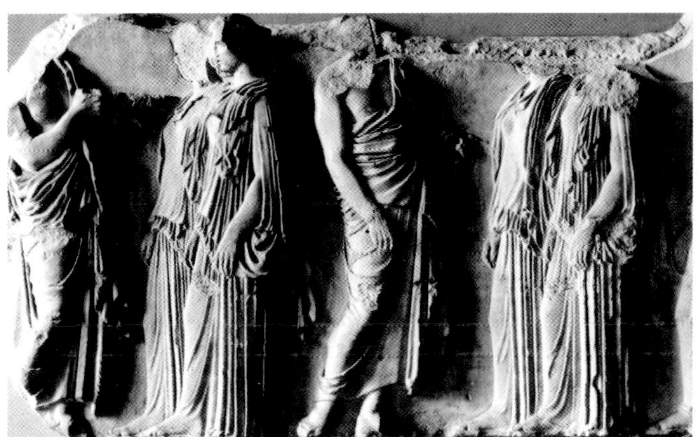

7-33. *Procession,* a portion of the east frieze, Parthenon. c. 440 B.C. Marble, height 43" (109.3 cm). Musée du Louvre, Paris

lenistic look of the three personifications. They represent not only a different level of reality but also a different, and less distinctly Roman, style from the Imperial procession. The acanthus ornament on the pilasters and the lower part of the wall, on the other hand, does not occur in Greek art, although the acanthus motif itself derives from Greece. The plant forms are graceful and alive. Yet the design as a whole, with its emphasis on symmetry, never violates the discipline of surface decoration. It thus serves as a foil for the spatially conceived reliefs above.

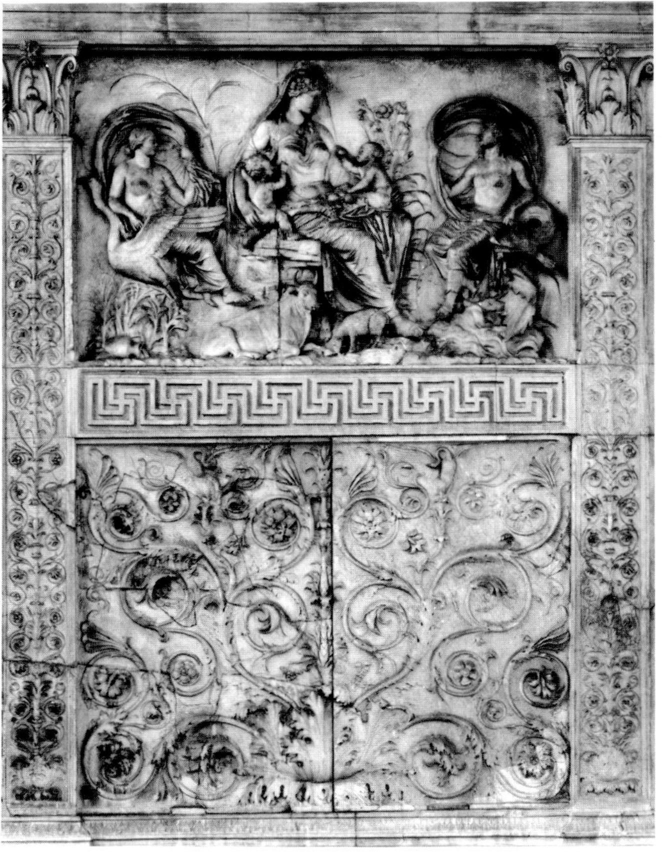

7-34. Allegorical and ornamental panels of the Ara Pacis

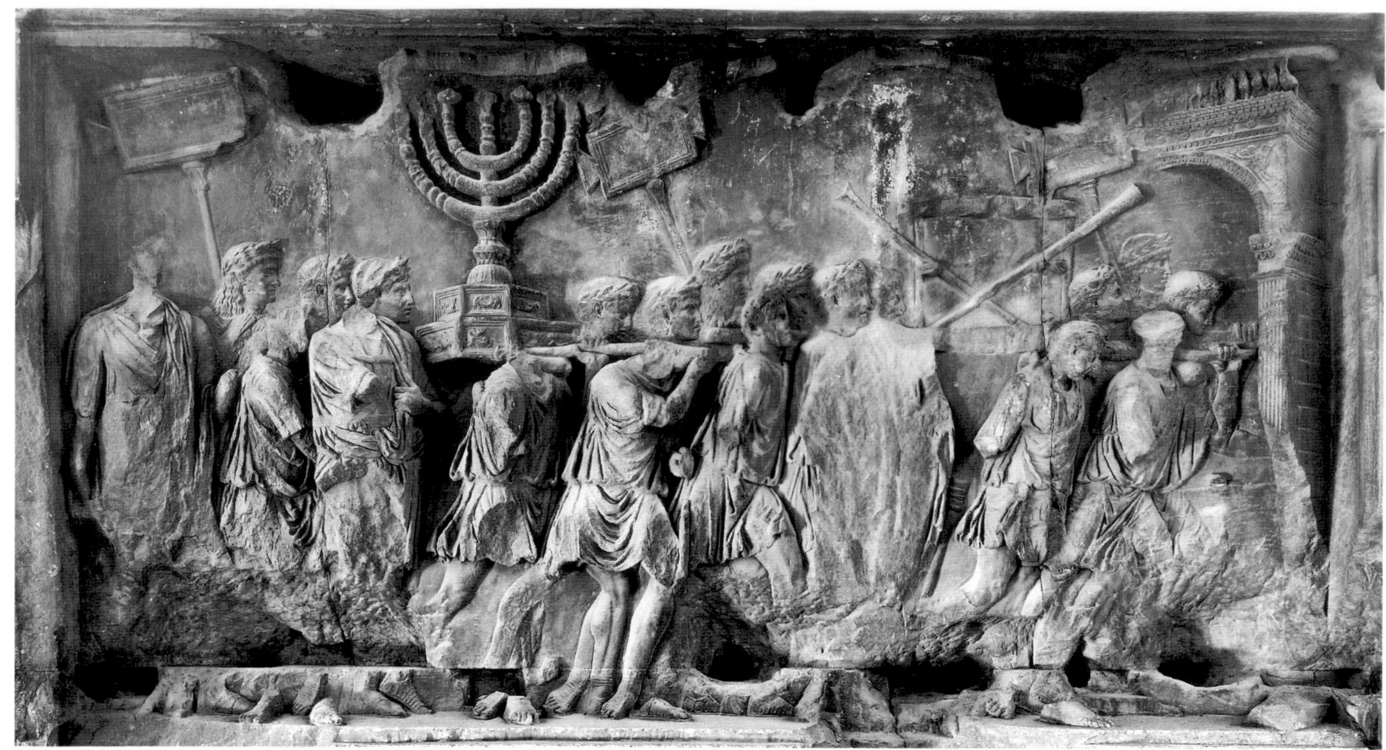

7-35. *Spoils from the Temple in Jerusalem.* Relief in passageway, Arch of Titus, Rome. 81 A.D. Marble, height 7'10" (2.4 m)

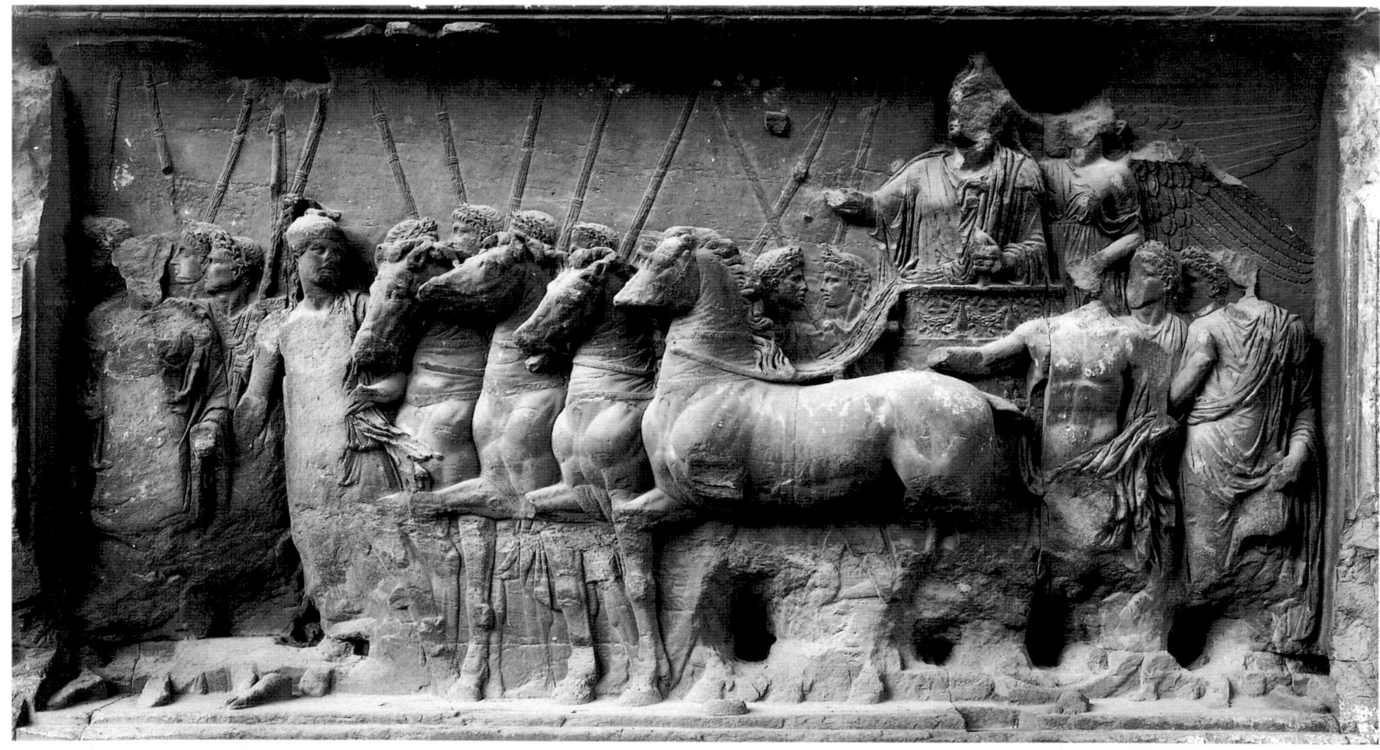

7-36. *Triumph of Titus.* Relief in passageway, Arch of Titus

THE ARCH OF TITUS. The spatial qualities of the Ara Pacis reliefs reached their most complete development in the two narrative panels on the arch built in 81 A.D. to commemorate the victories of the emperor Titus. One of them (fig. 7-35) shows part of the procession celebrating the conquest of Jerusalem. [See Primary Sources, no. 11, page 199.] The booty displayed includes the seven-branched menorah, or candlestick, and other sacred objects. The movement of a crowd of figures in depth is conveyed with striking success, despite the damaged surface. On the right, the procession turns away from us and disappears through a triumphal arch, which is placed obliquely to the background plane so that only the nearer half actually emerges from the background—a radical but effective compositional device. The other panel (fig. 7-36) avoids such experiments, although the number of layers of relief is equally great. Its design has a static quality, even though this scene is part of the same procession. The difference must be due to the subject: the emperor in his chariot, crowned by the winged Victory behind him. It seems that the sculptor's main concern was to display this image, rather than to keep the procession moving. Once we try to read the chariot and figures in terms of real space, we become aware of how contradictory the spatial relationships are. Four horses, shown in profile, move in a direction parallel to the bottom edge of the panel, but the chariot is not where it ought to be if they were really pulling it. Moreover, the emperor and most of the other figures are shown in frontal view, rather than in profile. These seem to be fixed conventions for representing the triumphant emperor that the artist felt must be respected, even though they were in conflict with the desire to create the kind of movement in space that was achieved so well in figure 7-35.

THE COLUMN OF TRAJAN. The conflict between the narrative or symbolic purposes of Imperial art and the desire for realistic treatment of space becomes fully evident in the Column of Trajan. The column was erected between 106 and 113 A.D. to celebrate that emperor's victorious campaigns against the Dacians (the inhabitants of what is now Romania). Freestanding columns had been used as commemorative monuments from Hellenistic times on; their source may have been the obelisks of Egypt. The Column of Trajan is distinguished not only by its great height (125 feet, including the base) but by the continuous spiral band of relief that covers its surface (fig. 7-37) and recounts in epic breadth the history of the Dacian wars. The column was crowned by a statue of the emperor (destroyed in the Middle Ages), and the base served as a burial chamber for his ashes. The design is often credited to Apollodorus of Damascus, who served as Trajan's military architect during the wars. If we could unwind the relief band, it would be 656 feet long, two-thirds the combined length of the three friezes of the Mausoleum at Halicarnassus and a good deal longer than the Parthenon frieze. In terms of the number of figures and the density of the narrative, however, our relief is by far the most ambitious frieze composition up to that time. It is also the most frustrating, for viewers must "run around in circles like a circus horse" (as one scholar put it) if they want to follow the narrative. Moreover, one can hardly see details above the fourth or fifth turn without binoculars.

One wonders for whom this pictorial account was intended. In Roman times, the monument formed the center of a small court flanked by libraries at least two stories tall within the Forum of Trajan, but even that arrangement does not answer our question. Nor does it explain the success of our column, which served as the model for several others. But let us take a closer look at the scenes that are visible in figure 7-37. In the center of the bottom strip, we see the upper part of a large river-god, the Roman descendant of Poseidon, who represents the Danube. To the left are some riverboats laden with supplies and a Roman town on the rocky bank. To the right, the Roman army crosses the river on a pontoon bridge. The second strip shows Trajan speaking to his soldiers (to the left) and the building of fortifications. The third depicts the building of a garrison camp and bridge as the Roman cavalry sets out on a reconnaissance mission (on the right). In the fourth strip, foot soldiers are crossing a stream (center); to the right, the emperor addresses his troops in front of a Dacian fortress. These scenes are a fair sampling of the events depicted on the column. Among the more than 150 episodes, actual combat occurs only rarely. The geographic, logistic, and political aspects of the campaign receive more attention, much as they do in Julius Caesar's famous account of his conquest of Gaul.

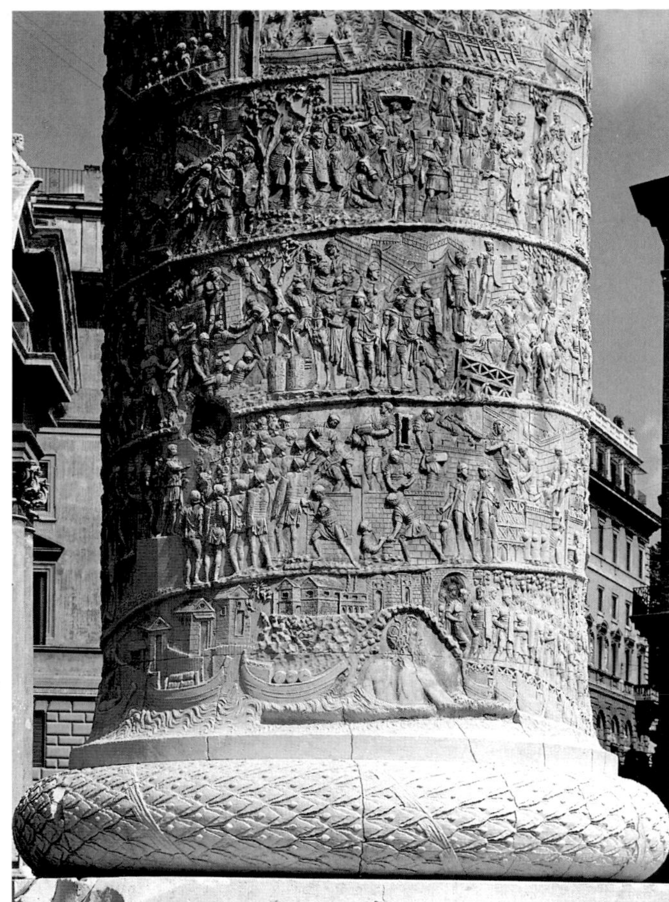

7-37. Lower portion of the Column of Trajan, Rome. 106–13 A.D. Marble, height of relief band approx. 50" (127 cm)

Only at one other time have we seen this matter-of-fact portrayal of military operations: Assyrian reliefs. Is there an indirect link between the two? And, if so, of what kind? The question is difficult to answer, especially since none of the panels showing military conquests that were carried in triumphal processions have survived (see page 174). Nor have the scrolls recording the Dacian wars, which may have been illustrated. Trajan actually conquered Assyria and the western part of the Parthian Empire, but only after the column had been erected. He died on his way back, and the territory was quickly ceded by his successor, Hadrian. Could Apollodorus, who came from the outer rim of the former Assyrian Empire, have known reliefs such as that in figure 3-19? At any rate, the spiral frieze on the Column of Trajan was a new and demanding framework for historic narrative, which imposed a number of difficult conditions upon the sculptor. Since there could be no inscriptions, the pictorial account had to be as explicit as possible. The spatial setting of each episode, therefore, had to be worked out with great care. Visual continuity had to be preserved without destroying the coherence of each scene. And the carving had to be much shallower than in reliefs such as those on the Arch of Titus. Otherwise, the shadows cast by the projecting parts would make the scenes unreadable from below.

Our artist has solved these problems with great success, but at a price. Landscape and architecture become "stage sets," and the ground on which the figures stand is tilted upward. These devices had already been used in Assyrian narrative reliefs. Here they appear once more, against the tradition of foreshortening and perspective space. Perhaps we are judging the Roman artist too harshly. Despite the testimony of literary sources that Greek Classical painters made great strides in treating illusionistic space (see pages 136–37), there is no direct evidence that they did so on the scale found here. Seen in this light, the Roman conquest of landscape and architectural space is a striking achievement, whatever its shortcomings. In another 200 years, this mode of pictorial description was to become dominant, and we shall find ourselves at the threshold of medieval art. In this respect, the relief band on the Column of Trajan foretells both the end of one era and the beginning of the next.

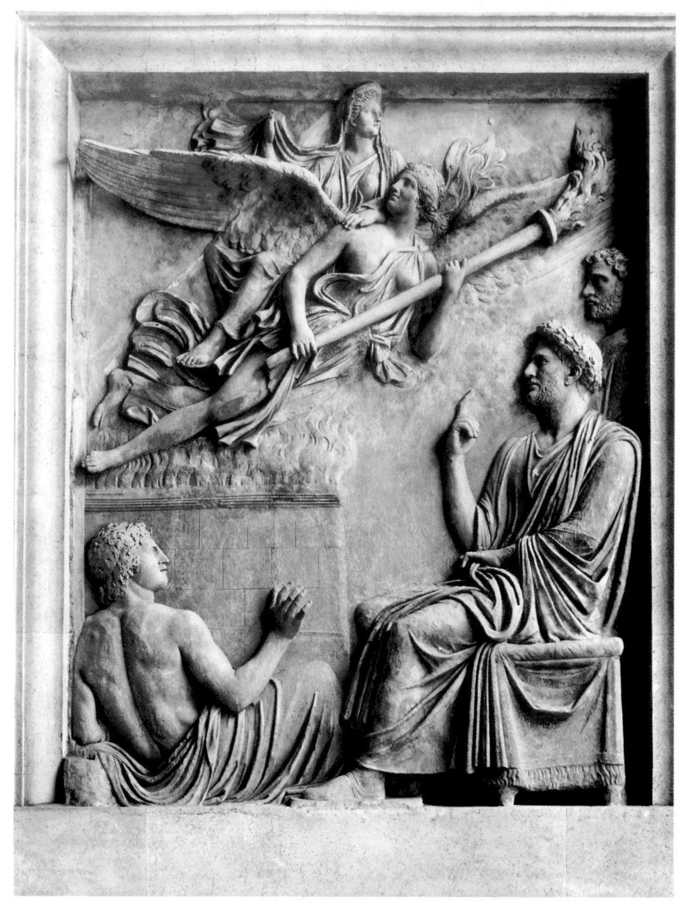

7-38. *Apotheosis of Sabina.* 136–38 A.D. Marble. Museo dei Conservatori, Rome

THE APOTHEOSIS OF SABINA. Trajan's successor, his cousin Hadrian, who was educated in Athens, led a Classical revival. He abandoned the age-old Roman custom of being clean-shaven and adopted the Greek fashion of wearing a beard as a sign of his admiration for the Hellenic heritage. Hadrianic reliefs relied on allegory, for largely personal reasons. First, he proclaimed the beautiful youth Antinous a god and erected cult statues of him as Apollo throughout the Empire. (One is depicted in a medallion on the Arch of Constantine, which was taken from a Hadrianic monument; see fig. 7-47, right). Then he had his wife, Sabina, deified. She was not the first Roman woman to be so honored. That distinction belonged to Livia, the wife of Augustus, whose portraits show her as a moral paragon, although, thanks to Suetonius, she is remembered chiefly for her intrigues. (She was proclaimed a goddess by Claudius I twelve years after her death.) In any event, the relief in figure 7-38 is the first of its kind. We see the deceased empress, wearing the crown of a goddess, borne to heaven from her funeral pyre by the female genius of Eternity (identified by her torch). Hadrian and the personification of the

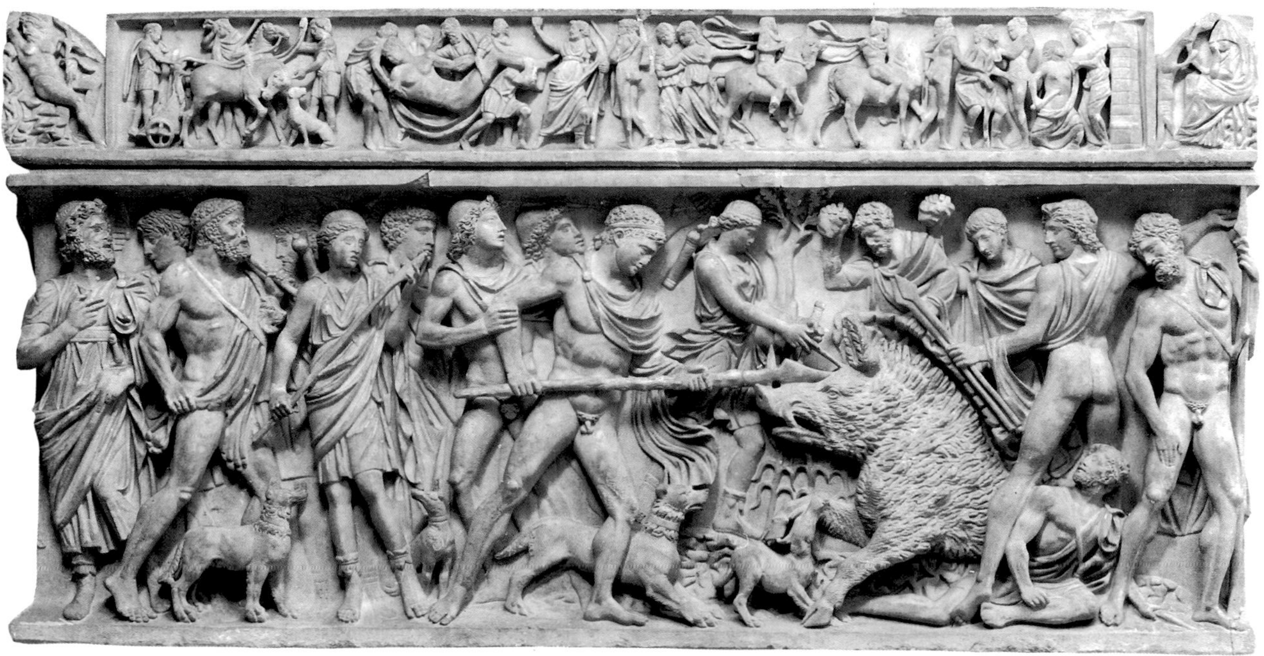

7-39. *Meleager Sarcophagus.* c. 180 A.D. Marble. Galleria Doria Pamphili, Rome

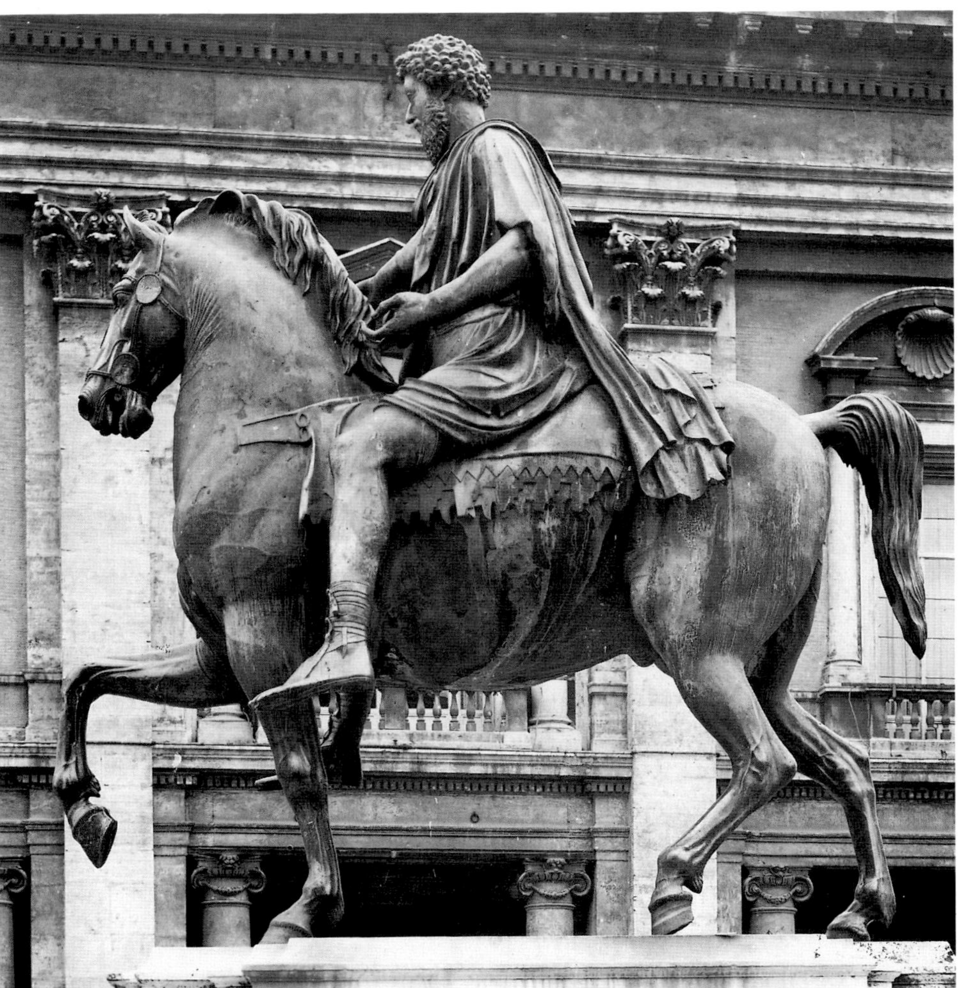

7-40. *Equestrian Statue of Marcus Aurelius.* 161–80 A.D. Bronze, over-lifesize. Piazza del Campidoglio, Rome

Campus Martius, where the royal cremation took place, witness the event to make it official. It is a strange sight, yet it is made plausible by the Classical style, which permits allegory and reality to mingle with surprising ease.

MELEAGER SARCOPHAGUS. The *Apotheosis of Sabina* denotes a major change in the attitude toward death that occurred in the time of Hadrian. Sarcophagi quickly replaced cinerary urns as part of a new belief in an afterlife. In response to the sudden demand for sarcophagi, patterns for decorating them were based at first on Greek examples. But new designs were soon passed from shop to shop, probably in illustrated manuscripts. Preferences changed over time. For example, under Marcus Aurelius battle sarcophagi were favored. Later, in the third century, biographical and historical scenes projected the deceased's ideal of life, often with moral overtones. But the most popular scenes were taken from Classical mythology. Since these occur on sarcophagi and nowhere else, they must have symbolic significance and not just antiquarian interest. Their purpose seems to have been to glorify the deceased through visual analogy to the legendary heroes of the past.

Here, too, Hadrian took the lead. A second medallion on the Arch of Constantine (see fig. 7-47, left) shows him slaying a wild boar. This relief is testimony not simply to his love of the chase but also to his courage in battle, for which hunting serves as a metaphor. A third medallion on the other side showing a sacrifice to Hercules equates great deeds with victory over death (see fig. 7-46, far right). This heroic analogy explains the prevalence of Meleager on sarcophagi. In Homer's account, Meleager saved Calydon from a huge boar that had been sent by Artemis to ravage his father's land but then died in the battle over its pelt. He thus served as an example of noble *virtus,* or virtue, a concept akin to the Greek *arete* (see page 101). For his heroism and death in the service of country, Meleager earned immortality. Figure 7-39 illustrates the finest example of the type. (The top shows the fallen Meleager being carried from the field of combat.) Its style is indebted, however distantly, to Skopas (see fig. 5-64), but now the poses are a bit stiff and the expressions are filled with the exaggerated pathos of Hellenistic sculpture. Typical of Roman reliefs is the crowding of the entire surface with figures (compare fig. 7-32).

LATER IMPERIAL PORTRAITS. A strong classicistic trend, often cool and formal, was continued in sculpture under Marcus Aurelius, who, like Hadrian, was a private man interested in Greek philosophy. We can sense this quality in his famous equestrian bronze statue (fig. 7-40), which is notable not only as the sole survivor from antiquity of this class of monument, but also as one of the few Roman statues that remained on public view throughout the Middle Ages. The image showing the mounted emperor as the all-conquering lord of the earth had been an established tra-

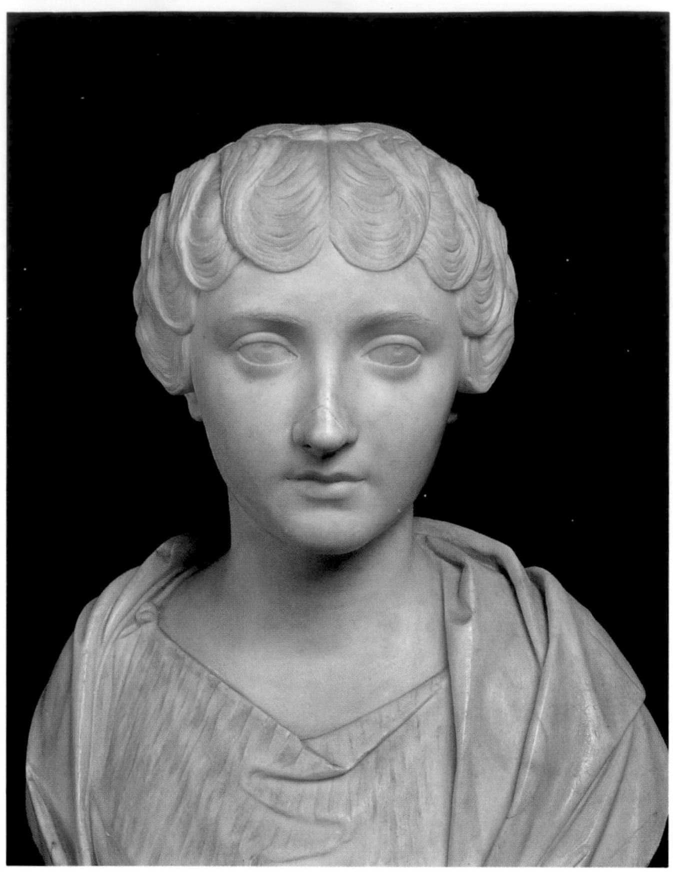

7-41. *Faustina the Younger.* c. 147–48 A.D.
Marble, height 23⅝" (60 cm). Museo Capitolino, Rome

dition ever since Julius Caesar permitted an equestrian statue of himself to be erected in the forum that he built. Marcus Aurelius, too, was meant to be seen as ever-victorious. According to medieval accounts, a small figure of a bound barbarian chieftain once crouched beneath the horse's right front leg. The powerful and spirited horse expresses this martial spirit. But the emperor himself is a model of stoic calm. Without weapons or armor, Marcus Aurelius appears as a bringer of peace rather than a military hero, for this is how he saw himself and his reign (161–180 A.D.).

A portrait of Marcus Aurelius' wife, Faustina the Younger (fig. 7-41), is cast in the same neo-Augustan mold as those of her husband. Although it is otherwise a clear likeness, her features have been subtly idealized in accordance with Greek sculpture, right down to the coiffure (compare the head of the *Dying Niobid* in fig. 5-50). In this way, the bust acclaims her as a model of Roman womanhood. Besides bearing him two sons, Faustina accompanied Marcus Aurelius on his military campaigns, which earned her the title Mother of the Camps. Her life embodied the feminine virtues that were important to the Romans, for which her husband later consecrated her a goddess: devotion to home and family, affection, respect, and piety, as well as beauty, grace, fertility, and chastity. The tunic and cloak worn by Faustina are signs of modesty that befit a Roman matron. The sculpture harks back to portraits of Livia, for it was during Augustus' reign that these virtues were defined, along with the legal status of women, although they were deeply rooted in Roman society. The portrait thus contains a flattering comparison to her great predecessor. Female members

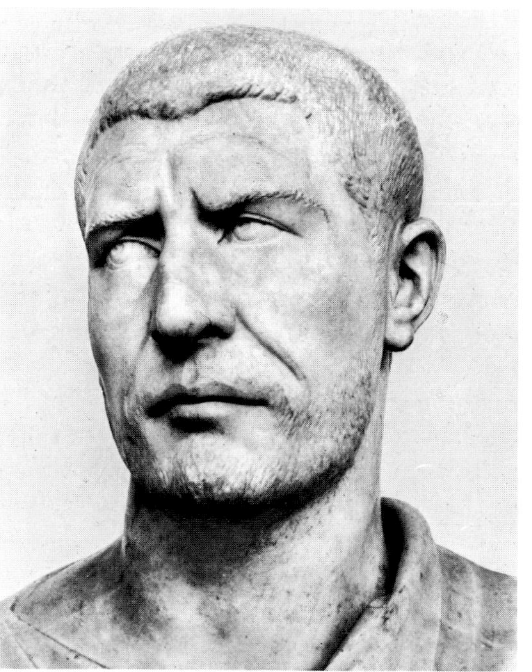

7-42. *Philippus the Arab.* 244–49 A.D.
Marble, lifesize. Musei Vaticani,
Braccio Nuovo, Città del Vaticano, Rome

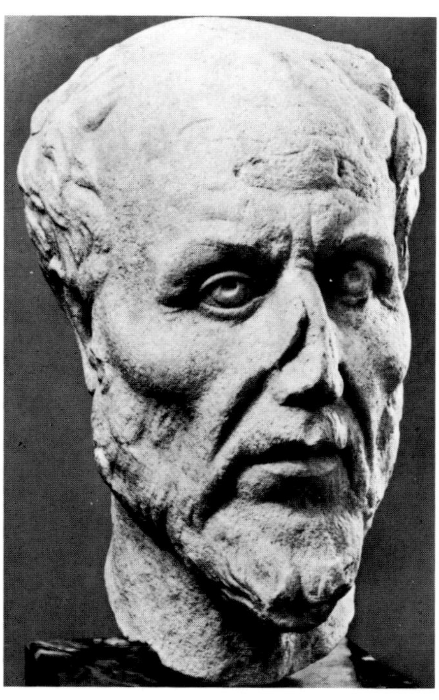

7-43. *Portrait Head* (probably Plotinus).
Late 3rd century A.D. Marble, lifesize.
Museum, Ostia

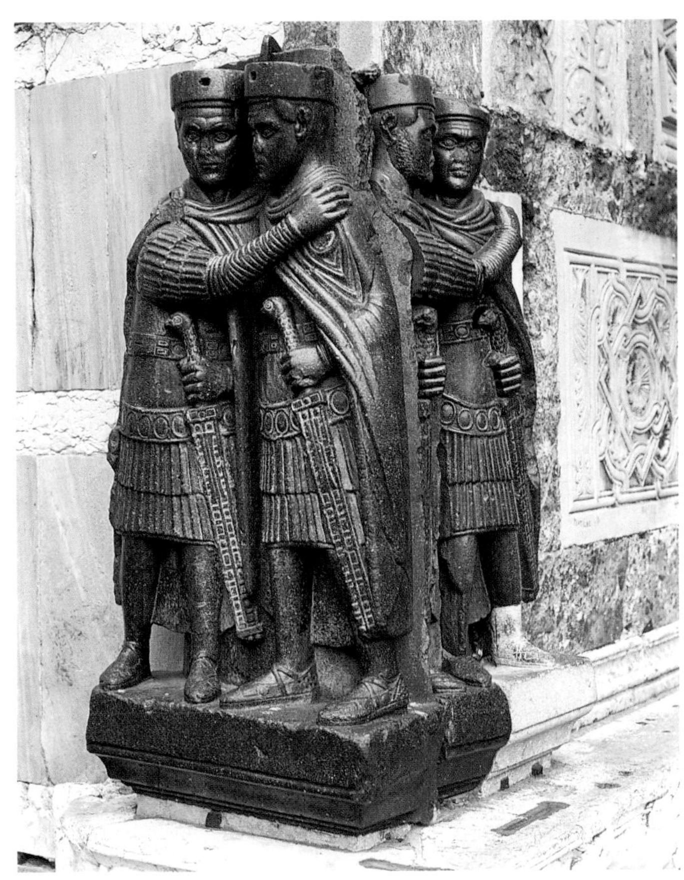

7-44. *The Tetrarchs.* c. 305 A.D. Porphyry, height 51" (129.5 cm). St. Mark's, Venice

of the aristocracy may have been subordinate to men, but they had a great deal of influence and sometimes independence as well. None had more power than the empress, who served as a model for other women and often determined matters of taste in fashion.

The reign of Marcus Aurelius was the calm before the storm. A period of chaos was ushered in by his decadent son Commodus, who was finally murdered in 192 A.D. The reforms of the short-lived Severan dynasty (193–235 A.D.) gave way to almost constant crisis, which plagued the Roman Empire for the remainder of the third century. Barbarians threatened the frontiers while internal conflicts undermined the authority of the emperor. Retaining the throne became a matter of naked force, succession by murder a regular habit. The "soldier emperors," who were mercenaries from the outlying provinces of the realm, followed one another at brief intervals. The portraits of some of these men, such as Philippus the Arab (fig. 7-42; see fig. 3-30), who reigned from 244 to 249 A.D., are among the most powerful likenesses in all of art. Their realism is as exact as that of Republican portraiture, but its aim is expressive rather than documentary. All the dark passions of the human mind—fear, suspicion, cruelty—are revealed here, with a directness that is almost unbelievable. The face of Philippus mirrors all the violence of the time. Yet it also moves us to pity. There is a psychological nakedness about it that recalls a brute creature, doomed and cornered. Clearly, the agony of the Roman world was not only physical but spiritual. That Roman art could create an image that reflects this crisis is a tribute to its continued vitality.

The results remind us of the head from Delos (see fig. 5-77). Let us note, however, the new means by which the impact of these portraits is achieved. We are struck, first of all, by the way expression centers on the eyes, which seem to gaze at some unseen threat. The engraved outline of the iris and the hollowed-out pupils, devices that do not appear in earlier portraits, serve to fix the direction of the glance. The hair, too, is rendered in un-Classical fashion as a close-fitting, textured cap. The beard has been replaced by a stubble that results from roughing up the surfaces of the jaw and mouth with short chisel strokes.

A somewhat later portrait, probably that of the Greek philosopher Plotinus, suggests a different aspect of the third-century crisis (fig. 7-43). Plotinus' thinking—abstract, speculative, and strongly tinged with mysticism—marked a retreat from concern with the beauty of the outer world, which he viewed as mere "images, traces, shadows." Instead, he favored "beautiful ways of life," an attitude that seems closer to the Middle Ages than to the Classical tradition of Greek philosophy. [See Primary Sources, no. 12, page 199.] This new frame of mind sprang from the same mood that, on a more popular level, was expressed in the spread of Oriental mystery cults throughout the Roman Empire. It is hard to say how close a likeness this head represents. The ascetic features, the intense eyes and tall brow, may portray inner qualities more accurately than outward appearance. According to his biographer, Plotinus was so contemptuous of the physical world that he refused to have any portrait made of himself. The body, he maintained, was an awkward enough likeness of the true, spiritual self. Why bother to make an even more awkward "likeness of a likeness"? Thus begins the dichotomy between body and soul that was to play such an important role in the High Renaissance (see page 437).

Such a view signals the end of portraiture as we have known it so far. If a physical likeness is worthless, a portrait becomes meaningful only as a visible symbol of the spiritual self. This attitude was foreshadowed in the first century A.D. by the widespread popularity of Epicureanism, which Pliny regarded as the death of portraiture because it advocated retiring from the world instead of achieving fame, thus negating ancestor worship. It is in these terms that we must view the statue of the Tetrarchs, who jointly ruled the four corners of the Roman Empire for a decade (fig. 7-44). To emphasize their equality, all are identical: they are the same height, wear the same clothes, and bear the same features, nominally those of the emperor Diocletian, who conceived this unique form of government. Each bearded Augustus embraces his Caesar, or junior partner, who was his designated successor and son-in-law. The sculpture is made of porphyry, an extremely hard Egyptian stone reserved for Imperial portraits because of its "royal" purple color. Yet the effect is not one of Imperial majesty and solidarity. Instead the figures appear huddled together, as if seeking strength against the turbulent times, to which they lent some measure of stability.

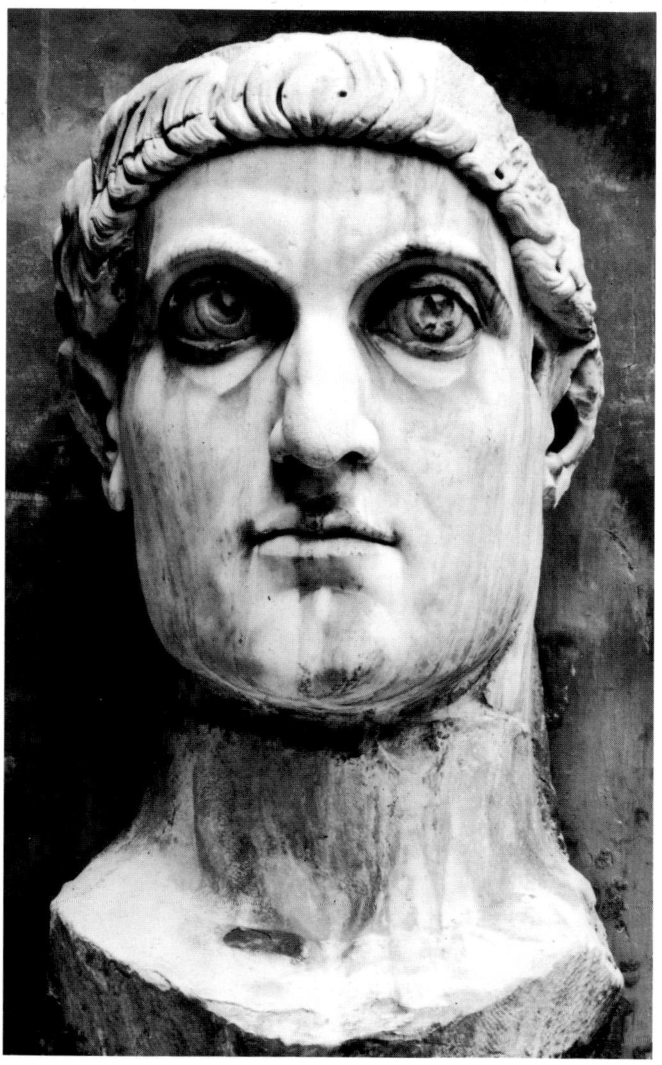

7-45. *Constantine the Great.* Early 4th century A.D. Marble, height 8' (2.4 m). Museo dei Conservatori, Rome

Stranger still is the head of Constantine the Great, the first Christian emperor and reorganizer of the Roman state, who was named a tetrarch in 307 but became sole ruler only in 324 (fig. 7-45). Although the head shows more individuality than those of the Tetrarchs, its face is not a true portrait. In fact, the head is one of several fragments of a huge statue from the apse of Constantine's basilica (see fig. 7-17). Although full-figure Imperial portraits, including other colossal statues of the period, generally show the ruler standing, this one probably depicted him seated nude in the manner of Jupiter, with a mantle draped across his legs. It is most likely the large statue mentioned by Bishop Eusebius, Constantine's friend and biographer, that held a cross-scepter, called a *labarum,* in its right hand. After Constantine's conversion in 312, this Imperial device, originally a Roman military standard, became a Christian symbol through the addition of the Chi Rho insignia within a wreath. (Chi and Rho are the first two letters of Christ's name in Greek.) Thus the colossal statue represented Constantine as a Christian ruler of the world, although the surviving hand points straight up. (The other hand most likely held an orb.) At the same time, it served as a cult statue to the emperor himself.

The head alone is eight feet tall. Everything is so out of proportion to the scale of ordinary people that we feel crushed by its size. The viewer's impression of being in the presence of some unimaginable power was deliberate. The portrait seems superhuman, only partly because of its enormous size. As an image of Imperial majesty, it is reinforced by the massive, immobile features out of which the huge eyes stare with hypnotic intensity. Instead of the Greek beard that had been in vogue since Hadrian's time, the face has the clean-shaven look of Trajan. For the rest of the fourth century, Roman emperors followed Constantine's example as the ideal Christian ruler (except for one, who sought a return to paganism). All in all, the colossal head conveys little of Constantine's appearance, but it tells us a great deal about his view of himself and his exalted office.

THE ARCH OF CONSTANTINE. Constantine's conception of his role is reflected in his triumphal arch (fig. 7-46), which was erected near the Colosseum between 312 and 315 A.D. One of the largest and most elaborate of its kind, it is decorated for the most part with sculpture taken from earlier monuments. This approach has often been viewed as being due to haste and to the poor state of the sculptural workshops of Rome at that time. These factors may have played a role, but there appears to be a conscious plan behind the way the earlier pieces were chosen. All of them come from a related group of monuments dedicated to Trajan, Hadrian, and Marcus Aurelius, and the portraits of these emperors have been reworked into likenesses of Constantine. This program conveys Constantine's view of himself as the restorer of Roman glory, the heir of the "good emperors" of the second century, who chose their successors based on merit rather than kinship.

The arch also contains a number of reliefs made especially for it, such as the friezes above the lateral openings. These show the new Constantinian style in full force. If we compare the medallions of figure 7-47, carved in Hadrian's time, with the relief just below them, they seem to belong to two different worlds. The scene

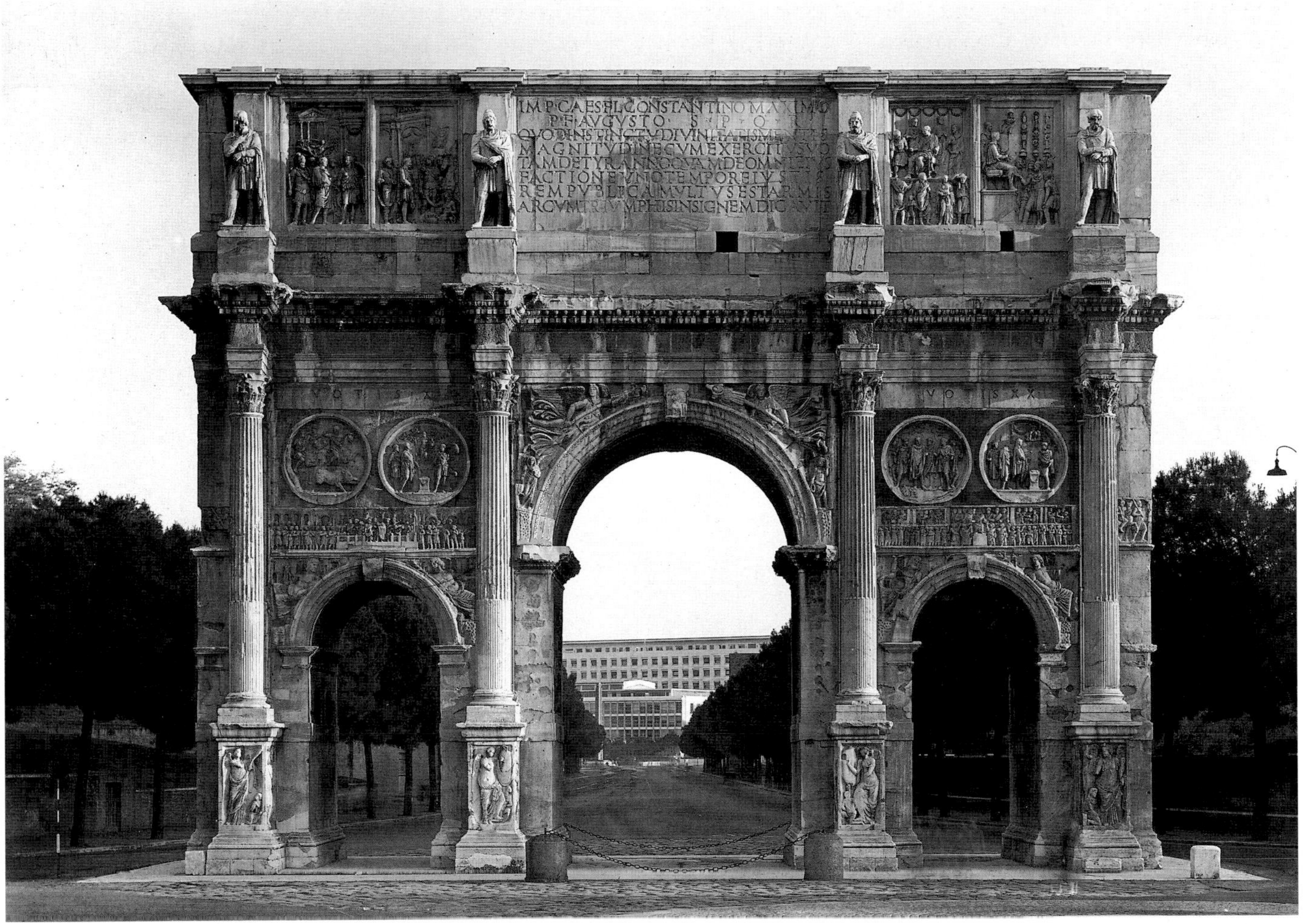

7-46. Arch of Constantine, Rome. 312–15 A.D.

depicts Constantine, after his entry into Rome in 312 A.D., speaking to the Senate and the people from the rostrum in the Forum.

The first thing we notice is the absence of the many devices developed since the fifth century B.C. for creating spatial depth. We find no oblique lines, no foreshortening, and almost no movement in the listening crowds. The architecture has been flattened out against the background, which thus becomes a solid, impenetrable surface. The rostrum and the people on or beside it form an equally shallow layer: the second row of figures appears as a series of heads above those of the first, while the figures themselves are oddly doll-like. The heads are very large, while the bodies seem not only dwarfish because of their stubby legs but also lack articulation. The use of contrapposto has disappeared completely, so that these figures no longer stand freely and by their own effort. Rather, they seem to dangle from invisible strings.

Judged from the Classical point of view, the features we have described so far are negative. Worse, they appear to represent the loss of many hard-won gains—a throwback to more primitive levels of expression. Yet such an approach does not help us understand the new style. The Constantinian panel cannot be explained as the result of a lack of ability, for it is far too consistent within itself to be regarded as simply a clumsy attempt to imitate earlier Roman reliefs. Nor can it be viewed as a return to Archaic art, since there is nothing in pre-Classical times that looks like it. No, the sculptor must have had a positive new purpose of his own. Perhaps we can approach it best by stressing the main feature of our relief: its sense of self-sufficiency.

The scene fills the available area completely. (Note how all the buildings are the same height.) Any suggestion that it continues beyond the frame is avoided. It is as if the artist had asked, "How can I get this entire ceremonial event into my panel?" In order to do so, an abstract order has been imposed upon the subject. The middle third of the strip is given over to the rostrum with Constantine and his entourage, the rest to the listeners and the buildings that identify the Roman Forum as the setting. They are all recognizable, even though their scale and proportions have been drastically adjusted. The symmetrical design also makes clear the unique status of the emperor. Constantine not only occupies the exact center, he is shown full-face. (His head, unfortunately, has been knocked off.) All the other figures turn their heads toward him to express their dependence on him. That the frontal pose is reserved for sovereigns, human or divine, is demonstrated by the seated figures at the corners of the rostrum, the only ones besides Constantine to face us directly. These figures are statues of the

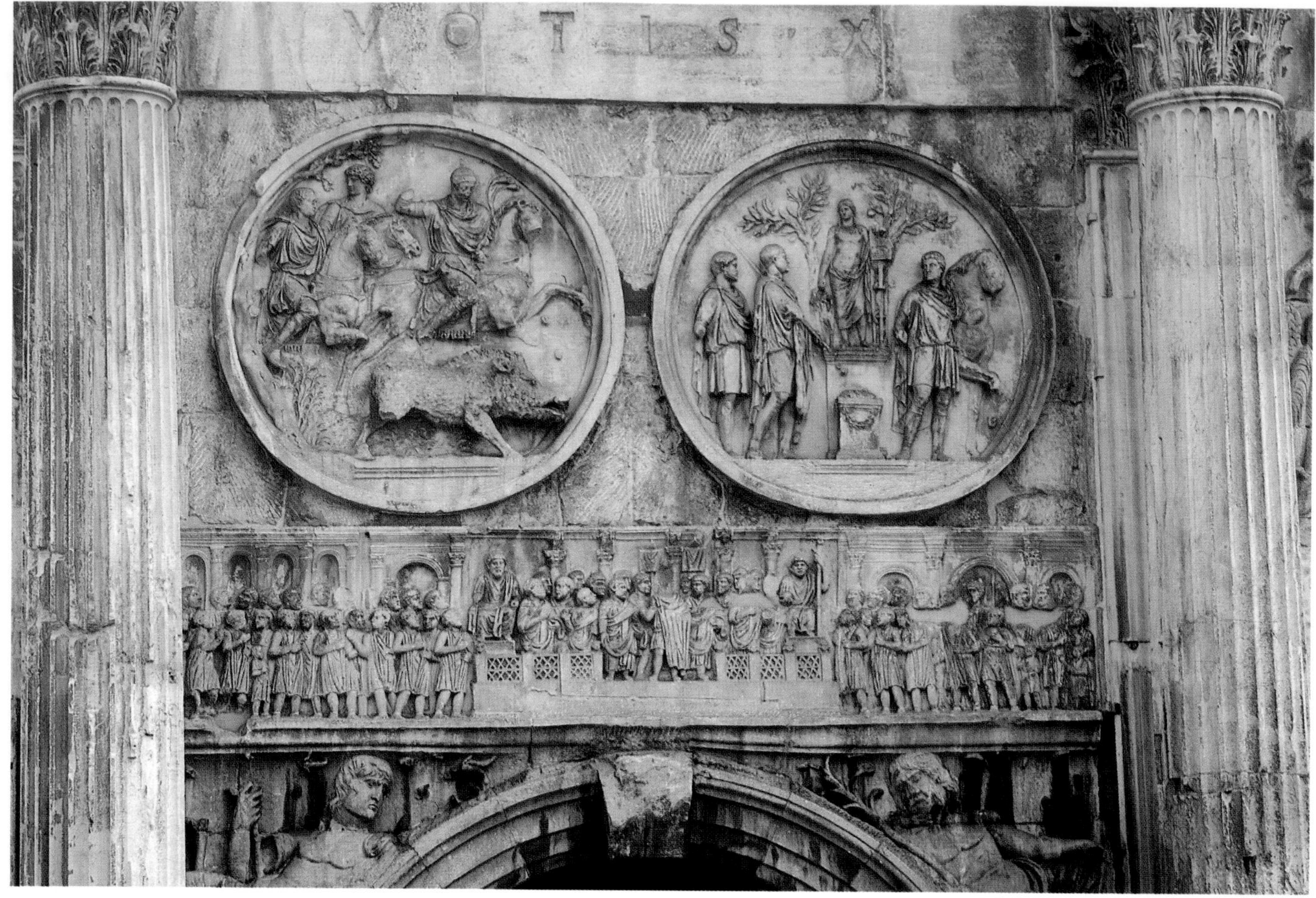

7-47. Medallions (117–38 A.D.) and frieze (early 4th century), Arch of Constantine

same "good emperors" we see elsewhere on the arch, Hadrian and Marcus Aurelius. Looked at in this way, our relief is a bold and original creation. It foreshadows a new vision that will become basic to the development of Christian art.

PAINTING

To modern viewers, painting tends to be the most exciting, as well as the most baffling, aspect of Roman art. It is exciting because it is the only large body of ancient painting after the Etruscan murals. Moreover, much of it came to light only in modern times and therefore has the charm of the unfamiliar. It is baffling because we know much less about it than we do about Roman architecture or sculpture. Almost all of the surviving works are wall paintings, and most of these come from Pompeii, Herculaneum, and other towns buried by the eruption of Mount Vesuvius in 79 A.D., or from Rome and its environs. Their dates cover a span of less than 200 years, from the end of the second century B.C. to the late first century A.D. What happened before then is largely a matter of guesswork, but after that time Roman painting seems to have stagnated. And since we have no original Classical Greek or Hellenistic wall paintings on Greek soil, except for a few Macedonian tombs from Alexander's time, it is far more difficult to single out the Roman element in painting than in sculpture or architecture.

Based in part on Vitruvius' discussion, four phases of Roman wall painting have been distinguished. However, the differences among them are not always clear, and there seems to have been a great deal of overlap in their sequence. [See Primary Sources, no. 4, page 196.] The earliest phase, known from a few examples of the late second century B.C., must have been widespread in the Hellenistic world, since examples of it have also been found in the eastern Mediterranean. Unfortunately, it is not very informative for us, as it consists entirely of the imitation of colored marble paneling. About 100 B.C., this so-called First Style began to be displaced by a far more ambitious style that sought to open up the flat surface of the wall by means of architectural perspectives and "window effects," including landscapes and figures.

The architectural vistas typical of the Second Style are represented by figure 7-48. Our artist is clearly a master of modeling and surface textures. The forms framing the vista—the richly decorated columns, moldings, and mask at the top—have an extraordinary degree of three-dimensional reality. They set off the distant view of buildings, which is flooded with light to convey a sense of space. But as soon as we try to enter this architectural maze, we are lost. The structures cannot be disentangled from each other, and their size and relationship are obscure. We quickly realize that the painter has no systematic grasp of spatial depth; the perspective is haphazard and inconsistent within itself. We were never intended to enter this space. Like a promised land, it remains forever beyond us.

When landscape takes the place of architectural vistas, foreshortening becomes less important. Now the virtues of the Roman painter's approach outweigh its drawbacks. This advantage can be seen most clearly in the Odyssey Landscapes, a continuous stretch of landscape subdivided into eight compartments by a framework of pilasters. Each section illustrates an adventure of Odysseus (Ulysses in Latin). Vitruvius tells us that such cycles were common. [See Primary Sources, no. 4, page 196.] However, the narrative has large gaps, which suggests that the scenes have been taken from a larger cycle. In the adventure with the Laestrygonians (fig. 7-49), the bluish tones create a feeling of light-filled space that envelops all the forms within this warm Mediterranean fairyland, in which the human figures seem to play a minor role. Only upon reflection do we realize how frail the illusion of consistency is. If we tried to map this landscape, we would find it just as ambiguous as the architectural perspective discussed above. Its unity is not structural but poetic.

The Odyssey Landscapes contrast with another approach to nature that we know from the murals in a room of the Villa of

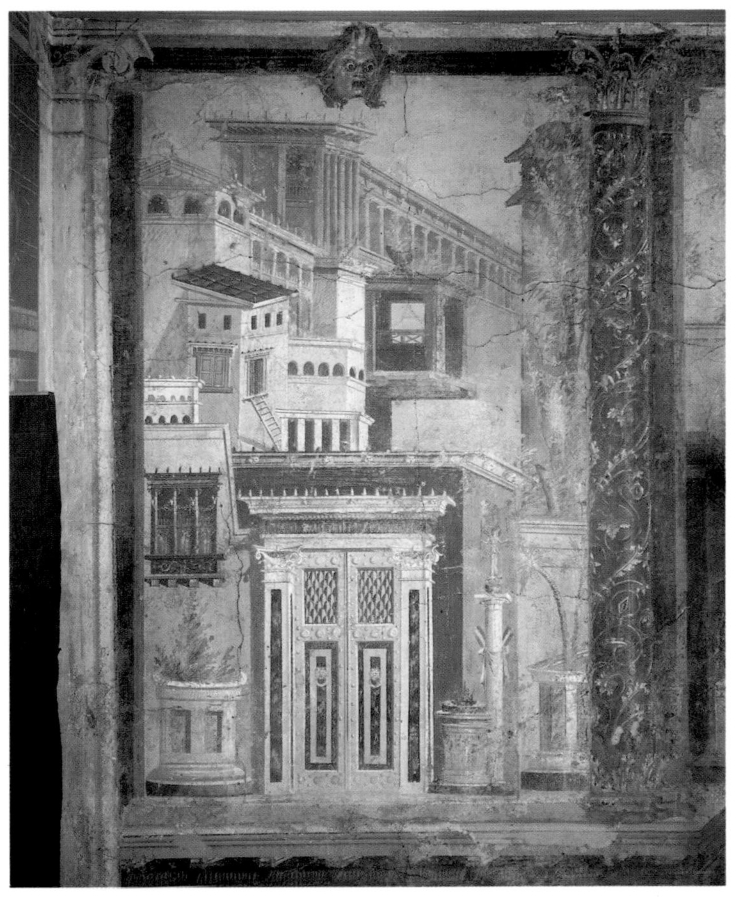

7-48. *Architectural View.* Wall painting from a villa at Boscoreale, near Naples. 1st century B.C. The Metropolitan Museum of Art, New York.
ROGERS FUND, 1903

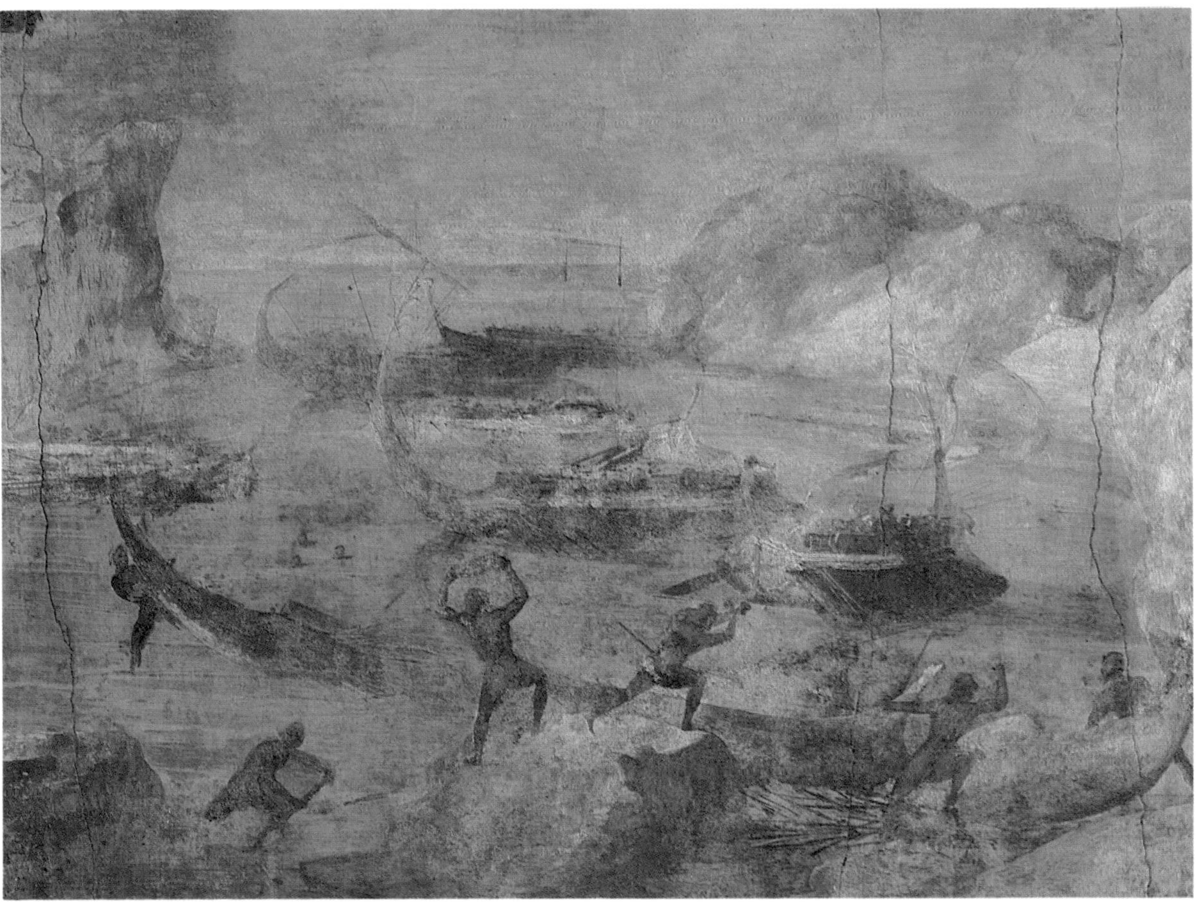

7-49. *The Laestrygonians Hurling Rocks at the Fleet of Odysseus.* Wall painting from a house on the Esquiline Hill, Rome. Late 1st century B.C. Biblioteca Apostolica Vaticana, Città del Vaticano, Rome

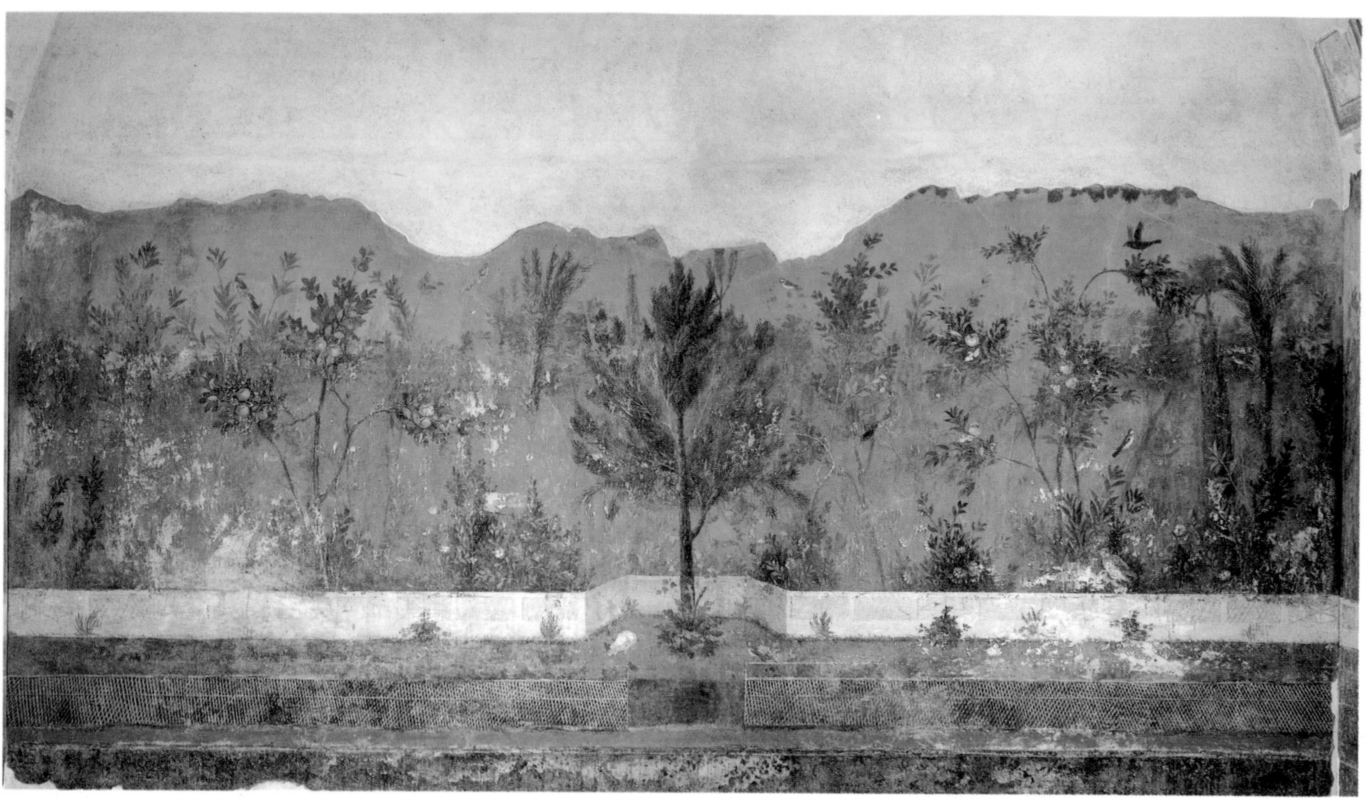

7-50. *View of a Garden.* Wall painting from the Villa of Livia at Primaporta. c. 20 B.C. Museo delle Terme, Rome

Livia at Primaporta (fig. 7-50). Their only antecedent lies not in Greek art but in Aegean painting (compare fig. 4-9). Here the architectural framework has been replaced by a view of a delightful garden full of flowers, fruit trees, and birds. These charming details have the same concreteness of color and texture as the architectural framework of figure 7-48. Their apparent distance from the beholder is also about the same: they seem to be within arm's reach. At the bottom is a low trellis, beyond it a narrow strip of lawn with a tree in the center, then a low wall. Just after that, the garden itself begins. However, we cannot enter it. Behind the front row of trees and flowers lies an opaque mass of greenery that shuts off our view as effectively as a dense hedge. This garden, then, is another promised land made only for looking. The wall has not really been opened up but merely pushed back a few feet and replaced by a wall of plants. It is this very limitation of spatial depth that gives the mural its coherence.

THE VILLA OF THE MYSTERIES. The great frieze in one of the rooms in the Villa of the Mysteries just outside Pompeii (fig. 7-51), like the garden view from the Villa of Livia, dates from the latter part of the first century B.C., when the Second Style was at its height. So far as the treatment of the wall space is concerned, the two works have more in common with each other than with other Second Style murals. Both are conceived in terms of rhythmic continuity and arm's-length depth. The frieze nevertheless has a grandeur of design that is nearly unique in Roman painting.

The figures have been placed on a narrow ledge of green against a regular pattern of red panels separated by strips of black, so as to create a kind of running stage on which they perform their strange ritual. Who are they, and what is the meaning of the cycle? Many details remain puzzling, but the frieze as a whole depicts various rites of the Dionysiac mysteries, a semisecret cult of very ancient origin that had been brought to Italy from Greece. The rituals are performed, perhaps as part of an initiation into womanhood or marriage, in the presence of Dionysus and Ariadne, with their train of satyrs and sileni. Thus human and mythical reality tend to merge into one. As a result all the figures have certain qualities in common: their dignity of bearing and expression, the firmness of body and drapery, and the rapt intensity with which they participate in the drama of the ritual.

The Third Style, from about 20 B.C. until at least the middle of the first century A.D., abandoned illusionism in favor of decorative surfaces with planes of intense color that were sometimes relieved by imitation panel paintings. By contrast, the Fourth Style, which prevailed at the time of the eruption of Mount Vesuvius in 79 A.D., was the most intricate of all. It united aspects of all three preceding styles to create an extravagant effect. The Ixion Room in the House of the Vettii at Pompeii (fig. 7-52) combines imitation marble paneling, framed mythological scenes that give the effect of panel pictures set into the wall, and fantastic architectural vistas seen through make-believe windows. The result is a somewhat disjointed compilation of motifs from various sources. This architecture has a strangely unreal and picturesque quality that is thought to reflect the architectural backdrops of the theaters of the time. It anticipates effects such as that of the Market Gate of Miletus (see fig. 7-23), which shares the same source.

A unique feature of Roman mural decoration is the still lifes that sometimes appear within the architectural schemes of the Fourth Style. These usually take the form of make-believe niches or cupboards, so that the objects, which are often displayed on two levels, remain close to us. Our example (fig. 7-53) is noteworthy for the rendering of the glass jar half-filled with water. The reflections are so carefully observed that we feel the painter must have copied them from an actual jar that was lit in just this way. But we cannot determine the source and direction of the light because the shadows cast by the various objects are not consistent with one another. Nor do we have the impression that the jar stands in a stream of light. Instead, the light seems to be imprisoned within the jar.

Clearly the Roman artist, despite striving for illusionistic effects, is no more systematic in the approach to light than in the handling of perspective. However real the details may seem, the work nearly always lacks unity overall. In the finest examples, however, other qualities compensate for this deficiency, so that we must not condemn the Roman artist to an inferior status. Like the preference for illusionistic space, the absence of a consistent view of the visible world should be thought of instead as a fundamental characteristic of Roman painting.

Greek Sources

There is no doubt that Greek designs were copied and that Greek paintings as well as painters were imported. It is tempting to link Roman paintings with lost works recorded by Pliny, Vitruvius, and others. *The Battle of Issos* (see fig. 5-60) is, however, one of the rare cases in which such a connection can be clearly demonstrated.

For the most part, Roman painting appears to have been a specifically Roman development. Despite the fact that the characters' names are given in Greek, there is no reason to assume a Greek origin for the Odyssey Landscapes any more than for the *View of a Garden* from the Villa of Livia. Likewise, still-life painting began in Greece, but even when certain Classical Greek motifs were adopted, the form in which we know it is distinctively Roman, as we can ascertain from the changes it underwent. Finally, the illusionistic tendencies that gained the upper hand in Roman murals during the first century B.C. represent a dramatic breakthrough that had no precedent in Greek art so far as we know.

The issue is more complex when it comes to narrative painting. Although not a trace of it exists, we can hardly doubt that Greek painting continued to evolve after the Classical era. In fact, narrative painting underwent a decline in the late Hellenistic period, when earlier panels were highly prized by collectors in the way

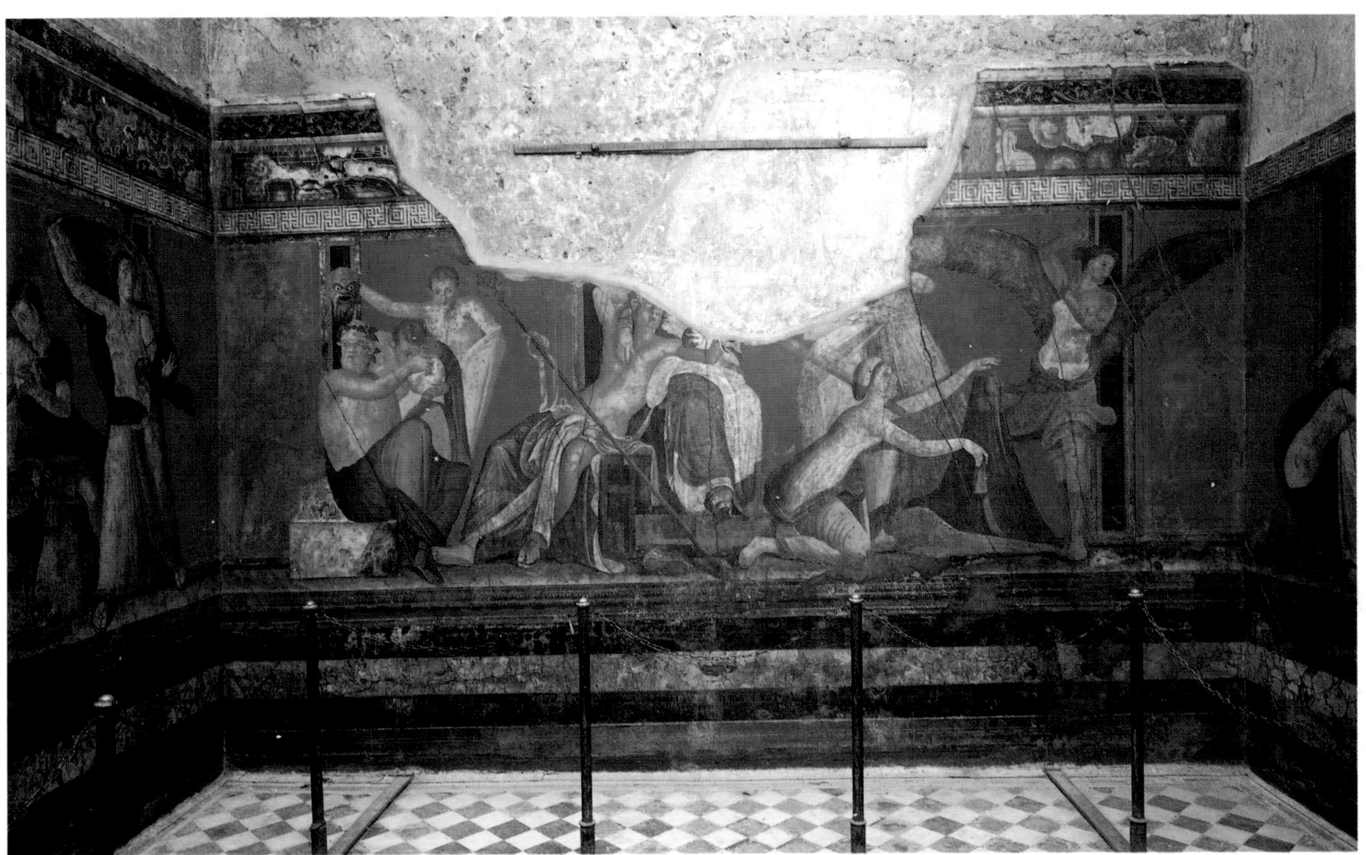

7-51. *Scenes of a Dionysiac Mystery Cult.* Mural frieze. c. 50 B.C. Villa of the Mysteries, Pompeii

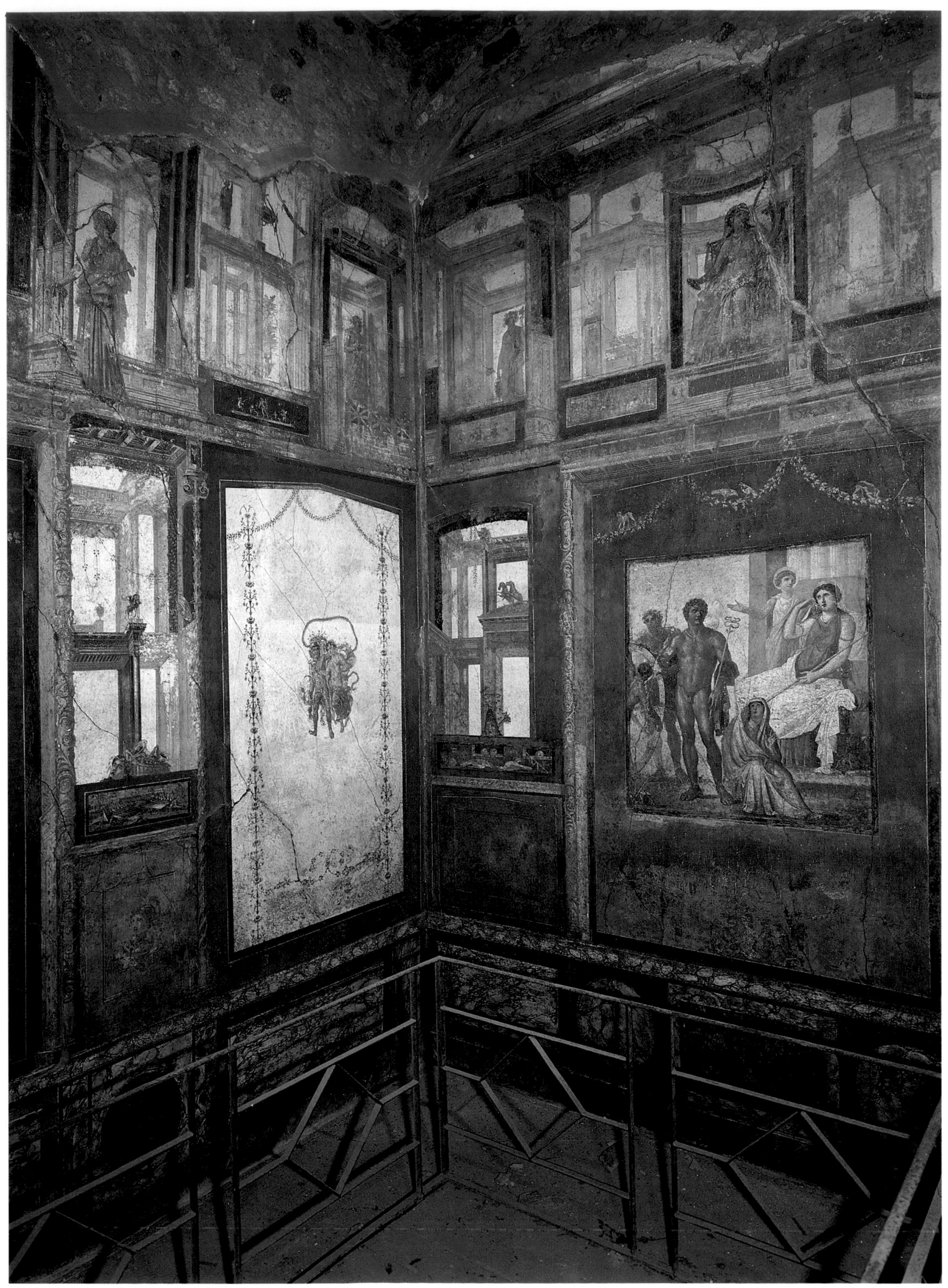

7-52. The Ixion Room, House of the Vettii, Pompeii. 63–79 A.D.

THEATER AND MUSIC IN ANCIENT ROME

According to contemporary sources, the Romans adopted Greek music, including its system of modes, with little modification. Judging from its wide range of instruments, however, Rome was a melting pot in music as it was in everything else. Many of these instruments were known to the Greeks as well. If the lyre and aulos were preferred by the Greeks, the trumpet and horn were the most characteristic instruments of the Romans. They were widely used in military campaigns, public parades, and festivals (compare fig. 7-35). Certain instruments were associated with particular cults, which thrived throughout the realm and were imported to Rome itself, such as that of Cybele, the Great Mother Goddess of Anatolia. The most common combination for celebrating rituals in Roman religions was flute-drum-cymbals.

Roman theater was very different in many respects from that of Greece, for its origins lay more in the region of Etruria. Tarquin the Elder, the Etruscan ruler of Rome between about 616 and 578 B.C., established the religious festivals known as *ludi Romani* (Roman games) to honor Jupiter each September. Plays were part of the program from the beginning and were always associated with religious festivals. He also introduced the Etruscan taste for spectacle and built the first Circus Maximus for horse races and similar events. Most Roman theater, in fact, fell into the category of modern carnival and circus acts, called *mimus,* or mime. The Roman writer Livy (59 B.C.–17 A.D.) states that the first theater performances were held in 364 B.C., when musicians and dancers were imported from Etruria to appease the gods during a plague. A late form of popular theater was pantomime (all mime)—introduced from Greece in 22 B.C.—which involved a single dancer who acted out all the roles of a tragedy by changing masks.

Serious drama began in 240 B.C., when Livius Andronicus, a freed Greek slave from south Italy, produced a Latin translation of two Greek plays for the *ludi Romani* and became the first writer of Greek-style tragedies in Latin. Because Roman tragedies reflected the stringent moral values of Republican Rome, they gradually died out during the Empire. The greatest author of comedies was Caecilius Statius (c. 219–168 B.C.) but, as with Livius Andronicus, none of his works is left. During the first century B.C., Roman comic theater was taken over by the Fabula Atellana (named for the town of Atella near Naples). It was a coarse variety of farce accompanied by music that relied on stock subjects with happy endings in the manner of late Greek comedy.

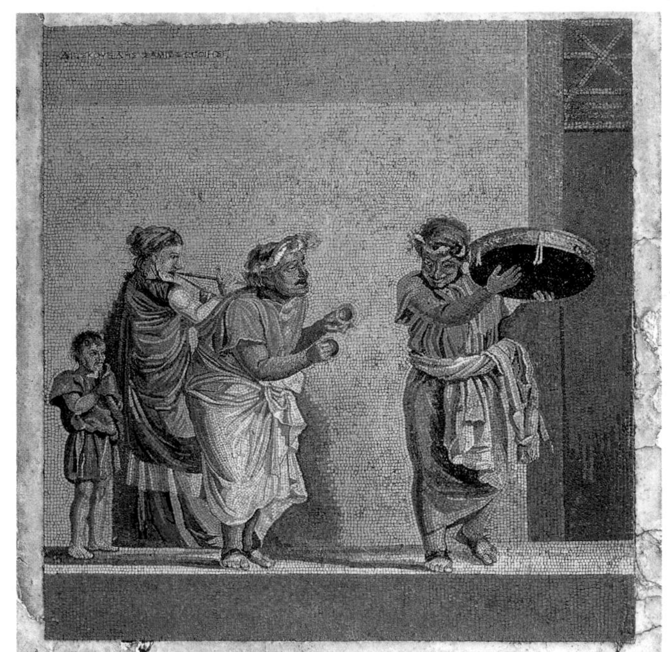

Scene from New Comedy (traveling musicians). 2nd century B.C. Mosaic from Pompeii, Villa of Cicero, 17 x 16⅛" (43.2 x 41 cm). Archaeological Museum, Naples

All that remains of Roman theater are 21 comedies by Plautus (c. 254–184 B.C.), six comedies by the freed African slave Terence (190–156 B.C.), and nine tragedies by Seneca (4 B.C.–65 A.D.), the teacher of the emperor Nero, which may never have been performed. These writers exercised enormous influence on sixteenth-century Elizabethan theater by providing models of plot and style that were used by William Shakespeare and Christopher Marlowe. Roman playwrights have fallen into unjust neglect today, especially Seneca, whose powerful dramas feature penetrating characterizations revealed in soliloquies that are fully the equal of Shakespeare's.

The architect and historian Vitruvius, writing in the late first century B.C., has left us a detailed account of Roman theater practices. He suggests that Roman architectural backdrops and painted scenery were considerably more elaborate than those of Greece. We can get a good idea of their probable appearance from the illusionistic treatment of architecture in Roman wall paintings (see fig. 7-52).

"Old Master" paintings are today. It was revived, Pliny tells us, around the middle of the first century B.C. by Timomachous of Byzantium, who "restored its ancient dignity to the art of painting." [See Primary Sources, no. 3, page 195.] This rebirth came around the same time as the frescoes in the Villa of the Mysteries (see fig. 7-51), which provide a test case of what is Roman in Roman painting. Many of the poses and gestures are taken from Classical Greek art, yet they lack the self-conscious quality that we call Classicism. An artist of great vision has filled these forms with new life. Our painter was the legitimate heir of the Greeks in the same sense that the finest Latin poets of the Augustan age were the legitimate heirs to the Greek poetic tradition.

Roman painting as a whole shows the same genius for adapting Greek examples to Roman needs as do sculpture and architecture. This is true even of seemingly reproductive or imitative works. The mythological panels that occur like islands in the Third and Fourth Styles (see fig. 7-52) sometimes give the impression of being copies after Hellenistic originals. In several cases, however, we possess more than one variant of the same composition derived ultimately from the same, presumably Greek, source.

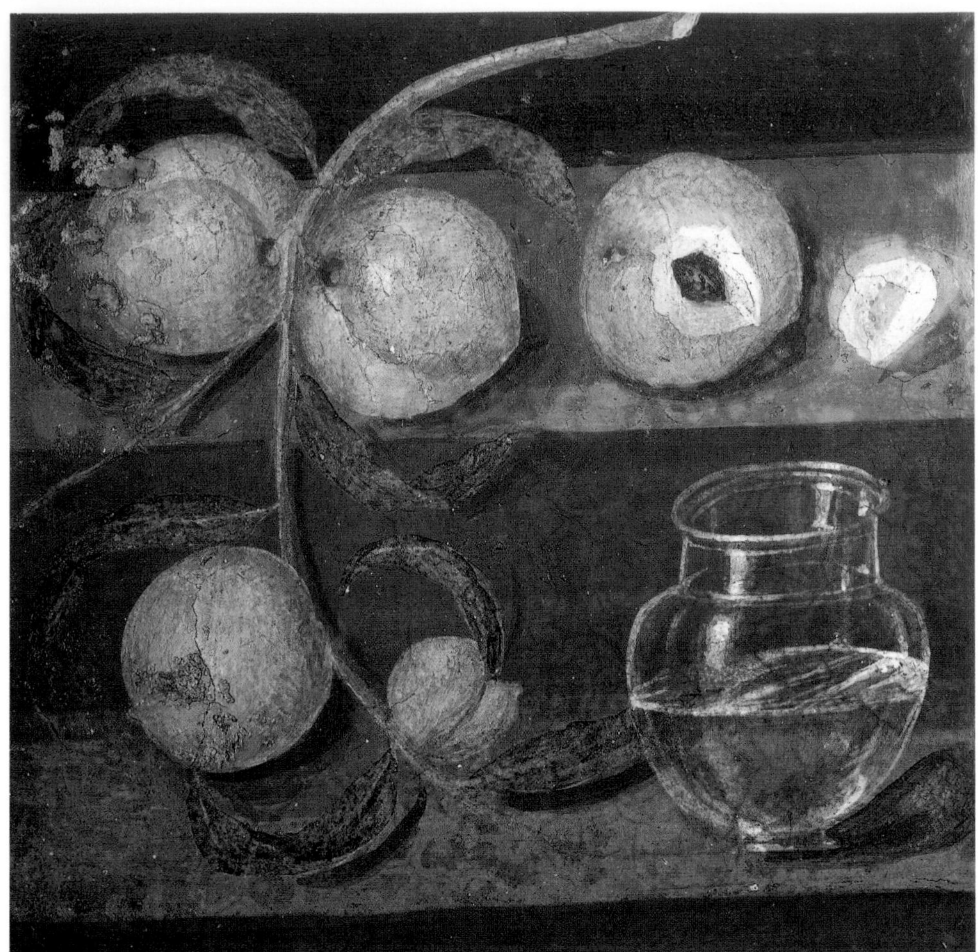

7-53. *Peaches and Glass Jar.* Wall painting from Herculaneum. c. 50 A.D. Museo Archeologico Nazionale, Naples

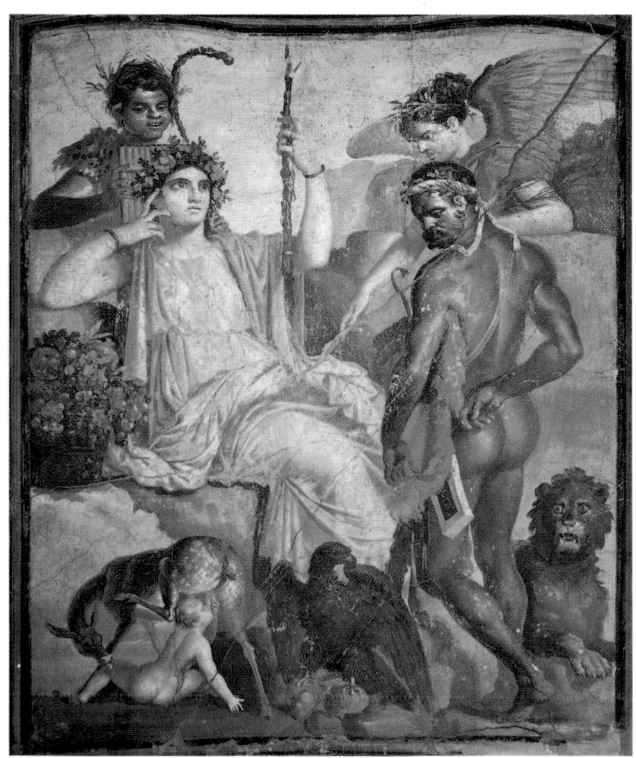

7-54. *Hercules and Telephus.* Wall painting from Herculaneum. c. 70 A.D. Museo Archeologico Nazionale, Naples

These variants attest to how readily the original was copied and changed. Moreover, a closer look shows that such panels, too, evolved in ways that reflect the changing taste of Roman artists and their patrons. Figures were freely altered and rearranged, often in very different settings, suggesting that they could be found in pattern books much like those for sarcophagi (see page 179). Thus, whatever their relation to the masterpieces of Greece that are lost to us forever, scenes such as Hermes overseeing the punishment of Ixion in figure 7-52 represent the eclectic Roman approach to painting, and it is likely that most were of recent vintage as well.

These pictures often have a rather disjointed character because they combine motifs from diverse sources. An example is the picture of Hercules discovering his infant son, Telephus, in Arcadia, from the basilica at Herculaneum (fig. 7-54). It may reflect a painting made in Pergamon, since a similar composition occurs in fragmentary form on the Great Altar (see pages 143–44). What shows that this scene is the work of a Roman painter is its unstable style. Almost everything has the look of a "quotation."

Not only the forms, but even the brushwork vary from one figure to the next. Thus the personification of Arcadia, seated in the center, seems as immobile and tightly modeled as a statue, whereas Hercules, although his pose is equally statuesque, exhibits a broader and more luminous technique. Or compare the Nemean Lion, emblem of Hercules, and the eagle of Jupiter, his father, which are painted in sketchy dabs, with the precise outlines of the doe and the child. The sparkling highlights on the basket of fruit are derived from yet another source: still lifes such as figure 7-53. And the mischievously smiling young Pan in the upper left-hand corner is composed of feathery brushstrokes that have an entirely different character. We recognize the same peculiarly Roman operating principle at work here as in the shifting decorative system of the Fourth Style as a whole, with its ambivalent perspective and inconsistent light.

PORTRAITS. Portrait painting, according to Pliny, was an established custom in Republican Rome that he considered to be in decline, along with the rest of painting. It served the ancestor cult as did the portrait busts discussed earlier (see page 171). None of these panels has survived, and the few portraits found on the walls of Roman houses in Pompeii may derive from a different, Hellenistic tradition. The only coherent group of painted portraits that has come down to us is from the Faiyum district in Lower Egypt. The earliest of them seem to date from the second century A.D. We owe them to the survival (or revival) of the ancient Egyptian custom of attaching a portrait of the deceased to the wrapped, mummified body. Originally, these portraits had been sculpted (compare fig. 2-29), but in Roman times they were replaced by painted ones such as the very fine wooden panel that is shown in figure 7-55.

The amazing freshness of its colors is due to the fact that it was done in a very durable medium called encaustic, which uses pigments suspended in hot wax. The mixture can be opaque and creamy, like oil paint, or thin and translucent. At their best, these portraits have an immediacy and a sureness of touch that have rarely been surpassed, thanks to the need to work quickly before the hot wax set. Our dark-haired boy is as solid and lifelike as anyone might wish. The style of the picture—and it does have style, otherwise we could not tell it from a snapshot—becomes apparent only when we compare it with other Faiyum portraits. Since they were produced quickly and in large numbers, they tend to have many elements in common. These include the emphasis on the eyes, the placing of the highlights and shadows, and the angle from which the face is seen. Over time, these elements would stiffen into a fixed type, but here they provide a flexible mold within which to cast an individual likeness. In this happy instance the intent was only to recall the personality of a beloved child. This way of painting was revived four centuries later in the earliest Byzantine icons, which were considered "portraits," of the Madonna and Child, Christ, and the saints.

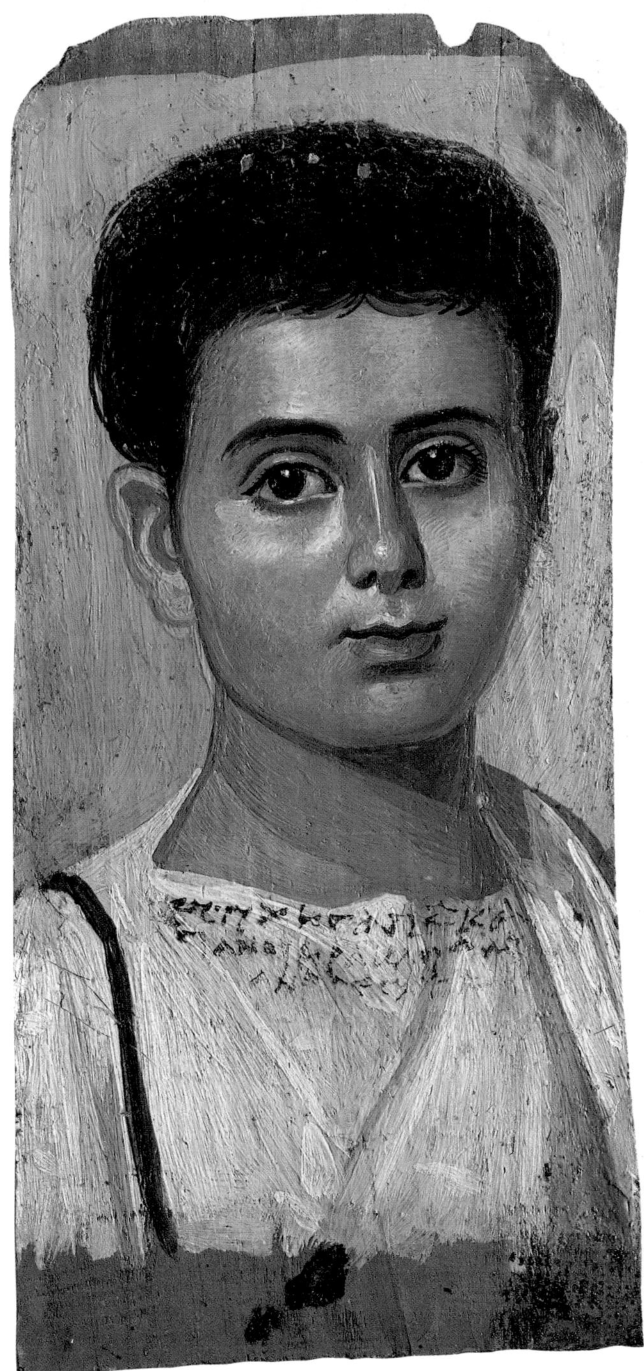

7-55. *Portrait of a Boy,* from the Faiyum, Lower Egypt. 2nd century A.D. Encaustic on panel, 15 3/8 x 7 1/2" (39 x 19 cm). The Metropolitan Museum of Art, New York

GIFT OF EDWARD S. HARKNESS, 1918

Primary Sources for Part One

The following is a selection of excerpts, in modern translations, from original texts by historians or writers from Egyptian times through the Roman era. These readings supplement the main text and are keyed to it. Their full citations are given in the Credits section at the end of the book.

1
The Book of the Dead

This text is an incantation from Plate III of the Papyrus of Ani in the British Museum, from the latter half of Dynasty XVIII. It accompanies the weighing of the soul illustrated in the closely related Papyrus of Hunefer (see fig. 2-31).

Saith Thoth the righteous judge of the cycle of the gods great who are in the presence of Osiris: Hear ye decision this. In very truth is weighed the heart of Osiris, is his soul standing as a witness for him; his sentence is right upon the scales great. Not hath been found wickedness [in] him any; not hath he wasted food offering in the temples; not hath he done harm in deed; not hath he let go with his mouth evil things while he was upon earth.

Saith the cycle of the gods great to Thoth [dwelling] in Hermopolis [the god's cult-center along the Nile in Upper Egypt]: Decreed is it that which cometh forth from thy mouth. Truth [and] righteous [is] Osiris, the scribe Ani triumphant. Not hath he sinned, not hath he done evil in respect of us. Let not be allowed to prevail Amemet [Ammut, the devourer of souls] over him. Let there be given to him cakes, and a coming forth in the presence of Osiris, and a field abiding in Sekhet-hetepu [Field of Peace] like the followers of Horus.

2
From *Cylinder A of Gudea*

Gudea's rebuilding of the temple, called Eninnu, to the god Ningirsu was recounted on three inscribed clay cylinders of about 2125 B.C. Cylinder A describes the construction of the temple. Gudea is presented as the architect, helped by Nidaba (goddess of writing, here representing the use of written sources) and Enki (god of builders).

For . . . Gudea . . . did Nidaba open
the house of understanding,
did Enki put right

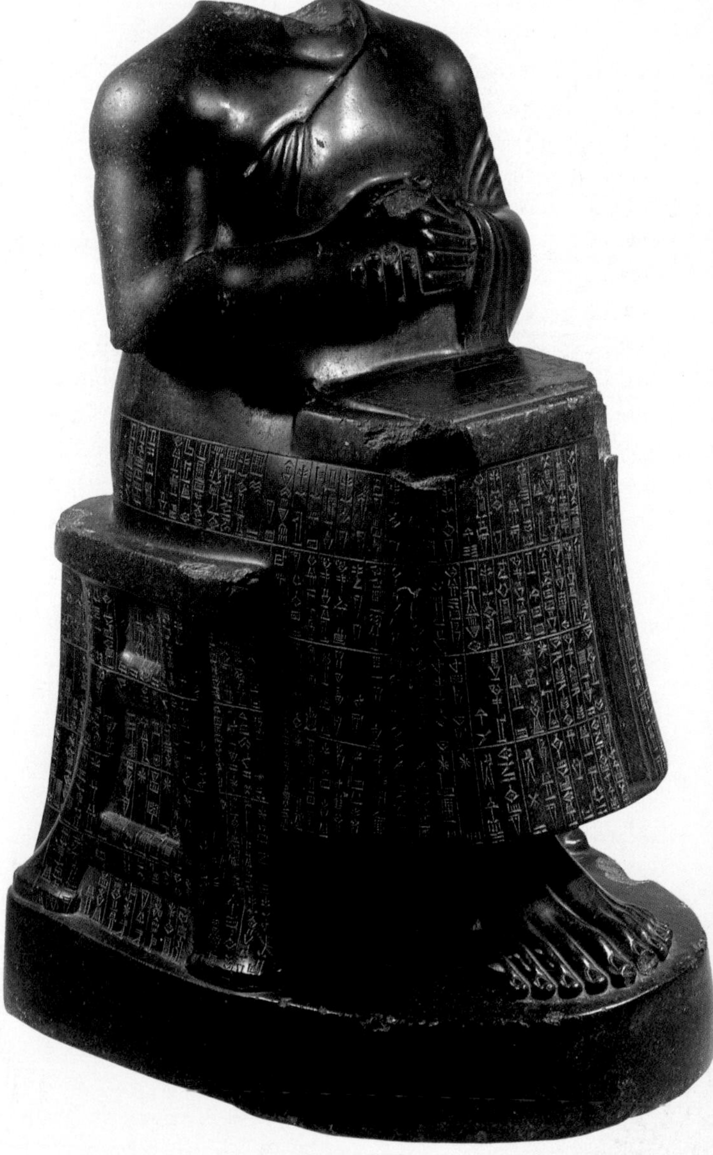

PS-2. *Gudea with Architectural Plan,* from Lagash (Telloh), Iraq. c. 2150. B.C. Diorite, height 29" (73.7 cm). Musée du Louvre, Paris

the design of the house.
To the house . . . did Gudea pace from south
to north on the fired [purified] mound, . . .
laid the measuring cord down
on what was a true acre,
put in pegs at its sides,
verified them himself.
It was cause of rejoicing
for him. . . .
In the brick-mold shed he performed
the pouring of water,
and the water sounded to the ruler
as cymbals and *alu* lyres playing for him;
on the brick pit and its bricks
he drenched the top layer,
hoed in honey, butter, and sweet princely oil; . . .
into the brick mold Gudea put the clay,
made "the proper thing" appear,
was establishing his name,
making the brick of the house appear. . . .
He placed the brick, paced off
the house,
laid out the plan of the house,
(as) a very Nidaba knowing the inmost
(secrets) of numbers,
and like a young man
building his first house,
sweet sleep came not unto his eyes;
like a cow keeping an eye on its calf,
he went in constant worry to the house—
like a man who eats food sparingly
he tired not from going. . . .
Gudea made Ningirsu's house
come out like the sun from the clouds,
had it grow to be like sparkling foothills;
like foothills of white alabaster
he had it stand forth to be marveled at . . .
the house's stretching out
along (substructure) walltops,
was like the heights of heaven
awe-inspiring;
the roofing of the house, like a white cloud,
was floating in the midst of heaven.
Its gate through which the owner entered
was like a lammergeier [vulture]
espying a wild bull,
its curved gateposts standing
at the gate
were like the rainbow
standing in the sky. . . .
It (the house) kept an eye on the country;
no arrogant one could walk
in its sight,
awe of Eninnu
covered all lands like a cloth.

3

PLINY THE ELDER (23–79 A.D.)

Natural History

The earliest preserved history of art appears in the work of the Roman naturalist and historian Pliny, who lived at the beginning of the Roman Imperial period and died in the eruption of Mount Vesuvius that destroyed Pompeii. Pliny says nothing about vase painting. For him the great era of painting began in the fifth century B.C., and its high point came in the fourth century B.C. Pliny lists the names and works of many artists who are otherwise unknown today. His anecdotes reveal the primacy placed on illusionism by Greeks and Romans. Pliny's work influenced Renaissance writers of art history, including Ghiberti and Vasari.

from Book 35 (on Greek painting)

The origin of painting is obscure. . . . All, however, agree that painting began with the outlining of a man's shadow; this was the first stage, in the second a single colour was employed, and after the discovery of more elaborate methods this style, which is still in vogue, received the name of monochrome. . . .

Four colours only—white from Melos, Attic yellow, red from Sinope on the Black Sea, and the black called 'atramentum'—were used by Apelles, Aetion, Melanthios and Nikomachos in their . . . works; illustrious artists, a single one of whose pictures the wealth of a city could hardly suffice to buy. . . .

Apollodoros of Athens [in 408–405 B.C.] was the first to give his figures the appearance of reality. [He] opened the gates of art through which Zeuxis of Herakleia passed [in 397 B.C.]. The story runs that Parrhasios and Zeuxis entered into competition, Zeuxis exhibiting a picture of some grapes, so true to nature that the birds flew up to the wall of the stage. Parrhasios then displayed a picture of a linen curtain, realistic to such a degree that Zeuxis, elated by the verdict of the birds, cried out that now at last his rival must draw the curtain and show his picture. On discovering his mistake he surrendered the prize to Parrhasios, admitting candidly that he had deceived the birds, while Parrhasios had deluded himself, a painter. . . .

Apelles of Kos [in 332–329 B.C.] excelled all painters who came before or after him. He of himself perhaps contributed more to painting than all the others together; he also wrote treatises on his theory of art. . . .

Nikomachos' . . . pupils were his brother Ariston, his son Aristeides and Philoxenos of Eretria, who painted for king Kassander the battle between Alexander and Dareios, a picture second to none [compare fig. 5-60].

from Book 34 (on bronze)

Besides his Olympian Zeus, a work which has no rival, Pheidias made in ivory the Athena at Athens, which stands erect in the Parthenon. . . . He is rightly held to have first revealed the capabilities of sculpture and indicatd its methods.

Polykleitos . . . made an athlete binding the diadem about his head, which was famous for the sum of one hundred talents which it realized. This . . . has been described as 'a man, yet a boy': the . . . spear-bearer [see fig. 5-42] as 'a boy, yet a man.' He also made the statue which sculptors call the 'canon,' referring to it as to a standard from which they can learn the first rules of their art. He is the only man who is held to have embodied the principles of his art in a single work. . . . He is considered to have brought the scientific knowledge of statuary to perfection, and to have systematized the art of which Pheidias had revealed the possibilities. It was his peculiar characteristic to represent his figures resting their weight on one leg; . . .

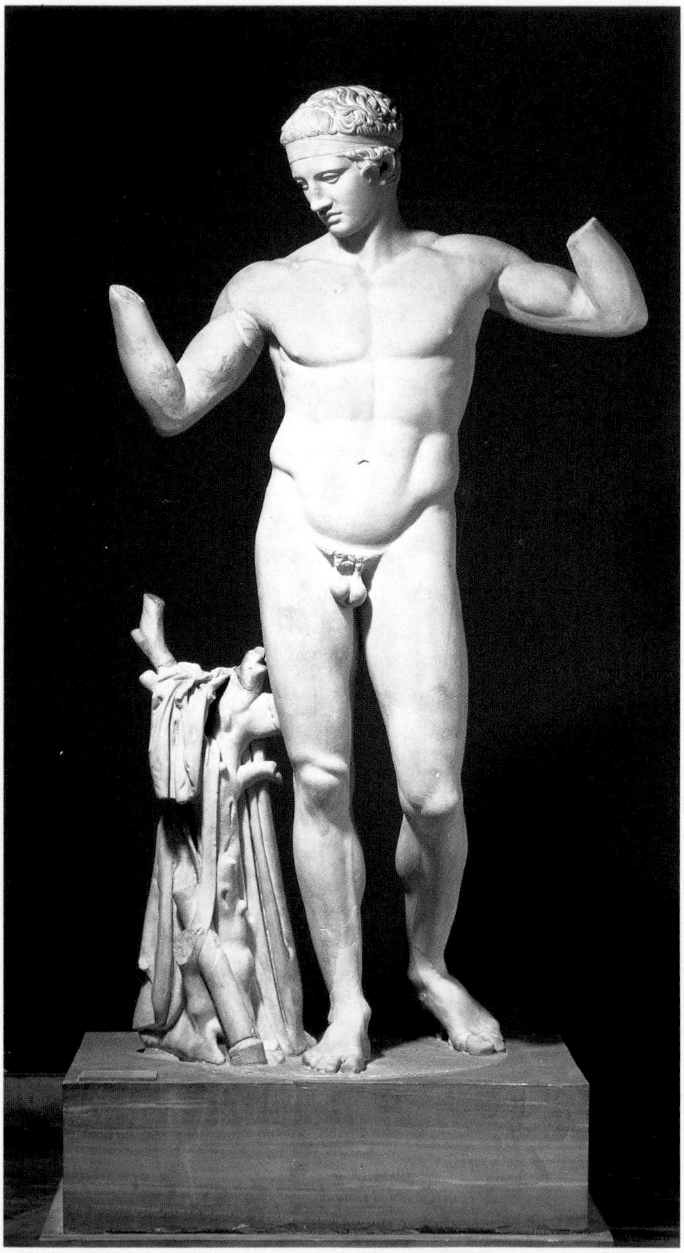

PS-3. Polykleitos. *Diadoumenos*. Roman marble copy (1st century B.C.) after bronze Greek original of c. 430 B.C., height 6'5" (1.95 m). Archeological Museum, Athens

Myron . . . [made an] athlete hurling the disk [see fig. 5-49], a Perseus, . . . and the Herakles which is near the great Circus in the temple of the great Pompeius. . . . He was more productive than Polykleitos, and a more diligent observer of symmetry. Still he too only cared for the physical form, and did not express the sensations of the mind. . . .

Lysippos produced more works than any other artist, possessing, as I have said, a most prolific genius. Among them is the man scraping himself [see fig. 5-70]. . . . In this statue the Emperor Tiberius took a marvellous delight, . . . he could not refrain from having the statue removed into his private chamber, substituting another in its place. . . . His chief contributions to the art of sculpture are said to consist in his vivid rendering of the hair, in making the heads smaller than older artists had done, and the bodies slimmer and with less flesh, thus increasing the apparent height of his figures. There is no word in Latin for the canon of symmetry which he was so careful to preserve, bringing innovations which had never been thought of before into the square canon of the older artists, and he often said that the difference between himself and them was that they represented men as they were, and he as they appeared to be. His chief characteristic is extreme delicacy of execution even in the smallest details.

from Book 36 (on marble)

The art of [marble] sculpture is much older than that of painting or of bronze statuary, both of which began with Pheidias. . . .

Praxiteles . . . outdid even himself by the fame of his works in marble. . . . Famous . . . throughout the whole world, is the Aphrodite which multitudes have sailed to Knidos to look upon [see fig. 5-67]. He had offered two statues of Aphrodite for sale at the same time, the second being a draped figure, which for that reason was preferred by the people of Kos with whom lay the first choice; the price of the two figures was the same, but they flattered themselves they were giving proof of a severe modesty. The rejected statue, which was bought by the people of Knidos, enjoys an immeasurably greater reputation. King Nikomedes subsequently wished to buy it from them, offering to discharge the whole of their public debt, which was enormous. They, however, preferred to suffer the worst that could befall, and they showed their wisdom, for by this statue Praxiteles made Knidos illustrious. . . .

Bryaxis, Timotheos, and Leochares were rivals and contemporaries of Skopas, and must be mentioned with him, as they worked together on the Mausoleion [figs. 5-63 and 5-64]. This is the tomb erected by Artemisia in honour of her husband Mausolos, . . . and its place among the seven wonders of the world is largely due to these great sculptors. The length of the south and north sides is 163 feet; the two facades are shorter, and the whole perimeter is 440 feet; its height is 25 cubits [37½ feet], and it has thirty-six columns. . . . The sculptures of the eastern front are carved by Skopas, those on the north by Bryaxis, on the south by Timotheos, and on the west by Leochares. . . . Above the colonnade is a pyramid, of the same height as the lower structure, consisting of twenty-four retreating steps rising into a cone. On the apex stands a chariot and four horses in marble made by Pythis. . . .

In the case of certain masterpieces the . . . number of the collaborators is an obstacle to their individual fame, since neither can one man take to himself the whole glory, nor have a number so great a claim to honour. This is the case with the Laokoon in the palace of the Emperor Titus, a work superior to all the pictures and bronzes of the world [compare fig. 5-76]. Out of one block of marble did the illustrious artists Hagesander, Polydoros, and Athanodoros of Rhodes, after taking counsel together, carve Laokoon, his children, and the wondrous coils of the snakes.

from Book 35 (on Roman painting)

Timomachos of Byzantium, in the period when Caesar was dictator [46–44 B.C.], painted an *Ajax* and a *Medea,* which were placed by Caesar, after he bought them for 80 talents, in the temple of Venus *Genetrix*. . . . Works by Timomachos which are equally praised are his *Orestes*, his *Iphigeneia among the Taurians,* his picture of *Lekythion* the trainer in agility, a family portrait of well-known people, and his picture of two men in Greek cloaks, whom he has painted as about to speak, one standing and the other seated. His art seems to have been exceptionally successful, however, in his painting of a *Gorgon*.

Women too have been painters: . . . Iaia of Kyzikos, who remained single all her life, worked at Rome. . . . She painted chiefly portraits of women, and also a large picture of an old woman at Naples, and a portrait of herself, executed with the help of a mirror. No artist worked more rapidly than she did, and her pictures had such merit that they sold for higher prices than those of [other] well-known contemporary painters, whose works fill our galleries.

4

VITRUVIUS (1ST CENTURY B.C.)
On Architecture

Vitruvius, like Pliny, was a Roman writer who admired the achievements of the Greeks. He was an architect under Julius Caesar and Augustus, and his treatise on architecture (c. 35–25 B.C.) reflects the classicizing taste of his time. Vitruvius' work was a principal source for Renaissance architects seeking the revival of antiquity. His account of the origin of the Greek orders is partly mythic, partly rational conjecture (see fig. 5-24).

from Book IV (on the Doric and Corinthian orders)

For in Achaea and over the whole Peloponnese, Dorus . . . was king; by chance he built a temple . . . at the old city of Argos, in the sanctuary of Juno. . . . Afterwards [Greeks in Ionia] . . . established a temple as they had seen in Achaea. Then they called it Doric because they had first seen it built in that style. When they wished to place columns in that temple, not having their proportions, . . . they measured a man's footstep and applied it to his height. Finding that the foot was the sixth part of the height in a man, they applied this proportion to the column. Of whatever thickness they made the base of the shaft they raised it along with the capital to six times as much in height. So the Doric column began to furnish the proportion of a man's body, its strength and grace. . . .

But the third order, which is called Corinthian, imitates the slight figure of a maiden; because girls are represented with slighter dimensions because of their tender age, and admit of more graceful effects in ornament. Now the first invention of that capital is related to have happened thus. A girl, a native of Corinth, already of age to be married, was attacked by disease and died. After her funeral, the goblets which delighted her when living, were put together in a basket by her nurse, carried to the monument, and placed on the top. That they might remain longer, exposed as they were to the weather, she covered the basket with a tile. As it happened the basket was placed upon the root of an acanthus. Meanwhile about spring time, the root of the acanthus, being pressed down in the middle by the weight, put forth leaves and shoots. The shoots grew up the sides of the basket, and, being pressed down at the angles by the force of the weight of the tile, were compelled to form the curves of volutes at the extreme parts. . . .

Workmen of old, . . . when they had put beams reaching from the inner walls to the outside parts, built in the spaces between the beams. . . . Then they cut off the projections of the beams, as far as they came forward, to the line and perpendicular of the walls. But since this appearance was ungraceful, they fixed tablets shaped as triglyphs now are, against the cut-off beams, and painted them with blue wax, in order that the cut-off beams might be concealed so as not to offend the eyes. Thus in Doric structures, the divisions of the beams being hidden began to have the arrangement of the triglyphs, and, between the beams, of metopes. Subsequently other architects in other works carried forward over the triglyphs the projecting rafters, and trimmed the projections. . . . In the Doric style the detail . . . of the triglyphs . . . arose from this imitation of timber work.

from Book V (on public buildings)

The sites of basilicas ought to be fixed adjoining the fora in as warm a quarter as possible, so that in the winter, business men may meet there without being troubled by the weather. And their breadth should be fixed at not less than a third, nor more than half their length, unless the nature of the site is awkward and forces the proportions to be changed. When the site is longer than necessary, the committee rooms are to be placed at the end of the basilica. . . . The columns of basilicas are to be of a height equal to the width of the aisle. The aisle is to have a width one third of the nave.

from Book VI (on private buildings)

We must go on to consider how, in private buildings, the rooms belonging to the family, and how those which are shared with visitors, should be planned. For into the private rooms no one can come uninvited, such as the bedrooms, dining-rooms, baths and other apartments which have similar purposes. The common rooms are those into which, though uninvited, persons of the people can come by right, such as vestibules, courtyards, peristyles and other apartments of similar uses. Therefore magnificent vestibules and alcoves and halls are not necessary to persons of a common fortune, because they pay their respects by visiting among others, and are not visited by others. . . . The houses of bankers and farmers of the revenue should be more spacious and imposing and safe from burglars. . . . For persons of high rank who hold office and magistracies, and whose duty it is to serve the state, we must provide princely vestibules, lofty halls and very spacious peristyles, plantations and broad avenues finished in a majestic manner.

from Book VII (on fresco wall painting)

For other apartments, that is, those used for spring, autumn, and summer, and also in atriums and peristyles, clearly defined principles for depicting objects were derived by the ancients from prototypes which really existed in nature. For a picture is an image of something which either really exists or at least can exist—for instance, men, actual buildings, ships, and other things from whose clearly defined and actually existent physical forms pictorial representations are derived by copying. Following this principle, the ancients, who first undertook to use polished wall surfaces, began by imitating different varieties of marble revetments in different positions, and then went on to imitate cornices, hard stones, and wedges arranged in various ways in relation to one another.

Later they became so proficient that they would imitate the forms even of buildings and the way columns and gables stood out as they projected from the background; and in open spaces, such as exedrae, because of the extensiveness of the walls, they depicted stage facades in the tragic, comic, or satyric style. Their walks, because of the extended length of the wall space, they decorated with landscapes of various sorts, modeling these images on the features of actual places. In these are painted harbors, promontories, coastlines, rivers, springs, straits, sanctuaries, groves, mountains, flocks, and shepherds. In places there are some designs done in the megalographic style representing images of the gods or narrating episodes from mythology, or, no less often, scenes from the Trojan war, or the wanderings of Odysseus over the landscape backgrounds, and other subjects, which are produced on the basis of similar principles from nature as it really is.

But these, which are representations derived from reality, are now scorned by the undiscriminating tastes of the present. For now there are monstrosities painted on stucco walls rather than true-to-life images based on actual things—instead of columns the structural elements are striated reeds; instead of gables there are ribbed appendages with curled leaves and volutes. Candelabra are seen supporting figures of small shrines, and, above the gables of these, many tender stalks with volutes grow up from their roots and have, without it making any sense whatsoever, little seated figures upon them. Not only that, but there are slender stalks which have little half-figures, some with human heads and some with beasts' heads [compare fig. 7-52].

Such things do not exist, nor could they exist, nor have they ever existed. Consequently it is the new tastes which have brought about a condition in which bad judges who deal with incompetent art have the power to condemn real excellence in the arts. For to what extent can a reed actually sustain a roof or a candelabrum the ornaments of a gable, or a tender, soft stalk support a seated figure, or at one time flowers and at another time half-figures be produced from roots and stalks? And yet upon seeing these false images they do not disapprove of them, but on the contrary they delight in them, nor do they give any attention to the question of whether any of these things could really exist or not. Minds obscured by weak powers of criticism are not able to make a valid judgment, with authority and with a rational understanding of what is proper, about what can exist. For pictures should not be given approbation which are not likenesses of reality; even if they are refined creations executed with artistic skill, they still should not, simply on the basis of these facts, immediately be judged as correct, unless their subjects demonstrate conceptual principles which are based on reality and are put into practice without deviations. . . .

But it will not be beyond the scope of our discussion to explain why a false method wins out over the truth. The reason is that what the ancients sought to achieve by laborious, painstaking diligence in their arts, the present age seeks to attain by colors and their alluring effect; and the impressiveness which the subtle skill of the artist used to contribute to works is now brought about by lavish expenditure on the part of the client, lest loss of subtlety be noted.

5

PLUTARCH (c. 46–AFTER 119 A.D.)

Parallel Lives of Greeks and Romans, from the lives of Perikles and Fabius Maximus

A Greek author of the Roman period, Plutarch wrote Parallel Lives *to show that ancient Greece matched or exceeded Rome in its great leaders. Comparing Perikles (d. 429 B.C.) with Fabius Maximus (d. 203 B.C.), he concludes that Perikles' buildings surpass all the architecture of the Romans. Plutarch is the only ancient source to say that Pheidias was the overseer of Perikles' works.*

But that which brought most delightful adornment to Athens, and the greatest amazement to the rest of mankind; that which alone now testifies for Hellas that her ancient power and splendour, of which so much is told, was no idle fiction,—I mean his construction of sacred edifices. . . . For this reason are the works of Perikles all the more to be wondered at; they were created in a short time for all time. Each one of them, in its beauty, was even then and at once antique; but in the freshness of its vigour it is, even to the present day, recent and newly wrought. Such is the bloom of perpetual newness, as it were, upon these works of his, which makes them ever to look untouched by time, as though the unfaltering breath of an ageless spirit had been infused into them.

His general manager and general overseer was Pheidias, although the several works had great architects and artists besides. Of the Parthenon, for instance, with its cella of a hundred feet in length, Callicrates and Ictinus were the architects. . . .

By the side of the great public works, the temples, and the stately edifices, with which Perikles adorned Athens, all Rome's attempts at splendour down to the times of the Caesars, taken together, are not worthy to be considered, nay, the one had a towering pre-eminence above the other, both in grandeur of design, and grandeur of execution, which precludes comparison.

6

PLATO (c. 427–347 B.C.)
The Republic, from Book X

At the end of his treatise on the ideal state, the philosopher Plato attacks poets and painters. He claims that painters are only imitators of appearances, rather than of essences (forms or ideas), and therefore dishonest; he concludes that they must be banished from the state. Implicit in this argument is a condemnation of the new illusionistic practices in Greek art. The treatise is written in Socratic dialogue form, which consists of a series of questions designed to elicit clear and rational answers.

"Could you tell me what imitation in general is? . . . We are, presumably, accustomed to set down some one particular form for each of the particular 'manys' to which we apply the same name. Or don't you understand?"

"I do."

"Then let's now set down any one of the 'manys' you please; for example, if you wish, there are surely many couches and tables."

"Of course."

"But as for *ideas* for these furnishings, there are presumably two, one of couch, one of table.

"Yes." . . .

"You could fabricate them quickly, . . . if you are willing to take a mirror and carry it around everywhere; quickly you will make the sun and the things in heaven; quickly, the earth; and quickly, yourself and the other animals and implements and plants. . . . "

"Yes," he said, "so that they look like they *are*; however, they surely *are* not the truth."

"Fine," I said, "and you attack the argument at just the right place. For I suppose the painter is also one of these craftsmen, isn't he?"

"Of course he is."

"But I suppose you'll say that he doesn't truly make what he makes. And yet in a certain way the painter too does make a couch, doesn't he?"

"Yes," he said, "he too makes what looks like a couch." . . .

"There turn out, then, to be these three kinds of couches: one that *is* in nature, which we would say, I suppose, a god produced. . . . And then one that the carpenter produced."

"Yes," he said.

"And the one that the painter produced, isn't that so?" . . .

"Now consider this very point. Toward which is painting directed in each case—toward imitation of the being as it is or toward its looking as it looks? Is it imitation of looks or of truth?"

"Of looks," he said.

"Therefore, imitation is surely far from truth; and, as it seems, it is due to this that it produces everything—because it lays hold of a certain small part of each thing, and that part is itself only a phantom. For example, the painter, we say, will paint for us a shoemaker, a carpenter, and the other craftsmen, although he doesn't understand the arts of any one of them. But, nevertheless, if he is a good painter, by painting a carpenter and displaying him from far off, he would deceive children and foolish human beings into thinking that it is truly a carpenter."

7

ARISTOTLE (384–322 B.C.)
The Politics, from Book VIII

The Politics *is a counterpart to Plato's* Republic, *a treatment of the constitution of the state. Books VII and VIII discuss the education prescribed for good citizens. Drawing is included as a liberal art—that is, a skill not only useful but also conducive to higher activities. Yet painting and sculpture are said to have only limited power to move the soul.*

There is a sort of education in which parents should train their sons, not as being useful or necessary, but because it is liberal or noble. . . . Further, it is clear that children should be instructed in some useful things—for example, in reading and writing—not only for their usefulness, but also because many other sorts of knowledge are acquired through them. With a like view they may be taught drawing, not to prevent their making mistakes in their own purchases, or in order that they may not be imposed upon in the buying or selling of articles [works of art], but perhaps rather because it makes them judges of the beauty of the human form. To be always seeking after the useful does not become free and exalted souls. . . .

The habit of feeling pleasure or pain at mere representations is not far removed from the same feeling about realities; for example, if any one delights in the sight of a statue for its beauty only, it necessarily follows that the sight of the original will be pleasant to him. The objects of no other sense, such as taste or touch, have any resemblance to moral qualities; in visible objects there is only a little, for there are figures which are of a moral character, but only to a slight extent, and all do not participate in the feeling about them. Again, figures and colours are not imitations, but signs, of character, indications which the body gives of states of feeling. The connexion of them with morals is slight, but in so far as there is any, young men should be taught to look . . . at [the works] of Polygnotus, or any other painter or sculptor who expresses character.

8

VERGIL (70–19 B.C.)

The Aeneid, from Book II

Vergil was the greatest Latin poet and the chief exponent of the Augustan age in literature. The Aeneid *is an epic poem about the hero Aeneas, who fled Troy when it was destroyed by the Greeks and settled in Italy. Book II tells of the fall of Troy, including the punishment by Minerva of Laocoön for trying to warn the Trojans against the trick wooden horse. The sculptural rendition of Laocoön shown in figure 5-76 closely resembles Vergil's description.* The Vatican Vergil *(see fig. 8-19) contains the complete* Aeneid *as well as other poetry by Vergil.*

Laocoön, by lot named priest of Neptune,
was sacrificing then a giant bull
upon the customary altars, when
two snakes with endless coils, from Tenedos
strike out across the tranquil deep. . . .
They lick their hissing jaws with quivering tongues.
We scatter at the sight, our blood is gone.
They strike a straight line toward Laocoön.
At first each snake entwines the tiny bodies
of his two sons in an embrace, then feasts
its fangs on their defenseless limbs. The pair
next seize upon Laocoön himself,
who nears to help his sons, carrying weapons.
They wind around his waist and twice around
his throat. They throttle him with scaly backs;
their heads and steep necks tower over him.
He struggles with his hands to rip their knots,
his headbands soaked in filth and in dark venom,
while he lifts high his hideous cries to heaven,
just like the bellows of a wounded bull.

9

LIVY (59 B.C.–17 A.D.)

From the Founding of the City, from Book I

Livy, a historian, was a contemporary of Vitruvius and Vergil and also moved in the circle of the emperor Augustus. His history of Rome begins with Aeneas and includes the legend of the she-wolf that suckled Romulus and Remus (compare fig. 6-9).

The Vestal [Virgin, Rhea Silvia] was ravished, and having given birth to twin sons, named Mars as the father of her doubtful offspring. . . . But neither gods nor men protected the mother herself or her babes from the king's cruelty; the priestess he ordered to be manacled and cast into prison, the children to be committed to the river. . . . The story persists that when the floating basket in which the children had been exposed was left high and dry by the receding water, a she-wolf, coming down out of the surrounding hills to slake her thirst, turned her steps towards the cry of the infants, and with her teats gave them suck so gently, that the keeper of the royal flock found her licking them with her tongue. . . . He carried the twins to his hut and gave them to his wife Larentia to rear.

10

POLYBIUS (c. 200–c. 118 B.C.)

Histories, from Book VI

Polybius was a Greek historian active during the Roman conquest of his homeland. His Histories *recount the rise of Rome from the third century B.C. to the destruction of Corinth in 146 B.C. In Book VI he considers cultural and other factors explaining Rome's success.*

Whenever any illustrious man dies, . . . they place the image of the departed in the most conspicuous position in the house, enclosed in a wooden shrine. This image is a mask reproducing with remarkable fidelity both the features and complexion of the deceased. On the occasion of public sacrifices they display these images, and decorate them with much care, and when any distinguished member of the family dies they take them to the funeral, putting them on men who seem to them to bear the closest resemblance to the original in stature and carriage. These representatives wear togas, with a purple border if the deceased was a consul or praetor, whole purple if he was a censor, and embroidered with gold if he had celebrated a triumph or achieved anything similar. They all ride in chariots preceded by the fasces, axes, and other insignia . . . and when they arrive at the rostra they all seat themselves in a row on ivory chairs. There could not easily be a more ennobling spectacle for a young man who aspires to fame and virtue. For who would not be inspired by the sight of the images of men renowned for their excellence, all together and as if alive and breathing? . . . By this means, by this constant renewal of the good report of brave men, the celebrity of those who performed noble deeds is rendered immortal. . . . But the most important result is that young men are thus inspired to endure every suffering for the public welfare in the hope of winning the glory that attends on brave men.

11

JOSEPHUS (37/8–c. 100 A.D.)
The Jewish War, from Book VII

The Jewish soldier and historian Josephus Flavius was born Joseph Ben Matthias in Jerusalem. He was named commander of Galilee during the uprising of 66–70 A.D. against the Romans in the reign of Nero. After surrendering, he won the favor of the general Titus Flavius Sabinus Vespasian and took the name Flavius as his own. Josephus moved to Rome, where he wrote an account of the war (75–79 A.D.) and Antiquities of the Jews (93 A.D.), which was later illustrated by Jean Fouquet (see fig. 15–18). The following passage from his history of the rebellion describes the triumphal procession into Rome following the Sack of Jerusalem in 70 A.D., which is depicted on the Arch of Titus (figs. 7-35, 7-36).

It is impossible to give a worthy description of the great number of splendid sights and of the magnificence which occurred in every conceivable form, be it works of art, varieties of wealth, or natural objects of great rarity. For almost all the wondrous and expensive objects which had ever been collected, piece by piece, from one land and another, by prosperous men—all this, being brought together for exhibition on a single day, gave a true indication of the greatness of the Roman Empire. For a vast amount of silver and gold and ivory, wrought into every sort of form, was to be seen, giving not so much the impression of being borne along in a procession as, one might say, of flowing by like a river. Woven tapestries were carried along, some dyed purple and of great rarity, others having varied representations of living figures embroidered on them with great exactness, the handiwork of Babylonians. Transparent stones, some set into gold crowns, some displayed in other ways, were borne by in such great numbers that the conception which we had formed of their rarity seemed pointless. Images of the Roman gods, of wondrous size and made with no inconsiderable workmanship, were also exhibited, and of these there was not one which was not made of some expensive material. . . .

The rest of the spoils were borne along in random heaps. The most interesting of all were the spoils seized from the temple of Jerusalem: a gold table weighing many talents, and a lampstand, also made of gold, which was made in a form different from that which we usually employ. For there was a central shaft fastened to the base; then spandrels extended from this in an arrangement which rather resembled the shape of a trident, and on the end of each of these spandrels a lamp was forged. There were seven of these, emphasizing the honor accorded to the number seven among the Jews. The law of the Jews was borne along after these as the last of the spoils. In the next section a good many images of Victory were paraded by. The workmanship of all of these was in ivory and gold. Vespasian drove along behind these and Titus followed him; Domitian rode beside them, dressed in a dazzling fashion and riding a horse which was worth seeing.

12

PLOTINUS (205–270 A.D.)
Enneads, from Book I.6, "On Beauty"

A Greek philosopher who taught in Rome, Plotinus was a Neoplatonist, the last great pagan expositor of the thought of Plato. Mystical in outlook, he conceived the cosmos as a hierarchical descent from the ineffable One (God) to matter. His reference to "images, traces, shadows" is a clear echo of Plato's argument in The Republic *and indicates his distrust of images. As the lowest form of existence in his scheme, matter could not be the site of true beauty. Plotinus' teachings were Christianized and transmitted to the Middle Ages by writers such as Pseudo-Dionysius.*

Beauty is mostly in sight, but it is to be found too in things we hear, in combinations of words and also in music . . . and for those who are advancing upwards from sense-perception ways of life and actions and characters and intellectual activities are beautiful, and there is the beauty of virtue. . . .

How can one see the "inconceivable beauty" which . . . does not come out where the profane may see it? Let him who can . . . leave . . . the sight of his eyes. . . . When he sees the beauty in bodies he must not run after them; we must know that they are images, traces, shadows, and hurry away to that which they image. For if a man runs to the image and wants to seize it as if it was the reality . . . [he] will, . . . in soul, . . . sink down into the dark depths where intellect has no delight, and stay blind in Hades. . . . Shut your eyes, and change to and wake another way of seeing, which everyone has but few use. . . .

First of all . . . look at beautiful ways of life: then at beautiful works, not those which the arts produce, but the works of men who have a name for goodness: then look at the souls of the people who produce the beautiful works.

Timeline One: Prehistory to 300 A.D.

	35,000–3500 B.C.	3500–3000 B.C.	3000–2500 B.C.
HISTORY AND POLITICS	**c. 35,000** First Paleolithic societies **c. 4000** Predynastic period in Egypt	**c. 3500–3000** Sumerian civilization, Mesopotamia **c. 3100** Narmer unites the Upper and Lower Kingdoms of Egypt. Beginning of Old Kingdom in Egypt (dynasties 1–6, until c. 2190); divine kingship of the pharaoh **c. 3000** Rise of early Aegean civilizations: Cretan, Cycladic, and Helladic periods	
RELIGION			
MUSIC, LITERATURE, AND PHILOSOPHY			**c. 3000–2500** *Epic of Gilgamesh,* early Sumerian heroic tale
SCIENCE AND TECHNOLOGY	**c. 8000** Husbandry and farming develop in the Near East	**c. 3500–3000** Wheeled carts in Sumer **c. 3500** Sailboats used on the Nile **c. 3300–3000** Invention of writing by Sumerians; use of potter's wheel and organic dyes	

PYRAMIDS AND POWER The pyramids, built in Egypt during the Old Kingdom, are artworks in which the connection of public architecture to political power, religious ideology, and the development of high technology is particularly clear. Intentionally grandiose, they were designed to impress the viewer with their monumentality and to represent the might and wealth of the pharaohs who built them. The newly centralized government placed power directly in the hands of the monarch, administered by an efficient bureaucracy able to mobilize tens of thousands of workers and apply accurate astronomical calculations and the latest in surveying techniques (such as the plumb line and the A-frame). The pyramids display a high degree of skill in their precise architecture and fine masonry. Built in as little as 30 years as tombs for Egypt's rulers, they and their attendant temples and sculptures express on a grand scale the contemporary idea of the divinity of the pharaoh.

"Venus" of Willendorf, c. 25,000–20,000 B.C.

Cave painting, Altamira, c. 15,000–10,000 B.C.

Female Head, Uruk, c. 3500–3000 B.C.

Inlay panel, Ur, c. 2600 B.C.

	2500–2000 B.C.	2000–1500 B.C.	1500–1000 B.C.
HISTORY AND POLITICS	**Sargon of Akkad, Akkadian ruler (r. 2340–2305),** unifies Mesopotamian region and organizes first empire, encompassing land in Persia, Africa, and the Aegean **c. 2125** Gudea rules in Mesopotamia; c. 2060–1950, Third Dynasty of Ur comes to power in Sumeria, ushering in a period of great cultural development **2040–1674** Middle Kingdom in Egypt. After a period of chaos, Egyptian pharaohs strengthen the country, institute a centralized government, and conquer neighboring Nubia (present-day Ethiopia)	**c. 2000–750** Bronze Age in Europe **c. 1760–1600** Babylonian Empire, founded by Hammurabi, flourishes	**c. 1500–1145** New Kingdom in Egypt (dynasties 18–20) **1478–1458** Queen Hatshepsut rules Egypt **c. 1450** Mycenaean forces conquer the Minoan city of Knossos on Crete **c. 1350** Assyrian Empire founded in Mesopotamia by Ashuruballit I; empire endures until 612 **Pharaoh Akhenaten (r. 1348–1336/5)** attempts radical alteration of Egyptian society. Deposed by Tutankhamen (r. 1336/5–1327) **c. 1319–1145** Ramesside period in Egypt (Dynasty 19), epitomized by Pharaoh Ramesses II, whose frequent wars against invaders bring about great expansion of Egyptian territory and influence **c. 1250 (traditional)** Moses and Israelites flee to Palestine from Egypt to escape persecution **1184 (traditional)** Attack on Troy in Asia Minor by united Greek armies under Agamemnon
RELIGION			**c. 1345** Akhenaten institutes a new monotheistic religion in Egypt **c. 1000** Hebrews in Palestine accept monotheism
MUSIC, LITERATURE, AND PHILOSOPHY	**c. 2350** *The Pyramid Texts,* early religious writings found on walls of Egyptian tombs	**c. 1900** *The Story of Sinuhe,* a Middle Kingdom Egyptian tale **c. 1760** Code of Hammurabi, first known legal document, carved on a stone monolith for the Babylonian king	**c. 1500** The Book of the Dead, first manuscripts (on papyrus), encapsulating Egyptian religious thought
SCIENCE AND TECHNOLOGY		**c. 2000** Iron used for tools and weapons in Asia Minor **c. 1725** Hyksos tribes introduce horse-drawn vehicles into Egypt **c. 1700** Babylonian mathematics flourish under Hammurabi: use of whole numbers, fractions, and square roots	**c. 1500** Chinese develop silk production **c. 1400** First Greek writing, known as Linear B, in general use in the Aegean

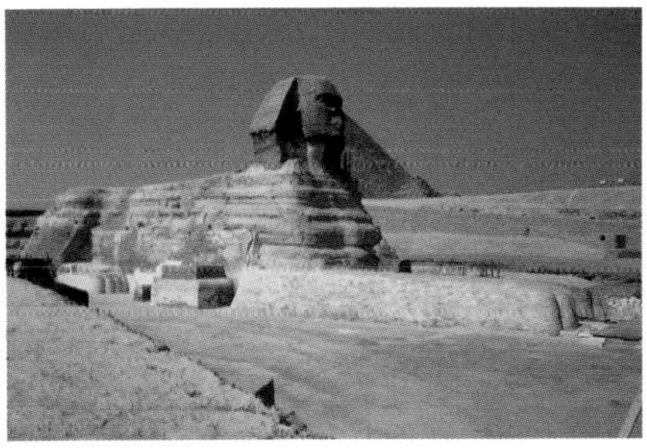

The Great Sphinx, Egypt, c. 2570–2544 B.C.

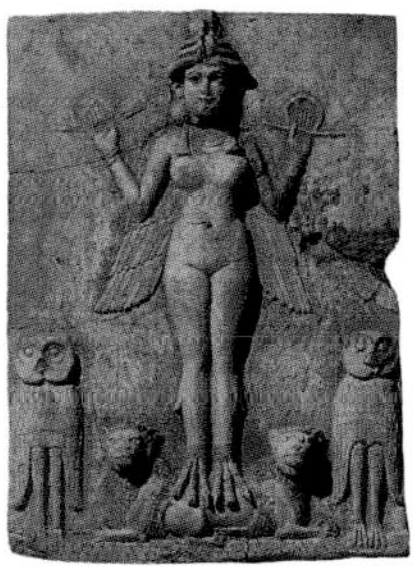

Inanna-Ishtar, Mesopotamia, c. 2025–1763 B.C.

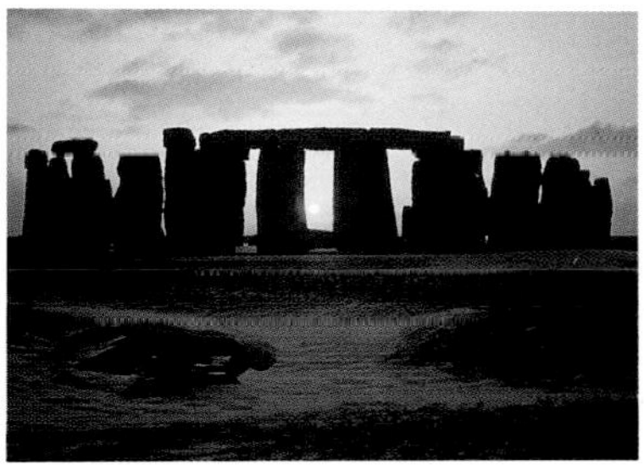

Stonehenge, England, c. 2000 B.C.

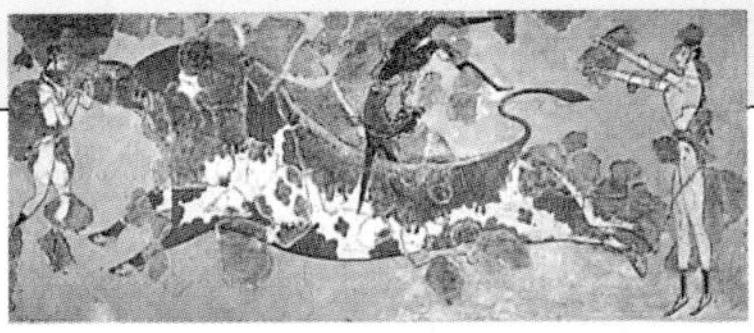

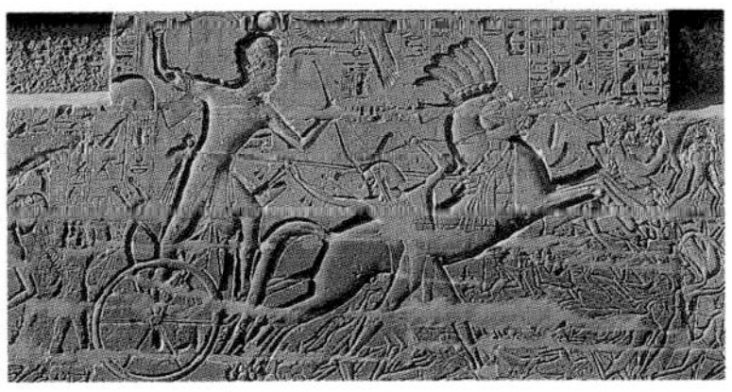

(TOP) *"The Toreador Fresco,"* Crete, c. 1500 B.C. (BOTTOM) *Sety I in a Chariot Charging the Libyans,* from the temple of Amun-Re at Karnak, Thebes, c. 1280 B.C.

Timeline One: Prehistory to 300 A.D.

	1000–600 B.C.	600–200 B.C.	200 B.C–1 A.D.
HISTORY AND POLITICS	**c. 1000–961** Israelite kingdom established by King David. Reign of his son, Solomon (961–922), is a time of legendary peace, justice, and stability **753 (traditional)** Founding of Rome by Romulus and Remus **By 700 (traditional)** Theseus unifies Athenian state **Nebuchadnezzar, Neo-Babylonian king (r. 605–562).** Under his rule the empire, based in Babylon, reaches its greatest extent, conquering Egypt (605) and Jerusalem (586)	**539** Persians conquer Babylonian Empire and Egypt (525). Expansion of Persian Empire **510** Roman Republic established **c. 510–508** Greece establishes the first government based on democratic principles **c. 499** Persians invade Greece; 490, defeated by Athenians at the Battle of Marathon **431–404** Peloponnesian War pits Greek city-states against one another; Athens is defeated by Sparta and its fleet destroyed at Syracuse **356–323** Alexander the Great leads Greek army in conquest of Egypt (323), Palestine, Phoenicia, and Persia (331) **264–201** Punic Wars waged between Rome and North Africa. Carthaginian general Hannibal marches from Spain and invades Italy (218), threatening Rome (211). He is defeated, and Roman expansion continues; Rome annexes Spain (201), by 147 dominates Asia Minor, Syria, Egypt, and Greece (146). Carthage destroyed (146)	**82–79** Sulla becomes first dictator of Roman state. Institutes substantial legal and legislative reforms **73–71** Slave rebellion led by the ex-gladiator Spartacus in Rome **51–30** Cleopatra, descendant of the Ptolemys, rules in Egypt **49–44** Julius Caesar (c. 101–44), Roman general, becomes dictator of Rome after a military career in the provinces. Assassinated by a group of senators who fear his usurpation of power **31** Sea battle of Actium, on the western coast of Greece, in which Julius Caesar's cousin Octavian defeats Marc Antony, a rival, and consolidates the Roman Empire under his control. Octavian takes the name Augustus Caesar and rules with Imperial powers, 27 B.C.–14 A.D. Golden Age of Rome, the *Pax Romana*. Henceforth Roman emperors are hereditary, although the senate retains some powers
RELIGION	**776** First Olympic Games, established as a religious festival in Olympia, Greece	**c. 563** Siddhartha (Gautama Buddha), founder of Buddhism, born in Nepal **c. 250** Mithraism, worship of an ancient Persian warrior hero, grows in Roman Empire	**4** Birth of Jesus Christ, crucified c. 30 A.D.
	Detail of *Ashurnasirpal II Killing Lions,* from the Palace of Ashurnasirpal II, Nimrud, Iraq, c. 850 B.C.	(LEFT) Marsyas Painter, red-figured pelike, Greece, c. 340 B.C. (RIGHT) *Nike of Samothrace,* c. 200–190 B.C.	*Imperial Procession,* from the Ara Pacis, Rome, c. 13–9 B.C.
MUSIC, LITERATURE, AND PHILOSOPHY	**c. 750–700 (traditional)** Homer composes the epics *Iliad* and *Odyssey*	**Confucius (551–c. 479),** Chinese philosopher **Pythagoras (c. 520),** Greek philosopher **c. 500–400** Greek drama: Aeschylus (523–456), Sophocles (496–406), Euripides (480–406), Aristophanes (c. 448–385) **c. 450–300** Classical Greek philosophy: Socrates (470–399), Plato (c. 427?–c. 347), Aristotle (384–322) **Demosthenes** (384–322), Greek philosopher and orator	**Cicero (106–43),** Roman statesman and orator **Vergil (70–19),** Roman author of *The Aeneid,* epic poem narrating the mythic origins of the Romans **Livy (59 B.C.–17 A.D.),** author of *From the Founding of the City,* a history of Rome **c. 50 Commentaries,** by Julius Caesar, details the progress of his wars in France **Ovid (43 B.C.–17 A.D.),** poet of *The Metamorphoses,* amorous and mythological tales
SCIENCE AND TECHNOLOGY	**c. 800** Adoption of the Phoenician alphabet, ancestor of modern European languages, by Greeks **c. 700–600** Phoenician sailors circumnavigate African continent; c. 700, horseshoes invented in Europe by Celtic tribes **c. 650** Coins for currency imported from Asia Minor to Greece	**c. 500** Greek advances in metalworking; invention of metal-casting and ore-smelting techniques **c. 300** Euclid, geometrician in Alexandria, writes *Elements,* fundamental text of mathematics and reasoning **Pytheas,** Greek explorer, travels the Atlantic coast of Europe, reaching points beyond Britain **Archimedes (287–212),** Greek mathematician	**c. 200** Standing army maintained by the Romans; development of the professional soldier; use of concrete as building material in the Roman Empire **c. 100** Earliest waterwheels **Vitruvius'** *On Architecture,* late-first-century B.C. manual of classical building methods and styles **46** Julius Caesar establishes the Julian calendar, in use until the 16th century A.D.

	1 A.D.–100 A.D.	100 A.D.–200 A.D.	200 A.D.–300 A.D.
HISTORY AND POLITICS	**Claudius (r. 41–54),** reluctant emperor of Rome, reconquers Britain **In the reign of the emperor Nero (r. 54–68),** a fire destroys most of Rome, which is soon rebuilt; first persecutions of Christians **79** Eruption of Mount Vesuvius in southern Italy; destruction of cities of Pompeii and Herculaneum by lava and ash **Emperor Trajan (r. 98–117)** brings the Roman Empire to its greatest expansion, venturing into Persian territory and northern Germany. The city of Rome has an estimated population of one million	**132–35** Jewish Diaspora begins; Jews expelled from Jerusalem **Marcus Aurelius, emperor of Rome (r. 161–80),** repulses the growing flood of Goth and Hun invaders from northern Europe	**285** Emperor Diocletian (r. 284–305) divides Roman Empire among four emperors in separate zones. Beginning of Roman decline, loss of territories, economic troubles, and political dissent

POMPEII The sudden destruction of Pompeii by lava from Mount Vesuvius in 79 B.C. preserved intact an entire city. Private houses, public buildings, shops, plumbing systems, and even bits of furniture were encased in lava and mud. Pompeii was a town of modest importance in first-century Rome; it thus affords a remarkable view of daily life—both high and low—in the Empire. Grooves in paved streets mark the passage of carts and chariots. On the walls of fine villas are brightly colored paintings; on those of cheaper lodgings are scrawled political slogans and graffiti. Among the finest wall paintings, otherwise rare, are those of the luxurious villas of wealthy Pompeiians decorated lavishly with complex architectural scenes, figures, and landscape vistas. With ornate mosaic floors and elegant architecture, the Pompeiian villas illustrate the refinement of aristocratic Roman life.

	1 A.D.–100 A.D.	100 A.D.–200 A.D.	200 A.D.–300 A.D.
RELIGION	**c. 45–50** St. Paul spreads Christianity in Asia Minor and Greece **St. Peter (died c. 64),** first bishop of Rome	**c. 130–68** Dead Sea Scrolls written; early manuscripts of Judaism and Christianity	**c. 250–302** Widespread persecution of Christians in Roman Empire
	Spoils from the Temple in Jerusalem, from the Arch of Titus, Rome, 81 A.D.	Pantheon, Rome, 118–125 A.D.	*Fayyum Portrait of a Boy,* Egypt, 2nd century A.D.
MUSIC, LITERATURE, AND PHILOSOPHY	**Seneca (4 B.C.–65 A.D.),** prominent Roman Stoic philosopher and adviser to Emperor Nero **Plutarch (c. 46–after 119),** Greek essayist, author of *Parallel Lives of Greeks and Romans* **c. 47–49** Epistles of St. Paul, written during his missionary work in Asia Minor **Tacitus (55–118),** Roman historian and political commentator		**Plotinus (205–70),** Neo-Platonic Greek philosopher and author of the *Enneads,* teaches in Rome
SCIENCE AND TECHNOLOGY	**c. 77** Pliny the Elder (23–79) writes his *Natural History,* an encyclopedic history, including a history of art **Ptolemy (85–160),** influential geographer and astronomer in Alexandria, popularizes the theory that the earth is at the center of the universe	**c. 100** Early glass-blowing techniques developed in Syria **Galen (c. 130–200),** Greek physician whose writings form the foundation of the study of human physiology	**By 200** More than 50,000 miles of paved roads built by Romans

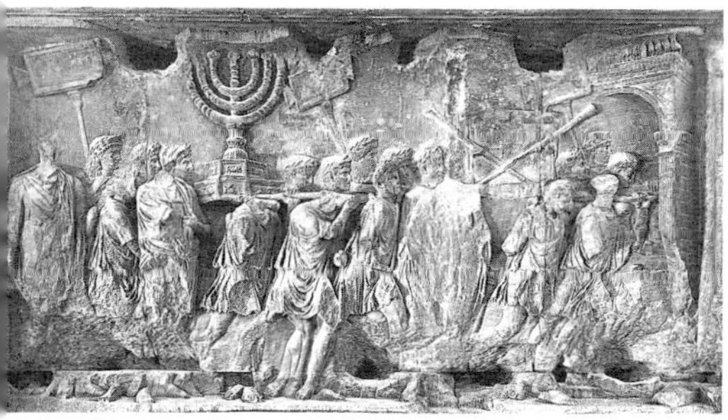

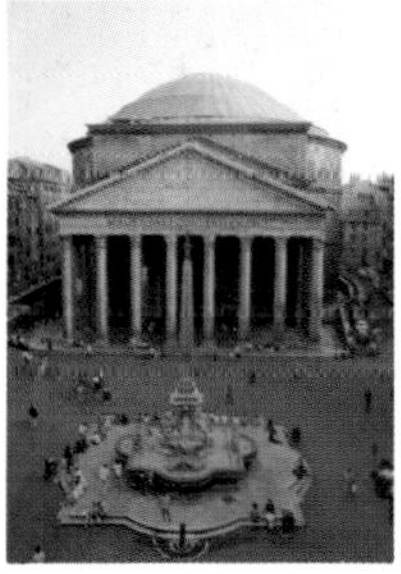

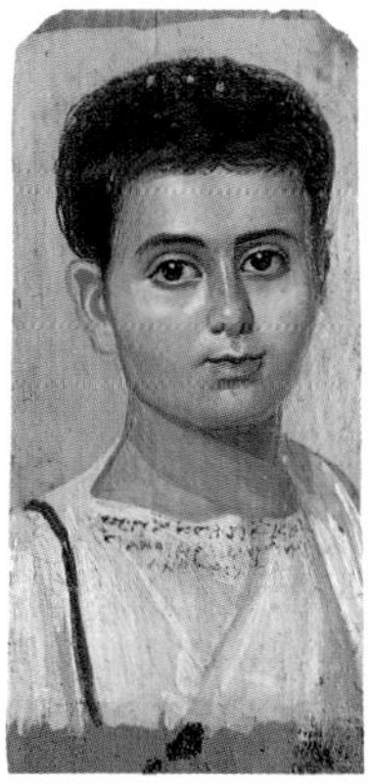

PART TWO

The Middle Ages

When we think of great Western civilizations of the past, we tend to do so in terms of the monuments that have come to symbolize them: the pyramids of Egypt, the ziggurats of Babylon, the Parthenon of Athens, the Colosseum of Rome. The Middle Ages would be represented by a Gothic cathedral—Notre-Dame in Paris, perhaps, or the cathedral of Chartres in France, or Salisbury Cathedral in England. We have many to choose from, but whichever one we pick, it will be well north of the Alps (although in an area that was once part of the Roman Empire). And if we were to spill a bucket of water in front of the cathedral of our choice, this water would eventually make its way to the English Channel rather than to the Mediterranean Sea. Here, then, we have perhaps the most important single fact about the Middle Ages—the center of gravity of European civilization has shifted to what had been the northern boundaries of the Roman world. The Mediterranean, which for so many centuries bound together all the lands along its shores, has become a border zone.

How did this dramatic shift come about? In 323 A.D. Constantine the Great made a fateful decision, the consequences of which are still felt today. He resolved to move the capital of the Roman Empire to the Greek town of Byzantium, which came to be known as Constantinople and today as Istanbul. Six years later, after a major building campaign, the transfer was officially completed. In taking this step, the emperor acknowledged the growing strategic and economic importance of the eastern provinces. The new capital also symbolized the new Christian basis of the Roman state, since it was in the heart of the most fully Christianized part of the Empire.

Constantine could hardly have foreseen that moving the seat of Imperial power would split the Empire. Less than 75 years later, in 395, the division of the realm into the Eastern and Western Empires was complete. Eventually that separation led to a religious split as well.

By the end of the fifth century, the bishop of Rome, who derived his authority from St. Peter, regained independence from the emperor. He then reasserted his claim as the pope, the head of the Christian Church. This claim to preeminence, however, was soon disputed by his Eastern counterpart, the patriarch of Constantinople. Differences in doctrine began to emerge and eventually the division of Christendom into a Western, or Catholic, and an Eastern, or Orthodox, Church became all but final. The differences between them went very deep. Roman Catholicism maintained its independence from state authority and became an international institution, reflecting its character as the Universal Church. The Orthodox Church, on the other hand, was based on the union of spiritual and secular authority in the person of the emperor, who appointed the patriarch. It thus remained dependent on the power of the State, requiring a double allegiance from the faithful. This tradition did not die even with the fall of Constantinople to the Ottoman Turks in 1453. The czars of Russia claimed the mantle of the Byzantine emperors, Moscow became "the third Rome," and the Russian Orthodox Church was as closely tied to the State as the Byzantine church had been.

Under Justinian (r. 527–65), the Eastern (or Byzantine) Empire reached new power and stability after riots in 532 nearly deposed him. In contrast, the Latin West soon fell prey to invading Germanic peoples: Visigoths, Vandals, Franks, Ostrogoths, and Lombards. By the end of the sixth century, the last vestige of centralized authority had disappeared even though the emperors at Constantinople did not give up their claim to the western provinces. Yet these invaders, once they had settled in their new lands, accepted the framework of late Roman, Christian civilization, however imperfectly. The local kingdoms they founded—the Vandals in North Africa, the Visigoths in Spain, the Franks in Gaul, the Ostrogoths and Lombards in Italy—were all Mediterranean-oriented, provincial states on the edges of the Byzantine Empire. They were subject to the pull of the Empire's military, commercial, and cultural power. As late as 630, after the Byzantine armies had recovered Syria, Palestine, and Egypt from the Sassanid Persians, the reconquest of the western provinces remained a serious possibility as well. Ten years later, the chance had ceased to exist, for an unforeseen new force—Islam—had made itself felt in the East.

Under the banner of Islam, the Arabs overran the African and Near Eastern parts of the Empire. By 732, a century after Mohammed's death, they had absorbed Spain and threatened to conquer southwestern France as well. In the eleventh century, the Turks occupied much of Asia Minor. Meanwhile the last Byzantine lands in the West (in southern Italy) fell to the Normans, from northwestern France. The Eastern Empire, with its domain reduced to the Balkan peninsula, including Greece, held on until 1453, when the Turks conquered Constantinople.

In the East, Islam created a new civilization stretching to the Indus Valley (now Pakistan). That civilization reached its highest point far more rapidly than did that of the medieval West. Baghdad, on the Tigris, was the most important city of Islam in the eighth century. Its splendor rivaled that of Byzantium. Islamic art, learning, and crafts were to have great influence on the European Middle Ages, from arabesque ornament, the manufacture of paper, and Arabic numerals to the transmission of Greek philosophy and science through the writings of Arab scholars. (The English language records this debt in words such as *algebra*.)

It would be difficult to exaggerate the impact of the rapid advance of Islam. The Byzantine Empire, deprived of its western Mediterranean bases, focused on keeping Islam at bay in the East. In the West, it retained only a precarious foothold on Italian soil. The European shore of the western Mediterranean, from the Pyrenees to Naples, was exposed to Arabic raiders from North Africa and Spain. Western Europe was thus forced to develop its own resources—political, economic, and spiritual.

The process was slow and difficult, however. The early medieval world was in a state of constant turmoil and therefore presents a constantly shifting picture. Not even the Frankish kingdom, which was ruled by the Merovingian dynasty from about 500 to 751 (when it was overthrown by the Carolingian king Pepin III), was able to impose lasting order. As the only international organization of any sort, Christianity was to play a critical role in promoting a measure of stability. Yet it, too, was divided between the papacy, whose influence was limited, and the monastic orders that spread quickly throughout Europe but remained largely independent of the Church in Rome.

This rapid spread of Christianity, like that of Islam, cannot be explained simply in institutional terms, for the Church did not perfectly embody Christian ideals. Moreover, its success was hardly guaranteed. In fact, its position was often precarious under Constantine's Latin successors. Instead, Christianity must have been extremely persuasive, in spiritual as well as moral terms, to the masses of people who heard its message. There is no other way to explain the rapid conversion of northern Europe. Heathen gods were as terrifying as those of the ancient Near East, reflecting the violent life of a warrior society.

Church and State gradually discovered that they could not live without each other. What was needed, however, was an alliance between a strong secular power and a united church. This link was forged when the Catholic Church, which had now gained the allegiance of the religious orders, broke its last ties with the East and turned for support to the Germanic north. There the leadership of Pepin III's son, Charlemagne, and his descendants—the Carolingian dynasty—made the Frankish kingdom into the leading power during the second half of the eighth century. Charlemagne usurped the territory of his brother, Carloman, from his heirs. He then conquered most of Europe from Spain to the North Sea to as far south as Lombardy. When Pope Leo III appealed to him for help in 799, Charlemagne went to Rome, where on Christmas Day, 800, the pope gave him the title of emperor—something that Charlemagne neither sought nor wanted.

In placing himself and all of Western Christianity under the protection of the king of the Franks and Lombards, Leo did not merely solemnize the new order of things. He also tried to assert his authority over the newly created Catholic emperor. He claimed that the emperor's legitimacy depended on the pope, based on the forged Donation of Constantine. (Before then it had been the other way around: the emperor in Constantinople had ratified the newly elected pope.) Although Charlemagne did not subordinate himself to the pope, this interdependence of spiritual and political authority, of Church and State, was to distinguish the West from both the Orthodox East and the Islamic South. Its outward symbol was the fact that though the emperor was crowned in Rome, he did not live there. Charlemagne built his capital at the center of his power, in Aachen, located in what is now Germany and close to France, Belgium, and the Netherlands.

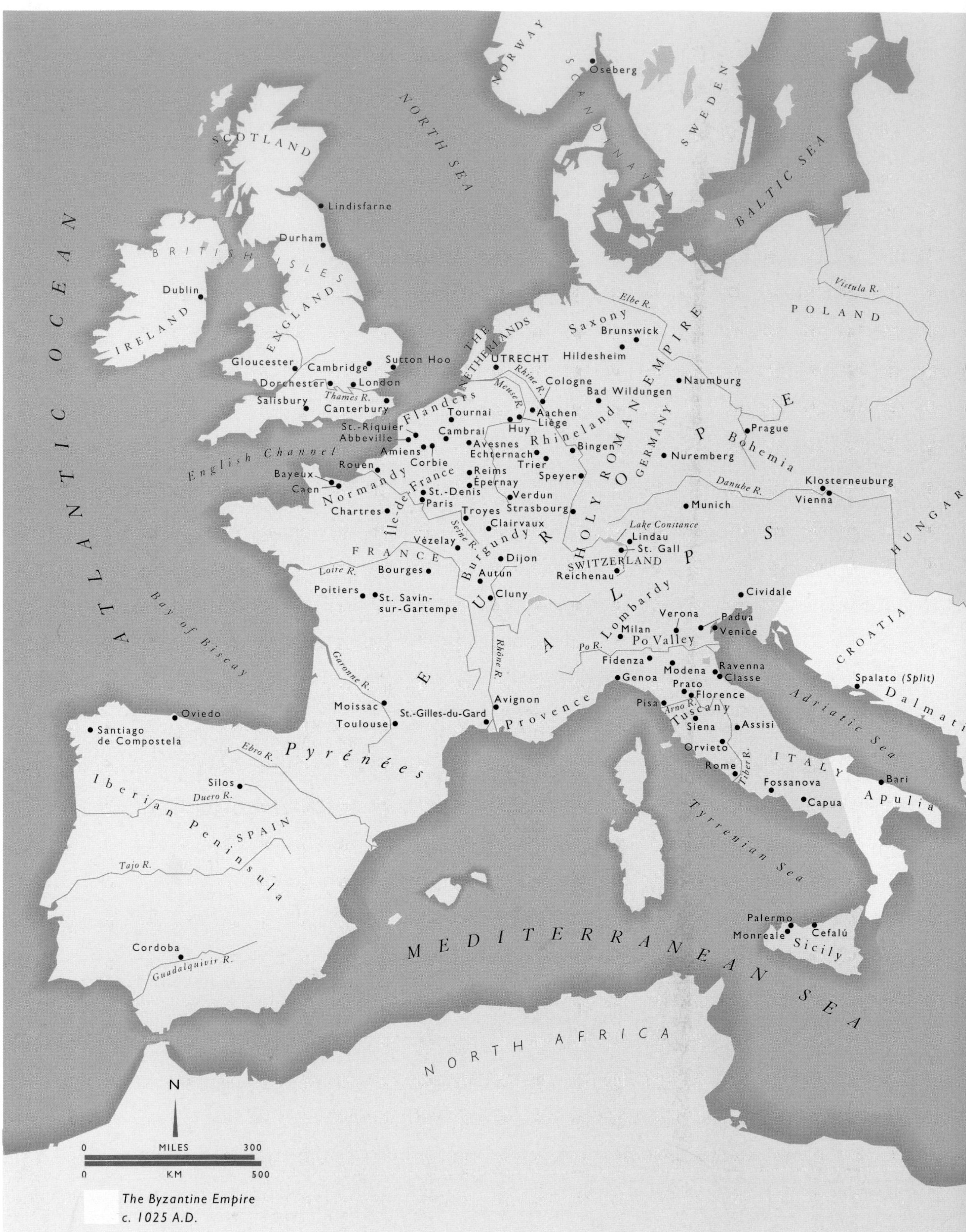
NORTH SEA
NORWAY
SCANDINAVIA
SWEDEN
BALTIC SEA
Oseberg
SCOTLAND
Lindisfarne
Durham
BRITISH ISLES
ATLANTIC OCEAN
Dublin
IRELAND
ENGLAND
Gloucester
Cambridge
Sutton Hoo
Dorchester
London
Thames R.
Salisbury
Canterbury
English Channel
THE NETHERLANDS
UTRECHT
Rhine R.
Meuse R.
Flanders
Tournai
St.-Riquier
Abbeville
Cambrai
Amiens
Corbie
Avesnes
Echternach
Rouen
Bayeux
Caen
Normandy
Île-de-France
Reims
Épernay
St.-Denis
Paris
Verdun
Chartres
Troyes
Strasbourg
Clairvaux
Seine R.
Vézelay
FRANCE
Loire R.
Bourges
Burgundy
Dijon
Autun
Cluny
Poitiers
St. Savin-sur-Gartempe
Bay of Biscay
Garonne R.
Rhône R.
Moissac
Toulouse
St.-Gilles-du-Gard
Avignon
Provence
Pyrénées
Ebro R.
Oviedo
Santiago de Compostela
Silos
Duero R.
Iberian Peninsula
SPAIN
Tajo R.
Cordoba
Guadalquivir R.
Elbe R.
Saxony
Brunswick
Hildesheim
Cologne
Bad Wildungen
Naumburg
Aachen
Liège
Huy
Rhineland
Bingen
Trier
Speyer
HOLY ROMAN EMPIRE
GERMANY
Nuremberg
Prague
Bohemia
Munich
Danube R.
Klosterneuburg
Vienna
HUNGARY
Vistula R.
POLAND
Lake Constance
Lindau
St. Gall
SWITZERLAND
Reichenau
ALPS
Lombardy
Cividale
Verona
Padua
Venice
Milan
Po Valley
Po R.
Fidenza
Modena
Ravenna
Classe
Genoa
Prato
Florence
Pisa
Arno R.
Tuscany
Siena
Assisi
Orvieto
Tiber R.
Rome
ITALY
Fossanova
Capua
Bari
Apulia
CROATIA
Spalato (Split)
Dalmatia
Adriatic Sea
Tyrrenian Sea
Palermo
Monreale
Cefalù
Sicily
MEDITERRANEAN SEA
NORTH AFRICA
N
0 MILES 300
0 KM 500
The Byzantine Empire c. 1025 A.D.

THE MIDDLE AGES

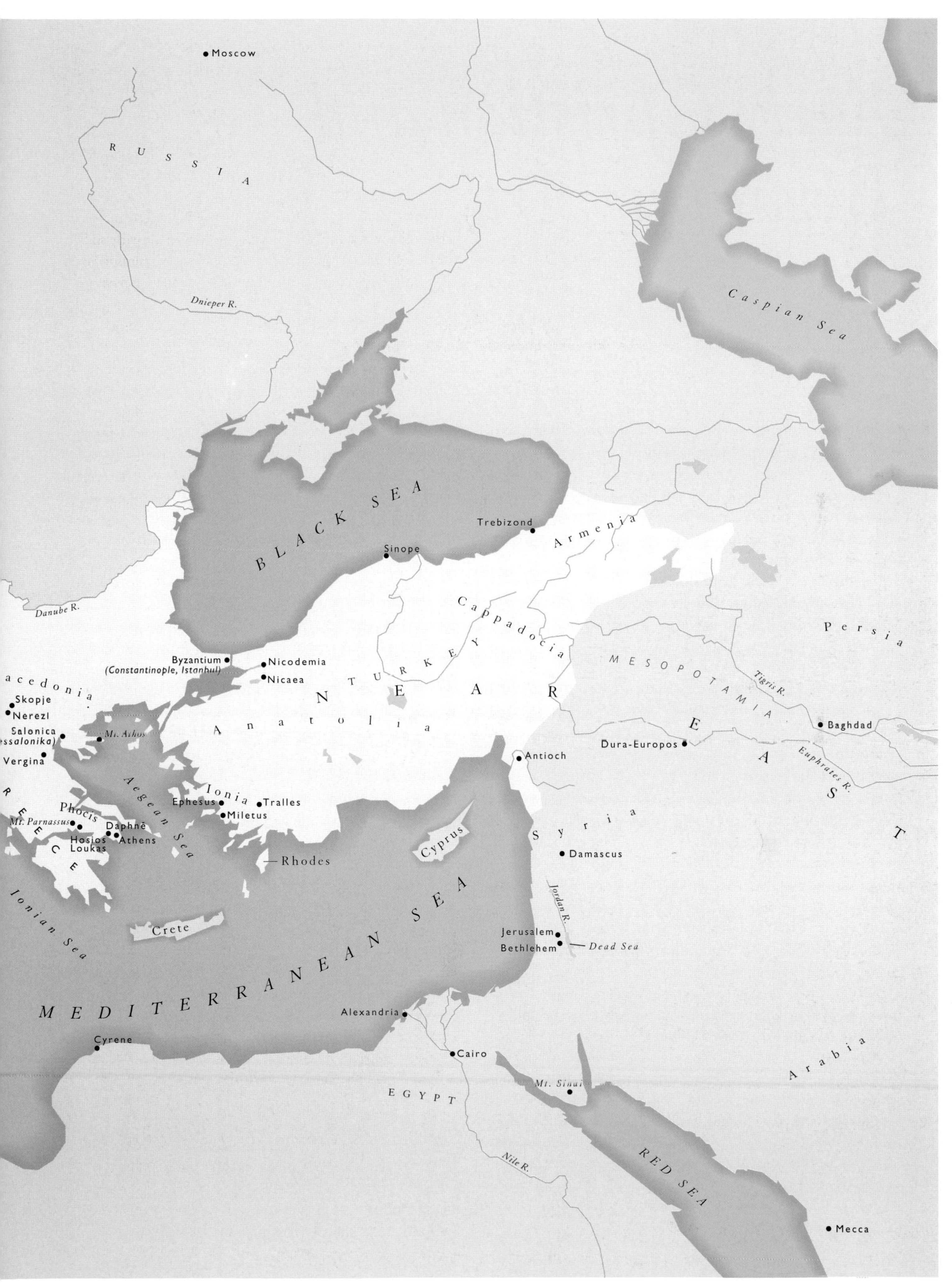
Moscow
RUSSIA
Dnieper R.
Caspian Sea
BLACK SEA
Trebizond
Armenia
Sinope
Danube R.
Cappadocia
Persia
Byzantium
(Constantinople, Istanbul)
Nicodemia
Nicaea
TURKEY
MESOPOTAMIA
Tigris R.
acedonia
Skopje
Nerezi
Salonica
ssalonika)
Vergina
Mt. Athos
NEAR EAST
Anatolia
Baghdad
Dura-Europos
Antioch
Euphrates R.
Aegean Sea
Ionia
Ephesus
Tralles
Miletus
Phocis
Mt. Parnassus
Daphnē
Hosios Loukas
Athens
Syria
Cyprus
Damascus
Rhodes
REECE
Ionian Sea
Jordan R.
Crete
Jerusalem
Bethlehem
Dead Sea
MEDITERRANEAN SEA
Alexandria
Cyrene
Cairo
Arabia
Mt. Sinai
EGYPT
Nile R.
RED SEA
Mecca

CHAPTER EIGHT

Early Christian and Byzantine Art

In the third century A.D. the Roman world was gripped by a spiritual crisis that reflected broad social turmoil as the empire fell apart. One result was the spread of Oriental mystery religions of various origins—Egyptian, Persian, Semitic. Their early development naturally centered in their home territory, the southeastern provinces and border regions of the empire. Although they were based on traditions that had existed long before Alexander conquered these ancient lands, the cults had been influenced by Greek ideas during the Hellenistic period. In fact, they owed their appeal to a blend of Oriental and Greek elements. At that time, the Near East was a vast melting pot where the competing faiths (including Judaism, Christianity, Mithraism, Manichaeism, Gnosticism, and many more) tended to influence each other.

As a result, all of these religions had a number of things in common. Among these were a claim to both exclusivity and universality, an emphasis on revealed truth, the hope of salvation, a chief prophet or messiah, a belief in a cosmic struggle of good against evil, a ritual of purification or initiation (such as baptism), and the duty to seek converts among unbelievers. The last faith of this type to develop was Islam, which was founded in the sixth century, and continues to dominate the Near East to this day.

It is difficult to trace the growth of the Graeco-Oriental religions under Roman rule. Many of them were underground movements that have left few tangible remains or texts. This is true of early Christianity as well. The Gospels of Mark, Matthew, Luke, and John (their likely chronological order) were probably written in the later first century and present somewhat varying pictures of Jesus and his teachings. In part, these reflect differences in doctrine between St. Peter, the first bishop of Rome, and St. Paul, the most important of the early converts and a tireless proselytizer. For the first three centuries after Christ, Christian congregations were reluctant to worship in public. Instead, their simple services took place in the houses of the wealthier members. At best, they made use of portable altars; there were few implements or vestments (special clothing worn by those conducting services). The new faith spread first to the Greek-speaking communities, notably Alexandria, then reached the Latin world by the end of the second century.

Even before it was declared a lawful religion in 261 by the emperor Gallienus, Christianity was rarely persecuted. It suffered chiefly under the tyrants Nero and Diocletian. In 309 Galerius, who succeeded Diocletian, issued an edict of toleration. Still, the new faith had little standing until the conversion of Constantine the Great in 312, despite the fact that by then nearly one-third of Rome was Christian.

According to Bishop Eusebius of Caesarea, based on the emperor's own account late in life, on the eve of the battle against Constantine's rival Maxentius at the Milvian Bridge over the Tiber River in Rome there appeared in the sky the sign of the cross with the inscription, "In this sign, conquer." The next night, Christ came to Constantine in a dream with the sign (which must have been the Chi Rho monogram, the *labarum*) and commanded him to copy it. He had the insignia inscribed on his helmet and on the military standards of his soldiers. After his victory, Constantine accepted the faith, if he had not done so already, although he was baptized only on his deathbed. The next year, 313, he and his fellow emperor, Licinius, issued the Edict of Milan, which proclaimed freedom of religion throughout the Empire.

Constantine never made Christianity the official state religion. Still, it had a special status under his rule. The emperor promoted it and helped shape its theology, partly in an effort to settle doctrinal disputes. Unlike the pagan emperors, Constantine could not be deified, but he did claim that his authority was granted by God. Thus he placed himself at the head of the Church as well as of the State. In doing so he adapted an ancient tradition: the divine kingship of Egypt and the Near East. Although there is no doubt that Constantine's faith was sincere, he set a pattern for future Christian rulers in using religion for personal and Imperial ends; for example by continuing to promote the cult of the emperor.

Eastern Religions

The area where the development of the Graeco-Oriental religions took place has seen so much war and destruction that major finds, such as the discovery of the Dead Sea Scrolls in 1947, are very rare. There is enough evidence, however, to indicate that the new faiths also gave birth to a new style in art, and that this style, too, blended Graeco-Roman and Oriental elements.

MITHRAS. *Mithras Slaying the Sacred Bull* (fig. 8-1) shows an early stage in this process. It depicts the central myth of the cult: the god Mithras captures and sacrifices the bull, which was associated with spring. He thus releases its vital life-giving forces to the snake, symbol of earth; the scorpion, the astrological sign of autumn, is shown sapping the bull's strength. Originally a minor figure in the pantheon of the Persian prophet Zoroaster (Zarathustra; c. 628–c. 551 B.C.), Mithras emerged as the chief deity of Persia. Mithraism spread from there and became the leading mystical sect of the Roman Empire during the second century, when our relief was carved. The image contains the main features of the religion: the struggle of good against evil and the triumph of life over death. These dualistic forces were represented by light and darkness, portrayed by the Roman sun-god Helios to the left and the moon goddess Luna (now missing) at the right.

The composition is indebted to Late Classical reliefs (compare fig. 5-64), in which similar Persian figures appear in hunting scenes and battles against the Greeks. Indeed, Helios is surprisingly like the head of the *Apollo Belvedere* (see fig. 5-69). Yet the relief has an exotic character that is unmistakably Oriental. This is evident not only in the subject and costume but also in the composition itself. The juxtaposition of hero and beast has an ancient history in the Near East. The clear layout, with its symbolic intent, also has roots in the same region (compare figs. 3-9 and 3-15). So, too, does the sympathetic portrayal of the splendid bull in its death throes, which is echoed in the struggling cows on the *Vaphio Cups* (see figs. 4-17 and 4-18).

The refined technique and Classical style indicate that the Mithraic relief was carved in Rome itself, where it was found. These features are nevertheless unusual. For the most part, the artists who wrestled with the task of coining images to express the contents of these faiths were not among the most gifted of their time. They were provincial craftsmen of modest ambition who drew upon whatever visual sources were available, adapting and combining them as best they could. Their efforts are often clumsy, yet it is here that we find the beginnings of a tradition that was to become basic to the development of medieval art.

DURA-EUROPOS. The most telling examples of this new compound style have been found in the Mesopotamian town of Dura-Europos on the upper Euphrates. This Roman frontier station was captured by the Persians under Shapur I about 256 A.D. (see page 79) and abandoned soon afterward. Its ruins have yielded the remains of sanctuaries of several religions, including Mithraism and Christianity. They are decorated with murals, all

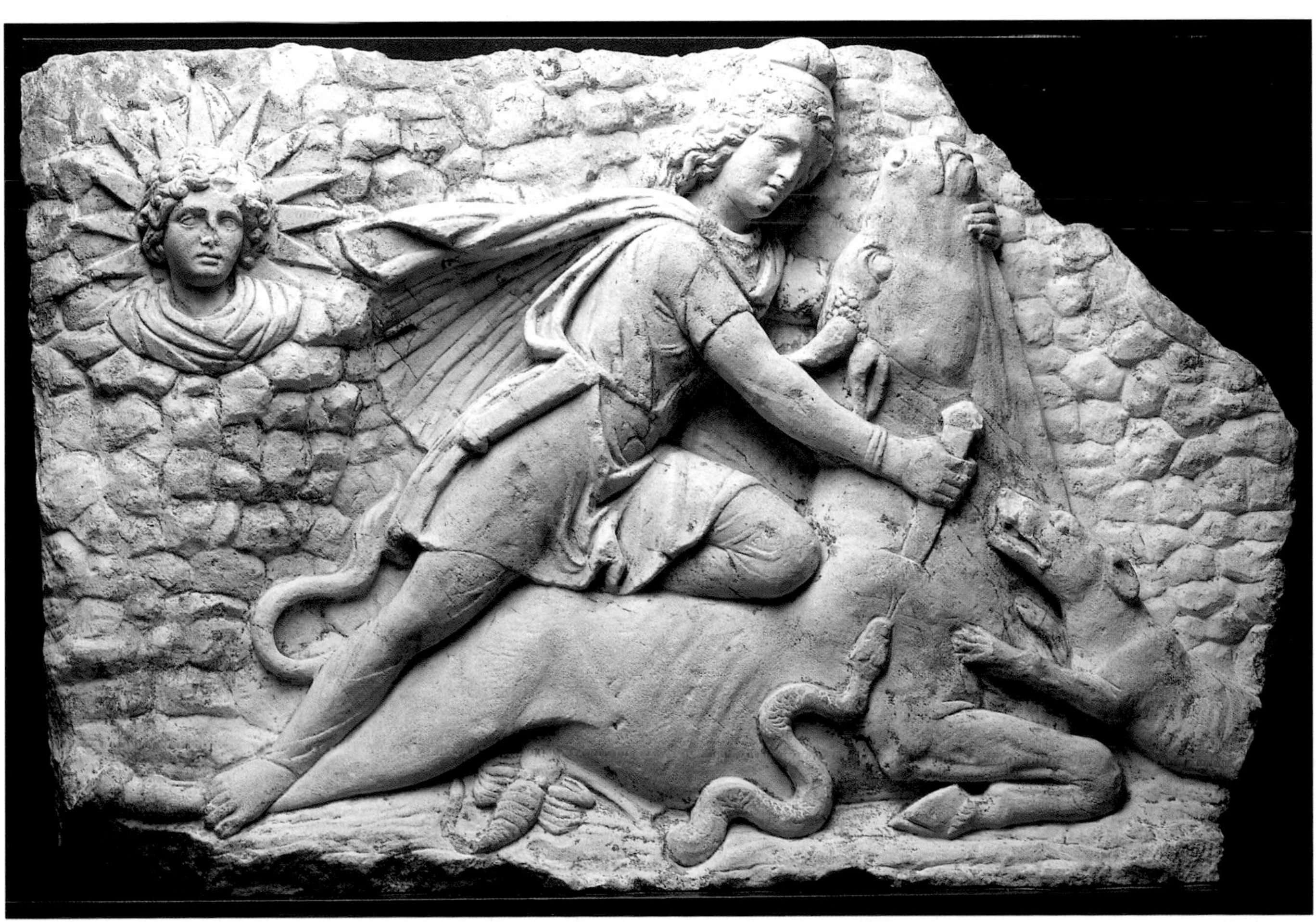

8-1. *Mithras Slaying the Sacred Bull.* c. 150–200 A.D. Limestone, 24 5/8 x 37 1/2" (62.5 x 95.2 cm). Cincinnati Art Museum

GIFT OF MR. AND MRS. FLETCHER E. NYCE

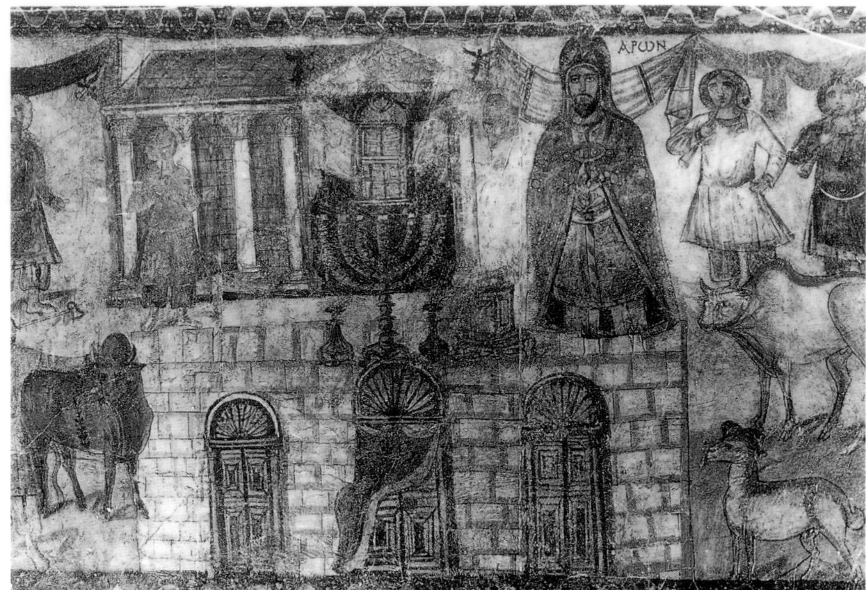

8-2. *The Consecration of the Tabernacle and Its Priests,* from the Assembly Hall of the Synagogue at Dura-Europos. 245–56 A.D. Mural, 4'8¼" x 7'8¼" (1.4 x 2.3 m). National Museum, Damascus, Syria

of which show essentially the same Graeco-Oriental character. The finest and best preserved are those from the assembly hall of a synagogue painted about 250 A.D. They have numerous compartments; the one shown here (fig. 8-2) depicts the consecration of the tabernacle.

It is characteristic of the melting-pot conditions described above that even Judaism was affected by them. The age-old injunction against images was relaxed so that the walls of the assembly hall could be covered with a detailed visual account of the history of the Chosen People and their Covenant with the Lord. The new attitude seems to have been linked with a tendency to change Judaism from a national to a universal faith by missionary activity among the non-Jewish population. (Interestingly, some of the inscriptions on the murals, such as the name Aaron in figure 8-2, are in Greek.) In any event, we may be sure that the artists who designed these pictures faced an unfamiliar task, just as did the painters who worked for the earliest Christian communities. They had to cast into visible form what had before been expressed only in words. How did they go about it?

Let us take a closer look at our illustration. We can read the details—animals, human beings, buildings, cult objects—without trouble, but their relationship is not clear. There is no action, no story, only an assembly of forms and figures that we are expected to be able to link together. The frieze in the Villa of the Mysteries (see fig. 7-51) presents a similar problem. There, too, the viewer is supposed to know what is represented. Yet it is much less puzzling, for the eloquent gestures and expressions make the figures meaningful even though we may not understand the context of the scenes.

If the synagogue painter is less persuasive, is it because of a lack of competence, or are there other reasons as well? The question is rather like the one we faced when discussing the Constantinian relief in figure 7-47, which resembles the synagogue mural in a number of ways. The synagogue painting shows the same sense of self-sufficiency by condensing the design for the sake of completeness, but the subject is far more demanding. The mural had to depict a historical event of great religious importance: the consecration of the tabernacle and its priests, which began the reconciliation of humanity and God, as described in the Holy Scriptures. And it had to do so in such a way as to suggest that this was a timeless, recurrent ritual. Thus the picture carries a wealth of significance that is far greater and more rigidly defined than that of the Dionysiac frieze or the Constantinian relief. Nor was there a tradition of Jewish religious painting that could help the artist visualize the scene.

No wonder our painter has made use of a sort of symbolic shorthand composed of images borrowed from older traditions. The tabernacle itself, for instance, is shown as a Classical temple simply because our artist could not imagine it as a tentlike structure of poles and goat's-hair curtains. The attendant and the red heifer in the lower left-hand corner are derived from Roman scenes of animal sacrifice; hence they show remnants of foreshortening that are not found among the other figures. Other echoes of Roman painting appear in the perspective view of the altar table next to the figure of Aaron. They can also be seen in the sometimes indifferent modeling and in the shadows attached to some of the figures. Did the painter still understand the purpose of these shadows? They seem to be empty gestures, since the rest of the picture reveals no awareness of either light or space in the Roman sense. Even the overlapping of some of the forms appears to be largely accidental.

The sequence of things in space is conveyed by other means. The seven-branched candlestick, or menorah, the two incense burners, the altar, and Aaron are to be seen as behind, rather than on top of, the wall. Their size, however, is based on their importance, not on their position in space. Aaron, as the main figure, is not only larger than the attendants but also more abstract. Because of its ritual meaning, his costume is shown in detail, at the cost of the body underneath. The attendants, on the other hand, still show some mobility and three-dimensional form. Their garments, surprisingly enough, are Persian, a sign not only of the odd mixture of civilizations in this border area but of possible artistic influences from Persia.

Our synagogue mural, then, combines—not very skillfully—a variety of elements that have in common only the religious message of the whole. In the hands of a great artist, this message might have been a stronger unifying force. Even then, however, the shapes and colors would have been an imperfect embodiment of the spiritual truth they were meant to serve. That, surely, was the outlook of the authorities who controlled the program and execution of the mural cycle. These pictures can no longer be understood in the framework of ancient art. They express an attitude that seems far closer to the Middle Ages. To sum up their purpose, we may quote a famous dictum justifying the pictorial representation of Christian themes: *Quod legentibus scriptura, hoc idiotis . . . pictura.* Translated freely it means: painting conveys the Word of God to the unlettered. [See Primary Sources, no. 14, page 364.]

EARLY CHRISTIAN ART

We do not know when and where the first Christian works of art were produced. None of the surviving examples can be dated earlier than about 200 A.D. In fact, we know little about Christian art before the reign of Constantine the Great, because little remains from the third century. The only Christian house found at Dura-Europos has murals that are far less extensive or developed than the synagogue frescoes. The painted decorations of the Roman catacombs, the underground burial places of the Christians, are the only sizable body of material, but these are only one of several kinds of Christian art that may have existed.

The Catacombs

The catacomb paintings tell us a good deal about the spirit of the communities that sponsored them, even though the lack of material from the eastern provinces of the Empire makes it difficult to judge their role in the development of Christian art. The burial rite and the safeguarding of the tomb were of vital concern to the early Christians, whose faith rested on the hope of eternal life in heaven. In the painted ceiling in figure 8-3, the imagery clearly expresses this otherworldly outlook, although the forms are still those of pre-Christian murals. The division of the ceiling into compartments is a highly simplified echo of the architectural schemes in Pompeian painting. The modeling of the figures, as well as the landscape settings, are also descended from Roman designs, though they have become debased by endless repetition. But the catacomb painter has little interest in the original meaning of the forms, which he has used to convey a new, symbolic content. Even the geometric framework shares in this task, for the great circle suggests the Dome of Heaven, inscribed with the Cross, the basic symbol of the faith. In the central medallion we see a youthful shepherd, with a sheep on his shoulders, in a pose that can be traced back as far as Greek Archaic art (compare fig. 5-12). He stands for Christ the Savior, the Good Shepherd who gives his life for his flock.

The semicircular compartments tell the story of Jonah. On the

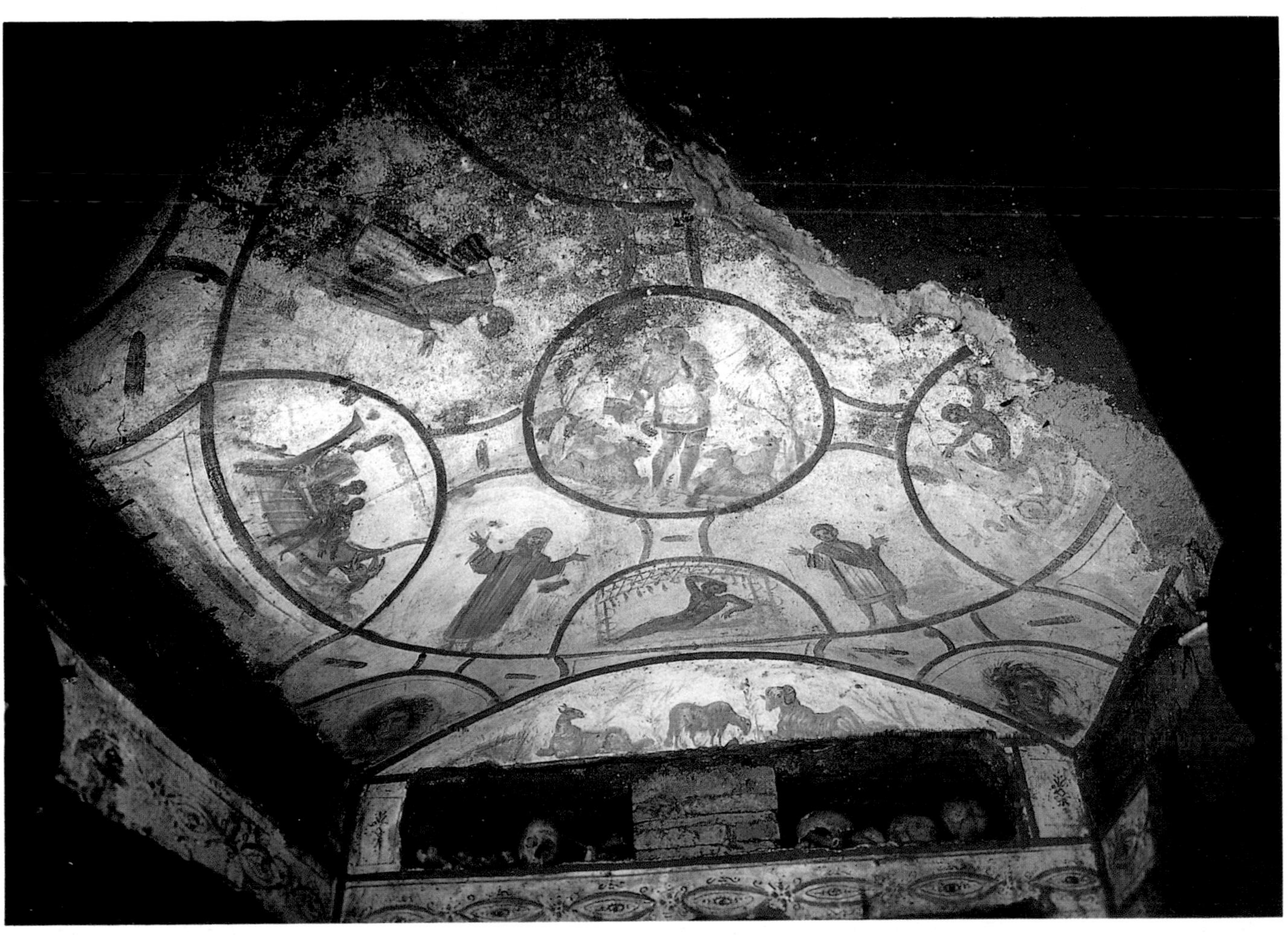

8-3. Painted ceiling. 4th century A.D. Catacomb of SS. Pietro e Marcellino, Rome

left he is cast from the ship, and on the right he emerges from the whale. At the bottom he is safe again on dry land, meditating upon the mercy of the Lord. This Old Testament miracle, often juxtaposed with New Testament miracles, enjoyed great favor in Early Christian art as proof of the Lord's power to rescue the faithful from the jaws of death. The standing figures with their hands raised in prayer (known as *orants*) may represent members of the Church. The entire scheme, though small in scale and unimpressive in execution, has a consistency and clarity that set it apart from its Graeco-Roman ancestors, as well as from the synagogue murals of Dura-Europos (see fig. 8-2). Here we have at least the promise of a monumental new form (compare fig. 8-49).

Architecture

Constantine's decision to make Christianity a legal religion of the Roman Empire had a profound impact on Christian art. Before then, the Church (*ecclesia*) was simply the congregation. (We will recall that the Greek word "ecclesia" originally meant the assembly of citizens; see page 122.) Now, almost overnight, an impressive setting had to be created for the faith, so that the Church might be visible to all. To do so, however, involved rethinking the meaning of the Church itself. It now became identified with its expression in architecture, something which we take for granted but for which there had been no need before. To meet the challenge, church leaders adapted existing types to new ends. Constantine devoted the full resources of his office to this task, and within a few years an astonishing number of large, imperially sponsored churches were built, not only in Rome but also in Constantinople, the Holy Land, and other important centers.

THE CHRISTIAN BASILICA. These structures were of a new type, now called the Early Christian basilica, that provided the basic model for the development of church architecture in western Europe. Although it has features of an assembly hall, temple, and private house, it cannot be wholly explained in terms of its sources. The Early Christian basilica as we know it owes its essential features—the long nave flanked by aisles and lit by clerestory windows, the apse, and the wooden roof— to the Imperial basilicas built during the previous hundred years, such as that at Leptis Magna (see figs. 7-19 and 7-20). The Roman basilica was not unique to Christianity, however. It had already been used by pagan cults and Judaism. Even so, it was a suitable model for Constantinian churches, since it combined the spacious interior needed to accommodate a large congregation with Imperial associations that proclaimed the privileged status of Christianity. But a church had to be more than an assembly hall. In addition to serving as a meeting place for the faithful, it was the sacred House of God, literally the Heavenly Jerusalem. As such, it was the Christian successor to the temples of old. In order to express this function, the basilica had to be redesigned. The plan of the Early Christian basilica was given a new focus, the altar, which was placed in front of the apse at the eastern end of the nave. The entrances, which in earlier basilicas had usually been on the flanks, were shifted to the western end. The Early Christian basilica was thus arranged along a single, longitudinal axis that is indebted to the layout of Greek temples, except that the latter faced eastward to greet the rising sun (compare fig. 5-32).

Unfortunately, none of the early Christian basilicas has survived in its original form. However, the plan of the greatest Constantinian church, Old St. Peter's in Rome, is known with a good deal of accuracy (fig. 8-4). Moreover, its appearance is preserved in an album from 1619 of detailed drawings with annotations by Jacopo Grimaldi that copy earlier ones, some of which also survive (figs. 8-5, 8-6). The church, begun as early as 319 and finished by 329, was built on the Vatican hill next to a pagan burial ground. It lies directly over the grave of St. Peter, which was marked by a shrine covered with a baldacchino that was placed on a platform and attached to the apse itself. [See Primary Sources, no. 15, page 364.] As such, St. Peter's served mainly as a martyrium of the apostle. ("Martyr" originally meant "witness" in Greek and only later came to denote someone willing to die for faith.) It was also a cemetery for the faithful who were buried along the nave. Funeral banquets, a custom which the Romans had inherited from the

THE LITURGY OF MASS

The central rite of many Christian churches is the Eucharist or communion service, a ritual meal that reenacts Jesus' Last Supper. In the Catholic Church and in a few Protestant churches, this service is known as the Mass (from the Latin words *Ite, missa est,* "Go, [the congregation] is dismissed" at the end of the Latin service). The Mass was first codified by Pope Gregory the Great about 600. Each Mass consists of the "ordinary"—those prayers and hymns that are the same in all Masses—and the "proper," the parts that vary, depending on the occasion. In addition to a number of specific prayers, the "ordinary" consists of five hymns: the *Kyrie Eleison* (Greek for "Lord have mercy on us"); the *Gloria in Excelsis* (Latin for "Glory in the highest"); *Credo* (Latin for "I believe," a statement of faith also called the Creed); *Sanctus* (Latin for "Holy"); and *Agnus Dei* (Latin for "Lamb of God"). The "proper" of the Mass consists of prayers, two readings from the New Testament (one from the Epistles and one from the Gospels); a homily, or sermon, on these texts; and hymns, all chosen specifically for the day.

Musical settings for the five "ordinary" hymns (also called a Mass) have been a major compositional form from 1400 into the twentieth century. However, these masses follow no set tradition and have considerable variety. Many of the greatest composers have written masses, including Josquin Des Prés, Bach, Haydn, Mozart, Beethoven, Verdi, Stravinsky, Britten, and Bernstein. These works often depart rather freely from liturgical requirements of the Mass, as they were written for special occasions, such as the Requiem Mass for the dead, the Nuptial Mass for weddings, and the Coronation Mass.

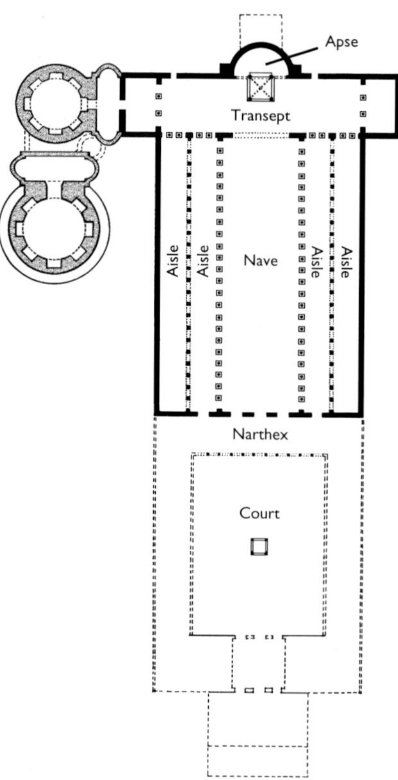

8-4. Plan of Old St. Peter's (after Frazer)

(Above Right) 8-5. Jacopo Grimaldi. *Facade of St. Peter's, Rome.* 1619. Drawing, Ms.: Barbarini Lat. 2733 fol. 133v. Vatican Library, Rome

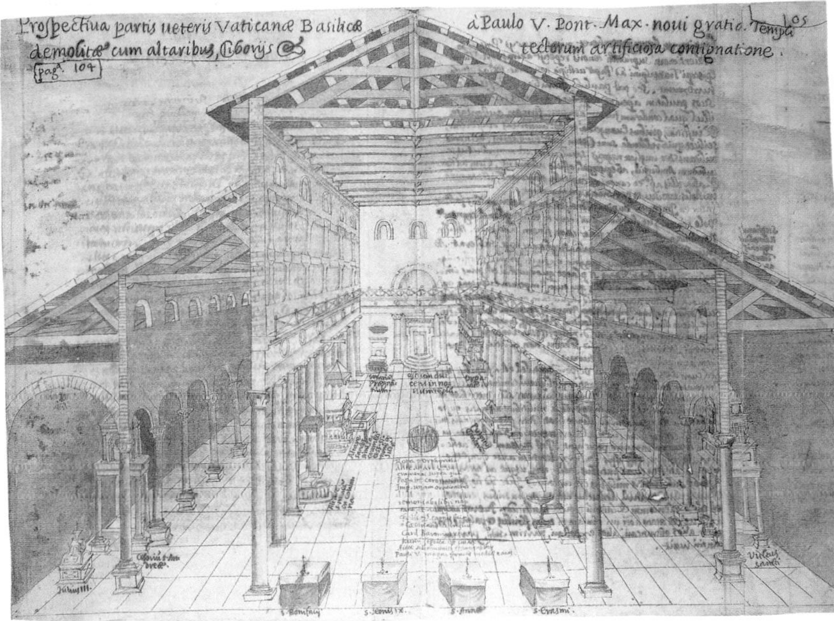

(Below Right) 8-6. Jacopo Grimaldi. *Interior of Old St. Peter's, Rome.* 1619. Drawing, Ms.: Barbarini Lat. 2733 fols. 104v–105r. Vatican Library, Rome

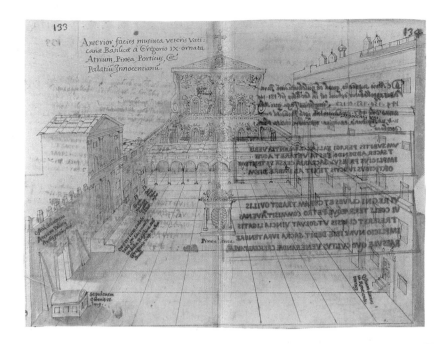

Etruscans (see figs. 6-2, 6-3), became Christianized and were held until the end of the fourth century. Other rituals were conducted from a portable altar placed before the shrine, using gold and silver implements donated by the emperor himself.

The basic plan follows the precedent set by the basilica of S. Giovanni in Laterano, Constantine's first major church, begun about 313 as the cathedral of the bishop of Rome. However, the apse in Old St. Peter's was at the west, not the east, end of the church. Before entering the church itself, we cross a colonnaded court, the atrium (a feature derived from the domus; see fig. 7-21), which was added toward the end of the fourth century. Only when we step from the entrance hall, the narthex, through the nave portal do we gain the view presented in figure 8-6. The steady rhythm of the nave arcade pulls us toward the "triumphal" arch at the western end, which frames the shrine of St. Peter and the apse beyond. As we come closer, we see that the shrine stands in a separate space placed at right angles to the nave and aisles to form a cross, the transept. This feature, which later became standard, is often left out in early basilican churches. Here it was sunken, perhaps to isolate the shrine from the rest of the church. Pairs of columns were used to create additional compartments, whose purpose is not known, at each end.

DOMED STRUCTURES. Another type of structure entered the tradition of Christian architecture in Constantinian times: round or polygonal buildings crowned with a dome. Known as central-plan churches, they developed out of Roman baths. (The design of the Pantheon, we will recall, was derived from the same source; see pages 164–65.) Similar structures had been built by Roman emperors such as Augustus and Hadrian to serve as monumental tombs, or mausoleums. In the fourth century, this type of building was given a Christian meaning in the baptisteries (where the bath became the sacred rite of baptism) and in the funerary chapels (where the hope for eternal life was expressed) that were

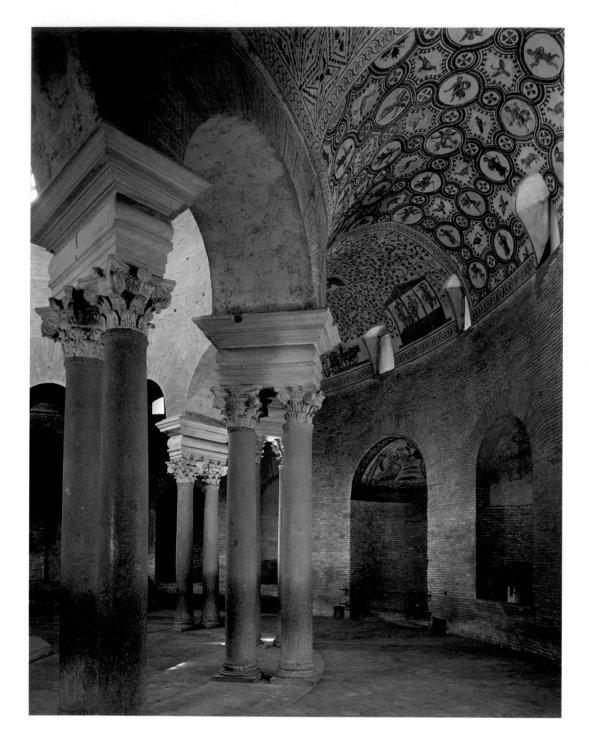

8-7. Interior,
Sta. Costanza, Rome.
c. 350 A.D.

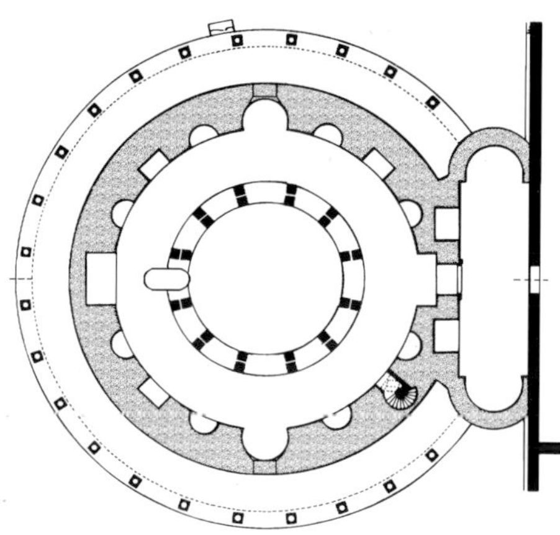

8-8. Plan of Sta. Costanza

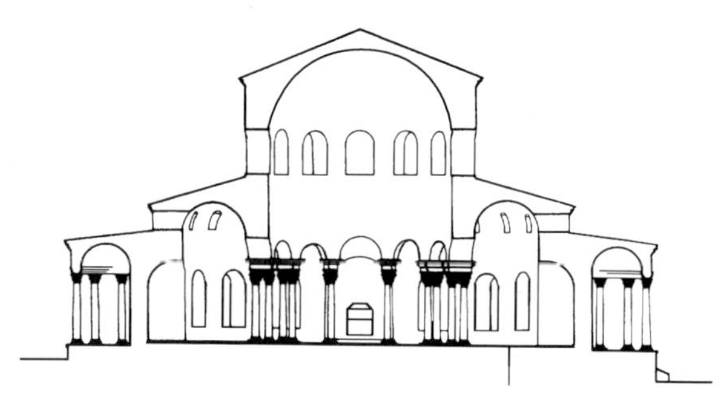

8-9. Section of Sta. Costanza

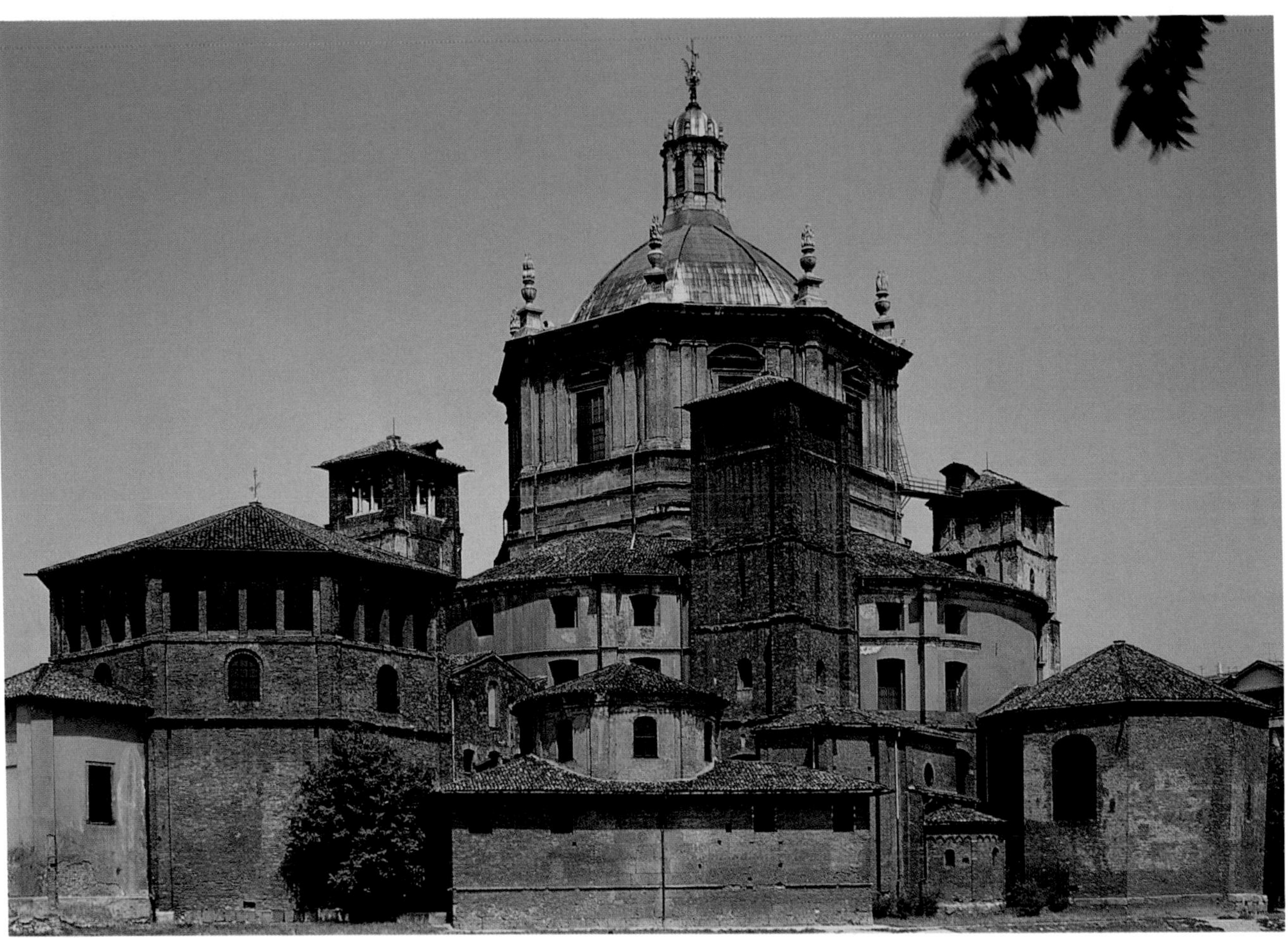

8-10. S. Lorenzo Maggiore, Milan, exterior from the southeast. c. 388–91 A.D.

linked with basilican churches. (St. Peter's was adjacent to a second-century circular tomb, and an Imperial mausoleum was attached to the south transept of the church around 400 A.D.) Because of these symbolic associations, central-plan churches were widely adopted. Most were derived from a handful of sacred sites, such as the Church of the Holy Sepulchre in Jerusalem, built by Constantine. But these served only as a point of departure, so that many liberties were taken with them. The sense of geometry was surprisingly loose. The shape could be round or polygonal. Only one or two major features and measurements were needed to link a building with its model. Symbolism even played an important role in the number of elements and their arrangement. For example, octagons, which had been used in Imperial mausoleums of the early fourth century such as Diocletian's and Galerius', were favored because the number eight was a symbol of resurrection: it signified the eighth day, the day of the new creation when the blessed shall attain the Heavenly Jerusalem. This free approach was typical of Early Christian architecture as a whole. Thus we find wide variation from building to building—not only among domed structures but basilican churches as well.

The finest surviving example of a central-plan church is Sta. Costanza (figs. 8-7–8-9), the mausoleum of Constantine's daughter Constantia. It was originally attached to the (now ruined) Roman church of St. Agnes Outside the Walls. In contrast to its predecessors, it shows a clear articulation of the interior space. A domed cylindrical core lit by clerestory windows—the counterpart of the nave of a basilican church—is surrounded by a ring-shaped "aisle" or ambulatory covered by a barrel vault. The mosaic decoration plays an important role in setting the mood. The motifs in the ambulatory are secular, but those in the two chapels are Christian. This striking contrast attests to how long the two forms coexisted. The distinction is blurred in the grape harvest above the entrance to the chapel in our illustration. It refers not only to the wine of the Eucharist (Jesus said, "I am the true vine") but also to the tree of life; thus it signifies the victory of eternal life over death for the Christian faithful.

S. LORENZO MAGGIORE. One building stands out for its daring originality: S. Lorenzo Maggiore in Milan (figs. 8-10–8-12). The plan is a quatrefoil with four corner towers, which were reworked during the Middle Ages. The two octagonal structures on the east and south ends seem to have been intended as a royal mausoleum and martyrium, though the church received its name long after it was finished. The walls are surely original, though the marble-and-stucco facing of the interior is missing, and the dome (as well as the supporting pillars) was rebuilt as an octagon in the sixteenth century. Several dates have been proposed for S. Lorenzo, but given its location just outside the city walls, it was most likely built as a palace church in 388–91, when the eastern emperor Theodosius the Great resided in Milan after defeating the western usurper Maximus. Although they would later squabble over issues of power and responsibility, Theodosius had already found

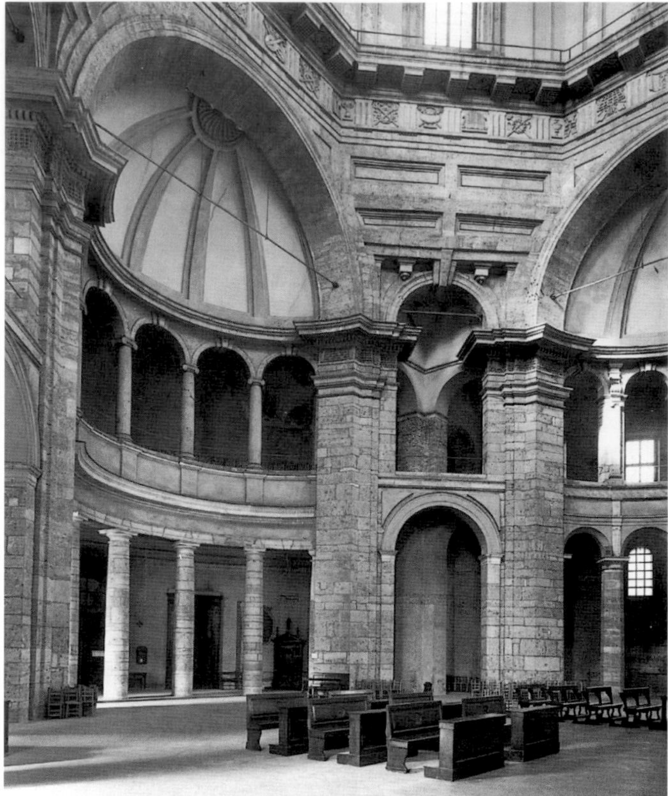

8-11. Interior, S. Lorenzo Maggiore

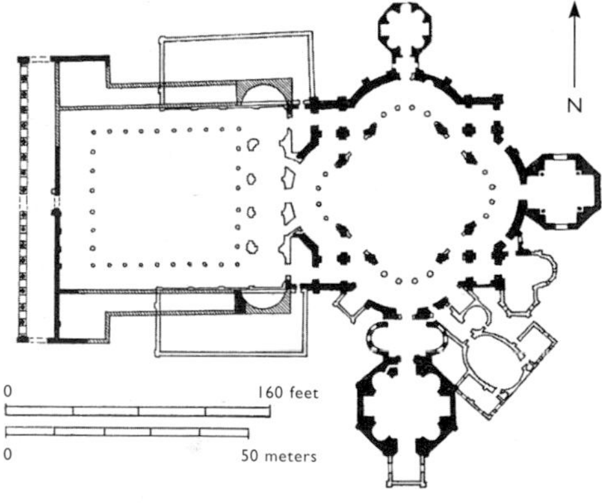

8-12. Plan of S. Lorenzo Maggiore (after Krautheimer)

Bishop Ambrose a willing ally during the ecumenical council of 381. (At that council the Nicene Creed was established as official Catholic dogma against the Arian "heresy," which taught that Jesus was not equal to God or made of the same substance, but a supernatural creature who was neither human nor divine.) At the time, Milan occupied a very important position. After Constantine moved his capital to Byzantium in 323, Milan served as the capital of the Western Empire. It was also the religious center of northern Italy, rivaling Rome. It was supplanted by Ravenna in 402, when the emperor Honorius was forced to withdraw from Milan.

S. Lorenzo is unlike any other church in Milan or in the entire Latin realm at the time, even though all of its elements can be traced to late Roman architecture. (The conch-shaped niches are similar to the apse of the basilica at Leptis Magna.) The central plan with its double shell and complex molding of space, the superb quality of construction, and the refined proportions of the noble interior—all suggest that S. Lorenzo was designed by an architect probably called from the east by Theodosius. It is thus of considerable importance because it gives us a glimpse of the great churches built by Constantine and his successors in Byzantium, none of which stands today.

Mosaics

We have not yet discussed an important aspect of Early Christian religious architecture: the contrast between exterior and interior. Such a contrast can be seen in the sixth-century church of S. Apollinare in Classe, which still retains its original appearance for the most part (figs. 8-13–8-15). (St. Apollinarus was the first bishop of Ravenna; Classe is the seaport of Ravenna.) Our view, taken from the west, shows the narthex but not the atrium, which was torn down a long time ago. (The round bell tower, or campanile, was added in medieval times.) As the plan shows, the church lacks a transept. The brick exterior is unadorned. It is only a shell whose shape reflects the space it encloses—the opposite of the Classical temple. This ascetic treatment of the exterior gives way to the utmost richness as we enter the church. Having left the everyday world behind, we find ourselves in a shimmering realm of light and color where precious marble surfaces and the brilliant glitter of mosaics evoke the spiritual splendor of the Kingdom of God.

The rapid growth of Christian architecture on a large scale had a revolutionary effect on Early Christian art. All of a sudden, huge wall surfaces had to be covered with images worthy of their monumental framework. Who was equal to this challenge? Certainly not the humble artists who had decorated the catacombs. They were replaced by masters of greater ability—probably recruited by officials of the Empire, as were the architects of the new basilicas. Unfortunately, so little of the decoration of fourth-century churches has survived that its history cannot be traced in detail.

WALL MOSAICS. Out of this process emerged a great new art form, the Early Christian wall mosaic, which to a large extent replaced the older and cheaper medium of mural painting. Mosaics—designs composed of small pieces of colored material set in plaster—had been used by the Sumerians as early as the third millennium B.C. to embellish architectural surfaces. The Hellenistic Greeks and the Romans, using small cubes of marble called *tesserae,* had refined the technique to the point that it could be used to copy paintings, as in *The Battle of Issos* (see fig. 5-60). But these were mostly floor mosaics, and the color scale, although rich in gradations, lacked brilliance, since it was limited to the various kinds of colored marble found in nature. The Romans also produced wall mosaics occasionally, but only for special purposes and on a limited scale.

The extensive and complex wall mosaics of Early Christian art thus are essentially without precedent. The same is true of their material, for they consist of tesserae made of colored glass. While the Romans knew of this material, they never made full use of it. Glass tesserae offered colors, including gold, of a far greater range

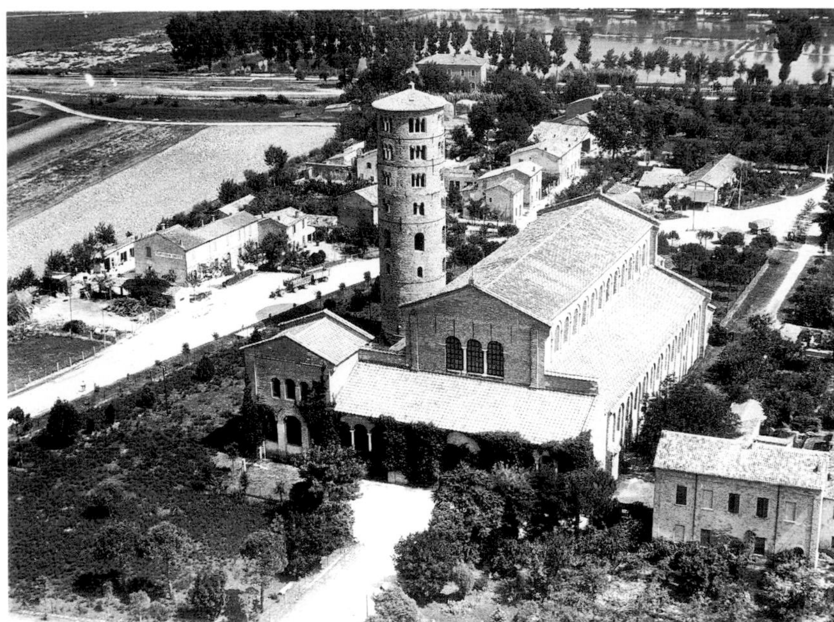

8-13. S. Apollinare in Classe, Ravenna, Italy. 533–49 A.D.

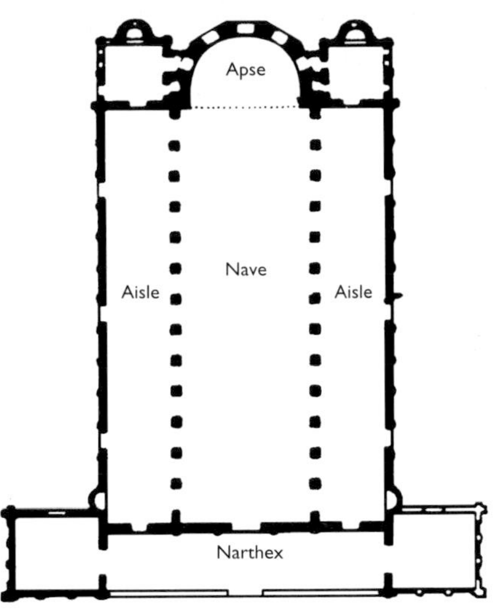

8-14. Plan of S. Apollinare in Classe (after De Angelis d'Ossat)

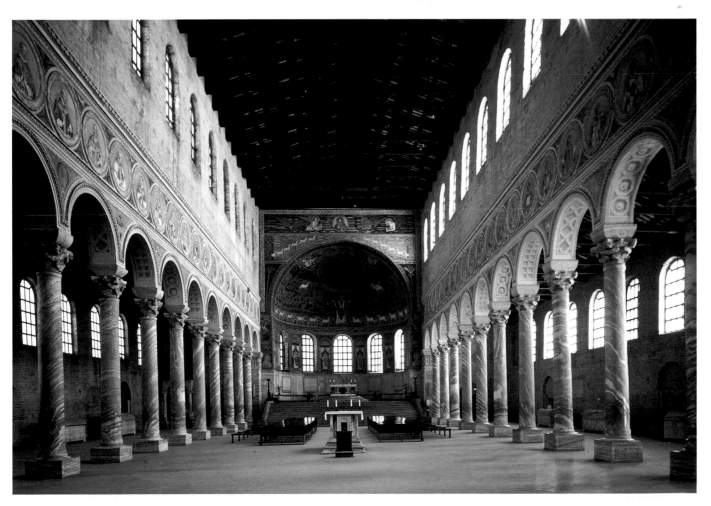

8-15. Interior (view toward the apse), S. Apollinare in Classe, Ravenna. 533–49 A.D.

and intensity than marble tesserae, but they lacked the fine gradations in tone needed to imitate painted pictures. Moreover, the shiny (and slightly irregular) faces of glass tesserae act as tiny reflectors, so that the overall effect is that of a glittering, immaterial screen rather than of a solid, continuous surface. All these qualities made glass mosaic the ideal material for the new architectural aesthetic of Early Christian basilicas.

The guiding principle of Graeco-Roman architecture had been to express a balance of opposing forces, rather like the balance within the contrapposto of a Classical statue. The result was

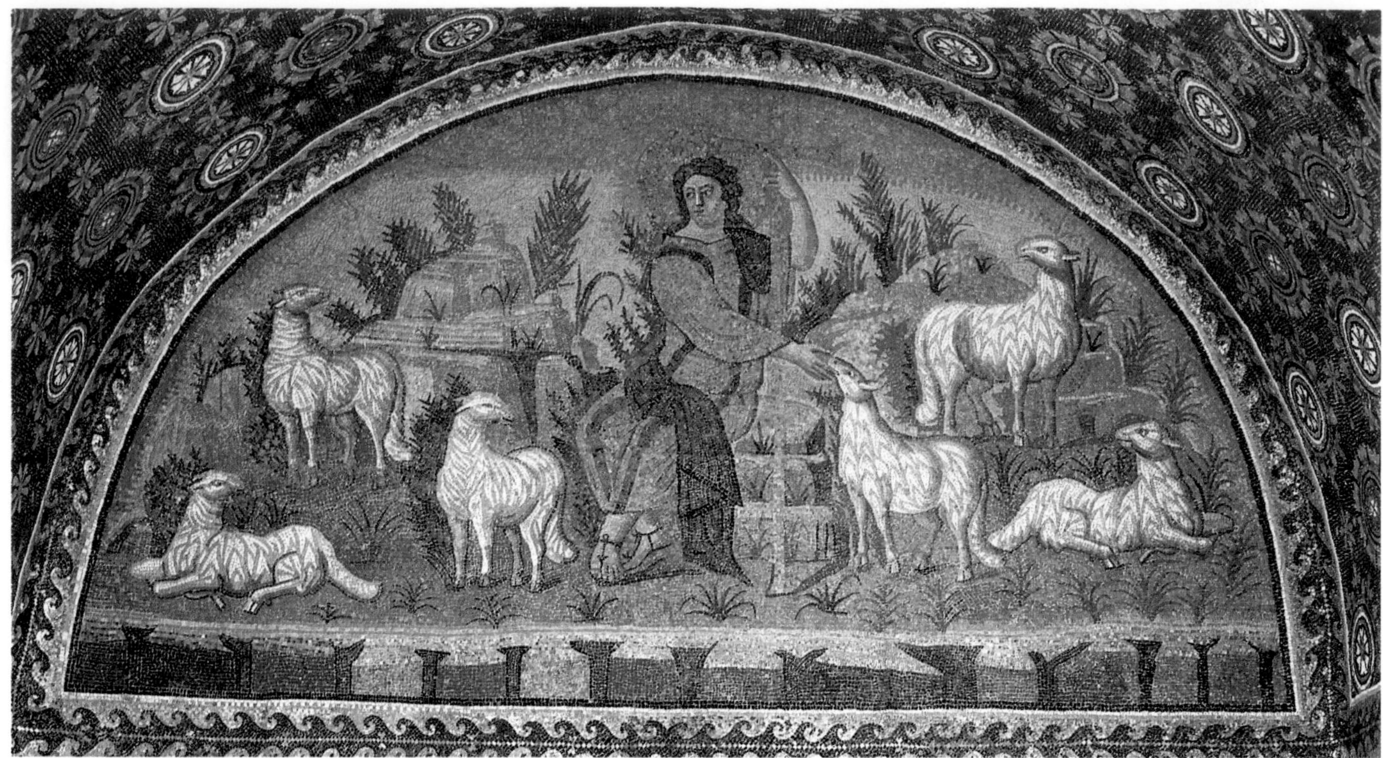

8-16. *Good Shepherd.* 425–50. Mosaic. Mausoleum of Galla Placidia, Ravenna

a muscular display of active and passive, supporting and supported members, whether these were structural or merely superimposed on a concrete core. Viewed in such terms, Early Christian architecture is strangely inexpressive, even antimonumental. The material structure is subservient to the creation of immaterial space. Walls and vaults seem like weightless shells, their actual thickness and solidity hidden rather than emphasized. The brilliant color, the brightness of gold, the severe geometric order of the images in a mosaic cycle such as that of S. Apollinare in Classe (see fig. 8-15) fit the spirit of these interiors to perfection. One might say, in fact, that Early Christian and Byzantine churches demand mosaics the way Greek temples demand architectural sculpture.

EARLY SOURCES. The development of Christian imagery was interwoven with that of architecture. The earliest church decorations probably consisted of ornamental designs in marble, plaster, stucco, or even gold. Soon, however, great pictorial cycles were spread over the nave walls, the triumphal arch, and the apse, first in painting, then in mosaic. Needless to say, the new art did not appear overnight. Much of the initial development seems to have occurred during the fifth century A.D. These cycles must have drawn upon sources that reflected the whole range of Graeco-Roman painting as well as the art of other centers of Christianity. Before Constantine's reign, there were large Christian communities in the great cities of North Africa and the Near East, such as Alexandria and Antioch. They had probably developed artistic traditions of their own, although few traces of them exist today. Paintings in an Orientalizing style similar to that of the murals in the synagogue at Dura-Europos (see fig. 8-2) may have decorated the walls of Christian places of worship in Syria and Palestine. (We recall that the earliest Christian congregations were formed by dissident members of the Jewish community.) Moreover, during the first or second century A.D., Alexandria, the home of a large, Hellenized Jewish colony, may have produced illustrations of the Old Testament in a style akin to that of Pompeian murals. We meet echoes of such scenes in Christian art later on, but we cannot be sure when or where they originated, or by what paths they entered the Christian tradition. The importance of Judaic sources for Early Christian art is hardly surprising: the new faith also incorporated many aspects of the Jewish service into its own liturgy. These included hymns, which would form the basis of medieval chants.

The heritage of the past was not only absorbed but also transformed both physically and spiritually. A characteristic example is the *Good Shepherd* mosaic (fig. 8-16) in the so-called mausoleum of Galla Placidia. (Galla Placidia was the sister of the emperor Honorius, who sponsored the first major building program in Ravenna. However, the building was probably originally intended as a chapel dedicated to the Spanish martyr St. Vincent.) The figure of the shepherd seated in a landscape expands the central subject of our catacomb painting (see fig. 8-3) by being both more elaborately and more formally treated. In accordance with the preference of the time, Christ is portrayed as a young man in the familiar pose of a philosopher. (We shall meet him again as a youthful philosopher in the *Sarcophagus of Junius Bassus;* see fig. 8-21.) The rest of his attributes, however, have been adapted from Imperial art, which provided a ready supply of motifs that was mined heavily in the early fifth century, when Christian imagery underwent intensive development. The halo was taken from representations of the emperor as sun-king, and even the cross had been an Imperial device.

CONTRASTS WITH GRAECO-ROMAN PAINTING. Roman mural painting used illusionistic devices to suggest a reality beyond the surface of the wall. Early Christian mosaics also denied the flatness of the wall surface, but here the goal was to achieve an "illusion of unreality," a luminous realm filled with celestial beings or symbols.

The Parting of Lot and Abraham (fig. 8-17) is a scene from the oldest and most important surviving cycle of this kind. It was done about 432–40 in the church of Sta. Maria Maggiore in Rome. In the left half of the scene, Abraham, his son Isaac, and the rest of his family depart for the land of Canaan. On the right, Lot and his clan, including his two small daughters, turn toward the city of Sodom. The task of the artist who designed our panel is similar to that of the sculptors of the Column of Trajan (see fig. 7-37). They needed to condense complex actions into a form that could be read at a distance. In fact, many of the same "shorthand" devices are employed, such as the formulas for house, tree, and city, or the trick of showing a crowd of people as a "grape-cluster of heads." But in the Trajanic reliefs, these devices could be used only to the extent that they allowed the artist to re-create actual historic events.

The mosaics in Sta. Maria Maggiore, on the other hand, depict the history of salvation. They begin with Old Testament scenes along the nave (in this instance from Genesis 13) and end with the life of Jesus as the Messiah on the arch across the nave. The scheme is not only a historical cycle but a symbolic program that presents a higher reality—the Word of God. Hence the artist need not be concerned with the details of historic narrative. Glances and gestures are more important than movement or three-dimensional form. The symmetrical composition, with its gap in the center, makes clear the significance of this parting. The way of righteousness is represented by Abraham, and the way of evil is signified by the city of Sodom, which was destroyed by the Lord.

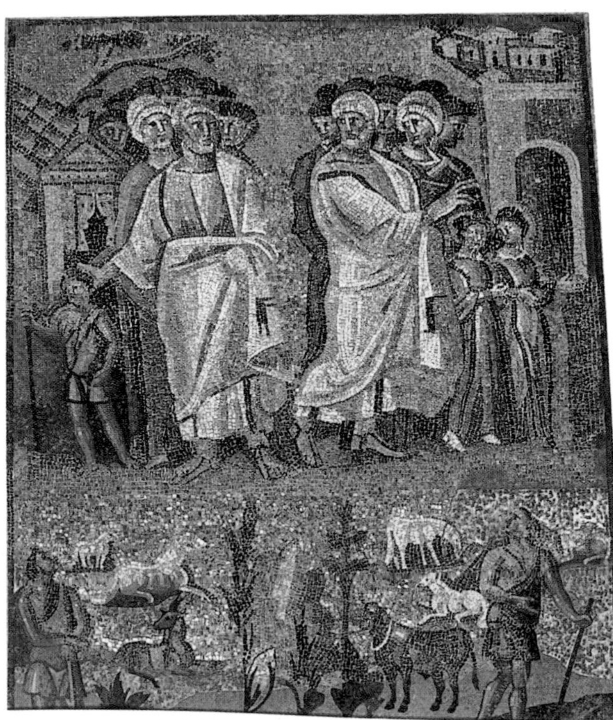

8-17. *The Parting of Lot and Abraham.* c. 432–40 A.D. Mosaic. Sta. Maria Maggiore, Rome

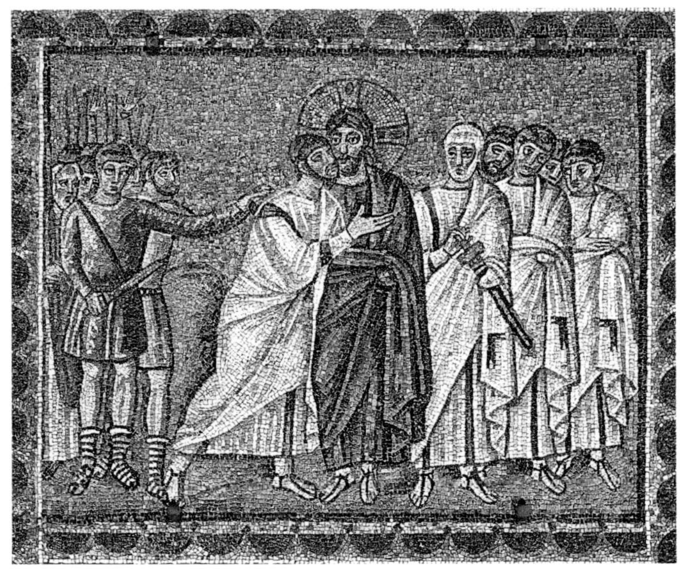

8-18. *The Betrayal of Christ.* c. 500 A.D. Mosaic. S. Apollinare Nuovo, Ravenna

S. APOLLINARE NUOVO, RAVENNA. The challenge of inventing a body of Christian imagery produced an extraordinary creative outpouring, and by 500 A.D. the process was largely complete. It had taken less than 175 years to lay the foundation for a new artistic tradition—a remarkably short time indeed! The earliest cycle of mosaics to survive intact (preceded by others in Rome) are those in S. Apollinare Nuovo in Ravenna. Originally a naval station on the Adriatic, Ravenna had become the capital first of the West Roman emperors in 402 and then, at the end of the century, of Theodoric, king of the Ostrogoths. Although Theodoric's Arian beliefs were considered heretical, his tastes were patterned after those of Constantinople, where he had spent a decade as a young man. Under Justinian, Ravenna became the main stronghold of Byzantine rule in Italy.

S. Apollinare Nuovo was built around 500 by Theodoric as his palace church. It received its present name only in the mid-ninth century, when the saint's relics were moved from S. Apollinare in Classe (see above). About 560 it was confiscated by Bishop Agnellus (with Justinian's blessing) and rededicated to St. Martin, a champion of orthodoxy. St. Martin replaced Theodoric at the head of the row of male martyrs leading from the palace at the west of the nave toward the enthroned Christ near the apse. A similar row of female martyrs ending in the Virgin Enthroned may also have been reworked at that time. The prophets, patriarchs, and apostles between the windows were left untouched, however.

It is the scenes depicting the ministry of Christ and the Passion that interest us. Although they have been placed on a narrow band above the clerestory, they are of great importance. The selection of subjects is somewhat unusual, perhaps reflecting Theodoric's Arian persuasion, but they generally center on events in which Jesus revealed his divinity through miracles and other acts—a reminder of the dual meaning of "martyr" (see above). In *The Betrayal of Christ* (fig. 8-18) he is literally revealed by the kiss of Judas. We immediately recognize the kinship with *The Parting of Lot and Abraham* at Sta. Maria Maggiore (fig. 8-17); and the figures betray their Roman ancestry as well (compare figs. 7-32 and

7-33). Yet we are struck not by any debt to the past but by the newness of the scene, which has no precedent in Greek or Roman art. Its originality lies not so much in the details as in the approach. The drama has a clarity that is surprisingly intense. Jesus and Judas are isolated between two equal groups of soldiers and disciples, so that we are forced to focus on the central event and, above all, its meaning. So persuasive is the result that the scene became "classic" in its own right: it is the ancestor of countless others not only in Byzantium but also in the West, from Giotto through El Greco and Van Dyck.

Roll, Book, and Illustration

From what sources did the designers of mosaic cycles such as those of Sta. Maria Maggiore and S. Apollinare Nuovo derive their compositions? They were certainly not the first to depict scenes from the Bible in extensive fashion (see box below). For certain subjects, they could have found models among the catacomb murals, but some prototypes may also have come from illustrated manuscripts. Because they were portable, manuscripts have been assigned an important role in disseminating religious imagery. In some cases there is no doubt that manuscript illustrations served as models for wall paintings. In others it is clear that they must have been derived from frescoes. But in many others the similarities between two pictures point to a common source that was probably a lost mural, not a manuscript.

Because it was founded on the Word of God as revealed in Holy Writ, the early Christian Church must have sponsored the duplicating of the sacred text on a large scale. Every copy of it was handled with a reverence quite unlike the treatment of any book in Graeco-Roman civilization. But when did these copies become works of pictorial art as well? And what did the earliest Bible illustrations look like?

Because books are frail things, we have only indirect evidence of their history in the ancient world. It begins in Egypt with the discovery of a suitable material, paperlike but more brittle, made from the papyrus plant (see pages 58–59; fig. 2-31). Books of papyrus were made in the form of rolls throughout antiquity. Not

VERSIONS OF THE BIBLE

The word "bible" is derived from the Greek word for books, since it was originally a compilation of a number of sacred texts. Over time, the books of the Bible came to be regarded as a unit, and thus the Bible is now generally considered a single book.

There is considerable disagreement between Christians and Jews, and among various Christian and Jewish sects, over which books should be considered canonical—that is, accepted as legitimate parts of the biblical canon, the standard list of authentic texts. However, every version of the Bible includes the Hebrew torah, or the Law (also called the Pentateuch, or Books of Moses), as the first five books. Also universally accepted by both Jews and Christians are the books known as the Prophets (which include texts of Jewish history as well as prophecy). There are also a number of other books known simply as the Writings, which include history, poetry (the Psalms and the Song of Songs), prophecy, and even folktales, some universally accepted, some accepted by one group, and some accepted virtually by no one. Books of doubtful authenticity are known as apocryphal books or, simply, Apocrypha, from a Greek word meaning obscure. The Jewish Bible or Hebrew Canon—the books that are accepted as authentic Jewish scripture—was agreed upon by Jewish scholars sometime before the beginning of the Christian era.

The Christian Bible is divided into two major sections, the Old Testament and the New Testament. The Old Testament contains many, but not all, of the Jewish scriptures, while the New Testament, originally written in Greek, is specifically Christian. It contains four gospels—each written in the first century A.D. by one of the Early Christian missionaries known as the four evangelists, Mark, Matthew, Luke, and John. The Gospels tell, from slightly different points of view, the story of the life and teachings of Jesus of Nazareth. They are followed by the Epistles, letters written by Paul and a few other Christian missionaries to various congregations of the church. The final book is the Apocalypse, by John the Divine, also called the Book of Revelation, which foretells the end of the world.

Jerome (342–420), the foremost scholar of the early Church, selected the books considered canonical for the Christian Bible from a large body of Early Christian writings. It was due to his energetic advocacy that the Church accepted the Hebrew scriptures as representing the Word of God as much as the Christian texts, and therefore worthy to be included in the Bible. Jerome then translated the books he had chosen from Hebrew and Greek into Latin, the spoken language of Italy in his time. This Latin translation of the Bible was—and is—known as the Vulgate because it was written in the vernacular (Latin *vulgaris*) language. The Vulgate remained the Church's primary text for the Bible for more than a thousand years. It was regarded with such reverence that in the fourteenth century, when early humanists first translated it into the vernacular languages of their time, they were sometimes suspected of heresy for doing so. The writings rejected for inclusion in the New Testament by Jerome are known as Christian Apocrypha. Although not canonical, some of these books, such as the Life of Mary and the Gospel of James, were nevertheless used by artists and playwrights during the Middle Ages as sources for stories to illustrate and dramatize.

BIBLICAL, CHURCH, AND CELESTIAL BEINGS

Much of Western art deals with biblical persons and celestial beings. Their names appear in titles of paintings and sculpture and in discussions of subject matter. Following is a brief guide to some of the most commonly encountered persons and beings in Christian art.

PATRIARCHS. Literally, heads of families, or rulers of tribes. The Old Testament patriarchs are Abraham, Isaac, Jacob, and Jacob's 12 sons. Patriarch may also refer to the bishops of the five chief bishoprics of Christendom: Alexandria, Antioch, Constantinople, Jerusalem, and Rome.

PROPHETS. In Christian art, prophets usually mean the Old Testament figures whose writings were seen to foretell the coming of Christ. The so-called major prophets are Isaiah, Jeremiah, and Ezekiel. The minor prophets are Hosea, Joel, Amos, Obadiah, Jonah, Micah, Nahum, Habakkuk, Zephaniah, Haggai, Zechariah, and Malachi.

TRINITY. Central to Christian belief is the doctrine that One God exists in Three Persons: Father, Son (Jesus Christ), and Holy Spirit. The Holy Spirit is often represented as a dove.

HOLY FAMILY. The infant Jesus, his mother Mary, and his foster father Joseph constitute the Holy Family. Sometimes Mary's mother, St. Anne, appears with them.

JOHN THE BAPTIST. The precursor of Jesus Christ, John is regarded by Christians as the last prophet before the coming of the Messiah, Jesus. John was an ascetic who baptized his disciples in the name of the coming Messiah; he recognized Jesus as that Messiah when he saw the Holy Spirit descend on Jesus when he came to John to be baptized.

EVANGELISTS. There are four: Matthew, John, Mark, and Luke—each an author of one of the Gospels. The first two were among Jesus' 12 apostles. The latter two wrote in the second half of the first century.

APOSTLES. The apostles are the 12 disciples Jesus asked to convert nations to his faith. They are Peter (Simon Peter), Andrew, James the Greater, John, Philip, Bartholomew, Matthew, Thomas, James the Less, Jude (or Thaddaeus), Simon the Canaanite, and Judas Iscariot. After Judas betrayed Jesus, his place was taken by Matthias. St. Paul (though not a disciple) is also considered an apostle.

DISCIPLES. See Apostles.

ANGELS AND ARCHANGELS. Beings of a spiritual nature, angels are spoken of in the Old and New Testaments as having been created by God to be heavenly messengers between God and human beings, Heaven and earth. Spoken of first by the apostle Paul, archangels, unlike angels, have names: Michael, Gabriel, and Raphael.

CHERUBIM AND SERAPHIM. The celestial hierarchy devised by Pseudo-Dionysius about 500 A.D. had cherubim (with four wings) and seraphim (six wings) at the peak, encircling the throne of God. After the Middle Ages, a cherub came to be represented as a rosy-cheeked, plump, and winged child.

SAINTS. Persons are declared saints only after death. The pope acknowledges sainthood by canonization, a process based on meeting rigid criteria of authentic miracles and beatitude. He ordains a public cult of the new saint throughout the Catholic Church. A similar process is followed in the Orthodox Church.

MARTYRS. Originally, martyrs (witnesses) referred to all the apostles. Later, it signified those persecuted for their faith. Still later, the term was reserved for those who died in the name of Christ.

POPE. Meaning "father," the term refers to the bishop of Rome, the spiritual head of the Roman Catholic Church. Today, the pope dwells in and heads an independent state, Vatican City, within the city of Rome. Throughout most of Christian history, the pope ruled a large territory that occupied much of central Italy. His chief attribute is a shepherd's staff; he dresses in white.

CARDINALS. Priests or higher religious officials chosen to help the pope administer the Church. They are of two types: those who live in Rome (the Curia) and those who remain in their dioceses. Together they constitute the Sacred College. One of their duties is to elect a pope after the death or removal of a sitting pope. They wear a red cassock (robe) and, depending on the occasion, one of three ceremonial hats.

DIOCESE. A territorial unit administered in the Western church by a bishop and in the Eastern Church by a patriarch. A cathedral is the diocese church and the seat of the bishop.

BISHOPS AND ARCHBISHOPS. A bishop is the highest order of minister in the Catholic Church, with his administrative territory being the diocese. Bishops are ordained by archbishops, who also have the authority to consecrate kings. Bishops carry an elaborately curved staff called a crozier and, on ceremonial occasions, wear a three-pointed hat.

PRIESTS AND PARISHES. Priests did not exist in the early Church because only bishops were authorized to offer the Eucharist and receive confession. As the Church grew, church officials called presbyters (elders), or priests, were designated by bishops to perform the Eucharist and ablutions in smaller administrative units, called parishes.

ABBOTS AND ABBESSES. Heads of large monasteries (called abbeys) and convents (nunneries).

MONKS AND NUNS. Men and women living in religious communities who have taken vows of poverty, chastity, and obedience to the rules of their orders.

CANONS AND CANONESSES. Men and women who live in religious communities but under less rigorous rules than monks and nuns.

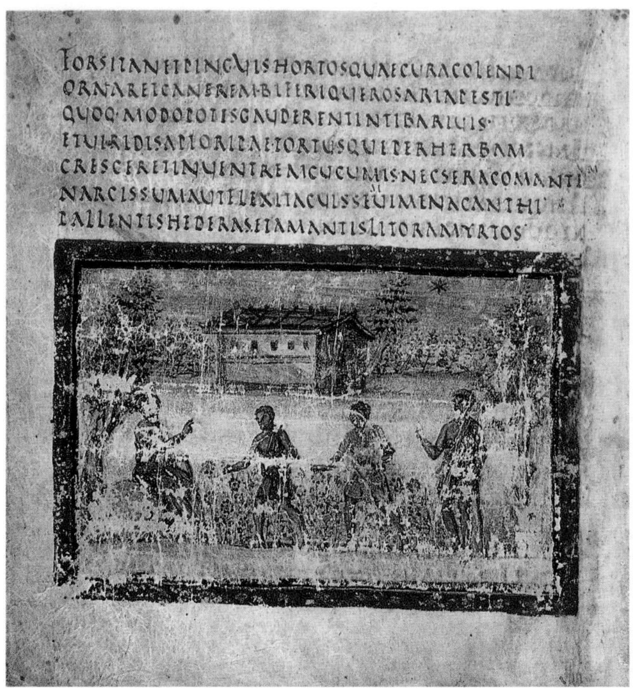

8-19. Miniature, from the *Vatican Vergil.* Early 5th century A.D. Biblioteca Apostolica Vaticana, Rome

until the second century B.C., in late Hellenistic times, did a better substance become available. This was parchment, or vellum (thin, bleached animal hide), which is far more durable than papyrus. It was strong enough to be creased without breaking and thus made possible the kind of bound book we know today, technically called a codex, which appeared sometime in the late first century A.D.

Between the second and the fourth century A.D., the vellum codex gradually replaced the roll. This change must have had an important effect on book illustration. As long as the roll form prevailed, illustrations seem to have been mostly line drawings, since layers of pigment would soon have cracked and come off in the process of rolling and unrolling. Only the vellum codex permitted the use of rich colors, including gold. Hence, it would make book illustration—or, as we usually say, manuscript illumination—the small-scale counterpart of murals, mosaics, and panel pictures. Some questions are still unanswered: When, where, and at what pace did book illumination develop? Were most of the subjects biblical, mythological, or historical? How much of a carryover was there from roll to codex?

THE VATICAN VERGIL. There can be little doubt that the earliest illuminations, whether Christian, Jewish, or classical, were strongly influenced by the illusionism of Hellenistic-Roman painting of the sort we met at Pompeii. One of the oldest illustrated manuscript books known, the *Vatican Vergil,* reflects this tradition, although the miniatures are far from inspired. The book was probably made in Italy about the time of the Sta. Maria Maggiore mosaics, to which it is closely linked in style. The picture (fig. 8-19), separated from the rest of the page by a heavy frame, has the effect of a window, and in the landscape we find remnants of deep space, perspective, and the play of light and shade. In striking contrast to earlier images, which are largely or completely independent of text, such manuscript illuminations are clearly subordinate to the written word. This approach was well suited to Christianity, which was based on the authority of sacred texts. Pictures took on a new role: to serve as illustrations or commentaries. This is the reason why manuscripts are unlikely sources for early Christian paintings and mosaics.

THE VIENNA GENESIS. The oldest illustrated Bible manuscripts discovered thus far appear to date from the early sixth century (except for one fragment of five leaves that seems to be related to the *Vatican Vergil*). They, too, contain echoes of the Hellenistic-Roman style, which has been adapted to religious narrative and often has a Near Eastern flavor that at times recalls the Dura-Europos murals (see fig. 8-2). The most important example, the *Vienna Genesis,* is a far more striking work than the *Vatican Vergil.* This Greek translation of the first book of the Bible achieves a sumptuous effect not unlike that of the mosaics we have seen. It is written in silver (now turned black) on purple vellum and adorned with brilliantly colored miniatures. Figure 8-20 shows a number of scenes from the story of Jacob. (In the foreground, for example, we see him wrestling with the angel, then receiving the angel's blessing.) The picture thus does not show a single event but a whole sequence. The scenes are strung out along a single U-shaped path, so that progression in space becomes progression in time. This method, known as continuous narration, has a history going back as far as ancient Egypt and Mesopotamia. Its appearance in miniatures such as ours may reflect earlier illustrations made for books in roll form: our picture certainly looks like a frieze turned back upon itself.

For manuscript illustration, the continuous method makes the most economical use of space. The painter can pack a maximum of narrative content into the area at his disposal. Our artist seems to have thought of his picture as a running account to be read like lines of text, rather than as a window that required a frame. The painted forms are placed directly on the purple background that holds the letters, making the entire page a unified field.

Sculpture

Compared to painting and architecture, sculpture played a secondary role in Early Christian art. The biblical prohibition of graven images in the Second Commandment was thought to apply particularly to large cult statues, the idols that were worshiped in pagan temples. [See Primary Sources, no. 13, page 364.] To escape the taint of idolatry, therefore, religious sculpture had to avoid lifesize representations of the human figure. It thus developed away from the spatial depth and massive scale of Graeco-Roman sculpture toward small-scale forms and lacelike surface decoration.

The earliest works of Christian sculpture are marble sarcophagi. These evolved from the pagan examples that replaced cinerary urns in Roman society around the time of Hadrian, when belief in an afterlife arose as part of a major change in the attitude toward death (see page 179). From the middle of the third century on, these stone coffins were made for the more important mem-

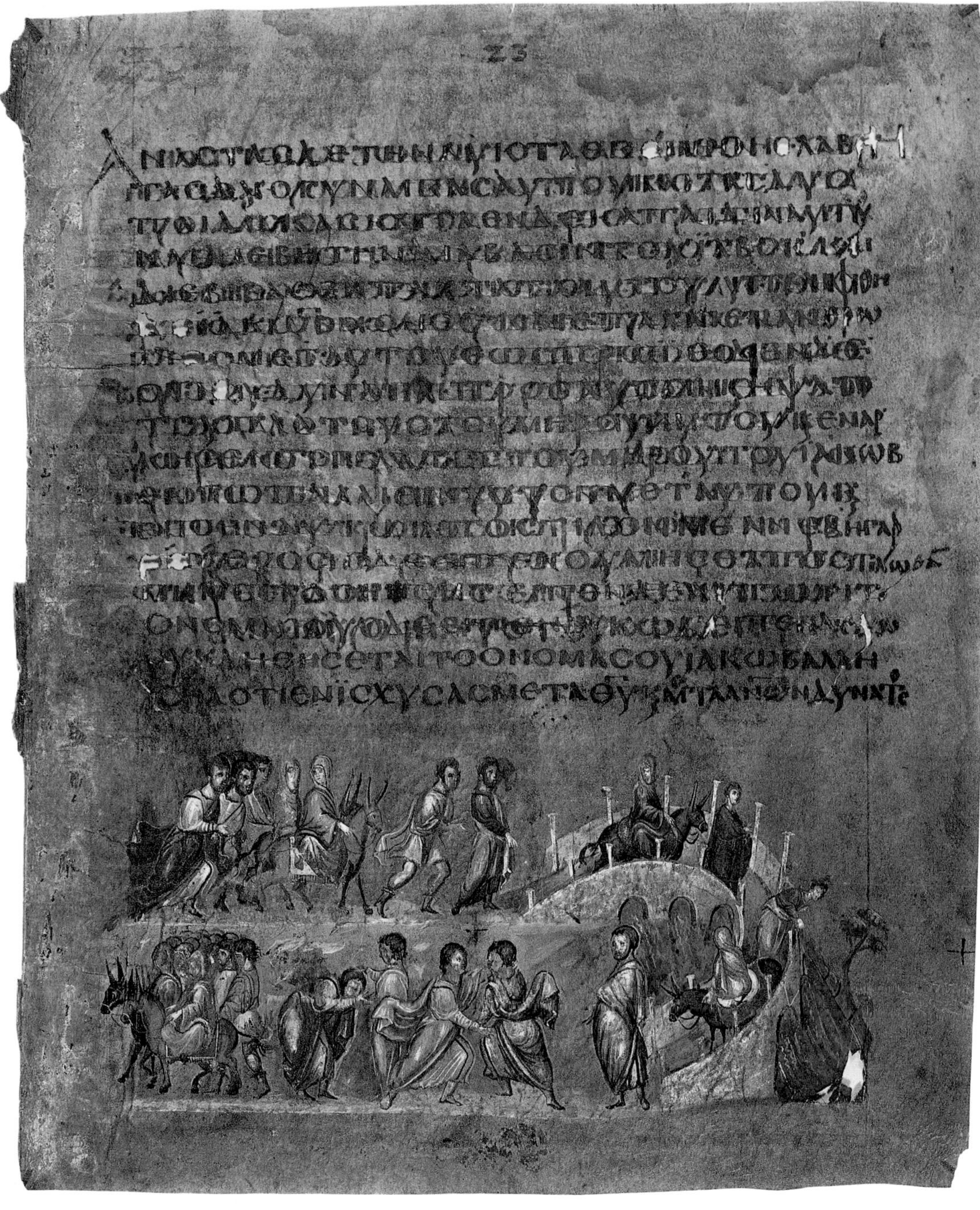

8-20. Page with *Jacob Wrestling the Angel,* from the *Vienna Genesis.* Early 6th century A.D. Tempera and silver on dyed vellum, 13¼ x 9½" (33.6 x 24.1 cm). Österreichische Nationalbibliothek, Vienna

bers of the Christian Church. Before the time of Constantine, they were decorated mainly with themes that are familiar from catacomb murals—the Good Shepherd, Jonah and the Whale, and so forth—but within a framework borrowed from pagan art. Not until a century later do we find a much broader range of subject matter and forms.

THE SARCOPHAGUS OF JUNIUS BASSUS. The finest Early Christian sarcophagus is the richly carved *Sarcophagus of Junius Bassus,* made for a prefect of Rome who died in 359 (fig. 8-21). Its colonnaded front, divided into ten square compartments, shows a mixture of Old and New Testament scenes. In the upper row we see (left to right) the Sacrifice of Isaac, St. Peter Taken Prisoner, Christ Enthroned Between Sts. Peter and Paul, and Christ Before Pontius Pilate (two compartments). In the lower row are the Misery of Job, the Temptation of Adam and Eve, Christ's Entry into Jerusalem, Daniel in the Lions' Den, and St. Paul Led to His Martyrdom. This choice, somewhat strange to the modern viewer, is characteristic of the Early Christian way of thinking, which stressed the divine rather than the human nature of Christ. Hence his suffering and death are merely hinted at. He appears before Pilate as a youthful, long-haired philosopher expounding the true wisdom (note the scroll). The martyrdom of the two apostles is shown in the same discreet fashion. The two central scenes are also devoted to Christ (see box pages 228–29). Enthroned above Jupiter as the personification of the heavens, he dispenses the Law to Sts. Peter and Paul. Below, he enters Jerusalem as Conquering Savior (compare fig. 7-40). Adam and

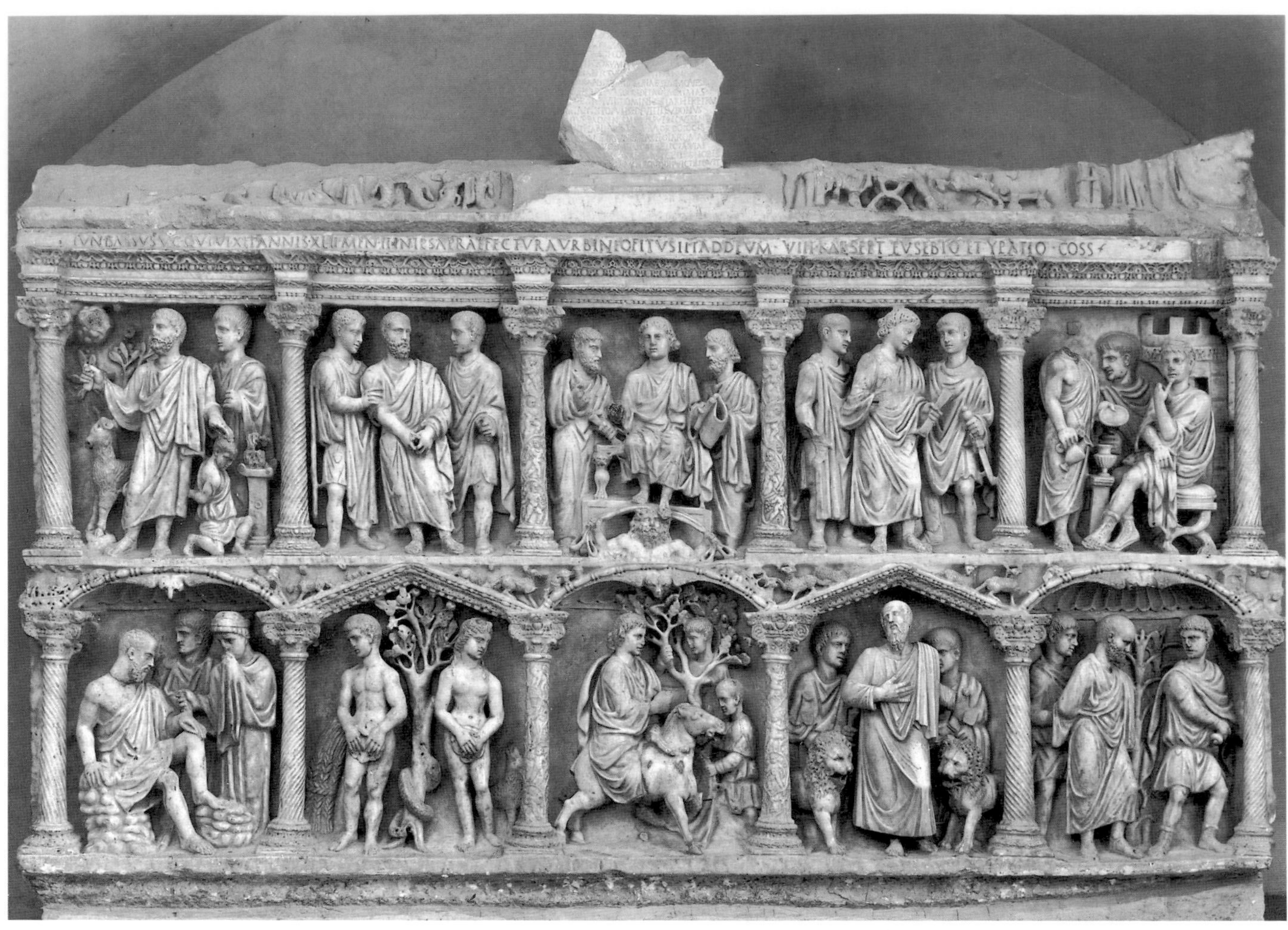

8-21. *Sarcophagus of Junius Bassus.* c. 359 A.D. Marble, 3'10½" x 8' (1.2 x 2.4 m). Museo Storico del Capitolino di S. Pietro, Rome

Eve, the original sinners, denote the burden of guilt redeemed by Christ. The Sacrifice of Isaac is an Old Testament prefiguration of Christ's sacrificial death and resurrection. Job and Daniel carry the same message as Jonah in the catacomb painting (see fig. 8-3): they fortify the hope of salvation.

When compared with the frieze on the Arch of Constantine, carved almost half a century before (see fig. 7-47), the *Sarcophagus of Junius Bassus* retains a veneer of classicism. The figures in their deep niches recall the statuesque dignity of the Greek and Roman tradition. (Compare Eve to the *Knidian Aphrodite* of Praxiteles; fig. 5-67.) Yet beneath this classicism we sense a kinship to the Constantinian style in the doll-like bodies, the large heads, and the passive air of scenes that would seem to call for dramatic action. The events and figures are no longer intended to tell their own story but to call to mind a symbolic meaning that unites them.

CLASSICISM. Classicizing tendencies of this sort seem to have recurred in Early Christian sculpture from the mid-fourth to the early sixth century. Their causes have been explained in various ways. During this period paganism still had many important followers, who may have fostered such revivals as a kind of rear-guard action. Recent converts (including Junius Bassus, who was not baptized until shortly before his death) often remained loyal to values of the past. Some Church leaders also sought to reconcile Christianity with the heritage of classical antiquity. They did so with good reason: Early Christian theology depended a great deal on the thinking of Greek and Roman philosophers, not only recent ones such as Plotinus (see fig. 7-43) but also Plato, Aristotle, and their predecessors. The Imperial courts, both East and West, remained aware of their links with pre-Christian times. They collected vast numbers of original Greek works and Roman copies, so that they became centers for classicizing tendencies. Whatever its roots in any given case, classicism remained important during this age of transition.

IVORY DIPTYCHS. This lingering tradition is found especially in a class of objects whose artistic importance far exceeds their physical size: ivory panels and other small-scale reliefs in precious materials. Designed for private ownership and meant to be enjoyed at close range, they often mirror a collector's taste. Such a refined aesthetic sense is not found among the large works sponsored by Church or State. The ivory in figure 8-22 forms the right half of a hinged two-leaved tablet, or diptych, that was carved about 390 to 400. It was probably made for a wedding between the Nicomachi and Symmachi, two aristocratic Roman families. (The other half is poorly preserved.) The conservatism of this piece is reflected not only in the pagan subject (a priestess of Bacchus and her assistant before an altar of Jupiter) but also in the design, which harks back to the era of Augustus (compare fig. 7-32). At first glance, we might well mistake it for a much earlier work. But we soon realize, from such details as the priestess's right foot overlapping the frame, that these forms are quotations from earlier examples. Although they have been reproduced with loving care, they are no longer fully understood. It is noteworthy that the pagan theme did not prevent our panel from being incorporated into the shrine of a saint many centuries later. Its cool perfection must have had an appeal for viewers in the Middle Ages.

Our second ivory (fig. 8-23) was done soon after 500 in the eastern Roman Empire. It shows a classicism that has become an eloquent vehicle for Christian content. The majestic archangel is a descendant of the winged Victories of Graeco-Roman art, down to the rich drapery (see fig. 5-57). Yet the power he heralds is not of this world, nor does he inhabit an earthly space. The niche against which he appears has lost all three-dimensional reality. Its relationship to him is purely symbolic and ornamental, so that he seems to hover rather than to stand (notice the position of the feet on the steps). It is this disembodied quality, conveyed through harmonious forms, that makes his presence so compelling.

PORTRAITURE. Monumental statuary, though discouraged by the Church, retained the support of the State, at least for a while. Emperors, consuls, and high officials erected portrait statues of themselves in public places as late as the reign of Justinian (527–65), and sometimes later than that. (The last recorded case is in the late eighth century.) During the latter half of the fourth century and the early years of the fifth, there was a revival of pre-

8-22. *Priestess of Bacchus.* Leaf of a diptych. c. 390–400 A.D. Ivory, $11\frac{3}{4}$ x $5\frac{1}{2}$" (30 x 14 cm). Victoria & Albert Museum, London

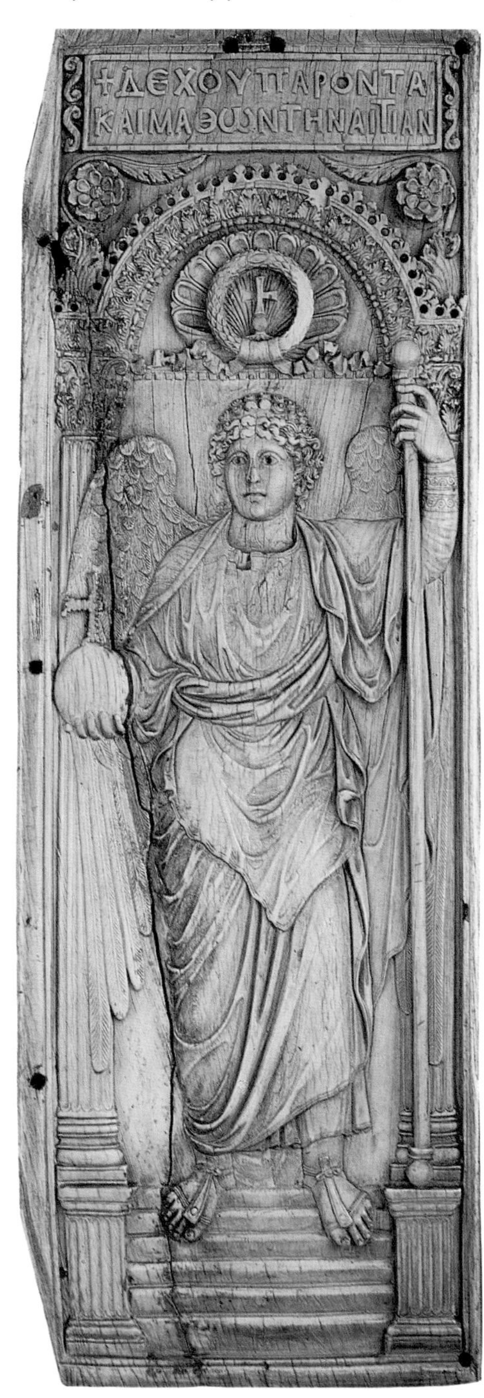

8-23. *The Archangel Michael.* Leaf of a diptych. Early 6th century A.D. Ivory, 17 x $5\frac{1}{2}$" (43.3 x 14 cm). The British Museum, London

Constantinian types and a renewed interest in individual appearances. From about 450 on, however, the outward likeness gives way to the image of a spiritual ideal. Sometimes these images were highly expressive, but they became increasingly impersonal. There would be no more portraits in the Graeco-Roman sense for almost a thousand years.

The process can be seen in the head of Eutropios from Ephesus (fig. 8-24), among the most striking of its kind. It reminds us of the sorrowful features of Plotinus and the colossal head of Constantine (see figs. 7-43 and 7-45). But both of these have a concreteness that seems almost overwhelming compared to the extreme attenuation of Eutropios. Here the face is frozen in visionary ecstasy, as if the sitter were a hermit saint. It looks, in fact, more like that of a specter than that of a being of flesh and

THE LIFE OF JESUS

Events in the life of Jesus, from his birth through his ascension to Heaven, are traditionally grouped in cycles, each with numerous episodes. The scenes most frequently depicted in European art are presented here.

INCARNATION CYCLE AND THE CHILDHOOD OF JESUS
These episodes concern Jesus' conception, birth, infancy, and youth.

ANNUNCIATION. The archangel Gabriel tells Mary that she will bear God's son. The Holy Spirit, shown usually as a dove, represents the Incarnation, the miraculous conception.

VISITATION. The pregnant Mary visits her older cousin, Elizabeth, who is to bear John the Baptist and who is the first to recognize the divine nature of the baby Mary is carrying.

NATIVITY. At the birth of Jesus, the Holy Family—Mary, his foster father Joseph, and the child—is usually depicted in a stable or, in Byzantine representations, in a cave.

ANNUNCIATION TO THE SHEPHERDS AND ADORATION OF THE SHEPHERDS. An angel announces the birth of Jesus to shepherds in the field at night. The shepherds then go to the birthplace to pay homage to the child.

ADORATION OF THE MAGI. The Magi, wise men from the East (called the three kings in the Middle Ages), follow a bright star for 12 days until they find the Holy Family and present their precious gifts to the Infant Jesus.

PRESENTATION IN THE TEMPLE. Mary and Joseph take the baby Jesus to the Temple in Jerusalem, where Simeon, a devout man, and Anna, a prophetess, foresee Jesus' messianic (savior's) mission and martyr's death.

MASSACRE OF THE INNOCENTS AND FLIGHT INTO EGYPT. King Herod orders all children under the age of two in and around Bethlehem killed to preclude his being murdered by a rival newborn king. The Holy Family flees to Egypt.

PUBLIC MINISTRY CYCLE

BAPTISM. John the Baptist baptizes Jesus in the Jordan River, recognizing Jesus' incarnation as the Son of God. This marks the beginning of Jesus' ministry.

CALLING OF MATTHEW. A tax collector, Matthew, becomes Jesus' first disciple (apostle) when Jesus calls to him, "Follow me."

JESUS WALKING ON THE WATER. During a storm, Jesus walks on the water of the Sea of Galilee to reach his apostles in a boat.

RAISING OF LAZARUS. Jesus brings his friend Lazarus back to life four days after Lazarus' death and burial.

DELIVERY OF THE KEYS TO PETER. Jesus names the apostle Peter his successor by giving him the keys to the kingdom of Heaven.

TRANSFIGURATION. As Jesus' closest disciples watch, God transforms Jesus into a dazzling vision and proclaims him to be his own son.

CLEANSING THE TEMPLE. Enraged, Jesus clears the Temple of moneychangers and animal traders.

PASSION CYCLE
The Passion (from *passio,* Latin for suffering) cycle relates Jesus' death, resurrection from the dead, and ascension into Heaven.

ENTRY INTO JERUSALEM. Welcomed by crowds as the Messiah, Jesus rides an ass into Jerusalem.

LAST SUPPER. At the Passover seder, Jesus tells his disciples of his impending death and lays the foundation for the Christian rite of the Eucharist: the taking of bread and wine in remembrance of Christ. (Strictly speaking, Jesus is called Jesus until he leaves his earthly physical form, after which he is called Christ.)

JESUS WASHING THE DISCIPLES' FEET. Following the Last Supper, Jesus washes the feet of his disciples to demonstrate humility.

AGONY IN THE GARDEN. In Gethsemane, the disciples sleep while Jesus wrestles with his mortal dread of suffering and dying.

BETRAYAL (ARREST). Disciple Judas Iscariot takes money to identify Jesus to Roman soldiers. Jesus is arrested.

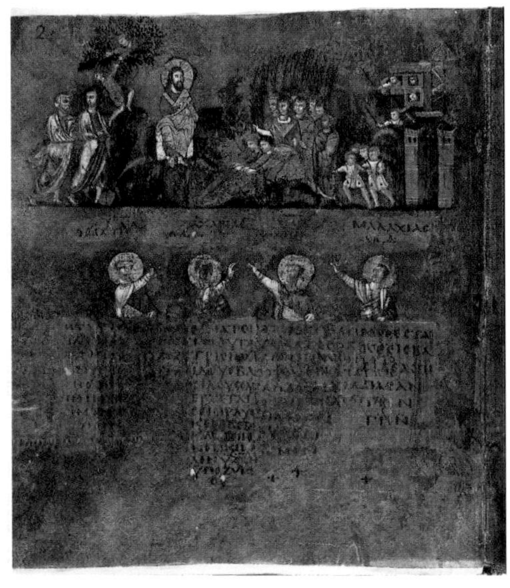

The Entry into Jerusalem, from the Codex Purpureus. 6th century. Illuminated parchment fol. 11. Diocesan Museum of Sacred Art, Duomo Rossano, Italy

blood. The avoidance of solid volumes has been carried so far that the features are for the most part indicated only by thin ridges or shallow lines. Their smooth curves emphasize the elongated oval of the head and thus reinforce its abstract, otherworldly character. Not only the individual person but the human body itself has ceased to be a tangible reality here—and with that the Greek tradition of sculpture in the round has reached the end of the road.

DENIAL OF PETER. As Jesus predicted, Peter, waiting outside the High Priest's palace, denies knowing Jesus three times, as Jesus is being questioned by the high priest, Caiaphas.

JESUS BEFORE PILATE. Jesus is questioned by the Roman governor Pontius Pilate regarding whether he calls himself King of the Jews. Jesus does not answer. Pilate reluctantly condemns him.

FLAGELLATION (SCOURGING). Jesus is whipped by Roman soldiers.

JESUS CROWNED WITH THORNS (THE MOCKING OF CHRIST). Pilate's soldiers mock Jesus by dressing him in robes, crowning him with thorns, and calling him King of the Jews.

CARRYING OF THE CROSS (ROAD TO CALVARY). Jesus carries the wooden cross on which he will be executed from Pilate's house to the hill of Golgotha, "the place of the skull."

CRUCIFIXION. Jesus is nailed to the cross by his hands and feet and dies after great physical suffering.

DESCENT FROM THE CROSS (DEPOSITION). Jesus' followers lower his body from the cross and wrap it for burial. Also present are the Virgin, the apostle John, and, in some accounts, Mary Magdalen.

LAMENTATION (*PIETÀ* OR *VESPERBILD*). The griefstricken followers gather around Jesus' body. In the *Pietà,* his body lies in the lap of the Virgin.

ENTOMBMENT. The Virgin and others place the wrapped body in a sarcophagus, or a rock tomb.

DESCENT INTO LIMBO (HARROWING OF HELL OR *ANASTASIS* IN THE ORTHODOX CHURCH). Christ descends to Hell, or limbo, to free deserving souls who have not heard the Christian message—the prophets of the Old Testament, the Kings of Israel, and Adam and Eve.

RESURRECTION. Christ rises from the dead on the third day after his entombment.

THE MARYS AT THE TOMB. As terrified soldiers look on, Christ's female followers (the Virgin Mary, Mary Magdalen, and Mary, mother of the apostle James) discover the empty tomb.

***NOLI ME TANGERE*, SUPPER AT EMMAUS, DOUBTING OF THOMAS.** In three episodes during the 40 days between his resurrection and ascent into Heaven, Christ tells Mary Magdalen not to touch him (*Noli me tangere*); shares a supper with his disciples at Emmaus; and invites the apostle Thomas to touch the lance wound in his side.

ASCENSION. As his disciples watch, Christ is taken into Heaven from the Mount of Olives.

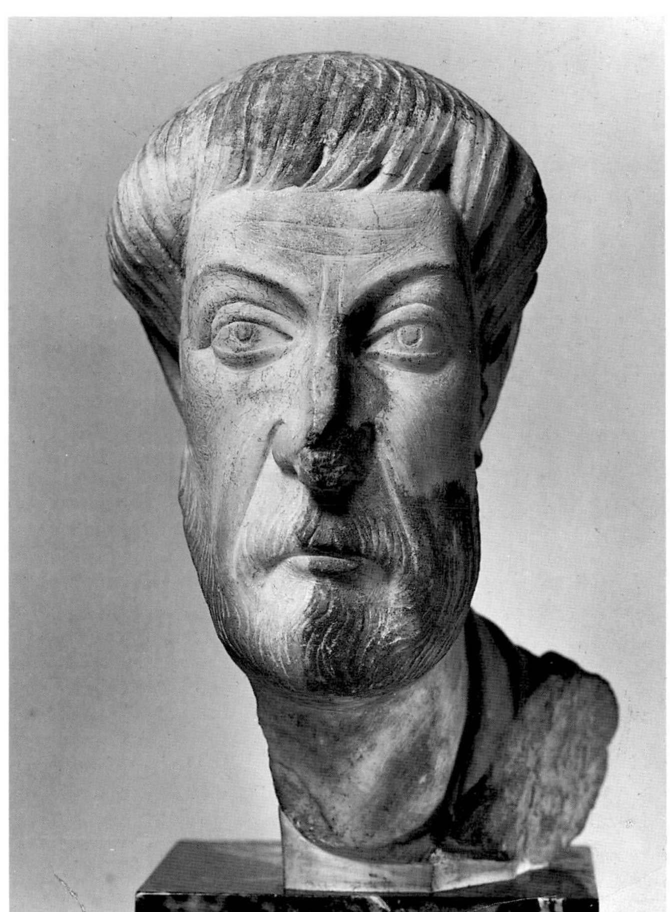

8-24. *Portrait of Eutropios.* c. 450 A.D. Marble, height 12½" (31.7 cm). Kunsthistorisches Museum, Vienna

BYZANTINE ART

Early Byzantine Art

There is no clear-cut line between Early Christian and Byzantine art. It could be argued that a Byzantine style (that is, a style linked to the Imperial court of Constantinople) can be seen in Early Christian art as early as the beginning of the fifth century, soon after the division of the Empire. However, we have avoided making this distinction. East Roman and West Roman—or, as some scholars prefer to call them, Eastern and Western Christian—characteristics are difficult to separate before the sixth century. Until that time, both areas contributed to the development of Early Christian art, but as the West declined, the leadership tended to shift to the East. This process was completed during the reign of Justinian. Constantinople not only reasserted its political dominance but became the artistic capital as well. Justinian himself was an art patron on a scale unmatched since Constantine's day. The works he sponsored have a grandeur that justifies the claim that his era was a golden age. They also display a unity of style that links them more strongly with the future development of Byzantine art than with the art of the past.

S. VITALE, RAVENNA. The finest Early Byzantine monuments survive not in Constantinople, where much has been destroyed, but in the town of Ravenna in Italy. The most important church of that time, S. Vitale, was begun by Bishop Ecclesius in 526, just before Theodoric's death. It was continued under Bishop Ursicinus and Bishop Victor, but built chiefly in 540–47 under Bishop Maximianus, who also consecrated S. Apollinare in Classe two years later (see figs. 8-13–8-15). S. Vitale is dedicated to a minor figure whose body was rediscovered by St. Ambrose at Bologna. Its structure is of a type derived mainly from Constantinople. Its plan shows only the barest remnants of the longitudinal axis of the Early Christian basilica. Toward the east is a cross-vaulted compartment for the altar, backed by an apse. On the other side is a narthex, whose odd, nonsymmetrical placement has never been fully accounted for. Otherwise the plan is octagonal with a domed central core (figs. 8-25–8-28), which makes it a descendant of the mausoleum of Sta. Costanza in Rome (see figs. 8-7–8-9). However, the intervening development seems to have taken place in the East,

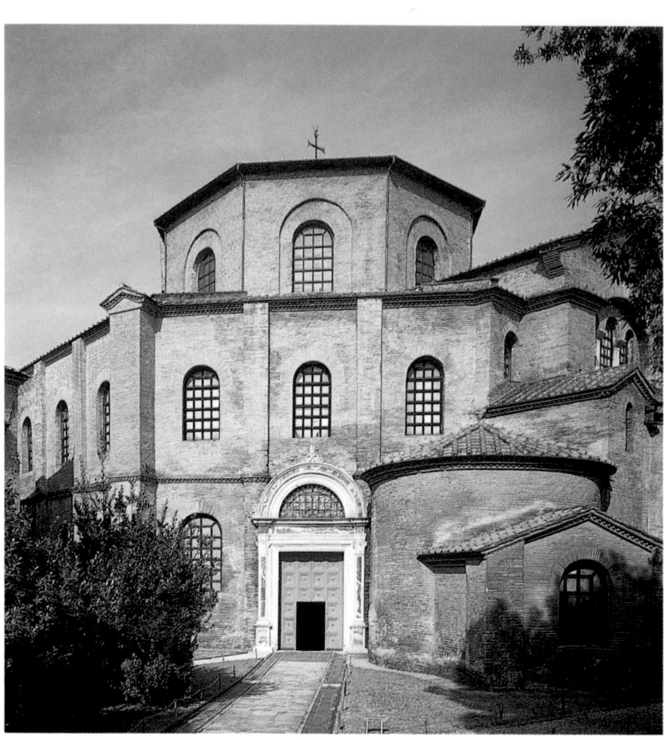

8-25. S. Vitale, Ravenna. 526–47 A.D.

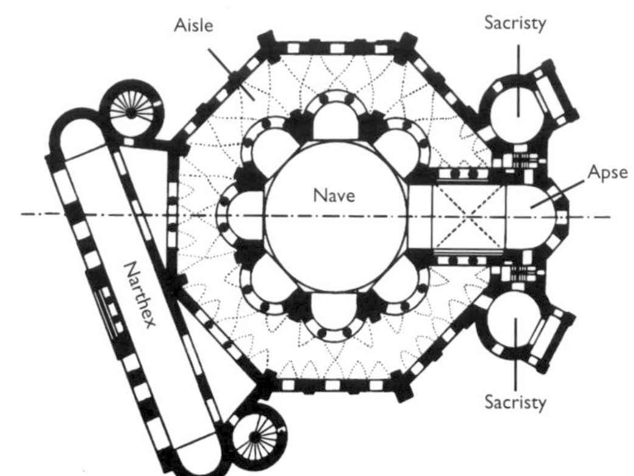

8-26. Plan of S. Vitale

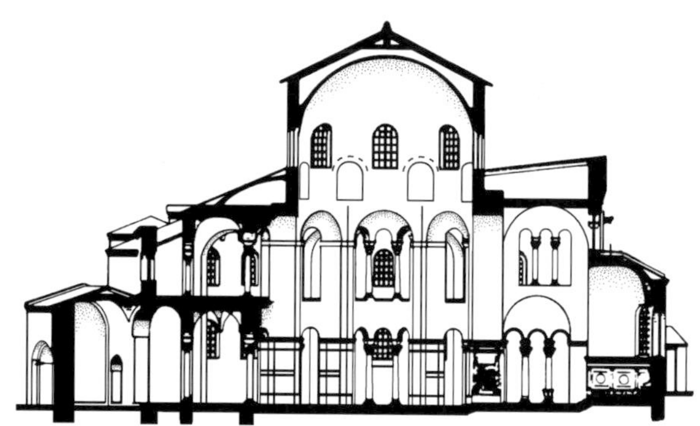

8-27. Transverse section of S. Vitale

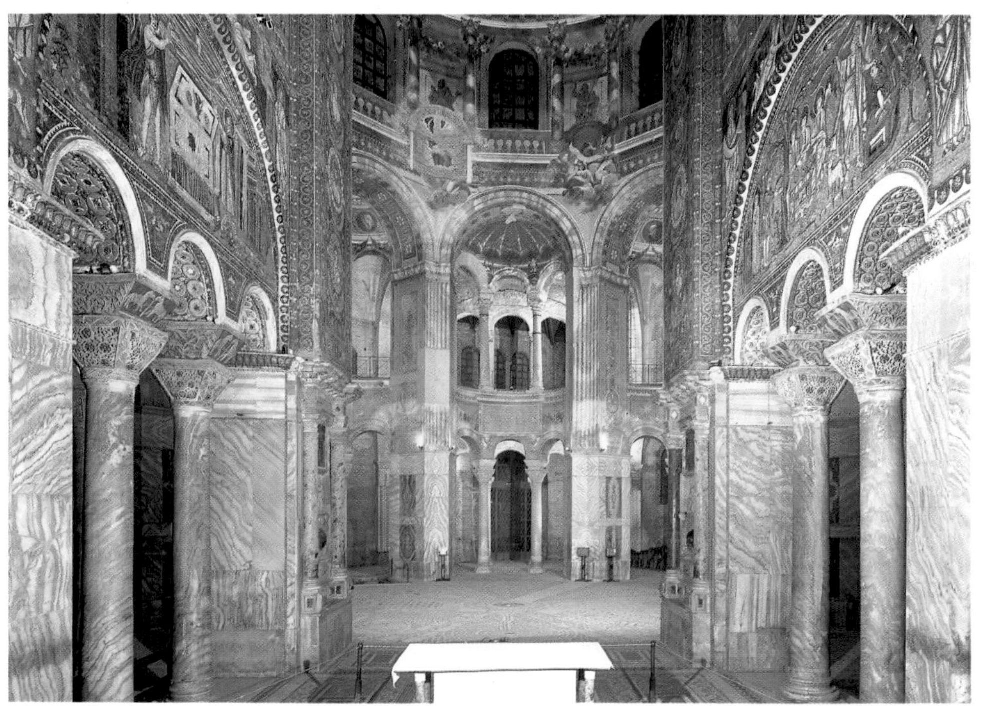

8-28. Interior (view from the apse into the choir), S. Vitale

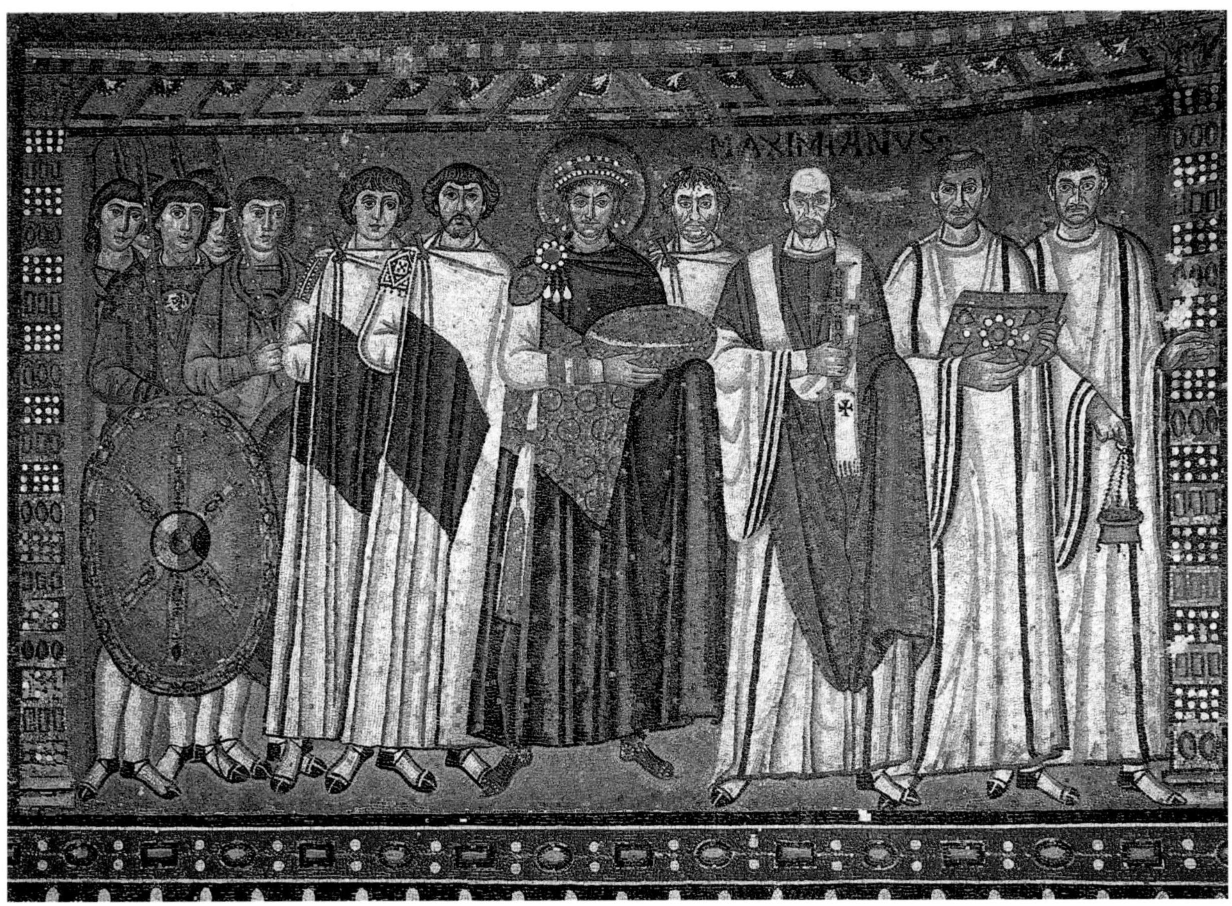

8-29. *Emperor Justinian and His Attendants.* c. 547 A.D. Mosaic. S. Vitale

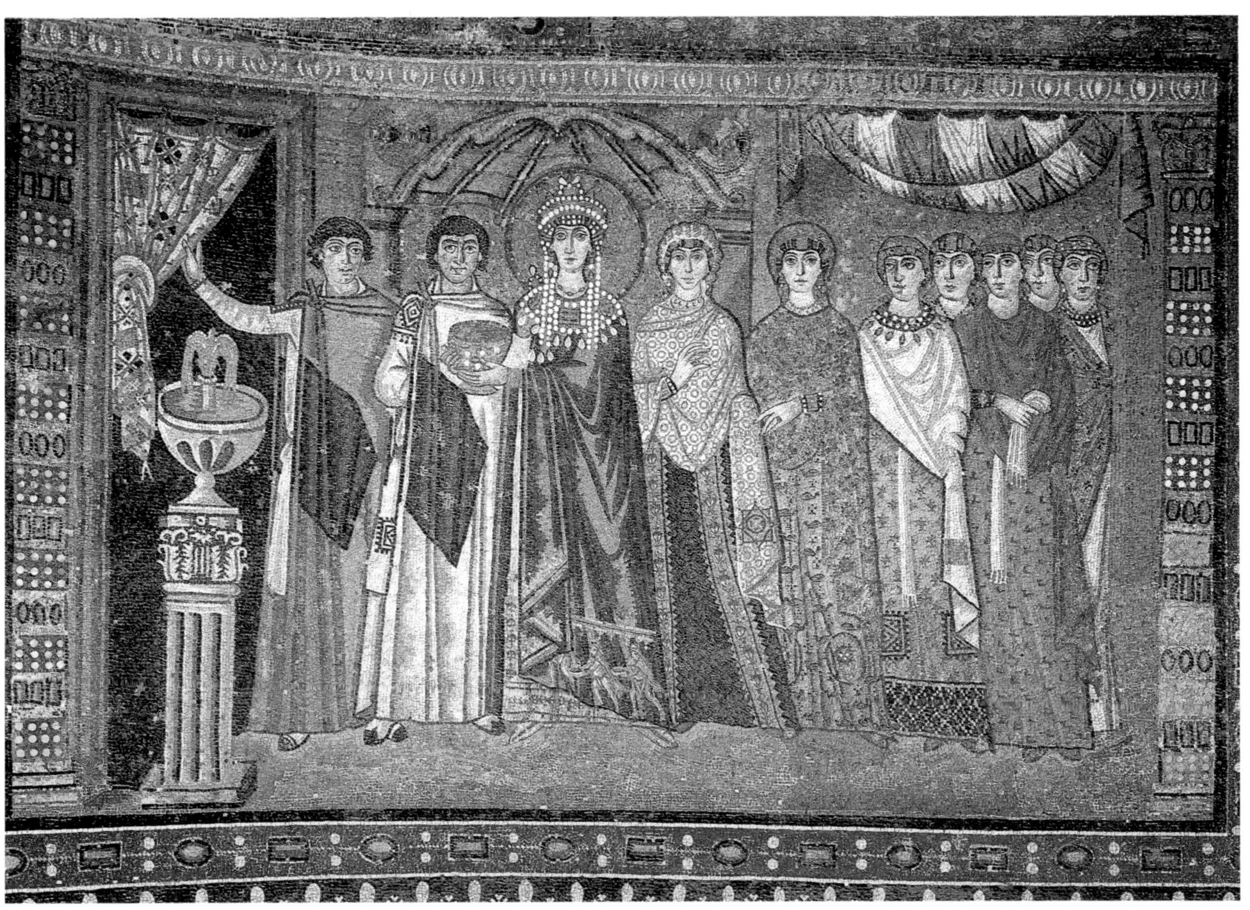

8-30. *Empress Theodora and Her Attendants.* c. 547 A.D. Mosaic. S. Vitale

where domed churches of various kinds had been built during the previous century.

When we recall S. Apollinare in Classe (see figs. 8-13–8-15), built at the same time on a straightforward basilican plan with funds from the same donor, we are struck by how different S. Vitale is. How did it happen that the East favored a type of church building (as distinct from baptisteries and mausoleums) so different from the basilica? A number of reasons have been suggested: practical, religious, political. All of them may be relevant, but none is fully persuasive. After all, the design of the basilica had been backed by the authority of Constantine; yet it was never as popular in the East as it had been in the West since early Imperial times. Moreover, it was Constantine who built the first central-plan churches in Constantinople, thereby helping to establish the preference for the type in the East. In any case, domed, central-plan churches were to dominate the world of Orthodox Christianity as thoroughly as the basilican plan dominated the architecture of the medieval West.

Compared to Sta. Costanza, S. Vitale is larger in scale and much richer in its spatial effect (see fig. 8-28). The circular nave is ringed by an aisle. Below the clerestory, this central space turns into a series of semicircular niches that penetrate into the aisle and thus link it to the nave in a new way. The aisle itself has a second story: the galleries may have been reserved for women. A new economy in the construction of the vaulting permits large windows on every level, which flood the interior with light. The complexity of the interior is matched by its lavish decoration.

S. Vitale's link with the Byzantine court can be seen in the two famous mosaics flanking the altar (figs. 8-29 and 8-30). They depict Justinian and his empress, Theodora, accompanied by officials, the local clergy, and ladies-in-waiting. Although they did not attend the actual event, the royal couple is shown as present at the consecration of S. Vitale. The purpose is to demonstrate their authority over Church and State, as well as their support for their archbishop, Maximianus, who at first was not unpopular with the citizens of Ravenna. In these large panels, whose design most likely came from the Imperial workshop, we find an ideal of beauty quite different from the squat, large-headed figures we met in the art of the fourth and fifth centuries.

We have caught a few glimpses of this new ideal (see figs. 8-3, 8-22, and 8-23), but only now do we see it complete. The figures are tall and slim, with tiny feet, small almond-shaped faces dominated by huge eyes, and bodies that seem to be capable only of ceremonial gestures and the display of magnificent costumes. There is no hint of movement or change. The dimensions of time and earthly space have given way to an eternal present in the golden setting of Heaven. Hence, the solemn, frontal images seem to belong to a celestial rather than a secular court. This union of political and spiritual authority reflects the "divine kingship" of the Byzantine emperor. Justinian and Theodora are portrayed as analogous to Christ and the Virgin. The embroidery on the hem of Theodora's mantle (see fig. 8-30) shows the three Magi carrying their gifts to Mary and the newborn King. Justinian (see fig. 8-29) is flanked by 12 companions—the equivalent of the 12 apostles. (Six are soldiers, crowded behind a shield with the monogram of Christ.)

Justinian, Theodora, and their neighbors were surely meant to be individual likenesses, and their features are indeed differentiated to some degree—especially those of Maximianus and Julianus Argentarius, the banker who underwrote the building. But the ideal has molded the faces as well as the bodies, so that they all resemble one another. We shall meet the same large dark eyes under curved brows, the same small mouths, and the same long, narrow noses countless times from now on in Byzantine art. As we turn from these mosaics to the interior space, we realize that it, too, shares the quality of dematerialized, soaring slenderness that endows the figures with an air of mute exaltation.

HAGIA SOPHIA, ISTANBUL. Among the surviving monuments of Justinian's reign in Constantinople, the most important by far is Hagia Sophia (Church of Holy Wisdom). The architectural masterpiece of its era, Hagia Sophia is one of the great creative triumphs of any age (figs. 8-31, 8-32, 8-34–8-36). The first church, begun by Constantine II and finished in 360, was destroyed during rioting in 404. Its replacement, built by Theodosius II within a decade, suffered the same fate in the riots of 532 that almost deposed Justinian, who immediately rebuilt it. Completed in only five years, Hagia Sophia achieved such fame that the names of the architects, too, were remembered: Anthemius of

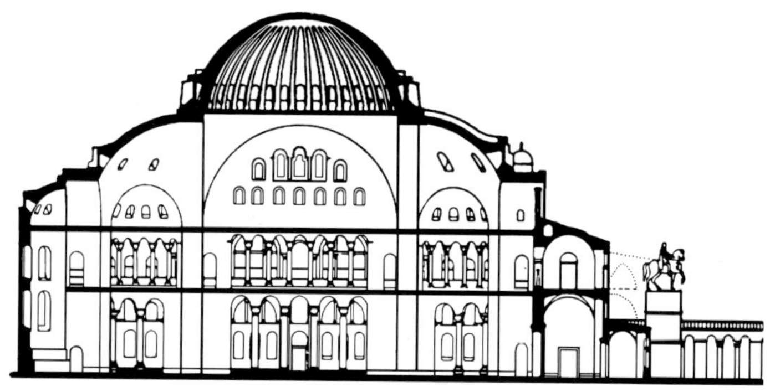

8-31. Section of Hagia Sophia (after Gurlitt)

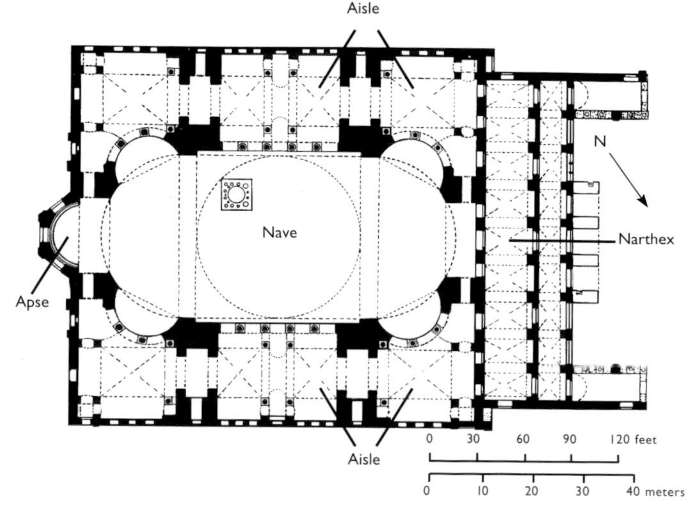

8-32. Plan of Hagia Sophia (after v. Sybel)

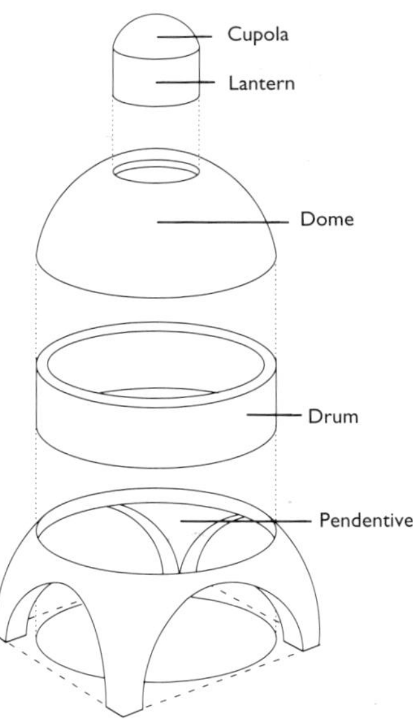

8-33. Parts of a dome

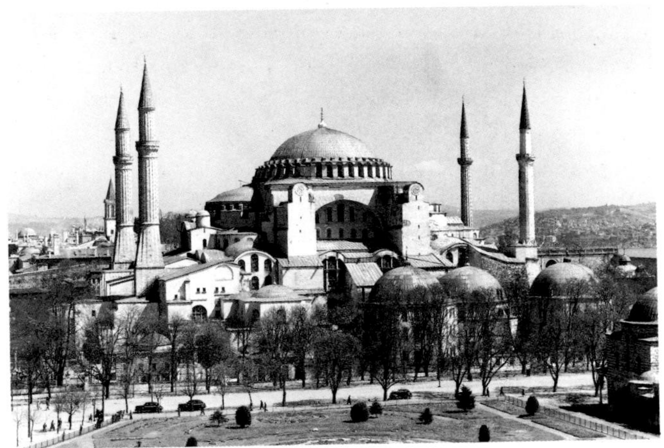

8-34. Anthemius of Tralles and Isidorus of Miletus. Hagia Sophia, Istanbul, Turkey. 532–37 A.D.

Tralles, an expert in geometry and the theory of statics and kinetics, and Isidorus of Miletus, who taught physics and wrote on vaulting techniques. After the Turkish conquest in 1453, the church became a mosque (the four minarets were added then) and the mosaic decoration was largely hidden under whitewash. Some of the mosaics were uncovered in the twentieth century, after the building was turned into a museum (see fig. 8-46).

The design of Hagia Sophia presents a unique combination of elements. It has the longitudinal axis of an Early Christian basilica, but the central feature of the nave is a vast square space crowned by a huge dome. At either end are half-domes, so that the nave has the form of a great ellipse. Attached to the half-domes are semicircular niches with open arcades, similar to those in S. Vitale. One might say, then, that the domed central space of Hagia Sophia has been inserted between the two halves of a divided central-plan church. The dome rests on four arches that carry its weight to the large piers at the corners of the square. Thus, the walls below the arches have no supporting function at all. The transition from the square formed by the arches to the circular rim of the dome is achieved by curved triangles called pendentives (see fig. 8-33). Hence, we speak of the entire unit as a dome on pendentives. This device, along with a new technique for building domes using thin bricks embedded in mortar, permits the construction of taller, lighter, and more economical domes than the older method (seen in the Pantheon, Sta. Costanza, and S. Vitale) of placing the dome on a round or polygonal base. Where or when the dome on pendentives was invented we do not know. Hagia Sophia is the earliest case we have of its use on a monumental scale, and it had a lasting impact. It became a basic feature of Byzantine architecture and, somewhat later, of Western architecture as well.

There is, however, still another element that entered into the design of Hagia Sophia. The plan, the buttressing of the main piers, and the huge scale of the whole recall the Basilica of Constantine (see figs. 7-16–7-18), the most ambitious achievement of Imperial Roman vaulted architecture and the greatest monument associated with a ruler for whom Justinian had particular admiration. Hagia Sophia thus unites East and West, past and future, in a single overpowering synthesis. Its massive exterior, firmly planted upon the earth like a great mound, rises by stages to a height of 184 feet—41 feet higher than the Pantheon—and therefore its dome, although its diameter is somewhat smaller (112 feet), stands out far more boldly. The dome improves on the Pantheon's, to which it is obviously indebted: the thinnest of ribs radiate from an oculus, which has been closed in, while the extremely lightweight construction made it possible to dispense with the rings altogether and to insert a row of windows around the base.

Once we are inside, all sense of weight disappears, as if the material, solid aspects of the structure had been banished to the outside. Nothing remains but a space that inflates, like so many sails, the apsidal recesses, the pendentives, and the dome itself. Here the architectural aesthetic we saw taking shape in Early Christian architecture (see pages 214–18) has achieved a new dimension. Even more than before, light plays a key role. The dome seems to float—"like the radiant heavens," according to a contemporary description—because it rests upon a closely spaced row of windows. The nave walls are pierced by so many openings that they have the transparency of lace curtains. Its purpose is clear. As Procopius, the court historian to Justinian, wrote: "Whenever one enters this church to pray, he understands at once that it is not by any human power or skill, but by the influence of God, that this work has been so finely turned. And so his mind is lifted up toward God and exalted, feeling that He cannot be far away, but must especially love to dwell in this place that He has chosen." [See Primary Sources, no. 16, pages 364–65.]

The glitter of the mosaics must have completed the "illusion of unreality." We can sense the new aesthetic even in ornamental

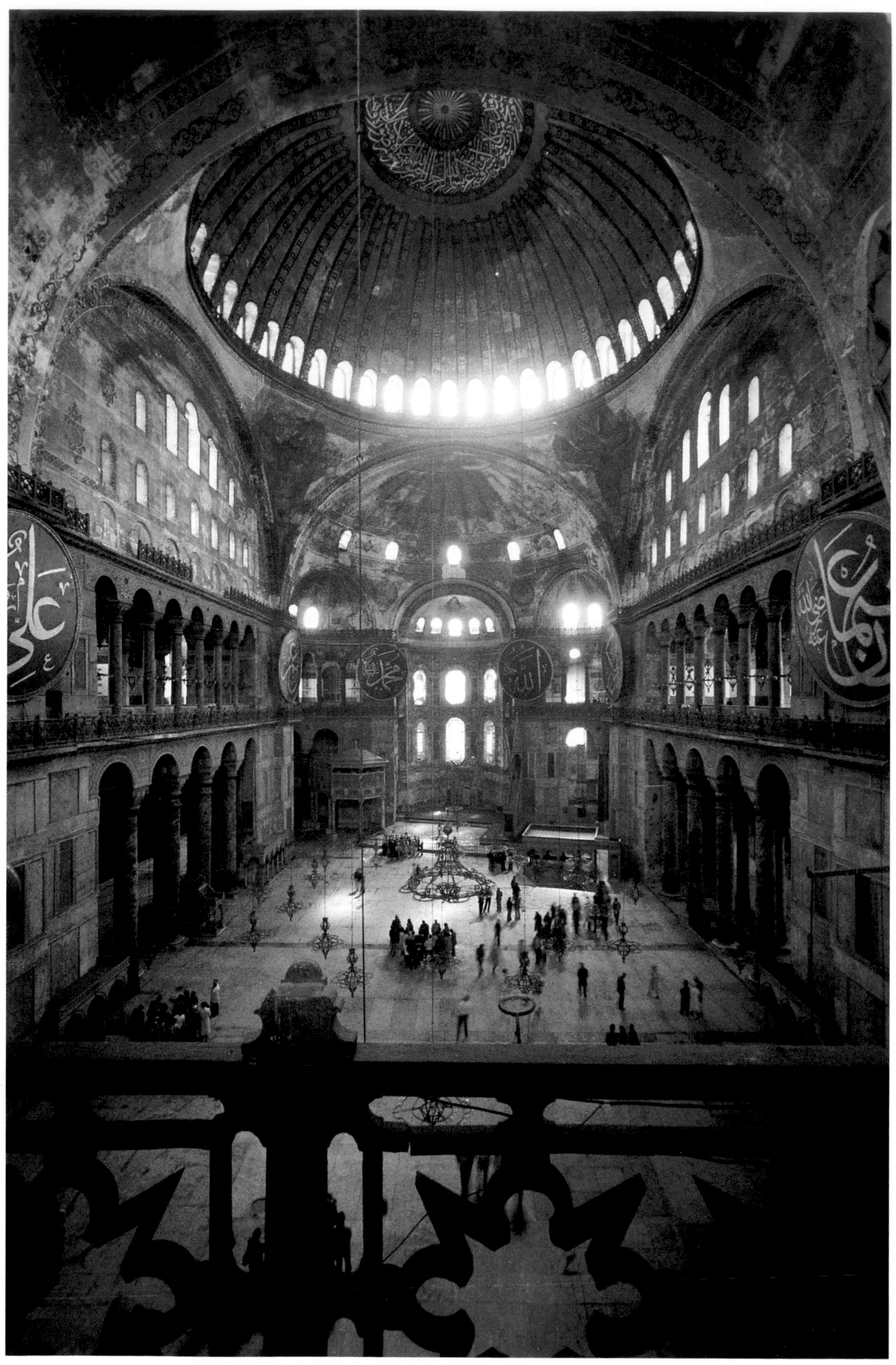

8-35. Interior, Hagia Sophia

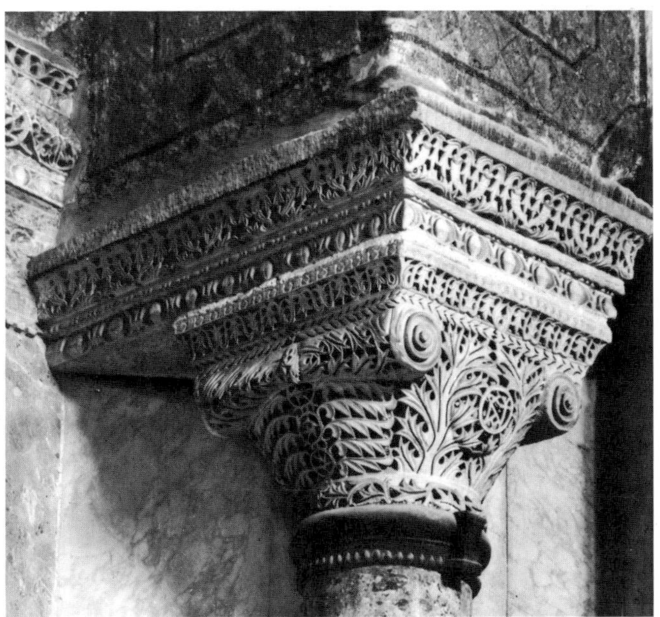

8-36. Capital, Hagia Sophia

details such as moldings and capitals (see fig. 8-36). The scrolls, acanthus leaves, and the like are motifs derived from classical architecture, but their effect is very different. Instead of actively cushioning the impact of heavy weight upon the shaft of the column, the capital has become a sort of openwork basket whose delicate surface pattern belies the strength and solidity of the stone.

THE THRONE OF MAXIMIANUS. Beyond architectural decorations and some sarcophagi, early Byzantine sculpture consists mainly of reliefs in ivory and silver, which survive in considerable numbers. Not surprisingly, they share characteristics with the capitals at Hagia Sophia, as we can see from the *Throne of Maximianus* (fig. 8-37). This magnificent episcopal chair (or *cathedra*) is covered with ivory panels (some are later replacements) that depict the infancy of Christ (on the backrest), the story of Joseph in Egypt (on the sides), and John the Baptist flanked by the four evangelists (on the front). They are embedded in strips of the most luxurious ornamentation covered with lacy foliage, including clusters of grapes, and inhabited by lions, stags, peacocks, and other creatures.

Considering its size, it is likely that the throne was the work of several people of outstanding ability who had been summoned to Constantinople from around the Empire by the court. It was probably a gift from Justinian to Maximianus, the archbishop of Ravenna, upon the dedication of S. Vitale. We are assured that it was made at the Byzantine court not only by its quality but also by the style of the Baptist and his companions, which echoes the classicism of *The Archangel Michael* (see fig. 8-23) yet also conforms to the aristocratic ideal of the S. Vitale mosaics (see figs. 8-29 and 8-30), with its flattened forms. The arcade with frontal figures, derived from sarcophagi, was to have a long life: it is found on nearly all metal reliefs and ivory carvings (especially book covers) throughout the Romanesque era.

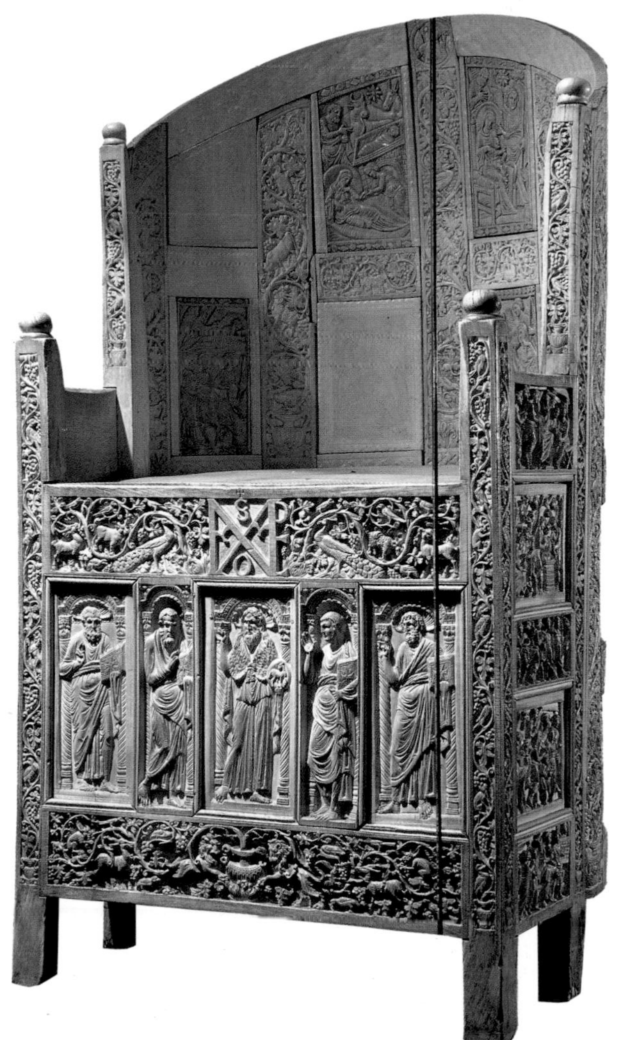

8-37. *Throne of Maximianus*. c. 547. Ivory over wood, 59 x 23½" (149.8 x 59.7 cm). Archiepiscopal Museum, Ravenna

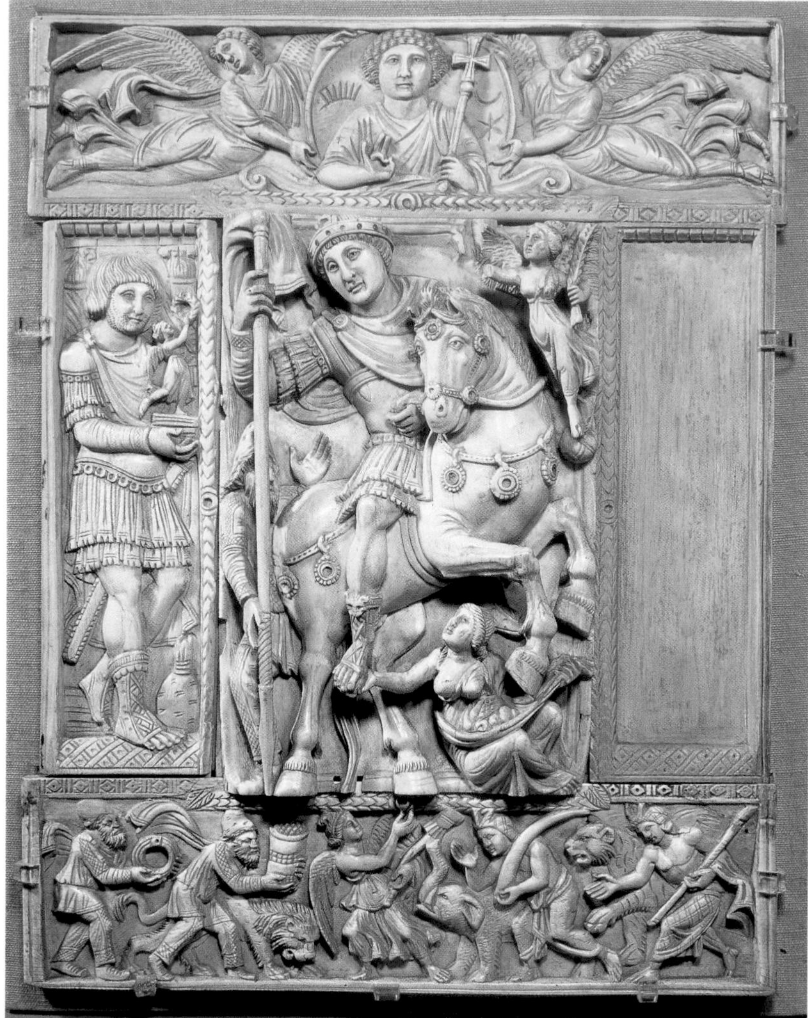

8-38. *Justinian as Conqueror.* c. 525–50 A.D. Ivory, 13½ x 10½" (34.2 x 26.8 cm). Musée du Louvre, Paris

THE JUSTINIAN DIPTYCH. The last vestiges of classicism can be seen in the beautifully carved diptych of Justinian as Conqueror (fig. 8-38), from about the same time as the throne, which celebrates Justinian's victories in Italy, North Africa, and Asia. The subject restates the allegorical scene on the breastplate of the *Augustus of Primaporta* in Christian terms (see fig. 7-28). The figure of Victory appears twice: above the emperor, to his right, and as a statuette held by the Roman general at the left, who no doubt was mirrored in the missing panel at the right. Scythians, Indians, even lions and elephants offer gifts and pay homage, while a figure personifying Earth supports Justinian's foot to signify his dominion over the entire world. His role as triumphant general and ruler of the Empire is blessed from Heaven by Christ (note the sun, moon, and star), whose image is carried in a medallion by two heraldically arranged angels. Despite their ancestry, the stubby figures are hardly classical in style. They remind us of Constantinian reliefs (compare fig. 7-47), but with an Oriental cast derived from the eastern provinces. The large head and bulging features of Justinian brim with the same energy as his charging steed. He is a far cry from the calm philosopher portrayed on the equestrian statue of Marcus Aurelius (see fig. 7-40), from which the image is derived.

ICONS. In the late sixth century, icons began to compete with relics as objects of personal, then public veneration. Icons are paintings of Christ, the Enthroned Madonna, or saints. From the beginning they were considered "portraits," and understandably so, for such pictures had developed in Early Christian times out of Graeco-Roman portrait panels. One of the chief arguments in their favor was the claim that Christ had appeared with the Virgin to St. Luke and permitted him to paint their portrait, and that other portraits of Christ or of the Virgin had miraculously appeared on earth by divine command. These "true" sacred images were considered to have been the source for the later, man-made ones. Little is known about their origins, for examples from before the Iconoclastic Controversy are extremely scarce (see below), but they no doubt developed in part from pagan icons, since both began to be painted around 200 A.D.

Of the few early examples, the most revealing is the *Virgin and Child Enthroned between Saints and Angels* (fig. 8-39). Like late Roman murals (see pages 184–87), it is painted in several styles. Its link with Graeco-Roman portraiture is clear not only from the use of encaustic (which was not used after the Iconoclastic Controversy) but also from the gradations of light and shade in the Virgin's face, which is similar in treatment to that of

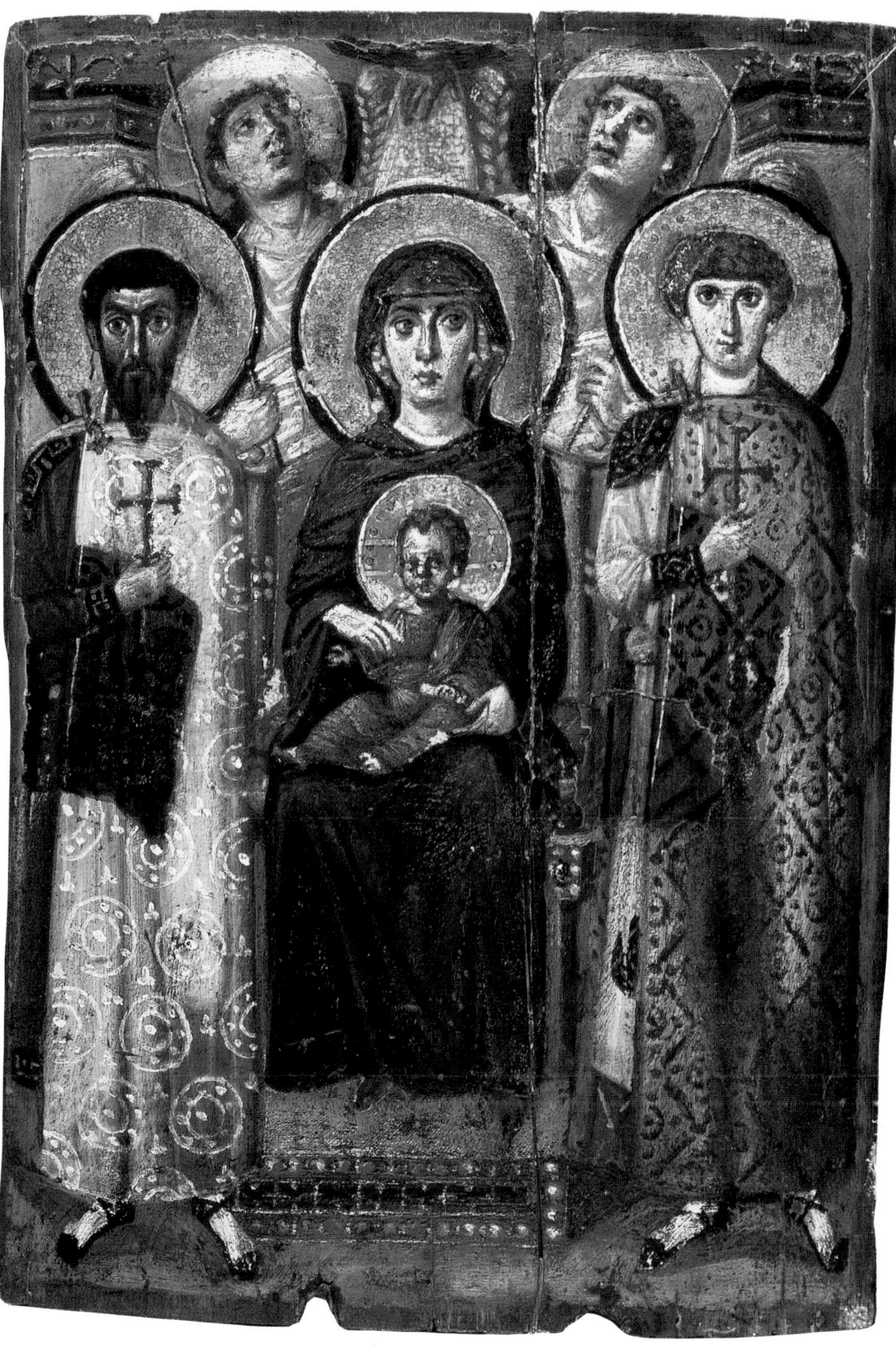

8-39. *Virgin and Child Enthroned between Saints and Angels.* Late 6th century A.D. Encaustic on panel, 27 x 19$^{3}/_{8}$" (68.5 x 49.2 cm). Monastery of St. Catherine, Mount Sinai, Egypt

the little boy in our Faiyum portrait (see fig. 7-55). She is flanked by the warrior saints Theodore on the left and George to the right, who recall the stiff figures that accompany Justinian in S. Vitale (see fig. 8-29). Typical of early icons, however, their heads are too massive for their doll-like bodies. Behind them are two angels who come closest to Roman art (compare the personification of Arcadia in fig. 7-54), although their lumpy features show that classicism is no longer a living tradition. Clearly these figures are quotations from different sources, so that the painting marks an early stage in the development of icons. Yet it is typical of the conservative icon tradition that the artist has tried to remain faithful to his sources, in order to preserve the likenesses of these holy figures. This icon, though not impressive in itself, is worthy of our attention because it is the earliest representation we have of the Madonna and Child. The motif itself was probably taken from the cult of Isis, which was popular in Egypt at the time of the Faiyum portraits. The regal Christ child probably evolved from images of the infant Dionysos. We note the stiff formality of the pose. To the Byzantines the Madonna was the regal mother, or bearer, of God (*Theotokos*), while Jesus is no mere infant but God in human form (*Logos*). [See Primary Sources, no. 18, pages 365–66.] Only later did she acquire the gentle maternal presence of the Virgin that is so familiar in Latin art (compare fig. 12-29).

Middle Byzantine Art

After the age of Justinian, the development of Byzantine art, not only painting and sculpture but architecture as well, was disrupted by the Iconoclastic Controversy, which began with an edict promulgated by Leo III in 726 prohibiting religious images. It raged for more than a hundred years between two hostile groups. The image-destroyers (Iconoclasts), led by the emperor and supported mainly in the eastern provinces, insisted on a literal interpretation of the biblical ban against graven images as leading to idolatry. They wanted to restrict religious art to abstract symbols and plant or animal forms. Their opponents, the Iconophiles, were led by the monks and centered in the western provinces, where the imperial edict was not very effective. The strongest argument in favor of icons proved to be Neo-Platonic: because Christ and his image are inseparable, the honor given to the image is transferred to him. [See Primary Sources no. 17, page 365.] The roots of the argument went very deep. On the plane of theology, they involved the basic issue of the relationship of the human and the divine in the person of Christ. Moreover, icons had come to replace the Eucharist as the focus of lay devotion because of the screen (*templon*) hung with icons separating the altar from the worshipers. Socially and politically, the conflict was a power struggle between Church and State, which in theory were united in the figure of the emperor. It came during a low point in Byzantine power, when the Empire had been greatly reduced in size by the rise of Islam. Iconoclasm seemed justified by Leo's victories over the Arabs, who were themselves iconoclasts. The controversy also caused an irreparable break between Catholicism and the Orthodox faith, although the two churches remained officially united until 1054, when the pope excommunicated the eastern patriarch for heresy.

If the edict could have been enforced throughout the Empire, it might well have dealt Byzantine religious art a fatal blow. It did succeed in greatly reducing the production of sacred images but failed to wipe it out entirely. Hence, after the victory of the Iconophiles in 843 under the empress Theodora there was a fairly rapid recovery. Spearheaded by Basil I the Macedonian, this restoration lasted from the late ninth to the eleventh century.

MONASTIC ARCHITECTURE. Byzantine architecture never produced another structure to match the scale of Hagia Sophia. The churches built after the Iconoclastic Controversy were initially modest in size and monastic in spirit. Most were built for small groups of monks living in isolated areas, although later monasteries erected in Constantinople under Imperial patronage were much larger and served social purposes by operating schools and hospitals. The two churches at the Monastery of Hosios Loukas in Greece are typical (figs. 8-40–8-42). (St. Luke of

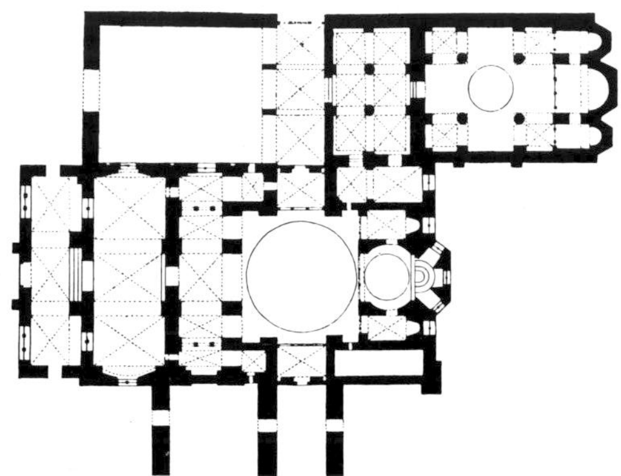

8-41. Plan of churches of the Monastery of Hosios Loukas (after Diehl)

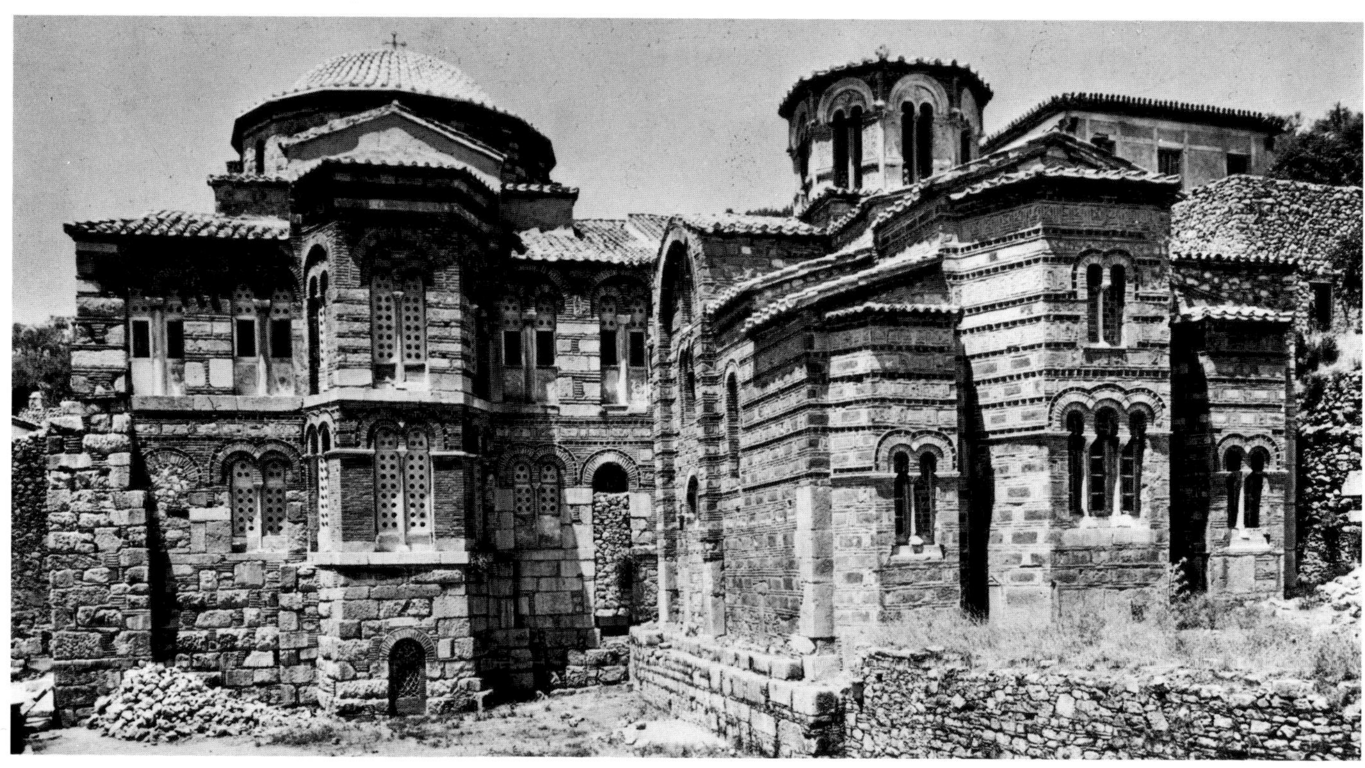

8-40. Churches of the Monastery of Hosios Loukas (St. Luke of Stiris), Greece. Early 11th century

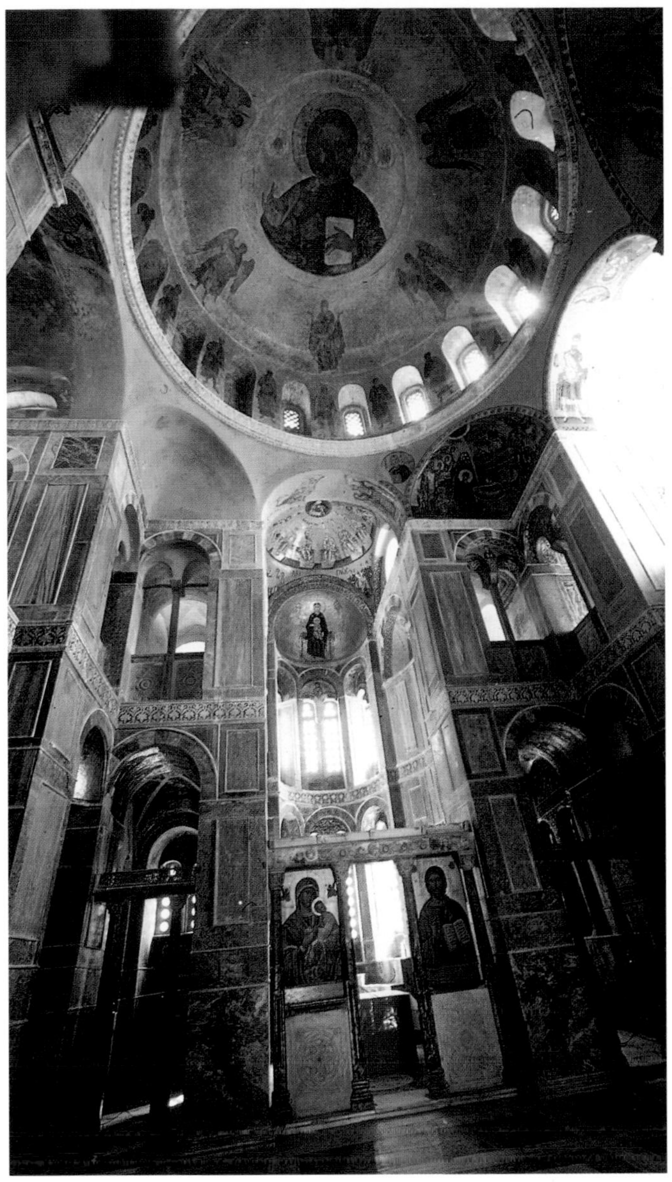

8-42. Interior, Katholikon, Hosios Loukas

Stiris was a much-venerated local hermit saint who died in 953.) The smaller of the two, the Panaghia Theotokos (All-Holy Mother of God), was built around 990 to replace the saint's martyrium. It served as the monastery's main church (*katholikon*) until the present Katholikon was erected early in the next century. They are joined at the hip, so to speak, in order to include St. Luke's grave. Both churches follow the usual Middle Byzantine plan of a Greek cross (that is, a cross with arms of equal length) contained in a square, with a narthex added on one side and an apse (sometimes with flanking chapels, as in the Panaghia) on the other. The central feature of such churches is a dome on a square base. It often rests on a cylindrical or octagonal drum with tall windows, which raises it high above the rest of the building. The monastery churches also show other features of later Byzantine architecture. One is a tendency toward more elaborate exteriors, in contrast to the severity we observed earlier (compare fig. 8-25). Another is a preference for elongated proportions, which was established by the Nea (New Church) completed by Basil I in Constantinople by 880. The full impact of this verticality, however, strikes us only when we enter the church (fig. 8-42 shows the interior of the Katholikon, on the left in figs. 8-40 and 8-41). The tall, narrow compartments produce both an unusually active space and a sense of crowdedness, almost of compression. This feeling is dramatically relieved as we raise our glance toward the luminous pool of space beneath the dome.

ST. MARK'S, VENICE. The largest and most lavishly decorated church of the period that survives today is St. Mark's in Venice, begun in 1063. The present structure is modeled on the Church of the Holy Apostles in Constantinople, which had been rebuilt by Justinian following the Nika riots and later destroyed; it replaced two earlier churches of the same name on the site. The Venetians had long been under Byzantine rule, and they remained artistically dependent on the East well after they had become politically and commercially powerful in their own right. St. Mark's, too, has the Greek-cross plan inscribed within a square, but here each arm

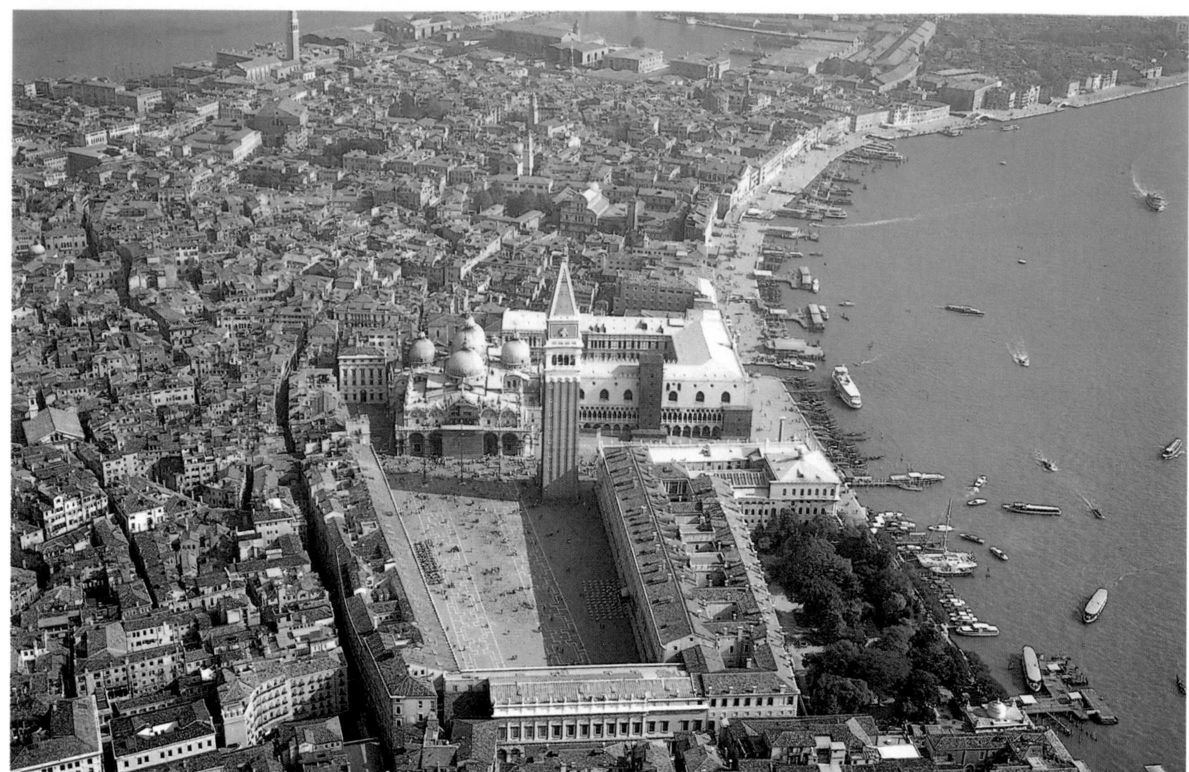

8-43. St. Mark's (aerial view), Venice. Begun 1063

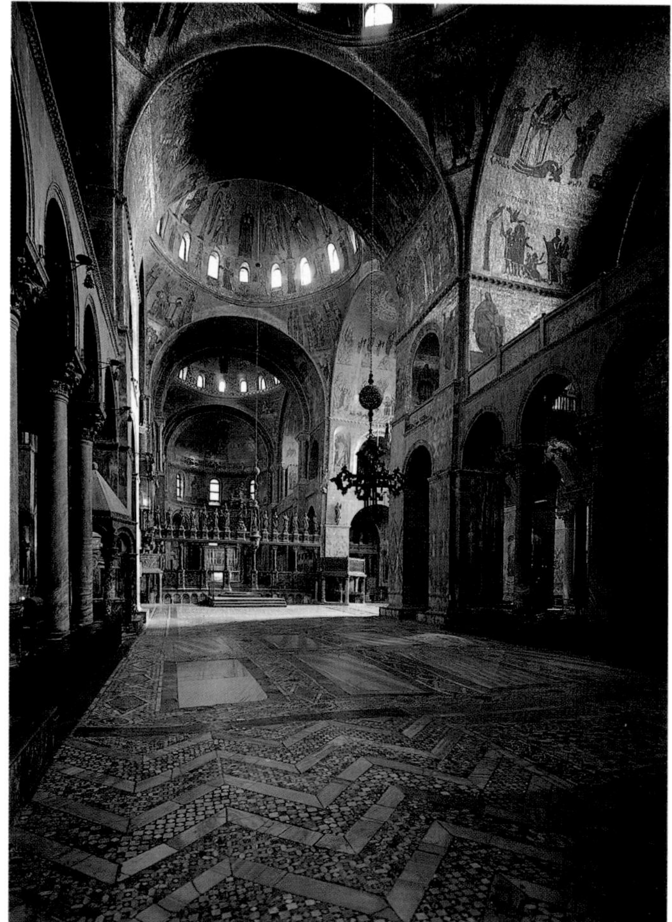

8-44. Interior, St. Mark's, Venice

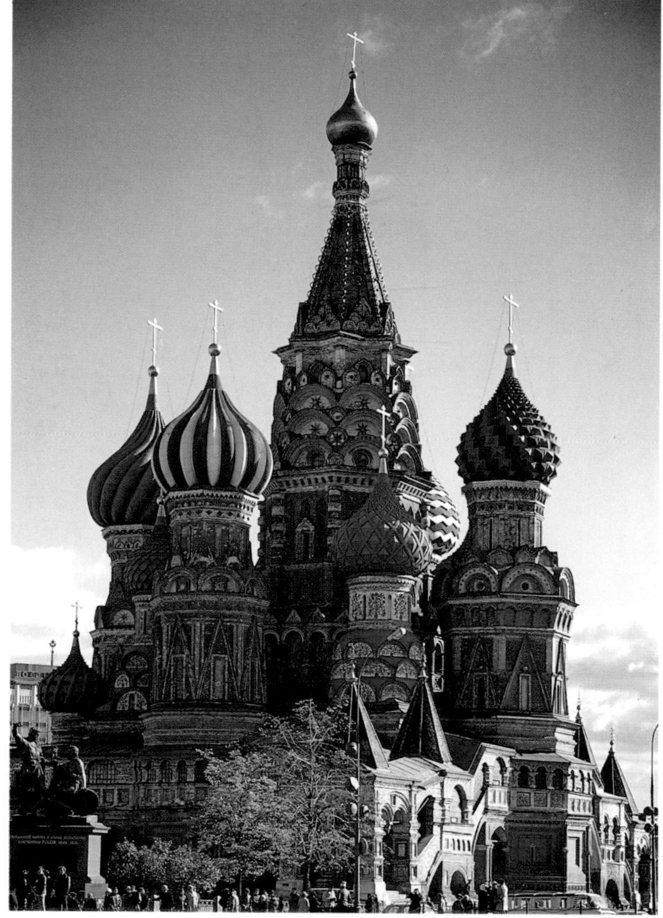

8-45. Cathedral of St. Basil, Moscow. 1554–60

of the cross is emphasized by a dome of its own (figs. 8-43 and 8-44). These domes are not raised on drums. Instead, they have been encased in bulbous wooden helmets covered by gilt copper sheeting and topped by ornate lanterns, so that they appear taller and more conspicuous at a distance. (They make a splendid landmark for seafarers.) The spacious interior, which is famous for its mosaics, shows that it was meant for the people of a large city rather than a small monastic community as at Hosios Loukas.

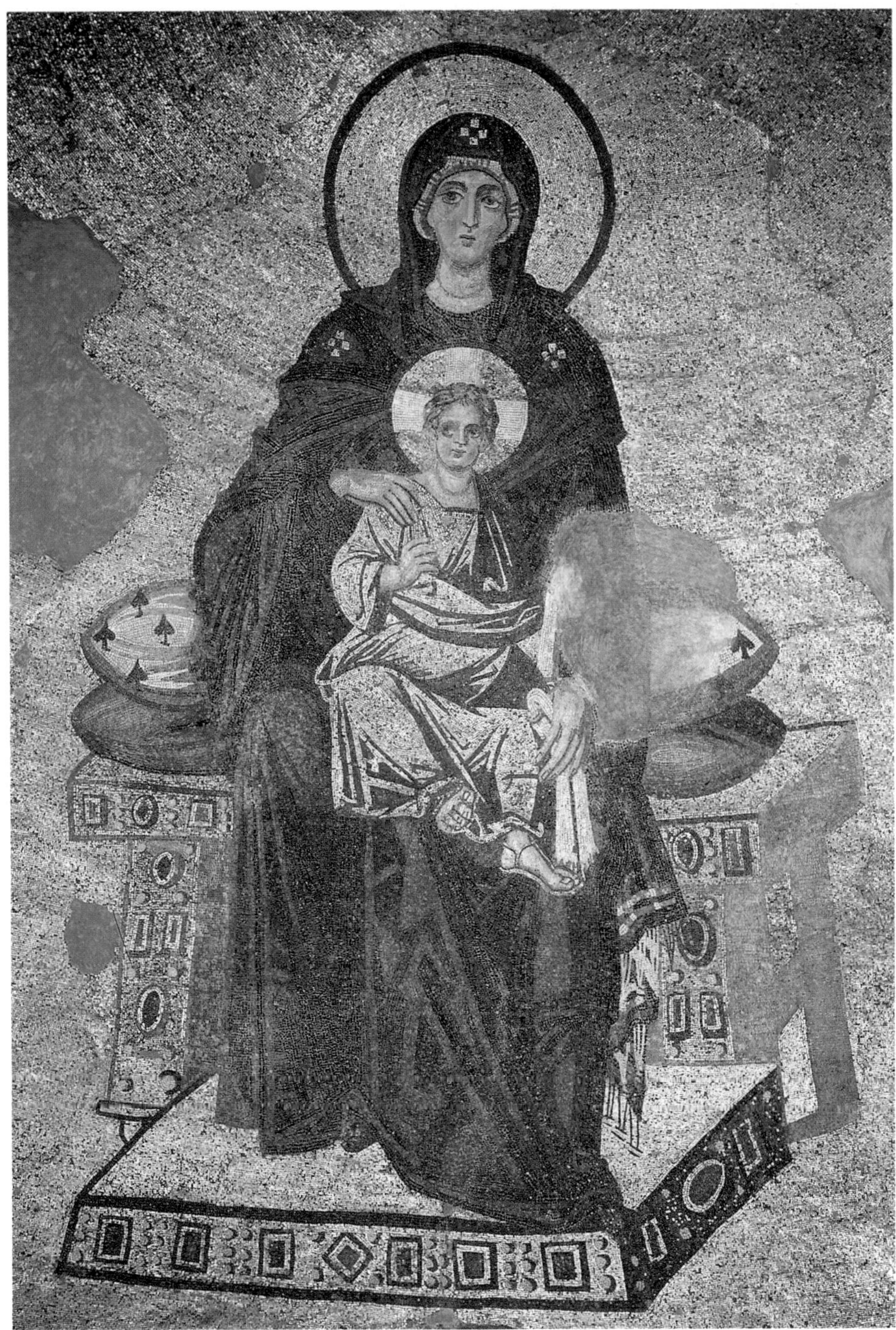

8-46. *Virgin and Child Enthroned.* c. 843–67. Mosaic. Hagia Sophia, Istanbul

ST. BASIL, MOSCOW. Byzantine architecture also spread to Russia, along with the Orthodox faith. There the basic type of the Byzantine church was transformed through the use of wood as a structural material. The most famous product of this native trend is the Cathedral of St. Basil adjoining the Kremlin in Moscow (fig. 8-45). Built during the reign of Ivan the Terrible, it seems as unmistakably Russian as that extraordinary ruler himself. The numerous domes have become fantastic towerlike structures as vividly patterned as the rest of the building. The total effect is extremely colorful. The church nevertheless conveys a sense of the miraculous that is derived from the more austere miracles of Byzantine architecture.

ORTHODOX REVIVAL. We know little about how the Byzantine artistic tradition managed to survive from the early eighth to the mid-ninth century, but survive it did. The most direct proof is the mosaic of the *Virgin and Child Enthroned* in Hagia Sophia (fig. 8-46). We know it was made sometime between the end of the Iconoclastic Controversy in 843 and 867, when it was unveiled to celebrate the triumph of Orthodoxy. It conforms to the earliest icon of the same subject (see fig. 8-39), and its subtle modeling and color are in the best tradition of Early Byzantine art. However, there is a new human quality in the fullness of the figures, the more relaxed poses, and their more natural expressions, which we have not seen before.

CLASSICAL REVIVAL. After Basil I reopened the university in Constantinople, there was a revival of classical learning, literature, and art. Much of it occurred in the early tenth century under Constantine VII, who was emperor in name only for most of his life, and consequently turned to classical scholarship and art. This renewed interest helps to explain the reappearance of Late Classical motifs in Middle Byzantine art. *David Composing the Psalms* (fig. 8-47) is one of eight full-page scenes in the so-called *Paris Psalter.* These scenes illustrating David's life introduce the Psalms (which David was thought to have composed). The psalter was probably illuminated about 900, although the temptation to date it earlier is almost irresistible. Not only do we find a landscape that recalls Pompeian murals, but the figures, too, are clearly derived from Roman models. David himself could well be mistaken for Orpheus charming the beasts with his music. His companions are even more surprising, since they are allegorical figures that have nothing to do with the Bible. The young woman next to David is Melody, the one coyly hiding behind a pillar is Echo, and the male figure with a tree trunk personifies the mountains of Bethlehem. The late date of the picture is evident only from certain qualities of style, such as the abstract zigzag pattern of the drapery covering Melody's legs.

DAPHNÉ. The *Paris Psalter* shows an almost antiquarian enthusiasm for the traditions of Classical art. Such a direct revival, however, is unusual. More often classicism is merged with the spiritualized ideal of human beauty we saw in the art of Justinian's reign. *The Crucifixion* mosaic in the Greek monastery church at Daphné (fig. 8-48) enjoys special fame. Its classical qualities are more fundamental, and more deeply felt, than those of the *Paris Psalter,* yet they are also completely Christian. There is no attempt to create a realistic spatial setting, but the composition has a balance and clarity that are truly monumental. Classical, too, is the heroic nudity of Christ, which emphasizes the Incarnation of the Logos (see pages 365–66). The statuesque dignity of the figures makes them seem extraordinarily organic and graceful compared to those of the Justinian mosaics at S. Vitale (see figs. 8-29 and 8-30).

The most important aspect of these figures' classical heritage, however, is emotional rather than physical. The gestures and facial expressions convey a restrained and noble suffering of the kind we first met in Greek art of the fifth century B.C. (see pages 131–32). We cannot say when and where this human interpretation of the Savior first appeared, but it seems to have developed in the wake of the Iconoclastic Controversy and reached its height during the Ducas and Comnene dynasties that ruled Byzantium from the middle of the eleventh through the late twelfth centuries. There are, to be sure, a few earlier examples of it, but none of them appeals to the emotions of the beholder so powerfully as the Daphné *Crucifixion.* To have introduced this compassionate view of Christ into sacred art was perhaps the greatest achievement of Middle Byzantine art.

Early Christian art had been quite devoid of this quality. It stressed the Savior's divine wisdom and power rather than his sacrificial death. Hence, the Crucifixion was depicted only rarely and without pathos, though with a like simplicity. Alongside the new emphasis on the Christ of the Passion, however, the image of the Pantocrator (Ruler of the Universe, as well as the All-Holder who contains everything) retained its importance. We recall this image from the *Sarcophagus of Junius Bassus* and above the apse of S. Apollinare in Classe (see figs. 8-21 and 8-15). Staring down from the center of the dome at Daphné is an awesome (though heavily restored) mosaic image of Christ the Pantocrator against a gold background (fig. 8-49). Its huge scale is emphasized by the much smaller figures of the 16 Old Testament prophets between the windows. Although the type descends from images of Zeus, the mature, bearded face of Jesus was first defined during the sixth century. It appeared in the Mandylion, a "true portrait" on cloth that, according to legend, Jesus sent to King Agbar. Later the Mandylion was the basis for the miraculous image that appeared on the veil (*sudarium*) of St. Veronica (from *vera icona,* or true image) when she wiped Jesus' face on the way to Calvary. Because of its historical "authenticity," the bearded Christ quickly replaced the youthful philosopher in art.

In the corners of the dome are four scenes that reveal the divine and human natures of Christ. The Annunciation (bottom left) is followed in counterclockwise order by the Birth, Baptism, and Transfiguration. The entire cycle represents a theological program that is in perfect harmony with the geometric relationship of the images. A strict order also governs the distribution of subjects throughout the rest of the interior. The basic scheme probably dates back to the time of Basil I, who built the Nea and ordered decorations added to Constantine's Church of the Holy Apostles, in Constantinople (both now destroyed). It was also at this time that Middle Byzantine imagery was defined. It was organized loosely along the lines of the 12 Great Feasts of the Orthodox church, which celebrate major events from the lives of Jesus and the Madonna. [See Primary Sources, no. 18, pages 365–66.] Taken together, they illustrate the Orthodox belief in the Incarnation as the redemption of original sin and the triumph over death.

HOSIOS LOUKAS. Byzantine art had managed somehow to preserve these and other biblical subjects from Early Christian times. In the eleventh century they enjoyed a revival, which thoroughly explored their narrative and pictorial potential. The *Nativity* in figure 8-50 from Hosios Loukas, which has the same composition as at Daphné but is somewhat earlier in date and in better condition, is more complex than previous examples. Instead of focusing simply on the Virgin and Child, the mosaicist used continuous narrative. The scene includes not only midwives bathing the newborn infant but also a host of angels, the Adoration of the Magi, and the Annunciation to the Shepherds. The great variety of poses and expressions lends a heightened sense of drama to the scene. Despite its schematic rendering, the mountainous landscape shows a new interest in illusionistic space as well. Missing only is the tender exchange of glances and gestures that is the most precious legacy of Daphné.

NEREZI. The emphasis on human emotions reaches its climax in the paintings at the church of St. Panteleimon in Nerezi, Macedonia. It was built by members of the Byzantine royal family and decorated by a team of artists from Constantinople. From the beginning of Byzantine art in the sixth century, mural painting

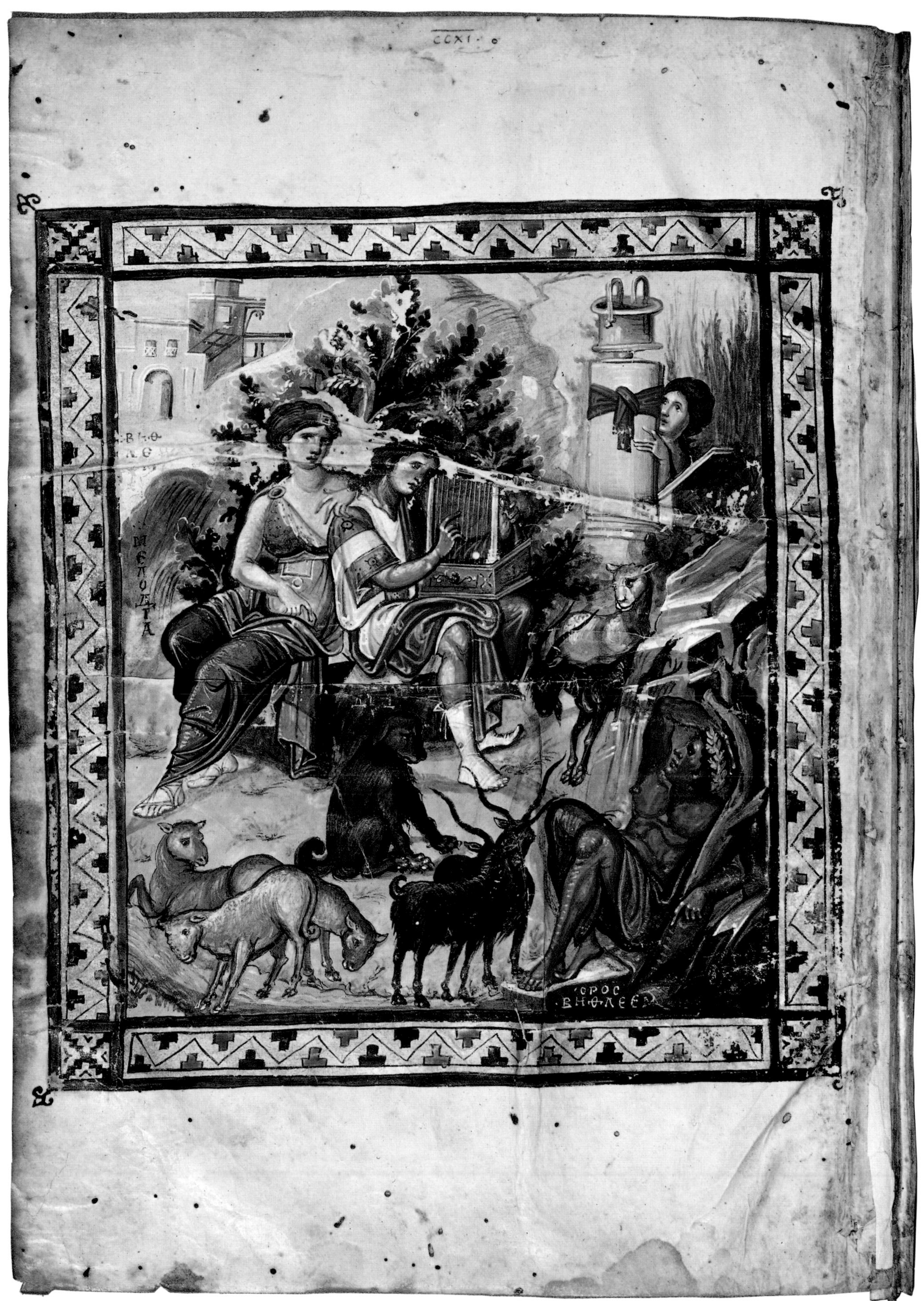

8-47. *David Composing the Psalms,* from the *Paris Psalter.* c. 900 A.D. 14⅛ x 10¼" (36 x 26 cm). Bibliothèque Nationale, Paris

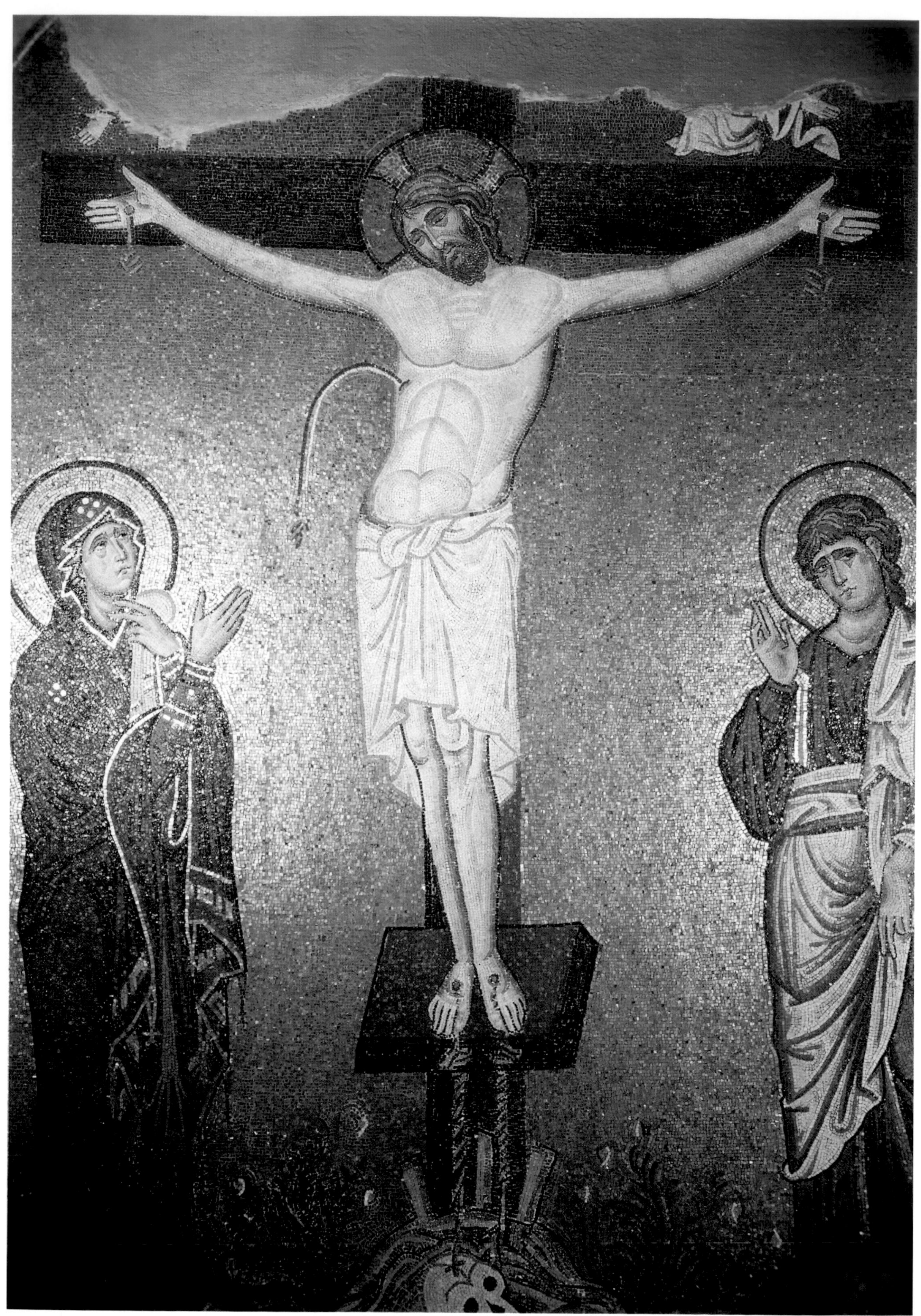

8-48. *The Crucifixion.* 11th century. Mosaic. Monastery Church, Daphné, Greece

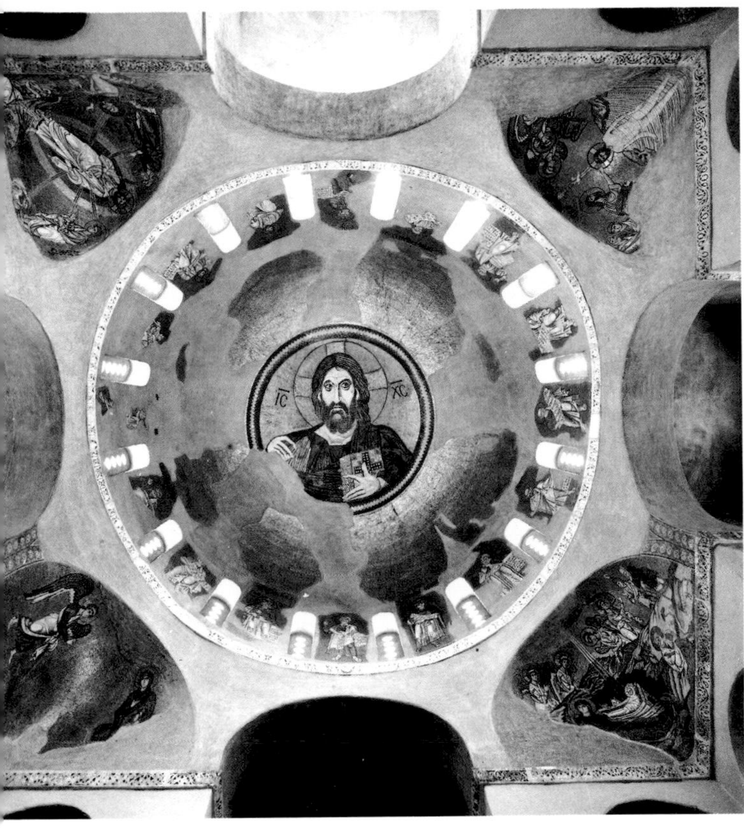

8-49. Dome mosaics. 11th century. Monastery Church, Daphné, Greece

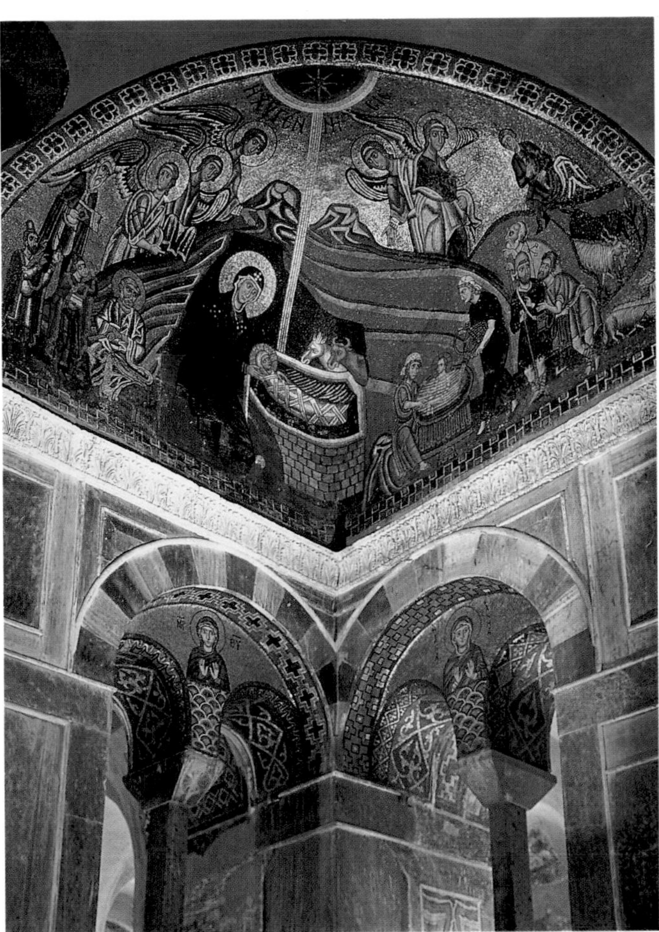

8-50. *Nativity.* Early 11th century. Mosaic. Monastery of Hosios Loukas

had served as a less expensive alternative to mosaic, which was preferred whenever possible. The two were closely linked, however, since mosaics were laid out in paint on fresh plaster each day before the tesserae were added. Thus the best painters participated fully in the new style and, in some cases, introduced innovations of their own. The artist responsible for the Lamentation over the dead Christ (fig. 8-51) was a great master who expanded on the latest advances. The gentle sadness of the Daphné *Crucifixion* has been replaced by a grief of almost unbearable intensity. The style remains the same, but its expressive qualities have been emphasized by subtle adjustments in the proportions and features. The subject seems to have been invented recently, for it does not occur in earlier Byzantine art. Even more than the Daphné *Crucifixion,* its origins lie in Classical art: in composition and mood, it echoes *Eos and Memnon* by Douris (see fig. 5-8). Yet nothing prepares us for the Virgin's anguish as she clasps her dead son or for the deep sorrow of St. John holding Christ's lifeless hand. We have entered a new realm of religious feeling that was to be explored further in the West.

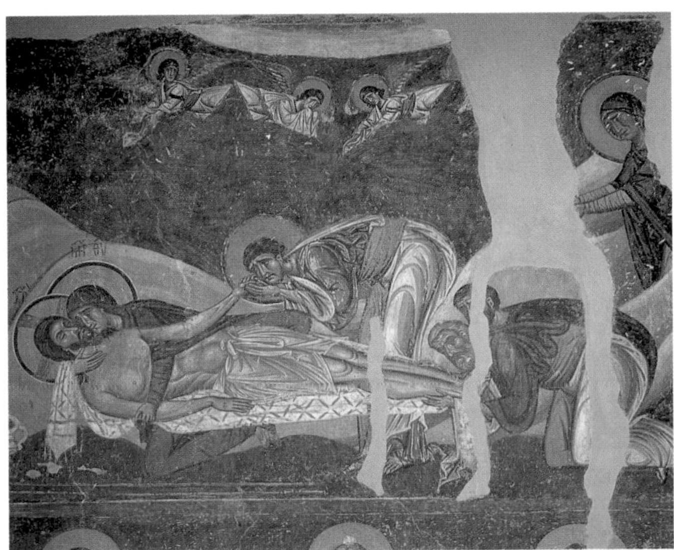

8-51. *Lamentation.* 1164. Fresco. Monastery of St. Panteleimon, Nerezi, Macedonia

MONREALE. The Byzantine manner was soon transmitted to Italy, where it was called the "Greek style" and had a decisive impact on Gothic painting (see page 343). Sometimes it was carried by miniature mosaic diptychs from Constantinople, but most often it was brought directly by visiting Byzantine artists. It first appeared in Sicily, a former Byzantine holding that was taken from the Muslims in 1091 by the Normans and united with southern Italy. The new style is seen throughout the magnificent churches and monasteries built in Palermo, the island's capital.

The Norman kings considered themselves the equals of the Byzantine emperors. Hence they called in teams of mosaicists

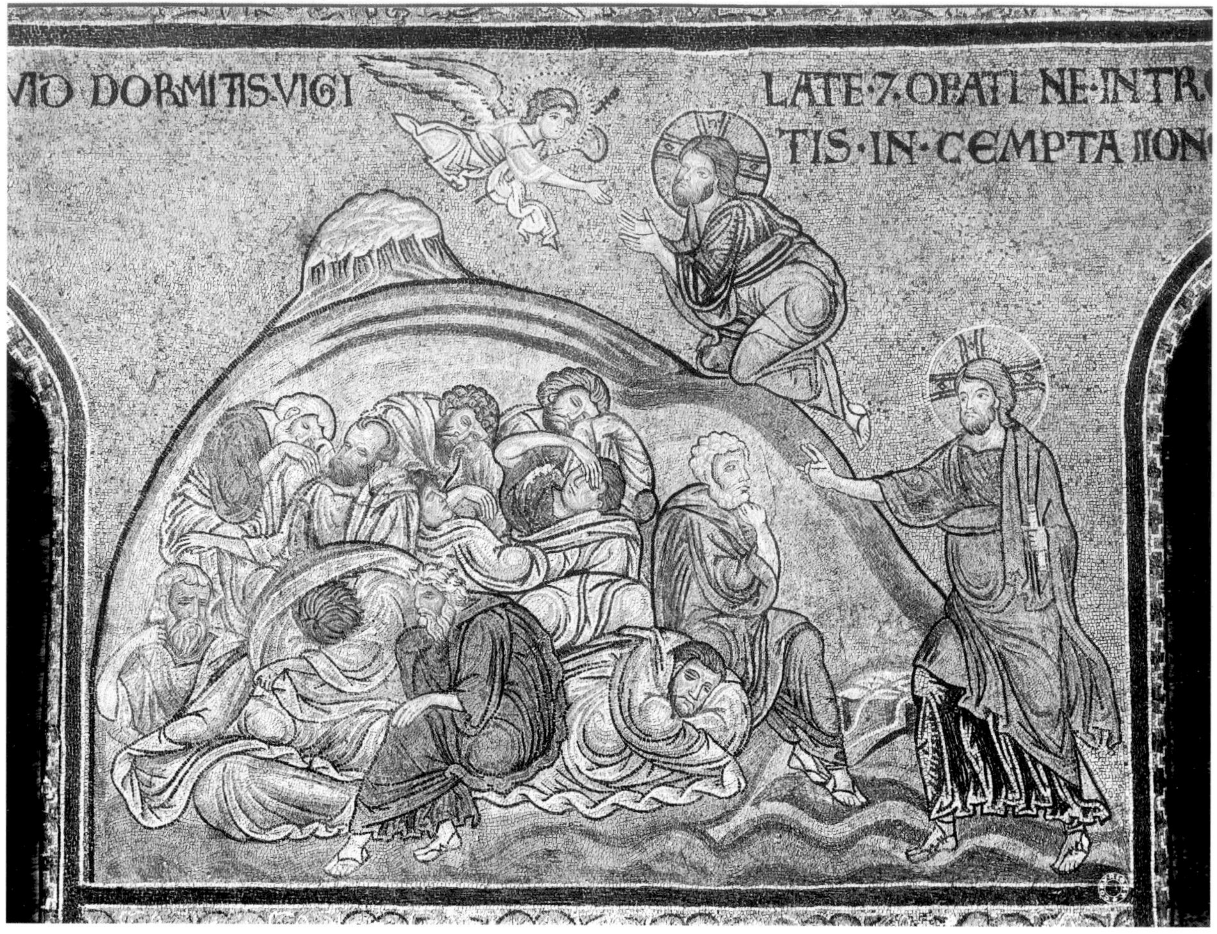

8-52. *Christ in the Garden of Gethsemane.* c. 1183. Mosaic. Cathedral, Monreale, Italy

from Constantinople to decorate their splendid religious buildings. The mosaics at the Cathedral of Monreale, the last to be executed, are in a thoroughly up-to-date Byzantine style, although the selection and distribution of subjects are largely Western. *Christ in the Garden of Gethsemane* (fig. 8-52) is a surprising premonition of El Greco's painting of the same subject (see fig. 14-11). The scene shows Christ being comforted by the angel of the Lord (above). Christ then admonishes Peter and the sleeping disciples (below), who appear enclosed by the mountain behind them in order to present the two events in a single image. Even more important than the striking composition is the attention paid to the figures, each of which is far more individualized than before. The artist's growing ability to investigate subtleties of characterization traces the progress of Byzantine art.

IVORIES. Monumental sculpture, as we saw earlier (see pages 224–25), tended to disappear completely from the fifth century on. In Byzantine art, large-scale statuary died out with the last Imperial portraits, and stone carving was confined almost entirely to architectural ornament (see fig. 8-36). But small-scale reliefs, especially in ivory and metal, continued to be produced in large numbers.

Their extraordinary variety of content, style, and purpose is suggested by the two examples shown here, both of which date from the tenth century. One is *The Harbaville Triptych,* a portable shrine with two hinged wings of the kind a high official might carry for his private worship while traveling (fig. 8-53). In the upper half of the center panel we see Christ Enthroned. On either side are St. John the Baptist and the Virgin, who plead for divine mercy on behalf of humanity. Below is John the Baptist, who is flanked by the four apostles arranged in strictly frontal view. Only in the upper tier of each wing is this formula relaxed. There we find an echo of Classical contrapposto in the poses of the two inner military saints. The exquisite refinement of this icon-in-miniature recalls the style of the Daphné *Crucifixion* (see fig. 8-48).

Our second example, slightly later in date, is the Veroli Casket (fig. 8-54), which was a wedding gift. Rather surprisingly, it is decorated with scenes of Greek mythology. Even more than the miniatures of the *Paris Psalter,* it reveals the antiquarian aspects of Byzantine classicism after the Iconoclastic Controversy. The subjects in the left panel—Helen and Castor, and Belerophon and the Nymph of Peirene—come from the world of mythology. The Sacrifice of Iphigenia in the right panel was derived from a famous drama by the Greek playwright Euripides. The panel shows a major change in style that features deep undercutting of the relief. The composition (which nevertheless remains curiously shallow) probably comes from an illustrated manuscript. Although quoted from ancient art, these knobby little figures, with their distinctive grape-cluster hair, are drained of all tragic emotion and reduced to a level of ornamental playfulness reflecting courtly taste.

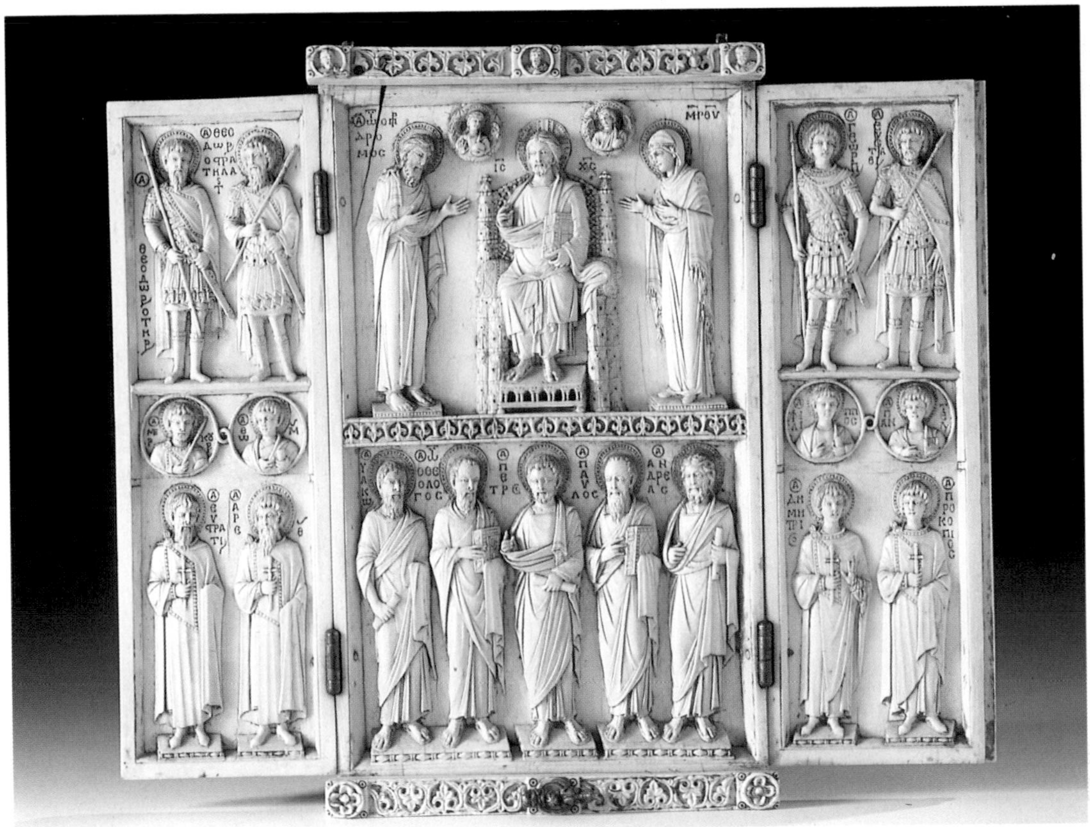

8-53. *The Harbaville Triptych.* Late 10th century. Ivory, 9½ x 11" (24.1 x 28 cm). Musée du Louvre, Paris

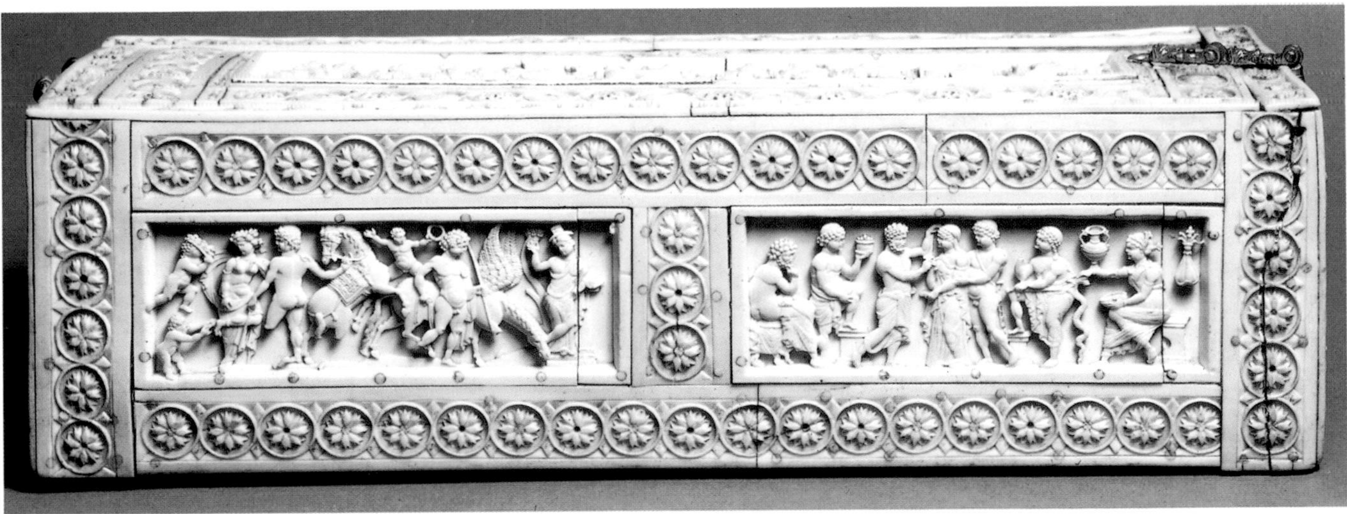

8-54. *The Sacrifice of Iphigenia.* Detail of ivory casket. 10th century. Victoria & Albert Museum, London

Late Byzantine Art

In 1204 Byzantium suffered an almost fatal defeat when the armies of the Fourth Crusade captured and sacked the city of Constantinople, instead of warring against the Turks. For more than 50 years, the core of the Eastern Empire remained in Western hands. Byzantium, however, survived this catastrophe. In 1261 it regained its independence under the Palaeologue dynasty, and the fourteenth century saw a last flowering of Byzantine painting before the Turkish conquest in 1453.

ICONS. The Crusades decisively changed the course of Byzantine art through contact with the West. The impact can be seen in the *Madonna Enthroned* (fig. 8-55), which unites elements of both, so that its authorship has been much debated. Because of the veneration in which they were held, icons had to conform to strict rules, with fixed patterns repeated over and over again. As a result, most of them are noteworthy more for exacting craftsmanship than for artistic inventiveness. Although painted at the end of the thirteenth century, our example reflects a much earlier type. There are echoes of Middle Byzantine art: in the graceful pose, the play of drapery folds, the tender melancholy of the Virgin's face. But these elements have become abstract, reflecting a new taste and style. The highlights on the drapery resemble sunbursts, in contrast to the soft shading of hands and faces. The total effect is neither flat nor spatial but transparent, so that the shapes look as if they were lit from behind. Indeed, the gold background and highlights are so brilliant that even the shadows never seem wholly opaque. This all-pervading radiance, we will recall, first appears in Early Christian mosaics. Panels such as this may, therefore, be viewed as the aesthetic equivalent of mosaics, and not simply as the descendants of the panel painting tradition. In fact, some of the most precious Byzantine icons are miniature mosaics attached to panels, and our artist may have been trained as a mosaicist rather than as a painter.

The style, then, is Late Byzantine—but with an Italian overlay, for example in the treatment of the faces, that is hard to explain. The elaborate throne, which looks like a miniature replica of the Colosseum (see fig. 7-10), no longer functions as a three-dimensional object, despite the foreshortening. The panel must have been painted by a Byzantine artist, not simply a Westerner trained in that tradition. However, this master may have worked either for a Western patron or in a Byzantine center under European control. (Cyprus, then controlled by the French, has been suggested.) Our painter might even have visited Italy or been active there, perhaps in Rome or Tuscany, where a neo-Byzantine style was well established (see page 343). Whatever position we adopt points to a profound shift in the relation between the two traditions: after 600 years of borrowing from Byzantium, Western art for the first time began to contribute something in return.

COVENANTS OLD AND NEW

By convention Western history is divided into two epochs separated by the birth of Jesus: B.C. (Before Christ) and A.D. (*Anno Domini,* "year of our Lord"), also called C.E. (Christian Era). To Christians, these periods correspond to the Old and New Testaments. Consequently they are also known as the Old Dispensation, which is the Covenant of the Ark, and the New Dispensation, the covenant represented by the cup of wine at the Last Supper, when Jesus said, "This is my blood of the new testament, which is shed for many." The Christian era is often termed the time of grace (*tempus gratia*), in contrast to the time of God's law as received by Moses (*tempus legem*).

The Covenant of the Ark bound the Israelites to worship Yaweh as their only god in exchange for being his chosen people. The ark consisted of the two tablets containing the Ten Commandments given to Moses on Mount Sinai; hence the Covenant of the Ark is also called the Covenant of Sinai. The ark resided at Shiloh in Canaan, the Promised Land, until it was brought by King David to Jerusalem, where it was later placed inside the tabernacle of the temple built by King Solomon. To many Christians, Jesus was the sacrificial lamb whose death atoned for the violation of the old covenant by the Jews, which it therefore replaced. To Muslims, Islam adds the Last Covenant, made between Muhammad and God, as revealed in the Koran.

(OPPOSITE) 8-55. *Madonna Enthroned.* Late 13th century. Tempera on panel, 32 1/8 x 19 3/8" (81.9 x 49.3 cm). National Gallery of Art, Washington, D.C.
ANDREW MELLON COLLECTION

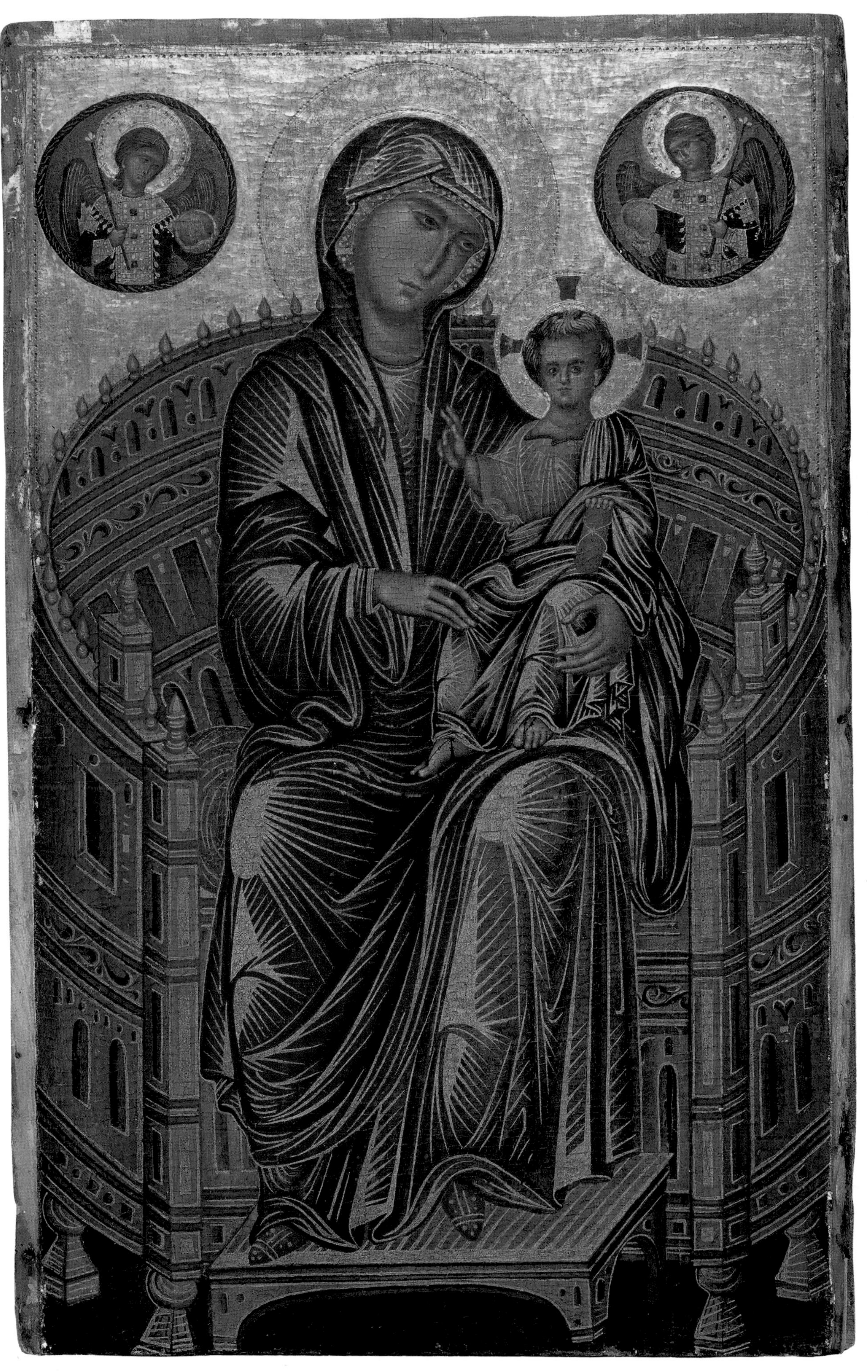

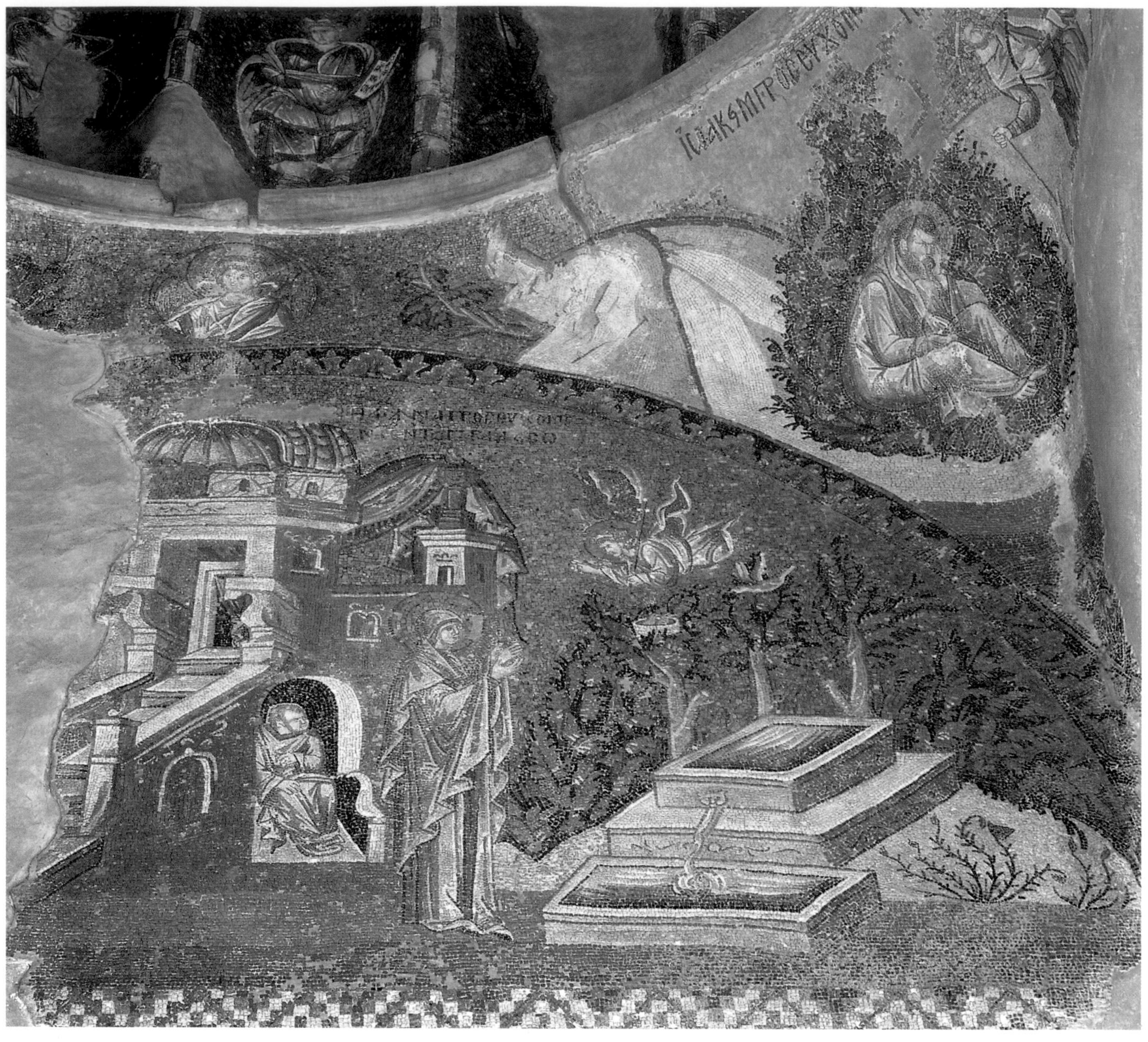

8-56. *Elizabeth at the Well.* c. 1310. Mosaic. Kariye Camii (Church of the Savior in the Chora Monastery), Istanbul

MOSAICS AND MURAL PAINTING. The finest surviving cycle of Late Byzantine mosaics is found in Istanbul's Kariye Camii, the former Church of the Savior in the Chora Monastery ("Chora" means "land" or "place"; "Camii" denotes a mosque, although the site is now a museum). Done about 1320, they represent the climax of the humanism that emerged in Middle Byzantine art. Like Constantine VII, Theodore Metochites, prime minister to the emperor Andronicus II, who restored the church and paid for its decorations, was a scholar and poet. *Elizabeth at the Well* (fig. 8-56) shows the growing Byzantine fascination with storytelling. As part of this lively narrative, the setting has blossomed into a full landscape, complete with illusionistic architecture. The scene revives a landscape style that had flourished in sixth-century secular mosaics and had been all but lost. Its illusionism is familiar to us from Pompeian painting, which was also preserved in manuscripts of the classical revival of the tenth century (compare fig. 8-47).

Equally impressive are the paintings in the mortuary chapel attached to Kariye Camii. Because of the Empire's greatly reduced resources, murals often took the place of mosaics, but at Kariye

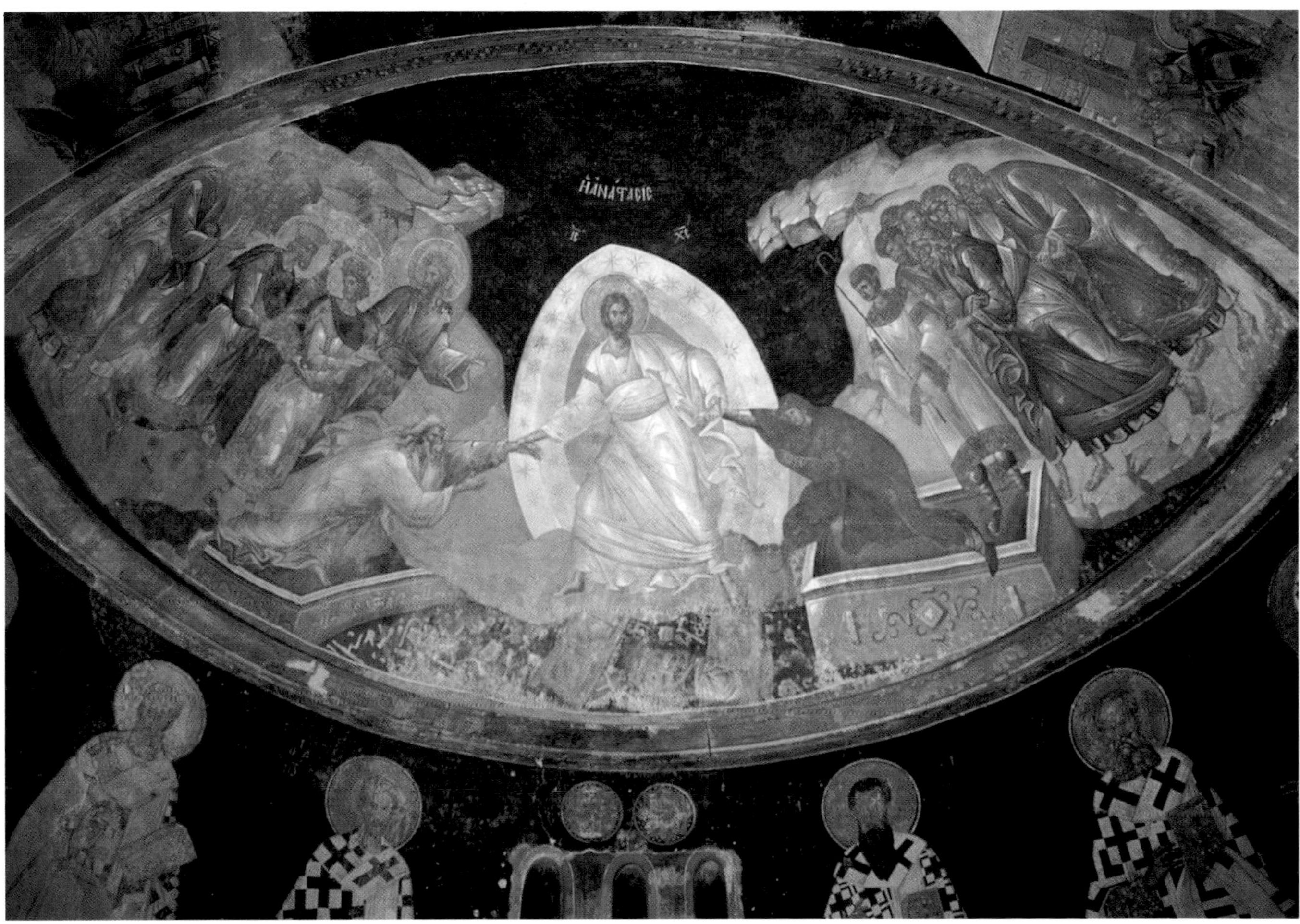

8-57. *Anastasis.* c. 1310–20. Fresco. Kariye Camii (Church of the Savior in the Chora Monastery), Istanbul

Camii they exist on an even footing. Figure 8-57 shows the Anastasis, which is Greek for resurrection. (The term means both to rise and to raise.) The scene depicts the traditional Byzantine image of this subject, which Western Christians call Christ's Descent into Limbo, or the Harrowing of Hell, to rescue souls. Surrounded by a radiant gloriole, the Savior has vanquished Satan and battered down the gates of Hell. (Note the bound Satan at his feet, in the midst of a profusion of hardware; the two kings to the left are David and Solomon.) What amazes us about the central group of Christ raising Adam and Eve from the dead is its dramatic force, a quality we would not expect from what we have seen of Byzantine art so far. Christ here moves with extraordinary physical energy, tearing Adam and Eve from their graves, so that they appear to fly through the air—a magnificently expressive image of divine triumph. Such dynamism had been unknown in the earlier Byzantine tradition. This style, which was related to slightly earlier developments in manuscript painting, was indeed revolutionary. Coming in the fourteenth century, it shows that 800 years after Justinian, when the subject first appeared, Byzantine art still had all its creative powers.

CHAPTER NINE

Early Medieval Art

Once established, the labels used for historical periods are almost impossible to change, even though they may no longer be suitable. The humanists who coined the term "Middle Ages" thought of the entire thousand years from the fifth to the fifteenth century as an age of darkness: an empty interval between classical antiquity and its rebirth, the Renaissance in Europe (see pages 205–207). Since then, our view of this period has changed completely. We no longer think of it as "benighted" but as a time of cultural change and creative activity. During the 200 years between the death of Justinian and the reign of Charlemagne, as we have already pointed out, the center of gravity of European civilization shifted northward from the Mediterranean Sea. At the same time, the economic, political, and spiritual framework of the Middle Ages began to take shape. We shall now see that the same centuries also gave rise to some important artistic achievements.

The Celtic-Germanic Style

THE ANIMAL STYLE. The Celtic-Germanic style was a result of the widespread migrations that took place after the fall of the Roman Empire. In 376 the Huns, who had advanced beyond the Black Sea from central Asia, became a serious threat to Europe. They pushed the Germanic Visigoths westward into the Roman Empire from the Danube. Then under Attila (d. 453) they invaded Gaul, homeland of the Celts in southwest Germany and eastern France, in 451. A year later they attacked Rome. Also in the fifth century the Angles and Saxons from today's Denmark and northern Germany invaded the British Isles, which had been colonized for centuries by Celts (see page 41). The Germanic peoples carried with them, in the form of nomads' gear, the artistic tradition known as the animal style. We have seen early examples of it in "Scythian gold" (see page 76 and fig. 3-24). The animal style, with its combination of abstract and organic shapes, of formal discipline and imaginative freedom, merged with the ornamental metalwork of the Celts, which had previously been affected by it (see fig. 1-22). The result was Celtic-Germanic art.

An excellent example of this "heathen" style is the gold-and-enamel purse cover (fig. 9-1) from the ship burial at Sutton Hoo of an East Anglian king (almost certainly Raedwald, who died around 625). On it are four pairs of symmetrical motifs. Each has its own distinctive character, an indication that they were assembled from different sources. One, the standing man between facing animals, has a very long history indeed. We first saw it in Mesopotamian art more than 3,200 years earlier (see fig. 3-9), and it is even older than that. The eagles pouncing on ducks bring to mind similar pairings of carnivore-and-victim in ancient bronzes. The design above them, at center, is of more recent origin. It consists of fighting animals whose tails, legs, and jaws are elongated into bands that form a complex interweaving pattern. The fourth, on the top left and right, uses interlacing bands as an ornamental device. This motif occurs in Roman and Early Christian art, especially along the southern shore of the Mediterranean. However, the combination of these bands with the animal style, as shown here, seems to be an invention of Celtic-Germanic art, not much before the date of our purse cover.

The chief medium of the style had been metalwork, in a variety of materials and techniques and sometimes of exquisitely refined craftsmanship. Such articles, small, durable, and eagerly sought after, account for the rapid diffusion of this idiom's repertory of forms. They spread not only geographically but also artistically: from metal into wood, stone, and even paint. We know from literary accounts that gold objects were plentiful. Since nothing else like it from the same period has been found elsewhere in England, however, it is far from clear whether the Sutton Hoo purse was made locally or, like "Scythian gold" (see pages 76–77), was of foreign origin, as were most of the luxury goods found at the mound.

Ship burials like those at Sutton Hoo and nearby Snape first began in Scandinavia, where the animal style flourished longer than anywhere else and where most wooden items have been found. The splendid animal head of the early ninth century in figure 9-2 is the terminal, or decorated end, of a post that was found in a buried Viking ship at Oseberg in southern Norway. Like the motifs on the Sutton Hoo purse cover, it is a composite. The basic shape of the head is surprisingly realistic, as are some of the details, such as the teeth, gums, and nostrils. But the surface is covered with

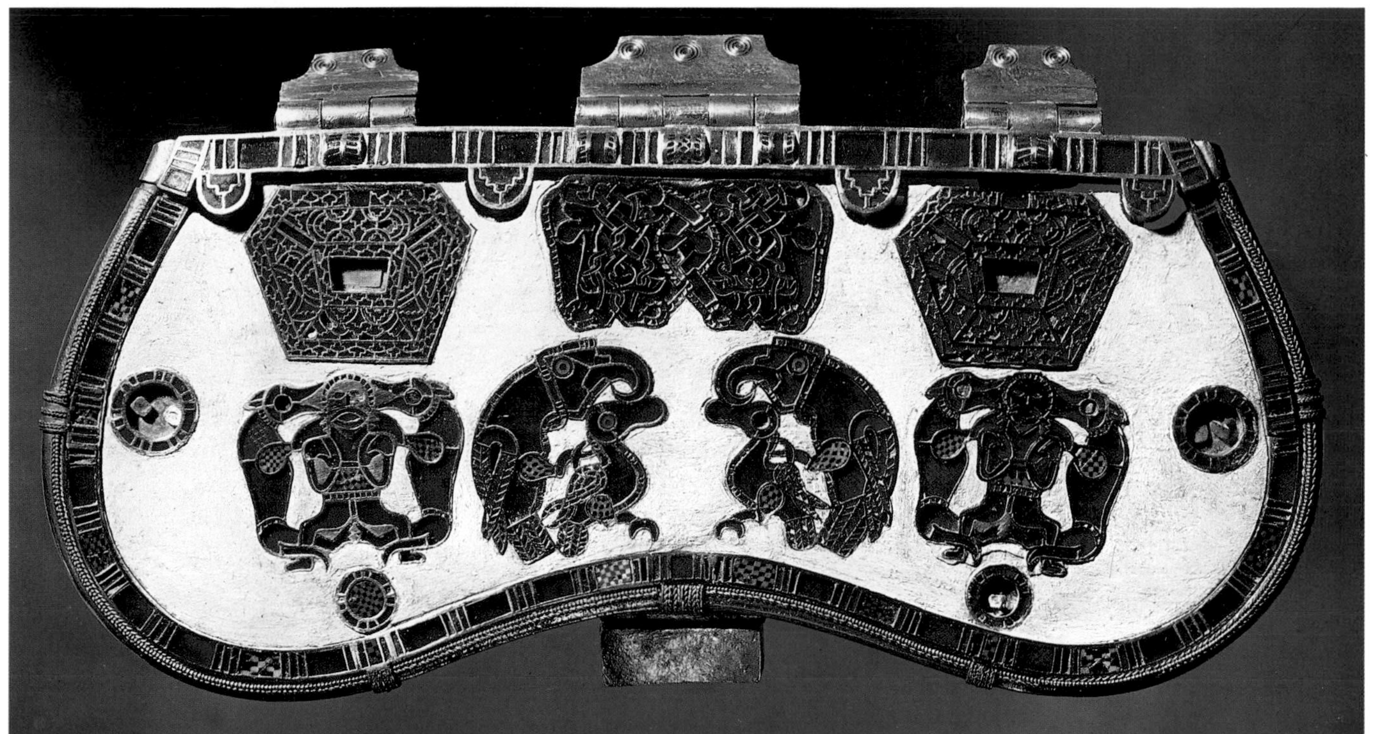

(ABOVE) 9-1. Purse cover, from the Sutton Hoo ship burial. 625–33 A.D. Gold with garnets and enamels, length 8" (20.3 cm). The British Museum, London

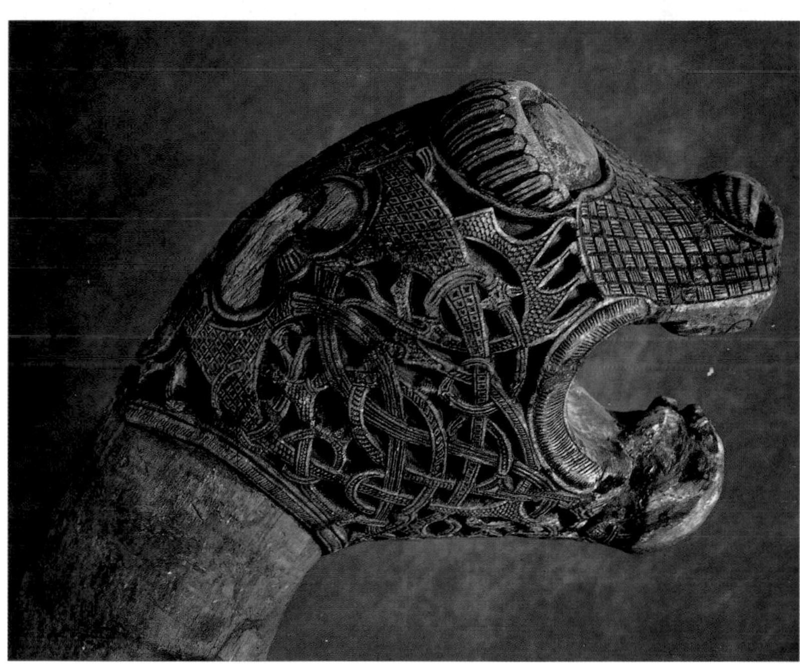

(RIGHT) 9-2. *Animal Head,* from the Oseberg ship burial. c. 825 A.D. Wood, height approx. 5" (12.7 cm). Institute for Art History and Classical Archaeology, University of Oslo, Norway

interlacing and geometric patterns derived from metalwork. Snarling monsters such as this used to rise from the prows of Viking ships, which gave them the character of mythical sea dragons.

The Hiberno-Saxon Style

The earliest Christian works of art made north of the Alps also reflected the Germanic version of the animal style. To understand how they came to be produced, however, we must first note the important role played by the Irish (Hibernians) in the early Middle Ages. During this period, the Irish were the spiritual and cultural leaders of western Europe. In fact, the period 600 to 800 A.D. deserves to be called the Golden Age of Ireland. Unlike their English neighbors, the Irish had never been part of the Roman Empire. Thus the missionaries who carried the Gospel to them from England in the fifth century found a Celtic society barbarian by Roman standards. The Irish readily accepted Christianity, which brought them into contact with Mediterranean civilization. However, they adapted what they had received in a spirit of vigorous local independence.

The institutional framework of the Roman Church, being essentially urban, was poorly suited to the rural Irish way of life. Irish Christians preferred to follow the example of the desert saints of Egypt and the Near East, who had left the temptations of

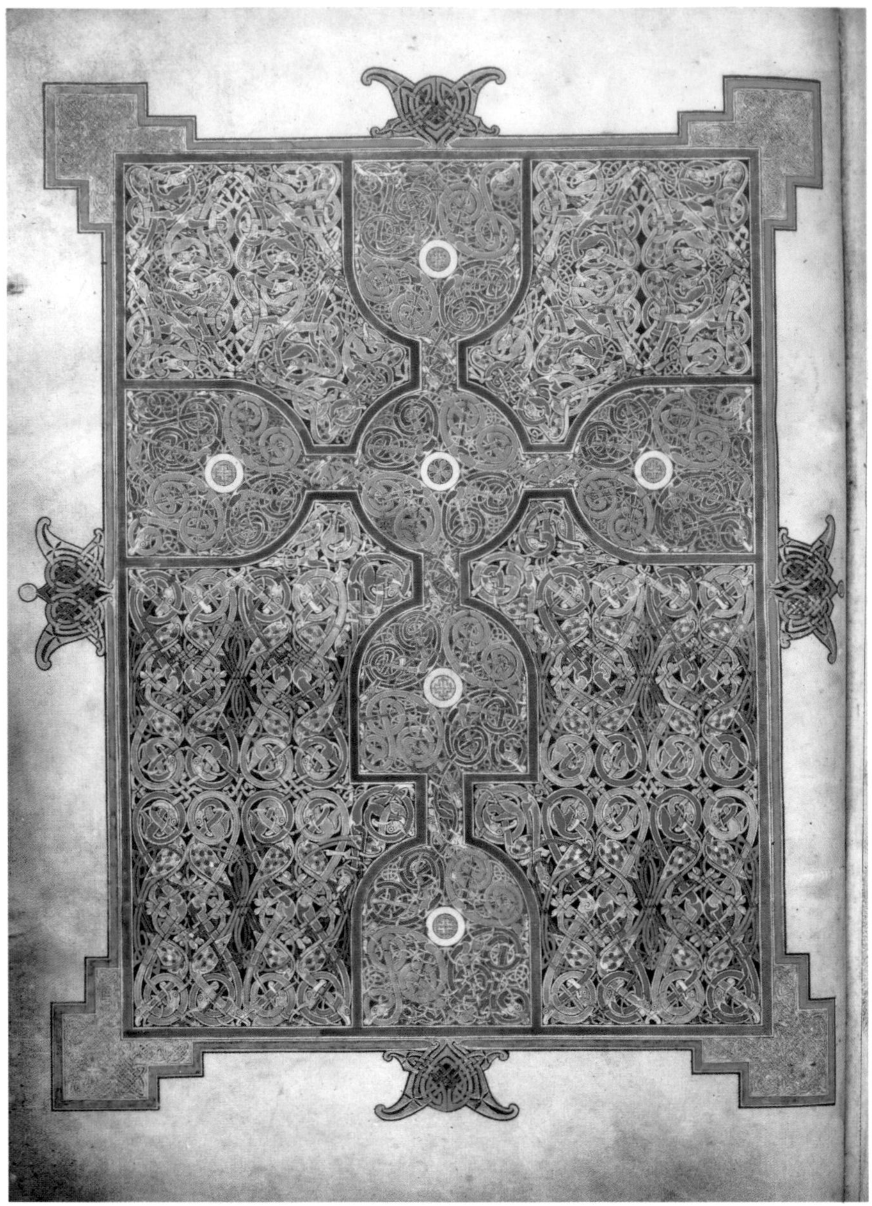

9-3. Cross page, from the *Lindisfarne Gospels.* c. 700 A.D. Tempera on vellum, 13½ x 9¼" (34.3 x 23.5 cm). The British Library, London

the city to seek spiritual perfection in the solitude of the wilderness, where groups of them founded the earliest monasteries (see pages 279–80). By the fifth century, monasticism had spread as far north as western Britain, but only in Ireland did the monks take over the leadership of the Church from the bishops.

Irish monasteries, unlike their Egyptian models, soon became centers of learning and the arts. They sent monks to preach to the heathen and to found monasteries not only in northern Britain but also on the European mainland, from present-day France to Austria. These Irish monks speeded the conversion of Scotland, northern France, the Netherlands, and Germany to Christianity. Further, they made the monastery a cultural center throughout the European countryside. The monasteries on the Continent were soon taken over by the monks of the Benedictine order, who were advancing north from Italy during the seventh and eighth centuries. Even so, Irish influence would be felt within medieval civilization for several hundred years.

MANUSCRIPTS. In order to spread the Gospel, the Irish monasteries had to produce copies of the Bible and other Christian books in large numbers. Their scriptoria (writing workshops) also became artistic centers. A manuscript containing the Word of God was looked upon as a sacred object whose beauty should reflect the importance of its contents. Irish monks must have known Early Christian illuminated manuscripts, but here, too, they developed an independent tradition instead of simply copying their models. While pictures illustrating biblical events held little interest for them, they devoted much effort to abstract decoration. The finest of these manuscripts belong to the Hiberno-Saxon style—a Christian form that evolved from heathen Celtic-Germanic art and flourished in the monasteries founded by Irishmen in Saxon England.

Thanks to a later *colophon* (inscription), we know a great deal about the origin of the *Lindisfarne Gospels,* including the translator and scribe, who presumably painted the illuminations as well.

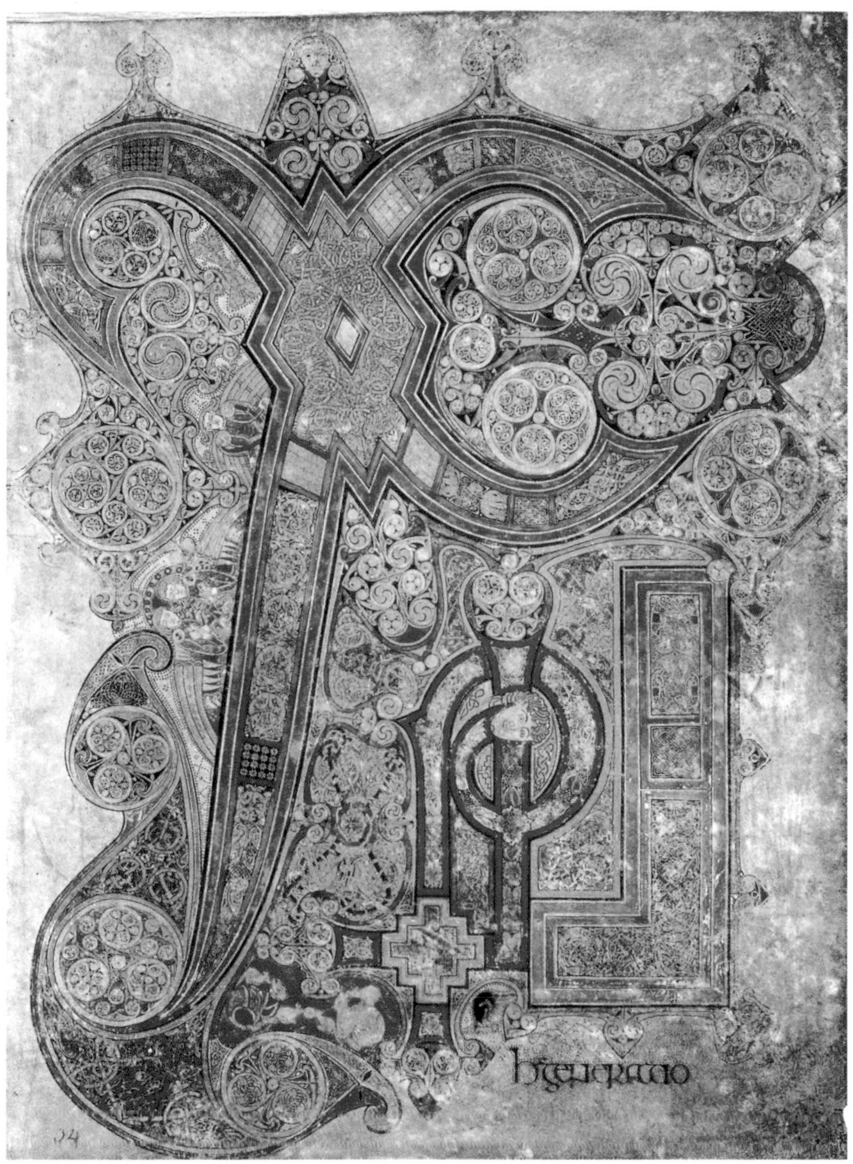

9-4. Chi-Rho page, from the *Book of Kells*. c. 800 A.D.?
13 x 9½" (33 x 24.1 cm). Trinity College Library, Dublin

[See Primary Sources, no. 19, page 366.] The Cross page (fig. 9-3) is a creation of breathtaking complexity. Working with the precision of a jeweler, the miniaturist has poured into the geometric frame an animal interlace so dense and yet so full of movement that the fighting beasts on the Sutton Hoo purse cover seem simple in comparison. It is as if these biting and clawing monsters had been subdued by the power of the Cross. In order to achieve this effect, our artist has had to work within a severe discipline by exactly following "rules of the game." These rules demand, for instance, that organic and geometric shapes must be kept separate. Within the animal compartments, every line must turn out to be part of an animal's body. There are other rules concerning symmetry, mirror-image effects, and repetitions of shapes and colors. Only by working these out by intense observation can we enter into the spirit of this mazelike world.

What was the origin of this complex style? From the beginning, Celtic art had favored a form of organic abstraction based mainly on plant motifs. This vocabulary was greatly enlarged during the later fourth century B.C. by Etruscan and other Italian artisans working for Celtic patrons. Many of the new forms they used emanated from Classical Greece. The vegetal style spread rapidly throughout the Celtic realm, where it became thoroughly integrated with existing motifs. It was subjected to a strict discipline using the compass, which continued to be used in Britain long after it was abandoned on the Continent. Yet nothing in earlier Celtic art prepares us for the elaboration found in Hibernian manuscripts, despite the persistence of plantlike forms.

The Irish manuscript style reached its climax a hundred years after the *Lindisfarne Gospels* in the *Book of Kells,* the most elaborate codex of Celtic art. Once called "the chief relic of the Western world," it was made at the monastery on the island of Iona and left incomplete when the island was invaded by Vikings between 804 and 807. Its many pages reflect a wide array of influences, from the Mediterranean to the English Channel. The justly famous Chi-Rho

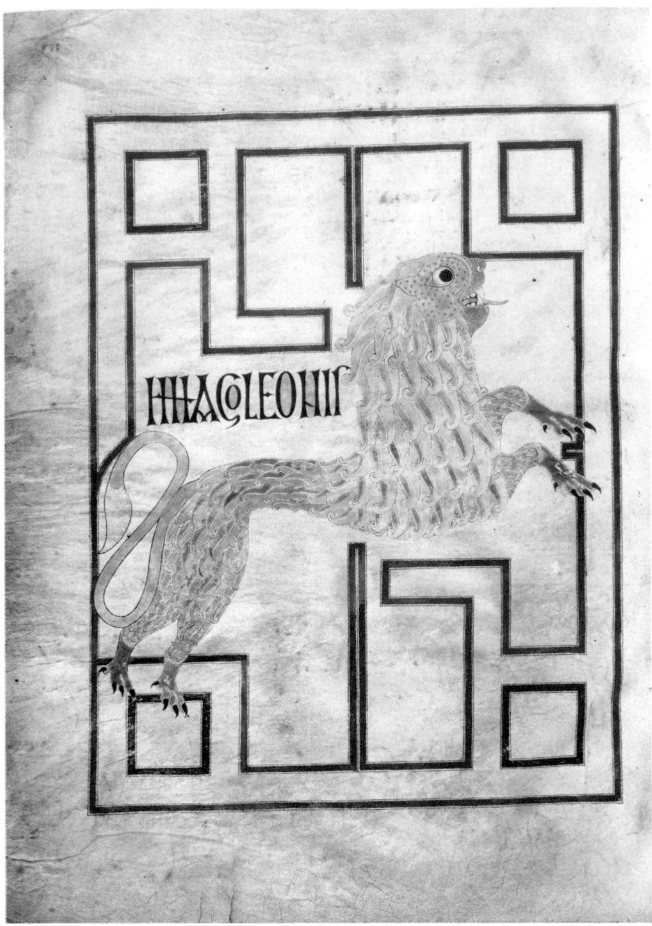

9-5. *Symbol of St. Mark,* from the *Echternach Gospels.* c. 690 A.D. $12\frac{3}{4}$ x $10\frac{3}{8}$" (32.4 x 26.4 cm). Bibliothèque Nationale, Paris

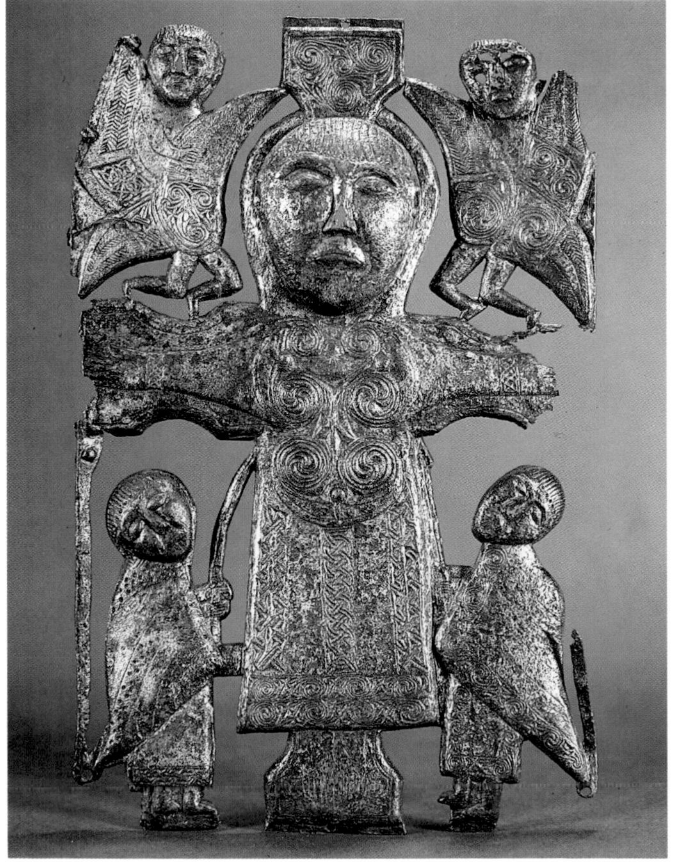

9-6. *Crucifixion,* plaque from a book cover (?). 8th century A.D. Bronze, height $8\frac{1}{4}$" (21 cm). National Museum of Ireland, Dublin

monogram (standing for Christ; fig. 9-4) has much the same swirling design as the Cross page from the *Lindisfarne Gospels.* But now the rigid geometry has been relaxed somewhat and, with it, the ban on images of humans. The top of the X-shaped Chi sprouts a thoroughly recognizable face, while along its shaft are three winged angels. And in a touch of enchanting fantasy, the tendril-like P-shaped Rho ends in a monk's head. More surprising still is the introduction of the natural world. Nearly hidden in the ornamentation, as if playing a game of hide-and-seek, are cats and mice, butterflies, even otters catching fish. No doubt they perform some symbolic function in order to justify their presence. Nevertheless, their appearance here is astounding.

Of the images in Early Christian manuscripts, the Hiberno-Saxon illuminators retained only the symbols of the four evangelists, since these could be readily translated into their ornamental style. These symbols—the man (St. Matthew), the lion (St. Mark), the eagle (St. John), and the ox (St. Luke)—were derived from the Revelation of St. John the Divine and assigned to the evangelists by St. Augustine. The lion of St. Mark in the *Echternach Gospels* (fig. 9-5), sectioned and patterned like the enamel inlays of the Sutton Hoo purse cover, is "animated" by the same curvilinear sense of movement we saw in the Chi-Rho page. Here again we see the masterly balance between the shape of the animal and the geometric framework (which includes the inscription, *imago leonis*). Thus tamed, as if caged within the manuscript page, he is nevertheless a worthy successor to the magnificent beasts in Assyrian lion hunts (compare fig. 3-20).

Celtic and Germanic artists showed little interest in the human figure for a long time. The bronze plaque of the *Crucifixion* (fig. 9-6), probably made for a book cover, shows a continuing emphasis on flat patterns, even when dealing with the image of a man. Although the composition is Early Christian in origin, the artist has treated the human frame as a series of ornamental compartments. The figure of Jesus is disembodied in the most literal sense: the head, arms, and feet are all separate elements joined to a central pattern of whorls, zigzags, and interlacing bands. Most fascinating of all are the faces: they hardly differ from those found on Celtic bronzes of fully 1,200 years earlier! Clearly, there is a wide gulf between the Celtic-Germanic and the Mediterranean traditions, a gulf that the Irish artist who modeled the *Crucifixion* saw no need to bridge.

The Lombard Style

The situation was much the same in Continental Europe. We even find it among the Lombards in northern Italy. The Germanic sculptor who carved the marble balustrade relief in the Cathedral Baptistery at Cividale (fig. 9-7) was just as perplexed as the Irish by the problem of representation. The evangelists' symbols are strange creatures indeed. All four of them have the same spidery front legs, and their bodies consist of nothing but head, wings, and (except for the angel) a little spiral tail. Apparently the artist did not mind violating their integrity by forcing them into their circular frames. On the other hand, the panel has a well-developed sense of ornament. The flat, symmetrical pattern is an effective piece of decoration, rather like an embroidered cloth. It may, in fact, have been derived in part from Oriental textiles.

9-7. Balustrade relief inscribed by the Patriarch Sigvald (762–76 A.D.), probably carved c. 725–50 A.D. Marble, approx. 36 x 60" (91.3 x 152.3 cm). Cathedral Baptistery, Cividale, Italy

CAROLINGIAN ART

The cultural achievements of Charlemagne's reign have proved far more lasting than his Empire, which began to fall apart even before his death in 814. This very page is printed in letters whose shapes are derived from the script in Carolingian manuscripts. The fact that these letters are known today as "Roman" rather than Carolingian recalls another aspect of the cultural reforms sponsored by Charlemagne: the collecting and copying of ancient Roman literature. The oldest surviving texts of many classical Latin authors are found in Carolingian manuscripts, which, until not long ago, were mistakenly considered Roman. Hence their lettering, too, was called Roman.

This interest in preserving the classics was part of an ambitious attempt to improve the education of the court and the clergy as part of a larger reform program. Charlemagne's goals were to improve the administration of his realm and the teaching of Christian truths. He summoned the best minds to his court, including Alcuin of York, the most learned scholar of the day, to restore ancient Roman learning and to establish a system of schools at every cathedral and monastery. The emperor, who could read but not write, took an active hand in this renewal, which went well beyond mere antiquarianism. He wanted to model his rule after the empire under Constantine and Justinian—not their pagan predecessors. To a great extent he succeeded. Thus the "Carolingian revival" may be termed the first, and in some ways most important, phase of a fusion of the Celtic Germanic spirit with that of the Mediterranean world.

Architecture

The word "architect" is derived from the Greek word for master builder and was defined in its modern sense of designer and theoretician by the Roman writer Vitruvius during the first century A.D. In the Middle Ages, however, it came to have different meanings. During the eighth century the distinction between design and construction—between theory and practice—became blurred. As a result, the term had nearly disappeared in northern Europe by the tenth century and was replaced by a new vocabulary, in part because the building trades were strictly separated under the guild system. When it was used, architect could apply not only to masons, carpenters, and even roofers but also to the person who commissioned or supervised a building. We know that in some instances the head abbot of a community of monks was the actual designer. As a result, the design of churches became increasingly subordinate to liturgical and practical considerations. Their actual appearance, however, was largely determined by an organic construction process. Roman architectural principles and construction techniques, such as the use of cement, had been largely forgotten. They were recovered only through cautious experimentation by builders, who were inherently conservative. Thus vaulting remained simple and was limited to short spans, mainly over aisles, if it was used at all.

Not until about 1260 did the theologian Thomas Aquinas revive Aristotle's definition of "architect" as the person who leads, as opposed to the artisan who makes. In doing so, he acknowledged a change that had occurred over the previous 150 years. During that time, the concept of *architectus* had been revived, thanks to the widespread copying of Vitruvius' ten books on architecture. However, it now had a different meaning, since architecture itself remained in the hands of master craftsmen. The stimulus may have been provided by the Crusades, which brought Westerners into contact with Byzantium, with its great libraries, as well as with Saracen architects, then among the most advanced in the world. Within a century the term "architect" was used by the humanist Petrarch to refer to the artist in charge of a project. Petrarch thus acknowledged what had become established practice in Florence, where first the painter Giotto and then the sculptors Andrea Pisano and Francesco Talenti were placed in charge of Florence Cathedral (see pages 323–24).

THE PALACE CHAPEL, AACHEN. The achievement of Charlemagne's famous Palace Chapel (figs. 9-8, 9-9, and 9-10) is all the more spectacular when seen in this light. On his visits to Italy, beginning with his son Pepin's baptism by Pope Hadrian in 781, Charlemagne had become familiar with the monuments of the Constantinian era in Rome and with those of the reign of Justinian in Ravenna. Charlemagne felt that his new capital at Aachen (the site was chosen for its mineral baths) must convey the majesty of empire through buildings of an equally impressive kind. To signify Charlemagne's position as a Christian ruler, his palace complex was modeled on the Lateran Palace in Rome, which had been given by Constantine to the pope. Charlemagne's palace included a basilica, the Royal Hall, which was linked to the Palace Chapel. The chapel itself was inspired in equal measure by the Lateran baptistery and S. Vitale (see figs. 8-25, 8-26, 8-27, and 8-28). The debt to the latter is especially clear in cross section (compare fig. 9-10 to fig. 8-27). To construct such a building on northern soil was a difficult undertaking, which was supervised by Einhard, Charlemagne's trusted adviser and biographer. Columns and bronze gratings had to be imported from Italy, and expert stonemasons must have been hard to find. The design, by Odo of Metz (probably the earliest architect north of the Alps known to us by name), is by no means a mere echo of S. Vitale but a vigorous reinterpretation. The piers and vaults have impressive massiveness, while the geometric clarity of the spatial units is very different from the fluid space of the earlier structure. These features, which are found in French buildings of the previous century, are a distinctly northern variant of Roman architecture.

Equally significant is Odo's scheme for the western entrance, now largely obscured by later additions and rebuilding (see fig. 9-8). At S. Vitale, the entrance consists of a broad, semidetached narthex with twin stair turrets, placed at an odd angle to the main axis of the church (see fig. 8-26). At Aachen, these elements have been molded into a tall, compact unit, in line with the main axis and attached to the chapel itself. This monumental structure, known as a westwork (from the German *Westwerk*), makes one of its first appearances here. It was originally flanked by a pair of round towers, thus anticipating the facade found on so many later medieval churches (compare fig. 9-21). Charlemagne's throne was placed in the tribune, as the gallery of the westwork is often called, behind the great window (later glassed in) above the entrance; there he could emerge into the view of people assembled in the atrium below. The throne faced an

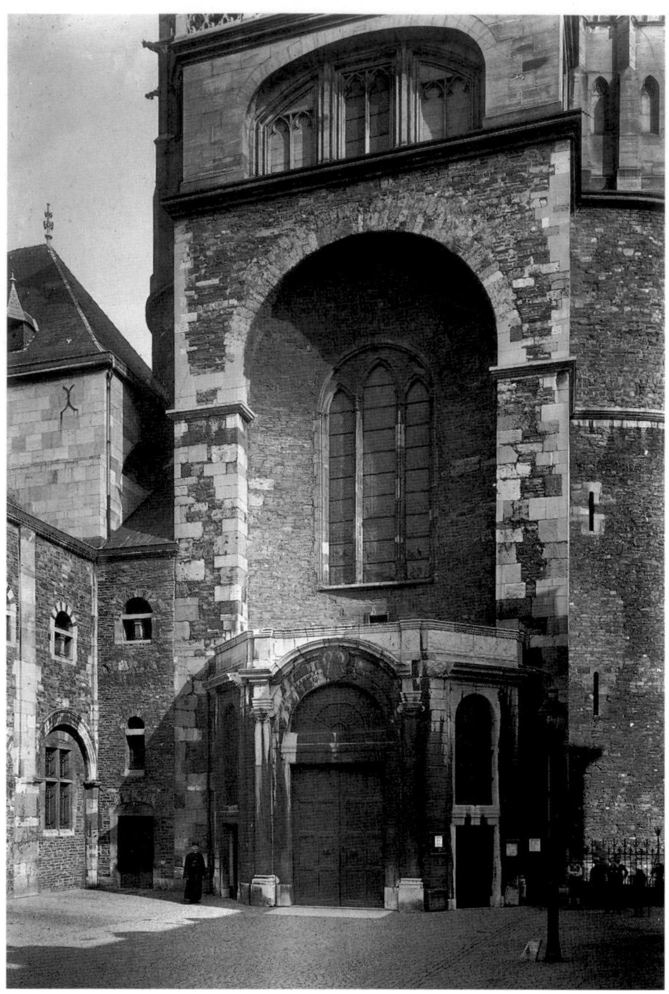

9-8. Entrance, Palace Chapel of Charlemagne, Aachen, Germany. 792–805 A.D.

GUILDS: MASTERS AND APPRENTICES

In the Middle Ages, the word "master" (Latin, *magister*) was a title conferred by a trade organization, or guild, on a member who had achieved the highest level of skill in the guild's profession or craft. In each city, trade guilds virtually controlled commercial life by establishing quality standards, setting prices, defining the limits of each guild's activity, and overseeing the admission of new members. The earliest guilds were formed in the eleventh century by merchants. Soon, however, craftsmen also organized themselves in similar professional societies, whose power continued well into the sixteenth century. Most guilds admitted only men, but some, such as the painters' guild of Bruges, occasionally admitted women as well. Guild membership established a certain level of social status for townspeople, who were neither nobility, clerics (people in religious life), nor peasantry.

A boy would begin as an apprentice to a master in his chosen guild, and after many years might advance to the rank of journeyman. In most guilds this meant that he was then a full member of the organization, capable of working without direction, and entitled to receive full wages for his work. Once he became a master, the highest rank, he could direct the work of apprentices and manage his own workshop, hiring journeymen to work with him.

In architecture, the master mason (sometimes called master builder) generally designed the building, that is, acted in the role of architect. In church building campaigns, teams of masons, carpenters (joiners), metalworkers, and glaziers (glassworkers) labored under the direction of the master builder.

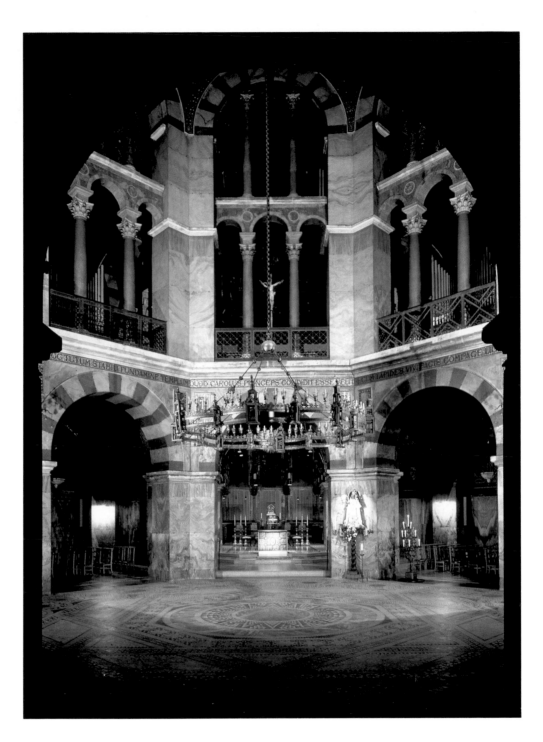

9-9. Interior of the Palace Chapel of Charlemagne, Aachen

(BELOW) 9-10. Cross section of the Palace Chapel of Charlemagne (after Kubach)

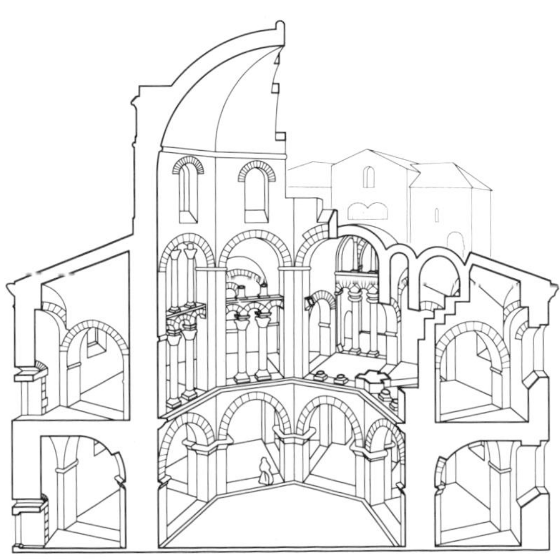

altar dedicated to Christ, who blesses the emperor from the dome mosaic. Thus, although contemporary documents say little about its function, the westwork seems to have served initially as a royal loge or chapel. But both here and elsewhere it may have been used for other purposes as the need arose.

CORVEY. An even more elaborate westwork formed part of the greatest basilican church of Carolingian times, that of the monastery of St.-Riquier (also called Centula), near Abbeville in northeastern France. Named for a monk who died in 645, it was established in 790 by Abbot Angilbert, a poet and scholar close to Charlemagne whose nickname at the court was Homer. The monastery has been destroyed, but its design is known from drawings and descriptions. Several innovations in the church would become of basic importance for the future. The westwork led into

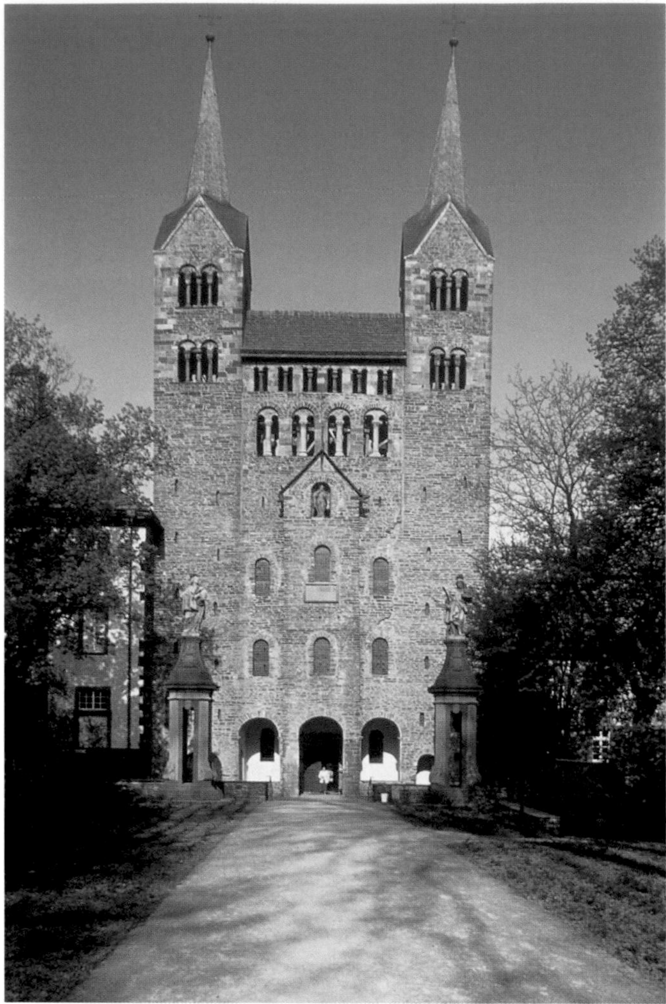

9-11. Facade, Abbey Church, Corvey. Late 9th century A.D., with later additions, Westphalia

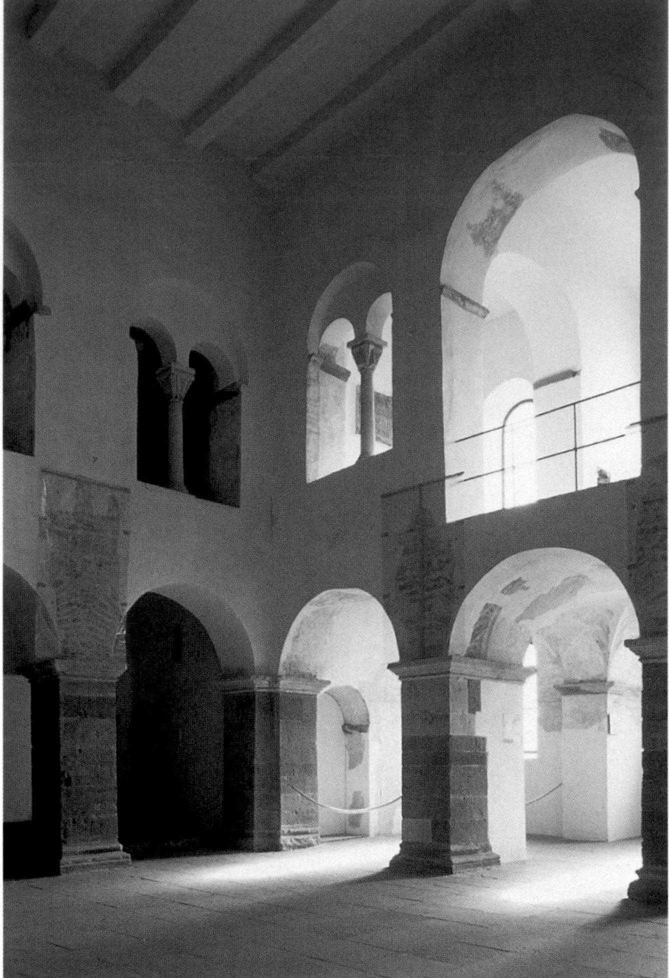

9-12. Western Tribune, Abbey Church, Corvey

a vaulted narthex, which was in effect a western transept. Its crossing (the area where the transept intersects the nave) was crowned by a tower, as was the crossing of the eastern transept. Both transepts, moreover, featured a pair of round stair towers. The church, one of three within the monastery, had several altars that were used at different stages of the worship service, as described by Angilbert himself. [See Primary Sources, nos. 20–21, page 367, and fig. PS-20] The monks followed *The Rule* established by St. Benedict of Nursia. [See Primary Sources, no. 22, pages 367–68.]

St.-Riquier was widely imitated in other Carolingian monastery churches, but these, too, have been destroyed or rebuilt in later times. The best-preserved is the abbey church at Corvey (figs. 9-11, 9-12), built in 873–85. Except for the upper stories, which date from around 1146, the westwork retains much of its original appearance. Even without these additions, it provided a suitably regal entrance. It is impressive not only because of its height but also because of its unadorned surfaces, which emphasize the clear geometry and powerful masses of the exterior. This wonderful simplicity is continued inside the church. Our view of the tribune shows the understated eloquence of Carolingian architecture at its finest. The east end of the church, now much altered, is also important for anticipating the apses with radiating chapels and ambulatories found on Romanesque churches (compare fig. 10-1).

PLAN OF A MONASTERY, ST. GALL. The importance of monasteries and their close link with the Imperial court are suggested by a unique document of the period, a large drawing on five sheets of vellum of a plan for a monastery preserved in the chapter library at St. Gall in Switzerland (fig. 9-13). Its basic features seem to have been determined at a council held near Aachen in 816–17 that established the Benedictines as the official order under the Carolingians. This copy was then sent by Abbot Haito of Reichenau to Gozbert, the abbot of St. Gall, for "you to study only" in rebuilding the monastery. We may therefore regard it as a standard plan, intended to be altered to meet local needs.

The monastery plan shows a complex, self-contained unit filling a rectangle about 500 by 700 feet. The main path of the entrance, from the west, passes between stables and a hostelry toward a gate. Here the visitor is admitted to a colonnaded semicircular portico flanked by two round towers—an early example of a westwork—that would have loomed above the low outer buildings. The plan emphasizes the church as the center of the monastic community. The church is a basilica, with a transept and choir in the east but an apse and altar at each end. The nave and aisles, which contain many other altars, do not form a single continuous space but are subdivided into compartments by screens. There are numerous entrances: two beside the western apse, others on the north and south flanks.

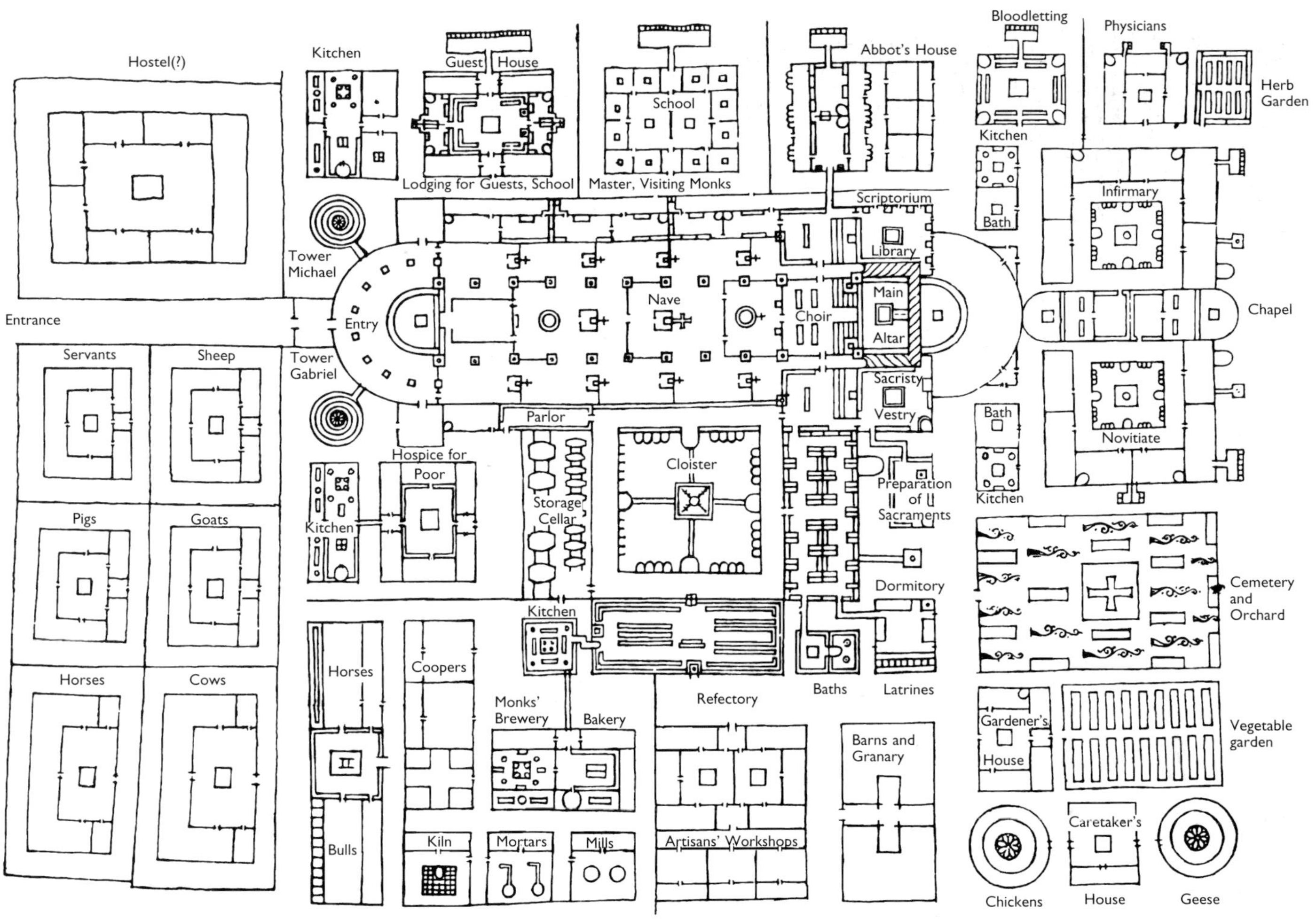

9-13. Plan of a monastery. Redrawn, with inscriptions translated into English from the Latin, from the original of c. 820 A.D. Red ink on parchment, 28 x 44⅛" (71.1 x 112.1 cm). Stiftsbibliothek, St. Gall, Switzerland

This arrangement reflects the functions of a monastery church, which was designed for the liturgical needs of the monks rather than for a lay congregation. Adjoining the church to the south is an arcaded cloister, around which are grouped the monks' dormitory (on the east side), a refectory (dining hall) and kitchen (on the south side), and a cellar. The three large buildings north of the church are a guesthouse, a school, and the abbot's house. To the east are the infirmary, a chapel and quarters for novices (new members of the community), the cemetery (marked by a large cross), a garden, and coops for chickens and geese. On the south side are workshops, barns, and other service buildings. There is no monastery exactly like this plan anywhere—even in St. Gall the design was not carried out as drawn. Yet the plan gives us a good idea of the layout of monasteries throughout the Middle Ages. [See Primary Sources, no. 22, pages 367–68.]

SPAIN. Outside of Germany, most early medieval churches were small in size, simple in plan, and provincial in style. The best examples, which are in Spain, owe their survival to their remote locations. Sta. Maria de Naranco (fig. 9-14) was built by Ramiro I about 848 as part of his palace near Oviedo. Like Charlemagne's Palace Chapel, it is an audience hall and chapel (it even included baths) but on a much more modest scale. Remarkably, it features

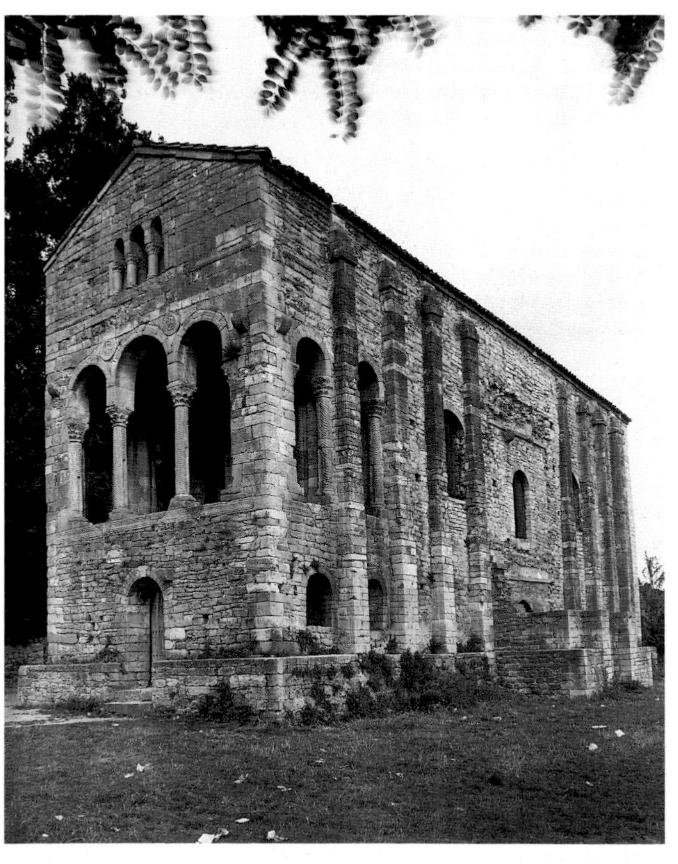

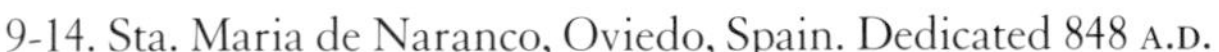

9-14. Sta. Maria de Naranco, Oviedo, Spain. Dedicated 848 A.D.

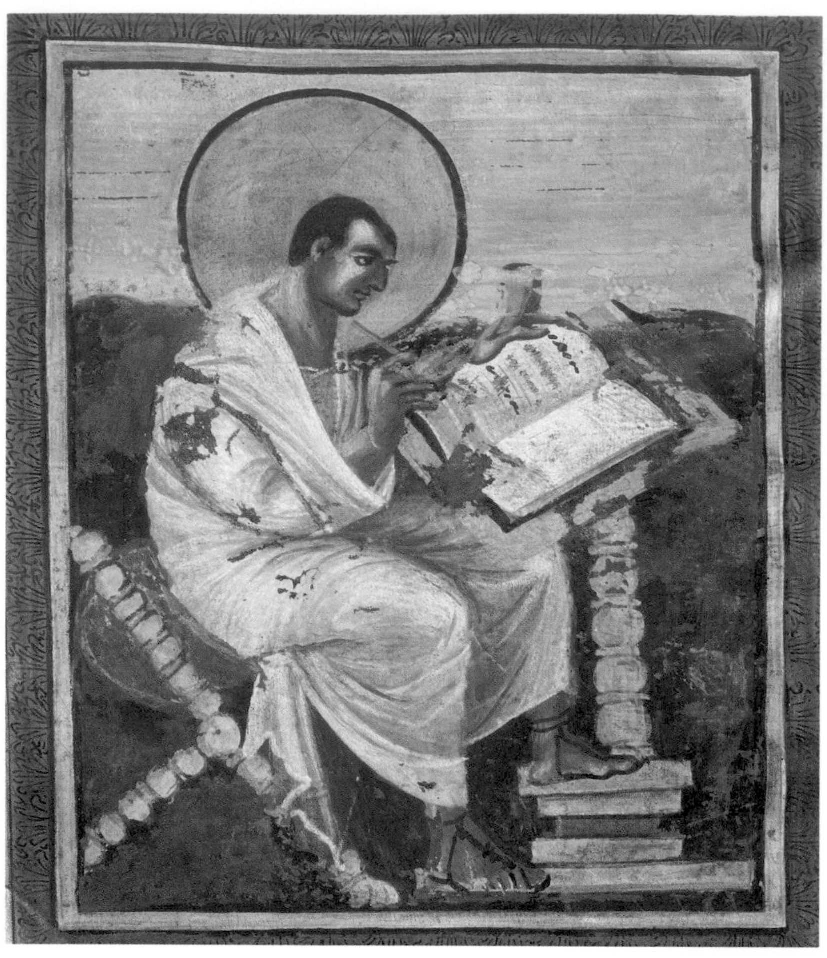

9-15. *St. Matthew,* from the *Gospel Book of Charlemagne.* c. 800–10 A.D. Ink and colors on vellum, 13 x 10" (33 x 25.4 cm). Kunsthistorisches Museum, Vienna

a tunnel vault along the upper story and arcaded loggias at either end that were clearly inspired by the interior of the Palace Chapel (see fig. 9-9). The construction, however, is more primitive. It was built of crudely carved, irregular blocks instead of the dressed masonry (called *ashlar*) found at Aachen. We need only glance at S. Apollinare in Classe (see fig. 8-13) to realize how much of the architectural past had been lost in only 300 years.

Manuscripts and Book Covers

THE GOSPEL BOOK OF CHARLEMAGNE. From the start, the fine arts played an important role in Charlemagne's cultural program. We know from literary sources that Carolingian churches contained murals, mosaics, and relief sculpture, but these have disappeared almost entirely. Illuminated manuscripts, carved ivories, and goldsmiths' work, on the other hand, have survived in considerable numbers. They demonstrate the impact of the Carolingian revival even more strikingly than the architectural remains of the period. The former Imperial Treasury in Vienna contains a Gospel Book said to have been found in the Tomb of Charlemagne and, in any case, closely linked with his court at Aachen. Looking at the picture of St. Matthew from that manuscript (fig. 9-15), we can hardly believe that such a work could have been executed in northern Europe about the year 800. Were it not for the large golden halo, the evangelist Matthew might almost be mistaken for a classical author's portrait like the one of Menander (fig. 9-16), painted at Pompeii almost eight centuries earlier. Whether Byzantine, Italian,

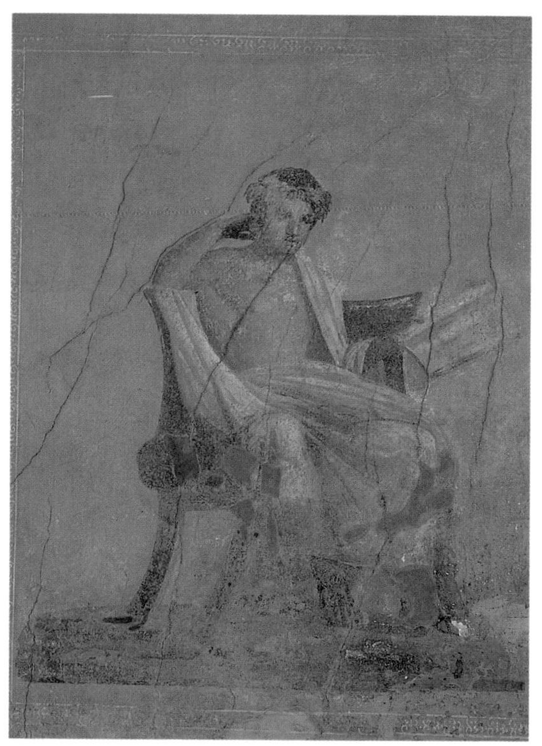

9-16. *Portrait of Menander.* c. 70 A.D. Wall painting. House of Menander, Pompeii

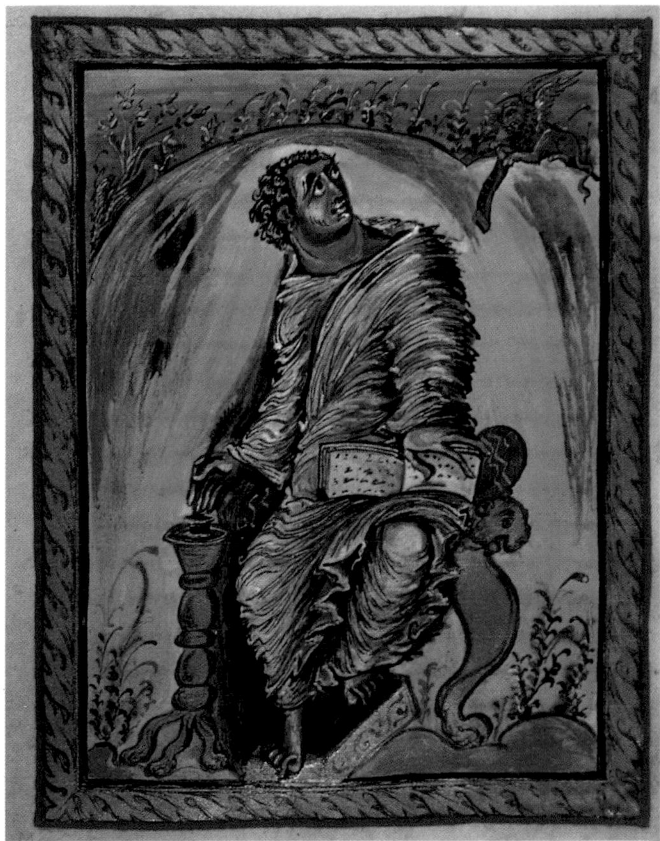

9-17. *St. Mark,* from the *Gospel Book of Archbishop Ebbo of Reims.* 816–35 A.D. Ink and colors on vellum, 10¼ x 8³⁄₁₆" (26 x 20.8 cm). Bibliothèque Municipale, Épernay, France

or Frankish, the artist clearly knew the Roman tradition of painting, down to the acanthus ornament on the wide frame, which emphasizes the "window" treatment of the picture.

THE GOSPEL BOOK OF ARCHBISHOP EBBO. This *St. Matthew* represents the first and most conservative phase of the Carolingian revival. It is comparable to a copy of the text of a classical work of literature. More typical is a miniature of St. Mark painted some three decades later for the *Gospel Book of Archbishop Ebbo of Reims* (fig. 9-17), which shows the classical model translated into a Carolingian idiom. It must have been based on an evangelist's portrait of the same style as the *St. Matthew,* but now the picture is filled with a vibrant energy that sets everything into motion. The drapery swirls about the figure, the hills heave upward, and the vegetation seems to be tossed about by a whirlwind. Even the acanthus pattern on the frame assumes a flamelike character. Matthew himself has been transformed from a Roman author setting down his thoughts into a man seized with the frenzy of divine inspiration, a vehicle for recording the Word of God. His gaze is fixed not upon his book but upon his symbol (the winged lion with a scroll), which transmits the sacred text. This dependence on the Word, so powerfully expressed here, characterizes the contrast between classical and medieval images of humanity. But the *means* of expression—the dynamism of line that distinguishes our miniature—recalls the passionate movement in ornamentation of Irish manuscripts (see figs. 9-3 and 9-5).

THE UTRECHT PSALTER. The Reims School also produced the most extraordinary of all Carolingian manuscripts, the *Utrecht Psalter* (fig. 9-18). It displays the style of the *Ebbo Gospels* in an even more energetic form, since the entire book is illustrated with pen drawings. That the artist has followed a much older model is indicated by architectural and landscape settings of the scenes, which recall those on the Column of Trajan (see fig. 7-37). It can also be seen in the use of Roman capital lettering, which had gone out of general use several centuries before. The wonderfully rhythmic quality of the draftsmanship, however, gives these sketches an expressive unity that could not have been present in the earlier pictures. Without it, the drawings of the *Utrecht Psalter* would carry little conviction, for the poetic language of the Psalms does not lend itself to illustration in the same sense as the narrative portions of the Bible.

The Psalms can be illustrated only by taking each phrase literally and then by visualizing it in some way. Thus the top of the page illustrates, "Let them bring me unto thy holy hill, and to thy tabernacles." Toward the bottom of the page, we see the Lord reclining on a bed, flanked by pleading angels. (The image is based on the words, "Awake, why sleepest thou, Oh Lord?") On the left, the faithful crouch before the Temple ("for . . . our belly cleaveth unto the earth"), and at the city gate in the foreground they are killed ("as sheep for the slaughter"). In the hands of a less imaginative and skillful artist, this procedure could well have turned into a tiresome charade. Here it has the force of a great drama.

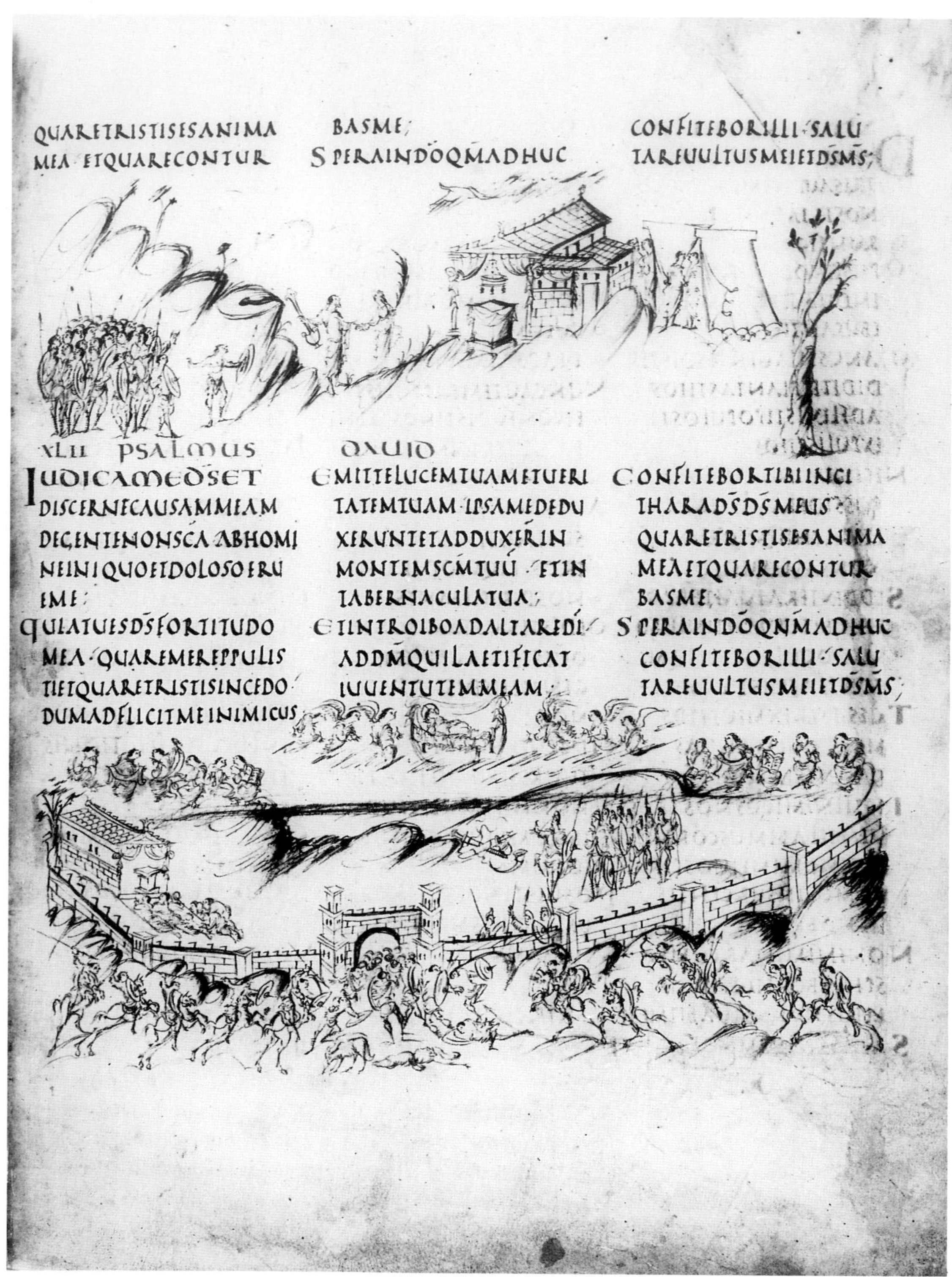

9-18. Illustrations to Psalms 43 and 44, from the *Utrecht Psalter.* c. 820–32 A.D. University Library, Utrecht, the Netherlands

THE LINDAU GOSPELS COVER. The style of the Reims School can still be felt in the reliefs of the front cover of the *Lindau Gospels* (fig. 9-19). This masterpiece of the goldsmith's art was made in the third quarter of the ninth century. It shows how splendidly the Celtic-Germanic metalwork tradition was adapted to the Carolingian revival. The clusters of semiprecious stones are not mounted directly on the gold ground. Instead, they are raised on claw feet or arcaded turrets, so that the light can penetrate beneath them to bring out their full brilliance. The crucified Jesus betrays no hint of pain or death. He seems to stand rather than to hang, his arms spread out in a solemn gesture. To endow him with the signs of human suffering was not yet conceivable, even though the means were at hand, as we can see from the expressions of grief among the small figures in the surrounding compartments.

OTTONIAN ART

Upon the death of Charlemagne's son, Louis I, in 843, the empire built by Charlemagne was divided into three parts by his grandsons: Charles the Bald, the West Frankish king, who founded the

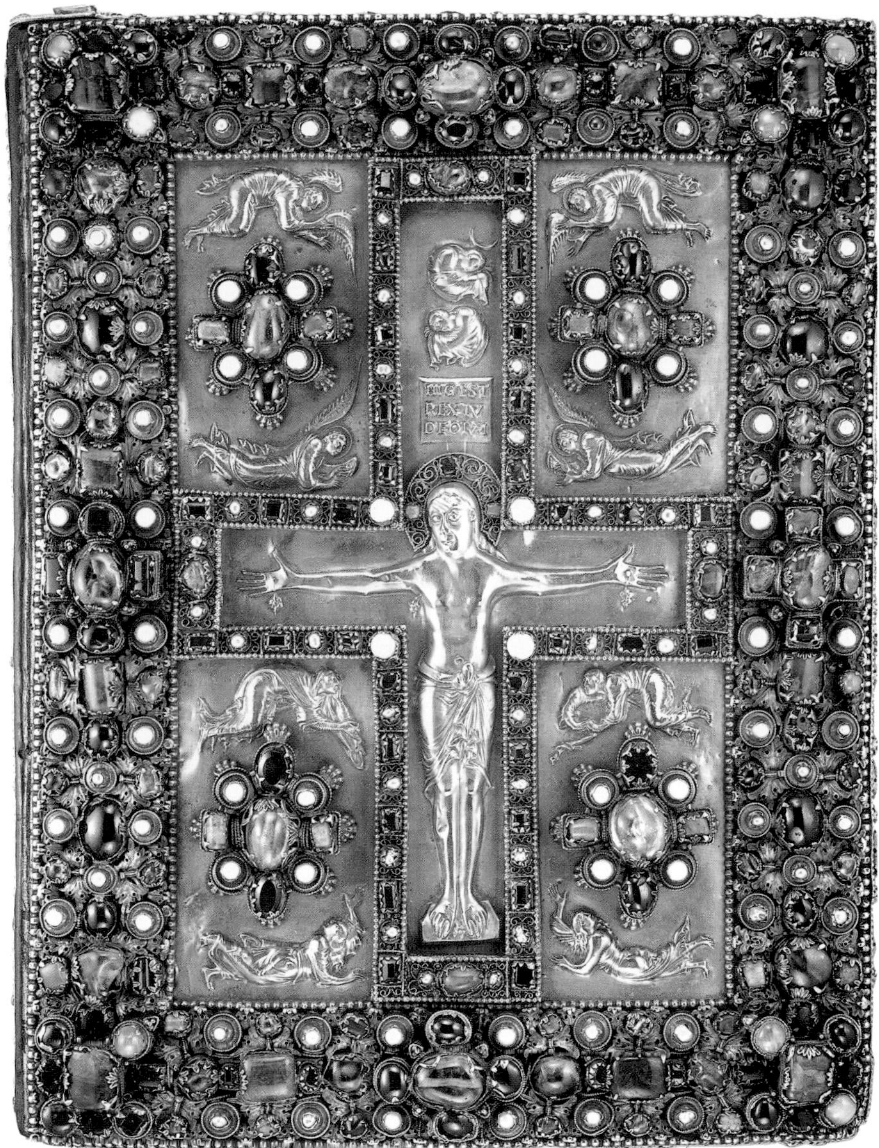

9-19. Front cover of binding, *Lindau Gospels*. c. 870 A.D. Gold and jewels, 13¾ x 10½" (35 x 26.7 cm). The Pierpont Morgan Library, New York

French Carolingian dynasty; Louis the German, the East Frankish king, who ruled an area roughly that of today's Germany; and Lothair I, who inherited the middle kingdom and the title of Holy Roman Emperor. By dividing the king's domain among his heirs, the Carolingian dynasty made the same fatal mistake as its predecessors, the Merovingians. Charlemagne had tried to impose unified rule by placing his friends in positions of power throughout the realm, but they became increasingly independent over time. During the late ninth and early tenth centuries this loose arrangement gave way to the decentralized political and social system, known today as feudalism, in France and Germany, where it had deep historical roots. Knights (originally cavalry officers) held fiefs, or feuds, as their land was called. In return, they gave military and other service to their lords, to whom they were linked through a complex system of personal bonds—termed *vassalage*—that extended all the way to the king. The land itself was worked by the large class of generally downtrodden peasants (serfs and esnes), who were utterly powerless.

The Carolingians finally became so weak that Continental Europe once again lay exposed. The Muslims attacked in the south. Slavs and Magyars advanced from the east, and Vikings from Scandinavia ravaged the north and west. The Vikings (the Norse ancestors of today's Danes and Norwegians) had been raiding Ireland and Britain by sea from the late eighth century on. Now they invaded northwestern France and occupied the area that ever since has been called Normandy. They soon adopted Christianity and Carolingian civilization, and their leaders were recognized as dukes nominally subject to the king of France. During the eleventh century, the Normans played a major role in shaping the political and cultural destiny of Europe. The duke of Normandy, William the Conqueror, became king of England following the invasion of 1066, while other Norman nobles expelled the Arabs from Sicily and the Byzantines from southern Italy.

In Germany, the center of political power had shifted north to Saxony after the death of the last Carolingian monarch in 911. Beginning with Henry I, the Saxon kings (919–1024) reestablished an effective central government. The greatest of them, Otto I, also revived the Imperial ambitions of Charlemagne. After marrying

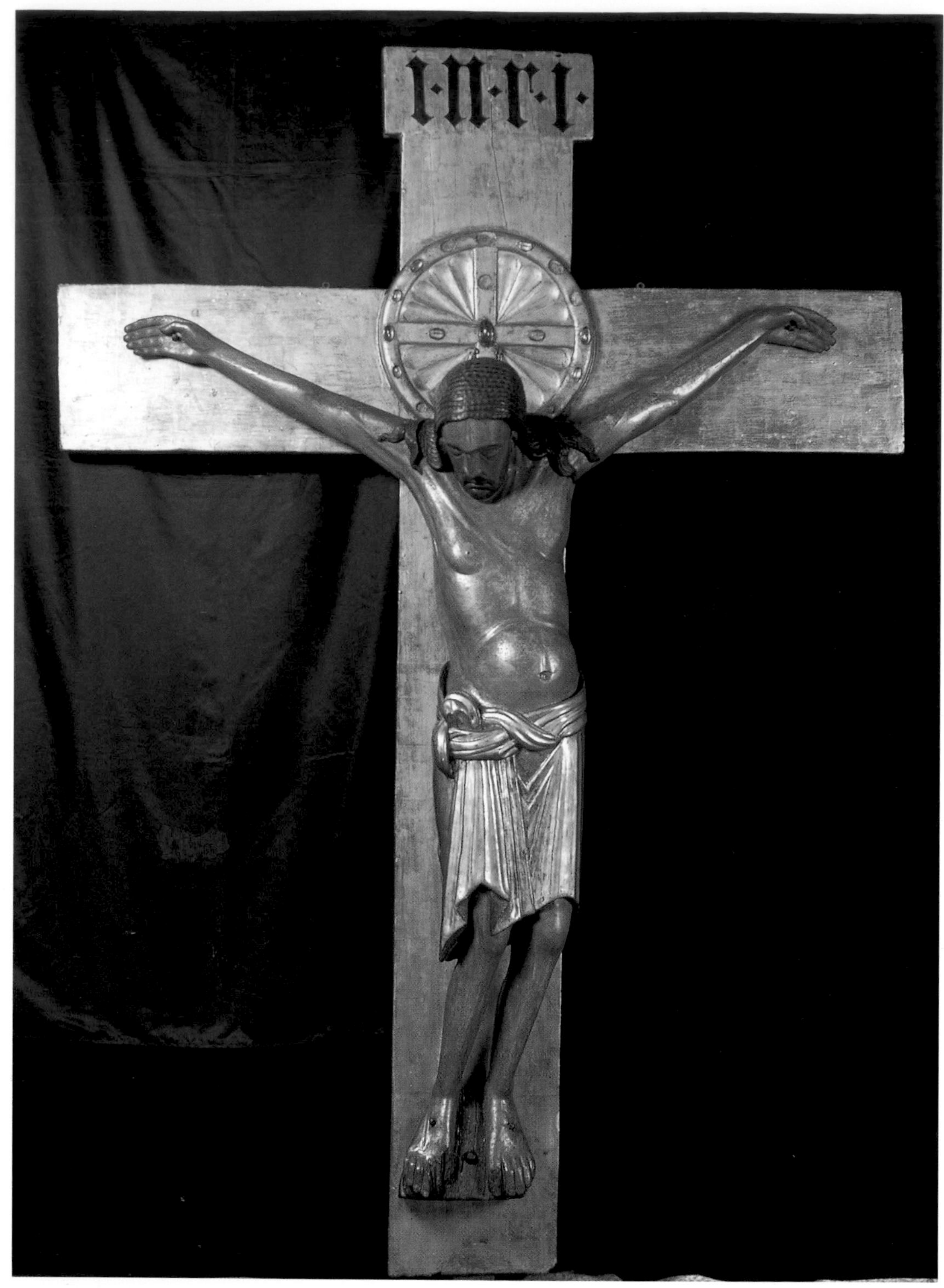

9-20. *The Gero Crucifix.* c. 975–1000 A.D. Wood, height 6'2" (1.88 m). Cathedral, Cologne, Germany

the widow of a Lombard king, he extended his rule over most of Italy. In 962 he was crowned emperor by Pope John XII, at whose request he conquered Rome and whom he later deposed for conspiring against him. From then on the Holy Roman Empire was to be a German institution. Perhaps we ought to call it a German dream, for Otto's successors were unable to maintain their claim to sovereignty south of the Alps. Yet this claim had important effects, since it led the German emperors into centuries of conflict with the papacy and local Italian rulers. North and South thus were linked in a love-hate relationship whose echoes are still felt today.

Sculpture

THE GERO CRUCIFIX. During the Ottonian period, from the mid-tenth century to the beginning of the eleventh, Germany was the leading nation of Europe, artistically as well as politically. German achievements in both areas began as revivals of Carolingian traditions but soon developed original traits.

The change of outlook is brought home to us if we compare the Christ on the cover of the *Lindau Gospels* with *The Gero Crucifix* (fig. 9-20) in the Cathedral at Cologne (carved for Archbishop Gero of

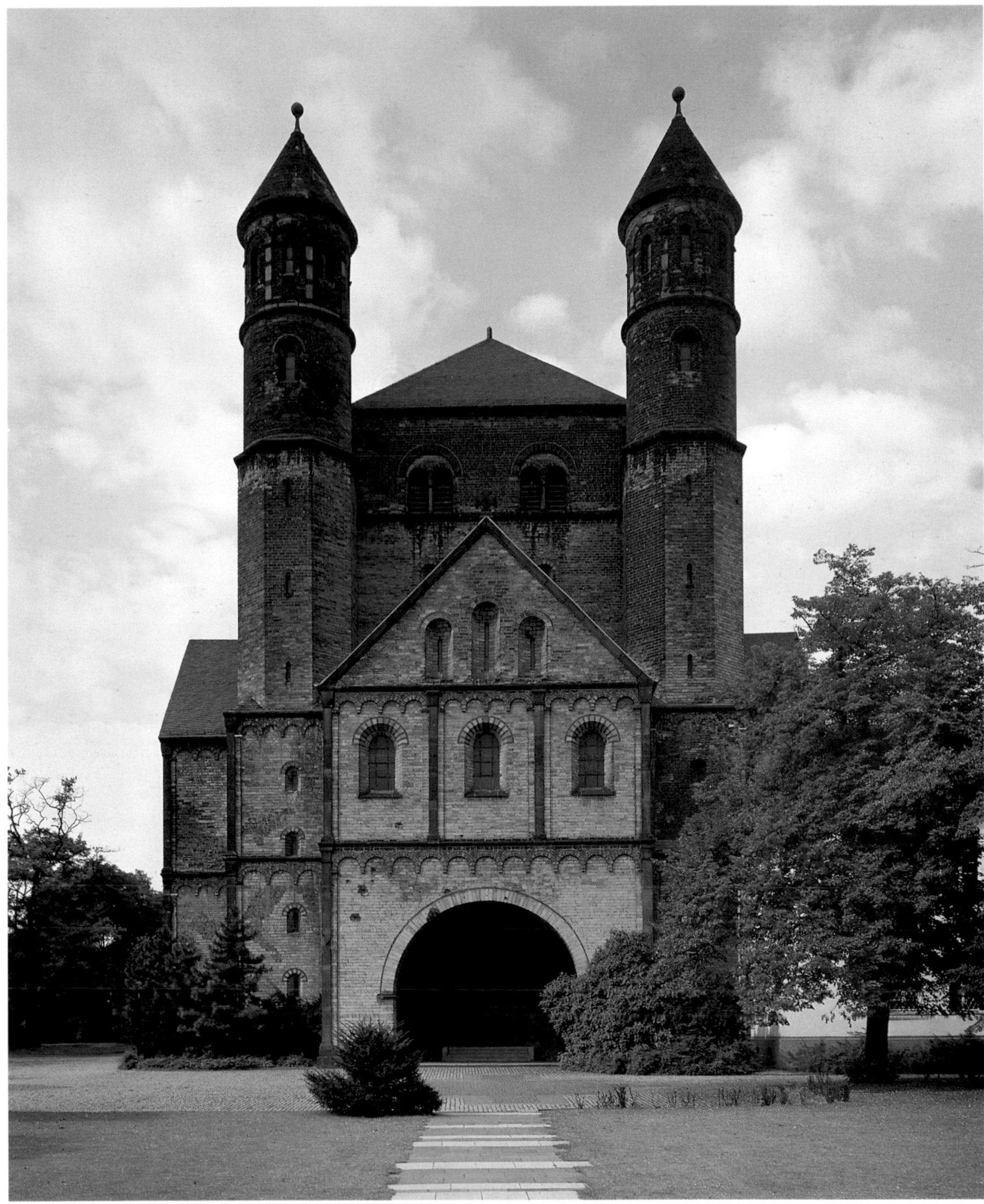

9-21. Westwork, St. Pantaleon, Cologne. Consecrated 980 A.D.

that city). The two works are separated by little more than a hundred years, but the contrast between them suggests a far greater span. In *The Gero Crucifix* we meet an image of the crucified Savior that is new to Western art. It is monumental in scale, carved in powerfully rounded forms, and filled with deep concern for the sufferings of the Lord. Particularly striking is the forward bulge of the heavy body, which makes the physical strain on arms and shoulders seem almost unbearable. The face, with its deeply incised features, has turned into a mask of agony, from which all life has fled.

How did the Ottonian sculptor arrive at this bold conception? *The Gero Crucifix* was clearly influenced by Middle Byzantine art, which had created the compassionate view of Christ on the cross (see fig. 8-48). Byzantine influence was strong in Germany at the time, for Otto II had married a Byzantine princess, thereby linking the two imperial courts. The source alone is not enough to explain the results. It remained for the Ottonian artist to translate the Byzantine image into large-scale sculptural terms and to replace its gentle pathos with expressive realism that has been the main strength of German art ever since.

The size and intensity of the figure signal an important religious development at the time. The individual was given a greater role in salvation, not merely through baptism and celebration of the Eucharist but through a personal union with Christ and identification with his sacrifice. The result was a rift between theology and mysticism that was not reconciled until a century later by St. Anselm of Canterbury.

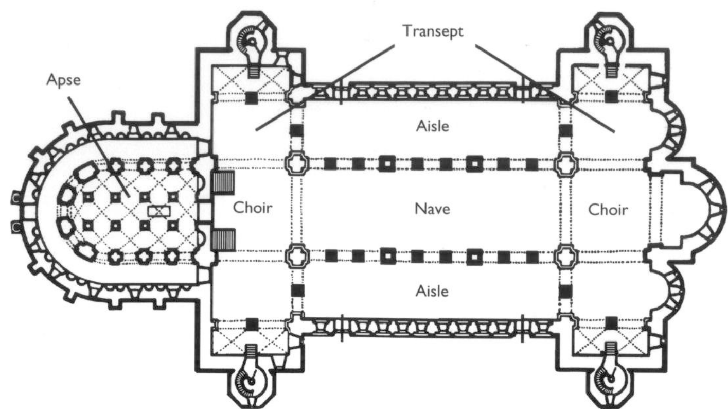

9-22. Reconstructed plan, Hildesheim Cathedral (St. Michael's), Germany. 1001–33 A.D. (after Beseler)

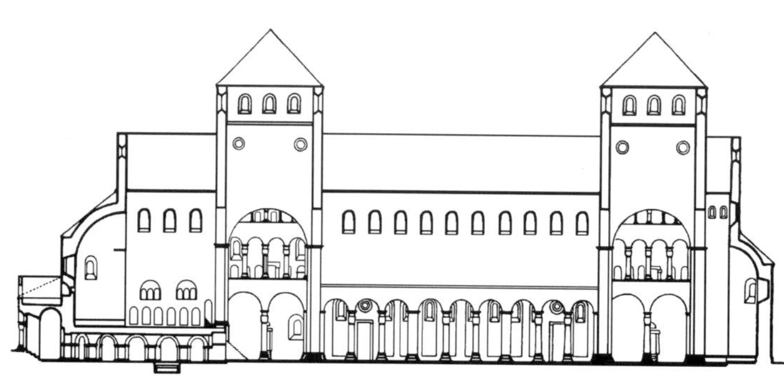

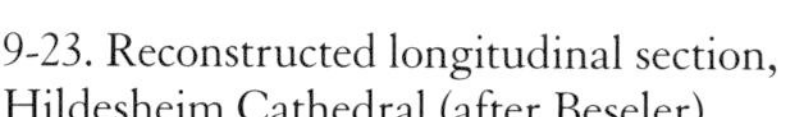
9-23. Reconstructed longitudinal section, Hildesheim Cathedral (after Beseler)

Architecture

ST. PANTALEON. Cologne was connected with the Imperial house through its archbishop, Bruno, the brother of Otto I, who left a strong mark on the city through the many churches he built or rebuilt. His favorite among these, the Benedictine abbey of St. Pantaleon, became his burial place as well as that of the wife of Otto II. Only the monumental westwork (fig. 9-21) retains its shape essentially unchanged. It is a massive and well-proportioned successor to Carolingian westworks, with the characteristic tower over the crossing of the western transept and a deep porch flanked by tall stair turrets [See fig. PS-20, page 366.]

ST. MICHAEL'S, HILDESHEIM. Judged in terms of surviving works, the most ambitious patron of architecture and art in the Ottonian age was Bernward, who became bishop of Hildesheim after having been court chaplain and a tutor of Otto III during the regency of the empress Theophano. His chief monument is another Benedictine abbey church, St. Michael's (figs. 9-22, 9-23, and 9-24). The plan, with its two choirs and lateral entrances, recalls that of the monastery church of St. Gall (see fig. 9-13). But in St. Michael's the symmetry is carried much further. Not only are there two identical transepts, with crossing towers and stair turrets (figs. 9-22 and 9-23), but the supports of the nave arcade, instead of being uniform, consist of pairs of columns separated by square piers. This alternate system divides the arcade into three equal units of three openings each. Moreover, the first and third units are correlated with the entrances, thus echoing the axis of the transepts. And since the aisles and nave are unusually wide in relation to their length, the architect's intention must have been to achieve a harmonious balance between the longitudinal and transverse axes throughout the structure.

The exterior as well as the choirs of Bernward's church have been disfigured by rebuilding. However, the restoration of the interior of the nave (figs. 9-23 and 9-24), with its great expanse of wall space between arcade and clerestory, retains the majestic feeling of the original design. (The capitals of the columns date from the twelfth century, the painted wooden ceiling from the thirteenth.) The western choir, as reconstructed in our plan, is especially interesting. Its floor was raised above the level of the rest of the church to make room for a half-subterranean basement chapel, or crypt. The crypt (apparently a special sanctuary of St. Michael) could be entered both from the transept and from the west. It was roofed by groin vaults resting on two rows of columns, and its walls were pierced by arched openings that linked it with the U-shaped corridor, or ambulatory, wrapped around it. This ambulatory must have been visible above ground, where it enriched the exterior of the choir, since there were windows in its outer wall. Such crypts with ambulatories, usually housing the venerated tomb of a saint, had been introduced into Western church architecture during Carolingian times. But the Bernwardian design stands out for its large scale and its careful integration with the rest of the building.

Metalwork

THE BRONZE DOORS OF BISHOP BERNWARD. We can gauge the importance Bernward himself attached to the crypt at St. Michael's from the fact that he commissioned a pair of rich-

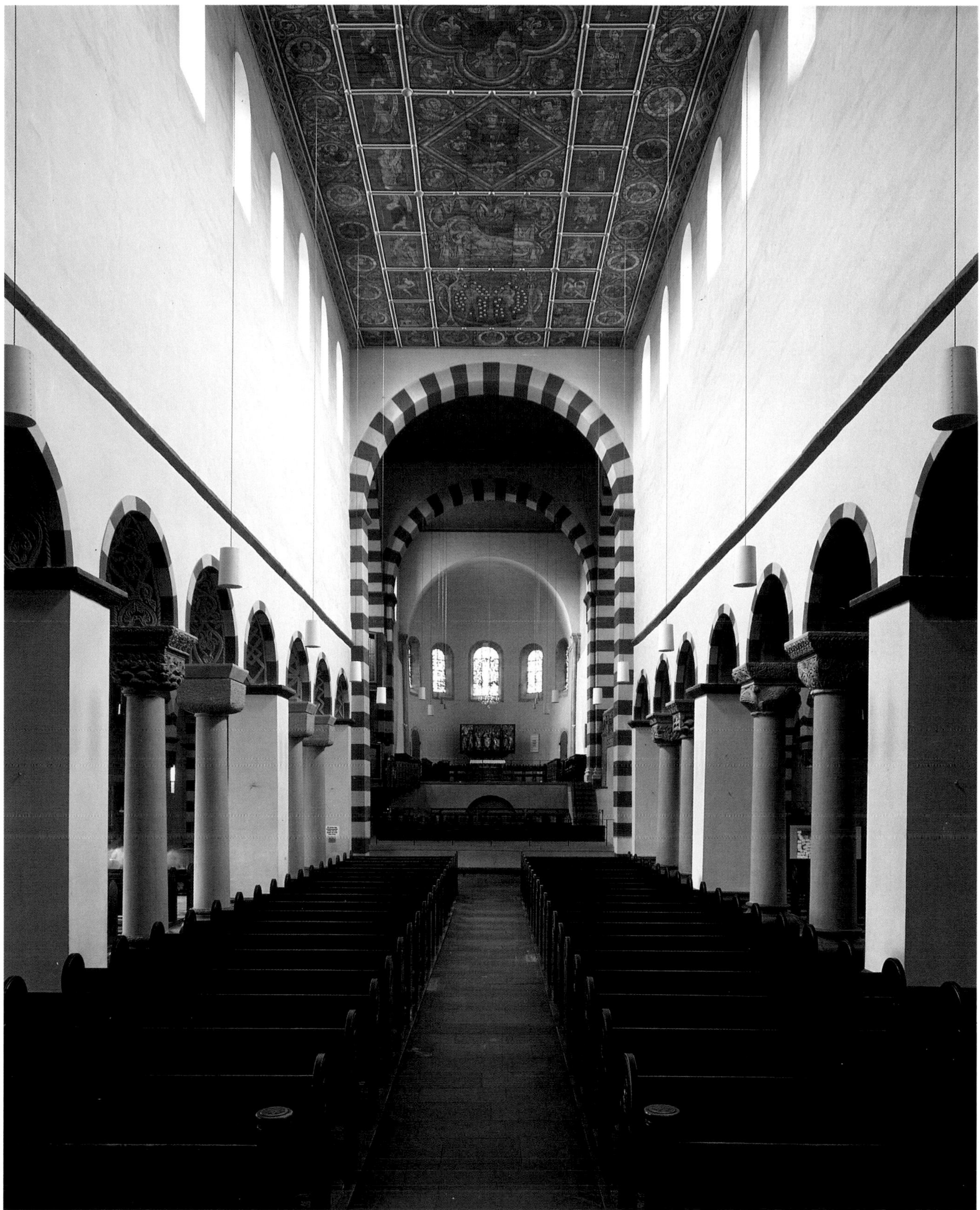

9-24. Interior (view toward the apse, after restoration of 1950–60), Hildesheim Cathedral

ly sculptured bronze doors that were probably meant for the two entrances leading from the transept to the ambulatory (fig. 9-25). They were finished in 1015, the year the crypt was consecrated. According to his biographer, Thangmar of Heidelberg, Bernward excelled in the arts and crafts. The idea may have come to him as a result of his visit to Rome, where he could have seen ancient Roman (and perhaps Byzantine) bronze doors. Bernward's doors, however, differ from earlier ones. They are divided into broad horizontal fields rather than vertical panels, and each field contains a biblical scene in high relief. The subjects, taken from Gen-

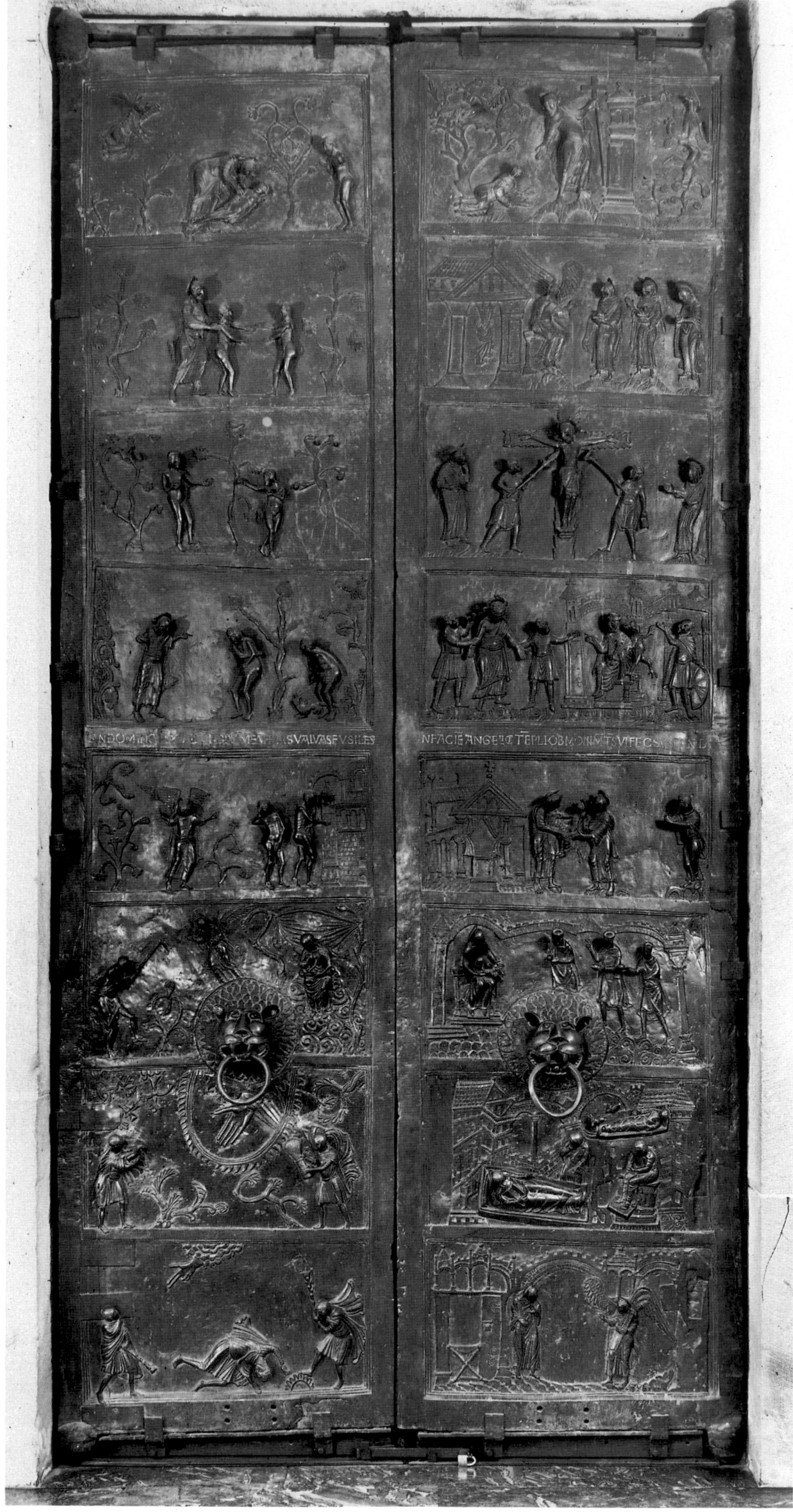

9-25. Doors of Bishop Bernward. 1015 A.D. Bronze, height approx. 16' (4.8 m). Hildesheim Cathedral

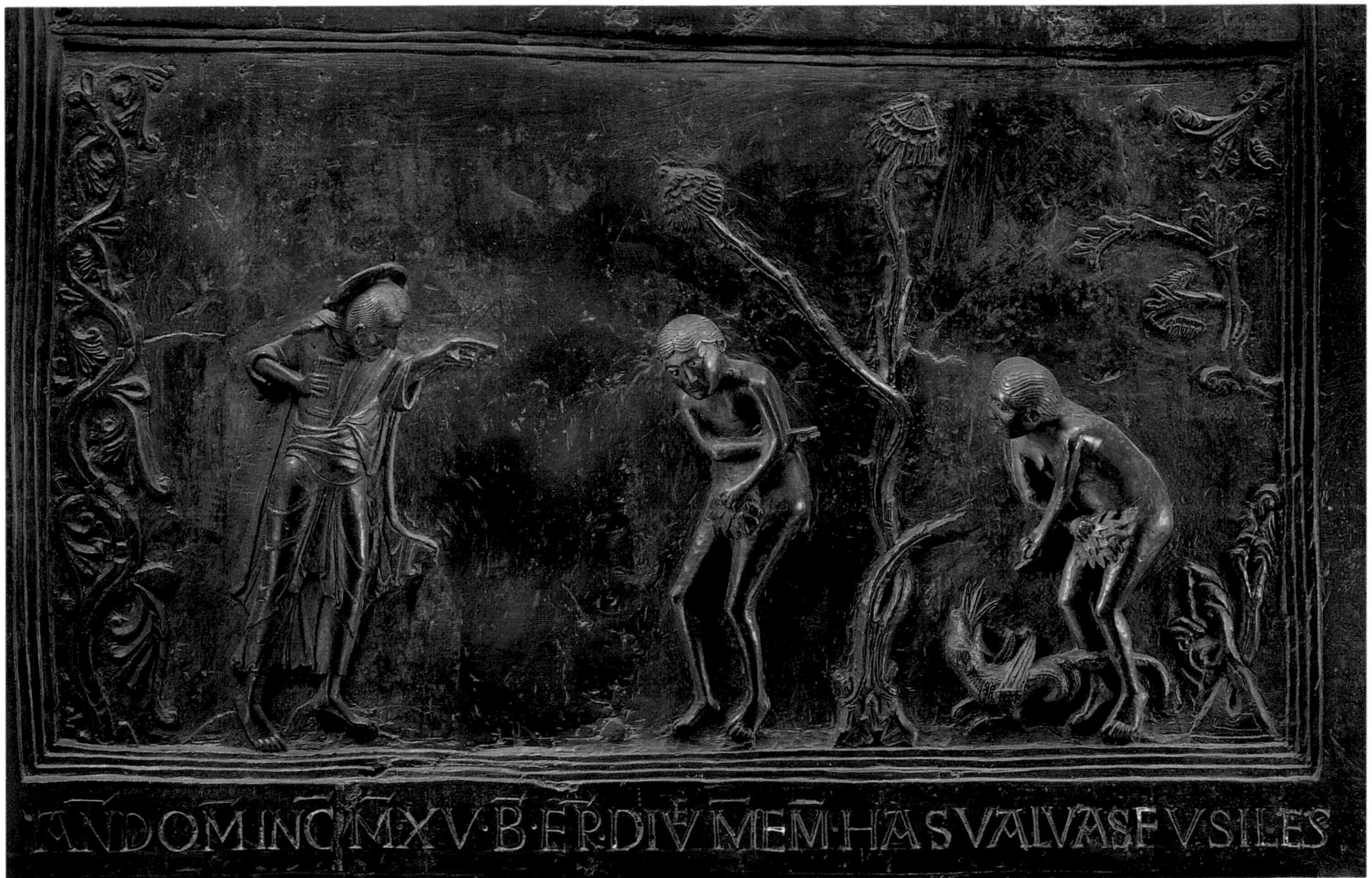

9-26. *Adam and Eve Reproached by the Lord,* from the Doors of Bishop Bernward. Bronze, approx. 23 x 43" (58.3 x 109.3 cm)

esis (left door) and the Life of Christ (right door), depict the origin and redemption of sin.

Our detail (fig. 9-26) shows Adam and Eve after the Fall. Below it, in inlaid letters notable for their classical Roman character, is part of the inscription, with the date and Bernward's name. In these figures we find none of the monumental spirit of *The Gero Crucifix.* They seem far smaller than they actually are, so that one might mistake them for a piece of goldsmith's work such as the *Lindau Gospels* cover (compare fig. 9-19). The composition must have been derived from an illuminated manuscript, since very similar scenes are found in medieval Bibles. Even the stylized bits of vegetation have a good deal of the twisting movement we recall from Irish miniatures. Yet this is no mere imitation. The story is conveyed with splendid directness and expressive force. The accusing finger of the Lord, seen against a great void of surface, is the focal point of the drama. It points to a cringing Adam, who passes the blame to his mate, while Eve, in turn, passes it to the serpent at her feet.

Manuscripts

THE GOSPEL BOOK OF OTTO III. The same intensity of glance and of gesture found in the Bernwardian bronze doors appears in Ottonian manuscript painting. Here Carolingian and Byzantine elements are blended into a new style of extraordinary scope and power. The most important center of manuscript illumination at that time was the Reichenau Monastery, located on an island in Lake Constance, on the borders of modern-day Germany, Switzerland, and Austria. Perhaps its finest achievement—and one of the great masterpieces of medieval art—is the *Gospel Book of Otto III.* Two full-page miniatures from it are reproduced here (figs. 9-27 and 9-28).

The scene of Jesus washing the feet of St. Peter contains strong echoes of ancient painting, transmitted through Byzantine art. (The subject is found at Hosios Loukas.) The soft pastel hues of the background recall the illusionism of Graeco-Roman landscapes (see figs. 7-49 and 7-50), and the architectural frame around Jesus is a late descendant of the kind of architectural perspectives we saw in the mural from Boscoreale (see fig. 7-48). The Ottonian artist has put these elements to a new use. What was once an architectural vista now becomes the Heavenly City, the House of the Lord filled with golden celestial space as against the atmospheric earthly space outside.

The figures have also been transformed. In ancient art, this composition had been used to depict a doctor treating a patient. Now St. Peter takes the place of the patient and Jesus that of the physician. (Jesus is still represented as a beardless young philosopher.) As a result, the emphasis has shifted from physical to spiritual action. This new kind of action is not only conveyed through glances and gestures, it also governs the scale of things. Jesus and St. Peter, the most animated figures, are larger than the rest, and Jesus' "active" arm is longer than his "passive" one. The eight apostles, who merely watch, have been compressed into a tiny space, so that we see little more than their eyes and hands. Even the fanlike Early Christian crowd from which this group is derived (see fig. 8-17) is less disembodied. The scene straddles two

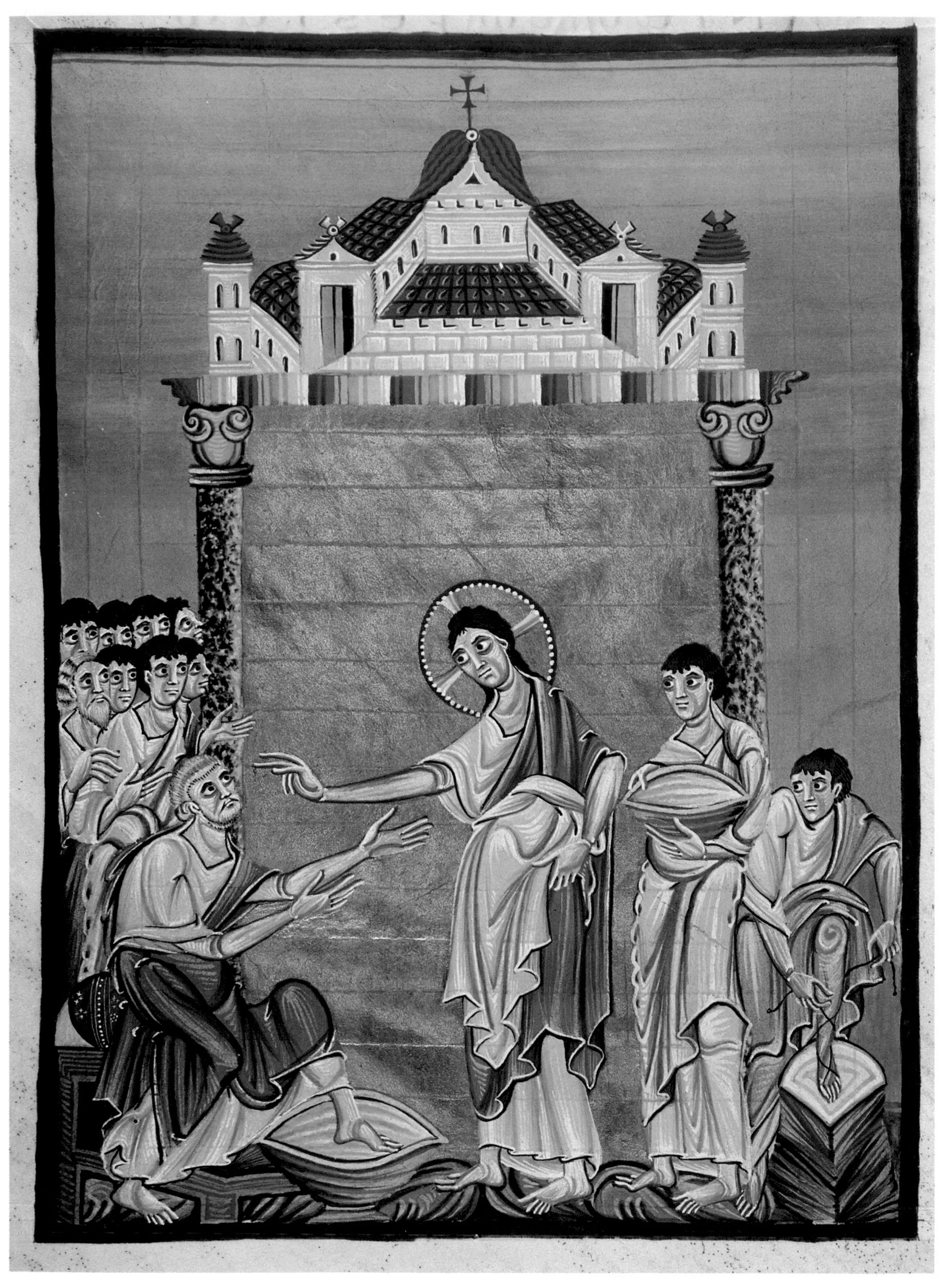

9-27. *Jesus Washing the Feet of Peter,* from the *Gospel Book of Otto III.* c. 1000 A.D. Tempera on vellum, 13 x 9$^{3}/_{8}$" (33 x 23.8 cm). Staatsbibliothek, Munich

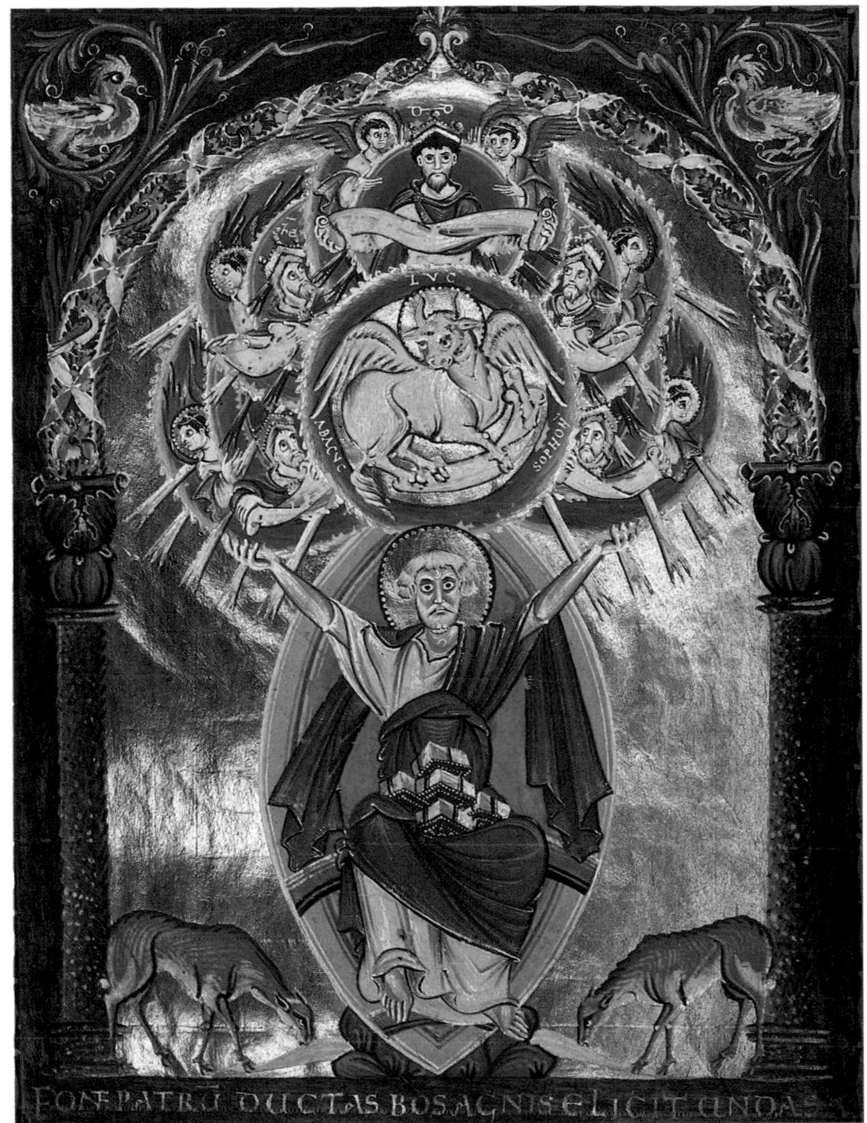

9-28. *St. Luke,* from the *Gospel Book of Otto III.* c. 1000 A.D. Tempera on vellum, 13 x 9⅜" (33 x 23.8 cm). Staatsbibliothek, Munich

9-29. *Moses Receiving the Law* and *The Doubting of Thomas.* Early 11th century. Ivory, each 9⅝ x 4" (24.5 x 10.2 cm). Staatliche Museen zu Berlin, Preussischer Kulturbesitz, Museum für Spätantike und Byzantische Kunst

eras. On the one hand, the nearly perfect blend of Western and Byzantine elements represents the culmination of the early medieval manuscript tradition. On the other, the expressive distortions look forward to Romanesque art, which incorporated them in heightened form.

The other miniature, the painting of St. Luke, is a symbolic image of overwhelming grandeur, despite its small size. Unlike his Carolingian predecessors (see figs. 9-15 and 9-17), the evangelist is not shown writing. Instead, his Gospel lies completed on his lap. Enthroned on two rainbows, he holds aloft an awesome cluster of clouds from which tongues of light radiate in every direction. Within it we see his symbol, the ox, surrounded by five Old Testament prophets and an outer circle of angels. At the bottom, two lambs drink the life-giving waters that spring from beneath his feet. The key to the design is in the inscription: *Fonte patrum ductas bos agnis elicit undas*—"From the source of the fathers the ox brings forth a flow of water for the lambs." St. Luke makes the prophets' message of salvation explicit for the faithful. The Ottonian artist has truly "illuminated" the meaning of this terse phrase.

IVORY DIPTYCHS. Closely related in style to the *Gospel Book of Otto III* is an ivory diptych with *Moses Receiving the Law* in the left panel and *The Doubting of Thomas* in the right (fig. 9-29). These two panels, which may have come from the abbey of Kues on the Mosel River, were probably made in nearby Trier, then a leading art center. It is certain that the artist was familiar with Byzantine ivories, among them the diptych of *Justinian as Conqueror* (see fig. 8-38), which was brought to Trier as early as the seventh century. Yet the artist, a great master, avoids the Byzantine influences that continued to find favor in Ottonian art. Instead, he prefers the physical distortions, fluid drapery, and architectural treatment seen in *Jesus Washing the Feet of Peter.* These devices are used to squeeze an amazing amount of action into the two scenes, which adopt the format of *The Archangel Michael* (see fig. 8-23) but depart entirely from its classicism. They also lend an impressive power to both panels that makes us feel the full force of the confrontation between mortal and God in divine and in human form: the awestruck Moses strains to receive the Ten Commandments from Heaven and Thomas reaches up to touch the wound of Christ.

CHAPTER TEN

Romanesque Art

Thus far almost all of our chapter headings and subheadings might serve equally well for a general history of civilization. Some are based on technology (for example, the Old Stone Age), others on geography, ethnology, or religion. Whatever the source, they have been borrowed from other fields, even though in our context they also designate artistic styles. There are only two important exceptions: Archaic and Classical are primarily terms of style. They refer to qualities of form rather than to the setting in which these forms were created. Why don't we have more terms of this sort? We do, as we shall see—but only for the art of the past 900 years.

Those who first thought of viewing the history of art as an evolution of styles began with the belief that ancient art evolved toward a single climax: Greek art from the age of Perikles to that of Alexander the Great. This style they called Classical (that is, perfect). Everything that came before was labeled Archaic, to indicate that it was still old-fashioned and tradition-bound; it was not yet Classical but striving in the right direction. The style of post-Classical times, on the other hand, did not deserve a special term, since it had no positive qualities of its own and was merely an echo or a decline of Classical art.

The early historians of medieval art followed a similar pattern. To them, the great climax was the Gothic style, from the thirteenth century to the fifteenth. For whatever was not yet Gothic they adopted the label Romanesque, which was first introduced in 1871. In doing so, they were thinking mainly of architecture. Pre-Gothic churches, they noted, were round-arched, solid, and heavy, compared to the pointed arches and the soaring lightness of Gothic structures. It was rather like the ancient Roman style of building, and "Romanesque" was meant to convey just that. The term is actually something of a misnomer. In one sense, all of medieval art before 1200 could be called Romanesque insofar as it shows any link with Roman tradition. Strictly speaking, however, it applies only to a small group of modest churches in northern Italy, southern France, and northern Spain. These structures do seem to be part of a revival around 950–1060 of the early Christian style under Constantine and Justinian, although the effect is rather superficial (compare figs. 8-13 and 8-25). This "First Romanesque," as it is sometimes known, was too limited and provincial, however, to account for the Romanesque itself. The same decorative vocabulary, moreover, had already been used on Ottonian churches (see fig. 9-21). What distinguishes the Romanesque proper is its amazing diversity and inventiveness, bespeaking a new spirit that is expressed in monumental architecture.

Carolingian art, we will recall, was brought into being by Charlemagne and his circle as part of a conscious revival. Even after his death it remained linked with his court. Ottonian art had a similarly narrow sponsorship. The Romanesque, in contrast, sprang up all over western Europe at about the same time. It consists of a large variety of regional styles, distinct yet closely related in many ways, and without a central source. In this respect, it resembles the art of the early Middle Ages rather than the Carolingian and Ottonian court styles that had preceded it. Its sources, however, include those styles, along with many other, less clearly traceable ones. They include Late Classical, Early Christian, and Byzantine elements, some Islamic influence, and the Celtic-Germanic heritage.

What welded these components into a coherent style during the second half of the eleventh century was not any single force but a variety of factors. The result was an upsurge of vitality throughout the West. The millennium came and went without the Apocalypse (described in the Book of Revelation of St. John the Divine) that many had predicted. Christianity had at last triumphed everywhere in Europe. The Vikings, still largely heathen in the ninth and tenth centuries when their raids terrorized the British Isles and the Continent, had entered the Catholic fold, not only in Normandy but in Scandinavia as well. In 1031 the Caliphate of Cordova had broken up into many small Muslim states, opening the way for the reconquest of the Iberian peninsula; and the Magyars had settled down in Hungary.

There was a growing spirit of religious enthusiasm that could be seen in the greatly increased numbers of people making pilgrimages to sacred sites and in the Crusades against the Muslims. Equally important was the reopening of Mediterranean trade routes by the navies of Venice, Genoa, Amalfi, Pisa, and Rimini. The revival of trade and travel linked Europe commercially and culturally, and urban life flourished as a result. The new pace of religious and secular life is vividly described in pilgrim guides of the time. [See Primary Sources, no. 23, pages 368–69.]

During the turmoil of the early Middle Ages, the towns of the Western Roman Empire had shrunk greatly. (The population of Rome, about one million in 300 A.D., fell to less than 50,000 at one point.) Some cities were deserted altogether. From the eleventh century on, they began to regain their former importance. New towns sprang up everywhere. Like the cities, they gained their independence, thanks to a new middle class of artisans and merchants, which established itself between the peasantry and the landed nobility and became an important factor in medieval society.

In many ways, then, western Europe between 1050 and 1200 became a great deal more "Roman-esque" than it had been since the sixth century. It recaptured some of the trade patterns, the urban quality, and the military strength of ancient Imperial times. To be sure, there was no central political authority. Even the empire of Otto I did not extend much farther west than modern Germany does. But to some extent the central spiritual authority of the pope took its place as a unifying force. The monasteries of the Cistercians and Benedictines rivaled the wealth and power of secular rulers. Indeed, it was now the pope who sought to unite Europe into a single Christian realm. In 1095 Pope Urban II called for the First Crusade to liberate the Holy Land from Muslim rule and to aid the Byzantine emperor against the advancing Turks. The army of Crusaders was more powerful than anything a secular ruler could have raised for the purpose. The pope's authority was spiritual, not just temporal, as he was forced to combat the heresies that grew throughout the Catholic realm. The pope's assertion of supremacy in dogma led to the final break (known as the Great Schism) with the Byzantine Orthodox church in 1054.

ARCHITECTURE

The most striking difference between Romanesque architecture and that of the earlier Middle Ages is the amazing increase in building activity. An eleventh-century monk, Raoul Glaber, summed it up well when he exclaimed that the world was putting on a "white mantle of churches." These churches were not only more numerous than those of the early Middle Ages, they were also larger, more richly articulated, and more "Roman-looking." Their naves now had stone vaults instead of wooden roofs. Their exteriors, unlike those of previous churches, were decorated with both architectural ornament and sculpture. Romanesque monuments of the first importance are distributed over an area that might well have represented the world—the Catholic world, that is—to Raoul Glaber: from northern Spain to the Rhineland, from the Scottish-English border to central Italy. The richest examples, the greatest variety of regional types, and the most adventurous ideas are to be found in France. If we add to this group the buildings, since destroyed or disfigured, whose original designs are known through archaeological research, we have a wealth of architectural invention unmatched by any previous era.

Southwestern France

ST.-SERNIN, TOULOUSE. We begin our survey of Romanesque churches with St.-Sernin, in the southern French town of Toulouse (figs. 10-1–10-3). It is one of a group of great churches of the "pilgrimage type," so called because they were built along the roads leading to the pilgrimage center of Santiago de Compostela in northwestern Spain. [See Primary Sources, no. 23, pages 368–69.] The plan is much more complex and more fully integrated than those of earlier structures such as Corvey, or St. Michael's at Hildesheim (see fig. 9-22). It is an emphatic Latin cross, with the center of gravity at the eastern end. Clearly this church was designed not only to serve a monastic community but also, like Old St. Peter's in Rome (see fig. 8-4), to accommodate large crowds of lay worshipers in its long nave and transept.

The nave is flanked by two aisles on each side. The inner aisle continues around the arms of the transept and the apse. This ambulatory circuit is anchored to the two towers of the truncated west facade, which was never completed as planned. The ambulatory, we will recall, had been a feature of the crypts of earlier churches such as St. Michael's. Now it is above ground, where it is linked with the aisles of the nave and transept. Chapels radiate from the apse and continue along the eastern face of the transept. (The apse, ambulatory, and apsidal chapels form a unit known as the pilgrimage choir.)

The plan also shows that the aisles of St.-Sernin are groin-vaulted throughout. Along with the features already noted, the use of vaulting imposes a high degree of regularity on the design. The aisles are made up of square bays, which serve as a basic module for the other dimensions. The nave and transept bays equal two such units, the crossing and the facade towers four units. The harmony conveyed by the repetition of these modules is perhaps the most striking feature of the pilgrimage church.

On the exterior, the interrelationship of elements is enhanced by different roof levels, which set off the nave and transept against the inner and outer aisles, the apse, the ambulatory, and the radiating chapels. The effect of careful articulation is increased by the buttresses, which reinforce the walls between the windows, to contain the outward thrust of the vaults. The windows and portals are further emphasized by decorative framing. The crossing tower was completed later, in Gothic times, and is taller than originally intended. The two facade towers, unfortunately, were never finished and remain stumps.

As we enter the nave, we are impressed with its tall proportions, the elaboration of the nave walls, and the indirect lighting. Together they create a sensation very different from the ample and serene interior of St. Michael's, with its simple and clearly separated blocks of space (see figs. 9-23 and 9-24). While the nave walls of St. Michael's look Early Christian (see fig. 8-6), those of

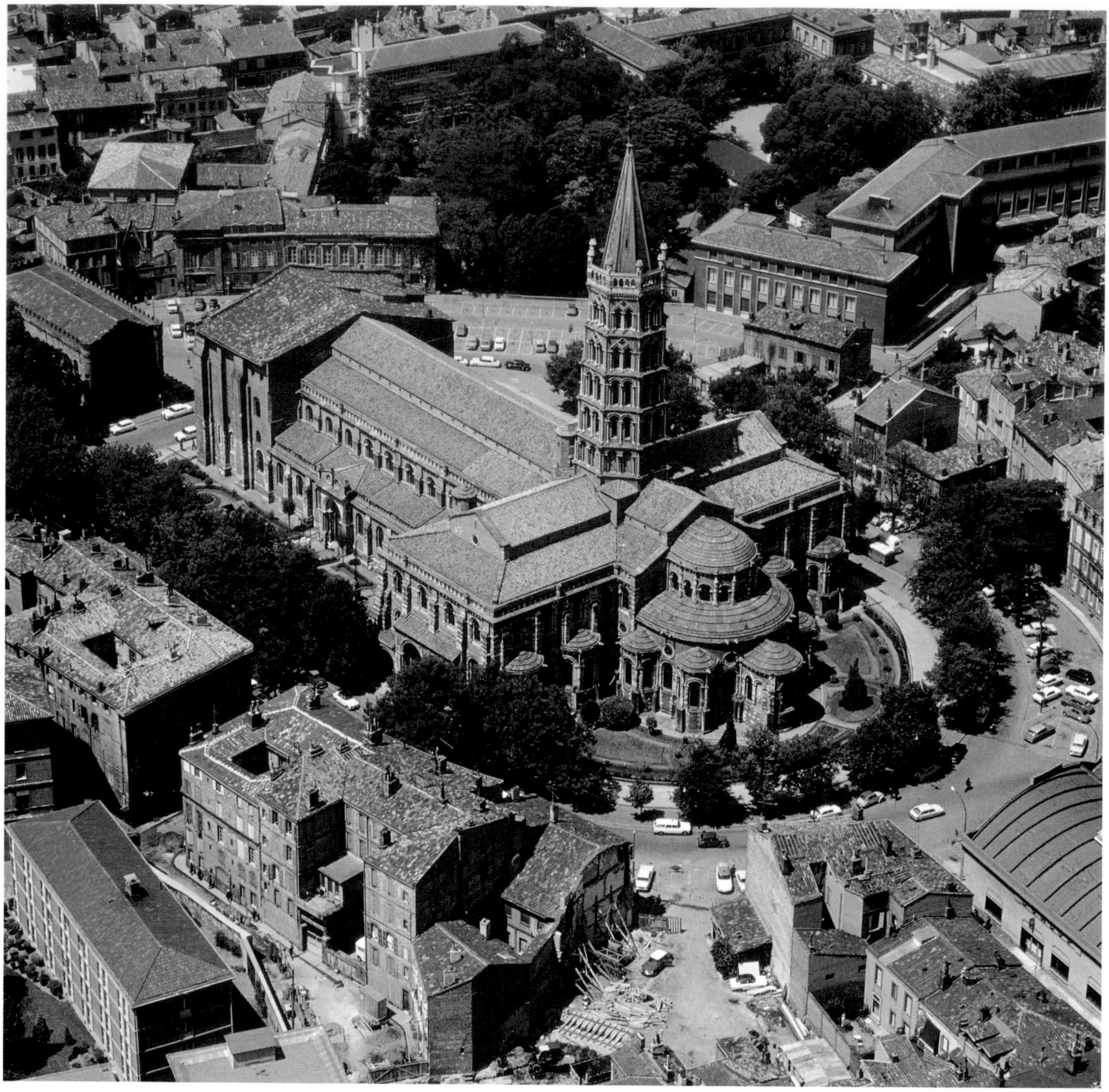

10-1. St.-Sernin, Toulouse, France (aerial view). c. 1070–1120

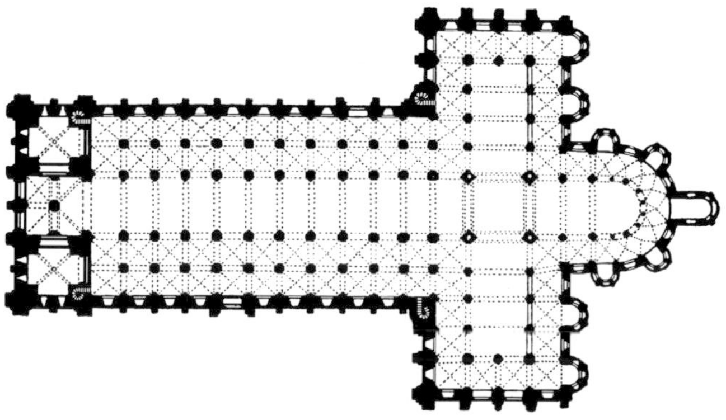

10-2. Plan of St.-Sernin (after Conant)

St.-Sernin seem more akin to structures such as the Colosseum (see fig. 7-11). The syntax of ancient Roman architecture—vaults, arches, engaged columns, and pilasters firmly knit together into a coherent order—has been recaptured here to a remarkable degree. Yet the forces expressed in the nave of St.-Sernin are no longer the physical, muscular forces of Graeco-Roman architecture but spiritual forces of the kind we have seen governing the human body in Carolingian and Ottonian miniatures. To a Roman viewer, the half-columns running the entire height of the nave wall would appear just as unnaturally drawn-out as the arm of Jesus in figure 9-27. The columns seem to be driven upward by some tremendous, unseen pressure, as if hastening to meet the transverse arches that subdivide the barrel vault of the nave. Their

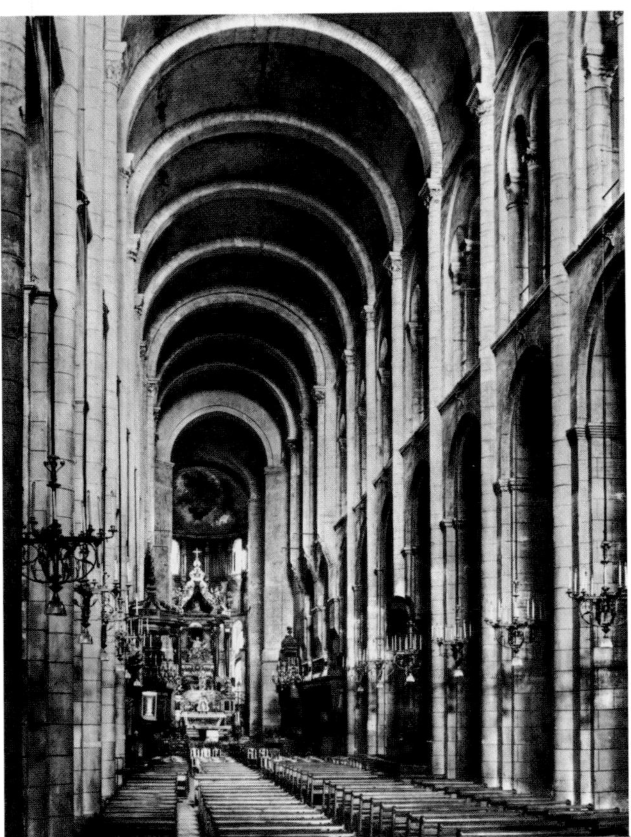

10-3. Nave and choir, St.-Sernin

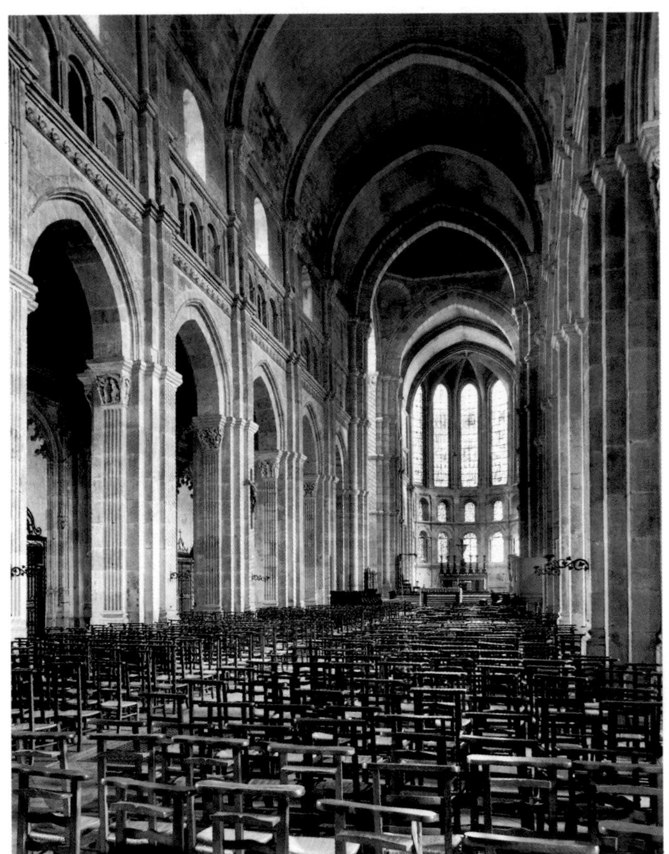

10-4. Nave wall, Autun Cathedral, France. c. 1120–32

insistently repeated rhythm propels us toward the eastern end of the church, with its light-filled apse and ambulatory (now obscured by a huge altar of later date).

We do not mean to suggest that the architect set out to achieve this effect. Beauty and engineering were inseparable. Vaulting the nave to eliminate the fire hazard of a wooden roof was not only a practical aim, it also provided a challenge to make the House of the Lord more impressive. Since a vault becomes more difficult to sustain the farther it is from the ground, every resource had to be strained to make the nave as tall as possible. However, for safety's sake there is no clerestory. Instead, galleries were built over the inner aisles to abut the lateral pressure of the nave vault. It was hoped that enough light would filter through them into the central space. St.-Sernin reminds us that architecture, like politics, is "the art of the possible"—and that its success, here as elsewhere, is measured by the degree to which the architect has explored the limits of what seemed possible, both structurally and aesthetically, under those particular conditions.

Burgundy and Western France

AUTUN CATHEDRAL. The builders of St.-Sernin would have been the first to admit that their answer to the problem of the nave vault was not a final one. The architects of Burgundy arrived at a more elegant solution, which can be seen in the Cathedral of Autun (fig. 10-4). The cathedral was begun by Bishop Étienne de Bage of the Cluniac order (see below) and consecrated in 1132. Here the galleries are replaced by a blind arcade (called a *triforium,* since it often has three openings per bay) and a clerestory. What made this three-story elevation possible was the use of the pointed arch for the nave vault. The pointed arch probably reached France from Islamic architecture, where it had been used for some time. By eliminating the part of the round arch that responds the most to the pull of gravity, the two halves of a pointed arch brace each other. The pointed arch thus exerts less outward pressure than the semicircular arch. Hence, not only can it be made as steep as possible, but the walls can be perforated. (For reasons of harmony, it also appears in the nave arcade, where it is not needed for further support.) The advances that grew out of this discovery were to make possible the soaring churches of the Gothic period (see, for example, figs. 11-12, 11-15, and 11-16).

Like St.-Sernin, Autun comes close to straining the limits of the possible. The upper part of the nave wall shows a slight outward lean under the pressure of the vault, a warning against any further attempts to increase the height of the clerestory or to enlarge the windows.

CLUNY. The largest structure ever built in Romanesque Europe was the third abbey church at Cluny. The order's rapid growth (see box, pages 279–80) can be seen in the fact that this great church, begun in 1088, was a replacement for the ample one finished only about 75 years earlier (which itself had been built beside the original wooden basilica of about 910). Unfortunately, Cluny III, as it is known, was destroyed after the French Revolution.

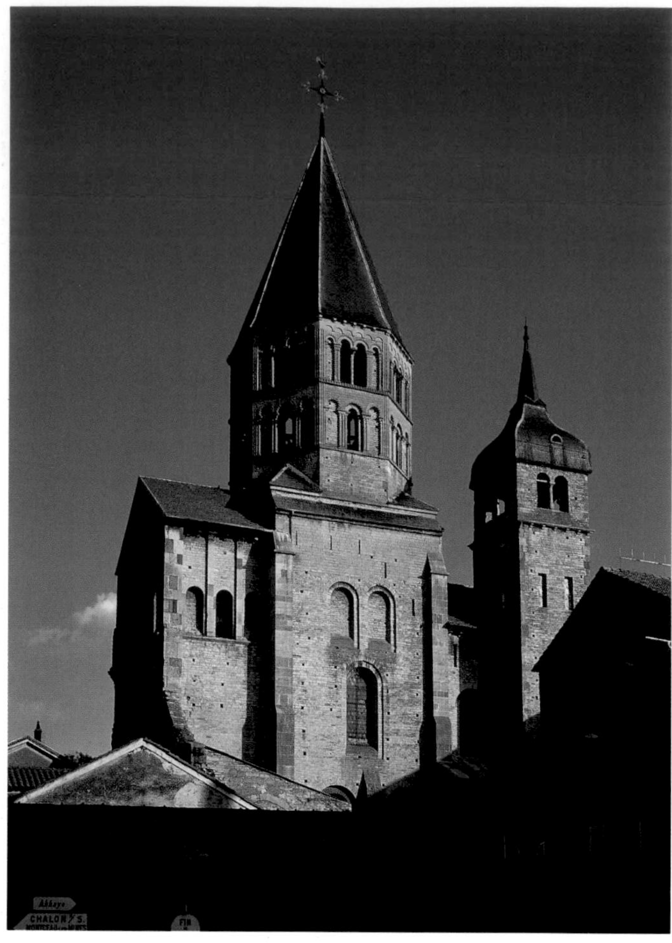

10-5. South Transept, Cluny III, 1088–1130

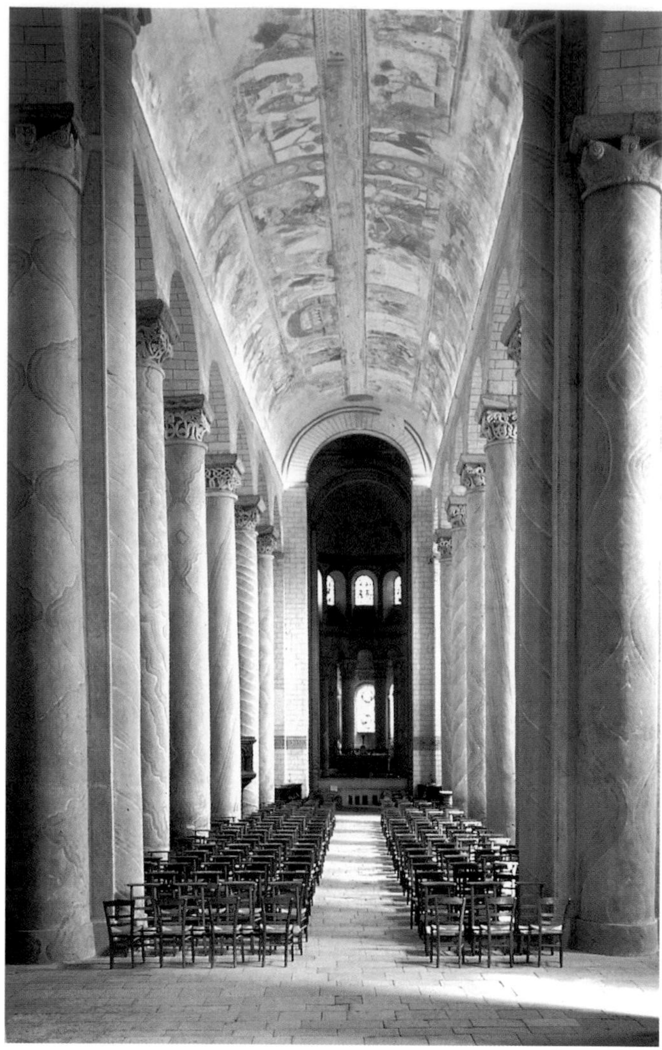

10-6. Choir (c. 1060–75) and nave (1095–1115), St.-Savin-sur-Gartempe, France

Only the south transept and its octagonal tower remain from what was once the most impressive massing of towers in all of Europe (fig. 10-5). They indicate the huge scale of the church as a whole, which was not to be surpassed until the Gothic. We can get a good idea of the interior if we combine the nave elevation of Autun with the barrel vault and apse of St.-Sernin, except that there was a second triforium in place of the clerestory.

HALL CHURCHES. A third type, called a "hall church," appears in the west of France. At St.-Savin-sur-Gartempe (fig. 10-6) the nave vault lacks the reinforcing arches, since it was designed to offer a continuous surface for murals (see fig. 10-36 for this cycle, the finest of its kind). Its weight rests directly on the nave arcade, which is supported by a majestic set of columns. Yet the nave is fairly well lit, for the two aisles are carried almost to the same height, and their outer walls have generously sized windows. At the eastern end of the nave, there is a pilgrimage choir beyond the crossing tower.

The nave and aisles of hall churches are covered by a single roof, as at St.-Savin. The west facade, too, tends to be low and wide and may become a richly sculptured screen. Notre-Dame-la-Grande at Poitiers (fig. 10-7), due west from St.-Savin, is noteworthy in this respect. The sculptural program is an exposition of

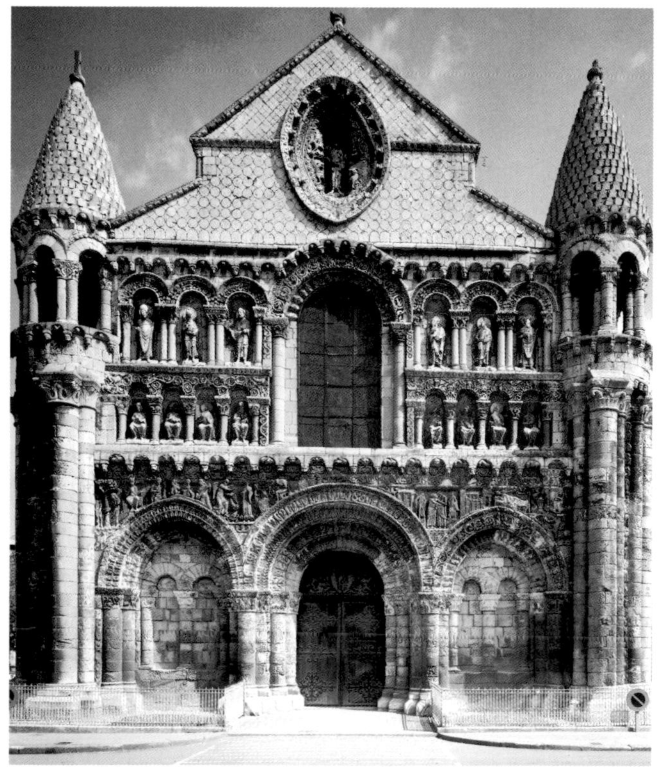

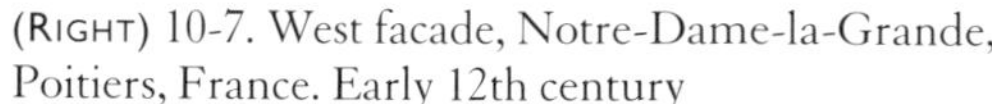

(RIGHT) 10-7. West facade, Notre-Dame-la-Grande, Poitiers, France. Early 12th century

MONASTICISM AND CHRISTIAN MONASTIC ORDERS

People of many times, places, and religious faiths have renounced the world and devoted themselves entirely to a spiritual way of life. Some have chosen to live alone as hermits, often in isolated places, where they have led harsh, ascetic existences. Others have come together in religious communities known as monasteries to share their faith and religious observance. Hermits have been especially characteristic of Hinduism, while the monastic life has been more common in Buddhism. Among the Jews of the first century B.C., there were both hermits, or anchorites (John the Baptist was one of these), and a kind of monasticism practiced by a sect known as the Essenes. Both forms are found in Christianity throughout most of its history as well. Their basis can be found in Scripture. On the one hand, Jesus urged giving up all earthly possessions as the road to salvation. On the other, the Book of Acts in the Bible records that his followers came together in their faith after the Crucifixion.

The earliest monasticism practiced by Christians was the hermit's life. It was chosen by a number of pious men and women who lived alone in the Egyptian desert in the second and third centuries A.D.This way of life was to remain fundamental to the Eastern Church, especially in Syria. But early on, communities emerged when colonies of disciples—both men and women—gathered around the most revered of the hermits, such as St. Anthony (fourth century), who achieved such fame as a holy man that he was pursued by people asking him to act as a divine intercessor on their behalf.

Monasteries soon came to assume great importance in early Christian life. (They included communities for women, which are often called convents or nunneries.) The earliest known monastery was founded by Pachomius along the Nile around 320, a community that blossomed into nine monasteries and two nunneries by the time of his death a quarter century later. Similar ones quickly followed in Syria, where monachism (monasticism) flourished until the 638 conquest by the Arabs. Syrian monasteries were for the most part sites along pilgrimage routes leading to the great monastery at Telanessa (present-day Qal'at Sim'ân), where Simeon Stylites (born 390) spent the last 30 years of his long life atop a tall column in almost ceaseless prayer.

Eastern monasticism was founded by Basil the Great (c. 330–379), bishop of Caesarea in Asia Minor. A remarkable man, he was the brother of Gregory of Nyssa and St. Macrina, successor to Eusebius as bishop of Caesarea. Along with his close friend Gregory Nazianzen, he was one of the four Fathers of the Greek Church. Basil's rule for this life established the basic characteristics of Christian monasticism: poverty, chastity, and humility. It emphasized prayer, scriptural reading, and work, not only within the monastery but also for the good of lay people in the world beyond its walls; as a result, monasticism now assumed a social role. One of the oldest rules in the West is that of St. Augustine of Hippo (354–430). He spread monasticism to Africa, where it proved short-lived due to the Vandal conquests.

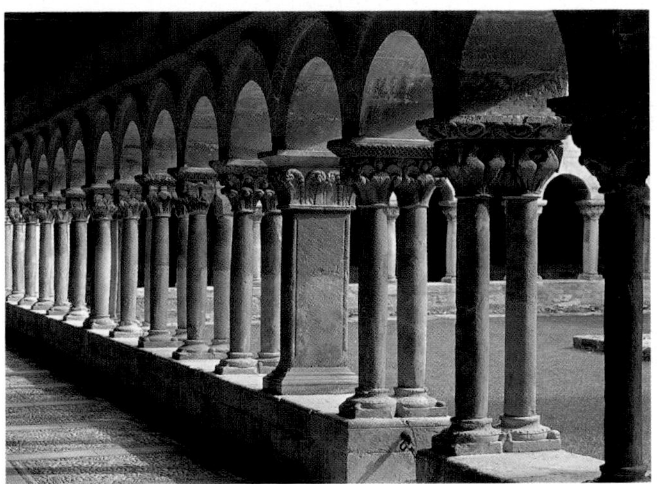

The cloister at Sto Domingo de Silos Monastery, Spain. c. 1085–1100

Monasticism had been brought even earlier to France by St. Martin of Tours (c. 316–397) around the middle of the fourth century and to Ireland by St. Patrick (c. 385–461) in the fifth century. Ireland wholeheartedly adopted a harsh form of anchoritism during the sixth century. Monasticism was established in England by St. Augustine (d. 604), first archbishop of Canterbury (not to be confused with the church doctor of the same name mentioned above), who went there in 597 at the request of Gregory the Great and enjoyed remarkable success in turning the country to Christianity.

The most important figure in Western monasticism was Benedict of Nursia (c. 480–c. 553), the founder of the abbey at Monte Cassino in southern Italy. His rule, which was patterned after Basil's, divided the monk's day into periods of private prayer, communal ritual, and labor and also required a moderate form of communal life, which was strictly governed. This was the beginning of the Benedictine order, the first of the great monastic orders (or societies) of the Western church. The Benedictines thrived with the strong support of Pope Gregory the Great, himself a former monk, who codified the Western liturgy and the forms of Gregorian chant (see pages 308–09).

Because of their organization and continuity, monasteries were considered ideal seats of learning and administration under the Frankish kings of the eighth century. They were supported even more strongly by Charlemagne and his heirs, who gave them land, money, and royal protection. As a result, they became rich and powerful, even exercising influence on international affairs. Monasteries and convents provided a place for the younger children of the nobility, and even talented members of the lower classes, to pursue challenging, creative, and useful lives as teachers, nurses, writers, and artists—opportunities that generally would have been closed to them in secular life (see "Hildegard of Bingen," page 298). Although they had considerable independence at first, the various orders eventually gave their loyalty to Pope Gregory the Great. They thereby became a major source of power for the papacy in return for its protection.

(box continues on following page)

MONASTICISM *(continued from preceding page)*

Through these linkages, Church and State over time became linked institutionally, to their mutual benefit, thereby promoting greater stability.

Besides the Benedictines, the other important monastic orders of the West included the Cluniacs, the Cistercians, the Carthusians, the Franciscans, and the Dominicans. The Cluniac order (named after its original monastery at Cluny, in France) was founded as a renewal of the original Benedictine rule in 909 by Berno of Baume and 12 brethren on farmland donated by William of Aquitaine. It quickly emerged as the leading international force in Europe, thanks to its unique charter, which made it answerable only to the papacy, then at a low ebb in its power. The order also enjoyed close connections to the Ottonian rulers. Indeed, under the abbots Odilo (r. 994–1049) and Hugh of Semur (r. 1049–1109), its authority became so great that it could determine papal elections and influence imperial policy. It also called for crusades and the reconquest of Spain.

Partly in reaction to the wealth and secular power of the Cluniac order and other Church institutions, the Cistercian order was founded in 1098 by Robert of Molesme as a return to the Benedictine rule. This order, headquartered at Cîteaux, reached its height under St. Bernard (1090–1153). His abbey in Clairvaux, settled with 12 brethren, overtook Cluny in population and power by the time of his death. Cistercian monasteries were deliberately located in remote places, where the monks would come into minimal contact with the outside world, and the rules of daily life were particularly strict. In keeping with this austerity, the order developed an architectural style known as Cistercian Gothic, recognizable by its geometric simplicity and lack of ornamentation (see pages 317 and 321).

The Carthusian order was founded by Bruno, an Italian monk, in 1084. Carthusians are in effect hermits, each monk or nun living alone in a separate cell, vowed to silence and devoted to prayer and meditation. The members of each house come together only for religious services and for communal meals several times a year. Because of the extreme austerity and piety of this order, several powerful dukes in the fourteenth and fifteenth centuries established Carthusian houses (charterhouses; French, *chartreuses*), so that the monks could pray perpetually for the souls of the dukes after they died. The most famous of these was the Chartreuse de Champmol, built in 1385 near Dijon, France, as the funerary church of Philip the Bold of Burgundy (see page 334) and his son, John the Fearless.

Eventually the conflict between poverty and work led to the creation of two orders of wandering friars: the Franciscans and the Dominicans. Founded with the blessing of Pope Innocent III, to whom they swore obedience, both orders became arms of papal policy. They grew with astonishing rapidity until they became rivals, due partly to their contrasting missions. The Franciscans were devoted to spiritual reform by living example, while the purpose of the Dominicans was to combat heresy. The Franciscan order was founded in 1209 by St. Francis of Assisi (c. 1181–1226) as a preaching community. Francis, who was perhaps the most saintly character since Early Christian times, insisted on a life of complete poverty, not only for the members personally but for the order as a whole. The Poor Clares, established by Francis and his friend St. Clare (1194–1253) near Assisi, was an order of nuns that followed the ascetic life while ministering to the sick. It, too, underwent spectacular growth, especially in Spain, where it was sponsored by the royal house. Franciscan monks and nuns were originally mendicant—that is, they begged for a living. This rule was revised in the fourteenth century.

The Dominican order was established in 1220 by St. Dominic (c. 1170–1221), a Spanish monk who had been a member of the Cistercians. Besides preaching, the Dominicans devoted themselves to the study of theology. They were considered the most intellectual of the religious orders in the late Middle Ages and the Early Renaissance. The Dominicans were well organized from the start. However, the Franciscan community did not become a formal order until a papal bull of 1230. It attained its greatest prominence under St. Bonaventure (1221–1274), who was, with the Dominican St. Thomas Aquinas (1225–1274), one of the great doctors (theologians) of the Church. The two even taught together at the University of Paris during the early 1250s.

Christian doctrine that is a feast for the eyes as well as the mind. The elaborately bordered arcades house large seated or standing figures. Below them a wide band of relief carving stretches across the facade. Essential to the rich sculptural effect is the doorway, which is deeply recessed and framed by a series of arches resting on stumpy columns. Taller bundles of columns enhance the turrets. Their conical helmets nearly match the height of the gable in the center, which rises above the actual height of the roof behind it.

Normandy and England

The next major development took place farther north, in Normandy, and for good reason. The duchy had been ruled by a series of weak Carolingians before being ceded to the Danes by the aptly named Charles the Simple in 911. It developed into the most dynamic force in Europe by the middle of the eleventh century under the Capetian dynasty, which was established when Hugh Capet was elected king in 987 and which ruled France for almost 350 years. Although it came late, Christianity was strongly supported by the Norman dukes and barons, who played an active role in monastic reform and founded numerous abbeys. Thus Normandy soon became a cultural center of international importance.

ST.-ÉTIENNE, CAEN. The architecture of southern France merged with local traditions to produce a new Norman school that evolved in an entirely different direction. The west facade of the abbey church of St.-Étienne at Caen (fig. 10-8), founded by William the Conqueror a year or two after his invasion of England in 1066, offers a striking contrast with that of Notre-Dame-la-Grande. The westwork proclaims this an Imperial church. Its closest ancestors are Carolingian churches built under royal patronage in the wake of St.-Riquier (see page 366). Like its predecessors, it has a minimum of decoration (compare fig. 9-12). Four huge buttresses divide the front of the church into three vertical sections. The vertical thrust continues in the two towers, whose height would be impressive even without the tall Early Gothic helmets. St.-Étienne is cool and composed: its refined proportions are meant to be appreciated by the mind rather than the eye. The interior is equally remarkable, but in order to understand its importance we must first turn to the extraordinary development of Anglo-Norman architecture in Britain during the last quarter of the eleventh century.

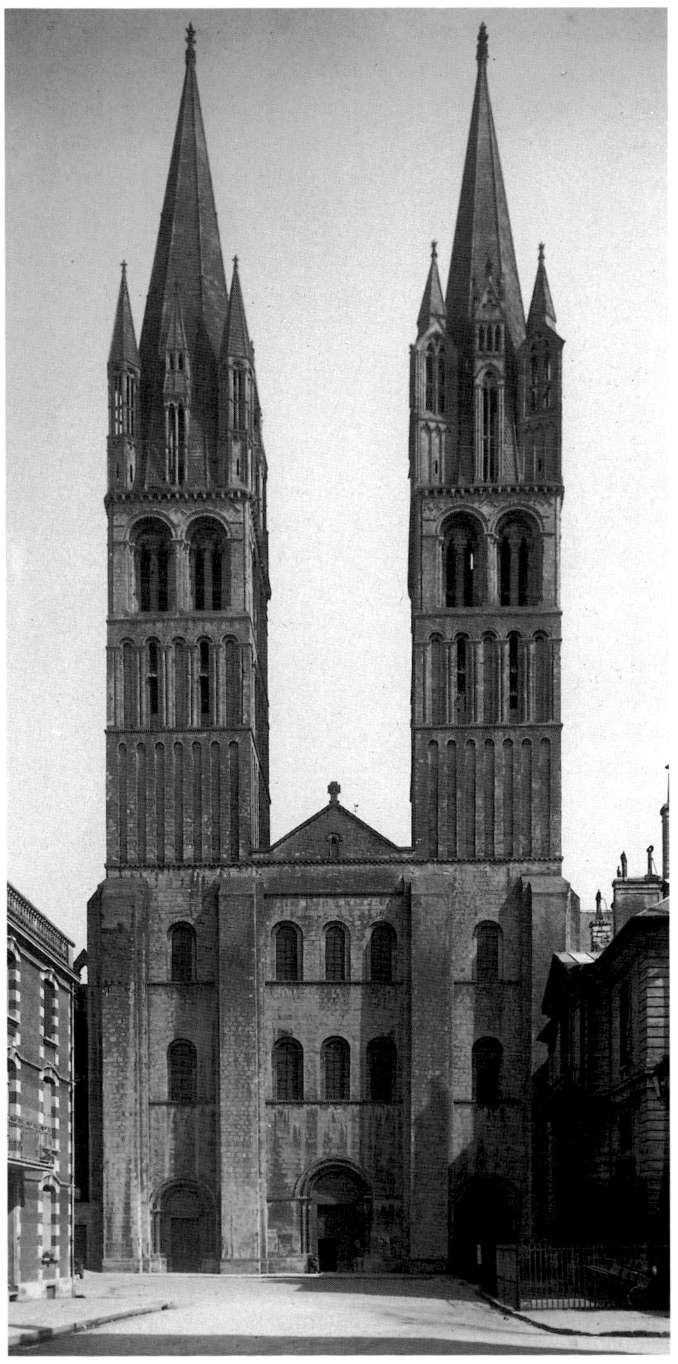

10-8. West facade, St.-Étienne, Caen, France. Begun 1068

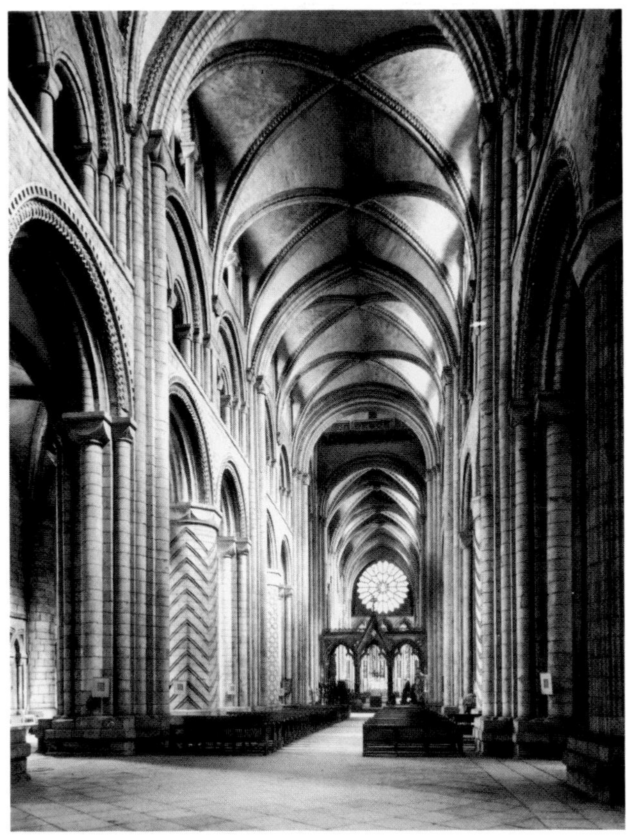

10-9. Nave (looking east), Durham Cathedral, England. 1093–1130

DURHAM CATHEDRAL. Its most ambitious work is the Cathedral of Durham (figs. 10-9–10-11), just south of the Scottish border, which was begun in 1093. Although its plan is more austere, it has a nave one-third wider than St.-Sernin's. Its overall length (400 feet) is also greater, making Durham one of the largest churches of medieval Europe. The nave may have been designed to be vaulted from the start. The vault over its eastern end had been completed by 1107, a remarkably short time, and the rest of the nave, following the same pattern, was finished by 1130. This vault is of great interest, for it represents the earliest systematic use of a ribbed groin vault over a three-story nave and thus marks a basic advance beyond the solution we saw at Autun.

Looking at the plan, we see that the aisles consist of the usual groin-vaulted compartments approaching a square. The bays of the nave, separated by strong transverse arches, are oblong and groin-vaulted in such a way that the ribs form a double-design. The vault thus is divided into seven sections rather than the usual four. Since the nave bays are twice as long as the aisle bays, the transverse arches occur only at the odd-numbered piers of the nave arcade. The piers therefore alternate in size. The larger ones are of compound shape (that is, bundles of column and pilaster shafts attached to a square or oblong core), the others cylindrical.

The easiest way to visualize the origin of this system is to imagine that the architect started out by designing a barrel-vaulted nave with galleries over the aisles and without a clerestory, as at St.-Sernin, but with the transverse arches spaced more widely. The realization suddenly dawned that putting groin vaults over the nave as well as the aisles would gain a semicircular area at the ends of each transverse vault that could be broken through to

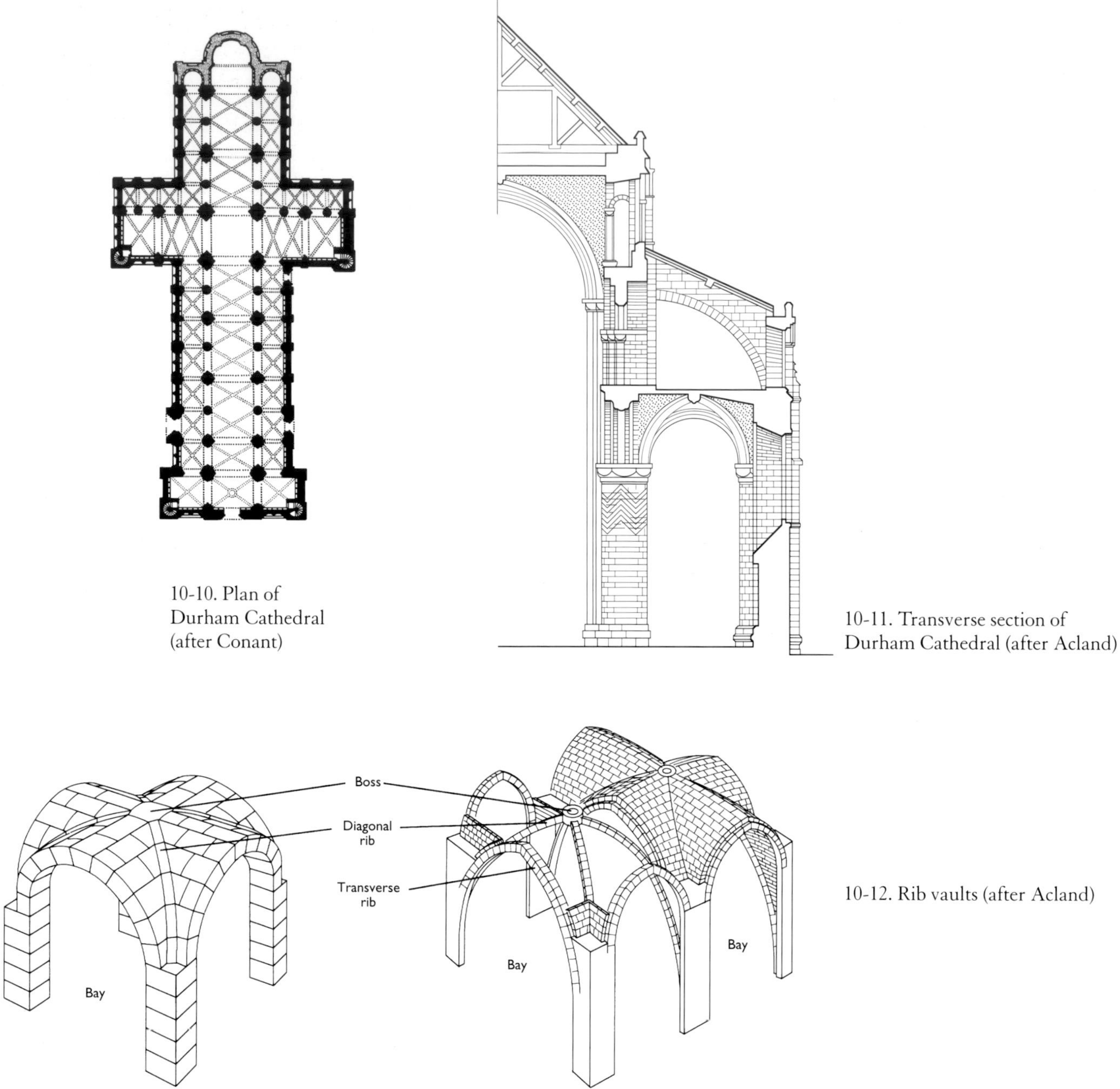

10-10. Plan of Durham Cathedral (after Conant)

10-11. Transverse section of Durham Cathedral (after Acland)

10-12. Rib vaults (after Acland)

make a clerestory, because it had no essential supporting functions (fig. 10-12, left). Each nave bay is intersected by two transverse barrel vaults of *oval* shape, so that it contains a pair of Siamese-twin groin vaults that divide it into seven compartments. The outward thrust and weight of the whole vault are concentrated at six securely anchored points on the gallery level. The ribs were needed to provide a stable skeleton for the groin vault, so that the curved surfaces between them could be filled in with masonry of minimum thickness. Thus both weight and thrust were reduced. We do not know whether this ingenious scheme was actually invented at Durham, but it could not have been devised much earlier, for it is still in an experimental stage. While the transverse arches at the crossing are round, those to the west of it are slightly pointed, indicating an ongoing search for improvements.

This system had other advantages as well. From an aesthetic standpoint, the nave at Durham is among the finest in all Romanesque architecture. The wonderful sturdiness of the alternating piers makes a splendid contrast with the dramatically lit, sail-like surfaces of the vault. This lightweight, flexible system for covering broad expanses of great height with fireproof vaulting, while retaining the ample lighting of a clerestory, marks the culmination of the Romanesque and the dawn of the Gothic.

ST.-ÉTIENNE, CAEN. Let us now return to the interior of St.-Étienne at Caen (fig. 10-13). It seems that the nave had been planned to have galleries and a clerestory, with a wooden ceiling. After the experience of Durham, it became possible, in the early twelfth century, to build a groined nave vault instead, with only slight changes in the wall design. But the bays of the nave here are approximately square. The double-X rib pattern therefore could be replaced by a single X with an additional transverse rib (see fig. 10-12, right), producing a groin vault with six sections instead of seven. These vaults are no longer separated by heavy transverse arches but by simple ribs. The result is another saving

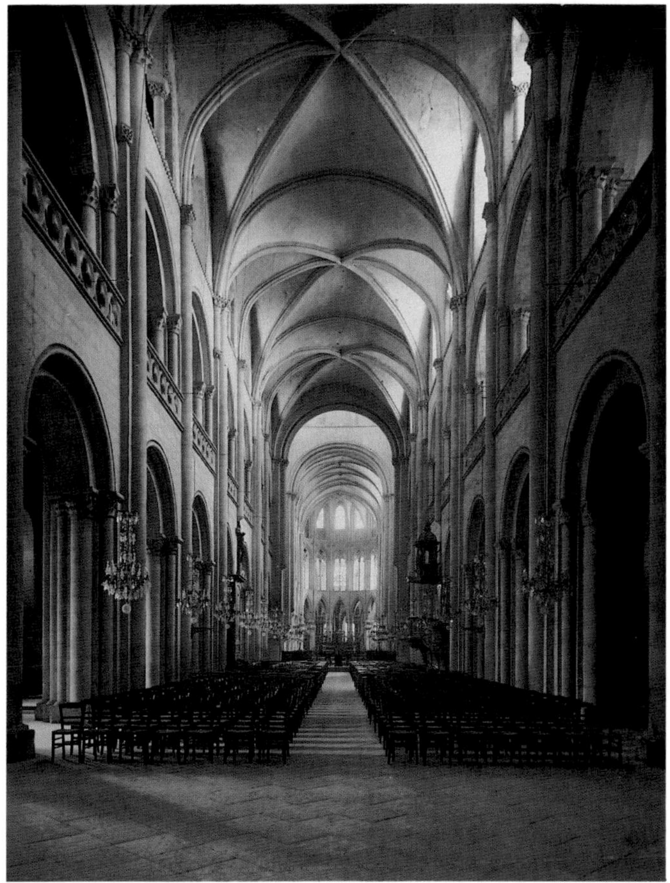

10-13. Nave (vaulted c. 1115–20), St.-Étienne, Caen

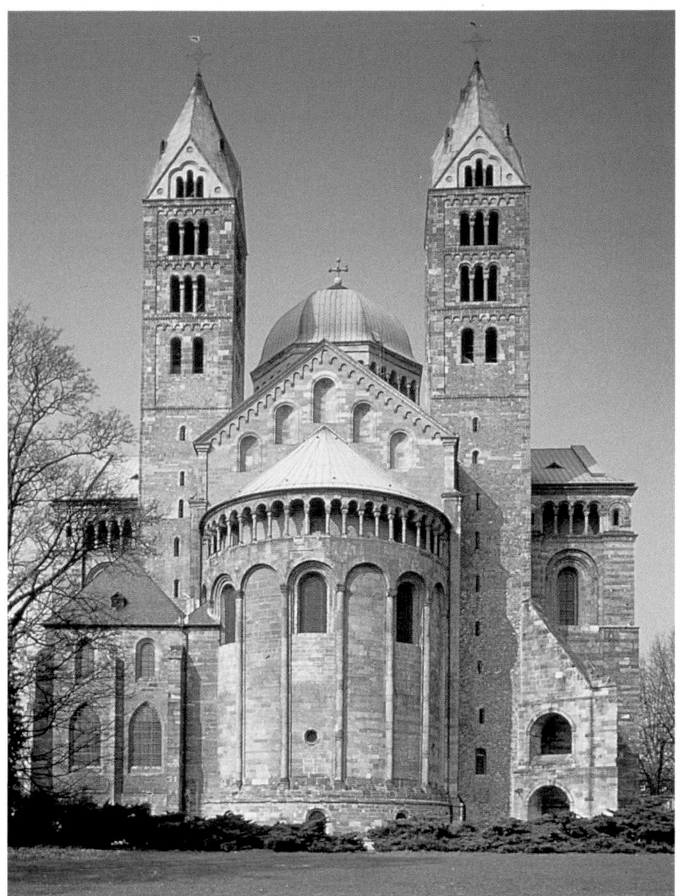

10-14. Speyer Cathedral, Germany, from the east. Begun 1030

in weight that also gives a stronger sense of continuity to the nave vault as a whole and makes for a less emphatic alternation of piers. Compared to Durham, the nave of St.-Étienne creates an impression of airy lightness akin to the quality of the Gothic choir that was added in the thirteenth century. In structural terms, too, we have here reached the point where Romanesque merges into Early Gothic.

Germany

SPEYER CATHEDRAL. German Romanesque architecture, centered in the Rhineland, was highly conservative. As an Imperial church, Speyer Cathedral reflects the Carolingian-Ottonian tradition. Begun about 1030, it was not completed until more than a century later. Speyer has a westwork (now covered by a modern reconstruction) and an equally monumental eastern grouping of crossing tower and paired stair towers (fig. 10-14). The effect reminds us of St. Pantaleon in Cologne, as do the tall proportions (compare fig. 9-21). The scale is so great as to dwarf every other church of the period. The nave, one-third taller and wider than that of Durham, has a large clerestory, since it was planned for a wooden roof. Only in the early twelfth century was it divided into square bays and covered with heavy, unribbed groin vaults. These, however, are closer to the Lombard rather than the Norman type. The architectural detail, though similar to St. Pantaleon's, is also kin to the First Romanesque in Lombardy, long a focus of German Imperial ambitions.

Lombardy

We might have expected central Italy, which had been part of the heartland of the Roman Empire, to have produced the noblest Romanesque of them all, since surviving classical originals were close at hand. There were a number of factors that prevented them from doing so. All of the rulers who sought to revive "the grandeur that was Rome," with themselves in the role of emperor, were in the north of Europe. The spiritual authority of the pope, reinforced by large territorial holdings, made Imperial ambitions in Italy difficult to achieve. New centers of prosperity and commerce, whether arising from seaborne trade or local industries, tended to consolidate a number of small principalities. They competed among themselves or aligned themselves from time to time with the pope or the German emperor if it seemed politically profitable. Lacking the urge to re-create the old Empire, and having Early Christian buildings as readily accessible as classical Roman ones, the Tuscans were content to continue what are basically Early Christian forms but enlivened them with decorative features inspired by pagan architecture.

S. AMBROGIO, MILAN. Instead, the lead in developing the Romanesque in Italy was taken by Lombardy, where ancient cities had once again grown large and prosperous. At the time when the Normans and Anglo-Normans were constructing their earliest ribbed-groined nave vaults, the same problem was being explored in and around Milan, which had devised a rudimentary system of

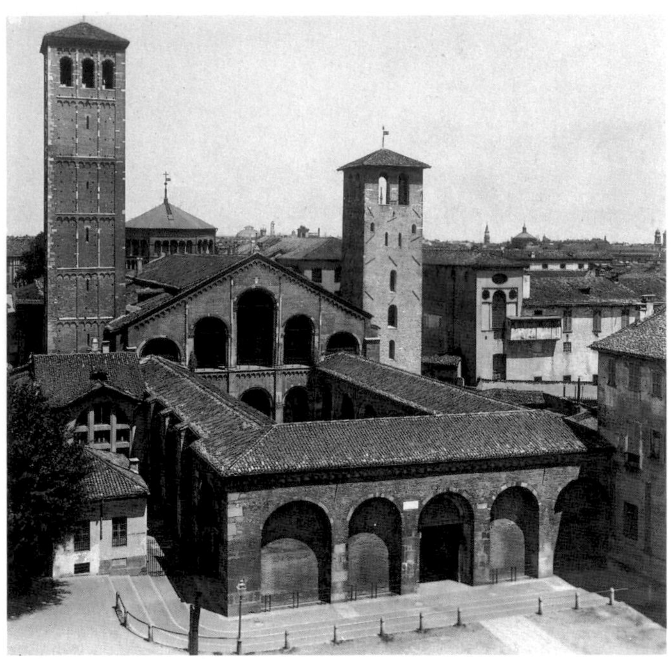

10-15. S. Ambrogio, Milan. Late 11th and 12th centuries

barrel vaulting during the so-called First Romanesque in the late ninth century. Lombard Romanesque architecture was both nourished and hindered by a building tradition that reached back to Roman and Early Christian times and included the monuments of Ravenna. This background lies behind one of its most important structures, S. Ambrogio in Milan (figs. 10-15 and 10-16). The site had been occupied by a church since the fourth century. The present building was begun in the late eleventh century, except for the apse and southern tower, which date from the tenth. The brick exterior, though more ornate and more monumental, follows the First Romanesque in recalling the proportions and the geometric simplicity of the Ravenna churches (see S. Apollinare in Classe and S. Vitale; figs. 8-13 and 8-25).

Upon entering the atrium, we encounter a handsome facade with deeply recessed arcades. Just beyond it are two bell towers, separate structures just touching the outer walls of the church. We have seen a round tower of this kind on the north side of S. Apollinare in Classe, probably the earliest surviving example, of the ninth or tenth century. Most of its successors are square, but the tradition of the freestanding bell tower, or campanile, remained so strong in Italy that they hardly ever became an integral part of the church itself.

The nave of S. Ambrogio is low and broad (it is some ten feet wider than that at Durham). It consists of four square bays separated by strong transverse arches. There is no transept, but the easternmost nave bay carries an octagonal, domed crossing tower or lantern. This feature was an afterthought, but we can easily see why it was added. The nave has no clerestory, and the windows of the lantern provide badly needed light. As at Durham, or Caen, there is a system of alternating piers, since the length of each nave bay equals that of two aisle bays. The latter are groin-vaulted, like the first three of the nave bays, and support galleries. The nave

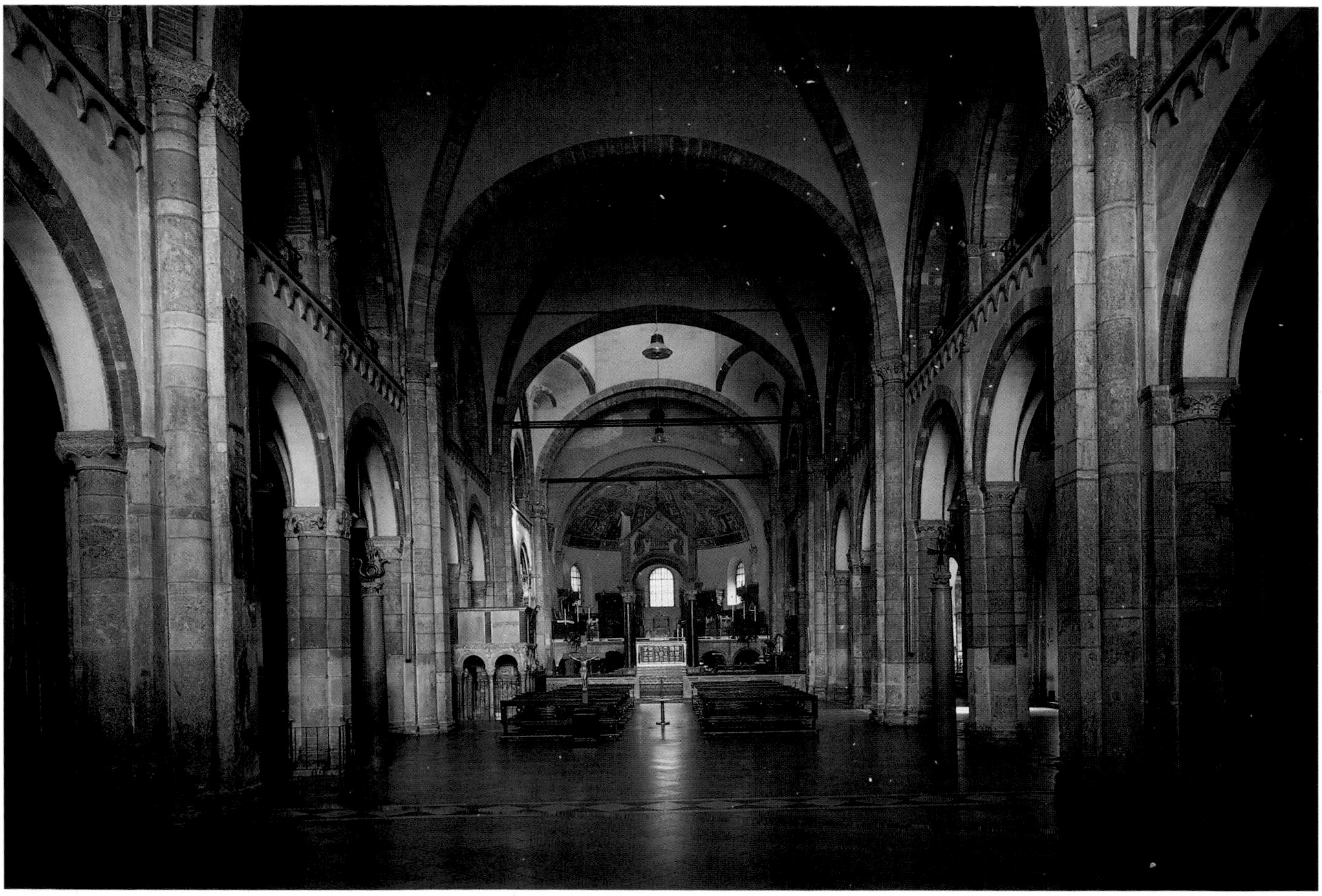

10-16. Interior, S. Ambrogio

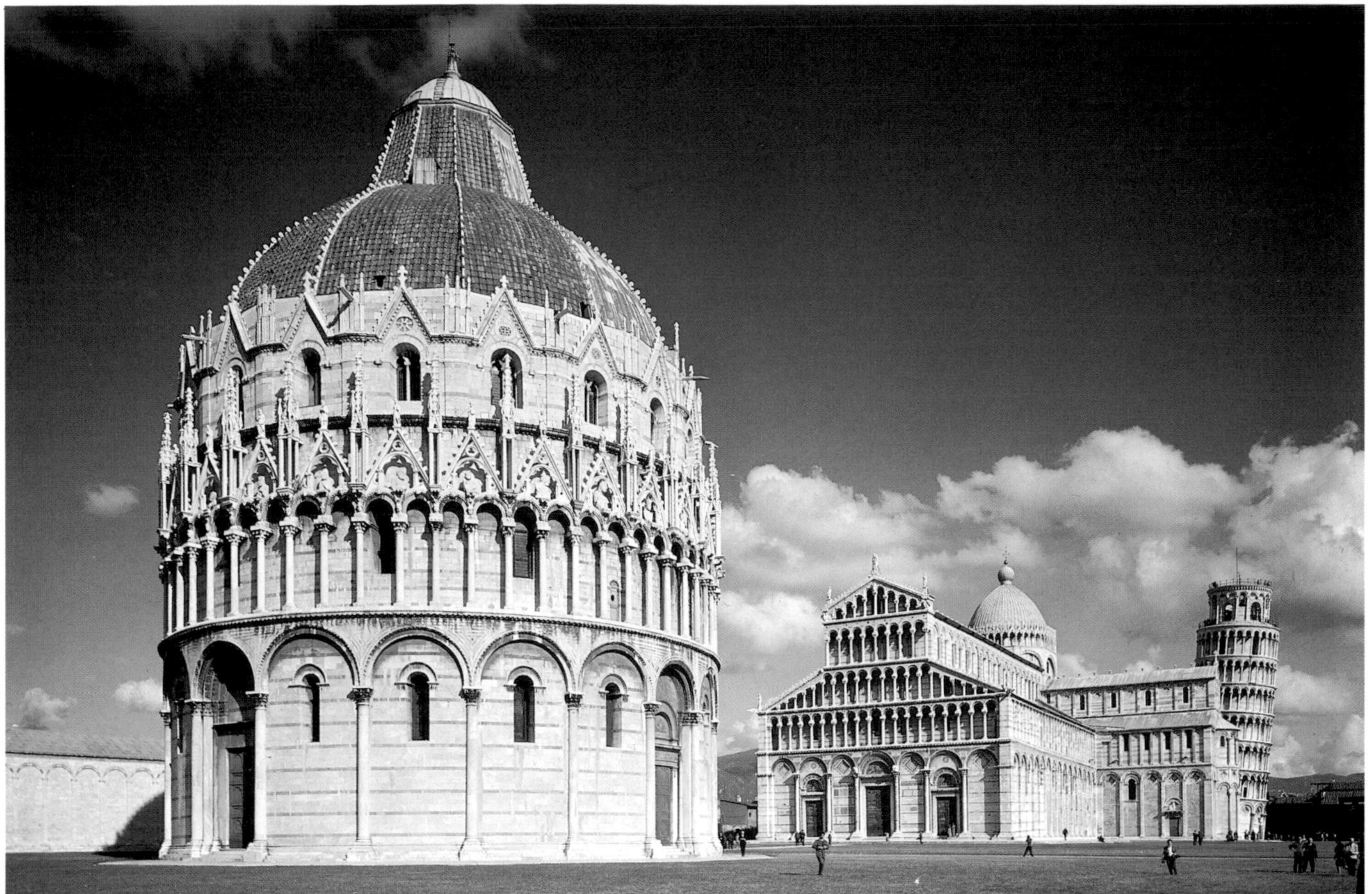

10-17. Pisa Baptistery, Cathedral, and Campanile (view from the west). 1053–1272

vaults, however, are quite different from those of northern churches. Made of brick and rubble, in a technique reminiscent of Roman groin vaults such as those in the Basilica of Constantine, they are a good deal heavier. The diagonal ribs, moreover, form true half-circles (at Durham and Caen, they are flattened), so that the vaults rise to a point high above the transverse arches. Apart from further increasing the height of the vault, this shape creates a domed effect and gives each bay the appearance of a separate unit.

On a smaller scale, the Milanese architect might have attempted a clerestory instead of galleries. But the span of the nave was determined by the width of the tenth-century apse. Moreover, Lombardy had a taste for ample interior proportions, like those of Early Christian basilicas (compare fig. 8-6), instead of height and light, as in contemporary Norman churches. Hence, there was no reason to experiment with more economical shapes and lighter construction. As a result, the ribbed groin vault in Lombardy never approached the proto-Gothic stage.

Tuscany

PISA CATHEDRAL. The most famous monument of the Tuscan Romanesque owes its fame to an accident. Because of poor foundations, the Leaning Tower of Pisa, designed by the sculptor Bonanno Pisano (active 1174–86), began to tilt even before it was completed (fig. 10-17). The tower is the campanile of Pisa Cathedral, which includes the church itself and the circular, domed baptistery to the west. This ensemble, built on an open site north of the city, reflects the wealth and pride of the city-republic of Pisa after its naval victory at Palermo in 1062.

Far more than Lombardy, with its strong northern ties, Tuscany remained conscious of its classical heritage throughout the Middle Ages. If we compare Pisa Cathedral with S. Apollinare in Ravenna and St.-Sernin in Toulouse (see figs. 8-13 and 10-1), we see that it is closely related to the latter in its scale and shape. However, the essential features and even the detached bell tower are still much as we see them in S. Apollinare. The basic plan of Pisa Cathedral is that of an Early Christian basilica, but it has been transformed into a Latin cross by the addition of two transept arms that resemble small basilicas with apses of their own. The crossing is marked by a dome. The rest of the church is wooden-roofed except for the aisles (four in the nave, two in the transept arms), which have groin vaults. The interior (fig. 10-18) has somewhat taller proportions than an Early Christian basilica, because there are galleries over the aisles, as well as a clerestory. Yet the classical columns supporting the nave and aisle arcades recall S. Apollinare in Classe (see fig. 8-15).

The only deliberate revival of the antique Roman style in Tuscan architecture was in the use of a multicolored marble "skin" on the exteriors of churches. Little of this is left in Rome because much of it was literally "lifted" to decorate later structures. However, the interior of the Pantheon still gives us some idea of it (see

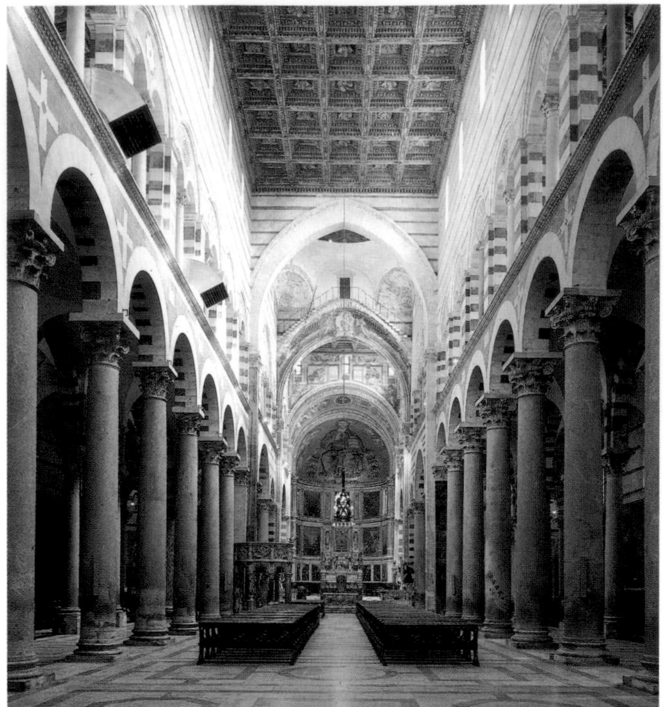

10-18. Interior, Pisa Cathedral

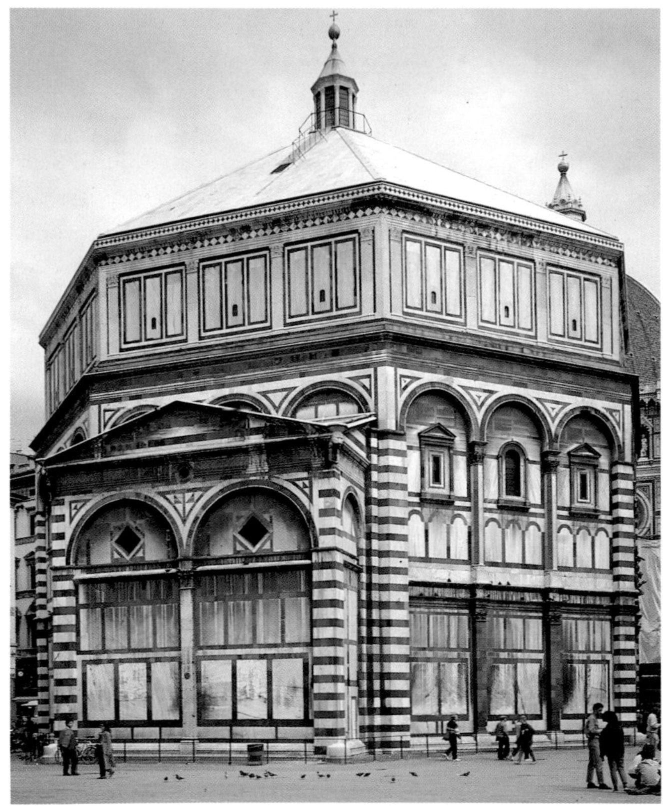

10-19. Baptistery of S. Giovanni, Florence. c. 1060–1150

fig. 7-12). We can recognize the desire to emulate such marble inlay in Pisa Cathedral and its companions. They are covered in white marble inlaid with horizontal stripes and ornamental patterns in dark-green marble. This decorative scheme is combined with blind arcades and galleries. The result is a lacelike richness of texture and color that is very different from the austere Early Christian exteriors. By now the time had long passed when a church was not allowed to compete with the outward splendor of classical temples.

THE BAPTISTERY OF S. GIOVANNI, FLORENCE. In Florence, which was to outstrip Pisa commercially and artistically, the greatest achievement of the Tuscan Romanesque is the baptistery (fig. 10-19), opposite the cathedral. It is a domed, octagonal structure of impressive size. Here the green-and-white marble paneling follows severe geometric lines, and the blind arcades are extraordinarily classical in proportion and detail. The entire building, in fact, has such a classical air that a few hundred years later, the Florentines believed it to have been originally a temple of Mars. Even today the debate over its date has not been settled to everyone's satisfaction. (According to some scholars, aspects of the present facade may actually date from the Early Renaissance.) We shall return to this baptistery a number of times, since it was to play an important role in the Renaissance.

SCULPTURE

The revival of monumental stone sculpture is even more surprising than the architectural achievements of the Romanesque era. Neither Carolingian nor Ottonian art had shown any tendencies in this direction. Freestanding statues all but disappeared from Western art after the fifth century. Stone relief survived only in the form of architectural ornament or surface decoration, with the depth of the carving kept to a minimum. Thus the only continuous sculptural tradition in early medieval art was that of sculpture-in-miniature: small reliefs and statuettes, in metal or ivory. Ottonian art, in works such as the bronze doors of Bishop Bernward (see fig. 9-25), had enlarged the scale of this tradition but not its spirit. Moreover, its truly large-scale sculptural efforts, such as *The Gero Crucifix* (see fig. 9-20), were limited almost entirely to wood. What little stone carving there was in western Europe before the mid-eleventh century hardly went beyond the artistic and technical level of the Sigvald relief (see fig. 9-7).

Southwestern France

Fifty years later, the situation had changed dramatically. We do not know exactly when and where the revival of stone sculpture began, but the earliest surviving examples are found in southwestern France and northern Spain, along the pilgrimage roads leading to Santiago de Compostela. The link with the pilgrimage traffic seems logical enough. Architectural sculpture, especially on the exterior of a church, is meant to appeal to the lay worshiper rather than to the members of a monastic community.

ST.-SERNIN, TOULOUSE. As in Romanesque architecture, the rapid development of stone sculpture shortly before 1100 coincides with the growth of religious fervor in the decades before the First Crusade. St.-Sernin at Toulouse contains several important examples that were probably carved about 1090, including the *Apostle* in figure 10-20. (This panel is now in the ambulatory; its

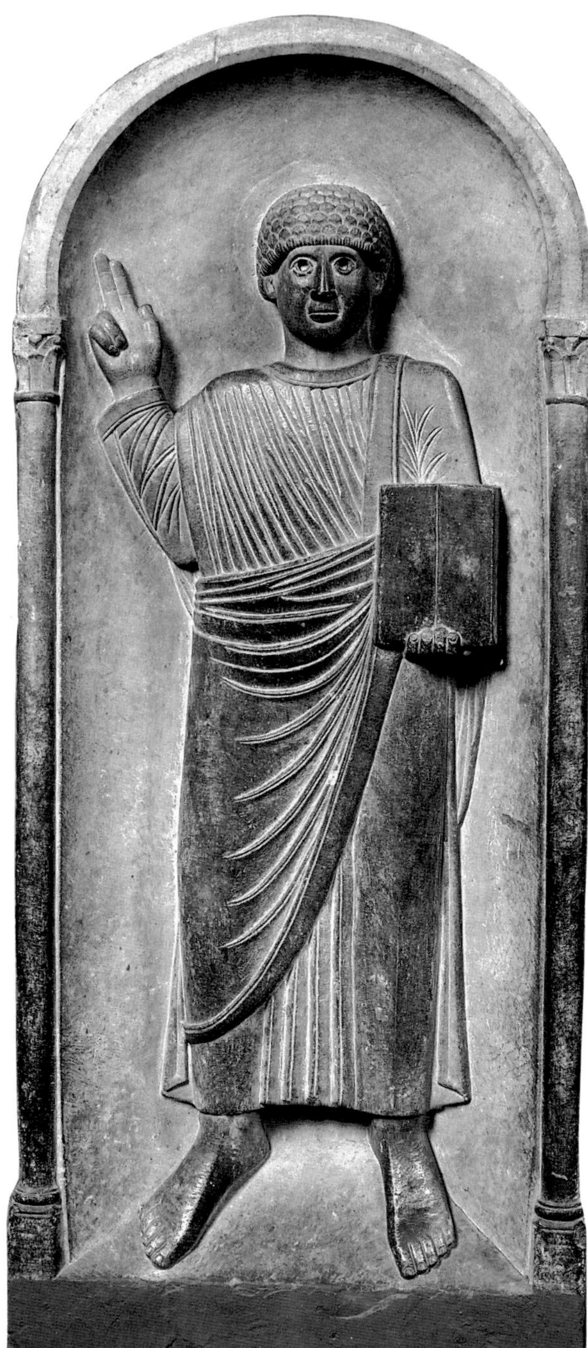

10-20. *Apostle.* c. 1090. Stone. St.-Sernin, Toulouse

original location is not certain, but it may have decorated the front of an altar.) Where have we seen its like before? The solidity of the forms has a strongly classical air, indicating that our artist must have had a close look at late Roman sculpture, of which there are numerous remains in southern France. But the solemn frontality of the figure and its placement in the architectural frame show that the design must be derived from a Byzantine source, probably an ivory panel descended from *The Archangel Michael* in figure 8-23.

In enlarging such a miniature, the carver of our relief has also reinflated it. The niche is a real cavity, the hair a round, close-fitting cap, the body severe and blocklike. Our *Apostle* has, in fact, much the same dignity and directness as the sculpture of Archaic Greece. The figure, which is somewhat more than half-lifesize, was not meant to be viewed only at close range. Its impressive bulk and weight "carry" over a considerable distance. This emphasis on massive volume hints at what may have been the main impulse behind the revival of large-scale sculpture. A stone-carved image, being tangible and three-dimensional, is far more "real" than a painted one. To the mind of a cleric steeped in abstract theology, this might seem irrelevant or even dangerous. For unsophisticated lay worshipers, any large sculpture had something of the quality of an idol, and it was this fact that gave it such great appeal.

ST.-PIERRE, MOISSAC. Another important early center of Romanesque sculpture was the abbey at Moissac, further north of Toulouse along the Garonne River. In figure 10-21 we see the magnificent trumeau (the center post supporting the lintel) and the western jamb of the south portal. (The parts of typical medieval portals are shown in fig. 10-22.) Both have a scalloped profile—apparently a bit of Moorish influence. The shafts of the half-columns applied to jambs and trumeau also follow this pattern, as if they had been squeezed from a giant pastry tube. Human and animal forms are treated with the same flexibility, so that the spidery prophet on the side of the trumeau seems perfectly adapted to his precarious perch. (Notice how he, too, has been fitted into the scalloped outline.) He even remains free to cross his legs in a dancelike movement and to turn his head toward the interior of the church as he unfurls his scroll.

But what of the crossed lions that form a symmetrical zigzag on the face of the trumeau—do they have a meaning? So far as we know, they simply "animate" the shaft, just as the interlacing beasts of Irish miniatures (from which they are descended) enliven the compartments they inhabit. In manuscript illumination, this tradition had never died out. Our sculpture has undoubtedly been influenced by it, just as the agitated movement of the prophet originated in miniature painting (see fig. 10-34). The crossed lions reflect another source as well. We can trace them through textiles to Persian metalwork (although not in this towerlike formation). They descend ultimately from the confronted animals of ancient Near Eastern art (see figs. 3-9 and 4-19). Yet we cannot fully account for their presence at Moissac in terms of their effectiveness as ornament alone. They belong to an extensive family of savage or monstrous creatures in Romanesque art that retain their demoniacal vitality even though they are forced, like our lions, to perform a supporting function. (A similar example may be seen in fig. 10-27.) Their purpose is thus not only decorative but expressive. They embody dark forces that have been domesticated into guardian figures or banished to a position that holds them fixed for all eternity, however much they may snarl in protest.

The south portal at Moissac shows the same richness of invention that St. Bernard of Clairvaux condemned in his letter of 1127 to Abbot William of St. Thierry about the sculpture of Cluny. [See Primary Sources, no. 24, page 369.] Although he did not object specifically to the role of art in teaching the unlettered, St. Bernard had little use for church decoration. He would surely have disapproved of the Moissac portal's excesses, which were clearly meant to appeal to the eye—as his grudging admiration for the cloister at Cluny attests.

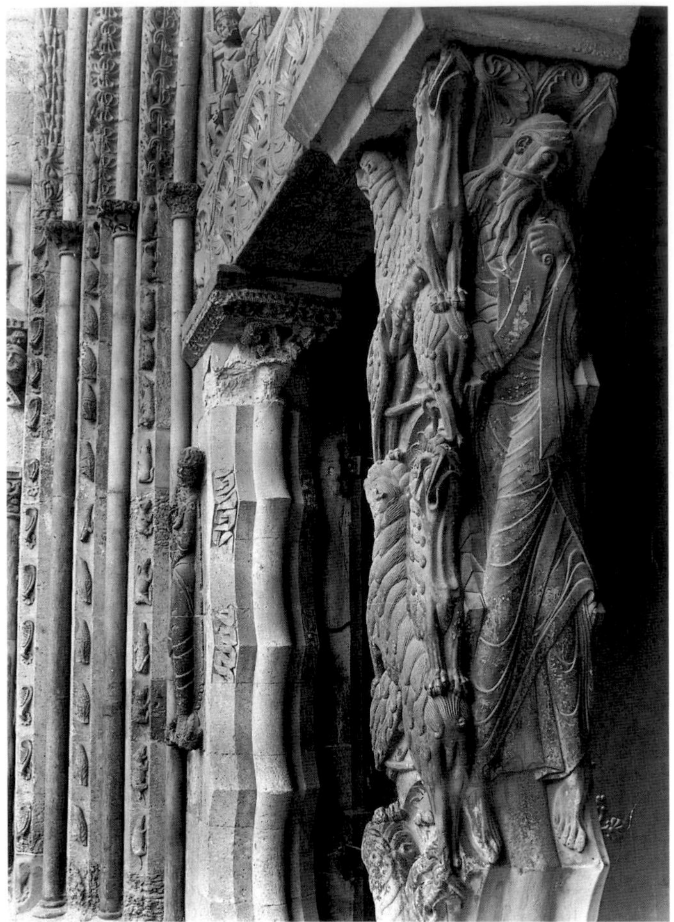

10-21. South portal (portion), St.-Pierre, Moissac, France. Early 12th century

In front of the portal at Moissac is a deep porch with lavishly sculptured sides. Within the arcade on the east flank (fig. 10-23) we see the *Annunciation* and *Visitation,* as well as the *Adoration of the Magi.* Other events from the early life of Christ are shown on the frieze above. Here we find the same thin limbs, the same eloquent gestures we saw in the prophet on the trumeau. (Note the wonderful play of hands in the *Visitation* and *Annunciation.*) Only the proportions of the bodies and the size of the figures vary with the architectural context. What matters is the vividness of the narrative, rather than consistency of treatment.

Burgundy

AUTUN CATHEDRAL. The tympanum (the lunette above the lintel) of the main portal of Romanesque churches usually holds a composition centering on the Enthroned Christ. Most often it shows the Apocalyptic Vision, or the Last Judgment, the most awesome scene of Christian art. At Autun Cathedral, this subject has been visualized with extraordinary force by Giselbertus (fig. 10-24), who probably based his imagery on a contemporary account rather than on the Revelation of St. John the Divine. The apostles, at the viewer's left, observe the weighing of souls, shown at the right. Four angels in the corners sound the trumpets of the Apocalypse. At the bottom, the dead rise from their graves in fear and trembling; some are already beset by snakes or gripped by huge, clawlike hands. Above, their fate quite literally hangs in the balance, with devils yanking at one end of the scales and angels at the other. The saved souls cling like children to the angels for

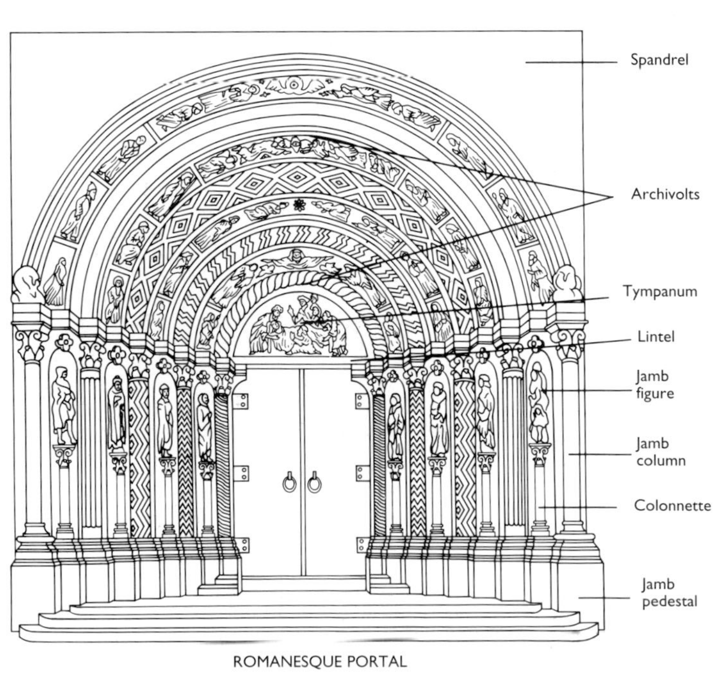

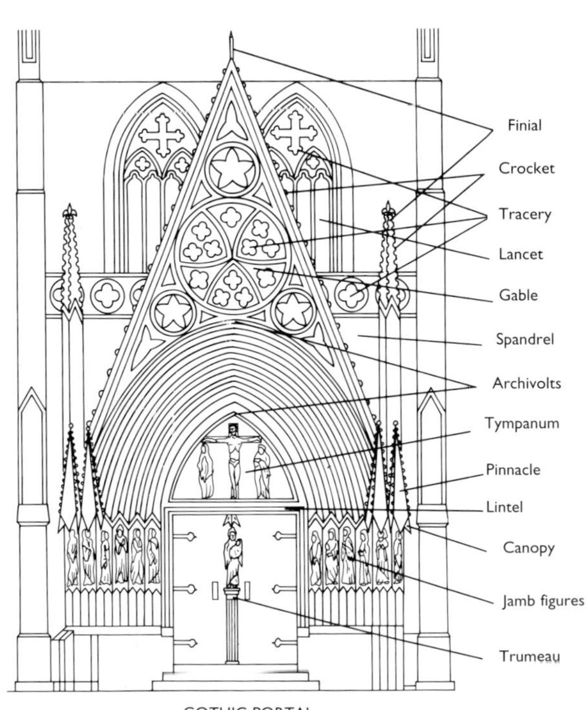

10-22. Romanesque and High Gothic portal ensembles

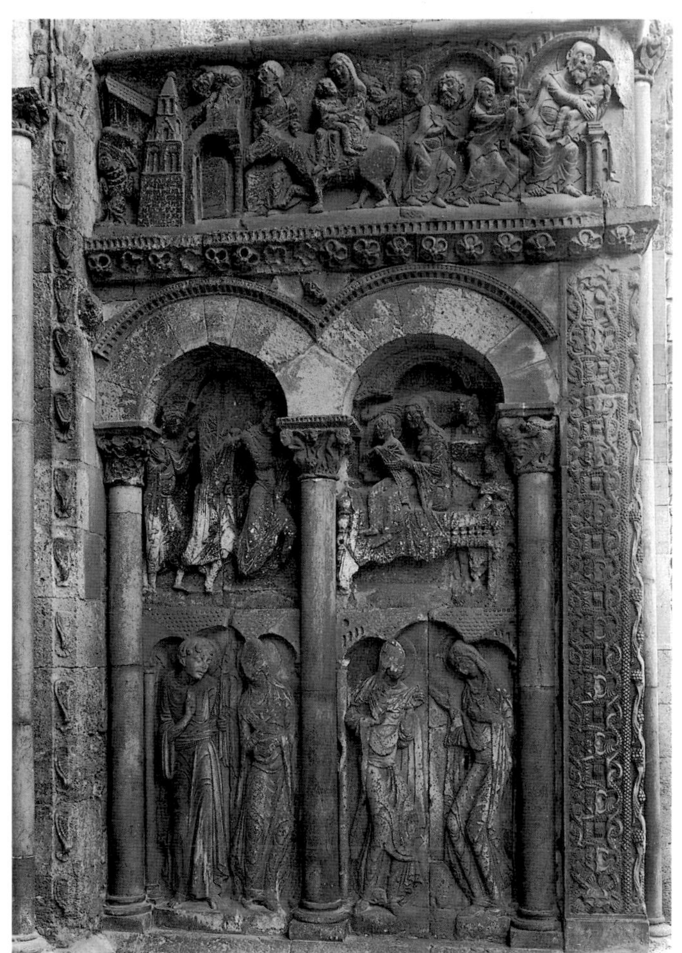

protection before their ascent to the Heavenly Jerusalem (far left), while the condemned, seized by grinning devils, are cast into the mouth of Hell (far right). These devils betray the same nightmarish imagination we saw in the Romanesque animal world. They are human in general outline but they have birdlike legs, furry thighs, tails, pointed ears, and savage mouths. No visitor, having "read in the marble" here (to quote St. Bernard of Clairvaux), could fail to enter the church in a chastened spirit.

The emergence of distinct artistic personalities in the twelfth century is rarely acknowledged, perhaps because it contradicts the widespread notion that all medieval art is anonymous. Giselbertus is not the only or even the earliest case. He is one of several Romanesque sculptors who are known to us by name, and not by accident. Their highly individual styles made theirs the first names worthy of being recorded since Anthemius of Tralles and Isidorus of Miletus 500 years earlier.

The work of Giselbertus is distinguished from that of his contemporaries by its unusually wide range. As at Moissac, it varies according to subject and location. His *Eve* (fig. 10-25) is as whimsical as the *Last Judgment* is terrifying. She is delicately plucking

(LEFT) 10-23. East flank, south portal, St.-Pierre, Moissac (the angel of the *Annunciation,* bottom left, is modern)

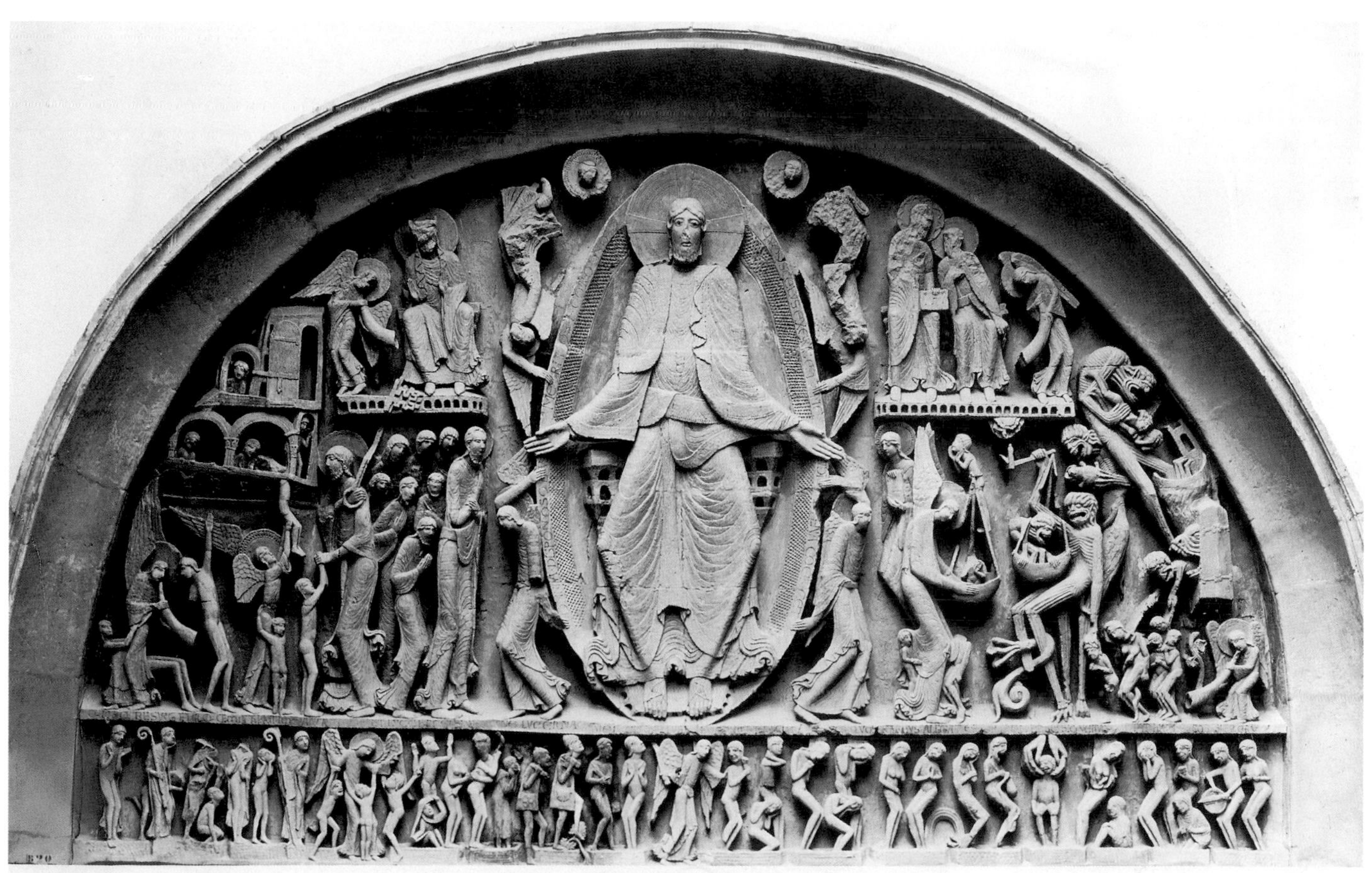

10-24. Giselbertus. *Last Judgment,* west tympanum, Autun Cathedral. c. 1130–35

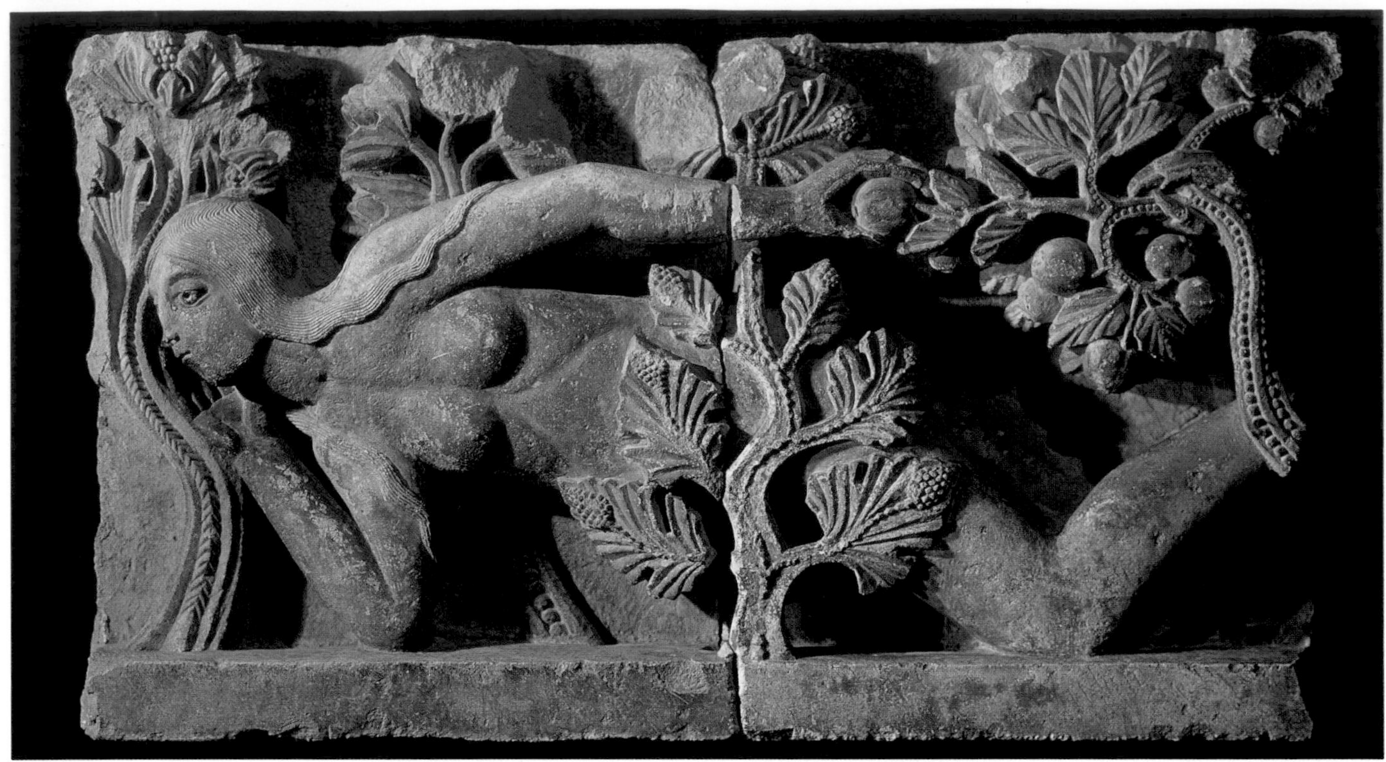

10-25. Giselbertus. *Eve,* right half of lintel, north portal from Autun Cathedral. 1120–1132. 28½ x 51" (72.4 x 129.5 cm). Musée Rolin, Autun

the apple from the Tree of Knowledge with an irresistible come-hither look at the missing Adam, who no doubt faced her. The languid pose, necessitated by the door lintel she adorns, allows Giselbertus to model her figure with captivating—and surprisingly sensual—beauty.

STE.-MADELEINE, VÉZELAY. Giselbertus began his career at Cluny (see pages 298–99). There he may have served as chief assistant to the unknown master who created perhaps the most beautiful of all Romanesque tympanums, that of Ste.-Madeleine in Vézelay, not far from Autun (fig. 10-26). [See Primary Sources,

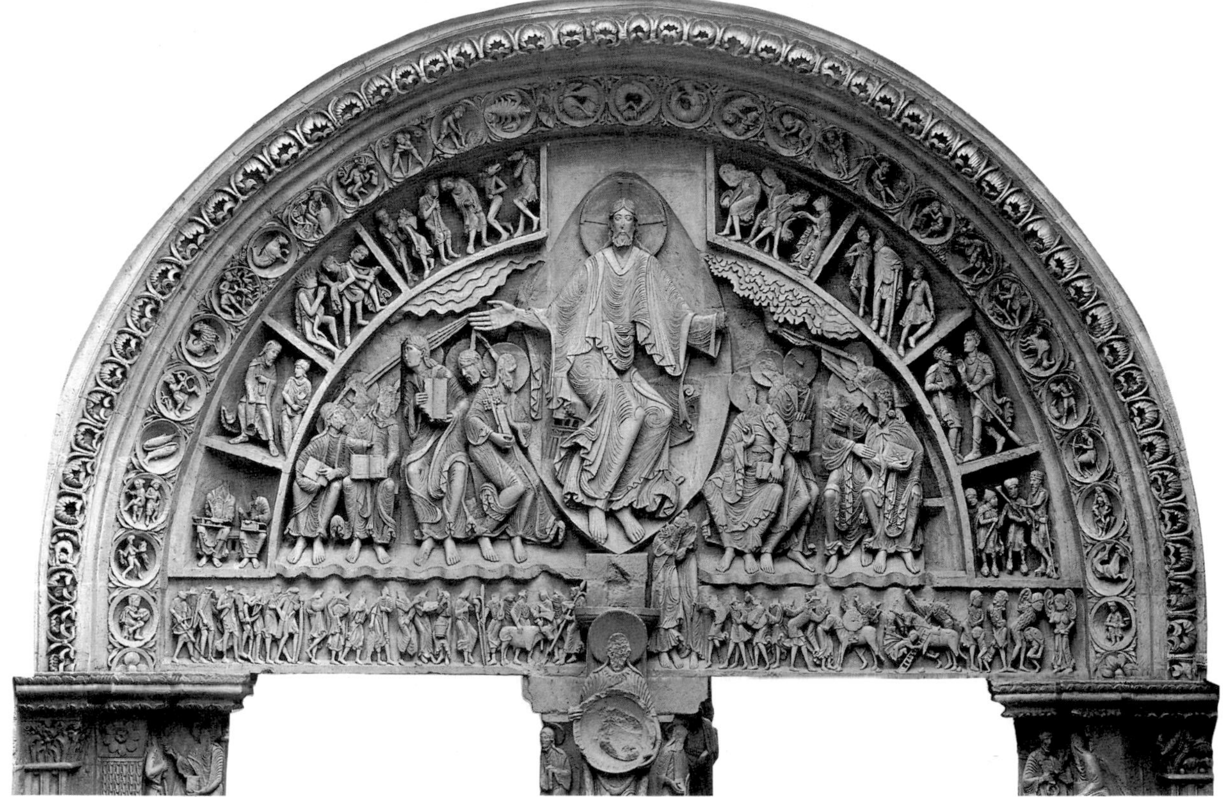

10-26. *The Mission of the Apostles,* tympanum of center portal of narthex, Ste.-Madeleine, Vézelay, France. 1120–32

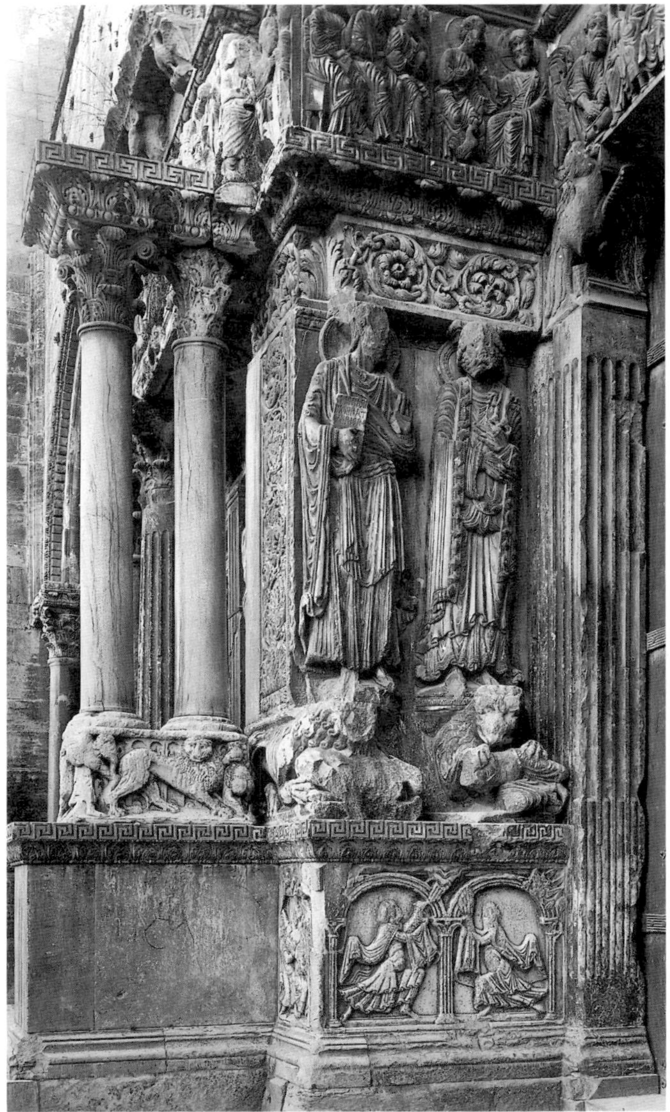

10-27. North jamb, center portal, St.-Gilles-du-Gard, France. Second quarter of the 12th century

no. 23, pages 368–69.] Its subject, the Mission of the Apostles, had a special meaning for this age of crusades, since it proclaims the duty of every Christian to spread the Gospel to the ends of the earth. From the hands of the majestic ascending Christ we see the rays of the Holy Spirit pouring down upon the apostles, all of whom hold copies of the Scriptures in token of their mission. The lintel and the compartments around the central group are filled with representatives of the heathen world, an encyclopedia of medieval anthropology which includes all sorts of legendary races. On the archivolt (the arch framing the tympanum) are the signs of the zodiac and the labors appropriate to every month of the year, to indicate that the preaching of the Faith is as unlimited in time as it is in space.

Romanesque Classicism

PROVENCE. The portal sculpture at Moissac, Autun, and Vézelay, although varied in style, has many qualities in common: intense expression, unbridled fantasy, and a nervous agility of form that owes more to manuscript illumination and metalwork than to the sculptural tradition of antiquity. The *Apostle* from St.-Sernin, in contrast, impressed us with its stoutly "Roman" flavor. The influence of classical monuments was particularly strong in Provence, the coastal region of southeastern France. This area had been part of the Graeco-Roman world far longer than the rest of the country and is full of splendid Roman remains. Perhaps for that reason, the Romanesque style persisted longer here than anywhere else.

Looking at the center portal of the church at St.-Gilles-du-Gard (fig. 10-27), one of the great masterpieces of Romanesque art, we are struck immediately by the classical flavor of the architectural framework, with its freestanding columns, meander patterns, and acanthus ornament. The two large statues, carved almost in the round, have a sense of weight and volume akin to that of the *Apostle* from St.-Sernin (see fig. 10-20). Being half a century later in date, however, they also display the richness of detail we have seen in intervening monuments. They stand on brackets supported by crouching beasts of prey, which also show a Roman massiveness, while the small figures on the base (Cain and Abel) recall the style of Moissac.

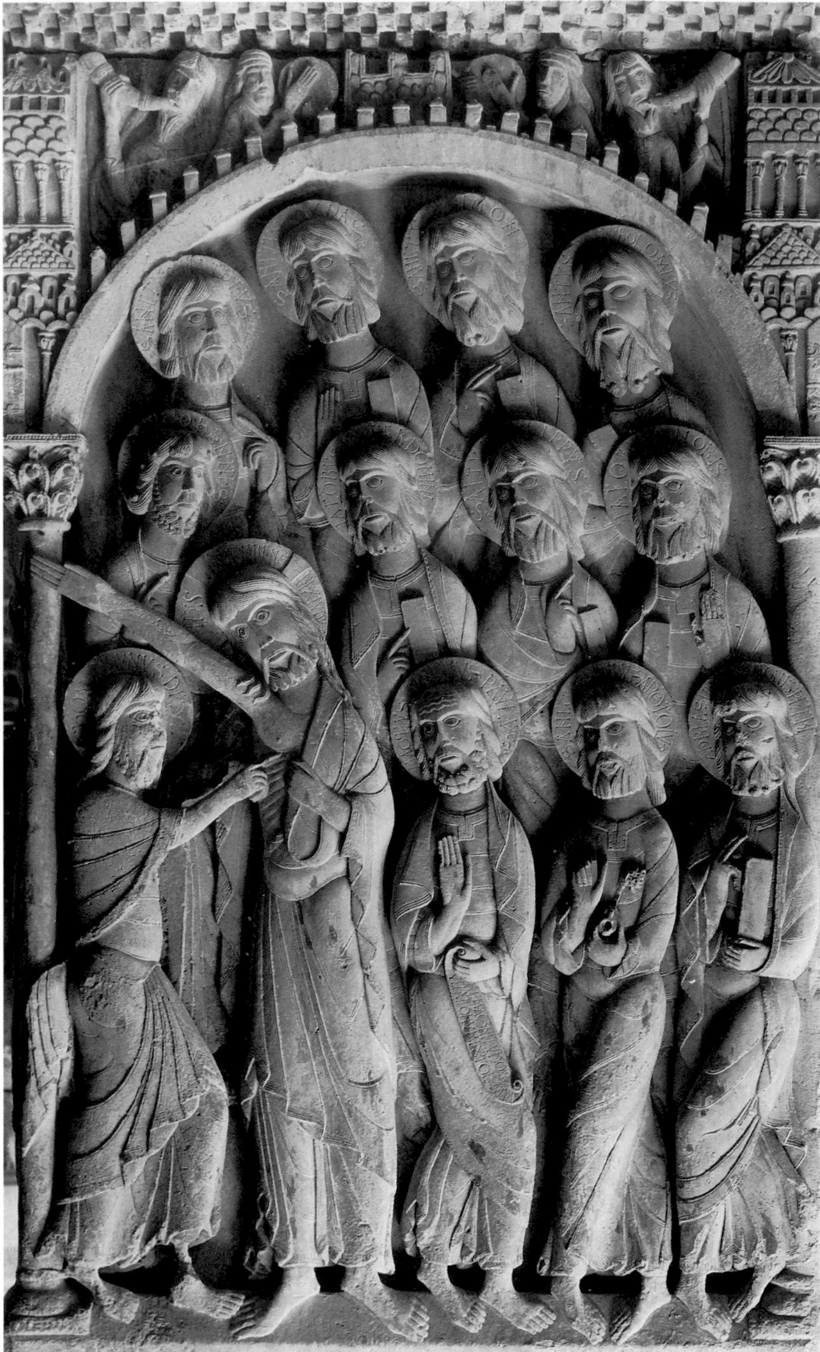

10-28. *The Doubting of Thomas.* c. 1130–40. Marble. Cloister, Sto. Domingo de Silos, Spain

Spain and Italy

STO. DOMINGO DE SILOS. The French style soon spread to Spain, first to Santiago de Compostela, where the sculpture has unfortunately been much rearranged, then to Sto. Domingo de Silos, which became an important destination in its own right, even though it lies some 60 miles off the pilgrimage route. Among the reliefs in the cloister of Sto. Domingo, which were probably carved in the second quarter of the twelfth century, is the splendid *The Doubting of Thomas* in figure 10-28. The composition, with apostles who all appear to have been cut from the same mold, is indebted to Ottonian art (compare fig. 9-27). The subtle carving owes something to France as well, in particular the corner piers of the cloister at Moissac. It shares other features found in Romanesque sculpture outside Spain: the elongated forms, angular poses, and emphatic gestures. Yet we cannot account for the appearance of this work solely in terms of external influences. *The Doubting of Thomas* is, in fact, highly original, and there is nothing like it elsewhere. Its unaffected plainness is both enchanting and deceptive—the stylization gives the scene an expressiveness that is as moving as it is direct. Like the Gregorian chants for which Silos is known, this relief is an eloquent testimony to faith. They share similar formal means as well: both rely on the repetition of unadorned motifs in simple cadence for their effect.

WILIGELMO. Although the French style quickly became international, it was modified through interaction with local tradition. We see this process in the work of Wiligelmo, whose reliefs from Genesis (fig. 10-29) on the facade of Modena Cathedral founded Romanesque sculpture in Italy. The scenes show a surprising kinship to the doors of Bishop Bernward at Hildesheim (see fig. 9-25).

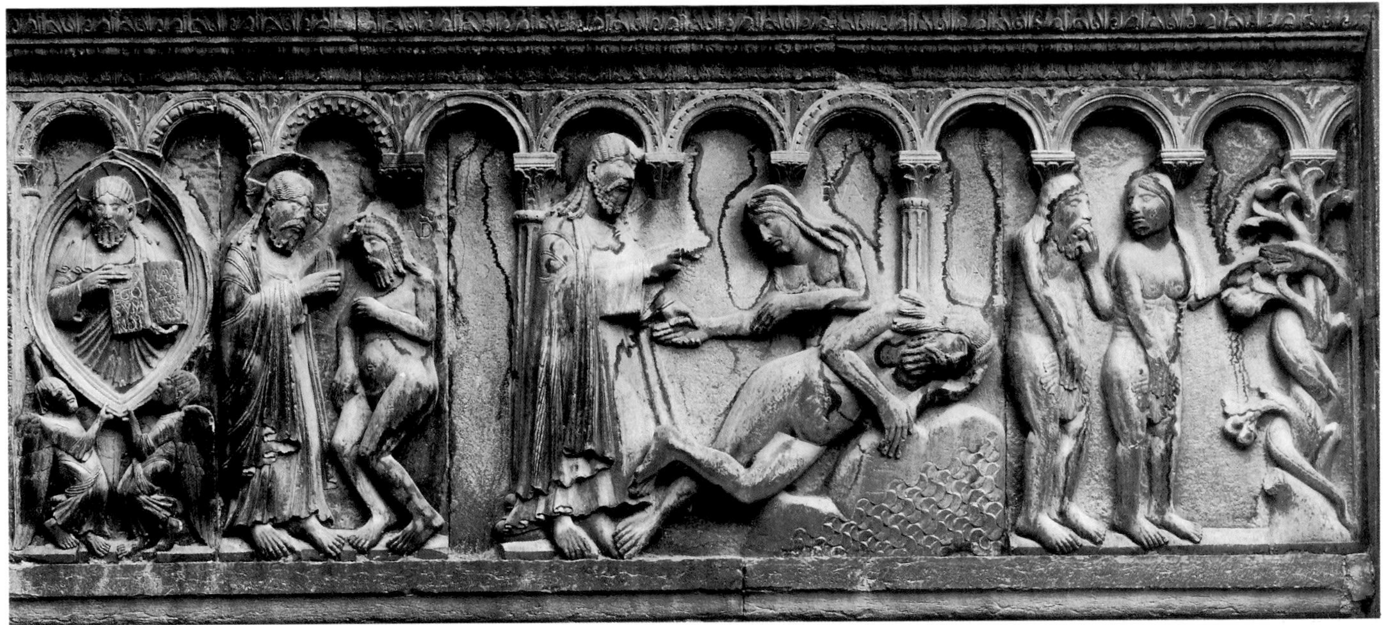

10-29. Wiligelmo. *Scenes from Genesis.* c. 1106–20. Marble, height approx. 36" (91.5 cm). Cathedral, Modena, Italy

The resemblance suggests that Wiligelmo perhaps came from Germany, where he may have been trained as a goldsmith under the name Wilhelm. If so, he must also have been familiar with the Romanesque style then emerging in Burgundy, as a glance at the frieze depicting the early life of Christ along the porch at Moissac attests (see fig. 10-23). Nevertheless, the figures show a knowledge of the nude that can have been gained only in Italy itself. Moreover, they have a massiveness derived from Early Christian ivory panels done in Italy that seems all the more astonishing if we compare them to the spindly Adam and Eve at Hildesheim, from which they descend. This solidity gives the scenes a solemn dignity, in contrast to the drama seen on Bernward's doors (compare fig. 9-26). The artist was proud of his work, and justly so. An inscription boasts, "Among sculptors, your work shines through, Wiligelmo." It is not surprising that Italian sculpture was revived by a German. The tradition had all but died out by the middle of the eighth century, while northern Italy remained in the hands of German rulers, who also acted as protectors of the papacy in Rome.

ANTELAMI. The nascent classicism of Wiligelmo reached its height toward the end of the twelfth century in the figure of King David from the facade of Fidenza Cathedral in Lombardy (fig. 10-30), by Benedetto Antelami, the greatest sculptor of Italian Romanesque art. As we have seen, artists' signatures are far from rare in Romanesque times. What sets Antelami apart is the fact that his work shows much more individuality than that of other artists. For the first time since the ancient Greeks, we can begin to speak (though with some hesitation) of a personal style. Unlike Wiligelmo, Antelami was at heart a monumental sculptor, not a relief carver. Thus his *King David* comes closer to the ideal of the freestanding statue than any medieval work we have seen so far. Whereas the *Apostle* from St.-Sernin is fixed to its niche, Antelami's *King David* stands physically free and even shows an attempt at classical contrapposto. To be sure, he would look awkward if placed on a pedestal in isolation. He demands the architectural

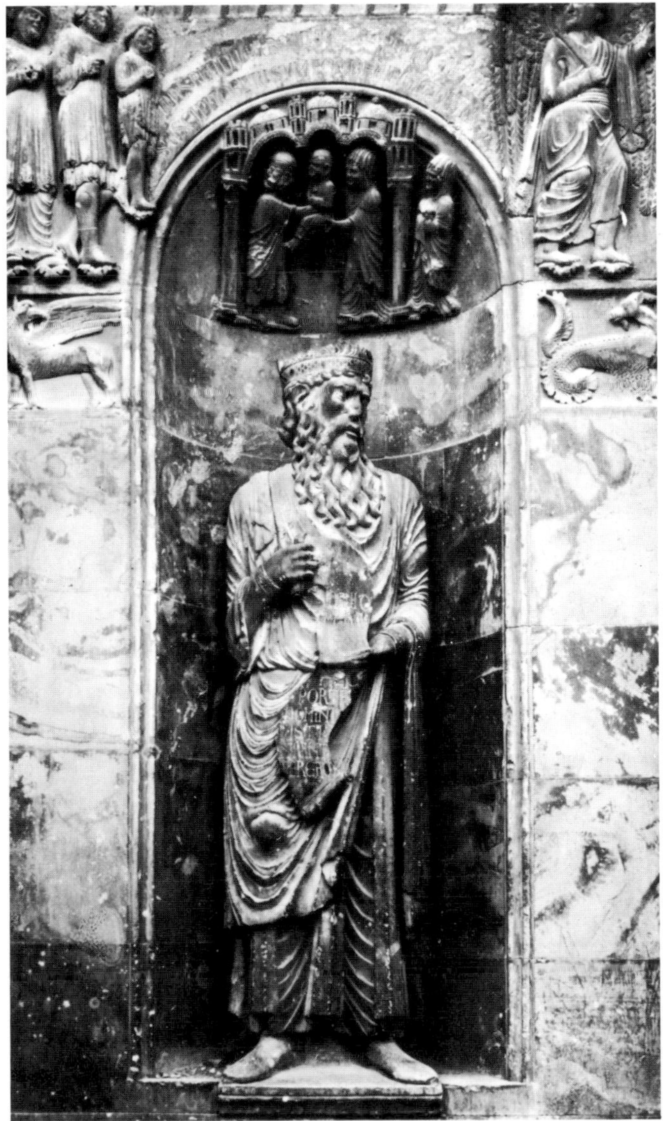

10-30. Benedetto Antelami. *King David.* c. 1180–90. West facade, Fidenza Cathedral, Italy

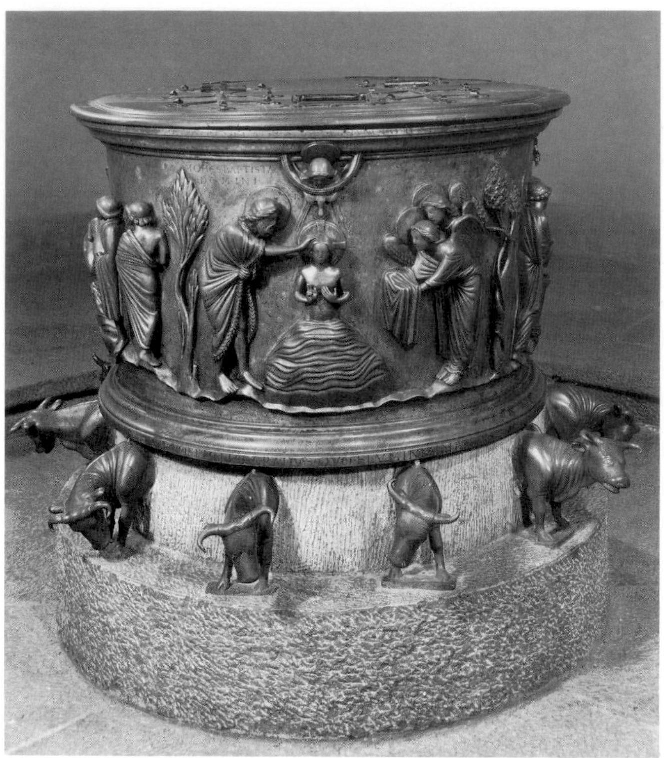

10-31. Renier of Huy. Baptismal Font. 1107–18. Bronze, height 25" (63.5 cm). St.-Barthélemy, Liège, Belgium

framework for which he was made, but far less than do the two statues at St.-Gilles-du-Gard, to which he is otherwise kin. Unlike the St.-Sernin *Apostle,* he is not part of a series of figures; his only companion is a second statue in a niche on the other side of the portal. We note, too, that the figure is lost in thought. Indeed, such expressiveness, new to Romanesque sculpture, is typical of Antelami's work. We shall meet it again in the statues of Donatello. The *King David* is an extraordinary achievement, especially if we consider that less than a hundred years separate it from the beginnings of the sculptural revival.

The Meuse Valley

The revival of individuality also took place in the valley of the Meuse River, which runs from northeastern France into Belgium and Holland. This region had been the home of the classicizing Reims style in Carolingian times (see figs. 9-17 and 9-18), and an awareness of classical sources pervades its art (called Mosan) during the Romanesque period. Here again the revival of individuality is linked with the influence of ancient art, although this influence did not lead to works on a monumental scale.

Mosan Romanesque sculptors excelled in metalwork. The baptismal font of 1107–18 in Liège (fig. 10-31) was done by the earliest artist of the region whose name we know: Renier of Huy. The vessel rests on 12 oxen (symbols of the 12 apostles), like Solomon's basin in the Temple at Jerusalem as described in the Bible. The reliefs make an instructive contrast with those of Bernward's doors (see fig. 9-26), since they are about the same height. Instead of the rough expressive power of the Ottonian panel, we find here a harmonious balance of design, a subtle control of the sculptured surfaces, and an understanding of organic structure that, in medieval terms, are amazingly classical. The figure seen from the back (beyond the tree on the left), with its graceful movement and Greek-looking drapery, might almost be taken for an ancient work.

Germany

THE LION MONUMENT. The only monumental freestanding statue of Romanesque art that has survived is that of an animal, and in a secular rather than a religious context. It is the lifesize bronze lion on top of a tall shaft that Duke Henry the Lion of Saxony had placed in front of his palace at Brunswick in 1166 (fig. 10-32). The ferocious animal personifies the duke, or at least the aspect of his personality that earned him his nickname. It brings to mind the lion of St. Mark from the *Echternach Gospels* (see fig. 9-5), and with good reason. Both are descended from the miniature beasts that decorate a Hallstatt bronze cauldron and from the monsters of Celtic art, which are derived from the Near East. We are also reminded of the Archaic bronze she-wolf of Rome (see fig. 6-9). Perhaps the resemblance is not a coincidence. The she-wolf was on public view in Rome at that time and must have had a strong appeal for Romanesque artists.

The more immediate relatives of the Brunswick lion, however, are the bronze water ewers in the shape of lions, dragons, griffins, and such that came into use in the twelfth century for the ritual washing of the priest's hands during Mass. These vessels,

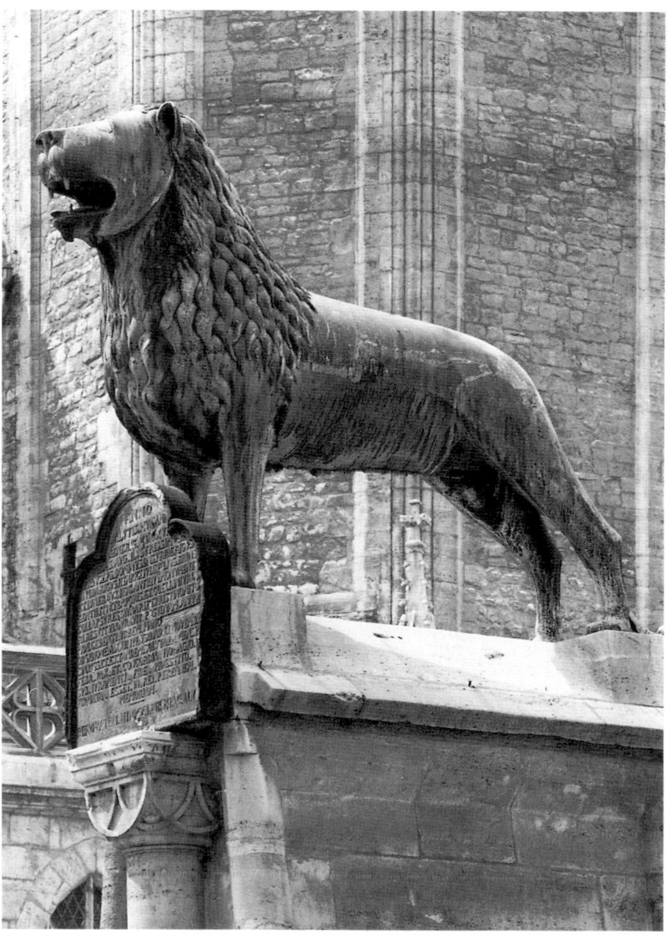

10-32. Lion Monument. 1166. Bronze, length approx. 6' (1.8 m). Cathedral Square, Brunswick, Germany

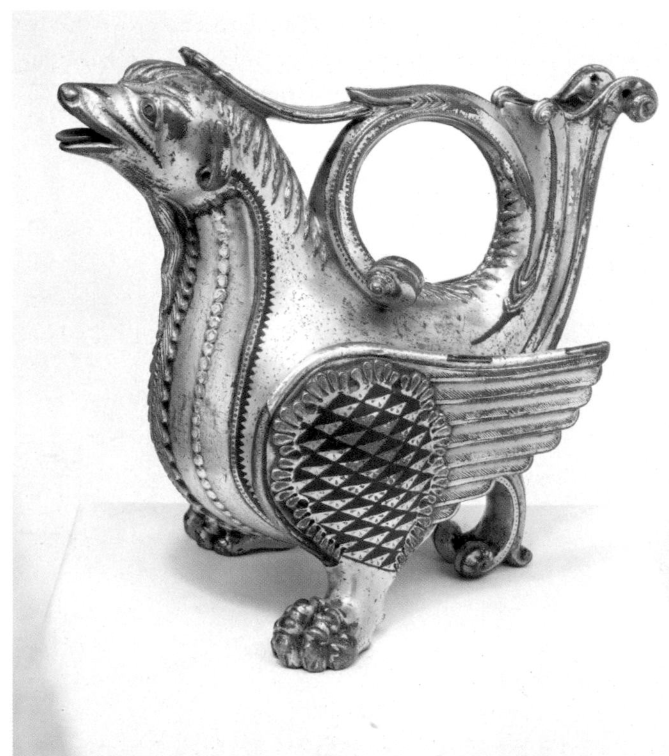

10-33. Ewer. Mosan. c. 1130. Gilt bronze, height 7¼" (18.5 cm). Victoria & Albert Museum, London

another instance of monsters serving the Lord, were of Near Eastern inspiration. The beguiling example in figure 10-33 betrays its descent from the winged beasts of Persian art, which were transmitted to the West through trade with the Islamic world.

PAINTING AND METALWORK

Unlike architecture and sculpture, Romanesque painting shows no revolutionary developments that set it apart from Carolingian or Ottonian art. Nor does it look more "Roman" than Carolingian or Ottonian painting. This does not mean, however, that in the eleventh and twelfth centuries painting was any less important than it had been during the earlier Middle Ages. The lack of dramatic change merely emphasizes the greater continuity of the pictorial tradition, especially in manuscript illumination.

France

THE GOSPEL BOOK, CORBIE. Soon after the year 1000 we find the beginnings of a painting style that corresponds to—and often anticipates—the monumental qualities of Romanesque sculpture. The new attitude can be seen in the *St. Mark* (fig. 10-34) from a Gospel Book probably done toward 1050 at the monastery of Corbie in northern France. The twisting movement of the lines, which pervades not only the figure of St. Mark but the winged lion, the scroll, and the curtain, recalls Carolingian miniatures of the Reims School such as the *Ebbo Gospels* (see fig. 9-17). This very resemblance helps us see the differences between the two works. In the Corbie manuscript, every trace of classical illusionism has disappeared. The fluid modeling of the Reims School, with its suggestion of light and space, has been replaced by firm contours filled in with bright, solid colors. As a result, the three-dimensional aspects of the picture are reduced to overlapped planes. Even Ottonian painting (see figs. 9-27 and 9-28) seems illusionistic in comparison. Yet by sacrificing the last remnants of modeling in terms of light and shade, the Romanesque artist has given his work a clarity and precision that had not been possible in Carolingian or Ottonian times. Only now can we truly say that the representational, the symbolic, and the decorative elements of the design are knit together into a unified structure.

This style avoids all pictorial effects—not only tonal values but the rendering of textures and highlights still found in Ottonian painting. For that very reason, however, it gains a new universality of scale. The evangelists of the *Ebbo Gospels,* the drawings of the *Utrecht Psalter,* and the miniatures in the *Gospel Book of Otto III* are made up of open, spontaneous flicks and dashes of brush or pen that have an intimate, handwritten flavor. They would look strange if copied on a larger scale or in another medium. The Cor-

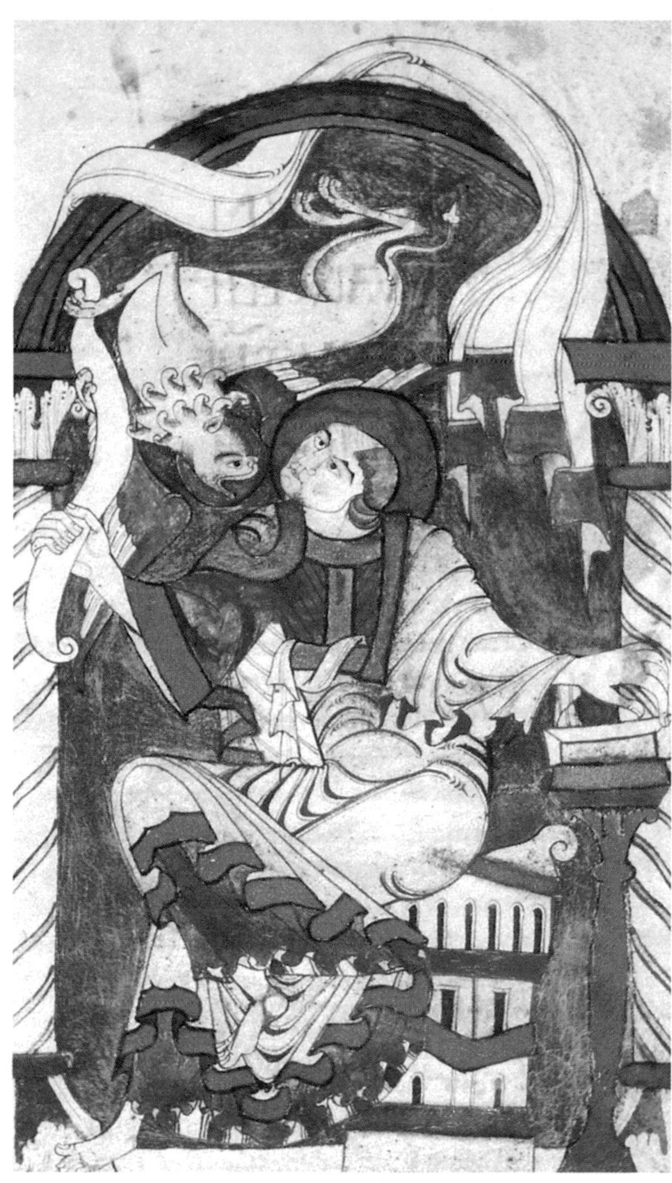

10-34. *St. Mark,* from a Gospel Book produced at Corbie. c. 1050. Bibliothèque Municipale, Amiens, France

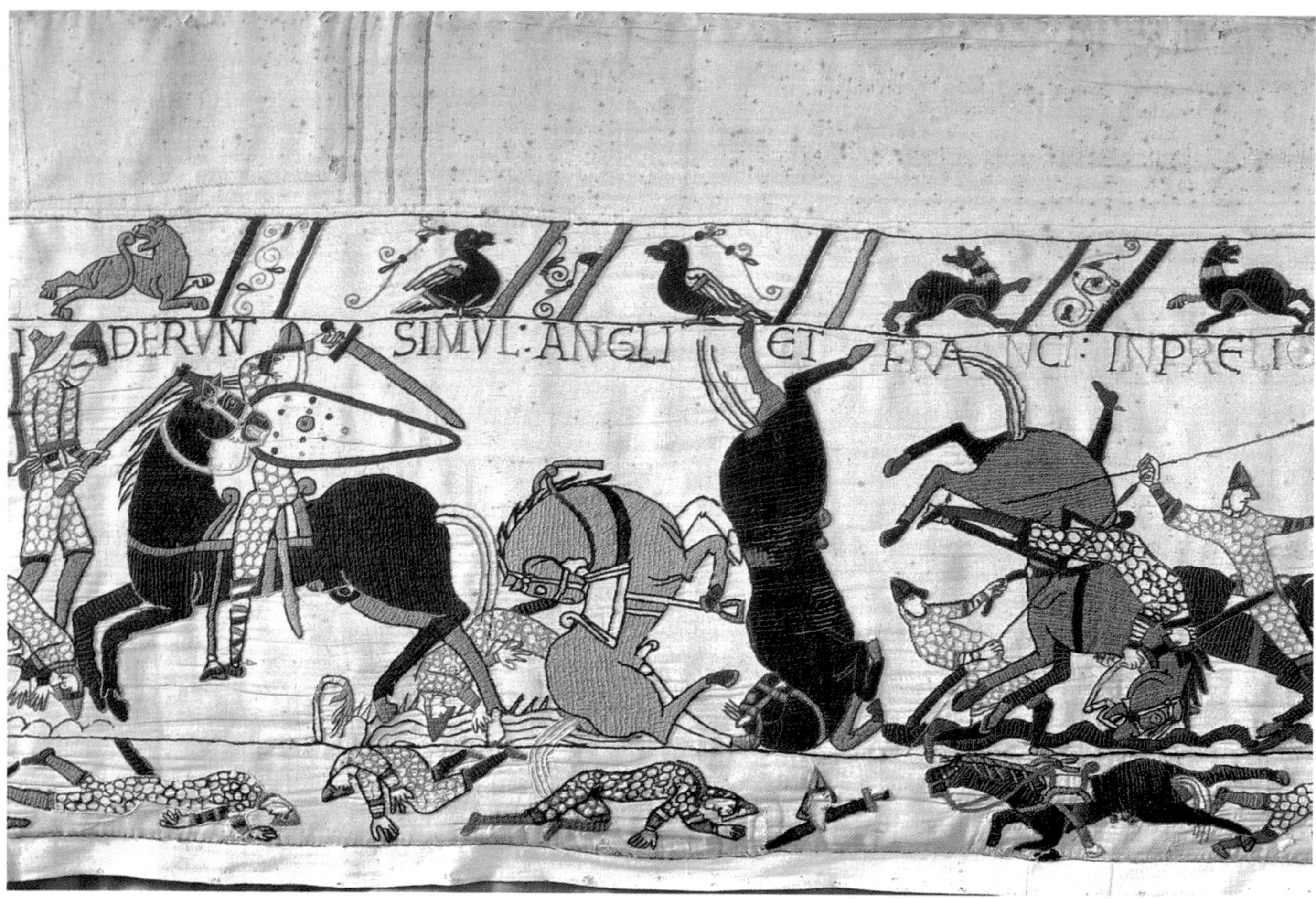

10-35. *The Battle of Hastings.* Detail of the *Bayeux Tapestry.* c. 1073–83. Wool embroidery on linen, height 20" (50.7 cm). Centre Guillaume le Conquerant, Bayeux, France

bie miniature, on the contrary, might be translated into a mural, a stained-glass window, a tapestry, or a relief panel without losing any of its essential qualities.

THE BAYEUX TAPESTRY. This monumentality is much the same as in the Vézelay tympanum (see fig. 10-26), where similar pleated drapery patterns are rendered in sculptural terms. It is found again in the *Bayeux Tapestry,* an embroidered frieze 230 feet long illustrating William the Conqueror's invasion of England. In our detail (fig. 10-35) depicting the Battle of Hastings, the designer has integrated narrative and ornament with complete ease. The main scene is framed by two border strips. The upper tier with birds and animals is purely decorative, but the lower one is full of dead warriors and horses and thus forms part of the story. Although it does not use the pictorial devices of classical painting, such as foreshortening and overlapping (see fig. 5-60), the tapestry gives us a vivid and detailed account of warfare in the eleventh century. The massed forms of the Graeco-Roman scene are gone, replaced by a new kind of individualism that makes each figure a potential hero, whether by force or by cunning. (Note how the soldier who has fallen from the horse with its hind legs in the air is, in turn, toppling his foe by yanking at the saddle girth of his mount.) The stylistic kinship with the Corbie manuscript can be seen in the lively somersaults of the horses, so like the pose of the lion in the miniature.

ST.-SAVIN-SUR-GARTEMPE. The firm outlines and strong sense of pattern found in the English Channel region are equally characteristic of Romanesque wall painting in southwestern France. *The Building of the Tower of Babel* (fig. 10-36) is part of the most impressive surviving cycle, which appears on the nave vault of the church at St.-Savin-sur-Gartempe (compare fig. 10-6). It is an intensely dramatic design, crowded with strenuous action. The Lord himself, on the far left, participates directly in the narrative as he addresses the builders of the huge structure. He is counterbalanced, on the right, by the giant Nimrod, the leader of the enterprise, who frantically hands blocks of stone to the masons atop the tower, so that the entire scene becomes a great test of strength between God and human. The heavy dark contours and the emphatic play of gestures make the composition easily readable from the floor below. Yet the same qualities occur in the illuminated manuscripts of the region, which can be equally monumental despite their small scale.

S. ANGELO IN FORMIS. Where did the idea come from to cover such a vast area with murals? Surely not from France itself, which had no tradition of monumental painting. It must have come from Byzantium (see fig. 8-57)—probably by way of Italy, which had strong ties to the East (see pages 218–22). Toward the end of the eleventh century, Greek artists decorated the newly constructed basilican church of the Benedictine monastery at

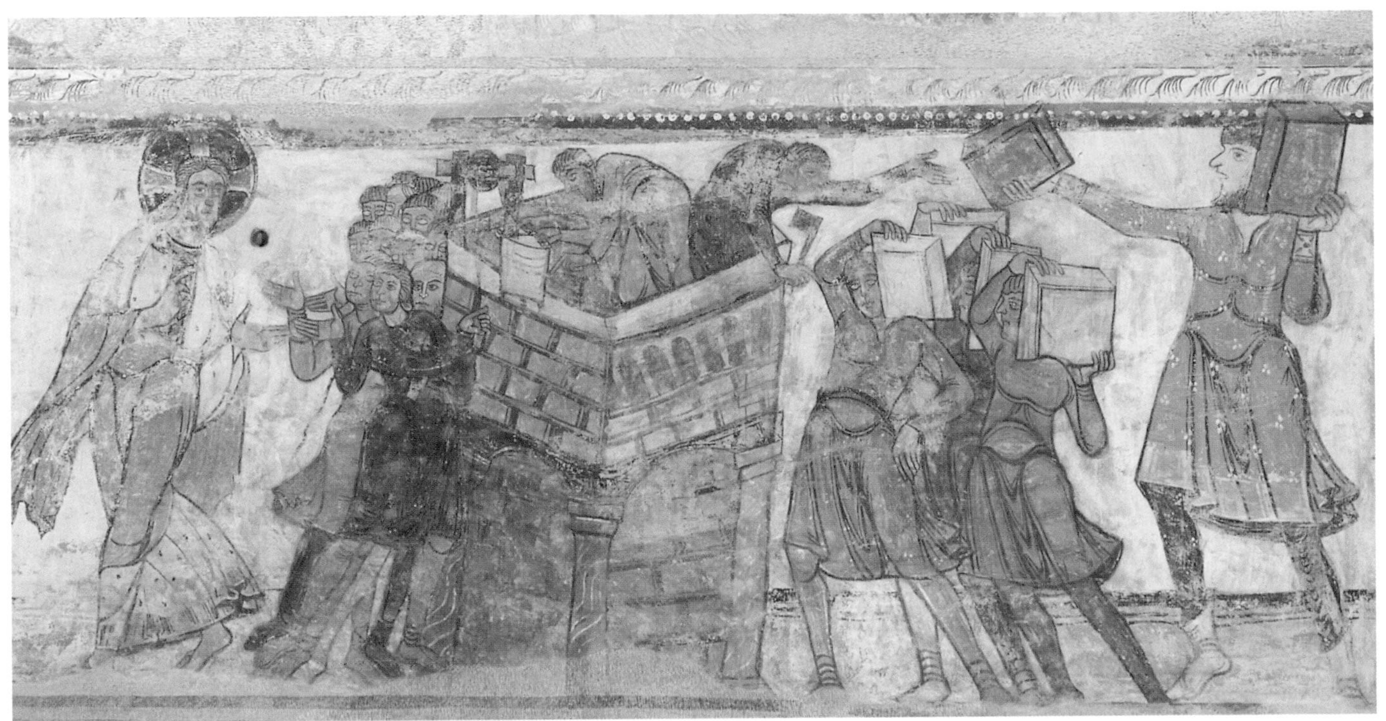

10-36. *The Building of the Tower of Babel.* Detail of painting on the nave vault, St.-Savin-sur-Gartempe. Early 12th century

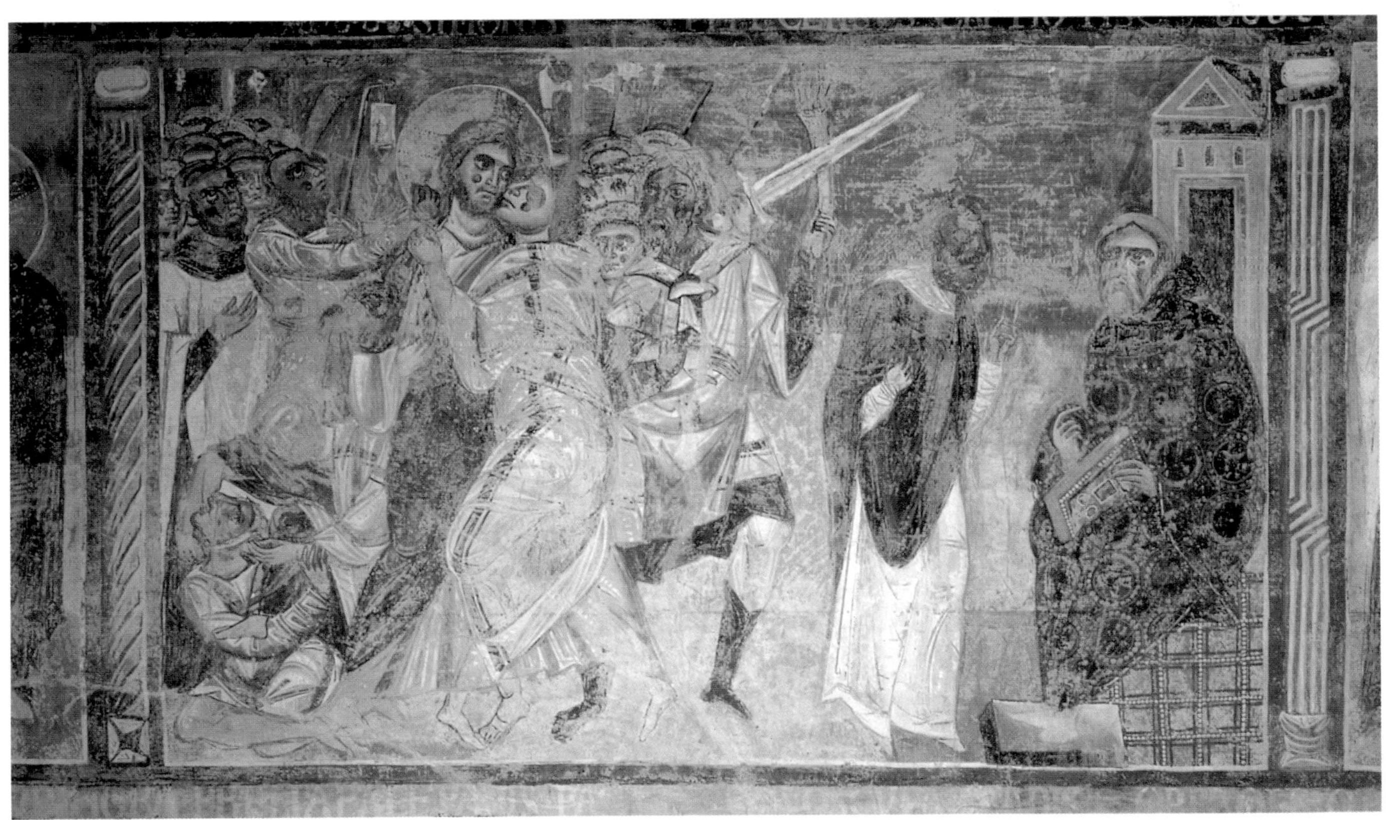

10-37. *The Arrest of Christ.* c. 1085. Fresco. S. Angelo in Formis, Capua, Italy

Monte Cassino with mosaics at the invitation of Abbot Desiderius (later Pope Victor III). Although they have been lost, their impact can be seen in the frescoes painted a short time later in the church of S. Angelo in Formis near Capua, also built by Desiderius. *The Arrest of Christ,* along the nave (fig. 10-37), is a counterpart to the mosaics and murals of Early Christian basilicas, whose splendor Desiderius sought to recapture. The painting shows its Byzantine heritage, but it has been adapted to Latin liturgical requirements and taste. What it lacks in sophistication this monumental style more than makes up for in expressive power. That quality appealed to Western artists, as it was in keeping with the vigorous art that emerged at the same time in the *Bayeux Tapestry.*

By the middle of the twelfth century Byzantine influence could be seen everywhere, from Italy and Spain in the south to

HILDEGARD OF BINGEN

The late tenth through the twelfth centuries witnessed the unprecedented rise of women, first as patrons of art and then as artists. This remarkable development began with the Ottonian dynasty, which forged an alliance with the Church by placing members of the ruling family in prominent positions. Thus Mathilde, Otto I's granddaughter, became abbess of the Holy Trinity convent at Essen in 974. Later, the sister, daughters, and granddaughter of Otto II also served as abbesses of major convents. Hardly less important, though not of royal blood, were Hrosvitha, canoness at the monastery of Gandersheim, who was the first woman dramatist we know of, and the two abbesses of Niedermünster, both named Uota. They paved the way for Herrad of Hohenberg (d. 1195), author of *The Garden of Delights,* an encyclopedia of knowledge and history compiled for the education of her sisters.

Most remarkable of all was the Benedictine abbess Hildegard of Bingen (1098–1179). Among the most brilliant women in history, she corresponded with leaders throughout Europe. In addition to a musical drama in Latin, the *Ordo Virtutum,* about the struggle between the forces of good and evil, she composed almost 80 vocal works that rank with the finest of the day. For her, musical harmony reflected the harmony of the universe. She also wrote some 13 books on theology, medicine, and science. She is known above all for her books of visions, which made her one of the great spiritual voices of her day. Although one (*To Know the Ways of God*) is now known only in facsimile (it was destroyed in 1945) and the other (*The Book of Divine Works*) in a later reproduction, it seems likely that the originals were executed under her direct supervision by nuns in her convent on the Rhine. It has also been argued that they were produced by monks at nearby monasteries.

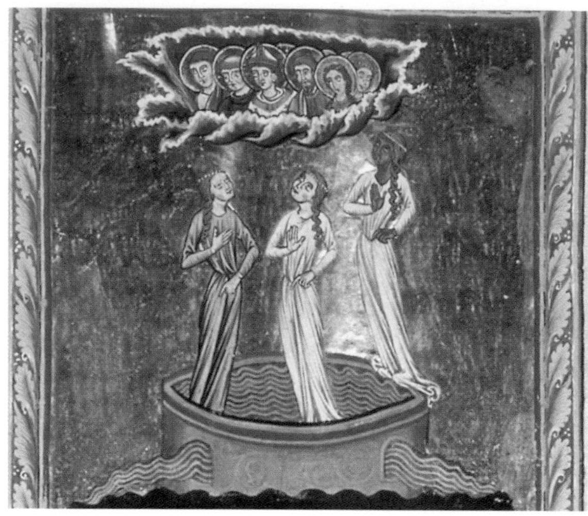

"The Fountain of Life," detail from *Liber divornum operum.* Vision 8. fol. 132r. 13th century. Tempera on vellum, 13 1/8 x 5 5/8" (33.3 x 14 cm). Biblioteca Statale di Lucca, Italy

That there were women artists from the twelfth century on is certain, although we know only a few of their names. [See Primary Sources, no. 39, page 375.] In one instance, an initial in a manuscript includes a nun bearing a scroll inscribed "Guda, the sinful woman, wrote and illuminated this book"; another book depicts Claricia, evidently a lay artist, swinging as carefree as any child from the letter Q she has decorated. Without these author portraits, we might never suspect the involvement of women illuminators.

France, Germany, and England in the north. How did it spread? Most likely the main conduit was the Benedictine order, then at the height of its power. A Byzantine style must have been a major feature of the decorations in the abbey church at Cluny, the seat of Benedictine monasticism in France. The Cluniac style is echoed in the early-twelfth-century frescoes at nearby Berzé-la-Ville, which have distinct Byzantine overtones that relate them directly to the paintings at S. Angelo in Formis.

The Channel Region

Although Romanesque painting, like architecture and sculpture, developed a wide variety of regional styles, its greatest achievements emerged from the monastic scriptoria of northern France, Belgium, and southern England. The works from this area are so closely related in style that at times we cannot be sure on which side of the English Channel a given manuscript was produced.

THE GOSPEL BOOK OF ABBOT WEDRICUS. The style of the miniature of St. John (fig. 10-38) has been linked with both Cambrai, France, and Canterbury, England. Here the abstract linear draftsmanship of the Corbie manuscript (see fig. 10-34) has been influenced by Byzantine art. (Note the ropelike loops of drapery, whose origin can be traced back to such works as *The Crucifixion* at Daphné in fig. 8-48 and even further, to the ivory leaf in fig. 8-23.) The energetic rhythm of the Corbie style has not been lost entirely, however. The controlled dynamics of every contour, both in the main figure and in the frame, unite the varied elements of the composition into a coherent whole. This quality of line betrays its ultimate source, the Celtic-Germanic heritage.

If we compare our miniature with one from the *Lindisfarne Gospels* (see fig. 9-3), we see how much the interlacing patterns of the early Middle Ages have contributed to the design of the St. John page. The drapery folds and the clusters of floral ornament have an impulsive yet disciplined aliveness that echoes the intertwined snakelike monsters of the animal style, even though the foliage is derived from the classical acanthus and the human figures are based on Carolingian and Byzantine models. The unity of the page is conveyed not only by the forms but by the content as well. St. John "inhabits" the frame in such a way that we could not remove him from it without cutting off his ink supply (offered by the donor of the manuscript, Abbot Wedricus), his source of inspi-

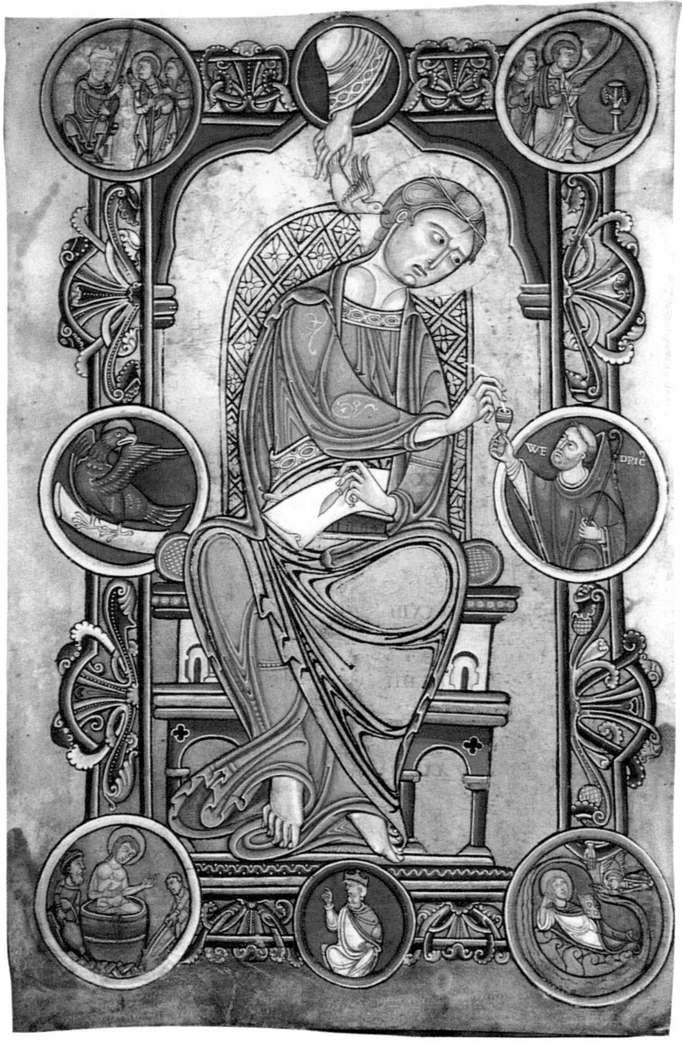

10-38. *St. John the Evangelist,* from the *Gospel Book of Abbot Wedricus.* c. 1147. Tempera on vellum, 14 x 9½" (35.5 x 24.1 cm). Société Archéologique et Historique, Avesnes-sur-Helpe, France

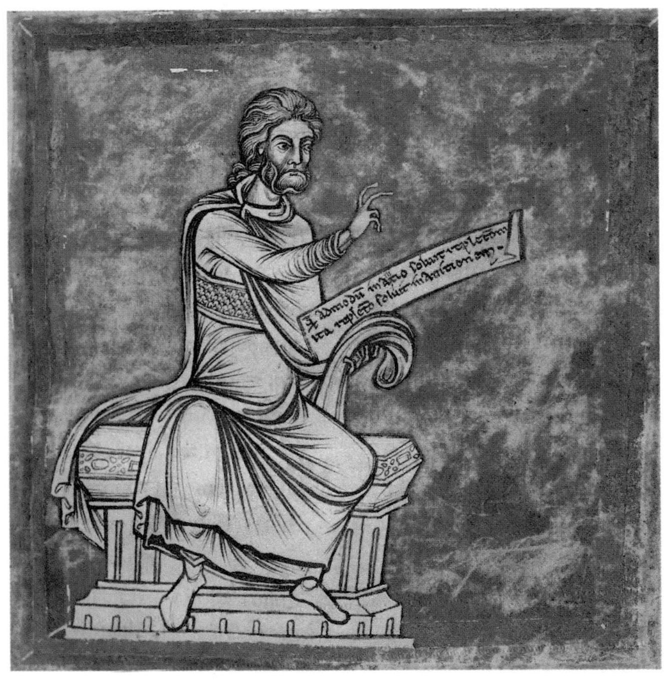

10-39. *Portrait of a Physician,* from a medical treatise. c. 1160. The British Museum, London

ration (the dove of the Holy Spirit in the hand of God), or his symbol (the eagle). The other medallions, less closely linked with the main figure, show scenes from the life of St. John.

PORTRAIT OF A PHYSICIAN. Soon after the middle of the twelfth century, an important change began to occur in Romanesque manuscript painting on both sides of the English Channel. The *Portrait of a Physician* (fig. 10-39), from a medical manuscript of about 1160, is quite different from the St. John miniature, although it was produced in the same region. Instead of abstract patterns, we find lines that describe three-dimensional shapes. The drapery folds no longer lead an ornamental life of their own but suggest the rounded volume of the body underneath. There is even a renewed interest in foreshortening. At last, then, we see an appreciation for the achievements of antiquity that is missing in the murals at S. Angelo in Formis and St.-Savin-sur-Gartempe. Here again, the lead was taken by Cluny, which was a major center of manuscript production.

This style, too, stemmed from Byzantine art, which saw a revival of classicism during the tenth and eleventh centuries. It may have been transmitted through Germany, where, as we have seen, Byzantine elements had long been present in manuscript painting (compare figs. 9-15 and 9-27). The physician, seated in the pose of Christ as philosopher, will remind us of David from the *Paris Psalter* (see fig. 8-47), but he has been utterly transformed. The sharp, deliberate lines look as if they had been engraved in metal, rather than drawn with pen or brush. Thus our miniature is the pictorial counterpart of the classicism we saw in the baptismal font of Renier of Huy at Liège (see fig. 10-31). In fact, it was probably also done at Liège.

NICHOLAS OF VERDUN. That a new way of painting should have originated in metalwork is not as strange as it might seem. The style's essential qualities are sculptural rather than pictorial. Moreover, metalwork (which includes not only cast or embossed sculpture but also engraving, enameling, and goldsmithing) had been a highly developed art in the Meuse Valley area since Carolingian times. Its greatest practitioner after Renier of Huy was Nicholas of Verdun, in whose work the classicizing, three-dimensional style of draftsmanship reaches full maturity. The Klosterneuburg Altar, which he completed in 1181 for provost Wernher, consists of numerous engraved and enameled

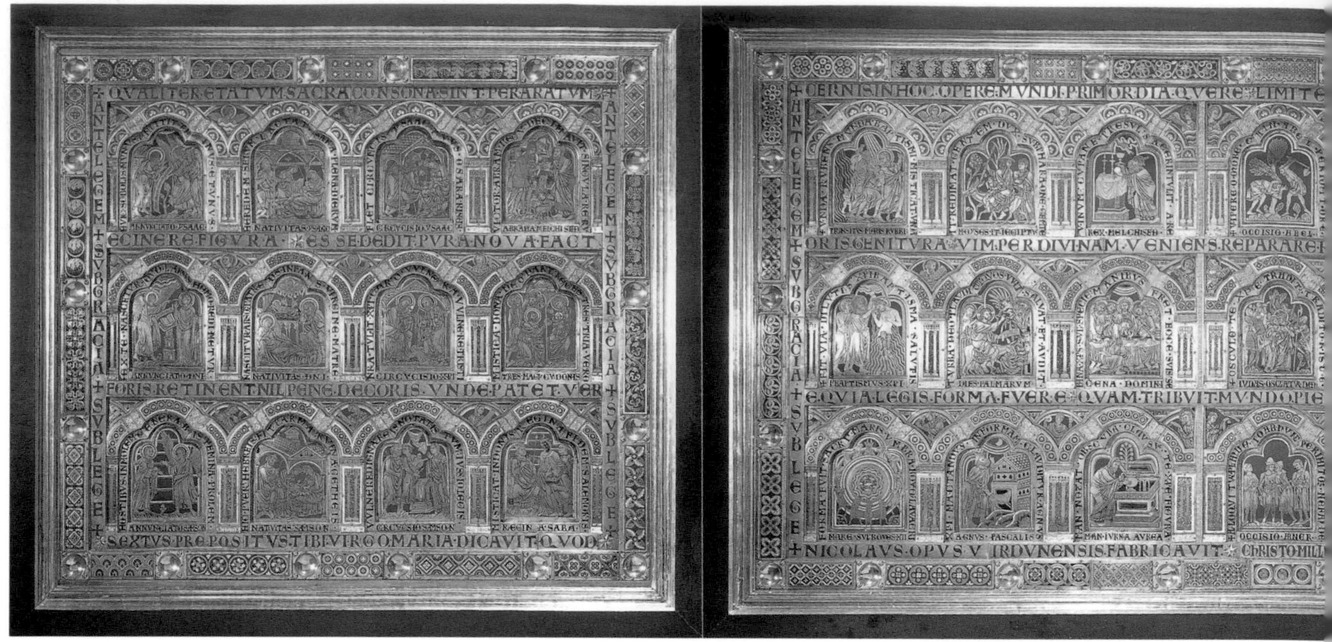

10-40. Nicholas of Verdun. *Klosterneuburg Altar.* 1181. Gold and enamel, height approx. 28" (71.1 cm). Klosterneuburg Abbey, Austria

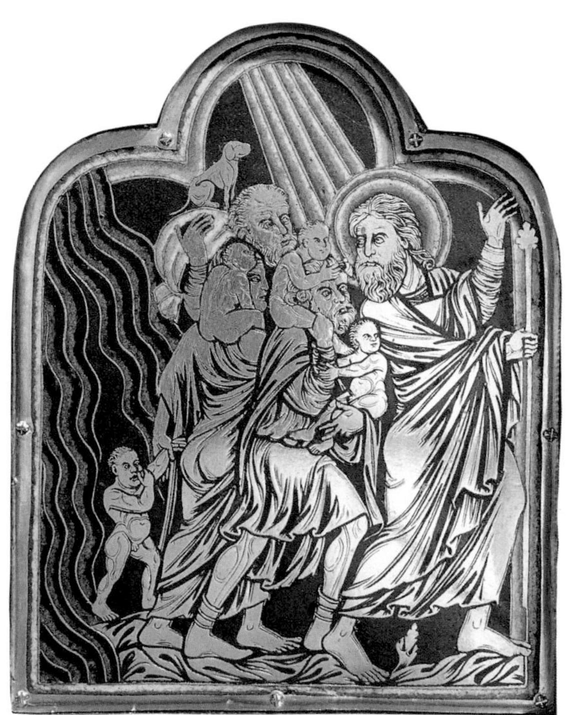

10-41. Nicholas of Verdun. *The Crossing of the Red Sea,* from the *Klosterneuburg Altar.* 1181. Enamel on gold plaque, height 5½" (14 cm). Klosterneuburg Abbey

plaques (fig. 10-40). They are laid out side by side like a series of manuscript illuminations from the Old and New Testaments in a complex program. Originally this work took the form of a pulpit, but after a fire in 1330 it was rearranged as a triptych. The plaques have a sumptuousness that recalls, on a miniature scale, the glittering play of light across mosaics (compare fig. 8-48). *The Crossing of the Red Sea* (fig. 10-41) clearly belongs to the same tradition as the Liège miniature. The figures, clothed in "wet" draperies familiar to us from Classical statues, have achieved such a high degree of organic structure and freedom of movement that we tend to think of them as forerunners of Gothic art rather than as the final phase of the Romanesque. Whatever we choose to call it, the style of the Klosterneuburg Altar was to have a profound impact on both painting and sculpture during the next 50 years (see figs. 11-44 and 11-45).

Equally revolutionary is the new expressiveness of the scene. All the figures, even the little dog perched on the bag carried by one of the men, are united through the exchange of glances and gestures within the tightly knit composition. Not since late Roman times have we seen such concentrated drama, although its intensity is unique to medieval art. Indeed, the astonishing humanity of Nicholas of Verdun's art is linked to an appreciation of the beauty of ancient works of art, as well as to a new regard for classical literature and mythology.

CARMINA BURANA. The reawakening of interest in humanity and the natural world throughout northwestern Europe sometimes was expressed as a greater readiness to acknowledge the enjoyment of sensuous experience. This aspect is reflected in poetry, such as the well-known *Carmina Burana,* composed during the later twelfth century by many of the leading poets of the day and preserved in an illuminated manuscript of the early thirteenth century that was produced at a Benedictine monastery in Upper Bavaria. That a collection of verse devoted largely, and at times very frankly, to the delights of nature, love, and drinking should have been embellished with illustrations is significant in itself (It also includes biting moral and satirical poems, as well as liturgical

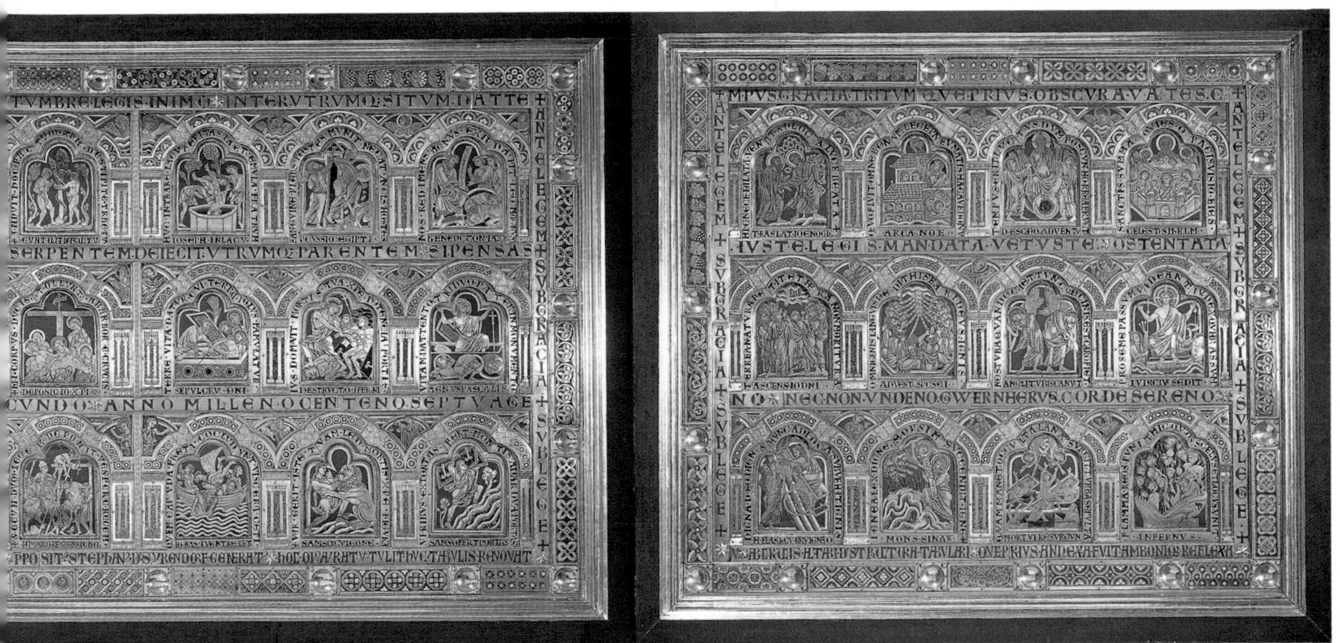

dramas.) We are even more surprised, however, to find that one of the miniatures (fig. 10-42), coupled with a poem praising summer, represents a landscape—the first, so far as we know, to appear in Western art since Late Classical times.

Echoes of ancient landscape painting, derived from Early Christian and Byzantine sources, can be found in Carolingian art (see figs. 9-17 and 9-18), but there they serve only as a background for the human figure. Later on, these remnants were reduced still further, even when the subject required a landscape setting. For example, the Garden of Eden on Bernward's doors (see fig. 9-26) is no more than a few twisted stems and bits of foliage. Thus the illustrator of the *Carmina Burana* must have been perplexed by how to depict the life of nature in summertime. He solved the problem in the only way possible at the time: by filling the page with a sort of anthology of Romanesque plant ornament interspersed with birds and animals.

The trees, vines, and flowers are so abstract that we cannot identify a single species. The birds and animals, probably copied from a zoological treatise, are far more realistic. Yet the plants have an uncanny vitality of their own. They seem to sprout and unfold as if the growth of an entire season were compressed into a few frantic moments. These giant seedlings convey the exuberance of early summer, of stored energy suddenly released, far more intensely than any normal vegetation could. Our artist has created a fairy-tale landscape, but his enchanted world evokes an essential underlying reality.

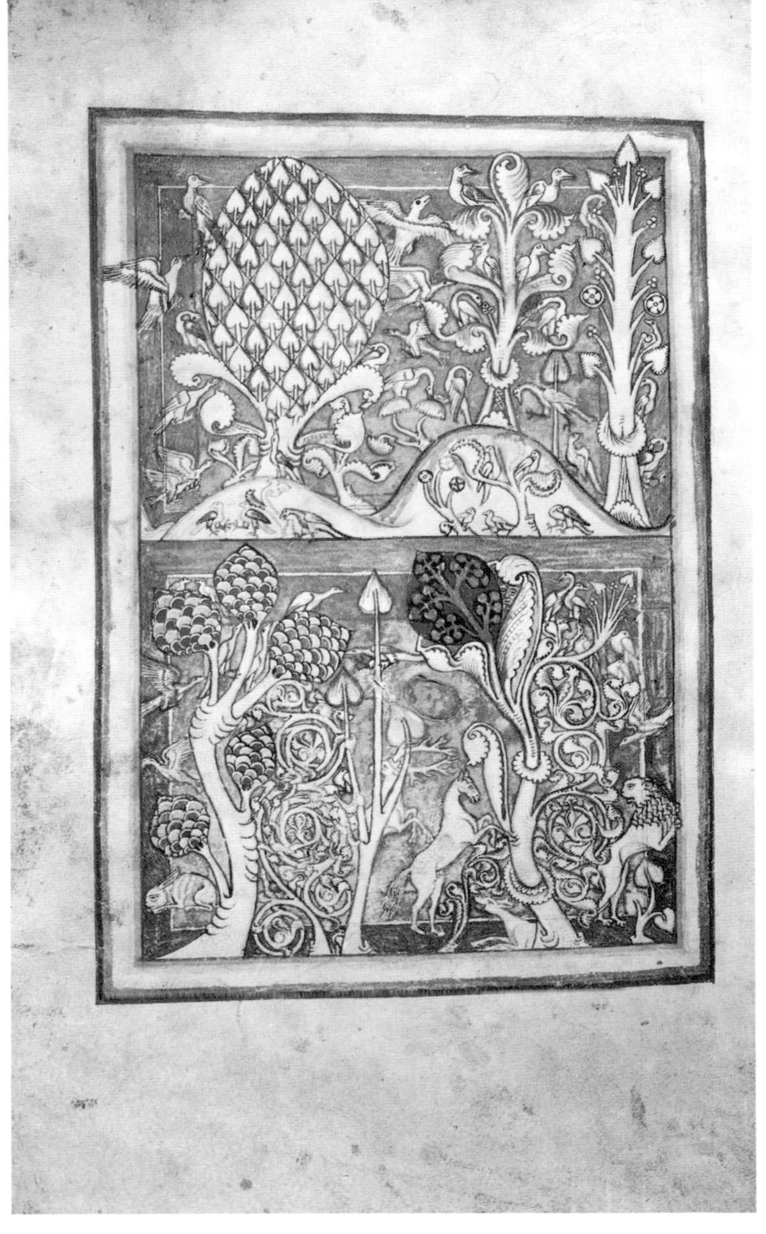

(RIGHT) 10-42. Page with *Summer Landscape,* from a manuscript of *Carmina Burana*. Early 13th century. 7 x 4⅞" (17.8 x 12.5 cm). Bayerische Staatsbibliothek, Munich

CHAPTER ELEVEN

Gothic Art

Time and space, we have been taught, are interdependent. Yet, although we tend to think of events as unfolding in time, we are not as aware of their unfolding in space. We visualize history as a stack of chronological layers, or periods, with each layer having a specific depth that corresponds to its length. For the more remote past, when our information is scanty, this simple image works reasonably well. It becomes less adequate as we draw closer to the present and our knowledge grows more precise. Thus we cannot define the Gothic era in terms of time alone; we must consider its changing surface area as well.

At the start, about 1140, this area was small indeed. It included only the province known as the Île-de-France (that is, Paris and vicinity), the royal domain of the French kings. A hundred years later, most of Europe had adopted the Gothic style, from Sicily to Iceland, with only a few Romanesque pockets left here and there. Through the Crusaders, the new style was even carried to the Near East. About 1450, the Gothic area began to shrink. (It no longer included Italy.) By about 1550, it had disappeared almost entirely. The Gothic layer, then, has a rather complicated shape. Its depth ranges from close to 400 years in some places to 150 in others. Moreover, this shape is not equally clear in all the visual arts.

The term "Gothic" was first coined for architecture, and it is in architecture that the characteristics of the style are most easily recognized. Although we speak of Gothic sculpture and painting, there is, as we shall see, some uncertainty about the exact limits of the Gothic style in these fields. This difference reflects the way the new style actually grew. It began with architecture, and for a century—from about 1150 to 1250, during the Age of the Great Cathedrals—architecture played the dominant role. Gothic sculpture, at first severely architectural in spirit, became less so after 1200. Its greatest achievements are between the years 1220 and 1420. Painting, in turn, reached a peak between 1300 and 1350 in central Italy. North of the Alps, it became the leading art from about 1400 on. Thus, in surveying the Gothic era as a whole, we find a gradual shift of emphasis from architecture to painting—from architectural to pictorial qualities. Early Gothic sculpture and painting both reflect the discipline of their monumental setting, while Late Gothic architecture and sculpture strive for "picturesque" effects.

Overlying this broad pattern is another one: international diffusion as against regional independence. Starting in the Île-de-France, Gothic art spread to the rest of France and to all Europe, where it came to be known as *opus modernum* or *opus francigenum* (modern or French work). In the course of the thirteenth century, the new style gradually lost its imported flavor, and regional variety began to appear. Toward the middle of the fourteenth century, there was a growing tendency for these regional styles to influence each other until, about 1400, an "International Gothic" style prevailed almost everywhere. Shortly thereafter, this unity broke apart. Italy, with Florence in the lead, created a radically new art, that of the Early Renaissance. North of the Alps, Flanders took the lead in the development of Late Gothic painting and sculpture. A century later, finally, the Italian Renaissance became the basis of another international style.

This development roughly parallels what happened in the political arena. Supported by shifting alliances with the papacy, the kings of France and England emerged as the leading powers at the expense of the Germans in the early thirteenth century, which was generally a time of peace and prosperity. Under these ideal conditions the new Franciscan and Dominican orders were established, and Catholicism found its greatest intellect, St. Thomas Aquinas, since St. Augustine and St. Jerome some 850 years earlier. After 1290, however, the balance of power quickly broke down. Finally, in 1305 the French pope Clement V moved the papacy to Avignon, France, where it remained for more than 70 years.

ARCHITECTURE

France

ST.-DENIS AND ABBOT SUGER. We can pinpoint the origin of the Gothic style with unusual accuracy. It was born between 1137 and 1144 in the rebuilding by Abbot Suger of the royal Abbey

Church of St.-Denis just outside the city of Paris. To understand how Gothic architecture arose at this particular spot, we must examine the relationship between St.-Denis, Suger, and the French monarchy. The kings of France derived their authority from the Carolingian tradition, although they belonged to the Capetian line (founded by Hugh Capet after the death of the last Carolingian in 987). But their power was eclipsed by that of the nobles who, in theory, were their vassals. The only area they ruled directly was the Île-de-France, and their authority was often challenged even there. Not until the early twelfth century did the royal power begin to expand. As chief adviser to Louis VI, Suger played a key role in this process. It was he who forged the alliance between the monarchy and the Church. This union brought the bishops of France (and the cities under their authority) to the king's side; the king, in turn, supported the papacy in its struggle against the German emperors.

Suger also engaged in "spiritual politics." By giving the monarchy religious significance and glorifying it as the strong right arm of justice, he sought to rally the nation behind the king. His plans for the abbey of St.-Denis must be viewed in this context. The church, founded in the late eighth century, enjoyed a dual prestige. It was both the shrine of St.-Denis, the Apostle of France and protector of the realm, and the chief memorial of the Carolingian dynasty. Both Charlemagne and his father, Pepin, had been consecrated as kings there. It was also the burial place of Charles Martel, Pepin, and Charles the Bald. Suger wanted to make the abbey the spiritual center of France, a pilgrimage church that would outshine all others and provide a focal point for religious as well as patriotic emotion. To achieve this goal, the old structure had to be enlarged and rebuilt. The great abbot himself wrote two accounts of the church and its rebuilding which, though incomplete, tell us a great deal. [See Primary Sources, nos. 25 and 26, pages 369–71.] Unfortunately, the west facade is sadly mutilated, and the choir at the east end, which Suger saw as the most important part of the church, retains its original appearance only in the ambulatory (figs. 11-1 and 11-2).

The ambulatory and chapels surrounding the apse are familiar elements from the Romanesque pilgrimage choir (compare fig. 10-2), but they have been integrated in a new way. Instead of being separate, the chapels are merged so as to form, in effect, a second ambulatory. Ribbed groin vaulting based on the pointed arch is used throughout. (In the Romanesque pilgrimage choir, only the ambulatory had been groin-vaulted.) As a result, the entire plan is held together by a new kind of geometric order. It consists of seven nearly identical wedge-shaped units fanning out from the center of the apse. (The central chapel, dedicated to the Virgin, and its neighbors on either side are slightly larger, presumably because of their greater importance.) We experience this double ambulatory not as a series of compartments but as a continuous (though articulated) space, whose shape is outlined for us by the network of slender arches, ribs, and columns that sustains the vaults.

What distinguishes this interior from earlier ones is its lightness, in both senses of the word. The architectural forms seem graceful, almost weightless, as against the massive solidity of the Romanesque. In addition, the windows have been enlarged to the point that they are no longer openings cut into a wall. Instead, they fill almost the entire wall area, so that they become translucent walls. If we look again at the plan, we see what makes this abundance of light possible. The outward pressure of the vaults is contained by heavy buttresses jutting out between the chapels. (In the plan, they look like stubby black arrows pointing toward the cen-

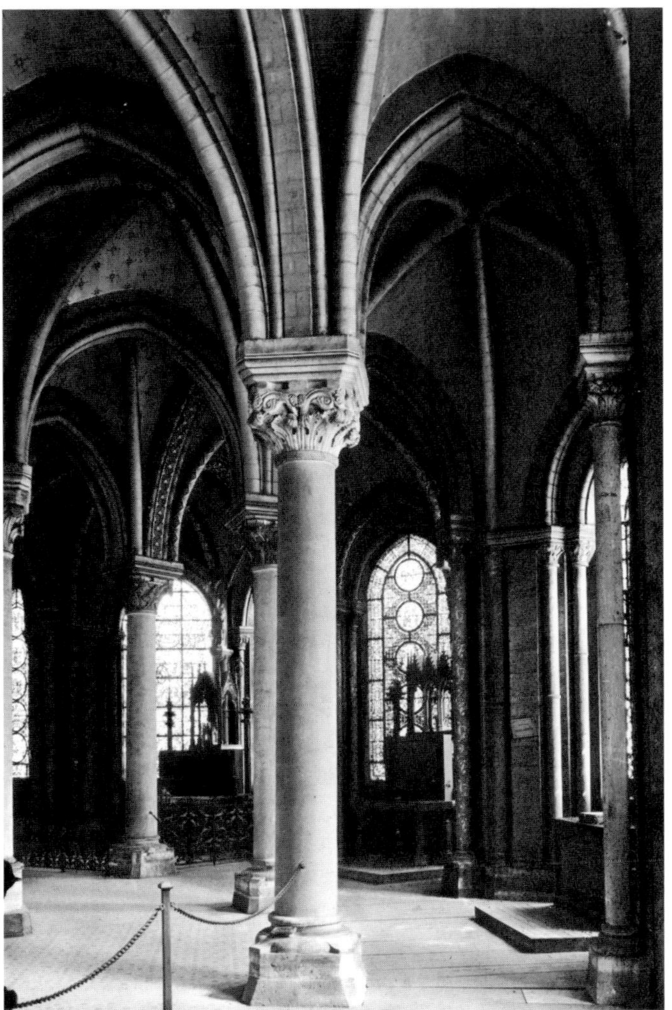

11-1. Ambulatory, Abbey Church of St.-Denis, Paris. 1140–44

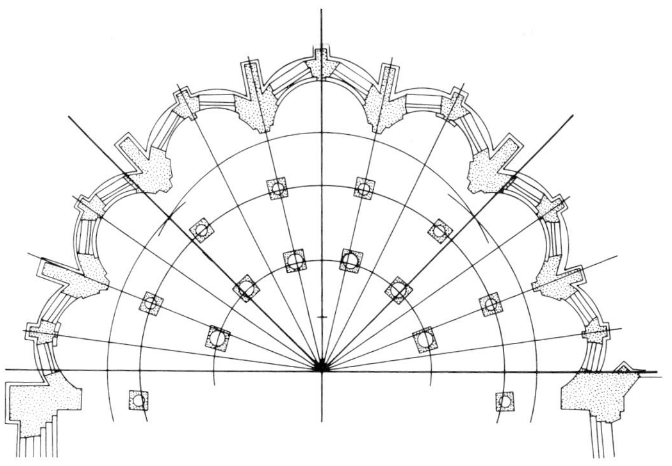

11-2. Plan of the choir and ambulatory of St.-Denis (Peter Kidson)

ter of the apse.) No wonder, then, that the interior appears so airy and weightless, since the heaviest parts of the structural skeleton are outside. The impression would be even more striking if we could see all of Suger's choir, for the upper part of the apse, rising above the double ambulatory, had very large, tall windows. The effect, from the nave, must have been similar to that of the somewhat later choir of Notre-Dame in Paris (see fig. 11-4).

SUGER AND GOTHIC ARCHITECTURE. In describing Suger's choir, we have also described the essentials of Gothic architecture. Yet none of the elements that entered into its design is really new. The pilgrimage choir plan, the pointed arch, and the ribbed groin vault can be found in regional schools of the French and Anglo-Norman Romanesque, although they were never combined in the same building until St.-Denis. The Île-de-France had not developed a Romanesque tradition of its own, so that Suger (as he himself tells us) had to bring together artisans from many different regions for his project. We must not conclude from this, however, that Gothic architecture was merely a synthesis of Romanesque traits. If it were only that, we would be hard pressed to explain the new spirit that strikes us so forcibly at St.-Denis: the emphasis on geometric planning and the quest for luminosity. Suger's account of the rebuilding of his church stresses both of these features as the highest values achieved in the new structure. "Harmony" (that is, the perfect relationship among parts in terms of mathematical proportions or ratios) is the source of all beauty, since it exemplifies the laws by which divine reason made the universe. Thus, it is suggested, the "miraculous" light that floods the choir through the "most sacred" windows becomes the Light Divine, a revelation of the spirit of God.

This symbolic interpretation of light and of numerical harmony was well established in Christian thought. It derived in part from the writings of a fifth-century Greek theologian who, in the Middle Ages, was believed to have been Dionysius the Areopagite, an Athenian disciple of St. Paul. Because of this identification, the works of another fifth-century writer, known as the Pseudo-Dionysius, gained great authority. In Carolingian France, moreover, Dionysius the disciple of St. Paul was identified both with the author of the Pseudo-Dionysian writings and with St.-Denis. Although these writings were available to Suger at St.-Denis, his debt to them seems rather general at best. Suger was not a scholar but a man of action who was conventional in his thinking. He probably consulted the contemporary theologian Hugh of St.-Victor, who was steeped in Dionysian thought, for the most obscure part of his program at the west end of the church.

This does not mean that Suger's own writings are simply a justification after the fact. On the contrary, he clearly knew his own mind. What, then, was he trying to achieve? Like the three blind men trying to describe an elephant by touching different parts of the animal, scholars have come to surprisingly little agreement. For Suger, the material realm was the stepping stone for spiritual contemplation. Thus the actual experience of dark, jewellike light that disembodies the material world lies at the heart of Suger's mystical intent: to be transported to "some strange region of the universe which neither exists entirely in the slime of earth nor entirely in the purity of Heaven."

SUGER AND THE MEDIEVAL ARCHITECT. The success of the choir design at St.-Denis is proved not only by its inherent qualities but also by its extraordinary impact. Every visitor, it seems, was overwhelmed by the achievement, and within a few decades the new style had spread far beyond the Île-de-France. The how and why of Suger's success are a good deal more difficult to explain. They involve a controversy we have met several times before—that of form versus function. To the advocates of the functionalist approach, Gothic architecture was the result of advances in engineering, which made it possible to build more efficient vaults, to concentrate their thrust at a few critical points, and thus to eliminate the solid walls of the Romanesque church. Suger, they argue, was fortunate in that his architect understood the principles of ribbed groin vaulting better than anybody else at that time. If the abbot chose to interpret the resulting structure as symbolic of Dionysian theology, he was simply expressing his enthusiasm over it in the abstract language of the churchman, so that his account does not help us to understand the origin of the new style.

As the integration of its parts suggests, the choir of St.-Denis is more rationally planned and constructed than any Romanesque church. The pointed arch (which can be "stretched" to reach any desired height regardless of the width of its base) has become an integral part of the ribbed groin vault. As a result, these vaults are no longer restricted to square or near-square compartments. They have a flexibility that allows them to cover areas of almost any shape (such as the trapezoids and pentagons of the ambulatory). The buttressing of the vaults, too, is more fully understood than before. How could Suger's ideas have led to these technical advances, unless we assume that he was a professionally trained architect? (Actually, architectural training as we know it did not exist at the time.) If we grant that he was not, can he claim any credit for the style of what he so proudly calls "his" new church? Oddly enough, there is no contradiction here. As we have seen (page 257), the term *architect* had a very different meaning from the modern one, which derives from Greece and Rome by way of the Italian Renaissance. To the medieval mind, the overall leader of the project, not the master builder responsible for its construction, was the "architect." As Suger's account makes abundantly clear, he shared this view, which is why he remains so silent about his helper.

Perhaps this is a chicken-and-egg question. The function of a church, after all, is not merely to enclose a maximum of space with a minimum of material but also to convey the religious ideas that lie behind it. For the master who built the choir of St.-Denis, the technical problems of vaulting must have been intertwined with such ideas, as well as with issues of form—beauty, harmony, and the like. As a matter of fact, the design includes elements that express function without actually performing it; for example, the slender shafts (called responds) that seem to carry the weight of the vaults to the church floor.

In order to know what concepts to convey, the medieval architect needed the guidance of religious authority. At a minimum, such guidance might be a simple directive to follow some established model. In Suger's case, however, it amounted to a more active role. It seems that he began with one master builder at the

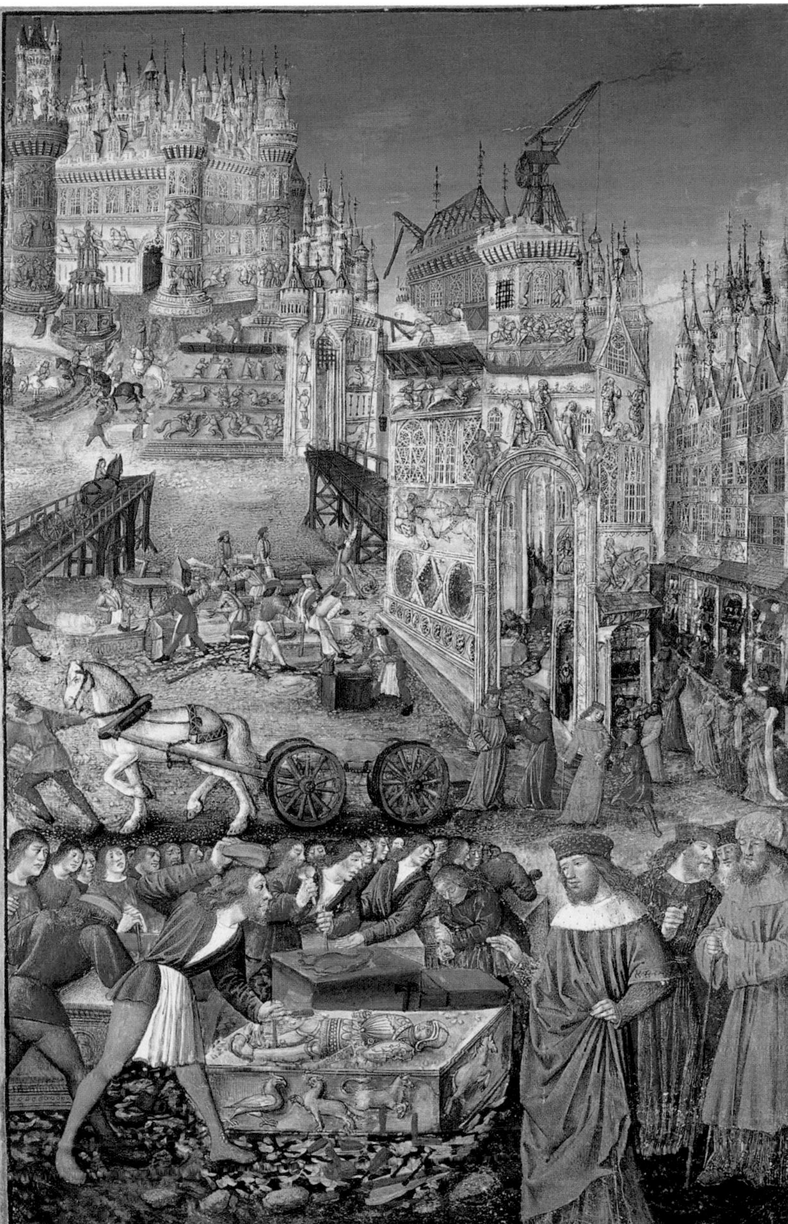

11-3. Jean Colombe. *King Priam Rebuilding Troy* (detail), detached miniature from *Histoire de la destruction de Troie la Grande,* after 1490. Tempera on vellum, 19⅝ x 13" (51 x 33 cm). Kupferstichkabinett Pergamon Museum, Berlin, Preussischer Kulturbesitz

west end but was disappointed with the results and had it torn down. This fact not only shows that Suger played a role in the design process but also confirms his position as the architect of St.-Denis in the medieval sense. Suger's views no doubt guided his choice of a second master of Norman background to translate them into the kind of structure he wanted, not simply as a matter of design preference. This great artist must have been singularly responsive to the abbot's objectives. Together, they created the Gothic. We have seen this kind of close collaboration between patron and architect before: it occurred between Djoser and Imhotep, Perikles and Pheidias, just as it does today.

CONSTRUCTING ST.-DENIS. Building St.-Denis was an expensive and complex task that required the combined resources of Church and State. Suger used stone from quarries near Pontoise for the ambulatory columns and lumber from the forest of Yveline for the roof. Both had to be transported by land and river over great distances, a slow and costly process. The master builder probably employed several hundred stonemasons and two or three times that many laborers. He was aided by advances in technology spurred by warfare. Especially important were better cranes powered by windlasses or treadwheels that used counterweights and double pulleys for greater efficiency. These devices were easily put up and taken down, allowing for lighter scaffolding suspended from the wall instead of resting on the ground. Such developments made possible the construction techniques illustrated in the border of figure 11-3 and were essential to building the new rib vaults.

NOTRE-DAME, PARIS. Although St.-Denis was an abbey, the future of Gothic architecture lay in the towns rather than in rural monastic communities. There had been a vigorous revival of urban life, we will recall, since the early eleventh century. This movement continued at a rapid pace, and the growth of the cities made itself felt not only economically and politically but in countless other ways as well. Bishops and the city clergy rose to new

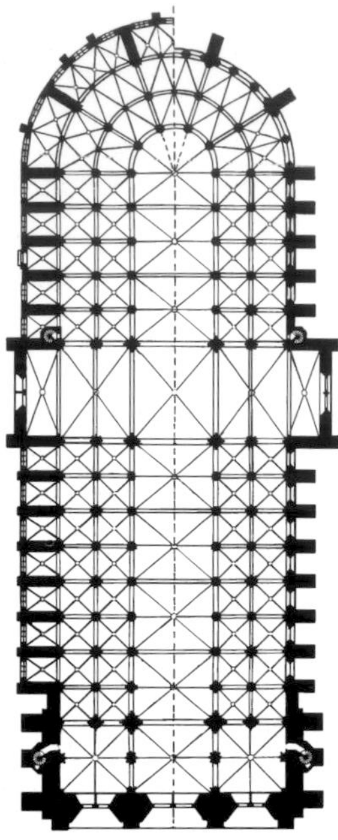

(LEFT) 11-4. Plan of Notre-Dame, Paris. 1163–c. 1250

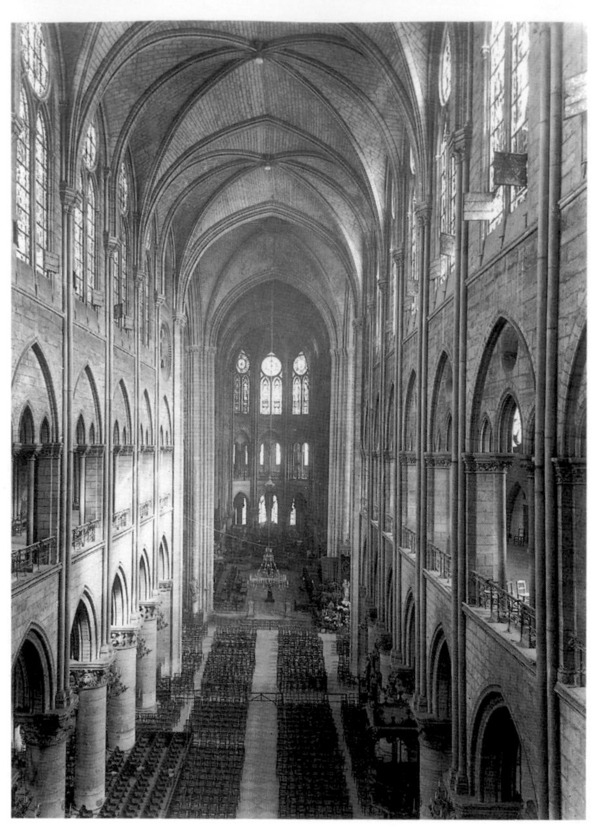

(RIGHT) 11-5. Nave and choir, Notre-Dame, Paris

(BELOW) 11-6. Notre-Dame (view from the southeast), Paris

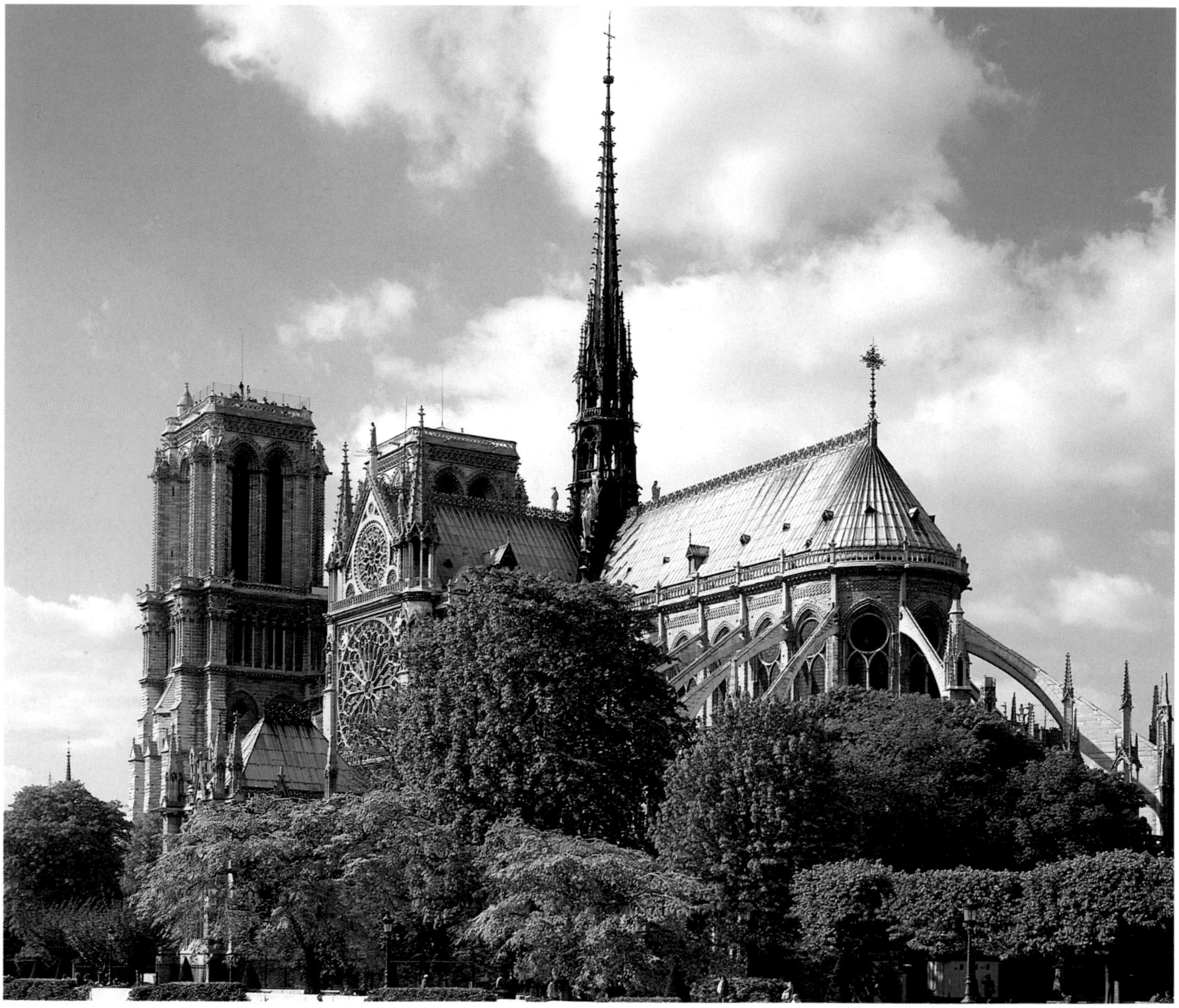

importance. Cathedral schools and universities took the place of monasteries as centers of learning. And the artistic efforts of the age culminated in the great cathedral churches. (A cathedral is the seat of a bishopric, or see.)

Notre-Dame ("Our Lady," the Virgin Mary) at Paris, begun in 1163, reflects the main features of Suger's St.-Denis more directly than does any other church (figs. 11-4–11-8). The plan (see fig. 11-4), with its emphasis on the long axis, is extraordinarily compact and unified compared to that of major Romanesque churches. The double ambulatory of the choir continues directly into the aisles, and the stubby transept barely exceeds the width of the facade. The six-part nave vaulting over squarish bays, although not identical with the "Siamese-twin" groin vaults in Durham Cathedral (see fig. 10-9), continues the kind of structural experimentation that was begun by the Norman Romanesque.

Inside (see fig. 11-5) we find other echoes of the Norman Romanesque in the galleries above the inner aisles and the columns of the nave arcade. Here, too, the use of pointed ribbed arches, pioneered in the western bays of the nave at Durham, occurs throughout the building. Yet the large clerestory windows and the lightness and slenderness of the forms create the weightless effect that we associate with Gothic interiors and make the nave walls seem thin. The vertical emphasis of the interior space is also Gothic. It depends less on the actual proportions of the nave—some Romanesque naves are equally tall relative to their width—than on the constant accenting of the verticals and the apparent ease with which the sense of height is attained. Romanesque interiors (such as that in fig. 10-3), by contrast, emphasize the great effort required in supporting the weight of the vaults.

In Notre-Dame, as in Suger's choir, the buttresses (the "heavy bones" of the structural skeleton) cannot be seen from the inside. (The plan shows them as massive blocks of masonry that stick out from the building like a row of teeth.) Above the aisles, these piers turn into flying buttresses—arched bridges that reach upward to the critical spots between the clerestory windows where the outward thrust of the nave vault is concentrated (see fig. 11-6). This method of anchoring vaults, characteristic of Gothic architecture, certainly owed its origin to functional considerations. Even the flying buttress, however, soon became aesthetically important. Its shape could express support (apart from actually providing it) in a variety of ways, according to the designer's sense of style (see fig. 11-7).

The most monumental aspect of the exterior of Notre-Dame is the west facade (see fig. 11-8). It retains its original appearance, except for the sculpture, which was badly damaged during the French Revolution and is for the most part restored. The design reflects that of the facade of St.-Denis, which was derived from Norman Romanesque facades such as that of St.-Étienne at Caen (see fig. 10-8). If we compare the latter with Notre-Dame, we see that they share some basic features. These include the pier but-

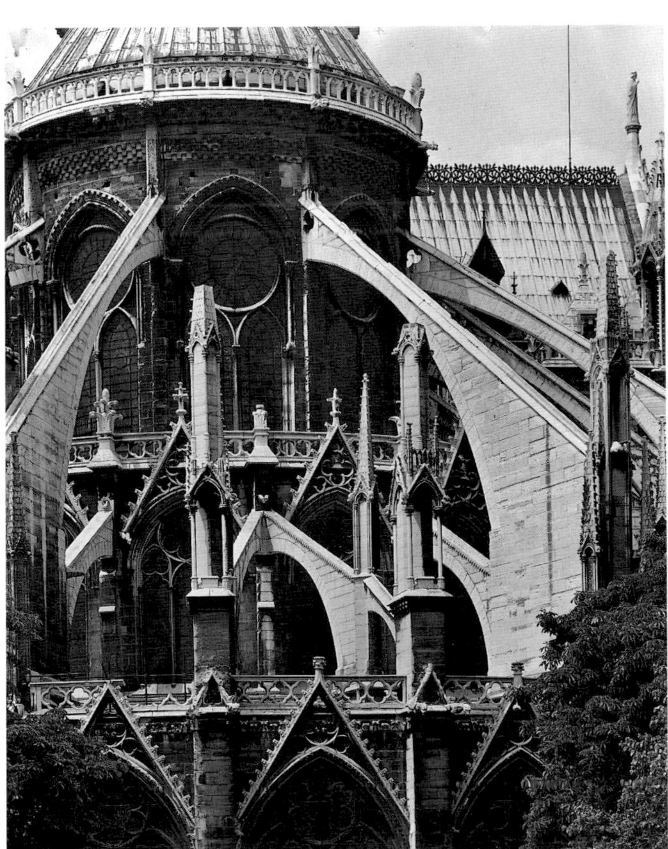

11-7. Flying arches and flying buttresses, Notre-Dame, Paris

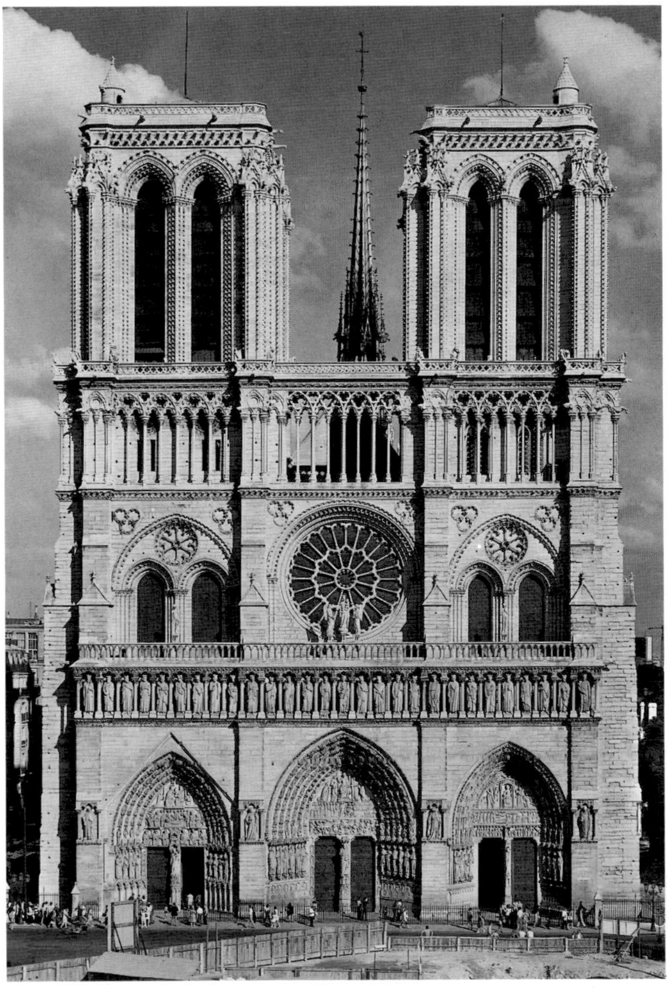

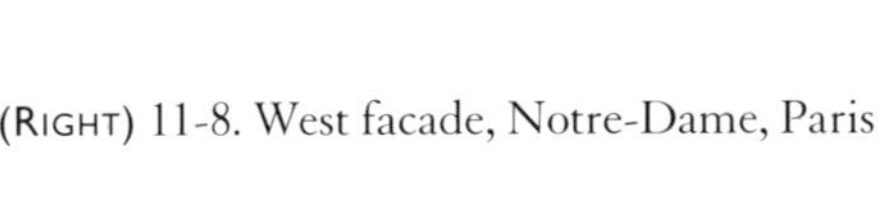

(RIGHT) 11-8. West facade, Notre-Dame, Paris

MEDIEVAL MUSIC AND THEATER

As in ancient Greece, music and theater were intimately connected during the Middle Ages. In fact, medieval theater was largely a direct outgrowth of music. The only musical texts that survive from the Middle Ages before the late eleventh century are religious. Like Early Christian visual art, they bring together Roman, Greek, Jewish, and Syrian elements. Early medieval pieces, or chants, were in the form of plainsong, a single, unaccompanied line of melody in free rhythm. Plainsong continued many of the features of the ancient Greek modes (see pages 125–26), thanks mainly to the philosopher Boethius (c. 480–524). His musical theories, set down around 500, were based on those of Pythagoras and other ancient Greek writers that are now mostly lost to us. By that time, however, Greek music was no longer a living tradition and had been modified by the Romans, so that its theories were adopted in different form.

One of the most important early medieval composers was Ambrose, a fourth-century bishop of Milan, who introduced an early variety of plainsong now known as Ambrosian chant. (He also converted the music-loving St. Augustine of Hippo to Catholicism.) Over the next two centuries, Ambrosian chant was developed further, especially by the choir of the papal chapel in Rome. Around 600, Pope Gregory the Great (590–604) codified the Church's liturgy (the prescribed form for various worship services and other rites), including the music to be sung in each kind of service and the prayer hours to be observed by the monastic orders. The plainsong style in use in Rome at the time, which is still sung in many Catholic services, is popularly known as Gregorian chant.

At first, medieval chant was sung in unison, one word to a note, but gradually more notes were added for some syllables. Eventually some of these multinote passages were developed into long musical phrases (*melismas*), until there were so many notes for each word that additional, often unrelated, texts could be inserted into the work. These interpolated texts (tropes, from the Latin *tropus,* for "added melody") ultimately developed into medieval drama. The introduction of dramatic elements was also an outgrowth of the interplay between two choruses (antiphons), or between a soloist and a choir (responses).

The growing complexity of medieval music gave rise to a new body of music theory—an organized code of rules comparable to the grammar of a spoken language. This effort reached its climax in the thirteenth century, when a system for musical notation was perfected. The development of this body of theory may also be compared to the evolution of architectural principles during the Romanesque and Gothic eras, when musicians sought a comprehensive structure for their work. Of the many centers of chant, the most important was the Cathedral of Notre-Dame in Paris, where a new type of polyphonic music (music in parts), called organum, developed from the late ninth to the thirteenth century. Organum might have two or more voices, which sang the same words and melody a set interval apart, often with a plainsong underpinning (*cantus firmus*). During the late twelfth century, these pieces became increasingly complex under Master Léonin and his pupil Master Pérotin, the first Western composers whose names and works we know. Eventually, around 1200 each voice was assigned its own text and melodic line. The resulting multivoiced composition, sometimes with instrumental accompaniment, was called a motet (from French *mot,* "word"). The motet had such appeal that it was quickly secularized by substituting vernacular verses (chiefly love poems) for religious texts.

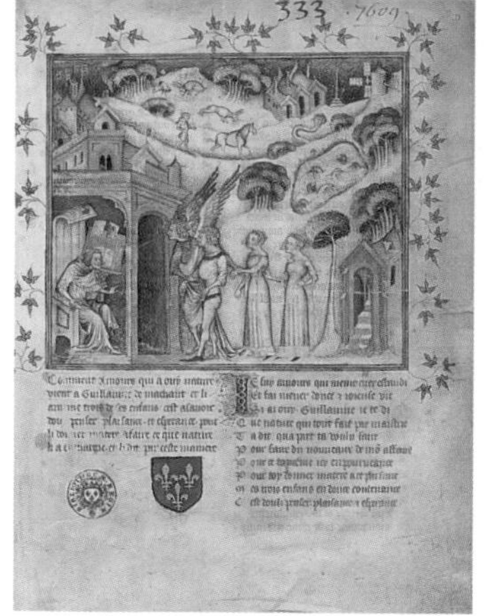

Maître aux Bouqueteaux. *Guillaume de Machaut in His Study (Amour Presenting Him to His Three Children).* 1370. A miniature from an illuminated manuscript page of Machaut's works, fol. D. Bibliothèque Nationale, Paris

Like Gothic architecture, the Notre-Dame style quickly spread throughout Europe. Although it lasted until about 1400 in some places, it was gradually replaced after 1325 by a new musical style. Called *ars nova* (new art), it featured polyphony and rhythms of ever-greater complexity and subtlety. Despite its name, *ars nova,* like the Gothic paintings of Giotto, remained rooted in the past while looking to the future. The greatest composer of *ars nova* was Guillaume de Machaut (c. 1300–1377). A cleric who served the kings of Bohemia and France, he was also considered the finest poet of his day. Thus he was a perfect blend of religious and secular talents characteristic of the Gothic era as a whole. Guillaume de Machaut was a new figure in European culture: the professional composer. During the twelfth and thirteenth centuries, courtly music had been composed by aristocratic amateurs (called *trouvères,* troubadours, or *Minnesingers*). They wrote songs chiefly on the theme of courtly love, but often

tresses that reinforce the corners of the towers and divide the facade into three main parts, the placing of the portals, and the three-story arrangement. The rich sculptural decoration, however, recalls the facades of western France (see fig. 10-7) and the carved portals of Burgundy, such as that at Vézelay.

Much more important are the qualities that distinguish Notre-Dame's facade from its Romanesque ancestors. Foremost among these is the way all the details have been integrated into a coherent whole. Here the meaning of Suger's emphasis on harmony, geometric order, and proportion becomes even more evident than in St.-Denis itself. This formal discipline can also be seen in the sculpture, which no longer shows the spontaneous (and often left the actual performance to minstrels, or *jongleurs*. Because of its sophistication, however, *ars nova* increasingly required professional musicians to compose and play it. The elaborate style of *ars nova* paralleled the rich ornamentation of Late Gothic architecture. It may also be seen as a musical counterpart to that late medieval blend of theology and philosophy known as Scholasticism.

Because of its pagan associations, theater was regarded as sinful by early Christianity. Actors were forbidden to become members of the Church or to receive the sacraments, although Theodora, the wife of the Byzantine emperor Justinian, had been a mime actress. Gradually, however, theater became associated with the great religious feasts, such as Christmas and Easter, although it, too, came eventually to rely on vernacular texts. Liturgical drama flourished at many of the same monasteries and churches that contributed to the development of medieval art and music, such as St. Gall in Switzerland. Theater and music shared many of the same subjects, such as the Passion cycle. The close relation between them is illustrated by the career of such composer–playwrights as Hildegard of Bingen (see box page 298). Another link of the two performing arts to religious life was architectural: music and drama were presented exclusively inside churches before 1200. Religious plays, acted by the priests and choirboys, often involved intricate self-contained architectural sets called mansions. In the early thirteenth century, performances became so elaborate and independent that they were moved outdoors to the churchyards, where they were taken over by civic institutions. At the same time, secular plays and farces illustrating moral lessons began to develop out of religious drama.

During the late Middle Ages, theater flourished as towns grew prosperous and the major guilds began to shoulder the costs of staging religious pageants. The dramas best known today date from the fourteenth century and later. They include the vast Corpus Christi cycle performed at York, England, the great Passion plays, and morality plays such as *Everyman*. These were community affairs, mounted in town squares, in which guild members assumed all the roles. Hence there was no clear distinction between religious and popular theater. The medieval tradition of music and theater continued well into the Renaissance, especially in the North. It culminated in Hans Sachs (1494–1576), the head of the shoemakers' guild in Nuremberg. A master singer and composer, he wrote thousands of songs, fables, verses, religious plays, and secular farces. Sachs was immortalized by Richard Wagner in his nineteenth-century German opera *Der Meistersinger*.

uncontrolled) growth so typical of the Romanesque. Instead, it has been assigned a precise role within the architectural framework. At the same time, the cubic solidity of the facade of St.-Étienne at Caen has been dissolved. Lacelike arcades and huge portals and windows break down the continuity of the wall surfaces, so that the total effect is that of a weightless openwork screen.

The rapid rate at which this tendency advanced during the first half of the thirteenth century can be seen by comparing the west front of Notre-Dame with the somewhat later facade of the south transept, visible in the center of figure 11-6. In the west facade, the rose window in the center is still deeply recessed. As a result, the stone tracery that subdivides the opening is clearly set off against the surrounding wall. On the transept, we can no longer distinguish the rose window from its frame because a network of tracery covers the entire area.

CHARTRES CATHEDRAL. Toward 1145 the bishop of Chartres, who befriended Abbot Suger and shared his ideas, began to rebuild his cathedral in the new style with the help of the faithful. [See Primary Sources, no. 27, page 371.] Fifty years later, a fire destroyed all but the west facade, which provided the main entrance, and the east crypt. A second rebuilding was begun in 1194 (fig. 11-9), and as the result of a huge campaign it was largely complete within the astonishingly brief span of 26 years. The basic design is so unified that it must have been planned by a single master builder. However, because the construction proceeded in stages and was never entirely finished, the harmony of the result is evolutionary rather than systematic. For example, the two west towers, though similar, are by no means identical. Moreover, their

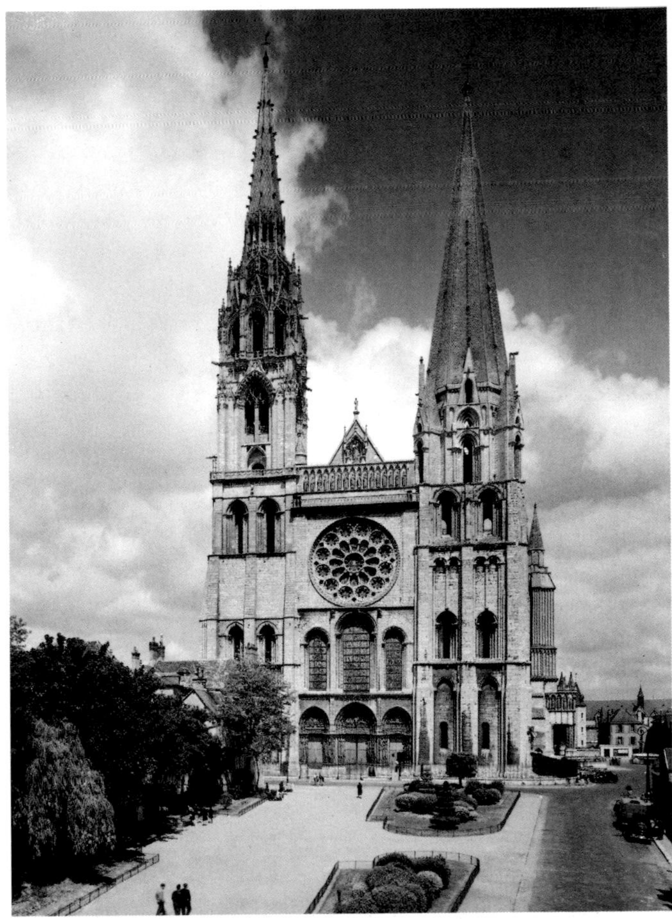

11-9. West facade, Chartres Cathedral (north spire is from 16th century). 1145–1220

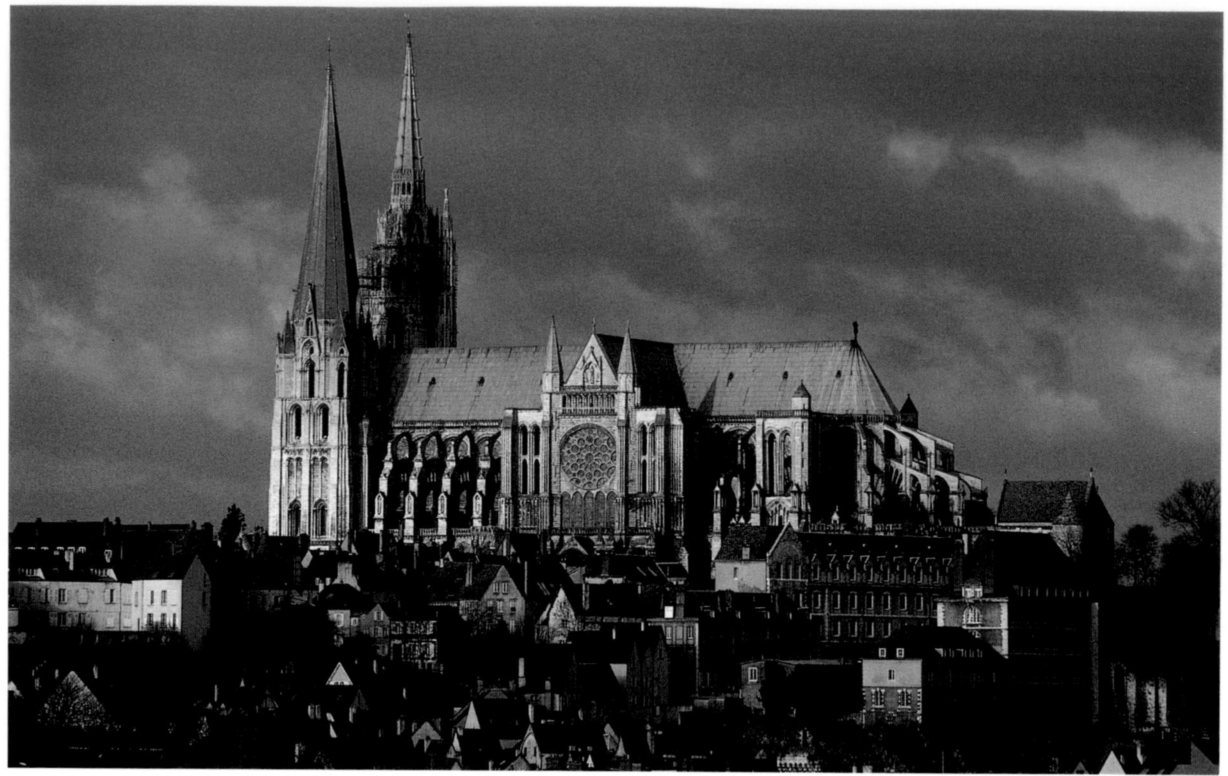

11-10. Chartres Cathedral

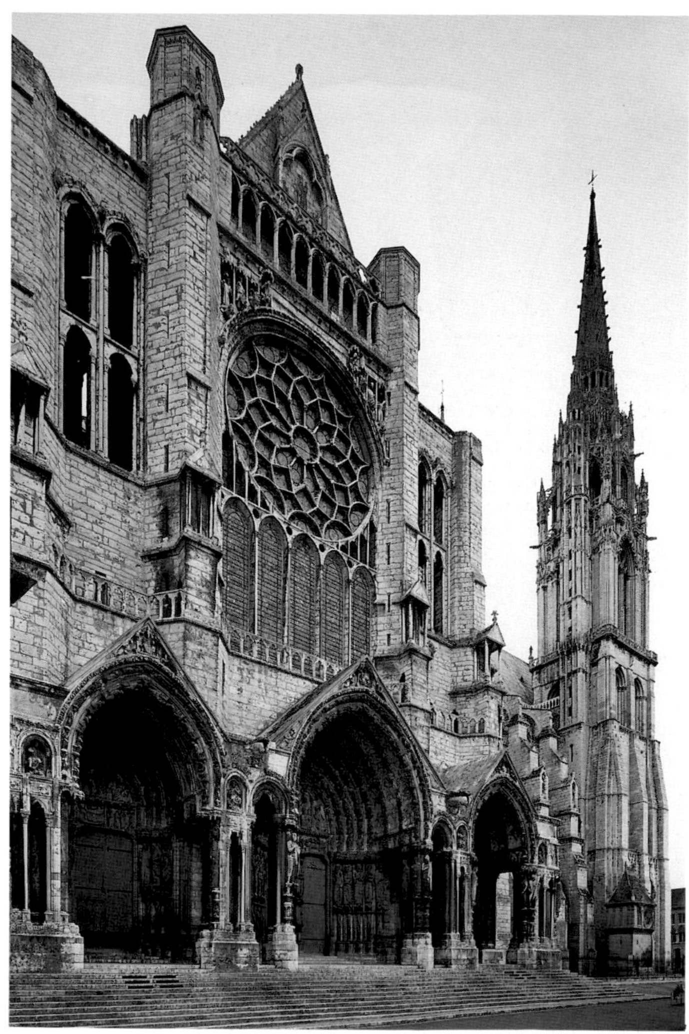

11-11. Portals, north transept, Chartres Cathedral (see also fig. 11-43)

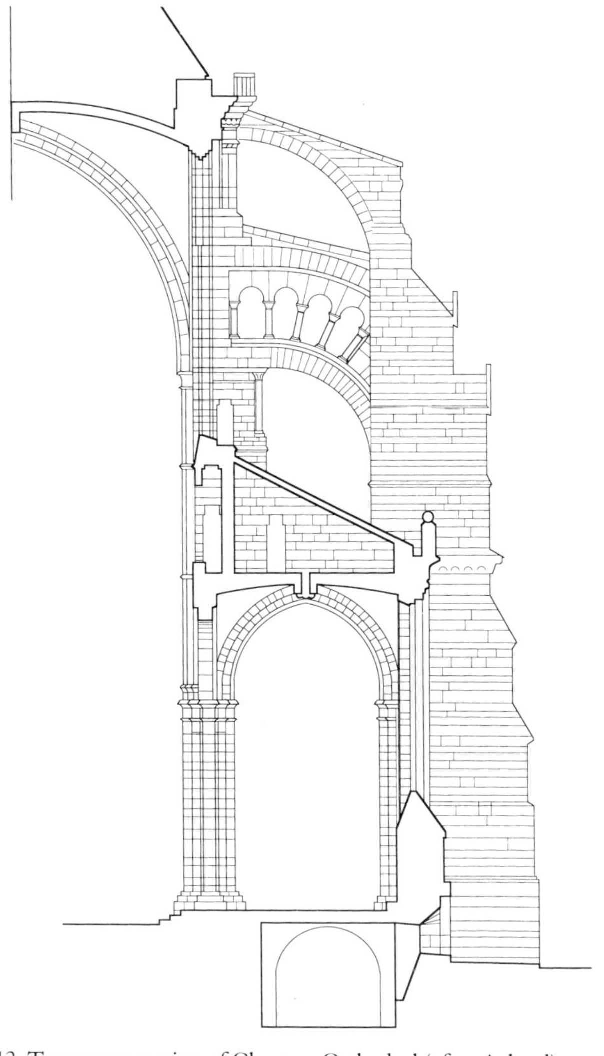

11-12. Transverse section of Chartres Cathedral (after Acland)

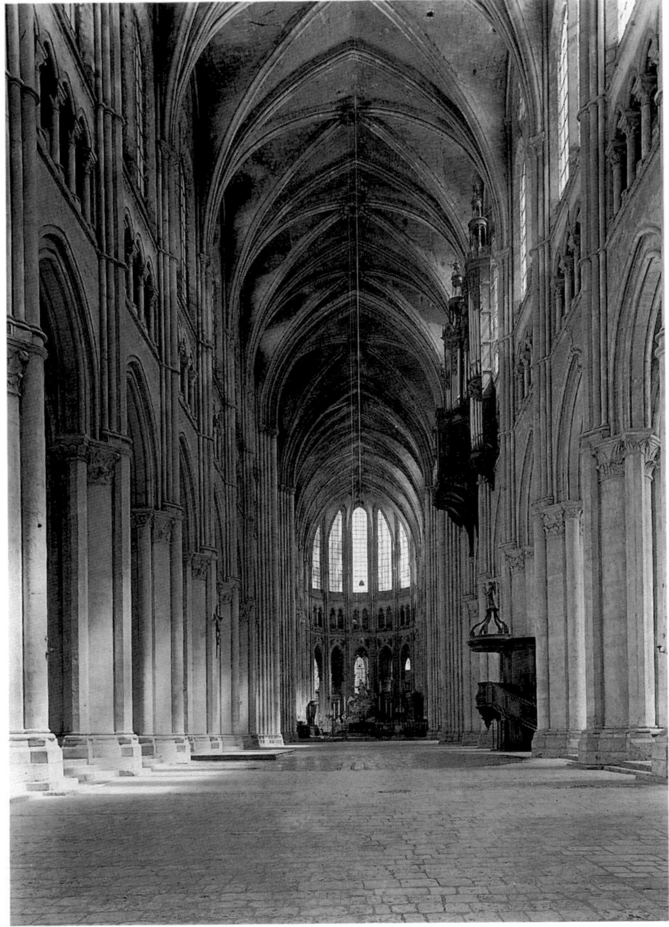

11-13. Nave and choir, Chartres Cathedral

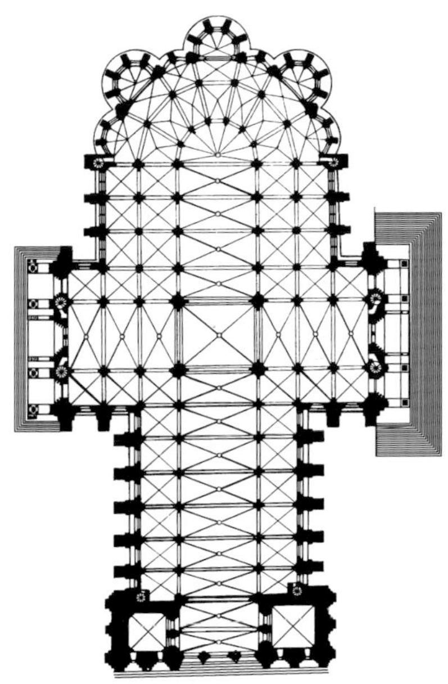

11-14. Plan, Chartres Cathedral

spires are very different: the north spire (on the left) dates from the early sixteenth century, nearly 300 years later than the other one.

The church was built on the highest point in town, and the spires can be seen for miles in the surrounding farmland (fig. 11-10). If the seven other spires had been completed as planned, Chartres would not have such strong directionality. Both arms of the transept have three deeply recessed portals lavishly decorated with sculpture and surmounted by an immense rose window over five smaller lancets (fig. 11-11). Perhaps the most striking feature of the flanks is the flying buttresses. They lend a powerfully organic presence to the apse at the east end, with its seven subsidiary chapels (figs. 11-10 and 11-12).

The west facade, divided into units of two and three, is a model of clarity. Its soaring verticality and punctuated surface are important in molding our expectations about the interior. The shape of the doors tells us that we will first enter a low chamber. As soon as we go into the narthex (the covered anteroom) we have left the temporal world behind. It takes some time for our eyes to adjust to the darkness of the interior. The noise of daily life has been shut out as well. At first, sounds are eerily muffled, as if swallowed up with the light by the void. Once we recover from this disorienting effect, we become aware of a glimmering light, which guides us into the cavernous church.

Designed one generation after the nave of Notre-Dame in Paris, the rebuilt nave (fig. 11-13) is the first masterpiece of the mature, High Gothic style. The openings of the pointed nave arcade are taller and narrower (see fig. 11-5). They are joined to a clerestory of the same height by a short triforium screening the galleries, which have been reduced to a narrow wall. Responds have been added to the columnar supports to stress the continuity of the vertical lines and guide our eye upward to the quadripartite vaults, which appear as diaphanous webs stretched across the slender ribs. Because there are so few walls, the vast interior space seems at first to lack clear boundaries. It is made to seem even larger by the sense of disembodied sound. The effect is so striking that it may well have been planned from the beginning with music in mind, both antiphonal choirs and large pipe organs, which had been in use for more than two centuries in some parts of Europe.

An alternating sequence of round and octagonal piers extends down the nave toward the apse, where the liturgy is performed. Beneath the apse is the crypt, which houses Chartres' most important possession: remnants of a robe said to have been worn by the Virgin Mary, to whom the cathedral is dedicated. The relic, which miraculously survived the great fire of 1194, drew pilgrims from all over Europe. To provide room for large numbers of visitors

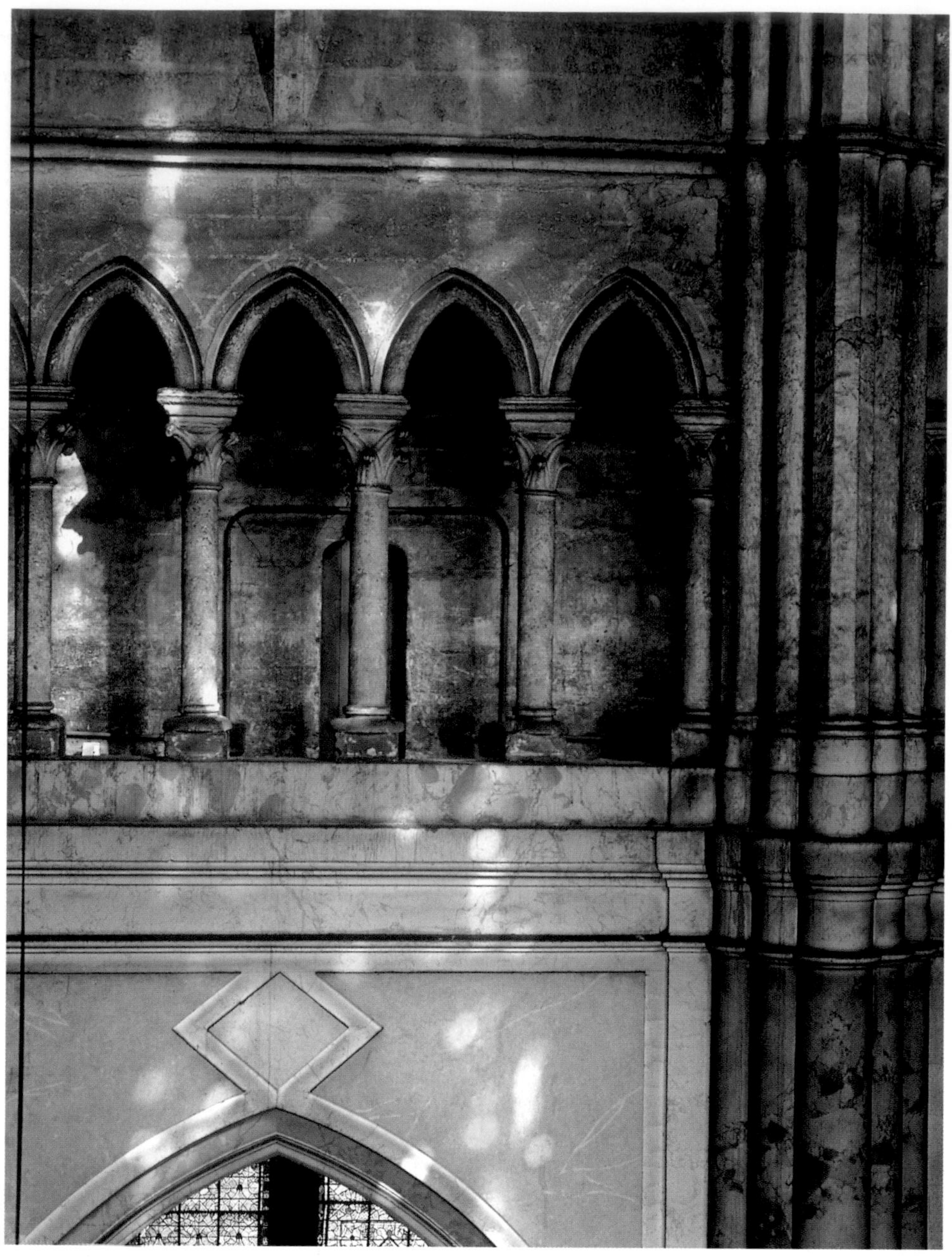

11-15. Triforium wall of the nave, Chartres Cathedral

without disturbing worshipers, there is a wide aisle running the length of the nave and around the transept. It is joined at the choir by a second aisle, forming an ambulatory that connects the apsidal chapels (see plan, fig. 11-14).

Alone among all major Gothic cathedrals, Chartres still retains most of its more than 180 original stained-glass windows (see fig. 11-67). The magic of the jewellike light from the clerestory is unforgettable to anyone who has experienced it (fig. 11-15). The windows admit far less light than one might expect. They act mainly as diffusing filters that change the quality of daylight, giving it the poetic and symbolic values so highly praised by Abbot Suger. The sensation of ethereal light dissolves the physical solidity of the church and, hence, the distinction between the temporal and the divine. The "miraculous light" creates the intensely mystical experience that lies at the heart of Gothic spirituality. (The aisles are darker because the stained-glass windows on the outer walls, though relatively large, are smaller and located at ground level, where they let in less light.)

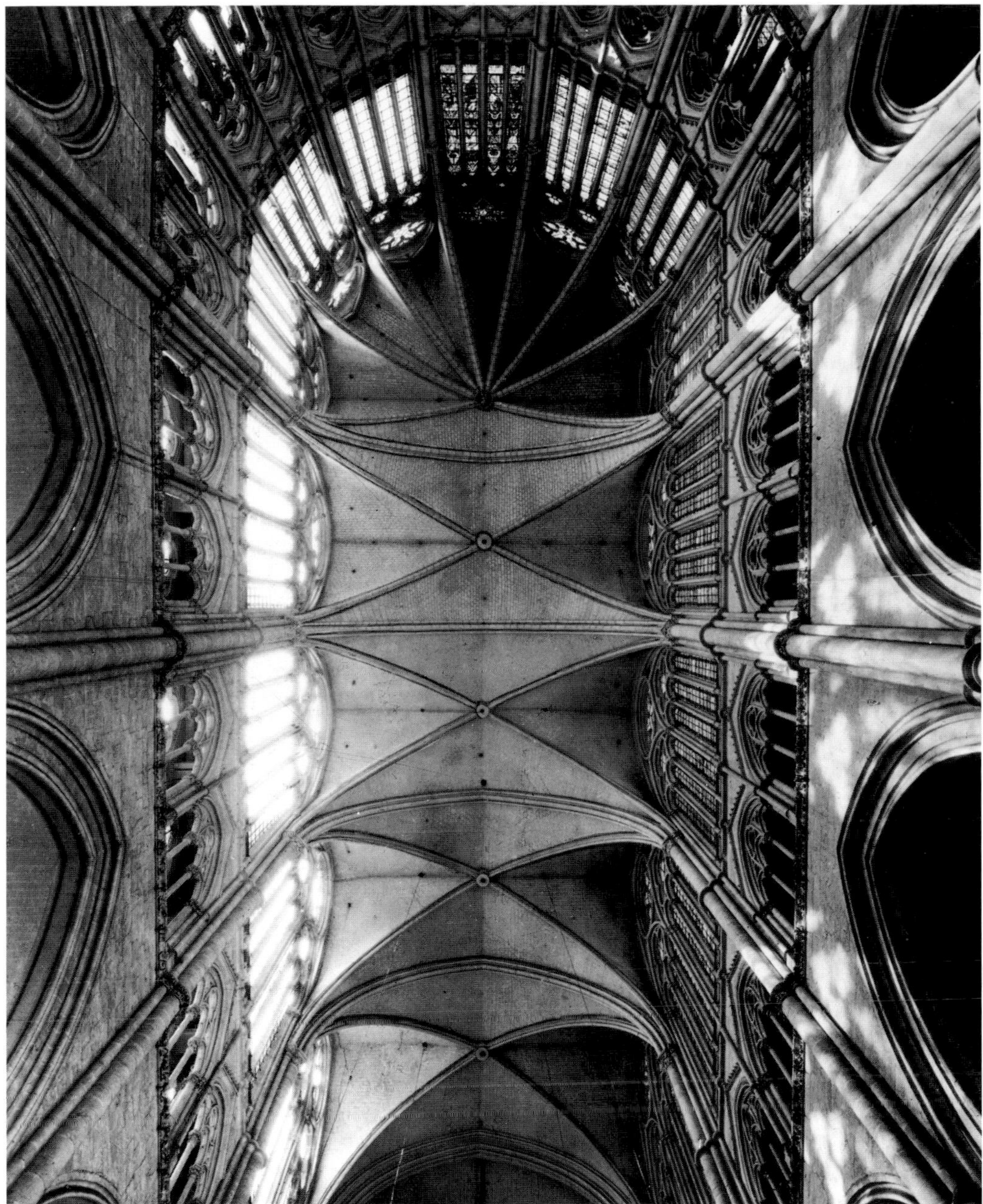

11-16. Choir vault, Amiens Cathedral. Begun 1220

AMIENS CATHEDRAL. The High Gothic style defined at Chartres reaches its climax a generation later in the interior of Amiens Cathedral (figs. 11-16 and 11-17). Breathtaking height is the dominant aim, in both technical and aesthetic terms. (The relatively swift progression toward verticality in French Gothic cathedral architecture is clearly seen in figure 11-18. Figure 11-19 shows how both height and large expanses of window were achieved.) At Amiens, skeletal construction is carried to its limits. The inner logic of the system is asserted in the shape of the vaults, which are as taut and thin as membranes, and in the expanded window area, which now includes the triforium, so that the entire wall above the nave arcade becomes a clerestory.

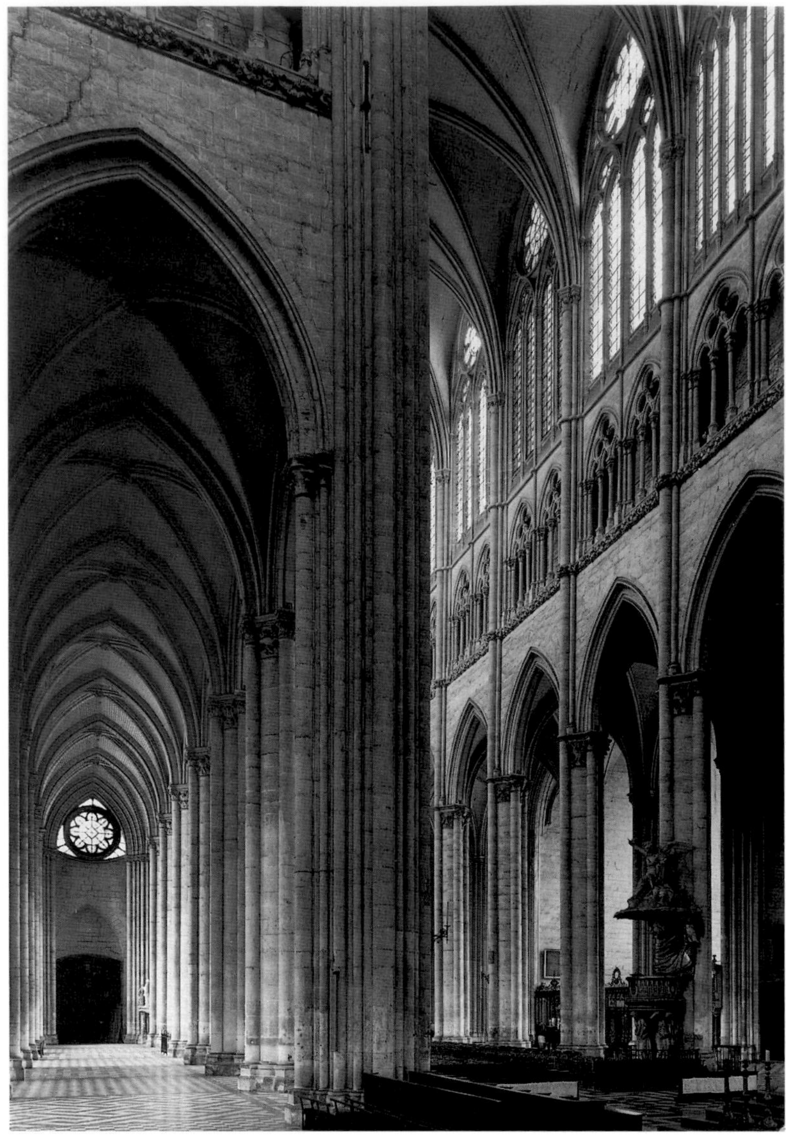

11-17. Nave and side aisle, Amiens Cathedral

(BELOW) 11-18. Comparison of nave elevations in same scale.
1) Notre-Dame, Paris
2) Chartres Cathedral
3) Reims Cathedral
4) Amiens Cathedral
(after Grodecki)

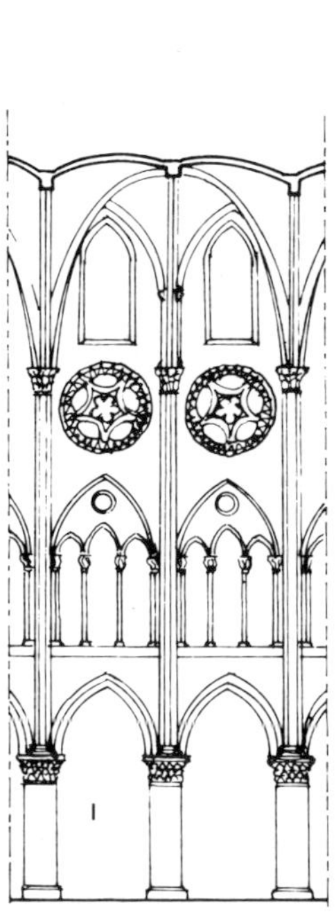

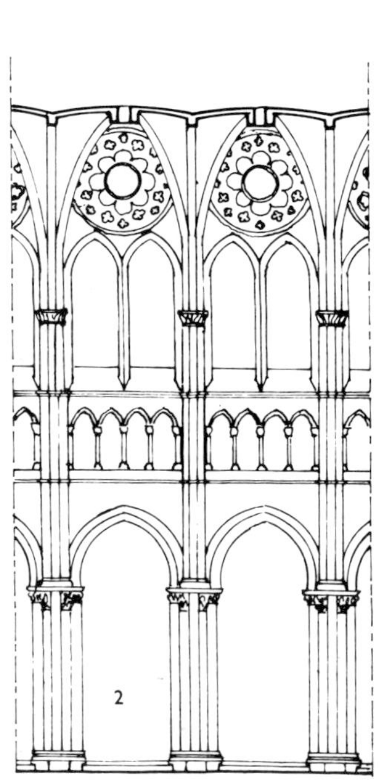

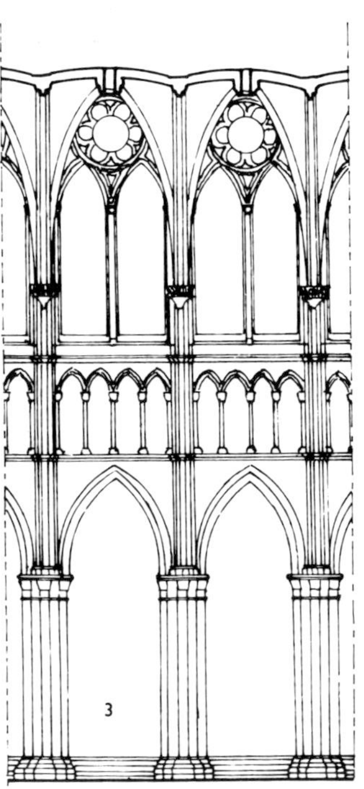

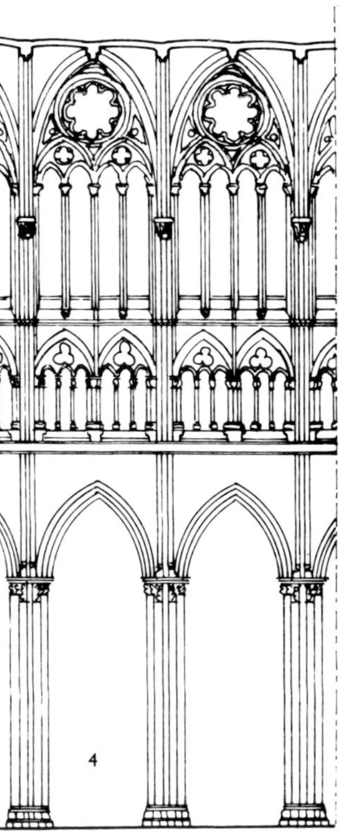

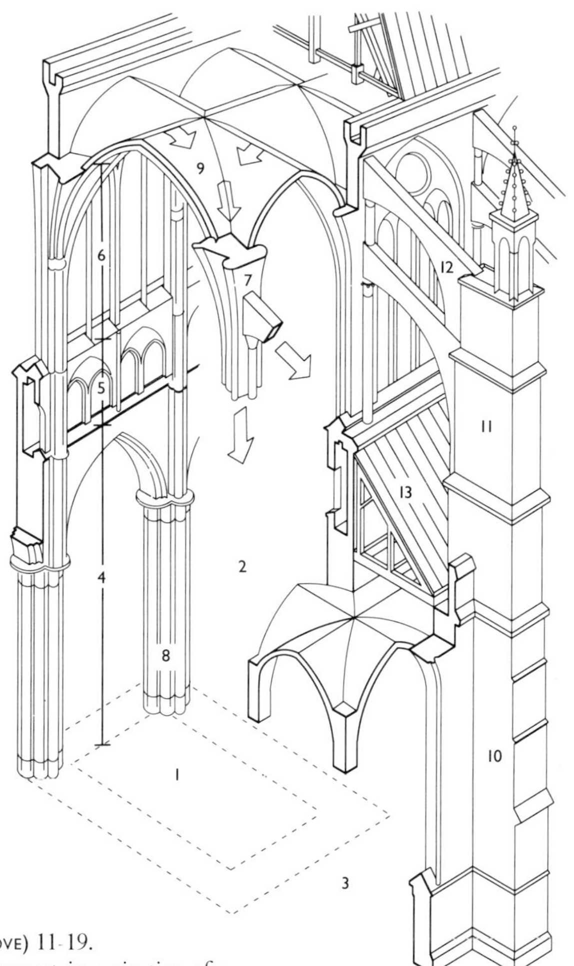

(ABOVE) 11-19. Axonometric projection of a High Gothic cathedral (after Acland).

1) Bay
2) Nave
3) Side aisle
4) Nave arcade
5) Triforium
6) Clerestory
7) Pier
8) Compound pier
9) Sexpartite vault
10) Buttress
11) Flying buttress
12) Flying arch
13) Roof

REIMS CATHEDRAL. The same emphasis on verticality and translucency can be traced in the development of the High Gothic facade. The most famous of these, at Reims Cathedral (fig. 11-20), makes an instructive contrast with the west facade of Notre-Dame in Paris, even though its basic design was conceived only about 30 years later. The two share many elements (as the Coronation Cathedral of the kings of France, Reims was closely linked to Paris), but in the later structure they have been reshaped into a very different ensemble. The portals, instead of being recessed, project forward as gabled porches, with windows in place of tympanums above the doorways. The gallery of royal statues, which in Paris forms a horizontal band between the first and second stories, has been raised until it merges with the third-story arcade. Every detail except the rose window has become taller and narrower than before. Pinnacles everywhere accentuate the restless upward movement. The sculptural decoration, by far the most lavish of its kind (see figs. 11-46 and 11-47), no longer remains in clearly marked-off zones. It has now spread to so many new perches, not only on the facade but on the flanks as well, that the exterior begins to look like a dovecote for statues.

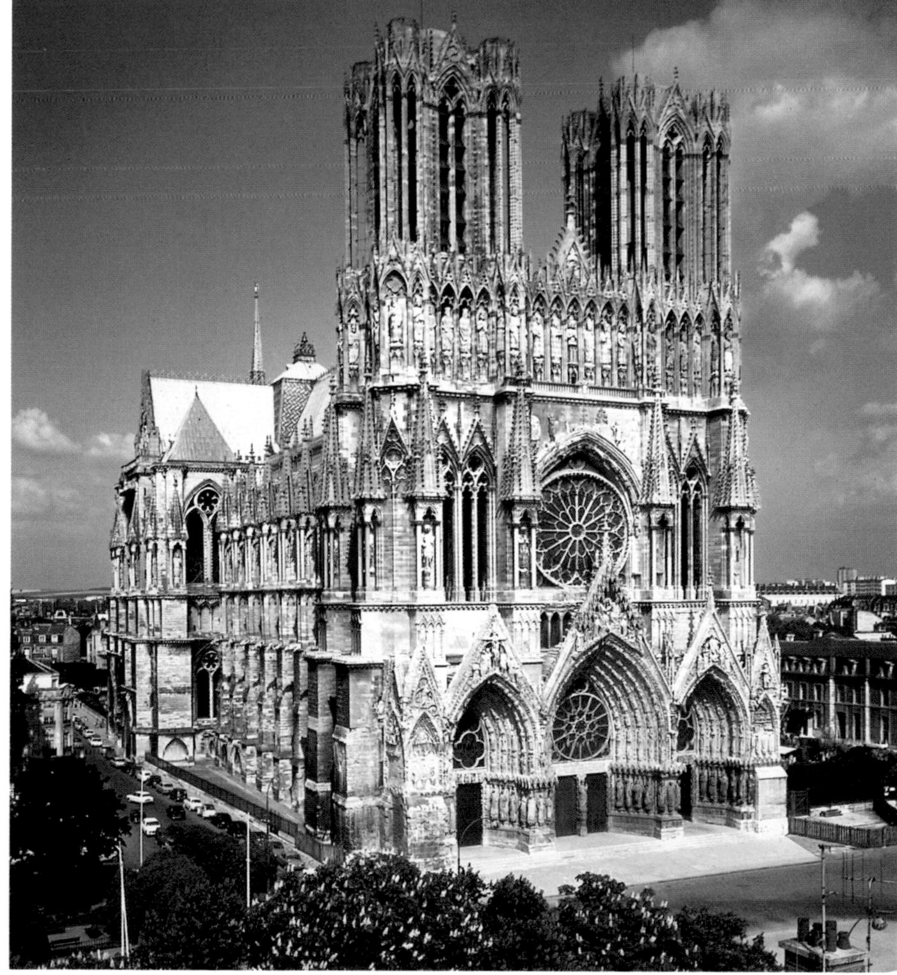

(RIGHT) 11-20. West facade, Reims Cathedral. c. 1225–99

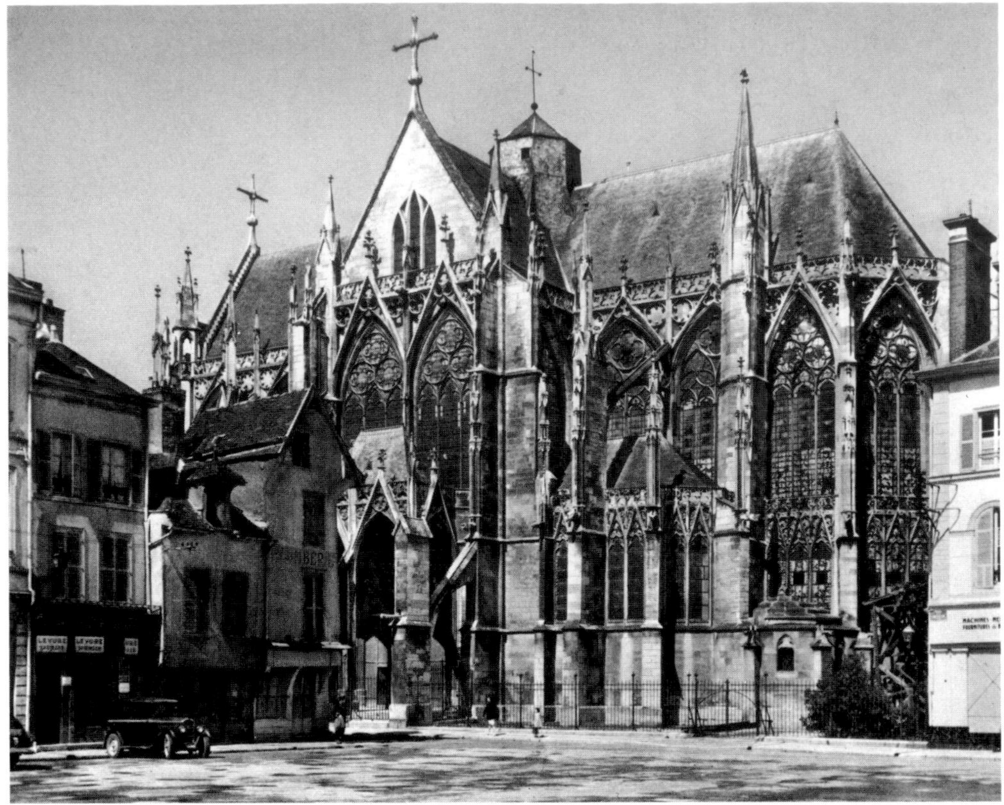

11-21. St.-Urbain, Troyes, France. 1261–75

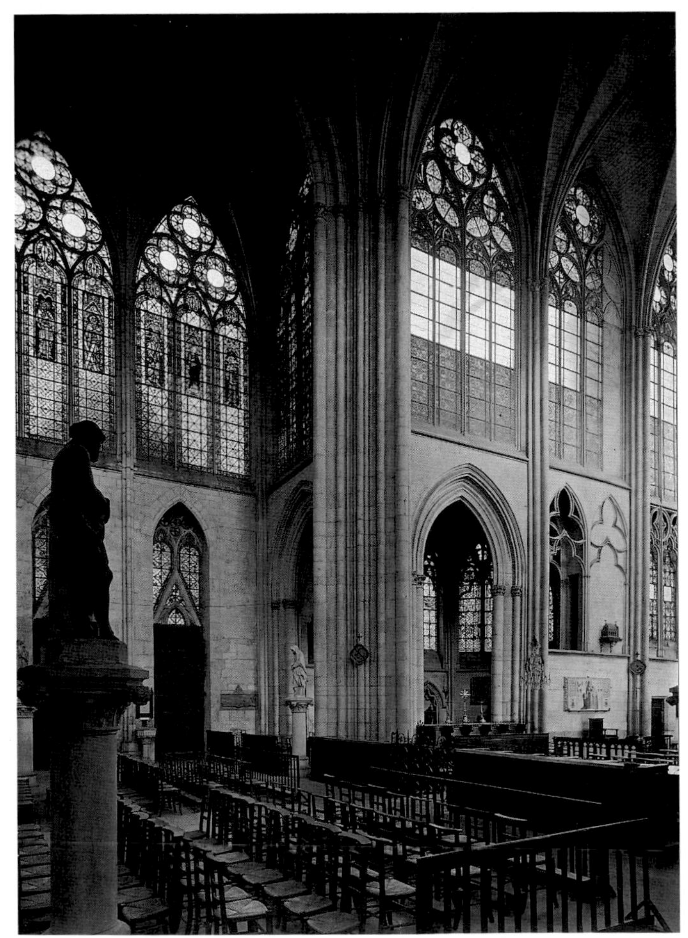

11-22. Interior toward northeast, St.-Urbain

LATER THIRTEENTH-CENTURY GOTHIC. The High Gothic cathedrals of France represent a concentrated effort rarely seen before or since then. They are truly national monuments. Their huge cost was borne by donations collected all over the country and from all classes of society. They are the tangible expression of the merging of religious and patriotic fervor that had been the goal of Abbot Suger. By the middle of the thirteenth century, this wave of enthusiasm had passed its crest. Work on the vast structures begun during the first half of the century now proceeded at a slower pace. New projects were fewer and generally far less ambitious. As a result, the highly organized teams of masons and sculptors that had formed at the sites of the great cathedrals during the preceding decades gradually broke up into smaller units.

A characteristic church of the later years of the century, St.-Urbain in Troyes (figs. 11-21 and 11-22), leaves no doubt that the heroic age of the Gothic style is past. Refinement of detail, rather than monumentality, has become the chief concern. By eliminating the triforium and simplifying the plan, the designer has created a delicate glass cage. (The choir windows begin ten feet above the floor.) It is sustained by flying buttresses so thin as to be hardly noticeable. The same spiny elegance can be felt in the architectural ornament.

FLAMBOYANT GOTHIC. In some ways, St.-Urbain anticipates the Late, or Flamboyant, phase of Gothic architecture. The beginnings of Flamboyant Gothic do seem to go back to the late thirteenth century, but its growth was delayed by the Hundred Years' War (1338–1453) with England. Hence we do not meet any

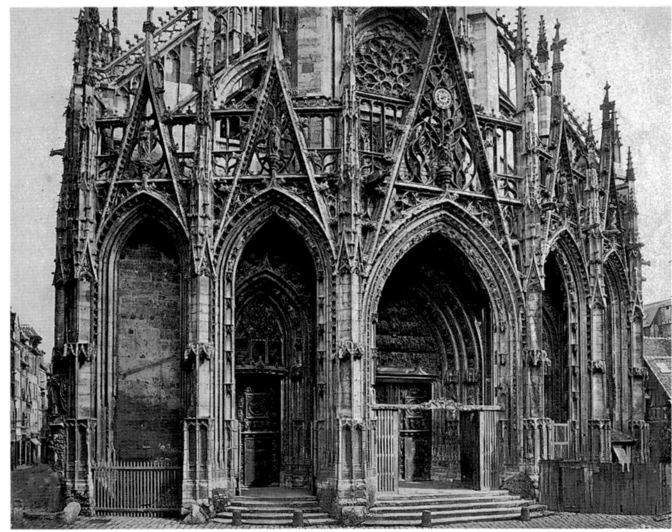

11-23. St.-Maclou, Rouen, France. Begun 1434

full-fledged examples of it until the early fifteenth century. Its name, which means flamelike, refers to the undulating patterns of curve and countercurve that are a main feature of Late Gothic tracery, as at St.-Maclou in Rouen (fig. 11-23). Structurally, Flamboyant Gothic shows no significant developments of its own. What distinguishes St.-Maclou from such churches as St.-Urbain in Troyes is its profuse ornament. The church was built largely between 1434 and 1470 by Pierre Robin; the facade was added by Ambroise Havel from 1500 to 1514. The architect has covered the structural skeleton with a web of decoration so dense and fanciful as to obscure it almost completely. It becomes a fascinating game of hide-and-seek to locate the "bones" of the building within this picturesque tangle of lines.

SECULAR ARCHITECTURE. Since our account of medieval architecture is mainly concerned with the development of style, we have confined our attention to religious structures. Churches were the most ambitious as well as the most representative efforts of the age. Secular building reflects the same general trends, but these are often obscured by the diversity of types, ranging from bridges and fortifications to royal palaces, from barns to town halls. Moreover, social, economic, and practical factors play a more important part here than in church design, so that the useful life of the buildings is apt to be much briefer and their chances of surviving lower. (Fortifications, for example, are often made obsolete by even minor advances in the technology of warfare.) As a result, our knowledge of secular structures of the pre-Gothic Middle Ages is fragmentary, and most of the surviving examples from Gothic times belong to the latter half of the period. This fact, however, is significant in itself. Nonreligious architecture, both private and public, became far more elaborate during the fourteenth and fifteenth centuries than it had been before.

The history of the Louvre in Paris provides a telling example. The original building, erected about 1200, followed the functional plan of the castles of that time. It consisted mainly of a stout tower (the donjon or keep) surrounded by a heavy wall. In the 1360s, King Charles V had a new one built as a royal residence. Although this second Louvre, too, has now disappeared, we know what it looked like from a miniature painted in the early fifteenth century (see fig. 11-94). There is still a defensive outer wall, but the structure behind it is much more like a palace than a fortress. Symmetrically laid out around a square court, it provided comfortable quarters for the royal household (note the countless chimneys), as well as lavishly decorated halls for state occasions.

England

The "royal French style of the Paris region" evoked an enthusiastic response abroad. Even more remarkable was its ability to adapt itself to a variety of local conditions. In fact, the Gothic monuments of England and Germany have become objects of intense national pride, and critics in both countries have claimed Gothic as a native style. A number of factors contributed to the rapid spread of Gothic art. Among these were the skill of French architects and stone carvers and the prestige of French centers of learning, such as the Cathedral School of Chartres and the University of Paris. Also important was the influence of the Cistercians, the reformed monastic order energized by St. Bernard of Clairvaux (see box pages 279–80).

In keeping with Bernard's ideals, Cistercian abbey churches were of a distinctive, severe type. Decoration of any sort was held to a minimum, and a square choir took the place of apse, ambulatory, and radiating chapels. For that very reason, however, Cistercian architects put special emphasis on harmonious proportions and exact craftsmanship. Their "anti-Romanesque" outlook (see pages 287–88) also led them to adopt certain basic features of the Gothic style, even though Cistercian churches remained strongly Romanesque in appearance. During the latter half of the twelfth century, as the reform movement gathered momentum, this austere Cistercian Gothic came to be known throughout western Europe.

Still, one wonders whether any of the explanations we have mentioned really go to the heart of the matter. The basic reason for the spread of Gothic art seems to have been the persuasive power of the style itself. It kindled the imagination and aroused religious feeling even among people far removed from the cultural climate of the Île-de-France.

That England was especially receptive to the new style is not surprising. Yet the English Gothic did not grow directly from the Anglo-Norman Romanesque. Rather, it emerged from the Gothic of the Île-de-France, which was introduced in 1175 by the French architect who rebuilt the choir of Canterbury Cathedral, and from that of the Cistercians. Within less than 50 years, it developed a well-defined character of its own, known as the Early English style, which dominated the second quarter of the thirteenth century. Although there was a great deal of building activity during those decades, it consisted mostly of additions to Anglo-Norman structures. Many English cathedrals had been begun about the same time as Durham (see figs. 10-9–10-11) but remained unfinished. They were now completed or enlarged. As a result, we find few churches that are designed in the Early English style throughout.

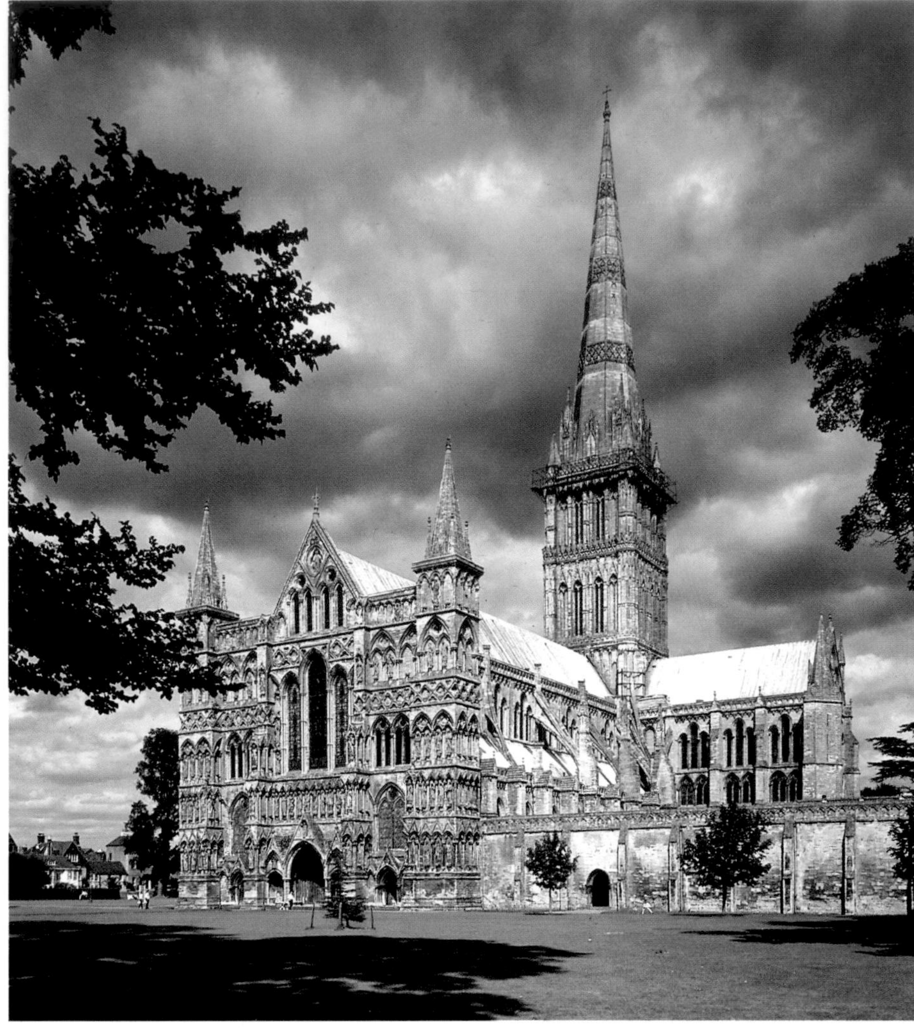

11-24. Salisbury Cathedral, England. 1220–70

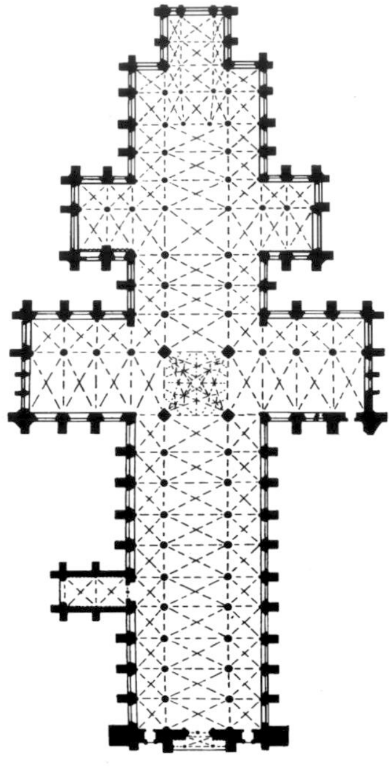

11-25. Plan of Salisbury Cathedral

SALISBURY CATHEDRAL. Among cathedrals, only Salisbury meets this requirement (figs. 11-24–11-26). We see immediately how different the exterior is from its counterparts in France—and how futile it would be to judge it by French Gothic standards. Compactness and verticality have given way to a long, low, sprawling look. (The crossing tower, which provides a dramatic unifying accent, was built a century later than the rest and is much taller than originally planned.) Since height is not the main goal, flying buttresses are used only as an afterthought. The west facade has become a screen wall, wider than the church itself and divided into horizontal bands of ornament and statuary. The towers have shrunk to stubby turrets. The plan, with its projecting double transept, retains the segmented quality of Romanesque structures, but the square east end derives from Cistercian architecture.

As we enter the nave, we recognize the same elements familiar to us from French interiors of the time, such as Chartres (see fig. 11-13). However, the English interpretation of these elements produces a very different effect. As on the facade, horizontal divisions are emphasized at the expense of the vertical. Hence we see the nave wall not as a succession of bays but as a series of arches and supports. These supports, carved of dark marble, stand out against the rest of the interior. This method of stressing their special function is one of the hallmarks of the Early English style. Another is the steep curve of the nave vault. The ribs ascend all the way from the triforium level. As a result, the clerestory gives the

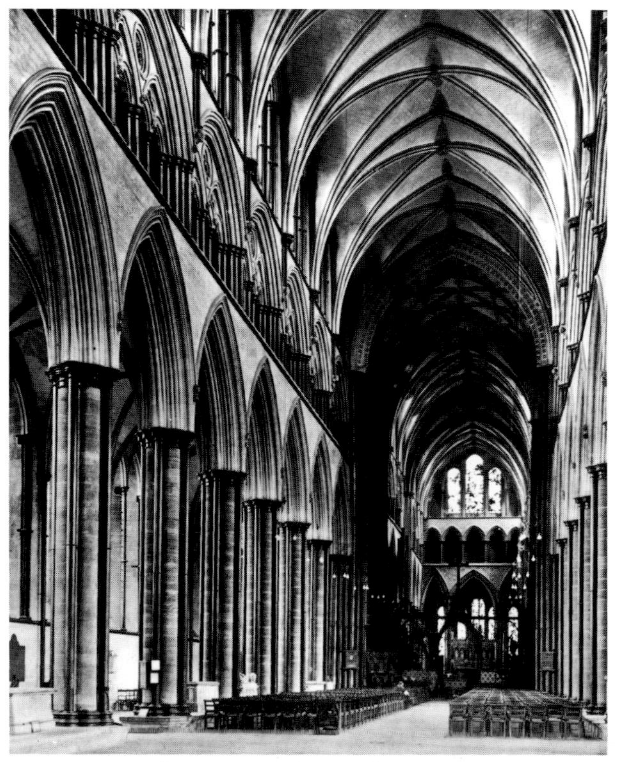

11-26. Nave and choir, Salisbury Cathedral

impression of being tucked away among the vaults. At Durham, more than a century earlier, the same treatment had been a technical necessity (compare fig. 10-11). Now it has become a matter of style, in keeping with the character of English Early Gothic as a whole. This character might be described as conservative in the positive sense. It accepts the French system but tones down its revolutionary aspects to maintain a strong sense of continuity with the Anglo-Norman past.

THE PERPENDICULAR STYLE. The contrast between the bold upward thrust of the crossing tower and the leisurely horizontal progression throughout the rest of Salisbury Cathedral suggests that English Gothic had developed in a new direction during the intervening hundred years. The change becomes very clear if we compare the interior of Salisbury with the choir of Gloucester Cathedral, built in the second quarter of the next century (fig. 11-27). Gloucester is a striking example of English Late Gothic, also called "Perpendicular." The name certainly fits, since we now find the dominant vertical accent that is absent in the Early English style. (Note the responds running in an unbroken line from the vault to the floor.) In this respect Perpendicular Gothic is much more akin to French sources, but it includes so many features we have come to know as English that it would look out of place on the Continent. The repetition of small uniform tracery panels recalls the bands of statuary on the west facade at Salisbury. The plan simulates the square east end of earlier English churches. And the upward curve of the vault is as steep as in the nave of Salisbury.

The ribs of the vaults, on the other hand, have taken on a new role. They have been multiplied until they form an ornamental network that screens the boundaries between the bays and thus makes the entire vault look like one continuous surface. This effect, in turn, emphasizes the unity of the interior space. Such

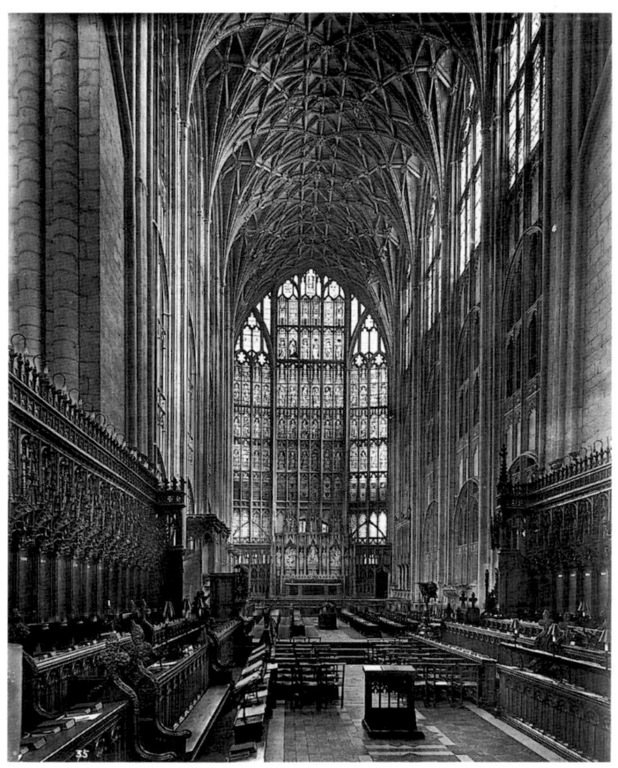

11-27. Choir, Gloucester Cathedral, England. 1332–57

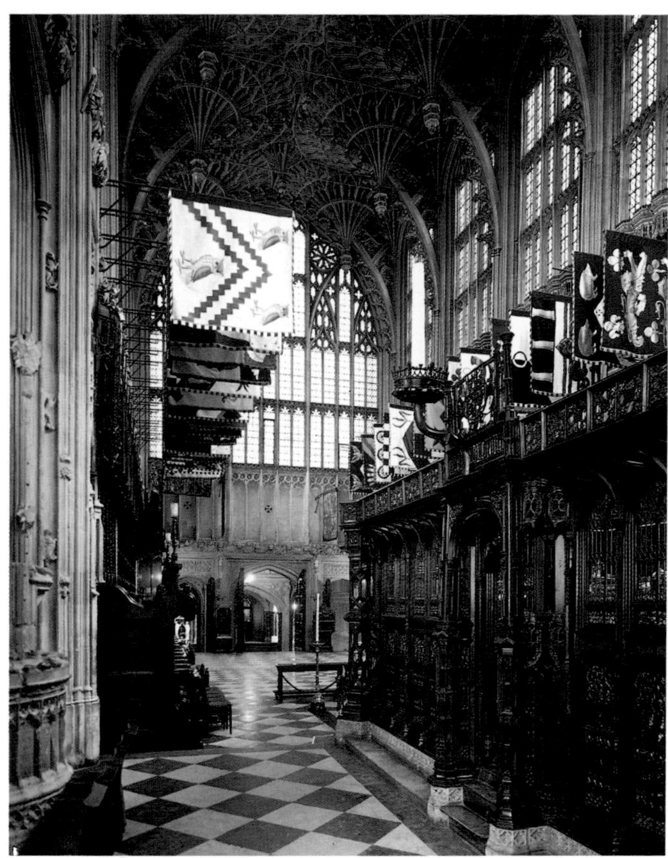

11-28. Chapel of Henry VII (view toward west), Westminster Abbey, London. 1503–19

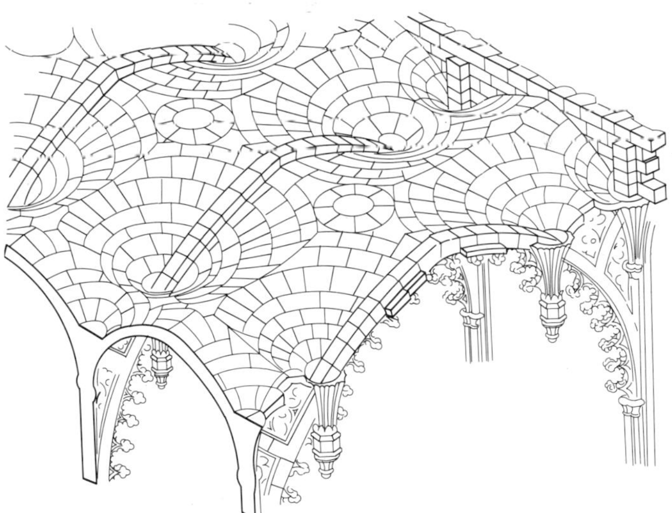

11-29. Diagram of vault construction, Chapel of Henry VII, Westminster Abbey (after Swaan)

elaboration of the "classic" four-part vault is characteristic of the so-called Flamboyant style on the Continent as well, but the English started it earlier and carried it to greater lengths. The climax is reached in the amazing pendant vault of Henry VII's Chapel at Westminster Abbey in the early years of the sixteenth century (figs. 11-28 and 11-29). With its lanternlike knobs hanging from conical "fans," this chapel merges ribs and tracery patterns in a dazzling display of architectural pageantry.

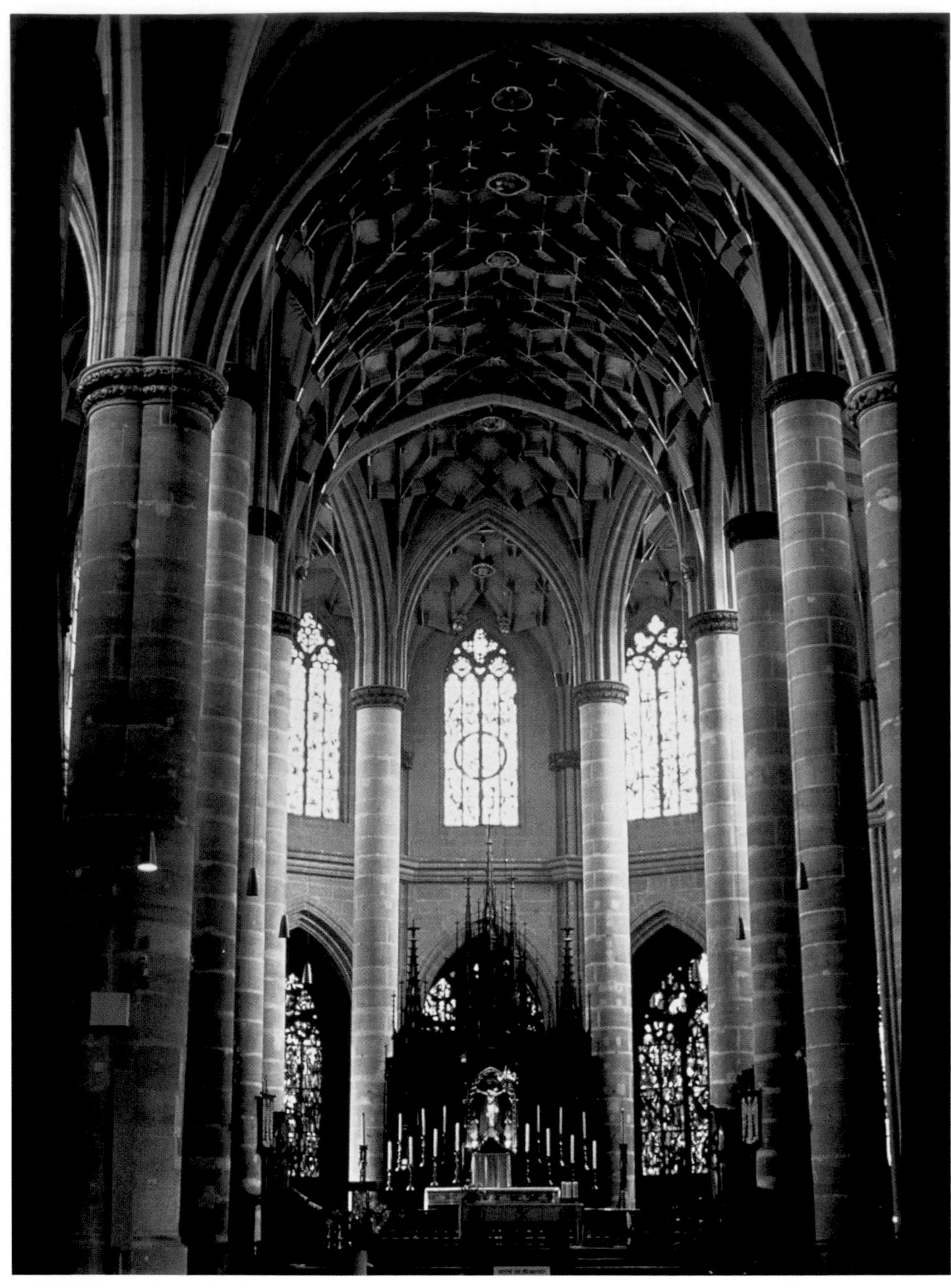

11-30. Choir, Heiligenkreuz, Schwäbish-Gmünd, Germany. After 1351

Germany

In Germany, Gothic architecture took root a good deal more slowly than in England. Until the mid-thirteenth century, the Romanesque tradition, with its persistent Ottonian elements, remained dominant, despite the growing acceptance of Early Gothic features. From about 1250 on, however, the High Gothic of the Île-de-France had a strong impact on the Rhineland. Cologne Cathedral (begun in 1248) is an ambitious attempt to carry the full-fledged French system beyond the stage of Amiens. However, it was not completed until modern times. Nor were any others like it ever built.

HALL CHURCHES. Far more typical of German Gothic is the hall church, or *Hallenkirche.* Such churches, with aisles and nave of the same height, stem from Romanesque architecture (see fig. 10-6). The type was favored in Germany, where its artistic possibilities were explored fully. Heiligenkreuz in Schwäbish-Gmünd (fig. 11-30) is one of many examples from central Germany. The space has a fluidity and expansiveness that enfold us as if we were standing under a huge canopy. There is no clear sense of direction to guide us. And the unbroken lines of the pillars, formed by bundles of shafts that diverge as they turn into lacy ribs covering the vaults, seem to echo the continuous movement that we feel in the space itself.

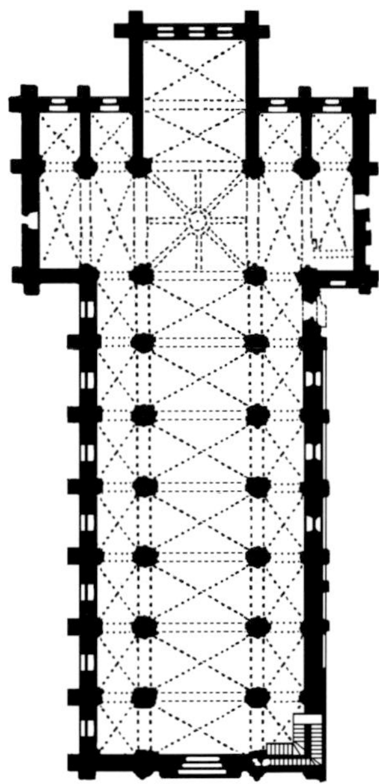

11-31. Plan of the Abbey Church of Fossanova

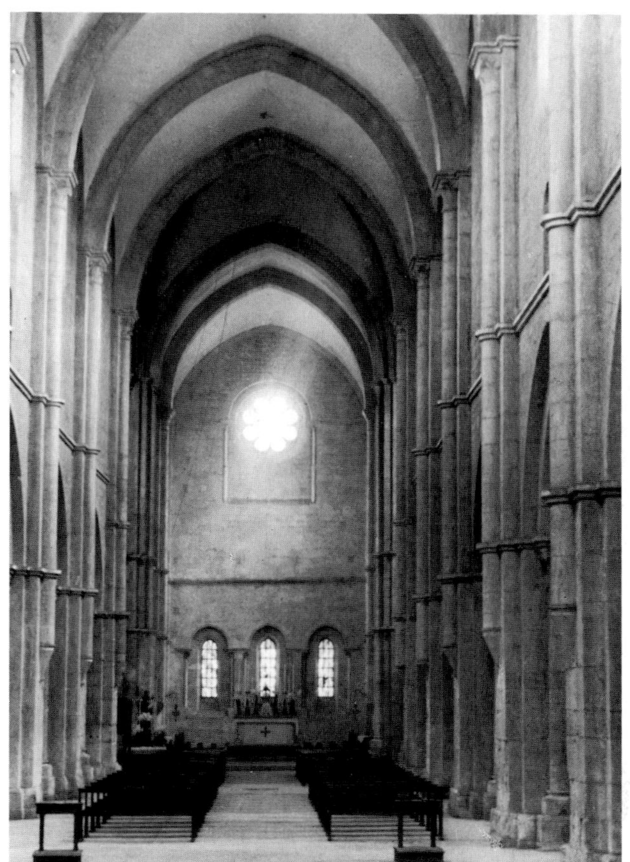

11-32. Nave and choir, Abbey Church of Fossanova, Italy. Consecrated 1208

Italy

Italian Gothic architecture stands apart from that of the rest of Europe. Judged by the standards of the Île-de-France, most of it hardly deserves to be called Gothic at all. Yet the Gothic in Italy produced beautiful and impressive structures that cannot be viewed as continuations of the local Romanesque. We must be careful, therefore, to avoid too rigid a standard in approaching these monuments, lest we fail to do justice to their blend of Gothic qualities and Mediterranean tradition. It was the Cistercians, rather than the cathedral builders of the Île-de-France, who provided the chief models for Italian architects. As early as the end of the twelfth century, Cistercian abbeys sprang up in both northern and central Italy, their designs patterned directly after those of the order's French monasteries.

ABBEY CHURCH, FOSSANOVA. One of the finest buildings is at Fossanova, some 60 miles south of Rome, which was consecrated in 1208 (figs. 11-31 and 11-32). Without knowing its location, we would be hard put to decide where to place it on a map—it might as well be Burgundian or English. The plan looks like a simplified version of Salisbury, and the finely proportioned interior resembles those of Cistercian abbeys of the French Romanesque and Gothic eras. There are no facade towers, only a lantern over the crossing, as befits the ideal of austerity prescribed by St. Bernard. The groin vaults, while based on the pointed arch, have no diagonal ribs. The windows are small, and the architectural detail retains a good deal of Romanesque solidity. Still, the flavor of the whole is unmistakably Gothic.

Churches such as the one at Fossanova made a deep impression upon the Franciscans, the monastic order founded by St. Francis of Assisi in the early thirteenth century (see pages 279–80). As mendicant friars dedicated to poverty, simplicity, and humility, they were the spiritual kin of St. Bernard. The severe beauty of Cistercian Gothic must have seemed to express an ideal closely related to theirs. Thus from the first their churches reflected Cistercian influence and played a leading role in establishing Gothic architecture in Italy.

STA. CROCE, FLORENCE. Sta. Croce in Florence, reputed to be designed by the sculptor Arnolfo di Cambio (c. 1245–c. 1310), may well claim to be the greatest of all Franciscan structures (figs. 11-33 and 11-34). It is also a masterpiece of Gothic architecture, even though it has wooden ceilings instead of groin vaults, except in the choir. There can be no doubt that this was a matter of deliberate choice, rather than of technical or economic necessity. The decision was made not simply on the basis of local practice. (Wooden ceilings, we will recall, were a feature of the Tuscan Romanesque.) It may also have sprung from a desire to evoke the simplicity of Early Christian basilicas and thus link Franciscan poverty with the traditions of the early Church. The plan, too,

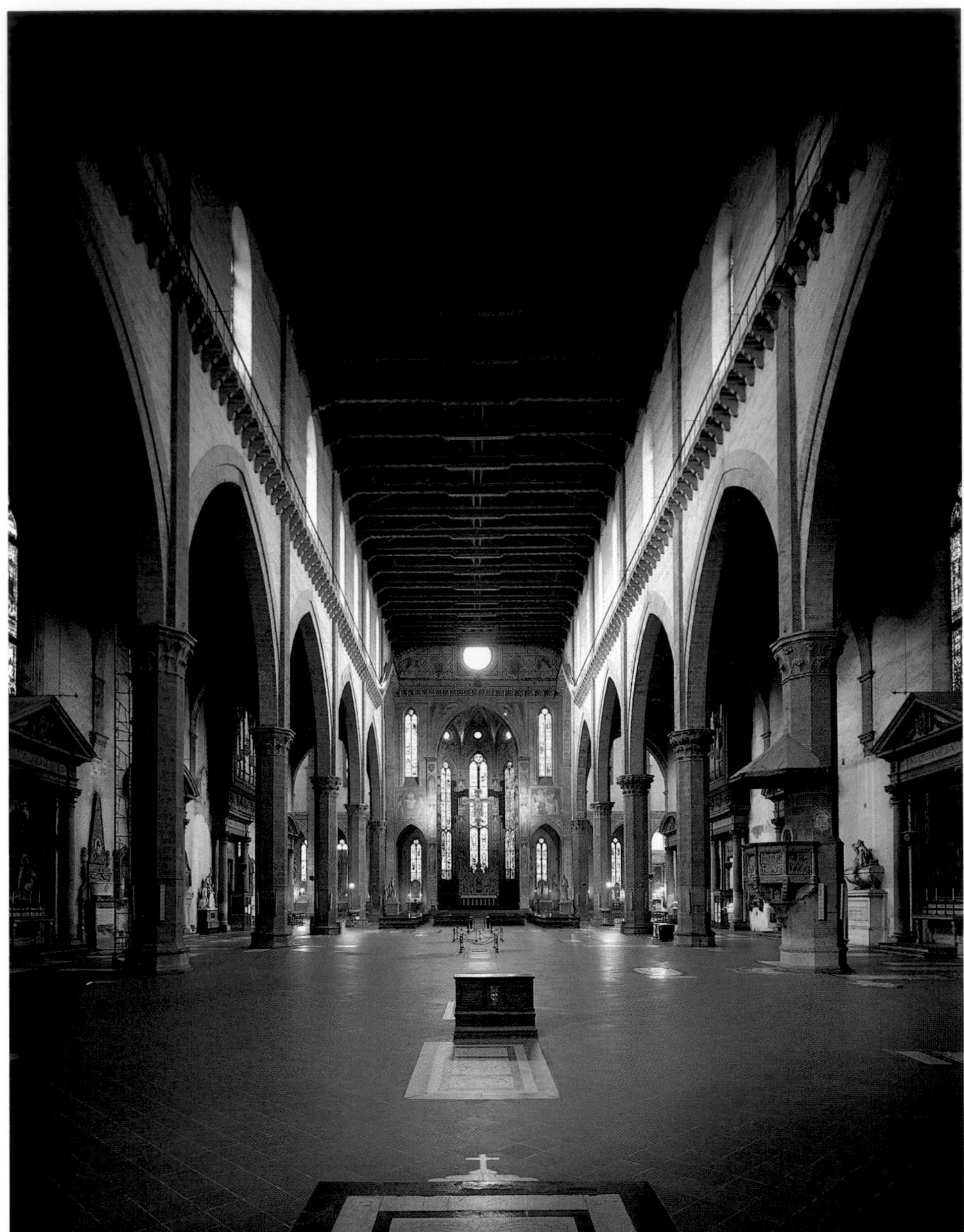

(LEFT) 11-33. Nave and choir, Sta. Croce, Florence. Begun c. 1295

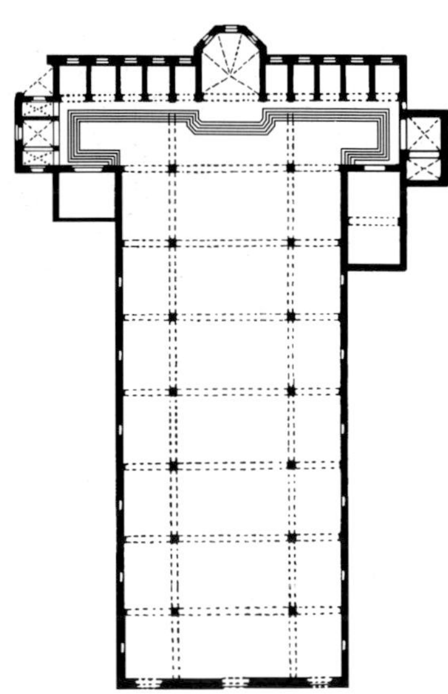

11-34. Plan of Sta. Croce

combines Cistercian and Early Christian features. We note, however, that it shows no trace of the Gothic structural system, except for the groin-vaulted apse. Hence, in contrast to Fossanova, there are no buttresses, since the wooden ceilings do not require them. The walls provide continuous surfaces. Indeed, Sta. Croce owes part of its fame to its murals. (Some of these can be seen on the transept and apse in our illustration.)

Why, then, do we speak of Sta. Croce as Gothic? Surely the use of the pointed arch is not enough to justify the term. But when we look at the interior we sense immediately that this space creates an effect fundamentally different from that of either Early Christian or Romanesque architecture. The nave walls have the weightless, "transparent" quality we saw in Northern Gothic churches, and the dramatic massing of windows at the eastern end conveys the dominant role of light as forcefully as Abbot Suger's choir at St.-Denis. Judged in terms of its emotional impact, Sta. Croce is Gothic beyond doubt. It is also profoundly Franciscan—and Florentine—in its monumental simplicity.

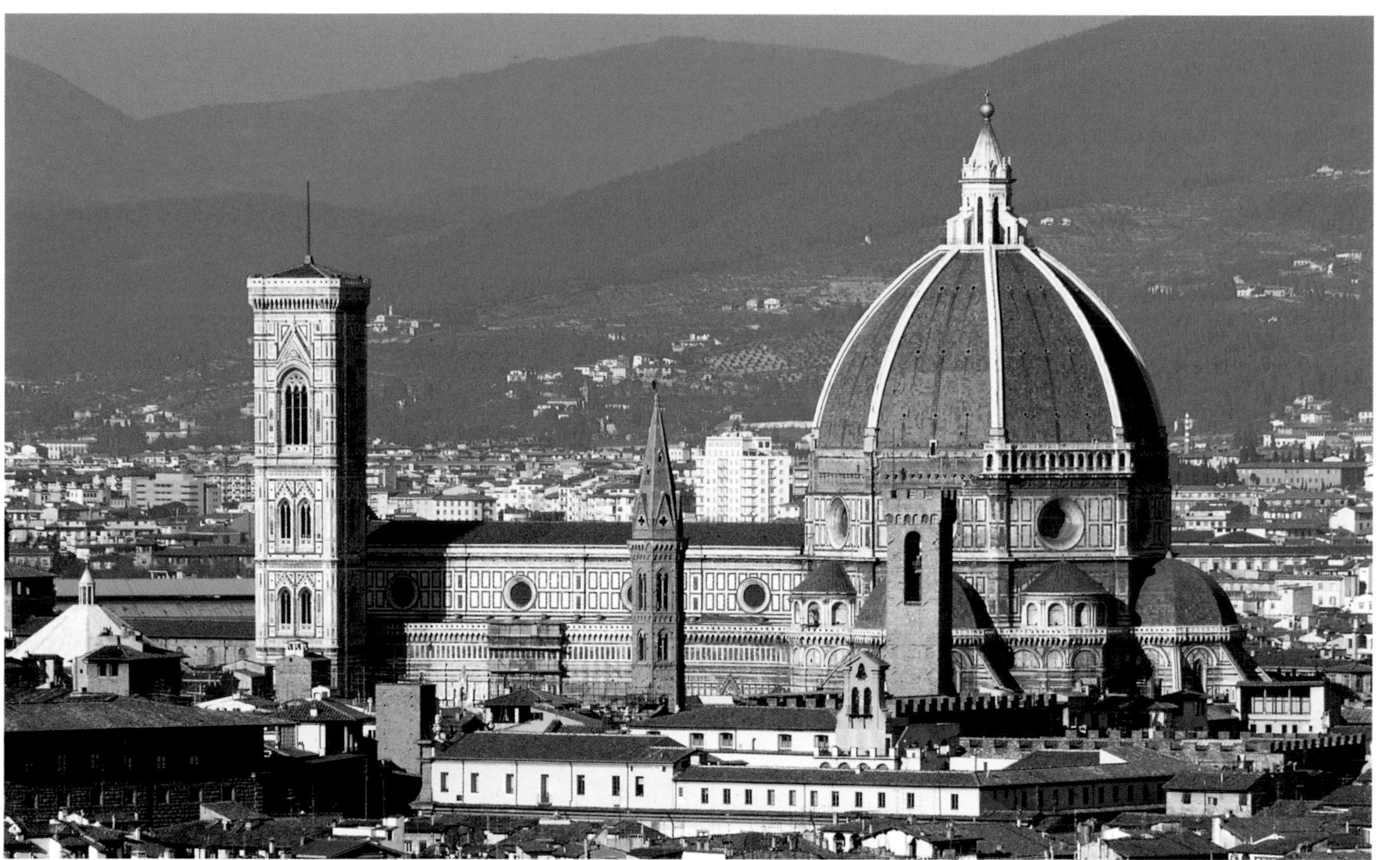

11-35. Florence Cathedral (Sta. Maria del Fiore). Begun by Arnolfo di Cambio, 1296; dome by Filippo Brunelleschi, 1420–36

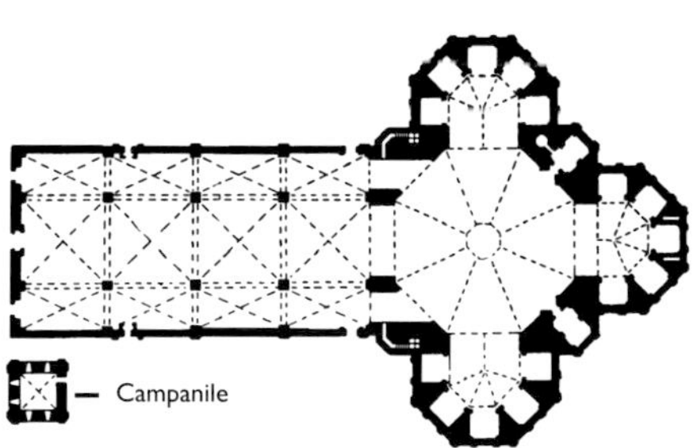

11-36. Plan of Florence Cathedral and Campanile

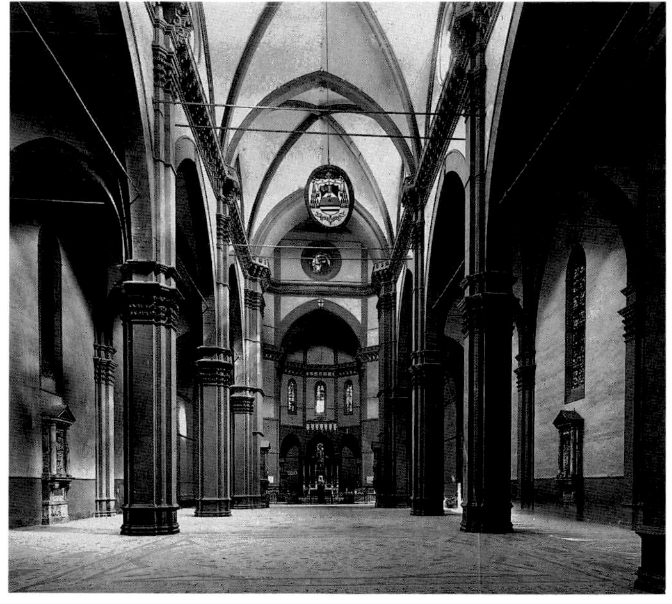

11-37. Nave and choir, Florence Cathedral

FLORENCE CATHEDRAL. At Sta. Croce the architect's main concern was an impressive interior. In contrast, Florence Cathedral was planned as a landmark to civic pride towering above the city (figs. 11-35 and 11-36). The original design, also by Arnolfo di Cambio, dates from 1296, a little after Sta. Croce was begun, and is not known in detail. Although somewhat smaller than the present building, it probably had the same basic plan. The building as we know it is based largely on a design by Francesco Talenti, who took over about 1343. The most striking feature is the octagonal dome with its subsidiary half-domes, a motif that can be traced to late Roman times (see figs. 7-13, 7-14, and 8-7–8-9). At first it may have been thought of as an oversize dome above the crossing of nave and transept, but it soon grew into a huge central pool of space that makes the nave look like an afterthought. The basic fea-

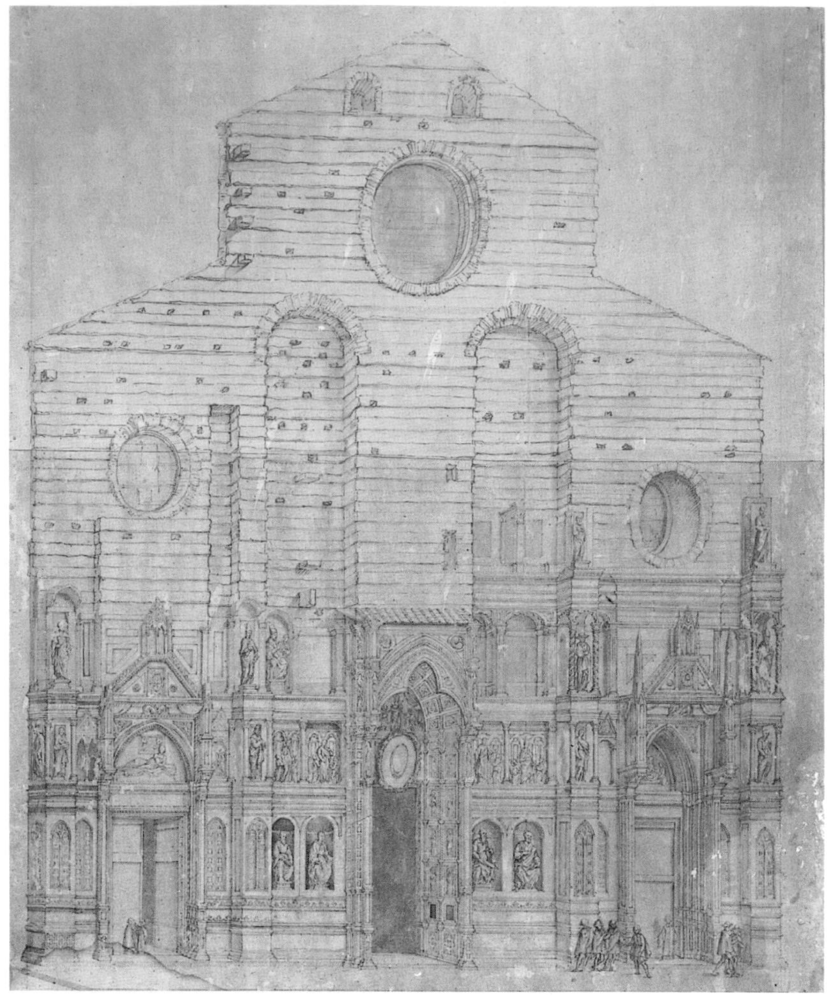

11-38. Bernardino Poccetti. Drawing of Arnolfo di Cambio's unfinished design for the facade of Florence Cathedral. c. 1587. Brown ink on canvas, 28⅜ x 22½" (72 x 57 cm). Museo dell'Opera di S. Maria del Fiore, Florence

tures of the dome were set by a committee of leading painters and sculptors in 1367. Because it posed enormous problems, however, the actual construction belongs to the early fifteenth century (see page 397).

Apart from the windows and the doorways, there is nothing Gothic about the exterior of Florence Cathedral. (Flying buttresses to sustain the nave vault may have been planned but proved unnecessary.) The solid walls, decorated with geometric marble inlays, are a perfect match for the Romanesque Baptistery nearby (see fig. 10-19). The interior, on the other hand, recalls Sta. Croce, even though the dominant impression is one of solemnity rather than lightness and grace. The ribbed groin vault of the nave rests directly on the nave arcade, so that width is emphasized instead of height. The architectural detail has a massive solidity that seems more Romanesque than Gothic (fig. 11-37). Thus the unvaulted interior of Sta. Croce reflects the spirit of the new style more than does the cathedral, which, on the basis of its structural system, ought to be the more Gothic of the two.

Typical of Italy, a separate campanile takes the place of the facade towers of Northern Gothic churches. It was begun by the great painter Giotto (see pages 346–50), who managed to finish only the first story, and continued by the sculptor Andrea Pisano (see page 338), who was responsible for the niche zone. The rest is the work of Talenti, who completed it by about 1360.

The west facade, so dramatic a feature in French cathedrals, never achieved the same importance in Italy. It is remarkable how few Italian Gothic facades were ever finished before the onset of the Renaissance. As we see them today, those of Sta. Croce and Florence Cathedral both date from the nineteenth century. Fortunately, Arnolfo's design for the cathedral is preserved in a drawing made by Bernardino Poccetti just before the facade was destroyed in 1587 (fig. 11-38). Only the bottom half of the decorations is shown in detail, but it gives us a clear idea of what an Italian Gothic facade would have looked like (though with some later alterations). Arnolfo devised an ornate scheme of pilasters and niches with sculptures to articulate the surface, which was further embellished by mosaics. The effect must have been a dazzling fusion of sculpture and architecture, of Classical severity and Gothic splendor.

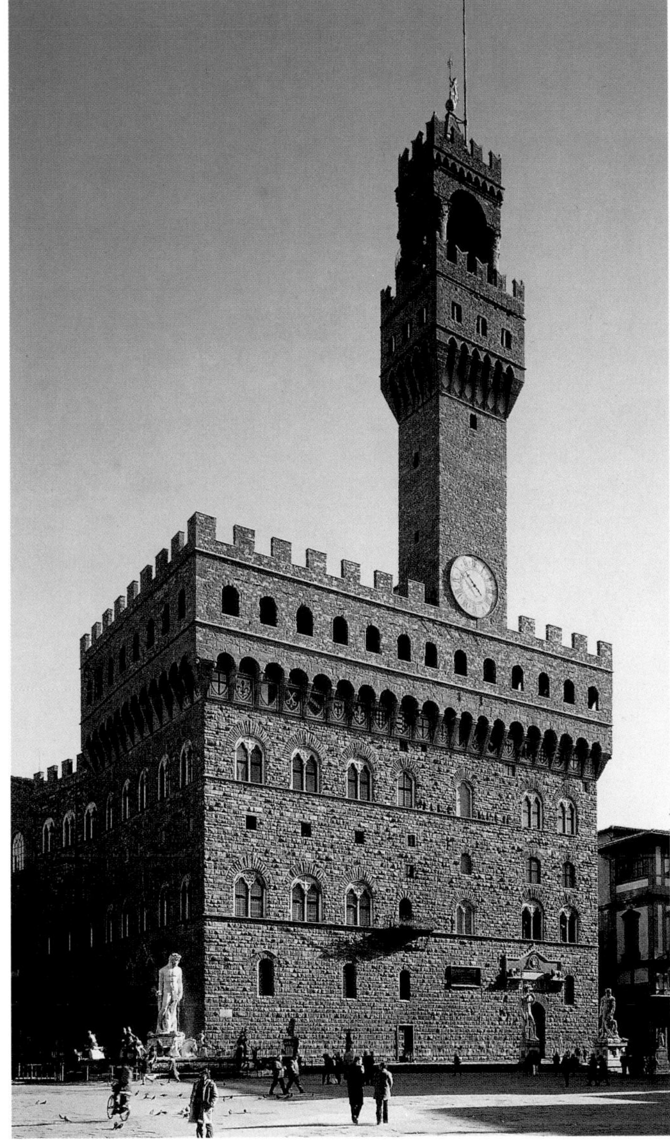

11-39. Palazzo Vecchio, Florence. Begun 1298

SECULAR ARCHITECTURE. The secular buildings of Gothic Italy also have a distinct local flavor. There is nothing in the cities of northern Europe to match the impressive grimness of the Palazzo Vecchio (fig. 11-39), the town hall of Florence. This structure is sometimes thought to be the work of Arnolfo di Cambio, who, as we have seen, was responsible for much of medieval Florence. Fortresslike structures such as this reflect the strife among political parties, social classes, and prominent families that pervaded the Italian city-states. The wealthy man's home (or *palazzo,* a term that denotes any large urban house) was quite literally his castle. It was designed both to withstand armed assault and to proclaim the owner's importance. The Palazzo Vecchio, while larger and more elaborate than any private house, follows the same pattern. Behind its battlemented walls, the city government could feel protected from angry crowds. The tall tower not only symbolizes civic pride but has a practical purpose: dominating Florence as well as the surrounding countryside, it served as a lookout against enemies from inside and outside the city. The Palazzo Vecchio nevertheless reflects the uncertainties of Florentine politics. It was begun in 1298, shortly after the antipapal Ghibelline faction was ousted by the Guelphs, but was given a slightly skewed shape in order not to intrude on the property of a family that briefly held power in the middle of the century.

Among Italian cities, Venice alone was ruled by a merchant aristocracy so firmly established that there was little internal strife. As a result, Venetian palazzi were not required to serve as fortresses but instead developed into graceful, ornate structures. The Ca' d'Oro (fig. 11-40) was built in the early fifteenth century for the merchant Marino Contarini, who spared no expense. It received its name ("house of gold") from the lavish gold leaf that once adorned the front facing the Grand Canal. The odd design in part reflects the different functions of the building. The ground floor was used as a shipping center and warehouse, while the second story is devoted mainly to a large reception hall, with several smaller ones to the right. Private quarters are found mainly on the upper floor. There is a touch of the Orient in the delicate latticework on the facade, even though most of the decorative vocabulary derives from the Late Gothic of northern Europe. Its rippling patterns, designed to be seen against their own reflection in the water of the Grand Canal, have the same fairy-tale quality we recall from the exterior of St. Mark's (see fig. 8-43).

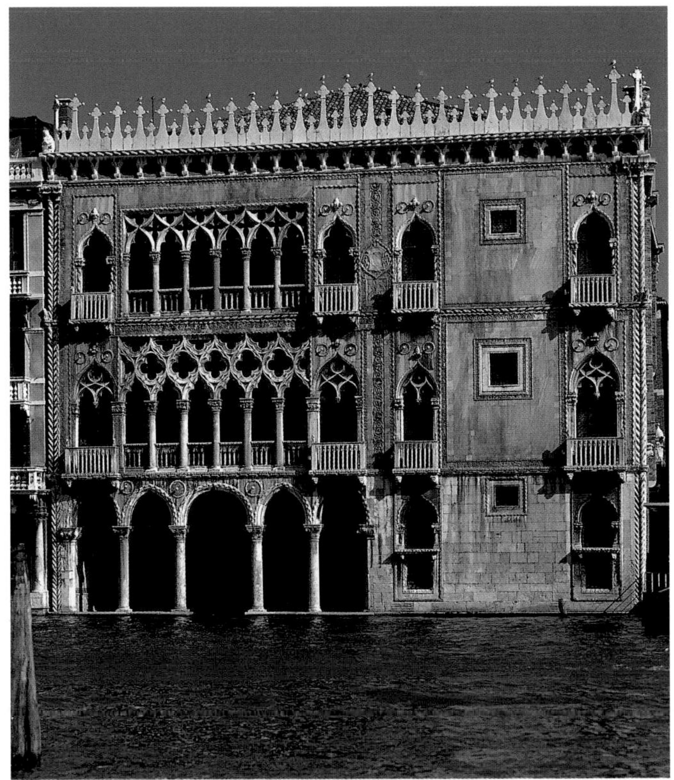

11-40. Ca' d'Oro, Venice. 1422–c. 1440

SCULPTURE

France

Abbot Suger must have attached considerable importance to the sculptural decoration of St.-Denis, although his story of the rebuilding of the church does not discuss it at length. The three portals of his west facade were far larger and more richly carved than those of Norman Romanesque churches. Unhappily, the trumeau figure of St.-Denis and the jamb statue-columns were removed in 1770–71 when the central portal was enlarged; worse still, the heads of the remaining figures were attacked by a mob during the French Revolution, and the metal doors melted down. As a consequence of these ravages and a series of clumsy restorations undertaken during the eighteenth and nineteenth centuries, we can gain only a general view of Suger's ideas about the role of sculpture within the total context of the structure he had envisioned.

CHARTRES CATHEDRAL, WEST PORTALS. Suger's concept, however, prepared the way for the splendid west portals of Chartres Cathedral (fig. 11-41). These were begun about 1145 under the influence of St.-Denis, but were even more ambitious. They may well be the oldest full-fledged example of Early Gothic sculpture. If we compare them with Romanesque portals, we are impressed with a new sense of order. It is as if all the figures had come to attention, conscious of their responsibility to the architectural framework. The dense crowding and frantic movement of Romanesque sculpture have given way to symmetry and clarity. The figures on the lintels, archivolts, and tympanums are no longer entangled but stand out as separate entities. As a result, the design carries much further than that of previous portals.

Especially striking is the novel treatment of the jambs (fig. 11-42), which are lined with tall figures attached to columns. Similar figures, we recall, had occurred on the jambs or trumeaux of Romanesque portals (see figs. 10-21 and 10-27), but they were reliefs carved into or protruding from the masonry of the doorway. The Chartres jamb figures, in contrast, are essentially statues, each with its own axis. They could, in theory at least, be detached from their supports. Here, then, we witness a development of truly revolutionary importance: the first step toward the reconquest of monumental sculpture in the round since the end of classical antiquity. Apparently this step could be taken only by borrowing the cylindrical shape of the column for the human figure, with the result that these statues seem more abstract than

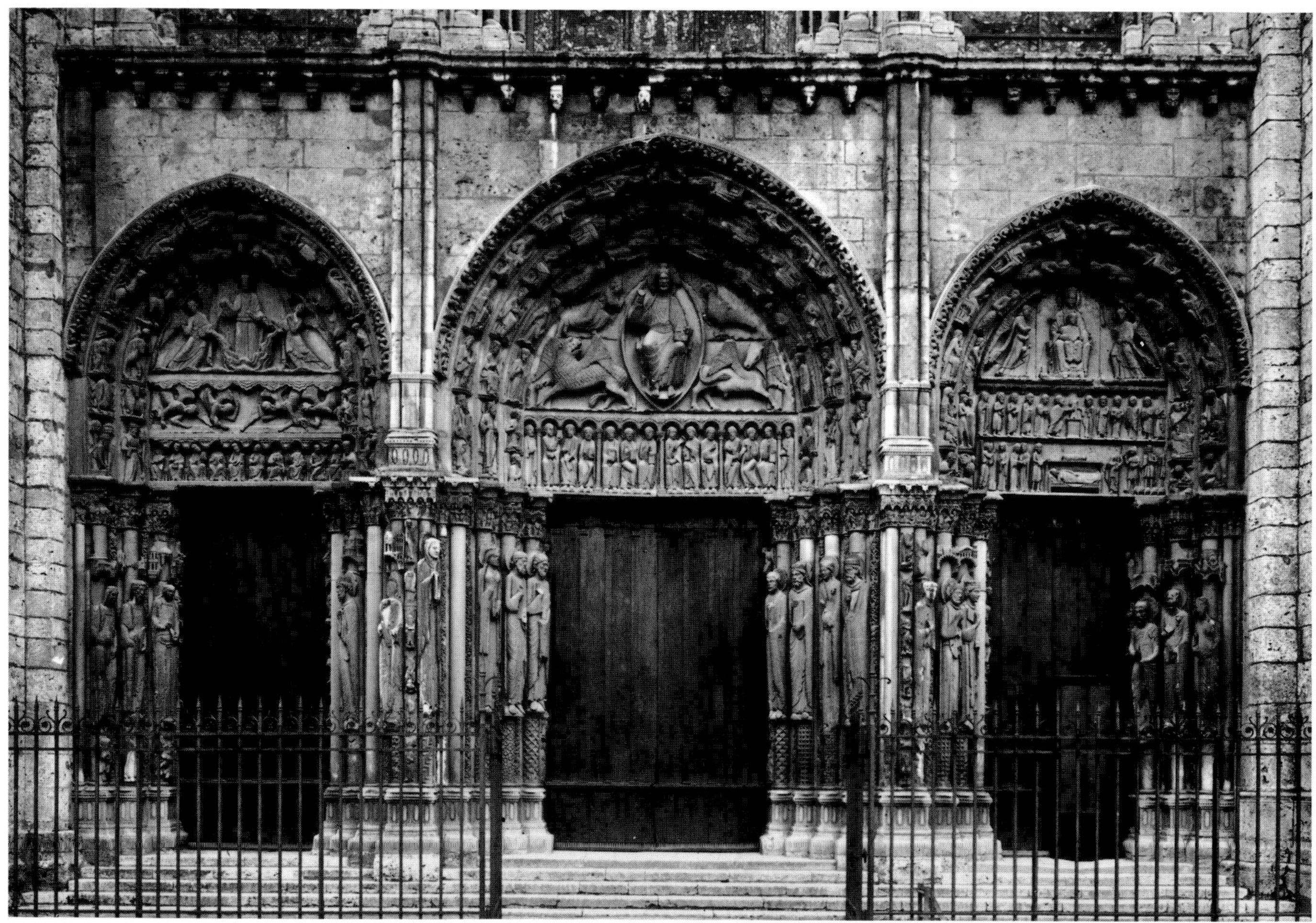

11-41. West portal, Chartres Cathedral. c. 1145–70

their Romanesque predecessors. Yet they will not retain their immobility and unnatural proportions for long. The very fact that they are round gives them a more emphatic presence than anything in Romanesque sculpture, and their heads show a gentle, human quality that bespeaks the fundamentally realistic trend of Gothic sculpture.

Realism is, of course, a relative term whose meaning varies according to circumstances. On the Chartres west portals, it appears to spring from a reaction against the fantastic and demoniacal aspects of Romanesque art. This response may be seen in the solemn spirit of the figures and their increased physical bulk (compare the Christ of the center tympanum with that at Vézelay, fig. 10-26). It also appears in the discipline of the symbolic program underlying the entire scheme. While an understanding of the subtler aspects of this program requires a knowledge of the theology of the Chartres Cathedral School, its main elements can be readily understood.

The jamb statues form a continuous sequence linking all three portals (see fig. 11-41). Together they represent the prophets, kings, and queens of the Bible. Their purpose is to acclaim the rulers of France as the spiritual descendants of Old Testament royalty and to stress the harmony of spiritual and secular rule, of priests (or bishops) and kings—ideals put forward by Abbot Suger. Christ himself is enthroned above the main doorway as Judge and Ruler of the universe. He is flanked by the symbols of the four evangelists, with the apostles below and the 24 elders of the Apocalypse in the archivolts. The right-hand tympanum shows Christ's incarnation: the Birth, the Presentation in the Temple, and the Infant Christ on the lap of the Virgin, who also stands for the Church. In the archivolts above are representations of the liberal arts as human wisdom paying homage to the divine wisdom of Christ. Finally, in the left-hand tympanum, we see the timeless Heavenly Christ (the Christ of the Ascension) framed by the ever-repeating cycle of the year: the signs of the zodiac and their earthly counterparts, the labors of the 12 months.

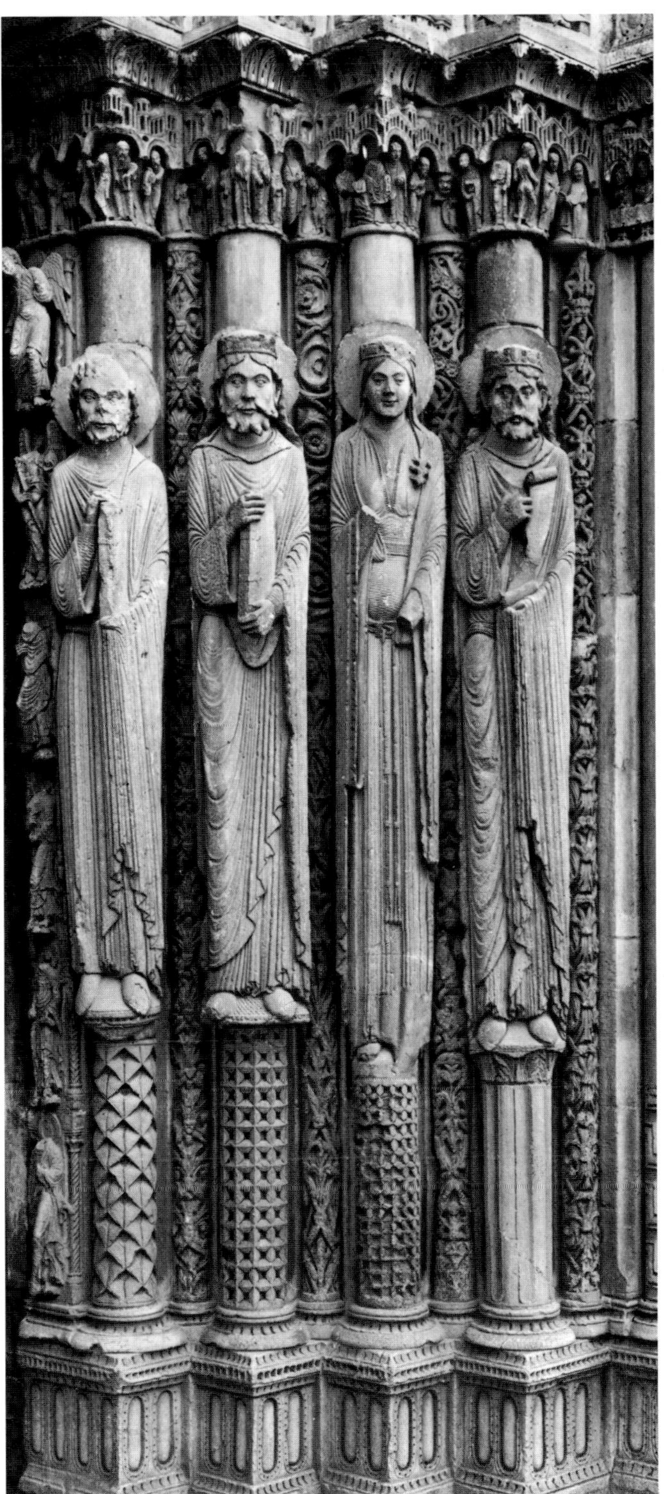

11-42. Jamb statues, west portal, Chartres Cathedral

CHARTRES CATHEDRAL, NORTH PORTALS. When Chartres Cathedral was rebuilt after the fire of 1194, the so-called Royal Portals of the west facade must have seemed small and old-fashioned in relation to the rest of the new structure. Perhaps for that reason, the two transept facades each received three large portals preceded by deep porches. The north transept (fig. 11-43) is devoted to the Virgin. She had already appeared over the right portal of the west facade in her traditional guise as the Mother of God seated on the Throne of Divine Wisdom (see fig. 11-41). Her new prominence reflects the growing importance of the cult of the Virgin, which had been actively promoted by the Church since the Romanesque era. The growth of Mariology, as it is known, was linked to a new emphasis on divine love, which was embraced by the faithful as part of the more human view that became increasingly popular during the Gothic era. The cult of the Virgin received special emphasis about 1204, when Chartres, which is dedicated to her, received the head of her mother, St. Anne, as a relic.

Our tympanum depicts events associated with the Feast of the Assumption (celebrated on August 15), when Mary was transported to Heaven. They are the Death (Dormition), Assumption, and Coronation of the Virgin, which, along with the Annunciation (see fig. 11-46), became the most frequent subjects relating to her life. The presence of all three here is extraordinary. It identifies Mary with the Church as the Bride of Christ and the Gateway to Heaven, in addition to her old role as divine intercessor. More important, it stresses her equality with Christ. Like him, she is transported to Heaven, where she becomes not only his companion (The Triumph of the Virgin) but also his Queen! Unlike earlier representations, which rely on Byzantine examples, these are

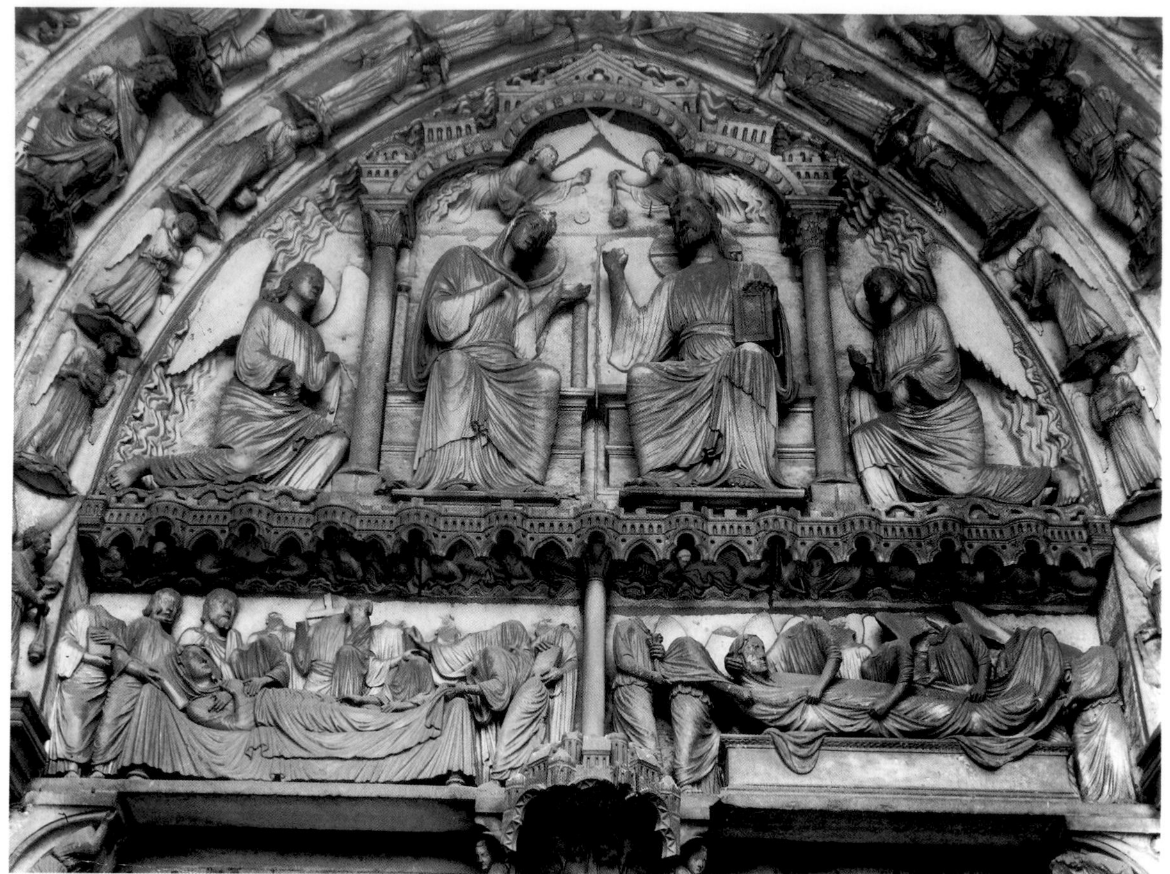

11-43. *Coronation of the Virgin* (tympanum), *Dormition and Assumption of the Virgin* (lintel), north portal, Chartres Cathedral. c. 1230

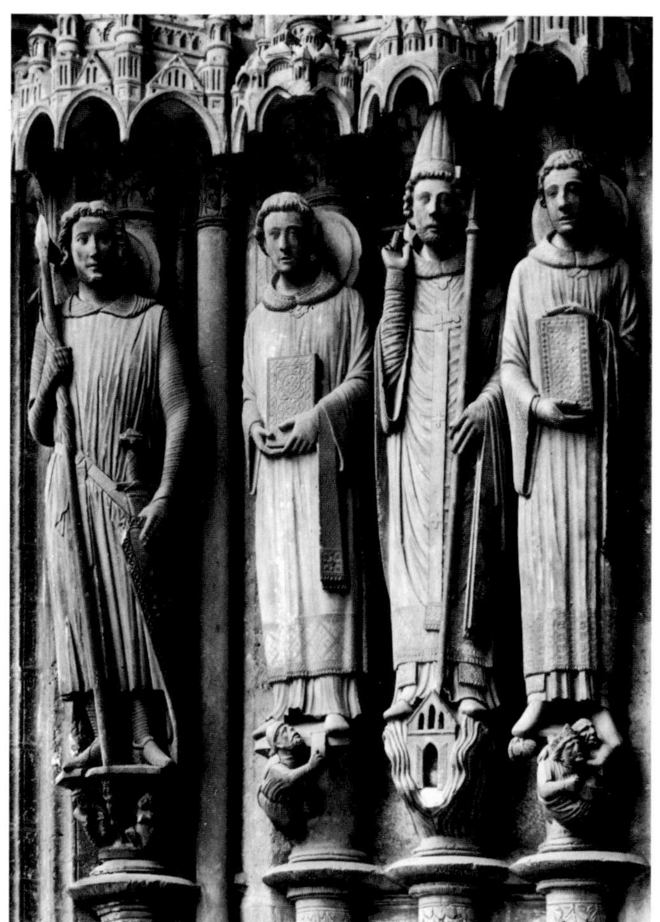

11-44. Jamb statues, south transept portal, Chartres Cathedral. c. 1215–20

of Western invention. The figures have a monumentality never found before in medieval sculpture. Moreover, the treatment is so pictorial that the scenes are independent of the architectural setting into which they have been crammed.

GOTHIC CLASSICISM. The *Coronation of the Virgin* represents an early phase of High Gothic sculpture. The jamb statues of these portals, such as the group shown in figure 11-44, show a similar evolution. By now, the interdependence of statue and column has begun to dissolve. The columns are quite literally put in the shade by the greater width of the figures, by the strongly projecting canopies, and by the elaborately carved bases of the statues.

In the three saints on the right, we still find echoes of the cylindrical shape of Early Gothic jamb statues, but even here the heads are no longer strictly in line with the central axis of the body. St. Theodore, the knight on the left, stands at ease, in a semblance of classical contrapposto. His feet rest on a horizontal platform, rather than on a sloping shelf as before, and the axis of his body, instead of being straight, describes a slight but perceptible S-curve. Even more surprising is the abundance of precisely observed detail in the weapons and in the texture of the tunic and chain mail. Above all, there is the organic structure of the body. Not since Imperial Roman times have we seen a figure as thoroughly alive as this. Yet the most impressive quality of the statue is not its realism, but the serene, balanced image that this realism conveys. In this ideal portrait of the Christian soldier, the spirit of the Crusades has been expressed in its most elevated form.

The style of the *St. Theodore* could not have evolved directly

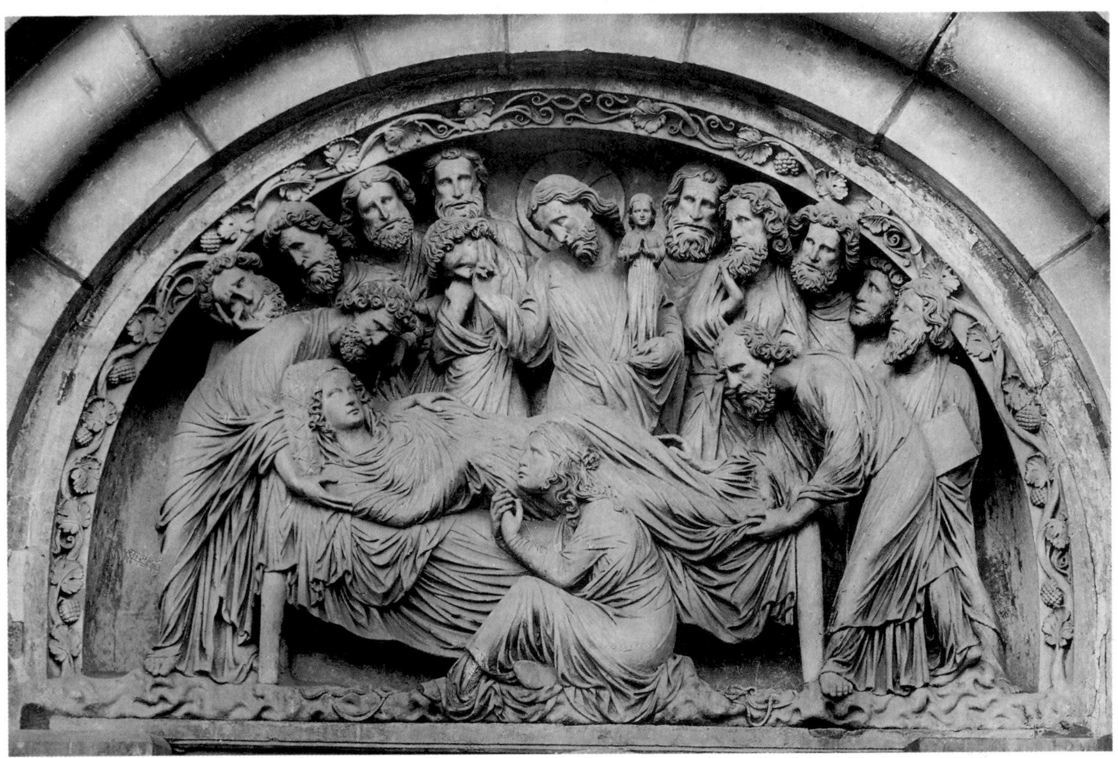

11-45. *Death of the Virgin,* tympanum of the south transept portal, Strasbourg Cathedral, France. c. 1220

from the elongated columnar statues of Chartres' west facade. It also incorporates another, equally important tradition: the classicism of the Meuse Valley, which we traced in the previous chapter from Renier of Huy to Nicholas of Verdun (compare figs. 10-31, 10-40, and 10-41). At the end of the twelfth century this trend, previously confined to metalwork and miniatures, began to appear in monumental stone sculpture as well and transformed it from Early Gothic to Classic High Gothic.

STRASBOURG CATHEDRAL. The link with Nicholas of Verdun is striking in the *Death of the Virgin* (fig. 11-45), a tympanum at Strasbourg Cathedral slightly later than the Chartres north transept portals. Here the draperies, the facial types, and the movements and gestures have a classical flavor that recalls the *Klosterneuburg Altar* (see fig. 10-40). What marks it as Gothic rather than Romanesque, however, is the deeply felt tenderness pervading the scene. We sense a bond of shared emotion among the figures, an ability to communicate by glance and gesture that surpasses even the Klosterneuburg Altar. This quality, too, has a long heritage reaching back to antiquity. It entered Byzantine art during the eleventh century as part of a renewed classicism (see figs. 8-48 and 8-51). Gothic expressiveness is unthinkable without such examples. But how much warmer and more eloquent it is at Strasbourg than at Chartres! What appears as merely one episode within the larger doctrinal statement of the earlier work now becomes the sole focus of attention. It serves as the vehicle for an outpouring of emotion that had never been seen in the art of Western Christendom.

REIMS CATHEDRAL. The climax of Gothic classicism is reached in some of the statues at Reims Cathedral. The most famous among them is the *Visitation* group (fig. 11-46, right). To have a pair of jamb figures enact a narrative scene such as this would have been inconceivable in Early Gothic sculpture. The fact that they can do so now shows how far the column has receded into the background. Now the S-curve resulting from the pronounced contrapposto is much more conspicuous than in the *St. Theodore.* It dominates the side view as well as the front view. The physical bulk of the body is further emphasized by horizontal folds pulled across the abdomen. The relationship of the two women shows the same warmth and sympathy we found in the Strasbourg tympanum, but their classicism is far more monumental. They remind us so strongly of ancient Roman matrons (compare fig. 7-32) that we wonder if the artist could have been inspired by large-scale Roman sculpture.

Because of the vast scale of the sculptural program, it was necessary to employ masters from other building sites. We therefore see several distinct styles among the Reims figures. Two of these styles, both clearly different from the classicism of the *Visitation,* appear in the *Annunciation* group (see fig. 11-46, left). The Virgin has a rigidly vertical body axis and straight, tubular folds meeting at sharp angles. This severe style was probably invented about 1220 by the sculptors of the west portals of Notre-Dame in Paris; from there it traveled to Reims as well as Amiens (see fig. 11-49, top center). The angel, in contrast, is remarkably graceful. We note the tiny, round face framed by curly locks, the emphatic smile, the strong S-curve of the slender body, and the richly

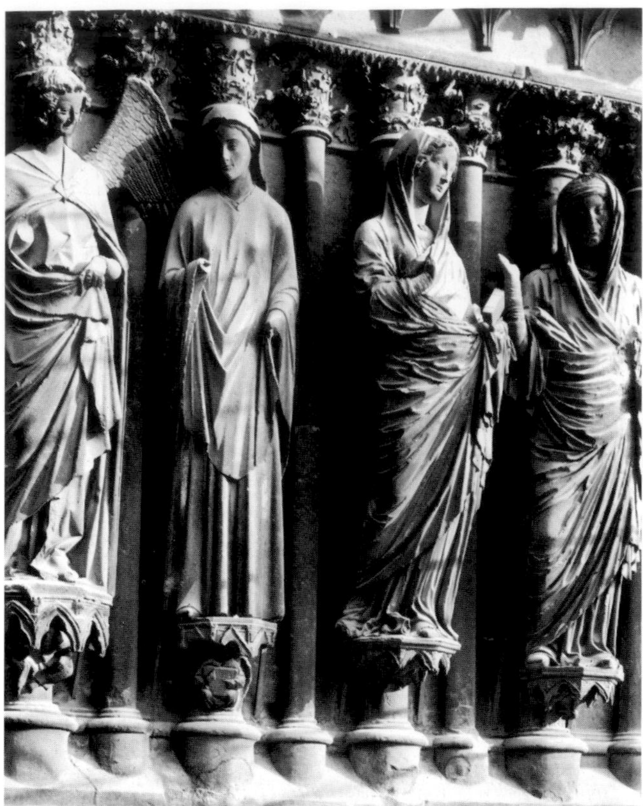

11-46. *Annunciation* and *Visitation,* west portal, Reims Cathedral. c. 1225–45

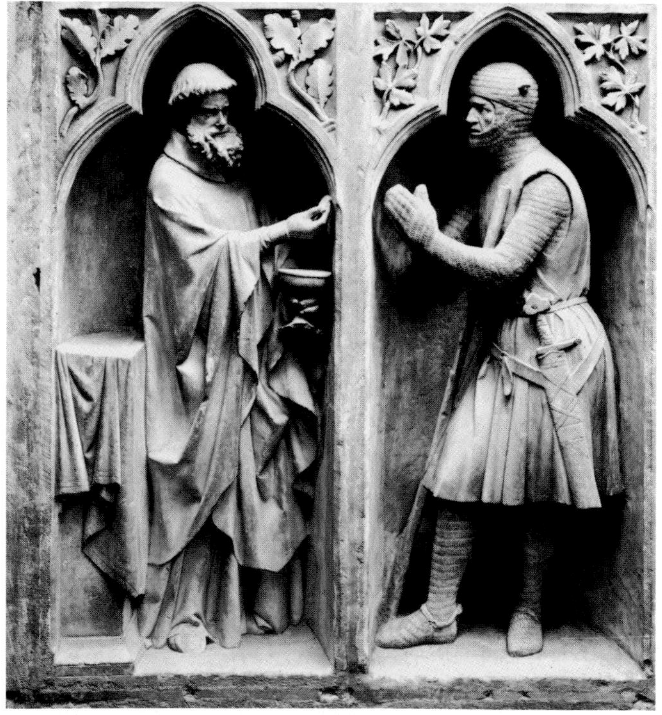

11-47. *Melchizedek and Abraham,* interior west wall, Reims Cathedral. After 1251

accented drapery. This "elegant style," created around 1240 by Parisian masters working for the royal court, spread far and wide during the following decades. In fact, it soon became the standard formula for High Gothic sculpture. We shall see its effect for many years to come, not only in France but abroad.

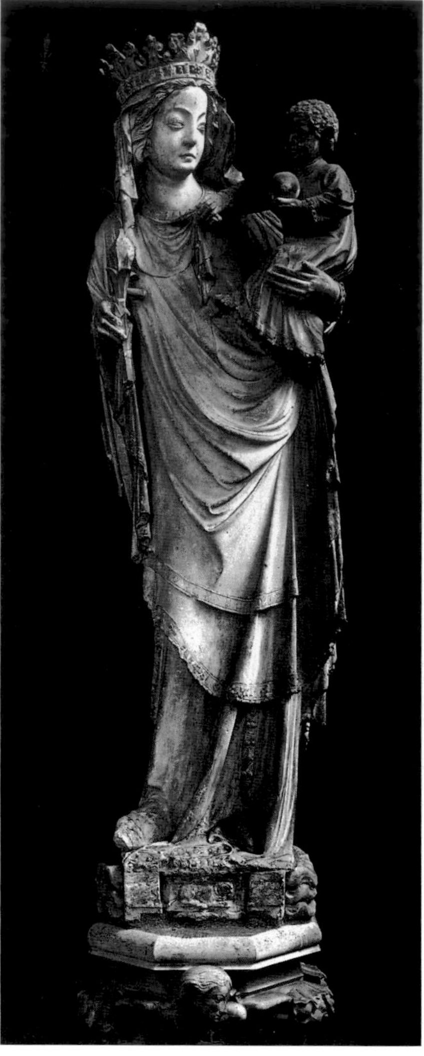

11-48. *The Virgin of Paris.* Early 14th century. Stone. Notre-Dame, Paris

A characteristic example of the elegant style is the group of *Melchizedek and Abraham,* carved shortly after the middle of the century for the interior west wall of Reims Cathedral (fig. 11-47). Abraham, in the costume of a medieval knight, recalls the vigorous realism of the *St. Theodore* at Chartres. Melchizedek, however, shows clearly his descent from the angel of the Reims *Annunciation.* His hair and beard are even more elaborately curled, and the draperies are more ample, so that the body almost disappears among the rich play of folds. The deep recesses and sharply projecting ridges betray a new awareness of effects of light and shadow that seem more pictorial than sculptural. The same may be said of the way the figures are placed in their cavernous niches.

THE VIRGIN OF PARIS. A half-century later every trace of classicism has disappeared from Gothic sculpture. The human figure now becomes strangely abstract. Thus the famous *Virgin of Paris* (fig. 11-48) in Notre-Dame Cathedral consists largely of hollows, and the projections have been reduced to the point where they are seen as lines rather than volumes. The statue is quite literally disembodied—its swaying stance no longer bears any relation to classical contrapposto. Compared to such unearthly grace, the angel of the Reims *Annunciation* seems solid and tangible indeed. Yet it contains the seed of the very qualities so strikingly expressed in *The Virgin of Paris.*

When we look back over the century and a half that separates

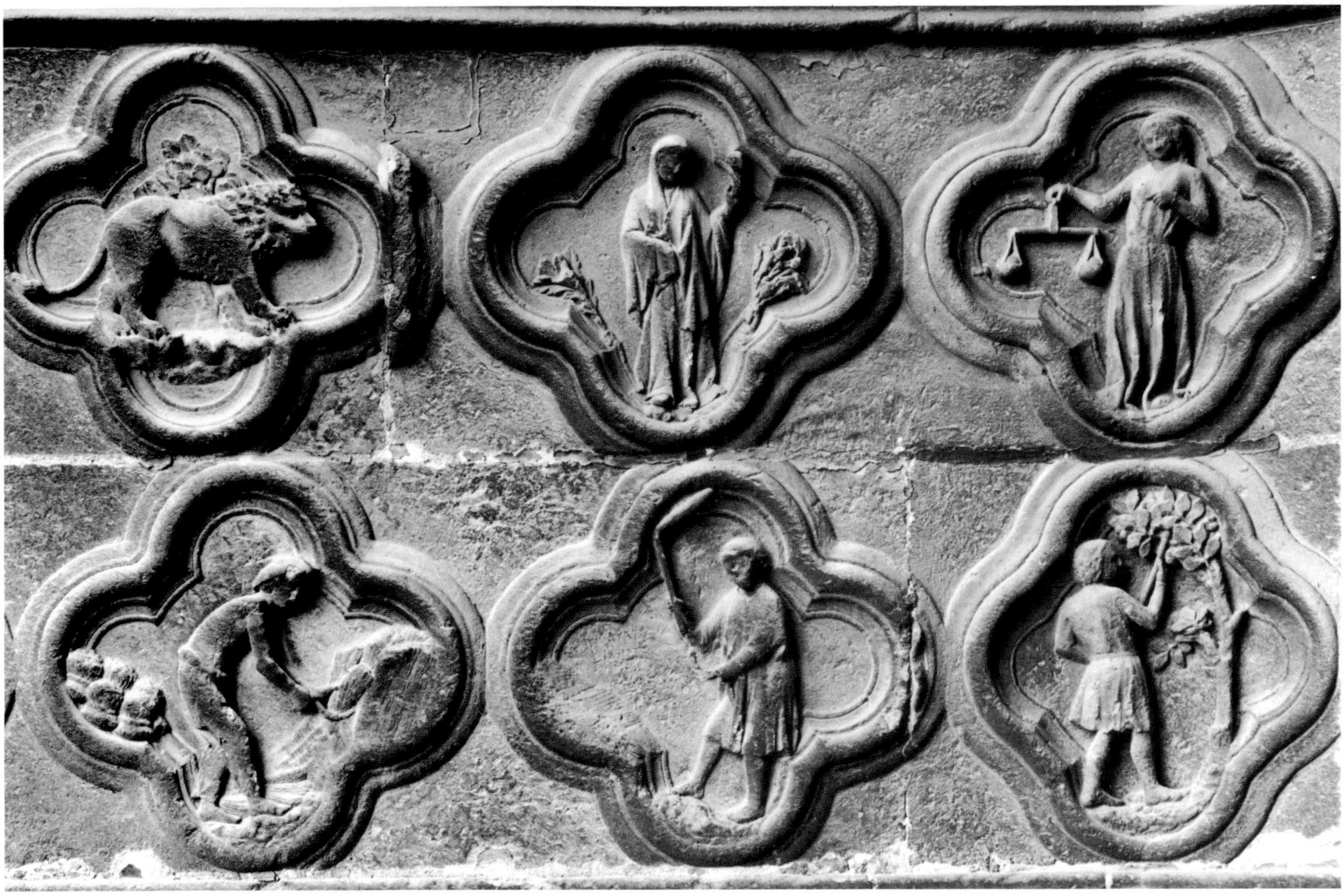

11-49. *Signs of the Zodiac* and *Labors of the Months (July, August, September)*, west facade, Amiens Cathedral. c. 1220–30

The Virgin of Paris from the Chartres west portals, we cannot help wondering what brought about this graceful manner. The new style was certainly encouraged by the royal court of France and thus had special authority. However, smoothly flowing, calligraphic lines came to dominate Gothic art, not just in France but throughout northern Europe from about 1250 to 1400. It is clear, moreover, that the style of *The Virgin of Paris* represents neither a return to the Romanesque nor a complete rejection of the earlier realistic trend.

Gothic realism had never been systematic. Rather, it had been a "realism of particulars," focused on specific details rather than on overall structure. Its most characteristic products are not the classically oriented jamb statues and tympanum compositions of the early thirteenth century but small-scale carvings, such as the *Labors of the Months* in quatrefoil frames on the facade of Amiens Cathedral (fig. 11-49), with their delightful scenes of everyday life. This keen interest in nature, which we first saw at the end of the Romanesque (see fig. 10-42), seems to have come from Byzantine art, where it appears some 200 years earlier, although its origins can be traced back to early Christian times, if not earlier (compare fig. 8-7). The same intimate kind of realism survives even within the formal framework of *The Virgin of Paris*. We see it in the Infant Christ, who appears here not as the Savior-in-miniature facing the viewer, but as a human child playing with his mother's veil. Our statue thus retains an emotional appeal that links it to the Strasbourg *Death of the Virgin* and to the Reims *Visitation*. It is this appeal, not realism or classicism as such, that is the essence of Gothic art.

England

The spread of Gothic sculpture beyond France began only toward 1200, so that the style of the Chartres west portals had hardly any echoes abroad. Once under way, however, it proceeded very quickly. England may well have led the way, as it did in evolving its own version of Gothic architecture. Unfortunately, so much English Gothic sculpture was destroyed during the Reformation that its development is difficult to study. Our richest materials are the tombs, which did not arouse the iconoclastic zeal of Protestants later on. They include a type that has no counterpart on the other side of the Channel (fig. 11-50). It shows the deceased, not in the quiet repose found on most medieval tombs, but as a fallen hero

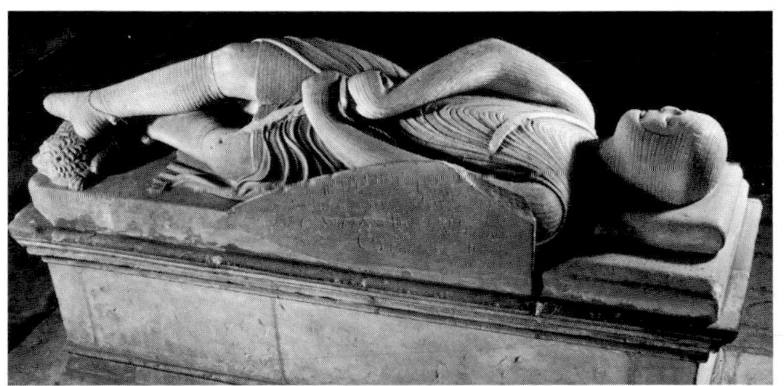

11-50. Tomb of a Knight. c. 1260. Stone. Dorchester Abbey, Oxfordshire, England

fighting to the last breath. According to an old tradition, these dramatic figures honor the memory of Crusaders who died in the struggle for the Holy Land. As the tombs of Christian soldiers, they carry a religious meaning that helps to account for their expressive power. Their agony, which recalls the *Dying Trumpeter* (see fig. 5-71), makes them among the finest achievements of English Gothic sculpture.

Germany

In Germany, the growth of Gothic sculpture can be traced more easily. From the 1220s on, German masters trained in the sculptural workshops of the French cathedrals brought the new style to their homeland, although German architecture at that time was still predominantly Romanesque. Even after the middle of the century, however, Germany did not produce the large statuary cycles like those of France. As a result, German Gothic sculpture tended to be less closely linked with its architectural setting. (The finest work was often done for the interiors of churches rather than for the exteriors.) This independence, in turn, permitted a greater expressive freedom than that of its French models.

THE NAUMBURG MASTER. These qualities are strikingly evident in the style of the Naumburg Master, an artist of real genius whose best-known work is the magnificent series of statues and reliefs of about 1240–50 for Naumburg Cathedral. The *Crucifixion* (fig. 11-51) forms the center of the choir screen; flanking it

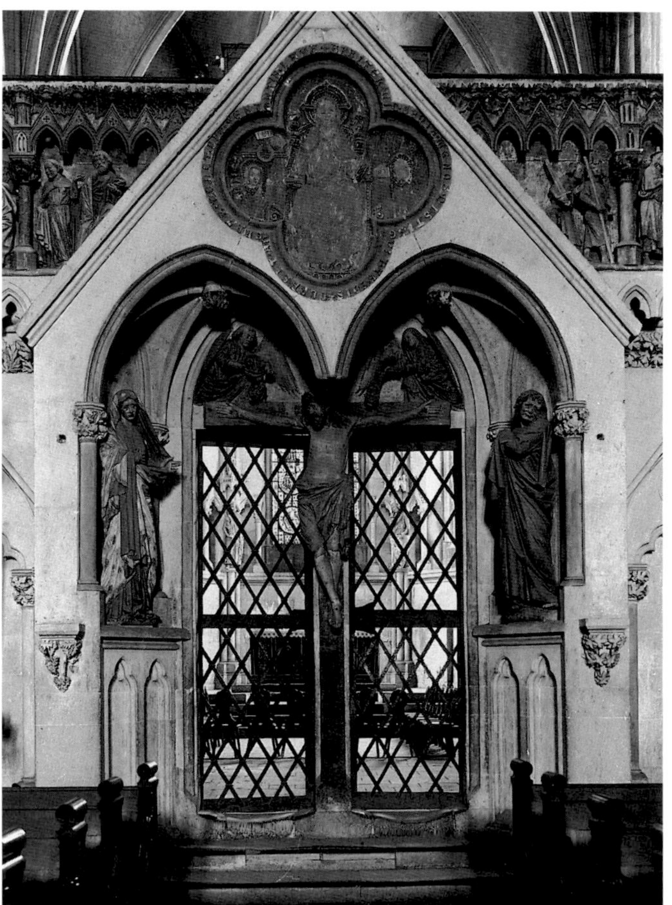

11-51. *Crucifixion,* on the choir screen, Naumburg Cathedral, Germany. c. 1240–50. Stone

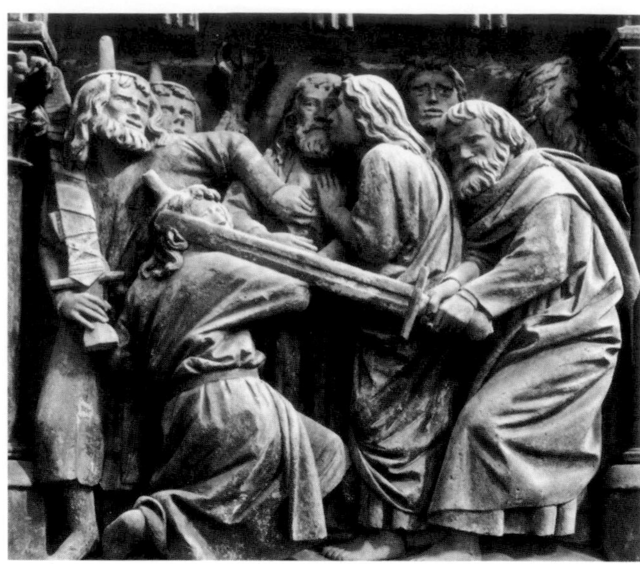

11-52. *The Kiss of Judas,* on the choir screen, Naumburg Cathedral. c. 1240–50. Stone

are statues of the Virgin and John the Baptist. Enclosed by a deep, gabled porch, the three figures frame the opening that links the nave with the sanctuary. Rather than placing the group above the screen, as was usual, our sculptor has brought the subject down to earth both physically and emotionally. The suffering of Christ thus becomes a human reality because of the emphasis on the weight and volume of his body. Mary and John, pleading with the viewer, convey their grief more eloquently than ever before.

The pathos of these figures is heroic and dramatic, as against the lyricism of the Strasbourg tympanum or the Reims *Visitation* (see figs. 11-45 and 11-46). If the classic High Gothic sculpture of France may be compared with Pheidias, the Naumburg Master might be termed the temperamental kin of Skopas (see pages 139–40). The same intensity dominates the Passion scenes, such as *The Kiss of Judas* (fig. 11-52), with its unforgettable contrast between the meekness of Christ and the violence of the sword-wielding St. Peter. Attached to the responds inside the choir are over-lifesized statues of nobles associated with the founding of the cathedral. These men and women were not of the artist's own time, so that they were only names in a chronicle to him. Yet the famous pair *Ekkehard and Uta* (fig. 11-53) are as individual and forceful as if they had been portrayed from life. They thus make an instructive contrast with the idealized portrait of *St. Theodore* at Chartres (see fig. 11-44, left).

THE PIETÀ. Gothic sculpture, as we have come to know it so far, reflects a desire to endow the traditional themes of Christian art with greater emotional appeal. Toward the end of the thirteenth century, this tendency gave rise to a new kind of religious imagery, designed for private devotion. It is often referred to by the German term *Andachtsbild* (contemplation image), since Germany played a leading part in its development. The most widespread type was a representation of the Virgin grieving over the dead Christ. It is called a *Pietà* after an Italian word derived from the Latin *pietas,* the root word for both pity and piety. No such scene occurs in the scriptural accounts of the Passion. The *Pietà*

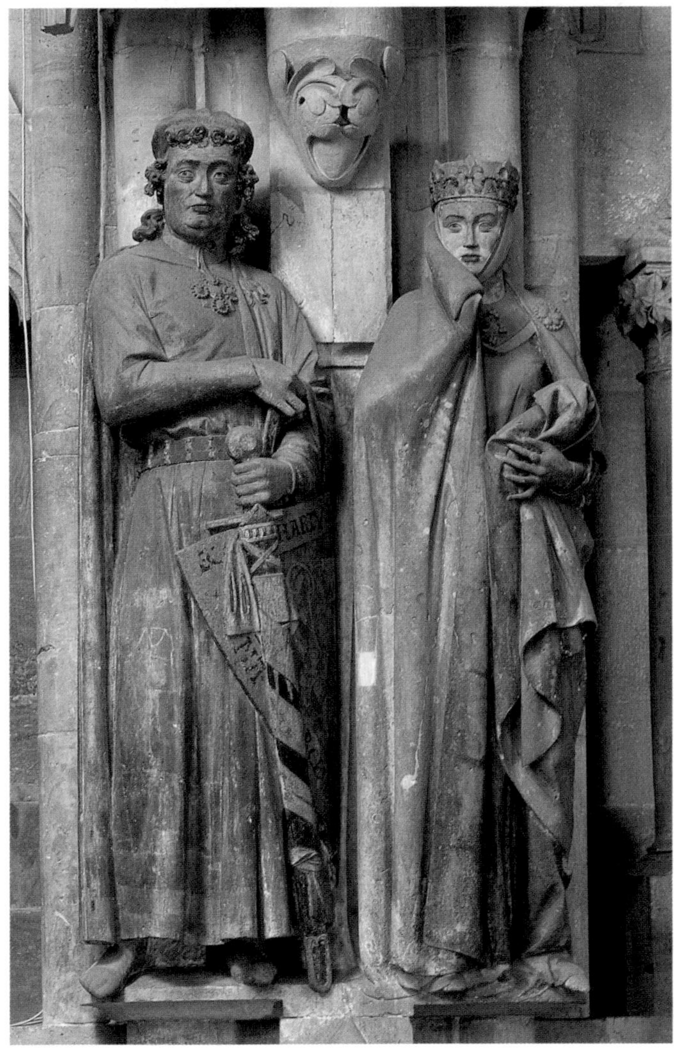

11-53. *Ekkehard and Uta.* c. 1240–50. Stone. Naumburg Cathedral

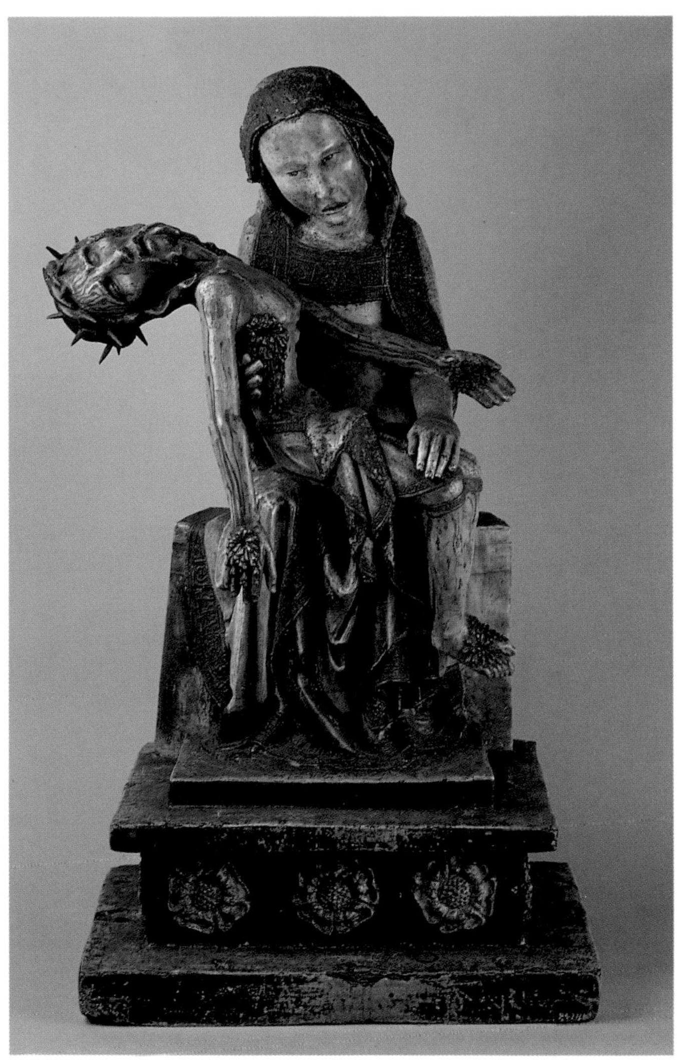

11-54. *Roettgen Pietà.* Early 14th century. Wood, height 34½" (87.5 cm). Rheinisches Landesmuseum, Bonn

unites two iconic types, the Madonna and Child and the Crucifixion. (These images were often paired once they became familiar to Western Europeans after the conquest of Constantinople in 1204.) We do not know where or when the *Pietà* was invented, but it portrays one of the Seven Sorrows of the Virgin. It thus forms a tragic counterpart to the motif of the Madonna and Child, one of her Seven Joys. [See Primary Sources, no. 28, page 371.]

The *Roettgen Pietà,* shown in figure 11-54, is carved of wood and vividly painted. Like most such groups, this large cult statue was meant to be placed on an altar. The style, like the subject, expresses the emotional fervor of lay religiosity, which emphasized a personal relationship with God as part of the tide of mysticism that swept fourteenth-century Europe. Realism here has become a means of expression to enhance its impact. The faces convey unbearable pain and grief; the wounds are exaggerated grotesquely; and the bodies and limbs have become puppetlike in their thinness and rigidity. The purpose of the work clearly is to arouse so overwhelming a sense of horror and pity that the faithful will share in Christ's suffering and identify their own feelings with those of the grief-stricken Mother of God. The ultimate goal of this emotional bond is a spiritual transformation that comprehends the central mystery of God in human form through compassion (which means "to suffer with").

At a glance, our *Pietà* would seem to have little in common with *The Virgin of Paris* (see fig. 11-48), which dates from the same period. Yet they share a lean, "deflated" quality of form and a strong emotional appeal to the viewer. Both features characterize the art of Northern Europe from the late thirteenth century to the mid-fourteenth. Only after 1350 do we again find an interest in weight and volume, coupled with a renewed desire to explore tangible reality as part of a change in religious sensibility.

France

SLUTER. The climax of this new trend came about 1400, during the period of the International Style (see pages 358–63). Its greatest representative was Claus Sluter, a sculptor of Netherlandish origin working at Dijon for the king's brother Philip the Bold, the duke of Burgundy. Between 1385 and 1393 Sluter decorated the portal of the Carthusian monastery known as the Chartreuse de Champmol (fig. 11-55). This work recalls the monumental statuary on thirteenth-century cathedral portals, but the figures have

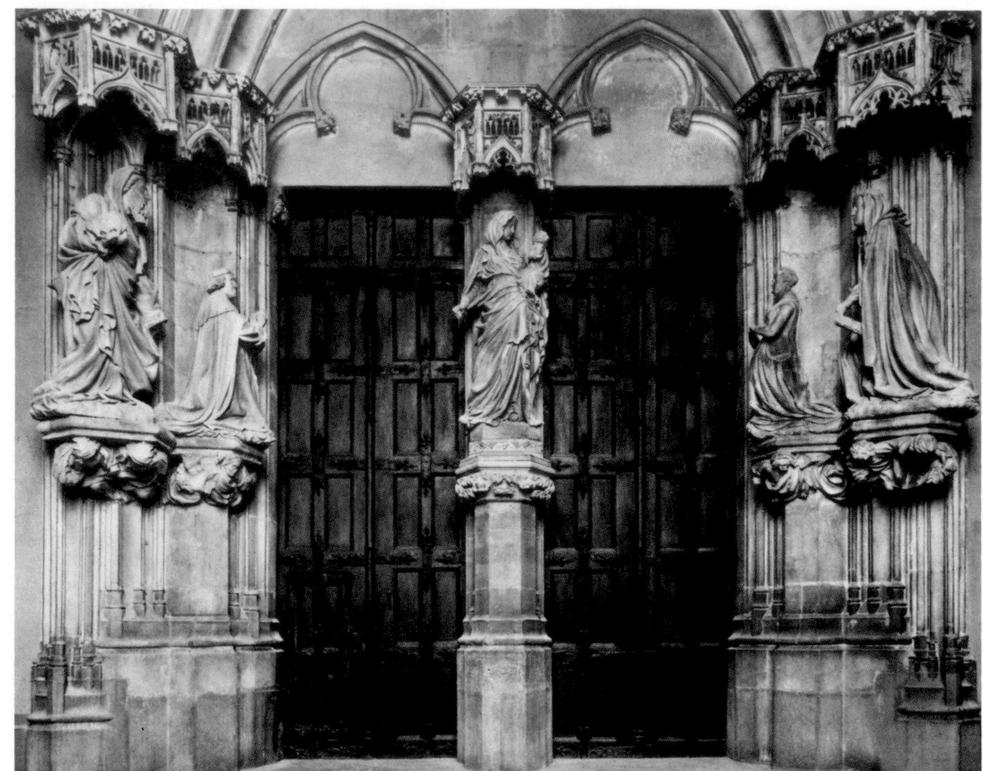

11-55. Claus Sluter. Portal of the Chartreuse de Champmol, Dijon, France. 1385–93. Stone

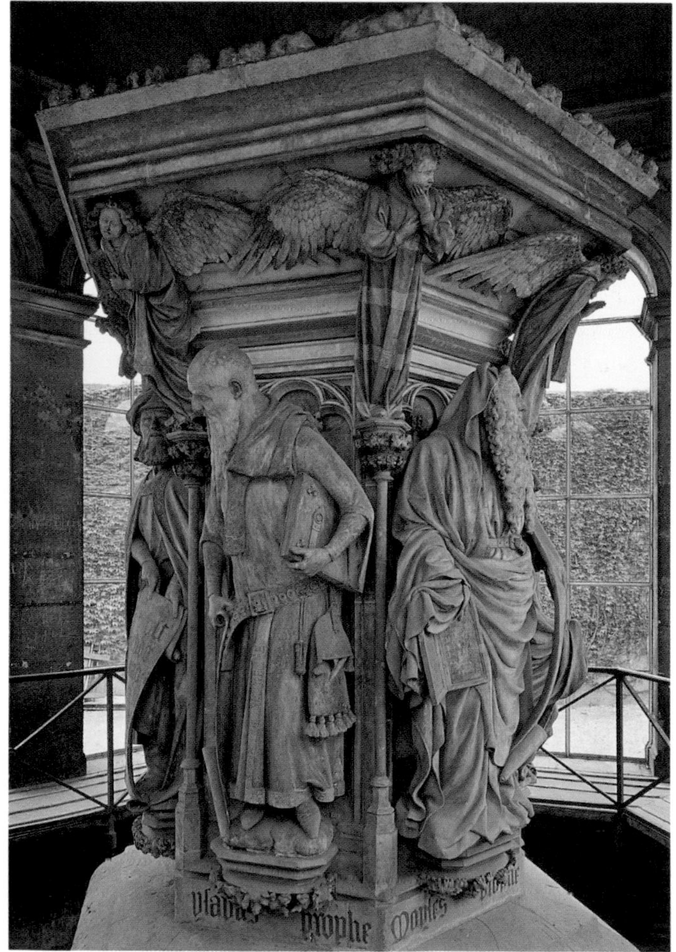

11-56. Claus Sluter. *The Moses Well.* 1395–1406. Stone, height of figures approx. 6' (1.8 m). Chartreuse de Champmol, Dijon

grown so large that they almost overpower their framework. The effect is due not only to their size and the bold three-dimensional carving but also from the fact that the jamb statues (showing the duke and his wife with their patron saints) are turned toward the Madonna on the trumeau. The five figures thus form a coherent unit, like the *Crucifixion* group at Naumburg. In both cases the sculptural composition has been superimposed on the shape of the doorway. It was not developed from it as at Chartres, Notre-Dame, or Reims. Significantly, the Champmol portal did not pave the way for a revival of architectural sculpture. Instead, it remained an isolated effort.

Sluter's other works belong to a different category that, for lack of a better term, we must label church furniture. It includes tombs, pulpits, and the like, which combine large-scale sculpture with a small-scale architectural setting. The most impressive of these is *The Moses Well* at the Chartreuse de Champmol (fig. 11-56). This symbolic well surrounded by statues of Old Testament prophets was at one time surmounted by a crucifix. The majestic Moses shows the same qualities we find in Sluter's portal statues. Heavy draped garments envelop the body like an ample shell. The swelling forms seem to reach out into the surrounding space as if trying to capture as much of it as possible. (Note the outward curve of the scroll, which reads: "The children of Israel do not listen to me.") The effect must have been enhanced greatly by the polychromy added by Jean Malouel (see pages 359–60), which has largely disappeared. At first glance, Moses seems to look forward to the Renaissance. (Compare Michelangelo's treatment of the same subject in fig. 13-13.) Only when we look more closely do we realize that Sluter remains firmly tied to the Gothic.

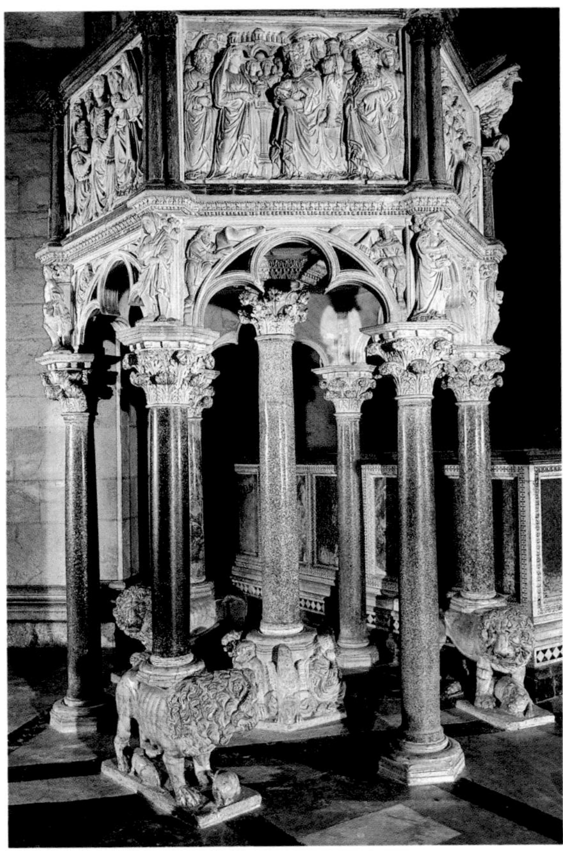

11-57. Nicola Pisano. Pulpit. 1259–60. Marble, height 15' (4.6 m). Baptistery, Pisa

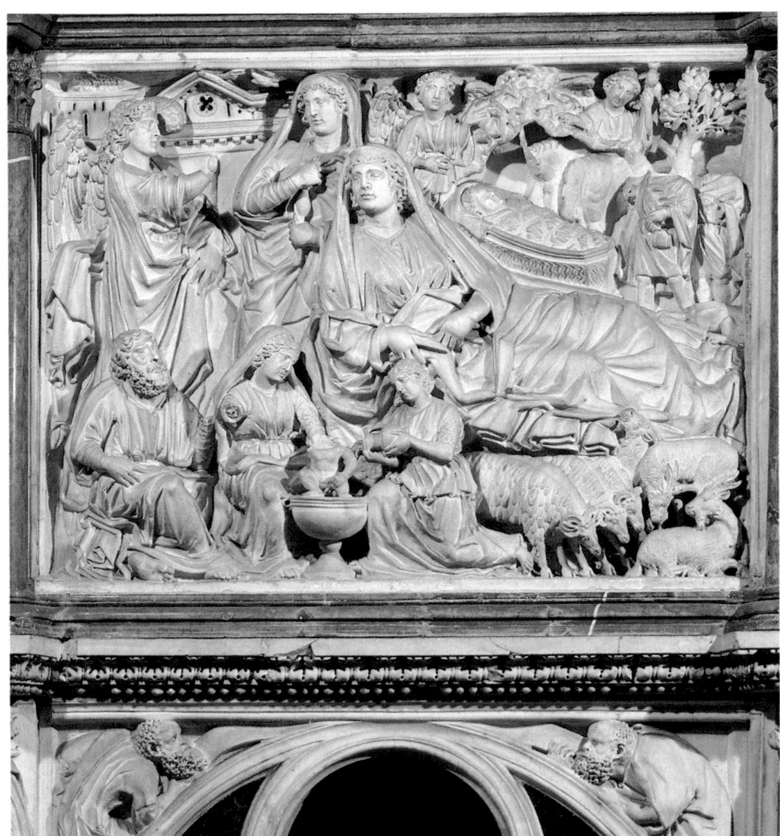

11-58. *Nativity,* detail of the pulpit by Nicola Pisano. Baptistery, Pisa

In the Isaiah (facing left), what strikes us is the precise and masterful realism of every detail, from the particulars of the costume to the texture of the wrinkled skin. The head, unlike that of Moses, has all the individuality of a portrait. Nor is this impression misleading: Sluter left us two splendid examples in the heads of the duke and duchess on the Chartreuse portal. It is this attachment to the specific that distinguishes his realism from that of the thirteenth century.

Italy

We have left a discussion of Italian Gothic sculpture to the last, for here, as in Gothic architecture, Italy stands apart from the rest of Europe. The earliest Gothic sculpture in Italy was probably produced in the extreme south, in Apulia and Sicily. This region was ruled by the German emperor Frederick II, who employed Frenchmen and Germans along with native artists at his court. Few of the works he sponsored have survived, but there is evidence that he favored a strongly classical style derived from the sculpture of the Chartres transept portals and the *Visitation* group at Reims (see figs. 11-43 and 11-46). This style not only provided a fitting visual language for a ruler who saw himself as the heir of the Caesars, it also blended easily with the classical tendencies in Italian Romanesque sculpture (see pages 291–94).

NICOLA PISANO. Such was the background of Nicola Pisano (c. 1220/5–1284), who went to Tuscany from southern Italy about 1250 (the year of Frederick II's death). Ten years later he completed the marble pulpit in the Baptistery of Pisa Cathedral (fig. 11-57). He has been described as "the greatest—and in a sense the last—of medieval classicists." Whether we look at the architectural framework or the sculptured parts of the pulpit, the classical flavor is so strong that the Gothic elements are at first hard to detect. But we do find such elements in the design of the arches and the shape of the capitals. They can also be seen in the standing figures at the corners, which look like small-scale descendants of the jamb statues on French Gothic cathedrals.

The most striking Gothic quality is the human feeling in the reliefs such as the *Nativity* (fig. 11-58). The dense crowding of figures, however, has no counterpart in Northern Gothic sculpture. The panel also shows the Annunciation and the shepherds in the fields receiving the glad tidings of the birth of Christ. The treatment of the relief as a shallow box filled almost to the bursting point with solid, convex shapes shows that Nicola Pisano must have been thoroughly familiar with Roman sarcophagi (compare fig. 7-39).

The figures atop the columns include an even more startling classical element: a nude male (fig. 11-59), instantly recognizable as Hercules by the lion cub on his shoulder and the skin of the Nemean lion he slew with his bare hands (compare fig. 5-6). But what is he doing here? He is the personification of Fortitude. Whenever we meet the unclothed body, from 800 to 1400, we may be sure, except for a few special cases, that such nudity has a moral significance. It may be negative (Adam and Eve or sinners in Hell) or positive (the nudity of the Christ of the Passion, of saints being martyred, or mortification of the flesh). Hercules' presence as one

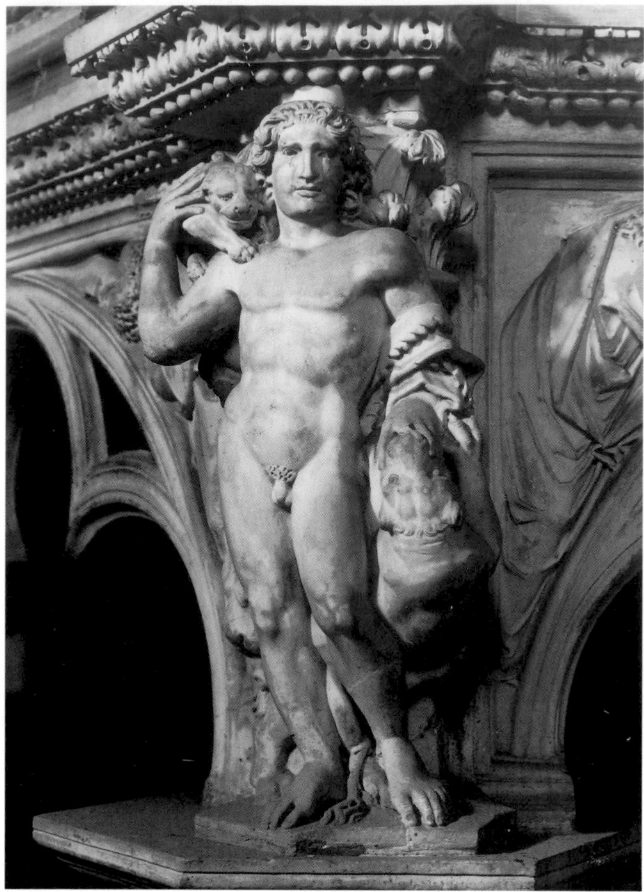

11-59. *Fortitude,* detail of the pulpit by Nicola Pisano

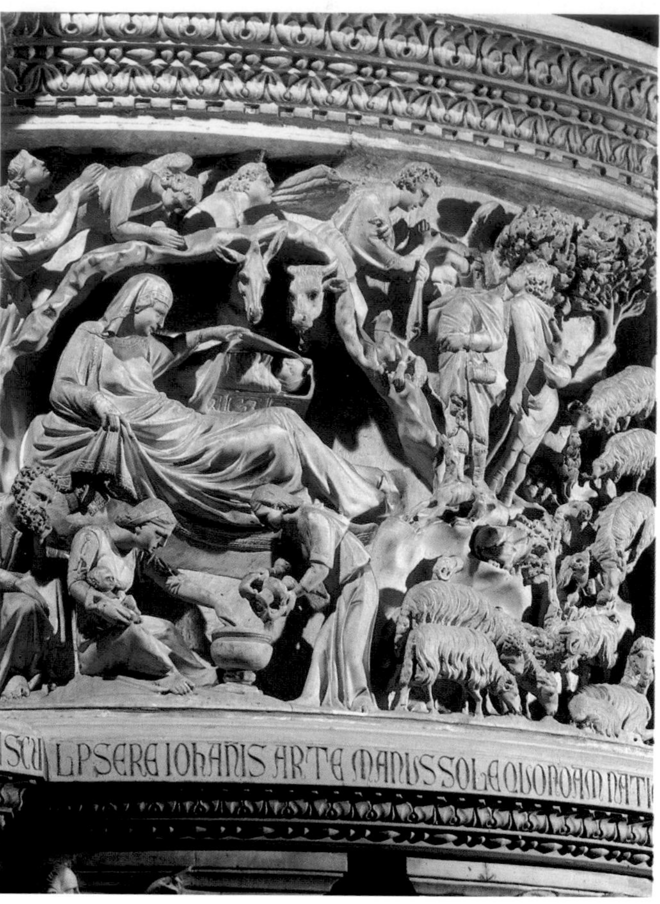

11-60. Giovanni Pisano. *The Nativity,* detail of pulpit. 1302–10. Marble. Pisa Cathedral

of the seven Cardinal Virtues was therefore perfectly acceptable to the medieval mind.

We may also be sure that such figures are derived, directly or indirectly, from classical sources, no matter how unlikely this may seem in some cases. Such is the case with Nicola's Hercules, who betrays his descent from Praxiteles' *Hermes* (see fig. 5-68). However, Hercules' nearest ancestors are miniature figures of Daniel in the lions' den on Early Christian sarcophagi of the fifth century, which have the same squat proportions. His appearance here is thus based on highly respectable sources. Like all medieval nudes, even the finest, it lacks the sensual appeal that we take for granted in every nude of classical antiquity. This quality was purposely avoided rather than unattainable. To the medieval mind the physical beauty of the ancient "idols," especially nude statues, embodied the insidious attraction of paganism. As seen in the bulging features and lumpy anatomy, Nicola's style remains Gothic despite his obvious fascination with antique sculpture.

GIOVANNI PISANO. Half a century later, Nicola's son Giovanni (1245/50–after 1314), who was an equally gifted sculptor, carved a marble pulpit for Pisa Cathedral. [See Primary Sources, no. 29, pages 371–72.] It has two inscriptions by the artist praising his ability but bemoaning the hostility to his work. This pulpit, too, includes a Nativity (fig. 11-60). Both panels have much in common, as we might expect, yet they also present a sharp—and instructive—contrast. Giovanni's slender, swaying figures, with their smoothly flowing draperies, recall neither classical antiquity nor the *Visitation* group at Reims. Instead, they reflect the elegant style of the royal court at Paris that had become the standard Gothic formula during the later thirteenth century. And with this change came a new treatment of relief. To Giovanni Pisano, space is as important as form. The figures are no longer tightly packed together. They are now spaced far enough apart to let us see the landscape setting, and each figure has its own pocket of space. Whereas Nicola's *Nativity* strikes us as a sequence of bulging, rounded masses, Giovanni's appears to be made up mainly of cavities and shadows.

Giovanni Pisano, then, follows the same trend toward disembodiment that we saw north of the Alps around 1300, only he does so in a more limited way. Compared to *The Virgin of Paris* (see fig. 11-48), his *Madonna* at Prato Cathedral (figs. 11-61 and 11-62) evokes memories of Nicola's style. The firmness of the modeling is emphasized by the strong turn of the head and the thrust-out left hip. We also note the heavy folds that anchor the figure to its base. Yet there can be no doubt that the Prato statue is derived from a French prototype that must have been rather like *The Virgin of Paris.* The back view, with its suggestion of "Gothic sway," reveals the connection more clearly than the front view, which hides the pose beneath a great swathe of drapery.

TOMBS. Italian Gothic church facades generally do not attempt to rival those of the French cathedrals. The French Gothic portal,

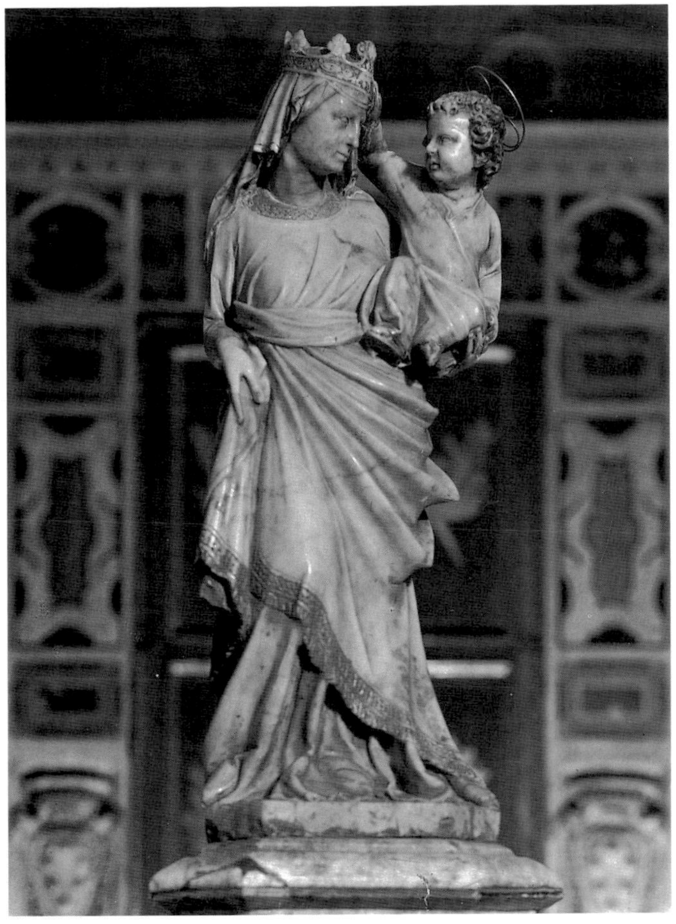

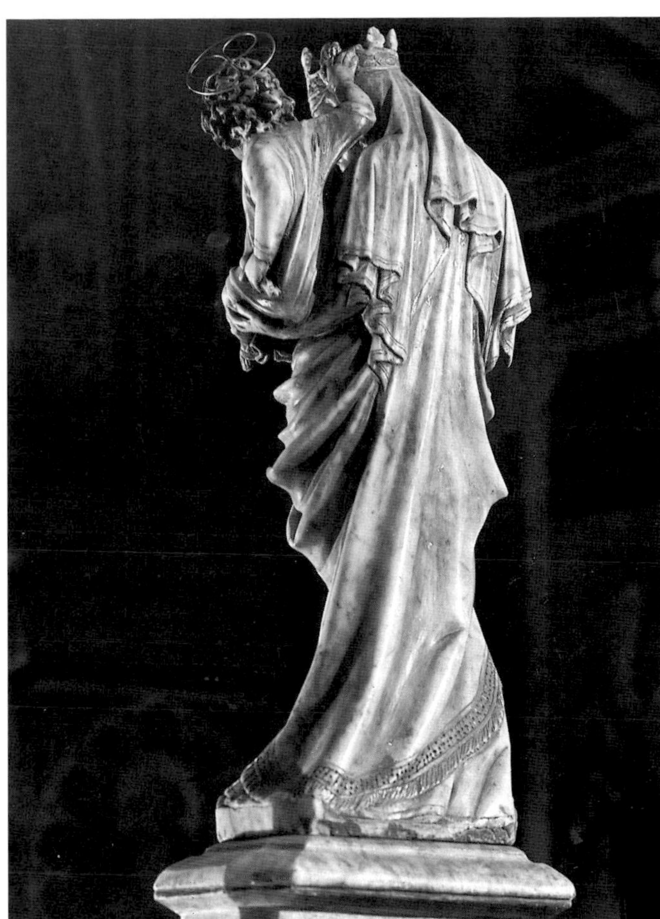

11-61, 11-62. Giovanni Pisano. *Madonna.* c. 1315. Marble, height 27" (68.7 cm). Prato Cathedral

with its jamb statues and richly carved tympanum, never found favor in the south. Instead, we often find a survival of Romanesque traditions of architectural sculpture, such as statues in niches or small-scale reliefs on wall surfaces (compare figs. 10-30 and 11-38). Italian Gothic sculpture excelled in the field that we have called church furniture—pulpits, screens, shrines, and tombs. Among the tombs, the most remarkable is the monument of Can Grande della Scala, the lord of Verona. This tall structure was built out-of-doors next to the church of Sta. Maria Antica and is now in the courtyard of the Castelvecchio. It consists of a vaulted canopy housing the sarcophagus; above there is a truncated pyramid, which supports an equestrian statue of the deceased (fig. 11-63). The ruler, astride his richly outfitted mount, is shown in full armor, sword in hand, as if he were standing on a windswept hill at the head of his troops. In a supreme display of self-confidence, he wears a broad grin. Clearly, this is no Christian soldier, no crusading knight, no embodiment of the ideals of chivalry, but a frank glorification of power.

Can Grande, remembered today mainly as the friend and protector of Dante, was an extraordinary figure. [See Primary Sources, no. 30, page 372.] Although he held Verona as a fief from the German emperor, he called himself "the Great Khan," thus asserting his claim to the absolute sovereignty of an Asiatic potentate. His freestanding equestrian statue—a form of monument that had traditionally been reserved for emperors (see fig. 7-40)—conveys the same ambition in visual terms.

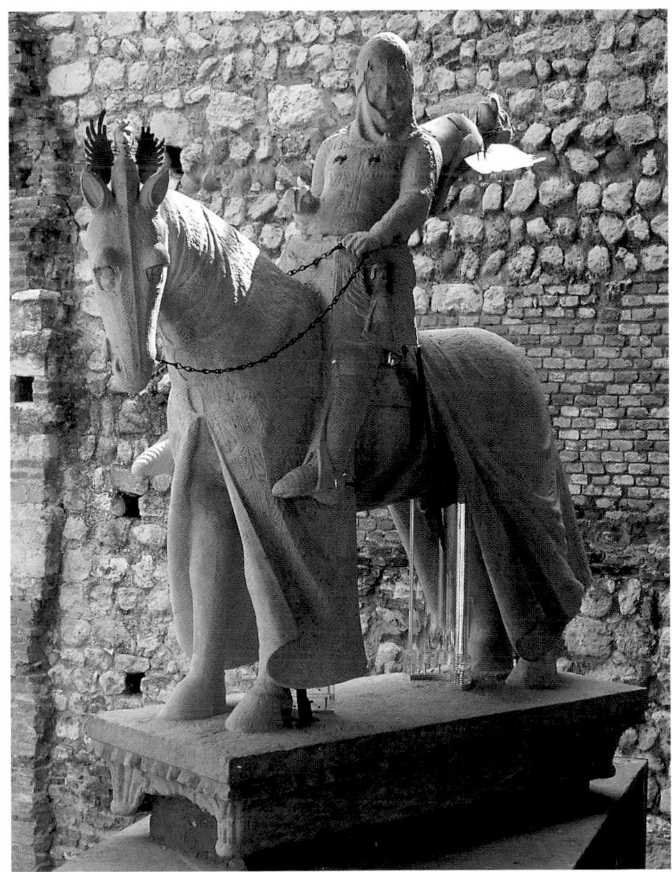

11-63. *Equestrian Statue of Can Grande della Scala,* from his tomb. 1330. Stone. Museo di Castelvecchio, Verona, Italy

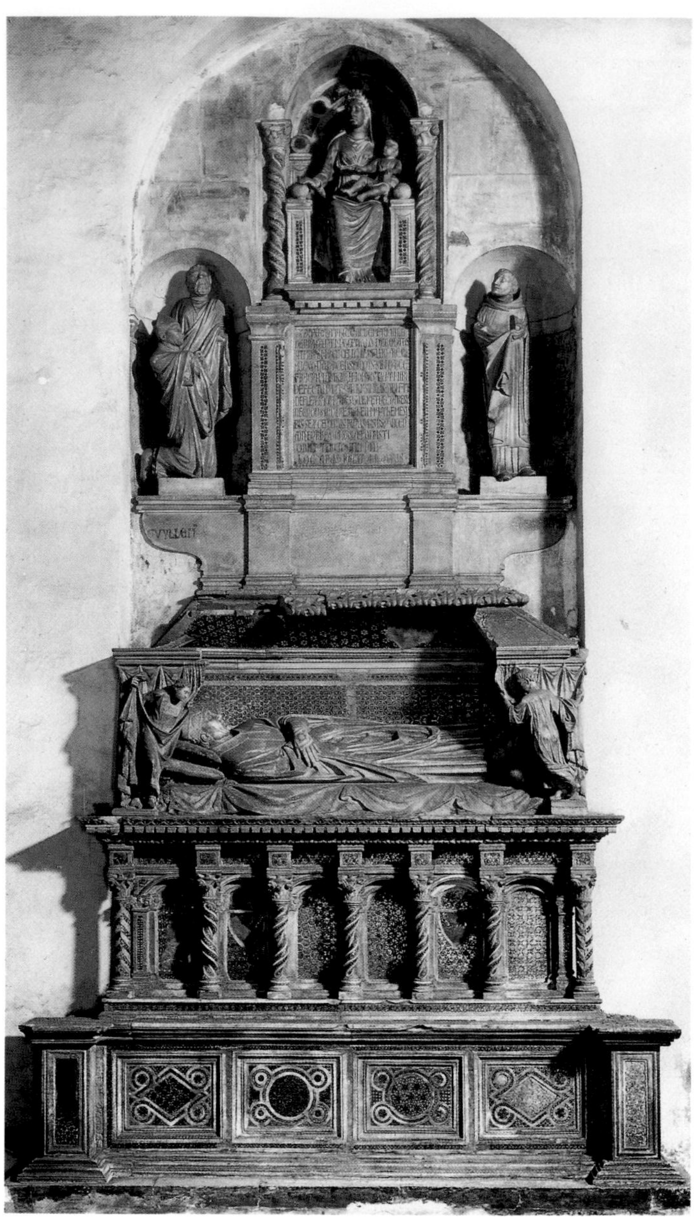

11-64. Arnolfo di Cambio. Tomb of Guglielmo de Braye. 1282. Marble. S. Domenico, Orvieto

ARNOLFO DI CAMBIO. The late thirteenth century saw the development of a new kind of tomb for leaders of the Catholic church. Its origins lie in French royal tombs, but the type spread quickly to Italy, where Arnolfo di Cambio gave it definitive form. Arnolfo had been an assistant to Nicola Pisano, under whom he developed a classicizing style that became even more emphatic after he moved to Rome. There he entered the employment of Charles of Anjou, which exposed him to French influences. The monument of Cardinal Guglielmo de Braye (fig. 11-64) reflects the artist's varied background. It combines several prototypes: a carved effigy resting on a sarcophagus and surmounted by a tableau of St. Mark presenting the deceased to the Virgin and Child. The tomb was originally housed in a tabernacle (now lost) rather than in its present shallow niche. Arnolfo's design proved so satisfying that it became the model followed by all other Italian sculptors for sepulchral monuments. Even without its architectural setting, the tomb has a grandeur befitting a prince of the church. The two angels solemnly closing the curtains add a human note that is as unexpected as it is touching.

GHIBERTI. During the later fourteenth century, Italy was especially hospitable to artistic influences from across the Alps, not only in architecture but in sculpture as well. These crosscurrents gave rise to the International Style about 1400. An outstanding representative of this style in Italian sculpture was Lorenzo Ghiberti (c. 1381–1455), a Florentine who as a youth must have had close contact with French art. We first encounter him in 1401–2, when he won a competition, later described in his *Commentaries,* for a pair of richly decorated bronze doors for the Baptistery of S. Giovanni in Florence. [See Primary Sources, no. 32, pages 372–73.] (It took him more than two decades to complete these doors, which fill the north portal of the building.) Each of the competing artists had to submit a trial relief, in a Gothic quatrefoil frame, depicting the Sacrifice of Isaac. Ghiberti's panel (fig. 11-65) strikes us first of all with the perfection of its craftsmanship, which reflects his training as a goldsmith. The silky shimmer of the surfaces and the wealth of beautifully articulated detail make it easy to understand why this entry was awarded the prize. If the composition seems somewhat lacking in dramatic force, that is characteristic of Ghiberti's calm, lyrical temper, which suited the taste of the period. Indeed, the figures, in their softly draped garments, have an air of courtly elegance even when they engage in acts of violence.

Ghiberti's doors were not the first ones on the Florence Baptistery. Some 70 years earlier Andrea da Pisano (no relation to Nicola or Giovanni Pisano; c. 1290–1348?) had received a commission for the south doors to rival those of Pisa Cathedral. In *The Baptism of Christ* (fig. 11-66), Andrea shows that he was an able follower of the painter Giotto (compare fig. 11-79). Ghiberti's doors are a direct outgrowth of Andrea's, which exercised great influence on Florentine art. But the differences are equally important. Andrea's reliefs must have seemed hopelessly old-fashioned to Ghiberti in their stiff, angular poses and simplified compositions. Although both artists were strongly influenced by French metalwork, Ghiberti's work shows the fluid grace and the tactile reality of International Style sculpture. These characteristics also grew out of French manuscript painting (compare fig. 11-89), whose intimacy appealed to Ghiberti.

However much his work may owe to French influence, Ghiberti shows himself to be thoroughly Italian in one respect: his admiration for ancient sculpture, which can be seen in the beautiful nude torso of Isaac. Here he revives a tradition of classicism that had reached its highest point in Nicola Pisano but had gradually died out during the fourteenth century. But Ghiberti is also the heir of Giovanni Pisano. In Giovanni's *Nativity* panel (see fig. 11-60) we noted a new emphasis on the spatial setting. Ghiberti's trial relief carries this tendency further and achieves a far more natural sense of recession. For the first time since classical antiquity, we experience the background of the panel not as a flat surface but as empty space from which the sculpted forms emerge, so that the angel in the upper right-hand corner seems to hover in midair. This pictorial quality relates Ghiberti's work to the painting of the International Style, where we find a similar concern with spatial depth and atmosphere (see pages 358–63). While not a revolutionary himself, he prepares the ground for the momentous changes that will mark the second decade of the fifteenth century in Florentine art and that we call the Early Renaissance.

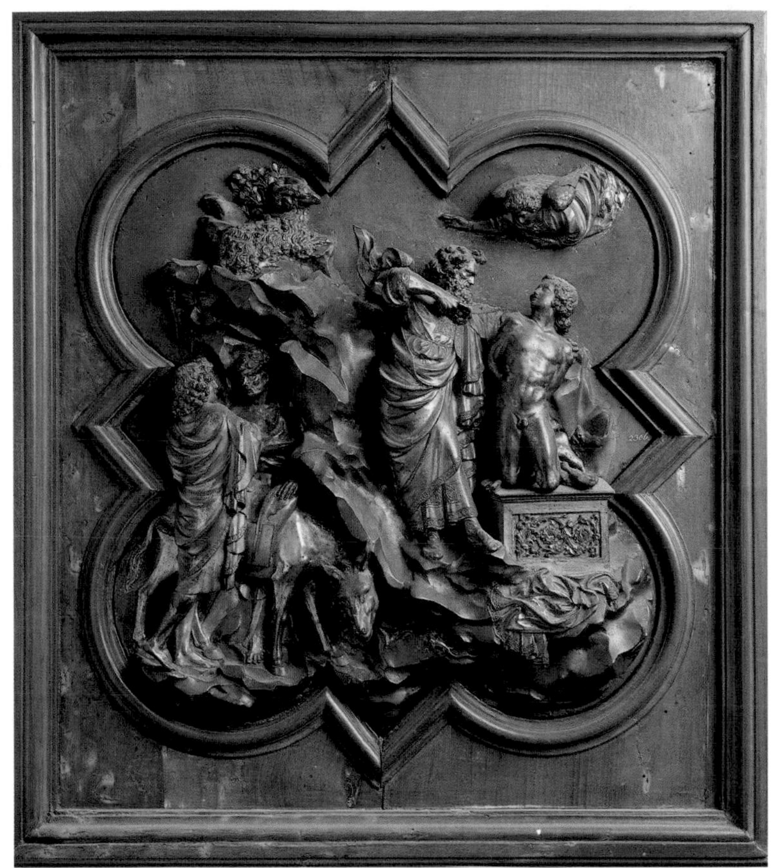

11-65. Lorenzo Ghiberti.
The Sacrifice of Isaac.
1401–2. Gilt bronze,
21 x 17" (53.3 x 43.4 cm).
Museo Nazionale del
Bargello, Florence

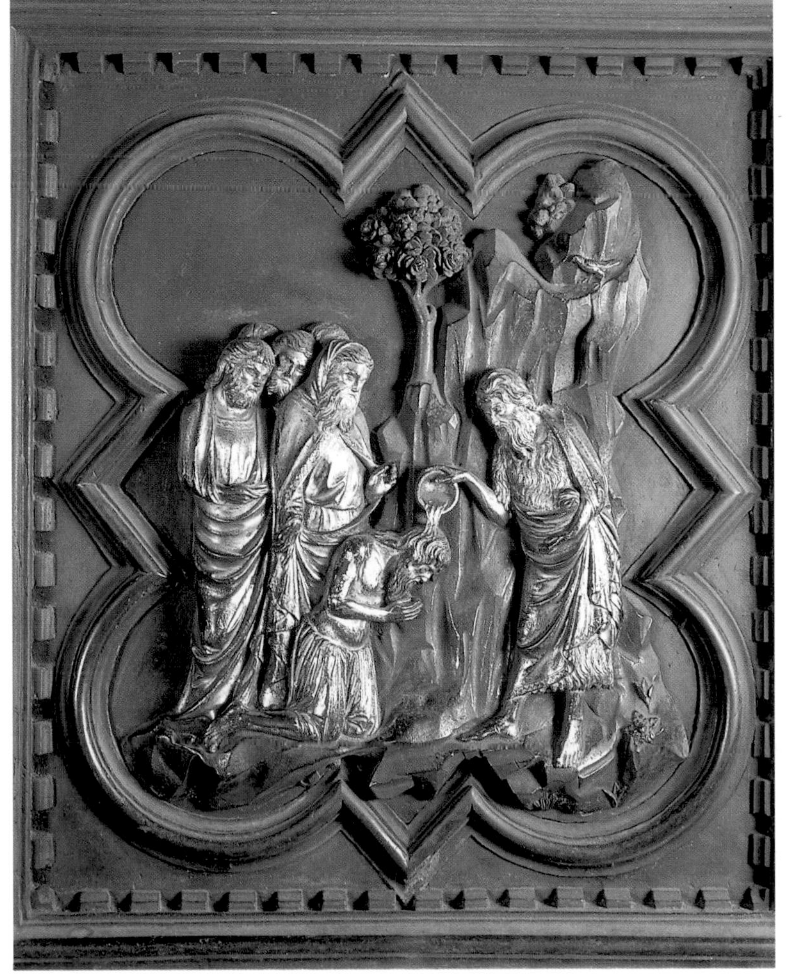

11-66. Andrea da Pisano.
The Baptism of Christ,
from the south doors,
Baptistery of S. Giovanni,
Florence. 1330–36.
Gilt bronze

PAINTING

France

STAINED GLASS. Although Gothic architecture and sculpture began so dramatically at St.-Denis and Chartres, Gothic painting developed at a rather slow pace in its early stages. The architectural style sponsored by Abbot Suger gave birth to a new conception of monumental sculpture almost at once, but it did not demand any radical change in painting. To be sure, Suger's account of the rebuilding of his church emphasizes the miraculous effect of stained-glass windows, with their "continuous light" flooding the interior. Stained glass was thus an integral element of Gothic architecture from the very beginning. Yet the technique of stained-glass painting had already been perfected in Romanesque times, and the style of stained-glass designs (especially single figures) sometimes remained surprisingly Romanesque for nearly another hundred years. Nonetheless, the "many masters from different regions" whom Suger assembled to execute the choir windows at St.-Denis faced a larger task and a more complex pictorial program than before.

During the next half-century, as Gothic structures became ever more skeletal and clerestory windows grew to huge size, stained glass displaced manuscript illumination as the leading form of painting. Since the production of stained glass was so closely linked with the great cathedral workshops, the designers were influenced more and more by architectural sculpture. The majestic *Notre Dame de la Belle Verrière* (fig. 11-67) at Chartres Cathedral is the finest early example of this process. The design recalls the relief on the west portal of the church (see fig. 11-41) but lacks some of its sculptural qualities. Moreover, it still betrays its Byzantine ancestry. By comparison, however, even the mosaic of the same subject in Hagia Sophia (see fig. 8-46) seems remarkably solid. The stained glass dissolves the group into a weightless mass that hovers effortlessly in indeterminate space.

The window consists of hundreds of small pieces of tinted glass bound together by strips of lead. The maximum size of these pieces was limited by the primitive methods of medieval glass manufacture, so that the design could not simply be "painted on glass." [See Primary Sources, no. 34, pages 373–74.] Rather, the window was painted *with* glass. It was assembled in somewhat the way one would put together a mosaic or a jigsaw puzzle, out of odd-shaped fragments cut to fit the contours of the forms. Only the finer details, such as eyes, hair, and drapery folds, were added by painting—or drawing—in black or gray on the glass surfaces. This process encourages an abstract, ornamental style, which tends to resist any attempt to render three-dimensional effects. Only in the hands of a great master could the maze of lead strips lead to such monumental figures.

The stained-glass workers who filled the windows of the great Gothic cathedrals also had to face the difficulties arising from the enormous scale of their work. No Romanesque painter had ever been called upon to cover areas so vast or so firmly bound into an architectural framework. The task required a degree of orderly planning that had no precedent in medieval painting.

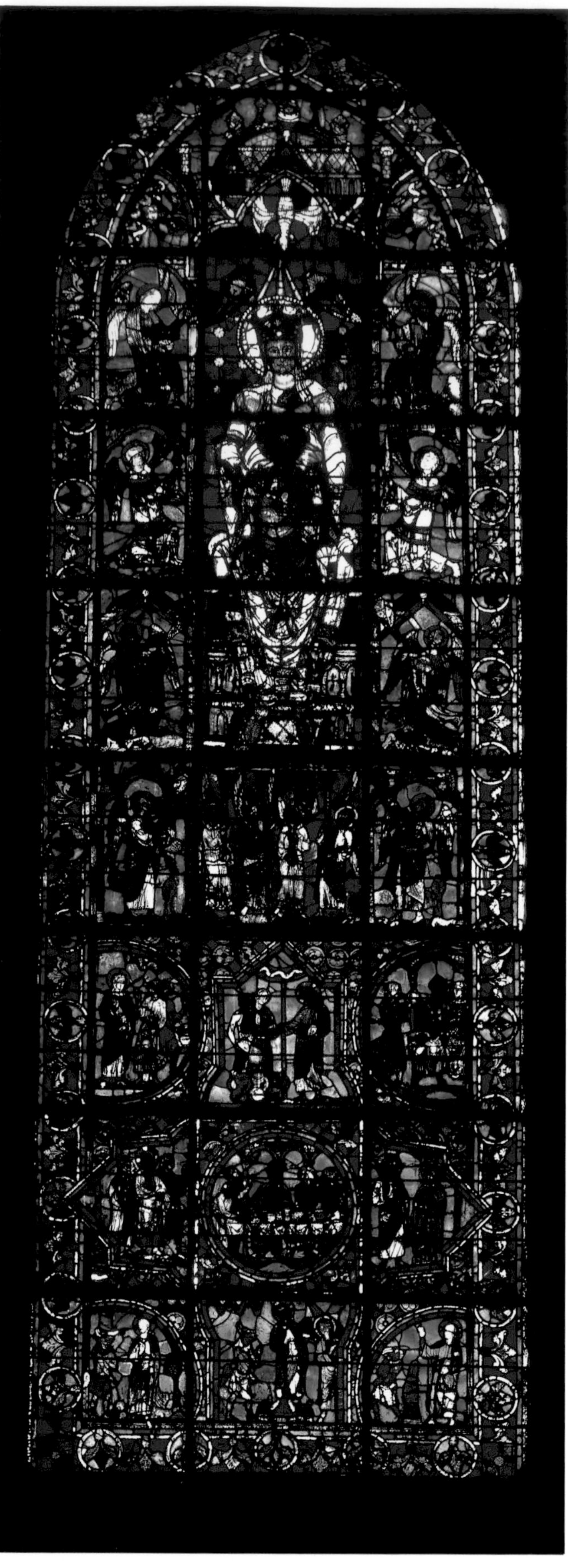

11-67. *Notre Dame de la Belle Verrière.* c. 1170. Stained-glass window, height approx. 14' (4.27 m). Chartres Cathedral

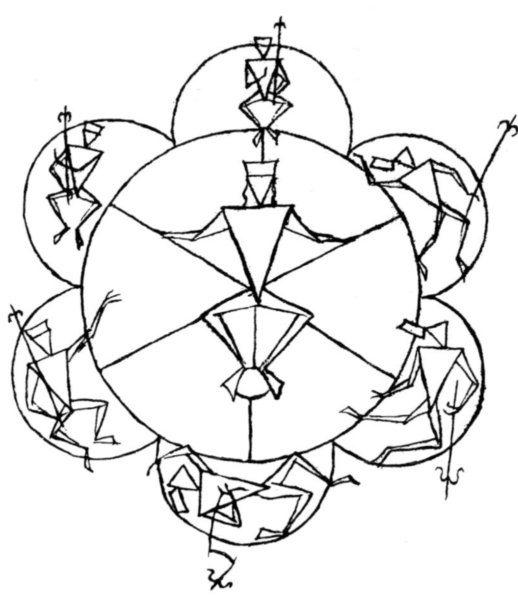

11-68. Villard de Honnecourt. *Wheel of Fortune.* c. 1240. Bibliothèque Nationale, Paris

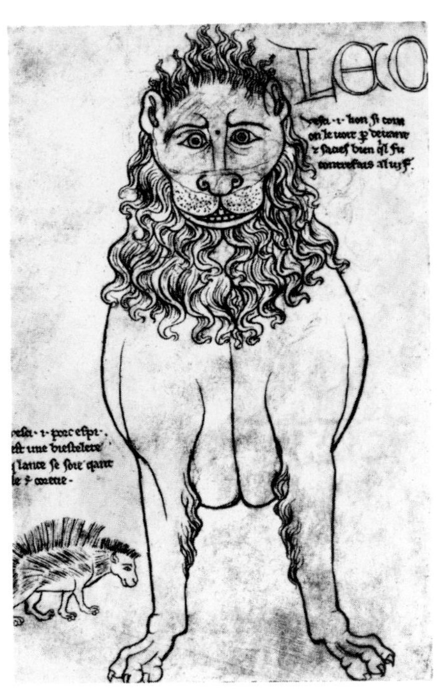

11-69. Villard de Honnecourt. *Front View of a Lion.* c. 1240. Bibliothèque Nationale, Paris

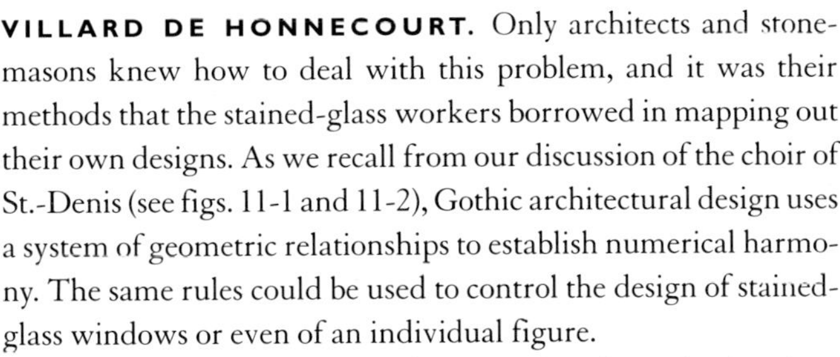

VILLARD DE HONNECOURT. Only architects and stonemasons knew how to deal with this problem, and it was their methods that the stained-glass workers borrowed in mapping out their own designs. As we recall from our discussion of the choir of St.-Denis (see figs. 11-1 and 11-2), Gothic architectural design uses a system of geometric relationships to establish numerical harmony. The same rules could be used to control the design of stained-glass windows or even of an individual figure.

We gain some insight into this procedure from the drawings in a notebook compiled about 1240 by the architect Villard de Honnecourt. What we see in the *Wheel of Fortune* (fig. 11-68) is not the final version of the design but the system of circles and triangles on which the image is based. The fundamental importance of these geometric schemes is illustrated by another drawing from the same notebook, the *Front View of a Lion* (fig. 11-69). According to the inscription, Villard has portrayed the animal from life. A closer look at the figure shows us that he was able to do so only after he had laid down a geometric pattern: a circle for the face (the dot between the eyes is its center) and a second, larger circle for the body. [See Primary Sources, no. 35, page 374.] To Villard, then, drawing from life meant something far different from what it does to us. It meant filling in an abstract framework with details based on direct observation.

The period 1200–1250 might be termed the golden age of stained glass. After that, as architectural activity declined and the demand for stained glass began to slacken, manuscript illumination gradually regained its former position of leadership. By then, however, miniature painting had been thoroughly influenced by both stained glass and stone sculpture, the artistic pacemakers of the first half of the century.

ILLUMINATED MANUSCRIPTS. The resulting change of style can be seen in figure 11-70, from a psalter done about 1260 for King Louis IX (St. Louis) of France. The scene illustrates I Samuel 11:2, in which Nahash the Ammonite threatens the Jews at Jabesh. We first notice the careful symmetry of the framework, which consists of flat, ornamented panels. The architectural setting is remarkably similar to the choir screen by the Naumburg Master (see fig. 11-51). It also recalls the canopies above the heads of jamb statues (see fig. 11-42) and the arched twin niches that enclose the relief of *Melchizedek and Abraham* at Reims (see fig. 11-47).

Against this two-dimensional background, the figures are "relieved" by smooth and skillful modeling. But their sculptural quality stops short at the outer contours, which are defined by heavy dark lines rather like the lead strips in stained-glass windows. The figures themselves show all the features of the elegant style originated about 20 years earlier by the sculptors of the royal court: graceful gestures, swaying poses, smiling faces, and neatly waved strands of hair (compare the *Annunciation* angel in figure 11-46 and *Melchizedek* in figure 11-47). Our miniature thus exemplifies the subtle and refined taste that made the court art of Paris the standard for all Europe. We find no trace of the expressive energy of Romanesque painting (see figs. 9-3 and 9-5).

MASTER HONORÉ. Until the thirteenth century, illuminated manuscripts had been produced in the scriptoria of monasteries. Now, along with many other activities that were once the special preserve of the clergy, it shifted to urban workshops organized by laymen, the ancestors of the publishing houses of today. Here again the workshops of sculptors and stained-glass painters may have set the pattern.

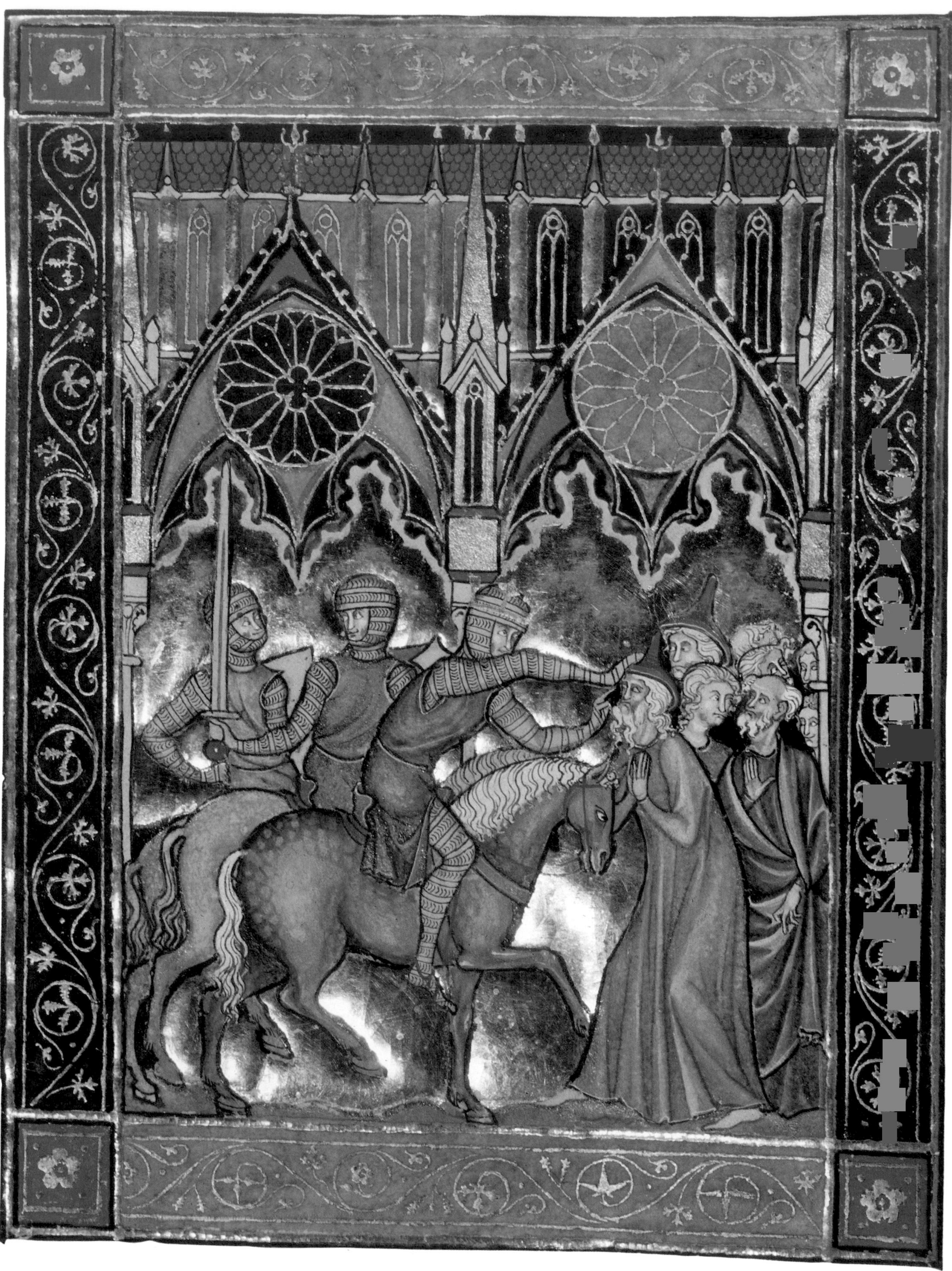

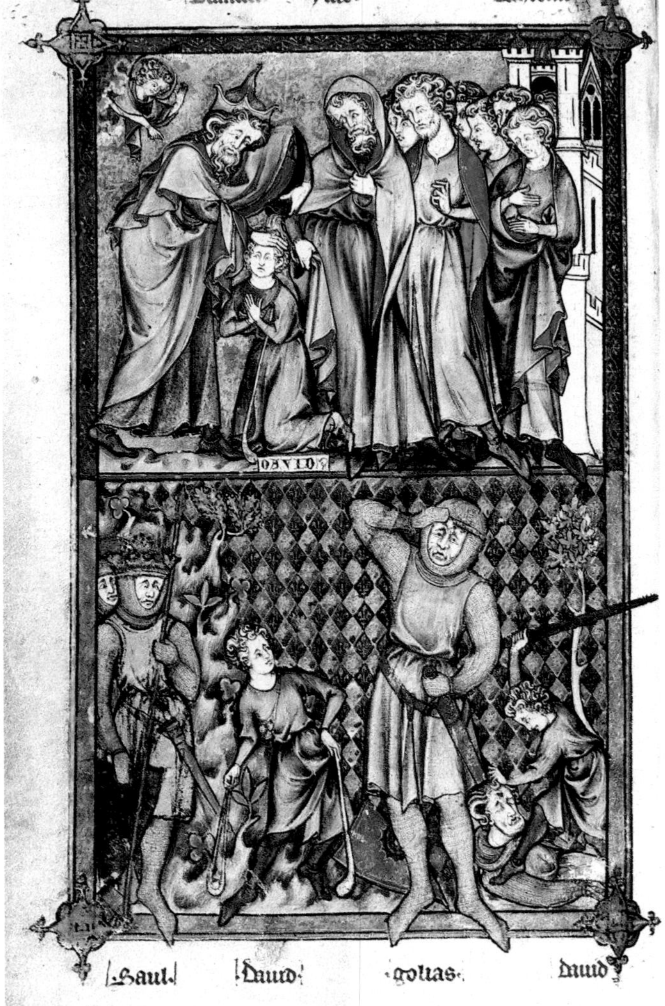

11-71. Master Honoré. *David and Goliath,* from the *Prayer Book of Philip the Fair.* 1295. Bibliothèque Nationale, Paris

Some of these new, secular illuminators are known to us by name. Among them is Master Honoré of Paris, who in 1295 did the miniatures in the *Prayer Book of Philip the Fair.* Our sample (fig. 11-71) shows him working in a style derived from the *Psalter of St. Louis.* Here, however, the framework no longer dominates the composition. The figures have become larger, and their relieflike modeling is more emphatic. They are even allowed to overlap the frame, a device that helps to detach them from the flat pattern of the background and thus introduces a certain, though very limited, spatial range into the picture.

Italy

Italian painting at the end of the thirteenth century produced an outpouring of creative energy as spectacular, and as far-reaching in its impact on the future, as the rise of the Gothic cathedral in France. A glance at Giotto's *Lamentation* (see fig. 11-79) will convince us that we are faced with a truly revolutionary development.

(Opposite) 11-70. *Nahash the Ammonite Threatening the Jews at Jabesh,* from the *Psalter of St. Louis.* c. 1260. 5 x 3½" (17.7 x 8.9 cm). Bibliothèque Nationale, Paris

How could a work of such intense dramatic power be conceived by a contemporary of Master Honoré? What were the conditions that made it possible? Oddly enough, as we look into the background of Giotto's art, we find that it arose from the same "old-fashioned" attitudes we met in Italian Gothic architecture and sculpture.

Medieval Italy, although strongly influenced by Northern art from Carolingian times on, had maintained contact with Byzantine civilization. As a result, panel painting, mosaic, and murals—media that had never taken firm root north of the Alps—were kept alive on Italian soil, though barely. Indeed, a new wave of influences from Byzantine art, which enjoyed a resurgence during the thirteenth century, overwhelmed the Romanesque elements in Italian painting at the very time when stained glass became the dominant pictorial medium in France.

There is a certain irony in the fact that this neo-Byzantine style appeared soon after the conquest of Constantinople by the armies of the Fourth Crusade in 1204. (One thinks of the way Greek art had once captured the taste of the Romans.) Pisa, whose navy made it a power in the eastern Mediterranean, was the first to develop a school of painting based on this "Greek manner," as the Italians called it. In some cases it was transplanted by Byzantine artists who had fled Constantinople during the Crusades. Giorgio Vasari later wrote that in the mid-thirteenth century, "Some Greek painters were summoned to Florence by the government of the city for no other purpose than the revival of painting in their midst, since that art was not so much debased as altogether lost."

There may be more truth to this statement than is often acknowledged. The Byzantine tradition had preserved Early Christian narrative art virtually intact. When transmitted to the West, this tradition led to an explosion of subjects and designs that had been essentially lost for nearly 700 years. Many of them, of course, had been available all along in the mosaics of Rome and Ravenna. There had also been successive waves of Byzantine influence throughout the early Middle Ages and the Romanesque period. Nevertheless, they lay dormant, so to speak, until interest in them was reawakened through closer relations with Constantinople, which enabled Italian painters to absorb Byzantine art far more thoroughly than ever before. During this same period, we recall, Italian architects and sculptors took a different course: untouched by the Greek manner, they were assimilating the Gothic style. Eventually, toward 1300, Gothic influence spilled over into painting as well, and its interaction with the neo-Byzantine produced the revolutionary new style.

TEMPERA. During the Gothic era altarpieces were painted on wood panel in tempera, an egg-based medium that dries quickly to form an extremely tough surface. The preparation of the panel was a complex, time-consuming process. First it was planed and coated with a mixture of plaster and glue known as gesso, which was sometimes reinforced with linen. Once the design had been drawn, the background was almost invariably filled in with gold leaf over red sizing. Then the underpainting, generally a green earth pigment (*terra verde*), was added. The image itself was painted in numerous layers of thin tempera with very fine brushes, a painstaking process that placed a premium on neatness, since few corrections were possible.

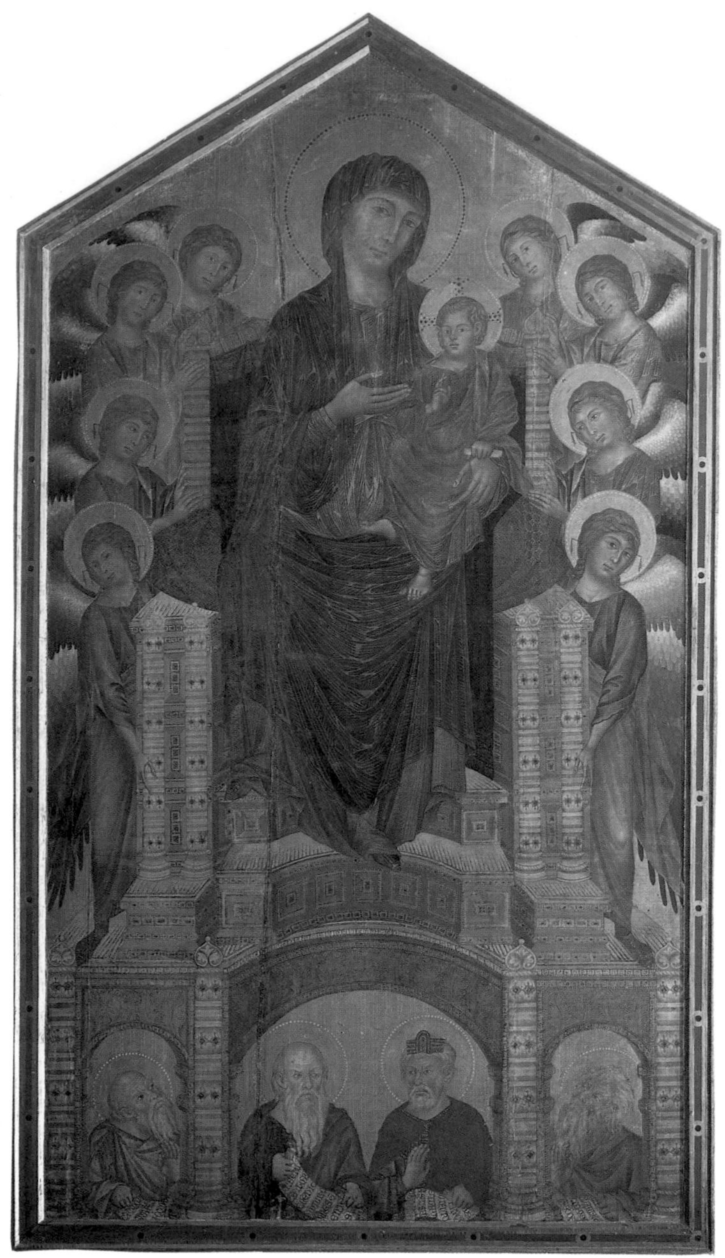

11-72. Cimabue. *Madonna Enthroned.* c. 1280–90. Tempera on panel, 12'7½" x 7'4" (3.9 x 2.2 m). Galleria degli Uffizi, Florence

CIMABUE. Among the most famous painters of the Greek manner was the Florentine master Cimabue (c. 1250–after 1300). Vasari claims that he was apprenticed to a Greek painter and that he became Giotto's teacher. His huge altar panel, *Madonna Enthroned* (fig. 11-72), rivals the finest Byzantine icons or mosaics (compare figs. 8-46 and 8-55). What distinguishes it from them is mainly a greater severity of design and expression, which befits its huge size. Panels on such a monumental scale had rarely been attempted in the East. Equally un-Byzantine is the picture's gabled shape and the way the throne of inlaid wood seems to echo it. The geometric inlays, like the throne's architectural style, remind us of the Florence Baptistery (see fig. 10-19).

DUCCIO. A quarter century later Duccio of Siena (c. 1255–before 1319) painted another *Madonna Enthroned* (fig. 11-73) for the main altar of Siena Cathedral. It was called the *Maestà* (majesty) to identify the Virgin's role as the Queen of Heaven surrounded by her court of saints and angels. [See Primary Sources, no. 36, page 374.] At first glance, the picture may seem much like Cimabue's, since both follow the same basic scheme. Yet the differences are important. They reflect not only contrasting personalities and local tastes—the gentleness of Duccio is characteristic of Siena—but also the rapid evolution of style.

In Duccio's hands, the Greek manner has become unfrozen. The rigid, angular draperies have given way to an undulating softness. The abstract shading-in-reverse with lines of gold is kept to a minimum. The bodies, faces, and hands are beginning to swell with three-dimensional life. Clearly, the heritage of Hellenistic-Roman illusionism that had always been part of the Byzantine tradition, however dormant or submerged, is asserting itself once more. But there is also a half-hidden Gothic element here. We sense it in the fluency of the drapery, the appealing naturalness of

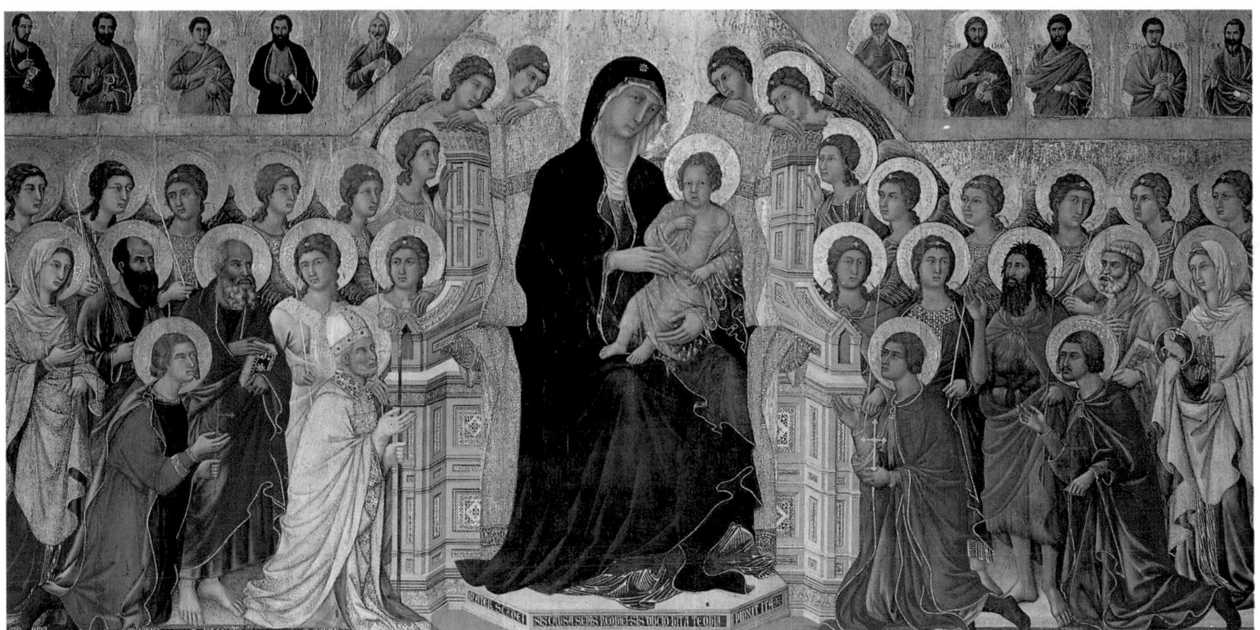

11-73. Duccio. *Madonna Enthroned,* center of the *Maestà Altar.* 1308–11. Tempera on panel, height 6'10½" (2.1 m). Museo dell'Opera del Duomo, Siena

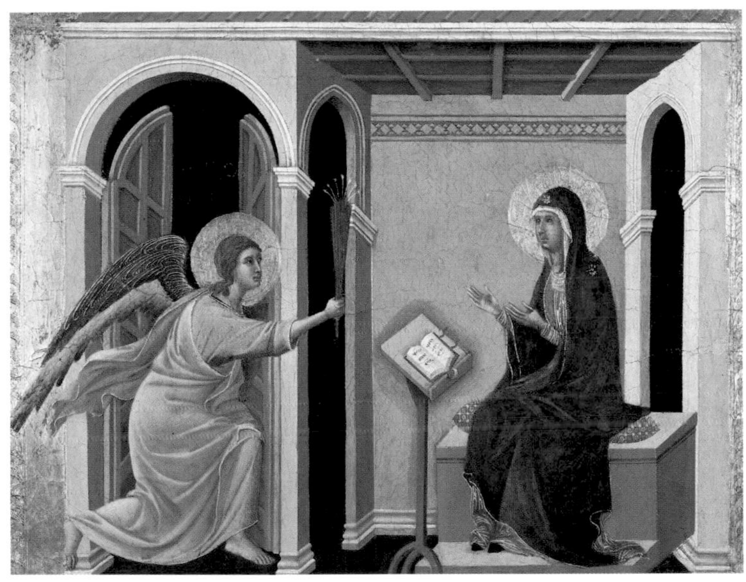

11-74. Duccio. *Annunciation of the Death of the Virgin,* from the *Maestà Altar*

the Infant Christ, and the tender glances by which the figures communicate with each other. The chief source of this Gothic influence must have been Giovanni Pisano (see page 336), who was in Siena from 1285 to 1295 as the sculptor–architect in charge of the cathedral facade.

On the reverse side of the *Maestà* are many small scenes from the lives of Christ and the Virgin. In these panels, Duccio's most mature works, the interaction of Gothic and Byzantine elements has given rise to a major new development. Here we see a new kind of picture space and, with it, a new treatment of narrative. The *Annunciation of the Death of the Virgin* (fig. 11-74) shows us something we have never seen before: two figures enclosed by an architectural interior.

Ancient painters and their Byzantine successors were unable to achieve this space. Their architectural settings always stay behind the figures, so that their indoor scenes tend to look as if they were taking place in an open-air theater, on a stage without a roof. Duccio's figures, in contrast, inhabit a space that is created and defined by the architecture, as if the artist had carved a niche into his panel. The origin of this spatial framework is derived from the architectural "housing" of Gothic sculpture (compare figs. 11-47 and 11-51). Northern Gothic painters, too, had tried to reproduce these architectural settings, but they could do so only by flattening them out completely (as in the *Psalter of St. Louis,* see fig. 11-70). Because they were trained in the Greek manner, the Italian painters of Duccio's generation, on the other hand, learned enough of the devices of Hellenistic-Roman illusionism (see fig. 7-52) to let them render such a framework without draining its

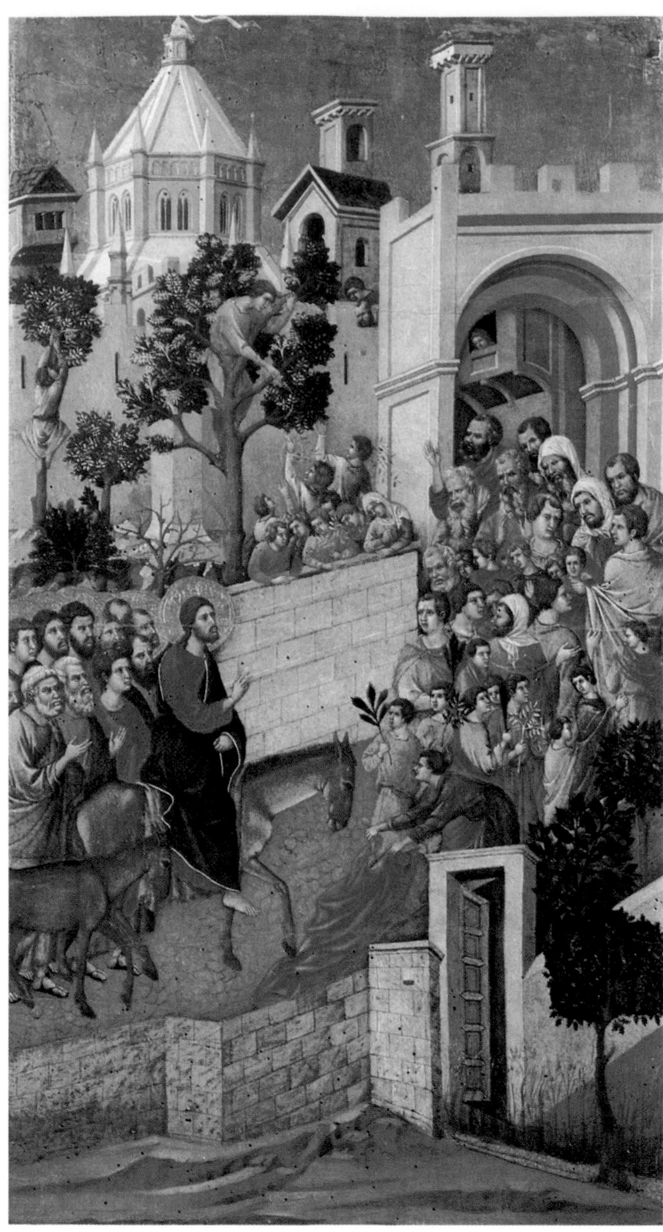

11-75. Duccio. *Christ Entering Jerusalem,* from the back of the *Maestà Altar.* 1308–11. Tempera on panel, 40½ x 21⅛" (103 x 53.7 cm). Museo dell'Opera del Duomo, Siena

three-dimensionality. Duccio, however, is not interested simply in space for its own sake. The architecture is used to integrate the figures within the drama more convincingly than ever before.

Even in the outdoor scenes on the back of the *Maestà,* such as *Christ Entering Jerusalem* (fig. 11-75), the architecture keeps its space-creating function. The diagonal movement into depth is conveyed not by the figures, which have the same scale throughout, but by the walls on either side of the road leading to the city, by the gate that frames the crowd, and by the structures beyond. Whatever the shortcomings of Duccio's perspective, his architecture is able to contain and enclose. For that reason, it seems more understandable than similar views in ancient or Byzantine art (compare figs. 7-48 and 8-56). The composition, which goes back to Early Christian times (see box pages 228–29), is otherwise based directly on a Byzantine example that was fully developed by the late tenth century.

GIOTTO. In Giotto (1267?–1336/7) we meet an artist of far bolder and more dramatic temper. Ten to 15 years younger than Duccio, Giotto was less close to the Greek manner from the start, despite his probable apprenticeship under Cimabue. [See Primary Sources, nos. 31 and 33, pages 372–373.] As a Florentine, he fell heir to Cimabue's sense of monumental scale, which made him a wall painter by instinct, rather than a panel painter. The art of Giotto is nevertheless so daringly original that its sources are far more difficult to trace than those of Duccio's style. Apart from his knowledge of the Greek manner as represented by Cimabue, the young Giotto seems to have been familiar with the work of the neo-Byzantine masters of Rome. Among them was Cimabue's contemporary Pietro Cavallini (documented 1272–1303), who worked in both mosaic and fresco. Cavallini's style is an astonishing blend of Byzantine, Roman, and Early Christian elements. The figures in his *Last Judgment* (fig. 11-76) are in the best up-to-date manner of

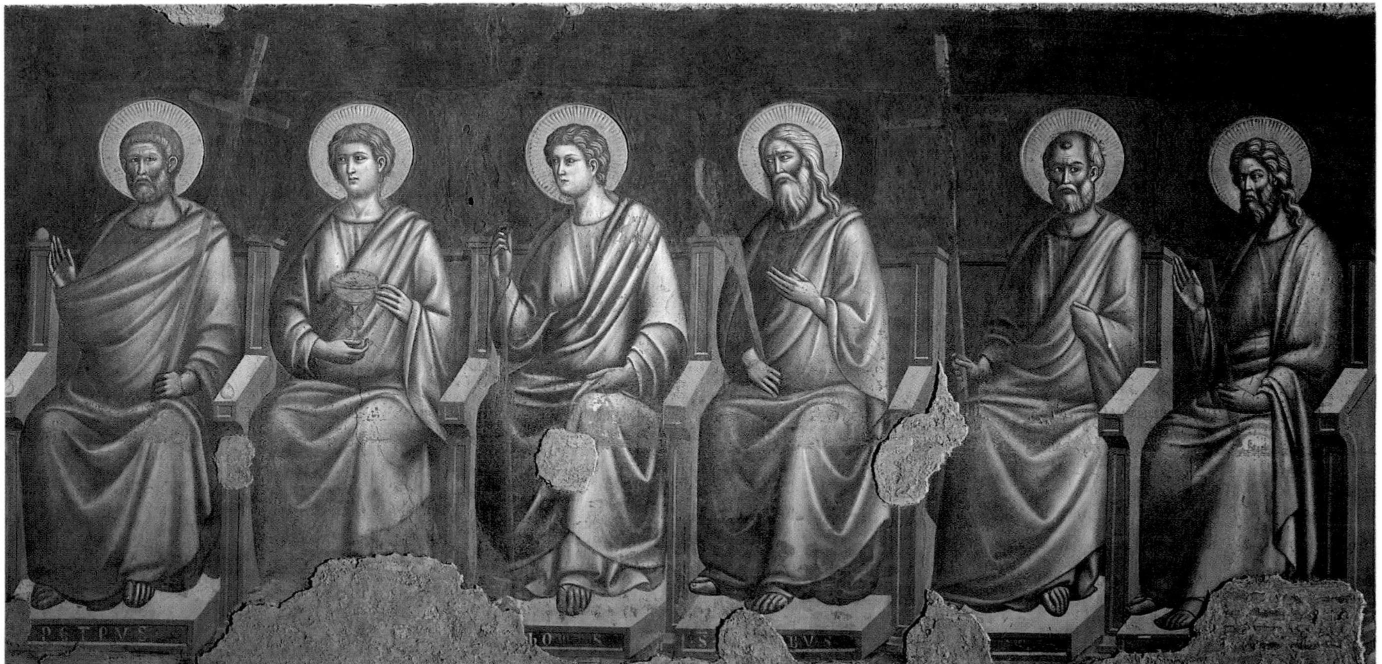

11-76. Pietro Cavallini. *Seated Apostles,* from *The Last Judgment.* c. 1290. Fresco. Sta. Cecilia in Trastevere, Rome

Late Byzantine art (compare the *Anastasis* in fig. 8-57), but he has modeled them in a soft daylight that must have come from exposure to antique wall painting (see fig. 7-54). (He was also a fresco restorer.) The result is an almost sculptural monumentality that is remarkably classical. Indeed, these saints have the same calm air and gentle gravity found on the *Sarcophagus of Junius Bassus* (see fig. 8-21), but with the relaxed naturalness of the Gothic.

Cavallini set an important example for Giotto. In Rome Giotto, too, must have become acquainted with Early Christian and ancient Roman mural painting. Classical sculpture likewise seems to have left an impression on him. More fundamental, however, was the influence of late medieval Italian sculptors: Nicola and Giovanni Pisano, and especially Arnolfo di Cambio. It was through them that Giotto came in contact with Northern Gothic art. The latter remains the most important of all the elements that entered into Giotto's style. Indeed, Northern works such as those in figure 11-53 and figure 11-61 are almost certainly the ultimate source of the emotional quality that characterizes his work.

Of Giotto's surviving murals, those in the Arena Chapel in Padua, painted in 1305–6, are the best preserved as well as the most characteristic. They are devoted mainly to events from the life of Christ, arranged in three tiers of narrative scenes (see fig. 11-78) that culminate in the *Last Judgment* at the west end of the chapel. Giotto depicts many of the same subjects that we find on the reverse of Duccio's *Maestà,* including *Christ Entering Jerusalem* (fig. 11-77). But where Duccio has enriched the traditional scheme, spatially as well as narratively, Giotto simplifies it. The two versions have much in common, since both ultimately derive from Byzantine sources. Giotto's painting, however, suggests the example of Byzantine mosaics done on Italian soil during the twelfth century, such as one in the Palatine Chapel at Palermo. The action proceeds parallel to the picture plane. Landscape, architecture, and figures have been reduced to a minimum. The austerity of Giotto's art is emphasized by the sober medium of fresco painting, with its limited range and intensity of tones. By contrast, Duccio's picture, which is executed in egg tempera on gold ground, has a jewel-like brilliance and sparkling colors. Yet Giotto's work has a far more powerful impact. It makes us feel so close to the event that we have a sense of being direct participants rather than distant observers.

How does the artist achieve this extraordinary effect? He does so, first of all, by having the entire scene take place in the foreground. Even more important, he presents it in such a way that the viewer's eye level falls within the lower half of the picture. Thus we can imagine ourselves standing on the same ground plane as the figures, even though we actually see them from well below. In contrast,

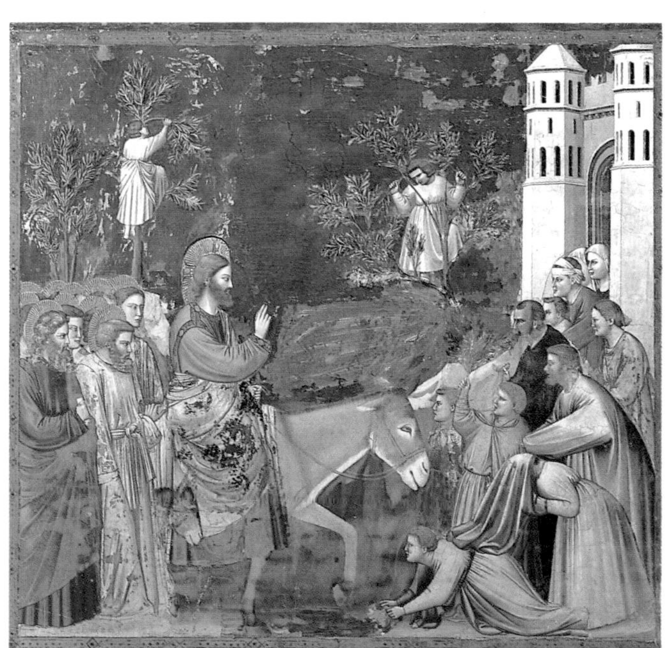

11-77. Giotto. *Christ Entering Jerusalem.* 1305–6. Fresco. Arena (Scrovegni) Chapel, Padua, Italy

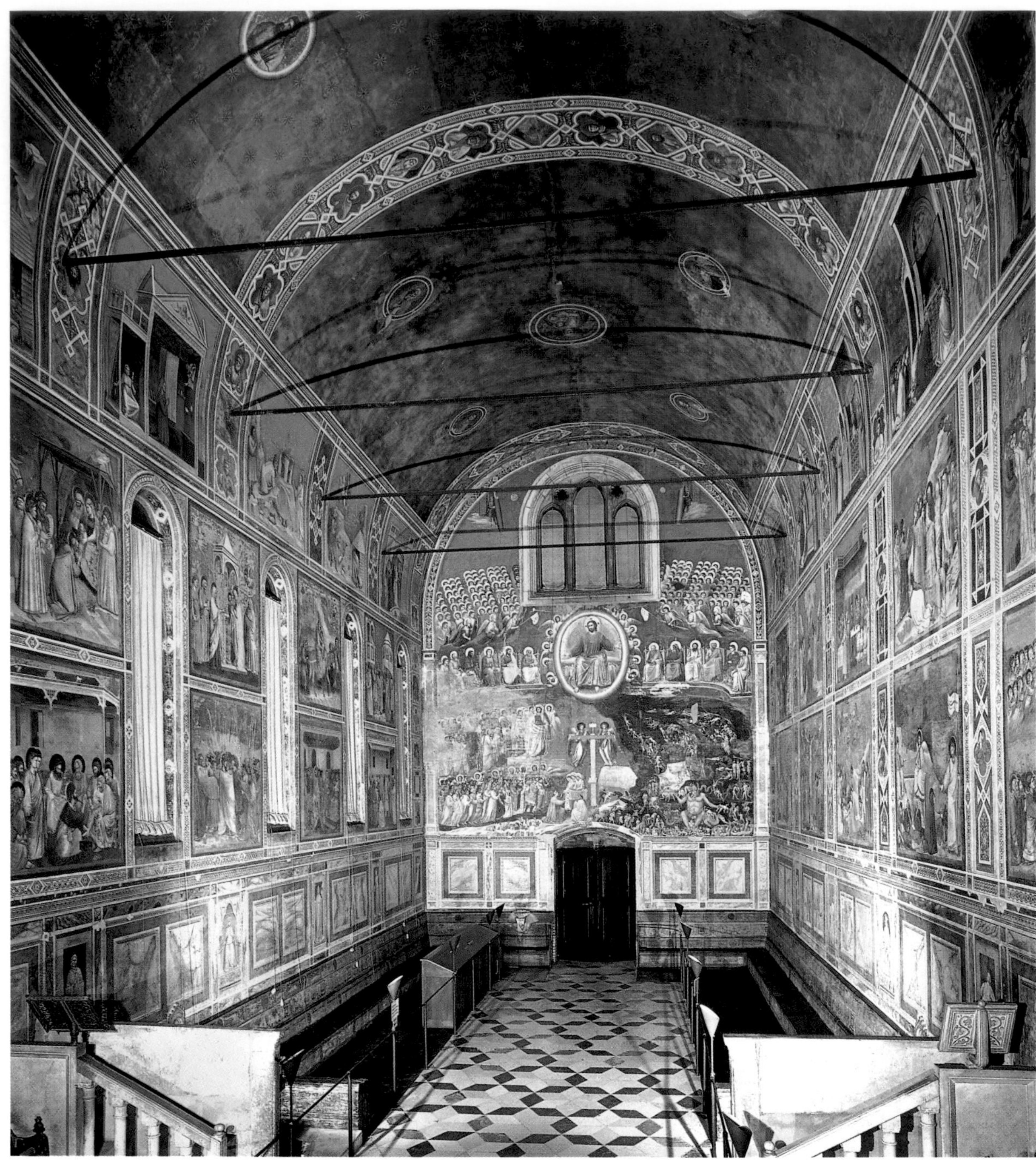

11-78. Interior, Arena (Scrovegni) Chapel, Padua, Italy. 1305–6

Duccio makes us survey the scene from above in "bird's-eye" perspective. The effects of this choice of viewpoint are far-reaching. Choice implies conscious awareness—in this case, awareness of a relationship in space between the beholder and the picture. Duccio does not yet treat his picture space as continuous with the viewer's space. Hence we have the feeling of floating above the scene. Even ancient painting at its most illusionistic does not tell us where we stand (see figs. 7-48 and 7-52) as Giotto does. Above all, Giotto gives his forms a strong three-dimensional reality that makes them seem as solid and tangible as sculpture in the round.

With Giotto it is the figures, rather than the framework, that create the picture space. As a result, this space is more limited than Duccio's. Its depth extends no further than the combined volumes of the overlapping bodies in the picture—but within its limits it is much more persuasive. To Giotto's contemporaries, the tactile quality of his art must have seemed a near-miracle. It was this characteristic that made them praise him as equal, or even superior, to the greatest of the ancient painters. His forms looked so lifelike that they could be mistaken for reality itself. Equally significant are the stories linking Giotto with the claim that painting is superior to sculpture. This was not an idle boast, as it turned out, for Giotto does indeed mark the start of what might be called "the era of painting" in Western art. The symbolic turning point is the year 1334, when he was appointed head of the Florence Cathedral workshop, an honor that until then had been reserved for architects or sculptors.

Giotto's aim was not simply to transplant Gothic statuary into painting. By creating a radically new kind of picture space, he had also sharpened his awareness of the picture surface. When we look at a work by Duccio (or his ancient and medieval predecessors), we tend to do so in installments, as it were. Our glance travels from detail to detail until we have surveyed the entire area. Giotto, on the contrary, invites us to see the whole at one glance. His large, simple forms, the strong grouping of his figures, and the limited depth of his "stage" give his scenes an inner coherence never found before. Notice how dramatically the massed verticals of the "block" of apostles on the left are contrasted with the upward slope formed by the welcoming crowd on the right, and how Jesus, alone in the center, bridges the gulf between the two groups. The more we study the composition, the more we come to realize its majestic firmness and clarity. Thus the artist has rephrased the traditional pattern of Christ's entry into Jerusalem to stress the solemnity of the event as the triumphal procession of the Prince of Peace.

Giotto's achievement as a master of design does not fully emerge from any single work. Only if we examine a number of scenes from the Padua fresco cycle do we see how closely each composition is attuned to the emotional content of the subject. *The Lamentation* (fig. 11-79) was clearly inspired by a Byzantine example similar to the Nerezi fresco (see fig. 8-51), which was known in Italy early on. The differences, however, are as important as the similarities. In its muted expression this *Lamentation* is closer to the Gothic *Death of the Virgin* on Strasbourg Cathedral (see fig. 11-45) than it is to the anguish conveyed so vividly by the Byzantine painter. The tragic mood, found also in religious texts of the era, is brought home to us by the formal rhythm of the design as much as by the gestures and expressions of the participants. [See Primary Sources, no. 28, page 371.] The low center of gravity, and the hunched figures convey the somber quality of the scene and arouse our compassion even before we have grasped the meaning of the event. With extraordinary boldness, Giotto sets off the frozen grief of the human mourners against the frantic movement of the weeping angels among the clouds. It is as if the figures on the ground were restrained by their obligation to maintain the stability of the composition while the angels, small and weightless as birds, do not share this duty.

Once again the impact of the drama is heightened by the simple setting. The descending slope of the hill acts as a unifying element. At the same time, it directs our glance toward the heads of Christ and the Virgin, which are the focal point of the scene. Even the tree has a twin function. Its barrenness and isolation suggest that all of nature shares in the sorrow over the Savior's death. Yet it also carries a more precise symbolic message: it alludes (as does Dante in a passage in *The Divine Comedy*) to the Tree of Knowledge, which the sin of Adam and Eve had caused to wither and which was to be restored to life through the sacrificial death of Christ.

What we have said of the Padua frescoes applies equally to the *Madonna Enthroned* (fig. 11-80), the most important of the few

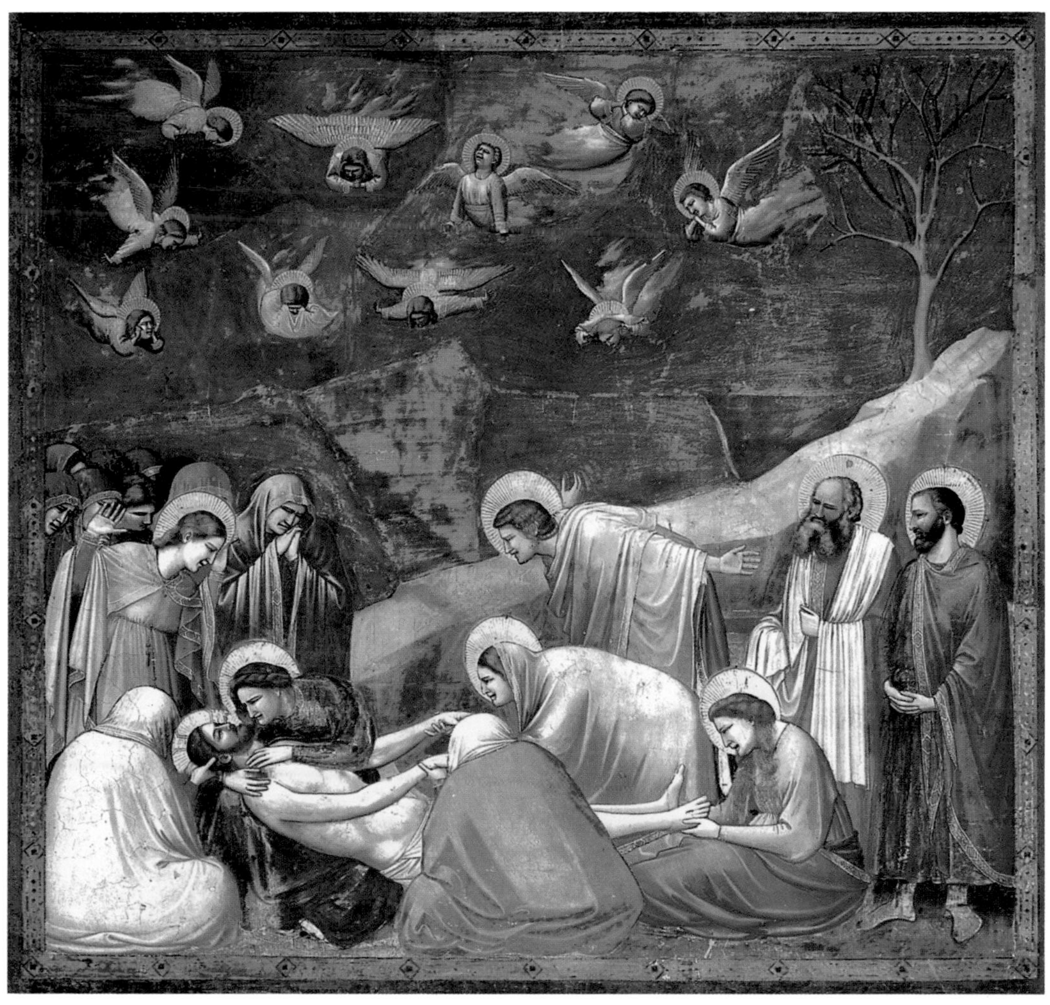

11-79. Giotto. *The Lamentation.* 1305–6. Fresco. Arena (Scrovegni) Chapel, Padua

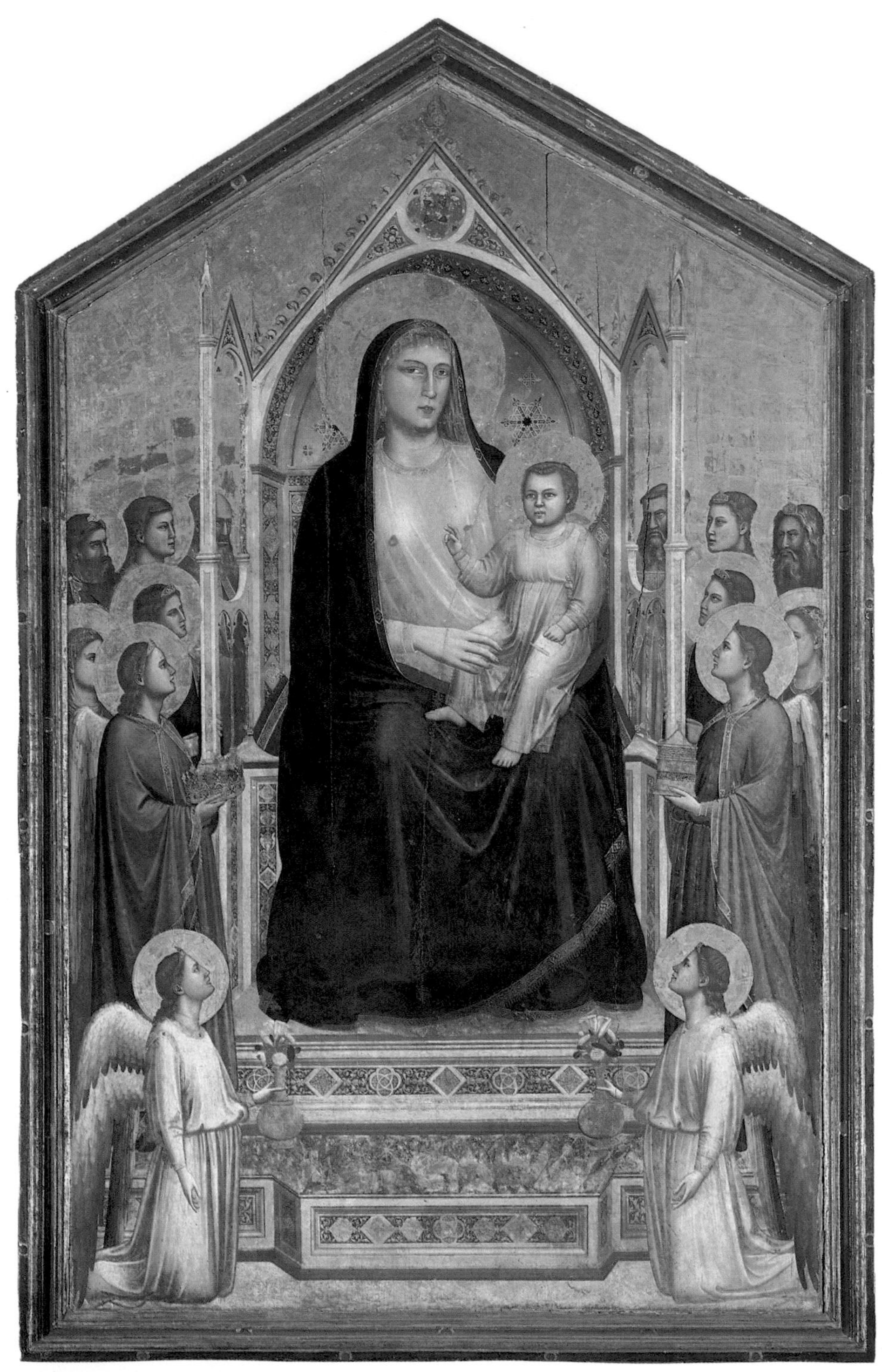

11-80. Giotto. *Madonna Enthroned.* c. 1310. Tempera on panel, 10'8" x 6'8" (3.3 x 2 m). Galleria degli Uffizi, Florence

panel paintings by Giotto. Done about the same time as Duccio's *Maestà,* it illustrates the striking differences between Florence and Siena. Its severity is clearly derived from Cimabue (see fig. 11-72). The figures, however, have the same sense of weight and volume that we saw in the frescoes in the Arena Chapel. Moreover, the picture space is just as persuasive—so much so, in fact, that the halos look like foreign bodies in it, despite the neutral gold background.

The throne, based on Italian Gothic architecture, has now become a nichelike structure. It encloses the Madonna on three sides and thus "insulates" her from the gold background. Its lavish ornamentation includes one feature of special interest: the colored marble surfaces of the base and of the quatrefoil within the gable. Such make-believe stone textures had been highly developed by ancient painters (see figs. 7-48 and 7-52), but the tradition had died out in Early Christian times. Its sudden reappearance here offers concrete evidence that Giotto was familiar with whatever ancient murals could still be seen in medieval Rome.

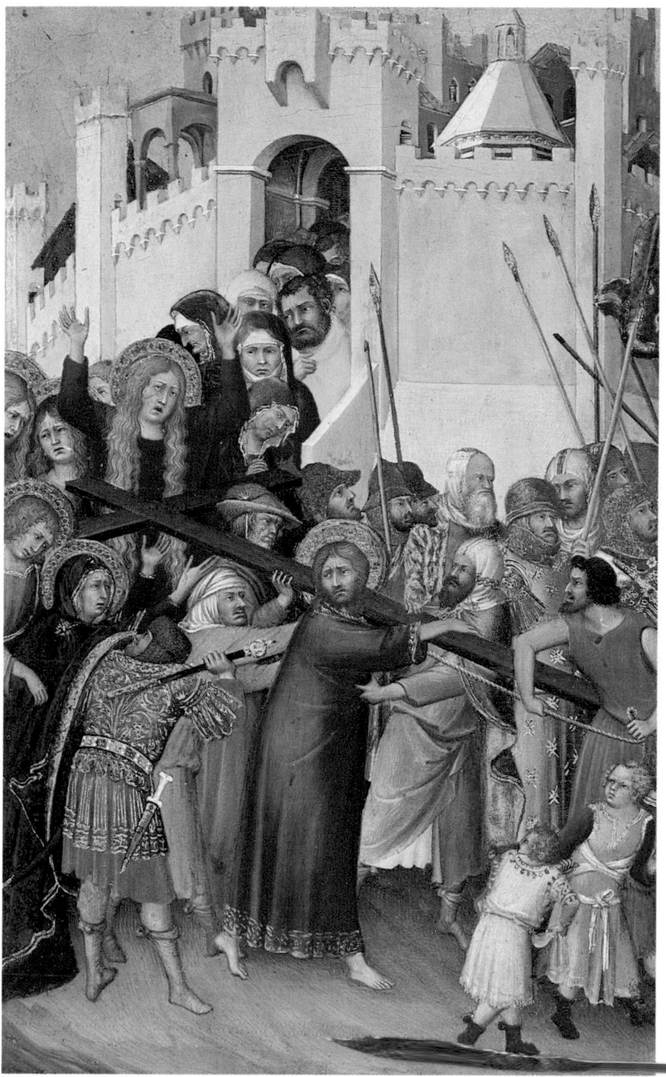

11-81. Simone Martini. *The Road to Calvary.* c. 1340. Tempera on panel, 9⅞ x 6⅛" (25 x 15.5 cm). Musée du Louvre, Paris

MARTINI. Few artists in the history of art equal Giotto as an innovator. His very greatness, however, tended to dwarf the next generation of Florentine painters. Their contemporaries in Siena were more fortunate in this respect, since Duccio never had the same overpowering impact. As a result, it was they, not the Florentines, who took the next decisive step in the development of Italian Gothic painting. Perhaps the most distinguished of Duccio's disciples was Simone Martini (c. 1284–1344), who painted the tiny but intense *The Road to Calvary* (fig. 11-81) about 1340. He spent the last years of his life in Avignon, the town in southern France that served as the residence of the popes during most of the fourteenth century. Our panel, originally part of a small altar, was probably done there, as it was commissioned by Philip the Bold of Burgundy for the Chartreuse de Champmol.

In its sparkling colors, and especially in the architectural background, it still echoes the art of Duccio (see fig. 11-75). On the other hand, the vigorous modeling of the figures, as well as their dramatic gestures and expressions, show the influence of Giotto. While Simone Martini is little concerned with spatial clarity, he is an acute observer. The sheer variety of costumes and physical types and the wealth of human activity create a sense of down-to-earth reality very different from both the lyricism of Duccio and the grandeur of Giotto.

THE LORENZETTI BROTHERS. This closeness to everyday life can also be seen in the work of the brothers Pietro and Ambrogio Lorenzetti (both died 1348?). However, it appears on a more monumental scale and is coupled with a keen interest in problems of space. The boldest spatial experiment is Pietro's *Birth of the Virgin* (fig. 11-82). In this triptych of 1342, the painted architecture has been related to the real architecture of the frame so closely that the two are seen as a single system. Moreover, the vaulted chamber, where the birth takes place, occupies two panels and continues unbroken behind the column that divides the center from the right wing. The left wing represents an anteroom which leads to a large and only partially seen space that suggests the interior of a Gothic church. What Pietro Lorenzetti achieved here is the outcome of a development that began three decades earlier in the work of Duccio (compare fig. 11-75): the conquest of pictorial space. Only now, however, does the painting surface take

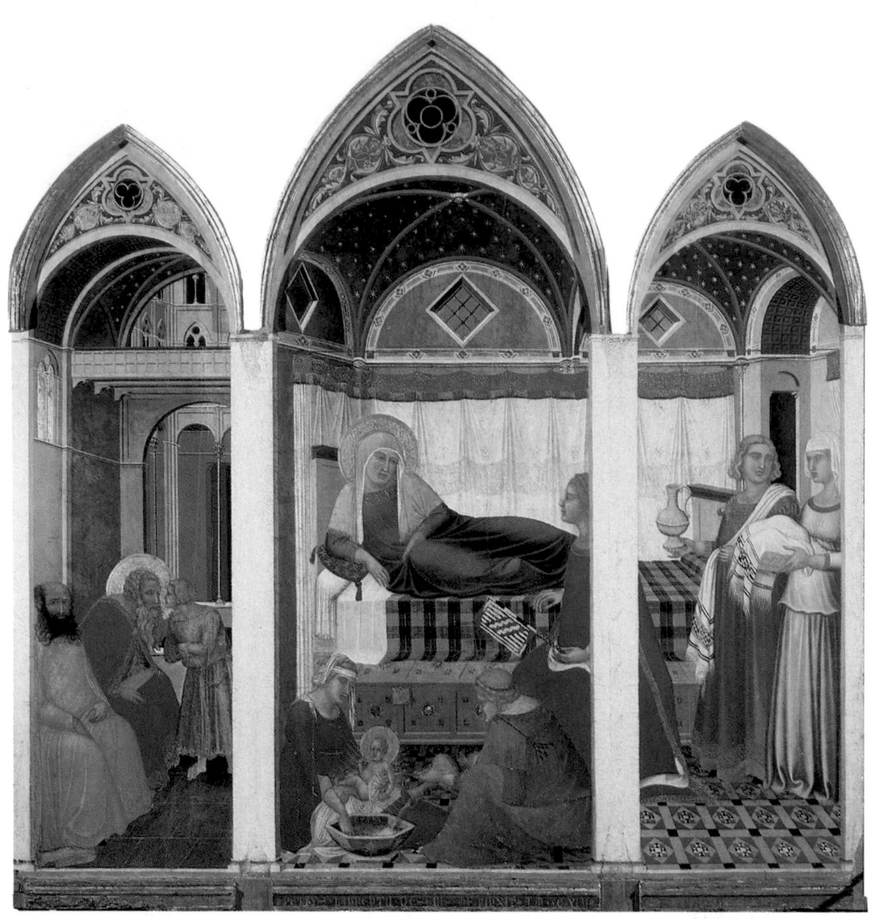

11-82. Pietro Lorenzetti. *Birth of the Virgin.* 1342. Tempera on panel, 6'1½" x 5'11½" (1.9 x 1.8 m). Museo dell'Opera del Duomo, Siena

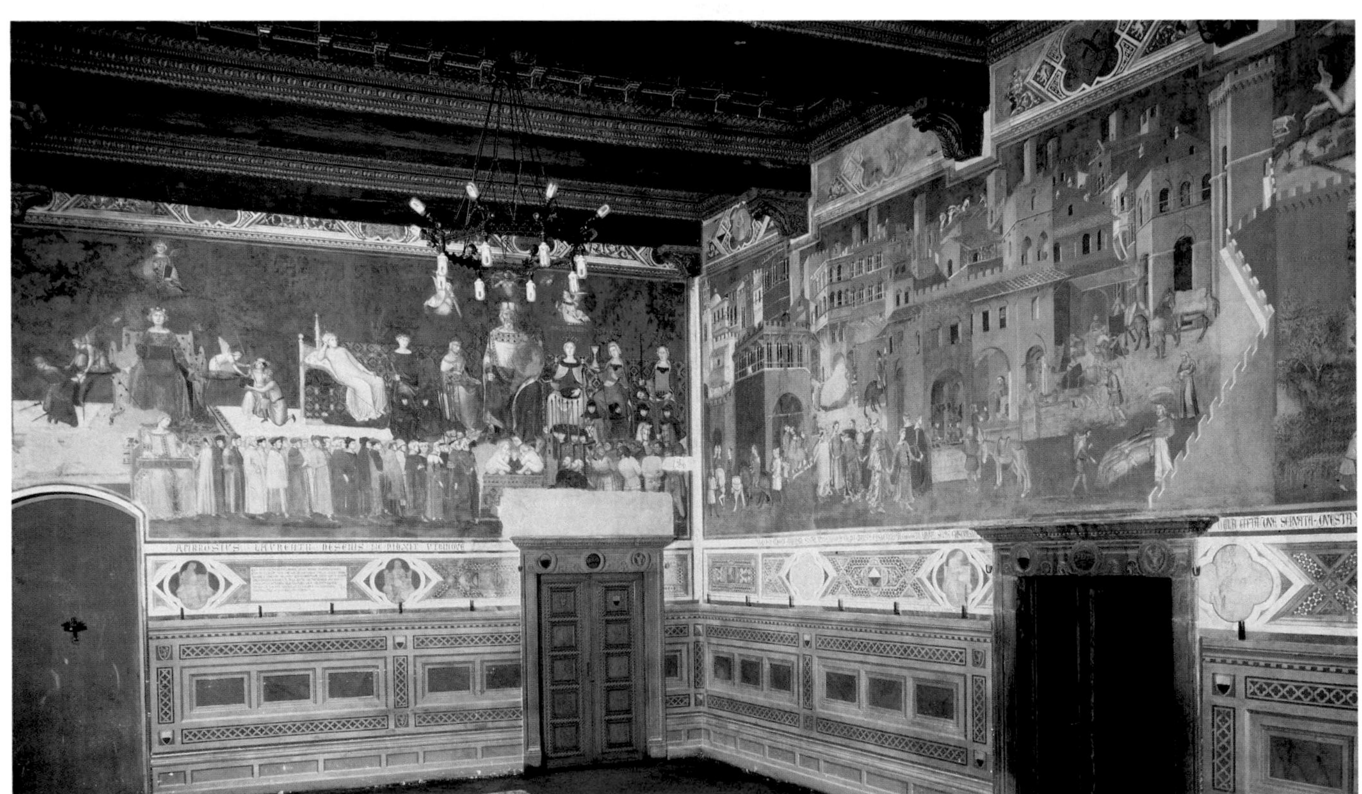

11-83. Ambrogio Lorenzetti. *The Commune of Siena* (left), *Good Government in the City,* and portion of *Good Government in the Country* (right). 1338–40. Frescoes in the Sala della Pace, Palazzo Pubblico, Siena

(Opposite Above) 11-84. Ambrogio Lorenzetti. *Good Government in the City.* Palazzo Pubblico, Siena
(Opposite Below) 11-85. Ambrogio Lorenzetti. *Good Government in the Country.* Palazzo Pubblico, Siena

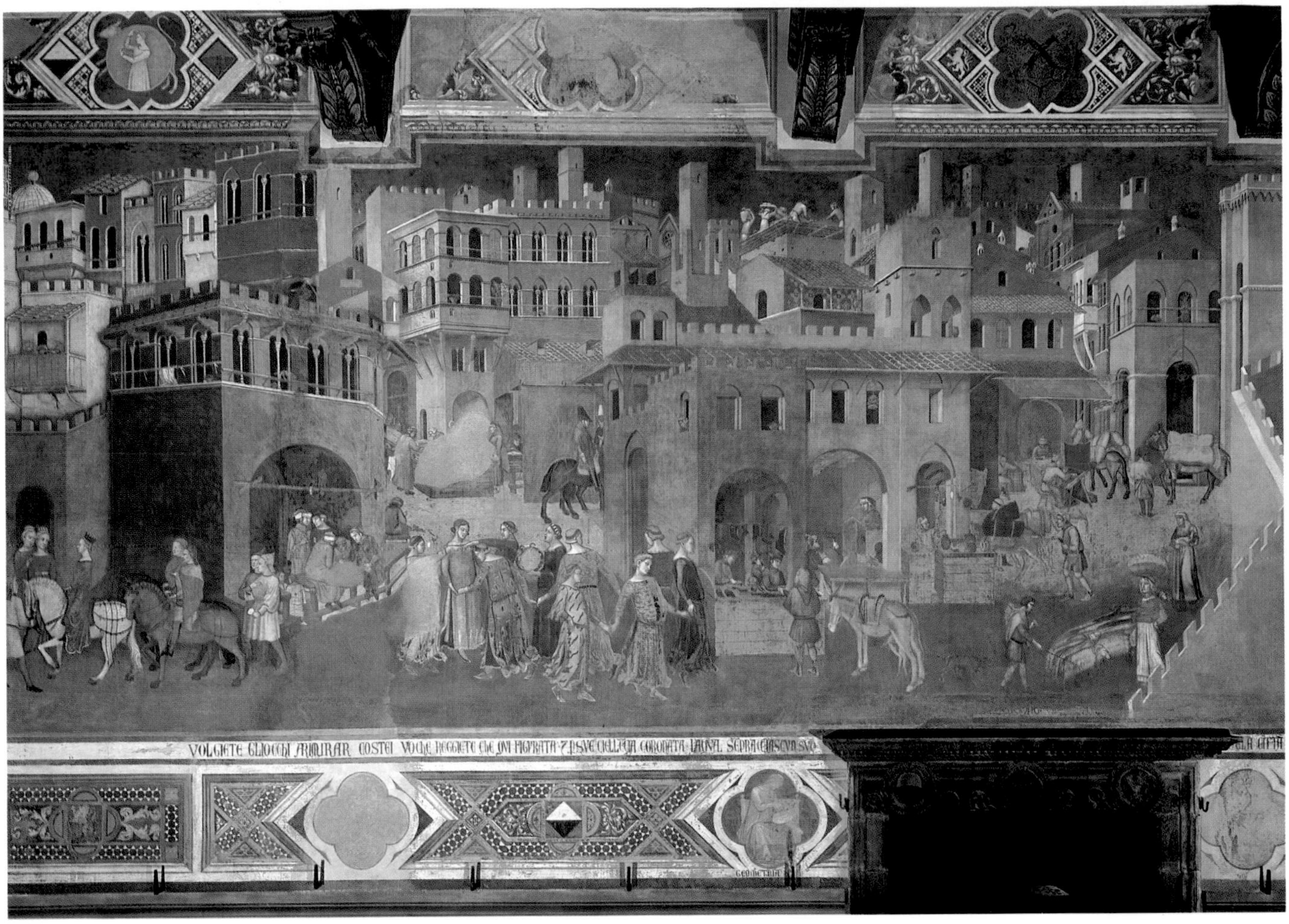

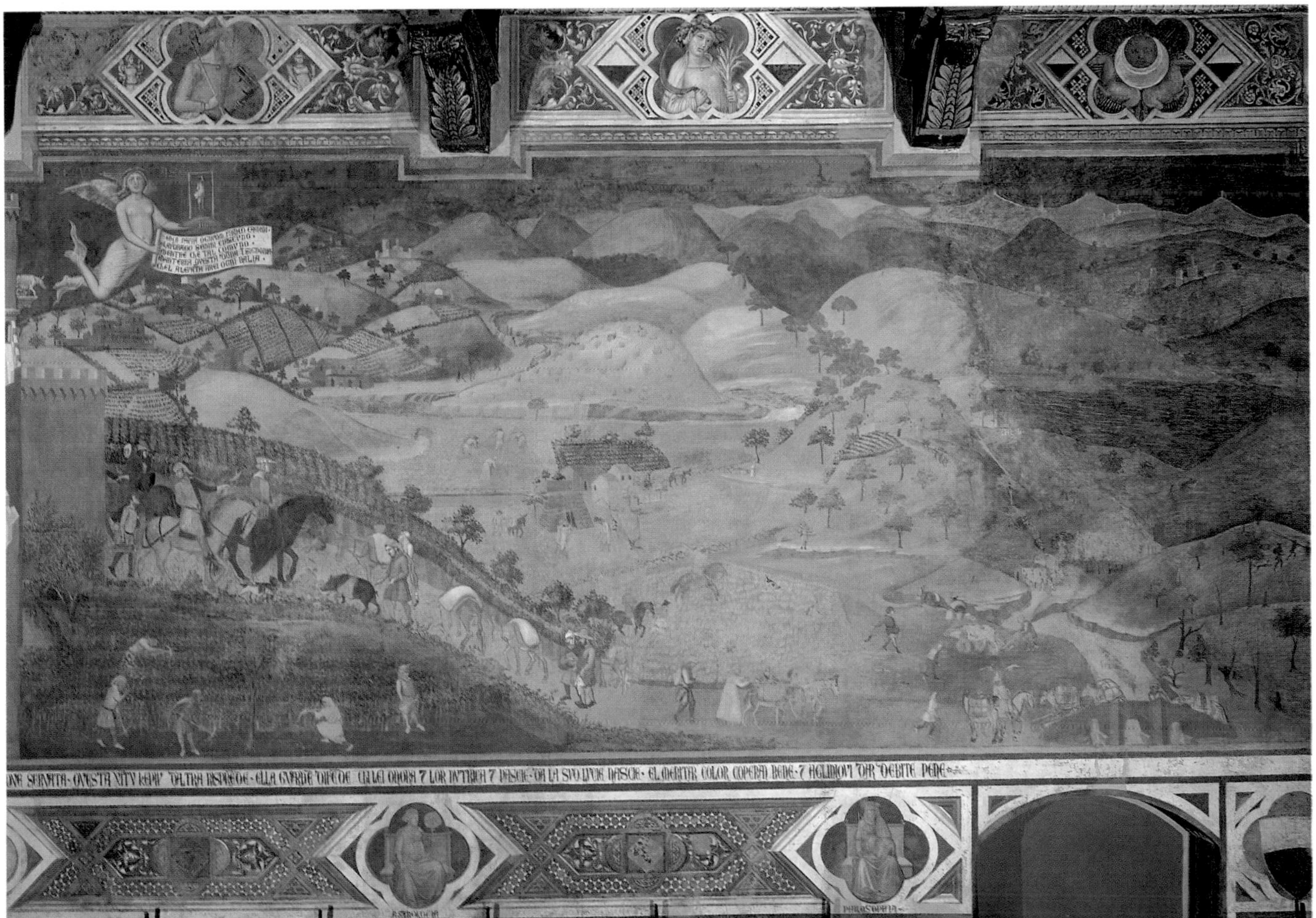

on the quality of a transparent window *through* which—not *on* which—we perceive the same kind of space we know from daily experience. Duccio's work alone does not explain Pietro's astonishing breakthrough. His achievement became possible, rather, through a combination of the *architectural* picture space of Duccio and the *sculptural* picture space of Giotto.

The same approach enabled Ambrogio Lorenzetti to unfold a view of the entire town before our eyes in his frescoes of 1338–40 in the Siena city hall (fig. 11-83). We are struck by the distance that separates this precise "portrait" of Siena from Duccio's Jerusalem (see fig. 11-75). Ambrogio's mural forms part of an allegorical program depicting the contrast of good and bad government. For example, the inscription under *Good Government in the City* (fig. 11-84) praises Justice and the many benefits that derive from her. [See Primary Sources, no. 37, page 374.] To the right on the far wall of figure 11-83, we see *The Commune of Siena* guided by Faith, Hope, and Charity and flanked by a host of other symbolic figures. To show the life of a well-ordered city-state, the artist had to fill the streets and houses with teeming activity. The bustling crowd gives the architectural vista its striking reality by introducing the human scale. On the right, outside the city walls, the *Good Government in the Country* fresco provides a view of the Sienese countryside fringed by distant mountains (fig. 11-85). It is a true landscape—the first since ancient Roman times. The scene is full of sweeping depth yet differs from its classical predecessors (such as fig. 7-49) in its orderliness, which gives it a domesticated air. The people here have taken full possession of nature: they have terraced the hillsides with vineyards and patterned the valleys with the geometry of fields and pastures. Ambrogio observes the peasants at their seasonal labors; his recording of this rural Tuscan scene is so characteristic that it has hardly changed during the past 600 years.

THE BLACK DEATH. The first four decades of the fourteenth century in Florence and Siena had been a period of political stability and economic expansion as well as of great artistic achievement. In the 1340s both cities suffered a series of catastrophes whose echoes were to be felt for many years. Banks and merchants went bankrupt by the score, internal upheavals shook the government, and there were repeated crop failures. Then, in 1348, the epidemic of bubonic plague—the Black Death—that spread throughout Europe wiped out more than half their urban population. Popular reactions to these events were mixed. Many people saw them as signs of divine wrath, warnings to a sinful humanity to forsake the pleasures of this earth. In such people the Black Death aroused a mood of otherworldly exaltation. To others, such as the gay company in Boccaccio's *Decameron,* the fear of death intensified the desire to enjoy life while there was still time. [See Primary Sources, no. 38, page 375.] These conflicting attitudes are reflected in the pictorial theme of the Triumph of Death.

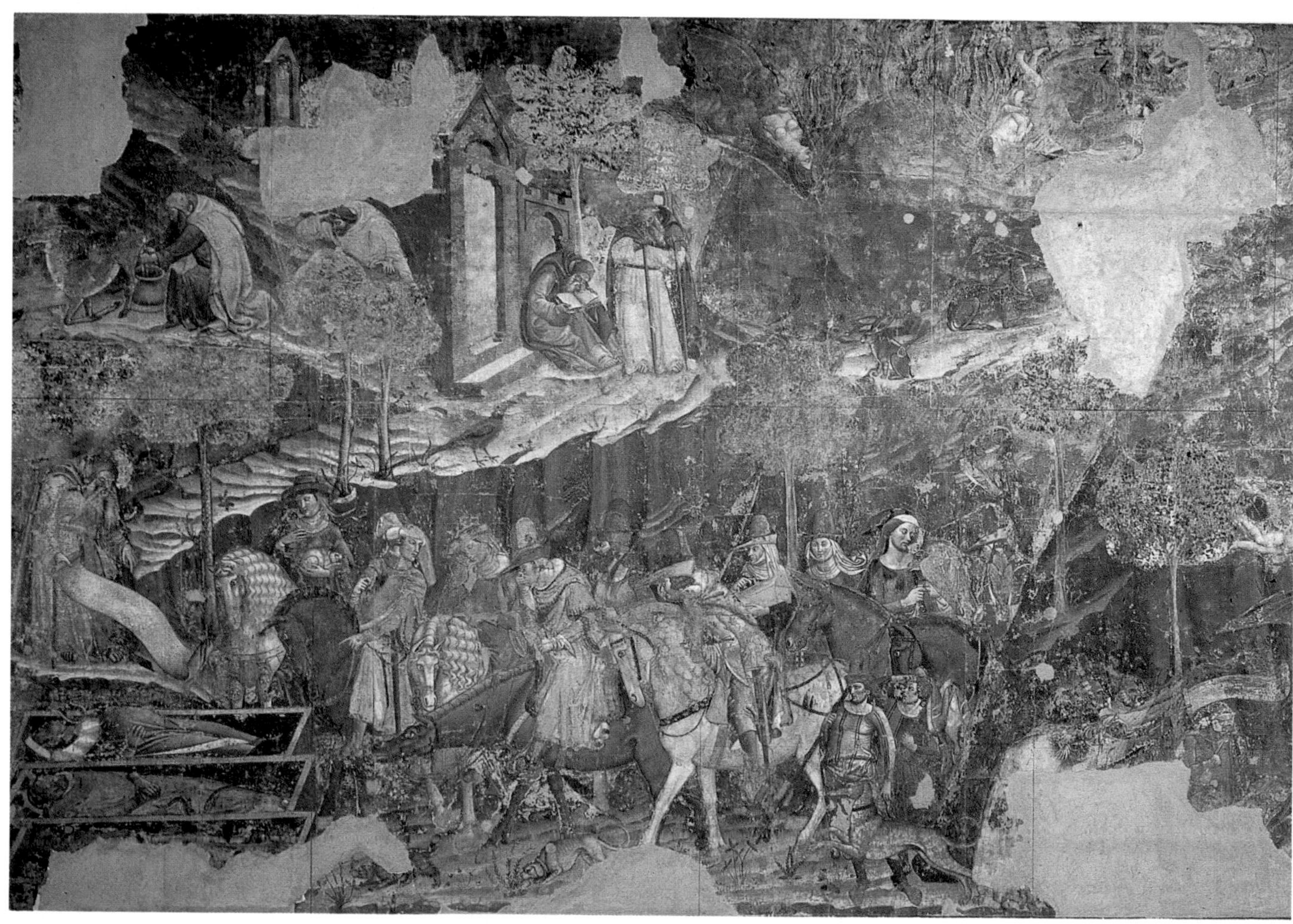

11-86. Francesco Traini(?). *The Triumph of Death* (detail). c. 1325–50. Fresco. Camposanto, Pisa

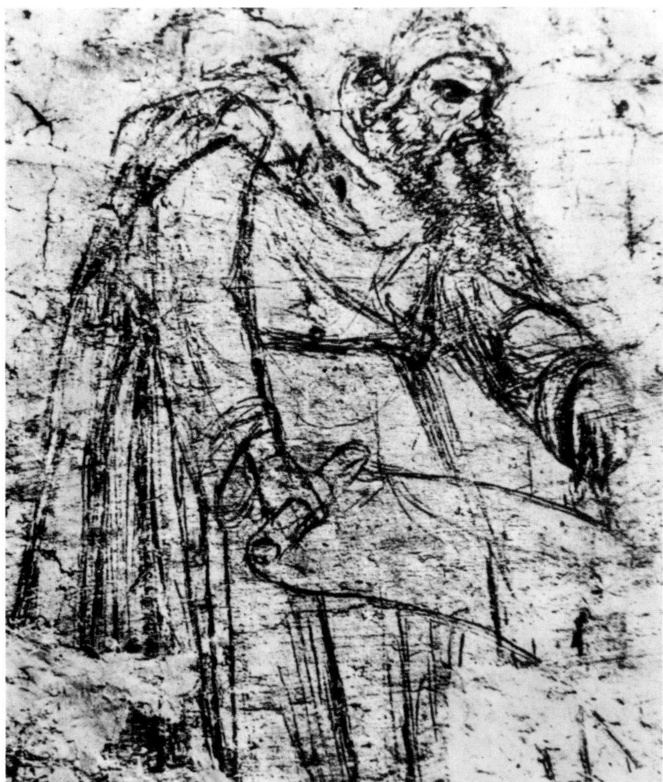

11-87. Francesco Traini. Sinopia drawing for *The Triumph of Death* (detail). Camposanto, Pisa

TRAINI. The most impressive version of this subject is an enormous fresco traditionally attributed to the Pisan master Francesco Traini (documented c. 1321–1363) in the Camposanto, the cemetery building next to Pisa Cathedral (fig. 11-86). In a particularly dramatic detail at the left, the elegantly costumed men and women on horseback have suddenly come upon three decaying corpses in open coffins. Even the animals are terrified by the sight and smell of rotting flesh. Only the hermit St. Macarius, having renounced all earthly pleasures, points out the lesson of the scene. His scroll reads: "If your mind be well aware, keeping here your view attentive, your vainglory will be vanquished and you will see pride eliminated. And, again, you will realize this if you observe that which is written." As the hermits in the hills above make clear, the way to salvation is through renunciation of the world in favor of the spiritual life. But will the living confront their own mortality, or will they, like the characters of Boccaccio, turn away from the shocking spectacle more determined than ever to pursue their hedonistic ways?

In the center lie dead and dying peasants who plead with Death, "the medicine for all pain, come give us our last supper." To the right are courtiers in a delightful landscape enjoying earthly pleasures as a female figure of death swoops down and angels and devils fight over the souls of the deceased in the sky overhead. Although the moral is clear, the artist's own sympathies seem curiously divided. His style, far from being otherworldly, recalls the realism of Ambrogio Lorenzetti, although the forms are harsher and more expressive. (The other half of the mural depicts a Last Judgment and vision of purgatory that are the most conventional aspects of the cycle.)

The fresco was badly damaged by fire in 1944 and had to be detached from the wall in order to save what was left of it. This procedure exposed the plaster underneath, on which the composition was sketched out (fig. 11-87). These drawings, of the same size as the fresco itself, are amazingly free. They reveal the artist's personal style more directly than the painted version, which was carried out with the aid of assistants. Because they are done in red, these drawings are called *sinopie* (an Italian word derived from ancient Sinope, in Asia Minor, which was famous as a source of brick-red earth pigment).

FRESCO PAINTING. *Sinopie* serve to introduce us to the standard technique of painting frescoes in the fourteenth century. After the first coat of plaster (*arriccio* or *arricciato*) had dried, the wall was divided into squares using a ruler or chalk lines tied to nails. The design was then brushed in with a thin ocher paint, and the outline developed further in charcoal, with the details being added last in sinopia. During the Renaissance, sinopie were replaced by cartoons: sheets of heavy paper or cardboard (*cartone*) on which the design was drawn in the studio. The design was then pricked with small holes and transferred to the wall by dusting ("pouncing") it with chalk. In the High Renaissance, however, the contours were often simply pressed through the paper with a stylus. Each section of the wall was covered with just enough fresh plaster (*intonaco*) to last the current session, in order for the water-based paints to sink in. (Some insoluble pigments could only be applied *a secco* to dry plaster.) Since the work had to be done on a scaffold, it was carried out from the top down, usually in horizontal strips about four by six feet in size. Needless to say, fresco painting was a slow process that required several assistants for large projects.

MASO DI BANCO, TADDEO GADDI. The artists who reached maturity around 1340 were not as innovative as the earlier painters we have discussed, but neither were they blind followers. At their best, they expressed the somber mood of the time with memorable intensity. The heritage of Giotto can be seen in tombs created about the same time for members of the Bardi family in Sta. Croce, Florence, by two of his foremost pupils (fig. 11-88). The larger of the two, probably by Maso di Banco (flourished 1341–1346), shows the dead man rising from his marble tomb to receive a personal Last Judgment from the risen Christ. The scene, with its eerie landscape and majestic Jesus, retains some of Giotto's grandeur without being simply derivative (compare fig. 11-78). The ensemble is among the first to combine painting and sculpture. The result is an astonishing mixture of temporal and visionary reality that expresses the hope—indeed, the expectation—of salvation and life after death.

The same theme is repeated in the tomb to the right by Taddeo Gaddi (1295/1300–1366). The deceased is painted on the side of the sarcophagus receiving the body of Jesus above her own sepulchre. The message is clear: by bearing witness to the Entombment, she shall rise again, just as Christ did. Like the other tomb, this one incorporates the image, widespread at the time, of Jesus as the Man of Sorrows whose suffering redeems humanity's sins and offers the promise of eternal life. Despite the debt to Giotto's

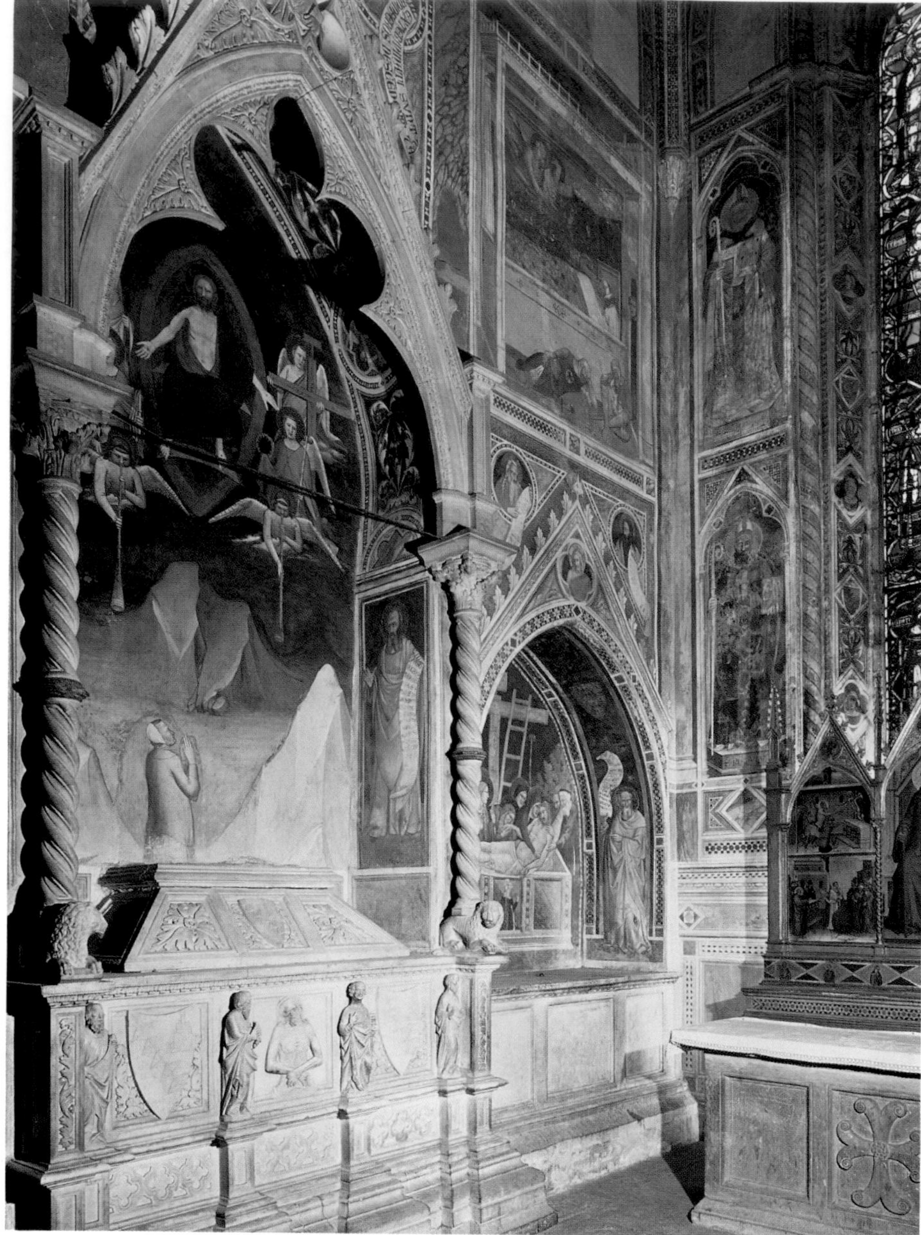

11-88. Maso di Banco (Att.) (left) and Taddeo Gaddi (right). Tombs of Members of the Bardi Family. c. 1335-45 and c. 1335-41. Bardi di Vernio Chapel, Sta. Croce, Florence

Lamentation (see fig. 11-79), Taddeo has begun to feel the influence of the Lorenzetti, which would soon be seen in the work of Maso and other Florentine artists as well.

North of the Alps

ILLUMINATED MANUSCRIPTS. What happened to Gothic painting north of the Alps during the latter half of the fourteenth century was determined in large part by the influence of the great Italians. Some examples of this influence can be found even earlier, such as the *Annunciation* in figure 11-89. This scene comes from a private prayer book—called a "book of hours"—illuminated by Jean Pucelle in Paris about 1325–28 for Jeanne d'Evreux, queen of France. The style of the figures recalls Master Honoré (see fig. 11-71), but the delicate *grisaille* (painting in gray) lends them a soft plasticity that was not explored by other artists for another 50 years. This is not Pucelle's only contribution: the architectural interior clearly derives from Duccio (see fig. 11-74). It had taken less than 20 years for the fame of the *Maestà* to spread from Tuscany to the Île-de-France.

In taking over the new picture space, however, Jean Pucelle had to adapt it to the special needs of a manuscript page, which lends itself far less readily than a panel to being treated as a window. The Virgin's chamber no longer fills the entire picture surface. It has become an airy cage that floats on the blank background (note the supporting angel on the right) like the rest of the ornamental framework, so that the entire page forms a harmonious unit. As we explore the details of this framework, we see that most of them have nothing to do with the religious purpose of the manuscript. The kneeling queen inside the initial D is surely meant to be Jeanne d'Evreux at her prayers, but who is the man with the staff next to her? He seems to be listening to the lute player perched on the tendril above him. The page is filled with other enchanting vignettes. A rabbit peers from its burrow beneath the girl on the left, and in the foliage leading up to the initial we find a monkey and a squirrel.

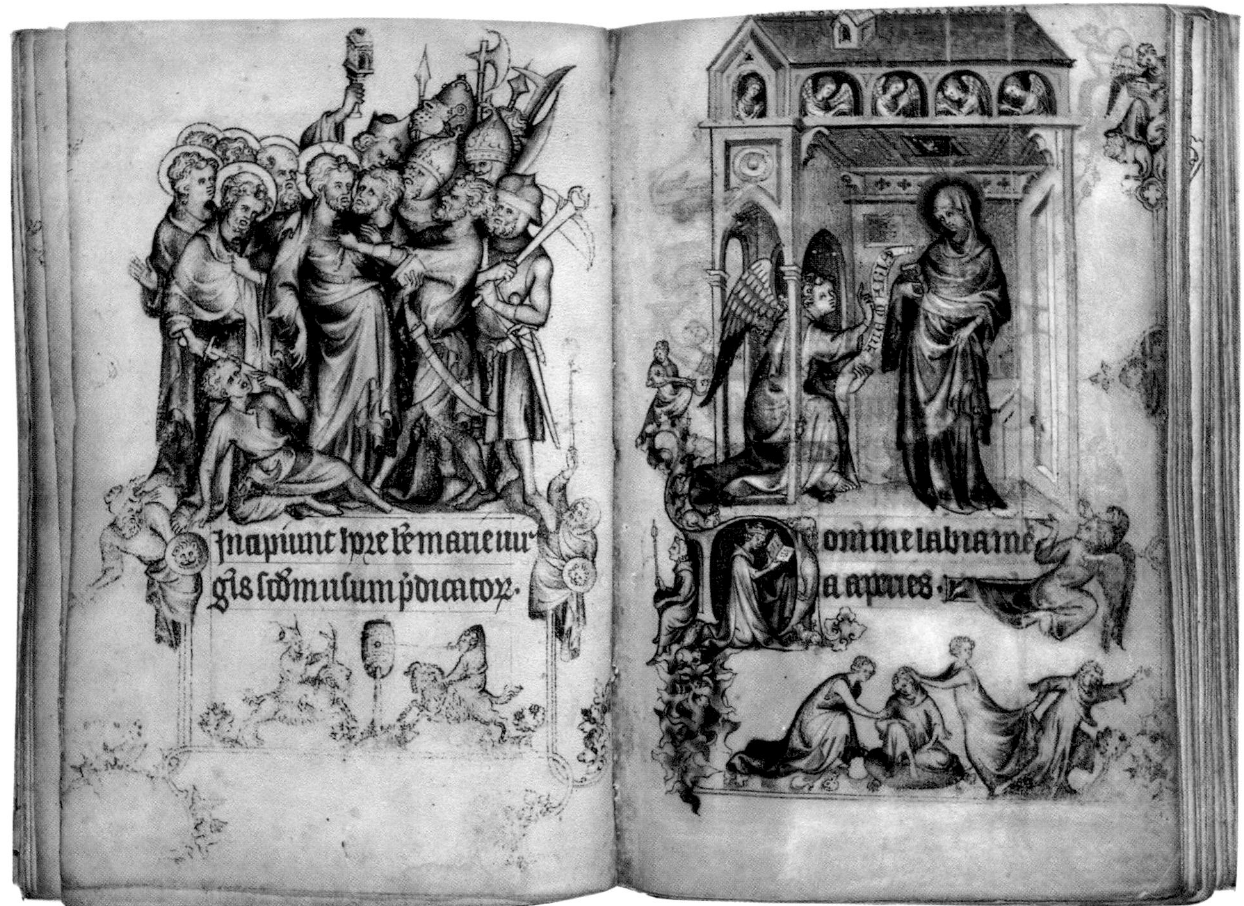

11-89. Jean Pucelle. *The Betrayal of Christ* and *Annunciation,* from the *Hours of Jeanne d'Evreux.* 1325–28. Tempera and gold leaf on parchment, each page, $3\frac{1}{2}$ x $2\frac{7}{16}$" (8.9 x 6.2 cm). Shown larger than actual size. The Metropolitan Museum of Art, New York

THE CLOISTERS COLLECTION, PURCHASE, 1954

DRÔLERIE. These fanciful marginal designs—or *drôleries*—are a characteristic feature of Northern Gothic manuscripts. They had originated more than a century before Jean Pucelle in the regions along the English Channel. From there they quickly spread to Paris and all the other centers of Gothic art. [See Primary Sources, no. 39, page 375.] Their subjects include a wide range of motifs: fantasy, fable, and grotesque humor, as well as scenes of everyday life, appear side by side with religious themes. The essence of drôlerie is its playfulness. In this special domain the artist enjoys an almost unlimited freedom, comparable to that traditionally claimed by the court jester, which accounts for the wide appeal of drôlerie during the later Middle Ages.

The innocent facade of Pucelle's drôlerie nevertheless hides a serious intent. The four figures at the bottom of the right-hand page are playing a game of tag called Froggy in the Middle, a reference to the Betrayal of Christ on the opposite page. We recognize this dramatic scene as a descendant of the mosaic in S. Apollinare Nuovo (see fig. 8-18). Below the *Betrayal* are two knights on goats jousting at a barrel. This image not only mocks courtly chivalry but also refers to Christ as a "scapegoat" and to the spear of Longinus that will pierce his side at the Crucifixion.

FRESCOES AND PANEL PAINTINGS. In the mid-fourteenth century, Italian influence became more important in Northern Gothic painting. Sometimes this influence was transmitted by Italian artists who were active on northern soil. An example is Simone Martini (see page 351), who worked at the palace of the popes near Avignon (see fig. 11-81).

One gateway of Italian influence was the city of Prague, the capital of Bohemia, thanks to Emperor Charles IV (1316–1378), the most remarkable ruler since Charlemagne. Charles received an excellent education in Paris at the French court of Charles IV, whose daughter he married and in whose honor he changed his name from Wenceslaus. He returned to Prague and in 1346 succeeded his father as king of Bohemia. As a result of Charles' alliance with Pope Clement VI, who resided at Avignon during what the humanist Petrarch called "the Babylon Captivity of the Papacy" (1309–77), Prague became an independent archbishopric. It was also through Clement's intervention that Charles was named Holy Roman Emperor by the German Electors at Aachen in 1349. This title was confirmed by coronations in Milan and Rome six years later. In exchange, Charles later supported Pope Urban V's return to Rome in 1367.

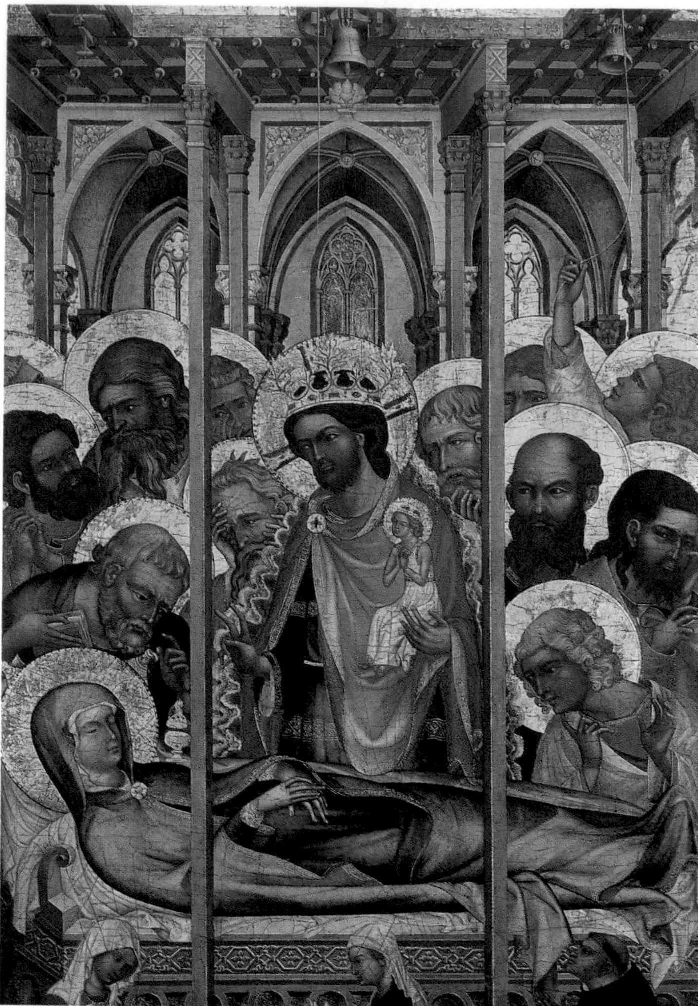

11-90. Bohemian Master. *Death of the Virgin*. 1355–60. Tempera on panel, 39⅜ x 28" (100 x 71 cm). Museum of Fine Arts, Boston

WILLIAM FRANCIS WARDEN FUND, SETH K. SWEETSER FUND, THE HENRY C. AND MARTHA B. ANGELL COLLECTION, JULIANA CHENEY EDWARDS COLLECTION, GIFT OF MARTIN BRIMMER, AND MRS. FREDERICK FROTHINGHAM; BY EXCHANGE

Like Charlemagne before him, Charles wanted to make his capital a center of learning. In 1348 he established a university along the lines of that in Paris, which attracted many of the best minds from throughout Europe. He also became a patron of the arts and founded an artists' guild. Prague soon became a cultural center second only to Paris itself. Charles was also impressed most by the art he saw during his two visits to Italy. (He is known to have commissioned works by several Italian painters.) Thus the *Death of the Virgin* (fig. 11-90), made by a Bohemian Master about 1355–60, brings to mind the works of the great Sienese painters. Its rich color recalls Simone Martini. The carefully articulated architectural interior further shows its descent from such works as Pietro Lorenzetti's *Birth of the Virgin* (see fig. 11-82), but it lacks the spaciousness of its Italian models. Also Italian is the vigorous modeling of the heads and the overlapping of the figures, which reinforces the three-dimensional quality of the design but raises the awkward question of what to do with the halos. (Giotto, we will recall, had faced the same problem in his *Madonna Enthroned*; compare fig. 11-80). Still, the Bohemian Master's picture is not just an echo of Italian painting. The gestures and facial expressions convey an intensity of emotion that represents the finest heritage of Northern Gothic art. In this respect, our panel is far more akin to the *Death of the Virgin* at Strasbourg Cathedral (see fig. 11-45) than to any Italian work.

The International Style

BROEDERLAM. Around 1400, the merging of Northern and Italian traditions gave rise to a single dominant style throughout western Europe. This International Style was not confined to painting—we have used the same term for the sculpture of the period—but painters clearly played the main role in its development. Among the most important was Melchior Broederlam (flourished c. 1387–1409), a Fleming who worked for the court of the duke of Burgundy in Dijon, where he would have known Simone Martini's *The Road to Calvary* (see fig. 11-81). Figure 11-91 shows the panels of a pair of shutters for an altar shrine that Broederlam painted in 1394–99 for the Chartreuse de Champmol. (The interior consists of an elaborately carved relief by Jacques de Baerze showing the Adoration of the Magi, the Crucifixion, and the Entombment.) Each wing is really two pictures within one frame. Landscape and architecture stand abruptly side by side, even though the artist has tried to suggest that the scene extends around the building.

Compared to paintings by Pietro and Ambrogio Lorenzetti, Broederlam's picture space seems naive in many ways. The architecture looks like a doll's house, and the details of the landscape are out of scale with the figures. Yet the panels convey a far stronger feeling of depth than we have found in any previous Northern work, thanks to the subtlety of the modeling. The softly rounded shapes and the dark, velvety shadows create a sense of light and air that more than makes up for any shortcomings of scale or perspective. This soft, pictorial quality is a hallmark of the International Style. It appears as well in the ample, loosely draped garments with their fluid curvilinear patterns of folds, which remind us of Sluter and Ghiberti (see figs. 11-56 and 11-65).

Broederlam's panels also show another feature of the International Style: its "realism of particulars." It is the same kind of realism we first saw in Gothic sculpture (see fig. 11-49) and somewhat later among the drôleries in the margins of manuscripts. We find it in the left panel in the carefully rendered foliage and flowers of the enclosed garden to the left, and in the contrast between the Gothic chamber and the Romanesque temple. We see it as well in the right panel, in the delightful donkey (obviously drawn from life), and in the rustic figure of St. Joseph, who looks and behaves like a simple peasant and thus helps to emphasize the delicate, aristocratic beauty of the Virgin. This painstaking detail gives Broederlam's work the flavor of an enlarged miniature rather than of a large-scale painting, even though the panels are more than five feet tall.

The expansion of subject matter during the International Style was linked to a comparable growth in symbolism. In the left panel, for example, the lily signifies Mary's virginity, as does the enclosed garden next to her. The contrasting Romanesque and Gothic architecture stands for the Old and New Testaments, respectively. This development paves the way for the elaboration of symbolic meaning that occurs 25 years later in works by Robert Campin.

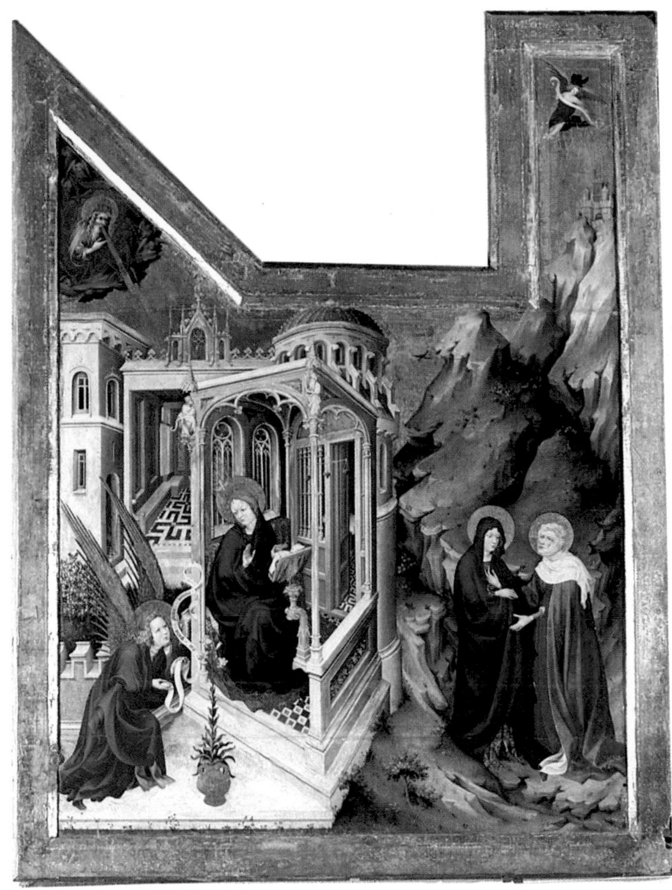
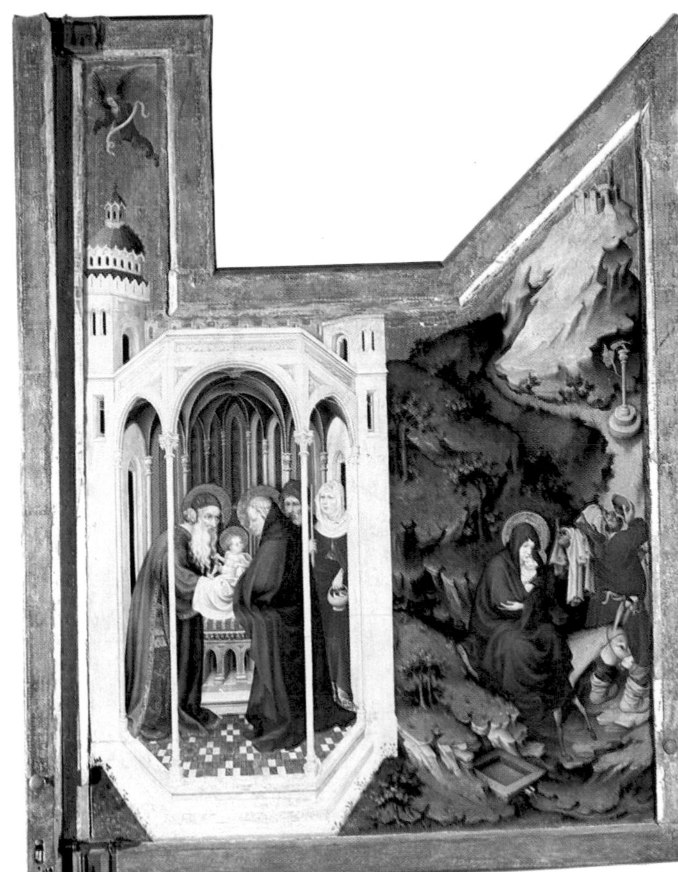

(ABOVE) 11-91. Melchior Broederlam. *Annunciation and Visitation; Presentation in the Temple;* and *Flight into Egypt.* 1394–99. Tempera on panel, each 65 x 49¼" (167 x 125 cm). Musée des Beaux-Arts, Dijon, France

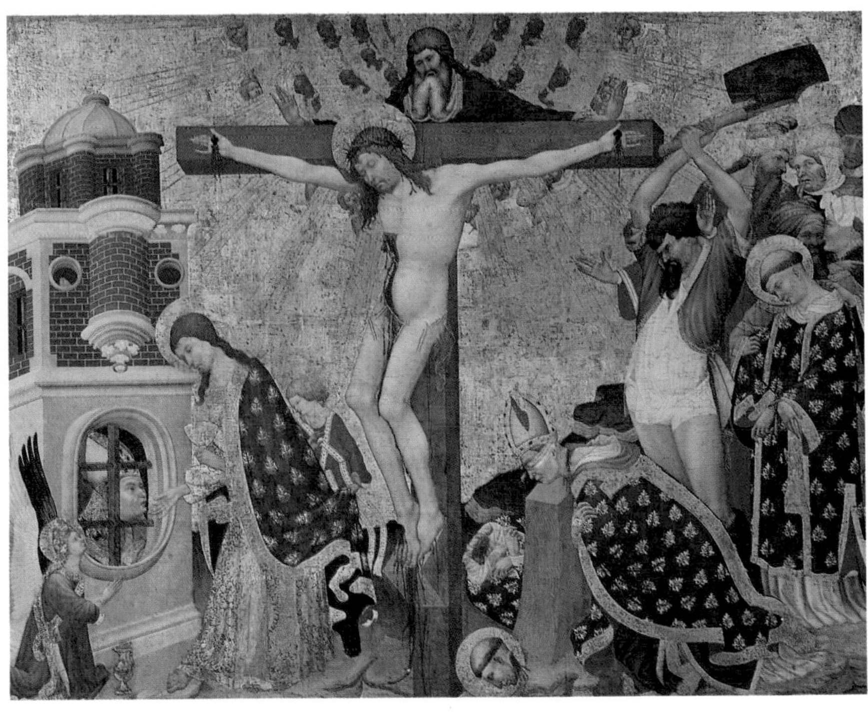

(RIGHT) 11-92. Jean Malouel and Henri Bellechose. *Martyrdom of St. Denis with the Trinity.* c. 1415. Tempera on panel, 5'3⅜" x 6'10⅝" (1.61 x 2.1 m). Musée du Louvre, Paris

MALOUEL AND BELLECHOSE. More monumental still is the somewhat later *Martyrdom of St. Denis* (fig. 11-92), also from the Chartreuse de Champmol. It was probably begun by the court painter Jean Malouel (Jan Maelwel; active 1386–1415) but completed after his death by his successor, Henri Bellechose (died 1440/44), who also was born in the Netherlands. The subject is unique: it equates Denis' martyrdom with the Crucifixion. At the left, Christ himself administers the last rites to Denis. To the right, we see the decapitation of the saint and his companions. Malouel also worked as an illuminator, but he was clearly a panel painter at heart. Although the diminutive prison is a remnant of manuscript illustrations, the figures combine French gracefulness with an impressive bulk that can have come only from Italian art (compare fig. 11-79). The more robust figures, such as the executioner,

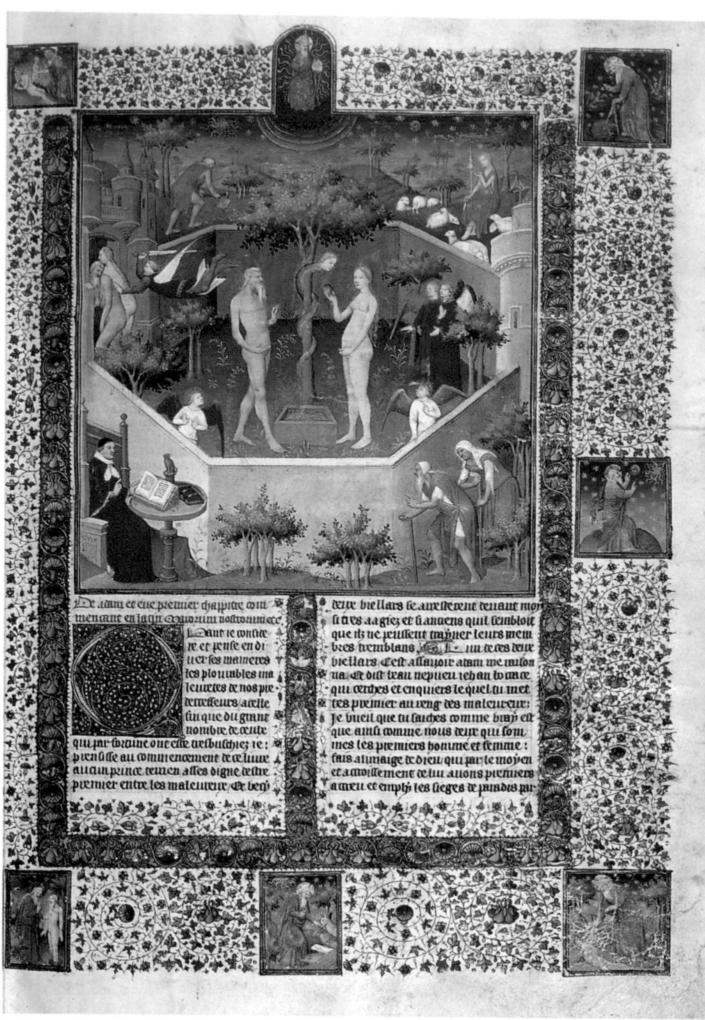

11-93. The Boucicaut Master. *The Story of Adam and Eve,* from Giovanni Boccaccio, *Des cas des nobles hommes et femmes* (The Fates of Illustrious Men and Women). Paris c. 1415. Gold leaf, gold paint, and tempera on vellum, 16¾ x 11½" (42.5 x 29.3 cm). The J. Paul Getty Museum, Los Angeles. Ms. 63, fol. 3

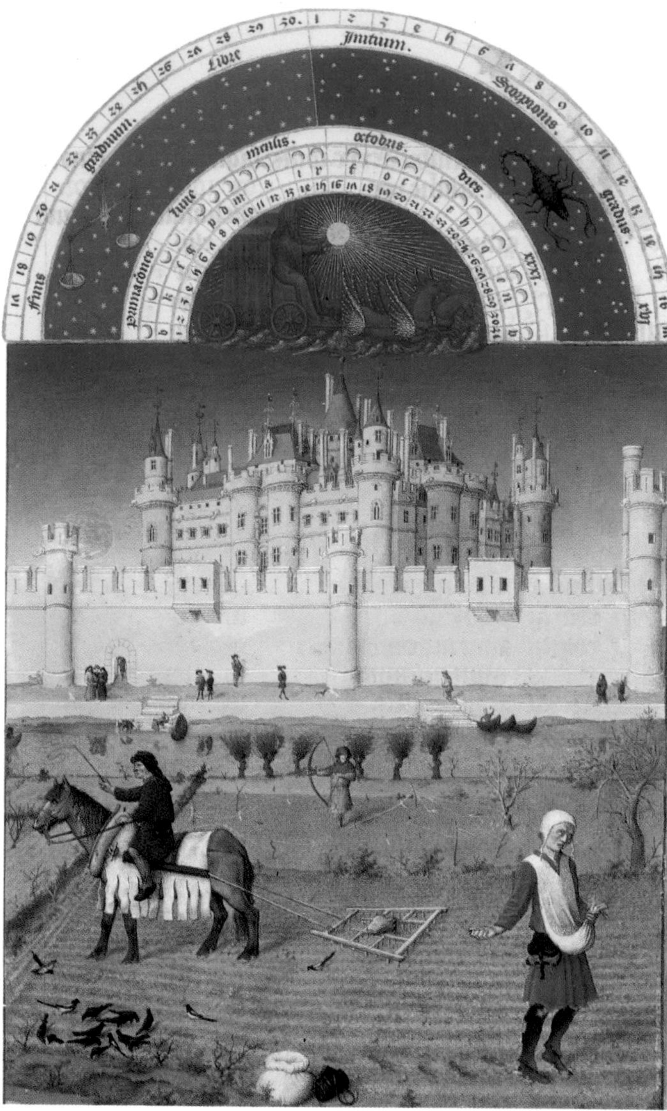

11-94. The Limbourg Brothers. *October,* from *Les Très Riches Heures du Duc de Berry.* 1413–16. 8⅞ x 5⅜" (22.5 x 13.7 cm). Musée Condé, Chantilly, France

were probably done by Bellechose, although the difference lies more in temperament than in style.

THE BOUCICAUT MASTER. Despite the growing importance of panel painting, book illumination remained the leading form of painting in northern Europe at the time of the International Style. Among the finest of the many manuscript painters employed by French courts was the Boucicaut Master, who may have been the Bruges artist Jacques Coen. In *The Story of Adam and Eve* (fig. 11-93) the promise of the Broederlam panels has been fulfilled. Landscape and architecture are united in deep, atmospheric space, although the perspective is skewed in order to reveal as much of the scene as possible. Even such intangible things as the starry sky have become paintable. Note, too, how the sky becomes lighter toward the horizon—the earliest known example of atmospheric perspective. Every detail, be it divine or natural, is rendered as if it were a miraculous revelation. Stemming from St. Augustine, who considered the temporal world a metaphor of the spiritual realm, this attitude represents a decisive change that soon leads to Late Gothic art.

THE LIMBOURG BROTHERS. The International Style reached its height in the luxurious book of hours known as *Les Très Riches Heures du Duc de Berry.* This volume was produced for the brother of the king of France, a man of far from admirable character but the most lavish art patron of his day. The artists were Pol de Limbourg and his two brothers. They were Flemings who were introduced to the court by their uncle, Jean Malouel. They must have visited Italy, for their work includes numerous motifs and whole compositions borrowed from the great masters of Tuscany.

The most remarkable pages of *Les Très Riches Heures* are those of the calendar, which depict the life of humanity and nature throughout the year. Such cycles, originally consisting of 12 single figures each performing an appropriate seasonal activity, were an established tradition in medieval art (compare fig. 11-49). Jean Pucelle had enriched the margins of the calendar pages of his

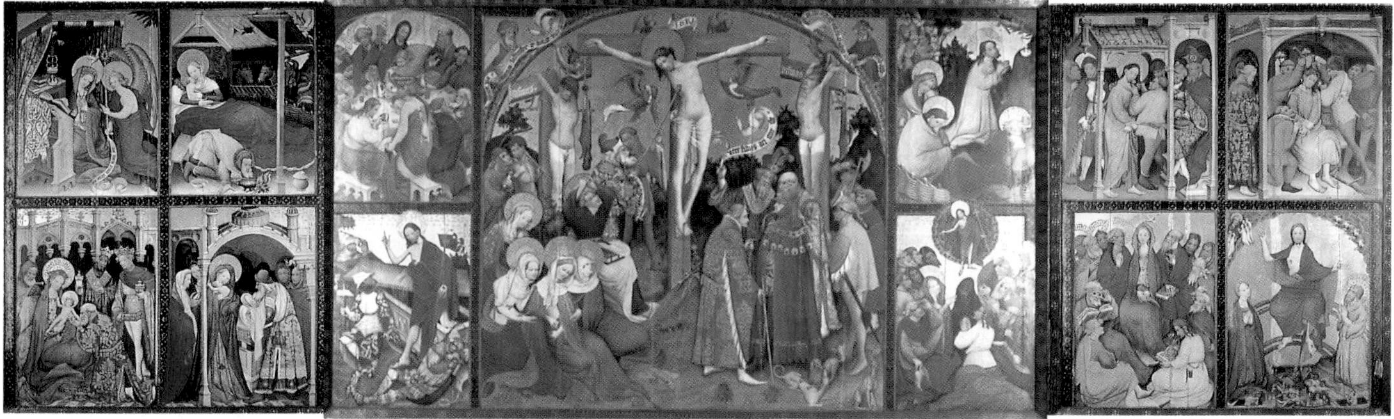

11-95. Konrad von Soest. *The Wildunger Altarpiece.* 1403? Panels, height 6'6¾" (2 m). Church, Bad Wildungen, Germany

books of hours with scenes showing the changing aspects of nature in addition to the labors of the months. The Limbourg brothers, however, combined these elements into a series of panoramas of human life in nature.

The illustration for the month of October (fig. 11-94) shows the sowing of winter grain. It is a bright, sunny day, and the figures—for the first time since classical antiquity—cast visible shadows on the ground. There is a wealth of realistic detail, such as the scarecrow in the middle distance and the footprints of the sower in the soil of the freshly plowed field. The sower is memorable in many ways. His tattered clothing, his unhappy air, go beyond mere description. Although peasants were often caricatured in Gothic art, the portrayal here is surprisingly sympathetic, as it is throughout this book of hours. He is meant to arouse our awareness of the miserable lot of the peasantry in contrast to the life of the aristocracy, symbolized by the castle on the far bank of the river. (The castle is a "portrait" of the Gothic Louvre, the most lavish structure of its kind at that time; see page 317.) Here, then, Gothic art transcends its "realism of particulars" to produce an encompassing vision of life that reflects the Limbourg brothers' knowledge of Italian art, as a glance at Ambrogio Lorenzetti's *Good Government* frescoes (see fig. 11-83) attests.

SOEST. The International Style spread to Germany from France and Bohemia mainly along the Rhine and Danube rivers until it eventually converged on Cologne and nearby Westphalia. The finest representative of this regional style was Konrad von Soest (active 1394–1422) of Dortmund. His *Wildunger Altarpiece* (fig. 11-95) is a truly international blend of elements drawn from throughout Europe. The Crucifixion is descended from Duccio's *Maestà* altar by way of Paris, which accounts for the willowy Christ and delicate Mary. Her grief is sweetly lyrical, in contrast to the despair of St. John behind her. The courtly throng to the left of Christ (the "sinister" side) is patently wicked, and the difference between the two groups could hardly be more telling. The side panels, however, are derived from Bohemian art. Densely packed with figures, they have a drama that is uniquely German but with the refinement characteristic of the International Style as a whole.

MASTER FRANCKE. This intensely expressive manner culminates in the paintings of Master Francke, a Netherlander who probably worked in Paris and Westphalia before settling in Hamburg as a member of the Dominican order. *Christ Carrying the Cross* (fig. 11-96) on the *Englandfahrer Altarpiece,* completed in 1424, has the physical brutality we saw in the Naumburg Master's *Kiss of Judas* (see fig. 11-52). Now it is matched by an expressive violence that makes us feel the full force of Jesus' suffering at the hands of the malevolent crowd, with its coarse, leering faces. Not until Hieronymus Bosch nearly a hundred years later will we again encounter such a pervasive sense of evil. Yet in the sorrowful faces to the left we can sense Master Francke's allegiance to the elegant manner of the International Style.

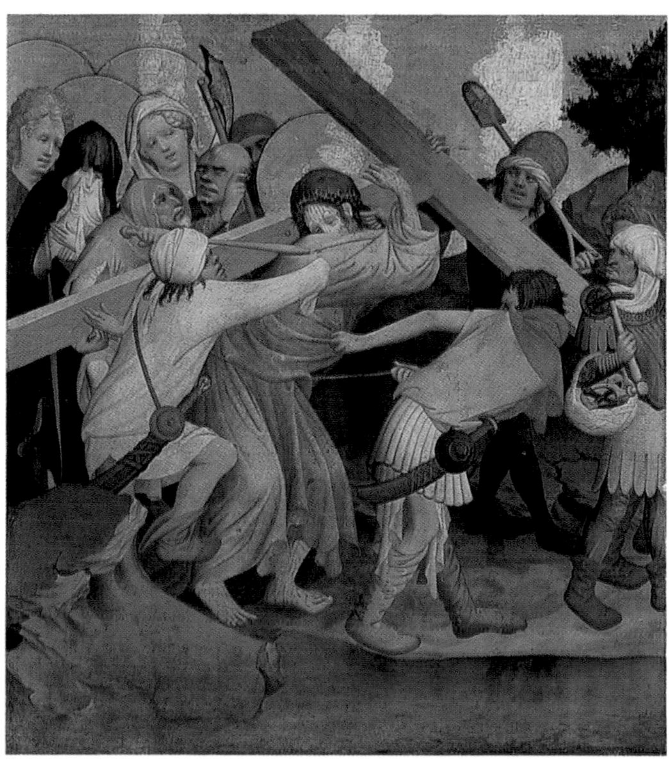

11-96. Master Francke. *Christ Carrying the Cross,* from the *Englandfahrer Altarpiece.* 1424. Panel, 39 x 35" (99 x 88.9 cm). Kunsthalle, Hamburg

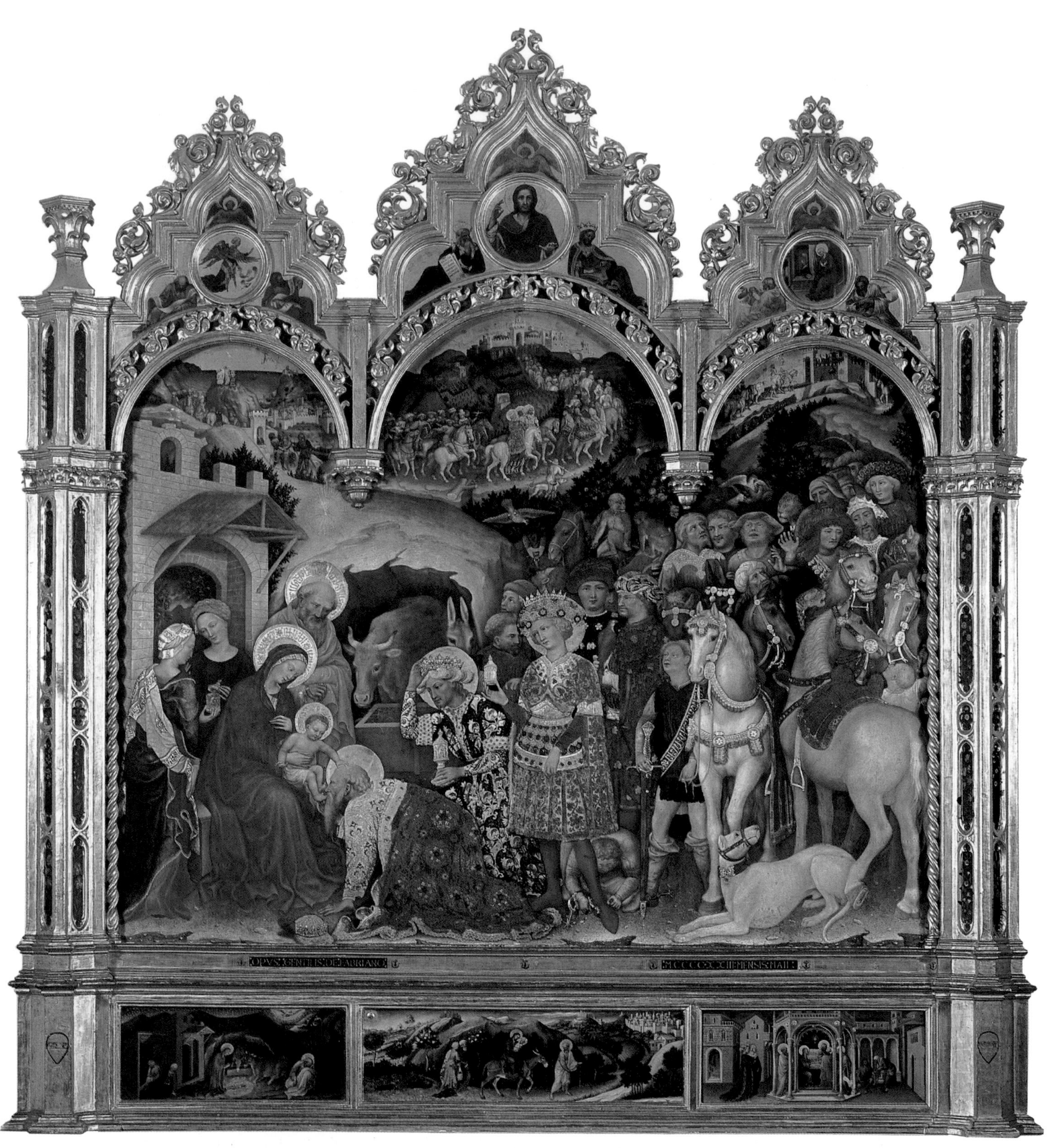

11-97. Gentile da Fabriano. *The Adoration of the Magi.* 1423. Tempera on panel, 9'10 ⅛" x 9'3" (3 x 2.8 m). Galleria degli Uffizi, Florence

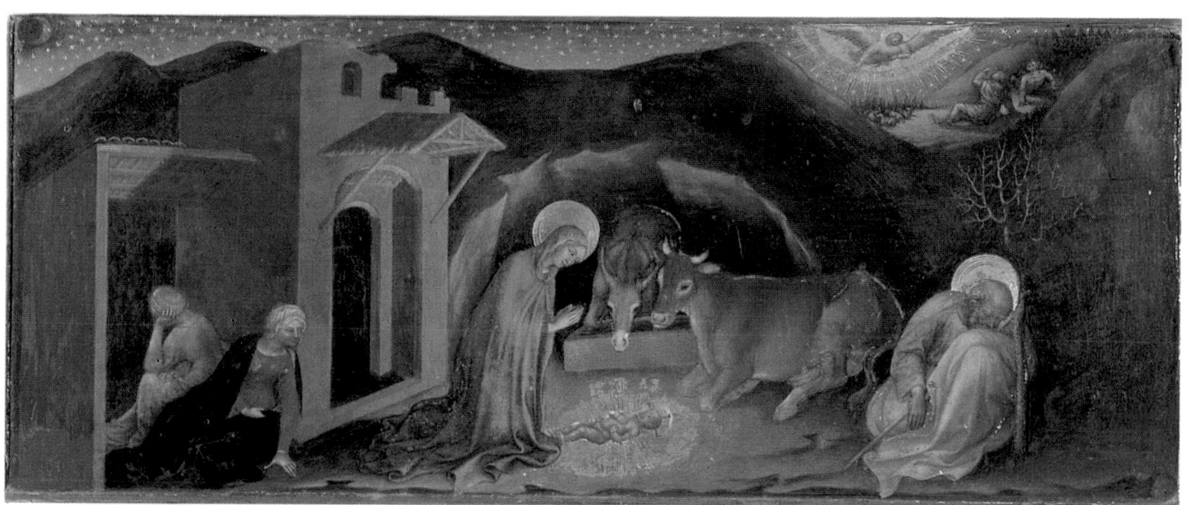

11-98. Gentile da Fabriano. *The Adoration of the Magi*. 1423. Tempera on panel, 9'10⅛" x 9'3" (3 x 2.8 m). Galleria degli Uffizi, Florence

GENTILE DA FABRIANO. Italy was also affected by the International Style, although it gave more than it received. The altarpiece with the three Magi and their train by Gentile da Fabriano (c. 1370–1427; fig. 11-97), the greatest Italian painter of the International Style, shows that he knew the work of the Limbourg brothers. The costumes here are as colorful, the draperies as ample and softly rounded, as in Northern painting. The Holy Family on the left seems almost in danger of being overwhelmed by the festive pageant pouring down from the hills in the distance. The foreground includes more than a dozen marvelously observed animals, not only the familiar ones but leopards, camels, and monkeys. (Such creatures were eagerly collected by the princes of the period, many of whom kept private zoos.) The Oriental background of the Magi is emphasized by the Mongolian facial cast of some of their companions. It is not these exotic touches, however, that mark this as the work of an Italian master, but something else, a greater sense of weight, of physical substance, than we find in Northern painting of the International Style.

Despite his love of detail, Gentile clearly is not a manuscript illuminator but a painter used to working on a large scale. The panels decorating the base, or predella, of the altarpiece have a monumentality that belies their small size. Gentile was thoroughly familiar with Sienese art. Thus the *Flight into Egypt* in the center panel is indebted to Ambrogio Lorenzetti's frescoes in the Siena city hall (see fig. 11-83). (The *Presentation in the Temple* to the right is based on another scene by the same artist that was also the source of Broederlam's depiction.) They show that Gentile, too, could achieve the delicate pictorial effects of a miniaturist when he wanted to.

Although he was not the first artist to depict it, the night scene in *The Nativity* in the left panel of the predella (fig. 11-98), partly based on the vision received by the fourteenth-century Swedish princess St. Bridget in Bethlehem, has an unprecedented poetic intimacy. The picture exhibits the new awareness of light as an independent factor, separate from form and color, that we first observed in the October page of *Les Très Riches Heures*. Even though the main sources of illumination are the divine radiance of the newborn Child ("the light of the world") and of the angel bringing the glad tidings to the shepherds in the fields, their effect is as natural as if the Virgin were kneeling by a campfire. (Note the strong cast shadows.) Yet the artistic possibilities this new world opened up were not to be explored fully until two centuries later, by Northern artists.

Primary Sources for Part Two

The following is a selection of excerpts, in modern translations, from original texts by poets, historians, religious figures, and artists of the Early Christian and Byzantine eras through the Middle Ages. These readings supplement the main text and are keyed to it. Their full citations are given in the Credits section at the end of the book.

13
The Holy Bible, Exodus 20: 1–5

Exodus, the second book of the Old Testament, is one of five books traditionally attributed to Moses (these five are the Hebrew Torah). Exodus tells of the departure of the Jews from Egypt in the thirteenth century B.C. In Chapter 20, God speaks to Moses on Mount Sinai and gives him the Ten Commandments. The second commandment pertains to images.

And the Lord spoke all these words: I am the Lord thy God, who brought thee out of the land of Egypt. . . .

Thou shalt not have strange gods before me.

Thou shalt not make to thyself a graven thing, nor the likeness of any thing that is in heaven above, or in the earth beneath, nor of those things that are in the waters under the earth.

Thou shalt not adore them, nor serve them.

14
POPE GREGORY I (r. 590–604)
From a letter to Serenus of Marseille

Bishop Serenus apparently moved to discourage excessive acts of devotion to paintings in his church by having the images destroyed. In this letter of 600 A.D., Pope Gregory the Great reprimands him, reminding him that images serve to teach those who cannot read. This remained the standard defense of figural painting and sculpture in the Western church throughout the Middle Ages.

Word has . . . reached us that you . . . have broken the images of the saints with the excuse that they should not be adored. And indeed we heartily applaud you for keeping them from being adored, but for breaking them we reproach you. . . . To adore images is one thing; to teach with their help what should be adored is another. What Scripture is to the educated, images are to the ignorant, who see through them what they must accept; they read in them what they cannot read in books. This is especially true of the pagans. And it particularly behooves you, who live among pagans, not to allow yourself to be carried away by just zeal and so give scandal to savage minds. Therefore you ought not to have broken that which was placed in the church not in order to be adored but solely in order to instruct the minds of the ignorant. It is not without reason that tradition permits the deeds of the saints to be depicted in holy places.

15
The Book of the Popes (Liber Pontificalis), from the life of Pope Sylvester I

This text is an official history of the Roman papacy from St. Peter (died c. 64 A.D.) to the twelfth century. Its biographies of the early popes were compiled from archival documents, for example, this list of gifts to Old St. Peter's by the emperor Constantine in the time of Pope Sylvester I (314–335 A.D.). Lavish imperial donations like these set a standard that subsequent popes and other prelates continued to match.

Constantine Augustus built the basilica of blessed Peter, the apostle, . . . and laid there the coffin with the body of the holy Peter; the coffin itself he enclosed on all sides with bronze. . . . Above he set porphyry columns for adornment and other spiral columns which he brought from Greece. He made a vaulted apse in the basilica, gleaming with gold, and over the body of the blessed Peter, above the bronze which enclosed it, he set a cross of purest gold, . . . He gave also 4 brass candlesticks, 10 feet in height, overlaid with silver, with figures in silver of the acts of the apostles, . . . 3 golden chalices, . . . 20 silver chalices, . . . 2 golden pitchers, . . . 5 silver pitchers, . . . a golden paten with a turret of purest gold and a dove, . . . a golden crown before the body, that is a chandelier, with 50 dolphins, . . . 32 silver lamps in the basilica, with dolphins, . . . for the right of the basilica 30 silver lamps, . . . the altar itself of silver overlaid with gold, adorned on every side with gems, 400 in number, . . . a censer of purest gold adorned on every side with jewels.

16
PROCOPIUS OF CAESAREA (6TH CENTURY)
From *Buildings*

Procopius was a historian during the reign of Emperor Justinian. He wrote an entire book (c. 550 A.D.?) about the fortifications, aqueducts, churches, and other public buildings constructed by Justinian throughout the Byzantine Empire. The book begins with the greatest of these, Hagia Sophia (see figs. 8-34–8-36).

The Emperor, disregarding all considerations of expense, . . . raised craftsmen from the whole world. It was Anthemius of Tralles, the most learned man in the discipline called engineering, . . . that ministered to the Emperor's zeal by regulating the work of the builders and preparing in advance designs of what was going to be built. He had as partner another engineer called Isidore, a native of Miletus. . . .

So the church has been made a spectacle of great beauty, stupendous to those who see it and altogether incredible to those who hear of it. . . . It subtly combines its mass with the harmony of its proportions, having neither any excess nor any deficiency, inasmuch as it is more pompous than ordinary [buildings] and considerably more decorous than those which are huge beyond measure; and it abounds exceedingly in gleaming sunlight. You might say that the [interior] space is not illuminated by the sun from the outside, but that the radiance is generated within, so great an abundance of light bathes this shrine all round. . . . In the middle of the church there rise four man-made eminences which are called piers, two on the north and two on the south, . . . each pair having between them exactly four columns. The eminences are built to a great height. . . . As you see them, you could suppose them to be precipitous mountain peaks. Upon these are placed four arches so as to form a square, their ends coming together in pairs and made fast at the summit of those piers, while the rest of them rises to an immense height. Two of the arches, namely those facing the rising and the setting sun, are suspended over empty air, while the others have beneath them some kind of structure and rather tall columns. Above the arches the construction rises in a circle. . . . Rising above this circle is an enormous spherical dome which makes the building exceptionally beautiful. It seems not to be founded on solid masonry, but to be suspended from heaven by that golden chain and so cover the space. All of these elements, marvellously fitted together in mid-air, suspended from one another and reposing only on the parts adjacent to them, produce a unified and most remarkable harmony in the work, and yet do not allow the spectators to rest their gaze upon any one of them for a length of time, but each detail readily draws and attracts the eye to itself. Thus the vision constantly shifts round, and the beholders are quite unable to select any particular element which they might admire more than all the others. No matter how much they concentrate their attention on this side and that, and examine everything with contracted eyebrows, they are unable to understand the craftsmanship and always depart from there amazed by the perplexing spectacle.

17

ST. THEODORE THE STUDITE (759–826 A.D.)

From *Second and Third Refutations of the Iconoclasts*

Theodore of the Stoudios monastery in Constantinople was a principal defender of icons against the Iconoclasts. He refuted their charges of idolatry by examining how an image is and is not identical to its prototype (the person portrayed). Some of his arguments reflect the Neo-Platonic theory expounded by Plotinus that the sense-world is related to the divine by emanation.

The holy Basil [St. Basil the Great, c. 329–379 A.D.] says, "The image of the emperor is also called 'emperor,' yet there are not two emperors, nor is his power divided, nor his glory fragmented. Just as the power and authority which rules over us is one, so also the glorification which we offer is one, and not many. Therefore the honor given to the image passes over to the prototype." . . . In the same way we must say that the icon of Christ is also called "Christ," and there are not two Christs; nor in this case is the power divided, nor the glory fragmented. The honor given the image rightly passes over to the prototype. . . .

Every image has a relation to its archetype; the natural image has a natural relation, while the artificial image has an artificial relation. The natural image is identical both in essence and in likeness with that of which it bears the imprint: thus Christ is identical with His Father in respect to divinity, but identical with His mother in respect to humanity. The artificial image is the same as its archetype in likeness, but different in essence, like Christ and His icon. Therefore there is an artificial image of Christ, to whom the image has its relation. . . .

It is not the essence of the image which we venerate, but the form of the prototype which is stamped upon it, since the essence of the image is not venerable. Neither is it the material which is venerated, but the prototype is venerated together with the form and not the essence of the image. . . .

If every body is inseparably followed by its own shadow, and no one in his right mind could say that a body is shadowless, but rather we can see in the body the shadow which follows, and in the shadow the body which precedes: thus no one could say that Christ is imageless, if indeed He has a body with its characteristic form, but rather we can see in Christ His image existing by implication and in the image Christ plainly visible as its prototype. . . .

By its potential existence even before its artistic production we can always see the image in Christ; just as, for example, we can see the shadow always potentially accompanying the body, even if it is not given form by the radiation of light. In this manner it is not unreasonable to reckon Christ and His image among things which are simultaneous. . . .

If, therefore, Christ cannot exist unless His image exists in potential, and if, before the image is produced artistically, it subsists always in the prototype: then the veneration of Christ is destroyed by anyone who does not admit that His image is also venerated in Him.

18

NICHOLAS MESARITES (c. 1163–AFTER 1214)

From *Description of the Church of the Holy Apostles*

The Church of the Holy Apostles in Constantinople, destroyed in the fifteenth century, was decorated with mosaics by the artist Eulalios in the twelfth century. The account written by the poet Constantinus Rhodius toward the end of his life is extremely lively, if slightly incomplete. (Certain standard subjects are omitted.) It essentially describes the program of the Twelve Great Feasts found in Middle and Late Byzantine mosaic and mural cycles.

The whole inner space has been covered with a mixture of gold and glass, as much as forms the domed roof and rise above the hollowed arches, down to [the revetment of] multicolored marbles and the second cornice. Represented here are the deeds and venerable forms which narrate the abasement of the Logos [Divine Word, God] and His presence among us mortals.

The first miracle is that of Gabriel bringing to a virgin maiden [the tidings of] the incarnation of the Logos and filling her with divine joy. . . .

The second is that of Bethlehem and the cave, the Virgin's giving birth without pain, the Infant, wrapped in swaddling clothes, reclining—O wonder—in a poor manger, the angels singing divine hymns, . . . the rustic lyre of the shepherds sounding the song of God's nativity.

The third is the Magi hastening from Persia to do homage to the all-pure Logos. . . .

The fourth is Simeon, the old man, bearing the infant Christ in his arms. . . . And that strange old prophetess Anna foretelling for all to hear the deeds which the infant was destined to accomplish [The Presentation in the Temple]. . . .

The fifth is the Baptism received from the hands of John by the stream of Jordan; the Father testifying to the Logos from above, and the Spirit coming down in the guise of a bird. . . .

Sixth, you may see Christ ascending the thrice-glorious mount of Tabor together with a chosen band of disciples and friends, altering His mortal form; His face shining with rays more dazzling than those of the sun, His garments a luminous white [The Transfiguration]. . . .

Next, you may see the widow's son, who had been brought on a bier to his tomb, returning alive and joyful to his house [The Raising of the Widow's Son of Nain]. . . .

Then again, Lazarus, who had been laid in his grave and had rotten four days long . . . leaping out of his tomb like a gazelle and returning once more to mortal life after escaping corruption.

Next, Christ mounted on a colt proceeding to the city of the God-slayers, the crowds, with branches and palm leaves acclaiming Him as the Lord when he arrives at the very gates of Zion. . . .

In addition to all the above wonders, you will see . . . Judas, that wretched man, betraying his Lord and teacher to be murdered . . . by an evil and abominable people. . . .

The seventh [actually, the eleventh] spectacle you will see among all these wonders is Christ's Passion [The Crucifixion]. . . . Christ naked, stretched out on the cross between two condemned criminals, . . . his hands and feet pierced with nails, hanging dead upon the wood of the cross . . . and this in the sight of His mother, the pure Virgin, and the disciple who is present at the Passion [St. Luke]. . . .

19

LINDISFARNE GOSPELS
Colophon

Colophons are notes written at the end of some manuscripts recording who wrote them, when, for whom, etc. The colophon at the end of the Lindisfarne Gospels *(c. 700 A.D.) was written some 250 years after the text, but most scholars believe that its information is accurate. It names the scribe, the binder, the maker of the metal ornaments on the binding, and the author of the English translation of the Latin text, but no painter. The painting seems to have been done by Eadfrith, the scribe.*

Eadfrith, Bishop of the Lindisfarne Church, originally wrote this book, for God and for Saint Cuthbert and . . . for all the saints whose relics are in the Island. And Ethelwald, Bishop of the Lindisfarne islanders, impressed it on the outside and covered it—as he well knew how to do. And Billfrith, the anchorite, forged the ornaments which are on it on the outside and adorned it with gold and with gems and also with gilded-over silver—pure metal. And Aldred, unworthy and most miserable priest, glossed it in English between the lines with the help of God and Saint Cuthbert. . . .

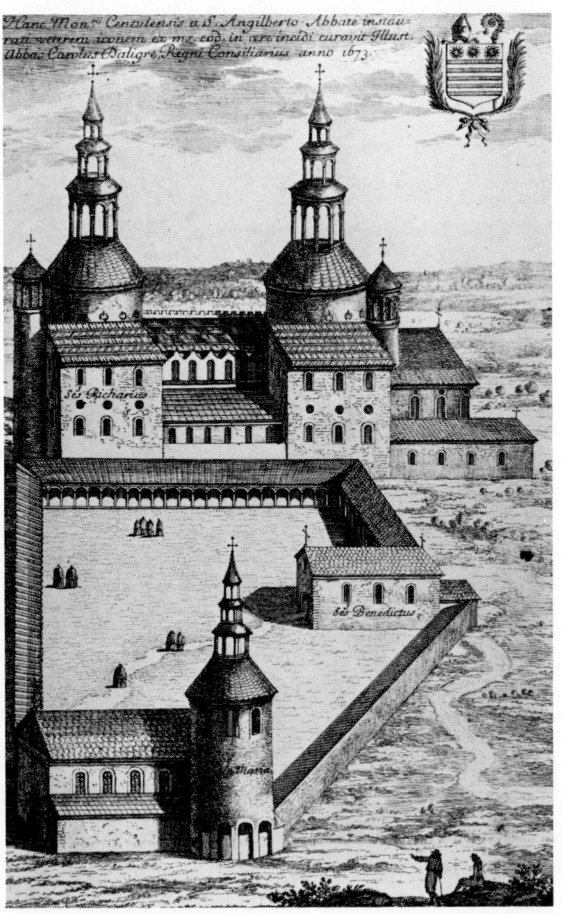

PS-20. Abbey Church of St.-Riquier (1673 engraving after a 1612 view by Petau, from an 11th-century manuscript illumination)

20

HARIULF (c. 1060–1143)

From *History of the Monastery of St.-Riquier*

Hariulf was a monk at St.-Riquier until 1105, when he became abbot of St. Peter's at Oudenbourg in Belgium.

The church dedicated to the Saviour and St. Richarius . . . was among all other churches of its time the most famous. . . . The eastern tower is close to the sepulchre of St. Richarius. . . . The western tower is especially dedicated to the Saviour. . . .

If one surveys the place, one sees that the largest church, that of St. Richarius, lies to the north. The second, somewhat smaller one, which has been built in honor of our Lady on this side of the river, lies to the south. The third one, the smallest, lies to the east. The cloisters of the monks are laid out in a triangular fashion, one roof extending from St. Richarius' to St. Mary's, one from St. Mary's to St. Benedict's and one from St. Benedict's to St. Richarius'. . . . The monastery is so arranged that, according to the rule laid down by St. Benedict, all arts and all necessary labors can be executed within its walls. The river flows through it, and turns the mill of the brothers.

21

ST. ANGILBERT (c. 750–814)

From *Customary for the Different Devotions*

Angilbert, a member of Charlemagne's court, became lay abbot of St.-Riquier in 781 and sponsored the monastery's rebuilding. His description reveals how the resident monks moved from one part of the basilica to another while chanting the devotions prescribed in The Rule *of St. Benedict.*

When the brethren have sung Vespers and Matins at the altar of the Saviour, then one choir should descend on the side of the holy Resurrection, the other one on the side of the holy Ascension, and having prayed there the processions should in the same fashion as before move singing towards the altars of St. John and St. Martin. After having prayed they should enter from both sides through the arches in the middle of the church and pray at the holy Passion. From there they should go to the altar of St. Richarius. After praying they should divide themselves again as before and go to the altars of St. Stephen and St. Lawrence and from there go singing and praying to the altar of the Holy Cross. Thence they should go again to the altar of St. Maurice and through the long gallery to the church of St. Benedict.

22

ST. BENEDICT OF NURSIA (c. 480–c. 553)

From *The Rule*

Monastic communities generally had a rule, or set of regulations, prescribing the discipline of their members' daily life. The Rule *written by St. Benedict for his community at Monte Cassino in southern Italy was admired by Pope Gregory the Great and by Charlemagne, who obtained an exact copy of it when he visited Monte Cassino in 787. The plan of St. Gall was part of a Carolingian effort to impose the Benedictine rule on all monasteries in France and Germany.* The Rule *requires complete renunciation of the world in order to maintain a routine of collective prayer and chanting seven times a day, about four hours of reading and meditation on the Bible, and some manual labor.*

Chapter 16: *The Day Office*

The prophet says: "Seven times daily I have sung Your praises" (Ps. 119:164). We will cleave to this sacred number if we perform our monastic duties at Lauds, Prime, Tierce, Sext, None, Vespers and Compline.

Chapter 17: *The number of psalms said in the Day Office*

Three psalms are to be chanted for Prime, each with a separate Gloria. An appropriate hymn is sung, before the psalms. . . . After the psalms a lesson from the apostle is recited, and the Hour is finished with the versicle, the Kyrie and dismissal. The Hours of Tierce, Sext and None are to be conducted in the same order.

Chapter 22: *How the monks are to sleep*

All the monks shall sleep in separate beds. . . . If possible they should all sleep in one room. However, if there are too many for this, they will be grouped in tens or twenties, a senior in charge of each group. Let a candle burn throughout the night. They will sleep in their robes, belted but with no knives, thus preventing injury in slumber. The monks then will always be prepared to rise at the signal and hurry to the Divine Office. But they must make haste with gravity and modesty.

The younger brothers should not be next to each other. Rather their beds should be interspersed with those of their elders. When they arise for the Divine Office, they ought encourage each other, for the sleepy make many excuses.

Chapter 48: *Daily manual labor*

Idleness is an enemy of the soul. Therefore, the brothers should be occupied according to schedule in either manual labor or holy reading. . . . From Easter to October, the brothers shall work at manual labor from Prime until the fourth hour. From then until the sixth hour they should read. After dinner they should rest (in bed) in silence. However, should anyone desire to read, he should do so without disturbing his brothers.

None should be chanted at about the middle of the eighth hour. Then everyone shall work as they must until Vespers. If conditions dictate that they labor in the fields (harvesting), they should not be grieved for they are truly monks when they must live by manual labor, as did our fathers and the apostles. Everything should be in moderation, though, for the sake of the timorous. . . .

All shall read on Saturdays except those with specific tasks. If anyone is so slothful that he will not or cannot read or study, he will be assigned work so as not to be idle.

Chapter 53: *The reception of guests*

The kitchen of the abbot and guests should be separate from that of the community so as not to disturb the brothers, for the visitors, of whom there are always a number, come and go at irregular hours. . . .

No one may associate or converse with guests unless ordered. If one meets or sees a guest, he is to greet him with humility . . . and ask a blessing. If the guest speaks, the brother is to pass on, telling the guest that he is not permitted to speak.

Chapter 55: *Clothing and shoes*

Each monk needs only two each of tunics and cowls, so he will be prepared for night wear and washing. Anything else is superfluous and should be banished. . . .

Bedding shall consist of a mattress, coverlet, blanket and pillow. The abbot will make frequent inspections of the bedding to prevent hoarding. Any infractions are subject to the severest discipline and, so that this vice of private ownership may be cut away at the roots, the abbot is to furnish all necessities: cowl, tunic, shoes, stockings, belt, knife, pen, needle, towel and writing tablet.

Chapter 57: *Artisans and craftsmen*

Craftsmen present in the monastery should practice their crafts with humility, as permitted by the abbot. But if anyone becomes proud of his skill and the profit he brings the community, he should be taken from his craft and work at ordinary labor. This will continue until he humbles himself and the abbot is satisfied. If any of the works of these craftsmen are sold, the salesman shall take care to practice no fraud. . . .

In pricing, they should never show greed, but should sell things below the going secular rate.

Chapter 66: *The porter of the monastery*

The monastery should be planned, if possible, with all the necessities—water, mill, garden, shops—within the walls. Thus the monks will not need to wander about outside, for this is not good for their souls.

23

From *Pilgrim's Guide to Santiago de Compostela*

The Pilgrim's Guide, *written in the mid-twelfth century, gives a vivid account of the routes and what was to be met along them by pilgrims to the shrine of the Apostle James in Compostela. Describing Ste.-Madeleine (the church of St. Mary Magdalen) at Vézelay (see fig. 10-26), the* Guide *recounts a medieval legend that Mary Magdalen journeyed to France after Christ's death and died in Aix-en-Provence.*

There are four roads which, leading to Santiago, converge to form a single road at Puente la Reina, in Spanish territory. One crosses Saint-Gilles [see fig. 10-27], Montpellier, Toulouse [see figs. 10-1–10-3] and the pass of Somport; another goes through Notre-Dame of Le Puy, Sainte-Foy of Conques and Saint-Pierre of Moissac [see figs. 10-21 and 10-23]; another traverses Sainte-Marie-Madeleine of Vézelay [see fig. 10-26], Saint Léonard in the Limousin as well as the city of Périgueux; still another cuts through Saint-Martin of Tours, Saint-Hilaire of Poitiers, Saint-Jean-d'Angély, Saint-Eutrope of Saintes and the city of Bordeaux. . . .

One needs three more days of march, for people already tired, to traverse the Landes of the Bordelais.

This is a desolate region deprived of all good: there is here no bread, wine, meat, fish, water or springs; villages are rare here. The sandy and flat land abounds none the less in honey, millet, panic-grass, and wild boars. If perchance you cross it in summertime, guard your face diligently from the enormous flies that greatly abound there and which are called in the vulgar wasps or horse-flies; and if you do not watch your feet carefully, you will rapidly sink up to the knees in the sea-sand copiously found all over.

Having traversed this region, one comes to the land of Gascon rich in white bread and excellent red wine. . . . The Gascons are fast in words, loquacious, given to mockery, libidinous, drunkards, prodigal in food. . . . However, they are well-trained in combat and generous in the hospitality they provide for the poor. . . .

They have the habit of eating without a table and of drinking all of them out of one single cup. In fact, they eat and drink a lot, wear rather poor clothes, and lie down shamelessly on a thin and rotten straw litter, the servants together with the master and the mistress.

On leaving that country, . . . on the road of St. James, there are two rivers. . . . There is no way of crossing them without a raft. May their ferrymen be damned! . . . They have the habit of demanding one coin from each man, whether poor or rich, whom they ferry over, and for a horse they ignominiously extort by force four. . . . When boarding . . . one must be most careful not to fall by chance into the water. . . .

Many times the ferryman, having received his money, has such a large troop of pilgrims enter the boat that it capsizes and the pilgrims drown in the waves. Upon which the boatmen, having laid their hands upon the spoils of the dead, wickedly rejoice.

St. Mary Magdalene

On the route that through Saint-Léonard stretches towards Santiago, the most worthy remains of the Blessed Mary Magdalene must first of all be rightly worshipped by the pilgrims. She is . . . that glorious Mary who, in the house of Simon the Leprous, watered with her tears the feet of the Savior, wiped them off with her hair, and anointed them with a precious ointment while kissing them most fervently. . . . It is she who, arriving after the Ascension of the Lord from the region of Jerusalem . . . went by sea as far as the country of Provence, namely the port of Marseille.

In that area she led for some years . . . a celibate life and, at the end, was given burial in the city of Aix. . . . But, after a long time, a distinguished man called Badilon, beatified in monastic life, transported her most precious earthly remains from that city to Vézelay, where they rest up to this day in a much honored tomb. In this place a large and most beautiful basilica as well as an abbey of monks were established [see fig. 10-26]. Thanks to her love, the faults of the sinners are here remitted by God, vision is restored to the blind, the tongue of the mute is untied, the lame stand erect, the possessed are delivered, and unspeakable benefices are accorded to many. Her sacred feast is celebrated on July 22.

The Stonecutters of the Church [of St. James] and the Beginning and Completion of Their Work

The master stonecutters that first undertook the construction of the basilica of the Blessed James were called Master Bernard the elder—a marvelously gifted craftsman—and Robert, as well as other stonecutters, about fifty in number, who worked assiduously under the most faithful administration of Don Wicart, the head of the chapter Don Segeredo, and the abbot Don Gundesindo, during the reign of Alphonso king of Spain and during the bishopric of Don Diego I, a valiant soldier and a generous man.

The church was begun in the year 1116 of the era. . . . And from the year that the first stone of the foundations was laid down until such a time that the last one was put in place, forty-four years have elapsed.

24

ST. BERNARD OF CLAIRVAUX (1090–1153)

From *Apologia to Abbot William of St.-Thierry*

Bernard of Clairvaux was a member of the Cistercians, an ascetic order founded in the eleventh century in opposition to the increasing opulence of the Benedictines. His letter to the Benedictine abbot William of St.-Thierry of about 1127 denounces all monastic luxury, especially the presence of art in cloisters. Like many others, Bernard believed that monks were spiritually superior to the "carnal" layfolk and so should not need material inducements to devotion.

As a monk, I put to monks the same question that a pagan used to criticize other pagans: "Tell me, priests," he said, "what is gold doing in the holy place?" I, however, say, . . . "Tell me, poor men, if indeed you are poor men, what is gold doing in the holy place?" For certainly bishops have one kind of business, and monks another. We [monks] know that since they [bishops] are responsible for both the wise and the foolish, they stimulate the devotion of a carnal people with material ornaments because they cannot do so with spiritual ones. But we who have withdrawn from the people, we who have left behind all that is precious and beautiful in this world for the sake of Christ, we who regard as dung all things shining in beauty, soothing in sound, agreeable in fragrance, sweet in taste, pleasant in touch—in short, all material pleasures— . . . whose devotion, I ask, do we strive to excite in all this? . . .

Does not avarice . . . cause all this . . . ? Money is sown with such skill that it may be multiplied. . . . The very sight of these costly but wonderful illusions inflames men more to give than to pray. In this way wealth is derived from wealth. . . . Eyes are fixed on relics covered with gold and purses are opened. The thoroughly beautiful image of some male or female saint is exhibited and that saint is believed to be the more holy the more highly colored the image is. People rush to kiss it, they are invited to donate, and they admire the beautiful more than they venerate the sacred. . . . What do you think is being sought in all this? The compunction of penitents, or the astonishment of those who gaze at it? O vanity of vanities . . . ! The Church is radiant in its walls and destitute in its poor. . . . It serves the eyes of the rich at the expense of the poor. The curious find that which may delight them, but those in need do not find that which should sustain them. . . .

But apart from this, in the cloisters, before the eyes of the brothers while they read what is that ridiculous monstrosity doing, an amazing kind of deformed beauty and yet a beautiful deformity? What are the filthy apes doing there? The fierce lions? The monstrous centaurs? The creatures, part man and part beast? The striped tigers? The fighting soldiers? The hunters blowing horns? You may see many bodies under one head, and conversely many heads on one body. On one side the tail of a serpent is seen on a quadruped, on the other side the head of a quadruped is on the body of a fish. Over there an animal has a horse for the front half and a goat for the back; here a creature which is horned in front is equine behind. In short, everywhere so plentiful and astonishing a variety of contradictory forms is seen that one would rather read in the marble than in books, and spend the whole day wondering at every single one of them than in meditating on the law of God. Good God! If one is not ashamed of the absurdity, why is one not at least troubled at the expense?

25

SUGER OF ST.-DENIS (1081–1151)

From *On the Consecration of the Church of St.-Denis*

Abbot Suger left two accounts of his rebuilding of the Abbey Church of St.-Denis: a booklet that describes the entire campaign from its conception to the consecration of the new east end on June 11, 1144; and a record of the precious outfittings, including the stained-glass windows, in a review of his accomplishments as abbot. In these excerpts from the first text (1144–47), Suger justifies his enlargement of the Carolingian building with reference to its overcrowding on religious holidays, and he recounts the auspicious discovery of a local quarry and the appearance of the workmen needed to execute his project. After rebuilding the west end of the Carolingian church, he destroyed its eastern apse and built a much larger, more elaborate choir over the old crypt. Suger notes as his principal innovation the radiating chapels filled with stained glass.

Through a fortunate circumstance . . . —the number of the faithful growing and frequently gathering to seek the intercession of the Saints—the [old] basilica had come to suffer grave inconveniences. Often on feast days, completely filled, it disgorged through all its doors the excess of the crowds as they moved in opposite directions, and the outward pressure of the foremost ones not only prevented those attempting to enter from entering but also expelled those who had already entered. At times you could see . . . that no one among the countless thousands of people because of their very density could move a foot; that no one, because of their very congestion, could [do] anything but stand like a marble statue, stay benumbed or, as a last resort, scream. The distress of the women . . . was so great and so intolerable that you could see . . . how they cried out horribly . . . how several of them, . . . lifted by the pious assistance of men above the heads of the crowd, marched forward as though upon a pavement; and how many others, gasping with their last breath, panted in the cloisters of the brethren to the despair of everyone. . . .

Through a gift of God a new quarry, yielding very strong stone, was discovered such as in quality and quantity had never been found in these regions. There arrived a skillful crowd of masons, stonecutters, sculptors and other workmen, so that—thus and otherwise—Divinity relieved us of our fears and favored us with Its goodwill by comforting us and by providing us with unexpected [resources]. I used to compare the least to the greatest: Solomon's riches could not have sufficed for his Temple any more than did ours for this work had not the same Author [God] of the same work abundantly supplied His attendants. The identity of the author and the work provides a sufficiency for the worker. . . .

Upon consideration, then, it was decided to remove that vault, unequal to the higher one, which, overhead, closed the apse containing the bodies of our Patron Saints, all the way [down] to the upper surface of the crypt to which it adhered; so that this crypt might offer its top as a pavement to those approaching by either of the two stairs, and might present the chasses [reliquaries] of the Saints, adorned with gold and precious gems, to the visitors' glances in a more elevated place. Moreover, it was cunningly provided that—through the upper columns and central arches which were to be placed upon the lower ones built in the crypt—the central nave of the old [church] should be equalized, by means of geometrical and arithmetical instruments, with the central nave of the new addition; and, likewise, that the dimensions of the old side-aisles should be equalized with the dimensions of the new side-aisles, except for that elegant and praiseworthy extension, in [the form of] a circular string of chapels, by virtue of which the whole [church] would shine with the wonderful and uninterrupted light of most luminous windows, pervading the interior beauty.

26

SUGER OF ST.-DENIS

From *On What Was Done Under His Administration*

St.-Denis was a Benedictine abbey, though its church was open to layfolk and attracted them in large numbers. The ostentatious embellishment of the church was the type of material display deplored by St. Bernard of Clairvaux. Suger's descriptions of it, recorded between 1144 and 1149, suggest a sensuous love of precious materials, but also a belief that contemplation of these materials could lead the worshiper to a state of heightened spiritual awareness. Like the Byzantine rationale for icons, the notion of "anagogical" transportation to another dimension is indebted to Neoplatonism.

We insisted . . . that the adorable, life-giving cross . . . should be adorned. . . . Therefore we searched around everywhere by ourselves and by our agents for an abundance of precious pearls and gems. . . . One merry but notable miracle which the Lord granted us in this connection we do not wish to pass over. . . . For when I was in difficulty for want of gems and could not sufficiently provide myself with more (for their scarcity makes them very expensive): then, lo and behold, [monks] from three abbeys of two Orders—that is, from Cîteaux and another abbey of the [Cistercian] Order, and from Fontevrault . . . offered us for sale an abundance of gems such as we had not hoped to find in ten years, hyacinths, sapphires, rubies, emeralds, topazes. Their owners had obtained them from Count Thibaut for alms; and he in turn had received them, through the hands of his brother Stephen, King of England [r. 1135–54], from the treasures of his uncle, the late King [Henry I, r. 1100–1135], who had amassed them throughout his life in wonderful vessels. We, however, freed from the worry of searching for gems, thanked God and gave four hundred pounds for the lot though they were worth much more. . . .

We hastened to adorn the Main Altar of the blessed Denis where there was only one beautiful and precious frontal panel from Charles the Bald [843–77], the third Emperor; for at this [altar] we had been offered to the monastic life. . . .

The rear panel, of marvelous workmanship and lavish sumptuousness (for the barbarian artists were even more lavish than ours), we ennobled with chased relief work equally admirable for its form as for its material. . . . Much of what had been acquired and more of such ornaments of the church as we were afraid of losing—for instance, a golden chalice that was curtailed of its foot and several other things—we ordered to be fastened there....

Often we contemplate ... these different ornaments both new and old.... When ... the loveliness of the many-colored gems has called me away from external cares, and worthy meditation has induced me to reflect, transferring that which is material to that which is immaterial, on the diversity of the sacred virtues: then it seems to me that I see myself dwelling, as it were, in some strange region of the universe which neither exists entirely in the slime of the earth nor entirely in the purity of Heaven; and that, by the grace of God, I can be transported from this inferior to that higher world in an anagogical manner....

We [also] caused to be painted, by the exquisite hands of many masters from different regions, a splendid variety of new windows....

Because [these windows] are very valuable on account of their wonderful execution and the profuse expenditure of painted glass and sapphire glass, we appointed an official master craftsman for their protection and repair.

27

ROBERT DE TORIGNY (d. 1186)

From *Chronicle*

Chartres Cathedral burned twice in the twelfth century, in 1134 and 1194. This contemporary notice of the rebuilding of the west front (see fig. 11-9) in the 1140s stresses the participation of masses of lay volunteers. This kind of piety was later referred to as the "cult of the carts."

In this same year, primarily at Chartres, men began, with their own shoulders, to drag the wagons loaded with stone, wood, grain, and other materials to the workshop of the church, whose towers were then rising. Anyone who has not witnessed this will not see the like in our time. Not only there, but also in nearly the whole of France and Normandy and in many other places, [one saw] everywhere . . . penance and the forgiveness of offenses, everywhere mourning and contrition. One might observe women as well as men dragging [wagons] through deep swamps on their knees, beating themselves with whips, numerous wonders occurring everywhere, canticles and hymns being offered to God.

28

From *Meditations on the Life of Christ*

This late-thirteenth-century text, addressed to a Franciscan nun, represents a long-standing tendency to embellish the New Testament account of Christ's life with apocryphal detail. Unlike earlier such embellishments, this one dwells especially on the emotions of the participants in the story. From the twelfth century on, worshipers (especially women) were encouraged to experience Scripture through visualization and emotion rather than as words alone. In its purpose the Meditations *is related to such two- and three-dimensional representations as in figures 11-79 and 11-54.*

Attend diligently and carefully to the manner of the Deposition. Two ladders are placed on opposite sides of the cross. Joseph [of Arimathea] ascends the ladder placed on the right side and tries to extract the nail from His hand. But this is difficult . . . and it does not seem possible to do it without great pressure on the hand of the Lord. . . . The nail pulled out, John makes a sign to Joseph to extend the said nail to him, that the Lady [Virgin Mary] might not see it. Afterwards Nicodemus extracts the other nail from the left hand and similarly gives it to John. Nicodemus descends and comes to the nail in the feet. Joseph supported the body of the Lord: happy indeed is this Joseph, who deserves thus to embrace the body of the Lord! . . . The nail in the feet pulled out, Joseph descends part way, and all receive the body of the Lord and place it on the ground. The Lady supports the head and shoulders in her lap, the Magdalen the feet at which she had formerly found so much grace. The others stand about, all making a great bewailing over Him: all most bitterly bewail Him, as for a first-born son.

After some little time, when night approached, Joseph begged the Lady to permit them to shroud Him in linen cloths and bury Him. She strove against this, saying, "My friends, do not wish to take my Son so soon; or else bury me with Him." She wept uncontrollable tears; she looked at the wounds in His hands and side, now one, now the other; she gazed at His face and head and saw the marks of the thorns, the tearing of His beard, His face filthy with spit and blood, His shorn head; and she could not cease from weeping and looking at Him. . . . The hour growing late, John said, "Lady, let us bow to Joseph and Nicodemus and allow them to prepare and bury the body of our Lord. . . ." She resisted no longer, but blessed Him and permitted Him to be prepared and shrouded.... The Magdalen ... seemed to faint with sorrow.... She gazed at the feet, so wounded, pierced, dried out, and bloody: she wept with great bitterness.... Her heart could hardly remain in her body for sorrow; and it can well be thought that she would gladly have died, if she could, at the feet of the Lord.

29

GIOVANNI PISANO

Inscriptions on the Pulpit in Pisa Cathedral

Giovanni Pisano's pulpit (1302–10) in Pisa Cathedral has two lengthy inscriptions, one of which is visible in figure 11-60. In the first inscription Giovanni praises his own talent; in the second, on the base of the pulpit, he laments that his work is not properly appreciated.

I praise the true God, the creator of all excellent things, who has permitted a man to form figures of such purity. In the year of Our

Lord thirteen hundred and eleven the hands of Giovanni, son of the late Nicola, by their own art alone, carved this work. . . . Giovanni who is endowed above all others with command of the pure art of sculpture, sculpting splendid things in stone, wood and gold . . . would not know how to carve ugly or base things even if he wished to do so. There are many sculptors, but to Giovanni remain the honours of praise. . . .

Giovanni has encircled all the rivers and parts of the world endeavouring to learn much and preparing everything with heavy labour. He now exclaims: 'I have not taken heed. The more I have achieved the more hostile injuries have I experienced. But I bear this pain with indifference and a calm mind.' That I (the monument) may free him from this envy, mitigate his sorrow and win him recognition, add to these verses the moisture (of your tears).

30

DANTE ALIGHIERI (1265–1321)

The Divine Comedy: Paradise, from Canto XVII

When Dante wrote the three books of The Divine Comedy, *he placed many of his contemporaries in Hell, Purgatory, and Paradise. In Paradise he meets his ancestor Cacciaguida, who describes Dante's exile from Florence for political reasons and his protection by Bartolommeo della Scala, father of Can Grande della Scala (see fig. 11-63). Dante stayed at Can Grande's court in Verona from 1314 to 1317.*

"Your first abode, your first refuge, will be the courtesy
of the great Lombard lord [Bartolommeo della Scala]
who[se coat of arms] bears the sacred bird [the eagle]
upon the ladder,

and he will hold you in such high regard
that in your give and take relationship
the one will give before the other asks.

With him you shall see one [Can Grande] who at his birth
was stamped so hard with this star's [Mars'] seal that all
of his achievements will win great renown.

The world has not yet taken note of him;
he is still very young, for Heaven's wheels
have circled round him now for just nine years.

But even before the Gascon [Pope Clement V] tricks proud
Henry [Emperor Henry VII, r. 1308–13],
this one [Can Grande] will show some of his mettle's
sparks by scorning wealth and making light of toil.

Knowledge of his munificence will yet
be spread abroad: even his enemies
will not be able to deny his worth.
Look you to him, expect from him good things.
Through him the fate of many men shall change,
rich men and beggars changing their estate.

Now write this in your mind but do not tell
the world"—and he said things concerning him
incredible even to those who see

them all come true. . . .

31

DANTE ALIGHIERI

The Divine Comedy: Purgatory, from Canto XI

In the first circle of Purgatory are those guilty of the sin of pride. Dante meets a famous manuscript illuminator who has learned the vanity of pride and the fleeting nature of fame, illustrated by the rapidity with which Giotto eclipsed Cimabue.

"Oh!" I said, "*you* must be that Oderisi,
honor of Gubbio, honor of the art
which men in Paris call 'Illuminating.' "

"The pages Franco Bolognese paints,"
he said, "my brother, smile more radiantly;
his is the honor now—mine is far less.

Less courteous would I have been to him,
I must admit, while I was still alive
and my desire was only to excel.

For pride like that the price is paid up here;
I would not even be here, were it not
that, while I still could sin, I turned to God.

Oh, empty glory of all human power!
How soon the green fades from the topmost bough,
unless the following season shows no growth!
Once Cimabue thought to hold the field
as painter; Giotto now is all the rage,
dimming the lustre of the other's fame."

32

LORENZO GHIBERTI (c. 1381–1455)

The Commentaries, from Book 2

Ghiberti's incomplete Commentaries *is an important early document of art history. The first book consists largely of extracts from Pliny and Vitruvius; the second is about art in Italy in the thirteenth and fourteenth cen-*

turies and ends with an account of Ghiberti's own work (fig. 11-65). Like Giovanni Pisano, Ghiberti was not reluctant to praise himself.

Whereas all gifts of fortune are given and as easily taken back, but disciplines attached to the mind never fail, but remain fixed to the very end, . . . I give greatest and infinite thanks to my parents, who . . . were careful to teach me the art, and the one that cannot be tried without the discipline of letters. . . . Whereas therefore through parents' care and the learning of rules I have gone far in the subject of letters or learning in philology, and love the writing of commentaries, I have furnished my mind with these possessions, of which the final fruit is this, not to need any property or riches, and most of all to desire nothing. . . . I have tried to inquire how nature proceeds . . . and how I can get near her, how things seen reach the eye and how the power of vision works, and how visual [word missing] works, and how visual things move, and how the theory of sculpture and painting ought to be pursued.

In my youth, in the year of Our Lord 1400, I left Florence because of both the bad air and the bad state of the country. . . . My mind was largely directed to painting. . . . Nevertheless . . . I was written to by my friends how the board of the temple of St. John the Baptist was sending for well-versed masters, of whom they wanted to see a test piece. A great many very well qualified masters came through all the lands of Italy to put themselves to this test. . . . Each one was given four bronze plates. As the demonstration, the board of the temple wanted each one to make a scene . . . [of] the sacrifice of Isaac. . . . These tests were to be carried out in a year. . . . The competitors were . . . : Filippo di ser Brunellesco, Simone da Colle, Niccolo D'Arezzo, Jacopo della Quercia from Siena, Francesco da Valdambrino, Nicolo Lamberti. . . . The palm of victory was conceded to me by all the experts and by all those who took the test with me. The glory was conceded to me universally, without exception. Everyone felt I had gone beyond the others in that time, without a single exception, with a great consultation and examination by learned men.

. . . The judges were thirty-four, counting those of the city and the surrounding areas; the endorsement in my favor of the victory was given by all, and by the consuls and board and the whole body of the merchants' guild, which has the temple of St. John the Baptist in its charge. It was . . . determined that I should do this bronze door for this temple, and I executed it with great diligence. And this is the first work; with the frame around it, it added up to about twenty-two thousand florins.

33

LORENZO GHIBERTI

The Commentaries, from Book 2

Ghiberti, and Vasari after him, traced the origins of modern painting to Giotto. Giotto is presented here as a natural genius and hence unfettered by the "Greek manner" of his teacher.

The art of painting began to arise [again] in Etruria. In a village near the city of Florence, called Vespignano, a boy of marvelous genius was born. He was drawing a sheep from life, and the painter Cimabue, passing on the road to Bologna, saw the boy sitting on the ground and drawing a sheep on a flat rock. He was seized with admiration. . . . And seeing he had his skill from nature, he asked the boy what his name was. He answered and said, I am called Giotto by name, my father is called Bondone and lives in this house close by. Cimabue went with Giotto to his father; he made a very fine appearance. He asked the father for the boy; the father was very poor. He handed the boy over to him and Cimabue took Giotto with him and he was Cimabue's pupil. He [Cimabue] used the Greek manner, and in that manner he was very famous in Etruria. And Giotto grew great in the art of painting.

He brought in the new art, . . . and many pupils were taught on the level of the ancient Greeks. Giotto saw in art what no others added. He brought in natural art, and grace with it. . . . He was . . . the inventor and discoverer of much learning that had been buried some six hundred years.

34

THEOPHILUS PRESBYTER

On Divers Arts, from Book II: "The Art of the Worker in Glass"

"Theophilus" may have been the pseudonym of Roger of Helmarshausen, a Benedictine monk and metalworker. Metalwork is the subject of the third book of this treatise, following books on painting and stained glass. Theophilus' text, written in the twelfth century, is the first in the Western tradition to give a practitioner's account of the technology of art production.

Chapter 17: *Laying Out Windows*

When you want to lay out glass windows, first make yourself a smooth flat wooden board. . . . Then take a piece of chalk, scrape it with a knife all over the board, sprinkle water on it everywhere, and rub it all over with a cloth. When it has dried, take the measurements . . . of one section in a window, and draw it on the board with a rule and compasses. . . . Draw as many figures as you wish, first with [a point made of] lead or tin, then with red or black pigment, making all the lines carefully, because, when you have painted the glass, you will have to fit together the shadows and highlights in accordance with [the design on] the board. Then arrange the different kinds of robes and designate the color of each with a mark in its proper place; and indicate the color of anything else you want to paint with a letter.

After this, take a lead pot and in it put chalk ground with water. Make yourself two or three brushes out of hair from the tail of a marten, badger, squirrel, or cat or from the mane of a donkey. Now take a piece of glass of whatever kind you have chosen, but larger on all sides than the place in which it is to be set, and lay it on the ground for that place. Then you will see the drawing on the board through the intervening glass, and, following it, draw the outlines only on the glass with chalk.

Chapter 18: *Glass Cutting*

Next heat on the fireplace an iron cutting tool, which should be thin everywhere except at the end, where it should be thicker. When the thicker part is red-hot, apply it to the glass that you want to cut, and soon there will appear the beginning of a crack. If the glass is hard [and does not crack at once], wet it with saliva on your finger in the place where you had applied the tool. It will immediately split and, as soon as it has, draw the tool along the line you want to cut and the split will follow.

35
VILLARD DE HONNECOURT (13TH CENTURY)
From *Sketchbook*

The first inscription below addresses the user of Villard's Sketchbook *and suggests what the book might be for. The others appear on the leaves shown in figures 11-68 and 11-69.*

Villard de Honnecourt greets you and begs all who will use the devices found in this book to pray for his soul and remember him. For in this book will be found sound advice on the virtues of masonry and the uses of carpentry. You will also find strong help in drawing figures according to the lessons taught by the art of geometry.

Here is a lion seen from the front. Please remember that he was drawn from life. This is a porcupine, a little beast that shoots its quills when aroused. Here below are the figures of the Wheel of Fortune, all seven of them correctly pictured.

36
AGNOLO DI TURA DEL GRASSO
From *History*

Duccio's Maestà *(figs. 11-73–11-75) stood on the main altar of Siena Cathedral until 1506, when it was removed to the transept. It was sawn apart in 1771, and some panels were acquired subsequently by museums in Europe and the United States. This local history of about 1350 describes the civic celebration that accompanied the installation of the altarpiece in 1311.*

This [the *Maestà*] was painted by master Duccio di Niccolò, painter of Siena, who was in his time the most skillful painter one could find in these lands. The panel was painted outside the Porta a Stalloreggi . . . in the house of the Muciatti. The Sienese took the panel to the cathedral at noontime on the ninth of June [1311], with great devotions and processions, with the bishop of Siena, . . . with all of the clergy of the cathedral, and with all the monks and nuns of Siena, and the Nove, with the city officials, the Podestà and the Captain, and all the citizens with coats of arms and those with more distinguished coats of arms, with lighted lamps in hand. . . . The women and children went through Siena with much devotion and around the Campo in procession, ringing all the bells for joy, and this entire day the shops stayed closed for devotions, and throughout Siena they gave many alms to the poor people, with many speeches and prayers to God and to his mother, Madonna ever Virgin Mary, who helps, preserves and increases in peace the good state of the city of Siena and its territory, . . . and who defends the city from all danger and all evil. And so this panel was placed in the cathedral on the high altar. The panel is painted on the back . . . with the Passion of Jesus Christ, and on the front is the Virgin Mary with her son in her arms and many saints at the side. Everything is ornamented with fine gold; it cost three thousand florins.

37
Inscriptions on the frescoes in the Palazzo Pubblico, Siena

The first inscription is painted in a strip below the fresco of Good Government *(see figs. 11-83–11-85), which is dated between 1338 and 1340. The second is held by the personification of "Security," who hovers over the landscape in figure 11-84.*

Turn your eyes to behold her,
you who are governing, [Justice] who is portrayed here,
crowned on account of her excellence,
who always renders to everyone his due.
Look how many goods derive from her
and how sweet and peaceful is that life
of the city where is preserved
this virtue who outshines any other.
She guards and defends
those who honor her, and nourishes and feeds them.
From her light is born
Requiting those who do good
and giving due punishment to the wicked.

Without fear every man may travel freely
and each may till and sow,
so long as this commune
shall maintain this lady [Justice] sovereign,
for she has stripped the wicked of all power.

38

GIOVANNI BOCCACCIO (1313–1375)

Decameron, from *The First Day*

The young people who tell the 100 stories of Boccaccio's Decameron *have fled Florence to escape the bubonic plague. At the beginning of the book, Boccaccio describes the horror of the disease and the immensity of the epidemic, as well as the social dissolution it produced.*

The years of the fruitful Incarnation of the Son of God had attained to the number of one thousand three hundred and forty-eight, when into the notable city of Florence, fair over every other of Italy, there came the death-dealing pestilence, . . . through the operation of the heavenly bodies or of our own iniquitous doings, being sent down upon mankind for our correction by the just wrath of God. . . . In men and women alike there appeared, at the beginning of the malady, certain swellings, either on the groin or under the armpits, whereof some waxed to the bigness of a common apple, others to the size of an egg, . . . and these the vulgar named plague-boils. From these two parts the aforesaid death-bearing plague-boils proceeded, in brief space, to appear and come indifferently in every part of the body; wherefrom, after awhile, the fashion of the contagion began to change into black or livid blotches. . . .

Well-nigh all died within the third day from the appearance of the aforesaid signs, this one sooner and that one later, and for the most part without fever or other complication. . . . The mere touching of the clothes or of whatsoever other thing had been touched or used by the sick appeared of itself to communicate the malady to the toucher. . . .

Well-nigh all tended to a very barbarous conclusion, namely, to shun and flee from the sick and all that pertained to them. . . . Some there were who conceived that to live moderately and keep oneself from all excess was the best defense; . . . they lived removed from every other, taking refuge and shutting themselves up in those houses where none were sick and where living was best. . . . Others, inclining to the contrary opinion, maintained that to carouse and make merry and go about singing and frolicking and satisfy the appetite in everything possible and laugh and scoff at whatsoever befell was a very certain remedy for such an ill. . . .

The common people (and also, in great part, . . . the middle class) . . . fell sick by the thousand daily and being altogether untended and unsuccored, died well-nigh all without recourse. Many breathed their last in the open street, by day and by night, while many others, though they died in their homes, made it known to the neighbors that they were dead rather by the stench of their rotting bodies than otherwise; and of these and others who died all about, the whole city was full. . . . The consecrated ground not sufficing for the burial of the vast multitude of corpses . . . there were made throughout the churchyards, . . . vast trenches, in which those who came . . . were laid by the hundred, . . . being heaped up therein by layers, as goods are stowed aboard ship. . . .

So great was the cruelty of heaven . . . that, between March and the following July, . . . it is believed for certain that upward of a hundred thousand human beings perished within the walls of the city of Florence. . . . Alas, how many great palaces, how many goodly houses, how many noble mansions, once full of families, of lords and of ladies, remained empty even to the meanest servant! How many memorable families, how many ample heritages, how many famous fortunes were seen to remain without lawful heir! How many valiant men, how many fair ladies, how many sprightly youths, . . . breakfasted in the morning with their kinsfolk, comrades and friends and that same night supped with their ancestors in the other world!

39

CHRISTINE DE PIZAN (c. 1363–c. 1430)

From *The Book of the City of Ladies*

Born in Venice but active in Paris and the courts of France, Christine de Pizan was a learned and well-known writer who championed the cause of women. This passage from her history of women (1404–5) mentions a manuscript illuminator who would have been a contemporary of the Limbourg brothers.

Regarding what you say about women expert in the art of painting, I know a woman today, named Anastasia, who is so learned and skilled in painting manuscript borders and miniature backgrounds that one cannot find an artisan in all the city of Paris—where the best in the world are found—who can surpass her, nor who can paint flowers and details as delicately as she does, nor whose work is more highly esteemed, no matter how rich or precious the book is. People cannot stop talking about her. And I know this from experience, for she has executed several things for me which stand out among the ornamental borders of the great masters.

Timeline Two: 300 to 1350

	300–600	600–700	700–750
HISTORY AND POLITICS	**Constantine the Great (r. 307–37)** reunites Roman Empire, moving capital to Constantinople, formerly Byzantium; 313, proclaims Edict of Milan, allowing religious toleration; c. 312, converts to Christianity. The religion spreads rapidly through the Roman world **410** Sack of Rome by the Visigoth Alaric **451** Attila, leader of the Huns, invades Gaul from eastern Europe and, in 452, Italy **476** Western Roman Empire falls, its territories divided among local rulers **c. 493** Theodoric, Eastern Roman Emperor, establishes Ostrogoth Kingdom in Italy **Justinian, Eastern Roman Emperor (r. 527–65)** with Empress Theodora. Their reign is marked by peace, legal reforms, and attempts to reunite the Empire **568** Lombard kingdom created in northern Italy	**600–800** Golden Age of Celtic culture **669–90** Theodore of Tarsus begins organization of English rival groups; period of Graeco-Roman cultural revival **697 (traditional)** First doge of Venice elected by governing council	**711–15** Conquest of North Africa and Spain by Muslims; much of the Mediterranean controlled by the Arabs **717** Leo III, Byzantine emperor (r. 717–41) defeats Arab invaders and establishes a period of peace; 726, his prohibition of images in churches sparks the Iconoclastic Controversy
RELIGION	**395** Christianity becomes official religion of the Roman Empire **432** St. Patrick (died c. 461) founds Celtic church in Ireland **529** St. Benedict (c. 480–c. 553) founds Benedictine monastic order		
MUSIC, LITERATURE, AND PHILOSOPHY	**Ammianus Marcellinus (c. 330–95),** Roman historian **Boethius (c. 480–524),** Roman philosopher whose *Consolation of Philosophy* held the struggle for knowledge to be the highest expression of love of God	**c. 600** Gregorian chants widely used in Catholic Mass **Isidore of Seville (d. 636),** encyclopedist **The Venerable Bede (673–735),** English writer and historian, primary member of Theodore of Tarsus' intellectual group	**Early 700s** *Beowulf,* English epic
SCIENCE, TECHNOLOGY, AND EXPLORATION	**c. 410** First records of alchemical experiments, in which science and myth are utilized to try to create gold from metal **c. 550** Procopius of Caesarea writes *Buildings,* on architecture and public works of the Byzantine Empire **c. 600** Chinese invent woodblock printing	**c. 600** Stirrup introduced in western Europe **604** First church bell made in Rome	

ICONOCLASM From the earliest days of Christianity, painted and carved images were used in churches as decorations, representing holy figures, biblical narratives, miracles, and other pious scenes. Such works of art have usually been considered precious and were sometimes venerated as holy themselves; but at some moments in history they have been attacked as idolatrous. In the eighth century the Byzantine emperor Leo III harshly criticized such images, placing himself in opposition to the pope, who declared them sacred. In 726 Leo issued a decree prohibiting images in churches. This touched off a power struggle between the Eastern emperor and the Western papacy. The controversy raised fundamental religious questions regarding the interpretation of the Bible and the divinity of Christ. In the course of it, Leo's followers, called Iconoclasts, destroyed much of the Byzantine art that existed at the time in churches, especially in the East. The Iconoclastic Controversy was no small event: cities revolted; battles were fought; and though the debate over artworks may have mainly been the excuse for a clash of the political forces of church and state, the importance of images—their power to move and stir people—should not be underestimated.

An effect of the ban on pious images was that artistic energies were temporarily channeled into secular and private art—for example, illuminated manuscripts for private use. The debate was settled in favor of holy images in 843, when image-worship was established by the pope as doctrinal. Grand cycles of mosaics like those formerly found in Byzantine churches reappeared slowly, and these displayed a new humanism derived from the secular, classicizing work of the Iconoclastic period.

Virgin and Child Enthroned Between Saints and Angels, Monastery of St. Catherine, Mount Sinai, late 6th century

750–800	800–850	850–900

HISTORY AND POLITICS

756 Pepin the Short, king of the Franks (r. 747–68), defeats the Lombards in Italy and destroys their kingdom. His gift of conquered central Italian lands to the pope (the Papal States) allows the papacy to be independent and earns France a privileged position

Charlemagne (r. 768–814), Pepin's successor, establishes control of most of Europe. His organization of European society into semi-autonomous regional centers (called marks) becomes the basis for feudal society; 800, crowned Holy Roman Emperor by the pope. Charlemagne's empire is divided after his death into eastern and western Frankish kingdoms (approximately present-day France and Germany)

Irene, first empress of Byzantium (r. 797–802)

800–900 Invasions by Scandinavian peoples in the North, Muslims in the Mediterranean, and Magyars from the East destabilize much of Europe, which suffers extended warfare

804–800 Vikings invade Ireland and, 856–75, British Isles. By 878, Danes control Scotland

c. 850–900 Angkor Thom, capital of the Khmer people, founded in what is now Cambodia. The moated city covers five square miles and has elaborate temples and palaces

c. 900 Toltec people settle in Mexico; they clash with the Maya in Yucatán

CHARLEMAGNE In the late eighth century, Charlemagne consolidated much of what is now France, Germany, Italy, and the Balkans into a single kingdom, with his court at Aachen in Germany. So much territory in the West had not been under one rule since Roman times. His coronation by the pope in Rome in 800 was clearly understood throughout Europe as a sign of his power over the papacy and the strength of his position. As such, it was seen as a threat by the Byzantine Empire in Constantinople and signaled the definitive division of the Christian world into two rival realms. Charlemagne was a great founder of schools, monasteries, and systems of civil administration. In the Carolingian period, named for his dynasty, the arts flourished as they often do in times of relative stability.

RELIGION

St. Angilbert (c. 750–814), monk at Charlemagne's court, rebuilds St.-Riquier Abbey

St. Boniface (d. 755) converts Germanic peoples to Christianity

St. Theodore the Studite (759–826) defends use of icons

Crucifixion, bronze plaque from a book cover(?), Ireland, 8th century

Chi-Rho page, from the *Book of Kells,* Ireland, c. 800?

Virgin and Child Enthroned, mosaic, Hagia Sophia, Constantinople, c. 843–67

Lindau Gospels, upper cover of binding, c. 870

MUSIC, LITERATURE, AND PHILOSOPHY

Hrabanus Maurus (784–856), German encyclopedist

c. 800 Carolingian schools chartered by Charlemagne, encouraging study of Latin texts

c. 800 First version of *The Thousand and One Nights,* a collection of Arabian stories of the court of Hārūn al-Rashīd

SCIENCE, TECHNOLOGY, AND EXPLORATION

822 Earliest documented church organ, Aachen

c. 850 Horse collar adopted in western Europe for draft work

860 Danish Vikings discover Iceland; c. 866, they attack England; c. 980, they find Greenland

Timeline Two: 300 to 1350

	900–950	950–1000	1000–1050
HISTORY AND POLITICS	**907** In China, the Five Dynasties period sees the land politically divided	**962** Otto I the Great, ruler of Germany (r. 936–73), defeats Magyar invaders and assumes crown of the Holy Roman Empire **Capetian kings (later, kings of France, 987–1792)** come to power in Frankish Kingdom with Hugh Capet (r. 987–96)	**1016** Normans arrive in Italy from northern France, establishing a kingdom in the south, 1071, by taking Bari; between 1072 and 1091 they take Sicily, evicting the Arabs who had possessed the island **First kings of Scotland:** Duncan I (r. 1034–40), murdered by the usurper Macbeth (r. 1040–57), himself defeated by Malcolm Canmore (r. 1057–93). Beginning of Anglicization of Scotland **Henry III the Black (r. 1039–56)** aggressively asserts German imperial authority by personally nominating new popes and mastering the duchies of Poland, Hungary, and Bohemia
RELIGION	**c. 900** Russia converts to Christianity under the Eastern Orthodox church **910** Abbey of Cluny founded in France. Cluniac organization of monasteries and reforming methods spread through Europe	**Bishop Bernward (bishop 993–1022)** makes Hildesheim, in Germany, a cultural and artistic center	
		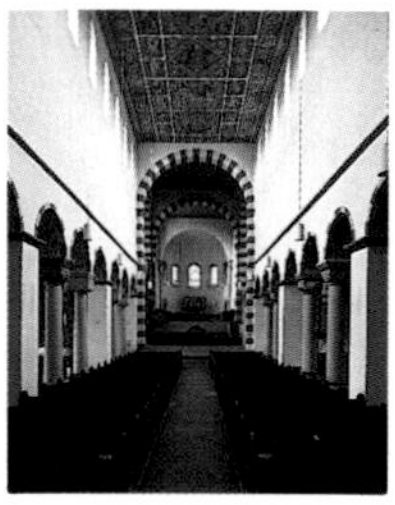 Interior, Hildesheim Cathedral, 1001–33 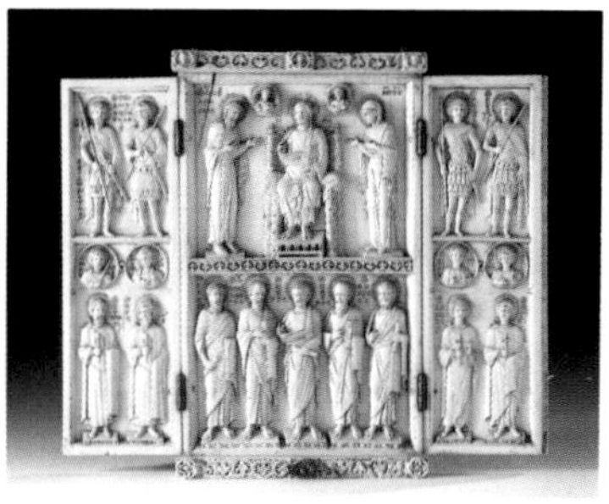 *The Harbaville Triptych,* ivory altar, late 10th century	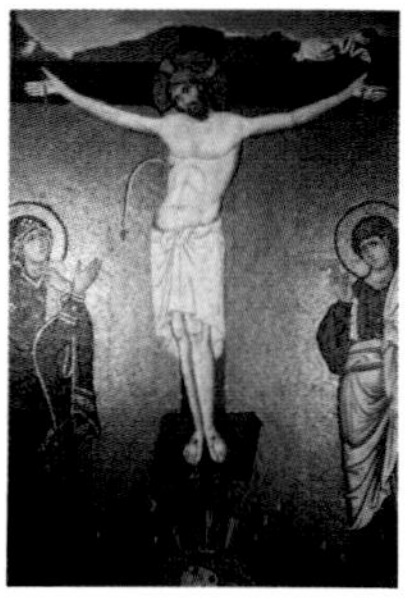 *The Crucifixion,* mosaic, Greece, 11th century
MUSIC, LITERATURE, AND PHILOSOPHY			**c. 1000** Ottonian revival in Germany **c. 1000** Development of modern music notation system in Europe **Solomon ibn Gabirol (1020–70),** Jewish poet and philosopher active in Muslim Spain
SCIENCE, TECHNOLOGY, AND EXPLORATION		**Ibn Sînâ (Avicenna) (980–1037?),** Arab physician and interpreter of Aristotle, active in Persia and the Middle East; chief medical authority of the Middle Ages	**c. 1000** Urban development of Europe begins; cities grow steadily in importance and size throughout the Middle Ages. Use of abacus for computation in Europe **1002** Leif Ericson sails to North America and establishes a settlement

MONASTERIES The great European monastic orders of the Middle Ages were founded during a time of weak governments and economic uncertainty; neither education nor literacy was common. Financed by kings, private patrons, and the papacy, abbeys such as Lindisfarne in England (635), Cluny (910) and Clairvaux (1115) in France, Hildesheim in Germany (1001–33), and Assisi in Italy (1209) were stable, self-contained societies in which strict religious observance was combined with intellectual and artistic experimentation, in a blend peculiar to the Middle Ages. Exempt from taxation, they became wealthy and powerful. Monastic life was dedicated to the furthering of Christian doctrine; this often meant not only pious works but the search for knowledge. Monks copied and wrote books; studied architecture, engineering, mathematics, medicine, and philosophy; painted frescos and panels and illuminated manuscripts.

	1050–1100	1100–1150	1150–1200
HISTORY AND POLITICS	**1066** French Normans under William the Conqueror, duke of Normandy, invade England and defeat local forces under King Harold at Battle of Hastings. William crowned king of England **1083** Henry IV, Holy Roman Emperor (ruler of Germany), invades Italy in a dispute with the pope; 1084, Rome sacked by Normans. Ensuing political chaos results in increased power of individual German principates and weakening of papacy **1096** First Crusade, called by Pope Urban II in 1095, to retake the Holy Land from the Muslims for Christianity. A disorganized mass of mostly French, Norman, and Flemish nobles and peasants, 30,000 or more, leaves Europe for Palestine in several waves; an estimated 12,000 are killed in Asia Minor; 1097–99, the crusading force takes Nicaea, Antioch, and Jerusalem, which they sack	**Foundation of the crusading orders of knighthood:** 1113, Knights Hospitalers; 1118, Templars; 1190, Teutonic Knights **1122** Suger becomes abbot of St.-Denis, near Paris, and adviser to kings Louis VI and Louis VII **1147–49** Second Crusade called, urged by the preaching of St. Bernard of Clairvaux; it achieves little. Suger is regent of France	**1171** Salah al-Din (Saladin), ruler of Egypt, dominates Damascus and captures Syria; 1187, he recaptures Jerusalem for Islam **1189–92** Third Crusade, a fruitless attempt to regain Jerusalem, led by Frederick I Barbarossa, Holy Roman Emperor; King Richard I the Lionhearted of England; and King Philip II of France, all of them rivals; the papacy is largely excluded. Project ends with capture of English king Richard I. The crusading armies, unable to oust Saladin from Palestine, conclude a pact with him that permits Christian pilgrims to visit Jerusalem unmolested
RELIGION	**1054** Final schism between Eastern (Orthodox) and Western (Catholic) Christian Churches **c. 1115** St. Bernard (1090–1153) heads the ascetic Cistercian order at the abbey of Clairvaux, in northern France		
MUSIC, LITERATURE, AND PHILOSOPHY	**c. 1050** *Chanson de Roland,* French epic tale **Hariulf (c. 1060–1143),** a monk at St.-Riquier, author of a history of the monastery **Peter Abelard (1079?–1144),** French Nominalist philosopher at the University of Paris, author of *Sic et Non,* a theological inquiry, and opponent of St. Bernard of Clairvaux	**c. 1100 Chrétien de Troyes,** French poet, writes Arthurian romances **Omar Khayyam (c. 1100),** Persian poet **Early 1100s** Troubadour poetry and music, a courtly, intricate style, often on the theme of love, popular in France and Italy **Ibn Rushd (Averroës) (c. 1126–98),** Spanish Muslim physician and philosopher, author of treatises on Plato and Aristotle	**c. 1160** *Nibelungenleid,* German epic **Nicholas Mesarites (c. 1163–after 1214),** Byzantine chronicler **Late 1100s** *Carmina Burana,* a collection of popular secular poems **Albertus Magnus (1192–1280),** German Scholastic philosopher **Matthew Paris (c. 1200–59),** French historian
SCIENCE, TECHNOLOGY, AND EXPLORATION	**1086** Domesday survey in England, first full census of a population, for taxation purposes. Domesday Book, containing collected data, compiled	**1100s** Moorish paper mills in operation; use in Italy of lateen sail for improved sailing; soap in widespread use; Theophilus Presbyter, German scholar, publishes manual on building and decorating a cathedral	**c. 1150** Crossbow, more effective than the standard bow and arrow, in widespread use **c. 1170** Leonardo of Pisa, Italian mathematician, introduces Hindu mathematics, geometry, and algebra **1180–1223** Philip II of France embarks on a rebuilding of Paris. Roads are paved, walls erected, and, c. 1200, the Louvre palace is begun **1193** First merchant guild, England

SUGER, ST.-DENIS, AND ARCHITECTURAL SYMBOLISM The prelate Suger, made abbot in 1122 of the Abbey Church of St.-Denis, was regent of France while King Louis VII was away on the Second Crusade. As such, his rebuilding of the church, begun c. 1140, was more than a simple architectural project. It set the standard for Gothic churches and is an early example of architecture used to represent political power and a philosophical idea.

The aesthetic design of the building has been attributed to Suger's interest in Scholasticism and Neoplatonism. Thus, the individual parts of the building support the entire structure, much as the individual believer upholds the Christian faith as a whole. St.-Denis was intended to be seen as the Christian universe in microcosm, an architectural experience of beauty through which the visitor comes to an emotional understanding of Christ. Technological innovations allowed the walls to be pierced with large windows that filled the interior with brilliant colored light. In Neo-Platonist terms, the stupendous stained-glass windows of the choir were meant not merely to illuminate the altar but to represent divine light itself, the ineffable spirit of God made visible.

In addition, as depository of holy relics and burial place of the kings of France, the Abbey Church had an important political function. Suger's new design served to glorify the nascent French state and to affirm the role of the monarch as defender of the faith. The building was thus created as a network of religious, aesthetic, and political ideas.

(LEFT) Speyer Cathedral, Germany, begun 1030
(RIGHT) *The Arrest of Christ,* fresco, S. Angelo in Formis, Capua, c. 1085

Timeline Two: 300 to 1350

	1200–1225	1225–1250	1250–1275
HISTORY AND POLITICS	**1202–4** Fourth Crusade sets out for Palestine in Venetian ships. Diverted to Christian Constantinople, crusaders sack the city; entire enterprise excommunicated by the pope; 1208–74, numerous other crusades shift possession of lands in the Middle East from one of the Western powers to another and confront the Muslims, who nevertheless hold Jerusalem from 1244 until 1917 **1206–23** Mongol ruler Genghis Khan crosses Asia and Russia, threatening Europe **1215** Magna Carta, a pact between the English monarch and the feudal barons, signed by King John. The document, limiting the absolute powers of the monarchy, is the genesis of a new constitution that places the law over the will of the king, contains new legal, religious, and taxation rights for the individual, including the right to a trial and other reforms, and establishes a parliament	**Louis IX, king of France (St. Louis, r. 1226–70),** leads Seventh and Eighth Crusades	**1254–73** Period of strife in Germany, with contested claims to the throne of the Holy Roman Empire, confirms fractured nature of individual German states and signals the end of the empire as a political power **By 1263** Papal grant to trade awarded to Teutonic Knights, originally a crusading order of chivalry. The order grows powerful in the absence of any strong monarch and controls much of Prussia, northern Germany, and parts of Lithuania and Poland. Founds numerous independent cities as a mercantile corporation; these later form part of the Hanseatic League of free trading cities of northern Europe **1271–95** The trader Marco Polo travels from Venice to the court of Kublai Khan. His journeys through India, China, Burma, and Persia open the first diplomatic relations between European and Asian nations
RELIGION	**1215** Fourth Lateran Council of bishops, in Rome, establishes major Catholic doctrines: transubstantiation, practice of confession, and worship of relics **1223** St. Francis of Assisi founds Franciscan monastic order, emphasizing poverty		
MUSIC, LITERATURE, AND PHILOSOPHY	**1200** Foundation of the University of Paris (called the Sorbonne after 1257); 1209, University of Valencia; 1242, University of Salamanca; these become centers for interchange between Arabs and Christians	**St. Thomas Aquinas (1225–74),** Italian Scholastic philosopher. His *Summa Theologica,* a founding text of Catholic teaching, examines the relationship between faith and intellect, religion and society	**Vincent of Beauvais (d. 1264),** French encyclopedist **Dante Alighieri (1265–1321),** author of *The Divine Comedy,* in Tuscan vernacular. The poem is immensely influential for the development of the Italian language **1266–83** *The Golden Legend,* a collection of apocryphal religious stories by the Italian prelate Jacopo da Voragine (c. 1228–98)
SCIENCE, TECHNOLOGY, AND EXPLORATION	**1200s** Use of coal gains over wood fuel; mining begins in Liège, France. Advances in seafaring: sternpost rudder and compass in use in Europe; spinning wheel and gunpowder introduced	**Roger Bacon (d. 1292),** English scientist who utilized observation and experiment in studying natural forces	

COURTLY LIFE AND THE INTERNATIONAL STYLE Intricate miniature illuminations, small personal diptychs, and precious, jeweled objects epitomize one aesthetic thread of the fourteenth century. The small scale and great elegance of these works reflect the rise, particularly in France, of a class of wealthy nobles whose refined taste and habit of traveling required art to be both beautiful and portable. Illuminated books of hours containing daily prayers, calendars, and parts of the Gospels were fashionable items that advertised the owner's wealth, piety, good taste, and connoisseurship. Contemporary with this graceful, decorative style was a parallel new style in literature—secular, romantic, and written in contemporary language, rather than the educated Latin of previous generations; the troubadour poets in Provençal, the *Roman de la Rose* in French, and much of Dante's and Petrarch's poetry in Italian are examples. Poems and paintings alike celebrate the sensual pleasures of the material world.

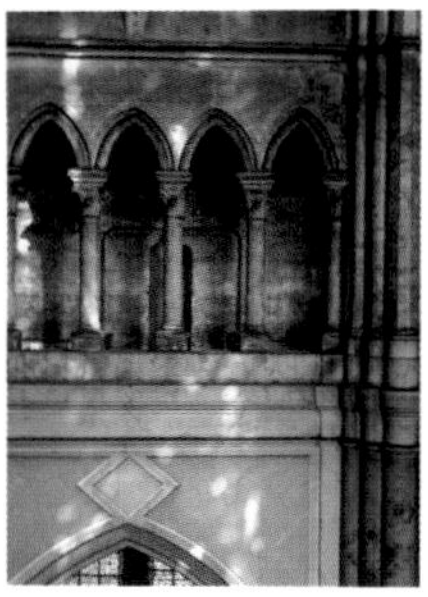

Interior, Chartres Cathedral, c. 1194–1220

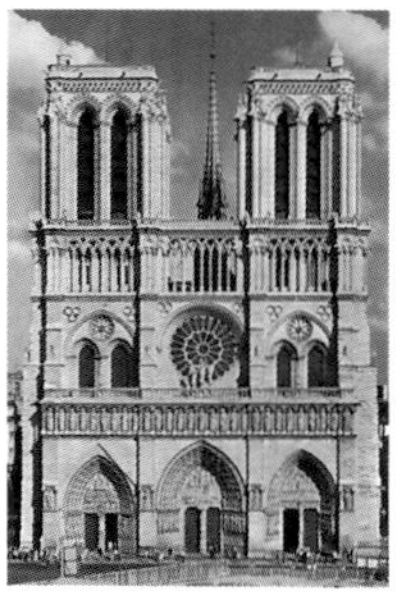

Notre-Dame, Paris, 1163–c. 1250

	1275–1300	1300–1325	1325–1350
HISTORY AND POLITICS	**1289** John of Montecorvino establishes a permanent Christian mission in China **1290** Jews expelled from England; 1306, from France **1295** King Edward I of England institutes the Model Parliament, first bicameral English parliament	**1302** First known convocation of French estates-general, parliamentary assembly of the crown, clergy, and commons, to support Philip IV the Fair in his struggle with Pope Boniface VIII over questions of papal authority **1305** Fearing political anarchy and desperate conditions in Rome, Pope Clement V establishes Avignon as the primary residence of the papacy; beginning of the so-called Babylonian Captivity (to 1376) **1310–13** Holy Roman Emperor Henry VII invades Italy to reestablish imperial rule	**1325** Foundation of the city of Tenochtitlán by the Aztecs **1338** Hundred Years' War between England and France begins (until 1453) **1347–50** Black Death in Europe. Bubonic plague kills an estimated one-third of population
RELIGION			
			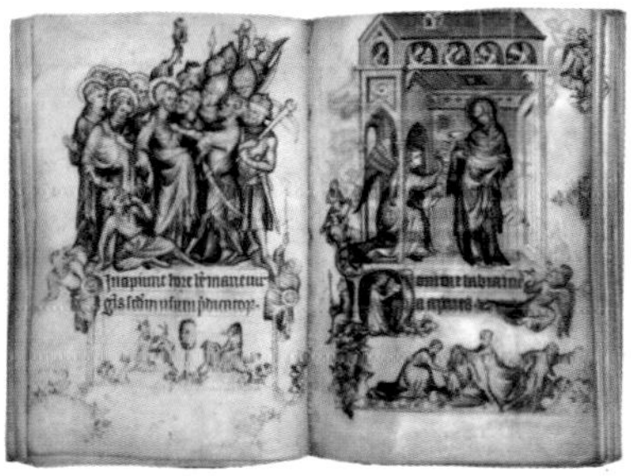 JEAN PUCELLE Illuminated pages from the *Hours of Jeanne d'Evreux,* Paris, 1325–28
MUSIC, LITERATURE, AND PHILOSOPHY	**c. 1297** Publication of Marco Polo's *Book of Various Experiences*. These enormously popular tales of travels in the Far East fostered a general interest in foreign lands	**c. 1300** The *Roman de la Rose,* satire on society written in vernacular French **William of Ockham (c. 1300–49),** English Nominalist philosopher, stresses mystical experience over rational understanding **Petrarch (1304–74),** Italian humanist scholar and poet **Giovanni Boccaccio (1313–75),** Italian author of *The Decameron,* a collection of tales	**1325–27 Ibn Batutah (1304–c. 1368),** Arab traveler and scholar, visits North Africa, the Mideast, and Persia; 1334, reaches India and later, 1342, China; his memoirs contain commentary on political and social customs **Franco Sacchetti (1332?–1400),** Italian poet and author of *Three Hundred Stories* **Geoffrey Chaucer (1340–1400),** English diplomat and author of *The Canterbury Tales*
SCIENCE, TECHNOLOGY, AND EXPLORATION	**Late 1200s** Arabic numerals introduced in Europe **c. 1286** Spectacles invented	**Early 1300s** Earliest cast iron in Europe; gunpowder first used for launching projectiles	**1335–45** Artillery first used on ships **1340** Francesco Pegolotti writes *The Merchant's Handbook,* an Italian manual for traders **1346** Longbow replaces crossbow: at the Battle of Crécy the English use it to defeat the French, including cavalry; greater participation of foot soldiers in warfare follows

EUROPE AND THE EAST The relationship of Christian European cultures to non-Christian nations had been alternately cordial and combative since the Muslim conquest of the Mideast and Spain in the eighth century. Arab scholarship and technology were commonly exchanged with those of Europe through trade and travel, and the crusades did much to increase knowledge of Arab culture in the West, but the regions farther to the East were little known. European contacts with Asia underwent a transformation in the late thirteenth century, after the Venetian trader Marco Polo, traveling to the courts of the Mongol emperor Kublai Kahn, China, India, and Persia, brought back the first accurate account of these places. As understanding of Asia grew, trade routes and trading colonies were established, as well as Christian missions. Lured by the prospect of great profit from trade in silk, exotic spices, and gold, as well as by adventure, merchants began to venture to these previously hostile nations in great numbers. Much of the zeal for the later crusades has been attributed not only to religious fervor but to the opportunity to open trade routes and mercantile contacts with Eastern countries. The effect on European culture was dramatic. The city of Venice became a thriving center for trade from the East, as did the Spanish coastal cities; these cities became not only mercantile but cultural centers for the exchange of arts and ideas. The influence of Asian taste can be seen in such images as the English heraldic lion, which is thought to derive from a Chinese dragon figure, no doubt woven in a precious silk textile.

PART THREE

The Renaissance through the Rococo

In discussing the transition from classical antiquity to the Middle Ages, we were able to point to a great crisis—the rise of Islam—marking the separation between the two eras. No comparable event sets off the Middle Ages from the Renaissance. The fifteenth and sixteenth centuries, to be sure, witnessed far-reaching developments: the fall of Constantinople and the Turkish conquest of southeastern Europe; the journeys of exploration that led to the founding of overseas empires in the New World, and in Africa and Asia, with the subsequent rivalry of Spain and England as the foremost colonial powers; and the deep spiritual crises of the Reformation and Counter-Reformation. None of these events, however great their effects, can be said to have produced the new era. By the time they happened, the Renaissance was well under way. Even if we disregard the few scholars who deny that the period existed at all, we are left with a wide range of views on the Renaissance. Perhaps the only essential point on which most experts agree is that the Renaissance had begun when people realized they were no longer living in the Middle Ages.

This statement is not as simpleminded as it sounds. It brings out the undeniable fact that the Renaissance was the first period in history to be aware of its own existence and to coin a label for itself. Medieval people did not think they belonged to an age distinct from classical antiquity. The past, to them, consisted simply of "B.C." and "A.D.," the era "under the Law" (that is, of the Old Testament) and the era "of Grace" (that is, after the birth of Jesus). From their point of view, then, history was made in Heaven rather than on earth. The Renaissance, by contrast, divided the past not according to the divine plan of salvation, but on the basis of human achievements. It saw classical antiquity as the era when civilization had reached the peak of its creative powers, and that was brought to an end by the barbarian invasions that destroyed the Roman Empire. Little was achieved during the thousand-year interval of "darkness" that followed. But now, at last, this "time in-between" or "Middle Age" had given way to a revival of all those arts and sciences that had flourished in antiquity. The present, the "New Age,"could thus be fittingly labeled a "rebirth"—*rinascita* in Italian (from the Latin *renascere,* to be reborn), *renaissance* in French and, by adoption, in English.

The origin of this revolutionary view of history can be traced back to the 1330s in the writings of the Italian poet Francesco Petrarca. Petrarch, as we call him, thought of the new era mainly as a "revival of the classics." In his view, it involved restoring Latin and Greek to their former purity and returning to the original texts of ancient authors. During the next two centuries, this concept of the rebirth of antiquity grew to include almost the entire range of cultural activity, including the visual arts. The latter, in fact, came to play a particularly important part in shaping the Renaissance, for reasons that we shall explore later.

The fact that this new view of history (to which we owe our concepts of the Renaissance, the Middle

Ages, and classical antiquity) arose in the mind of one man is itself a telling comment on the new era, although it was soon taken up by many others. Individualism—a new self-awareness and self-assurance—enabled Petrarch to proclaim, against all established authority, his own conviction that the "age of faith" was actually an era of darkness. In contrast, the "benighted pagans" of antiquity really represented the most enlightened stage of history. Such readiness to question traditional beliefs became a characteristic feature of the Renaissance as a whole. Humanism, to Petrarch, meant a belief in the importance of what we still call "the humanities" or "humane letters" (rather than divine letters, or the study of Scripture): the pursuit of learning in languages, literature, history, and philosophy for its own end, in a secular rather than a religious framework.

We must not assume, however, that Petrarch and his successors wanted to revive classical antiquity lock, stock, and barrel. By interposing the concept of "a thousand years of darkness" between themselves and the ancients, they acknowledged (unlike the medieval classicists) that the Graeco-Roman world was irretrievably dead. Its glories could be revived only in the mind, by nostalgic and admiring contemplation across the barrier of the "dark ages," by rediscovering ancient achievements in thought and art, and by attempting to compete with them on an ideal plane.

The aim of the Renaissance was not to duplicate the works of antiquity but to equal and, if possible, to surpass them. In practice, this meant that the authority granted to the ancient models was far from unlimited. Indeed, the most striking feature of the Renaissance is not the influence of the classical past, which was quickly absorbed, but its originality. Writers strove to express themselves with Ciceronian eloquence and precision, but not necessarily in Latin. Architects continued to build the churches required by Christian ritual, not to duplicate pagan temples. However, their churches were designed *all'antica,* "in the manner of the ancients," using forms based on the study of classical structures. The humanists, despite their enthusiasm for classical philosophy, did not become neo-pagans. Rather, they tried to reconcile the heritage of the ancient thinkers with Christianity.

The people of the Renaissance, then, found themselves in the position of the legendary sorcerer's apprentice who set out to emulate his master's achievements and in the process released far greater energies than he had bargained for. But since the master was dead, rather than merely absent, they had to cope with these unfamiliar powers as best they could, until they became masters in their own right. This process of forced growth was filled with crises and tensions. The Renaissance must have been an uncomfortable, though intensely exciting, time to live in. Yet these very tensions, it seems, called forth an outpouring of creative energy such as the world had never seen before. It is a paradox that the desire to return to the classics, based on a rejection of the Middle Ages, brought to the new era not the rebirth of antiquity but the birth of modern civilization.

As we narrow our focus from the Renaissance as a whole to the Renaissance in the fine arts, we are faced with some questions that are still under debate. When did Renaissance art begin? Did it, like

Gothic art, originate in a specific center or in several places at the same time? Should we think of it as one coherent style or as an attitude that might be embodied in more than one style?"Renaissance-consciousness," we know, was an Italian idea, and there can be no doubt that Italy played the leading role in the development of Renaissance art, at least until the early sixteenth century. This fact does not necessarily mean, however, that the Renaissance was confined to the South.

So far as architecture and sculpture are concerned, modern scholars agree with the traditional view, first expressed more than 500 years ago, that the Renaissance began soon after 1400 in Florence. For painting, however, an even older tradition claims that the new era began with Giotto, who, as Boccaccio wrote about 1350, "restored to light this art which had been buried for many centuries." We cannot disregard such testimony. Yet if we accept it at face value, we must assume that the Renaissance in painting dawned about 1300, a full generation before Petrarch. Giotto himself certainly did not reject the past as an age of darkness. After all, the two chief sources of his own style were the Byzantine tradition and the influence of Northern Gothic. The artistic revolution he created from these elements does not place him in a new era, since radical changes had occurred in medieval art before. Nor is it fair to credit this revolution to him alone, and not to Cimabue, Duccio, and the other great masters to whom he was linked. Petrarch was well aware of the achievements of all these artists—he wrote admiringly of both Giotto and Simone Martini—but he never claimed that they had restored to light what had been buried during the centuries of darkness. And, in fact, such a thing was inherently impossible because neither could have known Classical painting.

How, then, do we account for Boccaccio's statement about Giotto? We must understand that Boccaccio (1313–1375), a disciple of Petrarch, was concerned with advancing humanism in literature. In his defense of the status of poetry, he found it useful to draw analogies with painting. Had not the Roman poet Horace proclaimed that the two arts were alike in his famous dictum *ut pictura poesis*? Boccaccio thus cast Giotto in the role of "the Petrarch of painting," taking advantage of his already legendary fame. Boccaccio's view of Giotto as a Renaissance artist is, then, a bit of intellectual strategy, rather than a trustworthy reflection of Giotto's own attitude. Nevertheless, what he has to say interests us because he was the first to apply Petrarch's concept of "revival after the dark ages" to one of the visual arts, though somewhat prematurely.

Boccaccio's way of describing Giotto's achievement is also noteworthy. It was he who claimed that Giotto depicted every aspect of nature so truthfully that people often mistook his paintings for reality itself. Thus he implied that for painters the revival of antiquity meant absolute realism. This, as we shall see, would become a persistent theme in Renaissance thought. It justified the imitation of nature as part of the great movement "back to the classics" and tended to minimize the possible conflict between these two aims. After all, Classical Greek art was itself based on a synthesis of naturalism and ideal proportions.

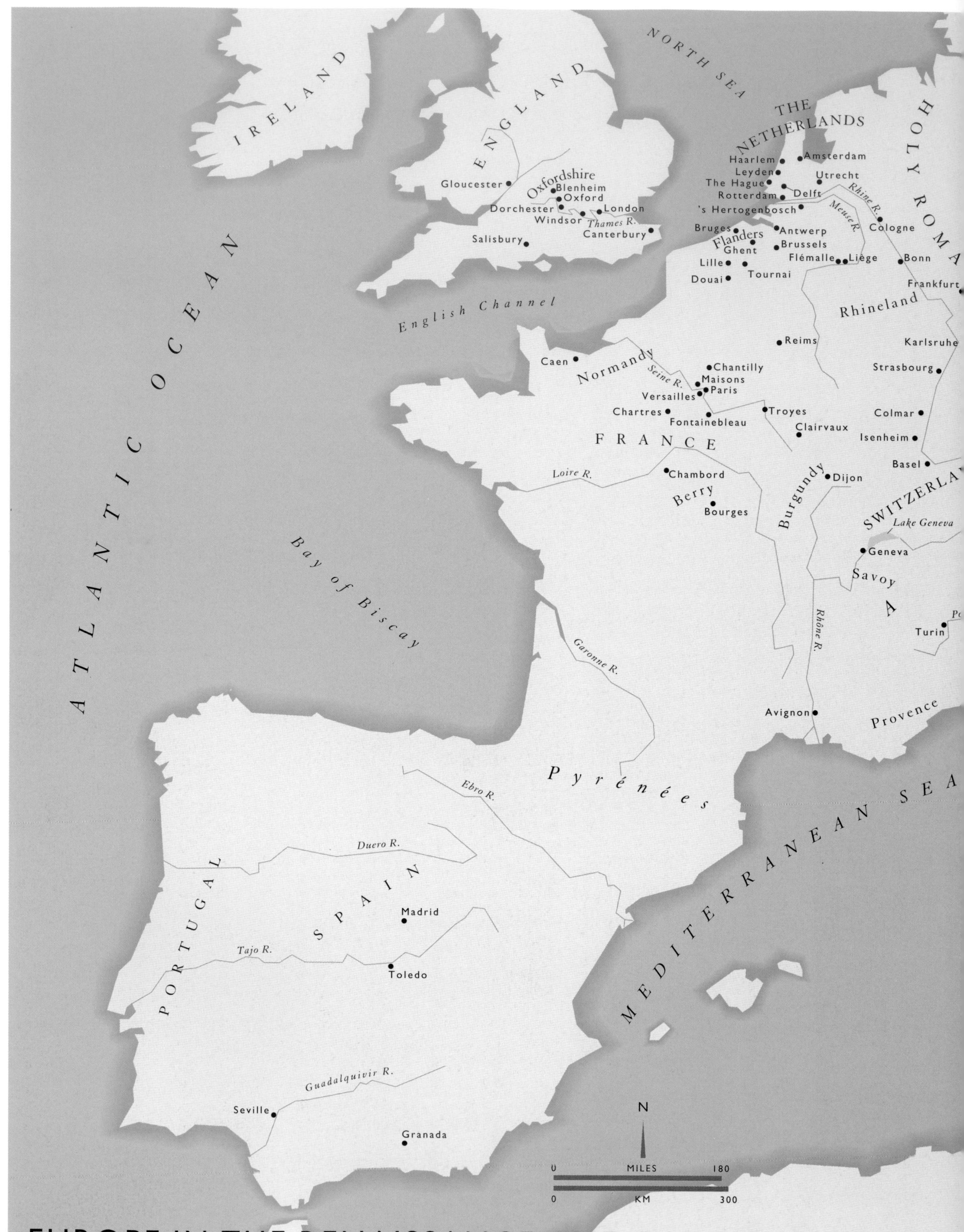

EUROPE IN THE RENAISSANCE AND BAROQUE

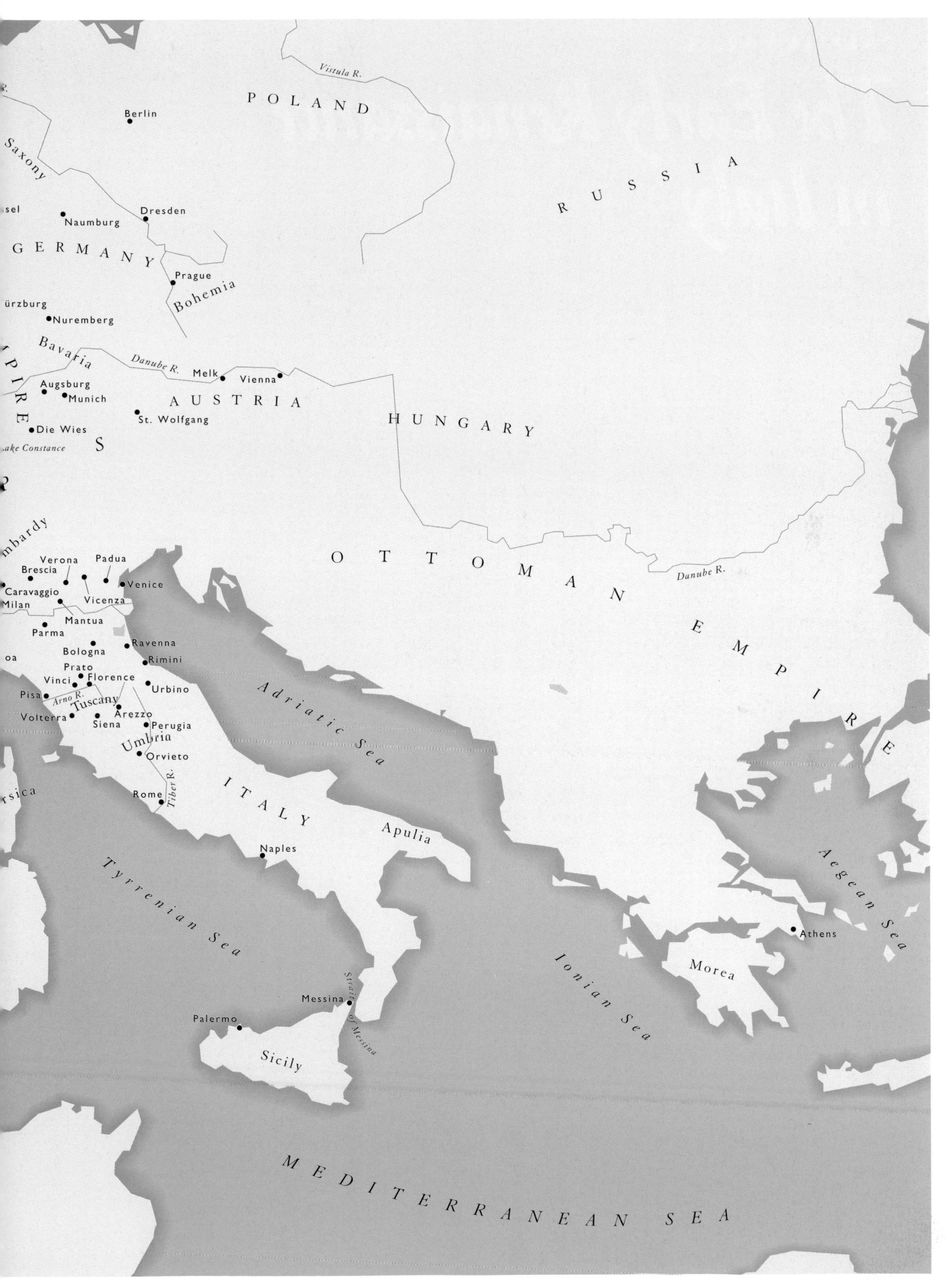

Vistula R.
POLAND
Berlin
Saxony
RUSSIA
Naumburg
Dresden
GERMANY
Prague
Bohemia
Nuremberg
Bavaria
Danube R.
Melk
Vienna
Augsburg
Munich
AUSTRIA
St. Wolfgang
Die Wies
HUNGARY
Verona
Padua
Brescia
Caravaggio
Venice
Milan
Vicenza
Mantua
Parma
OTTOMAN EMPIRE
Danube R.
Ravenna
Bologna
Rimini
Prato
Vinci
Florence
Urbino
Pisa
Arno R.
Tuscany
Arezzo
Volterra
Siena
Perugia
Umbria
Orvieto
Adriatic Sea
Rome
Tiber R.
ITALY
Apulia
Naples
Aegean Sea
Tyrrenian Sea
Athens
Ionian Sea
Morea
Strait of Messina
Messina
Palermo
Sicily
MEDITERRANEAN SEA

CHAPTER TWELVE

The Early Renaissance in Italy

There are a number of reasons that help explain why the Early Renaissance was born in Florence at the beginning of the fifteenth century, rather than in some other place or at some other time. Around 1400, Florence's independence was threatened by the powerful duke of Milan, who was trying to bring all of Italy under his rule. He already controlled the Lombard plain and most of the central Italian city-states. Florence was the only major obstacle to his ambition. The city put up a vigorous defense on three fronts: military, diplomatic, and intellectual. Of these, the intellectual was by no means the least important. The duke was admired by some as a new Caesar, bringing peace and order to the country. In opposition, Florence proclaimed itself the champion of freedom against unchecked tyranny.

This propaganda war was waged by humanists on both sides, but the Florentines gave by far the better account of themselves. Their writings, such as *Praise of the City of Florence* (1402–3) by Leonardo Bruni (see fig. 12-48), give new focus to the ideal of a rebirth of the classics. Speaking as a citizen of a free republic, Bruni asks why, among all the states of Italy, Florence alone had been able to defy the superior power of Milan. He finds the answer in her institutions, her cultural achievements, her geographical situation, the spirit of her people, and her descent from the city-states of ancient Etruria. Florence, he concludes, has taken on the same role of political and intellectual leadership as that of Athens at the time of the Persian Wars.

The patriotic pride, the call to greatness that can be seen in this image of Florence as the "new Athens" must have aroused a deep response throughout the city. Just when they were on the point of being overwhelmed by the forces of Milan, the Florentines began an ambitious campaign to finish the great artistic works begun a century before at the time of Giotto. Following the competition of 1401–2 for the bronze doors of the Baptistery of S. Giovanni, another major program continued the sculptural decoration of Florence Cathedral and other churches. At the same time, debate resumed over how to build the dome of the cathedral, the largest and most difficult project of all. The artistic campaign, which lasted more than 30 years, gradually petered out after the completion of the dome in 1436. Its total cost was comparable to that of rebuilding the Akropolis in Athens. The huge investment was not a guarantee of artistic quality, but it provided a splendid opportunity for the emergence of creative talent and a new style worthy of the "new Athens."

From the start, the visual arts were viewed as central to the rebirth of the Florentine spirit. Throughout antiquity and the Middle Ages, they had been classed with the crafts, or "mechanical arts." It cannot be by chance that the first appearance of the claim that they should be classed with the liberal arts occurs around 1400 in the writings of the Florentine chronicler Filippo Villani, a position later solidified by Alberti's treatise on painting (see Primary Sources, no. 40, page 612). A century later, this claim would be widely accepted throughout most of the Western world. What does it imply?

The liberal arts were defined by a tradition going back to Plato. They comprised the intellectual disciplines necessary for a "gentleman's" education: mathematics (including musical theory), dialectics, grammar, rhetoric, and philosophy. The fine arts were initially excluded because they were "handiwork"—they lacked a theoretical basis. During the early fourth century B.C., however, they were included in the liberal arts (see pages 135–36). Thus when Renaissance artists gained admission to this select group of humanists, they were viewed as people of ideas rather than mere manipulators of materials. Works of art came to be viewed more and more as the visible records of creative minds. This meant that works of art need not—indeed, should not—be judged only by the standards of craftsmanship. Soon anything that bore the imprint of a great master was eagerly collected—drawings, sketches, fragments, and unfinished pieces as well as finished works.

The outlook of artists changed as well. Now in the company of scholars and poets, they themselves often became learned and literary. They might write poems, autobiographies, or theoretical treatises. Another outgrowth of their new social status was that artists' personalities tended to develop in either of two contrasting ways. One was the person of the world, self-controlled, at ease in aristocratic society. The other was the solitary genius, secretive, subject to fits of melancholy, and likely to be in conflict with patrons. It is remarkable how quickly this modern view of art and artists took root in the Florence of the Early Renaissance. However, it did not immediately take hold everywhere, nor did it apply equally to all artists. England, for example, was slow to grant artists special status, and women in general were denied the training and opportunities available to men.

In addition to humanism and historical forces, individual genius played a decisive role in the birth of Renaissance art. It began with three men of exceptional ability—Filippo Brunelleschi, Donatello, and Masaccio. It is hardly a coincidence that these men knew one another. Moreover, they all faced the same task: to reconcile Classical form with Christian content. Yet each approached this problem in a unique way. Thanks to them, Florentine art retained leadership of the movement during the first half of the fifteenth century, which we now call the heroic age of the Early Renaissance. To trace its beginnings, we must discuss sculpture first because the sculptors had earlier and more plentiful opportunities to meet the challenge of the "new Athens."

FLORENCE: 1400–1450

Sculpture

GHIBERTI. The artistic campaign began with the competition for the Baptistery doors, and for some time it consisted mainly of sculptural projects. Ghiberti's trial relief does not differ greatly from the International Gothic (see fig. 11-65); nor do the doors themselves, even though it took another 20 years to complete them. Only in the trial panel can Ghiberti's admiration for ancient art, as shown by the torso of Isaac, be linked with the classicism of the Florentine humanists. Similar examples can be found in other Florentine sculpture around 1400. But such instances, isolated and small in scale, merely recapture what Nicola Pisano had done a century before (see fig. 11-58).

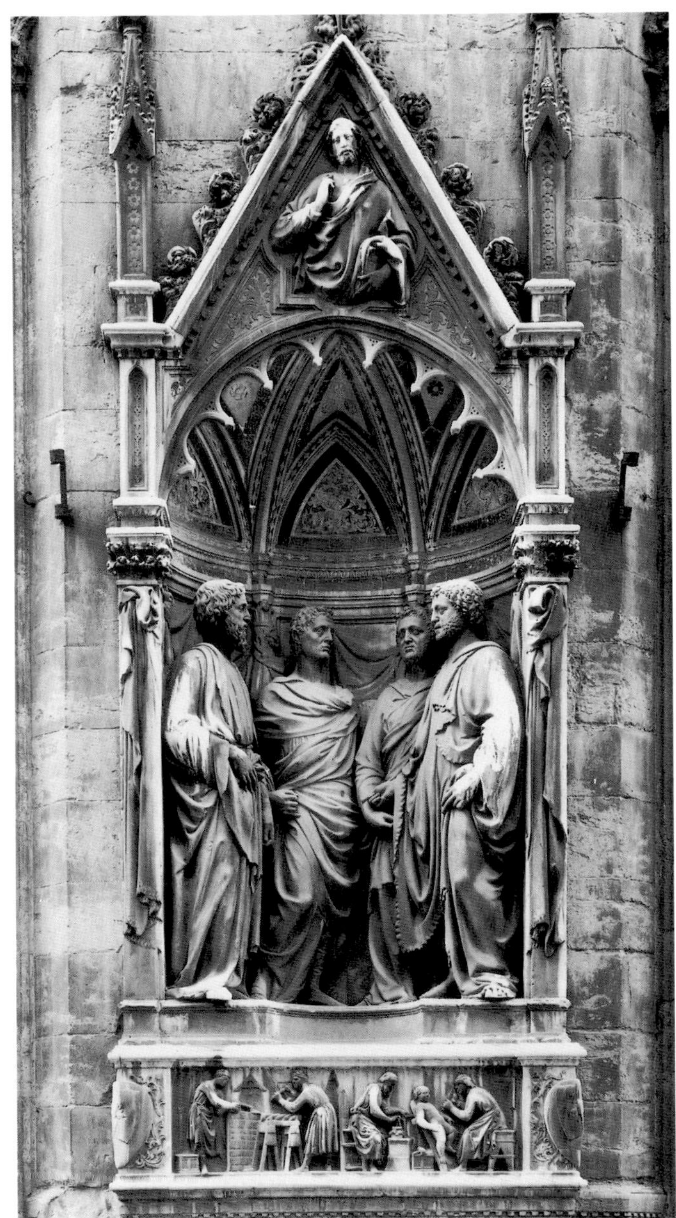

12-1. Nanni di Banco. *Four Saints (Quattro Coronati)*. c. 1410–14. Marble, about lifesize. Or San Michele, Florence

NANNI DI BANCO. A decade later this medieval classicism was surpassed by a somewhat younger artist, Nanni di Banco (c. 1384–1421). The four saints, called the *Quattro Coronati* (fig. 12-1), which he made about 1410–14 for one of the niches on the exterior of the church of Or San Michele, must be compared not with the work of Nicola Pisano but with the Reims *Visitation* (see fig. 11-46). The saints represent four Christian sculptors who were executed for not carving the statue of a pagan god ordered by Diocletian, a story that was later merged with that of four martyrs who refused to worship in the god's temple. The figures in both groups are about lifesize, yet Nanni's give the impression of being a good deal larger than those at Reims. Their monumental quality was beyond the range of medieval sculpture, even though Nanni depended less directly on ancient models. Only the heads of the second and third of the *Coronati* directly recall Roman sculpture—specifically, the portrait heads of the third century A.D. (see fig. 7-42). Nanni clearly was impressed by their realism and their agonized expressions. His ability to retain these qualities indicates a new attitude toward ancient art, one that unites classical form and content instead of separating them as medieval classicists had done.

DONATELLO. Early Renaissance art reestablished an attitude toward the human body similar to that of classical antiquity. Donatello, the greatest sculptor of his time, played a particularly important role in forming this new attitude. Born in 1386, several years after Nanni, Donatello died in 1466, surviving Nanni by 45 years. Among the founders of the new style, he alone lived well past the middle of the century. Together with Nanni, Donatello spent his early career working on commissions for Florence Cathedral and Or San Michele after completing his apprenticeship under Ghiberti. They often faced the same artistic problems, yet their personalities had little in common.

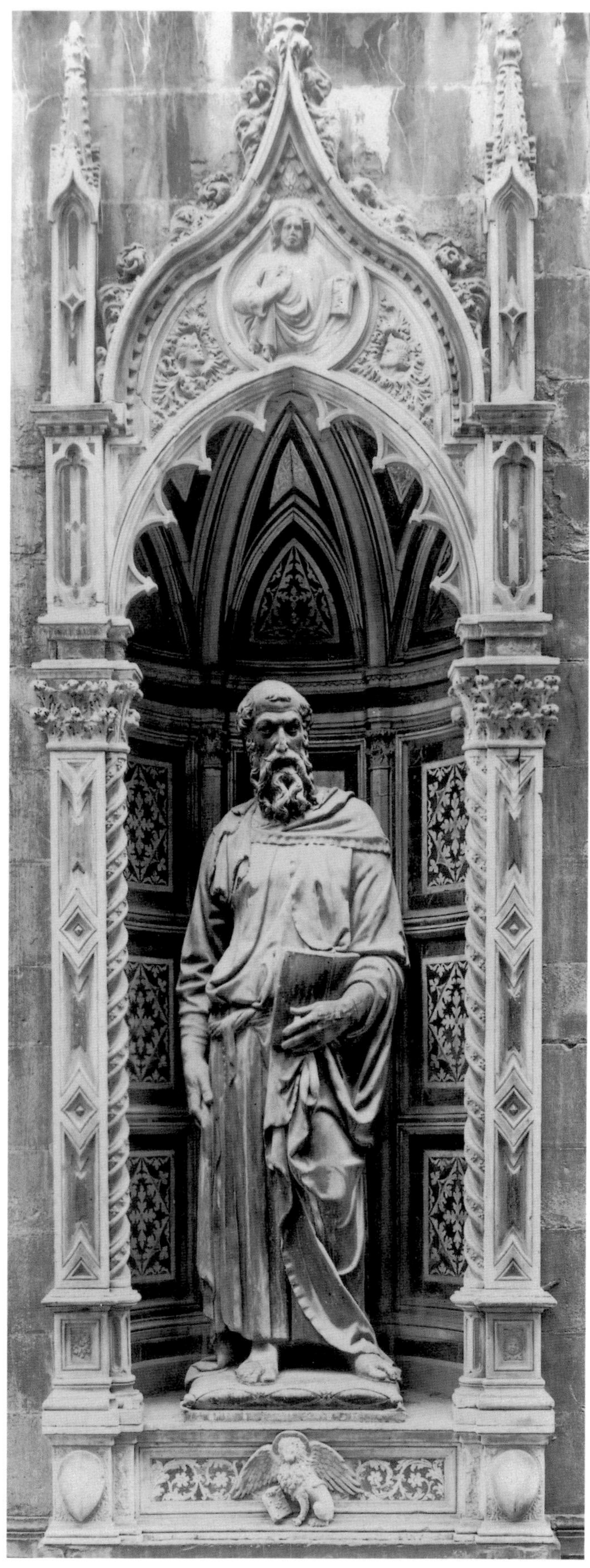

12-2. Donatello. *St. Mark*. 1411–13. Marble, 7'9" (2.4 m). Or San Michele, Florence

Their different approaches can be seen by comparing Nanni's *Quattro Coronati* with Donatello's *St. Mark* (fig. 12-2). Both are located in deep Gothic niches, but Nanni's figures, like Antelami's *King David* (see fig. 10-30), cannot be divorced from the architectural setting. Instead, they still seem attached, like jamb statues, to the pilasters behind them. The figure of *St. Mark*, however, would lose none of its authority if it were removed from the niche. Perfectly balanced, it is the first statue since antiquity that could stand by itself. To put it another way, it is the first statue to recapture the full meaning of the classical contrapposto. In one stroke, the young Donatello has mastered the central achievement of ancient sculpture. He treats the human body as an articulated structure, capable of movement, and its drapery as a separate element that is based on the shapes underneath rather than on patterns imposed from outside. Unlike the *Coronati*, *St. Mark* looks as if he could take off his clothes, yet he is not at all classical in appearance—that is, ancient motifs are not quoted as they are in Nanni's figures. Perhaps "classic" is a better word for him.

A few years later, about 1415–17, Donatello carved another statue for Or San Michele, the famous *St. George* (fig. 12-3). The niche is shallower than that of the *St. Mark*, so that the warrior saint actually protrudes from it slightly. Although encased in armor, his body and limbs are not rigid. His stance, with the weight placed on the forward leg, conveys his readiness for combat. (The right hand originally held a lance or sword.) The controlled energy of his body is reflected in his eyes, which seem to scan the horizon for the enemy. *St. George* is portrayed as the Christian Soldier in his Early Renaissance version, spiritually akin to the *St. Theodore* at Chartres (see fig. 11-44), but he is also the proud defender of the "new Athens."

Below *St. George*'s niche is a relief panel showing the hero's best-known exploit, the slaying of a dragon. (The maiden on the right is the princess whom the saint had come to free.) Here Donatello devised a new kind of relief that is shallow (called *schiacciato*, "flattened-out") yet creates an illusion of infinite depth. This had been achieved to some degree in Greek and Roman reliefs, as well as by Ghiberti (compare with figs. 5-58, 7-32–7-36, and 11-65). In all these cases, however, the actual carved depth is roughly proportional to the apparent depth of the space represented. The forms in the front plane are in very high relief, while more distant ones become progressively lower, seemingly immersed in the background. Donatello takes an entirely different approach. Behind the figures, the landscape consists of delicate surface modulations that cause the marble to catch light from varying angles. Every tiny ripple has a descriptive power that is much greater than its real depth. The sculptor's chisel, like a painter's brush, becomes a tool for creating shades of light and dark. Yet Donatello cannot have borrowed his landscape from any painting, for no painter at the time had achieved so coherent and atmospheric a view of nature.

Further evidence of Donatello's genius can be seen in the statues he made for the campanile of Florence Cathedral. When the campanile was built between 1334 and 1357, a row of tall Gothic niches was designed for statues (barely visible above the rooftops in fig. 11-35). In 1416 half of these niches were still empty, but in the next twenty years Donatello filled five of them. The most

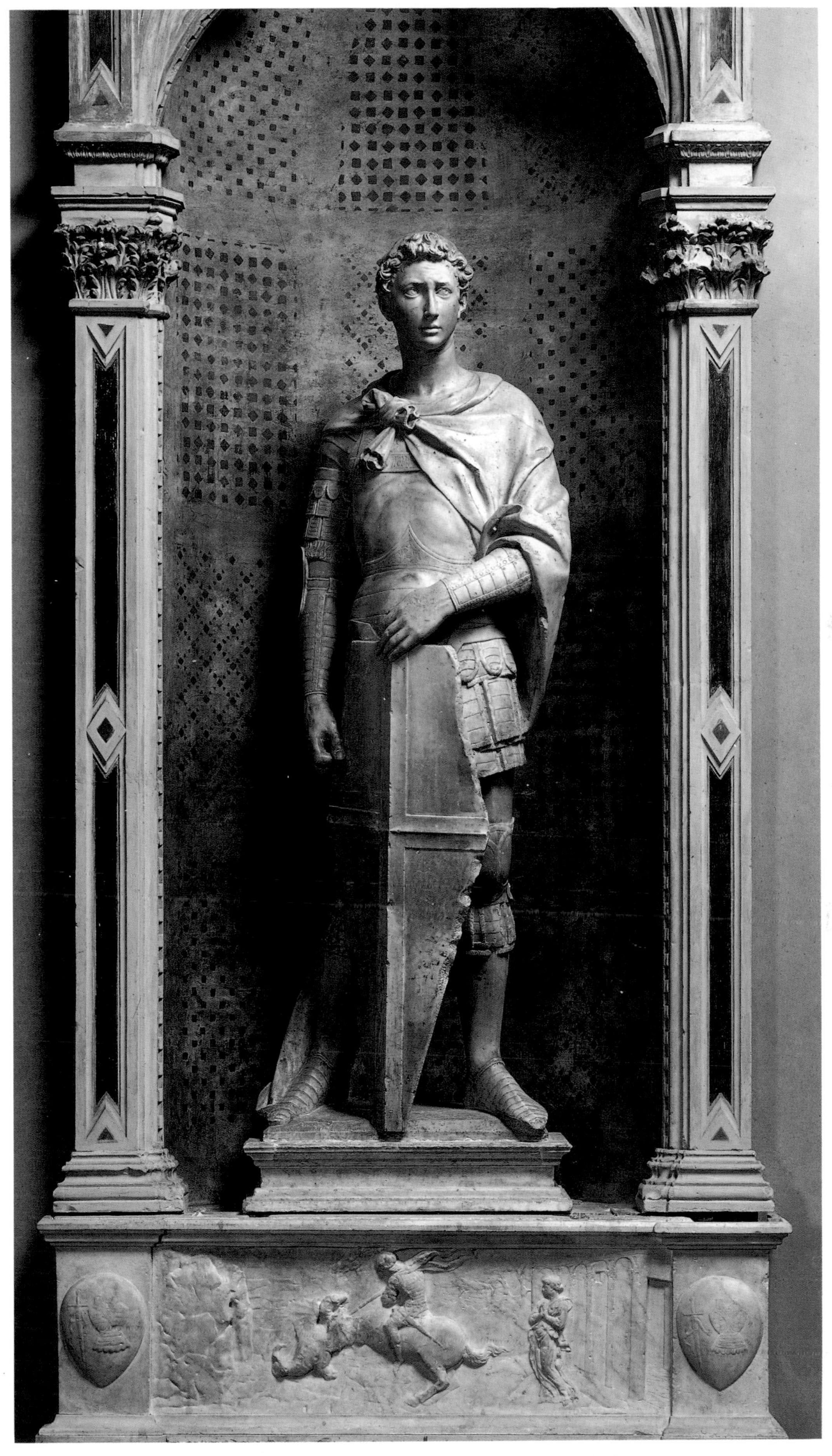

12-3. Donatello. *St. George* Tabernacle, from Or San Michele, Florence. c. 1415–17. Marble, height of statue 6'10" (2.1 m). Museo Nazionale del Bargello, Florence

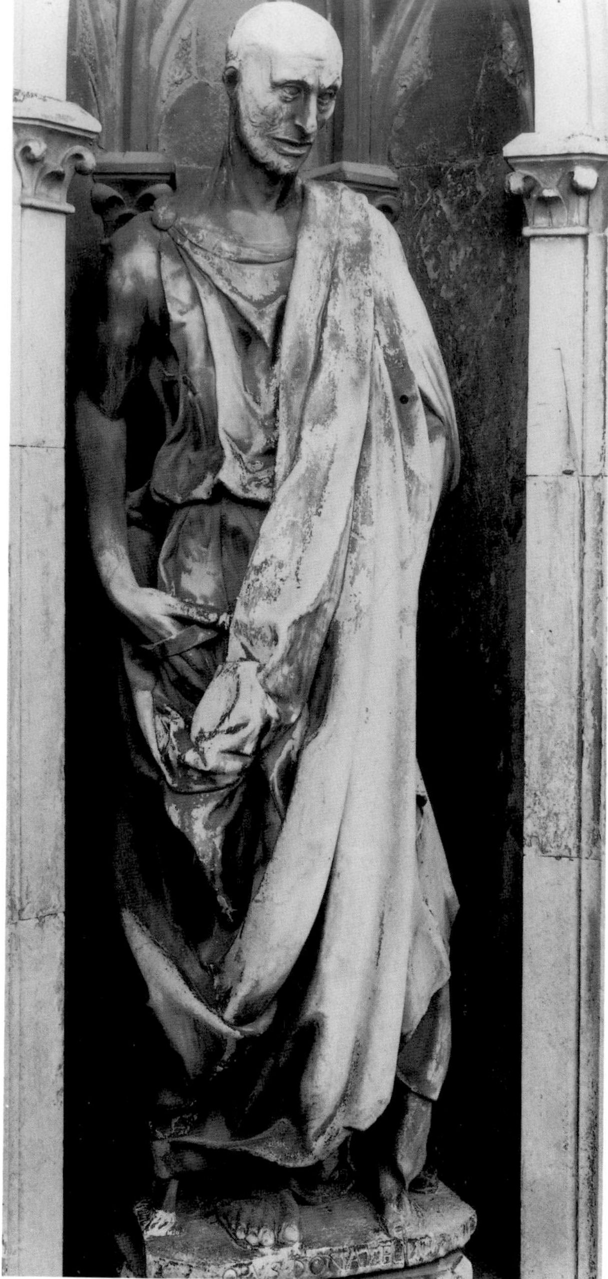

12-4. Donatello. *Prophet (Zuccone),* on the campanile of Florence Cathedral. 1423–25. Marble, height 6'5" (2 m). Original now in the Museo dell'Opera del Duomo, Florence

impressive statue in his series (fig. 12-4) is of an unidentified prophet who has been nicknamed *Zuccone* ("pumpkin-head"). Made a dozen years after the *St. Mark,* it is strikingly realistic, far more so than any ancient statue or its nearest rivals, the prophets on Sluter's *Moses Well* (see fig. 11-56). But what kind of realism have we here?

This is not the standard image of a prophet—a bearded old man in Oriental-looking costume, holding a large scroll. Rather, Donatello invented an entirely new type. Why did he not simply reinterpret the conventional image from a realistic point of view, as Sluter had done? Donatello obviously felt that the old type would not suit his purposes. But how did he conceive of the new one? Surely not by observing the people around him. More likely, he imagined the personalities of the prophets from what he had read about them in the Old Testament. He saw them as divinely inspired orators speaking to the multitudes. This, in turn, reminded him of the Roman orators he had seen in ancient sculpture. Hence the classical costume of the *Zuccone,* whose mantle falls from one shoulder like those of the patricians in figures 7-26 and 7-32. Hence, too, the prophet's head, ugly yet noble like those of Roman portraits of the third century A.D. (compare fig. 7-43).

Shaping these elements into a coherent whole was a difficult task that required an almost visible struggle. Donatello himself seems to have realized this: the *Zuccone* is the first of his surviving works that bears his signature. He is said to have sworn "by the Zuccone" and to have shouted at the statue while working on it, "Speak, speak, or the plague take you!"

Donatello had learned the technique of bronze sculpture as a youth by working under Ghiberti on the first Baptistery doors. By the 1420s, he began to rival his former teacher in that medium. *The Feast of Herod* (fig. 12-5), which he made about 1425 for the baptismal font of S. Giovanni (the Baptistery of Siena Cathedral), has the same exquisite surface finish as Ghiberti's panels (see fig. 11-65) but is much more expressive. By classical or medieval standards, the main scene is poorly composed. The focus of the drama (the executioner presenting the head of St. John to Herod) is far to the left, while the dancing Salome and most of the spectators are massed on the right and the center is empty. Yet we see at once why Donatello created this gaping hole. Far more than the witnesses' gestures and expressions, it conveys the impact of the shocking sight. Moreover, the centrifugal movement of the figures helps persuade us that the picture space does not end within the panel but continues in every direction. The frame thus becomes a window through which we see a segment of an unlimited reality. The arched openings within the panel frame additional segments of the same reality, luring us farther into the palace.

This architecture, with its round arches, its fluted columns and pilasters, is not Gothic at all. It reflects the new style launched by

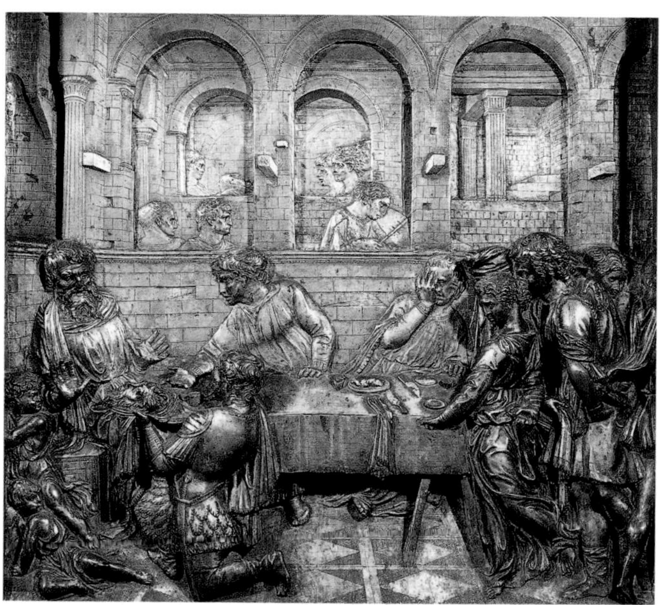

12-5. Donatello. *The Feast of Herod.* c. 1425. Gilt bronze, 23½" (59.7 cm) square. Baptismal font, Siena Cathedral

Filippo Brunelleschi (discussed below). More important, *The Feast of Herod* may be the earliest surviving example of a picture space using Brunelleschi's scientific perspective (see box, page 398). This perspective assumes an ideal vantage point, in which the viewer's eye is on a line perpendicular to the center of the panel. In the Baptistery, however, one must crouch low to see it correctly, as the basin to which the relief is attached is only a few feet high. Moreover, the building could not be built the way the artist has portrayed it. Why, then, did Donatello use scientific perspective? It was a convenient way to organize the image, which in fact shows the action as a continuous narrative. (Note that the Baptist's severed head is seen twice.)

DONATELLO'S DAVID. Donatello's bronze *David* (fig. 12-6) is equally revolutionary. It is the first freestanding lifesize nude statue since antiquity. In the Middle Ages it would have been condemned as an idol, and even in Donatello's day people must have felt uneasy about it, because for many years it remained the only work of its kind. The statue must have been meant for an open space. It probably stood on top of a column in the garden of Cosimo de' Medici, the most powerful figure in Florence, where it would have been visible from every side.

The key to the meaning of the statue is the helmet of Goliath, with its visor and wings. This form was derived from depictions of the Roman wind-god Zephyr, an evil figure who killed the young boy Hyacinth. We may assume that the helmet is a reference to the dukes of Milan, who had threatened Florence about 1400 and were warring against it once more in the mid-1420s. The statue thus is a patriotic public monument identifying David—weak but favored by the Lord—with Florence, and Goliath with Milan. David's nudity may be a reference to the classical origin of Florence; his wreathed hat, the opposite of Goliath's helmet, perhaps represents peace versus war.

Donatello chose to model an adolescent boy, not a full-grown youth like the athletes of Greece. The skeletal structure therefore is less fully enveloped in swelling muscles. Nor is the torso articulated according to the classical pattern (compare figs. 5-41 and 5-42). Rather, it is softly sensuous, like the cult statues of the Roman youth Antinous (compare fig. 7-47, right). *David* resembles an ancient statue mainly in its contrapposto. If the figure has a classical appearance, the reason lies in its expression, not anatomy. The lowered gaze signifies humility, which triumphs over the sinful pride of Goliath. It was inspired by Classical examples, which equate the lowered gaze with modesty and virtue (compare fig. 5-42). As in ancient statues, however, the body speaks to us more eloquently than the face, which by Donatello's standards strangely lacks individuality.

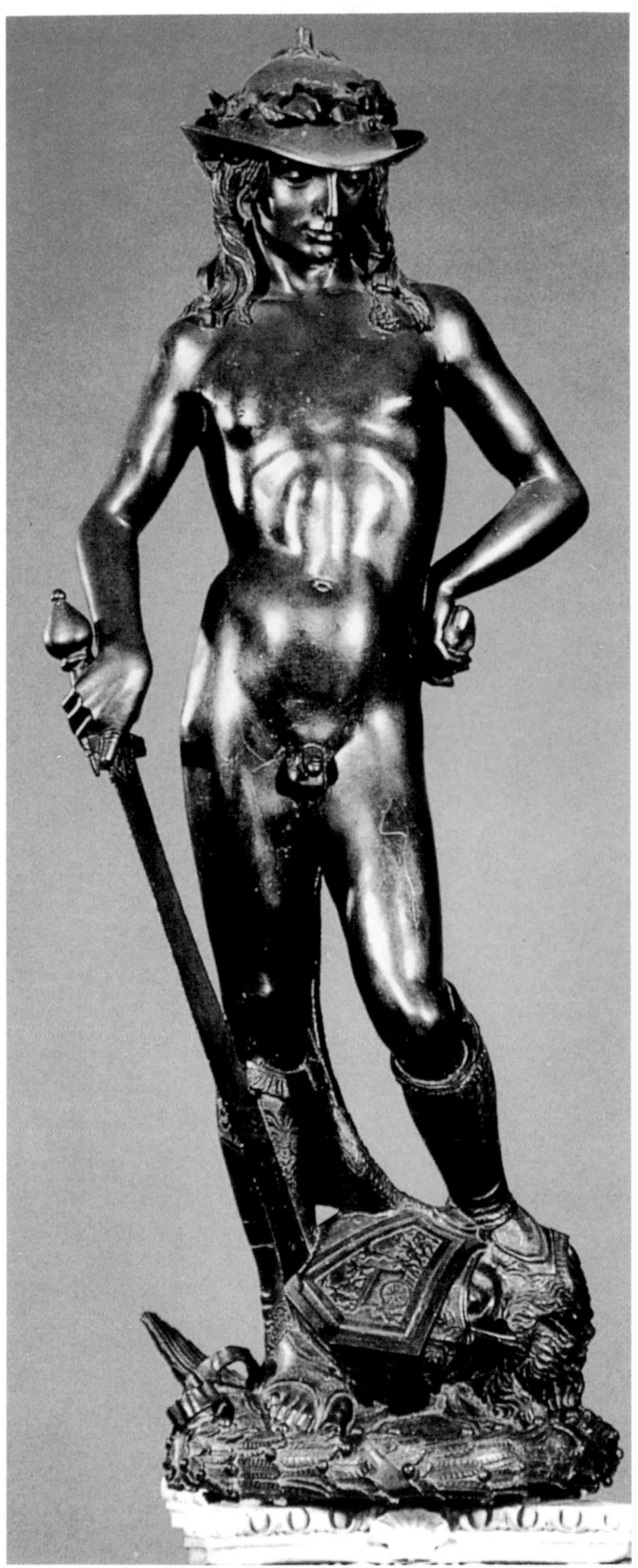

12-6. Donatello. *David.* c. 1425–30. Bronze, height 62¼" (158 cm). Museo Nazionale del Bargello, Florence

In 1443 Donatello was invited to Padua to produce his largest freestanding work in bronze: the *Equestrian Monument of Gattamelata.* This statue, which honored the recently deceased commander of the Venetian armies (fig. 12-7), is still in its original position on a tall pedestal near the facade of the church dedicated to St. Anthony of Padua. We may compare it with the mounted *Marcus Aurelius* in Rome and the *Can Grande* in Verona (see figs. 7-40 and 11-63). Like the *Marcus Aurelius,* the *Gattamelata* is impressive in scale and shares a sense of balance and dignity. The horse, a heavyset animal fit to carry a man in full armor, is so large that the rider must dominate it by authority rather than by force. The link with the *Can Grande,* though less obvious, is equally significant. Both statues were made to stand next to a church facade, and both are memorials to military figures. But the *Gattamelata* is

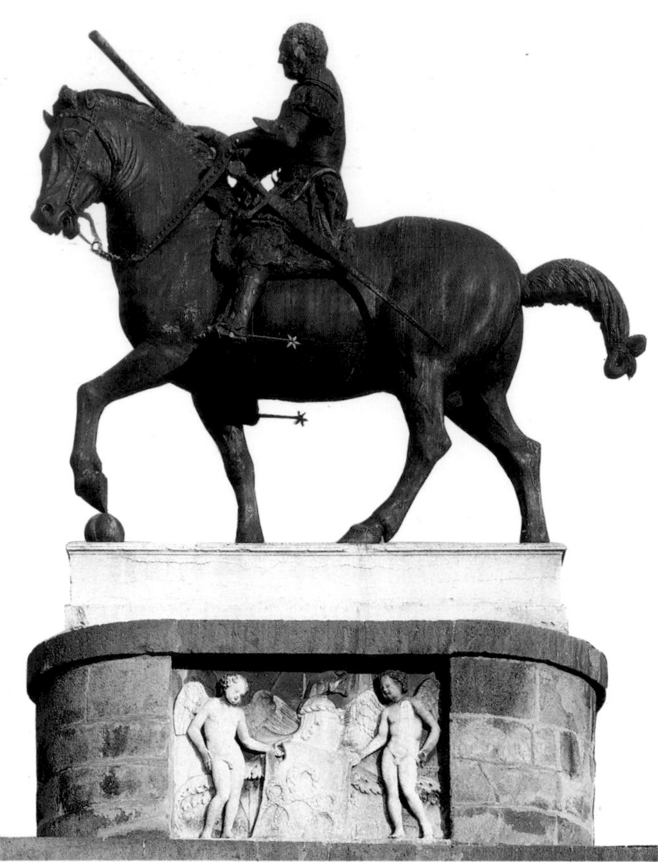

12-7. Donatello. *Equestrian Monument of Gattamelata.* 1445–50. Bronze, approx. 11 x 13' (3.35 x 3.96 m). Piazza del Santo, Padua

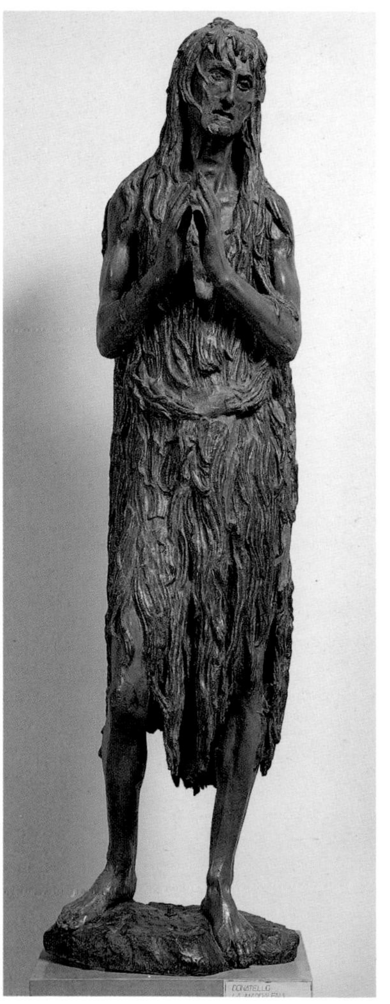

12-8. Donatello. *Mary Magdalen.* c. 1455. Wood, partially gilded, height 6'2" (1.88 m). Museo dell'Opera del Duomo, Florence

not part of a tomb. It was designed solely to commemorate a great soldier. Nor is it the self-glorifying statue of a sovereign; it is a monument authorized by the Republic of Venice. Donatello therefore has united the ideal with the real. The armor combines modern construction with classical detail; the head is that of an individual yet displays a truly Roman nobility of character.

When Donatello went home to Florence after a decade's absence, he must have felt like a stranger. The political and spiritual climate had changed, and so had the taste of artists and the public (see pages 388–89). His later sculpture (1453 to 1466) stands apart from the main trend. Its expressiveness exceeds anything Donatello had achieved before. The extreme individualism of these works confirms his reputation as the earliest "solitary genius" among the artists of the new age.

In contrast to the *David,* the *Mary Magdalen* (fig. 12-8) seems so far removed from Renaissance ideals that at first we are tempted to compare it with Gothic devotional images such as the Bonn *Pietà* (see fig. 11-54). Both give the viewer an almost physical shock. But when we look back at the *Zuccone* (see fig. 12-4), we realize that it is not very different from Donatello's earlier work. *Mary Magdalen* conveys deep religious feeling. Her ravaged features and wasted body make her the embodiment of penitence, so that we share her anguish and longing for redemption.

GHIBERTI. At the same time that Donatello made *The Feast of Herod,* Ghiberti was commissioned to do a second pair of bronze doors for the Baptistery in Florence (fig. 12-9), which are so beautiful that they were soon dubbed the "Gates of Paradise." They contain ten large reliefs in square frames, which create a larger field than the 28 small panels in quatrefoil frames of the earlier doors. They reveal the influence of Donatello and other pioneers of the Early Renaissance style. The only remnants of the Gothic style are seen in the figures, whose graceful classicism reminds us of the International Style. The *"Gates of Paradise"* show the pictorialism found in many Renaissance reliefs. The hint of spatial depth we saw in *The Sacrifice of Isaac* (see fig. 11 65) has grown in *The Story of Jacob and Esau* (fig. 12-10) into a complete setting that goes back as far as the eye can reach. We can imagine the figures leaving the scene, for the deep space of this "pictorial relief" does not require their presence. Ghiberti's spacious hall is a fine example of Early Renaissance architectural design. Like Donatello, Ghiberti presents his story in continuous narrative. (There are seven episodes in all.) Because *The Story of Jacob and Esau* is about a decade later than *The Feast of Herod* by Donatello, its perspective is more assured.

JACOPO DELLA QUERCIA. Outside Florence, the only major sculptor was Jacopo della Quercia of Siena (c. 1374–1438). Like Ghiberti, he changed his style from Gothic to Early Renaissance in mid-career, mainly through contact with Donatello. Had he grown up in Florence, he might have been one of the leaders of the new movement, but his highly individual art remained outside the main trend. It had no effect on Florentine art until the very end of the century, when the young Michelangelo fell under its spell.

Michelangelo's admiration was aroused by the scenes from Genesis framing the main portal of the church of S. Petronio in

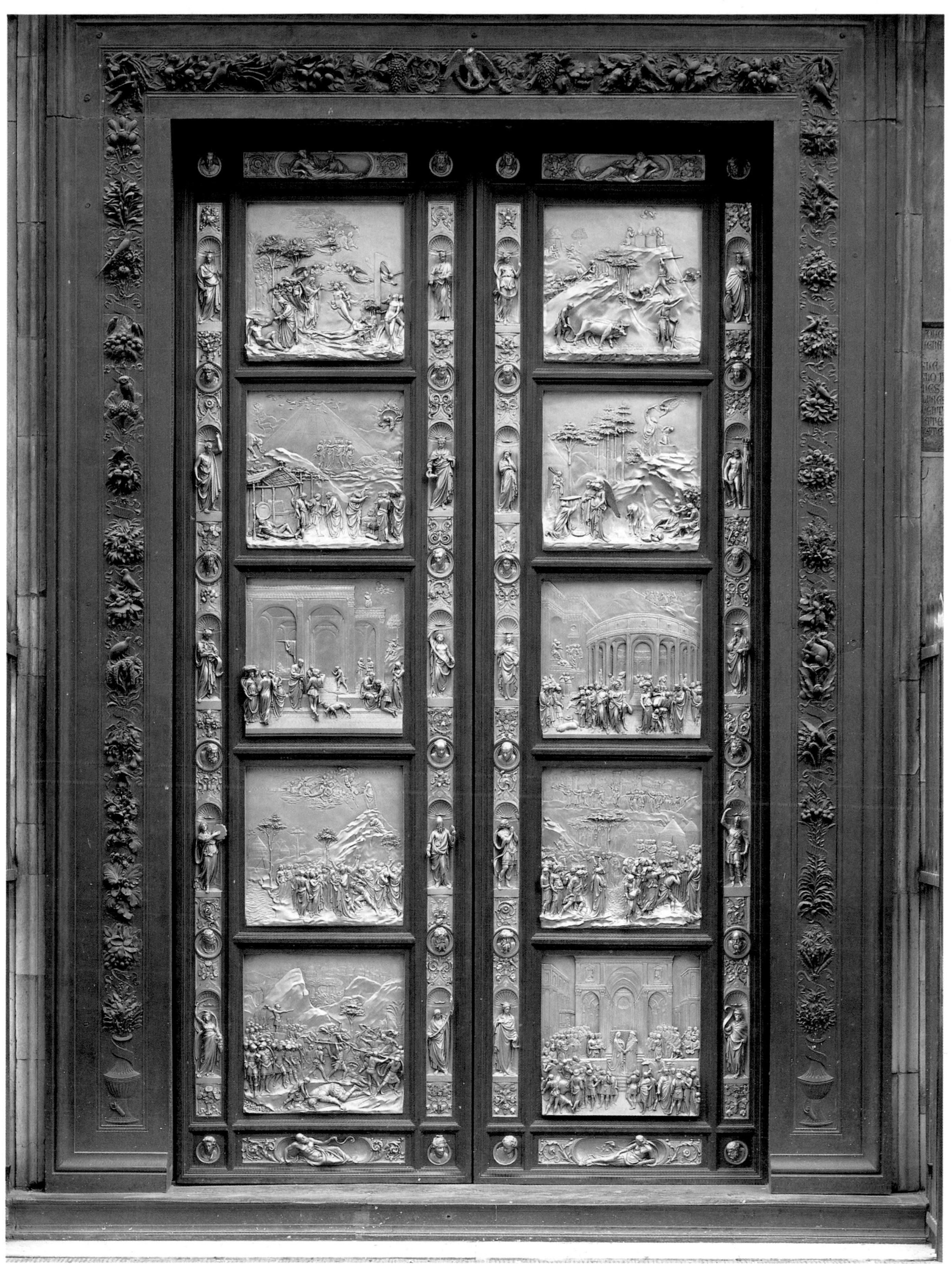

12-9. Lorenzo Ghiberti. *"Gates of Paradise,"* east doors of the Baptistery of S. Giovanni, Florence. c. 1435. Gilt bronze, height 15' (4.57 m)

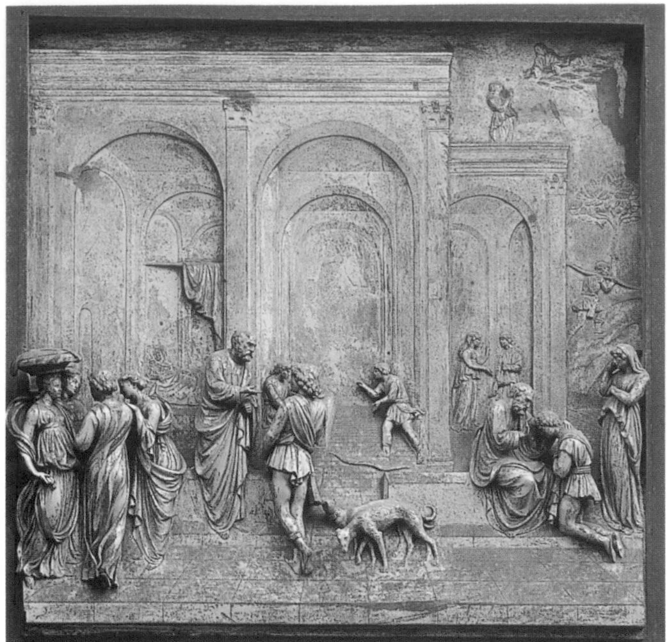

12-10. Lorenzo Ghiberti. *The Story of Jacob and Esau,* panel of the *"Gates of Paradise."* c. 1435. Gilt bronze, 31¼" (79.5 cm) square. Baptistery of S. Giovanni, Florence

Bologna. Among them was *The Creation of Adam* (fig. 12-11). The relief modeling of these panels is conservative—Jacopo had little interest in pictorial depth. Adam slowly rising from the ground, like a statue brought to life, recaptures the heroic beauty of a classical athlete. Here the nude body expresses the dignity and power of the individual as it did in classical antiquity. As he faces the Lord, Jacopo's Adam conveys a hint of the conflict that will lead to Original Sin. He will surely fall, but in a spirit of pride rather than as a mere victim of evil.

It is useful to compare Jacopo's *The Creation of Adam* with the work that probably inspired it, an *Adam in Paradise* from an Early Christian ivory diptych (fig. 12-12). The latter represents a classicizing trend that arose around 400 A.D. (compare fig. 8-22) as a final attempt to preserve the Greek ideal of physical beauty in a Christian context. Adam appears as the Perfect Man to whom God has granted "dominion . . . over every living thing," but the classic form has become a formula. Not until the fifteenth century would the beauty of the unclothed body be rediscovered. Jacopo's Adam is clearly nude, in the full classical sense.

Architecture

BRUNELLESCHI. Donatello did not create the Early Renaissance style in sculpture all by himself. The new architecture, in contrast, owed its existence to one person, Filippo Brunelleschi (1377–1446). Ten years older than Donatello, he, too, had begun his career as a sculptor. After losing the competition for the first Baptistery doors, he certainly went to Rome with Donatello. There he studied ancient structures and seems to have been the first person to take exact measurements of them. His discovery of scientific perspective (see box, page 398) may have grown out of his search for an accurate way of recording their appearance. We do not know what else he did during this period, but between 1417 and 1419 he again competed with Ghiberti, this time for the job of building the Florence Cathedral dome (see figs. 11-35 and 11-36). The dome had been designed half a century earlier, so only details

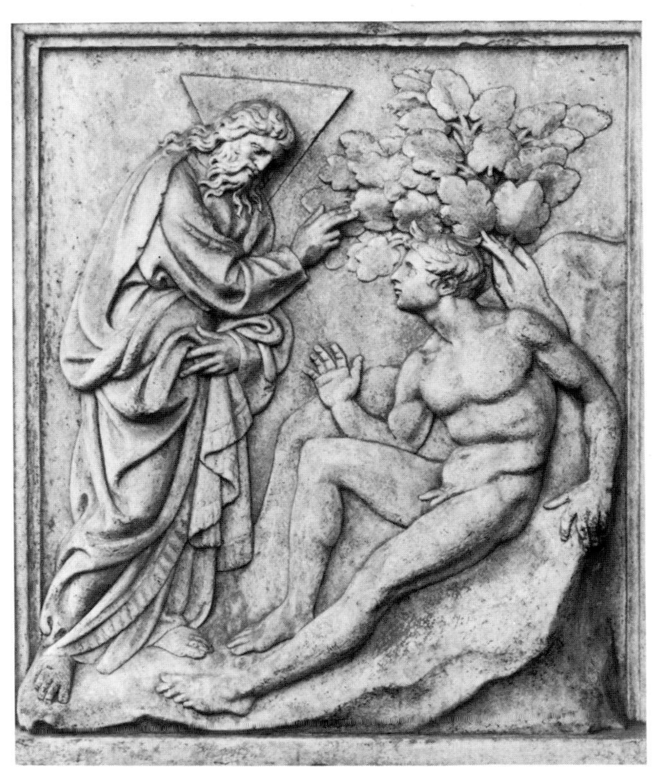

12-11. Jacopo della Quercia. *The Creation of Adam.* c. 1430. Marble, 34½ x 27½" (87.7 x 69.8 cm). Main portal, S. Petronio, Bologna

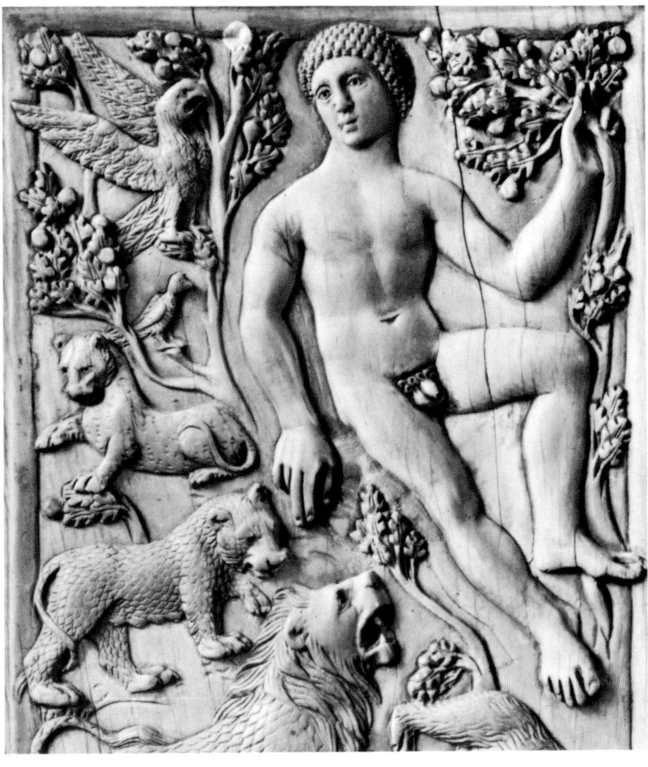

12-12. *Adam in Paradise,* detail of an ivory diptych. c. 400 A.D. Museo Nazionale del Bargello, Florence

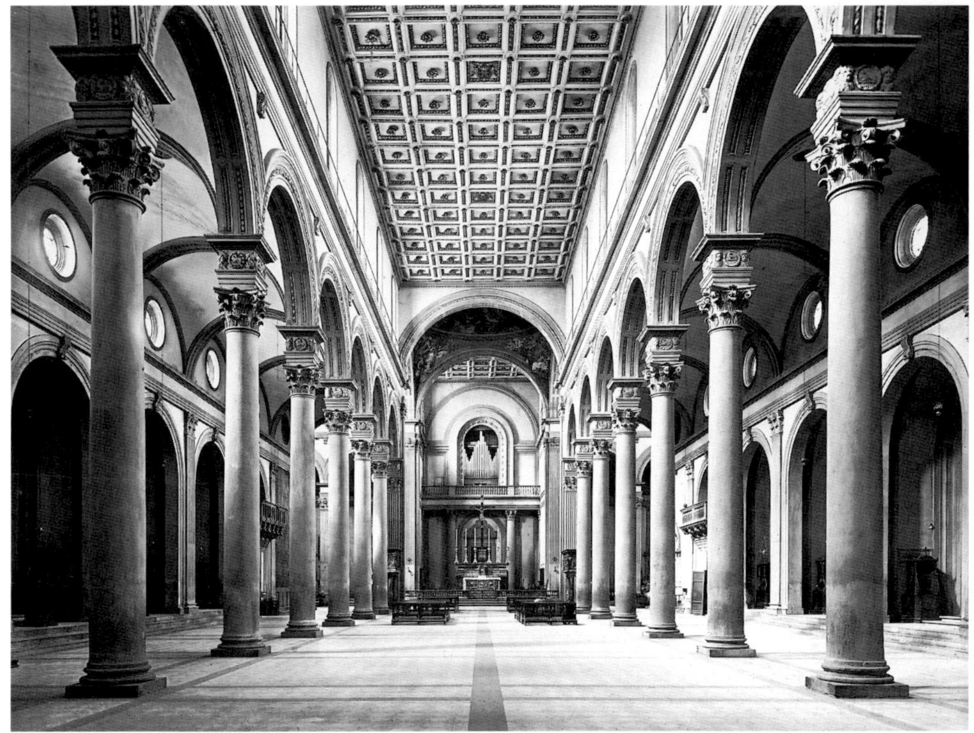

12-13. Filippo Brunelleschi. S. Lorenzo, Florence. 1421–69

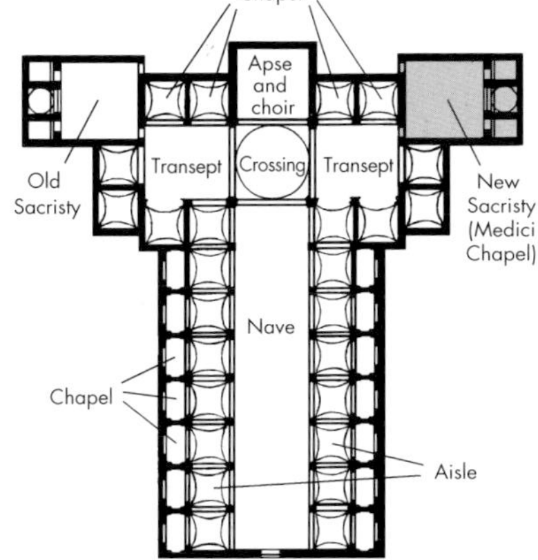

12-14. Plan of S. Lorenzo. Gray area indicates Michelangelo's later addition

could be changed, but its vast size posed a difficult problem of construction. Brunelleschi's proposals, although contrary to traditional practice, so impressed the authorities that this time he won. Thus the dome may be viewed as the first work of post-medieval architecture, as an engineering feat if not for style.

Brunelleschi's main achievement was to build the dome in two separate shells. They make use of a skeletal system inspired by the coffered dome of the Pantheon (see fig. 7-12). The two are ingeniously linked so as to reinforce each other, rather than forming a solid mass. Because the weight of the structure was lightened, Brunelleschi could dispense with the massive and costly wooden trusswork required by the older method of construction. Instead of having building materials carried up on ramps to the required level, he designed hoisting machines. Although Brunelleschi was neither a man of letters nor a scientist, his entire scheme reflects a bold, analytical mind that was willing to discard traditional solutions if better ones could be devised. This approach is very different from that of the Gothic stonemason–architects.

In 1419, while he was working out the final plans for the dome, Brunelleschi received his first opportunity to create buildings entirely of his own design. It came from the head of the Medici family, one of the leading merchants and bankers of Florence, who commissioned him to add a sacristy to the Romanesque church of S. Lorenzo. His plans for this sacristy (which was to serve also as a burial chapel for the Medici) were so successful that he was asked to develop a new design for the entire church. The construction, begun in 1421, was often interrupted, so that the interior was not completed until 1469, more than 20 years after the architect's death. The exterior remains unfinished to this day. Nevertheless, the building in its present form is essentially what Brunelleschi had envisioned about 1420. It represents the first full statement of his architectural aims (figs. 12-13 and 12-14).

At first glance, the plan may not seem very novel. Its general arrangement recalls that of Cistercian Gothic churches (see fig. 11-31), while the unvaulted nave and transept link it to Sta. Croce (see fig. 11-33). What distinguishes it is a new emphasis on symmetry and regularity. The entire design consists of square units. Four large squares form the choir, the crossing, and the arms of the transept. Four more are combined into the nave. Other squares, one-fourth the size of the large ones, make up the aisles and the chapels attached to the transept. (The oblong chapels outside the aisles were not part of the original design but were added some time after 1442.) As we study the plan, we see that Brunelleschi must have decided to make the floor area of the choir equal to four of the small square units. The nave and transept thus would be twice as wide as the aisles or chapels. In other words, Brunelleschi conceived S. Lorenzo as a grouping of "space blocks," the larger ones being simple multiples of a standard unit. Once we understand this, we realize how revolutionary he was. His clearly defined space compartments were a radical change from the Gothic architect's way of thinking. He was not concerned with the thickness of the walls between these compartments, so that the transept arms are slightly longer than they are wide, and the length of the nave is not four but four and one-half times its width.

In the interior, static order has replaced the flowing spatial movement of Gothic church interiors. S. Lorenzo does not sweep us off our feet. It does not even draw us forward after we have entered; we are content to remain near the door. From there our view seems to take in the entire structure, almost as if we were looking at a demonstration of scientific perspective (compare fig. 12-10).

The effect recalls the "old-fashioned" Tuscan Romanesque, such as Pisa Cathedral (see fig. 10-18), as well as Early Christian basilicas (compare fig. 8-6). These monuments, to Brunelleschi, exemplified the church architecture of classical antiquity. They inspired his use of round arches and columns, rather than piers, in the nave arcade. Yet these earlier buildings lack the lightness and precise articulation of S. Lorenzo. Their columns are larger and more closely spaced, tending to screen off the aisles from the nave. Only the arcade of the Florentine Baptistery is as graceful in its proportions as that of S. Lorenzo, but it is a *blind* arcade, without any supporting function (see fig. 10-19). The Baptistery was thought to have once been a classical temple. Hence, it was an appropriate source of inspiration for Brunelleschi.

Clearly, then, Brunelleschi did not revive the architectural forms of the ancients out of mere enthusiasm. The very quality that attracted him to them—their inflexibility—must from the medieval point of view have seemed their chief drawback. Unlike a medieval column, a classical column is strictly defined; its details and proportions can be varied only within narrow limits. (The ancients thought of it as an organic structure comparable to the human body.) The classical round arch, unlike any other arch (horseshoe, pointed, and so forth), has only one possible shape, a semicircle. The classical architrave, profiles, and ornaments are all subject to similarly strict rules. This is not to say that classical forms are completely rigid. If they were, they could not have persisted from the seventh century B.C. to the fourth century A.D. But the discipline of the Greek orders, which can be felt even in the most original Roman buildings, demands regularity and discourages arbitrary departures from the norm.

Without such "standardized" forms, Brunelleschi would have been unable to define his "space blocks" so clearly. With remarkable logic, he emphasizes the edges or "seams" of the units without disrupting their rhythmic sequence. To take one noteworthy example, consider the vaulting of the aisles. The transverse arches rest on pilasters attached to the outer wall (corresponding to the columns of the nave arcade), but between arch and pilaster there is a continuous architrave linking all the bays. We would expect these bays to be covered by unribbed groin vaults. Instead, we find a new kind of vault whose curved surface is formed from the upper part of a hemispherical dome. (Its radius equals half the diagonal of the square compartment.) Avoiding the ribs and even the groins, Brunelleschi has created a "one-piece" vault, strikingly simple and regular, in which each bay is a distinct unit.

At this point we may ask: If the new architecture consists of separate elements added together, be they spaces, columns, or vaults, how do they relate to each other? What makes the interior of S. Lorenzo seem so fully integrated? There is indeed a principle that accounts for the balanced nature of the design. For Brunelleschi, the secret of good architecture was to give the "right" proportions—that is, proportional ratios expressed in simple whole numbers—to all the major measurements of a building. The ancients had possessed this secret, he believed, and he tried to discover it when he measured their monuments. What he found, and exactly how he applied it, we do not know for sure. He may have been the first to discover what would be stated a few decades later in Leone Battista Alberti's treatise *On Architecture:* the mathematical ratios that determine musical harmony must also govern architecture, for they recur throughout the universe and thus are divine in origin. (See also box, page 125.)

Similar ideas, derived from the theories of the Greek philosopher Pythagoras, had been current during the Middle Ages, but they had never before been expressed so directly and simply. When Gothic architects "borrowed" the ratios of musical theory, they did so far less consistently. But even Brunelleschi's faith in harmonious proportions did not tell him how to allot these ratios to the parts of any given building. It left him many alternatives, and his choice was necessarily subjective. We may say, in fact, that the main reason S. Lorenzo strikes us as the product of a great mind is the individual sense of proportion that can be found in every detail.

In the revival of classical forms, Renaissance architecture found a standard vocabulary. The theory of harmonious propor-

SCIENTIFIC PERSPECTIVE

Although it is not certain, Brunelleschi probably invented linear, or scientific, perspective. The system is a geometric procedure for projecting space onto a plane, analogous to the way the lens of a camera projects a perspective image on film. Its central feature is the vanishing point, a single point toward which any set of parallel lines will seem to converge. If these lines are perpendicular to the picture plane, their vanishing point will be on the horizon, corresponding exactly to the position of the beholder's eye. Brunelleschi's discovery in itself was scientific rather than artistic, but it immediately became highly important to Early Renaissance artists. Unlike the intuitive perspective practices of the past, scientific perspective was objective, precise, and rational. In fact, it soon became an argument for upgrading the fine arts to liberal arts.

While empirical methods could also yield strikingly lifelike results, scientific perspective made it possible to represent three-dimensional space on a flat surface in such a way that all the distances remained measurable. This meant, in turn, that by reversing the procedure the plan could be derived from the perspective picture of a building. On the other hand, the scientific implications of the new perspective demanded that it be consistently applied, a requirement that artists could not always live up to, for practical as well as aesthetic reasons. Since the method presupposes that the beholder's eye occupies a fixed point in space, a perspective picture automatically tells us where we must stand to see it properly. Thus the artist who knows in advance that his work will be seen from above or below, rather than at ordinary eye level, can make his perspective construction correspond to these conditions. If, however, these are so abnormal that he must foreshorten his entire design to an extreme degree, he may disregard them and assume instead an ideal beholder, normally located. In 1435, Brunelleschi's discovery was described in *De Pictura,* the first Renaissance treatise on painting, by Leone Battista Alberti, who later became an important architect in his own right (see pages 412–14; Primary Sources, no. 40, page 612).

tions gave it a syntax that had been mostly absent in medieval architecture. This relative lack of flexibility should be viewed as an advantage. To take our linguistic analogy a bit further, we may draw a parallel between the "unclassical" flexibility of medieval architecture, expressed in numerous regional styles, and the equally "unclassical" attitude toward language that prevailed at the time, as found in its barbarized Latin and regional vernaculars, the ancestors of today's Western languages. The revival of Latin and Greek in the Renaissance did not stunt these languages. On the contrary, it made them so much more stable, precise, and articulate that before long Latin lost its dominant position as the language of intellectual discourse. It is not by chance that we can read Renaissance literature in Italian, French, English, or German without much trouble, while texts of a century or two earlier can often be understood only by scholars. Similarly, the revival of classical forms and proportions enabled Brunelleschi to transform the architectural "vernacular" of his region into a stable, precise, and articulate system. The principles on which his buildings were based soon spread to the rest of Italy and later to all of Northern Europe.

Among the surviving structures by Brunelleschi, not one escaped later alteration, not even the facade of the Pazzi Chapel (fig. 12-15). The chapel, begun about 1430, is an outgrowth of the Old Sacristy at S. Lorenzo some 11 years earlier. Brunelleschi (who died in 1446) could not have planned the front in its present form, which dates from about 1460 and remains incomplete. The

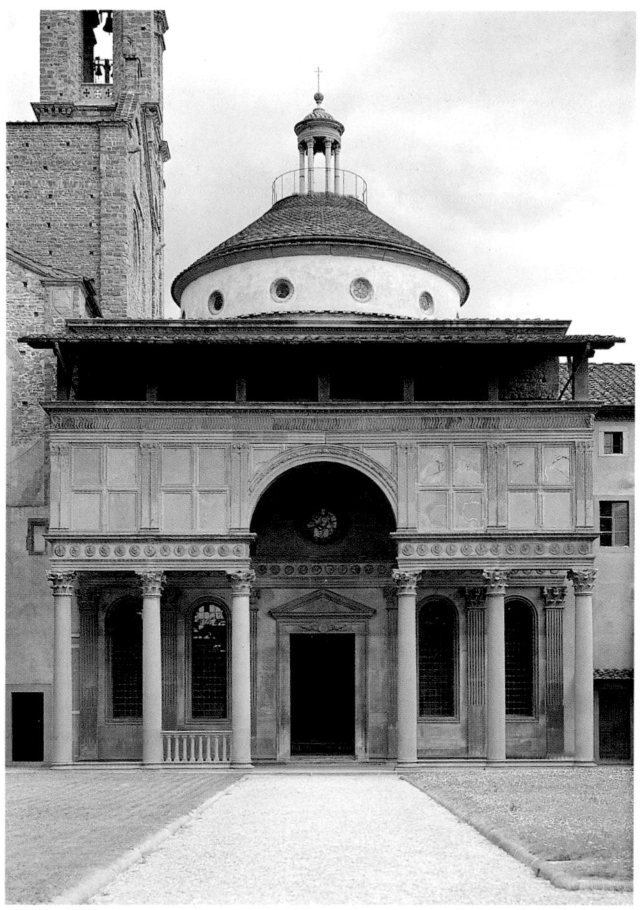

12-15. Filippo Brunelleschi and others. Pazzi Chapel, Sta. Croce, Florence. Begun 1430–33

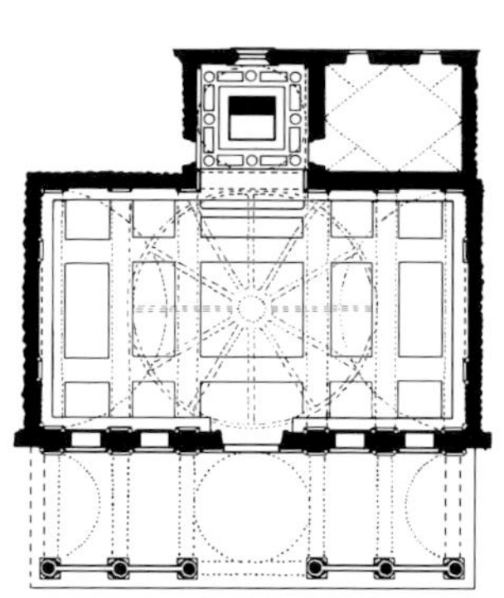

12-16. Plan of the Pazzi Chapel

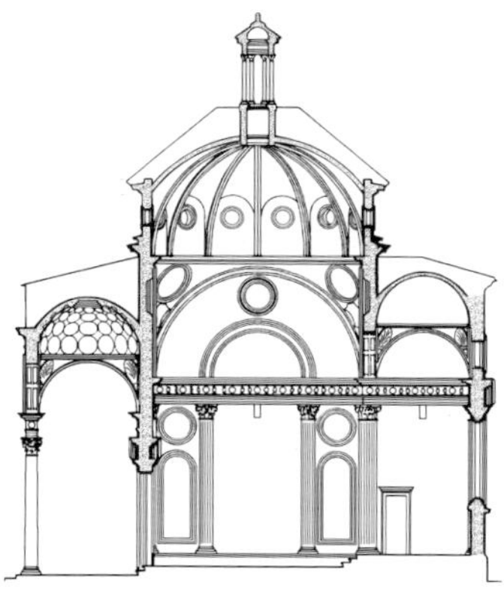

12-17. Longitudinal section of the Pazzi Chapel

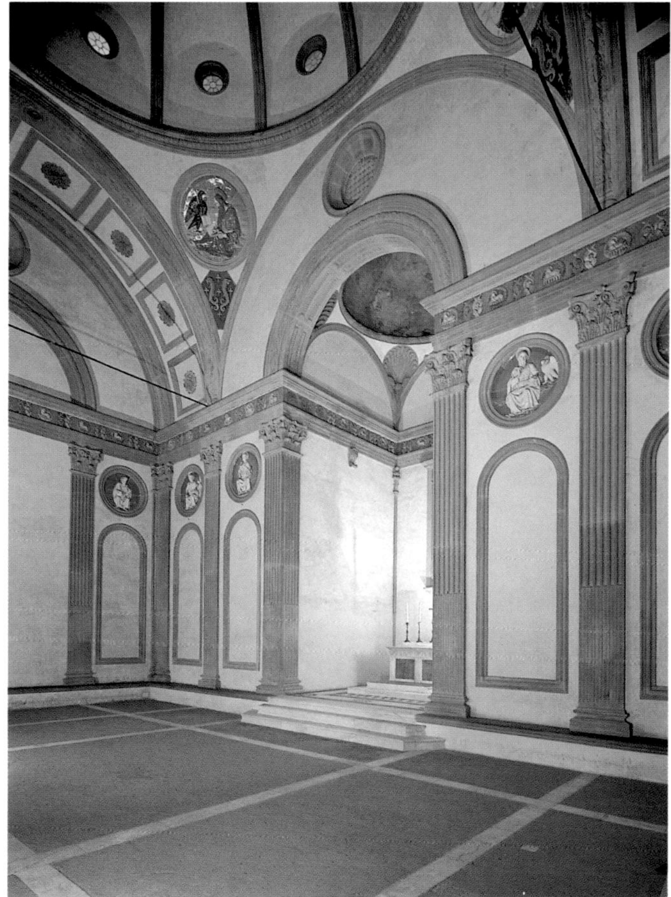

12-18. Interior of the Pazzi Chapel

chapel is totally unlike any medieval facade. A porch, similar to the narthex of Early Christian churches (see fig. 8-4), makes the facade appear to screen the rest of the structure. Another important innovation is the central arch linking two sections of a classical colonnade. It frames the portal and draws attention to the dome. The plan (fig. 12-16) shows us that the interrupted architrave supports two barrel vaults, which in turn help support a small dome.

Inside the chapel, we find the same motif on a larger scale: two barrel vaults flanking the dome. There is a third dome, like the one over the entrance but twice its diameter, above the square space housing the altar (figs. 12-17 and 12-18). The interior sur-

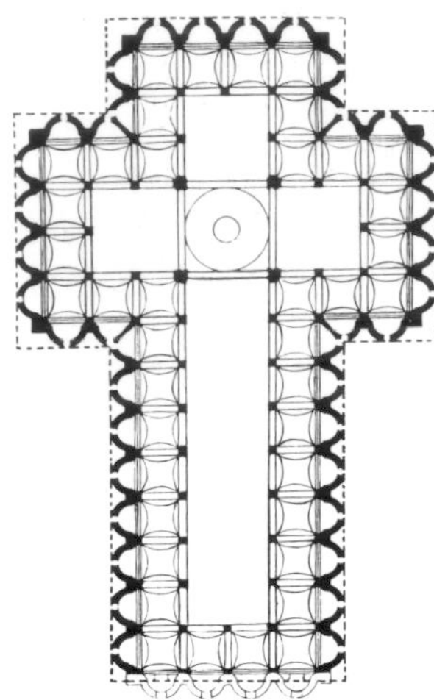
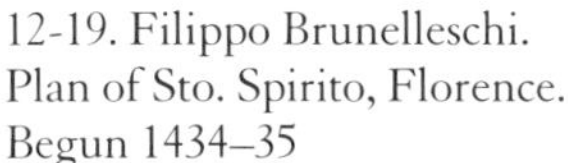

12-19. Filippo Brunelleschi. Plan of Sto. Spirito, Florence. Begun 1434–35

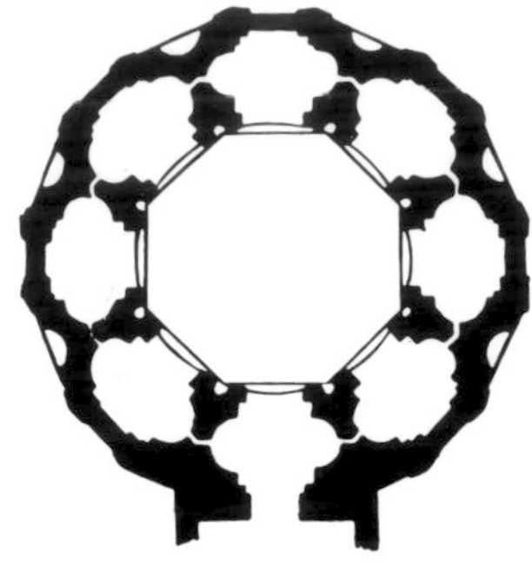

12-20. Filippo Brunelleschi. Plan of Sta. Maria degli Angeli, Florence. 1434–37

faces are articulated much as in S. Lorenzo, but their effect is richer and more festive. Here we also find some sculpture. On the four pendentives of the central dome are large roundels with reliefs of the evangelists. On the walls are 12 smaller reliefs of the apostles. These reliefs, however, are not essential to the design of the chapel. Brunelleschi provided the frames, but he may not have intended them to be filled with sculpture. Instead, they may very well have been planned "blind," like the recessed panels below them. In any case, the strong link between architecture and sculpture (never as strong in Italy as in Northern Europe during the Middle Ages) had been broken. Donatello had freed the statue from its setting, and Brunelleschi's conception of architecture as the visual counterpart of musical harmonies did not permit sculpture to play a more prominent role than the roundels in the Pazzi Chapel.

In the early 1430s, when the cathedral dome was nearing completion, Brunelleschi's career entered a new phase. His design for the church of Sto. Spirito (fig. 12-19) can be seen as a perfected version of S. Lorenzo. All four arms of the cross are alike, except that the nave is longer than the others. The entire structure is enveloped by an unbroken sequence of aisles and chapels. These chapels are the most surprising feature of Sto. Spirito. Brunelleschi had always avoided the apsidal shape, but now he used it to express the relationship between interior space and its boundaries more dynamically: the wall seems to bulge under the outward pressure of the space. Unhappily, this novel feature was later walled over. The interior elevation is a more systematic application of the proportions found in S. Lorenzo's, although the differences are not easily seen.

In the church of Sta. Maria degli Angeli, which Brunelleschi began about the same time as Sto. Spirito, this new direction reaches its logical conclusion (fig. 12-20). The domed, central-plan church—the first of the Renaissance—was inspired by the round and polygonal structures of Roman and Early Christian times. In many respects it perfects ideas explored in the Pazzi Chapel and the Old Sacristy. Because of financial problems, however, the church was not completed above the ground floor; we therefore cannot be sure of the design of the upper part, or even of some details in the plan. It is nevertheless clear that Brunelleschi has recaptured the ancient Roman principle of the "sculptured" wall. The dome was to rest on eight heavy piers that belong to the same mass of masonry from which the eight chapels have been "excavated." Both the wall and the space are charged with energy, and the plan reveals the precarious balance created by their pressures and counterpressures. In concept, Sta. Maria degli Angeli went so far beyond Brunelleschi's previous work that it must have bewildered his contemporaries. It had, in fact, no echoes until the end of the century.

MICHELOZZO. The massive "Roman" style of the church of Sta. Maria degli Angeli may explain why Brunelleschi's old patrons, the Medici, rejected his design for their new palace. Since the 1420s the family had gained such power that they were in practice, if not by law, the rulers of Florence. For that very reason they thought it wise to avoid ostentation. If Brunelleschi's plan for their palace followed the style of Sta. Maria degli Angeli, it would have been such a grand structure that the Medici felt that it might antagonize the public. They awarded the commission to a younger architect, Michelozzo (1396–1472). Construction began in 1444, two years before Brunelleschi's death.

Michelozzo's design for the Palazzo Medici-Riccardi (fig. 12-21) still recalls the fortresslike Florentine palaces of old (the windows on the ground floor were added by the Riccardi family in the seventeenth century). However, the type has been transformed (compare fig. 11-39). The three stories form a graded

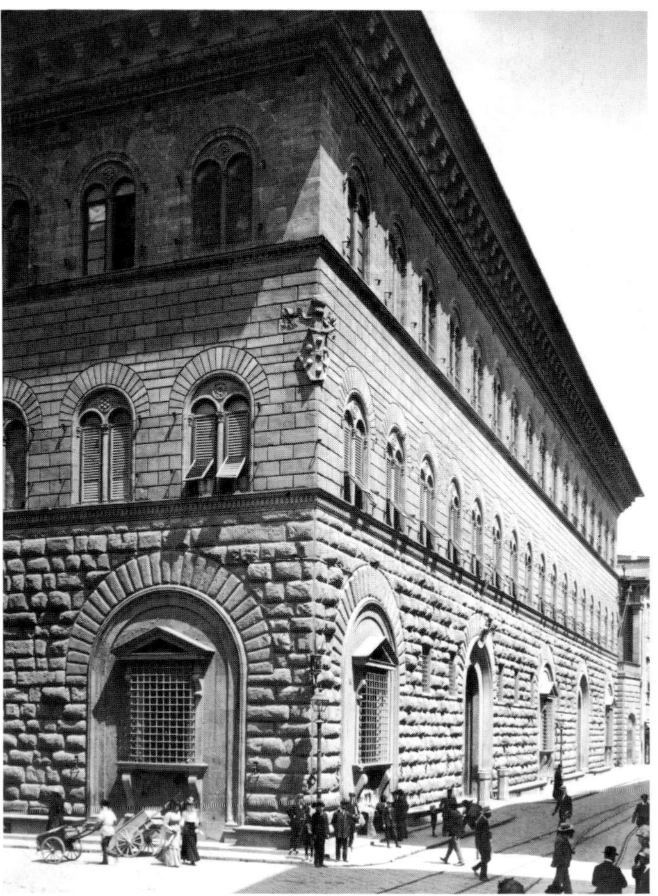

12-21. Michelozzo. Palazzo Medici-Riccardi, Florence. Begun 1444

sequence, each complete in itself. The lowest is built of rough-hewn, "rustic" masonry like the Palazzo Vecchio; the second has smooth-surfaced blocks with "rusticated" (indented) joints; and the third has an unbroken surface. On top of the structure rests, like a lid, a strongly projecting cornice like those of Roman temples. The change in style reflects a change in purpose: unlike Gothic palaces, which functioned partly as businesses and warehouses, the Palazzo Medici-Riccardi served mainly as a residence. It also proclaimed the family's status as discreetly as its imposing size permitted. Thus the large courtyard that dominates the interior is ceremonial rather than commercial.

Painting

MASACCIO. Early Renaissance painting did not appear until the early 1420s, a decade later than Donatello's *St. Mark* and some six years after Brunelleschi's first designs for S. Lorenzo. The new style was launched by a young genius named Masaccio (1401–1428), who was only 21 years old at the time and who died just six years later. The Early Renaissance was already well established in sculpture and architecture, making Masaccio's task easier than it would have been otherwise. His achievement was remarkable, nevertheless.

Masaccio's first mature work is a fresco of 1425 in Sta. Maria Novella (fig. 12-22). It shows the Holy Trinity in the company of the Virgin, St. John the Evangelist, and two donors who kneel on either side. The lowest section, linked with a tomb below, shows a skeleton lying on a sarcophagus. The inscription (in Italian) reads, "What you are, I once was; what I am, you will become." Here we seem to plunge into a new environment, one that brings to mind not the style of the recent past but the art of Giotto and his school, with its large scale, its severe composition, and its sculptural volume. Masaccio's allegiance to Giotto was only a starting point, however. For Giotto, body and drapery form a single unit, as if both had the same substance. In contrast, Masaccio's figures, like Donatello's, are "clothed nudes," whose drapery falls like real fabric. The Christ still adheres to the example set by Duccio's *Maestà* altarpiece, but the nearly sculptural treatment recalls an early *Crucifixion* by Brunelleschi that translates the same model into three dimensions. Like Donatello and Brunelleschi, Masaccio had a thorough knowledge of anatomy not seen since Roman art.

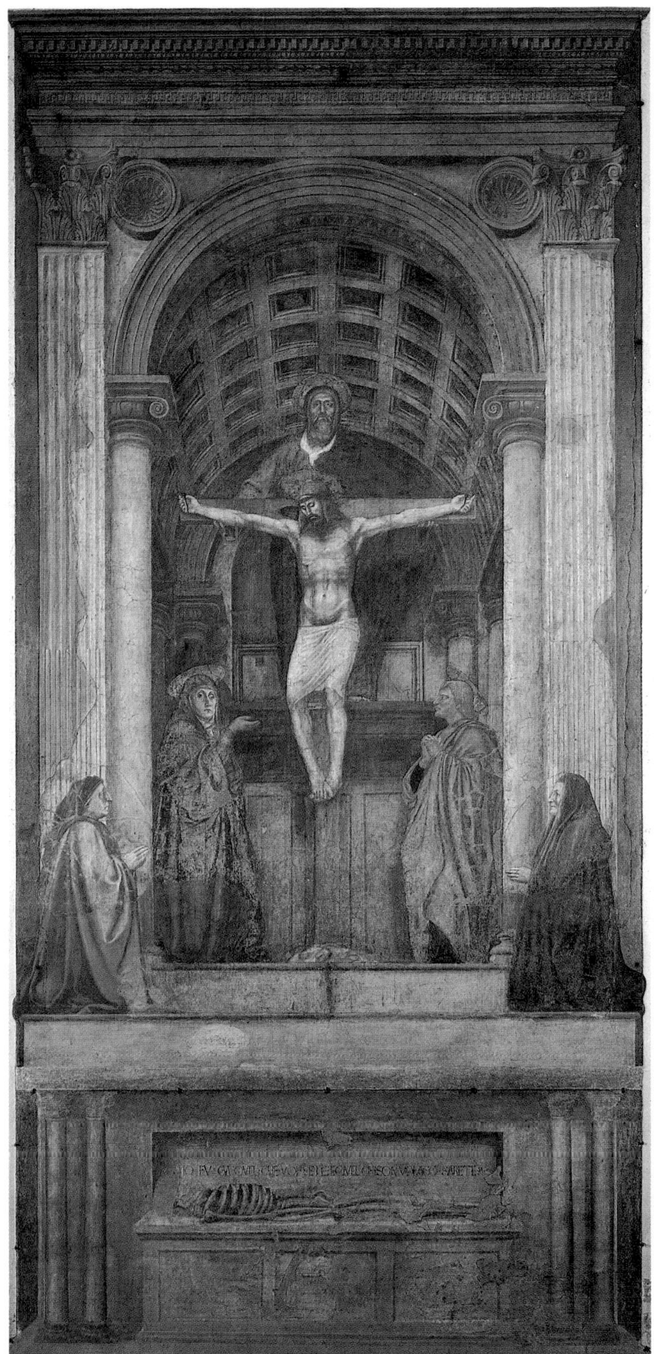

12-22. Masaccio. *The Holy Trinity with the Virgin, St. John, and Two Donors*. 1425. Fresco. Sta. Maria Novella, Florence

The up-to-date setting reveals the artist's understanding of Brunelleschi's new architecture and of scientific perspective. For the first time in history, we are given all the data needed to measure the depth of this painted interior, to draw its plan, and to duplicate the structure in three dimensions. It is, in short, the earliest example of a *rational* picture space. For Masaccio, like Brunelleschi, it must have also been a symbol of the universe ruled by divine reason. This barrel-vaulted chamber is not a niche but a deep space in which the figures could move freely if they so wished. As in Ghiberti's later relief panel *The Story of Jacob and Esau* (see fig. 12-10), the picture space is independent of the figures. They inhabit the space, but they do not create it. Take away the architecture and you take away the figures' space. We could go even further and say that scientific perspective depends on this particular kind of architecture, so different from the Gothic.

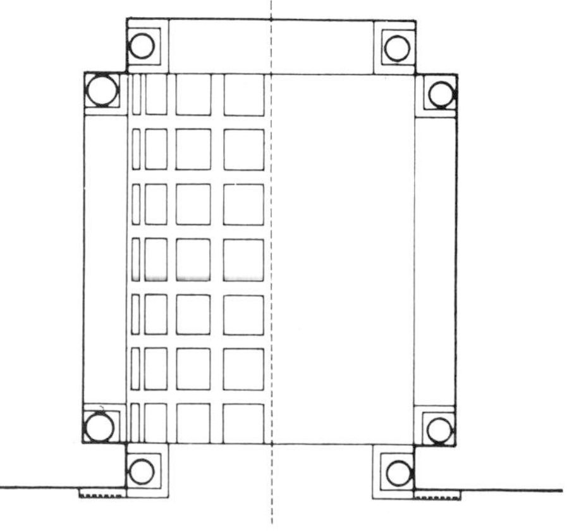

12-23. Plan of *The Holy Trinity*

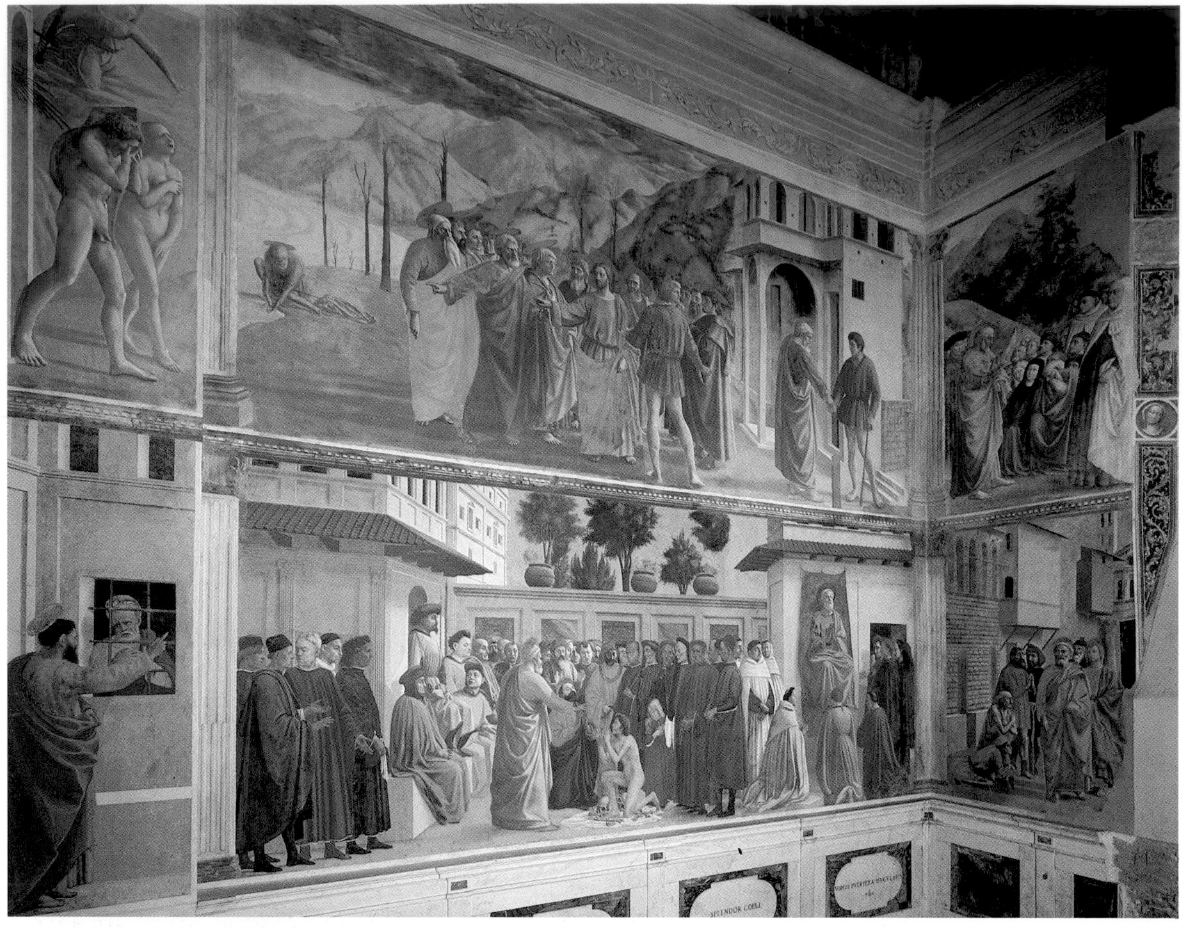

12-24.
Left wall of Brancacci Chapel, with frescoes by Masaccio. Sta. Maria del Carmine, Florence

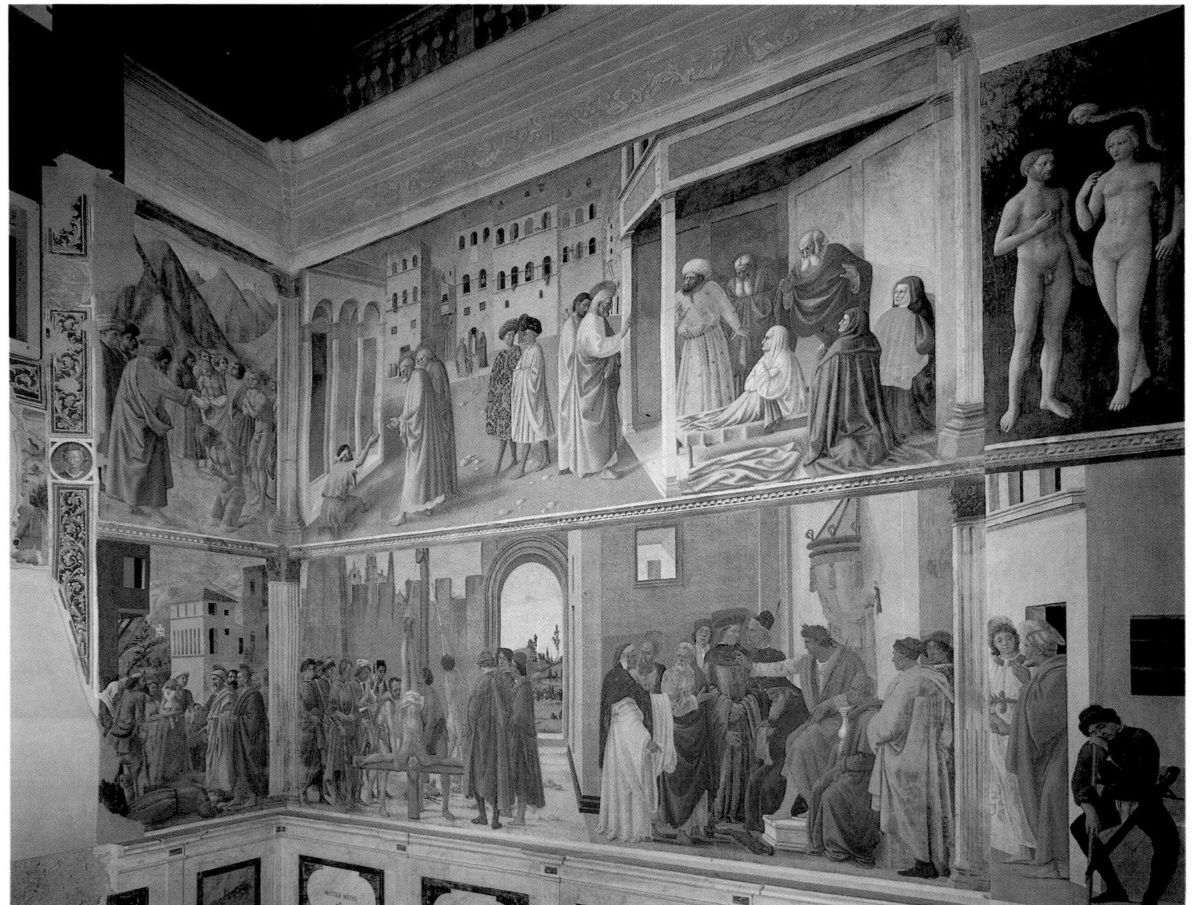

12-25.
Right wall of Brancacci Chapel, with frescoes by Masolino and Filippino Lippi. Sta. Maria del Carmine, Florence

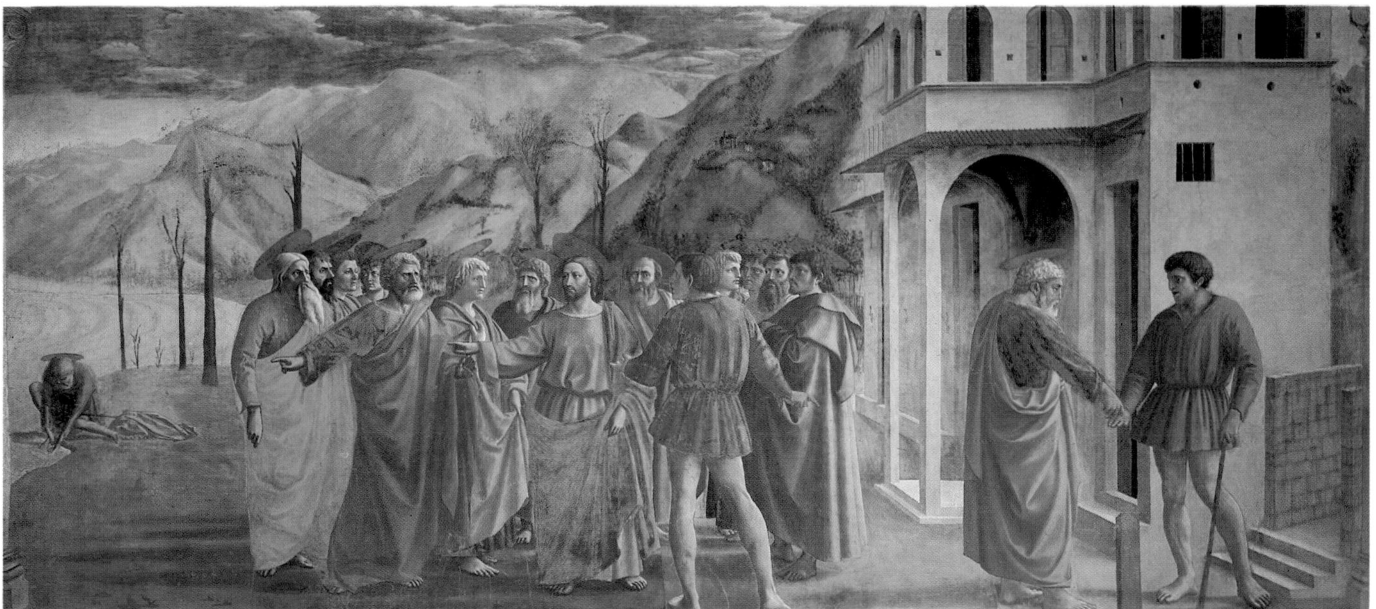

12-26. Masaccio. *The Tribute Money.* c. 1427. Fresco. Brancacci Chapel, Sta. Maria del Carmine, Florence

First we note that all the lines perpendicular to the picture plane converge toward a point below the foot of the Cross, on the platform that supports the kneeling donors. To see the fresco correctly, we must face this point, which is at normal eye level, somewhat more than five feet above the floor of the church. The figures within the chamber are five feet tall, slightly less than lifesize, while the donors, who are closer to us, are fully lifesize. The framework therefore is "lifesize," too, since it is directly behind the donors. The distance between the pilasters equals the span of the barrel vault, seven feet. The circumference of the arc over this span is 11 feet. That arc is subdivided by eight square coffers and nine ridges, the coffers being one foot wide and the ridges four inches wide. If we apply these data to the length of the barrel vault (it consists of seven coffers, the nearest of which is hidden behind the entrance arch), we find that the vaulted area is nine feet deep.

We can now draw a complete floor plan (fig. 12-23). However, the position of God the Father is puzzling at first. His arms support the Cross, close to the front plane, while his feet rest on a ledge attached to a wall. How far back is this surface? If it is the rear wall of the chamber, God would seem to be exempt from the laws of perspective. But unless the artist made a gross error in his perspective calculation, this cannot be so. Hence Masaccio must have intended to locate the ledge directly behind the Cross. The strong shadow that St. John casts on the wall beneath the ledge bears this out. What, then, is God standing on? It is likely that he is standing on the sepulchre of Christ, which is placed at a right angle to the wall and measures five and a half feet high by four feet wide and six or seven feet deep.

We realize, then, that *The Holy Trinity* is a restatement of the promise of eternal life in the Bardi Chapel frescoes by Maso di Banco and Taddeo Gaddi (see fig. 11-88). But in contrast to his Gothic predecessors, who combined painting with actual tomb sculpture, Masaccio has created an illusion that is far more convincing. This is so even though the niche is treated as a separate realm that the viewer, like the two donors, cannot enter. The rational pictorial space plays a key role in other ways. For Masaccio, as for Brunelleschi, it must have been a symbol of the universe ruled by divine reason. This attitude further explains the muted atmosphere, the calm gesture of the Virgin as she points to the Crucifixion, and the solemn grandeur of God the Father as he holds it effortlessly. The fervent hope of salvation portrayed in the Bardi Chapel (note the prayerful poses of the deceased) is presented here as a certitude based on reason as well as faith. Such, indeed, was the purpose of Renaissance humanism, in which the artist now assumed a position comparable to that of a philosopher.

The largest group of Masaccio's works to come down to us are frescoes in the Brancacci Chapel in Sta. Maria del Carmine (figs. 12-24 and 12-25), which are devoted to the life of St. Peter. The most famous of them is *The Tribute Money,* located in the upper tier (fig. 12-26). It depicts the story in the Gospel of Matthew (17:24–27) by the method known as "continuous narration" (see page 296). In the center, Christ instructs Peter to catch a fish, whose mouth will contain the tribute money for the tax collector. On the far left, in the distance, Peter takes the coin from the fish's mouth, and on the right he gives it to the tax collector. Since the lower edge of the fresco is almost 14 feet above the floor of the chapel, the artist could not assume an ideal vantage point. Instead, we must imagine that we are looking directly at the central vanishing point, which is located behind the head of Christ. Oddly enough, this feat is so easy that we take note of it only if we stop to analyze it. But then, any pictorial illusion is an imaginary experience. No matter how eager we are to believe in a picture, we never mistake it for reality, just as we never confuse a statue with a living thing.

If we could see *The Tribute Money* from the top of a ladder, the illusion of reality would not improve very much. The illusion does not depend mainly on scientific perspective. Masaccio controls the

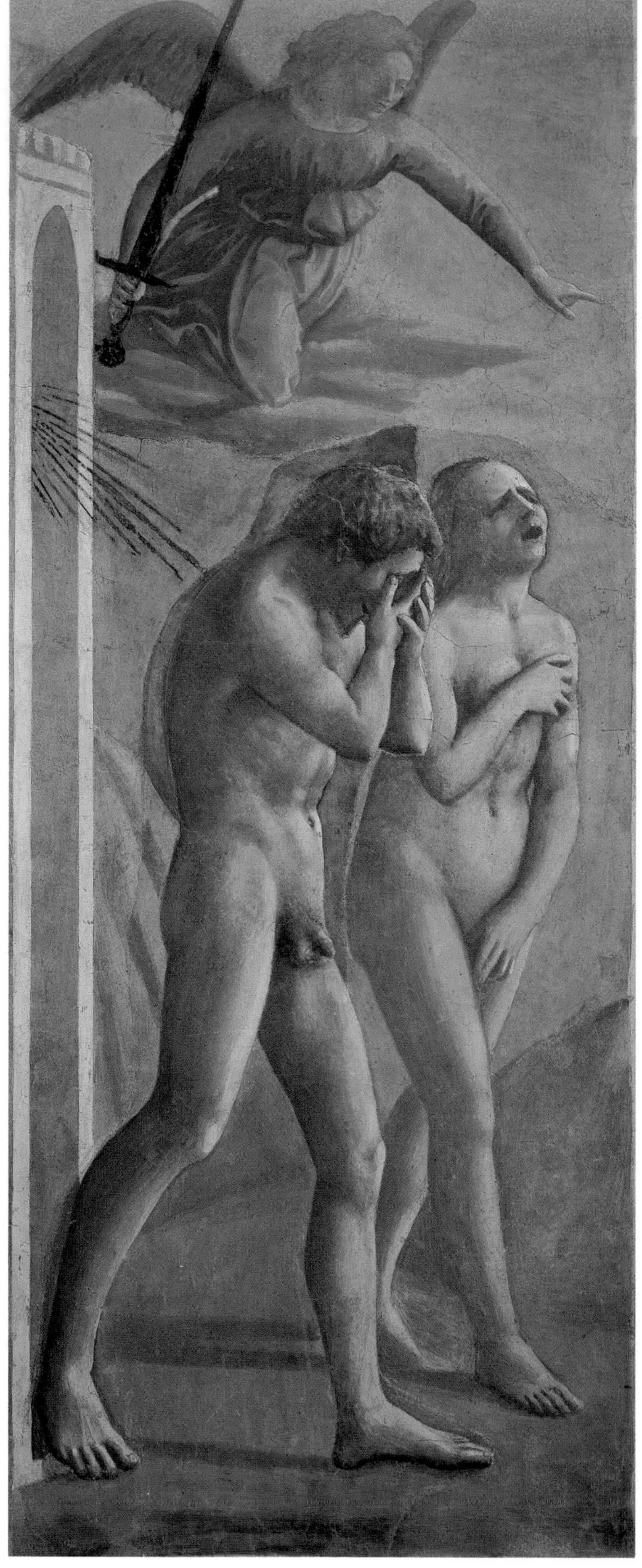

12-27. Masaccio. *The Expulsion from Paradise.* c. 1427. Fresco. Brancacci Chapel, Sta. Maria del Carmine, Florence flow of light (which comes from the right, where the window of the chapel is located). He also uses atmospheric perspective in the subtle tones of the landscape. We now recall Donatello's use of such a setting a decade earlier in his small relief of St. George (compare fig. 12-3).

The figures in *The Tribute Money,* even more than those in the *Trinity* fresco, display Masaccio's ability to merge the weight and volume of Giotto's figures with the new functional view of body and drapery. All stand in balanced contrapposto. Fine vertical lines scratched in the plaster establish the axis of each figure from the head to the heel of the engaged leg. In accord with this dignified approach, the figures seem rather static. The narrative is conveyed by intense glances and a few strong gestures, rather than by physical movement. But in another fresco in the same chapel, *The Expulsion from Paradise* (fig. 12-27), Masaccio proves that he can show the human body in motion. The tall, narrow format leaves little room for a spatial setting. The gate of paradise is barely indicated, and in the background are a few shadowy, barren slopes. Yet the soft, atmospheric modeling, and especially the forward-moving angel, boldly foreshortened, convey a sense of unlimited space. This scene is clearly akin to Jacopo della Quercia's Bolognese reliefs (see fig. 12-11). Masaccio's grief-stricken Adam and Eve, though less dependent on ancient models, are equally striking portrayals of the beauty and power of the nude human form.

It seems hard to believe that only a few years before, Gentile da Fabriano had completed *The Adoration of the Magi* (see fig. 11-97). Masaccio's style abandons the lyrical grace of the International Gothic. Yet he shared the work on the Brancacci Chapel with a much older artist, Masolino (documented 1423–d. 1440), who had been strongly influenced by Gentile. The two nevertheless worked together well and even collaborated on some of the frescoes (the head of Christ in *The Tribute Money* is by Masolino, for instance). However, Masolino continued to employ the International Style. Thus the figures in the upper tier of the right wall (see fig. 12-25) are simply larger versions of those in Pietro Lorenzetti's *Birth of the Virgin* (see fig. 11-82). The setting, too, remains Gothic in character, despite the scientific perspective (compare fig. 11-84). Masolino constructs a theatrical space that remains separate from his figures, whereas Masaccio's are closely tied to their surroundings.

Nowhere is the contrast between the two artists' styles more striking than in *The Temptation* by Masolino (visible in the upper right of fig. 12-25). This work forms an enchanting companion to the anguish in Masaccio's *Expulsion from Paradise.* Despite their contrapposto, the figures of Adam and Eve are no more classical than Adam in figure 12-12. In fact, they may be derived from a similar source, for Masolino was unable to treat the nude in convincing organic terms. In comparing these works, we see that Masaccio, like Donatello, captured the substance of antiquity without simply relying on its forms. Masaccio left for Rome before he could finish the Brancacci Chapel; Masolino's work, too, was interrupted for several years. It was finally finished near the end of the century by Filippino Lippi (1457/8–1504), who was responsible for the lower tier to either side.

While he preferred mural painting, Masaccio was skilled in panel painting. The many panels of his large altarpiece, or polyptych, made in 1426 for the Carmelite church in Pisa, are now dispersed among various collections. The center panel (fig. 12-28) is a more fully developed restatement of his earliest known work. The *Madonna Enthroned* is of the monumental Florentine type introduced by Cimabue and reshaped by Giotto (see figs. 11-72 and 11-80). The usual elements, including the gold ground, are present: a large, high-backed throne with angels on each side (here only two). Despite these traditional elements, the painting is revolutionary in several respects. The kneeling angels in Giotto's *Madonna* have become lute players seated on the lowest step of the throne. The Christ Child no longer blesses us but eats a bunch of grapes, a symbol of the Passion (the suffering of Jesus in his last days). (The grapes refer to wine, which represents the Savior's blood in the sacrament of the Eucharist.) Above all, the powerful proportions of the figures make them much more concrete and

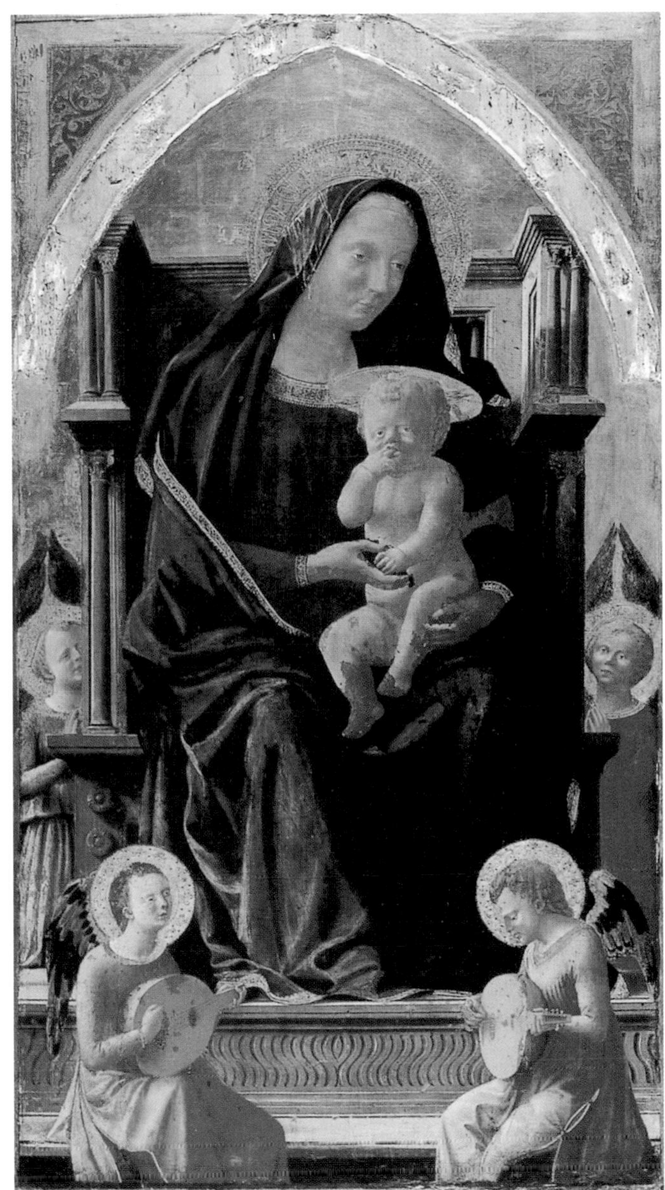

12-28. Masaccio. *Madonna Enthroned.* 1426. Oil on panel, 56 x 29" (142 x 73.6 cm). The National Gallery, London

REPRODUCED BY COURTESY OF THE TRUSTEES

impressive than any earlier ones, even Giotto's, although they are hardly beautiful by the standards of the International Style.

In light of the *Trinity* fresco, it is no surprise that Masaccio replaces Giotto's ornate but frail Gothic throne with a solid and austere stone seat in the style of Brunelleschi, or that he makes expert use of perspective. (Note especially the two lutes.) We are less prepared for the delicate and precise rendering of the light on the surfaces. Within the picture, sunlight enters from the left—not the glare of noon but the glow of the setting sun. (We can determine its exact angle from the shadows on the throne.) Hence there are no harsh contrasts between light and shade. The use of half-shadows results in a rich scale of transitional hues. The light retains its descriptive function while imposing a common tonality and mood on all the forms it touches.

TEMPERA AND OIL. These refinements were made possible by oil painting. The basic medium of medieval panel painting had been tempera, in which the finely ground pigments were mixed ("tempered") with diluted egg yolk. It produced a thin, tough, quick-drying coat that was well suited to the medieval taste for high-keyed flat color surfaces. However, in tempera the different tones on the panel could not be blended smoothly, and the continuous progression of values necessary for three-dimensional effects was difficult to achieve. Also, dark shades tended to look muddy. These were major drawbacks that were overcome by replacing the diluted egg yolk with oil. Medieval artists knew about oil, but they used it only for special purposes, such as coating stone surfaces or painting on metal. Its artistic potential was discovered around the 1420s by the Master of Flémalle and his contemporaries in the North (see pages 484–86). Oil, a viscous, slow-drying medium, can produce a variety of effects, from thin, translucent films (called "glazes") to the thickest impasto (that is, a thick, creamy layer of paint). The hues can also yield a continuous scale of tones, including velvety dark shades. Oil has a unique advantage over egg tempera, encaustic, and fresco: it allows artists to change their minds almost at will. Without oil, the conquest of visible reality would have been much more limited. The new medium spread quickly to Italy, where it became the foundation of modern painting. Although it continued to be mixed with tempera for some time, oil has been the basic medium ever since.

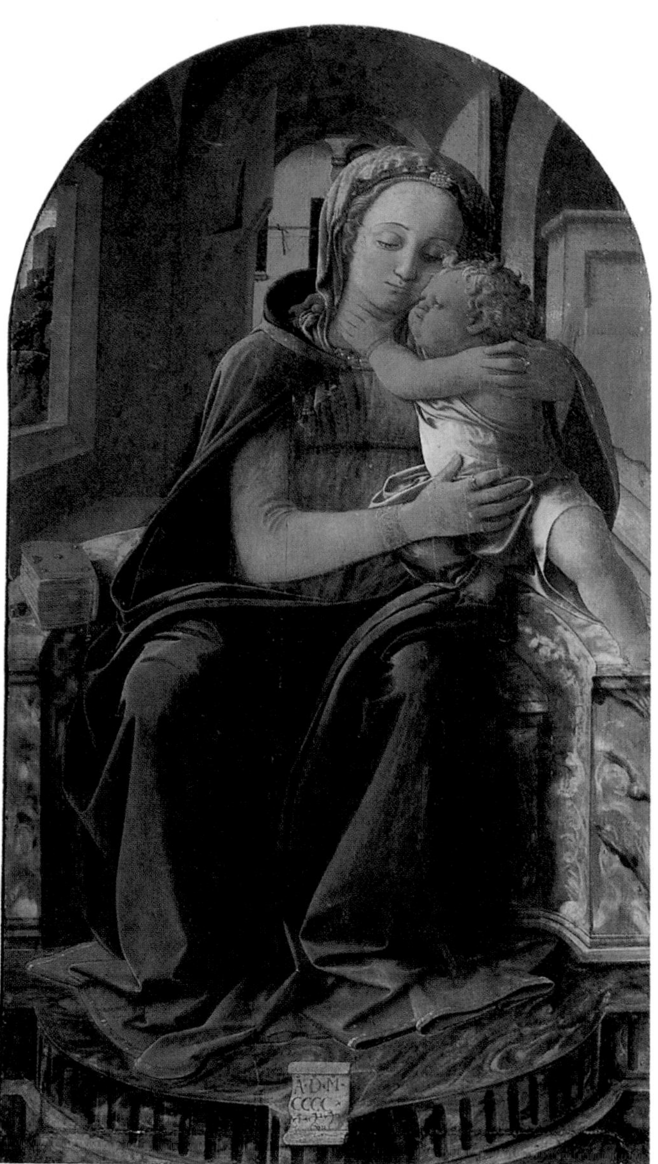

12-29. Fra Filippo Lippi. *Madonna Enthroned.* 1437.
Oil on panel, 45 x 25½" (114.7 x 64.8 cm).
Galleria Nazionale d'Arte Antica, Rome

FRA FILIPPO LIPPI. Masaccio's early death left a gap that was not filled for some time. Among the younger artists of his day, only Fra Filippo Lippi (c. 1406–1469) seems to have had close contact with him. ("Fra" means "brother"; Lippi was a friar.) Fra Filippo's earliest dated work, the *Madonna Enthroned* of 1437 (fig. 12-29), reminds us of Masaccio's *Madonna* in several ways: the lighting, the heavy throne, the massive figures, and the drapery folds over the Virgin's legs. But it does not have the same monumentality and severity. In fact, it seems cluttered, for Fra Filippo reduces the divine to the mundane. The background is a domestic interior (note the Virgin's bed on the right), and the patterned marble throne displays a prayer book and a scroll showing the date. Such a quantity of realistic detail, as well as the undisciplined perspective, indicates that Fra Filippo's artistic temperament was very different from Masaccio's. It also suggests that Fra Filippo must have seen Flemish paintings (perhaps during his visit to northeastern Italy in the mid-1430s).

Finally, we note the painter's interest in movement. We see it in the figures and, even more clearly, in parts of the drapery. The curly edge of the Virgin's headdress and the curved folds of her mantle streaming to the left, which accentuate her turn to the right, show an interest in graceful decorative effects that will later become an end in itself. Such effects are also found in the reliefs of Donatello and Ghiberti: compare Salome in *The Feast of Herod* (see fig. 12-5) and the maidens in the lower left-hand corner of *The Story of Jacob and Esau* (see fig. 12-10). It is not surprising that these two artists had such a strong effect on Florentine painting in the decade after Masaccio's death. Age, experience, and prestige gave them an authority unmatched by any painter active at the time. Their influence, and that of the Flemish masters, in altering Fra Filippo's outlook was important, since he lived until 1469 and played a key role in setting the course of Florentine painting during the second half of the century.

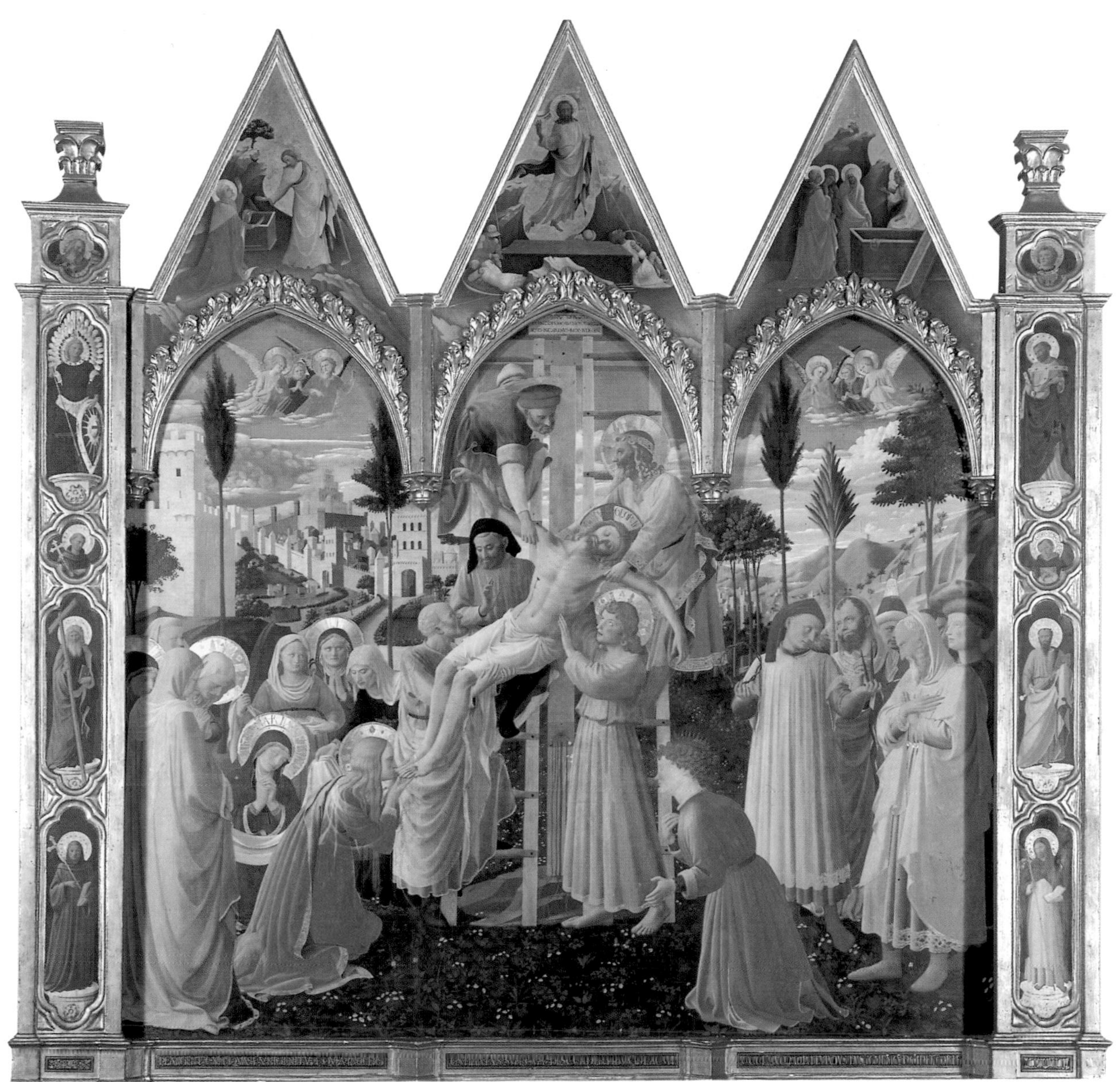

12-30. Fra Angelico. *Deposition.* Probably early 1440s. Oil on panel, 9'1/4" x 9'4 1/4" (275 x 285 cm). Museo di S. Marco, Florence

FRA ANGELICO. Fra Filippo's slightly older contemporary, Fra Angelico (c. 1400–1455), was also a friar, but unlike Fra Filippo he took his vows seriously and rose to a high position within his order. We sense his reverential attitude in the large *Deposition* (fig. 12-30), which was probably done for the same chapel as Gentile da Fabriano's *Adoration of the Magi* (see fig. 11-97). Fra Angelico took over the commission from Gentile's contemporary, Lorenzo Monaco. Lorenzo was responsible for the Gothic shape of the frame and its paintings, but he died before he could complete the altar. Some scholars date Fra Angelico's panel to about 1435, while others date it to the early 1440s. Either date may be correct, for Fra Angelico, like Ghiberti, developed slowly, and in his mature years his conservative style underwent very little change. We are clearly in a different world from Fra Filippo's. This *Deposition* is an object of devotion. Fra Angelico retains the very aspects of Masaccio that Fra Filippo had rejected: his dignity, directness, and spatial order. Thus Fra Angelico's dead Christ is the true heir of the monumental figure in Masaccio's *Trinity.*

Fra Angelico's art is something of a paradox. It combines Gothic piety (compare fig. 11-88) with Renaissance grandeur in an atmosphere of calm contemplation. The setting spreads behind the figures like a tapestry. The landscape, with the town in the distance, harks back to the *Allegory of Good Government* by Ambrogio Lorenzetti (see figs. 11-84 and 11-85). The artist also shows his awareness of the achievements of Northerners such as the Limbourg brothers (compare fig. 11-94): he evokes a brilliant sunlit day with striking success. Yet the scene does not seem at all Gothic. It has the same natural light that produces softly modeled forms in Masaccio's *Madonna Enthroned* (see fig. 12-28). This light fills the landscape with a sense of wonderment at God's creation, an effect that is wholly Renaissance in spirit. We shall meet it again in the work of Giovanni Bellini, which it anticipates in another respect: the beautiful, yet uninhabited city in the distance is surely the Heavenly Jerusalem (see fig. 12-63). At the same time, the bright, enamellike hues, though remnants of the International Style, look forward to the colorism of Domenico Veneziano.

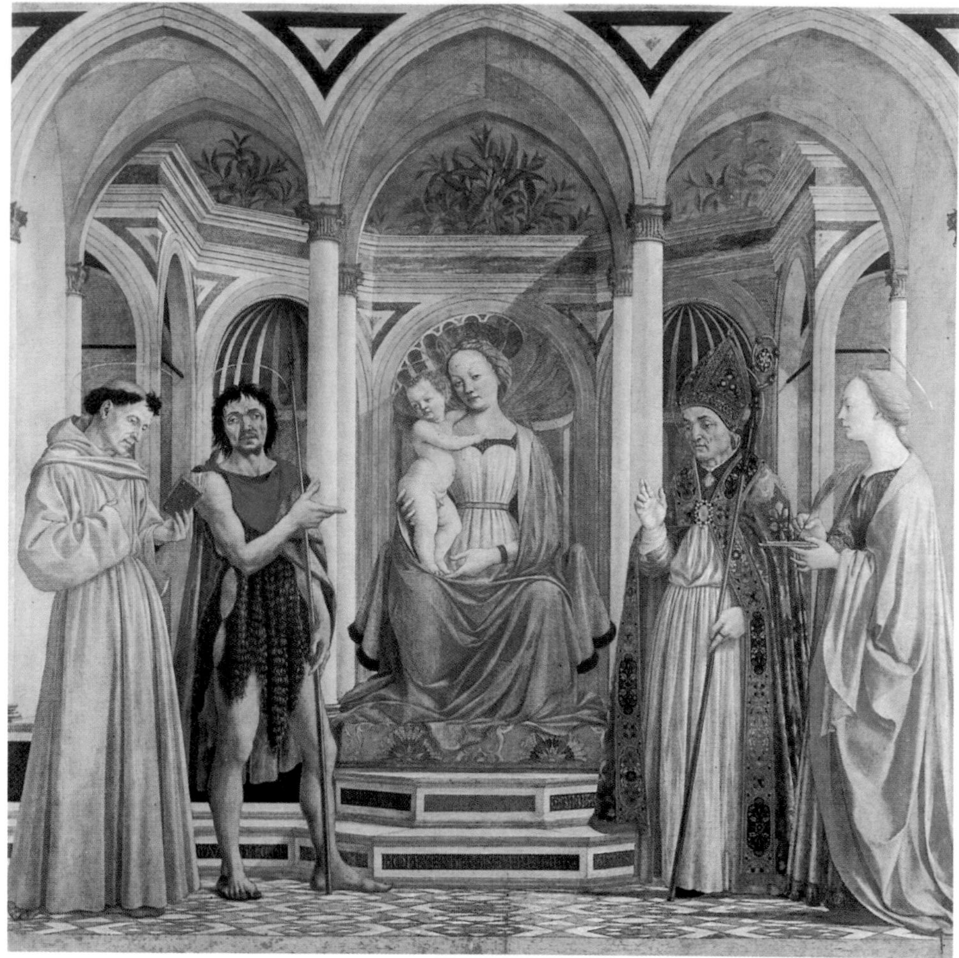

12-31. Domenico Veneziano. *Madonna and Child with Saints.* c. 1455. Oil on panel, 6'10" x 7' (2.08 x 2.13 m). Galleria degli Uffizi, Florence

DOMENICO VENEZIANO. In 1439 a gifted painter from Venice, Domenico Veneziano, settled in Florence. We can only guess at his age, training, and previous work. (He was probably born about 1410 and he died in 1461.) He must, however, have been in sympathy with the spirit of Early Renaissance art, for he quickly became an important artist in his new home. His *Madonna and Child with Saints,* shown in figure 12-31, is one of the earliest examples of a new kind of altar panel. This new type, the so-called *sacra conversazione* ("sacred conversation"), was popular from the mid-fifteenth century on. An enthroned Madonna is framed by architecture and flanked by saints who may converse with her, with the beholder, or among themselves.

Looking at Domenico's panel, we can understand the appeal of the sacra conversazione. The architecture and the space it defines are clear and tangible yet elevated above the everyday world. The figures, while echoing the formality of their setting, are linked with each other and with us by a fully human awareness. We are admitted to their presence, but they do not invite us to join them. Like spectators in a theater, we are not allowed "on stage." In Flemish painting, by contrast, the picture space seems a direct extension of the viewer's environment (compare fig. 15-1).

The basic elements of our panel were already present in Masaccio's *Holy Trinity* fresco. Domenico must have studied it carefully, for his St. John looks at us while pointing toward the Madonna, repeating the glance and gesture of Masaccio's Virgin. Domenico's perspective setting is worthy of the earlier master, although the slender proportions and colored inlays of his architecture are less Brunelleschian. His figures, too, are dignified like Masaccio's but without the same weight and bulk. The slim, sinewy bodies of the male saints, with their highly individualized, expressive faces, show Donatello's influence (see fig. 12-4).

In his use of color, however, Domenico owes nothing to Masaccio. He treats color as an integral part of his work, and the sacra conversazione is as noteworthy for its color scheme as for its composition. The blond tonality, its harmony of pink, light green, and white set off by spots of red, blue, and yellow, reconciles the brightness of Gothic panel painting with perspective space and natural light. A sacra conversazione is usually an indoor scene, but this one takes place in a kind of loggia (a covered open-air arcade) with sunlight streaming in from the right, as we can tell from the cast shadow behind the Madonna. The surfaces reflect the light so strongly that even the shadowed areas glow with color. Masaccio had achieved a similar effect in his *Madonna* of 1426, which Domenico surely knew. In this work the technique has been applied to a more complex set of forms and merged with Domenico's exquisite color sense. The influence of its distinctive tonality can be seen throughout Florentine painting of the second half of the century.

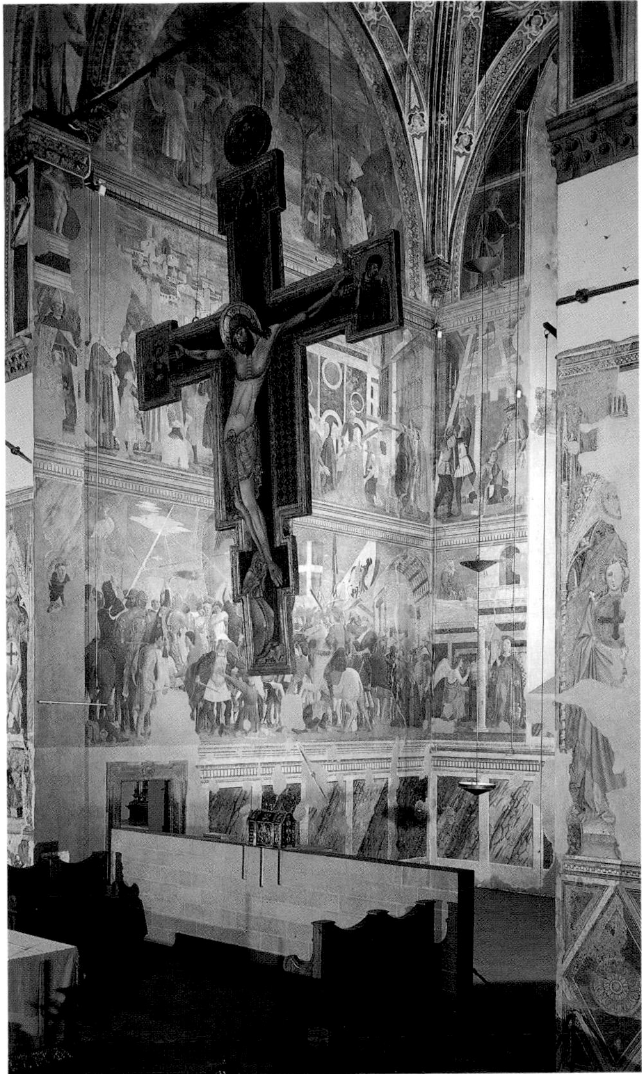

12-32. View into main chapel, with frescoes by Piero della Francesca. S. Francesco, Arezzo

PIERO DELLA FRANCESCA. When Domenico settled in Florence, he had a young assistant from southeastern Tuscany named Piero della Francesca (c. 1420–1492). Piero became his most important disciple and one of the great artists of the Early Renaissance. Surprisingly, however, he left Florence after a few years, never to return. The Florentines seem to have viewed his work as provincial and old-fashioned, and from their point of view they were right. Piero's style, even more than Domenico's, reflected the aims of Masaccio. He retained his allegiance to the founder of Italian Renaissance painting throughout his long career, while Florentine taste developed in a different direction after 1450.

Piero's most impressive work is the fresco cycle in the choir of S. Francesco in Arezzo, painted from about 1452 to 1459 (fig. 12-32). Its many scenes depict the legend of the True Cross (that is, the story of the Cross used for Christ's Crucifixion). The section in figure 12-33 shows the empress Helena, the mother of Constantine the Great, discovering the True Cross and the two crosses of the thieves who died beside Jesus. (All three had been hidden by enemies of the Faith.) On the left, they are being lifted out of the ground; on the right, the True Cross is identified by its power to bring a dead youth back to life.

Piero's link with Domenico is apparent in his colors. The tonality of this fresco, though less luminous than in Domenico's sacra conversazione, is similarly blond and evokes morning sunlight in much the same way. Since the light enters the scene at a low angle, in a direction almost parallel to the picture plane, it defines every shape and lends drama to the narrative. But Piero's figures have a harsh grandeur that recalls Masaccio, or even Giotto, more than Domenico. These men and women seem to belong to a lost heroic race, beautiful and strong—and silent. Their inner life is conveyed by glances and gestures, not by facial expressions. They have a gravity that makes them seem akin to Greek sculpture of the Severe style (see fig. 5-46).

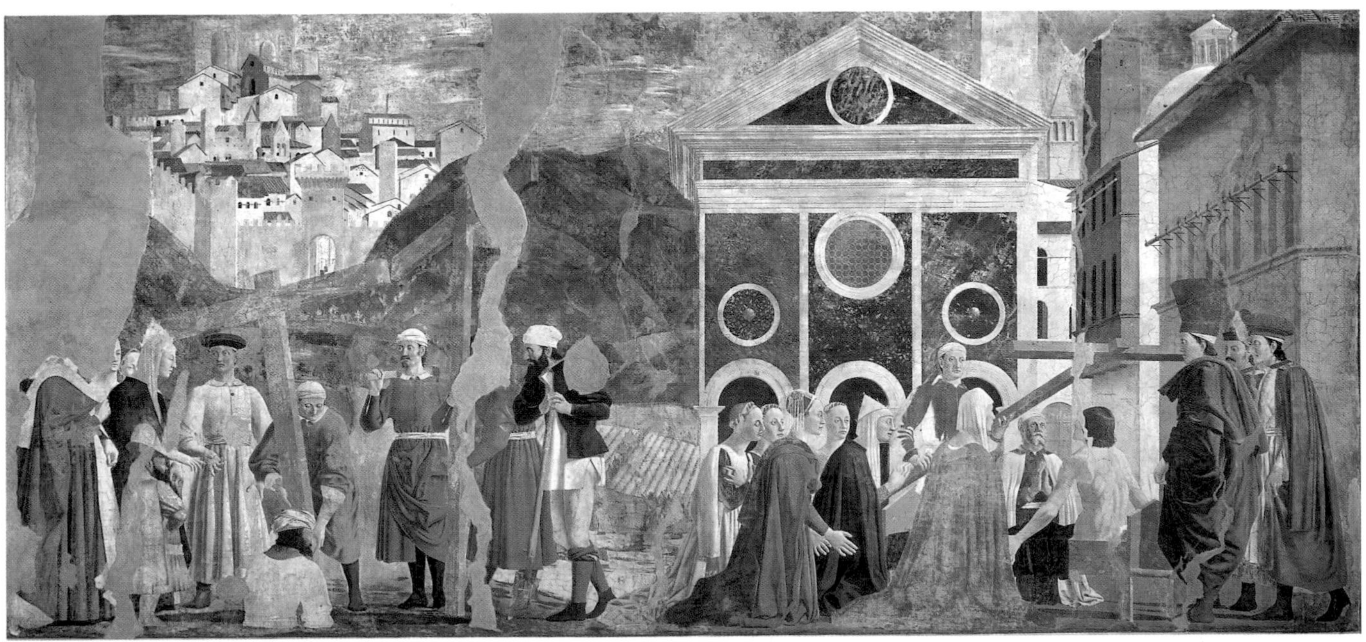

12-33. Piero della Francesca. *The Discovery and Proving of the True Cross.* c. 1455. Fresco. S. Francesco, Arezzo

How did Piero arrive at these images? They were born of his passion for perspective. More than any other artist of his day, Piero believed in scientific perspective as the basis of painting. In a mathematical treatise that was the first of its kind, he showed how it applied to stereometric bodies and architectural shapes, and to the human form. This mathematical outlook can be seen in all of his work. When he drew a head, an arm, or a piece of drapery, he saw them as variations or compounds of spheres, cylinders, cones, cubes, and pyramids. Thus he endowed the visible world with some of the clarity and permanence of stereometric bodies. Medieval artists, in contrast, built natural forms on geometric scaffolds (see fig. 11-68). We may regard Piero as the earliest ancestor of the abstract artists of our own time, for they, too, simplify natural forms. It is not surprising that Piero's fame is greater today than ever before.

UCCELLO. In mid-fifteenth-century Florence only one painter shared, and may have helped inspire, Piero's devotion to perspective: Paolo Uccello (1397–1475). His *Battle of San Romano* (fig. 12-34) may have influenced the battle scenes in Piero's frescoes at Arezzo (see fig. 12-32). Uccello's design also stresses stereometric shapes. The ground is covered with a gridlike design of discarded weapons and pieces of armor; they form a display of perspective studies that is neatly arranged so as to include one fallen soldier. The landscape, too, has been subjected to stereometric abstraction, matching the foreground. Despite these efforts, the panel lacks the order and clarity of Piero della Francesca's work. In the hands of Uccello, perspective produces strangely disturbing effects. What unites his picture is not its spatial structure but its surface pattern, which is reinforced by spots of brilliant color and lavish use of gold.

Uccello had been trained in the Gothic International Style. It was only in the 1430s that he was converted to the Early Renaissance outlook by the new science of perspective. He superimposed this technique on his earlier style like a straitjacket. The result is a fascinating but unstable mixture. As we study this panel, we realize that surface and space are more at war than the mounted soldiers, who get entangled with each other in all sorts of implausible ways.

CASTAGNO. The third dimension held no difficulties for Andrea del Castagno (c. 1423–1457), the most gifted Florentine painter of his day. Less subtle but more forceful than Domenico Veneziano, Castagno recaptures some of Masaccio's monumentality in his *Last Supper* (fig. 12-35). In this fresco, one of a set he painted in the refectory of the convent of S. Apollonia, the event is set in a richly paneled alcove that is designed as an extension of the real space. As in medieval representations of the subject, Judas sits

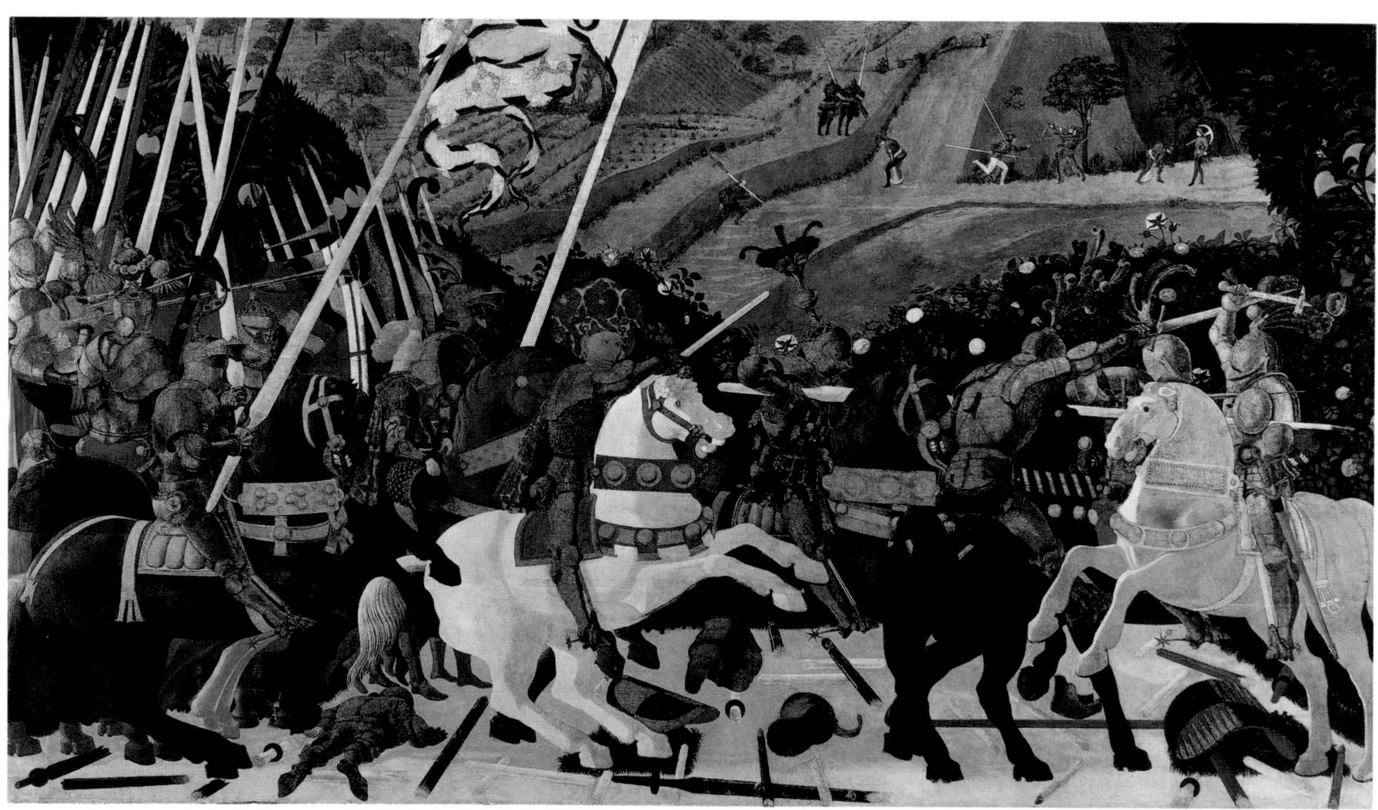

12-34. Paolo Uccello. *Battle of San Romano*. c. 1455. Tempera and silver foil on wood panel, 6' x 10'5¾" (1.8 x 3.2 m). The National Gallery, London

REPRODUCED BY COURTESY OF THE TRUSTEES

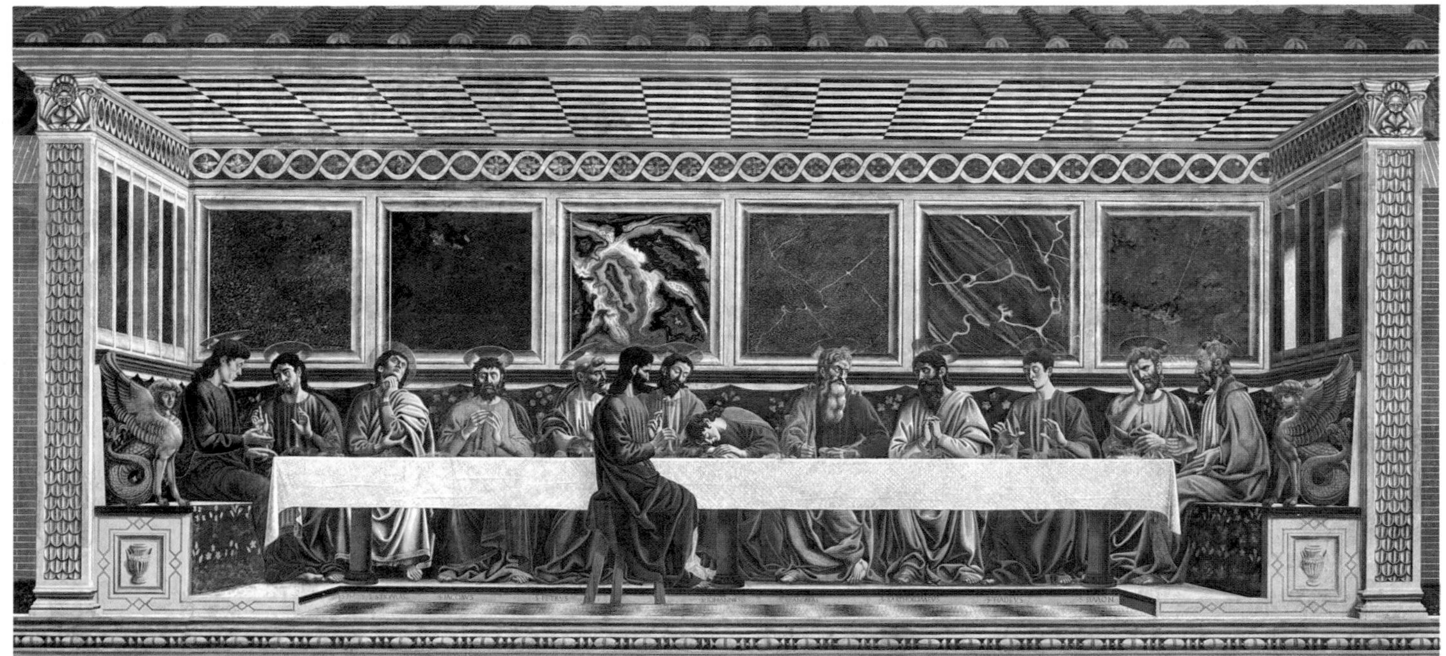

12-35. Andrea del Castagno. *The Last Supper.* c. 1445–50. Fresco. S. Apollonia, Florence

alone on the near side of the table. The symmetry of the architecture, emphasized by the colorful inlays, enforces a similar order among the figures and threatens to imprison them. There is so little communication among the apostles—only a glance here, a gesture there—that a brooding silence hovers over the scene.

Castagno, too, must have felt confined by a scheme imposed on him by the demands of both tradition and perspective. He used a daring device to break the symmetry and focus the drama of the scene. Five of the six marble panels on the wall behind the table are filled with subdued colored marble, but above the heads of St. Peter, Judas, and Christ its veining is so garish and explosive that a bolt of lightning seems to descend on Judas' head. When Giotto revived the ancient technique of illusionistic marble textures (see fig. 11-80), he could not have foreseen that it could have such expressive force.

Some five years after *The Last Supper,* between 1450 and 1457 (the year of his death), Castagno produced the *David* shown in figure 12-36. It is painted on a leather shield that was to be used only for display. Its owner probably wanted to convey an analogy between himself and the biblical hero, since David is here defiant as well as victorious. This figure differs greatly from the apostles of *The Last Supper.* Solid volume and statuesque immobility have given way to graceful movement, conveyed by both the pose and the windblown hair and drapery. The modeling of the earlier figures has been minimized. The forms are now defined mainly by their outlines, so that the *David* seems to be in relief rather than in the round. This dynamic linear style has its virtues, but it is far removed from Masaccio's. During the 1450s, the artistic climate of Florence changed greatly. Castagno's *David* is early evidence of the outlook that was to dominate during the second half of the century.

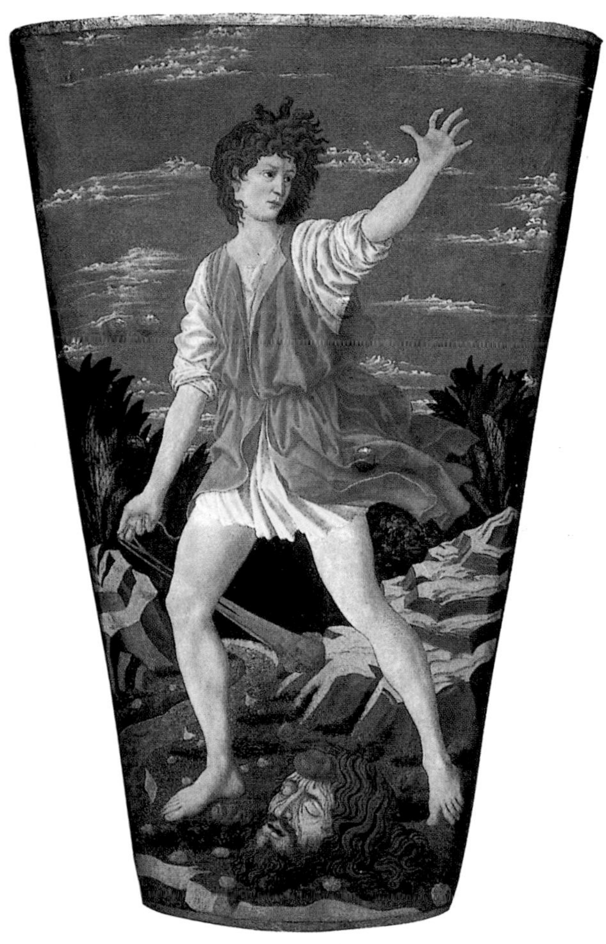

12-36. Andrea del Castagno. *David.* c. 1450–57. Leather, surface curved, height 45½" (115.8 cm). National Gallery of Art, Washington, D.C. Widener Collection

CENTRAL AND NORTHERN ITALY: 1450–1500

In the middle years of the fifteenth century, a younger generation of artists asserted itself in Florence. At the same time, the seeds planted by Florentine masters in other regions of Italy began to flower. (We recall Donatello's stay in Padua.) When some of these regions, notably the northeast, produced distinctive versions of the new style, Tuscany lost its central place in the artistic world.

Architecture

ALBERTI. In architecture, the death of Brunelleschi in 1446 brought to the fore Leone Battista Alberti (1404–1472). Like Brunelleschi's, Alberti's career had been long delayed, although in other ways the two men were very different. Until he was 40, Alberti seems to have been interested in the fine arts only as a scholar and theorist. He studied the monuments of ancient Rome, albeit casually at first, and wrote the first Renaissance treatises on sculpture and painting. He also began a third treatise, far more exhaustive than the others, on architecture—the first of its kind since Vitruvius', on which it is modeled. [See Primary Sources, no. 41, pages 612–13.] After about 1430, he was close to the leading artists of his day. (*On Painting* is dedicated to Brunelleschi and refers to "our dear friend" Donatello.) Alberti began to practice architecture as a dilettante, but in time he became a professional of outstanding ability. Highly educated in classical literature and philosophy, he was both a humanist and a person of the world.

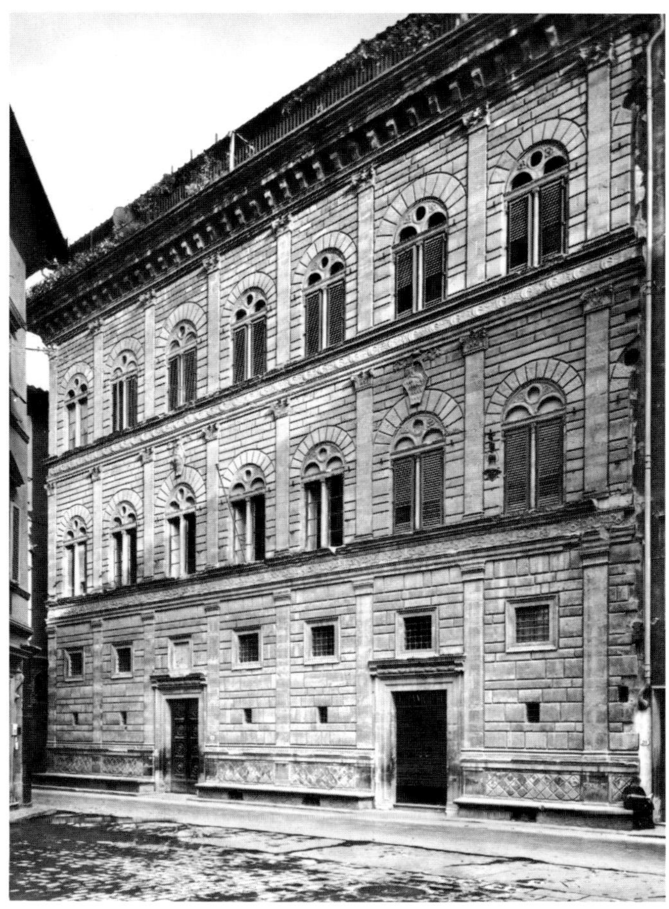

12-37. Leone Battista Alberti. Palazzo Rucellai, Florence. 1446–51

The design for the Palazzo Rucellai (fig. 12-37) may be Alberti's critique of the slightly earlier Medici Palace by Michelozzo (see fig. 12-21). Again we see three stories topped by a heavy cornice, but the articulation of the facade is more strict and classical. It consists of three orders of pilasters, separated by wide architraves, in imitation of the Colosseum (see fig. 7-11). Yet the pilasters are so flat that they remain part of the wall, and the facade seems to be one surface on which the artist projects a linear diagram of the Colosseum exterior.

To grasp the logic of this design, we must understand that Alberti was trying to resolve a fundamental issue of Renaissance architecture: how to apply a classical system to the exterior of a nonclassical structure. Whether Brunelleschi ever coped with this problem is hard to say. Only his exterior for the Pazzi Chapel survives (see fig. 12-15), but it has been altered, and it is too special a case to permit general conclusions. Be that as it may, Alberti's solution emphasizes the primacy of the wall surface and reduces the classical system to a network of incised lines.

For his first church exterior, Alberti tried a very different approach. Around 1450 Sigismondo Malatesta, lord of Rimini, commissioned him to turn the Gothic church of S. Francesco into a "temple of fame" and a burial site for himself, his wife, and members of his court. Alberti encased the older building in a Renaissance shell. The sides consist of deeply recessed arched niches containing stone sarcophagi (fig. 12-38). The facade has three similar niches: the large one framing the central portal and the other two (now filled in) intended to hold the sarcophagi of Sigismondo and his wife.

The facade niches are flanked by columns, a scheme based on the triumphal arches of ancient Rome (see fig. 7-46). Unlike the pilasters of the Palazzo Rucellai, these columns are not part of the wall. They project so strongly that we see them as separate from the wall, although they are partly embedded in it. Moreover, they are set on separate blocks, rather than on the platform supporting the walls. They would have nothing to support if the entablature did not project above each capital. As a result, the vertical divisions of the facade are more conspicuous than the horizontal ones; we expect each column to support an important element of the upper story. Yet Alberti planned only an arched niche (which remains incomplete) above the portal, with a window and framed by pilasters. Thus the second story does not fulfill the promise of the first. Perhaps Alberti would have altered this aspect of his design in the end, but the church was never finished, and the great dome, designed to be its crowning feature, was never built. Its appearance is known from a commemorative medal issued in 1450, the year the church was begun (fig. 12-39).

Like most of Alberti's work, S. Francesco was a remodeling project, which hampered his goal of superimposing a classical temple front on the traditional basilican church facade. Whereas the classical system of the Palazzo Rucellai is in danger of being devoured by the wall, that of S. Francesco retains too much of its ancient Roman character to fit the basilican shape. (For the medieval approach to this task, see the facade of Pisa Cathedral in fig. 10-17.) Only toward the end of his career did Alberti achieve this seemingly impossible feat: in the majestic facade of S. Andrea at Mantua (fig. 12-40), his last work, designed in 1470 at the behest

12-38. Leone Battista Alberti. S. Francesco, Rimini. Facade designed 1450

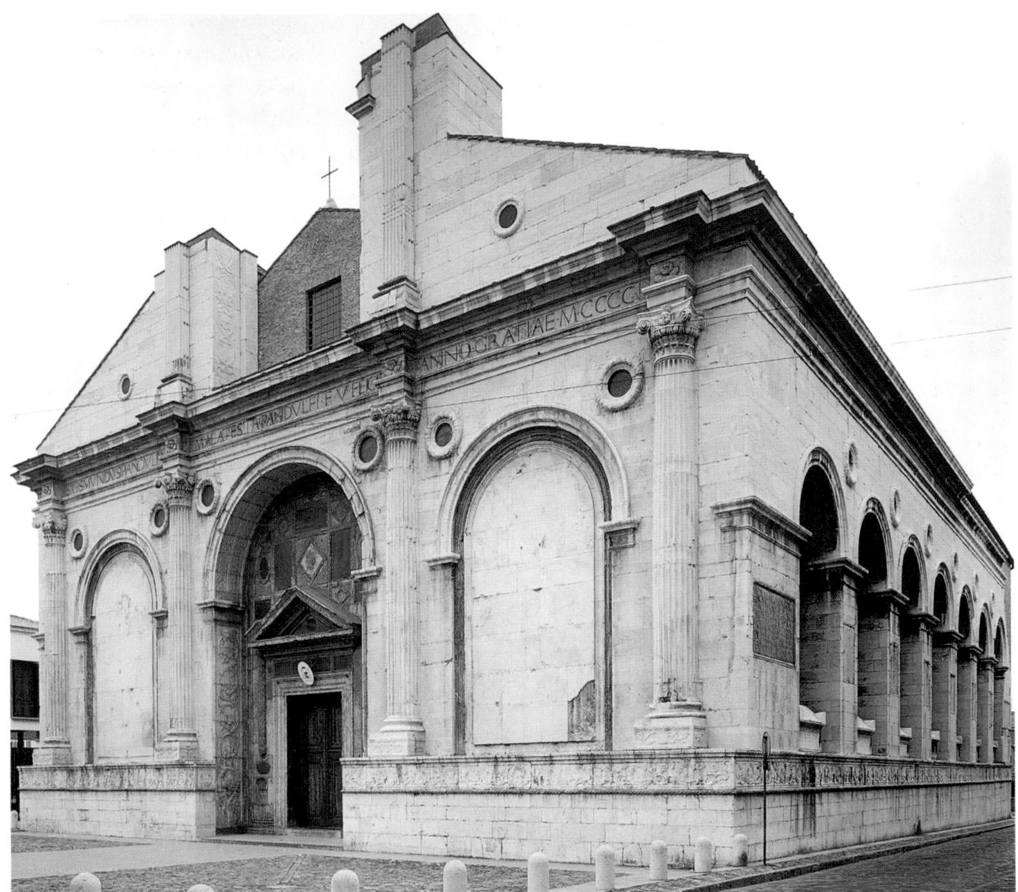

(BELOW) 12-39. S. Francesco, Rimini medal of 1450 by Matteo dei Pasti. Bronze, diameter 1 9/16" (4.0 cm). The British Museum, London

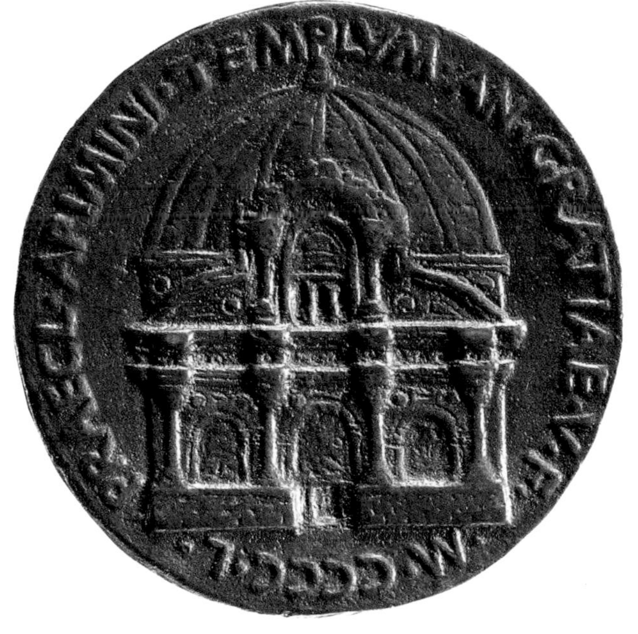

of Lodovico Gonzaga, Duke of Mantua. He superimposed the triumphal-arch motif, now with a huge center niche, upon a classical temple front and projected this combination onto the wall. He again uses flat pilasters that acknowledge the primacy of the wall surface. Unlike those of the Palazzo Rucellai, however, these pilasters are clearly set off from their surroundings. They are of two sizes. The smaller ones support the arch over the huge central niche. The larger ones are linked with the unbroken architrave and the strongly outlined pediment. They form what is known as a

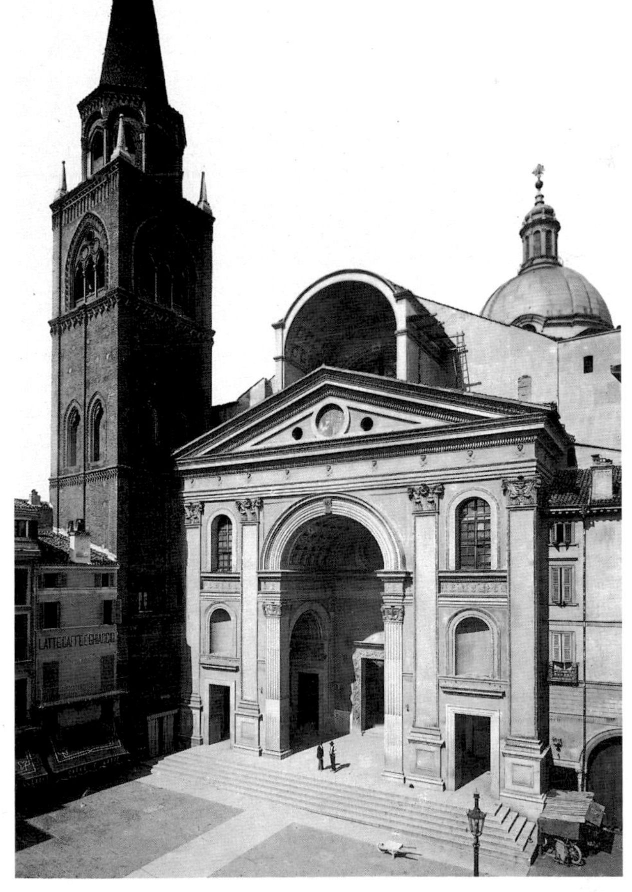

12-40. Leone Battista Alberti. S. Andrea, Mantua. Designed 1470

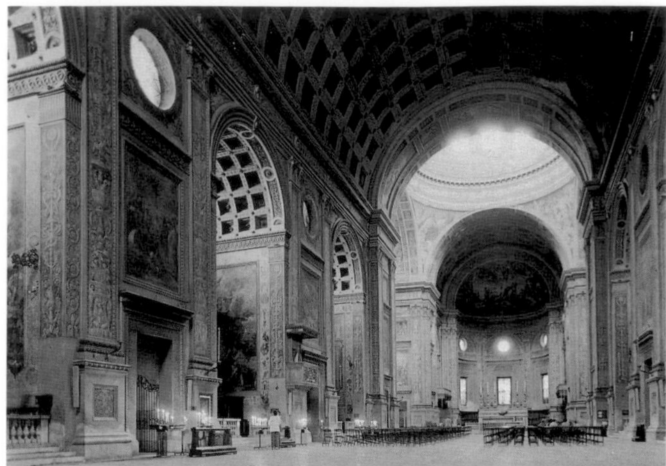

12-41. Leone Battista Alberti. Interior of S. Andrea

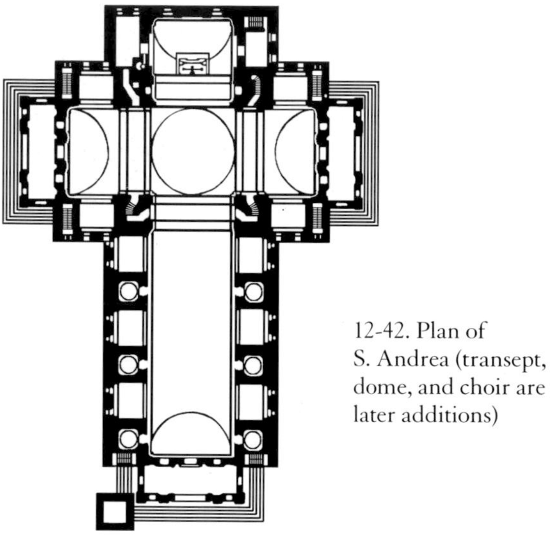

12-42. Plan of S. Andrea (transept, dome, and choir are later additions)

"colossal" order (meaning that it is more than one story high). It extends across all three stories of the facade wall, balancing the horizontal and vertical elements of the design.

So intent was Alberti on creating a coherent facade that he inscribed the entire design within a square, even though it is much lower than the nave of the church. (The effect of the west wall protruding above the pediment is more disturbing in photographs than at street level, where it can hardly be seen.) While the facade is distinct from the main body of the structure, it offers a "preview" of the interior, where the same colossal order, the same proportions, and the same triumphal-arch motif reappear on the walls of the nave (fig. 12-41).

When we compare the plan (fig. 12-42) with that of Brunelleschi's Sto. Spirito (see fig. 12-19), we are struck by how compact it is. Had the church been completed as planned, the difference would be even stronger, for Alberti's design had no transept, dome, or choir, only a nave ending in an apse. Following the example of the Basilica of Constantine (see figs. 7-16–7-18), the aisles are replaced by alternating large and small vaulted chapels. There is no clerestory. The colossal pilasters and the arches of the large chapels support a coffered barrel vault of impressive span (the nave is as wide as the facade). Here Alberti has drawn upon his memories of the massive vaulted halls in ancient Roman baths and basilicas, yet he interprets these models freely. No longer is their authority absolute; instead, they serve as a storehouse of motifs to be utilized at will. Freed from having to quote his sources literally, Alberti was able to create a structure that can truly be called a "Christian temple."

CENTRAL-PLAN CHURCHES. Because it occupies the site of an older basilican church (note the Gothic campanile next to the facade), S. Andrea does not conform to the ideal shape of sacred buildings as defined in Alberti's treatise *On Architecture.* There he explains that the plan of such structures should be either circular or derived from the circle (square, hexagon, octagon, and so forth). The reason is that the circle is the perfect, as well as the most natural, figure and therefore a direct image of divine reason. This claim rests, of course, on Alberti's faith in the God-given validity of mathematical proportions (discussed on page 398). He took to heart Virtuvius' belief that architecture must employ the same principles of symmetry and proportion as a "well-shaped man." (In support of this rule, Vitruvius pointed out that a man with arms and legs outstretched fits into a circle or square.) How could Alberti reconcile his belief in the central plan with historical evidence? After all, the standard form of both ancient temples and Christian churches was longitudinal. But, he reasoned, the basilican church plan became traditional only because the early Christians worshiped in private Roman basilicas. Since pagan basilicas were associated with the dispensing of justice (which originates from God), he granted that their shape has some relationship to sacred architecture. However, since they cannot rival the sublime beauty of the temple, their purpose is human rather than divine.

In speaking of temples, Alberti disregarded the standard form (see fig. 7-2) and relied instead on the Pantheon (see figs. 7-12–7-15), the round temple at Tivoli (see figs. 7-4 and 7-5), and the domed mausoleums, which he mistook for temples. Moreover, he asked, had not the early Christians themselves acknowledged the sacred nature of these structures by converting them to their own use? Here he could point to such buildings as Sta. Costanza (see figs. 8-7–8-9), the Pantheon itself (which had been used as a church ever since the early Middle Ages), and the Baptistery in Florence (then thought to be a former temple of Mars).

Alberti's ideal church must have such a harmonious design that it would be a revelation of divinity and would arouse pious contemplation in the worshiper. It should stand alone, above its surroundings. Light should enter through openings placed high, for only the sky should be seen through them. The fact that such a structure was not well suited to Catholic ritual meant little to Alberti. A church, he believed, must embody "divine proportion," which could be attained only by the central plan.

When Alberti set forth these ideas in his treatise, about 1450, he could have cited only Brunelleschi's unfinished Sta. Maria degli Angeli as a modern example of a central-plan church (see fig. 12-20). In 1460 he undertook a church in the shape of a Greek cross for the Duke of Mantua, but the result was unsatisfactory and the building likewise remained unfinished. Toward the end of the century, after his treatise became widely known, the central-plan church gained wide acceptance. Between 1500 and 1525 it reigned supreme in High Renaissance architecture.

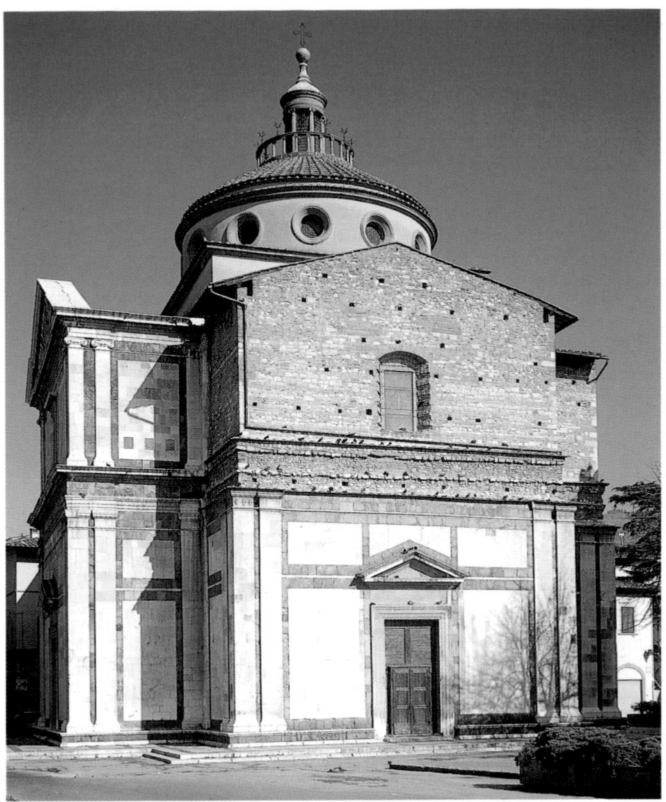

12-43. Giuliano da Sangallo. Sta. Maria delle Carceri, Prato. Begun 1485

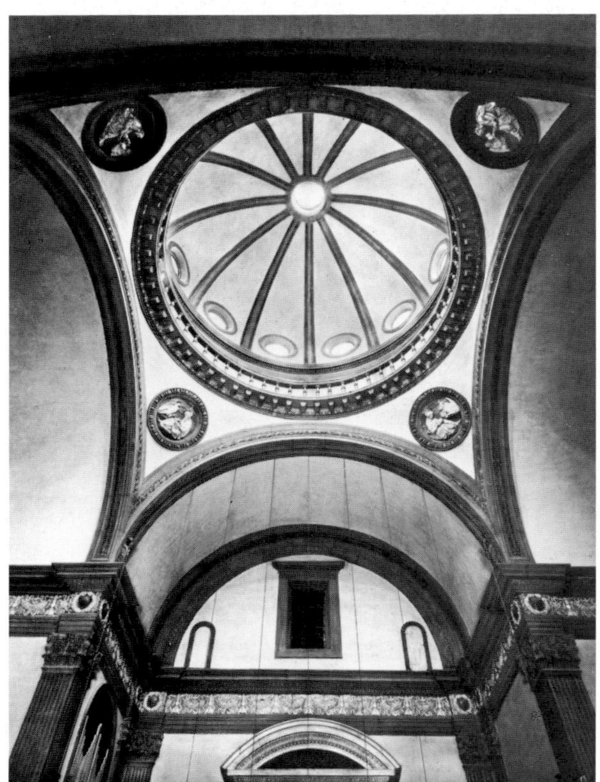

12-45. Interior of Sta. Maria delle Carceri

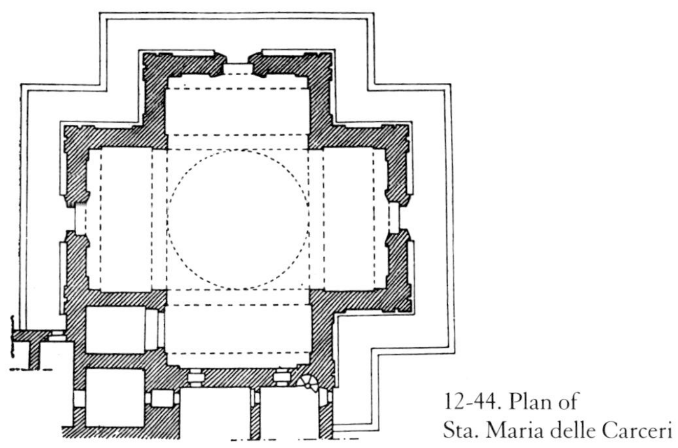

12-44. Plan of Sta. Maria delle Carceri

GIULIANO DA SANGALLO. It is no coincidence that Sta. Maria delle Carceri in Prato (figs. 12-43–12-45) was begun in 1485, the date of the first printed edition of Alberti's treatise. Its architect, Giuliano da Sangallo (c. 1443–1516), must have been an admirer of Brunelleschi. Many features of the plan and the interior recall the Pazzi Chapel (see figs. 12-16 and 12-17). The basic shape of his structure, however, conforms to Alberti's ideal. Except for the dome, the entire church would fit neatly inside a cube; its height (up to the drum) equals its length and width. By cutting into the corners of this cube, Giuliano has formed a Greek cross (a plan he preferred for its symbolic value). The arms are barrel-vaulted, and the dome rests on these vaults. Yet the dark ring of the drum does not quite touch the supporting arches, making the dome seem to hover weightlessly like the pendentive domes of Byzantine architecture (compare fig. 8-44). There can be no doubt that Giuliano wanted his dome to accord with the age-old tradition of the Dome of Heaven. The single round opening in the center and the 12 on the perimeter clearly refer to Christ and the apostles. Brunelleschi had anticipated this design in the Pazzi Chapel, but Giuliano's dome, which crowns a perfectly symmetrical structure, conveys its symbolic value far more strikingly.

Sculpture

Donatello left Florence for Padua in 1443. The effect of his ten-year absence was similar to that of Brunelleschi's death. However, while Alberti took Brunelleschi's place in architecture, there was no young sculptor of similar stature to take Donatello's. As a result, the other sculptors in the city gained greater prominence. Those who grew up under their influence brought about the changes that Donatello must have seen with dismay when he returned to Florence.

LUCA DELLA ROBBIA. Aside from Ghiberti, the only important sculptor in Florence after Donatello left was Luca della Robbia (1400–1482). He had come to prominence in the 1430s with the marble reliefs of the *Cantoria* (singers' pulpit) in the cathedral. The *Trumpet Players* panel shown here (fig. 12-46), like all of Luca's work, mixes sweetness with gravity, but it is unusual in its exuberance. Its style owes little to Donatello. Instead, it recalls the classicism of Nanni di Banco (see fig. 12-1), with whom Luca may have worked as a youth. We also sense a touch of Ghiberti here and there, as well as the influence of Roman reliefs (such as fig. 7-32).

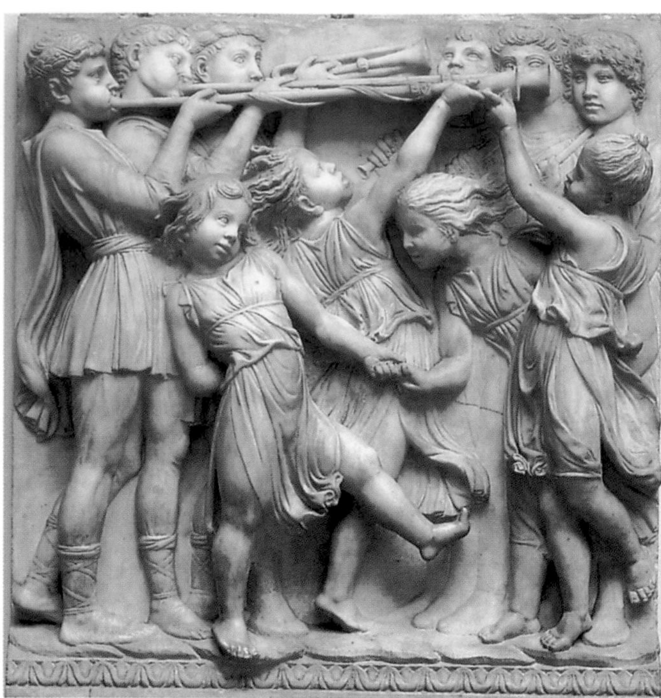

12-46. Luca della Robbia. *Trumpet Players,* from the *Cantoria.* c. 1435. Marble, 40⅝" x 36⅞" (103 x 93.5 cm). Museo dell'Opera del Duomo, Florence

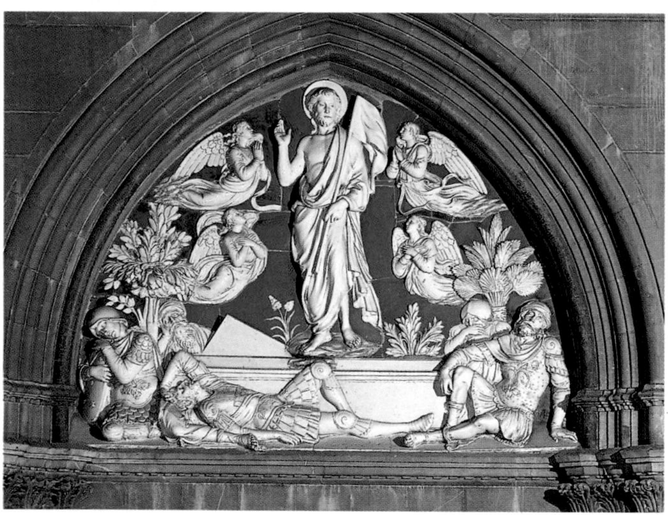

12-47. Luca della Robbia. *The Resurrection.* 1442–45. Glazed terracotta, 5'3" x 7'3½" (1.6 x 2.22 m). Museo Nazionale del Bargello, Florence

Unfortunately, Luca lacked a capacity for growth, despite his great gifts. So far as we know, he never did a freestanding statue, and the *Cantoria* remained his greatest achievement. For the rest of his long career he devoted himself to sculpture in terra-cotta, a cheaper and less demanding medium than marble. He covered this material with enamellike glazes to mask its surface and protect it from the weather. His finest works in this technique, which include *The Resurrection* in figure 12-47, have the dignity and charm of the *Cantoria* panels. The white glaze creates the effect of marble against the deep blue background of the lunette. Other colors were confined almost entirely to the decorative framework of the reliefs. This restraint, however, lasted only while he was in charge of his workshop. Later, the quality of the modeling declined and the simple harmony of white and blue often gave way to more vivid hues. At the end of the century, the Della Robbia shop had become a factory, turning out scores of small Madonna panels and garish altarpieces for village churches.

As Luca limited himself to terra-cotta, there was a shortage of marble sculptors in Florence during the 1440s. By the time Donatello returned, this gap had been filled by a group of men, most still in their twenties, from the hill towns north and east of Florence that had long supplied the city with stonemasons and carvers. Taking advantage of the unusual opportunities open to them, the most gifted of them developed into artists of considerable importance.

BERNARDO ROSSELLINO. The oldest of these, Bernardo Rossellino (1409–1464), seems to have begun as a sculptor and architect in Arezzo. He came to Florence about 1436 but received no major commissions until eight years later, when he was asked to design the Tomb of Leonardo Bruni (fig. 12-48). This great humanist and statesman had played a vital part in the city's affairs since the beginning of the century (see page 388). When he died in 1444, he received a grand funeral "in the manner of the ancients." His monument was probably ordered by the city government. Since Bruni had been born in Arezzo, his native town also wished to honor him and may have helped obtain the commission for Bernardo. (One wonders, however, what chance Bernardo would have had if Donatello had been available.)

Although Bruni's is not the earliest Renaissance tomb, it is the first to express the spirit of the new era. The references to antiquity contain many echoes of Bruni's funeral: the deceased lies on a bier supported by Roman eagles, his head wreathed in laurel and his right hand resting on a book (presumably his own *History of Florence,* rather than a prayer book). The monument is a fitting tribute to the man who, more than any other, had helped establish the historical perspective of the Florentine Early Renaissance. On the sarcophagus, two winged genii hold an inscription that is very different from those on medieval tombs. Instead of recording the name, rank, and age of the deceased and the date of his death, it refers only to his achievements: "At Leonardo's passing, history grieves, eloquence is mute, and it is said that the Muses, Greek and Latin alike, cannot hold back their tears." The religious aspect of the tomb is confined to the lunette, where the Madonna is adored by angels.

The monument may be viewed as an attempt to reconcile two contrasting attitudes toward death: the retrospective, commemorative outlook of the ancients (see page 138) and the Christian concern with afterlife and salvation. Bernardo's design, adapted from the Tomb of Guglielmo de Braye by Arnolfo di Cambio (see fig. 11-64), is well suited to this task. It balances architecture and sculpture within a compact framework. The two pilasters supporting a round arch resting on a strongly accented architrave recall the work of Alberti, who used this motif often. It is derived from the doorway to the Pantheon (see fig. 7-15), which accounts for its use in church portals such as that of S. Andrea in Mantua (see fig. 12-40). While Bernardo may have used it for aesthetic reasons, he may also have meant it to symbolize the gateway between one life and the next. Perhaps he even wanted us to associate the motif with the

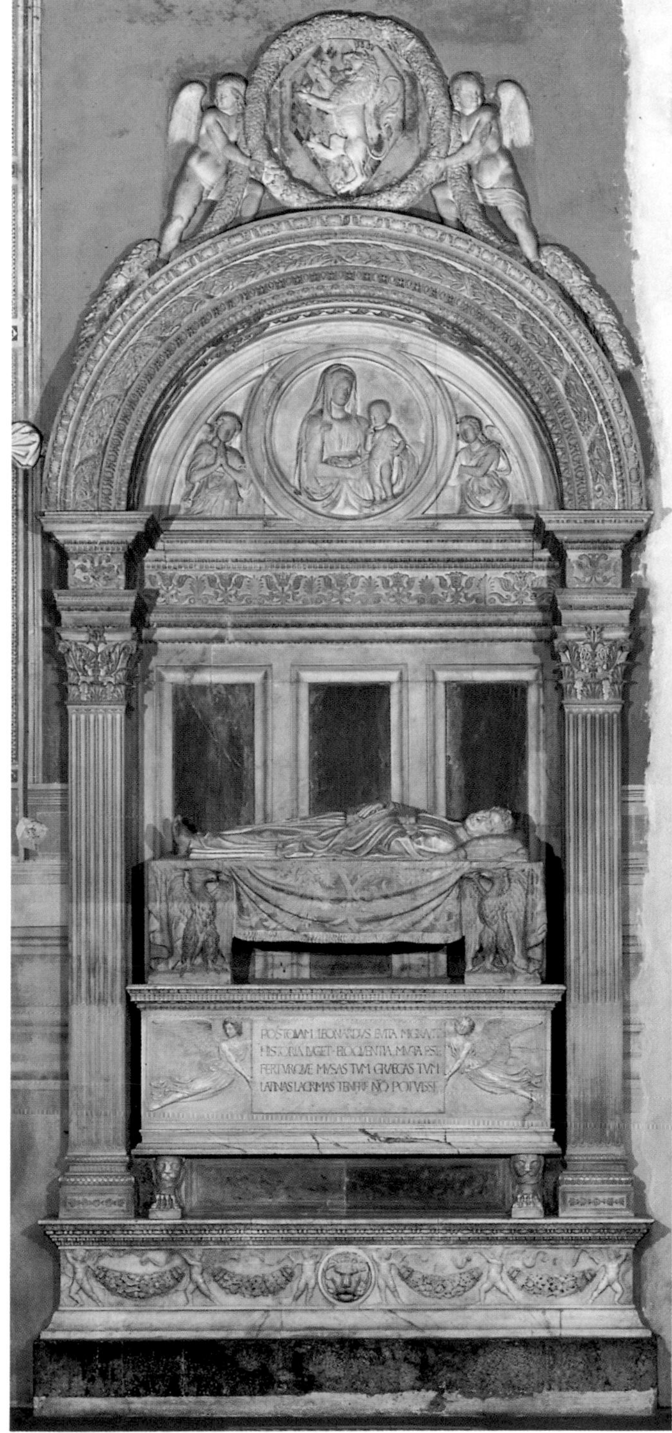

12-48. Bernardo Rossellino. Tomb of Leonardo Bruni. c. 1445–50. Marble, height 20' (6.1 m to top of arch). Sta. Croce, Florence

Pantheon, the "temple of the immortals" for both pagans and Christians. (Once dedicated to all the gods of the Roman world, it had been rededicated to all the martyrs when it became a church. In the High Renaissance it was to house the tombs of another breed of immortals: famous artists such as Raphael.)

All the tombs, tabernacles, and reliefs of the Madonna produced in Florence between 1450 and 1480 owe much to the Bruni monument. Nevertheless, its style is not easy to define, since its components vary a good deal in quality. Broadly speaking, it reflects the classicism of Ghiberti and Luca della Robbia; there are few echoes of Donatello. By the same token, we do not yet have a clear conception of Bernardo's style as a sculptor. He surely employed assistants here, as he did for later commissions. During the late 1440s, his workshop was the only training ground for young marble sculptors, such as his younger brother Antonio (1417–1470) and others of the same generation. Their share in Bernardo's sculptural projects is hard to pin down, however, for their personalities were not distinct until they began to work on their own.

DESIDERIO DA SETTIGNANO. Of the many sculptors who passed through the Rossellino shop, the most gifted was Desiderio da Settignano (1429/30–1464), who came from a family of stonemasons. But it was the influence of Donatello, to whom he was probably apprenticed in the early 1440s, that proved decisive. Indeed, his *St. John the Baptist* (fig. 12-49) was long thought to have been done by Donatello. Although Desiderio is

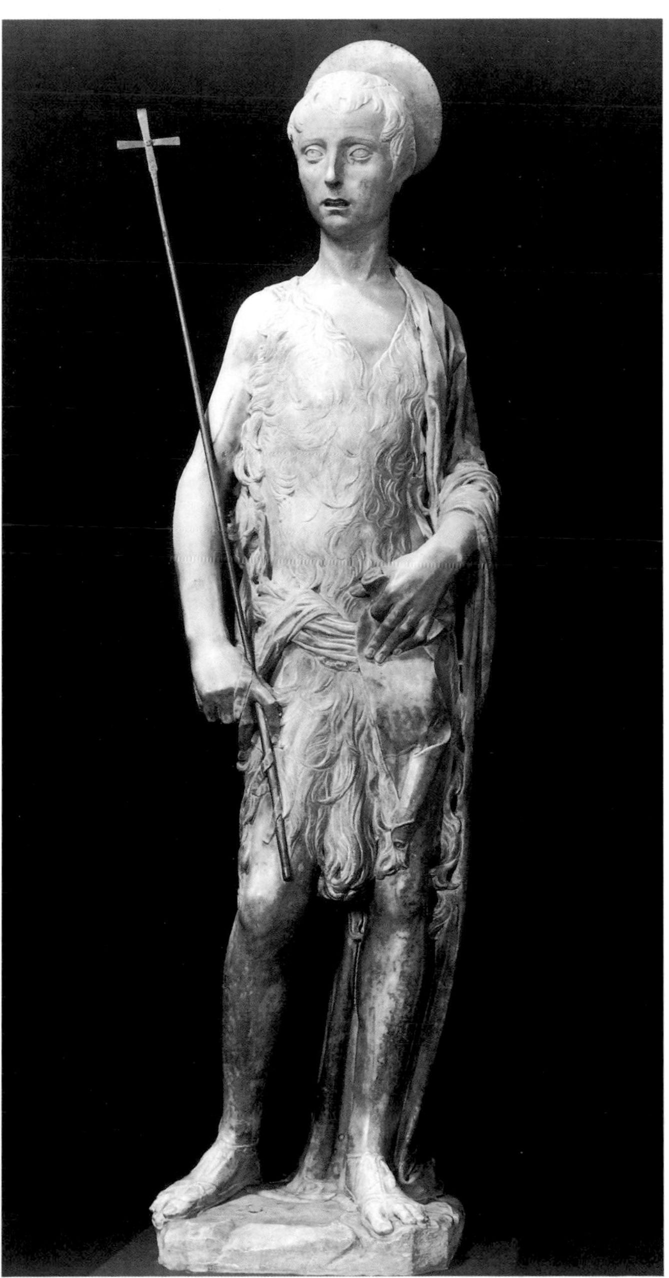

12-49. Desiderio da Settignano. *St. John the Baptist.* c. 1455–60. Marble, height 63" (160 cm). Museo Nazionale del Bargello, Florence

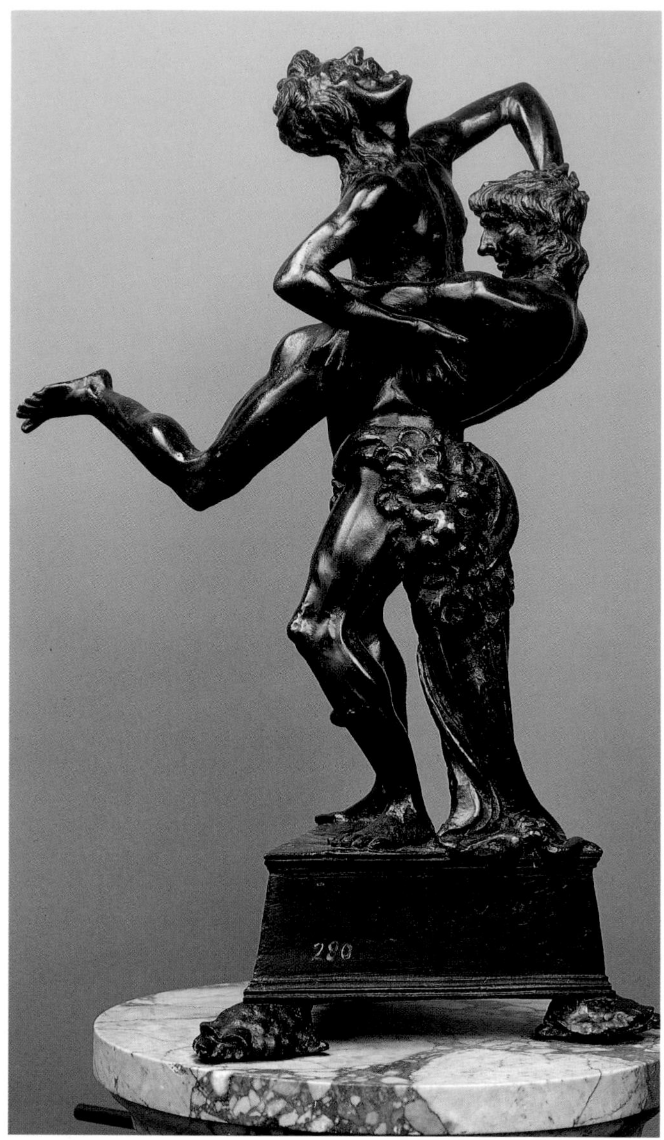

12-50. Antonio del Pollaiuolo. *Hercules and Antaeus.* c. 1475. Bronze, height 18" (45.8 cm, with base). Museo Nazionale del Bargello, Florence

remembered for his beautiful Madonnas and enchanting children, no other sculptor of the day was so attuned to the ascetic side of Donatello's later sculpture. Desiderio's *Baptist* was clearly inspired by Donatello's *Mary Magdalen* (see fig. 12-8); however, the differences are equally important, for Desiderio has magnified the figure's expressiveness by turning it inward. The young St. John has a disturbing, haunted look, as if torn by a spiritual experience of almost unbearable intensity. The effect is heightened by the subtlety of the carving, so refined that it is small wonder the statue passed as Donatello's.

POLLAIUOLO. By 1450 the great civic art campaign had come to an end in Florence, and artists had to depend mainly on private commissions. This put the sculptors at a disadvantage because of the high cost of making their work. Since there were few commissions for monuments, they created works of moderate size and price, such as bronze statuettes. The collecting of sculpture, common in ancient times, had ceased during the Middle Ages. The taste of kings, feudal lords, and others who could afford to collect for their own pleasure ran to gems, jewelry, goldsmith's work, illuminated manuscripts, and precious fabrics. The habit was revived in fifteenth-century Italy as part of the "revival of antiquity." Humanists and artists first collected ancient sculpture, especially small bronzes (such as fig. 5-78), of which there were many. Before long, artists began to cater to the demand by creating portrait busts and small bronzes "in the manner of the ancients."

A fine example of this kind is *Hercules and Antaeus* (fig. 12-50) by Antonio del Pollaiuolo (1431–1498). Pollaiuolo's style was very different from that of the marble carvers discussed above. He was trained as a goldsmith and metalworker, probably in the Ghiberti workshop, and was deeply impressed by the late styles of Donatello and Castagno, as well as by ancient art. From these sources, he developed the distinctive style that appears in our statuette. To create a freestanding group of two struggling figures, even on a small scale, was a daring idea. There is no precedent for this design among earlier statuary groups, ancient or Renaissance. Even bolder is the centrifugal force that can be felt in this composition. Limbs seem to move outward in every direction. We see the

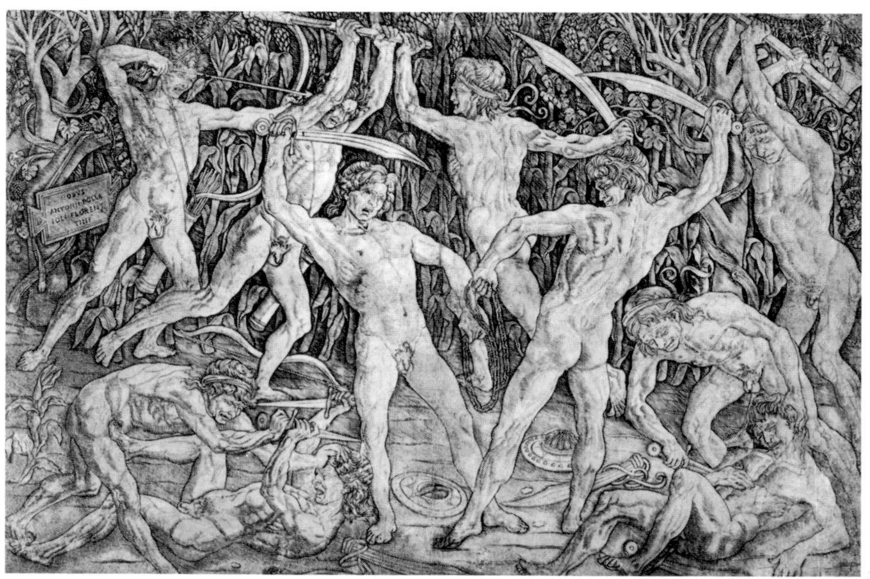

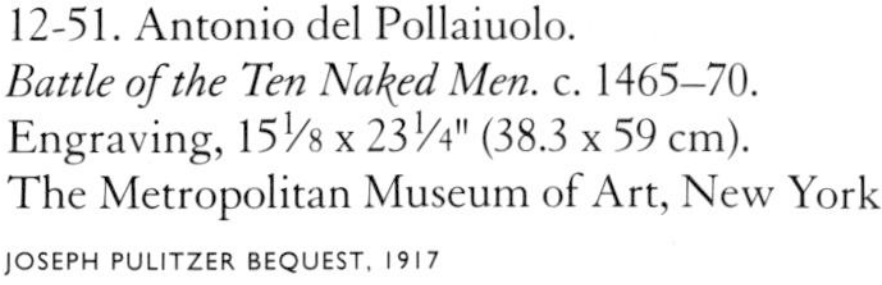

12-51. Antonio del Pollaiuolo. *Battle of the Ten Naked Men.* c. 1465–70. Engraving, 15⅛ x 23¼" (38.3 x 59 cm). The Metropolitan Museum of Art, New York

JOSEPH PULITZER BEQUEST, 1917

full complexity of their movements only when we view the statuette from all sides. Despite its violent action, the group is in perfect balance. To stress the central axis, Pollaiuolo in effect grafted the upper part of Antaeus onto the lower part of Hercules.

Pollaiuolo was a painter and engraver as well as a bronze sculptor, and we know that about 1465 he did a large picture of Hercules and Antaeus for the Medici, who also owned the statuette. (It has been lost but the design is preserved in a smaller copy.) For the first time, a sculptural group has been given the pictorial quality that could be seen in reliefs since the early years of the Renaissance.

Few of Pollaiuolo's paintings have survived, and only one engraving (see page 502), the *Battle of the Ten Naked Men* (fig. 12-51). This print, however, is of great importance, since it represents Pollaiuolo's most elaborate pictorial design. Its subject, undoubtedly a classical one, is not known for certain, but that matters little. The main purpose of the engraving obviously was to display the artist's mastery of the nude body in action. About 1465–70, when the print must have been produced, this was still a novel problem, and Pollaiuolo did more to solve it than any other master. An interest in movement, coupled with slender proportions and an emphasis on outline rather than on modeling, could be seen in Castagno's *David* (see fig. 12-36). Pollaiuolo also drew upon the action poses he found in certain types of Greek vases (compare fig. 5-62). But he realized that a full understanding of bodily movement demands a detailed knowledge of anatomy, down to the last muscle and sinew. And in fact these naked men have a "flayed" appearance, as if their skin had been stripped off to reveal the play of muscles underneath. So do the two figures of our statuette, though to a lesser degree.

Artists may have begun to study dissected cadavers as early as 1425, and the practice was almost certainly established during the 1450s by Andrea Mantegna (see page 426), among others. But this is the clearest evidence we have of a custom that was to be followed by artists throughout the High Renaissance. Equally novel are the facial expressions, which are as strained as the bodily movements. We have already seen contorted features in the work of Donatello and Masaccio (see figs. 12-5, 12-8, and 12-27). But the anguish they convey is internal. It does not arise from or accompany the physical action of Pollaiuolo's struggling nudes.

VERROCCHIO. Although Pollaiuolo did two large bronze tombs for St. Peter's in Rome during the late years of his career, he never had a chance to create a large-scale freestanding statue. For such works we must turn to Andrea del Verrocchio (1435–1488), the greatest sculptor of his day and the only one to share some of Donatello's range and ambition. A modeler as well as a carver (we have works of his in marble, terra-cotta, silver, and bronze), he combined elements from Antonio Rossellino and Antonio del Pollaiuolo into a unique style. He was also a respected painter and the teacher of Leonardo da Vinci (which is unfortunate, as he has been overshadowed ever since).

Like *Hercules and Antaeus* by Pollaioulo, Verrocchio's *The Doubting of Thomas* (fig. 12-52) is closely related to a painting: a *Baptism of Christ,* painted with the assistance of the young Leonardo. The result is a pictorialism unique in monumental sculpture of the Early Renaissance. In contrast to the *Quattro Coronati* of Nanni di Banco (see fig. 12-1), the subject is a narrative. Also, Verrocchio's group does not quite fit its niche on Or San Michele, for it replaced a figure by Donatello that had been moved. Hence, the statues have no backs so that they can fit in the shallow tabernacle, which acts as a foil rather than as a container.

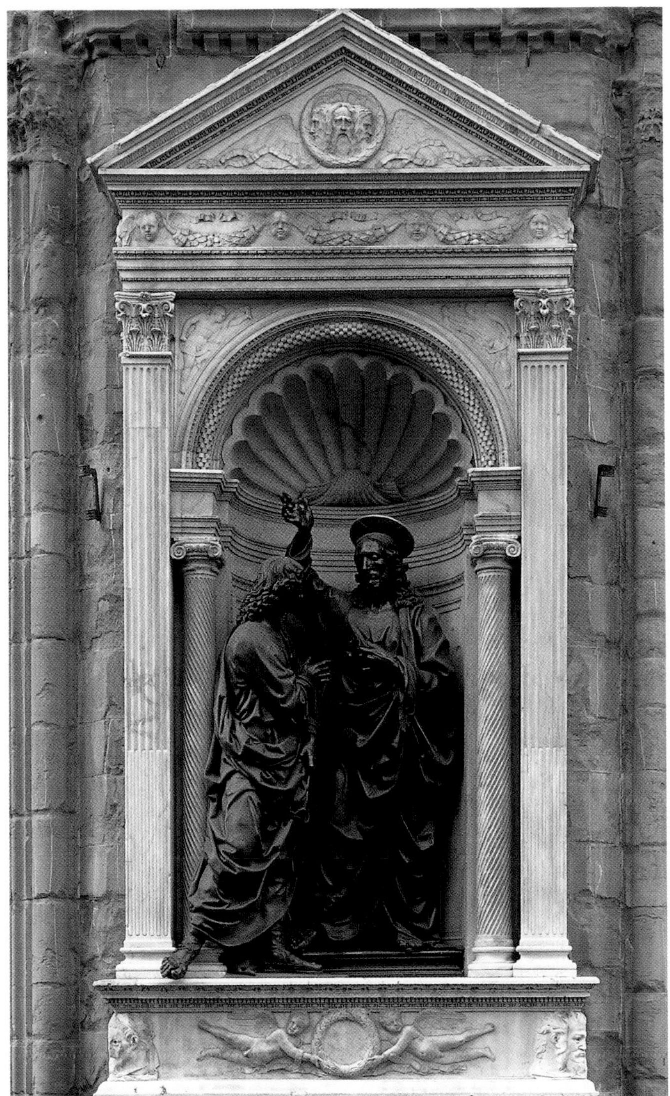

12-52. Andrea del Verrocchio. *The Doubting of Thomas.* 1465–83. Bronze, lifesize. Or San Michele, Florence

Although the biblical text is inscribed on the drapery, the drama is conveyed by the eloquent poses and bold exchange of gestures between Christ and Thomas. It is heightened by the active drapery, with its deep folds, which echo the contrasting states of mind. *The Doubting of Thomas* is of great importance in the history of sculpture. The work was admired for its great beauty, especially the head of Christ, which was to inspire Michelangelo. For Leonardo it served as a model of figures whose actions express the passions of the mind. Later it stimulated the sculpture of Bernini (compare fig. 17-29).

By coincidence, the crowning achievement of Verrocchio's career, as of Donatello's, was a bronze equestrian statue: the monument of a Venetian army commander, Bartolommeo Colleoni (fig. 12-53). Colleoni had asked for such a statue in his will, in which he left a large fortune to the Republic of Venice. He obviously knew the *Gattamelata* statue and wanted the same honor for himself. Verrocchio, too, must have viewed Donatello's work as the model for his own statue, yet he did not simply imitate it. Although perhaps less subtle, his version is no less impressive. The horse, graceful and spirited rather than robust and placid, conveys the same sense of anatomy-in-action that we saw in the nudes of Pollaiuolo. Its thin hide reveals every vein, muscle, and sinew, in contrast to the rigid surfaces of the armored figure bestriding it. Since the horse is also smaller in relation to the rider than Gattamelata's, Colleoni looms in the saddle as the very image of forceful dominance. Legs straight, one shoulder thrust forward, he surveys the scene before him with the same concentration we saw in Donatello's *St. George* (see fig. 12-3), but his lip is curled in contempt.

Neither *Gattamelata* nor *Colleoni* is a portrait in the specific sense of the term. Both idealize the personality that each artist associated with leadership in war. If *Gattamelata* conveys steadfast purpose and nobility, *Colleoni* radiates an almost frightening sense of power. As an image of self-assurance, it recalls the *Can Grande* (see fig. 11-63) rather than the *Gattamelata.* Perhaps Verrocchio visited the tomb of the Can Grande (who was well remembered in Florence as the patron of Dante) and decided to translate its arrogance into the style of his own day. In any case, Colleoni got a great deal more than he had asked for in his will.

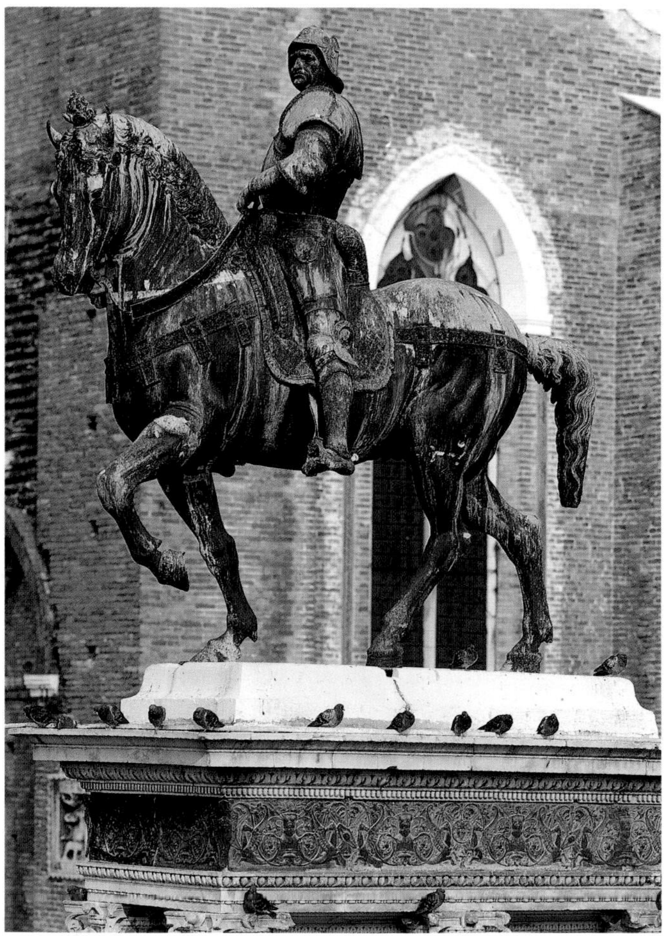

12-53. Andrea del Verrocchio. *Equestrian Monument of Colleoni.* c. 1483–88. Bronze, height 13' (3.9 m). Campo SS. Giovanni e Paolo, Venice

Painting

BOTTICELLI. In Florence, the trend established by Castagno's *David* stresses energetic, graceful movement and agitated linear contours over the stable monumentality of Masaccio's style. Its climax comes in the final quarter of the century, in the art of Sandro Botticelli (1444/5–1510). He was trained by Fra Filippo Lippi, whose *Madonna Enthroned* (see fig. 12-29) showed signs of linear movement, and was influenced by Pollaiuolo. Botticelli soon became the favorite painter of the so-called Medici circle—the group of nobles, scholars, and poets surrounding Lorenzo the Magnificent, the head of the Medici family and, for all practical purposes, the real ruler of the city.

Botticelli painted *The Birth of Venus* (fig. 12-54), his most famous picture, for the young prince Lorenzo de' Medici (it once hung in his summer villa). Its kinship with Pollaiuolo's *Battle of the Ten Naked Men* (see fig. 12-51) is unmistakable. The shallow modeling and the emphasis on outline produce an effect of low relief rather than of solid, three-dimensional shapes. Both works show little concern with deep space. The ornamental thicket forms a screen behind the naked men much like the grove on the right-hand side of the Venus. But the differences are just as striking. Botticelli obviously does not share Pollaiuolo's passion for anatomy. His bodies are drained of all weight and muscular power. Indeed, they seem to float even when they touch the ground. All this seems to deny the basic values of the founders of Early Renaissance art, yet the picture does not look medieval. The bodies, however ethereal, remain voluptuous. They are genuine nudes (see the discussion on pages 393 and 396) with full freedom of movement.

NEO-PLATONISM. Botticelli's *Venus* is derived from a variant of the *Knidian Aphrodite* by Praxiteles (see fig. 5-67). However, the subject was inspired by the Homeric *Hymn to Aphrodite,* which begins: "I shall sing of beautiful Aphrodite . . . who is obeyed by the flowery sea-girt land of Cyprus, whither soft Zephyr and the breeze wafted her in soft foam over the waves. Gently the golden-filleted Horae received her, and clad her in divine garments." Yet no single literary source accounts for the pictorial conception. It owes something as well to Ovid and the humanist poet Angelo Poliziano, who was, like Botticelli, a member of the Medici circle and may well have advised him on the painting, as he undoubtedly did on others.

The subject of the picture is clearly meant to be serious, even solemn. How could such images be justified in a Christian civilization without both the artist and his patron being accused of neo-paganism? To answer this question we must consider the meaning of the picture as well as the use of classical subjects in Early Renaissance art. During the Middle Ages, classical form had become divorced from classical subject matter. Artists could draw upon ancient poses, gestures, expressions, and types only by changing the identity of their sources. Philosophers became apostles, Orpheus turned into Adam, Hercules was now Samson. When medieval artists wanted to represent the pagan gods, they based their pictures on literary descriptions rather than visual models. This was the situation, by and large, until the mid-fifteenth cen-

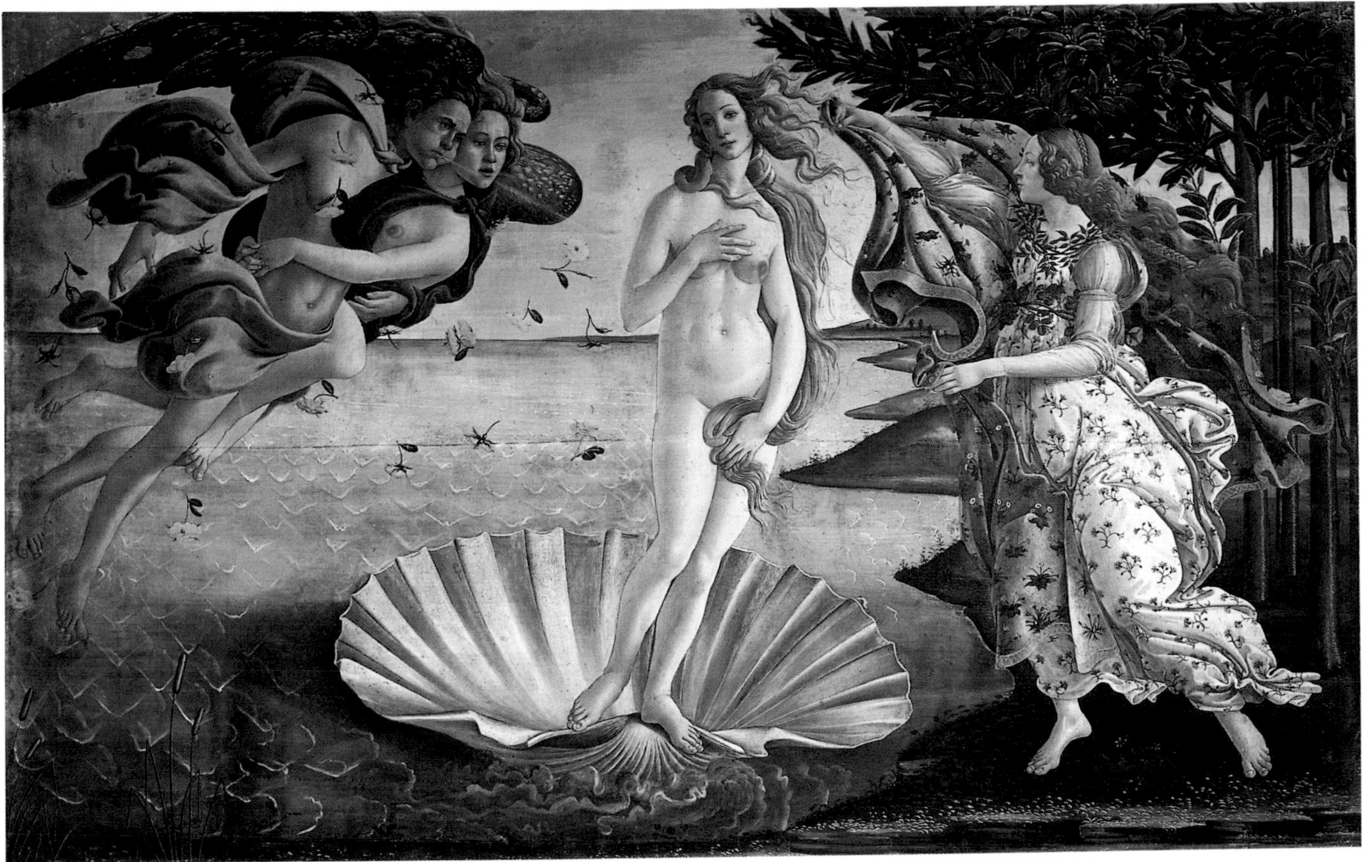

12-54. Sandro Botticelli. *The Birth of Venus*. c. 1480. Tempera on canvas, 5'8⅞" x 9'1⅞" (1.8 x 2.8 m). Galleria degli Uffizi, Florence

tury. Only with Pollaiuolo and Mantegna in northern Italy (see below) does classical form begin to rejoin classical content. Pollaiuolo's lost paintings of the Labors of Hercules (about 1465) mark the earliest case, so far as we know, of large-scale subjects from classical mythology depicted in a style inspired by ancient monuments.

In the Middle Ages, classical myths had at times been interpreted as allegories of Christian ideas, however remote the analogies might be. Europa carried off by the bull, for instance, could be declared to signify the soul redeemed by Christ. But such weak analogies were a poor excuse for reinvesting the pagan gods with their ancient beauty and strength. To fuse the Christian faith with ancient mythology, rather than merely relate them, required a stronger argument. This was provided by the Neo-Platonic philosophers. The best known of them was Marsilio Ficino, who enjoyed great prestige during the late fifteenth century and after. Ficino, who was also a priest, based his thought as much on the mysticism of Plotinus (see page 181) as on the works of Plato. He believed that the life of the universe, including human life, was linked to God by a spiritual circuit continuously ascending and descending, so that all revelation, whether from the Bible, Plato, or classical myths, was one. He also proclaimed that beauty, love, and beatitude, being phases of this same circuit, were one. Thus, Neo-Platonists could speak of both the "celestial Venus" (the nude Venus born of the sea, as in our picture) and the Virgin Mary as a source of "divine love" (meaning the recognition of divine beauty).

This celestial Venus, according to Ficino, dwells purely in the sphere of Mind. Her twin, the ordinary Venus, gives rise to "human love." Of her Ficino wrote to the Medici prince: "Venus . . . is a nymph of excellent comeliness, born of heaven and more than others beloved by God all highest. Her soul and mind are Love and Charity, her eyes Dignity and Magnanimity, the hands Liberality and Magnificence, the feet Comeliness and Modesty. The whole, then, is Temperance and Honesty, Charm and Splendor. Oh, what exquisite beauty! . . . a nymph of such nobility has been wholly given into your hands! If you were to unite with her in wedlock and claim her as yours she would make all your years sweet." In both form and content, this passage follows odes to the Virgin composed by medieval church fathers.

Once we know that Botticelli's picture has this quasi-religious meaning, it seems less surprising that the wind-god Zephyr and the breeze-goddess Aura on the left look so much like angels. It also makes sense that the Hora personifying Spring on the right, who welcomes Venus ashore, recalls the relationship of St. John to the Savior in the Baptism of Christ (compare fig. 10-31). As baptism is a "rebirth in God," so the birth of Venus evokes the hope for "rebirth" from which the Renaissance takes its name. Thanks to the fluidity of Neo-Platonic doctrine, the number of possible associations in our painting is endless. All of them, however, like the celestial Venus herself, "dwell in the sphere of Mind," and Botticelli's Venus would hardly be a fit vessel for them if she were less ethereal. Thus rather than being merely decorative, the highly stylized treatment of the surface is what elevates the picture to allegory.

A similar meaning can be assigned to *Primavera* (fig. 12-55), also painted for Lorenzo's country home. The large canvas was inspired by Poliziano's lighthearted poem about the birth of love in spring. Other elements cannot be explained by this source alone. They must have been derived from Ovid and the Roman poet Lucretius. We see Venus in her sacred grove, with Eros flying overhead. Her companions—the Three Graces and Hermes—are on the left, and on the right is Zephyr grasping for the nymph Chloris, whom he later transforms into Flora, the goddess of flowers. That the painting has a hidden meaning is suggested once more by the decorative treatment of the surface and the peculiar appearance of the groupings, which seem frozen despite their graceful rhythms.

According to one recent interpretation, *Primavera* can be understood on several levels based on Ficino's writings. It is, first, a metaphor of Platonic love between two friends: Mercury points the way to divine love in the guise of Venus, which is born of the Three Graces, symbolizing beauty. In contrast is physical love, represented by Flora, who was often thought of in lascivious terms during the Renaissance. On another level, the painting signifies the immortality of the soul through death and rebirth. This meaning arose by analogy of the Rape of Chloris to the Rape of Persephone, the subject of a poem by the Roman author Claudian that was popular among humanists at the time. Thus Venus becomes Demeter/Ceres of the Eleusian mysteries, with Mercury as the god of the dead. Eros is the vehicle of divine revelation, while the Three Graces stand for the soul. Finally, *Primavera* denotes the Last Judgment, in which Venus takes on the role of Mary the Divine Intercessor, Mercury becomes St. Michael, and Eros is the Holy Spirit. The Three Graces are seen as the Saved, as well the three virtues Faith, Hope, and Love. Zephyr depicts Satan snatching up the Damned, personified by Chloris. Flora, content with earthly pleasures, remains as unaware of her fate as the fashionable couples in Traini's *Triumph of Death* (see fig. 11-86). Even if we do not agree with every detail of this controversial reading, it accords well with Ficino's lofty Neo-Platonism. It also provides the most satisfactory explication to date of Botticelli's complex work by linking its content with that of *The Birth of Venus*.

Neo-Platonic philosophy and its expression in art were too complex to become popular outside its select and highly educated

EARLY ITALIAN RENAISSANCE THEATER AND MUSIC

Medieval theater continued with little change until around 1500 (see "Medieval Music and Theater," pages 308–09). Unlike other literary forms, theater was slow to show the influence of humanism, which dominated so much of Italian Renaissance intellectual life. This seems surprising, since the earliest humanist tragedy and comedy date from about 1390. (Both were written in Latin, and neither was actually performed.) Perhaps the main reason that new forms of drama were slow to develop in the Renaissance was the fact that the works of the Greek and Roman dramatists were only gradually rediscovered in the West. Although the plays of Seneca (see page 189) were known in the Middle Ages, Plautus' second-century B.C. comedies were not rediscovered until 1429. Further, when Constantinople fell to the Turks in 1453, fleeing Greek scholars brought the manuscripts of many previously unknown classical dramas with them to Italy. Renaissance theater was further revolutionized when the printing press was introduced into Italy in 1465. As a result, between 1471 and 1518 all of the known Greek and Roman plays were published.

Italian humanists were always interested more in philosophy and theory than in actual practice. Plautus' *Menaechmi* was first staged only in 1486, and then again five years later, but Seneca's *Hippolytus* had to wait until 1509. This emphasis on theory rather than practice also helped to inhibit the development of music, for Italy was slow to produce a composer of stature. Until the middle of the sixteenth century, the popes and the rulers of the Italian cities imported French and Flemish musicians to occupy all the important positions for composers in churches and at ducal courts. Since the goal of the humanists was to revive Latin and Greek, few of them were interested in writing poetry in Italian. Consequently, there were very few good writers for composers to work with, especially on secular motets and songs, which were fertile soil for experimentation. The first humanist to write extensively in Italian was Angelo Poliziano (1454–1494), a member of the Medici circle in Florence; his poetry inspired paintings by Botticelli and Raphael (see figs. 12-54 and 13-31). He also collaborated with the Flemish-born composer Heinrich Isaac (c. 1450–1517), and he wrote a play about the legendary Greek bard Orpheus with musical accompaniment in imitation of the antique; though the music is now lost, the stage design by the young Leonardo da Vinci still exists.

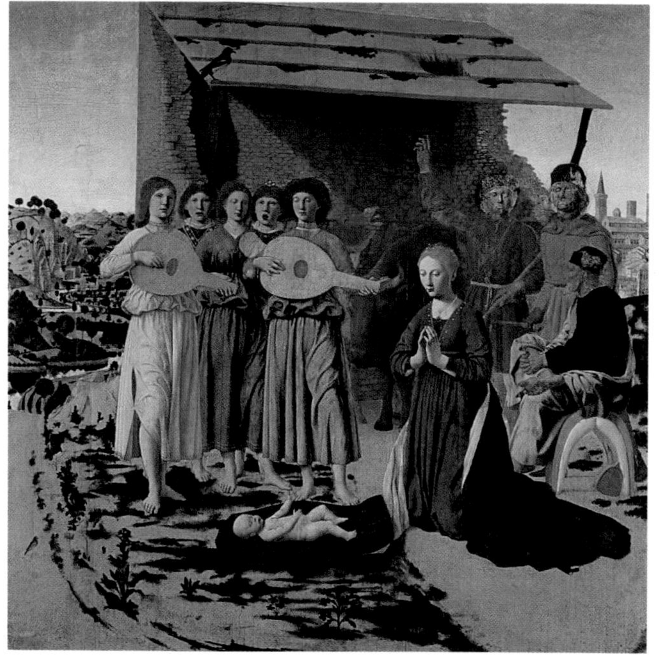

Piero della Francesca. *The Nativity.* Late 15th century. Oil on panel, 49¾ x 48¼" (126 x 123 cm). National Gallery, London

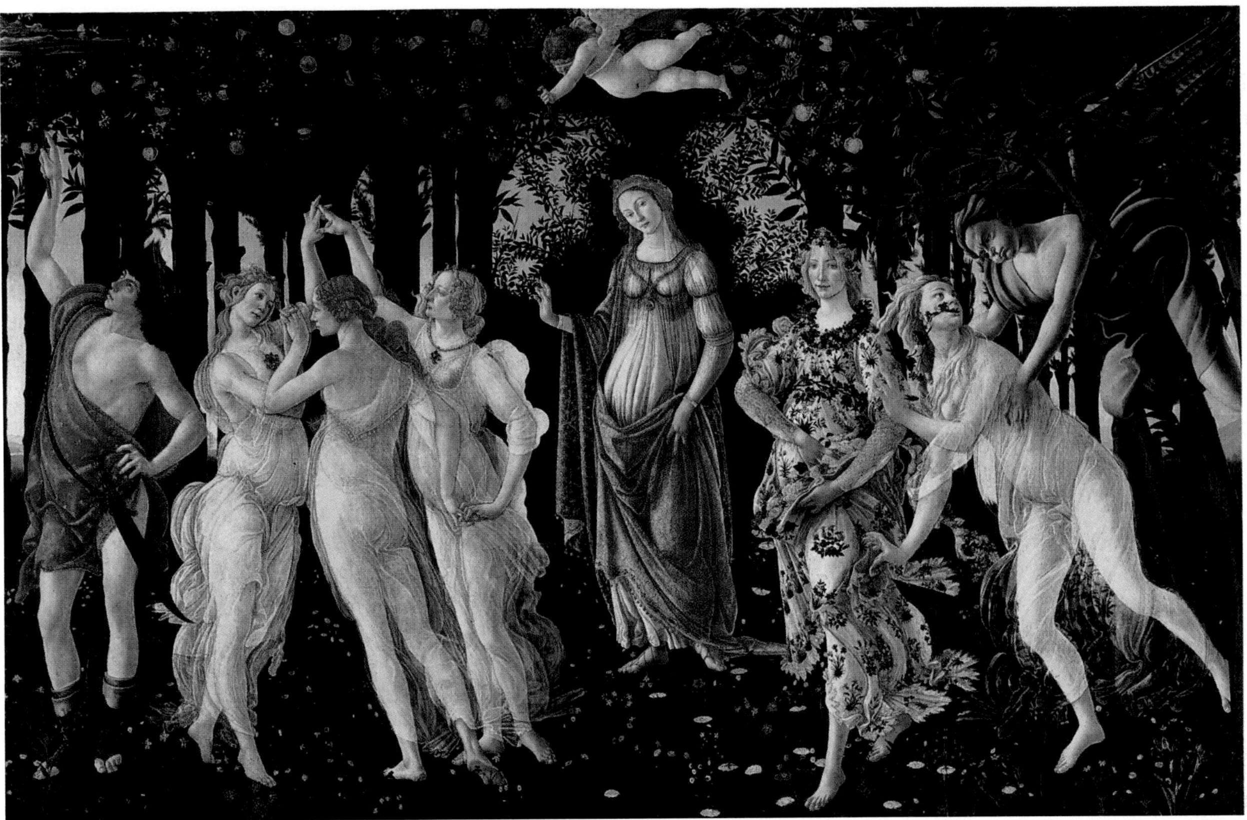

12-55. Sandro Botticelli. *Primavera.* c. 1482. Tempera on canvas. 6'8" x 10'4" (2.03 x 3.15 m). Galleria degli Uffizi, Florence

group of devotees. In 1494, the suspicions of ordinary people were aroused by the friar Girolamo Savonarola, an ardent advocate of religious reform. Savonarola gained a huge following with his sermons attacking the "cult of paganism" in the city's ruling circle. Botticelli himself may have been a follower of Savonarola. It is said that he burned a number of his "pagan" pictures. In his last works he returned to traditional religious themes, but with no major change in style. He seems to have given up painting after 1500, even though Savonarola's prediction that the world would be destroyed in that year was not fulfilled.

GHIRLANDAIO. The fresco cycles of Domenico Ghirlandaio (1449–1494), another contemporary of Botticelli, contain so many portraits that they almost serve as family chronicles of the wealthy patricians who sponsored them. Among his most touching individual portraits is the panel *An Old Man and His Grandson* (fig. 12-56). The attention to surface texture and facial detail emphasizes the old man's nose, which has been disfigured by rosacea. Ghirlandaio has shown the tender relationship between the little boy and his grandfather with unique understanding. Psychologically, our panel plainly bespeaks its Italian origin.

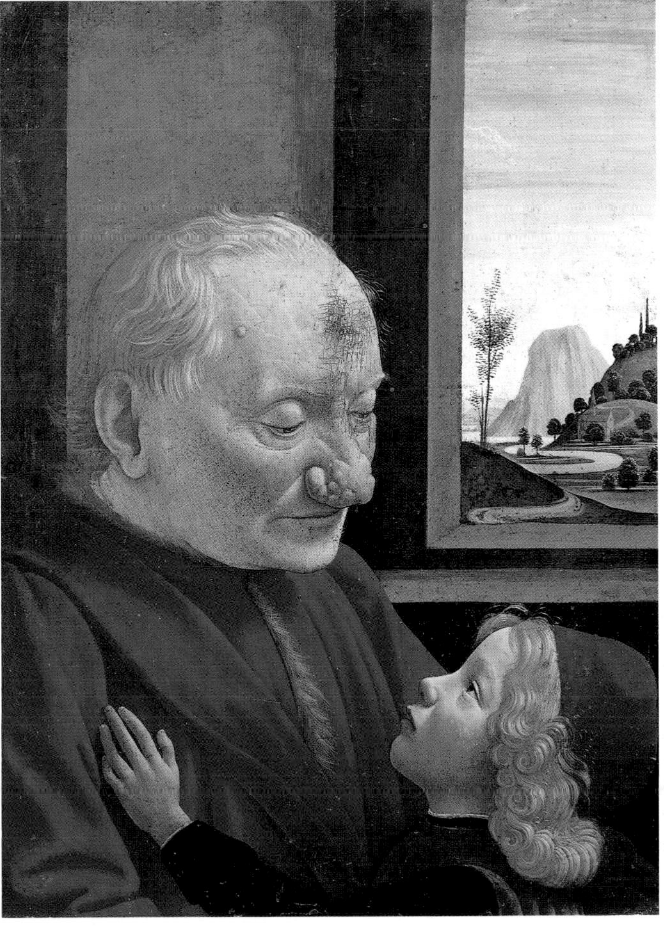

12-56. Domenico Ghirlandaio. *An Old Man and His Grandson.* c. 1480. Tempera and oil on wood panel, 24⅛ x 18" (61.2 x 45.5 cm). Musée du Louvre, Paris

PERUGINO. Rome, long neglected during the papal exile in Avignon (see page 351), once more became a major artistic center in the later fifteenth century. As the papacy regained power on Italian soil, the popes began to beautify both the Vatican and the city. They believed that the monuments of Christian Rome must outshine those of the pagan past. The most ambitious pictorial project of those years was the decoration of the walls of the recently

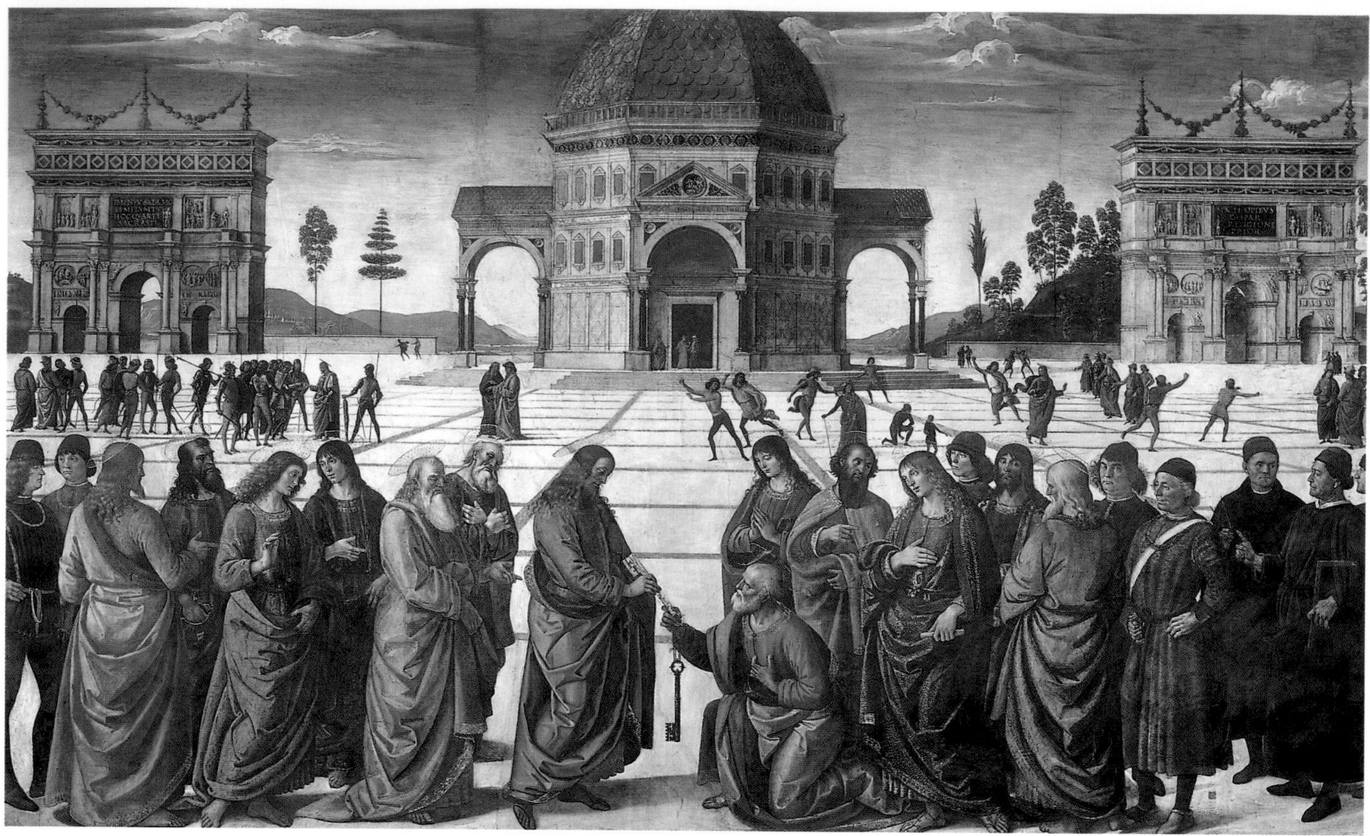

12-57. Pietro Perugino. *The Delivery of the Keys.* 1482. Fresco. Sistine Chapel, the Vatican, Rome

completed Sistine Chapel for Pope Sixtus IV. Begun around 1481–82, this large cycle consists of events from the life of Moses (left wall) and Christ (right wall), representing the old and new covenants (see box page 248). The artists include most of the important painters of central Italy, among them Botticelli and Ghirlandaio. If the Sistine murals do not, on the whole, present their best work, it is because these mostly young artists had little experience in monumental fresco painting, for which there had been few opportunities since the 1450s.

There is, however, one notable exception: *The Delivery of the Keys* (fig. 12-57) by Pietro Perugino (c. 1450–1523) is this artist's finest achievement. Born near Perugia in Umbria (the region southeast of Tuscany), Perugino maintained close ties with Florence. Early in his career he was strongly influenced by Verrocchio, as can be seen in the statuesque balance and solidity of his figures (compare fig. 12-52). The symmetrical design conveys the importance of the subject. The authority of St. Peter as the first pope, as well as of all those who followed him, rests on his having received the keys to the Kingdom of Heaven from Christ himself, in the same way that the Christian church in the background is built on the rock that is Peter. A number of Perugino's contemporaries, with highly individualized features, witness the solemn event. Equally striking is the vast expanse of the background. To the left, in the middle distance, is the moment when Jesus says, "Render to Caesar what is Caesar's"; to the right, the stoning of Christ. The inscriptions on the two Roman triumphal arches (modeled on the Arch of Constantine; see fig. 7-46) favorably compare Sixtus IV to Solomon, who built the Temple of Jerusalem where the Covenant of the Ark was later housed. The pair of arches flanks a domed structure representing the ideal church of Alberti's treatise *On Architecture.* Also Albertian is the mathematically exact perspective, which lends the view its spatial clarity, although in order to simplify the scheme the squares are far larger than those recommended by Alberti for such a piazza. This scene, so rational and intelligible in its construction, nevertheless achieves a stunning visionary effect. Despite its novel spatial qualities, Perugino's fresco in many respects continues the tradition of Piero della Francesca, who spent much of his later life working for Umbrian clients, notably the duke of Urbino. Also from Urbino, shortly before 1500, Perugino received a pupil whose fame would soon outshine his own: Raphael.

SIGNORELLI. The Sistine frescoes were completed by Luca Signorelli (1445/50–1523). Signorelli's background was similar to Perugino's, although his personality was more dramatic. Of provincial Tuscan origin, he had been a student of Piero della Francesca before coming to Florence in the 1470s. Like Perugino, he was impressed by Verrocchio, but he also admired the energy, expressiveness, and anatomic precision of Pollaiuolo's nudes. Signorelli combined these influences with Piero's solidity of form and mastery of perspective foreshortening to achieve an epic style that later had a lasting impact on Michelangelo. He reached the climax of his career just before 1500 with a cycle of frescoes on the walls of the S. Brizio Chapel in Orvieto Cathedral.

The commission from Pope Alexander VI was an important one; it was a reward for Orvieto's faithfulness to the Vatican. The cycle, whose subject is the end of the world, conforms to the typology established by St. Augustine. But it is also rooted in St.

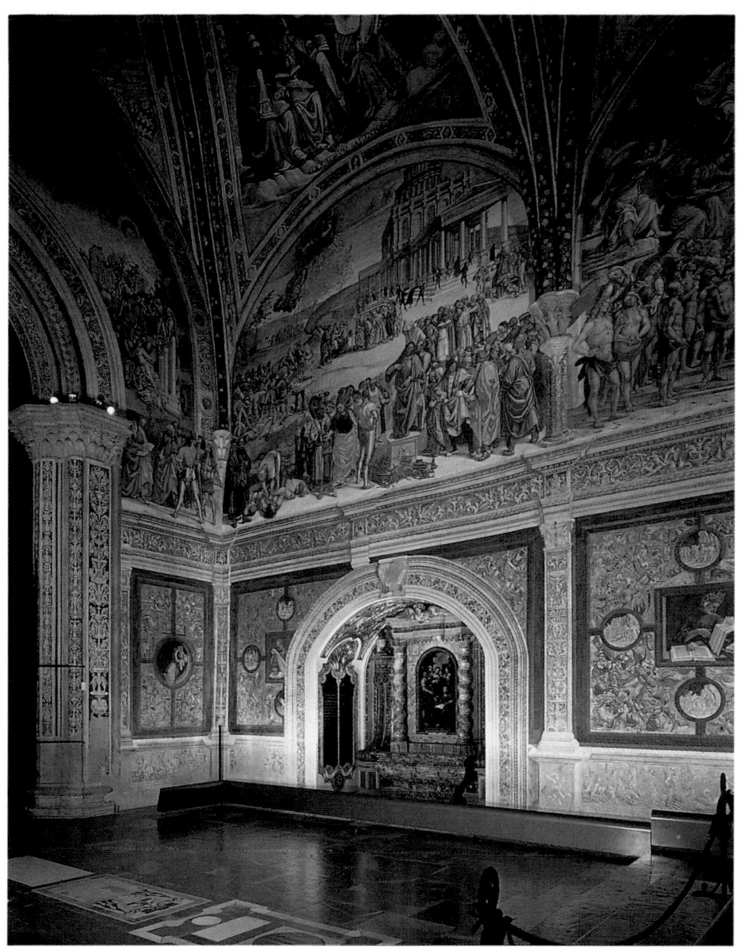

12-58. Luca Signorelli. *The Rule of the Antichrist.* 1499–1500. Fresco. S. Brizio Chapel, Orvieto Cathedral

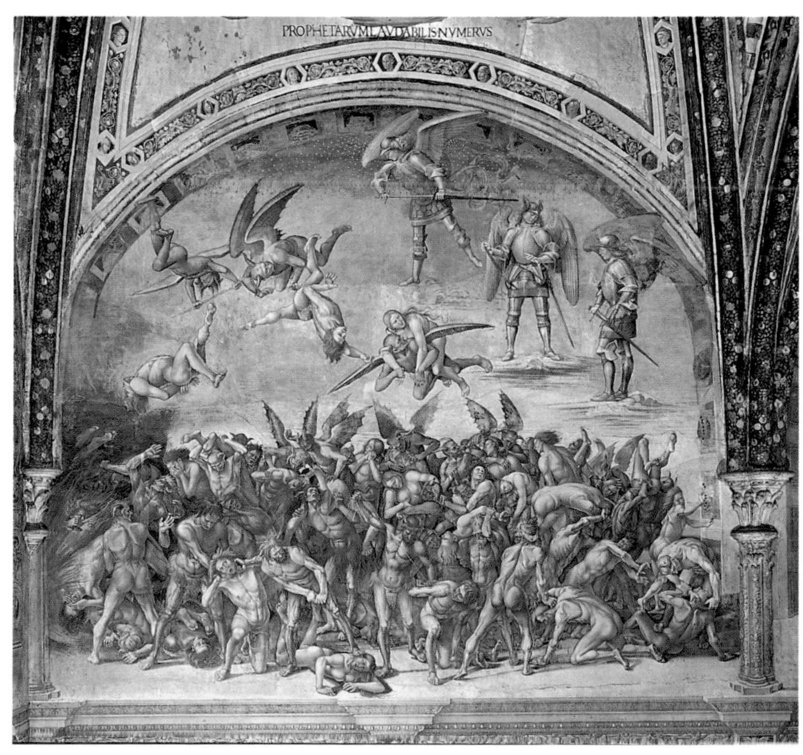

12-59. Luca Signorelli. *The Damned Cast into Hell.* 1499–1500. Fresco. S. Brizio Chapel, Orvieto Cathedral

Thomas Aquinas and Dante, as well as fifteenth-century Dominican theologians, especially St. Vincent Ferrer. The 1490s were a time of great hardship for Orvieto. It suffered from the plague, political unrest, economic decline, and fear of the Turks. (The Turks had crushed the Christian forces at Lepanto, Greece, in 1499—a defeat that was to be avenged in a second, more famous battle at the same site in 1571.) This turmoil is reflected in *The Rule of the Antichrist* (fig. 12-58), which is flanked by *The End of the World* and *The Coronation of the Elect.* The false Christ represents the chaos caused by political leaders and the "infidel" forces of

Islam. As Satan's chief ally, he rules the world before being defeated by St. Michael (seen in the upper left-hand corner). He appears before the third Temple of Solomon, the center of his evil realm, which is shown in a skewed view that contrasts with the rational calm of Perugino's *The Delivery of the Keys* (see fig. 12-57).

The most dynamic of the Orvieto frescoes is *The Damned Cast into Hell* (fig. 12-59). What strikes us most is not the harsh style, which befits the tumultuous scene. Nor is it Signorelli's use of the nude body as an expressive instrument, even though he goes far beyond earlier painters in this respect. Rather, it is the sense of tragedy that commands our attention. Signorelli's Hell, the exact opposite of Bosch's (compare fig. 15-14), is bathed in daylight; there are no monsters or machines of torture. The damned keep their dignity, and even the devils are less demonic. Even in Hell, it seems, the Renaissance faith in humanity does not lose its force.

VENICE AND PADUA. We turn now to the growth of Early Renaissance art in northern Italy. The International Style in painting and sculpture lingered there until mid-century, and architecture long retained a strongly Gothic flavor. As a result, there were hardly any major achievements in these fields. Between 1450 and 1500, however, a great painting tradition was born in Venice and its territories that was to flourish for the next three centuries. The Republic of Venice, although more oligarchic and oriented toward the East, had many ties with Florence. Hence it is not surprising that Venice, rather than Milan, became the center of Early Renaissance art in northern Italy.

MANTEGNA. Florentine masters had been carrying the new style to Venice and nearby Padua since the 1420s. Fra Filippo Lippi, Uccello, and Castagno had worked there. Still more important was Donatello's ten-year stay. Their presence, however, had little effect until shortly before 1450. At that time Andrea Mantegna (1431–1506) emerged as an independent master. He was trained by a minor Paduan painter, but his early career was shaped by his impressions of Florentine works and, we may assume, contact with Donatello. Next to Masaccio, Mantegna was the most important painter of the Early Renaissance. He, too, was a young genius, able to carry out commissions of his own by age 17. In the next decade he reached artistic maturity, and during the next half-century (he died at the age of 75) he broadened the range of his art. Yet he never abandoned the style he had developed in the 1450s.

The greatest achievement of Mantegna's early career, the frescoes in the Church of the Eremitani in Padua, was almost entirely destroyed by an accidental bomb explosion in 1944. *St. James Led to His Execution* (fig. 12-60) is the most dramatic scene of the cycle because of its daring "worm's-eye view" perspective, which is based on the viewer's actual eye level. (The central vanishing point is below the bottom of the picture, somewhat to the right of center.) As a result, the setting looms large, as in Masaccio's *Trinity* fresco (see fig. 12-22). Its main feature is a huge triumphal arch, which, although not a copy of any known Roman monument, looks so authentic that it might as well be.

Here Mantegna's devotion to the remains of antiquity shows his close ties to the humanists at the University of Padua, who had the same devotion to ancient literature. No Florentine painter or sculptor of the time could have conveyed such an attitude to him. The same desire for authenticity can be seen in the costumes of the Roman soldiers (compare fig. 7-27). It even extends to the use of "wet" drapery patterns, a Classical Greek invention that was adopted by the Romans (see fig. 7-32). But the tense figures, lean and firm, and especially their interaction, are derived from Donatello. Mantegna's subject hardly requires such a dramatic treatment. The saint, on the way to his execution, blesses a paralytic and commands him to walk. Through their glances and gestures, the bystanders express how deeply the miracle has stirred

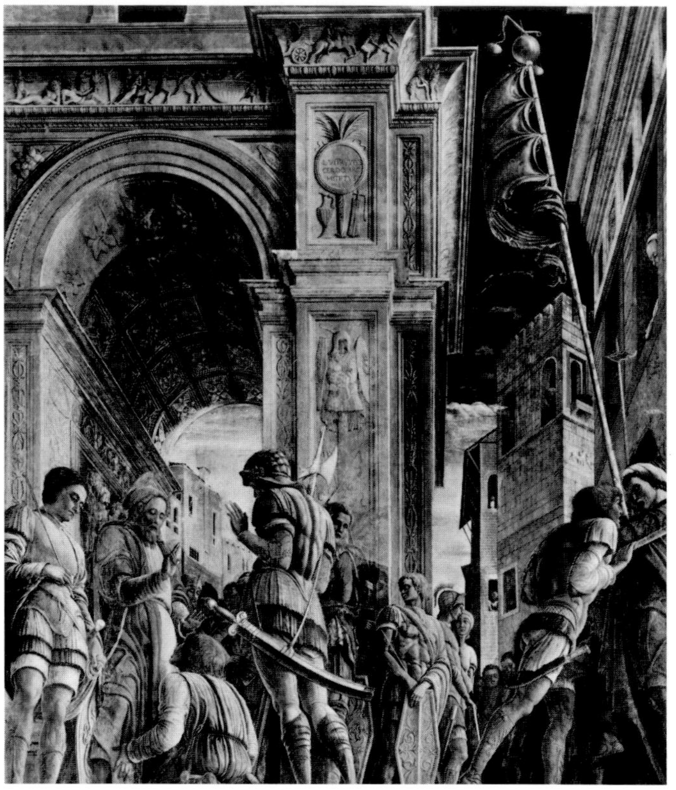

12-60. Andrea Mantegna. *St. James Led to His Execution.* c. 1455. Fresco. Ovetari Chapel, Church of the Eremitani, Padua. Destroyed 1944

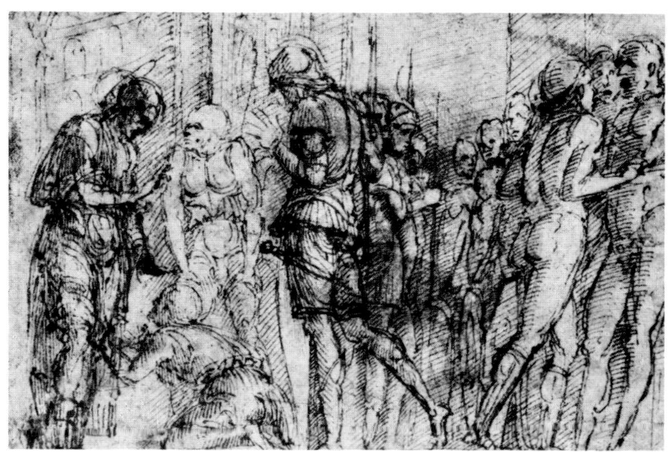

12-61. Andrea Mantegna. *St. James Led to His Execution.* c. 1455. Pen drawing, 6⅛ x 9¼" (15.7 x 23.5 cm). Collection G. M. Gathorne-Hardy, Donnington Priory, Newbury, Berkshire, England

them. The crowd generates an emotional tension that erupts in violence on the far right, where the spiral curl of the banner echoes the turbulence below.

By rare good luck, a sketch for this fresco has survived (fig. 12-61). This is the earliest known case of a drawing that permits us to compare the preliminary and final versions of such a design. (Among the drawings by earlier masters, none is related to a known picture in the same way.) This sketch differs from sinopie (full-scale drawings on the wall; see fig. 11-87) in its tentative quality. The composition has not yet taken full shape. The image is "unfinished" in both conception and the quick, shorthand style. We note, for example, that here the perspective is closer to normal, indicating that the artist worked out the exact scheme directly on the wall. Our drawing also offers proof of what we suspected in the case of Masaccio: that Early Renaissance artists conceived their compositions in terms of nude figures. The group on the right is still in that first stage; in the others, the outlines of the body show beneath the costume. But the drawing is also a work of art in its own right. The very quickness of its "handwriting" gives it an immediacy and force that are lost in the fresco.

On the evidence of these works, we would hardly expect Mantegna to be much concerned with light and color. Yet the *St. Sebastian* panel reproduced in figure 12-62, painted only a few years after the Paduan frescoes, shows that he was. In the foreground, we find classical remains (along with the artist's signature in Greek). The saint, too, looks more like a statue than a living body. But beyond we see an atmospheric landscape and a deep blue sky dotted with soft white clouds. The scene is bathed in warm late-afternoon sunlight, which creates a melancholy mood and makes the pathos of the dying saint even more poignant. The background shows the influence, direct or indirect, of the Van Eycks (compare fig. 15-2, left).

Some works of the great Flemish masters had surely reached Florence as well as Venice between 1430 and 1450. But in Venice they had a greater effect, evoking the interest in light-filled landscapes that became an important part of Venetian Renaissance painting.

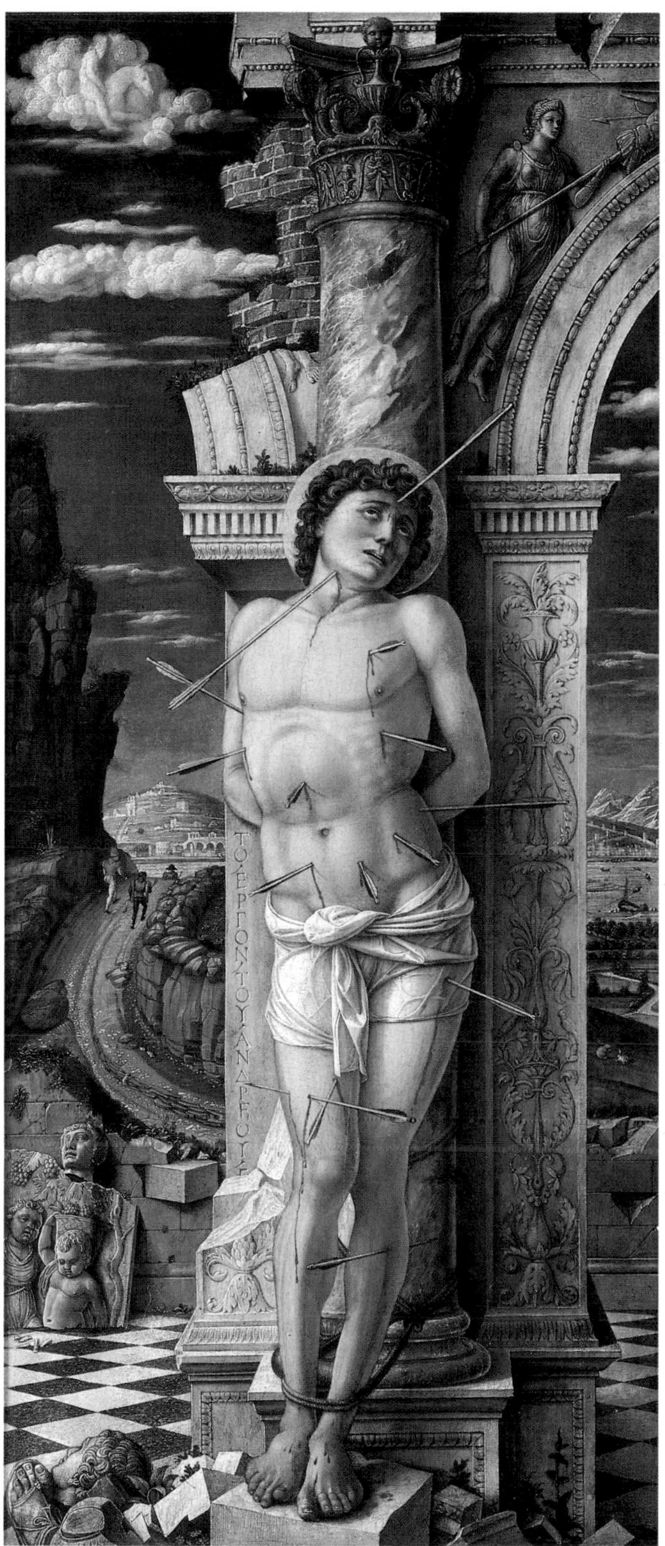

12-62. Andrea Mantegna. *St. Sebastian*. c. 1455–60. Tempera on panel, 26¾ x 11⅞" (68 x 30.6 cm). Kunsthistorisches Museum, Vienna

BELLINI. In the painting of Giovanni Bellini (c. 1431–1516), Mantegna's brother-in-law, we can trace the further growth of the Flemish tradition in the South. Bellini was slow to mature. His finest pictures, such as *St. Francis in Ecstasy* (fig. 12-63), date from the last decades of the century or even later. The subject is unique. The saint has left his wooden pattens behind and stands barefoot on holy ground, like Moses in the Lord's presence (see page 43). Despite the absence of the crucified seraph that appeared to him on Mount Alverna, the painting is often thought to show Francis receiving the stigmata (the wounds of Christ) on the Feast of the Holy Cross in 1224, although the marks on his hands are barely visible even in person. Instead, it most likely "illustrates" the Hymn of the Sun, which Francis composed the next year, after his annual fast at a hermitage near his hometown of Assisi. During that time he could not bear the sight of light and was plagued by mice. The monk finally emerged from his cell after the Lord assured him that he would enter the Kingdom of Heaven. We see him looking ecstatically up at the sun. (Note the direction of the shadows.) In the background is a magnificent expanse of Italian countryside. Yet this is no ordinary landscape. It represents the Heavenly Jerusalem, inspired by the Revelation of St. John the Divine. It lies across the river, separated from the everyday world by the bridge to the left. Behind looms Mount Zion, where the Lord dwells. How, then, shall we enter the gate to paradise, shown as a large tower?

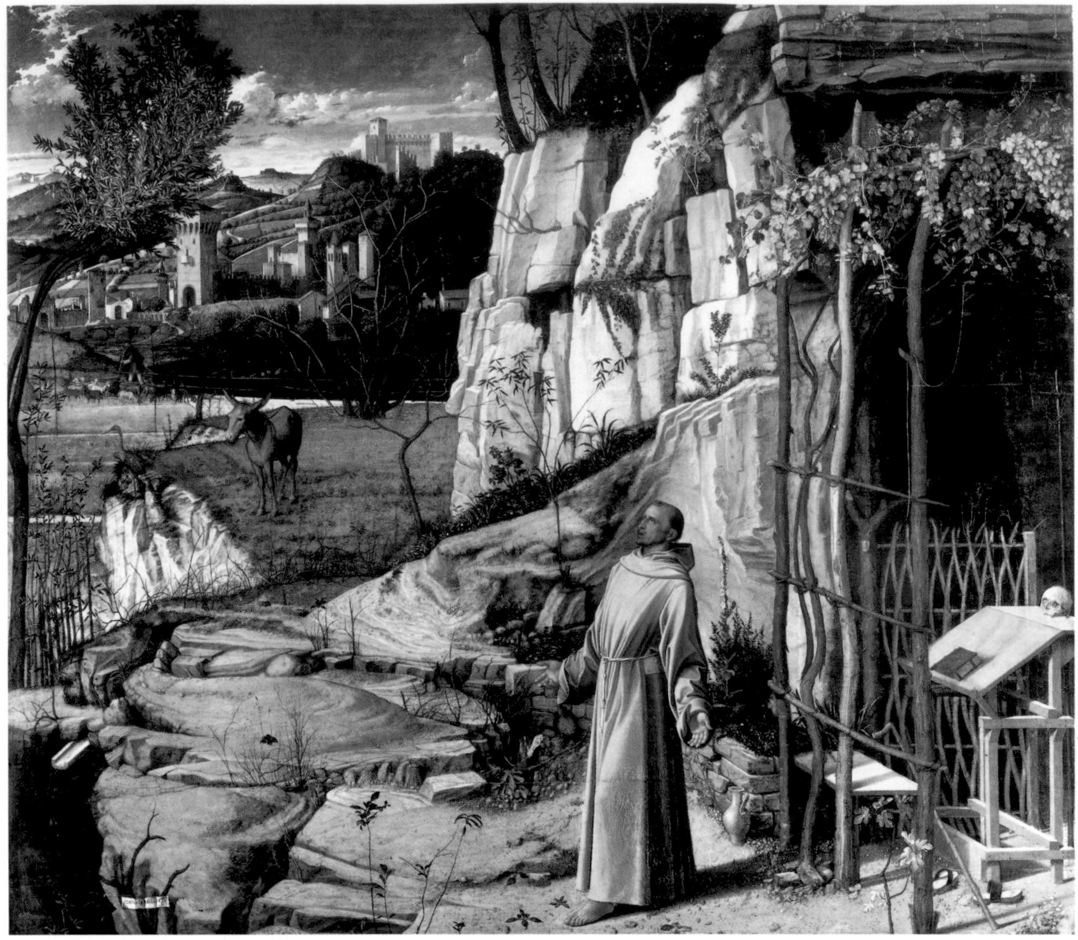

12-63. Giovanni Bellini. *St. Francis in Ecstasy.* c. 1485. Oil and tempera on panel, 49 x 55⅞" (124 x 141.7 cm). The Frick Collection, New York

COPYRIGHT THE FRICK COLLECTION

For Francis, the road to salvation lay in the ascetic life, symbolized by the cave, which also links him to St. Jerome, the first great hermit saint. The donkey stands for St. Francis himself, who referred to his body as Brother Ass, which must be disciplined. The other animals (hard to make out in our reproduction)—the heron, bittern, and rabbit—are, like monks, solitary creatures in Christian lore.

This iconography does not by itself explain the picture. More important is the treatment of the landscape. St. Francis is so small compared to the setting that he seems almost incidental. Yet his mystic rapture before the beauty of the visible world guides our own response to the view that is spread out before us, which is ample and intimate at the same time. St. Francis believed that the Lord had created nature for the benefit of humanity. The artist shares his reverence for the Lord's handiwork, which is expressed in the Hymn of the Sun:

> Be praised, my Lord, with all Your creatures,
> Above all Brother Sun,
> Who gives the day and by whom You shed light on us.
> And he is beautiful and radiant with great splendor.
> Of Thee, Most High, he is a symbol.

Bellini's contours are less brittle than Mantegna's. The colors are softer and the light more glowing. He also shares the concern of the great Flemings for every detail and its symbolism. Unlike the Northerners, however, he can define the viewer's spatial relationship to the landscape. The rock formations of the foreground are clear and firm, like architecture rendered by the rules of scientific perspective.

As the foremost painter of Venice, Bellini produced a number of altar panels of the sacra conversazione type. The last and most monumental one of the series is the *Madonna and Saints* in S. Zaccaria (fig. 12-64), done in 1505. Compared to Domenico's sacra conversazione of 50 years earlier (see fig. 12-31), the setting is simpler but no less impressive. We stand in the nave of a church looking toward the enthroned Madonna and Child in the apse, which fills most of the panel. The rest of the figures appear, however, under the vaulted canopy of the crossing, which is partly visible. The structure is obviously not a real church, for its sides are open and the scene is flooded with sunlight. (Domenico also placed his figures in a semi-outdoor setting.) The Madonna's high-backed throne and the music-making angel on its lowest step are derived (no doubt through many intermediaries) from Masaccio's *Madonna Enthroned* of 1426 (see fig. 12-28).

What distinguishes this altar from its Florentine ancestors is not only the spaciousness of the design but its calm, meditative mood. Instead of "conversation," we sense the figures' deep communion, which makes gestures unnecessary. We shall encounter this quality again and again in Venetian painting. Here we see it as if through a diffusing filter, for the artist has bathed the scene in a delicate haze. There are no harsh contrasts; light and shadow blend in almost imperceptible gradations; and colors glow with a new richness. In this magical moment, Bellini unites Florentine grandeur with Venetian intimacy.

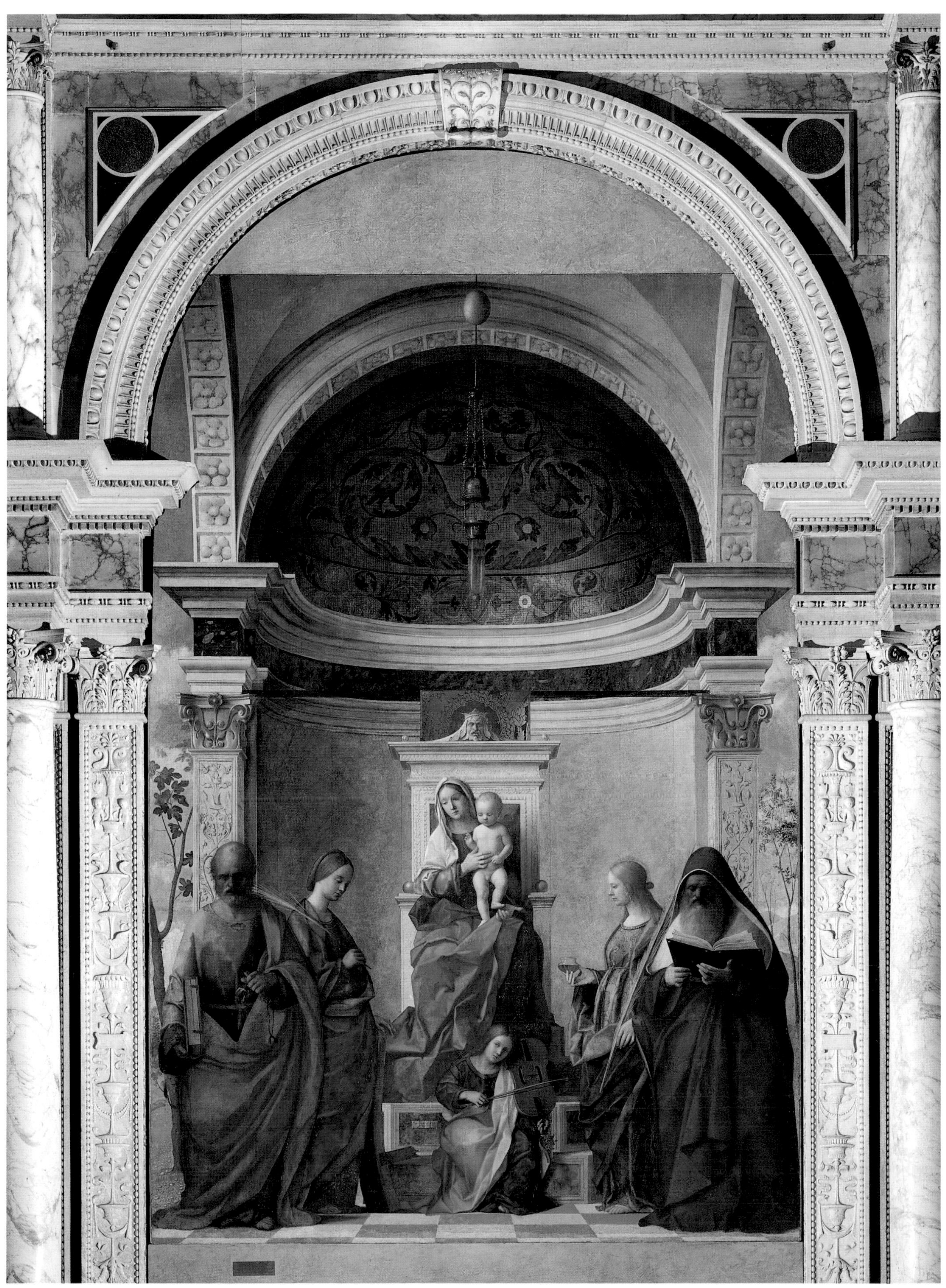

12-64. Giovanni Bellini. *Madonna and Saints.* 1505. Oil on panel, 16'5⅛" x 7'9" (5 x 2.4 m). S. Zaccaria, Venice

CHAPTER THIRTEEN

The High Renaissance in Italy

It used to be taken for granted that the High Renaissance followed the Early Renaissance as inevitably as night follows day. The great masters of the sixteenth century—Leonardo, Bramante, Michelangelo, Raphael, Giorgione, Titian—were thought to have shared the ideals of their predecessors but to have expressed them so completely that their names became synonyms for perfection. They represented the climax, the classic phase, of Renaissance art, just as Pheidias had brought the art of ancient Greece to its highest point. This view could also explain why these two classic phases, though 2,000 years apart, were so short. If art is assumed to develop along the pattern of a ballistic curve, its highest point cannot last more than a moment.

Since the 1920s, art historians have come to realize the drawbacks of this scheme. When we apply it literally, the High Renaissance becomes so brief that we wonder whether it happened at all. Moreover, it hardly helps our understanding of the Early Renaissance if we regard it as a "not-yet-perfect High Renaissance," any more than an Archaic Greek statue can be satisfactorily viewed from a Pheidian standpoint. Nor is it very useful to insist that the post-Classical phase, whether Hellenistic or "Late Renaissance," must be one of decline. The image of the ballistic curve has now been abandoned, and we have gained a less assured, but also less arbitrary, estimate of what, for lack of another term, we still call the High Renaissance.

In some basic respects, the High Renaissance was indeed the culmination of the Early Renaissance. In others, however, it was a major departure. Certainly the tendency to view artists as geniuses, rather than simply as artisans, was never stronger than during the first half of the sixteenth century. Plato's concept of genius—the spirit that enters poets and causes them to compose in a "divine frenzy"—had been broadened by Marsilio Ficino and his fellow Neo-Platonists to include architects, sculptors, and painters. For Giorgio Vasari, geniuses were set apart by "grace," in the sense of both divine grace, a gift from God, and gracefulness, which reflected it. To him, this concept had moral and spiritual significance, inspired in part by Dante's Inferno. Building further on Petrarch's scheme of history (see pages 383–84), he saw the High Renaissance as superior even to antiquity, because it belonged to the era of Christian grace that had not been revealed to the pagans (see box page 248). Thus in his *Lives of the Painters* (1550–68), Vasari praises the "gracious," virtuous personalities of Michelangelo, Leonardo, and Raphael as a way of accounting for their talent. Grace also served to justify his treatment of Michelangelo as the greatest artist of all time. This view remains with us to this day, although Michelangelo's character was far from admirable in all respects. [See Primary Sources, no. 42, page 613.]

What set these artists apart was the inspiration guiding their efforts, which was worthy of being called "divine," "immortal," and "creative." (Before 1500 *creating,* as distinct from *making,* was the privilege of God alone.) To Vasari, the painters and sculptors of the Early Renaissance, like those of the Late Gothic, had learned only to imitate nature. The geniuses of the High Renaissance, in contrast, had conquered nature by ennobling or transcending it. In actual fact, the High Renaissance remained thoroughly grounded in nature. Its achievement lay in the creation of a new classicism.

Faith in the divine origin of inspiration led artists to rely on subjective standards of truth and beauty. Whereas Early Renaissance artists felt bound by what they believed to be universal rules, such as the numerical ratios of musical harmony and the laws of linear perspective, their High Renaissance successors were less concerned with rational order than with visual effectiveness. They evolved a new drama and a new rhetoric to engage the emotions of the beholder, whether or not these were sanctioned by classical precedent. Indeed, the works of the great masters of the High Renaissance soon became classics in their own right. Their authority was equal to that of the most famous monuments of antiquity. At the same time, this cult of the genius had a profound effect on the artists themselves. It spurred them to ambitious goals, and prompted their patrons to support them. Since these ambitions often went beyond what was humanly possible, they were apt to be limited by external as well as internal difficulties. Artists were often left with a sense of having been defeated by malevolent fate.

Here we face a contradiction: if the creations of genius are viewed as unique by definition, they cannot be successfully imitated by lesser artists, however worthy they may seem of such imi-

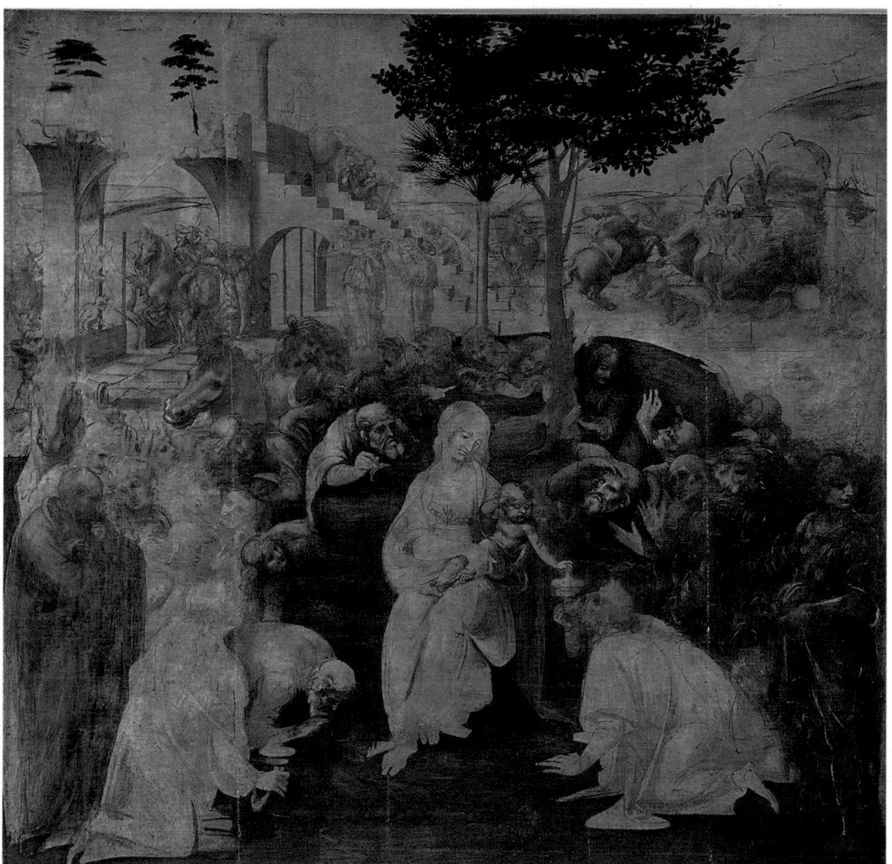

13-1. Leonardo da Vinci. *Adoration of the Magi.* 1481–82. Monochrome on panel, 8' x 8'1" (2.43 x 2.46 m). Galleria degli Uffizi, Florence

tation. Unlike the founders of the Early Renaissance, the leading artists of the High Renaissance did not set the pace for a broadly based "period style" that could be practiced on every level of quality. The High Renaissance produced surprisingly few minor masters. It died with those who had created it, or even before. Of the six great personalities mentioned above, only Michelangelo and Titian lived beyond 1520.

Conditions after that date were less favorable to the High Renaissance style than those of the first two decades of the sixteenth century. Yet the High Renaissance might well have ended soon anyway. Its harmonious grandeur was an inherently unstable balance of conflicting elements. Only these components, not the balance itself, could be transmitted to the artists who reached maturity after 1520. In pointing out the limited and precarious nature of the High Renaissance we do not mean to deny its tremendous impact upon later art. For most of the next 300 years, the great masters of the early sixteenth century loomed so large that the achievements of their predecessors seemed to belong to a forgotten era. Even when the art of the fourteenth and fifteenth centuries was finally rediscovered, people still saw the High Renaissance as the turning point and referred to all painters before Raphael as "the Primitives."

Leonardo da Vinci

One reason the High Renaissance deserves to be called a period is the fact that its key monuments were all produced between 1495 and 1520, despite the great differences in age of the artists who created them. Bramante, the oldest, was born in 1444, Raphael in 1483, and Titian about 1488–90. Yet the distinction of being the earliest High Renaissance master belongs to Leonardo da Vinci (1452–1519). Born in the little Tuscan town of Vinci, Leonardo was trained in Florence by Verrocchio. Conditions there must not have suited him. At the age of 30 he went to work for the duke of Milan as a military engineer, and only secondarily as an architect, sculptor, and painter.

ADORATION OF THE MAGI. Leonardo left behind, unfinished, the most ambitious work he had then begun, a large *Adoration of the Magi* (fig. 13-1), for which he had made several preliminary studies. The design of the ruins shows a geometric order and a precisely constructed perspective that recall Florentine painting in the wake of Masaccio rather than the style prevailing about 1480, which is reflected solely in the gracefulness of the Madonna and Child. Yet the structure is so peculiar as to heighten the contrast with the landscape. The result is a nearly hallucinatory space. Without the trees to anchor it, the composition would consist of two separate parts. The background cannot be explained in rational terms. What are we to make of the figures on the stairs of the wrecked building, or the combat of horsemen to either side?

The foreground is no less visionary. The main figures are contained within a triangle surrounded by the sweeping arc of onlookers. The scene is framed by a philosopher lost in thought to the left and by a young soldier on the right looking outside the picture to something that has caught his attention. They undoubtedly represent ideal types—but what do they signify? The contemplative and active lives surely, youth and old age as well, perhaps moral and

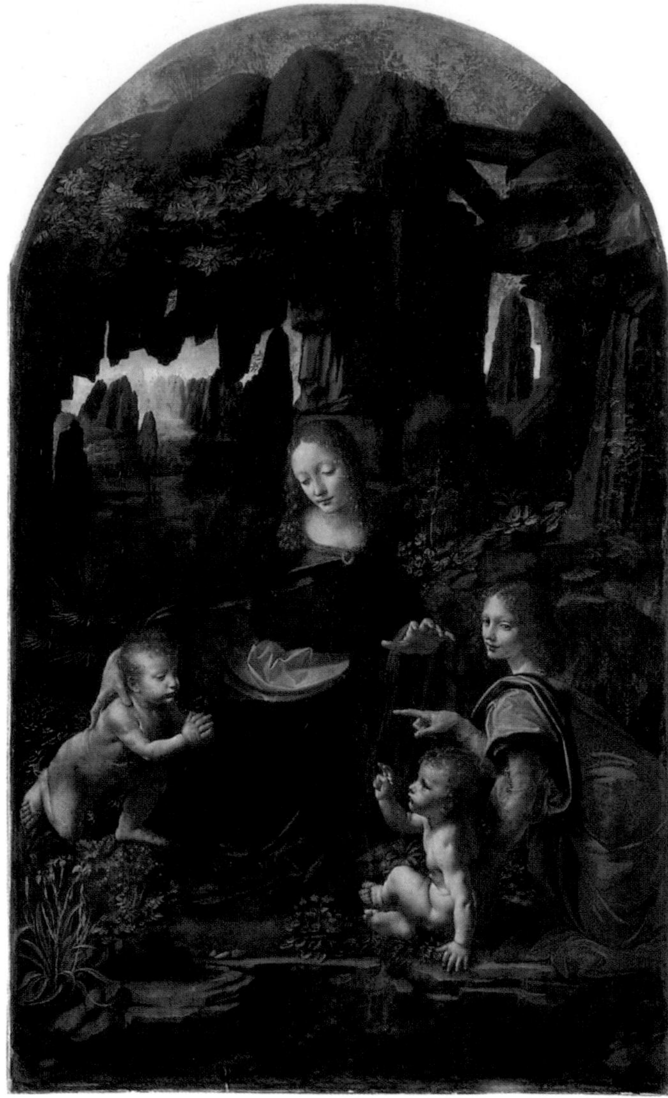

13-2. Leonardo da Vinci. *The Virgin of the Rocks*. c. 1485. Oil on panel transferred to canvas, 6'6" x 4' (1.9 x 1.2 m). Musée du Louvre, Paris

physical beauty, as one critic has suggested. Within these contrasts lies a duality of mind and body that Leonardo sought to resolve in his mature work. The assembly is as spellbinding as it is strange. The image foretells the future of Leonardo's work, and the figures already contain the seeds of those in his later paintings.

The most striking, and indeed revolutionary, aspect of the panel is the way it is executed, although Leonardo did not even complete the underpainting. The forms seem to materialize softly and gradually, never quite detaching themselves from a dusky realm. Leonardo, unlike Pollaiuolo or Botticelli, thinks not in terms of outlines but of three-dimensional bodies made visible in varying degrees by the incidence of light. In the shadows, these shapes remain incomplete. Their contours are only implied. In this method of modeling (called *chiaroscuro,* the Italian word for "light and dark"), the forms no longer stand abruptly side by side. Instead, they share in a new pictorial unity, for the barriers between them have been partially broken down. There is a comparable emotional continuity as well. The gestures and faces of the crowd convey with touching eloquence the reality of the miracle they have come to behold. We will recognize the influence of both Pollaiuolo and Verrocchio in the expressiveness of these figures. Leonardo may also have been impressed by the breathless shepherds in *The Portinari Altarpiece,* by the Flemish artist Hugo van der Goes, which had recently been brought to Florence (see fig. 15-12).

THE VIRGIN OF THE ROCKS. Soon after arriving in Milan, Leonardo painted *The Virgin of the Rocks* (fig. 13-2), another altar panel. This work suggests what the *Adoration* would have looked like had it been completed. The figures emerge from the semi-darkness of the grotto, enveloped in a moist atmosphere that delicately veils their forms. This fine haze, called *sfumato,* is more pronounced than similar effects in Flemish and Venetian painting. It imparts an unusual warmth and intimacy to the scene. It also creates a remote, dreamlike quality and makes the picture seem a poetic vision rather than an image of reality. In his notebooks Leonardo had much to say about the relation between art and literature. Called the *paragone,* it was rooted in Horace's statement that poetry is like painting (*ut pictura poesis*), which the High Renaissance reinterpreted to mean that painting ought to conform to poetry. [See Primary Sources, no. 41, pages 612–13.] The subject—the infant St. John adoring the Christ Child in the presence of the Virgin and an angel—is entirely new in art. The story of their meeting is one of the many legends that arose to satisfy curiosity about the "hidden" early life of Christ, which is hardly mentioned in the Bible. (According to a similar legend, St. John, about whom equally little is known, spent his childhood in the wilderness; hence he is shown wearing a hair shirt.)

Leonardo was the first to depict this scene, but the treatment is mysterious in many ways. The secluded setting, the pool in front, and the carefully rendered plant life hint at levels of meaning that are hard to define. How are we to interpret the relationships among the four figures, expressed in their gestures? Protective, pointing, blessing, they convey the wonderment of St. John's recognition of Christ as the Savior with infinite tenderness. The gap between these hands and St. John makes the exchange all the more striking. Although present in *The Doubting of Thomas* by Leonardo's teacher, Verrocchio (see fig. 12-52), the elegant gestures and the refined features are the first mature example of that High Renaissance "grace" signifying a spiritual state of being.

THE LAST SUPPER. Despite their originality, the *Adoration* and *The Virgin of the Rocks* do not yet differ clearly in conception from the paintings of the Early Renaissance. Leonardo's *The Last Supper,* produced a dozen years later, was the first statement of the ideals of High Renaissance painting (fig. 13-3). Unfortunately, the famous mural began to deteriorate a few years after its completion. The artist, dissatisfied with the limitations of the traditional fresco technique, experimented in an oil-tempera medium in plaster that did not adhere well to the wall. We thus need some effort to imagine its original splendor, even though the painting was recently restored. Yet what remains is more than sufficient to account for its tremendous impact. Viewing the composition as a whole, we are struck at once by its balanced stability. Only afterward do we realize that Leonardo achieved this balance by the reconciliation of competing, even conflicting, aims that no previous artist had attempted.

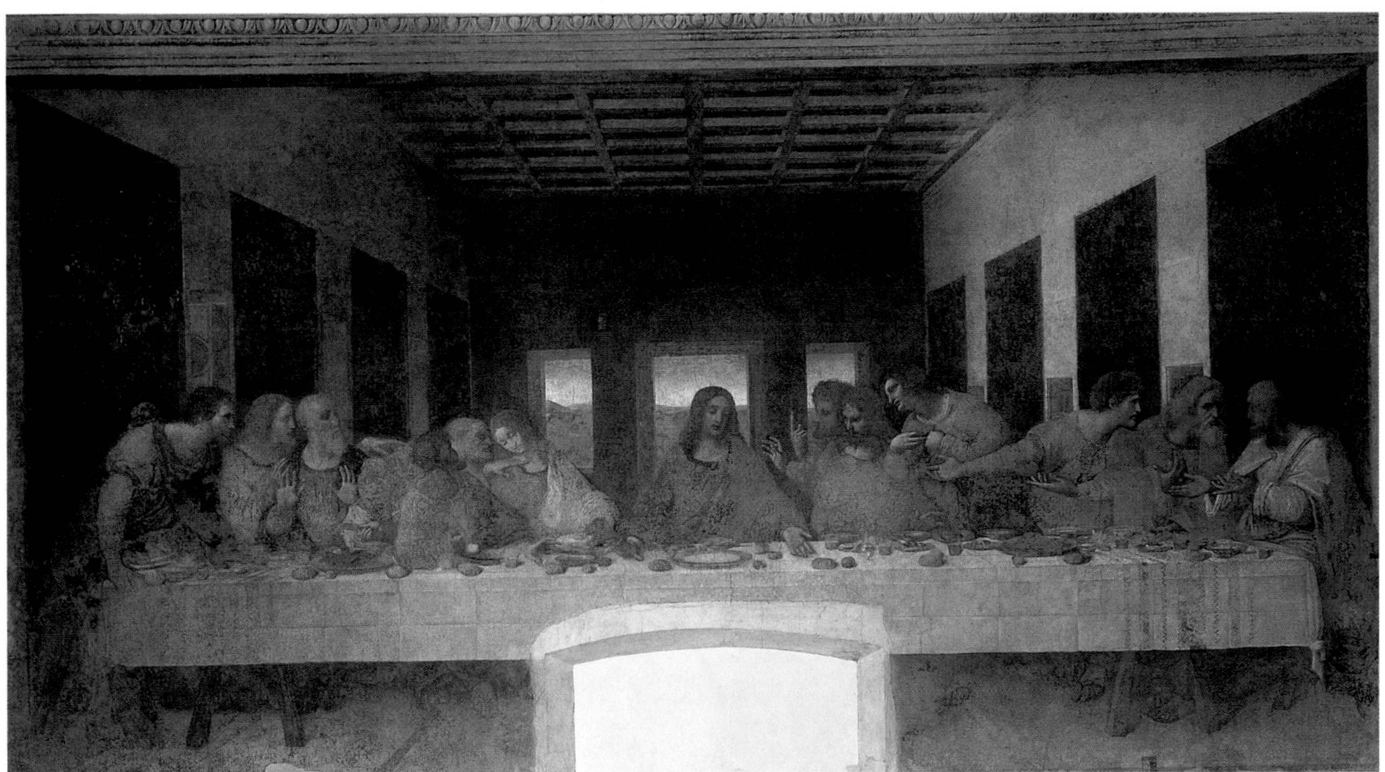

13-3. Leonardo da Vinci. *The Last Supper.* c. 1495–98. Tempera wall mural, 15'2" x 28'10" (4.6 x 8.8 m). Sta. Maria delle Grazie, Milan

A comparison with Castagno's *The Last Supper* (see fig. 12-35), painted half a century before, is particularly revealing here. In both cases the spatial setting seems like an annex to the real interior of the refectory (dining hall). But unlike Leonardo's, Castagno's architecture has an oppressive effect on the figures. The reason for this becomes clear when we realize that in the earlier work the space has been conceived independently. It was there before the figures entered and would equally suit another group of diners. As we know from a preliminary study, Leonardo began with the figural composition; the architecture plays no more than a supporting role.

The perspective is an ideal one. Leonardo's painting, high up on the refectory wall, assumes a vantage point some 15 feet above the floor and 30 feet back. This position is clearly impossible, yet we readily accept it. The central vanishing point, which governs our view of the interior, is located behind the head of Jesus in the exact middle of the picture and thus becomes charged with symbolic significance. Equally plain is the symbolic function of the main opening in the back wall: its projecting pediment acts as the architectural equivalent of a halo. We thus tend to see the perspective framework of the scene almost entirely in relation to the figures, rather than as a preexisting entity. We can easily test how vital this relationship is by covering the upper third of the picture. The composition then takes on the character of a frieze. The grouping of the apostles is less clear, and the calm triangular shape of Jesus becomes passive, instead of acting as a physical and spiritual force. At the same time, the perspective system helps to "lock" the composition in place. It thus gives the scene an eternal quality without making it look static.

The Savior has presumably just spoken the fateful words, "One of you shall betray me." The disciples are asking, "Lord, is it I?" We see nothing that contradicts this interpretation, but to view the scene as just one moment in a psychological drama does not do justice to Leonardo's aims, which went well beyond a literal rendering of the biblical narrative. He crowded the disciples together on the far side of the table, in a space too small for so many people. He clearly wanted to condense his subject, both physically (by the compact, monumental grouping of the figures) and spiritually (by presenting many levels of meaning at one time). Thus Jesus' gesture is one of submission to the divine will and of offering. It is a hint at Jesus' main act at the Last Supper, the institution of the Eucharist, in which bread and wine become his body and blood through transubstantiation. The apostles do not simply react to these words. Each reveals his own personality, his own relationship to the Savior. (Note that Judas is no longer segregated from the rest; his defiant profile sets him apart well enough.) Leonardo has carefully calculated each pose and expression so that the drama unfolds across the picture plane. The figures exemplify what the artist wrote in one of his notebooks, that the highest and most difficult aim of painting is to depict "the intention of man's soul" through gestures and movements of the limbs—a statement to be interpreted as referring not to momentary emotional states but to the inner life as a whole.

MONA LISA. In 1499, the duchy of Milan fell to the French, and Leonardo returned to Florence after brief trips to Mantua and Venice. He must have found the cultural climate very different from what he remembered. The Medici had been expelled, and the city was briefly a republic again until their return. For a while, Leonardo seems to have been active mainly as an engineer and surveyor. Then in 1503 the city commissioned him to do a mural

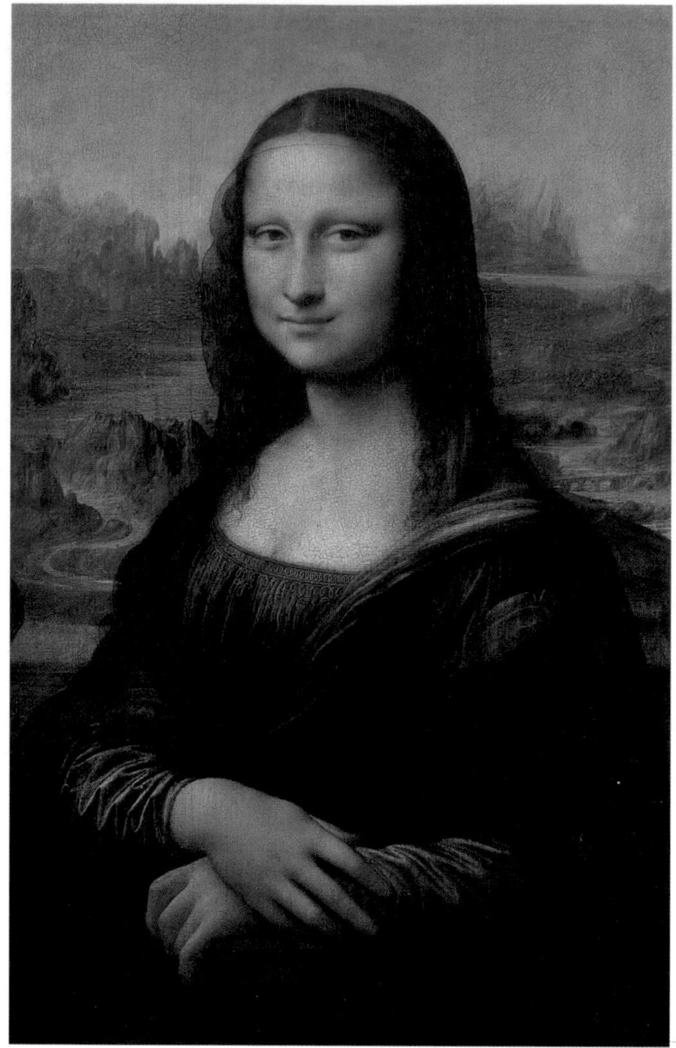

13-4. Leonardo da Vinci. *Mona Lisa.* c. 1503–5.
Oil on panel, 30¼ x 21" (77 x 53.5 cm). Musée du Louvre, Paris

of some famous event from the history of Florence for the council chamber of the Palazzo Vecchio. He chose the Battle of Anghiari, but in 1506 he abandoned the commission and returned to Milan at the request of the French. The painting is known only through various copies of the cartoon (including one by Peter Paul Rubens) that survived for more than a century.

While working on the mural, Leonardo also painted the *Mona Lisa* (fig. 13-4). [See Primary Sources, no. 42, page 613.] Here the sfumato of *The Virgin of the Rocks* is so perfected that it seemed miraculous to the artist's contemporaries. The forms are built from layers of glazes so thin that the panel seems to glow with a gentle light from within. But the fame of the *Mona Lisa* comes not from this subtlety alone. Even more intriguing is the sitter's personality. Why, among all the smiling faces ever painted, has this one been singled out as "mysterious"? Perhaps the reason is that, as a portrait, the picture does not fit our expectations. The features are too individual for Leonardo to have simply depicted an ideal type, yet they are so idealized that they blur the sitter's character. Once again the artist has brought two opposites into harmonious balance. The smile, also, may be read in two ways: as the echo of a momentary mood and as a timeless, symbolic expression akin to the "Archaic smile" of the Greeks (see figs. 5-14 and 5-15). The *Mona Lisa* seemingly embodies a maternal tenderness that was to Leonardo the essence of womanhood. Even the landscape, made up mainly of rocks and water, suggests elemental generative forces. Who was the sitter for this, the most famous portrait in the world? Her identity was a mystery until recently. We now know that she was the wife of a Florentine merchant born in 1479 and dead before 1556. This is not the only painting of the Mona Lisa: Leonardo also painted a nude version that once belonged to the king of France.

DRAWINGS. In his later years, Leonardo devoted himself more and more to his scientific interests. Art and science, we recall, were first united in Brunelleschi's discovery of systematic perspective. Leonardo's work is the climax of this trend. The artist, he believed, must know not only the rules of perspective but all the laws of nature. To him the eye was the perfect means of gaining such

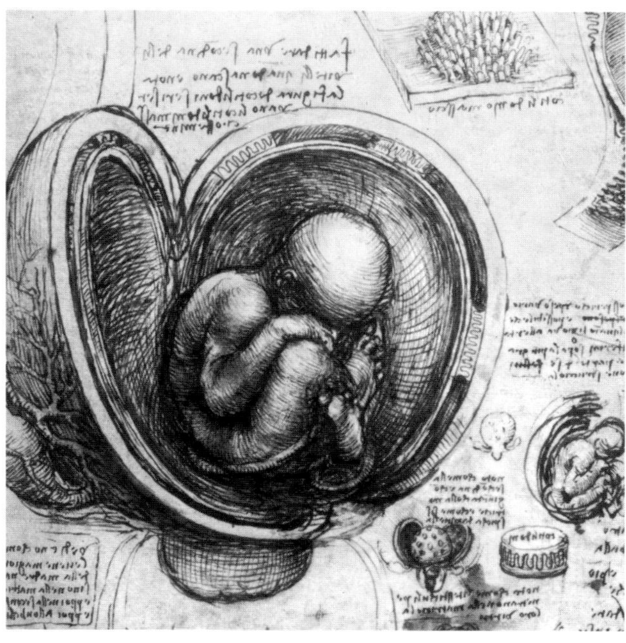

13-5. Leonardo da Vinci. *Embryo in the Womb.* c. 1510.
Detail of pen drawing, 11⅞ x 8⅜" (30.4 x 21.5 cm).
Windsor Castle, Royal Library

© 1991. HER MAJESTY QUEEN ELIZABETH II

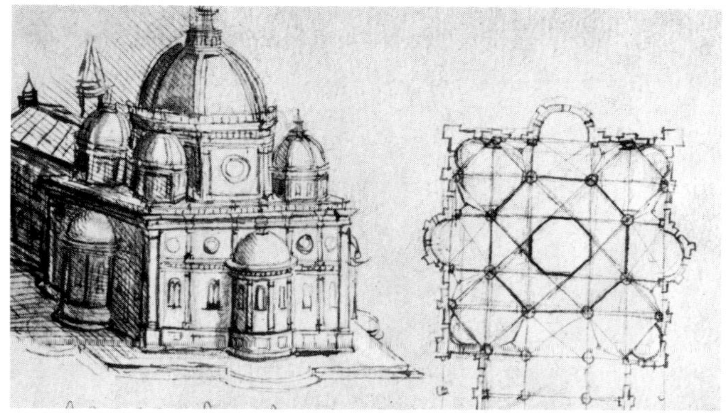

13-6. Leonardo da Vinci. *Project for a Church* (Ms. B). c. 1490.
Pen drawing. Bibliothèque de l'Arsenal, Paris

knowledge. The extraordinary range of his inquiries can be seen in the hundreds of drawings and notes that he hoped to turn into an encyclopedic set of treatises. How original he was as a scientist is still a matter of debate, but in one field there is no doubt of his importance: he created the modern scientific illustration, an essential tool for anatomists and biologists. A drawing such as the *Embryo in the Womb* (fig. 13-5) combines his own vivid observation with the analytic clarity of a diagram—or, to paraphrase Leonardo's own words, sight and insight.

Contemporary sources show that Leonardo was esteemed as an architect. He seems, however, to have been less concerned with actual building than with problems of structure and design. For the most part, the many architectural projects in his drawings were intended to remain on paper. Yet these sketches, especially those of his Milanese period, have great historic importance. In them we can trace the transition from the Early to the High Renaissance in architecture.

The domed, centrally planned churches of the type shown in figure 13-6 hold particular interest for us. The plan recalls Brunelleschi's Sta. Maria degli Angeli (see fig. 12-20), but the new relationship of the spatial units is more complex, while the exterior, with its cluster of domes, is more monumental than any Early Renaissance structure. In conception, this design stands halfway between the dome of Florence Cathedral and the most ambitious structure of the sixteenth century, the new basilica of St. Peter's in Rome (compare figs. 11-35, 13-9, and 13-10). It gives evidence, too, of Leonardo's close contact with the architect Donato Bramante (1444–1514).

Bramante

Bramante arrived in Milan around 1479, several years before Leonardo. A native of Urbino, he began his career as a fresco painter under the influence of Piero della Francesca and especially Andrea Mantegna. Thus he was already skilled at rendering architectural settings in correct perspective (compare figs. 12-33 and 12-60). His earliest work as a professional architect was the rebuilding of Sta. Maria presso San Satiro, which takes Brunelleschi and Alberti as its main points of departure. However, his east end for the Gothic church of Sta. Maria della Grazie, begun in 1492 for the Duke of Milan, has a complexity and grandeur that suggest the influence of Leonardo's drawings. It is likely that Leonardo, who was not a practicing architect but a military engineer, benefited in turn from Bramante, as well as others who were active in Milan.

THE TEMPIETTO. After Milan fell to the French in 1499, Bramante went to Rome, where he spent several years in a study of ancient buildings that was to transform him as an architect. Thus it was in Rome, during the last 15 years of his life, that he created High Renaissance architecture. The new style is shown fully formed in the Tempietto at S. Pietro in Montorio (fig. 13-7), commissioned by King Ferdinand and Queen Isabella of Spain and designed soon after 1500. This round chapel denotes a martyrium, for it marks the site of St. Peter's crucifixion. If the original plan had been carried out, the Tempietto would have appeared less isolated from its environment than it does today. It was intended to be surrounded by a circular, colonnaded courtyard set within a "molded" exterior space, a conception as bold and novel as the design of the chapel itself (fig. 13-8).

The nickname "little temple" is well deserved. In the three-step platform and the severe Doric order of the colonnade, classical temple architecture is more directly recalled than in any fifteenth-century building, and with good reason: it relies on the recently excavated Roman Temple of Hercules Victor. Moreover, it incor-

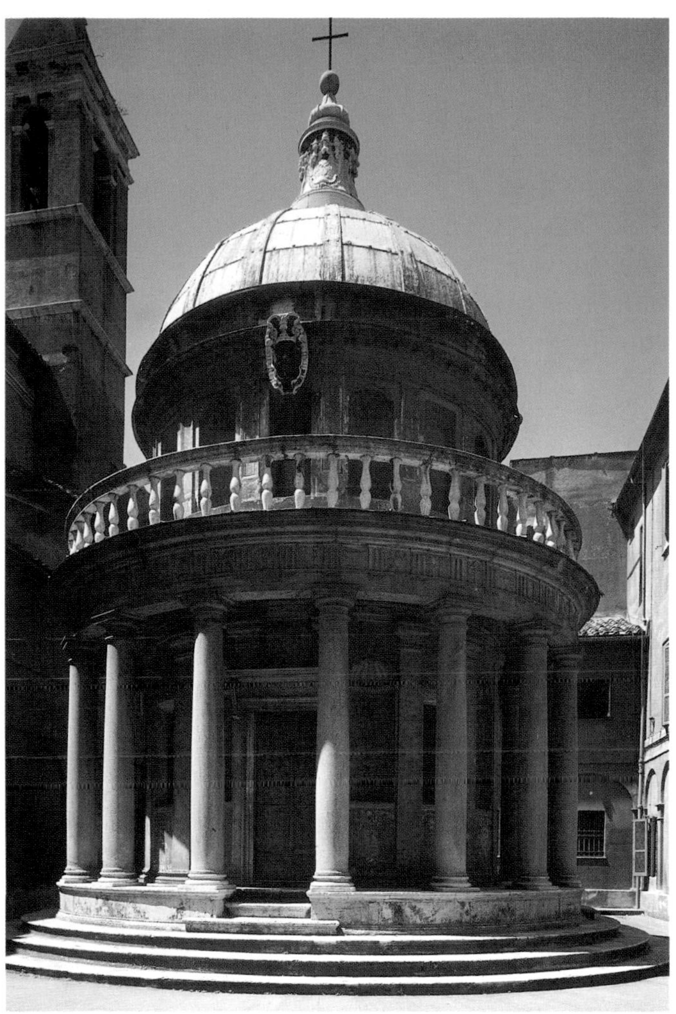

13-7. Donato Bramante. The Tempietto, S. Pietro in Montorio, Rome. 1502–11

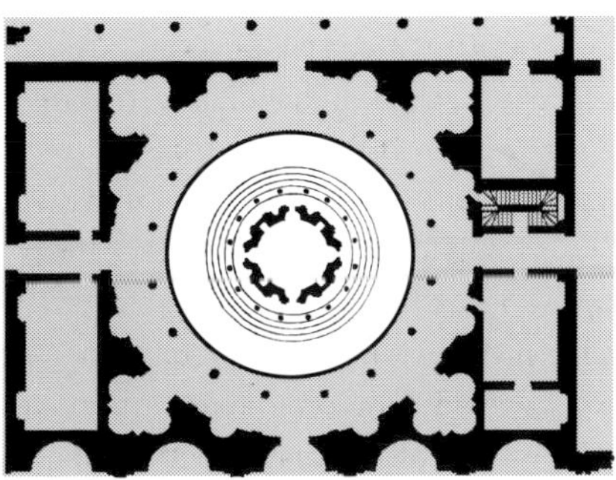

13-8. Plan of the Tempietto (after Serlio, in *Regole generali di Architettura*). Gray indicates unbuilt sections

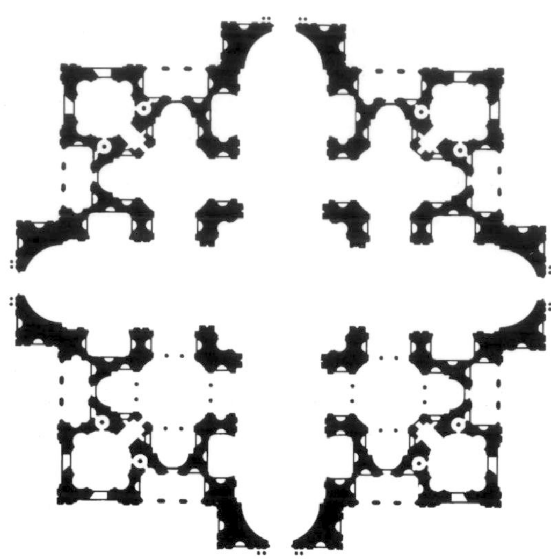

13-9. Donato Bramante. Original plan for St. Peter's, Rome. 1506 (after Geymuller)

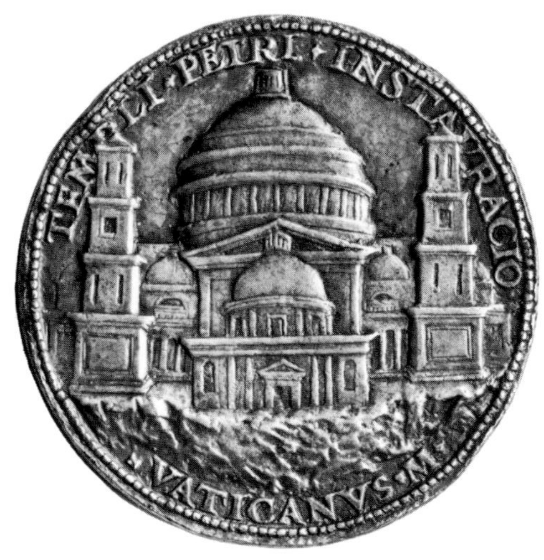

13-10. Caradosso. Bronze medal showing Bramante's design for St. Peter's. 1506. The British Museum, London

porates 16 ancient Roman columns that form the module on which the entire design is based. For example, the distance between them is four times their diameter, and they are placed two diameters from the wall. Equally striking is Bramante's use of the "sculptured wall" in the Tempietto itself and the courtyard, as seen in figure 13-8. Not since Brunelleschi's Sta. Maria degli Angeli have we seen such deeply recessed niches "excavated" from masses of masonry. These cavities are counterbalanced by the convex shape of the dome and by strongly projecting moldings and cornices. As a result, the Tempietto has a monumentality that belies its modest size.

The building, including the sculptural decoration in the metopes and frieze around the base, is a brilliant example of papal propaganda. The Tempietto proclaims Christ and the papal successors of St. Peter, who received his authority directly from the Lord (see fig. 12-57), as the direct heirs of ancient Rome. In this way, the Spaniard Pope Alexander VI asserted his claim to supremacy in both the spiritual and temporal realms. He was supported by the Spanish monarchy, then the most powerful in all of Europe.

ST. PETER'S, ROME. The Tempietto is the earliest of the great achievements that made Rome the center of Italian art during the first quarter of the sixteenth century. Most of them belong to the decade 1503–13, the papacy of Julius II. It was he who decided to replace the old basilica of St. Peter's, which was in poor condition, with a church so magnificent that it would overshadow all the monuments of ancient Imperial Rome. The task was given to Bramante, the foremost architect in the city. His original design of 1506 is known only from a plan (fig. 13-9) and from the medal commemorating the start of the building campaign (fig. 13-10), which shows the exterior in rather imprecise perspective. They are enough, however, to bear out the words Bramante reportedly used to define his aim: "I shall place the Pantheon on top of the Basilica of Constantine." The goal thus was to surpass the two most famous structures of Roman antiquity by a Christian building of a grandeur never seen before. Nothing less would have satisfied the ambitious Julius II, who wanted to unite all Italy under his command and thus gain a temporal power that matched his spiritual authority.

Bramante's design is indeed magnificent. A huge hemispherical dome, similar to that of the Tempietto, crowns the crossing of the barrel-vaulted arms of a Greek cross, with four lesser domes and tall corner towers at the angles. This plan fulfills all the demands laid down by Alberti for sacred architecture (see page 414). Yet it is strikingly different from anything envisioned by him (compare fig. 12-39). Based entirely on the circle and the square, it is so symmetrical that we cannot tell which apse was to hold the high altar. Bramante envisioned four identical facades like that on the medal of 1506, dominated by the same classical forms we saw in the Tempietto: domes, half-domes, colonnades, and pediments.

Inside the church, however, the sculptured wall reigns supreme. The plan shows no continuous surfaces, only great, oddly shaped "islands" of masonry that have been well described by one critic as giant pieces of toast half eaten by a voracious space. The actual size of these islands can be visualized only if we compare the measurements of Bramante's church with those of earlier buildings. S. Lorenzo in Florence, for instance, has a length of 268 feet, less than half that of the new St. Peter's (550 feet). Bramante's reference to the Pantheon and the Basilica of Constantine was no idle boast. His plan dwarfs these monuments, as well as every Early Renaissance church. (Each arm of the Greek cross has about the same dimensions as the Basilica of Constantine.)

How did he propose to build such an enormous structure? Cut stone and brick, the materials favored by medieval architects, would not do, for technical and economic reasons. Only concrete, as used by the Romans but largely forgotten during the Middle Ages, was strong and cheap enough (see page 159). By reviving this ancient technique, Bramante opened a new era in the history of architecture. Concrete permitted far more flexible designs than the building methods used by medieval masons. However, its possibilities were not exploited fully for some time. The construction of St. Peter's progressed so slowly that in 1514, when Bramante died, only the four crossing piers had been built. For the next three decades the project was carried on by architects trained under Bramante, who altered his design in a number of ways. A new and decisive phase in the history of St. Peter's began in 1546, when Michelangelo took charge, and the present appearance of the church (see fig. 13-27) is largely shaped by his ideas. But this must be considered in the context of Michelangelo's career as a whole.

Michelangelo

Nowhere is the concept of genius as divine inspiration—a superhuman power granted to a few individuals and acting through them—embodied more fully than in the life and work of Michelangelo (Michelangelo di Lodovico Buonarroti Simoni, 1475–1564). It was not only his admirers who viewed him in this light. He himself, steeped in Neo-Platonist tradition (see pages 420–21), accepted the idea of his genius as a living reality, although it seemed to him at times a curse rather than a blessing. What brings continuity to his long and stormy career is the sovereign power of his personality, his faith in the subjective rightness of everything he created. Conventions, standards, and traditions might be observed by lesser artists, but for him there was no higher authority than the dictates of his genius.

Unlike Leonardo, for whom painting was the noblest of the arts because it embraced every visible aspect of the world, Michelangelo was a sculptor to the core. More specifically, he was a carver of marble statues. Art, for him, was not a science but "the making of men," analogous (however imperfectly) to divine creation. Hence the limitations of sculpture that Leonardo condemned were virtues in Michelangelo's eyes. Only the "liberation" of real, three-dimensional bodies from recalcitrant matter could satisfy his urge. Painting, for him, should imitate the roundness of sculptured forms. Architecture, too, should share the organic qualities of the human figure.

Michelangelo's faith in the human image as the supreme vehicle of expression gave him a sense of kinship with Classical sculpture closer than that of any Renaissance artist. Among Italian masters, he admired Giotto, Masaccio, Donatello, and Della Quercia more than the men he knew as a youth in Florence. Of his training little is known. He was apprenticed to Ghirlandaio and carefully studied Masaccio's frescoes in the Brancacci Chapel (see figs. 12-24–12-26). Soon he was taken under the wing of Lorenzo de' Medici, which enabled him to study the antique statues in the garden of one of the family's houses. The collection was overseen by Bertoldo di Giovanni (c. 1420–1491), a pupil of Donatello, who was presumably taught the rudiments of sculpture by Michelangelo. From the beginning, Michelangelo was a carver rather than a modeler. The young artist's mind was decisively shaped by the cultural climate of Florence during the 1480s and 1490s, even though the troubled times led him to flee the city for Rome in 1496. Both the Neo-Platonism of Marsilio Ficino and the religious reforms of Savonarola affected him profoundly. These conflicting influences reinforced the tensions in Michelangelo's personality, his violent changes of mood, his sense of being at odds with himself and with the world. Just as he conceived his statues as human bodies released from their marble prison, so he saw the body as the earthly prison of the soul—noble, perhaps, but a prison nevertheless. This dualism of body and spirit endows his figures with extraordinary pathos. Although outwardly calm, they seem stirred by an overwhelming psychic energy that has no release in physical action.

PIETÀ. We sense none of these struggles in the *Pietà* commissioned in 1497 by a French cardinal for his tomb chapel in St. Peter's (fig. 13-11). The subject, of Northern origin (see pages 332–33), is rare, though not unknown, in Italy before this time. One of the Seven Sorrows of the Virgin, it owed its sudden popularity at the end of the fifteenth century to the growing veneration of Mary. Seated on Golgotha, the lovely and youthful Madonna stands for the Church and serves as the gateway to Heaven. This Lamentation lacks the pathos of the German *Andachtsbild* (compare fig. 11-54). We are meant to contemplate the central mystery of Christian faith—Jesus as God in human form who sacrificed himself to redeem our sins—with the same serenity as Mary herself. In spiritual as well as aesthetic terms, this *Pietà* still belongs to the fifteenth

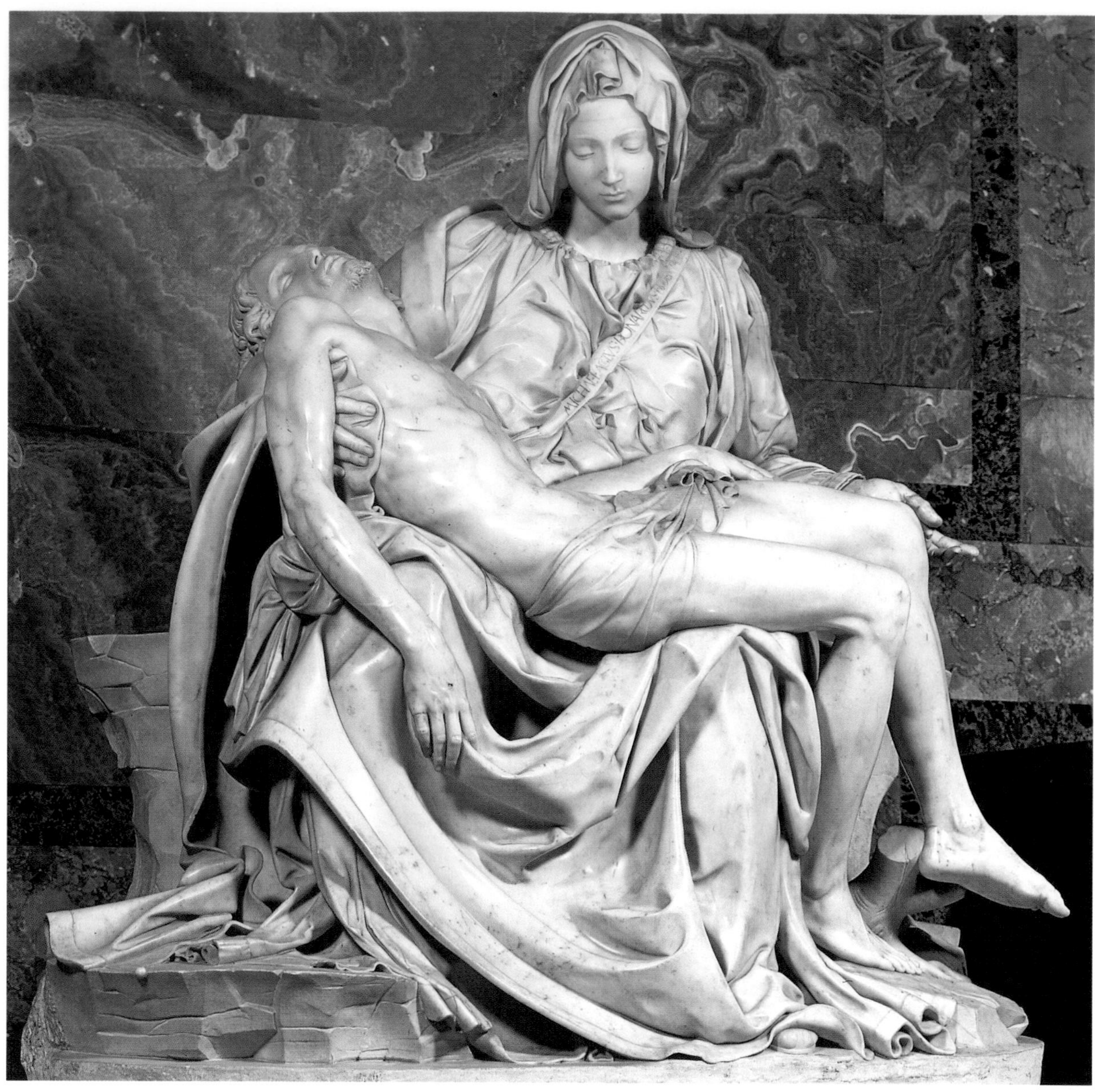

13-11. Michelangelo. *Pietà*. c. 1500. Marble, height 68½" (173.9 cm). St. Peter's, Rome

century. It is indebted to Jacopo della Quercia for the figure of the Virgin and to Andrea Verrocchio for the nobility of the faces and the ornamental treatment of the drapery. The cloak flowing like a river over the Madonna enables Michelangelo to resolve her physically and visually awkward relationship with her dead son. This problem seems to have been of little interest to the German Gothic artist, who instead used it to heighten the expressiveness of the figures. Michelangelo succeeded in his ambition to carve "the most beautiful work of marble in Rome, one that no living artist could better." To Vasari it "was a revelation of all the potentialities and force of the art of sculpture."

DAVID. The unique qualities of Michelangelo's art do not emerge fully until his *David* (fig. 13-12), the earliest monumental statue of the High Renaissance. Commissioned in 1501 as the symbol of the Florentine republic (see fig. 11-39), the huge figure was designed to be placed high above the ground, on one of the buttresses of Florence Cathedral. However, a committee of civic leaders and artists decided instead to put it in front of the Palazzo Vecchio.

We can well understand the decision. Because the head of Goliath has been omitted, Michelangelo's *David* looks challenging. He is not a victorious hero but the champion of a just cause. To Michelangelo, he embodied Fortitude—as did the "Herakles" on Nicola Pisano's pulpit (see fig. 11-59), which the *David* resembles in colossal form. Here, however, the figure has a civic rather than a moral significance. Vibrant with pent-up energy, he faces the world like Donatello's *St. George* (see fig. 12-3), although his nudity links him to the older master's bronze *David* as well. The style of the sculpture proclaims an ideal very different from the wiry slenderness of Donatello's youths. Michelangelo had just spent several years in Rome, where he had been deeply impressed with the emotion-charged, muscular bodies of Hellenistic sculp-

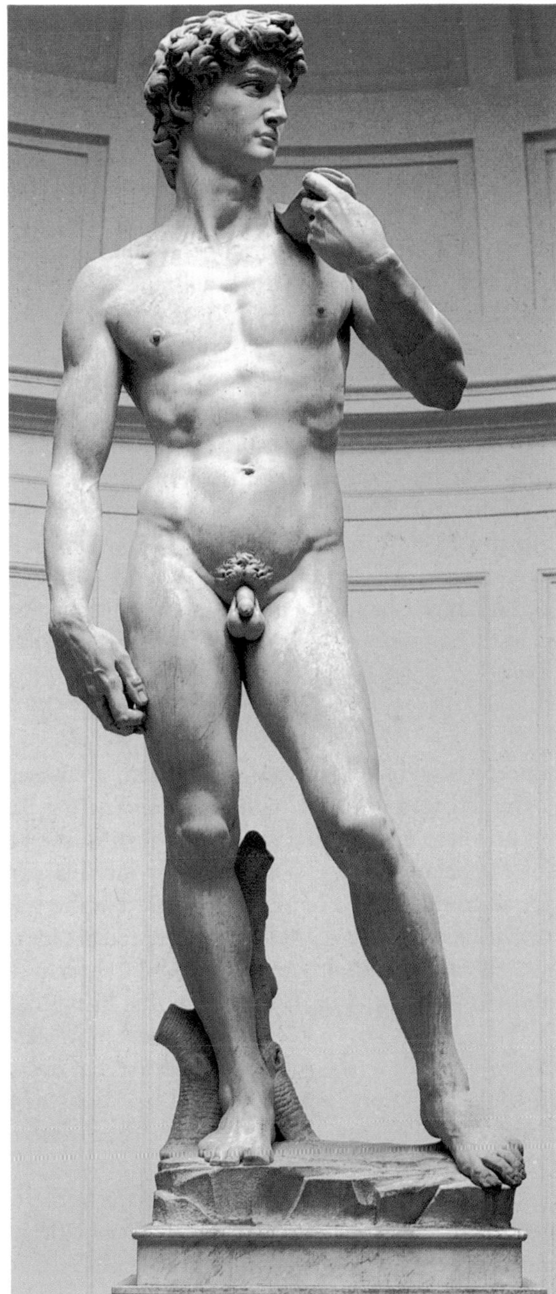

13-12. Michelangelo. *David.* 1501–4. Marble, height 13'5" (4.08 m). Galleria dell'Accademia, Florence

THE TOMB OF JULIUS II. This feature is seen again in the *Moses* (fig. 13-13) and the two *"Slaves"* (figs. 13-14 and 13-15) about ten years later. They were part of the ambitious sculptural program for the Tomb of Julius II, which would have been Michelangelo's greatest achievement if he had been able to carry it out as originally planned. The *Moses,* meant to be seen from below, has the awesome force called *terribilità*—a concept akin to the sublime. His pose, both watchful and meditative, suggests a man capable of wise leadership as well as towering wrath. We must not interpret the statue as showing a specific action or moment in time, though it is clear that Moses has just received the Ten Commandments. The position of the hands denotes awe in the presence of the Lord. The horns, a traditional attribute based on a mistranslation of the Hebrew word for "light" in the Vulgate (Latin Bible) that is also seen in Sluter's *Moses Well* (see fig. 11-56), signify the divine favor bestowed on Moses, whose face shone after he came down from Mount Sinai (Exodus 34). Whatever symbolic meaning the sculpture may have had was soon lost as Michelangelo reworked the plan of the tomb. (Originally *Moses* was to have been paired with a Saint Paul, who also "saw the light" of the Lord.)

The *"Slaves"* are more difficult to interpret. They seem to have belonged to a series representing the arts, now shackled by the death of their greatest patron. Later they came to signify the territories conquered by Julius II. In any event, Michelangelo has treat-

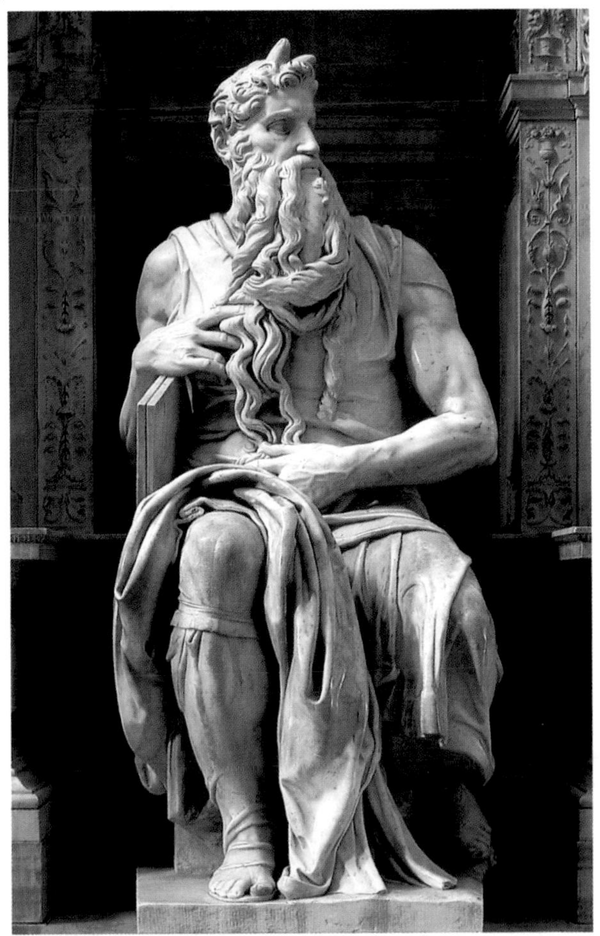

13-13. Michelangelo. *Moses.* c. 1513–15. Marble, height 7'8½" (2.35 m). S. Pietro in Vincoli, Rome

ture. Their heroic scale, their superhuman beauty and power, and the swelling volume of their forms became part of Michelangelo's own style and, through him, of Renaissance art in general.

Whereas his earlier work could sometimes be taken for ancient statues, in the *David* Michelangelo competes with antiquity on equal terms and replaces its authority with his own. This resolute individualism is partly indebted to Leonardo da Vinci, who had recently returned to Florence. (As with all of Michelangelo's great peers, they soon became rivals.) So is the expressive attitude of the figure, which conveys the "intention of man's soul." In Hellenistic works (compare fig. 5-74) the body "acts out" the spirit's agony, while the *David,* at once calm and tense, shows the action-in-repose that is so characteristic of Michelangelo.

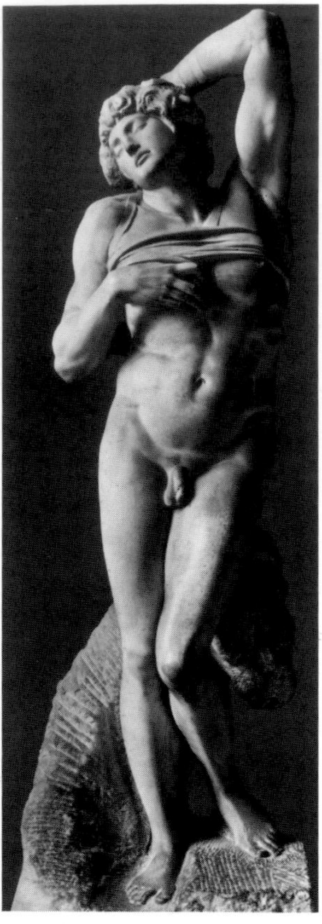

13-14. Michelangelo.
"The Dying Slave." 1513–16.
Marble, height 7'6" (2.28 m).
Musée du Louvre, Paris

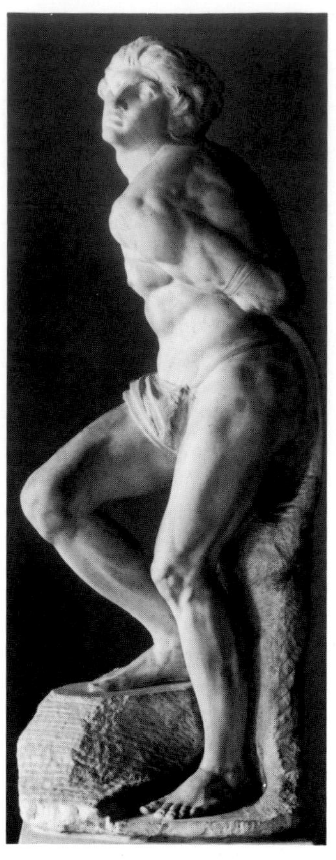

13-15. Michelangelo.
"The Rebellious Slave." 1513–16.
Marble, height 7' (2.13 m).
Musée du Louvre, Paris

ed the two figures as a contrasting pair. *"The Dying Slave"* (fig. 13-14) yields to his bonds, while *"The Rebellious Slave"* (fig. 13-15) struggles to free himself. In them we may see the influence of *The Laocoön Group* (see fig. 5-76), whose unearthing Michelangelo witnessed in 1506. Perhaps their meaning mattered less to him than their expressive content, which evokes the Neo-Platonic image of the body as the earthly prison of the soul. They represent the spiritual state of humanity, with all its conflicts, as reflected in one of the artist's own verses:

> He cannot act who by himself is bound
> And of himself no one is freely loosed.

The unfinished *Awakening Prisoner* (fig. 13-16), from a later plan for the tomb, provides invaluable insights into Michelangelo's artistic personality and working methods. For him, the making of a work of art was both joyous and painful, full of surprises, and not mechanical in any way. It appears that he started the process of carving a statue by trying to visualize a figure in the block as it came to him from the quarry. (At times he may even have done so while picking out his material on the spot.) At first Michelangelo did not see the figure any more clearly than one can see an unborn child inside the womb. He may have believed that he could see "signs of life" within the marble—a knee or an elbow pressing against the surface. To get a firmer grip on this dimly felt image, he made numerous drawings, and sometimes small models in wax or clay, before he dared to assault the "marble prison" itself. For that, he knew, was the final contest between himself and his material. We know that he drew the main view on the front of the block. Once he started carving, every stroke of the chisel would commit him more and more to a specific conception of the figure hidden in the block. The marble would permit him to free the figure whole only if his guess as to its shape was correct. In this way, by a flow of impulses back and forth between the mind and the partly shaped material, the artist gradually defined more and more of the image, until at last all of it had been given visible form. Sometimes he did not guess well enough. The stone refused to give up some essential part of its prisoner, and he left the work unfinished. Michelangelo himself came to appreciate the expressive qualities of incomplete works. Although he abandoned *Awakening Prisoner* for other reasons, every gesture seems to record the struggle for liberation and embody his inspiration even more faithfully than the *"Slaves."*

THE SISTINE CEILING. Julius II interrupted Michelangelo's work on the tomb at an early stage. He decided to enlarge St. Peter's, at first, it seems, to house his tomb, an idea that was soon abandoned. When the project was turned over to Bramante (see page 436), Michelangelo left Rome in anger. Two years later,

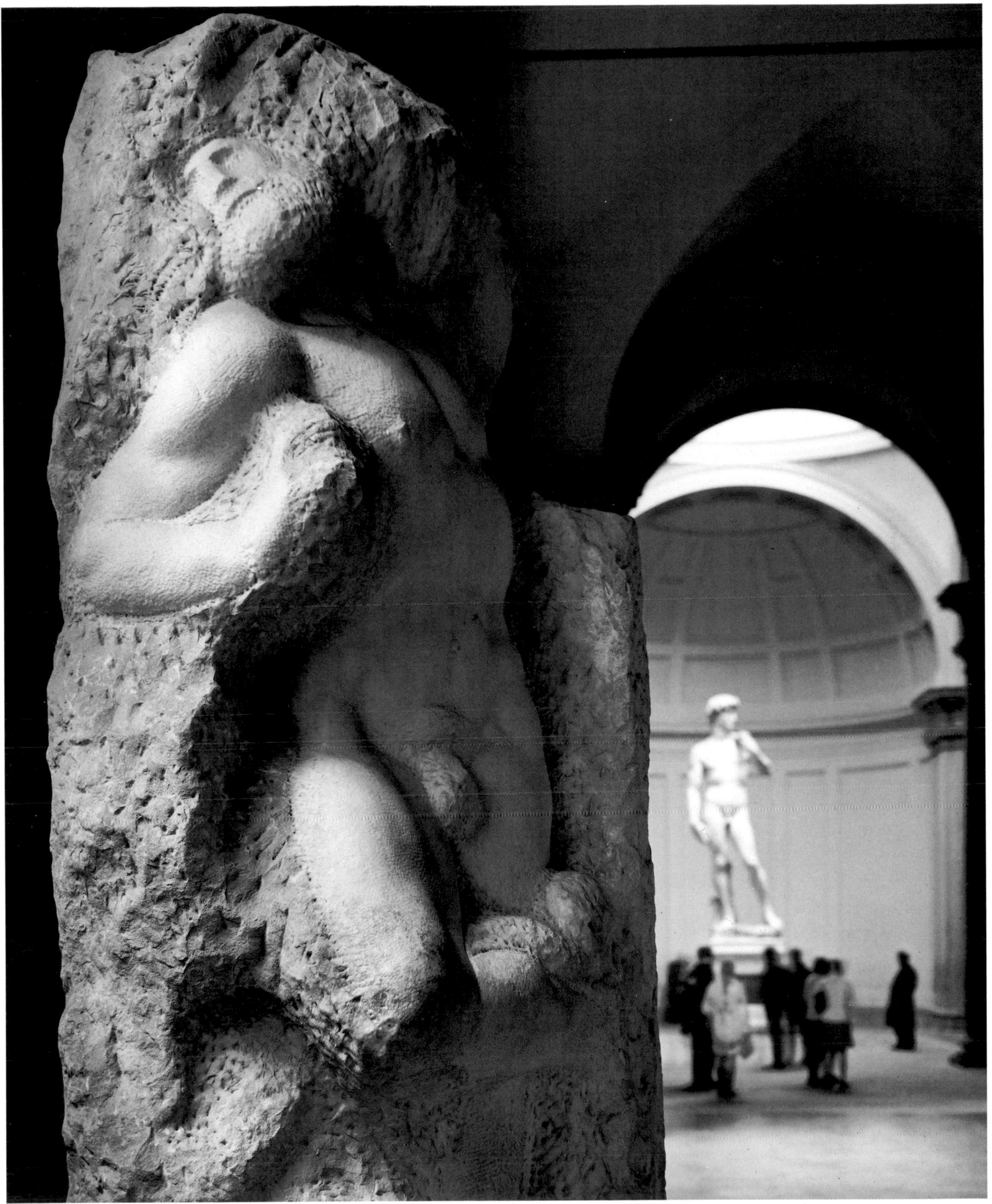

13-16. Michelangelo. *Awakening Prisoner*. c. 1525. Marble, height 8'11" (2.7 m). Galleria dell'Accademia, Florence the pope half-forced, half-coaxed him to return to paint frescoes on the ceiling of the Sistine Chapel in the Vatican (fig. 13-17). Driven by his desire to resume work on the tomb, Michelangelo finished the ceiling in four years, between 1508 and 1512. [See Primary Sources, no. 43, pages 613–15.] He produced a work of truly epochal importance. The ceiling is a huge organism with hundreds of figures distributed rhythmically within the painted architectural framework.

In the central area, subdivided by five pairs of girders, are nine scenes based on the Old Testament Book of Genesis, from the Creation of the World (at the far end of the chapel) to the Drunkenness of Noah. The theological scheme of these and other scenes, and the nude youths, medallions, prophets, and sibyls that accompany them, have not been fully explained. We know, however, that they link early history and the coming of Jesus. What greater theme could Michelangelo wish than the creation, destruction, and salvation of humanity? It is unclear how much responsibility he had for the program, but the subject matter of the ceiling fits his cast of mind so perfectly that his own desires cannot have conflicted strongly with those of his patron.

THEATER AND MUSIC DURING THE HIGH RENAISSANCE

Although the term applies specifically to art, the High Renaissance was intimately connected to literature, theater, and music. Indeed, these arts created the cultural climate that made the High Renaissance possible in the first place. The early sixteenth century ushered in the first great age of Italian literature since the time of Dante and Petrarch some 200 years earlier. It centered on the poet Ludovico Ariosto (1474–1533), whose masterpiece, *Orlando Furioso* (1532), used the story of the crusader knight Roland to glorify his patron, the d'Este family of Ferrara. As early as 1508, Ariosto had written the first comedy along classical lines in Italian: *The Chest,* which initiated the genre known as *commedia erudita* (learned or serious comedy). Even Niccolò Machiavelli (1469–1527), who is best known for his manual of power and courtly life, *The Prince* (published posthumously in 1532), wrote a comedy, *The Mandrake.* The first vernacular tragedy, *Sofonisba* (1515) by Giangiorgio Trissino (1478–1550), was written in the Greek style to combat the influence of Seneca, thus setting off a debate that was effectively won by partisans of Latin drama in 1541, when *Orbecche* by Giambattista Cinthio (1504–1573) became the first Italian tragedy actually to be produced.

The High Renaissance counterpart to Ariosto in music was the Fleming Josquin Des Prés (c. 1440–1521), who became the most celebrated composer of his time. Artistically he belonged to the same generation as Leonardo da Vinci, though he was even older. Despite his notorious artistic temperament, he was employed at one time or another by all the leading courts in Italy and France and enjoyed the patronage of no fewer than three popes. (He was present at the Vatican when Perugino and Botticelli were decorating the walls of the Sistine Chapel.) Josquin was regarded with much the same awe as Michelangelo came to be by his peers. The first true musical genius we know of, Josquin was a virtuoso equally at ease in secular and religious music. His work represented the perfect marriage of Flemish composition and Italian humanism, which, inspired by Greek accounts, sought unity between text and music. He thus found his ideal outlet in the song (*chanson*) and the motet, which made an entire realm of human action and feeling that lay outside the scope of the traditional Mass available to him. He cultivated a

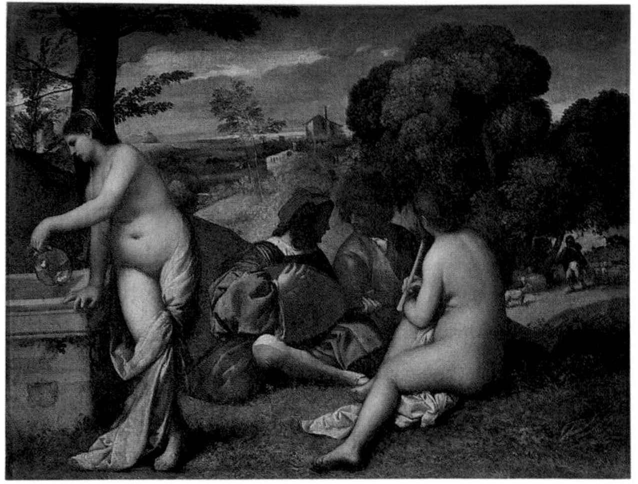

Titian. *Pastoral Concert.* c. 1509–10. Oil on canvas, 43¼ x 54⅜" (105 x 136.5 cm). Musée du Louvre, Paris

smooth, homogenous style that has aptly been compared to the art of Raphael as the embodiment of the classical ideal in its calm, balanced perfection. He was also important for beginning to lead music away from the system of modes used throughout the Middle Ages and Early Renaissance.

Josquin became famous throughout Europe, thanks not only to his travels but also to the invention of music publication using movable type by the Venetian Ottaviano Petrucci (1466–1539) in 1498, a development that proved as revolutionary as printing had been for books and printmaking. Petrucci enjoyed such success that during the 1520s and 1530s France, Germany, and the Netherlands emerged as rival centers of music publishing. The diffusion of music and ideas in print helped to elevate composers in humanist circles. Like artists, they now became "learned" and joined in debates over matters of theory with other intellectuals. Their status was further enhanced by the appearance of the first primers, which taught amateurs how to play instruments and set off a new wave of enthusiasm for music.

It is a sign of the growing importance of music that courts competed eagerly for the leading composers and musicians, who commanded high salaries. Moreover, the ideal prince or courtier was expected to cultivate some musical ability in addition to his other talents. That consummate courtier Leonardo da Vinci was himself an accomplished musician, as were Giorgione and Titian.

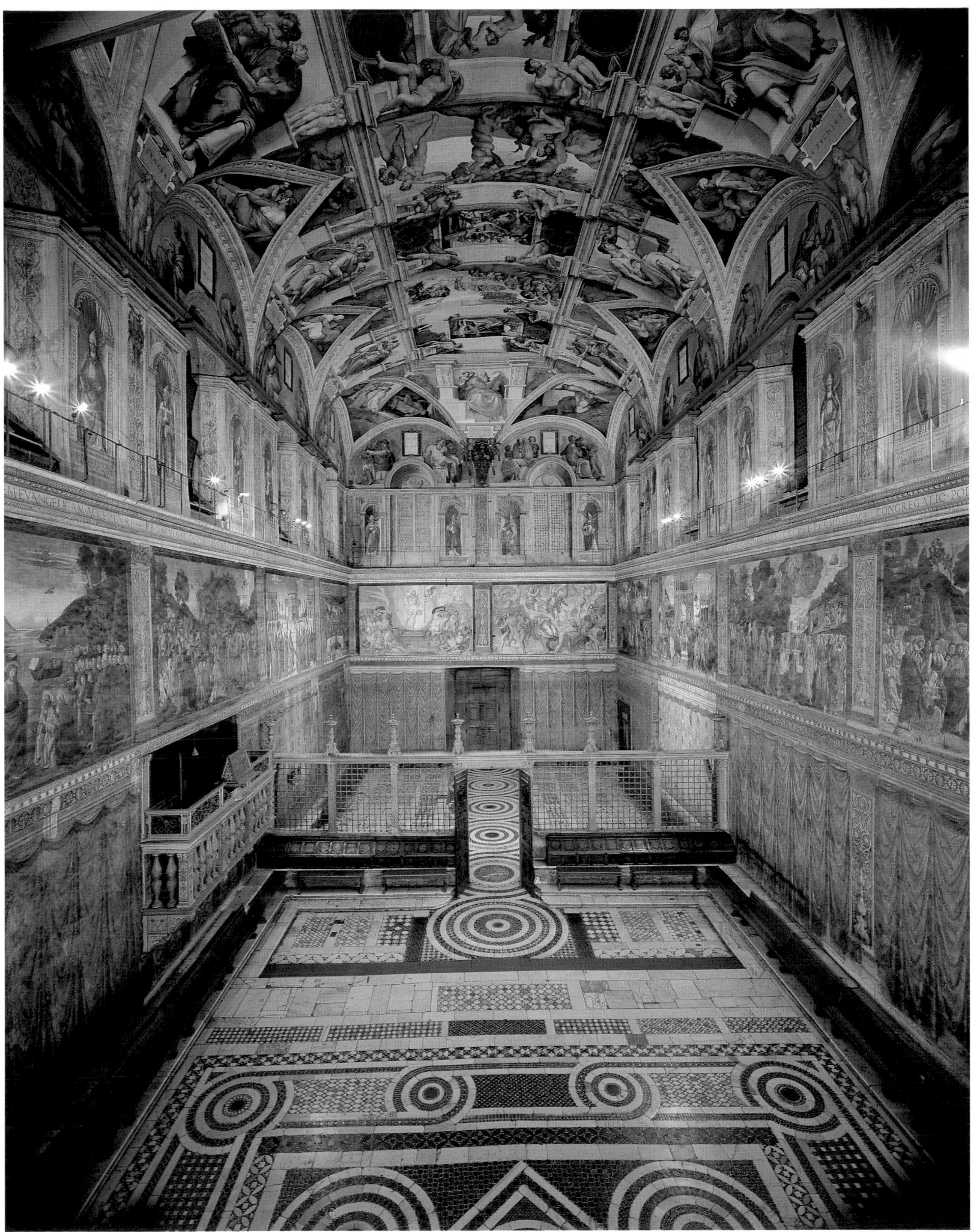

13-17. Interior of the Sistine Chapel showing Michelangelo's ceiling fresco. The Vatican, Rome

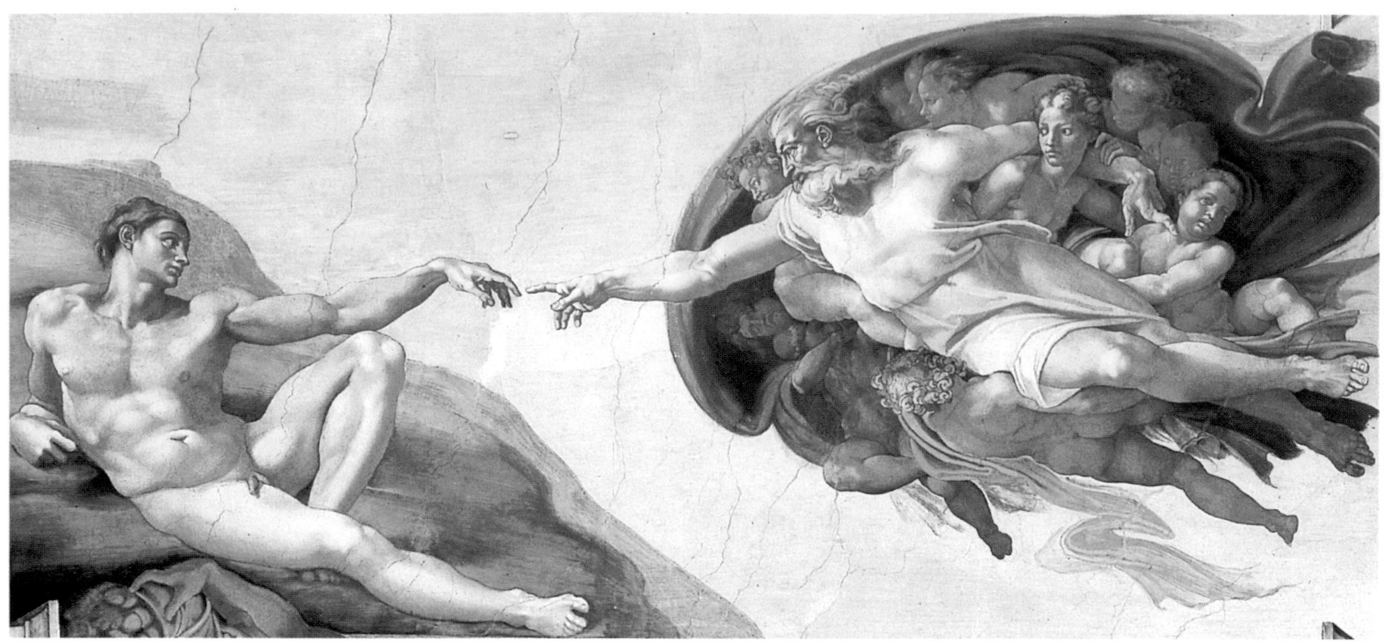

13-18. Michelangelo. *The Creation of Adam,* portion of the Sistine ceiling. 1508–12. Fresco

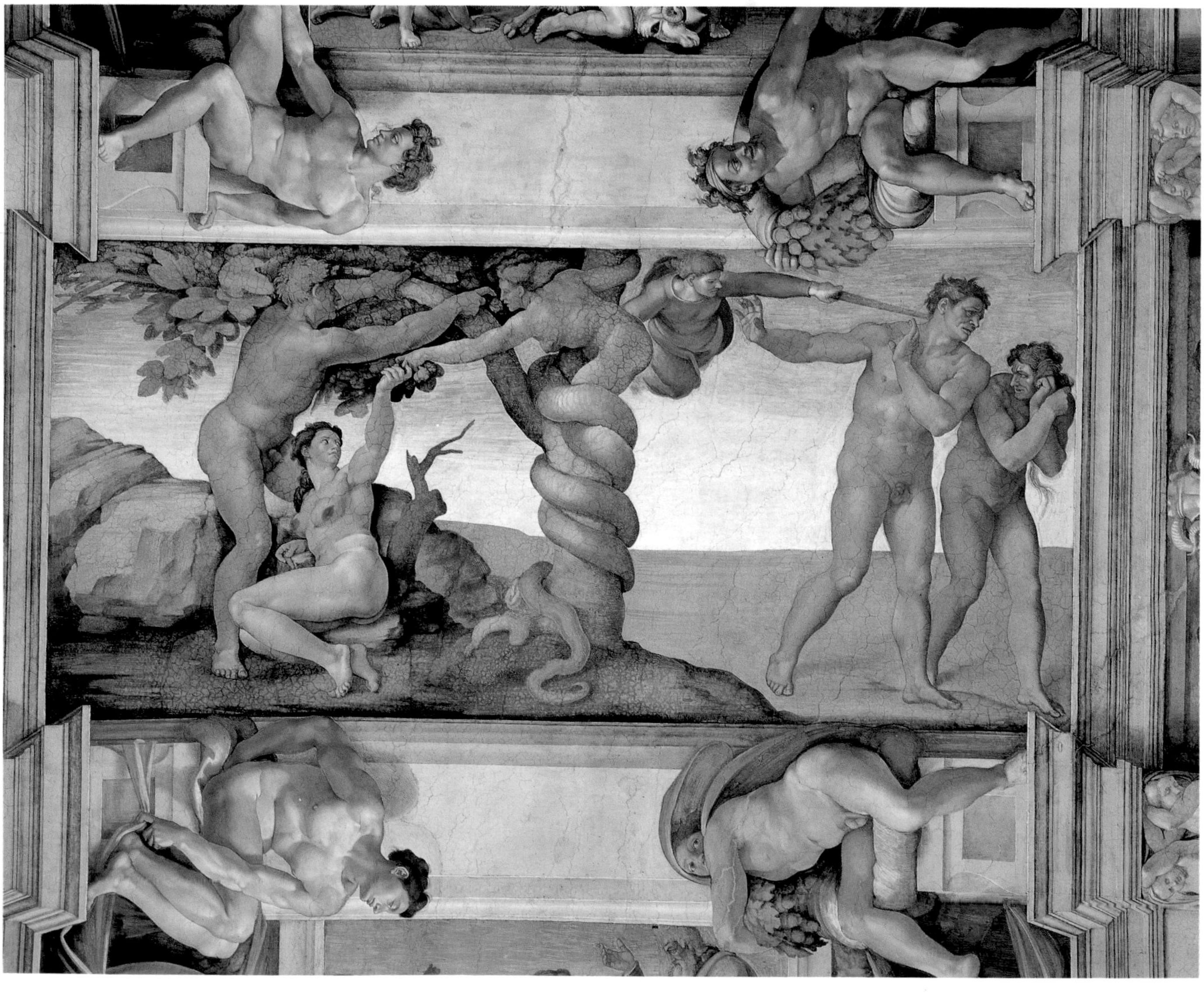

13-19. Michelangelo. *The Fall of Man* and *The Expulsion from the Garden of Eden,* portion of the Sistine ceiling. 1508–12. Fresco

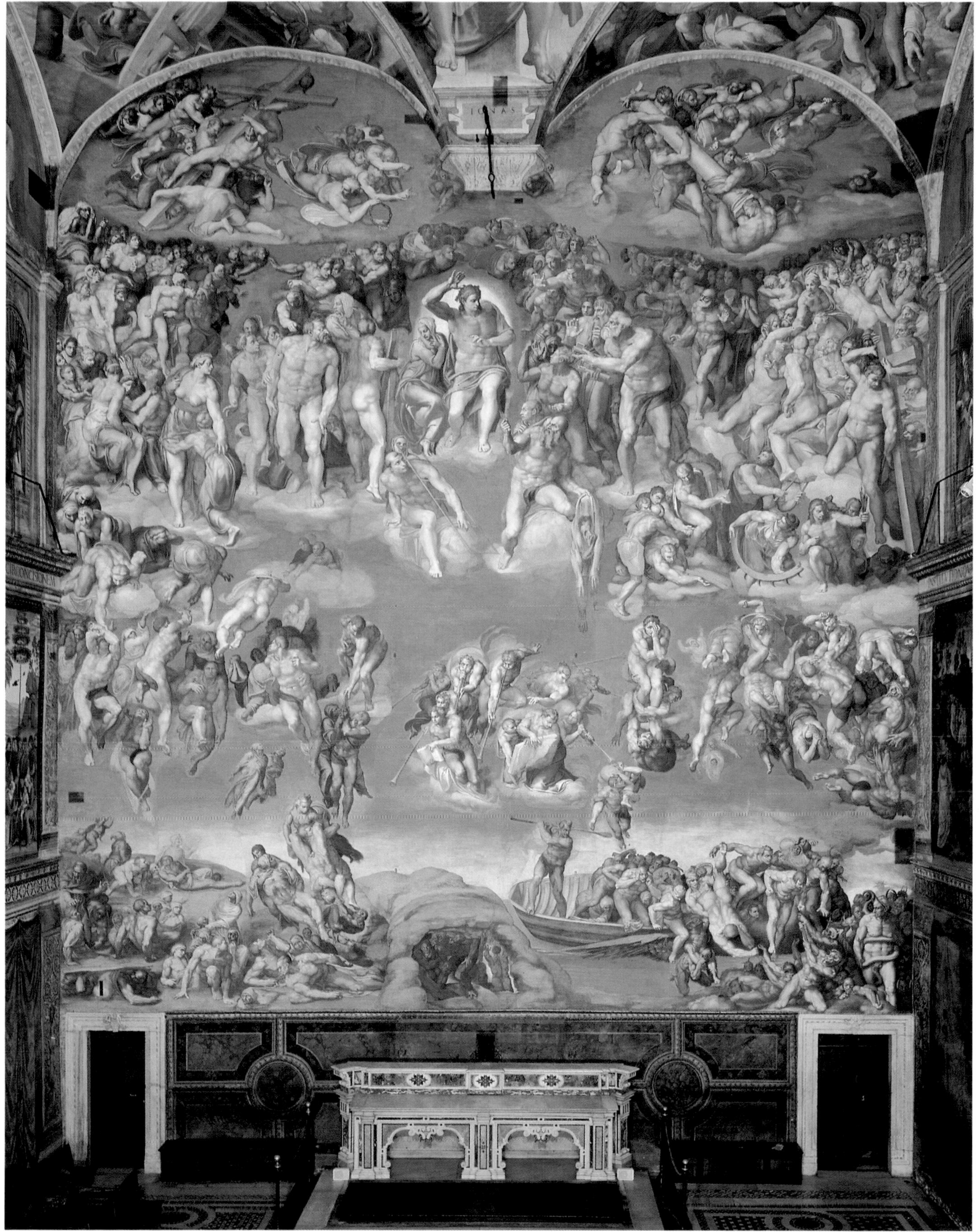

13-20. Michelangelo. *The Last Judgment.* 1534–41. Fresco. Sistine Chapel, the Vatican, Rome

A detailed survey of the ceiling would fill a book, and we shall have to be content with two of the four major scenes in the center portion. Of these, *The Creation of Adam* (fig. 13-18) must have stirred Michelangelo's imagination most deeply. It shows not the physical molding of Adam's body but the passage of the divine spark—the soul—and thus achieves a dramatic juxtaposition unrivaled by any other artist. Della Quercia had approached it in his relief panel (see fig. 12-11), which Michelangelo admired. But Michelangelo's design has a dynamism that contrasts the earthbound Adam, who has been likened to an awakening river-god (compare fig. 22-5), and the figure of God rushing through the sky. This relationship takes on even more meaning when we realize that Adam strains not only toward his Creator but toward Eve, whom he sees, yet unborn, in the shelter of the Lord's left arm.

Michelangelo has been regarded as a poor colorist, but the recent cleaning of the frescoes has revealed that this view is unjust. *The Fall of Man* and *The Expulsion from the Garden of Eden* (fig. 13-19) show the bold, intense hues that characterize the whole ceiling. The range of his palette is astonishing. Contrary to what had been thought, the heroic figures have none of the quality of painted sculpture. Full of life, they act out their epic roles in illusionistic "windows" that puncture the architectural setting. Michelangelo does not simply color the areas within the contours. Rather, he builds up his forms from broad and vigorous brushstrokes in the tradition of Giotto and Masaccio. In fact, *The Expulsion* is particularly close to Masaccio's (see fig. 12-27) in its intense drama. *The Fall,* by contrast, has an elegance that surely expresses not only beauty but a spiritual state as well.

Figure 13-19 also permits us to glimpse the nude youths that accompany the main sections of the ceiling. These wonderfully animated figures, which recur at regular intervals, play an important role in Michelangelo's design: they form a kind of chain linking the Genesis scenes. Yet their significance remains uncertain. Do they represent the world of pagan antiquity? Are they angels or images of human souls? They seem to be ideal beings, but ones who have not yet attained a state of grace and thus yearn for salvation. Whatever the answer, they clearly belong to the same category as the *"Slaves"* from the Tomb of Julius II, to which they are closely related visually and conceptually. Again the symbolic intent is overpowered by the expressiveness Michelangelo has poured into these figures.

THE LAST JUDGMENT. Michelangelo returned to the Sistine Chapel in 1534, more than 20 years after completing the ceiling fresco. At the time, the Western world was undergoing the spiritual and political crisis of the Reformation (see page 517). Michelangelo's religious beliefs had changed as well. We see the new mood with shocking directness as we turn from the radiant vitality of the ceiling fresco to the somber vision of *The Last Judgment* (fig. 13-20; shown here freshly cleaned), which illustrates Matthew 24:29–31.

How unlike the well-ordered, majestic treatment of Giotto (compare fig. 11-77), whose conception of Hell, in the lower right-hand corner, is still closely related to that on the west tympanum at Autun (see fig. 10-24). Michelangelo must have looked partly to Luca Signorelli's frescoes for Orvieto Cathedral (see fig. 12-58). In the Sistine Chapel, however, the agony has become essentially spiritual, as expressed through violent physical contortions within the turbulent atmosphere. The Blessed and Damned alike huddle together in tight clumps, pleading for mercy before a wrathful God. The only trace of classicism is the Apollo-like figure of the Lord. Straddling a cloud just below him is the apostle Bartholomew (fig. 13-21), holding a human skin to represent his martyrdom (he had been flayed). The face on that skin, however, is not the saint's but Michelangelo's own. In this grim self-portrait, so well hidden that it was noticed only in modern times, the artist has left a confession of guilt and unworthiness.

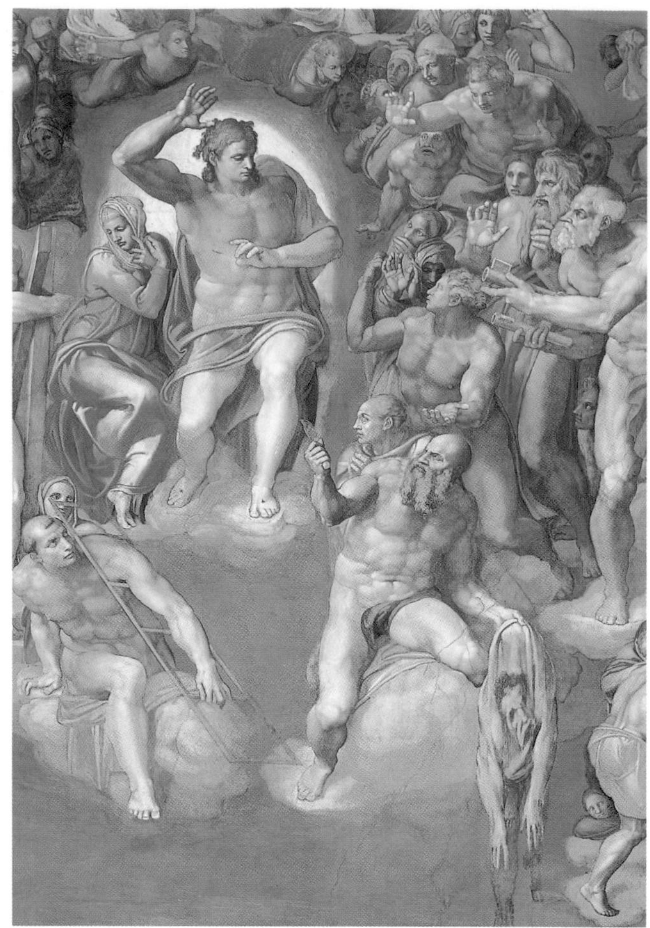

13-21. Michelangelo. *The Last Judgment* (detail, with self-portrait)

THE MEDICI CHAPEL. The time between the Sistine ceiling and *The Last Judgment* coincides with the papacies of Leo X (1513–21) and Clement VII (1523–34). Both were members of the Medici family and preferred to employ Michelangelo in Florence. His activities centered on the Medici church of S. Lorenzo. A century after Brunelleschi's revolutionary design for the sacristy (see pages 397–98), Leo X decided to build a matching structure, the New Sacristy. It was to house the tombs of Lorenzo the Magnificent, Lorenzo's brother Giuliano, and two younger members of the family, also named Lorenzo and Giuliano (see fig. 12-14). These tombs are nearly mirror images of each other. Michelangelo worked on this project for 14 years. He managed to complete the architecture and two of the tombs, those for the lesser Lorenzo and Giuliano (fig. 13-22). The New Sacristy was thus conceived

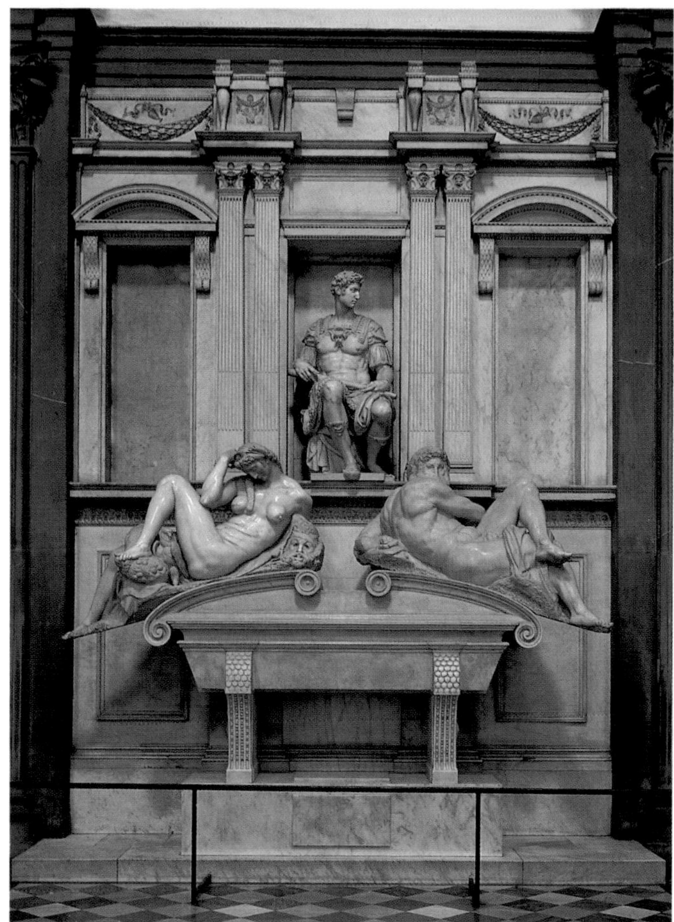

13-22. Michelangelo. Tomb of Giuliano de' Medici. 1524–34. Marble, height of central figure 71" (180.5 cm). New Sacristy, S. Lorenzo, Florence

as an architectural-sculptural ensemble. It is the only one of the artist's works in which the statues remain in the setting intended for them, although their exact placement is problematic.

Michelangelo's plans for the Medici tombs underwent many changes while the work was under way. Other figures and reliefs were designed, but never executed. The present state of the monuments can hardly be the final solution, but the dynamic process of design was halted when the artist left permanently for Rome in 1534.

The tomb of Giuliano remains a imposing visual unit, although the niche is too narrow and shallow to accommodate the seated figure comfortably. The triangle of statues is held in place by a network of verticals and horizontals whose slender, sharp-edged forms heighten the roundness and weight of the sculpture. The design still shows some kinship with such Early Renaissance tombs as that of Leonardo Bruni (see fig. 12-48), but the differences are more important. There is no inscription, and the effigy has been replaced by two allegorical figures—*Day* on the right and *Night* on the left. What is the meaning of this group? Some lines penned on one of Michelangelo's drawings suggest an answer. "Day and Night speak, and say: We with our swift course have brought the Duke Giuliano to death. . . . It is only just that the Duke takes revenge [for] he has taken the light from us; and with his closed eyes has locked ours shut, which no longer shine on earth."

Giuliano, the ideal image of the prince, is a younger and more pensive version of the *Moses.* The statue, in classical military garb, bears no resemblance to the deceased Medici. ("A thousand years from now, nobody will know what he looked like," Michelangelo is said to have remarked.) Originally the base of each tomb was to have included a pair of river-gods. The reclining figures, themselves derived from ancient river-gods (compare fig. 22-5), contrast in mood like the *"Slaves."* They embody action-in-repose more dramatically than any other works by Michelangelo. In the brooding menace of *Day,* whose face was left deliberately unfinished, and in the disturbed slumber of *Night,* the dualism of body and soul is expressed with unforgettable grandeur.

THE LAURENTIAN LIBRARY. The Tomb of Giuliano de' Medici is squeezed uncomfortably into an architectural framework that takes considerable liberties with classicism. The New Sacristy inspired Vasari to write that "all artists are under a great and permanent obligation to Michelangelo, seeing that he broke the bonds and chains that had previously confined them to the creation of traditional forms." However, his full powers as a creator of new architectural forms are displayed for the first time in the vestibule (fig. 13-23) to the Laurentian Library, adjoining S. Lorenzo. This library was built at the same time as the New Sacristy to house, for the public, the huge collection of books and manuscripts belonging to the Medici family.

By the standards of the 1520s, based on the classical ideal of Bramante, everything in the vestibule is wrong. The pediment above the door is broken. The pilasters of the niches taper down-

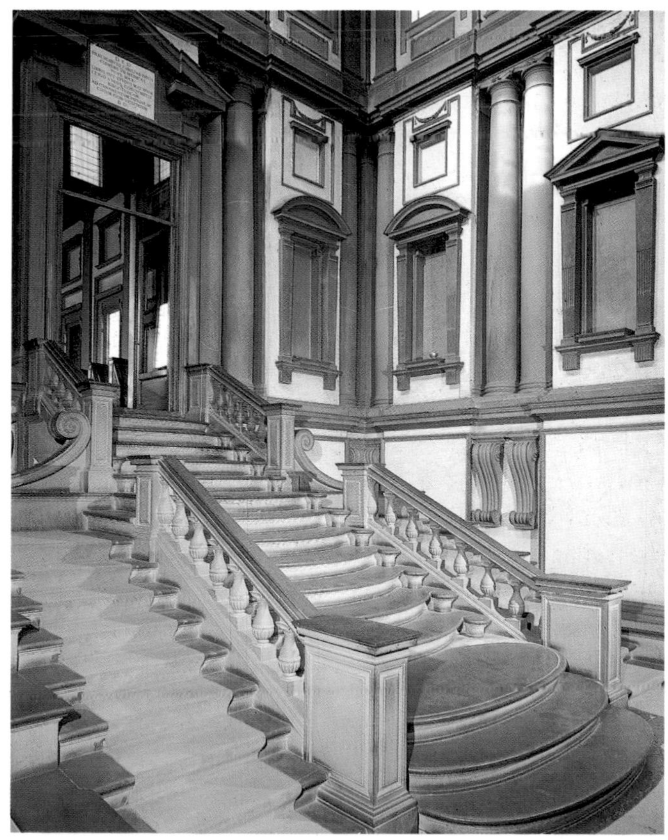

13-23. Michelangelo. Vestibule of the Laurentian Library, Florence. Begun 1524; stairway designed 1558–59

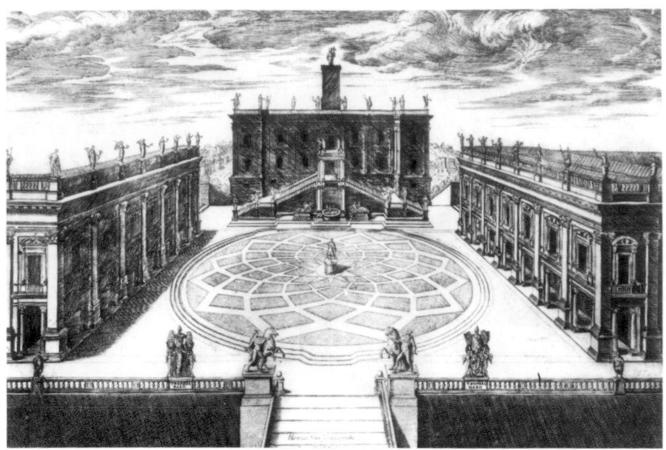

13-24. Michelangelo. The Campidoglio (engraving by Étienne Dupérac, 1569)

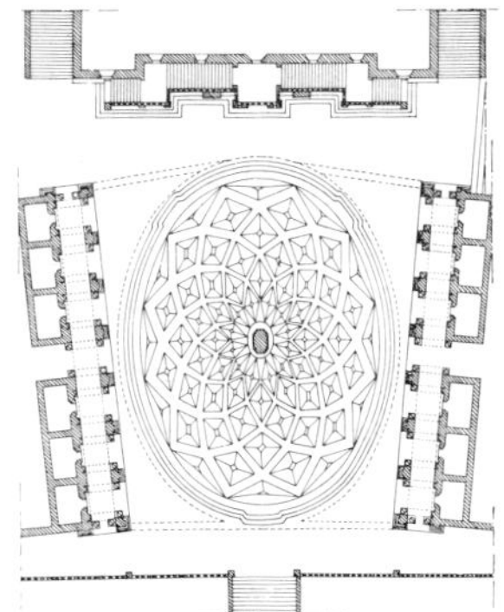

13-25. Plan of the Campidoglio, Rome

ward, and the columns belong to no recognizable order. The scroll brackets sustain nothing. Most paradoxical of all are the recessed columns. Although logical in structural terms—the columns support piers, which in turn support the roof beams—this feature flies in the face of convention. In the classical post-and-lintel system the columns (or pilasters) and entablature must project from the wall in order to stress their separate identities. The system could be reduced to a linear pattern (as in the Palazzo Rucellai; fig. 12-37), but no one before Michelangelo had dared to defy it by incorporating columns into the wall.

The purpose of these innovations is expressive rather than functional. The walls push inward between the columns to make the vestibule a kind of "compression chamber" where the viewer feels an almost physical stress. Our unease is heightened by the blank stare of the empty niches and by the nightmarish stairway, whose solution came to Michelangelo in a dream many years later. The steps, built from his design by Bartolommeo Ammanati (see pages 479–80), flow downward and outward so relentlessly that we wonder if we dare brave the current by mounting them.

THE CAMPIDOGLIO. During the last 30 years of Michelangelo's life, his main pursuit was architecture. In 1537–39, he received the most ambitious commission of his career: to reshape the Campidoglio, the top of Rome's Capitoline Hill, into a piazza with a monumental frame worthy of the site, which once had been the symbolic center of ancient Rome. At last he could plan on a grand scale, and he took full advantage of the opportunity. Although not completed until long after his death, the project was carried out essentially as he had designed it. The Campidoglio remains the most imposing civic center ever built, and it has served

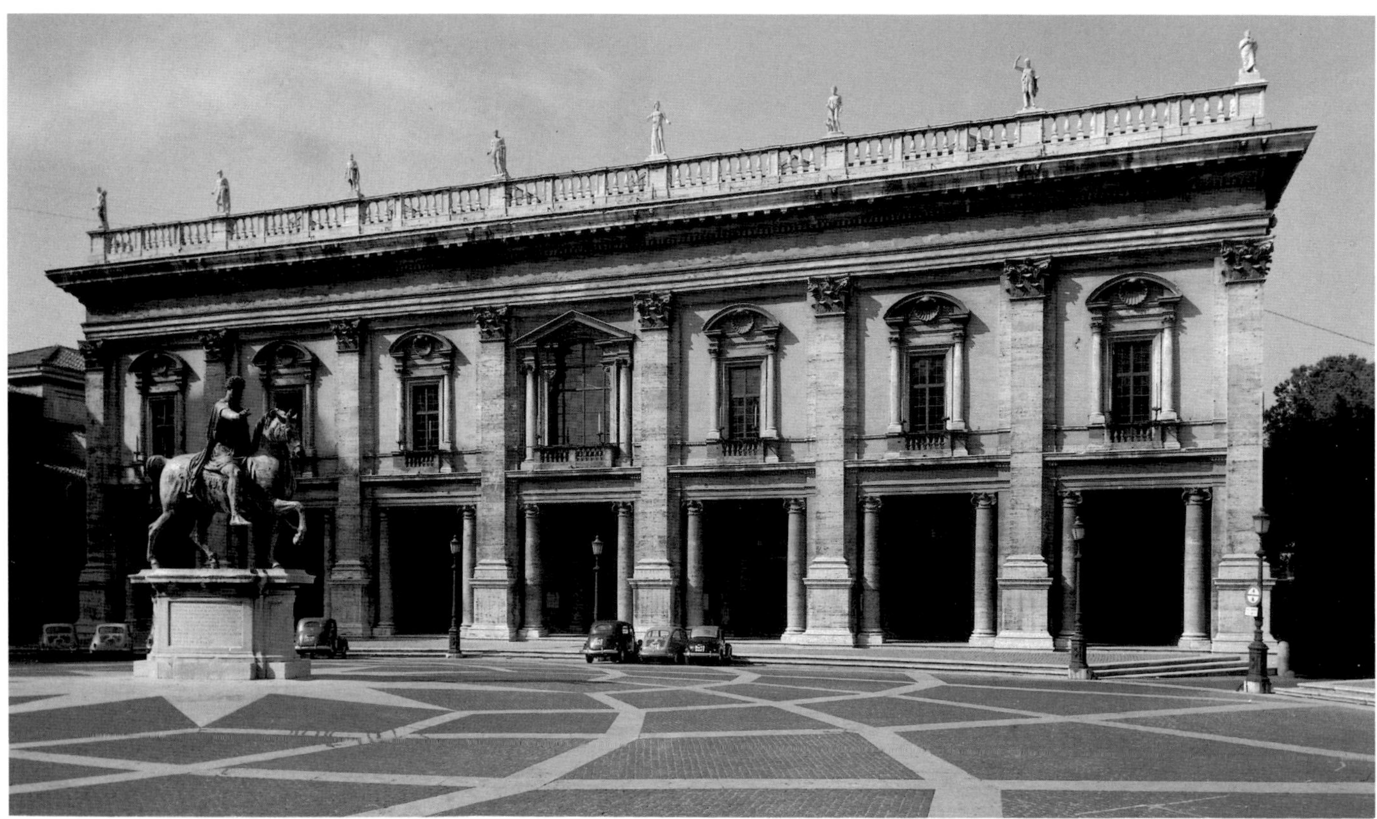

13-26. Michelangelo. Palazzo dei Conservatori, Campidoglio, Rome. Designed c. 1545

as a model for countless others. Pope Paul III transferred the equestrian monument of Marcus Aurelius (see fig. 7-40) to the Campidoglio, and Michelangelo designed its base. The statue became the focal point of his entire scheme, placed at the top of a gently rising oval mound that serves to integrate the space.

Three sides of the piazza are defined by palace facades. After ascending the flight of steps on the fourth side visitors thus find themselves in a huge "outdoor room." The effect cannot be seen in photographs. Even the best view, an engraving based on Michelangelo's design (fig. 13-24), conveys it imperfectly. The print shows the symmetry of the scheme and the sense of progression along the main axis toward the Senators' Palace. However, it distorts the shape of the piazza, which is not a rectangle but a trapezoid (fig. 13-25). This peculiarity was dictated by the shape of the existing site. The Senators' Palace and the Conservators' Palace on the right were older buildings that had to be preserved behind new exteriors, and they were placed at an angle of 80 instead of 90 degrees. But Michelangelo turned this problem into an asset. By adding a third structure that complements the Conservators' Palace in style and placement, he makes the Senators' Palace look larger than it is, so that it dramatically dominates the piazza.

The whole conception has the effect of a stage set: in the engraving, the "New Palace" on the left is only a show front with nothing behind it. Yet this facade and its twin are not shallow screens but three-dimensional structures (fig. 13-26). They combine voids and solids, horizontals and verticals in a way not found in any piece of architecture since Roman antiquity (compare fig. 7-23). They also share a striking feature: an open portico that links the piazza and facades, just as a courtyard is related to the arcades of a cloister.

The columns and stone beams of the porticoes are contained within a colossal order of pilasters that supports a heavy cornice topped by a balustrade. We have seen these elements on the facades of the Pazzi Chapel by Brunelleschi and Alberti's S. Andrea, and in the Tempietto of Bramante (see figs. 12-15, 12-40, and 13-7). But it was Michelangelo who welded them into a coherent system. For the Senators' Palace he used the colossal order and balustrade above a tall basement, which emphasizes the massiveness of the building. The single entrance at the top of the double-ramped stairway (see fig. 13-24) seems to gather all the spatial forces set in motion by the oval mound and the divergent flanks. It thus provides a dramatic climax for the visitor crossing the piazza.

ST. PETER'S. With the Campidoglio, the colossal order became firmly established. Michelangelo used it again on the exterior of St. Peter's (fig. 13-27). He took over the design of the church in 1546 upon the death of the previous architect, Antonio da Sangallo the Younger (the nephew of his friend Giuliano da Sangallo, but a rival nonetheless), whose work he completely recast. The system of the Conservators' Palace, with windows instead of open loggias and an attic instead of the balustrade, could be adapted to the jagged contour of the plan. Unlike Bramante's many-layered elevation (see fig. 13-10), the colossal order emphasized the compact body of the structure, thus setting off the dome more dramatically. The same desire for compactness and organic unity led

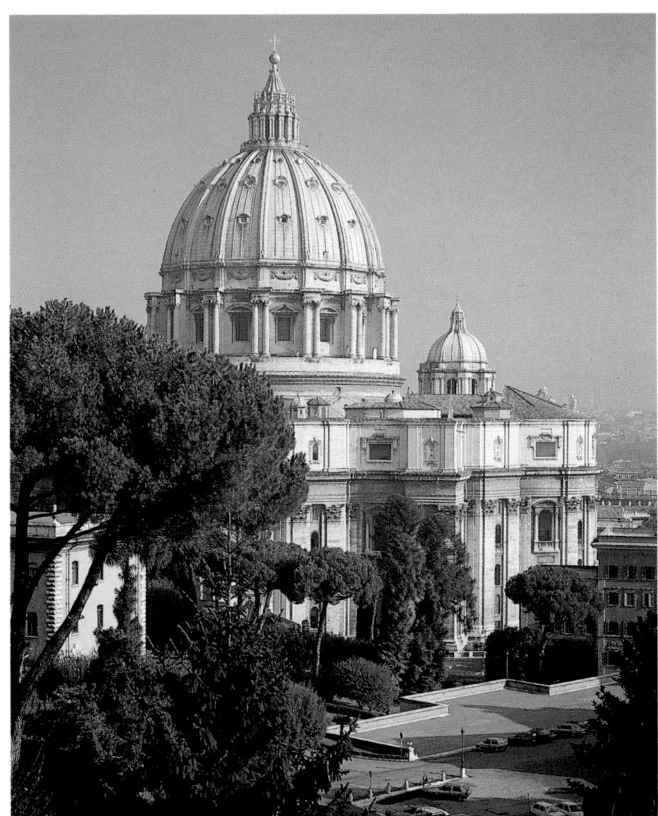

13-27. Michelangelo. St. Peter's, Rome, seen from the west. 1546–64 (dome completed by Giacomo della Porta, 1590)

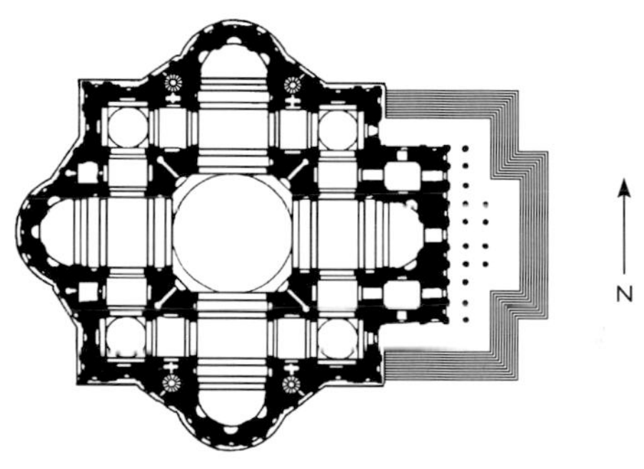

13-28. Michelangelo. Plan for St. Peter's

Michelangelo to simplify the interior, without changing its centralized character (fig. 13-28). He brought the complex spatial sequences of Bramante's plan (see fig. 13-8) into one cross-and-square. He further defined its main axis by modifying the exterior of the eastern apse and projecting a portico for it. This part of his design was never carried out. The dome, however, reflects his ideas in every important respect, although it was largely built after his death and has a steeper pitch.

Bramante had planned his dome as a stepped hemisphere above a narrow drum, which would have seemed to press down on the church. Michelangelo's plan, in contrast, has a powerful thrust that draws energy upward from the main body of the structure. This effect is created by the high drum, the strongly projecting buttresses accented by double columns, the ribs, the raised curve of the cupola, and the tall lantern. Michelangelo borrowed not only the double-shell construction but also the Gothic profile from the Florence Cathedral dome (see fig. 11-35), yet the effect is very different. The smooth planes of Brunelleschi's dome give no hint of the internal stresses. Michelangelo, however, gives a sculptured shape to these forces and relates it to the rest of the building. The impulse of the paired colossal pilasters below is taken up by the double columns of the drum, continues in the ribs, and culminates in the lantern. The logic of this design is so persuasive that few domes built between 1600 and 1900 were not influenced by it.

Michelangelo's magnificent assurance in handling such projects as the Campidoglio and St. Peter's seems to belie his portrayal of himself as a limp skin in *The Last Judgment.* It is indeed difficult to reconcile these contrasting aspects of his personality. Perhaps toward the end of his life he found greater fulfillment in architecture than in shaping human bodies, for we have no finished sculpture from his hand after 1545, when he at last completed the Tomb of Julius II. He devoted much of his final two decades to poetry and drawings of a religious and Neo-Platonic sort that are highly personal in their content. The statues undertaken for his own purposes, including a *Pietà* intended for his own tomb that he mutilated and partly reworked, show him groping for new forms, as if his earlier work had become meaningless to him.

Raphael

Whereas Michelangelo exemplifies the solitary genius, Raphael of Urbino (Raffaello Sanzio, 1483–1520) belongs to the opposite type: the artist as a person of the world. As a result, the two were natural antagonists. The contrast between them was as clear to their contemporaries as it is to us. Although each had his defenders, they enjoyed equal fame. Thanks to Vasari, Michelangelo's chief partisan, as well as to the authors of historical novels and fictionalized biographies, Michelangelo still fascinates people. Today, Raphael is usually discussed only by historians of art, although his life was also the subject of a fanciful account. The younger artist's career seems too much a success story, his work too marked by effortless grace, to match the tragic heroism of Michelangelo. Raphael also seems to have been less of an innovator than Leonardo, Bramante, and Michelangelo, whose achievements were basic to his. Nevertheless, he is the central painter of the High Renaissance. Our conception of the entire style rests more on his work than on any other artist's.

The genius of Raphael was a talent for synthesis that enabled him to merge the qualities of Leonardo and Michelangelo. The result was an art that was at once lyric and dramatic, pictorially rich and sculpturally solid. This power is already present in the Madonnas he painted in Florence (1504–8) after his apprenticeship with Perugino. The meditative calm of *La Belle Jardinière* (fig. 13-29) still reflects the style of his teacher (compare fig. 12-57). However, the forms are ampler and enveloped in sfumato. The Virgin, grave and tender, makes us think of the *Mona Lisa,* but without her mystery. The idealization of form already shows the grace and perfection that are the hallmarks of Raphael's style. The enigmatic gestures in *The Virgin of the Rocks* (see fig. 13-2) are replaced by a gentle, rhythmic interplay. In place of the intricate grouping, we find a stable pyramid whose severity is relieved by Mary's billowing cape. Most striking is the beautiful landscape

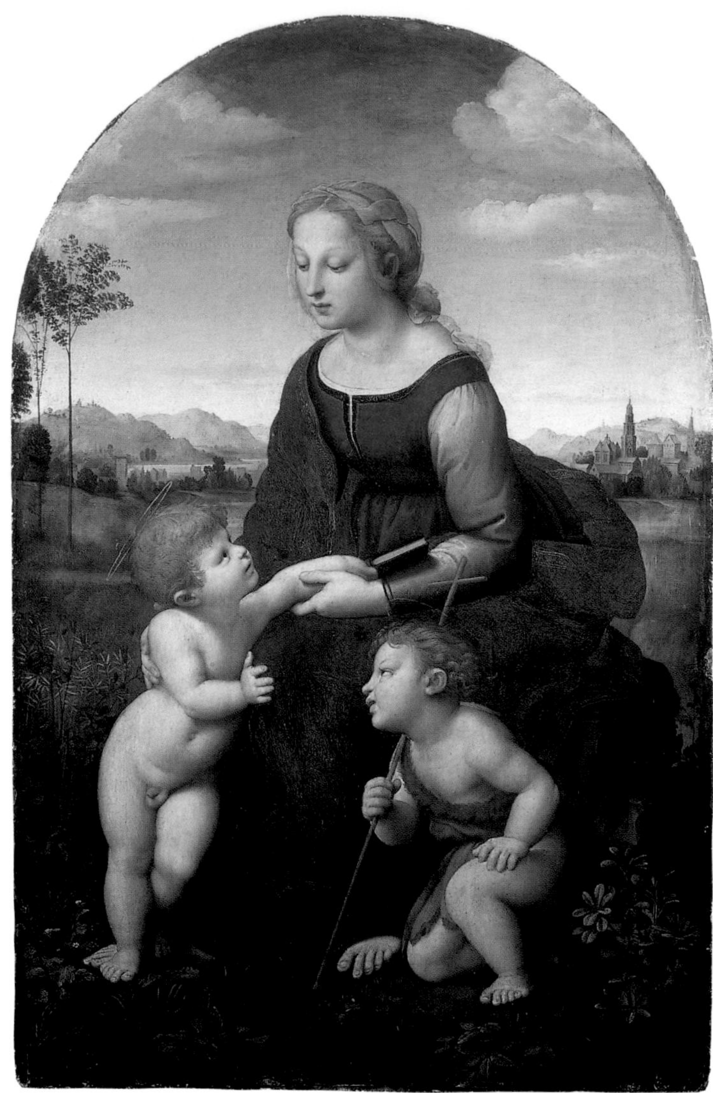

13-29. Raphael. *La Belle Jardinière.* 1507. Oil on panel, 48 x 31½" (122 x 80 cm). Musée du Louvre, Paris

which, unlike any by Leonardo, is carefully observed. The human forms, too, have a firmness that further attests to Raphael's devotion to nature.

THE STANZA DELLA SEGNATURA. One of the reasons *La Belle Jardinière* looks different from *The Virgin of the Rocks,* to which it is otherwise so clearly indebted, is Michelangelo's influence. Its full force can be felt only in Raphael's Roman works, however. In 1508, at the time Michelangelo began to paint the Sistine ceiling, Julius II summoned the younger artist from Florence at the suggestion of Bramante, who also came from Urbino. At first Raphael mined ideas he had developed somewhat earlier, but Rome transformed him as an artist, and he underwent an astonishing growth. This change is seen in the Stanza della Segnatura (Room of the Seal), the first in a series of rooms he was called on to decorate at the Vatican Palace. The stanza housed Julius II's personal library; only later did the tribunal of the seal (*segnatura*), presided over by Pope Paul III, meet there to dispense canon and civil law.

Raphael's cycle of frescoes on its walls and ceiling refers to the four domains of learning: theology, philosophy, law, and the arts.

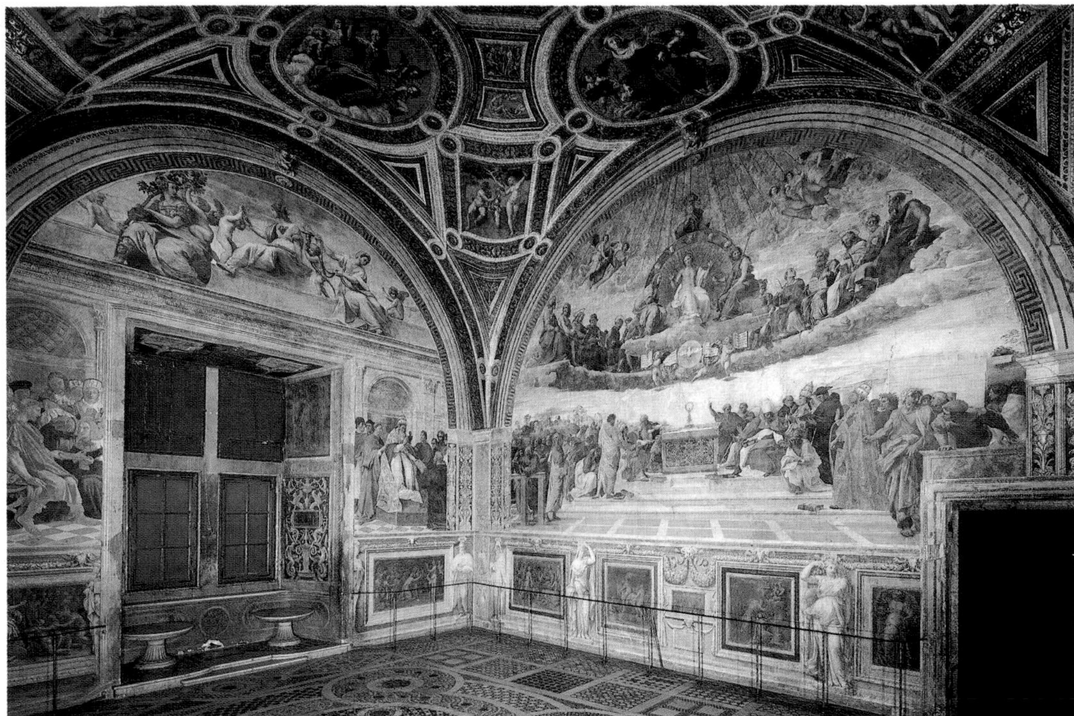

13-30. Stanza della Segnatura, with frescoes by Raphael. Vatican Palace, Rome

The program is derived in part from the Franciscan St. Bonaventure, who sought to reconcile reason and faith. It has roots as well in St. Thomas Aquinas, the Dominican chiefly responsible for reviving Aristotelian philosophy, who was influenced by Franciscan thought (see box pages 279–80). (Pope Julius II himself was a Franciscan, but there was also a major Dominican presence at the Vatican.) More generally, the Stanza represents a summation of High Renaissance humanism, for it attempts to unify all understanding into one grand scheme. Raphael probably had a team of scholars and theologians as advisers; yet the design is his alone.

To the right in our view (fig. 13-30) is *La Disputa,* or *Disputation over the Sacrament.* This was the first mural to be painted and the most important. Jesus sits enthroned in Heaven between the Virgin and St. John the Baptist. God the Father is behind him, with saints and prophets to either side, and the Holy Spirit hovering over the Eucharist below. Around the altar are church doctors, popes, artists, poets, and other personages, many of them unidentified. The title *La Disputa,* assigned in the seventeenth century, is misleading. The participants are not so much discussing as bearing witness to the Eucharist and its central place in the Catholic faith. The architectural space of the earthly realm is still treated in the geometric perspective of Perugino's *Delivery of the Keys* (see fig. 12-57), while the landscape makes subtle use of atmospheric perspective to emphasize the Host as the Light of the World. But it is the visionary space of the heavens that gives the mural a majesty in keeping with the sacred subject. The idea seems to have been inspired by the passage in Hebrews 12:1, "we also are encompassed about with so great a cloud of witnesses." It further embodies Bonaventure's quote from Ecclesiasticus (the apocryphal book Sirach), "In the highest heavens did I dwell, my throne on a pillar of cloud," as well as his definition of God, cited from Alan of Lille, "as an intelligible sphere whose center is everywhere and whose circumference is nowhere." Interestingly, the ratios of the circles are the musical intervals established by Pythagoras (see box page 125).

In the lunette over the door to the left are personifications of *The Three Legal Virtues*—Fortitude, Prudence, and Temperance. Beneath are *The Granting of Civil Law* (left) and *The Granting of Canon Law* (right), which attest to Julius II's activist view of the church militant. The opposite doorway depicts *Parnassus,* the sacred mountain of Apollo. The Muses appear in the company of the great poets from antiquity to the artist's own time. Humanists had regarded artistic inspiration as a means of revelation since the time of Dante and Petrarch. The painting reflects the papal court's dream of a Golden Age under Julius II, in which the Vatican Hill would become the new Parnassus. The message of the Stanza della Segnatura is that the philosophy of antiquity along with knowledge and the arts are forms of revelation that emanate from God. They lead to religious truth but are subordinate to it, just as civic law is subordinate to canon law. They are united by one of the most potent of all Christian concepts: *Logos* (the Word), which arises from the One and thus is absolute.

Of these frescoes, *The School of Athens* (fig. 13-31), facing *La Disputa,* has long been acknowledged as Raphael's masterpiece and the perfect embodiment of the classical spirit of the High Renaissance. Its subject is "the Athenian school of thought," a group of famous Greek philosophers gathered around Plato and Aristotle (fig. 13–32), each in a characteristic pose or activity. Raphael must have already looked at the Sistine ceiling, then nearing completion. He owes to Michelangelo the expressive energy, the physical power, and the dramatic grouping of his figures. Yet Raphael has not simply borrowed Michelangelo's gestures and poses. He has absorbed them into his own style and thus given them a different meaning. [See Primary Sources. no. 42, page 613.].

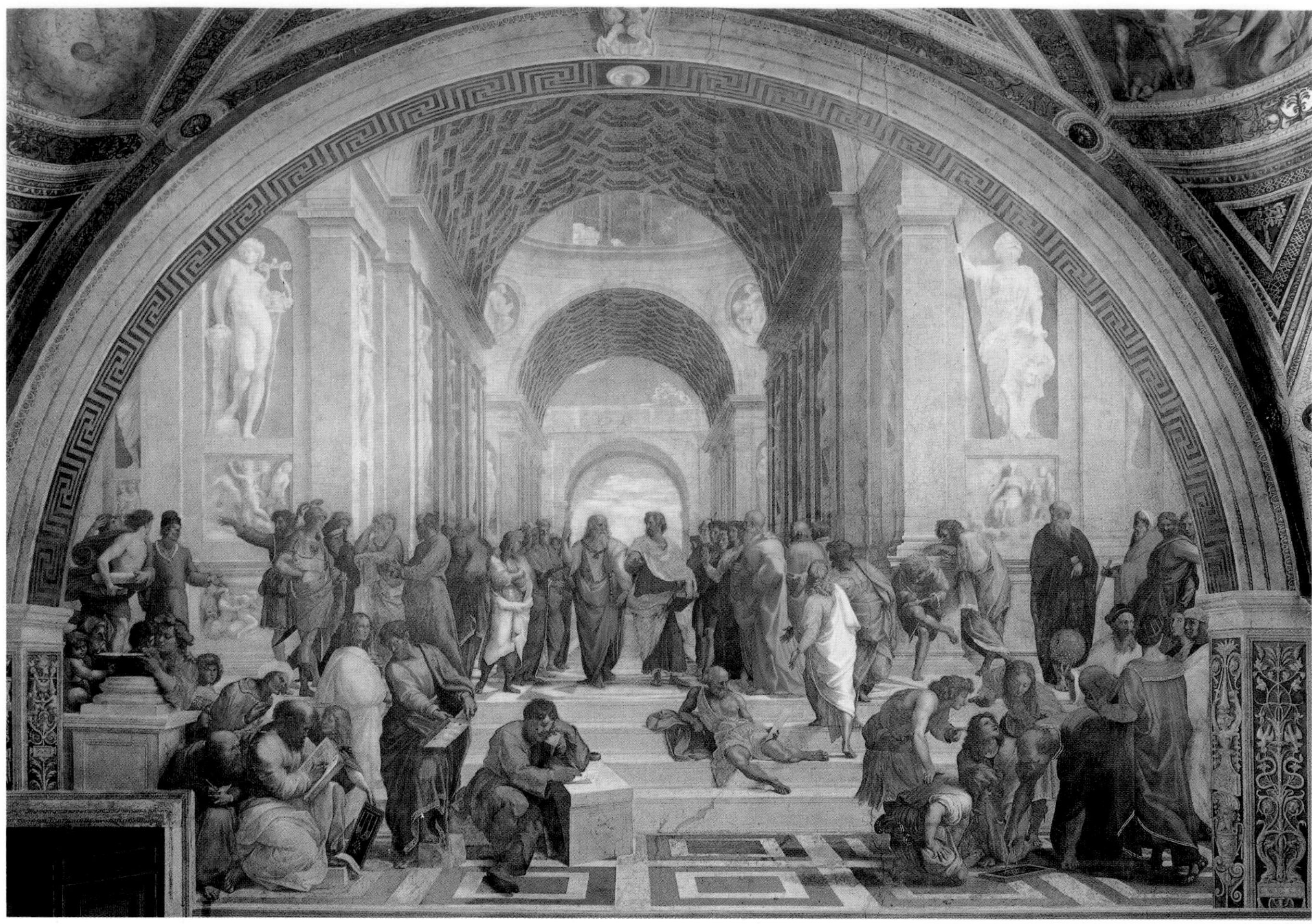

13-31. Raphael. *The School of Athens.* 1510–11. Fresco. Stanza della Segnatura, Vatican Palace, Rome

Body and spirit, action and emotion are now balanced harmoniously, and all members of this great assembly play their roles with magnificent, purposeful clarity. The total conception of *The School of Athens* suggests the spirit of Leonardo's *The Last Supper* (see fig. 13-3) rather than the Sistine ceiling. Raphael makes each philosopher reveal "the intention of his soul." He further distinguishes the relations among individuals and groups and links them in formal rhythm. The artist worked out the poses in a series of drawings, many of them from life. Also in the spirit of Leonardo is the symmetrical design, as well as the interdependence of the figures and their architectural setting. But Raphael's building plays a greater role in the composition than the hall of *The Last Supper.* With its lofty dome, barrel vault, and colossal statuary, it is classical in spirit, yet Christian in meaning. Inspired by Bramante, who, as Vasari informs us, helped him with the architecture, it seems like an advance view of the new St. Peter's. It bears a striking resemblance to drawings by the Northerner Maerten van Heemskerk in 1532–35 recording the great church under construction, from which it differs mainly in the decorative details. (Raphael developed into a skilled architect in his own right and succeeded Bramante at St. Peter's.) The dimensions and overall ground plan of the structure can be determined with considerable accuracy. This geometric precision, along with the spatial grandeur of the work as a whole, brings to a climax the tradition begun by Masaccio (see fig. 12-22). It was transmitted to Raphael by his teacher Perugino, who had inherited it from Piero della Francesca. What is new is the active role played by the architecture in creating narrative space. This innovation had a profound impact on the course of painting far beyond the sixteenth century.

The School of Athens has a complex program that reflects the most learned humanism of the day. We can give only the briefest account here. The building is in the shape of a simplified Greek cross to suggest the harmony of pagan philosophy and Christian theology. There are two huge niche sculptures. To the left is Apollo with a lyre, who reappears as the central figure in the mural *Parnassus.* To the right is Athena in her Roman guise as Minerva, goddess of wisdom and patron deity of the arts, who, in the words of the poet Dante, hastens the arrival of Apollo. The identity of most of the figures is not certain, but we can be sure that many incorporate portraits of Raphael's friends and patrons. At center stage Plato (whose face resembles Leonardo's) is holding his book of cosmology and numerology, *Timaeus,* which provided the basis for much of the Neo-Platonism that came to pervade Christianity. It presents a universe ruled by Divine Intelligence (*Nous*) instilled by the Demiurge, the giver of Forms, who takes over the chaos left by the Creator-God. Of particular importance is his theory of an ascending ladder of forms, which he called the Great Chain of Being. To Plato's proper left (the "sinister," or inferior side) his pupil Aristotle grasps a volume of his *Ethics,* which, like his science, is grounded in what is knowable in the material world.

Although Plato is his point of departure, he rejects his teacher's belief in Absolute Good arising from Forms as the Ideas of God. Instead, he takes a pragmatic approach based as much on psychology as philosophy. The tomes explain why one is pointing rhetorically to the heavens (the same gesture is found in *La Disputa*), the other to the earth. Thus stand reconciled the two most important Greek philosophers, whose approaches, although seemingly opposite, were deemed complementary by many Renaissance humanists. From the spatial construction of the two murals, it is clear that Raphael shows *The School of Athens* leading quite literally to *La Disputa:* if it were extended, the heavenly circle of saints and Old Testament figures in *La Disputa* would locate the ideal vantage point about 26 feet across the room, a little in front of *The School of Athens.*

To Plato's right (his "good" side) is his mentor Socrates, who was already viewed as a precursor of Jesus because he died for his beliefs (see fig. 21-2). He is addressing a group of disciples that includes the warrior Alcibiades. Standing before the steps are figures representing mathematics and physics (the lower branches of philosophy that are the gateway to higher knowledge). Raphael borrowed the features of Bramante for the head of Euclid, seen drawing or measuring two overlapping triangles with a pair of compasses in the foreground to the lower right. The diagram must be a reference to the star of David, who occupies an analogous position on the second level of *La Disputa.* These triangles, in turn, form the plan for the arrangement of the figures in the fresco.

On the other side is the bearded Pythagoras, for whom all things were numbers. He has his sets of numbers and harmonic ratios arranged on a pair of inverted tables that each achieve a total of the divine number ten. They refer in turn to the two tablets with the Ten Commandments held by Moses, who is found directly opposite in *La Disputa.* However, the format is also that of an inverted canonical table, thus giving a Christian meaning to a pagan concept. In addition to positing the One (a counterpart to god in Neo-Platonic thought), Pythagoras believed in a rational universe based on harmonious proportions, the foundation for much of Greek philosophy.

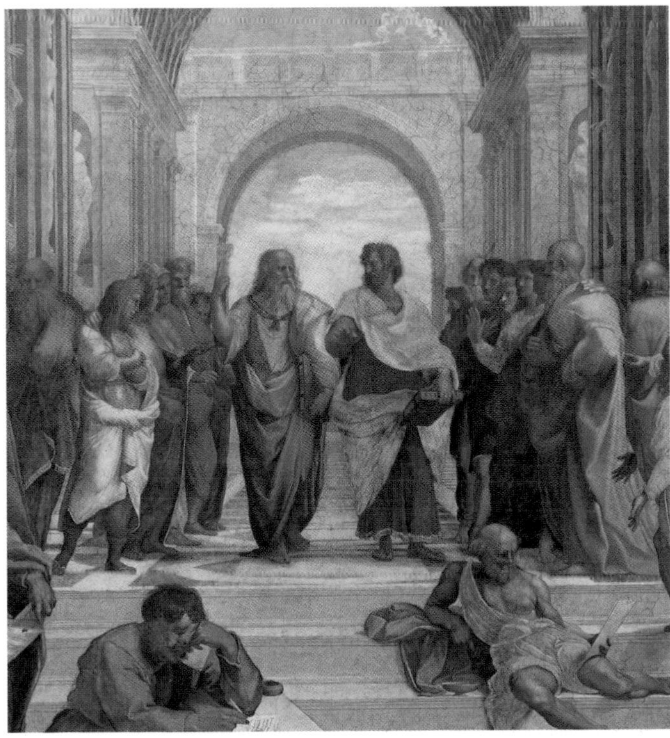

13-32. Raphael. *The School of Athens* (detail). 1510–11. Fresco. Stanza della Segnatura, Vatican Palace, Rome

This conviction was shared by the geographer, astronomer, and mathematician Ptolemy, seen from behind holding a terrestrial globe to the right of Euclid. He is shown crowned because he bore the same name as the Greek kings who ruled Egypt for 250 years after it was conquered by Alexander the Great (see page 61). (He is wrongly considered to be the astrologer Zoroaster by Vasari and by the seventeenth-century writer Pietro Bellori, who identified the relief above as Virtue seated beneath the Zodiac.) Ptolemy is linked to the scientist Aristotle and is paired in turn with a man holding a celestial globe. Modern scholars often identify the latter as Zoroaster, but more likely he is the Greek astronomer Hipparchus, whose catalog of the stars was the foundation of Ptolemy's astronomy. (He may also be the Roman geographer Strabo, who rejected Hipparchus' work). Next to them are two artists, perhaps Apelles and Protagoras. Vasari states that the man wearing a black hat is a self-portrait of Raphael. The other has generally been assumed to be Il Sodoma, the painter displaced by Raphael in the Stanza della Segnatura, but more likely he is Raphael's teacher, Perugino.

Despite their rivalry, Raphael added Michelangelo at the last minute as Heraclitus writing on the steps. Heraclitus, the first to posit *Logos* (later equated with Christ; see Primary Sources, no. 18, pages 365–66), was often paired with Diogenes the Cynic, shown lying at the feet of Plato and Aristotle, according to Vasari. Attempts to name other great philosophers who must have been included, such as the "hedonist" Epicurus and the Stoic Zeno, who were always paired, have proved too speculative to be of any real value, or are simply wrong. Be that as it may, the inclusion of so many artists among, as well as in the guise of, famous philosophers is testimony to the recently acquired—and hard-won—status of art as a learned profession.

GALATEA. Raphael rarely set so splendid a stage again. To create pictorial space, he relied increasingly on the movement of human figures rather than perspective vistas. In the *Galatea* of 1513 (fig. 13-33), the subject is again classical. The beautiful nymph Galatea, vainly pursued by the giant Polyphemus, belongs to Greek mythology. Like the verse by Angelo Poliziano that inspired it, the painting celebrates the lighthearted, sensuous aspect of antiquity, in contrast to the idealism of *The School of Athens.* While the latter presents an ideal view of the antique past, *Galatea* captures its pagan spirit as if it were a living force. The composition recalls Botticelli's *The Birth of Venus* (see fig. 12-54), a picture Raphael knew from his Florentine days, which shares a debt to Poliziano (see page 420). Yet their very resemblance emphasizes their profound differences. Raphael's full-bodied figures take on their dynamic spiral movement from the vigorous contrapposto of Galatea. In Botticelli's picture, the movement is not generated by the figures but imposed on them by the decorative, linear design, so that it remains on the surface of the canvas.

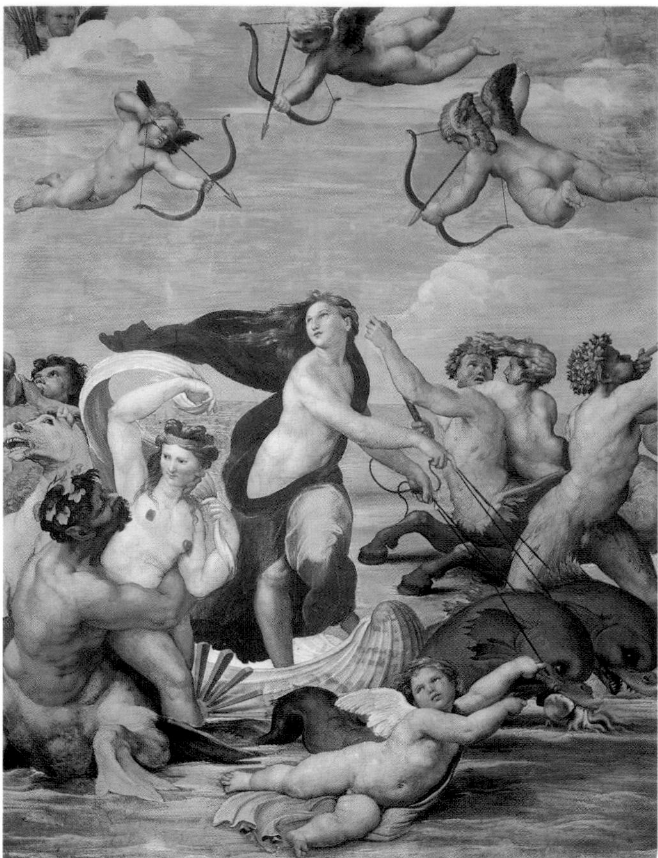

13-33. Raphael. *Galatea.* 1513. Fresco, 9'8⅛" x 7'4" (3 x 2.2 m). Villa Farnesina, Rome

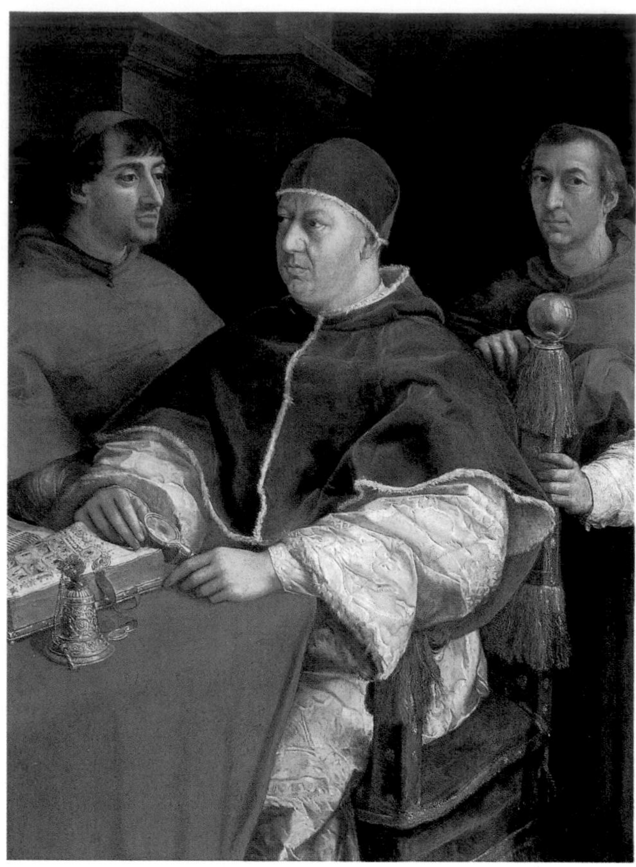

13-34. Raphael. *Pope Leo X with Giulio de' Medici and Luigi de' Rossi.* c. 1518. Oil on panel, 60⅝ x 46⅞" (154 x 119 cm). Galleria degli Uffizi, Florence

PORTRAITS. In his portraits, Raphael combined the realism of fifteenth-century portraits (such as fig. 12-56) with the human ideal of the High Renaissance, which in the *Mona Lisa* nearly overpowers the sitter's individuality. It is a tribute to his genius he did not flatter his subjects or impose conventions on them. Surely Pope Leo X (fig. 13-34) looks no more handsome here than he did in reality. The heavy-jowled features of this hedonistic pope have been recorded in detail, yet he has a commanding presence. His aura of power and dignity emanates more from his inner being than from his office. Raphael, we feel, has not falsified the sitter's personality but ennobled and focused it, as if he had observed Leo X in his finest hour. The contrast with the two cardinals, who lack this balanced strength, enhances the sovereign quality of the main figure. Even the pictorial treatment has this effect. Leo X has been set off from his companions and his presence heightened by intensified light, color, and texture.

LATER WORKS. When Leo X sent Michelangelo to Florence in 1516 to work on the Medici Chapel (see page 446), Raphael assumed undisputed leadership of art in Rome. He had already been named Bramante's successor at St. Peter's (Michelangelo was not put in charge of it until 30 years later) and had been appointed superintendent of antiquities. Now he was flooded with commissions and of necessity increasingly depended on his growing workshop. As a result, few of Raphael's later works, other than portraits such as that of Leo X, are entirely by his own hand. His reliance on assistants as well as the intervention of later restorers has partially obscured his achievement. The final phase of his brief career is nevertheless unusually rich and complex.

Raphael raised narrative painting to a new plane in a series of tapestry cartoons for the Sistine Chapel. They placed him in direct competition with Michelangelo and were consequently designed and executed entirely by his own hand. All are marked by a creative tension between grandiose rhetoric and high theater that pushes classicism to its limits and sometimes beyond. At times these forces coexist in an uneasy truce, but in *The Sacrifice at Lystra* (fig. 13-35) they are held in a state of dynamic equilibrium that is masterful. The painting greatly expands the pictorial and expressive range of Raphael's art. The scene, taken from Acts 14, shows Paul urging a crowd not to sacrifice animals in his honor after he had healed a cripple (to the far right in our illustration) and was mistaken for Mercury (hence the statue of the god at upper center in the background). The architectural setting, reconstructed from the antique with the passion of an archaeologist, is disposed linearly across the picture plane, partly in imitation of Roman reliefs (compare fig. 7-37). Besides framing the action, it plays an important expressive role by echoing the agitation of the surging crowd and the dignified strength of the saint and his companion, Barnabas.

Raphael has left a telling gap that not only highlights the figure of Mercury but also heightens the contrast between the two

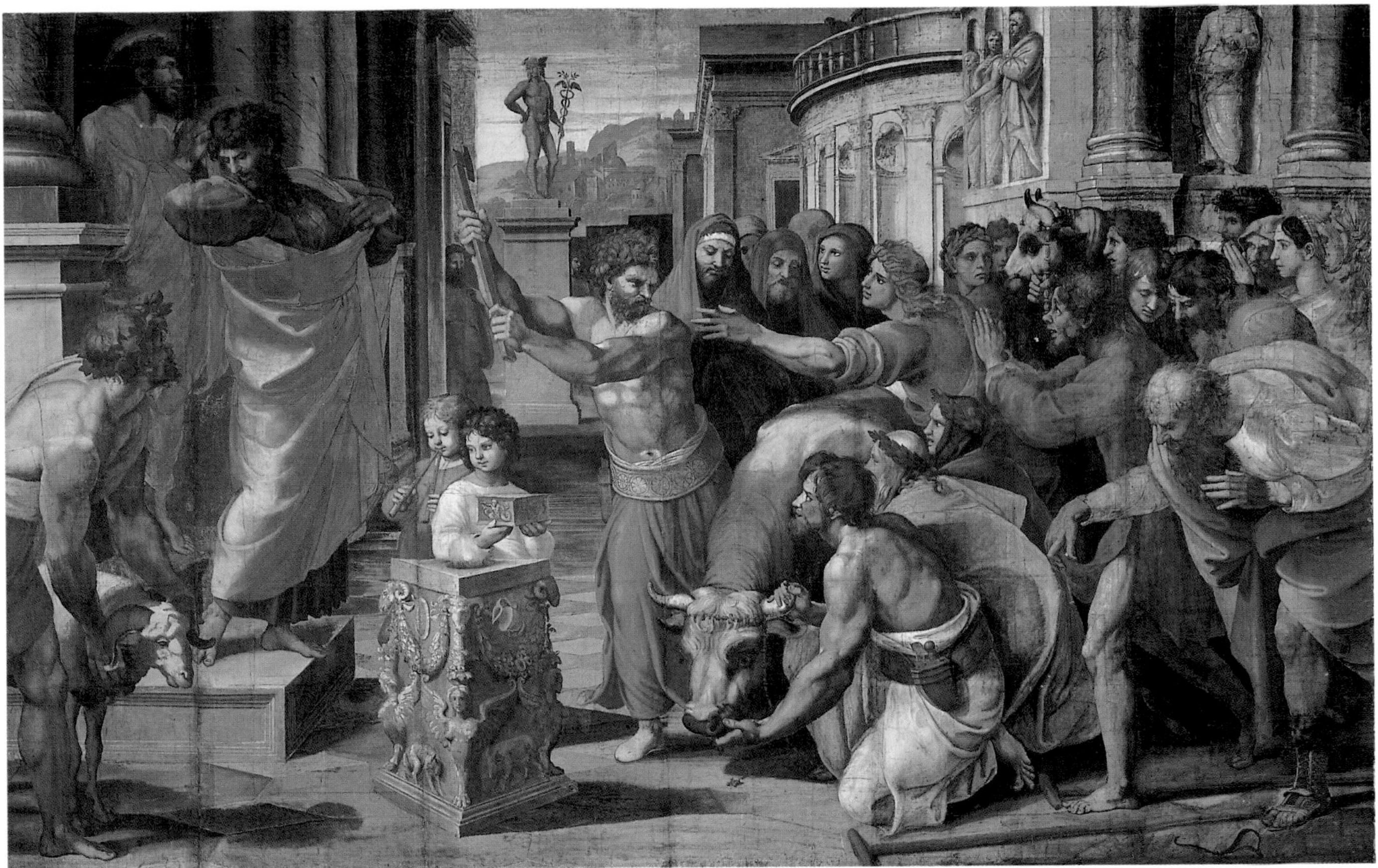

13-35. Raphael. *The Sacrifice at Lystra.* 1514–15. Tempera on paper, 11'5¾" x 17'8½" (3.5 x 5.4 m). Victoria & Albert Museum, London

groups. The drama differs from that of Leonardo and Michelangelo thanks to Raphael's unique power of concentration. In this work the artist has exhausted the possibilities of classicism. What steps he might have taken next we shall never know, as his life was cut short at the turning point of the High Renaissance. Yet it is significant that some of the leading Mannerists of the next generation emerged from his workshop.

Giorgione

The distinction between Early and High Renaissance art, so marked in Florence and Rome, is far less sharp in Venice. Giorgione (Giorgione da Castelfranco, 1478–1510), the first Venetian painter to belong to the new era, left the orbit of Giovanni Bellini only during the final years of his short career.

THE TEMPEST. Among his few mature works, *The Tempest* (fig. 13-36) is both the most unusual and the most enigmatic. There have been many attempts to explain this image. The most persuasive one is that the painting depicts Adam and Eve after the Fall. Their fate as decreed by God, whose voice is represented by the lightning bolt, is that man shall till the ground from which he was taken and that woman shall bring forth children in sorrow. Adam, dressed in Venetian costume, is seen resting from his labors. Eve, whose draped nudity signifies shame and carnal knowledge, suckles Cain, her firstborn son. In the distance is a bridge over the river surrounding the city of the earthly paradise, from which they have been expelled. Barely visible near the rock at river's edge is a snake, signifying the Temptation. The broken columns stand for death, the ultimate punishment of Original Sin.

The Tempest was probably commissioned by the merchant Gabriele Vendramin, one of Venice's greatest patrons of the arts, who owned the picture when it was first recorded in 1530. It certainly reflects the taste for learned humanist allegories in Venetian painting, whose subjects are often obscured, as here, by static poses and alien settings. The iconography does not tell us the whole story of *The Tempest,* however. It is the landscape, rather than Giorgione's figures, that interprets the scene for us. Belonging themselves to nature, Adam and Eve are passive victims of the thunderstorm that seems about to engulf them. The contrast to Bellini's *St. Francis in Ecstasy* (see fig. 12-63) is striking. Bellini's landscape is meant to be seen through the eyes of the saint, as a piece of God's creation. Despite its biblical subject, the mood in *The Tempest* is subtly, pervasively pagan. The scene is like an enchanted idyll, a dream of pastoral beauty soon to be swept away. In the past, only poets had captured this air of nostalgic reverie. Now, it entered the repertory of the painter. Indeed, the painting is very similar in mood to *Arcadia* by Jacopo Sannazaro, a pastoral poem about unrequited love that was popular in Giorgione's day. Thus *The Tempest* initiates what was to become an important new tradition.

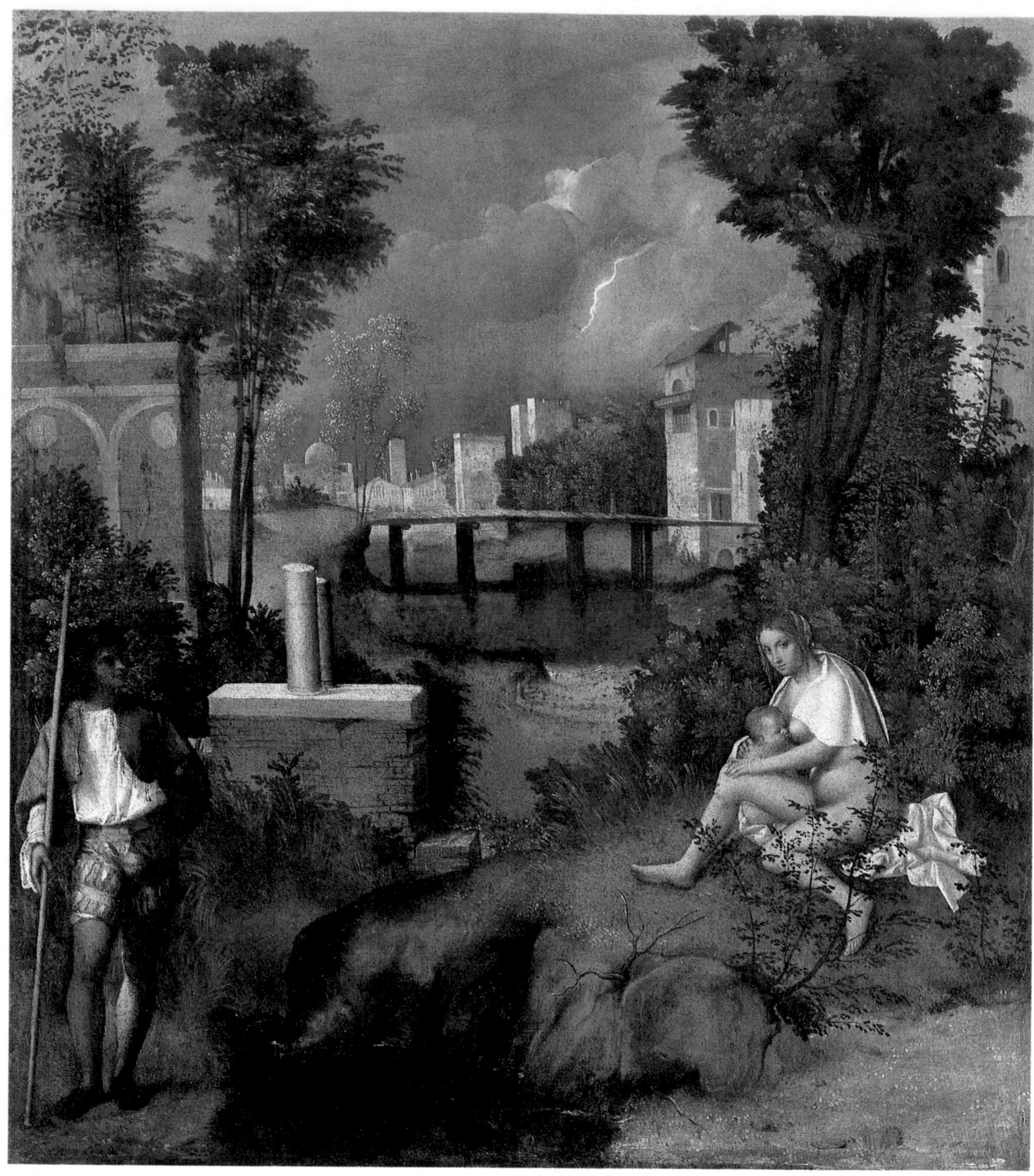

13-36. Giorgione. *The Tempest.* c. 1505. Oil on canvas, 31¼ x 28¾" (79.5 x 73 cm). Galleria dell'Accademia, Venice

Titian

Giorgione died before he could fully explore the sensuous, lyrical world he had created in *The Tempest.* This task was taken up by Titian (Tiziano Vecellio, 1488/90–1576), who was influenced by Bellini and then by Giorgione. An artist of incomparable ability, Titian was to dominate Venetian painting for the next half-century. [See Primary Sources, no. 43, pages 613–15.]

BACCHANAL. Titian's *Bacchanal* of about 1518 (fig. 13-37) is frankly pagan, inspired by an ancient author's description of such a revel. The landscape, rich in contrasts of cool and warm tones, has all the poetry of Giorgione, but the figures are of another breed. Active and muscular, they move with a joyous freedom that recalls Raphael's *Galatea* (see fig. 13-33). By this time, many of Raphael's compositions had been engraved (see fig. 22-4), and from these reproductions Titian became familiar with the Roman High Renaissance. A number of the participants in his *Bacchanal* also reflect the influence of classical art. Titian's approach to antiquity, however, is very different from Raphael's. He visualizes the realm of classical myths as part of the natural world, inhabited not by animated statues but by beings of flesh and blood. The figures of the *Bacchanal* are idealized just enough to persuade us that they belong to a long-lost golden age. They invite us to share their blissful state in a way that makes Raphael's *Galatea* seem cold and remote by comparison.

THE PESARO MADONNA. This festive quality reappears in many of Titian's religious paintings, such as the *Madonna with Members of the Pesaro Family* (fig. 13-38). Although the subject is a variant of the sacra conversazione, Titian has thoroughly trans-

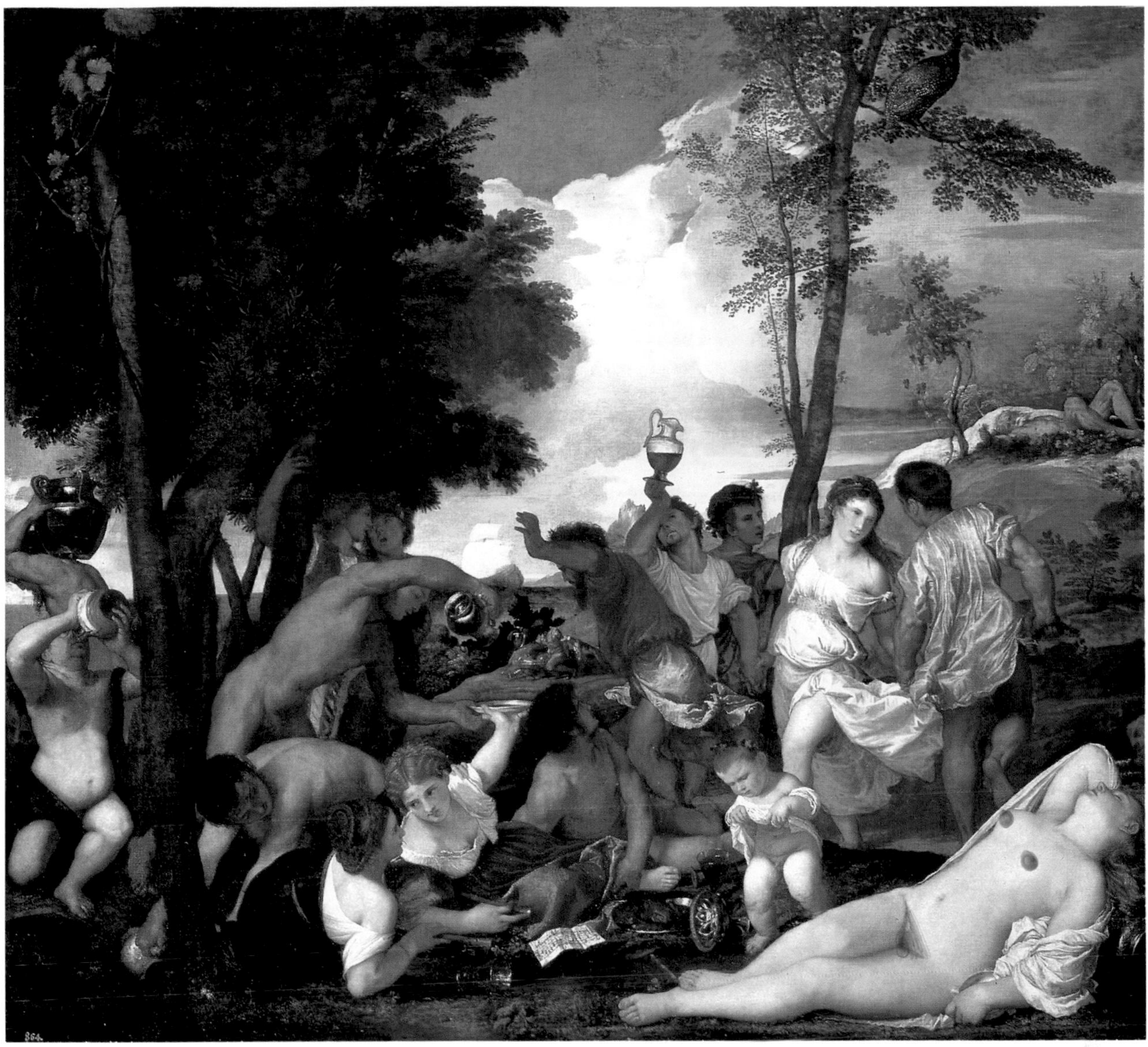

13-37. Titian. *Bacchanal.* c. 1518. Oil on canvas, 5'8⅞" x 6'4" (1.7 x 1.9 m). Museo del Prado, Madrid

formed it. For the first time, we feel that the participants are actually sharing in a dialogue. The Holy Family is no longer timeless and remote, as in Veneziano's prototype (compare fig. 12-31). The Infant Jesus is as natural as the child in the artist's *Bacchanal,* while the Virgin and St. Peter turn to the donor, Jacopo Pesaro, kneeling in devotion at the left. (St. Peter is identified by the key to the church near his foot, which was presented to him by Jesus; compare fig. 12-57.)

Much of the picture's effectiveness is due to the composition, which replaces the familiar frontal view with an oblique one that is far more active. The Virgin is enthroned in a barrel-vaulted hall that is open on either side. The setting is a High Renaissance counterpart of the architectural framework in Bellini's *Madonna and Saints* in S. Zaccaria (see fig. 12-64). The elevated columns, which are the key to the setting, represent the gateway to Heaven and are traditionally identified with Mary herself. They thus are a symbol of both eternal life and the Immaculate Conception (the belief that she was conceived without Original Sin). Because the view is diagonal, open sky and clouds fill most of the background. Except for the kneeling donors, every figure is in motion. The officer with the flag seems almost to lead a charge up the steps. (He is probably St. Maurice, namesake of the battle at Santa Maura where the Venetian navy, which included the papal fleet commanded by Pesaro, defeated the Turks in 1502—note the turbaned figure beside him.) Yet the design remains harmoniously self-contained despite the strong element of drama. Brilliant sunlight makes every color and texture sparkle, in keeping with the joyous spirit of the altar. The only hint of tragedy is the cross of the Passion held by two angel-putti. Hidden by clouds from the participants in the sacra conversazione but not from us, it adds a note of poignancy to the scene.

PORTRAITS. After Raphael's death, Titian became the most sought-after portraitist of the age. His immense gifts, evident in the donors' portraits in the *Pesaro Madonna,* are even more striking in the *Man with the Glove* (fig. 13-39). The dreamy intimacy of this portrait, with its soft outline and deep shadows, still reflects the style of Giorgione. Lost in thought, the young man seems unaware of us. The slight melancholy in his features has all the poetic appeal of *The Tempest.* The breadth and power of form, however, go far beyond Giorgione's. In Titian's hands, the possi-

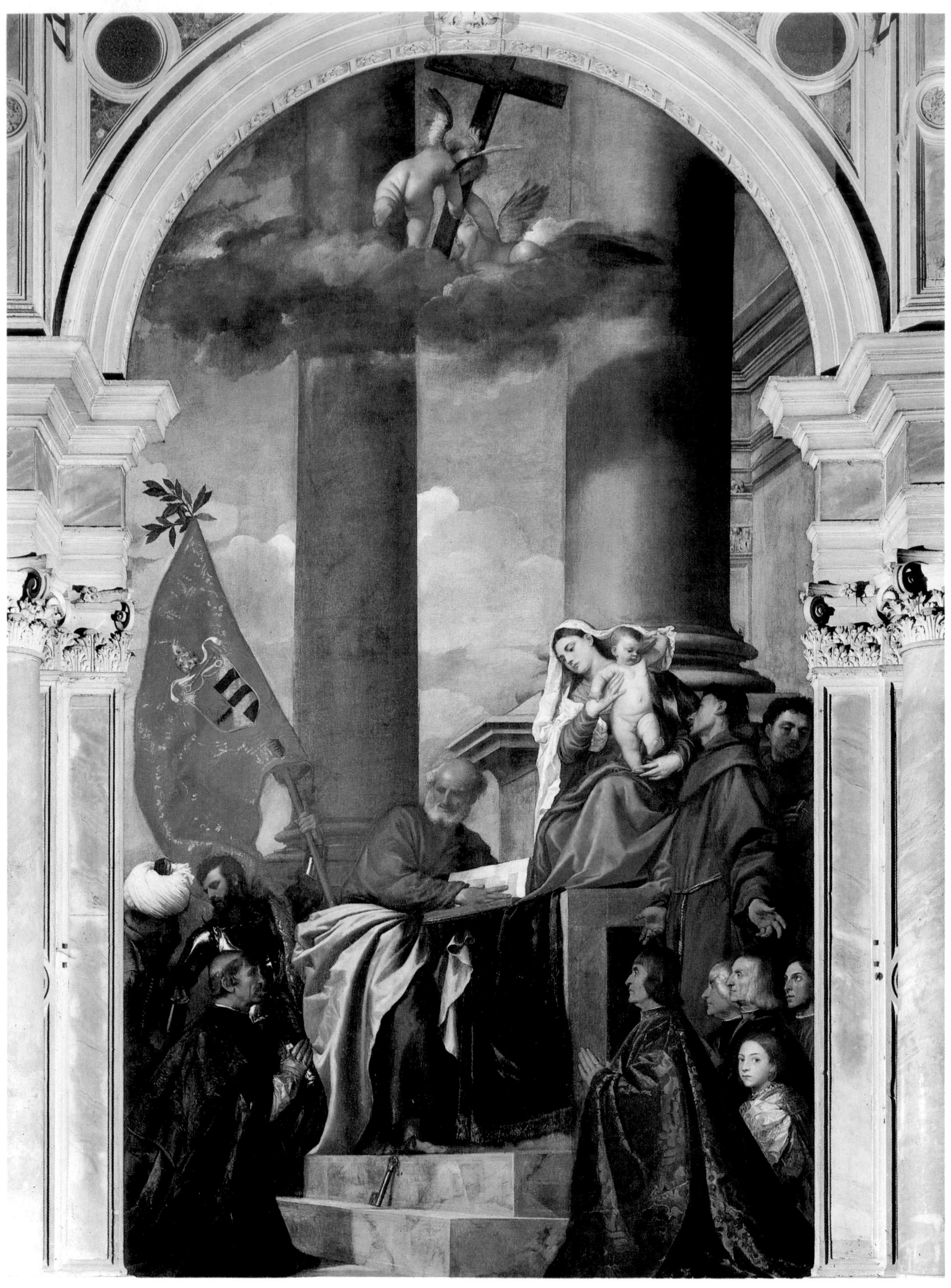

13-38. Titian. *Madonna with Members of the Pesaro Family.* 1526. Oil on canvas, 16' x 8'10" (4.9 x 2.7 m). Sta. Maria del Gloriosa dei Frari, Venice

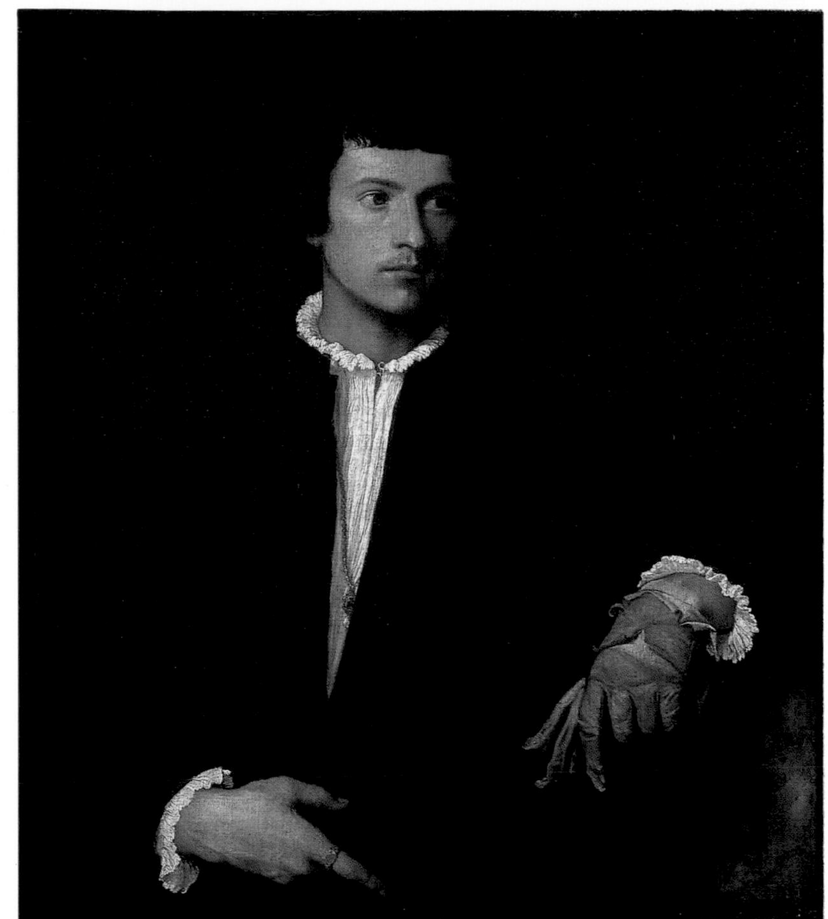

13-39. Titian. *Man with the Glove.* c. 1520. Oil on canvas, 39 ½ x 35" (100.3 x 89 cm). Musée du Louvre, Paris

(BELOW) 13-40. Titian. *Pope Paul III and His Grandsons.* 1546. Oil on canvas, 6'10" x 5'8" (2.1 x 1.7 m). Museo di Capodimonte, Naples

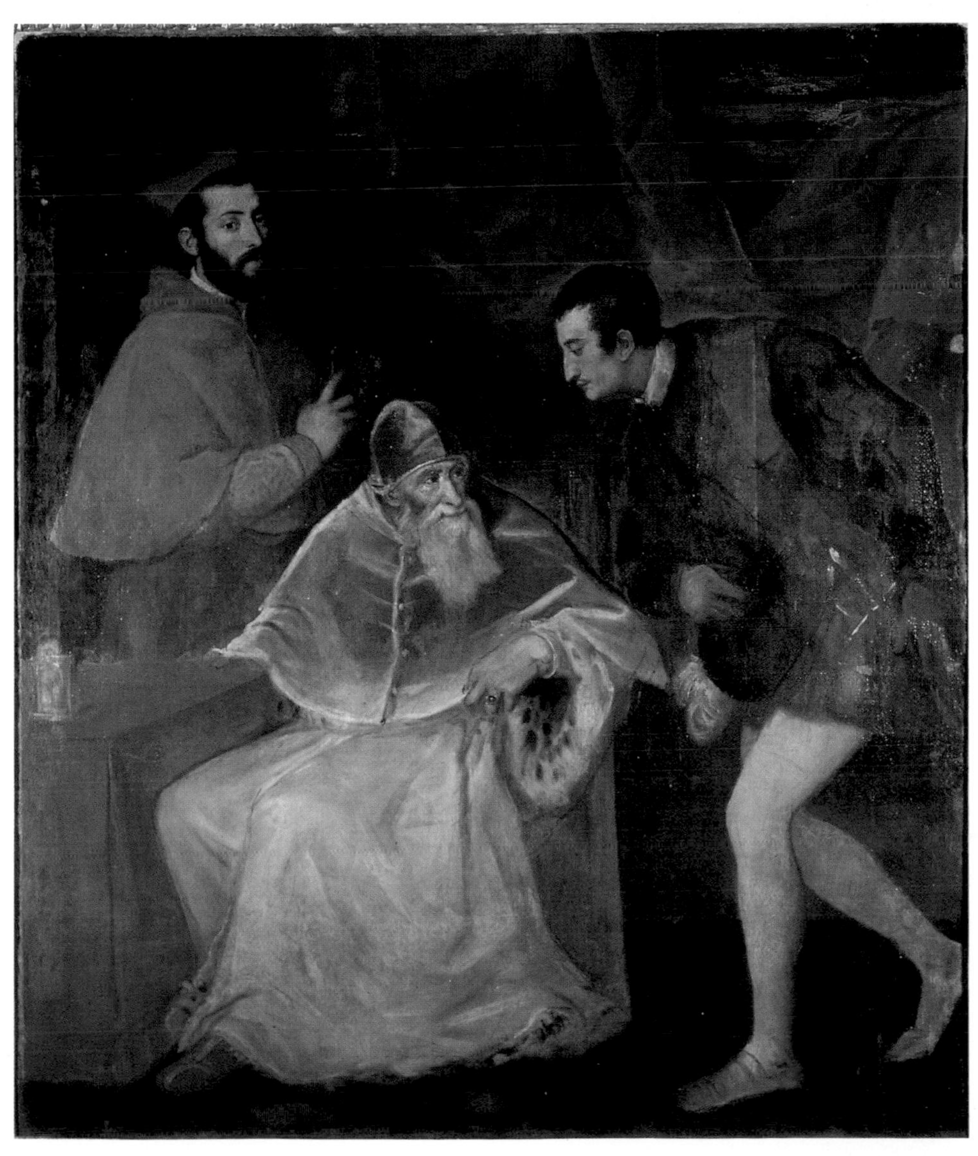

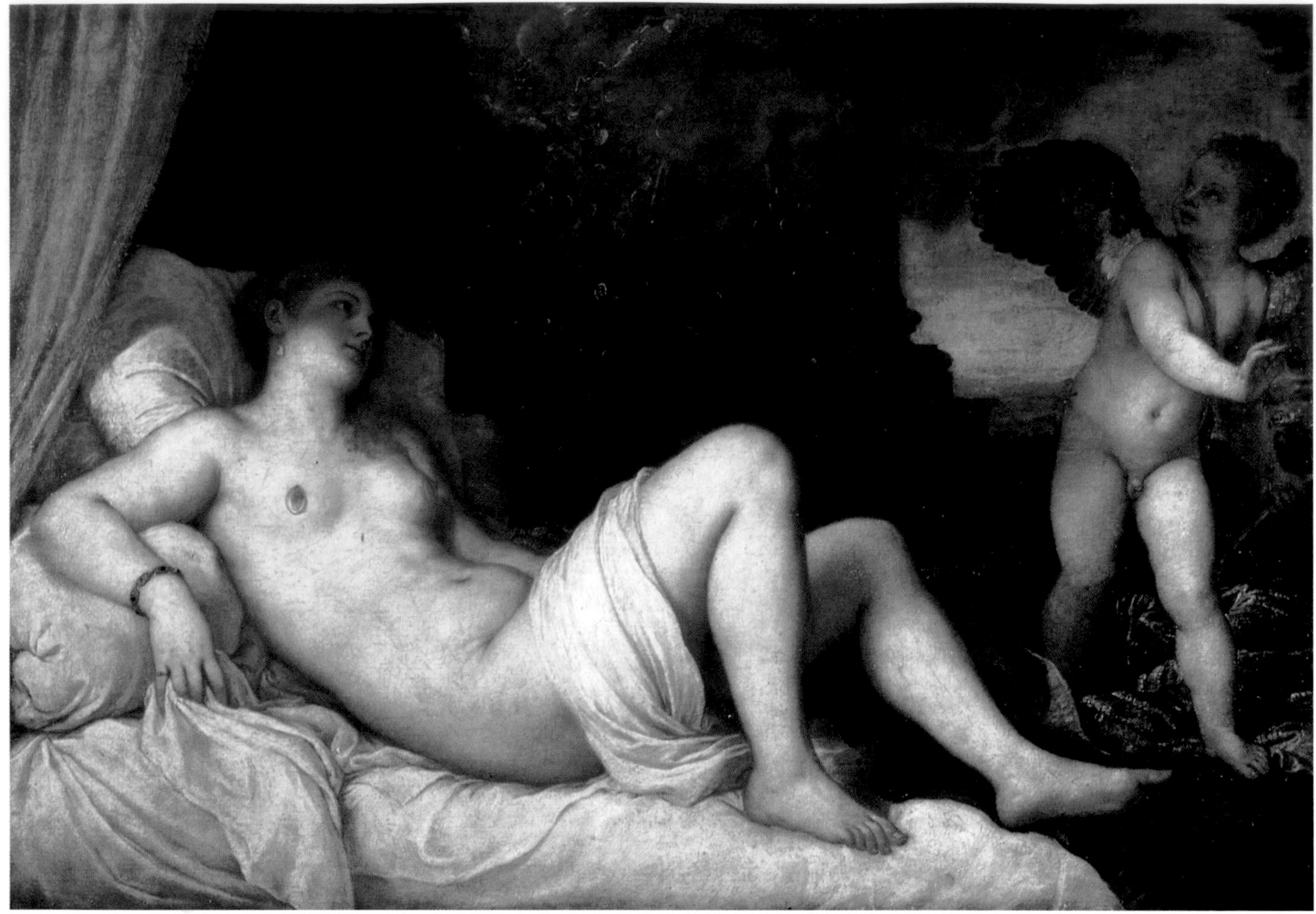

13-41. Titian. *Danaë.* c. 1544–46. Oil on canvas, 47¼ x 67¾" (120 x 172 cm). Museo e Gallerie Nazionale di Capodimonte, Naples

bilities of the oil technique—rich, creamy highlights and deep dark tones that are transparent and delicately modulated—now are fully realized, and the separate brushstrokes, hardly visible before, become increasingly free.

We can see the rapid pace of Titian's development by turning from the *Man with the Glove* to the papal group portrait *Pope Paul III and His Grandsons* (fig. 13-40), painted a quarter-century later. The composition is derived from Raphael's *Pope Leo X* (see fig. 13-34). The quick, slashing strokes here endow the entire canvas with the spontaneity of a sketch. (In fact, some parts are unfinished.) In the freer technique, Titian's uncanny grasp of human character also comes out. The tiny figure of the pope, shriveled with age, dominates his tall attendants with awesome authority. Comparing these two portraits by Titian, we see that the change of pictorial technique is not a surface phenomenon. It reflects a change of the artist's aim.

DANAË. The portrait of Julius II was painted in the middle of Titian's career during a long stay in Rome. *Danaë* (fig. 13-41), which dates from the same period, is a masterful display of the painterly use of sonorous color. By varying the consistency of his pigments, the artist was able to capture the texture of Danaë's flesh with uncanny accuracy, while distinguishing it clearly from bed sheets and covers. To convey these tactile qualities, Titian built up his surface in thin, transparent coats, known as glazes. The interaction between these layers produces unrivaled richness and complexity of color; yet the medium is so filmy that it becomes nearly as translucent as the cloud, in which guise Jupiter appears to the young woman, that trails off into the sky.

The figure shows the impact of Michelangelo's *Night* on the Tomb of Giuliano de' Medici (see fig. 13-22). After seeing the canvas in the artist's studio, Michelangelo is said to have praised Titian's coloring and style but criticized his design. [See Primary Sources, no. 42, page 613.] We can readily understand Michelangelo's discomfort, for Titian has rephrased his sculpture in utterly sensuous terms. Michelangelo, we know, made detailed drawings for his figures. Titian, too, was a fine draftsman and absorbed the influence of Michelangelo. But although he presumably worked out the essential features of his compositions in preliminary drawings, none have survived. Nor, it seems, did he transfer the design onto the canvas. Instead, he worked directly on the surface, making adjustments as he went along. Ever since Michelangelo and Titian, the merits of line versus color—of *disegno* and *colore*—have been the subject of intense debate. (The debate goes all the way back to ancient Greece; see page 136.) The role of color rests mainly on its sensuous and emotional appeal, in contrast to the more cerebral quality of line. Titian thus stands at the head of the coloristic tradition that descends through Rubens, Delacroix, and Van Gogh to the Expressionists of the twentieth century.

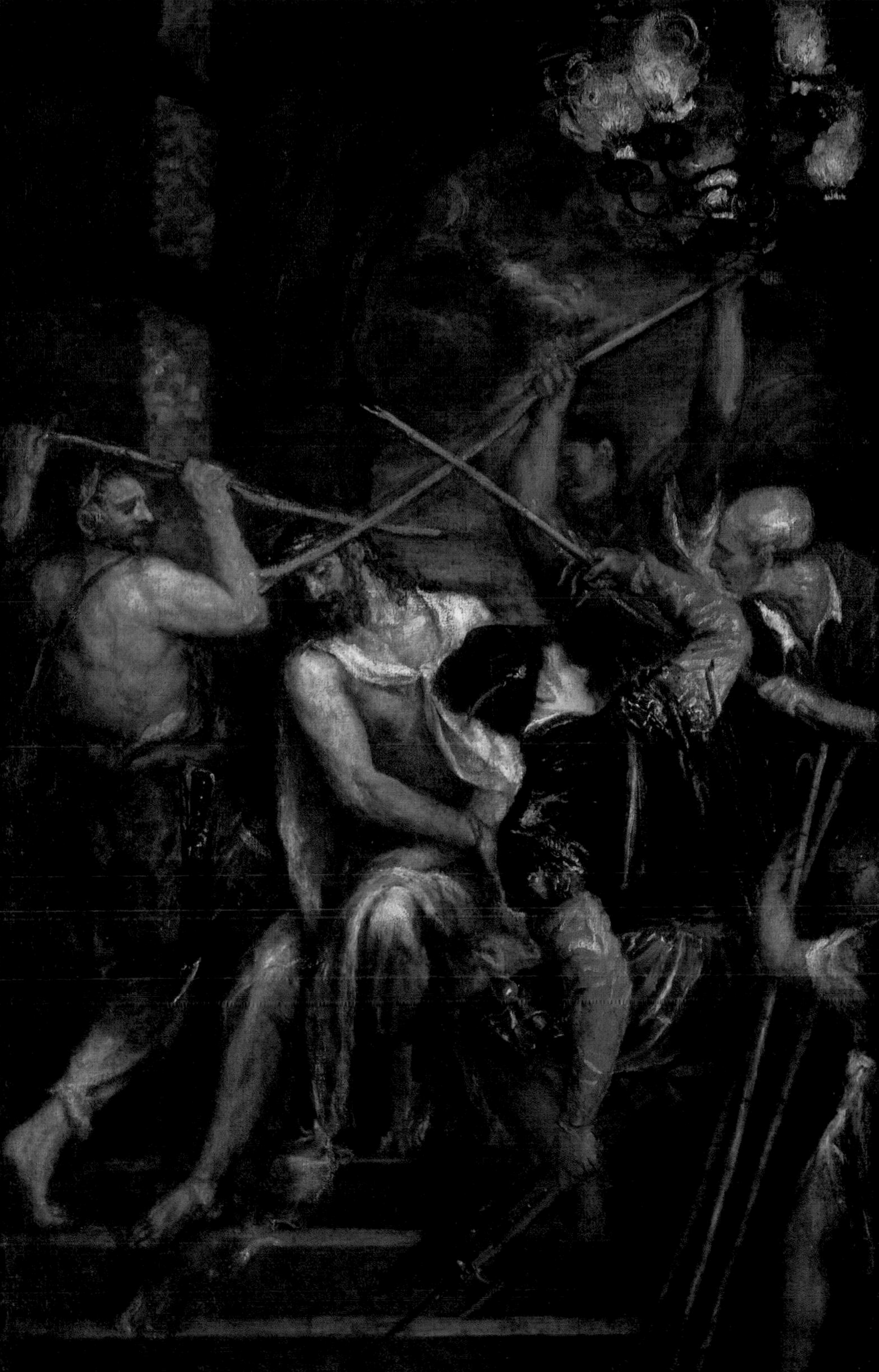

13-42. Titian. *Christ Crowned with Thorns*. c. 1570. Oil on canvas, 9'2" x 6' (2.8 x 1.8 m). Alte Pinakothek, Munich

LATE WORKS. The correspondence of form and technique that we have already seen in *Danaë* is even clearer in *Christ Crowned with Thorns* (fig. 13-42), the most awesome work of Titian's old age. To what does the canvas owe its power? Surely not only to its large scale or dramatic composition, although these are contributing factors. (The painting is a variant of one he had made a quarter-century earlier that is less successful.) The answer lies in the artist's technique. The shapes emerging from the semidarkness now consist wholly of light and color. Despite the heavy impasto, the shimmering surfaces have lost every trace of material solidity and seem translucent, as if aglow from within. The violent action has been miraculously suspended. What lingers in our minds is the mood of serenity arising from deep religious feeling rather than the drama. As a result, we contemplate not Jesus' physical suffering but its purpose: the redemption and salvation of humanity. The painting's ethereality reflects a widespread visionary tendency that was shared by other late-sixteenth-century Venetian artists. We shall meet it again in the work of Tintoretto and El Greco.

CHAPTER FOURTEEN

Mannerism and Other Trends

What happened after the High Renaissance? Eighty years ago the answer would have been that after the High Renaissance came the Late Renaissance, a term that implies a decline after the peak attained by Leonardo, Michelangelo, Raphael, Titian, and Bramante. This "decadent" phase lasted until the Baroque style emerged at the end of the sixteenth century. Today we take a far more positive view of the artists who reached maturity after 1520 and generally discard the term "Late Renaissance" as misleading. Yet we have still to agree on a name for the 75 years separating the High Renaissance from the Baroque. Since there was no single style in the years 1525 to 1600, why should this span be thought of as a period at all? This difficulty can be resolved by thinking of it as a time of crisis that gave rise to several competing tendencies rather than one dominant ideal. In fact, there is no clear dividing line among them, and we often find several contained in the work of an artist, which adds to the complexity of the era.

The great voyages of discovery that took place during the High Renaissance—Columbus' landing in the New World in 1492, Amerigo Vespucci's exploration of South America seven years later, and Magellan's voyage around the world beginning in 1519—had far-reaching consequences. The most immediate effect was the rise of the great European colonial powers, which vied with one another for commercial supremacy around the world. The Spanish (as well as the Portuguese) quickly established themselves in the Americas: Mexico was conquered by Hernán Cortés in 1519–21, Peru by Francisco Pizarro during the next decade. By 1585, Sir Walter Raleigh had founded the first English settlement in North America, and the French soon followed with outposts of their own. An unexpected effect was the explosion of knowledge as explorers brought back a host of natural and artistic wonders never before seen in Europe. Avid collectors formed Kunst- und Wunderkammern (literally, art and wonder rooms) to display exotic treasures from every corner of the earth. As Europeans struggled to assimilate the new discoveries into old categories of thought, the science inherited from ancient Greece and Rome was largely discarded by 1650 in favor of a new body of learning.

At almost the same time, the Protestant Reformation was launched by Martin Luther, a former Augustinian friar who had become professor of theology at the University of Wittenberg. At face value, the 95 theses he nailed to the Wittenberg Castle church door on All Saints' Eve in October 1517 were a broadside against the sale of indulgences promising redemption of sins. More fundamentally they were a wholesale attack on Catholic dogma, for Luther claimed that the Bible and natural reason were the sole bases of religious authority. Freed from traditional doctrine, the Protestant movement rapidly developed splinter groups. Within a few years the Swiss pastor Huldreich Zwingli wanted to reduce religion to its essentials by preaching an even more radical fundamentalism. He denounced the arts as distractions and denied the validity of even the Eucharist as a rite, which led to a split with Luther that was never healed. Even within Zwingli's camp there were rifts: the Anabaptists accepted only adult baptism.

What divided the reformers were the twin issues of grace and free will in attaining faith and salvation. These matters had been spelled out with the aid of the humanists, who initially had counted Luther and Zwingli among their number. Many of them, however, eventually turned against the Reformation because of its extreme views. By the time of Zwingli's death at the hands of the Catholic forces at the Battle of Kappel in 1531, the main elements of Protestant theology had been defined. They were codified around mid-century by John Calvin of Geneva, who tried to mediate between Luther and Zwingli while adopting the puritanical beliefs of the Anabaptists.

The Catholic church soon began a reform movement of its own, known today as the Counter-Reformation. After the Council of Trent in 1545–47, it was spearheaded by the Society of Jesus, the Jesuit order representing the Church militant, which had been founded by the Spanish saint Ignatius of Loyola in 1534. [See Primary Sources, no. 44, page 615.] The internal reforms were carried out mainly by Pope Paul IV after he ascended the throne of St. Peter in 1555, and by St. Carlo Borromeo, who initiated the model of reform as bishop of Milan five years later. Religious painting in Italy between 1520 and 1590 may be seen as a highly varied response to the spiritual crisis that culminated in the Counter-Reformation.

The Reformation and the Counter-Reformation soon became bound up in the political upheavals and social unrest sweeping Europe. Although they were sometimes passionate in their beliefs, rulers usually allied themselves with either movement depending on dynastic and economic self-interest. Thus Henry VIII of England established the Church of England in 1534 so that he could divorce his queen in the hope of producing a male heir. Later, Philip II of Spain embraced the Catholic cause to advance Hapsburg ambitions and cloaked his motives in the mantle of a crusade for the true faith.

PAINTING

Mannerism in Florence and Rome

Among the trends in art in the wake of the High Renaissance, Mannerism is the most significant, as well as the most problematic. In scope, the original meaning of the term was narrow and derogatory. It referred to a group of mid-sixteenth-century painters in Rome and Florence whose "artificial" style (*maniera*) was derived from certain aspects of the work of Raphael and Michelangelo. This phase has since been recognized as part of a wider movement that had begun around 1520. Keyed to a sophisticated taste, early Mannerism had appealed to a small circle of aristocratic patrons such as Cosimo I, the grand duke of Tuscany. The style soon became international as a number of events—including the plague of 1522 and, above all, the Sack of Rome by Spanish forces in 1527—drove many painters abroad, where most of the style's next phase developed.

This new phase, High Mannerism, was the assertion of a purely aesthetic ideal. Through formulaic abstraction, it became a style of utmost refinement that emphasized grace, variety, and virtuoso display at the expense of content, clarity, and unity. This taste for mannered elegance and bizarre conceits appealed to a narrow but cultured audience. In a larger sense Mannerism signaled a major shift in Italian culture. In part, it resulted from the High Renaissance quest for originality as a projection of the individual's personality, which had given artists license to explore their imaginations freely. While this investigation of new modes was ultimately healthy, the Mannerist style itself came to be regarded by many as decadent, and no wonder: given such subjective freedom, it produced extreme personalities that today seem the most "modern" of all sixteenth-century painters.

The formalism of High Mannerist art was part of a wider movement that placed inner vision, however private or fantastic, above the twin standards of nature and the ancients. Hence some scholars have broadened the definition of Mannerism to include the later style of Michelangelo, who would acknowledge no artistic authority higher than his own genius. Mannerism is often viewed as a reaction against the ideal created by the High Renaissance as well. Except for a brief initial phase, however, Mannerism did not consciously reject the tradition from which it stemmed. Although the subjectivity inherent in its aesthetic was unclassical, it was not deliberately anticlassical except in its more extreme forms. Even more important than Mannerism's anticlassicism is its insistent antinaturalism.

The relation of Mannerism to religious trends was equally paradoxical. Despite the intense religious feeling that informs many works by the first generation of artists, it has rightly been observed that Mannerism as a whole illustrates the spiritual bankruptcy of the age. In particular, the extreme worldliness of the second generation, the High Mannerists, was antithetical to both the Reformation, with its stern morality, and the Counter-Reformation, which demanded strict adherence to doctrine. However, after mid-century there was a Counter Mannerist trend, which adapted the vocabulary of Mannerism for Counter-Reformation ends. At the same time, the subjectivism of Mannerism came to be valued for its visionary power as part of a larger shift in religious outlook.

ROSSO. The first signs of disquiet in the High Renaissance appear shortly before 1520 in Florence. Art had been left in the hands of a younger generation that could refine but not further develop the styles of the great masters who had spent their early careers there. Having absorbed the lessons of the leading artists at one remove, the first generation of Mannerists was free to apply High Renaissance formulas to a new aesthetic divorced from its previous content. By 1521, Rosso Fiorentino (1495–1540), the most eccentric member of this group, expressed the new attitude in the

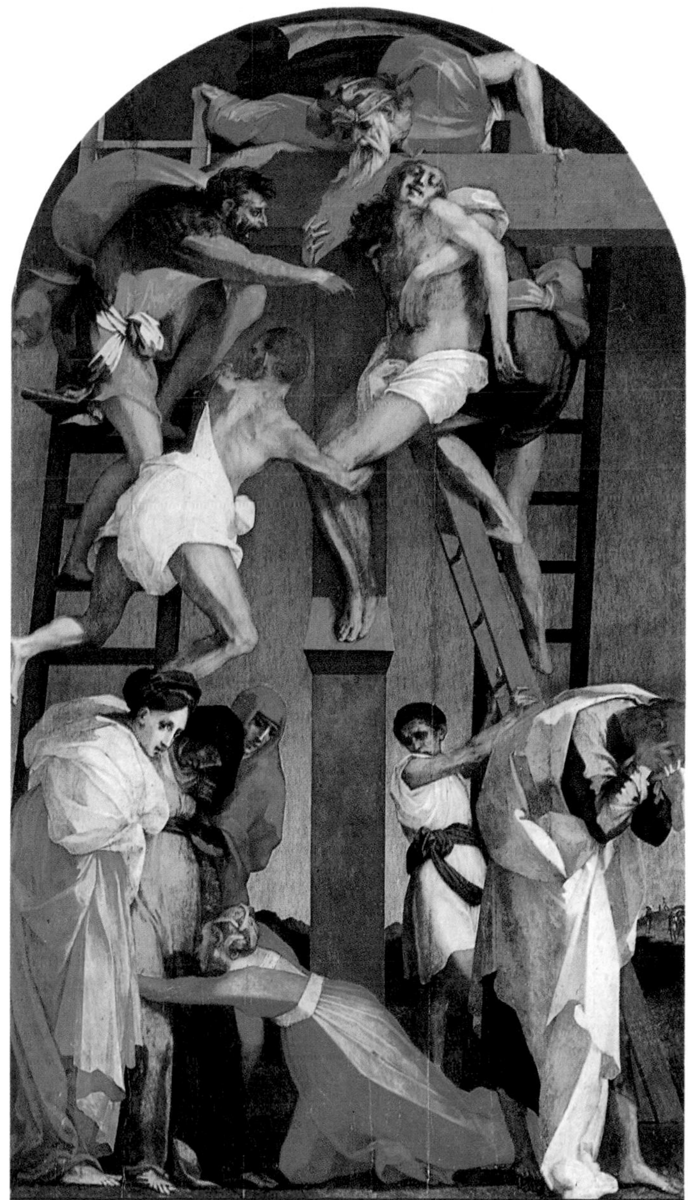

14-1. Rosso Fiorentino. *Descent from the Cross.* 1521. Oil on panel, 11' x 6'5½" (3.4 x 2 m). Pinacoteca Communale, Volterra

Descent from the Cross (fig. 14-1). Nothing has prepared us for the shocking impact of these spidery forms spread out against the dark sky. The figures are agitated yet rigid, as if frozen by a sudden icy blast. Even the draperies have brittle, sharp-edged planes. The acid colors and the light, brilliant but unreal, reinforce the nightmarish effect of the scene. Here is clearly a full-scale revolt against the classical balance of High Renaissance art: a profoundly disquieting, willful, visionary style that indicates a deep inner anxiety.

PONTORMO. Pontormo (1494–1556/7), a friend of Rosso's, had an equally strange personality. Introspective, headstrong, and shy, he worked only when and for whom he pleased. He would shut himself up in his quarters for weeks on end and refuse to see even his closest friends. His *Deposition* (fig. 14-2) reflects these aspects of his character. The painting contrasts sharply with Rosso's *Descent from the Cross* but is no less disturbing. Unlike Rosso's attenuated forms, Pontormo's have a nearly classical beauty and sculptural solidity inspired by Michelangelo, who in turn admired his art. (Compare the figure of Jesus to that in Michelangelo's *Pietà,* fig. 13-11.) Yet the figures are confined to a stage that is so claustrophobic as to cause acute discomfort in the viewer. The implausibility of the image, however, makes it convincing in spiritual terms. Indeed, this visionary quality is essential to its meaning, which is conveyed by formal means alone. We have entered a world of innermost contemplation in which every pictorial element responds to a purely subjective impulse. Everything is subordinate to the play of graceful rhythms created by the tightly interlocking forms. These patterns unify the surface and give the work a poignancy unlike any we have seen. Although they act in concert, the mourners are lost in a grief too personal to share with each other—or us. In this hushed atmosphere, anguish is transformed into a lyrical expression of exquisite sensitivity. The entire scene is as haunted as Pontormo's self-portrait just to the right of the swooning Madonna. The artist, moodily gazing into space, seems to shrink from the outer world, as if scarred by the trauma of some half-remembered experience, and into one of his own invention.

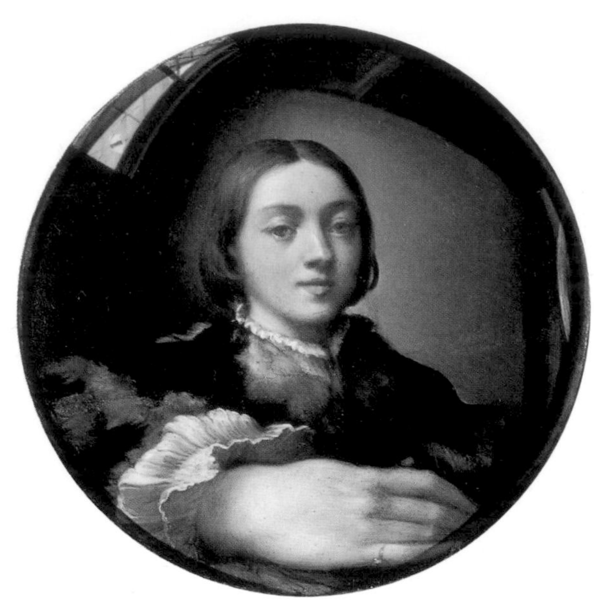

14-3. Parmigianino. *Self-Portrait.* 1524. Oil on panel, diameter 9⅝" (24.7 cm). Kunsthistorisches Museum, Vienna

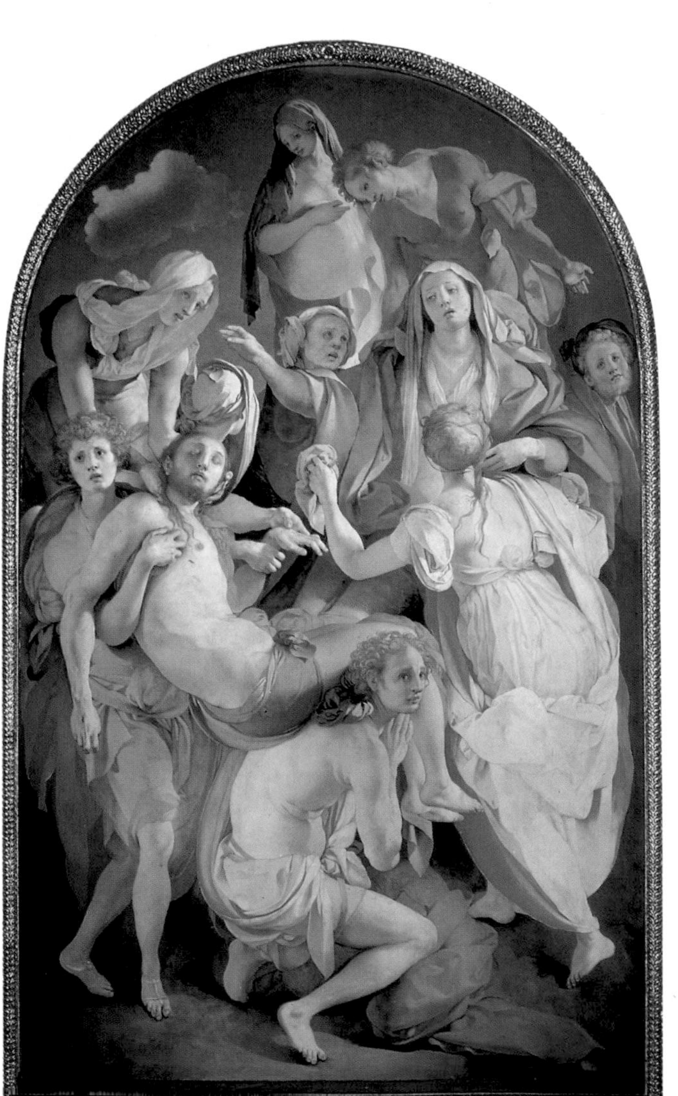

14-2. Pontormo. *Deposition.* c. 1526–28. Oil on panel, 10'3" x 6'4" (3.1 x 1.9 m). Sta. Felicita, Florence

PARMIGIANINO. The first phase of Mannerism was soon replaced by one less overtly anticlassical, less charged with subjective emotion, but equally far removed from the confident, stable world of the High Renaissance. The *Self-Portrait* (fig. 14-3) done as a demonstration piece by Parmigianino (Girolamo Francesco Maria Mazzuoli, 1503–1540) suggests no psychological turmoil. The artist's appearance is bland and well groomed. The features, painted with Raphael's smooth perfection, are veiled by a delicate Leonardesque sfumato. The distortions, too, are objective, not arbitrary, for the picture records what Parmigianino saw as he gazed at his reflection in a convex mirror. Earlier painters who used the mirror as an aid to observation had "filtered out" such distortions, except when the mirror image was contrasted with a direct view of the same scene (see fig. 15-8). But Parmigianino sub-

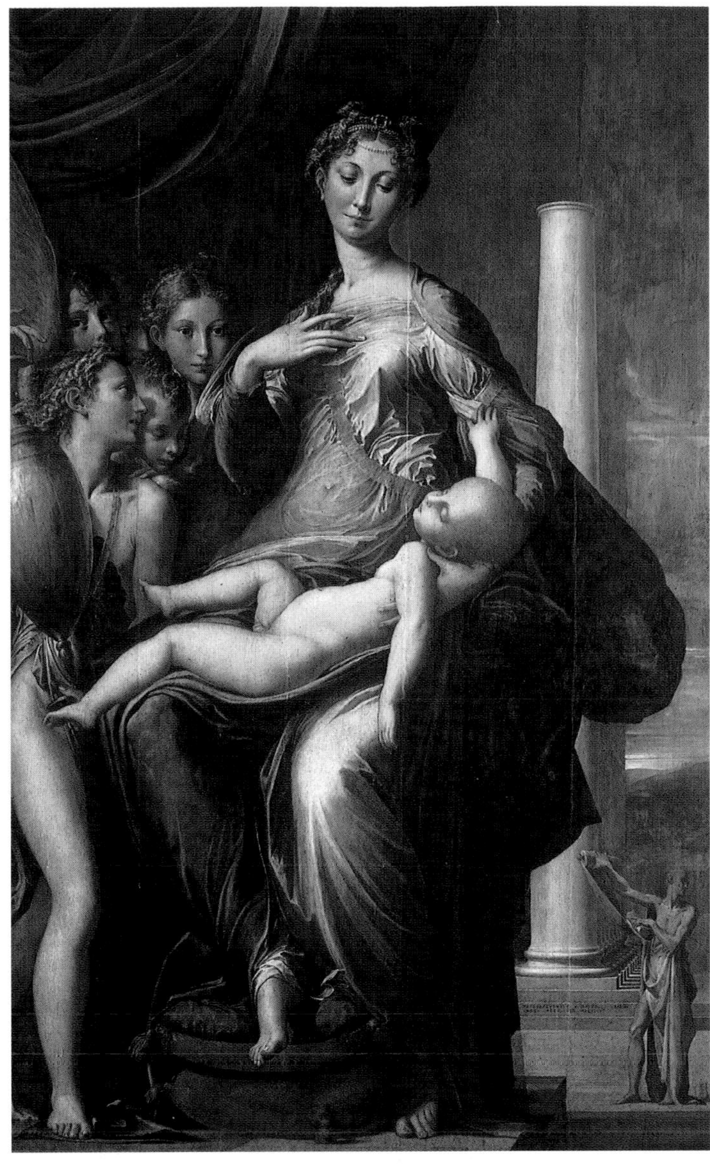

14-4. Parmigianino. *The Madonna with the Long Neck*. c. 1535. Oil on panel, 7'1" x 4'4" (2.2 x 1.3 m). Galleria degli Uffizi, Florence

stitutes his painting for the mirror itself, even using a specially prepared convex panel. Why was he so fascinated by his self-image? With his hand nearly touching the mirror, he becomes Narcissus (see page 156). The painting suggests an interest in magic as well. In the Renaissance the convex mirror was valued for its visionary effects, which seemed to reveal the future, as well as hidden aspects of the past and present. This concern may help to explain why Parmigianino's scientific detachment soon changed into its opposite. Vasari tells us that the artist, as he neared the end of his brief career (he died at 37), was obsessed with alchemy and became "a bearded, long-haired, neglected, and almost savage or wild man."

Parmigianino's strange imagination is evident in his most famous work, *The Madonna with the Long Neck* (fig. 14-4), which was painted after he had returned to his native Parma after several years in Rome. He had been deeply impressed with the rhythmic grace of Raphael's art (compare fig. 13-33), but he has transformed the older artist's figures into a remarkable new breed. The limbs, elongated and ivory-smooth, move with effortless languor, embodying an ideal of beauty as remote from nature as any Byzantine figure. The pose of the Christ Child balanced precariously on the Madonna's lap echoes that of a *Pietà* (compare fig. 13-11), indicating that he is fully aware of his death to redeem Original Sin. Although it is also found in Byzantine icons, this unusual device is Parmigianino's own invention and helps to explain the setting, which is not as arbitrary as it may seem. The gigantic column is a symbol often associated with the Madonna as the gateway to heaven and eternal life, as well as the Immaculate Conception (see page 457). It may also refer to the flagellation of Jesus during the Passion, thus reminding us of his sacrifice, which the tiny figure of a prophet foretells on his scroll. Visually, it serves to disrupt our perception of space, which is strangely disjointed. Parmigianino seems determined to prevent us from judging anything in this picture by the standards of ordinary experience. Here we approach the "artificial" style for which the term *Mannerism* was coined. *The Madonna with the Long Neck* is a vision of unearthly perfection, its cold elegance no less striking than the violence in Rosso's *Descent.*

Parmigianino is important as a printmaker as well as a painter. He was the first artist to seriously explore the possibilities of etching. Although the technique was introduced in the North shortly after 1510 (see page 502), it took the Italian Mannerists to appreciate the new medium. We can see why in Parmigianino's *The Entombment* (fig. 14-5). The print looks very much like the artist's ink drawings in its sketchlike immediacy, which conveys the agitation of the scene. Indeed, etching was ideally suited to the artist's individual style and nervous temperament—traits prized above all others by the Mannerists.

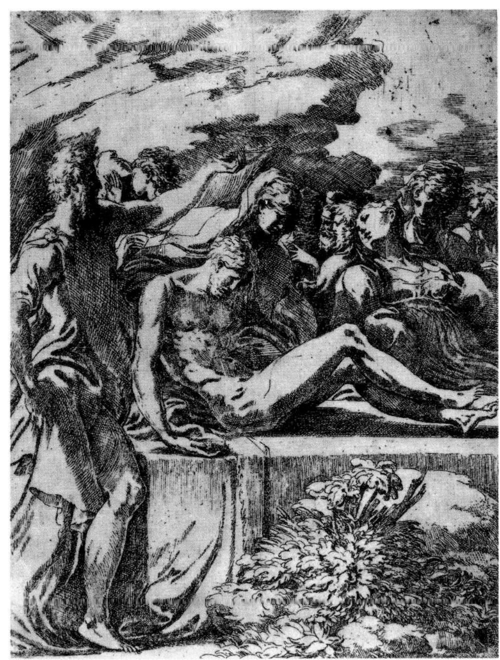

14-5. Parmigianino. *The Entombment*. c. 1535. Etching printed in brown ink, 12¼ x 9⅜" (31.3 x 23.8 cm). Los Angeles County Museum of Art

COLLECTION OF MARY STANSBURG RUIZ

MUSIC AND THEATER IN THE AGE OF MANNERISM

The music and theater of Italy between 1530 and 1600 reflect the same rich variety found in art. The most characteristic musical form after about 1530 was the madrigal, which was an outgrowth of French and Italian popular songs. It was similar to the motet in that all the voices were equally important, but it was livelier and more expressive. The madrigal was also closely connected to the resurgence of Italian poetry in the work of Ludovico Ariosto (see box page 442) and Torquato Tasso (1544–1595), Ariosto's successor as court poet to the ruling d'Este family of Ferrara. Like Ariosto, Tasso treated the Crusades in *Jerusalem Delivered* (1575), which remained the most popular poem of its kind through the seventeenth century. Although at first the best composers of madrigals were Flemish, after 1575 Italians dominated the form. Foremost among them was Carlo Gesualdo (c. 1560–1613), an aristocrat whose music was as bold and flamboyant as his personality. His madrigals, like those of Luca Marenzio (1553–1599), are full of complex verbal and musical conceits that make them counterparts to the paintings of the High Mannerists.

The church dignitaries at the Council of Trent (1545–63), which spearheaded the Counter-Reformation in the Catholic church, objected to the growing use of secular melodies in sacred music, as well as to elaborate polyphony that obscured the words of the liturgy. In response, Giovanni Palestrina (c. 1525–1594) based his masses on traditional Gregorian chants. In many respects, however, his works are the successors of Josquin Des Prés' in their seamless texture and the perfect balance of melodic and harmonic values—that is, the beauty both of the principal melody and the other notes that accompany it, known as harmony. Palestrina, who held all the important musical posts in Rome during his lifetime, had special authority because of the backing of the papacy, and his style became "classic": it was held up as a model for imitation into the twentieth century.

Venice, unlike Rome, was ruled by secular authorities, so that Venetian music differed greatly from that composed for the pope. The vast spaces of St. Mark's Church—which was the palace chapel of the Doges—encouraged the colorful music of Palestrina's contemporary, Andrea Gabrieli (1510–1586), who had studied under the Fleming Adrian Willaert (c. 1490–1562) and his nephew and pupil Giovanni Gabrieli (1557–1612). The compositions of the Gabrielis emphasized sensuous effects of sound over counterpoint (different melodic lines moving independently, or "counter" to each other). Giovanni was also the first composer to specify which instruments should play which parts, to include dynamic markings in his music as indications of loudness and softness, and to make use of harmonies that sound "modern" to our ears, although Palestrina had effectively abandoned the modes except insofar as they were an inescapable part of church music. Much of Giovanni's music was purely instrumental. Instrument-only music in the late sixteenth century began to achieve its independence from vocal music by adapting popular dance tunes, often treated as a theme with variations. Such dances had been performed for centuries, although they were rarely written down. This development coincided with the creation of new families of instruments, such as viols and recorders, whose ranges—soprano, contralto, tenor, and bass—approximated those of human voices. These instruments lent Late Renaissance music a wonderfully diverse and distinctive sound.

The principal theatrical performances in sixteenth-century Italy were public spectacles paid for by the aristocracy. They were an outgrowth of comic interludes (*intermezzi*), which were performed between the acts of dramas and featured such sensational scenery, costumes, music, dance, and special effects that they soon became more important than the plays themselves. The most splendid spectacles were produced in Florence to glorify the Medici family in allegorical terms: *Masque of the Genealogy of the Gods* (1566), with sets and costumes designed by Giorgio Vasari, and *The Battle of the Argonauts,* mounted in 1608 on the Arno River. These displays spurred the development of more elaborate and sophisticated scenery design at the Medici court under Bernardo Buontalenti (1536–1608) and his pupil Giulio Parigi

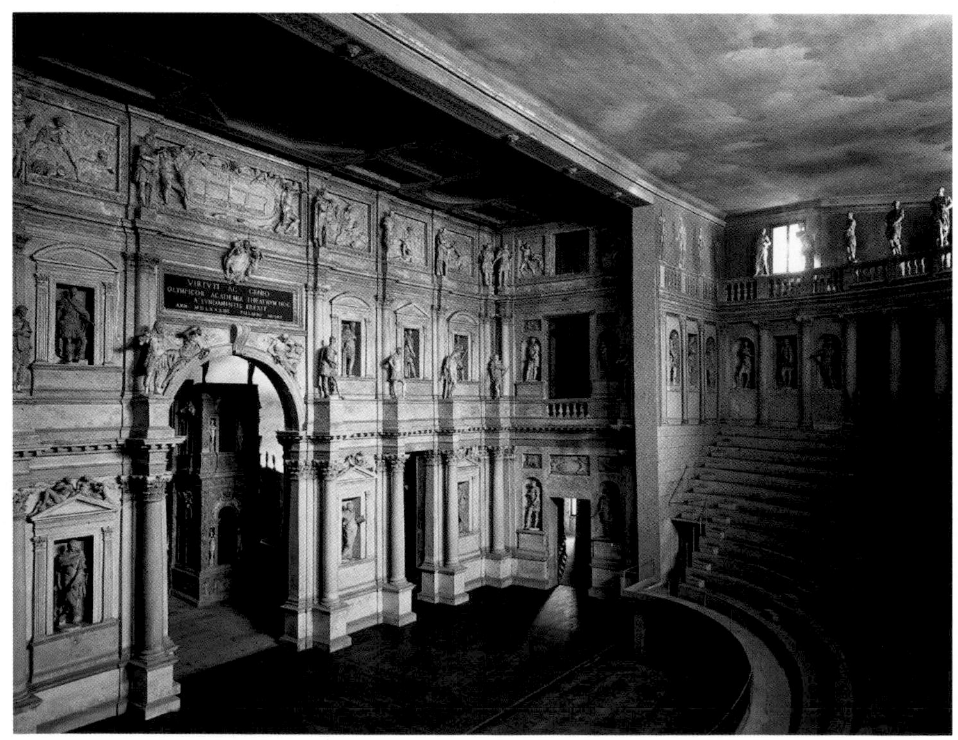

Andrea Palladio and Vincenzo Scamozzi. *Stage of the Teatro Olimpico, Vicenza.* c. 1585 (executed by Scamozzi)

(c. 1570–1635), as well as in Ferrara, Mantua, Urbino, Milan, Parma, and Rome. Scenography initially relied on the accounts of Roman theater in the architectural treatise of Vitruvius, which was published in 1486, the same year that the humanist antiquarian Pomponius Laetus (1424–1498) began to produce ancient plays at the Roman Academy. Even more important was the influence of Leon Battista Alberti's linear perspective (see Primary Sources, no. 40, page 612). Sebastiano Serlio (1475–1554) published an architectural treatise in 1545, which included a number of stage designs that made use of Alberti's perspective system to visualize Vitruvius' descriptions of Roman theaters. Serlio's designs proved so influential throughout Europe that they were often used to illustrate later editions of Vitruvius.

The occasional nature of dramatic presentations meant that few permanent theaters were built during the sixteenth century. The first court theater was erected by Buontalenti for the Medici in Florence. More important was the first public theater, built in 1565 in Venice, which immediately established its leadership in theater writing and production. Twenty years later the architect Andrea Palladio (see pages 480–82) designed a theater for the Olympic Academy in Vicenza, which opened with a performance of Sophocles' *Oedipus Rex.* Although the theater was soon abandoned, its construction is a measure of sixteenth-century interest in serious classical theater. The most popular form of theater was pastoral plays. These shared a common story line, in which a sophisticated young man or woman—in Torquato Tasso's *Aminta* (1573) this was actually the god Cupid—is forced by circumstance to spend some time among simple rural folk. The healthy manner of living and innocent goodness of the country people teach an important moral lesson and send the protagonist back to normal life refreshed in spirit.

After 1550, Renaissance theories of drama centered on Horace's *Art of Poetry* and Aristotle's *Poetics,* which had been published in a Latin translation in 1498. Drawing on these sources, Julius Caesar Scaliger (1484–1558) and Lodovico Castelvetro (1505?–1571) insisted that both tragedy and comedy be presented in five acts and that they obey the "unities" of time, space, and action sanctioned as inviolable rules by Classical precedent: the events portrayed had to take place in roughly the same time as it took to present them (or at least within one day); in a space approximately the size of the actual stage; and with the story line revolving around a single incident or problem. The new body of theory also promoted the concept of verisimilitude, incorporating realism, morality, and universality (typical, normative traits). These ideas in turn led to an insistence on decorum: strict adherence to what was considered appropriate to the age, sex, temperament, and social status of each character. Drama was further divided into tragedy and comedy along class lines. Tragedy involved the actions of noble, that is, aristocratic, characters while comedy was devoted to the buffooneries of the lower classes. However, the few plays written according to these rules met with a mixed reception in sixteenth-century Italy.

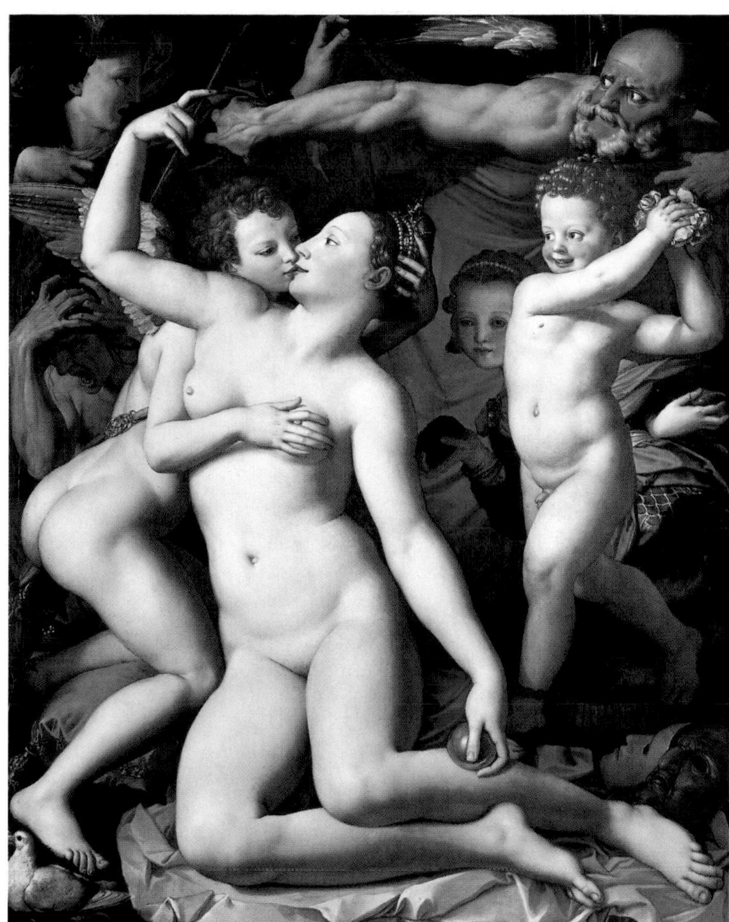

14-6. Agnolo Bronzino. *Allegory of Venus.* c. 1546. Oil on panel, 57½ x 45¼" (146.1 x 116.2 cm). The National Gallery, London

REPRODUCED BY COURTESY OF THE TRUSTEES

BRONZINO. High Mannerism is identified with the second generation of Mannerists. They transformed the styles of Rosso, Pontormo, and Parmigianino into one of cool perfection that filtered out the highly personal sensibilities of those artists. As a result, they produced few masterpieces. In their best works, however, formal beauty becomes the aesthetic counterpart to esoteric thought. Nowhere is this better seen than in the *Allegory of Venus* (fig. 14-6) by Agnolo Bronzino (1503–1572), Pontormo's favorite pupil. It was painted as a gift to Francis I of France from Cosimo I de' Medici. The central motif of Cupid embracing Venus was suggested by a lost *Triumph of Love* by Michelangelo that Pontormo and Bronzino are both known to have copied. However, as with so much else in High Mannerism, it has been corrupted in content and treatment. Father Time tears back the curtain from Fraud in the upper left-hand corner to reveal Venus and Cupid in an incestuous embrace, much to the delight of Folly, who is armed with roses, and the dismay of Jealousy, who tears her hair, as Pleasure, half-woman and half-snake, proffers a honeycomb. The moral is that folly blinds one to the jealousy and fraud of sensual love, which time reveals. The unmasking of this deceit revels in the very lasciviousness that it pretends to condemn. The painting is thus a perversion of the elevated humanism in Botticelli's *Birth of Venus* (see fig. 12-54). With its extreme stylization, Bronzino's

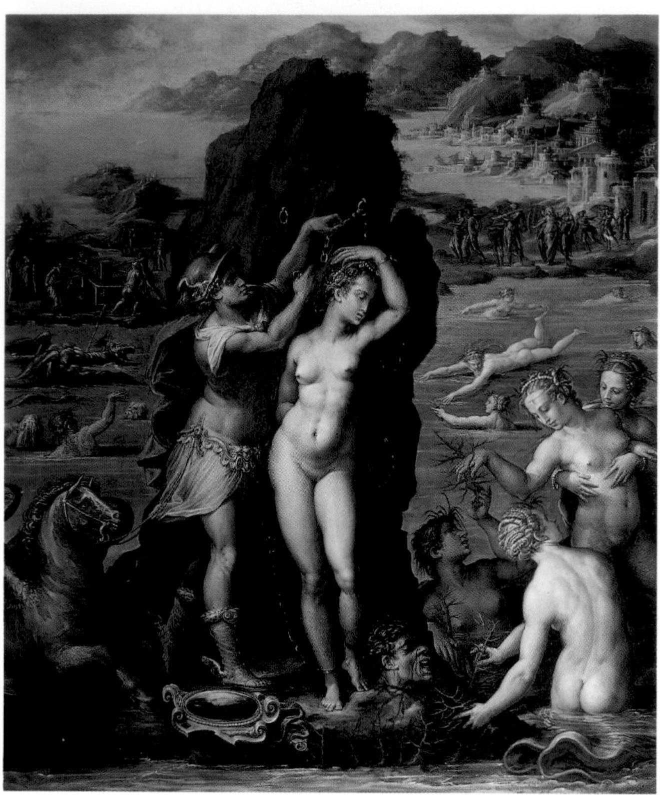

14-7. Giorgio Vasari. *Perseus and Andromeda*. 1570–72. Oil on slate, 45 1/2 x 34" (115.6 x 86.4 cm). Palazzo Vecchio, Florence

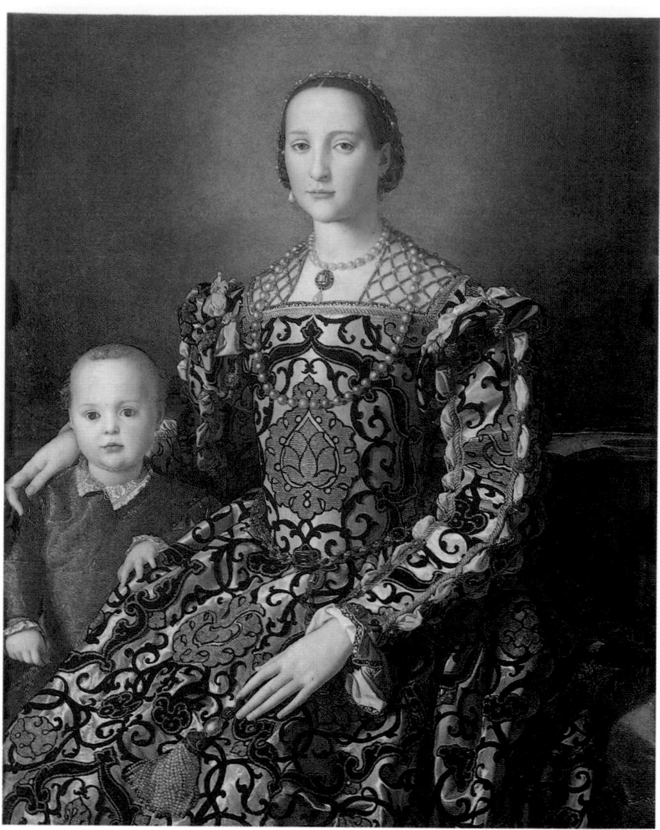

14-8. Agnolo Bronzino. *Eleanora of Toledo and Her Son Giovanni de' Medici*. c. 1550. Oil on panel, 45 1/4 x 37 3/4" (115 x 96 cm). Galleria degli Uffizi, Florence

subtle elegance proclaims an equally refined erotic ideal that reduces passion to a genteel exchange of serpentine gestures between figures as polished as marble.

VASARI. Bronzino's figures are indebted to Michelangelo in their sculptural quality (compare the Venus to *Night* in fig. 13-22). Those in *Perseus and Andromeda* (fig. 14-7) by Giorgio Vasari (1511–1574) owe more to Raphael. The debt is surprising, since Vasari esteemed Michelangelo above all others. The painting, one of his last works, is a play on Raphael's *Galatea* (see fig. 13-33). It forms part of Vasari's decorative scheme devoted to the four elements for the study of Francesco I de' Medici of Florence. The program, by the humanist Vincenzo Borghini, is devoted to the four elements. The artist has chosen to represent water with the story of coral, which according to legend was formed by the blood of the monster slain by Perseus when he rescued Andromeda. The subject provided an excuse to show voluptuous nudes, but here the story has become an enchanting fantasy. In keeping with this treatment, the Nereids, lighthearted versions of Raphael's mythological creatures, frolic with bits of coral they have discovered in the sea. Vasari's painting in turn spawned a host of imitations by minor artists in the waning years of Mannerism.

PORTRAITS. The Mannerists also produced splendid portraits in the same highly cultivated style. A superb example is Bronzino's painting of his main patron, Eleanora of Toledo (fig. 14-8), the wife of Cosimo I de' Medici. The sitter here appears as a member of an exalted social caste, not as an individual personality. Frozen behind the barrier of her ornate costume, Eleanora seems more akin to Parmigianino's *Madonna* (compare the hands) than to ordinary flesh and blood.

Mannerism in Venice

TINTORETTO. Mannerism did not appear in Venice until mid-century. There it became allied with the visionary tendencies we have already seen in Titian's late work. Its leading representative, Jacopo Tintoretto (1518–1594), was an artist of enormous energy and inventiveness. Judged by the conventional standards of Il Rosso, Pontormo, and Bronzino, he is not a Mannerist at all. Tintoretto reportedly wanted "to paint like Titian and to design like Michelangelo." However, his relationship to these two masters was as peculiar as Parmigianino's was to Raphael. *Christ Before Pilate* (fig. 14-9), one of his many huge canvases for the Scuola di San Rocco, the home of the Confraternity of St. Roch, provides a striking contrast with Titian's *Christ Crowned with Thorns* (see fig. 13-42). The bold brushwork, the glowing colors, and the sudden lights and shadows show what Tintoretto owed to the older artist. Indeed, the composition recalls Titian's *Madonna with Members of the Pesaro Family* (see fig. 13-38). Yet the total effect is unmistakably Mannerist. The feverish emotionalism of the flickering, unreal light, and the ghostly Christ, pencil-slim and motionless among the agitated Michelangelesque figures, remind us of Rosso's

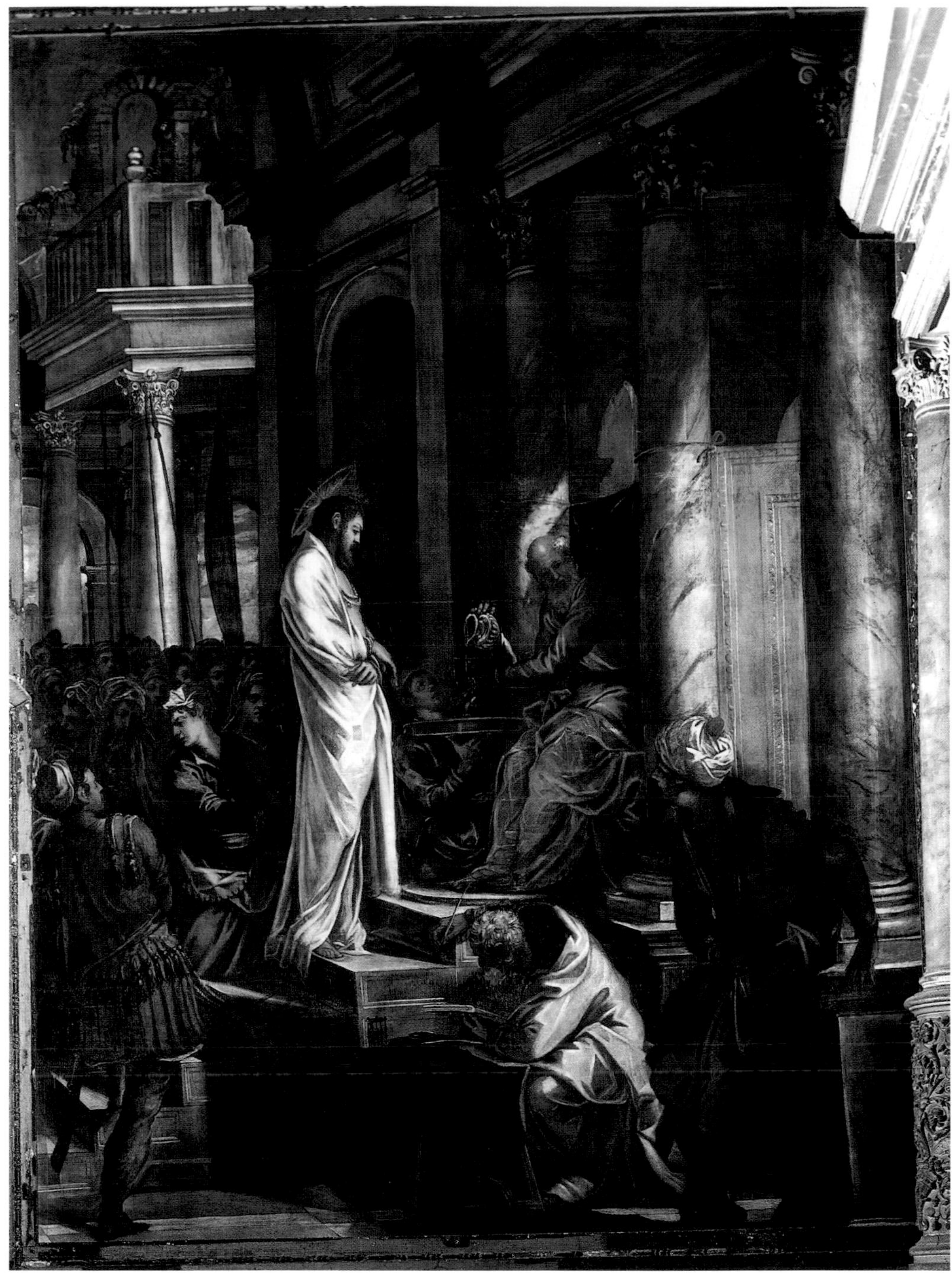

14-9. Jacopo Tintoretto. *Christ Before Pilate.* 1566–67. Wall painting, approx. 18'1" x 13'3½" (5.5 x 4.1 m). Scuola di San Rocco, Venice

Descent. There is, too, the suggestion of Raphael's influence—absorbed (like Michelangelo's) at second hand through prints and copies. His impact can be seen not only in individual figures, such as the seated scribe, but also in the strangely claustrophobic space (compare figs. 13-31 and 13-35).

The presentation is supremely theatrical. The fantastic setting with its deep space is very close to stage scenery of the time, notably the designs published by Sebastiano Serlio (see box page 467). The figures twist and turn in exaggerated poses to heighten the action as the crowd strains to see and hear what is going on. Occupying center stage in the midst of all this drama is Jesus, who faces Pilate with surprising calm. His stoic dignity emphasizes the Passion as the necessary fulfillment of this mission on earth to redeem humanity's sins through his sacrifice. His silence recalls the account in the Gospel of Matthew: "And when he was accused of the chief priests and elders, he answered nothing." Pilate washes "his hands before the multitude, saying, I am innocent of the blood of this just person." The turbaned figure in the foreground is Herod and the seated man in the white robe is the prophet Isaiah, who foretold the Passion in Book 53.

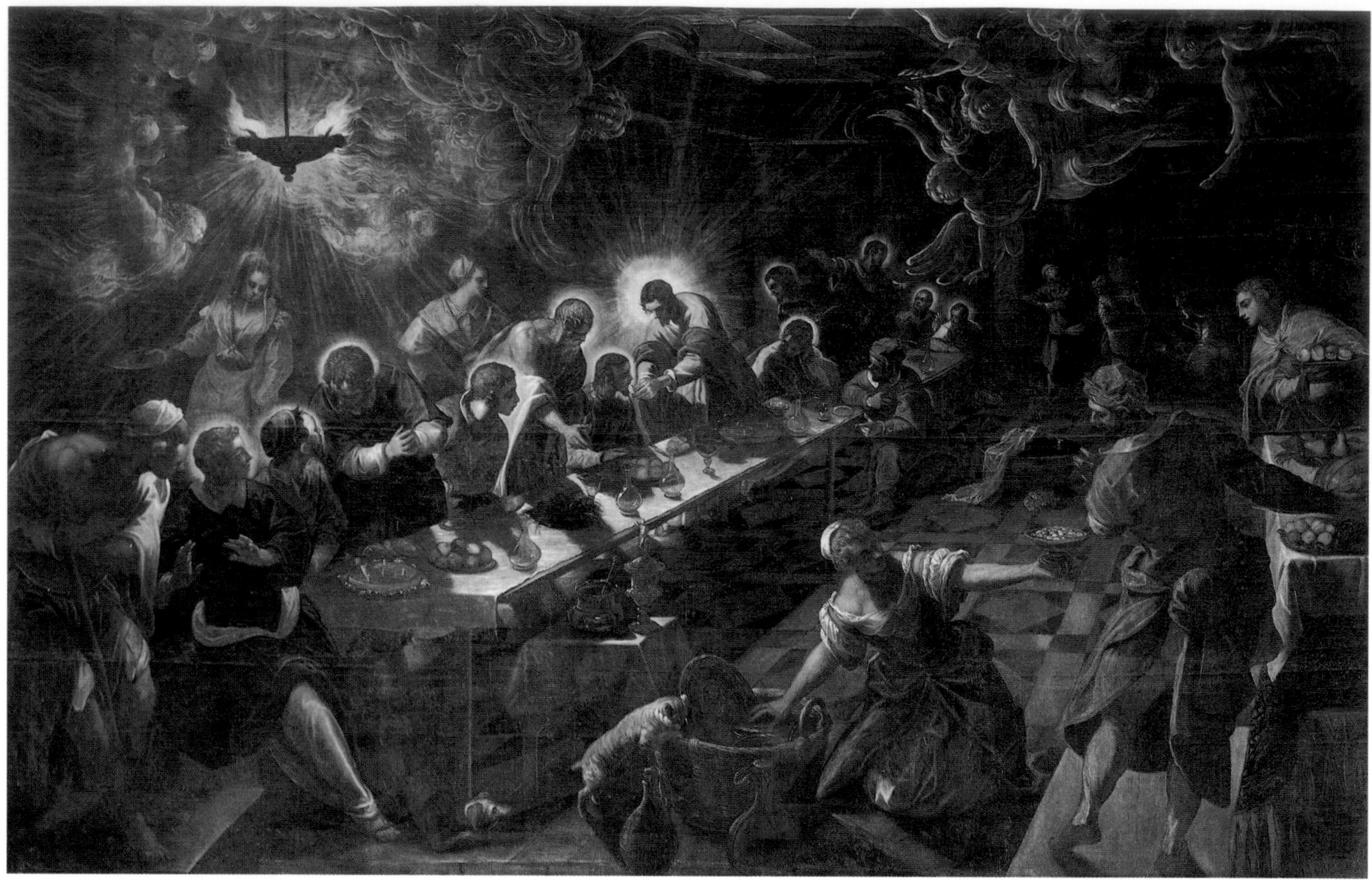

14-10. Jacopo Tintoretto. *The Last Supper.* 1592–94. Oil on canvas, 12' x 18'8" (3.7 x 5.7 m). S. Giorgio Maggiore, Venice

Tintoretto's final major work, *The Last Supper* (fig. 14-10), is also his most spectacular. At first, this canvas seems to deny the classic values of Leonardo's version (see fig. 13-3), painted almost exactly a century before. Christ, to be sure, is still at the center of the composition, but his small figure in the middle distance is distinguished mainly by the brilliant halo. In fact, this arrangement was designed to relate the scene to the space of the chancel of the church of S. Giorgio Maggiore (see figs. 14-27 and 14-28), for which it was commissioned. The painting was seen on the right wall by the faithful as they knelt to receive Communion, so that it receded less sharply than when viewed head on.

Tintoretto has gone to great lengths to give the event an everyday setting. The scene is cluttered with attendants, containers of food and drink, and animals. There are also celestial attendants who converge upon Christ just as he offers his body and blood, in the form of bread and wine, to the disciples. The smoke from the blazing oil lamp miraculously turns into clouds of angels, blurring the distinction between the natural and the supernatural and turning the scene into a magnificently orchestrated vision. Tintoretto barely hints at the human drama of Judas' betrayal, so important to Leonardo. Judas can be seen isolated on the near side of the table, but his role is so insignificant that he could almost be mistaken for an attendant. The artist's main concern has been to make visible the miracle of the Eucharist—the transubstantiation of earthly into divine food. The central importance of this institution to Catholic doctrine was forcefully reasserted during the Counter-Reformation.

EL GRECO. The last, and today most famous, Mannerist painter was also a product of the Venetian School. Domenikos Theotocopoulos (1541–1614), called El Greco, came from Crete, which was then under Venetian rule. His earliest paintings show that his training must have been from a Cretan artist still working in the Byzantine tradition. Soon after 1560 El Greco arrived in Venice and quickly absorbed the lessons of Titian, Tintoretto, and other artists. A decade later, in Rome, he came to know the art of Raphael, Michelangelo, and the central Italian Mannerists. In 1576/77 he went to Spain and settled in Toledo for the rest of his life. There he became a member of the leading intellectual circles of the city, then a major center of learning as well as the seat of Catholic reform in Spain. Although it provides the content of his work, Counter-Reformation theology does not account for the emotionalism that informs his painting. The spiritual tenor of El Greco's mature work was a response to mysticism, which was especially intense in Spain. Contemporary Spanish painting, however, was too provincial to affect him. His style had already been formed before he arrived in Toledo.

El Greco never forgot his Byzantine background. (Until the very end of his career, he signed his pictures in Greek.) *The Agony in the Garden* (fig. 14-11) builds on the Byzantine example seen in figure 8-52. However, it uses an irrational space to help conjure up a mystical vision representing a spiritual, rather than visual, reality. Jesus, isolated against a large rock that echoes his shape, is comforted by the angel bearing a golden cup, symbol of the Passion. The angel appears to kneel on a mysterious oval cloud, which envelops the sleeping disciples. In the distance to the right we see Judas and the soldiers coming to arrest the Lord. The composition is balanced by two giant clouds on either side. The entire landscape resounds with Jesus' agitation, represented by the sweep of supernatural forces. The elongated forms, eerie moonlight, and expressive colors help us to identify with his suffering.

The largest and most splendid of El Greco's major commissions, and the only one for a public chapel, is *The Burial of Count Orgaz* (figs. 14-12 and 14-13) in the church of Sto. Tomé. The program, which was given at the time of the commission, emphasizes the traditional role of good works in salvation and of the saints as intercessors with Heaven. The huge canvas honors a medieval benefactor who was so pious that St. Stephen and St. Augustine miraculously appeared at his funeral and lowered the body into its grave. The burial took place in 1323, but El Greco presents it as a contemporary event and even portrayed many of the local nobility and clergy among the attendants. The dazzling display of color and texture in the armor and vestments could hardly have been surpassed by Titian himself. Above, the count's soul (a cloudlike figure like the angels in Tintoretto's *Last Supper*) is carried to Heaven by an angel. The celestial assembly in the upper half of the picture is painted very differently from the group in the lower half: every form—clouds, limbs, draperies—takes part in the sweeping movement toward Christ. Here, even more than in Tintoretto's art, the entire range of Mannerism fuses into a single ecstatic vision.

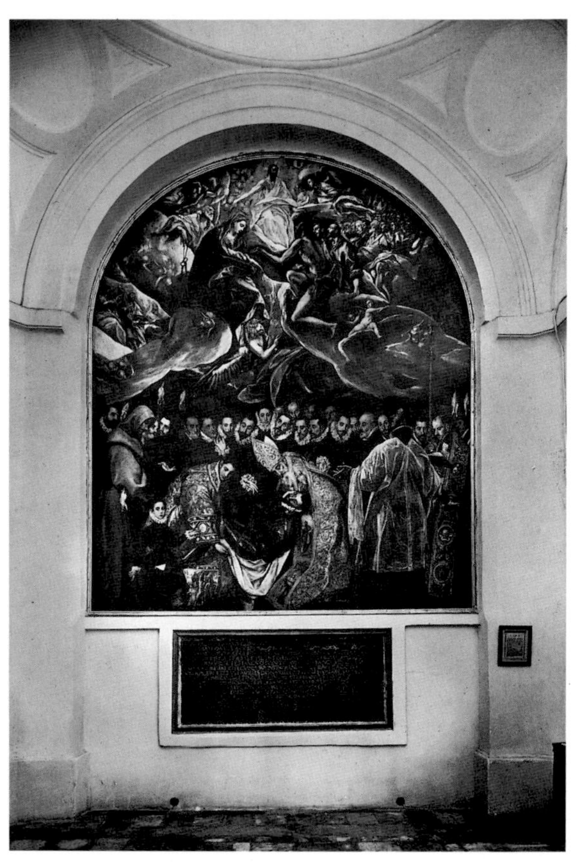

14-12. Chapel with *The Burial of Count Orgaz*. 1586. Sto. Tomé, Toledo, Spain

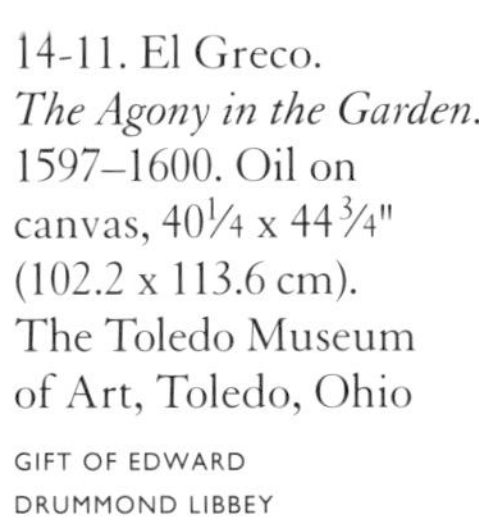

14-11. El Greco. *The Agony in the Garden*. 1597–1600. Oil on canvas, 40¼ x 44¾" (102.2 x 113.6 cm). The Toledo Museum of Art, Toledo, Ohio

GIFT OF EDWARD DRUMMOND LIBBEY

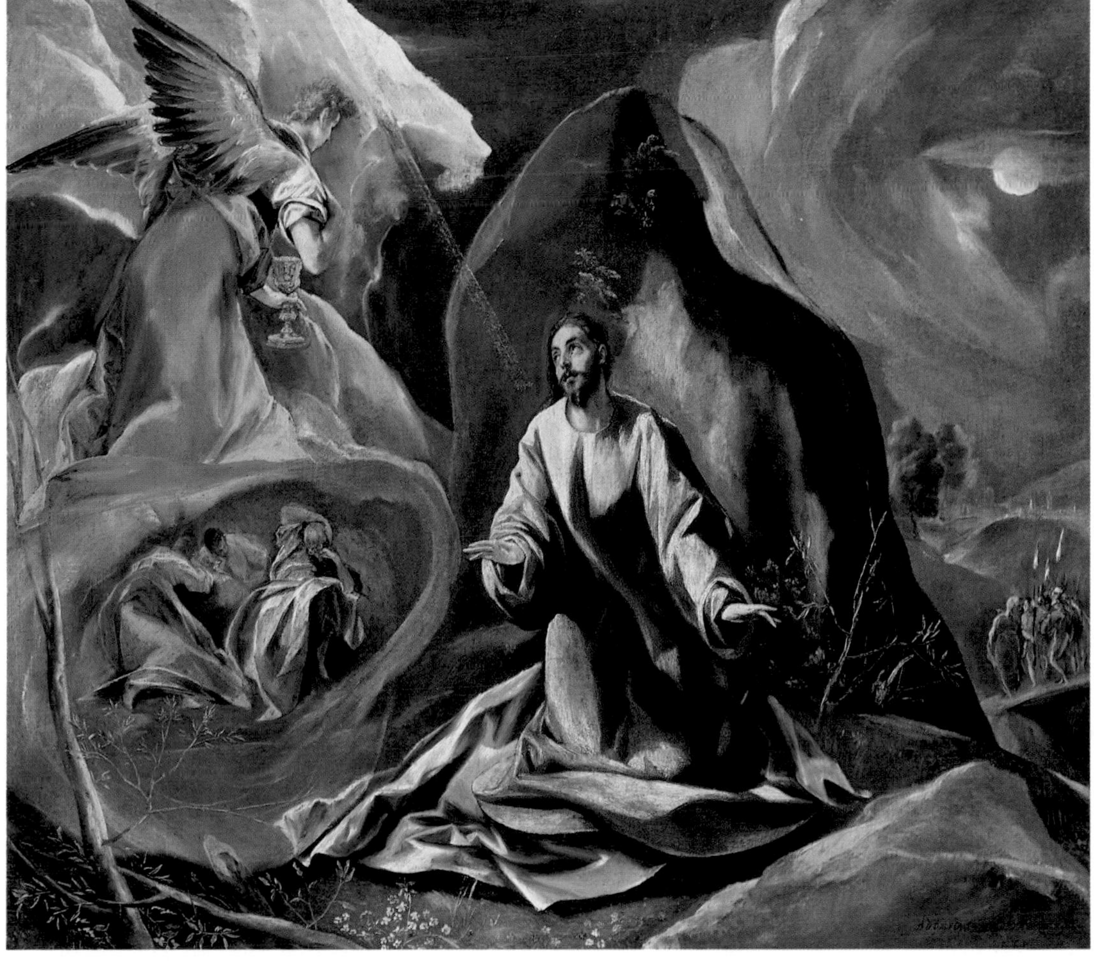

The full meaning of the work, however, becomes clear only when we see it in its original setting. Like a huge window, it fills one wall of its chapel. The bottom of the canvas is six feet above the floor, and as the chapel is only about 18 feet deep, we must look sharply upward to see the upper half of the picture. The foreshortening is calculated to achieve an illusion of boundless space above, while the figures in the lower foreground appear as on a stage. (Their feet are cut off by the molding just below the picture.) The large stone plaque set into the wall also belongs to the ensemble. It represents the front of the sarcophagus into which the two saints lower the body of the count and thus explains the action within the picture. The viewer, then, sees three levels of reality. The first is the grave itself, supposedly set into the wall at eye level and closed by an actual stone slab; the second is the reenactment of the miraculous burial; and the third is the vision of celestial glory witnessed by some of the participants. El Greco's task here was similar to Masaccio's in his *Trinity* mural (see fig. 12-22). But whereas Masaccio constructed the illusion of reality through a rational pictorial space that appears continuous with ours, El Greco has summoned an apparition that remains separate from its architectural surroundings.

El Greco has created a spiritual counterpart to his imagination. In contrast, Counter-Reformation images were given a convincing physical presence to convey their doctrinal message as clearly as possible. Every passage in *The Burial of Count Orgaz* is alive with the artist's peculiar religiosity, which is felt as a nervous exaltation occurring as the dreamlike vision is conjured up. This kind of mysticism is similar in character to the Spiritual Exercises of Ignatius of Loyola. St. Ignatius sought to make visions so real that they would seem to appear before the very eyes of the faithful. Such mysticism could be achieved only through fervent devotion. That effort is mirrored in the intensity of El Greco's work, which fully retains a feeling of spiritual struggle.

Although Mannerism spread to other cities, it did not become dominant outside Florence and Rome. Elsewhere it competed with other tendencies. In towns along the northern edge of the Lombard plain, such as Brescia and Verona, there were a number of artists who worked in styles based on Giorgione and Titian, but with a stronger interest in everyday reality.

SAVOLDO. One of the earliest and most attractive of these North Italian realists was Girolamo Savoldo (c. 1480–1550) from

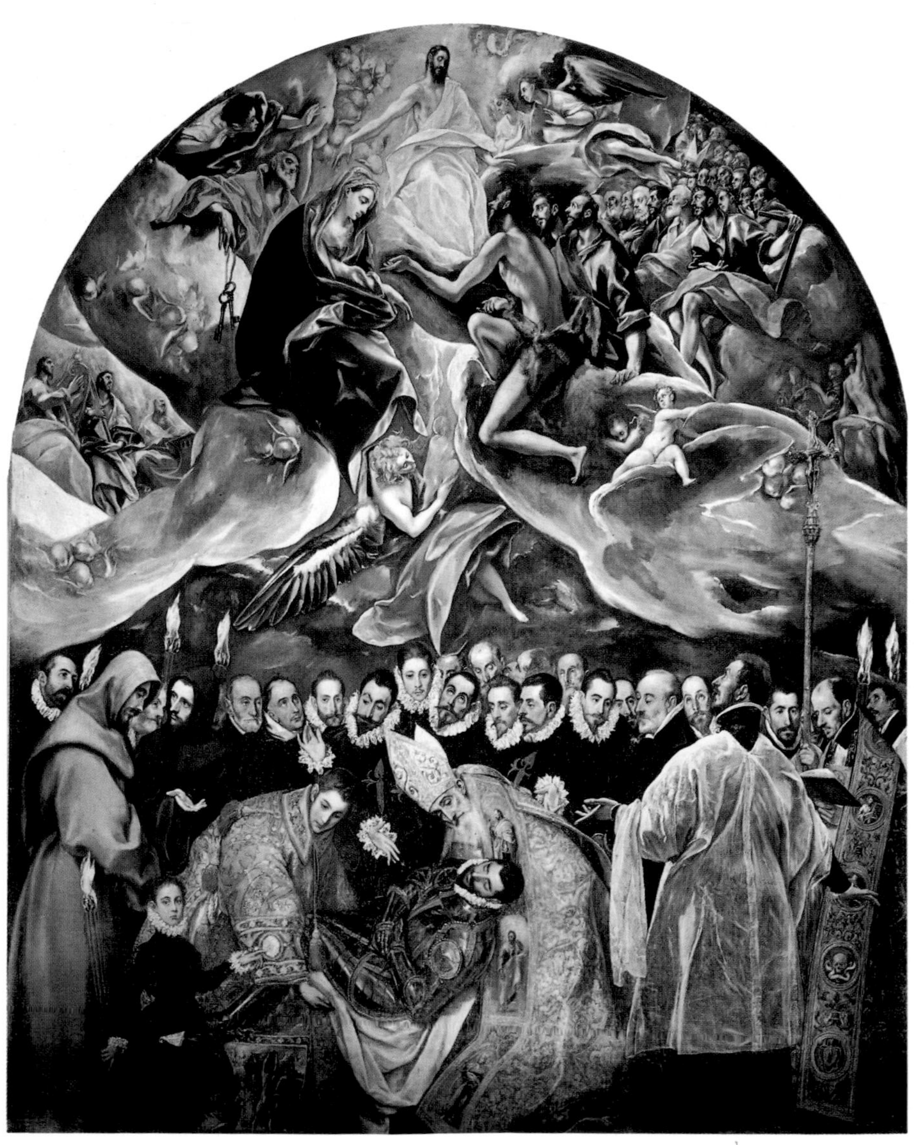

14-13. El Greco. *The Burial of Count Orgaz.* 1586. Oil on canvas, 16' x 11'10" (4.9 x 3.6 m). Sto. Tomé, Toledo, Spain

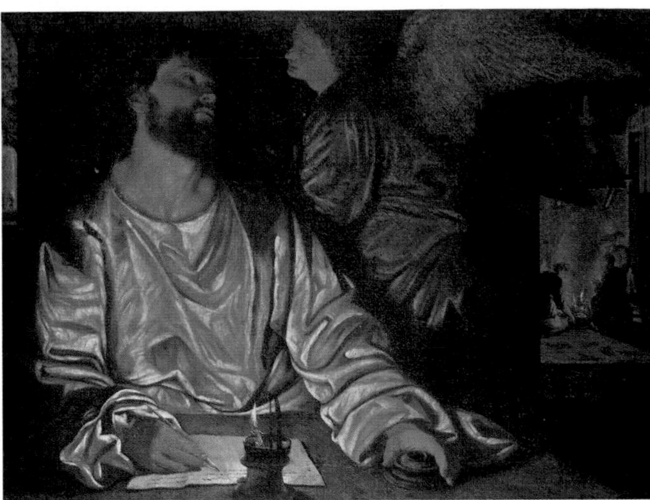

14-14. Girolamo Savoldo. *St. Matthew and the Angel.* c. 1535. Oil on canvas, 36¾ x 49" (93.3 x 124.5 cm). The Metropolitan Museum of Art, New York

MARQUAND FUND, 1912

Brescia. His *St. Matthew and the Angel* (fig. 14-14) must have been painted about the same time as Parmigianino's *Madonna with the Long Neck*. The style reflects Titian's influence (compare fig. 13-39), but Titian would never have placed Matthew in such a domestic setting. The humble scene in the background shows the saint's environment to be lowly indeed, and makes the presence of the angel dictating scripture to the illiterate saint doubly miraculous. This tendency to visualize sacred events among ramshackle buildings and simple people had been characteristic of Gothic painting, especially in the North, and Savoldo must have acquired it from that source. The nocturnal lighting, too, recalls such Gothic pictures as the *Nativity* by Gentile da Fabriano (see fig. 11-98). But whereas the main illumination in Gentile's panel is the divine radiance of the child, Savoldo uses an ordinary oil lamp for his similarly magic and intimate effect.

BASSANO. A different form of realism is found in the paintings of Jacopo da Ponte (c. 1510–1592), called Bassano after the town 30 miles northwest of Venice where he passed most of his career. He inevitably fell under the influence of Titian, but just as important to the formation of his style were prints by Germans such as Albrecht Dürer, who had twice visited Venice (see page 507), and by the Mannerists, notably Parmigianino. In *The Adoration of the Shepherds* (fig. 14-15), Bassano's most characteristic subject, the landscape will remind us of the setting in Titian's *Bacchanal*. The figures, however, show the impact of Parmigianino. Their interlocking rhythms, the gentle grace of the Madonna, the gesture of the Infant Christ, the seemingly arbitrary column, all can be found in *The Madonna with the Long Neck*. The pose of the shepherd doffing his hat, too, has its source in Parmigianino's etching *The Entombment*. The high-pitched color is Mannerist as well.

The role of Northern art seems less clear until we realize that the tender relationship between the Virgin and Child has an intimacy that can have come only from German prints (compare fig. 15-24), not Italian painting. The humble setting shows that Bassano must also have known a similar work by Martin Schongauer (see page 503). And the mountains in the distance find their nearest counterpart in the watercolor *Italian Mountains* (see fig. 16-4) that Dürer sketched on his way back from Venice, rather than any work by Titian. Unlike Dürer's, Jacopo's landscape is a "portrait," showing Mount Grappa near Bassano. *The Adoration of the Shepherds* is more than a synthesis of diverse sources, however. What is novel in all this is the pastoral quality of the scene. The artist includes peasants of the sort he must have met around his native town. Andrea Mantegna and the Fleming Hugo van der Goes had been among the few to show such simple people (see fig. 15-12). Yet for Bassano they were an essential feature of his work. His realism, then, is not one of specific details but of general type, which offsets the self-conscious artificiality of his style.

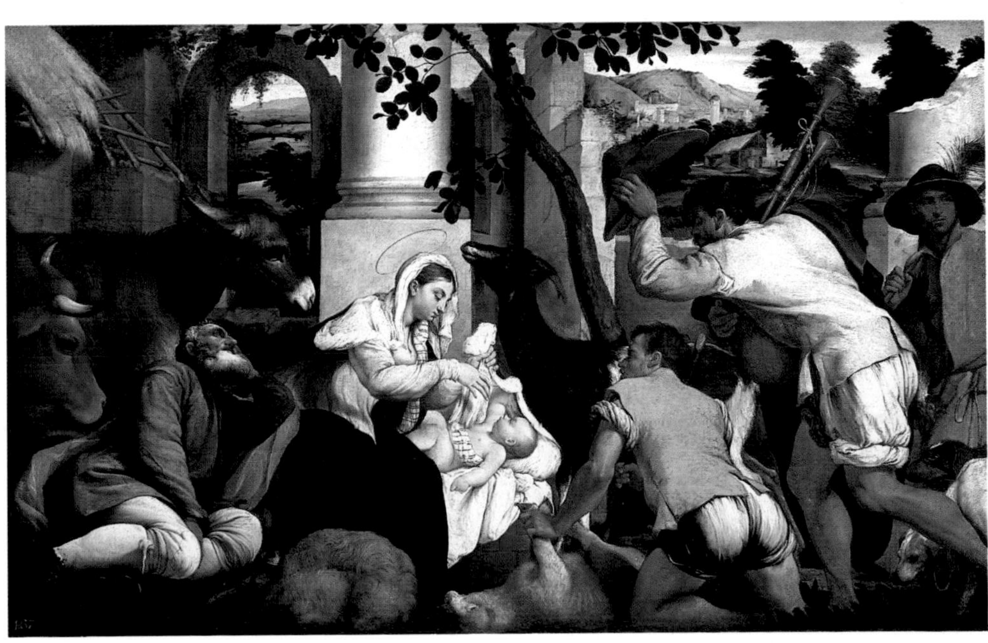

14-15. Jacopo Bassano. *The Adoration of the Shepherds.* 1542–47. Oil on canvas, 4'7" x 7'2¼" (1.39 x 2.19 m). The Royal Collection

© 1993. HER MAJESTY QUEEN ELIZABETH II

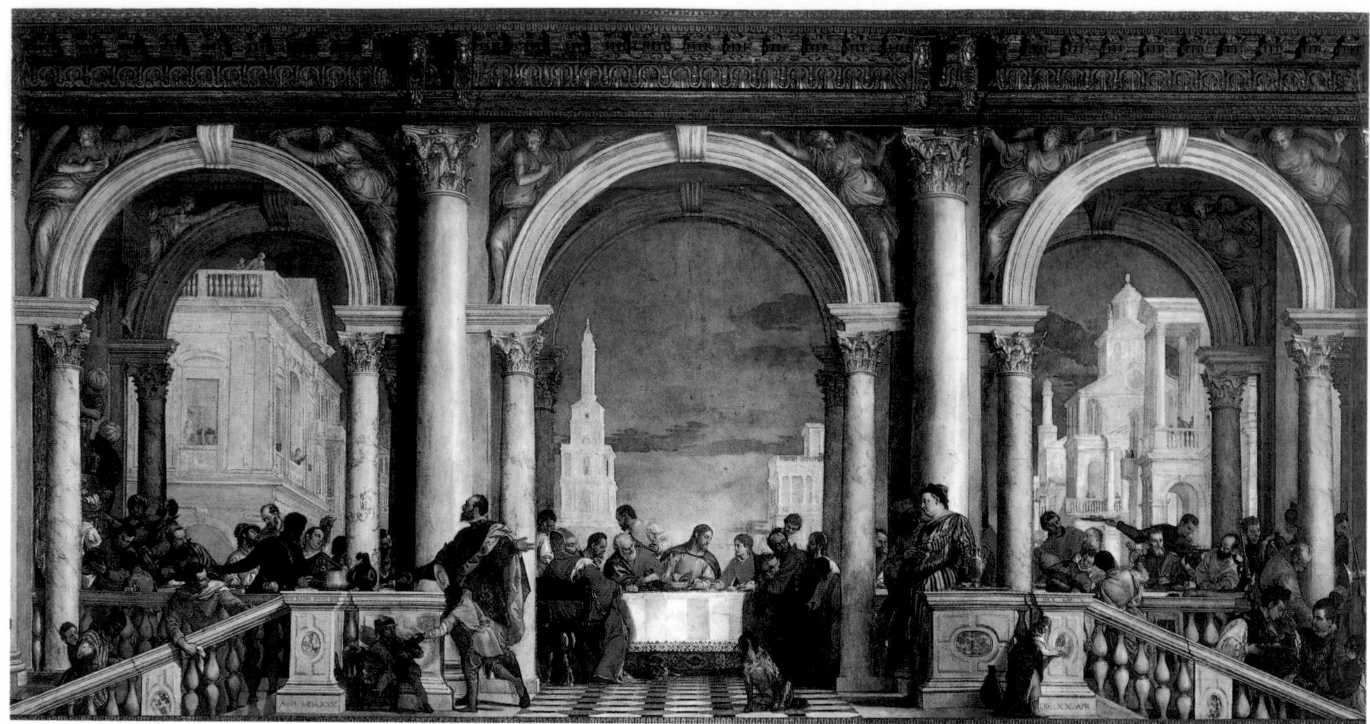

14-16. Paolo Veronese. *Christ in the House of Levi.* 1573. Oil on canvas, 18'2" x 42' (5.5 x 12.8 m). Galleria dell'Accademia, Venice

VERONESE. In the work of Paolo Veronese (Paolo Caliari, 1528–1588), North Italian realism takes on the splendor of a pageant. Born and trained in Verona, Veronese became, with Tintoretto, the most important painter in Venice. Both found favor with the public, although they worked in completely different styles. The contrast is evident if we compare Tintoretto's *The Last Supper* (see fig. 14-10) and Veronese's *Christ in the House of Levi* (fig. 14-16), which have similar subjects. Veronese avoids all reference to the supernatural. His symmetrical composition harks back to paintings by Leonardo and Raphael, while the festive mood recalls works by Titian of the 1520s. Hence, at first glance the picture looks like a High Renaissance work born 50 years too late. Missing, however, is the ideal conception of humanity that underlies the High Renaissance. Veronese paints a sumptuous banquet, a feast for the eyes, but not "the intention of man's soul."

We are not even sure which event from the life of Jesus he originally meant to depict. He gave the painting its present title only after he had been summoned by the religious tribunal of the Inquisition on the charge of filling his picture with "buffoons, drunkards, Germans, dwarfs, and similar vulgarities" unsuited to its sacred character. The account of this trial shows that the tribunal thought the painting represented the Last Supper, but Veronese's testimony never made clear whether it was the Last Supper or the Supper in the House of Simon. To him this distinction made little difference. In the end, he settled on a third title, *Christ in the House of Levi,* which allowed him to leave the offending incidents in place. He argued that they were no more objectionable than the nudity of Jesus and the Heavenly Host in Michelangelo's *The Last Judgment.*

The tribunal, however, failed to see the analogy on the grounds that "in the Last Judgment it was not necessary to paint garments, and there is nothing in those figures that is not spiritual." [See Primary Sources, no. 45, pages 615–16.] The Inquisition, of course, considered only the impropriety of Veronese's art, not its lack of spiritual depth. His refusal to admit the justice of the charge, his insistence on his right to include directly observed details, however "improper," and his indifference to the subject of the picture spring from an attitude so "extroverted" that it was not widely accepted until the nineteenth century. The painter's domain, Veronese seems to say, is the entire visible world, and here he will admit no authority other than his senses. Though tame by Mannerist standards, the presentation is highly theatrical, from the vast, stagelike space to the lavish costumes, which hardly differ from those in Venetian productions of the day. And just as it goes against the religious doctrines of the Counter-Reformation, the painting also violates the concept of decorum in contemporary dramatic theory (see box page 466–67).

Proto-Baroque Painting

A third trend that emerged about 1520 in northern Italy has been labeled Proto-Baroque, partly because it eludes convenient categories and partly because it embodies so many features that would later characterize the Baroque style. This tendency centers largely on Correggio, although later in the century it has a counterpart in architecture (see pages 482–83).

CORREGGIO. Correggio (Antonio Allegri da Correggio, 1494–1534), an extraordinarily gifted North Italian painter, spent most of his brief career in Parma, which lies to the west along the Lombard plain. As a result, he absorbed a wide range of influences: first from Leonardo and the Venetians, then from Michelangelo and Raphael. But their High Renaissance ideal of classical balance did not attract him for long. Correggio's work

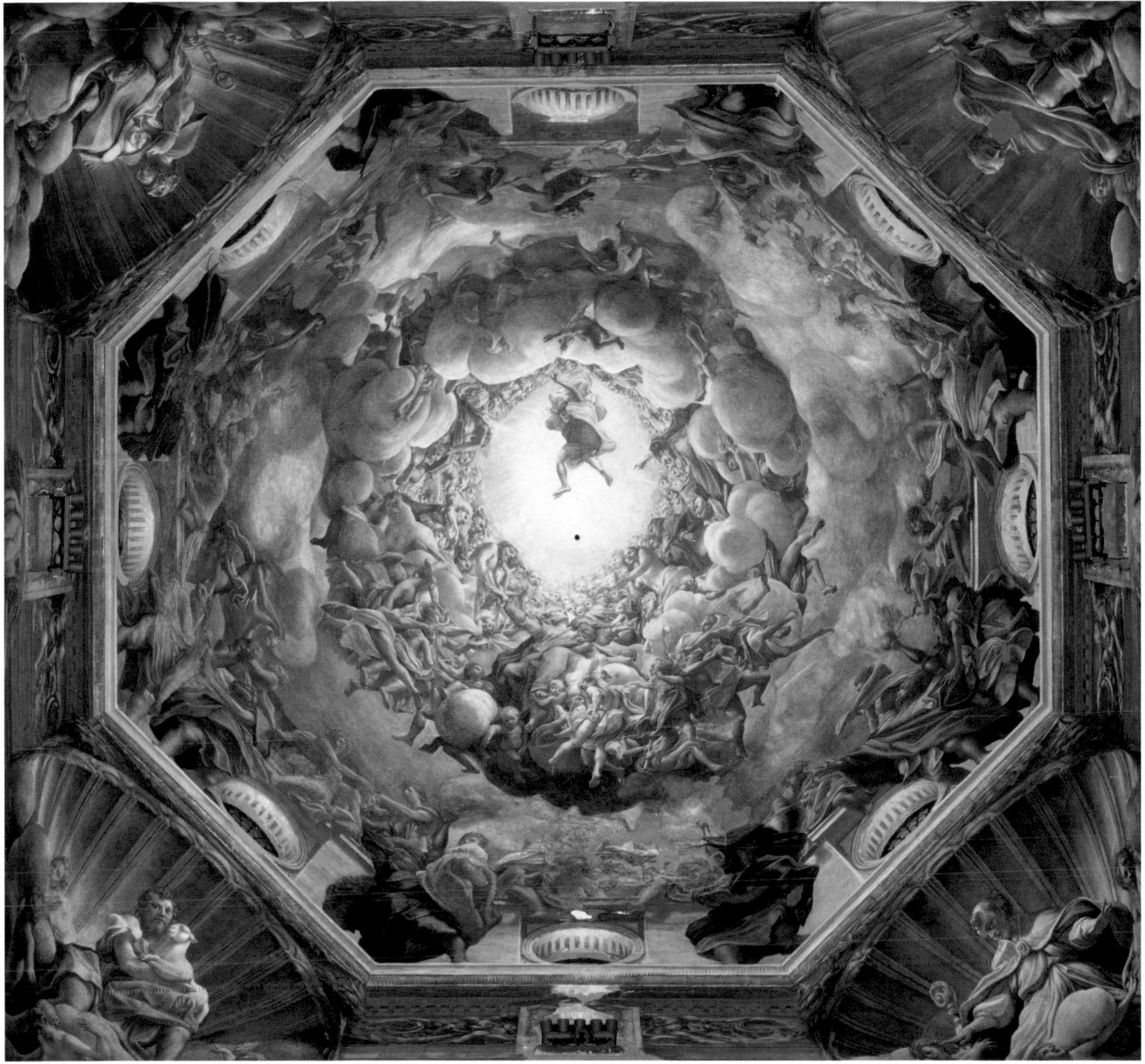

14-17. Correggio. *The Assumption of the Virgin*. Dome, Parma Cathedral, Parma, Italy. c. 1525. Fresco, diameter of base of dome 35'10" x 37'11" (10.93 x 11.56 m)

applies North Italian realism with the imaginative freedom of the Mannerists. (Surprisingly, we do not find any hint of his fellow townsman Parmigianino in his style.) His largest work, the fresco of *The Assumption of the Virgin* in the dome of Parma Cathedral (fig. 14-17), is a masterpiece of illusionistic perspective. A few years earlier he painted a similar dome, based on one by Andrea Mantegna (see pages 426–27), that is tame in comparison. Here the soaring figures that fill the vast, luminous space move with such ease that the force of gravity seems not to exist for them. Yet these are beings of flesh and blood, not spirits, and they delight in their weightless condition.

There was little difference between spiritual and physical ecstasy for Correggio, who thereby established an important precedent for Baroque artists such as Gianlorenzo Bernini (see page 547). We can see this by comparing *The Assumption of the Virgin* with his *Jupiter and Io* (fig. 14-18), part of a series depicting the loves of the classical gods. The nymph, swooning in the embrace of a cloudlike Jupiter, is the direct kin of the jubilant angels in the

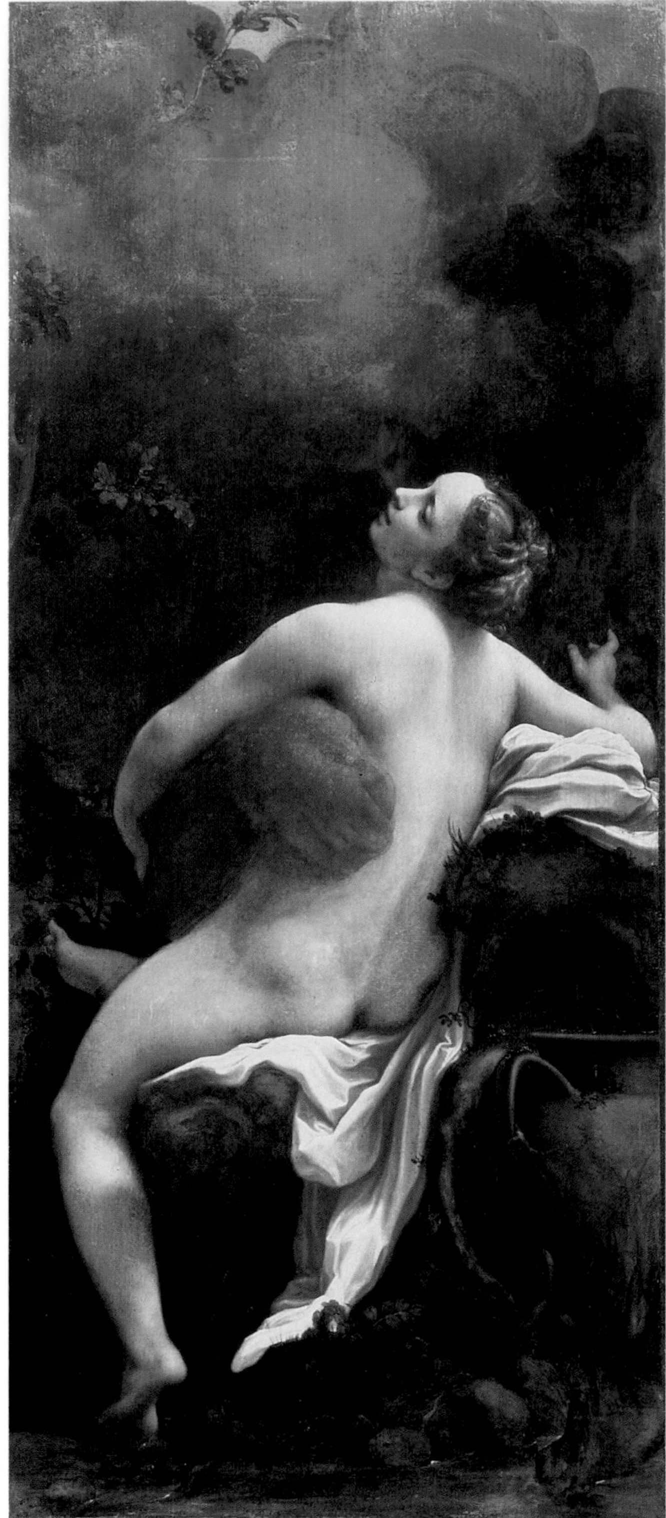

14-18. Correggio. *Jupiter and Io.* c. 1532. Oil on canvas, $64\frac{1}{2}$ x $27\frac{3}{4}$" (163.8 x 70.5 cm). Kunsthistorisches Museum, Vienna

fresco. The use of sfumato, combined with a Venetian sense of color and texture, produces a frank sensuality that far exceeds Titian's in his *Bacchanal* (see fig. 13-37). Correggio had no immediate successors, nor did he have any lasting influence on the art of his century. Toward 1600, however, his work began to be widely admired. For the next century and a half he was viewed as the equal of Raphael and Michelangelo, while the Mannerists, so important before, were largely forgotten.

SCULPTURE

Italian sculptors of the later sixteenth century fail to match the achievements of the painters. Perhaps Michelangelo's overpowering personality discouraged new talent in this field, but there was also a lack of major commissions outside of portraiture, as we can tell from the large number of small bronzes that were made during this period. In any case, the most interesting sculpture of this period was produced outside of Italy. After the death of Michelangelo in 1564 even the leading sculptor in Florence was a Northerner.

Mannerism

CELLINI. The second, elegant phase of Mannerism appears in countless sculptural examples in Italy and abroad. The best-known representative of the style is Benvenuto Cellini (1500–1571), a Florentine goldsmith and sculptor who owes much of his fame to his colorful autobiography. The gold saltcellar for Francis I of France (fig. 14-19), Cellini's only important work in precious metal that has survived, displays the virtues and limitations of his art. The main function of this lavish object is clearly as a conversation piece. Because salt comes from the sea and pepper from the land, the boat-shaped salt container is protected by Neptune. The pepper, in a tiny triumphal arch, is watched over by a personification of Earth. On the base are figures that represent the four seasons and the four parts of the day.

The saltcellar thus reflects the cosmic significance of the Medici tombs (compare fig. 13-22). But on this miniature scale Cellini's program turns into playful fancy on the same order as Vasari's *Perseus and Andromeda* (see fig. 14-7). Cellini wants to impress us with his ingenuity and skill. Earth, he wrote, is "fashioned like a woman with all the beauty of form, the grace and charm, of which my art was capable." The allegorical significance of the design is simply a pretext for this display of virtuosity. For instance, when he tells us that Neptune and Earth each have a bent and a straight leg to signify mountains and plains, form is completely divorced from content. Despite his admiration for Michelangelo, Cellini creates elegant figures that are as elongated, smooth, and languid as Parmigianino's (see fig. 14-4).

PRIMATICCIO. Parmigianino also influenced Francesco Primaticcio (1504–1570), Rosso's assistant and successor at the royal château of Fontainebleau. A man of many talents, Primaticcio designed the interior decoration of some of the main rooms, which combine painted scenes and a sculptured stucco framework. The section shown in figure 14-20 caters to the same aristocratic taste that admired the saltcellar of Cellini, who was Primaticcio's rival at the court of Francis I in 1540–45. The four maidens have no specific allegorical significance, although their role recalls the nudes of the Sistine ceiling. They seem to perform a task for which they are equally ill-fitted: they reinforce the piers that sustain the ceiling. These willowy caryatids epitomize the studied nonchalance of second-phase Mannerism. The painting is nearly lost in the luxurious ornamentation. Executed by assistants from Primaticcio's design, it shows Apelles painting the abduction of Campaspe by Alexander the Great, who gave his favorite concubine to the artist

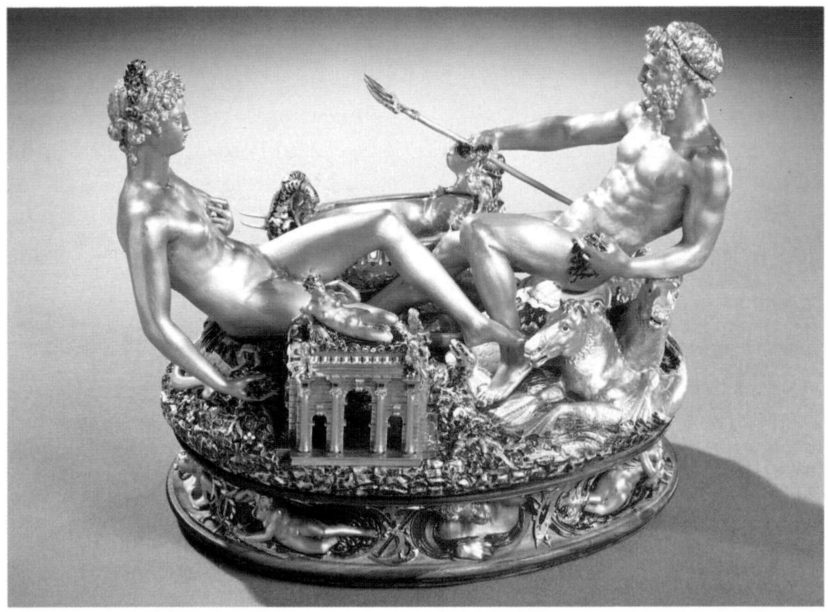

14-19. Benvenuto Cellini. *Saltcellar of Francis I.* 1539–43. Gold with enamel, $10^{1}/_{4}$ x $13^{1}/_{8}$" (26 x 33.3 cm). Kunsthistorisches Museum, Vienna

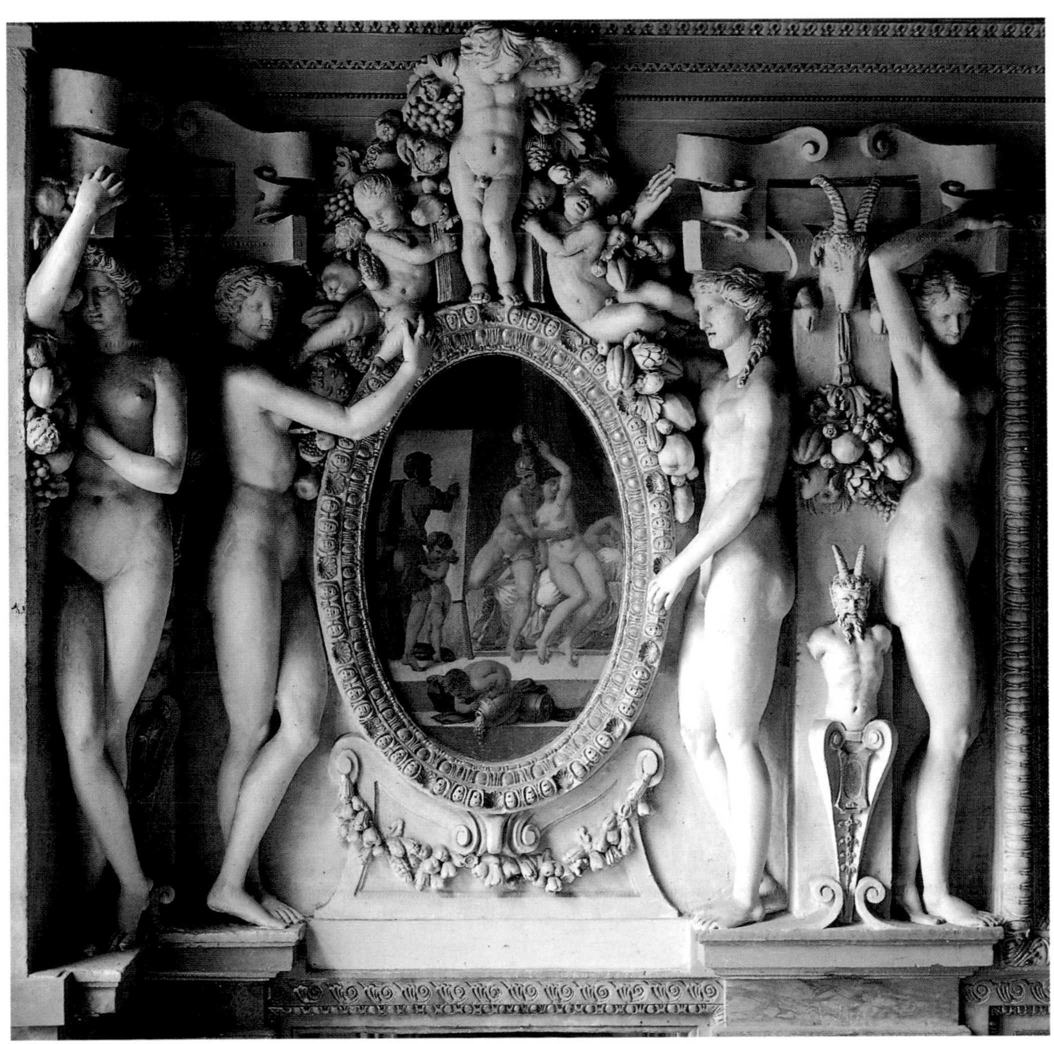

14-20. Francesco Primaticcio. *Stucco Figures.* c. 1541–45. Room of the Duchesse d'Estampes, Château of Fontainebleau, France

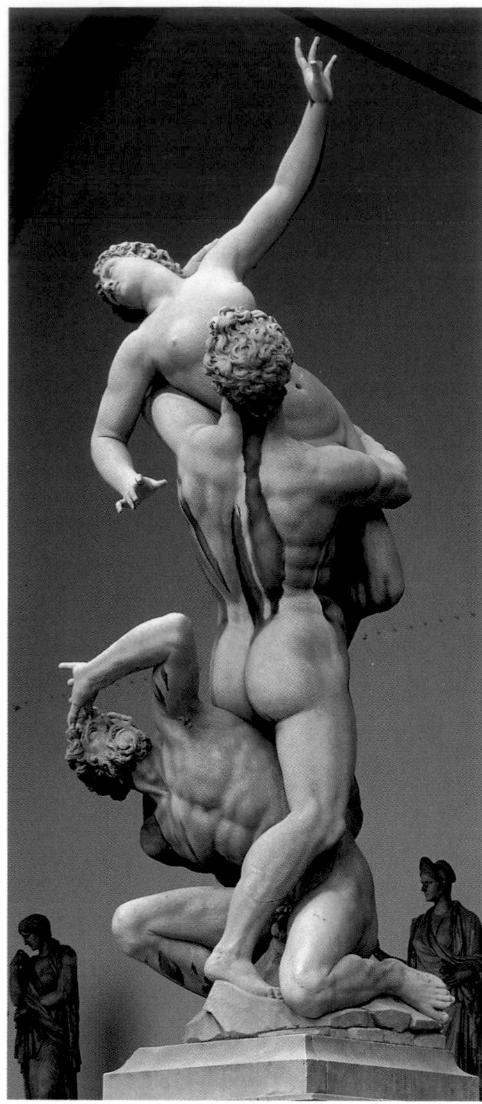

14-21. Giovanni Bologna. *The Abduction of the Sabine Woman.* Completed 1583. Marble, height 13'6" (4.1 m). Loggia dei Lanzi, Florence

when he fell in love with her. Such a heady mixture of violence and eroticism appealed greatly to the Mannerists. Yet the story was interpreted as a gesture of uncommon respect and nobility by the Roman historian Pliny, which justified the subject.

GIOVANNI BOLOGNA. Cellini, Primaticcio, and the other Italians employed by Francis I at Fontainebleau made Mannerism the dominant style in mid-sixteenth-century France. Their influence went far beyond the royal court. It reached Jean de Bologne (1529–1608), a gifted young sculptor from Douai in northern France, who went to Italy about 1555 for further training. He stayed and, under the Italianized name of Giovanni Bologna, became the most important sculptor in Florence during the last third of the century. His over-lifesize marble group, *The Abduction of the Sabine Woman* (fig. 14-21), was especially admired and still has its place of honor near the Palazzo Vecchio.

The subject, drawn from the legends of ancient Rome, seems an odd choice for statuary. According to the story, the city's founders, an adventurous band of men from across the sea, tried in vain to find wives among their neighbors, the Sabines. Finally, they resorted to a trick. Having invited the entire Sabine tribe into Rome for a festival, they attacked them, took the women away by force, and thus ensured the future of their race. Actually, the artist designed the group with no specific subject in mind. It was meant to demonstrate his ability while he was a student at the Academy of Design, founded by Vasari in 1562 under the patronage of Cosimo I de' Medici. He chose what seemed to him the most difficult feat, three figures of contrasting character united in a single action. When asked to identify the figures, the artist proposed *Andromeda,* but another member of the academy, Raffaello Borhini, suggested *The Rape of the Sabine Woman* as the most suitable title.

Here, then, is another artist who is noncommittal about subject matter, although his motive was different from Veronese's. Like Cellini, Bologna wished to display his virtuosity. His task was to carve in marble, on a massive scale, a sculptural composition that was to be seen from all sides. This had previously been attempted only in bronze and on a much smaller scale (see fig. 12-50). He has solved this formal problem brilliantly, but at the cost of insulating his group from the world of human experience. These figures, spiraling upward as if confined inside a tall, narrow cylinder, perform their well-rehearsed exercise with ease. Yet, like much Hellenistic sculpture (compare fig. 5-74), they lack emotional meaning. We admire their discipline but find no trace of pathos.

ARCHITECTURE

Mannerism

The term *Mannerism* was first coined to describe painting. We have had no difficulty in applying it to sculpture. But can it be usefully extended to architecture as well? And if so, what qualities must we look for? These questions have proved difficult to answer precisely. The reasons are all the more puzzling because the important Mannerist architects were leading painters and sculptors. Yet today only a few structures are generally considered to be Mannerist.

ROMANO. Such a building is the Palazzo del Te, in Mantua, by Giulio Romano (c. 1499–1566), Raphael's chief assistant. The courtyard facade (fig. 14-22) features unusually squat proportions and coarse rustication. The massive keystones of the windows have been "squeezed" up by the force of the triangular lintels. The effect is an absurd impossibility. There are no true arches except over the central doorway, which is surmounted by a pediment in violation of classical canon. Even more bizarre is how the triglyph midway between each pair of columns "slips" downward in defiance of all logic and accepted practice, creating the sense that the frieze might collapse before our eyes.

The reliance on gestures that depart from Renaissance norms does not in itself define Mannerism as an architectural period style. What, then, are the qualities we must look for? Above all, form is divorced from content for the sake of surface effect. The emphasis instead is on picturesque devices, especially encrusted decoration, with the occasional distortion of form and novel, even

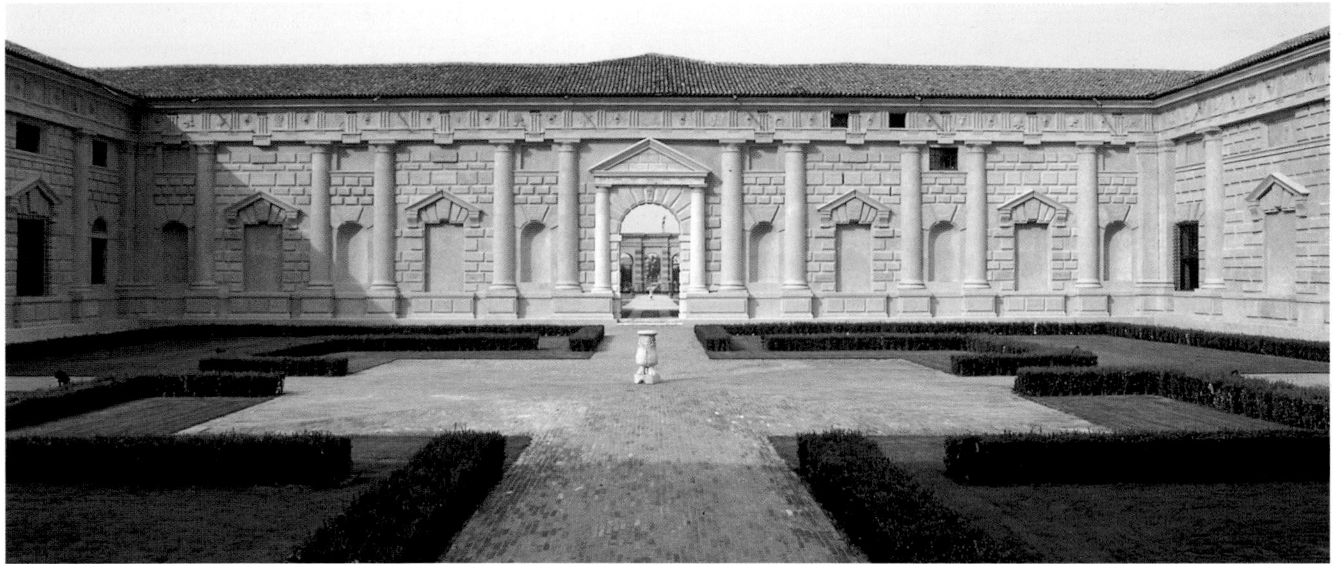

14-22. Giulio Romano. Courtyard of the Palazzo del Te, Mantua. 1527–34

illogical, rearrangement of space. Thus Mannerist architecture fails to integrate elements in a consistent way.

VASARI. We see many of these features in the Palazzo degli Uffizi in Florence designed by Giorgio Vasari, whom we have already met as a painter and biographer. It consists of two long wings (intended for offices, as the name Uffizi suggests) that face each other across a narrow court and are linked at one end by a loggia (fig. 14-23). The source of the "tired" scroll brackets and the odd combination of column and wall is the vestibule of the Laurentian Library. We will recall Vasari's praise for Michelangelo's unorthodox use of classical forms (see page 447). Does this mean that the Laurentian Library itself is Mannerist? The case can be argued both ways. On the one hand, Michelangelo's design subverts High Renaissance classicism as willfully as does Rosso's *Descent from the Cross* (see fig. 14-1). On the other, in the Laurentian Library these devices serve an expressive purpose that responds to the imperative of Michelangelo's genius, whereas in Vasari's design they are empty gestures. Whichever side one takes (they are not mutually exclusive), the differences in the results are plain enough. The Uffizi loggia lacks the sculptural power of its model. Instead, it forms a seemingly weightless screen that could just as well serve as a theater set. What is tense in Michelangelo's design becomes merely ambiguous. Vasari's architectural members seem as devoid of energy as the human figures in his *Perseus and Andromeda* (see fig. 14-7) and their relationships as deliberately "artificial."

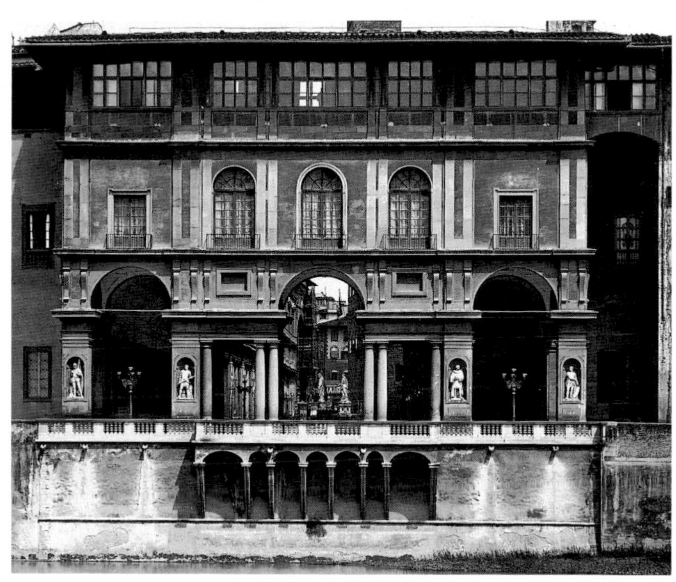

14-23. Giorgio Vasari. Loggia of the Palazzo degli Uffizi, Florence (view from the Arno River). Begun 1560

AMMANATI. The same is true of the courtyard of the Palazzo Pitti (fig. 14-24) by the sculptor Bartolommeo Ammanati (1511–1592), who collaborated with both Vasari and Michelangelo (see page 448). Here the three-story scheme of superimposed orders, derived from the Colosseum, has been overlaid with an extravagant pattern of rustication that "imprisons" the columns and reduces them to a passive role, despite the display of muscularity. These welts disguise rather than enhance the massiveness of

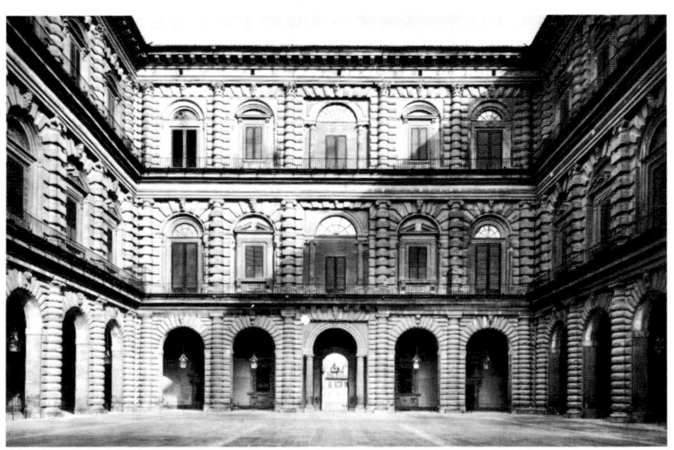

14-24. Bartolommeo Ammanati. Courtyard of the Palazzo Pitti, Florence. 1558–70

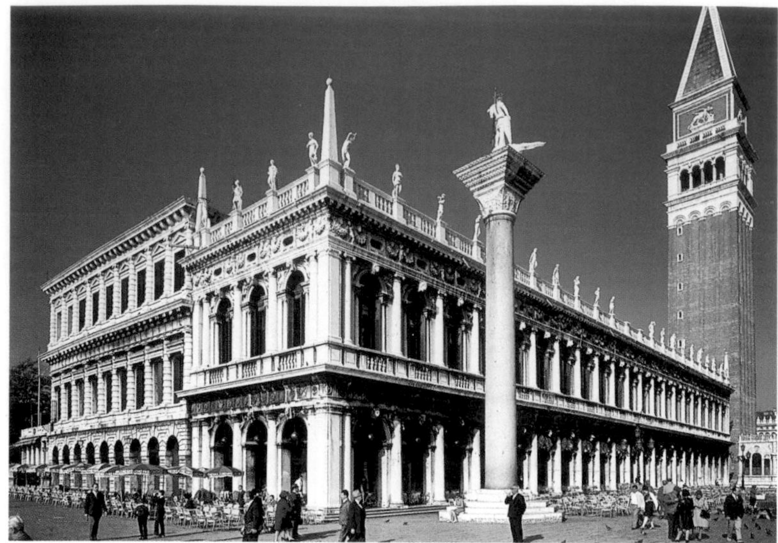

14-25 Jacopo Sansovino. Mint (left) and Library of St. Mark's, Venice. Begun c. 1535/7

the masonry, and the corrugated texture makes us think of the fancies of a pastry cook.

Ammanati had worked under Jacopo Sansovino in Venice, and the Palazzo Pitti stands in the same relation to Sansovino's Mint (fig. 14-25, left) as Vasari's Palazzo degli Uffizi does to Michelangelo's Laurentian Library.

Other Trends

SANSOVINO. We have not discussed the architecture of Venice since the Ca' d'Oro (see fig. 11-40), for it remained outside the mainstream of the Renaissance. Its essential characteristics were defined by Jacopo Sansovino (1486–1570), a minor Florentine sculptor from the circle of Raphael. He was called to Venice after the Sack of Rome in 1527 and established himself as the chief architect of the city. Not surprisingly, his buildings are sculptural in treatment. His masterpiece is the Library of St. Mark's (fig. 14-25), which forms part of a major reworking of the Piazzetta along the Grand Canal. The sculptural decoration is so luxurious that the building looks like a huge wedding cake. The street-level arcade consists of the Roman Doric order, inspired by the Colosseum (see fig. 7-10), while the upper story shows an elaborate treatment of the Ionic order (including triple-engaged columns) surmounted by a garlanded entablature. The structure is capped off by a balustrade, with lifesize statues over every column cluster and obelisks at each corner. The extravagant ornamentation, which set a new standard for lavish architecture, creates an effect of ponderous opulence that proclaims the Venetian republic as a new Rome. Sansovino's style was so authoritative that it enjoyed classic status and was followed in Venice for the remainder of the century. Nevertheless, it abandoned the logic of the High Renaissance.

Stranger still is the Mint to the left of the Library. Once again the facade has been penetrated wherever possible, but the results are even more massive. Though of equal height, the rusticated arcade seems barely able to sustain the weight of the upper two stories. (The top story was added belatedly around 1560.) The unique corkscrew columns and heavy cornices seem on the verge of Mannerism, but a glance at Ammanati's Pitti courtyard (see fig. 14-24) reveals the differences. Art historians have yet to find a term adequate to describe Sansovino's grandiose style.

PALLADIO. Most later sixteenth-century architecture can hardly be called Mannerist at all. Andrea Palladio (1518–1580), next to Michelangelo the most important architect of the century, belongs to the tradition of the humanist and theoretician Leone Battista Alberti (see page 412).

Although Palladio's career centered on his native Vicenza, a town near Venice, his buildings and theoretical writings brought him international status. Palladio believed that architecture must be governed by reason and by certain rules that were exemplified by the buildings of the ancients. He thus shared Alberti's basic outlook and his faith in the cosmic significance of numerical ratios (see page 414). But the two differed in how each related theory and practice. With Alberti, this relationship had been flexible, whereas Palladio believed quite literally in practicing what he preached. This view stemmed in part from the fact that he began his career as a stonemason and sculptor before entering the humanist circles of Count Giangiorgio Trissino of Vicenza at the age of 30. [See Primary Sources, no. 46, page 616.] As a result, his treatise *The Four Books of Architecture* (1570) is more practical than Alberti's, which helps to explain its huge success, while his buildings are linked more directly with his theories. It has even been said that Palladio designed only what was, in his view, sanctioned by ancient precedent. Indeed, the usual term for both Palladio's work and theoretical attitude is "classicistic." This term denotes a conscious striving for classic qualities, though the results are not necessarily classical in style.

Much of Palladio's architecture consists of town houses and country villas, which sometimes show the inspiration of Sansovino. The Villa Rotonda (fig. 14-26), one of Palladio's finest buildings, perfectly illustrates the meaning of his classicism. A country residence built near Vicenza for Paolo Almerico, it consists of a square block surmounted by a dome, with porches in the shape of temple fronts on all four sides. Alberti had defined the ideal church as a symmetrical, centralized design of this sort (see page 414). It is evident that Palladio found in the same principles the ideal country

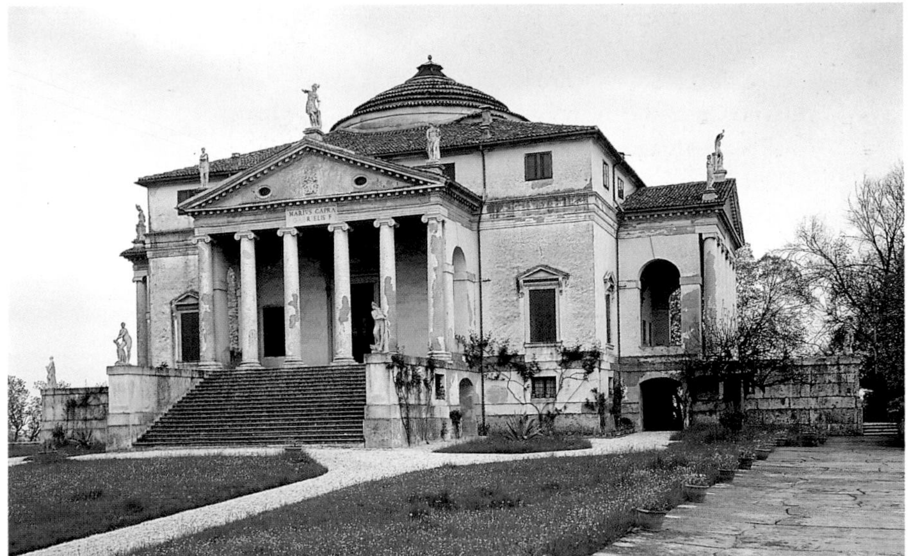

14-26. Andrea Palladio. Villa Rotonda, Vicenza. c. 1567–70

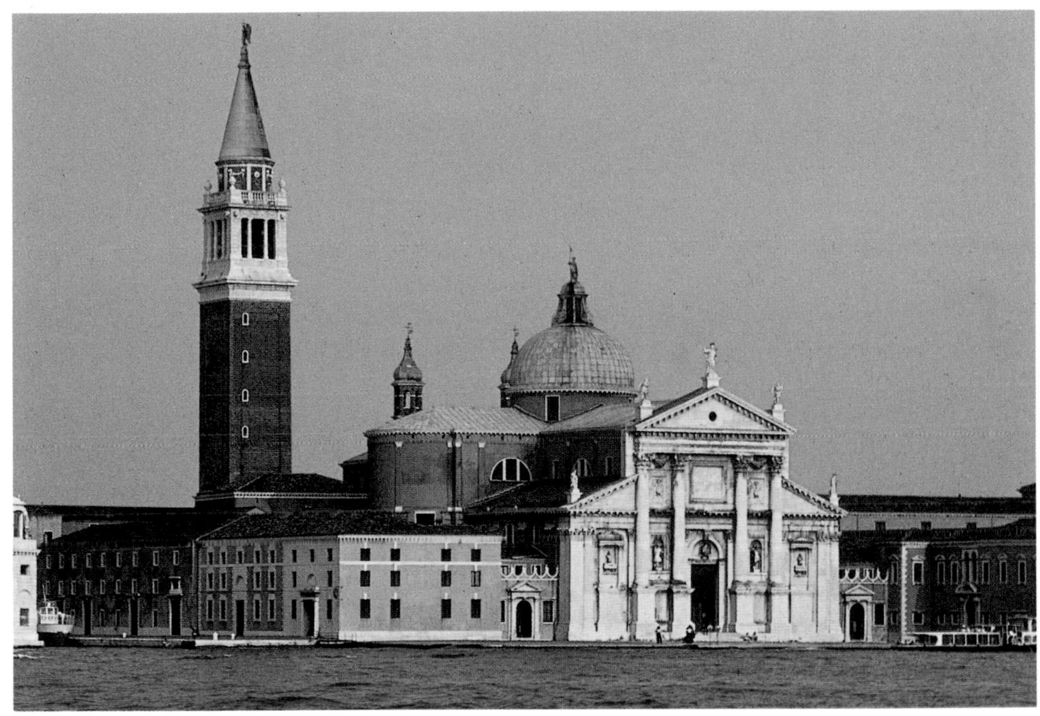

14-27. Andrea Palladio. S. Giorgio Maggiore, Venice. Designed 1565

14-28. Plan of S. Giorgio Maggiore

house. As he tells us in the second book on architecture, his design takes advantage of the pleasing views offered in every direction by the site. How could he justify such a secular context for the solemn motif of the temple front? Like Alberti, he interpreted the historical evidence in a selective fashion. He was convinced, on the basis of ancient literary sources, that Roman private houses had porticoes like these. (Excavations have since proved him wrong; see page 168.) But Palladio's use of the temple front here is not mere antiquarianism. He probably persuaded himself that it was legitimate because he regarded this feature as desirable for decorum—namely, appropriateness, beauty, and utility. This concept, embedded in the social outlook of the later sixteenth century, was similar to that introduced in theater by Salinger and Castelvetro (see box pages 466–67). Beautifully correlated with the walls behind and the surrounding vistas, the porches of the Villa Rotonda give the structure an air of serene dignity and festive grace that is enhanced by Lorenzo Vicentino's sculptures.

The facade of S. Giorgio Maggiore in Venice (fig. 14-27), of about the same date as the Villa Rotonda, adds to the same effect a new grandeur and complexity. Palladio's problem here was how to create a classical facade for a basilican church. He surely knew Alberti's solution at S. Andrea in Mantua (see fig. 12-40): a temple front enclosing a triumphal arch. But this design, although logical and compact, did not fit the cross section of a basilica. Palladio, again following what he believed to be ancient precedent, found a different answer. He superimposed a tall, narrow temple front on another low, wide one to reflect the different heights of nave and aisles. Theoretically, it was a perfect solution. In practice, however, he found that he could not keep the two systems as separate as he wished and still integrate them into a harmonious whole. This conflict, which makes parts of the design seem ambiguous, might almost be seen as Mannerist. The plan (fig. 14-28), too, suggests a duality, which in this case reflects the church's twofold purpose of serving a Benedictine monastery and a lay congregation. The main body of the church is strongly centralized—the transept is as long as the nave—but the longitudinal axis reasserts itself in the separate compartments for the main altar and the large choir beyond, where the monks worshiped.

Proto-Baroque Architecture

VIGNOLA AND DELLA PORTA. Palladio's authority as a designer keeps the conflicting elements in the facade and plan of S. Giorgio from actually clashing. In less assured hands, such a precarious union would break apart. The most widely accepted solution was developed in Rome by Giacomo Vignola (1507–1573) and Giacomo della Porta (c. 1540–1602), who had assisted Michelangelo at St. Peter's and were still using his architectural vocabulary. Il Gesù (Jesus) is a building with great importance for later church architecture. Since it was the mother church of the Jesuits, its design must have been closely supervised so as to conform to the aims of the militant order (see page 462). We may therefore view it as the architectural embodiment of the spirit of the Counter-Reformation.

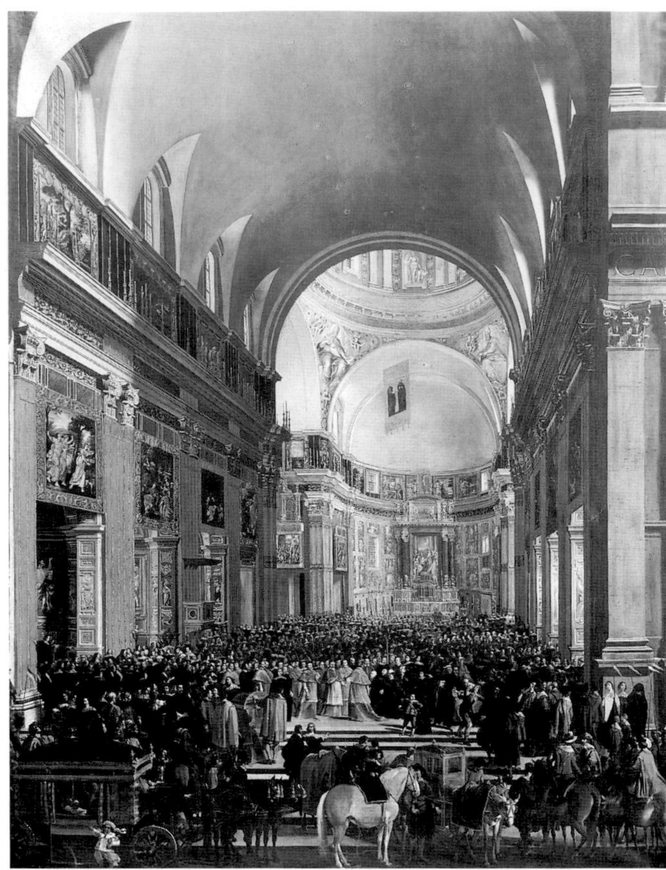

14-30. Andrea Sacchi and Jan Miel. *Urban VIII Visiting Il Gesù.* 1639–41. Oil on canvas. Galleria Nazionale d'Arte Antica, Rome

The planning of the structure began in 1550, only five years after the Council of Trent (see page 462). Michelangelo himself once promised a design but apparently never furnished it. The present ground plan, by Vignola, was adopted in 1568 (fig. 14-29). Il Gesù contrasts in almost every possible way with Palladio's S. Giorgio. It is a compact basilica dominated by its mighty nave. The aisles have been replaced by chapels, thus herding the congregation into one large, hall-like space directly in view of the altar. The attention of the audience is strongly directed toward altar and pulpit, as our view of the interior shows (fig. 14-30). (The painting depicts how the church would look from the street if the center part of the facade were removed. For the later, High Baroque decoration of the nave vault, see figure 17-13.) We also see here a feature that the ground plan cannot show: the dramatic contrast between the dim nave and the amply lighted eastern part of the church, thanks to the large windows in the drum of the dome. Light has been consciously exploited for its expressive possibilities—a novel device, "theatrical" in the best sense of the term—to give Il Gesù a stronger emotional focus than we have yet found in a church interior.

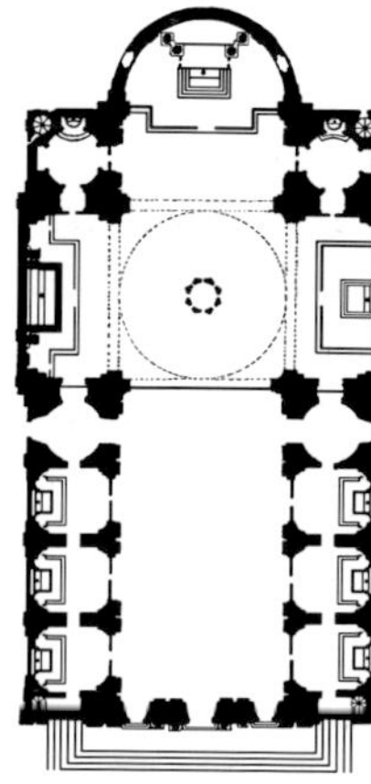

14-29. Giacomo Vignola. Plan of Il Gesù, Rome. 1568

Despite its originality, the plan of Il Gesù is not entirely new (see fig. 12-42). The facade by Giacomo della Porta (fig. 14-31) is as bold as the plan, although it, too, has earlier sources. The paired pilasters and broken architrave on the lower story are clearly derived from the colossal order on the exterior of St. Peter's (compare fig. 13-27), for it was Della Porta who completed Michelangelo's dome. In the upper story the same pattern recurs on a somewhat smaller scale, with four instead of six pairs of supports. The difference in width is bridged by two scroll-shaped buttresses, which hide the roofline. This device, taken from the facade of S. Maria Novella in Florence by Alberti, forms a graceful transition to the large pediment crowning the facade, which retains the classic proportions of Renaissance architecture. (The height equals the width.)

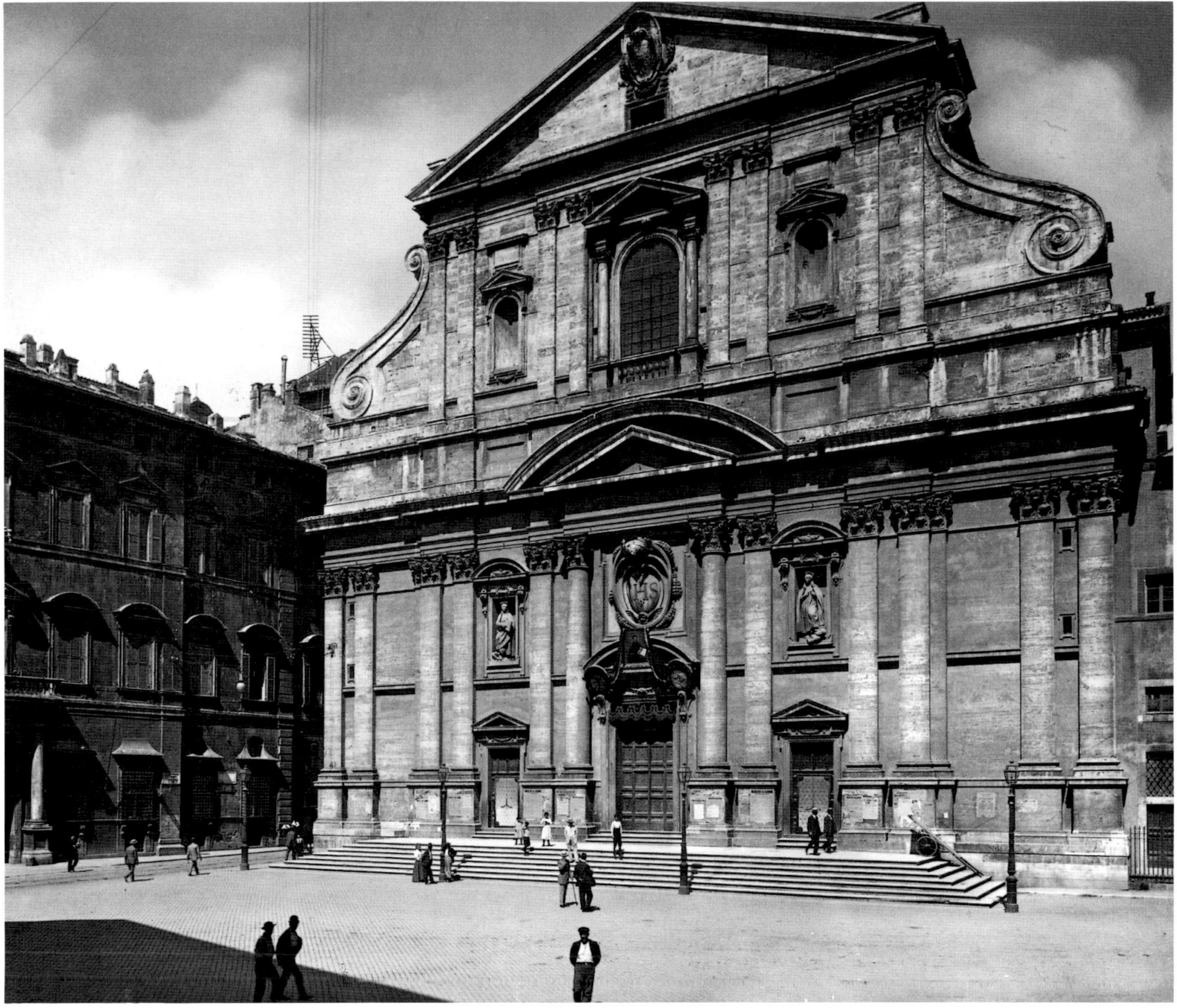

14-31. Giacomo della Porta. Facade of Il Gesù, Rome. c. 1575–84

What is fundamentally new here is the very element that was missing in the facade of S. Giorgio: the integration of all the parts into one whole. Della Porta, freed from classicistic scruples by his allegiance to Michelangelo, gave the same vertical rhythm to both stories of the facade. This rhythm is obeyed by all the horizontal members (note the broken entablature). In turn, the horizontal divisions determine the size of the vertical members (hence no colossal order). Equally important is the sculptural treatment of the facade, likewise inspired by Michelangelo, which places greater emphasis on the main portal. Its double frame—two pediments resting on coupled pilasters and columns—projects beyond the rest of the facade and gives strong focus to the entire design. Not since Gothic architecture has the entrance to a church received such a dramatic concentration of features. They attract the attention of the viewer outside the building in much the same way that the concentrated light beneath the dome channels the attention of the worshiper inside.

What are we to call the style of Il Gesù? It clearly has little in common with Palladio, and it shares with Vasari's architecture only the influence of Michelangelo. But this influence reflects two very different phases of the great master's career. The contrast between the Uffizi and Il Gesù is as great as the difference between the vestibule of the Laurentian Library and the exterior of St. Peter's. If we label the Uffizi Mannerist, the same term will not serve us for Il Gesù. As we shall see, the design of Il Gesù became basic to Baroque architecture. By calling it Proto-Baroque, we suggest both its great importance for the future and its special place in relation to the past.

CHAPTER FIFTEEN

"Late Gothic" Painting, Sculpture, and the Graphic Arts

Should we think of the Renaissance as one coherent style? Or should we view it as an attitude that might be embodied in more than one style? "Renaissance consciousness," we know, was an Italian idea. There can be no doubt that Italy played the leading role in the development of Renaissance art, at least until the early sixteenth century. This fact does not necessarily mean, however, that the Renaissance was confined to the South. When Boccaccio praised Giotto's imitation of nature, he could not know how many aspects of reality Giotto and his contemporaries had failed to investigate. These, we recall, were further explored by the painters of the International Style, although somewhat tentatively. To go beyond Gothic realism required a second revolution, which began in Italy and in the Netherlands about 1420. We must think of two events linked by a common aim—the conquest of the visible world—yet sharply divided in almost every other way.

The Italian, or Southern, revolution, which started in Florence and which we call the Early Renaissance, was more systematic. In the long run it was also more fundamental, since it included architecture and sculpture as well as painting. There are still many unanswered questions about the Northern revolution and its relation to the Renaissance as a whole. The new style emerged in Flanders around 1420, but we do not know why it took place at that particular time and in that particular area. This lack of a satisfactory explanation does not mean, however, that none is possible. Unless we believe in sheer fate or chance, we find it difficult to attribute it wholly to the great masters who gave birth to it. There must, we feel, be some link between their achievement and the social, political, and cultural setting in which they worked, but it has yet to be defined.

RENAISSANCE VERSUS "LATE GOTHIC" PAINTING

Many scholars treat fifteenth-century Northern painting as the counterpart of the Early Renaissance in Italy, because the Flemish artists had an impact that went far beyond their own region. In Italy they were admired as much as the leading Italian artists. Their intense realism had a marked influence on Early Renaissance painting, for the Italians, as we have already noted, associated the exact imitation of nature in painting with a "return to the classics." To Italian eyes, "Late Gothic" painting was clearly post-medieval.

Italian Renaissance art, however, made very little impression north of the Alps during the fifteenth century. Not until the final decades did humanism begin to play an important role in Northern thought, which it changed decisively. Nor do we find an interest in the art of classical antiquity before that time. Rather, the artistic and cultural environment of Northern painters clearly remained "Late Gothic." The term suggests the continuity with the worldview of the late Middle Ages. Moreover, the creators of the new style, unlike their Italian contemporaries, did not entirely reject the International Style. Instead, they took it as their point of departure, so that the break with the past was less abrupt in the North than in the South. Despite its great importance, their work may be seen as the final phase of Gothic painting. The term "Late Gothic" also reminds us that fifteenth-century architecture and sculpture outside Italy remained firmly rooted in the Gothic tradition.

We have, in fact, no satisfactory name for the new Flemish painting. Whatever we choose to call the style, we shall find that it has some justification. For the sake of convenience, we shall use the label, "Late Gothic." However, we will enclose it in quotation marks to indicate its doubtful status, as the term hardly does justice to the special character of Northern fifteenth-century art as a whole.

Netherlandish Painting

CAMPIN. The first, and perhaps most decisive, phase of the pictorial revolution in Flanders can be seen in the work of an artist formerly known as the Master of Flémalle (after the fragments of a large altar from Flémalle), who was undoubtedly Robert Campin, the foremost painter of Tournai. We can trace his career in documents from 1406 to his death in 1444, although it declined after his conviction in 1428 for adultery. His finest work is the *Mérode Altarpiece* (fig. 15-1), which he must have painted soon

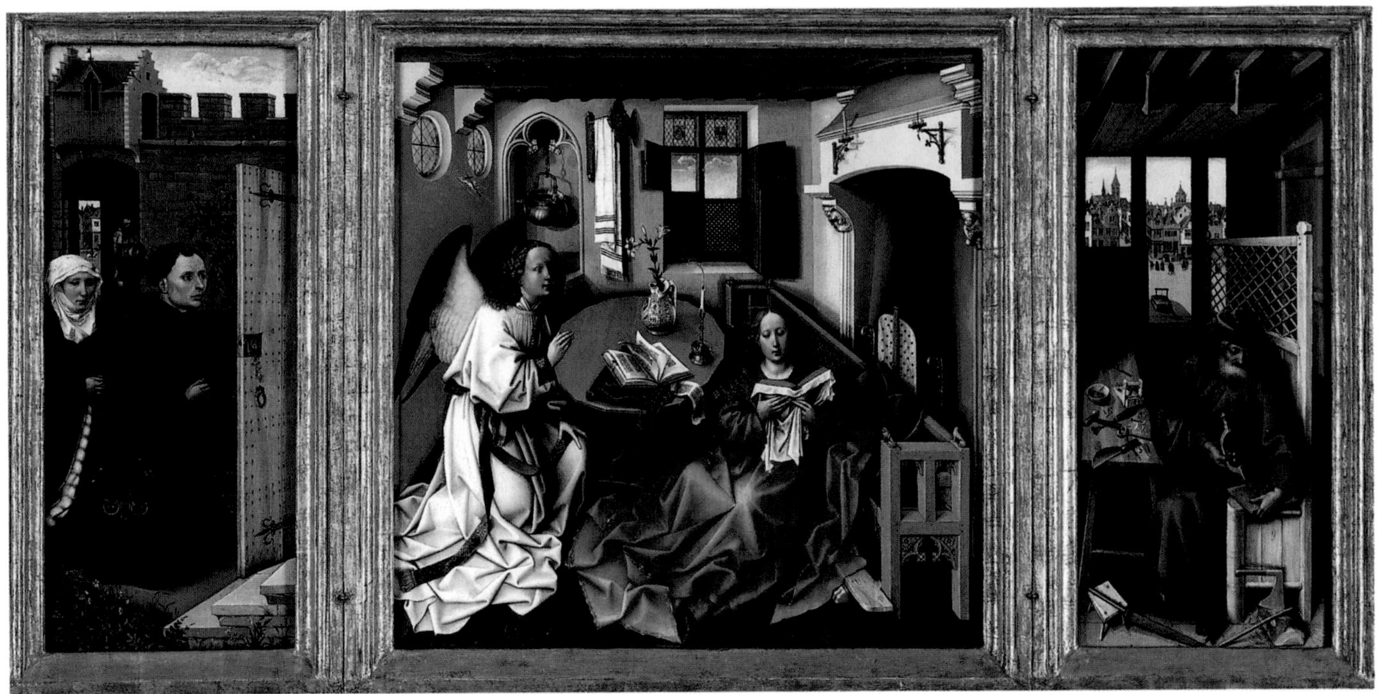

15-1. Robert Campin (Master of Flémalle). *Mérode Altarpiece*. c. 1425–30. Oil on panel, center 25 3/16 x 24 7/8" (64.3 x 62.9 cm); each wing approx. 25 3/8 x 10 7/8" (64.5 x 27.4 cm). The Metropolitan Museum of Art, New York. The Cloisters Collection, 1956

after 1425. If we compare it to the Franco-Flemish pictures of the International Style (see figs. 11-90–11-93), we see that it falls within the same tradition. Yet we also recognize in it a new pictorial experience. Here, for the first time, we have the sense of actually looking through the surface of the panel into a world that has all the essential features of everyday reality: unlimited depth, stability, continuity, and completeness. The painters of the International Style, even at their most daring, had never aimed at such consistency, and their commitment to reality was far from absolute. The pictures they created have the enchanting quality of fairy tales. The scale and relationship of things can be shifted at will, and fact and fancy mingle without conflict. Campin, in contrast, has tried to tell the truth, the whole truth, and nothing but the truth. To be sure, he does not yet do it with total ease. His objects, overly foreshortened, tend to jostle each other in space. But he defines every last detail of every object to make it as concrete as possible: its shape and size; its color, material, surface textures; its degree of rigidity; and its way of responding to light. The artist even distinguishes between the diffused light creating soft shadows and delicate gradations of brightness and the direct light entering through the two round windows, which produces the twin shadows sharply outlined in the upper part of the center panel and the twin reflections on the brass vessel and candlestick.

The *Mérode Altarpiece* transports us from the aristocratic world of the International Style to the household of a Flemish burgher. Campin was no court painter but a townsperson who catered to the tastes of well-to-do fellow citizens such as the two donors piously kneeling outside the Virgin's chamber. This is the earliest Annunciation in panel painting that occurs in a fully equipped domestic interior. It is also the first to honor Joseph, the humble carpenter, by showing him at work next door.

This bold departure from tradition forced our artist to confront a problem no one had faced before. He needed to transfer supernatural events from symbolic settings to an everyday environment without making them look either trivial or incongruous. He met this challenge by the method sometimes known as "disguised symbolism," which means that almost any detail within the picture, however casual, may carry a symbolic message. We saw its beginnings during the International Style in the *Annunciation* by Melchior Broederlam (see page 358), but his symbolism seems simple compared with the many hidden meanings in the *Mérode Altarpiece*. For example, the flowers are associated with the Virgin. In the left wing the roses denote her charity and the violets her humility, while in the center panel the lilies symbolize her chastity. The shiny water basin and the towel on its rack are not just household equipment. They are further attributes of Mary as the "vessel most clean" and the "well of living waters." Perhaps the most intriguing symbol of this sort is the candle next to the vase of lilies. It has been extinguished only moments before, as we can tell from the glowing wick and the curl of smoke. But why had it been lit in broad daylight, and what made the flame go out? Has the divine radiance of the Lord's presence overcome the material light? Or did the flame of the candle itself represent the divine light, now extinguished to show that God has become human, that in Jesus "the Word was made flesh"?

Clearly, the range of medieval symbolism has been greatly expanded. Yet it is so completely immersed in the world of everyday appearances that we often wonder whether a given detail carries a symbolic meaning. Scholars long wondered, for instance, about the boxlike object on Joseph's workbench (and a similar one on the ledge outside the open window). Finally they were identified as mousetraps that convey a specific theological message. According to

St. Augustine, God had to appear on earth in human form so as to fool Satan: "The Cross of the Lord was the devil's mousetrap."

Since it takes much scholarly ingenuity to explain this sort of iconography, we tend to think of the *Mérode Altarpiece* and similar pictures as puzzles. Yet we can enjoy them without knowing all their symbolism. But what about the patrons for whom these works were painted? Did they understand the meaning of every detail? They would have had no trouble with well-established symbols in our picture such as the flowers, and they probably knew the significance of the water basin. The message of the extinguished candle and the mousetrap could not have been common knowledge even among the well-educated, however.

These two symbols—and we can hardly doubt that they are symbols—appear for the first time in the *Mérode Altarpiece.* They must be unusual, too, for St. Joseph with the mousetrap has been found in only one other picture, and the freshly extinguished candle does not occur elsewhere, so far as we know. It seems that Campin introduced them into the visual arts, yet hardly any artists adopted them despite his great influence. If the candle and the mousetrap were difficult to understand even in the fifteenth century, why are they in our picture at all? Was the artist told to put them in by an exceptionally educated patron? This would be possible if it were the only case of its kind, but since there are countless instances of equally subtle or obscure symbolism in "Late Gothic" painting, it seems more likely that the initiative came from the artists, rather than from their patrons.

Campin either was a man of unusual learning or had contact with theologians or scholars who could supply him with the references that suggested the symbolic meanings of things such as the extinguished candle and the mousetrap. In other words, the artist did not simply continue the symbolic tradition of medieval art within the framework of the new realistic style. He expanded and enriched it by his own efforts. To him, even more than Broederlam (see page 358), realism and symbolism were interrelated. We might say that Campin needed a growing symbolic repertory because it encouraged him to explore features of the visible world that had not been depicted before, such as a candle just after it has been blown out or the interior of a carpenter's shop, which provided the setting for the mousetraps. For him to paint everyday reality, he had to "sanctify" it with spiritual significance.

This reverence for the physical world as a mirror of divine truths helps us to understand why in the Mérode panels the smallest details are rendered with the same attention as the sacred figures. The disguised symbolism of Campin and later painters was not grafted onto the new realistic style. It was ingrained in the creative process. Their Italian contemporaries must have sensed this, for they praised both the realism and the "piety" of the Flemish masters.

Campin's distinctive tonality makes the Mérode *Annunciation* stand out from earlier panel paintings (see figs. 11-81, 11-90, 11-91, and 11-97). The jewel-like brightness of the older works, their patterns of brilliant hues and lavish use of gold, have given way to a color scheme far less decorative but much more flexible and nuanced. The muted greens and bluish or brownish grays show a new subtlety, and the scale of intermediate shades is smoother and has a wider range. These effects are essential to the realistic style of Campin. They were made possible by the use of oil.

JAN AND HUBERT VAN EYCK. The full possibilities of oil were not discovered all at once, nor by any one artist. Campin contributed less than Jan van Eyck, a somewhat younger and much more famous artist who was long thought to have "invented" oil painting. [See Primary Sources, no. 47, pages 616–17.] We know a good deal about Jan's life and career. Born about 1390, he worked in Holland from 1422 to 1424, in Lille from 1425 to 1429, and thereafter in Bruges, where he died in 1441. Both a townsman and a court painter, he was highly esteemed by Duke Philip the Good of Burgundy, who occasionally sent him on diplomatic errands. After 1432, we can follow Jan's career through a number of signed and dated pictures.

The inscription on the frame of the great *Ghent Altarpiece* (see below) tells us that it was begun by Hubert van Eyck (who died in 1426) and completed by Jan in 1432. There are a number of "Eyckian" works, clearly older than the *Ghent Altarpiece,* that may have been painted by either or both of the two brothers. The most fascinating of these is a pair of panels showing *The Crucifixion* and *The Last Judgment* (fig. 15-2). Scholars agree that their date is between 1420 and 1425. The style of these paintings has many qualities in common with that of the *Mérode Altarpiece.* These include a total devotion to the visible world, an unlimited depth of space, and angular drapery folds, which are less graceful but far more realistic than the unbroken loops of the International Style. At the same time, the individual forms are not absolutely tangible, like those of Campin, and seem less "sculptural." The sweeping sense of space is the result not so much of foreshortening as of subtle changes of light and color. If we look closely at *The Crucifixion* panel, we see a gradual decrease in the intensity of local colors and in the contrast of light and dark, from the foreground figures to the far-off city of Jerusalem and the snowcapped peaks beyond. Everything tends toward a uniform bluish gray, so that the farthest mountain range merges imperceptibly with the color of the sky.

This optical phenomenon is known as "atmospheric perspective." The Van Eycks were the first to use it systematically, although the Boucicaut Master and the Limbourg brothers were aware of it (see figs. 11-93 and 11-94). The atmosphere is never wholly transparent. Even on the clearest day, the air between us and what we are looking at acts as a hazy screen that interferes with our ability to see distant shapes clearly. As we approach the limit of visibility, it swallows them completely. Atmospheric perspective is more essential to our perception of deep space than linear perspective, which records the decrease in the apparent size of objects as their distance from the viewer increases. It is effective not only in distant vistas. In *The Crucifixion* panel, even the foreground seems to be enveloped in a delicate haze that softens contours, shadows, and colors. Thus the entire scene has a continuity and harmony beyond the pictorial range of Campin.

How did the Van Eycks achieve this effect? It is difficult to determine their technical process, but there can be no doubt that they used the oil medium with extraordinary refinement. By alternating opaque and translucent layers of paint, called glazes, they were able to give their pictures a soft, glowing color that has never been equaled, probably because it depends as much on their individual sensibilities as it does on their skillful craftsmanship.

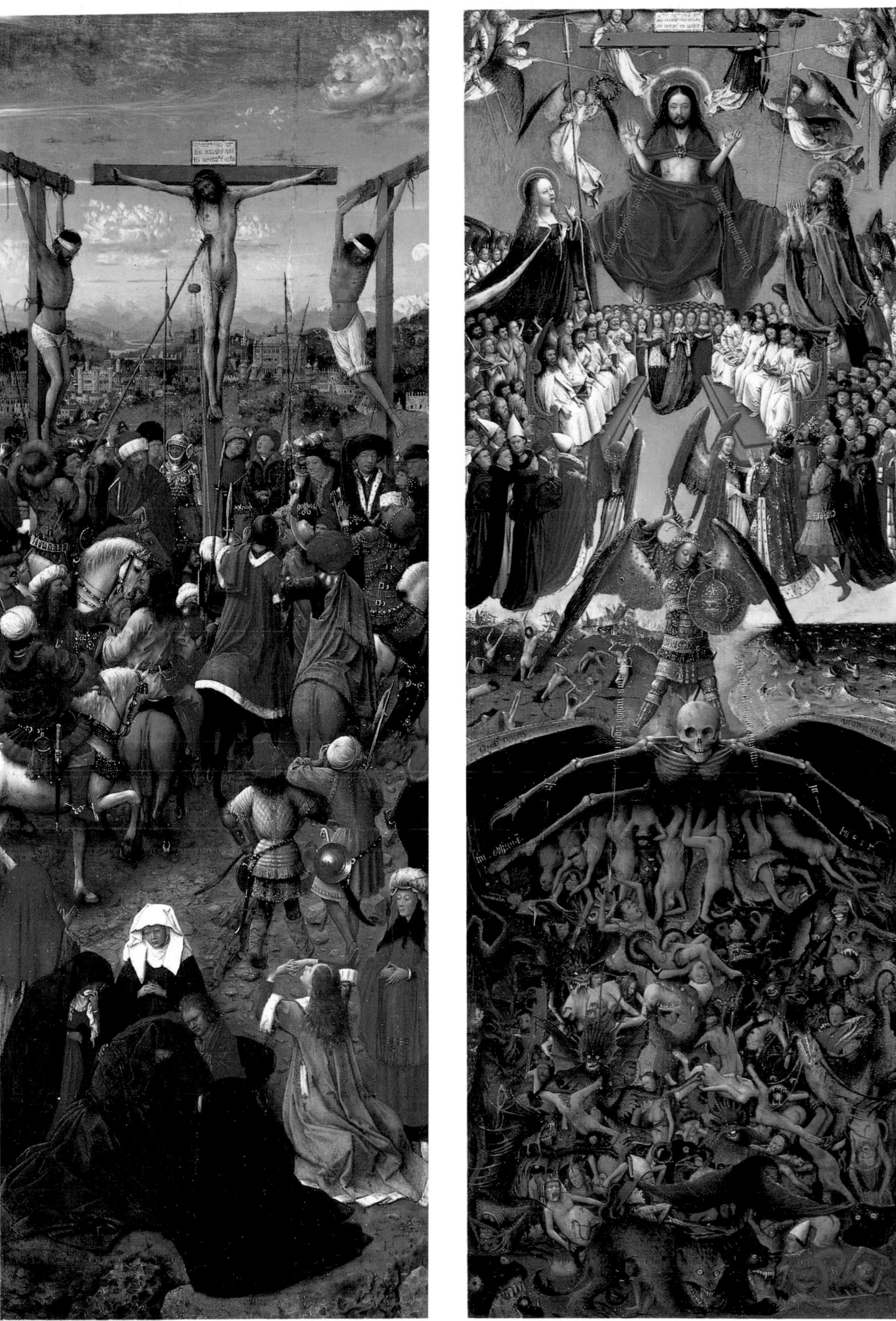

15-2. Hubert and/or Jan van Eyck. *The Crucifixion* and *The Last Judgment.* c. 1420–25. Tempera and oil on canvas, transferred from panel; each panel 22¼ x 7¾" (56.5 x 19.4 cm). The Metropolitan Museum of Art, New York

FLETCHER FUND, 1933

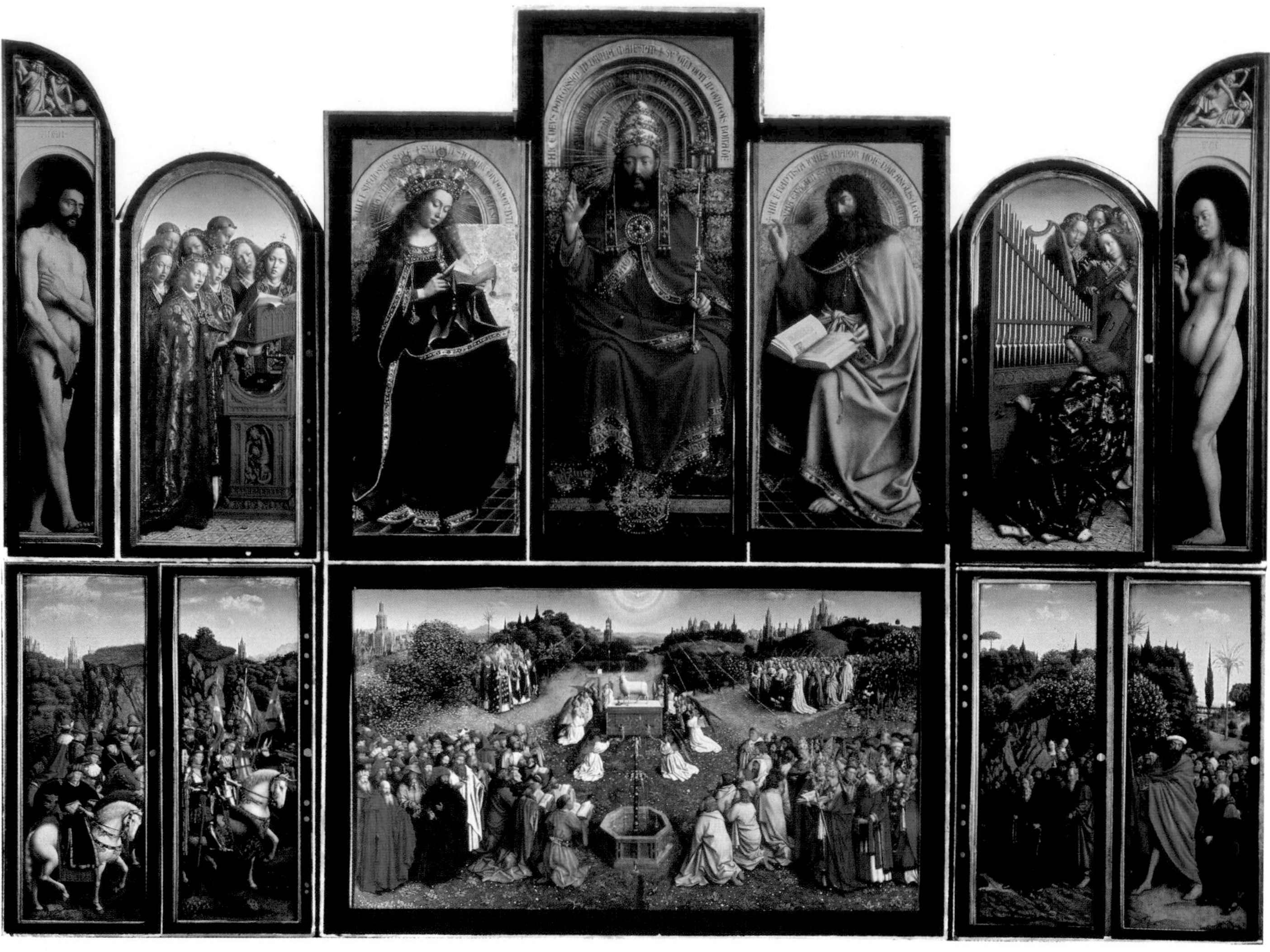

15-3. Hubert and Jan van Eyck. *Ghent Altarpiece* (open). Completed 1432. Oil on panel, 11'3" x 14'5" (3.4 x 4.4 m). Church of St. Bavo, Ghent, Belgium

Seen as a whole, *The Crucifixion* seems to lack drama, as if the scene were calmed by some magic spell. Only when we concentrate on the details do we become aware of the violent expressions in the faces of the crowd beneath the Cross, and the restrained but deeply touching grief of the Virgin Mary and her companions in the foreground. In *The Last Judgment* panel, this dual quality of the Eyckian style takes the form of two extremes. Above the horizon, all is order and calm symmetry; below it, on earth and in the realm of Satan, chaos prevails. The two states thus correspond to Heaven and Hell, contemplative bliss as against physical and emotional turbulence. The lower half, clearly, was the greater challenge to the artist's imaginative powers. The dead rising from their graves with frantic gestures of fear and hope, the damned being torn apart by monsters more terrifying than any we have seen before (compare fig. 10-24), all have the awesome reality of a nightmare. Yet it is "observed" with the same care as the natural world of *The Crucifixion* panel.

The *Ghent Altarpiece* (figs. 15-3, 15-4, and 15-6), the greatest monument of early Flemish painting, presents problems so complex that our discussion must be limited to essentials. We have already mentioned the inscription, which tells us that the work was begun by Hubert, who died in 1426, and completed by Jan in 1432. Its basic arrangement is a triptych—a central body with two hinged wings—the standard format of altarpieces. Each of the three units consists of four panels. And since the wings are also painted on both sides, the altarpiece has a total of 20 components of assorted shapes and sizes. It must originally have been placed in an elaborate architectural-style frame. The ensemble has been called a "super-altar," impressive but far from harmonious, that could not have been planned this way. Apparently Jan took over a number of panels left unfinished by Hubert, completed them, added some of his own, and assembled them at the behest of the wealthy donor, Jodicus Vyd, whose portrait we see on one of the outer panels of the altar.

To reconstruct this train of events, and to determine each brother's share, is an interesting but difficult game. Hubert remains a shadowy figure. His style, with retouches by Jan, can probably be found in the four central panels inside, although they did not belong together originally. The upper three, whose huge figures in the final arrangement crush the small ones below, seem to have been meant to form a self-contained triptych: the Lord between the Virgin Mary and St. John the Baptist. The lower panel and the four flanking it probably formed a separate altarpiece, the Adoration of the Lamb, symbolizing Jesus' sacrificial death. The two panels with music-making angels may have been planned as a pair of organ shutters.

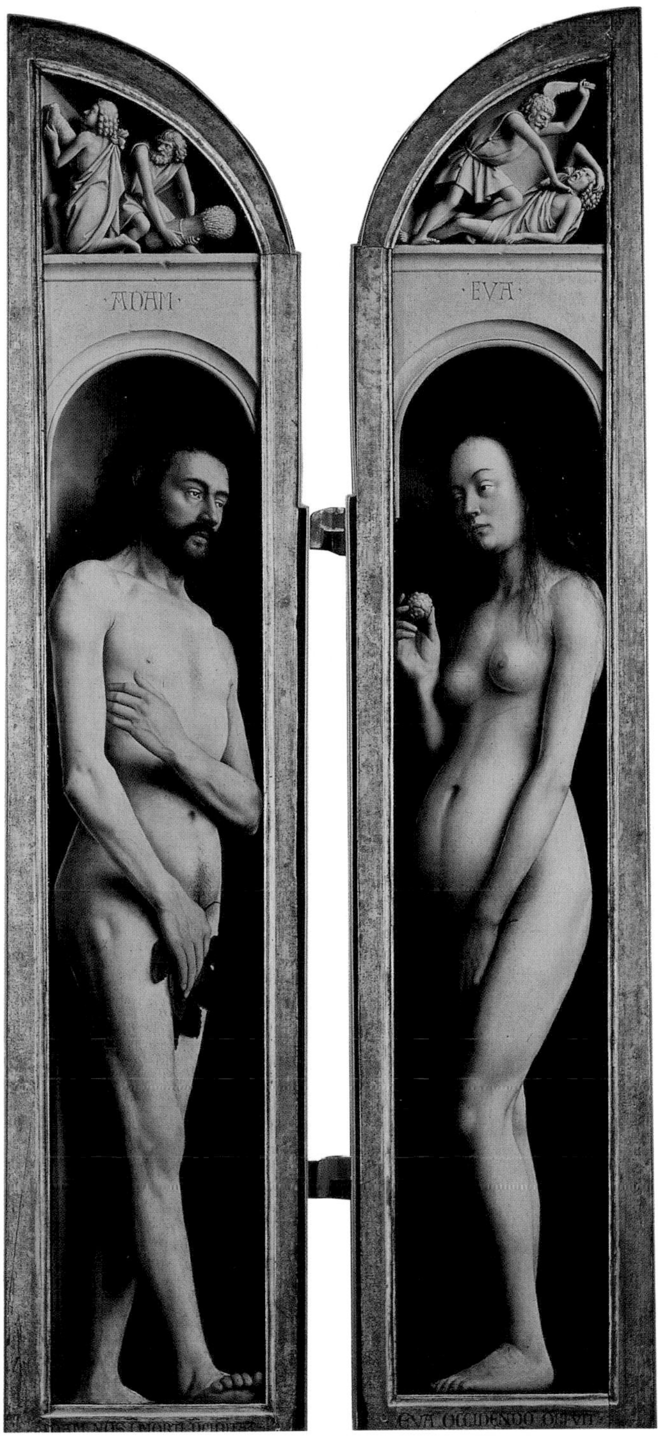

(LEFT) 15-4. *Adam* and *Eve*, details of *Ghent Altarpiece*, left and right wings

(BELOW) 15-5. *Adam*, from south transept, Notre-Dame, Paris. c. 1250. Stone, height 6'7¼" (2 m). Musée du Moyen Age, Hôtel de Cluny, Paris

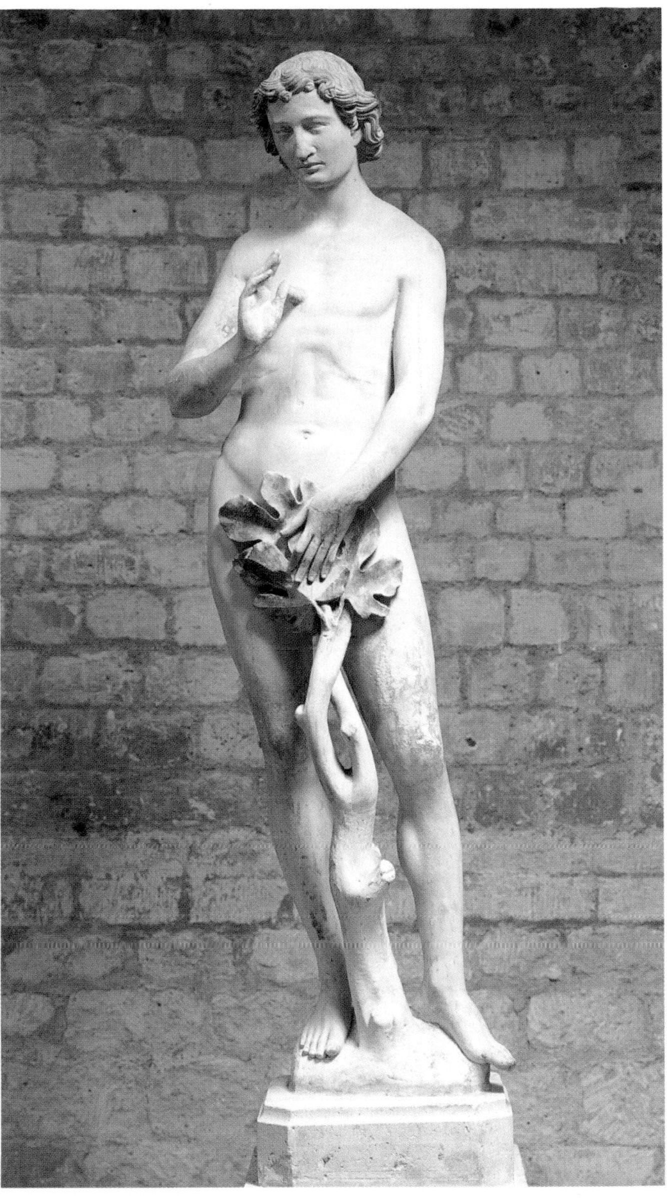

The two tall, narrow panels showing Adam and Eve (fig. 15-4) are certainly the most daring. These, the first monumental nudes of Northern panel painting (hardly less than lifesize), are magnificently observed and caressed by the most delicate play of light and shade. They were inspired by statues like the *Adam* in figure 15-5 (he was complemented by a missing Eve) from the middle of the thirteenth century, when Gothic realism was at its height (see page 331). Painting and sculpture were closely allied in the fifteenth century. Wood carvings and panel paintings were often combined in altars (see page 358). Moreover, both Campin and Van Eyck painted grisailles (pictures done entirely in gray tones) to simulate stone sculpture. (Note the small, expressive scenes above the *Adam* and *Eve* showing the story of Cain and Abel, which recall *The Kiss of Judas* on the Naumburg choir screen, fig. 11-52.) Still, Van Eyck's figures are revolutionary. Not only are they the first of their kind in painting, their degree of realism is not found before in any medium. Although they differ little in pose from their Gothic prototypes (compare fig. 11-93), they show a subtle shift in attitude. Their quiet dignity and prominent place in the altar suggest that, unlike the *Adam* from Notre-Dame, they should remind us not simply of Original Sin but also of our creation in God's own image. Actual evil, by contrast, is represented in the small, violently expressive scenes above, which show the story of Cain and Abel. Even more extraordinary is the fact that the *Adam* and *Eve* were designed specifically for their present positions in the ensemble. Jan van Eyck has established a new,

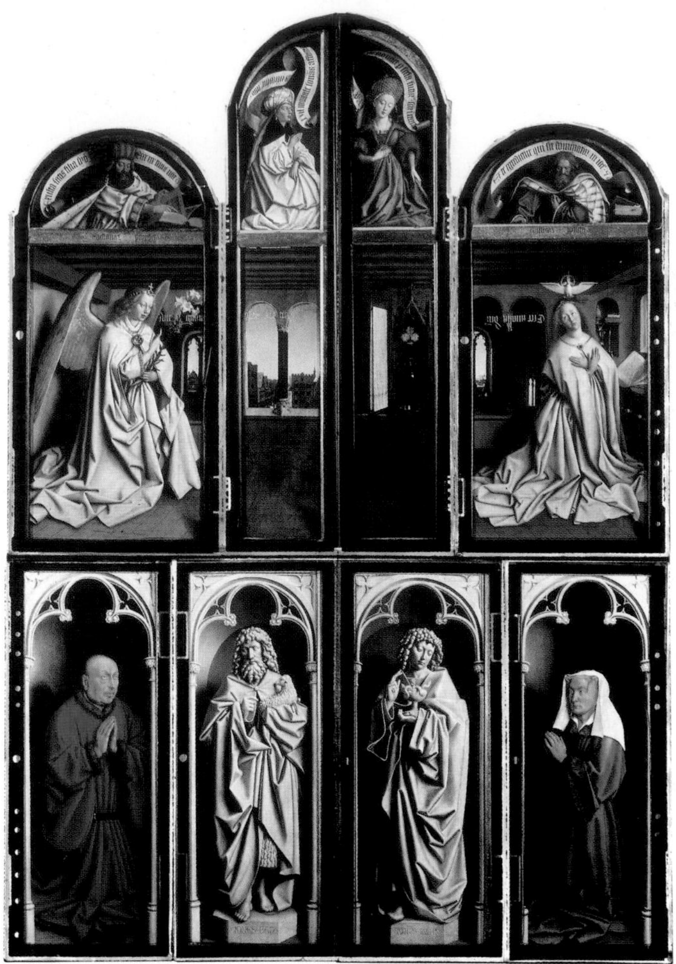

15-6. *Ghent Altarpiece* (closed)

direct relationship between picture space and real space by depicting the two figures as they would really appear to the spectator, whose eye level is below the bottom of the panels.

The outer surfaces of the two wings (fig. 15-6) seem to have been planned as one unit. Here, as we would expect, the largest figures are not above but are in the lower tier. The two St. Johns (painted in grays to simulate sculpture, like the scenes of Cain and Abel), the donor, and his wife, each in a separate niche, are the immediate kin of the *Adam* and *Eve* panels. The upper tier has two pairs of panels of different width. The artist has made a virtue of this awkward necessity by combining all four into one interior. Such an effect had first been created by Pietro Lorenzetti almost a century earlier (compare fig. 11-82). Not content with perspective devices alone, Jan heightens the illusion by painting the shadows cast by the frames of the panels on the floor of the Virgin's chamber. Interestingly enough, this Annunciation resembles, in its homely detail, the *Mérode Altarpiece*. It thus provides an important link between the two great pioneers of Flemish realism.

Donors' portraits of impressive individuality occupy prominent positions in both the Mérode and the Ghent altarpieces. A renewed interest in realistic portraiture had developed in the mid-fourteenth century, but until about 1420 its best achievements were in sculpture (see fig. 11-55). Painters usually confined themselves to profile views. Not until Campin, the first artist since antiquity to have real command of the human face in three-quarter view, did the portrait play a major role in Northern painting.

In addition to donors' portraits, we now begin to find a growing number of small likenesses whose intimacy suggests that they were keepsakes, pictorial substitutes for the real presence of the sitter. One of the most compelling is Jan van Eyck's *Man in a Red Turban* of 1433 (fig. 15-7), which may well be a self-portrait. (The slight strain about the eyes seems to come from gazing into a mirror.) The sitter is bathed in the same gentle, clear light as Adam and Eve on the *Ghent Altarpiece*. Every detail of shape and texture has been recorded with minute precision. Jan does not suppress the sitter's personality; yet this face, like all of Jan's portraits, remains a puzzle. It might be described as "even-tempered" in the most exact sense of the term. Its character traits are balanced against each other so perfectly that none can assert itself at the expense of the rest. Jan was fully capable of expressing emotion—we need only recall the faces of the crowd in *The Crucifixion* or the scenes of Cain and Abel in the *Ghent Altarpiece*. Hence the stoic calm of his portraits surely reflects his ideal of human character.

The Flemish cities of Tournai, Ghent, and Bruges, where the new style of painting flourished, rivaled those of Italy as centers of international banking and trade. Their foreign residents included many Italian businessmen. Jan van Eyck probably painted the portrait in figure 15-8 to celebrate the alliance of two of these families that were active in Bruges and Paris. It most likely shows the

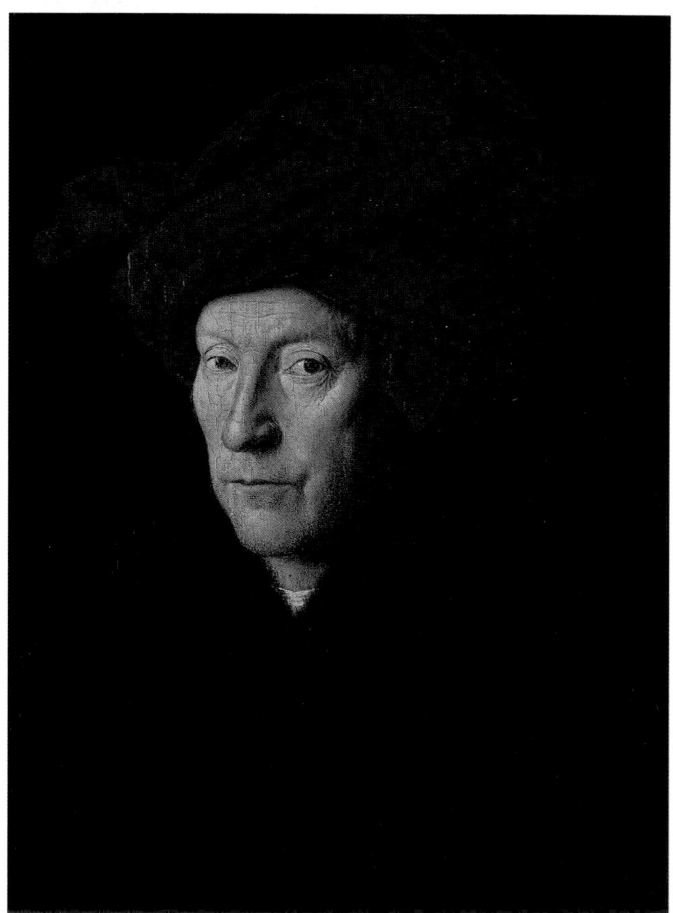

15-7. Jan van Eyck. *Man in a Red Turban (Self-Portrait?)*. 1433. Oil on panel, 10¼ x 7½" (26 x 19 cm). The National Gallery, London

REPRODUCED BY COURTESY OF THE TRUSTEES

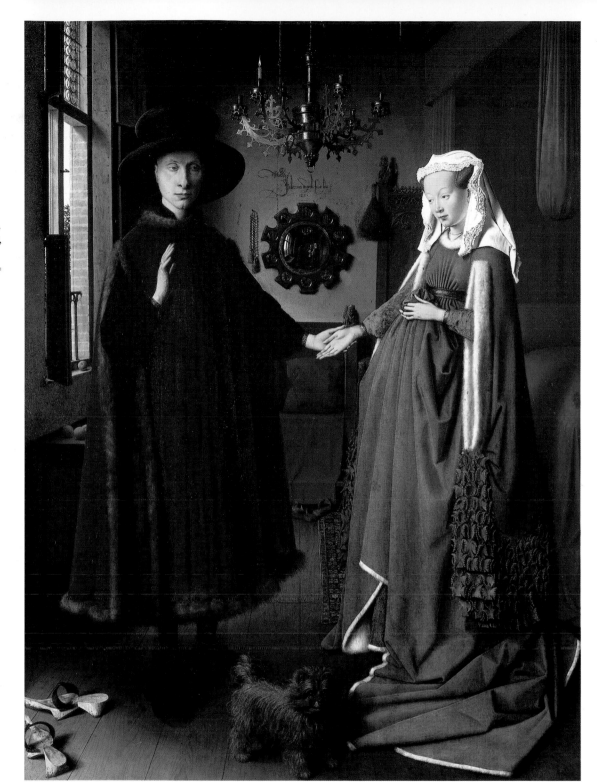

15-8. Jan van Eyck. *The Arnolfini Portrait.* 1434. Oil on panel, 33 x $22\frac{1}{2}$" (83.7 x 57 cm). The National Gallery, London

REPRODUCED BY COURTESY OF THE TRUSTEES

(BELOW RIGHT)
15-9. Jan van Eyck. *The Arnolfini Portrait* (detail)

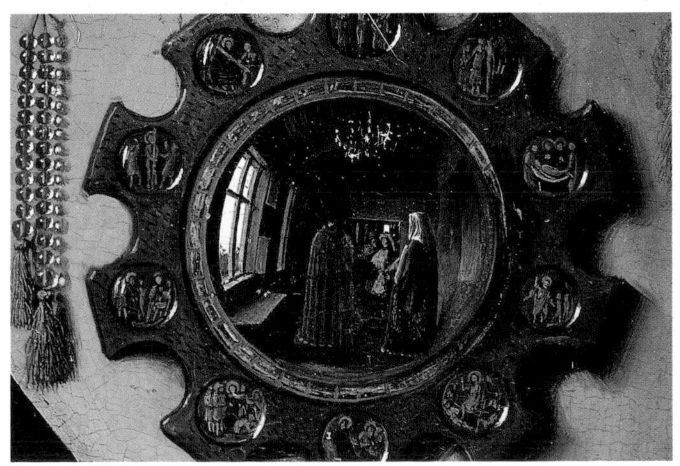

betrothal of Giovanni Arnolfini and Giovanna Cenami in the main room of the bride's house, rather than an exchange of marriage vows in the privacy of the bridal chamber, as usually thought. The young couple touches hands as he raises his right hand in solemn oath. (In accordance with Northern custom, the actual wedding no doubt took place later in front of a church, when the young couple's right hands were joined in holy matrimony.) They seem to be quite alone, but in the mirror behind them is the reflection of two other people who have entered the room (fig. 15-9). One of them is presumably the bride's father, who by tradition gives her to the groom. The other must be the artist, since the words above the mirror, in florid lettering, tell us that "Johannes de eyck fuit hic" (Jan van Eyck was here) in the year 1434.

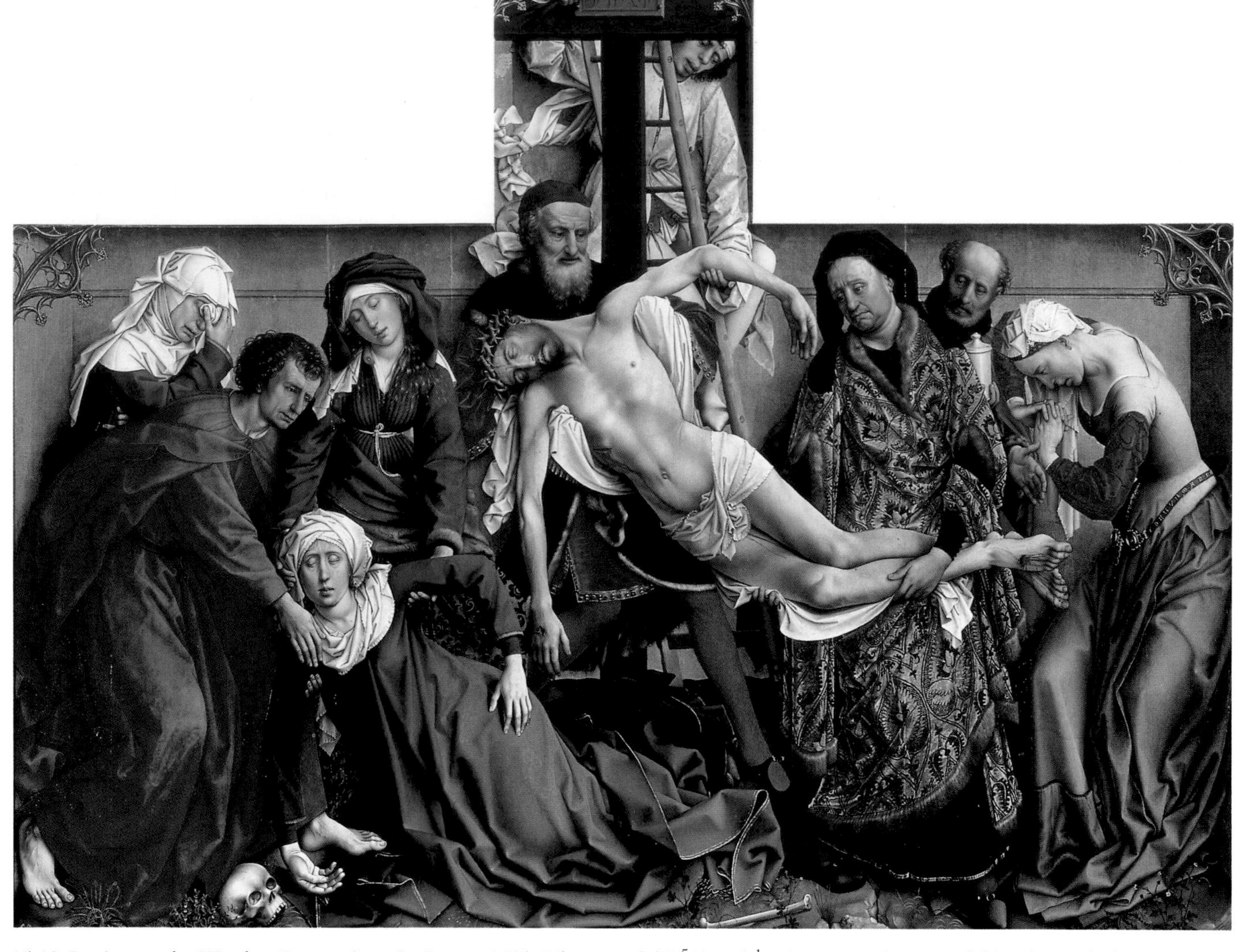

15-10. Rogier van der Weyden. *Descent from the Cross.* c. 1435. Oil on panel, 7'2 5/8" x 8'7 1/8" (2.2 x 2.6 m). Museo del Prado, Madrid

Jan's role, then, is that of a witness to the engagement, which also entailed a legal and financial contract between the two families. The picture claims to show exactly what he saw. Given its secular nature, we may wonder whether the picture is filled with the same sort of disguised symbolism as the *Mérode Altarpiece,* where the natural world contains the world of the spirit so completely that the two become one. Or does the realism serve simply as an accurate record of the event and its domestic setting? The elaborate bed, the main piece of furniture in the well-appointed living room of the day, was used not for sleeping but for greeting new mothers and paying final respects to the dead. May it not also refer to the physical consummation of marriage? Has the couple taken off their shoes merely as a matter of custom, or to remind us that they are standing on "holy ground"? (For the origin of the theme, see page 43.) By the same token, is the little dog a beloved pet or an emblem of fidelity? (In Latin, *fides* is the root for the words "dog," "fidelity," and "betrothal.") The other furnishings of the room pose similar questions. What is the role of the single candle in the chandelier, burning in broad daylight (compare page 485)? And is the convex mirror, whose frame is decorated with scenes from the Passion, not a Vanitas symbol (see fig. 15-9, page 491)? Jan was so intrigued by its visual effects that he included it in two other paintings as well.

ROGIER VAN DER WEYDEN. In the work of Jan van Eyck, the exploration of the reality made visible by light and color reached a level that was not to be surpassed for another two centuries. Rogier van der Weyden (1399/1400–1464), the third great master of early Flemish painting, set himself a different but equally important task: to recapture the emotional drama and pathos of the Gothic past within the framework of the new style. We see this greater expressive immediacy in his early masterpiece, *Descent from the Cross* (fig. 15-10), which dates from about 1435. Here the modeling is sculpturally precise, with angular drapery folds recalling those of his teacher, Robert Campin. The soft half-shadows and rich colors show his knowledge of Jan van Eyck, with whom he may also have been in contact. Yet Rogier is far more than a follower of the two older artists.

Whatever he owes to them (and it is clearly a great deal) he uses for his own purposes. The external events (in this case, the lowering of Jesus' body from the Cross) concern him less than the world of human feeling: "the inner desires and emotions . . . whether sorrow, anger, or gladness," in the words of an early account. The visible world in turn becomes a means toward that same end.

Rogier's art has been well described as "at once physically barer and spiritually richer than Jan van Eyck's." Judged for its expressive content, this *Descent* could well be called a Lamentation. The Virgin's swoon echoes the pose and expression of her son. So intense is her pain and grief that it inspires the same compassion in the viewer. Rogier has staged his scene in a shallow niche or shrine, not against a landscape. This bold device gives him a double advantage in heightening the effect of the tragic event. It focuses the viewer's attention on the foreground and allows the artist to mold the figures into a coherent group. It seems fitting that Rogier treats his figures as if they were colored statues, for the source of these grief-stricken gestures and faces is in sculpture rather than in painting. The panel descends from the Strasbourg *Death of the Virgin* (see fig. 11-45), to which it is very similar in both composition and mood.

Truly "Late Gothic," Rogier's art never departs from the spirit of the Middle Ages. Yet visually it belongs just as clearly to the new era, so that the past is restated in contemporary terms. Thus *The Miraflores Altarpiece* (fig. 15-11) is full of archaisms, yet it looks thoroughly up-to-date. By now the artist was in great demand, and his work involved the participation of assistants. Such is the case with our altar, named for the convent near Burgos that received it by 1445. (The composition is known in a second, equally fine version from his shop.) As the inscriptions on the scrolls tell us, the triptych celebrates the purity, faith, and perseverance of the Virgin, which are related in turn to the theme of her joys, sorrows, and glories.

A simulated portal provides the doorway into each scene, which is confined to the foreground of a small niche, despite the suggestion of deep space behind it. This old-fashioned device once again creates the impression of figures as colored sculpture in an architectural setting (see the Naumburg *Crucifixion,* fig. 11-51). The effect is increased by the reliefs lining the archivolts. These reliefs carry much of the narrative and symbolic burden by depicting events from the life of Jesus related to the subject below. The Virgin adoring the Christ Child in the left panel recalls a traditional Nativity (compare fig. 11-98). Because it is transferred to an indoor setting, this Madonna of Humility is also the Queen of Heaven. The center panel combines the Byzantine motif of the Last Kiss with the German *Pietà* (see fig. 11-54). However, the Final Appearance of Jesus to his Mother, in the right panel, is unusual in both subject and treatment. It recalls the more familiar *Noli me tangere,* where he appears to the Magdalen.

Like *The Deposition, The Miraflores Altarpiece* may be thought of as an enlarged Gothic *Andachtsbild* that is meant to be an object of spiritual devotion. The figures continue the aristocratic ideal of the International Style. Slender and elegant, they represent Rogier's definitive type. He uses them to convey a remarkable range of emotion not simply through gesture and expression but also through purely formal means—the precise quality of line, form, and color—which communicate their intent with powerful conviction.

Rogier was accessible to people who retained a medieval outlook. No wonder he set an example for countless other artists. When he died in 1464, after 30 years as the foremost painter of Brussels, his influence was supreme throughout Europe north of the Alps. Its impact continued to be felt almost everywhere outside Italy, in painting as well as sculpture, until the end of the fifteenth century.

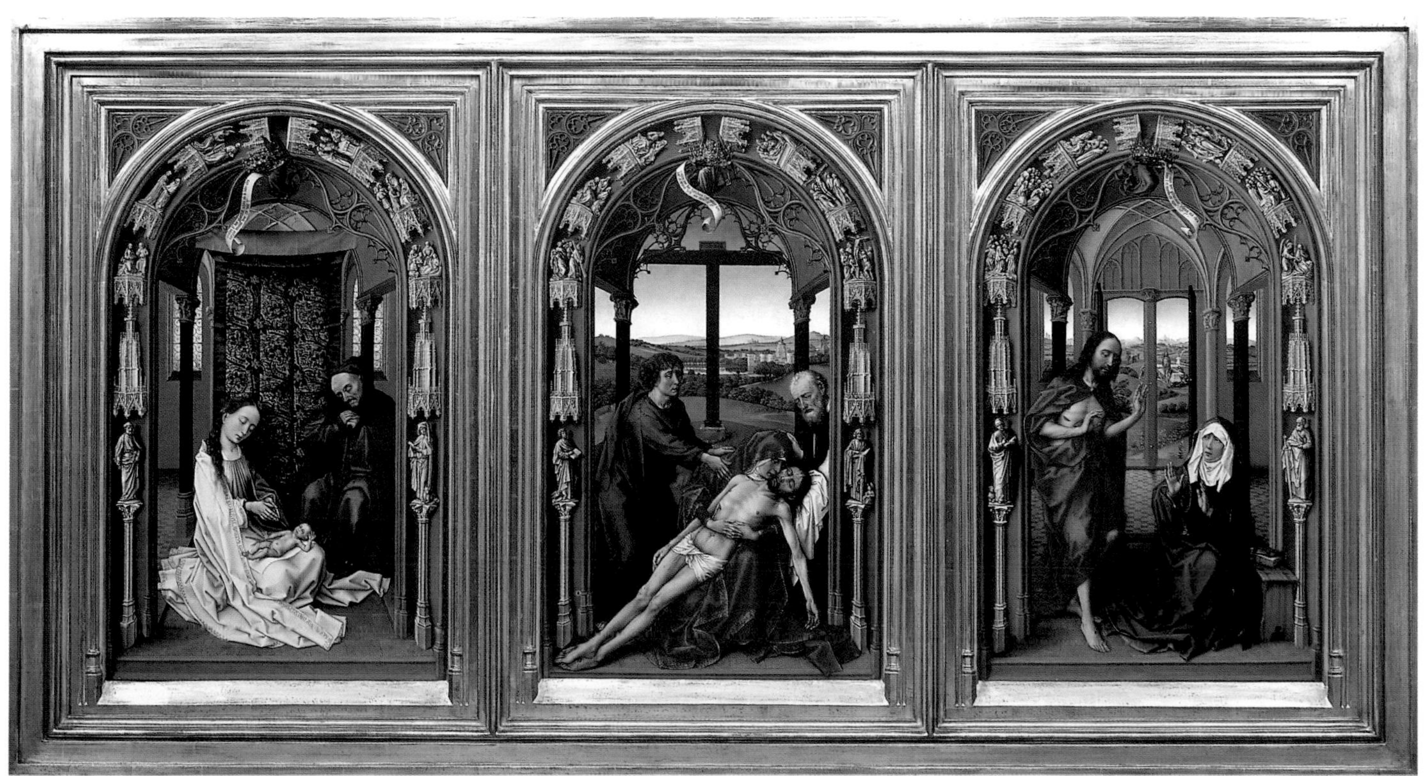

15-11. Rogier van der Weyden. *The Miraflores Altarpiece.* c. 1440–44. Oil on panel, each panel 28 x 16⅞" (71.1 x 42.8 cm). Staatliche Museen zu Berlin, Gemäldegalerie

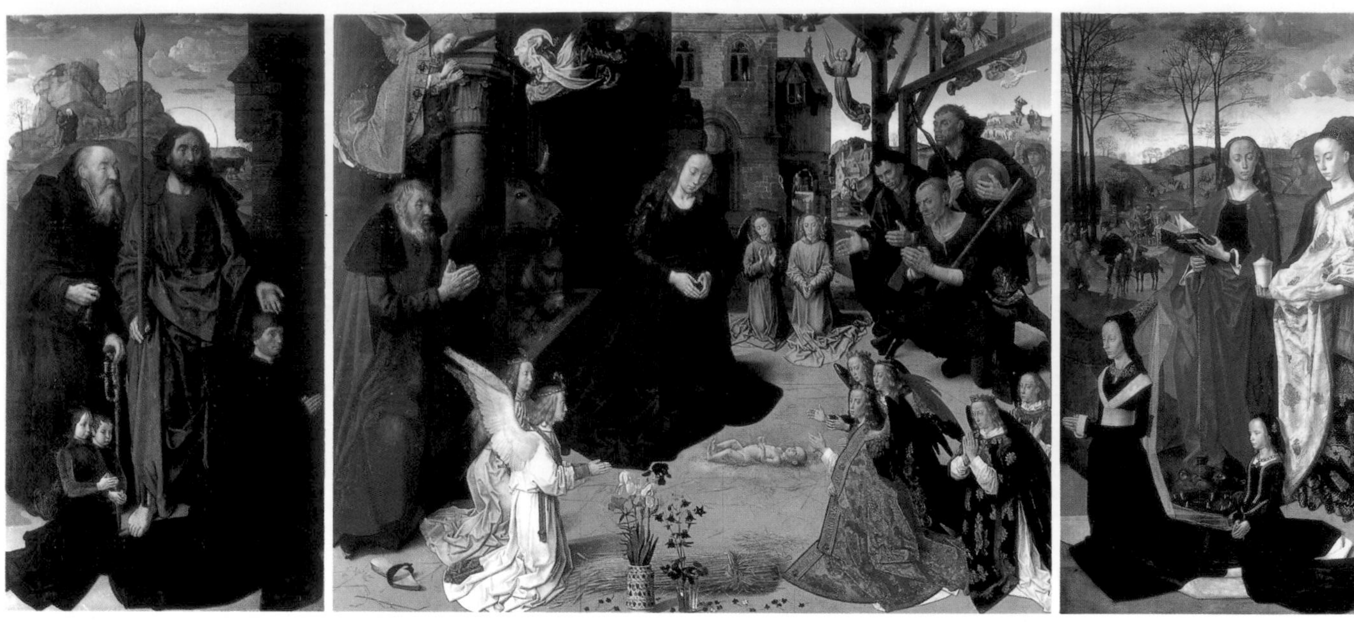

15-12. Hugo van der Goes. *The Portinari Altarpiece* (open). c. 1476. Tempera and oil on panel, center 8'3½" x 10' (2.5 x 3.1 m), wings each 8'3½" x 4'7½" (2.5 x 1.4 m). Galleria degli Uffizi, Florence

HUGO VAN DER GOES. Few of the artists who followed Rogier van der Weyden escaped from his shadow. To them his paintings offered a choice between intense drama and delicate restraint. The vast majority chose the latter, and their work is marked by a fragile charm. The most dynamic of Rogier's disciples was Hugo van der Goes (c. 1440–1482), an unhappy genius whose tragic end suggests an unstable personality. After a spectacular rise to fame in the cosmopolitan atmosphere of Bruges, he decided to enter a monastery as a lay brother in 1475, when he was nearly 35 years old. [See Primary Sources, no. 49, page 618.] He continued to paint for some time, but increasing fits of depression drove him to the verge of suicide, and seven years later he was dead.

The huge altarpiece commissioned in 1475 by Tommaso Portinari, an agent of the Medicis in Bruges, is Van der Goes' most ambitious work (fig. 15-12). There is a tension between the artist's devotion to the natural world and his concern with the supernatural that evokes a nervous and restless personality. Hugo has rendered a wonderfully spacious and atmospheric landscape with a wealth of precise detail. Yet the difference in the size of the figures seems to contradict this realism. In the wings, the kneeling members of the Portinari family are dwarfed by their patron saints, whose gigantic size marks them as being of a higher order. The latter figures are not meant to be "larger than life," however. They share the same huge scale with Joseph, the Virgin Mary, and the shepherds of the Nativity in the center panel, whose height is normal in relation to the architecture and to the ox and ass. The angels are on the same scale as the donors and thus appear abnormally small.

This change of scale stands outside the logic of everyday experience found in the setting the artist has provided for his figures. Although it originated with Rogier van der Weyden and has a clear symbolic purpose, Hugo exploited this variation for expressive effect. There is another striking contrast between the hushed awe of the shepherds and the ritual solemnity of all the other figures. These field hands, gazing in breathless wonder at the newborn Child, react to the miracle of the Nativity with a wide-eyed directness new to Flemish art. They were especially admired by the Italian painters who saw the work after Portinari brought it to Florence in 1483.

GEERTGEN TOT SINT JANS. During the last quarter of the fifteenth century there were no painters in Flanders comparable to Hugo van der Goes. The most original artists appeared farther

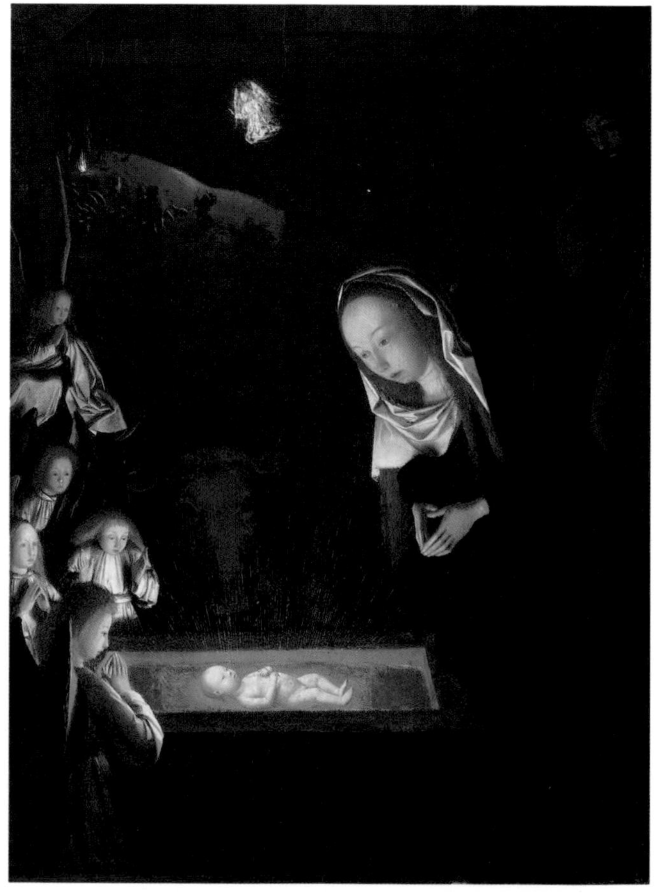

15-13. Geertgen tot Sint Jans. *Nativity.* c. 1490. Oil on panel, 13½ x 10" (34.3 x 25.7 cm). The National Gallery, London

REPRODUCED BY COURTESY OF THE TRUSTEES

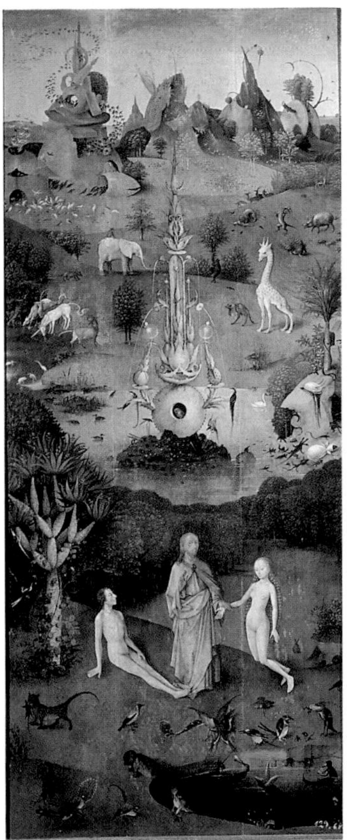
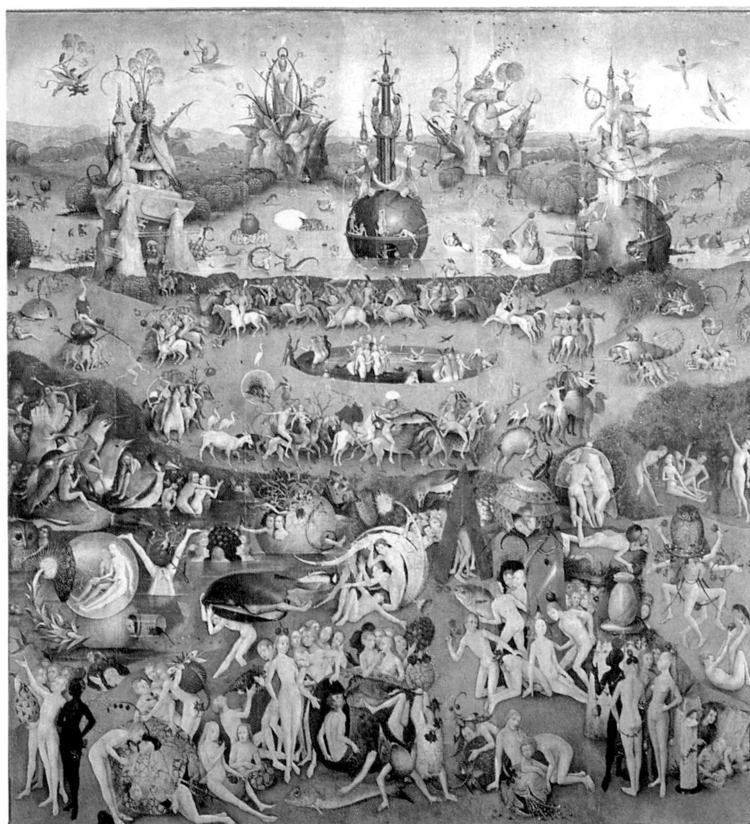
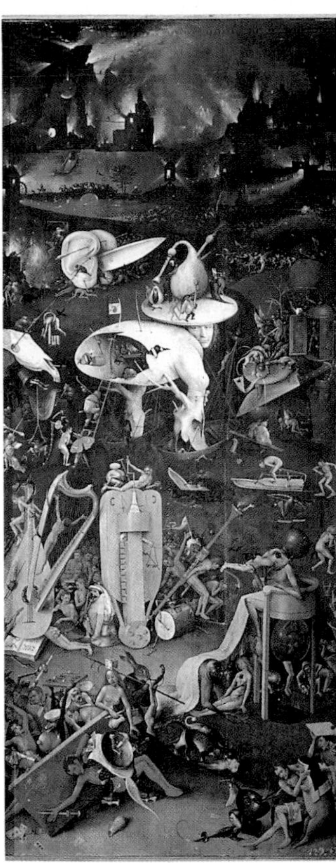

15-14. Hieronymus Bosch. *The Garden of Delights.* c. 1510–15. Oil on panel, center 7'2½" x 6'4¾" (2.19 x 1.95 m); wings, each 7'2½" x 3'2" (2.19 x .96 m). Museo del Prado, Madrid

north, in Holland. One of them, Geertgen tot Sint Jans of Haarlem, who died at the age of 28, about 1490–5, admired Hugo's work in Bruges. He then returned to his hometown to work for the Knights of St. John's, hence his name. The *Nativity* shown in figure 15-13 is as daring in its quiet way as the center panel of *The Portinari Altarpiece.* The idea of a nocturnal Nativity, illuminated mainly by radiance from the Christ Child, goes back to the International Style (see fig. 11-98). But Geertgen applies the pictorial discoveries of Jan van Eyck to give new reality to the scene. The magic effect of his little panel is enhanced by the smooth, simplified shapes that record the play of light with striking clarity. The heads of the angels, the Infant, and the Virgin are all as round as objects turned on a lathe, while the manger is a rectangular trough.

BOSCH. Another Dutch artist, Hieronymus Bosch, appeals to our interest in the world of fantasy. Little is known about Bosch except that he came from a family of painters named Van Aken, spent his life in the provincial town of 'sHertogenbosch, and died, an old man, in 1516. His most famous work, the triptych known as *The Garden of Delights* (fig. 15-14), is the richest and most puzzling of all. [See Primary Sources, no. 50, pages 618–19.] Of the three panels, only the left one has a clearly recognizable subject. It is the Garden of Eden, where the Lord introduces Adam to the newly created Eve. The airy landscape is filled with animals, including such exotic creatures as an elephant and a giraffe, as well as sinister hybrid monsters. The right wing, a nightmarish scene of burning ruins and instruments of torture, surely represents Hell. But what of the center panel? Here is a landscape much like that of the Garden of Eden, populated with countless nude men and women engaged in a variety of peculiar activities. In the center, they parade around a circular basin on the backs of all sorts of beasts. Many frolic in pools of water. Most of them are linked with huge birds, fruit, flowers, or marine animals. Only a few are openly engaged in lovemaking, but there can be no doubt that the birds, fruit, and the like are thinly disguised symbols of carnal desire. The delights in this "garden" are an unending repetition of the Original Sin of Adam and Eve, which dooms us in our life on earth to be prisoners of our appetites.

The picture's strange qualities stem in part from the fact that this is not a traditional altarpiece but a secular work. It was probably commissioned by Henry III of Nassau for his palace in Brussels, where it was hanging just after Bosch's death. (Henry would have been familiar with Bosch's work in 'sHertogenbosch, the royal summer residence.) Much of the imagery in *The Garden of Delights* derives from *The Romance of the Rose.* This allegorical poem on love, modeled loosely on Ovid's *Art of Love,* was begun around 1230–40 by Guillaume de Lorris (named for his hometown near Orléans) and greatly expanded around 1275 by Jean Chopinel, better known as Jean de Meun(g) for his birthplace, also in the vicinity of Orléans. It remained the most popular literary work in France for nearly three centuries. Bosch may well have known the version by Jean Molinet toward the end of the fifteenth century, but others would also have been available to Bosch. (It is most familiar to English-speaking peoples in Geoffrey Chaucer's translation of the later 1360s.)

There are many parallels between *The Garden of Delights* and

The Romance of the Rose. The title of Bosch's painting actually comes from the garden where the lover conquers his lady, whose symbol is the rose. As in the picture, the central feature is a fountain, where Narcissus fell in love with his reflection, thus giving rise to natural, or earthly, love. De Lorris' original poem begins in the garden after the Fall of Man. It is cast as a sexual nightmare that is further interpreted in de Meung's commentary covering a wide range of subjects, such as the sins of the clergy, which are treated in other works by Bosch as well. Both painting and poem use irony to teach moral lessons by horrid example. The difference is that in *The Romance of the Rose,* earthly love may lead to a higher, spiritual love and thus to divine love and redemption. Nowhere, however, does Bosch even hint that salvation is possible. Corruption, on the animal level at least, was already found in the Garden of Eden before the Fall; hence we are all destined for Hell, the Garden of Satan, with its grisly instruments of torture.

Bosch, then, has not simply illustrated *The Romance of the Rose* but interpreted it in highly personal terms, based in part on popular sayings of the day. We also know that the shapes of the fountains and many other forms were taken from treatises on astrology and alchemy, which Bosch would have known through his father-in-law, a well-to-do pharmacist. Astrology and alchemy united the humors with the zodiac in a scheme of good and evil paralleling that of the poem. In the context of *The Garden of Delights* they represent earthly knowledge, which is the corruption of spiritual knowledge, just as earthly love is the sinful opposite of divine love.

Swiss, German, and French Painting

After about 1430, the new realism of the Flemish masters began to spread into France and Germany. By the middle of the century, its influence prevailed everywhere in Northern Europe, from Spain to the Baltic. Among the countless artists (including many whose names are not known) who turned out provincial versions of Netherlandish painting, only a few were gifted enough to impress us with a distinctive personality.

WITZ. One of the earliest and most original of these masters was Conrad Witz of Basel (1400/10–1445/6). His altarpiece for Geneva Cathedral, painted in 1444, includes the panel shown in figure 15-15. To judge from the drapery, with its tubular folds and angular breaks, he must have had close contact with Campin. But the setting, rather than the figures, attracts our interest, and here the influence of the Van Eycks seems dominant. Witz, however, did not simply follow these great masters. An explorer himself, he knew more about the optical appearances of water than any other painter of his time, as we can see the bottom of the lake in the foreground. The landscape, too, is an original contribution. Representing a specific part of the shore of the Lake of Geneva, it is among the earliest landscape "portraits" that have come down to us.

FOUQUET. In France, the leading painter was Jean Fouquet (c. 1420–1481) of Tours. As the result of a lengthy visit to Italy around 1445, soon after he had completed his training, his work

MUSIC IN FIFTEENTH-CENTURY FLANDERS

The brilliance of the fifteenth-century Flemish painters had a close parallel in the field of music. After about 1420, the Netherlands produced a school of composers—Guillaume Dufay (c. 1400–1474), Johannes Ockeghem (c. 1420–1495), Josquin Des Prés (c. 1440–1521), and Adrian Willaert (c. 1490–1562)—so revolutionary as to dominate the development of music throughout Europe for the next 125 years. How much the new style was appreciated can be gathered from the words of the Flemish theorist Johannes Tinctoris (1446?–1511), who wrote of these composers in 1477: "Although it seems beyond belief, nothing worth listening to had been composed before their time." Except for the absence of any reference to the revival of antiquity, this remark, with its sweeping rejection of medieval music, shows a Flemish "Renaissance consciousness" much like that of the Italian humanists of the same period. In fact, Des Prés and Willaert held important positions in Italy, and Dufay had spent nearly a decade there early in his career. In Italy, during the High Renaissance, these Flemings were revered as the greatest composers of their day (see page 442). Their main contribution was the invention of the fugue: the passing of a short theme from one voice to another of equal weight (think of "Three Blind Mice"), a technique that was to become highly developed in the sixteenth century.

Tinctoris credited the English composer John Dunstable (c. 1385–1453), active in France between 1422 and 1435, with beginning a revolution that replaced the complexities of Gothic polyphony with a simpler style. Dufay carried Dunstable's innovations further by placing the main melody, which earlier had been sung by the tenor, in the soprano voice. This simple change gave greater prominence to the melodic line and emphasized its beauty. Dufay also led a movement to replace plainsong in sacred music with themes from secular songs, which were more flexible than chant and more appealing to contemporary taste. In the sixteenth century, these innovations evolved into a form called the parody mass, in which most of the themes were taken from popular songs, freely modified, and connected with newly composed passages. Ockeghem completed the musical revolution toward a more mellifluous style. Though less well known today than Dufay, Ockeghem was highly honored in his own time. The humanist Erasmus wrote of him, "His golden voice caressed the ears of the angels, and swayed the hearts of men to their depths," and his passing was mourned by his pupil Josquin in the lament "Nymphs of the Woods."

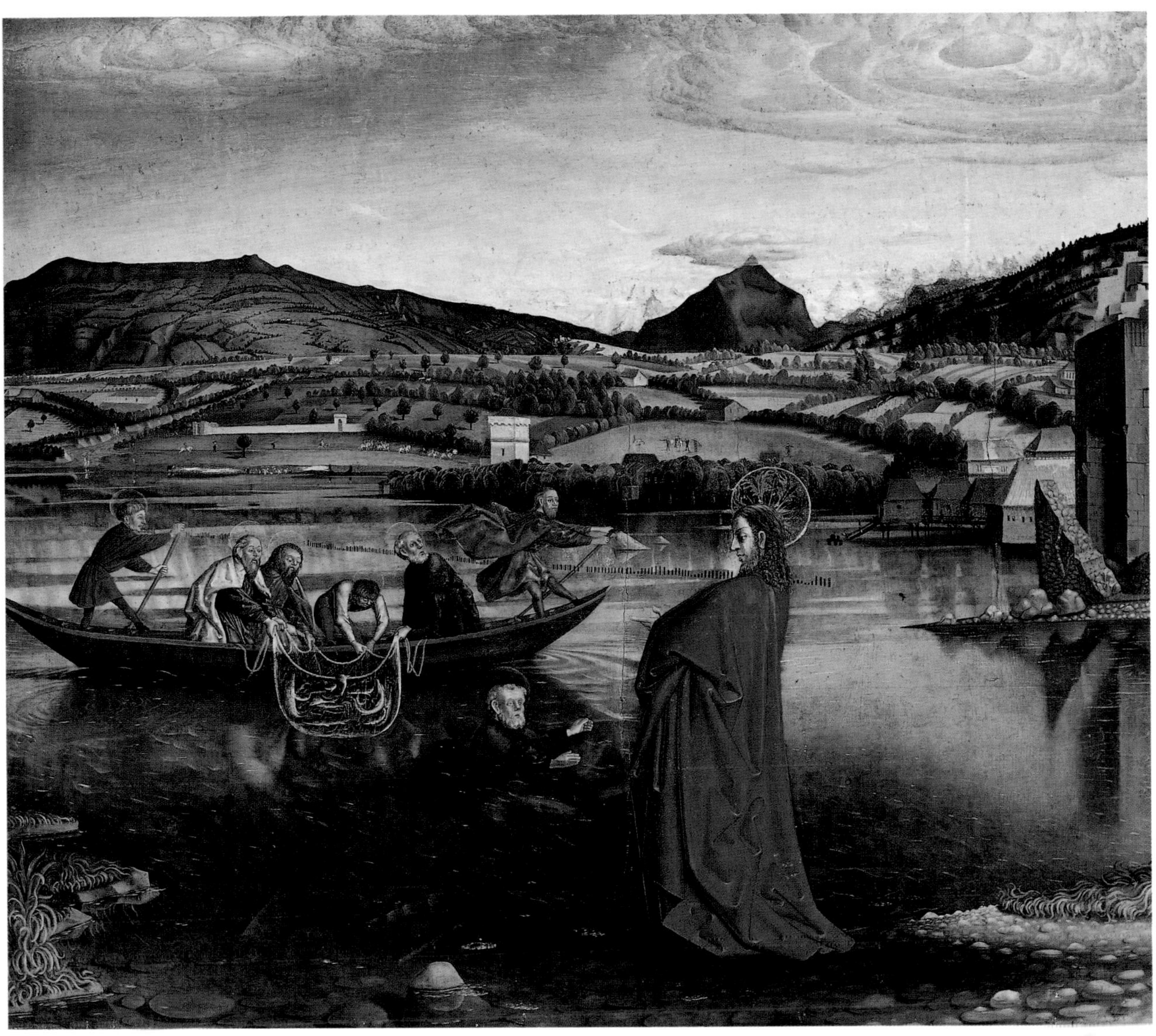

15-15. Conrad Witz. *The Miraculous Draught of Fishes.* 1444. Oil on panel, 51 x 61" (129.7 x 155 cm). Musée d'Art et d'Histoire, Geneva, Switzerland

remains basically Northern. *Étienne Chevalier and St. Stephen,* the left wing of the *Melun Diptych* (fig. 15-16), his most famous work, shows his mastery as a portraitist. The head of the saint seems no less individual than that of the donor. Italian influence can be seen in the style of the architecture and, less directly, in the statuesque solidity of the two figures. According to an old tradition, the Madonna in the right wing (fig. 15-17) is also a portrait—of Agnes Sorel, Charles VII's mistress. (Chevalier, the king's secretary and lord treasurer, served as executor of her estate upon her death in 1450, when our diptych may have been painted.) If so, it presents an idealized image of courtly beauty, as befits the Queen of Heaven, seen wearing a crown amidst a choir of angels. (Her bared, ample breast signifies the lactating Mary who nurtures the Infant Jesus.)

Here we see the beginnings of the tendency toward intellectual clarity and visual abstraction that were to become distinctive to French art. This emphasis extends to the background. The treatment of space is very different in the two panels, not out of disregard for visual perspective but in order to distinguish between the temporal and spiritual realms. Thus each half of the diptych is a self-contained world. In turn, pictorial space for Fouquet exists independently of the viewer's "real" space.

Manuscript painting continued to flourish on both sides of the Alps well into the sixteenth century, and Fouquet was the most famous illuminator of the day in the North. *The Fall of Jerusalem* (fig. 15-18) shows his debt to the Gothic. It comes from a copy of Josephus' *Les Antiquités Judaïques* that was started around 1410 for the duke of Berry and was completed by Fouquet some 60 years later. The scene, which closely follows Josephus' text [see Primary Sources, no. 11, page 199], depicts the forces of the Babylonian king Nebuchadnezzar under General Nebuzar-Adar overrunning the city and destroying the Temple of Solomon in 586 B.C. Fouquet's mastery of outdoor space and perspective is no less complete than in the *October* page of *Les Très Riches Heures du Duc de Berry* (see fig. 11-94). Yet Fouquet was more than an imitator of the Limbourg brothers, no matter how much he may have admired them.

The landscape is painted in the up-to-date style of Conrad Witz and presents a stunningly realistic evocation of a contemporary French town. It is hardly surprising that the page imitates

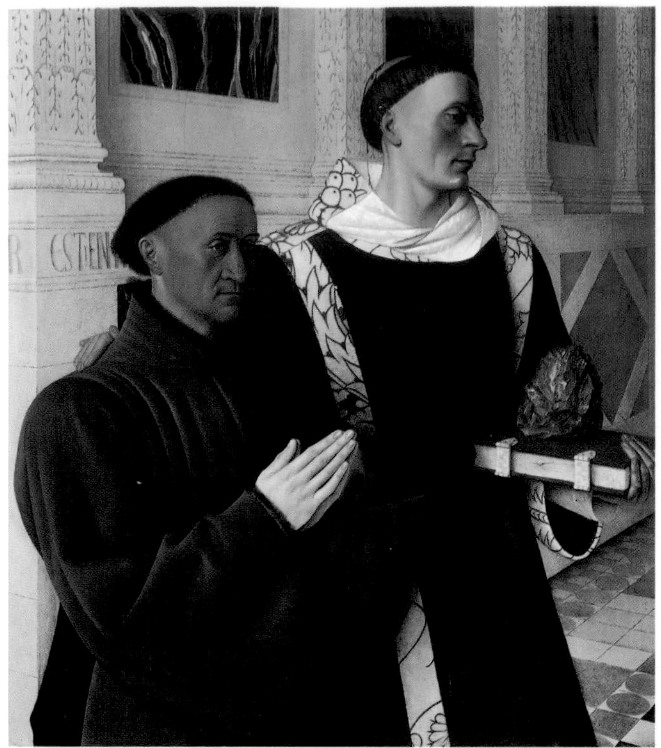

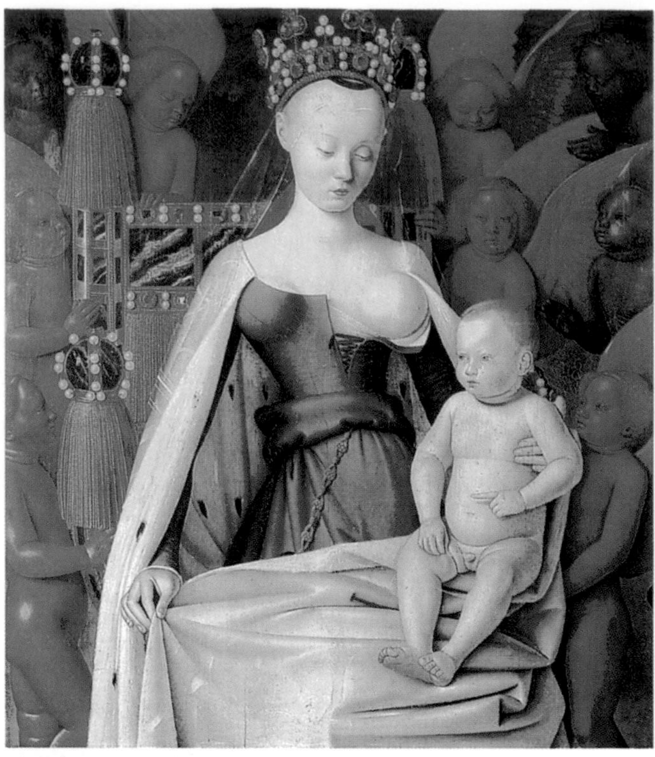

(Above Left) 15-16. Jean Fouquet. *Étienne Chevalier and St. Stephen,* left wing of the *Melun Diptych*. c. 1450. Oil on panel, 36½ x 33½" (92.7 x 85 cm). Staatliche Museen zu Berlin, Gemäldegalerie

(Above Right) 15-17. Jean Fouquet. *Madonna and Child,* right wing of the *Melun Diptych.* c. 1450. Oil on panel, 36⅝ x 33½" (93 x 85 cm). Musée Royal des Beaux-Arts, Antwerp, Belgium

(Left) 15-18. Jean Fouquet. *The Fall of Jerusalem,* from Josephus, *Les Antiquités Judaïques.* c. 1470–75. Illumination, 16⅞ x 11¾" (42.8 x 29.8 cm). Bibliothèque Nationale, Paris

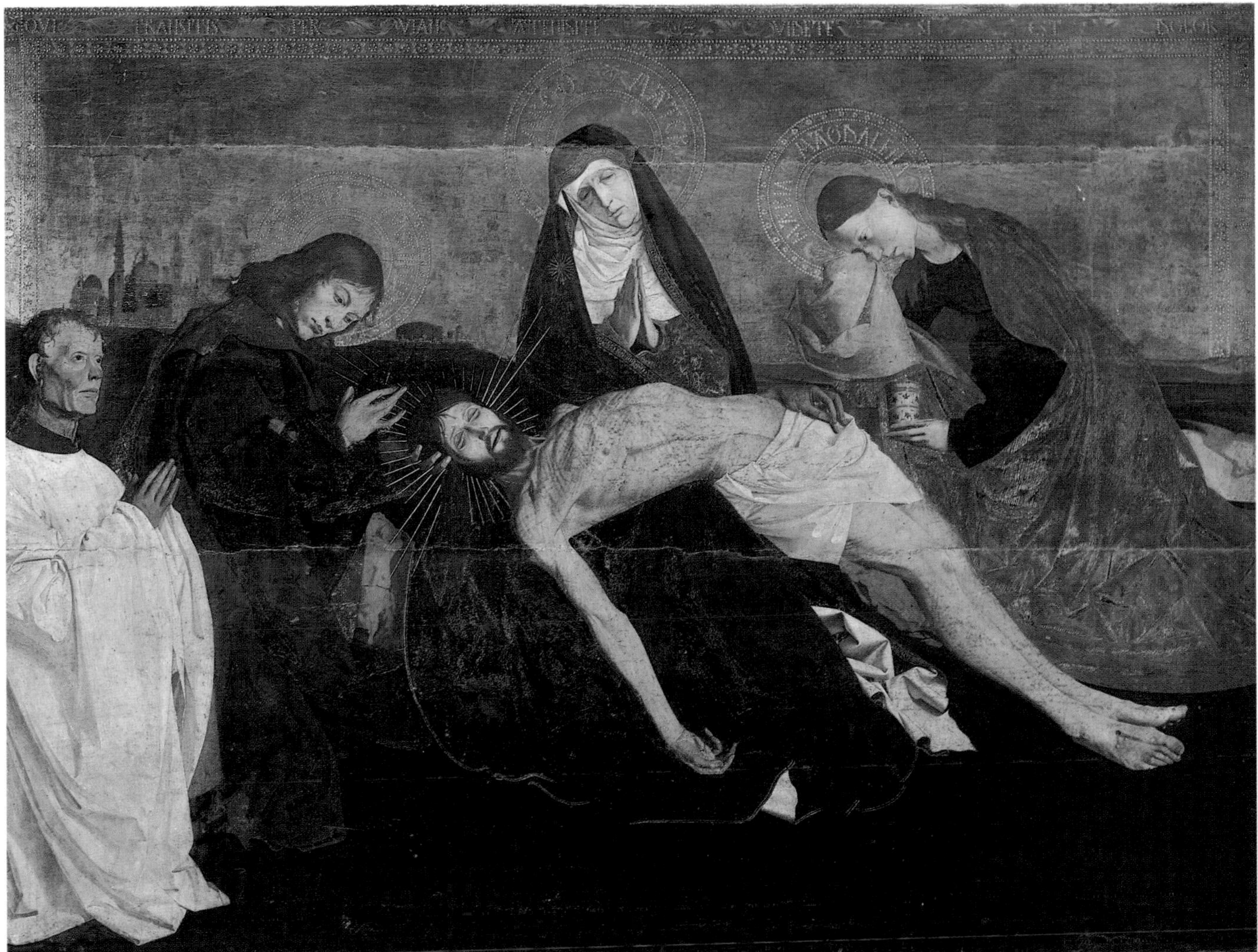

15-19. Enguerrand Quarton. *Avignon Pietà.* c. 1470. Oil on panel, 5'3¾" x 7'1⅞" (1.61 x 2.17 m). Musée du Louvre, Paris

effects found in panels, which had become the dominant form for painting. Yet the quality of the narrative itself belongs to the tradition of manuscript illustration. Even here Fouquet reveals himself an innovator. Precedents for the scene can be found in earlier illuminations, notably those by Jan van Eyck, who excelled as a manuscript painter. Yet, surprisingly, its closest relative is *The Building of the Tower of Babel* at St.-Savin-sur-Gartempe (see fig. 10-36), which presents a similar subject in reverse, so to speak. They share the same monumental spirit, despite the vast difference in size—truly a remarkable achievement!

QUARTON. A Flemish style influenced by Italian art also appears in the most famous of all fifteenth-century French pictures, the *Avignon Pietà* (fig. 15-19). As its name indicates, the panel comes from the extreme south of France and is attributed to an artist of that region, Enguerrand Quarton (c. 1410–c. 1466). He must have been familiar with the art of Rogier van der Weyden, for the figure types and the expressive content of the *Avignon Pietà* could be derived from no other source. At the same time, the magnificently simple and stable design is Italian rather than Northern. We first saw these qualities in the art of Giotto. Southern, too, is the bleak, featureless landscape that emphasizes the monumentality and isolation of the figures. The distant buildings behind the donor on the left have an unmistakably Islamic flavor, suggesting that the artist meant to place the scene in a Near Eastern setting. From these various features he has created an unforgettable image of pathos.

"LATE GOTHIC" SCULPTURE

If we had to describe fifteenth-century art north of the Alps in a single phrase, we might label it "the first century of panel painting." Panel painting was so dominant in the period between 1420 and 1500 that its standards apply to manuscript illumination, stained glass, and even sculpture. After the later thirteenth century, we will recall, the emphasis had shifted from architectural sculpture to the more intimate scale of devotional images, tombs, pulpits, and the like. Claus Sluter, whose art is so impressive in weight and volume, had briefly recaptured the monumental spirit of the High Gothic. However, he had no real successors, although echoes of his style can be felt in French art for the next 50 years.

It was the influence of Campin and Rogier van der Weyden

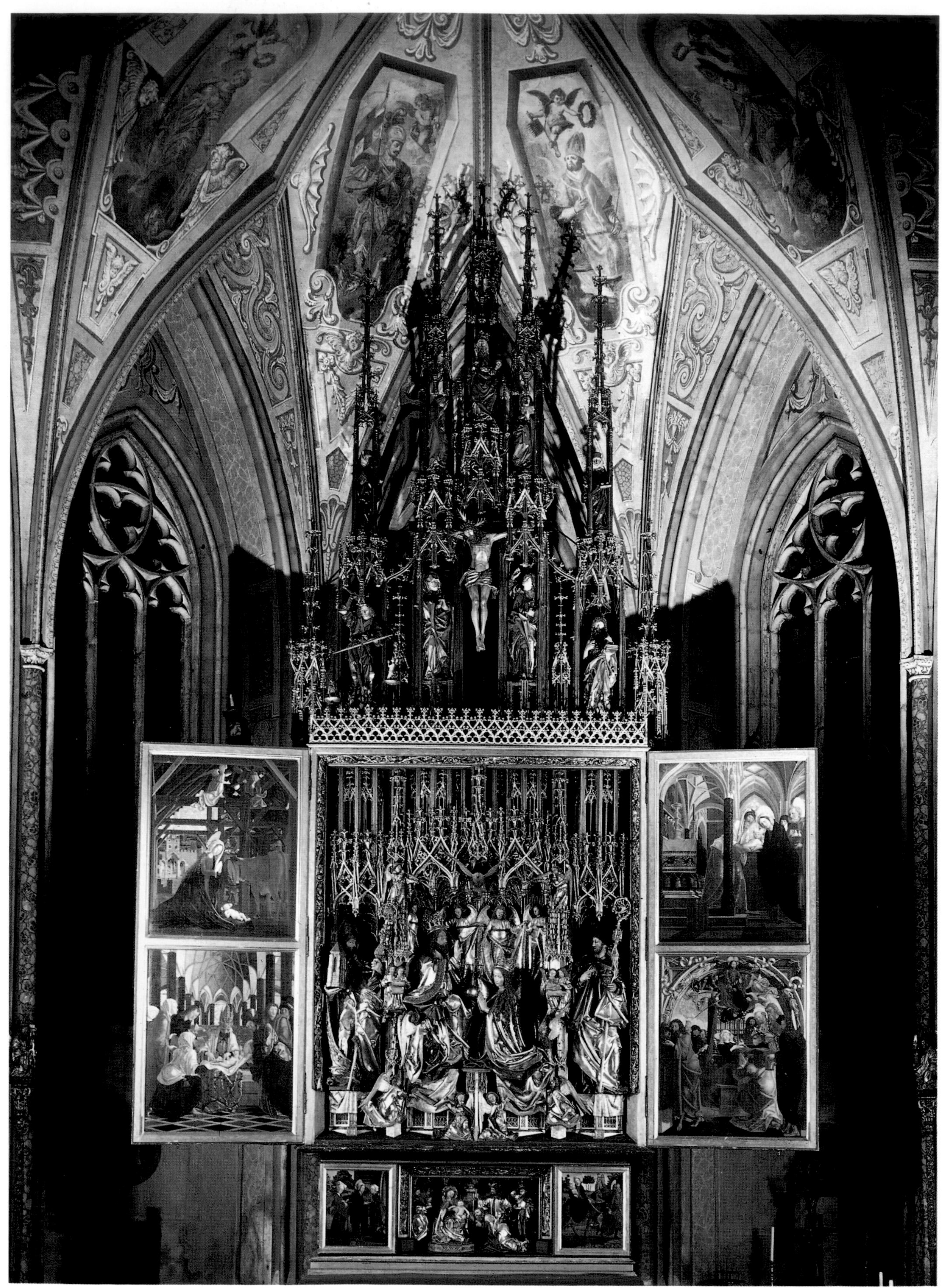

15-20. Michael Pacher. *St. Wolfgang Altarpiece*. 1471–81. Carved wood, figures about lifesize. Church of St. Wolfgang, Austria that ended the International Style in the sculpture of Northern Europe. The carvers, who quite often were also painters, began to reproduce the style of these artists in stone or wood and continued to do so until about 1500.

PACHER. The most important works of the "Late Gothic" carvers are wooden altar shrines, often large in size and intricate in detail. Such shrines were especially popular in the Germanic countries. One of the richest examples is the *St. Wolfgang Altarpiece* (fig. 15-20) by the Tyrolean sculptor and painter Michael Pacher (c. 1435–1498). [See Primary Sources, no. 51, page 619.] Its lavishly gilt and colored forms make a dazzling spectacle as they emerge from the shadows under Flamboyant canopies. We enjoy it, but in pictorial rather than sculptural terms. We have no sense of volume, either positive or negative. The figures and setting in the central panel, showing the Coronation of the Virgin, seem to melt into a pattern of twisting lines that permits only the heads to stand out as separate elements.

Surprisingly, when we turn to the paintings of scenes from the life of the Virgin on the interior of the wings, we enter a different realm, one that already commands the vocabulary of the Northern Renaissance. Here the artist provides a deep space in scientific perspective that takes the viewer's vantage point into account, so that the upper panels are represented slightly from below. The figures, strongly modeled by the clear light, seem far more "sculptural" than the carved ones, even though they are a good deal smaller. It is as if Pacher the sculptor felt unable to compete with Pacher the painter in rendering three-dimensional bodies and therefore chose to treat the Coronation of the Virgin in pictorial terms, by extracting the maximum of drama from contrasts of light and shade.

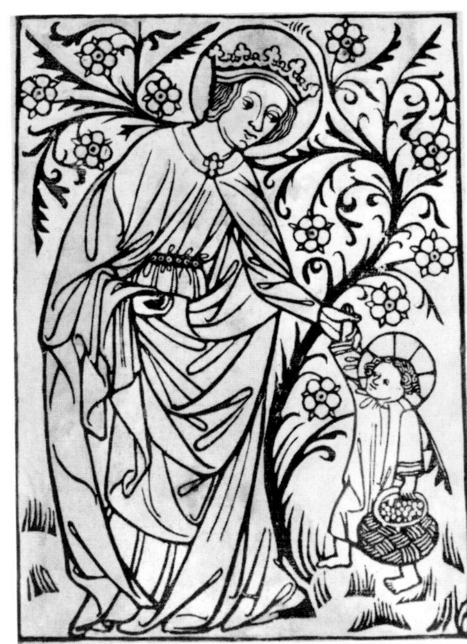

15-21. *St. Dorothy.* c. 1420. Woodcut, 10⅝ x 7½" (27 x 19 cm). Staatliche Graphische Sammlung, Munich

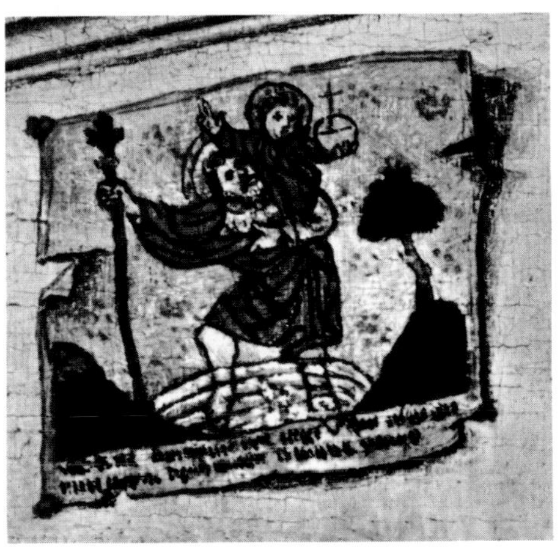

15-22. *Woodcut of St. Christopher,* detail from an *Annunciation* by Jacques Daret (?). c. 1435. Musées Royaux d'Art et d'Histoire, Brussels, Belgium

THE GRAPHIC ARTS

WOODCUTS. We must now take note of another important event north of the Alps: the development of printmaking. (For the various techniques of printing, for pictures as well as books, see box page 502.) The idea of printing pictorial designs from blocks of wood onto paper seems to have originated in Northern Europe at the very end of the fourteenth century. Many of the oldest surviving examples of such prints, called woodcuts, are German, others are Flemish, and some may be French; but all show the qualities of the International Style. The designs were probably furnished by painters or sculptors. The actual carving of the woodblocks, however, was done by specially trained artisans, who also produced woodblocks for textile prints. As a result, early woodcuts, such as the *St. Dorothy* in figure 15-21, have a flat, ornamental pattern. Forms are defined by simple, heavy lines, and there is little concern for three-dimensional effects, as indicated by the absence of hatching or shading. Since the outlined shapes were meant to be filled in with color, these prints often recall stained glass (compare fig. 11-67) more than the miniatures they replaced.

Despite their appeal to modern eyes, fifteenth-century woodcuts were popular art on a level that did not attract artists of great ability until shortly before 1500. A single woodblock yielded thousands of copies, to be sold for a few pennies apiece, so that for the first time in history anyone could own pictures. What people did with these prints is shown in figure 15-22, a detail from a Flemish *Annunciation* panel of about 1435. We see a tattered woodcut of St. Christopher is pinned up above the mantel. Perhaps it is a hint at the Virgin's journey to Bethlehem (St. Christopher was the patron saint of travelers), but it is also a symbol of her humility, for only the poor would have such a print on their walls. The *St. Christopher* woodcut has two lines of lettering—presumably a short prayer—at the bottom. Similar woodcuts combining image and text were sometimes assembled into popular picture books, called block books.

ENGRAVINGS. From the first, engravings appealed to a smaller and more sophisticated public. The oldest examples we know, dating from about 1430, already show the influence of the great Flemish painters. Their forms are systematically modeled with fine hatched lines and are often convincingly foreshortened. Nor do engravings share the anonymity of early woodcuts. Individual hands can be distinguished almost from the beginning, dates and initials appear soon after, and most of the important engravers of the last third of the fifteenth century are known to us by name. Although the early engravers were usually trained as goldsmiths, their prints are so closely linked to local painting styles that it is far

PRINTMAKING

The earliest printed books were produced in the Rhineland soon after 1450, and the technique spread quickly throughout Europe, with profound implications for Western civilization and literacy. Printed pictures were hardly less important, for without them the printed book could not have replaced the work of the medieval scribe and illuminator so quickly. The literary and pictorial aspects of printing were indeed closely linked from the start.

Johann Gutenberg (c. 1397–1468) is usually credited with inventing movable type, but the beginnings of printing actually lie in the ancient Near East 5,000 years ago. The Sumerians were the earliest "printers," for their relief impressions on clay from stone seals were carved with both pictures and inscriptions. From Mesopotamia the use of seals spread to India and eventually to China. The Chinese applied ink to their seals in order to impress them on wood or silk, and in the second century A.D. they invented paper. By the ninth century they were printing pictures and books from wooden blocks carved in relief, and 200 years later they developed movable type. Some of the products of Chinese printing surely reached the medieval West—although there is no direct evidence.

The technique of manufacturing paper, too, came to Europe from the East, though it gained ground as a cheap alternative to parchment very slowly. While printing on wood blocks was known in the later Middle Ages, it was used only for ornamental patterns on cloth. All the more astonishing, then, is the development, beginning about 1400, of a printing technology that within a century surpassed that of the Far East and proved of far wider cultural importance. After 1500, no basic changes were made in this field until the Industrial Revolution.

The printing technology of 1500 allowed for the reproduction of pictures by several methods, all developed in tandem with the printing of type.

WOODCUT: In a woodcut the design is cut into a woodblock so that the ridges will print. The thinner the ridges are, the more difficult they are to carve, and so this work was soon given over to specialists. Inscriptions are frequently found on early woodcuts, but to carve lines of text backward in relief on a wooden block must have been risky—a single slip could ruin an entire page. It is little wonder, then, that printers soon had the idea of putting each letter on its own small block. Wooden movable type carved by hand worked well for large letters but not for small ones, and the technique was too expensive for printing long texts such as the Bible. By 1450 this problem had been solved through the introduction of metal type cast from molds, and the stage was set for book production as it was practiced until very recently.

ENGRAVING: The success of metal type was no doubt attributable to the technical knowledge of armorers and especially goldsmiths, who had already entered the field of printmaking as engravers. The technique of engraving—of embellishing metal surfaces with incised pictures—was developed in classical antiquity (see fig. 6-11) and continued to be practiced throughout the Middle Ages (see fig. 10-41, where the engraved lines are filled in with enamel). Thus no new skill was required to engrave a plate that was to serve as the *matrix,* or recessed mold, for a paper print.

Engraved prints are more refined and flexible than woodcuts. In an engraving, lines are V-shaped grooves incised with a tool, called a burin, into metal plate, usually copper, which is relatively soft and easy to work with. The subsequent printing is done by rubbing ink into the grooves, wiping off the surface of the plate, covering it with a damp sheet of paper, and putting it through a press.

DRYPOINT: A variant of the technique of engraving is known as drypoint. It permitted artists to draw almost as freely as with a pen on a sheet of paper by scratching their designs into the copperplate with a fine steel needle. The needle, of course, did not cut grooves as deep as those made by the burin, so a drypoint plate wore out after a relative handful of impressions, whereas an engraved plate lasted through hundreds of printings. But the drypoint technique preserved the artist's personal "handwriting" and permitted soft, atmospheric effects—velvety shadows and delicate, luminous distances—unattainable with the burin.

ETCHING: Eventually creative printmakers came to prefer etching, often combined with drypoint, over the woodcut and engraving. The technique, too, must have originated with goldsmiths and armorers in the North. An etching is made by coating a copperplate with resin to make an acid-resistant "ground," through which the design is scratched with a needle, laying bare the metal surface underneath. The plate is then bathed in acid that etches (or "bites") the lines into the copper. The depth of these grooves varies with the strength and duration of the bath, and the biting is usually in stages. After a brief immersion in the acid bath the etcher applies a protective coating to the plate in those areas where the lines should be faint. The plate is then immersed until it is time to protect the next less delicate lines, and so on. To scratch a design into the resinous ground is, of course, an easier task than to scratch it into the copperplate itself. Hence an etched line is smoother and more flexible than a drypoint line. An etched plate is also more durable, yielding a far greater number of prints. But its chief virtue is its wide tonal range, including velvety dark shades not possible in a woodcut or an engraving.

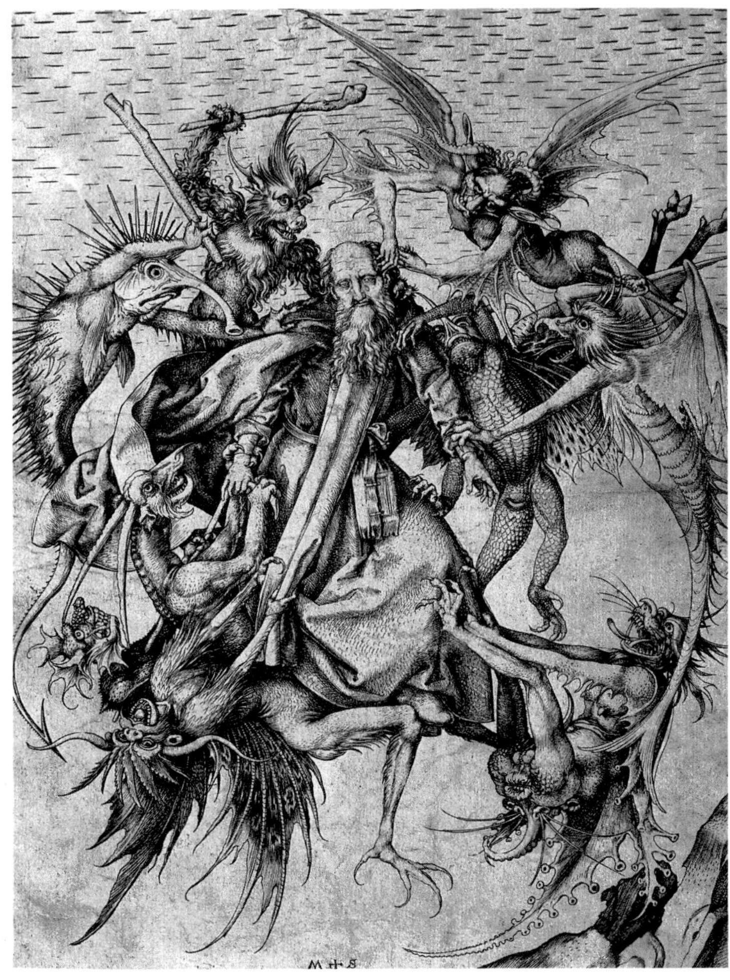

15-23. Martin Schongauer. *The Temptation of St. Anthony.* c. 1480–90. Engraving, 11½ x 8⅝" (29.2 x 21.8 cm). The Metropolitan Museum of Art, New York
ROGERS FUND, 1920

easier to determine their place of origin than it is for woodcuts. Especially in the Upper Rhine region, we can trace a continuous tradition of fine engravers from the time of Conrad Witz to the end of the century.

SCHONGAUER. The finest of the Upper Rhenish engravers was Martin Schongauer (c. 1430–1491). He was the first printmaker whom we also know as a painter, and the first to gain international fame. Schongauer might be called the Rogier van der Weyden of engraving. After learning the goldsmith's craft in his father's shop, he must have spent considerable time in Flanders, for he shows a thorough knowledge of Rogier's art. His prints are filled with motifs and expressive devices that reveal a deep affinity to the great Fleming. Yet Schongauer was a highly original artist in his own right. His finest engravings have a complexity of design, spatial depth, and richness of texture that make them equivalent to panel paintings. In fact, lesser artists often found inspiration in them for large-scale pictures. They were also copied by other printmakers.

The Temptation of St. Anthony (fig. 15-23), one of Schongauer's most famous works, masterfully combines intense expressiveness and formal precision, violent movement and ornamental stability. Schongauer was not to be surpassed by any later engraver in his range of tonal values, the rhythmic beauty of his engraved line, and his ability to render every conceivable kind of surface—spiky, scaly, leathery, furry—by varying the burin's attack upon the plate.

THE MASTER OF THE HOUSEBOOK. Schongauer had only one rival among the printmakers of his time, the Master of the Housebook (so called after a book of drawings attributed to him). Although he was probably of Dutch origin, he seems to have spent most of his career, from about 1475 to 1490, in the Rhineland. The very individual style of this artist is the opposite of Schongauer's. His prints—such as the *Holy Family by the Rosebush* (fig. 15-24)—are small, intimate in mood, and spontaneous, almost sketchy, in execution, which lends them a quaint charm that makes up for their naïveté. Even his tools were different from the standard engraver's equipment, which demanded a somewhat impersonal discipline. The Master of the Housebook instead scratched his designs into the copperplate with a fine steel needle, a technique known as drypoint. He was thus a pioneer in the use of a tool that was to become the supreme instrument of Rembrandt's graphic art a century and a half later.

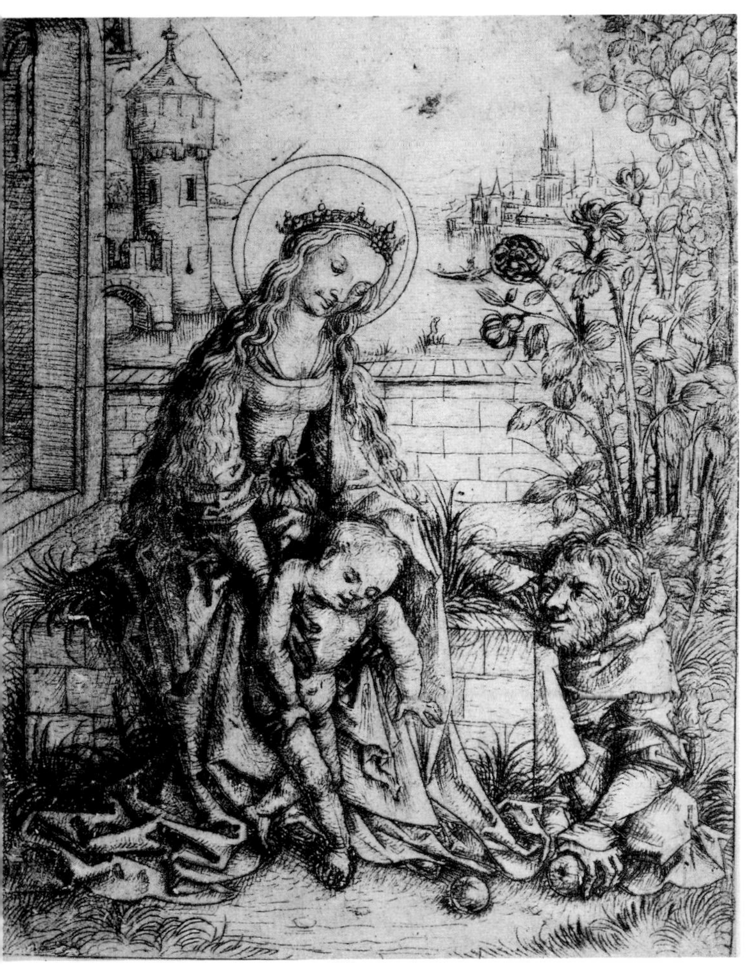

15-24. The Master of the Housebook. *Holy Family by the Rosebush.* c. 1480–90. Drypoint, 5⅝ x 4½" (14.2 x 11.5 cm). Rijksprentenkabinet, Rijksmuseum, Amsterdam

CHAPTER SIXTEEN

The Renaissance in the North

North of the Alps, as we have seen, most fifteenth-century artists were not influenced by Italian forms and ideas. Since the time of the Master of Flémalle and the Van Eycks they had looked to Flanders, rather than to Tuscany, for leadership. This relative isolation ended suddenly toward the year 1500. As if a dam had burst, Italian influence flowed northward in an ever wider stream, and Northern Renaissance art began to replace the "Late Gothic." That term, however, has a far less well-defined meaning than "Late Gothic," which at least refers to a single, clearly recognizable stylistic tradition, however questionable the name may be. The variety of trends north of the Alps is even greater than in Italy during the sixteenth century. Nor does Italian influence provide a common denominator, for this influence is itself diverse: Early Renaissance, High Renaissance, and Mannerist, all are to be found in regional variants from Lombardy, Venice, Florence, and Rome. Its effects, too, vary greatly. They may be superficial or profound, direct or indirect, specific or general. Still, we may speak for the first time of a Renaissance proper in the North. As in Italy, it is marked by an interest in humanism, albeit with equally inconsistent results. The "Late Gothic" tradition nonetheless remained very much alive, if no longer dominant. Its encounter with Italian art resulted in a conflict among styles that ended only when the Baroque emerged as an international movement in the early seventeenth century. Its course was decisively affected by the Reformation, which had a far greater impact on art north of the Alps than in Italy, but again with mixed results.

GERMANY

Painting and the Graphic Arts

It was in Germany, the home of the Reformation, where the first major stylistic developments took place during the first quarter of the century. Between 1475 and 1500, it had produced such important artists as Michael Pacher and Martin Schongauer (see figs. 15-20 and 15-23), but they hardly prepare us for the astonishing burst of creative energy that was to follow. The range of achievements of this period, which was as brief and brilliant as the Italian High Renaissance, is measured by the contrasting personalities of its greatest artists: Matthias Grünewald and Albrecht Dürer. Both died in 1528, probably at about the same age, although we know only Dürer's birth date (1471). Dürer quickly became internationally famous, while Grünewald, who was born about 1470–80, remained so obscure that his real name, Mathis Gothart Nithart, was discovered only at the end of the nineteenth century.

GRÜNEWALD. Grünewald's fame, like that of El Greco, has developed almost entirely within our own century. His main work, the *Isenheim Altarpiece,* is unique in the Northern art of his time in its ability to overwhelm us with the power of the Sistine ceiling. Long believed to be by Dürer, it was painted between 1509/10 and 1515 for the monastery church of the Order of St. Anthony at Isenheim, in Alsace, not far from the former abbey that now houses it in the city of Colmar.

The altarpiece is a carved shrine with two sets of movable wings, which give it three stages, or "views." The first of these views, when all the wings are closed, shows *The Crucifixion* in the center panel (fig. 16-1)—the most impressive ever painted. In one respect it is very medieval. Jesus' terrible agony and the desperate grief of the Virgin, St. John, and Mary Magdalen recall the older German *Andachtsbild* (see fig. 11-54). But the body on the Cross, with its twisted limbs, its many wounds, its rivulets of blood, is on a heroic scale that raises it beyond the human and thus reveals the two natures of Jesus. The same message is conveyed by the flanking figures. The three historic witnesses on the left mourn Jesus' death as a man, while John the Baptist, on the right, calmly points to him as the Savior. Even the background suggests this duality. Golgotha here is not a hill outside Jerusalem but a mountain towering above lesser peaks. The Crucifixion, lifted from its familiar setting, becomes a lonely event silhouetted against a ghostly landscape and a blue-black sky. Darkness is over the land, in accordance with the Gospel, yet light bathes the foreground with the force of revelation. This union of time and eternity, of reality and symbolism, gives Grünewald's *Crucifixion* its awesome grandeur.

When the outer wings are opened, the mood of the *Isenheim Altarpiece* changes completely (fig. 16-2). All three scenes in this

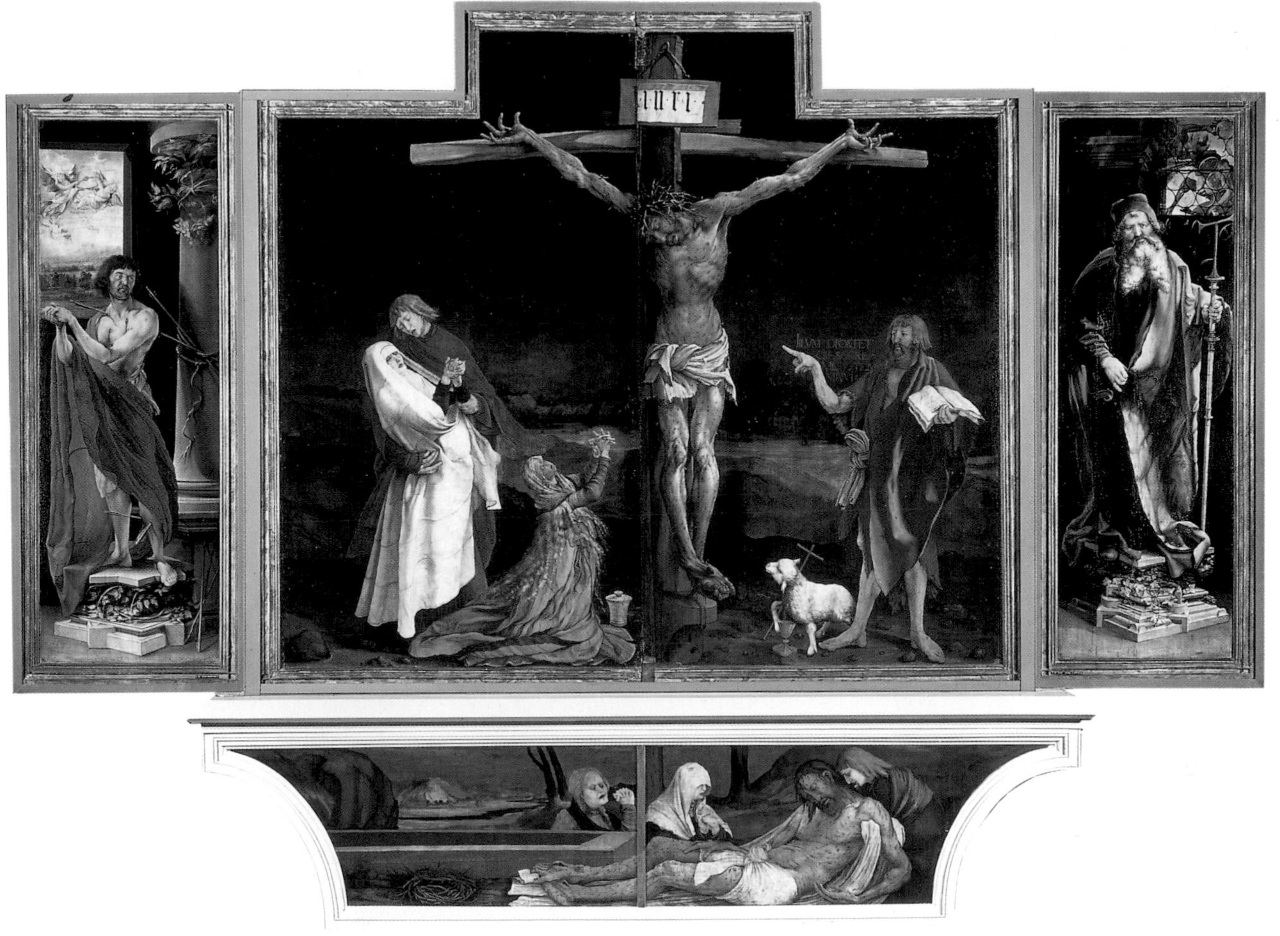

16-1. Matthias Grünewald. *St. Sebastian; The Crucifixion; St. Anthony Abbot;* predella: *Lamentation. Isenheim Altarpiece* (closed). c. 1509/10–15. Oil on panel, main body 9'9½" x 10'9" (2.97 x 3.28 m), predella 2'5½" x 11'2" (0.75 x 3.4 m). Musée Unterlinden, Colmar, France

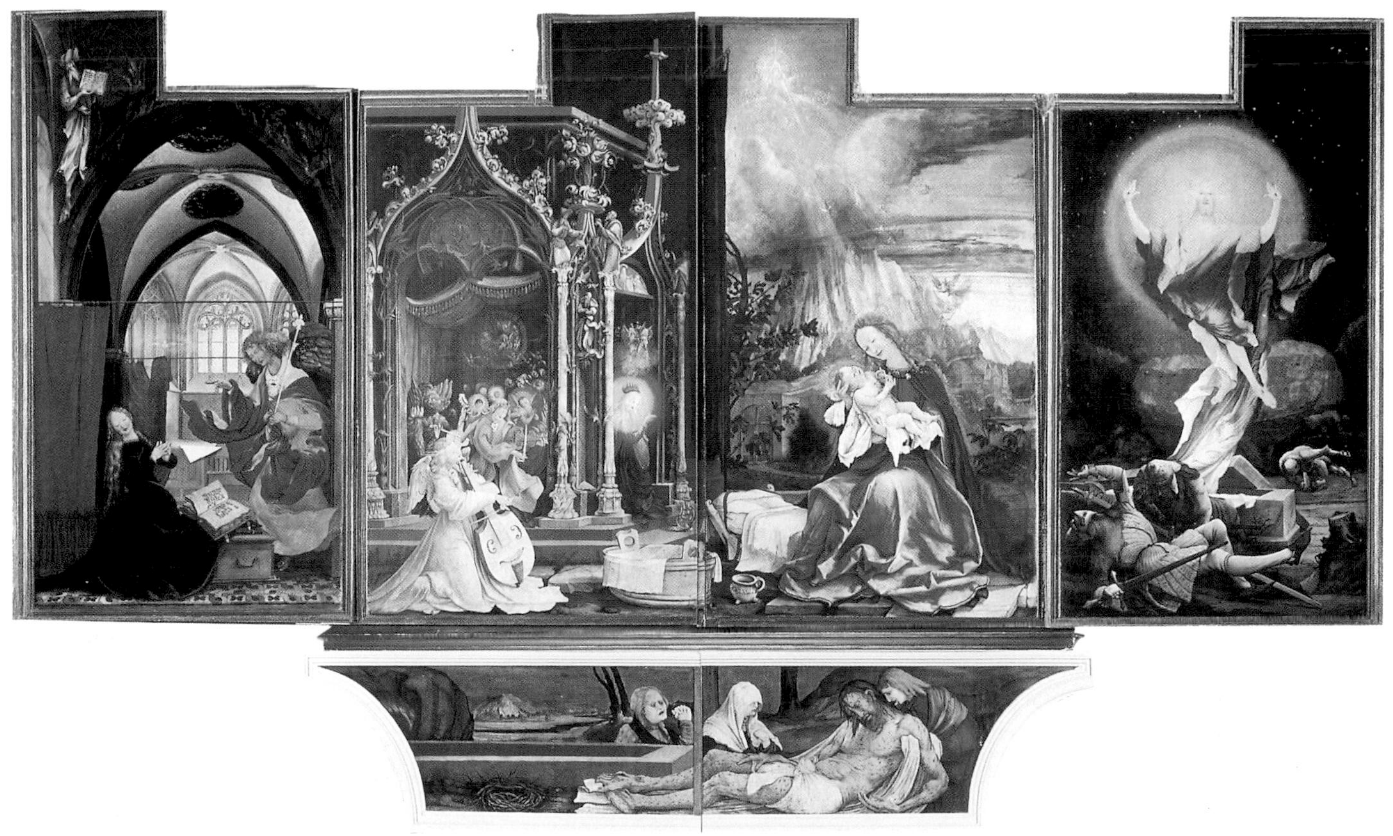

16-2. Matthias Grünewald. *The Annunciation; Madonna and Child with Angels; The Resurrection.* Second view of the *Isenheim Altarpiece.* c. 1509/10–15. Oil on panel, each wing 8'10" x 4'8" (2.69 x 1.42 m); center panel 8'10" x 11'2½" (2.69 x 3.41 m). Musée Unterlinden, Colmar,

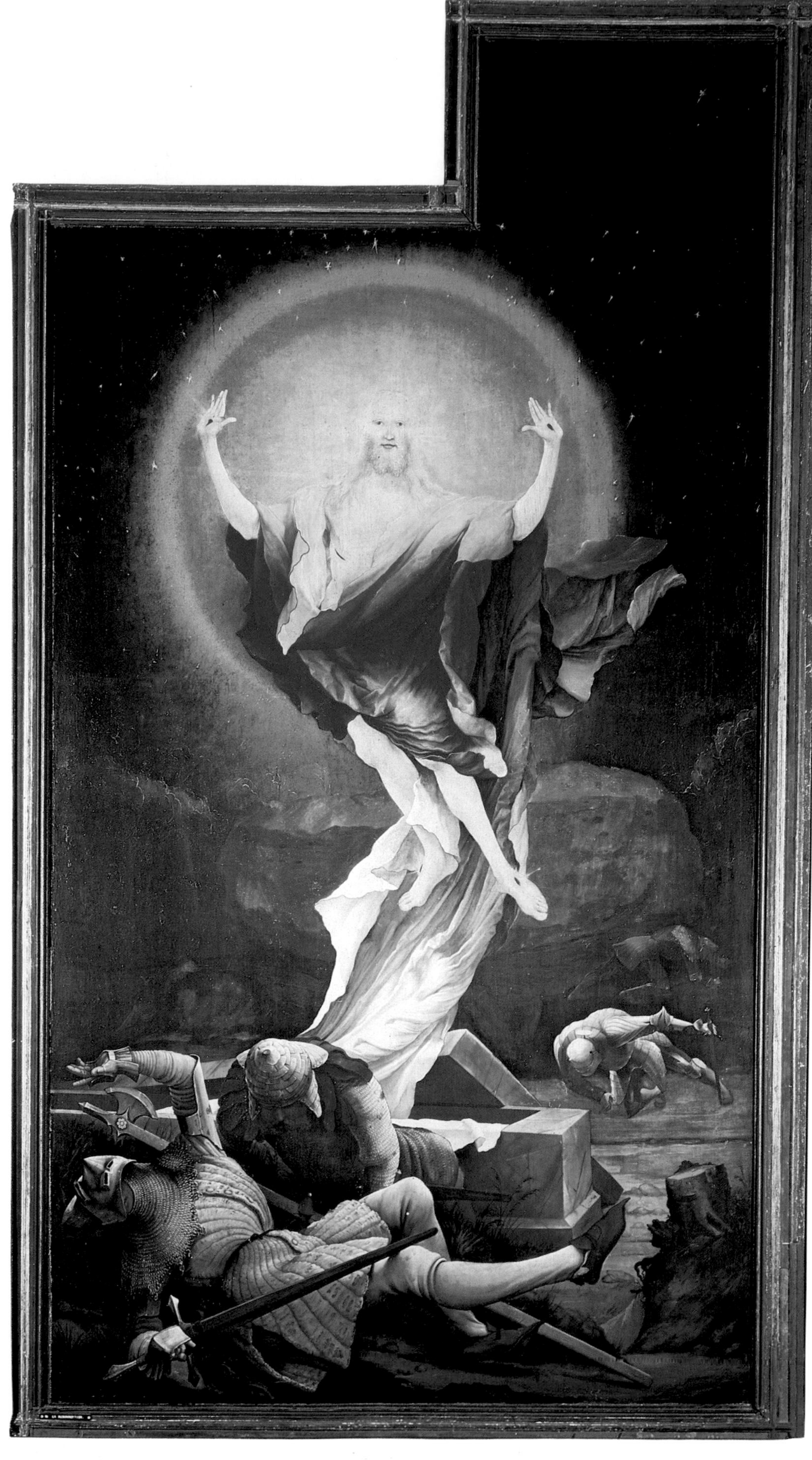

16-3. Matthias Grünewald. *The Resurrection,* from second view of the *Isenheim Altarpiece*

second view—the Annunciation, the Angel Concert for the Madonna and Child, and the Resurrection (fig. 16-3)—celebrate events as jubilant as the Crucifixion is austere. Most striking in comparison with "Late Gothic" painting is the sense of movement throughout these panels. Everything twists and turns as though it had a life of its own. The angel of *The Annunciation* enters the room like a gust of wind that blows the Virgin backward, and the Risen Jesus leaps from his grave with explosive force. This vibrant energy is matched by the ecstatic vision of heavenly glory in celebration of Jesus' birth, seen behind the Madonna and Child, who are surely the most tender and lyrical in all of Northern art.

In contrast to the brittle contours and angular drapery of "Late Gothic" art, Grünewald's forms are soft and fleshy. His light and color show a corresponding change. He employs the resources of his Flemish predecessors with extraordinary boldness and flexibility. The range of his color scale is matched only by the Venetians. Indeed, his use of colored light had no parallel at that time. Grünewald achieved unsurpassed miracles through light in the luminous angels of the Concert, the apparition of God the Father and the Heavenly Host above the Madonna, and the rainbow-hued radiance of the Risen Jesus.

How much did Grünewald owe to Italian art? Nothing at all, we are first tempted to say. Yet he must have learned from the Renaissance in more ways than one. His knowledge of perspective (note the low horizons) and the vigor of some of his figures cannot be explained by the "Late Gothic" tradition, and at times his pictures show architectural details of Southern origin. Perhaps the most important effect of the Renaissance on him, however, was psychological. We know little about his career, but he apparently did not lead the settled life of an artisan–painter controlled by guild rules. Like Leonardo, he was also an architect, an engineer, something of a courtier, and an entrepreneur. Moreover, he worked for many different patrons and stayed nowhere for very long. He was in sympathy with Martin Luther even though as a painter he depended on Catholic patronage. [See Primary Sources, no. 52, pages 619–20.]

In a word, Grünewald seems to have shared the free, individualistic spirit of Italian Renaissance artists. The daring of his pictorial vision likewise suggests that he relied on his own abilities. The Renaissance, then, had a liberating influence on him but did not change the basic cast of his imagination. Instead, it helped him to epitomize the expressive aspects of the "Late Gothic" in a uniquely intense and individual style.

DÜRER. For Albrecht Dürer (1471–1528), the Renaissance held a richer meaning. Attracted to Italian art while still a young journeyman, he visited Venice in 1494/5 (he was to go again in 1505) and returned to his native Nuremberg with a new view of the world and the artist's place in it. To him, the unbridled fantasy of Grünewald's art was "a wild, unpruned tree" (a phrase he used for painters who worked by rules of thumb, without theoretical foundations) that needed the discipline of the objective, rational standards of the Renaissance. Taking the Italian view that the fine arts belong among the liberal arts, he also adopted the ideal of the artist as a gentleman and humanistic scholar. By steadily cultivating his intellectual interests, he came to encompass an unprecedented

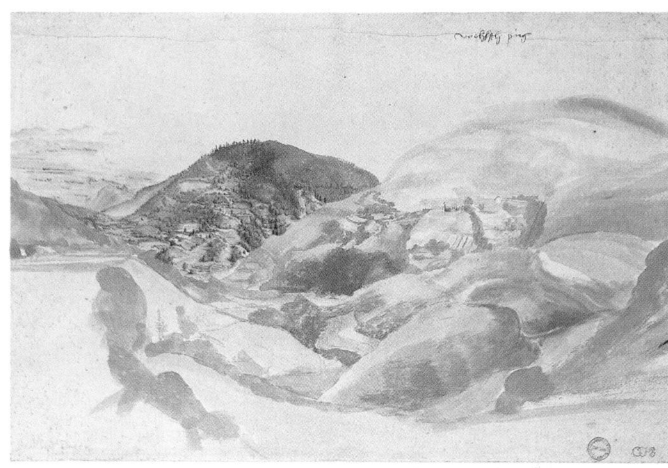

16-4. Albrecht Dürer. *Italian Mountains*. c. 1495 or 1505–6. Brush drawing in watercolor, 8¼ x 12¼" (21 x 31.2 cm). Ashmolean Museum, Oxford, England

variety of subjects and techniques. And as the greatest printmaker of the time, he had a wide influence on sixteenth-century art through his woodcuts and engravings, which circulated throughout Europe.

In Italy Dürer made copies after Mantegna and other Early Renaissance masters that show his eager grasp of their style. Equally remarkable are his watercolors painted on the way back from Venice, such as the one inscribed "Italian Mountains" (fig. 16-4). He was the first serious artist to work in watercolor, which gained new importance as a sketching medium thanks to his experiments. Yet Dürer did not record the name of the spot here or in his other sheets; the precise location had no interest for him. The title he jotted down seems exactly right, for this is not a "portraits" but a "study from the model." The calm rhythm of this panorama of softly rounded slopes conveys an organic view of nature that was matched in those years only by Leonardo's landscapes (compare the background in the *Mona Lisa;* see fig. 13-4).

After the breadth and lyricism of the *Italian Mountains,* the expressive violence of the woodcuts illustrating the Apocalypse is doubly shocking. This series was Dürer's most ambitious graphic work in the years following his return from Venice. The gruesome vision of *The Four Horsemen* (fig. 16-5) seems at first to return to the "Late Gothic" world of Martin Schongauer's *Temptation of St. Anthony* (see fig. 15-23). Yet the physical energy and full-bodied volume of these figures would have been impossible without Dürer's earlier experience in copying the works of such artists as Mantegna (compare fig. 12-60). At this stage, Dürer's style has much in common with Grünewald's. However, Dürer has redefined his medium—the woodcut—by enriching it with the linear subtleties of engraving. In his hands, woodcuts lose their former charm as popular art (see fig. 15-21). In its place, they gain the precise articulation of a mature graphic style. He set a standard that soon transformed the technique of woodcuts all over Europe.

Dürer was the first artist to be fascinated by his own image. In this respect he was more of a Renaissance personality than any Italian artist. His earliest known work, a drawing made at 13, is a self-portrait, and he continued to produce self-portraits through-

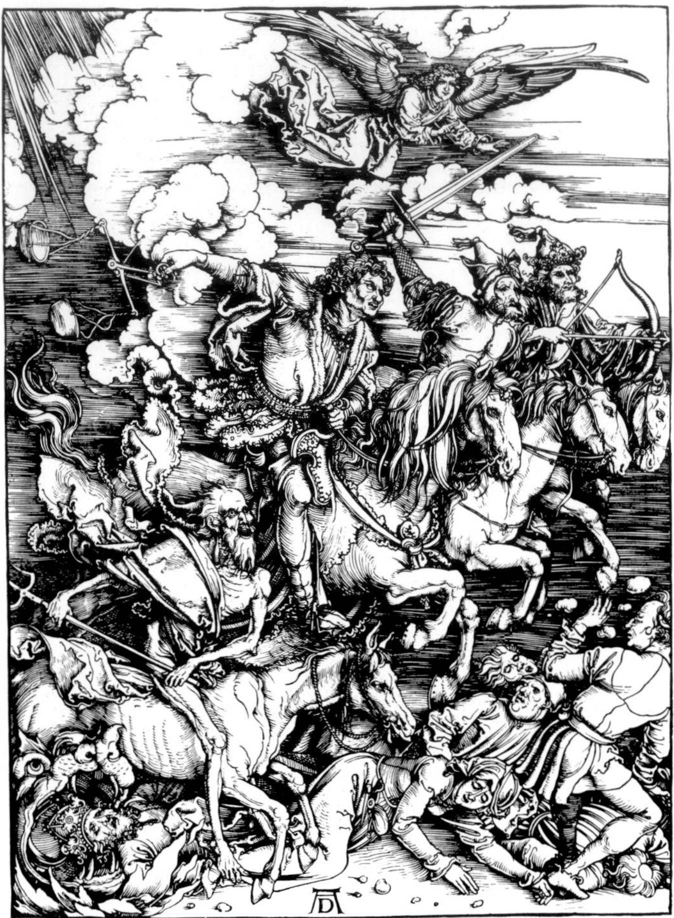

16-5. Albrecht Dürer. *The Four Horsemen of the Apocalypse.* c. 1497–98. Woodcut, 15½ x 11⅛" (39.3 x 28.3 cm). The Metropolitan Museum of Art, New York
GIFT OF JUNIUS S. MORGAN, 1919

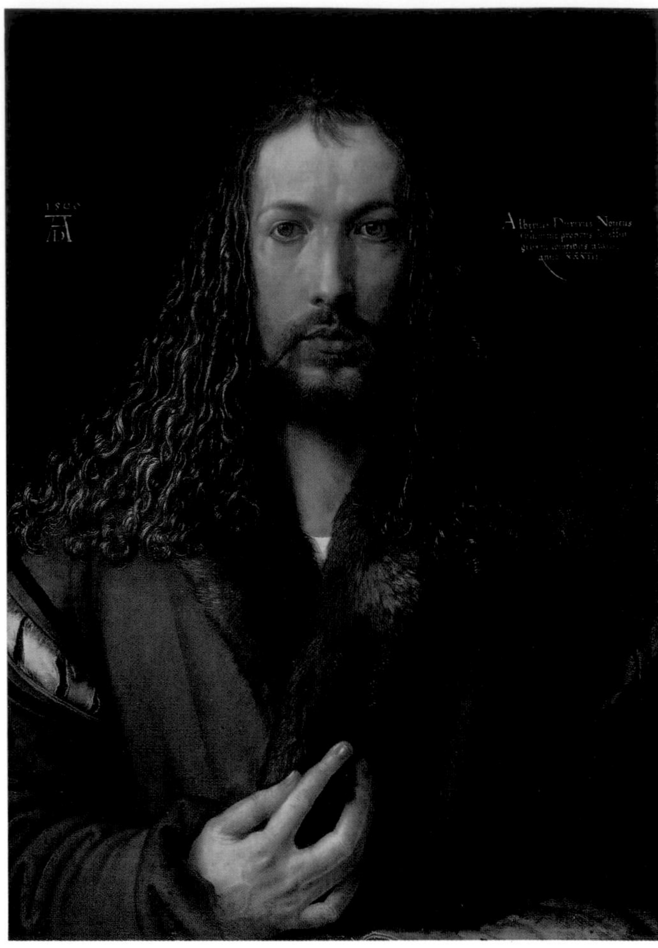

16-6. Albrecht Dürer. *Self-Portrait.* 1500. Oil on panel, 26¼ x 19¼" (66.3 x 49 cm). Alte Pinakothek, Munich

out his career. Most impressive, and uniquely revealing, is the panel of 1500 (fig. 16-6). In pictorial terms, it belongs to the Flemish tradition (compare Jan van Eyck's *Man in a Red Turban;* fig. 15-7). But the solemn pose and the idealization of the features have an authority that is beyond the range of ordinary portraits. The picture looks, in fact, like a secularized icon. It reflects not so much Dürer's vanity as the seriousness with which he viewed his mission as an artistic reformer.

The didactic aspect of Dürer's art is clearest in the engraving *Adam and Eve* of 1504 (fig. 16-7). Here the biblical subject serves as a pretext for the display of two ideal nudes: Apollo and Venus in a Northern forest (compare figs. 5-67 and 5-69). No wonder they look somewhat out of place. Unlike the picturesque setting and the animals in it, Adam and Eve are not observed from life. Instead, they are constructed according to what Dürer believed to be perfect proportions. [See Primary Sources, no. 53, page 620.] For the first time, both the form and the substance of the Italian Renaissance enter Northern art, but adapted to the unique cultural climate of Germany. That is why his ideal male and female figures,

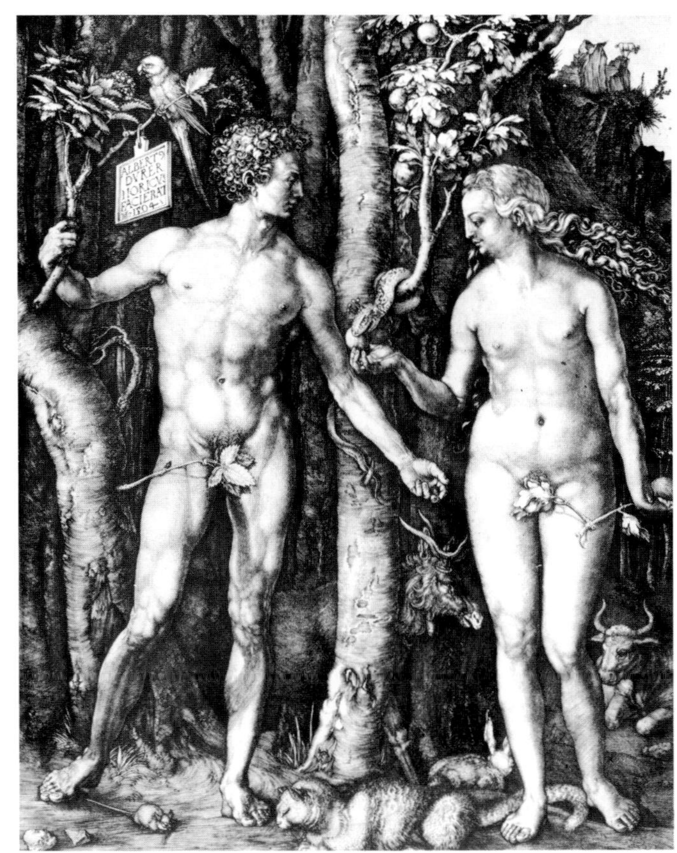

(RIGHT) 16-7. Albrecht Dürer. *Adam and Eve.* 1504. Engraving, 9⅞ x 7⅝" (25.2 x 19.4 cm). Museum of Fine Arts, Boston
CENTENNIAL GIFT OF LANDON T. CLAY

though very different from classical examples, were to become models in their own right to countless Northern artists.

The same approach, now applied to the body of a horse, is evident in *Knight, Death, and Devil* (fig. 16-8), one of the artist's finest prints. This time, however, there is no inconsistency. The knight on his mount, poised and confident as an equestrian statue, embodies an ideal that is both aesthetic and moral. He is the Christian Soldier steadfast on the road of faith toward the Heavenly Jerusalem, undeterred by the hideous rider threatening to cut him off or the grotesque devil behind him. The dog, a symbol of fidelity, loyally follows its master despite the lizards and skulls in their path. Italian Renaissance form, united with the heritage of "Late Gothic" symbolism (whether open or disguised), here takes on a new, characteristically Northern significance.

Dürer's convictions were essentially those of Christian humanism. He seems to have derived the subject of *Knight, Death, and Devil* from the *Manual of the Christian Soldier* by Erasmus of Rotterdam, the greatest of Northern humanists, whom he later met. It is the first of three engravings that were probably conceived as a unified program, as Dürer often sold them as a set. Taken together, they are an unusually personal statement. A *St. Jerome in His Study* complements the knight of action, who carries his faith into the world, with one who pursues his faith through private meditation.

The last of the suite, *Melencolia I* (fig. 16-9), is the very antithesis of the other two. One of the Four Temperaments, she holds the tools of geometry, yet is surrounded by chaos. She thinks but cannot act, while the infant scrawling on the slate, who symbolizes Practical Knowledge, can act but not think. This is, then, the melancholia of an artist, perhaps Dürer himself. He cannot achieve perfect beauty, which is known only to God, because he cannot extend his thinking beyond the limits of space and the physical world. This image comes from the humanist Marsilio Ficino, who viewed melancholia (to which he was himself subject) as the source of divine inspiration. He tied it to Saturn, the Mind of the World, which, as the oldest and highest of the planets, he deemed superior even to Jupiter, the Soul of the World. It is clear, however, that in contrasting the ineffectiveness of *Melencolia,* who derives her tools from Saturn, to the spiritual achievements of the knight and saint, Dürer asserts the superiority of faith over reason.

Dürer became an early and enthusiastic follower of Martin Luther, although, like Grünewald, he continued to work for Catholic patrons. His new faith can be sensed in the growing austerity of style and subject in his religious works after 1520. The climax of this trend is represented by *The Four Apostles* (fig. 16-10). These paired panels contain what has rightly been termed Dürer's artistic testament.

Dürer presented the panels in 1526 to the city of Nuremberg, which had joined the Lutheran camp the year before. These four apostles are fundamental to Protestant doctrine. John and Paul face one another in the foreground, with Peter and Mark behind. Quotations from their writings, inscribed below in Luther's translation, warn the city not to mistake human error and pretense for the will of God. They plead against Catholics and Protestant radicals alike. But in another, more universal sense, the figures represent the Four Temperaments and, by implication, the other cosmic quartets—

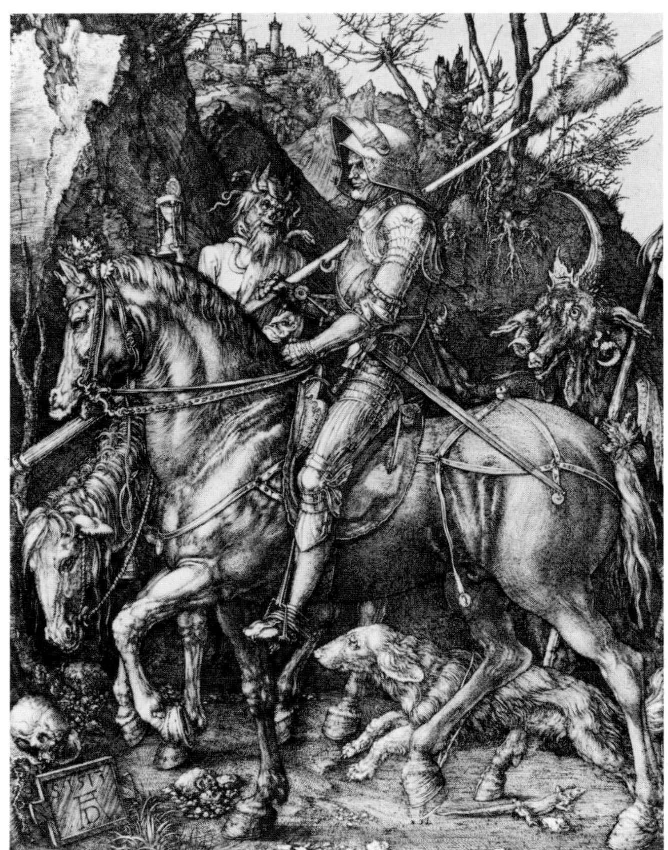

16-8. Albrecht Dürer. *Knight, Death, and Devil.* 1513. Engraving, $9\frac{7}{8} \times 7\frac{1}{2}$" (25.2 x 19.4 cm). Museum of Fine Arts, Boston

GIFT OF MRS. HORATIO GREENOUGH CURTIS IN MEMORY OF HER HUSBAND

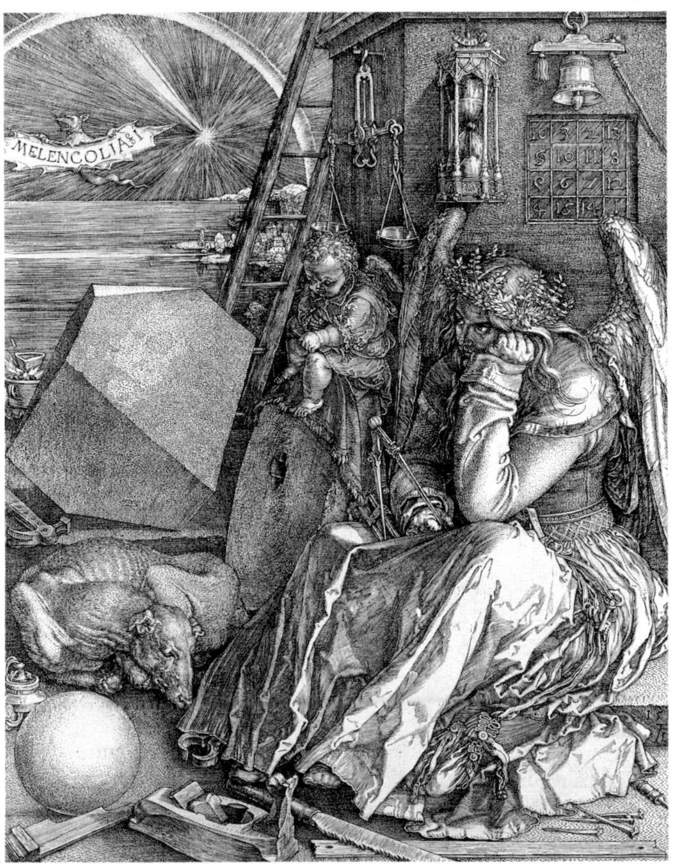

16-9. Albrecht Dürer. *Melencolia I.* 1514. Engraving, $9\frac{3}{8} \times 6\frac{5}{8}$" (23.8 x 16.8 cm). National Gallery of Art, Washington, D.C.

ROSENWALD COLLECTION

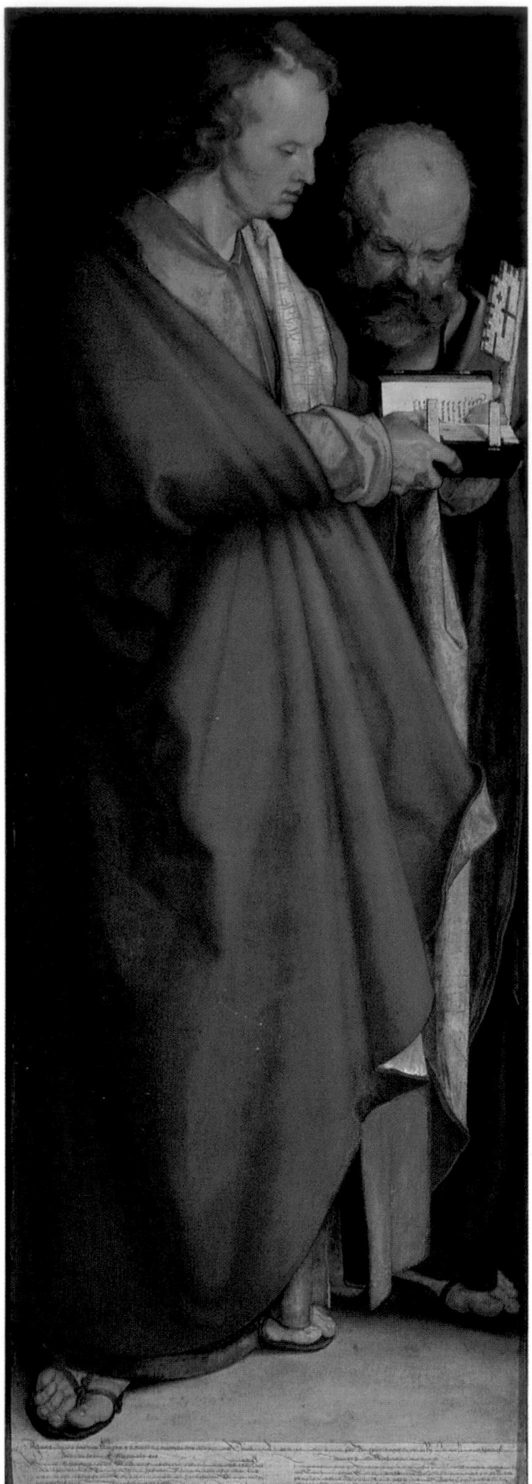

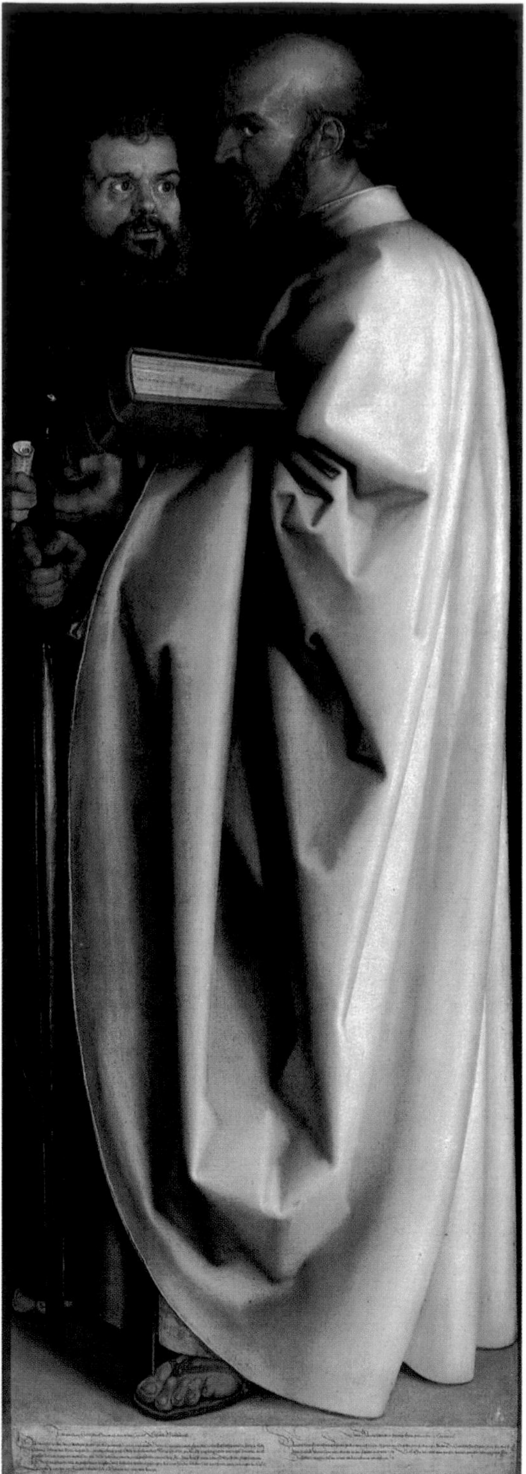

16-10. Albrecht Dürer. *The Four Apostles.* 1523–26. Oil on panel, each 7'1" x 2'6" (2.16 x .76 m). Alte Pinakothek, Munich

the seasons, the elements, the times of day, and the ages of life. Like the cardinal points of the compass, they encircle the Deity who is at the invisible center of this "triptych." In keeping with their role, the apostles have a severity and grandeur that we have not seen since Masaccio and Piero della Francesca. It is no coincidence that the style of *The Four Apostles* evokes the names of these great Italians. Dürer devoted a good part of his last years to the theory of art, including a treatise on geometry based on a thorough study of Piero della Francesca's discourse on perspective.

CRANACH THE ELDER. Dürer's hope for a monumental art embodying the Protestant faith was not fulfilled. Other German painters, notably Lucas Cranach the Elder (1472–1553), also tried to cast Luther's doctrines into visual form but did not create a viable tradition. On his way to Vienna around 1500, Cranach had probably visited Dürer in Nuremberg. In any event, he fell under the influence of Dürer's work, which he turned to for inspiration throughout his career. In 1504 Cranach left Vienna for Wittenberg, then a center of humanist learning. There he became court

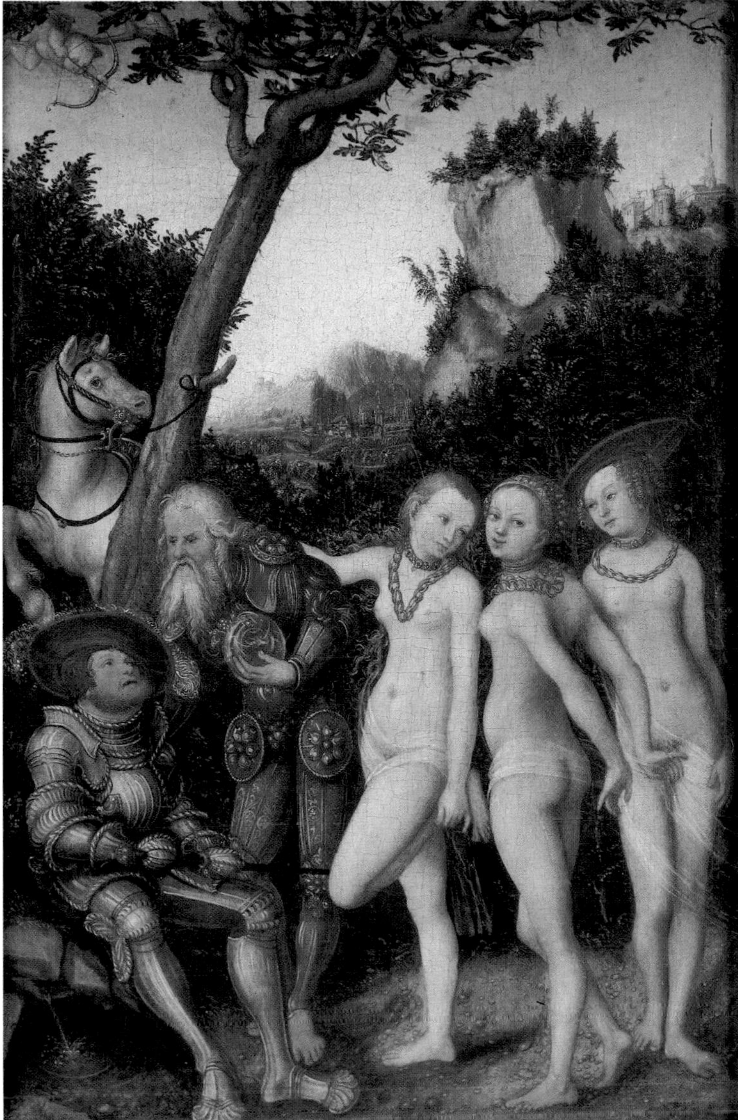

16-11. Lucas Cranach the Elder. *The Judgment of Paris.* 1530. Oil on panel, 13½ x 9½" (34.3 x 24.2 cm). Staatliche Kunsthalle, Karlsruhe, Germany

painter to Frederick the Wise of Saxony, as well as a close friend of Martin Luther, who even served as godfather to one of his children. Like Grünewald and Dürer, Cranach relied on Catholic patronage, but some of his altars have a Protestant content. Ironically, they lack the fervor of those he painted before his conversion. Efforts to embody Luther's doctrines in art were doomed, since the spiritual leaders of the Reformation looked upon religious images with indifference or, more often, hostility—even though Luther himself seems to have tolerated them. [See Primary Sources, no. 52, pages 619–20.]

Cranach is best remembered today for his portraits and his delightfully incongruous mythological scenes. In *The Judgment of Paris* (fig. 16-11), nothing could be less classical than the three coy damsels, whose wriggly nakedness fits the Northern background better than does the nudity of Dürer's *Adam and Eve.* Paris is a German knight clad in fashionable armor, indistinguishable from that of the nobles at the court of Saxony who were the artist's patrons. The playful eroticism, small size, and precise, miniature-like detail of the picture make it a collector's item, attuned to the tastes of a provincial aristocracy. Cranach's many portraits hardly differ from the doll-like creatures in *The Judgment of Paris.* Cranach's greatest contribution lies above all in the handling of the landscape, which lends Dürer's naturalism a lively fantasy through the ornate treatment of forms, such as the crinkly vegetation. Cranach had developed this manner soon after arriving in Vienna. It played a critical role in the formation of the Danube School, which culminated in the work of Albrecht Altdorfer (c. 1480–1538), a somewhat younger artist than Cranach who spent most of his career in Bavaria.

ALTDORFER. As remote from the classic ideal, but far more impressive, is Altdorfer's *The Battle of Issus* (fig. 16-12). We could not possibly identify the subject, Alexander's victory over Darius, without the text on the tablet suspended in the sky and the inscriptions on the banners (they were probably written by the Regensburg court humanist Aventinus) or the label on Darius' fleeing chariot. The artist has tried to follow ancient descriptions of the actual number and kind of combatants in the battle. To accomplish this, he adopts a bird's-eye view, traditional in Northern landscapes (compare fig. 15-14), so that the two leaders are lost in

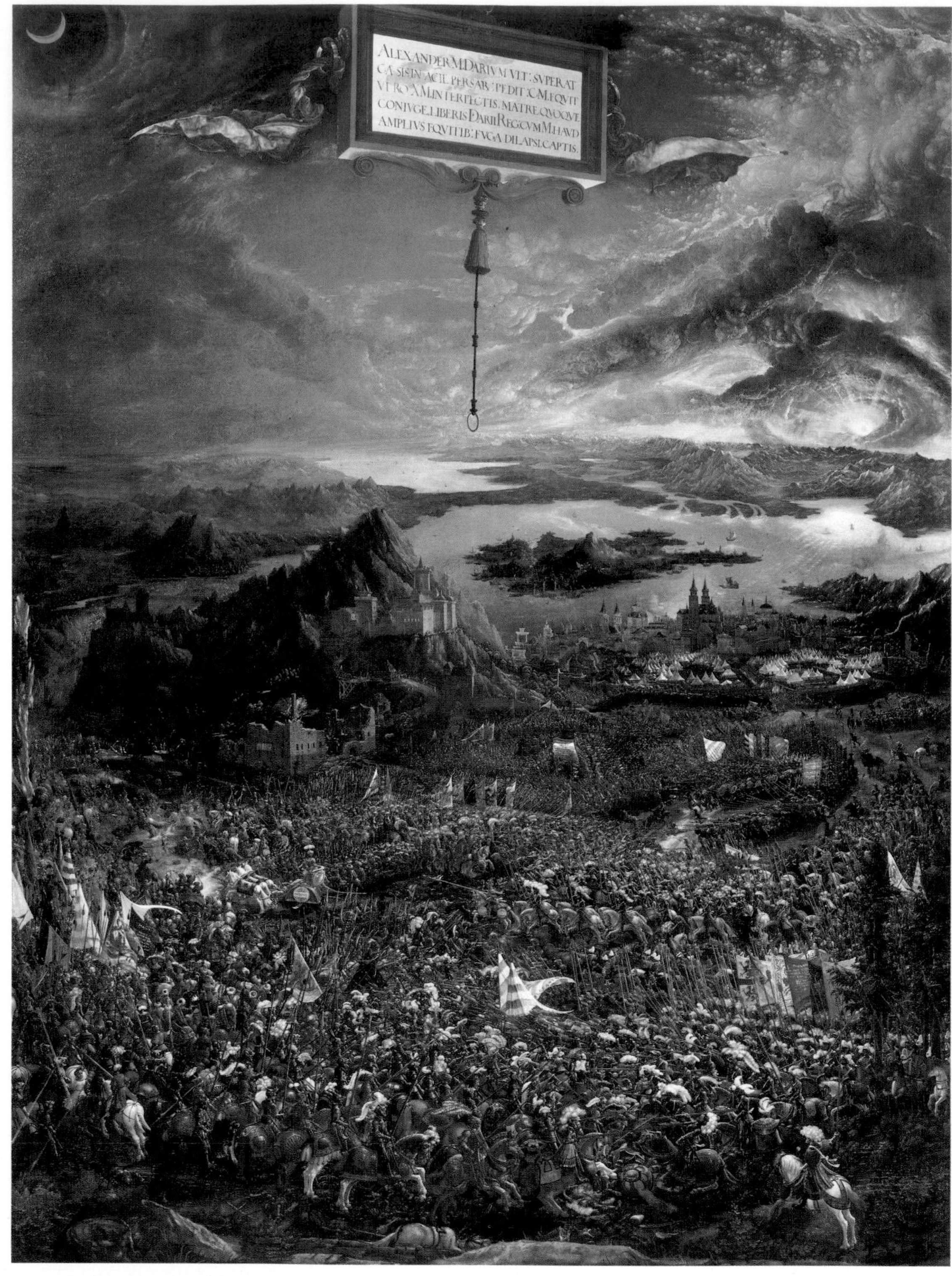

16-12. Albrecht Altdorfer. *The Battle of Issus.* 1529. Oil on panel, 62 x 47" (157.5 x 119.5 cm). Alte Pinakothek, Munich

the antlike mass of their own armies. (Contrast the Hellenistic depiction of the same subject in fig. 5-60.)

However, the soldiers' armor and the fortified town in the distance are unmistakably of the sixteenth century. The picture commemorates a battle that took place in 1529, the year this panel was painted. At that time the Turks tried unsuccessfully to invade Vienna after gaining control over much of eastern Europe. (They were to threaten the city repeatedly for another 250 years.) Neither the Hapsburg emperor Charles V nor Suleiman the Magnificent, the Turkish sultan, was present at this battle. Yet the painting acclaims Charles a new Alexander in his victory over Suleiman, the modern-day counterpart of Darius, who likewise became the ruler of a vast empire before his defeat at Issus.

To suggest its importance, Altdorfer treats the event as allegory. The sun triumphantly breaks through the clouds of the spectacular sky and "defeats" the moon, which represents the Turkish

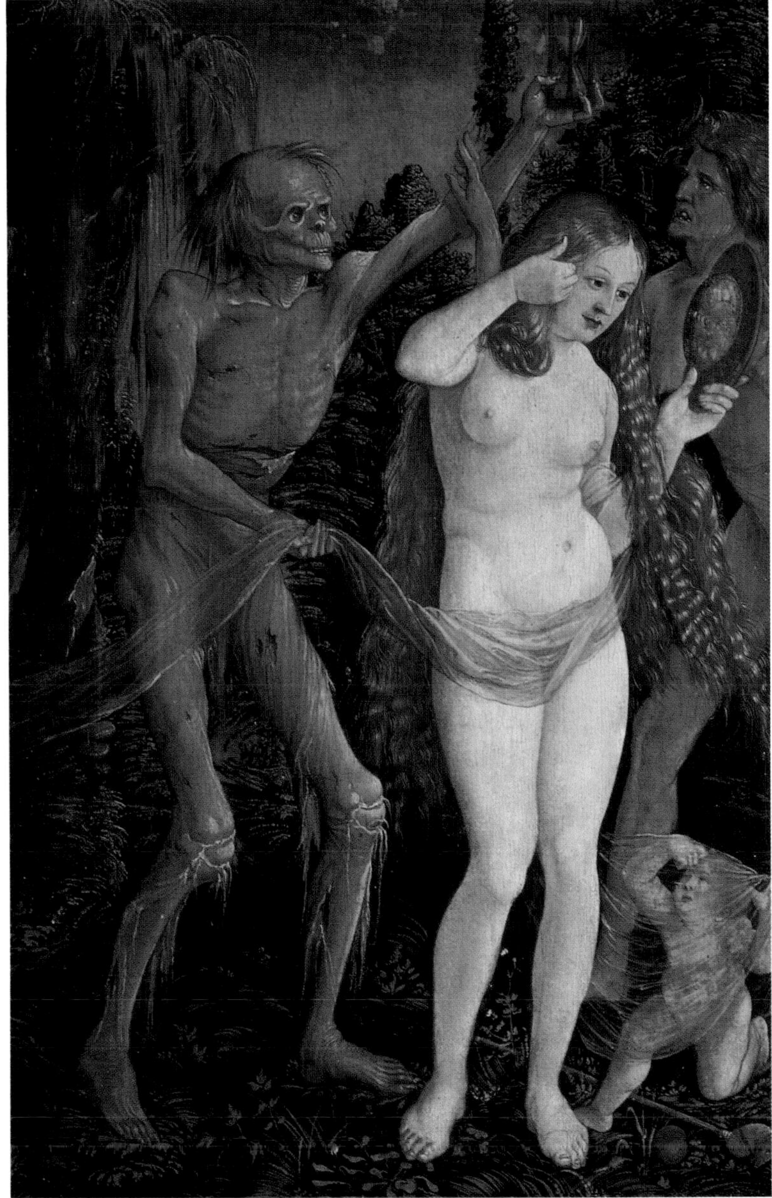

16-13. Hans Baldung Grien. *Death and the Maiden.* c. 1510. Oil on panel, $15\frac{3}{4} \times 12\frac{3}{4}$" (40 x 32.4 cm). Kunsthistorisches Museum, Vienna

Crescent. We have seen the same battle of good versus evil symbolized by the sun and moon in the Zoroastrian relief of *Mithras Slaying the Sacred Bull* (see fig. 8-1). The celestial drama above a vast Alpine landscape, correlated with the human contest below, raises the scene to the cosmic level. This turbulent sky is strikingly similar to the vision of the Heavenly Host above the Virgin and Child in the *Isenheim Altarpiece* (see fig. 16-2) by Grünewald, who influenced Altdorfer earlier in his career. Altdorfer may indeed be viewed as a later, and lesser, Grünewald. Although Altdorfer, too, was an architect, familiar with perspective and the Italian stylistic vocabulary, his paintings show the unruly imagination that is already familiar from the work of the older painter. But Altdorfer is also unlike Grünewald. He treats the human figure with ironic intent by making it incidental to the spatial setting. Tiny figures like the soldiers of *The Battle of Issus* also appear in his other late pictures, and he painted at least one landscape with no figures at all—the first "pure" landscape we know of since antiquity. (Dürer's sketch, *Italian Mountains,* fig. 16-4, is not a finished work of art.)

BALDUNG GRIEN. Altdorfer's fantastic landscape shares imaginative qualities found in paintings by Hans Baldung Grien (1484/5–1545). This former apprentice of Dürer spent much of his career in Strasbourg, which is not far from Isenheim and, like Nuremberg and Wittenberg, was a center of humanism. Yet he was fascinated above all with the magical and the demonic—the dark side of the Renaissance. Humanism and the occult may be viewed as two sides of the same coin. Since the late thirteenth century, humanists had been nearly as interested in the treatises of the ancients on magic as in their literature and learning. (In fact, the key text of Renaissance magic, the *Corpus Hermeticum,* was translated by the humanist Marsilio Ficino.) But whereas the occult appears rarely in Italian art, it was a source of constant fascination in the North. Nowhere is this better seen than in Baldung Grien's *Death and the Maiden* (fig. 16-13). Clearly based on Dürer's *Eve* (see fig. 16-7), she is the personification of Vanitas, signifying the triumph of Death over Beauty. Three ages of life—infancy, adulthood, old age—are repeated in the mirror. Yet although three heads stare out at the young woman, she examines her features serenely.

The painting illustrates the prophetic and demonic powers of the convex mirror. In antiquity, mirrors had often served as attributes of goddesses and sometimes of mortal women, such as brides. The motif of a woman contemplating her beauty reappeared in Gothic cycles of the Vices and Virtues. This moralizing tradition was revived after 1500 as part of a renewal of piety and mysticism during the Reformation. It was closely linked to resurgent occultism at a time when rationalism seemed inadequate to explain the world. Because of their association with light, mirrors have had mystical connotations throughout history, and reflected images were widely valued as a source of revelation. At the same time, supernatural qualities were attributed to them in folklore as a means of effecting hexes and other forms of black magic.

At first the convex mirror expressed the "Late Gothic" fascination with the visible world. We saw this in Jan van Eyck's *Arnolfini Portrait* (see fig. 15-8), which was painted within a few decades after mirrors began to be made from polished metal. After 1500 the convex mirror came to be used almost exclusively as a Vanitas symbol because of its extreme distortions, which heighten visionary reality; this aspect, too, had its origin in a work by Jan van Eyck. In Baldung Grien's painting, the characteristic image became a nude woman holding a convex mirror. It is used to convey a tragic vision of life to chilling effect through the striking contrast between the sensual nude and the grinning corpse, who holds an hourglass above her head as the horrified man vainly tries to stay the hand of Death.

Portraiture

HOLBEIN. Gifted though they were, Cranach and Altdorfer both evaded the main challenge of the Renaissance so bravely faced, if not always mastered, by Dürer: the human image. Their miniaturelike style set the pace for dozens of lesser masters. Perhaps the rapid decline of German art after Dürer's death was due to lack of ambition among artists and patrons alike. The career of Hans Holbein the Younger (1497–1543), the one painter of whom this is not true, confirms the general rule. The son of an important artist, he was born and raised in Augsburg, a center of international commerce in southern Germany that was particularly open to Renaissance ideas, but left at the age of 18 with his brother to seek work in Switzerland. Thanks in large part to the help of humanist patrons, by 1520 he was well established in Basel as a decorator, portraitist, and designer of woodcuts. Holbein took Dürer as his point of departure, but almost from the beginning his religious paintings and portraits show a keen interest in the Italian Renaissance, especially the latest tendencies from Venice and Rome.

Holbein's likeness of Erasmus of Rotterdam (fig. 16-14), painted soon after the famous author had settled in Basel, gives us a truly memorable image, at once intimate and monumental. This kind of profile view had been popular during the Early Renaissance and was adopted by Dürer late in his career. Here it is combined with a characteristically Northern emphasis on tangible reality to convey the sitter's personality that is nonetheless in keeping with High Renaissance ideas. The ideal of the humanist scholar, this doctor of humane letters has a calm rationality that lends him an intellectual authority formerly reserved for the Doctors of the Church. The similarity is intentional. Erasmus took as his model St. Jerome, who translated the Bible into Latin. In his biography of the saint, Erasmus praises him as "the best scholar, writer and expositor" who was "equally and completely at home in all literature, both sacred and profane" and "had the whole of Scripture by heart."

Holbein spent 1523–24 traveling in France, apparently with the intention of offering his services to Francis I. When he returned two years later, Basel was in the throes of the Reformation. Holbein then went to England, hoping for commissions at the court of Henry VIII. He brought with him the portrait of Erasmus (fig. 16-14) as a gift to the humanist Thomas More, who became his first patron in London. (Erasmus, in a letter recommending him to More, wrote: "Here [in Basel] the arts are out in the cold.") When Holbein returned to Basel in 1528, he saw Protestant mobs destroying religious images as "idols"; reluctantly, he abandoned Catholicism. Despite the entreaties of the city council, he left for London four years later and returned to Basel only once, in 1538, while traveling on the Continent as court painter to Henry VIII. (Henry had More beheaded in 1525 for refusing to consent to the Act of Supremacy, which made the king the head of the Church of England.) The city council made a last attempt to keep Holbein at home, but he had become an artist of international fame to whom Basel now seemed provincial indeed.

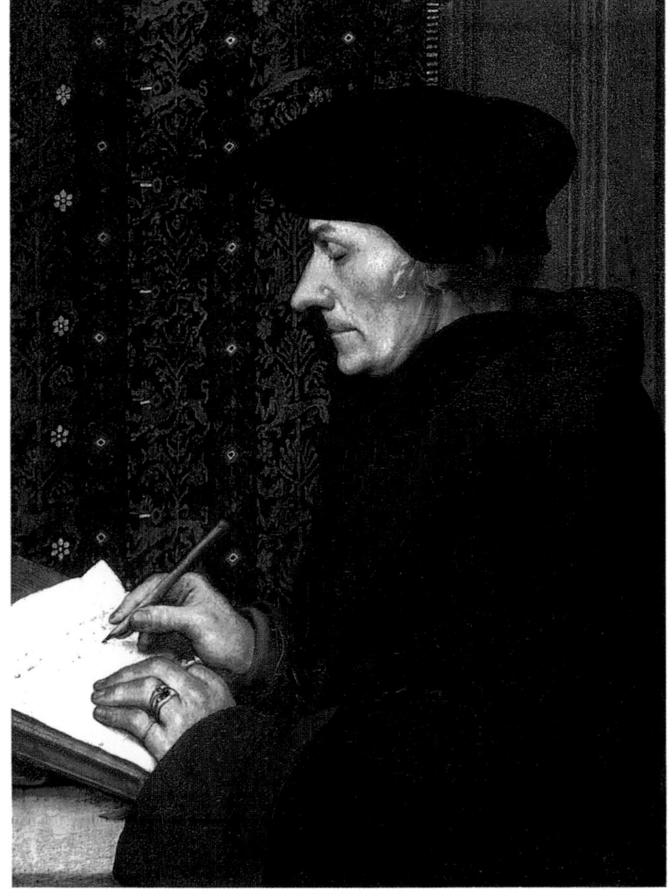

16-14. Hans Holbein the Younger. *Erasmus of Rotterdam*. c. 1523. Oil on panel, 16½ x 12½" (42 x 31.4 cm). Musée du Louvre, Paris

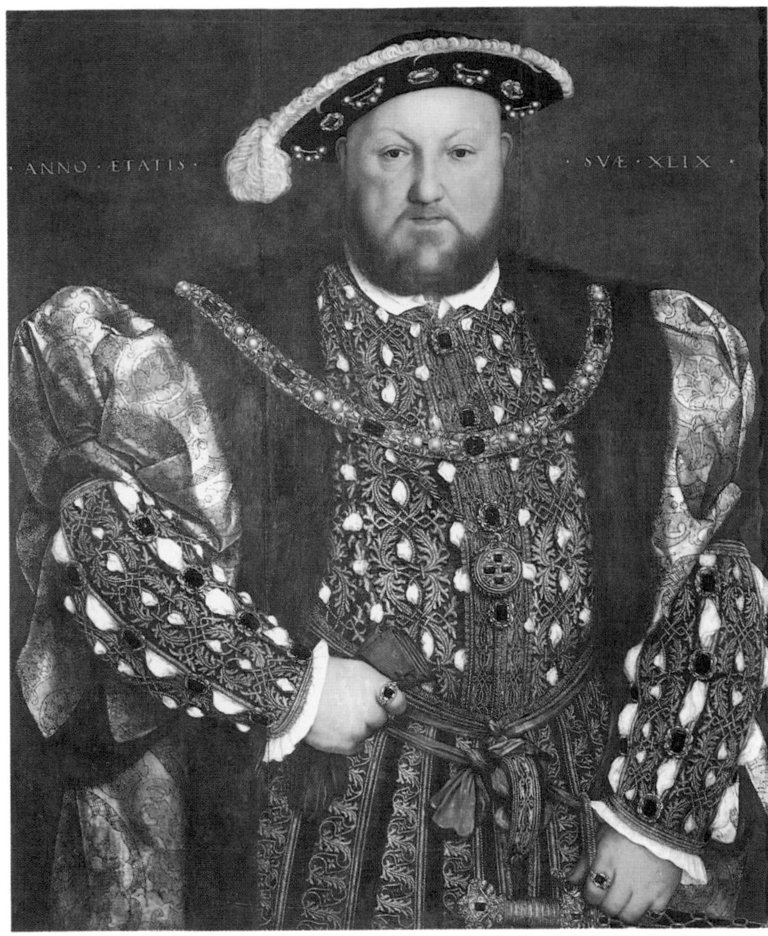

16-15. Hans Holbein the Younger. *Henry VIII.* 1540. Oil on panel, 32 1/2 x 29" (82.6 x 74.5 cm). Galleria Nazionale d'Arte Antica, Rome

Holbein's style, too, had gained an international flavor. His portrait of Henry VIII (fig. 16-15) has the rigid frontality of Dürer's self-portrait (see fig. 16-6), but its purpose is to convey the almost divine authority of the absolute ruler. The king's physical bulk creates an overpowering sense of his ruthless, commanding personality. The portrait shares with Bronzino's *Eleanora of Toledo* (see fig. 14-8) the immobile pose, the air of unapproachability, and the precisely rendered costume and jewels. Holbein's picture, unlike Bronzino's, does not reflect the Mannerist ideal of elegance. Both, however, clearly belong to the same kind of court portrait. The link between the two may lie in such French works as Jean Clouet's *Francis I* (fig. 16-16), which Holbein could have seen on his travels. (For more on Francis I as a patron of Italian Mannerists, see page 476.) The type seems to have developed at the royal court of France, where its ancestry can be traced back as far as Jean Fouquet (see fig. 15-16). Between 1525 and 1550 it spread to other regions as the embodiment of a new aristocratic ideal.

Although Holbein's pictures molded British taste in aristocratic portraiture for decades, he had no English disciples of real talent. The Elizabethan genius was more literary and musical than visual, and the demand for portraits in the later sixteenth century continued to be filled largely by visiting foreign artists.

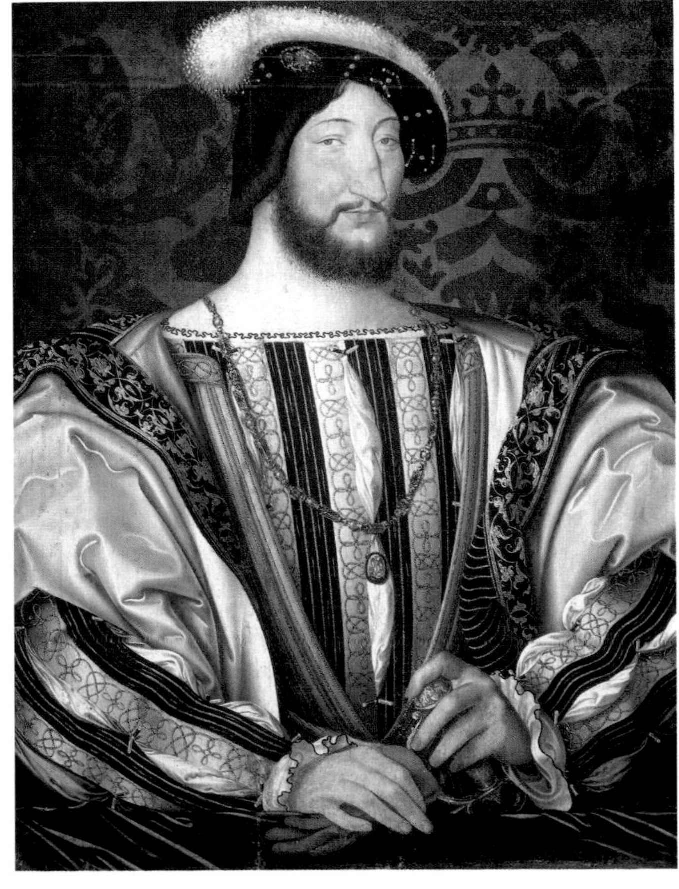

(RIGHT) 16-16. Jean Clouet. *Francis I.* c. 1525–30. Tempera and oil on panel, 37 3/4 x 29" (96 x 74.5 cm). Musée du Louvre, Paris

MUSIC AND THEATER IN THE NORTHERN RENAISSANCE

The most significant musical development of the Reformation was the introduction of congregational singing in the services of the Protestant churches. The reformer Martin Luther, himself a singer and composer, admired the sophisticated polyphony of Josquin Des Prés, whose music he retained for use by choirs in the Latin Mass. Luther also believed strongly in the educational value of music, and he wanted every member of the church to participate in the service by singing. So in 1524 he wrote a German Mass with chorales—simple hymns to be sung by the congregation—based on traditional chants and secular songs for use especially in parishes without professional choirs. The Swiss reformer John Calvin, on the other hand, objected to hymns based on new poems and insisted that only the Word of God be sung in church. The result was the Calvinist psalter: Old Testament psalms set to traditional melodies and generally sung in unison. Another form of Protestant music was the English anthem, a kind of motet that could be "full" (sung by the choir *a cappella,* "without accompaniment") or "verse" (for soloists with chorus and instruments).

In secular music, the most popular form throughout Northern Europe was the madrigal. Its chief exponent was Roland de Lassus (1532–1594), a Fleming who had lived in Italy as a youth, but spent most of his career in Munich. Widely regarded as the leading composer of his day, he was the equal of Giovanni Palestrina as a writer of religious music; but because his temperament was more secular, many of his religious compositions are parody masses (see page 496). In his later years he devoted himself chiefly to madrigals and motets. In its impulsive leaps, irregular rhythms, and dramatic harmonies, his style anticipates the bold brilliance of Carlo Gesualdo (see page 538). During the reign of Elizabeth I (1558–1603), the English developed a distinguished madrigal school under Thomas Morley (1557–c. 1602), Thomas Weelkes (c. 1575–1623), John Wilbye (1574–1638), and John Dowland (1563–1626), whose lute songs are sensitive settings of poems by Shakespeare and his contemporaries.

It is utterly remarkable that English theater developed into greatness during the late sixteenth century. Its tradition was deeply rooted in medieval religious drama, and secular theater reached back only to about 1520. When Queen Elizabeth suppressed religious theater in the 1570s, secular theater came to the fore under humanist influence at schools, universities, and inns—colleges where young men completed their education—despite the fact that theater was strictly regulated by the Master of the Revels. Yet neither the decline of religious theater nor the influence of the humanists can account satisfactorily for the enthusiastic support of theater throughout the realm—ten public outdoor theaters were built in London between 1567 and 1642, in addition to numerous private indoor theaters—or the sudden appearance of four very fine playwrights within just a few years. Thomas Kyd (1558–1594) inaugurated the theme of revenge with *The Spanish Tragedy* (c. 1587); Christopher Marlowe (1564–1593) presented the great morality play of the day in *Dr. Faustus* (c. 1588); John

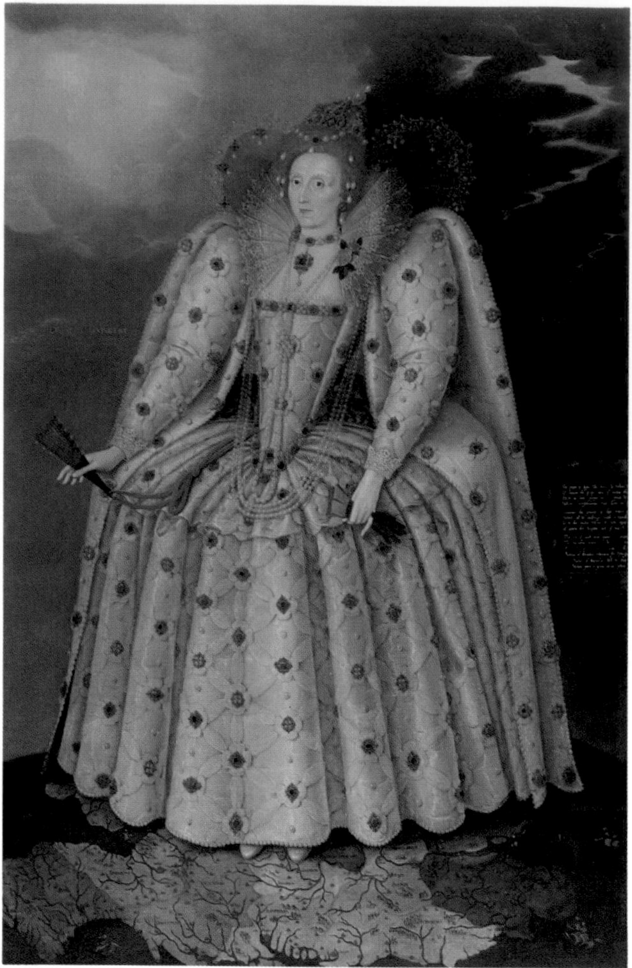

Marcus Gheeraerts the Younger. *Portrait of Elizabeth I.* c. 1592. Oil on canvas, 95 x 60" (241.3 x 152.4 cm). The National Portrait Gallery, London

REPRODUCED BY COURTESY OF THE TRUSTEES

Lyly (c. 1553–1606) used classical mythology to flatter the queen in *Endimion* (c. 1588); and Robert Greene (c. 1558–1592) helped to introduce the history, or chronicle, drama with *James IV* (c. 1591). Shortly before, William Shakespeare (1564–1616) had written *Henry VI* (1590). Of these playwrights, Shakespeare was incomparably the finest. His plays featured bold plots (many of them drawn from English history and patterned after Roman dramas), and they refrained from conventional moralizing and traditional happy endings in favor of tragedy of unrelenting darkness. His greatness lies in his use of blank verse (unrhymed, although metrical composition), which he perfected into a poetic language of infinite richness and subtlety able to express any thought or mood on a transcendent, indeed universal, plane.

Shakespeare's only serious rival in popularity was Ben Jonson (1572–1637), the leading classicist of the 1590s, whose theories followed those of Julius Caesar Scaliger and Lodovico Castelvetro (see box page 467). It was Jonson who published the first integrated edition of Shakespeare's works upon his death in 1616, thereby establishing the primacy of the playwright as a literary figure. Nevertheless, Jonson himself primarily wrote tragicomedies for reforming behavior based on Italian examples, which made him a great favorite at the court of James I, Elizabeth's successor.

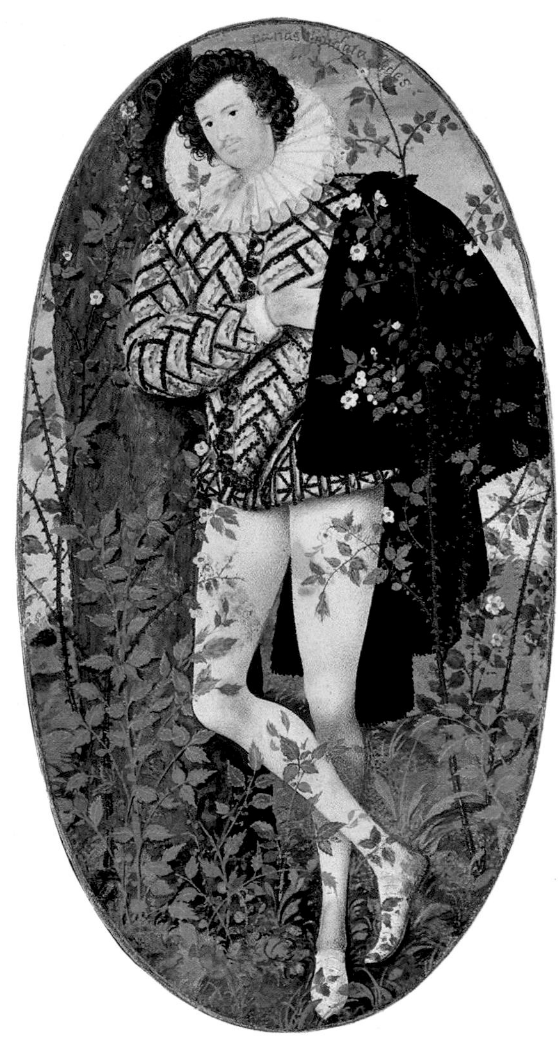

16-17. Nicholas Hilliard. *A Young Man Among Roses*. c. 1588. Oil on parchment, shown at actual size, 5⅜ x 2¾" (13.7 x 7 cm). Victoria & Albert Museum, London

HILLIARD. The most notable English painter of the period was Nicholas Hilliard (1547–1619), a goldsmith who also specialized in miniature portraits on parchment, tiny keepsakes often worn as jewelry. These "portable portraits" had been invented as cameos in antiquity and were revived in the fifteenth century. Holbein, too, produced miniature portraits, which Hilliard took as a model. We see this link with the older artist in the even lighting and the precise detail of *A Young Man Among Roses* (fig. 16-17). However, the proportions and the languorous grace of the pose come from Italian Mannerism, probably by way of Fontainebleau (compare figs. 14-7 and 14-20). Our lovesick youth is also descended from the fashionable attendants at the court of the duke of Berry. We can imagine him besieging his lady with sonnets and madrigals before presenting her with this token of devotion.

THE NETHERLANDS

Painting

The Netherlands in the sixteenth century had the most turbulent history of any country north of the Alps. When the Reformation began, they were part of the empire of the Hapsburgs under Charles V, who was also king of Spain. Protestantism quickly gained strength in the Netherlands, and attempts to suppress it led to revolt against foreign rule. After a bloody struggle, the northern provinces (today's Holland) emerged at the end of the century as an independent state. The southern ones (roughly corresponding to modern Belgium) remained in Spanish hands.

To be sure, the religious and political strife might have had catastrophic effects on the arts, yet this, astonishingly, did not happen. The art of the period does not equal that of the fifteenth century in brilliance, nor did it produce any pioneers of the Northern Renaissance comparable to Dürer and Holbein. This region absorbed Italian elements more slowly than Germany, but more steadily and systematically, so that instead of a few isolated peaks of achievement we find a continuous range. Between 1550 and 1600, their most troubled time, the Netherlands produced the major painters of Northern Europe, who paved the way for the great Dutch and Flemish masters of the next century.

Two main concerns, sometimes separate, sometimes interwoven, characterize Netherlandish sixteenth-century painting: to assimilate Italian art from Raphael to Tintoretto (albeit in an often dry and didactic manner), and to develop subjects that would supplement, and eventually replace, the traditional religious ones.

"MANNERISM" AND ROMANISM. When Flanders passed from Burgundy to Spain in 1482, Antwerp, with its deep harbor, replaced Ghent and Bruges as the political, commercial, and artistic capital of the Netherlands. Flemish artists spent the next quarter-century largely imitating earlier Netherlandish painting. Then, around 1507, we find two important new developments. "Antwerp Mannerism" is the misleading label applied to the school of largely anonymous painters that first arose in that city. Their preference for elongated forms, decorative surfaces, and arbitrary space seems to reassert Late Gothic tendencies, although the similarities are superficial. Actually, the style was not directly related to either the Renaissance or to Mannerism in Italy. Still, the term has some basis. It suggests the odd flavor of their work, for it was a "mannered" response to the "classics" by Jan van Eyck, Rogier van der Weyden, and their successors.

At almost the same time, a second group of Netherlandish artists, the so-called Romanists, began to visit Italy in the wake of Albrecht Dürer and returned home with the latest tendencies. The preceding generation of Flemish painters had already shown a growing interest in Renaissance art and humanism, but none ventured below the Alps, so that they assimilated both at second hand.

GOSSAERT. The greatest of the Romanists, Jan Gossaert (c. 1478–1532; nicknamed Mabuse, for his hometown), was also the first to travel south. In 1508 he accompanied Philip of Burgundy to Italy, where the Renaissance and antiquity made a deep impression on him. He nevertheless viewed this experience through Northern eyes. Except for their greater mon-

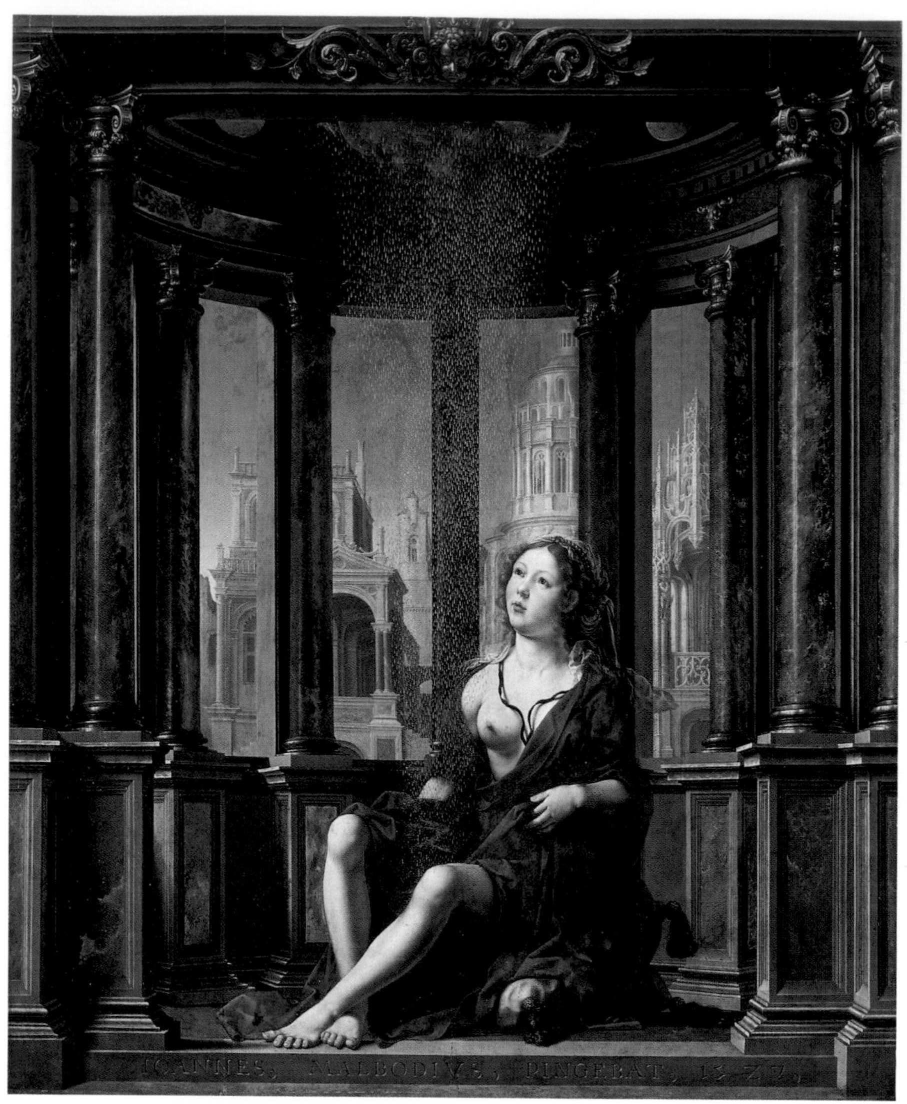

16-18. Jan Gossaert. *Danaë*. 1527. Oil on panel, 44½ x 37⅜" (113 x 95 cm). Alte Pinakothek, Munich

umentality, his religious subjects were based on fifteenth-century Netherlandish art, and he often found it easier to assimilate Italian classicism through the intermediary of Dürer's prints. *Danaë* (fig. 16-18), painted toward the end of Gossaert's career, is his most Italianate work. In true humanist fashion, the subject of Jupiter's seduction of the mortal is treated as a pagan equivalent of the Annunciation. Thus, the picture may be seen as a chaste counterpart to Correggio's *Jupiter and Io* (see fig. 14-18). Danaë's father had confined her to her chambers to guard her from suitors. The god enters, disguised as a shower of gold analogous to the stream of light in the *Mérode Altarpiece* (see fig. 15-1). Despite her partial nudity, Danaë appears as modest as the Virgin in any Annunciation. Indeed, she hardly differs in type from Gossaert's paintings of the Madonna and Child, inspired equally by Van Eyck and Raphael. She even wears the blue robe traditional to Mary as Queen of Heaven. The linear perspective of the architectural fantasy, compiled largely from Italian treatises, marks a revolution. Never before have we seen such a systematic treatment of space in the Netherlands.

STILL LIFE, LANDSCAPE, GENRE. Later religious art in the Netherlands combined Antwerp Mannerism and Romanism to produce a distinctive strain of Northern Mannerism that lasted until the end of the century. After 1550, however, narrative painting was increasingly replaced by secular themes: still life, landscape, and genre (scenes of everyday life). The process was gradual—it began around 1500 and was not complete until 1600—and was shaped less by the genius of individual artists than by the need to cater to popular taste as church commissions became scarcer. (Protestant iconoclastic zeal was particularly widespread in the Netherlands.) Still life, landscape, and genre had been part of the Flemish tradition since the Master of Flémalle and the brothers Van Eyck. In the *Mérode Altarpiece* (see fig. 15-1) we recall the objects grouped on the Virgin's table and the scene of Joseph in his workshop. We may also think of the outdoor setting of Van Eyck's *Crucifixion* (see fig. 15-2). But these elements were subordinate to the devotional purpose of the whole and often governed by the principle of disguised symbolism. Now they gained a new independence, until they became so dominant that the religious subject could be relegated to the background.

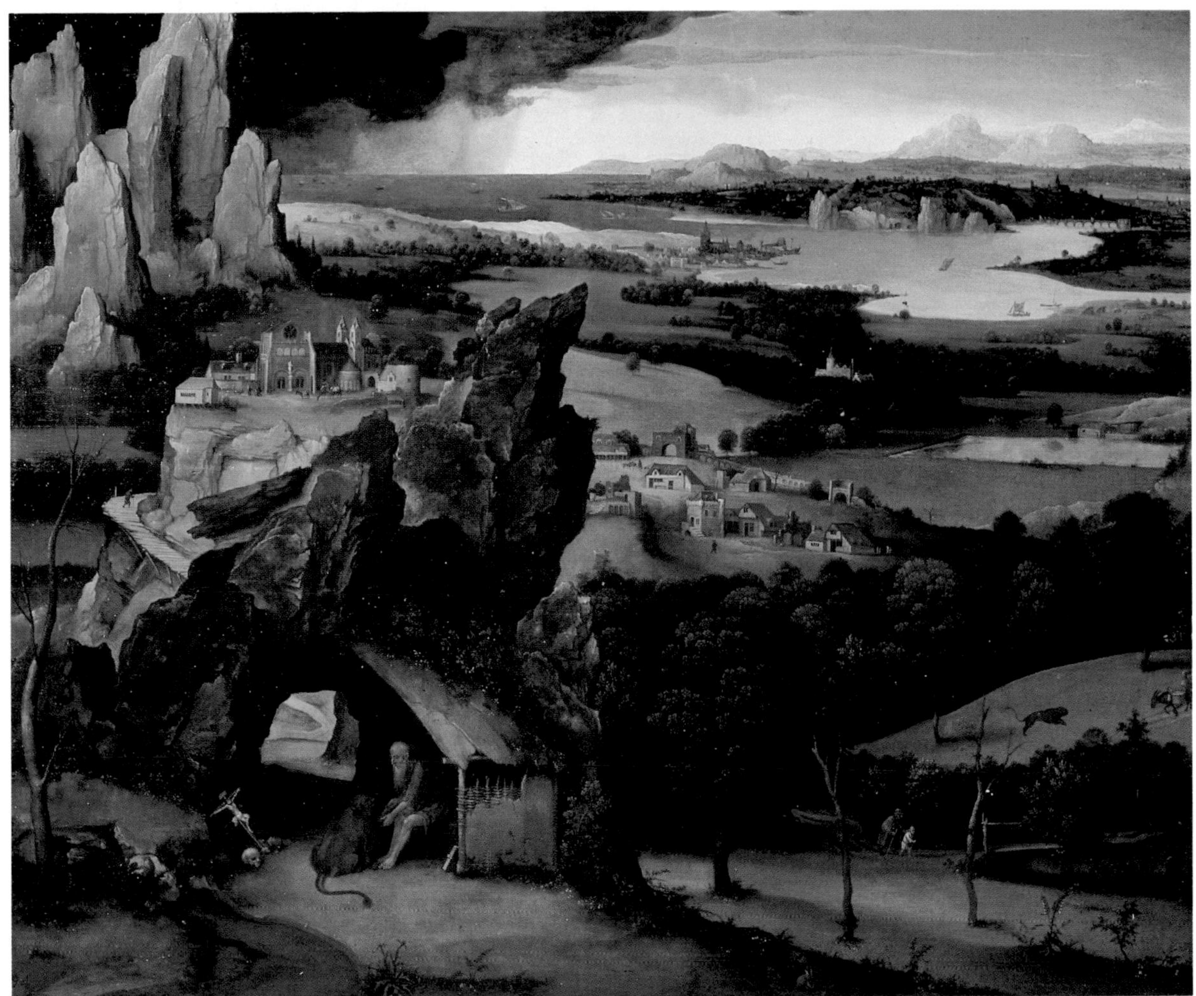

16-19. Joachim Patinir. *Landscape with St. Jerome Removing the Thorn from the Lion's Paw.* c. 1520. Oil on panel, 29 1/8 x 35 7/8" (74 x 91 cm). Museo del Prado, Madrid

PATINIR. We see the beginnings of this approach in the paintings of Joachim Patinir (c. 1485–1524). *Landscape with St. Jerome Removing the Thorn from the Lion's Paw* (fig. 16-19) shows that he is the heir of Bosch in both his treatment of nature and his choice of subject, but without the strange demonic overtones of *The Garden of Delights* (see fig. 15-14). Although the landscape dominates the scene, the figures are central to it in both visual and iconographic terms. The landscape has been constructed around the hermit in his cave, which could exist in another setting, whereas the picture would be incomplete without it. The painting is an allegory of the pilgrimage of life. It contrasts the way of the world with the road to salvation through ascetic withdrawal. (Note the two pilgrims wending their way up the hill to the right, past the lion hunt, which they do not notice.) The church on the mountain represents the Heavenly Jerusalem, which can be reached only by passing through the hermit's cave (compare fig. 12-63). Like Bosch, Patinir is ambivalent toward his subject. The vista in the background, with its well-kept fields and tidy villages, is enchanting in its own right. Yet, he seems to tell us, these temptations should not distract us from the path of righteousness.

AERTSEN. Pieter Aertsen (1508/9–1575) is remembered today mainly as a pioneer of still lifes. However, he seems to have first painted such pictures as a sideline, until he saw many of his altarpieces destroyed by iconoclasts. *The Meat Stall* (fig. 16-20), done a few years before he moved from Antwerp to Amsterdam, seems at first glance to be a purely secular picture. The tiny, distant figures are almost blotted out by the food in the foreground. There is little interest in selection or formal arrangement. The objects, piled in heaps or strung from poles, are meant to overwhelm us with their sensuous reality (the panel is nearly lifesize). Here the still life so dominates the picture that it seems independent of the religious subject in the background. The latter, however, is not merely a pretext for the painting; it must be important to the scene's meaning. In the distance to the left we see the Virgin on the Flight into Egypt giving bread to the poor, who are ignored by the faithful lined up for church. To the right is a tavern scene with the prodigal son.

The Northern Mannerists often relegated subject matter to a minor position within their compositions. This "inverted" perspective was a favorite device of Aertsen's younger contemporary, Pieter Bruegel the Elder, who treated it with ironic purpose in his

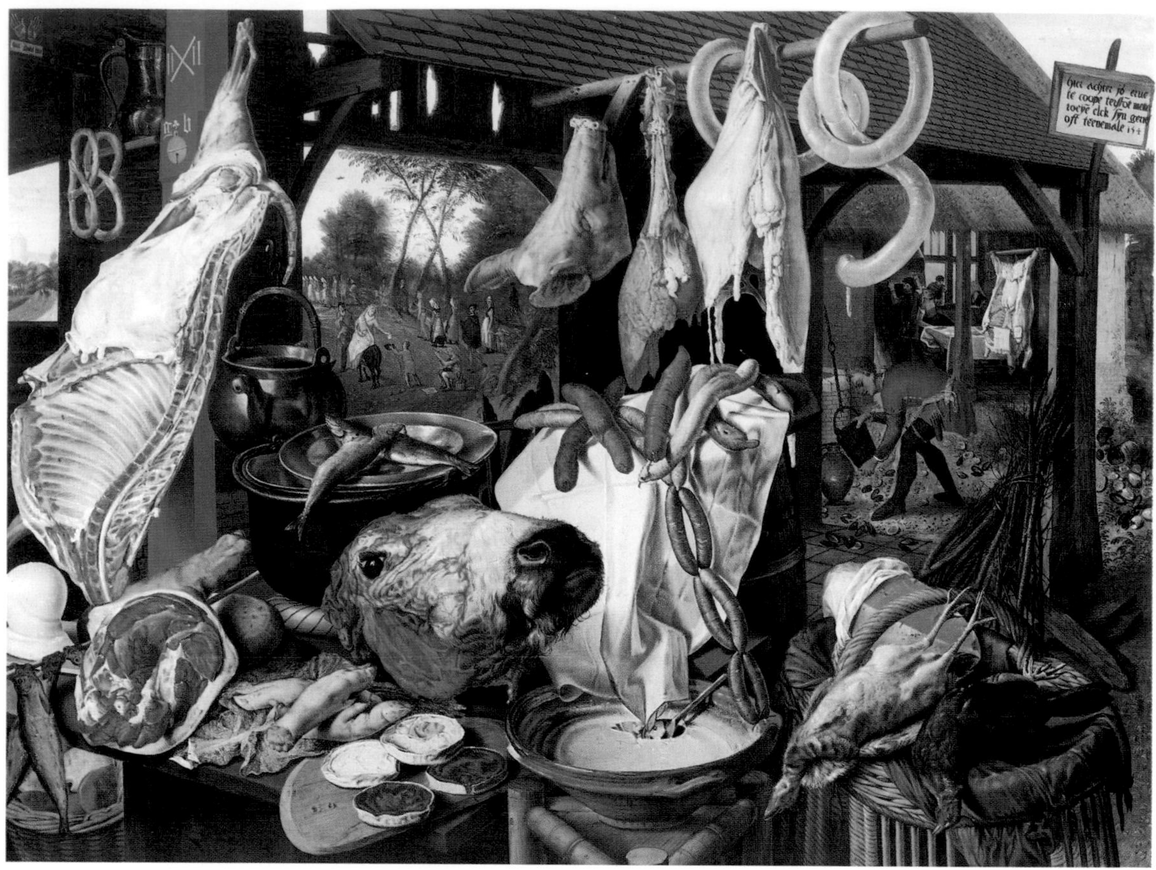

16-20. Pieter Aertsen. *The Meat Stall.* 1551. Oil on panel, 48½ x 59" (123.3 x 150 cm). University Art Collections, Uppsala University, Sweden

landscapes. Aertsen belonged to the same tradition, whose greatest representative was the humanist Erasmus of Rotterdam (see page 509). *The Meat Stall* is, then, a moralizing sermon on charity and gluttony. Not until around 1600 was this vision displaced as part of a larger change in worldview (see page 518). Only then did it no longer prove necessary to include religious or historical scenes in still lifes and landscapes.

BRUEGEL THE ELDER. The only genius among these Netherlandish painters, Pieter Bruegel the Elder (1525/30–1569), explored landscape and peasant life. Although his career was spent in Antwerp and Brussels, he may have been born near 'sHertogenbosch, the home of Hieronymus Bosch. Certainly Bosch's work impressed him deeply, and in many ways he is as puzzling to us as the older master. What were his religious convictions, his political sympathies? We know little about him, but his interest in folk customs and the daily life of humble people seems to have sprung from a complex philosophical attitude. Bruegel was highly educated, the friend of humanists, who, with wealthy merchants, were his main clients, although he also was patronized by the Hapsburg court. Yet he apparently never worked for the Church, and when he dealt with religious subjects he did so in a strangely ambiguous way.

His attitude toward Italian art is also hard to define. A trip to the South in 1552–53 took him to Rome, Naples, and the Strait of Messina, but the monuments that were admired by other Northerners seem not to have interested him. He returned instead with a sheaf of magnificent landscape drawings, especially Alpine views. He was probably much impressed by landscape painting in Venice, above all its integration of figures and scenery and the progression in space from foreground to background (see figs. 13-36 and 13-37).

Out of this experience came sweeping landscapes in Bruegel's mature style. *The Return of the Hunters* (fig. 16-21) is one of a set depicting the months. (He typically composed in series.) Such cycles, we recall, had begun with medieval calendar illustrations. Bruegel's winter scene shows its descent from *Les Très Riches Heures du Duc de Berry,* which was the first one ever painted so far as we know. Now, however, nature is more than a setting for human activities. It is the main subject of the picture. The seasonal tasks of men and women are incidental to the majestic annual cycle of death and rebirth that is the rhythm of the cosmos.

The *Peasant Wedding* (fig. 16-22) is Bruegel's most memorable scene of peasant life. These are stolid, crude folk, heavy-bodied and slow, yet their very clumsiness gives them a strange gravity that commands our respect. Painted in flat colors with little modeling and no cast shadows, the figures nonetheless have a weight and solidity that remind us of Giotto. Space is created in assured perspective, and the composition is as monumental and balanced as that of any Italian master. Why, we wonder, did Bruegel endow this commonplace ceremony with the solemnity of a biblical event? It is because he saw in the life of these rural people the natural condition of humanity. We know from his biographer, Carel van Mander (the "Netherlandish Vasari"), that Bruegel and his patron Hans Franckert often disguised themselves as peasants and joined in their revelries. [See Primary Sources, no. 48, pages

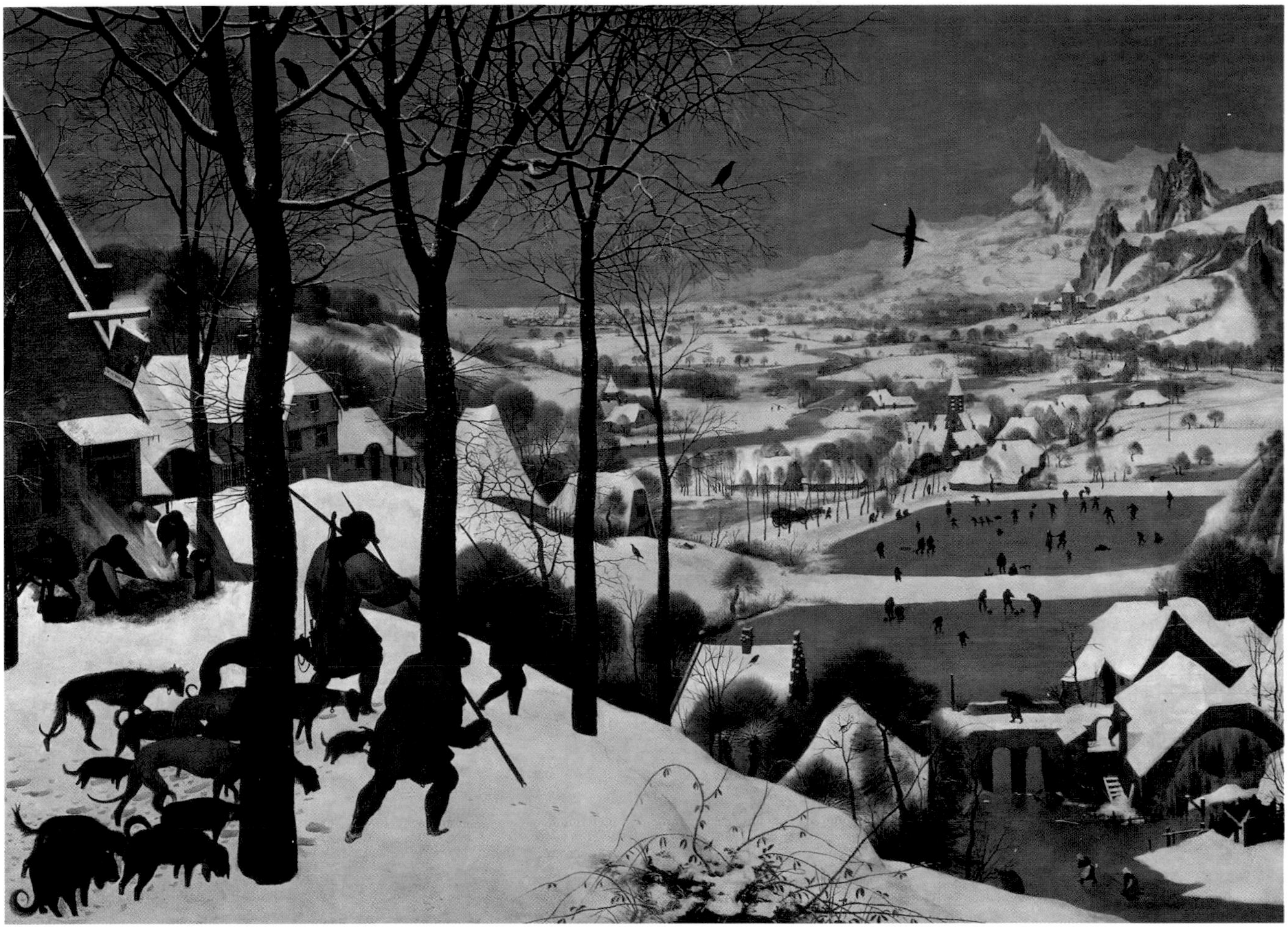

16-21. Pieter Bruegel the Elder. *The Return of the Hunters.* 1565. Oil on panel, 46½ x 63¾" (117 x 162 cm). Kunsthistorisches Museum, Vienna

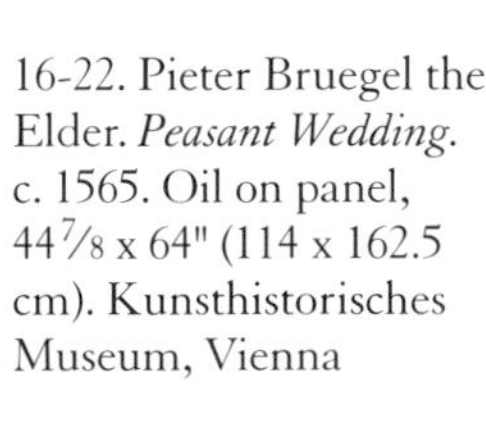

16-22. Pieter Bruegel the Elder. *Peasant Wedding.* c. 1565. Oil on panel, 44⅞ x 64" (114 x 162.5 cm). Kunsthistorisches Museum, Vienna

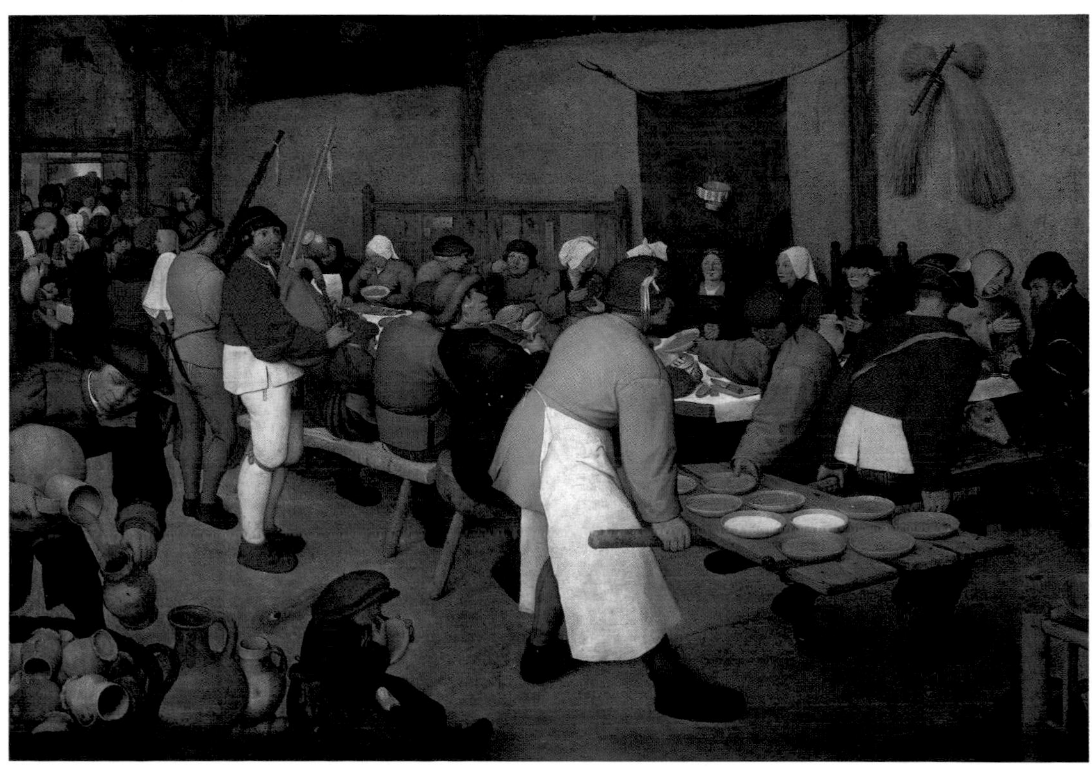

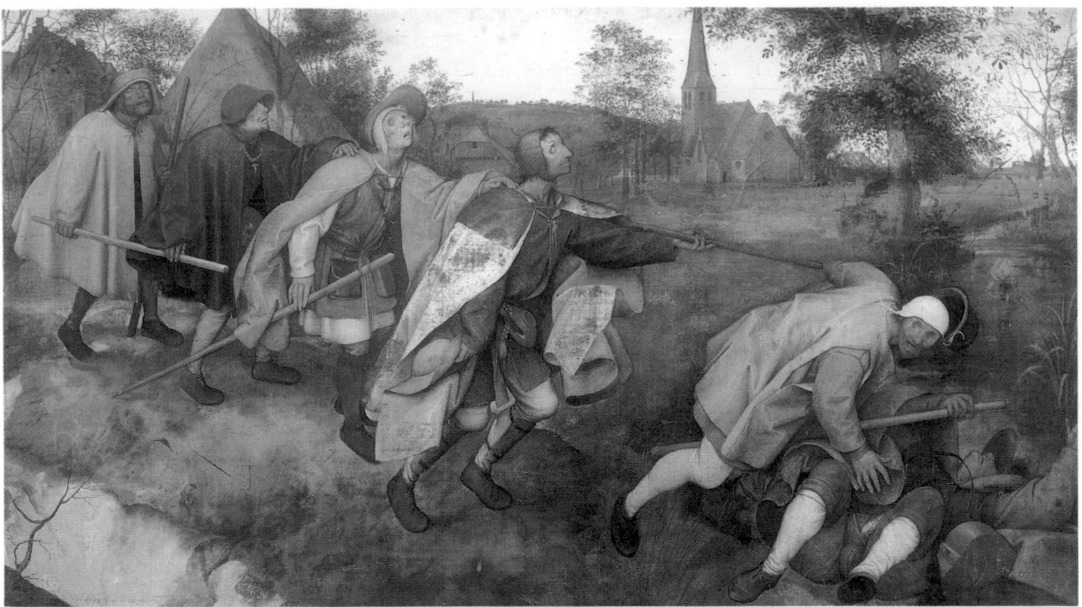

16-23. Pieter Bruegel the Elder. *The Blind Leading the Blind.* c. 1568. Oil on panel, 34½ x 60⅝" (85 x 154 cm). Museo di Capodimonte, Naples

617–18.] There Bruegel would draw them from life. In his hands, they become types whose follies he knew at first hand, yet whose dignity remains intact. For him, Everyman occupies an important place in the scheme of things.

Bruegel's philosophical detachment, which was shared by his fellow humanists, can also be seen in one of his last pictures, *The Blind Leading the Blind* (fig. 16-23). Its source is the Gospels (Matthew 15:12–19). Jesus, speaking of the Pharisees, says, "And if the blind lead the blind, both shall fall into the ditch." This parable recurs in humanistic as well as popular literature, and it appears in at least one earlier work. However, the tragic depth of Bruegel's image gives new urgency to the theme. He has used continuous narrative to ingenious effect. Each pose along the downward diagonal is more unstable than the last, thus leaving little doubt that everyone will end up in the ditch with the leader. (The gap between the two groups is especially telling.) Perhaps Bruegel found the meaning of the parable specially appropriate to his time, which was marked by religious and political fanaticism. Jesus continued: "Out of the heart proceed evil thoughts, murders . . . blasphemies." Could Bruegel have thought that this applied to the conflicts then raging over religious ritual?

FRANCE

Architecture and Sculpture

It took the Northern countries longer to absorb Italian forms in architecture and sculpture than in painting. France was more closely linked with Italy than the rest. We will recall that it had conquered Milan in 1499. Earlier King Francis I had shown his admiration for Italian art by inviting Leonardo to Fontainebleau before luring several of the leading Mannerists to France (see pages 476–78). As a result, France began to assimilate Italian art somewhat earlier than the other countries and was the first to achieve an integrated Renaissance style.

THE CHÂTEAU OF CHAMBORD. As we might expect, architects trained in the Gothic tradition could not adopt the Italian style all at once. They readily used its classical vocabulary, but its syntax gave them trouble for many years. At the Château of Chambord (fig. 16-24), however, the design, though greatly modified by later French builders, was originally by an Italian pupil of Giuliano da Sangallo, probably Domenico da Cortona. His was surely the plan of the center portion (fig. 16-25), which is quite unlike its French predecessors. This square block, whose source is the keep of medieval castles (see page 317), has a central staircase fed by four corridors. These form a Greek cross that divides the interior into four square sections. Each section is subdivided into one large and two smaller rooms and a closet. Together they form a suite (or apartment, in modern speech). The functional grouping of these rooms, imported from Italy, was to become a standard pattern in France. It is the starting point of all modern "designs for living." Yet the turrets, high-pitched roofs, and tall chimneys recall the old royal castle, the Louvre (see fig. 11-94), and the building is basically Gothic in style, despite the classical details.

LE BRETON. In 1528 Francis I, who built Chambord, decided to expand the medieval hunting lodge at Fontainebleau near Paris. What began as a modest enlargement soon developed into a vast palace. The design, though altered over the years, was largely the work of the stonemason Gilles Le Breton (d. 1553), whose father, Jean (d. 1543/44), had helped design Chambord. It included the Gallery of Francis I, which Rosso was called from Italy to decorate a few years later. The Cour du Cheval Blanc (Court of the White Horse, fig. 16-26) is typical of the project as a whole. The design must have evolved in an organic fashion: the wing is surprisingly asymmetrical, and the forms are inconsistent. (The Italianate staircase was built by Jean Androuet du Cerceau in 1634.) Nevertheless, Fontainebleau is the point of departure for nearly all French châteaux for the next 250 years. Indeed, visiting Italian architects had to adapt their designs to the French taste.

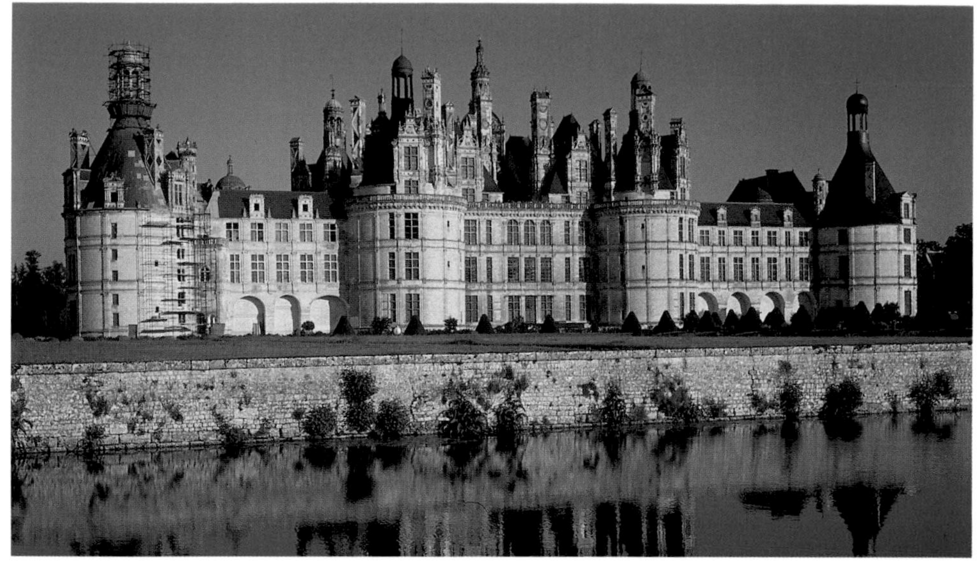

16-24. The Château of Chambord (north front), France. Begun 1519

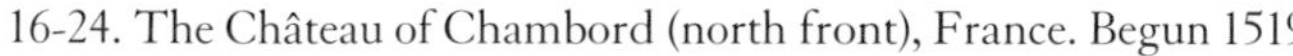

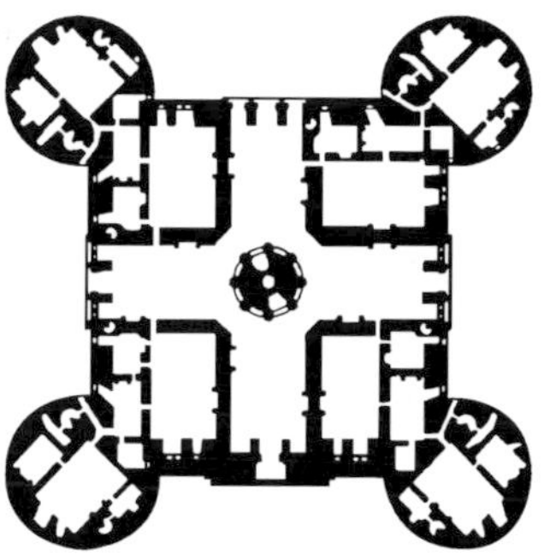

16-25. Plan of center portion, Château of Chambord (after Du Cerceau)

Thus classicism remained little more than a veneer applied to existing French prototypes, although later structures adhered to its principles more strictly.

This eclectic approach had such a strong appeal that it became, in effect, the basis of the national style. In his 1567 treatise, the architect Philibert de l'Orme (c. 1510–1570) actually proposed a new French classical order that was a variant of the five orders inherited from Greece and Rome. It added decorative bands to conceal the seams between column drums resulting from the limitations of French stone, which do not permit shafts as long as marble.

LESCOT. In 1546 Francis I decided to replace the Gothic royal castle, the Louvre, with a new palace on the old site. The project had barely begun at the time of his death, but his architect, Pierre Lescot (c. 1515–1578), continued it under Henry II and quadrupled the size of the court. This enlarged scheme was not completed for more than a century. Lescot built only the southern half of the court's west side (fig. 16-27), which represents its "classic" phase, so called to distinguish it from the style of such buildings as Chambord. This distinction is well justified. The Italian vocabulary of Chambord is based on the Early Renaissance, whereas Lescot drew on the work of Bramante and his successors. Lescot's design is classic in another sense as well. It is the finest surviving example of Northern Renaissance architecture.

The details of Lescot's facade do indeed have a surprising classical purity, yet we would not mistake it for an Italian building. Its distinctive quality comes not from a superficial use of Italian forms but from a genuine synthesis of the traditional château with the Renaissance palazzo. The classical orders (see figs. 12-37 and 14-24), the pedimented window frames, and the arcade on the ground floor are Italian. But the continuity of the facade is broken by three projecting pavilions that have taken the place of the château turrets. The high-pitched roof is also French. The vertical accents thus overcome the horizontal ones (note the broken architraves). This effect is heightened by the tall, narrow windows, which descend from the Gothic. Lescot's solution proved so satisfying that the need for a purer classicism was not felt until the completion of the Louvre 120 years later under Louis XIV (see fig. 19-10).

GOUJON. Equally un-Italian is the rich sculptural decoration covering almost the entire wall surface of the third story. These reliefs, beautifully adapted to the architecture, are by Jean Goujon (c. 1510–1565?), the finest French sculptor of the mid-sixteenth century, with whom Lescot often collaborated. Unfortunately, they have been much restored. To get a more precise idea of Goujon's style we must turn to the relief panels from the Fontaine des Innocents (fig. 16-28). These have survived intact, although their architectural framework by Lescot is lost. The graceful figures recall the Mannerism of Cellini (see fig. 14-19) and, even more, Primaticcio's decorations at Fontainebleau (see fig. 14-20). Like Lescot's architecture, they combine classical details of great purity with a slenderness that gives them a uniquely French air.

PILON. Germain Pilon (c. 1535–1590), the greatest sculptor of the later sixteenth century, was a more powerful artist. Whereas Goujon was mainly a relief carver, Pilon created monumental sculpture in the round in every medium. In his early years Pilon, too, learned a good deal from Primaticcio, but he openly acknowledged his debt to Mannerism instead of overlaying it with classicism. However, he soon developed his own manner by merging the School of Fontainebleau with elements taken from ancient sculpture, the Gothic tradition, and Michelangelo and his school. His main works are tombs, of which the earliest and largest was for Henry II and Catherine de' Medici (fig. 16-29). Primaticcio designed the architectural framework, an oblong, freestanding chapel on a platform decorated with bronze and marble reliefs. Pilon, it seems, was responsible for all the sculpture. On the top of the tomb are bronze figures of the king and queen kneeling in prayer, while inside the chapel the couple reappears as recumbent marble *gisants,* or nude corpses (fig. 16-30).

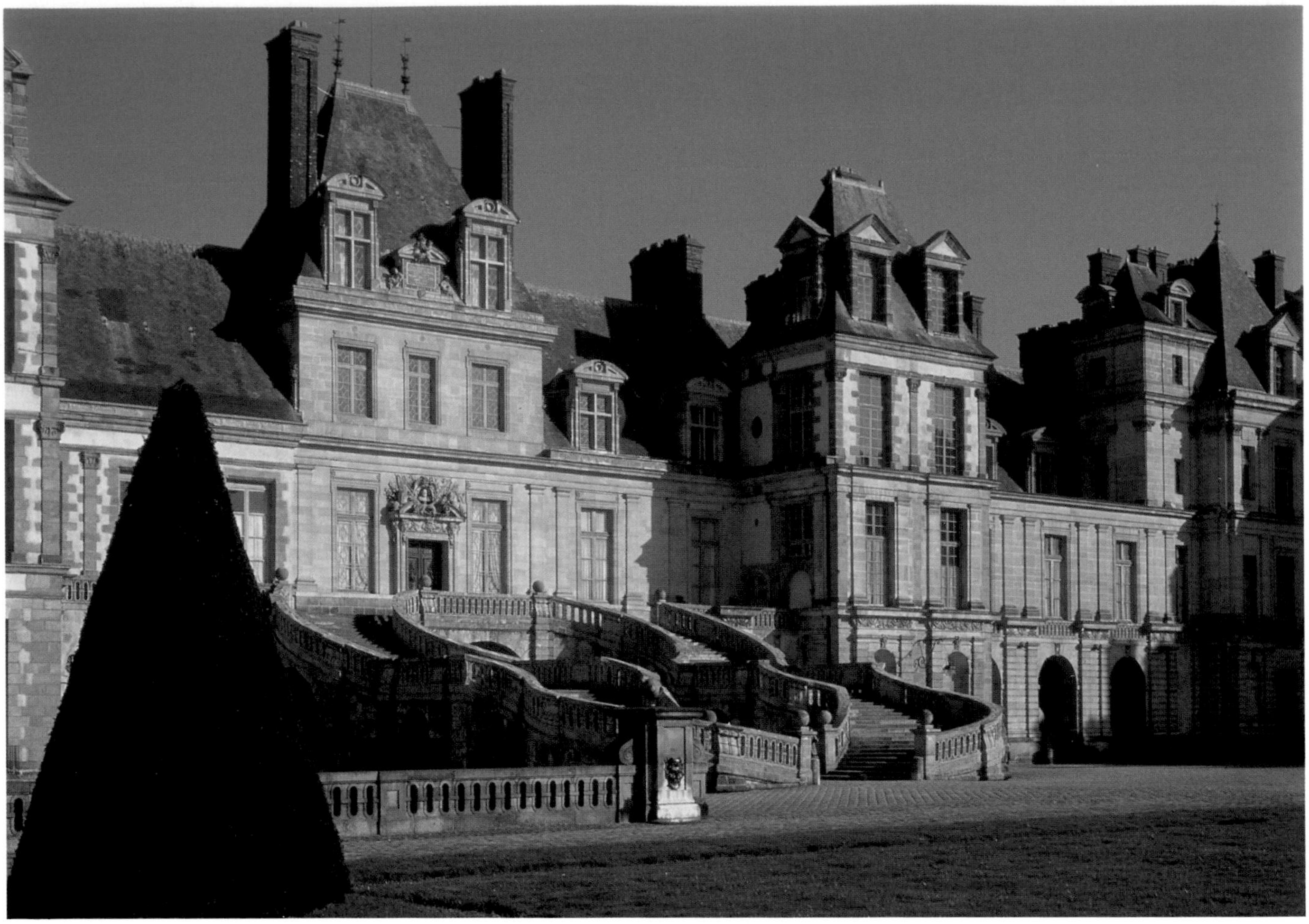

16-26. Gilles Le Breton, Court of the White Horse, Fontainebleau, 1528–40

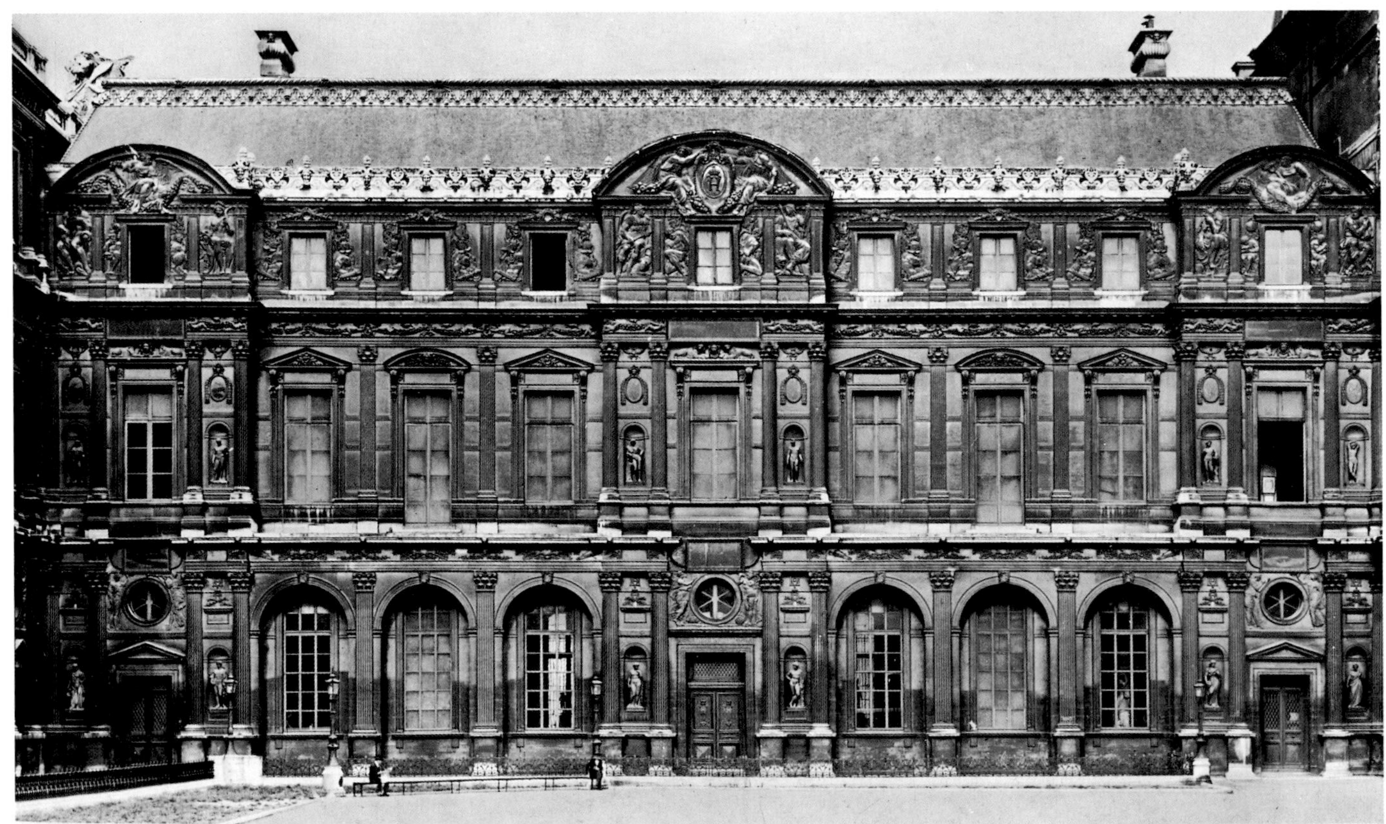

16-27. Pierre Lescot. Square Court of the Louvre, Paris. Begun 1546

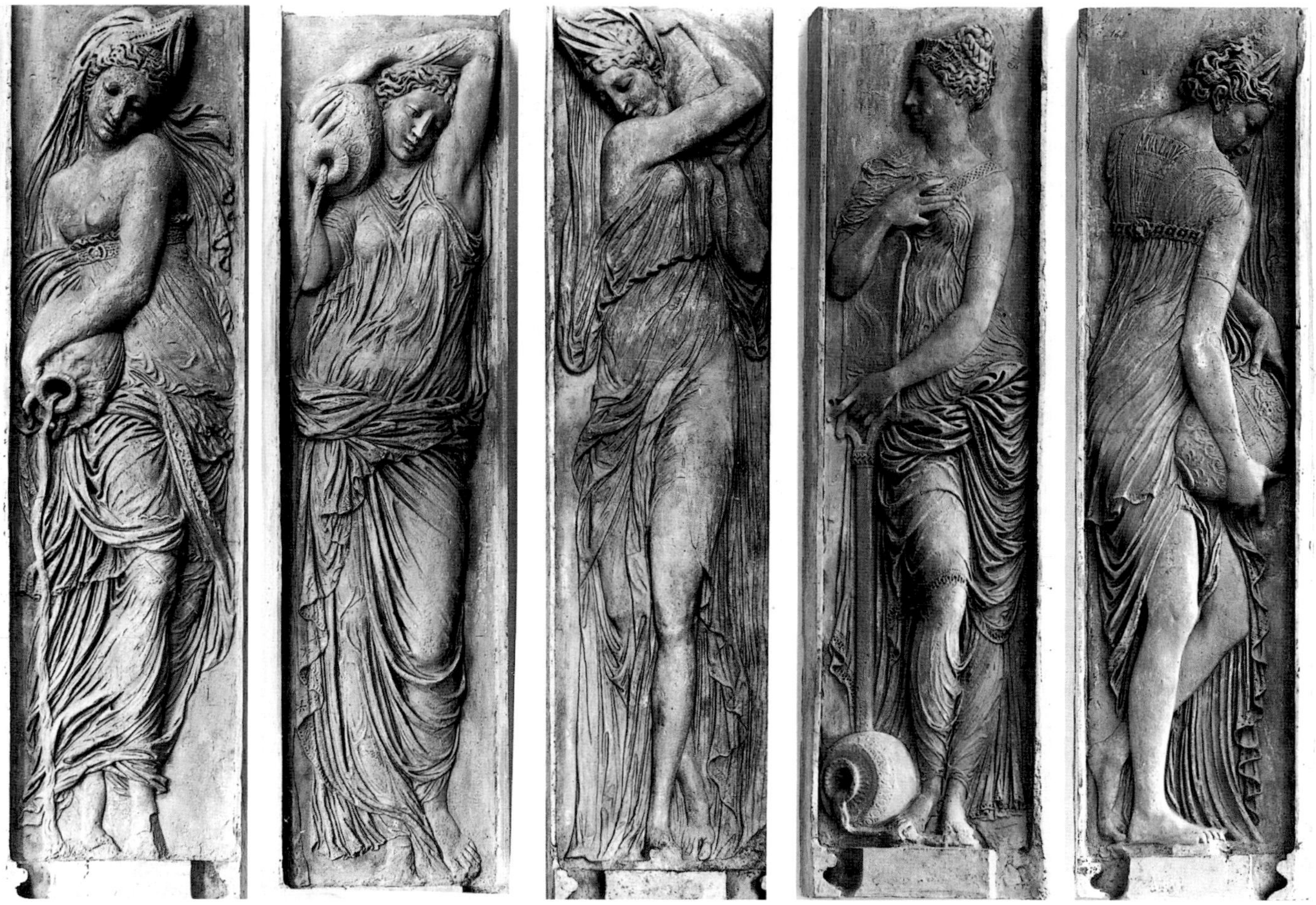

16-28. Jean Goujon. Reliefs from the Fontaine des Innocents, Paris. 1548–49

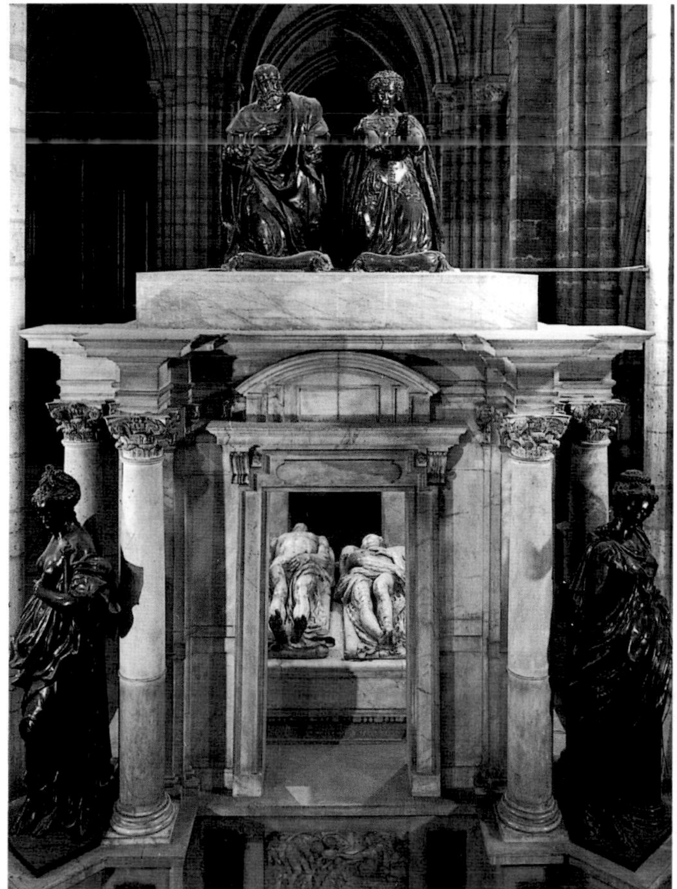

(LEFT) 16-29. Francesco Primaticcio and Germain Pilon. Tomb of Henry II. 1563–70. Abbey Church of St.-Denis, Paris

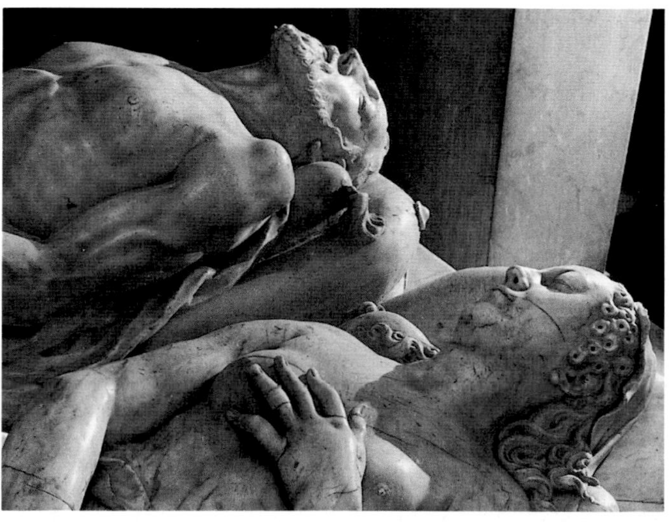

16-30. Germian Pilon. *Gisants* of the king and queen, detail of the Tomb of Henry II

This contrast of effigies had been a characteristic feature of Gothic tombs since the fourteenth century. The *gisant* expressed the transient nature of the flesh, usually by showing the body in an advanced stage of decay, with vermin sometimes crawling through its open cavities. That tradition remained popular in the North through the sixteenth century. How could this grim image be given Renaissance form without losing its emotional significance? Pilon's solution is brilliant. By idealizing the *gisants* he reverses their meaning, from the Gothic "prospective," which emphasizes the afterlife, to the classical "retrospective," which commemorates the deceased (see also page 416). The queen is in the pose of a classical Venus and the king is like the dead Christ. They evoke neither horror nor pity. Instead, they have the pathos of a beauty that continues even in death.

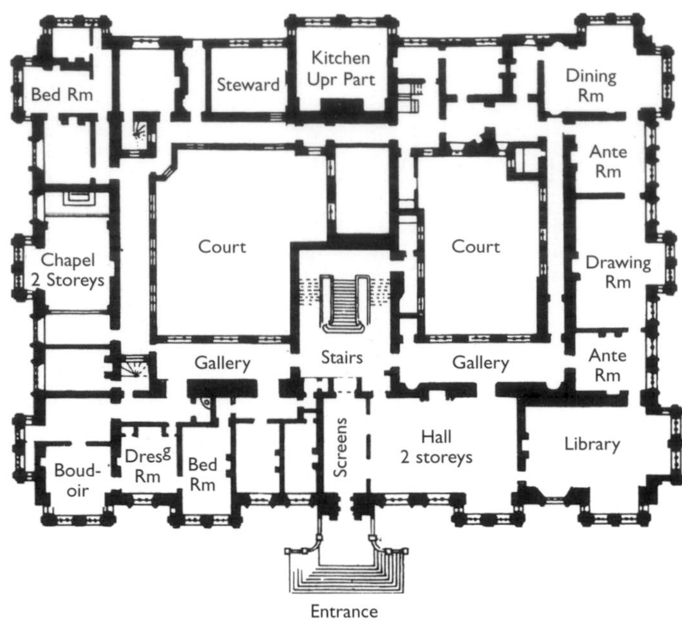

16-31. Plan of Longleat House, Wiltshire (after a plan from Sir Bannister Fletcher's *A History of Architecture)*

ENGLAND

Architecture

In England the form of "Late Gothic" known as the Perpendicular style (see fig. 11-28) proved extraordinarily persistent. Not until the middle of the sixteenth century did English architecture begin to absorb the stylistic vocabulary of the Italian Renaissance. It first appeared in 1563 with the publication of an architectural treatise by John Shute, which was based on a thorough study abroad of antique and contemporary architecture. Yet classicism was never applied consistently by Elizabethan architects. Instead, they relied on elements in pattern books from France, Italy, and Flanders, which they combined with the English vernacular tradition. Thus the Gothic lingered far longer in England than even in France. As late as 1600 the majority of English buildings still retained a "Perpendicular syntax"; that is to say, their stage of development corresponded to Chambord (see fig. 16-24). A major reason for this conservatism was the fact that English builders continued to be trained as masons and carpenters rather than as architects. They thus did not absorb the ideals of the Renaissance, merely its classical vocabulary, which they acquired almost entirely at second and third hand, beginning around 1550.

Perhaps the only mason worthy of the title of architect in the proper sense of the term was Robert Smythson (c. 1536–1614). He designed several of the Elizabethan "prodigy" houses—country mansions built at enormous cost solely for the purpose of entertaining Queen Elizabeth and her court. The first and finest of these is Longleat (fig. 16-32), which went through several building campaigns. Perfectly symmetrical on all four sides and beautifully proportioned, it avoids the picturesque medieval effects of earlier English architecture. Instead, it achieves a classical harmony that makes it the most beautiful building in all of Britain before the time of Inigo Jones (see pages 587–88). This classicism, French rather than Italian in character (compare fig. 16-26), surely reflects the taste of its owner, John Thynne. (Thynne had already erected a somewhat similar building for Protector Edward Somerset.) The plan (fig. 16-31) had been established by another mason. However, the first two stories as we now see them were largely the responsibility of Smythson working with a French sculptor, Allen Maynard (fl. 1563–c. 1584), who carved the chimney pieces and ornamentation.

Begun in 1572 after a fire destroyed most of the existing house, the building envisioned by Smythson and Maynard was largely completed in time for a visit by the queen in 1574, but the third story was added by Thynne after they finished their work a year later. (The stairs are from the next century; compare fig. 16-26.) In contrast to later prodigy houses by Smythson and his contemporaries, Longleat preserves its classical character by omitting the elaborate crowns then in vogue, which freely juxtaposed English and Flemish elements in wildly improbable combinations.

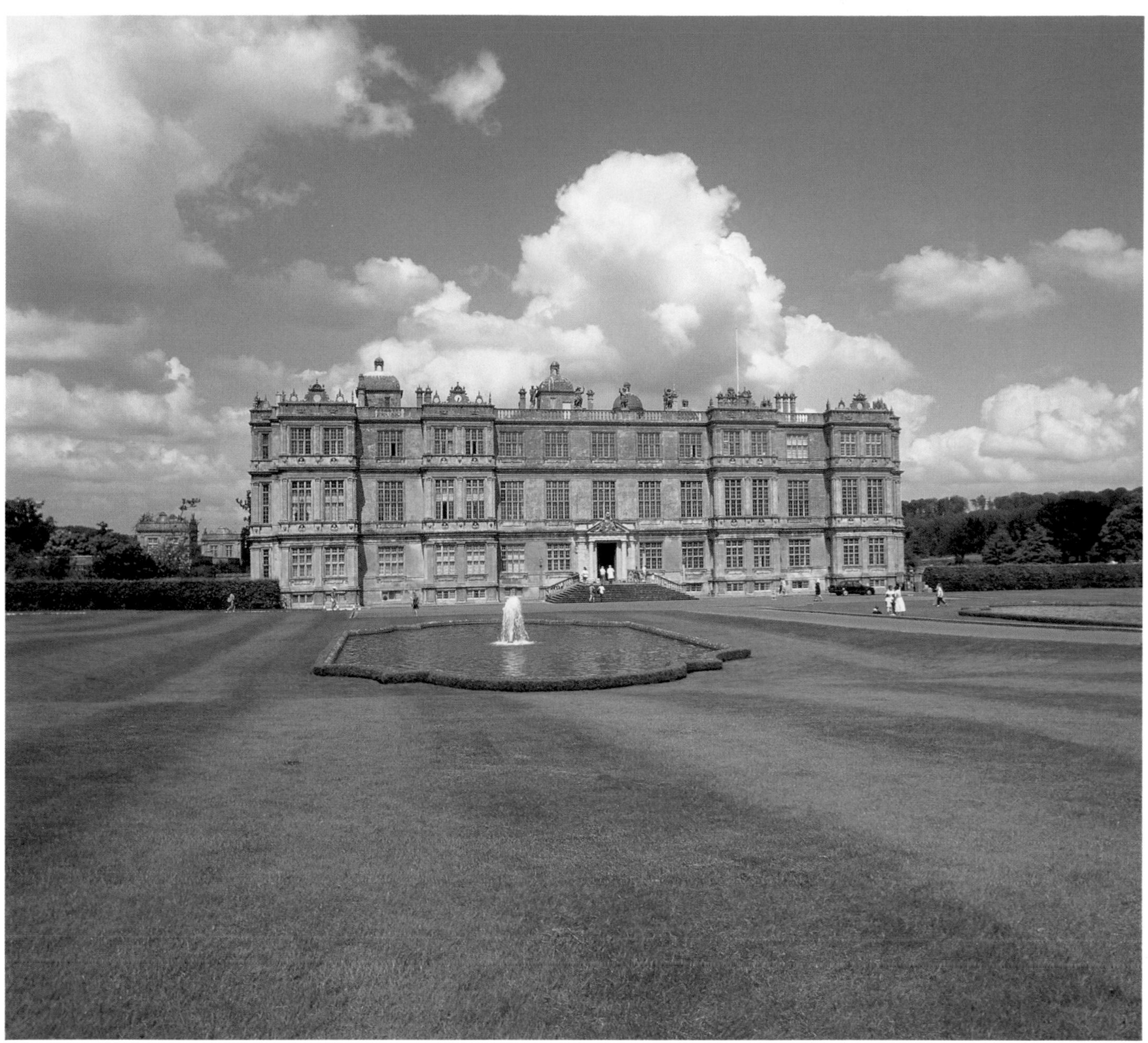

16-32. Robert Smythson, Allen Maynard, and others. Longleat, Wiltshire, England. 1572–80.

CHAPTER SEVENTEEN

The Baroque in Italy and Spain

What is Baroque? Like Mannerism, the term was originally coined to disparage the style it designates: it meant "irregular, contorted, grotesque." Art historians remain divided over its definition. Should Baroque be used only for the dominant style of the seventeenth century, or should it include other tendencies, such as classicism, to which it bears a complex relationship? Should the time frame include the period 1700 to 1750, known as the Rococo? More important, is the Baroque distinct from both Renaissance and modern? Although a good case can be made for viewing the Baroque as the final phase of the Renaissance, we shall treat it as a distinct era. The approach we choose is perhaps less important than understanding the factors that must enter into our decision.

The Baroque cannot be easily classified. It was a time full of contradictions and paradoxes, not unlike the present, which is why we find it so fascinating. It has been claimed that the Baroque style expresses the spirit of the Counter-Reformation. However, by 1600 Catholicism had regained much of its former territory, and Protestantism was on the defensive, so that neither side had the power to upset the new balance. In 1622 the heroes of the Counter-Reformation—Ignatius of Loyola, Francis Xavier (both Jesuits), Theresa of Avila, Filippo Neri, and Isidoro Agricola—were named saints (Carlo Borromeo had already been made one in 1610), thus beginning a wave of canonizations that lasted through the mid-eighteenth century. In contrast to the piety and good deeds of these reformers, the new princes of the Church who supported the growth of Baroque art were known mainly for their lives of worldly splendor.

Another reason why we should avoid placing too much emphasis on the Baroque's ties to the Counter-Reformation is that, unlike Mannerism, the new style was not specifically Italian, even though it was born in Rome during the final years of the sixteenth century. Nor was it confined to religious art. Baroque elements quickly entered the Protestant North, where they were applied primarily to secular subjects.

Equally problematic is the claim that Baroque is "the style of absolutism," reflecting the centralized state ruled by an autocrat of unlimited powers. Although absolutism reached its climax during the reign of Louis XIV in the later seventeenth century, it had been in the making since the 1520s (under Francis I in France, the Hapsburgs in Austria and Spain, and the Medici dukes in Tuscany). Moreover, Baroque art flourished in bourgeois Holland no less than in the absolutist monarchies, and the style sponsored under Louis XIV was a notably subdued, classicistic kind of Baroque.

It is nevertheless tempting to see the turbulent history of the era reflected in Baroque art, where the tensions of the era often seem to erupt into open conflict. The seventeenth century was one of almost continuous warfare, which involved almost every nation in a complex web of shifting alliances. The Thirty Years' War (1618–1648) was fueled by the ambitions of the kings of France, who sought to dominate Europe, and by those of the Hapsburgs, who ruled not only Austria and Spain but also the Netherlands, Bohemia, and Hungary. Although fought largely in Germany, the war eventually engulfed nearly all of Europe. After the Treaty of Westphalia ended the war and granted their freedom, the United Provinces—as the independent Netherlands was known—entered into a series of battles with England and France that lasted until 1679. Yet, other than in Germany, which was left in ruins, there is little correlation between these rivalries and the art of the period. In fact, the seventeenth century has been called the Golden Age of painting in France, Holland, Flanders, and Spain. Moreover, these wars had practically no effect on Baroque imagery. We see such an impact mainly in the etchings of Jacques Callot (see fig. 19-1), although we can also catch indirect glimpses of it in Dutch militia scenes, such as Rembrandt's *Night Watch* (see fig. 18-16).

It is also difficult to relate Baroque art to the science and philosophy of the period. A direct link did exist in the Early and High Renaissance, when an artist could also be a humanist and a scientist. During the seventeenth century, however, scientific and philosophical thought became too complex, abstract, and systematic for the artist to share. Gravitation and calculus could not stir the artist's imagination any more than Descartes' famous motto *Cogito, ergo sum* (I think, therefore I am).

There is nevertheless a relationship between Baroque art and science that, though subtle, is essential to an understanding of the age. The complex metaphysics of the humanists, which gave everything religious meaning, was replaced by a new physics. The change began with Copernicus, Kepler, and Galileo and culminated in Descartes and Newton. Their cosmology broke the ties between sensory perception and science. By placing the sun, not the earth (and humanity), at the center of the universe, it contradicted what our eyes (and common sense) tell us: that the sun revolves around the earth. Scientists now defined underlying relationships in mathematical and geometrical terms as part of the simple, orderly system of mechanics. Not only was the seventeenth century's worldview fundamentally different from what had preceded it, but its understanding of visual reality was forever changed by the new science, thanks to advances in optical physics and physiology. Thus we may say that the Baroque literally saw with new eyes.

The attack on Renaissance science and philosophy, which could trace their origins (and authority) back to antiquity, also had the effect of displacing natural magic, a precursor of modern science that included both astrology and alchemy. Unlike the new science, natural magic tried to control the world through prediction and manipulation; it did so by uncovering nature's "secrets" instead of her laws. However, because it was linked to religion and morality, it lived on in popular literature and folklore long afterward.

In the end, Baroque art was not simply the result of religious, political, or intellectual developments. Let us therefore think of it as one among other basic features that distinguish the period: the strengthened Catholic faith, the absolutist state, and the new science. These factors are combined in volatile mixtures that give Baroque its fascinating variety. Such diversity was well suited to express the expanding view of life. What ultimately unites this complex era is a reevaluation of humanity and its relation to the universe. Central to this image is the new psychology of the Baroque. Philosophers gave greater prominence to human passion, which encompassed a wider range of emotions and social levels than ever before. The scientific revolution leading up to Newton's unified mechanics responded to the same view, which presumes a more active role in people's ability to understand and affect the world around us. Remarkably, the Baroque remained an age of great religious faith, however divided it may have been in its loyalties. The interplay of passion, intellect, and spirituality may be seen as forming a dialogue that has never been truly resolved.

PAINTING IN ITALY

Around 1600 Rome became the fountainhead of the Baroque, as it had of the High Renaissance a century before, by attracting artists from other regions. The papacy patronized art on a large scale with the aim of making Rome the most beautiful city of the Christian world "for the greater glory of God and the Church." This campaign had begun as early as 1585, but the artists then on hand were Late Mannerists with little talent. Soon, however, it attracted ambitious young artists, especially from northern Italy. It was they who created the new style.

CARAVAGGIO. Foremost among them was a painter of genius, Michelangelo Merisi, called Caravaggio after his birthplace near Milan (1571–1610). His first important religious commission was for a series of three monumental canvases devoted to St. Matthew that he painted for the Contarelli Chapel in S. Luigi dei Francesi from 1599 to 1602 (fig. 17-1). As decorations they perform the same function that fresco cycles had in the Renaissance (compare fig. 12-32). Our view of the chapel includes *St. Matthew and the Angel,* in which the illiterate tax collector Matthew turns dramatically for inspiration to the angel who dictates the gospel. A third canvas is devoted to the saint's martyrdom. The main image, *The Calling of St. Matthew* (fig. 17-2), is remote from both Mannerism and the High Renaissance. Its only ancestor is the "North Italian realism" of artists such as Savoldo (see fig. 14-14). But Caravaggio's realism is of a new and radical kind. According to contemporary accounts, Caravaggio painted directly on the canvas from the live model. [See Primary Sources. no. 55, page 621.] He depicted the world he knew, so that his canvases are filled with ordinary people. Indeed, his pictures are often surprisingly autobiographical.

Never have we seen a sacred subject depicted so entirely in terms of contemporary lowlife. Matthew, the tax gatherer, sits with some armed men (who must be his agents) in a common Roman tavern as two figures approach from the right. The arrivals are poor people whose bare feet and simple garments contrast strongly with the colorful costumes of Matthew and his companions. For Caravaggio, however, naturalism is not an end in itself but a means of conveying profoundly religious content. Why do we sense a religious quality in this scene and not mistake it for an everyday event? The answer is that Caravaggio's North Italian realism is wedded to elements derived from his study of Renaissance art in Rome, which give the scene its surprising dignity. His style, in other words, is classical without being classicizing. The composition, for example, is spread across the picture surface and its forms are sharply highlighted, much as in a relief (see fig. 7-32). What identifies one of the figures as Christ? It is surely not the Savior's halo, the only supernatural feature in the picture, which is an inconspicuous gold band that we might well overlook. Our eyes fasten instead upon his commanding gesture, borrowed from Michelangelo's *Creation of Adam* (see fig. 13-18), which "bridges" the gap between the two groups and is echoed by Matthew, who points questioningly at himself.

Most decisive is the beam of sunlight above Jesus. It illuminates his face and hand in the gloomy interior, thus carrying his call across to Matthew. Without this light, so natural yet so charged with meaning, the picture would lose its power to make us aware of the divine presence. Caravaggio gives direct form to an attitude shared by certain saints of the Counter-Reformation: that the mysteries of faith are revealed not by speculation but through an inward experience that is open to all people. What separates the Baroque from the later Counter-Reformation is the externalization of the mystic vision, which appears to us complete, without any signs of the spiritual struggle in El Greco's art (see pages 470–72).

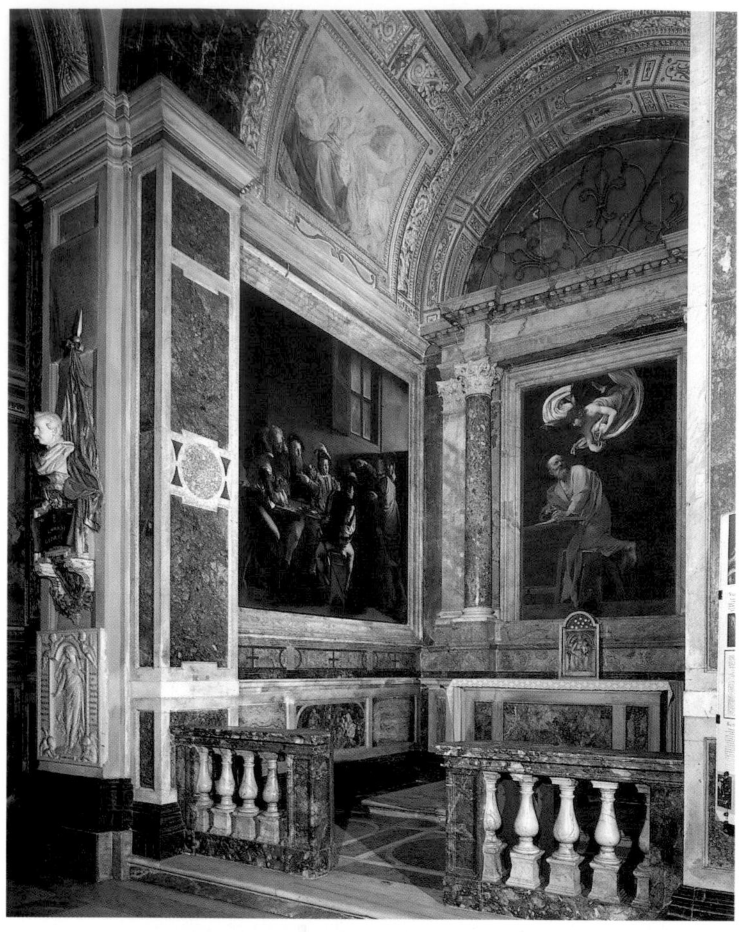

17-1. Contarelli Chapel, S. Luigi dei Francesi, Rome

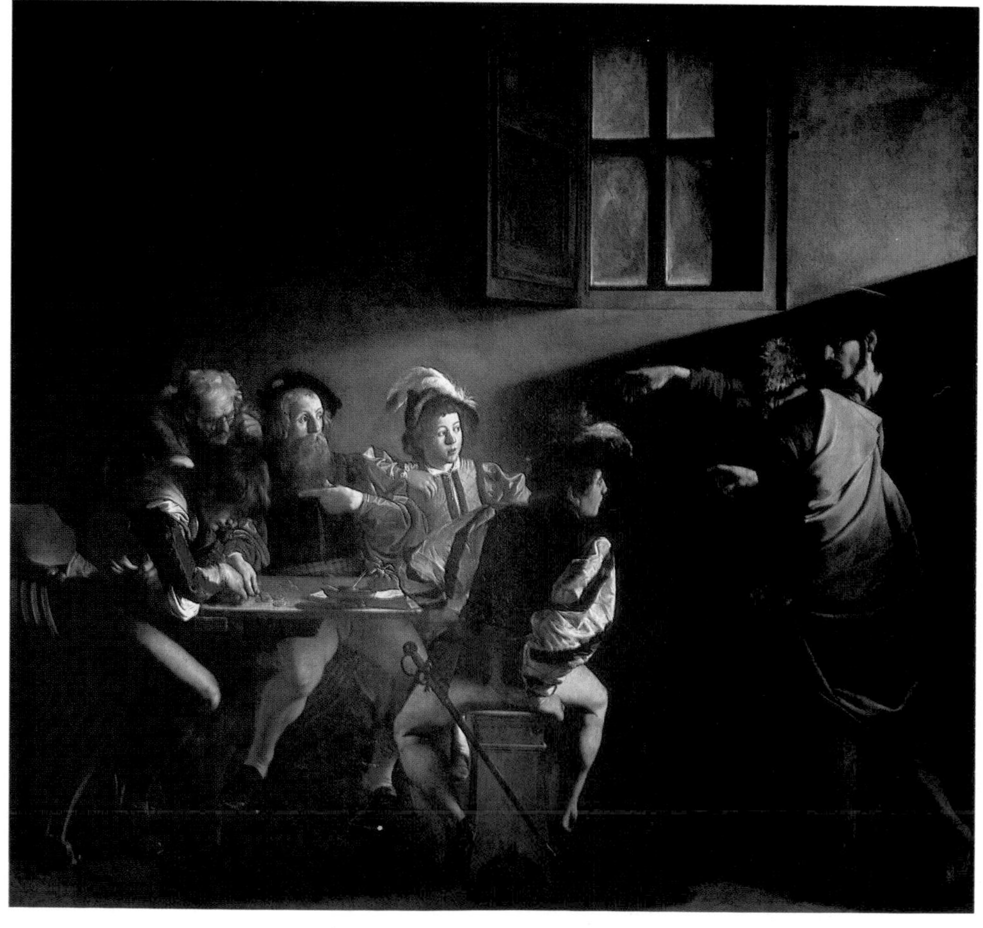

17-2. Caravaggio. *The Calling of St. Matthew.* c. 1599–1602. Oil on canvas, 11'1" x 11'5" (3.4 x 3.5 m). Contarelli Chapel, S. Luigi dei Francesi, Rome

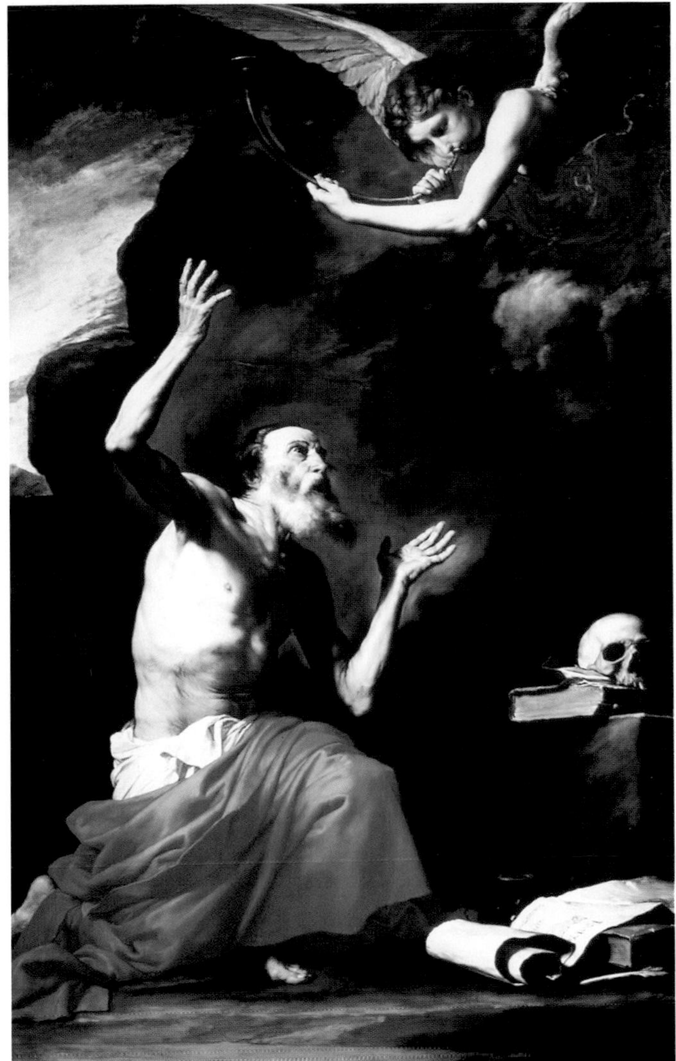

17-3. Jusepe Ribera. *St. Jerome and the Angel of Judgment.* 1626. Oil on canvas, 8'7⅛" x 5'4½" (2.62 x 1.64 m). Museo e Gallerie Nazionali di Capodimonte, Naples

Caravaggio's paintings have a "lay Christianity" that appealed to Protestants no less than to Catholics. This quality made possible his strong, though indirect, influence on Rembrandt, the greatest religious artist of the Protestant North. In Italy, Caravaggio's work was praised by artists and connoisseurs, but the ordinary people for whom it was intended resented meeting their own kind in these paintings. They preferred religious imagery of a more idealized sort. Conservative critics, moreover, regarded Caravaggio as lacking decorum: the propriety and reverence demanded of religious subjects. For these reasons, Caravaggism largely ran its course by 1630, when it was absorbed into other Baroque tendencies.

RIBERA. Caravaggio's style lived on only in Naples, then under Spanish rule, where the artist had fled from Rome after killing a man in a duel over a ball game. His main disciple in Naples was the Spaniard Jusepe Ribera (1591–1652), who settled there after having absorbed Caravaggio's style in Rome and who in turn spawned a school of his own. Especially popular were Ribera's paintings of saints, prophets, and ancient beggar–philosophers. Their asceticism appealed strongly to the otherworldliness of Spanish Catholicism. Such pictures also reflected the learned humanism of the Spanish nobility who ruled Naples and were the artist's main patrons. Most of Ribera's figures are middle-aged or elderly men who possess the unique blend of inner strength and intensity seen in *St. Jerome and the Angel of Judgment* (fig. 17-3), his masterpiece in this vein. The fervent characterization owes its expressive force to both the dramatic composition, inspired by Caravaggio (compare *St. Matthew and the Angel* in fig. 17-1), and the raking light, which gives the figure a powerful presence by heightening the realism and emphasizing the vigorous surface textures.

GENTILESCHI. So far, we have not discussed a named woman artist, although this does not mean that there were none. Pliny, for example, in his *Natural History* (Book 35) documents the names and work of women artists in Greece and Rome, and there are records of women manuscript illuminators during the Middle Ages (see box page 298). We must remember, however, that the vast majority of *all* artists remained anonymous until the late fourteenth century. As a result, it has been possible to identify only a few works by women before that time. Women began to emerge as distinct artistic personalities about 1550, but it was not until the Baroque era that they first played a major role in the arts. Because

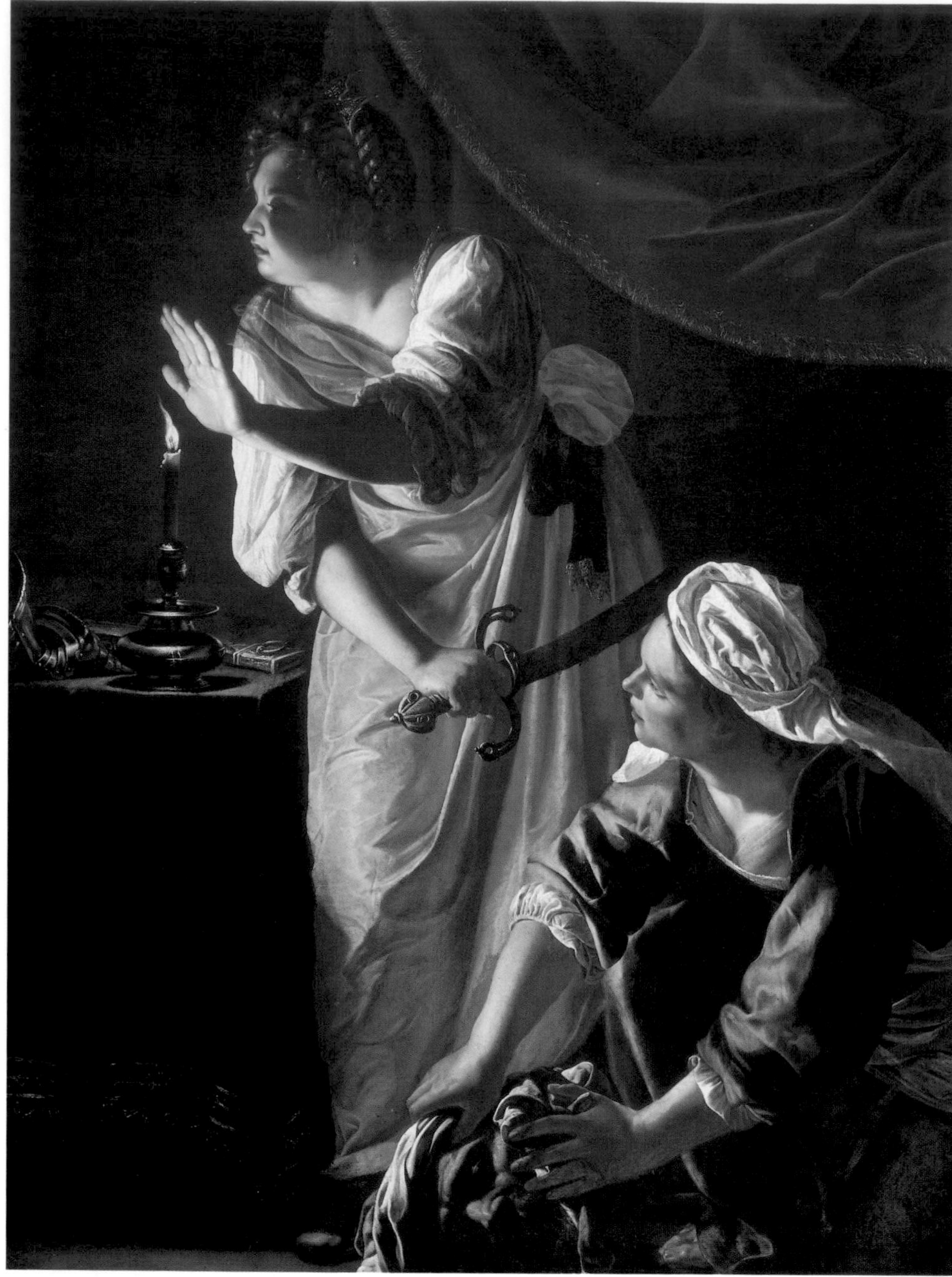

17-4. Artemisia Gentileschi. *Judith and Maidservant with the Head of Holofernes.* c. 1625. Oil on canvas, 6'1/2" x 4'7" (1.84 x 1.41 m). The Detroit Institute of Arts

GIFT OF LESLIE H. GREEN

it was difficult for them to obtain instruction in figure drawing and anatomy, they were effectively barred from painting narrative subjects. Hence until the middle of the nineteenth century women artists were largely restricted to painting portraits, genre scenes, and still lifes. Even so, many had successful careers and often became the equals or superiors of the men in whose styles they were trained. The exceptions to this rule were certain Italian women born into artistic families, for whom painting came naturally. The most important of them was Artemisia Gentileschi (1593–c. 1653).

She was born in Rome, the daughter of Caravaggio's follower Orazio Gentileschi, and became one of the leading painters of her day. She took great pride in her work but found the way difficult for a woman artist. [See Primary Sources, no. 54, page 620.] Her characteristic subjects are Bathsheba, the tragic object of King David's passion, and Judith, who saved her people by beheading the Assyrian general Holofernes. Both themes were popular during the Baroque era, which delighted in erotic and violent scenes. Artemisia's frequent depictions of these biblical heroines suggest an ambivalence toward men that was rooted in her turbulent life. While Gentileschi's early paintings of Judith take her father's and Caravaggio's work as their points of departure, our example (fig. 17-4) is a fully mature, independent work. The inner drama is hers alone, and it is no less powerful for its restraint. Rather than the beheading itself, the artist shows the instant after. Momentarily distracted, Judith gestures theatrically as her servant stuffs Holofernes' head into a sack. The object of their attention remains hidden from view, heightening the air of intrigue. The hushed, candlelit atmosphere creates a mood of mystery that conveys Judith's complex emotions with unsurpassed understanding.

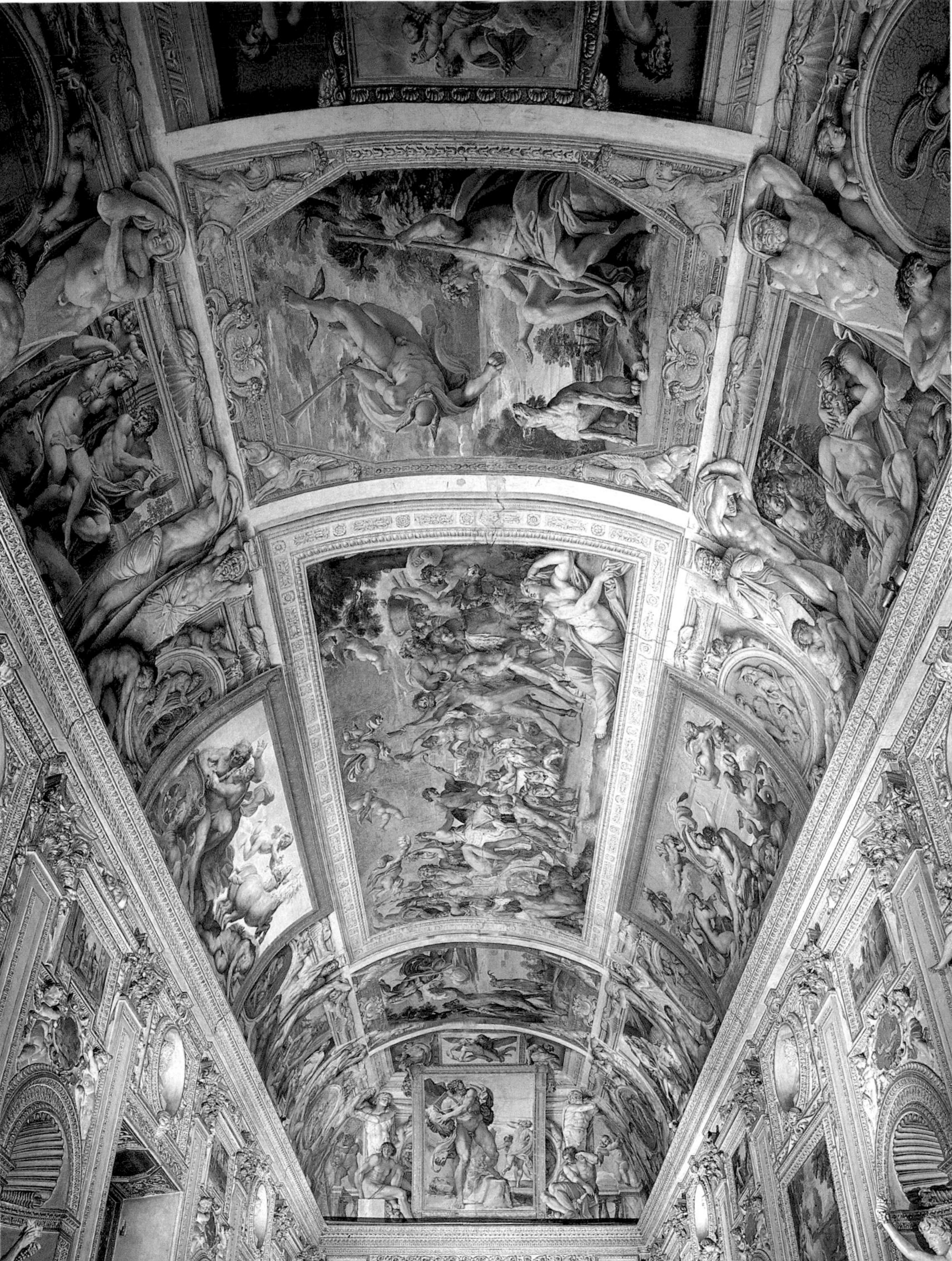

17-5. Annibale Carracci. Ceiling fresco. 1597–1601. Gallery, Palazzo Farnese, Rome

ANNIBALE CARRACCI. The conservative wishes of everyday people in Italy were met by artists who were less radical, and less talented, than Caravaggio. They took their lead instead from Annibale Carracci (1560–1609), who also had recently arrived in Rome. Annibale came from Bologna where, since the 1580s, he and two other members of his family had evolved an anti-Mannerist style based on North Italian realism and Venetian art. He was a reformer rather than a revolutionary. As with Caravaggio, who admired him, his experience of Roman classicism transformed his art. He, too, felt that art must return to nature, but his approach emphasized a revival of the classics, which to him meant the art of antiquity. Annibale also sought to emulate Raphael, Michelangelo, Titian, and Correggio. At his best, he was able to fuse these diverse elements, although their union always remained somewhat unstable.

Between 1597 and 1604 Annibale produced a vast ceiling fresco in the gallery of the Farnese Palace (fig. 17-5), his most ambitious work, which soon became so famous that it ranked behind

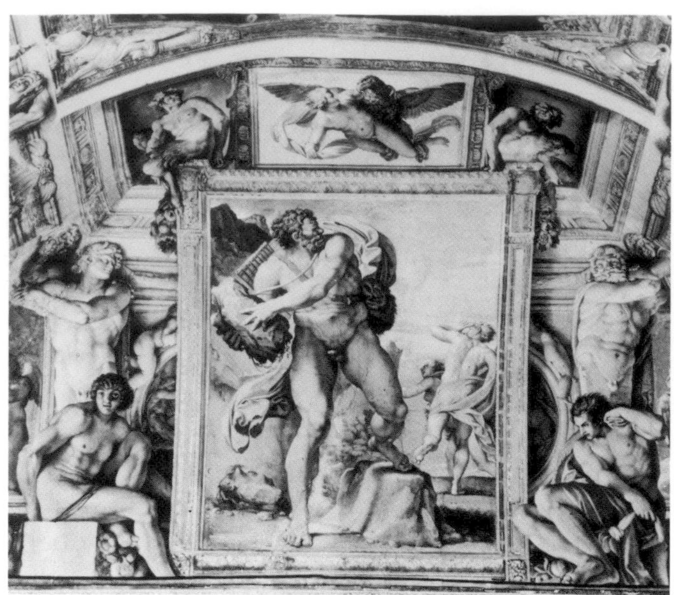

17-6. Annibale Carracci. Ceiling fresco (detail). Gallery Palazzo Farnese, Rome

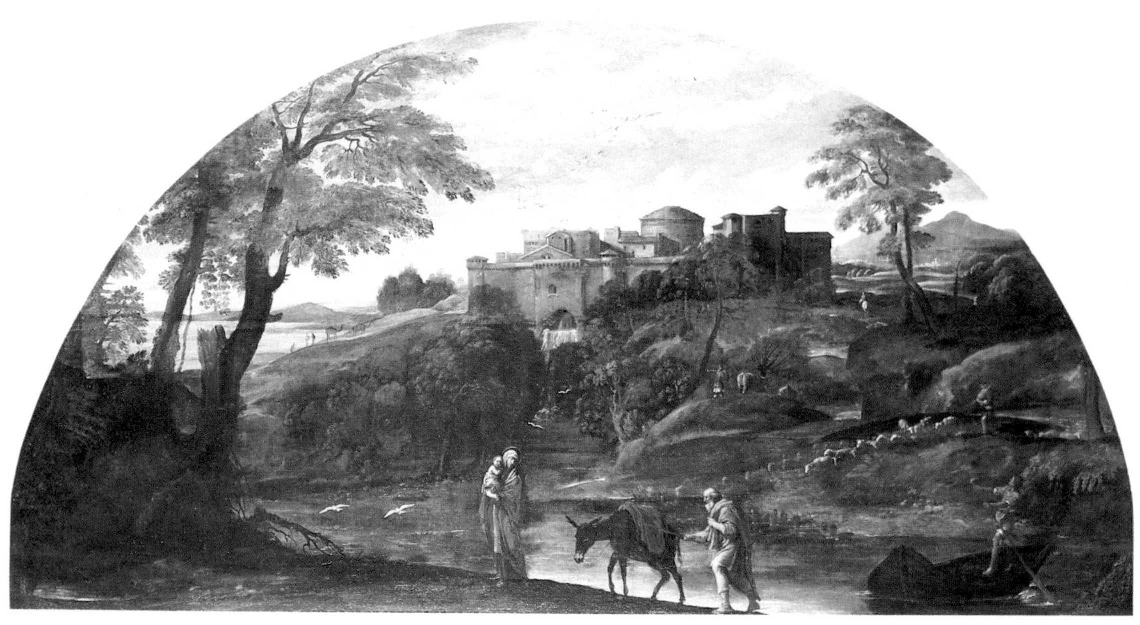

17-7. Annibale Carracci. *Landscape with the Flight into Egypt.* c. 1603. Oil on canvas, 4'1/4" x 8'2 1/2" (1.22 x 2.50 m). Galleria Doria Pamphili, Rome

only the murals of Michelangelo and Raphael. [See Primary Sources, no. 55, page 621.] Commissioned to celebrate a wedding in the Farnese family, it wears its humanist subject, the Loves of the Classical Gods, lightly. The narrative scenes, like those of the Sistine ceiling, are surrounded by painted architecture, simulated sculpture, and nude youths. But the fresco does not rely solely on Michelangelo's masterpiece. The style of the main panels recalls Raphael's *Galatea* (compare fig. 17–6 to fig. 13-33), with a strong debt to Titian (compare the *Bacchanal* in fig. 13-37). The whole is held together by an illusionistic scheme that reflects Annibale's knowledge of Correggio and the great Venetians. Carefully foreshortened and lit from below (as we can judge from the shadows), the nude youths and the simulated sculpture and architecture appear real. Against this background the mythologies are presented as simulated easel pictures, a solution adopted from Raphael. Each of these levels of reality is handled with consummate skill, and the entire ceiling has an exuberance that sets it apart from both Mannerism and High Renaissance art.

The sculptured precision of the Farnese Gallery does not do justice to the important Venetian element in Annibale Carracci's style. This aspect is most striking in his landscapes, such as the *Landscape with the Flight into Egypt* (fig. 17-7). Its pastoral mood and the soft light and atmosphere hark back to Giorgione and Titian (see figs. 13-36 and 13-37). The figures, however, play a far

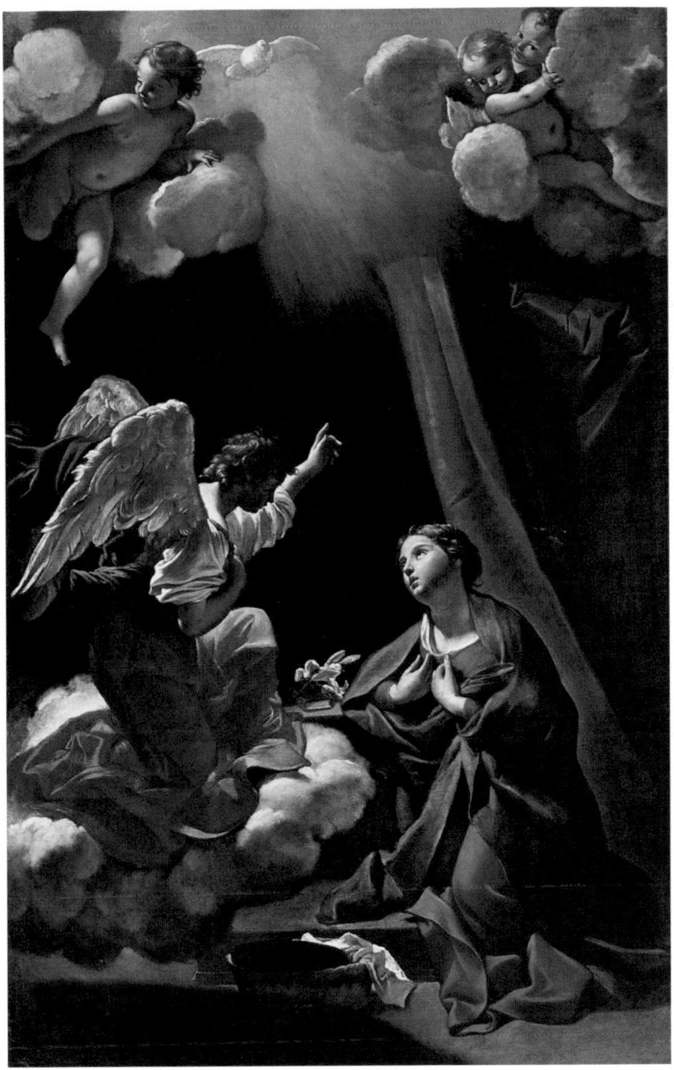

17-8. Giovanni Lanfranco. *Annunciation.* c. 1616. Oil on canvas, 9'8½" x 6' (2.96 x 1.83 m). S. Carlo ai Catinari, Rome

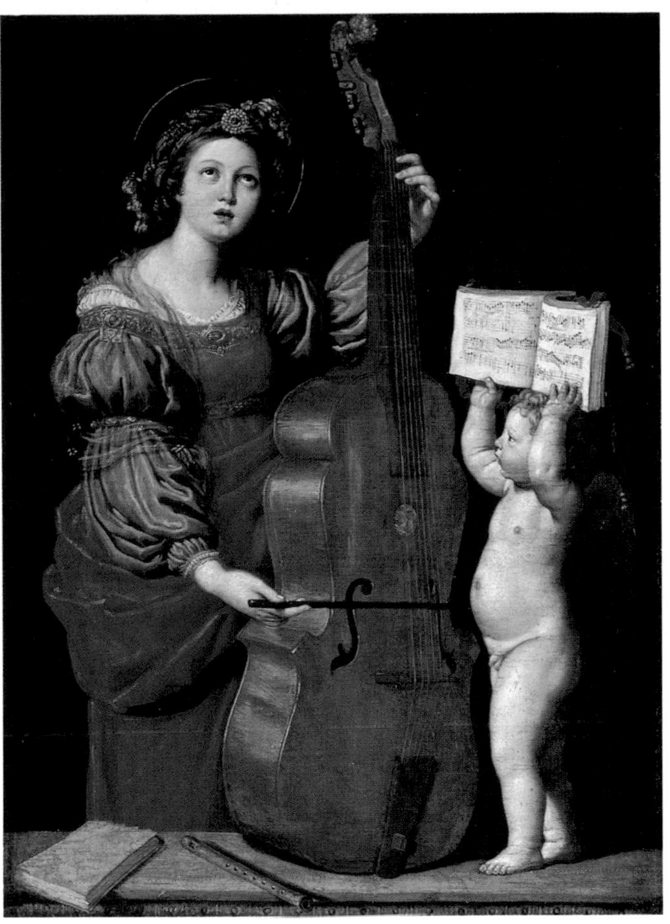

17-9. Domenichino. *St. Cecilia.* c. 1617–18. Oil on canvas, 62⅞ x 46⅛" (159 x 117 cm; enlarged). Musée du Louvre, Paris

less visible role here. They are as small and incidental as in any Northern landscape (compare fig. 16-21). Nor does the landscape in any way suggest the Flight into Egypt. It would be equally suitable for almost any story. Still, we feel that the figures could not be removed altogether, although we can imagine them replaced by others. This is not the untamed nature of Northern landscapes. The old castle, the roads and fields, the flock of sheep, the ferryman with his boat, all show that this "civilized," hospitable countryside has been inhabited for a long time. Hence the figures, however tiny, do not appear lost or dwarfed. Their presence is implied by the orderly, domesticated quality of the setting. This firmly constructed "ideal landscape" evokes a vision of nature that is gentle yet austere, grand but not awesome.

LANFRANCO; DOMENICHINO. The seeds of the reaction against Carracci's classicism were to be found within his own studio. The way was led by Giovanni Lanfranco (1582–1647), a native of Parma who worked for a while under Carracci. His *Annunciation* (fig. 17-8) unites Correggio's colorism with Caravaggio's drama. The result is an emotional style that signals the arrival of the High Baroque. Lanfranco's expressive intensity was the very opposite of the measured economy of Domenichino (1581–1641), Carracci's favorite pupil, who thought out every gesture and expression with impressive logic. Today, however, Domenichino is remembered more for his paintings of sweetly lyrical female figures, such as *St. Cecilia* (fig. 17-9), the patron saint of music. Inspired by Raphael, this subject inaugurates a long line of successors through the Rococo.

RENI; GUERCINO. Lanfranco won out over Domenichino in fresco decoration, where the main development of Baroque painting was to take place through the 1630s. Their rivalry was repeated by two other pupils of the Carracci: Guido Reni (1575–1642) and Guercino (Giovanni Francesco Barbieri; 1591–1666). Reni, who collaborated with Lanfranco for several years, exercised a widespread influence early on (Domenichino may have known Raphael's painting of St. Cecilia through a copy by Reni) and eventually assumed leadership of the Bolognese school. Guercino succeeded Reni upon his death, but only after making major concessions to his refined style.

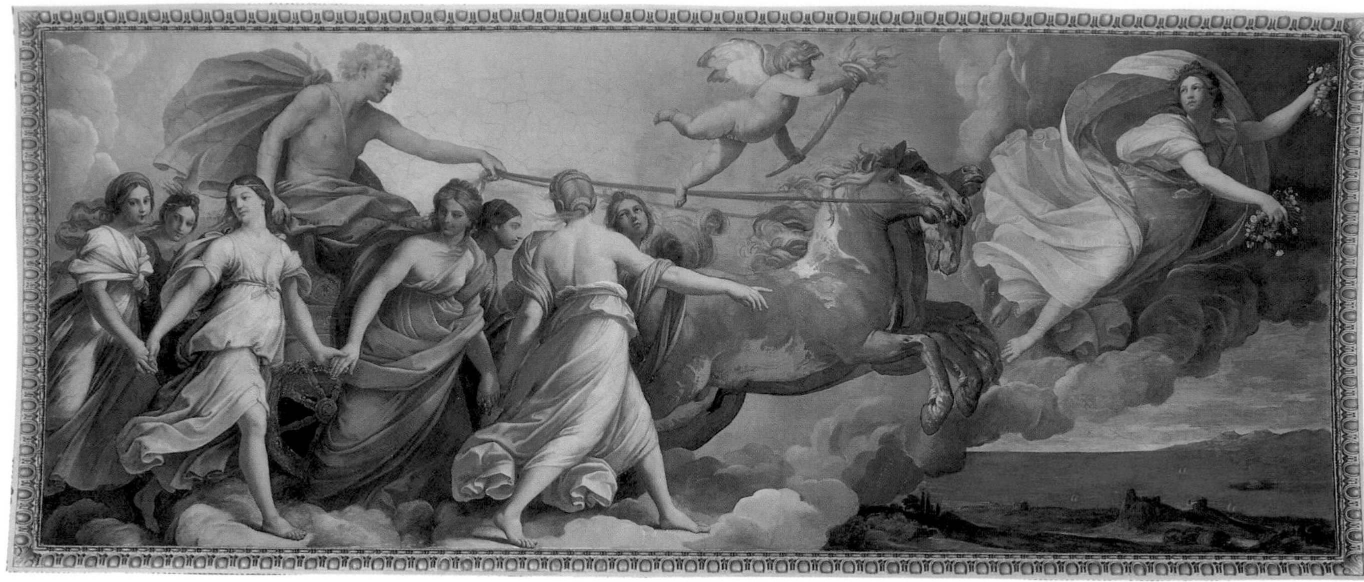

17-10. Guido Reni. *Aurora.* 1613. Ceiling fresco. Casino Rospigliosi, Rome

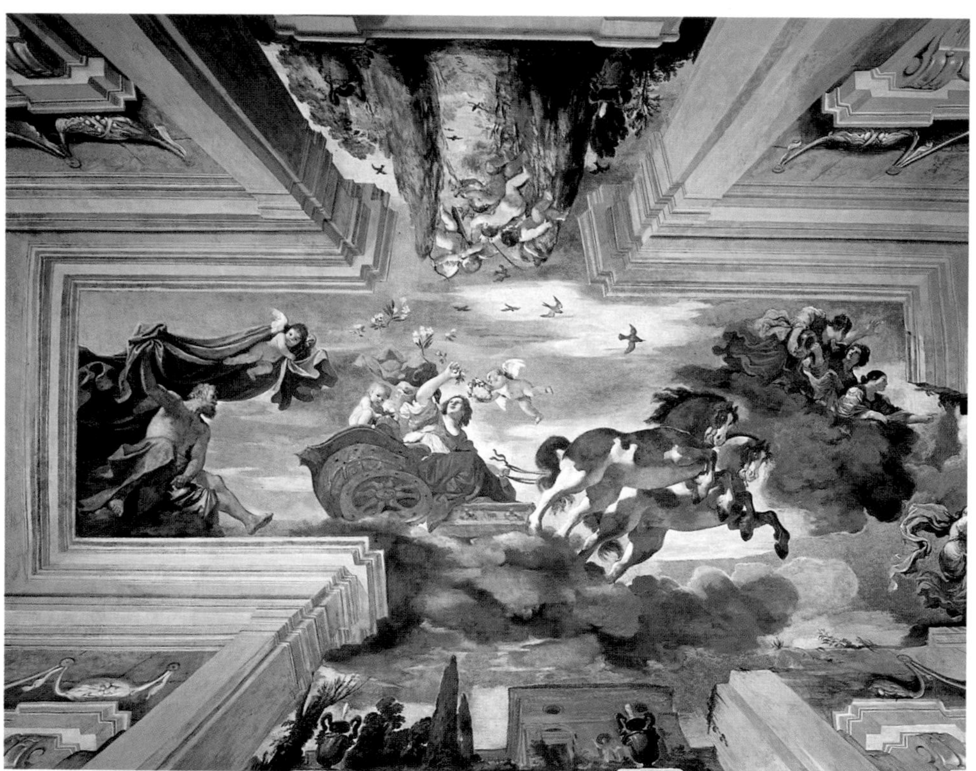

17-11. Guercino. *Aurora.* 1621–23. Ceiling fresco. Villa Ludovisi, Rome

To artists who were inspired by it, the Farnese Gallery seemed to offer two alternatives. Using the Raphaelesque style of the mythological panels, they could arrive at a deliberate, "official" classicism; or they could take their cue from the illusionism of the framework. The approach varied according to personal style and the conditions imposed by the site. Among the earliest examples of the first alternative is Reni's ceiling fresco *Aurora* (fig. 17-10), which shows Apollo in his chariot (the Sun) led by Aurora (Dawn). Here grace becomes the pursuit of perfect beauty. The relieflike design would seem like little more than a pallid reflection of High Renaissance art were it not for the glowing and dramatic light, which gives it an emotional force that the figures alone could never achieve. Hence this style is called Baroque classicism to distinguish it from all earlier forms of classicism, no matter how much it may be indebted to them.

The *Aurora* ceiling (fig. 17-11) painted less than ten years later by Guercino is the very opposite of Reni's. Here architectural perspective, combined with the pictorial illusionism of Correggio and the intense light and color of Titian, converts the entire surface into one limitless space, in which the figures sweep past as if driven by the winds. With this work, Guercino started what became a flood of similar visions characteristic of the High Baroque after 1630.

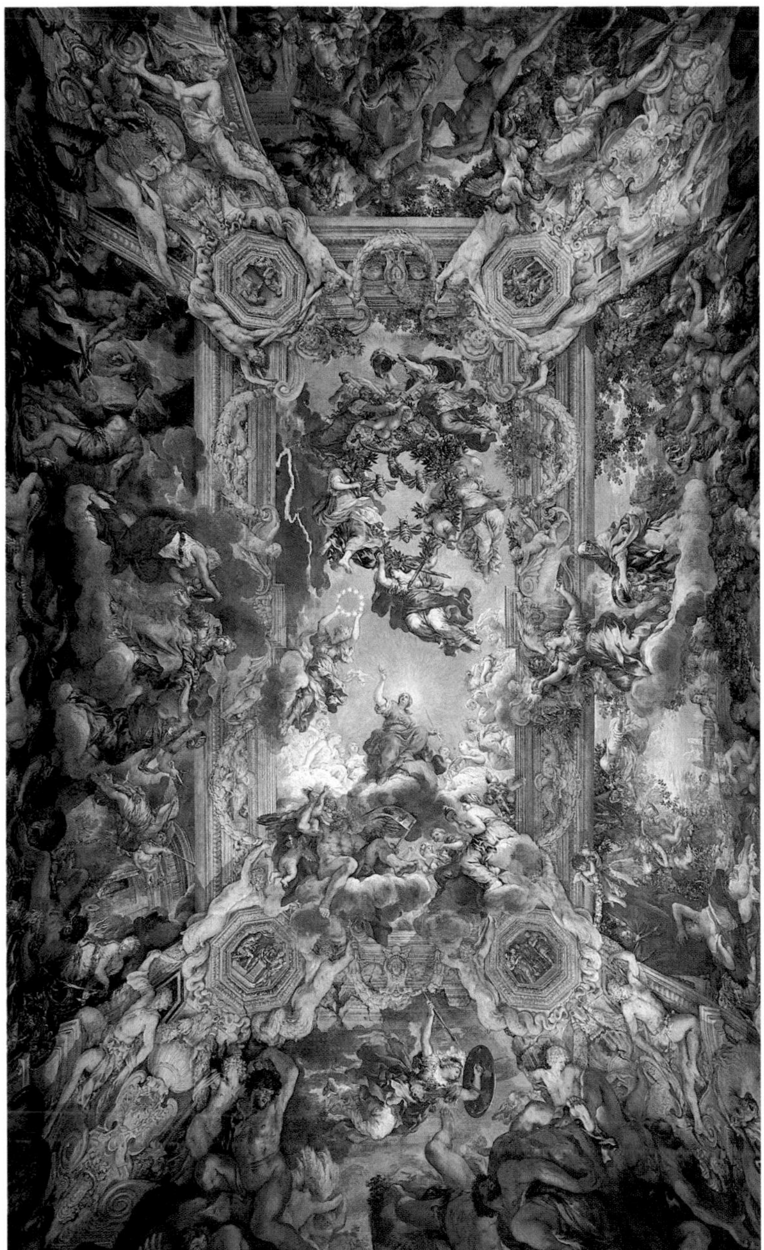

17-12. Pietro da Cortona. *Glorification of the Reign of Urban VIII.* 1633–39. Portion of ceiling fresco. Palazzo Barberini, Rome

DA CORTONA. The most overpowering of these illusionistic ceilings is the fresco by Pietro da Cortona (1596–1669) in the great hall of the Barberini Palace in Rome. This enormous painting glorifies the reign of the Barberini pope, Urban VIII (fig. 17-12), in the form of a complex allegory. As in the Farnese Gallery, the ceiling area is subdivided by a painted framework that simulates architecture and sculpture, but beyond it we now see the unbounded sky, as in Guercino's *Aurora.* Clusters of figures, perched on clouds or soaring freely, swirl above as well as below this framework. They create a dual illusion: some figures appear to hover inside the hall, close to our heads, while others recede into the distance. The effect is very similar to that of a domed ceiling painted by Lanfranco in Rome nearly a decade earlier, which was based directly on Correggio's *The Assumption of the Virgin* (see fig. 14-17).

Cortona's frescoes were the focal point for the rift between the High Baroque and Baroque classicism that grew out of the Farnese ceiling. The classicists asserted that art serves a moral purpose and must observe the principles of clarity, unity, and decorum. And, supported by a tradition based on Horace's adage *ut pictura poesis* (see page 432), they maintained that painting should follow the example of tragic poetry in conveying meaning through a minimum of figures whose movements, gestures, and expressions can be easily read. Cortona, though not anticlassical, presented the case for art as epic poetry, with many actors and episodes that expand on the central theme and create a magnificent effect. He was also the first to argue that art has a sensuous appeal that exists as an end in itself.

Although it took place largely on a theoretical level, the debate over illusionistic ceiling painting involved more than opposing approaches to telling a story and expressing ideas in art. The issue lay at the very heart of the Baroque. Illusionism allowed artists to overcome the apparent contradictions of the era by fusing separate

BAROQUE MUSIC IN ITALY

The most important contribution of the Baroque to music and theater was the invention of opera, which united all the theatrical elements of the period into a spectacular whole. It began modestly enough as a humanist exercise in Florence. Following the suggestion of Girolamo Mei of Rome, members of the Camerata of Florence, so called because it met *in camera* (behind closed doors) at the palace of Count Giorgio Bardi, set out to re-create ancient Greek drama, which they wrongly believed had been sung throughout a performance. Around 1590, Vincenzo Galilei (c. 1520–1591), the father of the astronomer Galileo, issued a polemic attacking the vocal counterpoint of madrigals as impersonal and artificial because it did not adhere to the Greek unity of text and music. Vincenzo experimented with monodies—short, dramatic monologues with continuo accompaniment—as part of an attempt to rediscover the power of music to move the soul. Along with the intermezzi that were performed between the acts of comedies, they were the direct forerunners of Baroque opera (short for *opera in musica,* "work in music"). The first opera was *Dafne,* produced privately in 1598 with a *libretto* (text) by Ottavio Rinuccini (1562–1621) and music mostly by Jacopo Peri (1561–1633). It was followed by *Euridice* from the same team, with additional arias by Giulio Caccini (c. 1546–1618), which was performed in 1600 in honor of the marriage of Henry IV and Marie de' Medici. Later that year and in 1601, Caccini and Peri, who were singers and professional rivals, published separate versions of the opera. Despite its limitations, the new declamatory style, called representative or theatrical style, made an extraordinary impression on listeners, and it was to remain the basis of classical opera in both Italy and France well into the eighteenth century.

Opera might nevertheless have remained of little more than antiquarian interest had it not been for Claudio Monteverdi (1567–1643). He has aptly been described as the "last great madrigalist and the first great opera composer." His *Orfeo,* produced in 1607 at Mantua with a libretto by Alessandro Striggio, enlarged the story of *Euridice* into the standard five acts demanded by the Roman poet Horace while increasing the variety of vocal music and giving a greater role to the instrumental accompaniment. Monteverdi was openly experimental. He was acutely aware of the conflict between the earlier style of the Netherlanders and the later Italian madrigalists such as Carlo Gesualdo (see page 516), and he fended off attacks by saying that he was working in an entirely new vein so that none of the old rules applied.

From then on, music took precedence over words in opera, which often emphasized extreme emotional states of mind (*affetti*) through violent contrasts, as did Baroque art. The future of the new form lay in Rome and Venice, which opened the first public opera house in 1637. Operas soon became wildly popular, not only in Italy but throughout Europe, and everyone vied for the services of the leading Italians. After 1650 the court in Vienna became the main center of theater and opera. Its zenith came with *The Golden Apple,* a huge spectacle staged there in 1668 to celebrate the wedding of Emperor Leopold I and the Infanta Margarita of

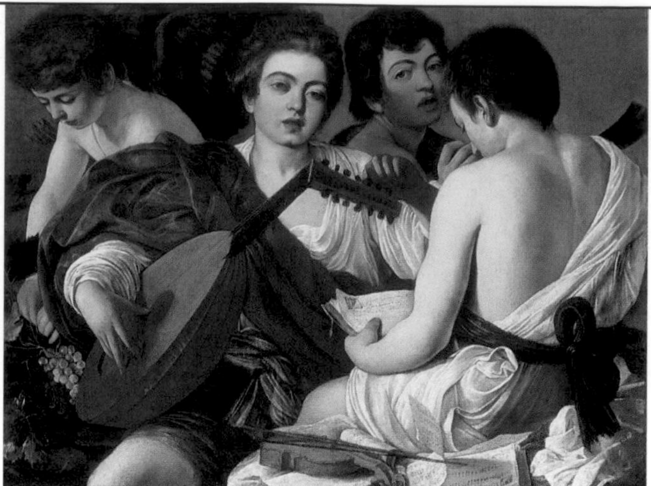

Caravaggio. *The Musicians.* c. 1595. Oil on canvas, 36¼ x 46⅝" (92.1 x 118.4 cm). The Metropolitan Museum of Art, New York

ROGERS FUND, 1952

Spain, with music by Pietro Antonio Cesti (1623–1669) and scenery by Ludovico Burnacini (1636–1707). The public wanted new operas as soon as they could be mounted, while star singers required virtuoso arias, solos to which they often added florid ornamentation to showcase their talents. Combined with the increasing emphasis on spectacle, these demands conspired to dilute opera as a dramatic form while the beauty of the music itself grew. The impact of opera was pervasive. Although it generally tried to adhere to tradition, even church music became operatic in the solo cantatas and oratorios of Giacomo Carissimi (1605–1674). These three vocal forms reached maturity in the compositions of Alessandro Scarlatti (1660–1725), who worked in Naples and Rome, so that he holds a position analogous to that of Francesco Solimena in painting (see page 540). In addition to being the outstanding Italian opera composer of his time, Scarlatti wrote religious music of great beauty. He was the pivotal figure in late Italian Baroque music, comparable in importance to Jean-Baptiste Lully of France (see box page 580).

The Baroque was the first period in which instrumental music equaled vocal music in stature. While continuing the practice of imitating different dance types, it also began to mimic vocal style. The two approaches are exemplified in the trio sonatas of Arcangelo Corelli (1653–1713). His chamber sonatas use dance movements, while the church sonatas in principle do not, although they were in fact often mixed. Both employ two violins and a continuo consisting of a lower viol and a keyboard instrument. When expanded to a full string orchestra, the trio sonata became the *concerto grosso* (grand concerto), the most characteristic type of Baroque instrumental music, which began as overtures to and during Mass. Corelli alternated sprightly, dancelike movements with slow ones that have a uniquely plaintive, bittersweet quality similar to the laments in Monteverdi's madrigals. Virtuoso touches of ornamentation are treated discretely so as not to disrupt the singing line, which for the most part is kept well within the range of the human voice. Each movement generally has one or two alternating melodies developed in clear progressions that became the basis for modern harmony.

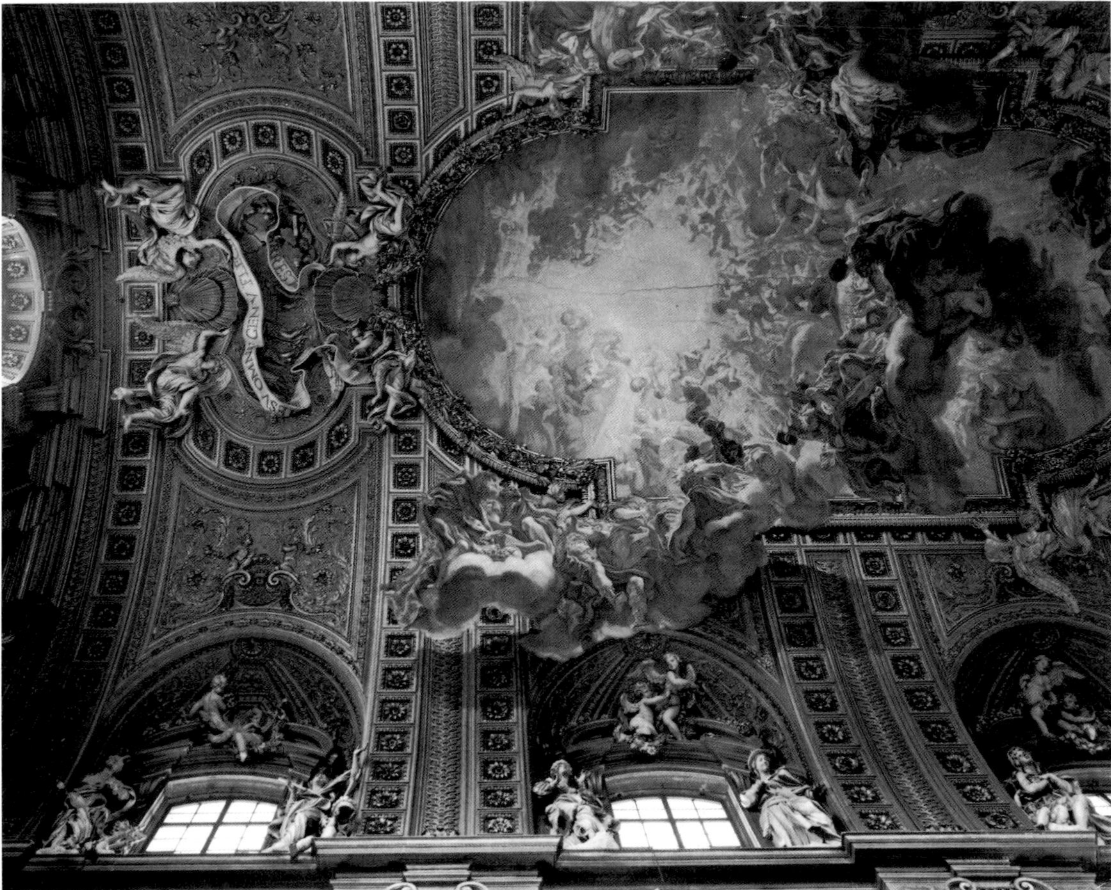

17-13. Giovanni Battista Gaulli. *Triumph of the Name of Jesus.* 1672–85. Ceiling fresco. Il Gesù, Rome

levels of reality into a pictorial unity of such overwhelming grandeur as to sweep aside any differences between them. Despite the intensity of the debate, in practice the two sides rarely came into conflict over easel paintings, where the differences between Cortona and Carracci's followers were not always so clear-cut. Surprisingly, Cortona found inspiration in Classical art and Raphael throughout his career. Nevertheless, the leader of the reaction against what were regarded as the excesses of the High Baroque was neither a fresco painter nor an Italian but a French artist living in Rome: Nicolas Poussin (see page 576), who, strangely enough, moved in the same antiquarian circle as Cortona early on but drew very different lessons from it.

IL GESÙ. It is a strange fact that few ceiling frescoes were painted after Cortona finished his *Glorification of the Reign of Urban VIII.* Ironically the new style of architecture fostered by Francesco Borromini and Guarino Guarini (see pages 542–45) provided few opportunities for adornment. But after 1670 such frescoes enjoyed a revival in older buildings, which reached its peak in the interior decoration of Il Gesù (fig. 17-13). Although his role in this case was only advisory, it is clear that the plan for this work must be by Gianlorenzo Bernini, the greatest sculptor–architect of the century (see below). At his suggestion, the commission for the ceiling frescoes went to Giovanni Battista Gaulli (1639–1709), his young protégé known as Baciccia. A talented assistant, Antonio Raggi (1624–1686), made the stucco sculpture. The program, which proved extraordinarily influential, is testimony to Bernini's imaginative daring. As in the Cornaro Chapel (see fig. 17-30), the ceil-

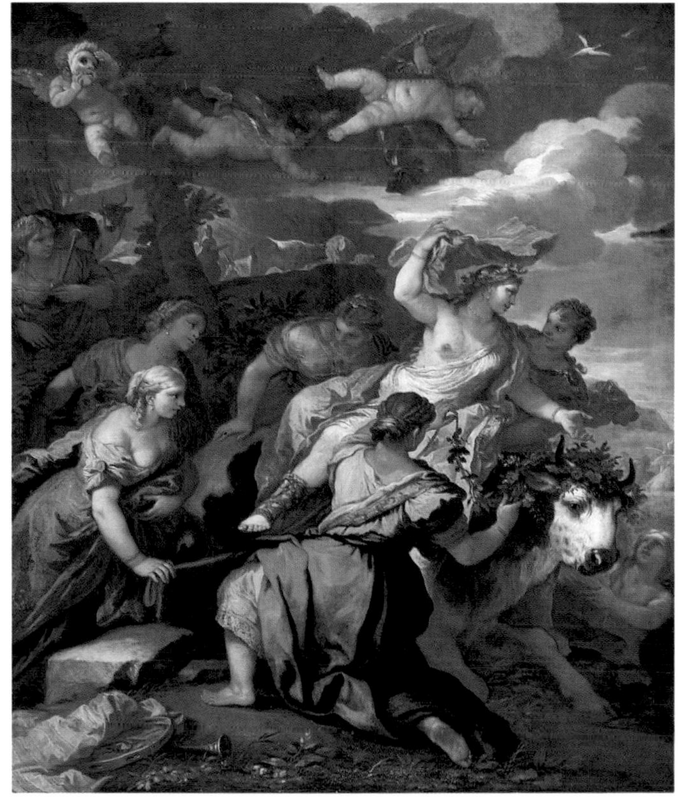

17-14. Luca Giordano. *The Abduction of Europa.* 1686. Oil on canvas, 7'5⅝" x 6'4¼" (2.27 x 1.93 m). Wadsworth Atheneum, Hartford, Connecticut

ELLA GALLUP SUMNER AND MARY CATLIN SUMNER COLLECTION

ing is treated as a single unit. The nave fresco, with its contrasts of light and dark that suggest a mystical vision, spills dramatically over its frame, then turns into sculptured figures. Here Baroque illusionism achieves its ultimate expression. [See Primary Sources. no. 54, page 620.]

GIORDANO. The greatest representative of the Late Baroque was the Neapolitan painter Luca Giordano (1634–1705). He began as an imitator of his teacher Ribera but became the successor to Pietro da Cortona as the leading decorative painter in Italy. Legendary for his speed, Giordano was a virtuoso whose remarkable facility resulted in a vast and varied output. *The Abduction of Europa* (fig. 17-14) shows his spontaneous approach at its best. The composition is based on one by Veronese that also was to inspire François Boucher (see page 596). The painting shares the graceful style of Cortona, but instead of the latter's blond palette, it favors a rich tonalism inherited from Lanfranco, who worked in Naples during the 1630s. Although he never fully accepted colorism, Giordano set the stage for the great Venetian painters of the eighteenth century, even in his professional life-style, which was largely spent on the move. He became the first in a line of great Italian artists, culminating in Tiepolo (see page 608), to be called to the Spanish court.

Gaulli and Giordano mark the final flowering of Baroque exuberance. By this time, the pendulum had swung in the opposite direction. Italian painting during the third quarter of the seventeenth century was marked by a conservative blend of the High Baroque and Baroque classicism. This led to an academic style that flourished in Rome and Naples, which were then closely linked. It was developed chiefly by Carlo Maratta (1625–1713) of Rome, the most admired artist of his day, and Francesco Solimena (1657–1747), Giordano's successor in Naples. Maratta may be regarded as a less doctrinaire counterpart to Charles Lebrun in France (see page 579). In contrast to his rival Gaulli (see fig. 17-13), he wanted to revive the grand manner of the Carracci by emphasizing individual figures through a clear, even light without abandoning Cortona's color and drama. As might be expected, the results of such a compromise were generally not impressive.

ARCHITECTURE IN ITALY

MADERNO. In architecture, the beginnings of the Baroque style cannot be defined as clearly as in painting. Carlo Maderno (1556–1629) was the most talented young architect to emerge in the vast ecclesiastical building program that got under way in Rome toward the end of the sixteenth century. In 1603 he was given the task of completing, at long last, the church of St. Peter's. Pope Clement VIII had decided to add a nave and narthex to the west end of Michelangelo's building (see fig. 13-28), thereby converting it into a basilica. The change of plan, which had already been proposed by Raphael in 1514, made it possible to link St. Peter's with the Vatican Palace to the right of the church (fig. 17-15). Maderno's design for the facade follows the pattern established by Michelangelo for the exterior of the church. It consists of a colossal order supporting an attic, but with a dramatic emphasis on the portals. The effect can only be described as a crescendo that builds from the corners toward the center. The spacing of the supports becomes closer, pilasters turn into columns, and the facade wall projects step-by-step.

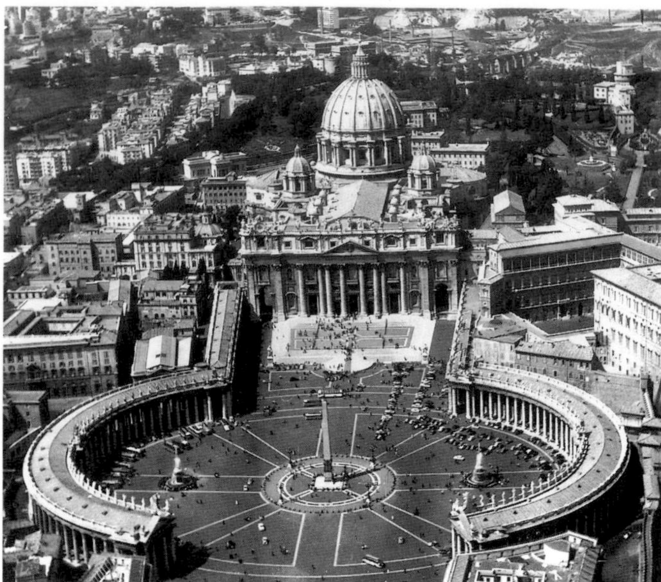

17-15. Aerial view of St. Peter's, Rome. Nave and facade by Carlo Maderno, 1607–15; colonnade by Gianlorenzo Bernini, designed 1657

This quickened rhythm had been hinted at a generation earlier in Giacomo della Porta's facade of Il Gesù (see fig. 14-31). Maderno made it the dominant principle of his facade designs, not only for St. Peter's but for smaller churches as well. In the process, he replaced the traditional concept of the church facade as one continuous wall surface, which was not yet challenged by the facade of Il Gesù, with the "facade-in-depth," dynamically related to the open space before it. The possibilities of this new treatment were not to be exhausted until 150 years later.

BERNINI. After Maderno's death in 1629, Gianlorenzo Bernini (1598–1680) was appointed to succeed him at St. Peter's. He molded the open space in front of the facade into a magnificent oval piazza. This "forecourt," which imposed a degree of unity on the sprawling Vatican complex, acts as an immense atrium framed by colonnades that Bernini himself likened to the motherly, all-embracing arms of the Church. The device itself is not new. It had been used at private villas designed by Vignola for the Farneses in the 1550s; but these were, in effect, belvederes opening onto formal gardens. What is novel is the idea of placing it at the main entrance to a building. Also new is the huge scale. For sheer impressiveness, this integration of the building with such a grandiose setting can be compared only with the ancient Roman sanctuary at Palestrina (see fig. 7-6).

The piazza can be thought of as a continuation on the exterior of the decoration program at St. Peter's that occupied Bernini at intervals during most of his long career. The enormous size of St. Peter's made the treatment of its interior a difficult task. How could its vastness be related to the human scale and given a measure of emotional warmth? Bernini began by designing the bronze canopy for the main altar under the dome (fig. 17-16). The tabernacle is a splendid fusion of architecture and sculpture. Four ornate, spiral-shaped columns support an upper platform. At its corners are stat-

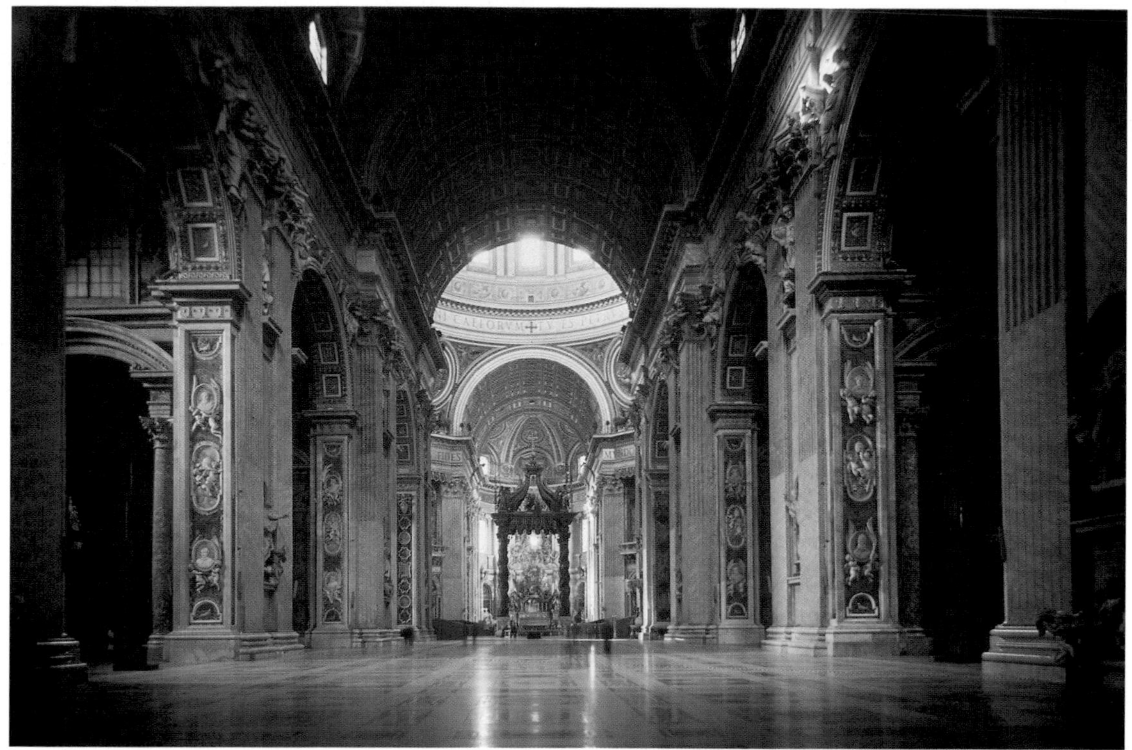

17-16. Carlo Maderno. Nave, with Bernini's Tabernacle (1624–33) at crossing, St. Peter's, Rome

ues of angels and vigorously curved scrolls, which raise high a cross above a golden orb, the symbol of the victory of Christianity over the pagan world. The entire structure is so alive with expressive energy that it strikes us as the epitome of Baroque style. Yet its most impressive feature, the corkscrew columns, had been invented in late antiquity and even employed on a much smaller scale in the old basilica of St. Peter's. Thus Bernini could claim the best possible precedent for his own use of the motif. This is not the only instance of a kinship between Baroque and ancient art. Several monuments of Roman architecture of the second and third centuries A.D. seem to anticipate the style of the seventeenth (see figs. 7-23 and 7-24).

CORTONA. Bernini considered himself Michelangelo's successor as both architect and sculptor. And like Michelangelo, he sometimes attacked rivals out of professional and personal jealousy. Thus he was harshly critical of Pietro da Cortona, who established himself as one of the leading architects in Rome with the church of Ss. Luca e Martina, fig. 17–17. Cortona, the son of a stone mason, began his career as an architect and turned to painting only later. He had intended to renovate the existing church of the Academy of St. Luke, the artist's guild, at his own expense to provide a tomb for himself. When the remains of St. Martina were discovered, the project came under the patronage of Cardinal Francesco Barberini, who ordered it completely rebuilt in 1635. The two-tiered facade, with its submerged columns and ornate dome, recalls Mannerist architecture by followers of Michelangelo in Florence, where Cortona began his career (compare fig. 13-23). The massing of elements, however, follows the example of Della Porta and Maderno, and the overall effect is strikingly Baroque. The facade has all the theatricality of a stage design. It disguises the plan of the church, a Greek

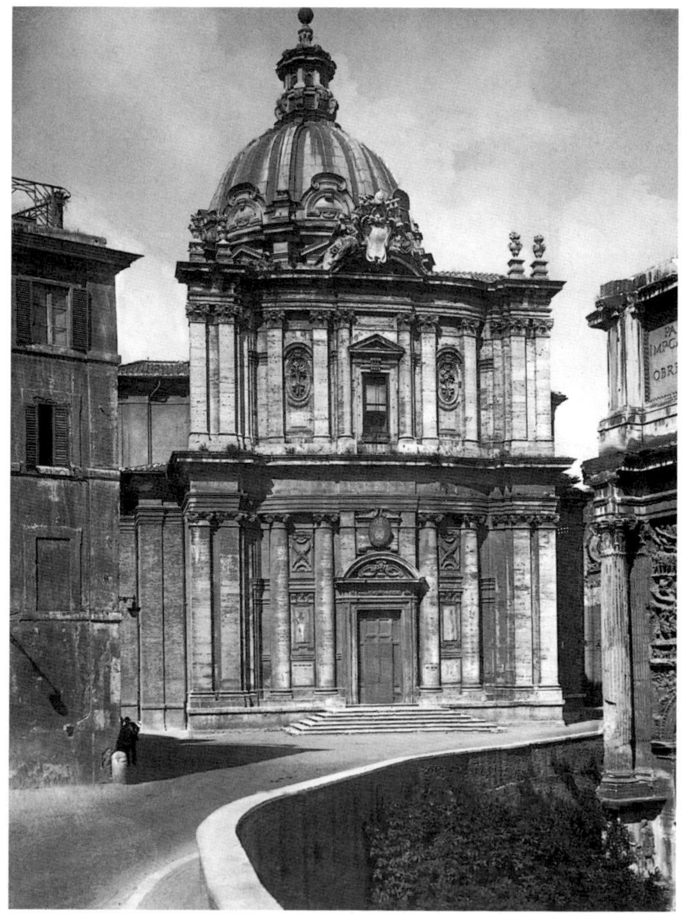

17-17. Pietro da Cortona. Facade of Ss. Martina e Luca, Rome. c. 1635–50

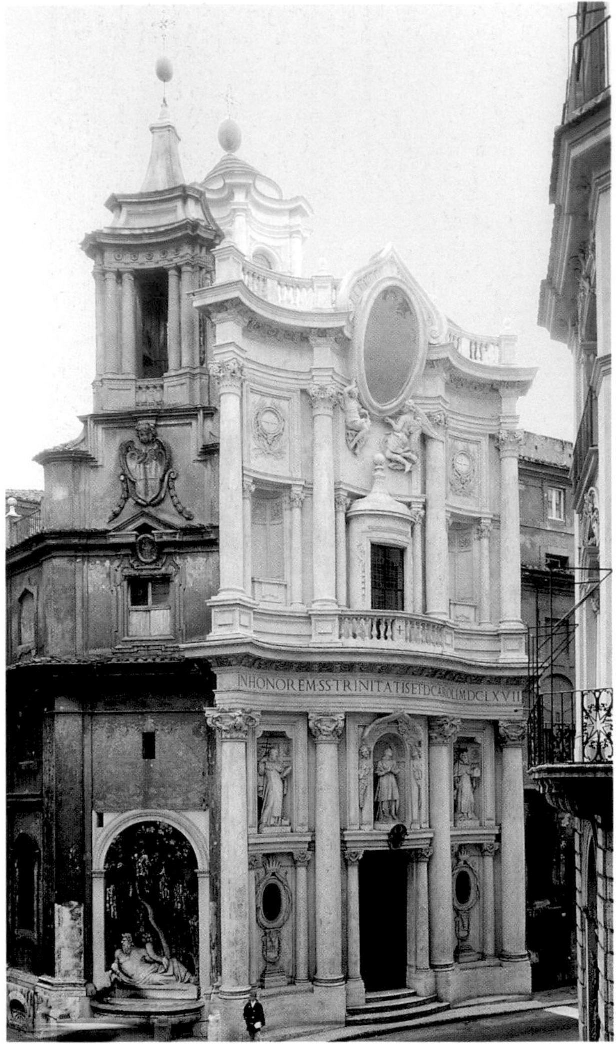

17-18. Francesco Borromini. Facade of S. Carlo alle Quattro Fontane, Rome. 1665–67

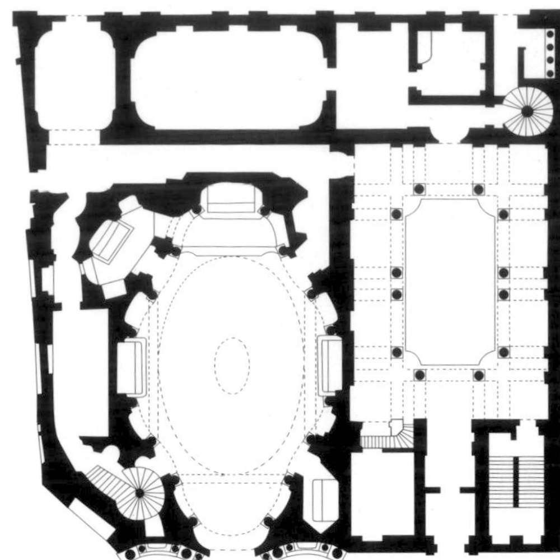

17-19. Plan of S. Carlo alle Quattro Fontane. Begun 1638

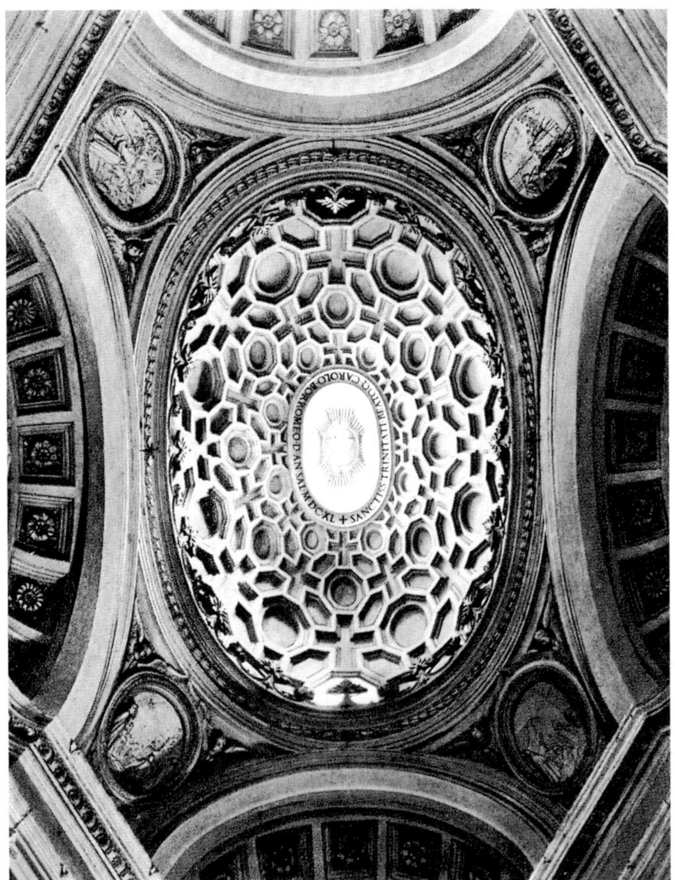

17-20. Dome of S. Carlo alle Quattro Fontane

cross with apses on each arm, although the grouping of the columns and pilasters is a preview of the interior. Moreover, the surface bows outward, showing a new malleability that was to become a characteristic feature of Italian Baroque architecture. Indeed, Cortona occupies a place of central importance. His S. Maria della Pace, begun in 1656, influenced the only major church Bernini built entirely himself, S. Andrea al Quirinale of two years later. And, as we shall see, he was to have a major impact on Borromini.

BORROMINI. As a personality, Bernini represents a type we first met among the artists of the Early Renaissance, a self-assured person of the world. His greatest rival in architecture, Francesco Borromini (1599–1667), who also started out at St. Peter's as an assistant to Maderno and then to Bernini himself, was the opposite: a secretive and emotionally unstable genius who died by suicide. The Baroque heightened the tension between the two types. The contrast between the two masters would be evident from their works alone, even without the accounts by their contemporaries. Both exemplify the climax of Baroque architecture in Rome, yet Bernini's design for the colonnade of St. Peter's is dramatically simple and unified, while Borromini's structures are extravagantly complex. Whereas the surfaces of Bernini's interiors are extremely rich, Borromini's, like Cortona's, are surprisingly plain. They rely on the architect's phenomenal grasp of spatial geometry to achieve their spiritual effects. Bernini himself agreed with those who denounced Borromini for flagrantly disregarding the classical tradition, enshrined in Renaissance theory and practice, that architecture must reflect the proportions of the human body.

In Borromini's first major project, the church of S. Carlo alle Quattro Fontane (figs. 17-18–17-20), it is the syntax, not the vocabulary, that is new and disquieting. The ceaseless play of concave and convex surfaces makes the entire structure seem elastic,

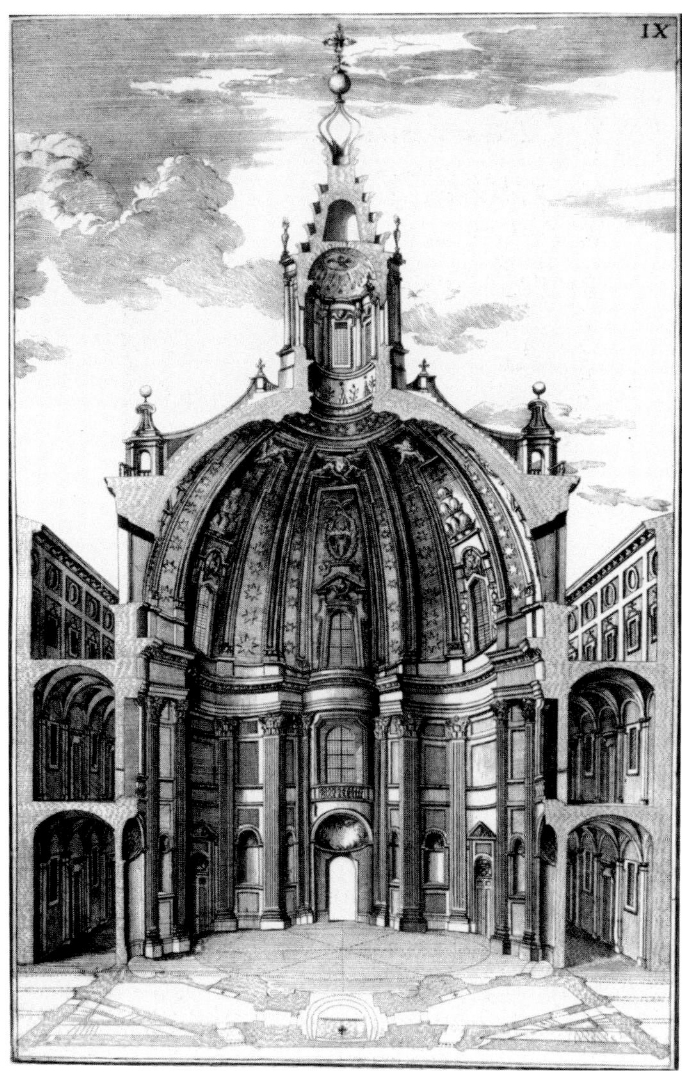

17-21. Francesco Borromini. Section, S. Ivo, Rome. Begun 1642

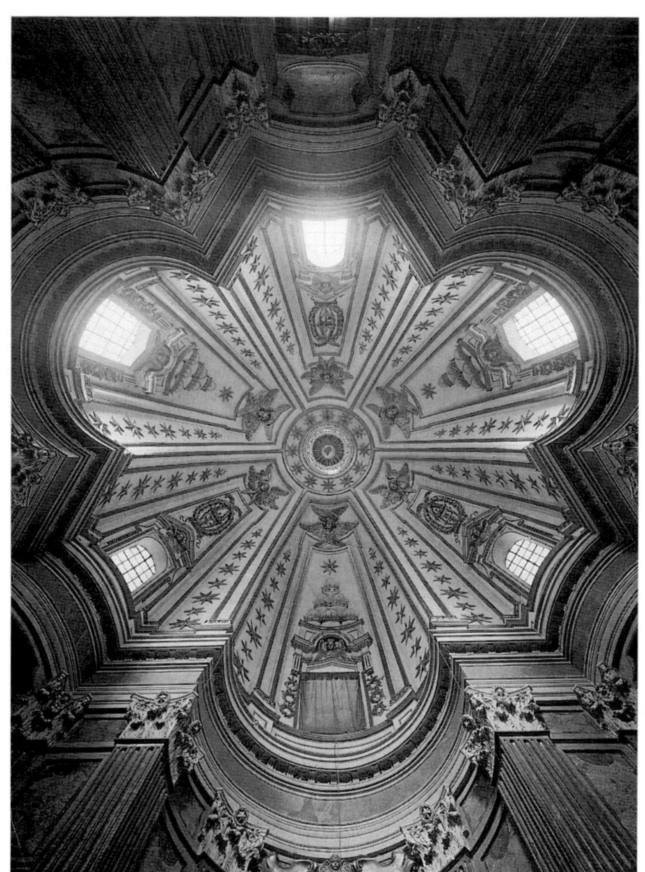

17-22. Dome of S. Ivo

"pulled out of shape" by pressures that no previous building could have withstood. The plan is a pinched oval that suggests a distended and half-melted Greek cross, as if it had been drawn on rubber. The inside of the coffered dome, too, looks "stretched": if the tension were relaxed, it would snap back to normal. The facade, designed almost 30 years later, shows the influence of Cortona's Ss. Martina e Luca, but here the pressures and counterpressures reach their maximum intensity. Borromini merges architecture and sculpture in a way that must have shocked Bernini. No such union had been attempted since Gothic art. S. Carlo alle Quattro Fontane established Borromini's fame. "Nothing similar," wrote the head of the religious order for which the church was built, "can be found anywhere in the world. This is attested by the foreigners who . . . try to procure copies of the plan. We have been asked for them by Germans, Flemings, Frenchmen, Italians, Spaniards, and even Indians."

The design of Borromini's next church, S. Ivo (figs. 17-21 and 17-22), is more compact and equally daring. Its plan, a star-hexagon, belongs to the central type. Here Borromini may have been thinking of octagonal structures, such as S. Vitale, Ravenna (compare figs. 8-25–8-28), but the result is completely novel. The space is not subdivided into a tall, domed "nave" ringed by

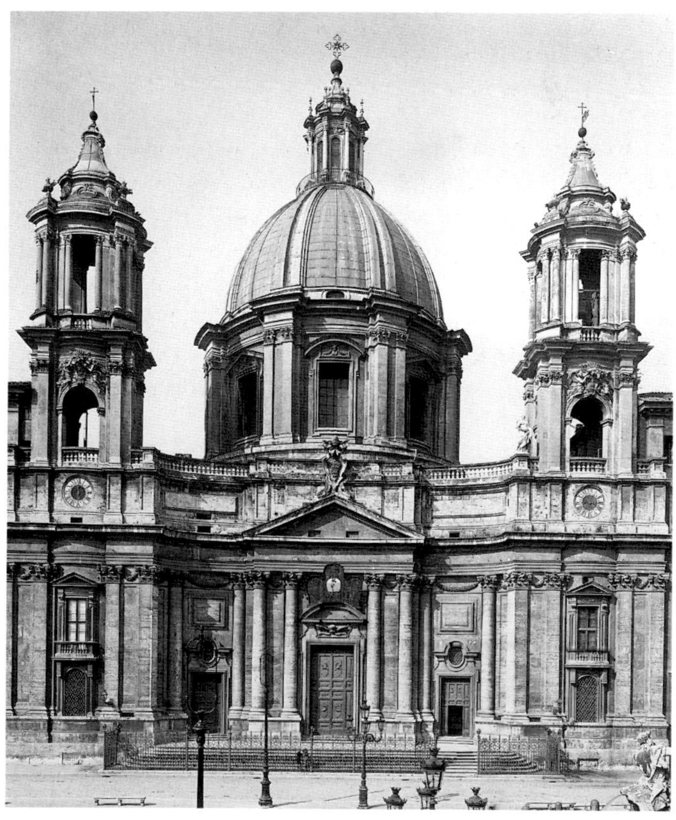

17-23 Francesco Borromini. S. Agnese in Piazza Navona, Rome. 1653–63

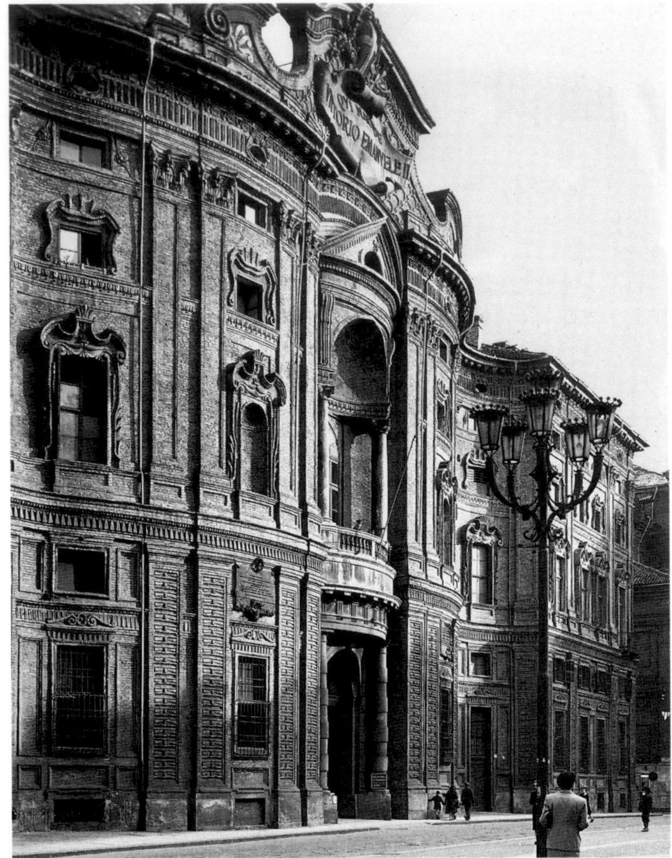

17-24. Guarino Guarini. Facade of Palazzo Carignano, Turin. Begun 1679

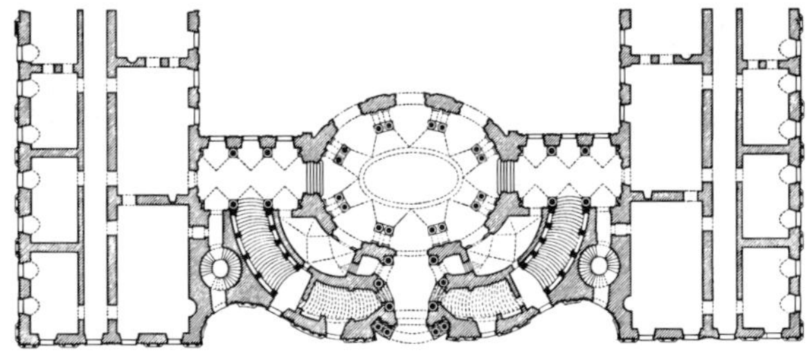

17-25. Plan of Palazzo Carignano

an ambulatory or chapels. Instead, Borromini covered all of it with one great dome that continues the star-hexagon pattern up to the circular base of the lantern. The entire design is again dominated by a concave-convex rhythm, which focuses our attention on the altar.

A third project by Borromini is of special interest as a High Baroque critique of St. Peter's. There was one problem that Maderno had been unable to solve: although his facade forms an impressive unit with Michelangelo's dome when seen from a distance, the dome is gradually hidden by the facade as we approach the church. Borromini designed the facade of S. Agnese in Piazza Navona (fig. 17-23) with this conflict in mind. Its lower part is adapted from the facade of St. Peter's, but it curves inward, so that the dome (a tall, slender version of Michelangelo's) functions as the upper part of the facade. The dramatic juxtaposition of concave and convex, so characteristic of Borromini, is emphasized by the two towers, which form a monumental group with the dome. Such towers were also originally planned for St. Peter's by Bramante (see fig. 13-10) and by Bernini, but they would have been freestanding. Once again Borromini joins Gothic and Renaissance features—the two-tower facade and the dome—into a remarkably "elastic" compound.

GUARINI. The new ideas introduced by Borromini were to be exploited not in Rome but in Turin, the capital of Savoy, which became the creative center of Baroque architecture in Italy toward the end of the seventeenth century. It was in 1666 that Guarino Guarini (1624–1683), Borromini's most brilliant successor, was called to Turin as an engineer and mathematician by the Duke of Savoy. Guarini was a Theatine monk whose genius was grounded in philosophy and mathematics. His design for the facade of the Palazzo Carignano (figs. 17-24 and 17-25) repeats on a larger scale the undulating movement of S. Carlo alle Quattro Fontane (see

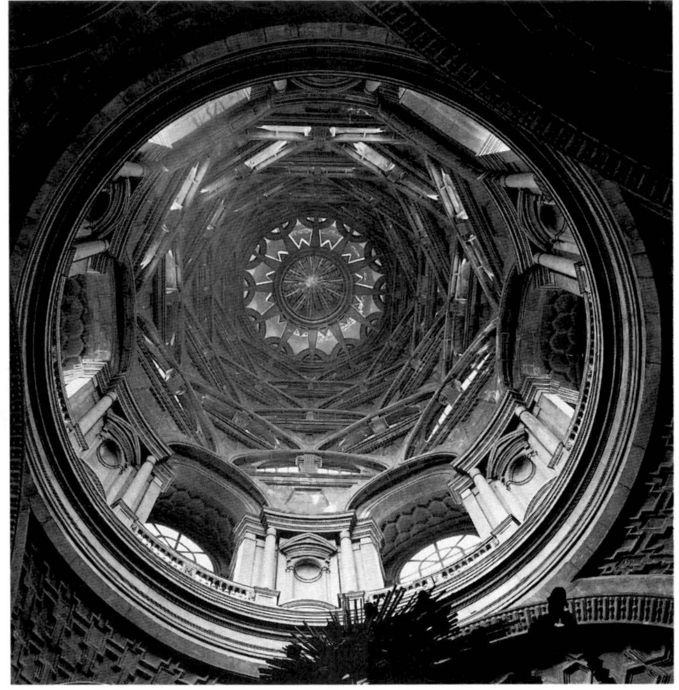

17-26. Guarino Guarini. Dome of Chapel of the Holy Shroud, Turin Cathedral. 1668–94

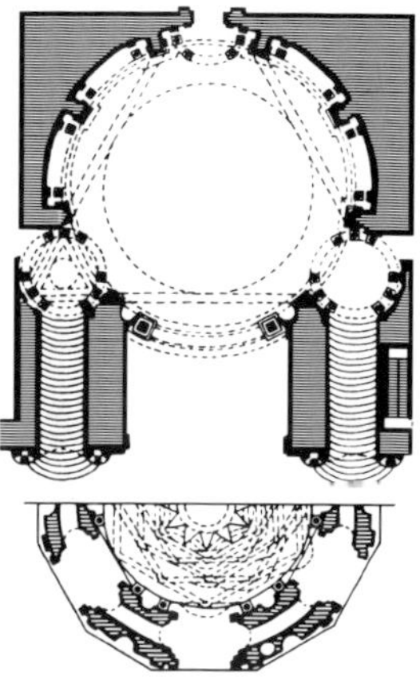

17-27. Plan of the Chapel of the Holy Shroud and of the dome

fig. 17-17), using a highly individual vocabulary. Incredibly, the exterior of the building is entirely of brick, down to the last detail, as was Borromini's Oratory of S. Filippo Neri (1637–40), which Guarini had seen during his novitiate in Rome in 1639–47.

Even more extraordinary is Guarini's dome of the Chapel of the Holy Shroud, a round structure attached to Turin Cathedral (figs. 17-26 and 17-27). The tall drum, with alternating windows and tabernacles, consists of familiar Borrominian motifs. Beyond it we enter a realm of pure illusion. The interior surface of the dome of S. Carlo alle Quattro Fontane, though dematerialized by light and a honeycomb of fanciful coffers, was still recognizable (see fig. 17-20). But here the surface has disappeared in a maze of ribs, inspired by Moorish architecture, which Guarini had studied while working in Messina, Sicily, during 1660–62. As a result, we find ourselves staring into a huge kaleidoscope. Above this seemingly endless funnel of space hovers the dove of the Holy Spirit within a 12-pointed star.

Guarini's dome retains the symbolic meaning of the Dome of Heaven (see page 415; see figs. 12-43–12-45). However, the objective harmony of the Renaissance has become subjective, a compelling experience of the infinite. If Borromini's style at times suggests a fusion of Gothic and Renaissance, Guarini takes the next step. In his writings, he contrasts the "muscular" architecture of the ancients with the effect of Gothic churches, which appear to stand only by means of some kind of miracle, and he expresses equal admiration for both. This attitude corresponds exactly to his own practice. By using the most advanced mathematical techniques of his day, he achieved miracles even greater than those of the seemingly weightless Gothic structures. He thus helped to pave the way for Soufflot and the rationalist movement in the next century (see pages 653–55).

SCULPTURE IN ITALY

BERNINI. We have already encountered Gianlorenzo Bernini as an architect. It is now time to consider him as a sculptor, although the two aspects are never far apart in his work. [See Primary Sources, no. 56, pages 621–22.] He was trained by his father, Pietro Bernini (1562–1629), a sculptor of considerable ability who worked in Florence, Naples, and Rome. Thus his work was a direct outgrowth of Mannerist sculpture in many respects, but these do not explain his revolutionary qualities.

As in the tabernacle for St. Peter's (see fig. 17-16), we can often see a strong relationship between Bernini's sculpture and that of antiquity. If we compare Bernini's *David* (fig. 17-28) with Michelangelo's (see fig. 13-12) and ask which is closer to the Pergamum frieze or *The Laocoön Group* (see figs. 5-74 and 5-76), our vote must go to Bernini. His figure shares with Hellenistic works that unison of body and spirit, of motion and emotion, that Michelangelo so consciously avoids. This does not mean that Bernini is more classical than Michelangelo. It shows, rather, that both the Baroque and the High Renaissance accepted the authority of ancient art, but each was inspired by a different aspect of antiquity.

Bernini's *David* is in no sense an echo of *The Laocoön Group*. What makes it Baroque is the implied presence of Goliath. Unlike earlier statues of David, Bernini's is conceived not as a self-contained figure but as half of a pair, his entire action focused on his adversary. Did Bernini, we wonder, plan a statue of Goliath to complete the group? He never did, nor did he need to, for his *David* tells us clearly enough where *he* sees the enemy. Consequently, the space between David and his invisible opponent is charged with energy—it "belongs" to the statue.

Bernini's *David* shows us what distinguishes Baroque sculpture from that of the two preceding centuries: its new, active relationship with the space it inhabits. It rejects self-sufficiency in favor of the illusion of forces implied by the action of the statue. Because it so often presents an "invisible complement" (like the Goliath of Bernini's *David*), Baroque sculpture is a tour de force. It attempts to achieve essentially pictorial effects that were traditionally outside the province of sculpture. Such a charging of space with energy is, in fact, a key feature of Baroque art. Caravaggio had achieved it in his *St. Matthew,* with the aid of a sharply focused

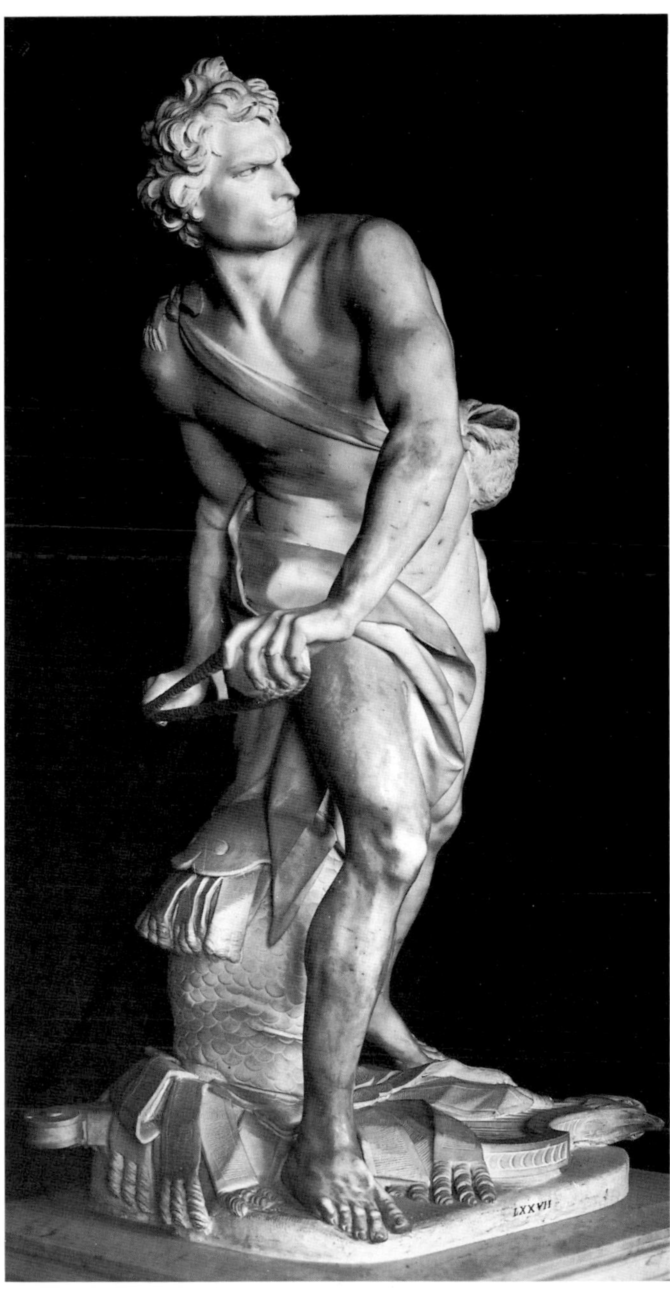

17-28. Gianlorenzo Bernini. *David.* 1623. Marble, lifesize. Galleria Borghese, Rome

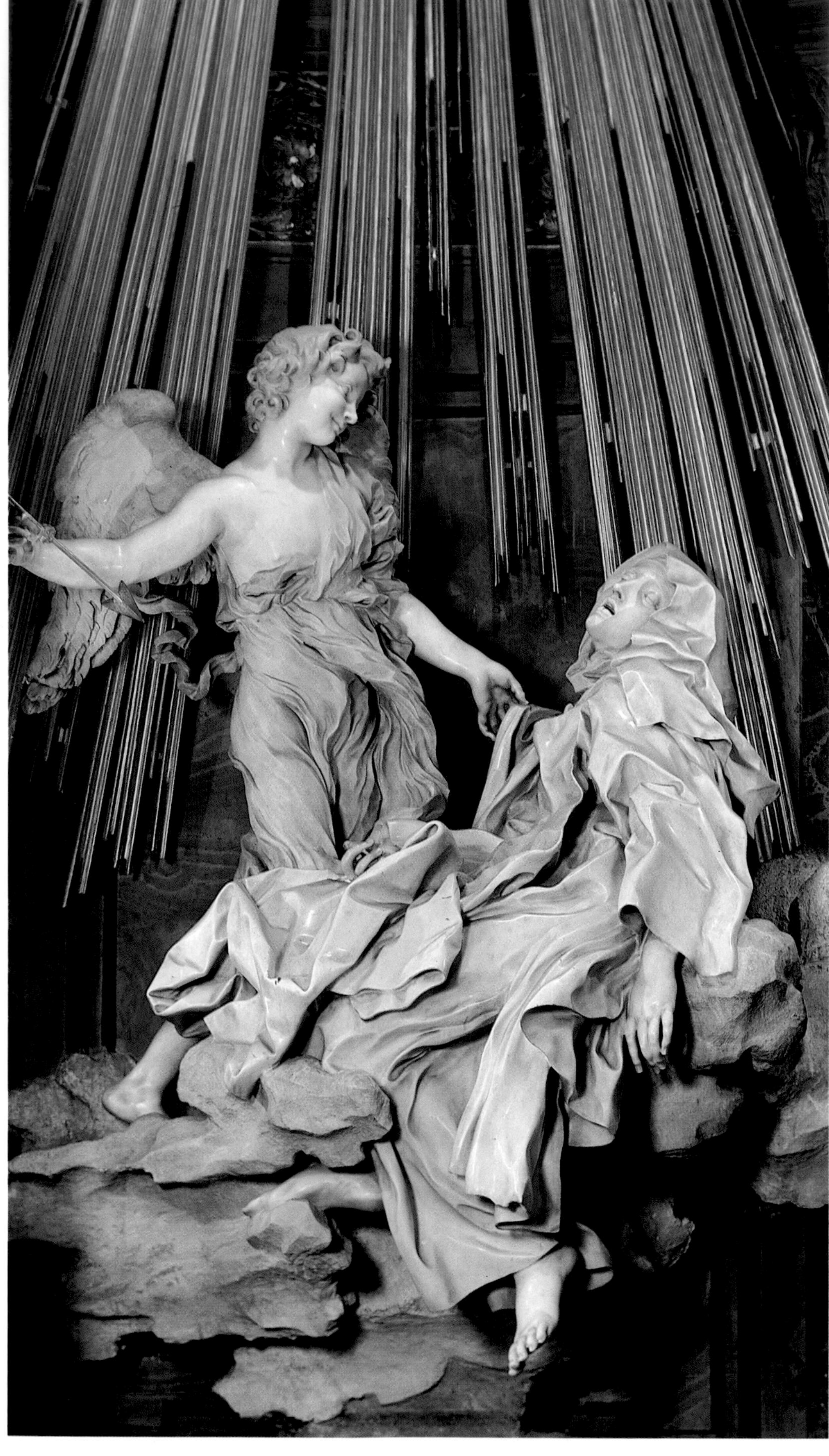

17-29. Gianlorenzo Bernini. *The Ecstasy of St. Theresa.* 1645–52. Marble, lifesize. Cornaro Chapel, Sta. Maria della Vittoria, Rome beam of light. Indeed, Baroque art does not make a sharp distinction between sculpture and painting. And as we have seen, the two may even be combined with architecture to form a compound illusion, like that of the stage.

In fact, Bernini had a passionate interest in the theater, and was an innovative scene designer. Thus he was at his best when he could merge architecture, sculpture, and painting in this way. His masterpiece in this vein is the Cornaro Chapel in the church of Sta. Maria della Vittoria containing the famous group called *The Ecstasy of St. Theresa* (fig. 17-29). Theresa of Avila, one of the great saints of the Counter-Reformation (see page 528), had described how an angel pierced her heart with a flaming golden arrow: "The pain was so great that I screamed aloud; but at the same time I felt such infinite sweetness that I wished the pain to last forever. It was not physical but psychic pain, although it affected the body as well to some degree. It was the sweetest caressing of the soul by God."

Bernini has made this visionary experience as sensuously real as Correggio's *Jupiter and Io* (see fig. 14-18). In a different context, the angel could be Cupid, and the saint's ecstasy is obvious. The two figures on their floating cloud are lit from a hidden window above so that they seem almost dematerialized. The viewer experiences them as visionary. The "invisible complement" here, less specific than David's but equally important, is the force that carries the figures toward Heaven, causing the turbulence of their drapery. Its divine nature is suggested by the golden rays, which come from a source high above the altar. In an illusionistic fresco by Guidebaldo Abbatini on the vault of the chapel, the glory of the heavens is revealed as a dazzling burst of light from which tumble clouds of jubilant angels (fig. 17-30). This celestial "explosion" gives force to the thrusts of the angel's arrow and makes the ecstasy of the saint believable.

To complete the illusion, Bernini even provides a built-in audience for his "stage." On the sides of the chapel are balconies resembling theater boxes that contain marble figures depicting members of the Cornaro family, who also witness the vision. Their space and ours are the same, and thus are part of everyday reality, while the saint's ecstasy, in its strongly framed niche, occupies a space that is real but beyond our reach. Finally, the ceiling fresco represents the infinite space of Heaven. We may recall that *The Burial of Count Orgaz* and its setting also form a whole that includes three levels of reality (see page 471). Yet there is a profound difference between the two chapels. El Greco's Mannerism evokes an ethereal vision in which only the stone slab of the sarcophagus is "real," in contrast to Bernini's Baroque theatricality, where the distinction nearly breaks down. It would be easy to dismiss *The Ecstasy of St. Theresa* as a theatrical display, but Bernini also was a devout Catholic who believed (as did Michelangelo) that he was inspired directly by God. Like the Spiritual Exercises of St. Ignatius, which Bernini practiced, his religious sculpture is intended to help the viewer identify with miraculous events through a vivid appeal to the senses.

Bernini was steeped in Renaissance humanism. Central to his sculpture is the role of gesture and expression in arousing emotion. While these devices were also important to the Renaissance (compare Leonardo), Bernini uses them with a freedom that seems anticlassical. However, he essentially followed the concept of decorum, and he planned his effects carefully, by varying them in accordance with his subject (see box page 549). Unlike the Frenchman Nicolas Poussin (whom he respected, as he did Annibale Carracci), Bernini did this for the sake of expressive impact rather than conceptual clarity. The approaches of the two artists were diametrically opposed as well. For Bernini, antique art served as no more than a point of departure for his own inventiveness, whereas for Poussin it served as a standard of comparison. It is nevertheless characteristic of the Baroque that Bernini's theories should be far more orthodox than his art. Thus he often sided with the classicists against his fellow High Baroque artists.

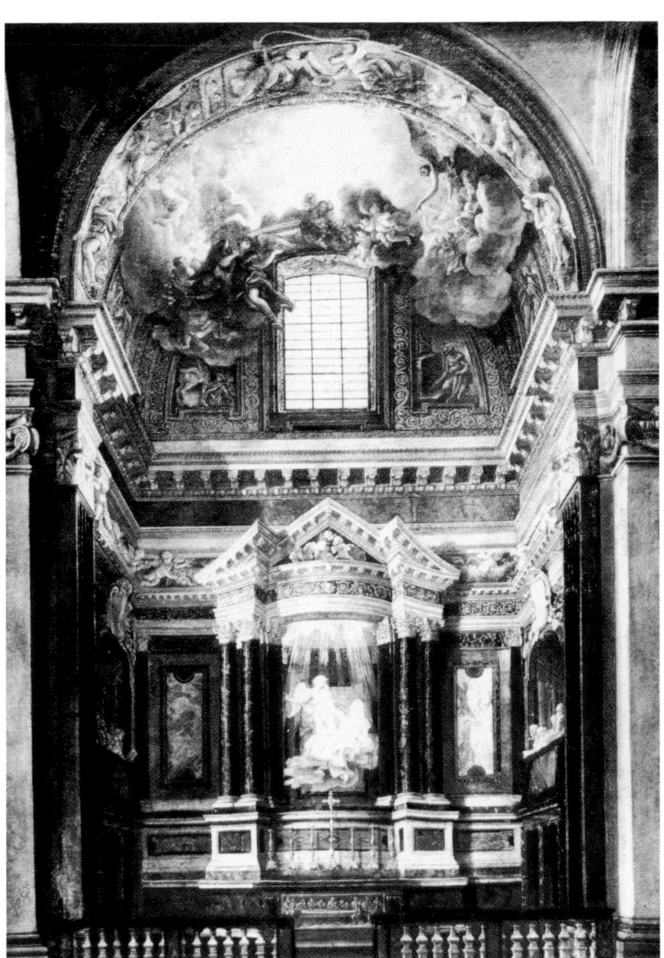

17-30. *The Cornaro Chapel.* 18th-century painting. Staatliches Museum, Schwerin, Germany

ALGARDI. It is no less ironic that Cortona was the closest friend of the sculptor Alessandro Algardi (1596–1654), who is regarded as the leading classical sculptor of the Italian Baroque and the only serious rival to Bernini in ability. His main contribution is *The Meeting of Pope Leo I and Attila* (fig. 17-31), done while he replaced Bernini at St. Peter's during the papacy of Innocent X. It revives a kind of high relief that now became widely popular. The scene depicts the defeat of the Huns from a threatened attack on Rome in 452, a fateful event in the early history of Christianity when its very survival was at stake. The subject is one that is familiar to us from antiquity: the victory over barbarian forces (compare fig. 5-71). Now, however, it is the church, not civilization, that triumphs, and the victory is spiritual rather than military.

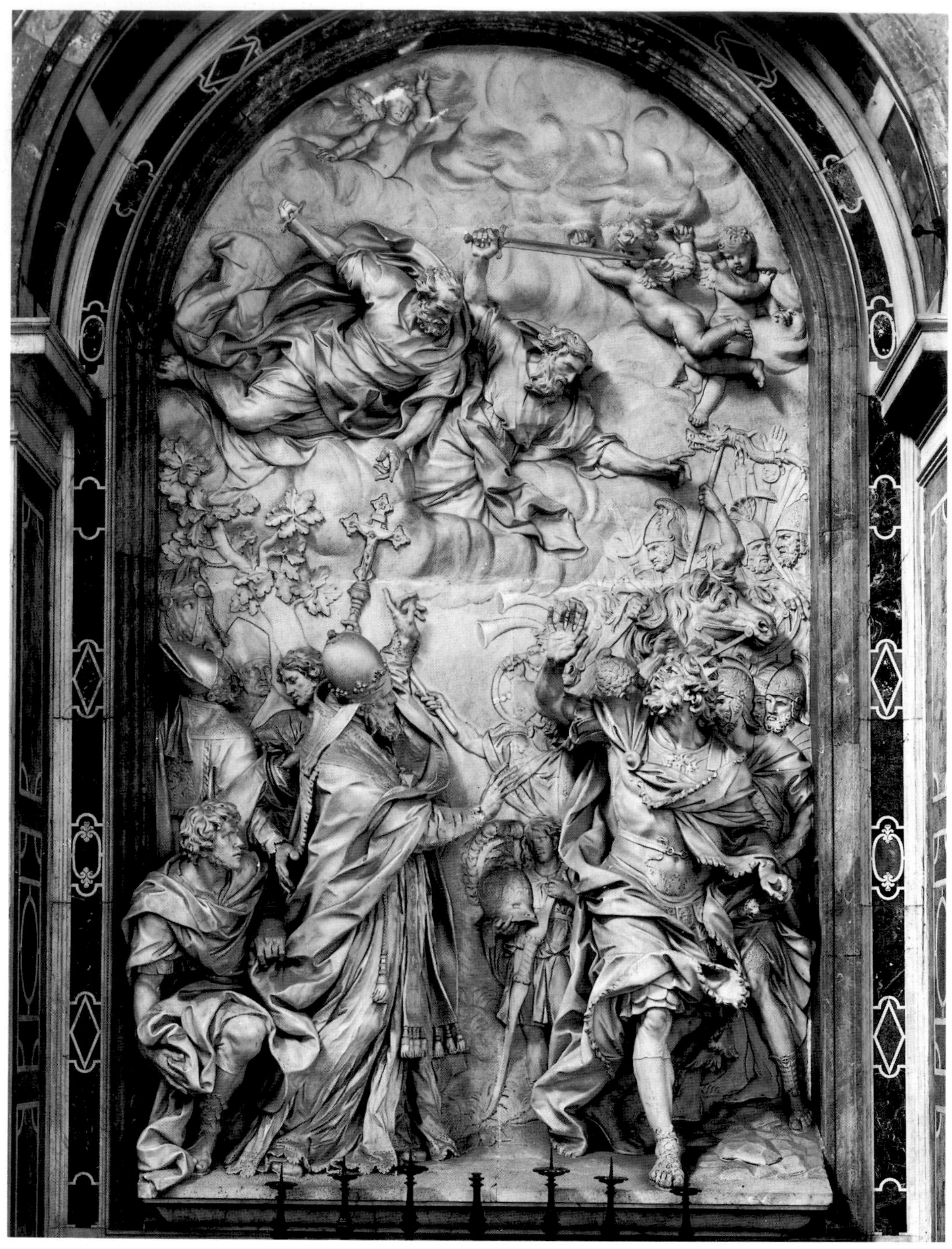

17-31. Alessandro Algardi. *The Meeting of Pope Leo I and Attila.* 1646. Marble, 28'1¾" x 16'2½" (8.5 x 4.9 m). St. Peter's, The Vatican, Rome

The commission was given for a sculpture because water condensation caused by the location in an old doorway of St. Peter's made a painting impossible. Never before had an Italian sculptor attempted such a large relief—it stands nearly 28 feet high. The problems posed by translating a pictorial conception (it had been treated by Raphael in one of the Vatican Stanze) into a relief on this gigantic scale were formidable. If Algardi has not succeeded in resolving every detail, his achievement is stupendous nonetheless. By varying the depth of the carving, he nearly convinces us that the scene takes place in the same space as ours. The foreground figures are in such high relief that they seem detached from the background. To accentuate the effect, the stage on which they are standing projects several feet beyond its surrounding niche. Thus Attila seems to rush out toward us in fear and astonishment as he flees the vision of the two apostles defending the faith. The result is surprisingly persuasive in both visual and expressive terms.

Such illusionism is, of course, quintessentially Baroque. So is the intense drama, which is heightened by the twisting poses and theatrical gestures of the protagonists. Algardi clearly was touched by Bernini's genius. Strangely enough, the relief is partly a throwback to an *Assumption of the Virgin* of 1606–10 in S. Maria Maggiore by Bernini's father, Pietro. Only in his observance of the three traditional levels of relief carving (low, middle, and high instead of continuously variable depth), his preference for frontal poses, and his restraint in dealing with the violent action can he be called a classicist, and then purely in a relative sense. Clearly, we must not draw the distinction between the High Baroque and Baroque classicism too sharply in sculpture any more than in painting.

PAINTING IN SPAIN

During the sixteenth century, at the height of its political and economic power, Spain had produced great saints and writers, but no artists of the first rank. Nor did El Greco's presence stimulate native talent. The reason is that the Catholic church, the main source of patronage, was extremely conservative, while the Spanish court and most of the aristocracy preferred to employ foreign painters, Titian above all, and held native artists in low esteem. Thus the main influences came from Italy and the Netherlands.

SANCHEZ COTÁN. Inspired by the example of Aertsen and his contemporaries in the Netherlands, Spanish artists began to develop their own versions of still life in the 1590s. We see the distinctive character of this tradition in the example (fig. 17-32) by Juan Sanchez Cotán (1561–1627). This minor religious artist is remembered today as one of the first and most remarkable members of the Toledo School of still-life painters. In contrast to the lavish display of food or luxury objects often found in Northern pictures, our painting has such a clear order and austere simplicity that we cannot help wondering what symbolic significance the artist meant to convey. The juxtaposition of direct sunlight and impenetrable darkness, of painstaking realism and abstract form, creates a memorable image in which even these humble fruits and vegetables become sacred examples of God's work.

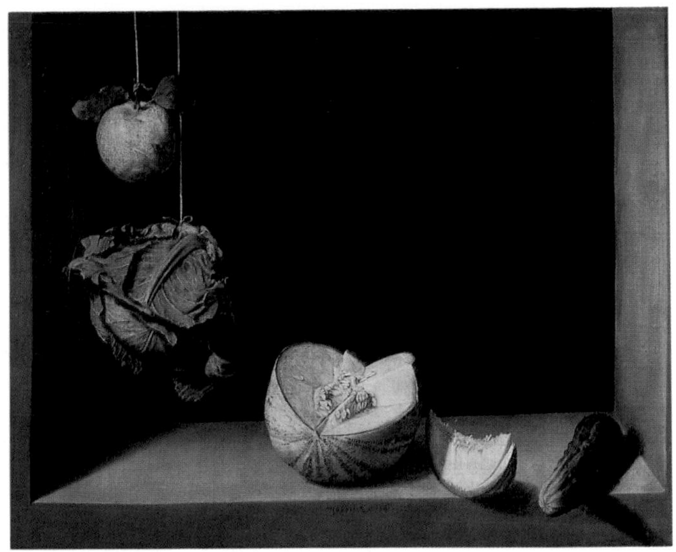

17-32. Juan Sanchez Cotán. *Quince, Cabbage, Melon, and Cucumber.* c. 1602. Oil on canvas, 27⅛ x 33¼" (68.8 x 84.4 cm). San Diego Museum of Art

GIFT OF MISSES ANNE R. AND AMY PUTNAM

Although he probably used contemporary North Italian paintings as his point of departure, Sanchez Cotán's still lifes make one think of Caravaggio, whose effect on Spanish art, however, is not found until considerably later. We do not know exactly how Caravaggism was transmitted. The likeliest source was Naples, where Caravaggio had fled, which was then under Spanish rule. His principal follower there was Jusepe Ribera (see page 531), but too little is known of his activity before about 1625 for us to trace

BAROQUE THEATER IN ITALY AND SPAIN

Besides the opera, the most popular form of Italian theater in the seventeenth century was the *commedia dell'arte,* which arose after 1570 as earlier sixteenth-century written farce declined. It then spread quickly throughout Europe, especially to France. The *commedia* actors improvised dialogue on a rough plot outline, taking the roles of stock characters—the innocent young girl, the impoverished youth, the braggart captain, the pedantic doctor—in age-old scenarios of love and intrigue. The comedic characters were clever servants, often called *zanni* ("Johnny" in the Venetian dialect—from which the English word *zany* is derived), who delighted their audiences by outwitting their masters and other figures of authority. The best known of these *zanni* were Harlequin, Mezzetin, and Pulcinella, whose name and huge nose survived into the twentieth century in the character of Punch of Punch-and-Judy puppet shows. The Italian *commedia* was also the source of modern slapstick and burlesque comedy. Its success depended on the close identification of the actors with their roles, which they rarely changed except in advanced age, so that they became one and the same in life and in art. Although the *commedia dell'arte* remained popular for 200 years, its heyday was over by 1650, when its creativity began to wane.

Under Philip III and Phillip IV the seventeenth century in Spain was the golden age of theater, as it was of art. It began around 1580 with the plays of Juan de la Cueva (c. 1543–1610) and Miguel de Cervantes (1547–1616), the author of *Don Quixote,* but its greatest writer was Lope de Vega (1562–1635), who claimed to have scripted more than 1,200 dramas and comedies. In its combination of worldliness and religion, Vega's work reflects the character and social order of Spain, which centered on the often-conflicting demands of love, honor, church, and responsibility among the social classes. The plots are lively and the writing fluid, but characters tend to be rather conventional because they conform to established codes. Tirso de Molina (1580–1648), a member of the Mercedarian order, was likewise prolific: he professed to have written 300 plays by 1621, of which 80 survive, but he is known primarily for introducing the legend of Don Juan in the *Trickster of Seville.* Vega's successor, Pedro Calderón de la Barca (1600–1681), wrote mainly cape-and-sword comedies for the court, which he served as Master of Revels, as well as religious dramas (called *autos sacramentales*) after he was ordained a priest toward the end of his life. Throughout the century, both types were performed at court and in public theaters by professional actors employed by local municipalities.

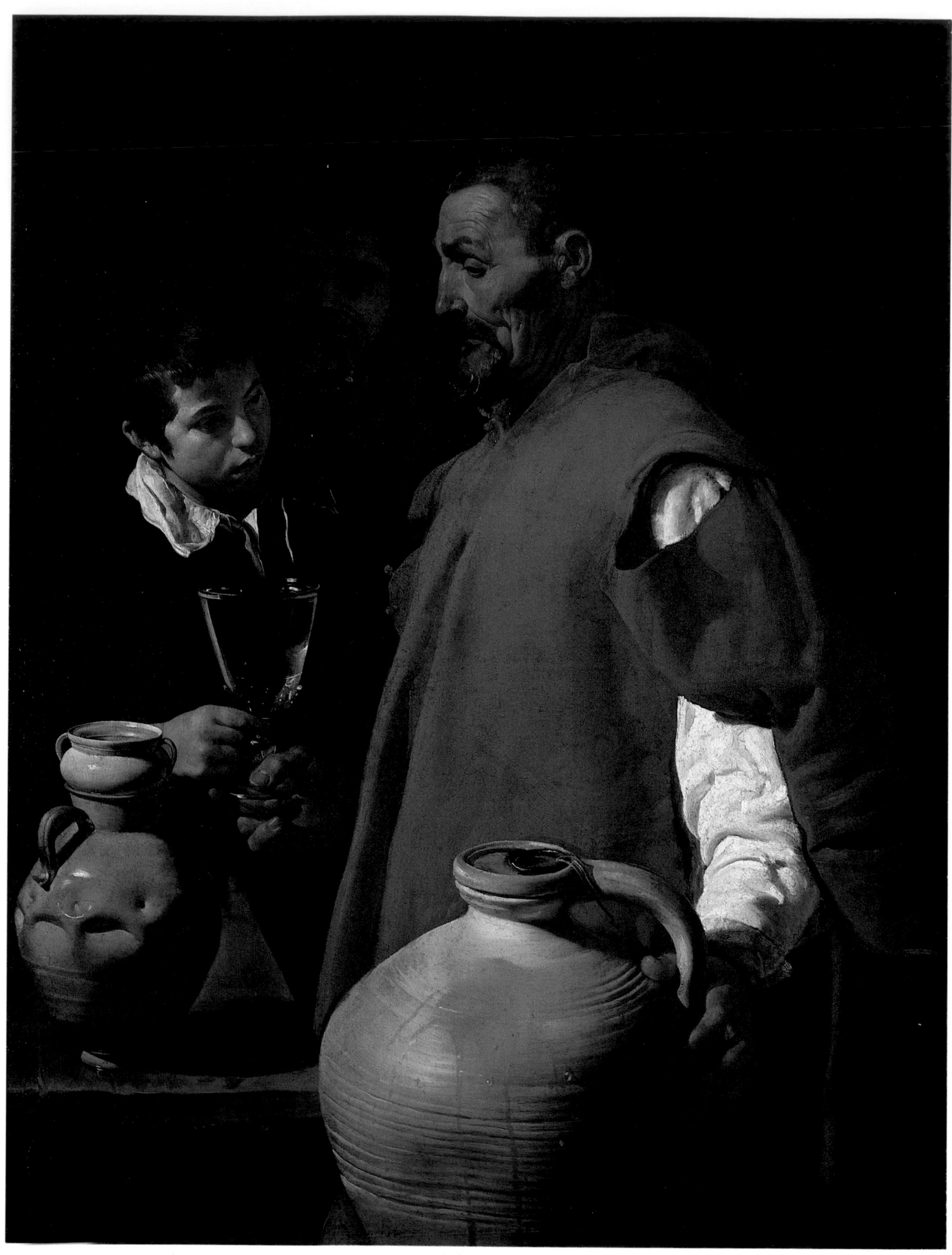

17-33. Diego Velázquez. *The Water Carrier of Seville.* c. 1619. Oil on canvas, $41\frac{1}{2}$ x $31\frac{1}{2}$" (105.3 x 80 cm). Wellington Museum, London
CROWN COPYRIGHT RESERVED

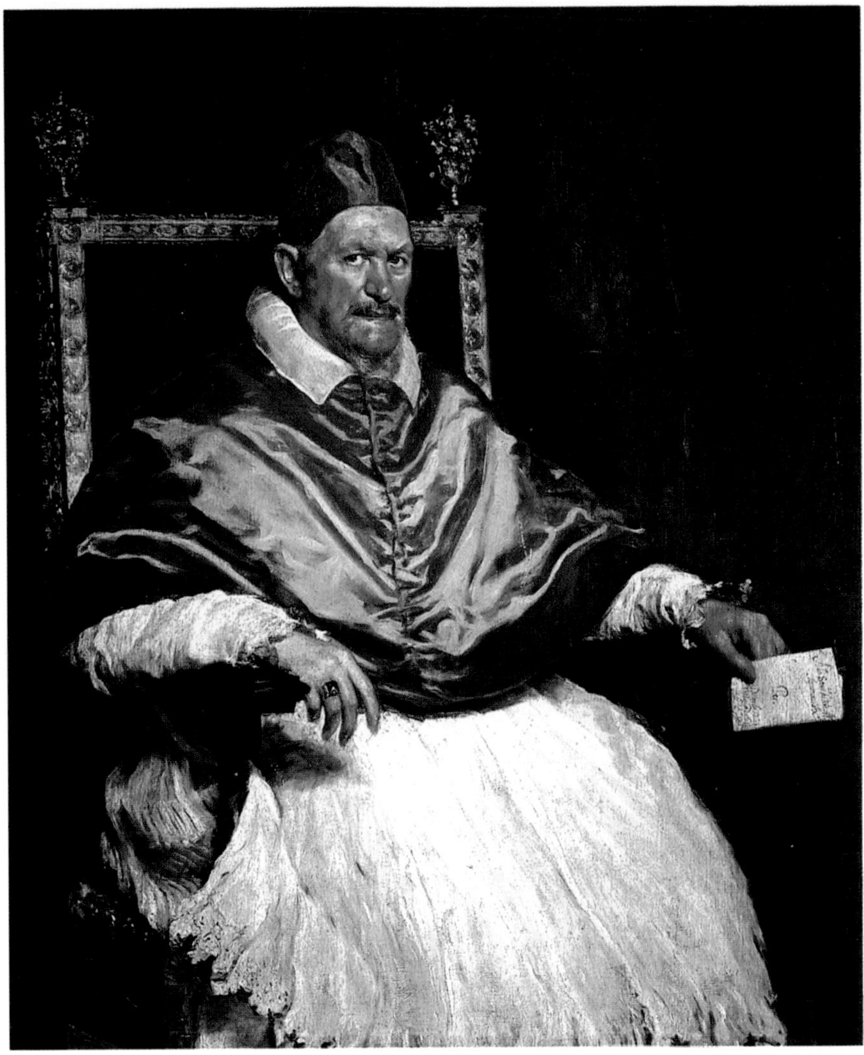

17-34. Diego Velázquez. *Pope Innocent X.* 1650. Oil on canvas, 55 x 45¼" (139.7 x 115 cm). Galleria Doria Pamphili, Rome

his influence on early Spanish Baroque art in detail. In any case, the impact of Caravaggism was felt especially in Seville, the home of the most important Spanish Baroque painters before 1640.

VELÁZQUEZ. Diego Velázquez (1599–1660) painted in a Caravaggesque vein during his early years in Seville. His interests at that time centered on scenes of people eating and drinking rather than religious themes. Known as *bodegónes,* such paintings are the distinctive Spanish counterparts of Dutch breakfast pieces (see fig. 18-24). They evolved from the paintings of tabletop displays brought to Spain by visiting Flemish artists in the early seventeenth century. *The Water Carrier of Seville* (fig. 17-33), which Velázquez painted at the age of 20, under the apparent influence of Ribera, already shows his genius. His powerful grasp of individual character and dignity gives this everyday scene the solemn spirit of a ritual—perhaps with good reason. The scene is related to Giving Drink to the Thirsty, one of the Seven Acts of Mercy, a popular theme among Caravaggesque painters of the day.

A few years later, Velázquez was appointed court painter to Philip IV, whose reign from 1621 to 1665 was the great age of painting in Spain. Much of the credit must go to the Duke of Olivares, who largely restored Spain's fortunes and supported an ambitious program of artistic patronage to proclaim the monarchy's greatness. Upon moving to Madrid, Velázquez quickly displaced the mediocre Florentines who had enjoyed the favor of Philip III and his minister, the Duke of Lerma. A skilled courtier, the artist soon became a favorite of the king, whom he served as chamberlain. Velázquez spent the rest of his life in Madrid painting mainly portraits of the royal family. The earlier of these still have the precise division of light and shade and the clear outlines of his Seville period, but after the late 1620s his work acquired a new fluency and richness.

During his visit to the Spanish court on a diplomatic mission in 1628, the Flemish painter Peter Paul Rubens (see page 555) helped Velázquez to discover the beauty of the many Titians in the king's collection. The magnificent portrait of Pope Innocent X (fig. 17-34), painted in 1650 while Velázquez was visiting Italy, is meant to evoke the great tradition of the papal portraits of Raphael (see fig. 13-34); however, its fluid brushwork and glowing color are derived from Titian (see fig. 13-40). The sitter's gaze, sharply focused on the viewer, conveys a passionate and powerful personality so characteristic of the Baroque.

The Maids of Honor (fig. 17-35) displays Velázquez' mature style at its fullest. Both a group portrait and a genre scene, it might be sub-

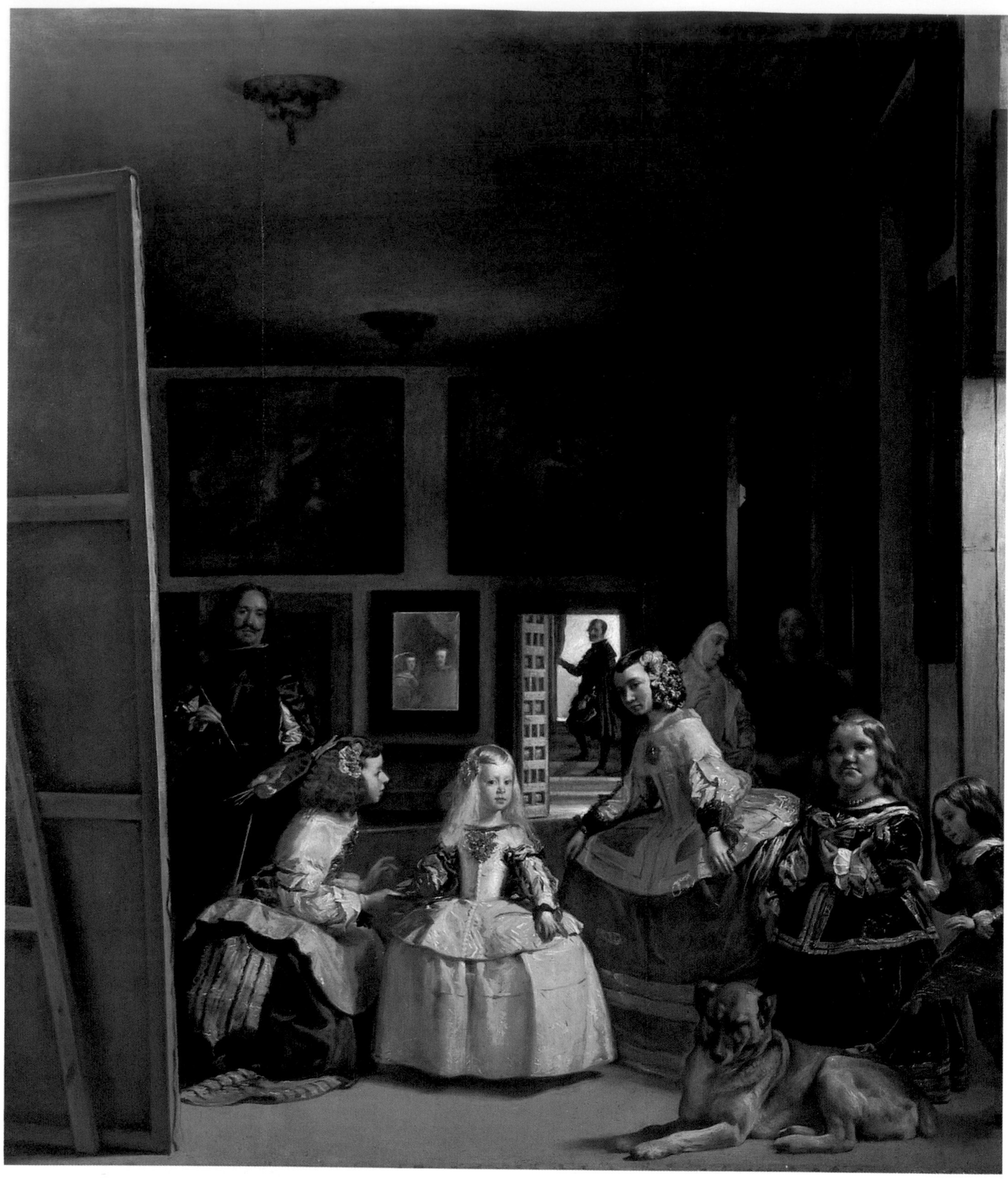

17-35. Diego Velázquez. *The Maids of Honor.* 1656. Oil on canvas, 10'5" x 9' (3.2 x 2.7 m). Museo del Prado, Madrid

titled "the artist in his studio," for Velázquez shows himself at work on a huge canvas. In the center is the Princess Margarita, who has just posed for him, among her playmates and maids of honor. The faces of her parents, the king and queen, appear in the mirror on the back wall. They have just stepped into the room, to see the scene exactly as we do. Through their presence the canvas celebrates Velázquez' position as royal painter and his knighthood in the Order of Santiago, whose red cross he proudly wears on his tunic.

The painting shows Velázquez' fascination with light. The varieties of direct and reflected light in *The Maids of Honor* are almost limitless. The artist challenges us to match the mirror image against the paintings on the same wall, and against the "picture" of the man in the open doorway. Although the side lighting and strong contrasts of light and dark still suggest the influence of Caravaggio, Velázquez' technique is far more subtle, with delicate glazes setting off the impasto of the highlights. The glowing col-

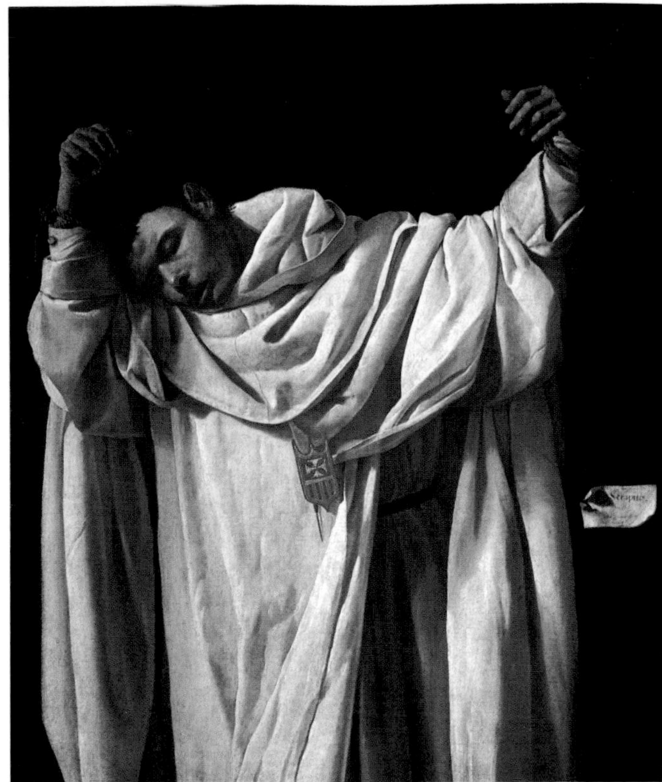

17-36. Francisco de Zurbarán. *St. Serapion.* 1628. Oil on canvas, 47½ x 41" (120.7 x 104.1 cm). Wadsworth Atheneum, Hartford, Connecticut

ELLA GALLUP SUMNER AND MARY CATLIN SUMNER COLLECTION

ors have a Venetian richness, but the brushwork is even freer and sketchier than Titian's. Velázquez explored the optical qualities of light more fully than any other painter of his time. His aim is to show the movement of light itself and the infinite range of its effects on form and color. For Velázquez, as for Jan Vermeer in Holland (see page 573), light *creates* the visible world. Velázquez could not have known the work of Vermeer (who was only 24 at the time), but he may have known domestic genre scenes by older Dutch painters. Looking at the open, sketchy brushwork in *The Maids of Honor,* we wonder if he could also have seen works by Frans Hals (compare fig. 18-11). However, unlike Hals, Velázquez does not try to capture time on the wing, even though the visual effects are fleeting. Rather, he suspends the moment to make the studio an ideal realm.

ZURBARÁN. Francisco de Zurbarán (1598–1664) stands out among the painters of Seville for his quiet intensity. His most important works were done for monastic orders and are filled with an ascetic piety that is uniquely Spanish. *St. Serapion* (fig. 17-36) shows an early member of the Mercedarians (Order of Mercy) who was brutally murdered by pirates in 1240 but canonized only a hundred years after this picture was painted. The canvas was placed as a devotional image in the funerary chapel of the order, which was originally dedicated to self-sacrifice.

The painting will remind us of Caravaggio. Zurbarán's saint, shown as a lifesize three-quarter-length figure, is both a hero and a martyr. The contrast between the white habit and the dark background gives the figure a heightened visual and expressive presence, so that the viewer contemplates the slain monk with a mixture of compassion and awe. Here pictorial and spiritual purity become one. The stillness creates a reverential mood that complements the stark realism. As a result, we identify with the strength of St. Serapion's faith rather than with his physical suffering. The absence of rhetorical pathos is what makes this image deeply moving.

MURILLO. The work of Bartolomé Esteban Murillo (1617–1682), Zurbarán's successor as the leading painter in Seville, is the most cosmopolitan, as well as the most accessible, of any Spanish Baroque artist. For that reason, he had countless followers, whose pale imitations obscure his real achievement. He learned as much from Northern artists, including Rubens and Rembrandt, as he did from Italians such as Reni and Guercino. The *Virgin and Child* in figure 17-37 unites these influences in an image that nevertheless retains an unmistakably Spanish character. The haunting expressiveness of the faces has a gentle pathos that lends a greater emotional appeal to Zurbarán's austere pietism. This human warmth, which became sentimentality in the work of lesser artists, reflects changes in religious outlook. It was also an attempt to inject new life into standard devotional images that had been reduced to formulas in the hands of some artists. The extraordinary sophistication of Murillo's brushwork and the subtlety of his color show the influence of Velázquez. There is a debt as well to the great Flemish Baroque painters Peter Paul Rubens and Anthony van Dyck (see fig. 18-5).

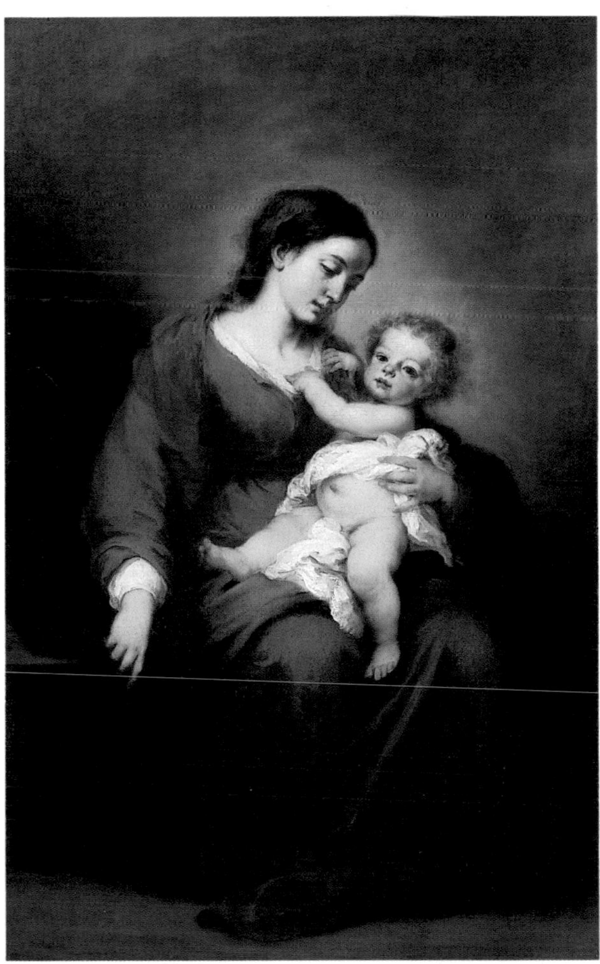

17-37. Bartolomé Esteban Murillo. *Virgin and Child.* c. 1675–80. Oil on canvas, 65¼ x 43" (165.7 x 109.2 cm). The Metropolitan Museum of Art, New York

ROGERS FUND, 1943

CHAPTER EIGHTEEN

The Baroque in Flanders and Holland

In 1581, the six northern provinces of the Netherlands, led by William the Silent of Nassau, declared their independence from Spain, capping a rebellion that had begun 15 years earlier against Catholicism and the attempt by Philip II to curtail local power. Spain soon recovered the southern Netherlands, called Flanders (now divided between France and Belgium); but after a long struggle the United Provinces (today's Holland) gained their autonomy, which was recognized by the truce declared in 1609. Although hostilities broke out again in 1621, the freedom of the Dutch was never again seriously in doubt; it was finally ratified by the Treaty of Münster, which ended the Thirty Years' War in 1648. The division of the Netherlands had very different effects on the economy, social structure, culture, and religion of the north and the south. After being sacked by Spanish troops in 1576, Antwerp, the leading port of the southern Netherlands, lost half its population. Although Brussels was the seat of government, Antwerp gradually regained its position as Flanders' commercial and artistic capital. As part of the Treaty of Münster, however, the Scheldt River leading to Antwerp's harbor was closed to shipping, thereby crippling trade for the next two centuries. Because Flanders continued to be ruled by Spanish regents, who viewed themselves as the defenders of the true faith, its artists relied on commissions from Church and State, although the aristocracy and wealthy merchants were also important patrons.

Holland, in contrast, was proud of its hard-won freedom. While the cultural links with Flanders remained strong, several factors encouraged the quick development of Dutch artistic traditions. Unlike Flanders, where all artistic activity radiated from Antwerp, Holland had a number of local schools of painting. Besides Amsterdam, the commercial capital, there were groups of artists in Haarlem, Utrecht, Leyden, Delft, and other towns. Thus Holland produced an almost bewildering variety of masters and styles.

The new nation was one of merchants, farmers, and seafarers, and its religion was Reformed Protestant, which was iconoclastic. Hence Dutch artists rarely had the large-scale commissions sponsored by Church and State that were available throughout the Catholic world. While city governments and civic bodies such as militias provided a certain amount of art patronage, their demands were limited. As a result, private collectors became the painter's chief source of support. This condition had already existed to some extent before (see page 518), but its full effect can be seen only after 1600. There was no shrinkage of output. On the contrary, the public developed such an appetite for pictures that the whole country became gripped by a kind of collector's mania. During a visit to Holland in 1641, the English traveler John Evelyn noted in his diary that "it is an ordinary thing to find a common farmer lay out two or three thousand pounds in this commodity. Their houses are full of them, and they vend them at their fairs to very great gain." The collector's mania caused an outpouring of artistic talent that can only be compared to that of Early Renaissance Florence. Pictures became a commodity, and their trade followed the law of supply and demand. Many artists produced for the market rather than for individual patrons. They were lured into becoming painters by hopes of success that often failed to materialize, and even the greatest masters were sometimes hard-pressed. (It was not unusual for an artist to keep an inn or run a small business on the side.) Yet they survived—less secure but freer.

FLANDERS

RUBENS. Although it was born in Rome, the Baroque style soon became international. The great Flemish painter Peter Paul Rubens (1577–1640) played a role of unique importance in this process. It might be said that he finished what Dürer had started a hundred years earlier: the breakdown of the artistic barriers between north and south. Rubens' father was a prominent Antwerp Protestant who fled to Germany to escape Spanish persecution during the war of independence (see page 517). The family returned to Antwerp after his death, when Peter Paul was ten years old, and the boy grew up a devout Catholic. Trained by local painters, Rubens became a master in 1598 but developed a personal style only when he went to Italy two years later.

During his eight years in the south, he absorbed the Italian tradition far more completely than had any Northerner before

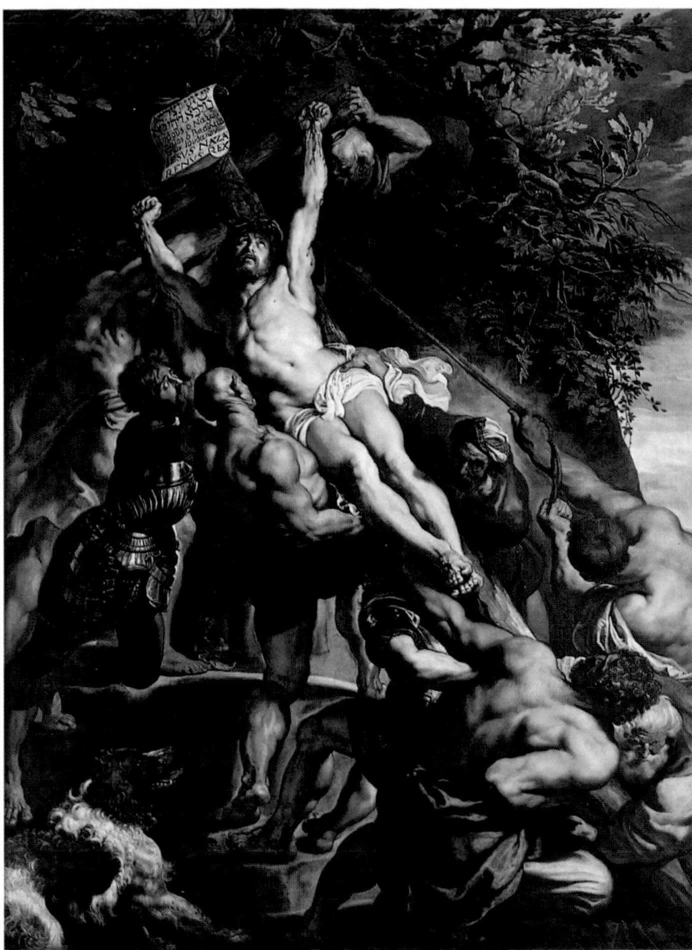

18-1. Peter Paul Rubens. *The Raising of the Cross.* 1609–10. Center panel of a triptych, 15'1" x 11'9⅝" (4.6 x 3.4 m). Antwerp Cathedral, Belgium

him. He studied ancient sculpture, the masterpieces of the High Renaissance, and the work of Caravaggio and Annibale Carracci. In fact, Rubens competed on even terms with the best Italians of his day and could well have made his career in Italy. When he returned to Flanders in 1608 because of his mother's illness, he meant the visit to be brief. His plans changed when he received a special appointment as court painter to the Spanish regent, which allowed him to set up a workshop in Antwerp that was exempt from local taxes and guild regulations. Rubens had the best of both worlds. Like Jan van Eyck (see page 486), he was valued at court not only as an artist but also as an adviser and emissary. Diplomatic errands gave him entrée to the royal households of the major powers, where he received commissions. Aided by a growing number of assistants, he was also free to carry out a huge volume of work for the city of Antwerp, for the Church, and for private patrons.

Rubens epitomized the Baroque ideal of the virtuoso for whom the entire universe is a stage. On the one hand, he was devoutly religious. On the other, he was a man of the world who succeeded in every arena by virtue of his character and ability. Rubens resolved the contradictions of the era through humanism, the union of faith and learning that was attacked by both the Reformation and the Counter-Reformation. In his paintings as well, Rubens reconciled seemingly incompatible forces. His enormous intellect and vitality enabled him to unite the natural and supernatural, reality and fantasy, learning and spirituality. Thus his epic canvases defined the scope and the style of High Baroque painting. They possess a seemingly boundless energy and inventiveness, that, like his heroic nudes, express life at its fullest. The presentation of this heightened existence required the expanded arena that only Baroque theatricality could provide. Rubens' sense of drama was as highly developed as Bernini's. At the same time, he could be the most human of artists.

The Raising of the Cross (fig. 18-1), the first major altarpiece Rubens painted after his return to Antwerp, shows how much he was indebted to Italian art. The muscular figures, modeled to show their physical power and passionate feeling, recall those of the Sistine ceiling and the Farnese Gallery, while the lighting suggests Caravaggio's. The panel nevertheless owes much of its success to Rubens' ability to combine Italian influences with Netherlandish ideas, which he updated in the process. The painting is more heroic in scale and conception than any previous Northern work, yet it is unthinkable without Rogier van der Weyden's *Descent from the Cross* (see fig. 15-10). Rubens is also a Flemish realist in such details as the foliage, the armor of the soldier, and the curly haired dog in the foreground. These varied elements, integrated with the utmost mastery, form a composition of tremendous dramatic force. The unstable pyramid of bodies, swaying precariously, bursts the limits of the frame in a characteristically Baroque way, making the viewer feel like a participant in the action.

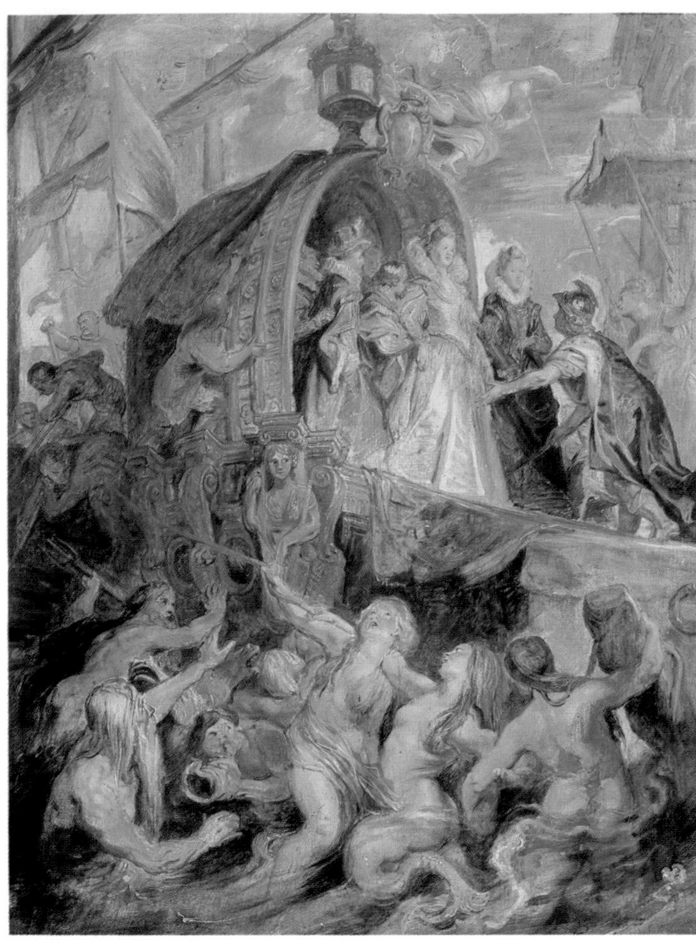

18-2. Peter Paul Rubens. *Marie de' Medici, Queen of France, Landing in Marseilles.* 1622–23. Oil on panel, 25 x 19¾" (63.5 x 50.3 cm). Alte Pinakothek, Munich

In the 1620s, Rubens' style reached its climax in his huge decorative schemes for churches and palaces. The most famous is the cycle in the Luxembourg Palace in Paris glorifying the career of Marie de' Medici, the widow of Henri IV and mother of Louis XIII. Our figure shows the artist's oil sketch for one episode: the young queen landing in Marseilles (fig. 18-2). This is hardly an exciting subject, yet Rubens has turned it into a spectacle of unprecedented splendor. As Marie de' Medici walks down the gangplank, Fame flies overhead sounding a triumphant blast on two trumpets, and Neptune rises from the sea with his fishtailed crew. Having guarded the queen's journey, they rejoice at her arrival. Everything flows together here in swirling movement: heaven and earth, history and allegory. Even drawing and painting come together, for Rubens used oil sketches like this one to prepare his compositions. Unlike earlier artists, he preferred to design his pictures in terms of light and color from the start. (Most of his drawings are figure studies or portrait sketches.) This unified vision, which had been explored but never fully achieved by the great Venetians, was Rubens' most precious legacy to later painters.

Around 1630, the drama of Rubens' earlier work changed to a late style of lyrical tenderness inspired by Titian, whose work Rubens discovered anew in the royal palace while he visited Madrid. *The Garden of Love* (fig. 18-3) is as glowing a tribute to life's pleasures as Titian's *Bacchanal* (see fig. 13-37). But these fashionable couples belong to the present, not to a golden age of the past, although they are playfully assaulted by swarms of cupids. The Garden of Love had been a feature of Northern painting ever since the courtly style of the International Gothic. The early versions, however, were genre scenes showing groups of young lovers in a garden. By merging this tradition with Titian's classical mythologies, Rubens has created an enchanted realm where myth and reality become one.

The picture must have had special meaning for him, since he had just married a beautiful girl of 16. (His first wife died in 1626.) He also bought a country house, Château Steen, and led the leisurely life of a squire. This change renewed his interest in landscape painting, which he had practiced only occasionally before. Here, too, the power of his genius is undiminished. In *Landscape with the Château Steen* (fig. 18-4), a magnificent open space sweeps from the hunter and his prey in the foreground to the mist-veiled hills along the horizon. As a landscapist, Rubens again creates a synthesis from his Northern and Southern sources, for he is the heir of both Pieter Bruegel and Annibale Carracci (compare figs. 16-21 and 17-6).

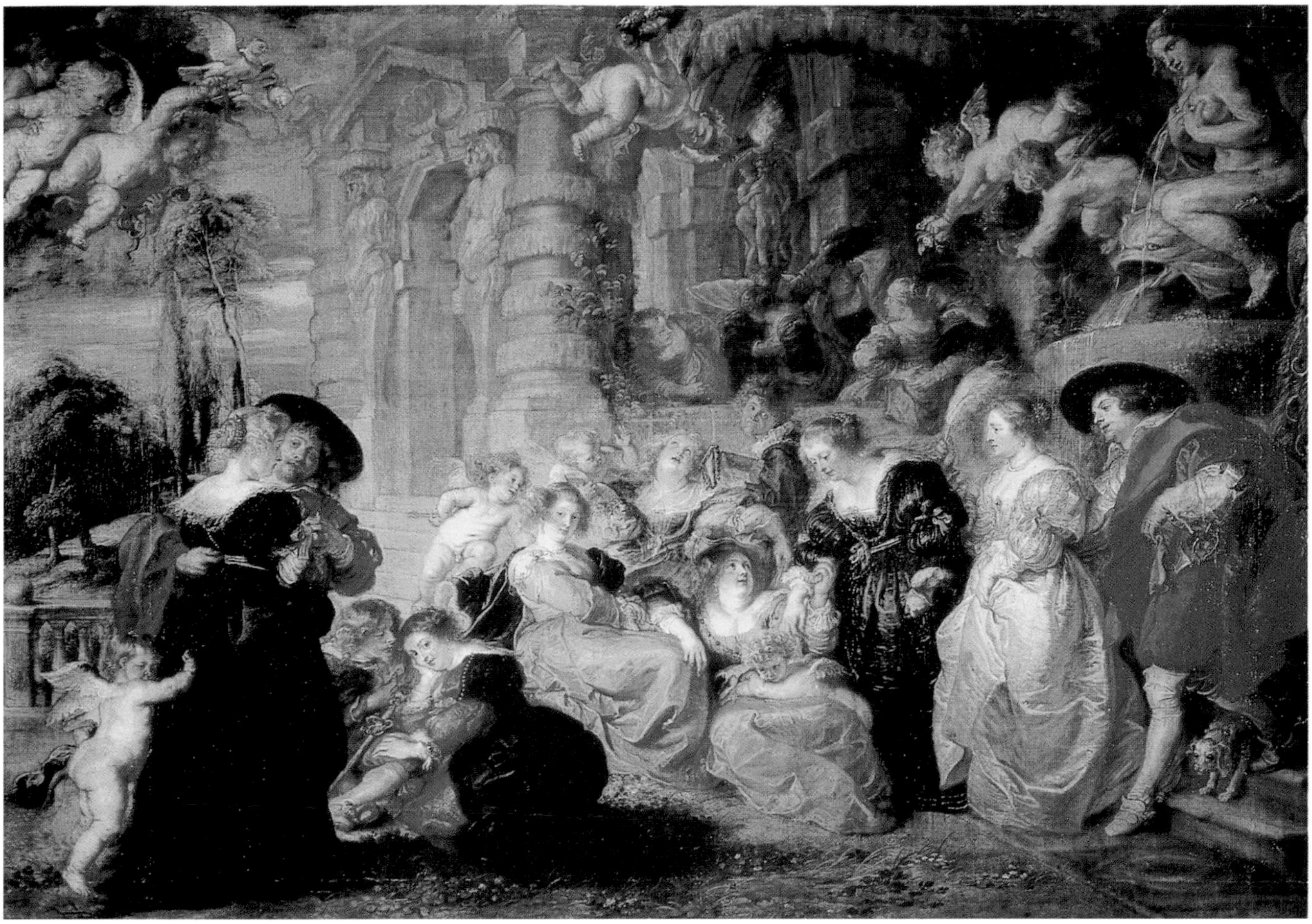

18-3. Peter Paul Rubens. *The Garden of Love.* c. 1638. Oil on canvas, 6'6" x 9'3½" (2 x 2.8 m). Museo del Prado, Madrid

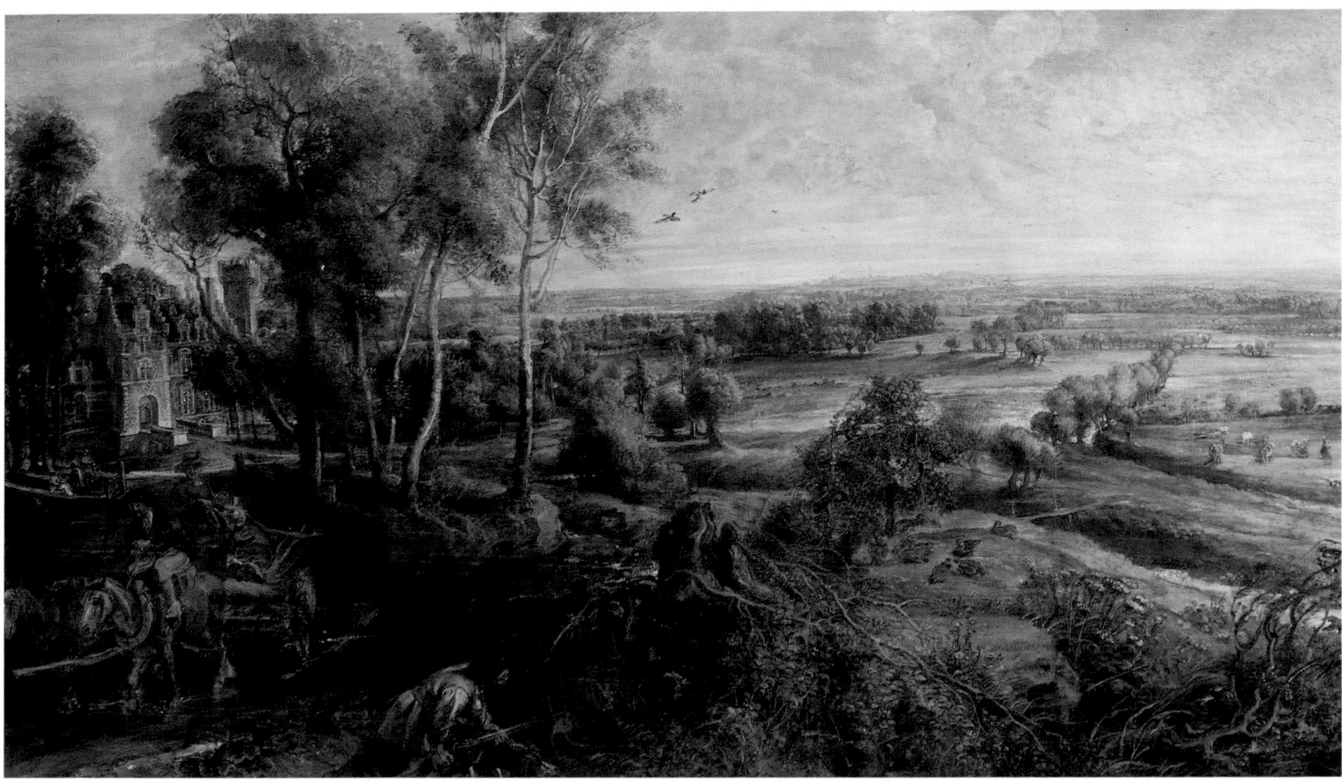

18-4. Peter Paul Rubens. *Landscape with the Château Steen.* 1636. Oil on panel, 4'5" x 7'9" (1.34 x 2.36 m). The National Gallery, London

REPRODUCED BY COURTESY OF THE TRUSTEES

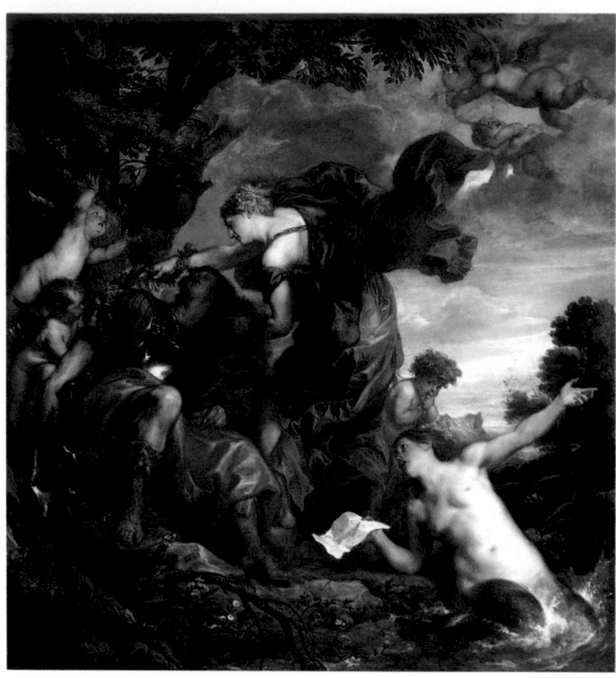

18-5. Anthony van Dyck. *Rinaldo and Armida*. 1629. Oil on canvas, 7'9" x 7'6" (2.36 x 2.24 m). The Baltimore Museum of Art
THE JACOB EPSTEIN COLLECTION

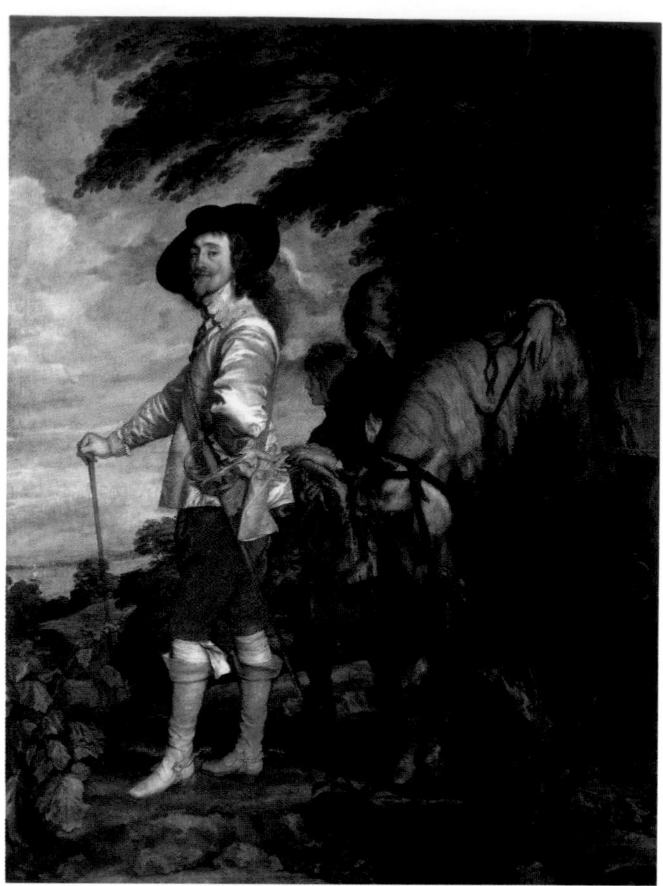

18-6. Anthony van Dyck. *Portrait of Charles I Hunting*. c. 1635. Oil on canvas, 8'11" x 6'11½" (2.7 x 2.1 m). Musée du Louvre, Paris

VAN DYCK. Besides Rubens, only one Flemish Baroque artist won international stature. Anthony van Dyck (1599–1641) was that rarity among painters, a child prodigy. Before he was 20, he had become Rubens' most valued assistant. But, like Rubens, he developed his mature style only after a stay in Italy.

Van Dyck's achievement as a history painter has been overshadowed by Rubens', yet it was of considerable importance in its own right. He was at his best in lyrical scenes of mythological love. *Rinaldo and Armida* (fig. 18-5) is taken from Torquato Tasso's immensely popular poem, *Jerusalem Freed* (1581), about the Crusades, which gave rise to a new courtly ideal throughout Europe and inspired numerous operas as well as paintings. Van Dyck shows the sorceress falling in love with the Christian knight she had intended to kill. The canvas reflects the conception of the English monarchy, for whom it was painted. Charles I, a Protestant, had married the Catholic Henrietta Maria, sister of his rival, the king of France. Charles found parallels in Tasso's epic. He saw himself as the virtuous ruler of a peaceful realm much like the Fortunate Isle where Armida brought Rinaldo. (Ironically, Charles' reign ended in civil war, and he was beheaded in 1649.) The artist tells his story of ideal love in the pictorial language of Titian and Veronese, but with an expressiveness and opulence that would have been the envy of any Venetian painter. The picture was so successful that it helped Van Dyck gain appointment to the English court two years later.

Van Dyck's fame rests mainly on the portraits he painted in London between 1632 and 1641. *Charles I Hunting* (fig. 18-6) portrays the king standing near a horse and two grooms against a landscape backdrop. Representing the sovereign at ease, it might be called a "dismounted equestrian portrait." It is less rigid than a formal state portrait, but hardly less grand, for the king remains in full command of the state, symbolized by the horse. The fluid movement of the setting complements the self-conscious elegance of the king's pose, which continues the stylized grace of Hilliard's portraits (compare fig. 16-17). Van Dyck has brought the Mannerist court portrait up to date, using Rubens and Titian as his points of departure. In the process, he created a new aristocratic portrait tradition that continued in England until the late eighteenth century and had considerable influence on the Continent as well.

JORDAENS. Jacob Jordaens (1593–1678) was the successor to Rubens and Van Dyck as the leading artist in Flanders. Although he was never a member of Rubens' studio, he turned to Rubens for inspiration throughout his career. His most characteristic subjects are mythological themes depicting the revels of nymphs and satyrs. Like his eating and drinking scenes, which illustrate popu-

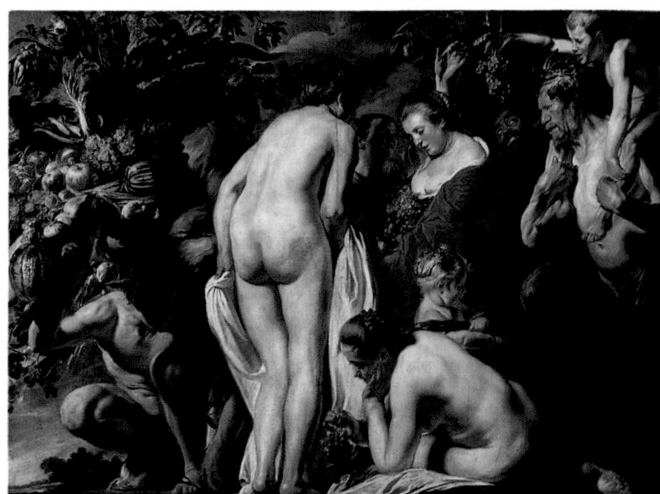

18-7. Jacob Jordaens. *Homage to Pomona (Allegory of Fruitfulness).* c. 1623. Oil on canvas, 5'10⅞" x 7'10⅞" (1.8 x 2.4 m). Musée Royaux d'Art et d'Histoire, Brussels

(BELOW) 18-8. Jan Brueghel the Elder. *Allegory of Earth.* c. 1618. Oil on copper, 18⅛ x 26⅜" (46 x 67 cm). Musée du Louvre, Paris

lar parables of an instructional and moralizing kind, they reveal him to be a close observer of people. These dwellers of the woods inhabit an idyllic realm, untouched by human cares. The painterly execution in *Homage to Pomona (Allegory of Fruitfulness)* (fig. 18-7) shows a strong debt to Rubens, yet the monumental figures lack Rubens' rhetoric and possess a calm dignity all their own.

JAN BRUEGHEL. Rubens' towering genius dominated Flemish painting. It touched every artist around him, including Jan Brueghel the Elder (1568–1625), the leader of the preceding generation, with whom he often collaborated. Brueghel was the principal heir to the tradition of his illustrious father, Pieter Bruegel the Elder (see page 520), whom he hardly knew. Jan also played an important role in the transition from Mannerism to the Baroque in the north. *Allegory of Earth* (fig. 18-8) shows one of his major contributions to Flemish art: the "paradise" landscape. It was part of a series devoted to the four elements, a common theme in Northern seventeenth-century painting, each with a biblical or mythological subject. Barely visible in the background is the expulsion of Adam and Eve from the Garden of Eden, a remnant of the Mannerist inverted perspective (see pages 518–19). Jan's enchanting vision of this innocent realm is made convincing by his meticulous realism. Like many older artists, he preferred small copperplates, which offered a smooth, hard surface ideally suited to his jewel-like style.

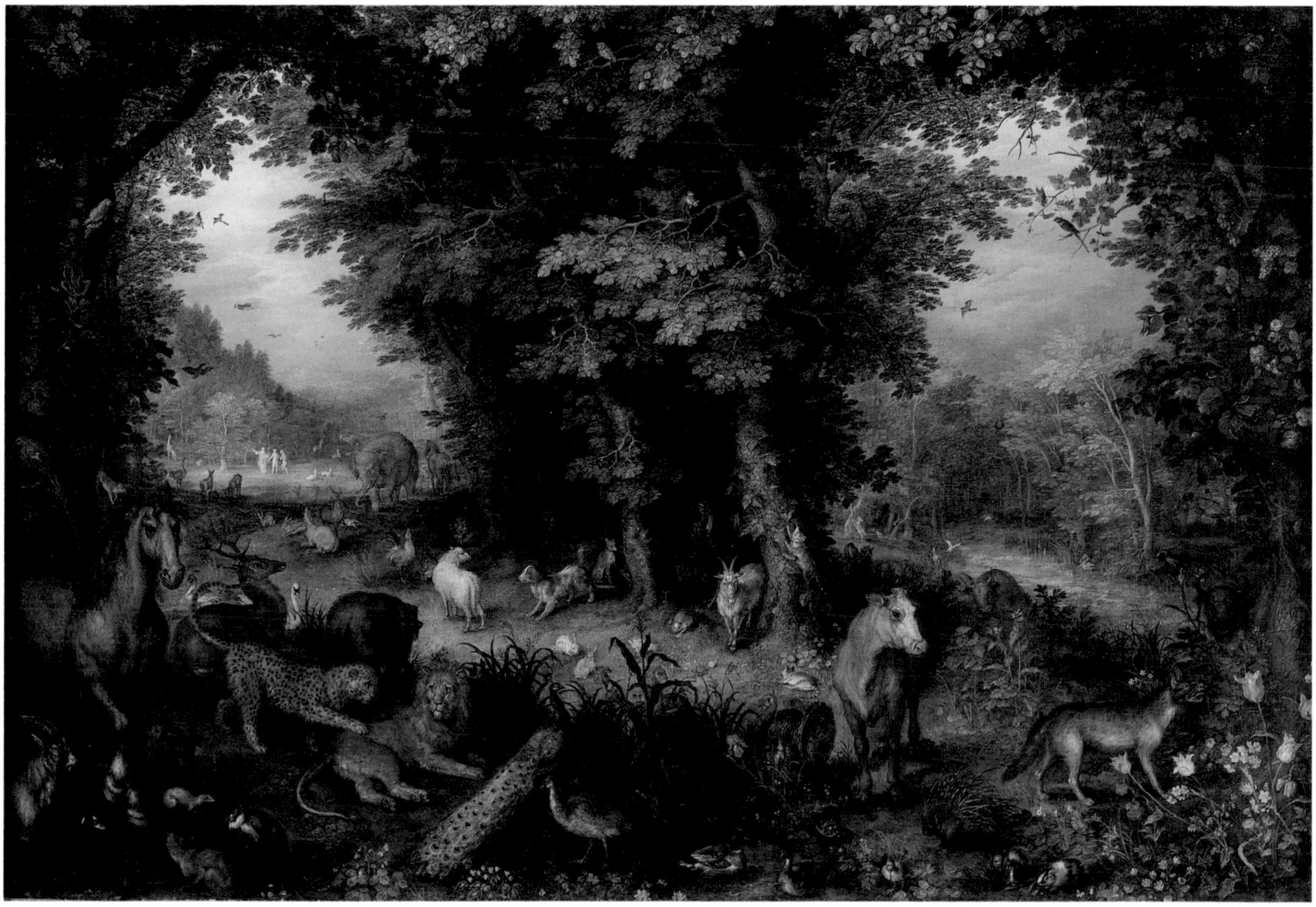

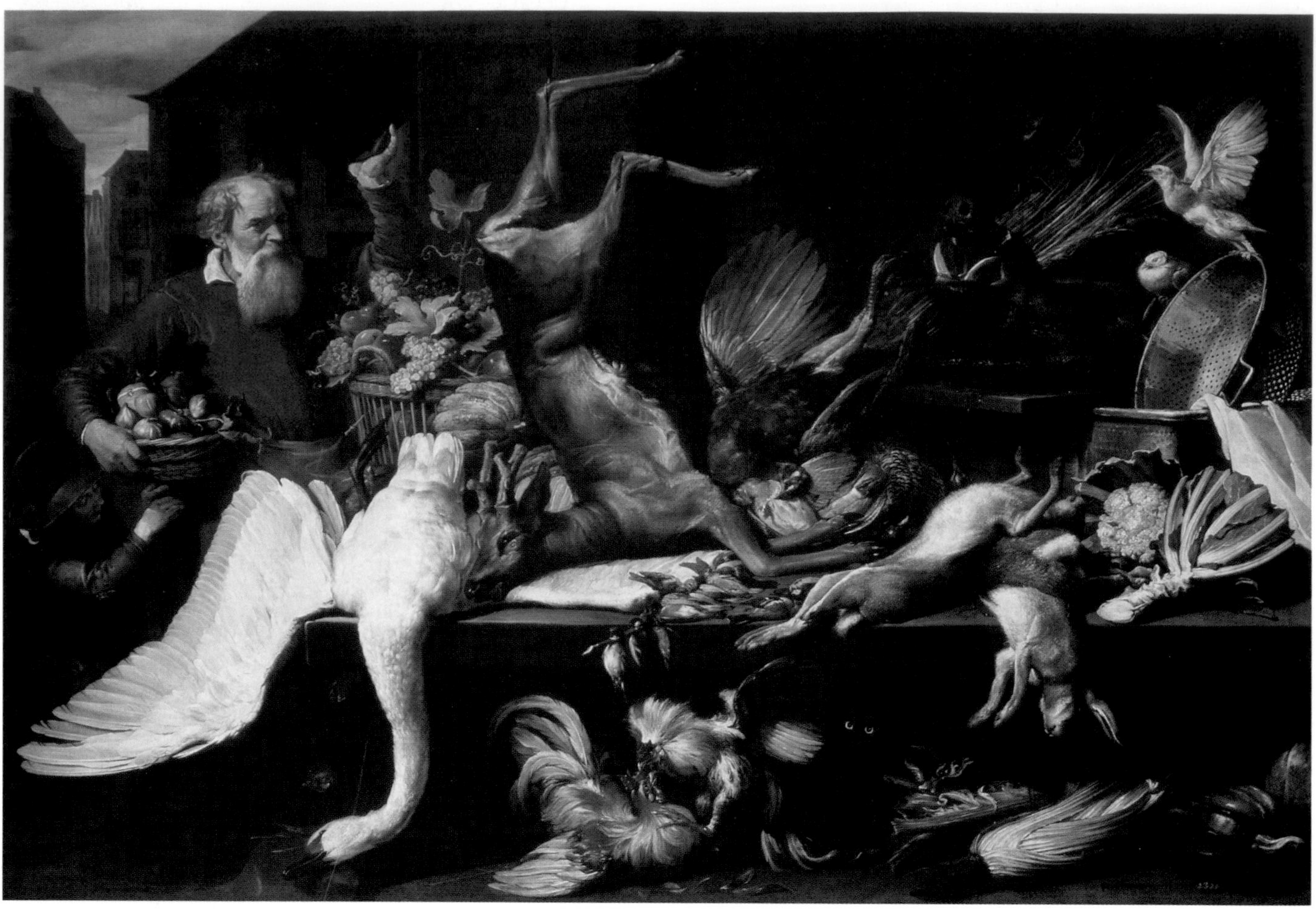

18-9. Frans Snyders. *Market Stall.* 1614. Oil on canvas, 6'11⅞" x 10'3⅝" (2.1 x 3 m). © 1991 The Art Institute of Chicago
CHARLES H. AND MARY F. S. WORCESTER FUND, 1981

SNYDERS. Brueghel also made an important contribution to flower painting. However, the development of the Baroque still life in Flanders was largely the responsibility of Frans Snyders (1579–1657), who studied with Jan's brother, Pieter Brueghel the Younger (1564–1638). Snyders concentrated on elaborate table still lifes piled high with food that express the Flemish gusto for life during the Baroque era. His splendid *Market Stall* (fig. 18-9) is a masterpiece of its kind. This early picture appeals frankly to the senses. The artist revels in the bravura application of paint, as seen in the varied textures of the game. The scene is further enlivened by the little drama of the youth picking the old man's pocket and the hens fighting in the foreground as a cat looks on from its safe retreat beneath the low bench.

Even here Rubens' influence can be felt: the composition descends from one Snyders painted with Rubens, based on the latter's design, shortly after both returned from Italy around 1609. *Market Stall* updates *The Meat Stall* of Pieter Aertsen (see fig. 16-20) into a Baroque style. Unlike Aertsen, Snyders subordinates everything to the ensemble, which is characteristically Baroque in its lavishness and immediacy. There is a fundamental difference in content as well. No longer is there a religious subject in the background. Although an emblematic meaning has been suggested, the painting celebrates a time of peace and prosperity after the truce of 1609, when hunting was resumed in the replenished game preserves.

HOLLAND

THE UTRECHT SCHOOL. The Baroque style came to Holland from Antwerp through the work of Rubens, and from Rome through direct contact with Caravaggio and his followers. Although most Dutch painters did not go to Italy, the majority of those who went in the early years of the century were from Utrecht, a town with strong Catholic traditions. It is not surprising that these artists were more attracted by Caravaggio's realism and "lay Christianity" than by Annibale Carracci's classicism. *The Calling of St. Matthew* by Hendrick Terbrugghen (1588–1629), the oldest and ablest of this group (fig. 18-10), reflects Caravaggio's

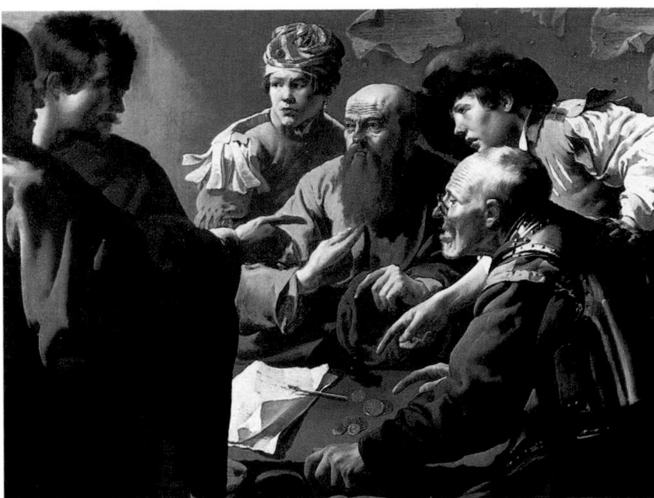

18-10. Hendrick Terbrugghen. *The Calling of St. Matthew.* 1621. Oil on canvas, 40 x 54" (101.5 x 137.2 cm). Centraal Museum, Utrecht, the Netherlands

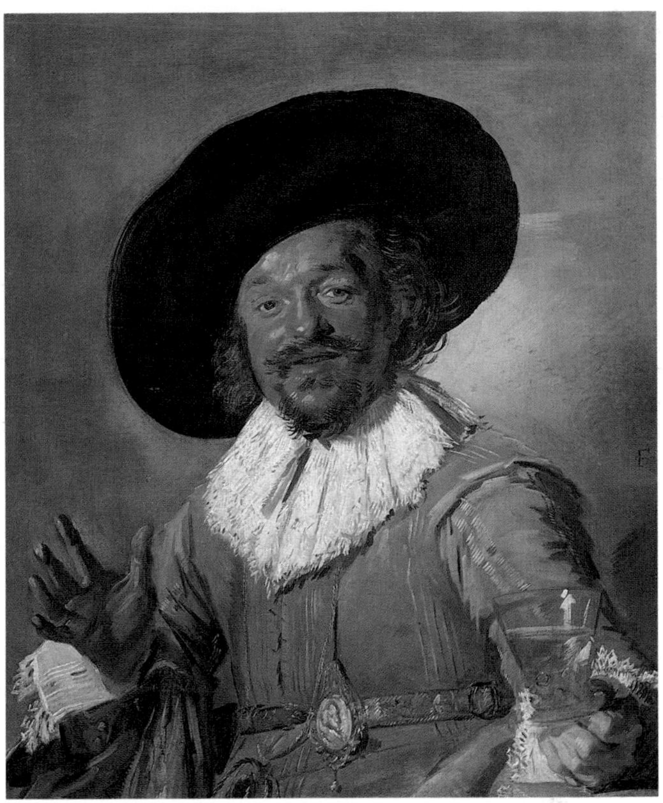

18-11. Frans Hals. *The Jolly Toper.* c. 1628–30. Oil on canvas, 31⅞ x 26¼" (81 x 66.6 cm). Rijksmuseum, Amsterdam

earlier version (see fig. 17-2) in the sharp light, the dramatic timing, and the everyday detail. Missing, however, is the element of grandeur and simplicity. While it produced few other major artists, the Utrecht School transmitted the style of Caravaggio to other Dutch masters, who then made better use of these new Italian ideas.

HALS. One of the first to profit from this experience was Frans Hals (1580/85–1666), the great portrait painter of Haarlem. He was born in Antwerp, and what little is known of his early work suggests the influence of Rubens. His mature style, however, is seen in *The Jolly Toper* (fig. 18-11), which perhaps represents "taste" from the allegory of the five senses. The painting combines Rubens' robustness with a focus on the "dramatic moment" that must be derived from Caravaggio via Utrecht. Everything here conveys complete spontaneity: the twinkling eyes and half-open mouth, the raised hand, the teetering wineglass, and—most important of all—the quick way of setting down the forms. Hals worked in dashing brushstrokes, each so clearly visible that we can almost count the total number of "touches." With this open, split-second technique, the completed picture has the immediacy of a sketch (compare our example by Rubens, fig. 18-2). The impression of a race against time is, of course, deceptive. Hals spent hours on this lifesize canvas, but he maintains the illusion of having done it all in the wink of an eye.

These qualities are even more forceful in the *Malle Babbe* (fig. 18-12), one of the artist's genre pictures. A lower-class counterpart of *The Jolly Toper,* this folk character, half witch (note the owl), half village idiot, screams insults at other guests in a tavern. Hals seems to share their attitude of cruel amusement rather than sympathy, but his portrayal is masterfully sharp and his lightninglike brushwork has the brilliance of incredible skill.

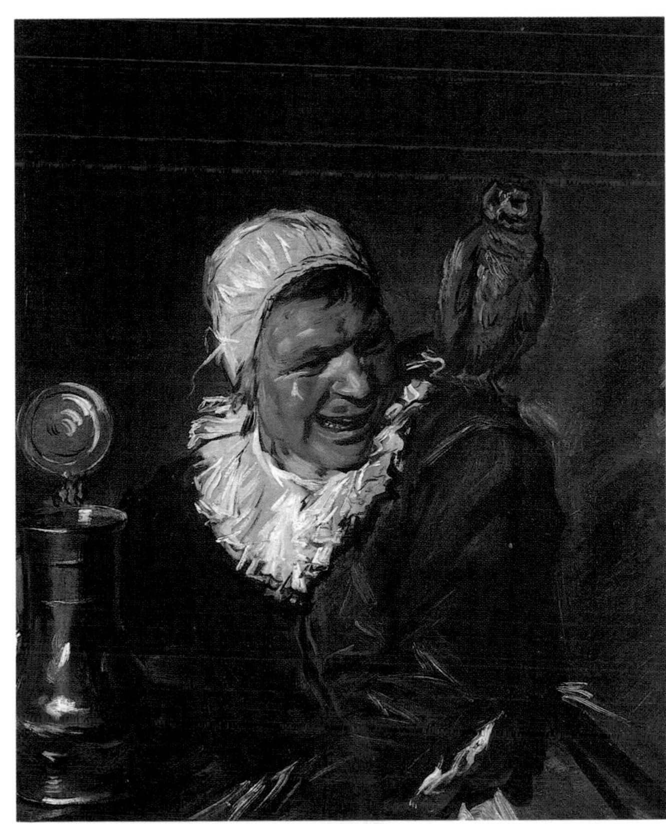

18-12. Frans Hals. *Malle Babbe.* c. 1650. Oil on canvas, 29½ x 25" (75 x 63.5 cm). Gemäldegalerie, Berlin

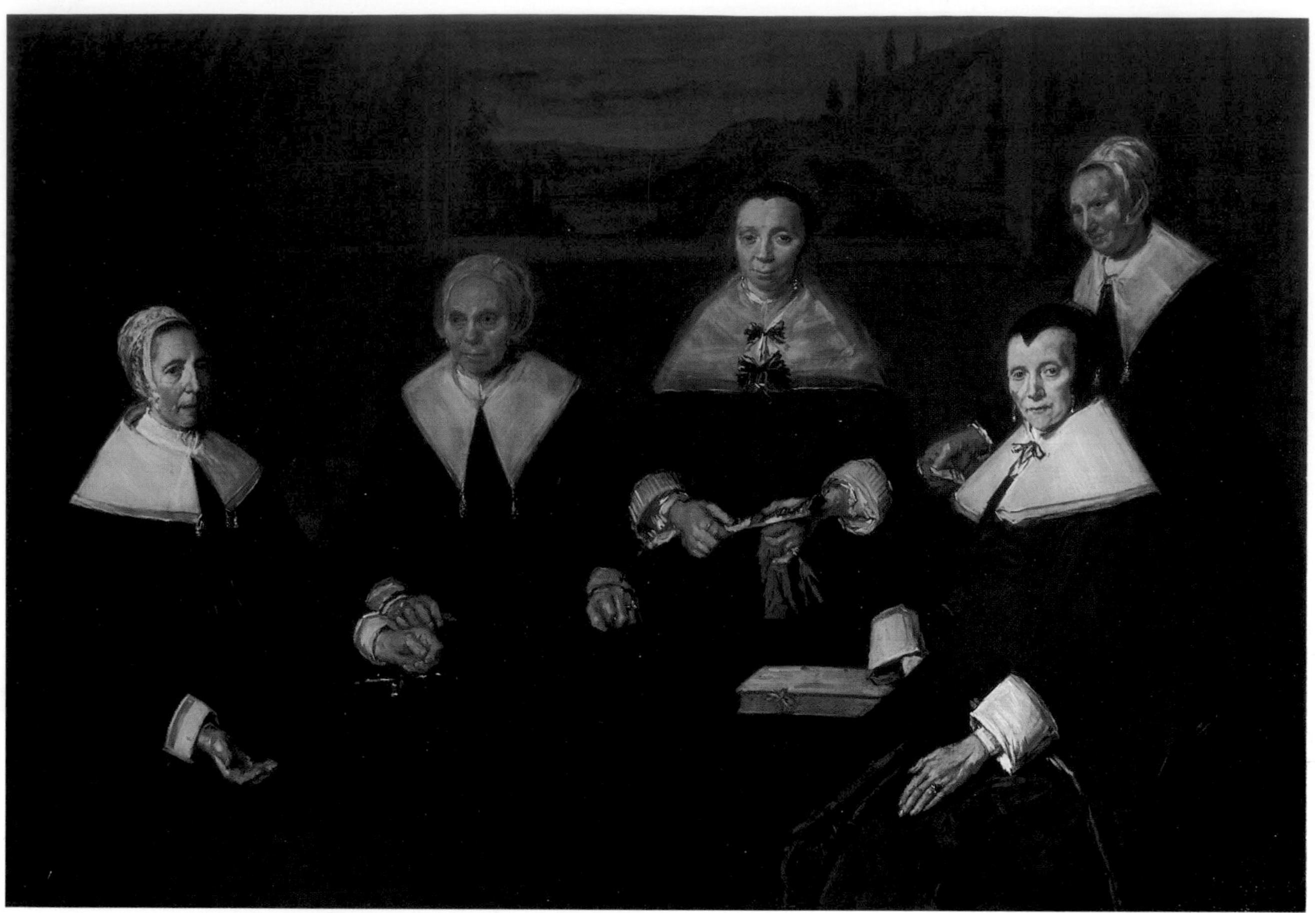

18-13. Frans Hals. *The Women Regents of the Old Men's Home at Haarlem.* 1664. Oil on canvas, 5'7" x 8'2" (1.70 x 2.49 m). Frans Halsmuseum, Haarlem, the Netherlands

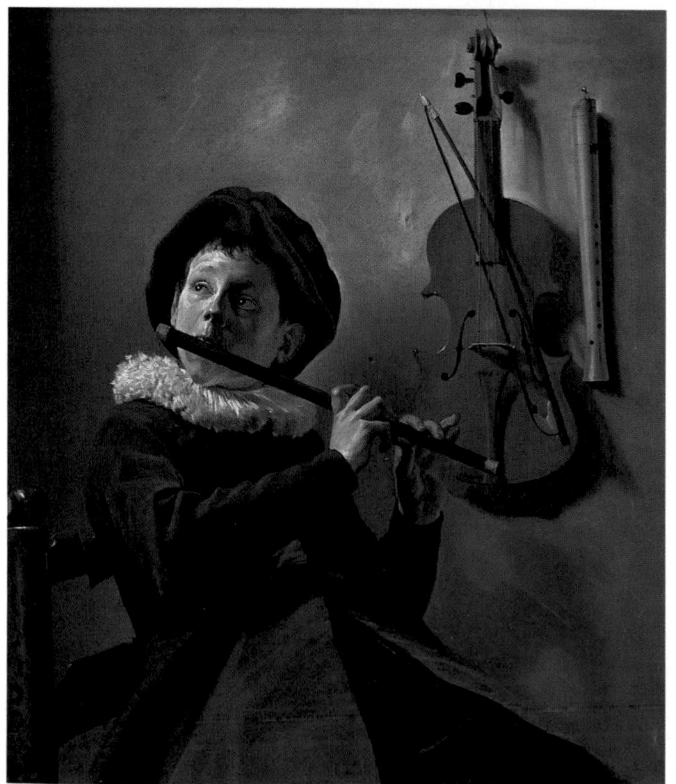

18-14. Judith Leyster. *Boy Playing a Flute.* 1630–35. Oil on canvas, 28 1/8 x 24 1/8" (73 x 62 cm). Nationalmuseum, Stockholm

In the artist's last canvases these pictorial fireworks are transformed into an austere style of great emotional depth. His group portrait *The Women Regents of the Old Men's Home at Haarlem* (fig. 18-13) has an insight into human character matched only in Rembrandt's late style (compare figs. 18-18 and 18-19). The experience of suffering and death has so etched the faces of these women that they seem themselves to have become images of death—gentle, inexorable, and timeless.

LEYSTER. Hals' virtuosity could not be readily imitated; hence, he had few followers. The most important among them was Judith Leyster (1609–1660), who was responsible for a number of works that once passed as Hals' own. Like many women artists before modern times, her career was curtailed by motherhood. (She married a fellow student of Hals.) Leyster's *Boy Playing a Flute* (fig. 18-14) is her masterpiece. Significantly, its style is closer to Terbrugghen's than to Hals'. The rapt musician is a memorable expression of lyrical mood. To convey this spirit, Leyster explored the poetic quality of light with an intensity that anticipates the work of Jan Vermeer a generation later (see page 573).

REMBRANDT. Like Hals, Rembrandt (1606–1669), the greatest genius of Dutch art, had indirect contact with Caravaggio through the Utrecht School. His earliest pictures, painted in his native Leyden, are small, sharply lit, and intensely realistic. Many deal with Old Testament subjects, a lifelong preference. They show both his greater realism and his new emotional attitude. Since the beginning of Christian art, episodes from the Old Testament had often been represented for the light they shed on Christian doctrine, rather than for their own sake. (The Sacrifice of Isaac, for example, "prefigured" the sacrificial death of Christ.) This perspective not only limited the choice of subjects, it also colored their interpretation. Rembrandt, by contrast, viewed the stories of the Old Testament in much the same lay Christian spirit that governed Caravaggio's approach to the New Testament: as direct accounts of God's ways with his human creations.

How strongly these stories affected him is clear in *The Blinding of Samson* (fig. 18-15). Painted in the High Baroque style he developed in the 1630s after moving to Amsterdam, it shows Rembrandt as master storyteller. The artist depicts the Old Testament world as full of Oriental splendor and violence, cruel yet seductive. The theatrical light pouring into the dark tent heightens the drama to the pitch of *The Raising of the Cross* (see fig. 18-1) by Rubens, whose work Rembrandt sought to rival.

Rembrandt was at this time an avid collector of Near Eastern objects, which serve as props in these pictures. He was now Amsterdam's most sought after portrait painter, and a man of considerable wealth. His famous group portrait known as *The Night Watch* (fig. 18-16), painted in 1642, shows a military company assembling for the visit of Marie de' Medici to Amsterdam. Although its members had each contributed toward the cost of the huge canvas (originally it was even larger), Rembrandt did not give them equal weight. He wanted to avoid the mechanically regular designs of earlier group portraits—a problem only Frans Hals had solved successfully. Instead, he made the picture a virtuoso performance filled with Baroque movement and lighting, which capture the excitement of the moment and give the scene unprecedented drama. Some of the figures were plunged into shadow, while others were hidden by overlapping. Legend has it that the people whose portraits he had obscured were not satisfied with the painting, but there is no evidence for this claim. On the contrary, we know that the painting was much admired in its time.

Like Michelangelo and, later, Van Gogh, Rembrandt has been the subject (one might say, the victim) of many fictionalized biographies. In these, the artist's fall from public favor is usually explained by the "catastrophe" of *The Night Watch.* It is true that his prosperity petered out in the 1640s, as he was replaced by other artists, including some of his own pupils. Yet his fortunes declined less suddenly and completely than his romantic admirers would have us believe. Certain important people in Amsterdam continued to be his friends and supporters, and he received some major public commissions in the 1650s and 1660s. Actually, his financial problems were due largely to poor management and his own stubbornness, which alienated his patrons.

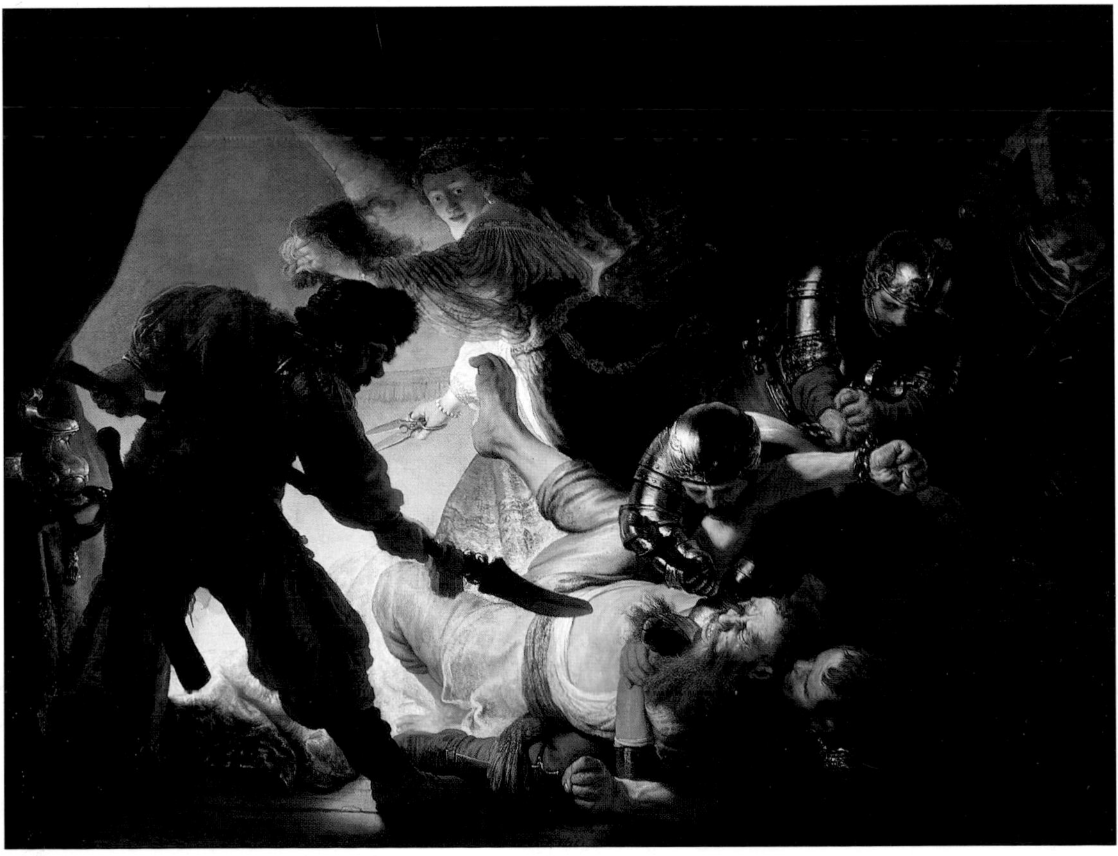

18-15. Rembrandt. *The Blinding of Samson.* 1636. Oil on canvas, 7'9" x 9'11" (2.4 x 3 m). Städelsches Kunstinstitut, Frankfurt

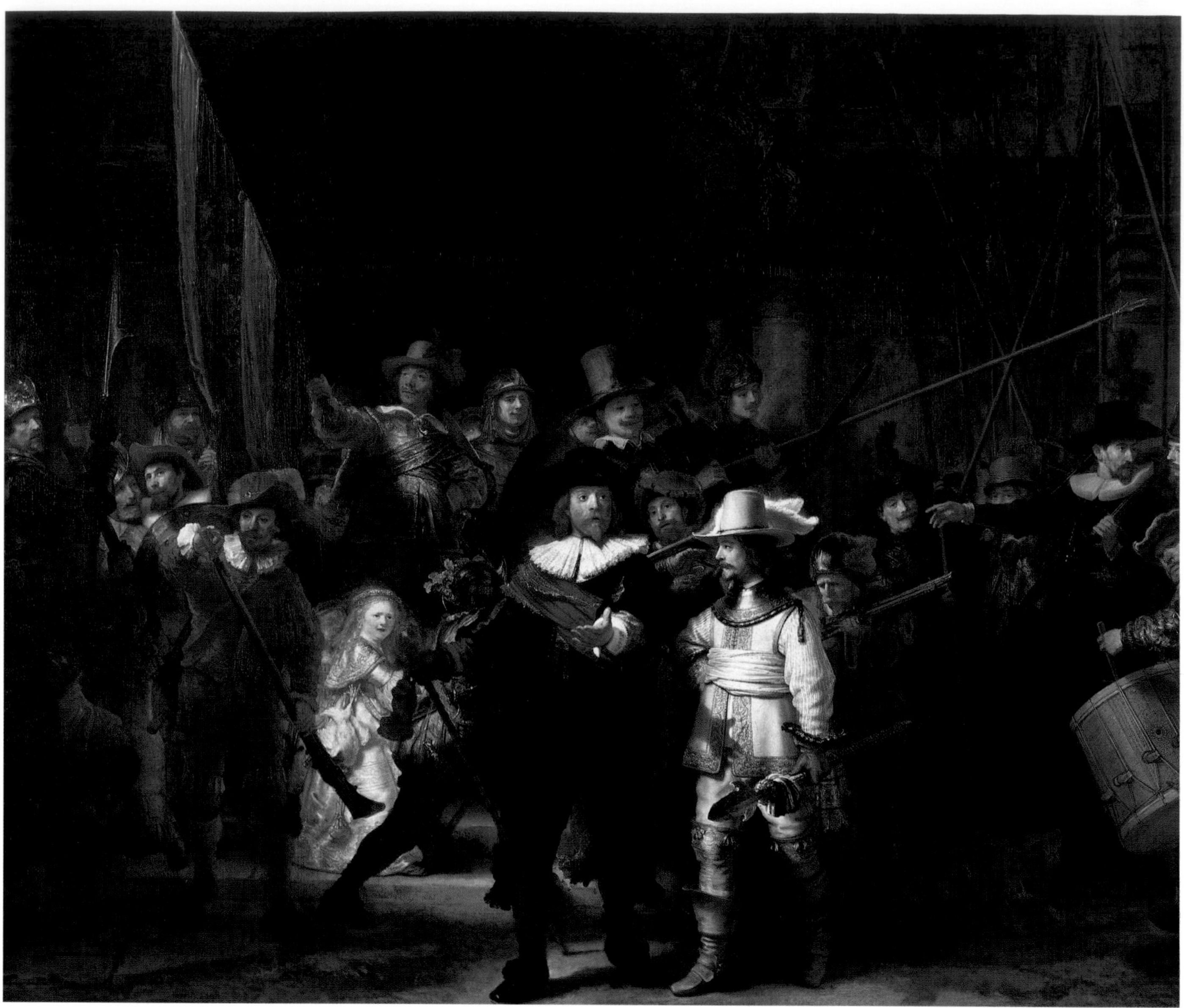

18-16. Rembrandt. *The Night Watch (The Company of Captain Frans Banning Cocq).* 1642. Oil on canvas, 12'2" x 14'7" (3.8 x 4.4 m). Rijksmuseum, Amsterdam

Still, the 1640s were a time of inner uncertainty and external troubles, especially his wife's death. Rembrandt's outlook changed profoundly: after about 1650, his style is marked by lyric subtlety and pictorial breadth. Some exotic trappings from the earlier years remain, but they no longer create an alien world. Rembrandt's etchings from these years, such as *Christ Preaching* (fig. 18-17), show this new depth of feeling. The sensuous beauty seen in *The Blinding of Samson* has yielded to a humble world of bare feet and ragged clothes. The scene is full of the artist's deep feeling of compassion for the poor and outcast who make up Christ's audience. Rembrandt had a special sympathy for the Jews, as heirs of the biblical past and as victims of persecution; they were often his models. This print strongly suggests some corner in the Amsterdam ghetto and surely incorporates observations of life from the drawings he made throughout his career. Here it is the magic of light that endows *Christ Preaching* with spiritual significance. Rembrandt's importance as a graphic artist is second only to Dürer's, although we get no more than a hint of his virtuosity from this single example.

In the many self-portraits Rembrandt painted over his long career, his view of himself reflects every stage of his inner development. It is experimental in the early Leyden years, disguised in the 1630s, and frank toward the end of his life. While our late example (fig. 18-18) is partially indebted to Titian's portraits (compare fig. 13-39), Rembrandt scrutinizes himself with the same typically Northern candor found in Jan van Eyck's *Man in a Red Turban* (see fig. 15-7). The bold pose and penetrating look bespeak a resigned but firm resolve in the face of adversity.

This approach helps to account for the dignity we see in the religious scenes that play so large a part in Rembrandt's work toward the end of his life. *The Return of the Prodigal Son* (fig. 18-19), created a few years before his death, may be his most moving painting. It is also his quietest—a moment stretching into eternity. So pervasive is the mood of tender silence that the viewer feels a kinship with this group. That bond is perhaps stronger and more intimate in this picture than in any earlier work of art. Here the understanding accumulated over a lifetime achieves a universal expression of sorrow and forgiveness.

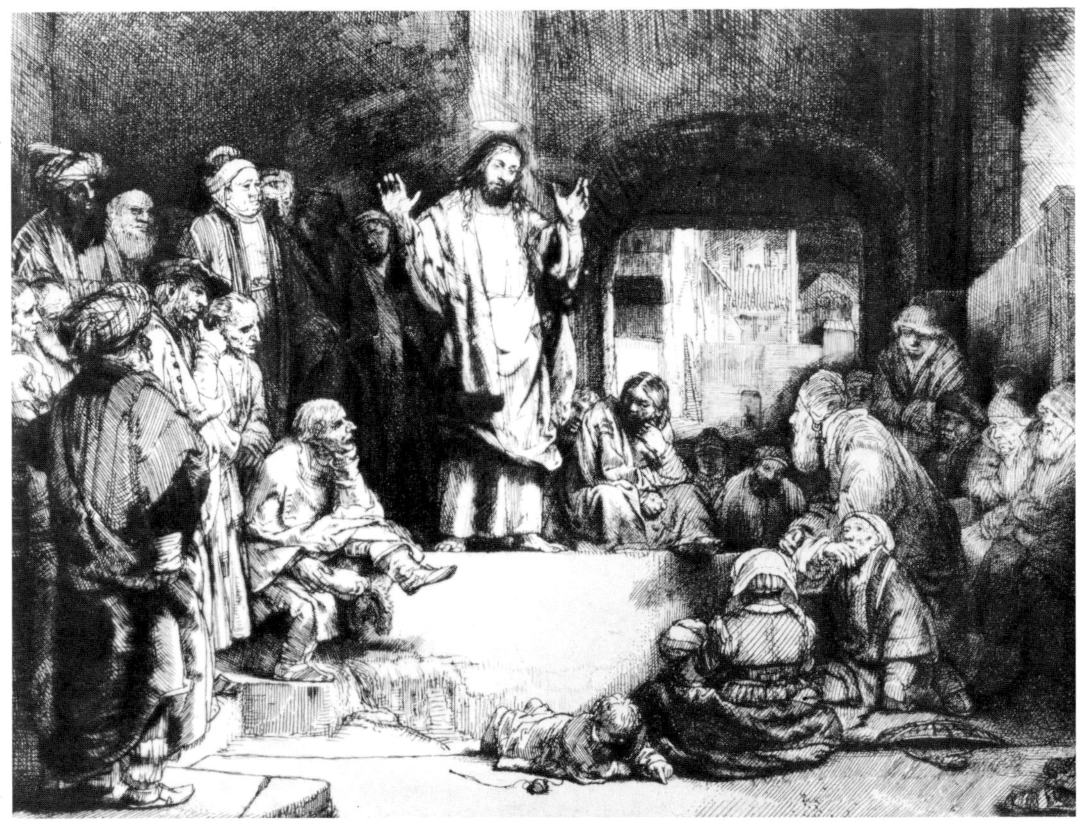

18-17. Rembrandt. *Christ Preaching.* c. 1652. Etching, $6\frac{1}{8}$ x $8\frac{1}{8}$" (15.6 x 20.6 cm). The Metropolitan Museum of Art, New York

BEQUEST OF MRS. H. O. HAVEMEYER, 1929

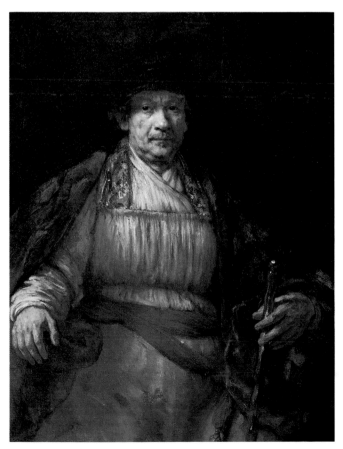

18-18. Rembrandt. *Self-Portrait.* 1658. Oil on canvas, $52\frac{5}{8}$ x $40\frac{7}{8}$" (133.6 x 103.8 cm). The Frick Collection, New York

COPYRIGHT THE FRICK COLLECTION

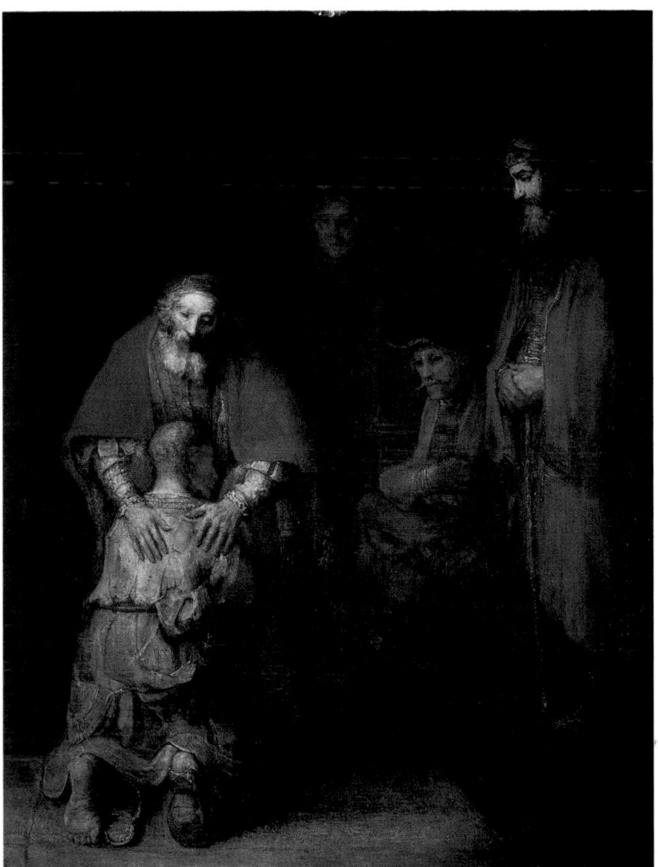

18-19. Rembrandt. *The Return of the Prodigal Son.* c. 1665. Oil on canvas, 8'8" x 6'$7\frac{3}{4}$" (2.6 x 2.1 m). Hermitage Museum, St. Petersburg

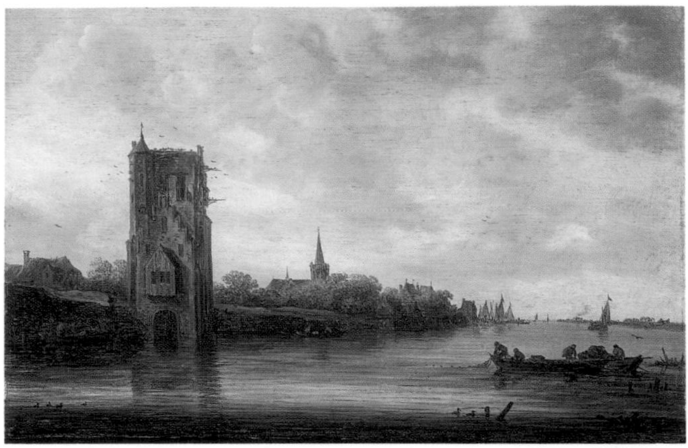

18-20. Jan van Goyen. *Pelkus-Poort.* 1646. Oil on panel, 14½ x 22½" (36.8 x 57.2 cm). The Metropolitan Museum of Art, New York

GIFT OF FRANCIS NEILSON, 1954

LANDSCAPES. Rembrandt's religious pictures demand an insight that was beyond the capacity of all but a few collectors. Most art buyers in Holland preferred subjects within their own experience: landscapes, architectural views, still lifes, everyday scenes. These types, we recall, emerged in the latter half of the sixteenth century (see page 518). As they became fully defined, artists began to specialize. The trend was not confined to Holland. We find it everywhere to some degree, but Dutch painting was its fountainhead, in both volume and variety.

VAN GOYEN. *Pelkus-Poort* (fig. 18-20) by Jan van Goyen (1596–1656) is the kind of landscape that enjoyed great popularity because its elements were so familiar: the distant town under an overcast sky seen through a moist atmosphere across an expanse of water. Such a view remains characteristic of the Dutch countryside to this day, and no one knew better than Van Goyen how to evoke the mood of these "nether lands," ever threatened by the sea.

Like other early Dutch Baroque landscapists, Van Goyen used only grays and browns highlighted by green accents, but within this narrow range he achieved an almost infinite variety of effects. The tonal landscape style in Holland was accompanied by radically simplified compositions in which the complex constructions of Northern Mannerism were reduced to orderly arrangements. Van Goyen's scene is based on a clear scheme of parallel bands surmounted by a triangle. He discovered what Annibale Carracci had already learned from Giorgione and the Venetians: that the secret to depicting landscape lay in geometry, which enabled the artist to gain visual control over nature as it did architecture.

CUYP. Other Northern artists absorbed this lesson in Rome, where they gathered in growing numbers. The Dutch Italianates who returned home in the 1640s brought with them new ideas that had an invigorating effect on landscape painting. Their impact can be seen in the work of Aelbert Cuyp (1620–1691), who never left his native soil. A follower of Van Goyen, he soon abandoned tonalism in favor of the radiant light in their views of the

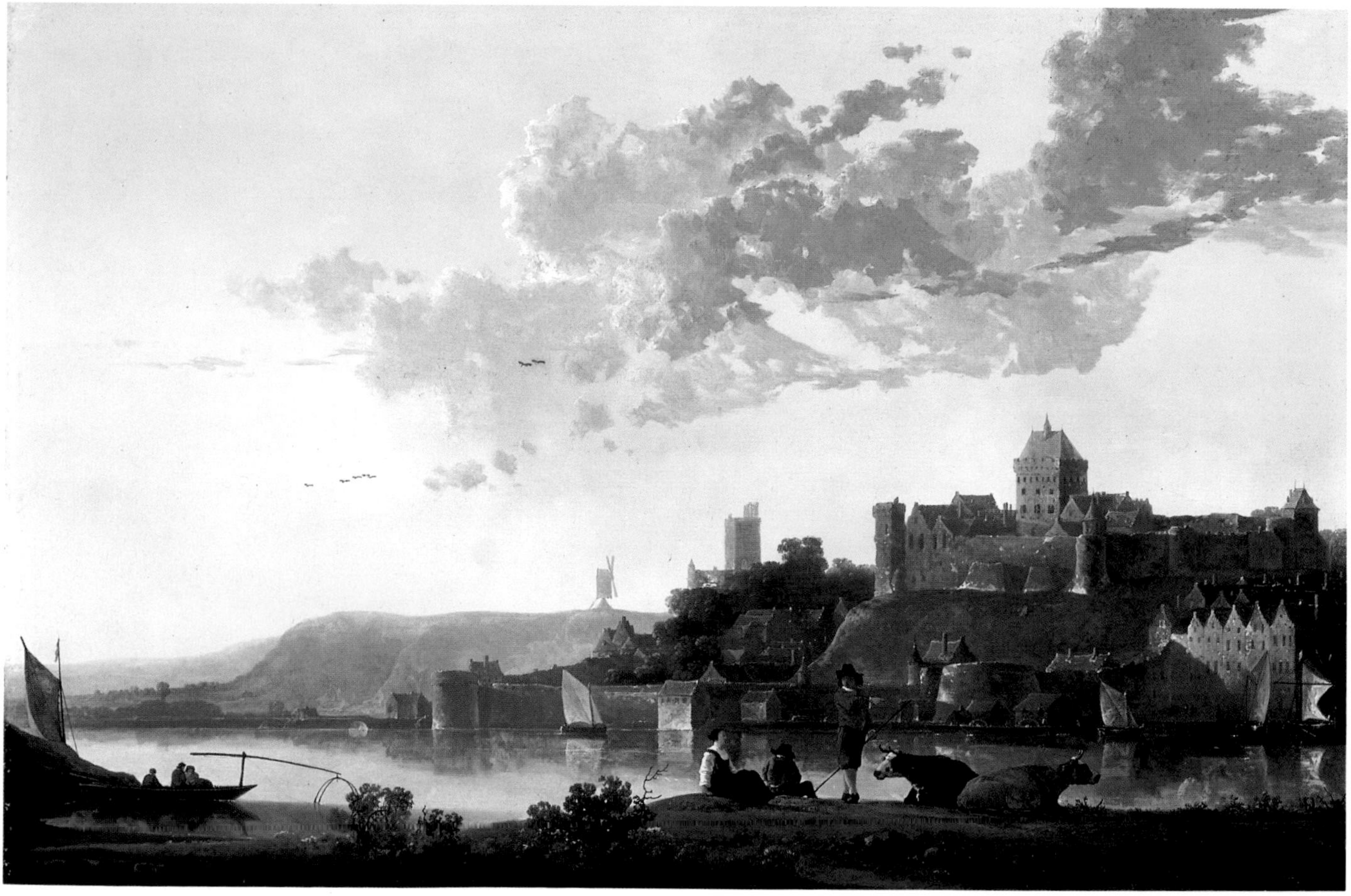

18-21. Aelbert Cuyp. *View of the Valkhof at Nijmegen.* c. 1655–65. Oil on panel, 19¼ x 29" (48.9 x 73.7 cm)

GIFT OF MRS. JAMES W. FESLER. © 1993 INDIANAPOLIS MUSEUM OF ART

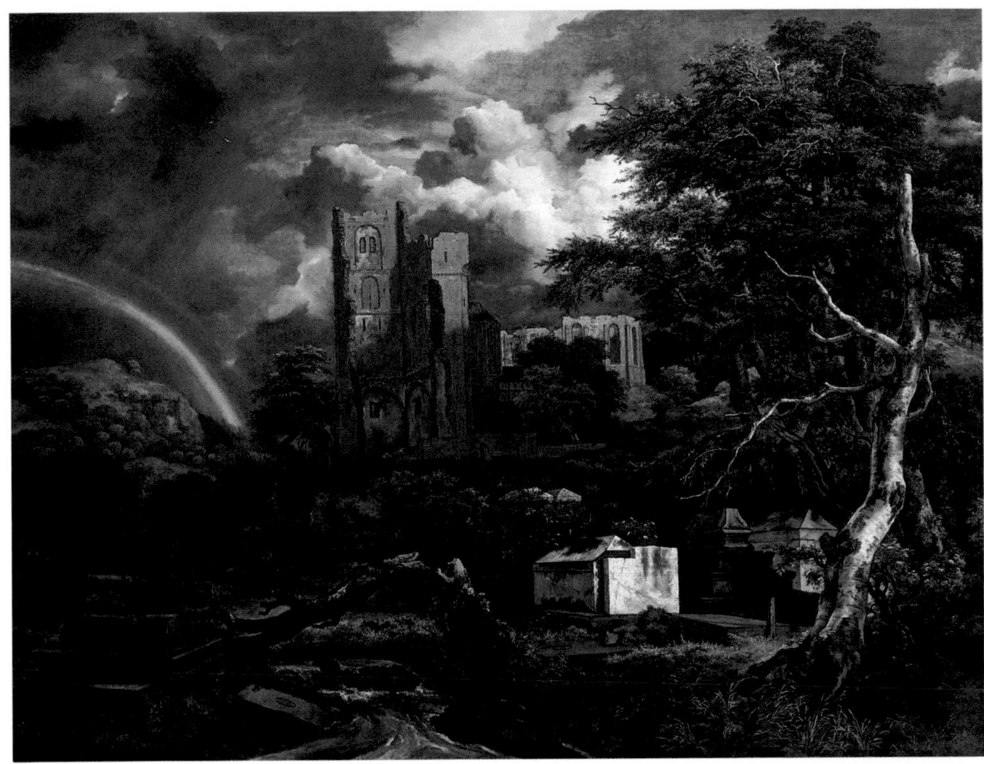

18-22. Jacob van Ruisdael. *The Jewish Cemetery*. 1655–60. Oil on canvas, 4'6" x 6'2½" (1.42 x 1.89 m). The Detroit Institute of Arts

GIFT OF JULIUS H. HAASS IN MEMORY OF HIS BROTHER, DR. ERNEST W. HAASS

(BELOW) 18-23. Pieter Saenredam. *Interior of the Choir of St. Bavo's Church at Haarlem*. 1660. Oil on panel, 27⅞ x 21⅝" (70.4 x 54.8 cm). Worcester Art Museum, Worcester, Massachusetts

CHARLOTTE E. W. BUFFINGTON FUND

Roman Campagna, which parallel the work of Claude Lorraine (see fig. 19-7). The golden light of late afternoon gives Cuyp's *View of the Valkhof at Nijmegen* (fig. 18-21) a poetic mood that suspends the scene in time and space. The nearly classical structure of the composition and cubic handling of the architecture heighten the sense of repose created by Cuyp's grasp of even the subtlest atmospheric effects.

RUISDAEL. Although nature was enjoyed for its own sake, it could also serve as a means of divine revelation through contemplation of God's work. Such is the case with *The Jewish Cemetery* (fig. 18-22) by Jacob van Ruisdael (1628/9–1682), the greatest Dutch landscape painter. Natural forces dominate this wild scene, which is imaginary except for the tombs, depicting the Jewish cemetery in Amsterdam. The thunderclouds passing over a deserted mountain valley, the medieval ruin, the torrent that has forced its way between ancient graves—all create a mood of melancholy. Nothing endures on this earth, the artist tells us: time, wind, and water grind all to dust—trees and rocks as well as the works of human hands. Even the elaborate tombs offer no protection from the same forces that destroy the church built in God's glory. In the context of this extended allegory, the rainbow may be understood as a sign of the promise of redemption through faith. Ruisdael's view of nature is thus the opposite of Annibale Carracci's "civilized" landscape (compare fig. 17-6). It harks back instead to Giorgione's tragic vision (see fig. 13-36). *The Jewish Cemetery* inspires that awe on which the Romantics, 150 years later, based their concept of the Sublime. The difference is that for Ruisdael, God remains separate from his creation, instead of a part of it.

SAENREDAM. Nothing at first seems further removed from *The Jewish Cemetery* than the painstaking *Interior of the Choir of*

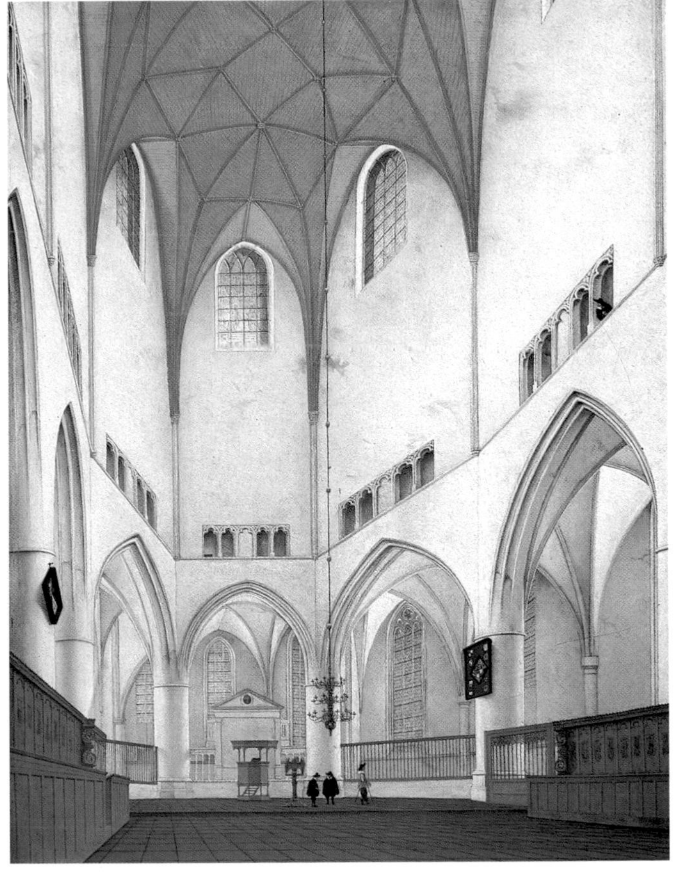

St. Bavo's Church at Haarlem (fig. 18-23), painted by Pieter Saenredam (1597–1665) at almost the same time. Yet it, too, is meant to serve as more than a mere record. (These architectural views were often freely invented as well.) The medieval structure, stripped of all furnishings and whitewashed under the Protestants, has acquired a crystalline spaciousness that invites spiritual contemplation.

MUSIC AND THEATER IN HOLLAND AND GERMANY

Dutch Protestant conservatism regarding music in the church inhibited the development of music in the Netherlands. The only important Dutch composer in the seventeenth century was Jan Sweelinck (1562–1621), who succeeded his father as organist of the Oude Kerk (Old Church) in Amsterdam. He was particularly noted for his psalm music. Sweelinck's strongest influence was felt not in Holland but in Germany, where his best pupils, such as Samuel Scheidt (1587–1654), George Frideric Handel's distinguished predecessor in Halle (see pages 604–05), were able to find employment and where a love of church music, fostered by Lutheranism, was widespread.

German music was largely under the sway of the Italians. Its chief representative was Heinrich Schütz (1585–1672), who studied with Giovanni Gabrieli in Venice (see page 466), then spent most of his career as *Kapellmeister* (Master of the Chapel) to the Elector of Saxony in Dresden, where he composed large quantities of extremely beautiful church music, including several oratorios—notably *The Seven Last Words of Christ* of 1645—that are important precursors of Johann Sebastian Bach's (see page 604). The most daring German composer of the time between Schütz and Bach was Heinrich von Biber (1644–1704), Kapellmeister to the Archbishop of Salzburg. A noted violinist, he was a Northern counterpart to Arcangelo Corelli (see page 538) and his writing, though technically more demanding, shares an alternately bittersweet plaintiveness and dancelike sprightliness. Biber made extensive use of different tunings (*scordatura,* "mistuning") to lend a varied character to the 15 "mystery" sonatas he composed for violin and continuo around 1675–76. These visionary works are musical meditations on the Catholic Rosary written to celebrate its feast in early October.

In contrast to its rich musical heritage, Germany had little to offer in the way of theater, which relied heavily on imported Italian and French players at the more affluent courts in Vienna, Dresden, and Munich, where opera proved the most popular theatrical form (see page 538). The situation was just the opposite in Holland, which enjoyed a lively theatrical life, especially in Amsterdam. Dutch theater was partly an outgrowth of the societies of rhetoricians (*rederijkers*) that had sprung up during the fifteenth century and partly of the Dutch Academy, which was founded in 1617 as a "Netherlandish training school." The theater also flourished because under these promising conditions Holland produced a number of gifted playwrights, notably Joost van den Vondel (1587–1679), at a time when rising nationalism placed new emphasis on the Dutch language. The plots often drew on the Old Testament to glorify the Dutch as a new "chosen people." These dramas were an important inspiration to artists, particularly Rembrandt. Many of his paintings, especially those from his early years, depict scenes drawn directly from these plays. Moreover, Rembrandt's use of exotic costumes and stage properties shows a deep love of drama that helps account, in part, for the theatricality of his work.

STILL LIFES. Still lifes exist above all to delight the senses, but even they can be tinged with a melancholy air. As a result of Holland's conversion to Calvinism, these visual feasts became vehicles for teaching moral lessons. Most Dutch Baroque still lifes treat the theme of Vanitas (the vanity of all earthly things). Overtly or implicitly, they preach the virtue of temperance, frugality, and hard work by warning the viewer to contemplate the brevity of life, the inevitability of death, and the passing of all earthly pleasures. The medieval tradition of imbuing everyday objects with religious significance was absorbed into vernacular culture though emblem books that, together with other forms of popular literature and prints, encompassed the prevailing ethic in words and pictures. The stern Calvinist sensibility is exemplified by such homilies as "A fool and his money are soon parted" (a saying that goes all the way back to ancient Rome) and is illustrated by flowers, shells, and other exotic luxuries. The very presence in Vanitas still lifes of precious goods, scholarly books, and objects appealing to the senses suggests an ambivalent attitude toward their subject. Such symbols usually take on multiple meanings that, although no longer comprehensible to us, were readily understood at the time. In their most elaborate form, these moral allegories become visual riddles that rely on the very learning they sometimes ridicule.

HEDA. The banquet (or breakfast) piece, showing the remnants of a meal, had Vanitas connotations almost from the beginning. The message may lie in such symbols as death's heads and extinguished candles or may be conveyed by less direct means. *Still Life* (fig. 18-24) by Willem Claesz. Heda (1594–1680) belongs to this widespread type. Food and drink are less emphasized here than luxury objects, such as crystal goblets and silver dishes, which are carefully juxtaposed for their contrasting shape, color, and texture. How different this seems from the piled-up foods of Aertsen's *The Meat Stall* (see fig. 16-20)! But virtuosity was not Heda's only aim. He reminds us that all is Vanity. His "story," the human context of these grouped objects, is suggested by the broken glass, the half-peeled lemon, and the overturned silver dish. The unstable composition, with its signs of a hasty departure, itself suggests transience. Whoever sat at this table has been suddenly forced to leave the meal. The curtain that time has lowered on the scene, as it were, gives the objects a strange pathos. The disguised symbolism of "Late Gothic" painting lives on here in a new form.

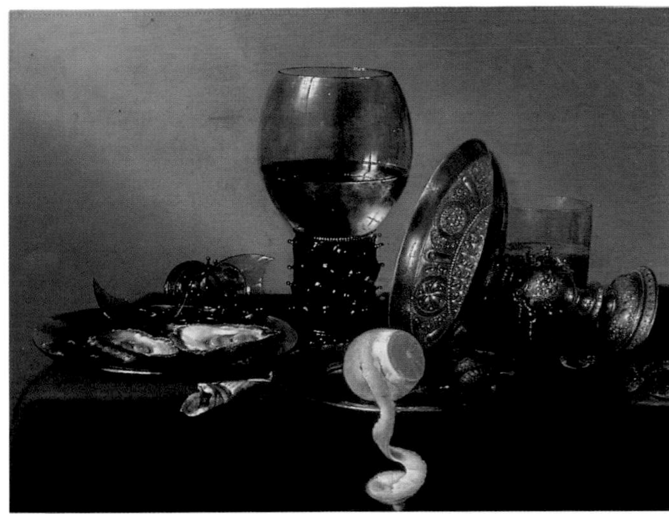

18-24. Willem Claesz. Heda. *Still Life.* 1634. Oil on panel, 16⅞ x 22⅞" (43 x 57 cm). Museum Boymans-van Beuningen, Rotterdam, the Netherlands

DE HEEM. The breakfast piece soon evolved into an even more lavish display known as the "fancy" still life for its visual splendor. This type reached its peak in the work of Jan de Heem (1606–1684). De Heem began his career in Protestant Holland, but he soon moved to Catholic Flanders. However, he traveled back and forth between the two countries and eventually returned to his native land. He was able to synthesize the sober Dutch tradition with the flamboyant manner of Frans Snyders into a unique style that had equal influence on both sides of the border. In *Still Life with Parrots* (fig. 18-25), he depicts delicious food, exotic birds, and luxurious goods from around the world. The result is a stunning tour de force. Despite the profusion of objects, the painting is unified by the balanced composition and colorful palette. In keeping with the theme of appetite, the viewer is meant to enjoy the visual abundance, which celebrates the work of the Lord and humanity. At the same time, the picture has a covert meaning. Many of these objects, including the oysters, melon, and shells (which commanded high prices), are also standard Vanitas symbols conveying an admonition to be temperate. Also present in *Still Life with Parrots* is the time-honored theme of the four elements,

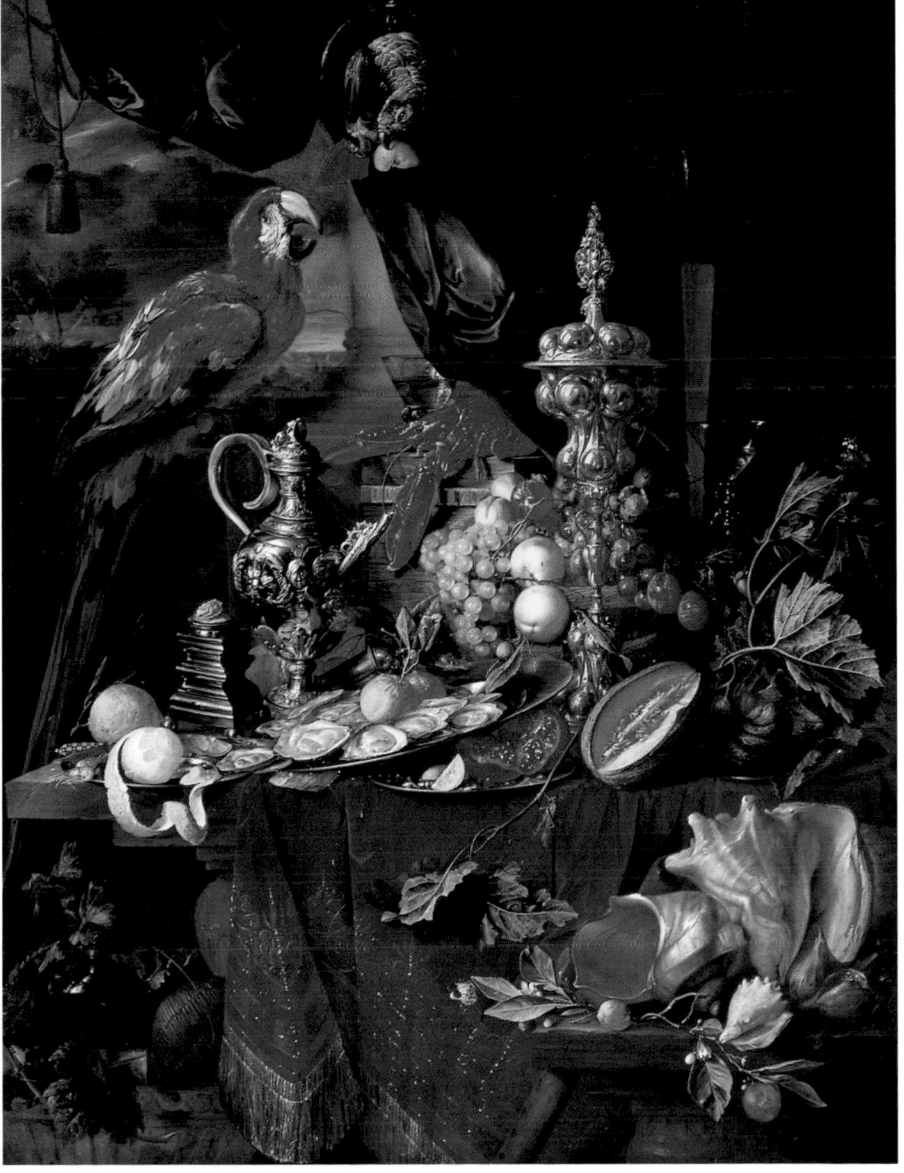

18-25. Jan de Heem. *Still Life with Parrots.* Late 1640s. Oil on canvas, 59¼ x 45½" (150.5 x 115.5 cm). John and Mable Ringling Museum of Art, Sarasota, Florida

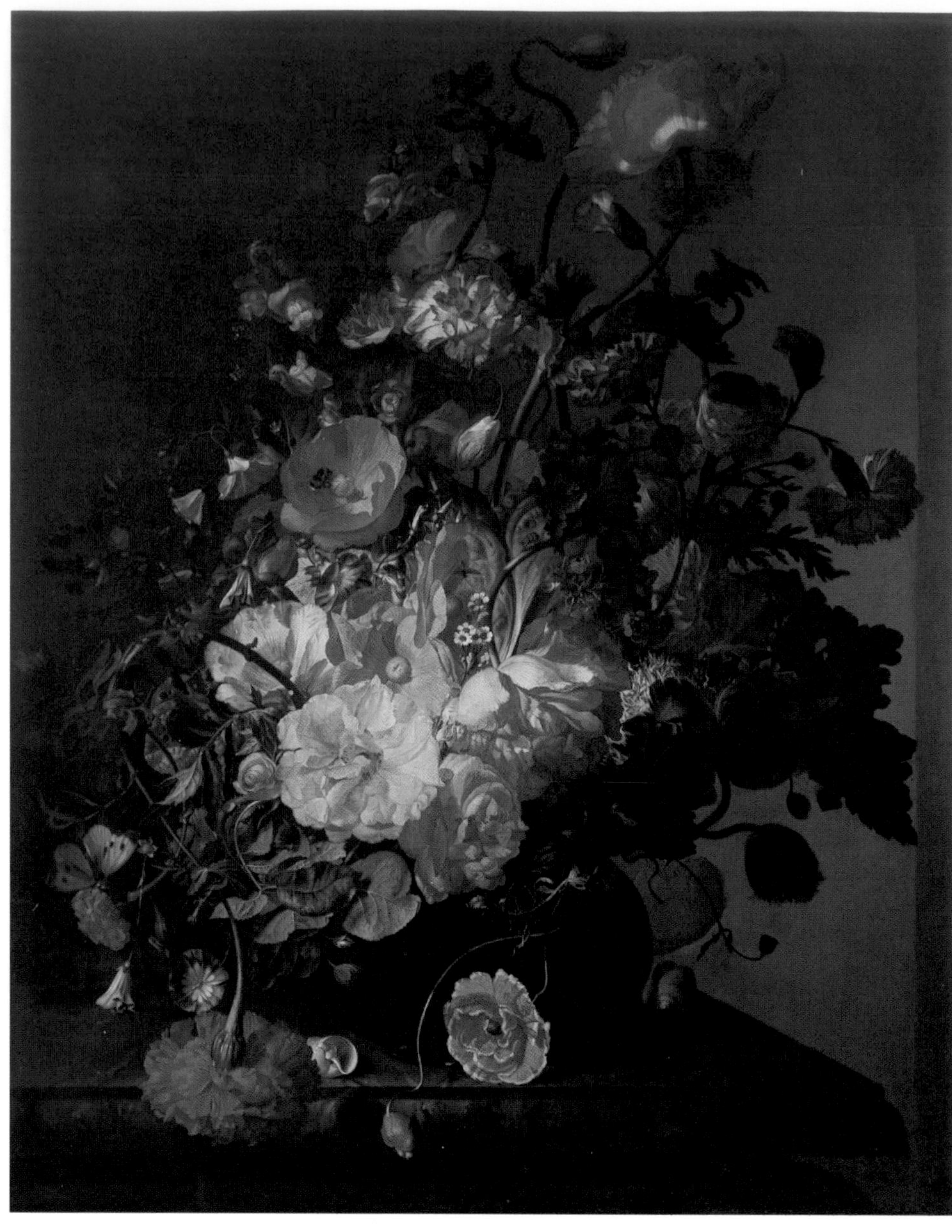

18-26. Rachel Ruysch. *Flower Still Life*. After 1700. Oil on canvas, 29¾ x 23⅞" (75.5 x 60.7 cm). The Toledo Museum of Art, Toledo, Ohio

PURCHASED WITH FUNDS FROM THE LIBBEY ENDOWMENT, GIFT OF EDWARD DRUMMOND LIBBEY

as well as traditional Christian imagery. The parrot is identified with the Madonna as the mother of Christ, while the grapes refer to the Eucharistic wine (and, hence, resurrection), as does the pomegranate, which stands for the Virgin's purity as well.

RUYSCH. De Heem also defined the High Baroque floral still life so completely that flower painters were to feel his impact for the next 200 years. Many of them were women, including his pupil Maria van Oosterwijck (1630–1693), who became a famous artist in her own right. Her achievements were soon outstripped by those of Rachel Ruysch (1664–1750), who shared honors with Jan van Huysum (1682–1749) as the leading Dutch flower painters of the day. Was Ruysch aware of the significance of every blossom, and of the butterflies, moths, and snails she put into the piece in figure 18-26, each of which has a symbolic meaning? By this time it is doubtful that she intended her bouquet to convey a moralizing message. Instead, the main purpose of the painting was surely to please the eye. She imparts such a sweeping vitality to the profusion of buds that they seem to leap from their vase.

STEEN. Genre scenes are as varied as landscapes and still lifes. They range from tavern brawls to refined domestic interiors. *The Feast of St. Nicholas* (fig. 18-27) by Jan Steen (1625/6–1679) is midway between these two extremes. St. Nicholas has just paid his pre-Christmas visit to the household, leaving toys, candy, and cake for the children. The little girl and boy are delighted with their presents. She holds a doll of St. John the Baptist and a bucket filled with sweets, while he plays with a golf club and ball. Everybody is jolly except their brother, on the left, who has received only a birch

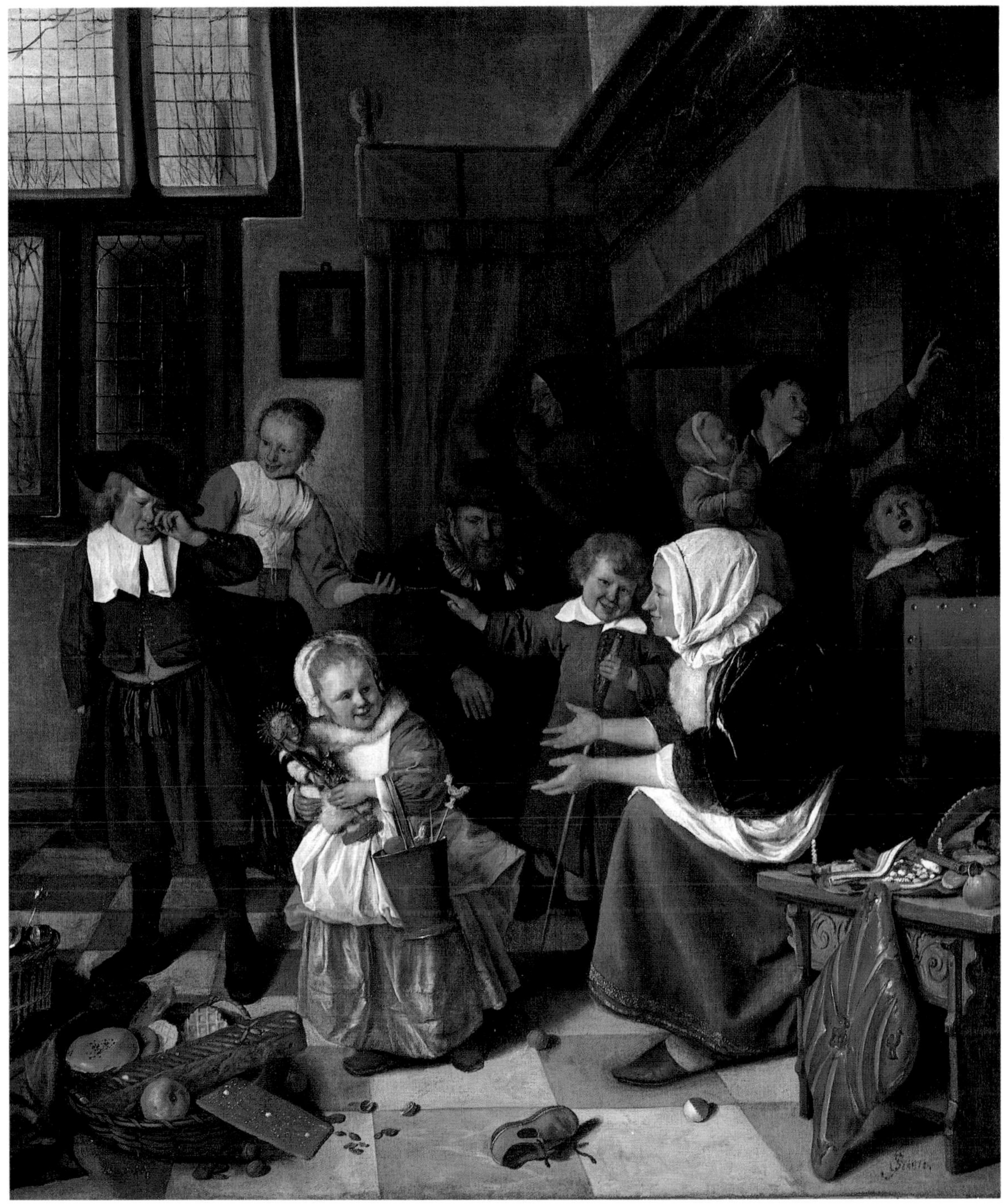

18-27. Jan Steen. *The Feast of St. Nicholas.* c. 1660–65. Oil on canvas, 32¼ x 27¾" (82 x 70.5 cm). Rijksmuseum, Amsterdam

rod (held by the maidservant) for caning naughty children. Soon his tears will turn to joy, however: his grandmother, in the background, beckons to the bed, where a toy is hidden.

Steen tells this story with relish, embroidering it with many delightful details. Of all the Dutch painters of daily life, he was the sharpest and the most good-humored observer. To supplement his earnings he kept an inn, which may explain his keen insight into human behavior. His sense of timing and his characterization often remind us of Frans Hals (compare fig. 18-12), while his storytelling stems from the tradition of Pieter Bruegel the Elder (compare fig. 16-22). Steen was also a gifted history painter, and although his pictures often contain parodies of well-known works by Italian artists, they usually convey a serious message as well. Thus the doll of St. John is meant to remind the viewer about the importance of spiritual matters over worldly possessions, no matter how delightful.

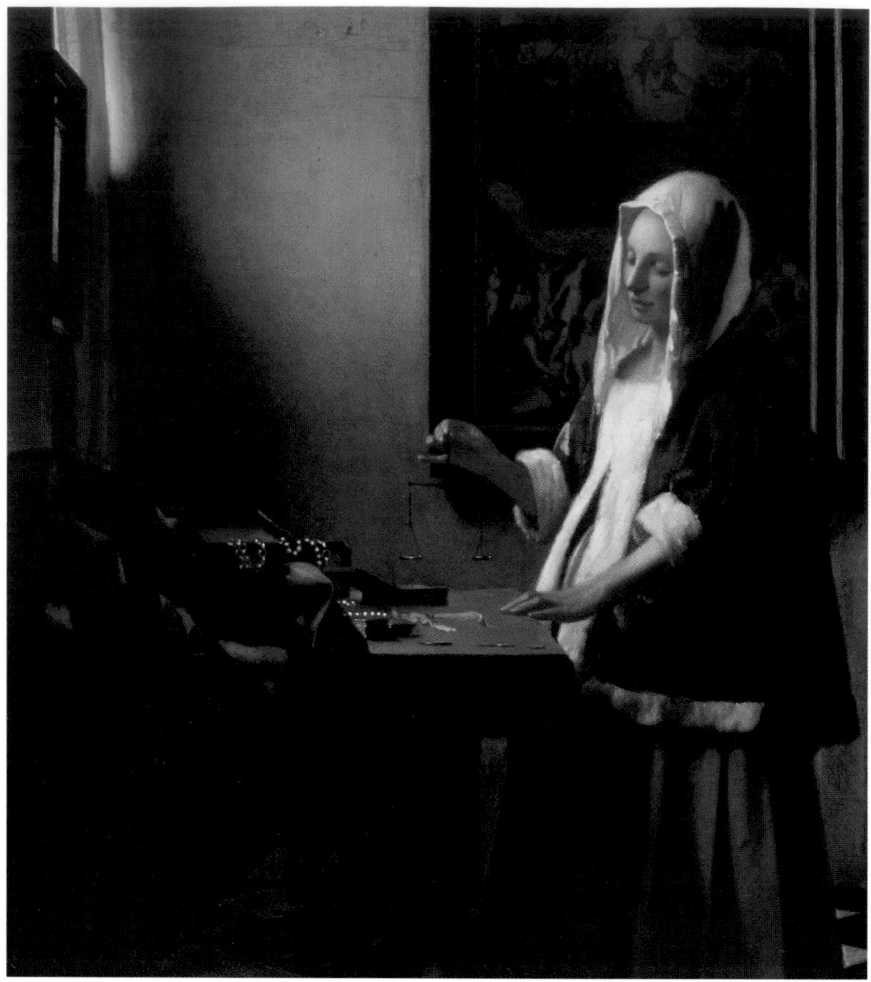

18-28. Jan Vermeer. *Woman Holding a Balance.* c. 1664. Oil on canvas, 16¾ x 15" (42.5 x 38.1 cm). National Gallery of Art, Washington, D.C.
WIDENER COLLECTION, 1942

VERMEER. In the genre scenes of Jan Vermeer (1632–1675), by contrast, there is hardly any narrative. Single figures, usually women, are seemingly engaged in everyday tasks. They exist in a timeless "still life" world, as if calmed by a spell. In *Woman Holding a Balance* (fig. 18-28), a young woman, richly dressed in the at-home wear of the day, is contemplating a balance in her hand, with strings of pearls and gold coins spread out on the table before her. The design is so perfect that we cannot move a single element without upsetting the delicate equilibrium. The vanishing point of the diagonals formed by the top of the mirror and the right side of the table lies near the juncture of the woman's hand and the picture frame. The bottom of the frame is actually lower on the right than on the left in order to guide our eye to the painting in the background, which depicts Christ at the Last Judgment, when every soul is weighed. Despite the obvious parallel of this subject to the woman's activity, the meaning is far from clear. The pans of the balance actually contain nothing, only beads of light.

What, then, is the woman doing? Is she weighing temporal against spiritual values? What accounts for her inner peace? Perhaps it is self-knowledge, symbolized here by the mirror. It may also be the promise of salvation through her faith. If so, light serves here not only to illuminate the scene but also to represent religious revelation. In the end, however, we cannot be sure, because Vermeer's approach to his subject proves as subtle as his pictorial treatment. He avoids any anecdote or symbolism that might limit us to a single interpretation. There can be no doubt, however, about his fascination with light. Vermeer's mastery of light's expressive qualities raises his concern for the reality of appearance to the level of poetry and includes all of its visual and symbolic possibilities. Here, then, we have found the real "meaning" of Vermeer's art. *Woman Holding a Balance* is also testimony to the artist's faith: he was a Catholic living in Protestant Holland, where his religion was officially banned, although worship in private houses was tolerated.

When there are two figures, as in *The Letter* (fig. 18-29), they do no more than exchange glances. The painting nonetheless does tell a story, but with unmatched subtlety. The "staged" entrance serves to establish our relation to the scene. We are more than bystanders: we become the bearer of the letter that has just been delivered to the young woman. Dressed in sumptuous clothing, she has been playing the lute, as if awaiting our visit. This instrument, filled with erotic meaning, traditionally signifies the harmony between lovers, who play each other's heartstrings. Are we, then, her lover? The amused expression of the maid suggests such an interest. Moreover, the lover in Dutch art and literature is often

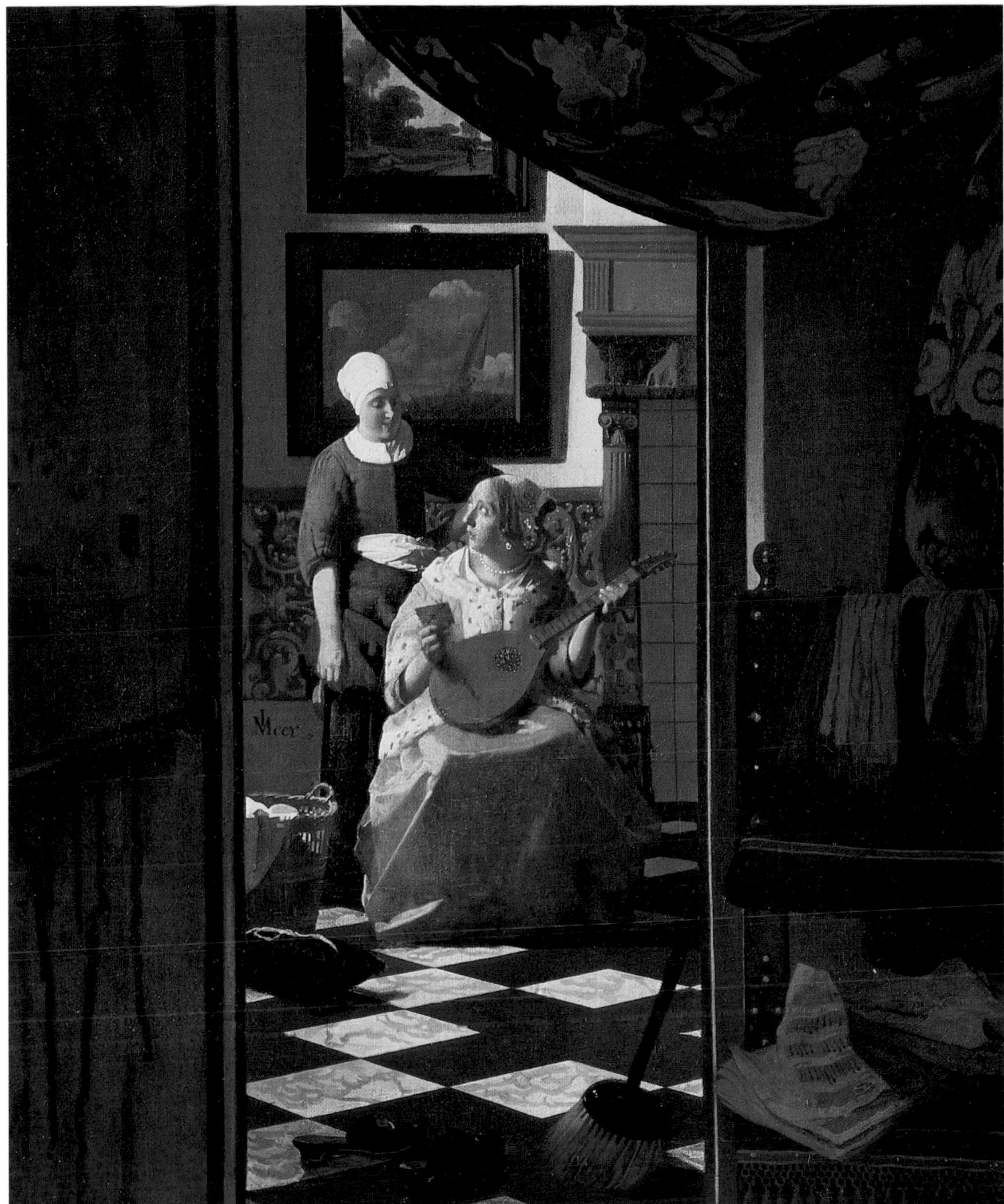

18-29. Jan Vermeer. *The Letter.* 1666. Oil on canvas, 17¼ x 15¼" (43.3 x 38.3 cm). Rijksmuseum, Amsterdam

compared to a ship at sea, whose calm waters shown in the painting on the wall indicate smooth sailing. As usual with Vermeer, however, the picture refuses to yield a final answer, since the artist has depicted the moment before the letter is opened.

Here, too, Vermeer's real interest centers on the role of light. The cool daylight that filters in from the left is the only active element, working its miracles upon all the objects in its path. As we look at *The Letter,* we feel as if a veil had been pulled from our eyes. The everyday world shines with jewel-like freshness, more beautiful than we have ever seen it before. No painter since Jan van Eyck *saw* as intensely as this. But Vermeer, unlike earlier artists, perceives reality as a mosaic of colored surfaces—more accurately, he translates reality into a mosaic as he puts it on canvas. We see *The Letter* not only as a perspective "window" but as a "field" made up of smaller fields. Rectangles predominate, carefully aligned with the picture surface; there are no "holes," no undefined empty spaces.

The interlocking shapes give Vermeer's work a uniquely modern quality in seventeenth-century art. How did he acquire it? Although there is considerable documentary evidence relating to his life, we know very little about his training. Some of his works show the influence of Carel Fabritius (1622–1654), the most brilliant of Rembrandt's pupils. Others suggest his contact with the Utrecht School. But none of these sources really explains the genesis of his style, which is so original that his genius was not recognized until about a century ago.

CHAPTER NINETEEN

The Baroque in France and England

FRANCE: THE AGE OF VERSAILLES

Under Henry IV (1553–1610), Louis XIII (1601–1643), and Louis XIV (1638–1715), France became the most powerful nation of Europe, militarily and culturally. These rulers were aided by a succession of extremely able ministers and advisers: the Duc de Sully, Cardinal Richelieu, Cardinal Mazarin, and Jean-Baptiste Colbert. By the late seventeenth century, Paris was vying with Rome to be the world capital of the major and minor arts. How did this change come about? Because of the Palace of Versailles and other vast projects glorifying the king of France, we are tempted to think of French art in the age of Louis XIV as the expression of absolute rule. This is true of the climactic phase of Louis' reign, 1660 to 1685, but by that time seventeenth-century French art had already attained its distinctive style.

The French are reluctant to call this style Baroque. To them, it is the Style of Louis XIV. Often they also describe the art and literature of the period as "classic." In this context, the word has three meanings. It is a synonym for "highest achievement," which implies that the Style of Louis XIV corresponds to the High Renaissance in Italy or the age of Pericles in ancient Greece. It also refers to the emulation of the forms and subject matter of classical antiquity. Finally, it suggests qualities of balance and restraint shared by ancient art and the Renaissance. The last two meanings describe what could more accurately be called "classicism." Since the Style of Louis XIV reflects Italian Baroque art, however modified, we may label it "Baroque classicism."

This classicism was the official court style between 1660 and 1685, but its origin was primarily artistic, not political. Sixteenth-century architecture, and to a lesser extent sculpture, in France were more closely linked with the Italian Renaissance than in any other Northern country. Painting, however, continued to be governed by the Mannerist style of the later school of Fontainebleau until after 1600 (see page 477). Classicism was also nourished by French humanism, with its intellectual heritage of reason and Stoic virtue, which reflected the values of the middle class, who dominated cultural and political life. These factors slowed the spread of the Baroque in France and altered its interpretation. Rubens' Medici cycle (see fig. 18-2), for example, had no effect on French art until the very end of the century. In the 1620s, when he painted it, the young artists in France were still assimilating the Early Baroque.

Printmaking

CALLOT. An important transitional figure among these neglected masters was Jacques Callot (1592/3–1635), an etcher and engraver whose work inspired both Georges de La Tour (see below) and the young Rembrandt. Much of his early career was spent at the court of Cosimo II de' Medici in Florence, where he mainly produced prints dealing with the theater, especially the commedia dell'arte (see box page 549). After he returned in 1621 to his native town of Nancy, his work underwent a major change. His prints now alternated between apocalyptic intensity, which allies him directly with Hieronymus Bosch, and extraordinary directness, which recalls the spirit of Pieter Bruegel the Elder; yet he belongs fully to his own time. Thus Callot's work looks as much to past tradition as it does to the art of the present. These qualities merge in *Great Miseries of War,* which appeared in 1633, the year Richelieu conquered Nancy. This series of etchings represents a distillation of Callot's experience of the Thirty Years' War, but it also has a moralizing purpose. *Hangman's Tree* (fig. 19-1) depicts soldiers paying for their crimes. The inscription reads: "Finally these thieves, sordid and forlorn, hanging like unfortunate pieces of fruit from this tree, experience the justice of Heaven sooner or later." The style is Mannerist, except in the group to the right, which exhibits the same naturalism as the Le Nains' (see below). This stark scene is far grimmer than Bosch's vision of Hell in *The Garden of Delights* (see fig. 15-14). The plate has a striking immediacy, gained from the artist's experience of the theater, that anticipates Goya's vivid imagery (see fig. 21-25).

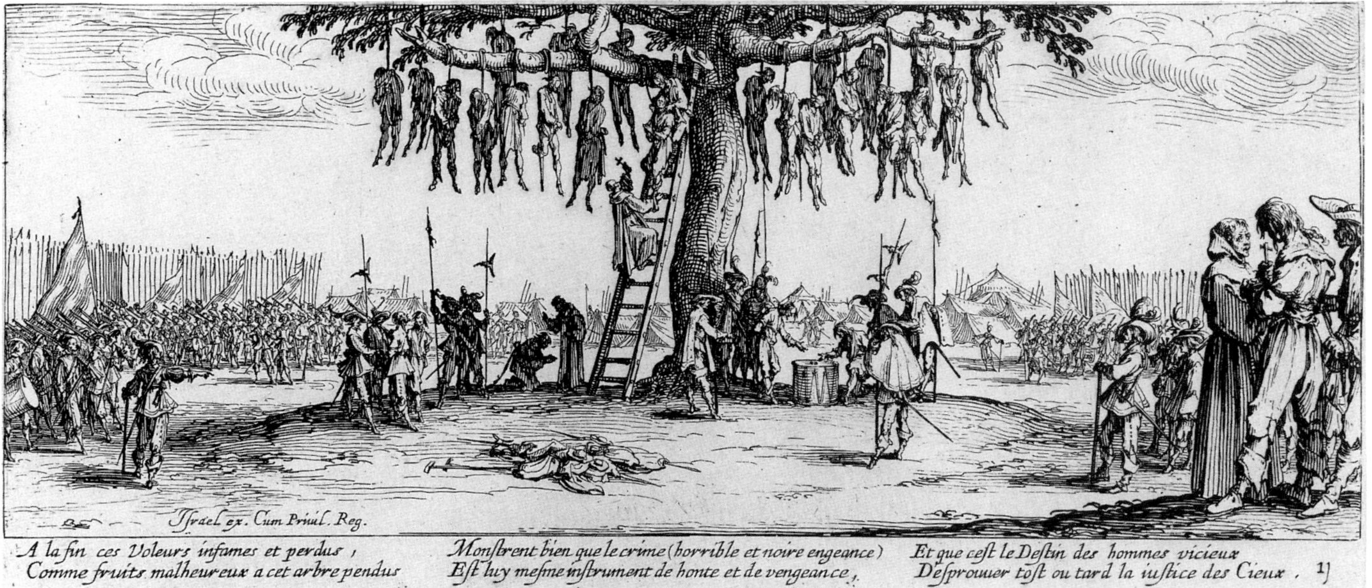

19-1. Jacques Callot. *Hangman's Tree,* from *Great Miseries of War.* 1633. Etching, $3\frac{1}{2}$ x 9" (9 x 23 cm). The British Museum, London

Painting

DE LA TOUR. Many early French Baroque painters were influenced by Caravaggio, although it is not clear how they absorbed his style. Most were minor artists toiling in the provinces, but a few developed highly original styles. The finest of them was Georges de La Tour (1593–1652), whose importance was recognized only in the nineteenth century. Although he spent his career in Lorraine in northeast France, he was by no means a simple provincial artist. Besides being named a painter to the king, he received important commissions from the governor of Lorraine. He began his career painting picturesque figures in the tradition of Callot. He then turned to elaborate stock scenes from contemporary theater derived largely from Caravaggio's Northern followers.

Although the latter are well painted, De La Tour would arouse little interest were it not for his mature religious pictures, which possess both seriousness and grandeur. *Joseph the Carpenter* (fig. 19-2) might be mistaken for a genre scene, but its devotional spirit has the power of Caravaggio's *The Calling of St. Matthew* (see fig. 17-2). De La Tour's intensity of vision lends each gesture, each expression its maximum significance within this spellbinding composition. The boy Jesus holds a candle, a favorite device with this artist, which lights the scene with an intimacy and tenderness that recall the *Nativity* by Geertgen tot Sint Jans (see fig. 15-13). De La Tour also shares Geertgen's tendency to reduce forms to a geometric simplicity that raises them above the everyday world, despite their apparent realism.

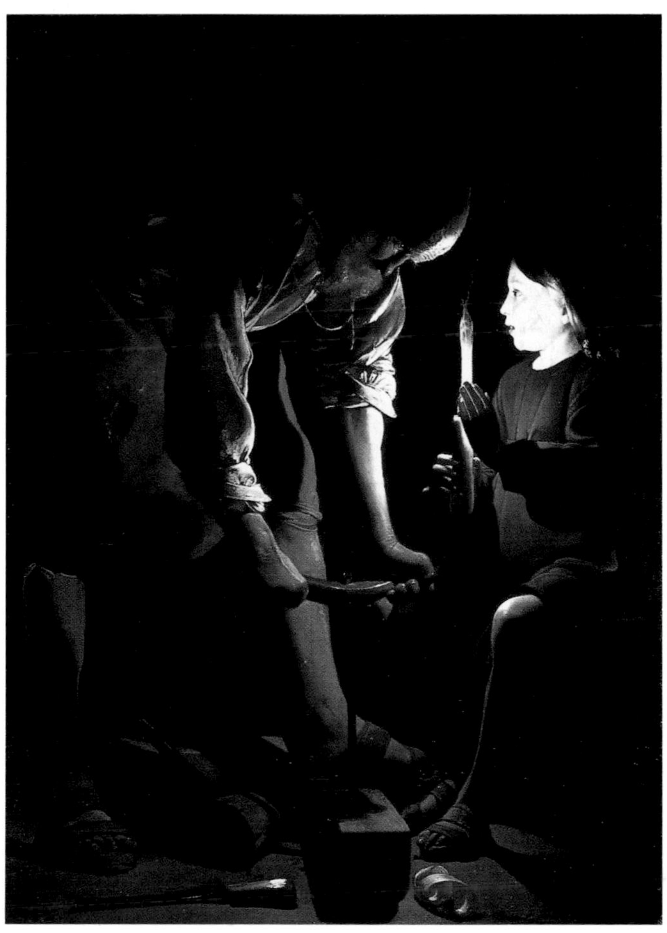

19-2. Georges de La Tour. *Joseph the Carpenter.* c. 1645. Oil on canvas, $51\frac{1}{8}$ x $39\frac{3}{4}$" (130 x 100 cm). Musée du Louvre, Paris

THE LE NAINS. Like Georges de La Tour, the three Le Nain brothers—Antoine, Louis, and Mathieu—were rediscovered in modern times, but they did not have to wait quite so long. Although their birth dates are not known, all must have been born in Laon during the first decade of the century. By 1629 they were in Paris, where the eldest two died of the plague in 1648. Despite the fact that they shared the same style, signed their pictures simply "Le Nain,"

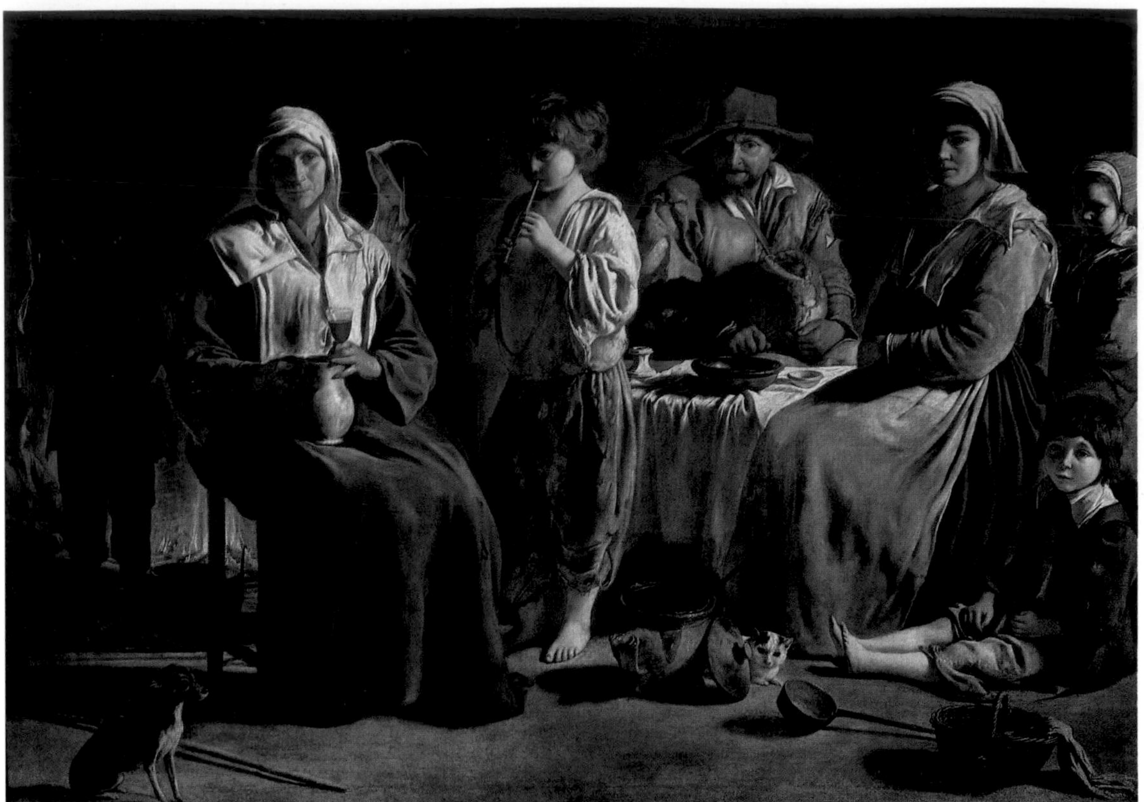

19-3. Louis Le Nain. *Peasant Family.* c. 1640. Oil on canvas, 44½ x 62½" (113 x 158.7 cm). Musée du Louvre, Paris

and worked on paintings together, each had a distinctive personality. Antoine was a miniaturist at heart, Louis the most severe, and Mathieu the most robust. Louis' *Peasant Family* (fig. 19-3) nevertheless exemplifies their "family" style and its virtues.

Like the peasant scenes of seventeenth-century Holland and Flanders, with which it has much in common, the picture stems from a tradition that goes back to Pieter Bruegel the Elder (see fig. 16-22). But whereas the Netherlandish scenes of lowlife are often humorous or satirical (see fig. 18-12), Le Nain gives them a human dignity and monumental weight that recall Velázquez's *The Water Carrier of Seville* but on a smaller scale (see fig. 17-32).

POUSSIN. Why were these artists forgotten so quickly? The reason is simply that classicism was supreme in France after the 1640s. The clarity, balance, and restraint of their art, when measured against other Caravaggesque painters, might be termed "classical," but none was a "classicist." The artist who did the most to bring about the rise of classicism was Nicolas Poussin (1593/4–1665). The greatest French painter of the century and the first French painter in history to win international fame, Poussin nevertheless spent almost his entire career in Rome. There, under the influence of Raphael, he developed the style that was to become the model for French painters of the second half of the century.

At first Poussin was inspired by Titian's warm, rich colors and by his approach to classical mythology. In *Cephalus and Aurora* (fig. 19-4) he portrays the ancient past as a poetic dream world, although the bliss of Titian's *Bacchanal* (see fig. 13-37) is now tinged with melancholy. Like many of his early works, this is a tale of frustrated love drawn from the Roman poet Ovid's *Metamorphoses,* a favorite source for Baroque artists. However, as is typical of Poussin, the picture departs from the text. Aurora, the goddess of dawn, tries to embrace the mortal Cephalus, who spurns her love out of faithfulness to his wife, Procris. Cephalus' fidelity is shown by the charming device of a putto holding up a portrait of Procris to his gaze. The sleeping river-god to the left signifies night. In the background, the sun-god Apollo waits by his chariot for daybreak (see also fig. 17-9).

The Abduction of the Sabine Women (fig. 19-5) must be understood in a very different way. It, too, shows the artist's allegiance to antiquity, but in style and attitude the two works are much farther apart than the several years' difference in date would suggest. *The Abduction of the Sabine Women* reveals the severe discipline of Poussin's intellectual style, which developed in response to what he regarded as the excesses of the High Baroque (see page 537). The strongly modeled figures are "frozen in action" like statues; many are, in fact, derived from Hellenistic sculpture. Poussin has placed them before reconstructions of Roman architecture that he believed to be archaeologically correct. The scene has a theatrical air, and with good reason. It was worked out by moving wax figurines around a miniature stagelike setting until it looked right to the artist. [See Primary Sources, no. 55, page 621.] Emotion is abundantly displayed, but it is so lacking in spontaneity that it fails to touch us. The attitude reflected here is clearly Raphael's (see figs. 13-31 and 13-32). More precisely, it is Raphael as filtered through Annibale Carracci and his school (compare figs. 17-5 and 17-9). The Venetian qualities of his early career have been consciously suppressed.

Poussin now strikes us as an artist who knew his own mind only too well. This impression is confirmed by the numerous let-

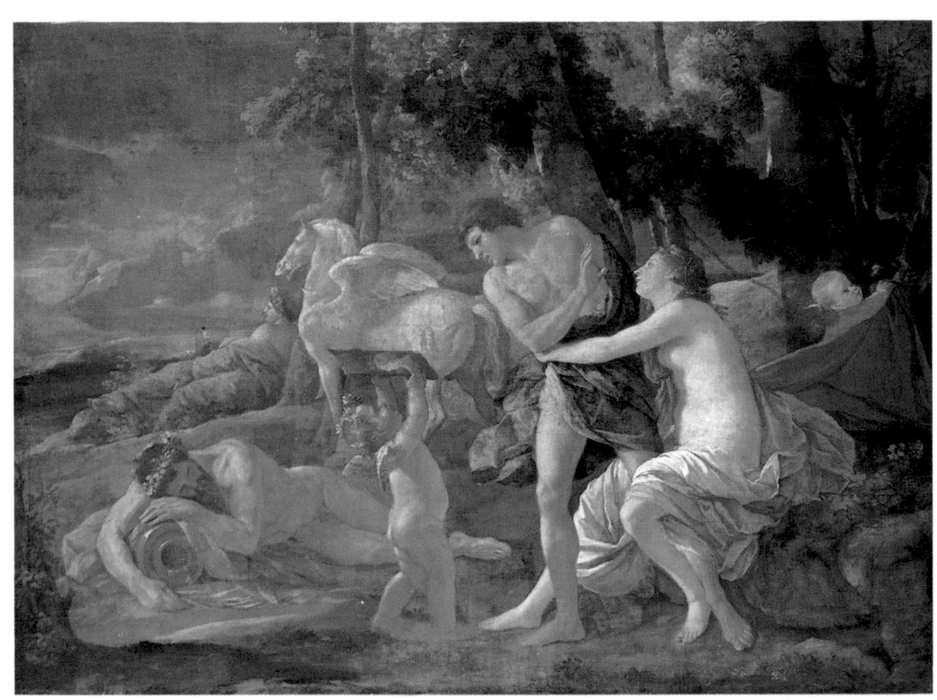

19-4. Nicolas Poussin.
Cephalus and Aurora. c. 1630.
Oil on canvas, 38 x 51"
(96.7 x 129.7 cm).
The National Gallery, London

REPRODUCED BY COURTESY OF THE TRUSTEES

(BELOW) 19-5. Nicolas Poussin.
The Abduction of the Sabine Women.
c. 1633–34. Oil on canvas,
5'7/8" x 6'10 5/8" (1.54 x 2.09 m).
The Metropolitan Museum of Art,
New York

HARRIS BRISBANE DICK FUND, 1946

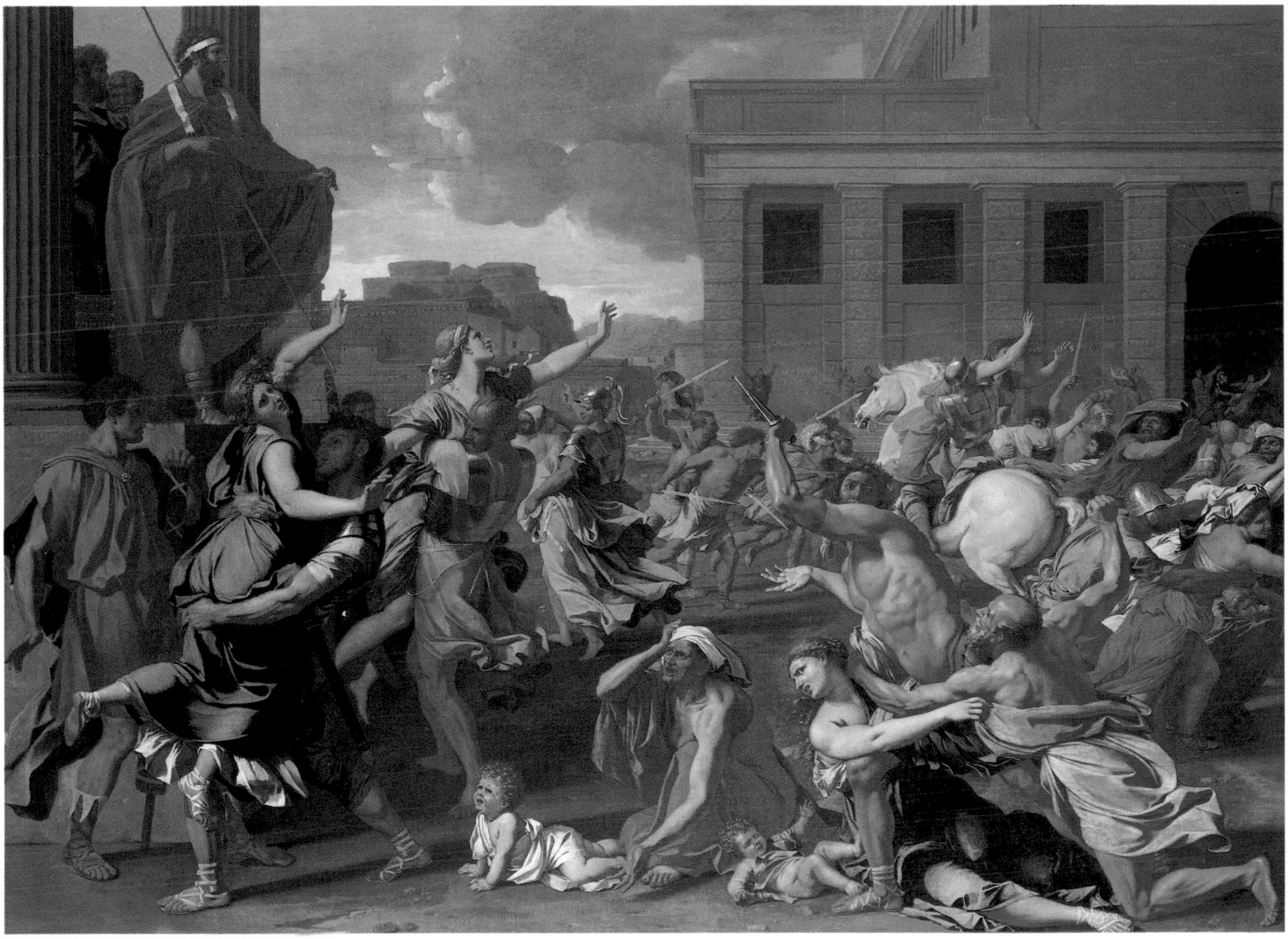

ters in which he stated his views to friends and patrons. The highest aim of painting, he believed, is to represent noble human actions. [See Primary Sources, no. 57, pages 622–23.] This is true even in *The Abduction of the Sabine Women,* which, ironically, was admired as an act of patriotism that ensured the future of Rome. (According to the accounts of Livy and Plutarch, the Sabines otherwise escaped unharmed, and the young women abducted by the Romans later became peacemakers between the two sides.) Be that

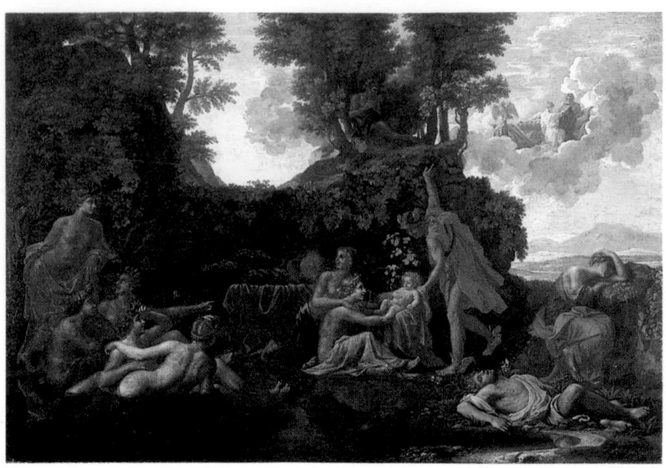

19-6. Nicolas Poussin. *The Birth of Bacchus.* c. 1657. Oil on canvas, 48¼ x 70½" (122.6 x 179.1 cm). Fogg Art Museum, Harvard University Art Museums, Cambridge, Massachusetts

GIFT OF MRS. SAMUEL SACHS IN MEMORY OF HER HUSBAND

as it may, such actions must be shown in a logical and orderly way—not as they really happened but as they would have happened if nature were perfect. To this end, art must strive for the general and typical. In appealing to the mind rather than the senses, the painter should suppress such incidentals as color and stress form and composition. In a good picture, the viewer must be able to "read" the emotions of each figure and relate them to the story.

These ideas were not new. We recall Horace's motto *ut pictura poesis* and Leonardo's statement that the highest aim of painting is to depict "the intention of man's soul" (see page 432). Before Poussin, however, no one made the analogy between painting and literature so close, or put it into practice so single-mindedly. His method accounts for the cold rhetoric in *The Abduction of the Sabine Women,* which makes the picture seem so remote.

Poussin also painted "ideal" landscapes with surprising success, for they have an austere beauty and somber calm. This severe rationalism lasted until about 1650, when he began to paint landscapes that return to the realm of mythology he had abandoned in middle age. They unite the Titianesque style of his early work with his later, Raphaelesque classicism. The result is a new kind of mythological landscape close in spirit to Claude Lorraine's (see below) but rich in personal associations and levels of meaning. Indeed, these late paintings have rightly been called transcendental meditations, for they contain archetypal imagery of universal meaning. *The Birth of Bacchus* (fig. 19-6), among his most profound works, takes up the great Stoic theme (which Poussin had treated twice as a young man) that death is to be found even in the happiest realm. The scene shows the moment when the infant (created by Jupiter's union with Semele, the moon-goddess, and born from his thigh) is brought by Mercury to the river-goddess Dirce for safekeeping, while the satyr Pan plays the flute in rapt inspiration. (Jupiter himself had been raised by sylvan deities.)

The picture is not beautifully executed. The act of painting became difficult for Poussin in old age, so that the brushwork is shaky. Yet he turned this difficulty to his advantage, and *The Birth of Bacchus* represents the purest expressiveness. Its serene lyricism conveys the joy of life on the one hand and forebodings of death on the other: to the right, the nymph Echo weeps over the dead Narcissus, the youth who spurned her love and drowned kissing his reflection. Like Cephalus and Aurora, the story of Echo and Narcissus is taken from Ovid, but now it is the meaning, not the narrative, that interests Poussin. He treats it as part of the eternal cycle of nature, in which the gods embody natural forces and the myths contain fundamental truths. Although he certainly drew on the pantheistic writings of Tommaso Campanella and the learned commentaries of the Stoic Natale Conti, it is the artist's personal understanding that brings these ideas to life.

CLAUDE LORRAINE. While Poussin developed the heroic qualities of the ideal landscape, the great French landscapist Claude Lorraine (1600–1682) brought out its idyllic aspects. He, too, spent almost his entire career in Rome. Like many Northerners, Claude explored the surrounding countryside, the Campagna, more thoroughly and affectionately than any Italian. Countless drawings made on the spot show his powers of observation. He also sketched in oils outdoors, the first artist known to have done so. Sketches, however, were only the raw material for his paintings. Claude's landscapes do not aim at topographic accuracy but evoke the poetic essence of a countryside filled with echoes of antiquity. Often, as in *A Pastoral Landscape* (fig. 19-7), the compositions have the hazy, luminous atmosphere of early morning or late afternoon. The space expands serenely, rather than receding step-by-step as in Poussin's landscapes. An air of nostalgia hangs over such vistas of past experience enhanced by memory. Hence they had a special appeal for the English, who had seen Italy only briefly or even not at all.

VOUET. At an early age Simon Vouet (1590–1649), too, went to Rome, where he became the leader of the French Caravaggesque painters. Unlike Poussin and Claude, however, he returned to France. Upon settling in Paris, he quickly shed all traces of Caravaggio's manner and developed a colorful style based on the Carraccis', which won such acclaim that Vouet was named First Painter to the king. He also brought with him memories of the great North Italian precursors of the Baroque. *The Toilet of Venus* (fig. 19-8) depicts a subject popular in Venice from Titian to Veronese. Vouet's figure also recalls Correggio's Io (see fig. 14-18), but without her frank eroticism. Instead, she has been given an elegant sensuousness far removed from Poussin's disciplined art.

The Toilet of Venus was painted about 1640, toward the beginning of Poussin's ill-fated sojourn in Paris, where he had gone at the invitation of Louis XIII. He met with no more success than Bernini was to have 20 years later (see page 586). After several years Poussin left, deeply disillusioned by his experience at the court, whose taste and politics Vouet understood far better. In one sense, their rivalry was to continue long afterward. Vouet's decorative style was the basis for the Rococo, but it was Poussin's classicism that soon dominated art in France. The two traditions vied with each other through the Romantic era, alternating in succession without either gaining the upper hand for long.

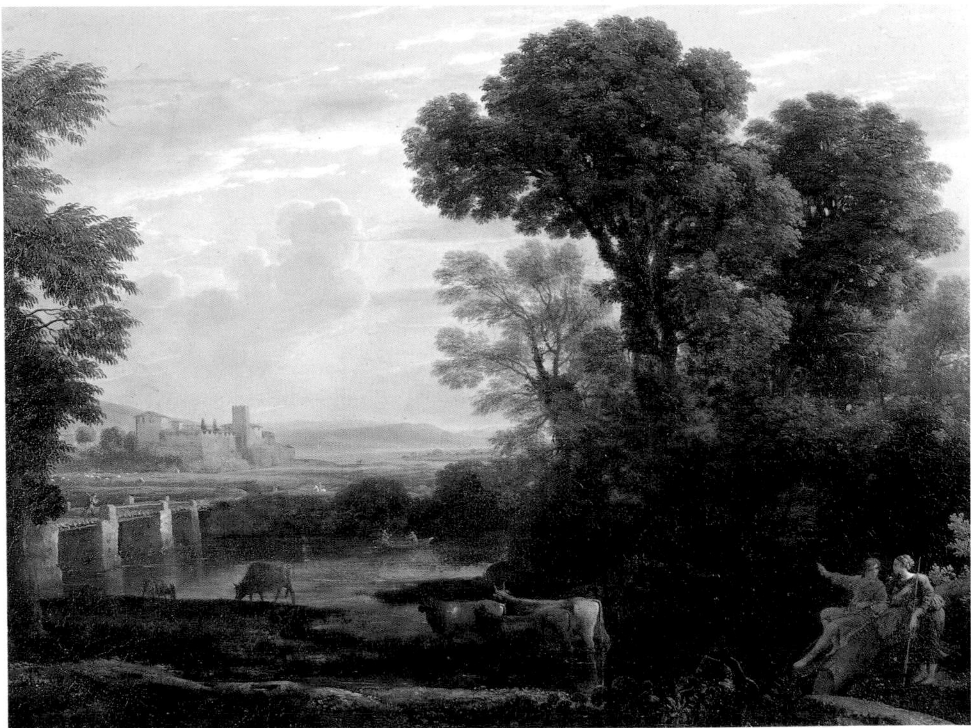

19-7. Claude Lorraine. *A Pastoral Landscape*. c. 1650. Oil on copper, 15½ x 21" (39.3 x 53.3 cm). Yale University Art Gallery, New Haven, Connecticut

LEO C. HANNA, JR., FUND

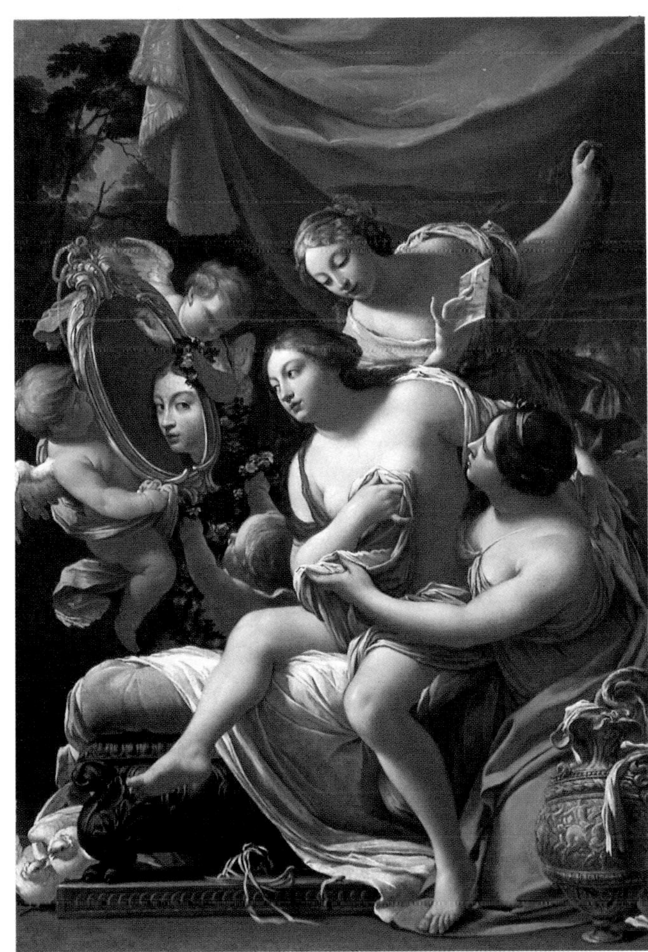

19-8. Simon Vouet. *The Toilet of Venus*. c. 1640. Oil on canvas, 65¼ x 45" (165.7 x 114.3 cm). The Carnegie Museum of Art, Pittsburgh

GIFT OF MRS. HORACE BINNEY HARE

THE ROYAL ACADEMY. When young Louis XIV took over the reins of government in 1661, Jean-Baptiste Colbert, his chief adviser, built the administrative apparatus to support the power of the monarch. In this system, aimed at subjecting the thoughts and actions of the entire nation to strict control from above, the visual arts had the task of glorifying the king. As in music and theater, which shared the same task, the official "royal style" was classicism. Centralized control over the visual arts was exerted by Colbert and the artist Charles Lebrun (1619–1690), who became supervisor of all the king's artistic projects. As chief dispenser of royal art patronage, Lebrun had so much power that for all practical purposes he was the dictator of the arts in France. His authority extended beyond the power of the purse. It also included a new system of educating artists in the officially approved style.

Throughout antiquity and the Middle Ages, artists had been trained by apprenticeship, and this practice still prevailed during the Renaissance. As painting, sculpture, and architecture gained the status of liberal arts, artists wished to supplement their "mechanical" training with theoretical knowledge. For this purpose, "art academies" were founded, patterned on the academies of the humanists. (The name *academy* is derived from the Athenian grove dedicated to the legendary hero Academus where Plato met with his disciples.) Art academies appeared first in Italy in the later sixteenth century as an outgrowth of literary academies. They seem to have been private associations of artists who met from time to time to draw from the model and discuss questions of art theory. These academies later became formal institutions that took over some functions from the guilds, but their teaching was limited and far from systematic.

This was the case as well with the Royal Academy of Painting and Sculpture in Paris, founded in 1648. But when Lebrun became its director in 1663, he established a rigid curriculum of

BAROQUE THEATER AND MUSIC IN FRANCE

The central fact of French culture in the seventeenth century was the taste for classicism, which had been established 50 years earlier. The Pléiade, a group of poets led by Pierre de Ronsard (1524–1585), was founded in 1550 to develop French literature along the lines of Greek and Roman poetry and plays, which had been published and studied since early in the century. Around the same time, court festivals became popular, as did *intermezzi* (also called *ballets de cour*), which combined song, dance, drama, and spectacle in the "antique" manner. Public theater was monopolized by the Confrérie de la Passion (Confraternity of the Passion), which was given control over secular drama. (Religious plays were banned in 1548.) These three factors—classical taste, antiquarianism, and court patronage—decisively shaped French theater and music. The preference for classicism and humanism was reinforced during the regency of Henry II's Italian queen, Catherine de' Medici (1560–74). However, the development of the arts was disrupted by the Wars of Religion between Catholics and Protestants that broke out in 1562. Hostilities continued until the Protestants were defeated in 1629 by the soldiers of Louis XIII under the direction of his chief minister, Cardinal Richelieu (1585–1642).

The end of the Wars of Religion placed Richelieu in a position of immense power. A highly cultivated man, he now turned his attention not only to governing France but also to patronage of the arts. In 1629, the same year that the Protestants were defeated, the French Academy, a small group of intellectuals, began to meet informally to discuss literature. At Cardinal Richelieu's behest, it became a state institution based on Italian models in 1636. The Academy required that theater teach moral lessons and adhere to the Italian concept of verisimilitude (see page 467). This was the first of a number of French academies that would be founded during the course of the seventeenth century to foster painting and sculpture, music, architecture, and even dance. These state-controlled academies oversaw the training of young artists and were responsible for awarding royal commissions. As time went on, the academies became increasingly authoritarian, eventually exercising rigid control over all of the arts.

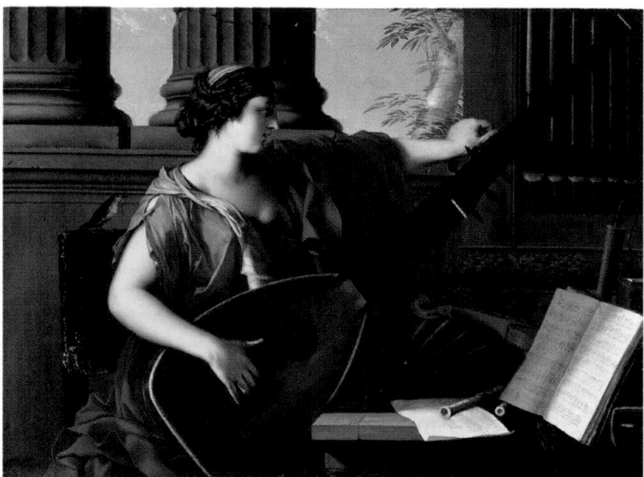

Laurent de la Hyre. *Allegory of Music*. 1645. Oil on canvas, 41⅝ x 56¾" (105.7 x 144.1 cm). The Metropolitan Museum of Art, New York

CHARLES B. CURTIS FUND, 1950

The first important French dramatist was Alexandre Hardy (c. 1572–1632), a prolific playwright who wrote some 700 tragicomedies (plays of serious subject that end happily) and pastoral plays for the Hôtel de Bourgogne, the only permanent playhouse in Paris before the end of the wars in 1629. Otherwise, plays were performed on tennis courts (*jeux de paume*), with a platform erected as a stage. In 1640 Cardinal Richelieu had a theater erected at his palace, the first in France to feature a proscenium (the arch separating the stage from the auditorium), an innovation from Italy that was soon to become standard throughout Europe. Richelieu took a particular interest in drama and personally employed five playwrights to work under his supervision. The only one to achieve lasting fame was Pierre Corneille (1606–1684), whose tragedies, drawn from ancient history and mythology, center on the hero who chooses death over dishonor. They are written in the ornate, emotional language that defined French classical drama before 1650. Yet when Corneille submitted *Le Cid* to the Academy for review the year it was founded, the play met with such harsh criticism that he stopped writing for four years. Corneille's younger brother, Thomas (1625–1709), was also a noted playwright whose finest works date from the 1670s.

French drama reached its zenith in the plays of Jean Racine (1639–1699), whose tragedies in the Greek manner revolved around the conflict of desire and duty, expressed in direct, simple language that quickly replaced the elaborate language of Pierre Corneille. Racine's plays embody the theories of Nicolas Boileau-Despréaux (1636–1711), who championed the three unities of action, time, and place and decorum in speech, manner, and moral behavior. Early in his career Racine had been befriended by Molière (Jean-Baptiste Poquelin, 1622–1673), whose plays marked the high tide of French comedy. *The Misanthrope* (1666) and *Tartuffe* (1664), influenced by the commedia dell'arte, which enjoyed great success in France, are masterpieces of cynical wit written in the 12-syllable Alexandrine couplets that had become the standard verse form of French theater. The Comédie Français, formed by royal decree in 1680 from Molière's troupe and that of the rival Hôtel de Bourgogne, was granted a monopoly on all dramas in French, with the sole exception of the commedia dell'arte (see page 549), which was eventually banned in 1697 for an imagined slight of the king's mistress.

Cardinal Jules Mazarin, Richelieu's successor, who was an Italian by birth, had an abiding love of opera, which he actively promoted. Soon after taking the reins of full power upon

Mazarin's death in 1661, Louis XIV began construction of a new palace at Versailles, outside Paris. Even before the palace was completed in 1682 Louis staged huge spectacles, such as *The Pleasure of the Enchanted Land* (1664), an allegory of his reign. The arts during the age of Louis XIV were meant to glorify the king, and classicism had an essential role to play. Classicism was favored not only because of its learned humanism and elevated moral tone but also because it suggested that France was the successor to Greece and Rome. In the debates after 1688 known as the Battle of the Ancients and the Moderns, French academicians even sought to show the supremacy of French culture by using it to replace antiquity as the new standard.

During the 1650s, Louis XIV appeared regularly in ballets, which became great spectacles. Thereafter he continued to enjoy ballets and operas by his court composer and dancing master, Jean-Baptiste Lully (1632–1687). Lully had initially collaborated with Corneille and Molière on comic ballets for the court, but Molière refused to work with Lully in 1672 because of the latter's unscrupulous practices. Lully then forged a partnership with the playwright Philippe Quinault (1635–1688) that lasted a decade, from *Atys* (1676) through *Armide* (1686), based on Torquato Tasso's *Jerusalem Freed.* Their work, which emphasized the unity between text and music, was comparable in character to the tragedies of Corneille and Racine. Because he clung to the Florence *camerata*'s ideal of emphatic declamation (see page 538), Lully composed music of measured and stately simplicity. He was also considered a revolutionary for introducing additional choruses and ballets to the opera, which lent the performances a greater pageantry that benefited greatly from the costumes designed by Jean Bérain (1637–1711). The results were sober and pompous, but also colorful—perfectly suited to life at Versailles. Lully occupied a position in French music comparable to that of Charles Lebrun in the arts. He was instrumental in founding the Royal Academy of Dance upon the king's retirement from active participation in ballets in 1661. In 1672, Lully merged the academies of music and dance to create the forerunner of the Opéra, the national opera company of France.

Lully was by far the most powerful force in French Baroque music. His only rival was Marc-Antoine Charpentier (1634–1704), a student of Carissimi, who as music director to the Jesuit order in Paris became the greatest French composer of religious music. Charpentier's secular music was also of high quality, particularly the opera *The Imaginary Illness* (1673), written with Molière after he had broken with Lully. The other major figure was the much younger François Couperin (1668–1733), organist to the king at Versailles, whose harpsichord and orchestral suites are notable for their lively invention. As a composer he straddled two eras: his most important compositions were written during the reign of Louis XV, although his music remained Late Baroque in style.

instruction in practice and theory based on a system of "rules." This set the pattern for all later academies, including the art schools of today. Much of this doctrine was derived from Poussin, with whom Lebrun had studied for several years in Rome, but it was carried to rationalist extremes. The Academy even devised a method for giving numerical grades to artists past and present in such categories as drawing, expression, and proportion. The ancients received the highest marks, of course, then came Raphael and his school, and Poussin. The Venetians, who "overemphasized" color, ranked low, with the Flemish and Dutch even lower. Subjects were also classified, from "history" (that is, narrative subjects, be they classical, biblical, or mythological) at the top to still life at the bottom.

Architecture

MANSART. Meanwhile, the foundations of Baroque classicism in architecture were laid by a group of designers of whom the best known was François Mansart (1598–1666). They form a continuous tradition with the sixteenth century that is unique in the history of architecture. The classicism introduced by Lescot at the Louvre (see fig. 16-27) reached its height around the middle of the sixteenth century under Henry II at the Château d'Anet, designed for Henry's mistress, Diane of Poitiers, by Philibert de l'Orme (see page 523); only the gateway, main entrance, and circular chapel are still intact. The tradition was continued at the Château of Ecouen by de l'Orme's chief disciple, Jean Bullant (c. 1520–1578), who is now known mainly for his books published in 1561 and 1563. The central position, however, was occupied by the du Cerceau family, which worked on the Louvre and other royal projects through the middle of the seventeenth century.

The du Cerceau dynasty began with Jacques Androuet du Cerceau the Elder (c. 1515–c. 1585), a contemporary of de l'Orme and Bullant. Du Cerceau spent about a decade in Rome absorbing the High Renaissance style of Bramante before returning home to publish a series of treatises dealing mainly with town houses and their decoration. These preserve designs for lost buildings by de l'Orme and other architects of the period. Du Cerceau's grandson, Salomon de Brosse (c. 1571–1626), continued the family style under the influence of Bullant. Mansart probably began his career under de Brosse in 1618; thus he belongs directly to this rich legacy. De Brosse's collaborators at the time included Mansart's brother-in-law, who may well have been responsible for the young man's training after the early death of his father. Mansart's talent was precocious, and within five years he had already established his reputation.

Apparently Mansart never visited Italy, but other French architects had already imported and adapted some aspects of the Roman Early Baroque. Chief among them was Jacques Lemercier (c. 1582–1654), who absorbed a rather dry and academic version of Vignola's and della Porta's church designs during his Roman stay of 1607 to 1614. His works for Cardinal Richelieu, including the enlargement of the Square Court of the Louvre in 1624, are uninspired adaptations of earlier designs by Lescot, du Cerceau, and de Brosse. Lemercier was soon replaced by Mansart, who was the first architect of genius since Lescot.

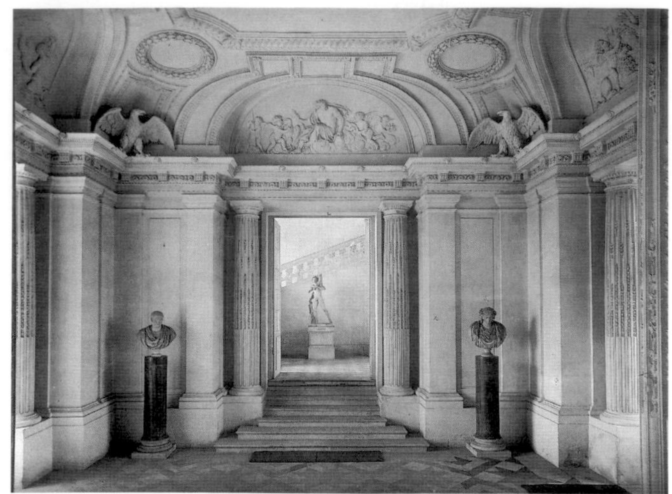

19-9. François Mansart. Vestibule of the Château of Maisons. 1642–50

Mansart clearly was familiar with the new Italian style. What he owed to it, however, is hard to determine. His most important buildings are châteaus, and in this field the French Renaissance tradition outweighed any Italian Baroque influences. For that reason his earlier designs are also the most classical. The Château of Maisons near Paris, built for the financier René du Longeuil in the 1640s, shows Mansart's mature style at its best. The exterior departs little from the precedents set by le Breton or de Brosse, although it possesses a classical logic and clarity that surpass any previous French design. It is the interior that breaks new ground. The vestibule leading to the grand staircase (fig. 19-9), among the most magnificent in all of French architecture, has a particularly beautiful effect, severe yet festive. On seeing the classically pure articulation of the white walls, one first thinks of Palladio (see page 480), whose treatise Mansart knew and admired. But sculpture is used here in a characteristically French way pioneered by de Brosse as an integral part of architectural design. The complex curves of the vaulting tell us that this structure, for all its classicism, belongs to the Baroque.

Mansart was at the height of his career at Maisons. Because of his difficult personality, however, in 1646 he was replaced after just a year at the church of the Val-de-Grâce in Paris by his chief rival, Lemercier. Lemercier then erected the most Baroque church ever built on French soil over Mansart's classical foundation. Mansart was also supplanted in the field of hôtels and châteaus by the younger and more adaptable Louis Le Vau (1612–1670). Le Vau was part of a team, including Charles Lebrun and the landscape architect André Le Nôtre (see below), called to the court by the king's minister, Colbert, in 1661 shortly before completing the château at Vaux-le-Vicomte outside Paris for the disgraced finance minister Nicolas Fouquet.

LOUIS XIV, COLBERT, AND THE LOUVRE. Mansart represents the early phase of French Baroque classicism. Its climactic stage, which may be compared with the heroic classicism of Poussin and Corneille (see page 580), began with the first great project Colbert directed, the completion of the Louvre. Work on the palace had proceeded intermittently for more than a century, along the lines of Lescot's design (see fig. 16-27). What remained to be done was to close the square court on the east side with an impressive facade. Colbert, however, was dissatisfied with the proposals of French architects, including Mansart, who submitted various designs not long before his death. He therefore invited Bernini to Paris in the hope that the most famous master of the Roman Baroque would do for the French king what he had already done for the Church. Bernini spent several months in Paris in 1665 and submitted three designs, all of them on a scale that would have engulfed the existing palace. After much argument, Louis XIV rejected these plans and turned over the problem to a committee of three: Charles Lebrun, his court painter;

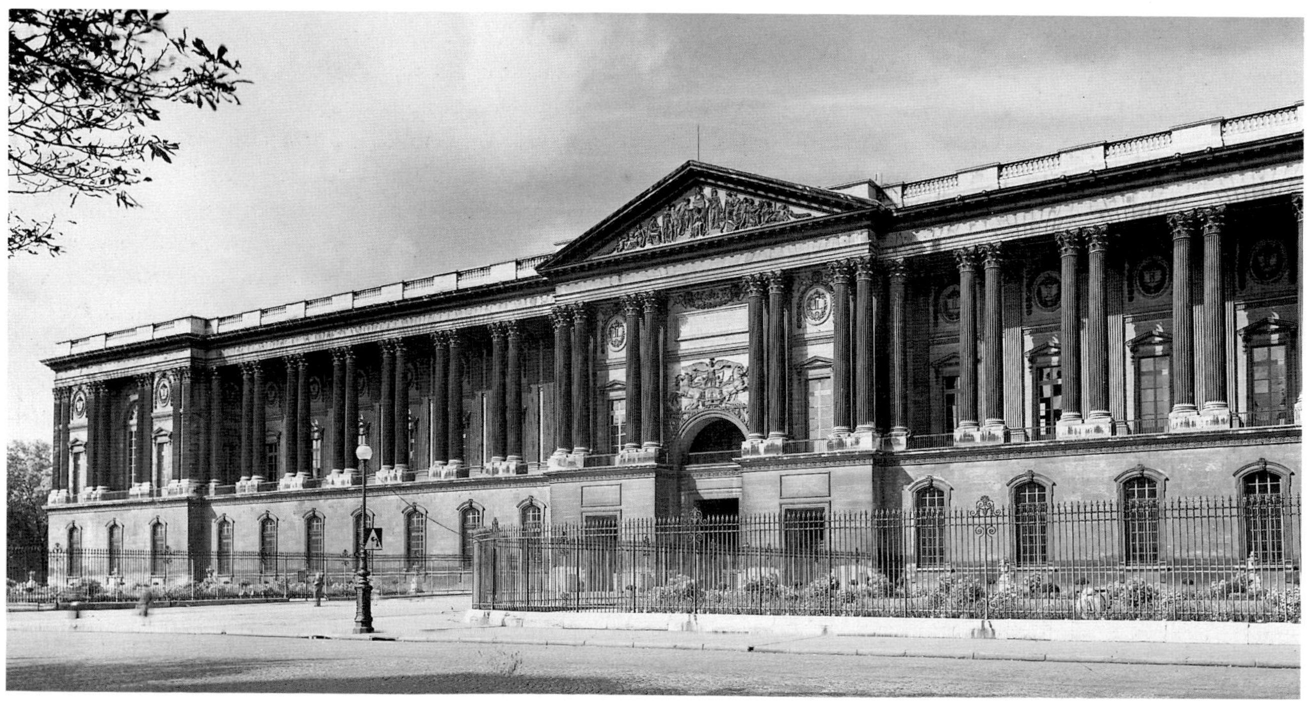

19-10. Claude Perrault. East Front of the Louvre, Paris. 1667–70

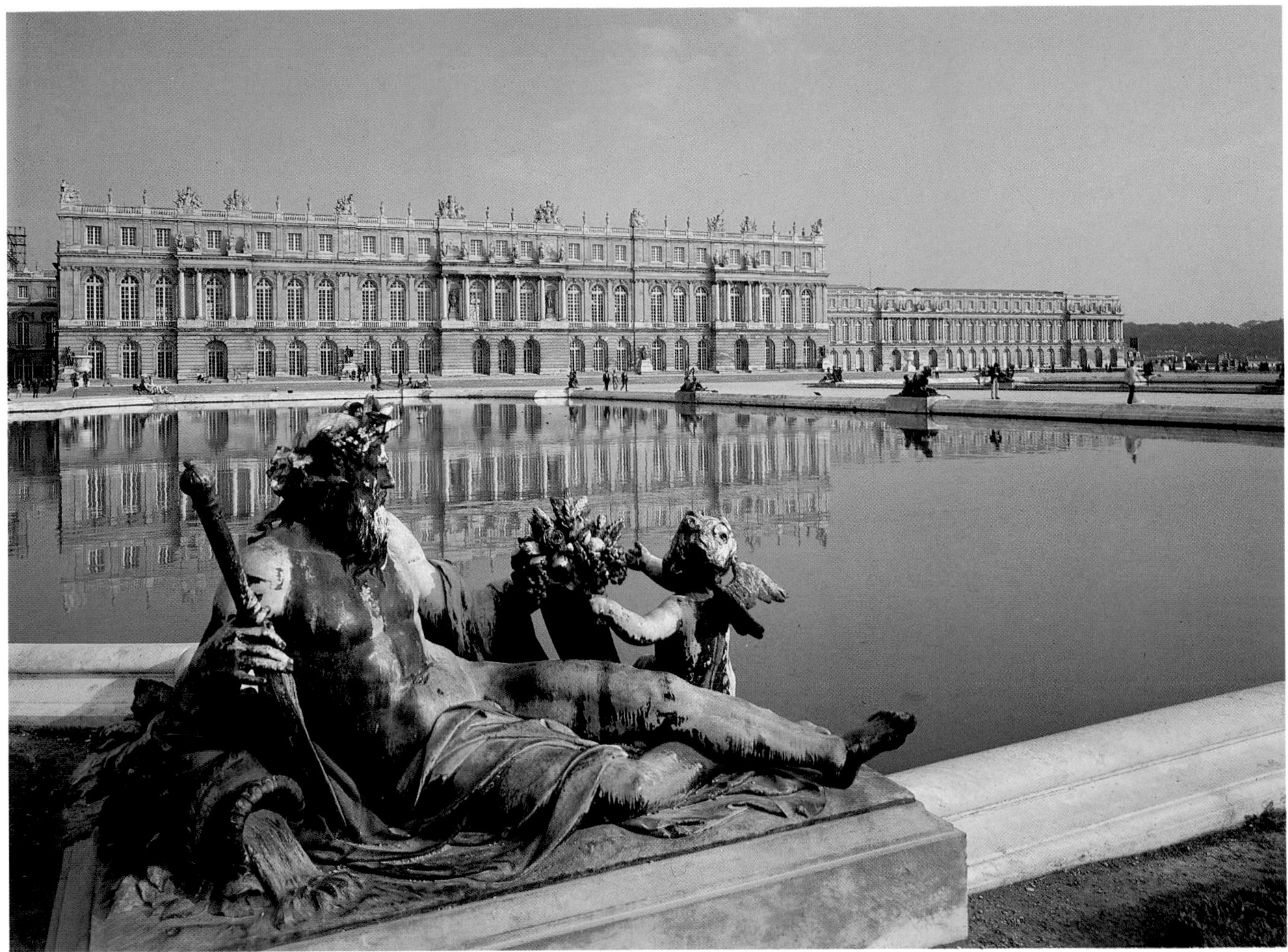

19-11. Louis Le Vau and Jules Hardouin-Mansart. Garden Front of the center block of the Palace of Versailles. 1669–85

Louis Le Vau, his court architect, who had already done much work on the Louvre (including the Gallery of Apollo, Queen's court, and south facade); and Claude Perrault (1613–1688), who was an anatomist and student of ancient architecture, not a professional architect. All three were responsible for the structure that was actually built (fig. 19-10), although Perrault is rightly credited with the major share. Certainly his supporters and detractors thought so at the time, and he was often called upon to defend its design. [See Primary Sources, no. 58, page 623.]

The center pavilion is a Roman temple front, and the wings look like the flanks of that temple folded outward. The temple theme required a single order of freestanding columns, but the Louvre had three stories. This problem was solved by treating the ground story as the podium of the temple and recessing the upper two behind the screen of the colonnade. The colonnade itself was novel and thus controversial in its use of paired columns, even though they were not needed for support.

The East Front of the Louvre signaled the victory of French classicism over the Italian Baroque as the royal style. It further proclaimed France the new Rome, both politically and culturally, by linking Louis XIV with the glory of the Caesars. The design combines grandeur and elegance in a way that fully justifies its fame. In some ways it suggests the mind of an archaeologist, but one who knew how to choose features of classical architecture that would be compatible with the older parts of the palace. This antiquarian approach was Perrault's main contribution. Perrault owed his position to his brother, Charles Perrault (1628–1703), who, as Colbert's Master of Buildings under Louis XIV, had helped to undermine Bernini during his stay at the French Court. [See Primary Sources, no. 58, page 623.] It is likely that Claude shared the views set forth some 20 years later in Charles' *Parallels Between the Ancients and Moderns* (see page 635), which claimed "that Homer and Virgil made countless mistakes which the moderns no longer make [because] the ancients did not have all our rules." Thus the East Front of the Louvre presents not simply a classical revival but a vigorous distillation of what Claude Perrault considered the eternal ideals of beauty, intended to surpass anything by the Romans themselves. Ironically, this great example proved to be too pure, even though it was attacked by strict classicists, and Perrault soon faded from favor.

THE PALACE OF VERSAILLES. The king's largest enterprise was the Palace of Versailles, located 11 miles from the center of Paris. It was built by Louis XIV to prevent a repeat of the civil rebellion known as the Fronde that occurred from 1648 to 1653 during his minority by forcing the aristocracy to live under royal control outside of Paris. It was begun in 1669 by Le Vau, who designed the elevation of the Garden Front (fig. 19-11) but died

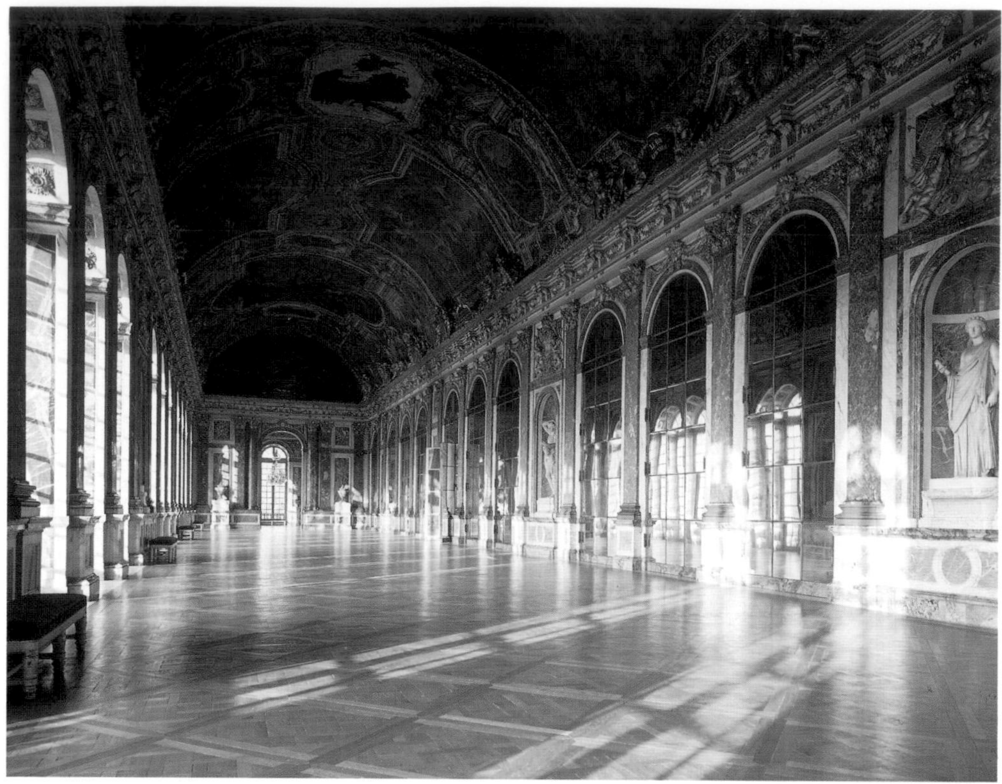

19-12. Hardouin-Mansart, Lebrun, and Coysevox. Galerie des Glaces (Hall of Mirrors), Palace of Versailles

(BELOW) 19-13. Hardouin-Mansart, Lebrun, and Coysevox. Salon de la Guerre, Palace of Versailles. Begun 1678

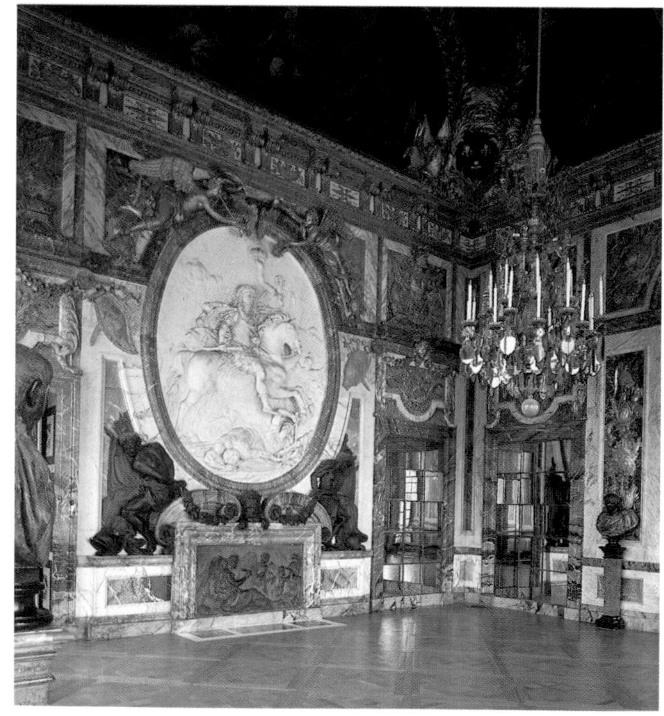

within a year. Under Jules Hardouin-Mansart (1646–1708), a great-nephew and pupil of François Mansart, the project was greatly expanded to accommodate the ever-growing royal household. The Garden Front, intended by Le Vau to be the main view of the palace, was stretched to an enormous length with no modification of the architectural elements. As a result, his original facade design, a less severe variant of the East Front of the Louvre, now looks repetitious and out of scale. The whole center block contains a single room, the famous Galerie des Glaces (Hall of Mirrors; fig. 19-12). At either end are the Salon de la Guerre (War) and its counterpart, the Salon de la Paix (Peace). The sumptuous effect of the Galerie des Glaces emulates the Gallery of Francis I at Fontainebleau, which was decorated by Rosso.

Baroque features, although not officially acknowledged, reappeared inside the Palace of Versailles. This shift reflected the king's own taste. Louis XIV was interested less in architectural theory and monumental exteriors than in the lavish interiors that would make suitable settings for himself and his court. Thus the man to whom he really listened was not an architect but the painter Lebrun. Lebrun's goal was in itself Baroque: to subordinate all the arts to the glorification of Louis XIV. To achieve it, he drew freely on his memories of Rome. The great decorative schemes of the Baroque that he saw there must also have impressed him. They stood him in good stead 20 years later, both in the Louvre and at Versailles. Although a disciple of Poussin, he had studied first with Vouet and became a superb decorator. Lebrun employed architects, sculptors, painters, and artisans to create ensembles of unprecedented splendor. The Salon de la Guerre at Versailles (fig. 19-13) is closer in many ways to the Cornaro Chapel than to the vestibule at Maisons (compare figs. 17-29 and 19-9). While Lebrun's ensemble is less adventurous than Bernini's, he has emphasized surface decoration just as much. And, as in so many Italian Baroque interiors, the separate components are less impressive than the effect of the whole.

THE GARDENS OF VERSAILLES. Apart from the magnificent interior, the most impressive aspect of Versailles is the park extending west of the Garden Front for several miles (fig. 19-14). Its design, by André Le Nôtre (1613–1700), is so strictly correlated with the plan of the palace that it continues the architectural space. Like the interiors, these formal gardens, with their terraces, basins, clipped hedges, and statuary, were meant to provide a suit-

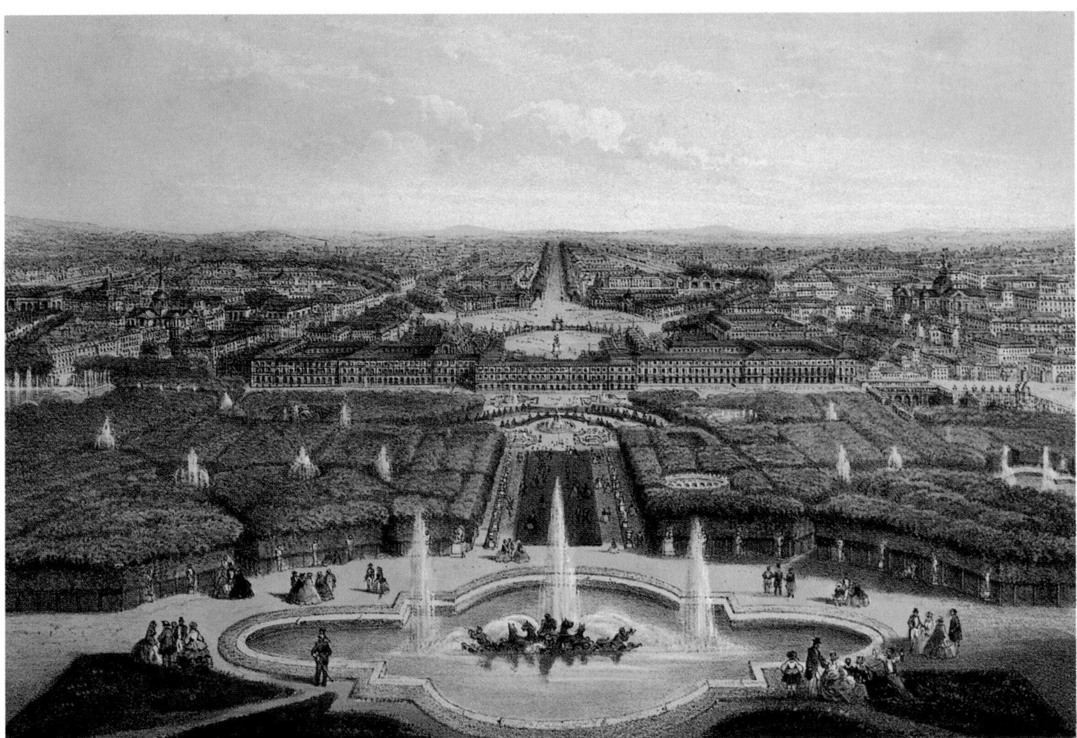

19-14. Charles Rivière. *Perspective View of the Château and Gardens of Versailles*. Lithograph after an 1860 photograph

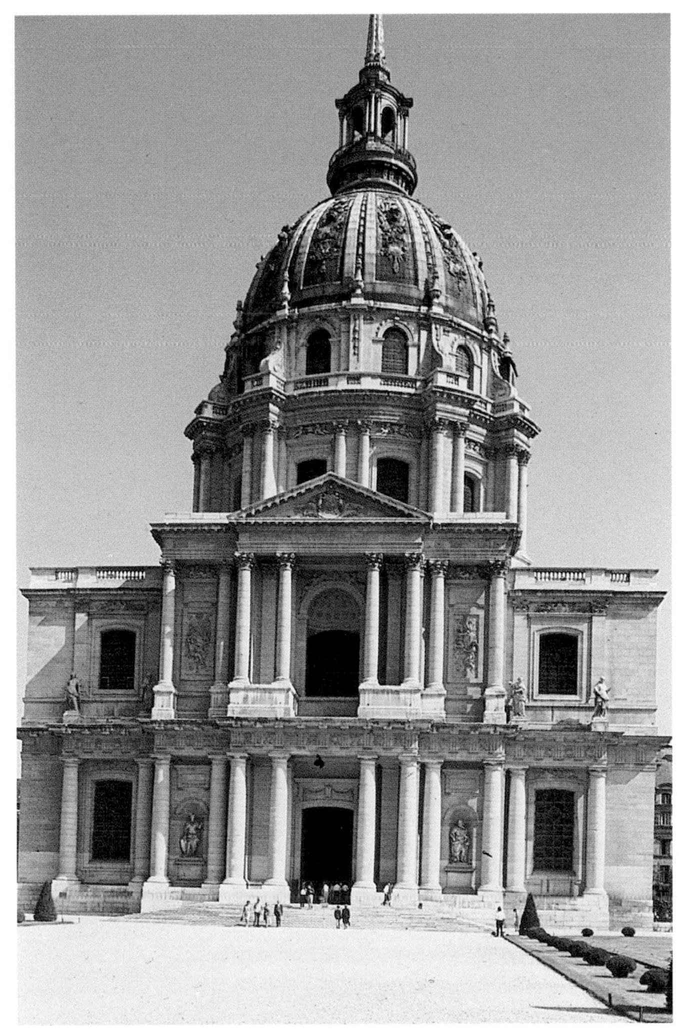

19-15. Jules Hardouin-Mansart. Church of the Invalides, Paris. 1680–91

able setting for the king's appearances in public. They form a series of "outdoor rooms" for the splendid fetes and spectacles that Louis XIV so enjoyed. The spirit of absolutism is even more striking in this geometric regularity imposed upon an entire countryside than it is in the palace itself. This kind of formal garden had its beginnings in Renaissance Florence but never on the scale achieved by Le Nôtre at Versailles and elsewhere.

HARDOUIN-MANSART. At Versailles, Jules Hardouin-Mansart worked as a member of a team, constrained by the design of Le Vau. His own style can be better seen in the Church of the Invalides (figs. 19-15 and 19-16), named after the institution for disabled soldiers of which it was a part. The building combines Italian Renaissance and Baroque features, but they have been interpreted in a distinctly French manner that stretches back to l'Orme's church for the castle at Anet (1549). The Invalides may be seen as Hardouin-Mansart's comment on its seventeenth-century predecessors in Paris: Lemercier's church of the College of the Sorbonne (1626), Mansart's Ste.-Marie de la Visitation (1632),

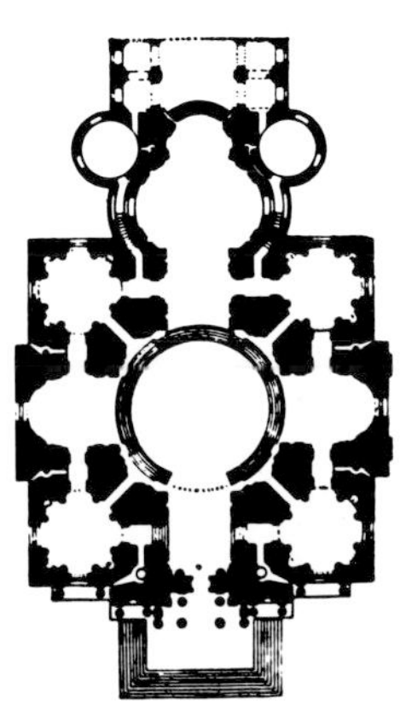

19-16. Plan of the Church of the Invalides

the Val-de-Grâce (see above), and Le Vau's church at the College of Four Nations (1662) on the Seine across from the Louvre. The Visitation is an unsatisfactory effort from just before Mansart's maturity. However, Hardouin-Mansart incorporated features found in his great-uncle's design for the Bourbon dynasty chapel at St.-Denis (1665). It may well be that the Invalides was intended to serve a similar purpose as Louis XIV's burial place.

In plan the Invalides consists of a Greek cross with four corner chapels. It is based (with various French intermediaries) on Michelangelo's plan for St. Peter's (see fig. 13-28). The only Baroque element is the oval choir. The dome, too, reflects the influence of Michelangelo (see fig. 13-27), but it consists of three shells, not the usual two, and the classicistic facade recalls the East Front of the Louvre. Nevertheless, the exterior as a whole is unmistakably Baroque. It breaks forward repeatedly in the crescendo effect introduced by Maderno (see fig. 17-14). And, as in Borromini's S. Agnese in Piazza Navona (see fig. 17-22), the facade and dome are closely linked. The dome itself is the most original, and the most Baroque, feature of Hardouin-Mansart's design. Tall and slender, it rises in one continuous curve from the base of the drum to the spire atop the lantern. On the first drum rests a second, narrower drum. Its windows provide light for the painted vision of heavenly glory inside the dome. The windows themselves are hidden behind a "pseudo-shell" with a large opening at the top, so that the Heavenly Glory seems mysteriously illuminated and suspended in space. Such bold "theatrical" lighting would do honor to any Italian Baroque architect.

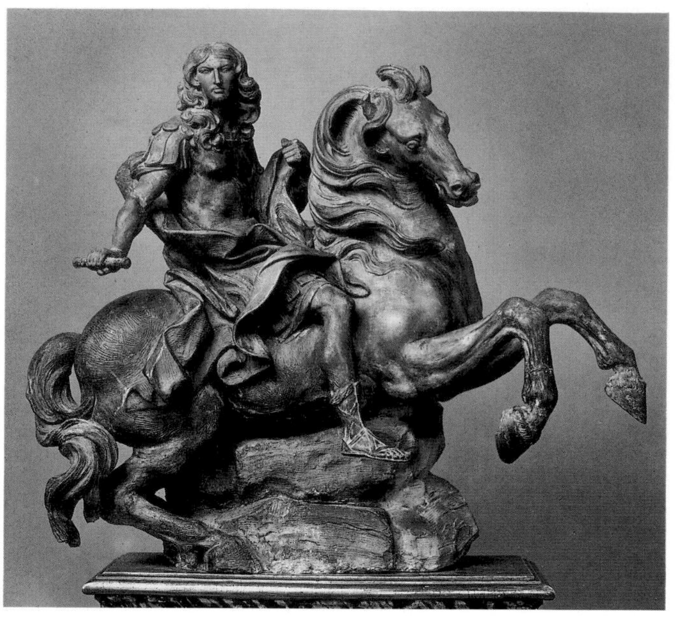

19-17. Gianlorenzo Bernini. *Model for Equestrian Statue of Louis XIV.* 1670. Terra-cotta, height 30" (76.3 cm). Galleria Borghese, Rome

Sculpture

Sculpture arrived at the official royal style in much the same way as architecture. While in Paris, Bernini carved a marble bust of Louis XIV. He was also commissioned to do an equestrian statue of the king, for which he made a terra-cotta model (fig. 19-17). However, the project shared the fate of Bernini's Louvre designs. Although he portrayed the king in classical military garb, the statue was rejected. Apparently the rearing horse, derived from Leonardo's design for the Battle of Anghiari (see page 434), was too dynamic to safeguard the dignity of Louis XIV. This decision was far-reaching. Equestrian statues of the king were later set up throughout France as symbols of royal authority. Bernini's design, had it succeeded, might have set the pattern for these monuments. Adopted instead was a timid variation on the equestrian portrait of Marcus Aurelius (see fig. 7-40) executed in the 1680s by François Girardon (1628–1715), which was destroyed during the French Revolution.

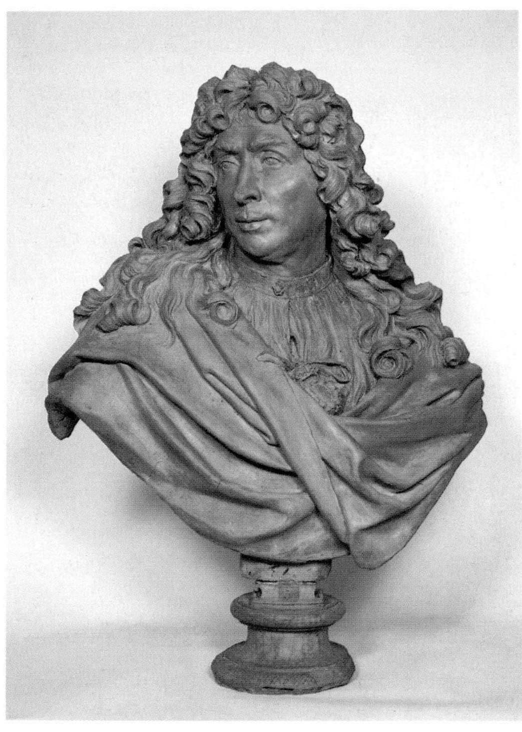

19-18. Antoine Coysevox. *Charles Lebrun.* 1676. Terra-cotta, height 26" (66 cm). The Wallace Collection, London

REPRODUCED BY PERMISSION OF THE TRUSTEES

COYSEVOX. Bernini's influence can nevertheless be felt in the work of Antoine Coysevox (1640–1720), one of the sculptors Lebrun employed at Versailles. The victorious Louis XIV in Coysevox's large stucco relief for the Salon de la Guerre (see fig. 19-13) retains the pose of Bernini's equestrian statue, although with a certain restraint. Coysevox is the first in a long line of distinguished French portrait sculptors. His bust of Lebrun (fig. 19 18) repeats the general outlines of Bernini's model of Louis XIV. The face, however, shows a realism and subtle characterization that are Coysevox's own.

PUGET. Coysevox approached the Baroque in sculpture as closely as Lebrun would permit. Pierre-Paul Puget (1620–1694), the most talented and most Baroque of seventeenth-century French sculptors, had no success at court until after Colbert's death, when Lebrun's power was on the decline. *Milo of Crotona* (fig. 19-19),

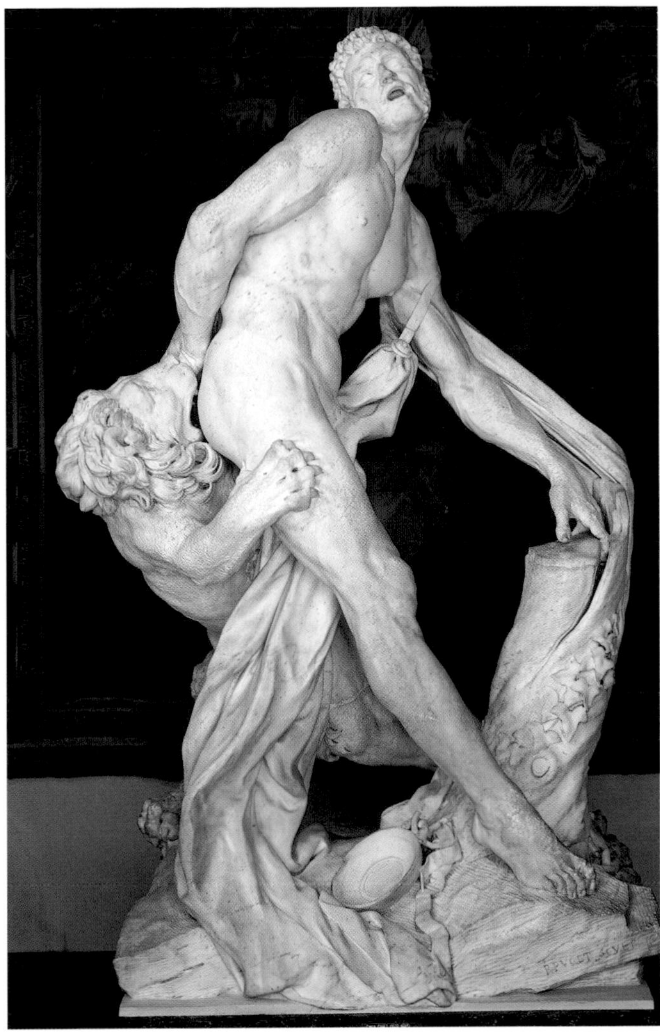

19-19. Pierre-Paul Puget. *Milo of Crotona*. 1671–83. Marble, height 8'10½" (2.7 m). Musée du Louvre, Paris

Puget's finest statue, can be compared to Bernini's *David* (see fig. 17-27). Puget's composition is more contained than Bernini's, but the agony of the hero has such force that its impact is almost physical. The internal tension fills the statue with an intense life that also recalls *The Laocoön Group* (see fig. 5-76). That, one suspects, is what made it acceptable to Louis XIV.

ENGLAND

The English made no significant contribution to Baroque painting and sculpture. They were content with feeble offshoots of Van Dyck's portraiture by imported artists such as the Dutch-born Peter Lely (1618–1680) and his German successor, Godfrey Kneller (1646–1723). The English achievement in architecture, however, was of genuine importance. This accomplishment is all the more surprising in light of the fact that England did not produce any buildings of note after the Late Gothic until the "prodigy" houses of Elizabethan times (see page 526; fig. 16-32).

JONES. The first English architect of genius was Inigo Jones (1573–1652), whose work evolved from the country house tradition. He was also the leading English theatrical designer of the day. When he went to Italy about 1600 and again in 1613, he was influenced by the Baroque stage designs of Giulio Parigi (see page 549). Surprisingly, he returned a disciple of Palladio (who had designed the theater of the Olympic Academy in Vicenza, one of the earliest of its kind; see page 466). In 1615 Jones was appointed Surveyor of the King's Works, a post he held until 1643. The Banqueting House he built at Whitehall Palace in London (fig. 19-20) for the masques and other entertainment he presented at the court

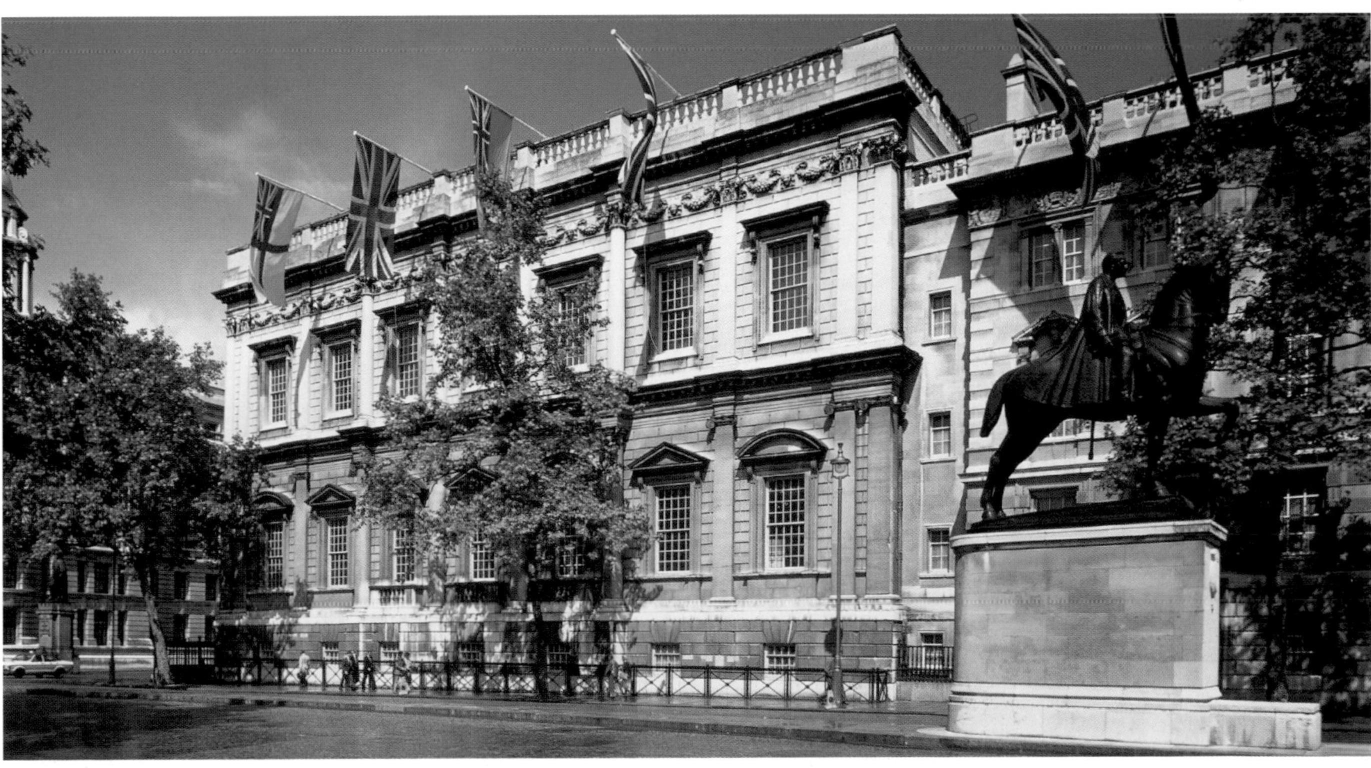

19-20. Inigo Jones. West front of the Banqueting House, Whitehall Palace, London. 1619–22

BAROQUE THEATER AND MUSIC IN ENGLAND

In England, court masques adapted from Italian court pageants played a similar role to the French *ballets de cour* in that they promoted an idealized vision of monarchy presented through allegory and myth expressed in elegant speeches, music, and dance. Many of these masques were created for James I by the playwright Ben Jonson (1572–1637) and staged by Inigo Jones, who became Surveyor of the King's Works in 1615 (see pages 587–88). Upon the overthrow in 1642 of Charles I by the Puritans—whose religious views demanded the most austere social standards—all theaters were closed, and remained so during the Commonwealth, the Puritan period of rule led by Oliver Cromwell; they were reopened only when the monarchy was restored in 1660. The Restoration, as the reign of the new king, Charles II, came to be known, was a period of great creativity for theater and music. There was an almost immediate demand for new plays, which were supplied by John Dryden (1631–1700), whose work was influenced by Shakespeare and the classical Roman authors. The later plays by Dryden and William D'Avenant (1606–1668), Jonson's successor at court, are rather stilted, moralizing tragedies about people of noble birth. Comedy fared better, while adhering to the same goal of moral instruction. *The Rover: or the Banished Cavalier* (1677) by Mrs. Aphra Behn (1640–1689) and *The Way of the World* (1700) by William Congreve (1670–1729) and Sir John Vanbrugh (best known as the architect of Blenheim Palace; see fig. 19-25) are uproarious comedies of manners that reflect the cynicism—and what later critics would call the licentiousness—of the age. The Restoration marked a revolution in English theater: not only did women begin to write plays but they also appeared on the legitimate stage for the first time. Some became enormously successful: one, Nell Gwyn, soon retired from the stage to become Charles II's mistress.

Theater gave rise to a new class of stage music by the leading composer of the Restoration, Henry Purcell (1659–1695). During the Commonwealth, English operas were plays set to music, which managed to avoid the ban against theater because they were considered concerts. This practice continued even during the Restoration. Thus *Venus and Adonis,* by Henry Purcell's teacher John Blow (1649–1708), is essentially a masque in disguise. A large part of Purcell's output is theater music, such at *The Fairy Queen* (1692), which is a free adaptation of Shakespeare's *A Midsummer Night's Dream* (not Edmund Spencer's epic poem *The Faerie Queen,* published in 1596, which is an allegory of love and honor). The closest Purcell came to opera was *Dido and Aeneas* (1689), which is basically a concert opera reputedly composed for a girls' boarding school but perhaps given as a court entertainment instead. In the following decade, Purcell found an eager collaborator in Dryden, who supplied the composer with his finest "plays" set to music: notably *King Arthur* (1691), *Oedipus* (1692), and *The Indian Queen* (1695). Blow and Purcell also wrote numerous odes for the royal family and to celebrate other occasions, as well as many church anthems and a considerable body of chamber music and keyboard works.

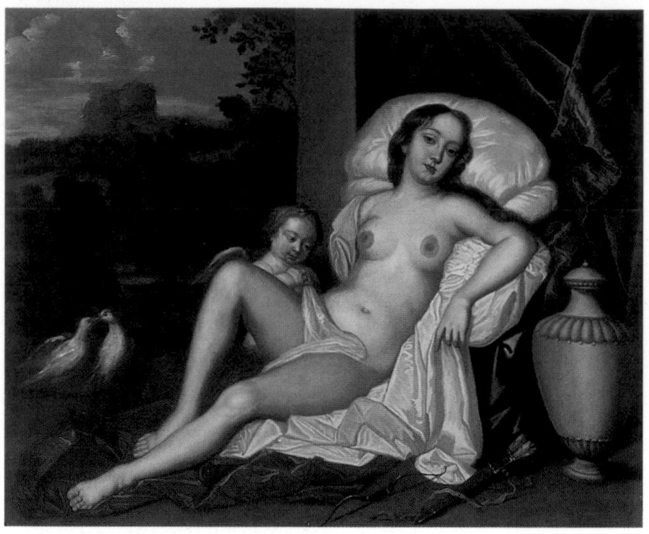

Sir Peter Lely. *Portrait of Nell Gwyn as Venus with Her Son Charles Beauclerk as Cupid.* 17th century. Oil on canvas, 47⅝ x 58½" (121 x 148.6 cm). Army and Navy Club, London

conforms in every way to the principles in Palladio's treatise, although it does not copy any specific building by Palladio. It is essentially a Vitruvian "basilica" (a double cube with an apse for the king's throne) treated as a Palladian villa, but with a breadth and consistency that remind us of Longleat (see fig. 16-32). Symmetrical and self-sufficient, it is, for its date, more like a Renaissance palazzo than any other building north of the Alps. Jones' spare style, supported by Palladio's authority as a theorist, stood as a beacon of classicist orthodoxy in England for 200 years.

WREN. This classicism can be seen in some parts of St. Paul's Cathedral (figs. 19-21–19-23) by Sir Christopher Wren (1632–1723), the great English architect of the late seventeenth century. Note the second-story windows and especially the dome, which looks like Bramante's Tempietto much enlarged (see fig. 13-7). St. Paul's is in other ways an up-to-date Baroque design that reflects a thorough knowledge of the Italian and French architecture of the day. Wren came close to being a Baroque counterpart of the Renaissance artist–scientist. An intellectual prodigy, he first studied anatomy, then physics, mathematics, and astronomy, and was highly esteemed by Sir Isaac Newton. His serious interest in architecture did not begin until he was about 30. However, it is characteristic of the Baroque as opposed to the Renaissance that there seems to be no direct link between his scientific and artistic ideas. It is hard to determine whether his technological knowledge affected the shape of his buildings.

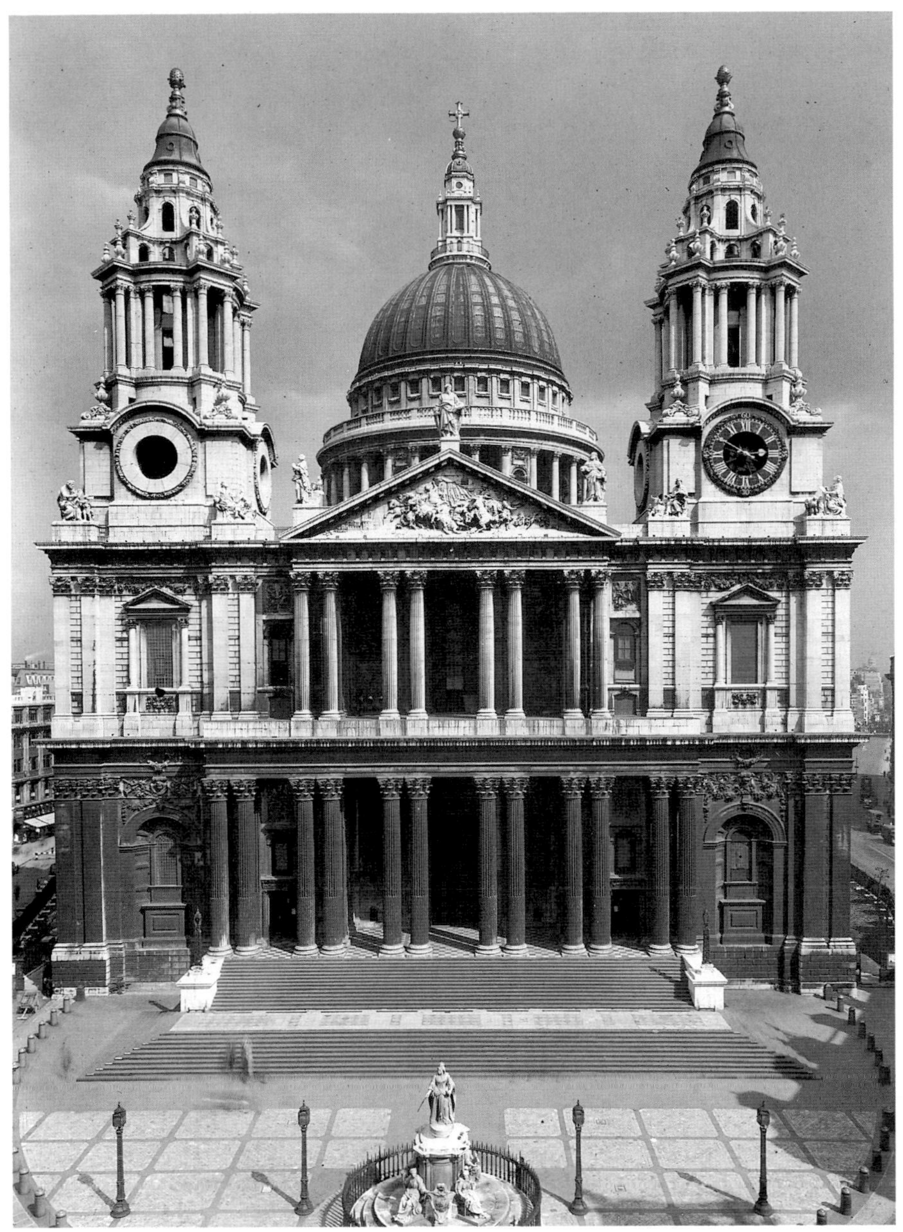

19-21. Sir Christopher Wren. Facade of St. Paul's Cathedral, London. 1675–1710

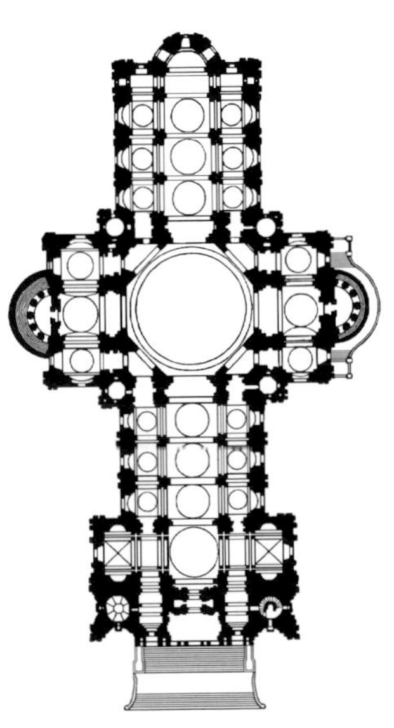

19-22. Plan of St. Paul's Cathedral

If the great London fire of 1666 had not destroyed the Gothic cathedral of St. Paul and many lesser churches, Wren might have remained an amateur architect. But after the catastrophe, he was named to the short-lived royal commission for rebuilding the city, and a few years later he began his designs for St. Paul's. [See Primary Sources, no. 59, page 623.] Wren favored central-plan churches and originally conceived St. Paul's in the shape of a Greek cross (fig. 19-24), based on Michelangelo's plan of St. Peter's (see fig. 13-28), with a huge domed crossing. This idea was evidently inspired by a design by Inigo Jones, who had been involved with the restoration of the Gothic St. Paul's earlier in the century. Wren's proposal was nevertheless rejected by church authorities in favor of a conventional basilica.

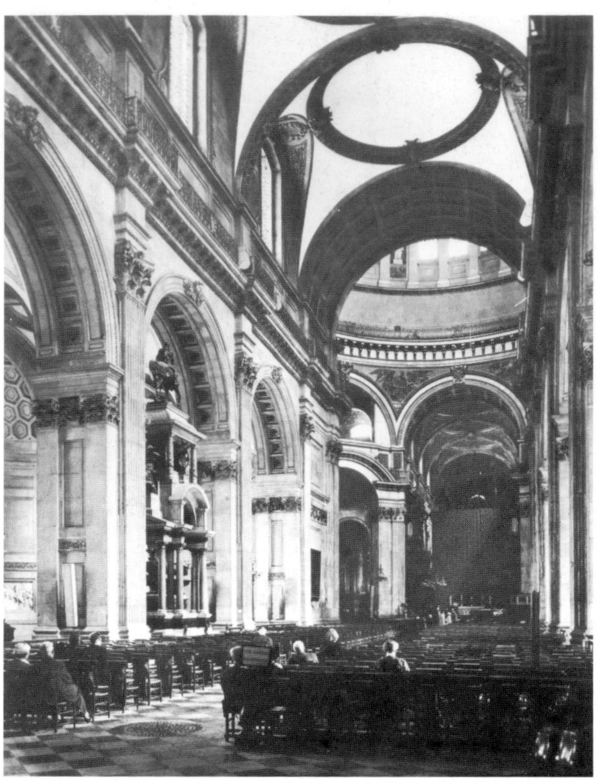

19-23. Interior of St. Paul's Cathedral

The tradition of Inigo Jones provided no more than a starting point for Wren. On his only trip abroad in 1665–66, Wren had visited Paris at the time of the dispute over the completion of the Louvre. He must have sided with Perrault, whose design for the East Front is clearly reflected in the facade of St. Paul's. St. Paul's also bears a striking resemblance to Hardouin-Mansart's Church of the Invalides (see fig. 19-15), which inspired the tripartite construction of the dome. Despite his belief that Paris provided "the best school of architecture in Europe," Wren was not indifferent to the Roman Baroque. He must have wanted the new St. Paul's to be the St. Peter's of the Church of England: more sober and not so large, but just as impressive. His dome, like that of St. Peter's, has a diameter as wide as nave and aisles combined, but it rises high above the rest of the structure and dominates even our close view of the facade. Wren ingeniously hid the buttresses supporting the dome behind a thick wall, which further helps to brace them. The lantern and the upper part of the clock towers also suggest that he knew Borromini's S. Agnese in Piazza Navona (see fig. 17-22), probably from drawings or engravings. The final result reflects not only the complex evolution of the design but also some needless changes made late in the construction by the commission overseeing it, which dismissed Wren in 1718.

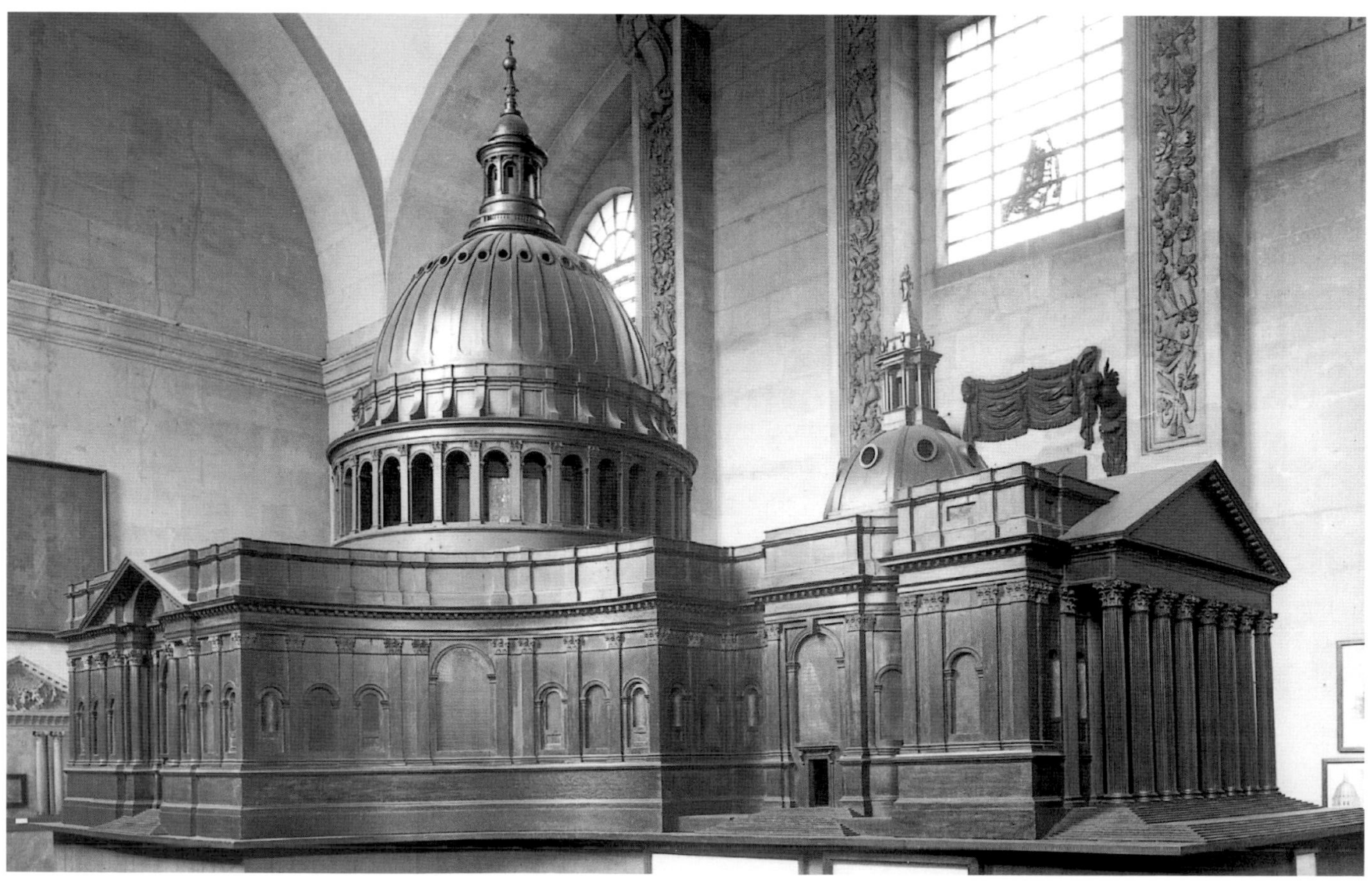

19-24. William Clere. The "Great Model" for St. Paul's Cathedral by Sir Christopher Wren. 1673. Wood, 13 x 14 x 17' (3.98 x 4.26 x 5.24 m). Conway Library, The Courtauld Institute Library, London

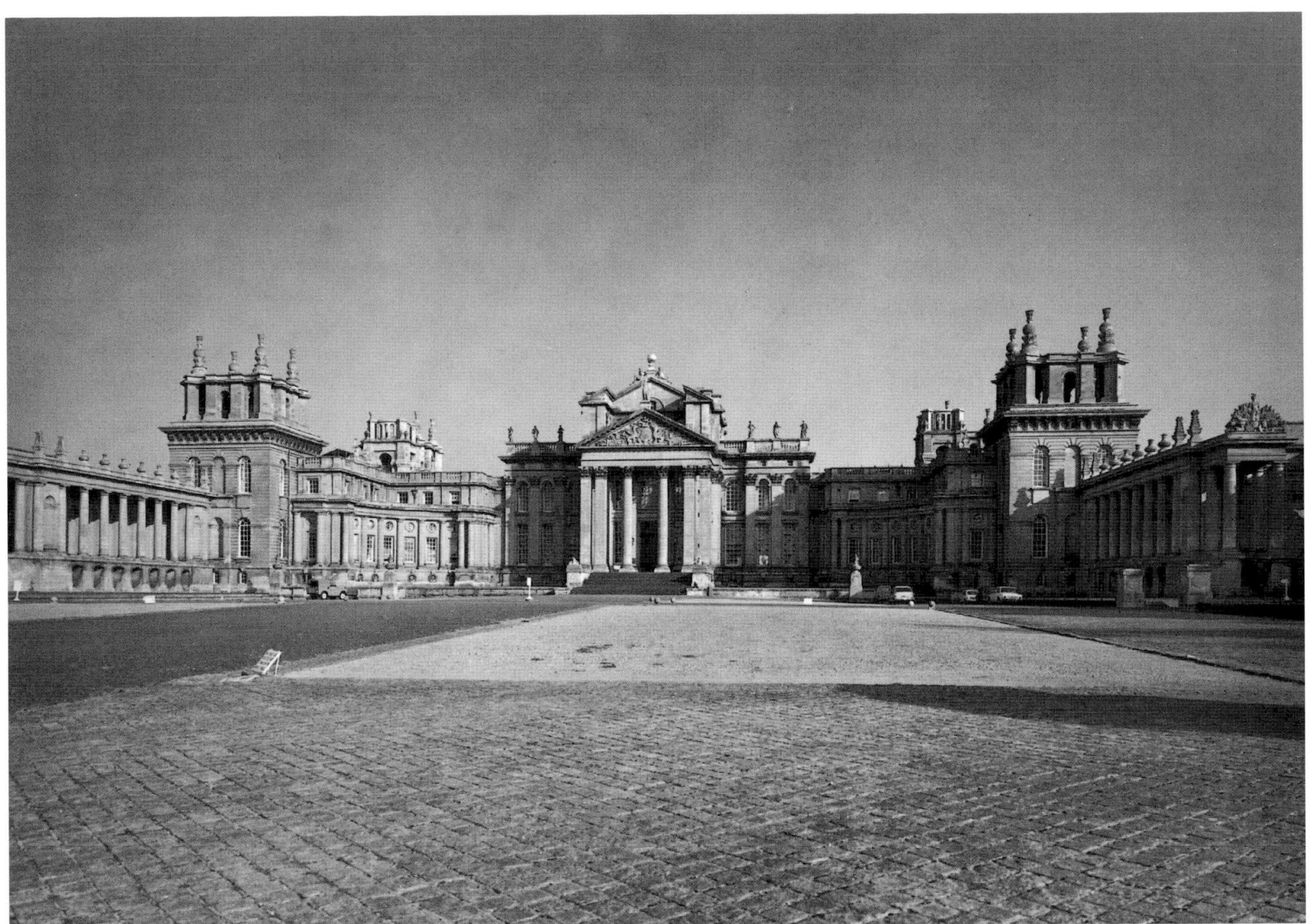

19-25. Sir John Vanbrugh. Blenheim Palace, Woodstock, England. Begun 1705

VANBRUGH. The marriage of English, French, and Italian Baroque elements is even more evident in Blenheim Palace (fig. 19-25). This grandiose structure was designed by Sir John Vanbrugh (1664–1726), a gifted amateur, with the aid of Nicholas Hawksmoore (1661–1719), Wren's most talented pupil. Vanbrugh owed his position to the Earl of Carlisle, which established him as Wren's rival and eventual successor. Blenheim, though it was his greatest work, caused Vanbrugh enormous problems. In the end he was left out in the cold like Wren, and the building had to be completed by Hawksmoore. It nevertheless shows no sign of this turbulent history. Blenheim skillfully combines the masses of an English castle with the breadth of a country house such as Longleat (see fig. 16-32); the rambling character of a French château such as Fontainebleau (see fig. 16-26); and a facade inspired, interestingly enough, by Wren. However, when we compare the facade of Blenheim and its framing colonnade with the piazza of St. Peter's (see fig. 17-14) we can see that Vanbrugh's kinship was even closer to Bernini. The main block uses a colossal Corinthian order to wed a temple portico with a Renaissance palace (compare fig. 13-26), while the wings rely on a low-slung Doric order. Such an eclectic approach, extreme even by the relaxed standards of the period, is maintained in the details. Vanbrugh, like Inigo Jones, had a strong interest in the theater. (He was a popular playwright.) The effect has both a theatricality and a massiveness that make Blenheim a fitting counterpart to Versailles (see fig. 19-11) as a symbol of English power. Designed mainly for show and entertainment, it was presented by a grateful nation to the Duke of Marlborough for his victories over French and German forces at the battle of Blenheim in 1704 during the War of Spanish Succession.

CHAPTER TWENTY

The Rococco

Much as the Baroque is often considered the final phase of the Renaissance, so the Rococo has been treated as the end of the Baroque: a long twilight, delicious but decadent, that was cleaned away by the Enlightenment and Neoclassicism. In France, the Rococo is linked with Louis XV, because it roughly corresponds to his life span (1710–1774). However, it cannot be identified with the State or the Church any more than can the Baroque, even though these continued to provide the main patronage. Moreover, the essential characteristics of Rococo style were created before the king was born. Its first symptoms begin as much as 50 years earlier, during the Late Baroque. Hence the view of the Rococo as the final phase of the Baroque is well founded. As the philosopher François-Marie Voltaire pointed out, the eighteenth century lived in the debt of the past. In art, Poussin and Rubens cast their long shadows over the period. The controversy between their partisans, in turn, goes back much further to the debate between the supporters of Michelangelo and of Titian over the merits of design versus color. In this sense, the Rococo, like the Baroque, still belongs to the Renaissance world.

To overemphasize the similarities and stylistic debt of the Rococo to the Baroque, however, risks ignoring a fundamental difference between them. What is it? In a word, it is fantasy. If the Baroque presents theater on a grand scale, the Rococo stage is smaller and more intimate. At the same time, the Rococo is both more lighthearted and tender-minded, marked equally by playful whimsy and wistful nostalgia. Its artifice evokes an enchanted realm that presents a diversion from real life. Because the modern age is the product of the Enlightenment, the Rococo is still often criticized for its unabashed escapism and eroticism. To its credit, however, the Rococo discovered the world of love and broadened the range of human emotion in art to include the family as a major theme for the first time.

FRANCE

THE RISE OF THE ROCOCO. After the death of Louis XIV in 1715, the administrative machine that Colbert (see page 579) had created ground to a stop. The nobility, formerly attached to the court at Versailles, were now freer from royal control. Many of them chose not to return to their châteaus in the provinces but to live in Paris, where they built elegant town houses, known as hôtels. Hôtels had been used as city residences by the landed aristocracy since about 1350, but during the seventeenth century they developed into social centers. As state-sponsored building activity was declining, the field of "design for private living" took on new importance. These city sites were usually cramped and irregular, so that they offered few opportunities for impressive exteriors. Hence the layout and decor of the rooms became the architects' main concern. The hôtels demanded a style of interior decoration that was less grandiose than Versailles'. They required instead an intimate style that would give greater scope to individual fancy uninhibited by classicistic rules. To meet this need, French designers created the Rococo from Italian gardens and interiors. (In France it is often called "the Style of Louis XV," even though it was defined largely during the regency phase of 1717 to 1723.) The name fits well: it was coined from *coquillage* and *rocaille* (echoing the Italian *barocco*), which referred to the playful decoration of grottoes with irregular shells and stones.

The Decorative Arts

It was in the decorative arts that the Rococo flourished first and foremost. We have not discussed the decorative arts until now because their conservative nature tended to limit creativity except in a few unusual cases. The latter half of the seventeenth century was a time of change in French design. A central role was played by Colbert, who in the 1660s acquired the Gobelins (named after the brothers who founded them) for the Crown. He turned them into a royal workshop that supplied luxurious furnishings, including tapestries, to the court under the direction of Charles Lebrun. After 1688 the War of the League of Augsburg forced the Crown to economize. Reduced spending at the Gobelins gradually loosened central control of the decorative arts and opened the way to new stylistic developments. The situation paralleled the decline of the Academy's dominance over the fine arts, which gave rise to the Rococo in painting (see page 579).

This change does not explain the excellence of French decor, however. Crucial to its development was the importance assigned to designers: their engravings established new standards of design that were expected to be followed by artisans, who thereby lost much of their independence. Let us note, too, the collaboration of architects, who became more involved in interior decoration. Along with sculptors, who often created the ornamentation, they helped raise the decorative arts to the level of the fine arts, thus establishing a tradition that continued into modern times. The decorative and fine arts were most clearly joined in major furniture. French cabinetmakers known as *ébénistes* (after ebony, their preferred wood veneer) helped to bring about the revolution in interior decor by introducing new materials and techniques. Many of these upstarts came originally from Holland, Flanders, Germany, and even Italy.

The decorative arts played a unique role during the Rococo. Hôtel interiors were more than collections of objects. They were total environments put together with great care by discerning collectors and the talented architects, sculptors, decorators, and dealers who catered to their taste. A room, like an item of furniture, could involve the services of a wide variety of artisans—cabinetmakers, wood carvers, gold- and silversmiths, upholsterers, and porcelain makers. All were dedicated to producing the ensemble, even though each craft was a separate specialty subject to strict regulations. Together they fueled the hunger for novelty that swept Europe.

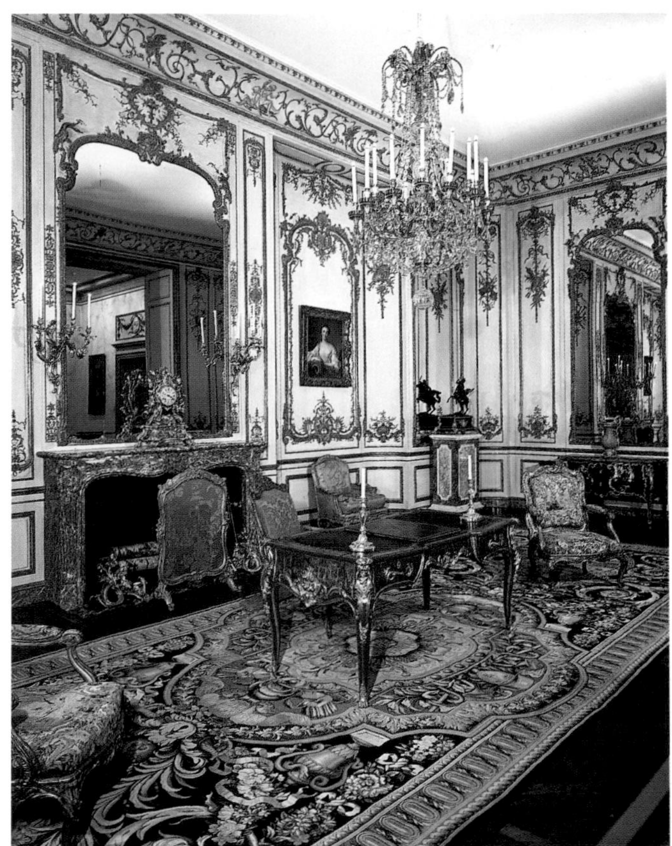

20-1. Nicolas Pineau. Room from the Hôtel de Varengeville, Paris. c. 1735. The Metropolitan Museum of Art, New York

WRIGHTSMAN COLLECTION

PINEAU. Almost none of these rooms has survived intact. Most have been destroyed, heavily altered, or dispersed. Even so, we can get a good idea of their appearance by the reconstruction of one such room from the Hôtel de Varengeville, Paris, designed about 1735 by Nicolas Pineau (1684–1754) for the Duchesse de Villars (fig. 20-1). To create a sumptuous effect, the walls and ceiling are encrusted with ornamentation and the elaborately carved furniture is adorned with gilt bronze. Everything swims in a sea of swirling patterns united by the most sophisticated sense of design and materials the world has ever known. Here there is no clear distinction between decoration and function in the clock on the mantel and the statuette in the corner. The painting, too, has been thoroughly integrated into the room.

Sculpture

CLODION. Because so much of it was done to adorn interiors, French Rococo sculpture generally took the form of small groups in a "miniature Baroque" style, designed to be viewed at close range. A typical example is *Satyr and Bacchante* (fig. 20-2) by Claude Michel (1738–1814), known as Clodion. Its coquettish eroticism is a playful echo of the ecstasies of Bernini, whose work Clodion studied during a nine-year stay in Italy (compare fig. 17-28). Although he undertook several large cycles in marble, Clodion was by nature a modeler who was at his best working on a small scale. He could work miracles with terra-cotta, and he reigned supreme in this intimate medium.

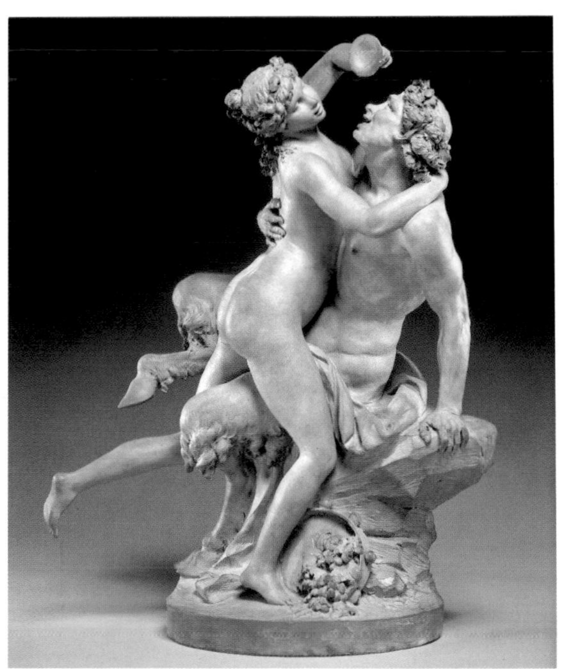

20-2. Claude Michel, known as Clodion. *Satyr and Bacchante.* c. 1775. Terra-cotta, height 23¼" (59 cm). The Metropolitan Museum of Art, New York

BEQUEST OF BENJAMIN ALTMAN, 1913

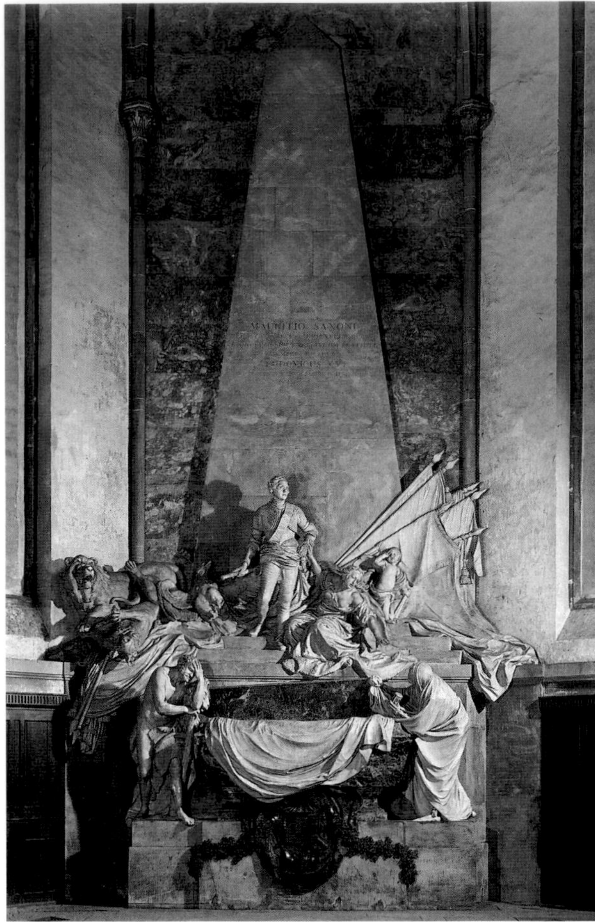

20-3. Jean-Baptiste Pigalle. Tomb of the Maréchal de Saxe. 1753–76. Marble. St. Thomas, Strasbourg, France

PIGALLE. There were few monumental commissions for French Rococo sculptors. Lifesize statues were confined largely to decorative figures of nymphs, goddesses, and the like, making them counterparts to the mythological creatures in the paintings of Boucher and his followers (see below). However, the Tomb of the Maréchal de Saxe (fig. 20-3) by Jean-Baptiste Pigalle (1714–1785), Clodion's teacher and the most gifted sculptor of the era, recaptures some of the grandeur of the Baroque. The Maréchal steps from a pyramid denoting immortality toward a casket held open for him by the figure of Death, as France tries in vain to intervene. He is mourned by the grief-stricken Hercules to the left, representing the French army, and, to the right, the weeping infant personifying the Genius of War, who extinguishes his torch before the fallen military standards. The strange menagerie to the left stands for the nations defeated by the Maréchal in combat: Holland, England, and the Holy Roman Empire. If the allegory strikes us as heavy-handed, there can be no denying the effectiveness of the presentation, which is among the most astonishing in all of sculpture. The poses show the classicism required for official French art, but the spirit of the whole is unmistakably Baroque. Pigalle has mounted a tableau worthy of Bernini, whose works he studied during several years in Rome as a young man. The restraint also suggests the example of Algardi (see pages 545–48). The pyramid is not a three-dimensional structure but a low relief built against the wall of the church, while the steps leading up to it and the figures on them are in the round, like actors performing before a backdrop. We must therefore view the monument as a kind of theatrical performance in marble. The artist has even set it apart from its surroundings by creating an elevated "stage space" that projects forcefully outward.

Painting

"POUSSINISTES" VERSUS "RUBÉNISTES." It is not surprising that the strict system of the French Academy (see page 579) did not produce any major artists. Even Charles Lebrun, as we have seen, was far more Baroque in practice than we would expect from his classicistic theory. The rigidity of the official doctrine gave rise to a reaction that vented itself as soon as Lebrun's authority began to wane. Toward the end of the century, the members of the Academy formed two factions over the issue of drawing versus color: the "Poussinistes" (or conservatives) against the "Rubénistes." The conservatives defended Poussin's view that drawing, which appealed to the mind, was superior to color, which appealed to the senses. The Rubénistes (many of whom were of Flemish descent) favored color, rather than drawing, as being more true to nature. They also pointed out that drawing, admittedly based on reason, appeals only to the expert few, whereas color appeals to everyone. This argument had important implications. It claimed that the layperson should be the judge of artistic values and challenged the Renaissance notion that painting, as a liberal art, could be appreciated only by the educated mind.

WATTEAU. By the time Louis XIV died in 1715, the power of the Academy had long been overcome, and the influence of Rubens and the great Venetians was everywhere. The greatest of the young artists working in the "Rubéniste" manner was Jean-Antoine Watteau (1684–1721). Watteau's paintings broke many academic rules, and his subjects did not conform to any established type. To make room for Watteau, the Academy invented the new category of *fêtes galantes* (elegant fetes or entertainments). The term refers to the fact that the artist's work mainly shows scenes of fashionable people or comedy actors in parklike settings. Watteau often interweaves theater and real life, so that no clear distinction can be made between the two. *A Pilgrimage to Cythera* (fig. 20-4), painted as his reception piece for the Academy, is an evocation of love that includes elements of classical mythology. Accompanied by swarms of cupids, young couples have come to Cythera, the island of love, to pay homage to Venus, whose garlanded image appears on the far right. The action unfolds in the foreground from right to left, like a continuous narrative, which tells us that they are about to board the boat. Two lovers are still engaged in their tryst; behind them, another couple rises to follow a third pair down the hill as the young woman casts a wistful look back at the goddess' sacred grove.

As a fashionable conversation piece, the scene recalls Rubens' *The Garden of Love* (compare fig. 18-3), but Watteau has added a touch of poignancy that lends it a poetic subtlety reminiscent of Giorgione and Titian (see figs. 13-36 and 13-41). Watteau's figures, too, lack the vitality of Rubens'. Slim and graceful, they move with the assurance of actors who play their roles so well that they touch

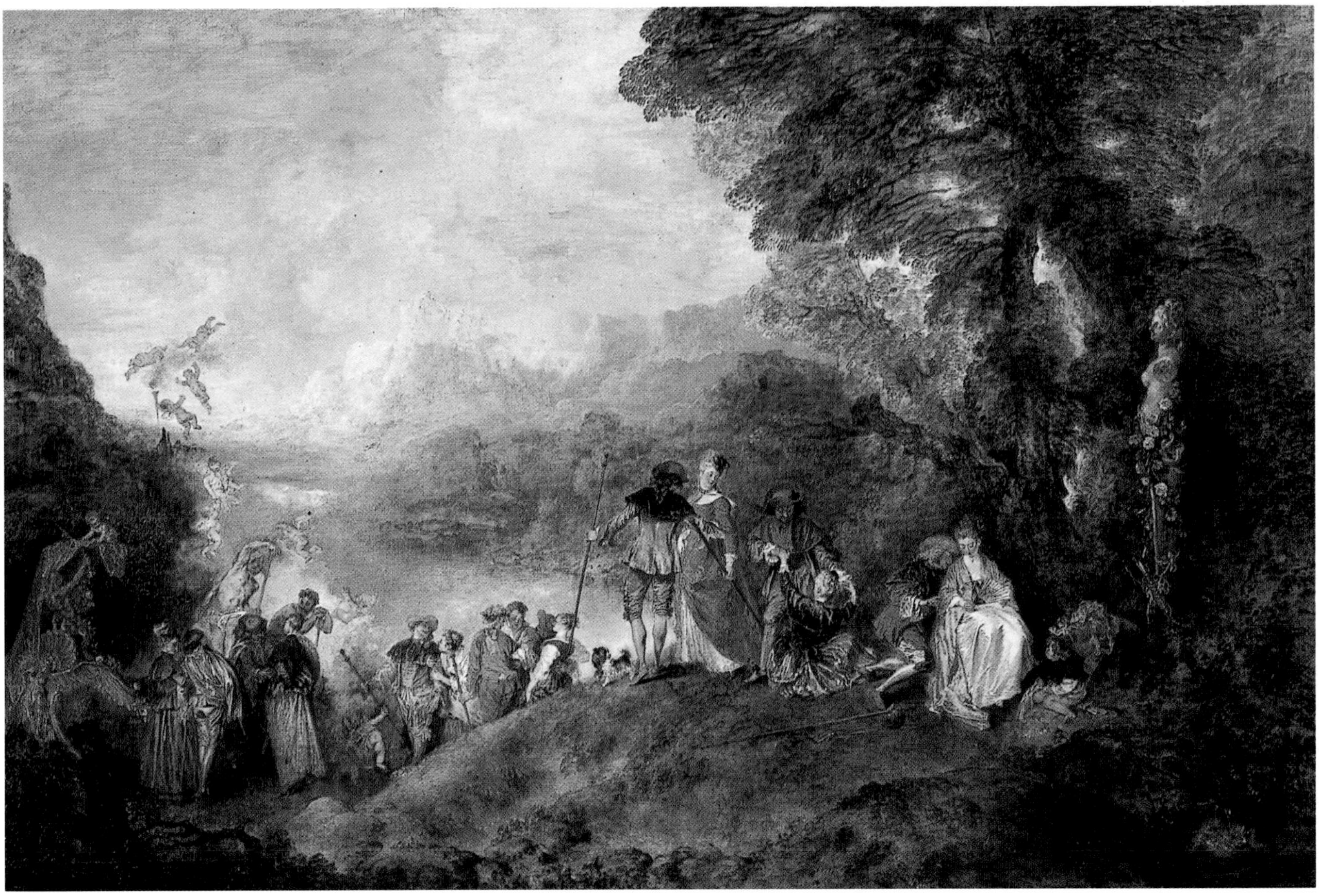

20-4. Jean-Antoine Watteau. *A Pilgrimage to Cythera.* 1717. Oil on canvas, 4'3" x 6'4½" (1.3 x 1.9 m). Musée du Louvre, Paris

us more than reality ever could. They recapture an earlier ideal of "mannered" elegance.

Many of Watteau's paintings center on the commedia dell'arte. His treatment of this Italian theme is all the more remarkable because the commedia dell'arte was officially banned in France from 1697 until 1716 (see page 610). Shortly before his death, Watteau painted perhaps his most moving work: *Pierrot* (fig. 20-5), traditionally known as *Gilles* after a similar stock character in the commedia dell'arte. It was probably done as a sign for a café owned by a friend of the artist who retired from the stage after achieving fame in the racy role of the clown. The performance has ended, and the actor has stepped forward to face the audience. The other characters, all highly individualized, are probably likenesses of friends from the same circle. Yet the painting is more than a portrait or an advertisement. Watteau approaches his subject with incomparable human understanding and artistic genius. Pierrot is lifesize, so that he confronts us as a full human being, not simply as a stock character. In the process, Watteau transforms him into Everyman, with whom he evidently identified himself—a merging of identity basic to the commedia dell'arte. The face and pose have a poignancy that suggests, among other things, a subtle sense of alienation. Like the rest of the actors, except the doctor on the donkey who looks mischievously at us, he seems lost in his own thoughts. Still, it is difficult to define his mood, for the expression is as elusive as it is eloquent.

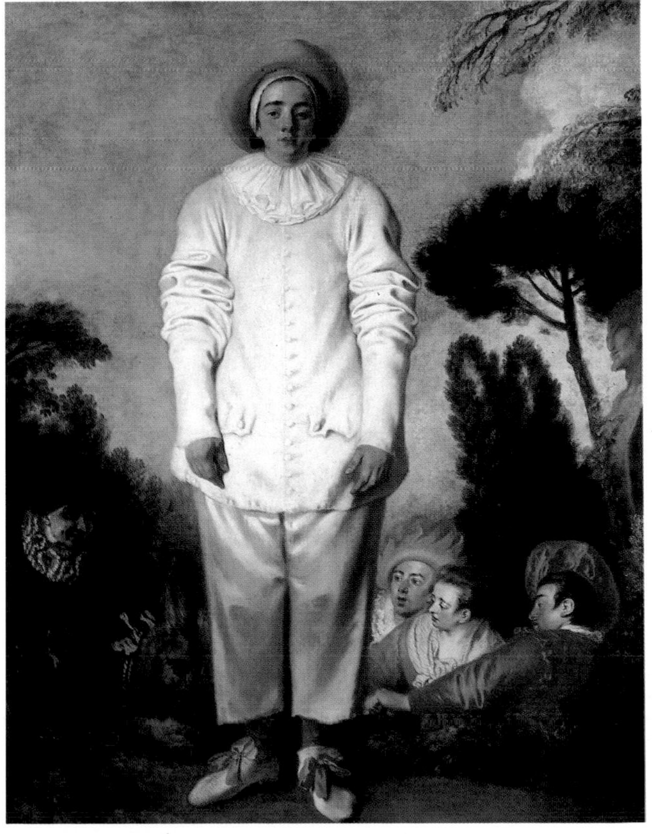

20-5. Jean-Antoine Watteau. *Gilles and Four Other Characters from the Commedia dell'Arte (Pierrot)*. c. 1719. Oil on canvas, 72½ x 58⅜" (184 x 149 cm). Musée du Louvre, Paris

BOUCHER. The work of Watteau signals a shift in French art to the Rococo. Although the term originally applied to the decorative arts, it suits the playful character of French painting before 1765 equally well. By about 1720 even history painting becomes intimate in scale and ebullient in style and subject. The finest painter in this vein was François Boucher (1703–1770), who epitomizes the age of Madame de Pompadour, the mistress of Louis XV. *The Toilet of Venus* (fig. 20-6), which was painted for her private retreat, is full of silk and perfume. Compared to Vouet's sensuous goddess (see fig. 19-8), from which she is descended, Boucher's *Venus* has been transformed into a coquette of enchanting beauty. In this cosmetic land, she is an eternally youthful Venus with the same rosy skin as the cherubs who attend her. If Watteau elevated human love to the level of mythology, Boucher raised playful eroticism to the realm of the divine. What Boucher lacks in the emotional depth that distinguishes Watteau's art he makes up for in his understanding of the fantasies that enrich people's lives.

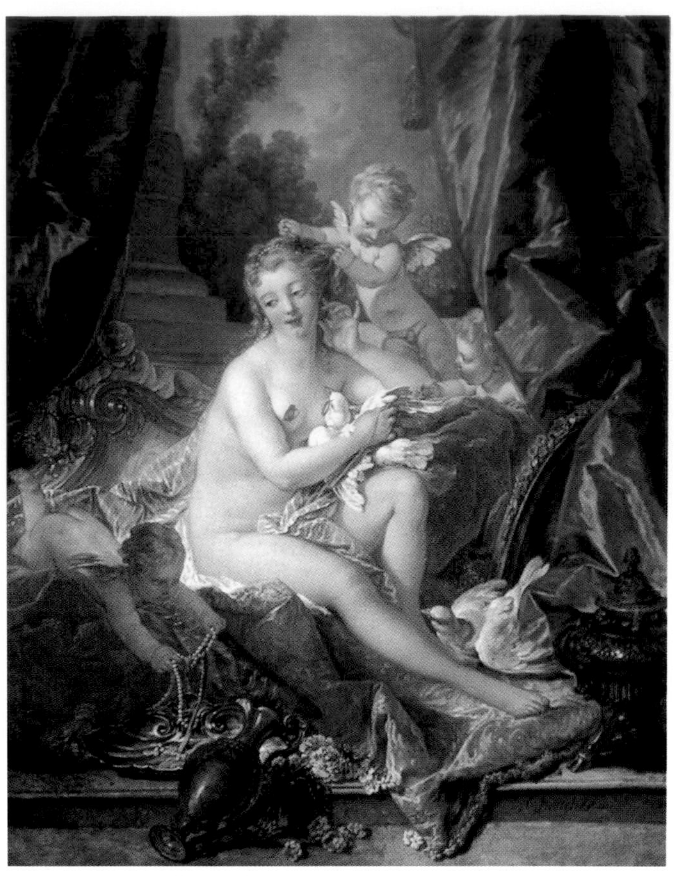

20-6. François Boucher. *The Toilet of Venus.* 1751. Oil on canvas, 43 x 33½" (109.2 x 85.1 cm). The Metropolitan Museum of Art, New York

BEQUEST OF WILLIAM K. VANDERBILT

FRAGONARD. *Bathers* (fig. 20-7), by Jean-Honoré Fragonard (1732–1806), Boucher's star pupil, shows him to be an even franker Rubéniste than Boucher. He paints with a fluid breadth and spontaneity that recalls Rubens' oil sketches and even paraphrases the Flemish master's figures (see fig. 18-2). They move with a floating grace that also links him with Tiepolo, whose work he had admired during a long stay in Italy (compare fig. 20-24). Fragonard's paintings are diverse, ranging from erotic fantasies to intimate studies and pastoral landscapes, all marked by the extraordinary virtuosity that made him the finest pure painter of his generation. He had the misfortune to outlive his era. His pictures became outmoded as the French Revolution approached, and he was reduced to poverty after 1789. Later he was supported only by a curatorship to which he was appointed in 1793 by Jacques-Louis David (see pages 641–42), who recognized his achievement, although their styles were diametrically opposed. He died, virtually forgotten, in the heyday of the Napoleonic era.

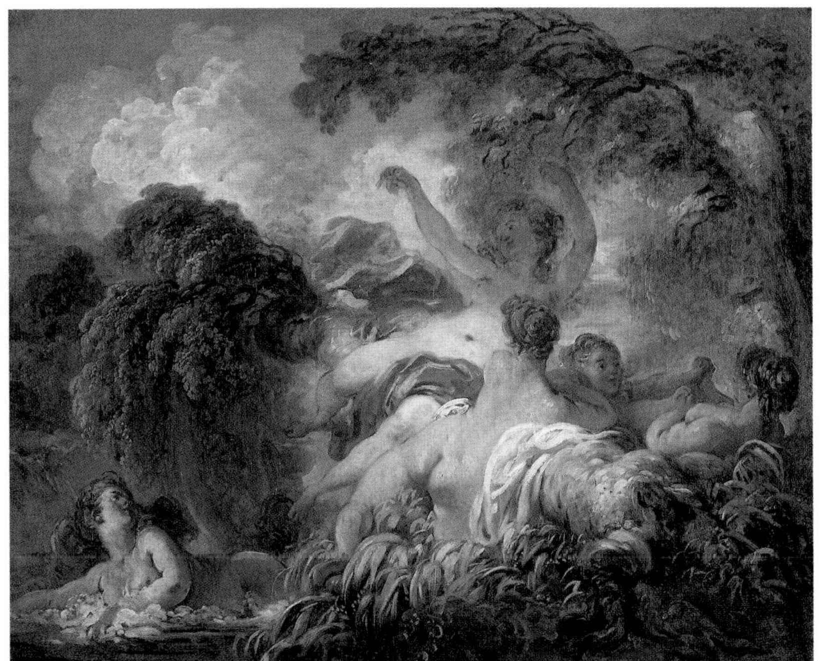

20-7. Jean-Honoré Fragonard. *Bathers.* c. 1765. Oil on canvas, 25¼ x 31½" (64 x 80 cm). Musée du Louvre, Paris

CHARDIN. The style Fragonard practiced with such mastery was not the only one open to him and the other French painters of his generation. His art might have been different if he had followed that of his first teacher, Jean-Baptiste-Siméon Chardin (1699–1779). The Rubénistes had cleared the way for a renewed interest in still-life and genre paintings by Dutch and Flemish masters. This revival was spurred by the presence of numerous artists from the Netherlands, especially Flanders, who settled in France in growing numbers after about 1550 but maintained ties to their native lands. Chardin is the finest French painter in this vein. Yet he is far removed in spirit and style, if not in subject matter, from any Dutch or Flemish painter. Indeed, he is more akin to Le Nain and Sanchez Cotán (see pages 575–76 and 549). His paintings act as moral statements, not by conveying symbolic messages as Baroque art often does (see page 568), but by affirming the rightness of the existing social order and its values. To the rising middle class who were the artist's patrons, his genre scenes and kitchen still lifes proclaimed the virtues of hard work, frugality, honesty, and devotion to family.

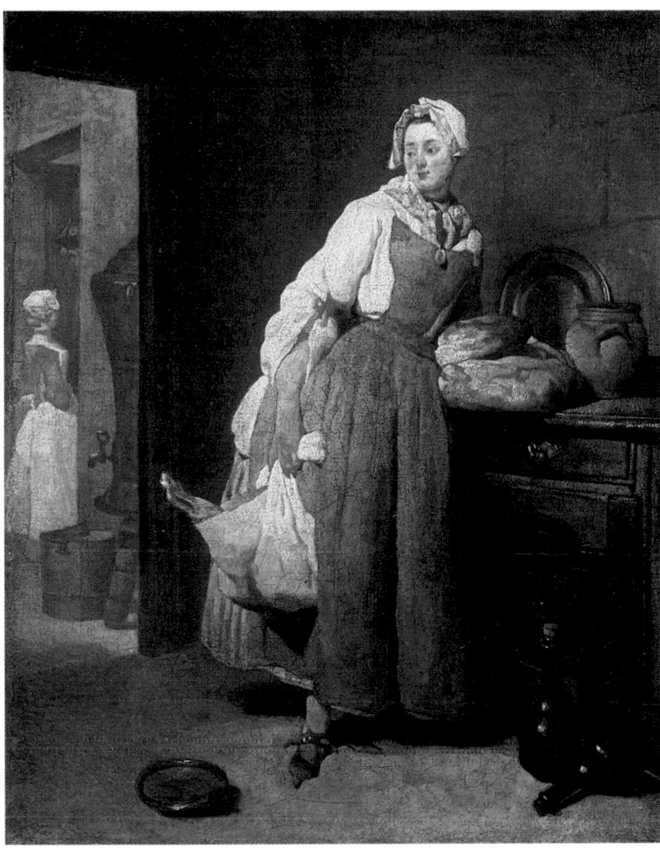

20-8. Jean-Baptiste-Siméon Chardin. *Back from the Market*. 1739. Oil on canvas, 18½ x 14¾" (47 x 37.5 cm). Musée du Louvre, Paris

Back from the Market (fig. 20-8) shows life in a Parisian middle-class household. Here we find such feeling for the beauty hidden in everyday life and so clear a sense of spatial order that we can compare him only to Vermeer (see fig. 18-28). However, Chardin's technique is quite unlike any Dutch artist's. His brushwork renders the light on colored surfaces with a creamy touch that is both analytical and lyrical. To reveal the inner nature of things, he summarizes forms and subtly alters their appearance and texture, rather than describing them in detail.

Chardin's genius discovered poetry in even the most humble objects and endowed them with timeless dignity. His still lifes usually depict the same modest environment, avoiding the "object appeal" of their Dutch predecessors. In *Kitchen Still Life* (fig. 20-9), we see only the common objects that belong in any kitchen: earthenware jugs, a casserole, a copper pot, a piece of raw meat, smoked herring, two eggs. But how important they seem, each so firmly placed in relation to the rest, each so worthy of the artist's—and our—scrutiny! Despite his concern with formal problems, evident in the beautifully balanced design, Chardin treats these objects with a respect close to reverence. Beyond their shapes, colors, and textures, they are to him symbols of the life of common people.

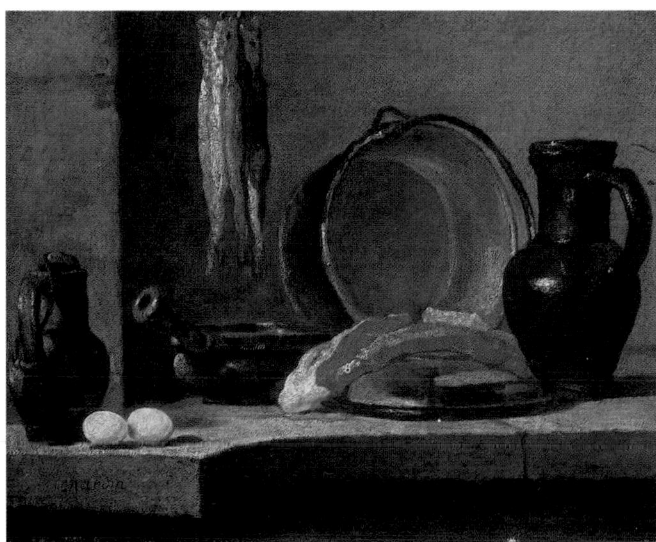

20-9. Jean-Baptiste-Siméon Chardin. *Kitchen Still Life*. c. 1731. Oil on canvas, 12½ x 15⅜" (32 x 39 cm). Ashmolean Museum, Oxford

BEQUEATHED BY MRS. W. F. R. WELDON

VIGÉE-LEBRUN. It is from portraits that we can gain the clearest understanding of the French Rococo, for the transformation of the human image lies at the heart of the age. In portraits of the aristocracy, men were endowed with the illusion of character as an attribute of their noble birth. But the finest Rococo portraits were those of women, hardly a surprising fact in a society that idolized love and feminine beauty. Indeed, one of the finest artists in this vein was herself a beautiful woman: Marie-Louise-Elisabeth Vigée-Lebrun (1755–1842), who has left us a fascinating autobiography. [See Primary Sources, no. 60, page 624.]

Throughout Vigée's long life she enjoyed great fame, which took her to every corner of Europe, including Russia, when she fled the French Revolution. *The Duchesse de Polignac* (fig. 20-10), painted a few years after Vigée had become the portraitist for Queen Marie Antoinette, amply demonstrates her ability. The duchesse is a descendant of Domenichino's *St. Cecilia* (see fig. 17-8). She has the youthful loveliness of Boucher's *Venus* (see fig. 20-6), made all the more persuasive by the artist's ravishing treatment of her clothing. At the same time, there is a sense of transience in the lyrical mood that exemplifies the Rococo's whimsical theatricality. Interrupted

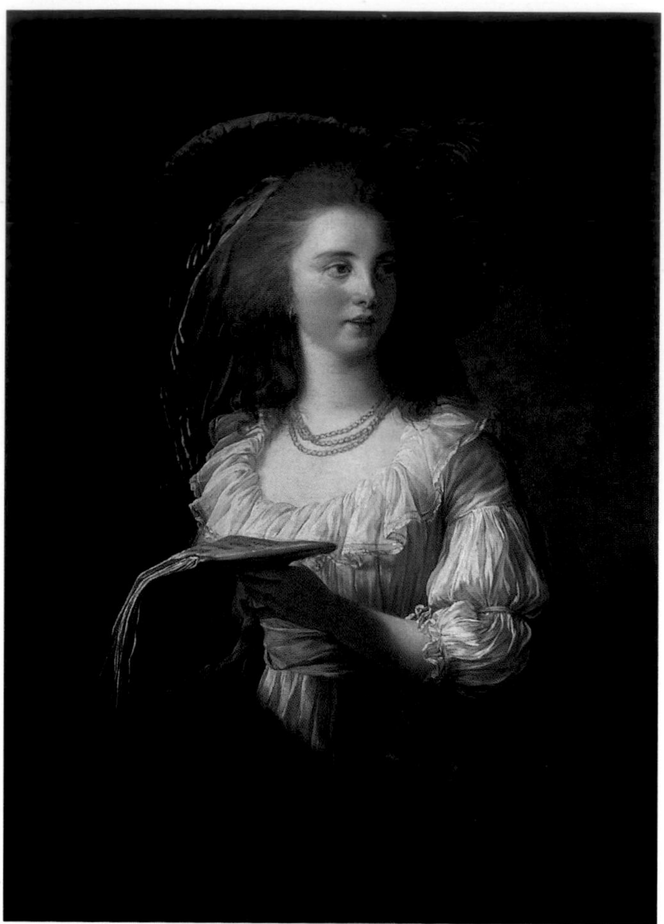

20-10. Marie-Louise-Elisabeth Vigée-Lebrun. *The Duchesse de Polignac*. 1783. Oil on canvas, 38¾ x 28" (98.3 x 71 cm)

© THE NATIONAL TRUST WADDESDON MANOR

in her singing, the duchesse becomes a real-life counterpart to the poetic creatures in Watteau's *A Pilgrimage to Cythera* (see fig. 20-4) by way of the delicate sentiment she shares with the girl in Chardin's *Back from the Market* (see fig. 20-8).

ENGLAND

Painting

Across the English Channel, the Venetians were the dominant artists for more than a half-century (see page 610). However, the French Rococo had a major, though unacknowledged, effect. In fact, it helped to bring about the first school of English painting since the Middle Ages that had more than local importance.

HOGARTH. The earliest of these painters, William Hogarth (1697–1764) was the first English artist of genius since Nicholas Hilliard (see fig. 16-17). He began as an engraver and soon took up painting. Although he must have learned something about color and brushwork from Venetian and French examples, as well as Van Dyck, his work is so original that it has no real precedent. He made his mark in the 1730s with a new kind of picture, which he described as "modern moral subjects . . . similar to representations on the stage." It follows the vogue for sentimental comedies, such as those by Sir Richard Steele, that sought to teach moral lessons through satire (see box page 610). In the same vein is John Gay's *The Beggar's Opera* of 1728 [see box page 605], a social and political satire that Hogarth illustrated in one of his paintings. Hogarth wished to be judged as a dramatist, he said, even though his "actors" could only "exhibit a dumb show." These pictures, and the prints he made from them for sale to the public, came in sets, with certain details repeated in each scene to unify the sequence. Hogarth's "morality plays" teach, by bad example, solid middle-class virtues. They show a country girl who succumbs to the temptations of fashionable London; the evils of corrupt elections; and aristocratic rakes who live only for pleasure and marry wealthy women of lower status for their fortunes, which they soon dissipate. Hogarth is probably the first artist in history to become a social critic in his own right.

In *The Orgy* (figs. 20-11 and 20-12), from *The Rake's Progress,* the young wastrel is overindulging in wine and women. It is set in a famous London brothel, the Rose Tavern. The girl adjusting her shoe in the foreground is preparing for a vulgar dance involving the silver plate and candle behind her; to the left a chamber pot

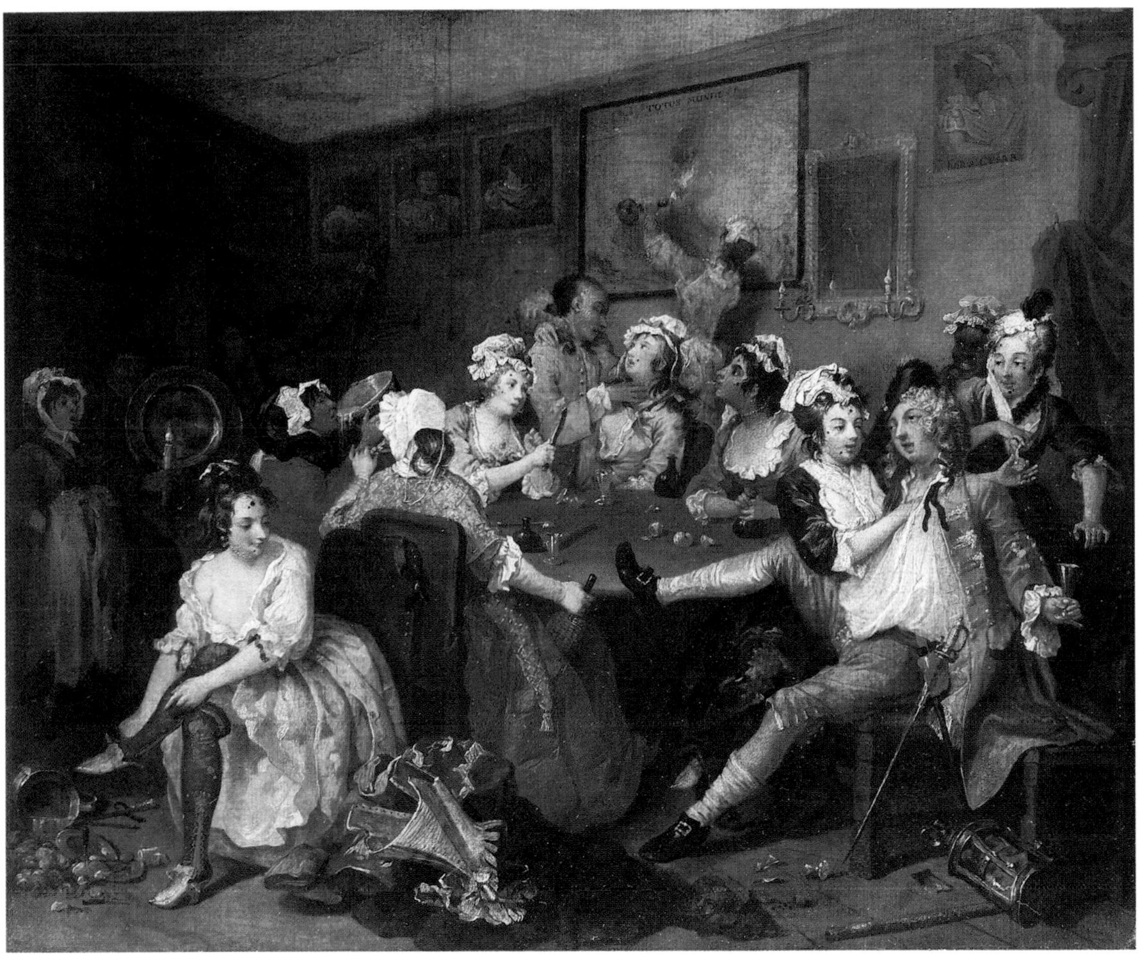

20-11. William Hogarth. *The Orgy,* Scene III of *The Rake's Progress*. c. 1734. Oil on canvas, 24½ x 29½" (62.2 x 74.9 cm). Sir John Soane's Museum, London

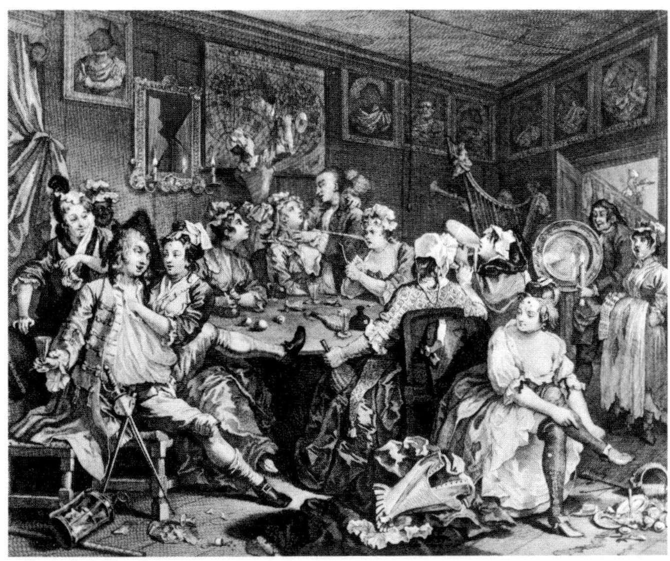

20-12. William Hogarth. *He Revels (The Orgy),* Scene III of *The Rake's Progress*. 1735. Engraving. The Metropolitan Museum of Art, New York

HARRIS BRISBANE DICK FUND, 1932

spills its contents over a chicken dish; and in the background a singer holds sheet music for a coarse song of the day. (The rogue is later arrested for debt, enters into a marriage of convenience, turns to gambling, goes to debtor's prison, and dies in an insane asylum.) The scene is so full of visual clues that a full account would take pages, as well as constant references to other plates in the series. However literal-minded, the picture has great appeal. Hogarth combines some of Watteau's sparkle with Jan Steen's narrative gusto (compare figs. 20-4 and 18-27) and entertains us so well that we enjoy his sermon without being overwhelmed by its message. The link to Steen is no accident. A succession of Dutch genre painters were active in England during the late seventeenth and early eighteenth centuries and helped establish the tradition there during Hogarth's lifetime.

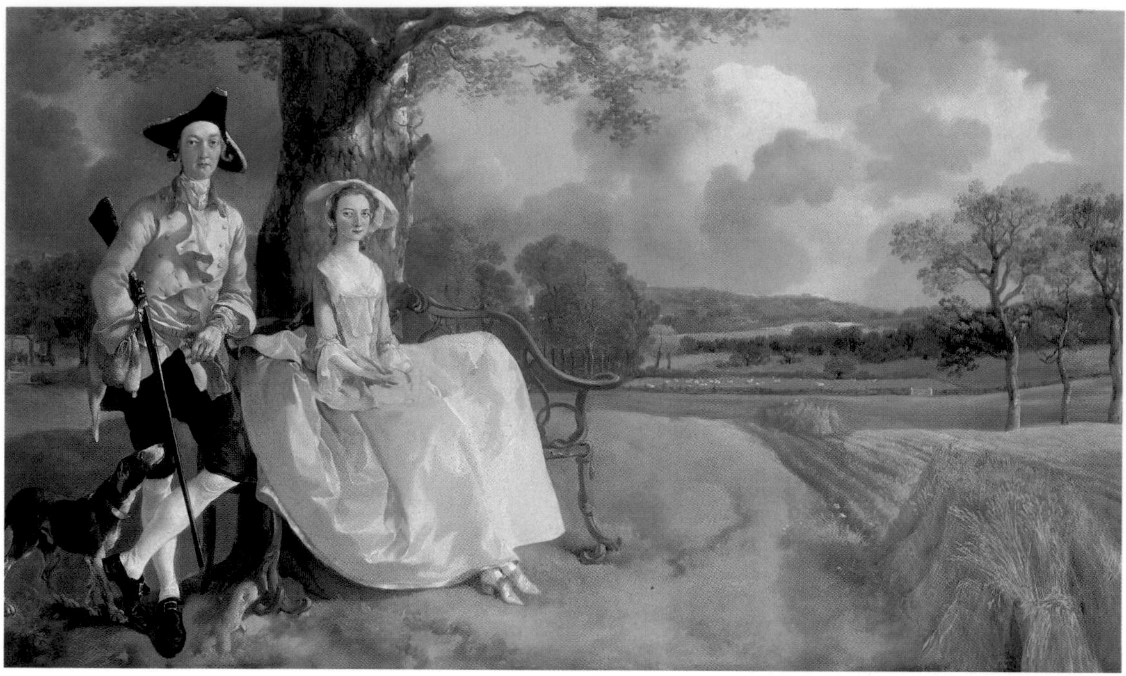

20-13. Thomas Gainsborough. *Robert Andrews and His Wife*. c. 1748–50. Oil on canvas, 27½ x 47" (69.7 x 119.3 cm). The National Gallery, London

REPRODUCED BY COURTESY OF THE TRUSTEES

GAINSBOROUGH. Portraiture remained the only constant source of income for English painters. Here, too, eighteenth-century England produced a style that differed from Continental traditions. Hogarth was a pioneer in this field as well. The greatest master, however, was Thomas Gainsborough (1727–1788), who began by painting landscapes but ended as the favorite portraitist of British high society. His early paintings, such as *Robert Andrews and His Wife* (fig. 20-13), have a lyrical charm that is not always found in his later pictures. The outdoor setting, though indebted to Watteau, was largely invented by Francis Hayman (1708–1766), whom Gainsborough came to know while an art student in London. Gainsborough soon surpassed Hayman and even painted the backgrounds in some of the latter's works during the 1750s. Compared to Van Dyck's artifice in *Portrait of Charles I Hunting* (see fig. 18-6), this country squire and his wife are unpretentiously at home in their setting. The landscape is derived from Ruisdael and his school but has a sunlit, hospitable air never achieved (or desired) by the Dutch masters. The casual grace of the two figures, which affect an air of naturalness, indirectly recalls Watteau's style. The newlywed couple—she dressed in the fashionable attire of the day, he armed with a rifle to denote his status as a country squire (hunting was a privilege of wealthy landowners)—do not till the soil themselves. The painting nevertheless conveys the gentry's closeness to the land, from which the English derived much of their sense of national identity. (Many private estates had been created in 1535, when Henry VIII broke with the Catholic church and distributed its property to his supporters.) Out of this attachment to place was to develop a feeling for nature that became the basis for English landscape painting, to which Gainsborough himself made an important early contribution.

Gainsborough spent most of his career working in the provinces, first in his native Suffolk, then in the resort town of Bath. Toward the end of his career, he moved to London, where his work underwent a major change. The splendid portrait (fig. 20-14) of the famous actress Mrs. Siddons (see box page 610) has the virtues of Gainsborough's late style: a cool elegance that trans-

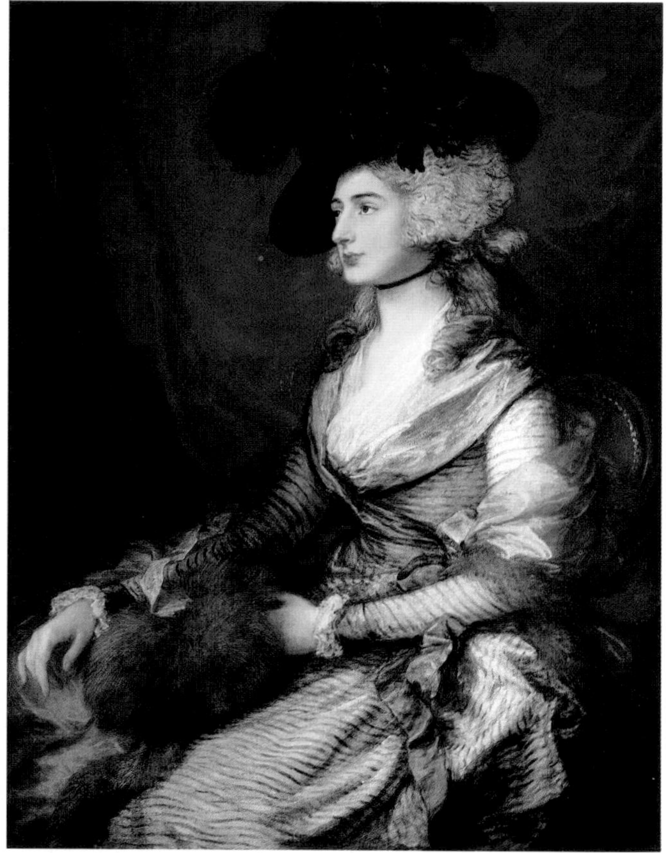

20-14. Thomas Gainsborough. *Mrs. Siddons*. 1785. Oil on canvas, 49½ x 39" (125.7 x 99.1 cm). The National Gallery, London

REPRODUCED BY COURTESY OF THE TRUSTEES

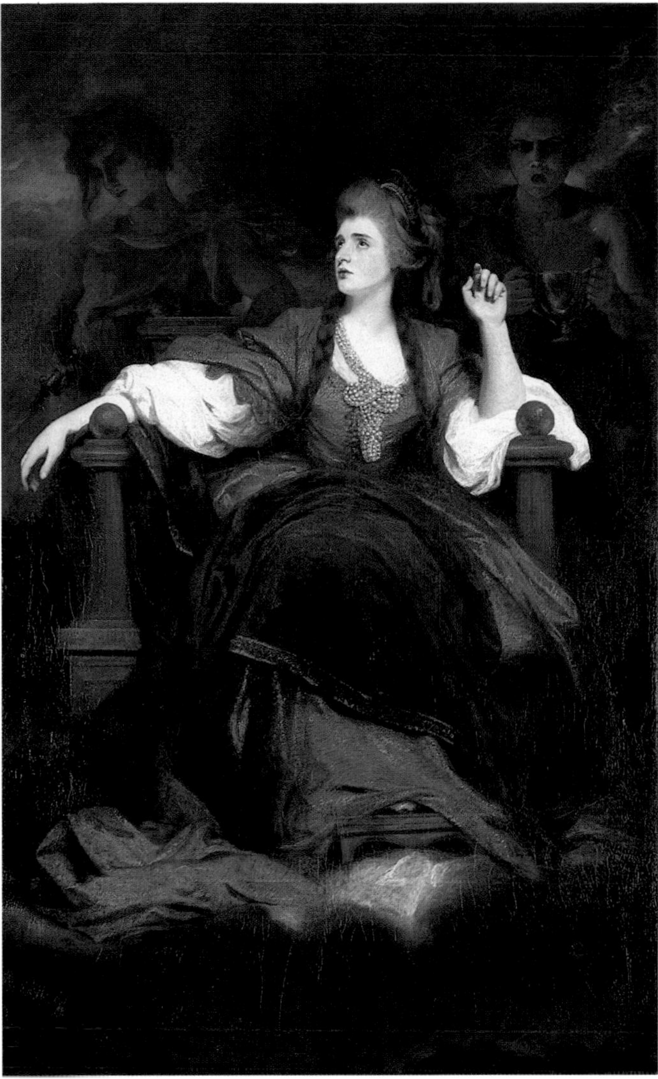

20-15. Sir Joshua Reynolds. *Mrs. Siddons as the Tragic Muse*. 1784. Oil on canvas, 7'9" x 4'9 1/2" (2.36 x 1.46 m). Henry E. Huntington Library and Art Gallery, San Marino, California

lates Van Dyck's aristocratic poses into late-eighteenth-century terms, and a fluid, translucent technique reminiscent of Rubens' that renders the glamorous sitter, with her fashionable attire and coiffure, to ravishing effect.

REYNOLDS. Gainsborough painted Mrs. Siddons in a conscious attempt to outdo his great rival on the London scene, Sir Joshua Reynolds (1723–1792), who had portrayed the same sitter as the Tragic Muse (fig. 20-15). Reynolds, a less adept painter, had to rely on pose and expression to suggest the aura of character that Gainsborough was able to convey through color and brushwork alone. Reynolds, who had been president of the Royal Academy since its founding in 1768, championed the academic approach to art, which he had acquired during two years in Rome. [See Primary Sources, no. 61, page 624.] In his *Discourses* he set forth what he felt were necessary rules and theories. His views were essentially those of Lebrun, tempered by British common sense, and like Lebrun, he found it difficult to live up to his theories in practice. Although he preferred history painting in the grand style, most of his works are portraits "enabled" by allegorical additions or disguises like those in his picture of Mrs. Siddons. His style owed a good deal more to the Venetians, to the Flemish Baroque, and even to Rembrandt (note the lighting in his *Mrs. Siddons*) than he was willing to admit, although he often recommended following the example of earlier masters.

Reynolds was generous enough to praise Gainsborough, whom he outlived by a few years, and whose instinctive talent he must have envied. He eulogized him as one who saw with the eye of a painter rather than a poet, even if the compliment was left-handed. Gainsborough's paintings epitomized the Enlightenment philosopher David Hume's idea that painting must incorporate both nature and art. Gainsborough himself was a simple and unpretentious person who exemplified Hume's "natural man," free of excessive pride or humility. Reynolds' approach, on the other hand, as stated in his *Discourses,* was based on Horace's saying, *ut pictura poesis*. His use of poses from the antique was intended to elevate the sitter from an individual to a universal type through association with the great art of the past and the noble ideals it embodied. This heroic model was closely related to the writings of the playwright Samuel Johnson and the practices of the actor David Garrick, both of whom were friends of Reynolds. (Garrick sat for portraits by Hogarth and Gainsborough, as well as Reynolds.) In this, Reynolds was the opposite of Gainsborough. Yet, for all of the differences between them, the two artists had more in common, artistically and philosophically, than they cared to admit.

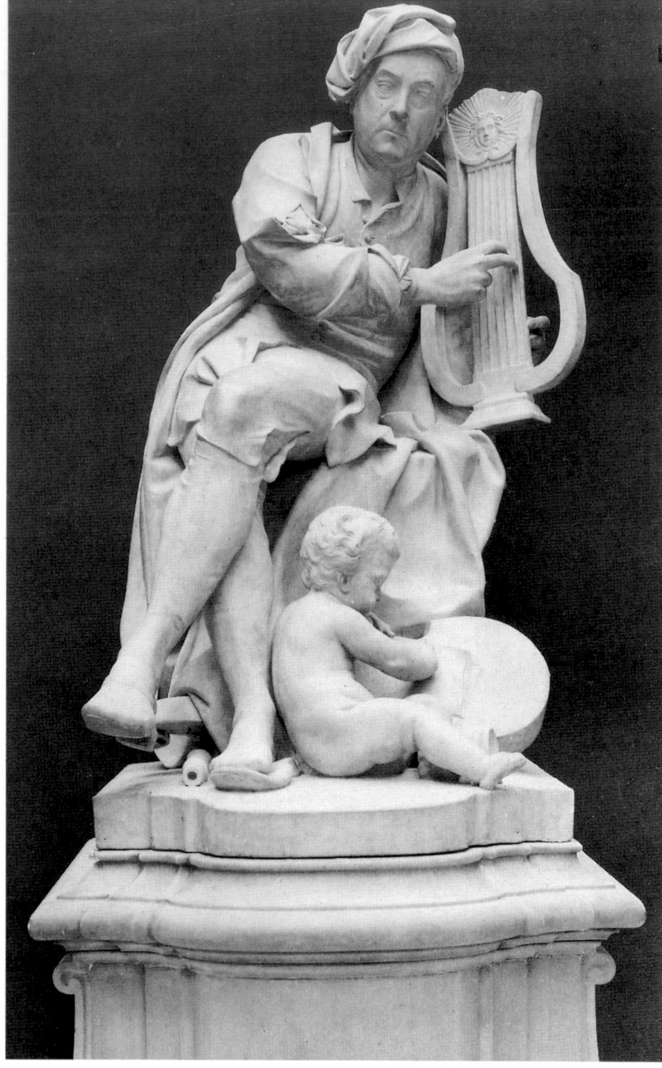

20-16. Louis-François Roubiliac. *George Frideric Handel*. 1738. Marble, lifesize. Victoria & Albert Museum, London

Reynolds and Gainsborough looked back to Van Dyck, drawing different lessons from his example. Both emphasized, in varying degrees, the visual appeal and technical skill of their paintings. Moreover, their portraits of Mrs. Siddons are clearly related to the Rococo style of France—note their resemblance to Vigée's *Duchesse* (see fig. 20-10)—yet they remain distinctly English in character. Hume and Johnson were similarly linked by their skepticism. If anything, Johnson's writings, which inspired Reynolds, were more pessimistic than Hume's, which generally advocated a tolerant and humane ethical system.

Sculpture

English sculpture has not been discussed in these pages since that of the thirteenth century (see fig. 11-50). During the Reformation a great deal of sculpture was destroyed. This vandalism had so chilling an effect that for 200 years there was too little demand for statuary to sustain more than the most modest local production. With the rise of a vigorous English school of painting, however, sculptural patronage grew as well. During the eighteenth century, when portraits of famous people were all the rage, England set an example for the rest of Europe in creating the "monument to genius." Statues were set up in public places to honor cultural heroes such as Shakespeare, a privilege that in the past had been reserved for heads of state.

ROUBILIAC. One of the earliest and most delightful of these statues is the monument to the great composer George Frideric Handel (fig. 20-16) by the French-born Louis-François Roubiliac (1702–1762). It was also the first to be made of a culture hero within his lifetime. (The next to achieve this distinction was Voltaire in France a generation later; see fig. 21-12). Roubiliac (portrayed in fig. 21-6) carved the figure in 1738 for the owner of Vauxhall Gardens in London, a pleasure park with dining facilities and an orchestra stand where Handel's music was often performed. The statue thus served two purposes: homage and advertising. Handel is in the guise of Apollo, the god of music, playing a classical lyre, while a putto at his feet writes down the divine music. But Handel is a domestic Apollo, in slippers and dressing gown, with a soft beret on his head instead of a wig. These attributes mark him as a man of arts and letters. Although Roubiliac shows that he is well aware of the Baroque sculptural tradition, the informality of his *Handel* seems uniquely English. Touches such as the right foot resting upon rather than inside the slipper (an allusion to the composer's gouty big toe?) suggest that he sought advice from William Hogarth, with whom he was on excellent terms (see pages 598–99). *Handel* was Roubiliac's first big success in his adopted homeland, and it became the ancestor of countless monuments to cultural heroes everywhere (see fig. 22-32).

GERMANY AND AUSTRIA

Rococo was a refinement in miniature of the curvilinear, "elastic" Baroque of Borromini and Guarini. Thus, it could readily be united with architecture in central Europe, where the Italian style had taken firm root. It is not surprising that the Italian style received such a warm response there. In Austria and southern Germany, ravaged by the Thirty Years' War, the number of new buildings remained small until near the end of the seventeenth century. The Baroque was an imported style, practiced mainly by visiting Italians. Not until the 1690s did native designers come to the fore. There followed a period of intense activity that lasted more than 50 years and gave rise to some of the most imaginative creations in the history of architecture. These monuments were built to glorify princes and prelates who generally deserve to be remembered only as lavish patrons of the arts. Rococo architecture in central Europe is larger in scale and more exuberant than in France. Moreover, painting and sculpture are more closely linked with their settings. Palaces and churches are decorated with ceiling frescoes and sculpture unsuited to domestic interiors, however lavish, although they reflect the same taste that produced the Hôtel de Varengeville.

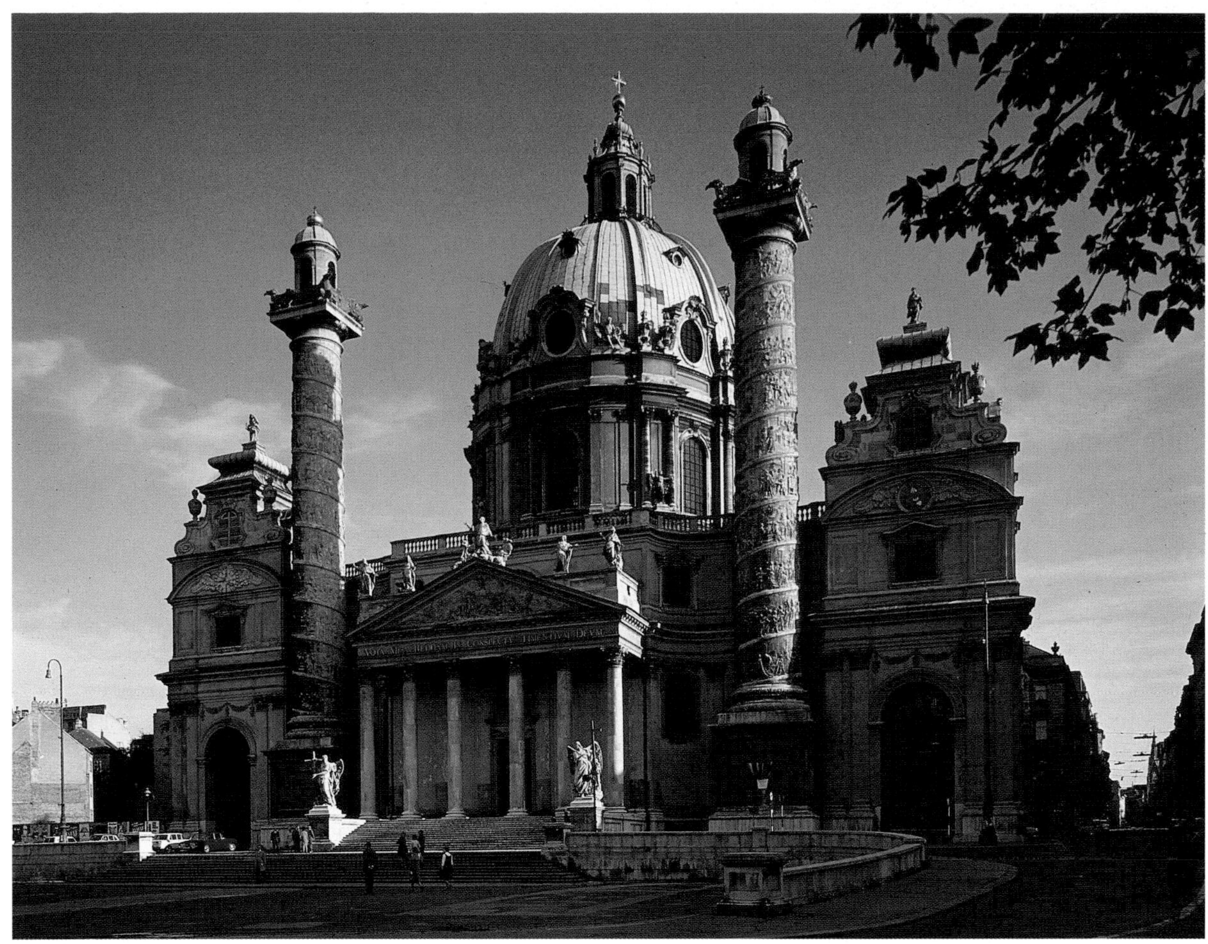

20-17. Johann Fischer von Erlach. Facade of St. Charles Borromaeus (Karlskirche), Vienna. 1716–37

FISCHER VON ERLACH. The Austrian Johann Fischer von Erlach (1656–1723), the first great architect of the Rococo in central Europe, is a transitional figure closely linked to the Italian tradition. He had studied in Rome with Carlo Fontana (1634–1714), whose buildings embody the same compromise between the High Baroque and Baroque classicism found in Italian painting toward the end of the seventeenth century. Fischer von Erlach, however, was a genius who represents the decisive shift of the center of architecture from Italy to north of the Alps. His church of St. Charles Borromaeus in Vienna (figs. 20-17 and 20-18) combines the facade of Borromini's S. Agnese and the Pantheon portico (see figs. 17-22 and 7-15). Here we find a pair of huge columns, derived from the Column of Trajan (see fig. 7-37) and decorated with scenes from the life of the saint, instead of facade towers, which have become corner pavilions reminiscent of those on the Louvre court (compare fig. 16-27). The church celebrates his patron, the emperor Charles VI, as a Christian ruler. It reminds us that the Turks, who menaced Austria and Hungary, had been defeated at the siege of Vienna only in 1683, thanks mainly to the intervention of John III of Poland, and that they remained a serious threat as late as 1718.

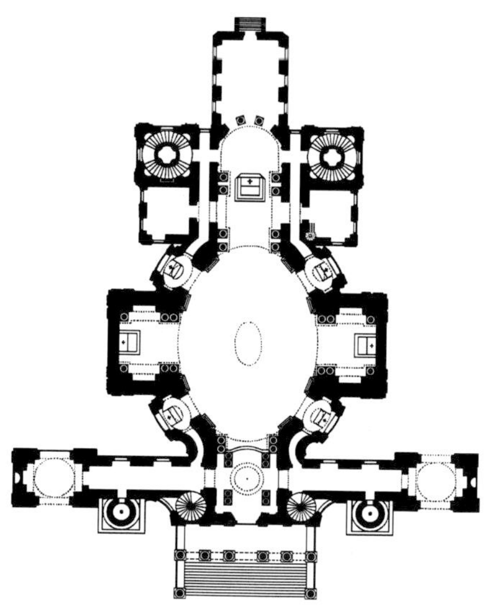

20-18. Plan of St. Charles Borromaeus

The extraordinary breadth of this ensemble is due to the site itself (see fig. 20-18). It obscures the equally long main body of the

ROCOCO MUSIC

Although music after 1700 was the direct outgrowth of the previous century, it not only had a different sound but it was dominated by a handful of great composers. They were nevertheless surrounded by many others of equal ability who began to form recognizable schools. These phenomena were interrelated. They were made possible by the international circulation of printed scores and musical treatises and the codification of the modern major–minor harmonic system (see "Modern Harmony," page 606). Of course, we have encountered great composers before; yet when we listen to their music, it does not sound "modern" to our ears, no matter how beautiful or intricate it may be on its own terms.

The earliest of these eighteenth-century giants was Antonio Vivaldi (1678–1741). The son of a violinist at St. Mark's in Venice, he trained for the priesthood but was allowed to leave after one year for health reasons. From then on, he was employed chiefly as head of the Conservatory of the Pietà orphanage for girls. His vast body of work in virtually every instrumental and vocal form shows enormous versatility, one of the chief characteristics of the Rococo. Like the other great composers of the time, he was under constant pressure, due to his responsibilities and popularity, to write new music. He was, for example, the most successful composer of operas in Venice. He claimed to have written 90 in all; of the 20 that survive relatively intact, some show signs of haste. (One of them was composed in only five days!) Nevertheless, *Orlando Furioso* (1727), inspired by Ariosto's epic poem, is unquestionably a masterpiece that is much superior to Handel's better-known opera of the same title (1733) and his *Alcina* (1735), based on the same story. Today Vivaldi is known almost exclusively for his concertos, which number nearly 500, the large majority of them for the violin, of which *The Four Seasons,* set to verses probably written by Vivaldi himself, is justly the most famous.

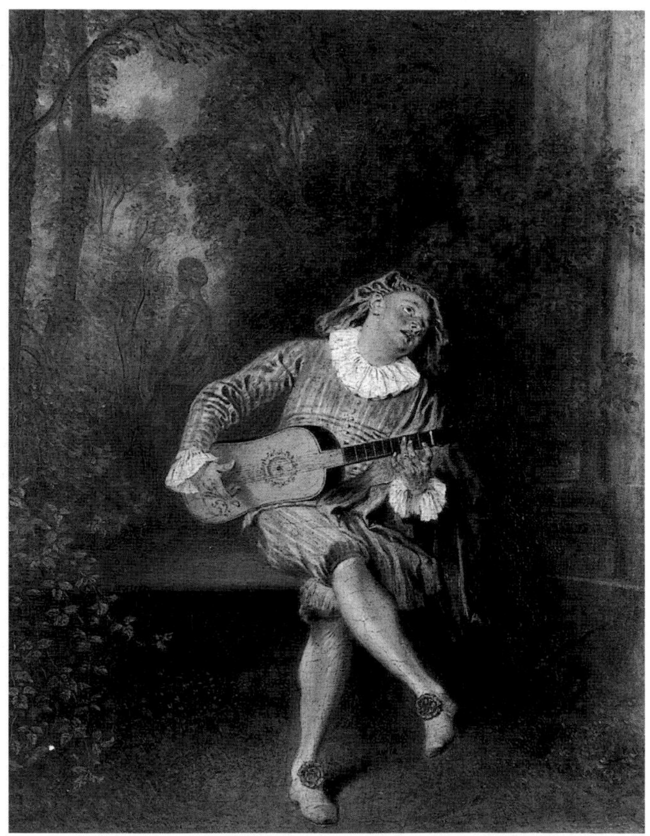

Jean Antoine Watteau. *Mezzetin*. 1718. Oil on canvas, 21¾ x 17" (55.3 x 43.2 cm). The Metropolitan Museum of Art, New York
MUNSEY FUND, 1942

Johann Sebastian Bach (1685–1750), trained as an organist and violinist, spent part of his early career as a court composer, then settled down as music director at the church of St. Thomas in Leipzig, a position that made huge demands on him for new music. As an organist, he was indebted to a virtuoso tradition that began in Italy with Girolamo Frescobaldi (1583–1643) and continued in Germany with Dietrich Buxtehude (1637–1707), whom he went out of his way to hear in Lübeck. Bach was influenced early on by Italian music, which helped to shape his sense of melody and harmony. His keyboard compositions show the impact of François Couperin as well (see box pages 580–81). Bach's music balances melody and polyphony, harmony and counterpoint, expressive power and supreme rationality. The instrumental works are built largely on fugues and variations, for he believed completely in his system of counterpoint, even when it forced unsatisfactory results. He is remembered chiefly for choral music, including the justly celebrated *Mass in B Minor,* several oratorios, which are nearly miniature operas, and voluminous cantatas, most of them early works. They owe their character to the revolution brought about in 1700 by Erdmann Neumeister (1671–1756) of Hamburg, a theologian and poet who introduced a new kind of sacred poetry, which he called a "cantata." It effectively reconciled the difference between the Lutheran chorale and Calvinist psalm by alternating biblical passages with original texts that expand on the scripture's meaning by offering personal responses and meditations.

Bach was hardly the most famous or prolific German composer of his time. That honor belonged to his friend Georg Philipp Telemann (1681–1767), who worked for a while in Leipzig but spent most of his life in Hamburg. New issues of his compositions were eagerly sought after, for they show the fertile imagination of Vivaldi, the technical mastery of Bach, and the cosmopolitan flair of Rameau. This is especially true of his overtures (which are really dance suites), trio sonatas, quartets, and concertos. These are combined in his justly celebrated *Tafelmusik* (1733) which, rather than being entertainment music for banquets (as the meaning of the German word *Tafel* suggests), are three chamber suites (or "productions") following a set format that shows off Telemann's mastery of every form.

George Frideric Handel (1685–1759), an admirer of Telemann, was likewise famous throughout almost his entire career. Born at Halle in Saxony, he first worked in Hamburg, then visited Italy between 1706 and 1710, when he met Arcangelo Corelli, Alessandro Scarlatti (1659–1725), and his son Domenico Scarlatti (1685–1757), a brilliant composer of harpsichord sonatas. The stay in Italy was decisive to Handel's formation, for it was there that he learned to compose operas and adopted the lyrical manner that distinguishes his work. Upon his return to Germany, he was appointed music director at Hanover but soon went to London on a leave of absence and never really returned. As fate would have it, the elector of Hanover then became King George I of England, and he continued to support Handel in London. Handel was both a composer and an impresario who made and lost fortunes in Italian opera. His masterpiece in this vein is *Julius Caesar,* put on in 1724. Four years later, however, John Gay's *The Beggar's Opera* (1728), a social and political satire written in English at the suggestion of the author Jonathan Swift (1667–1745), took England by storm. *The Beggar's Opera* used familiar songs culled from a variety of sources (including Purcell) and arranged by the German-born Johann Christoph Pepusch (1667–1752), who had settled in London in 1700 and no doubt enjoyed creating this spoof of his rival's music. (Ironically, the libretto for Handel's first opera was written by Gay with the poet Alexander Pope, a member of Lord Burlington's circle.) Handel, who by this time had become an English citizen, now turned increasingly to oratorios in his adopted tongue, though he continued to compose operas for another decade. The oratorios have a drama that makes them virtually concert operas, not church music, although many are based on biblical subjects. Their extroverted character expresses the confidence of the English as the new chosen people. His instrumental music, such as the *Concerti Grossi Opus 6,* is extremely appealing in its poetry and stateliness.

After failing to achieve success in Paris early in his career, Jean-Philippe Rameau (1683–1764) made his mark as a theorist in 1722 with the *Treatise on Harmony,* then returned the following year to Paris, where he gained the backing of a major patron and began to write operas, which established his reputation and earned him the support of the court. His style has the clarity and grace of Watteau and the intelligence of Voltaire. Despite the fact that Rameau's operas, such as *The Gallant Indes* (1735; a "heroic ballet" in several episodes) and *Castor and Pollux* (1737), are the direct descendants of Jean-Baptiste Lully's, they were attacked by the latter's supporters for their variety and drama. Ironically, the Lullyists later championed him against Italian opera, whose cause was being promoted by the Enlightenment philosopher Jean-Jacques Rousseau on the grounds that French was not fit for singing! Nevertheless, the revival of *Castor and Pollux* in 1754, after it had been heavily reworked by the composer, was an outstanding success that marked the defeat of Italian opera. The declamatory style satisfied the Lullyists, while the brilliant inventiveness, especially of the instrumental writing, pleased Rameau's partisans, who proclaimed the opera his masterpiece.

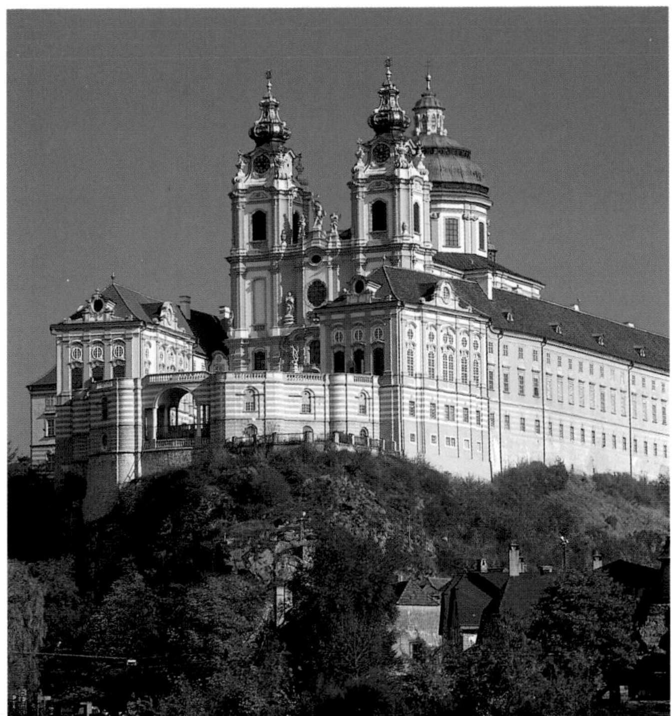

20-19. Jakob Prandtauer. Monastery Church, Melk, Austria. Begun 1702

church, which is a large oval with side chapels and a deep choir. With the inflexible elements of Roman Imperial art embedded into the elastic curvatures of his church, Fischer von Erlach expresses, more boldly than any Italian architect of the time, the power of the Christian faith to transform the art of antiquity. Indeed, it was now Italy's turn to respond to the North. The Superga, a monastery church overlooking Turin that was begun only a year later by Filippo Juvarra (1678–1736), another pupil of Fontana, was clearly influenced by Fischer von Erlach's design and by the Monastery of Melk.

PRANDTAUER. The Monastery Church of Melk (fig. 20-19) was designed by Jakob Prandtauer (1660–1726). A stonemason rather than an architect by training, he supervised every phase of the construction. It owes much of its monumental effect to its site on the crest of a cliff above the Danube, from which it rises like a vision of heavenly glory. The polychromed buildings form a tightly knit unit that centers on the church. The wings, housing the library and imperial hall, are joined at the west by curving arms, which meet at a high balcony that provides a dramatic view onto the world beyond the monastery. The interior was left to other architects but the magnificent library, rivaling the finest of the age, is his.

MODERN HARMONY

The development of eighteenth-century music was made possible by the codification of the modern system of harmony, which, after a gradual development over approximately 300 years, was spelled out in its final form in the *Treatise on Harmony* (1722) by the French composer Jean-Philippe Rameau. This system was based on the "tempered" diatonic scale, a progression of notes derived by equally spacing ("tempering") 12 tones within an octave (in essence, the black-and-white keys of a piano). The tonal distance, or interval, between any two of these one-twelfth-octave tones is called a semitone or "half step." Twice that interval is called a whole tone or "whole step." The diatonic system includes two principal scales, the major scale—the familiar "do-re-mi" that music students practice—and a modification of it called the minor scale. Both major and minor scales include a specific progression of five whole tones and two semitones, which start from the tonic, the note on which the scale is based, to the same note an octave above it. Like Greek modes, the major and minor scales communicate emotional qualities. Generally, a listener experiences the major scale as positive and optimistic and the minor scale as somber or plaintive.

The tempered scale allowed a keyboard to include a number of octaves, which in turn increased the range of music that could be written for keyboard instruments. The 48 pieces that Johann Sebastian Bach wrote in his *Well-Tempered Clavier* (1722, 1744) were one of the first series of compositions that exploited the possibilities of the newly expanded keyboard.

Another feature of the system as defined by Rameau were chords, sets of notes based on specific tones of the scale, sounded together in accompaniment to the melody. The major chord, for example, is derived from the major scale. It is made up of the tonic, the third note of the scale, and the fifth note of the scale. The chords for each scale were intended to create a full multivoice sound that is pleasing to the ear. Rameau's rules defined which chords were to be used in which musical circumstances; however, it was also understood that a composer might "break" the rules to create a deliberately discordant effect, or dissonance, for expressive purposes. Such dissonances were almost always "resolved" back to the notes of the scale in which the work was being played.

We need not be schooled in music theory to appreciate the virtues of the new system, which are readily apparent to the ear: its orderliness and flexibility, which not only permitted the fullest development of counterpoint but created new melodic possibilities as well. Modern harmony was an essential precondition for the work of the great composers of the eighteenth and nineteenth centuries, and it remained the basis of Western music composition until the end of World War I, when avant-garde composers began to seek other modes of musical expression.

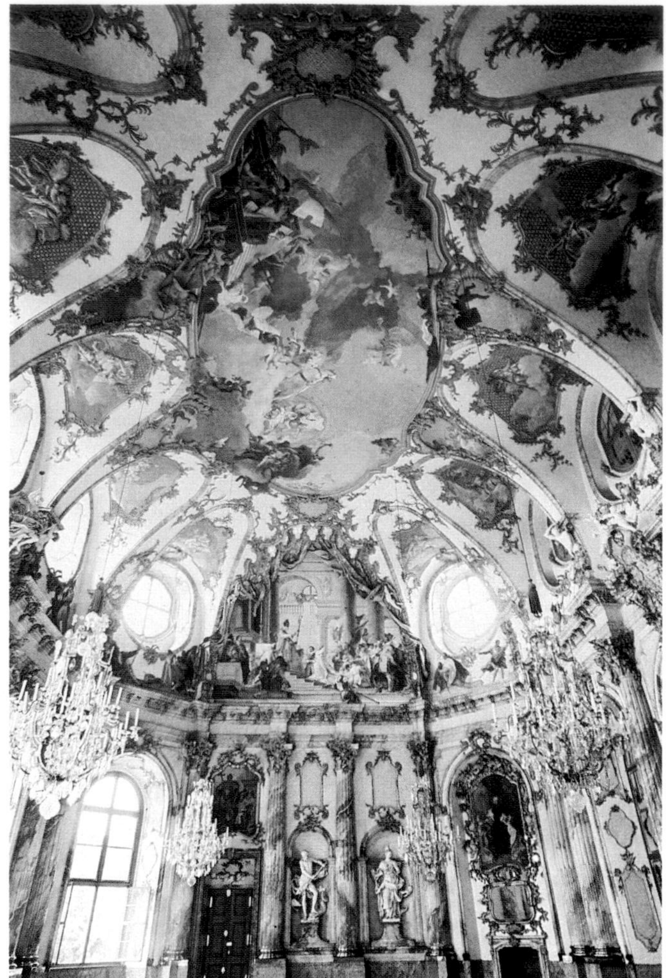

20-20. Balthasar Neumann. The Kaisersaal, Residenz, Würzburg, Germany. 1719–44. Frescoes by Giovanni Battista Tiepolo, 1751

NEUMANN. The next generation of architects favored lightness and elegance. Chief among them was Balthasar Neumann (1687–1753). Trained as a military engineer, he was named a surveyor for the Episcopal Palace in Würzburg after his return from a visit to Milan in 1720. The design is not wholly his. The basic plan was already established by one Johann Maximilian von Welsch (1671–1745), and although Neumann greatly modified it, he was required to consult the leading architects of Paris and Vienna in 1723. The final result is a skillful blend of the latest German, French, and Italian ideas. The breathtaking Kaisersaal (fig. 20-20) is a great oval hall decorated in the favorite color scheme of the mid-eighteenth century: white, gold, and pastel shades. The number and aesthetic role of structural members such as columns, pilasters, and architraves are now minimized. Windows and vault segments are framed by continuous, ribbonlike moldings, and the white surfaces are covered with irregular ornamental designs. These lacy, curling motifs, the hallmark of the French style (see fig. 20-1), are happily combined with German Rococo architecture. (The basic design recalls an early interior by Fischer von Erlach.)

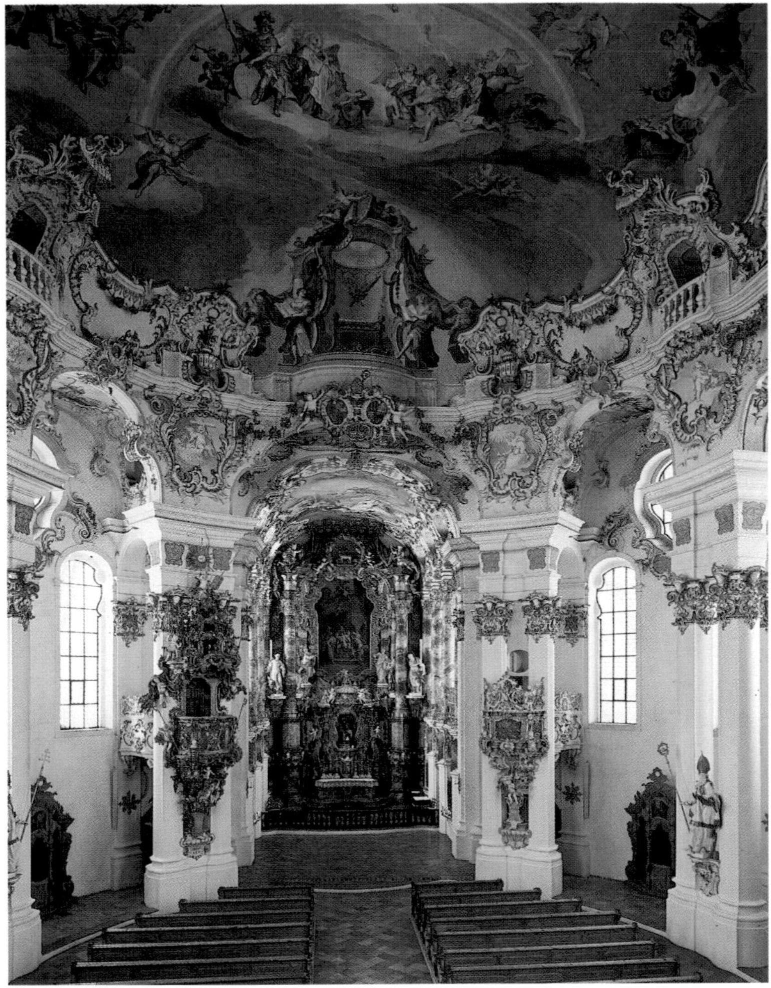

20-21. Dominikus Zimmermann. Interior of Die Wies, Upper Bavaria, Germany. 1745–54

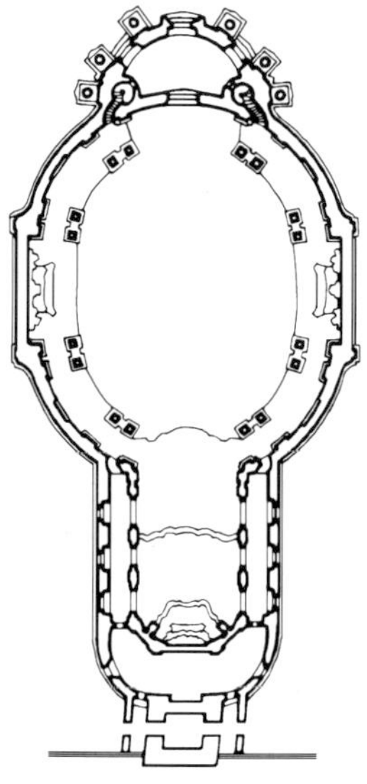

20-22. Plan of Die Wies

ZIMMERMANN. A contemporary of Balthasar Neumann, Dominikus Zimmermann (1685–1766) created what may be the finest spatial design of the mid-eighteenth century: the Bavarian pilgrimage church nicknamed "Die Wies" ("The Meadow"; figs. 20-21 and 20-22). The exterior is so plain that the interior seems overwhelming. It owes its richness to the fact that the architect and his brother, Johann Baptist Zimmermann (1680–1758), who was responsible for the frescoes, were trained as stucco workers. Like St. Charles Borromaeus, its main shape is oval, but since the ceiling rests on paired, freestanding supports, the spatial configuration is more fluid and complex. As a result, we are reminded of a German Gothic Hallenkirche. Even the Rococo decor tends to break up the surface in a way that recalls the webbed vaults found in mature Hallenkirchen (see fig. 11-30). Here Guarini's prophetic revaluation of Gothic architecture has become reality.

ITALY

Just as the style of architecture invented in Italy achieved its climax north of the Alps, much of the Italian Rococo took place in other countries. The timid style of the Late Baroque in Italy was transformed during the first decade of the eighteenth century by the rise of the Rococo in Venice, which had been an artistic backwater for a hundred years. The Italian Rococo is distinguished from the Baroque by a renewed appreciation of Veronese's colorism and pageantry but with an airy sensibility that is new. The first artist to formulate this style was Sebastiano Ricci (1659–1734), who began his career as a stage painter and became an important artist only in mid-career. His skill at blending a Venetian painterly manner with High Baroque illusionism made Ricci and later his Venetian followers the leading decorative painters in Europe between 1710 and 1760. They were active in every major center throughout Europe, especially London and Madrid. They were not alone: many artists from Rome and other parts of Italy also worked abroad.

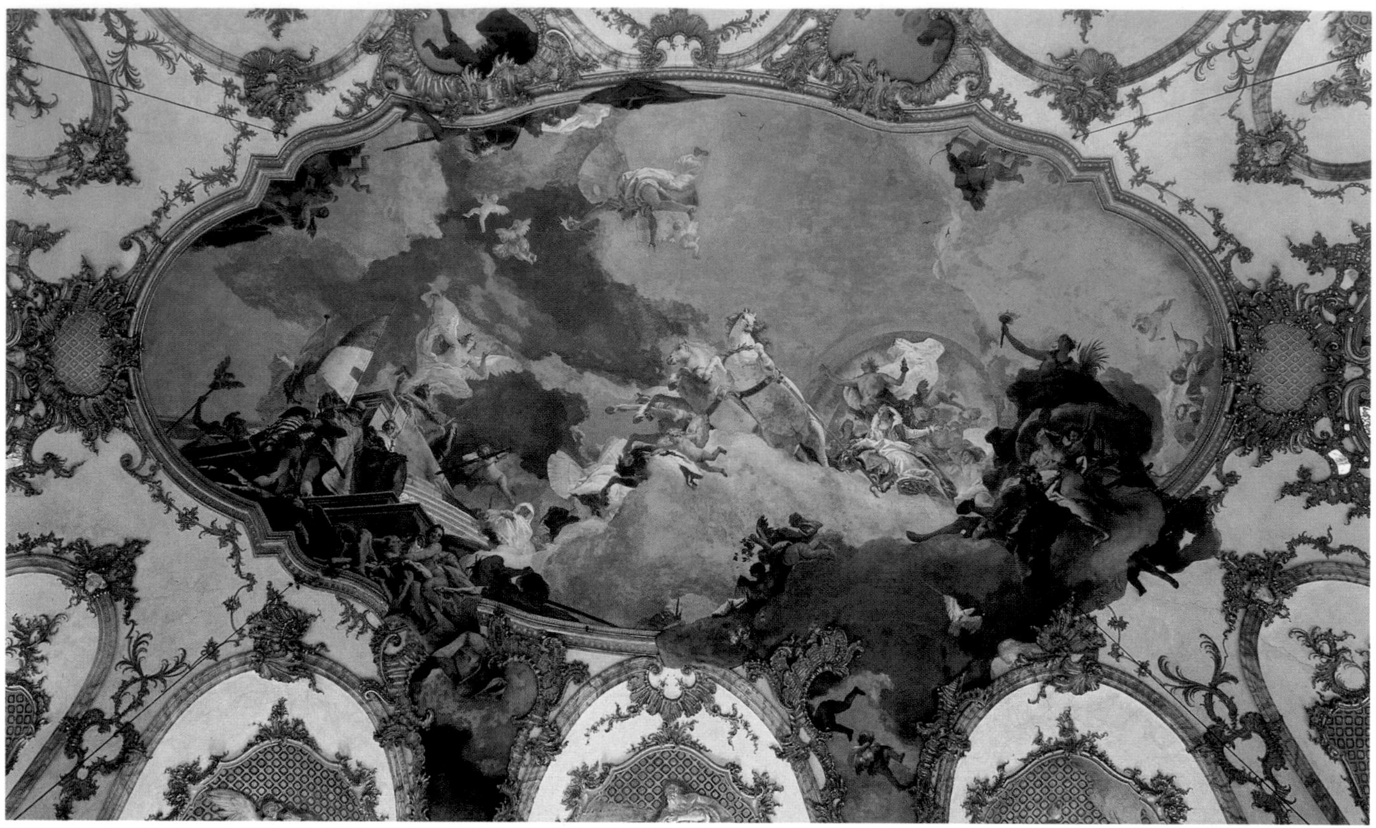

20-23. Giovanni Battista Tiepolo. Ceiling fresco (detail). 1751. The Kaisersaal, Residenz, Würzburg

TIEPOLO. The last and most refined stage of Italian illusionistic ceiling decoration can be seen in the works of Giovanni Battista Tiepolo (1696–1770). In his mastery of light and color, his grace and masterful touch, and his power of invention, Tiepolo easily surpassed his fellow Venetians. These qualities made him famous far beyond his home territory. When Tiepolo painted the Würzburg frescoes (figs. 20-23 and 20-24; and see fig. 20-20), his powers were at their height. The tissuelike ceiling so often gives way to illusionistic openings that we no longer feel it to be a spatial boundary. These openings do not, however, reveal avalanches of figures propelled by dramatic bursts of light, like those of Roman ceilings (compare fig. 17-12). Rather, we see blue sky and sunlit clouds, and an occasional winged creature soaring in this limitless expanse. Only along the edges of the ceiling are there solid clusters of figures (fig. 20-23).

At one end, replacing a window (see fig. 20-20), is *The Marriage of Frederick Barbarossa* (see fig. 20-24). As a public spectacle, it is as festive as *Christ in the House of Levi* (see fig. 14-16) by Veronese. The artist has followed Veronese's example by putting the event (which took place in the twelfth century) in a contemporary setting. Its allegorical fantasy is literally revealed by the carved putti opening a gilt-stucco curtain onto the wedding ceremony. The result is a display of theatrical illusionism worthy of Bernini. Unexpected in this lively procession is the element of classicism, which gives an air of noble restraint to the main figures in keeping with the solemnity of the occasion.

Tiepolo later became the last in the line of Italian artists, beginning with Luca Giordano (see pages 539–40), invited to work at the Royal Palace in Madrid. There he encountered the German painter Anton Raphael Mengs, a champion of the classical revival whose presence signaled the end of the Rococo (see page 640).

GIAQUINTO. The artist replaced by Mengs was Corrado Giaquinto (1703–1765), who left because of ill health. The only serious rival to Tiepolo, he can be viewed as the last great painter in both Naples, where he trained under Francesco Solimena, and Rome, where he passed most of his career, for the two schools were closely related (see page 540). At the Spanish court, where his power was similar to Lebrun's (see pages 579, 581), Giaquinto was hailed as the successor to Giordano, whose work had a decisive impact on his art. *Justice and Peace* (fig. 20-25) clearly resembles Giordano's *The Abduction of Europa* (see fig. 17-13), but with overtones of Boucher's style (see fig. 20-6). The painting unites the best of both worlds: the monumentality of Italy and the charm of France. What sets it apart is its ravishing beauty. The seemingly effortless brushwork and bold palette are unique to Giaquinto. No other painter of the Rococo could apply such a daring array of hues with such creamy consistency.

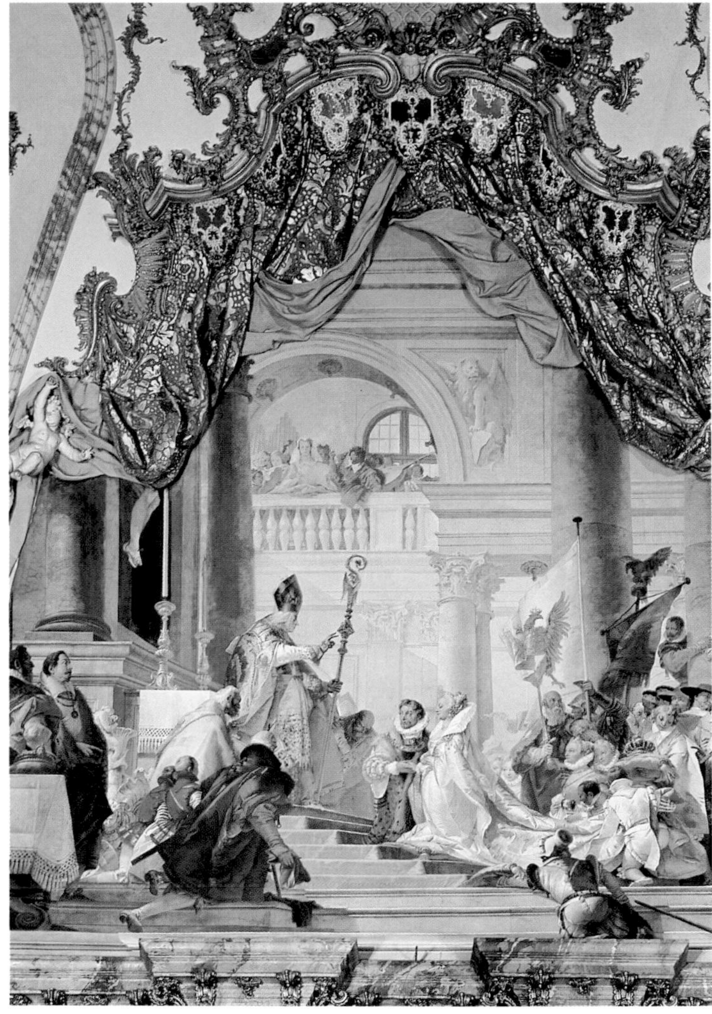

20-24. Giovanni Battista Tiepolo. *The Marriage of Frederick Barbarossa* (partial view). 1752. Fresco. Kaisersaal, Residenz, Würzburg

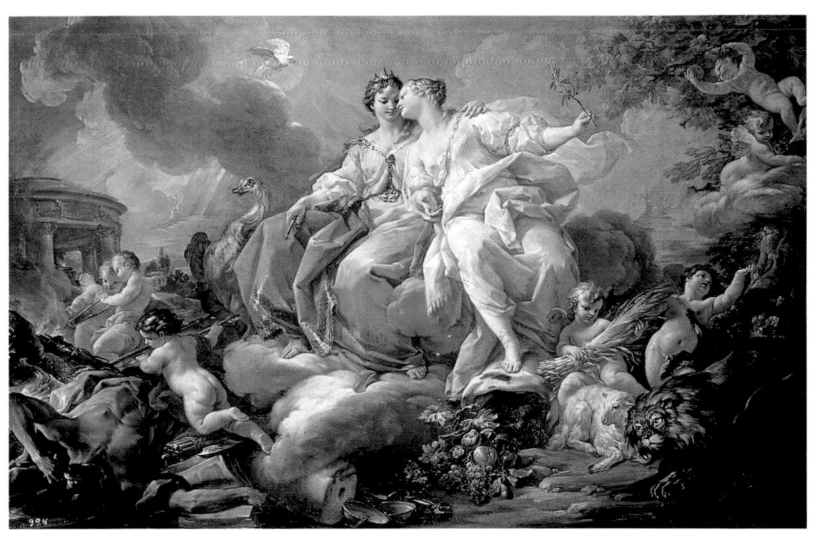

20-25. Corrado Giaquinto. *Justice and Peace*. c. 1753–54. Oil on canvas, 7'1" x 13'11 1/4" (2.16 x 4.25 m). Museo del Prado, Madrid

ROCOCO THEATER

Theater throughout the Rococo period was marked by sentimentality, usually with a moralizing theme. In England this trend began with *Love's Last Shift* by Colley Cibber (1671–1757), which was presented even before the attacks of Jeremy Collier (1650–1726) in 1698 on the morality of the theater. The net result was a more conservative kind of domestic drama for the middle class, exemplified by *The Conscious Lovers* (1722) by Sir Richard Steele (1672–1729), in which people recant the folly of their ways. As a consequence of the political satires by Henry Fielding (1707–1754), which offended the prime minister, Sir Robert Walpole, theater was further constrained by the Licensing Act of 1737, which imposed strict censorship. England, which had been influenced by Molière and Racine during the seventeenth century, now made an important contribution to French theater. The counterpart to Steele's plays in France were the "tearful comedies" of Philippe Destouches (1680–1754), who served as a diplomat in London in 1716, Pierre-Claude Nivelle de La Chaussée (1692–1754), and Pierre Marivaux (1688–1763). Tragedy enjoyed a final resurgence in the plays of the writer and philosopher Voltaire (François-Marie Arouet, 1694–1778), who sought to liberalize classical drama after living as a refugee from 1726 to 1729 in England, where he came to know all the leading intellectuals and developed an admiration for Shakespeare. His later plays are no less sentimental than those of his peers, but the growing emphasis on spectacle led him in 1759 to banish spectators from the stage for the first time. Comedy was left in the hands of the Comédie Italienne, created in 1716 when the commedia dell'arte was invited back to France by the Duc d'Orléans upon the death of his brother, Louis XIV. In Italy, by contrast, the energies of the playwrights were absorbed by the mania for opera. The principal exception was Carlo Goldoni (1707–1793), a Venetian dramatist whose vivid comedies deliberately imitated those of Molière.

The major contributions of Rococo theater thus lay not in writing but in stagecraft: scenic design and acting. With the increased demand for spectacle, many artists were trained or employed as scenographers, including François Boucher and Canaletto. The affinity was natural, since the backgrounds in many paintings came to look increasingly like set designs after 1700. Boucher's pupil, Philippe-Jacques de Loutherbourg (1740–1812), who also trained under the scene designer Louis-René Boquet (1717–1814), brought French practices with him to England, where many painters, including Hogarth's father-in-law, James Thornhill (1676–1734), George Lambert (c. 1699–1765), and Francis Hayman (1708–1776), regularly worked for the theater.

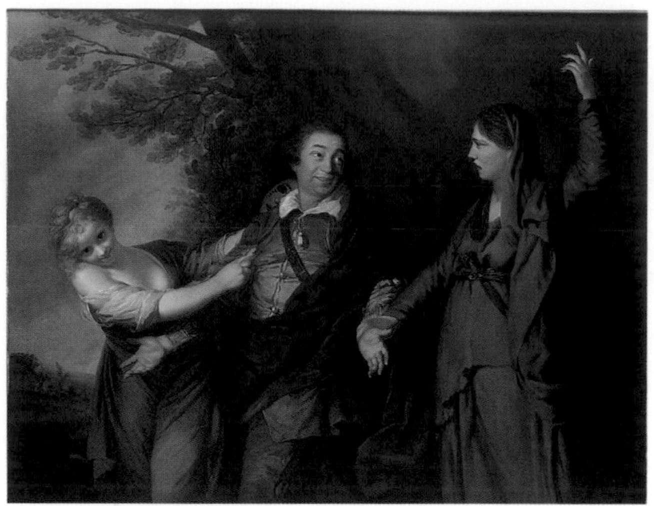

Sir Joshua Reynolds. *Garrick Between Tragedy and Comedy.* 1761. Oil on canvas, 48½ x 72" (125.2 x 182.9 cm). Collection the Royal National Theatre, London

De Loutherbourg, who became a friend of Thomas Gainsborough, had been invited to England by the actor David Garrick (1717–1779) to supervise scene painting at his Drury Lane Theater, and both men introduced a number of innovations in the theater, especially in improved lighting. Garrick, whose portrait was painted by all the leading artists of the day, including Hogarth, Reynolds, and Gainsborough, dominated the English stage after his debut in 1741 and played a major role in theatrical reform on the Continent following his visits to France in 1763 and Italy and Germany two years later. Like Voltaire, he removed spectators from the stage. Nevertheless, Garrick had several rivals, chief among them Charles Macklin (1697?–1797) and Samuel Foote (1720–1777), who established the Haymarket as a rival to Drury Lane and Covent Garden, the two legitimate theaters in London. These three men were among the first English actors to show an awareness of period dress, which was also taken up by the French theater. Voltaire's main actor, Henri-Louis Lekain (1729–1778), and his leading lady, Mademoiselle Clairon (1723–1803), became the first French actors to use authentic costumes as part of the trend toward greater realism in theater.

Women had been acting in the Comédie-Française since the 1690s, but they never achieved the status of English actresses. Thus, Adrienne Lecouvreur (1692–1730), who was the first to adopt formal court costumes for tragic heroines, was buried anonymously the same year that Anne Oldfield (1683–1730) was interred in Westminster Abbey. After 1780 the reigning actress was Sarah Siddons (1755–1831), the sister of the great impresario John Philip Kemble (1757–1823); like Garrick, she sat for both Gainsborough and Reynolds (see figs. 20-14 and 20-15). During the early decades of the eighteenth century, a number of women in England also became successful playwrights.

CANALETTO. During the eighteenth century, landscape in Italy evolved a new form in keeping with the character of the Rococo: *veduta* (view) painting. Its beginnings can be traced back to the seventeenth century with the many foreigners, such as Claude Lorraine (see fig. 19-7), who specialized in depicting Rome's environs. After 1720, however, it took on a specifically urban identity. The most famous of the vedutists was Canaletto (Giovanni Antonio Canal, 1697–1768) of Venice. His pictures were great favorites with the British, who bought them as souvenirs of the grand tours of Italy, then so popular. Indeed, he

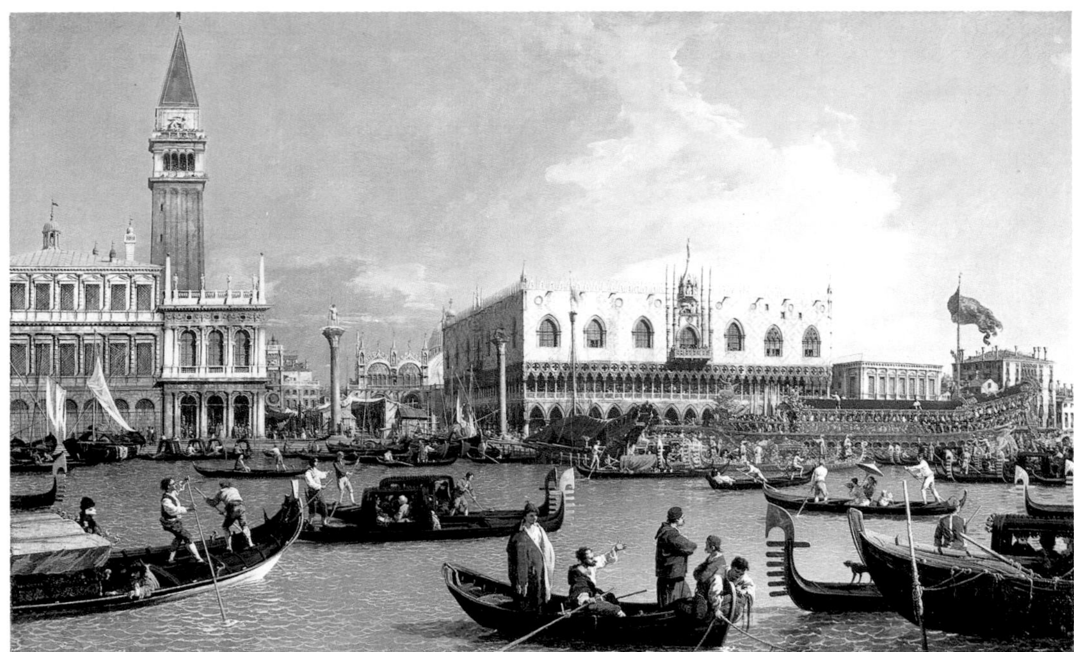

20-26. Canaletto. *The Bucintoro at the Molo*. c. 1732. Oil on canvas, 30¼ x 49½" (77 x 126 cm). The Royal Collection

© 1993 HER MAJESTY QUEEN ELIZABETH II

enjoyed such success with clients from England that he later became one of several Venetian artists to spend long sojourns in London. *The Bucintoro at the Molo* (fig. 20-26) was one of a series of paintings commissioned by Joseph Smith, an English entrepreneur living in Venice. These served both to decorate Smith's house and to introduce Canaletto's work to prospective buyers. Smith later issued them as a suite of etchings to meet the demand for mementos of Venice by those who could not afford an original canvas by the artist.

Canaletto's landscapes are, for the most part, topographically accurate. However, he was not above tampering with the truth. While he usually made only slight adjustments for the sake of the composition, he would sometimes treat scenes with considerable freedom or create composite views. He may have used a mechanical or optical device (perhaps a camera obscura, a forerunner of the photographic camera) to render some of his views, although he was a skilled draftsman who hardly needed such aids. In any event, they fail to account for the sparkle of his pictures and his sure sense of composition. These features sprang in part from his training as a scenographer, which also helps to explain the liveliness of his paintings. He often included vignettes of daily life in Venice that lend a human interest to his scenes and make them fascinating cultural documents as well. *The Bucintoro at the Molo* shows a favorite subject: the Doge returning on his magnificent barge to the Piazza San Marco from the Lido (the city's island beach) on Ascension Day after celebrating the Marriage of the Sea. Canaletto has captured the festive air surrounding this great public celebration, which is presented as a brilliant theatrical display.

PIRANESI. Canaletto shared his background as a designer of stage sets with Ricci (see above) and with Giovanni Panini (1691–1765), his fellow vedutist in Rome who had a passion for classical antiquity (see fig. 7-12). They, in turn, are the forerunners of another Roman artist, Giovanni Battista Piranesi (1720–1778), whose *Prison Caprices* (fig. 20-27) are rooted in contemporary designs for theater and opera. Unlike the prints after Canaletto's paintings, these masterful etchings were intended as original works of art from the beginning; thus, they have a gripping power. In Piranesi's imagery, the play between reality and fantasy, so fundamental to the theatrical Rococo, has been transformed into a romanticized vision of despair as terrifying as any nightmare. His bold imagination appealed greatly to many artists of the next generation, on whom he exercised a decisive influence.

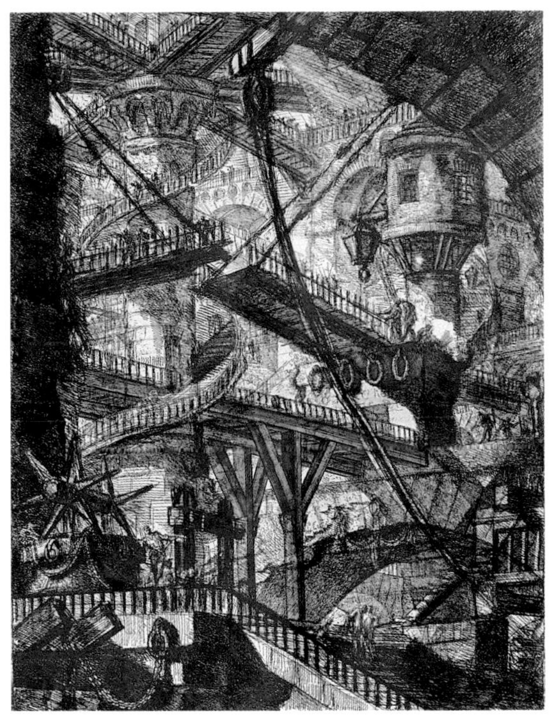

20-27. Giovanni Battista Piranesi. *Tower with Bridges*, from *Prison Caprices*. 1760–61. Etching, 21¾ x 16⅜" (55.2 x 41.6 cm). The Metropolitan Museum of Art, New York

ROGERS FUND

Primary Sources for Part Three

The following is a selection of excerpts, in modern translations, from original texts by artists, architects, religious figures, and historians from the Renaissance period through the Rococo period. These readings supplement the main text and are keyed to it. Their full citations are given in the Credits section at the end of the book.

40
LEONE BATTISTA ALBERTI (1404–1472)
From *On Painting*

Alberti's On Painting, *published in 1435, and his* On Sculpture, *which appeared in 1464, are among the most influential and revealing documents of the Early Renaissance. Alberti's was the first published account of linear perspective, though its relation to the system invented by Brunelleschi is problematic.*

I first draw a rectangle of right angles, where I am to paint, which I treat just like an open window through which I might look at what will be painted there, and then I decide how large I want the people in my picture, and I divide the length of a man of this size into three, which is proportionate to a two-foot measurement [a *braccio*], since a normal man measures almost six feet. And I mark these two-foot units on the bottom line of my rectangle, as many of them as it will take, and this line is for me proportional to the horizontal quantity I originally saw. Then inside the rectangle, where I like, I mark a point which will be where the middle ray hits, and I call it the midpoint. This should not be higher above the bottom line than a man I would paint there, so that the viewer and the things seen will appear to be on a level with each other. Then I draw straight lines from the midpoint to the divisions already marked in the bottom line. These lines will show how each transverse quantity might change from the one before almost to infinity. . . .

As for the transverse quantities . . . I take a little space and in it draw a straight line similar to the bottom line and divide it similarly, then above it I put a point, straight above one end of it, as high as the midpoint is above the bottom line, and thence I draw lines to each point in the first line. Then I fix the distance I want from the eye to the painting, and so draw a perpendicular line cutting every line it finds, and the places where I find all my parallels to be drawn, that is, the squares of the pavement in the painting. . . . When I have done this, I draw a horizontal straight line in the painting, parallel to the lower ones, passing through the midpoint, as a boundary that can be passed only by quantities higher than the observer's eye.

41
LEONE BATTISTA ALBERTI
From *On Architecture*

Modeled on Vitruvius' treatise on architecture (first century B.C.), On Architecture *was completed in 1452 but not published until 1485, after Alberti's death.*

The most expert Artists among the Ancients . . . were of [the] opinion that an Edifice was like an Animal, so that in the formation of it we ought to imitate Nature. . . . It is manifest that in those [animals] which are esteemed beautiful, the parts or members are not constantly all the same, . . . but we find that even in those parts

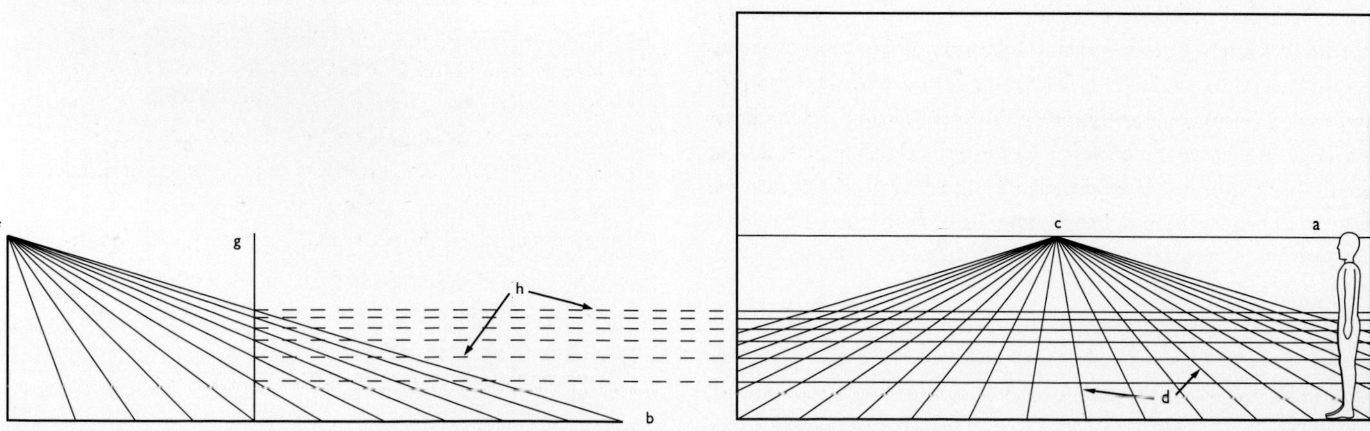

PS-40. Design of Leone Battista Alberti's Perspective Construction, according to recent discoveries:
a) height of human being; b) base line; c) vanishing point; d) orthagonals; e) "little space"; f) distance point; g) vertical intersection; h) transversals

wherein they vary most, there is something inherent and implanted which tho' they differ extremely from each other, makes each of them be beautiful. . . . But the judgment which you make that a thing is beautiful, does not proceed from mere opinion, but from a secret argument and discourse implanted in the mind itself. . . . There is a certain excellence and natural beauty in the figures and forms of buildings, which immediately strike the mind with pleasure and admiration. It is my opinion that beauty, majesty, gracefulness and the like charms, consist in those particulars which if you alter or take away, the whole wou'd be made homely and disagreeable. . . . There is . . . something . . . which arises from the conjunction and connection of these other parts, and gives the beauty and grace to the whole: which we will call Congruity, which we may consider as the original, of all that is graceful and handsome. . . . Wherever such a composition offers itself to the mind either by the conveyance of the sight, hearing, or any of the other senses, we immediately perceive this Congruity: for by Nature we desire things perfect, and adhere to them with pleasure when they are offered to us; nor does this Congruity arise so much from the body in which it is found, or any of its members, as from itself and from Nature, so that its true Seat is in the mind and in reason. . . . This is what Architecture chiefly aims at, and by this she obtains her beauty, dignity and value.

42

LEONARDO DA VINCI (1452–1519)

From his undated manuscripts

Leonardo, the consummate High Renaissance man, wrote on a variety of intellectual topics. The comparison of the arts, or Paragone, *was a common subject in High Renaissance scholarship.*

He Who Depreciates Painting Loves Neither Philosophy nor Nature

If you despise painting, which is the sole imitator of all visible works of nature, you certainly will be despising a subtle invention which brings philosophy and subtle speculation to bear on the nature of all forms—sea and land, plants and animals, grasses and flowers—which are enveloped in shade and light. Truly painting is a science, the true-born child of nature. For painting is born of nature; to be more correct we should call it the grandchild of nature, since all visible things were brought forth by nature and these, her children, have given birth to painting. Therefore we may justly speak of it as the grandchild of nature and as related to God.

A Comparison Between Poetry and Painting

The imagination cannot visualize such beauty as is seen by the eye, because the eye receives the actual semblances or images of objects and transmits them through the sense organ to the understanding where they are judged. But the imagination never gets outside the understanding; . . . it reaches the memory and stops and dies there if the imagined object is not of great beauty; thus poetry is born in the mind or rather in the imagination of the poet who, because he describes the same things as the painter, claims to be the painter's equal! . . . The object of the imagination does not come from without but is born in the darkness of the mind's eye. What a difference between forming a mental image of such light in the darkness of the mind's eye and actually perceiving it outside the darkness!

If you, poet, had to represent a murderous battle you would have to describe the air obscured and darkened by fumes from frightful and deadly engines mixed with thick clouds of dust polluting the atmosphere, and the panicky flight of wretches fearful of horrible death. In that case the painter will be your superior, because your pen will be worn out before you can fully describe what the painter can demonstrate forthwith by the aid of his science, and your tongue will be parched with thirst and your body overcome by sleep and hunger before you can describe with words what a painter is able to show you in an instant.

On Painting and Poetry

Poetry is superior to painting in the presentation of words, and painting is superior to poetry in the presentation of facts. . . . For this reason I judge painting to be superior to poetry. But as painters did not know how to plead for their own art she was left without advocates for a long time. For painting does not talk; but reveals herself as she is, ending in reality; and Poetry ends in words in which she eloquently sings her own praises.

43

GIORGIO VASARI (1511–1574)

From *The Lives of the Most Excellent Italian Architects, Painters, and Sculptors from Cimabue to Our Times*

Vasari was inspired to write The Lives *by his patron, Cardinal Farnese, later Pope Paul III. The book, first published in 1550 and expanded in 1568, was based on interviews conducted throughout Italy. Vasari personally knew many of the artists about whom he wrote, including Michelangelo, whom he idolized at the expense of others, most notably Raphael, who becomes his rival's student—a claim effectively refuted by Pietro Bellori at the end of the seventeenth century. Although art historians have spent entire careers disproving details of Vasari's narrative, they remain the starting point for the study of Italian Renaissance art. Because of the length of the biographies, only brief excerpts are possible here.*

This marvellous and divinely inspired Leonardo . . . would have been proficient at his early lessons if he had not been so volatile and unstable; for he was always setting himself to learn many things only to abandon them almost immediately. . . . Clearly, it was because of his profound knowledge of painting that Leonardo started so many things without finishing them; for he was convinced that his hands, for all their skill, could never perfectly express the subtle and wonderful ideas of his imagination. . . .

For Francesco del Giocondo Leonardo undertook to execute the portrait of his wife, Mona Lisa. He worked on this painting for four years, and then left it still unfinished. . . . If one wanted to see how faithfully art can imitate nature, one could readily perceive it from this head; for here Leonardo subtly reproduced every living detail. . . . Leonardo also made use of this device: while he was painting Mona Lisa, who was a very beautiful woman, he employed singers and musicians or jesters to keep her full of merriment and so chase away the melancholy that painters usually give to portraits. As a result, in this painting of Leonardo's there was a smile so pleasing that it seemed divine rather than human; and those who saw it were amazed to find that it was as alive as the original.

. . . Raphael Sanzio of Urbino, an artist as talented as he was gracious, . . . was endowed by nature with the goodness and modesty to be found in all those exceptional men whose gentle humanity is enhanced by an affable and pleasing manner, expressing itself in courteous behaviour at all times and towards all persons. . . . Raphael [had] the finest qualities of mind accompanied by such grace, industry, looks, modesty, and excellence of character as would offset every defect, no matter how serious, and any vice, no matter how ugly. . . .

At the time when Raphael determined to change and improve his style he had never studied the nude as intensely as it requires, for he had only copied it from life, employing the methods he had seen used by Perugino, although he gave his figures a grace that he understood instinctively. . . . Nonetheless, Raphael realized that in this manner he could never rival the accomplishments of Michelangelo, and...being unable to compete with Michelangelo in the branch of painting to which he had set his hand, resolved to emulate and perhaps surpass him in other respects. So he decided not to waste his time by imitating Michelangelo's style but to attain a catholic excellence in the other fields of painting. . . .

When Michelangelo had finished the statue [of Pope Julius II, later destroyed], Bramante, the friend and relation of Raphael and therefore ill-disposed to Michelangelo, seeing the Pope's preference for sculpture, schemed to divert his attention, and told the Pope that it would be a bad omen to get Michelangelo to go on with his tomb, as it would seem to be an invitation to death. He persuaded the Pope to get Michelangelo, on his return, to paint the vaulting of the Sistine Chapel. In this way Bramante and his other rivals hoped to confound him, for by taking him from sculpture, in which he was perfect, and putting him to colouring in fresco, in which he had had no experience, they thought he would produce less admirable work than Raphael. . . . Thus, when Michelangelo returned to Rome, the Pope was disposed not to have the tomb finished for the time being, and asked him to paint the vaulting of the chapel. Michelangelo tried every means to avoid it, and recommended Raphael. . . . At length, seeing that the Pope was resolute, [he] decided to do it. . . . Michelangelo then made arrangements to do the whole work singlehanded. . . . When he had finished half, the Pope . . . daily became more convinced of Michelangelo's genius, and wished him to complete the work, judging that he would do the other half even better. Thus, singlehanded, he completed the work in twenty months, aided only by his mixer of colours. He sometimes complained that owing to the impatience of the Pope he had not been able to finish it as he would have desired, as the Pope was always asking him when he would be done. On one occasion Michelangelo replied that he would be finished when he had satisfied his own artistic sense. "And we require you to satisfy us in getting it done quickly," replied the Pope, adding that if it was not done soon he would have the scaffolding down. . . . Michelangelo wanted to retouch some parts of the painting *a secco,* as the old masters had done on the scenes below...in order to heighten the visual impact. The Pope, learning that this ornamentation was lacking...wanted him to go ahead. However, he lacked the patience to rebuild the scaffolding, and so the ceiling stayed as it was. . . .

Gian. Bellini and other painters of [Venice], through not having studied antiquities, employed a hard, dry and laboured style, which Titian acquired. But in 1507 arose Giorgione, who began to give his works more tone and relief, with better style, though he imitated natural things as best he could, colouring them like life, without making drawings previously, believing this to be the true method of procedure. He did not perceive that for good composition it is necessary to try several various methods on sheets, for invention is quickened by showing these things to the eye, while it is also necessary to a thorough knowledge of the nude. . . .

On seeing Giorgione's style Titian abandoned that of Bellini, although he had long practised it, and imitated Giorgione so well that in a short time his works were taken for Giorgione's. . . . Titian's methods in these paintings differ widely from those he adopted in his youth. His first works are executed with a certain fineness and diligence, so that they may be examined closely, but these are done roughly in an impressionist manner, with bold strokes and blobs, to obtain the effect at a distance. This is why many in trying to imitate him have made clumsy pictures, for if people think that such work can be done without labour they are deceived, as it is necessary to retouch and recolour them incessantly, so that the labour is evident. The method is admirable and beautiful if done judiciously, making paintings appear alive and achieved without labour.

. . . In 1546, at the summons of Cardinal Farnese, [Titian] went to Rome where he found Giorgio Vasari who . . . was working for the cardinal on the hall of the Palazzo della Cancellaria. The cardinal recommended Titian to Vasari, who then lovingly kept him company and took him to see the sights of Rome. After Titian had rested for some days he was given rooms in the Belvedere [Palace] so that he could set his hand to painting once more the portrait of Pope Paul. . . . Then one day Michelangelo and Vasari went along to visit Titian in the Belvedere, where they saw a painting he had finished of a woman, representing Danäe, who had in her lap Jove transformed into a rain of gold; and naturally, as one would do with the artist present, they praised it warmly. After they had gone, they started to discuss Titian's method and Buonarrotti commended it highly, saying that his colouring and his style pleased him very much, but that it was a shame that in Venice they did not learn to draw well from the beginning and that those painters did not pursue their studies with more method. For the truth was, he went on, that if Titian had been assisted by art and design as much as he was by nature, and especially in reproducing living subjects, then no one could achieve more or work better, for he had a fine spirit and a lively and entrancing style.

44
From the Canons and Decrees of the Council of Trent

The Catholic church responded to the growth in northern Europe of independent "Reformed" churches (inaugurated by Martin Luther's 1517 critique of the Church) by attempting to stop the Reformation and win back the territories and peoples lost to the Roman Church. These various measures of the sixteenth and early seventeenth centuries are collectively called the Counter-Reformation. One agency of this development was the Council of Trent, a series of three meetings of church leaders in 1545–47, 1551–52, and 1562–63. The following is from one of the council's last edicts, dated December 3–4, 1563, a response to ongoing Protestant attacks against religious images.

The holy council commands all bishops and others who hold the office of teaching and have charge of the *cura animarum,* that in accordance with the usage of the Catholic and Apostolic Church, received from the primitive times of the Christian religion, and with the unanimous teaching of the holy Fathers and the decrees of sacred councils, they above all instruct the faithful diligently in matters relating to intercession and invocation of the saints, the veneration of relics, and the legitimate use of images.... Moreover, that the images of Christ, of the Virgin Mother of God, and of the other saints are to be placed and retained especially in the churches, and that due honor and veneration is to be given them; not, however, that any divinity or virtue is believed to be in them by reason of which they are to be venerated, or that something is to be asked of them, or that trust is to be placed in images, as was done of old by the Gentiles who placed their hope in idols; but because the honor which is shown them is referred to the prototypes which they represent, so that by means of the images which we kiss and before which we uncover the head and prostrate ourselves, we adore Christ and venerate the saints whose likeness they bear. That is what was defined by the decrees of the councils, especially of the Second Council of Nicaea, against the opponents of images.

Moreover, let the bishops diligently teach that by means of the stories of the mysteries of our redemption portrayed in paintings and other representations the people are instructed and confirmed in the articles of faith, which ought to be borne in mind and constantly reflected upon; also that great profit is derived from all holy images, not only because the people are thereby reminded of the benefits and gifts be stowed on them by Christ, but also because through the saints the miracles of God and salutary examples are set before the eyes of the faithful, so that they may give God thanks for those things, may fashion their own life and conduct in imitation of the saints and be moved to adore and love God and cultivate piety. But if anyone should teach or maintain anything contrary to these decrees, let him be anathema.

If any abuses shall have found their way into these holy and salutary observances, the holy council desires earnestly that they be completely removed, so that no representation of false doctrines and such as might be the occasion of grave error to the uneducated be exhibited.... Finally, such zeal and care should be exhibited by the bishops with regard to these things that nothing may appear that is disorderly or unbecoming and confusedly arranged, nothing that is profane, nothing disrespectful, since holiness becometh the house of God.

45
From a session of the Inquisition Tribunal in Venice of Paolo Veronese

Because of the liberal religious atmosphere of Venice, Veronese was never required to make the various changes to his painting of the Last Supper *(see fig. 14-16) asked for by the tribunal of the Inquisition in this interrogation. All parties seem to have been satisfied with a mere change of title to* Supper in the House of Levi *(now* Christ in the House of Levi).

Today, Saturday, the 18th of the month of July, 1573, having been asked by the Holy Office to appear before the Holy Tribunal, Paolo Caliari of Verona, ... Questioned about his profession:
Answer: I paint and compose figures.

Q: Do you know the reason why you have been summoned?

A: No, sir.

Q: Can you imagine it?

A: I can well imagine.

Q: Say what you think the reason is.

A: According to what the Reverend Father, the Prior of the Convent of SS. Giovanni e Paolo, ... told me, he had been here and Your Lordships had ordered him to have painted [in the picture] a Magdalen in place of a dog. I answered him by saying I would gladly do everything necessary for my honor and for that of my painting, but that I did not understand how a figure of Magdalen would be suitable there....

Q: What picture is this of which you have spoken?

A: This is a picture of the Last Supper that Jesus Christ took with His Apostles in the house of Simon....

Q: At this Supper of Our Lord have you painted other figures?

A: Yes, milords.

Q: Tell us how many people and describe the gestures of each.

A: There is the owner of the inn, Simon; besides this figure I have made a steward, who, I imagined, had come there for his own pleasure to see how the things were going at the table. There are many figures there which I cannot recall, as I painted the picture some time ago. . . .

Q: In this Supper which you made for SS. Giovanni e Paolo what is the significance of the man whose nose is bleeding?

A: I intended to represent a servant whose nose was bleeding because of some accident.

Q: What is the significance of those armed men dressed as Germans, each with a halberd in his hand? . . .

A: We painters take the same license the poets and the jesters take and I have represented these two halberdiers, one drinking and the other eating nearby on the stairs. They are placed there so that they might be of service because it seemed to me fitting, according to what I have been told, that the master of the house, who was great and rich, should have such servants.

Q: And that man dressed as a buffoon with a parrot on his wrist, for what purpose did you paint him on that canvas?

A: For ornament, as is customary.

Q: Who are at the table of Our Lord?

A: The Twelve Apostles.

Q: What is St. Peter, the first one, doing?

A: Carving the lamb in order to pass it to the other end of the table.

Q: What is the Apostle next to him doing?

A: He is holding a dish in order to receive what St. Peter will give him.

Q: Tell us what the one next to this one is doing.

A: He has a toothpick and cleans his teeth. . . .

Q: Did anyone commission you to paint Germans, buffoons, and similar things in that picture?

A: No, milords, but I received the commission to decorate the picture as I saw fit. It is large and, it seemed to me, it could hold many figures.

Q: Are not the decorations which you painters are accustomed to add to paintings or pictures supposed to be suitable and proper to the subject and the principal figures or are they for pleasure—simply what comes to your imagination without any discretion or judiciousness?

A: I paint pictures as I see fit and as well as my talent permits.

Q: Does it seem fitting at the Last Supper of the Lord to paint buffoons, drunkards, Germans, dwarfs, and similar vulgarities?

A: No, milords.

Q: Do you not know that in Germany and in other places infected with heresy it is customary with various pictures full of scurrilousness and similar inventions to mock, vituperate, and scorn the things of the Holy Catholic Church in order to teach bad doctrines to foolish and ignorant people?

A: Yes that is wrong. . . .

After these things had been said, the judges announced that the above named Paolo would be obliged to improve and change his painting within a period of three months from the day of this admonition and that according to the opinion and decision of the Holy Tribunal all the corrections should be made at the expense of the painter and that if he did not correct the picture he would be liable to the penalties imposed by the Holy Tribunal. Thus they decreed in the best manner possible.

46

ANDREA PALLADIO (1518–1580)

From *The Four Books of Architecture*

Published in 1570, Palladio's The Four Books of Architecture *made an enormous impression on his European contemporaries. His book provided the basis for much French and English architecture of the seventeenth and eighteenth centuries.*

Guided by a natural inclination, I gave myself up in my most early years to the study of architecture: and as it was always my opinion, that the ancient Romans, as in many other things, so in building well, vastly excelled all those who have been since their time, I proposed to myself Vitruvius for my master and guide, who is the only ancient writer of this art, and set myself to search into the reliques of all the ancient edifices, that, in spight of time and the cruelty of the Barbarians, yet remain; and finding them much more worthy of observation, than at first I had imagined, I began very minutely with the utmost diligence to measure every one of their parts; of which I grew at last so sollicitous an examiner, (not finding any thing which was not done with reason and beautiful proportion) that I have very frequently not only travelled in different parts of Italy, but also out of it. . . .

Whereupon perceiving how much this common use of building was different from the observations I had made upon the said edifices, and from what I had read in Vitruvius, Leon Battista Alberti, and in other excellent writers . . . it seemed to me a thing worthy of a man, who ought not to be born for himself only, but also for the utility of others, to publish the de-signs of those edifices, (in collecting which, I have employed so much time, and exposed myself to so many dangers) and concisely to set down whatever in them appeared to me more worthy of consideration; and moreover, those rules which I have observed, and now observe, in building; that they who shall read these my books, may be able to make use of whatever will be good therein, and supply those things in which . . . I shall have failed; that one may learn, by little and little, to lay aside the strange abuses, the barbarous inventions, the superfluous expence, and (what is of greater consequence) avoid the various and continual ruins that have been seen in many fabricks. . . .

47

CAREL VAN MANDER (1548–1606)

From *The Painter's Treatise*

Van Mander's biographies of distinguished Dutch and Flemish painters, published in 1604, are a counterpart to the lives of Italian artists by Giorgio Vasari, which first appeared in 1550. Van Mander, a painter himself, begins his biographies with Jan van Eyck because he was considered the inventor of oil painting and consequently the originator, with his brother Hubert, of the Netherlandish tradition of painting. Among the works described by Van Mander are the Ghent Altarpiece (see figs. 15-3, 15-4, 15-6) and a painting that is probably The Arnolfini Portrait *(see figs. 15-8 and 15-9).*

It is supposed that the art of painting with a glue and egg medium [tempera painting] was imported into the Netherlands from Italy, because, as we have noted in the biography of Giovanni of Cimabue, this method was first used in Florence, in 1250. . . .

According to the people of Bruges, Joannes [Jan] was a learned man, clever and inventive, who studied many subjects related to painting: He examined many kinds of pigment; he studied alchemy and distillation. At length, he worked out a method of varnishing his egg and glue paintings with oil, so that these shining and lustrous pictures exceedingly delighted all who saw them. . . .

Joannes had painted a panel on which he had spent much time. . . . He varnished the finished panel according to his new invention and placed it in the sunlight to dry. . . . The panel burst at the joints and fell apart. Joannes . . . took a resolve that the sun should not damage his work ever again.

Accordingly, . . . he set himself to discover or invent some kind of varnish which would dry within the house, away from the sunlight. He had already examined many oils and other similar materials supplied by nature, and had found that linseed oil and nut oil had the best drying ability of them all. . . .

Joannes found, after many experiments, that colors mixed with these oils could be handled easily, that they dried well, became hard, and, once dry, could resist water. The oil made the color appear more alive, owing to a lustre of its own, without varnish. And what surprised and pleased him most was that paint made with oil could be applied more easily and mixed more thoroughly than paint made with egg and glue. . . .

Joannes . . . had created a new type of painting, to the amazement of the world. . . . This noble discovery, of painting with oil, was the only thing the art of painting still needed to achieve naturalistic rendition.

If the ancient Greeks, Apelles and Zeus [Zeuxis] had come to life again in this country and had seen this new method of painting, they would not have been any less surprised than if war-like Achilles [had] witnessed the thunder of cannon fire. . . .

The most striking work which the Van Eyck brothers did together is the altar-piece in the church of St John, in Ghent. . . .

The central panel of the altar-piece represents a scene from the Revelation of St John, in which the elders worship the Lamb. . . . In the upper part, Mary is represented; she is being crowned by the Father and the Son. . . .

Next to the figure of Mary are little angels singing from sheets of music. They are painted so exquisitely and so well that one can detect readily, from their facial expressions, who is singing the higher part, the high counter part, the tenor part, and the bass. . . .

Adam and Eve are represented. One may observe that Adam has a certain fear of breaking the command of the Lord, for he has a worried expression. . . .

The altar painting of the Van Eyck brothers was shown only to a few personages of high standing or to someone who would reward the keeper very well. Sometimes it was shown on important holidays, but then there was usually such a crowd that it was difficult to come near it. Then the chapel containing the altarpiece would be filled with all kinds of people—painters young and old, every kind of art lover, swarming like bees and flies around a basket of figs or raisins. . . .

Some Florentine merchants sent a splendid painting, made in Flanders, by Joannes to King Alphonso I of Naples. . . . A huge throng of artists came to see this marvelous painting, when it reached Italy. But although the Italians examined the picture very carefully, touching it, smelling at it, scenting the strong odor produced by the mixture of the colors with oil, and drawing all kinds of conclusions, the secret held until Antonello of Messina, in Sicily, went to Bruges to learn the process of oil-painting. Having mastered the technique, he introduced the art into Italy, as I have described in his biography. . . .

Joannes had once painted in oil two portraits in a single scene, a man and a woman, who give the right hand to each other, as if they had been united in wedlock by *Fides*. This little picture came through inheritance into the hands of a barber in Bruges. Mary, aunt of King Philip of Spain and widow of King Louis of Hungary, . . . happened to see this painting. The art loving princess was so pleased with this picture that she gave a certain office to the barber which brought him a yearly income of a hundred guilders.

48

CAREL VAN MANDER

From *The Painter's Treatise*

Van Mander's biography of Pieter Bruegel the Elder remains an important source of information about the artist, whose talent he appreciated fully.

He did a great deal of work [in Antwerp] for a merchant, Hans Franckert, a noble and upright man, who found pleasure in Breughel's company and met him every day. With this Franckert, Breughel often went out into the country to see peasants at their fairs and weddings. Disguised as peasants they brought gifts like the other guests, claiming relationship or kinship with the bride or groom. Here Breughel delighted in observing the droll behavior of the peasants, how they ate, drank, danced, capered, or made love, all of which he was well able to reproduce cleverly and pleasantly. . . . He represented the peasants—men and women of the Campine and elsewhere—naturally, as they really were, betraying their boorishness in the way they walked, danced, stood still, or moved.

. . . When the widow of Pieter Koeck [van Aelst, with whom van Mander says Breughel studied] was living in Brussels, he courted her daughter who . . . he had often carried about in his arms, and married her. The mother, however, demanded that

Breughel should leave Antwerp and take up residence in Brussels, so as to give up and put away all thoughts of his former girl. And this indeed he did. He was a very quiet and thoughtful man, not fond of talking, but ready with jokes when in the company of others. . . . He left behind him two sons who are also good painters. One is called Pieter. He was a pupil of Gillis van Coninxloo. . . . Jan, who had learned the use of water color from his grandmother, the widow of Pieter van Aelst, was instructed in the art of painting in oils by Pieter Goedkindt. . . .

49

GASPAR OFHUYS (c. 1456–1523)

From an account of the illness of Hugo van der Goes

Gaspar Ofhuys entered the "Red Cloister" monastery near Brussels together with Hugo van der Goes in 1475. Ofhuys was perhaps jealous of the special privileges Van der Goes enjoyed because of his status as a painter, and intimates that his mental illness was an affliction brought on by the sin of pride. This sin was often attributed to artists in the Middle Ages.

About five or six years after he had taken the vows it fell to our brother [Hugo van der Goes] to make a journey which—if I remember right—took him to Cologne. . . . Hugo, during one night of his journey home, was seized by a strange illness of his mind; he uttered unceasing laments about being doomed and sentenced to eternal damnation. He even wanted to lay murderous hands on himself and had to be prevented by force from doing so. Because of this strange illness that journey came to an extremely sad end. However, thanks to efficient help, Brussels was safely reached, and prior Thomas was immediately summoned. When he saw and heard all that had happened he suspected that Hugo was vexed by the same illness which had befallen King Saul; and remembering that Saul was relieved when David played the harp he at once permitted plenty of music to be made in the presence of Hugo and also other soothing performances to be arranged in order to chase away those fantasies. But with all this, Hugo's health did not improve; he continued to rave and to pronounce himself a child of perdition. In this sad state he came home to the monastery. . . .

We can speak of two possible assumptions concerning the illness of our painter-brother converse. The first is that it was a natural one, a kind of frenzy. There exist various natural species of this disease: sometimes it is caused by "melancholy" victuals, sometimes by imbibing strong wine; then again by passions of the soul such as anxiety, sadness, overwork, or fear. . . . As regards those passions of the soul, I know for certain that this converse brother was much afflicted by them. For he was deeply troubled by the thought of how he could ever finish the works of art he wanted to paint, and it was said at that time that nine years would hardly suffice for it. . . .

The second possibility of explaining this disease is that it was sent by Divine Providence which, as it is written in the second Epistle of St. Peter, ch. 3, "is long-suffering to us-ward, not willing that any should perish, but that all should come to repentance." For this converse brother was highly praised in our order because of his special artistic achievements—in fact, he thus became more famous than he would have been outside our walls; and since he was only human—as are all of us—the various honors, visits, and accolades that came to him made him feel very important. Thus, since God did not want him to perish, He in His compassion sent him this humiliating disease which indeed made him very contrite. This our brother understood very well, and as soon as he had recovered he became most humble.

50

FRAY JOSÉ DE SIGÜENZA (1544?–1606)

From the *History of the Order of St. Jerome*

The works of Hieronymus Bosch were collected by the Spanish king Philip II (r. 1556–98) and were displayed in his Escorial Palace near Madrid, where Sigüenza was the librarian. The interpretation of Bosch's work was as difficult then as it is today and caused just as much disagreement. This passage is Sigüenza's attempt to interpret the painting that we call The Garden of Delights *(see fig. 15-14).*

Among these German and Flemish pictures . . . there are distributed throughout the house many by a certain Geronimo Bosch. Of him I want to speak at somewhat greater length for various reasons: first, because his great inventiveness merits it; second, because they are commonly called the absurdities of Geronimo Bosque by people who observe little in what they look at; and third, because I think that these people consider them without reason as being tainted by heresy. . . .

The difference that, to my mind, exists between the pictures of this man and those of all others is that the others try to paint man as he appears on the outside, while he alone had the audacity to paint him as he is on the inside. . . .

The . . . painting has as its basic theme and subject a flower and the fruit of [a] type that we call strawberries. . . . In order for one to understand his idea, I will expound upon it in the same order in which he has organized it. Between two pictures is one large painting, with two doors that close over it. In the first of the panels he painted the Creation of Man, showing how God put him in paradise, a delightful place . . . and how He commands him as a test of his obedience and faith not to eat from the tree, and how later the devil deceived him in the form of a serpent. He eats and, trespassing God's rule, is exiled from that wondrous place and deprived of the high dignity for which he was created. . . . This is [shown] with a thousand fantasies and observations that serve as warnings. . . .

In the large painting that follows he painted the pursuits of man after he was exiled from paradise and placed in this world, and he shows him searching after the glory that is like hay or straw, like a plant without fruit, which one knows will be cast into the oven the next day, . . . and thus uncovers the life, the activities, and the thoughts of these sons of sin and wrath, who, having forgotten the commands of God . . . strive for and undertake the glory of the flesh. . . .

In this painting we find, as if alive and vivid, an infinite number of passages from the scriptures that touch upon the evil ways of man, . . . many allegories or metaphors that present them in the guise of tame, wild, fierce, lazy, sagacious, cruel, and bloodthirsty beasts of burden and riding animals. . . . Here is also demonstrated the transmigration of souls that Pythagoras, Plato, and other poets . . . displayed in the attempt to show us the bad customs, habits, dress, disposition, or sinister shades with which the souls of miserable men clothe themselves—that through pride they are transformed into lions; by vengefulness into tigers; through lust into mules, horses, and pigs; by tyranny into fish; by vanity into peacocks; by slyness and craft into foxes; by gluttony into apes and wolves; by callousness and evil into asses; by stupidity into sheep; because of rashness into goats. . . .

One can reap great profit by observing himself thus portrayed true to life from the inside. . . . And he would also see in the last panel the miserable end and goal of his pains, efforts, and preoccupations, and how . . . the brief joys are transformed into eternal wrath, with no hope or grace.

51
From the contract for the St. Wolfgang Altarpiece

It took Michael Pacher ten years (1471–81) to complete this elaborate altarpiece for the pilgrimage church of St. Wolfgang. The altarpiece is still in its original location (see fig. 15-20).

Here is recorded the pact and contract concerning the altar at St. Wolfgang, concluded between the very Reverend, Reverend Benedict, Abbot of Mondsee and of his monastery there, and Master Michael, painter of Bruneck, on St. Lucy's day of the year 1471.

ITEM, it is first to be recorded that the altar shall be made conforming to the elevation and design which the painter has brought to us at Mondsee, and to its exact measurements.

ITEM, the predella shrine shall be guilded on the inside and it shall show Mary seated with the Christ Child, Joseph, and the Three Kings with their gifts; and if these should not completely fill the predella shrine he shall make more figures or armored men, all gilt.

ITEM, the main shrine shall show the Coronation of Mary with angels and gilt drapery—the most precious and the best he can make.

ITEM, on one side St. Wolfgang with mitre, crozier, church, and hatchet; on the other St. Benedict with cap, crozier, and a tumbler, entirely gilded and silvered where needed.

ITEM, to the sides of the altar shall stand St. Florian and St. George, fine armored men, silvered and gilded where needed.

ITEM, the inner wings of the altar shall be provided with good paintings, the panels gilded and equipped with gables and pinnacles, representing four subjects, one each. . . .

ITEM, the outer wings—when the altar is closed—shall be done with good pigments and with gold added to the colors; the subject from the life of St. Wolfgang. . . .

ITEM, at St. Wolfgang, while he completes and sets up the altar, we shall provide his meals and drink, and also the iron work necessary for setting up the altar, as well as help with loading wherever necessary.

ITEM, the contract is made for the sum of one thousand two hundred Hungarian guilders or ducats. . . .

ITEM, if the altar is either not worth this sum or of higher value, and there should be some difference of opinion between us, both parties shall appoint equal numbers of experts to decide the matter.

52
MARTIN LUTHER (1483–1546)
From *Against the Heavenly Prophets in the Matter of Images and Sacraments*

Luther inaugurated the Protestant Reformation movement in 1517 with a public critique of certain Church practices, especially the sale of indulgences. His actions soon inspired a number of similar reformers in the north, some of whom were more extreme in their denunciations of the conventional artistic and musical trappings of the Church. The ideas of one of these, Andreas Bodenstein, inspired this writing of 1525.

I approached the task of destroying images by first tearing them out of the heart through God's Word and making them worthless and despised. . . . For when they are no longer in the heart, they can do no harm when seen with the eyes. But Dr. Karlstadt [Andreas Bodenstein], who pays no attention to matters of the heart, has reversed the order by removing them from sight and leaving them in the heart. . . .

I have allowed and not forbidden the outward removal of images, so long as this takes place without rioting and uproar and is done by the proper authorities. . . . And I say at the outset that according to the law of Moses no other images are forbidden than an image of God which one worships. A crucifix, on the other hand, or any other holy image is not forbidden. Heigh now! you breakers of images, I defy you to prove the opposite! . . .

Thus we read that Moses' Brazen Serpent remained (Num. 21:8) until Hezekiah destroyed it solely because it had been worshiped (II Kings 18:4). . . .

However, to speak evangelically of images, I say and declare that no one is obligated to break violently images even of God, but everything is free, and one does not sin if he does not break them with violence. . . .

Nor would I condemn those who have destroyed them, especially those who destroy divine and idolatrous images. But images for memorial and witness, such as crucifixes and images of saints, are to be tolerated. This is shown above to be the case even in the Mosaic law. And they are not only to be tolerated, but for the sake of the memorial and the witness they are praiseworthy and honorable, as the witness stones of Joshua (Josh. 24:26) and of Samuel (I Sam. 7:12).

53

ALBRECHT DÜRER (1471–1528)

From the draft manuscript for *The Book on Human Proportions*

Dürer made two trips to Italy and was exposed to the new art theories being discussed there, which impressed him greatly. He did not accept them uncritically, however. His rethinking of Italian ideas often appears only in preliminary form, in drafts such as this one, written in 1512–13.

How beauty is to be judged is a matter of deliberation. . . . In some things we consider that as beautiful which elsewhere would lack beauty. "Good" and "better" in respect of beauty are not easy to discern, for it would be quite possible to make two different figures, neither of them conforming to the other, one stouter and the other thinner, and yet we scarce might be able to judge which of the two may excel in beauty. What beauty is I know not, though it adheres to many things. When we wish to bring it into our work we find it very hard. We must gather it together from far and wide, and especially in the case of the human figure. . . . One may often search through two or three hundred men without finding amongst them more than one or two points of beauty which can be made use of. You therefore, if you desire to compose a fine figure, must take the head from some and the chest, arm, leg, hand, and foot from others. . . .

Many follow their taste alone; these are in error. Therefore let each take care that his inclination blind not his judgment. For every mother is well pleased with her own child. . . .

Men deliberate and hold numberless differing opinions about these things and they seek after them in many different ways, although the ugly is more easily attained than the beautiful. Being then, as we are, in such a state of error, I know not how to set down firmly and with finality what measure approaches absolute beauty. . . .

It seems to me impossible for a man to say that he can point out the best proportions for the human figure; for the lie is in our perception, and darkness abides so heavily within us that even our gropings fail. . . .

However, because we cannot altogether attain perfection, shall we therefore wholly cease from our learning? This bestial thought we do not accept. For evil and good lie before men, wherefore it behooves a rational man to choose the better.

54

ARTEMISIA GENTILESCHI (1593–c. 1653)

From a letter to Don Antonio Ruffo

Being a woman in what was considered until very recently a man's field was not easy, as this letter of November 13, 1649, only begins to suggest. Ruffo was one of Artemisia's patrons.

I have received a letter of October 26th, which I deeply appreciated, particularly noting how my master always concerns himself with favoring me, contrary to my merit. In it, you tell me about that gentleman who wishes to have some paintings by me, that he would like a Galatea and a Judgment of Paris, and that the Galatea should be different from the one that Your Most Illustrious Lordship owns. There was no need for you to urge me to do this, since by the grace of God and the Most Holy Virgin, they [clients] come to a woman with this kind of talent, that is, to vary the subjects in my painting; never has anyone found in my pictures any repetition of invention, not even of one hand.

As for the fact that this gentleman wishes to know the price before the work is done, . . . I do it most unwillingly. . . . I never quote a price for my works until they are done. However, since Your Most Illustrious Lordship wants me to do this, I will do what you command. Tell this gentleman that I want five hundred ducats for both; he can show them to the whole world and, should he find anyone who does not think the paintings are worth two hundred scudi more, I won't ask him to pay me the agreed price. I assure Your Most Illustrious Lordship that these are paintings with nude figures requiring very expensive female models, which is a big headache. When I find good ones they fleece me, and at other times, one must suffer [their] pettiness with the patience of Job.

As for my doing a drawing and sending it, I have made a solemn vow never to send my drawings because people have cheated me. In particular, just today I found . . . that, having done a drawing of souls in Purgatory for the Bishop of St. Gata, he, in order to spend less, commissioned another painter to do the painting using my work. If I were a man, I can't imagine it would have turned out this way. . . .

I must caution Your Most Illustrious Lordship that when I ask a price, I don't follow the custom in Naples, where they ask thirty and then give it for four. I am Roman, and therefore I shall act always in the Roman manner.

55

GIOVANNI PIETRO BELLORI (1613–1696)

From *Lives of the Modern Painters, Sculptors, and Architects*

Unlike Vasari's Lives, *Bellori's book is more selective and critical. He often ignores or gives minimal treatment to those artists and architects who offended his classical taste. Bellori's account was published in Rome in 1672.*

When the divine Raphael with the ultimate outlines of his art used its beauty to the summit, restoring it to the ancient majesty of all those graces and enriching the merits that once made it most glorious in the presence of the Greeks and the Romans, painting was most admired by men and seemed descended from Heaven. But since things of the earth never stay the same, and whatever gains the heights inevitably must with perpetual vicissitude fall back again, so art, which from Cimabue and Giotto had slowly advanced over the long period of two hundred and fifty years, was seen to decline rapidly and from a queen become humble and common. Thus, with the passing of that happy century, all of its beauties quickly vanished. The artists, abandoning the study of nature, corrupted art with the *maniera,* that is to say, with the fantastic idea based on practice and not on imitation. This vice, the destroyer of painting, first began to appear in masters of honored acclaim. It rooted itself in the schools that later followed. . . .

Thus, when painting was drawing to its end. . . . It pleased God that in the city of Bologna, the mistress of sciences and studies, a most noble mind was forged and through it the declining and extinguished art was reforged. He was that Annibale Carracci, of whom I now mean to write. . . .

Annibale continued in the [Farnese] gallery [see fig. 17-5] . . . ordering various myths toward an end: the theme . . . is human love governed by Heaven. Thus the theme of love . . . displays its power, subjecting the breasts of the strong, the chaste, and the savage: the loves, that is to say, of Hercules, Diana, and of Polyphemus. . . . The amours of Jupiter, Juno, Aurora, and Galatea reveal its power in the universe. The white wool that Diana receives from the god Pan and the golden apples given to Paris by Mercury are the gifts by which Amor sways human minds, and the discords provoked by beauty. The Bacchanal is the symbol of drunkenness, the source of impure desires. And since the end of all irrational pleasures is sorrow and punishment, . . . he painted Andromeda bound to the rock to be devoured by the sea monster, symbolizing that the soul bound to emotion becomes the food of vice if Perseus—that is to say, reason and the love of the worthy—does not come to her assistance.

Now [Caravaggio] began to paint according to his own genius. He not only ignored the most excellent marbles of the ancients and the famous paintings of Raphael, but he despised them, and nature alone became the object of his brush. . . . [He] was making himself more and more notable for the color scheme which he was introducing, not soft and sparingly tinted as before, but reinforced throughout with bold shadows and a great deal of black to give relief to the forms. He went so far in this manner of working that he never brought his figures out into the daylight, but placed them in the dark brown atmosphere of a closed room, using a high light that descended vertically over the principal parts of the bodies while leaving the remainder in shadow in order to give force through a strong contrast of light and dark. The painters then in Rome were greatly impressed by his novelty and the younger ones especially gathered around him and praised him as the only true imitator of nature. Looking upon his works as miracles, they outdid each other in following his method. . . .

. . Having thought up his inventions, [Poussin] then made a rough sketch of what he had in mind; he then made small wax models, half a hand's breadth in height, of all the figures striking their attitudes, and then constructed the story of the fable in relief in order to study the natural effects of the light and the shadow of the bodies. He then made larger models, which he dressed, so as to make a separate study of their attire and the folds of material on the naked form, and for this purpose he used fine canvas, or wet cambric, with just a few pieces of cloth providing a variety of colors. Thus he gradually sketched nude life studies, and the drawings emanating from his imaginings were done with simple lines, using simple chiaroscuro watercolours, which nonetheless effectively conveyed movement and expression. He continually sought action in historical subjects, and maintained that it was the painter himself who had the right to choose the subject matter and that he should avoid subjects that had no meaning. . . . He read Greek and Latin histories and made notes, which he then used when the occasion arose.

56

FILIPPO BALDINUCCI (1625–1696)

From *The Life of Bernini*

In 1681 Baldinucci, a Florentine theorist and scholar, was commissioned by Queen Christina of Sweden, who spent her life in Rome after converting to Catholicism, to write a biography of Bernini shortly after his death. Carefully researched, it is still the main source of information about the artist.

The opinion is widespread that Bernini was the first to attempt to unite architecture with sculpture and painting in such a manner that together they make a beautiful whole. This he accomplished by removing all repugnant uniformity of poses, breaking up the poses sometimes without violating good rules, although he did not bind himself to the rules. . . . He knew from the beginning that his strong point was sculpture. Thus, although he felt a great inclination toward painting, he did not wish to devote himself to it altogether. . . . Bernini declared that painting was superior to sculpture, since sculpture shows that which exists with more dimensions, whereas painting shows that which does not exist, that is, it shows relief where there is no relief and gives an effect of distance where there is none. . . . [I]t is not surprising at all that a man of Bernini's excellence in the three arts, whose common source is drawing, also possessed in high measure the fine gift of composing excellent and most ingenious theatrical productions. . . . Bernini was, then, outstanding in dramatic actions and in composing plays. He put on many productions, which were highly applauded for scope and creativity. . . . Bernini's ability to blend his talents in the arts for the invention of stage machinery has never been equalled in my opinion.

57

NICOLAS POUSSIN (c. 1593–1665)
From an undated manuscript

Poussin's ideas on art were central to the formation of the French Academy in 1648 and, because of the preeminence of that academy, therefore to the entire European academic movement of the seventeenth through the nineteenth centuries.

The magnificent manner consists of four things: subject, or topic, concept, structure and style. The first requirement, which is the basis for all the others, is that the subject or topic should be great, such as battles, heroic actions and divine matters. However, given the subject upon which the painter is engaged is great, he must first of all make every effort to avoid getting lost in minute detail, so as not to detract from the dignity of the story. He should describe the magnificent and great details with a bold brush and disregard anything that is vulgar and of little substance. Thus the painter should not only be skilled in formulating his subject matter, but wise enough to know it well and to choose something that lends itself naturally to embellishment and perfection. Those who choose vile topics take refuge in them on account of their own lack of ingenuity. Faintheartedness is therefore to be despised, as is baseness of subject matter for which any amount of artifice is useless. As for the concept, it is simply part of the spirit, which concentrates on things, like the concept realized by Homer and Phidias of Olympian Zeus who could make the Universe tremble with a nod of his head. The drawing of things

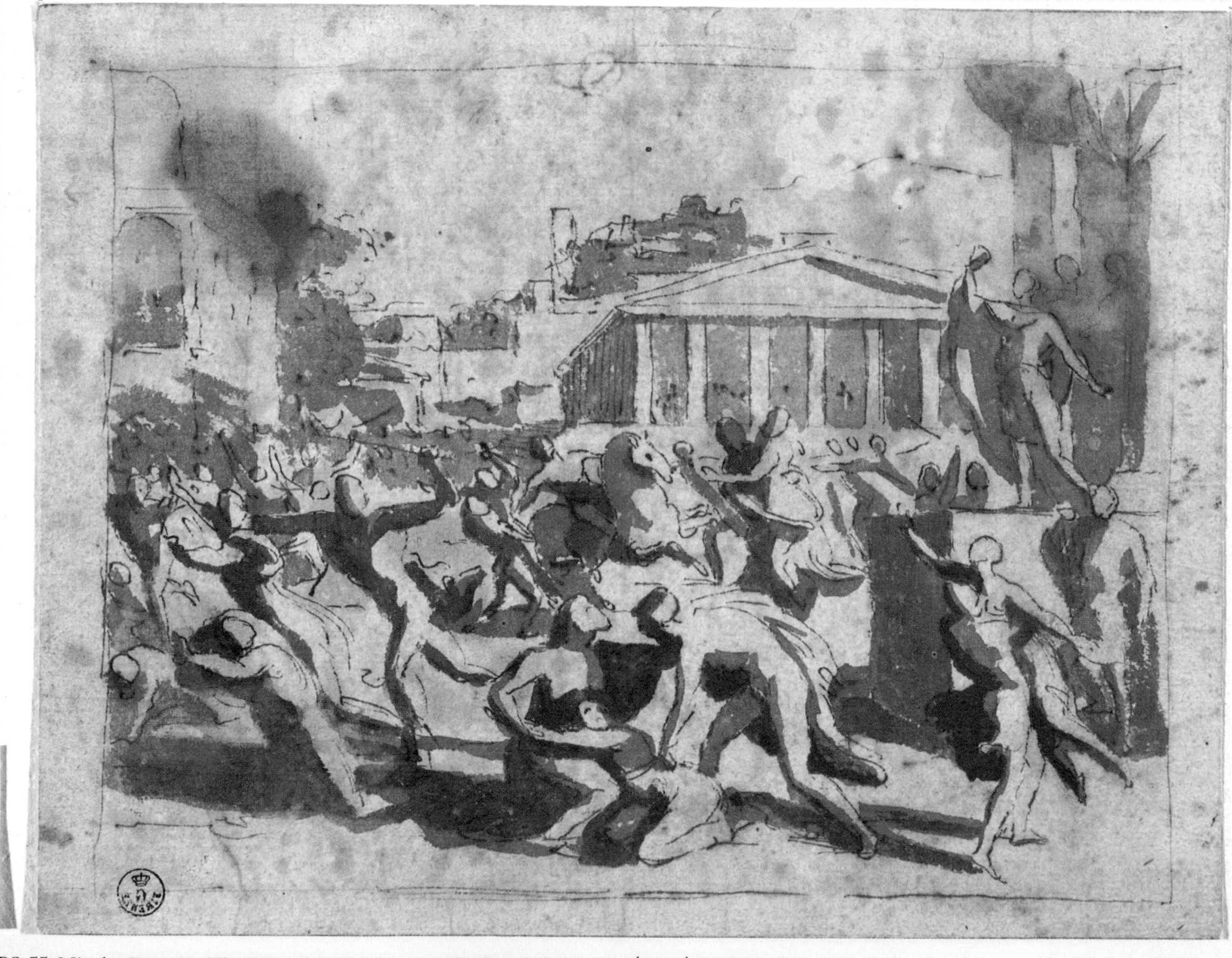

PS-55. Nicolas Poussin. *The Rape of the Sabines.* c. 1630. Brush drawing, 6¼ x 8⅛" (16.1 x 20.7 cm). Archive of Drawings and Prints, Uffizi Gallery, Florence

should be such that it expresses the concept of the things themselves. The structure, or composition of the parts, should not be studiously researched, and not sought after or contrived with effort but should be as natural as possible. Style is a particular method of painting and drawing, carried out in an individual way, born of the singular talent at work in its application and in the use of ideas. This style, and the manner and taste emanate from nature and from the mind.

58

CHARLES PERRAULT (1628–1703)

From *Memoirs of My Life*

Charles Perrault, a poet, critic, and adviser to Colbert on arts and letters, helped his brother, Claude, get the assignment to design the East Front of the Louvre (see fig. 19-10).

Since the Cavaliere Bernini's design was not very well conceived, and could only be carried out to the shame of France, I made a listing of only a few of the incongruities with which it was ridden, because I thought it inappropriate to point out too many of them the first time. I sent this memorandum to Monsieur Colbert, who was then at Saint-Germain. The first time he came to Paris, after having received my list, he had me step into the garden with him, and even cut short the audience he was granting to someone else, in order to talk to me. . . .

"You did well," he told me; "continue doing so, because one cannot be too well informed on a matter of this importance. I don't understand," he added, "how this man believes he can give us a design in which so many things are misunderstood."

From that moment on, Monsieur Colbert undoubtedly saw that he had approached the wrong party, but he believed he had to follow through on his gamble. Perhaps he thought also that with good advice, he could redirect the Cavaliere to the right way of doing things, and that by showing him his mistakes, he would have him produce something excellent; but he still did not know the Cavaliere. . . .

I am persuaded that as an architect he hardly excelled at all, except with the decor and machinery of the theater. . . .

59

SIR CHRISTOPHER WREN (1632–1723)

From *Proposals for Rebuilding the City of London After the Great Fire*

The manner of building in the city of London, practised in the former ages, was commonly with timber, a material easily procured, and at little expense when the country was overburthened with woods. This often subjected the town to great and destructive fires, sometimes to the ruin of the whole, as happened, for instance, in the year 1083, and reign of William the Conquerer. . . . Notwithstanding these incidents, this mode continued until the two fatal years 1665 and [166]6; but then the successive calamities of plague and fire gave all people occasion seriously to reflect on the causes of the increase of both to that excessive . . . closeness of buildings, and combustible materials; and hence the wishes for the necessary amendment of both, by widening the streets, and building with stone and brick, became universal.

Some intelligent persons went farther, and thought it highly requisite the city in the restoration should rise with beauty, by the straightness and regularity of buildings, and convenience for commerce, by the well disposing of streets and public places, and the opening of wharfs, &c. which the excellent situation, wealth, and grandeur of the metropolis of England did justly deserve. . . . In order therefore to a proper reformation, Dr. Wren (pursuant to the royal commands) immediately after the fire, took an exact survey of the whole area . . . and designed a plan or model of a new city in which the deformity and inconveniences of the old town were remedied. . . .

The observations of a late critic (allowing for some mistakes in his description of [my] scheme for rebuilding the city) are judicious and right.

"Towards the end of King James the First's reign, and in the beginning of his son's, taste in architecture made a bold step from Italy to England at once, and scarce staid a moment to visit France by the way. From the most profound ignorance in architecture, the most consummate night of knowledge, Inigo Jones started up, a prodigy of art, and vied even with his master, Palladio himself. From so glorious an outset there was not any excellency that we might not have hoped to attain; Britain had a reasonable prospect to rival Italy. . . . But in the midst of these sanguine expectations, the fatal civil war commenced. . . . What followed was all darkness and obscurity. . . .

"Wren was the next genius that arose, to awake the spirit of science. . . .

"The fire of London furnished the most perfect occasion that can ever happen in any city, to rebuild it with pomp and regularity. This Wren foresaw, and . . . offered a scheme for that purpose, which would have made it the wonder of the world. He proposed to have laid out one large street from Aldgate to Temple Bar, in the middle of which was to have been a large square, capable of containing the new church of St. Paul [see figs. 19-21–19-24], with a proper distance for the view all round it; whereby that huge building would not have been cooped up, as it is at present, in such a manner as nowhere to be seen to advantage at all; but would have had a long and ample vista at each end. . . . He further proposed to rebuild all the parish churches in such a manner as to be seen at the end of every vista of houses. . . . Lastly, he proposed to build the houses uniform, and supported on a piazza, . . . and by the waterside . . . he had planned a long and broad wharf . . . with proper warehouses for merchants between, to vary the edifices, and make it at once one of the most beautiful and most useful ranges of structure in the world. But the hurry of rebuilding, and the disputes about property, prevented this glorious scheme from taking place."

60

MARIE-LOUISE-ELISABETH VIGÉE-LEBRUN (1755–1842)

From the *Memoirs of Vigée-Lebrun*

Vigée-Lebrun published three volumes of memoirs (1835 and 1837) when she was in her eighties. Female portraits and the painting of flowers were considered the most appropriate subjects for women artists in the eighteenth and nineteenth centuries.

M. Le Brun asked for my hand in marriage. Nothing could have been further from my thoughts than my marrying Le Brun. . . . I was then twenty years old; I had few worries about my future since I was already earning a substantial amount of money. In short, I had no inclination to wed at all. . . . Finally, I accepted, goaded on by the desire to escape the torment of living with my stepfather. . . . So little inclined was I to sacrifice my freedom, that even as I approached the church on my wedding day, I was still asking myself, "Shall I say yes or no?" Alas, I said yes and merely exchanged my old problems for new ones. . . . His overwhelming passion for extravagant women, combined with a love of gambling, decimated both his fortune and my own, of which he made very free use. So, by the time I left France in 1789 I had less than twenty francs to my name, in spite of the fact that I had earned more than a million from my work: he had squandered the lot! . . .

When I finally announced my marriage officially . . . I was not as downcast as I might have been, for I still had my beloved painting. I was overwhelmed with commissions from every quarter and although Le Brun took it upon himself to appropriate my earnings, this did not prevent him from insisting that I take pupils in order to increase our income even further. I consented to this demand without really taking time to consider the consequences and soon the house was full of young ladies learning how to paint "eyes, noses and faces." I was constantly correcting their efforts and was thus distracted from my own work, which I found very irritating indeed. . . .

I believe the strain of having to leave my precious brushes for several hours each day only increased my eagerness to paint. I refused to leave my easel until nightfall and the number of portraits I painted at this period is quite astonishing. As I had a horror of the current fashion, I did my best to make my models a little more picturesque. I was delighted when, having gained their trust, they allowed me to dress them after my fancy. No-one wore shawls then, but I liked to drape my models with large scarves, interlacing them around the body and through the arms, which was an attempt to imitate the beautiful style of draperies seen in the paintings of Raphael and Dominichino. . . .

Happy as I was at the idea of becoming a mother, after nine months of pregnancy, I was not in the least prepared for the birth of my baby. The day my daughter was born, I was still in the studio, trying to work on my *Venus Binding the Wings of Cupid* in the intervals between labour pains.

61

SIR JOSHUA REYNOLDS (1723–1792)

From "A Discourse, Delivered at the Opening of the Royal Academy, January 2, 1769"

An Academy, in which the Polite Arts may be regularly cultivated, is at last opened among us by Royal Munificence. This must appear an event in the highest degree interesting, not only to the Artists, but to the whole nation.

It is indeed difficult to give any other reason, why an empire like that of Britain, should so long have wanted an ornament so suitable to its greatness, than that slow progression of things, which naturally makes elegance and refinement the last effect of opulence and power. . . .

The principal advantage of an Academy is, that . . . it will be a repository for the great examples of the Art. These are the materials on which Genius is to work, and without which the strongest intellect may be fruitlessly or deviously employed. By studying these authentick models, that idea of excellence which is the result of the accumulated experience of past ages may be at once acquired, and the tardy and obstructed progress of our predecessors, may teach us a shorter and easier way. The Student receives, at one glance, the principles which many Artists have spent their whole lives in ascertaining. . . . How many men of great natural abilities have been lost to this nation, for want of these advantages? . . .

Raffaelle, it is true, had not the advantage of studying in an Academy; but all *Rome,* and the works of Michael Angelo in particular, were to him an Academy. . . .

One advantage, I will venture to affirm, we shall have in our Academy, which no other nation can boast. We shall have nothing to unlearn. . . .

But as these Institutions have so often failed in other nations . . . I must take leave to offer a few hints, by which those errors may be rectified. . . .

I would chiefly recommend, that an implicit obedience to the *Rules of Art,* as established by the practice of the great Masters, should be exacted from the *young* Students. That those models, which have passed through the approbation of ages, should be considered by them as perfect and infallible Guides; as subjects for their imitation, not their criticism.

I am confident, that this is the only efficacious method of making a progress in the Arts; and that he who sets out with doubting, will find life finished before he becomes master of the rudiments. For it may be laid down as a maxim, that he who begins by presuming on his own sense, has ended his studies as soon as he has commenced them. Every opportunity, therefore, should be taken to discountenance that false and vulgar opinion, that rules are the fetters of Genius.

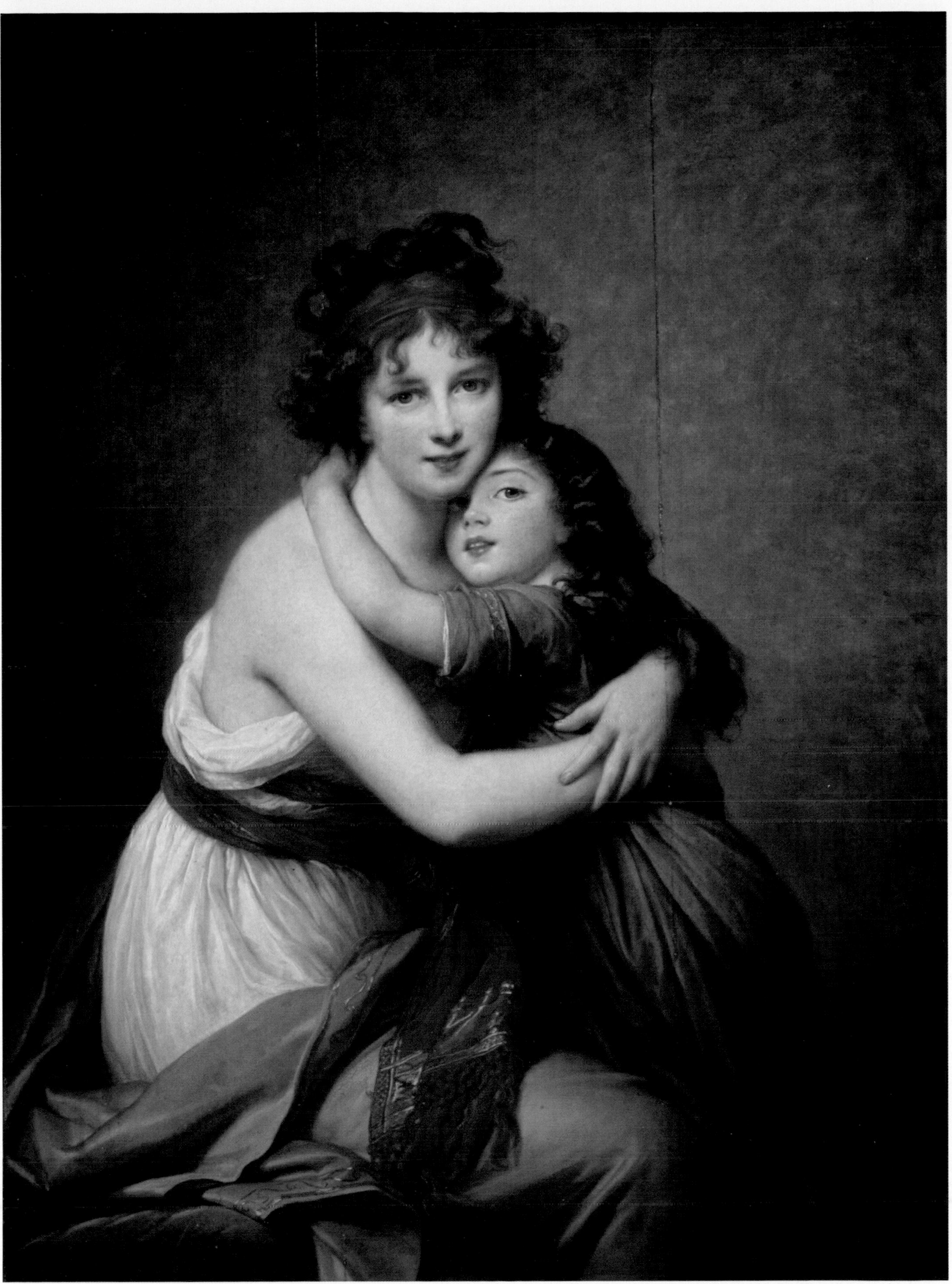

PS-60. Elizabeth-Louise Vigée-LeBrun. *Self-Portrait with Her Daughter, Julie.* c. 1789. Oil on canvas, 51$^{3}/_{16}$ x 37" (130 x 94 cm). Musée du Louvre, Paris

Timeline Three: 1350 to 1800

History and Politics

1350–1375

1356 Edward, the "Black Prince," son of Edward III of England, defeats the French at Poitiers and takes prisoner Jean le Bon, king of France

c. 1358 Foundation of the powerful Hanseatic League of Baltic mercantile cities

Peasant uprisings: 1358, Jacquerie revolt in France; 1381, Wat Tyler's rebellion in England, London sacked

1368 In China, the Buddhist monk Chu Yüan-chang leads a peasants' revolt, driving the Mongols out of Beijing and founding the Ming dynasty, taking the title Hungwu

Timur (Tamerlane, c. 1369–1405), Mongol leader with capital at Samarkand, establishes the Timurid Empire, conquering much of the Mideast and Persia and invading India

1375–1400

1400–1425

1410 Teutonic Knights defeated by Poles and Lithuanians at battle of Tennenberg, ending their sole jurisdiction over Prussia

Philip the Good of Burgundy (r. 1419–67) inherits the Northern Provinces; including Holland, Flanders, and Luxembourg, it is one of the largest and richest holdings in Europe and a threat to France

SOURCES OF RENAISSANCE NEO-PLATONISM Neo-Platonic ideas of harmony, balance, proportion, and spirituality appeared in Western thought throughout the Middle Ages, but the source texts of Plato, Plotinus, and their followers were little known. In 1394 the Greek scholar Manuel Chrysoloras visited Italy from Constantinople and remained to teach Greek in Florence. In 1439 other Greek scholars from the Byzantine Empire attended the ecclesiastical Council of Florence, which attempted to unite the Eastern and Western churches, and they further exposed local writers and artists to the intellectual heritage of classical Greece, especially its idealism. The work

Religion

1350–1375

1375–1400

1378 Papal court returns to Rome from Avignon. Great Papal Schism begins, in which several candidates compete for the papacy

c. 1382 John Wycliffe, English theologian and religious reformer, initiates first complete translation of the Bible into English

1400–1425

1405–15 Jan Hus, influenced by Wycliffe, leads the Hussite movement to reform the church in Bohemia and denounces sale of indulgences; 1415, burned at the stake as a heretic at the Council of Constance

1417 Pope Martin V ends Great Schism

Visual Arts

BOHEMIAN MASTER
Death of the Virgin, Prague, 1355–60

Florence Cathedral, begun by Arnolfo di Cambio, 1296; dome by Filippo Brunelleschi, 1420–36

CLAUS SLUTER
The Moses Well, Dijon, 1395–1406

DONATELLO
St. Mark, 1411–13

GENTILE DA FABRIANO
The Adoration of the Magi, Italy, 1423

Music, Literature, and Philosophy

1350–1375

1361 Foundation of the University of Pavia in northern Italy

Christine de Pisan (c. 1363–c. 1430), French writer of poems on courtly love, best known for her spirited defense of women in *The Book of the City of Ladies*, c. 1404–5

Leonardo Bruni (1370–1444), prominent humanist and classical scholar in Florence, author of *Praise of the City of Florence,* 1402–3

1375–1400

1395–98 Manuel Chrysoloras, a Byzantine Greek scholar, teaches Greek in Florence; translates Plato's *Republic* into Latin; author of first Greek grammar used in western Europe

1400–1425

Leone Battista Alberti (1404–72) writes influential treatises *On Painting,* 1435, *On Architecture,* 1452, and *On Sculpture,* 1464

Science, Technology, and Exploration

1350–1375

1355 Death of Jacopo Dondi (b. 1298), creator of an early clock run by weights

1375–1400

1375 Charles V of France commissions the *Carta catalana,* an accurate map of Europe, North Africa, and western Asia

Prince Henry the Navigator of Portugal (1394–1460) sponsors exploration, especially of the African coasts, an observatory, a school of navigation, and improvements in ship design, the compass, and cartography

1398 Cennino Cennini writes the *Libro dell' arte,* a technical manual for painters

1400–1425

1406 King Edward IV of England founds the Society of Merchant Adventurers to encourage trade and commerce

1407 Establishment of Bank of St. George, first public bank, in Genoa

1410 Ptolemy's *Geography* translated into Latin

c. 1413 Pictorial perspective invented in Italy by Filippo Brunelleschi of the Early Renaissance architects Leone Battista Alberti (1404–72) and Filarete (c. 1400–c. 1469) reflects this influence to a certain degree.

After the fall of Constantinople to the Turks in 1453, many scholars fled permanently to the West. Their ideas, and the precious manuscripts they brought, stimulated interest in humanist studies. Neo-Platonism was particularly influential at the erudite Florentine court of Lorenzo de' Medici, known as the Platonic Academy. The philosopher Marsilio Ficino (1433–99) and the artists Sandro Botticelli (1444/5–1510) and Michelangelo (1475–1564) were prominent members of this circle.

	1425–1450	1450–1475	1475–1500
HISTORY AND POLITICS	**1438** Hapsburg rule of the Holy Roman Empire (later Germany and Austria) begins (until 1806) **By 1450** Medici family, founded by Cosimo the Elder (1389–1464), gains power in Florence; 1469–92, Lorenzo the Magnificent virtually rules the city	**1453** Constantinople falls to the Turkish army of Mohammed II; Ottoman Empire founded **Matthias the Just (r. 1458–90)** establishes Hungary as dominant power in central Europe **1469** Marriage of Ferdinand of Aragon and Isabella of Castile unites Spain	**1477** French army defeats Charles the Bold of Burgundy at Nancy. Northern Provinces pass to Maximilian, Hapsburg emperor; 1488, Flemish cities revolt against his rule **1478** Pazzi Conspiracy in Florence; Giuliano de' Medici assassinated during Easter mass, and Pazzi family decimated in revenge; 1480, turmoil among Tuscan city-states quelled by Lorenzo's leadership **1492** Defeat of Muslim Grenada by the Spanish Christian powers; 1502, expulsion of Jews and Moors **1493–94** Territories of South America divided between Spain and Portugal by the pope **1494** Medici rulers expelled for the first time from Florence; a republic declared **1495–96** Charles VIII of France invades Italian peninsula and claims the kingdom of Naples; repulsed by the Holy League (the papacy, Spain, and Holy Roman Empire)
RELIGION	**1431** Joan of Arc burned at the stake in Rouen, accused of heresy and witchcraft **1439** Council of Florence attempts to reunite the Eastern Orthodox church with the Western Catholics; its success is short-lived	**1464** Pope Pius II, humanist and patron of learning, dies during a failed crusade against the Turks **Pope Sixtus IV (r. 1471–84)** condemns the excesses of the Spanish Inquisition and tries to reunite Russian church with Rome	**1494** Rise in Florence of Fra Girolamo Savonarola (1452–98), monk and religious radical advocating moral and governmental reform; 1498, he is burned at the stake for heresy
	(LEFT) JAN VAN EYCK *Arnolfini Portrait,* detail, 1434 (RIGHT) LORENZO GHIBERTI Panel of the *"Gates of Paradise,"* c. 1435	HUGO VAN DER GOES *The Portinari Altarpiece,* center panel, c. 1476	SANDRO BOTTICELLI *The Birth of Venus,* c. 1480
MUSIC, LITERATURE, AND PHILOSOPHY	**François Villon (born c. 1431),** French poet **Marsilio Ficino (1433–99),** humanist and philosopher, undertakes a translation of Plato, under the patronage of the Medici in Florence **Josquin Des Prés (c. 1440–1521),** Flemish composer of madrigals **Pope Nicholas V (r. 1447–55)** founds Vatican Library	**Desiderius Erasmus of Rotterdam (c. 1466–1536),** scholar and satirical author (*Praise of Folly,* 1509), epitomizes the humanist intellectual concerns of the Northern Reformation	**1481** A commentary on Dante's *Divine Comedy* is published, with illustrations by Botticelli and a preface by Marsilio Ficino **1494** Sebastian Brant (1458?–1521), German humanist, writes *The Ship of Fools,* a satirical poem
SCIENCE, TECHNOLOGY, AND EXPLORATION	**c. 1425** Discovery and proliferation in northern Europe of the technique of painting with oil **c. 1440** Earliest record of a suction pump	**c. 1450** Movable type for printing invented in Germany (by Johann Gutenberg?); books become more readily available; literacy gradually spreads **Leonardo da Vinci (1452–1519)** performs dissections of human cadavers; his experiments in hydraulics, mechanics, engineering, flight, and optics, recorded in coded manuscripts, address a dazzling range of intellectual and scientific problems	**1487–88** Bartholomew Diaz of Portugal rounds Cape of Good Hope and circumnavigates African continent **1490** First Latin edition of Galen's works on medicine published in Venice **1492** Columbus lands in the Bahamas **1497–1501** Voyages of Vasco da Gama and Pedro Cabral establish Portuguese dominance of trade with India, utilizing both Atlantic and Pacific sea passages

Timeline Three: 1350 to 1800

	1500–1525	1525–1550	1550–1575
HISTORY AND POLITICS	**Francis I of France (r. 1515–47),** a popular king. His rich and cultured court introduces Italian ideas and art to the North **1519–21** The Spaniard Hernán Cortés defeats Aztecs in Mexico; 1532, Francisco Pizarro conquers Peru **Charles V of Spain** elected Holy Roman Emperor (r. 1519–56); founder of Hapsburg Dynasty **Suleiman I, Turkish sultan (r. 1520–66),** raids the European continent, threatening Hungary, Austria, and Italy; begins a gradual Turkish conquest of the eastern Mediterranean islands over the next century **1524–25** Peasants' War in Germany, inspired by Martin Luther	**1527** Henry VIII of England, seeking a divorce from his first wife, Catherine of Aragon, breaks with the Catholic church; 1534, his Act of Supremacy establishes the Church of En-gland and confiscates Catholic church property **1527** Charles V of Spain sacks Rome, demoralizing the Italian states and signaling the end of Roman dominance **1533–84** Ivan the Terrible rules in Russia	**Wars of Lutheran against Catholic princes in Germany;** 1555, Peace of Augsburg lets each sovereign decide the religion of his subjects **1556** Philip II reigns in Spain; territories include lands in the Americas, Italy, France, and the Netherlands as well as the Iberian peninsula **Elizabeth I (r. 1558–1603)** succeeds to the English throne, fostering a period of prosperity, international trade, and exploration **1562–98** Henry IV's persecution of Protestants in France leads to religious wars **1568–1648** The Netherlands revolt against Spain; 1579, Union of Utrecht affirms the unification of the northern Netherlands; 1581, they declare independence from Spain **1571** Battle of Lepanto, off the Greek coast. Spanish and Venetian fleets defeat the Turks, beginning the decline of Turkish naval power
RELIGION	**1517** Martin Luther (1483–1546) posts "95 Theses," against Catholic practice of selling indulgences, on door of Wittenberg church, signaling the beginning of the Protestant Reformation	**1534** Ignatius of Loyola (1491–1556) founds Society of Jesus (Jesuits) **1541** John Calvin (1509–64) brings Reformation to the Swiss city of Geneva. His writings establish the rigorous Calvinist branch of Protestantism **1545** Pope Paul III (r. 1534–49), in response to the threat of Protestantism, calls the Council of Trent, the first major conference on church reform. Its tenets provide the basis for the Catholic Counter-Reformation, including a number of rules for artists depicting religious subjects. The council meets periodically until 1563	**1560** John Knox, Scottish minister, founds Presbyterian branch of Protestant church

MICHELANGELO
David, 1501–4

HIERONYMUS BOSCH
The Garden of Delights, center panel, c. 1510–15

PONTORMO
Deposition, c. 1526–28

TITIAN
Christ Crowned with Thorns, c. 1570

	1500–1525	1525–1550	1550–1575
MUSIC, LITERATURE, AND PHILOSOPHY	**Sir Thomas Wyatt (1503–42),** English poet and courtier under Henry VIII, translates Petrarch's sonnets and creates the English sonnet form **1516 Ludovico Ariosto (1474–1533),** Italian poet and diplomat, publishes *Orlando Furioso,* an epic poem	**1528** Baldassare Castiglione (1478–1529) writes *The Book of the Courtier* **1532** Niccolò Machiavelli (1469–1527) writes *The Prince,* examining Renaissance political practice and thought **1534** François Rabelais (1483–1553) authors the satires *Gargantua* and *Pantagruel* **1547** Henry Howard translates Vergil's *Aeneid* into English blank verse	**1550** Giorgio Vasari (1511–74), Italian painter, publishes *The Lives of the Artists* **Felix Lope de Vega (1562–1635),** Spanish poet and playwright **William Shakespeare (1564–1616),** English dramatist and poet **Ben Jonson (1572–1637),** English dramatist and poet; **John Donne (1573–1631),** English master of metaphysical poetry and prose
SCIENCE, TECHNOLOGY, AND EXPLORATION	**1501** Amerigo Vespucci, a Florentine navigator in the service of Portugal, explores coast of Brazil **1511** First road map of Europe **1513** The Spaniard Vasco Nuñez de Balboa crosses Panama and finds the Pacific Ocean **1516** Portuguese sailors reach China; 1543, Japan **1519–22** Ferdinand Magellan of Portugal circumnavigates the globe	**1543** Nicolaus Copernicus (1473–1543), Polish astronomer, publishes theory of the solar system in which the planets revolve around the sun; beginning of modern astronomy **1543** Andreas Vesalius (1514–64), court physician to Emperor Charles V, publishes first scientific study of human anatomy based on dissections	**1556** Georgius Agricola (1494–1555) publishes *De re metallica,* on metallurgy **1569** Gerhard Mercator (1512–94) designs correct projection of the earth onto a flat map for accurate navigation charts **c. 1572** Tycho Brahe (1546–1601), Danish astronomer, produces a catalogue of stars; Johannes Kepler (1571–1630), German astronomer, discovers the elliptical orbits of the planets

	1575–1600	1600–1625	1625–1650
HISTORY AND POLITICS	**1588** Spanish Armada, aiming to attack England, defeated by English navy	**1607** Colony of Jamestown, Virginia, first permanent settlement in North America, founded by English; 1620, Pilgrims arrive at Plymouth, in New England **1613** Romanov dynasty comes to power in Russia (deposed 1917) **1618–48** Thirty Years' War; much of Protestant Europe erupts in political and religious struggles against Catholic regimes	**1625** Charles I rules England. Disputes with Parliament and autocratic measures lead, in 1642, to Civil War; 1649, Charles beheaded, ending the war and founding the Commonwealth (1649–53) under Oliver Cromwell **1630–42** Large-scale emigration of English settlers to North American colonies: 16,000 arrive in Massachusetts **1639** Japanese enforce policy of isolation from all Europeans, except a token Dutch trading post **1648** Treaty of Westphalia ends Thirty Years' War; Spain acknowledges the sovereignty of the northern Netherlands
RELIGION			**Publications of Cornelius Jansenius (*Augustinus,* 1640)** lead to conflict with Jesuits. Preoccupied with internal strife, the papacy loses its dominant position in European politics

THE PROTESTANT REFORMATION The history of European Christianity before the Renaissance was punctuated by periodic movements to reform corrupt practices within the Catholic church. In the Middle Ages these were usually local and short-lived. But the fifteenth century saw the spread of literacy and education, growing economic power, a much-envied rise in the wealth of the papacy, and persistent quarrels between the pope and secular princes; these forces made criticism of the Church especially fierce. In 1517, the German cleric Martin Luther proclaimed his "95 Theses" condemning abuses of the Church and sparked a popular revolt, soon joined by rulers who saw the pope as a rival and who coveted the vast territories held by the papacy. The movement grew dramatically, especially in northern Europe. What had begun as a protest with mixed political, pious, and social aims developed into a detailed reformulation of the Christian religion itself; this restructuring is generally called Protestantism.

Protestantism focused on the relationship of the individual believer to God and was characterized by an austerity of taste that signified a rejection of the corrupt and worldly opulence of Rome. Use of images in churches was strictly prohibited. Renaissance taste for the personal, the contemporary, and the material was to some degree a product of Protestant culture, which patronized secular arts. For this new market, artists began to create small images for personal use. A new vocabulary of subject matter developed: landscape, still life, and scenes of daily life. In the North such paintings were sold directly to the public in a free-market system, rather than solely by patronage or commission.

ARTEMISIA GENTILESCHI
Judith and Maidservant with the Head of Holofernes, c. 1625

JACQUES CALLOT
Detail of *Hangman's Tree,* from *Great Miseries of War,* 1633

	1575–1600	1600–1625	1625–1650
MUSIC, LITERATURE, AND PHILOSOPHY	**1588** St. Theresa of Avila writes *Interior Castle,* a visionary text; Michel de Montaigne, French thinker, writes *Essays* **1590** Edmund Spenser, English poet, publishes *The Faerie Queene*	**1604** Carel van Mander publishes biographical history of Dutch and Flemish painting **1605** Miguel de Cervantes Saavedra (1547–1616) writes *Don Quixote* **1607** Claudio Monteverdi's *Orpheus* is performed in Mantua, one of the first operas **Baruch Spinoza (1632–77),** Dutch philosopher	**Molière (1622–73)** and **Jean Racine (1639–99),** French playwrights **1636** Pierre Corneille (1606–84), French dramatist, writes *Le Cid* **1637** René Descartes (1596–1650), French philosopher and scientist, writes *Discourse on Method* **1649** Francisco Pacheco (1564–1654), Spanish historian, publishes *The Art of Painting*
SCIENCE, TECHNOLOGY, AND EXPLORATION	**c. 1575** Potatoes, maize, tobacco, cocoa, coffee imported from the Americas to Europe **1578** Li Shih-chen, Chinese physician, publishes an illustrated compendium of medicines **1582** Pope Gregory XIII reforms the calendar, aligning it more accurately with astronomy; in order to do so, he decrees that Thursday, October 4, be followed by Friday, October 15	**c. 1600** Invention of the telescope and microscope, based on new lens-grinding techniques developed in Holland **1610** Galileo Galilei (1564–1642), in Italy, first uses the telescope to view the stars and planets; his conclusions support the Copernican system and are banned by the Catholic church in 1633	**1628** William Harvey, English physician (1575–1657), describes the circulation of blood **1636** Founding of Harvard College, Boston **1642** Blaise Pascal (1623–62) invents first adding machine **Antonio Stradivari (1644–1737),** Italian designer of fine stringed instruments **1648** Royal Academy of Painting and Sculpture founded in Paris

Timeline Three: 1350 to 1800

	1650–1675	1675–1700	1700–1725
HISTORY AND POLITICS	**1652–54** Naval and mercantile competition between English and Dutch leads to war **1659** Louis XIV of France marries Maria Teresa, daughter of Philip IV of Spain; 1661, establishes autocratic regime (r. 1661–1715) with his influential adviser Jean-Baptiste Colbert **1660** Parliament proclaims Charles II king, restoring English monarchy **1666** Great Fire in London destroys more than 450 acres of the city **1672–78** France and England wage war against the Netherlands. William III of Orange beats back invasion of French forces	**1679** English Parliament passes Habeas Corpus Act, which sets foundation for fair judicial procedure and prisoners' rights **1685** Louis XIV revokes Edict of Nantes (1598), which had granted Protestants some religious freedom. Mass emigration of educated Protestants ensues, a blow to French industry and commerce. In England, James II, a Catholic, succeeds to the throne and attempts to restore Catholicism **1688** The so-called Glorious Revolution in England: James II flees; Parliament passes Declaration of Rights, limiting the power of the monarchy **1689** Protestants William III of Orange and Mary rule England; new laws protect freedom of religion, establish annual parliaments, and guarantee individual liberty **Peter the Great (r. 1689–1725)** rules Russia, with a program of westernization **1692** Witchcraft trials in Salem, Massachusetts	**1701** Frederick III crowns himself king of Prussia. Prussia gains international power through military strength **1702–13** War of Spanish Succession: extinction of the Hapsburg line in Spain leads to war among major European powers. At conclusion, Philip of Anjou, grandson of Louis XIV, takes the Spanish throne as Philip V; beginning of Bourbon rule in Spain **1704** Defeat of French at Blenheim by English and allies, led by John Churchill, Duke of Marlborough **1707** Union of England and Scotland as the United Kingdom of Great Britain **Louis XV (r. 1715–74)**, king of France, consolidates absolute power of the monarchy
RELIGION	**c. 1667** Russian church changes liturgy and ritual to conform to Greek practice. Secession from the church of the conservative "Old Believers" **1668** Society of Friends (Quakers) officially established in England	**1682** Louis XIV's Four Articles are adopted in France, placing secular power over religious authority. Vehemently opposed by Pope Innocent XI (r. 1676–89)	**John Wesley (1703–91)**, with his brother, Charles, founds the Methodist branch of Protestantism in England **1721** Peter the Great reforms Russian church government

DIEGO VELÁZQUEZ
The Maids of Honor, 1656

FRANS HALS
The Women Regents of the Old Men's Home at Haarlem, 1664

BARTOLOMÉ ESTEBAN MURILLO
Virgin and Child, c. 1675–80

SIR CHRISTOPHER WREN
Facade of St. Paul's Cathedral, London, 1675–1710

RACHEL RUYSCH
Flower Still Life, after 1700

	1650–1675	1675–1700	1700–1725
MUSIC, LITERATURE, AND PHILOSOPHY	**1667** John Milton (1608–74), English poet, writes *Paradise Lost* **Joseph Addison (1672–1719)**, English essayist, editor with the writer and statesman **Sir Richard Steele (1672–1729)** of the *Spectator,* a literary and satirical periodical **1672** Giovanni Pietro Bellori (1613–96), Italian commentator on Baroque art, publishes *Lives of the Modern Painters*	**John Locke (1632–1704)**, founder of English school of empirical philosophy **Baroque composers:** Alessandro Scarlatti (1659–1725) and Antonio Vivaldi (1678–1741), Italian; Johann Sebastian Bach (1685–1750) and George Frideric Handel (1685–1759), German **François-Marie Voltaire (1694–1778)**, French critical writer	**1711** Alexander Pope (1688–1744), English poet, writes *The Rape of the Lock* **David Hume (1711–76)**, Scottish philosopher **Jean-Jacques Rousseau (1712–78)**, French philosopher and novelist **Denis Diderot (1713–84)**, editor of first *Encyclopedia,* in France **Johann Joachim Winckelmann (1717–68)**, German art theorist and antiquarian
SCIENCE, TECHNOLOGY, AND EXPLORATION	**1662** Royal Society of London founded by Charles II, a forum for scientific activity for two centuries; 1662, Boyle's Law describes the properties of gas pressure **1663** Charles Lebrun, at Royal Academy in Paris, institutes strict guidelines for art **1665** In England Robert Hooke publishes his discovery of cells and microorganisms **1673** Pendulum clock invented by the Dutchman Christiaan Huygens	**1687** Isaac Newton (1642–1727) publishes theory of the laws of motion, including the principle of gravity, in England; 1704, his *Optics* investigates the nature and behavior of light **1698** Steam engine invented in England by Thomas Savery	**1705** Edmund Halley (1656–1742), in England, discovers similarities in the paths of comets **Benjamin Franklin (1706–90)**, American statesman and inventor, invents bifocal lens, lightning rod, and Franklin stove and publishes observations on electricity in Philadelphia **1717** Temperature gradation system proposed by Gabriel Fahrenheit in Holland

	1725–1750	1750–1775	1775–1800
HISTORY AND POLITICS		**1756–66** Seven Years' War: England and Prussia fight Austria and France on land and sea and throughout the colonies; called the French and Indian Wars in North America; 1759, French defeated at Quebec **Catherine the Great (r. 1762–96)** increases the power, territory, and influence of Russia	**1775–83** American Revolution: 1776, Declaration of Independence; 1787–88, United States Constitution ratified **1789** French Revolution begins. Declaration of a National Assembly dedicated to producing a constitution. Mobs storm Bastille prison and riot in Paris; 1792, French monarchy is abolished; 1793, Louis XVI is beheaded. European states declare war against the French Republic, whose radical ideas are feared to encourage unrest **1793–95** Reign of Terror in France, dominated by Maximilien Robespierre, with as many as 350 executions per month **1793–95** Partition of Poland by Russia, Prussia, and Austria completely erases the country **1796–97** Napoleon Bonaparte's Italian campaign conquers most of Italy; after his Egyptian campaign (1798–99), his reputation as soldier and diplomat is established; 1799, he controls France
RELIGION			**1793** French government, under Robespierre, outlaws the worship of God; Cult of Reason established **1798** Napoleon abolishes papal rule and establishes a French-dominated Roman Republic in the Papal States
MUSIC, LITERATURE, AND PHILOSOPHY	**1726** Jonathan Swift (1667–1745), Irish political satirist, writes *Gulliver's Travels*	**1755** Samuel Johnson (1709–84) compiles a *Dictionary of the English Language* **Wolfgang Amadeus Mozart (1756–91)**, innovative Austrian composer of symphonies, operas, and church music **1774** Johann von Goethe (1749–1832) publishes *The Sorrows of Young Werther* in Germany, extolling naturalism and sentimentality; it inspires numerous suicides	**1776** Adam Smith (1723–90), Scottish economist, writes *The Wealth of Nations* **1781** Immanuel Kant (1724–1804), German critical philosopher, writes the *Critique of Pure Reason* **1792** Mary Wollstonecraft (1759–1836) writes *Vindication of the Rights of Women,* first English feminist treatise
SCIENCE, TECHNOLOGY, AND EXPLORATION	**1744** Geographical survey of France begun, the first such topographical survey **1745** Discovery of Pompeii and Herculaneum **1749** George Leclerc (1707–88) writes a treatise on natural history in England	**1753** Carl Linnaeus, Swedish botanist (1707–78), writes the *Species Plantarum,* the definitive modern classification system for plants **1764** Invention of the spinning jenny and cotton gin (1793) hastens mechanization of textile production **1768–79** Captain James Cook (1728–79) explores the islands of the Pacific **1774** Joseph Priestly (1733–1804), English chemist, isolates oxygen	**1783** First flight in a hot-air balloon, France **1789** Antoine Lavoisier (1743–94) publishes his systematic study of chemistry in France **1790–1801** Revolutionary government of France institutes metric system **1798** Edward Jenner (1749–1823) demonstrates first vaccination against smallpox **1798** Alois Senefelder (1771–1834), Hungarian inventor, develops lithography

THE ENLIGHTENMENT The European eighteenth century was a time of colonial expansion and development of new methods in industry, farming, financial markets, and government. Constitutions and parliamentary systems weakened monarchs and the church and offered the vote to broader populations. English parliamentary monarchy, American representative democracy, and the various forms of the French government after the Revolution were all attempts to remake the political system more inclusively, while radical discoveries in the sciences and technology encouraged a new definition of society itself. Thinkers such as Rousseau, Hume, Voltaire, Diderot, Kant, and Swift sought to use reason and scientific method in their inquiries and took experience as the measure of knowledge. Coupled with this skeptical, modernist attitude was a taste for sentimentality and idealism, expressed as a commitment to the perfectibility of humanity. This led, in public life, to reforms in education, medicine, taxation, and religious tolerance, as well as movements to abolish slavery. The Neoclassical and Romantic movements in art are both a reflection of and reaction to this impulse.

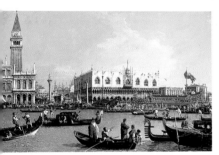

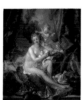

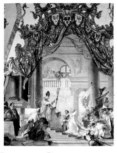

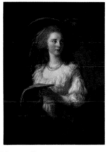

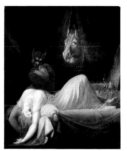

CANALETTO
The Bucintoro at the Molo, c. 1732

FRANÇOIS BOUCHER
The Toilet of Venus, 1751

GIOVANNI BATTISTA TIEPOLO
The Marriage of Frederick Barbarossa, 1752

MARIE-LOUISE-ELISABETH VIGÉE-LEBRUN
The Duchesse de Polignac, 1783

(LEFT) JOHN HENRY FUSELI
The Nightmare, c. 1790
(RIGHT) FRANCISCO GOYA, *The Sleep of Reason Produces Monsters,* from *Los Caprichos,* c. 1798

PART FOUR

The Modern World

Art history, according to the classical model of Johann Winckelmann, unfolds in an orderly progression in which one phase follows another as inevitably as night follows day. In addition, the concept of period style implies that the arts march in lockstep, sharing the same characteristics and developing according to the same inner necessity. The thoughtful reader will already suspect, however, that any attempt to synthesize the history of art and place it into a broader context must mask a welter of facts that do not conform to such a systematic model and may, indeed, call it into question. So far as the art of the distant past is concerned, we may have little choice but to see it in larger terms, since so many facts have been erased that we cannot possibly hope to reconstruct a full and accurate historical record. Hence it is arguably the case that any reading is an artificial construct inherently open to question. As we approach the art of our times, these become more than theoretical issues. They take on a new urgency as we try, perhaps vainly, to understand modern civilization and how it came to be this way.

It is suggestive of the difficulties facing the historian that the period which began 250 years ago has not acquired a name of its own. Maybe this does not strike us as peculiar at first. We are, after all, still in its midst. Considering how promptly the Renaissance coined a name for itself, however, we may well wonder why no key concept comparable to the "rebirth of antiquity" has yet emerged. It is tempting to call this "The Age of Revolution," for it has been characterized by rapid and violent change. It began with revolutions of two kinds: the Industrial Revolution, symbolized by the invention of the steam engine; and a political revolution, under the banner of democracy, inaugurated in America and France.

Both of these revolutions are still going on. Industrialization and democracy are sought over much of the world. Western science and Western political thought (and, in their wake, all the other products of modern civilization: food, dress, art, music, literature) will eventually belong to all peoples, although they have been challenged by other ideologies that command allegiance—nationalism, religion, even tribalism. Industrialization and democracy are so closely linked today that we tend to think of them as different aspects of one process, with effects more far-reaching than any basic shift since the Neolithic Revolution 10,000 years ago. Still, the twin revolutions are not the same. Indeed, we cannot discern a common impulse behind these developments, despite attempts to relate them to the rise of capitalism. The more we try to explain their relationship and trace their historic roots, the more paradoxical they seem. Both are founded on the idea of progress. But whereas progress in science and technology during the past two centuries has been more or less continuous and measurable, we can hardly make this claim for our pursuit of happiness, however we choose to define it. Here, then, is a fundamental conflict that continues to this very day.

If we nevertheless accept "The Age of Revolution" as a convenient name for the era as a whole, we must still make a distinction for the twentieth century. For lack of a better word, we shall call it *modernity.* It is a problematic term, *modernity*. What is it? When did it begin? These questions are not unlike those posed by the Renaissance, and so perhaps is the answer. No matter how many different opinions there may be about the nature of the beast—and scholars remain deeply divided over the issues—the modern era clearly began when people acquired "modern consciousness." Around 1900, men and women in the Western world became aware that the character of the new age in which they were living was defined by the machine, which brought with it a different sense of time and space, as well as the promise of a new kind of humanity and society.

It is difficult for us to appreciate from our vantage point just how radical the technological revolution seemed to people of the time, for it has since become commonplace and has been outstripped by even more far-reaching changes. The advances that took place in science, mathematics, engineering, and psychology during the 1880s and 1890s laid the foundation for the Machine Age. The diesel and turbine engines, electric motor, tire, automobile, light bulb, phonograph, radio, box camera: all these were invented before 1900, and the airplane shortly thereafter. They forever transformed the quality of life—its very feel—but it was not until these changes reached a "critical mass" in the opening years of this century that their sweeping magnitude was fully realized. Of course, this was by no means the first time that people have felt modern, which simply means contemporary. Yet modern consciousness has been so fundamental to our identity that we can hardly hope to understand civilization for the past 100 years without it.

The word *modern* has its origins in the early medieval *modernus,* meaning that which is present, of our time, and, by extension, new or novel. In contrast *antiquity* lacked a comparable expression, even though the word *modern* derives ultimately from the Latin *modo* (now). As this odd fact suggests, modernity is based on the Christian view of history as a break in time (before and after Christ), instead of the concept of recurring cycles that had prevailed in Greece and Rome. It is to Petrarch that we owe the idea of history as a succession of periods, which he separated into eras of light, dark, and rebirth. For him, history was linear and progressive, permitting humanity to play an active part in shaping its outcome. Petrarch's veneration for antiquity was indebted partly to Bernard of Chartres, who in the early twelfth century argued that we are puny dwarfs who see farther than our predecessors because we are standing on the shoulders of giants. However, such a position did not allow the authority of the past, no matter how great, to go unchallenged. The end of the twelfth century witnessed the first dispute between disciples of ancient versus modern poetry; ever since, literature and criticism have taken the lead in framing the central issues of modernity. The controversy was revived in late-seventeenth-century France by Charles Perrault as the Quarrel of Ancients and Moderns (satirized by the English writer Jonathan Swift in *The Battle of the Books*). Throughout the debate, *modern* generally held negative connotations, for it was taken as the opposite of *classic,* whose original antonym in Latin was "vulgar." Yet not even the most conservative voices recommended the slavish imitation of antiquity. Moreover, the moderns saw themselves as adhering to eternal values even more faithfully than had the ancients themselves! As Christians, they held the advantage over the ancients on another count as well, since religious truth was deemed superior to scientific truth or aesthetic beauty, the only area where the pagans had excelled.

The nineteenth century gave birth to two conflicting views of modernity that have continued to compete with each other to this day: one based on scientific and material progress, which arose out of the Enlightenment, with its belief in reason and freedom, and that is identified with the middle class; and a radical alternative regarding the bourgeoisie as the enemy of culture—in a word, philistines. Although its roots lie in eighteenth-century German thought, the second of these is a peculiarly Romantic notion first formulated by the French writer Stendhal (Marie-Henri Beyle). Not only did he relate modernity specifically to Romanticism as a reaction against classicism, he regarded the Romantic as a warrior in the service of modernity. But why should modernity need such a warrior in the first place? Because the times were slow to accept the new, which could therefore only be validated by the future, not the present. We will recognize in Stendhal's warrior the forerunner of the avant-garde.

It was, nevertheless, Charles Baudelaire who gave modernity its current meaning. "Modernity," he wrote, "is the transitory, the fugitive, the contingent, the half of art, of which the other half is the eternal and the immutable." And "since all centuries and all peoples have had their own form of beauty, so inevitably we have ours. The particular element in each manifestation comes from the emotions; and just as we have our own particular emotions, so we have our own beauty." Perceptively, he located the source of that beauty in urban existence: "The life of our city is rich in poetic and marvelous subjects. We are enveloped and steeped as though in an atmosphere of the marvelous; but we do not notice it." In this he relied partly on his fellow critic Théophile Gautier, who said that modern beauty is based on accepting modern civilization as it is. To do so, however, artists must go against tradition and rely on their own imaginations, which requires taking enormous risks.

Baudelaire had the distinction of being the first to use mechanical metaphors for beauty in place of the organic ones favored by the Romantics. He further denounced the material progress of modern civilization, thereby helping to create the schism between modernity and modernism. What is the difference between them? Paradoxically, modernism looks to the future, whereas modernity is concerned with the present, which can stand in the way of progress. To artists, modernism is a trumpet call that both asserts their freedom to create in a new style and provides them with the mission to define the meaning of their times—and even to reshape society through their art. To be sure, artists have always responded to the changing world around them, but rarely have they risen to the challenge as they have under the banner of modernism, or with so fervent a sense of personal cause.

This is a role for which the "avant-garde" (literally, vanguard) is hardly sufficient. Although both arose as part of the decadent movement toward the end of the nineteenth century, the term *avant-garde,* like *modernism,* has a long history reaching back to the Middle Ages. The term originated in French warfare and was first applied to the arts in the sixteenth century but began to acquire its modern definition only under the Romantics. The Socialist reformer Comte de Saint-Simon included artists with scientists and industrialists in the elite group that would rule the ideal state, because as people of imagination they can foresee the future and therefore help to create it. As Baudelaire realized, however, there is an inherent contradiction between Romantic individualism and the discipline necessary for political action. Although its scope was subsequently limited mainly to culture, the avant-garde has sometimes played an active part in politics. Despite the fact that they are closely linked, the avant-garde is by no means synonymous with—and is even antithetical to—modernism. We shall find that the two have held very different meanings for different artists—and produced surprisingly different results in each of the visual arts. Both run counter to their times. But whereas modernism remains dedicated to a utopian vision of the future that stems from the Enlightenment, the avant-garde is bent solely on the destruction of bourgeois modernity. Judged by this standard, few of the twentieth-century's leading artists have been members of a self-styled avant-garde.

Today, having cast off the framework of traditional authority which confined and sustained us before, we can act with a latitude both frightening and exhilarating. The consequences of this freedom to question all values are everywhere around us. Our knowledge about ourselves is now vastly greater, but this has not reassured us as we had hoped. In a world without fixed reference points, we search constantly for our own identity and for the meaning of human existence, individual and collective.

Because modern civilization lacks the cohesiveness of the past, it no longer proceeds by readily identifiable periods; nor are there clear period styles to be discerned in art or in any other form of culture. Instead, we find a continuity of another kind: movements and countermovements. Spreading like waves, these "isms" defy national, ethnic, and chronological boundaries. Never dominant anywhere for long, they compete or merge with one another in endlessly shifting patterns. Hence our account of modern art is guided more by movements than by countries. Only in this way can we hope to do justice to the fact that modern art, all regional differences notwithstanding, is as international as modern science.

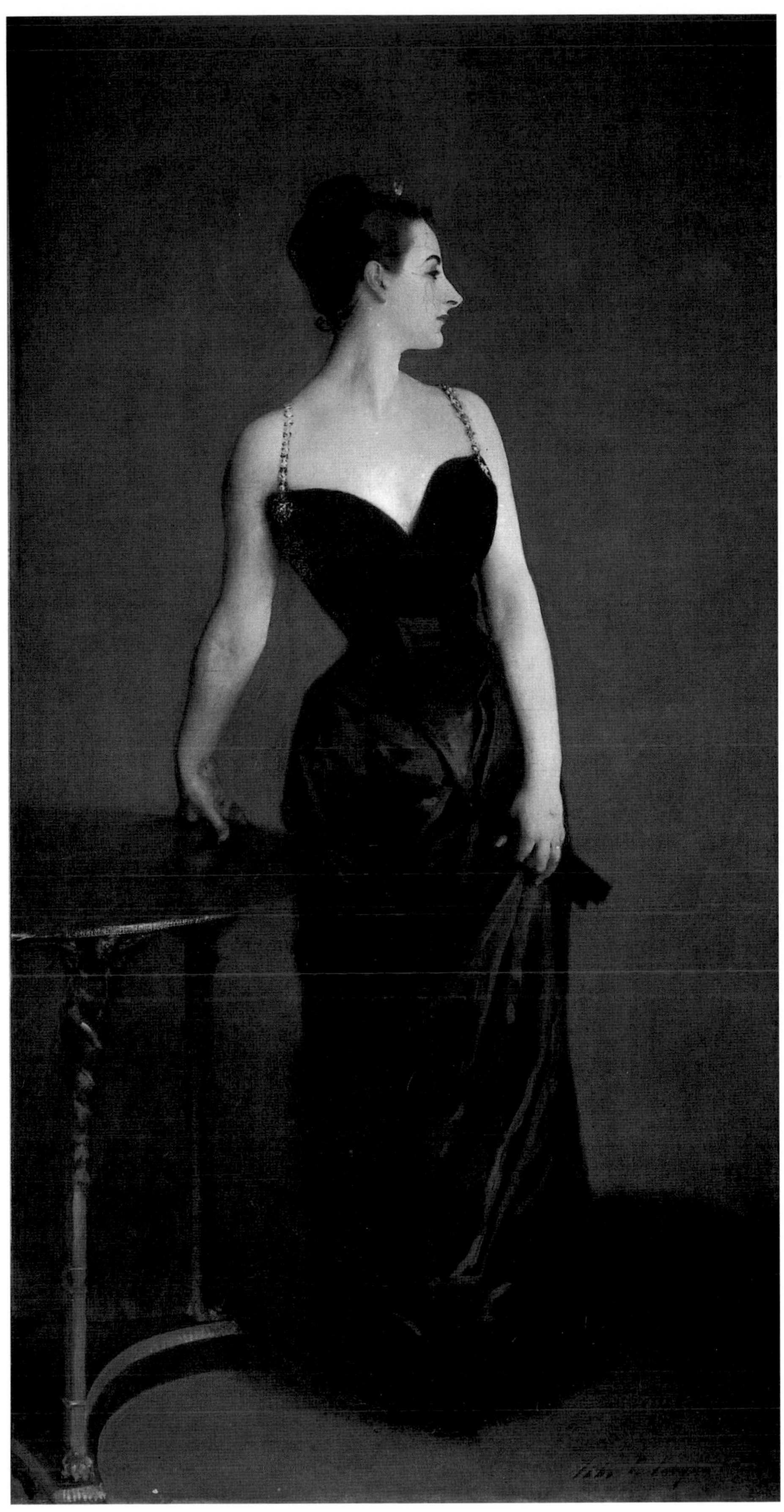

John Singer Sargent. *Madame X (Madame Pierre Gautreau)*. 1884. Oil on canvas, 82⅛ x 43¼" (208.6 x 109.9 cm). The Metropolitan Museum of Art, New York

A.H. HEARN FUND, 1916

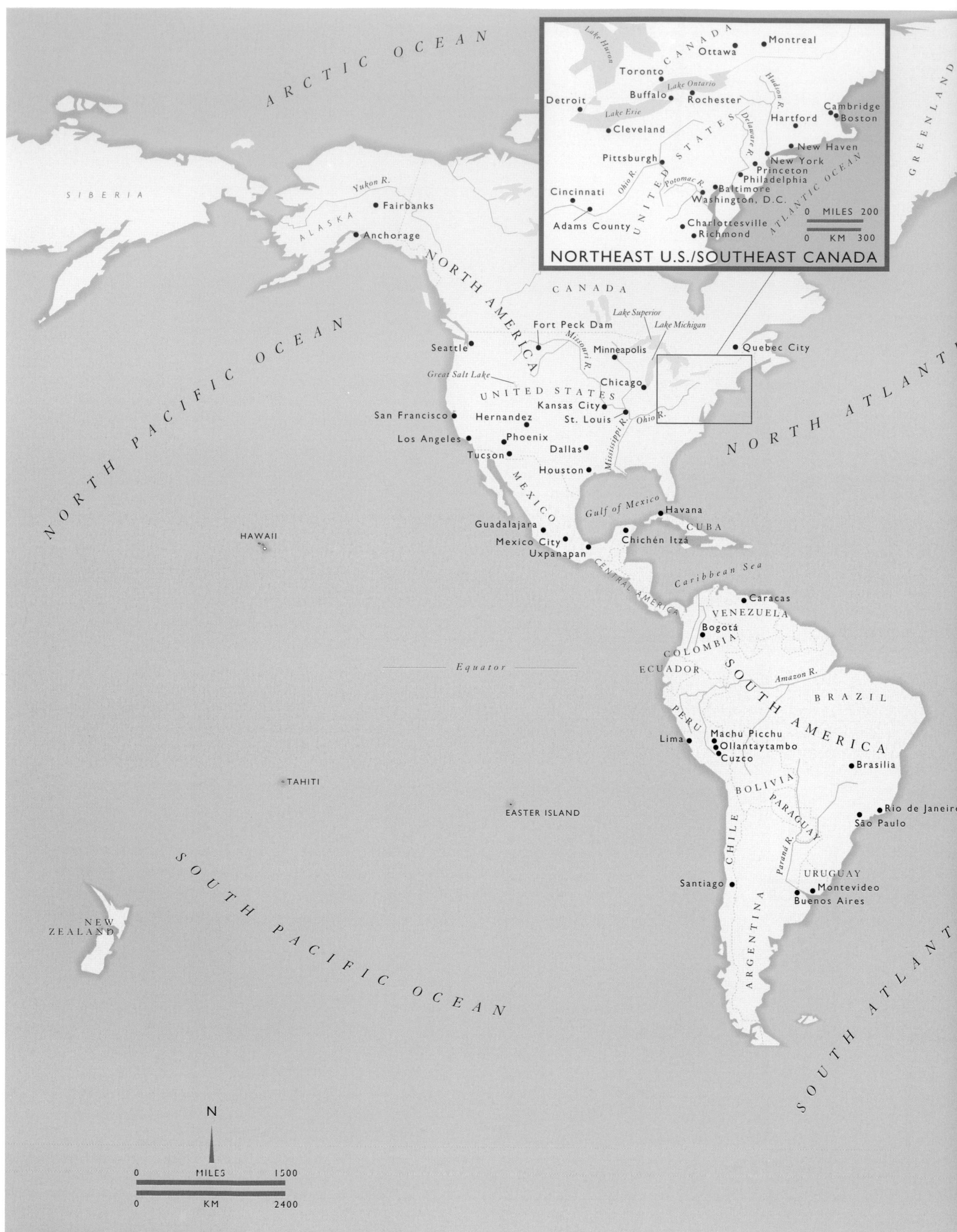
ARCTIC OCEAN
SIBERIA
ALASKA
Yukon R.
Fairbanks
Anchorage
NORTH AMERICA
CANADA
Lake Superior
Lake Michigan
Fort Peck Dam
Missouri R.
Seattle
Minneapolis
Quebec City
Great Salt Lake
Chicago
UNITED STATES
Kansas City
St. Louis
Ohio R.
Mississippi R.
San Francisco
Hernandez
Los Angeles
Phoenix
Tucson
Dallas
Houston
MEXICO
Gulf of Mexico
Havana
CUBA
Guadalajara
Mexico City
Uxpanapan
Chichén Itzá
CENTRAL AMERICA
Caribbean Sea
Caracas
VENEZUELA
Bogotá
COLOMBIA
ECUADOR
Equator
SOUTH AMERICA
Amazon R.
BRAZIL
PERU
Lima
Machu Picchu
Ollantaytambo
Cuzco
Brasilia
BOLIVIA
PARAGUAY
Rio de Janeiro
São Paulo
CHILE
Paraná R.
URUGUAY
Santiago
Montevideo
Buenos Aires
ARGENTINA
NORTH PACIFIC OCEAN
HAWAII
TAHITI
EASTER ISLAND
SOUTH PACIFIC OCEAN
NEW ZEALAND
NORTH ATLANTI
SOUTH ATLANT
GREENLAND
Lake Huron
CANADA
Ottawa
Montreal
Toronto
Lake Ontario
Hudson R.
Buffalo
Rochester
Detroit
Lake Erie
Cambridge
Boston
Hartford
Cleveland
Delaware R.
New Haven
Pittsburgh
New York
Princeton
Philadelphia
UNITED STATES
Ohio R.
Potomac R.
Baltimore
Cincinnati
Washington, D.C.
ATLANTIC OCEAN
Adams County
Charlottesville
Richmond
0 MILES 200
0 KM 300
NORTHEAST U.S./SOUTHEAST CANADA
N
0 MILES 1500
0 KM 2400

THE MODERN WORLD

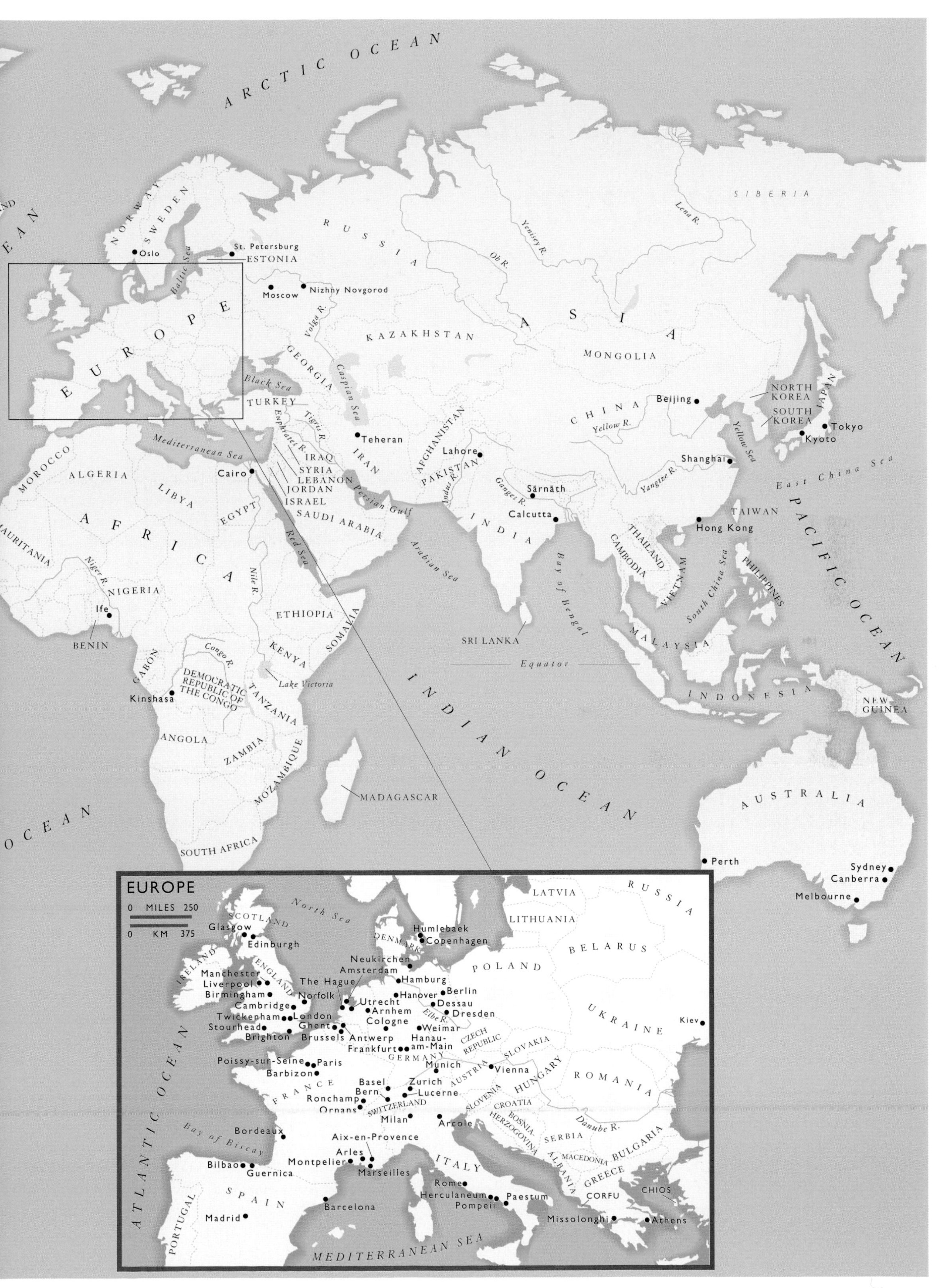

ARCTIC OCEAN
EUROPE
ASIA
AFRICA
INDIAN OCEAN
PACIFIC OCEAN
AUSTRALIA
RUSSIA
SIBERIA
NORWAY
SWEDEN
Oslo
St. Petersburg
ESTONIA
Baltic Sea
Moscow
Nizhny Novgorod
Volga R.
Ob R.
Yenisey R.
Lena R.
KAZAKHSTAN
MONGOLIA
GEORGIA
Caspian Sea
Black Sea
TURKEY
Tigris R.
Euphrates R.
IRAQ
SYRIA
LEBANON
JORDAN
ISRAEL
Teheran
IRAN
AFGHANISTAN
PAKISTAN
Lahore
Indus R.
Ganges R.
Sārnāth
Calcutta
INDIA
CHINA
Yellow R.
Beijing
NORTH KOREA
SOUTH KOREA
JAPAN
Tokyo
Kyoto
Yellow Sea
Shanghai
Yangtze R.
East China Sea
TAIWAN
Hong Kong
THAILAND
CAMBODIA
VIETNAM
South China Sea
PHILIPPINES
MALAYSIA
INDONESIA
NEW GUINEA
Equator
SRI LANKA
Bay of Bengal
Arabian Sea
Persian Gulf
SAUDI ARABIA
Red Sea
Mediterranean Sea
Cairo
EGYPT
LIBYA
ALGERIA
MOROCCO
MAURITANIA
Niger R.
NIGERIA
Ife
BENIN
Nile R.
ETHIOPIA
SOMALIA
KENYA
Congo R.
Lake Victoria
GABON
DEMOCRATIC REPUBLIC OF THE CONGO
Kinshasa
TANZANIA
ANGOLA
ZAMBIA
MOZAMBIQUE
MADAGASCAR
SOUTH AFRICA
OCEAN
Perth
Sydney
Canberra
Melbourne
EUROPE
0 MILES 250
0 KM 375
North Sea
SCOTLAND
Glasgow
Edinburgh
IRELAND
ENGLAND
Manchester
Liverpool
Birmingham
Norfolk
Cambridge
Twickenham
London
Stourhead
Brighton
DENMARK
Humlebaek
Copenhagen
Neukirchen
Amsterdam
Hamburg
The Hague
Utrecht
Hanover
Berlin
Dessau
Arnhem
Elbe R.
Dresden
Cologne
Ghent
Weimar
Brussels
Antwerp
Hanau-am-Main
Frankfurt
GERMANY
CZECH REPUBLIC
SLOVAKIA
LATVIA
LITHUANIA
BELARUS
POLAND
UKRAINE
Kiev
Poissy-sur-Seine
Paris
Barbizon
FRANCE
Basel
Bern
Zurich
Lucerne
Munich
AUSTRIA
Vienna
HUNGARY
ROMANIA
Ronchamp
Ornans
SWITZERLAND
SLOVENIA
CROATIA
BOSNIA HERZEGOVINA
SERBIA
Danube R.
Milan
Arcole
Bay of Biscay
Bordeaux
Aix-en-Provence
Arles
Montpelier
Marseilles
ITALY
MACEDONIA
BULGARIA
ALBANIA
GREECE
Bilbao
Guernica
SPAIN
Barcelona
Rome
Herculaneum
Paestum
Pompeii
CORFU
CHIOS
Missolonghi
Athens
Madrid
PORTUGAL
ATLANTIC OCEAN
MEDITERRANEAN SEA

CHAPTER TWENTY-ONE

Neoclassicism and Romanticism

The history of the two movements to be dealt with in this chapter covers roughly a century, from about 1750 to 1850. Paradoxically, Neoclassicism has been seen as the opposite of Romanticism on the one hand and as no more than one aspect of it on the other. The problem is that the two terms are not directly comparable. Neoclassicism was a new revival of Classical antiquity, although one that was not necessarily more consistent than earlier classicisms. Moreover, it was linked, at least initially, to Enlightenment thought. Romanticism, in contrast, refers not to a specific style but to an attitude of mind that manifested itself in a number of ways, including classicism. Romanticism, therefore, is a far broader concept and thus harder to define. To complicate matters further, the Neoclassicists and early Romantics were exact contemporaries, who in turn overlapped the preceding generation of Rococo artists. David and Goya, for example, were born within a few years of each other. And in England the leading representatives of the Rococo, Neoclassicism, and Romanticism—Reynolds, West, and Fuseli—shared many of the same ideas; nor were they always separated by clear differences in style or approach. Finally, Romanticism lasted far longer in sculpture and architecture than it did in painting: it persisted well into the era of Realism and Impressionism, with remnants lingering as late as 1900.

NEOCLASSICISM

The Enlightenment

The modern era was born during the American Revolution of 1776 and the French Revolution of 1789. These political upheavals were preceded by a revolution of the mind that had begun half a century earlier. Its standard-bearers were those thinkers of the Enlightenment in England, France, and Germany—David Hume, Voltaire, Jean-Jacques Rousseau, and Heinrich Heine, to name only the most important—who proclaimed that all human affairs ought to be ruled by reason and the common good, rather than by tradition and established authority. In the arts, as in economics, politics, and religion, this rationalist movement turned against the prevailing practice, the ornate and aristocratic Rococo. In the mid-eighteenth century, there was a widespread call for a return to reason, nature, and morality in art. Because they eluded precise definition, such terms proved highly problematic. Nevertheless, this demand in effect meant a return to the ancients. After all, had not the classical philosophers been the original "apostles of reason"? The first to formulate this view was Johann Joachim Winckelmann, the German art historian and theorist who popularized the concept of the "noble simplicity and calm grandeur" of Greek art (in *Thoughts on the Imitation of Greek Works . . . ,* published in 1755). [See Primary Sources, no. 62, page 926.] His ideas deeply impressed two painters then living in Rome, the German Anton Raphael Mengs (1728–1779) and the Scotsman Gavin Hamilton (1723–1798). Both had strong antiquarian leanings but otherwise limited artistic ability. This shortcoming may explain why they accepted Winckelmann's doctrine so readily. Mengs' importance lies principally in his role as a proselytizer of the "Winckelmann program," since most of his paintings are weak paraphrases of Italian art. He left Rome in 1761 after painting his major work, a ceiling fresco of Parnassus inspired by Raphael, and went to Spain, where he vied with the aging Tiepolo (see page 608).

It is a measure of Italy's decline that artistic leadership passed to the Northerners who gathered in Rome. The only Roman painter who could compete on even terms with the foreigners was Pompeo Batoni (1708–1787), a splendid technician who continued the eclectic classicism of Carlo Maratta (see page 540) but is remembered today chiefly for portraits of his English patrons. This vacuum helps to account for the astonishing success of Mengs and Hamilton. Toward the end of Batoni's career the Italian school was eclipsed once and for all by the French Academy in Rome under Joseph Marie Vien (1716–1809), its head from 1775 to 1781. To French artists, a return to the classics meant, of course, the style of Poussin and the "academic" theory of Lebrun, com-

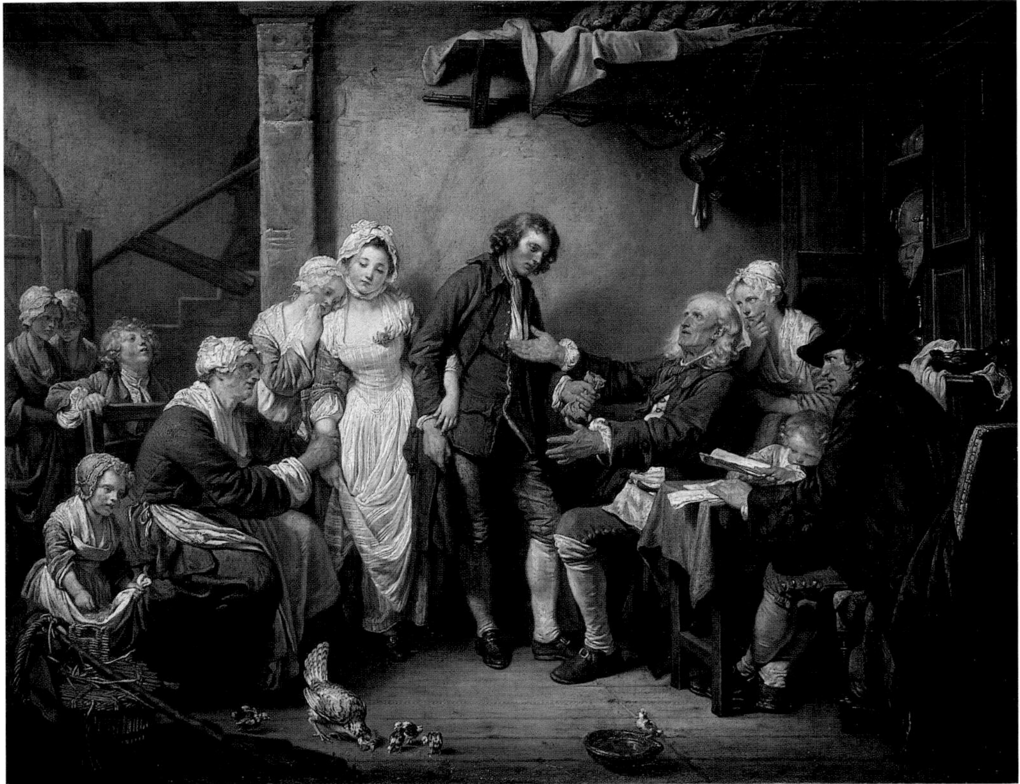

21-1. Jean-Baptiste Greuze. *The Village Bride.* 1761. Oil on canvas, 36 x 46½" (91.4 x 118.1 cm). Musée du Louvre, Paris

bined with a maximum of archaeological detail from newly discovered ancient sculpture and the excavations of Pompeii. Vien himself was a minor artist who reduced history painting to genre scenes of ancient life, but he was a gifted teacher. It was his pupils who would establish French painting as the self-proclaimed guardian of the great tradition of Western art.

PAINTING

France

GREUZE. In France, the anti-Rococo trend in painting was at first a matter of content rather than style, which accounts for the sudden fame around 1760 of Jean-Baptiste Greuze (1725–1805). *The Village Bride* (fig. 21-1), like his other paintings of those years, is a scene of lower-class family life. What distinguishes it from earlier genre paintings (compare fig. 18-27) is its contrived, stagelike character, borrowed from Hogarth's "dumb show" narratives (see figs. 20-11 and 20-12). But Greuze had neither wit nor satire. His pictorial sermon illustrates the social gospel of Jean-Jacques Rousseau that the poor, in contrast to the immoral aristocracy, are full of "natural" virtue and honest sentiment. Everything is intended to remind us of this point, from the theatrical gestures and expressions of the actors to the smallest detail: one of the chicks gathered around the hen in the foreground has left the brood and sits alone on a saucer, like the bride who is about to leave her own "brood." *The Village Bride* was acclaimed a masterpiece. The loudest praise came from Denis Diderot, that apostle of Reason and Nature. Here at last was a painter with a social mission who appealed to the viewer's moral sense, instead of merely giving pleasure like the frivolous artists of the Rococo! In his first flush of enthusiasm, Diderot accepted the narrative of Greuze's pictures as "noble and serious human action" in Poussin's sense. [See Primary Sources, no. 63, page 926.] Diderot's extravagant praise of Greuze is understandable. *The Village Bride* is a pictorial counterpart to Diderot's own melodramas (see box page 651).

DAVID. Greuze was less successful at painting historical subjects, and Diderot modified his views later, when a far more gifted and rigorous "Neo-Poussinist" appeared on the scene: Jacques-Louis David (1748–1825). A disciple of Vien, David had developed his Neoclassical style in Rome during the years 1775 to 1781. Upon his return to France, he quickly established himself as the leading Neoclassical painter. He overshadowed all others by far, so that our conception of the movement is largely based on his work. In *The Death of Socrates* (fig. 21-2) of 1787, David seems more "Poussiniste" than Poussin himself (compare fig. 19-5). The composition unfolds parallel to the picture plane like a relief, and the figures are as solid and immobile as statues. David has added one unexpected element. The lighting, sharply focused and casting

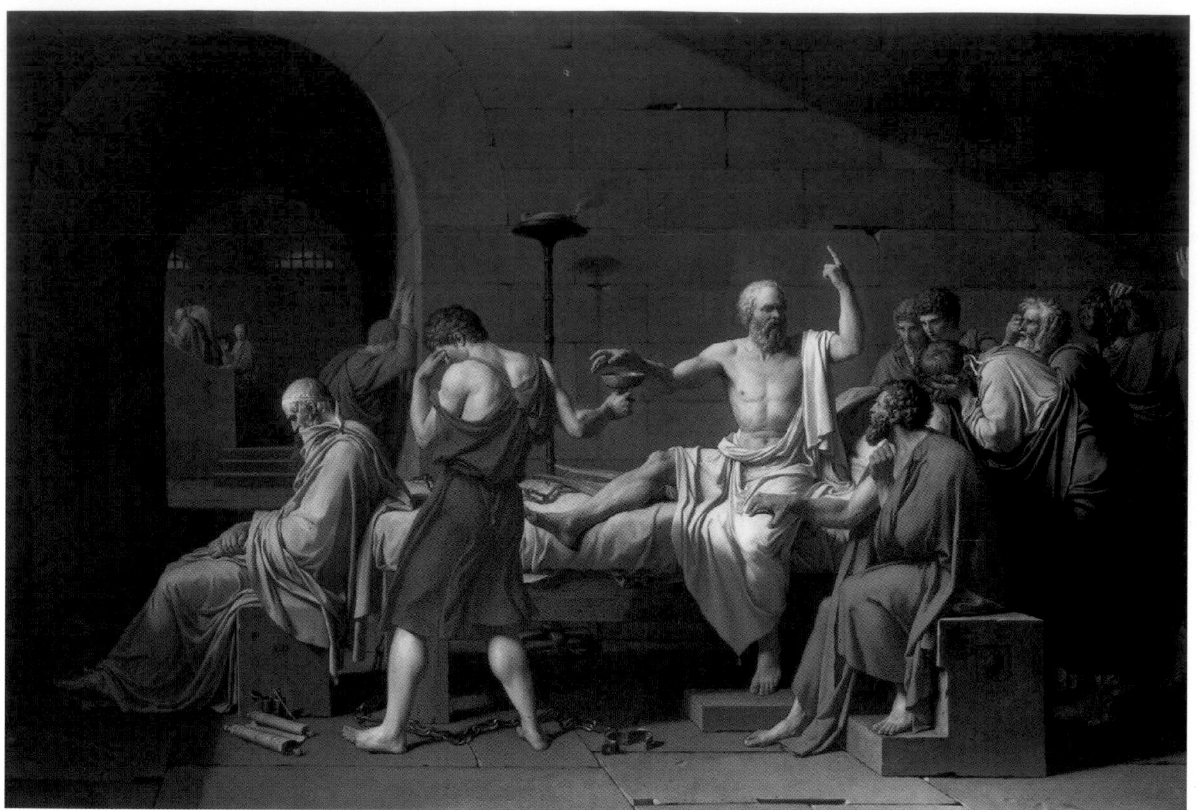

21-2. Jacques-Louis David. *The Death of Socrates.* 1787. Oil on canvas, 4'3" x 6'5¼" (1.3 x 1.96 m). The Metropolitan Museum of Art, New York. Wolfe Fund, 1931

CATHERINE LORILLARD WOLFE COLLECTION

precise shadows, is derived from Caravaggio. So is the firmly realistic detail. (Note the hands and feet, the furniture, the texture of the stone surfaces.) As a result, the picture has a lifelike quality that is astonishing in such a doctrinaire statement of the new style. The very harshness of the design suggests that David was passionately involved in the issues of his age, artistic as well as political. Refusing to compromise his principles, Socrates was convicted of a trumped-up charge and sentenced to death. He is shown about to drink poison from the cup. Thus he becomes not only an example of Ancient Virtue but also the founder of the "religion of Reason." Here he is a Christlike figure amid his 12 disciples, although fewer people were actually present at his death and his wife is omitted from the scene.

David took an active part in the French Revolution. For some years he had artistic control comparable only to Lebrun's a century before (see pages 579 and 581). During this time he painted his greatest picture, *The Death of Marat* (fig. 21-3). David's deep emotion has made a masterpiece from a subject that would have embarrassed a lesser artist. Marat, one of the political leaders of the Revolution, had been murdered in his bathtub. He was required to sit in water to relieve a painful skin condition and did his work there, with a wooden board serving as his desk. One day a young woman named Charlotte Corday burst in with a personal petition and plunged a knife into his chest while he read it. David has composed the scene with a simplicity and directness that are awe-inspiring. The canvas, which was planned as a public memorial to the martyred hero, combines devotional image and historical account. Classical art could offer little guidance for such a work, even though the slain figure probably was derived from an antique source. The artist has drawn on the Caravaggesque tradition of religious art even more than in *The Death of Socrates.* It is no accident that his Marat reminds us so strongly of Zurbarán's *St. Serapion* (see fig. 17-36).

England

WEST. The martyrdom of a secular hero was first immortalized by Benjamin West (1738–1820) in *The Death of General Wolfe* (fig. 21-4). Largely self-taught, West went to Rome from Pennsylvania in 1760 and caused a sensation, since no American painter had appeared in Europe before. He relished his role of frontiersman. On being shown the *Apollo Belvedere* (see fig. 5-69) he reportedly exclaimed, "How like a Mohawk warrior!" He also quickly absorbed the lessons of Neoclassicism, so that he was in command of the most up-to-date style when he left a few years later. West stopped in London for what was intended to be a brief stay on his way home but decided to remain there. He enjoyed phenomenal success and became the most important history painter in England. West was a founding member of the Royal Academy, then its president after the death of Reynolds. His career was thus European rather than American, but he always took pride in his New World background.

The Death of General Wolfe, West's most famous work, represents an event that had aroused considerable feeling in London.

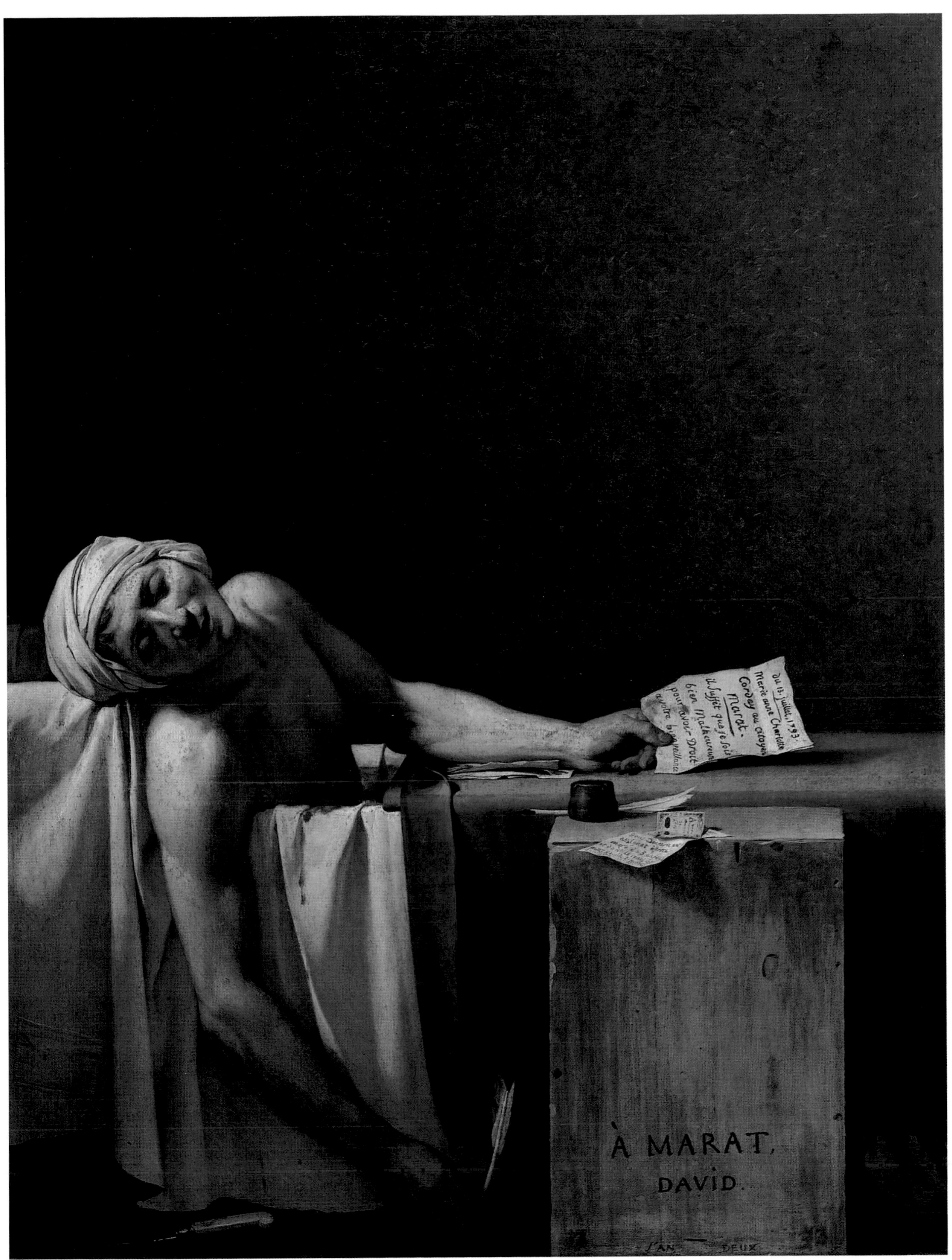

21-3. Jacques-Louis David. *The Death of Marat.* 1793. Oil on canvas, 65 x 50½" (165 x 128.3 cm). Musées Royaux des Beaux-Arts de Belgique, Brussels

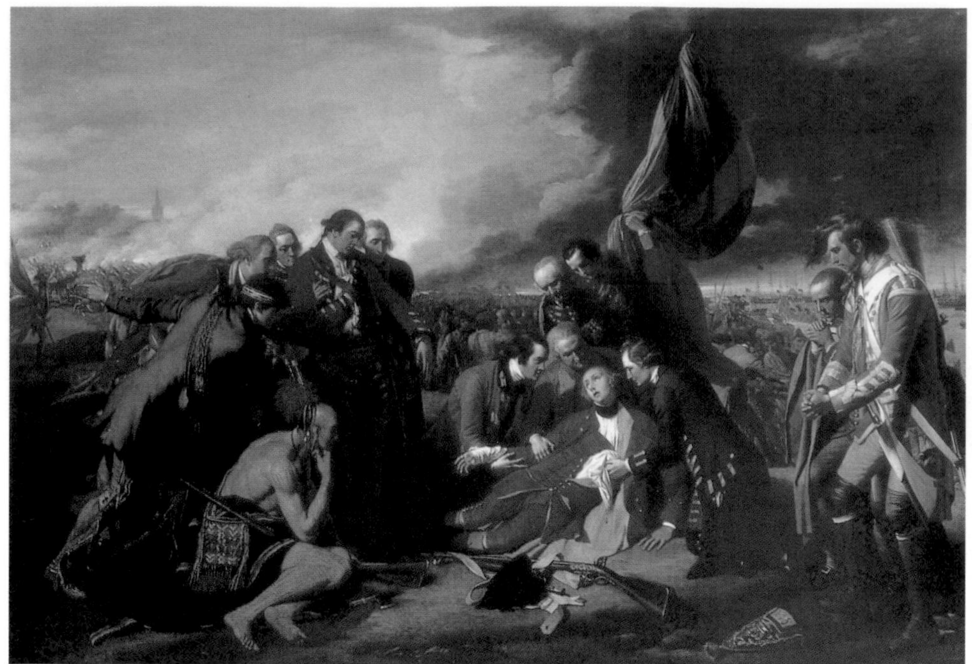

21-4. Benjamin West. *The Death of General Wolfe.* 1770. Oil on canvas, 4'11½" x 7' (1.51 x 2.13 m). National Gallery of Canada, Ottawa

GIFT OF THE DUKE OF WESTMINSTER

Wolfe's death in 1759 occurred in the siege of Quebec during the French and Indian War. When West decided to represent this event 11 years later, two methods were open to him. He could give a factual account with the maximum of historic accuracy, or he could use "the grand manner," based on Poussin's ideal of history painting (see pages 537 and 539), with figures in "timeless" classical costume. Although he had been influenced by Mengs and Hamilton, he did not follow them in this painting—he knew the American scene too well for that. Instead, he merged the two approaches. His figures wear contemporary dress, and the figure of the Indian places the scene in the New World. Yet all the attitudes and expressions are "heroic." The composition, in fact, recalls the lamentation over the dead Christ (see fig. 11-79). The artist has dramatized it with Baroque lighting, drama, and brushwork (see fig. 18-1). West thus endowed the death of a modern military hero with both the classical pathos of "noble and serious human actions," as defined by academic theory, and the trappings of a real event. He created an image that expresses an attitude basic to modern times: the shift of allegiance from religion to nationalism. No wonder his picture had countless successors during the nineteenth century.

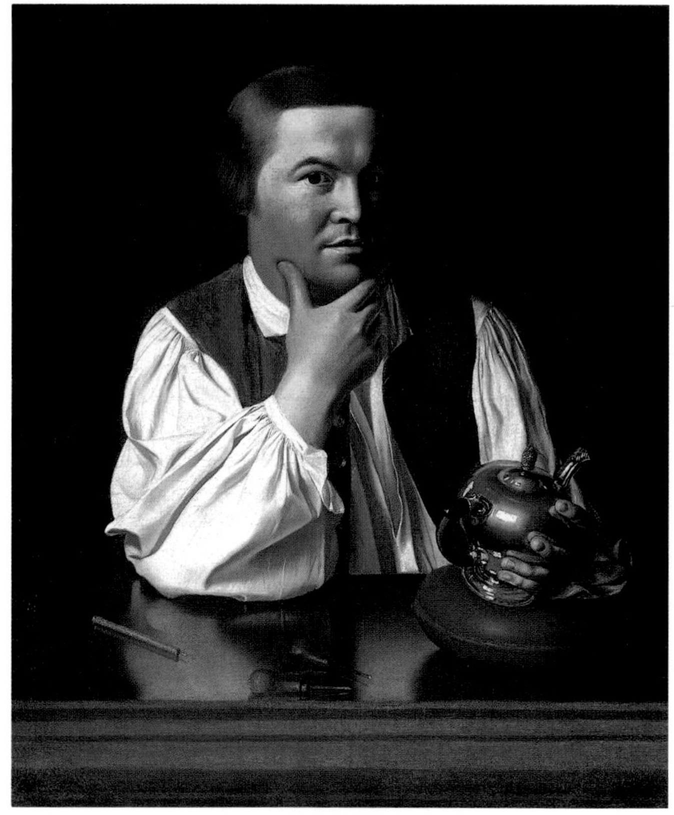

21-5. John Singleton Copley. *Paul Revere.* c. 1768–70. Oil on canvas, 35 x 28½" (88.9 x 72.3 cm). Museum of Fine Arts, Boston

GIFT OF JOSEPH W., WILLIAM B., AND EDWARD H. R. REVERE

COPLEY. West's gifted countryman, John Singleton Copley of Boston (1738–1815), moved to London just two years before the American Revolution. As New England's outstanding portrait painter, he had adapted the formulas of the British portrait tradition to the cultural climate of his hometown. *Paul Revere,* painted around 1768–70 (fig. 21-5), is deservedly his most famous painting in this vein. Silversmith, printmaker, businessman, and patriot, Revere has acquired legendary status thanks to Henry Wadsworth Longfellow's famous poem about his midnight ride. Copley's painting, in turn, has become virtually an American icon. It has generally been treated as a workingman's portrait, so to speak. However, this is not Revere's working outfit but his best

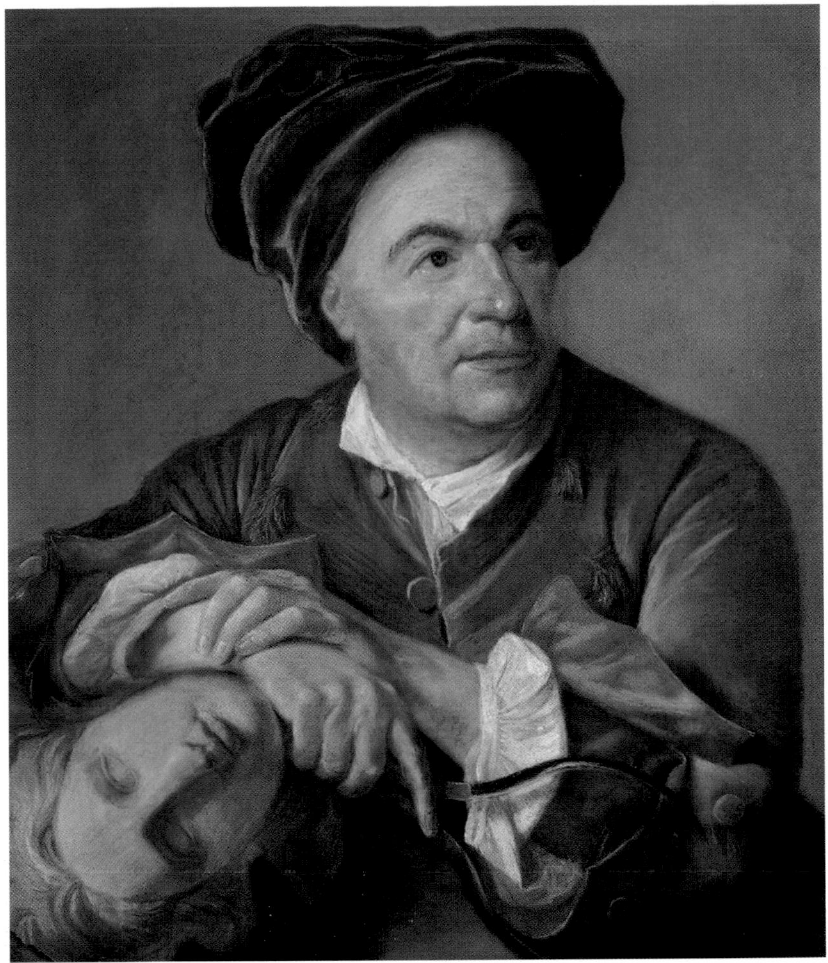

21-6. Francis Xavier Vispré (attr.). *Portrait of Louis-François Roubiliac.* c. 1750. Pastel on paper laid on canvas, 24½ x 21½" (62.2 x 54.6 cm). Yale Center for British Art, New Haven, Connecticut

PAUL MELLON COLLECTION

business clothes. Revere looks out at us with astonishing directness, as if he were examining us with the same intensity as we see him. The thoughtful mood is heightened by the sharp light, which gives him an unusually forceful presence. Revere is a thinker who possesses an active intelligence, and we will recognize the pose of hand on chin as an old device used since antiquity to represent philosophers. Clearly, this is no ordinary craftsman. Why, then, did Copley show Revere at a workbench with his engraving tools spread out before him? And why is he holding a teapot as the object of his contemplation and offering it to us for our inspection? Revere's work as a silversmith is not a sufficient explanation, natural as it might seem.

Paul Revere belongs to a type of informal portrait that originated in France in the early eighteenth century and soon became popular as well in England. Reserved originally for artists, writers, and the like, it soon gave rise to a variant showing a sculptor at work in his studio with his tools prominently displayed (fig. 21-6). Sometimes an engraver is seen instead. There is another source as well: moralizing portraits, the descendants of pictures of St. Jerome, that show the sitter holding or pointing to skulls, much as Revere has the teapot in his hand. Copley was surely familiar with such images from the portrait engravings he collected, although the exact sources for the Revere painting remain unknown. Copley transformed Revere from a craftsman into an artist–philosopher, and with good reason. Revere's portrait probably dates from around the time of his first engravings. The painter and the silversmith must have known each other well, for the artist endowed his portrait with a penetrating characterization. (Copley ordered various pieces of silver, and even false teeth, from Revere.) The painting thus stands as a compelling tribute to a fellow artist—and as an invaluable document of colonial culture. In Europe, Copley was at last able to attain his ideal of history painting in the manner of West. His most memorable work is *Watson and the Shark* (fig. 21-7). As a young man, Watson had been dramatically rescued from a shark attack while swimming in Havana harbor, but not until he met Copley did he decide to have this gruesome experience memorialized. Perhaps he thought that only a painter newly arrived from America would do full justice to the exotic flavor of the incident. Copley, in turn, must have been fascinated by the task of translating the story into pictorial terms. Fol-

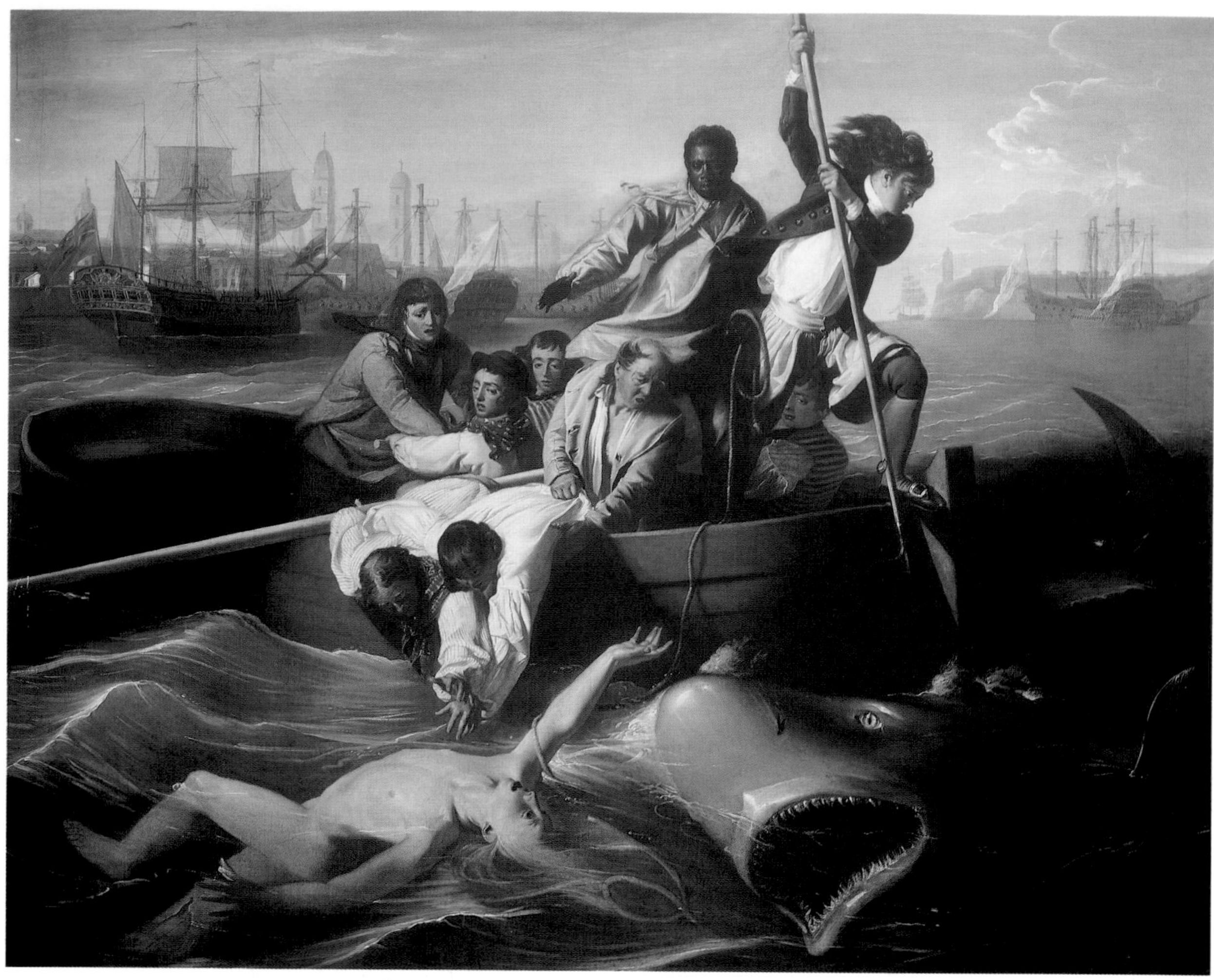

21-7. John Singleton Copley. *Watson and the Shark*. 1778. Oil on canvas, 7'6 1/4" x 6'1/2" (2.29 x 1.84 m). Museum of Fine Arts, Boston

GIFT OF MRS. GEORGE VON LENGERKE MEYER

lowing West's example, he made every detail as authentic as possible (here the black man has the same purpose as the Indian in *The Death of General Wolfe*) and utilized all the expressive resources of Baroque painting to invite the beholder's participation. The composition is indebted partially to a hunting scene by Rubens. Copley may also have remembered representations of Jonah and the Whale, which include the elements of his scene, except that the action is reversed. (The prophet is thrown overboard into the jaws of the sea monster.) The shark becomes a monstrous embodiment of evil; the man with the boat hook recalls an Archangel Michael fighting Satan; and the nude youth, resembling a fallen gladiator, flounders helplessly between the forces of doom and salvation. This kind of moral allegory is typical of Neoclassicism as a whole, and despite its charged emotion, the picture has the same logic and clarity found in David's *The Death of Socrates*.

KAUFFMANN. One of the leading Neoclassicists in England was the Swiss-born painter Angelica Kauffmann (1741–1807). A founding member of the Royal Academy, she spent 15 years in London among the group that included Reynolds and West, whom she had met in Winckelmann's circle in Rome (see page 640). From the antique this disciple of Mengs developed a delicate style admirably suited to the interiors of Robert Adam (see page 657), which she was often commissioned to decorate. Kauffmann's most ambitious works are narrative paintings, of which the artist John Henry Fuseli (see page 674) observed, "Her heroines are herself." *The Artist in the Character of Design Listening to the Inspiration of Poetry* (fig. 21-8) combines both aspects of her art. The subject must have held particular meaning for her. It is eloquent testimony to women's struggle to gain recognition in the arts. The artist has assumed the guise of Design, suggesting her strong sense of identification with the muse. The painting became a prototype of the allegorical "friendship" pictures showing two female figures that remained popular into the Romantic era (see fig. 21-54).

STUBBS. George Stubbs (1724–1806), who painted portraits of racehorses (and sometimes their owners) for a living, developed a new type of animal picture full of feeling for the grandeur and violence of nature that looks forward to Romanticism. On a visit to North Africa, he is said to have seen a horse killed by a lion. Certainly this image haunted his imagination. *Lion Attacking a Horse* (fig. 21-9) can be seen as an animal counterpart to Copley's *Watson*

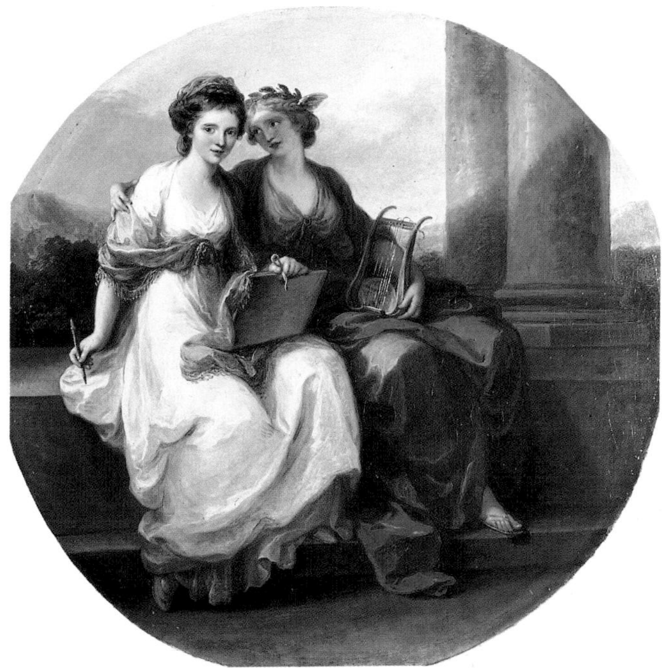

21-8. Angelica Kauffmann. *The Artist in the Character of Design Listening to the Inspiration of Poetry.* 1782. Oil on canvas, diameter 24" (61 cm). The Iveagh Bequest, Kenwood, London

and the Shark, and it has similar allegorical overtones. People have no place in this realm. The artist identifies himself emotionally with the horse, whose pure whiteness contrasts so dramatically—and symbolically—with the sinister rocks of the lion's domain. Thunderclouds racing across the sky reinforce the mood of doom. The horse, frightened also by the approaching storm, seems doubly defenseless against these forces of destruction. We respond to the horse with the same mixed fascination and horror as we do to Watson.

Stubbs' depiction of animals with nearly human action and emotion was the beginning of a larger investigation so characteristic of the Enlightenment. He later made a series of drawings for a book of comparative anatomy—including one that could well be used to illustrate Plato's famous observation that humans are featherless bipeds. In them he emphasized the similarities in physiology and psychology between people and animals. His scientific curiosity and comprehensive approach relate him to Diderot's attempt to unite all knowledge and philosophy in his massive *Encyclopédie.*

THE PICTURESQUE AND THE SUBLIME. Picturesque landscape painting was as distinctive to the Enlightenment as the English garden (see page 652), to which it was closely related. As the term implies, the picturesque was a way of looking at nature through the eyes of landscape painters. The scenery of Italy and the idyllic landscapes of Claude contributed to the English appreciation of nature. In expressing emotions inspired by these examples, English nature poets such as James Thomson further validated the aesthetic response to nature, often through references to mythology. The picturesque was soon joined by wilder scenes reflecting a taste for the sublime—that delicious sense of awe experienced before grandiose nature. The idea had been around since the beginning of the eighteenth century, but it was defined once and for all by Edmund Burke in *Inquiry into the Origin of Our Ideas of the Sublime and the Beautiful* of 1756, which held that the sublime is the opposite of beauty. After touring the rugged lake region of England in 1780, the Reverend William Gilpin claimed that the picturesque lay somewhere between Burke's extremes, since it is neither vast nor smooth but finite and rough. The picturesque later came to include a topographical mode as well as a rustic mode. It nevertheless remained a way of manipulating nature to conform to artistic examples.

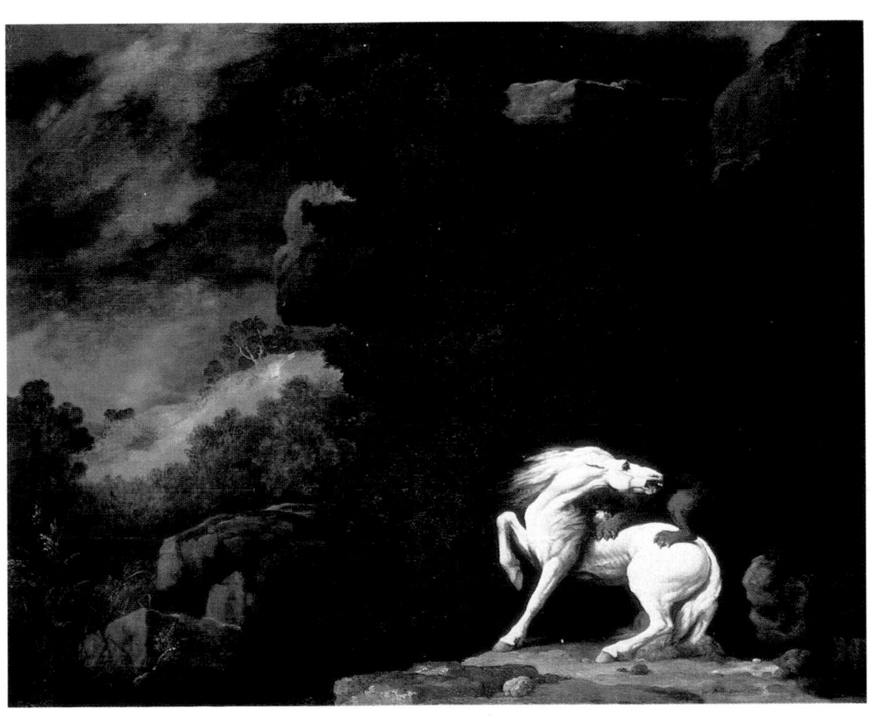

21-9. George Stubbs. *Lion Attacking a Horse.* 1770. Oil on canvas, 40⅛ x 50¼" (102 x 127.6 cm). Yale University Art Gallery, New Haven, Connecticut

GIFT OF THE YALE UNIVERSITY ART GALLERY ASSOCIATES

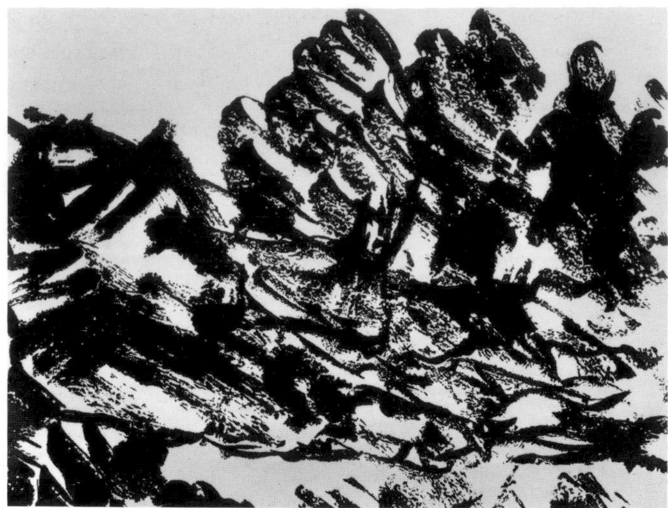

21-10. Alexander Cozens. *Landscape,* from *A New Method of Assisting the Invention in Drawing Original Compositions of Landscape.* 1784–86. Aquatint. The Metropolitan Museum of Art, New York

ROGERS FUND, 1906

COZENS. Alexander Cozens (c. 1717–1786), who helped to originate the picturesque, soon tired of these models. He felt they could produce only conventional variations on a standard theme. The direct study of nature, important though it was, could not be the new starting point either. It did not supply the imaginative, poetic quality that for him constituted the essence of landscape painting. As a teacher, Cozens developed what he called "a new method of assisting the invention in drawing original compositions of landscape," which he published, with illustrations such as figure 21-10, shortly before his death. Leonardo da Vinci, Cozens noted, had observed that an artist could stimulate his imagination by trying to find recognizable shapes in the stains on old walls. Why not then produce such chance effects on purpose, to be used in the same way? Crumple a sheet of paper, smooth it. Then, while thinking generally of landscape, blot it with ink, using as little conscious control as possible. (Our example is such an "ink-blot landscape.") With this as the point of departure, representational elements may be picked out among the blots and developed into a finished picture. Cozens' blotscape, then, is not a work of nature but a work of art. Even though only half-born, it shows a highly individual graphic manner.

Because it relies on art, the Cozens method still falls within the picturesque, while the all-embracing scope of his attempt places it within the Enlightenment, with its love of systems. It has far-reaching implications, theoretical as well as practical, but these could hardly have been understood by his contemporaries, who regarded the "blot-master" as ridiculous. Nevertheless, the method was not forgotten. Its memory was kept alive partly by its very notoriety. The two great masters of Romantic landscape in England, John Constable and William Turner, both benefited from it, although they differed in almost every other way.

SCULPTURE

The history of Neoclassical sculpture does not simply follow that of painting. Neoclassicism, which in painting is sometimes hard to distinguish from Romanticism, stands out far more clearly in sculpture. Unlike painters, Neoclassical sculptors were overwhelmed by the authority granted since Winckelmann to ancient statues, which were praised as supreme manifestations of the Greek genius. Like the *Apollo Belvedere* (see fig. 5-69), most of them were in fact mechanical Roman copies of no great distinction after Hellenistic pieces. (Goethe, upon seeing the newly discovered late Archaic sculpture from Aegina, pronounced it clumsy and inferior; see figs. 5-22 and 5-23.)

When Winckelmann published his essay advocating the imitation of Greek works, enthusiasm for classical antiquity was already well established among the intellectuals of the Enlightenment. In Rome from 1760 on, the restoring of ancient sculpture and its sale, especially to wealthy visitors from abroad, was a flourishing business. To these patrons, "classics" such as the *Apollo Belvedere* or *The Laocoön Group* (see fig. 5-76), to cite only two of the most famous, belonged to a different world. They were admired as embodiments of an aesthetic ideal, undisturbed by the demands of time and place. To enter this world, the modern sculptor set himself the goal of creating "modern classics"—sculpture demanding to be judged on a basis of equality with its ancient predecessors. This was not just a matter of style and subject matter. It meant that sculptors had to hope that critical acclaim would establish such works as modern classics and attract buyers. The original plaster permitted them to present major works to the public without investing in expensive marble or bronze. Plaster sculpture thus became a feature at the Salons, the exhibitions sponsored by the French Academy, where success was crucial for young artists. Without the original plaster, the Neoclassic revolution in sculpture would have been impossible to accomplish.

If Paris was the artistic capital of the Western world, Rome during the second half of the eighteenth century became the birthplace and spiritual home of Neoclassicism. As we have seen, however, the new style was pioneered by the resident foreigners from north of the Alps, rather than Italians. That Rome should have been an even stronger magnet for sculptors than for painters is hardly surprising. Rome offered an abundance of sculptural monuments but only a meager choice of ancient painting. (The city also had many skilled artisans in both marble and bronze.) In the shadow of these monuments, Northern sculptors trained in the Baroque tradition awakened to a new conception of what sculpture ought to be. They paved the way for Antonio Canova, whose success as the creator of modern classics was the ultimate fulfillment of their ambitions (see pages 686–87).

England

The leading role of Anglo-Roman artists prior to 1780 in the formulation of Neoclassicism was a result of England's enthusiasm for classical antiquity since the early years of the century. This precocious appreciation was political, philosophic, and literary. Because it was motivated by a new nationalism, this admiration

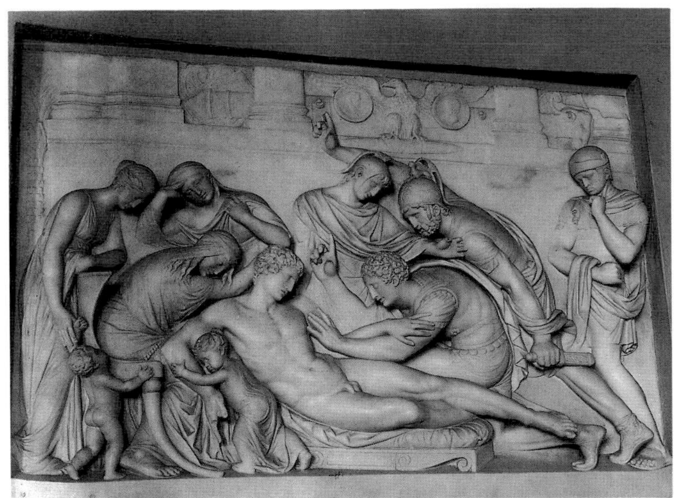

21-11. Thomas Banks. *The Death of Germanicus.* 1774. Marble, height 30" (76.2 cm). Holkham Hall, Norfolk, England

BY KIND PERMISSION OF THE EARL OF LEICESTER AND THE TRUSTEES OF THE HOLKHAM ESTATE

soon turned into a demand that England become "the principal seat of the arts" as well.

BANKS. Thomas Banks (1735–1805) came closest to achieving the sculptor's goal of creating modern classics. Little is known of Banks' career before he went to Rome in 1772 for seven years on a traveling fellowship from the Royal Academy. *The Death of Germanicus* (fig. 21-11) of 1774, a large relief, shows his close study of classical sources, yet it is not in the least archaeological in flavor. While the facial types and drapery treatment derive from classical sources, the strained poses, the pronounced linear rhythms, and the emotional intensity of the scene have no counterpart in ancient sculpture. They reflect, rather, Banks' admiration for the two chief Anglo-Roman painters, Gavin Hamilton (who had treated the same subject) and Henry Fuseli (see page 674).

Unfortunately, Banks found little demand for his "new classics" on his return to England, although they were enthusiastically received by the recently established Royal Academy. He was thus forced to seek commissions for funerary monuments, which were the main source of steady employment for sculptors in England.

France

HOUDON. Jean-Antoine Houdon (1741–1828), unlike most of his contemporaries, built his career on portrait sculpture. He would have been glad to accept state commissions had they been available; however, he soon discovered his special gift for portraits, for which there was a growing demand. Indeed portraiture proved the most viable field for Neoclassic sculpture. How else could modern artists rise above the quality of the Greek and Roman classics?

Houdon's portraits retain the acute sense of individual character introduced by Coysevox (see fig. 19-18), and they established entirely new standards of physical and psychological realism that reflected Enlightenment ideals. Houdon, more than any other artist of his time, knew how to give these ideals visible form while still relying on Rococo devices. His portraits have an apparent lack of style that is deceptive. His style consists of the uncanny ability to make all his sitters into Enlightenment personalities while remaining conscientiously faithful to their individual features. He even managed this on the rare occasions when he had to make portrait busts of figures long dead, or when he had to work from a death mask only.

With Voltaire, he was more fortunate. Houdon modeled him from life a few weeks before the famous author's death in May 1778 and then made a death mask as well. From these studies he created *Voltaire Seated* (fig. 21-12), which was immediately acclaimed as towering above all others of its kind. The original plaster has not survived, but a terra-cotta cast from it, retouched by Houdon, offers a close approximation. As contemporary critics quickly pointed out, the *Voltaire Seated* was a "heroicized" likeness. The sculptor enveloped the frail old man in a Roman toga and even added some hair he no longer had so as to justify the classical headband. Yet the effect is not disturbing, for Voltaire wears the toga as casually as a dressing gown. His facial expression and the turn of his head, so reminiscent of Rococo portraiture (compare fig. 20-10 of about the same time), suggest the atmosphere of an intimate conversation. Thus Voltaire is not cast

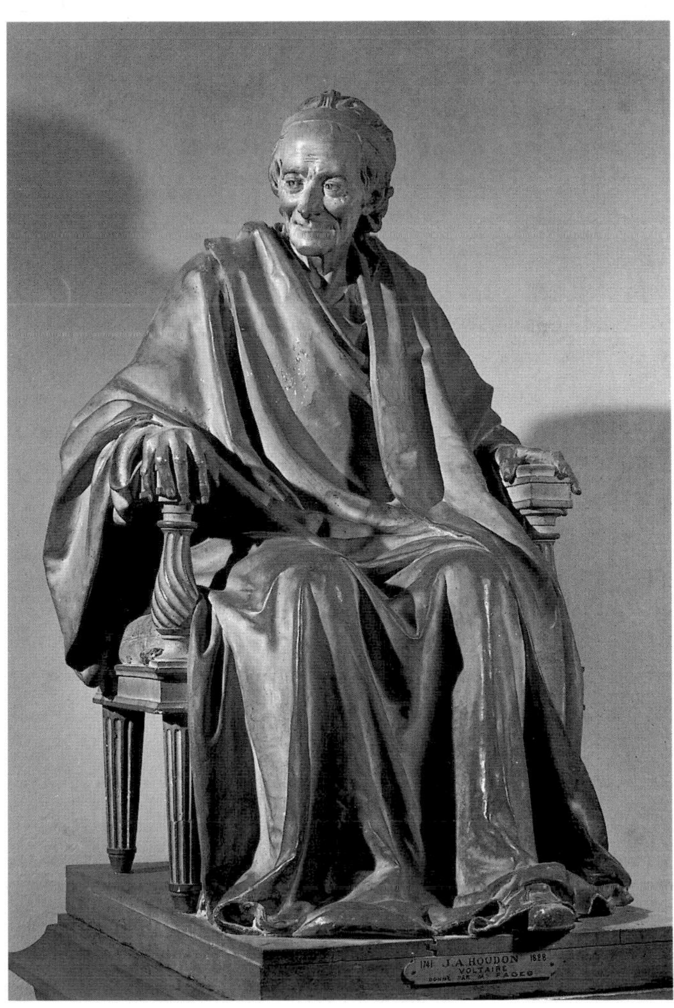

21-12. Jean-Antoine Houdon. *Voltaire Seated.* 1781. Terra-cotta model for marble original, height 47" (119.3 cm). Musée Fabre, Montpellier, France

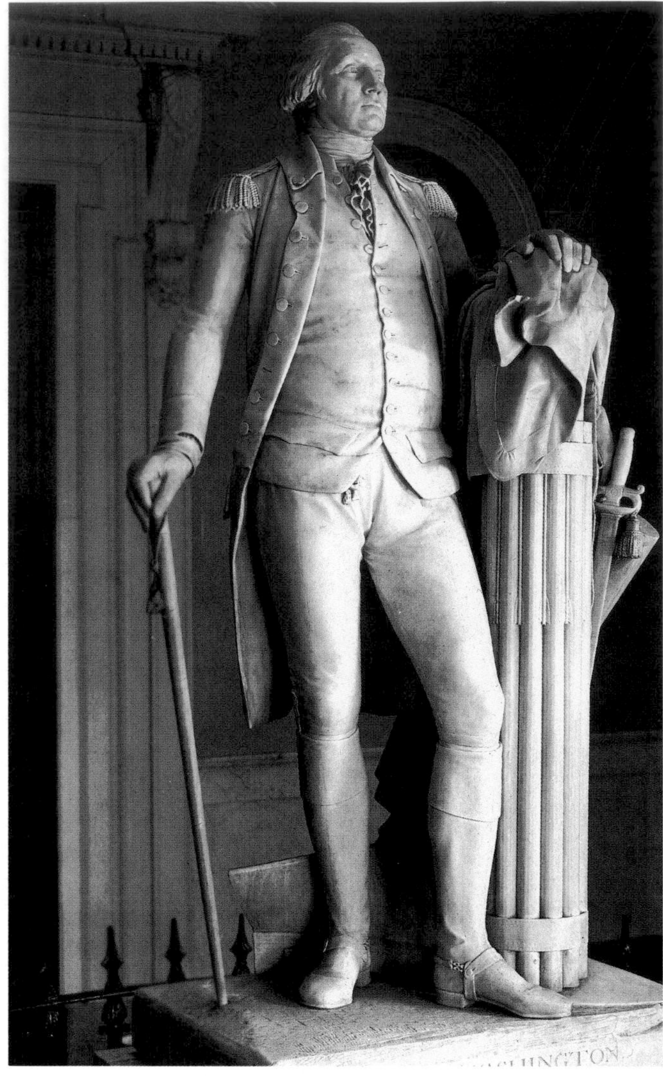

21-13. Jean-Antoine Houdon. *George Washington.* 1788–92. Marble, height 6'2" (1.88 m). State Capitol, Richmond, Virginia

in the role of classical philosopher—he becomes the modern counterpart of one, a modern classic in his own right! In him, we recognize ourselves. Voltaire is the image of modern man: unheroic, skeptical, with his own idiosyncratic mixture of rationality and emotion. That is surely why Voltaire strikes us as so "natural." We are, after all, the heirs of the Enlightenment, which coined this ideal type.

Aside from *Voltaire Seated,* the Virginia *George Washington* (fig. 21-13) is Houdon's finest effort. In 1778, the year he portrayed Voltaire, Houdon became a Freemason and modeled Benjamin Franklin. Replicas of the Franklin bust spread the artist's fame in the New World. American colonial sculpture hardly existed aside from weather vanes, tombstone carvings, and cigar-store Indians. Public monuments were few and were imported from England rather than produced at home. Thus the newborn Republic had to look to France for a sculptor to immortalize its first president. After all, it could not be entrusted to an Englishman. There was, it seems, no contact with British sculpture from 1776 until after the fall of Napoleon. Thus when the Virginia legislature decided to commission a marble statue of George Washington, the natural choice was Houdon. Houdon insisted on coming over to model his sitter directly, and in October 1785, he spent two weeks at Mount Vernon as Washington's guest. The figure was finally erected in the rotunda of the State Capitol 11 years later.

Houdon initially made two versions, one in classical and one in modern costume, the final form of the statue. Even the latter, though thoroughly up-to-date in detail, has a classical pose, and we can feel the chill breath of the *Apollo Belvedere* (see fig. 5-69), as it were, on the tranquil, smooth surfaces. By this time, Washington no longer held public office; he was simply a gentleman farmer. Houdon has given him a general's uniform, but the sword, no longer needed in peacetime, is suspended from a bundle of 13 rods (the fasces, representing the original states of the Union) and his right hand rests on a cane. Behind his feet is a plow, the symbol of peace. These attributes, with their classical allusions, blend easily with the contemporary dress, and the contrapposto stance of the figure is so natural that the beholder is hardly aware of its antique origin. The statue is more than a record of Washington's physical appearance. Above all, Houdon has created a powerful impression of Washington's character within the framework of the personality type of the Enlightenment. Far more than any other portrait, Houdon's statue, and the busts associated with it, determined how the nation visualized the Father of His Country.

ARCHITECTURE

England

THE PALLADIAN REVIVAL. England was the birthplace of Neoclassicism in architecture, as it had been in the forefront of painting and sculpture. The earliest sign of this attitude was the Palladian revival. It was sparked by the publication of Colin Campbell's (1676–1729) treatise *Vitruvius Brittanicus* (1715–17, 1725), which advocated a return to the style of Palladio and Inigo Jones and rejected Wren's. However, it was the wealthy amateur Richard Boyle, Lord Burlington (1694–1753), who emerged as the leader of the movement in the 1720s. To accomplish his designs, he employed his friend William Kent (c. 1685–1748), a painter–decorator among his considerable entourage of artists and writers. (Their number included the poet Alexander Pope, who urged a classical reform of literature.) Palladio appealed to the English partly because his designs for villas were well-suited to English country houses and partly because his style accorded with the Rule of Taste promoted by the Enlightenment philosopher Anthony Ashley Cooper, Third Earl of Shaftesbury. What distinguishes the Palladian revival from earlier classicisms, however, is less its external appearance than its motivation. Instead of merely reasserting the superior authority of the ancients, it claimed to satisfy the demands of reason and thus to be more "natural" than the Baroque. At the time the Baroque style was identified with papist Rome by English Protestants, with absolutist France by George I, and with Tory policies by the Whig opposition. Thus began an association between Neoclassicism and liberal politics that was to continue through the French Revolution. The appeal to reason found support in Palladio himself, who decried abuses "contrary to natural reason" on the grounds that "architecture, as well as all other arts, being an imitation of

NEOCLASSICAL THEATER

In France, around the middle of the eighteenth century, the philosopher and encyclopedist Denis Diderot (1713–1784) attempted to add domestic tragedy and the comedy of virtue (the so-called middle genres) to the accepted classifications of theater through his sentimental plays *The Illegitimate Son* (1757) and *The Father of a Family* (1758). They were quickly forgotten, with good reason. The only important French playwright of the later Enlightenment was Pierre-Augustin Caron de Beaumarchais (1732–1799), whose comedies *The Barber of Seville* (1775) and *The Marriage of Figaro* (1783) became the basis for operas by Rossini and Mozart. While the *Barber* is a lighthearted farce derived from the commedia dell'arte about the triumph of young lovers over lecherous old men, *Figaro* was a critique of the aristocracy, whose ranks Beaumarchais joined, thanks to the wealth he amassed through his inventions and business ventures.

Neoclassicism in German theater was represented chiefly by the playwright, critic, and university professor Johann Christoph Gottsched (1700–1766), who modeled his plays on French examples and who based his ideas on the classical theories of the French critic Nicolas Boileau (1636–1711); however, their success depended heavily on his close association with the actress Caroline Neuber (1697–1760). His theories were attacked by Gotthold Ephraim Lessing (1729–1781) in *Laokoon* (1766) and in the journal *Hamburgische Dramaturgie* (1767–68). Lessing argued that the goal of drama is to arouse compassion, thereby fulfilling an important moral and social function. Although he belittled his own work, Lessing's plays, such as *Minna von Barnhelm* (1767), embody his principles very capably.

Lessing helped pave the way for the *Sturm und Drang* (Storm and Stress) period (1770–87), which constituted a rebellion against the restrictions of the Neoclassical drama and Enlightenment philosophy and was the first attempt to create a distinctive German form of theater. Although this literary movement took its name from a play of that title (1776) by F. M. Klinger, it centered on the young poet Johann Wolfgang von Goethe (1749–1832), whose drama *Goetz van Berlichingen* (1773), inspired by the memoirs of a famous sixteenth-century German knight, launched the movement in theater. The extreme subjectivity of *Sturm und Drang* writing was epitomized by Goethe's novel *The Sorrows of Young Werther,* published the following year. *Sturm und Drang* in theater was poorly received but widely discussed; it was finally legitimized by August von Kotzebue (1761–1819), who became the most popular playwright in Europe. The late eighteenth century was notable for the establishment of national theaters throughout Germany, as well as Austria; important examples are the Hamburg National Theater, which employed Lessing as its artistic adviser (dramaturge) when it opened in 1767, and the Burgtheater in Vienna in 1776.

After the publication of *The Sorrows of Young Werther,* which established his reputation, Goethe was invited to the court in Weimar, where he spent the rest of his career and even served as minister of state for ten years. During a sojourn to Italy in 1786–88 he became a convert to classicism and rejected *Sturm und Drang.* In 1791 he was appointed director of the theater at Weimar, in which he showed little interest until he became friends with the poet Friedrich von Schiller (1759–1805). Schiller had written some early dramas before turning to the study of history, which led to a professorship at the university in Jena, not far from Weimar. The friendship was so close that Schiller moved to Weimar in 1799. From then until his death he wrote his great dramas, which were a direct outgrowth of his abiding interest in history. They center on the Thirty Years' War, about which he wrote the first major treatise, particularly on General Albrecht Wallenstein (1583–1634). His other plays concern William Tell, Mary Stuart, and Joan of Arc. Under Goethe and Schiller, Weimar became home to the leading theater on the Continent. They argued that theater should transform experience through harmony and grace rather than create an illusion of real life; hence, they instituted stylized conventions designed to lead the viewer to ideal truth.

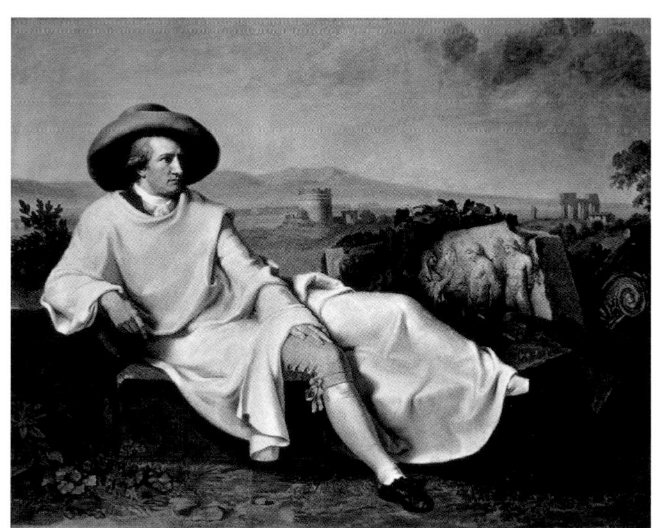

Johann Heinrich Wilhelm Tischbein. *Goethe in the Campagna.* 1787. Oil on canvas, 64 5/8" x 81 1/8" (164 x 206 cm). Stadelsches Kunstinstitut, Frankfurt

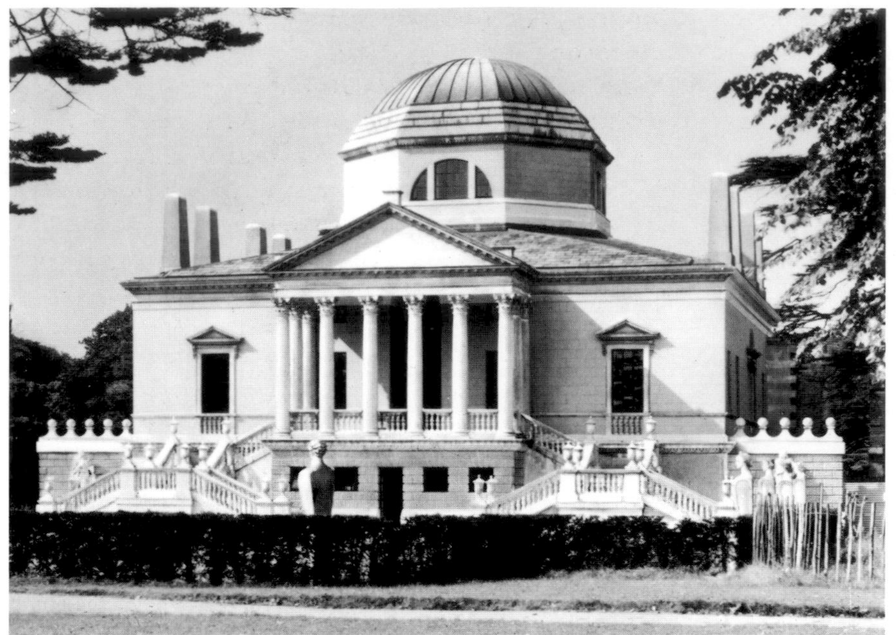

21-14. Lord Burlington and William Kent. Chiswick House, near London. Begun 1725

nature, can suffer nothing that either alienates or deviates from that which is agreeable to nature."

This rationalism helps to explain the abstract, segmented look of Chiswick House on Burlington's estate (fig. 21-14). Adapted by Burlington and Kent from the Villa Rotonda (see fig. 14-26), as well as other Italian sources, it is compact, simple, and geometric—the antithesis of the Baroque pomp of Blenheim Palace (see fig. 19-25). The concept was not new to England. It had been used on a larger scale just a couple of years earlier at Mereworth Castle by Campbell. Chiswick is at once bolder and more rigorous, yet less derivative than Mereworth. Campbell himself acknowledged Burlington as "not only a great Patron of all Arts, but the first Architect." The exterior surfaces are flat and unbroken, the ornament is meager, and the temple portico juts out abruptly from the blocklike body of the structure. The interior, probably by Kent, is more luxurious, in the manner of Jones, but with a clarity that looks forward to Robert Adam.

THE ENGLISH GARDEN. Should such a villa be set in a geometric, formal garden, like Le Nôtre's at Versailles (see fig. 19-11)? Lord Burlington and Kent maintained that such a setting would be unnatural, hence contrary to reason. At Chiswick they invented what became known all over Europe as "the English landscape garden." It was carefully planned to look unplanned, with winding paths, irregularly spaced clumps of trees, and little lakes and rivers instead of symmetrical basins and canals. The "reasonable" garden must seem as unbounded, as full of surprise and variety, as nature itself. It must, in a word, be "picturesque," a term that applies equally well to Burlington's villa, which would look out of place in other surroundings. English landscape architects now took the landscapes of Claude Lorraine (see fig. 19-7) as their source of inspiration. A standard feature was the inclusion of little temples half concealed by the shrubbery, or artificial ruins, "to draw sorrowful reflections from the soul."

Such sentiments were not new. They had often been expressed before in poetry and painting. But to project them onto nature itself, through planned irregularity, was a new idea. The landscape garden, a work of art intended not to look like a work of art, blurred the long-established boundary between artifice and reality. It thus set an important precedent for the revival styles to come. After all, the landscape garden stands in the same relation to nature as a synthetic ruin to an authentic one, or a Neoclassic or Neo-Gothic building to its ancient or medieval model. When the fashion spread to the other side of the Channel, it was welcomed not only as a new way to lay out gardens but as a vehicle of Romantic emotion.

STOURHEAD. Of all the landscape gardens laid out in England in the mid-eighteenth century, the one at Stourhead most nearly retains its original appearance. Its creators, the banker Henry Hoare and the designer Henry Flitcroft (1697–1769), were both enthusiastic followers of Lord Burlington and William Kent. Stourhead is unique not only for its fine preservation but also for the owner's active role in planning every detail of its development.

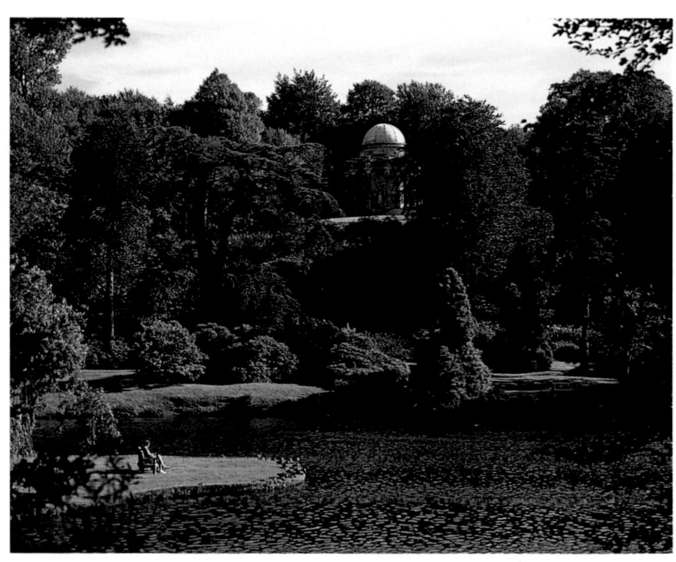

21-15. Henry Flitcroft and Henry Hoare. Landscape garden with Temple of Apollo, Stourhead, England. 1744–65

Our view (fig. 21-15) is across a small lake made by damming the river Stour. High on the far shore is the Temple of Apollo modeled on the recently discovered Temple of Venus at Baalbek. Other focal points at Stourhead are a grotto, a Temple of Venus, a Pantheon, a genuine Gothic cross, and a neomedieval tower built to commemorate King Alfred the Great, the "Father of His People."

France

THE RATIONALIST MOVEMENT. The rationalist movement came somewhat earlier in France so far as theory is concerned but was first realized in actual buildings only in the middle years of the century. It was made up of several factions that were united by their rejection of the Rococo as heavy and ornate. Structural Rationalism was initiated by the pro-Greek rigorists, who were theorists rather than practicing architects. The first, Abbé Jean-Louis de Cordemoy (fl. 1706–12), argued in his *New Treatise on All Architecture* (1708, 1714) against the representative and expressive use of architectural elements. He favored a simple, clear system based on freestanding columns surmounted by an entablature and stripped of all unnecessary ornament. For him good architecture depended not on Vitruvius' utility, solidity, and beauty but on order, arrangement, and appropriateness (akin to the concept of decorum). He therefore warned against the unnecessary use of classical elements. He was further important for helping to initiate the French fascination with the Gothic by calling for an architecture combining classical forms and Gothic construction principles. The idea was first introduced cautiously by the great classicist Claude Perrault, who wrote, "Gothic architecture may not be the best kind, but it is not to be rejected out of hand [simply because things are] different in Gothic and ancient architecture. And (here comes the heresy) Gothic is not therefore to be thought the worse for it." Perrault's proposal in 1676 for a new church of St. Geneviève featured a classical peristyle surmounted by a barrel vault—a design so prophetic that several churches were later erected along those very lines.

De Cordemoy was an early but inconsistent voice. The central figure was the Jesuit Abbé Marc-Antoine Laugier (1713–1769), whose *Essay on Architecture* (1753) acknowledged a debt to de Cordemoy's treatise but was far more systematic. The difference was essentially one of a perceptive critic as against a true philosopher of the Enlightenment, whose faith in reason was complete. Following Vitruvius, Laugier accepted that the beautiful in architecture, as in art, must proceed from nature. And like Jean-Jacques Rousseau, he believed that early people lived in an idyllic state of harmony with nature. In needing shelter from the elements, they built primitive huts of trees using the simplest possible—and therefore the "truest"—system of vertical and horizontal elements. This post-and-lintel method Laugier believed to be the forerunner of the columns and entablatures found in Classical Greek architecture, where every element performed an unambiguous role and ornament was held to a minimum (compare page 123). He therefore rejected the Roman use of arches and pilasters, as well as compound orders. Despite his insistence on clarity and logic, Laugier, too, was fascinated by the lightness, gracefulness, and spaciousness of Gothic architecture. He proposed a union of these two ideal systems in which glass would fill the voids between columns.

Laugier was probably familiar with the ideas of the Franciscan theologian Carlo Lodoli (1690–1761) of Venice, who was an even purer structuralist. Lodoli argued that architecture was a science based on the nature of materials, specifically stone, and the laws of statics. Designs should be determined by function (the relationship between structure and purpose) and representation (the way material is disposed to fulfill the intended purpose). Beauty would thus proceed not from aesthetics but from the dictates of materials. To him the Greek orders, and by extension Roman and Renaissance architecture, were dishonest because they substituted marble for wood. The only true models of masonry architecture were Stonehenge and Egyptian temples, even though they employed the same post-and-lintel system as Greek architecture.

The actual attack on the Rococo style began in 1737 with a treatise by the architect Jacques-François Blondel (1705–1774), the leader of the traditionalists. He argued for a return to the French classical style of Perrault and Mansart out of nostalgia for the age of Louis XIV. The offensive was joined eight years later by the theorist Abbé Jean-Bernard Leblanc, whose *Letters from England* (1745) endorsed a Neoclassical style under the influence of Lord Burlington's ideas. The antiquarians, centering on the collector the Comte de Caylus, attracted the younger generation French architects who returned from studies in Rome during the 1740s and '50s filled with new ideas based on antiquity, as well as the Renaissance. The most prominent was Jean-Laurent Legeay (c. 1710–c. 1786), a visionary who influenced first Piranesi in Rome (see page 611) and then Boullée in Paris (see below) after being appointed to a position at the Academy in 1742. The archaeological Neoclassicists of the 1760s proved even more radical. Chief among them were Marie-Joseph Peyre (1730–1785) and Charles-Louis Clérisseau (1721–1820), a pupil of Blondel who was also inspired by Piranesi and Johann Winckelmann (see page 640). They believed that the Romans had perfected the Greek orders by extending and combining them in boldly imaginative ways.

It is characteristic of the Enlightenment that utility and necessity replaced beauty, which came to be measured by reason, not aesthetics. However, practicing architects found it difficult, even impossible, to adhere to such an approach in every respect, and they mounted a vigorous counteroffensive. The net effect was that French architecture in the 1750s and '60s was dominated by the conscious return to the Style of Louis XIV but was "corrected" and overlaid with new ideas of such astonishing boldness that they provided the foundation for modern architecture.

SOUFFLOT. The first great monument of the rationalist movement was the Panthéon in Paris (fig. 21-16) by Jacques-Germain Soufflot (1713–1780). It was begun in 1757 as the Church of Ste.-Geneviève, but secularized during the Revolution. The architect owed his position to his close relationship with the Marquis de Marigny, the brother of Louis XV's mistress, Madame du Pompadour, with whom he toured Italy in 1749–51. Upon his return, he settled in Lyons, the home of Laugier, where he quickly established himself among the leading architects of the day. As with so much else in eighteenth-century France, the Church of Ste.-

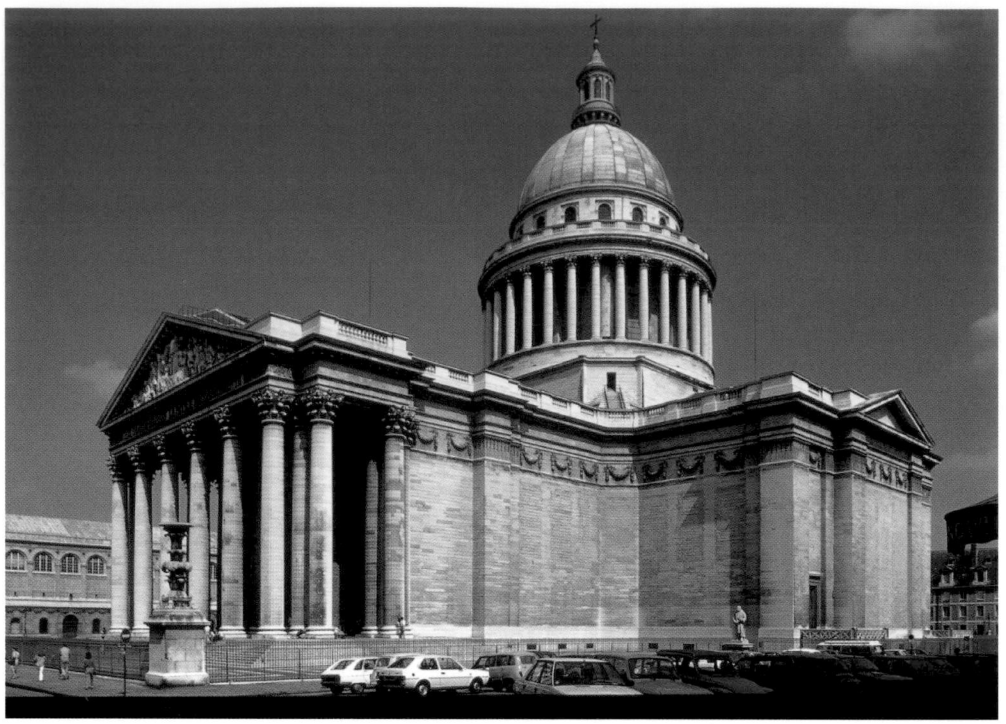

21-16. Jacques-Germain Soufflot. The Panthéon (Ste.-Geneviève), Paris. 1757–92

Geneviève looks back to the preceding century, in this case Hardouin-Mansart's Church of the Invalides (see fig. 19-15). The huge east portico, however, is modeled directly on Perrault's Louvre facade (see fig. 19-10), as well as ancient Roman temples. (Soufflot had spent seven years studying architecture in Italy as a winner of the French Academy's Prix de Rome at the beginning of his career.) The plan, unusual for France, is in the shape of a Greek cross. Although Hardouin-Mansart's Invalides also uses a Greek-cross plan (see fig. 19-16), the overall shape strongly suggests a debt to Wren's initial proposal for St. Paul's in London (see fig. 19-24). From the beginning, however, Soufflot intended his church to have long arms and to treat the interior as a classical colonnade surmounted by an entablature rather than as a traditional arcade. He eventually resolved to enlarge the dome. This decision posed formidable problems of vaulting, which he solved with characteristic ingenuity. Interestingly enough, the dome in its final form is also derived from Wren's St. Paul's (see fig. 19-21), not Hardouin-Mansart's Invalides, as one might expect, which further indicates England's new importance for Continental architects. Although he never crossed the Channel, Soufflot had personal ties to England and could easily have known Wren's designs from engravings issued in 1726 and 1756. The English connection also helps to explain why the smooth, sparsely decorated surfaces are more akin to those of Chiswick House (which was published by its codesigner, William Kent, in his book on Inigo Jones of 1727) than to any French building. It is an indication of the appeal Chiswick offered to French rationalists that Voltaire had admired it during his English sojourn of 1721–26.

From this coolly precise exterior we would never suspect that Soufflot also had a strong interest in Gothic churches. He admired them, not for the seeming miracles they performed, but for their structural elegance—a rationalist version of Guarini's point of view (see fig. 17-26). Ste.-Geneviève fulfills Soufflot's ideal, conceived early in his career, "to combine the classic orders with the lightness so admirably displayed by certain Gothic buildings." In this regard, he was responding partly to Laugier and other theorists who advocated a union of these seemingly incompatible styles. Soufflot studied Gothic architecture and its proportions in detail. He even constructed a special device to test the strength of stone in order to understand the Gothic structural system, which he used to support the massive dome. However, the buttresses at the four corners remain completely hidden from view by a parapet in order not to disturb the insistent classicism inside and out.

Ste.-Geneviève remains the great architectural statement of the rationalist movement. Unfortunately, the windows were walled in at the suggestion of the critic–theorist Antoine Quatremère de Quincy (1755–1849) in 1791–93 to make the building more "appropriate" for a national monument. The remodeling destroyed the light-filled interior and emphasized the abstract severity of the facade. Soon after being rededicated as the Panthéon, it received the ashes of the Enlightenment philosophers Voltaire and Rousseau and eventually those of the author Victor Hugo. As the Panthéon, the building underwent numerous modifications during the nineteenth century that reflect the turbulent politics of the era. At the direction of Napoleon, Soufflot's pupil Jean-Baptiste Rondelet (1743–1829) redesigned the marble flooring and made changes to the crypt so that it could accommodate the remains of military heroes. Under the Restoration the building was reconsecrated as a church and a fresco, *The Apotheosis of Louis XVIII,* was added to the dome by Antoine-Jean Gros (see page 663). Finally, during the July Monarchy it was restored to its role as the Panthéon, and the pediment was replaced in the 1830s with an entirely new one by Pierre-Jean David d'Angers (1788–1856) representing "The Nation Distributing with the Help of Liberty and History Laurel Wreaths to Great Men."

BOULLÉE. Étienne-Louis Boullée (1728–1799) was half a generation younger than Soufflot and even more daring. He began as a painter and retired early, but though he built little other than private residences, his teaching at the Royal Academy, where he was Legeay's student and successor, helped to create a tradition of visionary architecture that flourished during the last third of the century and the early years of the next. [See Primary Sources, no. 64, page 927.] Boullée's ideal was an architecture of "majestic nobility," an effect he sought to achieve by combining huge, simple masses. Most of his designs were for structures on a scale so enormous that they could hardly be built even today. His ideas were strongly influenced by the theories of Jacques-François Blondel, with whom he also studied, particularly the concept of varying the compositions of different building types according to their social character.

Boullée hailed the sphere as the perfect form, since no trick of perspective can alter its appearance (except, of course, its apparent size). Thus he designed a memorial to Isaac Newton as a gigantic hollow sphere mirroring the universe (fig. 21-17). "O Newton!" he exclaimed, "I conceived the idea of surrounding you with your discovery, and thus, somehow, of surrounding you with yourself." The interior was to be bare, apart from an empty sarcophagus symbolizing the mortal remains of the great man. However, the surface of its upper half would be pierced by countless small holes, points of light meant to create the illusion of stars. Bathed in deep shadow, Boullée's plan for the memorial to Newton has a striking pictorialism inspired in part by the *Prison Caprices* of Piranesi (see fig. 20-27). Plans such as this have a utopian grandeur that dwarfs the boldest ambitions of earlier architects. Largely forgotten during most of the nineteenth century, Boullée was rediscovered in the early twentieth, when architects again dared to "think the unthinkable."

LEDOUX. Although he, too, was a pupil of Blondel, Claude-Nicolas Ledoux (1736–1806) was the opposite of Boullée. He was an architect who built much and turned to theory only late in his career. Yet his work quickly developed visionary qualities that are readily apparent in his most important achievement, the 50 tollgates he designed for the new walls around Paris in 1785–89, of which only four still exist. (The rest were dismantled during the French Revolution.) Our example (fig. 21-18) shows a remarkable sense of geometry placed at the service of an extraordinary imagination. Ledoux has mounted a huge rotunda on a square base, which is entered through a Greek portico supported by pillars instead of columns. (All four sides are identical in appearance.) Although the structure was derived from antiquity via Palladio, the effect is anything but classical. Visually the portico seems almost crushed by the burden of the rotunda, whose massiveness is barely relieved by the strangely medieval-looking screen of arches over paired columns (compare fig. 10-17). The radically simplified forms and decidedly odd proportions are a critique of all earlier examples of the same type, from the Pantheon (see fig. 7-15) through Soufflot's Ste.-Geneviève (see fig. 21-16). (See also figs. 12-15, 14-26, 19-15, and 21-14.) The building, nearly Mannerist in its gestures, is among the most peculiar of any before Frank Lloyd Wright's Guggenheim Museum (see fig. 26-39), which may be regarded as its descendant.

Neoclassicism and the Antique

The mid-eighteenth century was greatly stirred by two experiences: the rediscovery of Greek art as the original source of classic style, and the excavations at Herculaneum and Pompeii in 1738 and 1748, which for the first time revealed the daily life of the ancients and the full range of their arts and crafts. Richly illustrated books about the Akropolis at Athens, the temples at Paestum, and the finds at Herculaneum and Pompeii were published in England and France. Archaeology caught everyone's imagination. From this came a new style of interior decoration. The Greek phase of this revival proved necessarily limited, as only a narrow range of household furnishings was known at second hand from paintings and sculpture, such as the *Grave Stele of Hegeso* (see fig. 5-58). When they wanted to work in a Greek style, designers turned chiefly to architecture, whose vocabulary could be readily adapted to large

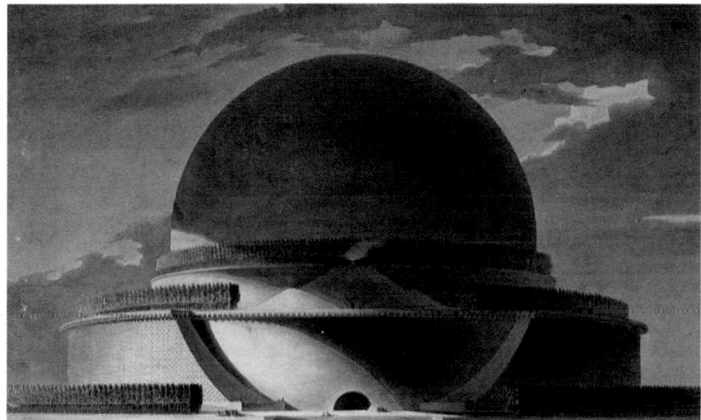

21-17. Étienne-Louis Boullée. *Project for a Memorial to Isaac Newton.* 1784. Ink and wash drawing, 15½ x 25½" (39.4 x 64.8 cm). Bibliothèque Nationale, Paris

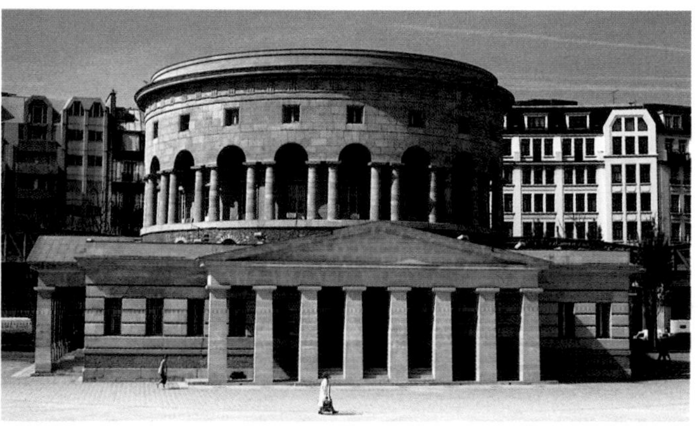

21-18. Claude-Nicolas Ledoux. Barrière de Villette (after restoration), Paris. 1785–89

NEOCLASSICAL MUSIC

Neoclassicism and *Sturm und Drang* (see box page 651) were also important to music. The leading representative of the former was Christoph Willibald Glück (1714–1787). Glück wrote two operas, *Orfeo ed Euridice* (1762) and *Alceste* (1767) with the poet Raniero Calzabigi (1714–1795), who was influenced by Rameau's operas during a sojourn in Paris. They sought to correct the excesses of Italian opera through "a beautiful simplicity" and to "confine music to its proper function of serving the poetry for the expression and the situation of the plot." Though originally produced in Vienna, which had become the opera capital of Europe, the two operas enjoyed greater success in Paris, where classicism was an uninterrupted tradition. Glück's operas have a nobility and depth of feeling that hark back to Monteverdi, and a classicism and pageantry worthy of Lully and Rameau. The subject of both works is the immortality of love, which conquers even death. Alceste, who was willing to die so that her husband, King Admetes, could live, was seen as a paradigm of conjugal love. Thanks in good measure to the opera's popularity, Jean-François Peyron (1744–1814), the only serious rival of Jacques-Louis David (see pages 641–42), made it the subject of his first important commission from Louis XVI in 1785. (The painting is now in the Louvre.)

Carl Philipp Emanuel Bach (1714–1788), a son of Johann Sebastian Bach, served for nearly 30 years at the Berlin court of Frederick the Great (1712–1786), himself a very able composer. Unlike his illustrious father, the younger Bach loathed counterpoint. The widespread reaction against the complexities of counterpoint may be likened to the call for natural morality by Bach's exact contemporary, the philosopher Jean-Jacques Rousseau (1712–1778). Bach nevertheless adopted a conservative style that suited his patron's taste. Upon being appointed music director of Hamburg, one of the most important posts in Germany, he felt free to pursue a direct, expressive style that sometimes shows a debt to his predecessor there, Georg Philipp Telemann. His first Hamburg symphonies exemplify *Sturm und Drang* in music: they are full of extremes, with brooding, sighing, slow movements sandwiched between dynamic fast ones characterized by irregular rhythms and emotional outbursts that startle the listener. Their limitation, and it is a significant one, is the composer's disregard for form, which prevented him from developing them further.

Sturm und Drang also influenced the middle symphonies written by Franz Joseph Haydn (1732–1809) from 1771 to 1774. He spent almost his entire career at the estate of the Esterházys south of Vienna, where he had a small but excellent ensemble of instrumentalists and singers in the service of an enlightened if demanding patron. Haydn became the most famous composer of his era and was called to Paris (1785–86) and London (1790, 1794), where he created symphonies of unrivaled sophistication and richness. He was no less a master of the string quartet, for which he wrote many compositions, all marked by unprecedented variety, formal mastery, and refined feeling. Haydn remained a person of his times: the late oratorios—*The Creation* (1798), based on Milton's *Paradise Lost,* and *The Seasons* (1801), adapted from James Thomson's poem (1726–30) of the same name—maintain the late-eighteenth-century view of an orderly cosmos created by a benevolent god.

Haydn became a close friend of Wolfgang Amadeus Mozart (1756–1791), despite their great differences in age, temperament, and outlook. A child prodigy, Mozart received a rigorous training from his father, Leopold (1719–1787), who took him on tour throughout the great courts of Europe, where he was exposed to the full range of contemporary music. Mozart failed in his efforts to gain a major court appointment; deprived of this measure of security, he became a prolific composer for the open market, putting the stamp of his individual genius on everything he wrote. His finest quartets are the six dedicated to Haydn, who declared him the greatest composer alive, while the late symphonies blaze new territory that foreshadow those of the young Beethoven. His numerous concertos for piano, of which he was a virtuoso, combine enchanting lyricism with brilliant technical display. Mozart was a supreme vocal composer, and it is the singing quality of the human voice that underlies his mature work, regardless of instrument. He was also a master of compositional technique, including counterpoint (he had discussed Bach's music with his successor at Leipzig), and his compositions depend for much of their success on their formal perfection. Indeed, for Mozart, form was the vehicle of expression, which it served to contain, so that there was an ideal, "classical" balance between the two. He was fully sympathetic with the Enlightenment. Its philosophy both informs and burdens his operas, including his acknowledged masterpieces, *The Marriage of Figaro* (1787), based on the play by Beaumarchais, and *Don Giovanni* (1787). Both are a new type of comic opera, called *opera buffa* to distinguish it from traditional serious operas (*opera seria*), but unlike others of their kind, they have a wonderful humanity and substantial content, thanks in part to the librettos by Mozart's collaborator, Lorenzo Da Ponte (1749–1838).

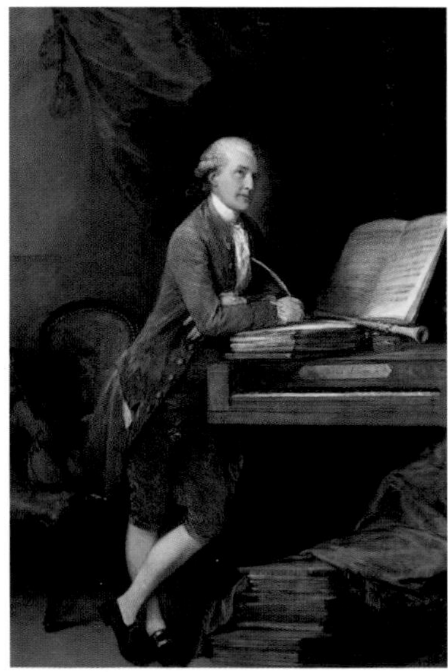

Thomas Gainsborough. *Portrait of Johann Christian Fischer.* 1780. Oil on canvas, 90 x $59^{1}/_{2}$" (228.6 x 150.5 cm). The Royal Collection, London

© HER MAJESTY ELIZABETH II

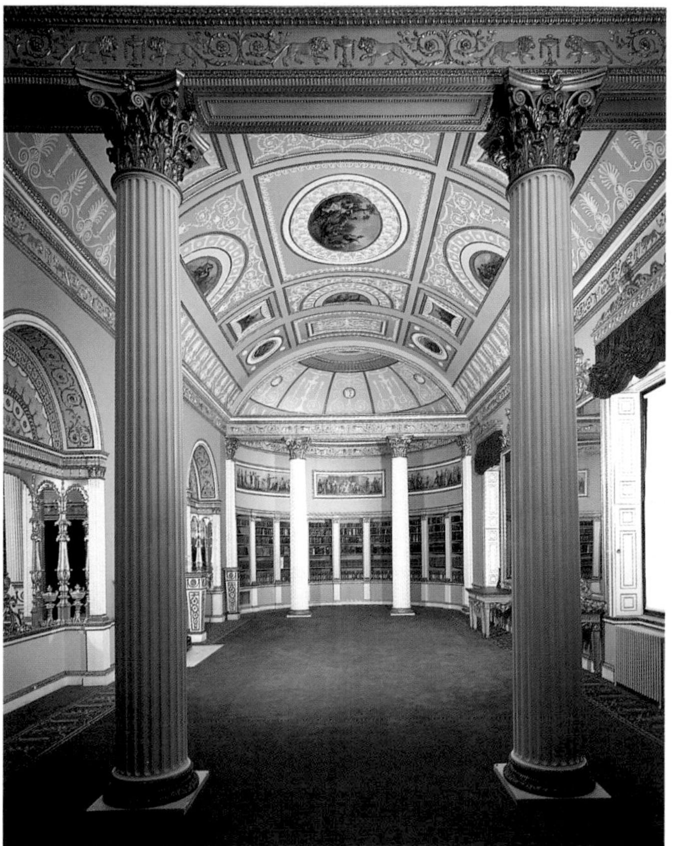

21-19. Robert Adam. The Library, Kenwood, London. 1767–69

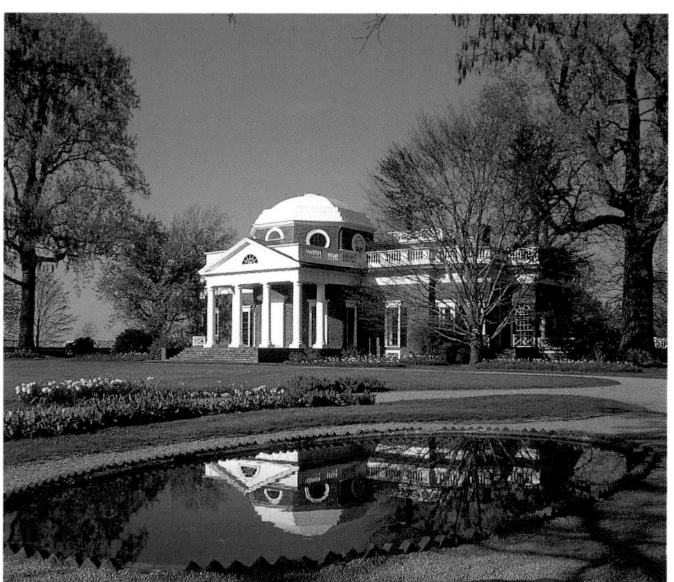

21-20. Thomas Jefferson. Monticello, Charlottesville, Virginia. 1770–84; 1796–1806

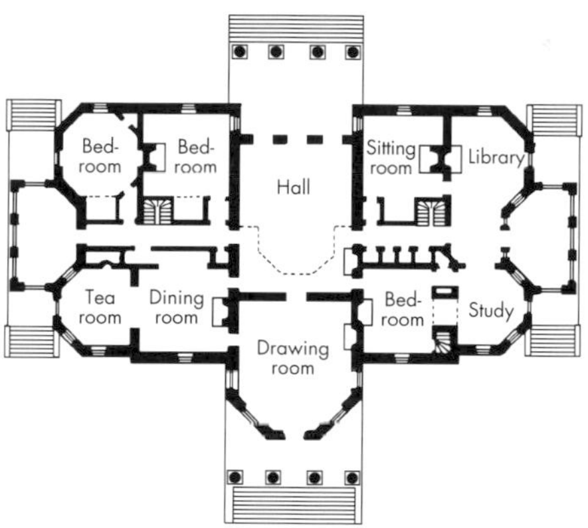

21-21. Plan of Monticello

pieces of furniture where it was combined with Roman elements. Thus it was, for the most part, a classicism of particulars.

ADAM. The Neoclassical style was epitomized by the work of the Englishman Robert Adam (1728–1792). His friendship with Piranesi in Rome reinforced Adam's goal of arriving at a personal style based on the antique without slavishly imitating it. He was also influenced by Clérisseau, with whom he measured the palace of Diocletian at Split (see fig. 7-24). His genius is seen most fully in the interiors he designed in the 1760s for palatial homes, which take the style of Lord Burlington and William Kent as their point of departure. Most are remodelings of or additions to existing homes. Because he commanded an extraordinarily wide vocabulary, including the Gothic, each room is different in both shape and design. Yet the syntax, which treats classicism with remarkable richness and flexibility, remains distinctive to him. The library wing he added to Kenwood (fig. 21-19) shows Adam at his finest. It is covered with a barrel vault connected at either end to an apse that is separated by a screen of Corinthian columns. The basic scheme, clearly Roman in inspiration (compare fig. 7-21), comes from Palladio (see pages 480–82). Amazingly, it had been anticipated more than 40 years earlier by Johann Fischer von Erlach (see pages 603 and 605), who no doubt used the same source.

Adam was concerned above all with movement, but this idea must be understood not in terms of Baroque dynamism or Rococo ornamentation but in the careful balance of varied shapes and proportions. The play of semicircles, half-domes, and arches lends an air of festive grace. The library thus provides an apt setting for "the parade, the convenience, and the social pleasures of life," since it was also a room "for receiving company." This intention was in keeping with Adam's personality, which was at ease with the aristocratic circles in which he moved. The room owes much of its charm to the paintings by Antonio Zucchi (1762–1795), later the husband of Angelica Kauffmann, who also worked for Adam, and to the stucco ornament by Adam's plasterer Joseph Rose, which was adapted from newly discovered Roman examples. The color, too, was in daring contrast to the stark white that was widely preferred for interiors at the time. The effect, stately yet intimate, echoes the delicacy of Rococo interiors (Adam had stayed in Paris in 1754 before going to Rome) but with a characteristically Neoclassic insistence on planar surfaces, symmetry, and geometric precision.

JEFFERSON. The Palladianism launched by Lord Burlington spread overseas to the American colonies, where it became known as the Georgian style. An example of great distinction is the house of Thomas Jefferson (1743–1826), Monticello (figs. 21-20 and 21-21). Built of brick with wood trim, it is not so doctrinaire in design as Chiswick House. (Note the less compact plan and the numerous windows.) It nevertheless stands as a monument to the Enlightenment ideals of order and harmony, with which Jefferson was fully in sympathy. The original plan was adapted from a book of English designs, then gradually modified as Jefferson was exposed to other treatises. The scheme of about 1770 featured an Ionic portico placed over a Doric one and surmounted by a pediment. However, the building was remodeled during Jefferson's presidency, and in its final form Monticello has a facade inspired by Palladio (compare fig. 14-26), though the plan itself was modified only slightly. There is a clear separation between the private quarters in the wings and the public areas for receiving and entertaining visitors, which are described by the porch and dome.

Instead of using the Corinthian order favored by Lord Burlington, Jefferson chose the Roman Doric, which Adam had helped to legitimize, although the late eighteenth century came to favor the heavier and more austere Greek Doric. Jefferson was linked indirectly to Adam through Clérisseau, whom he came to know while serving as the American ambassador to France in 1784–88 and whose help he sought in designing the state capitol of Virginia in Richmond in 1785. Jefferson thought out every detail of Monticello, including its relation to the rest of the plantation. Thus the building is carefully placed in its setting, thanks to Jefferson's study of landscape gardening during a visit to England.

THE ROMANTIC MOVEMENT

Of all the "isms" found in Western art of the past two centuries, Romanticism has always been the most difficult to define. It deserves to be termed an "ism" only because its followers (or at least some of them) thought of themselves as being part of a movement. But none of them has left us anything approaching a definition. Romanticism, it seems, was a certain state of mind rather than the conscious pursuit of a goal. If we try to analyze this state of mind, it breaks down into a series of attitudes, none of which, taken individually, is unique to Romanticism. It is only their particular combination that seems characteristic of the Romantic movement.

How did Romanticism come about? The Enlightenment, paradoxically, liberated not only reason but also its opposite. It helped to create a new wave of emotionalism that was to last for the better part of a half-century and came to be known as Romanticism. The word derives from the late-eighteenth-century vogue for medieval tales of adventure (such as the legends of King Arthur or the Holy Grail), called "romances" because they were written in a Romance language, not in Latin. This interest in the long-neglected "Gothick" past was the sign of a general trend. Those who shared a hatred of the established social order and religion—against established values of any sort—could either try to found a new order based on their faith in the power of reason, or they could seek release in a craving for emotional experience. Their common goal was a desire to "return to Nature." The rationalist acclaimed nature as the ultimate source of reason, while the Romantic worshiped it as unbounded, wild, and ever-changing. The Romantic believed that evil would disappear if people were only to behave "naturally" and give their impulses free rein. In the name of nature, the Romantics acclaimed liberty, power, love, violence, the Greeks, the Middle Ages, or anything else that aroused them, although actually they exalted emotion as an end in itself. This attitude has motivated some of the noblest, as well as vilest, acts of our era. In its most extreme form, Romanticism could be expressed only through direct action, not through works of art. No artist, then, can be a wholehearted Romantic, for the creation of a work of art demands some detachment, self-awareness, and discipline. What William Wordsworth, the great Romantic poet, said of poetry in 1798—that it is "emotion recollected in tranquility"—applies also to the visual arts.

To cast fleeting experience into permanent form, Romantic artists needed a style. But since they were in revolt against the old order, this could not be the established style of the time. It had to come from some phase of the past to which they felt linked by "elective affinity" (another Romantic concept). Romanticism thus favored the revival not of one style, but of a potentially unlimited number of styles. In fact, the rediscovery and use of forms that previously had been neglected or scorned evolved into a stylistic principle in itself. Revivals became the "style" of Romanticism in art, as it did, to a degree, in literature.

Seen in this context, Neoclassicism was simply the first phase of Romanticism, a revival that continued all the way through the nineteenth century, although it came to represent conservative taste. Perhaps it is best, then, to think of them as two sides of the same modern coin. If we maintain the distinction between them, it is because, until about 1800, Neoclassicism overshadowed the other Romantic revivals, and because of the Enlightenment's dedication to the cause of liberty as against the cult of the individual represented by the Romantic hero.

PAINTING

It is one of the many contradictions of Romanticism that, despite the desire for unhindered freedom of individual creativity, it became art for the rising professional and commercial class. The upper middle class dominated nineteenth-century society and replaced state commissions and aristocratic patronage as the most important source of support for artists. Painting remains the greatest creative achievement of Romanticism in the visual arts because, being less expensive, it was less dependent than architecture or sculpture on public approval. It held a greater appeal for the individualism of the Romantic artist as well. Moreover, it could better accommodate the themes and ideas of Romantic literature. Romantic painting was not essentially illustrative. Nevertheless, literature, past and present, now became a more important source of inspiration for painters than ever before. It provided a new range of subjects, emotions, and attitudes. Romantic poets, in turn, often saw nature with a painter's eye. Many had a strong interest in art criticism and theory. Some, notably Johann Wolfgang von Goethe and Victor Hugo, were capable draftsmen. And William Blake cast his visions in both pictorial and written form (see page 675). Art and literature thus have a complex relationship within the Romantic movement.

Spain

GOYA. We begin with the great Spanish painter Francisco Goya (1746–1828), David's contemporary and the only artist of the age who may be called a genius without hesitation. When Goya first arrived in Madrid in 1766, he found both Mengs and Tiepolo working there. He was much impressed with Tiepolo (see page 608), whom he must have recognized immediately as the greater of the two. Goya's early works are in a delightful late Rococo vein that reflects the influence of Tiepolo, as well as the French masters of the Rococo. (Spain had produced no painters of significance for more than a century.) He ignored the growing Neoclassic trend during his brief visit to Rome five years later.

In the 1780s, however, Goya became more of a libertarian. His involvement with Enlightenment thought is best seen in his etchings, which made him the most important printmaker since Rembrandt. Published in series at intervals throughout his career, they ridicule human folly from the same moral viewpoint as Hogarth. But what a vast difference separates the two artists! Although suggested by proverbs and popular superstitions, many of Goya's prints defy exact analysis. He created terrifying scenes such as *The Sleep of Reason Produces Monsters* from the series *Los Caprichos* of the late 1790s (fig. 21-22). The subtitle, added later, expanded on its meaning. "Imagination abandoned by reason produces impossible monsters; united with her, she is the mother of the arts." The artist, shrinking from the assault of his visions, suffers from the same disorder as the figure in Dürer's *Melencolia I* (see fig. 16-9), but his paralysis is psychological rather than conceptual. The image belongs to that realm of imagined horror that we will meet in Fuseli's *The Nightmare* (see fig. 21-43) but is infinitely more compelling. Goya's etching owes part of its success to the technique of aquatint, which he was the first to exploit fully, although he did not invent it (see box below).

Goya surely sympathized with the French Revolution and not with the king of Spain, who had joined other monarchs in war against the young Republic. Yet he was highly regarded at court,

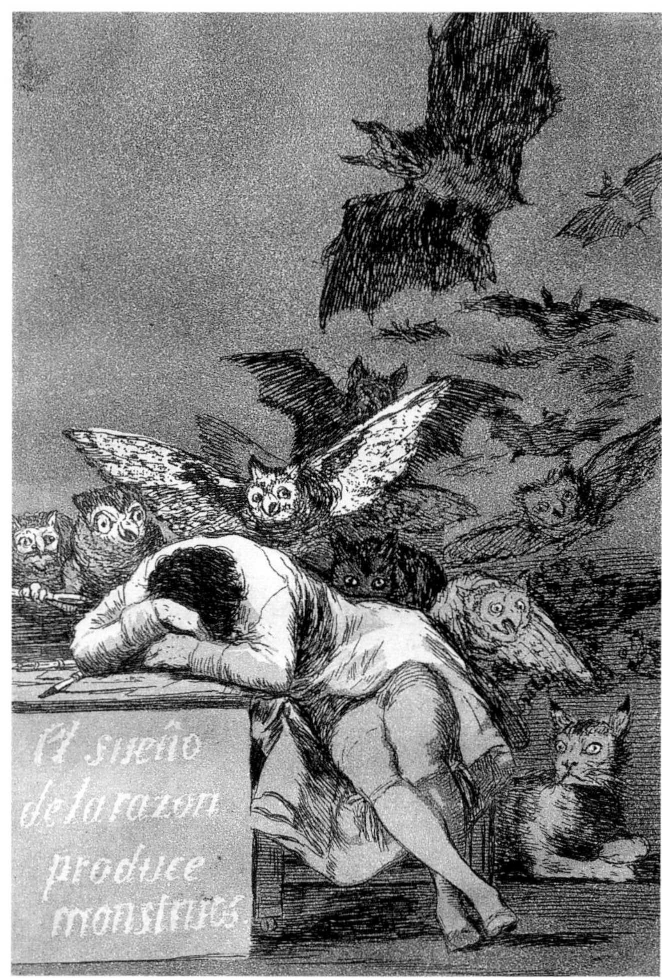

21-22. Francisco Goya. *The Sleep of Reason Produces Monsters,* from *Los Caprichos.* c. 1798. Etching and aquatint, 8½ x 6" (21.6 x 15.2 cm). The Metropolitan Museum of Art, New York

GIFT OF M. KNOEDLER & CO., 1910

NEW PRINTMAKING TECHNIQUES

During the eighteenth century, the range of printmaking was enlarged by the addition of two techniques on copperplates. The first, aquatint, is an extension of etching. It involves melting resin powder on the plate, which leaves a fine crackle pattern exposed to the acid bath. The result is an even, medium tone similar to that of a wash drawing. The other, called mezzotint, is found almost exclusively in portrait and other reproductive engravings. It utilizes a cylindrical rocker covered with tiny teeth to pit the surface of the plate, providing velvety grays and rich blacks on the finished print.

The first completely new print medium, however, was lithography. Invented in Germany shortly before 1800 by Alois Senefelder, it is the most important of the planographic processes, that is, processes that produce prints from a flat surface. Using a greasy crayon or ink, called *tusche,* the artist draws or brushes the design onto a special lithographic stone; alternatively, it can be transferred from paper. (Zinc and aluminum plates have also been used for lithographic printing.) Once the design is fixed by an acid wash, the surface is dampened, then rolled with oily ink, which adheres to the greasy design but is repelled by water. The print is made by pressing moistened paper under light pressure against the stone. Because this technique allows for a limitless number of prints to be pulled relatively cheaply, lithography has been closely associated from the beginning with commercial printing and the popular press.

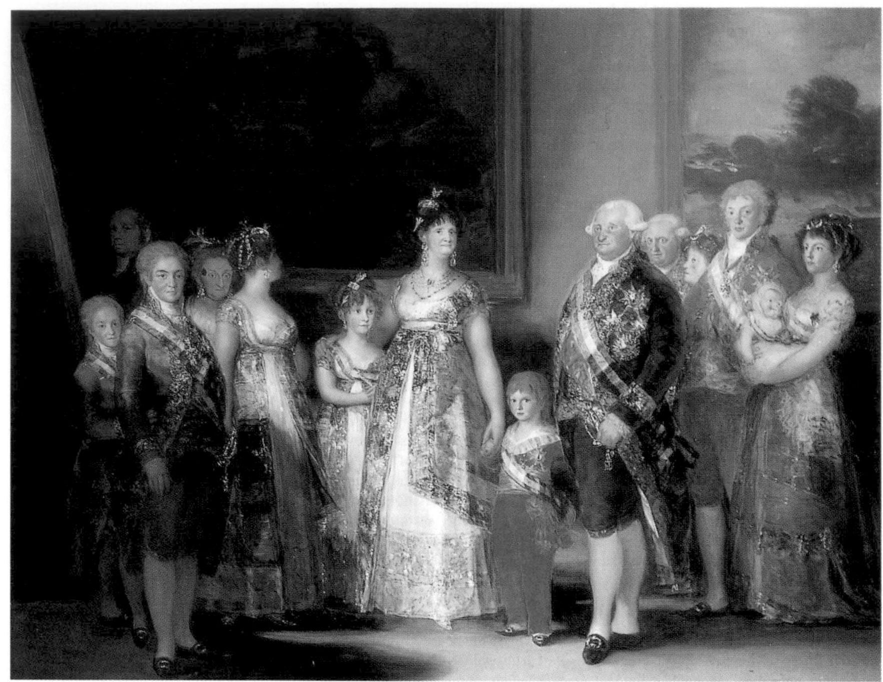

21-23. Francisco Goya. *The Family of Charles IV.* 1800. Oil on canvas, 9'2" x 11' (2.79 x 3.35 m). Museo del Prado, Madrid

where he was appointed painter to the king in 1799. Goya now abandoned the Rococo for a Neo-Baroque style based on Velázquez and Rembrandt, the masters he had come to admire most. It is this Neo-Baroque style that announces the arrival of Romanticism.

The Family of Charles IV (fig. 21-23), Goya's largest royal portrait, echoes Velázquez' *The Maids of Honor* (see fig. 17-35). The entire clan has come to visit the artist, who is painting in one of the picture galleries of the palace. As in the earlier work, shadowy canvases hang behind the group and the light pours in from the side, although its subtle gradations owe as much to Rembrandt as to Velázquez. The brushwork has a sparkle, the color a radiance, rivaling that of *The Maids of Honor.* Goya does not use the Caravaggesque Neoclassicism of David, but his painting has more in common with David's work than we might think. Like David, he practices a revival style and, in his way, is equally devoted to the unvarnished truth: he uses the Neo-Baroque of Romanticism to unmask the royal family.

Psychologically, *The Family of Charles IV* is almost shockingly modern. No longer shielded by the polite conventions of Baroque court portraiture, the inner being of these individuals has been laid bare with pitiless honesty. They are like a collection of ghosts. We see the frightened children, the bloated king, and—in a master stroke of sardonic humor—the grotesquely vulgar queen, posed like Velázquez' Princess Margarita. (Note the left arm and the turn of the head.) How could Goya get away with this? Was the royal family so dazzled by the splendid painting of their costumes that they failed to realize what he had done to them? Goya, we realize, must have painted them as they saw themselves, while unveiling the deeper truth for all the world to see.

When Napoleon's armies occupied Spain in 1808, Goya and many other Spaniards hoped that the conquerors would bring the liberal reforms so badly needed. The barbaric behavior of the French troops crushed these hopes and generated a popular resistance of equal savagery. Many of Goya's works from 1810 to 1815 reflect this bitter experience. The greatest is a pair of large paintings done in 1814 at his request for the newly restored King Ferdinand VII. Their purpose was to commemorate the heroic actions of the Spanish people during the struggle for independence from France. Goya chose two events that ignited the prolonged guerrilla war against the occupying forces. *The Second of May, 1808* (fig. 21-24) shows a group of Madrid citizens attacking a detachment of French troops. The soldiers took revenge by murdering the family of bankers (to whom the artist was related by marriage) and servants of the house from which the shot that killed the Mamaluke (on horseback) was fired. *The Third of May, 1808* (fig. 21-25) represents the execution of rioters the following night. It is doubtful that Goya witnessed either incident, since he made little attempt at topographical accuracy. In characteristically Romantic fashion, he has taken liberties with both scenes for the sake of a higher, "poetic" truth. Together these canvases are the models for the scenes of violence and combat taken up by the French painters Théodore Géricault and Eugène Delacroix (compare figs. 21-28 and 21-33). In *The Second of May, 1808,* the blazing color, and broad, fluid brushwork are more strongly Neo-Baroque than ever in order to heighten the drama. In *The Third of May, 1808,* the dramatic nocturnal light, so reminiscent of El Greco (compare fig. 14-11), gives the picture the emotional intensity of religious art, but these martyrs are dying for Liberty, not the Kingdom of Heaven. Nor are their executioners the agents of Satan but of

21-24. Francisco Goya. *The Second of May, 1808.* 1814. Oil on canvas, 8'9" x 11'4" (2.67 x 3.45 m). Museo del Prado, Madrid

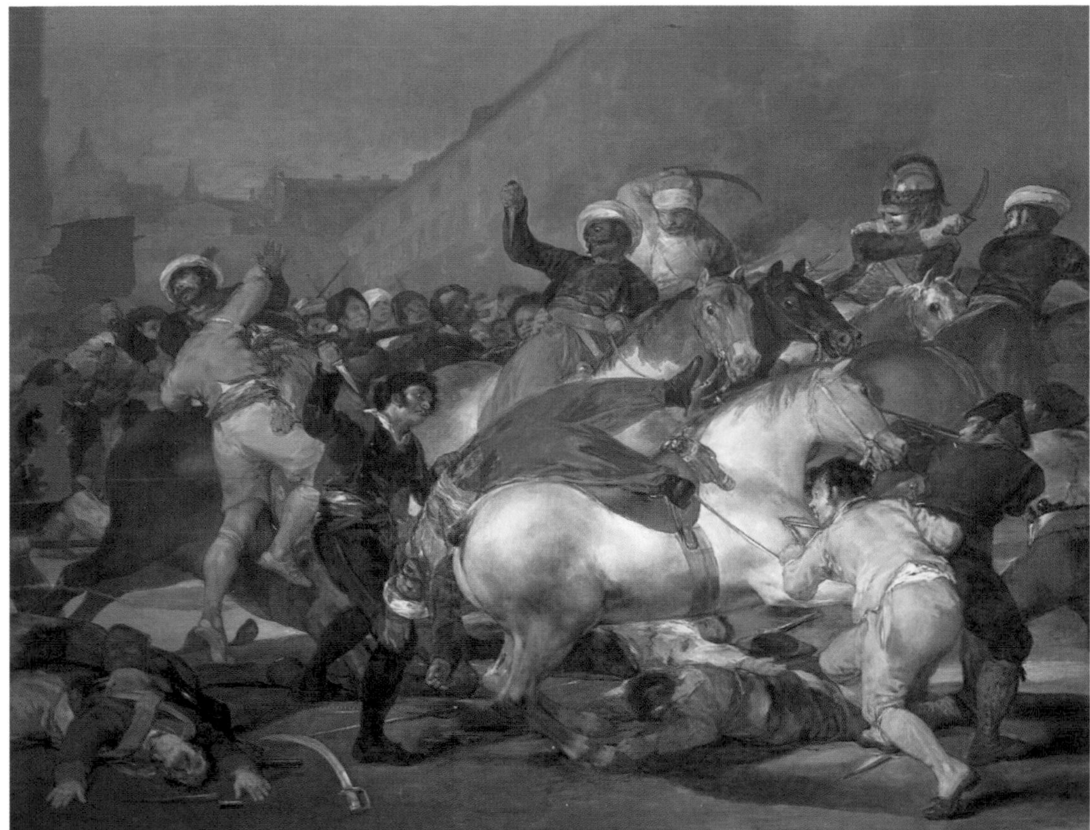

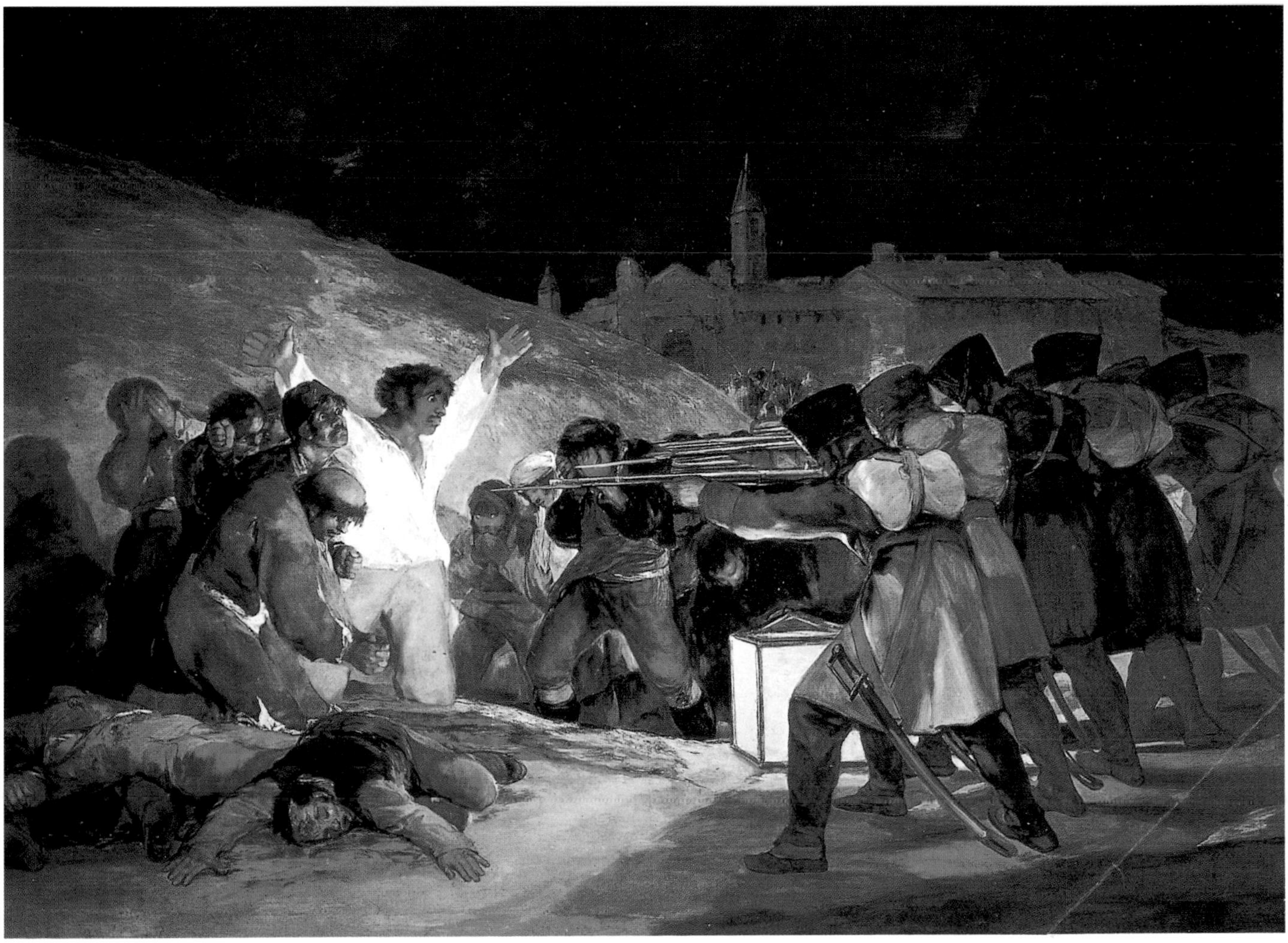

(BELOW) 21-25. Francisco Goya. *The Third of May, 1808.* 1814. Oil on canvas, 8'9" x 13'4" (2.67 x 4.06 m). Museo del Prado, Madrid

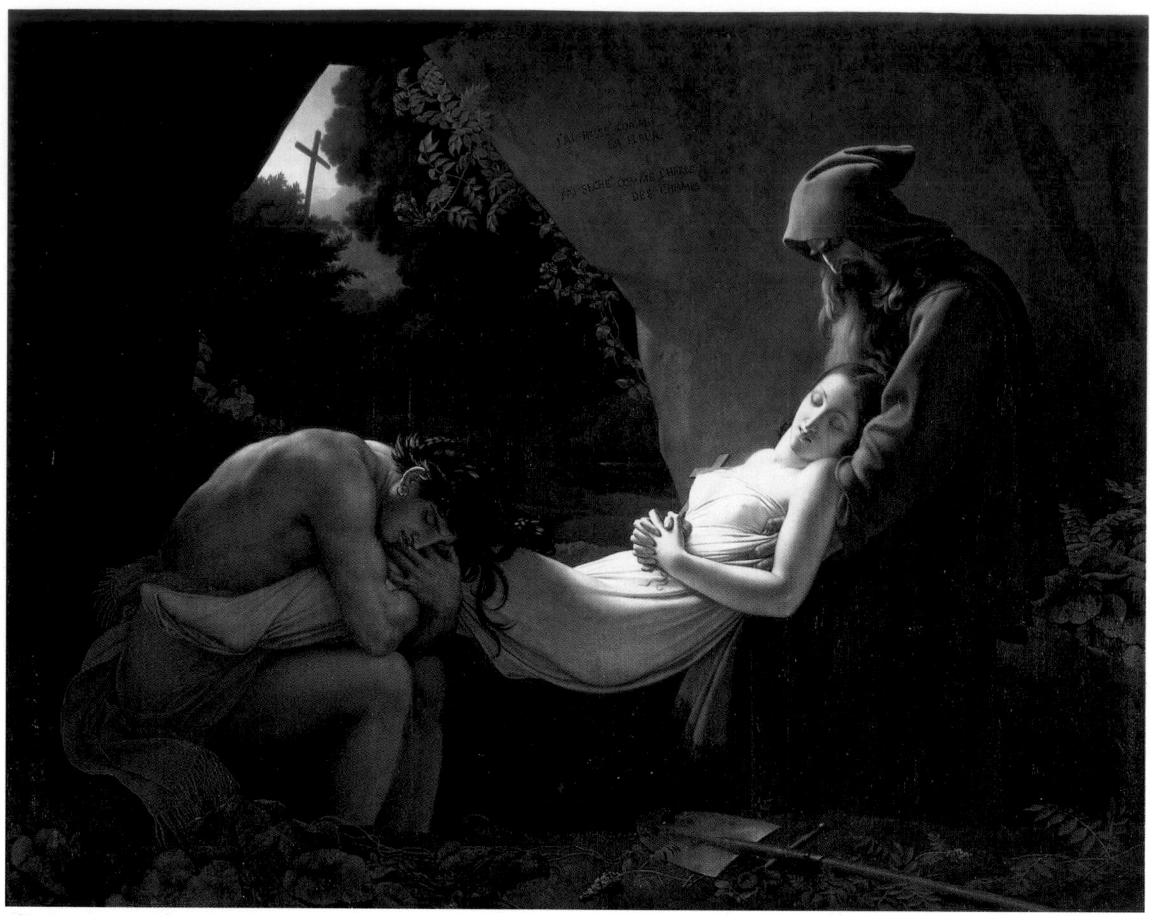

21-26. Anne-Louis Girodet-Trioson. *The Funeral of Atala.* 1808. Oil on canvas, 5'5$\frac{3}{4}$" x 6'10$\frac{5}{8}$" (1.67 x 2.10 m). Musée du Louvre, Paris

political tyranny. They are a formation of faceless killers, completely indifferent to their victims' despair and defiance. The same scene was to be repeated countless times in modern history. With the prophecy of genius, Goya created an image that has become a terrifying symbol of our era.

After the defeat of Napoleon, the Spanish monarchy brought a new wave of repression, and Goya withdrew more and more into a private world. Finally, in 1824, he went into voluntary exile. After a brief stay in Paris, Goya settled in Bordeaux, where he died. His importance for the Neo-Baroque Romantic painters of France is affirmed by Delacroix, the greatest of them all (see pages 666–69), who said that the ideal style would be a combination of Michelangelo's and Goya's art. Later, Édouard Manet turned to him as a source as well.

France

GIRODET. By 1795 Neoclassicism had largely run its course and rapidly lost its purity and rigor. Within a few years French Romantic painting began to emerge among the Primitif faction of Jacques-Louis David's studio. These rebellious students simplified his severe Neoclassicism still further by turning to the linear designs of Greek and Etruscan vase painting and the unadorned style of the Italian Early Renaissance. At the same time, they undermined it by preferring subjects whose appeal was primarily emotional rather than intellectual. Their sources were not the classical authors such as Horace or Ovid but the Bible, Homer, Ossian (the legendary Gaelic bard whose poems were forged by James Macpherson in the eighteenth century), and Romantic literature—anything that excited the imagination. The ablest, as well as most radical, member of the group was Anne-Louis Girodet-Trioson (1767–1824), whose *Funeral of Atala* (fig. 21-26) has all the hallmarks of the Primitif style. Without abandoning his teacher's demanding technique, he reduces the composition to a rhythmic play of lines across the picture plane. The artist emphasizes simple shapes with strong contours, which are further accentuated by the strong highlights. The scene is taken from the wildly popular *Atala, or The Love of Two Savages in the Desert* by François-René de Chateaubriand, one of the first Romantic authors and later foreign minister of France. The unfinished novel, published as excerpts in 1801, has the character of a classical idyll, but with a Romantic taste for the exotic and a religious theme that reflects the Catholic renewal in France. These elements are readily apparent in Girodet's canvas, which treats the burial of the virtuous young woman in the cave like the entombment of a Christian martyr. (Note the cross on the hillside.) Yet unlike the secular martyrdom memorialized by David in *The Death of Marat,* the painting is a celebration of sentiment. Girodet uses an eerie light to evoke an elegiac mood that is his real aim.

GROS. With its exciting glamour and its adventurous conquests in remote parts of the world, the reign of Napoleon (which lasted from 1799 to 1815, with one interruption) gave rise to French Romanticism. David became an ardent admirer of Napoleon and executed several large pictures glorifying the emperor. As a portrayer of the Napoleonic myth, however, he was partially eclipsed by artists who had been his students. They found the style of David too confining and fostered a Baroque revival to capture the excitement of the age. Antoine-Jean Gros (1771–1835), David's favorite pupil, shows us Napoleon as a Christlike leader and healer (fig. 21-27). During the siege of Jaffa on the Mediterranean coast in 1799, the bubonic plague broke out. To calm the panic that followed, the general entered the pesthouse and walked fearlessly among the patients—an event that soon became legendary. The painting is a carefully calculated piece of propaganda that ignores the fact that Napoleon had ordered the execution of hundreds of prisoners. The central group is a play on the doubting of St. Thomas (see figs. 9-29 and 12-52), but now the roles are reversed. This simple but ingenious device raises Napoleon to an almost godlike status even before he became emperor toward the end of 1804, the year the picture was painted. The focus is on the general's courage in touching the sick and the dying. (Note the officer covering his face with a kerchief against the odor.) Many of the figures are paraphrased from Michelangelo's *Last Judgment* (see fig. 13-20). The burning ruins in the background heighten the apocalyptic aura of the scene. But what really excited the artist's imagination was the alien surroundings. Napoleon's conquests opened up Egypt and the Near East for the first time in centuries and led to the European colonization of North Africa. *Napoleon in the Pesthouse at Jaffa* is one of the first symptoms of Orientalism: the Romantic fascination with the Arab world that preoccupied European artists and writers throughout most of the nineteenth century. The artist cannot resist dwelling on the foreign costumes and architecture, which curiously paraphrase the classical setting in an early canvas by his master, David.

After Napoleon's empire collapsed, David spent his last years in exile in Brussels. There his major works were playfully amorous subjects, which were drawn from ancient myths and legends and painted in a coolly sensuous Neo-Mannerist style he had developed in Paris. He turned his pupils over to Gros, whom he urged to return to Neoclassic orthodoxy. Much as Gros respected his teacher's doctrines, his emotional nature drew him to the color and drama of the Baroque. He remained torn between academic principles and his pictorial instincts. Consequently, he never achieved David's authority and ended his life by suicide.

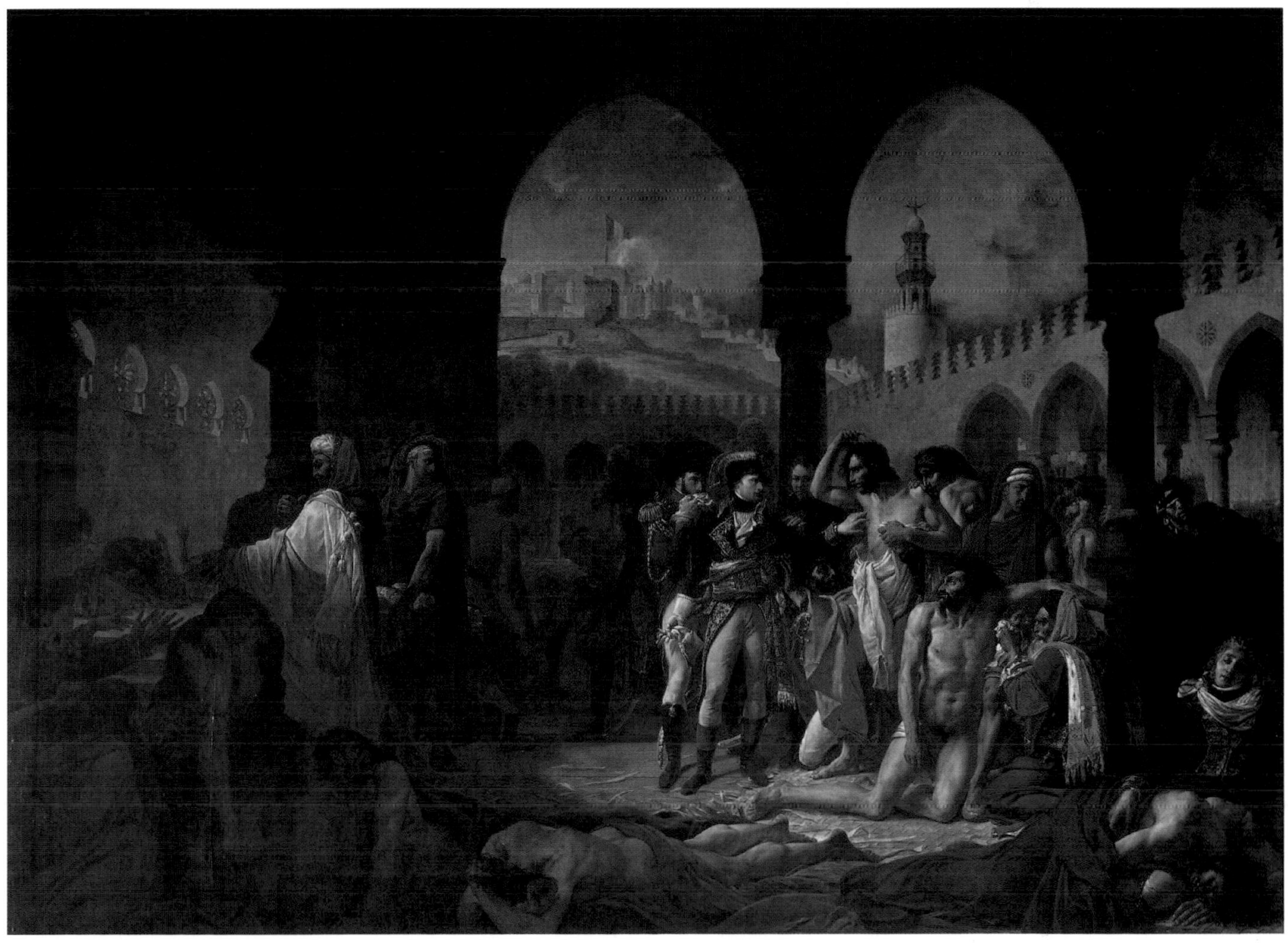

21-27. Antoine-Jean Gros. *Napoleon in the Pesthouse at Jaffa, 11 March 1799.* 1804. Oil on canvas, 17'5½" x 23'7½" (5.32 x 7.20 m). Musée du Louvre, Paris

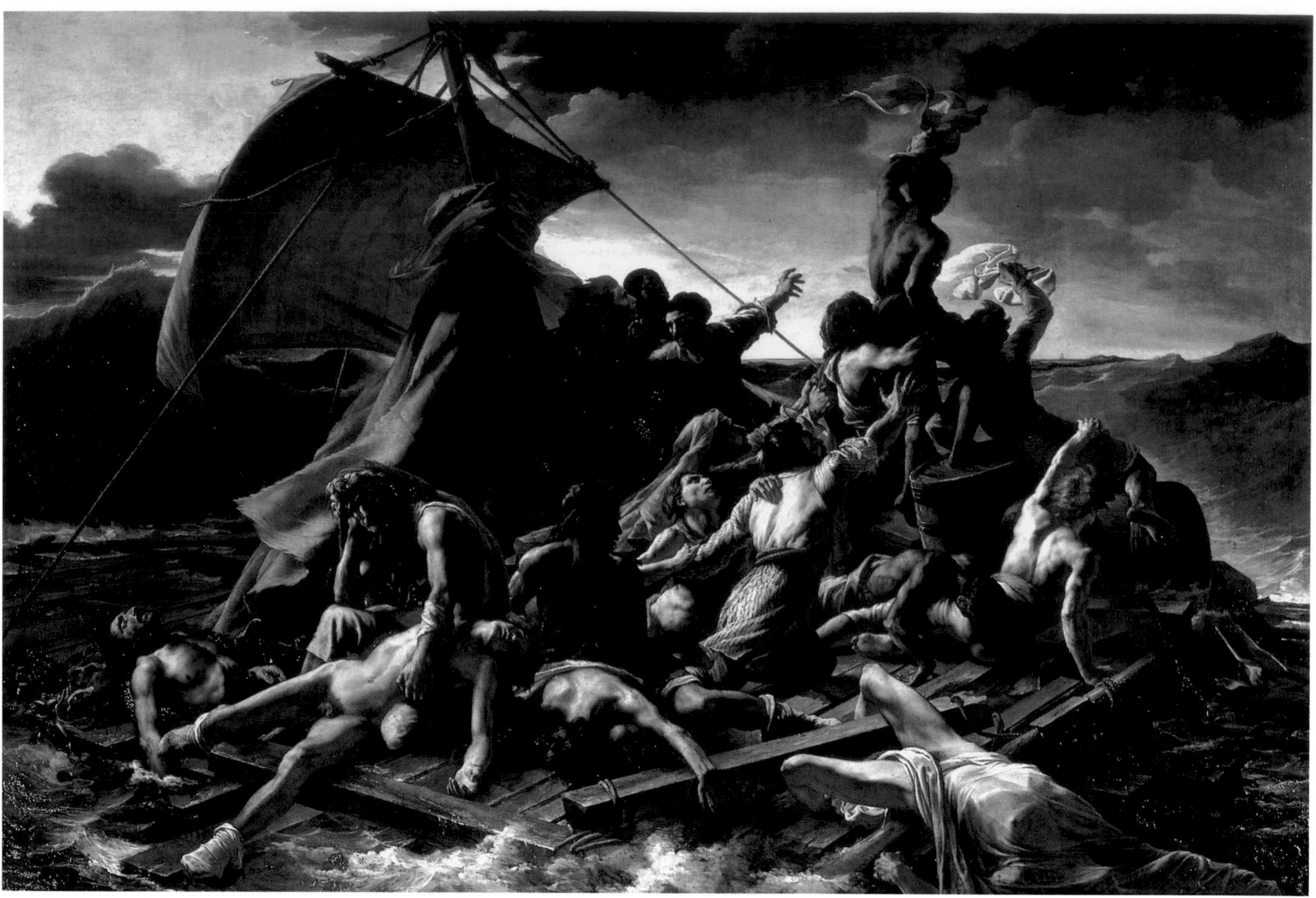

21-28. Théodore Géricault. *The Raft of the "Medusa."* 1818–19. Oil on canvas, 16'1" x 23'6" (4.9 x 7.16 m). Musée du Louvre, Paris

GÉRICAULT. The Neo-Baroque trend initiated in France by Gros aroused the imagination of many talented younger artists. The chief heroes of Théodore Géricault (1791–1824), apart from Gros, were Michelangelo and the great Baroque masters. He painted his most ambitious work, *The Raft of the "Medusa"* (fig. 21-28), in response to a political scandal and a modern tragedy of epic proportions. The *Medusa,* a government vessel, had foundered off the West African coast with hundreds of men on board. Only a handful were rescued after many days on a makeshift raft that had been set adrift by the ship's heartless captain and officers. The event attracted Géricault's attention because, like many French liberals, he opposed the monarchy that was restored after Napoleon. He went to extraordinary lengths in trying to achieve a maximum of authenticity. He interviewed survivors, had a model of the raft built, even studied corpses in the morgue. This search for uncompromising truth is like David's, and *The Raft* is indeed remarkable for its powerfully realistic detail. Yet these preparations were subordinate in the end to the spirit of heroic drama that dominates the canvas. Géricault depicts the moment when the rescue ship is first sighted. From the bodies of the dead and dying in the foreground, the composition is built up to a climax in the group that supports the frantically waving black man, so that the forward surge of the survivors parallels the movement of the raft itself. In 1820 the artist took the monumental canvas on a traveling exhibit to England, in the hope that this theme of "man against the elements" would have strong appeal across the Channel, where Copley had painted *Watson and the Shark* 40 years before (see fig. 21-7).

Géricault's numerous studies for *The Raft of the "Medusa"* had taught him how to explore extremes of the human condition scarcely touched by earlier artists, even Gros. He went now not only to the morgue, but to the insane asylum of Paris. There he became a friend of Dr. Georget, a pioneer in modern psychiatry, and painted for him a series of portraits of individual patients to illustrate various types of derangement, such as that in figure 21-29. The study has an immediacy that recalls Frans Hals, but Géricault's sympathy toward his subject makes his work contrast tellingly with *Malle Babbe* (see fig. 18-12). This ability to see the victims of mental disease as fellow human beings, not as accursed or bewitched outcasts, is one of the noblest fruits of the Romantic movement.

Goya, too, had ventured into an insane asylum a few years earlier but rendered it as a madhouse in keeping with his pessimistic view of human nature. The two artists shared other subjects that few had taken up before, including horses and blacksmiths. Géricault, himself an enthusiastic horseman, later became interested in the British animal painters such as George Stubbs (see pages 646–47) during his stay in England. Sadly, he was to die at an early age following a riding accident.

INGRES. The leadership of David's school ultimately fell to his pupil Jean-Auguste-Dominique Ingres (1780–1867). In 1806 he went to Italy and remained for 18 years, so that he largely missed out on the formation of Romantic painting in France. After his return he became the high priest of the Davidian tradition, which he defended from the attacks of younger artists. [See Primary Sources, no. 65, page 928.] What had been a revolutionary style only half a century before now became rigid dogma, endorsed by the government and backed by the weight of conservative opinion.

Ingres is usually called a Neoclassicist, and his opponents Romantics. Actually, both factions stood for aspects of Romanticism after 1800: the Neoclassic phase, with Ingres as the last important survivor, and the Neo-Baroque, announced in France by Gros' *Napoleon in the Pesthouse at Jaffa.* Indeed, the two seem so interrelated that we should prefer a single name for both if a suitable one could be found. ("Romantic Classicism," which is appropriate only to the classical camp, has not won wide acceptance.) The two sides seemed to revive the old quarrel between Poussinistes and Rubénistes (see page 594). The original Poussinistes had never quite practiced what they preached, and Ingres' views, too, were far more doctrinaire than his pictures. He always held that drawing was superior to painting, yet his canvas *Odalisque with a Slave* (fig. 21-30) reveals an exquisite sense of color. Instead of merely tinting his design, he sets off the petal-smooth

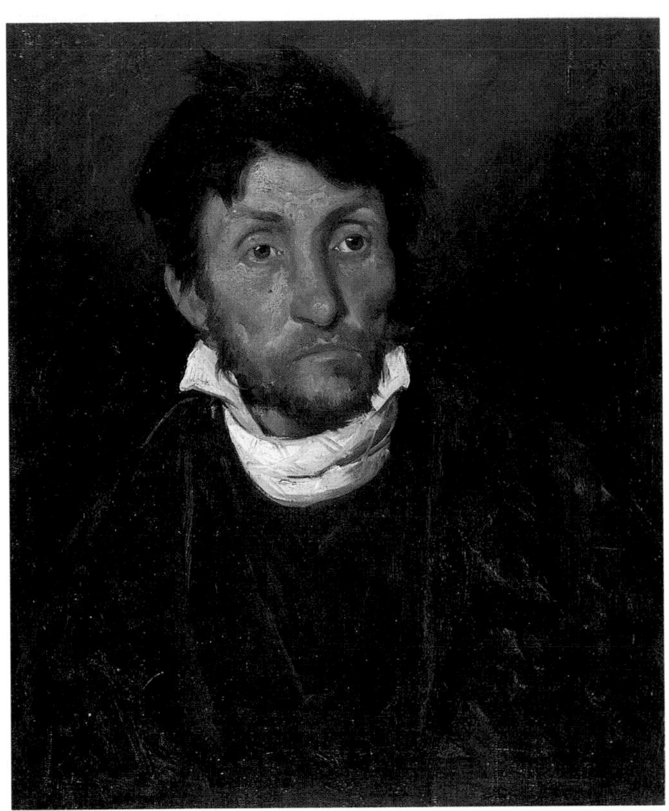

21-29. Théodore Géricault. *The Madman.* 1821–24. Oil on canvas, 24 x 20" (61 x 50.8 cm). Museum voor Schone Kunsten, Ghent, Belgium

(Below) 21-30. Jean-Auguste-Dominique Ingres. *Odalisque with a Slave.* 1839–40. Oil on canvas, 28⅜ x 39½" (72.1 x 100.3 cm). Fogg Art Museum, Harvard University Art Museums, Cambridge, Massachusetts

GRENVILLE L. WINTHROP REQUEST

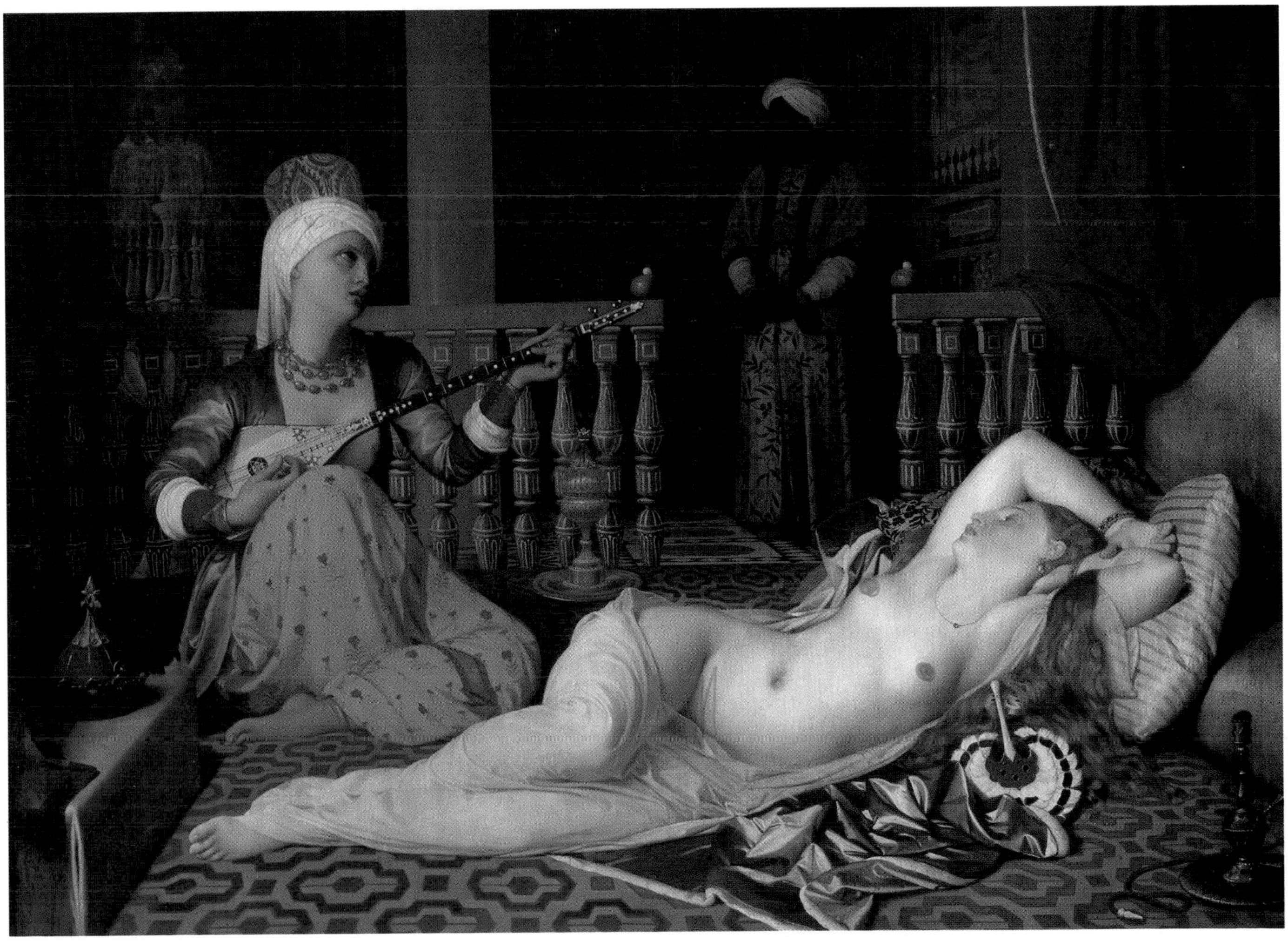

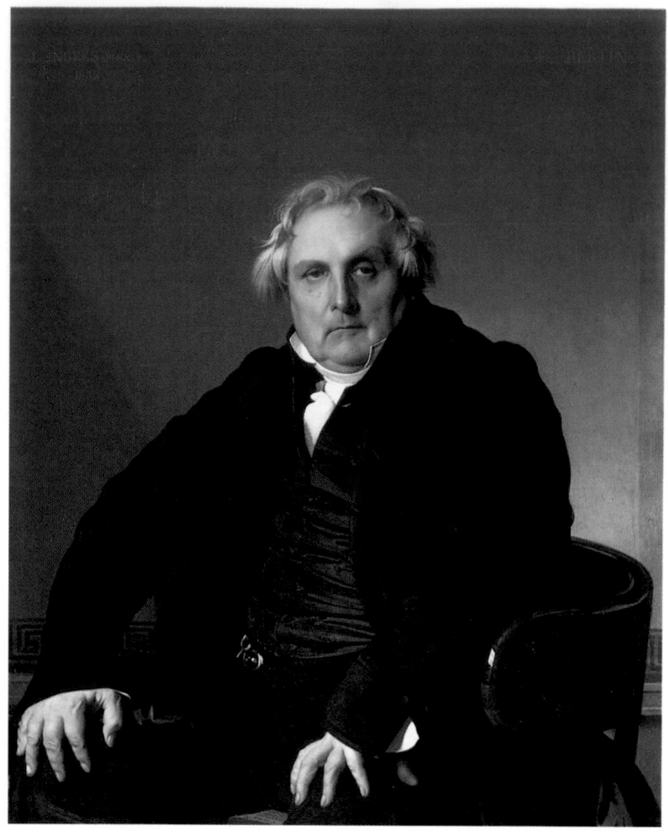

21-31. Jean-Auguste-Dominique Ingres. *Louis Bertin.* 1832. Oil on canvas, 46 x 37½" (116.8 x 95.3 cm). Musée du Louvre, Paris

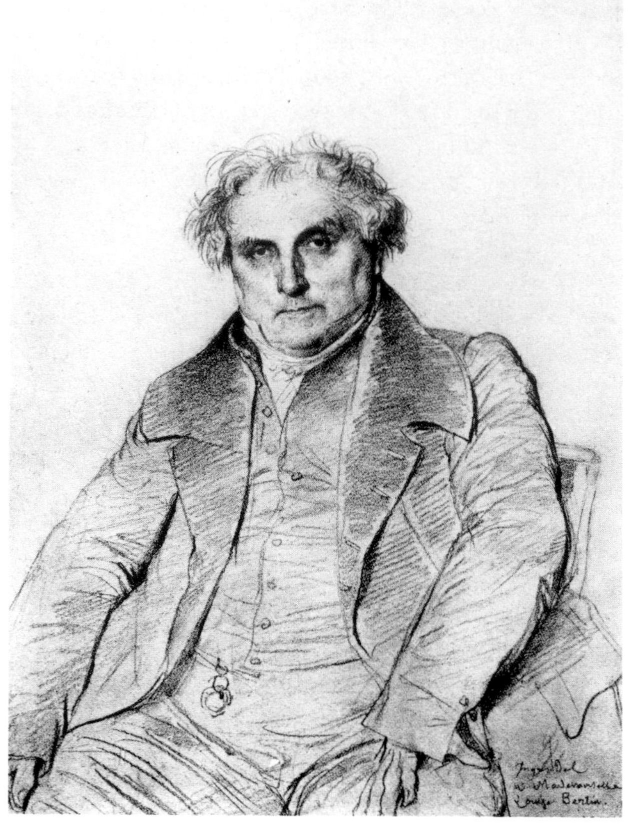

21-32. Jean-Auguste-Dominique Ingres. *Louis Bertin.* 1832. Pencil drawing. Musée du Louvre, Paris

limbs of this Oriental Venus (*odalisque* is a Turkish word for a harem slave girl) with a dazzling array of transparent tones and rich textures. The poetic mood, filled with the enchantment of the *Thousand and One Nights,* is just as important as the finely balanced composition in holding the picture together. The exotic subject is characteristic of the Romantic movement. Despite Ingres' professed worship of Raphael, this nude hardly embodies a classical ideal of beauty. Her elongated proportions, languid grace, and strange mixture of coolness and voluptuousness remind us of Parmigianino's figures (compare fig. 14-4). Whether he admitted it or not, Ingres was just as Romantic as his great rival Eugène Delacroix, only in a different way (compare fig. 21-34).

History painting as defined by Poussin remained Ingres' lifelong ambition, but he had great difficulty with it. Portraiture, which he pretended to dislike, was his strongest gift and his steadiest source of income. He was, in fact, the last great professional in a field soon to be dominated by the camera. Ingres' *Louis Bertin* (fig. 21-31) at first glance looks like a kind of "super-photograph," but this impression is deceptive. Comparing it with the preliminary pencil drawing (fig. 21-32), we realize how much interpretation the portrait contains. The drawing, quick, sure, and precise, is a masterpiece of detached observation, but the painting endows the sitter with a massive presence and forceful personality. Bertin's pose is shifted slightly to the left, his jacket open to lend the figure greater weight. The position of his powerful hands, which are barely indicated in the drawing, has been adjusted to convey an almost lionlike strength. Ingres further uses the Caravaggesque Neoclassicism he had inherited from David to introduce slight changes of light and to selectively emphasize certain features in the face that subtly alter its expression, which now has an almost frightening intensity.

Only Ingres among the Romantics could unify psychological depth and physical accuracy so completely. His followers focused on physical accuracy alone, competing vainly with the camera. The Neo-Baroque Romantics, in contrast, emphasized the psychological aspect to such a degree that their portraits tended to become records of the artist's private emotional relationship with the sitter. These are often interesting and moving, but they are no longer portraits in the proper sense of the term.

DELACROIX. The year 1824 was crucial for French painting. Géricault died after a riding accident. The first showing in Paris of works by the English Romantic painters, especially John Constable, was a revelation to many French artists (see pages 675–77). Ingres returned to France from Italy and had his first public success. And Eugène Delacroix (1798–1863) established himself as the foremost Neo-Baroque Romantic painter. For the next quarter-century, he and Ingres were bitter rivals, and their polarity, fostered by supporters, dominated the artistic scene in Paris. [See Primary Sources, no. 66, page 928.]

To critics, who had recently begun to struggle with the problem of defining Romanticism in art, Delacroix seemed the first indisputably Romantic painter, and his work did indeed crystallize the issues. As a result, Romanticism, which previously had been identified largely with Madame de Staël (see box page 682), now became virtually synonymous with modernism. Delacroix occupied a position at its artistic center comparable to that of Victor Hugo and Stendhal in literature and Hector Berlioz in music (see boxes on pages 682 and 690–91). Delacroix, like his model Rubens, is an extremely challenging artist, so that it is not easy to take the full measure of his accomplishments. Although he studied with a important pupil of David, his early paintings reflect his admiration for Gros (who nevertheless called *The Massacre at Chios* "the massacre of painting" when it was exhibited in 1824) and for Géricault, whom he knew well.

The first work to show him as a mature master is *The Death of Sardanapalus* (fig. 21-33), inspired by Lord Byron's drama in free verse of 1821. Delacroix was above all a literary painter. (He also became the most original—and controversial—illustrator of the age.) If the military hero inspired the early Romantics, it was the cultural hero who touched the imagination of the generation that arose in the mid-1820s. The glamorous days of Napoleon and his empire were now only a memory, so that Delacroix had either to go to some remote place or turn to exotic history and literature for the kind of subject that excited his imagination. He often chose those writers favored by other Romantic artists: Dante, Shakespeare, Goethe, Scott. But he was inspired above all by Byron, the archetype of the Romantic, whose valiant death as commander of a regiment at Missolonghi in 1824 during the Greek war of independence from the Turks was mourned by Delacroix as a tragedy. The artist's fascination with all things English was fired by the flood of literature that began to be published in French translations in 1816. It was further kindled by his friendship with Géricault and Gros' pupil Richard Bonington (1802–1828), who also helped to awaken his interest in the Orient. This enthusiasm was cemented when Delacroix, who had learned English as a schoolboy, visited London in 1825.

His journal records that when stuck for a subject, he would turn to the same authors again and again for inspiration. "I should want to spread out some good thick, fat paint on a brown or red canvas. What I would need, then, in finding a subject is to open a book that can inspire me and let its mood guide me. There are those that never fail. The same with engravings. Dante, Lemartine, Byron, Michelangelo." Exactly this sort of thing seems to have happened with the *Sardanapalus,* which, strangely enough, does not illustrate the final scene in Lord Byron's literary play. It instead evokes his death as the artist imagined it. However, Delacroix's vision of the Orient was based almost entirely on Byron's poetry: "The Giaour," "The Bride of Abydos," and "The Siege of Corinth" (which inspired one of Berlioz's operas, as did "The Corsair").

The picture has the apocalyptic intensity of Michelangelo's

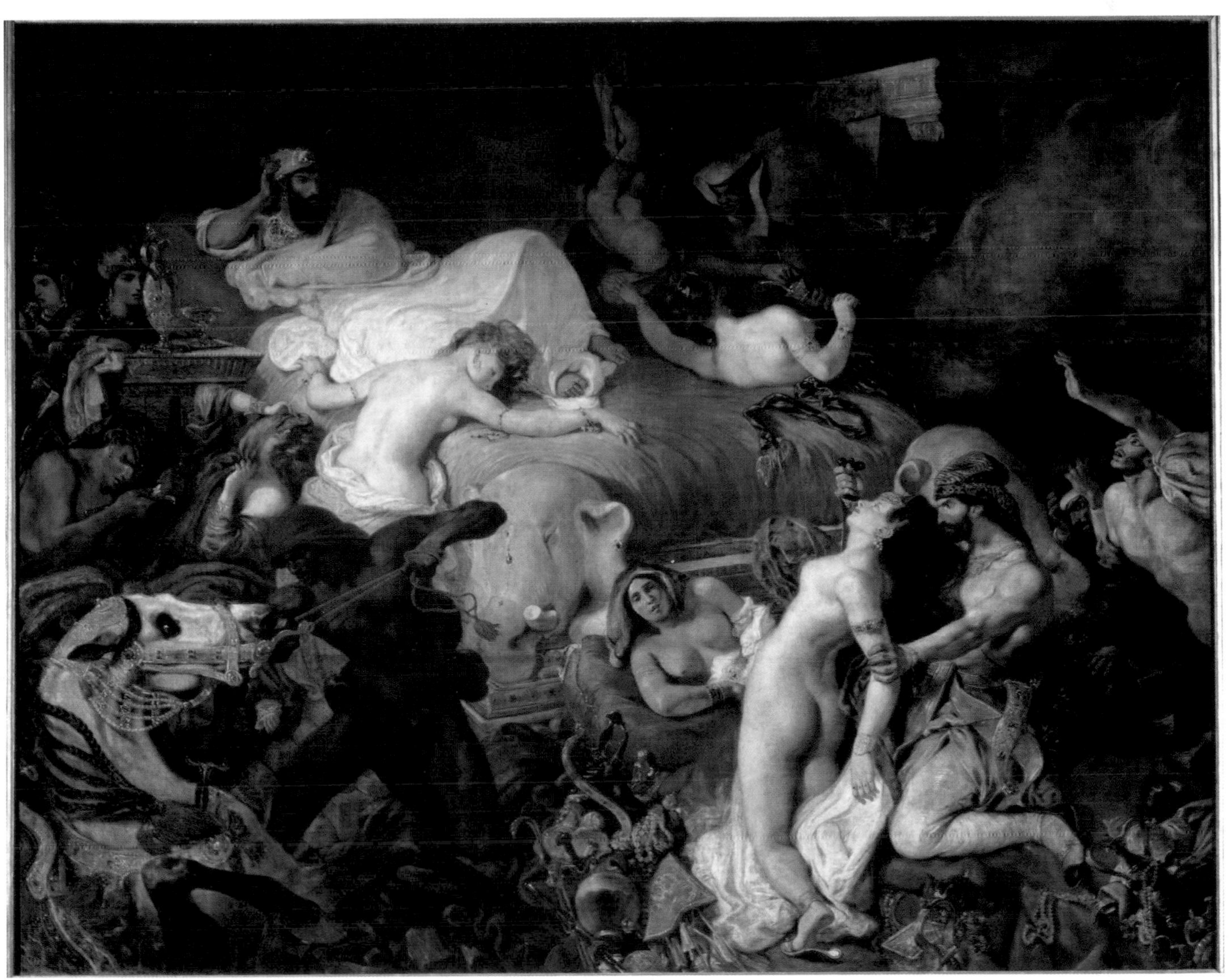

21-33. Eugène Delacroix. *The Death of Sardanapalus.* 1827. Oil on canvas, 12'1½" x 16'2⅞" (3.69 x 4.94 m). Musée du Louvre, Paris

Last Judgment (see fig. 13-20), the nearly superhuman power of Rubens' *Raising of the Cross* (see fig. 18-1), and the extraordinary freedom of Velazquez' late works (see fig. 17-34). Such sources have been combined into an intoxicating mixture of sensuousness and cruelty. As in Rubens' painting, the sea of writhing figures is loosely organized along a rising diagonal. In both, virtually every square inch is covered with action, save for a glimpse onto the distant background. The rich color and fluid brushwork show Delacroix to be a Rubéniste of the first order. Earlier he had maintained the primacy of line to enclose form. Here he is more concerned with setting up linear rhythms across the canvas, which requires him to adjust contours in response to one another. As a result, there is a ceaseless movement in which the main organizing role is played by the cascades of red cloth. No wonder the painting was severely criticized by conservatives for its poor draftsmanship and inconsistent space, for it violates every classical rule. Delacroix realized its flaws but was willing to sacrifice everything for the sake of effect. While we do not quite accept the scene as authentic, we revel in the sheer splendor of the painting.

Delacroix's sympathy with the Greeks did not prevent him from sharing the enthusiasm of fellow Romantics for the Orient. He was enchanted by a visit in 1832 to North Africa, where he found a living counterpart of the violent, chivalric, and picturesque past evoked in Romantic literature. His sketches from this trip supplied him with a large repertory of subjects: harem interiors, street scenes, lion hunts. It is fascinating to compare his *Women of Algiers* (fig. 21-34) with Ingres' *Odalisque with a Slave* (see fig. 21-30). In his version, Ingres also celebrates the exotic world of the Near East—alien, seductive, and violent—but how different the result! Delacroix's is based on studies made during an actual visit to a harem in Algiers. The painting has an authenticity even in the details that is clearly missing in Ingres' aromatic confection, even though the Arab women were carefully posed using a model in the studio and the costumes were reworked. No less important, the intense colors and bright light of northern Africa made an indelible impression on the artist, whose palette underwent a major change.

Delacroix's creativity reached its peak in the years around 1840. During this extraordinarily fertile period, he established many of the great themes that would preoccupy him for the rest of his career. Thereafter he introduced only a few new subjects—*The Abduction of Rebecca* (fig. 21-35) among them. Taken from Sir Walter Scott's novel *Ivanhoe,* it shows the beautiful Jewish woman being taken from the burning castle of Front-de-Boeuf by two Saracen slaves of

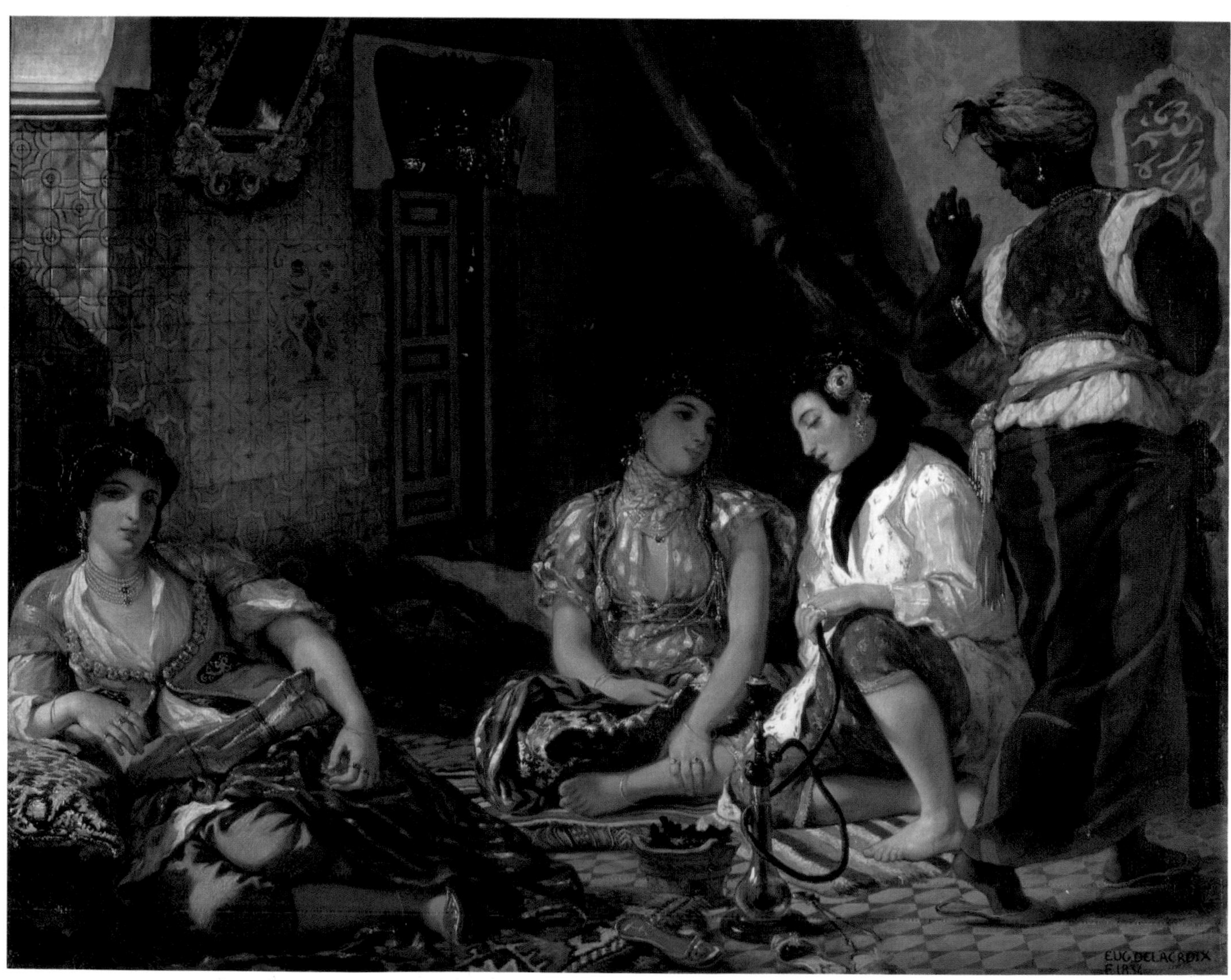

21-34. Eugène Delacroix. *Women of Algiers*. 1834. Oil on canvas, 70⅞ x 90⅛" (180 x 229 cm). Musée du Louvre, Paris

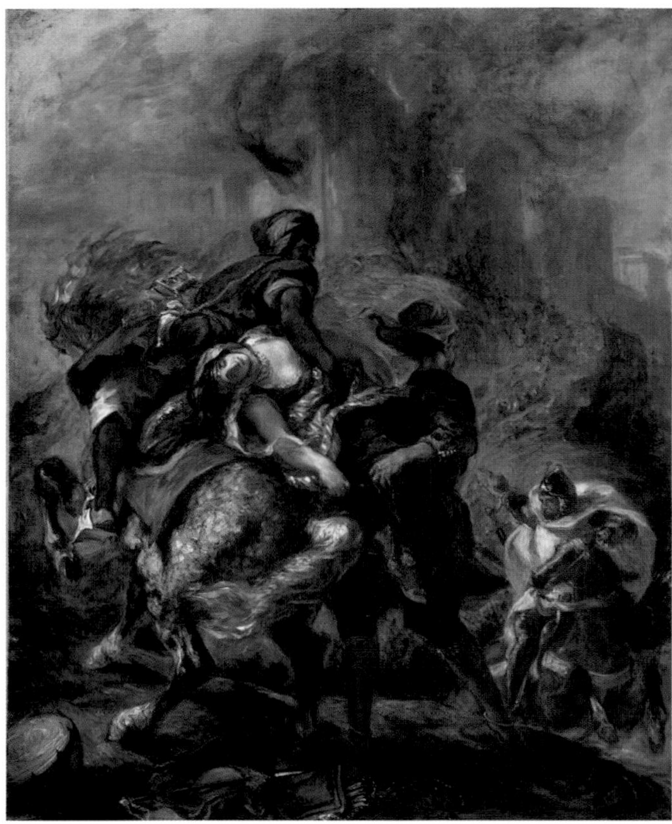

21-35. Eugène Delacroix. *The Abduction of Rebecca*. 1846. Oil on canvas, 39½ x 32¼" (100.3 x 81.9 cm). The Metropolitan Museum of Art, New York

CATHERINE LORILLARD WOLFE COLLECTION, WOLFE FUND, 1903

the Knight Templar Bois-Gilbert. Although Delacroix harbored doubts about the literary quality of Scott's work, it provided the violent subjects so dear to his own Romantic sensibility, and he treated it often. The scene is remarkably similar to Oriental combats inspired by Lord Byron's poems. What mattered to the artist was its exotic quality. The painting shows Delacroix at the height of his powers. It is the direct outgrowth of the change initiated by the *Women of Algiers*. The color is lighter and more expressive. Above all, the brushwork has a nervous energy that animates the entire surface. Not since Rubens have we seen such virtuosity. How did he achieve it? Ironically, at the very moment that his inventiveness seemed to wane, he turned his attention to the formal qualities of art. He arrived, in fact, at pure painting.

When it was exhibited at the Salon of 1846, the painting was favorably reviewed by the young critic Charles Baudelaire:

> The admirable thing about *The Abduction of Rebecca* is the perfect ordering of its colors, which are intense, close-packed, serried and logical; the result of this is a thrilling effect. With almost all painters who are not colorists, you will always notice vacuums, that is to say great holes, produced by tones which are below the level of the rest, so to speak. Delacroix's painting is like nature: it has a *horror vacuii*.

Baudelaire devoted a long section of his Salon review to Delacroix, whose art he worshiped and understood more deeply than any other critic of the day. He noted perceptively, "Delacroix had decorations to paint, and he solved the great problem. He discovered pictorial unity without doing harm to his trade as a colorist. We have the Palais Bourbon to bear witness to this extraordinary *tour de force*." This commission, which occupied the artist between 1838 and 1847, brought him into renewed contact with the tradition of Western art. His work now showed a preference for classical and biblical themes, without abandoning his earlier subjects. He was, as Baudelaire observed, that rarity in the nineteenth century: an artist who could paint moving religious works, even though he was not a believer himself. The time frame of the Bourbon Palace decorations coincides with a general crisis of tradition that gripped French art beginning in about 1840 and climaxing eight years later, when revolution was in the air everywhere. Delacroix came to be seen, with Ingres, as the last great representative of the mainstream of European painting. Baudelaire put it best: "Delacroix is the latest expression of progress in art. Heir to the great tradition . . . and a worthy successor of the old masters, he has even surpassed them in his command of anguish, passion and gesture! But take away Delacroix, and the great chain of history is broken and slips to the ground. It is true that the great tradition has been lost, and that the new one is not yet established." There is every indication that Delacroix himself was aware of his new status. Contrary to Baudelaire, however, Delacroix does stand at the head of a new tradition. Not only did the Impressionists take his palette and technique as their point of departure, but he became, in effect, the founder of what later came to be called Expressionism. Thus the course of modern art is unthinkable without him.

DAUMIER. The later work of Delacroix reflects the attitude that eventually doomed the Romantic movement: its growing detachment from contemporary life. History, literature, the Bible, and the Near East were the realms of the imagination where he sought refuge from the turmoil of the Industrial Revolution. It is ironic that Honoré Daumier (1808–1879), one of the few Romantic artists who did not shrink from reality, remained practically unknown as a painter in his day. A biting political cartoonist, he contributed satirical drawings to various Paris weeklies for most

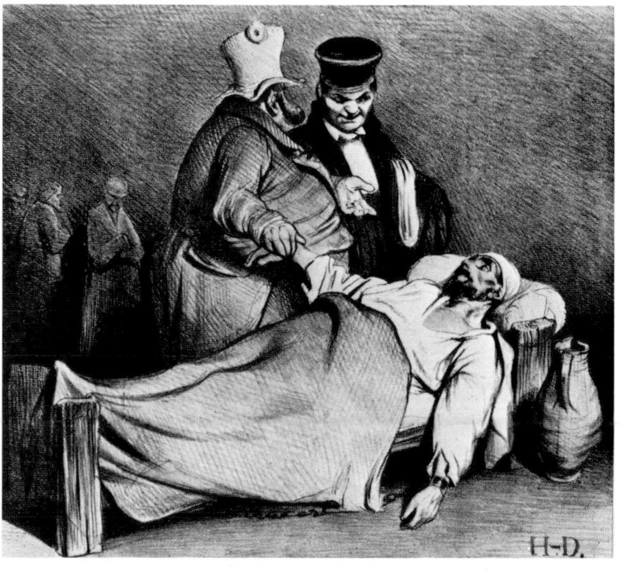

21-36. Honoré Daumier. *It's Safe to Release This One!* 1834. Lithograph

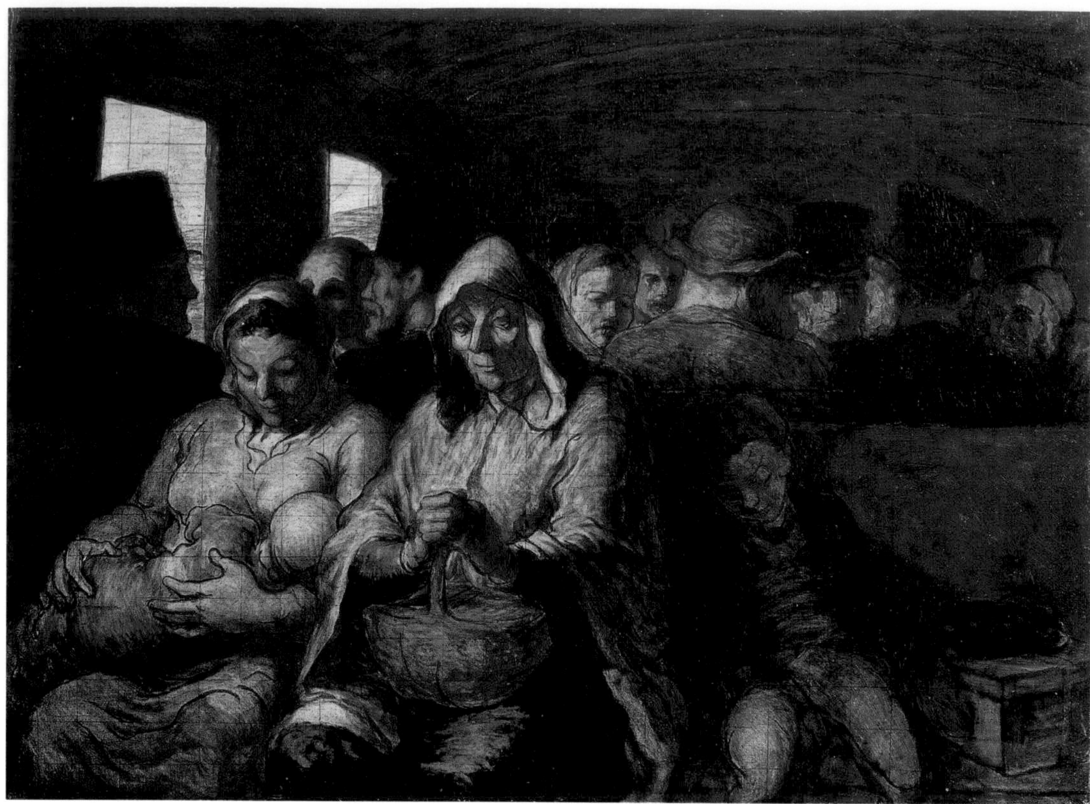

21-37. Honoré Daumier. *The Third-Class Carriage.* c. 1862. Oil on canvas, 25¾ x 35½" (65.4 x 90.2 cm). The Metropolitan Museum of Art, New York

BEQUEST OF MRS. H. O. HAVEMEYER, 1929. THE H. O. HAVEMEYER COLLECTION

of his career. Nearly all of Daumier's cartoons were done with lithography (see box page 659). He turned to painting in the 1840s but found no public for his work. Only a few friends encouraged him and, a year before his death, arranged his first solo exhibition. Thus his pictures had little impact during his lifetime.

Although Daumier is sometimes called a realist, his work falls entirely within the range of Romanticism. The neat outlines and systematic crosshatching in Daumier's early cartoons (fig. 21-36) show his conservative training. He quickly developed a bolder and more personal style of draftsmanship, however, and his paintings of the 1850s and 1860s have the full pictorial range of the Neo-Baroque. Their subjects vary widely. Many show aspects of everyday urban life that also occur in his cartoons, now viewed with a painter's eye rather than from a satirist's angle. In *The Third-Class Carriage* (fig. 21-37), Daumier's forms reflect the compactness of Millet's (compare fig. 21-41) but are painted so freely that they must have seemed raw and "unfinished" even by Delacroix's standards. Yet the power of the image derives from this very freedom. Daumier's concern is not for the visible surface of reality but for the emotional meaning behind it. In *The Third-Class Carriage,* he has captured a peculiarly modern human condition: "the lonely crowd." The only thing these people have in common is the fact that they are traveling together in a railway car. Although they are physically crowded, they take no notice of one another, for each is alone with his or her own thoughts. Daumier explores this state with an insight into character and a breadth of human sympathy worthy of Rembrandt, whose work he admired. His feeling for the dignity of the poor also suggests the Le Nains, who had recently been rediscovered by French critics. Indeed, the old woman on the left in Louis Le Nain's *Peasant Family* (see fig. 19-3) seems the direct ancestor of the central figure in *The Third-Class Carriage.*

LANDSCAPE PAINTING. Thanks to the cult of nature, landscape painting became the most characteristic form of Romantic art. While it arose out of the Enlightenment, the Romantic landscape lies outside the descriptive and emotional range of the eighteenth century. The Romantics believed that God's laws could be seen written in nature. Their faith, known as pantheism, was based not on rational thought but on subjective experience, and the appeal to the emotions rather than the intellect made those lessons all the more compelling. In order to express the feelings inspired by nature, the Romantics transcribed landscape as faithfully as possible, in contrast to the Neoclassicists, who forced landscape to conform to prescribed ideas of beauty and linked it to historical subjects. At the same time, the Romantics felt equally free to modify nature's appearance as a means of evoking heightened states of mind in accordance with dictates of the imagination, the only standard they ultimately recognized. Landscape inspired the Romantics with passions so exalted that only in the hands of the greatest history painters could the human figure equal nature in power.

COROT. The first and undeniably greatest French Romantic landscape painter was Camille Corot (1796–1875). In 1825 he went to Italy for two years and explored the countryside around Rome, like a latter-day Claude Lorraine. What Claude recorded in his drawings—the quality of a particular place at a particular time—Corot made into paintings, small canvases done on the spot in an hour or so (fig. 21-38). In size and immediacy, these quickly exe-

21-38. Camille Corot. *View of Rome: The Bridge and Castel Sant'Angelo with the Cupola of St. Peter's.* 1826–27. Oil on paper mounted on canvas, 10½ x 17" (22 x 38 cm). Fine Arts Museums of San Francisco

MUSEUM PURCHASE, ARCHER M. HUNTINGTON FUND

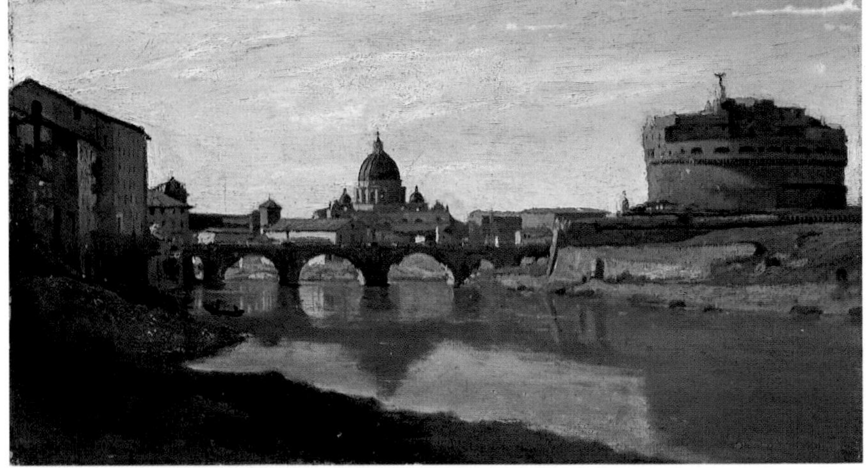

(BELOW) 21-39. Camille Corot. *Morning: Dance of the Nymphs.* 1850. Oil on canvas, 38⅝ x 51⅝" (97.1 x 130 cm). Musée d'Orsay, Paris

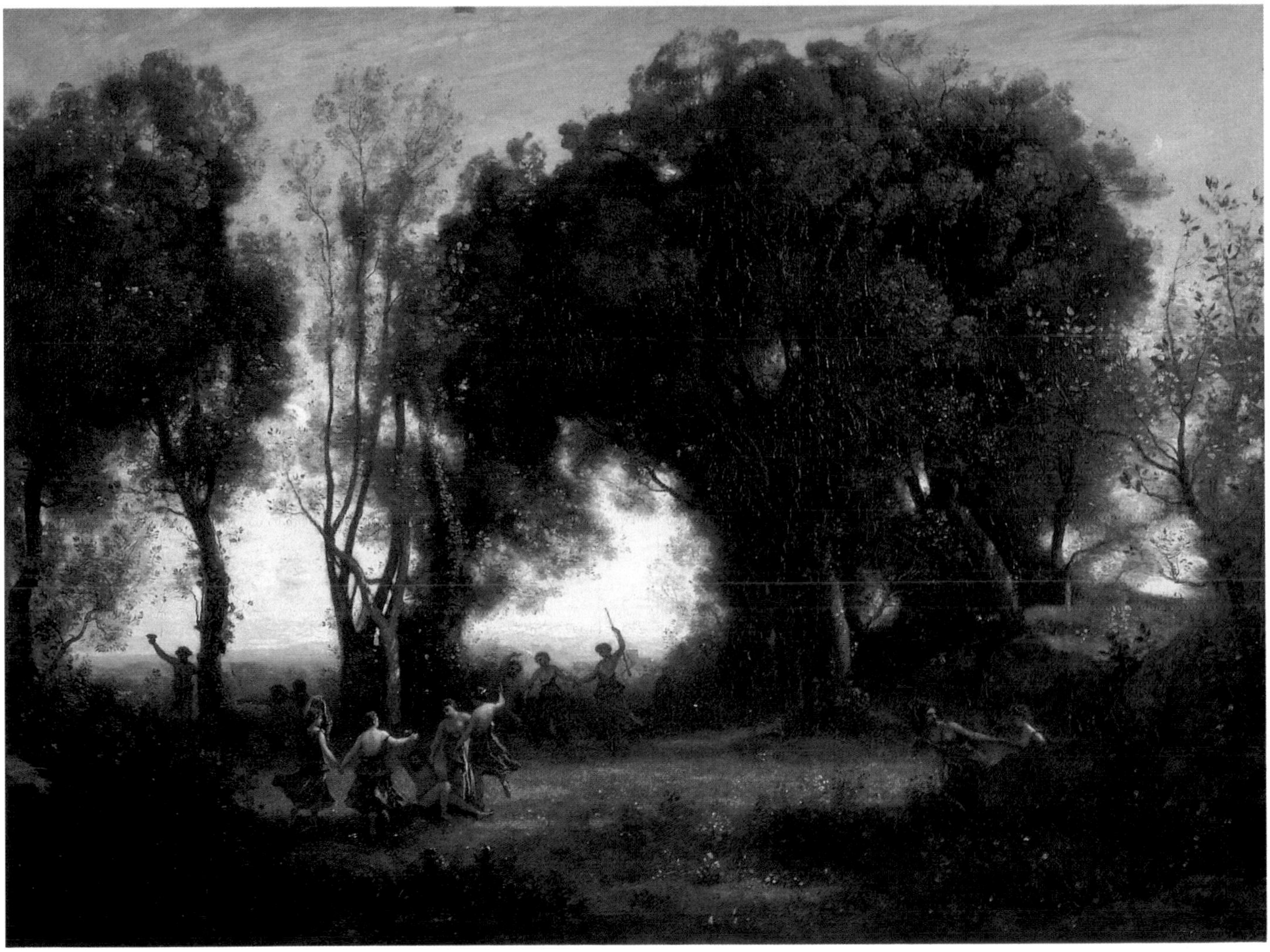

cuted pictures are analogous to Constable's oil sketches, yet they stem from different traditions. If Constable's view of nature, which emphasizes the sky as "the chief organ of sentiment," is derived from Dutch seventeenth-century landscapes, Corot's instinct for architectural clarity and stability recalls Poussin and Claude. But he, too, insists on "the truth of the moment." His exact observation and his readiness to seize upon any view that attracted him during his excursions show the same commitment to direct visual experience that we find in the English artist. The Neoclassicists had also painted oil sketches out-of-doors. Unlike them, Corot did not transform his sketches into idealized pastoral visions. His willingness to accept them as independent works of art marks him unmistakably as a Romantic.

After returning from his second visit to Italy in 1834, Corot began to paint historical landscapes that combined stylistic and topographical features from Italy and the North. But during the 1840s he gradually developed a unique style that appears in its definitive form in *Morning: Dance of the Nymphs* (fig. 21-39). The

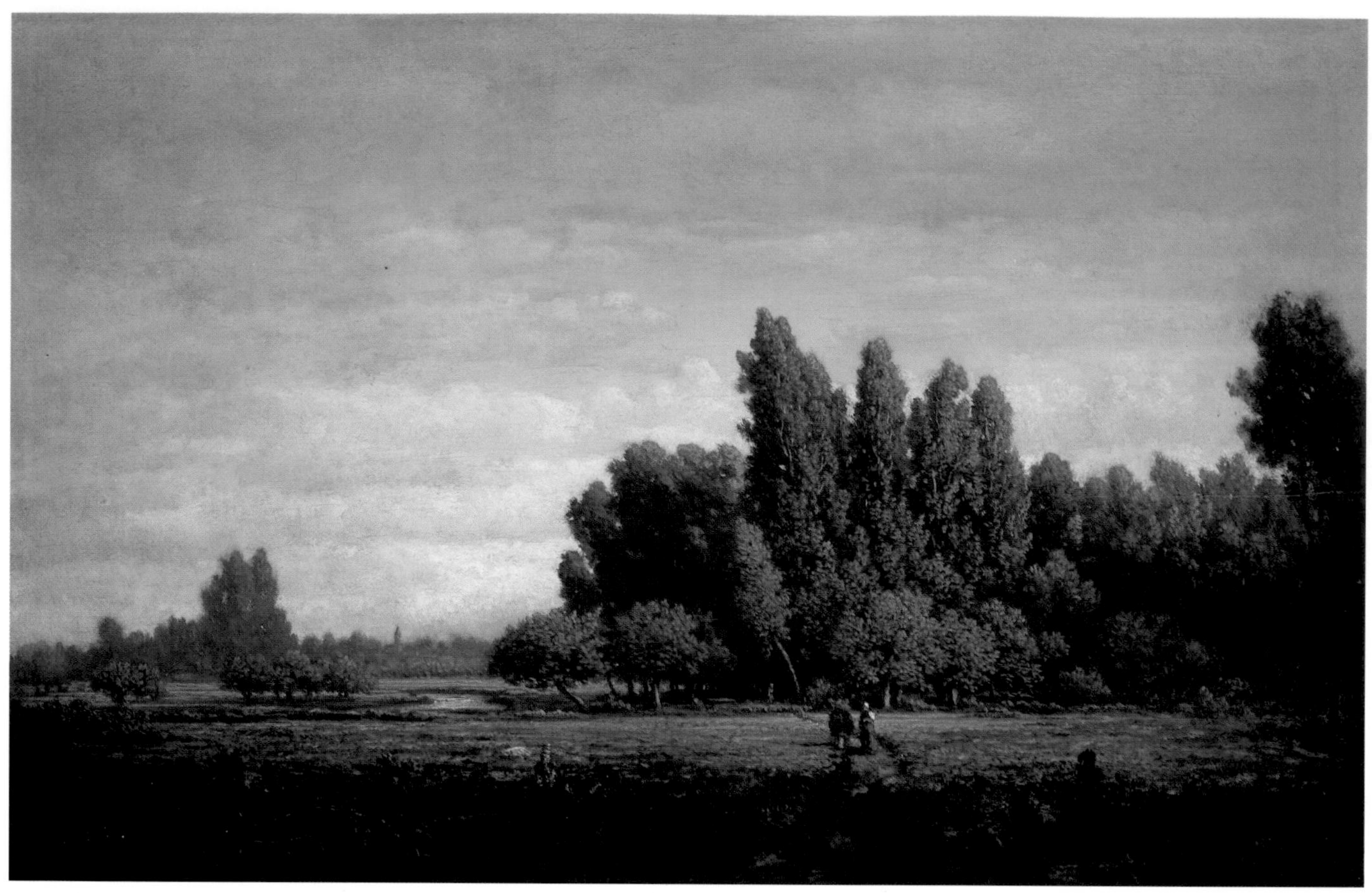

21-40. Théodore Rousseau. *A Meadow Bordered by Trees*. c. 1840–45. Oil on panel, 16⅜ x 24⅜" (41.6 x 61.9 cm). The Metropolitan Museum of Art, New York

BEQUEST OF ROBERT GRAHAM DUN, 1911

canvas has rightly been called a souvenir of the opera, especially the ballets traditional in Parisian productions which Corot habitually sketched. He found in them a common bond of feeling with painting that provided inspiration for his work. The landscape shows a new unity between the figures and their setting. The silvery light creates a veiled atmosphere that envelops the forms and lends the painting a poetic mood reminiscent of that in Poussin's late works (see fig. 19-6). In this way, Corot reconciles romantic sentiment and classical content.

Morning: Dance of the Nymphs was the outgrowth of the crisis of tradition in French art and of a personal crisis. When he painted it, Corot was approaching old age with considerable anxiety, and in Poussin he discovered a kindred spirit burdened with similar fears. Thus it was Corot's own development that enabled him to unlock the secret of the late Poussin and learn how to interpret nature in a deeply personal way.

ROUSSEAU. Corot's early fidelity to nature was an important model for the Barbizon School, though he was not actually a member. This group of younger painters, centering on Théodore Rousseau (1812–1867), settled in the village of Barbizon on the edge of the forest of Fontainebleau near Paris to paint landscapes and scenes of rural life. Enthused by Constable, whose work had been exhibited in Paris in 1824, they turned to the Northern Baroque landscape as an alternative to the Neoclassical tradition. From Ruisdael's example (see fig. 18-22), Rousseau learned how to give his encrusted forms and gnarled trees a sense of inner life. It was, however, the hours of solitary contemplation in the forest of Fontainebleau that made it possible for him to unlock nature's secrets. *A Meadow Bordered by Trees* (fig. 21-40) is a splendid example of his landscapes, which are filled with a simple reverence that admirably reflects the rallying cry of the Romantics—sincerity.

MILLET. Jean-François Millet (1814–1875) became a member of the Barbizon School in 1848, the year revolution swept France and the rest of Europe. Although he was no radical, *The Sower* (fig. 21-41) was championed by liberal critics because it was the very opposite of the Neoclassical history paintings endorsed by the establishment. Millet's archetypal image nonetheless has a self-consciously classical flavor that reflects his admiration for Poussin. Blurred in the hazy atmosphere, this "hero of the soil" is a timeless symbol of the unending labor that the artist viewed as the peasant's inescapable lot. (Could Millet have known the pathetic sower from the October page of *Les Très Riches Heures du Duc de Berry*? Compare fig. 11-94.) Ironically, the painting monumentalizes a rural way of life that was rapidly disappearing as a result of the Industrial Revolution. For that very reason, however, the peasant was seen as the chief victim of the evils arising from the Machine Age.

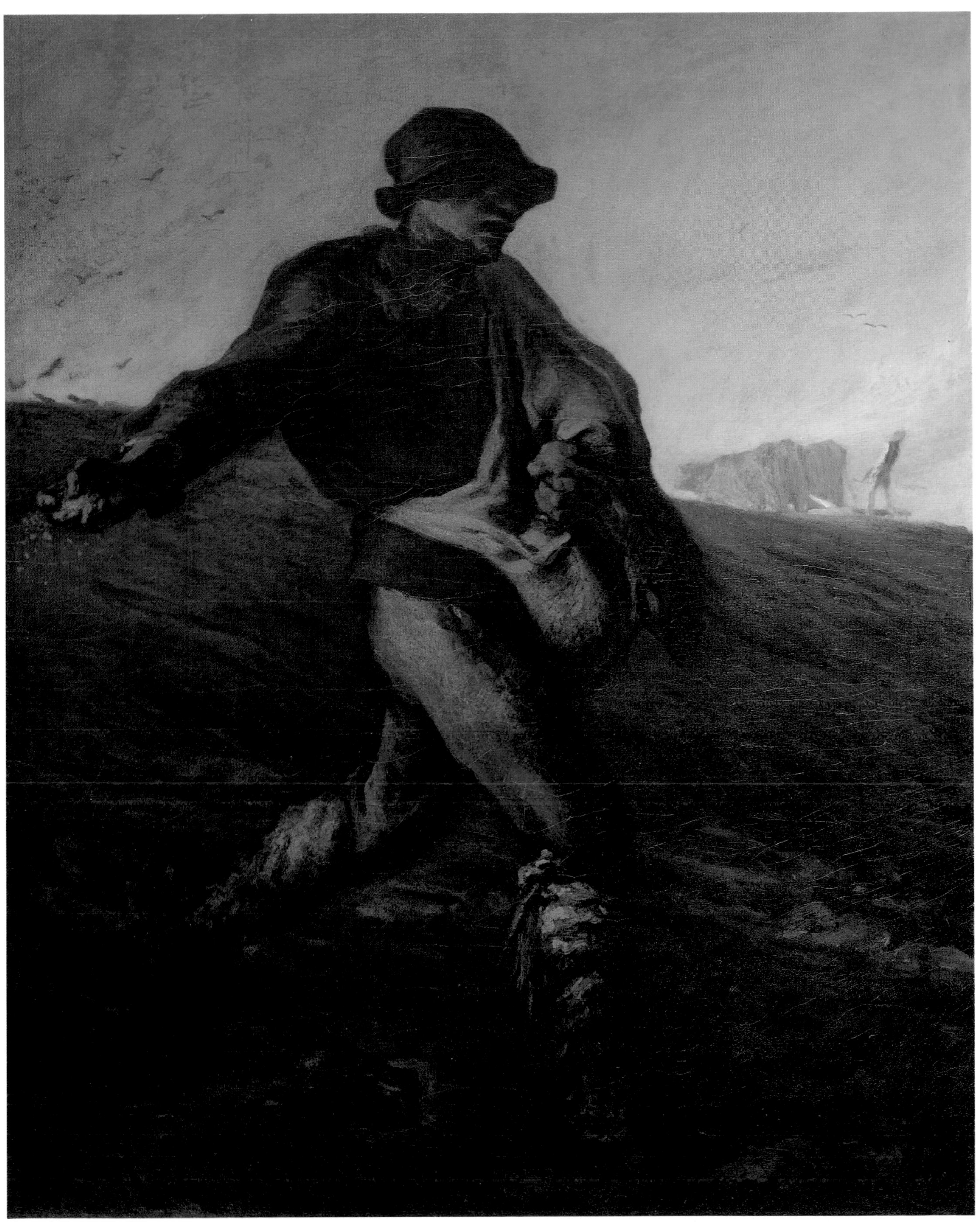

21-41. Jean-François Millet. *The Sower.* c. 1850. Oil on canvas, 40 x $32\frac{1}{2}$" (101.6 x 82.6 cm). Museum of Fine Arts, Boston

GIFT OF QUINCY ADAMS SHAW THROUGH QUINCY A. SHAW, JR., AND MRS. MARION SHAW HAUGHTON

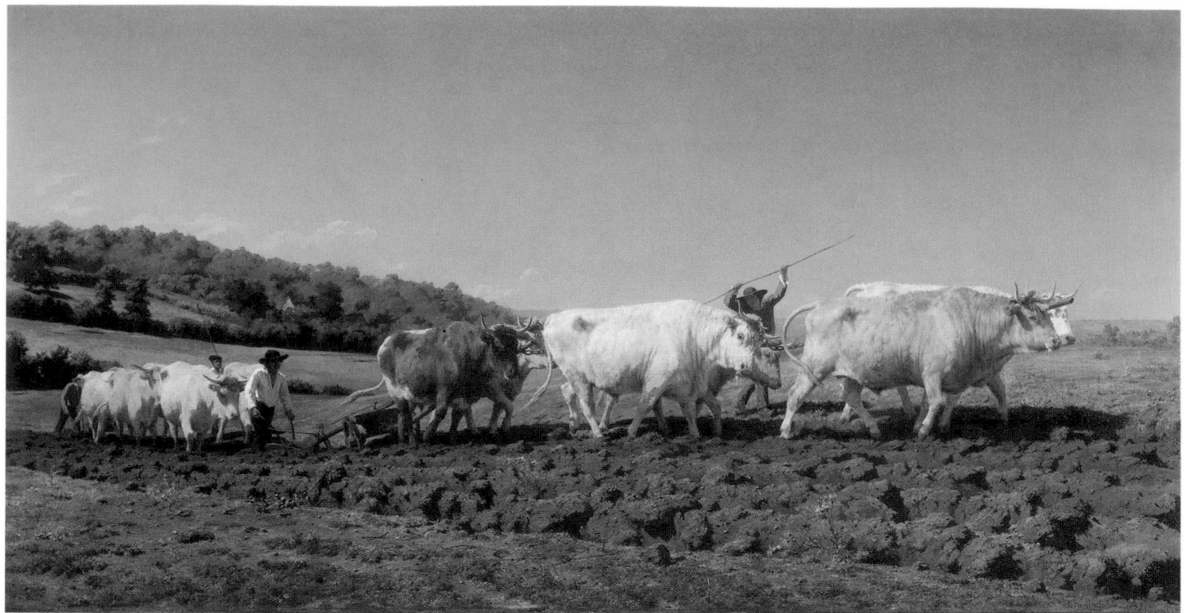

21-42. Rosa Bonheur. *Plowing in the Nivernais.* 1849. Oil on canvas, 5'9" x 8'8" (1.75 x 2.64 m). Musée d'Orsay, Paris

BONHEUR. The Barbizon School generally advocated a return to nature as a way of fleeing the social ills brought on by industrialization and urbanization. Despite their conservative outlook, these artists were raised to a new prominence in French art by the popular revolution of 1848. That same year Rosa Bonheur (1822–1899), also an artist who worked outdoors, received a French government commission that led to her first great success. She established herself as a leading painter of animals—and eventually as the most famous woman artist of her time. [See Primary Sources, no. 67, page 929.] Her painting *Plowing in the Nivernais* (fig. 21-42) was exhibited the following year, after a winter spent making studies from life. The theme of humanity's union with nature had already been popularized in the country romances of George Sand, among others (see box page 682). Bonheur's picture shares Millet's reverence for peasant life, but the real subject here, as in all her work, is the animals within the landscape. She depicts them with a convincing naturalism that later placed her among the most influential realists.

England

FUSELI. England was as precocious in fostering Romanticism as it had been in promoting Neoclassicism. In fact, one of its first representatives, John Henry Fuseli (1741–1825), was a contemporary of West and Copley. This Swiss-born painter (originally named Füssli) had an extraordinary impact on his time, more perhaps because of his adventurous and forceful personality than the quality of his work. Ordained a minister at 20, he left the Church by 1764 and went to London in search of freedom. Encouraged by Reynolds, he spent the 1770s in Rome, where he met Gavin Hamilton and studied classical art. Fuseli, however, based his style on Michelangelo and the Mannerists, not on Poussin and the antique. A German acquaintance of those years described him as "extreme in everything, Shakespeare's painter." Shakespeare and Michelangelo were indeed his twin gods. He even envisioned a Sistine Chapel, with Michelangelo's figures transformed into

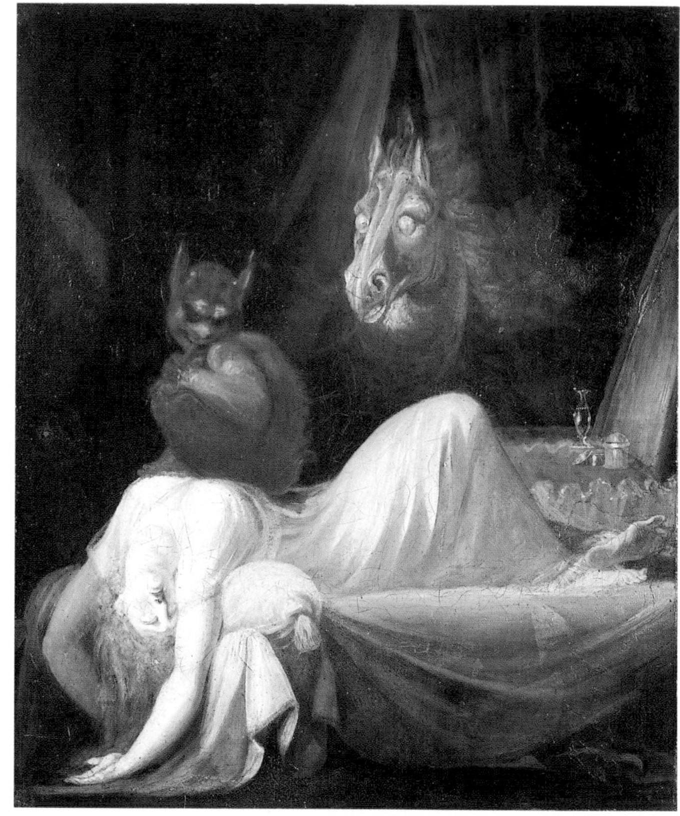

21-43. John Henry Fuseli. *The Nightmare.* c. 1790. Oil on canvas, 29½ x 25¼" (74.9 x 64.1 cm). Freies Deutsches Hochstift-Frankfurter Goethe-Museum, Frankfurt

Shakespearean characters. The sublime would be the common denominator for "classic" and "Gothic" Romanticism. This concept marks Fuseli as a transitional figure. He espoused many of the same Neoclassical theories as Reynolds, West, and Kauffmann (he translated Winckelmann's writings into English) but bent their rules virtually to the breaking point.

We see this mixture in *The Nightmare* (fig. 21-43). The sleep-

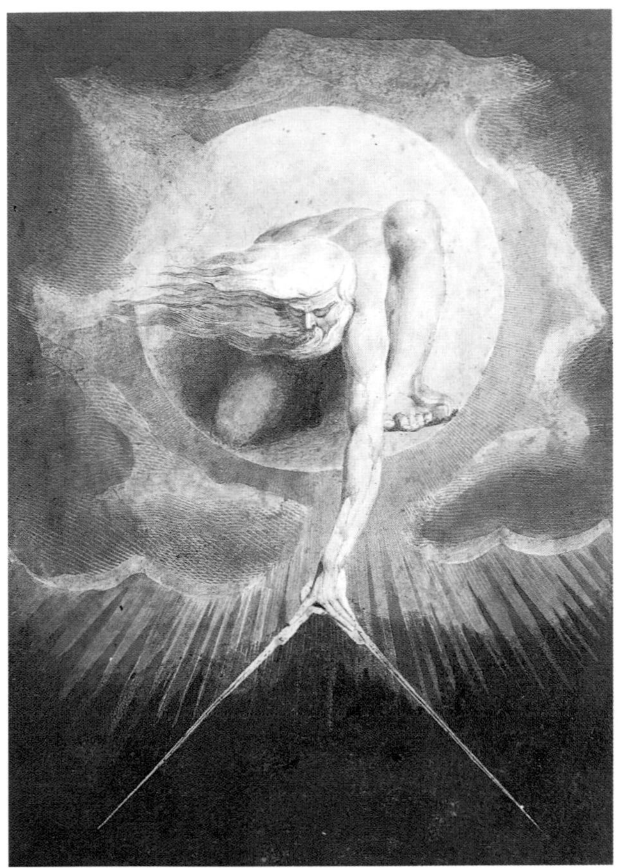

21-44. William Blake. *The Ancient of Days,* frontispiece of *Europe, A Prophesy.* 1794. Metal relief etching, hand-colored illustration, 9⅛ x 6⅝" (23.2 x 16.8 cm). Library of Congress, Washington, D.C.
LESSING J. ROSENWALD COLLECTION

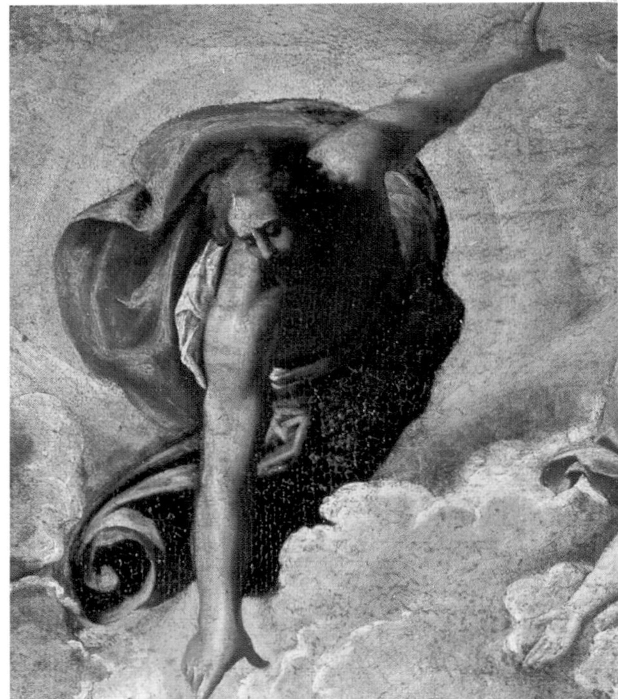

21-45. Taddeo Zuccaro. *The Conversion of St. Paul* (detail). c. 1555. Oil on canvas. Galleria Doria Pamphili, Rome

ing woman, more Mannerist than Michelangelesque, is Neoclassical in style. The grinning devil and the luminescent horse, however, come from the demon-ridden world of medieval folklore, while the Rembrandtesque lighting reminds us of Reynolds (compare fig. 20-15). Here the Romantic quest for terrifying experiences leads not to physical violence but to the dark recesses of the mind. What was the genesis of *The Nightmare*? Nightmares often have strong sexual overtones, sometimes openly expressed, at other times disguised. We know that Fuseli originally conceived the subject not long after his return from Italy. He had fallen violently in love with a friend's niece who soon married a merchant, much to the artist's distress. We may see in the picture a projection of his "dream girl," with the demon taking the artist's place while the impassioned horse, a well-known erotic symbol, looks on.

BLAKE. Fuseli later befriended the poet–painter William Blake (1757–1827), who had an even greater creativity and stranger personality than his own. A recluse and visionary, Blake produced and published his own books of poems with engraved text and hand-colored illustrations. Though he never left England, he acquired a large repertory of Michelangelesque and Mannerist motifs from engravings, as well as through the influence of Fuseli. He also conceived a tremendous admiration for the Middle Ages and came closer than any other Romantic artist to reviving pre-Renaissance forms. (His books were meant to be the successors of illuminated manuscripts.)

These elements are all present in Blake's memorable image *The Ancient of Days* (fig. 21-44). The muscular figure, radically foreshortened and fitted into a circle of light, is taken from Mannerist sources (fig. 21-45), while the symbolic compasses come from medieval representations of the Lord as Architect of the Universe. We might therefore expect the Ancient of Days to signify Almighty God. In Blake's esoteric mythology, however, he stands rather for the power of reason, which the poet regarded as ultimately destructive, since it stifles vision and inspiration. To Blake, the "inner eye" was all-important; he felt no need to observe the visible world around him.

CONSTABLE. It was in landscape rather than in narrative scenes that English painting reached its fullest expression. During the eighteenth century, landscape paintings consisted largely of imaginary scenes conforming to Northern and Italian Baroque examples. John Constable (1776–1837) admired both Ruisdael and Claude, yet he opposed all flights of fancy. Landscape painting, he believed, must be based on observable facts. It should aim at "embodying a pure apprehension of natural effect." Toward that end, he painted countless oil sketches outdoors. These were not the first such studies. However, he was more concerned than his predecessors with the

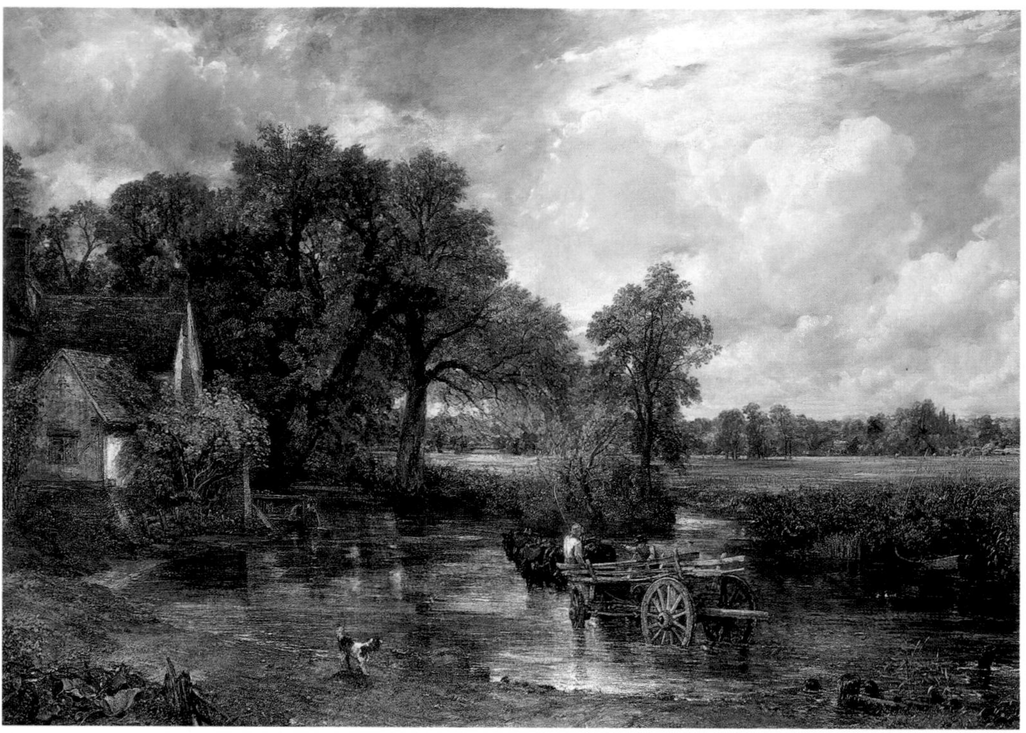

21-46. John Constable. *The Haywain.* 1821. Oil on canvas, 4'3¼" x 6'1" (1.3 x 1.85 m). The National Gallery, London

REPRODUCED BY COURTESY OF THE TRUSTEES

intangible qualities—sky, light, and atmosphere—rather than the concrete details of the scene. Often the land served as no more than a foil for the ever-changing drama overhead, which he studied with a meteorologist's accuracy. In order to record these fleeting effects, he arrived at a painting technique as broad, free, and personal as that of Cozens' "ink-blot landscapes," even though his point of departure was nature, not the imagination.

All of Constable's pictures show familiar views of the English countryside. It was, he later claimed, the scenery around his native Stour Valley that made him a painter. [See Primary Sources, no. 68, page 929.] Although he painted the final versions in his studio, he prepared them by making oil studies based on sketches from nature. The sky, to him, was a mirror of those sweeping forces so dear to the Romantic view of nature. It remained "the key note, standard scale, and the chief organ of sentiment." In *The Haywain* (fig. 21-46), he has caught a particularly splendid moment, as a great expanse of wind, sunlight, and clouds plays over the spacious landscape. The earth and sky have become vehicles of sentiment imbued with the artist's poetic attitude. At the same time, there is an intimacy in this monumental composition that reveals Constable's deep love of the countryside. This new, personal note is characteristically Romantic. Since Constable has painted the landscape with such conviction, we see the scene through his eyes and accept it as real, even though it looks back to paintings by Gainsborough and Ruisdael.

In 1829 a marked change came over Constable's work. Deeply affected by his wife's death a year earlier, he was subject to dark moods. *Salisbury Cathedral from the Meadows* (fig. 21-47), begun that summer, is his most personal statement. When the canvas was exhibited two years later, he added nine lines from *The Seasons* by the eighteenth-century poet James Thomson that reveal its meaning: the rainbow is a symbol of hope after a storm that follows on the death of the young Amelia in the arms of her lover Celadon. Although a political intent has sometimes been attributed to the landscape, there can be little doubt of its autobiographical significance. To the left of the huge ash tree, a symbol of life, is a cenotaph, an emblem of death. To the right stands the great church, one of Constable's major themes, a symbol of faith and resurrection. The rainbow, added late in the composition's development and inspired by Ruisdael's *The Jewish Cemetery* (see fig. 18-22), suggests the artist's renewed optimism. Thus the painting reflects his changing state of mind.

Constable continued to work on *The Rainbow,* as he called it, on and off for several more years. He attached great importance to the canvas. He regarded the painting as the fullest expression of his art and felt it would be considered his finest work by future generations. It is indeed an astonishing achievement. The amazingly free application of paint (much of it done with a palette knife) and rich, somber color convey an agitation not seen before in his landscapes. All nature is caught up in the fury of a catastrophic event beyond human comprehension. Every leaf, every branch acts as an index of feeling, expressing the artist's turbulent emotions. Once again it is the sky that provides the keynote: now the storm has clearly passed. No other painter before or since was able to capture the clash of the elements with such power. Even

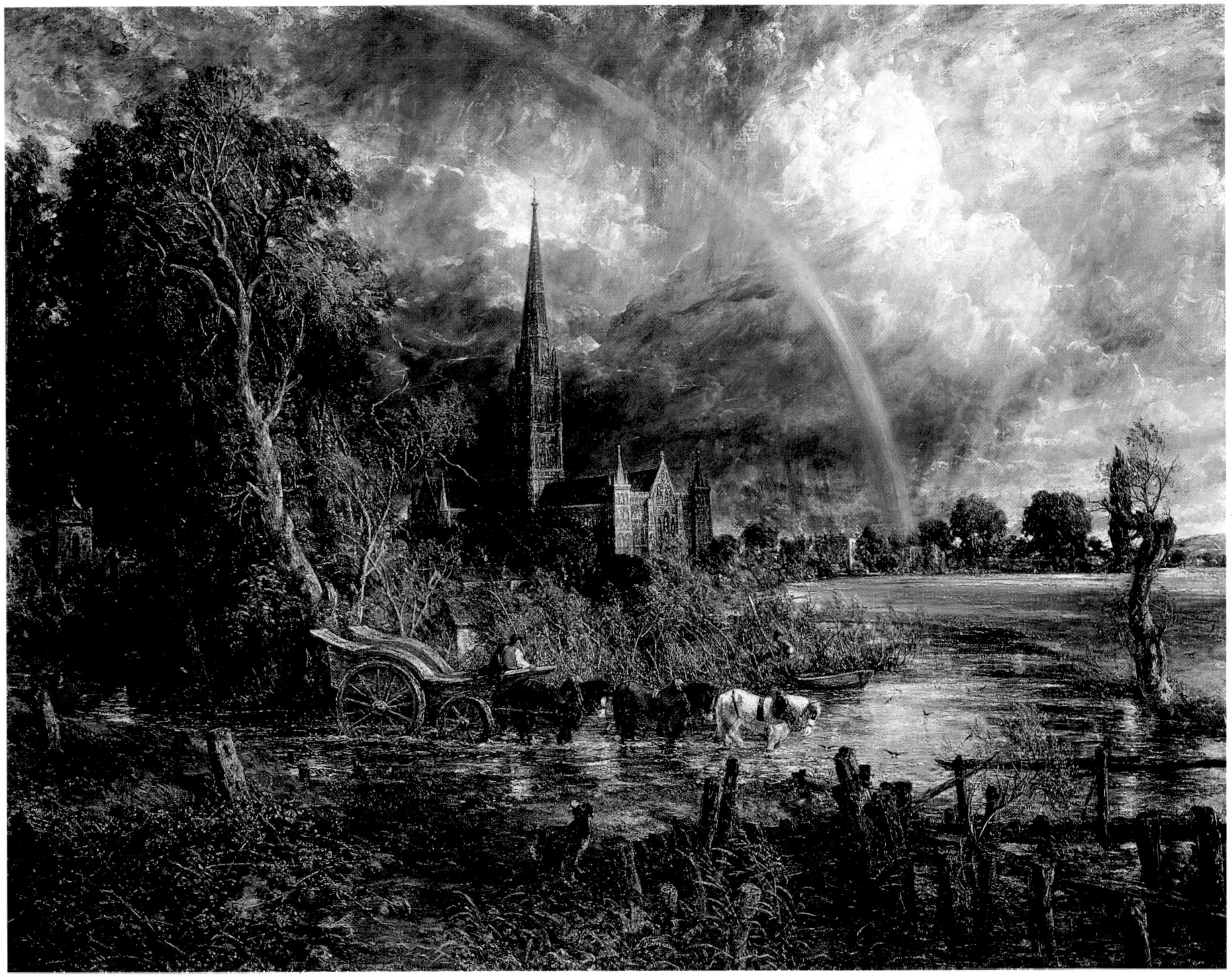

21-47. John Constable. *Salisbury Cathedral from the Meadows.* 1829–34. Oil on canvas, 59¾ x 74¾" (151.8 x 189.9 cm).
PRIVATE COLLECTION, ON LOAN TO THE NATIONAL GALLERY, LONDON

paintings by Constable's great rival Joseph Mallord William Turner seem tame by comparison.

TURNER. Joseph Mallord William Turner (1775–1851) arrived at a style that Constable disdainfully but accurately described as "airy visions, painted with tinted steam." Turner began as a watercolorist, and the use of translucent tints on white paper may help to explain his obsession with colored light. Like Constable, he made extensive studies from nature (though not in oils), but the scenery he selected satisfied the Romantic taste for the picturesque and the sublime—mountains, the sea, or places linked with historic events. In his full-scale pictures he often changed these views so freely that they became unrecognizable.

Many of Turner's landscapes are linked with literary themes and bear such titles as *The Destruction of Sodom* or *Snowstorm: Hannibal Crossing the Alps* or *Childe Harold's Pilgrimage: Italy.* When they were exhibited, he would add appropriate quotations from ancient or modern authors to the catalogue. Sometimes he would make up some lines himself and claim to be "citing" his own unpublished poem, "Fallacies of Hope." Yet these canvases are the opposite of history painting as defined by Poussin. The titles indeed indicate "noble and serious human actions," but the tiny figures, who are lost in the seething violence of nature, suggest the ultimate defeat of all endeavor—"the fallacies of hope."

The Slave Ship (fig. 21-48) is one of Turner's most spectacular visions and illustrates how he translated his literary sources into "tinted steam." First entitled *Slavers Throwing Overboard the Dead and Dying—Typhoon Coming On,* the painting has several levels of meaning. Like Géricault's *The Raft of the "Medusa"* (see fig. 21-28), which had been exhibited in England in 1820, it has to do, in part, with a specific incident that Turner had read about.

When an epidemic broke out on a slave ship, the captain threw his human cargo overboard because he was insured against the loss of slaves at sea, but not by disease. Turner also thought of a relevant passage from James Thomson's poem *The Seasons* that describes how sharks follow a slave ship during a typhoon, "lured

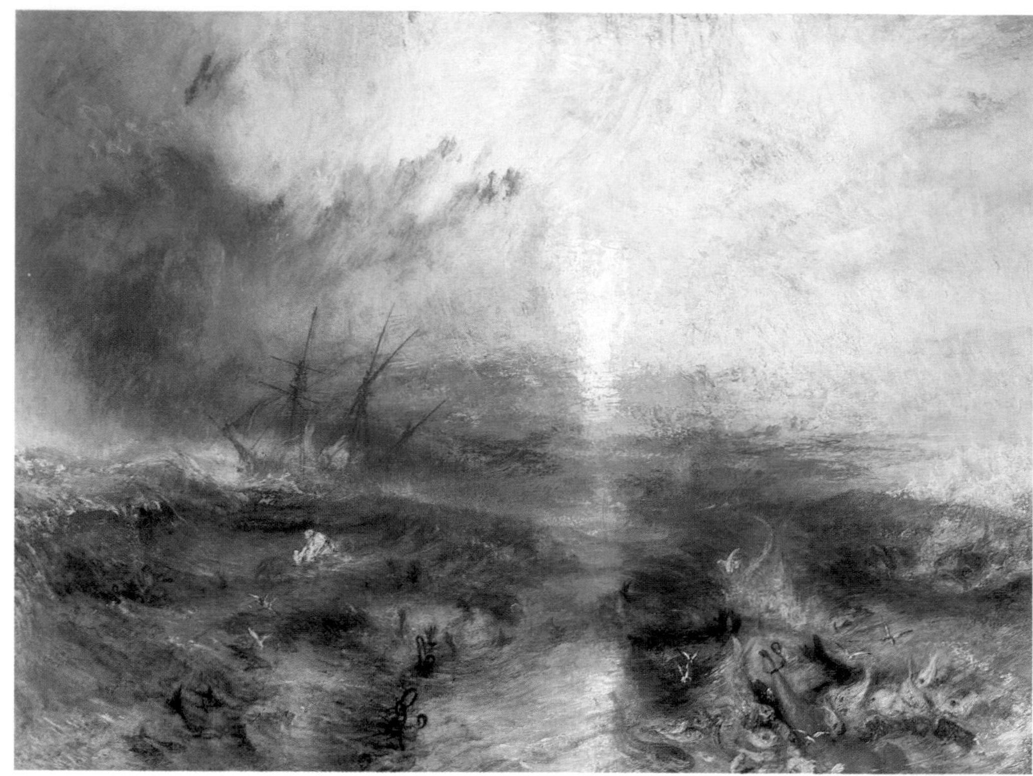

21-48. Joseph Mallord William Turner. *The Slave Ship*. 1840. Oil on canvas, 35¾ x 48" (90.8 x 121.9 cm). Museum of Fine Arts, Boston

HENRY LILLIE PIERCE FUND (PURCHASE)

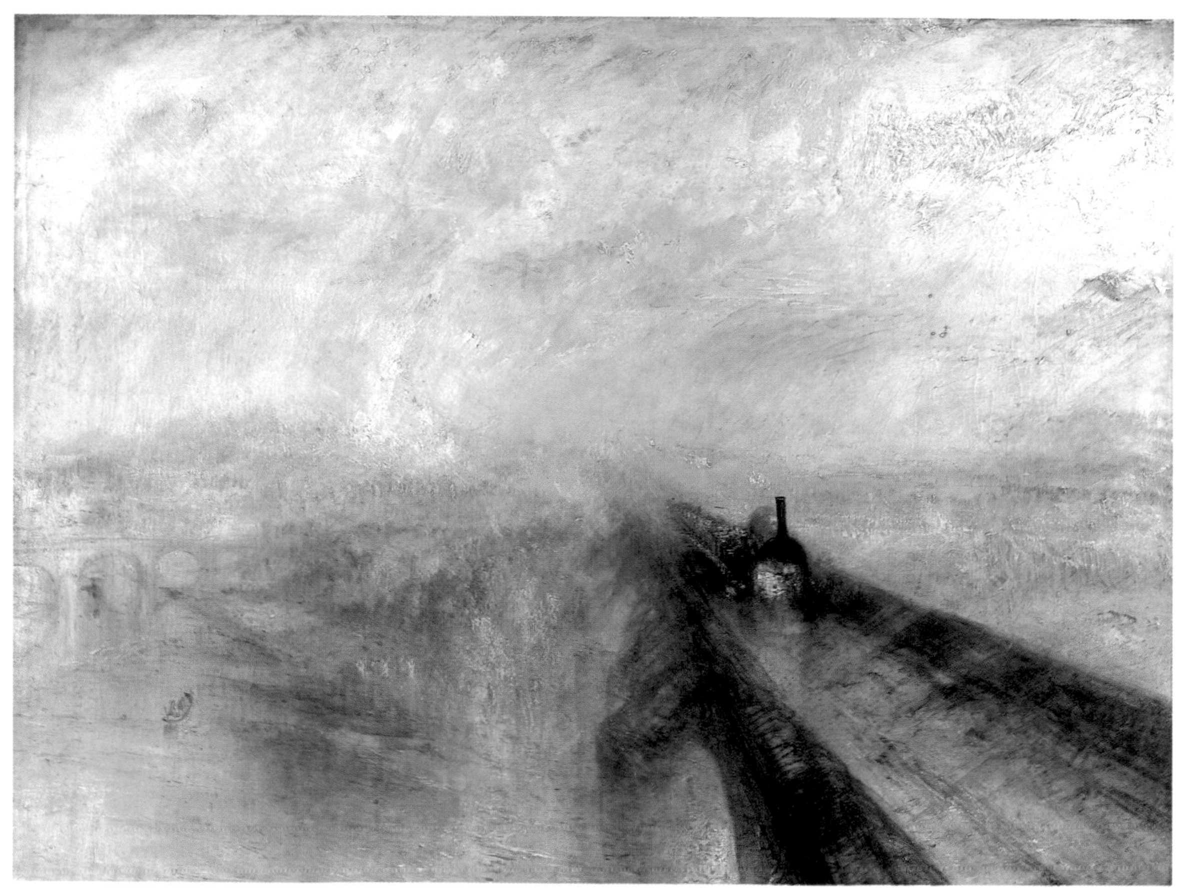

21-49. Joseph Mallord William Turner. *Rain, Steam and Speed—The Great Western Railway*. 1844. Oil on canvas, 35¾ x 48" (90.8 x 122 cm). The National Gallery, London

REPRODUCED BY COURTESY OF THE TRUSTEES

by the scent of steaming crowds, or rank disease, and death." But what is the relation between the slaver's action and the typhoon? Are the dead and dying slaves being cast into the sea against the threat of the storm, perhaps to lighten the ship? Is the typhoon nature's retribution for the captain's greed and cruelty? Of the many storms at sea that Turner painted, none has quite this apocalyptic quality. A cosmic catastrophe seems about to engulf everything, not merely the "guilty" slaver but the sea itself, with its crowds of fantastic and oddly harmless-looking fish.

While we still feel the force of Turner's imagination, most of us enjoy the tinted steam for its own sake rather than as a vehicle of the awesome emotions the artist meant to evoke. Even in terms of the values he himself acknowledged, Turner strikes us as "a virtuoso of the Sublime," led astray by his own enthusiasm. He must have been pleased by praise from the theorist John Ruskin, who saw in *The Slave Ship* (which he owned), "the true, the beautiful, and the intellectual"—all qualities that raised Turner above older landscape painters in his eyes. Still, Turner may have come to wonder if his tinted steam had its intended effect. Soon after finishing *The Slave Ship,* he read in his copy of Goethe's *Color Theory,* recently translated into English, that yellow has a "gay, softly exciting character," while orange-red suggests "warmth and gladness." These are hardly the emotions that would be aroused by *The Slave Ship* in a viewer who did not know its title. Interestingly enough, Turner soon modified his approach to take Goethe's ideas into account. He even painted a pair of canvases about the Deluge that were meant to illustrate Goethe's theory of positive (light and warm) and minus (dark and cold) colors. They nevertheless hardly differ from the rest of his work.

Many of Turner's paintings originated in watercolors called "color beginnings" that are as abstract as American Color Field Painting (see page 817). However, they always retained a basis in the artist's actual experiences. Turner seems to have sought out the unusual. *Rain, Steam and Speed—The Great Western Railway* (fig. 21-49) shows the recently completed Maidenhead railway bridge looking across the Thames River toward London. It was painted after Turner had stuck his head out of a window on the Exeter express for some nine minutes during a rainstorm. One could hardly ask for a more vivid impression of speed and atmospheric turbulence. Yet, in a touch of delicious irony, he has added a hare (barely visible in our illustration) racing ahead of the oncoming train. The train pursues the hare, which runs vainly ahead just as the hound chases its prey.

WATERCOLORS. Turner was the greatest watercolorist of his time. Watercolors were first introduced into Britain by visiting Northerners, who had used them as a means of recording on-the-spot observations since the time of Dürer (see fig. 16-4). The English soon made the medium their own. Because they became an indispensable part of the genteel person's education, watercolors are often thought of as an amateur's medium. After the middle of the eighteenth century, however, they attracted gifted painters such as Thomas Gainsborough (see page 600). Important contributions were made by Alexander Cozens' talented son, John Robert Cozens (1752–1797), who was the first to introduce poetic melancholy into watercolors, and Thomas Girtin (1752–1802), Turner's brilliant contemporary, who during his brief career revolutionized the English landscape by investing it with a Romantic mood. The full potential of watercolors was realized only in the nineteenth century, when artists such as Turner and Constable, who turned to them late in his career, greatly extended the range of subjects, techniques, and expression. Many of the most famous watercolorists are all but forgotten today, while others, such as John Sell Cotman (1782–1842), who were largely ignored, are now seen as major artists.

COTMAN. Cotman started out in London, where he moved in the same circles as Turner. However, most of his career was spent as a drawing master in the north of England, as much out of a weakness in his character as out of the force of circumstances. Although he achieved modest local recognition as a leader of the Norwich landscape school, he died in obscurity and was only rediscovered in the 1920s, when his highly unusual style suddenly appeared remarkably modern. Cotman's watercolors are notable for an economy of means that endows even the simplest subject with monumentality and dignity. His formalism grew out of the landscape tradition of Nicolas Poussin and Claude Lorraine, but he was no classicist. And although he was affected by the Dutch and Flemish Baroque artists who so influenced Constable, Cotman's watercolors are among the most original creations of the English Romantic landscape school during its early phase.

Durham Cathedral (fig. 21-50), a watercolor painted in the studio from nature studies, bears the stamp of his genius. The artist has concentrated on the essential elements, so that the scene is

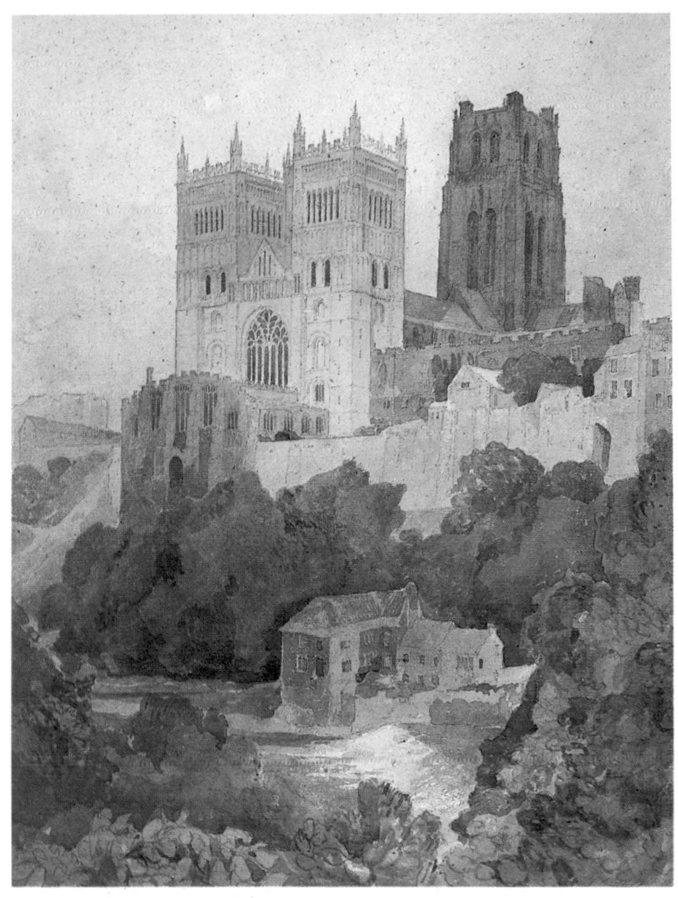

21-50. John Cotman. *Durham Cathedral.* 1805. Watercolor on paper, 17 1/4 x 13" (43.8 x 33 cm). The British Museum, London

reduced to a flat, nearly abstract pattern. The result is an expressiveness of astonishing intensity. Cotman emphasizes the massiveness of the great church, which looms over the house below as if threatening to crush it. The landscape shows the English Romantic fascination with the Gothic. It inspired the artist with much the same sentiment found in Ruisdael's *The Jewish Cemetery* (see fig. 18-22). Did Cotman intend it as a testimony of his personal faith? Of man's works, he seems to say, only the cathedral, a house of worship, will endure. Yet we know surprisingly little about his beliefs.

Germany

FRIEDRICH. In Germany, as in England, landscape was the finest achievement of Romantic painting. The underlying ideas, too, were often strikingly similar. About 1800 German artists rediscovered the Gothic, which they regarded as their native heritage. For the most part, this "Gothic Revival" remained limited in subject matter and scope, but in the hands of Caspar David Friedrich (1774–1840), the most important German Romantic artist, it acquired a haunting mystery. A devout Protestant, he had a pantheistic love of nature, which he imbued with deep religious feeling. In *Abbey in an Oak Forest* (fig. 21-51) all is death—the ancient graves, the barren trees, and ruined church silhouetted against the somber winter sky at twilight. We contemplate the forlorn scene with the same hushed reverence as the solemn procession of monks. Hardly distinguishable from the tombstones, they seek the crucifix enshrined in the arched portal, which offers eternal life to the faithful. The frozen stillness is in marked contrast to the painting by Ruisdael that probably inspired it (similar to fig. 18-22). Infinitely lonely, the bleak landscape is a reflection of the artist's own melancholy.

When Friedrich painted *The Polar Sea* (fig. 21-52), he may have known of Turner's "Fallacies of Hope." In an earlier picture on the same theme (now lost) he had inscribed the name "Hope" on the crushed vessel. In any case, he shared Turner's attitude toward human fate. The painting, too, was inspired by a specific event, to which the artist gave symbolic significance: a dangerous moment in William Parry's Arctic expedition of 1819–20. One wonders how Turner might have depicted this scene. Perhaps it would have been too static for him. Friedrich, however, was attracted by this very immobility. He has visualized the piled-up slabs of ice as a kind of megalithic monument to human defeat built by nature itself. There is no hint of tinted steam—the very air seems frozen—nor any subjective handwriting. We look right through the paint-covered surface at a reality that seems created without the painter's intervention.

This technique, impersonal and exacting, is peculiar to German Romantic painting. It stems from the early Neoclassicists, but the Germans, whose tradition of Baroque painting was weak, adopted it more wholeheartedly than the English or the French. Friedrich learned this approach at the Royal Academy in Copenhagen, and although in his hands it yielded extraordinary effects, the results proved disappointing for most German artists, who lacked his lofty imagination.

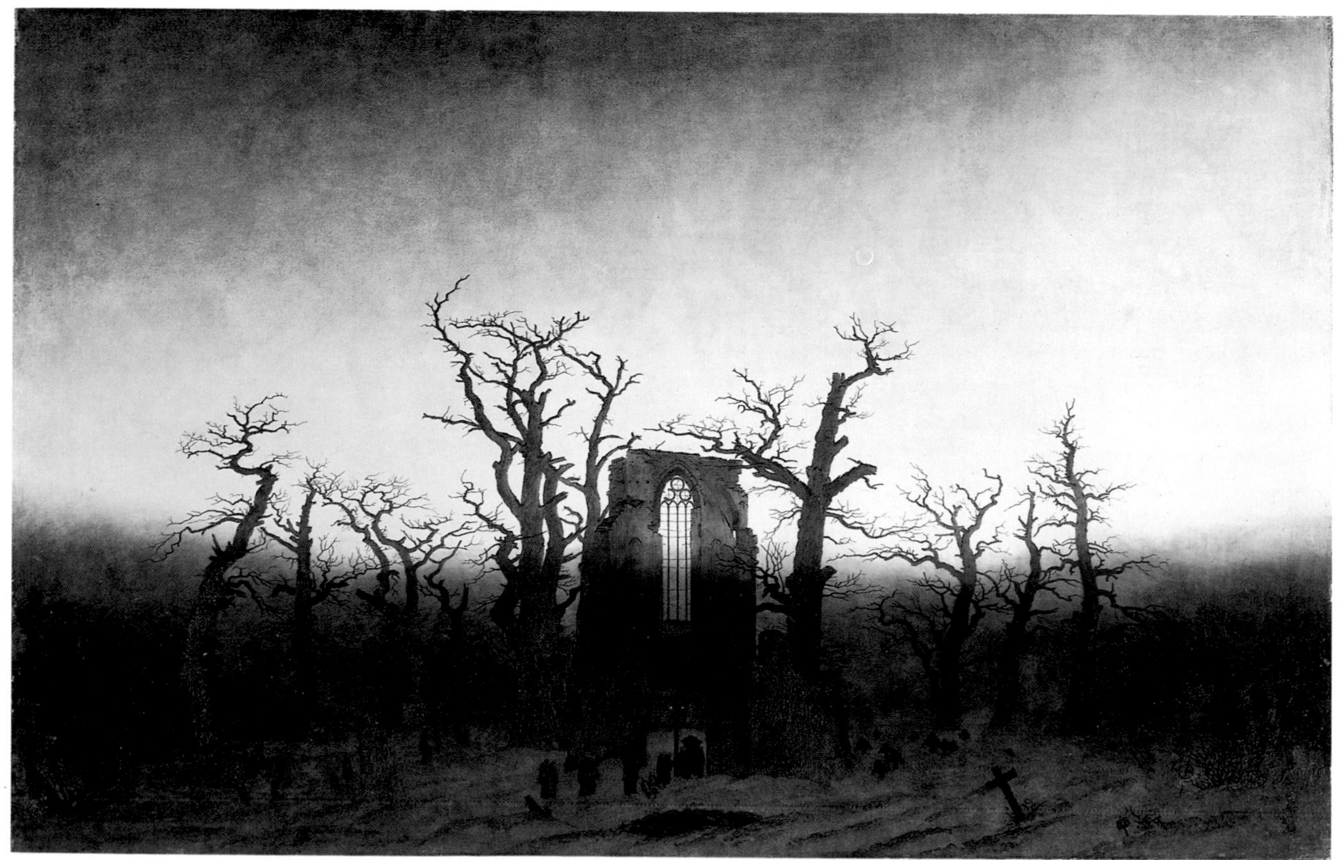

21-51. Caspar David Friedrich. *Abbey in an Oak Forest.* 1809–10. Oil on canvas, 44 x 68½" (111.8 x 174 cm). Schloss Charlottenburg, Berlin

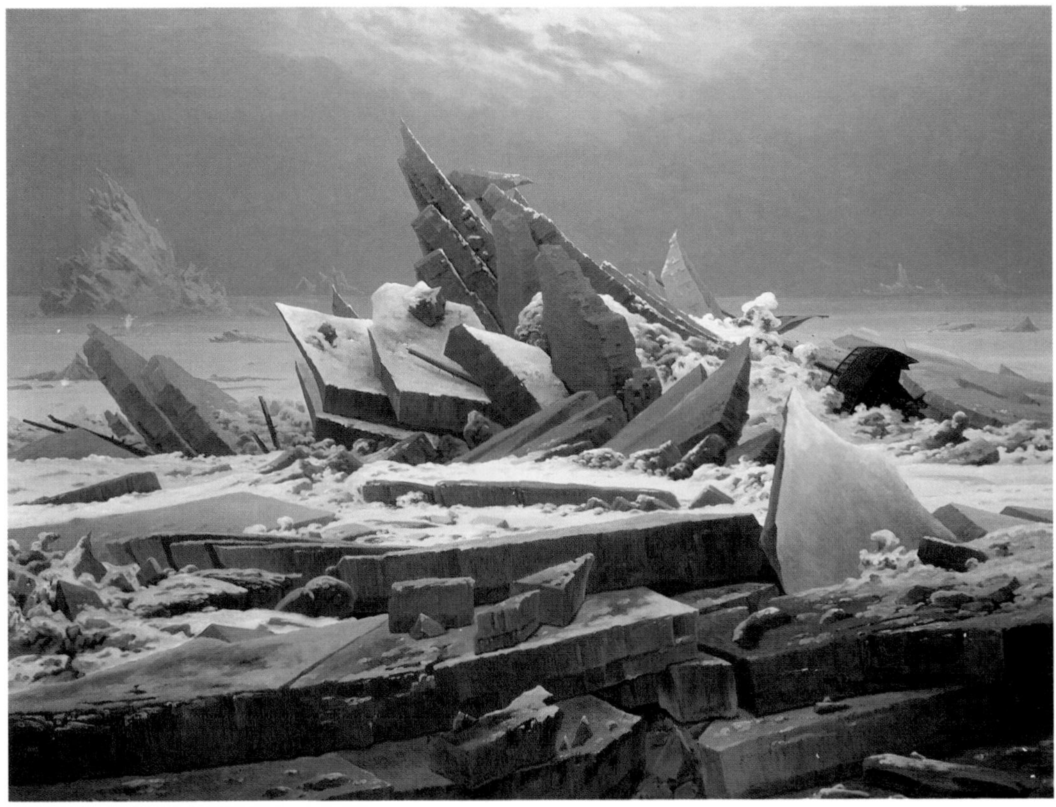

21-52. Caspar David Friedrich. *The Polar Sea.* 1824. Oil on canvas, 38½ x 50½" (97.8 x 128.3 cm). Kunsthalle, Hamburg, Germany

RUNGE. Philipp Otto Runge (1777–1810), who attended the Copenhagen academy soon after Friedrich, shared many of the same ideas but expressed them very differently. His most important work was a series of four allegorical landscapes devoted to the times of day, which occupied him throughout his brief career and was left incomplete at his death. The paintings incorporate an ambitious program having several levels of meaning. They stand for, among other things, the seasons and the ages of life. The set was intended for a Gothic chapel of Runge's own design, where poetry and music by his friends would be heard.

Morning, the only picture to be finished, was later cut up and survives only in fragments, but a slightly earlier, smaller version (fig. 21-53) gives a good idea of its appearance. The landscape represents spring and childhood. Within Runge's program, it also signifies "the boundless illumination of the universe." Aurora–Venus (combining the rising sun and the morning star) hovers over the Christlike infant as child genii sprout from a lily above. (Flowers in Runge's personal system become symbols of universal life through emotional identification with their forms.) The decorated frame, inspired by medieval manuscripts (compare fig. 10-38), expands on the meaning of the central image. The light of revelation, eclipsed by darkness below, liberates the soul trapped beneath the earth within the roots of the bulb. Above, the soul rises as a genius from the lily to the heavens and is transformed into an angel.

Morning is an extraordinary synthesis of Classical mythology and Christian faith, Romantic attitudes and Neoclassical technique. Painting for Runge was a deeply spiritual act revealing the divinity of nature. To him, this elevated conception required

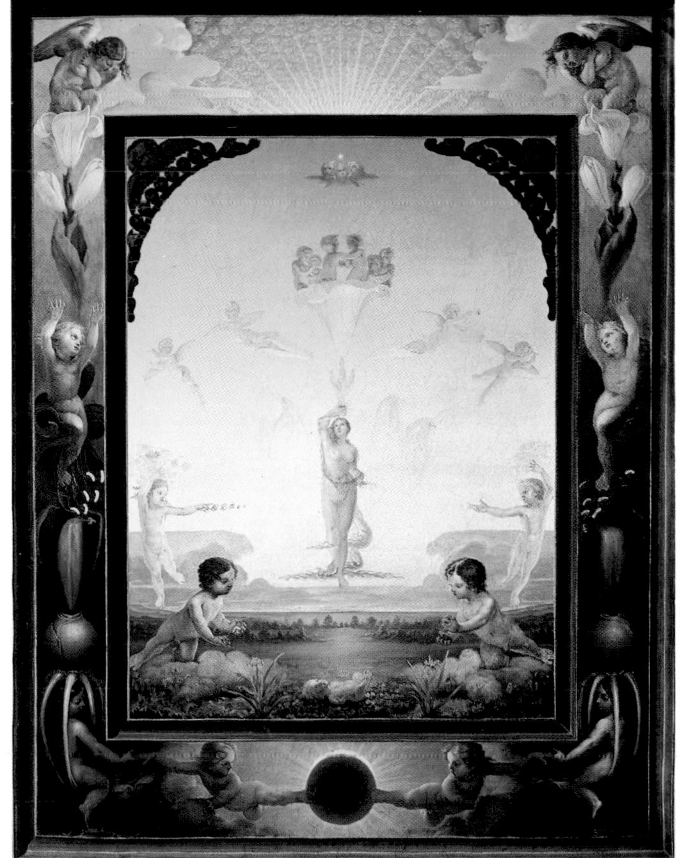

21-53. Philipp Otto Runge. *Morning.* 1808. Oil on canvas, 42⅞ x 33⅝" (109 x 85.4 cm). Kunsthalle, Hamburg

THE ROMANTIC MOVEMENT IN LITERATURE AND THE THEATER

Romanticism in art had an exact counterpart in literature and the theater. It was inextricably entwined with Johann Wolfgang von Goethe, whose dramatic poem *Faust* (Part 1, 1808; Part 2, 1832) remains the greatest monument of the Romantic movement. Goethe was interested in a vast range of subjects, including botany and architecture. His book on color theory (1810), which constituted an attack on Newtonian optics, exercised widespread influence on painters. He was also a gifted amateur musician who conducted operas and wrote librettos, as well as lyrical poems that inspired some of the finest songs by Beethoven and Schubert. Romanticism in the theater began in Germany just before the turn of the nineteenth century as an outgrowth of the work of Friedrich von Schiller and Goethe. It centered on August Wilhelm von Schlegel (1767–1845), the editor of the literary journal *Athenäum* from 1798 to 1800, and his brother Friedrich (1772–1829), a noted philosopher. Together they promoted Romanticism as an all-embracing vision. An early admirer of Shakespeare, whose plays he began to translate, August Schlegel emphasized mood and character over plot in literature and championed the revival of such medieval works as the twelfth-century German epic *Nibelungenlied (The Song of the Niebelungs).* The Schlegels were part of a small, tightly knit group that included Ludwig Tieck (1773–1853), who completed the job of translating Shakespeare after August's death. Tieck, who wrote both comedies and tragedies, was also an important theorist, especially later in life, and exercised considerable influence on German Romantic painting through his friendship with Philipp Otto Runge (see pages 681 and 683). In the heady early days of Romanticism he collaborated with Wilhelm Heinrich Wackenroder (1773–1798), who stated that "the Gothic church and the Greek temple are equally pleasurable in the sight of God." Medievalism, with its reverence for Christian ideals, was also taken up in 1799 by the writer Novalis (Friedrich von Hardenberg, 1772–1801). The writings of the Schlegel circle inspired not only the landscape painter Caspar David Friedrich but also the Nazarenes, who were to establish the mainstream of German Romantic art (see pages 680 and 683). Though he was generally overlooked during his lifetime, the finest playwright of the early nineteenth century in Germany was Heinrich von Kleist (1777–1811), a poet and novelist, whose tragedies and comedies are filled with the conflict of extreme emotions typical of Romanticism.

German ideas were first introduced into France by Madame de Staël (Germaine Necker, 1760–1817), the daughter of Louis XVI's finance minister and the wife of the Swedish ambassador to France, who detested Napoleon. She went into exile in Germany, where she wrote *Of Germany,* which presented many of the Schlegels' theories. The book, initially suppressed upon its publication in 1810, was reissued after Napoleon's exile to Elba in 1813. Equally important for French Romanticism was the enthusiasm for all things English, which reached its height during the following decade. The novels of Sir Walter Scott sparked the taste for medieval legends, while an English troupe caused a sensation in Paris with its performances of Shakespeare four years after his plays had been declared superior to Racine's by Marie-Henri Beyle, known as Stendhal, in 1823.

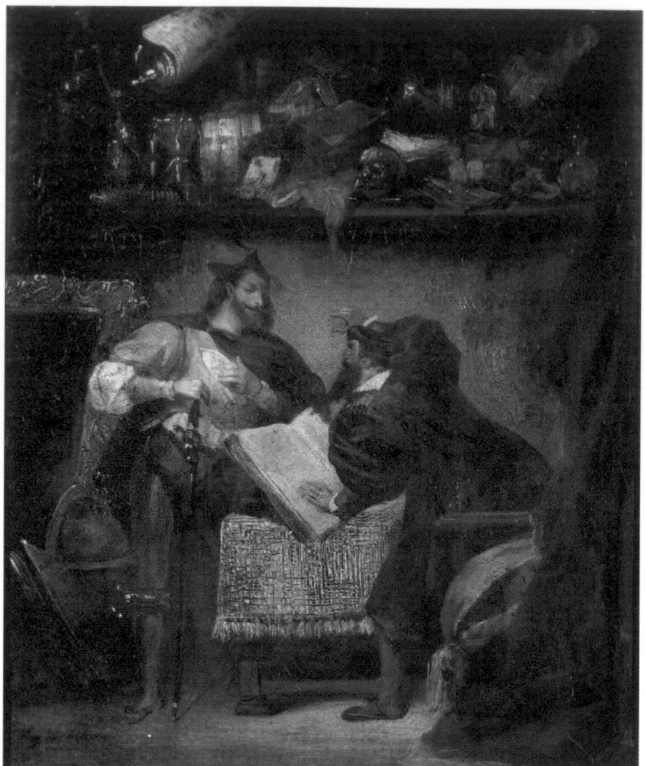

Eugène Delacroix. *Mephistopheles Appears Before Faust.* 1826–27. Oil on canvas, 17 7/8 x 14 7/8" (45.5 x 37.7 cm). The Wallace Collection, London

The central figure among the French Romantics was the novelist Victor Hugo (1802–1885). The introduction to his play about Oliver Cromwell (1827), the puritan who ruled England after the execution of King Charles II, was a broadside attack on classical drama. In 1830 Hugo's drama *Hernani* announced the triumph of Romanticism. It reversed the shopworn triumph of young lovers (so dear to classical French theater) by ending in tragedy and broke from the stilted literary conventions of French drama by altering the length of the poetic line. Perhaps fittingly, it was the failure of Hugo's *The Burgraves* in 1843 that signaled the end of Romantic theater. The other leading dramatist of the 1830s was Alexandre Dumas the Elder (1802–1870), who wrote a number of successful historical and domestic plays before turning to the novels for which he is best known today: *The Three Musketeers* (1844) and *The Count of Monte Cristo* (1845). George Sand (Amandine-Aurore-Lucile Dupin Dudevant, 1804–1876), who adopted a male pen name to help gain acceptance of her work, was a favorite novelist as well as a prolific playwright. Her apartment was also host to one of the most glittering *salons*—gatherings of writers, artists, and musicians that formed the center of cultural life in nineteenth-century Europe.

It was popular theater that enjoyed the greatest success, fueled by the huge growth of cities spawned by the Industrial Revolution. Much of it took the form of bourgeois melodramas, which owed their appeal to their simple plots and morality. New kinds of spectacle were made possible by the same technology that gave rise to the Industrial Revolution itself, for example, the invention in 1816 of gaslight and limelight, which involved heating lime with compressed oxygen and compressed hydrogen. They were superseded by Thomas Edison's invention of the electric light in 1879, which led to the improved carbon arc lamp a year later. Among the favorite spectacles were large paintings of panoramas and dioramas, which created special effects through changes of light and color. The leader in this field was Louis Daguerre, who was also an important scene designer before he turned to the invention of photography (see page 702).

In England, all the important Romantic poets tried their hand at plays but with little success: Samuel Taylor Coleridge (1772–1834), William Wordsworth (1770–1850), John Keats (1795–1821), Percy Bysshe Shelley (1792–1822), and even Robert Browning (1812–1889). The most important among them was Lord Byron (George Gordon, 1788–1824), the very prototype of the Romantic writer. His impact was immediate—Delacroix painted canvases inspired by Byron's dramas *Marino Faliero* and *Sardanapalus* (see fig. 21-33)—and lasted well beyond his own brief lifetime. The novelist Sir Walter Scott (1771–1832) also wrote plays, but mainly his novels were adapted to the stage by others to great acclaim. The most popular productions in England were translations of middle-class plays by the German Kotzebue; these were superseded by the works of George Bulwer-Lytton (1803–1873)—famous for the opening "It was a dark and stormy night"—who invented the "gentlemanly" melodrama that gave an air of Victorian respectability to the theater.

Philadelphia was the theater capital in the United States, as it was of art, before 1815. The most important house, the Chestnut Street Theater, was designed by the great English architect Inigo Jones. New York City soon superseded Philadelphia. The close ties between art and theater in America are illustrated by William Dunlap (1766–1839), who was the nation's leading playwright before turning to painting in 1812; toward the end of his long life he also wrote the first histories of American theater and art. Many artists, particularly aspiring younger ones along the frontier, found their first employment painting stage scenery. As in Europe, the growth of cities in America created a demand for larger and more numerous theaters around the country. Especially popular were Native American and Yankee plays as symbols of the young nation. They were soon joined by African-American minstrel shows (the term *Jim Crow* comes from a song introduced by Thomas D. Rice in 1829), which featured the "end men" Tambo and Bones, and a "middle" man who functioned as a master of ceremonies. The 1840s saw the rise of a new type, the city boy, who was often pitted against his country cousin.

abstraction to express the poetic idea. The artist communicates his intent through the stylized forms and symmetrical composition. More generally, *Morning* represents the mystical yearning of the soul for the infinite so dear to the German Romantic. This ecstatic vision, the "chord" of harmony, as he put it, is depicted using the same method as Friedrich's. Every detail has been precisely observed. The picture surface, transparent as glass, makes us look at nature with the same innocence as the newborn child. As a result, the landscape has an appealing simplicity, despite the complexity of its program. In the end, it is the painting technique that validates Runge's ideas and makes them convincing.

THE NAZARENES. In 1809 a group of young German painters at the Vienna Academy banded together to form the Guild of St. Luke, after the artists' guilds of old. They equated simplicity with pious virtue and avoided all virtuosity, which worked against the heartfelt sincerity that was their goal. Two years later they decided to lead the life of artist–monks at an abandoned monastery near Rome, where they became known as the Nazarenes. At first their paintings and drawings had a striking purity, achieved by imitating the painstaking precision of the old German masters and the style of the Early Renaissance. Over time their work suffered from the Neoclassic emphasis on form at the expense of color and from increasingly inflated rhetoric. The Nazarene movement gradually petered out as its members died or returned to Germany, where they established the mainstream of German Romanticism.

OVERBECK. The Nazarenes were at their best in intimate subjects, such as *Italia and Germania* (fig. 21-54) by Friedrich Overbeck (1789–1869). This manifesto by the movement's "priest" expresses the North's long-standing love-hate relationship with the South. It shows personifications of the two countries, so different in every respect, reconciled in tender friendship. The painting is at once a nostalgic reminiscence of the artist's homeland and a celebration of the beauty he found around him in Rome, here

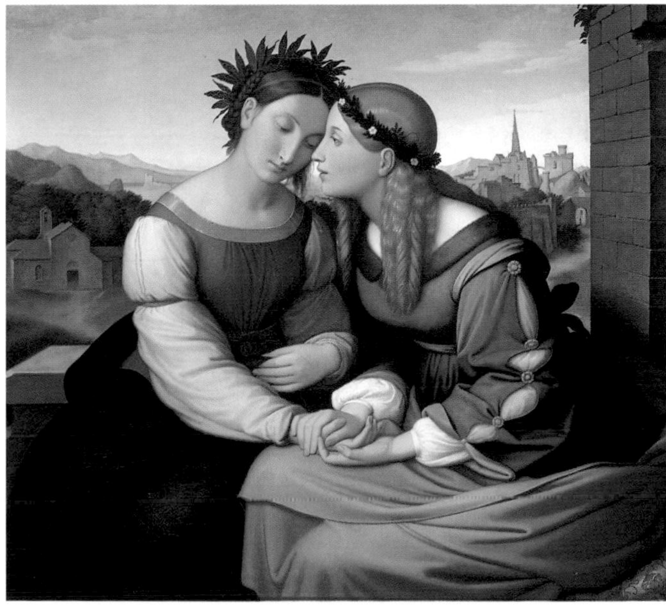

21-54. Friedrich Overbeck. *Italia and Germania*. 1811–28. Oil on canvas, 37 3/4 x 41 7/8" (96 x 106.4 cm). Bayerische Staatsgemäldesammlungen, Neue Pinakothek, Munich

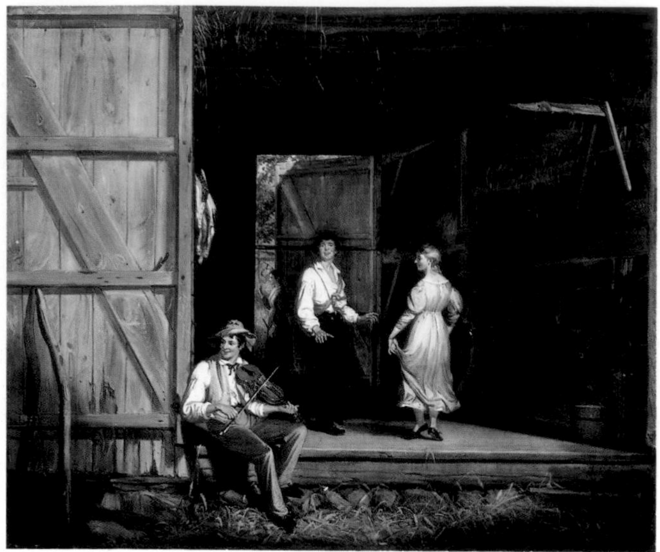

21-55. William Sidney Mount. *Dancing on the Barn Floor.* 1831. Oil on canvas, 25 x 30" (63.5 x 76.2 cm). Collection of The Museums at Stony Brook

GIFT OF MR. AND MRS. WARD MELVILLE

united in harmony and mutual respect. Its source was Angelica Kauffmann's self-portrait (see fig. 21-8) by way of German portraiture.

United States

Painting following the American Revolution was dominated by followers of Benjamin West, who took every young artist from the New World under his wing. Strangely enough, the only ones to enjoy much success were portraitists such as Gilbert Stuart (1755–1828). Using the fashionable conventions of Joshua Reynolds, they conferred the aura of established aristocracy on the Federalists, who were only too eager to forget the recent revolutionary past enshrined by the history painters. What Americans wanted was an art based not on the past but on the present. Romantic painting in the United States rode the tidal wave of nationalism fostered by Jacksonian democracy. Collectors now began to support artists who could articulate their vision of the United States. For perhaps the only time in the country's history, artists, patrons, and intellectuals shared a common point of view.

MOUNT. During the 1820s, America found its history painting in genre scenes descended from Dutch and English examples. The first native genre painter of real talent, William Sidney Mount (1808–1868), spent his career on rural Long Island, which provided him with a rich vein of subjects. Although he began as a history painter, Mount quickly turned to scenes of everyday life, which he imbued with the humor of Jan Steen. *Dancing on the Barn Floor* (fig. 21-55), one of his first efforts, projects the ideal of America as a land of contentment in which its fun-loving people enjoy a simple, happy life as the fruit of their honest labor. The carefully observed violinist testifies to the artist's love of music, his favorite theme. This ingenious inventor and theoretician wrote considerable "fiddle" music himself and later patented a violin of unusual design.

THE HUDSON RIVER SCHOOL. At about the same time, Americans began to discover landscape painting. Before then, settlers were far too busy carving out homesteads to pay much attention to the poetry of nature's moods. The attitude toward landscape began to change only as the surrounding wilderness was gradually tamed. The spread of civilization allowed Americans for the first time to see nature as the escape from urban life that had long inspired European painters. As in England, the contribution of the poets proved essential to shaping American ideas about nature. By 1825 they were calling on artists to depict the wilderness as the most distinctive feature of the New World and its emerging culture. Pantheism virtually became a national religion during the Romantic era. While it could be frightening, nature was everywhere and was believed to play a special role in determining the American character. Led by Thomas Cole (1801–1848), the founder of the Hudson River School, which flourished from 1825 until the Centennial celebration in 1876, American painters elevated the forests and mountains to symbols of the United States.

COLE. Like many early American landscapists, Cole came from England, where he was trained as an engraver, but he learned the basics of painting from an itinerant artist in the Midwest. After a summer sketching tour up the Hudson River, he invented the means of expressing the elemental power of the country's primitive landscape. He did so by transforming the formulas of the English picturesque into Romantic hymns based on the direct observation of nature. Because he also wrote poetry, Cole was uniquely able to create a visual counterpart to the literary ideas of the day. His painting *View of Schroon Mountain, Essex County, New York, After a Storm* (fig. 21-56) shows the peak rising majestically like a pyramid from the forest below. It is treated as a symbol of permanence surrounded by death and decay, signified by the autumnal foliage, passing storm, and dead trees. Stirred by sublime emotion, the artist has heightened the dramatic lighting behind the mountain, so that the broad landscape becomes a revelation of God's eternal laws.

BINGHAM. *Fur Traders Descending the Missouri* (fig. 21-57) by George Caleb Bingham (1811–1879) shows this close identification with the land in a different way. The picture, both a landscape and a genre scene, is full of the vastness and silence of the wide-open spaces. The two trappers in their dugout canoe, gliding downstream in the misty sunlight, are entirely at home in this idyllic setting. Bingham portrays the United States as a benevolent Eden in which settlers assume their rightful place. Rather than being dwarfed by a vast and often hostile continent, these hardy pioneers live in an ideal state of harmony with nature, symbolized by the waning daylight. The picture reminds us of how much Romantic adventurousness went into the westward expansion of the United States. The scene owes much of its haunting charm to the silhouette of the black cub chained to the prow and its reflection in the water. This masterstroke adds a note of primitive mystery that we shall not meet again until the work of Henri Rousseau (see pages 753–54).

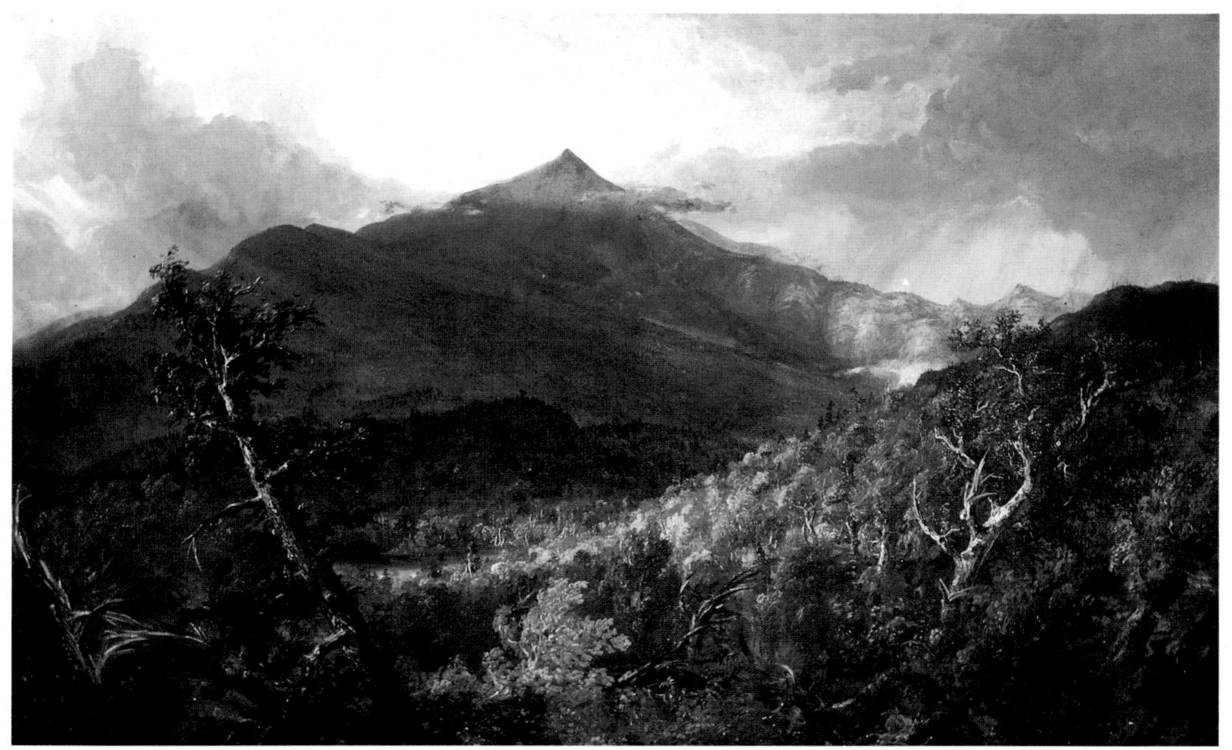

21-56. Thomas Cole. *View of Schroon Mountain, Essex County, New York, After a Storm.* 1838. Oil on canvas, 39 3/8 x 63" (100 x 160 cm). The Cleveland Museum of Art

HINMAN B. HURLBUT COLLECTION

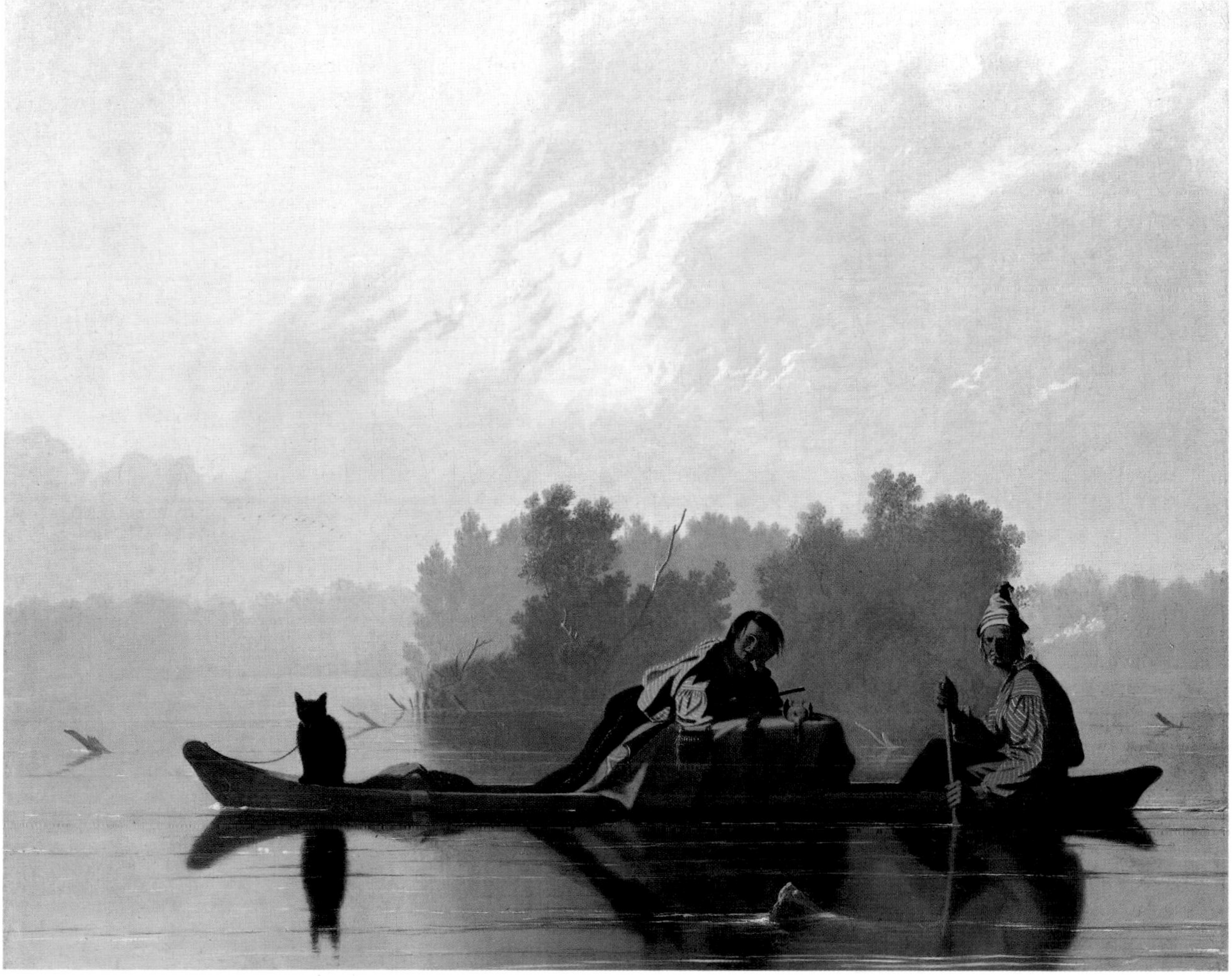

21-57. George Caleb Bingham. *Fur Traders Descending the Missouri.* c. 1845. Oil on canvas, 29 x 36 1/2" (73.7 x 92.7 cm). The Metropolitan Museum of Art, New York

MORRIS K. JESUP FUND, 1933

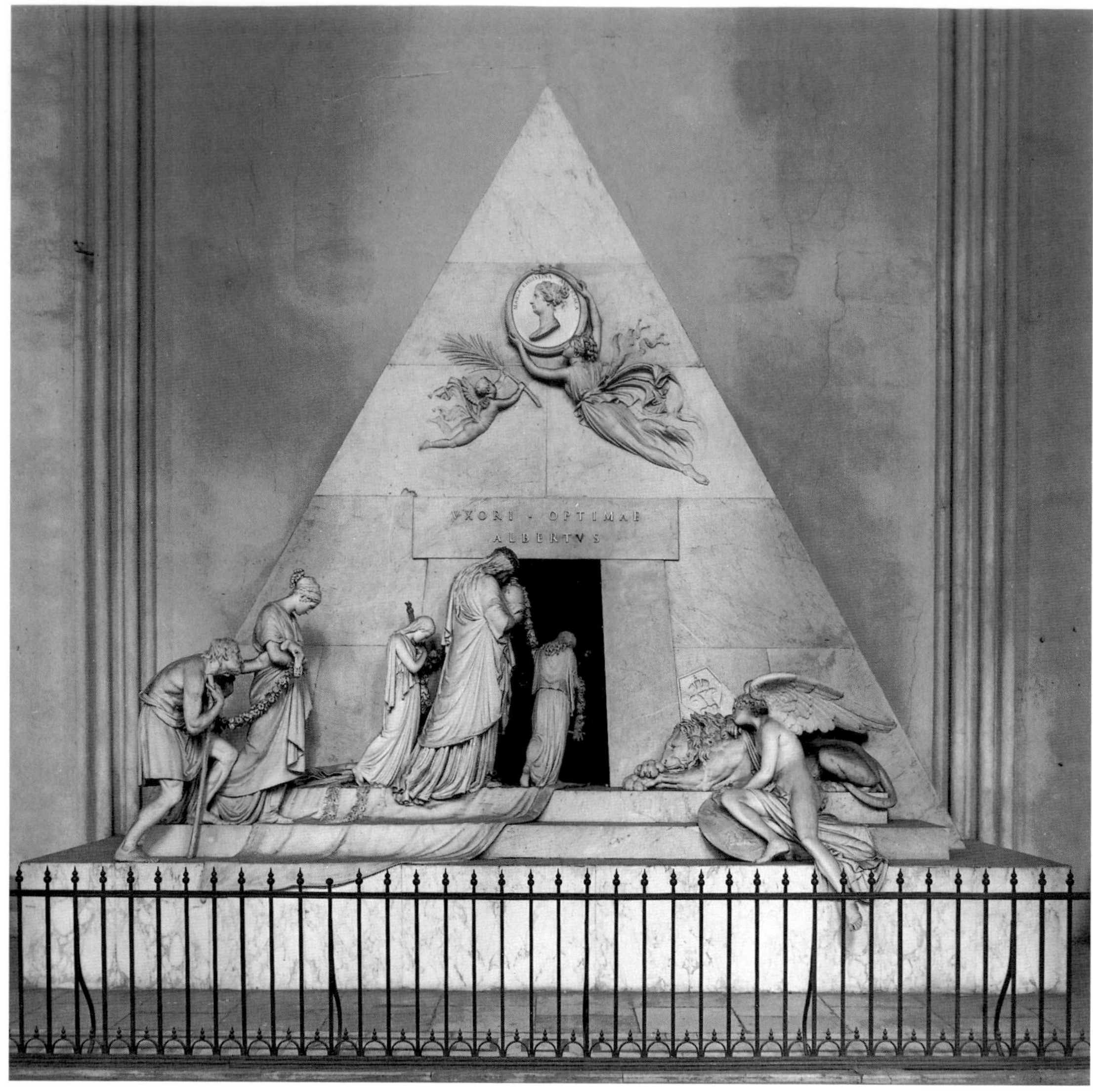

21-58. Antonio Canova. Tomb of the Archduchess Maria Christina. 1798–1805. Marble, lifesize. Augustinerkirche, Vienna

SCULPTURE

In attempting to define Romanticism in sculpture, we are immediately struck by an extraordinary fact. In contrast to the abundance of theoretical writings that accompanied Neoclassical sculpture from Winckelmann on, there exists only one piece of writing that sets forth a general theory of sculpture from the Romantic point of view: Baudelaire's essay of 1846, "Why Sculpture Is Boring," which occupies only a few pages of his long review of the Salon of that year. Actually, Baudelaire is less concerned with the state of French sculpture at that moment, which strikes him as deplorable, than he is with the limitations of sculpture as a medium. To him, there can be no such thing as Romantic sculpture. Every piece of sculpture is a "fetish" whose objective existence prevents the artist from making it a vehicle for expressing his subjective view of the world, his personal sensibility. It can overcome this limitation only if it is placed in the service of architecture, where it becomes part of a larger whole, such as a Gothic cathedral. As soon as it is detached from this context, sculpture returns to its primitive status. Fortunately, Baudelaire's theory was not taken at face value by either artists or patrons. It does suggest the difficulty Romantic sculptors had in finding a self-image they could live with. The unique virtue of sculpture—its solid, space-filling reality (its "idol" quality)—was not compatible with the Romantic temperament. The rebellious and individualistic urges of Romanticism could find expression in rough, small-scale sketches but rarely survived the laborious process of translating the sketch into a permanent, finished monument.

Italy

CANOVA. At the beginning of the Romantic era, we find an adaptation of the Neoclassical style to new ends by sculptors, led by Antonio Canova (1757–1822). He was not only the greatest sculptor of his generation, he was the most famous artist of the Western world from the 1790s until long after his death. Both his work and his personality became a model for every sculptor during those years. Canova's meteoric rise led to numerous commis-

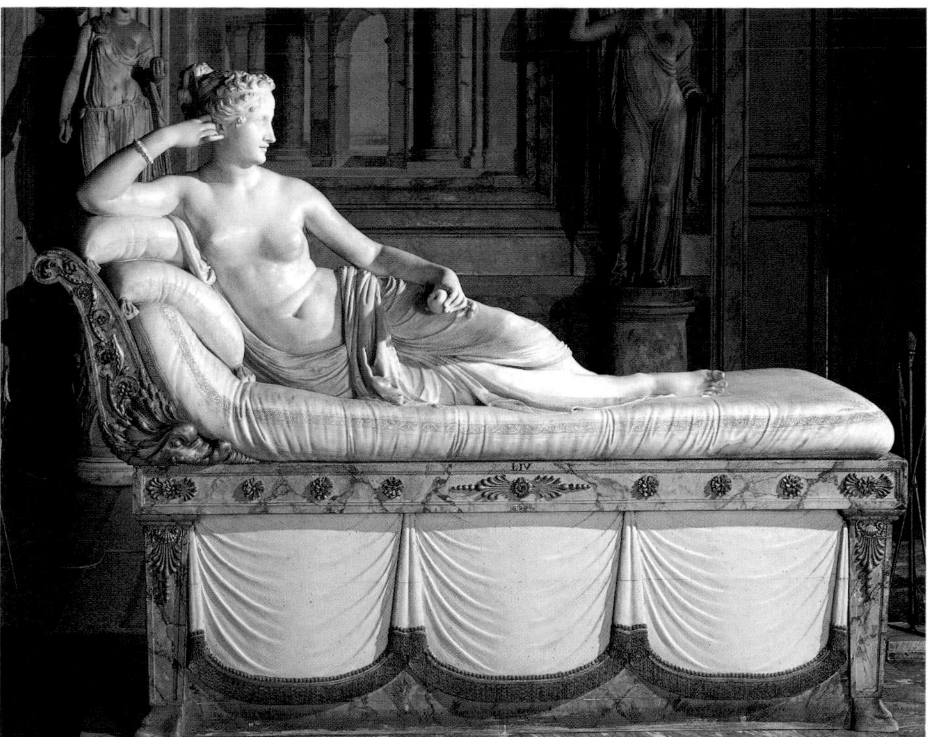

21-59. Antonio Canova. *Pauline Borghese as Venus.* 1808. Marble, lifesize. Galleria Borghese, Rome

sions. The Tomb of Maria Christina, archduchess of Austria, in the Church of the Augustinians in Vienna (fig. 21-58) is remarkable as much for its "timeless" beauty as for its gently melancholy sentiment. It was commissioned by her husband soon after her death in 1798. Its framework had been anticipated in a monument to Titian planned by Canova several years before. This ensemble, in contrast to the tombs of earlier times (such as fig. 12-48), does not include the real burial place. Moreover, the deceased appears only in a portrait medallion framed by a snake biting its own tail, a symbol of eternity, and sustained by two floating genii. Presumably, but not actually, the urn carried by the woman in the center contains her ashes. This is an ideal burial service performed by mostly allegorical figures: a mourning winged genius on the right, and the group about to enter the tomb on the left, who represent the Three Ages of Life. The slow procession, directed away from the beholder, stands for "eternal remembrance." All references to Christianity are conspicuously absent.

Canova must have known of Pigalle's tomb for the Maréchal de Saxe (see fig. 20-3), which looks forward to that of the archduchess in so many respects. The differences are equally striking, however. Canova's design looks surprisingly like a very high relief. Most of the figures are seen in strict profile, so that they seem to hug the wall plane despite the deep space. Gestures are kept to a minimum, and the allegorical trappings that clutter Pigalle's monument have been swept away, so that nothing distracts us from the solemn ritual being acted out before us. It is this intense concentration that distinguishes Canova's Romantic classicism from the Baroque classicism of Pigalle.

Canova's friends included Jacques-Louis David (see pages 641–42), who helped to spread his fame in France. In 1802, Canova was invited to Paris by Napoleon, who wanted his portrait done by the greatest sculptor of the age. With Napoleon's approval, he made a colossal nude figure in marble showing the conqueror as a victorious and peace-giving Mars. (Fittingly enough, the statue was given to the Duke of Wellington after he defeated Napoleon at Waterloo.) Not to be outdone, Napoleon's sister Pauline Borghese had Canova sculpt her as a reclining Venus (fig. 21-59). The statue is so obviously idealized as to quiet any gossip. We recognize it as a forerunner, more classically proportioned, of Ingres' *Odalisque* (see fig. 21-30). She is equally characteristic of early Romanticism, which incorporated Rococo eroticism but in a less sensuous form. Strangely enough, Pauline Borghese seems less three-dimensional than the painting. She is designed like a "relief in the round," for front and back view only. Her charm comes almost entirely from the fluid grace of her contours.

THORVALDSEN. Canova remained the model for every ambitious sculptor for most of the nineteenth century. However, the Napoleonic era was not favorable for those who wanted to be like him: independent, obligated to no single patron, free to create "modern classics." The only one who achieved that goal was Bertel Thorvaldsen (1770–1844), a Dane who came to Rome in 1797 on a scholarship from the Royal Academy in Copenhagen and became Canova's successor. For all of Europe except France and Spain, he remained the model of sculptural perfection until the 1850s. Germans, Scandinavians, and many Italians viewed him as more "truly Greek" than Canova. Although he established his reputation early, Thorvaldsen had to live through some difficult years before he could feel artistically and financially secure.

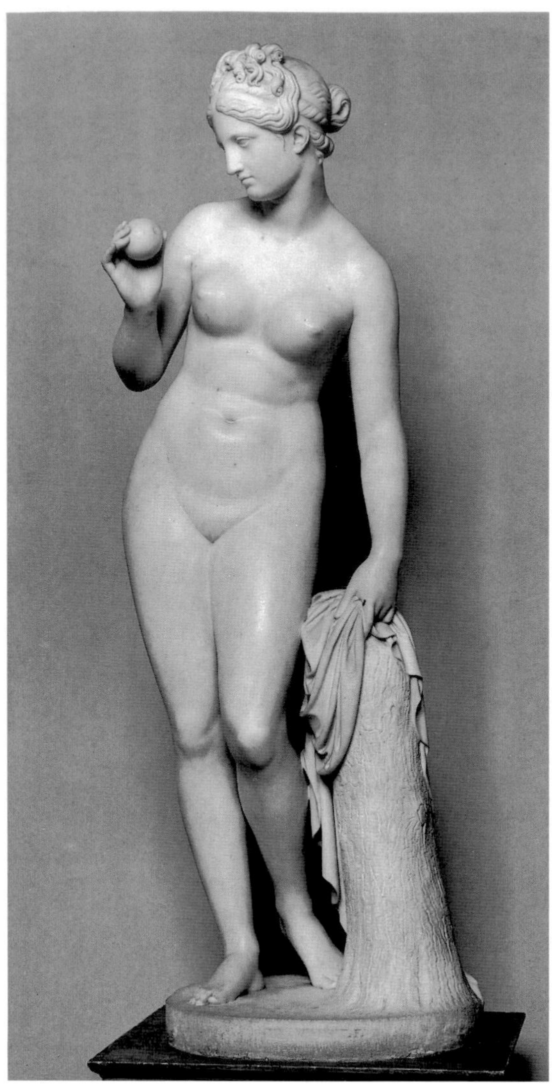

21-60. Bertel Thorvaldsen. *Venus.* 1813–16. Marble, lifesize. Thorvaldsens Museum, Copenhagen

Thorvaldsen became the first to revive the most heroic phase of Greek art, but he soon underwent a basic change not only of style but of outlook. His *Venus* (fig. 21-60) is closer to a living model than to any ancient source, though its immediate ancestor is a statue by Houdon. Thorvaldsen shows her in a moment of triumph, holding the golden apple awarded by Paris in the beauty contest that started the Trojan War. Yet she contemplates the apple in a way that might lead us to mistake her for an Eve tempted, were it not for the garment in her left hand. The statue shows Thorvaldsen's new emphasis on poetic sentiment, as well as his reawakened religious feeling, which he shared with the young German painters in Rome known as the Nazarenes, many of whom were his friends (see page 683). Thus his *Venus* is far more Romantic than Neoclassic, despite its style.

France

It was in France that the main development of Romantic sculpture took place. Although the doctrine of the Academy came to be broadened and modified in the course of time, its core lasted until Rodin late in the century. This core might be defined as the belief that the human body is nature's noblest creation and hence the sculptor's noblest subject. Translated into practice, this idea meant that every student of sculpture received a rigorous training. The course of study was especially demanding at the Paris École des Beaux-Arts. In 1819 it opened as the successor to both the Académie Royale de Peinture et Sculpture and the Académie Royale d'Architecture under the Académie des Beaux-Arts, which in turn was part of the Institut de France. Since the level of teaching at the École was far higher in sculpture than it was in painting, the limitations of the academic sculptural tradition became apparent only much later. The Romantic reaction against the ideal of the "modern classic" asserted itself in the sculpture sections of the French Salons right after the Revolution of 1830, which brought about the fall of the restored Bourbon regime. However, antiacademic tendencies did not become dominant until the last two decades of the century, when Michelangelo, Rodin's ideal, at last won out over Canova. What ultimately destroyed the modern classic was the cult of the fragmentary and the unfinished.

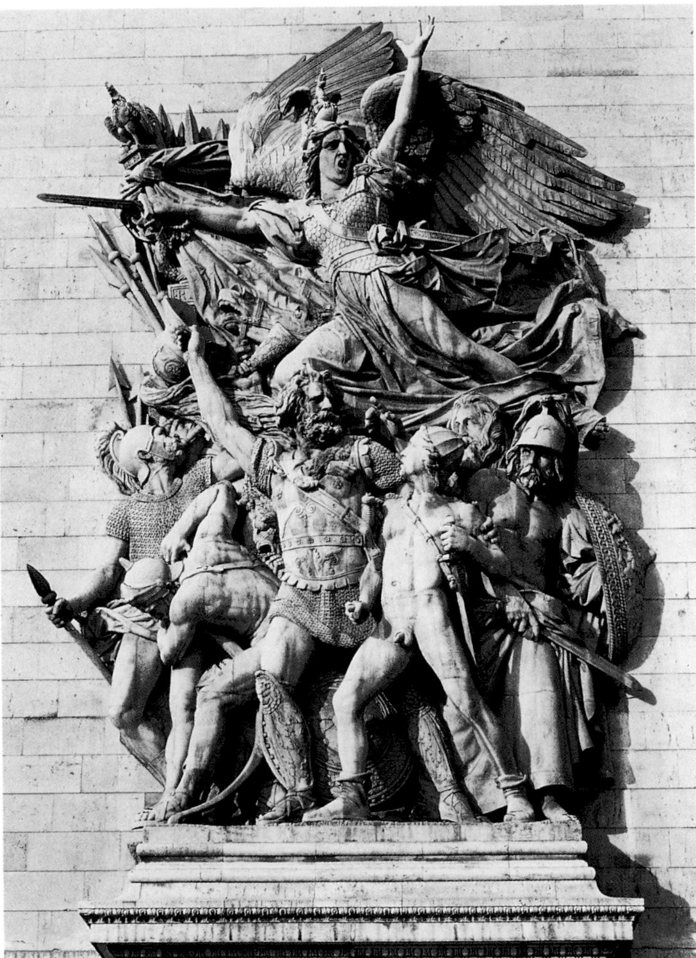

21-61. François Rude.
La Marseillaise. 1833–36.
Stone, approx. 42 x 26'
(12.8 x 7.9 m).
Arc de Triomphe, Paris

That the Romantic "rebellion" started so much later in sculpture than in painting also attests to how closely the medium was linked to politics in nineteenth-century France. Artists were often passionately involved in politics, but because the state remained the largest single source of commissions, the fortunes of the sculptors were more directly affected than those of the painters by changes in regime. French sculpture was by no means dominated by its social and political environment. Yet, to the extent that it was a public art, sculpture responded to the pressure of these forces, directly or indirectly, far more than did painting. It was shaped by them in varying degrees, depending on local circumstances. Thus we cannot understand its development without reference to the changing politics around it.

RUDE. François Rude (1784–1855), who enthusiastically took Napoleon's side after the emperor's return from Elba, sought refuge in Brussels from Bourbon rule, as had Jacques-Louis David, whom he knew and revered. After returning to Paris, Rude must have felt that artistically he had reached a dead end and decided to strike out in new directions. He acquired a new interest in the French Renaissance tradition of the School of Fontainebleau and Giovanni Bologna (see pages 476–78), which would eventually lead him back to Claus Sluter. This rediscovery of national sculptural traditions, so characteristic of Romantic revivalism, was part of a new nationalism, which was also illustrated by a passion for historic portraits as "morally elevating for the public."

These concerns are manifest in Rude's masterpiece, *The Departure of the Volunteers of 1792,* commonly called *La Marseillaise* (fig. 21-61). It was carved for Napoleon's unfinished triumphal arch on the Place de l'Étoile. The new king, Louis-Philippe, and his energetic minister of the interior, Adolphe Thiers, saw the arch's completion as an opportunity to demonstrate that his government was one of national reconciliation. Hence the sculptural program had to offer something to every segment of the French political spectrum. Rude was fortunate in getting a commission for one of the four groups that flank the opening. He raised his subject—the French people rallying to defend the Republic against attack from abroad—to the level of mythic splendor. The volunteers surge forth, some nude, others in classic armor, inspired by the great forward movement of the winged genius of Liberty above them. No wonder the work incited an emotional response that made people identify the group with the national anthem itself. For Rude, the group had a deeply felt personal meaning: his father had been among those volunteers. When the arch was officially unveiled in 1836, there was almost unanimous agreement that Rude's group made the other three pale into insignificance. Despite its great public acclaim, *The Departure* failed to gain Rude the official honors he so clearly deserved. He found himself more and more in opposition to the regime, and his most important works between 1836 and 1848 were direct expressions of his Bonapartist political beliefs.

ROMANTICISM IN MUSIC

Many music historians still view the early nineteenth century as part of the Classical period. To them, the Romantic era proper did not arrive until the 1860s, by which time Romanticism in art had run its course. Music proved the ideal Romantic art form because it was widely believed to allow the fullest expression of pure feeling, without the hindrance of literal meaning or the reality of appearance. The archetype of the early Romantic composer was Ludwig van Beethoven (1770–1827). He sympathized strongly with the American and French revolutions, which fed his restless Romantic spirit, and in his personal relations he bowed to no one, least of all to his aristocratic patrons. Nevertheless, he was closest spiritually to Goethe, a member of the previous generation whom he revered. His early works still belong to the Neoclassical period of music (see box page 656), but his style has more affinities with that of C. P. E. Bach than of Mozart or Haydn, with whom he nominally studied for four years. Beethoven was a virtuoso whose only rival at the piano was Mozart's pupil Johann Nepomuk Hummel (1778–1837), who introduced the cascades of notes that were to become characteristic of Romanticism. Like Mozart, Beethoven was a universal genius. Beethoven greatly expanded the expressive range of the forms he inherited. His works are more explosive and dynamic, louder and more grandiose. By emphasizing content over form, he pushed the boundaries of classical music to their limits, and sometimes beyond. Mercilessly self-critical, he composed far fewer works than his predecessors, but with few exceptions they are substantial contributions to the literature. In addition to the famous nine symphonies, on which his public reputation rests, there are 31 sonatas for piano, an instrument that was at once personal and symphonic in his hands, and 17 quartets that are the most profound utterances in all of chamber music. The most striking aspect of Beethoven's music is its novelty, which made it controversial to many of his contemporaries, such as the composer Carl Maria von Weber (1786–1826), who was his harshest critic. It features heroic expression counterbalanced by melting lyricism. No other composer could scale the heights or plumb the depths of the soul to such stirring effect. Extremely public during his youth and early maturity, his music became increasingly private over time, perhaps as the result of his growing deafness, which was largely complete by 1816, as well as his troubled personal life. Yet its complexity was a consistent outgrowth of the composer's personality and makes the late works demanding for interpreter and listener alike.

Beethoven was the essential point of departure for most Romantic composers of the next generation. Yet, no matter how awed they were by his commanding presence, they remained independent personalities determined to make their own contributions.

The dreamy sensibility of Franz Schubert (1797–1828) found its ideal outlet in German art songs (*Lieder;* singular, *Lied*), inspired by the poetry of Goethe and Schiller among others, which he wrote in vast quantity and variety and that occasionally provides a glimpse of the stormy side of his personality. Lieder remained the heart and soul of his chamber music, which is pure enchantment: the first piano trio, the octet, and the last three quartets, including the well-known *Death and the Maiden,* which is based on one of his most memorable songs. Schubert's piano sonatas in turn present an ideal combination of intimate lyricism and large scale, although he had some difficulty handling extended symphonic form itself.

Orchestral writing presented no difficulties to Felix Mendelssohn-Bartholdy (1809–1847). Like Mozart, he was a child prodigy who was writing significant music by late adolescence. (His sister, Fanny, was also gifted and remains unjustly neglected.) His five symphonies and numerous overtures are notable for their vitality and colorism, which "paint" vivid images in sound. Mendelssohn, too, was stirred by literature, above all by the plays of Shakespeare. For an 1843 production by Ludwig Tieck he set Shakespeare's *A Midsummer Night's Dream* to music that perfectly captures its impish spirit. Mendelssohn, like Schubert, succumbed early to syphilis (the AIDS of the time), which also claimed the lives of numerous other people in the arts.

The most characteristic music of Robert Schumann (1810–1856) was piano and vocal music. But although he lacked the facility for orchestration of his friend Mendelssohn, his four symphonies were of major importance for the next generation of German composers. They breathe an innocence and love of nature that make them the musical counterparts of Romantic landscape paintings. Schumann was also inspired by Romantic writers and undertook a series of large-scale vocal works: incidental music for *Manfred* (1849), incorporating the poem by Lord Byron; the opera *Genoveva* (1850), taken from Ludwig Tieck's drama; and *Scenes from Faust* (1853), based on Goethe's poetry. Schumann's wife, Clara Wieck (1819–1896), was also an excellent pianist and composer, but she put her career second to her husband's, so that only recently has her music come to the fore. Schumann died young after suffering from two years of madness, perhaps brought on by syphilis.

The only composer to equal Beethoven's heroic stature was the Frenchman Hector Berlioz (1803–1869), whose music employs the full force of a very large orchestra. Despite being mainly self-taught, Berlioz was a masterful composer in thorough command of orchestration—the technique of specifying which instruments should play which parts of a musical composition. Berlioz's music is programmatic, that is, it tells a story, or at least suggests a sequence of incidents, and this emphasis on story line over pure form is one of his most Romantic qualities. Berlioz's *Symphonie fantastique* (1830) is a morbid account of unrequited love. Shakespeare made a deep impression on him, and his most successful work is a dramatic realization of *Romeo and Juliet* (1839). No one, not even Verdi and Tchaikovsky later in the century, understood better the magic of love or the power of tragedy in Shakespeare. Although they were little performed during his lifetime, Berlioz's operas were important for successfully reviving the grand tradition of Lully and Rameau.

Paris was the opera capital of Europe during the first half of the nineteenth century. The most prolific and popular composer of opera was Giacchino Rossini (1792–1868), who adapted his Italian style to suit the French taste. While his operas generally have ridiculous plots, the music itself is beautiful and, given a libretto of quality, the result is a masterpiece: *The Barber of Seville* (1816), based on Beaumarchais' play, and *William Tell* (1829), Rossini's last opera, inspired by Schiller's drama of 1804. By the time he arrived in Paris in 1824, Rossini had the field to himself. His only potential rival, Luigi Cherubini (1760–1842), another Italian who had settled there in 1788, turned his attention largely to church music after 1813. A later academic counterpart to Christoph Willibald Glück (see page 656), Cherubini provided the classical antithesis to Rossini's unabashed Romanticism. During his day, he was regarded as the equal of Beethoven, whose is known to have admired him. Indeed, Beethoven's lone opera, *Fidelio,* was influenced by Cherubini's "rescue" operas. *Medea* (1797), based on the Greek tragedy by Euripides, remains Cherubini's finest achievement, though modern performances are marred by a later orchestration of the spoken dialogue.

With Rossini's departure for Paris in 1824, Italian opera was left in the capable hands of Gaetano Donizetti (1797–1848). Most of his 70 operas are potboilers, but the finest ones have spirited drama and appealing music. *Lucia di Lammermoor* (1835), freely adapted from a historical novel by Sir Walter Scott (see box page 682), might be considered the perfect opera: it spins its tale through a succession of glorious arias that bring the characters, centering on a tragic heroine of epic proportions, vividly to life. Donizetti's style largely determined the character of Italian opera before Giuseppe Verdi. His chief competition, Vincenzo Bellini (1801–1835), died too young to achieve his full potential only a few years after writing *Norma* and *La Somnambula* in 1831.

Among the most unusual musical personalities of the Romantic movement was the Polish composer Frédéric Chopin (1810–1849), who was drawn to Paris. A celebrated virtuoso of the piano, Chopin introduced a wide range of new types of composition for the keyboard, most of them—such as the *polonaise* and the *mazurka*—based on the national music of Poland, although John Field (1782–1837) helped to pave the way for his nocturnes, and there is a debt to Schubert and Mendelssohn as well. These compositions are so free and inventive that they seem to be entirely new forms spun as if by magic from Chopin's endlessly fertile imagination. Though mostly small in scale, they yielded not only poetic intimacy, at which he excelled, but also heroic grandeur. Chopin and his companion, the novelist George Sand (see box page 682), sat for a famous portrait by Delacroix.

For Chopin, music remained an expressive vehicle first, a technical display second. With the Italian violinist Niccolò Paganini (1782–1840), who also spent much of his life in Paris, virtuosity became an end in itself, which greatly enlarged the scope of violin playing. He was one of the first great music stars to be idolized by an adoring public. Paganini became the model in turn for the Hungarian pianist Franz Liszt (1811–1886), a friend of Chopin who came to Paris for a while but later traveled widely.

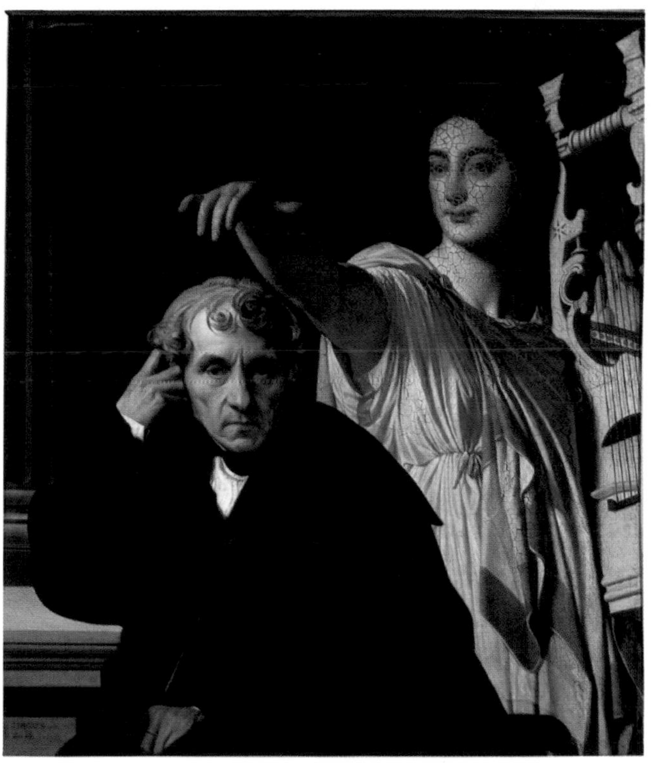

Jean-Auguste-Dominique Ingres. *Cherubini and the Muse of Lyric Poetry.* 1842. Oil on canvas, 41⅜ x 37" (105.1 x 94 cm). Musée du Louvre, Paris

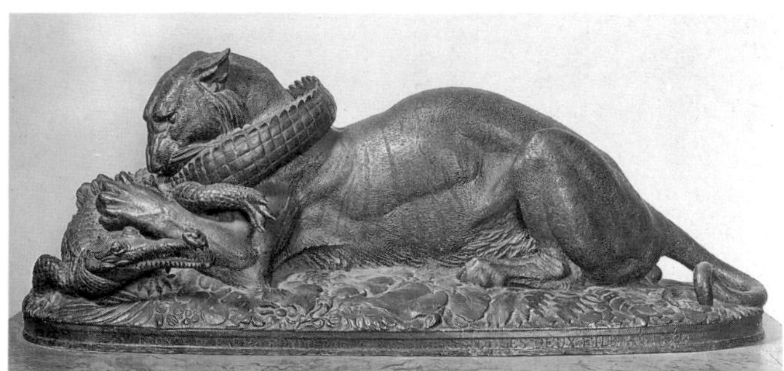

21-62. Antoine-Louis Barye. *Tiger Devouring a Gavial of the Ganges*. 1831–32. Bronze, length 39½" (100.3 cm). Musée du Louvre, Paris

BARYE. *La Marseillaise* brings to mind certain paintings by Delacroix and, in fact, its ultimate source is pictorial. In a similar way, Stubbs' *Lion Attacking a Horse* (see fig. 21-9) is the forerunner of animal groups by Antoine-Louis Barye (1795–1875). Barye followed in his father's footsteps as a goldsmith but spent all his free hours at the Paris zoo, sketching live animals and studying their anatomy. He also became a friend of Delacroix, who shared these interests and sometimes treated the same themes. Barye scored his first public success at the Salon of 1831 with the plaster model of *Tiger Devouring a Gavial of the Ganges* (fig. 21-62). His group displays a realism based on thorough scientific knowledge. What really impressed critics and public alike was the ferocity of the tiger, the pitiless display of "nature red in tooth and claw" so exciting to the Romantic imagination. Animal combats had a long tradition in Western art going all the way back to classical antiquity. These followed well-established formal conventions that governed both the choice of animals and their compositional relationship. Barye disregarded all such precedents. Not only did he study his animals directly from nature, he chose exotic species and unusual combinations, no matter how implausible. (Gavials are unlikely prey for tigers.) What counted was the group's expressive power, intensified here by the compact monumentality of design.

PRÉAULT. Besides bringing Rude and Barye into prominence, the Salons of the early 1830s served as showcases for sculptors still in their twenties. What separated them from the generation of their teachers was that none was old enough to have experienced the Napoleonic era. As it happened, there was not a single first-rate artist in this group. Auguste Préault (1809–1879), the most interesting of them, may have been the first to earn the title "a genius without talent," as he was called by one of his contemporaries. His ambitious relief titled *Tuerie (Slaughter)* (fig. 21-63), sent to the Salon of 1834, shows that his interest centered on extreme physical and emotional states. He submitted the panel as

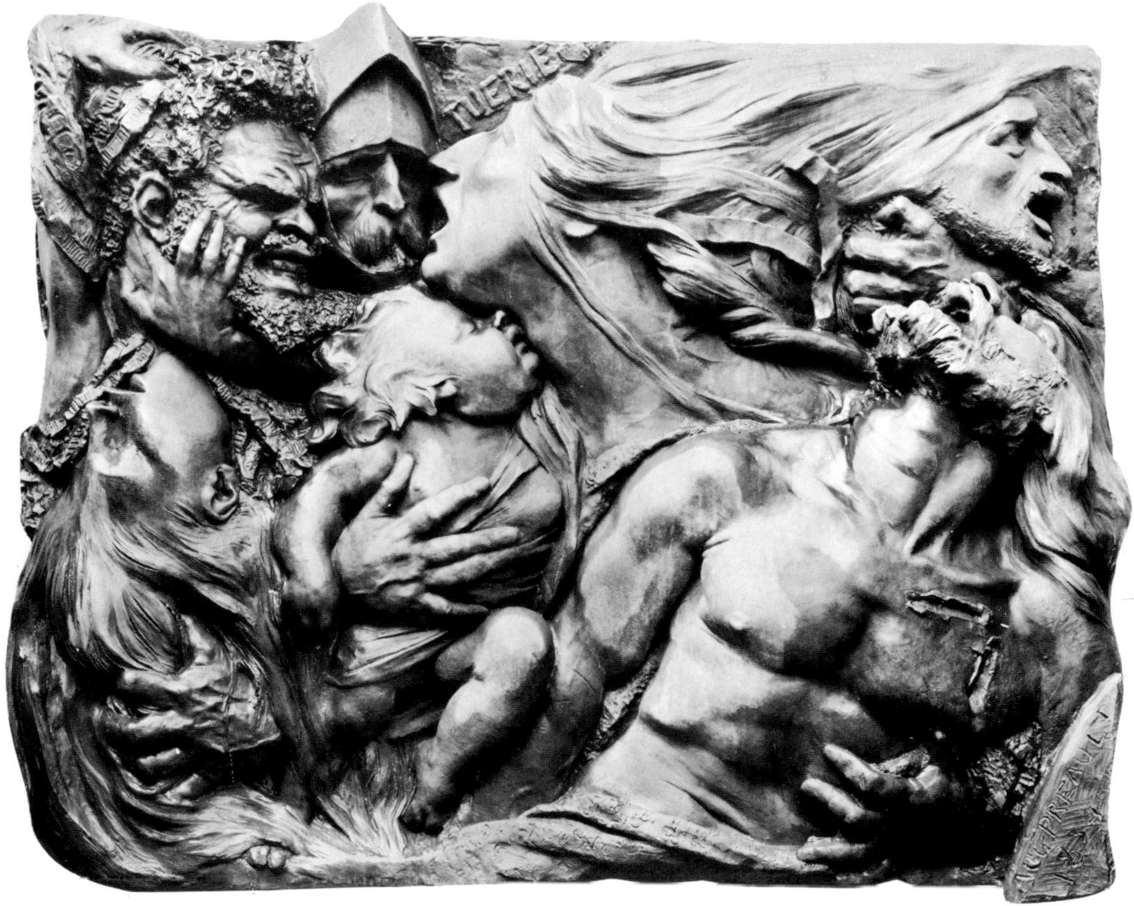

21-63. Auguste Préault. *Tuerie (Slaughter)*. 1834. Bronze, 43 x 55" (109.2 x 139.7 cm). Musée des Beaux-Arts, Chartres, France

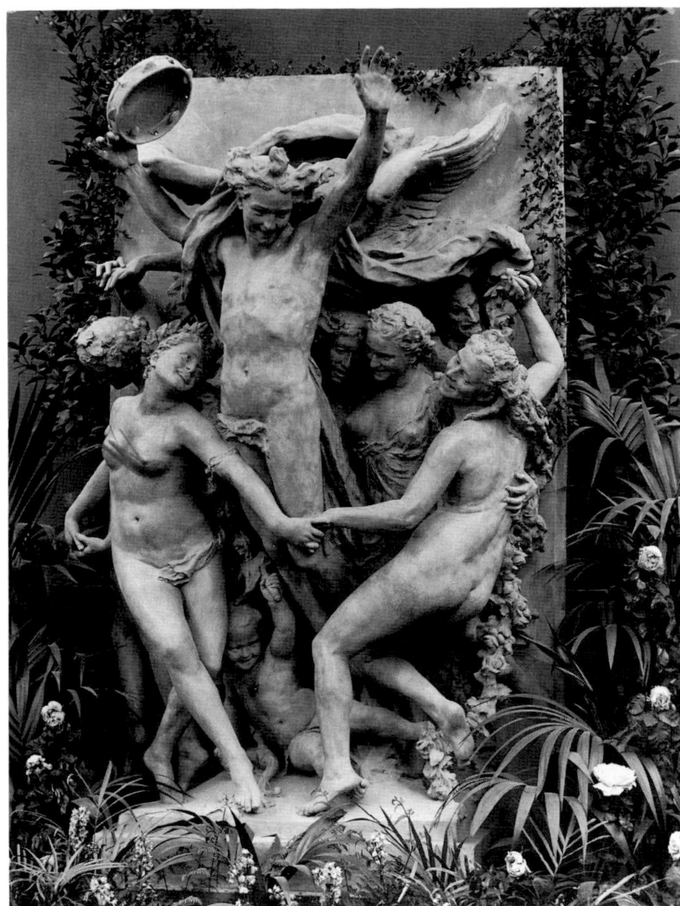

21-64. Jean-Baptiste Carpeaux. *The Dance*. 1867–69. Plaster model, approx. 15' x 8'6" (4.6 x 2.6 m). Musée de l'Opéra, Paris

the fragment of a larger composition, probably to ease it past the jury. The design is actually quite self-contained, even though every figure in it is indeed a fragment, except for the baby. The style of *Tuerie* must be termed Neo-Baroque, yet it is brimming with a physical and emotional violence far beyond anything found in Baroque art. Its expressive distortions and its irrational space, filled to the bursting point with writhing shapes, evoke memories of Gothic sculpture. In fact, the helmeted knight's face next to that of the screaming mother hints that the subject itself—some dread apocalyptic event beyond human control—is medieval. But in true Romantic fashion, Préault does not define it.

Tuerie established Préault's reputation as the prototype of the Romantic sculptor. It was acclaimed by avant-garde critics as a radical attack on the rules of classical relief. (What conservatives thought of it can easily be imagined.) Its very extremism, however, condemned *Tuerie* to being a dead end. Neither Préault nor anyone else could make it the starting point of a new development.

CARPEAUX. If the high tide of Romanticism is to be found among the French sculptors born during the first decade of the century, those born during the second may, with some hesitation, be designated late Romantics, but we again look in vain for a major talent among them. The third decade, in contrast, saw the birth of several important sculptors. Of these, the greatest and best known was Jean-Baptiste Carpeaux (1827–1875). Carpeaux's masterpiece came at the end of the Second Empire, which succeeded the short-lived Second Republic in 1852. In 1861 Carpeaux's old friend, the architect Charles Garnier, began the Paris Opéra (see pages 699–701) and entrusted him with one of the four sculptural groups across the facade. *The Dance* (fig. 21-64) perfectly matches Garnier's Neo-Baroque architecture. (The plaster model in our illustration is both livelier and more precise than the final stone group, visible in fig. 21-77, lower right.) The group created a scandal after its unveiling in 1869. The nude dancing bacchantes around the winged male genius in the center were denounced as drunk, vulgar, and indecent—and small wonder, for their coquettish gaiety derives from small Rococo groups such as Clodion's (see fig. 20-2). But unlike Clodion's, Carpeaux's enormous figures (they are 15 feet tall) look undressed rather than nude because of their naturalism, so that we do not accept them as inhabiting the realm of mythology. Public opinion insisted that the group be replaced. After the war with Germany ended in 1871, the old complaints were forgotten and *The Dance* was recognized as a masterpiece. It is as obviously superior to the other three Opéra groups by more conservative sculptors as Rude's *La Marseillaise* is to its neighbors on the Arc de Triomphe. (Carpeaux had studied for a while with Rude.) *The Dance* established the Beaux-Arts style in sculpture for the rest of the century, much as Garnier's Opéra did in architecture (see pages 699–701).

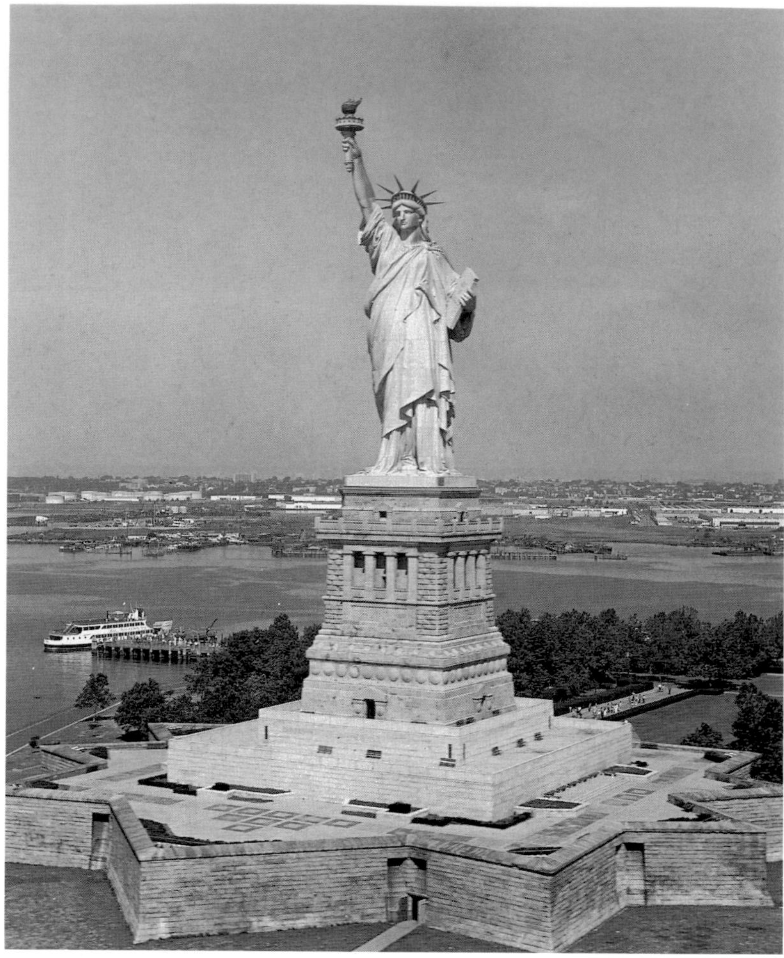

21-65. Auguste Bartholdi. *Statue of Liberty (Liberty Enlightening the World).* 1875–84. Copper sheeting over metal armature, height of figure 151'6" (46 m). Liberty Island, New York Harbor

BARTHOLDI. To defy established society, its values and institutions, was easier for writer and painters than for sculptors. To the latter, the late nineteenth century offered enormous opportunities for official commissions. It is a safe guess that the great majority of monuments in the Western world were produced, or at least begun, between 1872 and 1905. The most ambitious of these was the *Statue of Liberty* (or, to use its official title, *Liberty Enlightening the World;* fig. 21-65) by Auguste Bartholdi (1834–1904).

This monument in memory of French support for America during the War of Independence was a gift of the French people, not of the government. Its enormous cost was raised by public subscription, which took ten years. It was placed on a tall pedestal built with funds raised by the American public. Bartholdi developed the *Statue of Liberty* from a previous concept for a gigantic lighthouse in the form of a woman holding a lamp that was intended to be erected at the northern entry to the Suez Canal. All he had to do was exchange the Egyptian headdress for a radiant crown and the lantern for a torch. The final model shows an austere, classically draped young woman holding the torch in her raised right hand and a tablet in her left. She steps on the broken shackles of tyranny with her left foot, on which her weight rests. The right leg is set back, so that the figure seems to be advancing when viewed from the side but looks stationary from the front. As a piece of sculpture, the *Statue of Liberty* is less original than one might think. Formally and iconographically, it derives from a well-established ancestry reaching back to Canova and beyond. Its conservatism is, however, Bartholdi's conscious choice. He sensed that only a "timeless" statue could embody the ideal he wanted to glorify.

The figure, which stands more than 150 feet tall, presented severe structural problems that called for the skills of an architectural engineer. Bartholdi found the ideal collaborator in Gustave Eiffel, the future builder of the Eiffel Tower (see pages 733–34 and fig. 22-38). The project took more than a decade to complete. The *Statue of Liberty* was inaugurated at last in the fall of 1886. Its fame as the symbol—one is tempted to say "trademark"—of the United States has been worldwide ever since.

ARCHITECTURE

Given the individualistic nature of Romanticism, we might expect the range of revival styles to be widest in painting, the most personal and private of the visual arts, and narrowest in architecture,

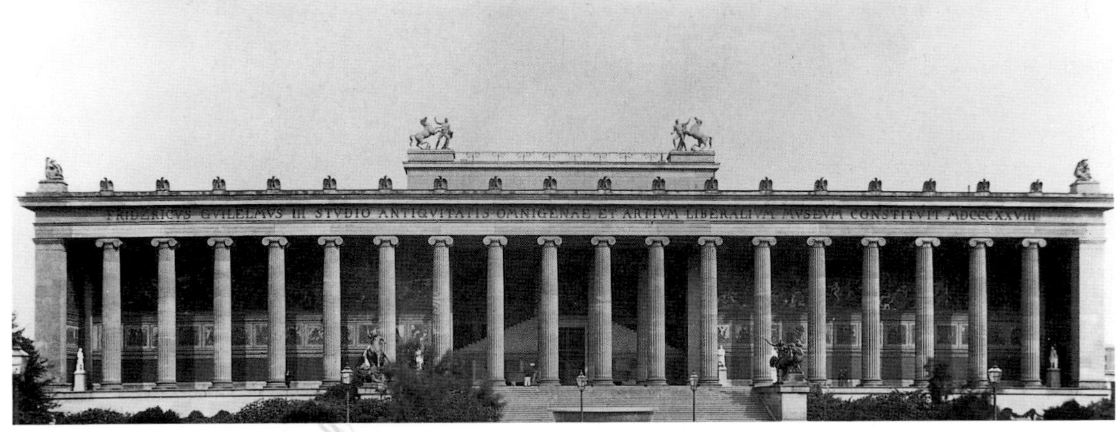

21-66. Karl Friedrich Schinkel. Altes Museum, Berlin. 1824–28

the most communal and public. Yet the opposite is true. Painters and sculptors were unable to abandon Renaissance habits of representation and never really revived medieval art or ancient art before the Classical Greek era. Architects were not subject to this limitation, however. Consequently, the revival styles lasted longer in architecture than in the other arts because it was free to draw on a wider range of sources.

The Classical Revival

The "Greek revival" phase of Neoclassicism was pioneered on a small scale in England but was quickly taken up everywhere. The Greek Doric was believed to embody more of the "noble simplicity and calm grandeur" of classical Greece than did the later, less "masculine" orders. Greek Doric was also the least flexible order; hence, particularly difficult to adapt to modern purposes. Only rarely could Greek Doric architecture furnish a direct model for Neoclassical structures. We instead find variations of it combined with elements taken from the other Greek orders.

SCHINKEL. The Altes Museum (Old Museum; fig. 21-66) by Karl Friedrich Schinkel (1781–1841) is a spectacular example of the Greek revival. The main entrance resembles a Doric temple seen from the side (see fig. 5-28), but with Ionic columns strung across a Corinthian order (compare fig. 5-24). Strictly speaking, it is like a Greek stoa (see page 122). The plan is based on one published in a contemporary treatise by the French architect Jean-Nicolas Durand (1760–1834), a pupil of Boullée and professor at the recently established engineering school in Paris. Durand reduced classical architecture to a set of geometric formulas based on function and economy. Schinkel's building, however, has none of Durand's frank utilitarianism. On the contrary, it is notable for its bold design and refined proportions. Schinkel, an architect of great ability, began as a painter in the style of Caspar David Friedrich (see page 680). He then worked as a stage designer before being appointed to the Berlin public works office, which he later headed. (He owed his appointment to Wilhelm von Humboldt, the Prussian statesman and Minister of Education, who was a friend of Goethe and Schiller; see box page 682.) Hence he knew how to instill architecture with Romantic associations and a theatrical flair worthy of Piranesi. Schinkel's first love was the Gothic, but although most of his public buildings are in a Neoclassical style, they retain a strong element of the picturesque. He could admire both styles because he shared the Enlightenment belief in the moral and educational functions of architecture. Here the measured rhythm of the monumental facade establishes a contemplative mood appropriate to viewing the art of antiquity. The Altes Museum expresses the veneration of ancient Greece in the land of Winckelmann and Mengs. To the poet Goethe, Greece remained the peak of civilization. The Altes Museum is, furthermore, testimony to the informed attitude that gave rise to art museums, galleries, and academies on both sides of the Atlantic during the nineteenth century. At the same time, the Greek style served the imperial ambitions of Prussia, which emerged as a major power at the Congress of Vienna in 1815. The imposing grandeur of the Altes Museum proclaims Berlin as the new Athens, with Kaiser Wilhelm III as a modern Perikles.

VON KLENZE. Schinkel was the tutor and friend of Crown Prince Friedrich Wilhelm, an amateur architect who wanted to combine Greek and Gothic architecture into a new style expressing his dream of a united Germany. This same ambition was shared by Crown Prince Ludwig of Bavaria, an ally of Napoleon who nevertheless conceived a monument to German unity during a visit to occupied Berlin in 1807. To achieve his vision, Ludwig turned to another Prussian, Leo von Klenze (1784–1864). Like Schinkel he had been a pupil of Friedrich Gilly (1772–1800) in Berlin. Von Klenze was actually the first to design a Neoclassical museum as a temple of art: the Glyptothek in Munich (1816), which houses the sculpture from Aegina (see figs. 5-22 and 5-23), followed by the Alte Pinakothek (1822), which holds the collection of Old Master paintings. Such an association could find support in the Classical past, specifically the small pinakotheke (picture gallery) at the entrance to the Akropolis. Whereas Schinkel merely referred to a plan by Durand, von Klenze actually studied with him, as well as with Napoleon's architects Percier and Fontaine (see page 701).

In 1821 von Klenze designed his masterpiece Walhalla, over-

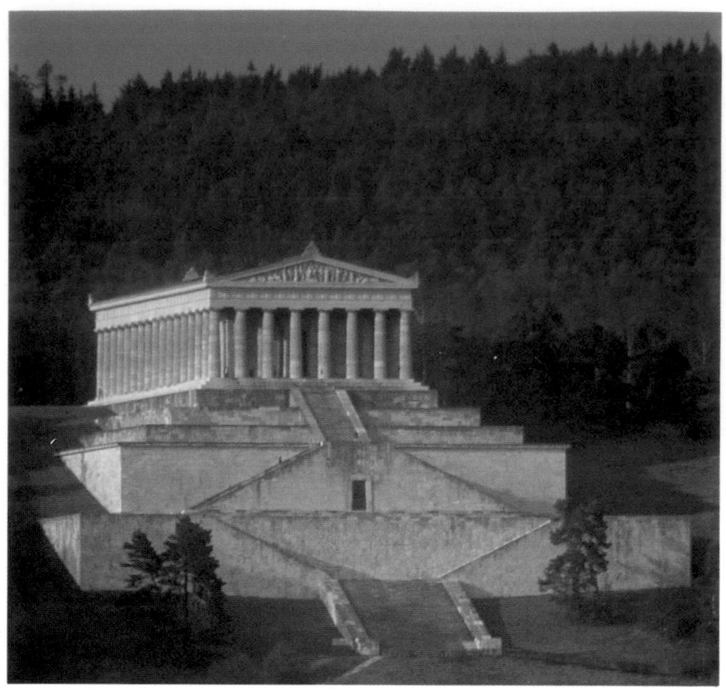

21-67. Leo von Klenze. Walhalla, near Regensburg, Germany. 1821–42

looking the Danube near Regensburg (fig. 21-67). Named for the resting place of heroes in ancient Teutonic mythology, it served as a pantheon of German notables whose portrait busts lined the interior. The design owes a great deal to a proposed monument to Frederick the Great by Gilly, which was as grandiose as anything conceived by Boullée, but it has been tamed by the academic classicism von Klenze absorbed in Paris. The building nevertheless fulfills its intended purpose, as stated by Prince Ludwig himself: "The Walhalla was erected so that the German might depart from it more German and better than when he had arrived."

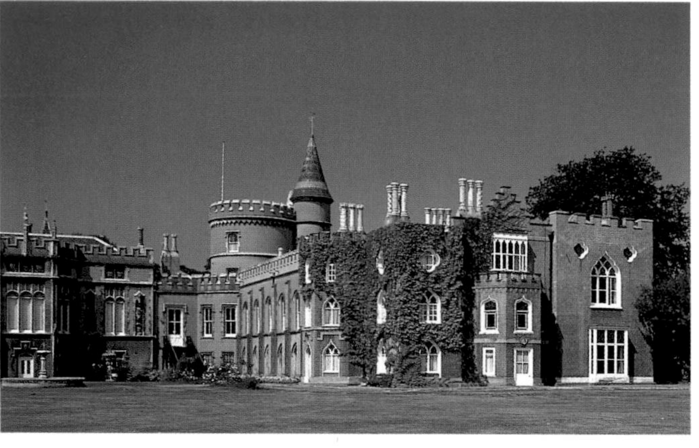

21-68. Horace Walpole, with William Robinson and others. Strawberry Hill, Twickenham, England. 1749–77

The Gothic Revival

It is characteristic of Romanticism that at the time architects launched the classical revival, they also started a Gothic revival. The appeal of the Gothic was chiefly as a means for creating picturesque effects and as a way of expressing Romantic feeling. After 1800, the choice between classical and Gothic modes was more often resolved in favor of Gothic. Nationalist sentiment, strengthened by the Napoleonic wars, became an important factor. England, France, and Germany each believed that Gothic expressed its national genius. The French theorist Eugène Viollet-le-Duc (1814–1879), a structural rationalist at heart, preferred it because it was "true according to the program and true according to the methods of construction." But certain English writers, notably John Ruskin (1800–1900), regarded Gothic as superior for ethical or religious reasons on the grounds that it was "honest" and "Christian."

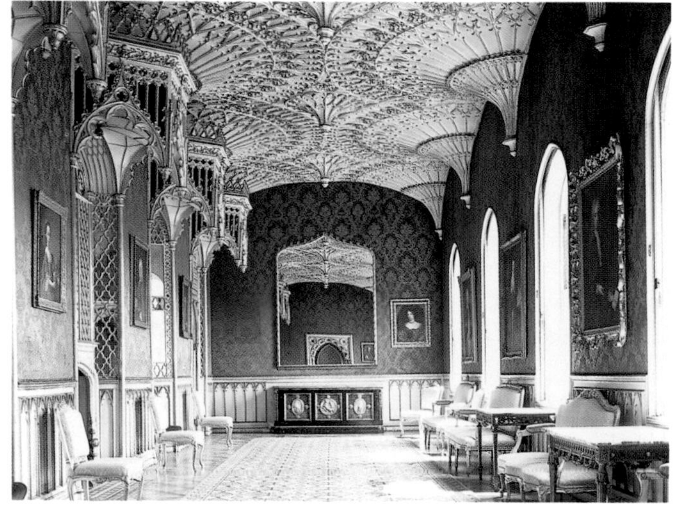

21-69. Interior of Strawberry Hill

WALPOLE. England played a key role in the Gothic revival, as it did in the development of Romantic literature and painting. Gothic forms had never wholly disappeared in England. They

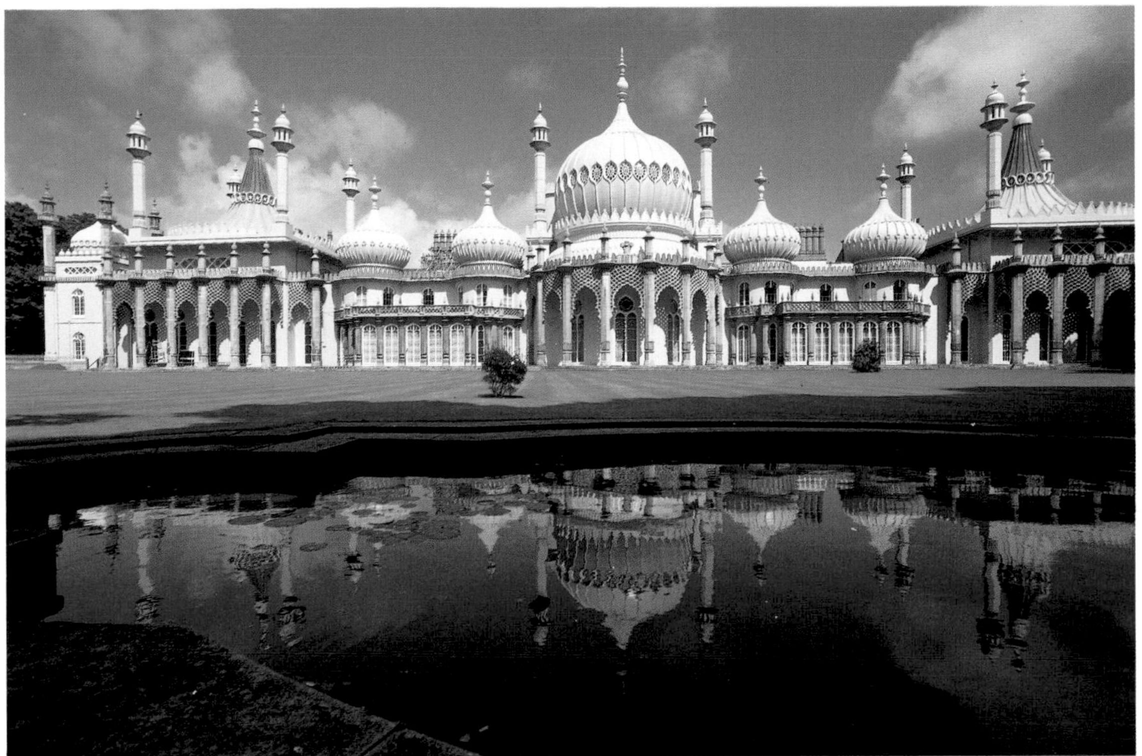

21-70. John Nash. The Royal Pavilion, Brighton, England. 1815–18

were used on occasion for special purposes, even by Sir Christopher Wren and Sir John Vanbrugh (see pages 588–91), but these were survivals of an authentic, if outmoded, tradition. The conscious revival was begun by William Kent in the 1730s, partly at the prompting of Robert Walpole, one of the most important politicians of the day. It soon became linked with the cult of the picturesque, and with the vogue for medieval (and pseudomedieval) romances. Horace Walpole (1717–1797), Robert's son, started the medieval craze with the publication in 1764 of his novel *The Castle of Otranto: A Gothic Story.* It was in this spirit that he enlarged and "gothicized" Strawberry Hill, his country house outside London (figs. 21-68 and 21-69). The process, which began midway in the eighteenth century, took more than 25 years and involved Walpole's circle of friends. Those who worked on the project included John Chute (1701–1776), William Robinson (c. 1720–1775), Richard Bentley (1708–1782), Thomas Pitt (c. 1737–1793), and Robert Adam, who was responsible for the round tower. The rambling structure has a studied irregularity, due mainly to Chute, that is decidedly picturesque. Inside, most of the elements were faithfully copied or adapted from authentic Gothic sources. The gallery in figure 21-69, designed by Pitt in 1759–62 with fireplaces by Chute, is a splendid imitation of the English Perpendicular style found in the chapel of Henry VII at Westminster Abbey (compare fig. 11-28), with its conical vaults. The richly brocaded yet dainty wall surfaces look almost as if they were decorated with lace-paper doilies. Although Walpole associated the Gothic with the pathos of the Sublime, he acknowledged that the house was "pretty and gay." This playfulness, so free of dogma, gives Strawberry Hill its special charm. Gothic here is still an "exotic" style. It appeals because it is strange. But for that very reason it must be "translated," like a medieval romance or like the Chinese motifs that crop up in Rococo decoration.

NASH. The Romantic imagination saw the Gothic and the mysterious East in much the same light. The masterpiece in this vein is the Royal Pavilion at Brighton (fig. 21-70), created half a century later by John Nash (1752–1835). The greatest architect of the English picturesque, he mastered the full range of revival styles, which here have been combined to brilliant effect. This "stately pleasure dome" is a cream-puff version of the Taj Mahal. Over a Neo-Palladian building Nash imposed a cast-iron armature supporting a facade of sheet-iron domes, minarets, and lacy screens. Chinese and even Gothic motifs were thrown in for good measure. Hence the style was known as Indian Gothic.

LATROBE. By 1800 the Gothic was a fully acceptable alternative to the Greek revival as a style for major churches. The result was often a mixture in keeping with the eclectic bent of Romanticism. Benjamin Latrobe (1764–1820), an Anglo-American who under Jefferson became the most influential architect of "Federal" Neoclassicism, submitted a design in each style among the seven or eight he worked up for the cathedral in Baltimore. In this respect he may be called a disciple of the English architect John Soane (1753–1837), who also worked in a variety of revival styles. The Neoclassic one was chosen, but it might just as well have been the Neo-Gothic. The present building is, in fact, a combination of

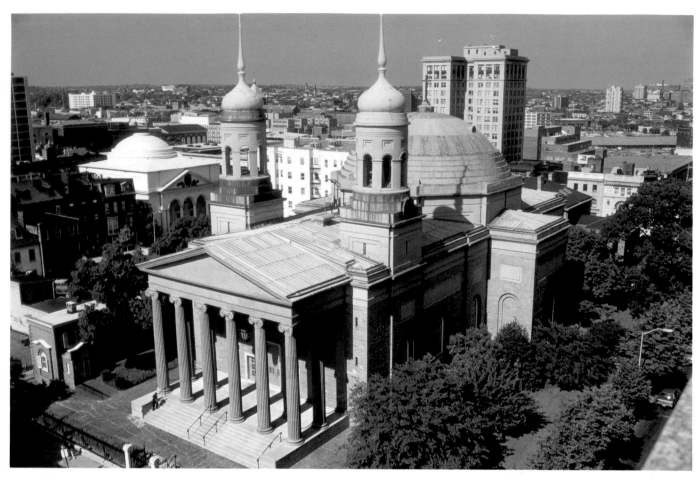

21-71. Benjamin Latrobe. Baltimore Cathedral (Basilica of the Assumption), Baltimore, Maryland. Begun 1805

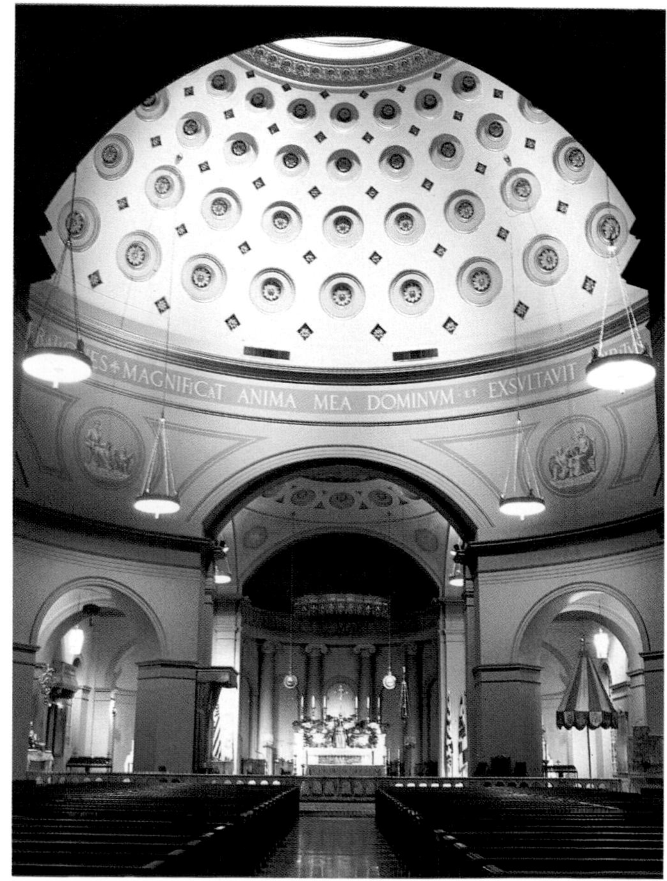

21-72. Interior of Baltimore Cathedral

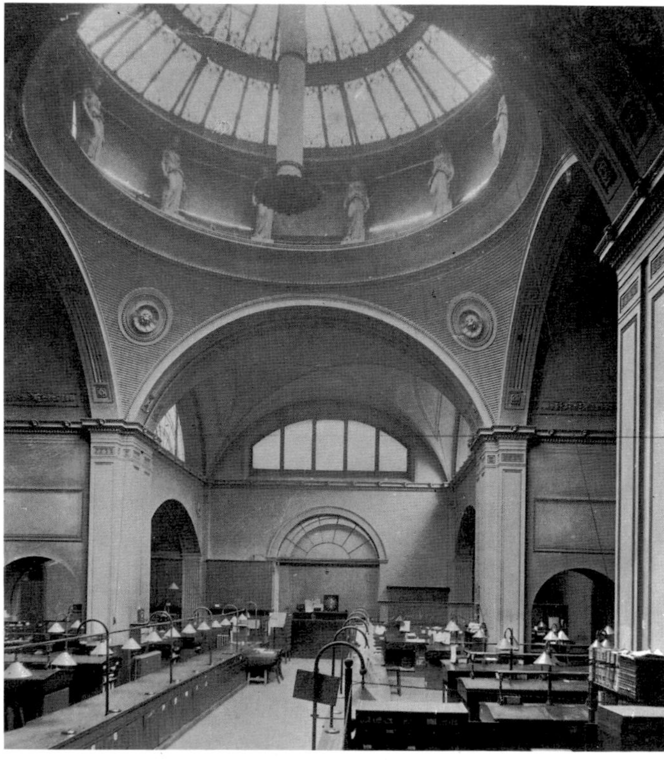

21-73. Sir John Soane. Consols' Office, Bank of England, London. 1794. Destroyed the two. The exterior (fig. 21-71) has walls that resemble Soufflot's Panthéon (see fig. 21-16), which also provided the model for Latrobe's initial design in the shape a Greek cross. It, too, features a dome and a temple front but adds bell towers of disguised Gothic-Baroque ancestry. (The bulbous crowns are not his work.)

The interior (fig. 21-72) is far more distinguished. It was inspired by the domed and vaulted spaces of ancient Rome, especially the Pantheon (see fig. 7-12). Latrobe, however, was not interested in archaeological correctness. The "muscularity" of Roman structures has been subdued. The delicate moldings, profiles, and coffers are derived straight from Robert Adam (compare fig. 21-19). They are no more than linear accents that do not disturb the continuous, abstract surfaces. Here Latrobe shows how much he had learned from Soane's masterpiece, the Bank of England in London, before his departure for America in 1796. Unfortunately, the bank was largely destroyed in 1927, but it is still known from photographs (fig. 21-73). Like Adam, Soane was enthused by Piranesi's epic architectural fantasies, which he joined with the latest French theories. Soane's eclecticism is seen in the "Byzantine" dome on pendentives (compare fig. 8-35), which he used to picturesque effect. Soane relied heavily on the designs and advice of his teacher, George Dance (1741–1825), but was a far more capable architect.

In Latrobe's interpretation, the spatial qualities of ancient architecture have acquired the visionary character of Boullée's memorial to Isaac Newton (see fig. 21-17)—vast, pure, sublime. The seemingly weightless interior nearly presents that combination of classic form and Gothic lightness first proposed by Soufflot. It also shows the free and imaginative look of the mature Neoclassic style when handled by a gifted architect. Had the Gothic design been chosen, the exterior might have been more striking, but the interior probably less impressive. Like most Romantic architects seeking the sublime, Latrobe viewed Gothic churches "from the outside in"—as mysterious, looming structures silhouetted against the sky—but based his spatial fantasy on Roman monuments.

BARRY AND PUGIN. The largest monument of the Gothic revival is the Houses of Parliament in London, designed by Sir Charles Barry (1785–1860) and A. N. Welby Pugin (1812–1852) (fig. 21-74). As the seat of government and a focus of patriotic feeling, it presents a curious mixture: repetitious symmetry governs the main body of the structure and picturesque irregularity its silhouette. The building imposes Pugin's Gothic vocabulary, inspired by the English Perpendicular style (compare fig. 11-28), onto the classically conceived structure by Barry, with results that satisfied neither. Nevertheless, the Houses of Parliament admirably convey the grandeur of Victorian England at the height of its power.

Neo-Renaissance and Neo-Baroque Architecture

GARNIER. Meanwhile, the stylistic alternatives were continually increased for architects by other historical revivals. When the Renaissance, then the Baroque, returned to favor by mid-century, the revival movement had come full circle: Neo-Renaissance and Neo-Baroque replaced the Neoclassical. This final phase of historicism dominated French architecture during the years 1850 to 1875 and lingered through 1900. It is epitomized in the Paris Opéra (figs. 21-75–21-77), designed by Charles Garnier (1825–1898). He had graduated from the École des Beaux-Arts

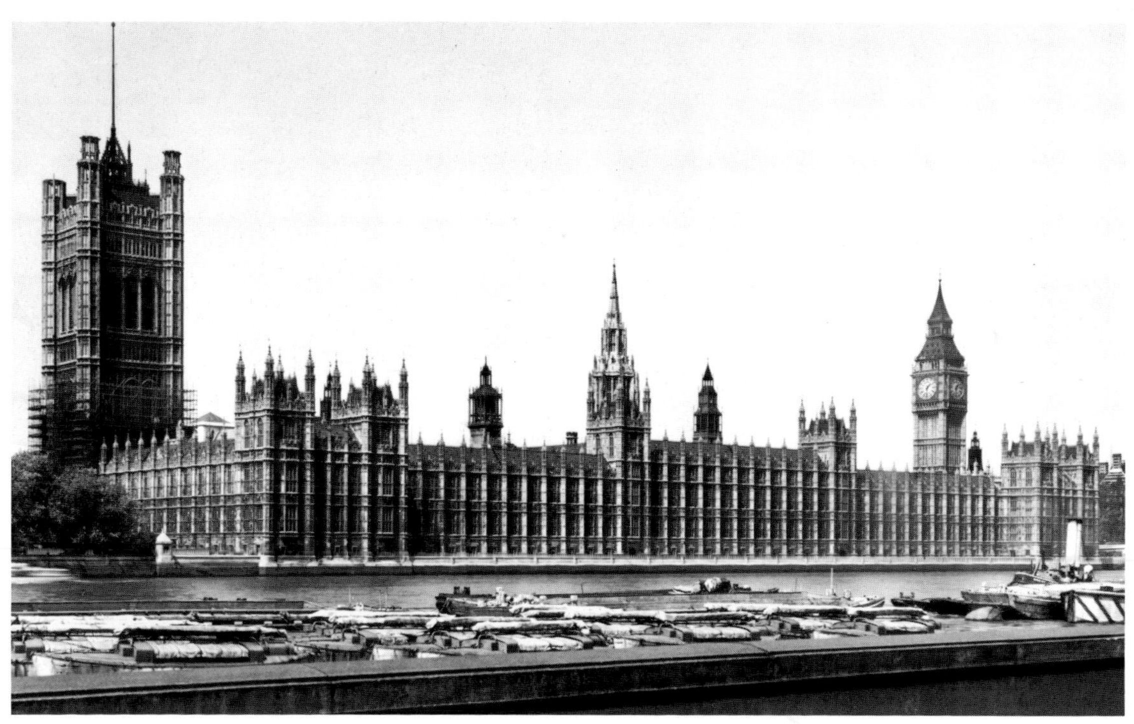

21-74. Sir Charles Barry and A. N. Welby Pugin. The Houses of Parliament, London. Begun 1836

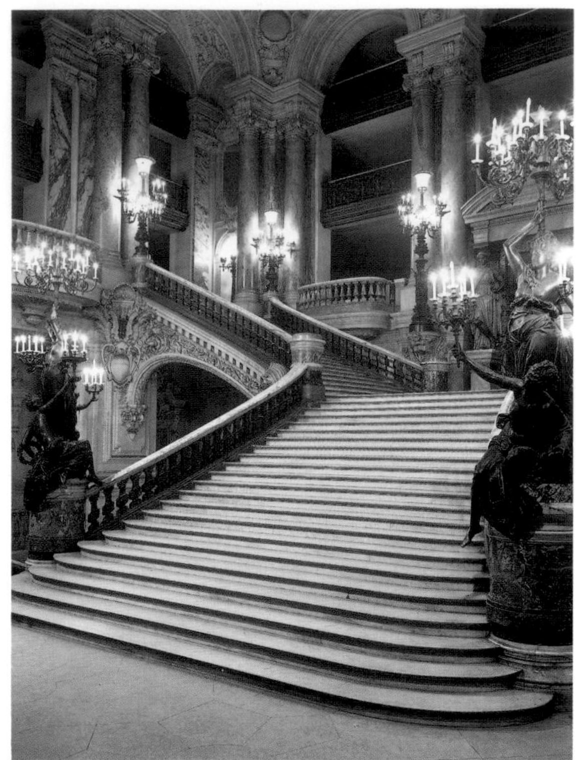

(LEFT) 21-75. Charles Garnier. Grand Staircase, the Opéra, Paris. 1861–74

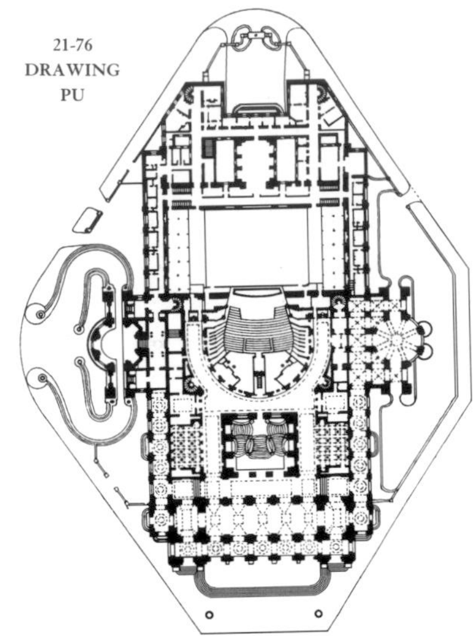

21-76. Plan of the Opéra

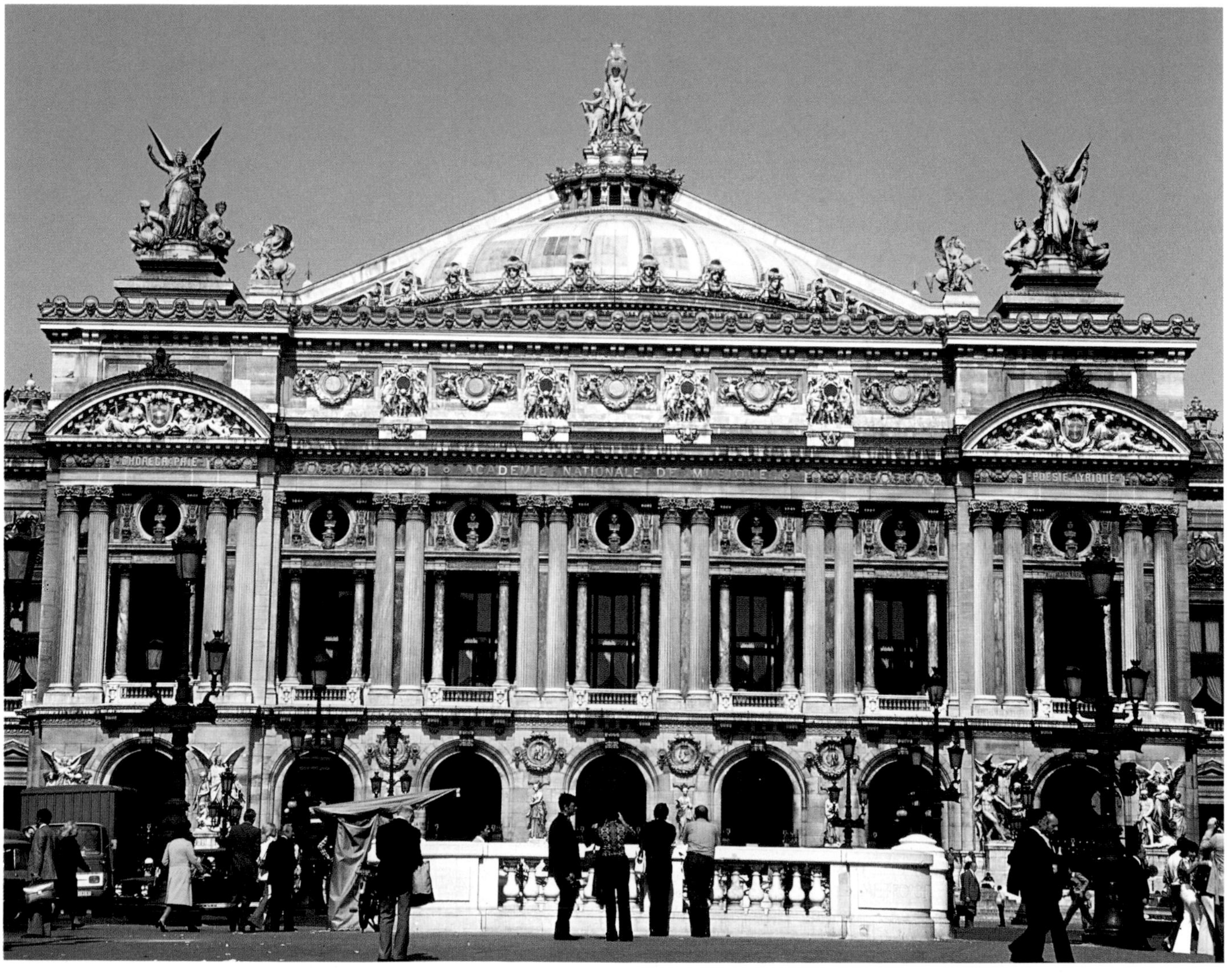

21-77. The Opéra

and won the Prix de Rome, which enabled him to spend six years studying in Italy and Greece. The Opéra was the culmination of Baron Georges-Eugène Haussmann's plan to modernize Paris under Napoleon III. It is the focal point for a series of main avenues that converge on it from all sides. Although the building was not completed until after the fall of the Second Empire, its extravagance typified the Beaux-Arts style of the new Paris at its height. The building is a masterpiece of eclecticism. The fluid curves of the Grand Staircase, for example, recall the Vestibule of the Laurentian Library (see fig. 13-23). The massing of the main entrance for those arriving on foot is reminiscent of Lescot's Square Court of the Louvre (see fig. 16-27). But the paired columns of the facade, "quoted" from Perrault's East Front of the Louvre (see fig. 19-10), are combined with a smaller order, in a fashion suggested by Michelangelo's Palazzo dei Conservatori (see fig. 13-26). The rear entrance consists of a temple front. On the east side is the emperor's entrance with a sweeping staircase like that of the Cour de Cheval Blanc at Fontainebleau (see fig. 16-26), and on the west side, a carriage entrance. The Opéra used the latest building materials and techniques, including iron. The stagecraft, too, was state-of-the-art. Garnier nevertheless went to great lengths to conceal the technology, which for him remained a means, not a principle.

The Opéra consciously suggests a palace of the arts combined with a temple of the arts. The theatrical effect captures the festive air of a crowd gathering before the opening curtain. Its Neo-Baroque quality derives more from the abundance of sculpture—including Carpeaux's *The Dance* (see fig. 21-64)—and ornament than from its architectural vocabulary. The whole building looks "overdressed," its luxurious vulgarity so naive as to disarm all criticism. It reflects the taste of the capitalist tycoons, newly rich and powerful, who saw themselves as the heirs of the old aristocracy. For a display of comparable extravagance, we must turn to Sansovino's Library of St. Mark's (see fig. 14-25), which celebrates the wealth of Venice. Small wonder, then, that captains of industry found the styles before the French Revolution more appealing than Neoclassical or Neo-Gothic.

DECORATIVE ARTS

THE EMPIRE STYLE. During the Romantic era the decorative arts followed much the same course as architecture, with which they were intertwined, but they were, if anything, even more eclectic. The revival sparked by the discoveries at Pompeii and Herculaneum reached its climax during the early nineteenth century with the Empire style. This late form of Neoclassicism spread throughout Europe in the wake of Napoleon's conquests. As the term suggests, the style drew heavily on Roman art and associated Napoleon with the Caesars by borrowing imperial imagery. At first, Roman examples were copied more or less faithfully, but such imitations are the least important contribution of the Empire style. Far more interesting are the free adaptations of those sources to glorify the Bonapartes. These often incorporate Egyptian motifs to commemorate Napoleon's invasion in 1798, which opened up the Middle East.

PERCIER AND FONTAINE. We have already caught a glimpse of the Empire style in the bed of Canova's Pauline Borghese as Venus (see fig. 21-59). We see it at its fullest in the Château de Malmaison, Napoleon's private residence near Paris, which was remodeled after 1798 by the architects Charles Percier (1764–1838) and Pierre-François Fontaine (1762–1853). They were also entrusted with its furnishings, and their book on interior decoration, printed in 1812, set the standard for the Empire style. The bedroom of Napoleon's wife, Joséphine, reveals her taste for the ornate, which was characteristic of the Empire style as a whole (fig. 21-78). Its lavish splendor tells us a great deal about the First Empire and its ambitions. As at Versailles (see fig. 19-13), the decor here serves the purpose of propaganda, for this is a state bedroom. (The empress usually slept in an ordinary one nearby.) The remarkable bed—made by François-Honoré Jacob-Desmalter (1770–1841), the leading furniture manufacturer under Napoleon, after a design by Percier and Fontaine—became the centerpiece of a total redecoration in 1810. Ordered previously, it continued to proclaim Joséphine as empress even after her marriage had been annulled earlier that year. The ornamentation incorporates swans and cornucopias, standard Napoleonic devices, while the canopy resembles a military tent surmounted by an imperial eagle. Nearby is a tripod washstand, with basin and jug, based on Pompeiian examples. Like everything else about the bedroom, it is faithful to archaeological fact in details. Yet nothing in antiquity looked like this, and the effect is surprisingly close to the style of Louis XVI on the eve of the French Revolution.

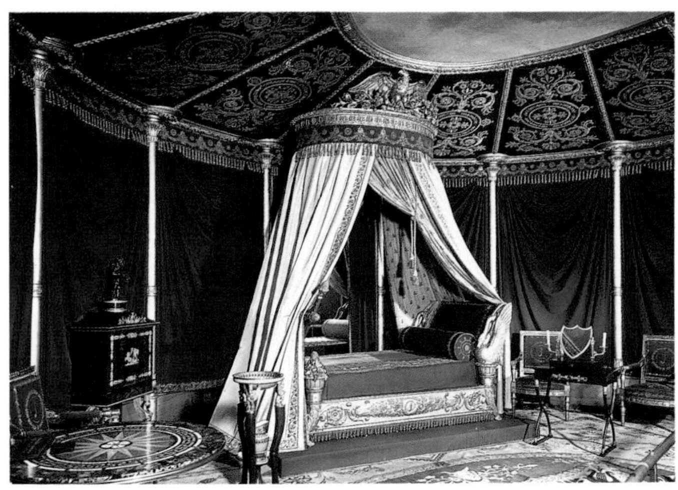

21-78. François-Honoré Jacob-Desmalter (after a design by Charles Percier and Pierre-François Fontaine). Bedroom of Empress Joséphine Bonaparte. c. 1810. Château de Malmaison, Rueil-Malmaison, France

THE INDUSTRIAL REVOLUTION. The rise of the Industrial Revolution led to the degeneration of the decorative arts. Everything from porcelain and silverware to drapery and furniture became mass-produced to meet the needs of the rapidly expanding middle class. Despite attempts to preserve the craftsmanship of the past, the machine won out after the Revolution of 1848. This decline was also seen in the standards of design, which catered to the largest number of customers. During the Restoration and Second Empire, the decorative arts were intended to evoke the earlier glory of France through indiscriminate imitation. There were even revivals of revival styles! By 1840 furnishings began to disappear in a sea of bric-a-brac that provided a luxurious setting for the wealthy. Only rarely did the decorative arts rise above the ordinary. Among the few exceptions are the enormous torchères for the Grand Staircase of the Paris Opéra (see fig. 21-75) by the gifted sculptor Albert-Ernest Carrier-Belleuse (1824–1887). In the end, however, the only thing that could reverse the trend was another revolution in the decorative arts: the Arts and Crafts Movement (see pages 734–35).

PHOTOGRAPHY

Is photography art? The fact that we still pose the question testifies to the continuing debate. The answers have varied with the changing definition and understanding of art. In itself, of course, photography is simply a medium, like oil paint or pastel, used to make art and has no inherent claim to being art. After all, what distinguishes any art from a craft is why, not how, it is done. But photography shares creativity with art because, by its very nature, its performance necessarily involves the imagination. Any photograph, even a casual snapshot, represents both an organization of experience and the record of a mental image. The subject and style of a photograph thus tell us about the photographer's inner and outer worlds. Furthermore, photography participates in the same seek-and-find process as painting or sculpture. Photographers may not realize what they respond to until after they see the image in printed form.

Like woodcut, etching, engraving, and lithography, photography is a form of printmaking that is dependent on mechanical processes. But in contrast to the other graphic mediums, photography has always been tainted as the product of a new technology. Apart from pushing a button or lever, or setting up special effects, no active intervention is required of the artist's hand to guide an idea. For this reason, the camera has usually been considered to be little more than a recording device. Photography, however, is by no means a neutral medium. Its reproduction of reality is never completely faithful. Whether we realize it or not, the camera alters appearances. Photographs reinterpret the world around us, making us see it in new terms.

Photography and painting represent parallel responses to their times and have generally expressed the same worldview. Sometimes the camera's power to extend our way of seeing has been realized first by the painter's creative vision. The two mediums nevertheless differ fundamentally in their approach. Painters communicate their understanding through techniques that represent their cumulative response over time, whereas photographers recognize the moment when the subject before them corresponds to the mental image they have formed of it.

It is hardly surprising that photography and art have enjoyed an uneasy relationship from the start. Artists have generally treated the photograph as something like a preliminary sketch, as a convenient source of ideas or record of motifs to be fleshed out and incorporated into a finished work. Academic painters found the detail provided by photographs to be in keeping with their own precise naturalism. Many other kinds of artists resorted to photographs without always admitting it. Photography has in turn been heavily influenced throughout its history by the painter's mediums. Photographs are often still judged according to how well they imitate paintings and drawings. To understand photography's place in the history of art, we must recognize the medium's particular strengths and inherent limitations.

The Founders of Photography

In 1822 a French inventor named Joseph Nicéphore Niépce (1765–1833) succeeded in making the first permanent photographic image, although his earliest surviving example (fig. 21-79) dates from four years later. He then joined forces with a younger man, Louis-Jacques-Mandé Daguerre (1789–1851), who had invented an improved camera. After ten more years of chemical and mechanical research, the daguerreotype, using positive exposures, was unveiled publicly in 1839, and the age of photography was born. The announcement spurred the Englishman William Henry Fox Talbot (1800–1877) to complete his own photographic process, involving a paper negative from which positives could be made, which he had been pursuing independently since 1833.

What motivated the earliest photographers? They were searching for an artistic medium, not for a practical device. Though Niépce was a research chemist rather than an artist, his achievement was an outgrowth of his efforts to improve the lithographic process. Daguerre was a skilled painter, and he probably turned to the camera to heighten the illusionism of his huge painted dioramas, which were the sensation of Paris during the 1820s and 1830s. Fox Talbot saw in photography a substitute for drawing, as well as a means of reproduction, after using a camera obscura as a tool to sketch landscapes while on a vacation. The interest that all of the founders had in the artistic potential of the medium they had created is reflected in their photographs. Daguerre's first picture (fig. 21-80) imitates a type of still life originated by Chardin, while Fox Talbot's *Sailing Craft* (fig. 21-81) looks like the English marine paintings of his day.

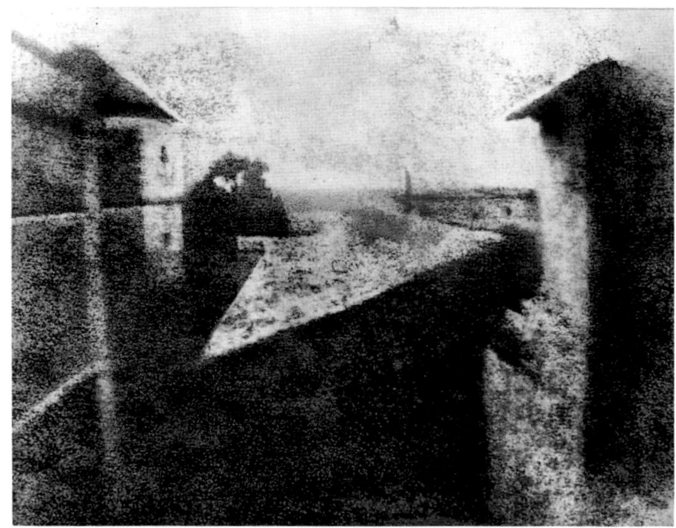

21-79. Joseph Nicéphore Niépce. *View from His Window at Le Gras.* 1826. Heliograph, 6½ x 7⅞" (16.5 x 20 cm). Gernsheim Collection, Harry Ransom Research Center, University of Texas at Austin

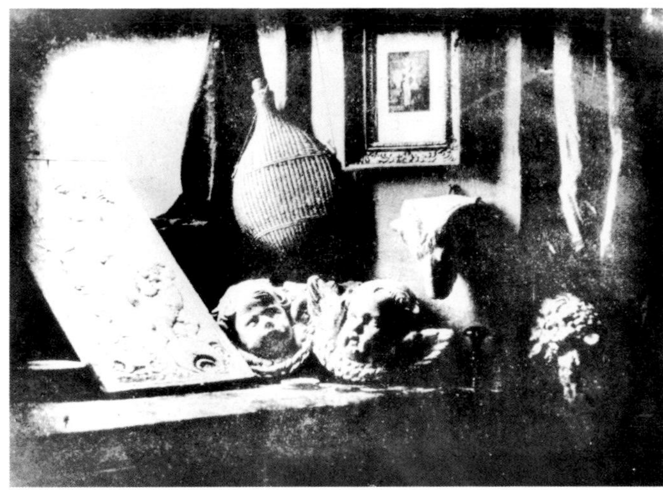

21-80. Louis-Jacques-Mandé Daguerre. *Still Life.* 1837. Daguerreotype, 6½ x 8½" (16.5 x 21.7 cm). Société Française de Photographie, Paris

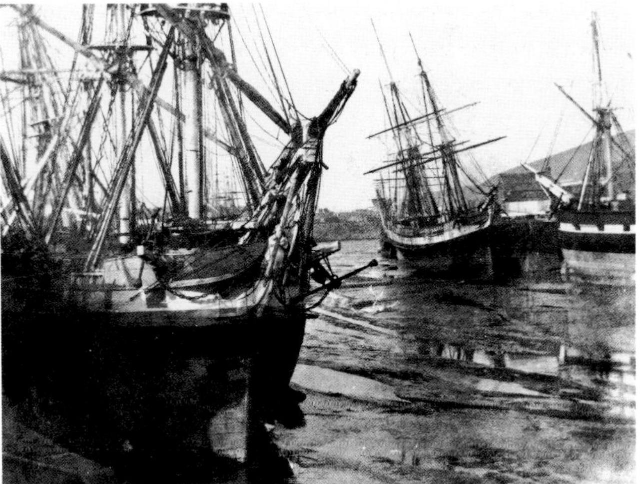

21-81. William Henry Fox Talbot. *Sailing Craft.* c. 1845. Calotype. Science Museum, London

That the new medium should have a mechanical aspect was particularly appropriate. It was as if the Industrial Revolution, having forever altered civilization's way of life, now had to invent its own method for recording itself, although the transience of modern existence was not captured by "stopping the action" until the 1870s. Photography underwent a rapid series of improvements, including better lenses, glass-plate negatives, and new chemical processes that provided faster emulsions and more stable images. Since many of the initial limitations of photography were overcome around mid-century, it would be misleading to tell the early history of the medium in terms of technological developments, important though they were.

The basic mechanics and chemistry of photography had been known for a long time. The camera obscura, a box with a small hole in one end, dates back to antiquity. In the sixteenth century it was widely used for visual demonstrations. The camera was fitted with a mirror and then a lens in the Baroque period, which saw major advances in optical science culminating in Newtonian physics. By the 1720s it had become an aid in drawing architectural scenes. At the same time, silver salts were discovered to be light-sensitive.

Why, then, did it take another hundred years for someone to put this knowledge together? Much of the answer lies in the nature of scientific revolutions, which as a rule combine old technologies and concepts with new ones. (They do this in response to changing worldviews that they, in turn, influence.) Photography was neither inevitable in the history of technology nor necessary to the history of art; yet it was an idea whose time clearly had come. If we try for a moment to imagine that photography had been invented a hundred years earlier, we will find this to be impossible simply on artistic, let alone technological, grounds. The early eighteenth century was too devoted to fantasy to be interested in the literalness of photography. Rococo portraiture, for example, was more concerned with providing a flattering image than an accurate likeness. Hence the camera's straightforward record would have been totally out of place. Even in architectural painting, extreme liberties were often taken with topographical truth (see pages 610–11).

The invention of photography was a response to the artistic urges and historical forces that underlie Romanticism. Much of the impulse came from a quest for the True and the Natural. The desire for "images made by Nature" can already be seen, on the one hand, in Cozens' ink-blot compositions (see fig. 21-10), which were "natural" because they were made by chance; and, on the other, in the late-eighteenth-century vogue for silhouette portraits (traced from the shadow of the sitter's profile), which led to attempts to record such shadows on light-sensitive materials. David's harsh realism in *The Death of Marat* (see fig. 21-3) had already proclaimed the cause of unvarnished truth. So did Ingres' *Louis Bertin* (see fig. 21-31), which established the standards of physical reality and character portrayal that photographers would follow. [See Primary Sources, no. 69, pages 929–30.]

Portraiture

Like lithography, which was invented in 1797, photography met the growing demand for images of all kinds. By 1850, large numbers of the middle class were having their likenesses painted, and it was in portraiture that photography found its readiest acceptance. Soon after the daguerreotype was introduced, photographic studios sprang up everywhere, especially in America, and multi-image *cartes de visites,* invented in 1854 by Adolphe-Eugène Disdéri, became ubiquitous. Anyone could have a portrait taken cheaply and easily. In the process, the average person became memorable. Photography thus became an outgrowth of the democratic values fostered by the American and French revolutions. There was also keen competition among photographers to get the famous to pose for portraits.

NADAR. Gaspard Félix Tournachon (1820–1910), better known as Nadar, managed to attract most of France's leading personalities to his studio. Like many early photographers, he started out as an artist but came to prefer the lens to the brush. He initially used the camera to capture the likenesses of the 280 sitters whom he caricatured in an enormous lithograph, *Le Panthéon Nadar.* The

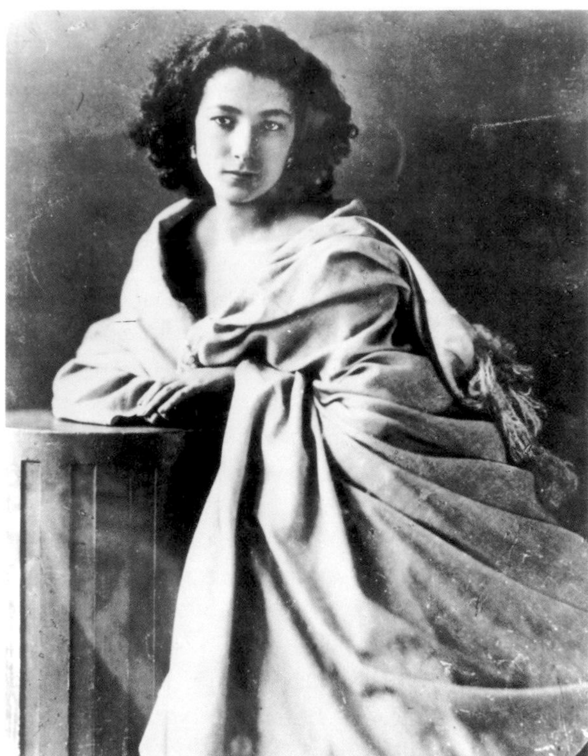

21-82. Nadar. *Sarah Bernhardt.* 1859. George Eastman House, Rochester, New York

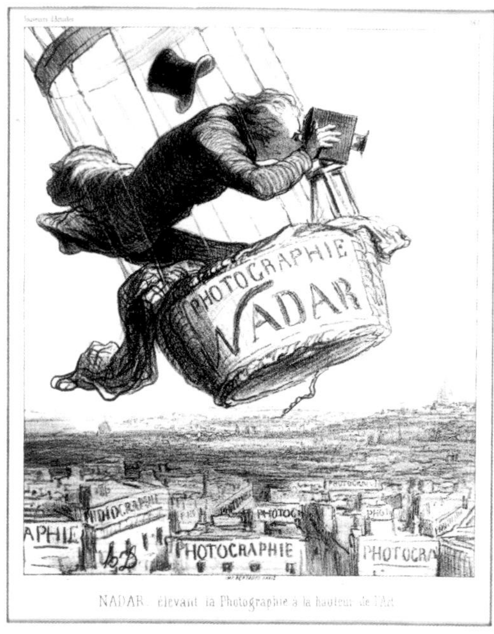

21-83. Honoré Daumier. *Nadar Elevating Photography to the Height of Art.* 1862. Lithograph. George Eastman House, Rochester, New York

actress Sarah Bernhardt posed for him several times, and his photographs of her (fig. 21-82) are the direct ancestors of modern glamour photography (compare fig. 27-11). With her romantic pose and expression, she is a counterpart to the soulful maidens found throughout nineteenth-century painting. Nadar has treated her in remarkably sculptural terms. Indeed, the play of light and sweep of drapery are reminiscent of the sculptured portrait busts that were so popular with collectors at the time.

The Restless Spirit

Early photography reflected the outlook and temperament of Romanticism. Indeed, the entire nineteenth century had a pervasive curiosity and an abiding belief that everything could be discovered. While this fascination sometimes showed a serious interest in science—witness Darwin's voyage on the *Beagle* from 1831 to 1836—it typically took the form of a restless quest for new experiences and places. Photography had a remarkable impact on the imagination of the period by making the rest of the world widely available, or by simply revealing it in a new way. Sometimes the search for new subjects was close to home. Nadar, for example, took aerial photographs of Paris from a hot-air balloon. This feat was wittily parodied by Daumier (fig. 21-83), whose caption, "Nadar Elevating Photography to the Height of Art," expresses the prevailing skepticism about the aesthetics of the new medium.

A love of the exotic was fundamental to Romantic escapism, and by 1850 photographers began to cart their equipment to faraway places. The same restless spirit that we saw in George Caleb Bingham's *Fur Traders Descending the Missouri* (see fig. 21-57) also drew photographers to the frontier. They documented the westward expansion of the United States, often for the U.S. Geological Survey, with pictures that have primarily historical interest today.

O'SULLIVAN. An exception is the landscape photography of Timothy O'Sullivan (c. 1841–1882), who often preferred scenery that contemporary painters had overlooked. He practically

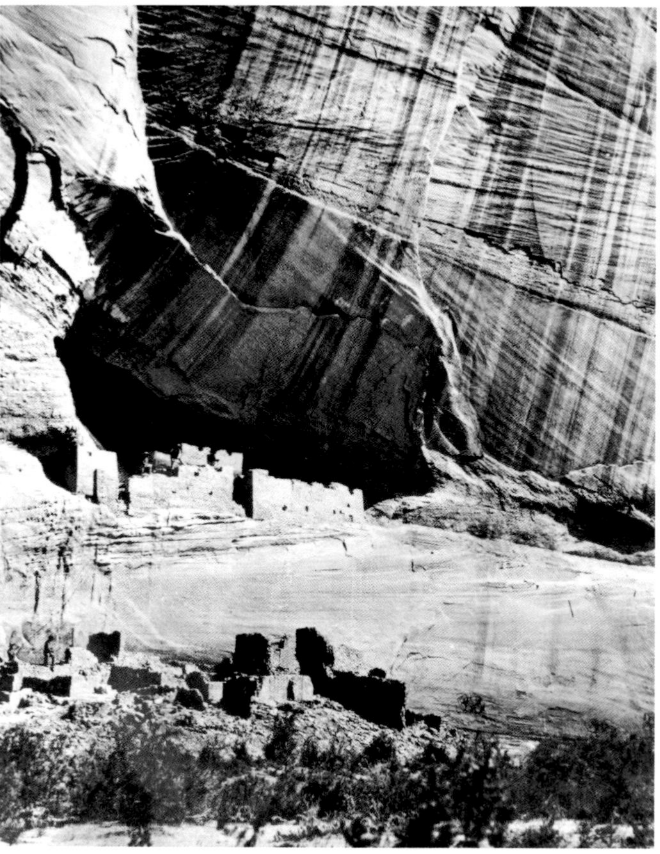

21-84. Timothy O'Sullivan. *Ancient Ruins in the Cañon de Chelle, N.M., in a Niche 50 Feet Above the Present Cañon Bed* (now Canyon de Chelly National Monument, Arizona). 1873. Albumen print. George Eastman House, Rochester, New York

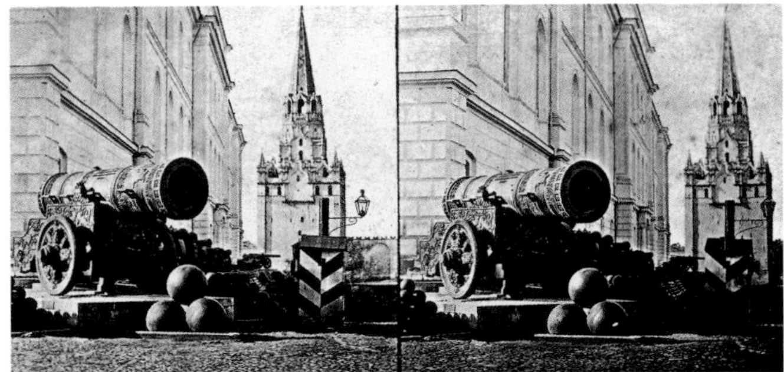

21-85. *Tsar Cannon Outside the Spassky Gate, Moscow* (cast 1586; presently inside the Kremlin). Second half of 19th century. Stereophotograph
COURTESY CULVER PICTURES

invented his own aesthetic in photographing the *Cañon de Chelle* (fig. 21-84), which conforms to no established pictorial type. The view filling the entire photograph allows no visual escape and lends the scene an awesome force. The composition is held together by the play of lines of the displaced strata of the rock, which creates a strikingly abstract design. O'Sullivan's control of tonal relations is so masterful that even color photographs taken since then of the same site have far less impact.

Stereophotography

The unquenchable thirst for vicarious experiences accounts for the great popularity of stereoscopic photographs. Invented in 1849, the two-lens camera produced two photographs comparable to the slightly different images perceived by our two eyes. When seen through a special viewer called a stereoscope, stereoptic photographs fuse to create a remarkable illusion of three-dimensional depth. Two years later, stereoscopes became the rage at the Crystal Palace exposition in London (see fig. 22-36). Countless thousands of double views, such as that in figure 21-85, were taken over the next 50 years. Virtually every corner of the earth became accessible to practically any household, with a vividness second only to being there.

Stereophotography was an important breakthrough. Its binocular vision marked a major departure from perspective in the pictorial tradition and demonstrated for the first time photography's potential to enlarge vision. Nevertheless, this success waned, except for special uses. People were simply too accustomed to viewing pictures as if with one eye. Later on, when the halftone plate was invented in the 1880s for reproducing images on a printed page, stereophotographs revealed another drawback. As our illustration shows, they were unsuitable for this kind of reproduction. From then on, single-lens photography was closely linked with the mass media of the day.

Photojournalism

Basic to the rise of photography was the widespread nineteenth-century sense that the present was already history in the making. Only with the advent of the Romantic hero did great acts, other than martyrdom, become popular subjects for contemporary painters and sculptors. It is hardly surprising that photography was invented a year after the death of Napoleon, who had been the subject of more paintings than any previous secular leader. At about the same time, Géricault's *The Raft of the "Medusa"* (see fig. 21-28) and Delacroix's *The Massacre at Chios* signaled a decisive shift in the Romantic attitude toward representing contemporary events. This outlook brought with it a new kind of photography: photojournalism.

BRADY. Its first great representative was Mathew Brady (1823–1896), who covered the Civil War in the United States. Other wars had already been photographed, but Brady and his 20 assistants (including Timothy O'Sullivan) were able to bring home the horrors of that war with unprecedented directness, despite using cameras too slow and cumbersome to show actual combat.

GARDNER. *Home of a Rebel Sharpshooter, Gettysburg* (fig. 21-86) by Alexander Gardner (1821–1882), who left Brady to form his own photographic team in 1863, is a landmark in the history of art. Never before had both the grim reality and the significance of death on the battlefield been conveyed so fully in a single image. Compared with the heroic act celebrated by Benjamin West (see fig. 21-4), this tragedy is as anonymous as the slain soldier himself. The photograph is all the more convincing for having the same harsh realism found in David's *The Death of Marat* (see fig. 21-3), and the limp figure, hardly visible between the rocks framing the scene, is no less touching. In contrast, the paintings and engravings by the artists—notably Winslow Homer (see page 723)—who illustrated the Civil War for magazines and newspapers were mostly genre scenes that kept the reality of combat safely at arm's length.

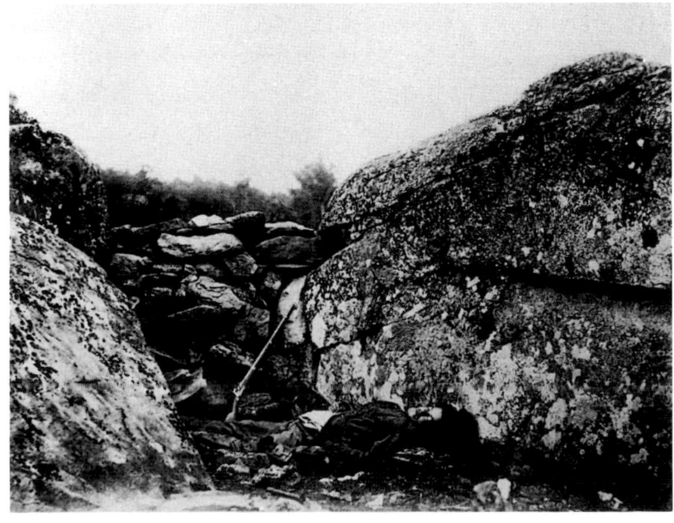

21-86. Alexander Gardner. *Home of a Rebel Sharpshooter, Gettysburg.* July 1863. Wet-plate photograph. Chicago Historical Society

CHAPTER TWENTY-TWO

Realism and Impressionism

PAINTING

France

"Can Jupiter survive the lightning rod?" asked Karl Marx, not long after the middle of the nineteenth century. The question, suggesting that the ancient god of thunder and lightning was now threatened by science, sums up the difficulty we felt in the sculptor Carpeaux's *The Dance* (see fig. 21-64). The French poet and art critic Charles Baudelaire addressed the same problem when, in 1846, he called for paintings that expressed "the heroism of modern life." [See Primary Sources, no. 70, page 930.] At that time only one painter was willing to make an artistic doctrine of this demand: Baudelaire's friend Gustave Courbet (1819–1877).

COURBET AND REALISM. Courbet was born in Ornans, a village near the French-Swiss border, and remained proud of his rural background. He had begun as a Neo-Baroque Romantic in the early 1840s. By 1848, under the impact of the revolutionary upheavals then sweeping through Europe, he had come to believe that the Romantic emphasis on feeling and imagination was merely an escape from the realities of the time. Truth and sincerity became the rallying cry of the Realists, their motto Baudelaire's precept, "It is necessary to be of one's time." Modern artists must rely on direct experience—they must be Realists. "I cannot paint an angel because I have never seen one," Courbet said. [See Primary Sources, no. 71, page 930.] As a descriptive term, *realism* is not very precise. For Courbet, it meant something akin to the realism of Caravaggio (see page 529). As an admirer of Louis Le Nain and Rembrandt, Courbet had, in fact, strong links with the Caravaggesque tradition. Moreover, his work, like Caravaggio's, was denounced for its supposed vulgarity and lack of spiritual content. What ultimately defines Courbet's Realism, however, and distinguishes it from Romanticism, is his devotion to radical (as against merely liberal) politics. His Socialist views were the result of his close friendship with the theorist Pierre-Joseph Proudhon, ten years his senior, who was from the same region in southern France, and they colored his entire outlook. Although Socialism did not determine the specific content or appearance of Courbet's pictures, it does help to account for his choice of subject matter and style, which went against the grain of tradition.

Burial at Ornans (fig. 22-1), from 1849, fully embodies Courbet's programmatic Realism. Here is a picture that disregards the academic hierarchy by treating an apparent genre scene with the same seriousness and monumentality as a history painting. In addition it was executed with a heavy impasto that violated accepted standards of finish so that it had a hostile reception from the public and most critics. Courbet asked 50 people to pose for him in his studio. He painted them lifesize, solidly and matter-of-factly. The canvas is very much larger than anything by Millet, and with none of his overt pathos or sentiment (compare fig. 21-41). Its nearest relatives are Dutch group portraits of the seventeenth century. *Burial at Ornans* rivals Rembrandt's *The Night Watch* (see fig. 18-16) in scale and ambition. Courbet has adopted the Dutch master's dark palette and thick brushwork as well. The picture consciously avoids any trace of Baroque dynamism, however. It has instead a classical gravity worthy of Masaccio and Raphael (see fig. 12-26 and fig. 13-31). In contrast to other funerary scenes, such as El Greco's *The Burial of Count Orgaz* (see fig. 14-13), this is not the apotheosis of a great man or woman (compare also fig. 7-38). In fact, the identity of the deceased is never revealed—nor is it important—though the painting is sometimes said to have been inspired by the funeral of Courbet's grandfather. It is not even a religious scene, let alone about death. The real subject is the gathering as social ritual, to which the burial itself seems almost incidental. The composition is divided into three groups of clergy, men, and women, each of whom is carefully observed. Many of the faces are partially obscured, however, so that they remain as anonymous as the person they have come to mourn. The artist's main intention was to record the dress and customs of his hometown. By rigorously excluding anything that might distract our attention, he prevents us from reading any further significance into the painting. Yet, strangely enough, it has a grandeur and solemnity that are deeply

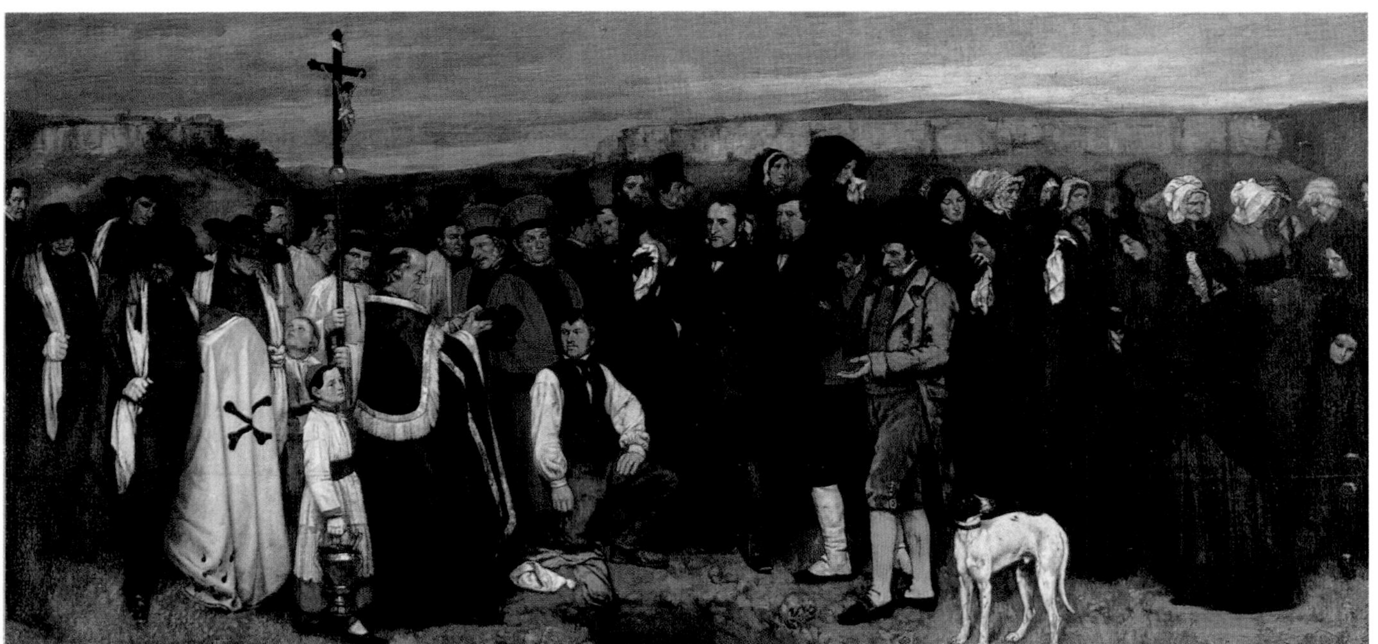

22-1. Gustave Courbet. *Burial at Ornans.* 1849–50. Oil on canvas, 10'3½" x 21'9½" (3.13 x 6.64 m). Musée d'Orsay, Paris

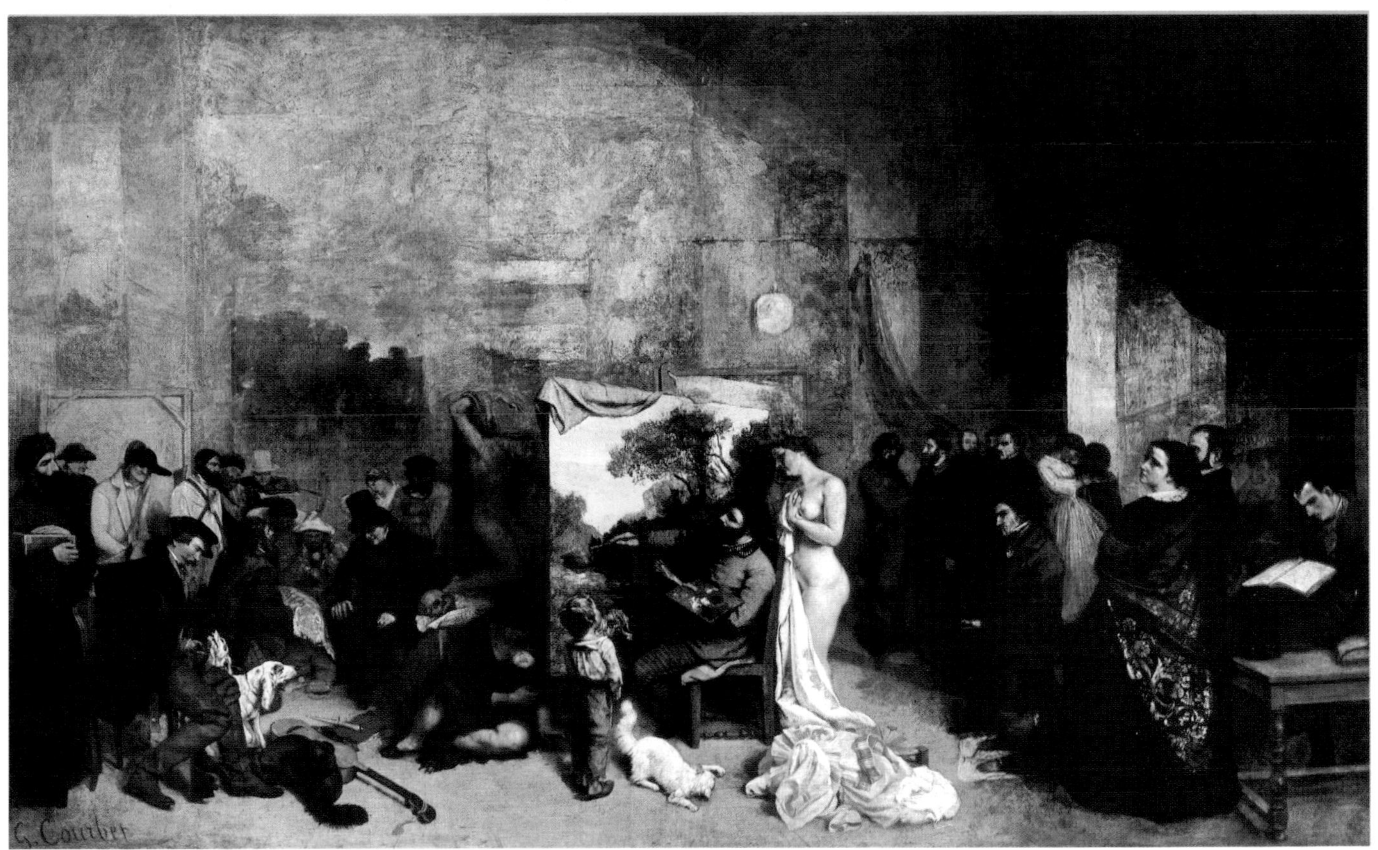

22-2. Gustave Courbet. *Studio of a Painter: A Real Allegory Summarizing My Seven Years of Life as an Artist.* 1854–55. Oil on canvas, 11'10" x 19'7" (3.6 x 6 m). Musée d'Orsay, Paris

moving, precisely because of the factual presentation. In this way, *Burial at Ornans* fulfills Baudelaire's "heroism of modern life."

During the 1855 Paris Exposition, where works by Ingres and Delacroix were prominently displayed, Courbet brought attention to his pictures by organizing a private exhibition in a large shed and by distributing a "manifesto of Realism." The show, which included *Burial at Ornans,* centered on another huge canvas entitled *Studio of a Painter: A Real Allegory Summarizing My Seven Years of Life as an Artist* (fig. 22-2). (Fittingly enough, the two paintings now hang opposite each other in the Musée d'Orsay in Paris.)

"Real allegory" is something of a teaser. Allegories, after all, are unreal by definition. Courbet meant either an allegory couched in the terms of his particular Realism (discussed below), or one that did not conflict with the "real" identity of the figures or objects embodying it.

The framework is familiar: Courbet's composition clearly belongs to the type seen in Velázquez' *The Maids of Honor* and Goya's *The Family of Charles IV* (see figs. 17-35 and 21-23). But now the artist has moved to the center, and the visitors here are his guests, not royal patrons who enter whenever they wish. He has invited them specially for a purpose that becomes evident only upon further thought. The picture does not yield its full meaning unless we take the title seriously and consider Courbet's relation to this assembly.

There are two main groups. On the left are "the people." They are types rather than individuals, drawn largely from the artist's home environment at Ornans: hunters, peasants, workers, a Jew, a priest, a young mother with her baby. On the right we see groups of portraits representing the Parisian side of Courbet's life: clients, critics, intellectuals. (The man reading is Baudelaire.) All of these people are strangely passive, as if they are waiting for something to happen. Some are quietly conversing among themselves; others seem lost in thought. Yet hardly anybody looks at Courbet. They are not his audience but a representative sampling of his social environment.

Only two people watch the artist at work: a small boy, intended to suggest "the innocent eye," and the nude model. What is her role? In a more conventional picture, we would identify her as Inspiration, or Courbet's Muse, but she is no less "real" than the others here. Courbet probably meant her to be Nature, or that undisguised Truth which he proclaimed to be the guiding principle of his art. (Note the emphasis on the clothing she has just taken off.) Significantly enough, the center group is lighted by clear, sharp daylight, but the background and the side figures are veiled in semidarkness. This underlines the contrast between the artist—the active creator—and the world around him that waits to be brought to life.

MANET AND THE "REVOLUTION OF THE COLOR PATCH." Courbet's *Studio* helps us to understand a picture that shocked the public even more: *Luncheon on the Grass* (fig. 22-3), showing a nude model accompanied by two gentlemen in frock

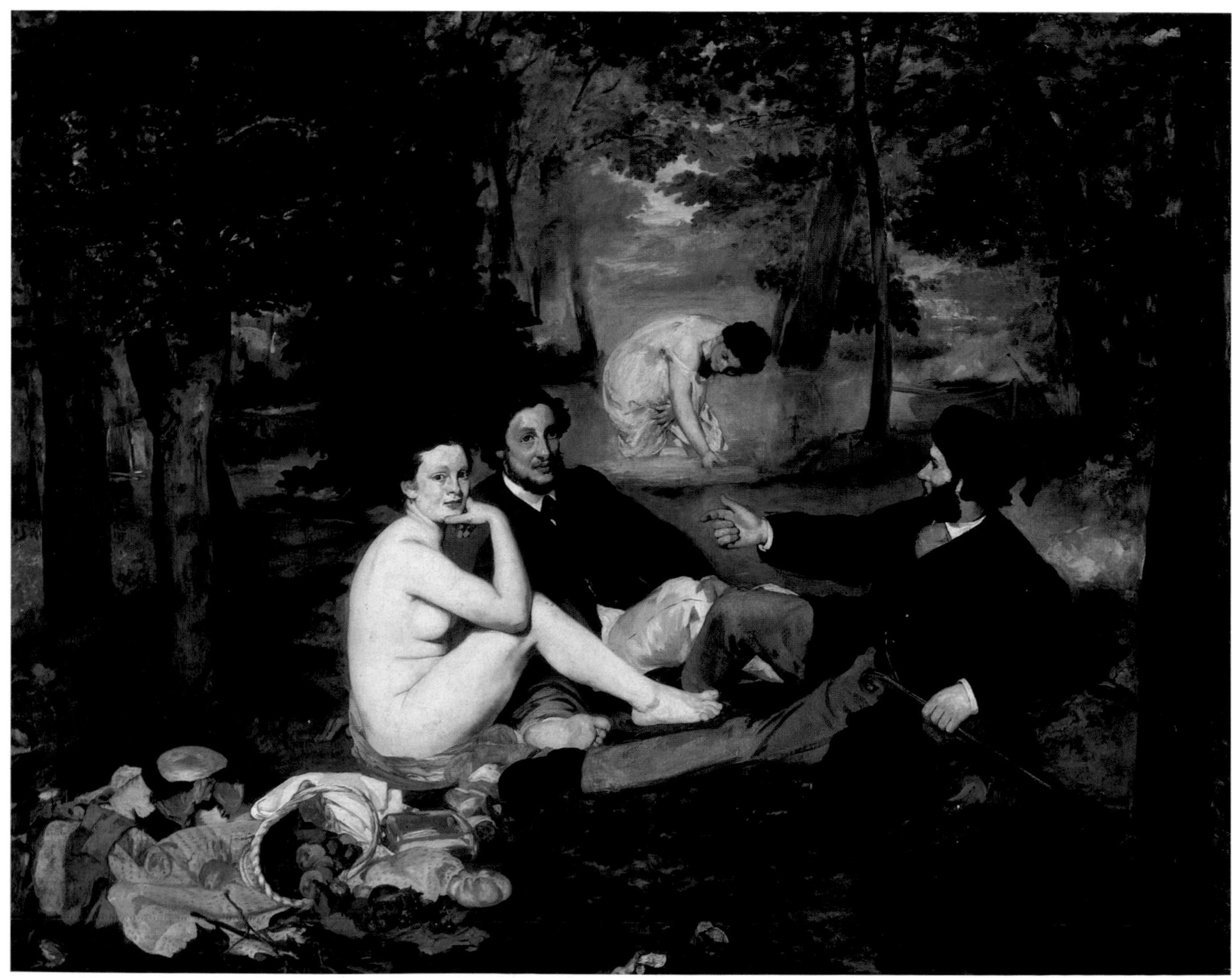

22-3. Édouard Manet. *Luncheon on the Grass (Le Déjeuner sur l'herbe)*. 1863. Oil on canvas, 7' x 8'10" (2.1 x 2.6 m). Musée d'Orsay, Paris

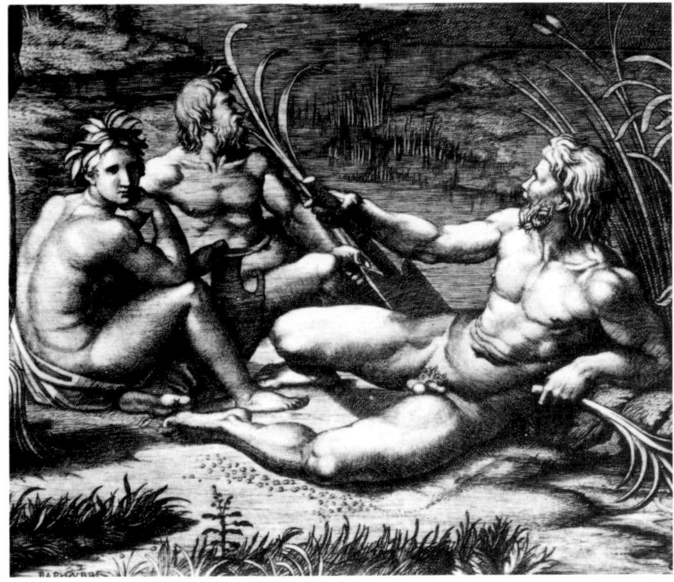

22-4. Marcantonio Raimondi, after Raphael. *The Judgment of Paris* (detail). c. 1520. Engraving. The Metropolitan Museum of Art, New York

ROGERS FUND, 1919

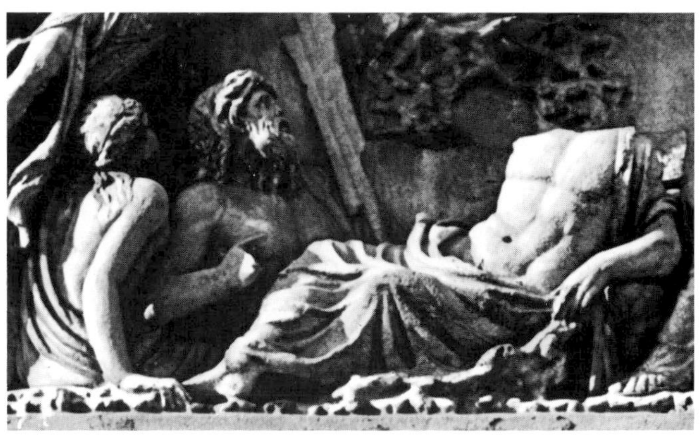

22-5. *River Gods*. Detail of Roman sarcophagus. 3rd century A.D. Villa Medici, Rome

GIVEN ANONYMOUSLY

coats, by Édouard Manet (1832–1883). Manet was the first to grasp Courbet's full importance; his *Luncheon,* among other things, is a tribute to the older artist. There is a long tradition of such outdoor picnic scenes stretching back to a work by Titian in the Louvre that Manet copied while an art student. He nevertheless offended contemporary morality by juxtaposing the nude and nattily attired figures in an outdoor setting without allegorical intent. Even worse, the neutral title offered no "higher" significance. The group has so formal a pose that Manet certainly did not intend to depict an actual event. Instead it derives from a classical source (figs. 22-4 and 22-5), while the girl bathing in a landscape setting was inspired by a painting of *Diana Bathing* by Watteau. (Manet originally titled his canvas *The Bath,* which would have shocked the public even more.) The unembarrassed gaze and frank realism of the nude are not simply a witty parody of classical art. Far more than Courbet's *Studio of a Painter, Luncheon on the Grass* fulfills all the conditions set down in "The Heroism of Modern Life" by Baudelaire. [See Primary Sources, no. 70, page 930.] By borrowing freely from the past and clothing his figures in modern urban dress, Manet both updated tradition and gave fresh meaning to the nude. These, he seems to say, are the gods and goddesses of today, and they are no less worthy of our attention—or respect—than those of the past. Nevertheless, the scene fits neither everyday experience nor mythology. Perhaps the meaning of the canvas lies in this very denial of plausibility. For that reason, Manet could be championed by two seemingly opposite literary giants: the Realist novelist Émile Zola, who found in the artist's paintings a counterpart to his own writings; and the Symbolist poet Stephane Mallarmé, who appreciated Manet's economy and artfulness.

As a visual manifesto of artistic freedom, the *Luncheon* is much more revolutionary than Courbet's *Studio.* It asserts the painter's privilege to combine whatever elements he pleases for aesthetic effect alone. The nudity of the model is "explained" by the contrast between her warm, creamy flesh tones and the cool black-and-gray of the men's attire. To put it another way, the world of painting has "natural laws" that are different from those of everyday reality, and the painter's first loyalty is to his canvas, not to the outside world. Here begins an attitude that became a bone of contention between progressives and conservatives for the rest of the century. It was later summed up in the doctrine of Art for Art's Sake (see page 721). Manet himself refrained from such controversies. His work nevertheless attests to his lifelong devotion to "pure painting": to the belief that brushstrokes and color patches themselves—not what they stand for—are the artist's primary reality. From among the painters of the past, he found that Hals, Velázquez, and Goya had come closest to this ideal. He admired their broad, open technique, their preoccupation with light and color values. Many of his canvases are, in fact, "pictures of pictures": they translate into modern terms those older works that particularly fascinated him. Yet he always filtered out the expressiveness or symbolism of his models to avoid distracting the viewer's attention from the pictorial structure. His paintings always have an emotional reserve that can easily be mistaken for emptiness unless we understand its purpose.

Courbet is said to have remarked that Manet's pictures were as flat as playing cards. Looking at *The Fifer* (fig. 22-6), we can see what he meant. Painted three years after the *Luncheon,* it has very little modeling, no depth, and hardly any shadows. (There are a few, actually, but it takes a real effort to find them.) The figure looks three-dimensional only because its contour renders the forms in realistic foreshortening. Otherwise Manet avoids all the methods invented since Giotto's time for transforming a flat surface into a pictorial space. The undifferentiated light-gray back-

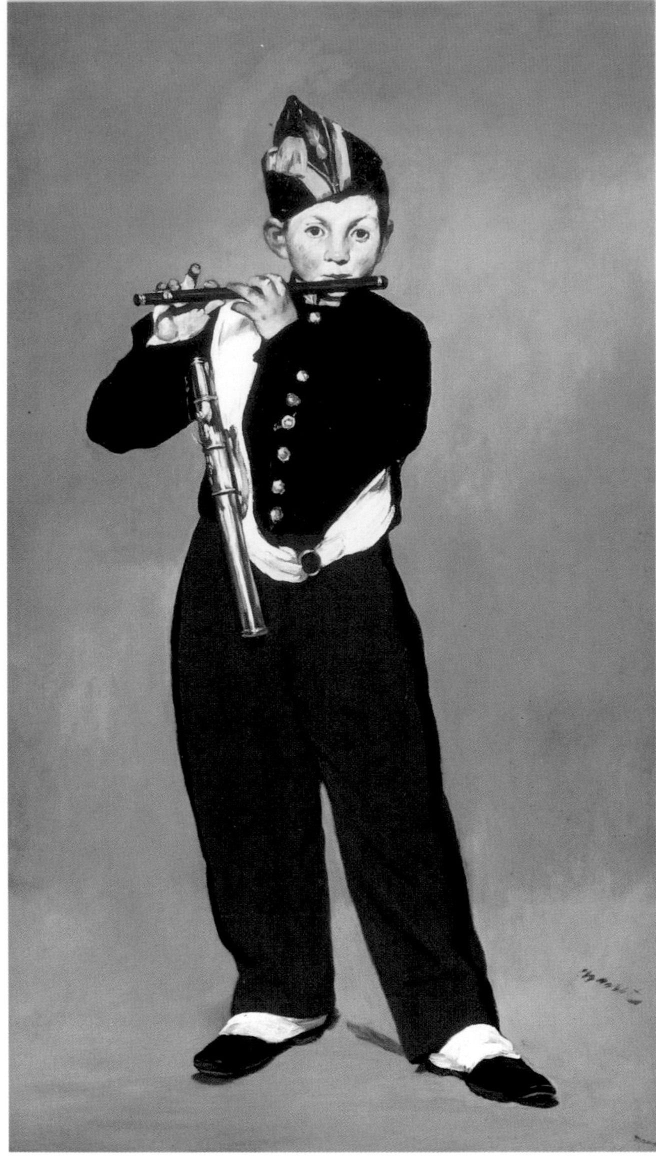

22-6. Édouard Manet. *The Fifer.* 1866. Oil on canvas, 63 x 38¼" (160 x 97.5 cm). Musée d'Orsay, Paris

ground seems as near to us as the figure, and just as solid. If the fifer stepped out of the picture, he would leave a hole, like the cutout shape of a stencil.

Here, then, the canvas itself has been redefined. It is no longer a "window" but a screen made up of flat patches of color, like a child's jigsaw puzzle. How radical a step this is can be readily seen if we compare *The Fifer* to Delacroix's *The Death of Sardanapalus* (see fig. 21-33) and to a Cubist work such as Picasso's *Three Dancers* of 1925 (see fig. 24-28). The structure of Manet's painting obviously resembles that of Picasso's, whereas Delacroix's still follows the "window" tradition of the Renaissance. In hindsight, we realize that the revolutionary qualities of Manet's art could already be seen in the *Luncheon,* even if they were not yet so obvious. The three figures lifted from Raphael's group of river-gods form a unit nearly as shadowless and stencillike as *The Fifer.* They would be more at home on a flat screen, and the chiaroscuro of their present setting, which is inspired by the landscapes of Courbet, no longer fits them.

What brought about this "revolution of the color patch"? We do not know, and Manet himself surely did not reason it out beforehand. It is tempting to think that he was spurred to create the new style by the challenge of photography. The "pencil of nature," then known for a quarter-century, had demonstrated the objective truth of Renaissance perspective, but it established a standard of representational accuracy that no handmade image could hope to rival. Painting needed to be rescued from competition with the camera. Manet accomplished this by insisting that a painted canvas is, above all, a material surface covered with pigments—that we must look *at* it, not *through* it. Unlike Courbet, he gave no name to the style he had created. When his followers began calling themselves Impressionists, he refused to adopt the term for his own work. His aim was to be accepted as a Salon painter, a goal that eluded him until late in life.

MONET AND IMPRESSIONISM. The word *Impressionism* was coined in 1874 after a hostile critic had looked at a picture entitled *Impression: Sunrise* by Claude Monet (1840–1926). It certainly fits Monet better than it does Manet. Monet had adopted Manet's concept of painting and applied it to landscapes done outdoors. Monet's *On the Bank of the Seine, Bennecourt* of 1868 (fig. 22-7) is flooded with sunlight so bright that conservative critics claimed it made their eyes hurt. In this flickering network of color patches, shaped like mosaic tesserae, the reflections on the water are as real as the banks of the Seine. [See Primary Sources, no. 72, page 931.] Even more than *The Fifer,* Monet's painting is a "playing card." Were it not for the woman and the boat in the foreground, the picture would be just as effective upside down. The mirror image here serves a purpose opposite that of earlier mirror images (compare fig. 15-15). Instead of adding to the illusion of real space, it strengthens the unity of the actual painted surface. This inner coherence sets *On the Bank of the Seine, Bennecourt* apart from Romantic "impressions" such as Constable's *The Haywain* (see fig. 21-46) or Corot's *View of Rome* (see fig. 21-38), even though all three share the same on-the-spot immediacy.

In the late 1860s and early 1870s Monet and his friend Auguste Renoir (1841–1919) worked together to develop Impressionism into a fully mature style, one that proved ideally suited to painting outdoors. Monet's *Red Boats, Argenteuil* (fig. 22-8) captures to perfection the intense sunlight of Argenteuil along the Seine near Paris where the artist was spending his summers. Now the flat brushstrokes have become flecks of paint, which convey an extraordinary range of visual effects. The amazingly free brush weaves a tapestry of rich color inspired by the late paintings of Delacroix. Despite its spontaneity, Monet's technique retains an underlying logic in which each color and brushstroke has its place. As an aesthetic, then, Impressionism was hardly the straightforward realism it at first seems. However, it remained an intuitive approach, even in its color, although the Impressionists were familiar with many of the optical theories that were to provide the basis for Seurat's Divisionism (see pages 740–41).

PISSARRO. The method that Monet and Renoir evolved was soon adopted by other members of the group. The landscapes of Camille Pissarro (1830–1903) have a straightforward naturalism

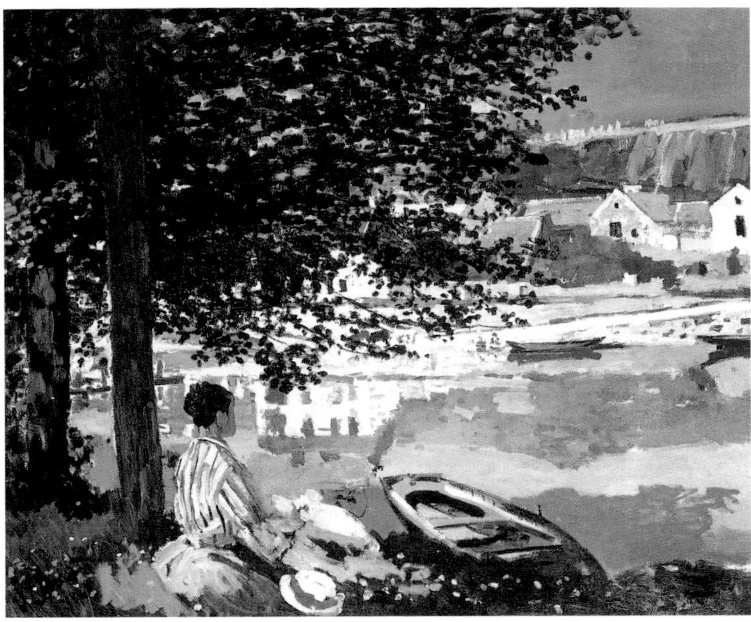

22-7. Claude Monet. *On the Bank of the Seine, Bennecourt.* 1868. Oil on canvas, 32⅛ x 39⅝" (81.5 x 100.7 cm). The Art Institute of Chicago

MR. AND MRS. POTTER PALMER COLLECTION

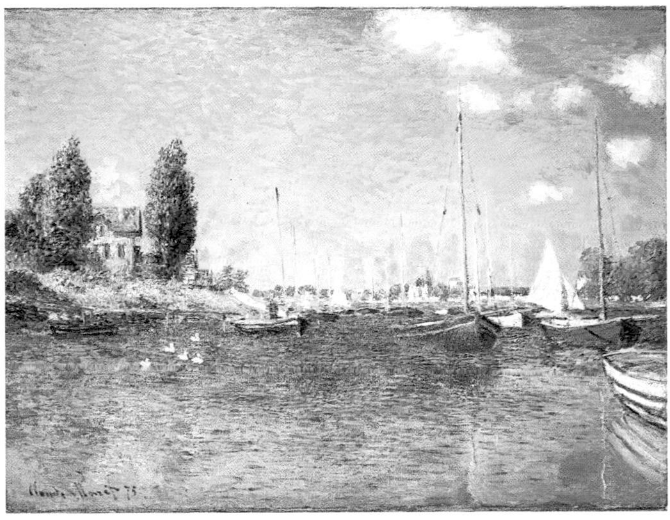

22-8. Claude Monet. *Red Boats, Argenteuil.* 1875. Oil on canvas, 23½ x 31⅝" (59.7 x 80.3 cm). Fogg Art Museum, Harvard University Art Museums, Cambridge, Massachusetts

BEQUEST OF COLLECTION OF MAURICE WERTHEIM, CLASS OF 1906

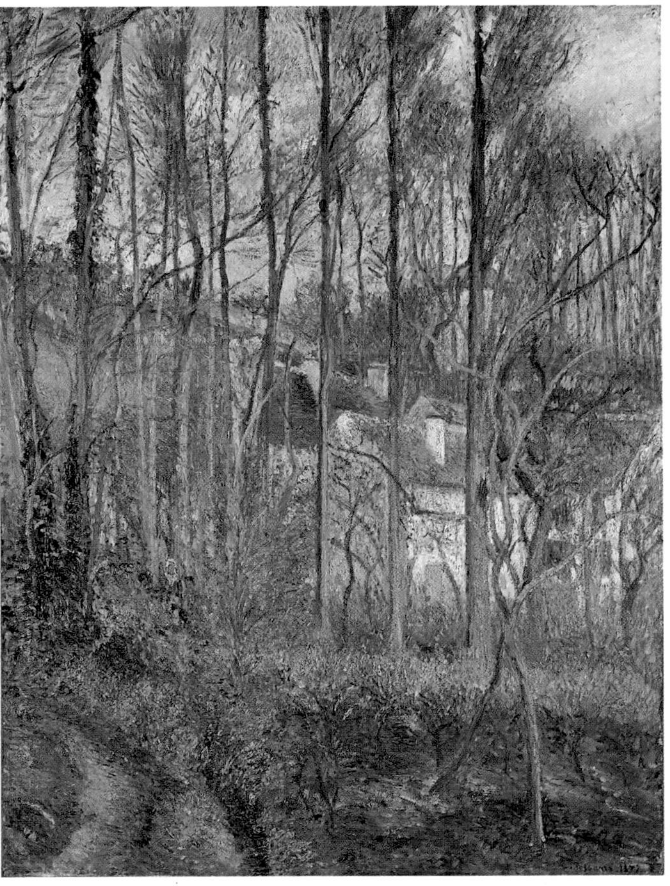

22-9. Camille Pissarro. *The Côte des Boeufs at l'Hermitage, near Pontoise.* 1877. Oil on canvas, 45¼ x 34½" (114.9 x 87.6 cm). The National Gallery, London

REPRODUCED BY COURTESY OF THE TRUSTEES

that places him close to the Barbizon School, and a firm, almost classical structure that was shared by his friend Paul Cézanne (see pages 736–39). We see these qualities in *The Côte des Boeufs at l'Hermitage, near Pontoise* (fig. 22-9). The painting has a real feel for rural life and scenery, which concerned Pissarro more than any other Impressionist. The artist makes no attempt to beautify the overgrown landscape, which evokes the rebirth of life in early springtime though the tangled network of forms embedded in the dense surface texture. Yet the majestic procession of trees and the blocklike buildings establish a clear structure that lends the picture a timeless dignity.

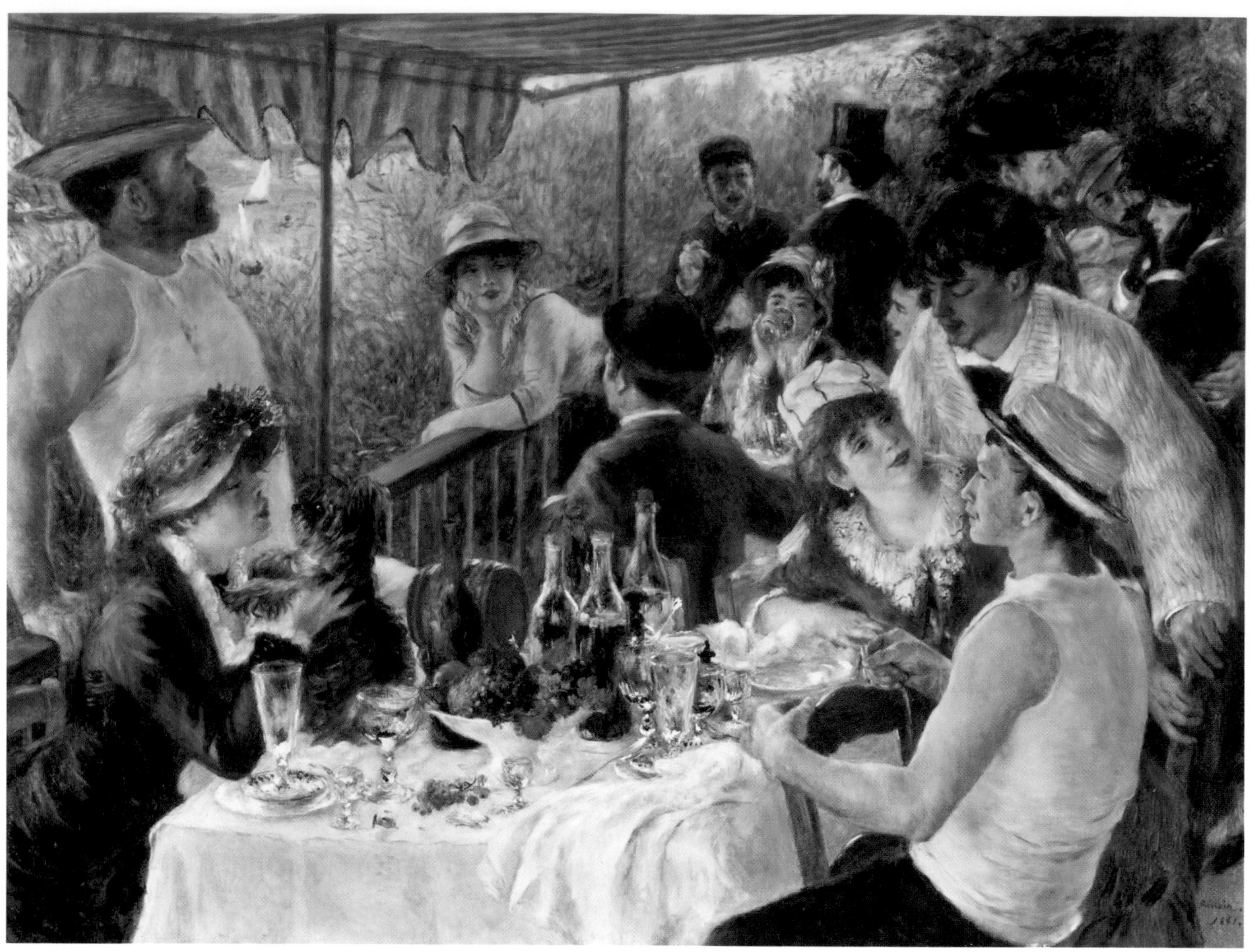

22-10. Auguste Renoir. *Luncheon of the Boating Party, Bougival.* 1881. Oil on canvas, 51 x 68" (129.5 x 172.7 cm). The Phillips Collection, Washington, D.C.

RENOIR. The Impressionist painters answered Baudelaire's call to artists to capture the "heroism of modern life" by depicting its dress and its pastimes. Scenes from the world of entertainment—dance halls, cafés, concerts, the theater—were favorite subjects for them. These carefree views of bourgeois pleasure are flights from the cares of daily life. Although he helped to create the Impressionist landscape style, Renoir began as a figure painter who took Manet as his point of departure, and his finest works after 1875 focus on people. *Luncheon of the Boating Party, Bourigval* (fig. 22-10) is filled with the joy of life. The painting is a masterful orchestration of color and light aided by the lively brushwork. (Note the reflections on the glasses and bottles.) The group of merrymakers, all friends of the artist, has an air of spontaneity worthy of Steen or Hogarth (compare figs. 18-27 and 20-11). Yet the composition is actually controlled by a strong underlying geometry. This firm structure lends stability to the apparent informality and fixes the viewer's position, so that we become participants in the festive gathering. Thus we have no difficulty imagining ourselves leaning against a railing and observing the scene with the same casualness as the man in the straw hat. (The young woman with a dog was soon to become Renoir's wife.)

MANET AND IMPRESSIONISM. Such spontaneity came less easily to Manet. In 1869, however, he became a convert to Impressionism under Monet's influence and soon developed into the greatest of all the Impressionists. His last major picture, *A Bar at the Folies-Bergère* (fig. 22-11), was painted about the same time as Renoir's *Luncheon of the Boating Party, Bougival,* with which it has much in common. The canvas is a virtuoso display. It shows a single figure as calm and as firmly set within the rectangle of the canvas as the fifer (see fig. 22-6), but the background is no longer neutral. A huge shimmering mirror image now fills most of the picture. The mirror, close behind the barmaid, shows the whole interior of the nightclub. The artist, however, denies the three-dimensionality of the scene by taking certain liberties. For example, the reflection of the barmaid and customer is shown off to one

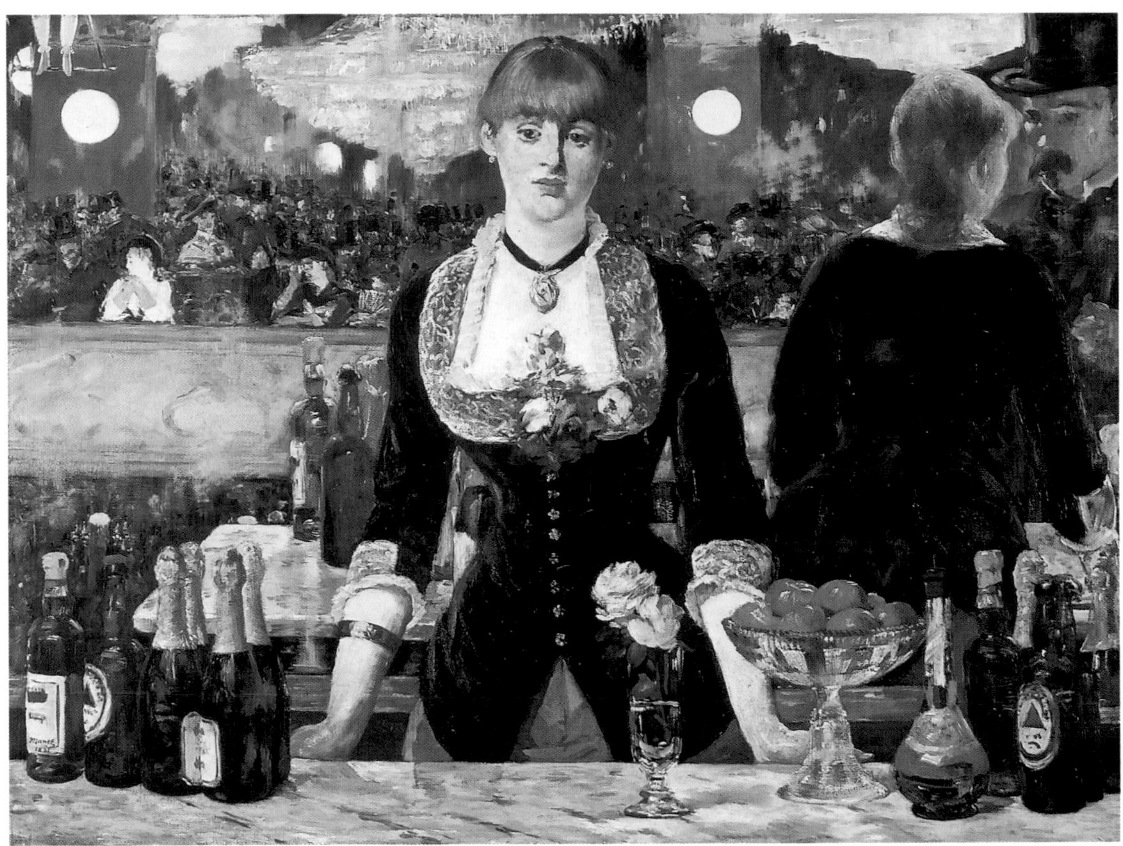

22-11. Édouard Manet. *A Bar at the Folies-Bergère*. 1881–82. Oil on canvas, 37½ x 51" (95.3 x 129.7 cm). Courtauld Institute Galleries, Home House Trustees, London

side, something that is obviously impossible and creates a subtle aura of unreality. The foreground is just as fascinating. Manet was a superb still-life painter. Here he creates a miniature self-contained world in the water glass with a rose and the fruit bowl filled with oranges with only a few deft strokes of the brush. The barmaid's attitude, detached and touched with melancholy, contrasts poignantly with the liveliness of her setting, which she is not permitted to share. For all its gaity, the mood of the canvas reminds us of Daumier's *The Third-Class Carriage* (see fig. 21-37).

DEGAS. Edgar Degas (1834–1917), too, had a deep understanding of human character that lends significance even to seemingly casual scenes such as *The Glass of Absinthe* (fig. 22-12). He makes us look steadily at the disenchanted pair in his café scene, but out of the corner of our eye, so to speak. The design of this picture at first seems as unstudied as a snapshot—Degas practiced photography, though it was not yet capable of capturing an instant on the fly—but a longer look shows us that everything here dovetails precisely. The zigzag of empty tables between us and the unfortunate couple reinforces their brooding loneliness, for example. Compositions as boldly calculated as this set Degas apart from other Impressionists.

A wealthy aristocrat by birth, he had been trained in the tradition of Ingres, whom he greatly admired. When he joined the Impressionists, Degas did not abandon his early loyalty to draftsmanship, and he always stood slightly outside the movement by refusing to adopt its name. His finest works were often done in pastels (powdered pigments molded into sticks), which allowed him to create effects of line, tone, and color simultaneously. *Prima Ballerina* (fig. 22-13) shows the advantages of this flexible medium. The oblique view of the stage, from a box near the proscenium arch, has been shaped into another deliberately off-center composition. The dancer floats above the steeply tilted floor like a butterfly caught in the glare of the footlights.

The Tub (fig. 22-14), of a decade later, is another oblique view, but now severe, almost geometric, in design. The tub and the

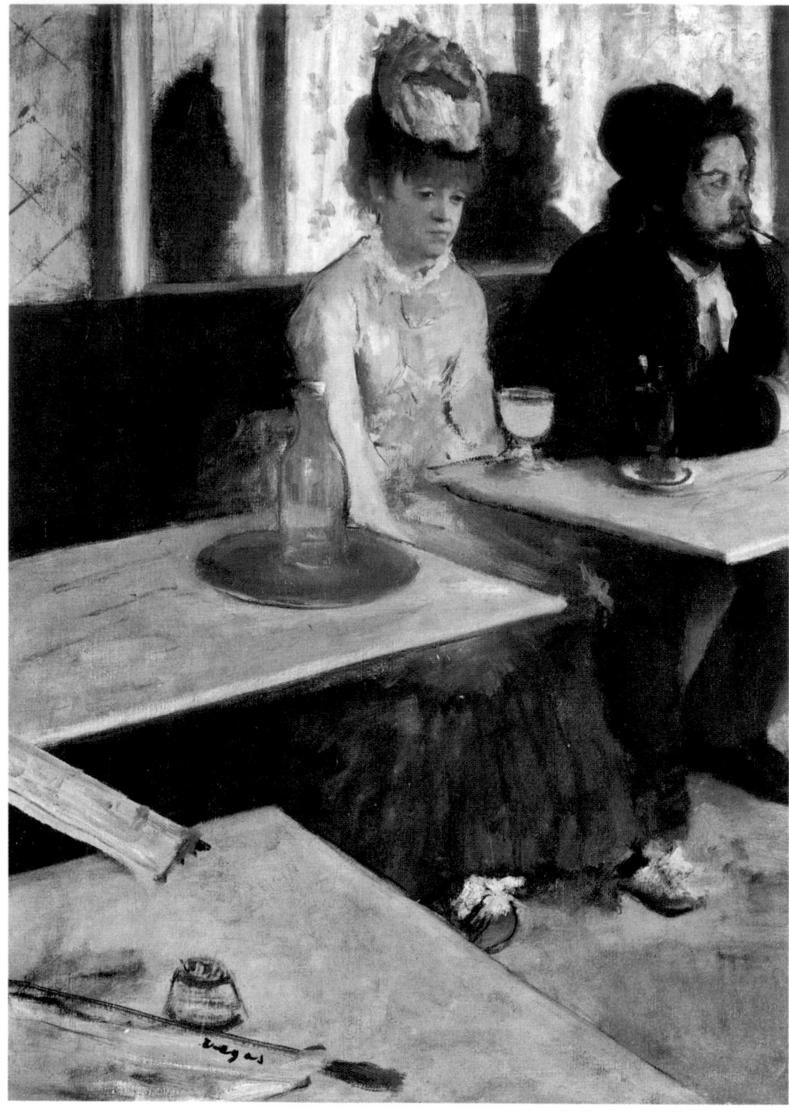

22-12. Edgar Degas. *The Glass of Absinthe.* 1876. Oil on canvas, 36 x 27" (91.3 x 68.7 cm). Musée d'Orsay, Paris

(Opposite) 22-13. Edgar Degas. *Prima Ballerina.* c. 1876. Pastel, 23 x 16½" (58.3 x 42 cm). Musée d'Orsay, Paris

crouching woman, both strongly outlined, form a circle within a square, and the rest of the rectangular format is filled by a shelf so sharply tilted that it almost shares the plane of the picture. Yet on this shelf Degas has placed two pitchers that are hardly foreshortened at all. (Note how the curve of the small one fits the handle of the other.) Here the tension between the "2-D" surface and "3-D" depth comes close to the breaking point. *The Tub* is Impressionist only in its shimmering, luminous colors. Its other qualities are more characteristic of the 1880s, the first Post-Impressionist decade, when many artists showed a renewed concern with problems of form (see Chapter 23).

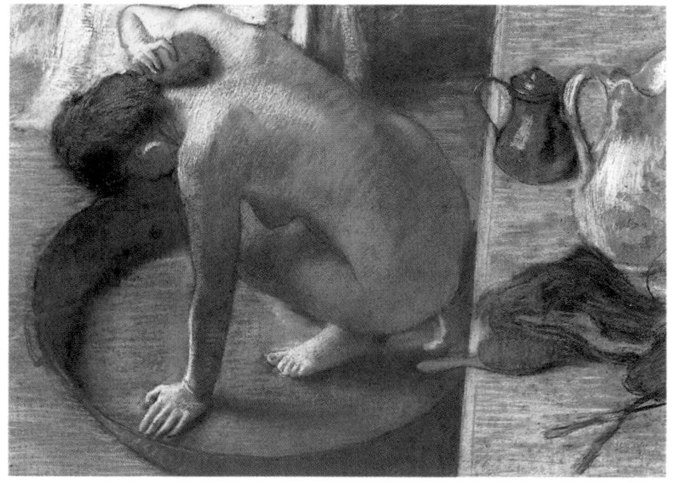

22-14. Edgar Degas. *The Tub.* 1886. Pastel, 23½ x 32⅜" (59.7 x 82.3 cm). Musée d'Orsay, Paris

MORISOT. The Impressionists' ranks included several women of great ability. The subject matter of Berthe Morisot (1841–1895), a member of the group from its beginning, was the world she knew: the domestic life of the French upper middle class, which she depicted with understanding. Morisot's early paintings, centering on her mother and her sister Edma, were influenced at first by Manet, whose brother she later married, but they have a subtle sense of alienation. Her mature work is altogether different in

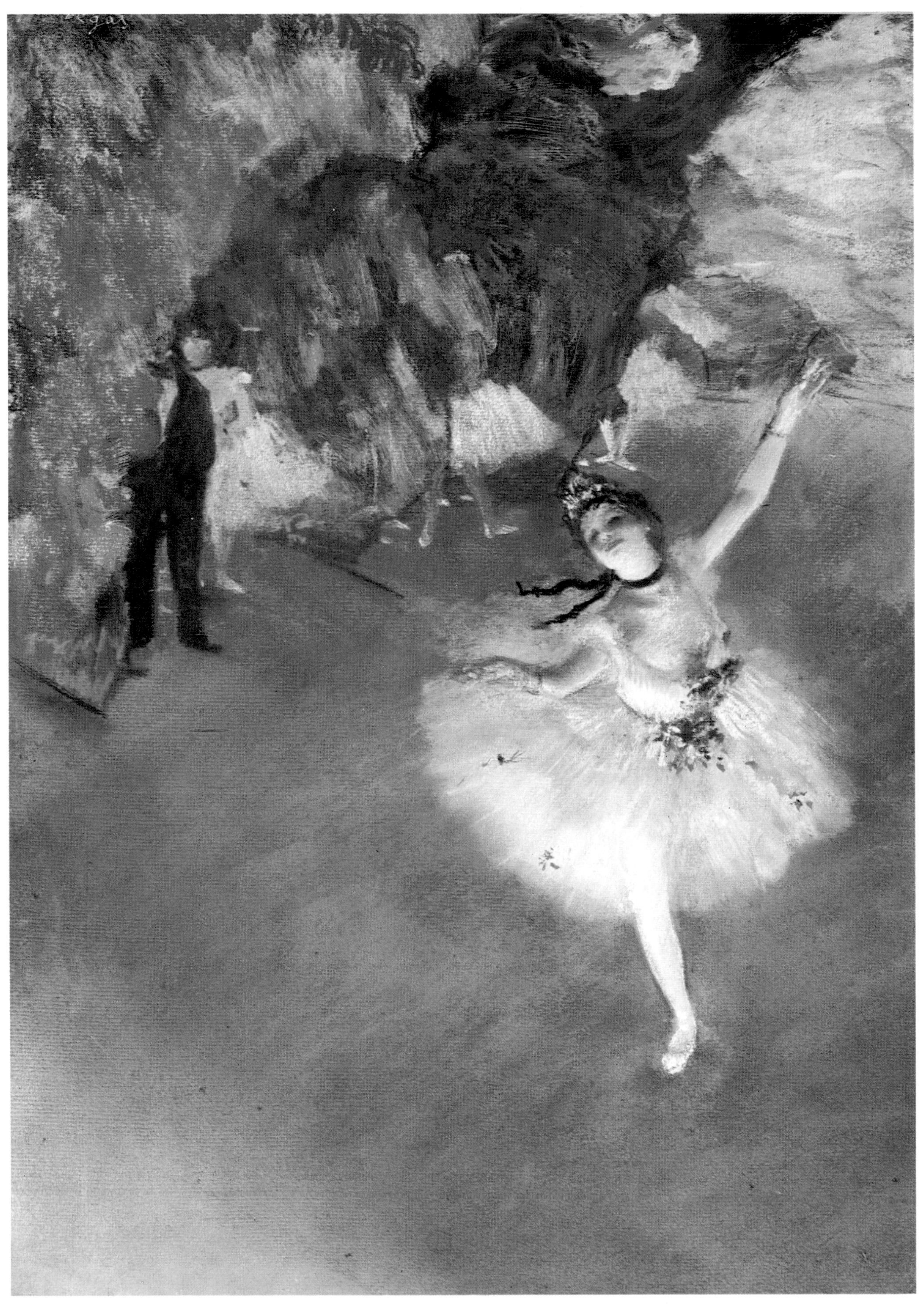

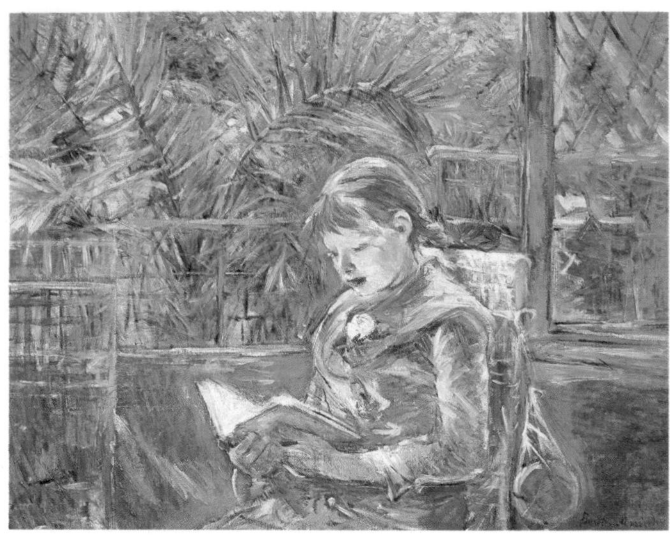

22-15. Berthe Morisot. *La Lecture (Reading)*. 1888. Oil on canvas, 29¼ x 36½" (74.3 x 92.7 cm). Museum of Fine Arts, St. Petersburg, Florida

GIFT OF FRIENDS OF ART IN MEMORY OF MARGARET ACHESON STUART

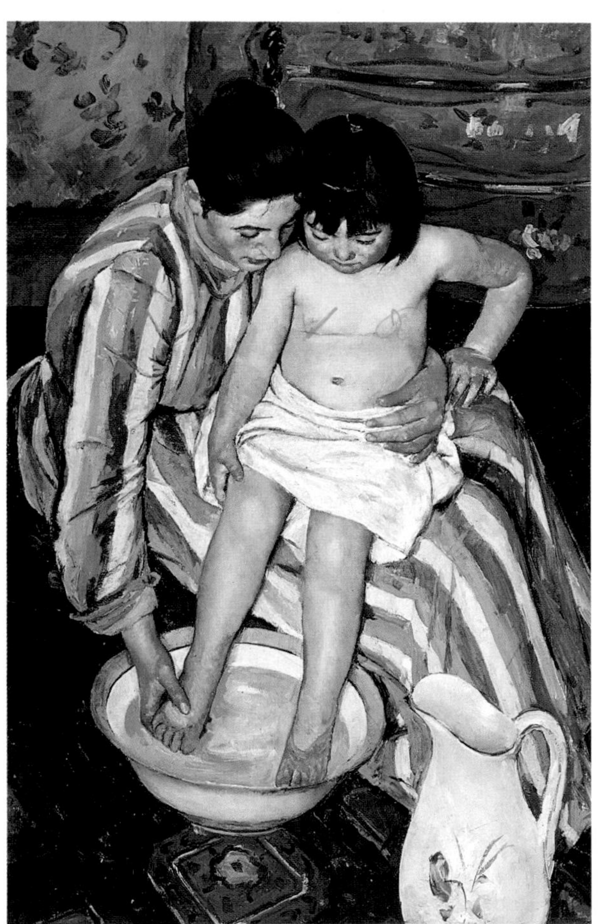

22-16. Mary Cassatt. *The Bath*. 1891–92. Oil on canvas, 39½ x 26" (100.3 x 66 cm). The Art Institute of Chicago

ROBERT A. WALLER COLLECTION

character. The birth of her daughter Julie in 1878 marked a change in her art, which reached its height during the following decade. Her painting of a little girl reading in a room overlooking the artist's garden (fig. 22-15) shows her light-filled style at its best. Morisot applied her virtuoso brushwork with a sketchlike brevity that omits unessential details yet conveys a complete impression of the scene. The figure is fully integrated within the formal design, which is enhanced by the pastel hues. Morisot's painting radiates an air of contentment free of the sentimentality that often affects genre paintings of the period.

CASSATT. Surprisingly, Americans were the first patrons of the Impressionists, responding to the new style sooner than Europeans did. At a time when no French museum would have them, Impressionist works entered public collections in the United States, and American painters such as James McNeill Whistler (see below) and Mary Cassatt (1845–1926) were among the earliest followers of Manet and his circle. Cassatt joined the Impressionists in 1877 and became a tireless champion of their work. She had received a standard academic training in her native Philadelphia but had to struggle to overcome traditional barriers. Though painting was viewed as an unsuitable occupation for a woman, like Morisot, she was able to pursue her career as an artist because she was independently wealthy. Cassatt was helped to gain early acceptance for Impressionist paintings in the United States through her social contacts with wealthy private collectors. Although she never married or had children, maternity provided the thematic and formal focus of most of her work. Cassatt developed a highly accomplished individual style. *The Bath* (fig. 22-16) is characteristic of her mature work around 1890. The oblique view, simplified color forms, and flat composition show the impact of her mentor Degas, as well as her study of Japanese prints. Despite the complexity of its design, the painting has a directness that lends simple dignity to motherhood.

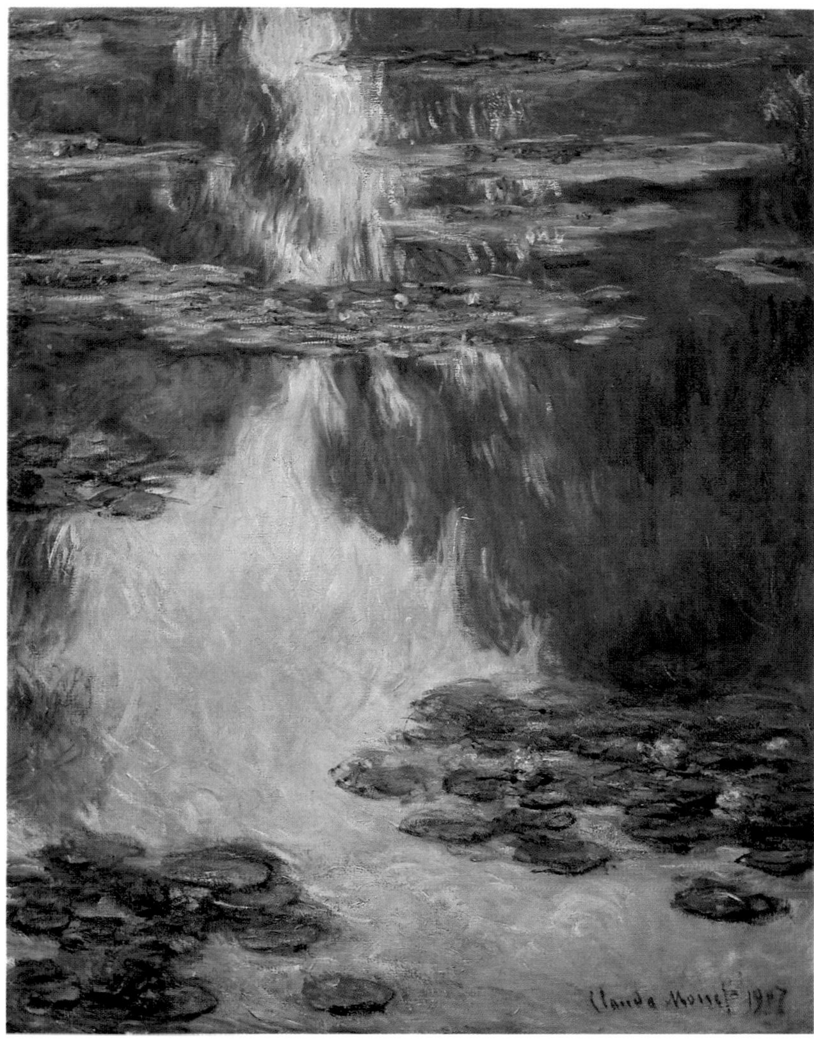

22-17. Claude Monet. *Water Lilies*. 1907. Oil on canvas, 36½ x 29" (92.7 x 73.7 cm). Kawamura Memorial Museum of Art, Sakura City, Chiba Prefecture, Japan

MONET'S LATER WORKS. By the mid-1880s Impressionism had become widely accepted. Its technique was imitated by conservative painters and practiced as a fusion style by a growing number of artists worldwide. Ironically, the movement now underwent a deep crisis. Manet died in 1883. Renoir, already beset by doubts, moved toward a more classical style. Racked by internal dissension fostered by Degas, the group held its last show in 1886. At that time Pissarro abandoned Impressionism altogether for several years in favor of Seurat's Divisionism (see pages 740–41). Among the major figures of the movement, only Monet remained faithful to the Impressionist view of nature. Although his work became more subjective over time, he never ventured into fantasy, nor did he forsake the basic approach of his earlier landscapes.

About 1890 Monet began to paint pictures in series, showing the same subject under different conditions of light and atmosphere. These tended increasingly to resemble Turner's "airy visions, painted with tinted steam," as Monet concentrated on the effects of colored light. (He had visited London and knew Turner's work; see pages 677–79.) His *Water Lilies* (fig. 22-17) is a fascinating sequel to *On the Bank of the Seine* (see fig. 22-7), painted almost 40 years earlier. The surface of the pond now takes up the entire canvas, so that the effect of a weightless screen is stronger than ever. The artist's brushwork, too, has greater variety and a more individual rhythm. While the scene is still based on nature, this is no ordinary landscape but one entirely of his making. On the estate at Giverny given to him late in life by the French government, the artist created a self-contained world for purely personal and artistic purposes. The subjects he painted there are as much reflections of his imagination as they are of reality. They convey a very different sense of time as well. Instead of the single moment captured in *On the Bank of the Seine,* his *Water Lilies* summarizes a shifting impression of the pond in response to the changing water as breezes play across it.

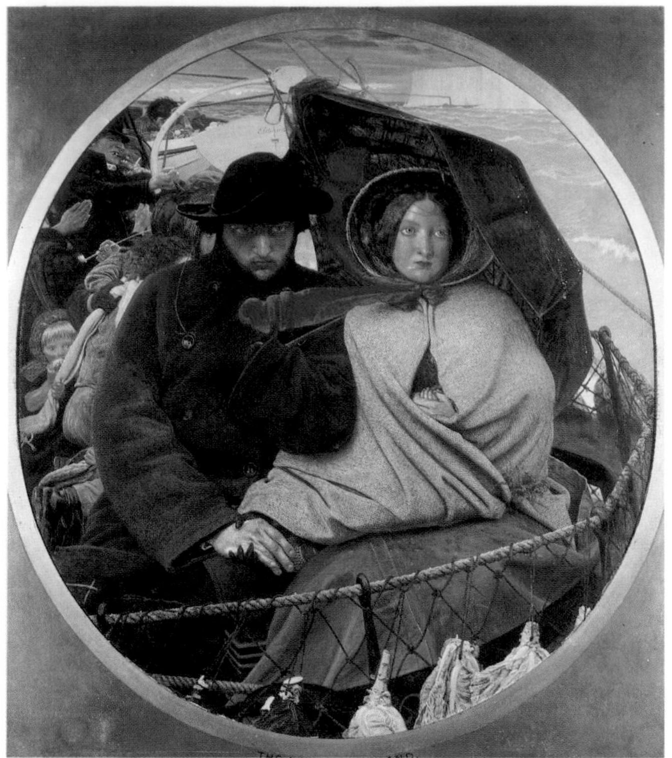

22-18. Ford Madox Brown. *The Last of England.* 1852–55. Oil on panel, 32½ x 29½" (82.5 x 74.9 cm). City Museum and Art Gallery, Birmingham, England

BY PERMISSION BIRMINGHAM MUSEUM AND ART GALLERY

England

REALISM. By the time Monet came to admire his work, Turner's reputation was at a low ebb in his own country. In 1848, when Courbet launched his revolutionary doctrine of Realism, a concern with "the heroism of modern life" arose independently in English painting, although the movement lacked a leader of Courbet's stature and boldness.

Perhaps the best-known example of English Realism is *The Last of England* (fig. 22-18) by Ford Madox Brown (1821–1893), a picture that enjoyed enormous popularity throughout the latter half of the nineteenth century in the English-speaking world. The subject—a group of emigrants as they set out on their long overseas journey—may be less obvious today than it once was; nor does it carry the same emotional charge. There can be no question, however, that the artist has treated an important theme taken from modern experience, and that he has done so with touching seriousness.

The painting is intended to dramatize the conditions that made the emigrants decide to leave England. The pathos of the scene may strike us as a bit theatrical: note the contrast between the brooding young family in the foreground (Brown used himself, his wife, and daughter as the models) and the "good riddance" gesture of the man at the upper left. We recognize its source in the "dumb shows" of Hogarth, whom Brown admired (see fig. 20-11). Brown's style, however, has nothing in common with Hogarth's. Its extreme precision of detail strikes us as almost photographic. There is no hint of personal "handwriting" in the scene. Brown had developed this painstaking technique some years earlier, after he met the Nazarenes, the group of German painters in Rome who practiced what they regarded as a "medieval" style (see page 683). He in turn taught it to his three pupils who together in 1848 helped to found the artists' society called the Pre-Raphaelite Brotherhood: William Holman Hunt (1827–1910), John Everett Millais (1829–1896), and Dante Gabriel Rossetti (1828–1882).

THE PRE-RAPHAELITES. Brown himself never actually joined the Pre-Raphaelites, but he shared their basic aims: to do battle against the frivolous art of the day by having "genuine ideas to express" and by producing "pure transcripts . . . from nature," an objective inspired by the writings of John Ruskin. As the name of the Brotherhood proclaims, its members took their inspiration from the "primitive" masters of the fifteenth century. To that extent, they belong to the Gothic revival, which had long been an important aspect of the Romantic movement. What set the Pre-Raphaelites apart from Romantics like the Nazarenes was a desire to reform the ills of modern civilization through art. This ambition was inspired by Chartism, the democratic working-class movement that reached its peak in the revolutionary year 1848.

HUNT. *The Awakening Conscience* (fig. 22-19) by William Holman Hunt, the artist who remained truest to the Brotherhood's ideals, is perhaps the quintessential Pre-Raphaelite statement. It, too, is a morality play in the tradition of Hogarth. The painting addresses a very real social problem of the time, although Hunt treated it as a personal crisis. Inspired by an episode in Charles

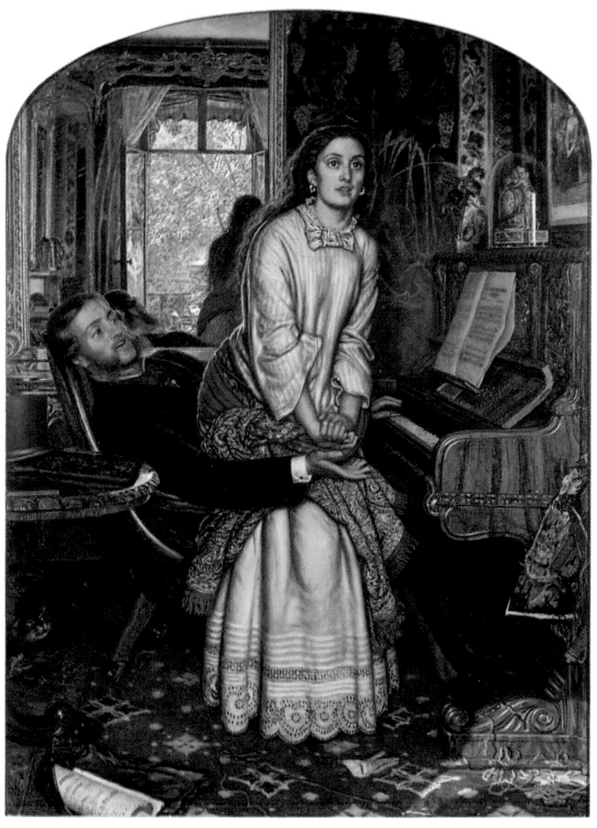

22-19. William Holman Hunt. *The Awakening Conscience.* 1853. Oil on canvas, 30 x 20" (76.2 x 50.8 cm). The Tate Gallery, London

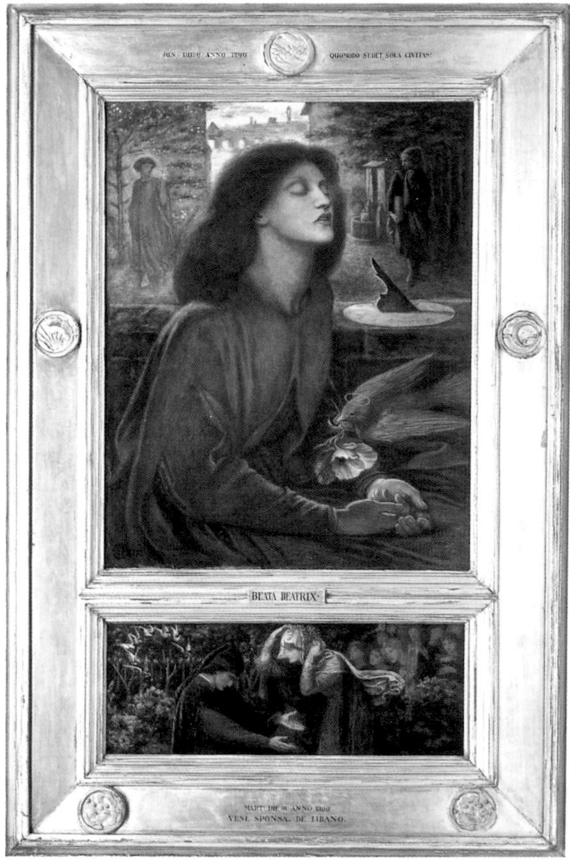

22-20. Dante Gabriel Rossetti. *Beata Beatrix.* 1872. Oil on canvas, 34 1/2 x 27 1/4" (87.5 x 69.3 cm); predella 10 1/2 x 27 1/4" (26.5 x 69.3 cm). The Art Institute of Chicago

CHARLES L. HUTCHINSON COLLECTION

Dickens' *David Copperfield,* it shows a young woman stirred to the realization by the music she sings that she has been living in sin. The scene is presented in obsessive detail, which is filled with symbolic meaning. The print above the piano, for example, shows Christ and the Woman Taken into Adultery, while the light reflected in the mirror is that of religious revelation. Here the artist looked to the example of Jan van Eyck's *Arnolfini Portrait* (see fig. 15-8), which had recently been acquired by the National Gallery in London.

ROSSETTI. Unlike Hunt, Dante Gabriel Rossetti was not concerned with social issues. He thought of himself instead as a reformer of aesthetic sensibility. The vast majority of his work consists of watercolors or pastels showing women taken from literary sources, but all bear a striking resemblance to his wife, Elizabeth Siddal. *Beata Beatrix* (fig. 22-20), created as a memorial to Siddal, imposes her features on the wife of his namesake, the Italian poet Dante, whose account of her death inspired the painting. Rossetti explained the program in considerable detail: "The picture illustrates the 'Vita Nuova,' embodying symbolically the death of Beatrice as treated in that work. The picture is not intended at all to represent death, but to render it under the semblance of a trance.... I have introduced ... the figures of Dante and Love passing through the street and gazing ominously on one another, conscious of the event; while the bird, a messenger of death, drops the poppy between the hands of Beatrice. She, through her shut lids, is conscious of a new world." In this version, the artist has expressed the hope of seeing his beloved Elizabeth again by adding a second panel showing Dante and Beatrice meeting in Paradise and inscribing the dates of their deaths on the frame. For all its apparent spirituality, the painting has an aura of repressed eroticism that is the hallmark of Rossetti's work. It exerted a powerful influence on other Pre-Raphaelites as well.

BURNE-JONES. Rossetti's pupil Edward Burne-Jones (1833–1898) came to be identified most completely with the Brotherhood in the public's mind, although he was too young to have been a member. *The Wheel of Fortune* (fig. 22-21) is an allegorical painting that was initially planned as part of a large pseudotriptych devoted to the story of Troy. The project, which remained unfinished, was based on a poem by William Morris that likewise was never completed. It was divided into four sections representing Fortune, Fame, Oblivion, and Love. The figures chained to the wheel of fortune, from which they cannot

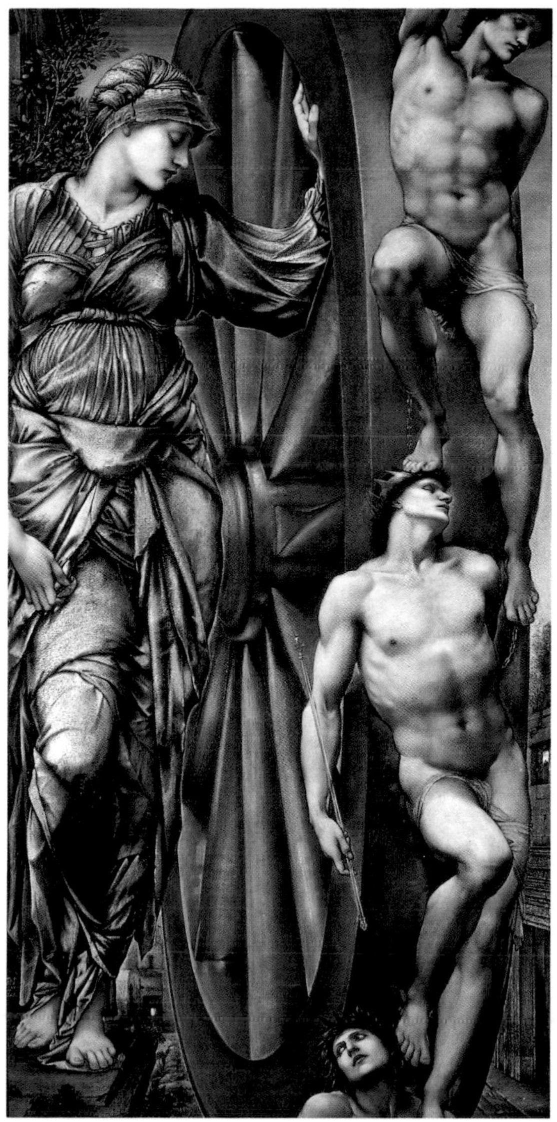

22-21. Edward Burne-Jones. *The Wheel of Fortune.* 1877–83. Oil on canvas, 6'6 3/4 x 3'3 3/8" (2 x 1 m). Musée d'Orsay, Paris

NATIONALISM IN MID-NINETEENTH-CENTURY MUSIC

In the mid-nineteenth century, composers turned for inspiration to their native heritages. The fascination with folk music, as well as folklore, was an outgrowth of nationalism, an intrinsic part of Romanticism that became nearly universal after mid-century. Among the first to take up this interest was Johannes Brahms (1833–1897), an equally ardent nationalist and fervent admirer of Count Otto von Bismarck, the Prussian minister who unified Germany. Although he was one of the first composers to show an interest in folk music, Brahms owed much to his teacher, Robert Schumann, for whose widow, Clara, he developed an abiding but unrequited love (see page 690). Brahms' development was slow: his first symphony was not completed until 1876, but it is cast in the heroic mold of Beethoven. No other composer of his generation wrote masterpieces in such a wide range of music. The works are characteristically intense, with writing high in the string sections, but with slow movements of astonishingly tender lyricism. They are nevertheless without the bombast found in the work of other composers from the same time and are held together by a thorough command of composition and a strong, classical structure.

Brahms was one of the first to appreciate the Czech composer Antonin Dvořák (1841–1904), whose career he encouraged. Whereas Brahms' music is alternately brooding and rapturous, Dvořák's is almost uniformly sunny and uniquely Czech in flavor—he called himself proudly "a happy Bohemian." Love of nature and homeland fill his music. Dvořák was proud of his national music, but he was affected by that of other cultures, especially during his sojourn in New York as head of the National Conservatory of Music (1892–95), when he produced his celebrated *New World Symphony* and *American Quartet.* He left behind a body of chamber music even more substantial than Brahms' and a splendid cello concerto that is the greatest of its kind. The late tone poems, inspired mostly by folk tales, became important models for the next generation of Czech composers centering on Leo Janáček (1854–1928).

Perhaps the most distinctive national school was to be found in Russia. The group known as "The Five" sought to infuse their music with the sound of their country and often took folk melodies as the basis for their work. They also revived the system of modes, which had remained intact in Orthodox music and was indigenous to large parts of Russia. The most original member of the Russian school was Modest Moussorgsky (1839–1881), despite his being the least trained. His opera *Boris Godunov* (1868–72), written about the same time as Aleksei Tolstoy's drama but taken from an earlier play by Aleksandr Pushkin (1799–1837) and a history of Russia by Nikolai Karamzin, is the undisputed masterpiece of the entire movement.

The greatest Russian composer remains Peter Ilyich Tchaikovsky (1840–1893), who began as a student of the traditionalist Anton Rubinstein (1829–1894) but was decisively influenced early in his career by "The Five." The tone poems, all based on literature, pulsate with Romantic yearning and adventure, while the six symphonies, several of which incorporate Russian themes, are programmatic—especially the last three, which are virtually autobiographical. Indeed, the final one (the *Pathétique*) is a valedictory statement of the composer's life, with its struggles and triumphs. Its undeniable Russian elements notwithstanding, Tchaikovsky's music owes its enduring appeal to its internationalism. Despite its physical isolation, Russia was closely linked to the musical capitals of western Europe. Thus, Tchaikovsky's three great ballets build on the French tradition and possess a sophistication that is extraordinarily cosmopolitan. Two of them are based on folk tales retold by the brothers Grimm and were written for Marius Petipa (1819–1910), under whom Russian ballet reached its zenith.

With Richard Wagner (1813–1883), nationalist rhetoric came to express the growing expansionist mood of Germany that led ultimately to the rise of Nazism during the 1930s. Wagner manned the barricades in Dresden during the revolutionary upheavals that struck Europe throughout 1848–49 and was forced into exile for 13 years, until he won the support of Ludwig II of Bavaria. His operas, such as *Tristan and Isolde* (1859), written under the influence of the philosophy of Arthur Schopenhauer (1788–1860), and the enormous four-part cycle *The Ring of the Nibelungen* (1853–74), which dates from about the same time as Christian Hebbel's plays, expand greatly on medieval Germanic legends. Wagner's goal was a total work of art that united music, literature, and theater. His texts reflect the influence of Goethe in their literary, declamatory style. One of Wagner's characteristic devices is the leitmotif (pronounced

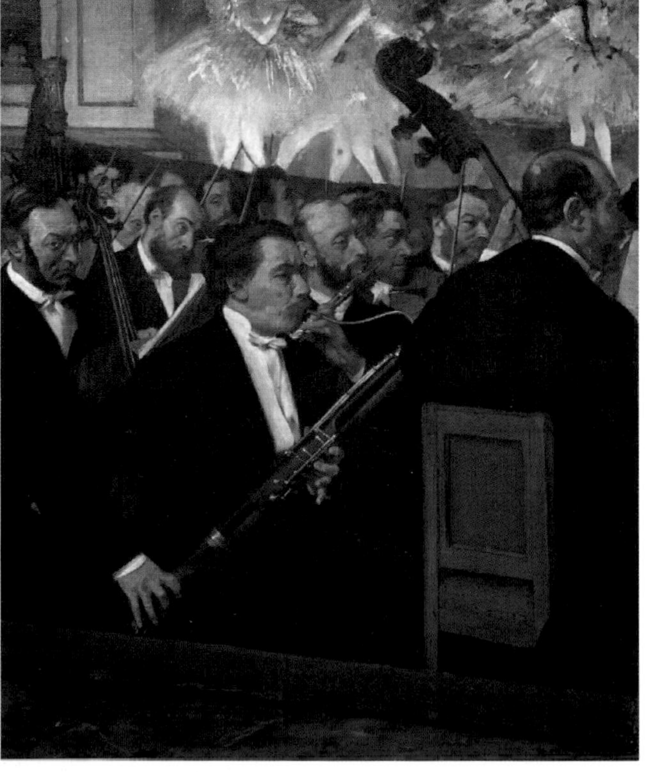

Edgar Degas. *Orchestra of the Opera.* c. 1870. Oil on canvas, 22¼ x 18³⁄₁₆" (56.5 x 46.2 m). Musée d'Orsay, Paris

"light moteef," from German, "leading motif"), a melodic line that represents a person, idea, or situation. If, for example, the music brings together the leitmotif for Tristan with one that signifies Fate, the informed listener understands that Tristan is being drawn toward his destiny. Add the motif for Isolde and we know that his fate is intertwined with hers. Music of such sophistication demanded a highly educated audience, which the prosperous cities of nineteenth-century Europe could readily supply.

Despite the enormous demands Wagner placed on singers, it was the orchestra that carried the largest part of the musical burden. His highly unconventional orchestration techniques and integrated drama set an important example for the Italian composer Giuseppe Verdi (1813–1901), who nevertheless denied their influence. Verdi's early operas often have patriotic subjects espousing the cause of Italian independence (the *risorgimento*). Although his arias remained vehicles of virtuoso singing, the last five operas broke decisively with the style of Donizetti and Bellini under the influence of Wagner's integrated approach. Dating from 1862 to 1893, they are the finest in culmination of the entire Italian tradition stretching back to Monteverdi. Like Berlioz and Tchaikovsky, Verdi was attracted above all to the plays of Shakespeare—*Macbeth, Othello,* and *The Merry Wives of Windsor*—which brought out the best in him.

As in art and architecture, revivalism was an important factor in music, although it never became a guiding principle. Mendelssohn resuscitated Bach's *St. Matthew Passion,* Wagner rediscovered Palestrina and Glück (his very antitheses as composers), while Brahms helped to prepare complete editions of the works of Handel, C. P. E. Bach, and Mozart that mark the beginning of modern musicology.

escape, include a slave, a king, and a poet. The composition was inspired by an altarpiece by Mantegna, while Dame Fortune reflects his admiration for Botticelli's figures, such as those in figure 12-54. The figures also show the impact of the sibyls and nudes on the ceiling of the Sistine Chapel (see fig. 13-19), which the artist studied in detail during a visit to Rome, as well as Michelangelo's "slaves" (compare figs. 13-14–13-16). The artist's principal interest, however, lies in the decorative design. Inspired by Early Renaissance paintings, it has the flatness and luxuriance of a tapestry. Even more than Whistler's, Burne-Jones' work represents an escape from reality into a dreamlike world of heightened beauty and rarefied feeling.

WHISTLER. James Abbott McNeill Whistler (1834–1903) came to Paris from America in 1855 to study painting. Four years later he moved to London, where he spent the rest of his life, but he visited France during the 1860s and was in close touch with the rising Impressionist movement. *Arrangement in Black and Gray: The Artist's Mother* (fig. 22-22), his best-known painting, reflects the influence of Manet in its emphasis on flat areas, while the likeness has the austere precision of Degas. Its fame as a symbol of our latter-day "mother cult" is a paradox of popular psychology that would have horrified Whistler, who wanted the canvas to be appreciated for its formal qualities alone.

A witty, sharp-tongued advocate of Art for Art's Sake, he thought of his pictures as comparable to pieces of music and called them "symphonies" or "nocturnes." [See Primary Sources, no. 73, page 931.] The boldest example, painted about 1874, is *Nocturne in Black and Gold: The Falling Rocket* (fig. 22-23). Without an explanatory subtitle, we would have real difficulty making it out. No French painter had yet dared to produce a picture so "nonrepresentational," so reminiscent of Cozens' "blotscapes" and Turner's "tinted steam" (see figs. 21-10 and 21-48). It was this canvas, more than any other, that prompted John Ruskin to accuse

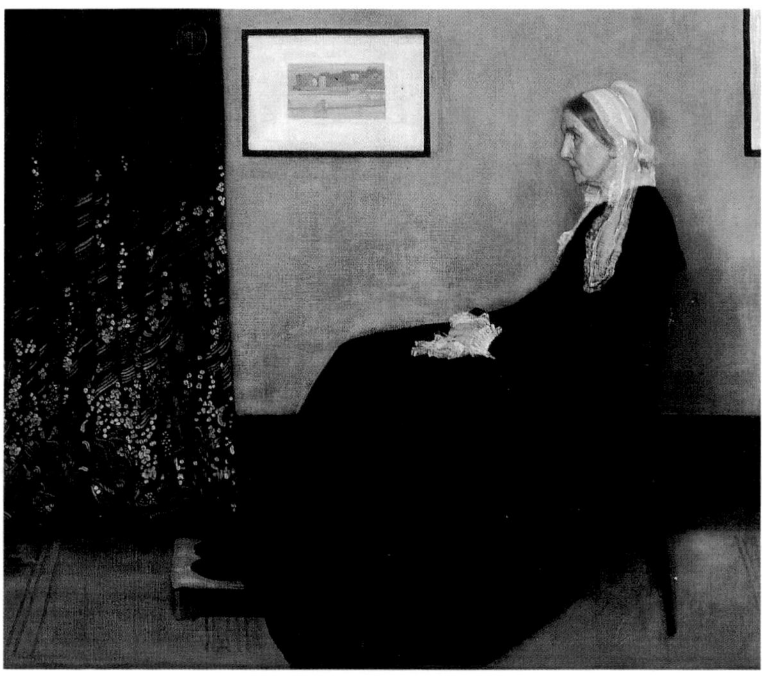

22-22. James Abbott McNeill Whistler. *Arrangement in Black and Gray: The Artist's Mother.* 1871. Oil on canvas, 57 x 64½" (144.6 x 163.8 cm). Musée d'Orsay, Paris

22-23. James Abbott McNeill Whistler. *Nocturne in Black and Gold: The Falling Rocket.* c. 1874. Oil on panel, 23¾ x 18⅜" (60.2 x 46.8 cm). The Detroit Institute of Arts

GIFT OF DEXTER M. FERRY, JR.

Whistler of "flinging a pot of paint in the public's face." (Since the same critic had highly praised Turner's *The Slave Ship,* we must conclude that what Ruskin admired was not the tinted steam itself but the Romantic feeling behind it.)

During Whistler's subsequent suit for libel, he offered a definition of his aims that seems to be particularly applicable to *The Falling Rocket:* "I have perhaps meant rather to indicate an artistic interest alone in my work, divesting the picture from any outside sort of interest.... It is an arrangement of line, form, and color, first, and I make use of any incident of it which shall bring about a symmetrical result." The last phrase has special significance, since Whistler acknowledges that in using chance effects, he does not look for resemblances but for a purely formal harmony. While he rarely practiced what he preached to quite the same extent as he did in *The Falling Rocket,* his statement reads like a prophecy of American abstract painting (see fig. 24-60).

United States

THE AMERICAN BARBIZON SCHOOL. After the Civil War, the United States underwent unprecedented industrial growth, immigration, and westward expansion. These changes led to not only a new range of social and economic problems but also to a different outlook and taste. As the United States became more like the Old World, Americans traveled abroad in growing numbers and found their cultural models in Europe, particularly in France, which led to a new cosmopolitanism in art. There was an equally dramatic shift in the attitude toward nature. The uneasy balance between civilization and nature shifted once and for all in favor of progress by the end of the Centennial Celebration in 1876. The loss of the twin Romantic visions of the virgin wilderness and a pastoral Eden left nature as little more than a sentimental vestige to be preserved in parks. Since landscape ceased to be a teacher of moral truths as well, the viewer was left only with a personal reaction to a total impression of scenery. In this way, the mystery of nature retained its spiritual significance but required a different mode of expression. The American Barbizon painters answered the need for a new form of landscape by turning inward. Their canvases embody the altered mentality of the United States by evoking a poetic state of mind with ever-increasing freedom.

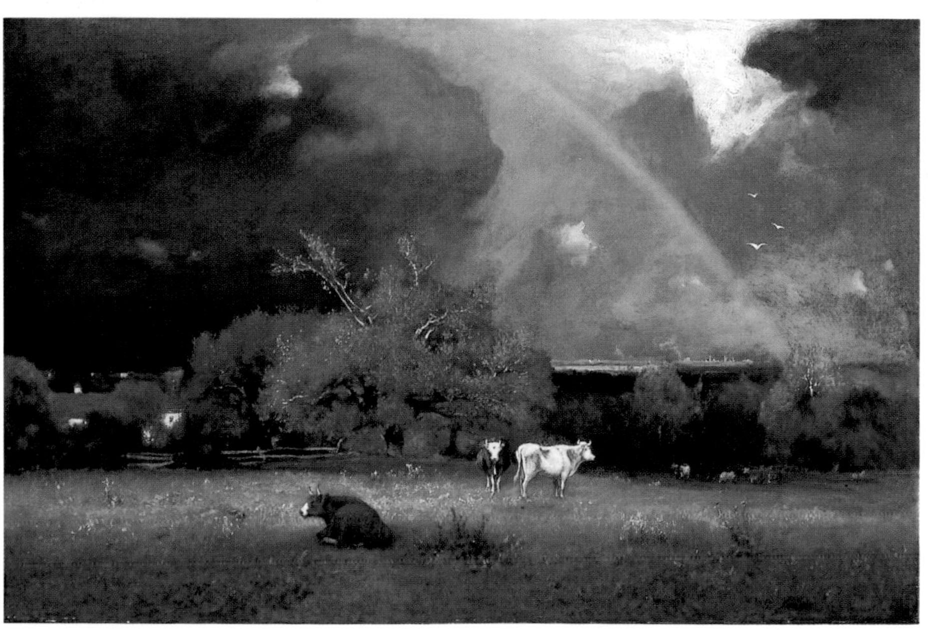

22-24. George Inness. *The Rainbow.* c. 1878–79. Oil on canvas, 30¼ x 45¼" (76.8 x 114.9 cm). © 1993 Indianapolis Museum of Art

GIFT OF GEORGE E. HUME

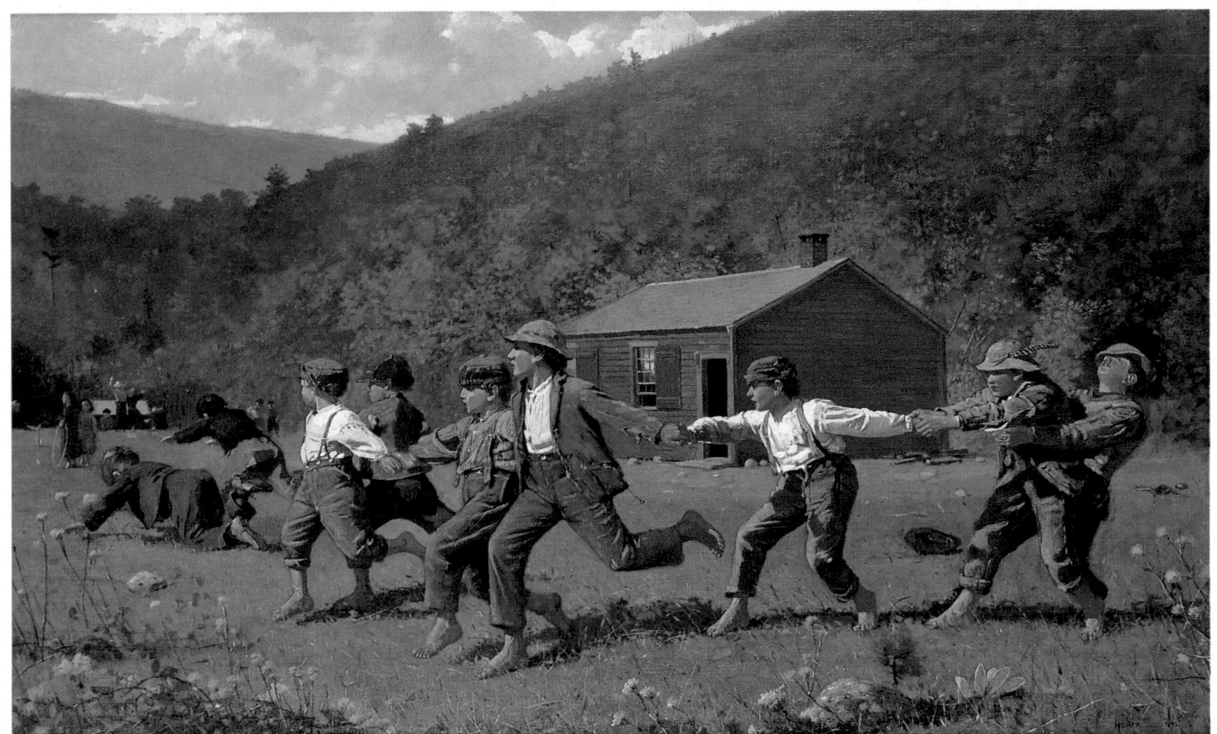

22-25. Winslow Homer. *Snap the Whip.* 1872. Oil on canvas, 22¼ x 36½" (56.5 x 92.7 cm). The Butler Institute of Art, Youngstown, Ohio

INNESS. The leader of the American Barbizon School was George Inness (1825–1894), who had been deeply impressed by the work of Théodore Rousseau and his followers during a visit to France. *The Rainbow* (fig. 22-24) shows one of the storm scenes so characteristic of this artist. The contrast of nature's bounty with the tumultuous sweep of cosmic forces is reminiscent of Cole's *View of Schroon Mountain* (see fig. 21-56). Instead of depicting the wilderness, however, this former member of the Hudson River School has followed a rustic scene by Millet. Inness endowed his landscape with a sense of divine presence by freely rearranging nature according to formulas that act as indexes of personal feelings. Deeply religious, he had converted to the spiritualism of Emanuel Swedenborg, who believed in an immaterial but light-filled realm of departed souls that is visually similar and parallel to our own. Although only a few of his landscapes have a specific symbolic meaning, rainbows had spiritual significance for Inness. Swedenborg's ideas confirmed and intensified his approach, which relied increasingly on light and color to impart his vision of a deeper reality lying hidden from people's eyes but not their souls.

HOMER. The far more gifted Winslow Homer (1836–1910) was a pictorial reporter during the Civil War and continued as a magazine illustrator until 1875. He went to Paris in 1866 but arrived too soon to feel its full impact. French art, however, had an important effect on his work. *Snap the Whip* (fig. 22-25) conveys a nostalgia for a simpler era of America before the Civil War (see fig. 21-57). We are carried back to the innocent time of Mark Twain's *Tom Sawyer* and *Huckleberry Finn.* The sunlit scene might be called "pre-Impressionist." Its fresh delicacy lies halfway between Corot and Monet (compare figs. 21-38 and 22-7). The air of youthful innocence relies equally on the composition, which was inspired by the bacchanals then popular in French art (compare fig. 21-64). Homer's sophisticated design shows the same subtle understanding of motion as Bruegel's *The Blind Leading the Blind* (see fig. 16-23), which also ends in a fallen figure.

EAKINS. Thomas Eakins (1844–1916) arrived in Paris from Philadelphia about the same time as Homer. He went home four years later, after receiving a conventional academic training but with decisive impressions of Velázquez and Courbet. Elements from both these artists are combined in *William Rush Carving His Allegorical Figure of the Schuylkill River* (fig. 22-26; compare figs. 17-35 and 22-2). Eakins had encountered stiff opposition for advocating traditional life studies at the Pennsylvania Academy of the Fine Arts. To him, Rush was a hero for basing his 1809 statue for the Philadelphia Water Works on the nude model, though the figure itself was draped in a classical robe. Eakins no doubt knew contemporary European paintings of sculptors carving from the nude; these were related to the theme of Pygmalion and Galatea popular at the time among academic artists. Conservative critics nevertheless denounced *William Rush Carving His Allegorical Figure of the Schuylkill River* for its nudity, despite the presence of the chaperon knitting quietly to the right. To us the painting's declaration of unvarnished truth seems a courageous fulfillment of Baudelaire's demand for pictures that express the heroism of modern life.

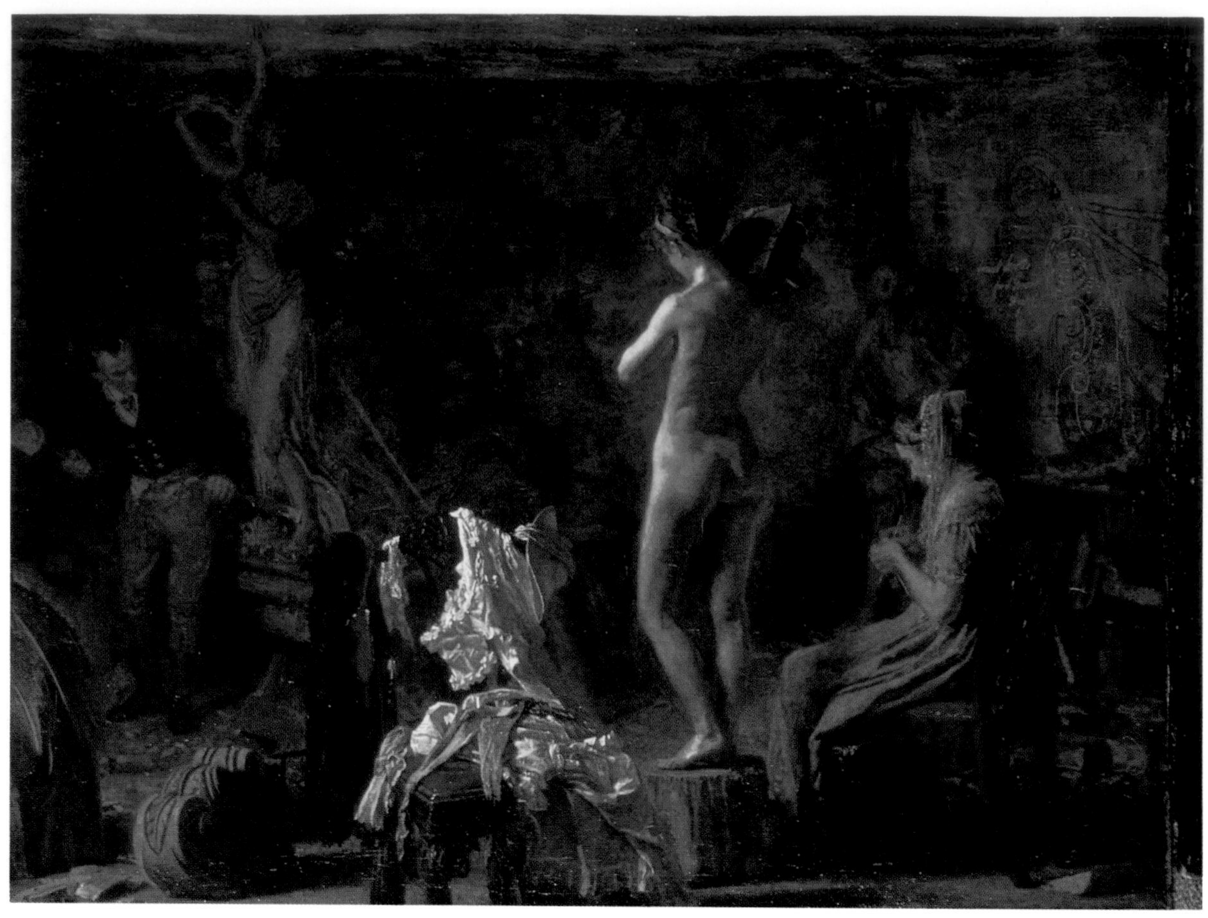

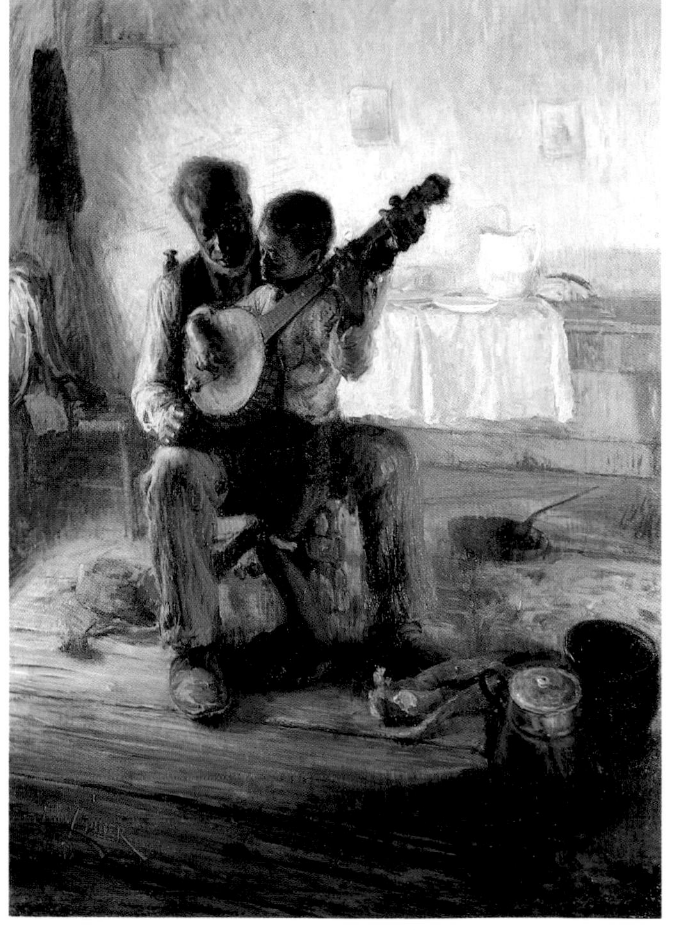

(ABOVE) 22-26. Thomas Eakins. *William Rush Carving His Allegorical Figure of the Schuylkill River.* 1877. Oil on canvas, 20⅛ x 26½" (51.1 x 67.3 cm). Philadelphia Museum of Art

GIVEN BY MRS. THOMAS EAKINS AND MISS MARY A. WILLIAMS

(LEFT) 22-27. Henry O. Tanner. *The Banjo Lesson.* c. 1893. Oil on canvas, 48 x 35" (121.9 x 88.9 cm). Hampton University Museum, Hampton, Virginia

TANNER. Thanks in large part to Eakins' enlightened attitude, Philadelphia became the leading center of minority artists in the United States. Eakins encouraged women and blacks to study art seriously at a time when professional careers were closed to them. African-Americans had no chance to enter the arts before Emancipation, and after the Civil War the situation improved only gradually. Henry O. Tanner (1859–1937), the first important black painter, studied with Eakins in the early 1880s. Tanner's masterpiece, *The Banjo Lesson* (fig. 22-27), painted after he moved permanently to Paris, bears Eakins' unmistakable influence. Avoiding the mawkishness of similar subjects by other American painters, the scene is rendered with the same direct realism as *William Rush Carving His Allegorical Figure of the Schuylkill River.*

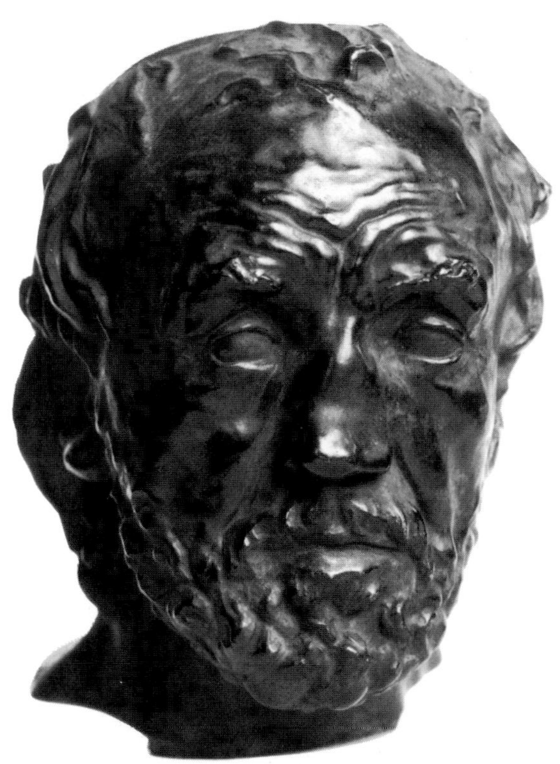

22-28. Auguste Rodin. *The Man with the Broken Nose.* 1864. Bronze, height $9\frac{1}{2}$" (24 cm). Rodin Museum, Philadelphia Museum of Art

SCULPTURE

Impressionism, it is often said, revitalized sculpture no less than painting. The statement is at once true and misleading. Auguste Rodin (1840–1917), the first sculptor of genius since Bernini, redefined sculpture during the same years that Manet and Monet redefined painting. However, he did not follow these artists' lead. How indeed could the effect of such pictures as *The Fifer* or *On the Bank of the Seine* be reproduced in three dimensions and without color?

RODIN. What Rodin did accomplish can be seen in the first piece he tried to exhibit at the Salon, *The Man with the Broken Nose* of 1864 (fig. 22-28). (It was rejected on the grounds that it conformed to no established category of sculpture.) Earlier, he had worked briefly under Carrier-Belleuse and Barye, whose influence may help to explain the vigorous surface (compare fig. 21-62). These welts and wrinkles produce, in polished bronze, an ever-changing pattern of reflections. But is this effect borrowed from Impressionist painting? Does Rodin actually dissolve three-dimensional form into flickering patches of light and dark? These fiercely exaggerated shapes pulsate with sculptural energy, and they retain this quality under whatever conditions the piece is viewed. Rodin did not work directly in bronze. He modeled in wax or clay. How, then, could he calculate in advance the reflections on the cast bronze surfaces of the casts made from these models?

His working method was intended not to capture elusive optical effects but to emphasize the process of "growth"—the miracle of dead matter coming to life in the artist's hands. As the color patch for Manet and Monet is the primary reality, so are the malleable lumps from which Rodin builds his forms. Conservative critics rejected *The Man with the Broken Nose* and Impressionist painting on the same grounds: it was "unfinished," a mere sketch.

The Man with the Broken Nose was Rodin's confession of aesthetic faith. Later on, he said of it: "That mask determined all my future work." The head, on which he had worked for about a year, represented a revolutionary insight. What matters in sculpture is not whether it is "finished" or "complete" but whether it conveys to the beholder the way it grew. *The Man with the Broken Nose* certainly does, and that is why Rodin thought of it as the cornerstone of his entire future oeuvre. He was the first to make of "unfinishedness" an aesthetic principle that governed both his handling of surfaces and the whole shape of the work. (*The Man with the Broken Nose* is not a bust but a head "broken off" at the neck.) By discovering the independence of the fragment, he rescued sculpture from mechanical naturalism just as Manet rescued painting from photographic realism.

Despite the sculptural revolution that Rodin announced with such daring at 24, he still believed that the sculptor's noblest task was to show the nude human form, although it could now be done in fragmentary form. He also continued to believe that the sculptor's purpose was to create "new classics"—that is, works free from the dictates of the patron and demanding to be judged on their own terms—without regard to traditional standards of beauty and ugliness. [See Primary Sources, no. 74, page 931.] When in 1880 he was at last given a major commission, the entrance of the École des Arts Décoratifs in Paris, Rodin developed an ambitious ensemble called *The Gates of Hell,* which, characteristically, he never finished. The symbolic program was inspired by Dante's *Inferno,* but it was equally indebted to Baudelaire's *The Flowers of Evil.* Its common denominator is a tragic view of the human condition: guilty passions, desire forever unfulfilled here and in the beyond, the vain hope of happiness. The perceptive critic Gustave Geffroy, writing of *The Gates of Hell* in 1889, defined their subject as the endless reenactment of the sufferings of Adam and Eve. Indeed, Rodin had tried in 1881 to persuade the government to let him flank *The Gates* with statues of the two.

The Gates of Hell served as the framework for countless smaller pieces that he eventually made into independent works. The most famous of these autonomous fragments is *The Thinker* (fig. 22-29). The figure was intended for the lintel of *The Gates,* where it could contemplate the panorama of despair below him. It recalls a statue by Carpeaux of another subject from *The Inferno,* Ugolino and his sons. The ancestry of *The Thinker* can be traced back much further, however. It descends, indirectly, from the first phase of Christian art. (The pensive man seated at the left in the Byzantine ivory in figure 8-54 reflects an Early Christian source.) It also includes the action-in-repose of Michelangelo's superhuman bodies (see figs. 13-15, 13-19, and 13-22), the tension in Puget's *Milo of Crotona* (see fig. 19-19, especially the feet), and the expressive dynamism of *The Man with the Broken Nose.*

Who is *The Thinker*? In the context of *The Gates of Hell,* he was originally conceived as a generalized image of Dante, the poet who in his mind's eye sees what goes on all around him. Once Rodin decided to detach him from *The Gates,* he became *The Poet-*

Thinker and finally just *The Thinker.* But what kind of thinker? Partly Adam, no doubt (though there is also a different Adam by Rodin, another "outgrowth" of *The Gates*), partly Prometheus, and partly the brute imprisoned by the passions of the flesh. Rodin wisely refrained from giving him a specific name, for the statue fits no preconceived identity. In this new image of a man, form and meaning are one, instead of being separated as in Carpeaux's *The Dance* (see fig. 21-64). Carpeaux's naked figures pretend to be nude, while *The Thinker,* like the nudes of Michelangelo, is no longer bound to the undressed model.

The Kiss (fig. 22-30), an over-lifesize group in marble, also evolved from *The Gates.* It was meant to be Dante's Paolo and Francesca, but Rodin rejected it as unsuitable. Evidently he realized that *The Kiss* shows the ill-fated pair succumbing to their illicit desire for each other here on earth, not as tortured souls in Hell. Knowing its original title helps us to understand a striking aspect of the group: passion reigned in by hesitancy, for the embrace is not yet complete. Less powerful than *The Thinker,* it exploits another kind of artful unfinishedness. Rodin had been impressed by the struggle of Michelangelo's *"Slaves"* against the remnants of the blocks that imprison them (compare fig. 13-16). *The Kiss* was planned from the start to include the mass of rough-hewn marble to which the lovers are attached and which thus becomes symbolic of their earthbound passion. The contrast of textures emphasizes the veiled, sensuous softness of the bodies.

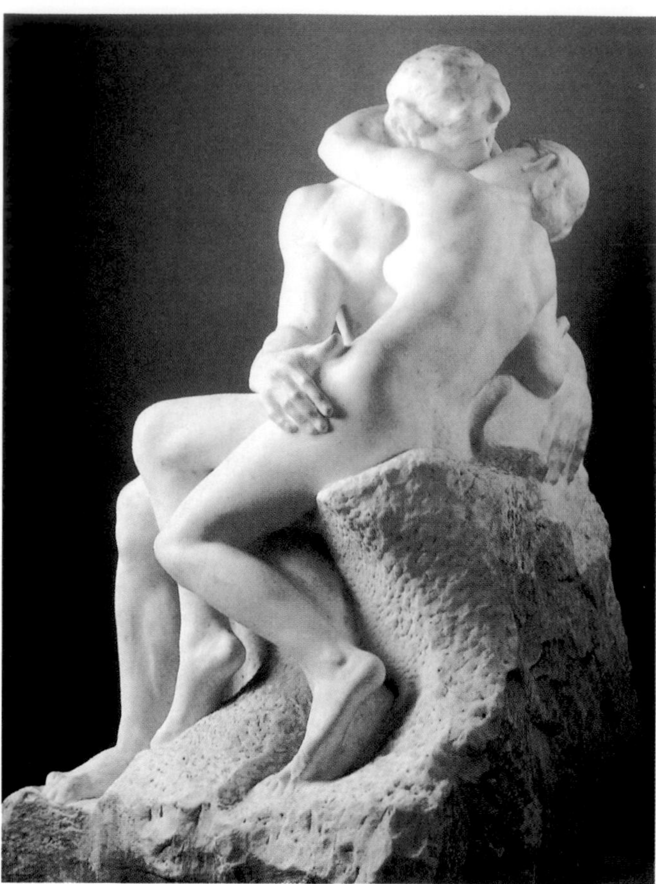

22-30. Auguste Rodin. *The Kiss.* 1886–98. Marble, over-lifesize. Rodin Museum, Paris

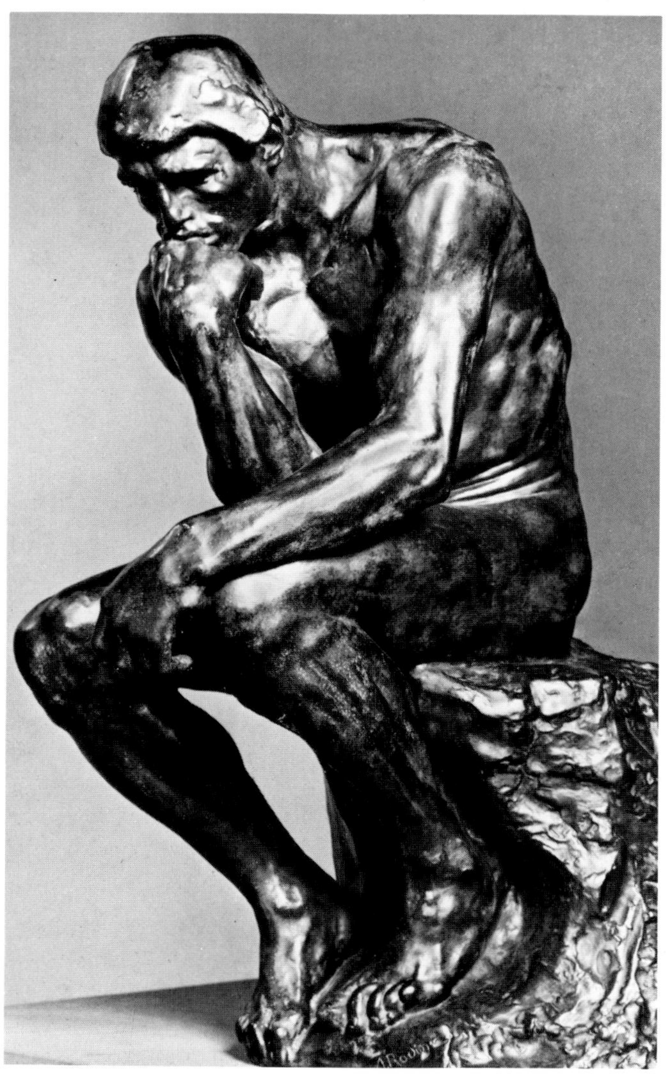

22-29. Auguste Rodin. *The Thinker.* 1879–89. Bronze, height 27½" (69.8 cm). The Metropolitan Museum of Art, New York

GIFT OF THOMAS F. RYAN, 1910

Rodin, however, was by instinct a modeler, not a carver like Michelangelo. His greatest works were intended to be cast in bronze. Even these, however, reveal their full strength only when we see them in plaster casts made directly from Rodin's clay originals. The *Monument to Balzac* was his last, as well as most daring and controversial, creation (fig. 22-31). The sculpture was rejected by the writers' association that had commissioned it and remained in plaster for many years. He had been asked at the insistence of the author Émile Zola to take over the project when the first sculptor died after producing only a sketch. He declared it to be "the sum of my whole life. . . . From the day of its conception, I was a changed man." Outward appearance did not pose a problem (Balzac's features were well known). But Rodin wanted far more than that. He was searching for a way to cast Balzac's whole personality into visible form, without the addition of allegorical figures, which were the usual props of monuments to genius. The final version gives no hint of the many alternative solutions he tried. (More than 40 have survived.) The element common to them all is that Balzac is standing in order to express the virile energy Rodin saw in his subject.

The final sculpture shows the writer clothed in a long dressing gown—described by his contemporaries as a "monk's robe"—

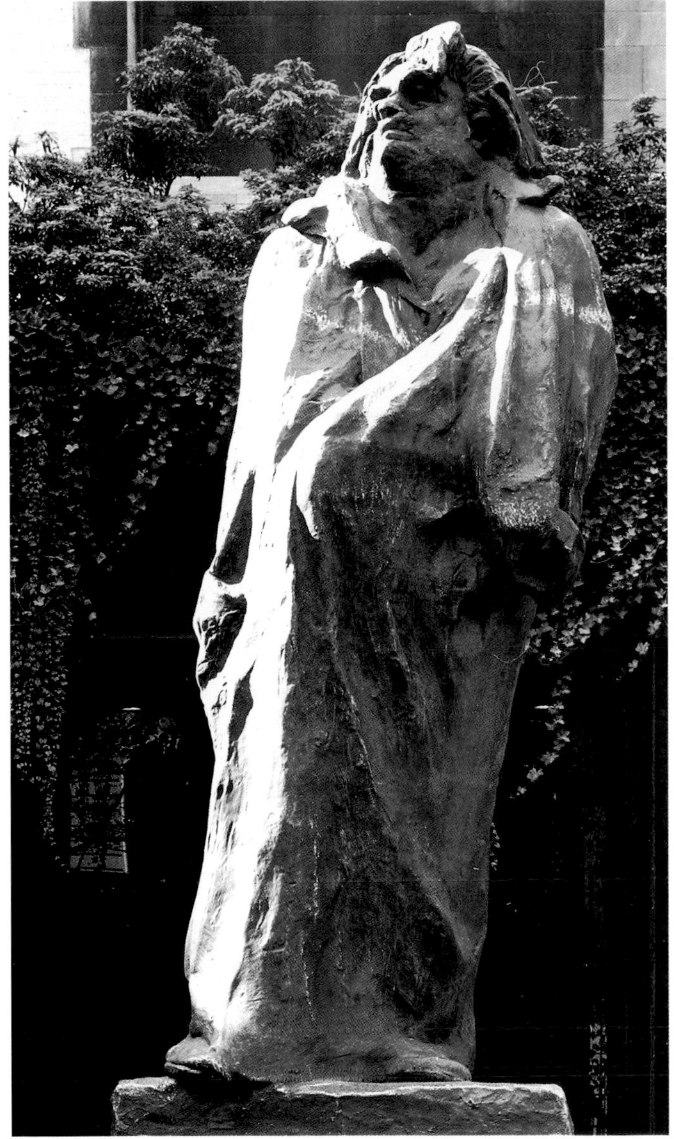

22-31. Auguste Rodin. *Monument to Balzac*. 1897–98. Bronze (cast 1954), height 9'3" (2.82 m). The Museum of Modern Art, New York
PRESENTED IN MEMORY OF CURT VALENTIN BY HIS FRIENDS

which he liked to wear while working at night. Here was a "timeless" costume that permitted Rodin to conceal and simplify the contours of the body. Seized by a sudden creative impulse, Balzac awakens in the middle of the night. Before he settles down to record his thoughts on paper, he hastily throws the robe over his shoulders without putting his arms through the sleeves. But, of course, Balzac is not about to write. He looms before us with the awesome power of a phantom, completely unaware of his surroundings. The entire figure leans backward to stress its isolation from the beholder.

The statue is larger than life, physically and spiritually: it has an overpowering presence. Like a huge monolith, the man of genius towers above the crowd. He shares "the sublime egotism of the gods" (as the Romantics put it). From a distance we see only the great bulk of the figure. The head thrusts upward—one is tempted to say erupts—with elemental force from the mass formed by the shroudlike cloak. When we are close enough to make out the features clearly, we sense beneath the arrogance an inner agony that stamps *Balzac* as the kin of *The Man with the Broken Nose*.

To this day, the *Balzac* remains a startling sight. Rodin had indeed reached the outer limits of his art, as he himself realized. The question remains, Why did he never have it cast in bronze, even though a wealthy private collector offered to pay for it? Its compact shape certainly lent itself to a marble statue, and it may be that he visualized the monument as one all along.

CLAUDEL. Rodin employed various assistants throughout his career. One of them, Camille Claudel (1864–1943), has been recognized in recent years as an important artist in her own right. Claudel entered Rodin's studio as a 19-year-old, and for the next decade she was his artistic collaborator and mistress. Her sculpture is strongly in her mentor's style, and the best ones might be mistaken for his. Much of her work is autobiographical. *Ripe Age*

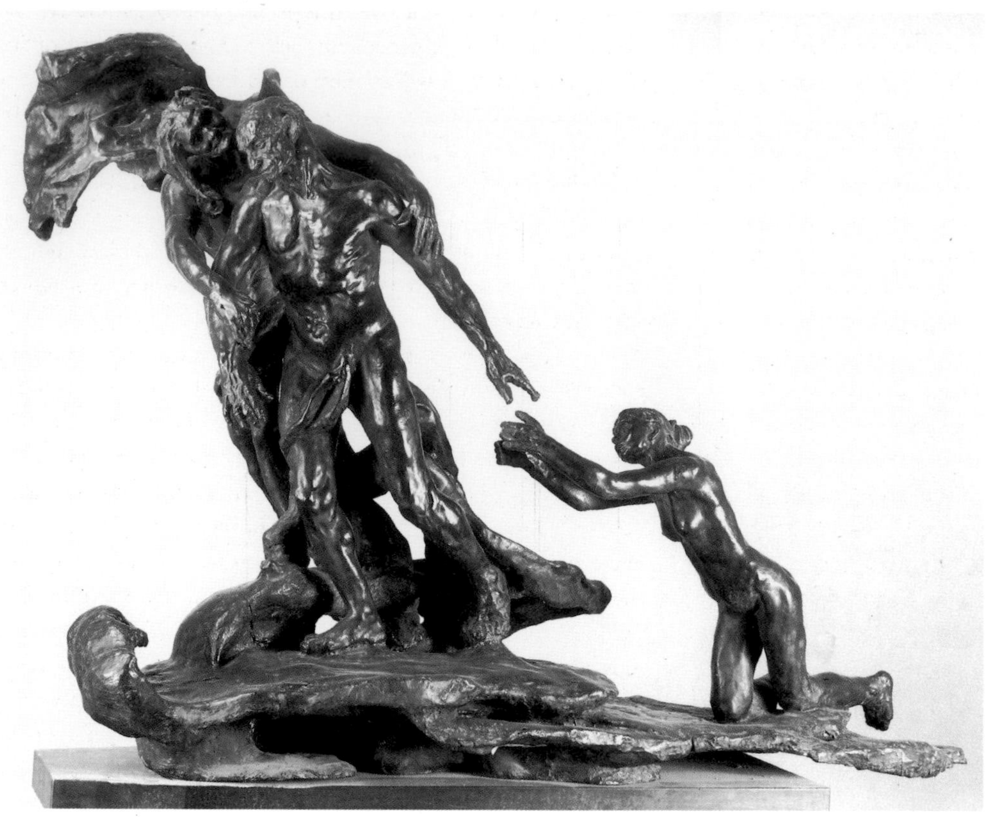

(LEFT) 22-32. Camille Claudel. *Ripe Age*. c. 1907. Bronze, 34½ x 20½" (87.6 x 21.9 cm). Musée d'Orsay, Paris

(BELOW) 22-33. Edgar Degas. *The Little Fourteen-Year-Old Dancer*. 1878–80. Bronze with gauze tutu and satin hair ribbon, height 38" (96.5 cm). Norton Simon Art Foundation, Pasadena, California

(fig. 22-32) depicts a grisly Rodin, whose features are clearly recognizable, being led away reluctantly by his longtime companion, Rose Beuret, whom Claudel sought to replace in his affections. Beuret is shown as a sinister, shrouded figure who first appears in Claudel's work as Clotho, one of the three Fates, ironically caught in the web of life she has woven. The nude figure is a self-portrait of Claudel, which likewise evolved from an earlier work, *Entreaty*.

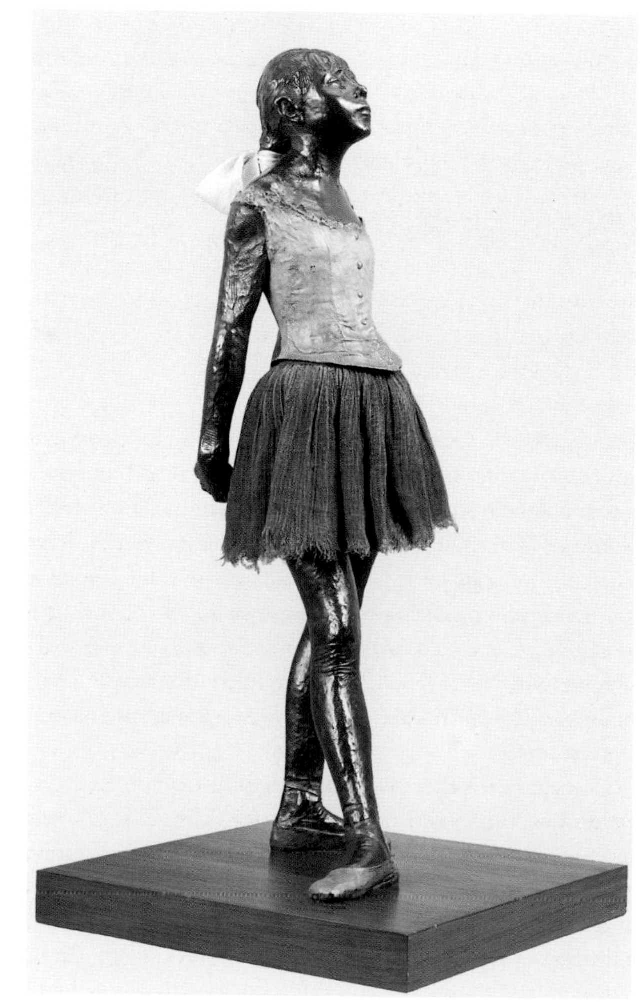

DEGAS. The fundamental difference between painting and modeling is illustrated by the fact that only Degas among the Impressionists produced sculpture. He made dozens of small-scale wax figurines that explore the same themes as his paintings and drawings. (Renoir's late sculptures were actually done by an assistant according to his instructions and thus do not qualify, since they are not by his own hand.) These are private works made for his own interest. Few of them were exhibited during the artist's lifetime, and none were cast until after his death in this century. During the 1870s there was a growing taste for casts made from artists' working models. It reflected the same appreciation for spontaneity and inspiration found in drawings and oil sketches, which had long appealed to collectors. This preference, which dates back to Rodin's ideal, Michelangelo, was essentially an outgrowth of the Romantic cult of originality, not of Impressionism. It was felt that quick, unfinished, even fragmentary works conveyed the force of the artist's vision more directly than any finished piece could. For the first time, sculptors felt emboldened to violate time-honored standards of naturalism and craftsmanship for statuettes and to leave the impress of their fingers on the soft material as they molded it. Nevertheless, when Degas showed the wax original of *The Little Fourteen-Year-Old Dancer* at the Impressionist exhibitions of 1880 and 1881, the public was scandalized by its lack of traditional finish and uncompromising observance of unvarnished truth, although the response from critics was less harsh. The sculpture, reproduced here in a posthumous cast (fig. 22-33), is nearly as rough in texture as the slightly smaller nude study from life on which it is based.

Instead of sculpting her costume, Degas used real cotton and silk, a revolutionary idea for the time but something the Romantics, with their insistent naturalism, must often have felt tempted to do. Degas was intrigued by the tension between the concrete surface and the abstract but powerfully directional forces beneath it. The ungainliness of the young adolescent's body is subtly emphasized by her pose, that of a dancer at "stage rest." In Degas' hands it becomes an extremely stressful one, so full of sharply contrasting angles that no dancer could maintain it for more than a few moments. Yet, rather than awkwardness, the statuette conveys a simple dignity and grace that are irresistible. The openness of the stance, with hands clasped behind the back and legs pointing in opposite directions, demands that we walk around the dancer to arrive at a complete image of it. As we view the sculpture from different angles, the surface provides a constantly shifting impression of light akin to that in Degas' numerous paintings and pastels of the ballet (compare fig. 22-13).

ARCHITECTURE

For more than a century, from the mid-eighteenth to the late nineteenth, architecture had been dominated by a succession of "revival styles" (see pages 695–701). This term, we will recall, does not imply that earlier forms were slavish copies; the best work of the time has both individuality and high distinction. Moreover, as we have seen, each successive phase of revivalism mirrored a different facet of Neoclassical and Romantic thought. Yet the architecture of the past, however freely interpreted, proved in the long run to be inadequate to the practical demands of the Industrial Age. (See box pages 764–65.) The problem became one not simply of how to utilize a host of new inventions in the most utilitarian of structures such as factories and warehouses but also how to apply them to stores, apartments, libraries, and other city buildings that formed the bulk of construction.

LABROUSTE. A famous early example is the Bibliothèque Ste.-Geneviève in Paris by Henri Labrouste (1801–1875). He entered the École des Beaux-Arts in 1819, the year it opened, and was quickly recognized for his brilliance. In 1824 he won the Prix de Rome and spent five years in Italy studying classical architecture on a government stipend. Labrouste's radical ideas established him among the leaders of the younger generation following his return during the turbulent year 1830, when the French government was overthrown. The Bibliothèque Ste.-Geneviève was his first important commission, and it made his reputation. The exterior (fig. 22-34) represents the early Beaux-Arts style at its finest. It conforms to the historicism prevalent at mid-century. The facade is drawn chiefly from Italian Renaissance banks, libraries, and churches (compare fig. 12-38), but the two-tiered elevation also looks back to Perrault's East Front of the Louvre (see fig. 19-10). To identify the building as a library, Labrouste inscribed the names of great writers around the facade. (The letters were originally painted red for legibility.) What led him to use this simple but ingenious device was first of all the library's location just behind Soufflot's church of Ste.-Geneviève, which, it will be recalled, had been secularized during the French Revolution and renamed the Panthéon (see fig. 21-16). Labrouste, in effect, has turned his library into a pantheon as well—but one dedicated to literary, not national, heroes. This facade has also been interpreted as an expression of Auguste Comte's positivism, in which the rows of names act like so many rows of newsprint, with embossed decoration, to denote the library as the setting for human activity.

The reading room (fig. 22-35), by contrast, recalls the nave of a French Gothic cathedral (compare fig. 11-17). The combination of the classical and the Gothic again pays homage to Soufflot, whose goal was to combine them. Barrel vaults supported by columns, though derived from Romanesque churches (see fig. 10-6), were introduced into Renaissance libraries by Michelozzo (see pages 400–01) and soon became a common feature of reading rooms. The type was revived by Boullée in a characteristically visionary project for a huge library in the Palais Mazarin surmounted by a coffered vault. There can be little doubt, in fact, that Labrouste's design is partly indebted to Boullée's. Barrel-vaulted libraries enjoyed renewed popularity in England and on the Continent during the 1830s (compare also fig. 21-19). To Labrouste, barrel vaults undoubtedly looked "Gothic." (The term "Romanesque" had not yet been invented.) They had the further advantage of acquiring Renaissance literary associations through the addition of the classical columns.

Labrouste's enthusiasm for the Gothic arose from his contact with the writer Victor Hugo, who consulted him on technical questions for his novel *Notre-Dame de Paris (The Hunchback of Notre-Dame)*. Hugo believed that architecture was originally a form of writing, which had reached its zenith in the Greek and Gothic eras. In a similar vein, Labrouste once wrote that the Temple of Hera at Paestum (see fig. 5-26) had been "covered with painted notices, serving as a book." Hugo, and most likely Labrouste himself, was strongly influenced by the Socialist followers of Saint-Simon (see page 636). They regarded Greek and Gothic architecture as ideal "organic" phases, to be succeeded by a third one expressing a new social philosophy, moral values, and religious beliefs. Such egalitarian ideas, further shaped by Charles Fourier, were appropriate to

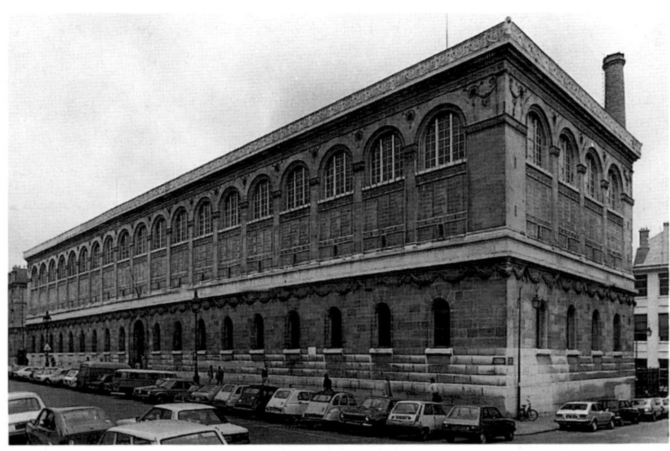

22-34. Henri Labrouste. Bibliothèque Ste.-Geneviève, Paris. 1843–50

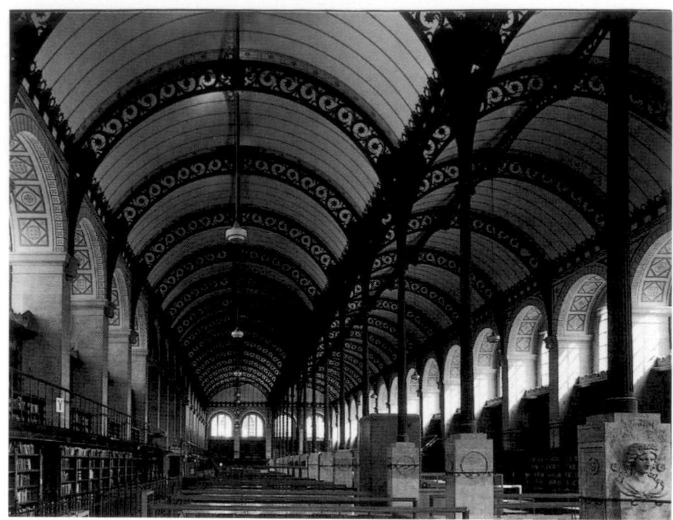

22-35. Henri Labrouste. Reading Room, Bibliothèque Ste.-Geneviève

the library, which was for general use by the public. But why did Labrouste choose cast-iron columns and arches? Cast iron was not necessary to provide support for the two barrel roofs—this could have been done using other materials—but to complete the building's symbolic program. With the Bibliothèque Ste.-Geneviève he announced that technology would provide the new tradition to succeed the Classical and the Gothic.

Labrouste boldly left the interior iron skeleton uncovered, rather than disguising it. His solution does not fully integrate the two systems but lets them coexist. The iron supports, shaped like Corinthian columns, are as slender as the new material permits. Their collective effect is that of a space-dividing screen that denies their structural importance. To make them appear weightier, Labrouste has placed them on tall pedestals of solid masonry, instead of directly on the floor. Aesthetically the arches presented greater difficulty, since there was no way to make them look as powerful as their masonry ancestors. Here Labrouste has gone to the other extreme, perforating them with lacy scrolls as if they were pure ornament, so that the vaulting has a fanciful and delicate quality. This daring architectural (as against merely structural) use of exposed iron members created a sensation and placed Labrouste in the forefront of French architecture, though it had already been tried 30 years earlier in England (see page 765). The reading room featured another innovation as well. It was the first of its kind to be lit by gas, making it usable at night. Although iron was later replaced by structural steel and ferroconcrete, Labrouste's wedding of historicism and engineering proved so satisfying that most libraries, railroad stations, and the like were indebted to the Bibliothèque Ste.-Geneviève, directly or indirectly, for the remainder of the century.

The authority of historic modes nevertheless had to be broken if the industrial era was to produce a truly contemporary style. It proved extraordinarily persistent, however. Labrouste, pioneer though he was of cast-iron construction, could not think of architectural supports as anything but columns having proper capitals and bases, rather than as metal rods or pipes (see pages 757–59). The "architecture of conspicuous display" practiced by Garnier (see pages 699–701) was divorced, even more than were the previous revival styles, from the needs of the present. It was only in structures that were not considered "architecture" at all that new building materials and techniques could be explored without these restrictions.

PAXTON. Within a year of the completion of the Bibliothèque Ste.-Geneviève, the Crystal Palace (fig. 22-36) was built in London. A pioneering achievement far bolder in conception than

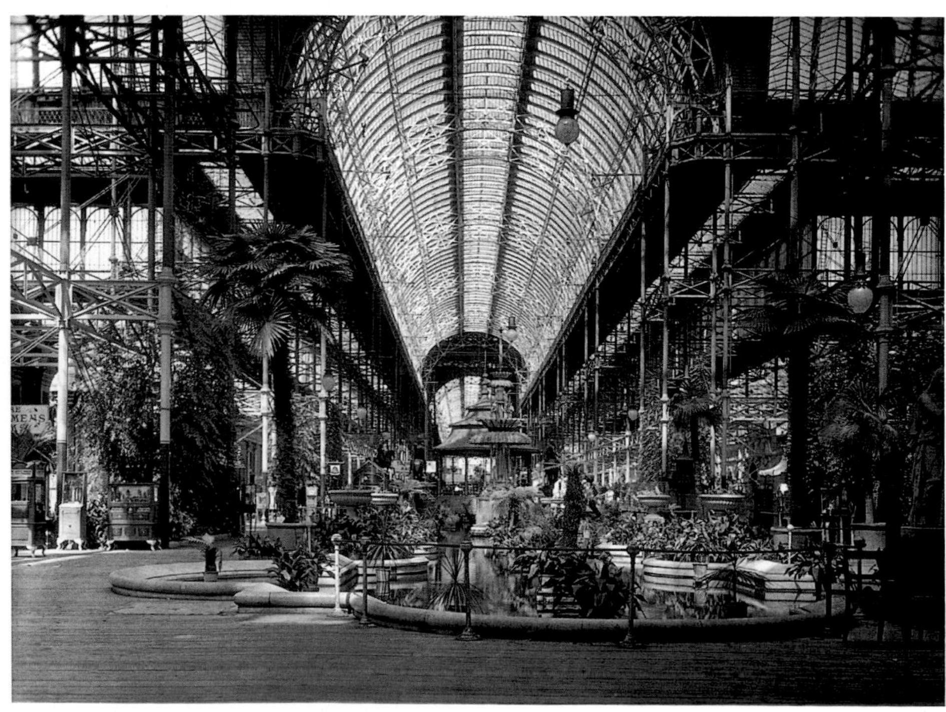

22-36. Sir Joseph Paxton. The Crystal Palace, London. 1851; reerected in Sydenham 1852; destroyed 1936

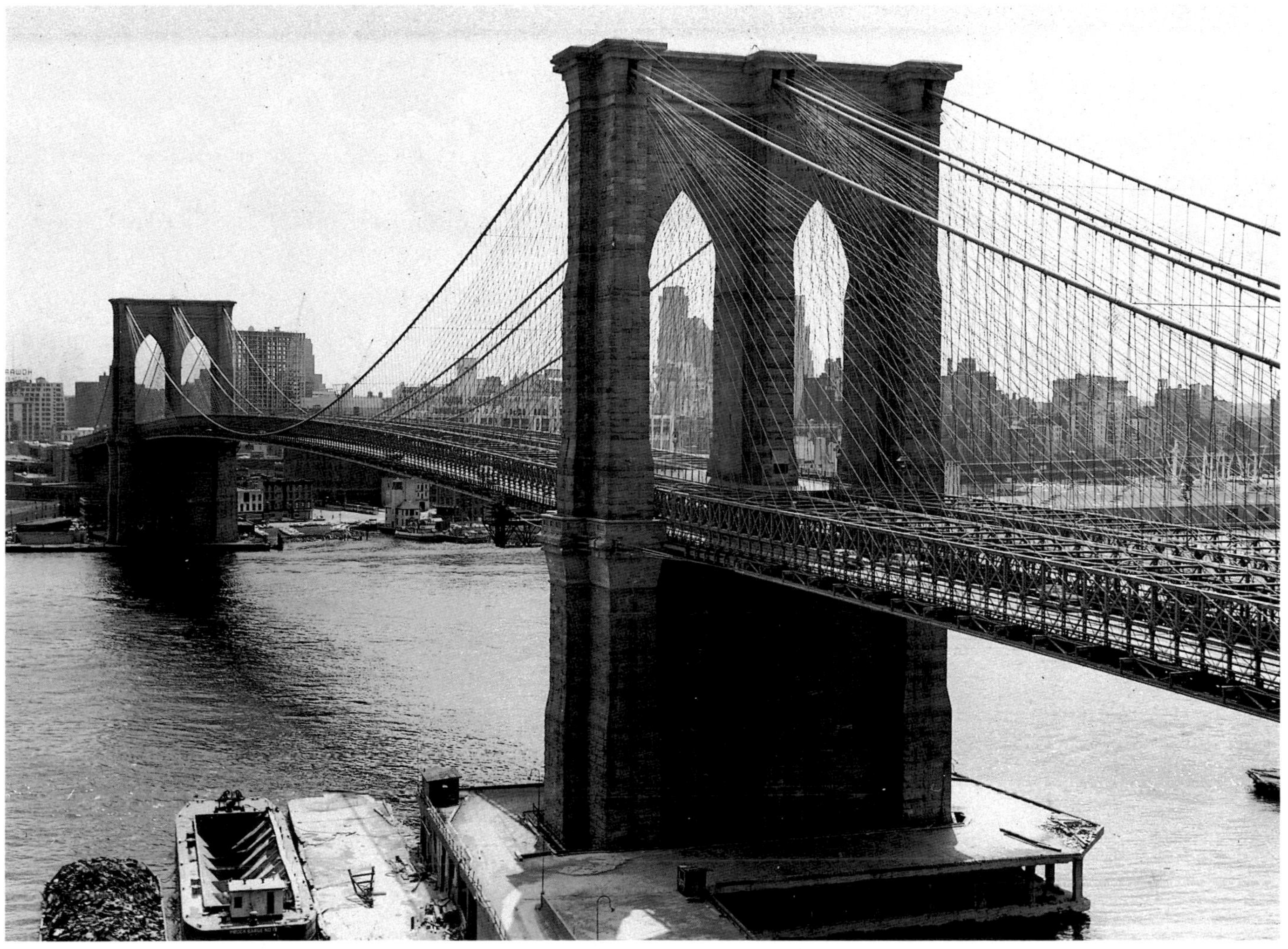

22-37. John and Washington Roebling. The Brooklyn Bridge, New York. 1867–83

Labrouste's library, the Crystal Palace was designed to house the first of the great international expositions that continue in our day. Its designer, Sir Joseph Paxton (1801–1865), was an engineer and builder of greenhouses. The Crystal Palace was, in fact, a gigantic greenhouse—so large that it enclosed some old trees growing on the site—with its iron skeleton freely on display. In exhibition buildings, ease and cost of construction were paramount, since they were not intended to stay up for very long. Paxton's design was such a success that it set off a wave of similar buildings for commercial purposes, such as public markets. However, the notion that products of engineering might have beauty, not just utility, made very slow headway, even though it found supporters from the mid-nineteenth century on. Hence most such buildings were adorned with decorations that follow the eclectic taste of the period.

ROEBLING. Only rarely could an engineering feat express the spirit of the times. One of the few to do so was the Brooklyn Bridge, built by John (1806–1869) and Washington (1837–1926) Roebling (fig. 22-37), which was referred to, appropriately enough, as America's Arch of Triumph. It remains one of the outstanding achievements of the Industrial Revolution. The massive towers nevertheless incorporate aspects of Egyptian, Roman, and Gothic architecture (note the pointed arches) to express a combination of eternal strength, civic pride, and soaring spirituality. Small wonder it was celebrated by poets and artists alike (see fig. 24-36).

REALISM IN MID-NINETEENTH-CENTURY THEATER

Realism was the dominant style in mid-nineteenth-century theater, as it was in painting. In part, theatrical Realism was a reflection of the pragmatic character of the Industrial Revolution. Its principal theorist was the French philosopher Auguste Comte (1798–1857), the founder of a system of thought known as Positivism, which called for a material explanation of truth based on objective observation and scientific analysis. As in art, Realism in drama covered a wide range of tendencies, from simple adherence to historic fact, social reality, or physical appearance to highly emotional treatments that have much in common with Romanticism.

The Realist playwright best known today is Alexandre Dumas the Younger (1824–1895), whose drama *Camille* (1852) was the first to treat the now-familiar theme of the prostitute with a heart of gold. While a modern audience might find Camille somewhat melodramatic, in its own time the play was considered an unflinching depiction of life at the fringes of Parisian society. In response to the criticism of *Camille* contained in *Olympe's Marriage* (1855) by Émile Augier (1820–1889), Dumas abandoned Realism three years later in *The Demi-Monde,* his first attempt at social and moral criticism. The most popular playwright of the period was Victorien Sardou (1831–1908), whose drama *La Tosca* (1887) was later turned into a well-known opera by the Italian composer Giacomo Puccini (see box page 747). This story of love, treachery, and revenge during the Italian struggle for independence was an important starring role for the great British tragic actress Sarah Bernhardt (1844–1923; see fig. 21-82). A gifted sculptor as well, Bernhardt specialized in tragic heroines such as Camille and Adrienne Lecouvreur. Her only rival was the English actress Ellen Terry (1847–1928), who came from a long line of actors. She was the leading lady to Henry Irving (1838–1905), by far the most important actor and manager in England during the later nineteenth century, who commissioned Edward Burne-Jones (see page 719) and other prominent artists to design stage sets for him. Irving was knighted in 1895, while Terry was made a Dame Commander of the British Empire only in 1925.

Germany produced few major dramatists during the third quarter of the century. Instead, it was content to rely on the plays of Shakespeare, Goethe, and Schiller and on translations of Sardou and the younger Dumas. Vienna became the main theater center under Heinrich Laube (1806–1884), a former member of Young Germany, and Franz Dingelstedt (1814–1881), who had produced Christian Friedrich Hebbel's (1813–1863) trilogy *The Nibelungen* in 1861 at Weimar. A fascination with old Germanic legends that was fueled by growing nationalism helped to make historical accuracy the goal of German theater. The chief contributors to theater in Germany at this time were Duke George II of Saxe-Meiningen (1826–1914) and his wife, the actress Helene Franz (1839–1923), who elevated the quality of acting through careful preparation and emphasis on ensemble. Attention was also paid to costumes and scenery.

Russian authors of the time had a particular affinity for psychological Realism. The first Russian professional playwright, Aleksandr Ostrovsky (1823–1886), had an abiding interest in characters and their relationships. However, the major plays were written by the great novelists of the era. Ivan Turgenev (1818–1883) wrote a number of dramas that are remarkable for their portrayal of their characters' inner lives and complex relationships. Leo Tolstoy (1828–1910) also tried his hand at plays, notably *The Power of Darkness,* which was produced in 1895, some 30 years after it was written. Aleksei Tolstoy (1817–1875), a distant relative, established himself as the leading Realist with a strong interest in the history of Russia. *The Death of Ivan the Terrible* and *Tsar Boris,* both of 1870, were based on the historical research of Nikolai Karamzin (1766–1826), which did much to stimulate Russian nationalism.

In the United States, the favorite dramas before the Civil War were various adaptations of the novel *Uncle Tom's Cabin* by Harriet Beecher Stowe (1811–1896). This portrayal of the life of slaves on southern plantations helped fuel abolitionist sentiment. The years before the war were also a time of great actors. The Englishman William Burton (1804–1860) headed the finest company in New York, the undisputed theater capital of America, although the Boston Museum also staged many plays after 1850. Burton had been preceded by another English performer, Junius Booth (1796–1852), whose son Edwin Booth (1833–1893) became the greatest actor America has ever produced. Unfortunately, the family remains notorious for another son, John Wilkes Booth (1838–1865), the assassin of President Abraham Lincoln. The most popular form of theater was the burlesque extravaganza. Over time it came to appeal mainly to men by featuring beautiful women, although striptease was added only in 1929. Vaudeville, a more genteel form of family entertainment that reached its height between 1890 and 1930, was defined largely by Tony Pastor (1837–1908).

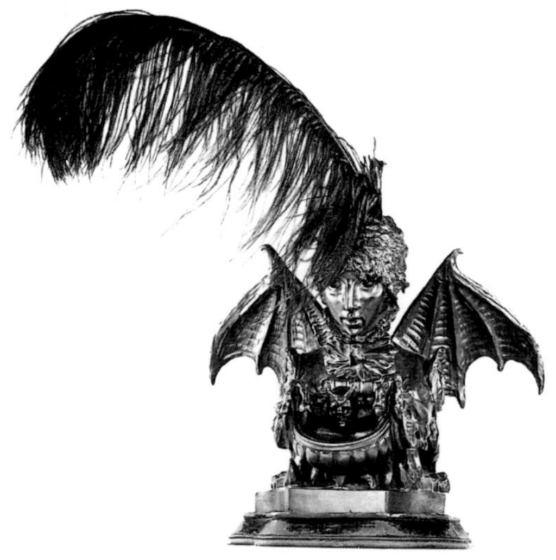

Sarah Bernhardt. *Fantastic Inkwell, Self-Portrait as a Sphinx.* After 1880. Patinated bronze. Height: 12½" (31.8 cm); base: 7½" (19.1 cm). Museum of Fine Arts, Boston

HELEN AND ALICE COLBURN FUND

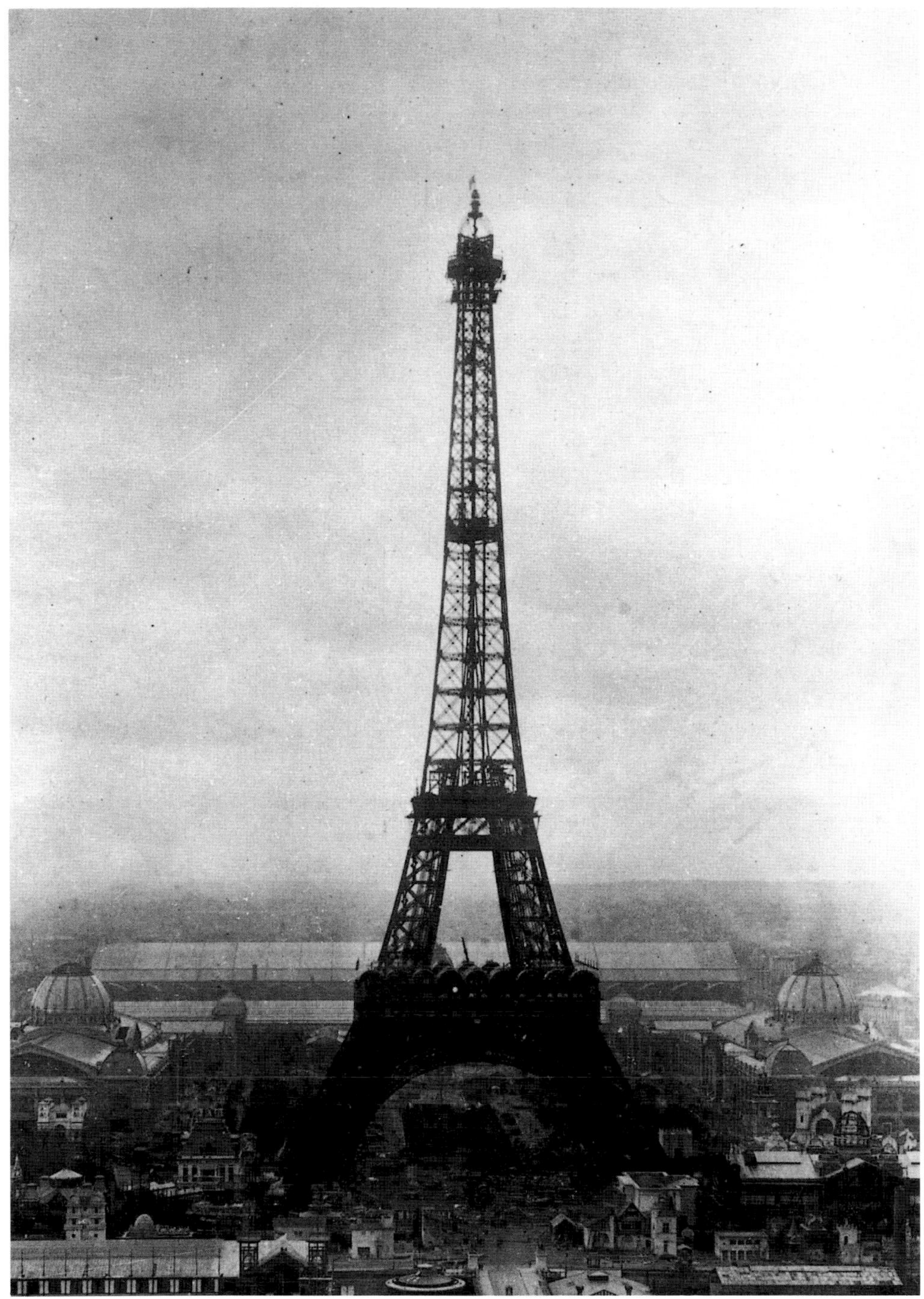

22-38. Gustave Eiffel. The Eiffel Tower, Paris. 1887–89

EIFFEL. What was needed for products of engineering to be accepted as architecture was a structure that would capture the world's imagination through its bold conception. The breakthrough came with the Eiffel Tower, named after its designer, Gustave Eiffel (1832–1923). As shown in a contemporary photograph (fig. 22-38), it was erected at the entrance to the Paris World's Fair of 1889, where it, too, served as a triumphal arch of science and industry. It has become such a visual cliché beloved of tourists—much like the *Statue of Liberty,* which also involved Eiffel (see fig. 21-65)—that we can hardly appreciate what a revolutionary impact it had at the time. [See Primary Sources, no. 75, page 932.] The tower, with its frankly technological aesthetic, so dominates the city's skyline even now that it provoked a storm of protest by the leading intellectuals of the day. Eiffel used the same principles of structural engineering that he had already applied successfully to bridges. Yet it is so novel in appearance and so daring in construction that nothing like it has ever been built, before or since.

The Eiffel Tower owed much of its success to the fact that for a small sum anyone could take its elevators to see a view of Paris that was previously reserved for the privileged few able to afford hot-air balloon rides (see fig. 21-83). It thus helped to define a distinctive feature of modern architecture, one that it shares with

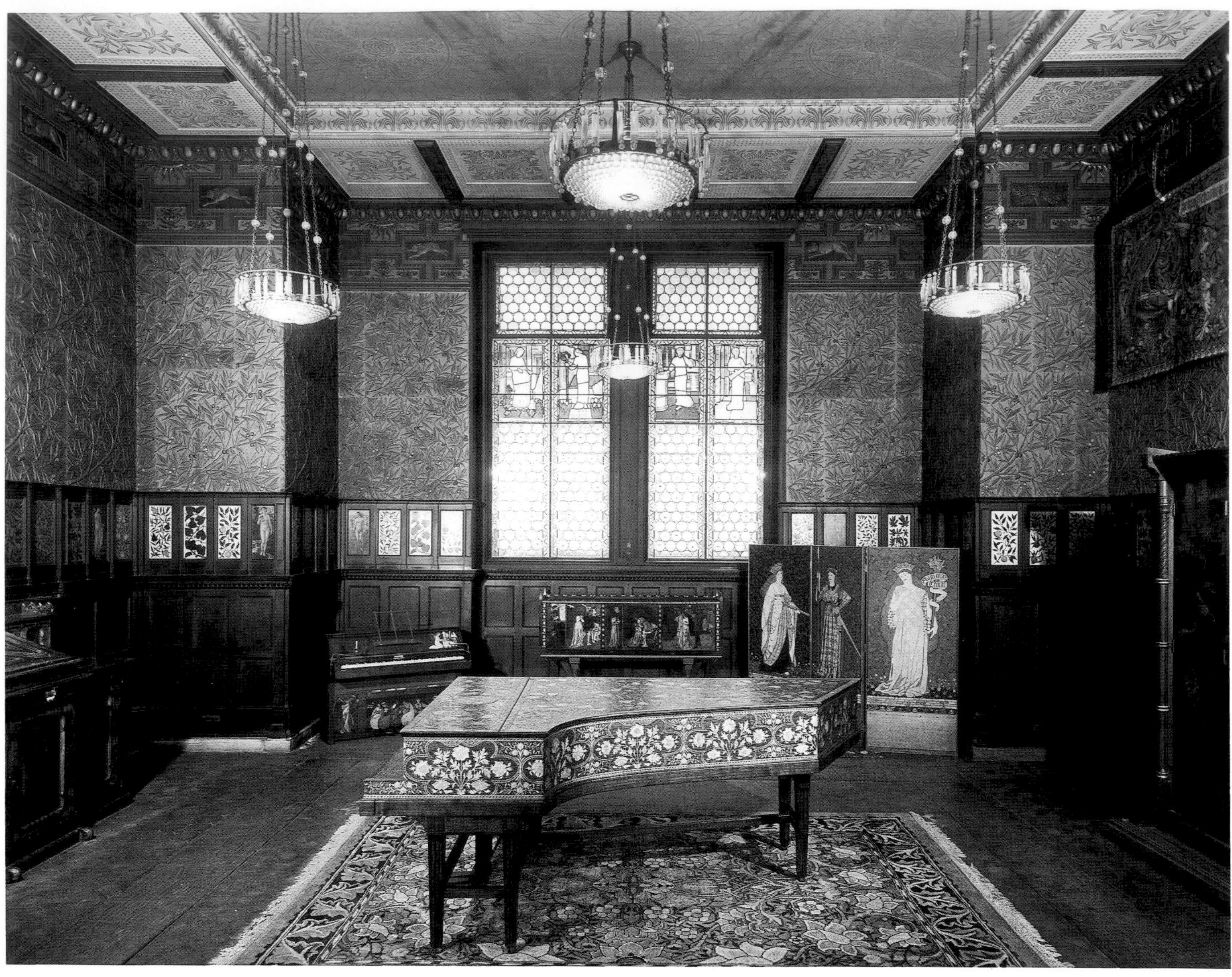

22-39. William Morris (Morris & Co.). Green Dining Room. 1867. Victoria & Albert Museum, London

modern technology as a whole: it acts on large masses of people without regard to social or economic class. Although this capacity, which was shared only by the largest churches and public buildings of the past, has also served the aims of political extremists at both ends of the spectrum, modern architecture has tended by its very nature to function as a vehicle of democracy. We can readily understand, then, why the Eiffel Tower quickly became a popular symbol of Paris itself. It could do so, however, precisely because it serves no practical purpose whatsoever.

DECORATIVE ARTS

MORRIS. The decorative arts played an unusually important role in England during the second half of the nineteenth century. William Morris (1834–1896), the early leader in what came to be known as the Arts and Crafts Movement, started out with William Holman Hunt as a student of the Pre-Raphaelite painter Rossetti but soon shifted his interest to "art for use"—domestic architecture and interior decoration such as furniture, tapestries, and wallpapers. He wanted to displace the shoddy products of the Machine Age by reviving the handicrafts of the preindustrial past, an art "made by the people, and for the people, as a happiness to the maker and the user."

Morris was an apostle of simplicity. Architecture and furniture ought to be designed in accordance with the nature of their materials and working processes; surface decoration must be flat rather than illusionistic. His interiors (fig. 22-39) are total environments that create an effect of quiet intimacy. Despite Morris' self-proclaimed championship of the medieval tradition, he never imitated its forms directly but tried to capture its spirit. His achievement was to invent the first original system of ornament since the Rococo.

Through the many enterprises he sponsored, as well as his skill as a writer and publicist, Morris became a tastemaker without equal in his day. Toward the end of the century, his influence had spread throughout Europe and America. Nor was he content to reform the arts of design alone. He saw them, rather, as a lever by which to reform modern society as a whole. As a result, he played an important part in the early history of Fabian socialism (the gradualist kind invented in England as an alternative to the revolutionary socialism of the Continent).

WHISTLER. In the 1860s the reform ideas of William Morris began to affect domestic architecture and decoration. The boldest innovations, however, came not from members of his immediate circle but from Whistler and his followers. Whistler himself created one of the masterpieces of nineteenth-century design: the Peacock Room (fig. 22-40), which housed the blue-and-white porcelain collection of his patron Frederick Leyland. What began as a modest project to remedy the previous decorations soon grew into an ambitious overhaul by Whistler, who spared no expense to achieve his lavish scheme while Leyland was away. The results were inevitably mixed, as the room embodied fundamentally the same sensibility as Morris' Green Dining Room (see fig. 22-39). The fanciful decorations, with gilt everywhere, nevertheless exemplify the Aesthetic Movement, which sought refuge from the tawdry reality of the Industrial Revolution by retreating into a realm of pure beauty. The peacock motif, which reflects Whistler's fascination with Japanese art, seems a singularly appropriate symbol of his aestheticism, which regarded beauty as an end in itself, without regard to social responsibility.

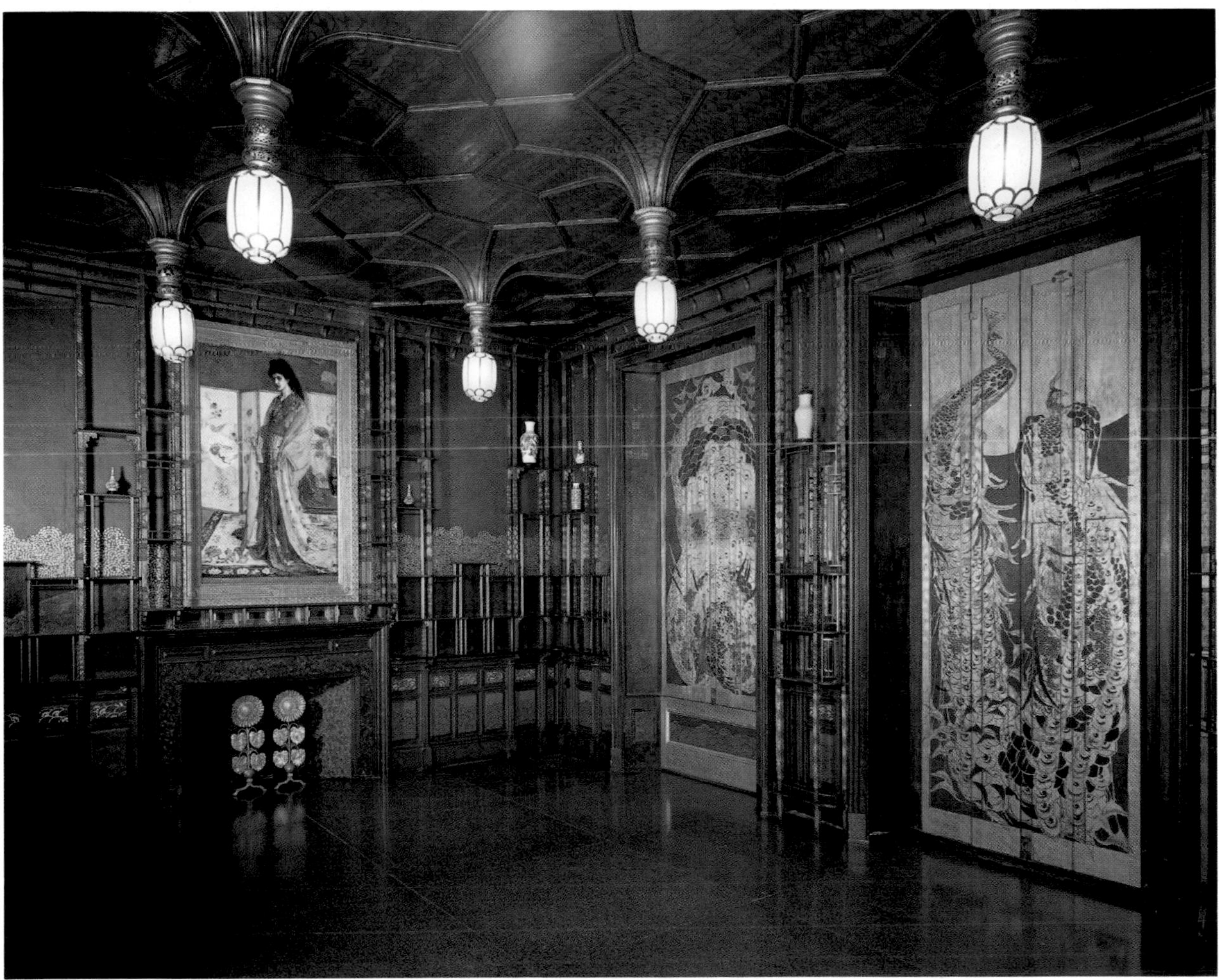

22-40. James Abbott McNeill Whistler. *Harmony in Blue and Gold: The Peacock Room.* 1876–77. Oil color and gold on leather and wood. The Freer Gallery of Art, Smithsonian Institution, Washington, D.C.

CHAPTER TWENTY-THREE

Post-Impressionism, Symbolism, and Art Nouveau

PAINTING

Post-Impressionism

In 1882, just before his death, Édouard Manet was made a knight of the Legion of Honor by the French government. This event marks the turn of the tide. Impressionism had gained wide acceptance among artists and the public, but by the same token it was no longer a pioneering movement. When the Impressionists held their last group show four years later, the future already belonged to the "Post-Impressionists." Taken literally, this colorless label applies to all painters of significance in the 1880s and 1890s. In a more specific sense, it designates a group of artists who passed through an Impressionist phase but became dissatisfied with the limitations of the style and pursued a variety of directions. Because they did not share one common goal, we have no more descriptive term for them than Post-Impressionists. In any event, they were not "anti-Impressionists." Far from trying to undo the effects of the "Manet Revolution," they wanted to carry it further. Thus Post-Impressionism is just a later stage, though a very important one, of the development that had begun in the 1860s with such pictures as Manet's *Luncheon on the Grass.*

CÉZANNE. Paul Cézanne (1839–1906), the oldest of the Post-Impressionists, was born in Aix-en-Provence, near the Mediterranean coast. There he formed a close friendship with the writer Émile Zola, later a champion of the Impressionists. A man of intensely emotional temperament, Cézanne came to Paris in 1861 filled with enthusiasm for the Romantics. Delacroix was his first love among painters, and he never lost his admiration for him. Cézanne, however, quickly grasped the nature of the "Manet Revolution." He also completely transformed it. *A Modern Olympia* (fig. 23-1) was painted in response to a work by Manet entitled *Olympia* featuring a prostitute whose frank nakedness scandalized the art world. As in *Luncheon on the Grass* (see fig. 22-3), executed by Manet the same year, Cézanne's nude shares the company of a man wearing contemporary clothing; his features are plainly those of Cézanne himself (see fig. 23-2). Like many of his early works, *A Modern Olympia* is sexually charged, albeit in a curiously ambivalent way that suggests why he never formed a lasting relationship. While the setting is a boudoir, the picture is one of the first to treat what was to become one of the favorite themes in modern art: the artist and his model, a subject often full of erotic overtones. The artist sits in silent adoration of the young woman, whose sumptuous surroundings suggest that she is indeed a modern goddess. Yet the relationship between the two figures is strange indeed. Although separated in space, they are placed so near each other on the picture plane that she seems almost to recoil from his dark presence! Equally disturbing is the brushwork, which communicates the turbulent passion repressed by the seemingly impassive artist in the picture. Never before have we seen such brusqueness, not even in Cézanne's ideal, Delacroix. The subtitle *The Pasha* pays homage to the Orientalism of Delacroix, whose *The Death of Sardanapalus* (see fig. 21-33) nevertheless has a sensuousness absent from Cézanne's *Olympia.* This artist-as-potentate can admire, but not possess, his "harem girl."

After passing through this Neo-Baroque phase, Cézanne began to paint bright outdoor scenes with Pissarro, but he never shared his fellow Impressionists' interest in "slice-of-life" subjects, in movement and change. About 1879, when he painted the *Self-Portrait* in figure 23-2, he had decided "to make of Impressionism something solid and durable, like the art of the museums." His Romantic impulsiveness of the 1860s gave way to a patient, disciplined search for harmony of form and color. Every brushstroke is like a building block, firmly placed within the pictorial architecture, which creates a subtle balance of "2-D" and "3-D." (Note how the pattern of wallpaper in the background frames the rounded shape of the head.) The colors, too, are deliberately con-

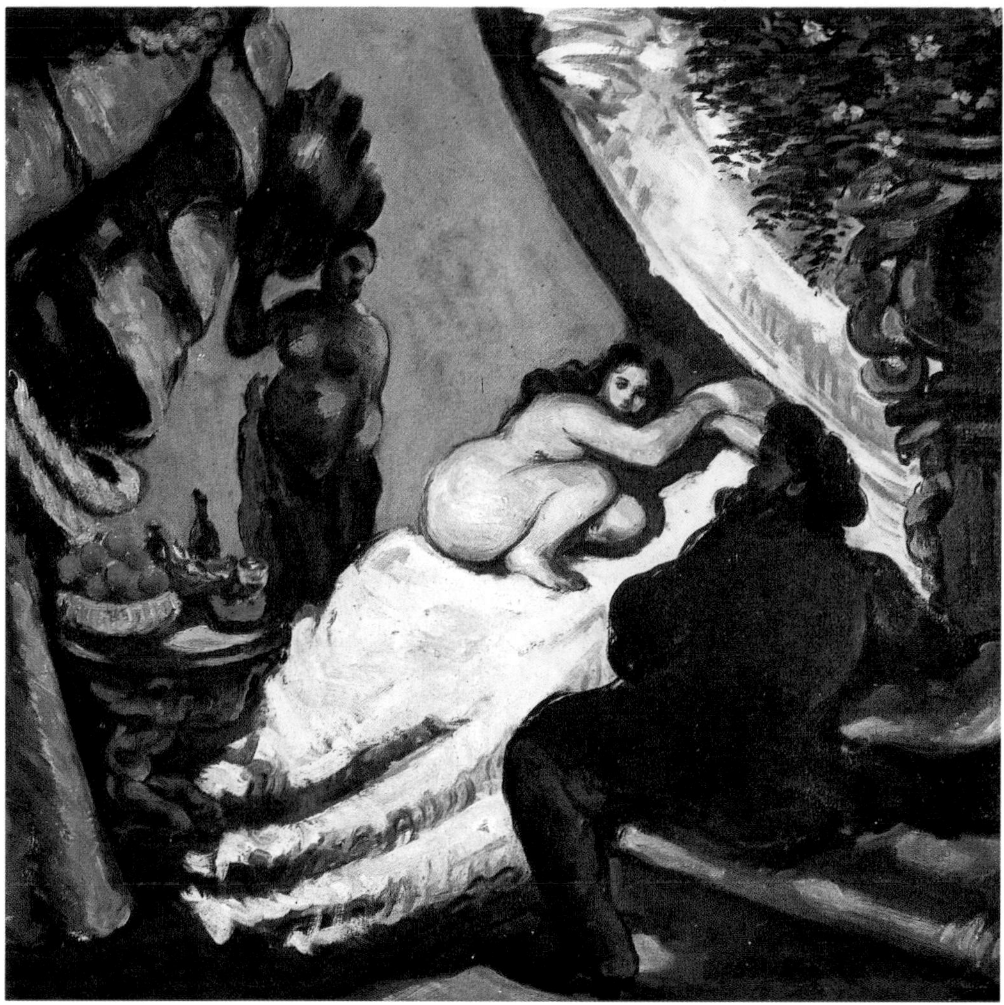

23-1. Paul Cézanne. *A Modern Olympia (The Pasha)*. Early 1870s. Oil on canvas, 22 x 21⅝" (56 x 55 cm). Private collection

trolled so as to produce "chords" of warm and cool tones that echo throughout the canvas.

In Cézanne's still lifes, such as *Still Life with Apples in a Bowl* (fig. 23-3), this quest for the "solid and durable" can be seen even more clearly. Not since Chardin have simple everyday objects assumed such importance in a painter's eye. The ornamental backdrop is again integrated with the three-dimensional shapes, and the brushstrokes have a rhythmic pattern that gives the canvas its shimmering texture. We also notice aspects of Cézanne's mature style that are more evident here than in the *Self-Portrait* and may puzzle us at first. The forms are deliberately simplified and outlined with dark contours. Also the perspective is "incorrect," for both the fruit bowl and the horizontal surfaces seem to tilt upward. The longer we study the picture, the more we realize the rightness of these apparently arbitrary distortions. When Cézanne took these liberties with reality, his purpose was to uncover the permanent qualities beneath the accidents of appearance. All forms in nature, he believed, were based on the cone, the sphere, and the cylinder. [See Primary Sources, no. 76, page 932.] This order underlying reality was the true subject of his pictures, but he had to reinterpret it to fit the separate, closed world of the canvas.

To apply this method to landscape became the greatest challenge of Cézanne's career. From 1882 on, he lived in isolation near his hometown of Aix-en-Provence, exploring its surroundings as Claude Lorraine and Camille Corot had explored the Roman countryside. One feature, the distinctive shape of a mountain called Mont Ste.-Victoire, seemed to obsess him. Its craggy profile looming against the blue Mediterranean sky appears in a long series of compositions, such as the monumental late work in figure 23-4. There are no hints of human presence here—houses and roads would only disturb the lonely grandeur of the view. Above the wall of rocky cliffs that bar our way like a chain of fortifications, the mountain rises in triumphant clarity, infinitely remote yet as solid as the shapes in the foreground. For all its architectural stability, the scene is alive with movement. But the forces at work here have been brought into balance, subdued by the greater power of the artist's will. This disciplined energy, distilled from the trials of a stormy youth, gives Cézanne's mature style its enduring strength.

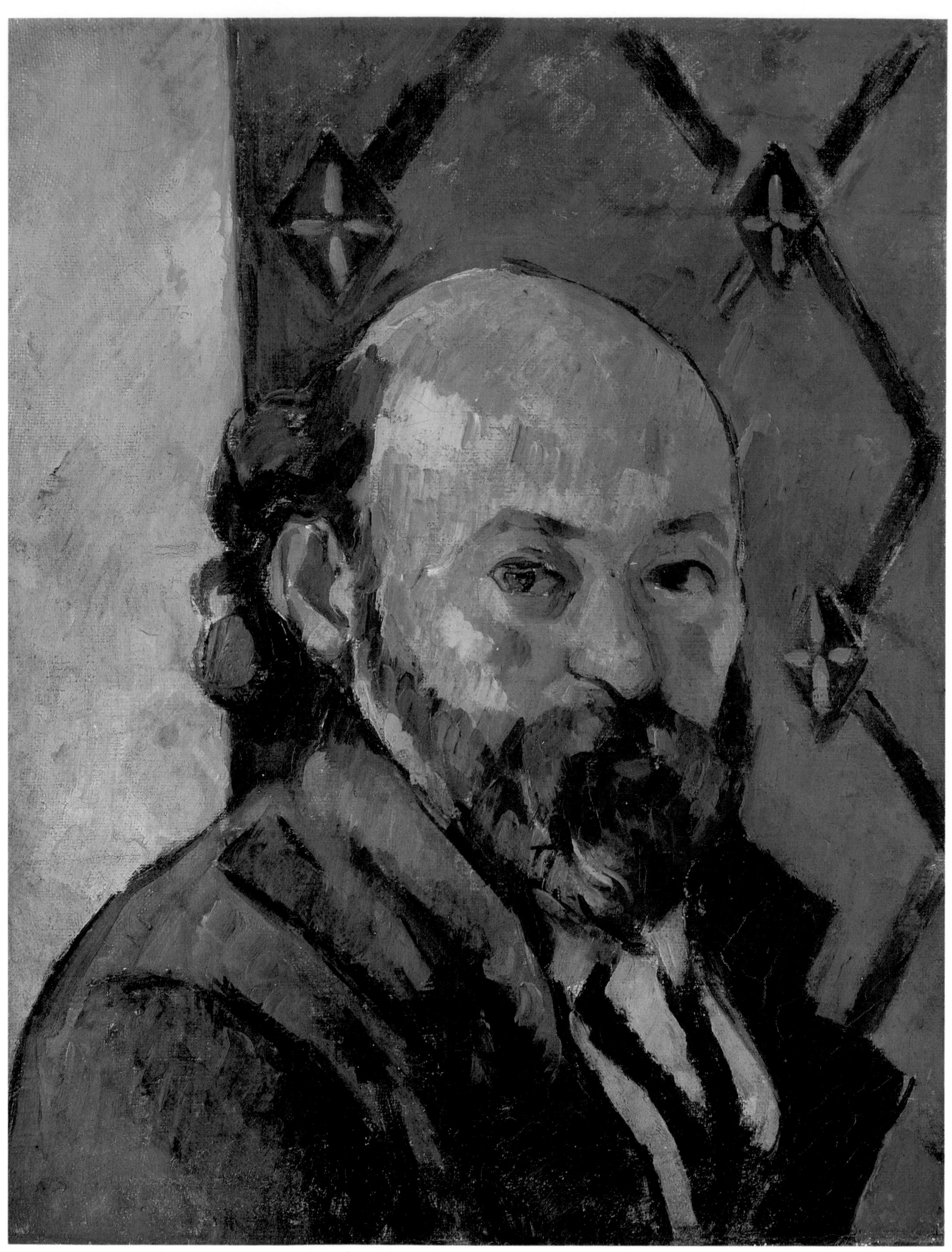

23-2. Paul Cézanne. *Self-Portrait.* c. 1879. Oil on canvas, 13¾ x 10⅝" (35 x 27 cm). The Tate Gallery, London

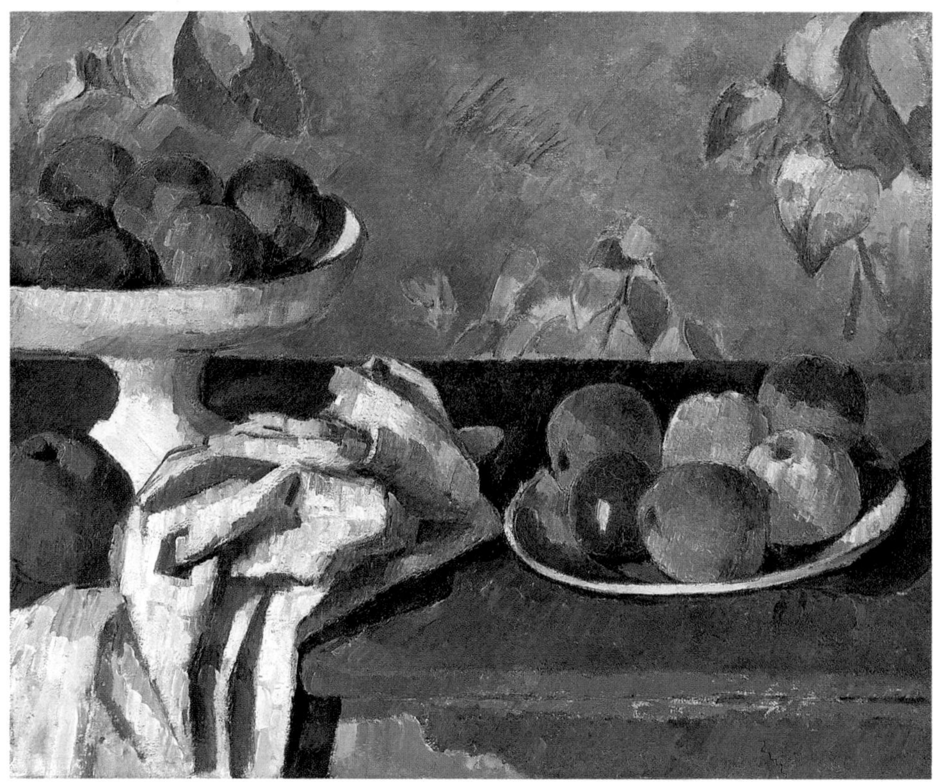

23-3. Paul Cézanne. *Still Life with Apples in a Bowl*. 1879–82. Oil on canvas, 17⅛ x 21¼" (43.5 x 54 cm). Ny Carlsberg Glyptotek, Copenhagen, Denmark

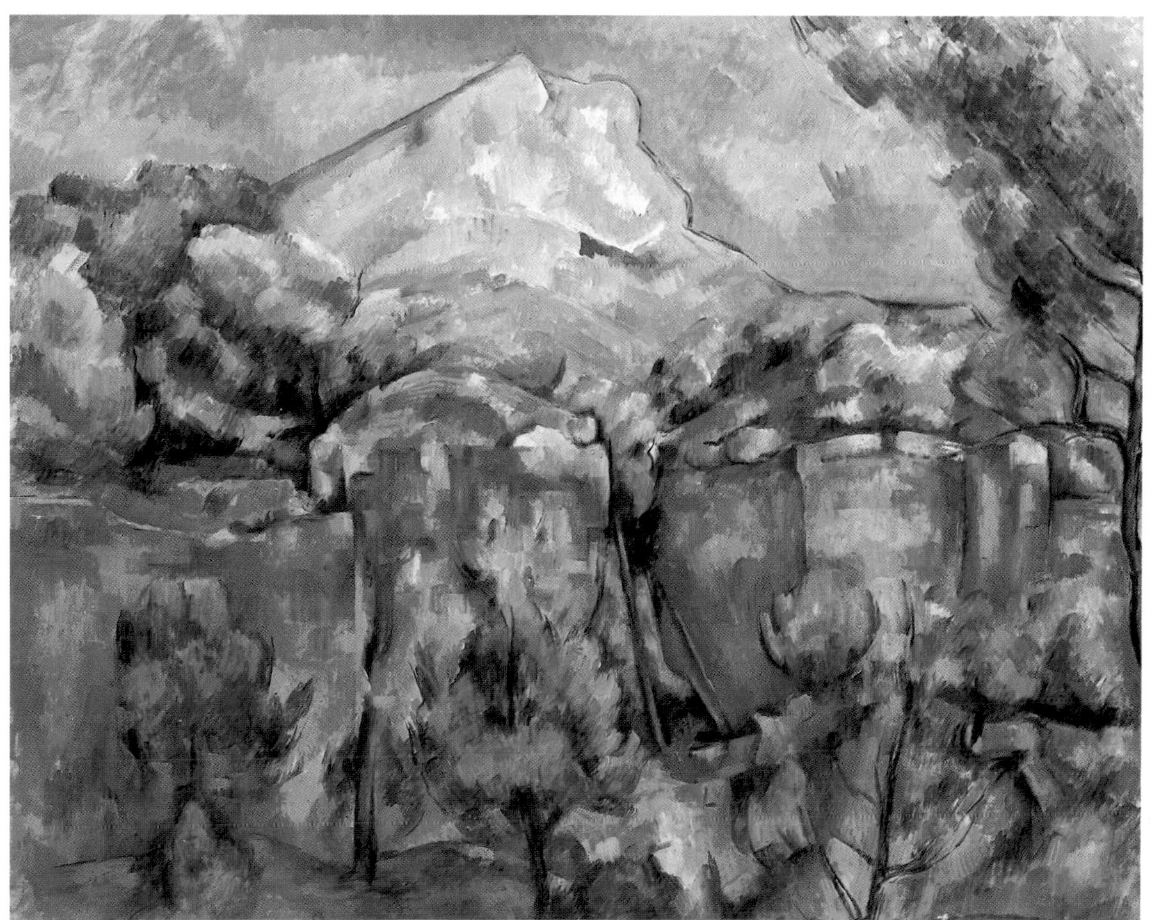

23-4. Paul Cézanne. *Mont Ste.-Victoire Seen from Bibemus Quarry*. c. 1897–1900. Oil on canvas, 25½ x 31½" (65.1 x 80 cm). The Baltimore Museum of Art

THE CONE COLLECTION, FORMED BY DR. CLARIBEL CONE AND MISS ETTA CONE OF BALTIMORE, MARYLAND

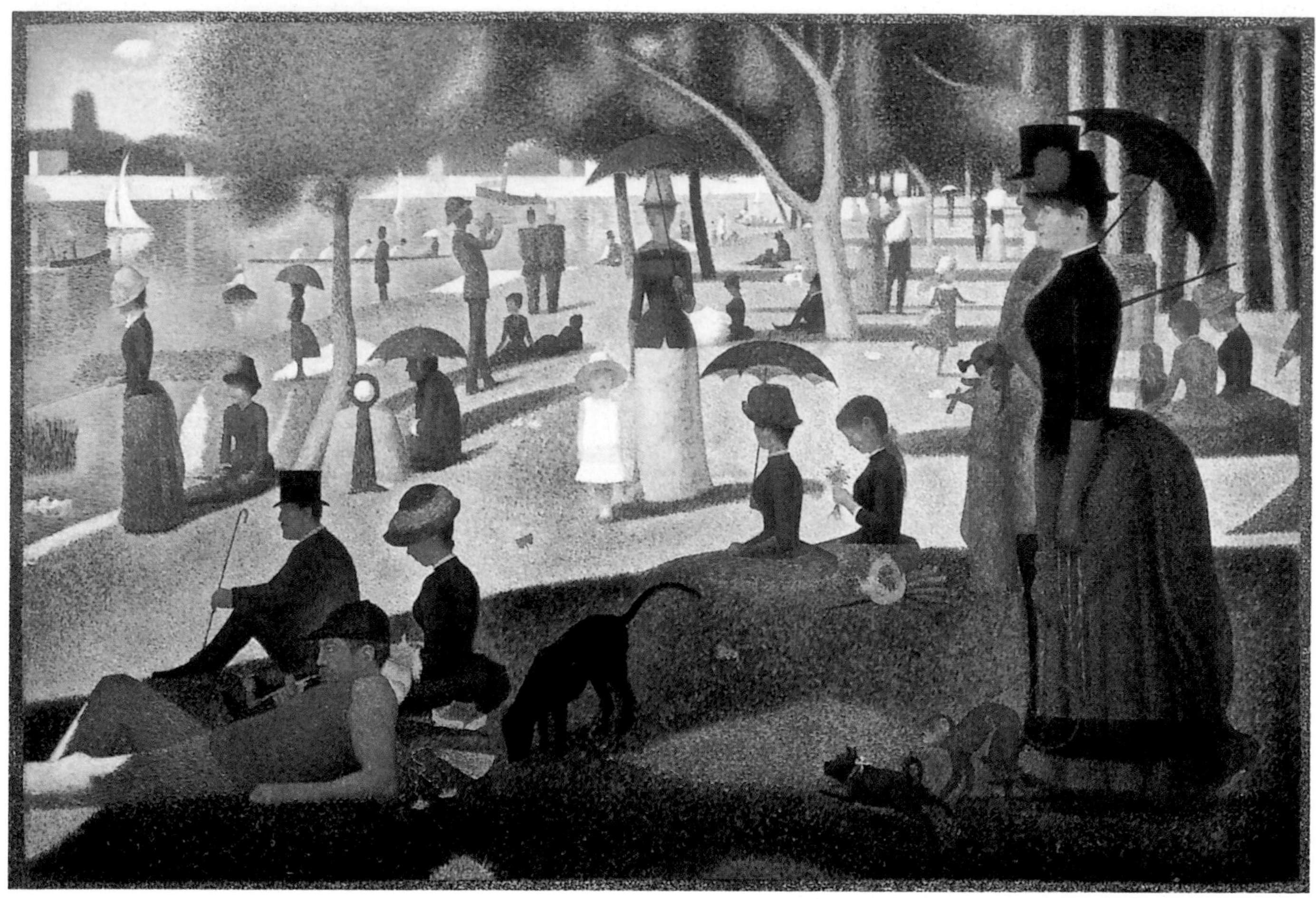

23-5. Georges Seurat. *A Sunday Afternoon on the Island of La Grande Jatte.* 1884–86. Oil on canvas, 6'10" x 10'1¼" (2.08 x 3.08 m). The Art Institute of Chicago

HELEN BIRCH BARTLETT MEMORIAL COLLECTION

SEURAT. Georges Seurat (1859–1891) shared Cézanne's aim to make Impressionism "solid and durable," but he went about it very differently. His goal, he once stated, was to make "modern people, in their essential traits, move about as if on friezes, and place them on canvases organized by harmonies of color, by directions of the tones in harmony with the lines, and by the directions of the lines." Seurat's career was as brief as those of Masaccio, Giorgione, and Géricault and his achievement just as remarkable. Although he participated in the last Impressionist show, it is an indication of the Post-Impressionist revolution that thereafter he exhibited with an entirely new group, the Society of Independents.

Seurat devoted his main efforts to a few very large paintings. He would spend a year or more on each of them, making endless series of preliminary studies before he felt sure enough to tackle the final version. *A Sunday Afternoon on the Island of La Grande Jatte* (fig. 23-5), his greatest masterpiece, had its origin in this painstaking method. The subject is the kind that had long been popular among Impressionist painters. Impressionist, too, are the brilliant colors and the effect of intense sunlight. Otherwise, however, the picture is the very opposite of a quick "impression." The firm, simple contours and the relaxed, immobile figures give the scene a stability that recalls Piero della Francesca (see fig. 12-33) and shows a clear awareness of Puvis de Chavannes (see pages 748–50).

In *La Grande Jatte,* modeling and foreshortening are reduced to a minimum. Moreover the figures appear mostly in either strict profile or in frontal views, as if Seurat had adopted the rules of ancient Egyptian art. He has fitted them into the composition as tightly as the pieces of a jigsaw puzzle. So exactly are they fixed in relation to one another that not a single one could be moved by even a millimeter. Frozen in time and space, they act out their roles with ritualized solemnity, in contrast to the joyous abandon of the relaxed figures in Renoir's *Luncheon of the Boating Party, Bougival* (see fig. 22-10), who are free to move about in the open air. Thus we read this cross section of Parisian society as timeless, despite the period costumes. No wonder the picture remains so spellbinding more than a century after it was painted.

Even the brushwork demonstrates Seurat's passion for order and permanence. The canvas surface is covered with systematic, impersonal "flicks" that make Cézanne's architectural brushstrokes seem dynamic and temperamental by comparison. These tiny dots of brilliant color were supposed to merge in the beholder's eye and produce intermediary tints more luminous than those mixed on the palette. This procedure was variously known as

Neo-Impressionism, Pointillism, or Divisionism (the term preferred by Seurat). The actual result, however, did not follow the theory. Looking at *La Grande Jatte* from a comfortable distance (seven to ten feet from the original), we find that it does not achieve the desired effect. The dots do not disappear but are as clearly visible as the tesserae of a mosaic (compare figs. 8-29 and 8-30). Seurat himself must have liked this unexpected effect, which gives the canvas the quality of a shimmering, translucent screen. Otherwise he would have reduced the size of the dots.

The painting has a dignity and simplicity that suggest a new classicism, but it is a distinctly modern classicism based on scientific theory. Seurat adapted the laws of color discovered by Eugène Chevreul, O. N. Rood, and David Sutter as part of a comprehensive approach to art. Like Degas, he had studied with a follower of Ingres, and his theoretical interests grew out of this experience. He came to believe that art must be based on a system. With the help of his friend Charles Henry (who was, like Rood and Sutter, an American), he formulated a series of artistic "laws" based on early experiments in the psychology of visual perception. These principles helped him to control every aesthetic and expressive aspect of his paintings. But, as with all artists of genius, Seurat's theories do not really explain his pictures. It is the pictures, rather, that explain the theories. In fact, the theories were devised, along with their "proofs," to support Seurat's paintings.

Strange as it may seem, color was an accessory to form in Seurat's work: the very opposite of the Impressionists' technique. Much of his output is drawings done in conté crayon—made of graphite and clay—which provides rich, velvety blacks (fig. 23-6). These sheets have a haunting mystery in contrast to the festive colors of his paintings. In examples such as ours, Seurat's forms achieve a machinelike quality through rigorous abstraction. This is the first expression of a peculiarly modern outlook leading to Futurism (see pages 783 and 785). Seurat's systematic approach to art has the logic of modern engineering, which he and his followers hoped would transform society. This social consciousness was linked to a form of anarchism descended from that of Courbet's friend Proudhon and contrasts with the general political indifference of the Impressionists. The fact that Seurat shared the same subject matter with the Impressionists serves only to emphasize further the basic difference in attitude.

Toward the end of his brief career, Seurat's paintings acquired a new liveliness, seen in *Chahut* (fig. 23-7). True, everything is held very precisely in place by a system of vertical and horizontal lines that defines the canvas as a self-contained rectilinear field. Only in the work of Vermeer have we encountered a similar "area-consciousness" (compare fig. 18-28). But while these dancers move in lockstep, the decorative arabesques within the flat design have an unexpected energy. Consciously or unconsciously, Seurat here moves close to the world of commercial art. The speckled surface resembles the cheap offset printing then coming into use. The subject and composition, too, directly anticipate the posters of Henri de Toulouse-Lautrec—even in the marvelous wit and insight with which the facial expressions are observed.

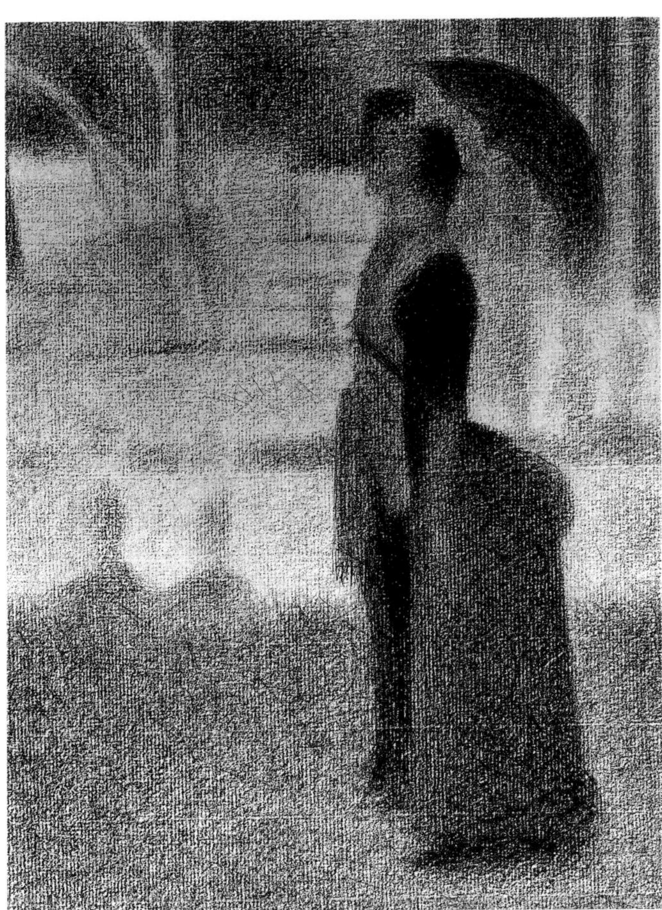

23-6. Georges Seurat. *The Couple*. c. 1884–85. Conté crayon on paper, 11½ x 9" (29.2 x 22.8 cm). Private collection, Paris

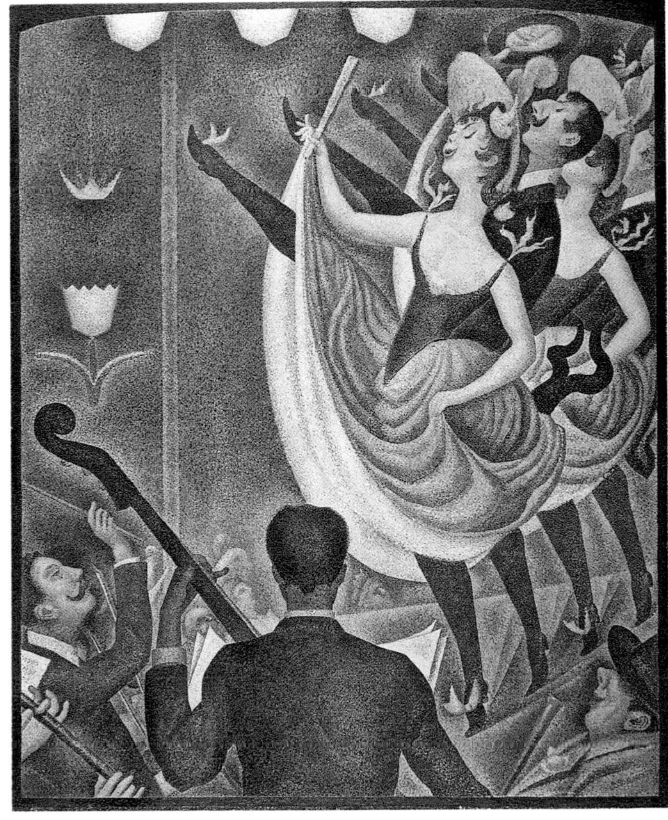

23-7. Georges Seurat. *Chahut*. 1889–90. Oil on canvas, 66½ x 54¾" (169 x 139 cm). Rijksmuseum Kröller-Müller, Otterlo, Holland

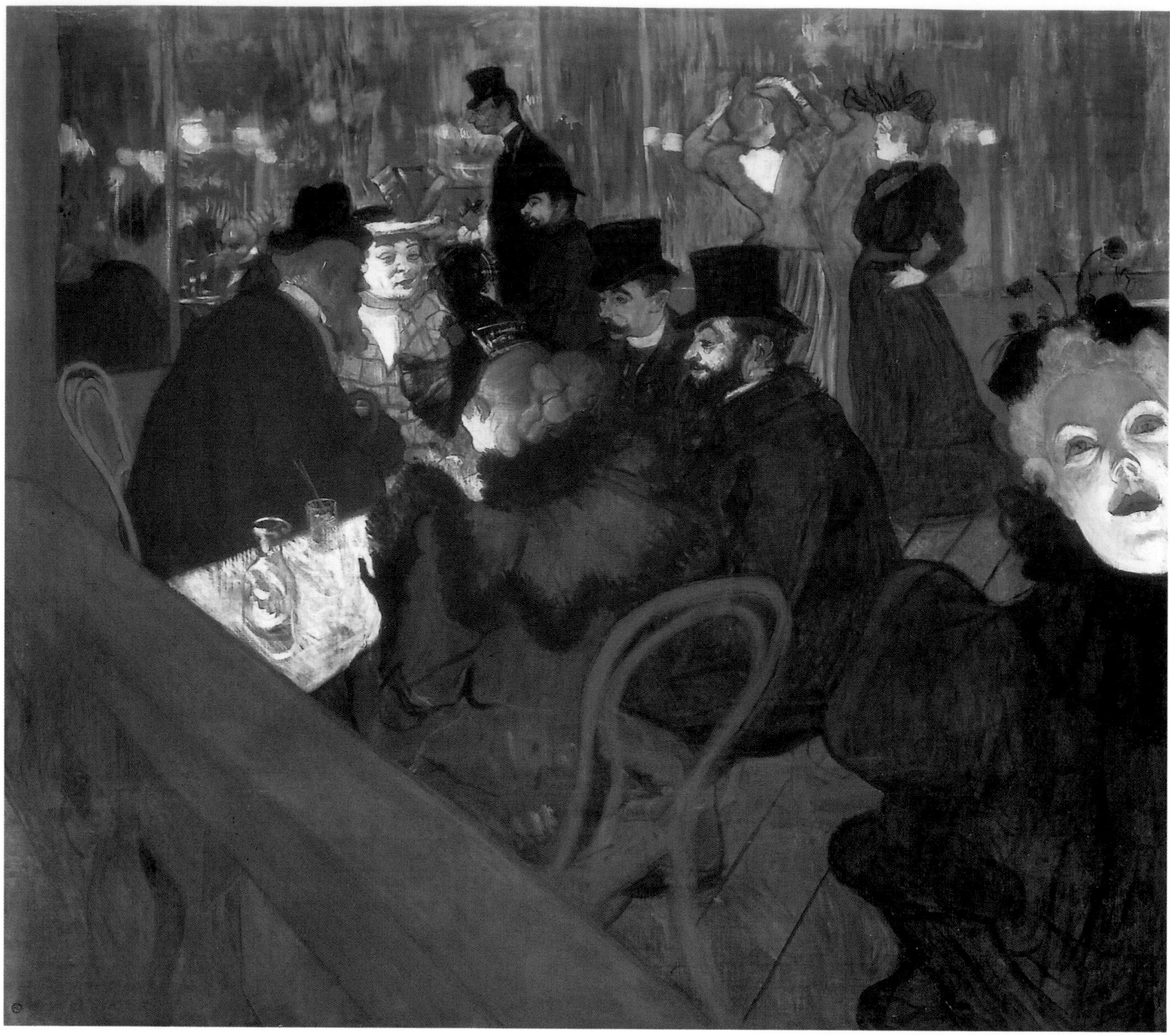

23-8. Henri de Toulouse-Lautrec. *At the Moulin Rouge.* 1893–95. Oil on canvas, 48⅜ x 55½" (123 x 141 cm). The Art Institute of Chicago
HELEN BIRCH BARTLETT MEMORIAL COLLECTION

TOULOUSE-LAUTREC. Born a dwarf, Henri de Toulouse-Lautrec (1864–1901) was an artist of superb talent who led a dissolute life in the night spots and brothels of Paris and died of alcoholism. He was a great admirer of Degas, and his *At the Moulin Rouge* (fig. 23-8) recalls the zigzag pattern in Degas' *The Glass of Absinthe* (see fig. 22-12). Yet this view of the well-known nightclub is no Impressionist "slice of life." Toulouse-Lautrec sees through the gay surface of the scene. He views performers and customers alike with a sharp eye for character—including his own: he is the tiny, bearded man next to the very tall man in the back of the room. The large areas of flat color and the emphatic, smoothly curving outlines reflect the influence of Gauguin (compare fig. 23-13). The Moulin Rouge that Toulouse-Lautrec shows has an atmosphere so joyless and oppressive that we have to wonder if the artist did not regard it as a place of evil. Strangely enough, this scene, no less than Manet's *Luncheon on the Grass* (see fig. 22-3), fulfills Baudelaire's "heroism of modern life." It includes "the spectacle of fashionable life and of thousands of roaming existences—criminals and kept women—drifting about in the undergrounds of a great city." [See Primary Sources, no. 70, page 930.]

If his paintings inevitably bring to mind Degas and Gauguin, Toulouse-Lautrec is without precedent as a graphic artist. His posters, done in a distinctive style, are ideally suited to inexpensive lithography, which enforces an equal economy of form and color. His first poster, *La Goulue* (fig. 23-9), which established his fame, lends this seedy demimonde an air of glamour that is at once captivating and mysterious. As advertising it set a standard that has rarely been matched. The design is wed to the text so seamlessly that they cannot live without each other.

VAN GOGH. While Cézanne and Seurat were converting Impressionism into a more severe, classical style, Vincent van Gogh (1853–1890) followed the opposite direction. He believed that Impressionism did not provide the artist with enough freedom to

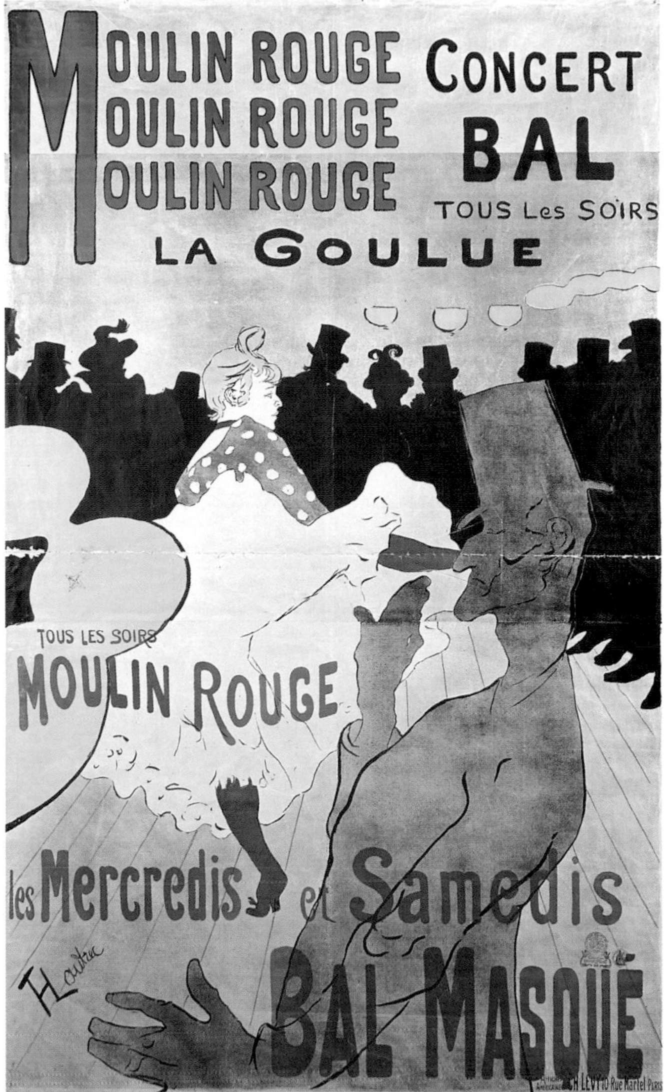

23-9. Henri de Toulouse-Lautrec. *La Goulue.* 1891. Colored lithographic poster, 6'3" x 3'10" (1.90 x 1.16 m)

express his emotions. Since this was his main concern, he is sometimes called an Expressionist, although the term ought to be reserved for certain twentieth-century painters (see page 770). Van Gogh, the first great Dutch master since the seventeenth century, did not become an artist until 1880. As he died only ten years later, his career was even briefer than Seurat's. His early interests were in literature and religion. Profoundly dissatisfied with the values of industrial society and filled with a strong sense of mission, he worked for a while as a lay preacher among poverty-stricken coal miners in Belgium. This same intense feeling for the poor dominates the paintings of his early period, 1880 to 1885. In *The Potato Eaters* (fig. 23-10), the last and most ambitious work of those years, there remains a naive clumsiness that comes from his lack of conventional training. This awkwardness only adds to the expressive power of his style. [See Primary Sources, no. 77, page 932.] We are reminded of Daumier and Millet (see figs. 21-37 and 21-41) and of Rembrandt and Le Nain (see figs. 18-19 and 19-3). For this peasant family, the evening meal has the solemn importance of a ritual.

When he painted *The Potato Eaters,* Van Gogh had not yet discovered the importance of color. A year later in Paris, where his brother Theo had a gallery devoted to modern art, he met Degas,

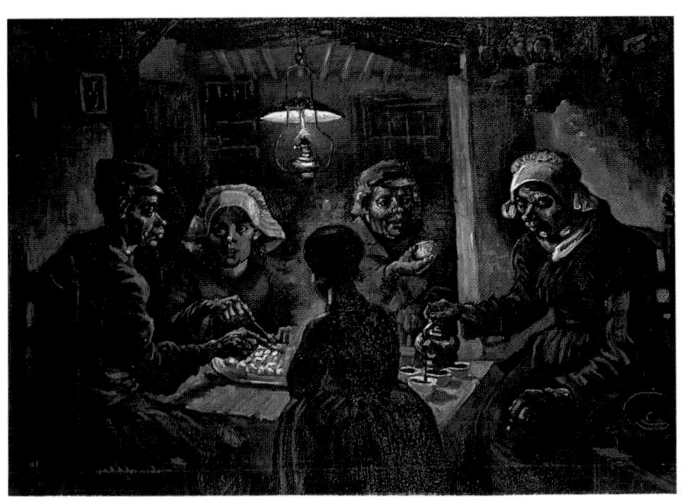

23-10. Vincent van Gogh. *The Potato Eaters.* 1885. Oil on canvas, 32¼ x 45" (82 x 114.3 cm). Vincent van Gogh Foundation/ Van Gogh Museum, Amsterdam

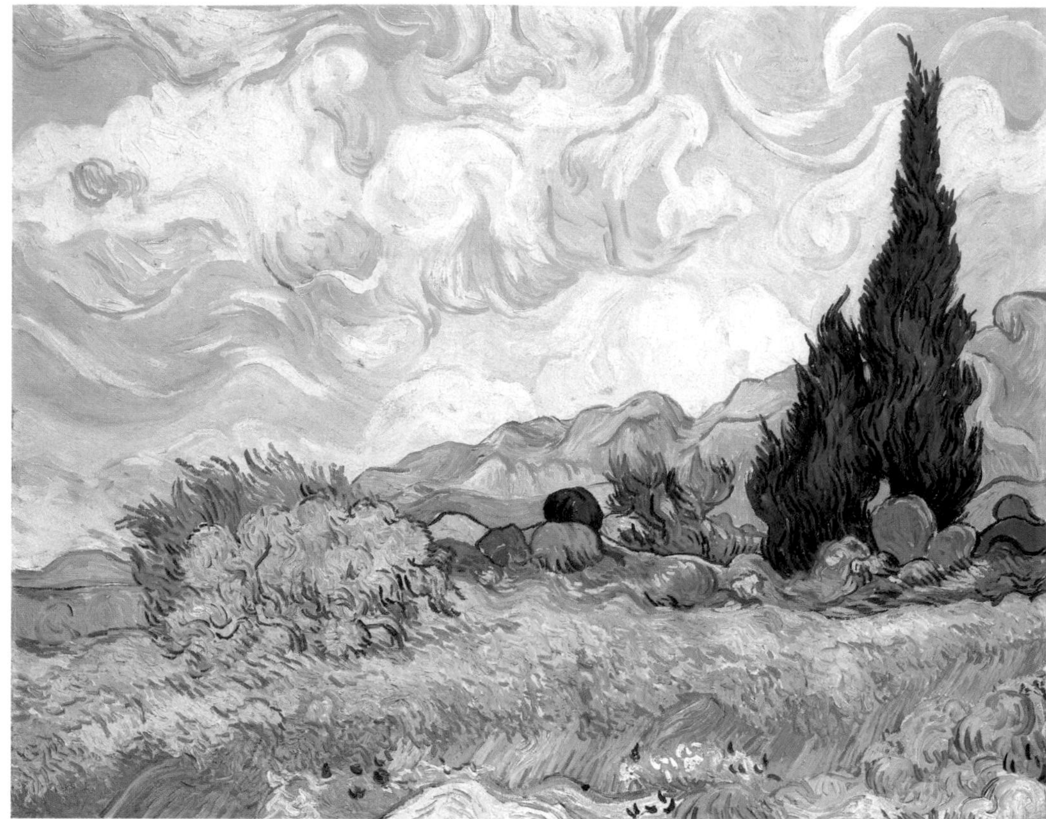

23-11. Vincent van Gogh. *Wheat Field and Cypress Trees.* 1889. Oil on canvas, 28½ x 36" (72.4 x 91.4 cm). The National Gallery, London

REPRODUCED BY COURTESY OF THE TRUSTEES

Seurat, and other leading French artists. Their effect on him was electrifying. His pictures now blazed with color, and he even experimented briefly with the Divisionist technique of Seurat. This phase, however, lasted less than two years. Although it was vitally important for his development, he had to merge it with the style of his earlier years before his genius could fully unfold. Paris had opened his eyes to the sensuous beauty of the visible world and had taught him the pictorial language of the color patch. Painting nevertheless continued to be a vessel for his personal emotions. To investigate a deeper spiritual reality with these new means, he went to Arles, in the south of France. It was there, between 1888 and 1890, that he produced his greatest canvases.

Like Cézanne, Van Gogh now devoted his main energies to landscape painting, but the sun-drenched Mediterranean countryside evoked a very different response in him. He saw it filled with ecstatic movement, not architectural stability and permanence. In *Wheat Field and Cypress Trees* (fig. 23-11), both earth and sky pulsate with an overpowering turbulence. The wheat field resembles a stormy sea, the trees spring flamelike from the ground, and the hills and clouds heave with the same wavelike motion. The dynamism in every brushstroke makes of each one not merely a deposit of color but an incisive graphic gesture. The artist's personal "handwriting" is an even more dominant element than in the canvases of Daumier (compare fig. 21-37). Yet to Van Gogh it was the color, not the form, that determined the expressive content of his pictures. The letters he wrote to his brother include many eloquent descriptions of his choice of hues and the emotional meanings he attached to them. He had learned about Impressionist color from Pissarro, but his personal color symbolism probably stemmed from discussions with Paul Gauguin (see below), who stayed with Van Gogh at Arles for several months. (Yellow, for example, meant faith or triumph or love to Van Gogh, while carmine was a spiritual color and cobalt a divine one. Red and green, on the other hand, stood for the terrible human passions.) Although he admitted that his desire "to exaggerate the essential and to leave the obvious vague" made his colors look arbitrary by Impressionist standards, he remained deeply committed to the visible world. [See Primary Sources, no. 78, page 933.]

Compared to Monet's *On the Bank of the Seine* (see fig. 22-7), the colors of *Wheat Field and Cypress Trees* are stronger, simpler, and more vibrant but in no sense "unnatural." They speak to us of that "kingdom of light" Van Gogh had found in the South and of his mystic faith in a creative force animating all forms of life—a faith no less ardent than the sectarian Christianity of his early years. His *Self-Portrait* (fig. 23-12) will remind us of Dürer's (see fig. 16-6), and with good reason: the missionary had now become a prophet. His emaciated, luminous head with its burning eyes is set off against a whirlpool of darkness. "I want to paint men and women with that something of the eternal which the halo used to symbolize," Van Gogh had written in an attempt to define for his brother the human essence that was his aim in pictures such as this. At the time of the *Self-Portrait,* he had already begun to suffer from a severe form of mental illness that made painting increasingly difficult for him. Despairing of a cure, he committed suicide a year later, for he felt very deeply that art alone made his life worth living.

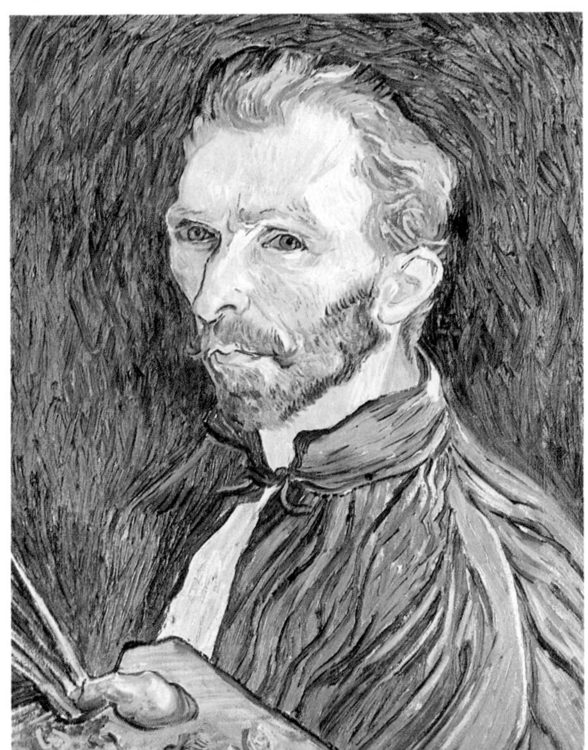

23-12. Vincent van Gogh. *Self-Portrait.* 1889. Oil on canvas, 22½ x 17" (57.2 x 43.2 cm). Collection Mrs. John Hay Whitney, New York

GAUGUIN. The search for religious feeling also played an important part in the work, if not in the life, of another great Post-Impressionist, Paul Gauguin (1848–1903). He began as a prosperous stockbroker in Paris and as an amateur painter and collector of modern pictures. At the age of 35, however, he became convinced that he must devote himself entirely to art. He quit his business career, separated from his family, and by 1889 was the central figure of a new movement called Synthetism or Symbolism.

Gauguin started out as a follower of Cézanne and once owned one of his still lifes. He then developed a style that, though less intensely personal than Van Gogh's, was in some ways an even bolder advance beyond Impressionism. Gauguin believed that Western civilization was spiritually empty because industrial society had forced people into an incomplete life dedicated to material gain, while their emotions were neglected. To rediscover this hidden world of feeling, Gauguin left Paris in 1886 to live among the peasants of Brittany at Pont-Aven in western France. There, two years later, he met the painters Émile Bernard (1868–1941) and Louis Anquetin (1861–1932), who had rejected Impressionism and had begun to evolve a new style that they called Cloissonism (after an enamel technique), for its strong outlines. Gauguin incorporated their approach into his own and emerged as the most forceful member of the Pont-Aven group, which quickly came to center on him.

The Pont-Aven style was first developed fully in the works Gauguin and Bernard painted there during the summer of 1888. Gauguin noticed particularly that religion was still part of the everyday life of the country people. In pictures such as *The Vision After the Sermon (Jacob Wrestling with the Angel)* (fig. 23-13), he tried to depict their simple, direct faith. Here at last is what no

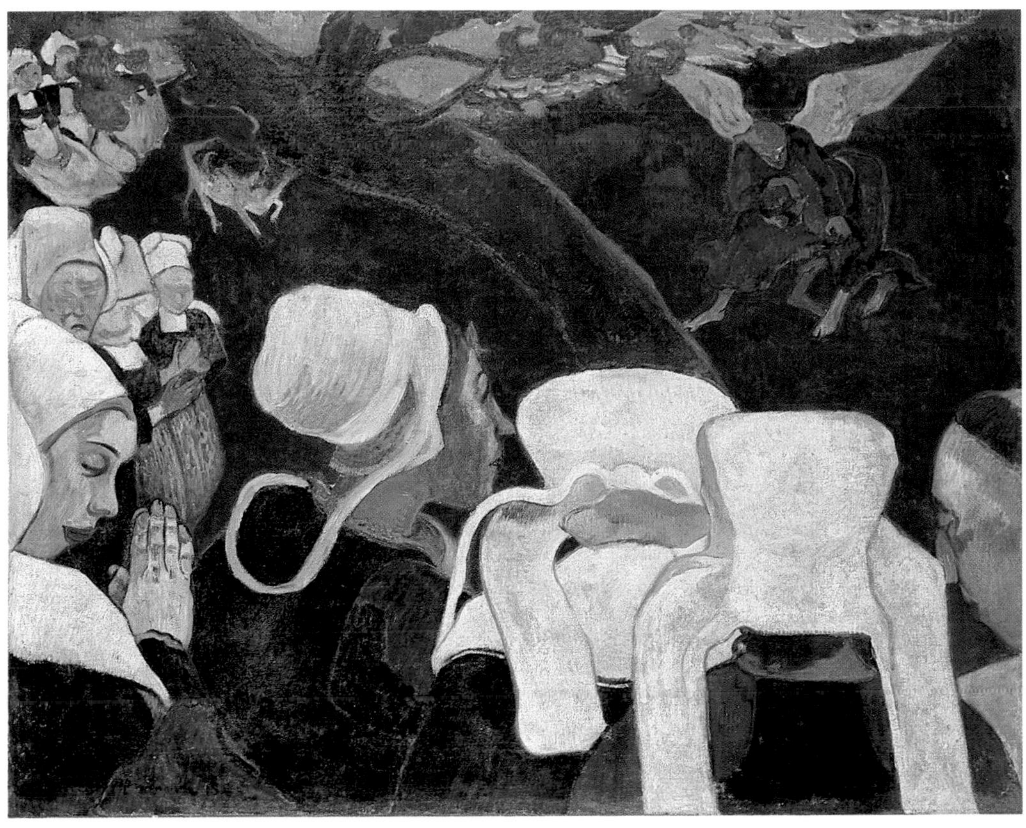

23-13. Paul Gauguin. *The Vision After the Sermon (Jacob Wrestling with the Angel).* 1888. Oil on canvas, 28¾ x 36½" (73 x 92.7 cm). The National Galleries of Scotland, Edinburgh

Romantic artist had achieved: a style based on pre-Renaissance sources. Modeling and perspective have given way to flat, simplified shapes outlined heavily in black, while the brilliant colors are equally "unnatural." This style, inspired by folk art and medieval stained glass, is meant to re-create both the imagined reality of the vision and the trancelike rapture of the peasant women. The painting fulfills the goal of Synthetism: by treating the canvas in this decorative manner, the artist has turned it from a representation of the external world into an aesthetic object that projects an inner idea without using narrative or literal symbols. Yet we sense that Gauguin remained an outsider, although he tried to share this experience. He could paint pictures about faith but not from faith.

Two years later, Gauguin's search for the unspoiled life led him even farther afield. He went to Tahiti—he had already visited Martinique in 1887—as a sort of "missionary in reverse," to learn from the natives instead of teaching them. [See Primary Sources, no. 79, page 933.] He spent the rest of his life in the South Pacific and returned home only once, from 1893 to 1895. Yet he never found the virgin Eden he was seeking. Indeed, he often had to rely on the writings and photographs of those who had recorded its culture before him. Nonetheless his Tahitian canvases envision an ideal world filled with the beauty and meaning he pursued so futilely in real life.

His masterpiece in this vein is *Where Do We Come From? What Are We? Where Are We Going?* (fig. 23-14), painted as a summation of his art shortly before he was driven by despair to attempt suicide. Even without the suggestive title, we would recognize the painting's allegorical purpose from its monumental scale, the carefully thought-out poses and placement of the figures in the tapestry-like landscape, and their pensive air. Although Gauguin intended the surface to be the sole conveyer of meaning, we know from his letters that the huge canvas represents an epic cycle of life. The scene unfolds from right to left. It begins with the sleeping girl, continues with the beautiful young woman (a Tahitian Eve) in the center picking fruit, and ends with "an old woman approaching death who seems reconciled and resigned to her thoughts." Gauguin has cast the answer to his title in distinctly Western terms. In effect, the picture constitutes a variation on the three ages of life found in *Death and the Maiden* by Hans Baldung Grien (see fig. 16-13). The mysterious Maori god overseeing everything is a counterpart to the figure of Death in Baldung Grien's painting.

MUSIC IN THE POST-IMPRESSIONIST ERA

The late nineteenth century presents a welter of musical tendencies no less perplexing than the diversity found in Post-Impressionism. Strictly speaking, the term *Impressionism* cannot be applied to music because music, by its very nature, cannot describe, it can only evoke. The term has nevertheless often been used to characterize the works of the Frenchman Claude Debussy (1862–1918), such as *La Mer* (1905), which successfully conveys the contrasting moods of the sea. In reality, however, his compositions are much closer in spirit to Symbolist poetry. (His closest friends, such as Pierre Louÿs, were writers.) This is especially evident in his lone opera, *Pelléas et Mélisande* (1893–1902), which was derived from a play by the Franco-Belgian Symbolist Maurice Maeterlinck (1862–1949); despite the vast difference between them, the opera reveals a debt to Wagner's music, which Debussy first heard at Bayreuth in 1888. Early in his career, Debussy summered in Russia as the guest of Tchaikovsky's patron, Madame von Meck, and it must have been at that time that he first became interested in modes, as well as other "lost" and exotic musical forms. This interest was reinforced by hearing Javanese music at the Universal Exposition in Paris in 1889. As a consequence, he began to employ such unusual devices as the pentatonic scale (the five black notes on the piano), which in his later years pushed conventional tonalism virtually to its breaking point.

Symbolism also touched Debussy's fellow "Impressionist," Maurice Ravel (1875–1937), particularly in such early works as *Gaspard de la nuit* (1908) for piano, which was inspired by a poem by Aloysius Bertrand (1807–1841). It also underlies the enchanting *Mother Goose,* originally composed that same year as a piano duet for the daughters of a close friend and later orchestrated as a ballet: the choice of stories and their musical treatment revel in the realm of dreams and other emanations of the subconscious, despite the air of childlike innocence.

The music of Debussy and Ravel was in many respects the conscious antithesis of Neo-Romanticism, that late phase of

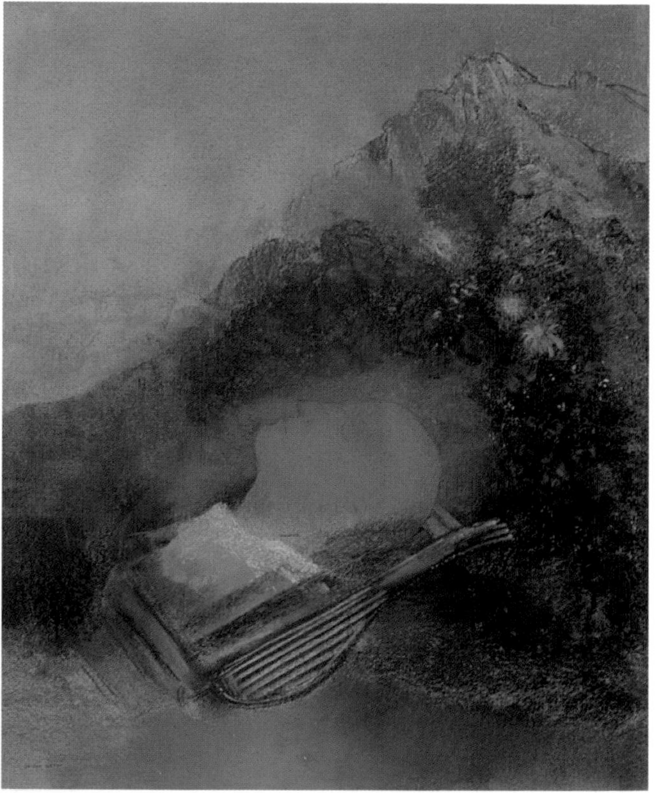

Odilon Redon. *Orpheus*, c. 1903–10. Pastel on paper, 27 1/8 x 22 3/8" (68.8 x 56.8 cm). The Cleveland Museum of Art

GIFT FROM J. H. WADE, 1926

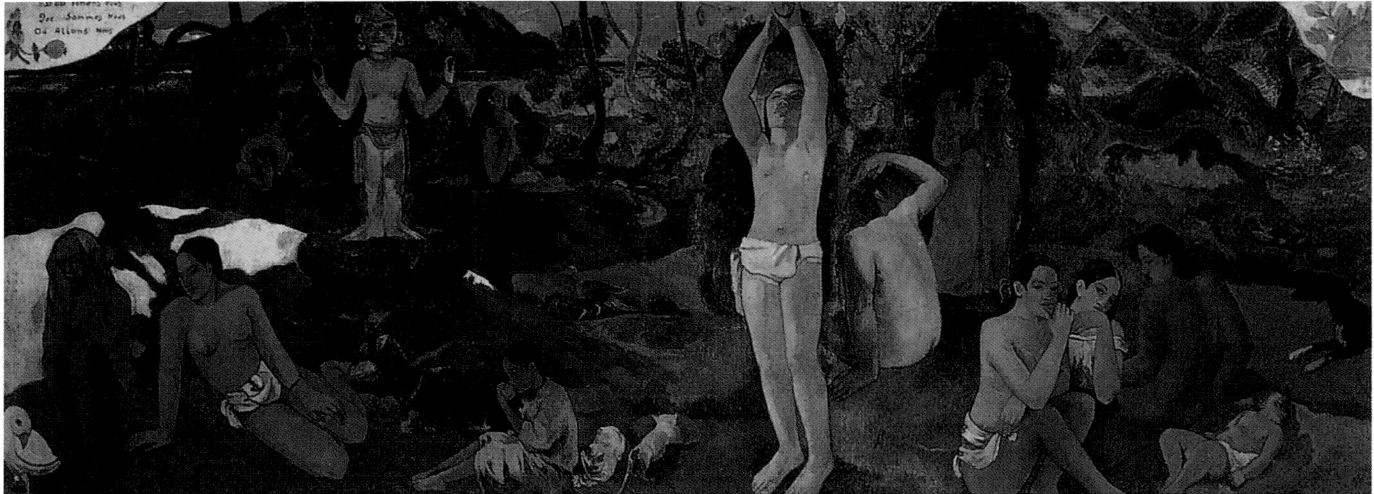

23-14. Paul Gauguin. *Where Do We Come From? What Are We? Where Are We Going?* 1897. Oil on canvas, 4'6¾" x 12'3½" (1.3 x 3.7 m). Museum of Fine Arts, Boston
ARTHUR GORDON TOMPKINS RESIDUARY FUND

Romanticism that is identified particularly with the German composers Gustav Mahler (1866–1911) and Richard Strauss (1864–1949). Strauss started out as a classicist but through his friendship with the poet Alexander Ritter (1833–1896) became a disciple of Wagner and Liszt. While pursuing a career as a conductor, he first gained fame for his tone poems, such as *Death and Transfiguration* (1889). From 1905 on, however, Strauss devoted himself primarily to operas, notably *Der Rosenkavalier* (*The Cavalier of the Rose;* 1911), which, like all his finest efforts, was the result of his collaboration with the Austrian Neo-Romantic poet and dramatist Hugo von Hofmannsthal (1874–1929). The composer later supported the Nazis and served for a while as head of musical affairs under Hitler, although he was officially exonerated of collaboration shortly before his death.

If Strauss represents the final glory of German Romanticism, the symphonies and orchestrated song cycles by his friend and fellow conductor Gustav Mahler of Vienna can be seen as the musical counterpart to the morbid sensitivity of Gustav Klimt and the Vienna Secession movement, with which he was personally involved. His works' enormous scale makes huge demands on orchestra and chorus alike, while the extremes of hypersensitive introspection and almost hysterical bombast go beyond the expressive limits of Romanticism. Mahler's late works, sparser in character, were the point of departure for the next generation of Viennese composers, whose work he encouraged: Arnold Schoenberg, Anton Webern, and Alban Berg, who were to revolutionize twentieth-century music (see boxes on pages 780, 808).

This fact points to an anomaly, namely, that a number of Late Romantics had the unfortunate fate of living well beyond the advent of modern music. Both Ravel and the Finnish composer Jean Sibelius (1865–1957) responded by virtually ceasing to write music after 1925. Sibelius was a throwback to the nationalist composers of the mid-nineteenth century. His early works are tone poems, based on Nordic legends, that are filled with a brooding melancholy. His major contribution, however, lies in the seven symphonies, which build short motifs into large structures of decidedly unconventional form that nearly stand Romanticism on its ear. Although passionate at times, his compositions lack the lush, sentimental appeal of those by the other great nationalist composer of the era, the Russian Sergei Rachmaninov (1873–1943), who wrote piano concertos as showcases for his virtuosity, in addition to three symphonies that follow in a direct line of descent from Tchaikovsky's.

Just as there was no true Impressionism in music, so the term *realism* in late-nineteenth-century opera is something of a misnomer. It was applied to a small group of operas—including *Carmen* (1875) by Georges Bizet (1838–1875) and *Pagliacci* (1892) by Ruggiero Leoncavallo (1858–1919), which is often produced on the same bill with *Cavalleria Rusticana* (1889) by Pietro Mascagni (1863–1945)—set in contemporary Europe that are nonetheless sentimental melodramas. *La Bohème* (1896) and *Tosca* (1900) by Giacomo Puccini (1858–1924), Verdi's successor as the leading composer of this genre in Italy, partake of this *verismo,* as it was called, although they are set earlier in the century; however, they owe their success to their combination of melting lyricism and pungent drama. The later operas, such as *Madame Butterfly* (1904) and *Girl of the Golden West* (1910), based on successful melodramas by the American playwright David Belasco (c. 1853–1931), exploit the European taste for the exotic, although they were failures initially. Belasco's plays, however, were considered examples of realism by audiences in the United States, to whom their setting and moral meaning were instantly recognizable. Their realism was heightened by spectacular staging and special effects.

Moreover Gauguin painted the composition in response to Puvis de Chavannes' classical allegories, especially *The Sacred Grove* (see fig. 23-16, left). Gauguin tells us that the real secret to the central mystery of life lies in this primitive Eden, not in some mythical past.

The renewal of Western art and civilization as a whole, Gauguin believed, must come from "the Primitives." He advised other Symbolists to avoid the Greek tradition and to turn instead to Persia, the Far East, and ancient Egypt. The idea of primitivism itself is not new. It stems from the Romantic myth of the Noble Savage, proclaimed by the thinkers of the Enlightenment more than a century before. Its ultimate source is the age-old tradition of an earthly paradise where human societies once dwelled—and might perhaps live again—in a state of nature and innocence. But no one before Gauguin had gone as far to put the doctrine of primitivism into practice. His pilgrimage to the South Pacific has more than a purely private meaning. It symbolizes the end of the 400 years of colonial expansion that had brought almost the entire globe under Western domination.

Symbolism

Van Gogh's and Gauguin's discontent with the spiritual ills of Western civilization was part of a widely shared sentiment at the end of the nineteenth century. It reflected an intellectual and moral upheaval that rejected the modern world and its materialism in favor of irrational states of mind. A preoccupation with decadence, evil, and darkness pervaded the artistic and literary climate. Even those who saw no escape analyzed their predicament in fascinated horror. Yet, paradoxically, this very awareness proved to be a source of strength that gave birth to the remarkable movement known as Symbolism.

Symbolism in art was at first an outgrowth of the literary movement that arose in 1885–86 with Jean Moréas and Gustave Kahn at its helm. Reacting against the Naturalism of the novelist Émile Zola, they asserted the primacy of subjective ideas and championed the *poètes maudits* (the doomed poets) Stéphane Mallarmé and Paul Verlaine. There was a natural sympathy between the Pont-Aven painters and the Symbolist poets, and in a long article defining Symbolism published in April 1892, the writer G. Albert Aurier insisted on Gauguin's leadership. However, unlike Post-Impressionism, which was a stylistic tendency, Symbolism was a general outlook, one that allowed for a wide variety of styles—whatever would embody its peculiar frame of mind.

THE NABIS. Gauguin's Symbolist followers, who called themselves Nabis (from the Hebrew word for "prophet"), were less remarkable for creative talent than for their ability to spell out and justify the aims of Post-Impressionism in theoretical form. One of them, Maurice Denis, coined the statement that was to become the first article of faith for modernist painters of the twentieth century: "A picture—before being a war horse, a female nude, or some anecdote—is essentially a flat surface covered with colors in a particular order." He added that "every work of art is a transposition, a caricature, the passionate equivalent of a received sensation." The theory of equivalents gave the Nabis their independence from Gauguin: "We supplemented the rudimentary teaching of Gauguin by substituting for his over-simplified idea of pure colors the idea of beautiful harmonies, infinitely varied like nature; we adapted all the resources of the palette to all the states of our sensibility; and the sights which caused them became to us so many signs of our own subjectivity. We sought equivalents, but equivalents in beauty!"

VUILLARD. We can now understand why paintings by the Nabis soon came to look so different from Gauguin's. They became involved with decorative projects that, like Whistler's Peacock Room (see fig. 22-40), participate in the late-nineteenth-century's retreat into a world of beauty. The pictures of the 1890s by Édouard Vuillard (1868–1940), the most gifted member of the Nabis, share this quality. They are mostly domestic scenes, small in scale and intimate in effect. These combine the flat planes and emphatic contours of Gauguin (see fig. 23-13) with the shimmering Divisionist "color mosaic" and geometric surface organization of Seurat (see fig. 23-7). The seemingly casual view of his mother's corset-shop workroom in *The Suitor* (fig. 23-15) has a delicate balance of "2-D" and "3-D" effects. Indeed, Vuillard probably derived his flat patterns from the fabrics themselves. The picture's quiet magic makes us think of Vermeer and Chardin (compare figs. 18-28 and 20-8), whose subject matter, too, was the snug life of the middle class.

In both subject and treatment, the painting has counterparts as well in Symbolist literature and theater: the poetry of Paul Verlaine, the novels of Stéphane Mallarmé, and the productions of Aurélian-Marie Lugné-Poë, for whom Vuillard designed stage sets (see box page 757). It evokes a wide range of feelings through purely formal means that could never be conveyed by naturalism alone. The Nabis established an important precedent for Matisse a decade later (see fig. 24-2). By then, however, the movement had disintegrated as its members became more conservative. Vuillard himself turned more to naturalism, and he never recaptured the delicacy and daring of his early canvases.

PUVIS DE CHAVANNES. The Symbolists discovered that there were some older artists, descendants of the Romantics, whose work, like their own, placed inner vision above the observation of nature. Many of the Symbolists, as well as other Post-Impressionists, found inspiration in the classicism of Pierre-Cécile Puvis de Chavannes (1824–1898), a follower of Ingres who became the leading muralist of his day. Rejecting academic conventions, he pursued a radical simplification of style, which at first seemed out of place but was soon hailed by critics and artists of every outlook. The effectiveness of the murals he executed in the 1880s for the museum at Lyons (fig. 23-16) depends in large part on Puvis' formal devices—the compressed space, schematic forms, and restricted palette—which imitate in oil the chalky surface of old frescoes. The antinaturalism of his style emphasizes the allegorical quality of the scene, which has a gravity and mystery missing from other mural paintings by his contemporaries. Storytelling is replaced by nostalgia for an idealized, mythical past. The stiff, ritualistic poses freeze time and convey a poetry that is both melancholy and serene. Puvis' economy of means was intended to present his ideas with maximum clarity, but it has just the opposite effect: it heightens the suggestiveness of his paintings. His popularity

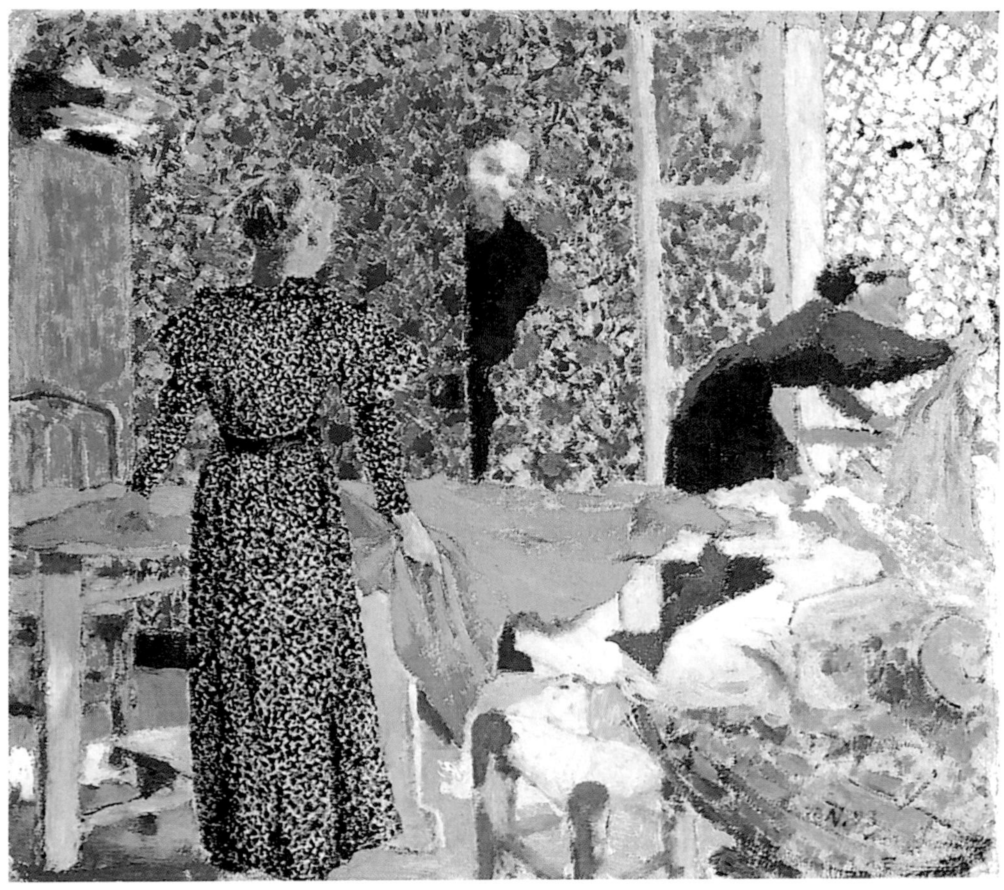

23-15. Édouard Vuillard. *The Suitor.* 1893. Oil on millboard panel, 12½ x 14" (31.8 x 35.6 cm). Smith College Museum of Art, Northampton, Massachusetts

PURCHASED, DRAYTON HILLYER FUND, 1938

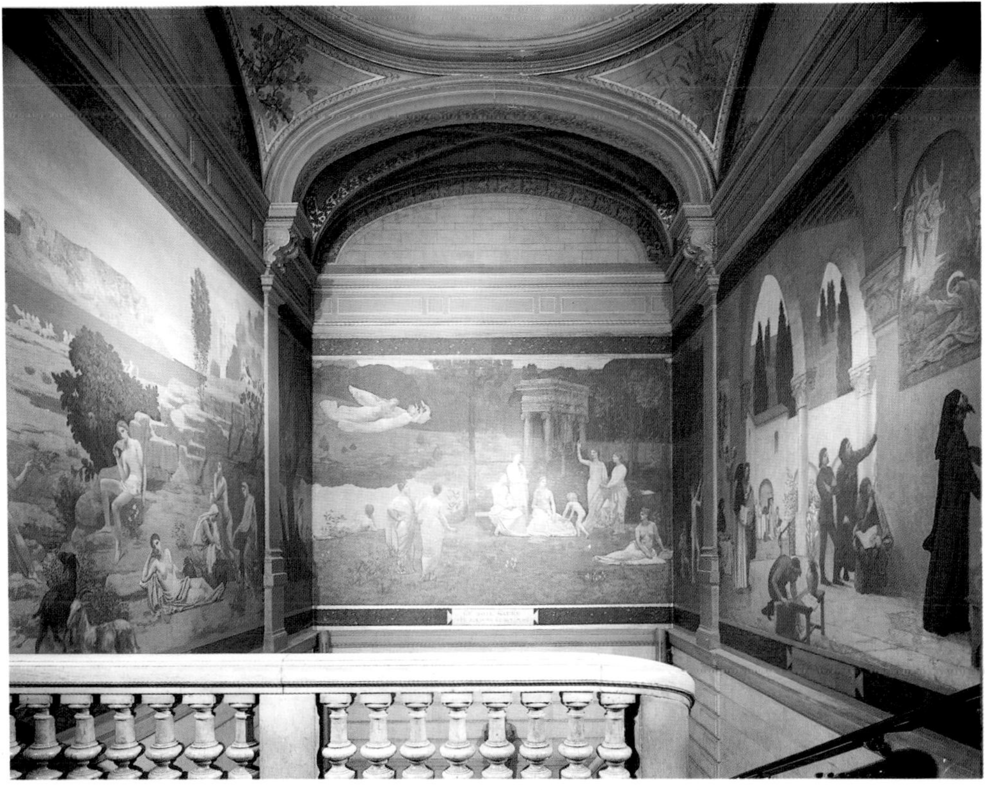

23-16. Pierre-Cécile Puvis de Chavannes. *The Sacred Grove,* c. 1883–84; *Vision of Antiquity,* c. 1888–89; and *Christian Inspiration,* c. 1888–89. Painting cycle, Grand Staircase, Musée des Beaux-Arts, Lyons, France

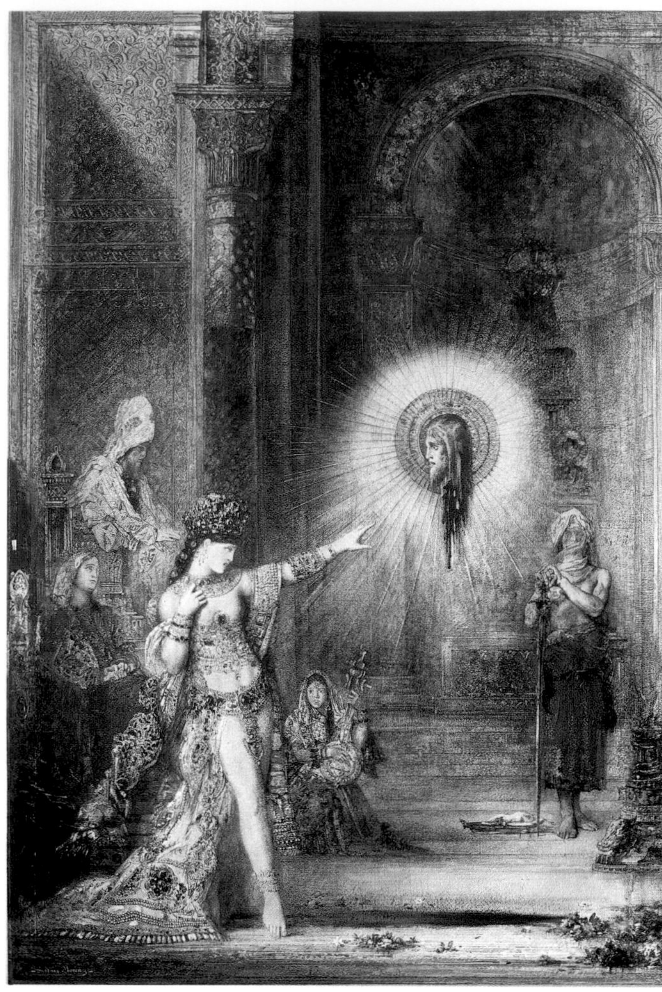

23-17. Gustave Moreau. *The Apparition (Dance of Salomé)*. c. 1876. Watercolor, 41¾ x 28⅜" (106 x 72 cm). Musée du Louvre, Paris

resulted precisely from this ambiguity, which allowed a wide variety of interpretation. Symbolists from Gauguin through the young Picasso could thus claim him as one of their own. Nevertheless, Puvis vehemently protested any association with the Symbolist movement.

MOREAU. One of the Symbolists, Gustave Moreau (1826–1898), a recluse who admired Delacroix, created a world of personal fantasy that has much in common with the medieval reveries of the English Pre-Raphaelites Rossetti and Burne-Jones. *The Apparition* (fig. 23-17) shows one of his favorite themes. The head of John the Baptist, in a blinding light, appears to the dancing Salomé. The painting combines the dreams of Oriental splendor and cruelty so dear to the Romantic imagination with a belief in the supernatural. Moreau summons up this exotic realm through the odalisque-like sensuousness of the girl, the stream of blood pouring from the severed head, and the vast, mysterious space of the setting, which suggests an exotic temple rather than Herod's palace. Moreau gained recognition only late in life. Suddenly, his art was in tune with the times. During his last six years, he even held a professorship at the conservative École des Beaux Arts, the successor of the official art academy that had been founded under Louis XIV (see page 579). There he attracted the most gifted students, among them such future modernists as Matisse and Rouault.

BEARDSLEY. How prophetic Moreau's work was of art at the end of the century can be seen from a comparison with Aubrey Beardsley (1872–1898), a gifted young Englishman whose elegant black-and-white drawings were the height of "decadent" taste. They include an illustration (fig. 23-18) for Oscar Wilde's *Salomé* (see box page 757) that might well be the final scene of the drama depicted by Moreau: Salomé has taken up John's severed head and triumphantly kissed it. Beardsley's erotic meaning is plain. Salomé is passionately in love with John and has asked for his head because she could not have him any other way. Even though Moreau's intent remains ambiguous, the parallel is striking. There are formal similarities as well, such as the "stem" of trickling blood from which John's head rises like a flower. Yet Beardsley's *Salomé* cannot be said to derive from Moreau's. The sources of his style are English—specifically, the graphic art of the Pre-Raphaelites—with a strong Japanese influence.

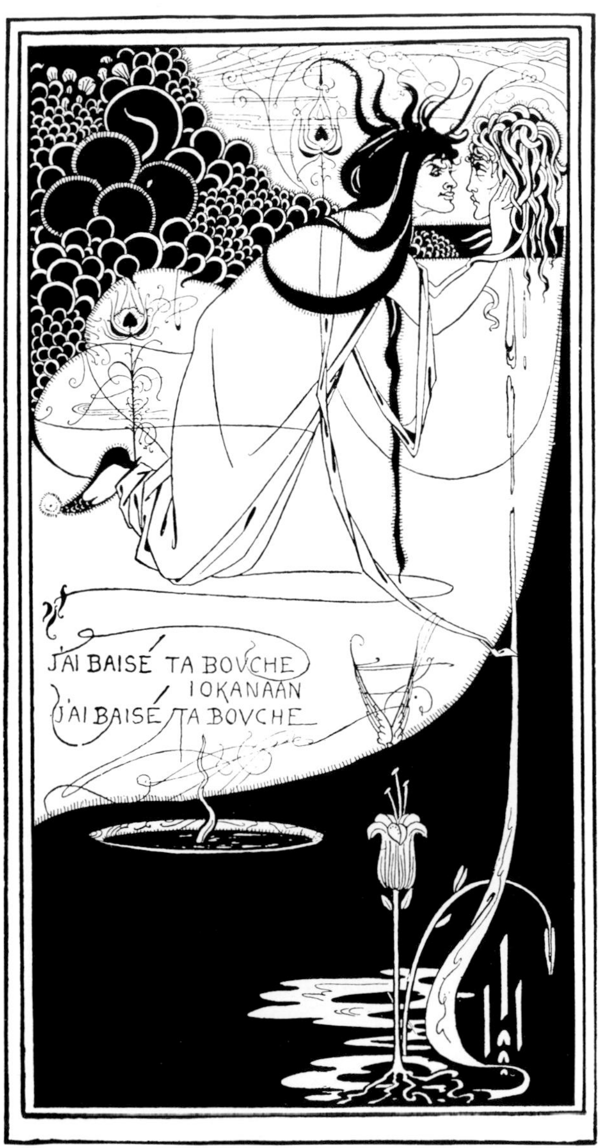

23-18. Aubrey Beardsley. *Salomé*. 1892. Pen drawing, $10^{15}/_{16}$ x $5^{13}/_{16}$" (27.8 x 14.8 cm). Aubrey Beardsley Collection. Manuscripts Division, Department of Rare Books and Special Collections, Princeton University Library, New Jersey

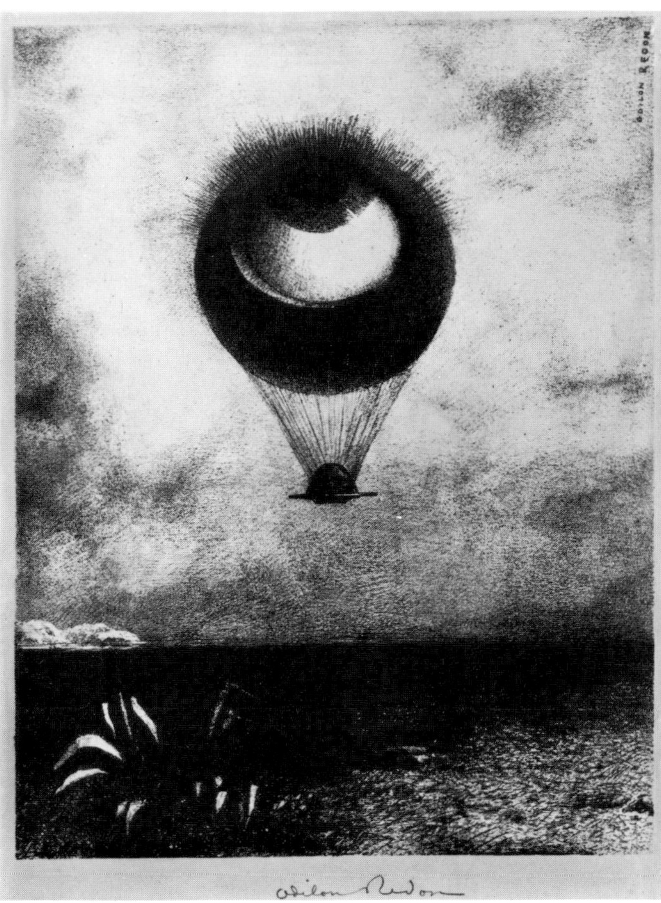

23-19. Odilon Redon. *The Eye Like a Strange Balloon Mounts Toward Infinity,* from the series *Edgar A. Poe.* 1882. Lithograph, $10\frac{1}{4}$ x $7\frac{11}{16}$" (25.9 x 19.6 cm). The Museum of Modern Art, New York
GIFT OF PETER H. DEITSCH

REDON. Another solitary artist whom the Symbolists discovered and claimed as one of their own was Odilon Redon (1840–1916). Like Moreau, he had a haunted imagination, but his imagery was even more personal and disturbing. A master of etching and lithography, he drew inspiration from the fantastic visions of Goya (see fig. 21-22) as well as Romantic literature. The lithograph shown in figure 23-19 is one of a set he issued in 1882 and dedicated to Edgar Allan Poe. The American poet had been dead for 33 years, but his tormented life and his equally tortured imagination made him the very model of the *poète maudit* (doomed poet). His works, excellently translated by Baudelaire and Mallarmé, were greatly admired in France. Redon's lithographs do not illustrate Poe. They are, rather, "visual poems" in their own right, evoking the macabre, hallucinatory world of Poe's imagination. In our example, the artist has revived an ancient device, the single eye representing the all-seeing mind of God. But, in contrast to the traditional form of the symbol, Redon shows the whole eyeball removed from its socket and converted into a balloon that drifts aimlessly in the sky. The disquieting visual puzzles in Redon's lithographs express the pessimism of a troubled mind struggling to find meaning. Only after 1900 did this general outlook give way to a new serenity filled with spiritual overtones.

ENSOR. In the paintings of the Belgian artist James Ensor (1860–1949), a cynical view of the human condition reaches obsessive intensity and for much the same reason. In *Christ's Entry into Brussels in 1889* (fig. 23-20), the demon-ridden world of Bosch and Schongauer has come to life again in modern form (compare figs. 15-14 and 15-23). The painting, showing the Second Coming of

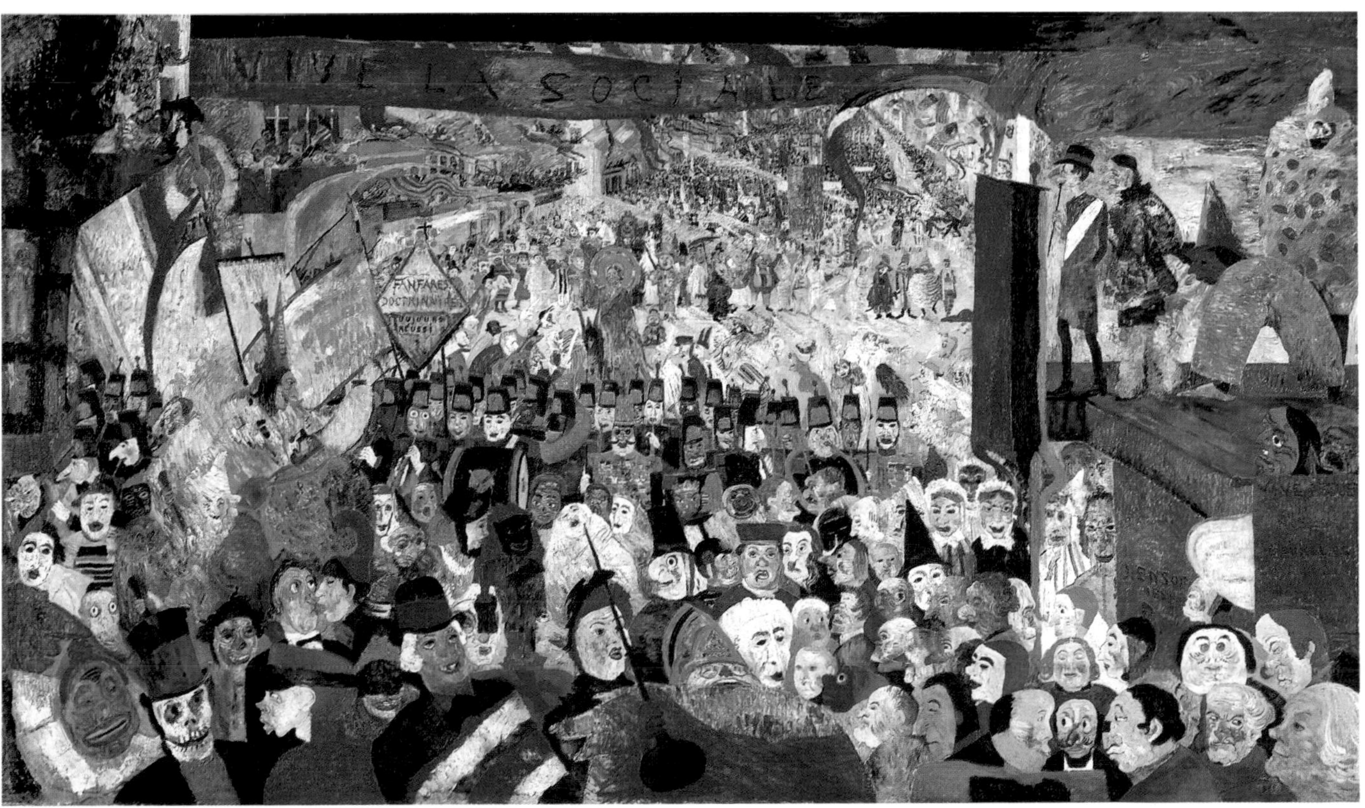

23-20. James Ensor. *Christ's Entry into Brussels in 1889.* 1888. Oil on canvas, 8'$6\frac{1}{2}$" x 14'$1\frac{1}{2}$" (2.6 x 4.3 m). Collection of the J. Paul Getty Museum, Malibu, California

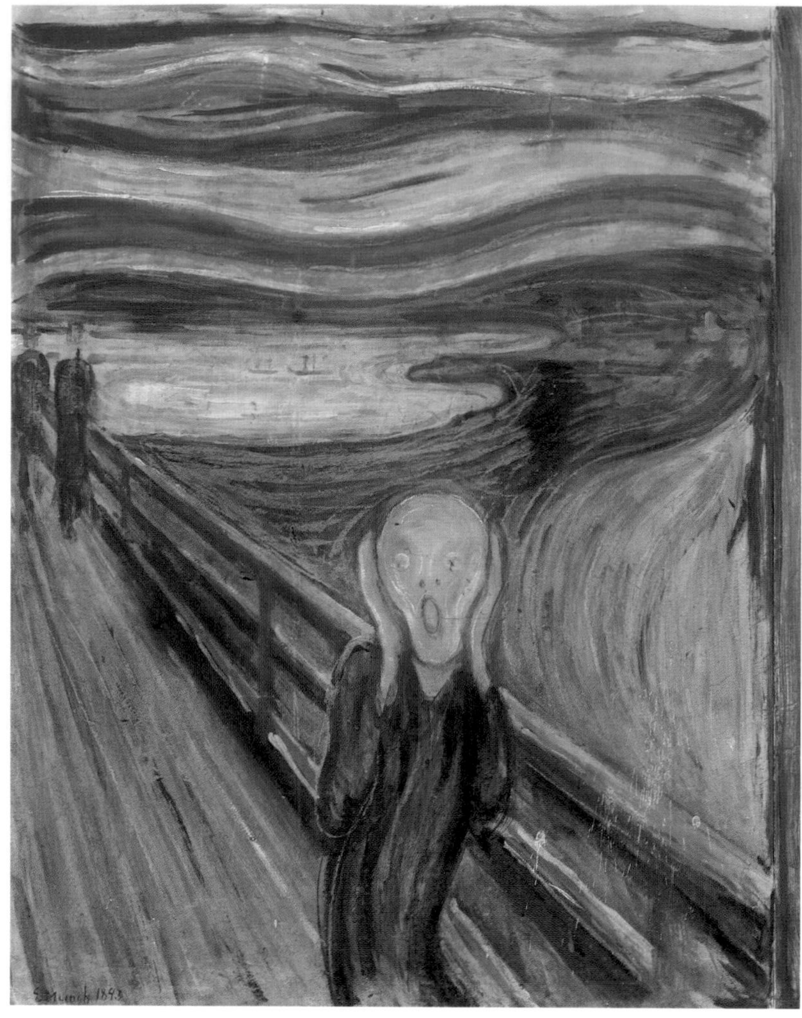

23-21. Edvard Munch. *The Scream*. 1893. Tempera and casein on cardboard, 36 x 29" (91.4 x 73.7 cm). Nasjonalgalleriet, Oslo, Norway

Christ in contemporary Belgium, is a grotesque parody of a subject familiar to us since the Late Gothic (compare figs. 11-75 and 11-77). Here Christ is virtually lost in a sea of leering faces, which are treated as the personification of evil. As we examine these masks we become aware that they are the crowd's true faces, revealing the depravity ordinarily hidden behind the facade of everyday appearances. At the time, Ensor identified with Christ, whose suffering he felt paralleled his own at the hands of hostile critics and an indifferent public. Later, when his art began to gain wide acceptance, he abandoned this bitter attitude.

MUNCH. Something of the same morbid quality is found in the early work of Edvard Munch (1863–1944). A far more gifted artist, he came to Paris from Norway in 1889 and based his starkly expressive style on Toulouse-Lautrec, Van Gogh, and Gauguin. *The Scream* (fig. 23-21) shows the influence of all three. It is an image of fear: the terrifying, unreasoned fear we feel in a nightmare. Unlike Goya and Fuseli (see figs. 21-22 and 21-43), Munch visualizes this experience without the aid of frightening apparitions, and it is more persuasive for that very reason. [See Primary Sources, no. 80, page 933.] The rhythm of the long, wavy lines seems to carry the echo of the scream into every corner of the picture, making of earth and sky one great sounding board of fear.

KLIMT. Munch's pictures generated such controversy when they were exhibited in Berlin in 1892 that a number of young radicals broke from the artists association and formed the Berlin Secession, which took its name from a similar group that had been founded in Munich earlier that year. The Secession quickly became a loosely allied international movement. In 1897 it spread to Austria, where Gustav Klimt (1862–1918) established the Vienna Secession with the purpose of raising the level of quality of the arts and crafts in Austria through close ties to Art Nouveau (see pages 757–58). *The Kiss* (fig. 23-22) by Klimt expresses a different kind of anxiety from Munch's *The Scream*. The image will remind us of Beardsley's *Salomé* (see fig. 23-18), but here the barely suppressed eroticism has burst into desire. (It shows the artist with his lover Emilie Flöge.) Engulfed in robes inspired by Byzantine mosaics (compare figs.

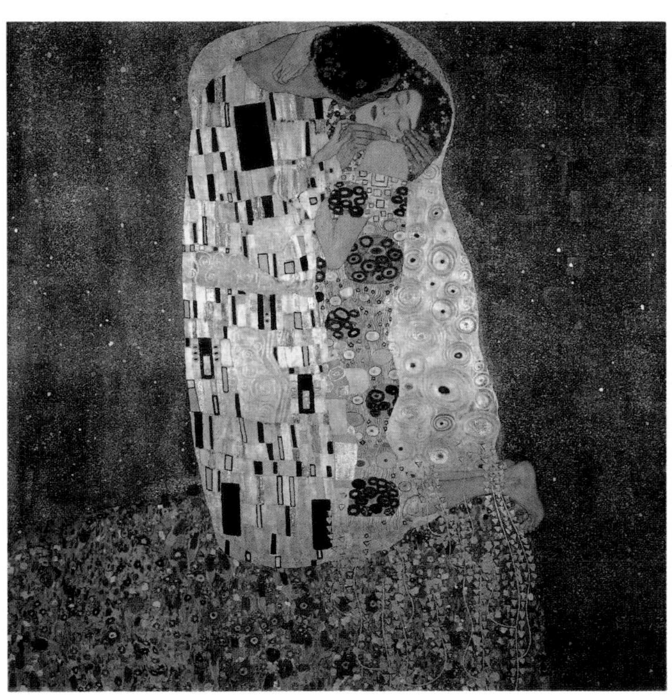

23-22. Gustav Klimt. *The Kiss.* 1907–8. Oil on canvas, 70⅞ x 70⅞" (180 x 180 cm). Österreichische Galerie, Vienna

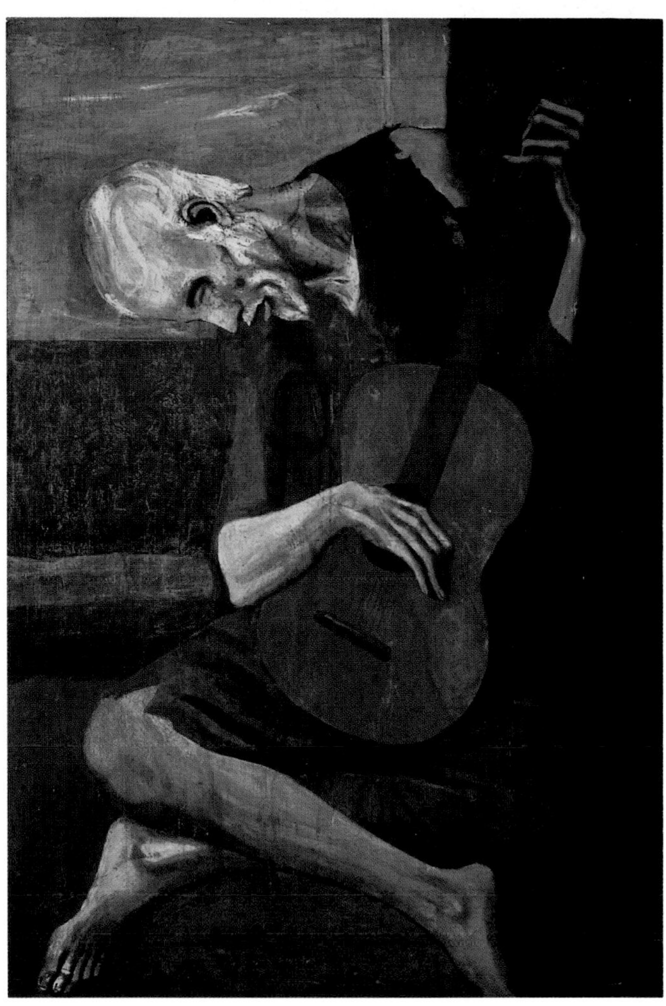

23-23. Pablo Picasso. *The Old Guitarist.* 1903. Oil on panel, 48⅜ x 32½" (122.9 x 82.6 cm). The Art Institute of Chicago

HELEN BIRCH BARTLETT MEMORIAL COLLECTION

8-29 and 8-30) that create an illusion of rich beauty, the angular figures embrace in a moment of passion. The atmosphere is nevertheless strangely oppressive, emphasizing the anxiety of their joyless existence.

PICASSO'S BLUE PERIOD. When he came to Paris from his native Spain in 1900, Pablo Picasso (1881–1973) felt the spell of the same artistic atmosphere that had given rise to the style of Munch. His so-called Blue Period (the term refers to the prevailing color of his canvases as well as to their mood) consists almost exclusively of pictures of beggars and outcasts, such as *The Old Guitarist* (fig. 23-23). These victims of society have a pathos that reflects the artist's own sense of isolation. Yet they convey poetic melancholy more than outright despair. The aged musician accepts his fate with a resignation that seems almost saintly, and the elongated grace of his limbs reminds us of El Greco (compare fig. 14-13). *The Old Guitarist* is a strange union of Mannerism and the art of Gauguin and Toulouse-Lautrec, imbued with the personal gloom of a 22-year-old genius.

ROUSSEAU. A few years later, Picasso and his friends discovered a painter who until then had attracted no attention, although he had been exhibiting his work since 1886. He was Henri Rousseau (1844–1910), a retired customs collector who had started to paint in middle age without training of any sort. His ideal—which, fortunately, he never achieved—was the dry academic style of the followers of Ingres. Rousseau is that paradox, a folk artist of genius. How else could he have done a picture like *The Dream* (fig. 23-24)? What goes on in the enchanted world of this canvas needs no explanation because none is possible. Perhaps for that very reason its magic becomes believably real to us. Rousseau himself described the scene in a little poem:

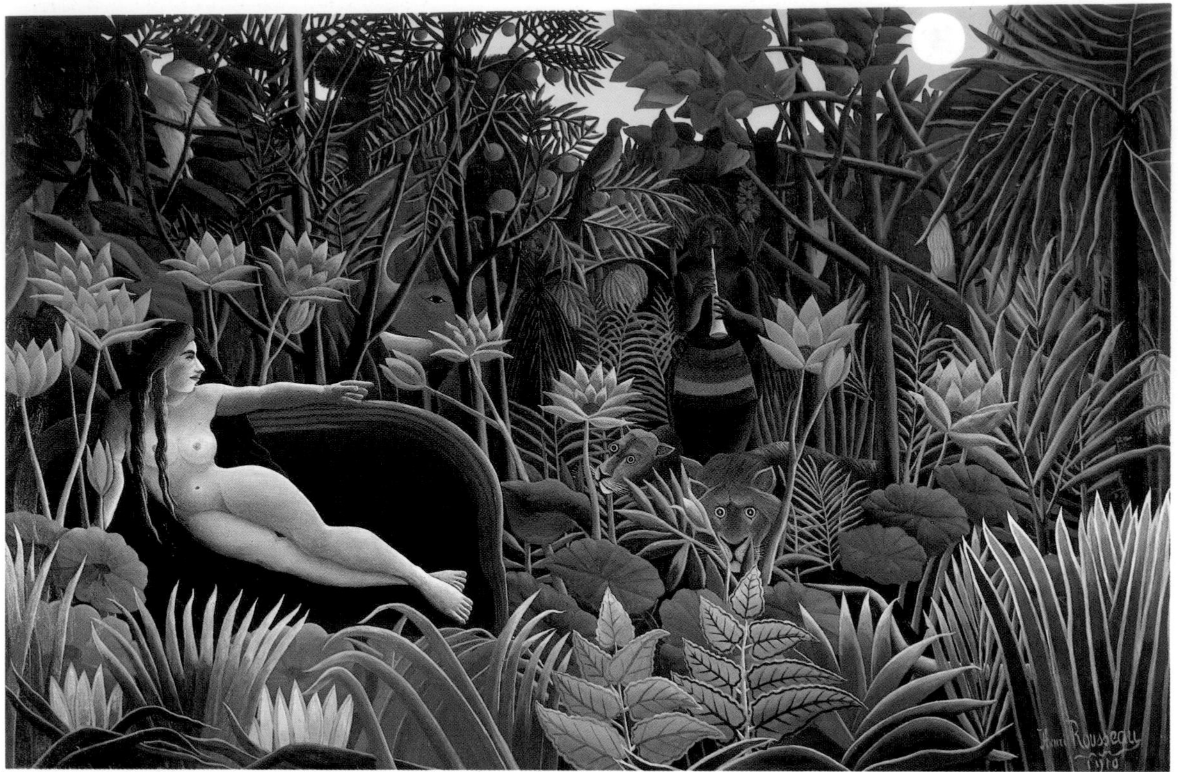

23-24. Henri Rousseau. *The Dream.* 1910. Oil on canvas, 6'8½" x 9'9½" (2.05 x 2.96 m). The Museum of Modern Art, New York
GIFT OF NELSON A. ROCKEFELLER

Yadwigha, peacefully asleep
Enjoys a lovely dream:
She hears a kind snake charmer
Playing upon his reed.
On stream and foliage glisten
The silvery beams of the moon.
And savage serpents listen
To the gay, entrancing tune.

Here at last was the innocent directness of feeling that Gauguin thought so necessary for the age. Picasso and his friends were the first to recognize this quality in Rousseau's work. They honored him as the godfather of twentieth-century painting.

MODERSOHN-BECKER. The inspiration of primitivism that Gauguin had traveled so far to find was discovered by Paula Modersohn-Becker (1876–1907) in the village of Worpswede, near her family home in Bremen, Germany. Among the artists and writers who gathered there was the Symbolist lyric poet Rainer Maria Rilke, Rodin's friend and briefly his personal secretary. Rilke had visited Russia and been deeply impressed with what he viewed as the purity of Russian peasant life. His influence on the colony at Worpswede affected Modersohn-Becker, whose last works are direct forerunners of modern art. Her gentle but powerful *Self Portrait* (fig. 23-25), painted the year before her early death, presents a transition to Expressionism from the Symbolism of Gauguin and his followers, which she absorbed during several

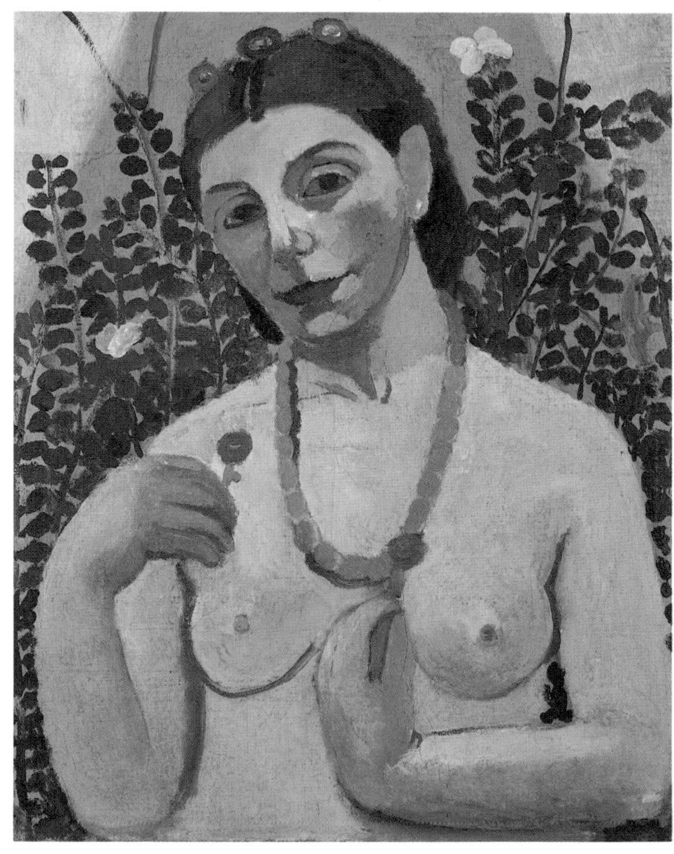

23-25. Paula Modersohn-Becker. *Self-Portrait.* 1906. Oil on canvas, 24 x 19¾" (61 x 50.2 cm). Öffentliche Kunstsammlung Basel, Kunstmuseum, Switzerland

stays in Paris. The color has the intensity of Matisse and the Fauves (see pages 770–71). At the same time, her deliberately simplified treatment of forms parallels the experiments of Picasso, which led to *Les Demoiselles d'Avignon* (see fig. 24-13).

SCULPTURE

MAILLOL. In sculpture, there was nothing comparable to Post-Impressionism, but a form of Symbolism appeared around 1900. Younger French sculptors who had been trained under the dominant influence of Rodin were ready by then to go their own separate ways. The finest of these, Aristide Maillol (1861–1944), began as a Symbolist painter, although he did not share Gauguin's anti-Greek attitude. Maillol admired the simplified strength of early Greek sculpture but rejected its later phases. The *Seated Woman* (fig. 23-26) evokes memories of the Archaic and Severe styles rather than those of Pheidias and Praxiteles. Thus Maillol might be called a "classic primitivist." The solid forms and clearly defined volumes also recall Cézanne's statement that all natural forms are based on the cone, the sphere, and the cylinder. But the most notable quality of the figure is its harmonious, self-sufficient repose, which the outside world cannot disturb. A statue, Maillol thought, must above all be "static": structurally balanced like a piece of architecture. It must represent a state of being that is detached from external circumstance, with none of the restless, thrusting energy of Rodin's work. In this respect, the *Seated Woman* is the exact opposite of *The Thinker* (see fig. 22-29). Maillol later gave it the title *La Méditerranée—The Mediterranean*—to suggest the source from which he drew the timeless serenity of his figure.

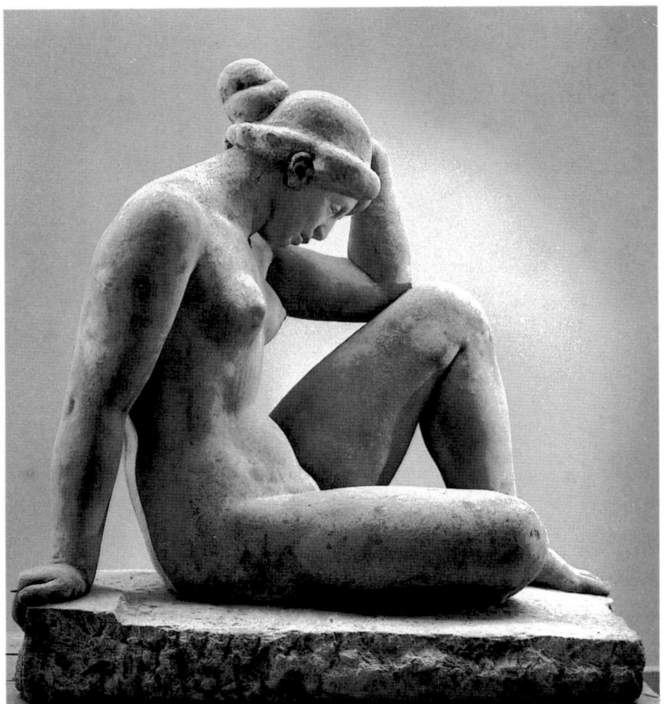

23-26. Aristide Maillol. *Seated Woman (La Méditerranée)*. c. 1901. Stone, height 41" (104.1 cm). Collection Oskar Reinhart, Winterthur, Switzerland

MEUNIER. If Maillol sought to transcend his epoch, the Belgian Constantin Meunier (1831–1905) was thoroughly immersed in it. Politically and socially, Belgium exemplified all the tensions of the later nineteenth century. A conservative government, insensitive to the extremes of wealth and poverty in the country, seemed determined to suppress all protests or attempts at reform. The workers' movement thus had a late start. Not until 1885 were labor unions strong enough to found the Belgian Workers' Party. By that time, many writers and artists had become supporters of social reform. Meunier began as a painter but soon began to model in clay. From 1885 until the end of his life, his output was made up almost entirely of sculpture. The change was motivated by his search for a more "monumental" medium. The heroism of labor, its pride and its pathos, was to be his theme as a sculptor. He treated it with the seriousness of his earlier religious subjects. He shared this concern with Vincent van Gogh, who had an unforgettable experience of human misery in the mining district of Belgium (see page 743). Meunier's lifesize *Bust of a Puddler* (fig. 23-27) has an air of pathos, of noble suffering appropriate to a "martyr of labor." It also shows Meunier's considerable debt to Rodin, for whom he always expressed the greatest admiration.

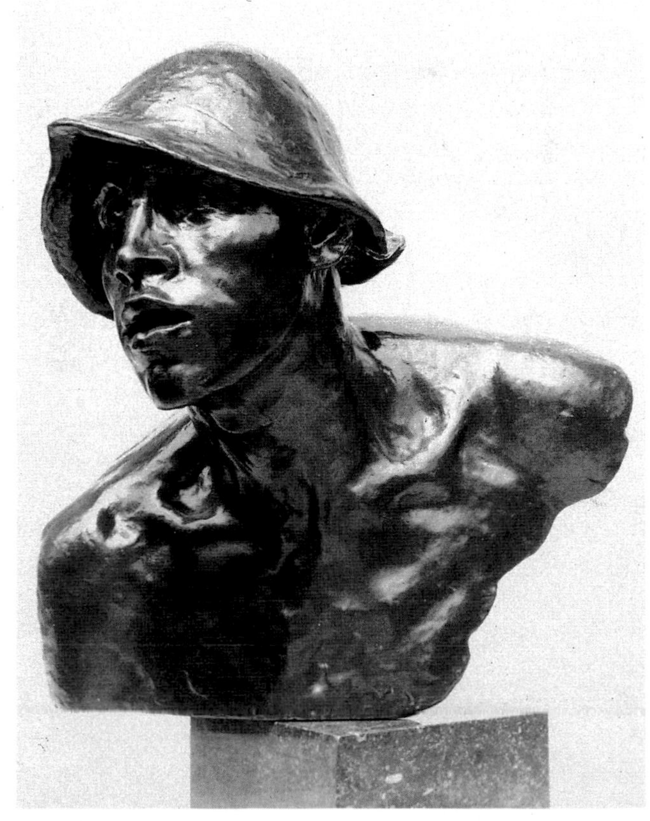

23-27. Constantin Meunier. *Bust of a Puddler.* c. 1885–90. Bronze, lifesize. Private collection

THEATER IN THE POST-IMPRESSIONIST ERA

The major competing tendencies of the late nineteenth century were Realism and Symbolism, which were sometimes found in the work of the same author. The most important Realist was the French novelist Émile Zola (1840–1902). Inspired by Charles Darwin's theory of evolution and Auguste Comte's socialism, he argued that the dramatist should observe the human condition with the detachment of the scientist and illustrate the "inevitable laws of heredity and environment." However, Zola's plays, like those of the Goncourt brothers, were more important in theory than in practice, and Realism found its main expression in the plays of Henri Becque (1837–1899), which are pessimistic to the point of cynicism. Even so, Realism's success depended in the end on the determination of André Antoine (1858–1943), who established the Théâtre Libre (Free Theater) in 1887 and a decade later the Théâtre Antoine, both of which became proving grounds for Realist drama and experimental staging techniques until Antoine was appointed head of the state-supported Odéon in 1906.

Antoine also mounted productions of foreign playwrights, notably the Norwegian Henrik Ibsen (1828–1906), who first established his reputation with verse–dramas about the legendary past, notably *Peer Gynt* (1867), which is still considered the great national saga of Norway. In the 1870s, however, he turned to Realism in such plays as *The Doll's House* (1879), then began making greater use of Symbolism beginning with *The Wild Duck* (1884). The basic theme of his mature works nevertheless remained the same: the conflict between duty and self, which finally sees the consequences of its actions in a moment of revelation. However, Ibsen's treatment of this theme changed considerably over time, almost reversing itself: whereas at first he condemned excessive devotion to duty, in the end he came to criticize unbridled self-interest.

Like the Norwegian painter Edvard Munch, Ibsen enjoyed considerable influence in Germany, thanks in part to the productions mounted by Otto Brahm (1856–1912), who was president of the Freie Bühne (Free Theater) in Berlin in 1889–94 and then director of the Deutsches Theater (German Theater) for a decade before taking over the Lessing Theater until his death. The most important German playwright associated with the Freie Bühne was Gerhart Hauptmann (1862–1946), whose drama *The Weavers* (1892) shows the same social conscience as the early paintings of Van Gogh (see fig. 23-10) and the sculpture of Constantin Meunier (see fig. 23-27). Psychological, not social, realism was the particular interest of Arthur Schnitzler (1862–1931), whose major play, *Anatol* (1893), follows the ideas of his friend Sigmund Freud, the founder of modern psychiatry, in treating human sexuality through a series of affairs that inevitably give way to boredom because ego gratification cannot give rise to enduring love. Owing in good measure to heavy government funding, it was in Germany that most of the major technical innovations in stagecraft were devised, including the revolving stage, the elevator stage, the rolling platform, and the sliding platform.

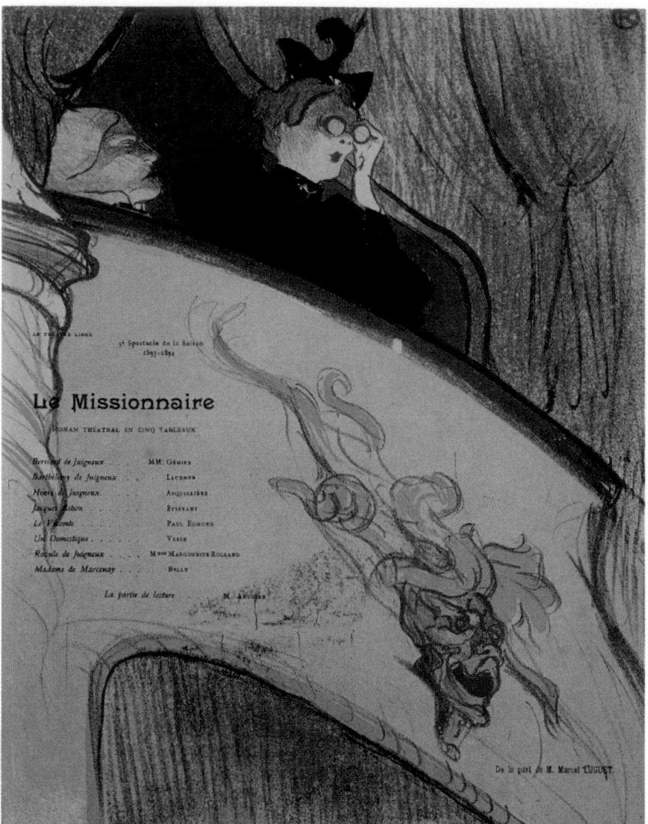

Henri de Toulouse-Lautrec. *Le Missionnaire.* 1894.
Four-color lithograph on wove paper, sheet: $12^{1}/_{16}$ x $9^{7}/_{16}$" (30.6 x 24 cm). National Gallery of Art, Washington, D.C.
GIFT OF THE ALTAS FOUNDATION

In England, the counterpart of the Théâtre Libre and the Freie Bühne was the Independent Theater, where George Bernard Shaw (1856–1950) first achieved critical acclaim in 1892. Shaw used sharp wit to illustrate philosophical propositions in the guise of national and social issues. His belief in human progress through moral persuasion and exercise of free choice found its highest expression in *Man and Superman* (1901), in which a socialist intellectual representing man as spiritual creator outwits his rivals but succumbs to a woman who exemplifies the life force.

The leading Realist in Russia at the turn of the century was Anton Chekhov (1860–1904), whose fame rests on the four plays about ennui in the upper class that he wrote for the Moscow Art Theater during the last five years of his life, especially *The Three Sisters* (1901). Like Chekhov, who befriended him, Maxim Gorky (1868–1936) was at first better known as a writer of short stories; his plays, likewise written mainly for the Moscow Art Theater and centering on class conflict, reflect his political activism.

The antithesis of Zola's Realism was the Symbolism of Stéphane Mallarmé (1842–1898), a poet who was affected by Edgar Allan Poe's macabre writings, Charles Baudelaire's poetry and art criticism, and Richard Wagner's operas. Mallarmé proposed theater that evoked the mystery of life through poetic metaphor. Symbolism was championed first by the short-lived Théâtre d'Art of Paul Fort (1872–1962) and then by the Théâtre de l'Oeuvre under Aurélian-Marie Lugné-Poë (1869–1940). Lugné-Poë drew many of his ideas about scenery from his friends Édouard Vuillard, Maurice Denis, and Pierre Bonnard, whom he also employed to create sets, along with Odilon Redon and Henri de Toulouse-Lautrec (see pages 751 and 742). The most important French dramatist associated with Lugné-Poë was the Belgian-born Maurice Maeterlinck (1862–1949), whose masterpiece, *Pelléas et Mélisande* (1892), which was to inspire Debussy's opera ten years later (see box page 746), relies heavily on symbolic devices to create an air of mystery. Lugné-Poë also staged *Ubu Roi* by Alfred Jarry (1873–1907), which sparked a riot on opening night in 1896. Originally written as a schoolboy satire of a chemistry teacher, this play about an unscrupulous bourgeois king and his wife who give in to every appetite and depraved whim later exercised great influence on the absurdist theater of the Surrealists. A year later Lugné-Poë abandoned Symbolism out of admiration for Ibsen, whose dramas offered far richer content.

After establishing his reputation as a Realist in the late 1880s with *Miss Julie,* the Swedish playwright August Strindberg (1849–1912) began to write "dream plays" in which he tried, as he put it, "to imitate the disconnected but seemingly logical form of the dream. Anything may happen; everything is possible and probable. Time and space do not exist. But one consciousness reigns above them all—that of the dreamer." Unlike Schnitzler's plays, Strindberg's dramas arose not from Freudian theory but from the dramatist's own bout with madness during the 1890s, when he was living in Berlin, from which he recovered with the aid of Emanuel Swedenborg's spiritualist belief in a higher reality.

Closely related to Strindberg as a dramatist was the German Benjamin Franklin Wedekind (1864–1918), whose two major plays, *Earth Spirit* and *Pandora's Box* (both 1895), deal with frankly sexual themes through the prostitute Lulu, who inspired the subject of Alban Berg's unfinished opera (see box page 808). After becoming disillusioned with the power of words, Hugo von Hofmannsthal (1874–1929) actually gave up theater almost entirely to write librettos for Richard Strauss' operas (see box page 747). Another leader in the reaction against Realism was the Swiss-born Adolphe Appia (1861–1928), who emphasized the staging of Wagner's operas through three-dimensional scenery and carefully calculated light effects that made full use of recent advances in lighting technology.

The only serious experiment with Symbolism by an English dramatist was *Salomé* (1892) by Oscar Wilde (1856–1900), but it can hardly be called an English play. It had been written in French during the previous decade and was published in Paris with illustrations by Aubrey Beardsley (see fig. 23-18). Moreover, the work, which was banned in England until 1931, was first produced in Paris by Lugné-Poë in 1896 with Sarah Bernhardt in the lead role. Wilde was otherwise a writer of extremely clever, albeit conventional, comedies; his main connection to Symbolism was his involvement with the Aesthetic Movement, whose dandyism he personified.

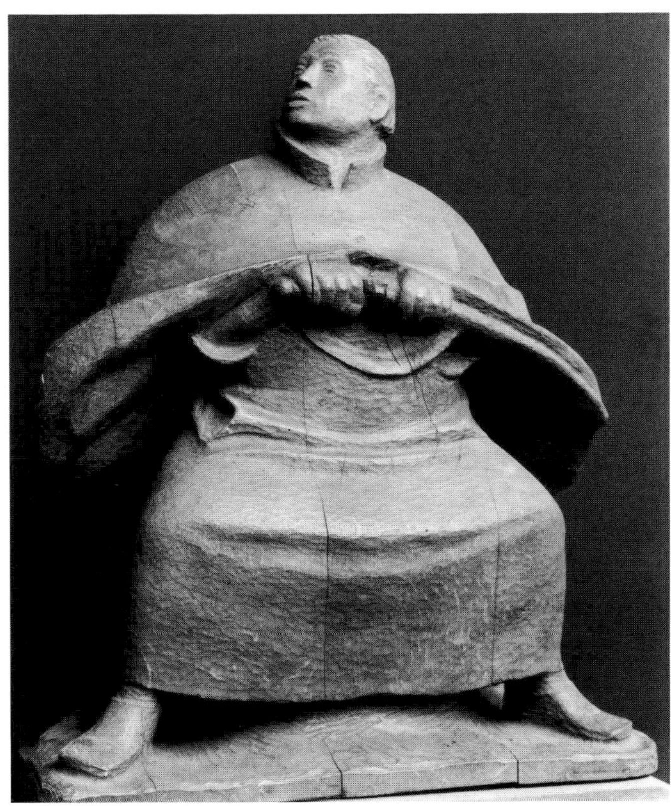

23-28. Ernst Barlach. *Man Drawing a Sword.* 1911. Wood, height 31" (78.7 cm). Private collection

BARLACH. The German sculptor Ernst Barlach (1870–1938), who reached maturity in the years before World War I, was a "Gothic primitivist." What Gauguin had experienced in Brittany and the tropics, Barlach found by going to Russia: the simple humanity of a preindustrial age. Human beings, to Barlach, are humble creatures at the mercy of forces beyond their control; they are never masters of their fate. His figures, such as *Man Drawing a Sword* (fig. 23-28), embody elementary emotions—wrath, fear, grief—that seem imposed upon them. When they act, they are unaware of their own impulses. These figures do not fully emerge from the material substance (often, as here, a massive block of wood). Their clothing is like a hard chrysalis that hides the body, as in medieval sculpture. The range of Barlach's art is severely restricted in both form and emotion, yet within these limits its quiet intensity is not easily forgotten.

ARCHITECTURE

Art Nouveau

During the 1890s and early 1900s a movement usually known as *Art Nouveau* arose in Europe and America. It takes its name from the shop opened in Paris in 1895 by the entrepreneur Siegfried Bing, who employed most of the leading designers of the day and helped to spread their work everywhere. By that time, however, the movement had already been in full force for several years. Art Nouveau has various other names as well: it is called *Jugendstil* (Youth Style) in Germany and Austria, *Stile Liberty* (after the well-known London store that helped to launch it) in Italy, and *Modernista* in Spain. Like Post-Impressionism and Symbolism, Art Nouveau is not easy to characterize. It was primarily a decorative style, inspired by Rococo forms and based on sinuous curves that often suggest organic shapes. Its favorite pattern was the whiplash line; its typical shape, the lily. There was also a severely geometric side that proved of even greater significance in the long run. The ancestor of Art Nouveau was the ornament of William Morris and the Japonist enthusiasm of Whistler. It was also related to the styles of Gauguin, Beardsley, Munch, and Klimt, among others. In turn it was allied to such varied outlooks as aestheticism, socialism, and symbolism.

The goal of Art Nouveau was to raise the crafts to the level of the fine arts, thereby abolishing the distinction between them. In this respect, it was meant to be a "popular" art, available to everyone. Yet it often became so extravagant as to be affordable only to the wealthy few. Art Nouveau had a profound impact on public taste, and its widespread influence on the applied arts can be seen in wrought-iron work, furniture, jewelry, glass, typography, and even women's fashions. Historically Art Nouveau may be regarded as a prelude to modernism, but its preciousness was perhaps the most obvious symptom of the anxiety that afflicted the Western world at the end of the nineteenth century. Hence it is worthy of our attention as our own culture passes through a similar transition.

Although it is usually thought of in terms of the decorative arts, Art Nouveau had an important impact on architecture. As a style of decoration it did not translate readily on a large scale. Indeed, it was aptly called book-decoration architecture for the origin of its designs, which were best suited to two-dimensional surface effects. But in the hands of architects seeking a modern yet national style, Art Nouveau produced impressive results. Thus the authority of the "revival styles" was undermined once and for all in Europe.

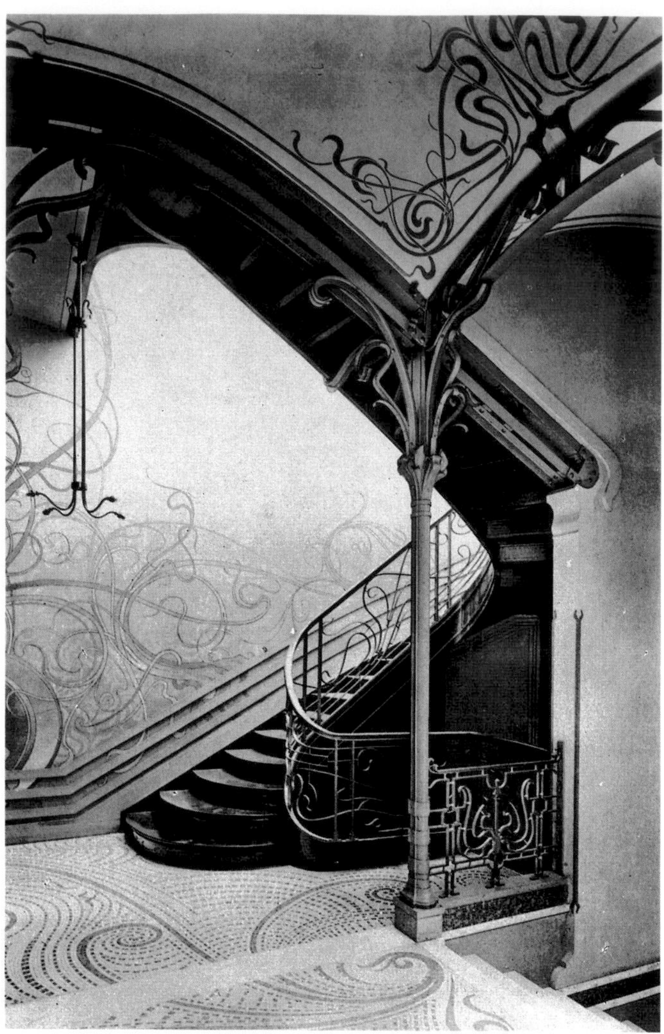

23-29. Victor Horta. Interior Stairwell of the Tassel House, Brussels. 1892–93

HORTA. The first architect to explore the full potential of Art Nouveau was Victor Horta (1861–1947), the founder of the movement in Brussels. After studying in Paris, Horta brought the latest ideas back to Belgium. There he gained the patronage of wealthy industrialists who were surprisingly liberal in their political and cultural views. The stairwell in Tassel House (fig. 23-29), built in 1892–93 for a mathematics professor, has an amazingly fluid grace. Horta has made maximum use of wrought iron, which could be drawn out into almost any shape, but his interior presents no structural advance. The supporting role of the column is frankly acknowledged, although it has been made as slender as possible. In a charming play on the Corinthian capital (compare fig. 5-37), it sprouts ribbonlike tendrils that dissolve the arches—an effect that is enhanced by continuing the vegetal motif in the vault above. Similarly the bannister, which is light and supple, uncoils with taut springiness. The linear patterns extend to the floor and walls, which further integrate the space visually. The ensemble has a litheness and airiness that make the Grand Staircase of Garnier's Opéra seem heavy and vulgar (see fig. 21-75).

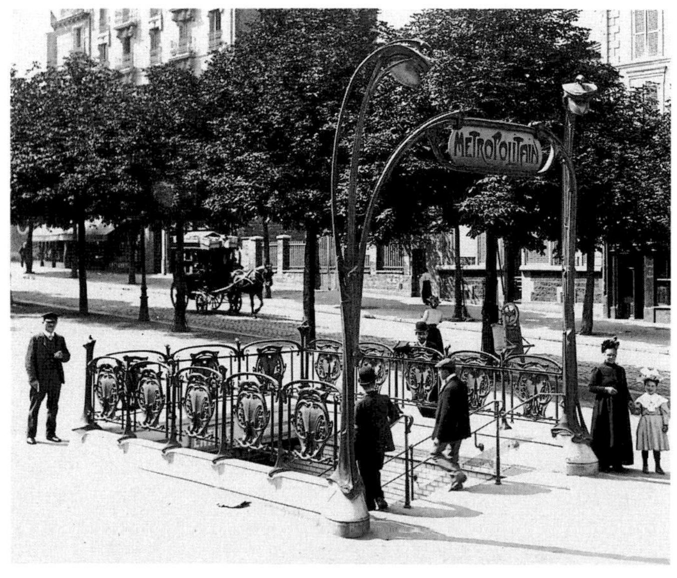

23-30. Hector Guimard. Métro Station, Paris. 1900

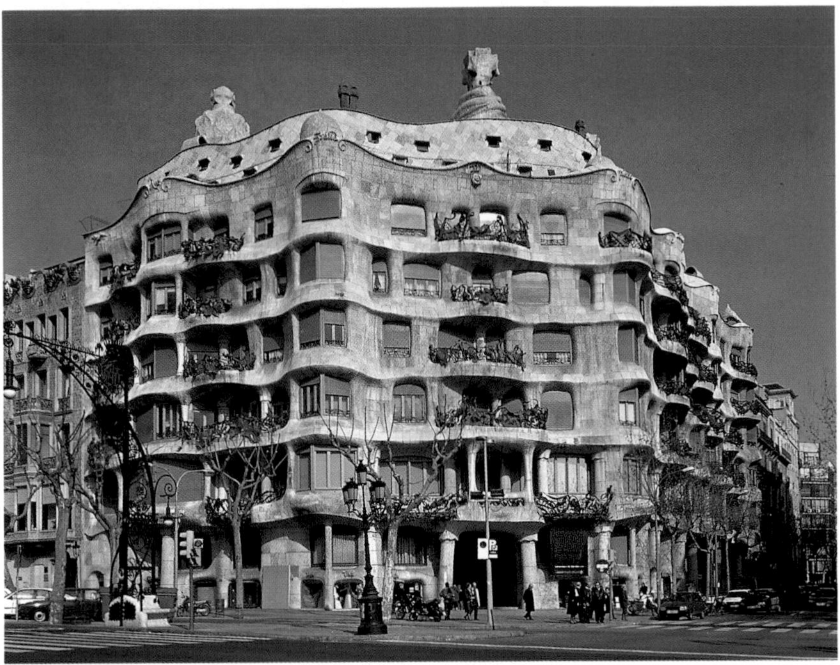

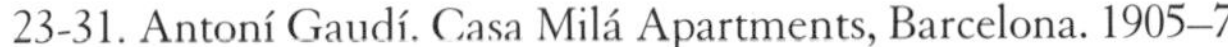

23-31. Antoní Gaudí. Casa Milá Apartments, Barcelona. 1905–7

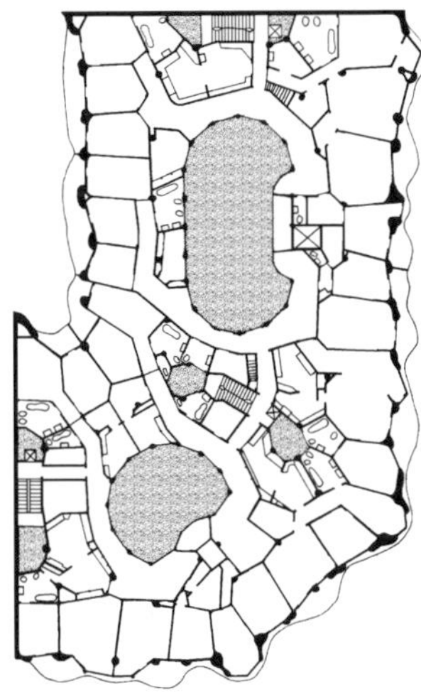

23-32. Floor plan of typical floor, Casa Milá

GUIMARD. Although Art Nouveau's designs lie mainly on the surface, the same devices could be turned into independent three-dimensional forms whose role was essentially sculptural. The entrances for the Métro (the Paris subway) designed in 1900 for the Paris Exposition by Hector Guimard (1867–1942) are just such a case (fig. 23-30). Like Horta, whose work he admired, Guimard was a designer rather than an engineer, and it is this background in the applied arts that makes these stations appealing even today. The functional purpose is so thoroughly disguised by the fanciful forms that we readily overlook their role in providing safety and light, which comes from the plantlike posts springing like strange hybrids from the sidewalk.

GAUDÍ. The most remarkable instance of Art Nouveau in architecture is the Casa Milá in Barcelona (figs. 23-31 and 23-32), a large apartment house by Antoní Gaudí (1852–1926), who began his career working in the Gothic Revival style. It shows an almost maniacal avoidance of all flat surfaces, straight lines, and symmetry. As a result, the building looks as if it had been freely modeled of some flexible substance, even though the structure is built of steel. The "skin" is not stucco or cement, as we might suppose, but cut stone. The softly rounded facade, with its "eroded" openings, undulates as freely as Guarini's Palazzo Carignano (see fig. 17-24). The roof has the rhythmic motion of a wave, while the chimneys seem to have been squeezed from a pastry tube. The Casa Milá expresses one man's fanatical devotion to the ideal of "natural" form. It could never be repeated, let alone developed further. Rather, its combination of modern structure and old-fashioned craftsmanship was an attempt at architectural reform from the edges rather than from the center.

MACKINTOSH. Gaudí represents one extreme of Art Nouveau architecture. The Scot Charles Rennie Mackintosh (1868–1928) represents another. Although they stood at opposite poles, both strove for the same goal—a contemporary style independent of the past. Mackintosh's basic outlook was so close to the functionalism of Louis Sullivan (see below) that at first glance his work hardly seems to belong to Art Nouveau at all. The north facade of the Glasgow School of Art (fig. 23-33), designed as early as 1896 while Mackintosh was an assistant in the firm of Honeyman and Keppie,

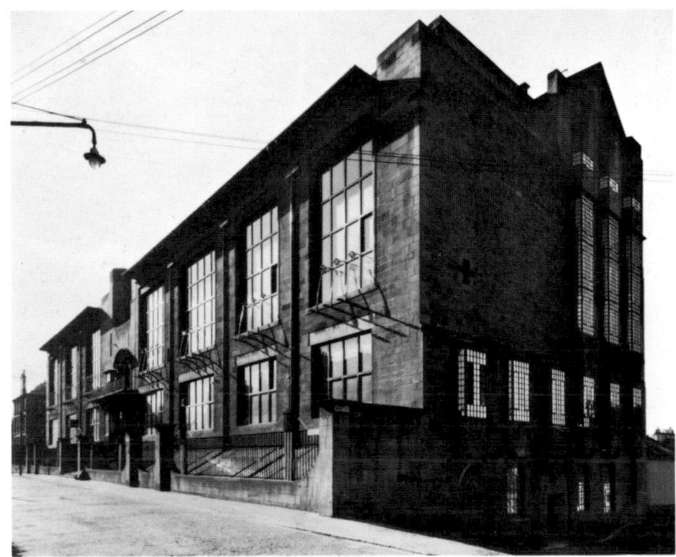

23-33. Charles Rennie Mackintosh. North facade of the Glasgow School of Art, Glasgow, Scotland. 1896–1910

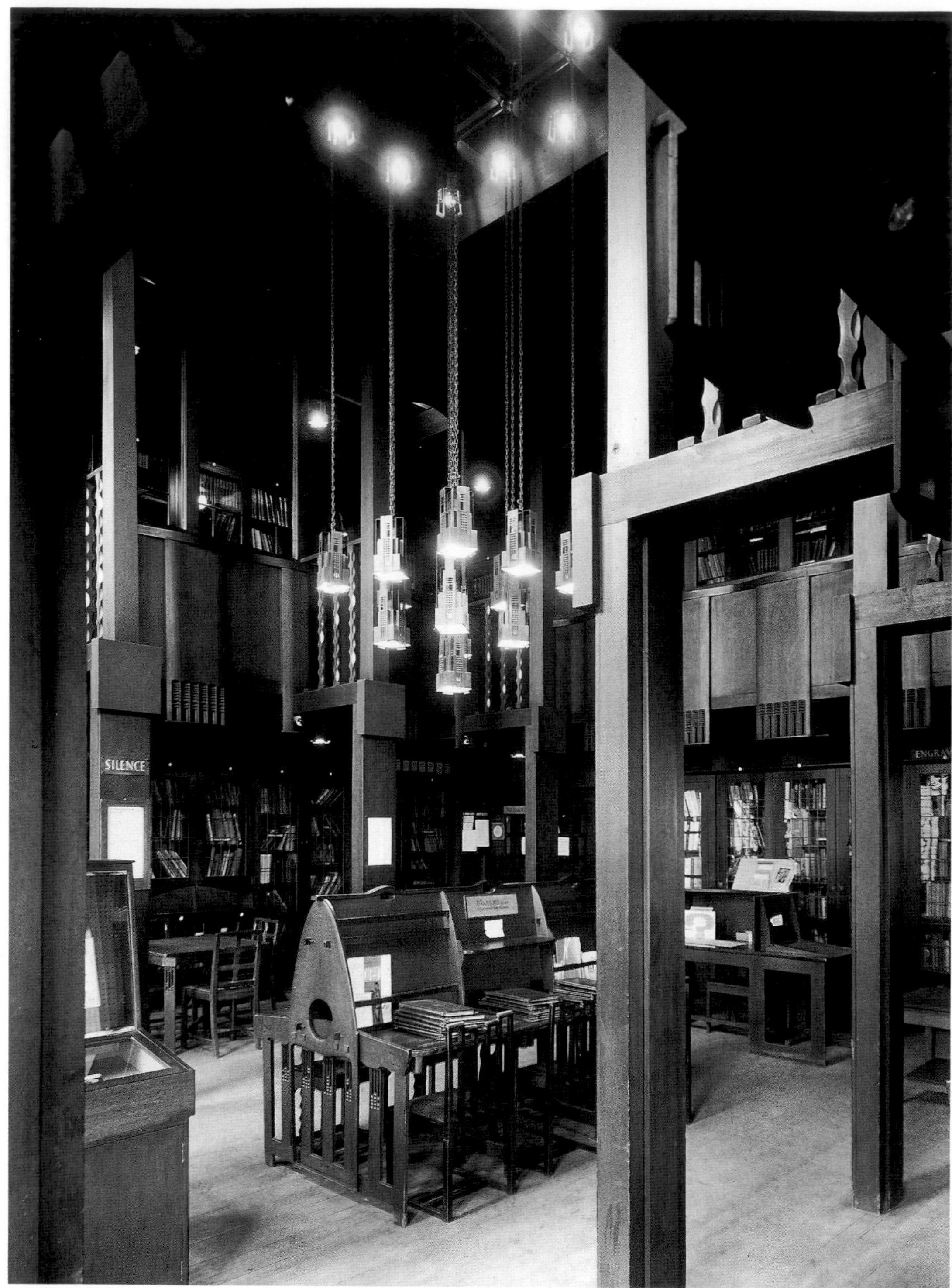

23-34. Interior of the Library, Glasgow School of Art

might be mistaken for a building done 30 years later. Huge, deeply recessed studio windows have replaced the walls, leaving only a framework of undecorated cut stone (which he preferred for its mass). The center bay, however, is "sculptured" in a style related to Gaudí's, despite its preference for angles over curves. Another Art Nouveau feature is the wrought-iron grillwork (here with a minimum of ornament). Even more surprising is the two-story library (fig. 23-34). With its rectangular wooden posts and lintels supporting the balcony, it anticipates early-twentieth-century interiors.

VAN DE VELDE. Through architectural magazines and exhibitions, Mackintosh's work came to be widely known abroad. Its structural clarity and force had a profound effect on one of the leaders of Art Nouveau in Belgium, Henry van de Velde (1863–1957). He began as a Divisionist painter but, under the influence of William Morris, became a designer of posters, furniture, silverware, and glass first for Siegfried Bing in Paris, then in Berlin. After 1900, he worked mainly as an architect. In 1908 Van de Velde founded the Weimar School of Arts and Crafts in Ger-

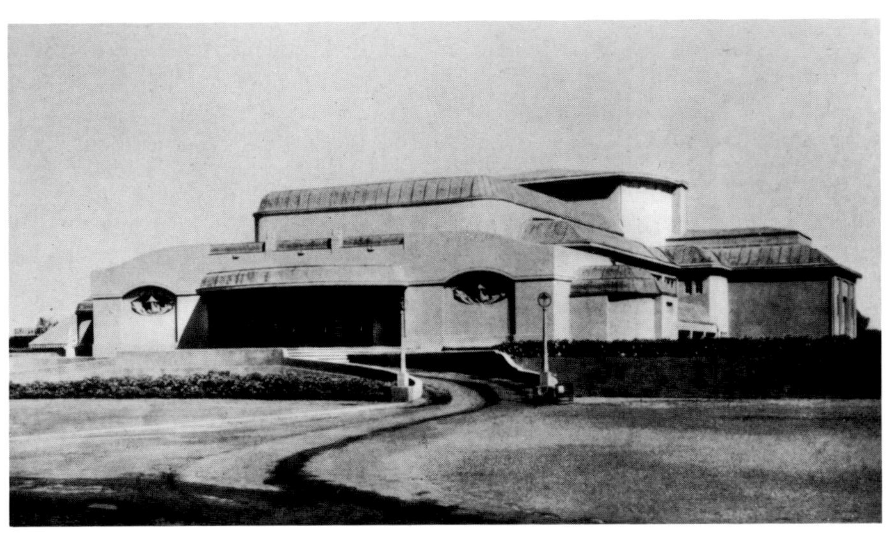

23-35. Henry van de Velde. Theater, Werkbund Exhibition, Cologne. 1914. Destroyed

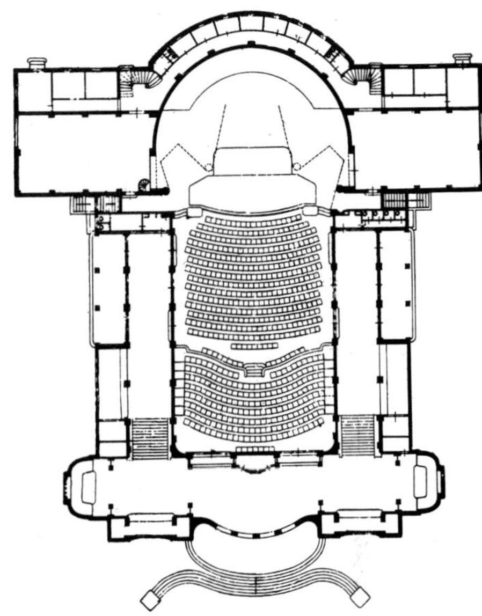

23-36. Plan of the Theater, Werkbund Exhibition

many, which became famous after World War I as the Bauhaus (see page 868). His most ambitious building (figs. 23-35 and 23-36), the theater he designed in Cologne for an exhibition sponsored by the Werkbund (arts and crafts association) in 1914, makes a striking contrast with the Paris Opéra (see figs. 21-76 and 21-77). Whereas the older building tries to evoke the splendors of the Louvre, Van de Velde's exterior is a tightly stretched, plain "skin" that covers—and reveals—the individual units of the internal space. So great is the difference that it seems almost incredible that the Opéra should have been completed only 40 years before. Van de Velde's theater, constructed of concrete, bears a curious resemblance to Mesopotamian ziggurats (compare fig. 3-4), which had greatly impressed him during a visit to the Middle East and Greece in 1903. He held theater as sacred, for to him it was the ultimate expression of social and spiritual life—a conception that was influenced heavily by the director Max Reinhardt and the stage designer Edward Gordon Craig (see box page 756).

United States

The search for a modern architecture first began in earnest around 1880. It required wedding the ideas of William Morris and a new machine aesthetic, tentatively explored some 15 years earlier in the decorative arts, to new construction materials and techniques. The process itself took several decades, during which architects experimented with a variety of styles. It is significant that its symbol was the skyscraper and that its first home was Chicago, then a flourishing metropolis not burdened by allegiance to the styles of the past.

RICHARDSON. The Chicago fire of 1871 had opened enormous opportunities to architects from older cities such as Boston and New York. Among them was Henry Hobson Richardson (1838–1886), who profited as a young man from studies at the École des Beaux-Arts and contact with Labrouste in Paris (see fig. 22-35). Most of his work along the eastern seaboard shows a massive Neo-Romanesque style. There are still echoes of this historicism in his last major project for Chicago, the Marshall Field Wholesale Store designed in 1885 (fig. 23-37). The huge structure filled an entire city block. In its symmetry and the treatment of masonry, it may remind us of Italian Early Renaissance palaces (see fig. 12-21) as interpreted through the Beaux-Arts style (compare fig. 22-34). Yet the complete lack of ornament proclaims its utilitarian purpose.

Warehouses and factories as commercial building types had a history dating back to the later eighteenth century. Richardson must have been familiar with this tradition, which on occasion had produced impressive "stripped-down" designs (fig. 23-38). In con-

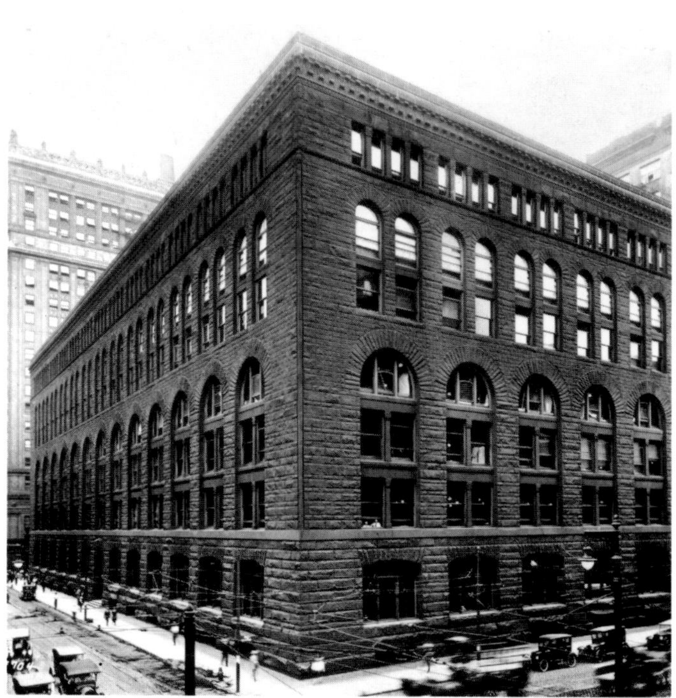

23-37. Henry Hobson Richardson. Marshall Field Wholesale Store, Chicago. 1885–87. Demolished 1930

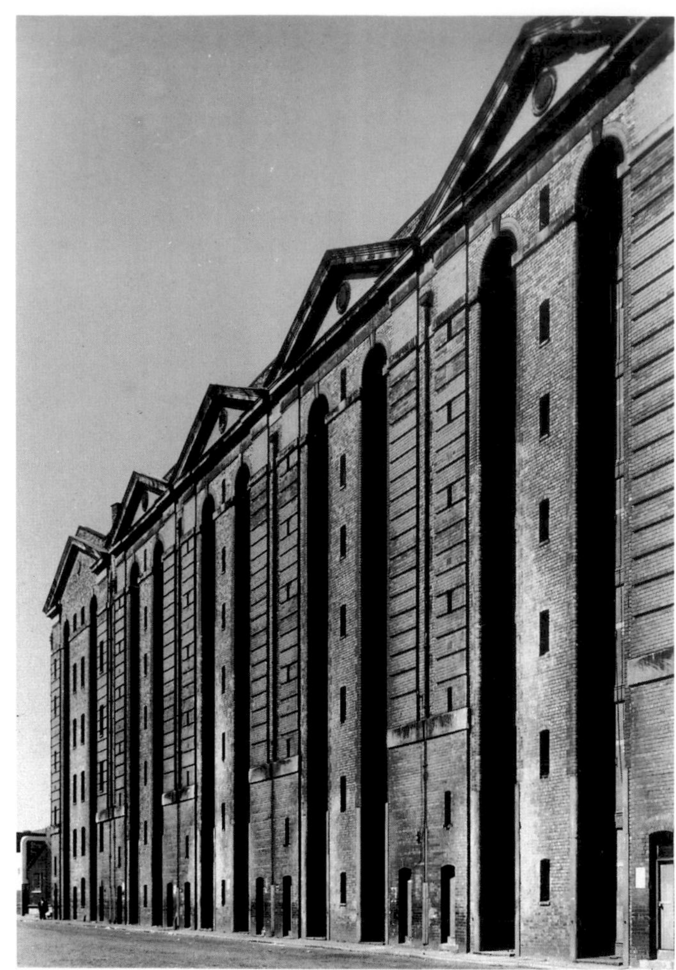

23-38. Warehouses on New Quay, Liverpool. 1835–40

trast to those earlier structures, however, the walls of the Marshall Field Wholesale Store do not present a continuous surface pierced by windows. Except for the corners, which have the effect of heavy piers, they show a series of superimposed arcades, like a Roman aqueduct (see fig. 7-9). This impression is strengthened by the absence of ornament and the thickness of the masonry. (Note how deeply the windows are recessed.) These arcaded walls are as functional and self-sustaining as their ancient predecessors. They give the building a sense of strength and dignity unrivaled in any earlier commercial structure. Behind them is an iron skeleton that actually supports the seven floors, but the exterior does not depend on it, either structurally or aesthetically.

SULLIVAN. Richardson's Marshall Field building stands midway between the old and the new. It embodies, with utmost severity and logic, a concept of monumentality derived from the past, but its opened-up walls, divided into vertical "bays," look forward to the work of Louis Sullivan (1856–1924), who also received training at the École des Beaux-Arts. In 1879 Sullivan became an assistant to the engineer Dankmar Adler (1844–1900); two years later they formed a partnership that lasted until 1895. The Wainwright Building in St. Louis (fig. 23-39), their first skyscraper, was built only five years after the Marshall Field Store. It, too, is monumental but in a very untraditional way. The organization of the exterior reflects and expresses the internal steel skeleton. Their total effect of the slender, continuous brick piers that rise between the windows from the base to the attic is that of a vertical grating encased by the corner piers and by the emphatic horizontals of attic and mezzanine.

This is, of course, only one of the many possible "skins" that could be stretched over the structural framework. What counts is that we immediately feel this wall is derived from the skeleton underneath, that it is not self-sustaining. "Skin" is perhaps too weak a term to describe this brick casing. To Sullivan, who often thought of buildings as comparable to the human body, it was more like the "flesh" and "muscle" attached to the "bone," yet capable of an infinite variety of expressive effects. He coined the phrase "form follows function," but to him it meant something very different from the modernist creed of the twentieth century: "It is the pervading law of all things organic, and inorganic, of all things physical and metaphysical, of all things human and all things superhuman, of all true manifestations of the head, of the heart, of the soul, that the life is recognizable in its expression, that form ever follows function." Clearly he intended a flexible relationship between the two, not rigid dependence. [See Primary Sources, no. 81, pages 933–34.]

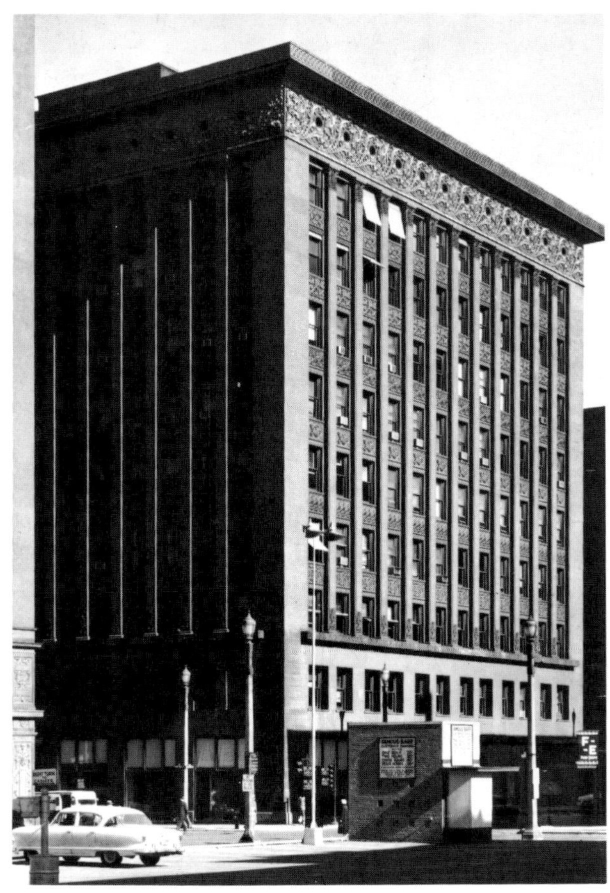

23-39. Louis Sullivan. Wainwright Building, St. Louis, Missouri. 1890–91. Destroyed

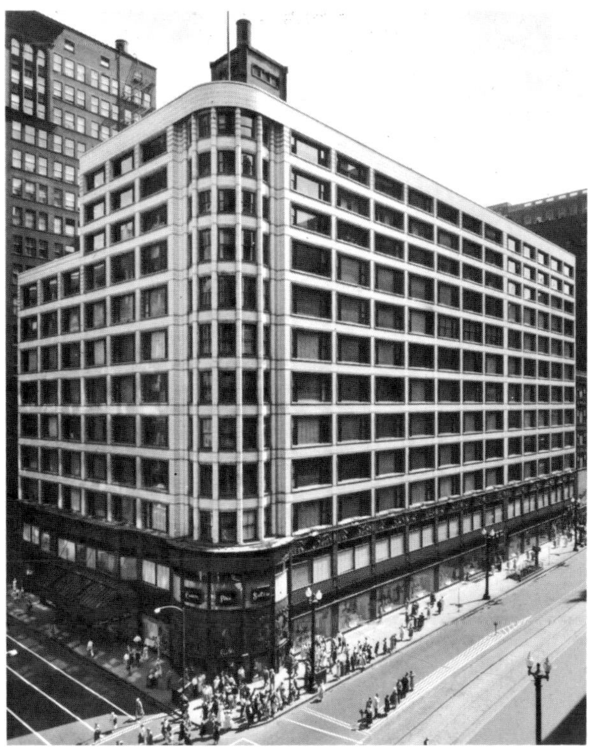

23-40. Louis Sullivan. Schlesinger and Mayer Department Store, Chicago. 1899–1904

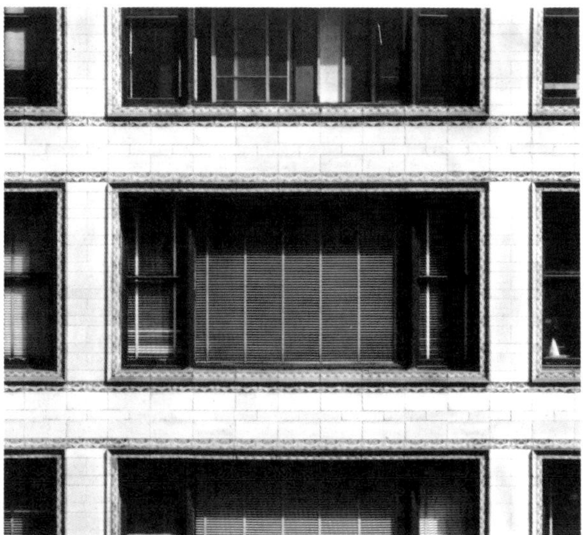

23-41. Detail of facade, showing window, Schlesinger and Mayer Department Store

The range of Sullivan's invention becomes evident if we compare the Wainwright Building with his last building, the Schlesinger and Mayer (later the Carson, Pirie, Scott and Company) Department Store in Chicago, begun nine years later (fig. 23-40). The white terra-cotta on the upper stories follows the grid of the steel frame far more closely, and the overall effect, enhanced by the simple molding around the windows (fig. 23-41), is one of lightness and crispness rather than of harnessed energy. The contrast between the horizontal continuity of the sides and the vertical accent at the corner has been subtly calculated to provide a clear terminus to the facade.

Sullivan's buildings are based on a lofty idealism inspired by the poetry of Walt Whitman and the philosophy of Friedrich Nietzsche. Their ornamentation remains firmly rooted in the nineteenth century, even as they point the way to modern architecture. From the beginning his geometry carried a spiritual meaning, derived partly by the theosopher Emanuel Swedenborg, that centered on birth, flowering, decay, and regeneration. It was tied to a highly original style of decoration embodying Sullivan's theory that ornament must give expression to structure—not by reflecting it literally but by interpreting the same concepts through organic abstraction. The soaring verticality of the Wainwright Building, for example, stands for growth, which is developed further by the vegetative motifs of the moldings along the cornice and between the windows. The clean articulation of the windows on the upper stories of the Schlesinger and Meyer building gives way on the ground floor and mezzanine to a lavish display of ironwork (designed largely by George G. Elmslie using Sullivan's system) that increases the storefront's attraction to shoppers.

THE MATERIALS OF MODERN ARCHITECTURE

After about 1780, in the world of commercial architecture we find the gradual introduction of new materials and techniques that were to have a profound effect on architectural style by 1900. Of these by far the most important was iron, which was used as early as the fourth millennium B.C. and began to be made on a large scale beginning in the fourteenth century. Pig iron, smelted in blast furnaces, can be poured into molds to make cast iron, which has relatively high amounts of carbon and impurities (slag), so that it is brittle. Wrought iron, introduced around 1820, is soft and malleable (hence its name) but, having less carbon and slag, possesses greater tensile strength, making it ideal for bolts, ties, and trusses. Steel is an even stronger alloy of iron and small amounts of carbon that is also ductile and corrosion-resistant. (Technically, most nineteenth-century steel was really a form of wrought iron, since it lacked other elements, such as nickel, chromium, and aluminum, which were added after 1900 for greater hardness.) It was handmade until the 1850s, when the Englishman Henry Bessemer and the American William Kelly independently invented a commercial process to remove the impurities by introducing oxygen, which also heated the iron in a converter of steel lined with silica. The open-hearth furnace, devised in 1864 by William and Frederick Siemens, used regenerative preheating of air to smelt a combination of iron ore and pig iron at extremely high temperatures. The only major advances since then are the basic-oxygen process and the electric furnace.

Cast iron was first mass-produced for rails by Abraham Darby in 1767. Fires at textile mills led to the use of cast-iron pillars in the 1780s, then beams during the following decade. Cast-iron columns were also introduced in churches as early as the 1780s; soon the structural elements of churches were being built almost entirely of iron, for example, St. George at Everton, erected in 1812–13 by the architect Thomas Rickman and iron founder John Cragg, which uses an extremely sophisticated structural system, including tension rods, to tie it together (see illustration on next page). Cast iron has the advantage of being stronger and more fire-resistant than wood, but it is subject to corrosion and, being an excellent heat conductor, expands and contracts, thereby causing condensation that further contributes to the problem of rust. Iron and steel proved especially useful for bridge spans. The first iron bridge was built in 1777–79 at Coalbrookdale by Abraham Darby III from a design by the architect Thomas F. Pritchard. Construction was greatly improved during the first half of the nineteenth century by the introduction of new truss systems and the riveted I-beam. Within a few decades of their first appearance, iron columns and arches became the standard means of supporting roofs over the large spaces required by railroad stations. The first railway shed, built in 1830, was a modest structure using straight beams; the arch became an important form only in the 1840s, as rail lines became increasingly common first throughout Europe and then in America, and large terminals began to be erected.

Because it can be manufactured with great consistency, iron can be used in predictable ways that can be calculated by using standard mathematical formulas. This property gave rise to new structural systems (notably those by James Bogardus in the 1840s and '50s) that are extremely stable yet lightweight, though they almost always remained completely hidden from view. Technology produced a fundamental change in the practice of architecture, which became increasingly dependent on engineering. As a consequence, the tradition of artists and gifted amateurs practicing as architects was over by 1880. The triumph of the iron age was announced at the Universal Exposition held in Paris in 1889 by the Hall of Machines, designed by Charles Dutert with the engineering team of Contamin, Pierron, and Charton, which is seen behind the Eiffel Tower in figure 22-38. The tower itself was a miracle of engineering, manufacturing, and construction. In addition to being extremely lightweight, it was precast so precisely that no fabrication or cutting was done on the site, only riveting, and planned so carefully that not a single worker was killed. (Interestingly enough, Eiffel added the arches at the base, similiar to those on his bridges, to assure the viewer that the tower would stand, though they were not structurally necessary.) By this time, iron was already being rapidly supplanted by steel. Steel mills sprang up everywhere after 1865 to serve the rail industry, but it was not until the 1880s that long rolled-steel beams began to be produced in large quantities, thanks to the widespread use of the open-hearth furnace. This innovation in turn made possible steel-frame construction, essential to skyscrapers, whose potential was first explored during the same decade in New York and Paris and then in Chicago.

The difficulty with iron and steel is that they rust and can be damaged by fire. To overcome these limitations, they were embedded in concrete, to make ferroconcrete, which is fire- and water-resistant but has low tensile strength and is subject to erosion. Ferroconcrete thus unites the best of both materials. Concrete is made by heating limestone and clay until they almost fuse, then grinding and mixing them with water and stone, sand or gravel. Used widely by the Romans, it was rediscovered in

PHOTOGRAPHY

Documentary Photography

During the second half of the nineteenth century, the press played a leading role in the social movement that brought the harsh realities of poverty to the public's attention. The camera became an important instrument of reform through the photodocumentary, which tells the story of people's lives in a pictorial essay. It responded to the same conditions that had stirred Courbet (see pages 706–08), and its factual reportage likewise fell within the Realist tradition. Before then, photographers had been content to present romanticized images of the poor like those in genre paintings of the day. The first photodocumentary was John Thomson's illustrated sociological study *Street Life in London,* published in 1877. To get his pictures, he had to pose his figures, since exposures took minutes, not a split second, as they do today.

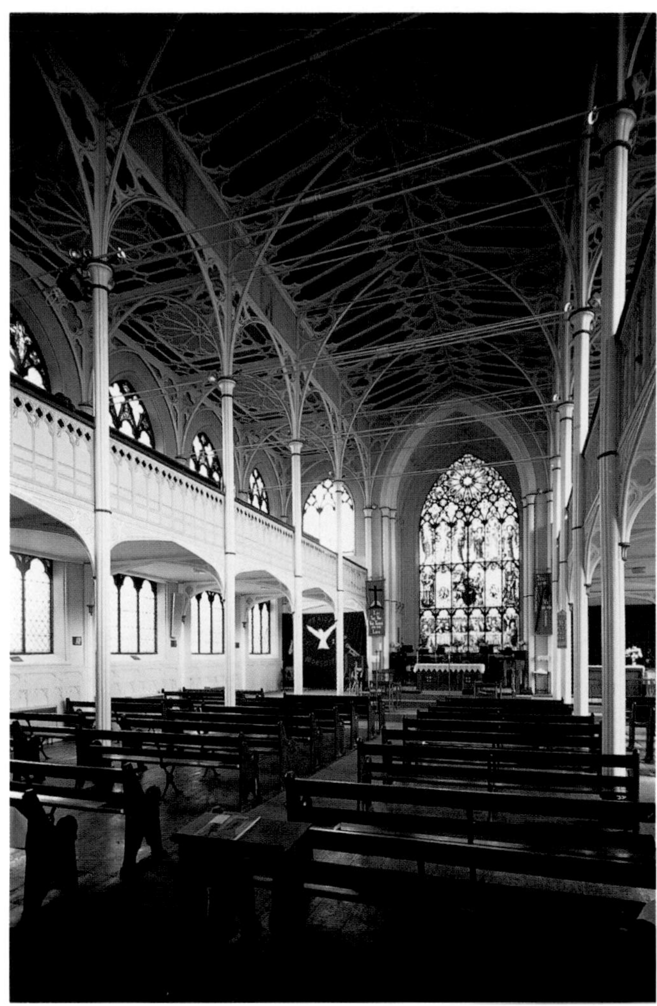

Thomas Rickman and John Cragg. Interior, St. George's Church, Everton, Liverpool, England. 1812–13

1774 by John Smeaton of England. Portland Cement, which is stronger and more durable, was invented in 1824 by another Englishman, Joseph Aspdin. The process of making it is similar to that of concrete but uses different materials. Lime, silica, alumina, sulfates, and iron oxide are heated until they nearly coalesce before being ground up and mixed with gypsum. Though a concrete house was built as early as 1837 by J. B. White of England, cement did not become widely adopted until the 1850s and '60s for sewer systems. It nevertheless remained too expensive for large-scale use before the early 1900s.

Ferroconcrete incorporating tension rods was first patented in 1856 by François Coignet. Iron beams were substituted in patents issued in 1867 and 1878 to Joseph Monier, whose system was improved further by Gustav Adolf Wayss in his important publication of 1887. In 1892 the Belgian François Hennebique replaced iron with steel and enclosed girders in cement for the first time to protect them from fire and corrosion, as well as from the chemical fumes found in factories; equally important, he combined all supports, walls, and ceilings into a single unit using hooked connections that were far more stable. The final step was taken in the early 1900s by Eugène Freyssinet, who recalculated all the formulas for reinforced concrete and in the process invented prestressed concrete, which enables curved supports to carry much greater loads and counteracts deterioration of the concrete itself under pressure.

As important as these developments were, modern architecture would not have been possible without others that we now take for granted. Plate glass was introduced in the 1820s, followed by cheaper sheet glass around 1835. The repeal of the excise tax on glass in 1845 in England finally made sheet glass an affordable material on a large scale. Used in conjunction with cast iron, ever-larger panes of glass gave rise to the modern storefront, which became ubiquitous after mid-century. Massive windows, used serially, were also incorporated first into department stores and eventually into skyscrapers from the late 1870s onward. Equally essential to the skyscraper was the invention of the passenger elevator by Elisha Otis in 1857. The humble brick became an important building material in the 1850s with the advent of the modern kiln, which produced it cheaply in vast quantities. Other amenities included gas lighting (1840s), toilets (c. 1870), electricity (1880s), telephones (1880s), and central heat (1890s).

Finally, we should mention rubber. It was limited chiefly to waterproofing as the result of a process for applying it to fabrics devised by Samuel Peale in 1791, though it was the chemist Charles Mackintosh who opened the first factory in Glasgow in 1823; its widespread use as insulation and other applications was made possible only in 1839, when Charles Goodyear, relying on the work of the German chemist Friedrich Ludersdorf and the American chemist Nathaniel Hayward, discovered vulcanization, which involved cooking the rubber with sulfur to prevent it from melting in hot weather and becoming brittle in cold weather. Synthetic rubber was initially developed in Germany during World War I because natural rubber was hard to come by, but it was not commercially viable until after 1930, when the chemistry of polymers was finally understood by Wallace Hume Carothers of America and Hermann Staudinger of Germany. The result was neoprene (1931), Buna (1935), butyl rubber (1940), and GR-S (government rubber–styrene, used in World War II).

RIIS. The invention of gunpowder flash ten years later allowed Jacob Riis (1849–1914) to rely for the most part on the element of surprise. Riis was a police reporter in New York City, where he learned at first hand about the crime-infested slums and their appalling living conditions. He kept up a steady campaign of illustrated newspaper exposés, books, and lectures, which in some cases led to major revisions of the city's housing codes and labor laws. Even today, his photographs' unflinching realism has lost none of its force. Certainly it would be difficult to imagine a more nightmarish scene than *Bandits' Roost* (fig. 23-42). With good reason we sense a pervasive air of danger in the eerie light. The notorious gangs of New York City's Lower East Side looked for their victims by night and killed them without hesitation. The motionless figures seem to look us over with the practiced casualness of hunters coldly sizing up potential prey.

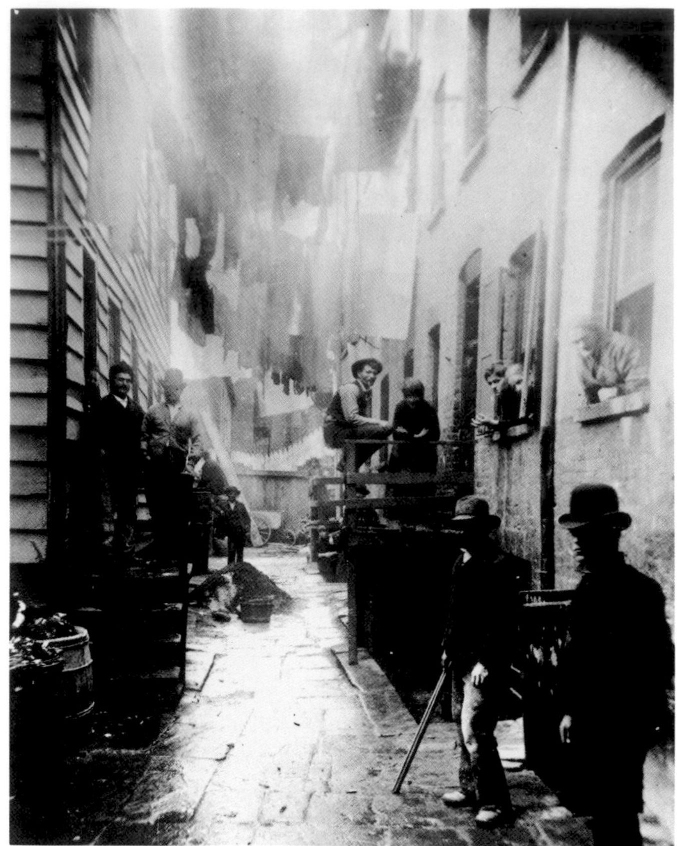

(LEFT) 23-42. Jacob Riis. *Bandits' Roost.* c. 1888. Gelatin-silver print. Museum of the City of New York

(BELOW) 23-44. Henry Peach Robinson. *Fading Away.* 1858. Combination print. Royal Photographic Society, London

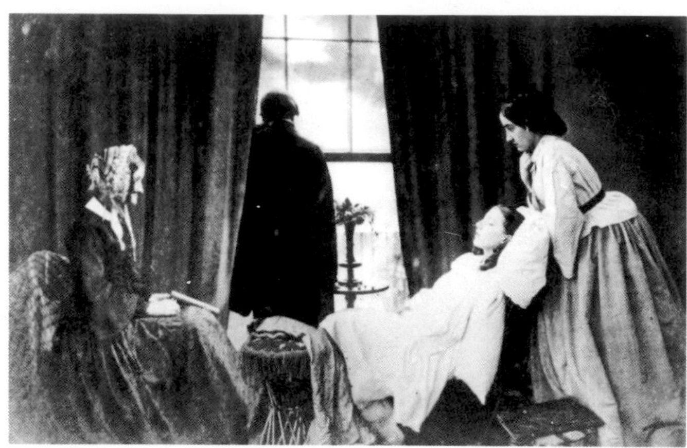

(RIGHT) 23-43. Oscar Rejlander. *The Two Paths of Life.* 1857. Combination albumen print, 16 x 31" (40.6 x 78.7cm). George Eastman House, Rochester, New York

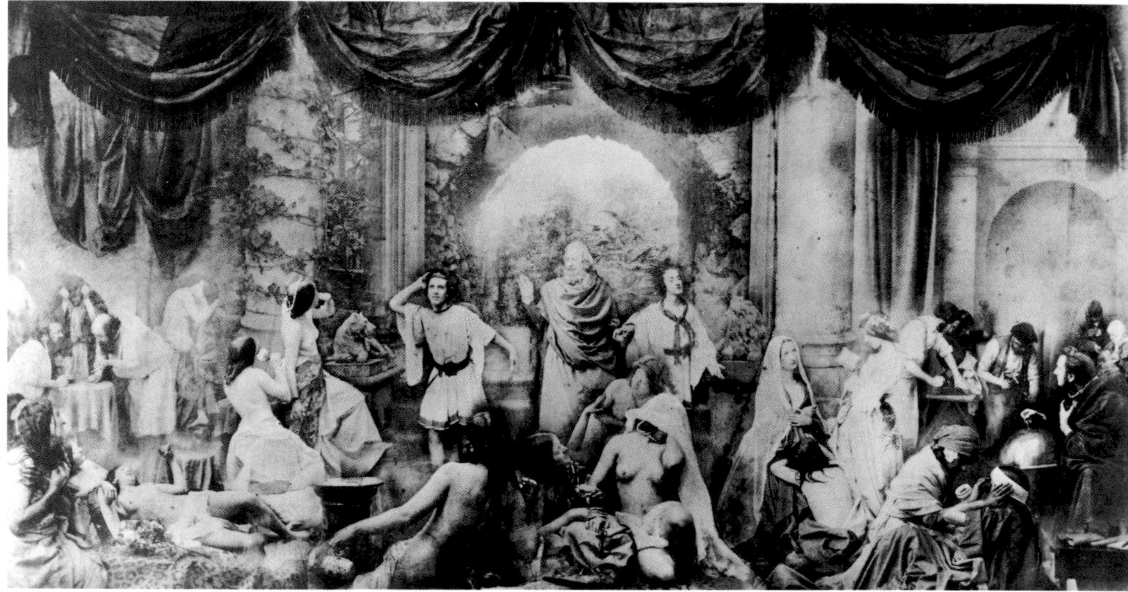

Pictorialism

The raw subject matter and realism of documentary photography had little impact on art and were avoided by most other photographers as well. England, through such organizations as the Photographic Society of London, founded in 1853, became the leader of the movement to convince doubting critics that by imitating painting and printmaking, photography could indeed be art. To Victorian England, beauty meant art with a high moral purpose or noble sentiment, preferably in a classical style.

REJLANDER. *The Two Paths of Life* (fig. 23-43) by Oscar Rejlander (1818–1875) fulfills these ends by presenting an allegory descended from Hogarth's *Rake's Progress* series (see figs. 20-11 and 20-12). This amazing photomontage, almost three feet wide, combines 30 negatives through composite printing. We see a young man (in two images) choosing between the paths of virtue and vice, the latter represented by a half-dozen nudes. The picture created a sensation in 1857, and Queen Victoria herself purchased a print. Rejlander, however, never enjoyed the same success again. He was the most adventurous photographer of his time and soon turned to other subjects less in keeping with popular taste.

ROBINSON. The mantle of art photography fell to Henry Peach Robinson (1830–1901), who became the most famous photographer in the world. He established his reputation with *Fading Away* (fig.

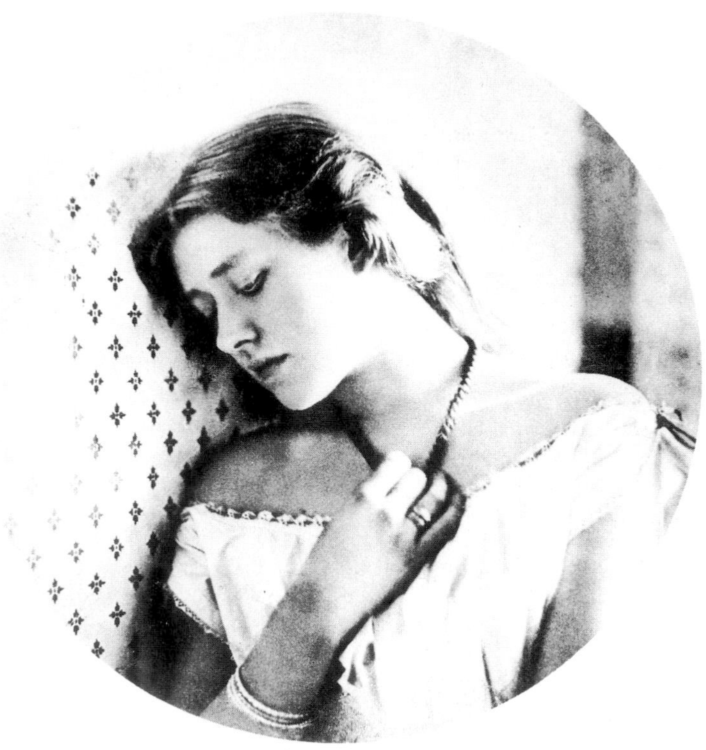

23-45. Julia Margaret Cameron. *Ellen Terry, at the Age of Sixteen.* c. 1863. Carbon print, diameter 9½" (24 cm). The Metropolitan Museum of Art, New York
ALFRED STIEGLITZ COLLECTION, 1949

23-44), which appeared a year after Rejlander's *The Two Paths of Life.* With six lines from Shelley's "Queen Mab" printed below on the mat, the photograph is typical of Robinson's sentimental scenes. Like *The Two Paths of Life,* it is a photomontage but made of only five negatives. The scene is as carefully staged as any Victorian melodrama. At first Robinson made detailed drawings before photographing the individual components. He later renounced multiple-negative photography but still tried to imitate contemporary genre painting in his pictures. When treating elevated subject matter he continued to distinguish between fact and truth, which to him was a mixture of the real and the artificial.

CAMERON. The photographer who pursued ideal beauty with the greatest passion was Julia Margaret Cameron (1815–1879). An intimate friend of leading poets, scientists, and artists, she took up photography at the age of 48 when she was given a camera. She went on to create a remarkable body of work. In her own day Cameron was known for her allegorical and narrative pictures, but now she is remembered chiefly for her portraits of the men who shaped Victorian England. Many of her finest photographs, however, are of the women who were married to her closest friends. An early study of the actress Ellen Terry (fig. 23-45; see box page 732) has the lyricism and grace of the Pre-Raphaelite aesthetic that shaped Cameron's style (compare fig. 22-20).

Naturalistic Photography

EMERSON. The attack against art photography was taken up by Peter Henry Emerson (1856–1936), who became the bitter enemy of Robinson. Emerson championed what he called naturalistic photography, based on scientific principles and Constable's landscapes. Nevertheless he, too, contrasted realism with truth, which he defined in terms of sentiment, aesthetics, and the selective arrangement of nature. Using a single negative, Emerson composed his scenes with the greatest care. The results were sometimes similar to Robinson's, which of course he never acknowledged. Most of Emerson's work was devoted to scenes of rural and coastal life and are not far removed from early documentary photographs.

In his best prints, nature predominates. He was a master at distributing tonal masses across a scene, and his photographs (fig. 23-46) are equivalent to fine English landscape paintings of the period. Although the effect is rarely apparent in his work, Emerson advocated putting the lens slightly out of focus, in the belief that the eye sees only the central area of a scene sharply. When he gave up this idea a few years later, he decided that photography was indeed science instead of art because it was machine-made, not personal.

Photo-Secession

The issue of whether photography could be art came to a head in the early 1890s with the Secession movement (see page 752). In 1893 the Linked Ring was founded in London as a rival to the renamed Royal Photographic Society of Great Britain. Stimulated by Emerson's ideas, the Secessionists wanted a pictorialism independent of science and technology. They steered a course between academicism and naturalism by imitating every form of late Romantic art that did not involve narrative. Equally incompatible with their aims were Realist and Post-Impressionist painting, then at their zenith. In the group's approach to photography as Art for Art's Sake, the Secession had the most in common with Whistler's aestheticism.

To resolve the dilemma between art and mechanics, the Secessionists tried to make their photographs look as much like paintings as possible. Rather than resorting to composite or multiple images, however, they exercised total control over the printing process, chiefly by adding special materials to their printing paper

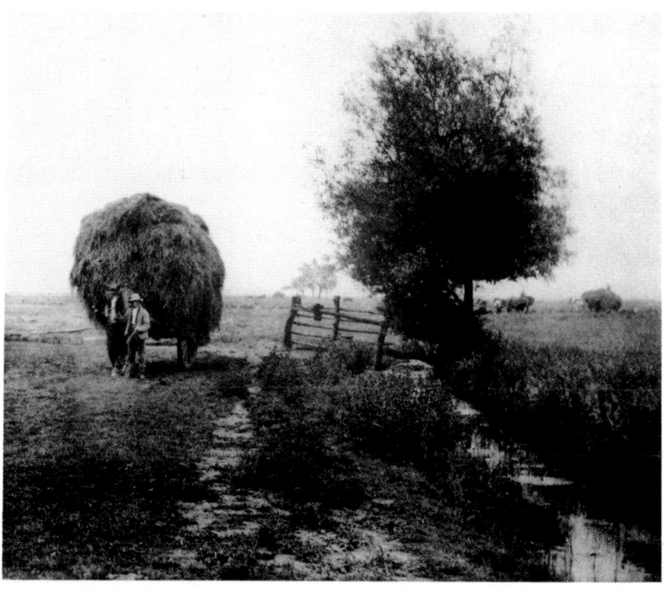

23-46. Peter Henry Emerson. *Haymaking in the Norfolk Broads.* c. 1890. Platinum print. Société Française de Photographie, Paris

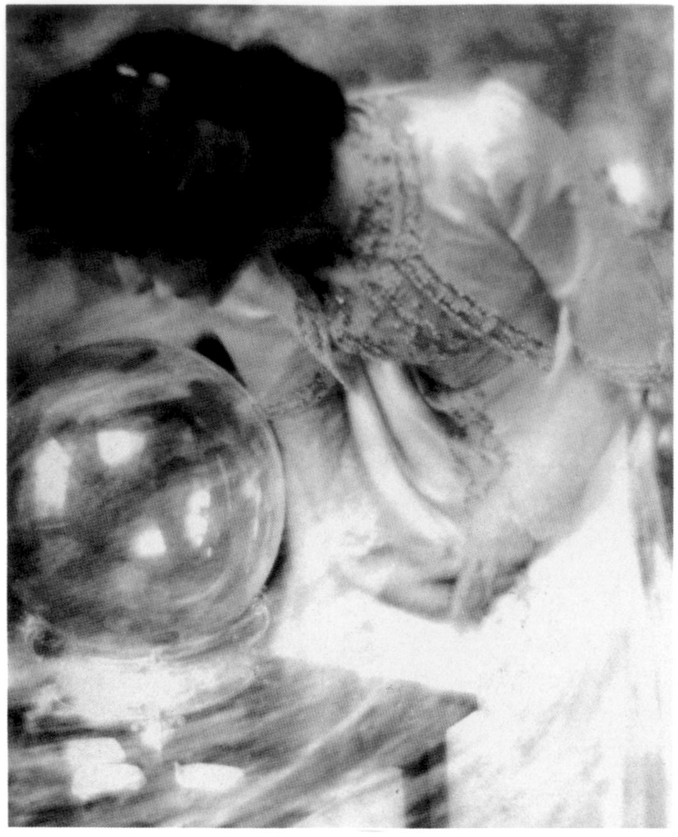

in order to create different effects. Pigmented gum brushed on coarse drawing paper yielded a warm-toned, highly textured print that in its way approximated Impressionist painting. Paper impregnated with platinum salts was especially popular among the Secessionists because of its clear grays. *The Magic Crystal* (fig. 23-47) by Gertrude Käsebier (1854–1934) uses a platinum print of unmatched tonal subtlety to create an ethereal atmosphere, in which spiritual forces seem to visibly sweep across the photograph.

STEICHEN. The Linked Ring had close ties with America through Käsebier and Alfred Stieglitz, who opened his Photo-Secession gallery in New York in 1905. [See Primary Sources, no. 82, page 934.] Among his protégés was the young Edward Steichen (1879–1973), whose photograph of Rodin in his sculpture studio (fig. 23-48) is without doubt the finest achievement of the entire Photo-Secession movement. The head in profile contemplating *The Thinker* expresses the essence of the confrontation between the sculptor and his work of art. His brooding introspection hides the inner turmoil evoked by the monument to Victor Hugo which rises dramatically like a ghost in the background. Not since *The Creation of Adam* by Michelangelo (see fig. 13-18), who was Rodin's ideal, have we seen a more telling use of space or an image that penetrates the mystery of creativity so deeply.

The Photo-Secession movement achieved its goal of gaining wide recognition for photography as an art form, but by 1907 its approach was regarded as stilted. Though the movement lasted for a few more years, it was becoming clear that the future of photography did not lie in the imitation of painting, which was then being reformed by modernists. Yet the legacy of the Photo-Secession was valuable, despite its limitations, for it taught photographers much about the control of composition and the response to light.

Motion Photography

MUYBRIDGE. An entirely new direction was charted by Eadweard Muybridge (1830–1904), the father of motion photography.

(Above) 23-47. Gertrude Käsebier. *The Magic Crystal.* c. 1904. Platinum print. Royal Photographic Society, Bath

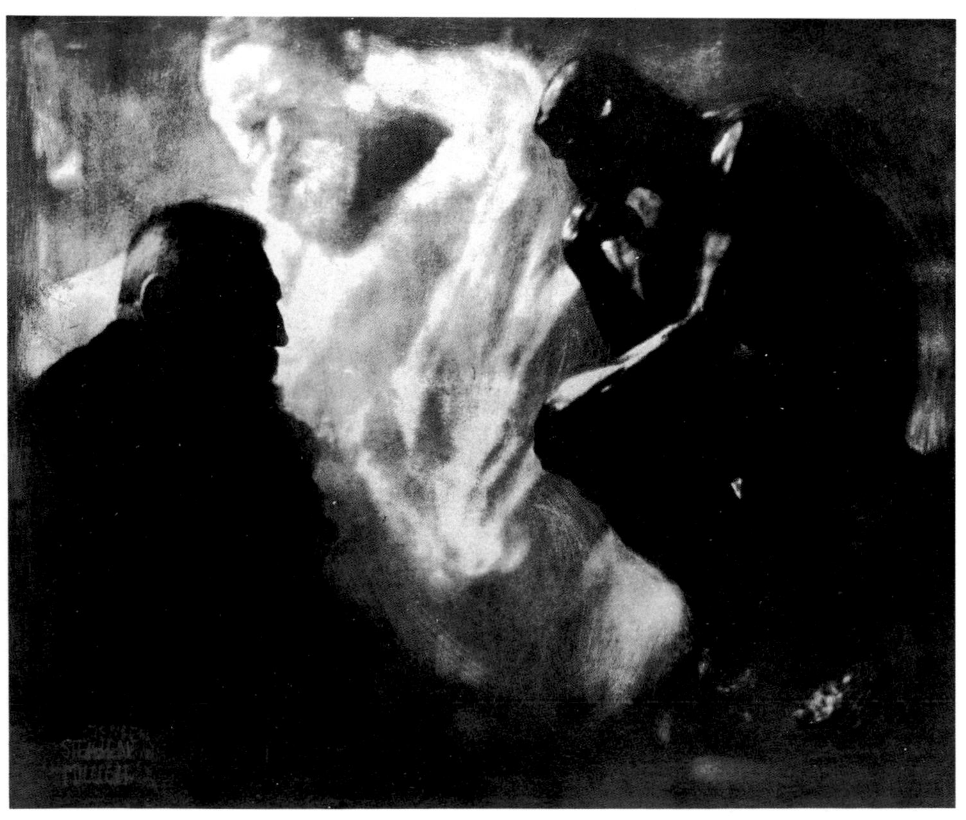

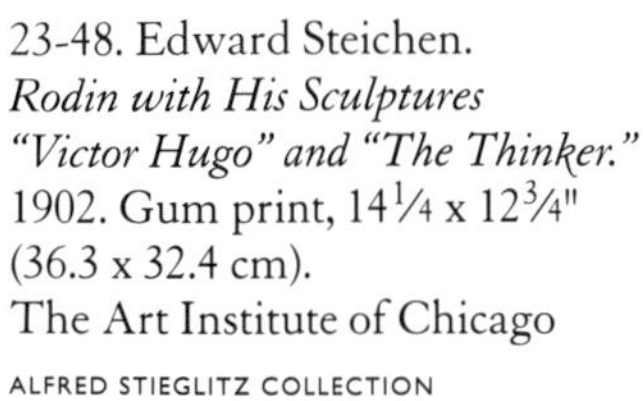

23-48. Edward Steichen. *Rodin with His Sculptures "Victor Hugo" and "The Thinker."* 1902. Gum print, 14¼ x 12¾" (36.3 x 32.4 cm). The Art Institute of Chicago
ALFRED STIEGLITZ COLLECTION

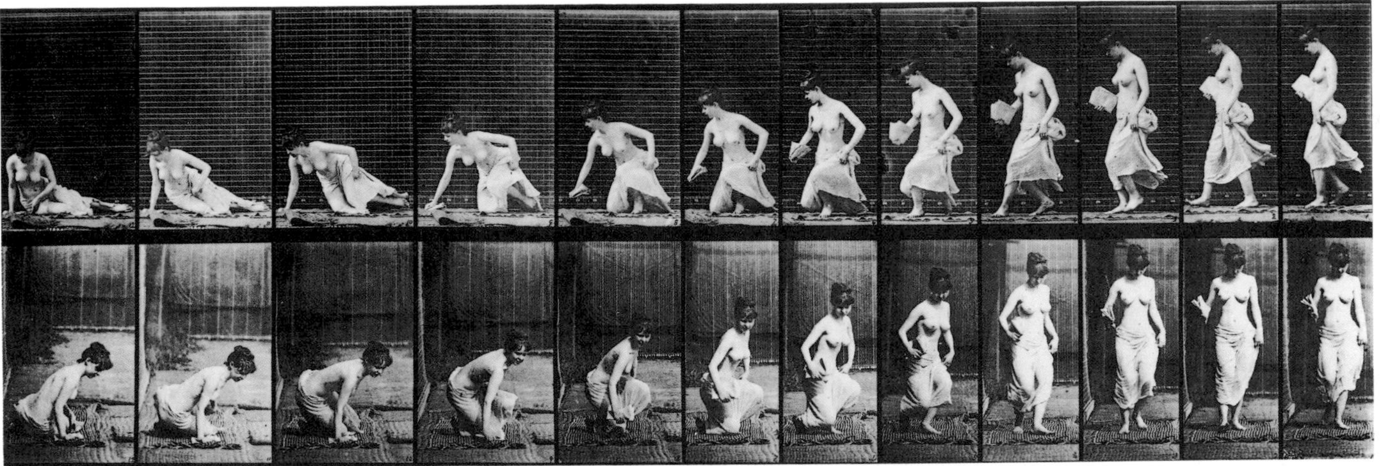

23-49. Eadweard Muybridge. *Female Semi-Nude in Motion,* from *Human and Animal Locomotion,* vol. 2, pl. 271. 1887. George Eastman House, Rochester, New York

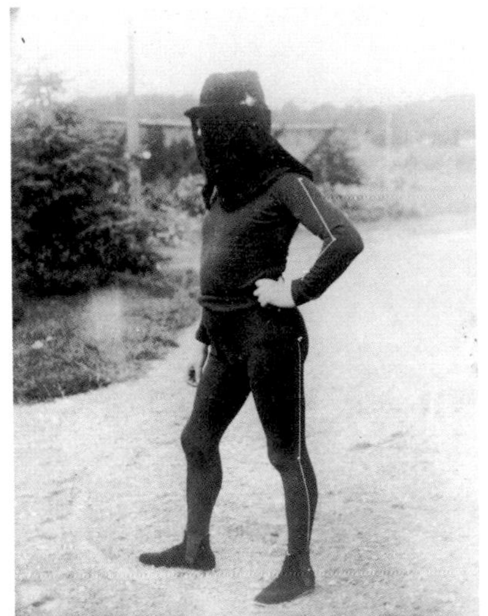

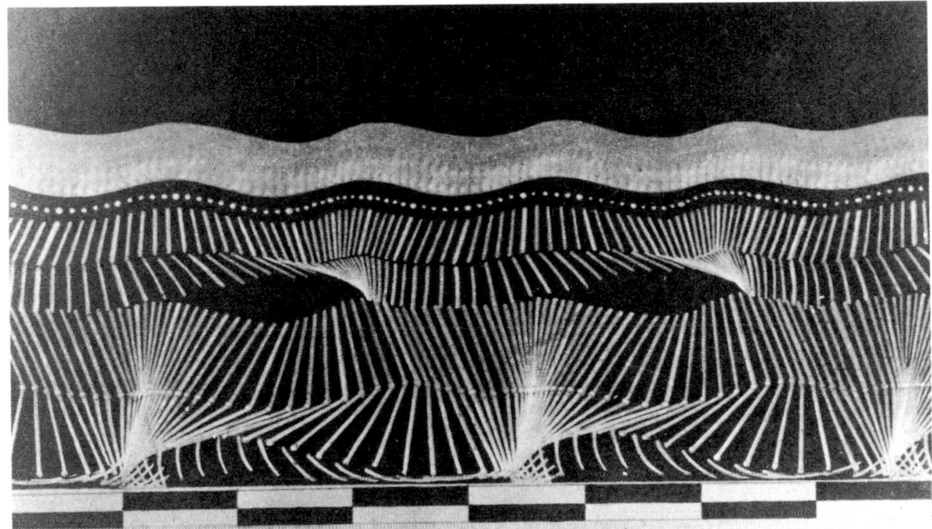

23-50a and b. Étienne-Jules Marey. *Man in Black Suit with White Stripes Down Arms and Legs, Walking in Front of a Black Wall.* c. 1884. Chronophotograph

He wedded two different technologies in devising a set of cameras capable of photographing action at successive points. Photography had grown from such marriages, for example, earlier when Nadar used a hot-air balloon to take aerial shots of Paris (see fig. 21-83). After some trial efforts, Muybridge managed in 1877 to get a set of pictures of a trotting horse that forever changed artistic depictions of the horse in movement. Of the 100,000 photographs he devoted to the study of animal and human locomotion, the most astonishing were those taken from several vantage points at once (fig. 23-49). The idea was surely in the air, for the art of the period occasionally shows similar experiments, but Muybridge's photographs must nevertheless have come as a revelation to artists. The simultaneous views present an entirely new treatment of motion across time and space that challenges the imagination. Like a complex visual puzzle, they can be combined in any number of ways that are endlessly fascinating.

Muybridge left it to others to pursue these possibilities further. Much of his later work was conducted at the University of Pennsylvania in Philadelphia with the support of Thomas Eakins, then the head of the Academy of the Fine Arts. Eakins was already adept at using a camera, and it provided the subjects for several of his paintings. Soon his interest in science led him to take up motion photography as well. Unlike Muybridge's succession of static images, Eakins' multiple exposures show sequential motion on one plate. In the end, however, photography for Eakins was simply a means of depicting figures more realistically.

MAREY. It was Étienne-Jules Marey (1830–1904) who developed motion photography into an art. A noted French physiologist, Marey (like Muybridge, with whom he was in direct contact) saw the camera as a tool for demonstrating the mechanics of bodily movement. Soon he began to use it so creatively that his photographs have a perfection not equaled for another 60 years (compare fig. 27-23). Indeed, his multiple exposure of a man walking (fig. 23-50a and b) satisfies both scientific and aesthetic truth in a way that Emerson and the Secessionists never imagined.

The photographs of Muybridge and Marey convey a uniquely modern sense of dynamics reflecting the new tempo of life in the Machine Age. However, because the gap was then so great between scientific fact on the one hand and visual perception and artistic representation on the other, their far-reaching aesthetic implications were first realized by the Futurists (see pages 783 and 785).

CHAPTER TWENTY-FOUR

Twentieth-Century Painting

PAINTING BEFORE WORLD WAR I

In our account of art in the modern era, we have already discussed a succession of "isms": Neoclassicism, Romanticism, Realism, Impressionism, Post-Impressionism, Divisionism, and Symbolism. There are many more to be found in twentieth-century art—so many, in fact, that nobody has made an exact count. These "isms" can form a serious obstacle. They may make us feel that we cannot hope to understand the art of our time unless we become familiar with numerous obscure doctrines. Actually, we can disregard all but the most important "isms." Like the terms we have used for the styles of earlier periods, they are merely labels to help us sort things out. If an "ism" fails the test of usefulness, we need not keep it. This is true of many "isms" in contemporary art. The movements they designate either cannot be seen very clearly as separate or have so little importance that they are of interest only to the specialist. It has always been easier to invent new labels than to create a movement in art that truly deserves a new name.

Still, we cannot do without "isms" altogether. Since the start of the modern era, the Western world (and, increasingly, the rest of the world) has faced the same basic problems everywhere, and local artistic traditions have steadily given way to international trends. Among these we can distinguish three main currents, each made up of a number of "isms," that began among the Post-Impressionists and have developed greatly in our own century: Expressionism, Abstraction, and Fantasy. The first stresses the artist's emotional attitude toward himself and the world; the second focuses on the formal structure of the work of art; and the third explores the realm of the imagination, especially its spontaneous and irrational sides. We must not forget, however, that feeling, order, and imagination are all present in every work of art. Without imagination, it would be deadly dull; without some degree of order, it would be chaotic; without feeling, it would leave us unmoved.

These currents are not mutually exclusive, and we shall find them interrelated in many ways. An artist's work often belongs to more than one, which may in turn embrace a wide range of approaches, from the realistic to the completely nonrepresentational (or *nonobjective*). Our three currents, then, do not correspond to specific styles but to general attitudes. They represent parallel responses to the realization, intuitive as well as intellectual, that after 1900 people were living in a different age. Expressionism is concerned mainly with the human community; Abstraction is interested in the structure of reality; and Fantasy is occupied with the labyrinth of the mind. We shall also find that Realism, which is concerned with the appearance of the world around us, has continued to exist independently of the other three, especially in the United States, where art has often pursued a separate course. These strands bear a shifting relation to one another that reflects the complexity of modern life. To be understood, they must be seen in their proper historical context. Beginning in the mid-1930s, however, the distinction between them begins to break down, so that after 1945 it is no longer meaningful to trace their evolutions separately.

In examining twentieth-century art, we shall find it anything but tidy. On the contrary, we quickly discover that the visual arts are like soldiers marching to different drummers. A purely chronological approach would reveal just how out of step they have generally been with one another—but at the cost of losing sight of the internal development of each. Does this mean that the other visual arts other than painting have shared none of the same concerns? No, that is not the case either. The three main currents we outlined above—Expressionism, Abstraction, and Fantasy—may be found as well in sculpture, architecture, and photography before 1945. But they are present in different measure and do not always carry the same meaning. For that reason, the parallels between them should not be overemphasized.

EXPRESSIONISM

The Fauves

The twentieth century may be said to have begun five years late so far as painting is concerned. Between 1901 and 1906, several comprehensive exhibitions of the work of Van Gogh, Gauguin, and Cézanne were held in Paris, as well as in Germany. For the first time the achievements of these masters became available to a broad public. The young painters who had grown up in the "deca-

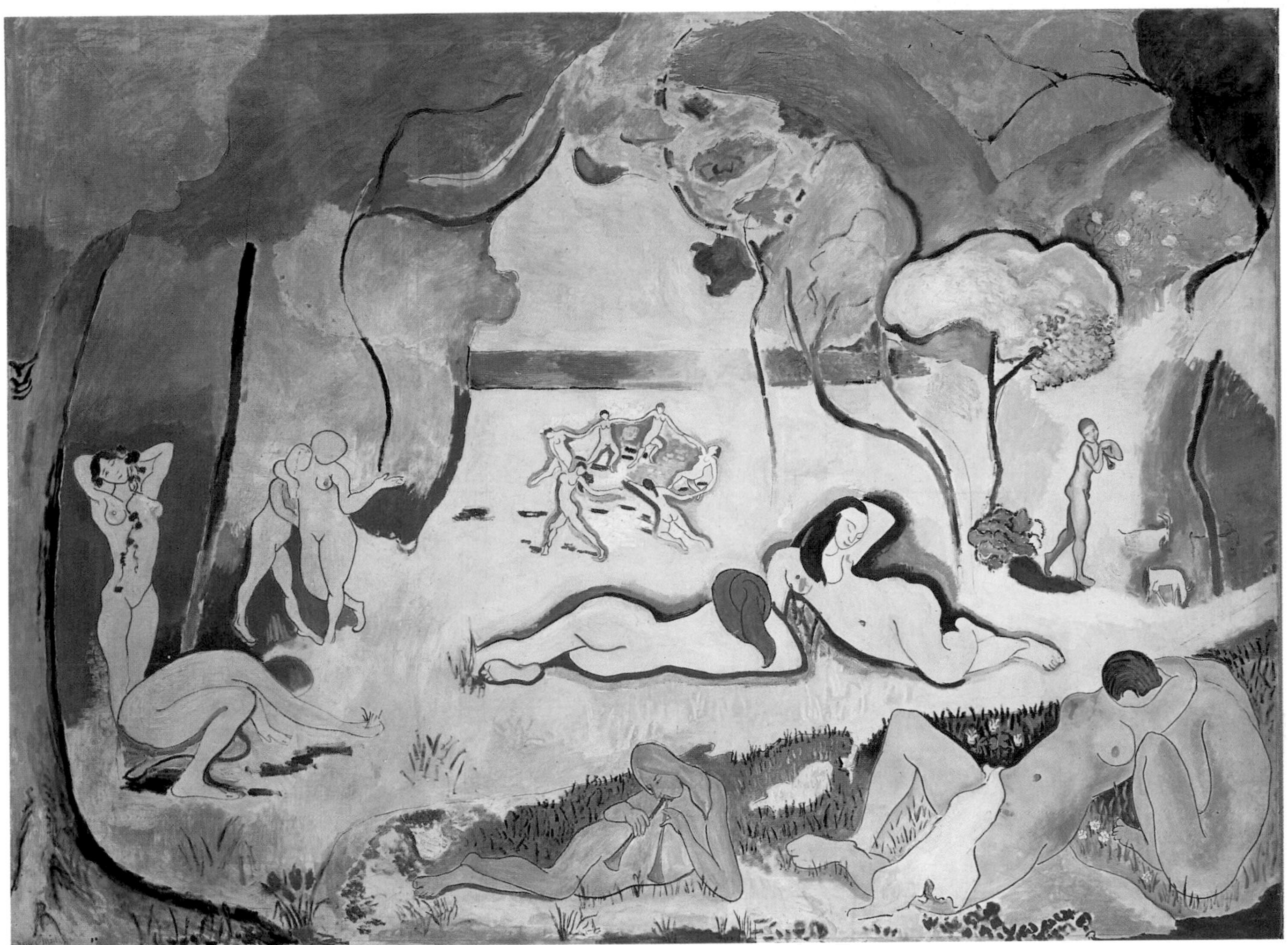

24-1. Henri Matisse. *The Joy of Life.* 1905–6. Oil on canvas, 5'8½" x 7'9¾" (1.74 x 2.38 m). The Barnes Foundation, Merion, Pennsylvania

dent," morbid mood of the 1890s (see page 750) were profoundly impressed by what they saw. Several of them formulated a radical new style, full of the violent color of Van Gogh and the bold distortions of Gauguin, which they manipulated freely for pictorial and expressive effects. When their work first appeared in 1905, it so shocked the conservative critic Louis Vauxcelles that he dubbed these artists *Fauves* (wild beasts), a label they wore with pride. Actually, it was not a common program that brought them together but their shared sense of liberation and experiment. As a movement, Fauvism included a number of loosely related individual styles, and the group dissolved after a few years. Most of its members were unable to sustain their inspiration or to adapt successfully to the challenges posed by Cubism. It was nevertheless a decisive breakthrough, for it constituted the first unquestionably modern movement of the twentieth century in both style and attitude, one to which every important painter before World War I admitted a debt.

MATISSE. Its leader was Henri Matisse (1869–1954), the oldest of the founders of twentieth-century painting. *The Joy of Life* (fig. 24-1), probably the most important picture of his long career, sums up the spirit of Fauvism better than any other single work. It obviously derives its flat planes of color, the heavy undulating outlines, and the "primitive" flavor of its forms from Gauguin (see fig. 23-14). Even its subject suggests the vision of humanity in a state of Nature that Gauguin had sought in Tahiti. But we soon realize that Matisse's figures are not Noble Savages under the spell of a native god. The subject is a pagan scene in the classical sense: a bacchanal like Titian's (compare fig. 13-37). The poses of the figures have a classical origin for the most part, and behind the apparently careless draftsmanship lies a profound knowledge of the human body. (Matisse, a pupil of Gustave Moreau, had been trained in the academic tradition.) What makes the picture so revolutionary is its radical simplicity, its "genius of omission." Everything that possibly can be has been left out or stated indirectly. The scene nevertheless retains the essentials of plastic form and spatial depth. What holds the painting together is its firm underlying structure. (Matisse admired Cézanne and owned one of his paintings.)

Painting, Matisse seems to say, is not a representation of observed reality but the rhythmic arrangement of line and color on a flat plane. But it is not only that. How far can the image of nature be pared down without destroying its basic properties and thus reducing it to mere surface ornament? "What I am after, above all," he once explained, "is expression. . . . [But] . . . expression does not consist of the passion mirrored upon a human face. . . . The whole arrangement of my picture is expressive. The place-

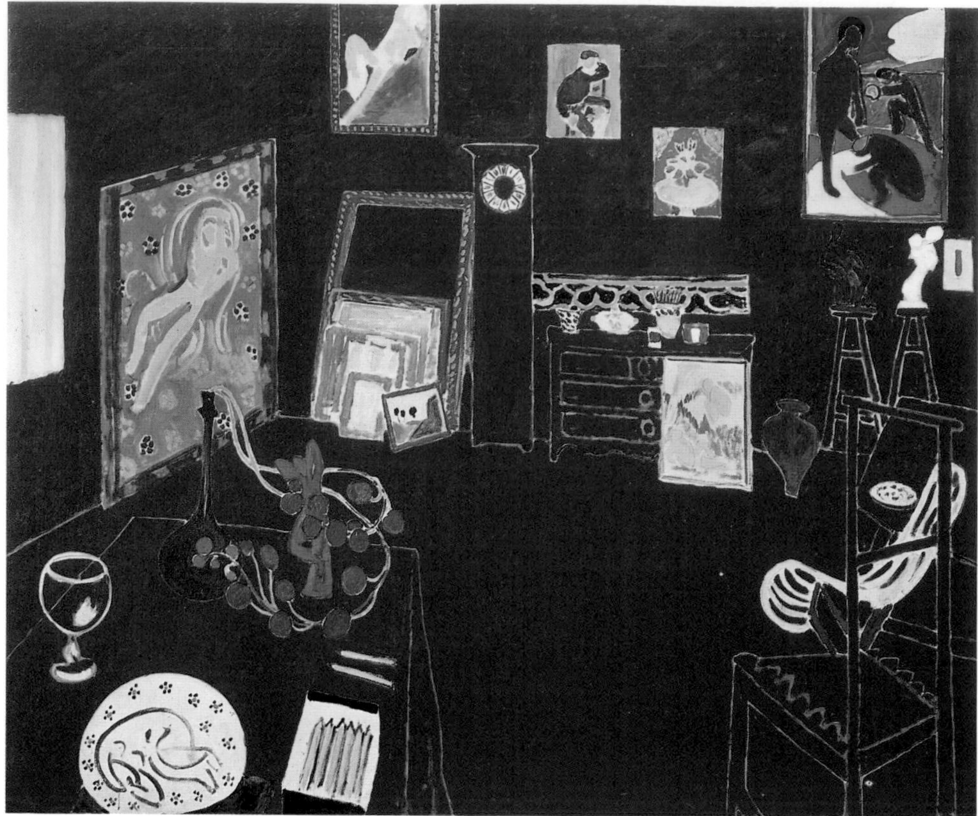

24-2. Henri Matisse. *The Red Studio.* 1911. Oil on canvas, 5'11¼" x 7'2¼" (1.81 x 2.19 m). The Museum of Modern Art, New York

MRS. SIMON GUGGENHEIM FUND

ment of figures or objects, the empty spaces around them, the proportions, everything plays a part." [See Primary Sources, no. 83, pages 934–35.] What, we wonder, does *The Joy of Life* express? Exactly what its title says. Whatever his debt to Gauguin, Matisse was never stirred by the same agonized discontent with the decadence of civilization. He instead shared the untroubled outlook of the Nabis, with whom he had previously associated, and the canvas owes its decorative quality to their work (compare fig. 23-15). He was concerned above all with the act of painting. This to him was an experience so profoundly joyous that he wanted to transmit it to the beholder.

Matisse's "genius of omission" is seen again in *The Red Studio* (fig. 24-2). By reducing the number of tints to a minimum, he makes color an independent structural element. The result is to emphasize the radical new balance he struck between the "2-D" and "3-D" aspects of painting. Matisse spreads the same flat red color on the tablecloth and wall as on the floor, yet he distinguishes the horizontal from the vertical planes with complete assurance using only a few lines. Equally bold is Matisse's use of pattern. He harmonizes the relation of each element with the rest of the picture by repeating a few basic shapes, hues, and decorative motifs in a seemingly casual, but perfectly calculated, array around the edges of the canvas. Cézanne had pioneered this integration of surface ornament into the design of a picture (see fig. 23-2), but here Matisse makes it a mainstay of his composition.

ROUAULT. The other important member of the Fauves, Georges Rouault (1871–1958), would hardly have agreed with Matisse's definition of "expression." For him this had still to include, as it had in the past, "the passion mirrored upon a human face"—as we can tell from his *Head of Christ* (fig. 24-3). The expressiveness does not reside only in the "image quality" of the face. The savage slashing brushstrokes speak eloquently of the artist's rage and compassion. If we cover the upper third of the picture, it is no longer a recognizable image. Yet the expressive effect is hardly diminished.

Rouault was the true heir of Van Gogh's and Gauguin's concern for the corrupt state of the world. However, he hoped for spiritual renewal through a revitalized Catholic faith. His pictures, whatever their subject, are personal statements of that ardent hope. Trained in his youth as a stained-glass worker, he was better prepared than the other Fauves to share Gauguin's enthusiasm for medieval art. Rouault's later work, such as *The Old King* (fig. 24-4), has glowing colors and broad, black-bordered shapes inspired by Gothic stained-glass windows (compare fig. 11-67). Within this framework he retains a good deal of the pictorial freedom we saw in the *Head of Christ,* which he uses to express his profound understanding of the human condition. The old king's face conveys a mood of resignation and inner suffering that reminds us of Rembrandt, Daumier, and Van Gogh.

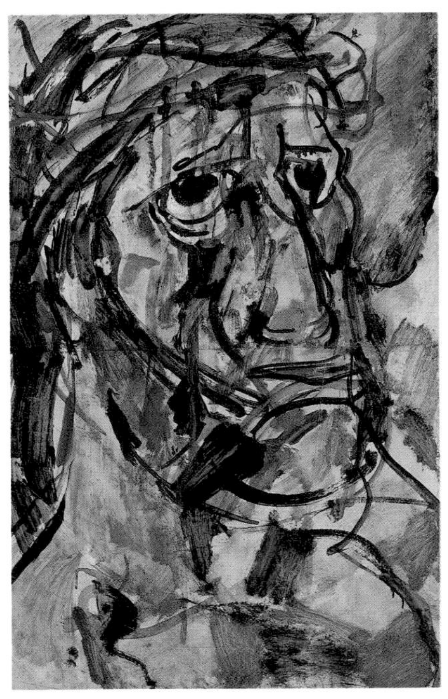

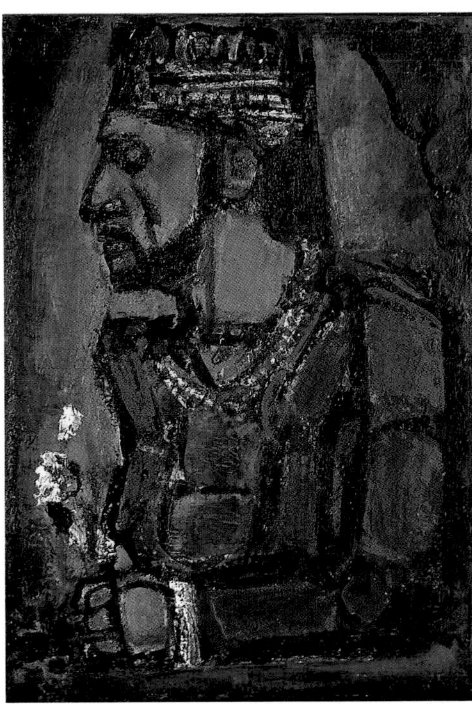

(FAR LEFT) 24-3. Georges Rouault. *Head of Christ.* 1905. Oil on paper, mounted on canvas, 39 x 25¼" (99.1 x 64.2 cm). The Chrysler Museum, Norfolk, Virginia

GIFT OF WALTER P. CHRYSLER, JR.

(LEFT) 24-4. Georges Rouault. *The Old King.* 1916–37. Oil on canvas, 30¼ x 21¼" (76.8 x 54 cm). The Carnegie Museum of Art, Pittsburgh

PATRONS ART FUND

German Expressionism

Fauvism had a decisive influence on the Expressionist movement that arose at the same time in Germany. Because Expressionism had historically been especially appealing to the Northern mind, it lasted far longer in Germany. There it proved broader and more varied than in France. For these reasons, Expressionism is sometimes applied to German art alone, but such a limit ignores the close ties and numerous similarities between the two movements. The two branches were not separated by any fundamental difference in style or content, although German Expressionism was characterized by greater emotional extremes and a more spontaneous approach. Conversely, Fauvism was for the most part less openly neurotic and morbid.

DIE BRÜCKE. Expressionism in Germany began with *Die Brücke* (The Bridge), a group of like-minded painters who lived in Dresden in 1905. Through its totally bohemian life-style, *Die Brücke* cultivated a sense of imminent disaster that is one of the hallmarks of the modern avant-garde. Their early work not only reveals the direct impact of Van Gogh and Gauguin but also shows elements derived from Munch, who was then living in Berlin and who deeply impressed the German Expressionists. It was an exhibition of Matisse that proved decisive, however. *Self-Portrait with Model* (fig. 24-5) by Ernst Ludwig Kirchner (1880–1938), the group's leader, reflects Matisse's simplified, rhythmic line and loud color. Yet the contrast between the coldly aloof artist and the brooding model, who looks as if she has been violated, has a peculiar expressiveness that can have come only from Munch, whose work was often fraught with a palpable sexual tension.

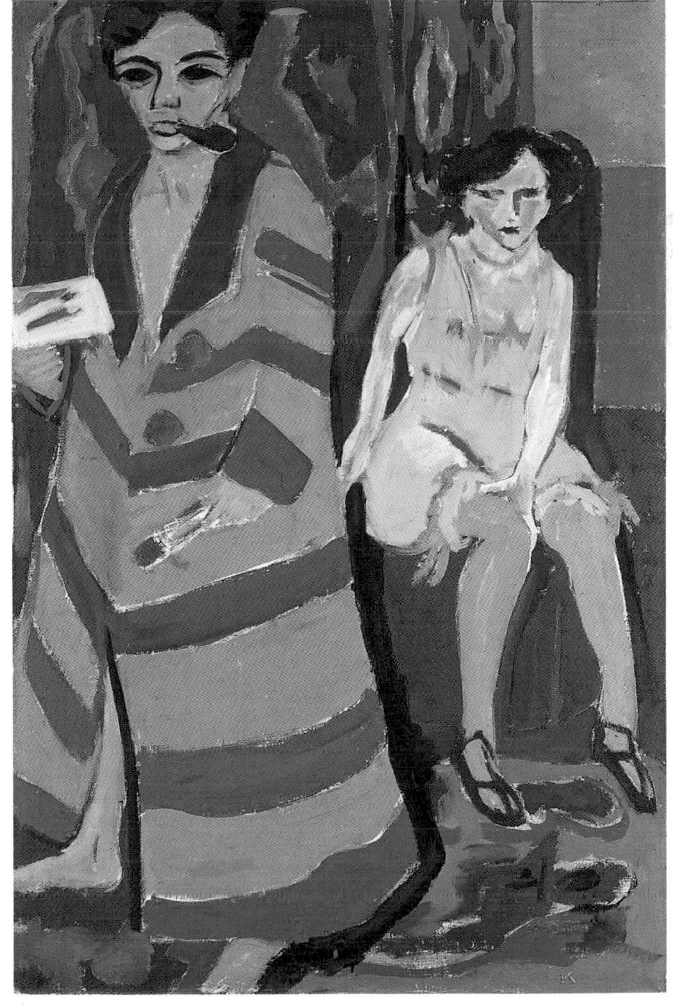

24-5. Ernst Ludwig Kirchner. *Self-Portrait with Model.* 1907. Oil on canvas, 59¼ x 39⅜" (150.5 x 100 cm). Kunsthalle, Hamburg

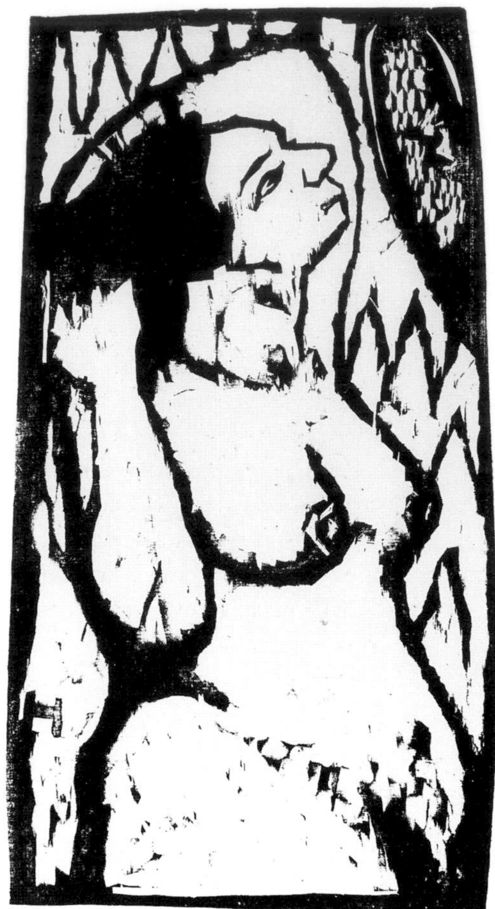

24-6. Erich Heckel. *Woman Before a Mirror.* 1908.
Woodcut, 16 5/8 x 8 7/8" (42.2 x 22.5 cm).
Brücke Museum, Berlin

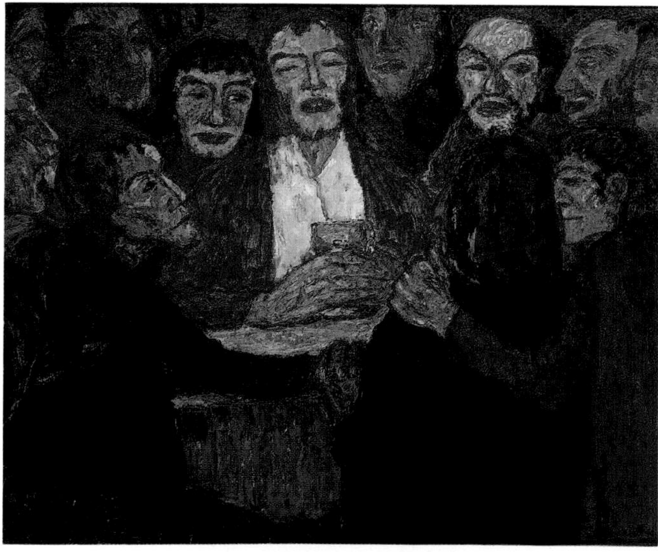

24-7. Emil Nolde. *The Last Supper.* 1909.
Oil on canvas, 32 1/2 x 41 3/4" (82.6 x 106.1 cm).
Stiftung Seebull Ada und Emil Nolde,
Neukirchen, Schleswig, Germany

HECKEL. The artists of *Die Brücke* were idealists who sought to revive German art. Toward that end, they took up woodcuts, which they regarded as a uniquely national medium. The first to do so was Kirchner, but the finest printmaker of the group was Erich Heckel (1883–1970). Under the influence of ethnographic art and Gauguin's woodcuts, Heckel's prints, such as *Woman Before a Mirror* (fig. 24-6), imitate the straightforward manner of the early German "primitives" (compare figs. 15-21 and 16-5) rather than the example of Dürer that originally inspired *Die Brücke.* Heckel's woman before a mirror is "primitive" in another sense as well: her ponderous fleshiness lends her the primeval quality of ancient fertility goddesses (see fig. 1-12), but with a sensuous charm that is utterly disarming.

NOLDE. One *Brücke* artist, Emil Nolde (1867–1956), stands somewhat apart. Older than the rest, he was already working in an Expressionist style when he was invited in 1906 to join the movement, which he left two years later. Nolde shared Rouault's preference for religious subjects, and his figures show a like sympathy for the suffering of humanity. The thickly encrusted surfaces and deliberately clumsy draftsmanship of *The Last Supper* (fig. 24-7) reject pictorial refinement in favor of the kind of primeval, direct expression inspired by Gauguin. Ensor's grotesque masks, too, come to mind (see fig. 23-20), as does the blocklike monumentality of Barlach's peasants (see fig. 23-28). But it is the impact of ethnographic art that we feel the most. Nolde admired the "primitive" artist's ability "to express delight in form and the love of creating it," the "absolute originality, the intense and often grotesque expression of power and life in very simple forms."

KOKOSCHKA. Another artist of highly individual talent was the Austrian painter Oskar Kokoschka (1886–1980), who began his career as a member of the Vienna Secession (see page 752). In 1910, he was invited to Berlin by Herwarth Walden, the publisher of *Der Sturm* (The Storm), which soon attracted members of *Die Brücke* and *Der Blaue Reiter* (see below). His main contribution is the portraits he painted before World War I, such as the moving *Self-Portrait* in figure 24-8. Like Van Gogh, Kokoschka saw himself as a visionary, a witness to the truth and reality of his inner experiences (compare fig. 23-12). We may find in this tortured psyche an echo of the cultural climate that also produced Sigmund Freud.

Kokoschka's most memorable work, *The Bride of the Wind* (fig. 24-9), celebrates his love for Alma Mahler, the "muse" who inspired so many of Germany's and Austria's leading cultural figures. (Besides the composer–conductor Gustave Mahler, she married the poet Franz Werfel and the architect Walter Gropius.) Based on Romantic paintings of Dante's tragic lovers Paolo and Francesca, it was originally conceived as Tristan and Isolde after Wagner's opera but received its present title from the poet Georg Trakl. The awesome canvas is a monument to the power of love: echoing the impassioned brushwork, the entire universe resounds in a great chord of exaltation at the pair's embrace. Its ecstatic vision forms a fascinating contrast to Gustav Klimt's *The Kiss* (see fig. 23-22). The painting achieves that state of mind when "one's perception reaches out towards the Word, towards awareness of the vision," which was Kokoschka's ideal. "It is love, delighting to lodge itself in the mind."

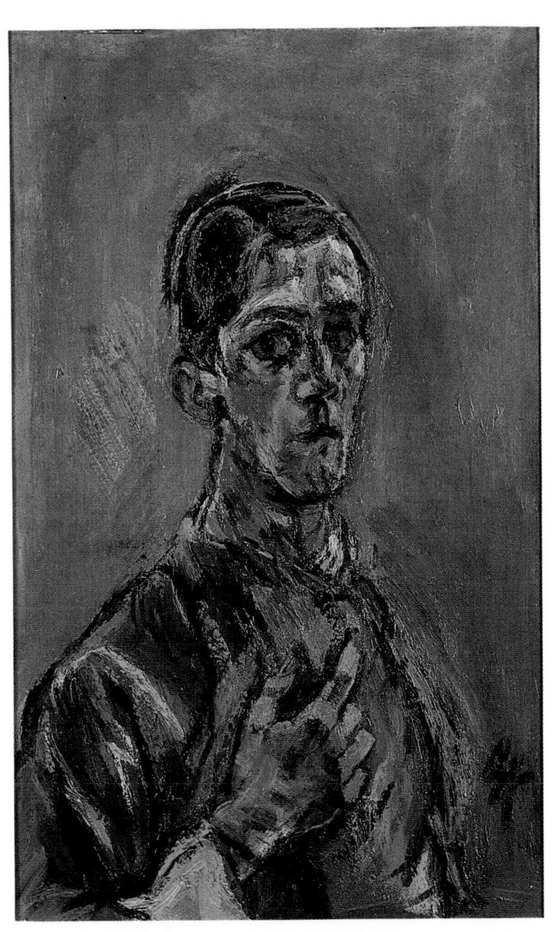

(LEFT) 24-8. Oskar Kokoschka. *Self-Portrait.* 1913. Oil on canvas, 32" x 9½" 81.7 x 49.7cm). The Museum of Modern Art, New York PURCHASE

KANDINSKY. The most daring and original step beyond Fauvism was taken in Germany by a Russian, Wassily Kandinsky (1866–1944), the leading member of a group of Munich artists called *Der Blaue Reiter* (The Blue Rider) after one of his early paintings. Formed in 1911, it was a loose alliance united only by its mystical tendencies. Kandinsky began to give up representation as early as 1910 and abandoned it altogether several years later. Using the rainbow colors and the free, dynamic brushwork of the Paris Fauves, he created a completely nonobjective style charged with extraordinary energy. These works have titles as abstract as their forms: our example, one of the most striking, is called *Sketch I for "Composition VII"* (fig. 24-10). Perhaps we should avoid the term *abstract,* because it is often taken to mean that the artist has analyzed and simplified visible reality into geometric forms. (Com-

(BELOW) 24-9. Oskar Kokoschka. *The Bride of the Wind.* 1914. Oil on canvas, 5'11¼" x 7'2⅝" (1.81 x 2.20 m). Öffentliche Kunstsammlung Basel, Kunstmuseum, Switzerland

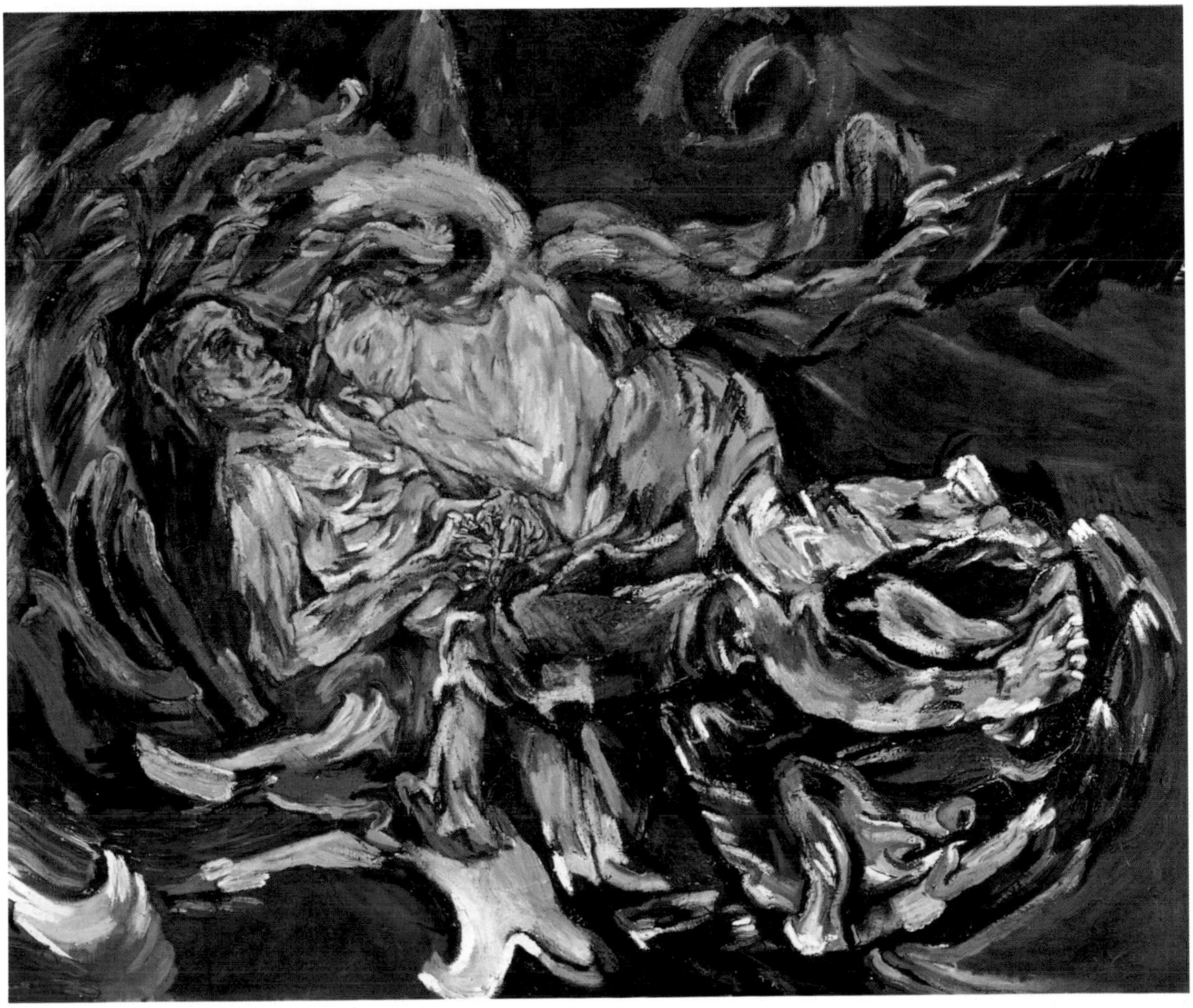

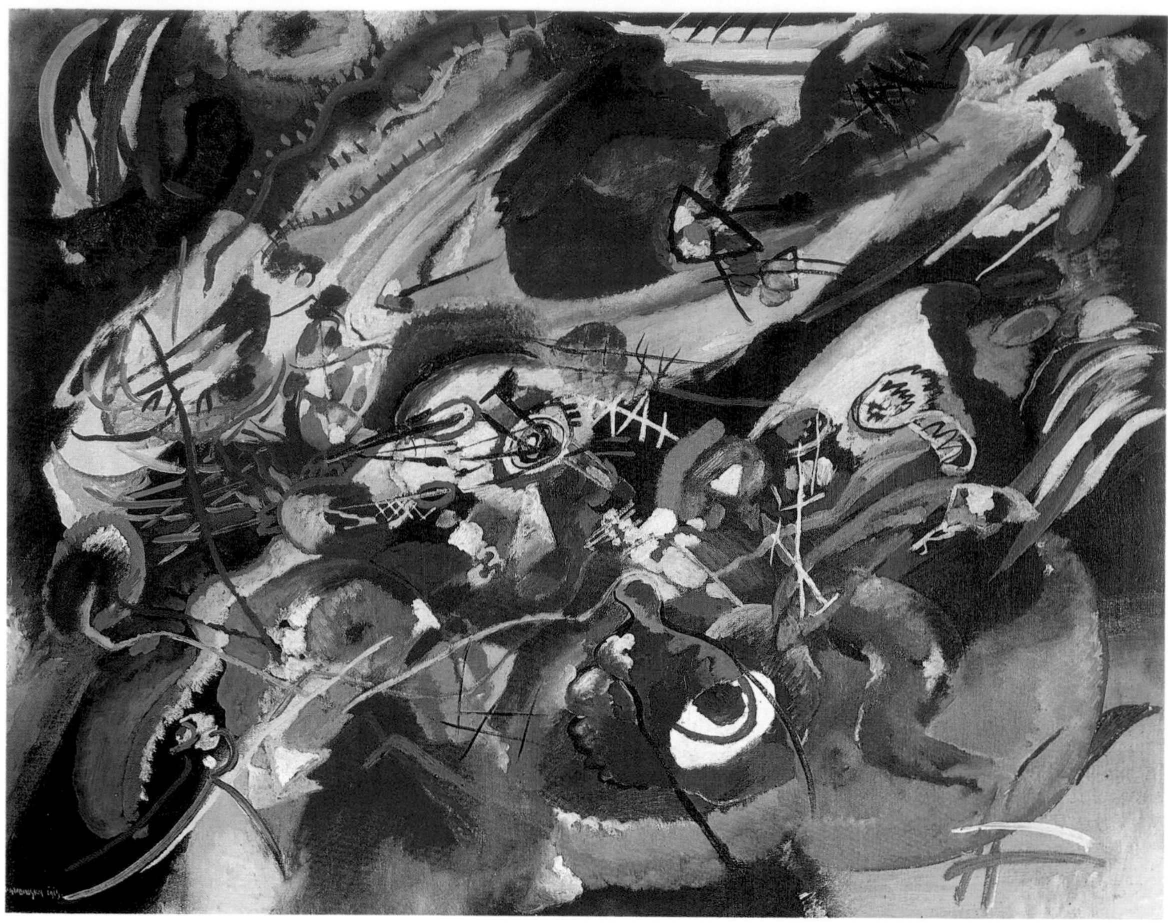

24-10. Wassily Kandinsky. *Sketch I for "Composition VII."* 1913. Oil on canvas, 30¾ x 39⅜" (78 x 100 cm). Private collection

pare Cézanne's assertion that all natural forms are based on the cone, sphere, and cylinder.) Kandinsky did indeed derive his shapes from the world around him—landscapes that he freely invented—but by transforming rather than reducing them. (Not until after his return from Russia in 1922 were the implications of his discussion of form fully realized when he adopted geometric abstraction; see page 794.)

Kandinsky's aim is made clear in the first part of his book *Concerning the Spiritual in Art,* written in 1910 but published in 1912. His intention was to charge form and color with a purely spiritual meaning (as he put it), one that expressed his deepest feelings, by eliminating all resemblance to the physical world. [See Primary Sources, no. 84, page 935.] To him, the only reality that mattered was the artist's inner reality. Kandinsky regarded the Symbolists as his ancestors. Like Gauguin, he wanted to create an art of spiritual renewal. But in contrast to Rouault or Nolde, he had no specific spiritual program, though his views were similar to those of the theosophist Rudolf Steiner, who influenced many early modern artists in Germany. Kandinsky, like Steiner, believed that humanity had lost touch with its spirituality through attachment to material things, and he sought to rekindle a dreamlike consciousness through his art.

The second part of the book is concerned exclusively with the formal aspects of painting, above all color. Kandinsky studied the color theories of Seurat and his followers (see page 741), as did many other Expressionists, but the meaning he gave to specific hues was no less individual than Van Gogh's. Kandinsky's theory of color relationships is strikingly similar to the tonal relationships spelled out in *Theory of Harmony* (1911) by the Expressionist composer Arnold Schoenberg (see box page 780), an ally of *Der Blaue Reiter* with whom the artist was in close contact.

What does all this have to do with Kandinsky's paintings themselves? The character of his art is best summed up by his later statement: "Painting is the vast, thunderous clash of many worlds, destined, through a mighty struggle, to erupt into a totally new world, which is creation. And the birth of a creation is much akin to that of the Cosmos. There is the same vast and cataclysmic quality belonging to that mighty symphony—the Music of the Spheres."

Kandinsky's antinaturalism was inherent in Expressionist theory from the very beginning. Whistler, too, had spoken of "divesting the picture from any outside sort of interest." He even anticipated Kandinsky's "musical" titles (see fig. 22-23). But it was the liberating influence of the Fauves that permitted Kandinsky to put this approach into practice. (When the upper third of Rouault's *Head of Christ* in figure 24-3 is covered, we recall, the rest becomes a nonrepresentational composition strangely similar to Kandinsky's in its slashing brushwork and charged forms.)

How valid is the analogy between painting and music? Although Kandinsky was careful to acknowledge the differences between the two art forms, he sought painting that, like music, was absolute because it was divorced entirely from the

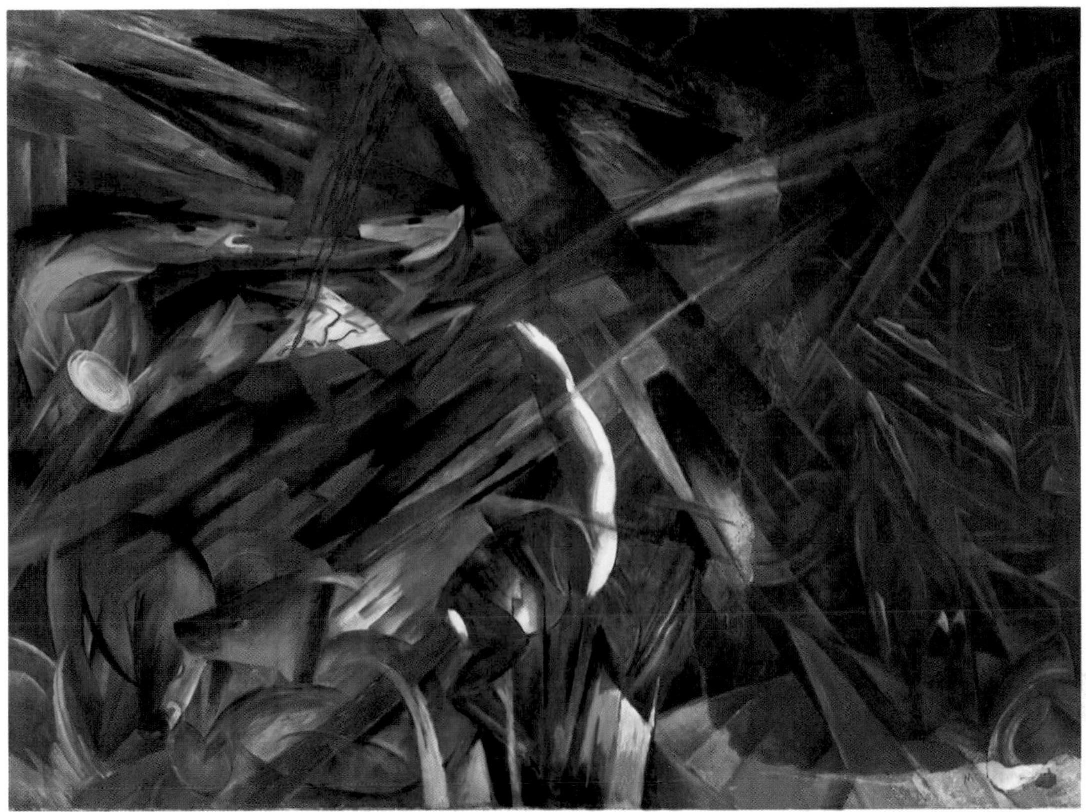

24-11. Franz Marc. *Animal Destinies.* 1913. Oil on canvas, 6'4½" x 8'7" (1.94 x 2.62 m). Öffentliche Kunstsammlung Basel, Kunstmuseum, Switzerland

"objective," material realm. While acknowledging that music can say far more than words, Schoenberg (who was also a competent painter) wrote, "I cannot unreservedly agree with the distinction between color and pitch. I find that a note is perceived by its color, one of whose dimensions is pitch. Color, then, is the great realm, pitch one of its provinces. . . . If the ear could discriminate between differences of color, it might be feasible to invent melodies that are built of colors." When a painter like Kandinsky carries such an approach through so completely, does he really lift his art to another plane? Kandinsky's advocates like to point out that representational painting has a "literary" content, and they object to such dependence on another art. But they do not explain why the "musical" content of nonobjective painting should be more desirable. They think music is a higher art than literature or painting because it is inherently nonrepresentational. This point of view has an ancient tradition that goes back to Plato and includes Plotinus, St. Augustine, and their medieval successors.

The case is difficult to argue, and it does not matter whether this theory is right or wrong, for the proof of the pudding is in the eating, not in the recipe. Kandinsky's—or any artist's—ideas are not important to us unless we are convinced of the importance of the work itself. The painting reproduced here has such vitality that it impresses us with its radiant freshness and feeling, even though we may be uncertain what exactly the artist has expressed.

MARC. The subject matter of Franz Marc (1880–1916), another member of *Der Blaue Reiter,* was the unconscious life of animals in nature. Motivated by the pantheistic feeling of the Romantics, which was heightened by his association with Kandinsky, the artist's paintings represent humanity's desire to return to a state of harmony with the universe—a central concept of Rudolf Steiner's theosophy. Marc's color symbolism is as personal as that of Van Gogh, who had inspired his early work (see page 744). He wrote: "Blue is the masculine principle, robust and spiritual. Yellow is the feminine principle, gentle, serene, sensual. Red is matter, brutal and heavy." But it was the Orphism of Robert Delaunay (see page 783), with whom he formed a friendship in 1912, that showed Marc the full potential of color to express his mystical beliefs. Later that year, Futurism enabled him to depict the dynamism of nature by creating rhythms that echo those of the cosmos, or so he believed. In *Animal Destinies* (fig. 24-11), Marc's poetic vision attained apocalyptic intensity. With its interpenetrating crystalline forms looking like so many pieces of jagged stained glass, the picture is even more powerful than Stubbs' *Lion Attacking a Horse* (see fig. 21-9). Both paintings evoke terrifying forces of nature that overwhelm uncomprehending beasts. Here the artist was indeed on the verge of depicting the "higher" symbolic reality he sought. A year later he abandoned representation almost entirely for an abstract style no less advanced than Kandinsky's. Soon, however, he was drafted into World War I, which claimed his life.

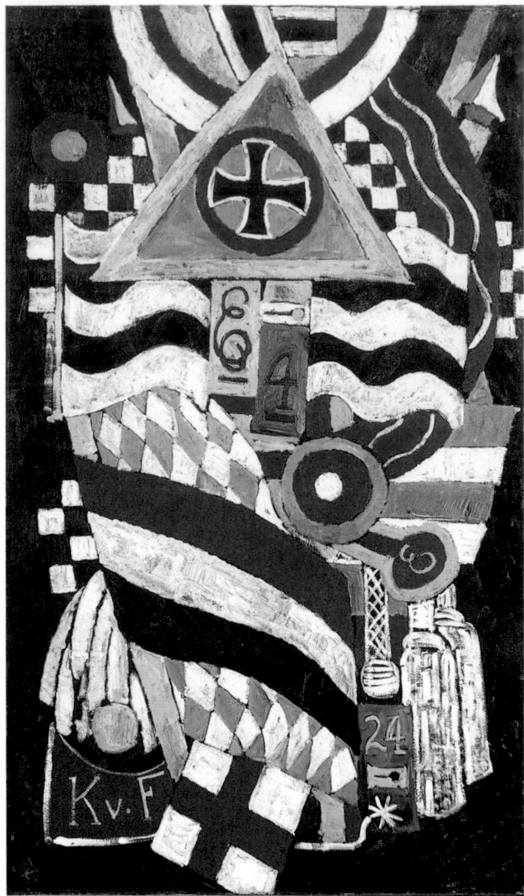

24-12. Marsden Hartley. *Portrait of a German Officer.* 1914. Oil on canvas, 68¼ x 41⅜" (173 x 104 cm). The Metropolitan Museum of Art, New York

THE ALFRED STIEGLITZ COLLECTION, 1949

HARTLEY. Americans became familiar with the Fauves through exhibitions from 1908 on. After the pivotal Armory Show of 1913, which introduced the latest European art to New York, there was a growing interest in the German Expressionists as well (see page 773). The driving force behind the modernist movement in the United States was the photographer Alfred Stieglitz (see page 892), who almost single-handedly supported many of its early members. To him, modernism meant abstraction and its related concepts. Among the most important works by the Stieglitz group are the canvases painted by Marsden Hartley (1887–1943) in Munich during the early years of World War I under the direct influence of Kandinsky. *Portrait of a German Officer* (fig. 24-12) is a masterpiece of design from 1914, the year Hartley was invited to exhibit with *Der Blaue Reiter.* He had already been introduced to Futurism and several offshoots of Cubism, including Orphism (see page 783), which he used to discipline Kandinsky's supercharged surface. The emblematic image is an allusion to Hartley's lover, who was killed during World War I. It includes the insignia, epaulets, Maltese cross, and other details from an officer's uniform of the day.

ABSTRACTION

The second of our main currents is Abstraction. When discussing Kandinsky, we said that the term is usually taken to mean the process (or the result) of analyzing and simplifying observed reality into geometric shapes. Literally, it means "to draw away from, to separate." Actually, abstraction goes into the making of any work of art, whether the artist knows it or not, since even the most painstakingly realistic portrayal can never be an entirely faithful replica. The process was not conscious and controlled, however, until the Early Renaissance, when artists first analyzed the shapes of nature in terms of mathematical bodies (see page 410). Cézanne and Seurat revived this approach and explored it further. They are the direct ancestors of the abstract movement in twentieth-century art. The difference, as one critic has noted, is that for the latter, abstraction has been both a premise and a goal, not simply a reductive refinement. Abstraction has been the most distinctive and consistent feature of modern painting, to which even its most outspoken opponents have responded.

PICASSO'S *DEMOISELLES D'AVIGNON*. It is difficult to imagine the birth of modern abstraction without Pablo Picasso. About 1905, stimulated as much by the Fauves as by the retrospective exhibitions of the great Post-Impressionists, he gradually abandoned the melancholy lyricism of his Blue Period (see fig. 23-23) for a more robust style. He shared Matisse's enthusiasm for Gauguin and Cézanne, but he viewed these masters very differently. In 1907 he produced his own counterpart to *The Joy of Life* (see fig. 24-1), a monumental canvas (fig. 24-13) so challenging that it outraged even Matisse. (They nevertheless remained lifelong friends and rivals who learned much from each other's example.) The title, *Les Demoiselles d'Avignon* (The Young Ladies of Avignon), which came from Picasso's friend André Salmon, does not refer to the town of that name but to Avignon Street in a notorious section of Barcelona near where the artist grew up. When Picasso started the picture, it was to be a temptation scene in a brothel, but he ended up with a composition of five nudes and a still life. But what nudes! Their savage aggressiveness makes Matisse's generalized figures in *The Joy of Life* seem incredibly innocent.

The three on the left are angular distortions of classical figures, but the violently dislocated features and bodies of the other two have all the "barbaric" qualities of ethnographic art. Following Gauguin's lead, the Fauves had discovered African and Oceanic sculpture and had introduced Picasso to this material. Nonetheless it was Picasso, not the Fauves, who used primitivist art as a battering ram against the classical conception of beauty. Not only the proportions but the organic integrity and continuity of the human body are denied here, so that the canvas (in the apt description of one critic) "resembles a field of broken glass."

Picasso, then, has destroyed a great deal. What has he gained in the process? Once we recover from the initial shock, we begin to see that the destruction is quite methodical. Everything—the figures as well as their setting—is broken up into angular wedges or facets. These, we will note, are not flat but shaded in a way that gives them a certain three-dimensionality. We cannot always be sure whether they are concave or convex. Some look like chunks of solidified space, others like fragments of translucent bodies. They constitute a unique kind of matter, which imposes a new integrity and continuity on the entire canvas. *Les Demoiselles,* unlike *The Joy of Life,* can no longer be read as an image of the

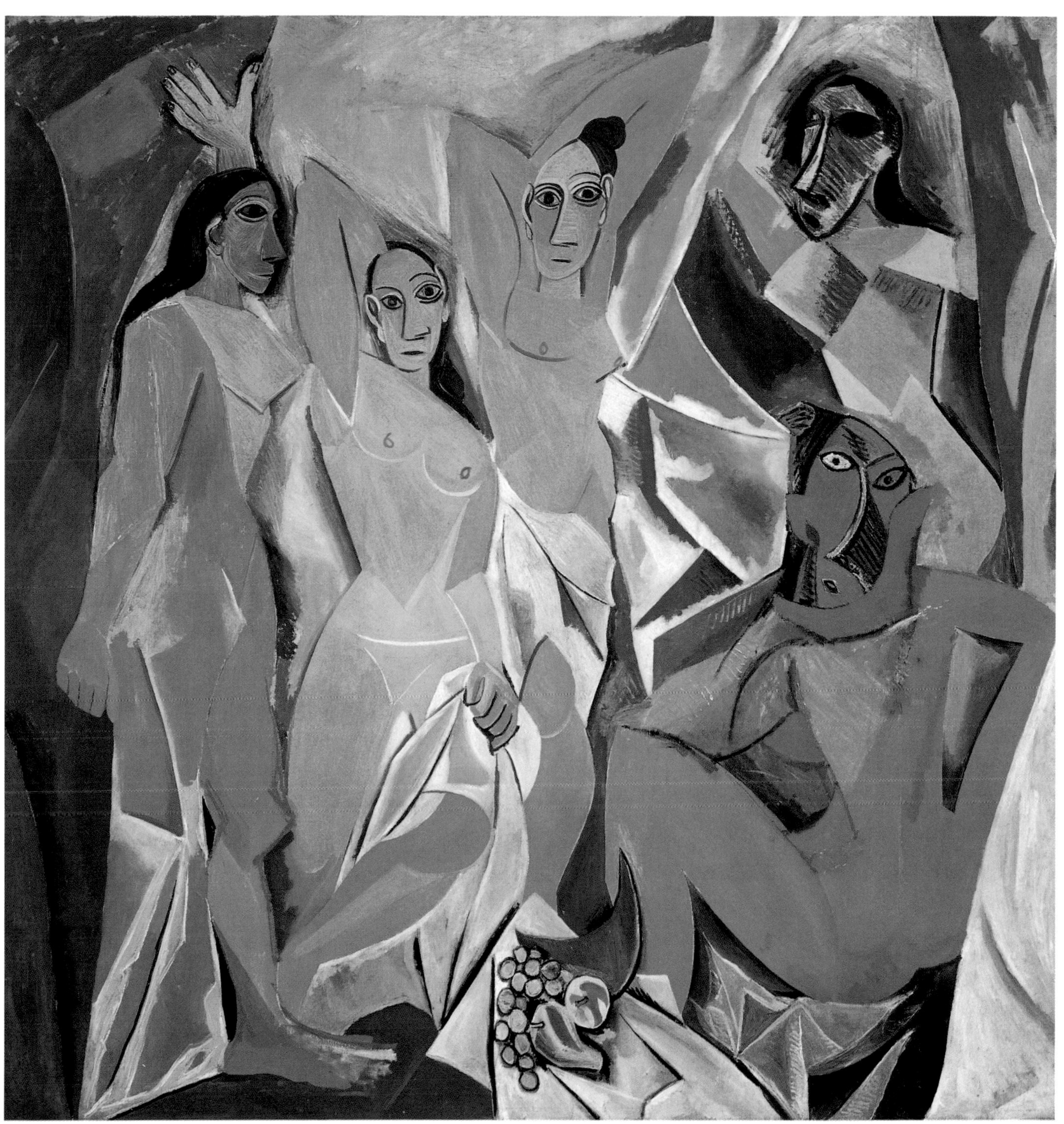

24-13. Pablo Picasso. *Les Demoiselles d'Avignon*. 1907. Oil on canvas, 8' x 7'8" (2.44 x 2.34 m). The Museum of Modern Art, New York

ACQUIRED THROUGH THE LILLIE P. BLISS BEQUEST

MUSIC BEFORE WORLD WAR I

Just as the art of the twentieth century was distinguished by abstraction from an early date, so its music has often been marked by atonality, a rejection of the major and minor diatonic scales, the rules of harmony in general, and especially the importance of the tonic (the first tone of the scale in which a given piece was written; see box page 606). From about 1550, most European music had centered around the tonic note, in effect a musical "home base" to which the melody tended to return. However, a frequent return to the tonic note is not actually required by the rules of harmony or the tempered scale (see page 606)—a fact that had already been exploited by a number of German Romantic composers, starting with Wagner, who emphasized chromaticism (musical color) at the expense of tonality (which stresses the importance of the tonic). It was almost inevitable that the final break with tonality would be made by a post-Romantic.

The final step was taken by Arnold Schoenberg (1874–1951). The hypersensitive content of his early work, like Mahler's, sometimes brings to mind the world of neurosis explored by his great contemporary in Vienna Sigmund Freud, the pioneer of modern psychology. His *Transfigured Night* (1899) has the sensuality of the famous Liebestod duet in Wagner's opera *Tristan and Isolde.* Schoenberg, an Expressionist by inclination, later became a friend of Kandinsky and a capable artist in his own right. Schoenberg, however, moved almost immediately into complete atonality and dissonance with *Erwartung* (Expectation), a one-act stage work for soprano that stands the Liebestod on its ear thematically and musically. In 1912 he took the further step of abandoning the pitches used in normal singing for "speech-song" (German, *Sprechstimme*) in the song-cycle *Pierrot Lunaire.* Commissioned and first performed by the actress Albertine Zehme, it was based partly on the performance practices of contemporary German melodrama and cabaret, with which Schoenberg was thoroughly familiar, having written a cycle of cabaret songs at the beginning of his career. Schoenberg nevertheless continued to make use of other traditional composition techniques of composition, which he used to build into pieces of extraordinary intricacy.

If any one event announced the arrival of twentieth-century music, it was the ballet *The Rite of Spring* (1913) by the Russian-born composer Igor Stravinsky (1882–1971), the last of three scores commissioned in 1910–13 by the impresario Sergei Diaghilev for his Ballets Russes (see box page 784). While a pupil of the nationalist composer Nikolai Rimsky-Korsakov (1844–1908) in St. Petersburg, Stravinsky had revealed a striking gift for melody in the Russian tradition and an unusual sense of rhythm. These were evident in his first two ballets, *The Firebird* and *Petrushka,* which created a sensation in Paris because of their exoticism. The primitivism and overt eroticism of *The Rite of Spring* caused a famous riot at its premiere, although there is evidence that it was staged. Stravinsky was the musical counterpart to Picasso as a giant of his time. Indeed, not only was *The Rite* similar to Picasso's *Les Demoiselles d'Avignon* (see fig. 24-13) in its impact, but Stravinsky's rhythmic "cells" were analogous to the facets in Analytic Cubism: both served as building blocks to create dynamic compositions of unprecedented complexity. Like Picasso, Stravinsky turned to classicism after 1920, cultivating a lean style that stressed clarity and balance while rejecting any concession to Romanticism. His position in music was comparable to Picasso's in art: until the end of World War II, he was by far the leading composer in the world. The culmination of this phase of Stravinsky's career are the *Symphony in C* (1940) and *Symphony in Three Movements* (1945), which restored melody and rhythm to prominence in his work. Finally, toward the end of his long life, he successfully adopted the serialism of his contemporary Arnold Schoenberg, who emerged as the world's most influential composer only after 1945.

external world. Its world is its own, analogous to nature but constructed along different principles. Picasso's revolutionary "building material," compounded of voids and solids, is hard to describe with any precision. After seeing an exhibition of paintings by Picasso's friend Georges Braque in 1909, Louis Vauxcelles, the same critic who named Fauvism, dubbed the new style Cubism after Matisse described them as consisting of little cubes.

Analytic Cubism

That *Les Demoiselles* owes anything to Cézanne may at first seem incredible. However, Picasso had studied Cézanne's late work (such as fig. 23-4) with great care, finding in Cézanne's abstract treatment of volume and space the structural units from which to derive the faceted shapes of Analytic (or Facet) Cubism. The link is clearer in *Portrait of Ambroise Vollard* (fig. 24-14)—Vollard was one of the leading print publishers and dealers of the time—which Picasso painted three years later. The facets are now small and precise, more like prisms, and the canvas has the balance and refinement of a fully mature style.

Contrasts of color and texture, so pronounced in *Les Demoiselles,* are now reduced to a minimum; the subdued tonality of the picture approaches monochrome, so as not to compete with the design. The structure has become so complex and systematic that it would seem wholly intellectual if the "imprismed" sitter's face did not emerge with such dramatic force. Indeed, this is as com-

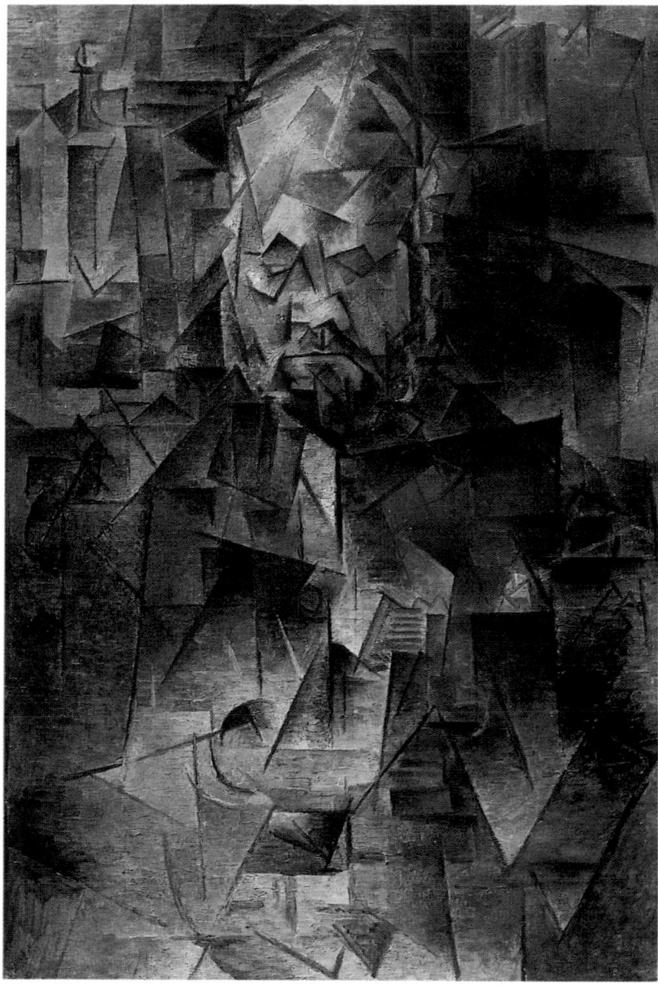

24-14. Pablo Picasso. *Portrait of Ambroise Vollard.* 1910. Oil on canvas, 36¼ x 25⅝" (92 x 65 cm). The Pushkin State Museum of Fine Arts, Moscow

manding a portrait as Ingres' *Louis Bertin* (see fig. 21-31), one that fully conveys the power of Vollard's complex personality. There is no trace of the "barbaric" distortions in *Les Demoiselles;* they had served their purpose. Cubism had become an abstract style within the purely Western sense, but it was not any more removed from observed reality. Picasso may have been playing an elaborate game of hide-and-seek with nature, but he still needed the visible world to stimulate his creative powers. The nonobjective realm held no appeal for him, then or later.

Synthetic Cubism

By 1910 Cubism was well established as an alternative to Fauvism. Picasso had been joined by a number of other artists, notably Georges Braque (1882–1963), who had started out as a Fauve painter and then helped to create Cubism. The two collaborated so intimately that their work at that time is difficult to tell apart. Both of them (it is not clear to whom the chief credit belongs) initiated the next phase of Cubism, which was even bolder than the first. Usually called Synthetic Cubism because it puts forms back together, it is also known as Collage Cubism, after the French word for "paste-up," the technique that started it all. We see its beginnings in Picasso's *Still Life with Chair Caning* of 1912 (fig. 24-15). Most of the painting consists of facets. Because they were already abstract signs, the letters could not be translated into prismatic shapes. But beneath the still life is a piece of imitation chair caning, which was pasted onto the canvas, and the picture is "framed" by a piece of rope. This inclusion of found materials has a most remarkable effect: the abstract still life appears to rest on a real surface (the chair caning) as if it were on a tray, and the reality of this tray is further emphasized by the rope.

Within a year, Picasso and Braque were producing still lifes composed almost entirely of cut-and-pasted scraps of material, with only a few painted lines added to complete the design. In *Le Courrier* by Braque (fig. 24-16) we recognize strips of imitation wood graining, part of a tobacco wrapper with a contrasting stamp, half the masthead of a newspaper, and a bit of newsprint made into a playing card (the ace of hearts). Why did Picasso and Braque suddenly prefer the contents of the wastepaper basket to brush and paint? In wanting to explore their new concept of the picture as a tray on which to "serve" the still life, they found the best way was to put real things on the tray. The ingredients of a collage actually play a double role. They have been shaped and combined, then drawn or painted upon to give them a representational meaning, but they do not lose their original identity as scraps of material—they remain "outsiders" in the world of art.

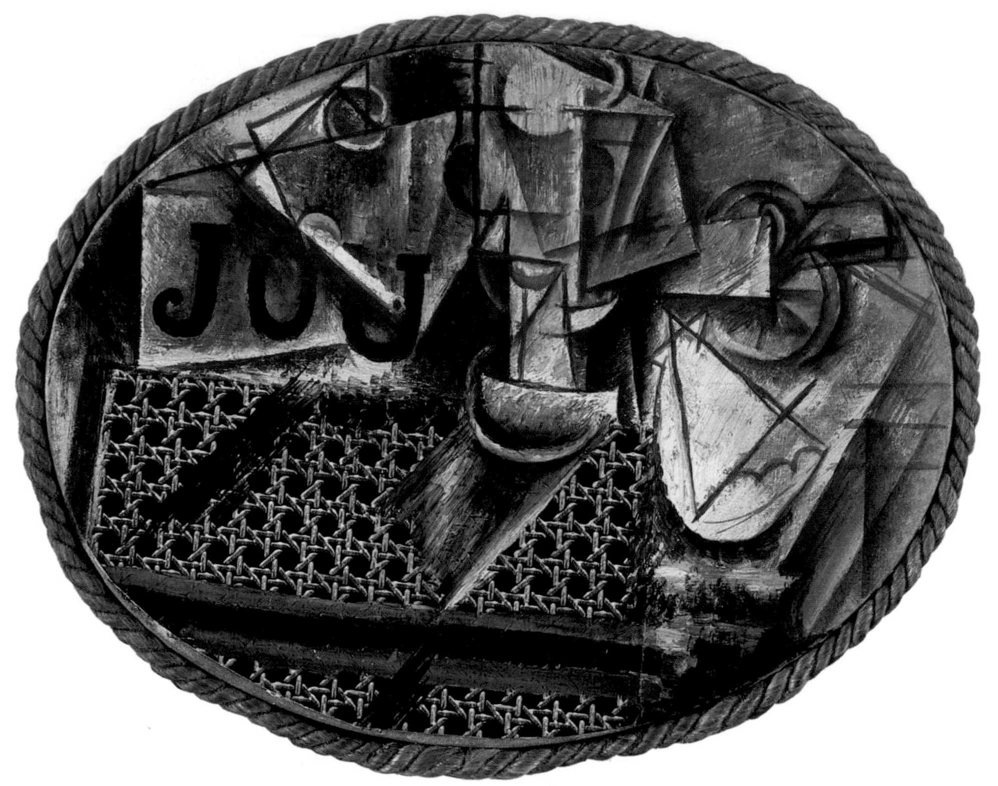

24-15. Pablo Picasso. *Still Life with Chair Caning.* 1912. Collage of oil, oilcloth, and pasted paper simulating chair caning on canvas, 10½ x 13¾" (26.7 x 35 cm). Musée Picasso, Paris

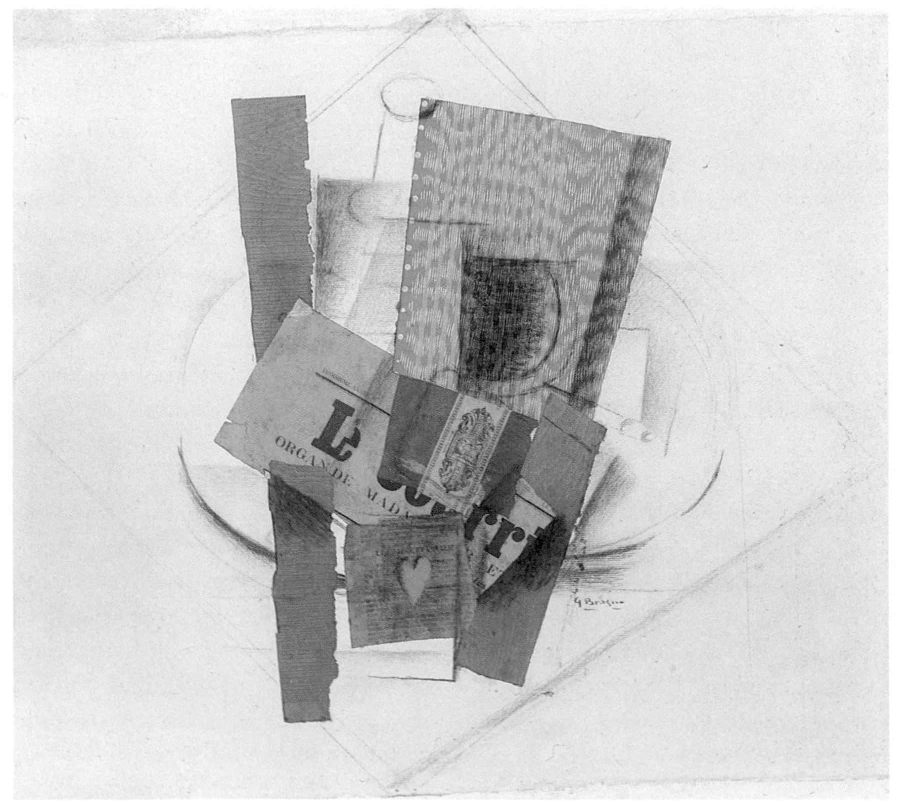

24-16. Georges Braque. *Newspaper, Bottle, Packet of Tobacco (Le Courrier).* 1914. Collage of charcoal, gouache, pencil, ink, and pasted paper on cardboard, 20⅝ x 25" (52.4 x 63.5 cm). Philadelphia Museum of Art

A. E. GALLATIN COLLECTION

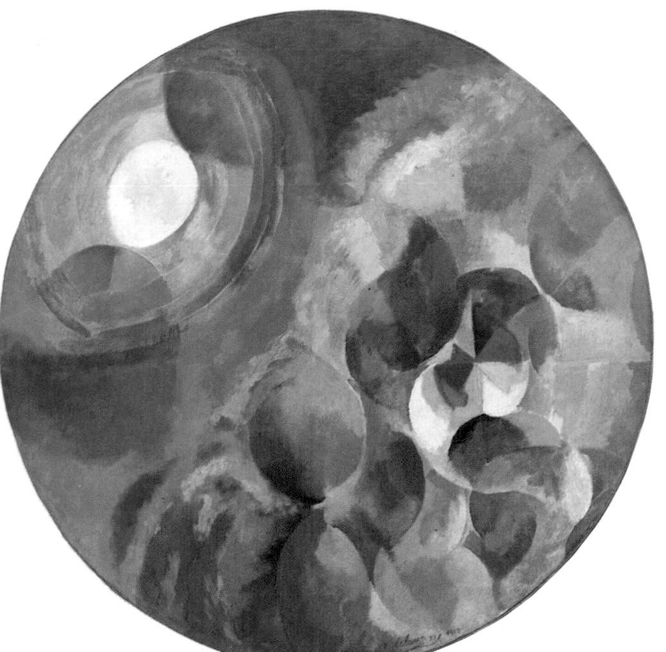

24-17. Robert Delaunay.
Simultaneous Contrasts: Sun and Moon.
1913. Oil on canvas, diameter 53" (134.5 cm).
The Museum of Modern Art, New York
MRS. SIMON GUGGENHEIM FUND

Their function is both to represent (to be a part of an image) and to present (to be themselves). In this latter capacity, they give the collage a self-sufficiency that no Analytic Cubist picture can possibly have. A tray, after all, is a self-contained area, detached from the rest of the physical world. Unlike a painting, it cannot show more than is actually on it.

The difference between the two phases of Cubism may also be defined in terms of picture space. Analytic Cubism retains a certain kind of depth, so that the painted surface acts as a window through which we still perceive the remains of the perspective space of the Renaissance. Though fragmented and redefined, this space lies behind the picture plane and has no visible limits. Potentially, it may even contain objects that are hidden from our view. In Synthetic Cubism, on the contrary, the picture space lies in front of the plane of the "tray." Space is not created by illusionistic devices, such as modeling and foreshortening, but by the actual overlapping of layers of pasted materials. The integrity of the nonperspective space is not affected when, as in *Le Courrier,* the apparent thickness of these materials and their distance from each other are increased by a bit of shading here and there. Synthetic Cubism, then, offers a basically new space concept, the first since Masaccio. It is a true landmark in the history of painting.

Before long Picasso and Braque discovered that they could maintain this new pictorial space without the use of pasted materials. They only had to paint as if they were making collages. World War I, however, put an end to their collaboration and delayed the further development of Synthetic Cubism, which thus reached its height in the following decade.

Orphism

The Cubism of Picasso and Braque was little concerned with color—an issue addressed finally by Robert Delaunay (1885–1941) and his wife, Sonia Delaunay-Terk (1885–1979). They evolved a totally abstract style called Orphism (after the legendary Orpheus) by the poet Apollinaire (1880–1918), the chief theorist of the movement. Following the concepts of Chevreul, Seurat, and Gauguin, the Delaunays wanted to produce pure color harmonies as independent of nature as music. Late in 1912, Delaunay began to paint his series *Simultaneous Contrasts* (fig. 24-17), in which the swirling movement is meant to evoke the rhythms pulsating throughout the universe. The idea was in the air. At almost the same time the Czech painter Frantisek Kupka (1871–1957), working independently in Paris, came to the identical solution. It was soon taken up as well by the Americans Stanton Macdonald-Wright (1890–1973) and Morgan Russell (1886–1953), who were also active in Paris and who called their movement Synchromism. Orphism proved to be short-lived, however. Even the Delaunays were able to maintain this nonobjective style for only a few years and soon turned to Futurism. Nevertheless, the movement was of great importance. Among its early members were Marcel Duchamp and his brother Raymond Duchamp-Villon. In addition to Franz Marc, it affected Fernand Léger, Marc Chagall, and even Paul Klee.

Futurism

As originally conceived by Picasso and Braque, Cubism was a formal discipline of subtle balance applied to traditional subjects: still life, portraiture, the nude. Other painters, however, saw in the new style a strong kinship with the geometric precision of engineering that made it uniquely attuned to the dynamism of modern life. The short-lived Futurist movement in Italy represents this attitude. In 1909–10 its disciples, led by the poet Filippo Tom maso Marinetti, issued a series of manifestos violently rejecting the past and exalting the beauty of the machine. [See Primary Sources, no. 85, page 935.]

At first they used techniques developed from Post-Impressionism to convey the surge of industrial society, but these were otherwise static compositions, still dependent upon repre-

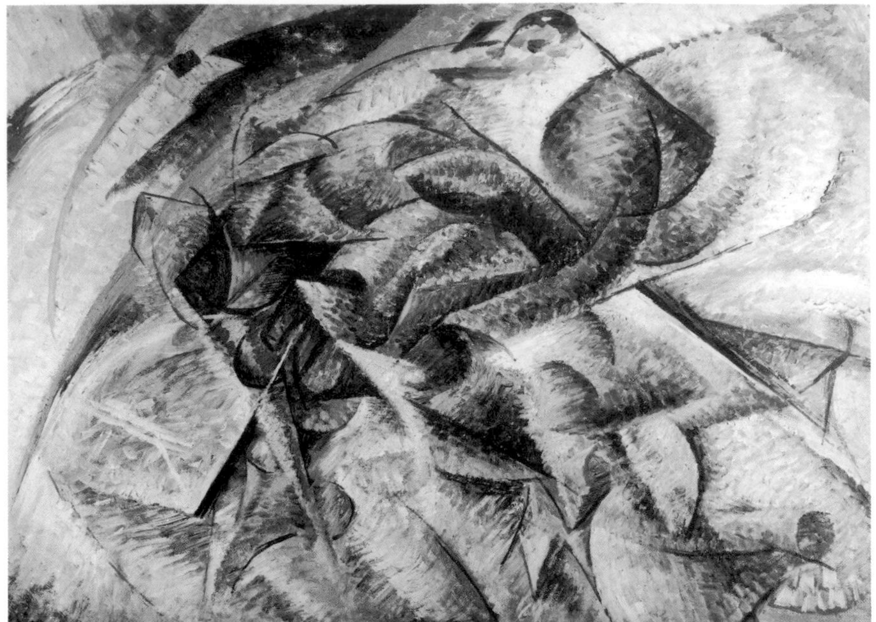

24-18. Umberto Boccioni. *Dynamism of a Cyclist.* 1913. Oil on canvas, 27 5/8 x 37 3/8" (70 x 95 cm). Collection Gianni Mattioli, Milan

THEATER BEFORE WORLD WAR I

By far the most adventurous theater before World War I was to be found in Russia, thus preparing the way for even more radical experiments after the Russian Revolution of 1917. The most famous of the Russian reformers remains Konstantin Stanislavsky (1863–1938), who was a cofounder of the Moscow Art Theater with Vladimir Nemirovich-Danchenko (1858–1943). Stanislavsky's legacy is clouded by a lack of fully authentic texts, but in general he placed greatest emphasis on the actor, despite the fact that he never adopted the "star" system. Stanislavsky insisted on a rigorous training of body, voice, and mind based on a thorough understanding of stagecraft, reality, and the drama itself, so that the action would unfold naturally and convincingly, though he was by no means a Realist. Stanislavsky's theories were later practiced in the modified America form known as "method acting" (see box page 819).

The key figure in early Russian modernism, however, was Vsevelod Meyerhold (1874–1940), who considered the director to be the main creative force in the theater. He was employed by every Russian avant-garde theater, including Stanislavsky's Moscow Art Theater, but never lasted very long in any position because his experiments were regarded as too bold. For example, he dispensed with the theatrical curtain and set his productions in symbolic scenery or even on a bare stage. Alexander Tairov (1885–1950) adopted a centrist position: like Stanislavsky, he stressed the importance of the actor but followed Meyerhold in treating the play as the point of departure for the director's creativity. At the same time, he maintained that there is no relationship between art and life and that theater should be like the sacred dances of ancient temples. The ritual effect of his productions, which stressed unity of word, music, and dance, was similar in intent to Classical Greek theater. At the opposite end of the spectrum was the equally innovative Nikolai Evreinov (1879–1953), whose "monodramas," such as *The Theater of the Soul* (1912), sought to lead the audience to a greater understanding by drawing on what he believed was humanity's innate theatricality, which leads people to seek a higher reality.

The Russians had a great impact on French theater. The first to exercise his influence was Sergei Diaghilev (1872–1929), whose publication *The World of Art* promoted Symbolist art, literature, and theater. The ballet company he took to Paris in 1909 met with such success that he formed the Ballets Russes, featuring the great dancer Vasily Nijinsky (1890–1950), the choreography of Mikhail Fokine (1880–1942), the music of Igor Stravinsky and his teacher Nikolai Rimsky-Korsakov, and the designs of Aleksandr Benois (1870–1960) and Léon Bakst (1866–1924). With the onset of the Russian Revolution the company remained in Paris; it later employed Picasso, Braque, and De Chirico, among other artists, as stage and costume designers.

Under Russian influence, Jacques Rouché (1862–1957) launched the periodical *Modern Theater* simultaneously with the Théâtre des Arts in 1910. His ideas were to bear fruit at the Paris Opéra, where he was appointed director four years later and remained until 1936. It was at the Théâtre des Arts that Jacques Copeau (1879–1949), who became the leading figure in French theater between the wars, got his start. He adopted the opposite position of Meyerhold's in arguing that only the actor was essential and that the director's primary responsibility was the faithful translation of the script into a "poetry of the theater." And whereas Rouché thought primarily in visual terms, Copeau argued for a return to the bare stage.

For all of its inventiveness, early-twentieth-century theater contributed little in the way of new plays. The main impetus in sentational images. By adopting the simultaneous views of Analytic Cubism in *Dynamism of a Cyclist* (fig. 24-18), Umberto Boccioni (1882–1916), the most original of the Futurists, was able to communicate the energy of rapid pedaling across time and space far more tellingly than if he had actually depicted the human figure. In traditional art the subject could be seen in only one time and place. In the flexible vocabulary provided by Cubism, Boccioni found the means of expressing what Albert Einstein had defined in 1905 in his special theory of relativity—the twentieth century's new sense of time, space, and energy. Moreover, Boccioni suggests the unique quality of the modern experience. With his pulsating movement, the cyclist has become an extension of his environment, from which he is now indistinguishable.

Cubo-Futurism

As its name implies, Cubo-Futurism took its style from Picasso and Braque and based its theories on Futurist tracts. The movement arose in Russia a few years before World War I as the result of close contacts with the leading European art centers. The Russian Futurists were, above all, modernists. They welcomed industry, which was spreading rapidly throughout Russia, as the foundation of a new society and the means for conquering that old Russian enemy, nature. Unlike the Italian Futurists, however, the Russians rarely glorified the machine, least of all as an instrument of war.

Central to Cubo-Futurist thinking was the concept of *zaum,* a term that has no counterpart in English. Invented by Russian poets, *zaum* was a "trans-sense" (as opposed to the Dadaists' nonsense; see page 798) language based on new word forms and syntax. In theory, *zaum* could be understood universally, since it was thought that meaning was implicit in the basic sounds and patterns of speech. When applied to painting, *zaum* provided the artist with complete freedom to redefine the style and content of art. The picture surface was now seen as the sole conveyer of meaning through its appearance. Hence the subject of a work of art became its visual elements and their formal arrangement. However, because Cubo-Futurism was concerned with means, not ends, it failed to provide the actual content that is found in

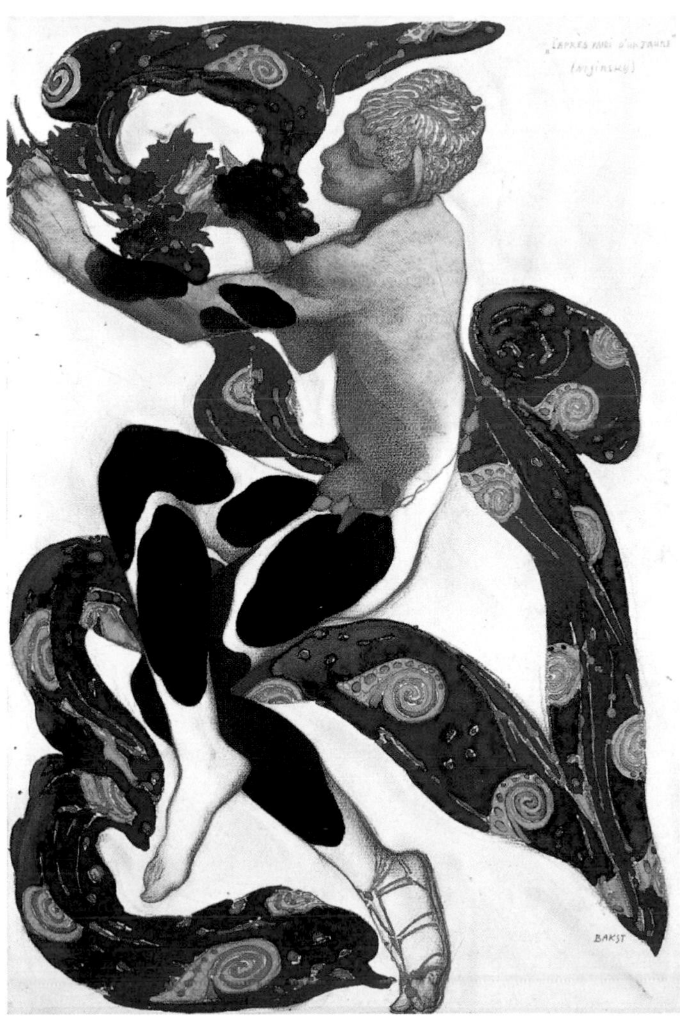

Leon Bakst. *Nijinsky in L'Après-midi d'un Faune* (costume design). 1912. Watercolor, paper, and gouache, sheet: 15⅜ x 10½" (39.1 x 26.7 cm). Wadsworth Atheneum, Hartford, Connecticut

THE ELLA GALLUP SUMNER AND MARY CATLIN SUMNER COLLECTION FUND, 1935

dramatic writing came from Ireland. There plays with a Gaelic focus were produced by the Irish National Theater Society, better known as the Abbey Theater, where it was housed after 1904. The most important playwrights were the poet William Butler Yeats (1865–1939), Lady Augusta Gregory (1863–1935), and John Millington Synge (1871–1909). Yeats' early work sprang from the writing of the French Symbolists he had met in Paris. He was primarily concerned with restoring the importance of writing to theater; thus, his poetic-mythic approach was the opposite of Lady Gregory's, whose style was realistic-domestic. It was Yeats who convinced Synge to return from Paris to write about Irish peasant life. Synge successfully synthesized the best features of Yeats and Lady Gregory in the two finest dramas staged by the Abbey: *Riders to the Sea* (1904) and *The Playboy of the Western World* (1907). Synge was fearless in tackling controversial subjects that went against customary beliefs—*Playboy* caused riots wherever it played—but the real secret of his success was his unique form of poetic prose.

In England, the most important theorist was the director and designer Edward Gordon Craig (1872–1966), the son of Ellen Terry and Edward Goodwin, whose thinking laid the ground for many of the key concepts of modern directing. Like Meyerhold, he conceived of the director as an artist who created theater as a work of art independent of the drama itself by utilizing lights and simply painted screens. No one, however, had more impact on theater than Max Reinhardt (1873–1943), who succeeded Otto Brahm as director of the Deutsches Theater in Berlin. He realized that each play demanded a different approach, without adhering to any single system. In place of the conventions of the day he insisted that the director rethink and control every detail of the production, which was prepared in close collaboration with his actors and designers.

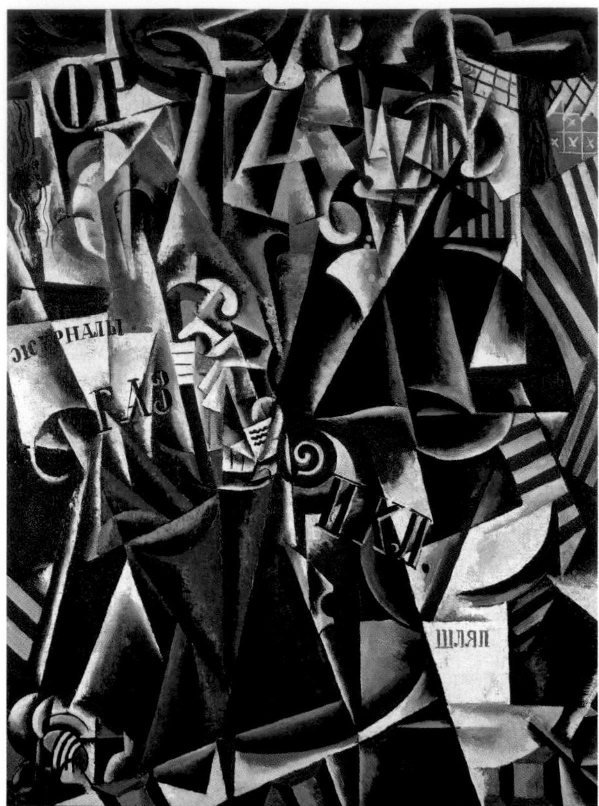

24-19. Liubov Popova. *The Traveler.* 1915.
Oil on canvas, 56 x 41½" (142.2 x 105.4 cm).
Norton Simon Art Foundation, Pasadena, California

24-20. Kazimir Malevich. *Suprematist Composition: White on White.* 1918. Oil on canvas, 31¼ x 31¼" (79.4 x 79.4 cm).
The Museum of Modern Art, New York

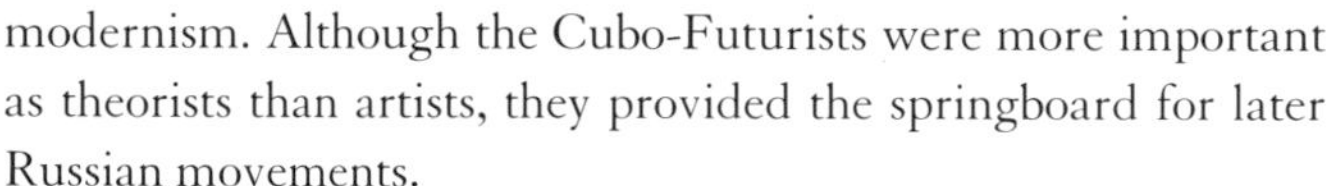

modernism. Although the Cubo-Futurists were more important as theorists than artists, they provided the springboard for later Russian movements.

The new world envisioned by the Russian modernists redefined the roles of man and woman, and it was in Russia that women emerged as artistic equals in a way that was not achieved in Europe or America until considerably later. The finest painter of the Cubo-Futurists was Liubov Popova (1889–1924), who studied in Paris in 1912 and visited Italy in 1914. The combination of Cubism and Futurism that she absorbed abroad is seen in *The Traveler* (fig. 24-19). The treatment of forms remains essentially Cubist, but the painting shares the Futurist obsession with representing dynamic motion in time and space. The jumble of image fragments creates the impression of objects seen in rapid succession. The tumultuous interaction of forms with their environment across the plane nearly extends the painting into the surrounding space. At the same time, the strong modeling draws attention to the surface and gives it a relieflike quality that is enhanced by the vigorous texture.

Suprematism

The first purely Russian art of the twentieth century was Suprematism. It was devised by Kazimir Malevich (1878–1935), who wanted to reduce painting to a "supreme" reality—an independent abstraction in itself—based on geometry; hence the movement's name. According to the artist, Suprematism was also a philosophical color system. His space was an intuitive one, with both scientific and mystical overtones. The flat plane replaces volume, depth, and perspective. Each side or point represents one of the three dimensions, while the fourth side stands for the fourth dimension, time. Like Einstein's theory of relativity, the formula $E=mc^2$, Suprematism had an elegant simplicity that belied the intense effort required to synthesize a complex set of ideas and reduce them to a fundamental "law." The relation between art and science is closer than we might think, for despite the differences in approach, they are united by the imagination. In fact, the key to solving the theory of relativity came to Einstein as a visual image.

Malevich's Suprematist painting of a black quadrilateral within a white border had much the same impact on Russian artists in 1915 that Einstein's theory had on scientists: it unveiled a world never seen before, one that was unmistakably modern. Later, Malevich began to tilt his quadrilaterals and to simplify his paintings still further in search of the ultimate work of art. These efforts culminated in *Suprematist Composition: White on White* (fig. 24-20), his most famous composition, which limits art to its fewest possible components. It is tempting to dismiss such a radical extreme as an absurd reduction. Seen in person, however, the canvas is surprisingly persuasive. The shapes, created by two subtly different shades of white, have a visionary purity that makes other paintings seem needlessly complex.

FANTASY

Our third current, Fantasy, follows a less clear-cut course than the other two, since it depends on a state of mind more than on any particular style. The one thing all painters of Fantasy have in common is the belief that imagination, "the inner eye," is more important than the outside world. We must be careful how we use the term *fantasy*. It originated in psychoanalytic theory and meant something very different in the early twentieth century than it does now. It was thought of as mysterious and profound, anything but the lighthearted and superficial entity we take it for today.

Why did private fantasy come to loom so large in early-twentieth-century art? There were several causes. First, the rift that developed between reason and imagination in the wake of rationalism tended to break down the heritage of myth and legend that had been the channel of private fantasy in earlier times. Second, the artist had greater freedom—and insecurity—within society, giving him a sense of isolation and favoring an introspective attitude. Then, too, the Romantic cult of emotion prompted the artist to seek out subjective experience and to accept its validity. Needless to say, this process took time. We saw the trend beginning at the end of the eighteenth century in the art of Goya and Fuseli (see figs. 21-22 and 21-43). In early-nineteenth-century painting, private fantasy was still a minor current, but by 1900 it had become a major one, thanks to Symbolism on the one hand and the naive vision of artists such as Henri Rousseau on the other.

DE CHIRICO. The heritage of Romanticism can be seen most clearly in the astonishing pictures painted in Paris just before World War I by the Italian artist Giorgio de Chirico (1888–1978), such as *Mystery and Melancholy of a Street* (fig. 24-21). Illuminated by the cold light of the full moon, this deserted square, with its tilted perspective and rapidly diminishing arcades, has all the poetry of Romantic reverie—but it also has a strangely sinister air. This is an "ominous" scene in the full sense of the term: everything here suggests an omen, a portent of unknown and disquieting significance. The artist himself could not explain the incongruities in these paintings—the empty furniture van or the girl with the hoop—that trouble and fascinate us. De Chirico called this *Metaphysical Painting:* "We who know the signs of the metaphysical alphabet are aware of the joy and the solitude which are enclosed by a portico, by the corner of a street, or even in a room, on the surface of a table, or between the sides of a box.... The minutely accurate and prudently weighed use of surfaces and volumes constitutes the canon of the metaphysical aesthetic." [See also Primary Sources, no. 86, page 935.] Later, after he had returned to Italy, De Chirico adopted a conservative style and disowned his early works. As if embarrassed at having put his dream world on display, he nevertheless secretly continued to paint copies to meet commercial demand.

CHAGALL. The power of nostalgia, so evident in *Mystery and Melancholy of a Street,* also dominates the work of Marc Chagall (1887–1985), a Russian who went to Paris in 1910. *I and the Village* (fig. 24-22) weaves dreamlike memories of Russian folk tales, Jewish proverbs, and the look of Russia into a glowing Cubist vision:

> But please defend me against people who speak of "anecdote" and "fairy tales" in my work. A cow and woman to me are the same—in a picture both are merely elements of a composition [which] have different values of plasticity, but not different poetic values. In the large cow's head in *I and the Village* I made a small cow and woman milking visible through its muzzle

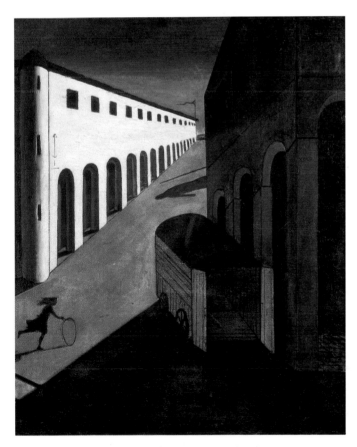

24-21. Giorgio de Chirico. *Mystery and Melancholy of a Street.* 1914. Oil on canvas, 34¼ x 28½" (87 x 72.4 cm). Private collection

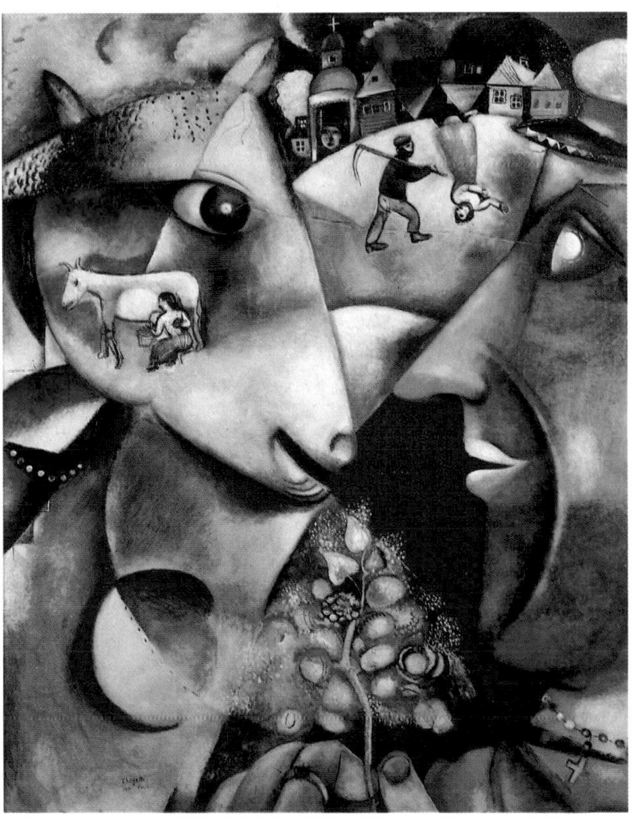

24-22. Marc Chagall. *I and the Village.* 1911. Oil on canvas, 6'3⅝" x 4'11½" (1.92 x 1.51 m). The Museum of Modern Art, New York

MRS. SIMON GUGGENHEIM FUND

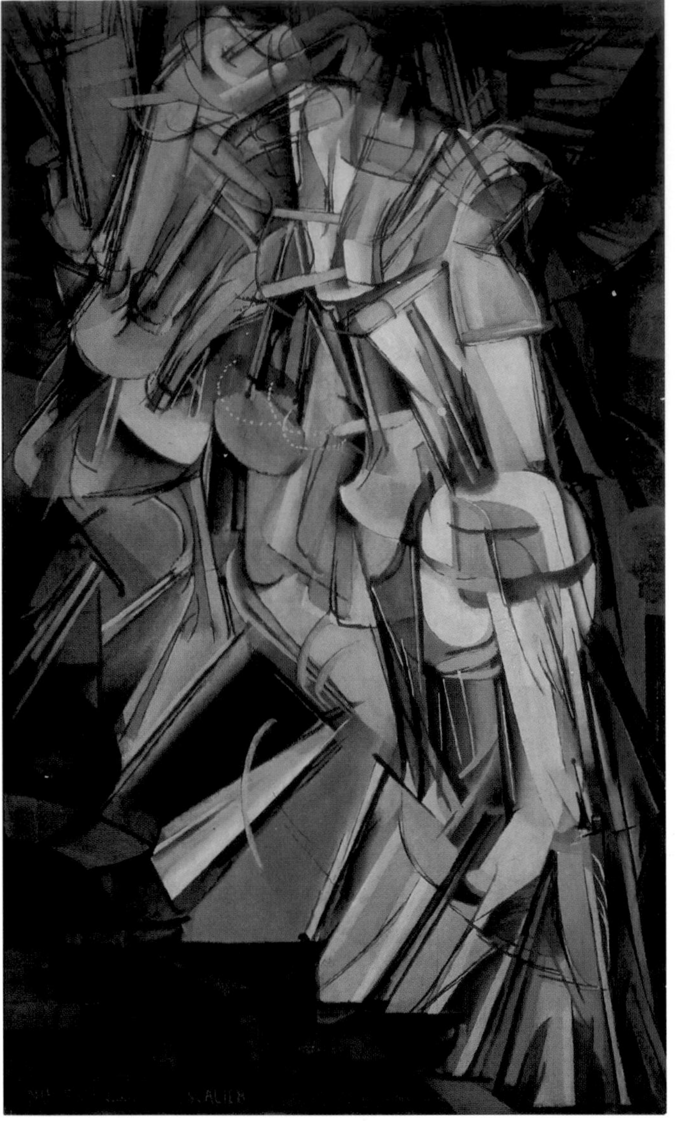

24-23. Marcel Duchamp. *Nude Descending a Staircase No. 2.* 1912. Oil on canvas, 58 x 35" (147.3 x 89 cm). Philadelphia Museum of Art

LOUISE AND WALTER ARENSBERG COLLECTION

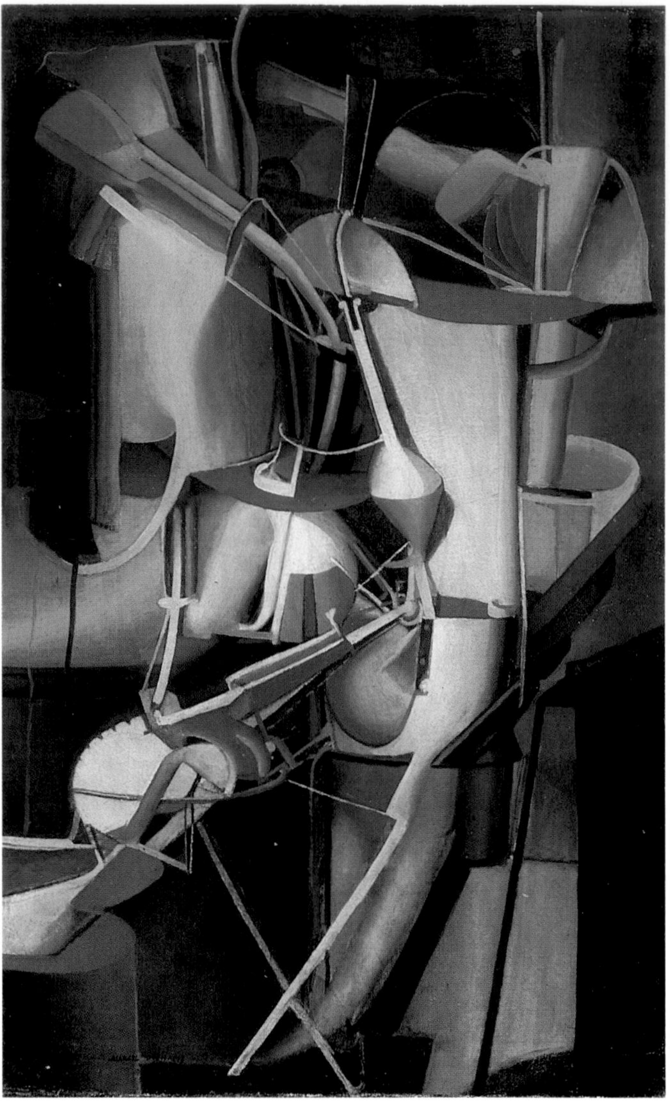

24-24. Marcel Duchamp. *The Bride.* 1912. Oil on canvas, 35⅛ x 21¾" (89.4 x 55.2 cm). Philadelphia Museum of Art

LOUISE AND WALTER ARENSBERG COLLECTION

> because I needed that sort of form, there, for my composition. Whatever else may have grown out of these compositional arrangements is secondary. The fact that I made use of cows, milkmaids, rooster, and provincial Russian architecture as my source forms is because they are part of the environment from which I spring.

The experiences of Chagall's childhood were so important to him that his imagination shaped and reshaped them for years.

DUCHAMP. In Paris shortly before World War I we encounter another artist of Fantasy, the Frenchman Marcel Duchamp (1887–1968). After basing his early style on Cézanne, he created a dynamic version of Analytic Cubism, similar to Futurism, by superimposing successive phases of movement on one another, much like multiple-exposure photography (see fig. 23-50a and b). His *Nude Descending a Staircase* (fig. 24-23) caused a scandal at the Armory Show because it went against all traditional notions of what a nude should look like. Although his objective was simply to paint "a static representation of movement," this parody of the human figure already shows the ironic wit that was to underlie his later work.

Duchamp's development soon took a far more disturbing turn. In *The Bride* (fig. 24-24) from 1912, we look in vain for any resemblance, however remote, to the human form. What we see instead is a mechanism that seems part motor, part distilling apparatus. It is beautifully engineered to serve no purpose whatsoever. The title cannot be irrelevant: by lettering it right onto the canvas, Duchamp has emphasized its importance. Yet it remains truly puzzling. Evidently the artist intended the machine as a kind of modern fetish that acts as a metaphor of human sexuality. He satirizes the scientific outlook on humanity by "analyzing" the bride until she is reduced to a complicated piece of plumbing that seems utterly dysfunctional, physically and psychologically. Thus the picture represents the negative counterpart of the glorification of the machine, so stridently proclaimed by the Futurists. We may further see in Duchamp's pessimistic outlook a response to the gathering forces that were soon to be unleashed in World War I, toppling the political order that had been created 100 years earlier at the Congress of Vienna following Napoleon's final defeat.

REALISM

THE ASH CAN SCHOOL. In America, the first wave of change was initiated by the Ash Can School, which flourished in New York just before World War I. Centering on Robert Henri, who had studied with a pupil of Thomas Eakins at the Pennsylvania Academy, this group of artists consisted mainly of former illustrators for Philadelphia and New York newspapers. They were fascinated with the teeming life of the city slums and found an endless source of subjects in the everyday urban scene, to which they brought a reporter's eye for color and drama. Despite the socialist philosophy that many of them shared, theirs was not an art of social commentary but one that felt the pulse of the city, in which they discovered vitality and richness while ignoring poverty and squalor. To capture these qualities they relied on rapid execution, inspired by Baroque and Post-Impressionist painting. This lends their canvases a sense of directness and spontaneous observation.

BELLOWS. Although not among its founders, George Bellows (1882–1925) became the leading representative of the Ash Can School in its heyday. His masterpiece, *Stag at Sharkey's* (fig. 24-25), shows why. No painter in America before Jackson Pollock had expressed such heroic energy. *Stag at Sharkey's* reminds us of Eakins' *William Rush Carving His Allegorical Figure of the Schuylkill River* (see fig. 22-26) for it continues the same Realist tradition. Both place us in the scene as if we were present and use the play of light to pick out the figures against a dark background. Bellows' paintings were fully as shocking as Eakins' had been. Most late-nineteenth-century American artists had all but ignored urban life in favor of landscapes and genteel interiors. Compared with these, the subjects and surfaces of the Ash Can pictures had a disturbing rawness.

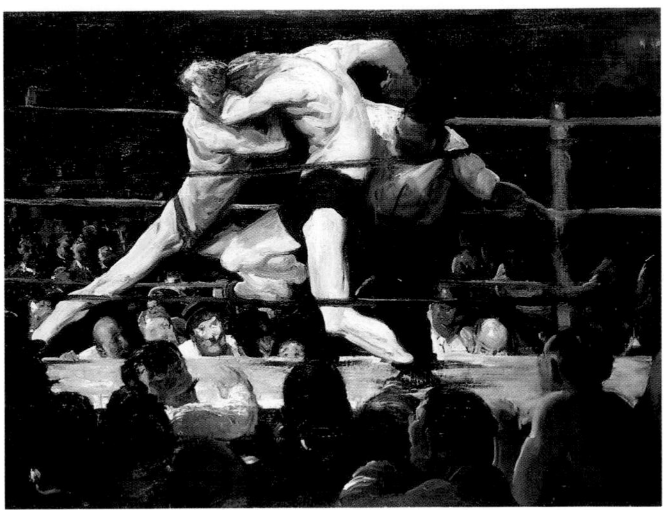

24-25. George Bellows. *Stag at Sharkey's*. 1909. Oil on canvas, 36¼ x 48¼" (92.1 x 122.6 cm). The Cleveland Museum of Art

HINMAN B. HURLBUT COLLECTION

THE ARMORY SHOW. The Ash Can School was quickly eclipsed by the rush toward a more radical modernism set off by the Armory Show. Held in New York in 1913, it was an outgrowth of the Independents Show three years earlier, which had showcased the talents of a group of rising young artists known as the Eight. The Armory Show was intended to foster a "new spirit in art" by introducing the public to the latest trends from Europe and the United States. The exhibition began with a survey of French painting from the Romantics to the Post-Impressionists and featured the Symbolists. The modern section was also heavily French, with a major emphasis on Matisse and Picasso. There were curious lapses as well: Orphism had a prominent place while German Expressionism was poorly represented and Futurism was omitted completely. The selection of sculpture was haphazard at best. American art, which made up by far the largest part of the exhibition, included works by members of the Ash Can School, the Stieglitz Group, and the Eight. While it failed to promote the interests of its organizers, the Armory Show did succeed in its goal of introducing a new cosmopolitanism into the American art scene. It also proved a success with collectors, who bought an astonishing number of works from the exhibition.

PAINTING BETWEEN THE WARS

The Founders

As we examine painting between the wars, we shall find anything but an orderly progression. World War I had totally disrupted the evolution of modernism, and its end unleashed an unprecedented outpouring of art after a four-year creative lull. The responses were equally varied. Because they were already fully formed artists, the founders of modern painting—Picasso, Braque, Matisse, Kirchner, and Kandinsky—followed very different paths from those who had not yet reached maturity by 1914. Responding only to the dictates of their imaginations, they broke the rules they had established earlier; hence their development defies convenient categories. Rather than a simple linear development, we must think in terms of multiple layers of varying depths that bear a shifting relation to one another.

PICASSO. We begin with Picasso, whose genius towers over the period. As a Spanish national living in Paris, he was not involved in World War I, unlike many French and German artists who served in the military and even lost their lives. This was a time of quiet experimentation that laid the foundation for Picasso's art over the next several decades. The results did not become fully apparent, however, until the early 1920s, following a period of intense development. *Three Musicians* (fig. 24-26) shows the fruit of that labor. It utilizes the "cut-paper style" of Synthetic Cubism so consistently that we cannot tell from the reproduction whether it is painted or pasted. The canvas revives a favorite theme of the artist's early years, the Italian commedia dell'arte (see box page 610). The shapes are locked together as tightly as the pieces of a jigsaw puzzle to create a colorful, almost jaunty composition. The effect is by no means lighthearted, however. On the contrary, the painting is a haunting evocation of the tragic mood following World War I. The somber palette invests the scene with grave solemnity. These musicians wear mysterious masks, like those of a primitive rite, which lend them a peculiar anonymity that is almost frightening. The piece they play must be anything but joyous.

By now, Picasso was internationally famous. Cubism had spread throughout the Western world. It influenced not only other painters but sculptors and even architects. Yet Picasso was already striking out in a new direction. Soon after the invention of Synthetic Cubism, he had begun to do drawings in a realistic manner reminiscent of Ingres. By 1920 he was working simultaneously in two separate styles: the Synthetic Cubism of the *Three Musicians* and a Neoclassical style, of strongly modeled, heavy-bodied figures such as his *Mother and Child* (fig. 24-27). To many of his admirers, this seemed a kind of betrayal. But in retrospect the reason for Picasso's double-track performance is clear. Having reached the limits of Synthetic Cubism, he wanted to resume contact with the Classical tradition. In fact, Picasso had never entirely abandoned the "art of the museums." *Mother and Child* was part

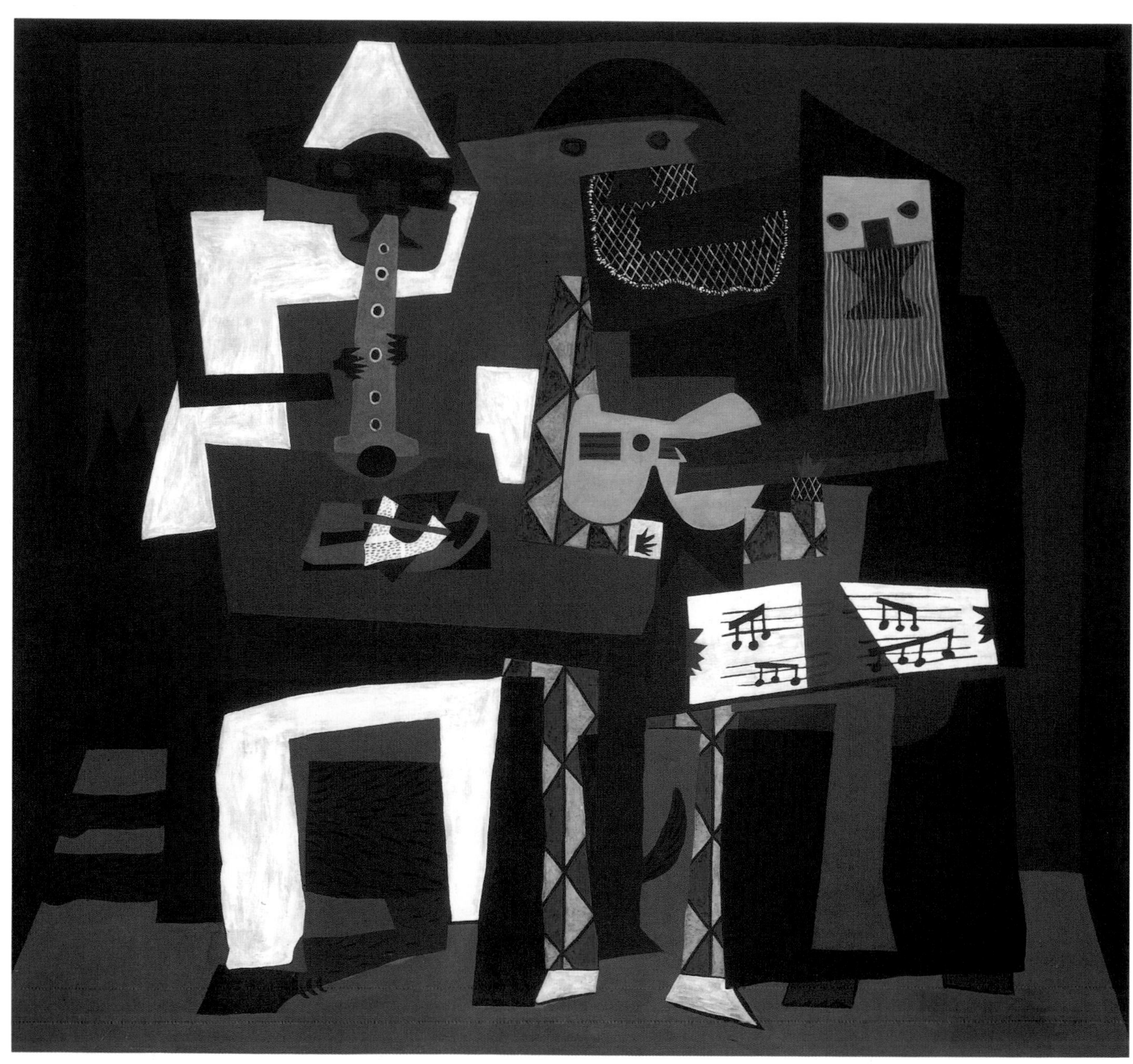

24-26. Pablo Picasso. *Three Musicians*. Summer 1921. Oil on canvas, 6'7" x 7'3¾" (2 x 2.3 m). The Museum of Modern Art, New York
MRS. SIMON GUGGENHEIM FUND

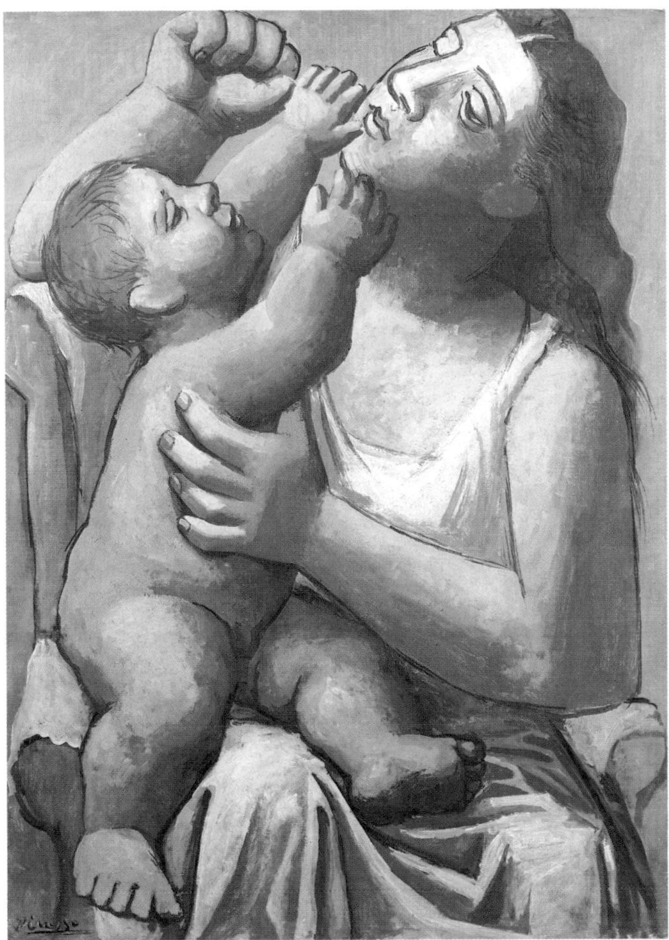

24-27. Pablo Picasso. *Mother and Child.* 1921–22. Oil on canvas, 38 x 28" (96.7 x 71 cm). The Alex L. Hillman Family Foundation, New York

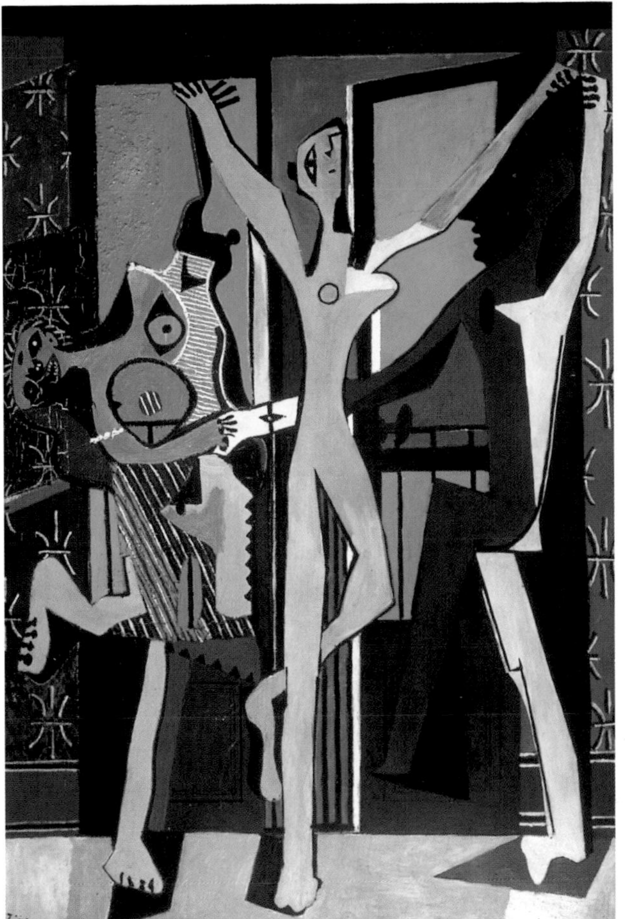

24-28. Pablo Picasso. *Three Dancers.* 1925. Oil on canvas, 7'1½" x 4'8¼" (2.15 x 1.43 m). The Tate Gallery, London

of a much broader return to classicism by artists who felt a need to reaffirm their belief in an orderly world following the cataclysmic upheavals of World War I. The figures in *Mother and Child* have a mock-monumental quality that suggests colossal statues rather than flesh-and-blood human beings, yet the theme is treated with surprising tenderness. The forms are carefully dovetailed within the frame, not unlike the way the *Three Musicians* is put together.

A few years later the two tracks of Picasso's style began to converge into an extraordinary synthesis that was to become the basis of his art. The *Three Dancers* of 1925 (fig. 24-28) shows how he accomplished this seemingly impossible feat. Structurally, the picture is pure Synthetic Cubism. It even includes painted imitations of specific materials, such as patterned wallpaper and samples of various fabrics cut out with pinking shears. The figures, a wildly fantastic version of a classical scheme (compare the dancers in Matisse's *The Joy of Life,* fig. 24-1), are an even more violent assault on convention than the figures in *Les Demoiselles d'Avignon.* Human anatomy is here simply the raw material for Picasso's incredible inventiveness. Limbs, breasts, and faces are handled with the same freedom as the fragments of external reality in Braque's *Le Courrier* (see fig. 24-16). Their original identity no longer matters. Breasts may turn into eyes, profiles merge with frontal views, shadows become substance, and vice versa in an endless flow of metamorphoses. They are "visual puns," offering wholly unexpected possibilities of expression—humorous, grotesque, macabre, even tragic.

Three Dancers marks a transition to Picasso's experiment with Surrealism (see page 798). He had been in close contact with the Surrealists since 1923; his art, in turn, was a point of departure for them. Yet he denied he was affected by Surrealism until a decade later, and with good reason. His prodigious imagination notwithstanding, he did not practice automatism; hence his work did not arise spontaneously from the subconscious. Instead, the paintings of the 1920s addressed formal concerns in the free transformation of objects, which was worked out with great care.

Three Dancers is one of the few canvases from this period that is so boldly expressive. It is only with *Girl Before a Mirror* of 1932 (fig. 24-29) that he began to reinvest his paintings with the psychological content that had marked his early work. In fact, the picture is an outgrowth of two canvases from 1905–6. The motif of a young woman contemplating her beauty goes all the way back to antiquity, but rarely has it been depicted with such disturbing overtones. Picasso's girl is anything but serene. On the contrary, she reaches out to touch the image in the mirror with a gesture of longing and apprehension. We all feel a jolt when we unexpectedly see ourselves in a mirror, which often gives back a reflection that upsets our self-conception. Picasso here suggests this visionary truth in several ways. He has treated his shapes much like the enclosed, flat panes of a stained-glass window. Just as a real mir-

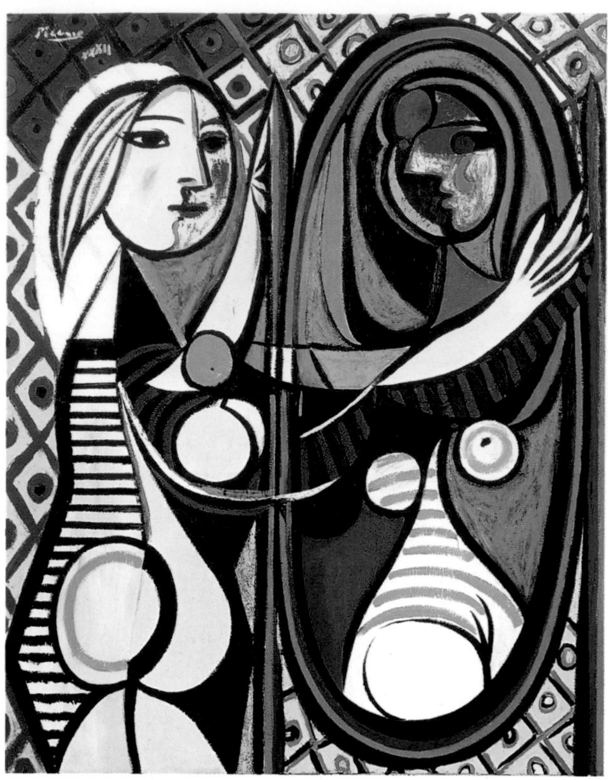

24-29. Pablo Picasso. *Girl Before a Mirror.* March 1932. Oil on canvas, 64 x 51¼" (162.3 x 130.2 cm). The Museum of Modern Art, New York
GIFT OF MRS. SIMON GUGGENHEIM

ror introduces changes of its own and does not reflect the simple truth, so this one alters the way the girl looks, revealing a deeper reality. She appears not so much to be examining her physical appearance as to be exploring her sexuality. Her face is divided into two parts, one with a somber expression, the other with a masklike appearance whose color nevertheless betrays passionate feeling. The mirror is a sea of conflicting emotions signified above all by the color scheme of her reflection. Framed by strong blue, purple, and green hues, her features stare back at her with fiery intensity. Clearly discernible is a tear on her cheek. But it is the masterstroke of the green spot, shining like a beacon in the middle of her forehead, that conveys the anguish of the girl's confrontation with her inner self. Picasso was probably aware of the theory that red and green are complementary colors that intensify each other. However, this "law" can hardly have dictated his choice of green to stand for the girl's psyche. That was surely determined as a matter of pictorial and expressive necessity.

Although Picasso never developed into a true adherent of Surrealism, the impact of his fellow Spaniard Joan Miró (see page 800) can be seen in the biomorphism of his mural *Guernica* (fig. 24-30). Picasso did not show any interest in politics during World War I or the 1920s, but the Spanish Civil War stirred him to ardent partisanship with the Loyalists. The mural, executed in 1937 for the Pavilion of the Spanish Republic at the Paris International Exposition, has truly monumental grandeur. It was inspired by the terror-bombing of Guernica, the ancient capital of the Basques in northern Spain. The painting does not represent the event itself. Rather, it evokes the agony of total war with a series of powerful images.

The destruction of Guernica was the first demonstration of the technique of saturation bombing that was later used on a huge scale during the course of World War II. The mural was thus a prophetic vision of doom. The symbolism of the scene resists exact interpretation, despite its several traditional elements: the mother and her dead child are the descendants of the *Pietà* (see fig. 11-54), the woman with the lamp recalls the *Statue of Liberty* (see fig. 21-65), and the dead fighter's hand, still clutching a broken sword, is a familiar emblem of heroic resistance. We also sense the contrast between the menacing, human-faced bull, which we know Picasso intended to represent the forces of brutality and darkness, and

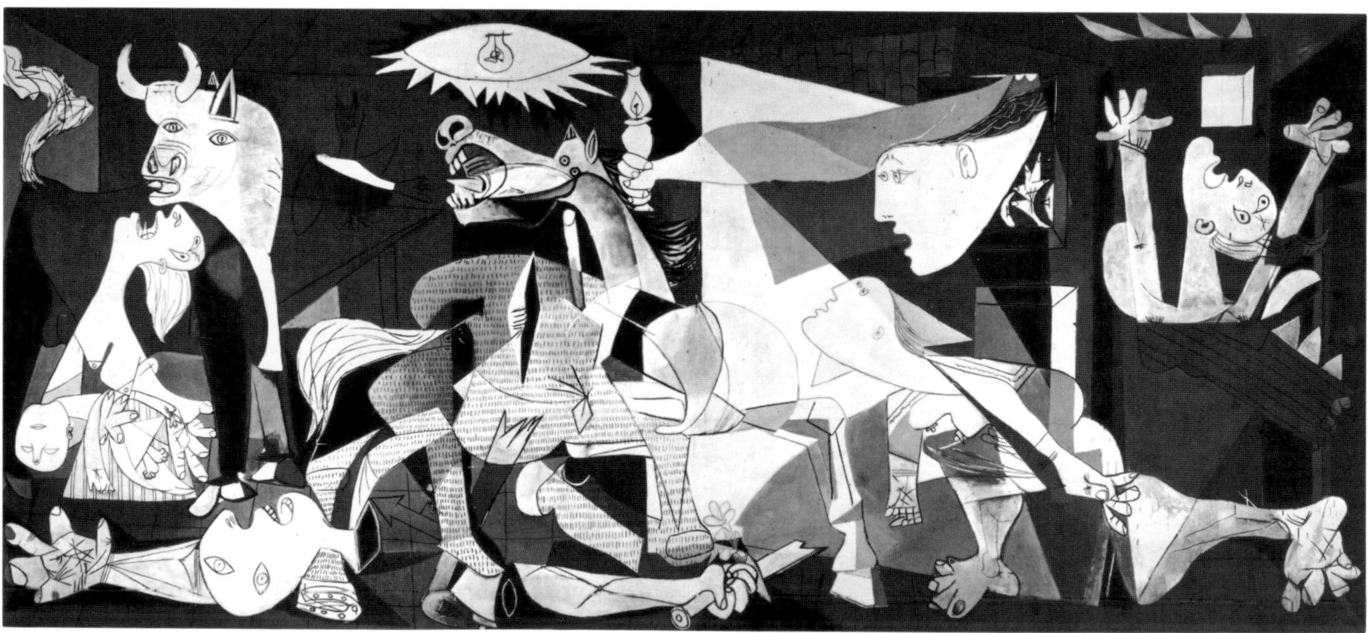

24-30. Pablo Picasso. *Guernica.* 1937. Oil on canvas, 11'6" x 25'8" (3.5 x 7.8 m). Museo Nacional Centro de Arte Reina Sofía, Madrid. On permanent loan from the Museo del Prado, Madrid

the dying horse, which stands for the people. He insisted, however, that the mural was not a political statement about fascism, though "there is a deliberate appeal to people, a deliberate sense of propaganda."

These figures owe their terrifying eloquence to what they are, not to what they mean. The anatomical dislocations, fragmentations, and transformations, which in the *Three Dancers* seemed fantastic, now express the stark reality of unbearable pain. The ultimate test of the validity of collage construction (here shown in superimposed flat "cutouts" restricted to black, white, and gray) is that it could express such overpowering emotions.

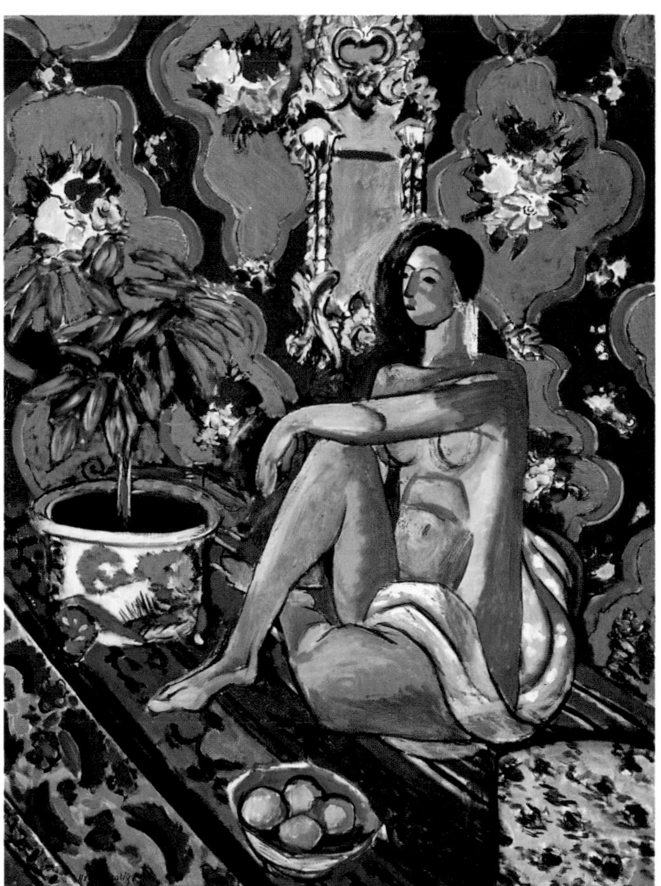

24-31. Henri Matisse. *Decorative Figure Against an Ornamental Background.* 1927. Oil on canvas, 51⅛ x 38½" (129.9 x 97.8 cm). Musée National d'Art Moderne, Paris

MATISSE. From 1911 on, Matisse was influenced increasingly by Cubism, but after the war he, like Picasso, returned to the Classical tradition. The lessons he absorbed from Cubism nevertheless had a far-reaching effect on his style. We see this in *Decorative Figure Against an Ornamental Background* (fig. 24-31). The painting has a new richness. At the same time, there is an underlying discipline resulting from his study of Cubism. The carpet provides a firm geometric structure for organizing the composition so that everything has its place, although the system itself is entirely intuitive. Only in this way could Matisse control all the elements of his complex picture. It is among the finest in a long series of odalisques (harem girls) that Matisse painted during the 1920s and 1930s. In them the artist emerges as the heir of the French tradition, which he had absorbed through his teacher Gustave Moreau (see page 750). The visual splendor would be worthy of Delacroix himself. Yet in the calm pose and strong contours of the figure, Matisse reveals himself to be a classicist at heart, more akin to Ingres than to the Romantics (compare figs. 21-30 and 21-33). The picture has overtones of Degas (see fig. 22-14), who had been trained by a disciple of Ingres and thus formed an important link in the chain of tradition. It breathes the classical serenity of *Seated Woman* by Matisse's friend Maillol (see fig. 23-26), who early in his career had also been inspired by Gauguin. Nevertheless, Matisse's is a distinctly modern classicism.

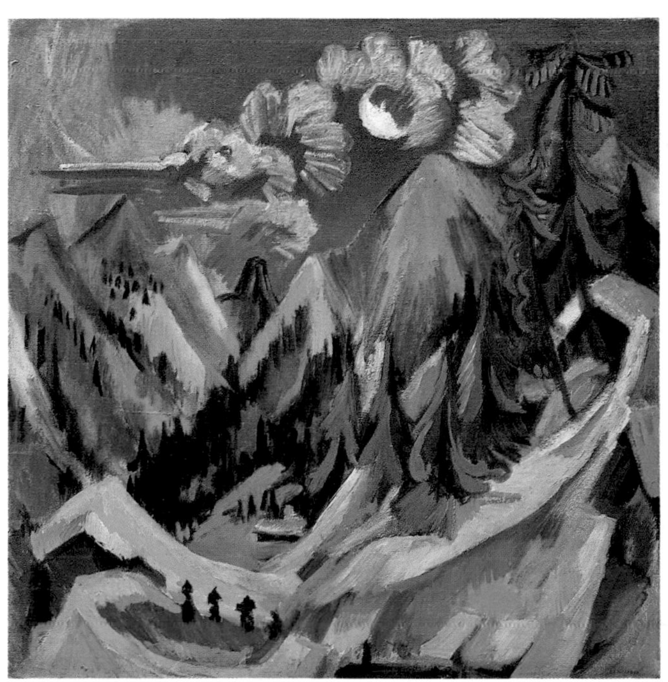

24-32. Ernst Ludwig Kirchner. *Winter Landscape in Moonlight.* 1919. Oil on canvas, 47⅝ x 47⅝" (121 x 121 cm). The Detroit Institute of Arts

GIFT OF CURT VALENTIN IN MEMORY OF THE ARTIST ON THE OCCASION OF DR. WILLIAM R. VALENTINER'S SIXTIETH BIRTHDAY

KIRCHNER. Kirchner, too, was influenced by Cubism after 1911, when he joined the other members of *Die Brücke* in Berlin. Four years later he was drafted into World War I, which ruined his physical and mental health. Released from the army after six months to recover from tuberculosis, he moved to Switzerland, where he turned increasingly to landscapes, as did many other German Expressionists following the war. *Winter Landscape in Moonlight* (fig. 24-32), painted in the Swiss Alps, is filled with a sense of peace and wonderment before nature. The painting has the ecstatic rhythms of the young Kandinsky (compare fig. 24-10), whose work Kirchner came to know while participating in exhibitions of *Der Blaue Reiter* following the dissolution of *Die Brücke*.

KANDINSKY. Kandinsky himself spent the war years in Russia, where he participated enthusiastically in the revolution and played an important role in shaping artistic policy. When his teaching reforms met with growing hostility, he returned to Germany in 1921 and soon accepted an invitation from Walter

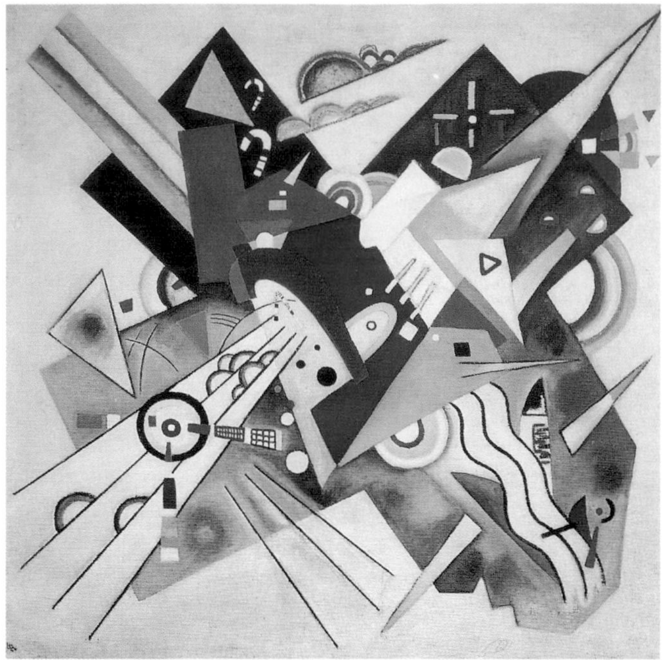

24-33. Wassily Kandinsky. *Accented Corners, No. 247.* 1923. Oil on canvas, 51¼ x 51¼" (130 x 130 cm). Private collection

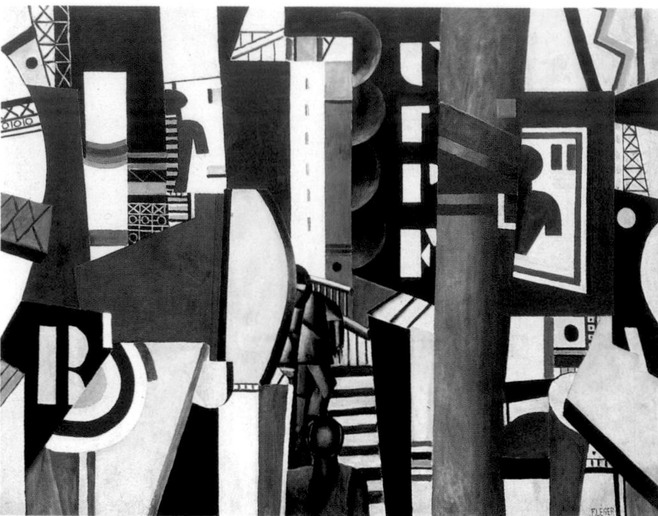

24-34. Fernand Léger. *The City.* 1919. Oil on canvas, 7'7" x 9'9" (2.31 x 2.98 m). Philadelphia Museum of Art

A. E. GALLATIN COLLECTION

Gropius to teach at the Bauhaus (see page 868). Although he had begun to experiment with a more geometric style in Russia under the influence of Constructivism and other related avant-garde movements (see page 839), some of which shared his mystical tendencies, his output was small. It was only after Kandinsky assumed his position at Weimar that he adopted geometric abstraction once and for all. The lessons and exercises he developed for his students helped to crystallize his theories of form and structure. These he set out systematically in *Point and Line to Plane,* published in 1926, which spells out concepts that were present only in elementary form in his earlier book, *Concerning the Spiritual in Art* (see page 776). His development was reinforced by the presence at the Bauhaus after 1923 of Laszlo Moholy-Nagy, who came from a Constructivist background, although his approach was otherwise the opposite of Kandinsky's (see pages 900–01). Looking at a typical example of Kandinsky's work from this time (fig. 24-33), we seem to have entered a different world from that of his earlier work (see fig. 24-10). Only when we analyze the painting do we realize that it embodies the same clash of cosmic forces. The artist has clarified the shapes and lines of force that had been buried in a sea of swirling forms. Yet the attitude is still the same, and he admitted that he remained a Romantic to the end. (Later, his forms became increasingly biomorphic in the manner of Miró; see page 800.)

Abstraction

Picasso's abandonment of strict Cubism signaled the broad retreat of abstraction after 1920. The utopian ideals associated with it had been largely dashed by "the war to end all wars." In retrospect, abstraction can be seen as a necessary phase through which modern painting had to pass, but it was not essential to modernism as such, even though it has been perhaps the dominant tendency of the twentieth century.

LÉGER. The Futurist spirit continued to find followers on both sides of the Atlantic. Buoyant with optimism and pleasurable excitement, *The City* (fig. 24-34) by the Frenchman Fernand Léger (1881–1955) creates a vision of a mechanized utopia that reflects his Communist political views. This beautifully controlled industrial landscape is stable without being static and reflects the clean geometric shapes of modern machinery. In this instance, the term *abstraction* applies more to the choice of design elements and their manner of combination than to the shapes themselves, since these are "prefabricated" entities, except for the two figures on the staircase.

DEMUTH. The modern movement in America proved short-lived. One of the few artists to continue working in an abstract vein after World War I was Charles Demuth (1883–1935). A member of the Stieglitz group (see pages 892–94), he had been friendly with Duchamp and the exiled Cubists in New York during World War I. A few years later, under the impact of Futurism, he developed a style known as Precisionism to depict urban and industrial architecture. Influences from all of these movements can be seen in *I Saw the Figure 5 in Gold* (fig. 24-35). The title is taken from the poem "The Great Figure" by Demuth's friend William Carlos Williams, whose name also forms part of the design as "Bill," "Carlos," and "W. C. W." In the poem the figure 5 appears on a red fire truck, while in the painting it has become the dominant feature, thrice repeated to reinforce its echo in our memory as the fire truck rushes on through the night:

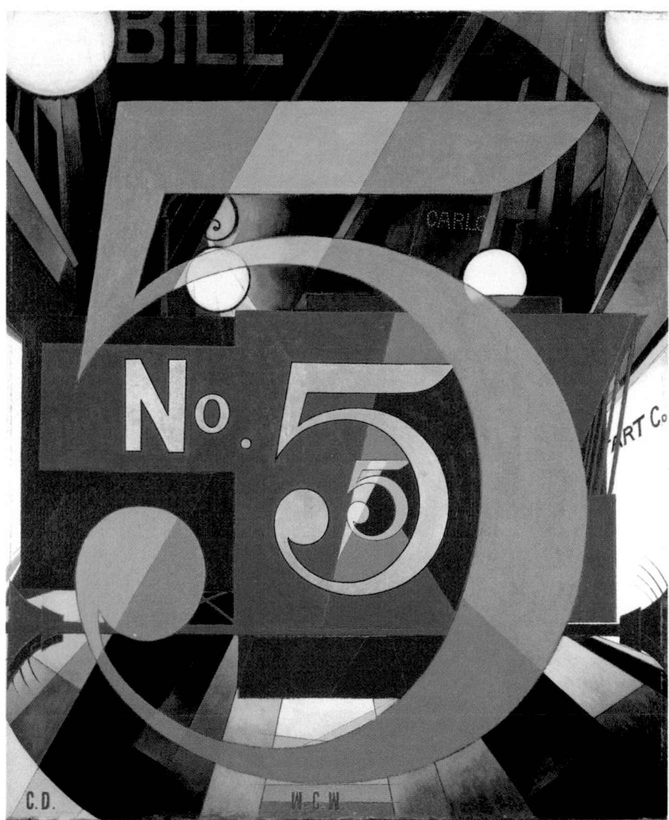

24-35. Charles Demuth. *I Saw the Figure 5 in Gold.* 1928. Oil on composition board, 36 x 29¾" (91.4 x 75.6 cm). The Metropolitan Museum of Art, New York

THE ALFRED STIEGLITZ COLLECTION, 1949

Among the rain
and lights
I saw the figure 5 in gold
on a red
firetruck
moving
tense
unheeded
to gong clangs
siren howls
and wheels rumbling
through the dark city

STELLA. Poetry was central as well to *Brooklyn Bridge* (fig. 24-36) by the Italian-American Joseph Stella (1877–1946). To Stella, who emigrated to America as a young man, the bridge became a symbol of his adopted land, which provided his boldest theme. He wrote in his autobiography: "To realize this towering imperative vision in all its integral possibilities . . . I appealed for help to the soaring verse of Walt Whitman and to the fiery Poe's plasticity. Upon the swarming darkness of the night, I rung all the bells of alarm with the blaze of electricity scattered in lightnings down the oblique cables, the dynamic pillars of my composition, and to render more pungent the mystery of the metallic apparition, through the green and red glare of the signals I excavated here and there caves as subterranean passages to infernal recesses." His painting achieves what a contemporary critic perceptively called the apo-

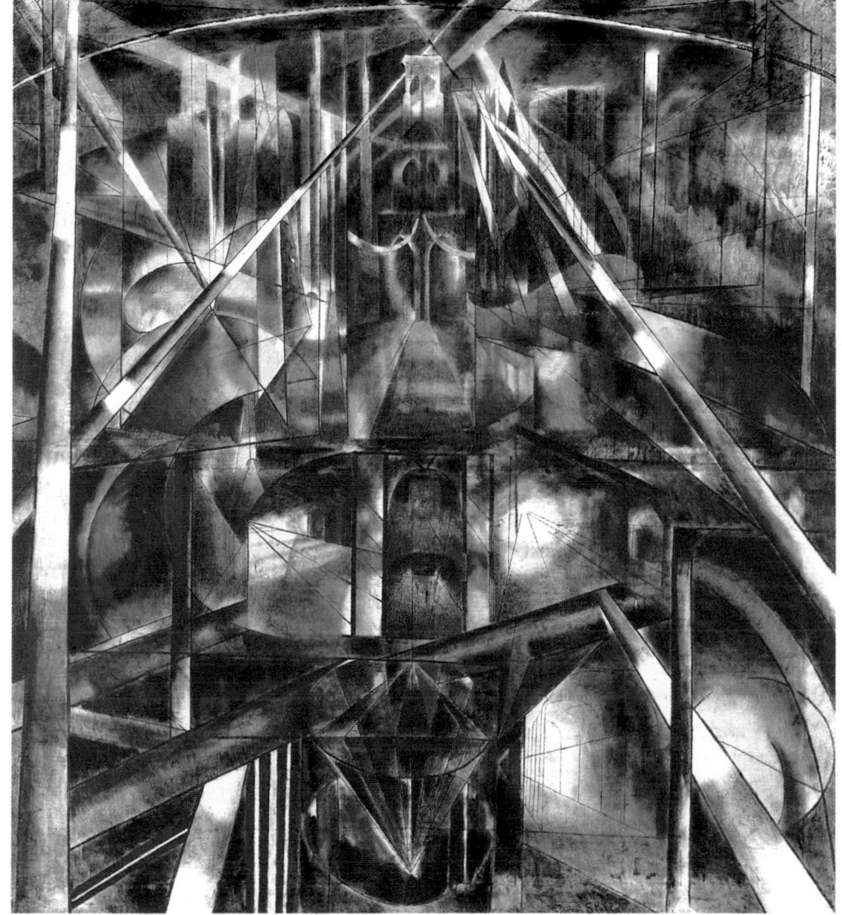

24-36. Joseph Stella. *Brooklyn Bridge.* 1917. Oil on bedsheeting, 7' x 6'4" (2.13 x 1.93 m). Yale University Art Gallery, New Haven, Connecticut

GIFT OF COLLECTION SOCIÉTÉ ANONYME

theosis of the bridge through a synthesis of Futurism, which he had been exposed to during a visit to Paris in 1912, and Precisionism, which he experimented with as early as 1917. With its maze of luminescent cables, vigorous diagonal thrusts, and crystalline cells of space, the painting is a striking visual counterpart to Hart Crane's famous hymn of 1930, "To Brooklyn Bridge":

> O harp and altar, of the fury fused,
> (How could mere toil align thy choiring strings!)
> Terrific threshold of the prophet's pledge,
> Prayer of pariah, and the lover's cry,—
> Again the traffic lights that skim thy swift
> Unfractioned idiom, immaculate sigh of stars,
> Beading thy path—condense eternity:
> And we have seen night lifted in thine arms.

MONDRIAN. The most radical abstractionist of our time was a Dutch painter nine years older than Picasso, Piet Mondrian (1872–1944). He arrived in Paris in 1912 as a mature Expressionist in the tradition of Van Gogh and the Fauves. Under the influence of Analytic Cubism, his work soon underwent a complete change, and within the next decade Mondrian developed an entirely nonrepresentational style that he called Neo-Plasticism. The short-lived movement as a whole is also known as De Stijl, after the Dutch magazine advocating his ideas, which were formulated with Theo van Doesburg (1883–1931) and Bart van der Leck (1876–1958). [See Primary Sources, no. 87, page 936.] Mondrian became the center of the abstract movement in Paris, where he returned in 1919 and remained until the onset of World War II. Indeed, the School of Paris in the 1930s was made up largely of foreigners like him—especially the Abstraction-Création group, which included artists of every outlook. As a result, the differences between the various movements soon became blurred, although Mondrian himself remained true to his principles

Composition with Red, Blue, and Yellow (fig. 24-37) shows Mondrian's style at its most severe. He restricts his design to horizontals and verticals and his palette to the three primary hues—red, yellow, and blue—plus black and white. Representation is completely eliminated. Yet his canvases remain paintings in every sense of the term. Mondrian never hid his brushwork or the texture of the canvas, and the colors have surprising density. Like Kandinsky, Mondrian was affected by theosophy, albeit the distinctive Dutch branch founded during World War I by the mathematician M. J. H. Schoenmaekers. Unlike Kandinsky, however, he did not strive for pure, lyrical emotion. His goal, he asserted, was "pure reality," which he defined as equilibrium "through the balance of unequal but equivalent oppositions," especially between line and color. [See Primary Sources, no. 88, page 936.] "Plastic" for Mondrian, as for many other early-twentieth-century artists, meant the formal structural relationships underlying both art and nature. The term Neo-Plasticism itself was coined by Schoenmaekers, for whom yellow symbolized the vertical movement of the sun's rays; blue, the horizontal line of the earth's orbit around the sun; and red, the union of both. For all of their analytic calm, Mondrian's paintings are highly idealistic. He believed, "When we realize that equilibriated relationships in society signify what is just, then we shall realize that in art, likewise, the demands of life press forward when the spirit of the age is ready."

24-37. Piet Mondrian. *Composition with Red, Blue, and Yellow.* 1930. Oil on canvas, 20 x 20" (50.8 x 50.8 cm). Private collection

COURTESY OF THE MONDRIAN ESTATE/HOLTZMAN TRUST/MBI NY

Perhaps we can best understand what he meant by equilibrium if we think of his work as "abstract collage" that uses black bands and colored rectangles instead of recognizable fragments of chair caning and newsprint. He was interested solely in relationships and wanted no distracting elements or accidental associations. By establishing the "right" relationship among his bands and rectangles, he transforms them as thoroughly as Braque transformed the snippets of pasted paper in *Le Courrier* (see fig. 24-16). How did he discover the "right" relationship? And how did he determine the shape and number for the bands and rectangles? In Braque's collage, the ingredients are to some extent "given" by chance. Apart from his self-imposed rules, however, Mondrian constantly faced the problem of unlimited possibilities. He could not change the relationship of the bands to the rectangles without changing the bands and rectangles themselves. When we consider his task, we begin to realize its infinite complexity.

Looking again at *Composition with Red, Blue, and Yellow,* we find that when we measure the various units, only the proportions of the canvas itself are truly rational, an exact square. Mondrian has arrived at all the rest "by feel" and must have undergone endless trial and error. How often, we wonder, did he change the dimensions of the red rectangle to bring it and the other elements into self-contained equilibrium? Strange as it may seem, Mondrian's exquisite sense for nonsymmetrical balance is so specific that critics well acquainted with his work have no difficulty in distinguishing fakes from genuine pictures. Designers who work with nonfigurative shapes, such as architects and typographers, are likely to be most sensitive to this quality. Mondrian has had a greater influence on them than on artists (see Chapter 26).

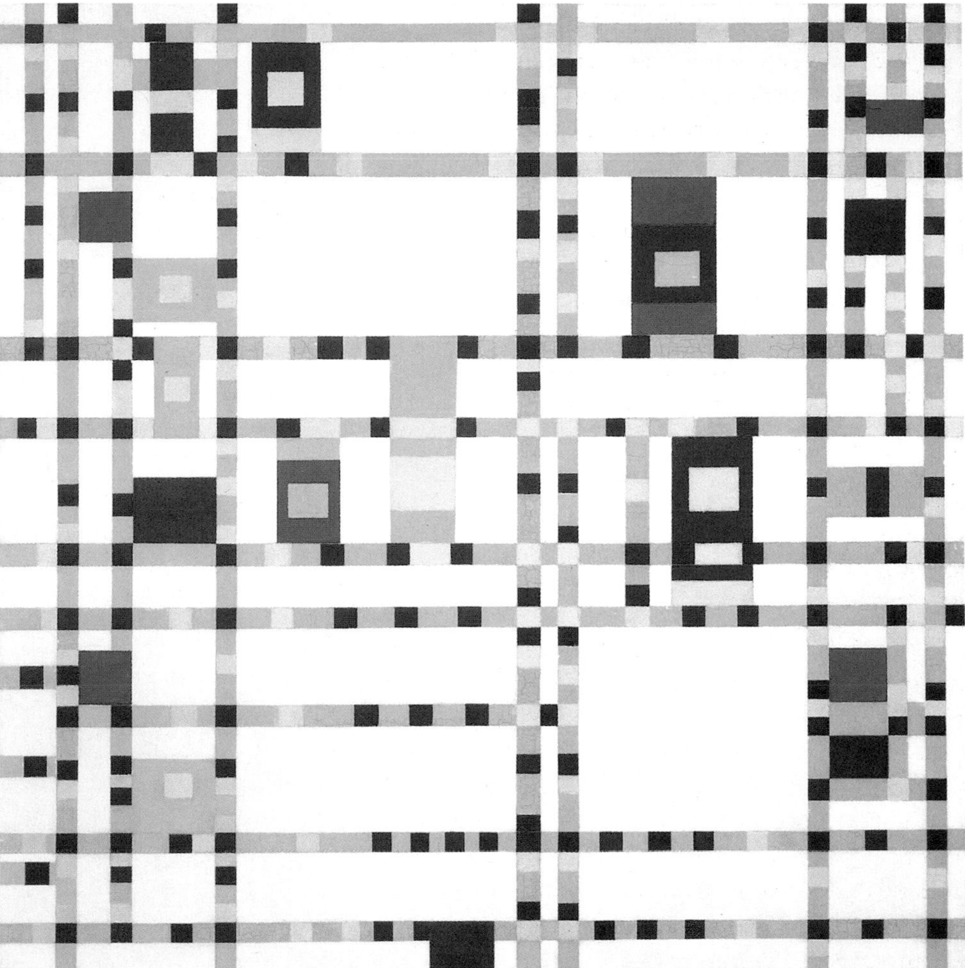

24-38. Piet Mondrian. *Broadway Boogie Woogie.* 1942–43. Oil on canvas, 50 x 50" (127 x 127 cm). The Museum of Modern Art, New York

At the beginning of World War II, Mondrian left Paris for London and then New York, where he arrived in 1940. He now began to give to his works such titles as *Trafalgar Square* or *Broadway Boogie Woogie* (fig. 24-38), which hint at some degree of relationship, however indirect, with observed reality. *Broadway Boogie Woogie* immortalizes Mondrian's fascination with the culture he found in America. The artist uses white and the three primary colors to signify radiant light. The play of color evokes with striking success the jaunty rhythms of music and light found in New York's nightclub district during the jazz age. As in a medieval manuscript decoration (see fig. 9-3), the composition relies entirely on surface pattern. *Broadway Boogie Woogie* seems as flat as the canvas it is painted on. Although Mondrian abandons his system of black lines, he has laid out his colored "tiles" along a grid system that closely resembles a city map.

This sense of order seems typically Dutch. If we analyze the surface geometry in Jan Steen's *The Feast of St. Nicholas* (see fig. 18-27), we find that it is basically similar to *Broadway Boogie Woogie.* Each part of the room is treated as a separate element to be integrated into the design as a whole. Thus, although Steen used three-dimensional space, the problems he faced in composing his work were not so very different from those confronted by Mondrian 200 years later.

NICHOLSON. Mondrian had a number of followers among painters. By far the most original was the English artist Ben Nicholson (1894–1982). A rigorous abstractionist, he bent Mondrian's rules without breaking them in his painted reliefs (fig. 24-39).

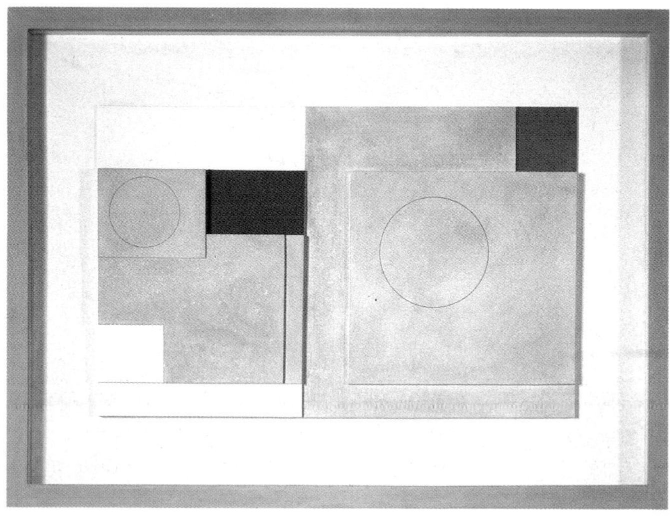

24-39. Ben Nicholson. *Painted Relief.* 1939. Synthetic board mounted on plywood, painted, 32⅞ x 45" (83.5 x 114.3 cm). The Museum of Modern Art, New York

GIFT OF H. S. EDE AND THE ARTIST BY EXCHANGE

These also show the inspiration of his wife, the sculptor Barbara Hepworth (see page 846). The overlapping shapes violate the integrity of the rectangle and overcome the tyranny of the grid maintained by Mondrian. The geometry is further enlivened by the introduction of the circle. Yet Nicholson's work, too, relies on the delicate balance of elements. The effect is enhanced by the subdued palette and matte finish, which create harmonies of the utmost refinement. Indeed, Mondrian's primary colors seem astonishingly bright and exuberant in comparison.

Fantasy

DADA. Out of despair over the mechanized mass killing of World War I, a number of artists in Zurich and New York (including Marcel Duchamp) simultaneously launched a protest movement called Dada (or Dadaism), which then spread to other cities in Germany and France. The term, which means "hobbyhorse" in French, was reportedly picked at random from a dictionary, although it had actually been used as the title of a Symbolist journal. As an infantile, all-purpose word, however, it perfectly fitted the spirit of the movement. Dada has often been called nihilistic, and it was indeed the very prototype of an avant-garde movement. Its declared purpose was to make clear to the public at large that all established values—political, moral, or aesthetic—had been rendered meaningless by the catastrophe of the Great War. Dada's program was closely linked to Communism, which it hoped would overthrow bourgeois society and substitute a proletarian paradise. Such political activism was the norm. Between 1915 and 1950 most avant-garde artists on both sides of the Atlantic, even Picasso, were associated with Communism or Socialism at one time or another.

During its short life (c. 1915–22) Dada preached nonsense and anti-art with a vengeance. [See Primary Sources, no. 89, page 937.] As Hans Arp wrote, "Dadaism carried assent and dissent ad absurdum. In order to achieve indifference, it was destructive." Marcel Duchamp once "improved" a reproduction of Leonardo's *Mona Lisa* with a moustache and the abbreviation LHOOQ, which when pronounced in French makes an off-color pun. Not even modern art was safe from the Dadaists' assaults. One example exhibited a toy monkey inside a frame with the title *Portrait of Cézanne*. Yet Dada was not a completely negative movement. In its calculated irrationality there was also liberation, a voyage into unknown provinces of the creative mind. The only law respected by the Dadaists was that of chance, and the only reality, that of their imagination.

ERNST. Although their most characteristic art form was the readymade (see pages 841–42), the Dadaists adopted the collage technique of Synthetic Cubism for their purposes. Figure 24-40 by the German Dadaist Max Ernst (1891–1976), an associate of Duchamp, is largely composed of snippets from illustrations of machinery. The caption pretends to enumerate these mechanical ingredients which include (or add up to) "1 Piping Man." Actually, there is also a "piping woman." These offspring of Duchamp's prewar *Bride* (see fig. 24-24) stare at us blindly through their goggles.

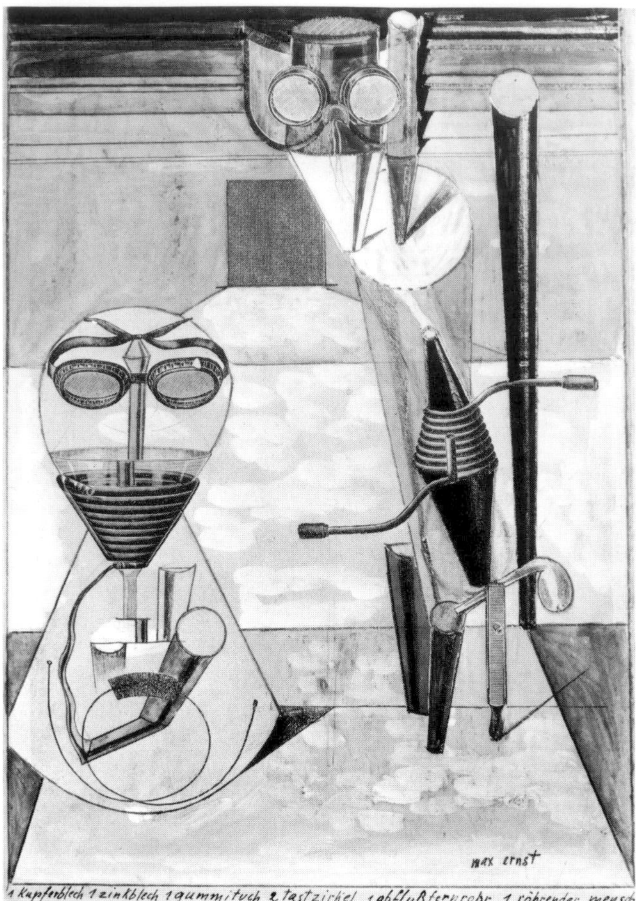

24-40. Max Ernst. *1 Copper Plate 1 Zinc Plate 1 Rubber Cloth 2 Calipers 1 Drainpipe Telescope 1 Piping Man*. 1920. Collage, 12 x 9" (30.5 x 23 cm). Estate of Hans Arp

SURREALISM. In 1924, after Duchamp's retirement from Dada, a group led by the poet André Breton founded Dada's successor, Surrealism, which also took up Communism. They defined their aim as "pure psychic automatism . . . intended to express . . . the true process of thought . . . free from the exercise of reason and from any aesthetic or moral purpose." [See Primary Sources, no. 90, page 937.] Surrealist theory was filled with concepts borrowed from psychoanalysis, and its rhetoric cannot always be taken seriously. The notion that a dream can be transferred by "automatic handwriting" directly from the unconscious mind to the canvas, bypassing the conscious awareness of the artist, did not work in practice. Some degree of control was unavoidable. Nevertheless, Surrealism gave rise to several novel techniques for stimulating and exploiting chance effects.

ERNST'S DECALCOMANIA. Max Ernst, the most inventive member of the group, often combined collage with "frottage." (Frottage involves making rubbings from pieces of wood, pressed flowers, and other relief surfaces—the process we all know from the children's pastime of rubbing with a pencil on a piece of paper covering, say, a coin.) In *La Toilette de la Mariée* (fig. 24 41), he has produced fascinating shapes and textures by another technique: "decalcomania" (the transfer, by pressure, of oil paint to the can-

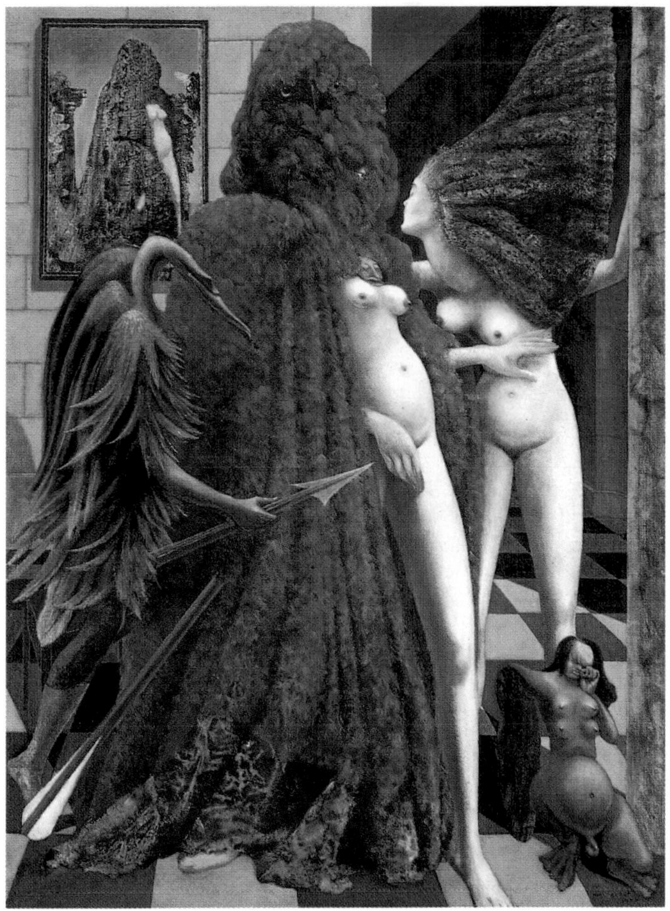

24-41. Max Ernst. *La Toilette de la Mariée.* 1940. Oil on canvas, 51 x 37⅞" (129.5 x 96.2 cm). Peggy Guggenheim Collection, Venice

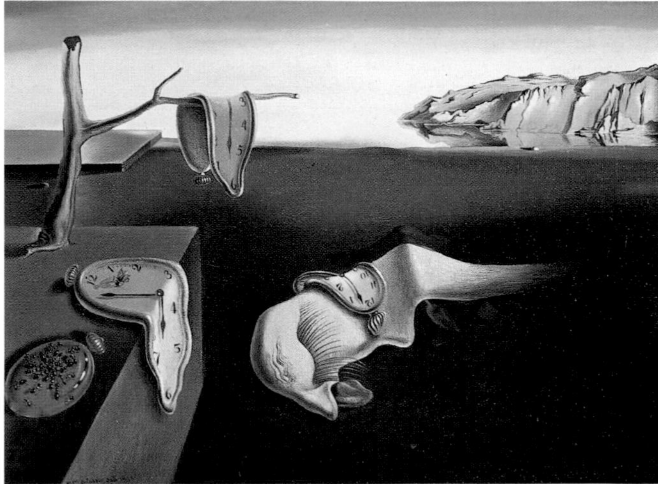

24-42. Salvador Dalí. *The Persistence of Memory.* 1931. Oil on canvas, 9½ x 13" (24.1 x 33 cm). The Museum of Modern Art, New York

GIVEN ANONYMOUSLY

vas from some other surface). This procedure is in essence another variant of that recommended by Leonardo da Vinci and Alexander Cozens (see fig. 21-10). Ernst certainly found, and further developed, an extraordinary wealth of images among his stains. The end result has some of the qualities of a dream, but it is a dream born of a strikingly Romantic imagination.

DALÍ. The same can be said of *The Persistence of Memory* (fig. 24-42) by Salvador Dalí (1904–1989). The most notorious of the Surrealists because of his self-promotion, he used a painstaking realism to render a "paranoid" dream in which time, forms, and space have been distorted in a frighteningly convincing way.

MAGRITTE. The Belgian artist René Magritte (1898–1967) also employed detailed realism but for completely different ends. Although he found his early inspiration in the work of De Chirico, his style comes from the tradition of Magic Realism that flourished in Belgium in the late nineteenth and early twentieth centuries. Magritte's goal was "poetic painting." His illusionistic pictures transform objects into images having completely different meaning through astonishing metamorphoses, changes in scale, juxtapositions, and the like. *Les Promenades d'Euclid* (fig. 24-43) shows one of his favorites devices, the picture within a picture. The title, added after the fact through free association, only compounds the mystery of the painting by failing to explain it. This divorce of word and image prevents us from finding any literal (or literary) meaning. The painting's charm lies not simply in this visual and verbal puzzle but in the presentation itself: the beautifully simple, abstract design and the artist's way of subtly heightening reality while ultimately denying its plausibility.

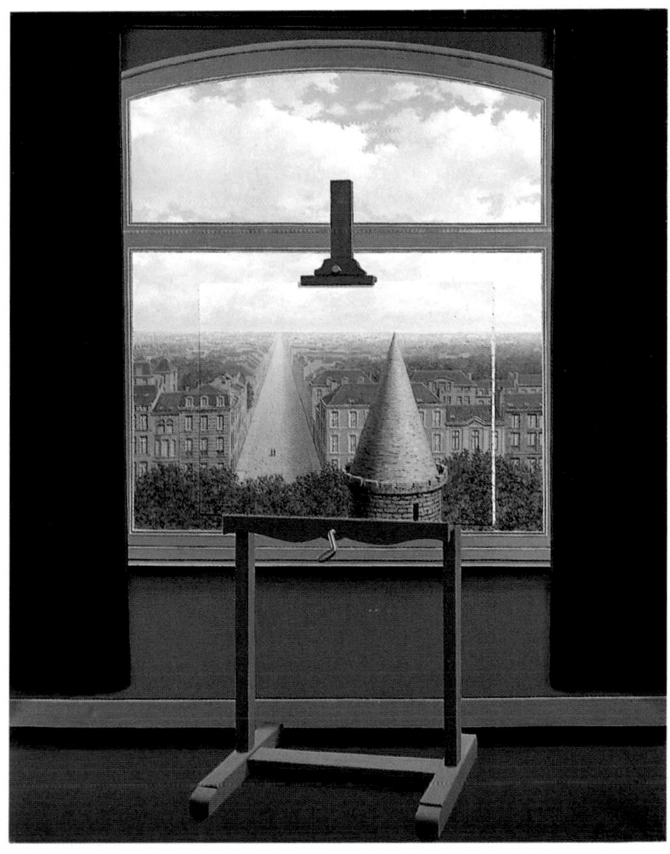

24-43. René Magritte. *Les Promenades d'Euclid.* 1955. Oil on canvas, 64⅛ x 51⅛" (163 x 130 cm). The Minneapolis Institute of Arts

THE WILLIAM HOOD DUNWOODY FUND

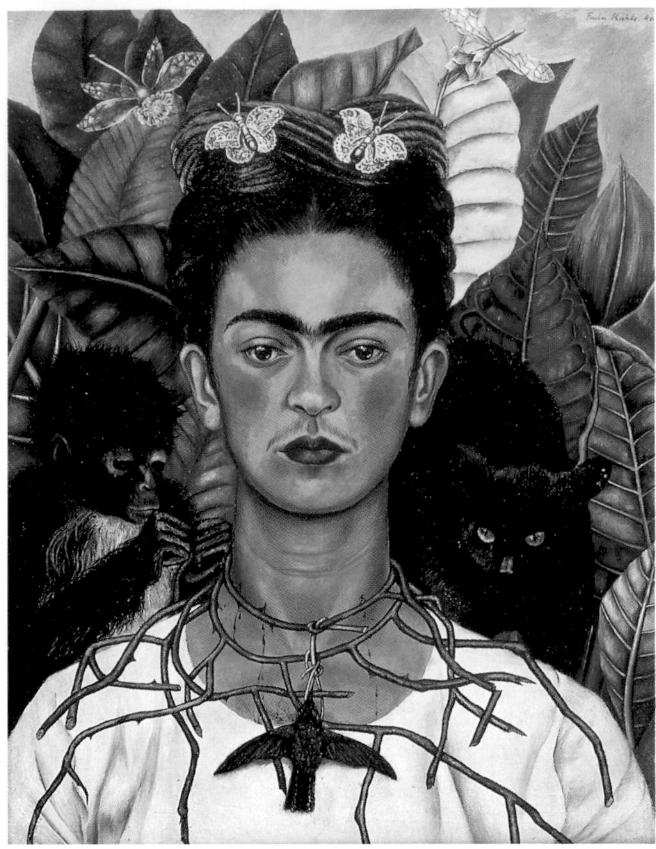

24-44. Frida Kahlo. *Self-Portrait with Thorn Necklace.* 1940. Oil on canvas, 24½ x 18¾" (62 x 47.5 cm). Art Collection, Harry Ransom Research Center, University of Texas at Austin

KAHLO. A number of women, Meret Oppenheim among them (see page 842), were associated with the Surrealist movement. Today the best known is Frida Kahlo (1910–1954), who was first discovered by the poet André Breton during a visit to Mexico in 1938 and then rediscovered in recent years by feminist art historians. She owes her reputation as much to her troubled life as to her work, for they are inseparable. Her paintings are frankly autobiographical. However they are presented in such enigmatic terms and are so full of personal meaning that the exact circumstances must be known in order to understand their content. *Self-Portrait with Thorn Necklace* (fig. 24-44) is similar to traditional Mexican religious images. It was painted in 1940, when her tempestuous marriage to the painter Diego Rivera (1886–1957) was interrupted by divorce for a year. The necklace, an allusion to the crown of thorns worn by Christ during the Passion, is a symbol of her humiliation. From it hangs a dead hummingbird, a traditional amulet worn in Mexico by people seeking love. On her shoulders are two demons in the guise of the artist's pets: death, who appears as a black cat, and the devil, seen as a monkey. She is shown as a martyr to love hoping for a resurrection like the Lord's, as signified by the butterflies overhead. In context, it seems likely that Kahlo was thinking of suicide.

MIRÓ. Surrealism also has a boldly imaginative branch. Some works by Picasso, such as *Three Dancers* (see fig. 24-28), have affinities with it, and its greatest representative was also Spanish: Joan Miró (1893–1983), who painted the striking *Composition*

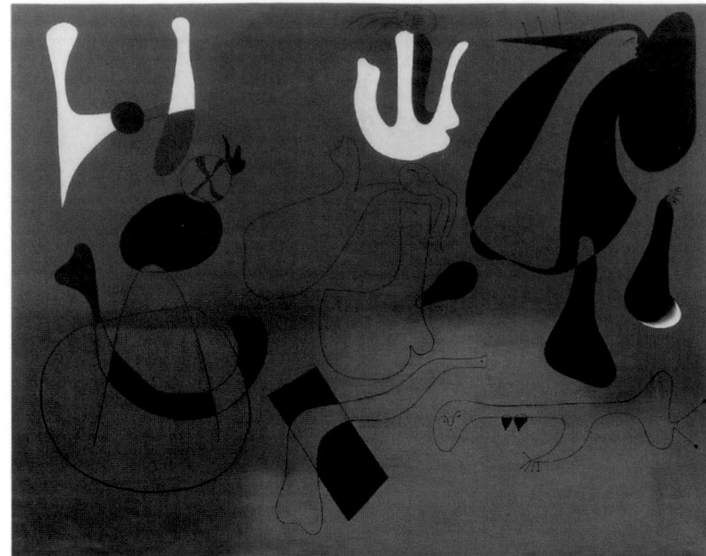

24-45. Joan Miró. *Composition.* 1933. Oil on canvas, 51¼ x 63½" (130.5 x 161.3 cm). Wadsworth Atheneum, Hartford, Connecticut
ELLA GALLUP SUMNER AND MARY CATLIN SUMNER COLLECTION

(fig. 24-45). His style has been labeled "biomorphic abstraction," since his designs are fluid and curvilinear, like organic forms, rather than geometric. Actually, "biomorphic concretion" might be a more suitable name. Like the sculptures of Hans Arp (see page 842), the shapes in Miró's pictures have their own vigorous life. They seem to change before our eyes, expanding and contracting like amoebas until they approach human individuality closely enough to please the artist. Their spontaneous "becoming" is the very opposite of abstraction as we defined it above (see page 778). Once he conceived his forms, however, Miró subjected them to a formal discipline no less rigorous than that of Cubism. (In fact, he began as a Cubist and turned to Surrealism only in 1924, five years after moving to Paris.)

KLEE. Miró's work shows the impact of the German-Swiss painter Paul Klee (1879–1940). Klee in turn was decisively influenced early in his career by *Der Blaue Reiter* and shared many of the same ideas as his friends Kandinsky and Marc. He was fascinated, for example, with music and was himself a talented violinist. His theories of art have much in common with those of Kandinsky. (They were colleagues at the Bauhaus.) He nevertheless went in the opposite direction. Instead of a higher reality, he wanted to illuminate a deeper one from within the imagination. Thus natural forms are essential to his work, but as pictorial metaphors conveying hidden meaning rather than as representations of nature. He was affected, too, by Cubism and Orphism, but ethnographic art and the drawings of small children held an equally vital interest for him.

During World War I, he molded these elements into a pictorial language of his own, marvelously economical and precise. *Twittering Machine* (fig. 24-46), a delicate pen-and-ink drawing tinted with watercolor, demonstrates the unique flavor of Klee's art. With a few simple lines, he has created a ghostly mechanism that simultaneously mocks our faith in the miracles of the Machine Age and our sentimental appreciation of bird song. It is the quality of the line itself that evokes the raspy sound made by this strange device.

The little contraption is not without its sinister aspect: the heads of the four sham birds look like fishermen's lures, as if they might entrap real birds. It thus condenses into one striking invention a complex set of ideas about present-day civilization.

The title has an essential role. It is characteristic of the way Klee worked that the picture, no matter how appealing, does not reveal its full content unless the artist tells us what it means. The title, in turn, needs the picture. The witty concept of a twittering machine does not kindle our imagination until we are shown such a thing. This interdependence is familiar to us from cartoons, but Klee lifts it to the level of high art without giving up the playful character of these verbal–visual puns. To him art was a language of signs, of shapes that are images of ideas: as the shape of a letter is the image of a specific sound or an arrow is the image of the command, "This way only." He also realized that in any conventional system the sign is no more than a "trigger." The instant we perceive it, we automatically give it meaning without stopping to consider its shape. Klee wanted his signs to be perceived as visual facts yet also to act as "triggers."

How did Klee create the *Twittering Machine*? His writings confirm what we can sense from the drawing itself. He started with a point, which grew organically into a line that became a plane and then evolved into spaces; taken together these define the form. This process, though based on "pure artistic craftsmanship," gives the drawing its air of fresh inspiration and accounts for its whimsical character: "The legend of the childishness of my drawing must have originated from those linear compositions of mine in which I tried to combine a concrete image . . . with the pure representation of the linear element. Always combined with the more subconscious dimensions of the picture."

Toward the end of his life, Klee became absorbed in the study of ideographs of all kinds, such as hieroglyphics, hex signs, and the mysterious markings in prehistoric caves—simplified representational images that appealed to him because they had the twin quality he strove for in his own graphic language. This "ideographic style" is clearly stated in figure 24-47, *Park near Lu(cerne)*. As a lyric poet may use the plainest words, these deceptively simple shapes sum up a wealth of experience and sensation: the innocent gaiety of spring, the clipped orderliness peculiar to captive plant life in a park. Has it not also a relationship, in spirit if not in fact, with the Romanesque *Summer Landscape* in the manuscript of *Carmina Burana* (see fig. 10-42)? Klee's attitude soon changed. Shortly before his death, the artist's horror over World War II led him to abandon this lighthearted approach in favor of a pessimistic manner similar to Miró's darkest fantasies of the same time.

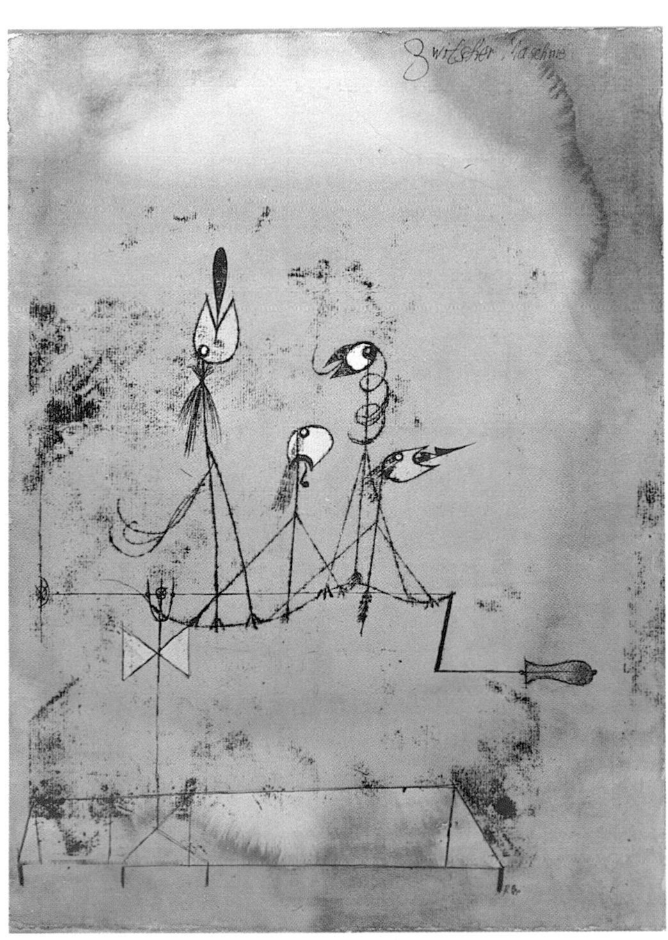

24-46. Paul Klee. *Twittering Machine*. 1922. Watercolor and pen and ink on oil transfer drawing on paper, mounted on cardboard, 25 1/4 x 19" (64.1 x 48.3 cm). The Museum of Modern Art, New York

PURCHASE

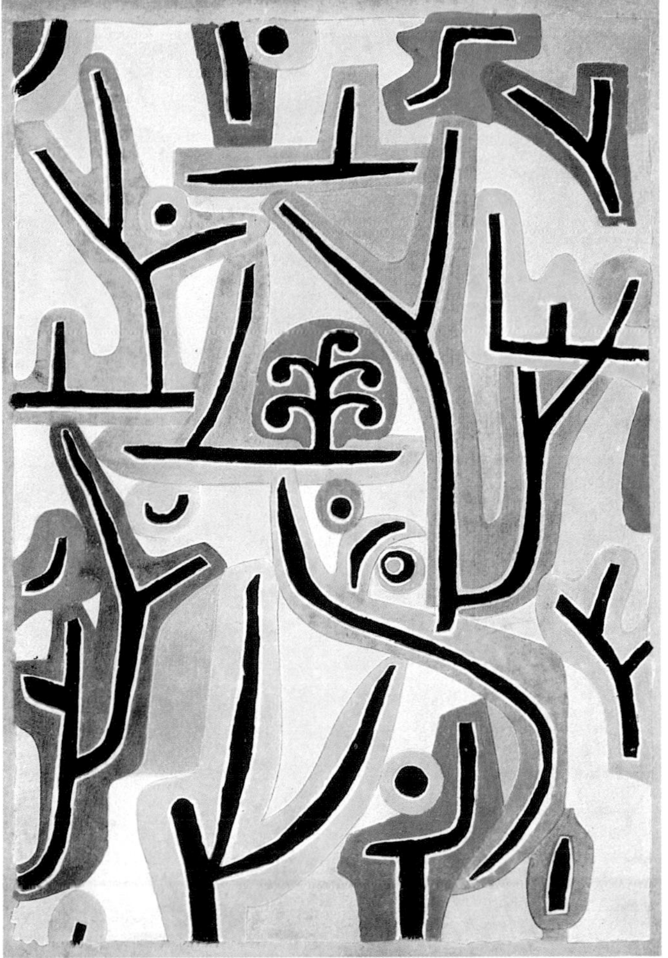

24-47. Paul Klee. *Park near Lu(cerne)*. 1938. Oil and newsprint on burlap, 39 1/2 x 27 1/2" (100.3 x 69.7 cm). Fondation Paul Klee, Kunstmuseum, Bern, Switzerland

COPYRIGHT 1986 COSMOPRESS, GENEVA

THEATER BETWEEN THE WARS

German Expressionism in art had a counterpart in Expressionist drama, which compressed as much emotion as possible into a play, eliminating anything not needed to convey the central message of the piece. It initially took the form of subjective truth and utopian vision in *The Beggar* (1912) by Reinhard Sorge (1892–1916) but soon turned to antiwar sentiment in *One Race* (1918) by Fritz von Unruh (1885–1970). Expressionist theater was also promoted by Herwarth Walden (1878–1941), publisher of the journal *Der Sturm,* which attracted many of the leading painters to Berlin, including Oskar Kokoschka, who was also a dramatist. The trilogy *Gas* (1917–20) by Georg Kaiser (1878–1945) characteristically expressed utopian ideals by reducing its characters to symbols of social forces, such as the Engineer and the Billionaire's Son.

Under the Weimar Republic (1920–33), Germany was the most vibrant center of theater in all of Europe, with a dazzling variety that reflected the turmoil of the postwar years. The most important German drama produced between the wars was *Man and the Masses* (1921) by Ernst Toller (1893–1939), featuring a kaleidoscopic production by the director Jürgen Fehling (1890–1968). The play already shows the pessimism that led to the decline of Expressionism a few years later. In its place rose Epic Theater, promoted by Erwin Piscator (1893–1966), who championed proletarian drama. He instituted a deliberately episodic style of drama that, in contrast to Expressionism, encouraged psychological distance in the viewer through using divided stages, incorporating film clips, and having characters speak to the audience directly. These devices, later to become standard, thus broke the traditional theatrical illusion that the audience is watching actual events as they are taking place.

The main exponent of Epic Theater was Bertholt Brecht (1898–1956), a confirmed Communist who spent much of his career in exile in America. He remains best known for *The Three Penny Opera* (1928), with cabaret-style music by Kurt Weill (1900–1950), which is even more profoundly cynical than the original opera by John Gay on which it is based (see page 605). The collaborations of Brecht and Weill are, in effect, modern-day morality plays but with an anticapitalist bent. Brecht's best play, however, is *Mother Courage and Her Children* (1938–39), the story of the destruction of a family during the Thirty Years' War. It provoked viewers to think about its meaning by setting contemporary events in the past (a process known as historification) and presenting them as a series of disjointed episodes, while adding strange effects to induce a sense of alienation.

The 1920s were also a time of technical innovation in Germany. The Bauhaus conducted important experiments under its longtime director Walter Gropius, who devised a stage that could be reconfigured to place the audience in the center of the action. Oskar Schlemmer (1888–1943), head of the theater workshop, designed abstract costumes that made actors into architectural units to be placed at will within the stage space by rigorously controlling their every movement. *Neue Sachlichkeit* (New Objectivity) also found an outlet in theater in documentary dramas dealing with a variety of social issues, but the only playwright of this genre of note was Ferdinand Bruckner (1891–1958).

In France, the major contribution was Surrealist theater. In addition to Jarry's *Ubu Roi, The Breasts of Tiresias* (1903–17) by Guillaume Apollinaire (1880–1918) was the early prototype of Surrealist drama, mingling popular theater with music and dance in an illogical free form. The poet Jean Cocteau (1892–1963) used many of these devices in *Parade* (1917), a ballet presented by Diaghilev's Ballets Russes that was one of the great collaborations of the time, with costumes by Picasso and music by Erik Satie (1866–1925). Cocteau's finest efforts were restatements of Classical Greek dramas transposed to modern times and treated with all kinds of Surrealist effects. He also worked for the Ballet Suédois (Swedish Ballet), a rival company active in the early 1920s that attracted the painters Léger and De Chirico.

Although the Surrealists mounted numerous absurdist events in the 1920s and '30s, the most important work was done by André Breton's disciple Antonin Artaud (1896–1948) after he abandoned Surrealism in 1931. Rather than appealing to the mind, his Theater of Cruelty rejected language as impotent and mounted a concerted assault on all the senses to drain the "abscesses" of civilization by "providing the spectator with the true sources of his dreams, in which his taste for crime, his erotic obsessions, his savagery . . . would surge forth." Surrealism also stimulated Henri-René Lenormand (1882–1951) to write *Time Is a Dream* (1919) and *The Eater of Dreams* (1922), whose distortions of time and space anticipate effects seen later in Dalí's *The Persistence of Memory* (see fig. 24-42). Perhaps the most interesting Surrealist play was *No Exit* (1944), written during World War II by the existentialist philosopher Jean-Paul Sartre (1905–1980). It is a drama about interpersonal relations in which a man and two women pursue each other vainly as they seek self-validation in the eyes of others, whom they try to control but who in turn have their own agenda. Sartre's "theater of situations" sought to "explore the state of man in its entirety, and to present to modern man a portrait of himself" through his choices and actions.

Although it was short-lived, Italian Futurism was notable for its extreme rejection of traditional staging through the use of multimedia techniques to promote its glorification of the machine, achieve simultaneous effects, and break down barriers between the arts. World War I saw the equally brief Theater of the Grotesque in the plays of Luigi Chiarelli (1880–1947). By far the greatest Italian playwright of the century was Luigi Pirandello (1867–1936), a novelist who turned his hand to drama only after 1910. *Six Characters in Search of an Author* (1921) intermixes fantasy and reality so completely that truth becomes entirely subjective and unknowable, since it varies according to the perspective of each character and spectator. The finest dramatist in Spain was the novelist and poet Federico García Lorca (1898–1936). He worked with the theater group La Barraca in the early 1930s to create updated versions of popular theater dealing with the time-honored Spanish themes of love and honor, as did Alejandro Casona (1903–1966), who directed a similar touring group, the People's Theater.

After the revolution, theater in Russia continued to be a hotbed of experimentation. The most powerful director was Meyerhold, who now emphasized biomechanics—machinelike movement—as the chief means of expression. His sets, designed by the Constructivists, were the most boldly imaginative the world has ever seen. In 1918 Meyerhold collaborated on *Mystery Bouffe* with Kazimir Malevich and Vladimir Mayakovsky (1893–1930)—the only true literary genius produced by the Communist Revolution in which Malevich, like Tatlin, believed wholeheartedly. However, Mayakovsky's last plays, such as *The Bedbug* (1929), were acerbic satires on Soviet bureaucracy that were received so badly that he committed suicide. Yevgeny Vakhtangov (1883–1922), who trained many of the leaders of the next generation, managed to successfully combine the seemingly opposite approaches of Meyerhold and Stanislavsky.

Theater thrived in England after World War I. Not since the Elizabethan era were there so many great directors and actors or so many major theaters. The list of legendary stars includes Tyrone Guthrie, Barry Jackson, Laurence Olivier, John Gielgud, Michael Redgrave, Alec Guinness, Elsa Lanchester, Charles Laughton, and Sybil Thorndike, to name only the most famous. English playwriting of the time is remembered now chiefly for comedies by the novelist W. Somerset Maugham (1874–1965) and Noël Coward (1899–1973), who was a consummate man of the theater. There was considerable dramatic writing by serious authors as well. A notable example is *I Have Been Here Before* (1937) by the novelist J. B. Priestley (1894–1984), which deals with the effect of previous incarnations on the present. The poet W. H. Auden (1907–1973) and the novelist Christopher Isherwood (1904–1986) collaborated on several plays in expressionistic verse, including *The Dog Beneath the Skin* (1935), which was presented at the Group Theater. The American-born poet T. S. Eliot (1888–1965) was also a founder of the Group Theater, which staged his *Sweeney Agonistes* (1932), an "Aristophanic melodrama" that he considered a poem in dialogue, and *Murder in the Cathedral* (1935), about the death of Thomas à Becket. Both were attempts to restore verse to theater using popular forms and music-hall techniques, though Eliot abandoned this approach toward the end of the decade. The early dramas written for the Abbey Theater in the mid-1920s by Sean O'Casey (1880–1964) dealt with the impact of the Irish rebellion on people's lives, but his style later veered toward Expressionism in the pacifist play *The Silver Tassie* (1928), which led to a break with the Abbey, despite support from Yeats.

In the United States, new groups sprang up everywhere, many of them later subsidized by the government during the Great Depression under the Federal Theater Project. Stagecraft underwent radical changes at the hands of the designers Lee Simonson (1888–1967) and Robert Jones (1887–1954) and the producers Arthur Hopkins (1878–1950) and Norman Bel Geddes (1893–1958), all of whom were well versed in the latest European techniques. The Group Theater, begun in 1931 by Lee Strasberg (1901–1982) and others along the lines of the Moscow Art Theater, included such stars as Stella Adler (1904–1992) and Elia Kazan (b. 1909). It was also the golden age of Hollywood films. Orson Welles, Laurence Olivier, Vivien Leigh, John Gielgud, Elsa Lanchester, Vincent Minelli, and Judy Garland were among the actors and directors who were equally successful on stage and screen.

For the first time in its history, America had writers who were fully the equal of those in Europe, and many of them wrote for the stage. The finest was unquestionably Eugene O'Neill (1888–1953), the son of the actor James O'Neill (1846–1920), whose powerful dramas *Desire Under the Elms* (1925), *Mourning Becomes Electra* (1931), and *The Iceman Cometh* (1940/46) remain the great American classics of the era. Their only rivals are the plays written by Clifford Odets (1906–1963) in 1935 for the Group Theater—*Waiting for Lefty, Awake and Sing,* and *Paradise Lost*—all scripted in intense, graphic language. Odets' most popular work remains *Golden Boy* (1937), about a young violinist who becomes a boxer to earn money, which is a thinly veiled reference to his own decision to move to Hollywood, where his talents soon petered out. The novelist John Steinbeck (1902–1968) adapted three of his books for the stage. The best is *Of Mice and Men,* done in collaboration with George S. Kaufman (1889–1961), a story of strength, weakness, and human dignity among migrant workers in a Midwest farming town during the Depression. Maxwell Anderson (1888–1959) achieved critical acclaim during the 1930s when he won the Pulitzer Prize for *Both Your Houses* (1933) and the Drama Critics' Circle Award for *Winterset* (1935). Much of his work dealt with war or the great monarchs and political leaders of the past. Other notable contributions to the American theater were *Street Scene* (1929) by Elmer Rice (1892–1967), about oppression and dehumanization; *The Time of Your Life* (1939) by William Saroyan (1908–1981), a witty and colorful story about life in San Francisco; *Mulatto* (1935) by Langston Hughes (1902–1967), the great writer of the Harlem Renaissance; and *The Cradle Will Rock* (1937) by Marc Blitzstein (1905–1964), whose rejection by the Federal Theater Project led Orson Welles and John Houseman (1902–1988) to form the Mercury Theater.

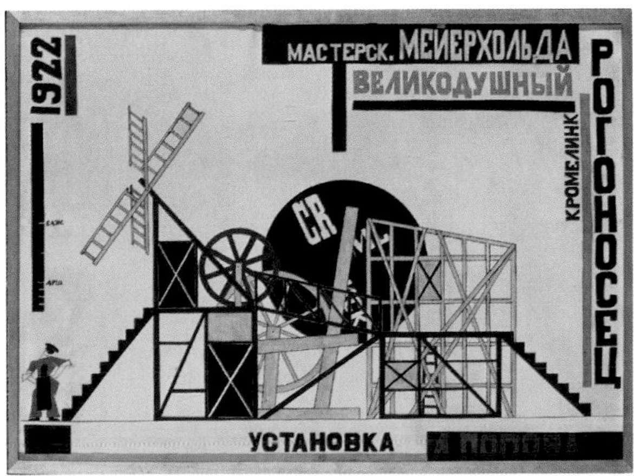

Liubov Popova. Set design for the *Magnanimous Cuckold.* 1922. India ink, gouache, and collage on varnished paper, 19 5/8 x 27 1/8" (50 x 69 cm). Trétiakov Gallery, Moscow

GIFT OF GEORGE COSTAKIS

Expressionism

KOLLWITZ. The experience of World War I filled German artists with a deep anguish at the state of modern civilization, which found its principal outlet in Expressionism. The work of Käthe Kollwitz (1867–1945) consists almost exclusively of prints and drawings comparable to those of Kokoschka, whom she admired. Her graphics had their sources in the nineteenth century. Munch, Klimt, and the German artist Max Klinger (1857–1920) were early inspirations, as was her friend Ernst Barlach (see page 757). However, Kollwitz pursued a resolutely independent course by devoting her art to themes of inhumanity and injustice. To articulate her social and ethical concerns, she adopted an intensely expressive yet naturalistic style that is as unrelenting in its bleakness as her choice of subjects. Gaunt mothers and exploited workers provided many of Kollwitz's themes, but her most impassioned statements were reserved for war. World War I, which cost her oldest son his life, made her an ardent pacifist. Her lithograph *Never Again War!* (fig. 24-48) is an unforgettable image of protest.

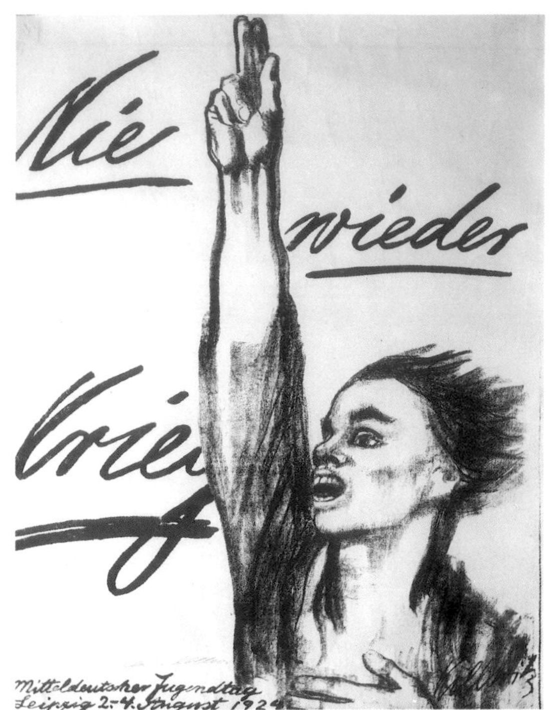

24-48. Käthe Kollwitz. *Never Again War!* 1924. Lithograph, 37 x 27½" (94 x 70 cm). Courtesy Galerie St. Etienne, New York

GROSZ. George Grosz (1893–1959), a painter and graphic artist who had studied in Paris in 1913, joined the Dadaist movement in Berlin after the end of the war. Inspired by the Futurists, he used a dynamized form of Cubism to develop a savagely satiric style that expressed the disillusionment of his generation. In *Germany, a Winter's Tale* (fig. 24-49), the city of Berlin forms the kaleidoscopic and chaotic background for several large figures, which are superimposed on it as in a collage. They include the marionette-like "good citizen" at his table and the sinister forces that molded him: a hypocritical clergyman, a brutal general, and an evil schoolmaster. This, Grosz tells us, is the decadent world of the bourgeoisie that he, like many German intellectuals, hoped would be overthrown by Communism. His bitter parodies are counterparts to the Expressionist dramas of Georg Kaiser and also participate in the nihilism of the early Dadaist plays by Berthold Brecht, who shared a Marxist outlook (see box page 784).

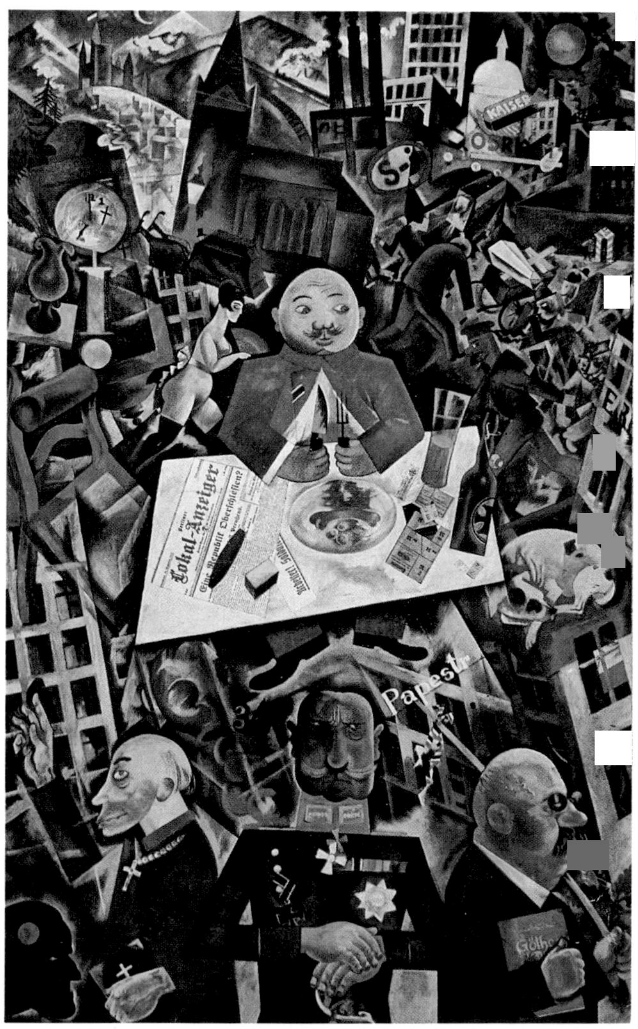

24-49. George Grosz. *Germany, a Winter's Tale.* 1918. Formerly Collection Garvens, Hannover, Germany

BECKMANN. Max Beckmann (1884–1950), a robust descendant of *Die Brücke* artists, did not become an Expressionist until after he had lived through World War I, which filled him with such despair at the state of modern civilization that he took up painting to "reproach God for his errors." *The Dream* (fig. 24-50) is a mocking nightmare, a tilted, zigzag world as disquieting as those in Bosch's *Hell* (see fig. 15-14). It is crammed with maimed, puppetlike figures that reflect the artist's experience in the army medical corps. We see the handless swimmer, carrying a fish, who climbs a ladder that leads only to another ladder on the ceiling; the crippled clown whose open hat protects his eyes but not his head from the nonexistent sun; the woman singing ecstatically to herself as she plays a stringless cello; and the beggar frantically cranking his hurdy-gurdy and blaring his trumpet to this unreceptive audience. (Note the mirror that reflects nothing and the lantern that illuminates nothing.) All are blind except the blond girl in the center. Evidently a recent arrival, to judge from her trunk, she observes everything with detachment and gestures as if to say,

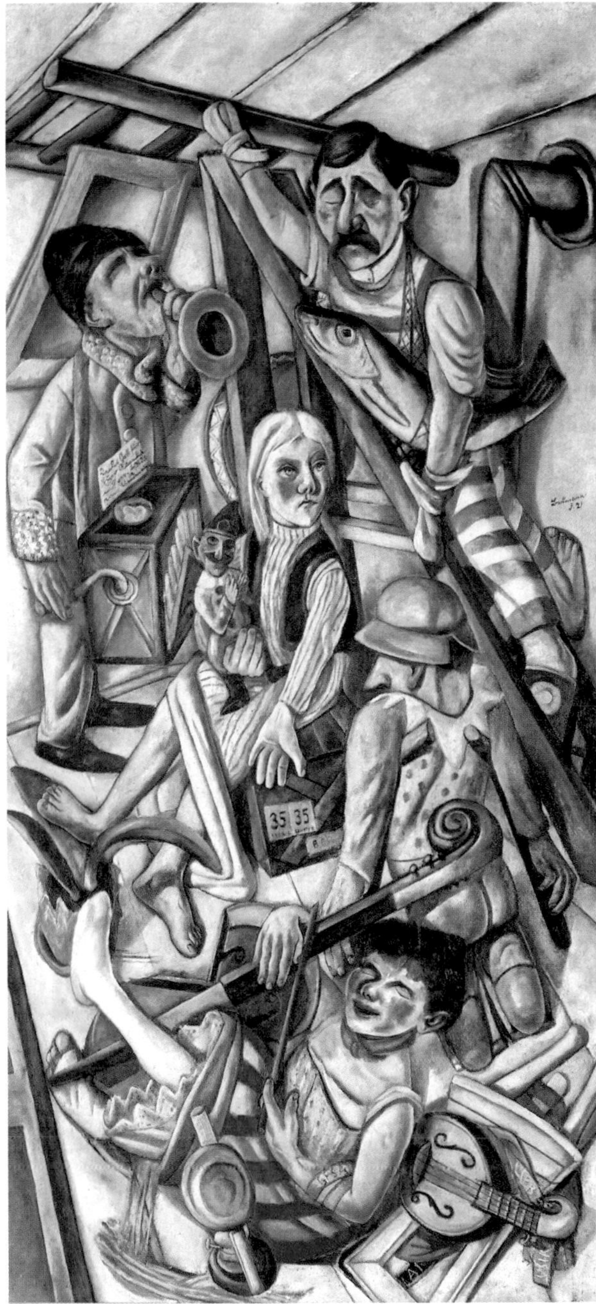

24-50. Max Beckmann. *The Dream.* 1921. Oil on canvas, 71 x 35" (180.3 x 89 cm). Collection Morton D. May, St. Louis, Missouri

"Behold this Ship of Fools," while the puppet she holds mockingly applauds the absurd performance. Her innocence is underscored by the plant, which rudely pushes aside her dress as she tries to stop its advance with one foot. The forms show the inspiration of early German prints, which Beckmann shared with the members of *Die Brücke* (compare figs. 15-21–15-24).

The claustrophobic space, derived from the same source, is essential to the image, which radiates an oppressive aura. It was, he said, "how I defend myself against the infinity of space . . . the great spatial void and uncertainty that I call God." [See Primary Sources, no. 91, pages 937–38.] Beckmann has created a powerful image whose meaning is conveyed by evocative symbolism which is necessarily subjective. How indeed could Beckmann have expressed the chaos in Germany after that war with the worn-out language of traditional symbols? "These are the creatures that haunt my imagination," he seems to say. "They show the true nature of the modern condition—how weak we are, how helpless against ourselves in this proud era of so-called progress."

Some elements from this grotesque and sinister sideshow recur in altered form more than a decade later in the wings of Beckmann's triptych *Departure* (fig. 24-51), a painting that reflects his admiration for Grünewald (compare figs. 16-1 and 16-2). The right panel incorporates a blind man holding the fish, a lantern, and a mad musician. The left panel shows a scene of almost unimaginable torture. What are we to make of these brutal images? We know from letters written by the artist and a close friend that they represent life itself as endless misery filled with all kinds of physical and spiritual pain. The woman trying to make her way in the dark with the aid of the lamp is carrying the corpse of her memories, evil deeds, and failures, from which no one can

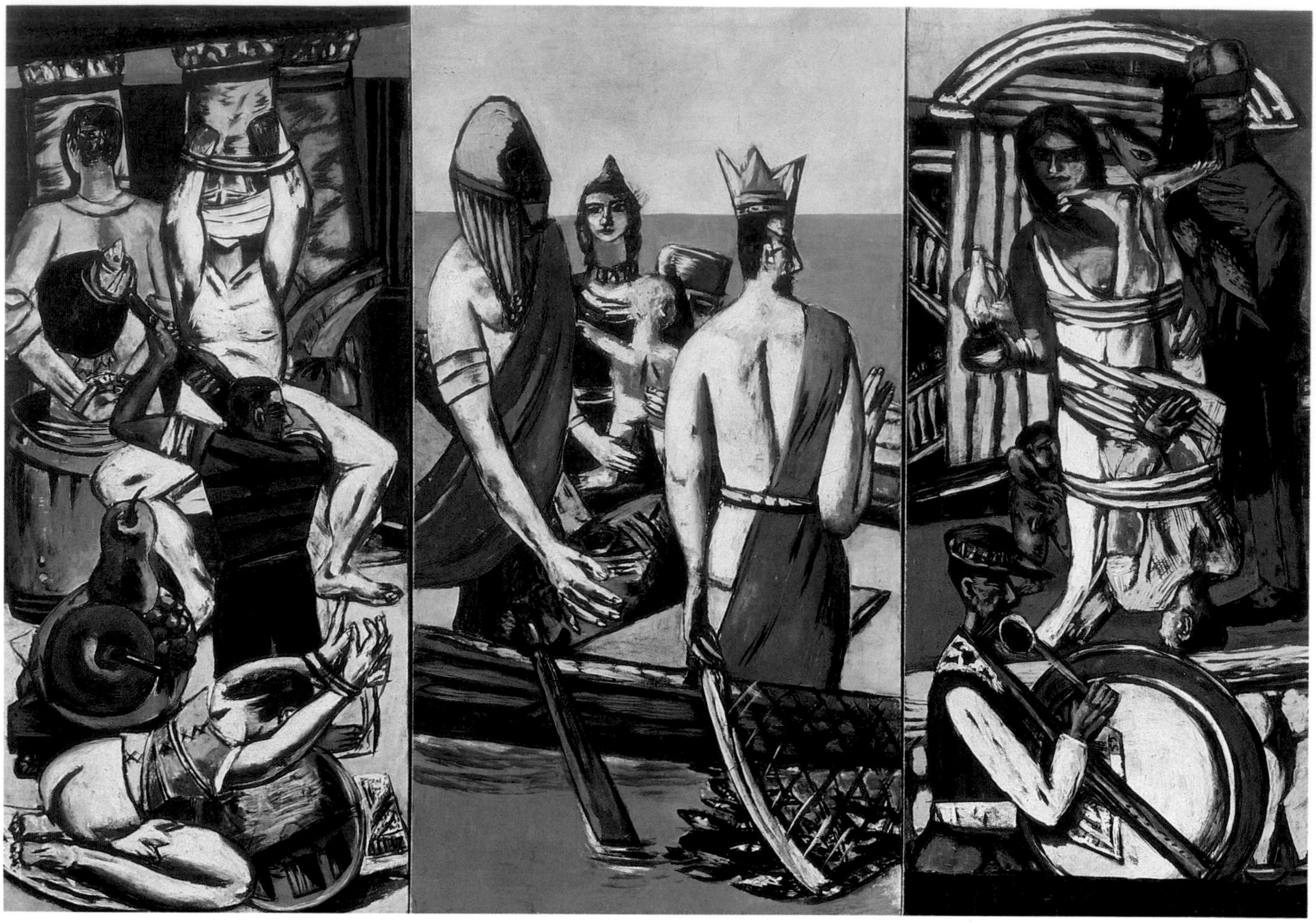

24-51. Max Beckmann. *Departure.* 1932–33. Oil on canvas, center panel 7'1¾" x 3'9⅜" (2.15 x 1.15 m); side panels each 7'1¾" x 3'3¼" (2.15 x 1 m). The Museum of Modern Art, New York

GIVEN ANONYMOUSLY BY EXCHANGE

ever be free so long as life beats its drum. The center panel signifies the departure from life's illusions to the reality behind appearances. The crowned figure seen from behind recalls the legendary Fisher King from the legend of the Holy Grail, whose health and that of his land is restored by Parsifal.

Departure proved remarkably prophetic. It was completed when the artist was on the verge of leaving his homeland under Nazi pressure. The topsy-turvy quality of the two wing scenes, full of mutilations and meaningless rituals, captures well the flavor of Hitler's Germany. The stable design of the center panel, in contrast, with its expanse of blue sea and its sunlit brightness, conveys the hopeful spirit of an embarkation for distant shores. After living through World War II in occupied Holland under the most difficult conditions, Beckmann spent the final three years of his life in America.

DOVE. After 1920 in the United States, most of the original members of the Stieglitz group concentrated on landscapes, which they treated in representational styles derived from Expressionism. Alone among them, Arthur G. Dove (1880–1946) consistently maintained a form of abstraction, one loosely related to Kandinsky's. The difference between the two artists is that Dove wanted to reveal the inner life of nature whereas Kandinsky tried to rid his images of readily recognizable subject matter. Dove was a natural-born painter, with a sure touch and flawless sense of design. His paintings possess a monumental spirit that belies their often modest size. *Foghorns* (fig. 24-52) epitomizes the intelligence and economy of his mature landscapes. To evoke the diffusion of sound, Dove utilized the simple but ingenious device of irregular concentric circles of color that grow paler as they radiate outward.

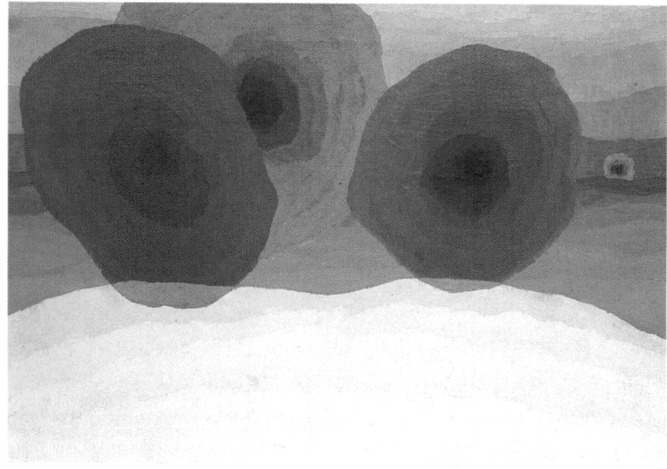

24-52. Arthur G. Dove. *Foghorns.* 1929. Oil on canvas, 18 x 26" (42.7 x 66 cm). Colorado Springs Fine Arts Center

ANONYMOUS GIFT

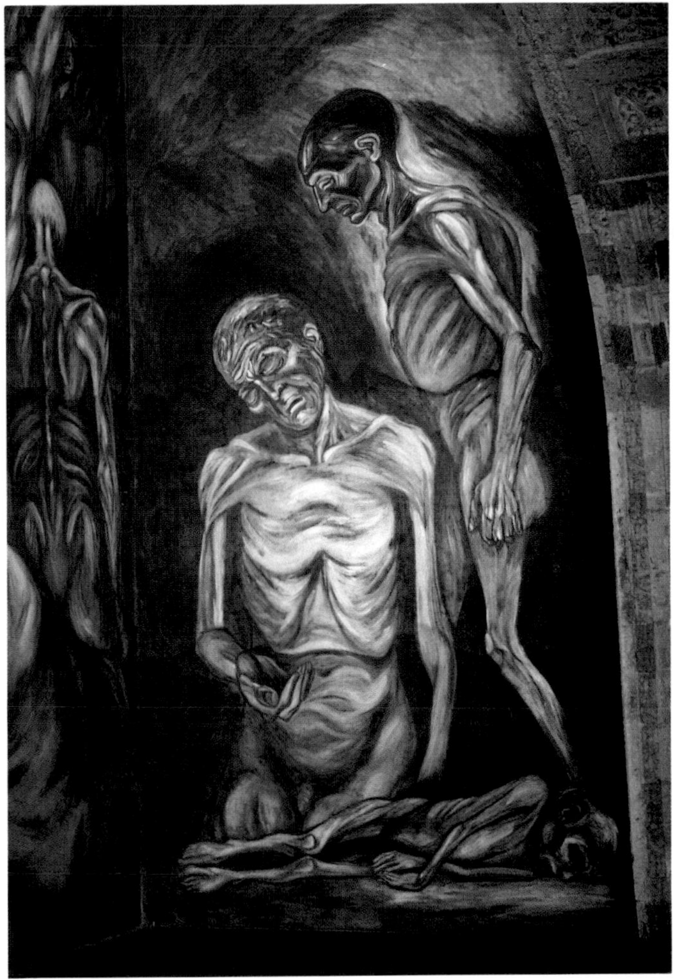

24-53. José Clemente Orozco. *Victims.* Detail of fresco cycle. 1936. University of Guadalajara, Mexico

Realism

DIX. In 1923 the director of the Mannheim museum in Germany organized an exhibition with the title *Die Neue Sachlichkeit* (The New Objectivity; sometimes also known as Magic Realism). This, he explained, was "a label for the new realism bearing a socialist flavor. Cynicism and resignation are the negative side of New Objectivity; the positive side expresses itself in the enthusiasm for immediate reality." Its principal representatives were George Grosz, who by this time had abandoned his slashing style for a more realistic manner no less biting in its sarcasm, and Max Beckmann, whose naturalism was simply a means for expressing his disillusionment. But it was the meticulous realism of Otto Dix (1891–1969), another Expressionist who had also been a member of Dada, that defined the main characteristics of the New Objectivity. Its roots lay in German Renaissance art and the Romanticism of Runge, which Dix used to expose the ills of modern Germany with obsessive detail. Dix's best works are his portraits, such as that of Dr. Mayer-Hermann (fig. 24-54). The image has a supernatural clarity that lends an almost nightmarish intensity to this image of a doctor seated impassively before his instruments, which echo his bulbous shape. In the process, they have acquired the alien quality of the devices in Max Ernst's *1 Piping Man* (see fig. 24-40), so that they become strangely menacing. For an equally compelling portrayal, we must turn to Ingres' *Louis Bertin* (see fig. 21-31). That Dix compares favorably is testimony to his powers of

OROZCO. During the 1930s, the center of Expressionism in the New World was Mexico. The Mexican Revolution began in 1911 with the fall of the dictator Porfirio Díaz and continued for more than two decades. It inspired a group of young painters to search for a national style incorporating the great native heritage of Pre-Columbian art. They also felt that their art must be "of the people," expressing the spirit of the revolution in large mural cycles in public buildings. Although each developed his own distinctive style, they shared a common point of departure: the Symbolist art of Gauguin, which had shown how non-Western forms could be integrated into the Western tradition. The flat, decorative quality of Symbolism was well suited to murals. However, the involvement of these painters in the political turmoil of the day often led them to overburden their works with ideology. The artist freest of this imbalance between form and subject matter was José Clemente Orozco (1883–1949), a passionately independent artist who refused to get embroiled in factional politics. The detail from the mural cycle at the University of Guadalajara (fig. 24-53) illustrates his most powerful trait: a deep humanitarian sympathy with the silent, suffering masses.

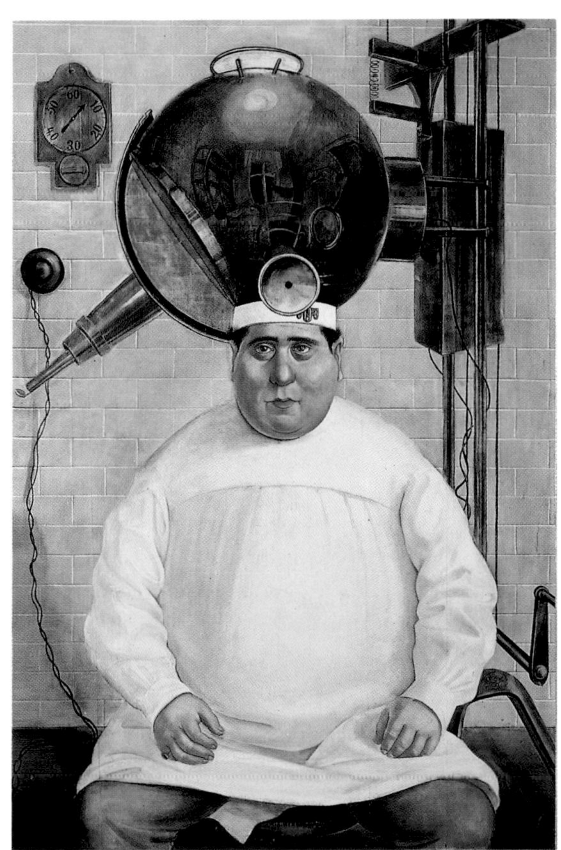

24-54. Otto Dix. *Dr. Mayer-Hermann.* 1926. Oil and tempera on wood, 58¾ x 39" (149.2 x 99.1 cm). The Museum of Modern Art, New York

GIFT OF PHILIP JOHNSON

MUSIC BETWEEN THE WARS

In 1923 Arnold Schoenberg (see also box page 780) had made the decisive final step from dissonance to complete atonality when he took another step and produced his first "serial" works based on the so-called "twelve-tone row" (also called the "series") utilizing the same devices he had been working with for some time. Each row uses all the notes of the tempered scale just once, except for a few "free" notes that do not conform to the sequence. It thus constitutes a self-contained musical realm representing the final overthrow of tonalism. By subjecting it to various traditional techniques for modification and extension (including such devices as retrogrades, inversions, and transpositions), the row can be built into a large-scale composition without repeating any sequence. Serialism was, then, simply a means of organizing Schoenberg's compositions, which were often conventional in form, notably the concertos for cello, violin, and piano written between 1932 and 1942. Although others were to extend its principles, he always stressed the personal nature of his work, which was no less individual than that of his contemporaries. He remained an Expressionist at heart. *A Survivor from Warsaw* (1948), written after the composer had fled Austria and settled in California (as did Stravinsky), conveys the nightmare of the Holocaust with almost unbearable anguish. By this time he had emerged as the most influential composer in the West. Even Stravinsky adopted serialism toward the end of his long life. The two composers were frequently at odds, yet the similarities in practice are often more striking than the differences in theory. Both remained rooted in tradition while pursuing parallel concerns. Early on Schoenberg's music had a dissonance and liveliness comparable to Stravinsky's, while in the late 1920s it acquired an equal astringency.

Needless to say, Schoenberg's music made extraordinary demands on musician and listener alike. Yet he was able to attract talented disciples almost as soon as he settled in Vienna in 1903. Chief among them was Anton Webern (1883–1945), who, like Gustav Mahler before him, was better known as a conductor during his lifetime. Webern's mature compositions, all small in scale, are miracles of rigor, conciseness, and purity. For more than a decade his music retained aspects of Schoenberg's expressionism, making it a counterpart to the hypersensitive manner of his friend Oscar Kokoschka. Hence, serialism initially had little impact on his style and, as with Schoenberg, was little more than a convenient means of organizing his music more coherently. However, he gradually began to apply its principles to other aspects of music, not just tone rows. Much of Webern's work consists of songs and choral music that treat the voice as simply another instrument, for he was as devoted to his serial system as Bach had been to counterpoint. At first Webern's literary sources differed little in character from Mahler's, but his terse atonality can be regarded as the antidote to the inflated rhetoric of his predecessor's song cycles, such as *The Youth's Magic Horn.* Despite their serial technique, Webern's later songs are remarkably successful settings of mystical poems by his friend Hildegard Jone.

The main contributions of Alban Berg (1885–1935), Schoenberg's other important pupil, are the Expressionist operas *Wozzeck* (1923), based on the play by Georg Büchner, and the unfinished *Lulu* (1935), derived from two plays of 1895 by Franklin Wedekind. Both are emotionally harrowing explorations of the dark side of human existence in a world of unrelenting evil: *Wozzeck* becomes a terrifying symbol of modern man trapped by forces he cannot comprehend that ultimately destroy him, while *Lulu* traces the descent of the protagonist into prostitution and her murder at the hands of Jack the Ripper as a tragic metaphor for the unbridled lust and avarice in contemporary society. In Berg's vocal writing one can still hear the last vestiges of Wagnerian opera, stripped of its mythical trappings so that it evokes a disturbing, yet haunting, vision of twentieth-century life. His string quartet and *Lyric Suite* are outstanding contributions to the chamber music literature.

The most important composer to emerge between the world wars was Béla Bartók (1881–1945). In 1905 he met the composer Zoltán Kodály (1882–1967); together they began to collect the ethnic music of Hungary and ran the Budapest Academy of Music. While utilizing folk melodies, rhythms, and modes, Bartók incorporated the complex rhythms and the percussive effects of Stravinsky, as well as the dissonance and atonality of Schoenberg. His music was intensely personal, uniting Expressionism and Surrealism to convey the searing emotionalism apparent in the opera *Bluebeard's Castle* (1918), the ballet *The Mandarin Prince* (1926), and especially the six string quartets (1908–39), which equal Beethoven's in profundity and innovation. Bartók was a famous piano virtuoso, whose three concertos (1926–45) exploit the full percussive potential of that instrument. The final piano concerto and the *Concerto for Orchestra* (1943) are more melodic and accessible to a wide audience without diluting the composer's unique vision.

The Czech composer Leoš Janáček (1854–1928) did not achieve prominence until the last decade or so of his life, when most of his best music was also written. Because of the language barrier, his late operas, such as *The Makrouplos Affair* and *From the House of the Dead,* present serious obstacles for performance that have hindered their wider acceptance, but they are comparable to Bartók's *Bluebeard's Castle* in their fervent nationalism, uncompromising tough-mindedness, and innovativeness. More accessible are the orchestral pieces: the justly famous *Sinfionetta* (1926) combines swirling passion with brilliant, imaginative touches that make it one of the greatest masterpieces of the twentieth century.

The Russian piano virtuoso Sergei Prokoviev (1891–1953) began his career as a member of the avant-garde with two dissonant concertos for piano, although the heart of his music remained melody coupled with strong rhythm, as the two violin concertos make abundantly clear. He left for Europe following the Russian Revolution of 1917. Soon after his return to Russia in 1934, he composed his great ballet *Romeo and Juliet* and an orchestral fairy tale for children, *Peter and the Wolf.* Although he tried his best to meet the demands of Soviet authorities for propaganda music in such works as the Fifth Symphony (1944), he suffered terrible privation and repression, as did the younger Dmitri Shostakovich (1906–1975), whose wartime symphonies are rousing public works but whose private works—notably the string quartets and piano sonatas—are uncompromising in their integrity. Fittingly enough, no one today listens to the composers who were approved by Russian officials.

The most prominent German composer to emerge after World War I was Paul Hindemith (1895–1963), who nevertheless occupies a problematic place in history. His finest works are the chamber music pieces—mostly in the form of concertos for various instruments—from the 1920s, which have the vitality of a young composer reveling in his growing mastery. Thereafter Hindemith became increasingly absorbed by theory and pedagogy. Over time, he devised a comprehensive, yet still modern, tonal system that reflected his moral and spiritual idealism. The fullest statements of the composer's principles are *The Life of the Virgin (Das Marienleben)* (1948), which is a complete reworking of the song cycle for soprano after poems by Rainer Maria Rilke that had first appeared 25 years earlier; and *The Harmony of the Universe* (1951), which is based on a poem by Hindemith himself on the life of the seventeenth-century astronomer Johannes Kepler, whose treatise bears the same title. Although these works undeniably achieve the complete integration he sought, they lack the lively interest of his early works, which he was able to revive only occasionally, for example, the Symphony in B-flat (1951) for concert band.

The United States produced two composers of note during the first part of the twentieth century: Charles Ives (1874–1954) and Henry Cowell (1897–1965). Ives received a conventional academic music training at Yale University, but even before then he had begun to experiment with effects that were to become the hallmarks of his music. They reach their height in Symphony no. 4 (1916), which employs several themes played simultaneously in different keys by different groups under separate conductors that create a clashing, kaleidoscopic effect; and in the Concord Sonata for piano (1920), which uses elbows as well as wood blocks to play the notes. Ives was nevertheless a gifted melodist. *Three Places in New England* (1914) is a consciously American piece in its choice of themes and alternately festive and haunting atmosphere.

Ives did little composing after 1918. He spent the rest of his life as a successful insurance salesman and shared his music with only a few friends, such as Cowell and Carl Ruggles (1876–1971). Cowell, like Ives, was a pioneer in experimental music for the piano. He wrote several pieces for "prepared piano," an instrument made ready for performance by having objects attached to or placed on its strings, some of which might also be tuned unconventionally. He was the first American composer to show a consistent interest in the music of other cultures, which he incorporated into his numerous symphonies. Ruggles was a resolute individualist whose few works, such as *Sun Treader* (1932), deal with Symbolist themes. Although their treatment sometimes has a nearly post-Romantic massiveness, they consistently show an obsession with perfection of form and sound achieved through the most concentrated means. (He once spent the afternoon repeating the same note on the piano in search of "the perfect C.")

Aaron Copland (1900–1990) studied under Nadia Boulanger (1887–1979) during the early 1920s in Paris, where he came under the influence of Stravinsky. Upon his return to the United States, he adopted themes and rhythms inspired by jazz. Enthused by liberal ideology, he sought to create music that would speak to all the people, not simply those of one region. As a result, Copland, more than any other composer, defined our concept of "American" music across a wide spectrum, including Latin, Mexican, Appalachian, and Western. His three ballets—*Billy the Kid* (1838), *Rodeo* (1942), and above all *Appalachian Spring* (1944)—are justifiably popular works that combine touching lyricism with rhythmic vivacity of almost irresistible appeal. Copland's work also includes a number of challenging serious works, such as *Variations* for piano (1930) and the Third Symphony (1946), composed in the Neoclassical manner of Stravinsky.

England also had an important school of composers before 1945, starting with the Victorian Romantic Edward Elgar (1857–1934). Elgar's cantata, *A Dream of Gerontius* (1900), based on a poem about a soul's journey to heaven by the theologian John Henry Newman, conveys the idealism of the English school, which reaches all the way back to George Frideric Handel (see pages 604–05), although Elgar himself largely retired in bitter disillusionment after completing his well-known cello concerto in 1919. Equally characteristic was the love of nature found in the work of Gustav Holst (1874–1934), best-known for *The Planets* (1916). Perhaps the finest composer representative of the English school between the wars was Ralph Vaughan Williams (1872–1958), whose numerous symphonies and varied compositions, such as the *Serenade to Music* (1938), set to a text from Shakespeare's *Merchant of Venice,* epitomize English lyricism.

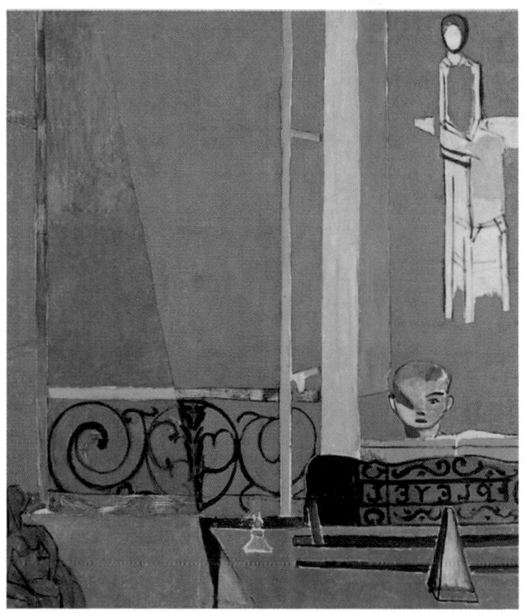

Henri Matisse. *Piano Lesson.* 1916. Oil on canvas, 8'½" x 6'11¾" (245.1 x 212.7 cm). The Museum of Modern Art, New York

MRS. SIMON GUGGENHEIM FUND

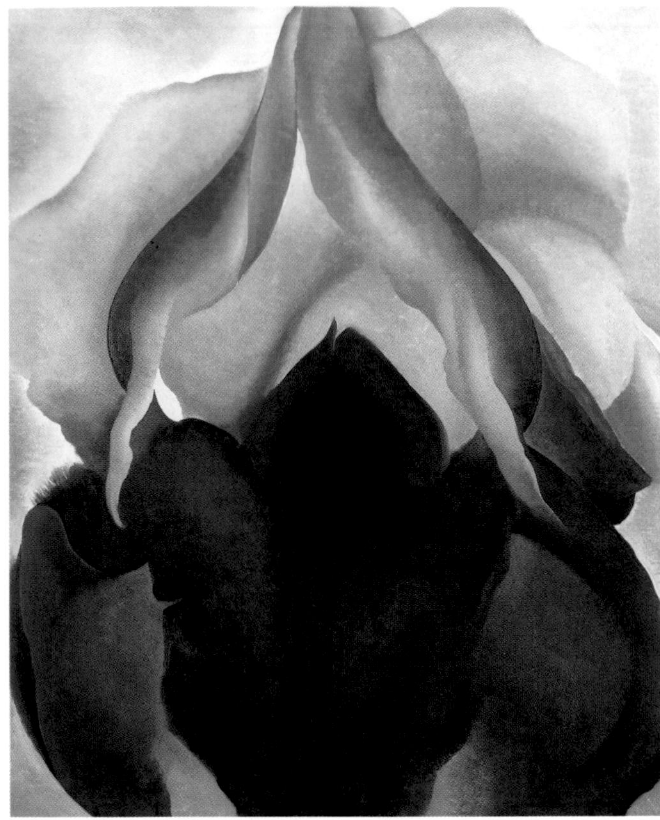

24-55. Georgia O'Keeffe. *Black Iris III.* 1926. Oil on canvas, 36 x 29⅞" (91.4 x 75.9 cm). The Metropolitan Museum of Art, New York

THE ALFRED STIEGLITZ COLLECTION, 1949

characterization. It also attests to his desire to extend "those forms of expression already present in the Old Masters. For me, the object is primary and determines the form. I have therefore always felt it vital to get as close as possible to the thing I see." Such an approach was necessary for Dix because the object both stood for and provided the subject of art.

O'KEEFFE. The New Objectivity soon gave way to realism for its own sake tinged with Romantic nostalgia as part of a widespread conservative reaction on both sides of the Atlantic. The most important representative of the naturalism found in American art as a whole during the 1920s was Georgia O'Keeffe (1887–1986). Throughout her long career, she covered a wide range of subjects and styles. Like Arthur Dove, she practiced a form of organic abstraction indebted to Expressionism, but she also adopted the Precisionism of Charles Demuth (see page 794), so that she is sometimes considered an abstract artist. Her work often combined aspects of both approaches: as she absorbed a subject into her imagination, she would alter and simplify it to give it a personal meaning. Nonetheless, O'Keeffe remained a realist at heart. *Black Iris III* (fig. 24-55) is the kind of painting for which she is best known. The image is marked by a strong sense of design unique to her. The decorative quality of the flower is deceptive, however. Observed close up and magnified to large scale, it is a thinly disguised symbol of female sexuality.

AMERICAN SCENE PAINTING. The dominance of realism during the 1930s signaled the retreat of progressive art everywhere in response to the economic depression and social turmoil that gripped both Europe and the United States. Often realism was linked to the reassertion of traditional values. Most American artists split into two camps, the Regionalists and the Social Realists. The Regionalists sought to revive idealism by updating the American myth, which was defined, however, largely in midwestern terms. The Social Realists, on the other hand, captured the dislocation and despair of the Depression era and were often concerned with social reform. Although bitterly opposed to each other, both movements drew freely on the Ash Can School (see page 789).

HOPPER. The one artist who appealed to all factions, including that of the few remaining modernists, was a former pupil of Robert Henri, Edward Hopper (1882–1967). He focused on what has since become known as the "vernacular architecture" of American cities—storefronts, movie houses, all-night diners—which no one else had thought worthy of an artist's attention. *Early Sunday Morning* (fig. 24-56) finds a haunting sense of loneliness in the familiar elements of an ordinary street. Its quietness, we realize, is temporary; there is hidden life behind these facades. We almost expect to see one of the window shades raised as we look at them. Apart from its poetic appeal, the picture also shows great formal discipline. We note the careful placement of the fireplug

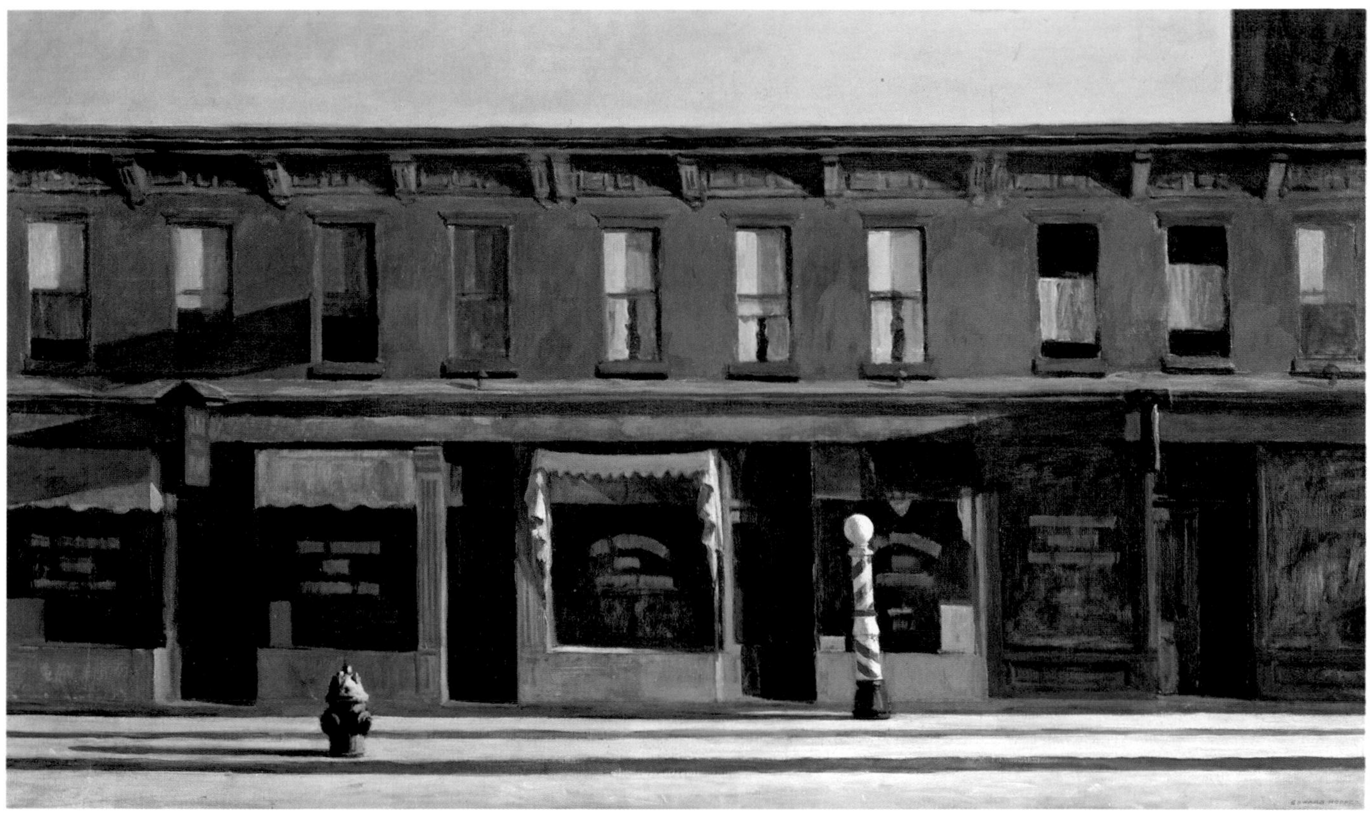

24-56. Edward Hopper. *Early Sunday Morning.* 1930. Oil on canvas, 35 x 60" (88.9 x 152.4 cm). Whitney Museum of American Art, New York

and barber pole, the subtle variations in the treatment of the row of windows, the precisely calculated slant of sunlight, and the delicate balance of verticals and horizontals. Obviously, Hopper was aware of Mondrian.

LAWRENCE. The 1920s brought about a cultural revival among African Americans known as the Harlem Renaissance. Although its promise was shattered by the economic disaster of the Great Depression, this brief flowering, which included literature and music, produced the first black artists to gain national recognition. By far the most famous remains Jacob Lawrence (1917–2000), who rose to prominence around 1940. Motivated by rage at the injustices inflicted on African Americans, Lawrence treated historical themes and the major social issues of the day. His series *From Every Southern Town . . .* (fig. 24-57) focuses on the great exodus of blacks from the South. Despite its small size, our panel has an impressive monumentality, thanks to the simplified forms and flat colors. So powerful was Lawrence's impact that his art continues to define African-American painting for many people, although he retired in 1983.

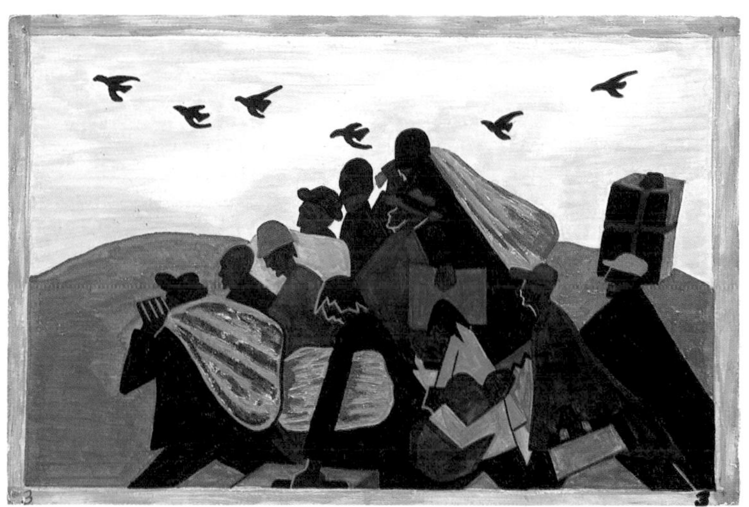

24-57. Jacob Lawrence. *The Migration of the Negro,* panel 3, from the series *From Every Southern Town Migrants Left by the Hundreds to Travel North.* 1940–41. Tempera on Masonite, 11½ x 17½" (29.2 x 44.4 cm). The Phillips Collection, Washington, D.C.

PAINTING SINCE WORLD WAR II

Abstract Expressionism: Action Painting

Having survived the most serious economic calamity and the greatest threat to civilization in all of history, the world now faced a potentially even greater danger: nuclear holocaust. This central fact conditioned the entire Cold War era, which came to an end only with the fall of Communism in Russia in 1985. Ironically, it was also a period of unprecedented prosperity in much of the West but not in the rest of the world, which, with the notable exception of Japan, struggled until recently to compete successfully.

The painting that prevailed for about 15 years following the end of World War II arose in direct response to the anxiety brought on by these historical circumstances. The term *Abstract Expressionism* is often applied to this style, which was initiated by artists living in New York City. Under the influence of Surrealism and existentialist philosophy, Action painters, the first of the Abstract Expressionists, developed a new approach to art. Painting became a counterpart to life itself. It was seen as an ongoing process in which artists faced considerable risks and overcame the dilemmas confronting them through a series of conscious and unconscious decisions in response to both internal and external demands. The Color Field painters in turn dissolved the frenzied gestures and intense hues of the Action painters in broad forms of poetic color that partly reflect the influence of Oriental mysticism. In a sense, Color Field Painting resolved the conflicts expressed by Action Painting. They are, however, two sides of the same coin, separated by the thinnest differences of approach.

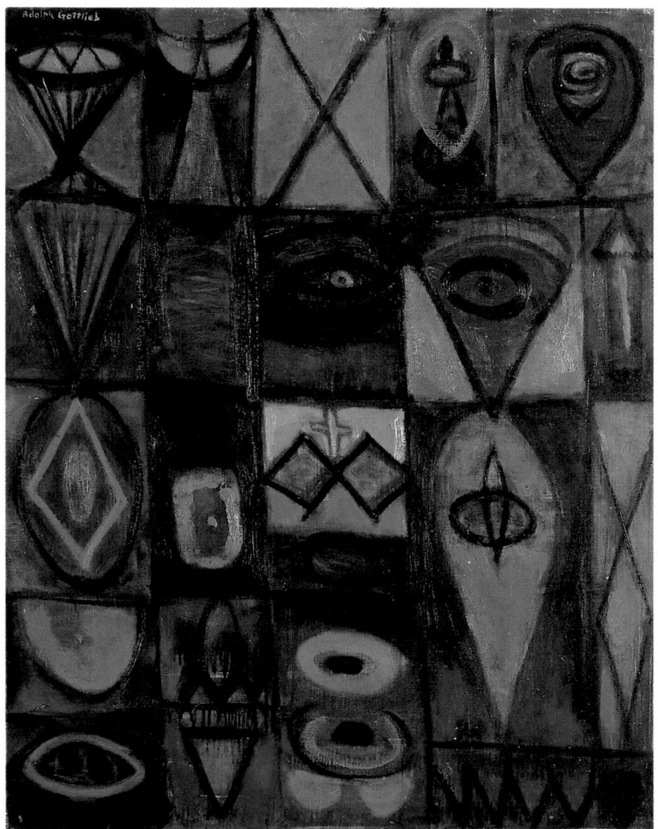

24-58. Adolph Gottlieb. *Descent into Darkness.* 1947.
Oil on Masonite, 30 x 25" (76.2 x 63.5 cm).
Smith College Museum of Art, Northampton, Massachusetts
ACQUIRED BY EXCHANGE, 1951

GOTTLIEB. During World War II, the poet André Breton and other Surrealists found refuge in New York, where their work was enthusiastically received by critics and exhibited at museums and galleries such as Peggy Guggenheim's Art of This Century. Soon the early Abstract Expressionists developed their own form of Surrealism that allowed them to convey their sense of horror at the pervasive evil of a chaotic world. Distraught by the carnage of the war, they became mythmakers who sought to create images that expressed their sense of impending disaster. They were strongly affected by the theory of the collective subconscious formulated by Freud's disciple Carl Jung, who believed that universal archetypes are imbedded in our psyches.

The breakthrough came in a discussion between Adolph Gottlieb (1903–1974) and Mark Rothko (1903–1970), who suggested they try Classical themes. Gottlieb then began to paint pictographs based on Sophocles and the other Greek tragedians. Pictographs are a form of picture writing found in prehistoric art; no longer intelligible to us, they nevertheless exercise a mysterious, instinctive appeal. Few prehistoric images, however, have the impact of Gottlieb's pictographs (fig. 24-58), which conjure up something more elemental than even the most ancient relic. The canvas owes its power to his uncanny ability to cast the viewer back into the dark, primitive realm of the subconscious. Painted in an uncompromisingly severe style, it radiates a menacing evil that is a truly frightening evocation of the war. Composed in a grid system derived from Mondrian, the painting has Surrealist forms influenced by the grimmest works of Picasso, Miró, and Klee from the same years. At face value the picture seems a confusing jumble of human anatomy cut up and reassembled by a lunatic. It demands to be read section by section, yet it does not yield a literal meaning. Instead, the accumulation of intuitive responses through free association provides an experience at once overwhelming and profoundly disturbing.

GORKY. Arshile Gorky (1904–1948), an Armenian who came to America at 16, was the pioneer of the movement and the single most important influence on its other members. It took him 20 years, painting first in the manner of Cézanne, then in the vein of Picasso, to arrive at his mature style. We see it in *The Liver Is the Cock's Comb* (fig. 24-59), his greatest work. The enigmatic title suggests Gorky's close contact with the Surrealists during the war. Gorky developed a personal mythology that underlies his work; each form represents a private symbol within this hermetic realm. Everything here is in the process of turning into something else. The treatment reflects his own experience in camouflage, gained from a class he conducted during the war. The biomorphic shapes clearly owe much to Miró (see fig. 24-45), while their spontaneous handling and the glowing color reflect Gorky's enthusiasm for Kandinsky (see fig. 24-10). Yet the dynamic interlocking of the forms, their aggressive power of attraction and repulsion are uniquely his own.

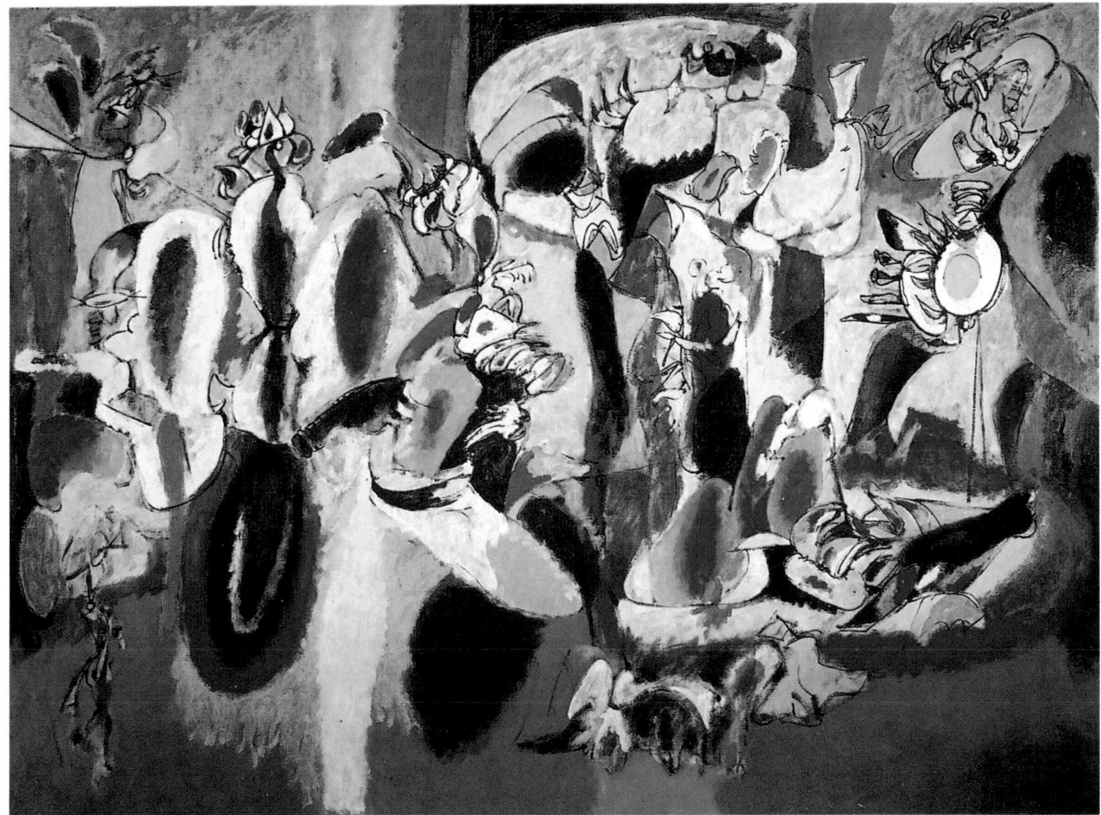

24-59. Arshile Gorky. *The Liver Is the Cock's Comb.* 1944. Oil on canvas, 6'1¼" x 8'2" (1.86 x 2.49 m). Albright-Knox Art Gallery, Buffalo, New York

GIFT OF SEYMOUR H. KNOX, 1956

POLLOCK. The most important of the Action painters proved to be Jackson Pollock (1912–1956). His huge canvas entitled *Autumn Rhythm: Number 30, 1950* (fig. 24-60) was executed mainly by pouring and spattering the colors instead of applying them with a brush. [See Primary Sources, no. 92, page 938.] The result, especially when viewed at close range, suggests both Kandinsky and Max Ernst (compare figs. 24-10 and 24-41). Kandinsky's nonrepresentational Expressionism and the Surre-

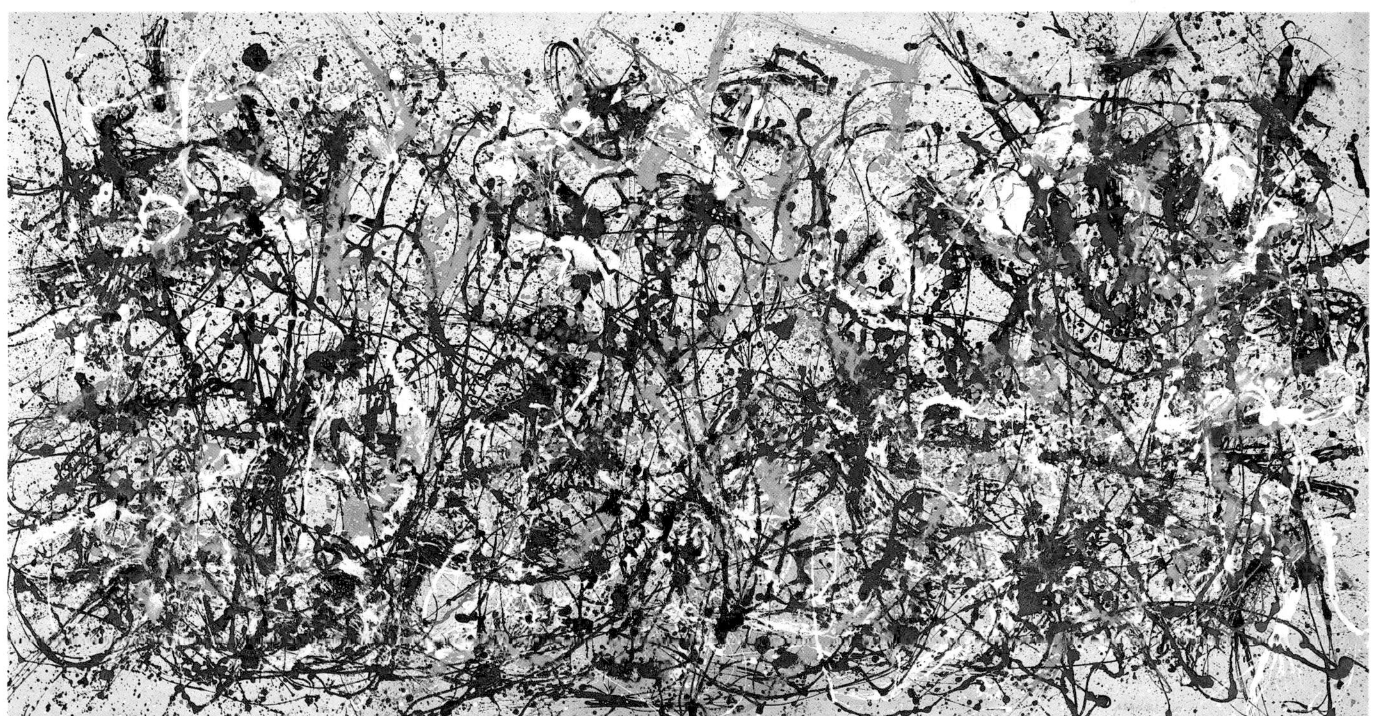

24-60. Jackson Pollock. *Autumn Rhythm: Number 30, 1950.* 1950. Oil on canvas, 8'8" x 17'3" (2.64 x 5.26 m). The Metropolitan Museum of Art, New York

GEORGE A. HEARN FUND, 1957

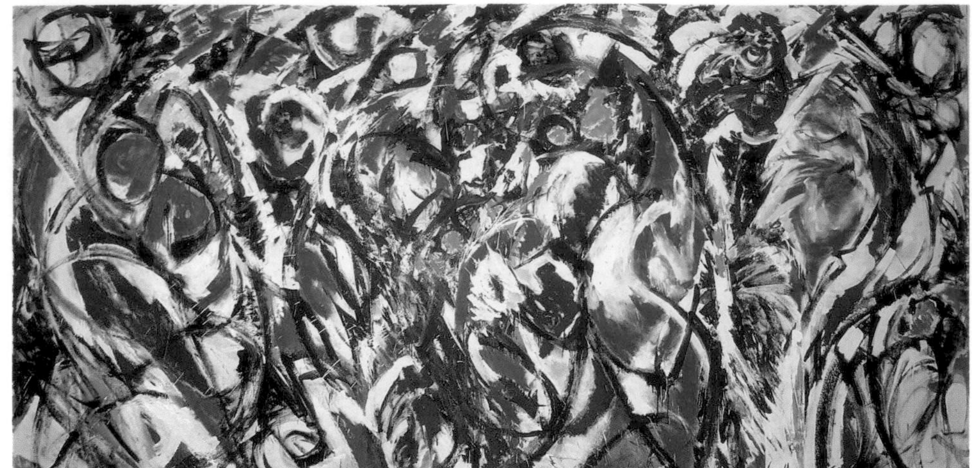

24-61. Lee Krasner. *Celebration*. 1959–60. Oil on canvas, 7'8¼" x 16'4½" (2.3 x 4.9 m). Private collection

COURTESY ROBERT MILLER GALLERY, NEW YORK

alists' exploitation of chance effects are indeed the main sources of Pollock's work, but they do not account for his revolutionary technique and the emotional appeal of his art. Why did Pollock "fling a pot of paint in the public's face," as Ruskin had accused Whistler of doing? It was surely not to be more abstract than his predecessors, for the strict control implied by abstraction is exactly what Pollock relinquished when he began to dribble and spatter. Rather, he came to regard paint itself not as a passive substance to be manipulated at will but as a storehouse of pent-up forces for him to release.

The actual shapes visible in our illustration were largely determined by the internal dynamics of his material and his process: the viscosity of the paint, the speed and direction of its impact upon the canvas, its interaction with other layers of pigment. The result is a surface so alive, so sensuously rich, that all earlier American painting looks pale in comparison. Pollock did not simply "let go" and leave the rest to chance when he "aimed" the paint at the canvas instead of "carrying" it on the tip of his brush. He released the forces within the paint by giving it a momentum of its own. He himself was the source of energy for these forces, and he "rode" them as a cowboy might ride a wild horse, in a frenzy of psychophysical action. He did not always stay in the saddle, yet the thrill of this contest, which strained his entire being, was well worth the risk. Our metaphor, though crude, points up the main difference between Pollock and his predecessors: his total commitment to the act of painting. Hence his preference for huge canvases that provide a "field of combat" large enough for him to paint not merely with his arms but with the motion of his whole body.

The term *Action Painting* conveys the essence of this approach far better than does Abstract Expressionism. To those who complain that Pollock was not sufficiently in control of his medium, we reply that this loss was more than offset by a gain. There is a new continuity and expansiveness in the creative process that gave his work its distinctive mid-twentieth-century stamp. Pollock's drip technique, however, was not in itself essential to Action Painting, and he stopped using it in 1953.

KRASNER. Lee Krasner (1908–1984), who was married to Pollock, never abandoned the brush, although she was unmistakably influenced by Pollock. She struggled to establish her artistic identity, emerging from his shadow only after undergoing several changes in direction and destroying much of her early work. After Pollock's death, she succeeded in doing what he had been attempting to do for the last three years of his life: to reintroduce the figure into Abstract Expressionism while retaining its automatic handwriting. The potential had always been there in Pollock's work. We can easily imagine wildly dancing people in *Autumn Rhythm* (compare fig. 24-60). In *Celebration* (fig. 24-61), Krasner defines these rudimentary shapes from within the tangled network of lines by using the broad gestures of Action Painting to suggest human forms without actually depicting them.

DE KOONING. The work of Willem de Kooning (1904–1997), another prominent member of the group and a close friend of Gorky, always retains a link with the world of images, whether or not it has a recognizable subject. In some paintings, such as *Woman II* (fig. 24-62), the image emerges from the jagged welter of brushstrokes as insistently as it does in Rouault's *Head of Christ* (see fig. 24-3). De Kooning shares with Pollock the furious energy of the painting process, the sense of risk, of a challenge successfully—but barely—met. In reality, the artist worked on the canvas for two years, constantly repainting it until he got it right. What are we to make of his wildly distorted *Woman II*? It is as if the flow of psychic impulses in the process of painting has unleashed this nightmarish specter from deep within the artist's subconscious, much as it did in Adolph Gottlieb's pictographs (compare fig. 24-58). For that reason, he has sometimes been accused of being a woman-hater, a charge he denied. Rather, his figure is like a primordial goddess, cruel yet seductive, who represents the primitive side of our makeup. We have met her before, for example, in *"The Mistress of the Animals"* from Thera (see fig. 4-8). De Kooning's woman was actually intended as a humorous caricature of modern movie stars such as Marilyn Monroe. Yet he shared with Max Beckmann an Old World horror of empty space, which to him signified the existential void. Only

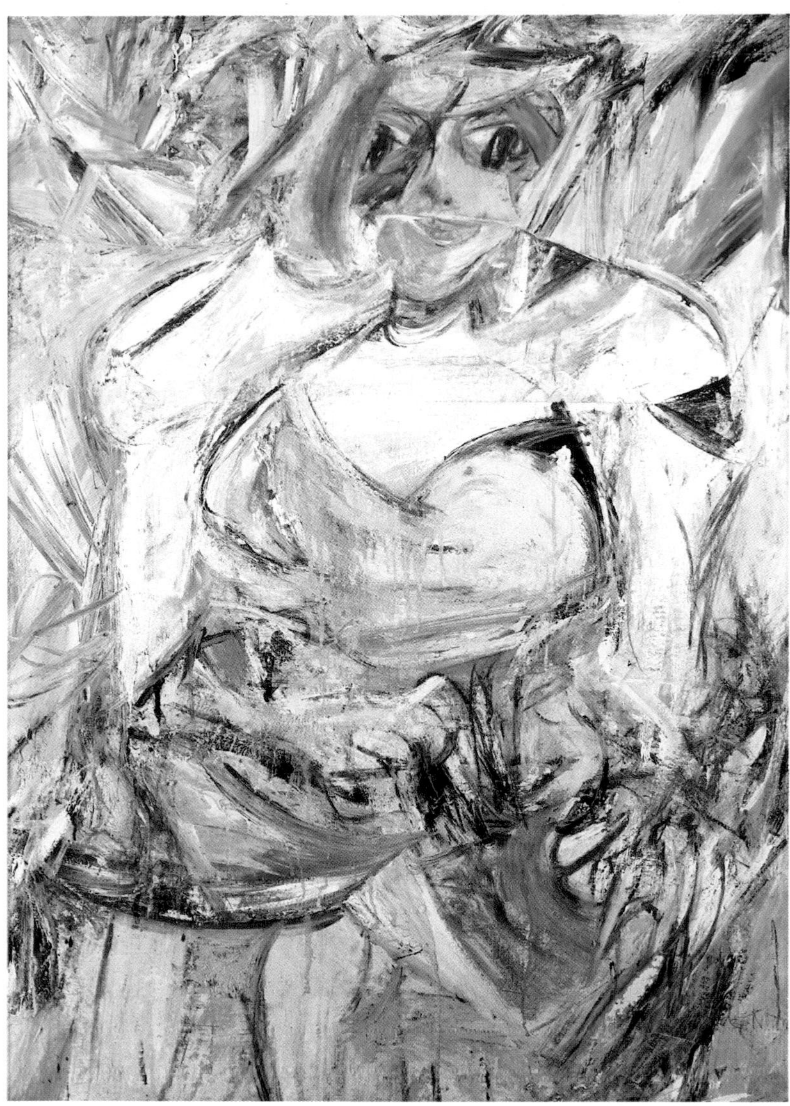

24-62. Willem de Kooning. *Woman II*. 1952. Oil on canvas, 59 x 43" (149.9 x 109.2 cm). The Museum of Modern Art, New York
GIFT OF MRS. JOHN D. ROCKEFELLER 3RD

after he moved to Long Island from the confines of New York City was he able to overcome this deep-seated anxiety.

Expressionism in Europe

Action Painting marked the international coming-of-age for American art. The movement had a powerful impact on European art, which in those years had nothing to show of comparable force and conviction. One French artist, however, was of such amazing originality as to constitute a movement all by himself: Jean Dubuffet, whose first exhibition soon after the Liberation electrified and antagonized the Paris art world.

DUBUFFET. As a young man Dubuffet (1901–1985) had formal instruction in painting, but he responded to none of the various trends he saw around him nor to the art of the museums. All struck him as divorced from real life, and he turned to other pursuits. Only in middle age did he experience the breakthrough that permitted him to discover his creative gifts. Dubuffet suddenly realized that for him true art had to come from outside the ideas and traditions of the artistic elite, and he found inspiration in the art of children and the insane. The distinction between "normal" and "abnormal" struck him as no more justifiable than established notions of "beauty" and "ugliness." Not since Marcel Duchamp (see pages 788–89) had anyone attempted so radical a critique of art.

Dubuffet made himself the champion of what he called *l'art brut,* "art-in-the-raw," but he created something of a paradox besides. While extolling the directness and spontaneity of the amateur as against the refinement of professional artists, he became a professional artist himself. Duchamp's questioning of established values had led him to cease artistic activity altogether, but Dubuffet became incredibly prolific, second only to Picasso in output. Compared with the work of Paul Klee, who had first utilized the style of children's drawings (see pages 800–01), Dubuffet's art is "raw" indeed. Its stark immediacy, its explosive, defiant presence, are the opposite of Klee's discipline and economy. Did Dubuffet perhaps fall into a trap of his own making? If his work merely imitated the *art brut* of children and the insane, would not these self-chosen conventions limit him as much as those of the artistic elite?

We may be tempted to think so on first sight of *Le Métafisyx*

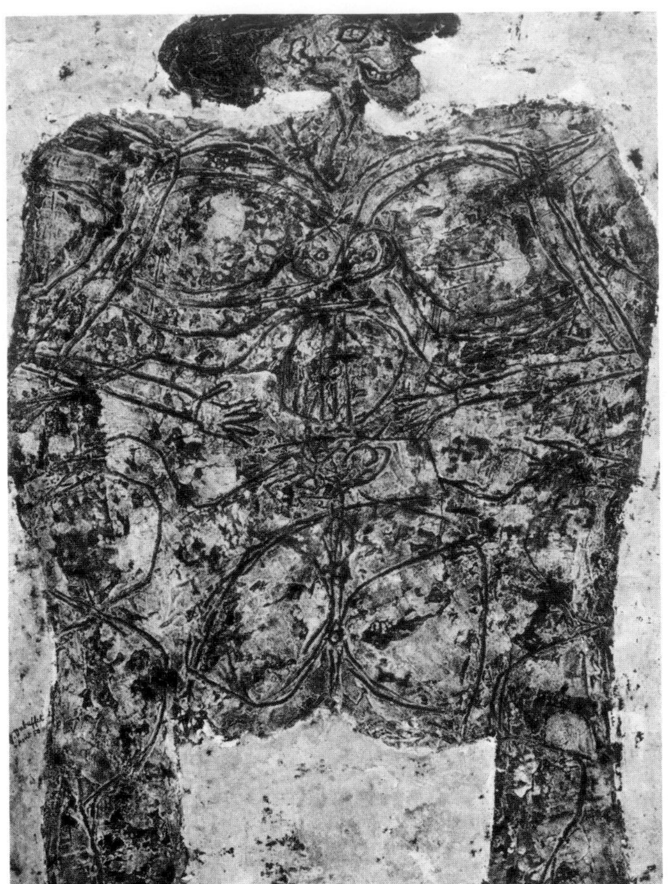

24-63. Jean Dubuffet. *Le Métafisyx,* from the *Corps de Dames* series. 1950. 45¾ x 35¼" (116.2 x 89.5 cm). Private collection

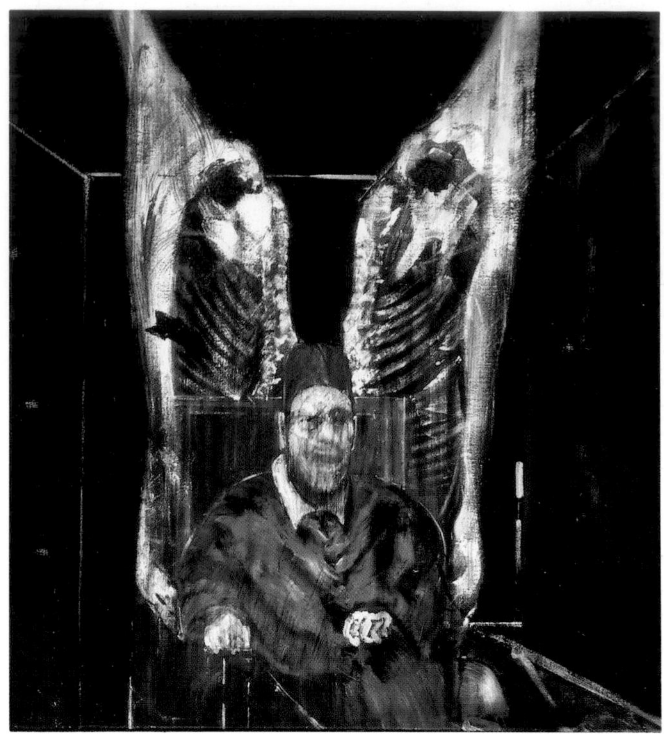

24-64. Francis Bacon. *Head Surrounded by Sides of Beef.* 1954. Oil on canvas, 50¾ x 48" (129 x 122 cm). The Art Institute of Chicago

HARRIOTT A. FOX FUND

(fig. 24-63) from his *Corps de Dames* series. Even De Kooning's wildly distorted *Woman II* (see fig. 24-62) seems gentle when matched against this shocking assault on our inherited sensibilities. The paint is as heavy and opaque as a rough coating of plaster, and the lines describing the blocklike body are scratched into the surface like graffiti made by an untrained hand. Appearances are deceiving, however. The fury and concentration of Dubuffet's attack should convince us that his demonic female is not "something any child can do." In an eloquent statement the artist explained the purpose of images such as this: "The female body . . . has long . . . been associated with a very specious notion of beauty which I find miserable and most depressing. Surely I am for beauty, but not that one. . . . I intend to sweep away everything we have been taught to consider—without question—as grace and beauty [and to] substitute another and vaster beauty, touching all objects and beings, not excluding the most despised. . . . I would like people to look at my work as an enterprise for the rehabilitation of scorned values, and . . . a work of ardent celebration."

BACON. The English artist Francis Bacon (1909–1992) was allied not with Abstract Expressionism, though he was clearly related to it, but with the Expressionist tradition. For his power to translate sheer anguish into visual form he had no equal among twentieth-century artists except perhaps Rouault (see page 772). Bacon often derived his imagery from other artists. He freely combined several sources while transforming them in order to give them new meaning. *Head Surrounded by Sides of Beef* (fig. 24-64) reflects Bacon's obsession with Velázquez' *Pope Innocent X* (compare fig. 17-34), a picture that haunted him for some years. It is, of course, no longer Innocent X we see here but a screaming ghost, inspired by a scene from Sergei Eisenstein's film *Battleship Potemkin,* that is materializing out of a black void. The two glowing sides of beef are taken from a painting by Rembrandt. Knowing the origin of the imagery does not help us to understand it, however. Nor does comparison with earlier works such as Grünewald's *The Crucifixion,* Fuseli's *The Nightmare,* Ensor's *Christ's Entry into Brussels in 1889,* or Munch's *The Scream,* which are its ancestors (see figs. 16-1, 21-43, 23-20, and 23-21). Bacon was a gambler, a risk taker, in real life as well as in the way he worked. What he wanted were images that, in his own words, "unlock the deeper possibilities of sensation." Here he competes with Velázquez, but on his own terms, which are to set up an almost unbearable tension between the shocking violence of his vision and the luminous beauty of his brushwork.

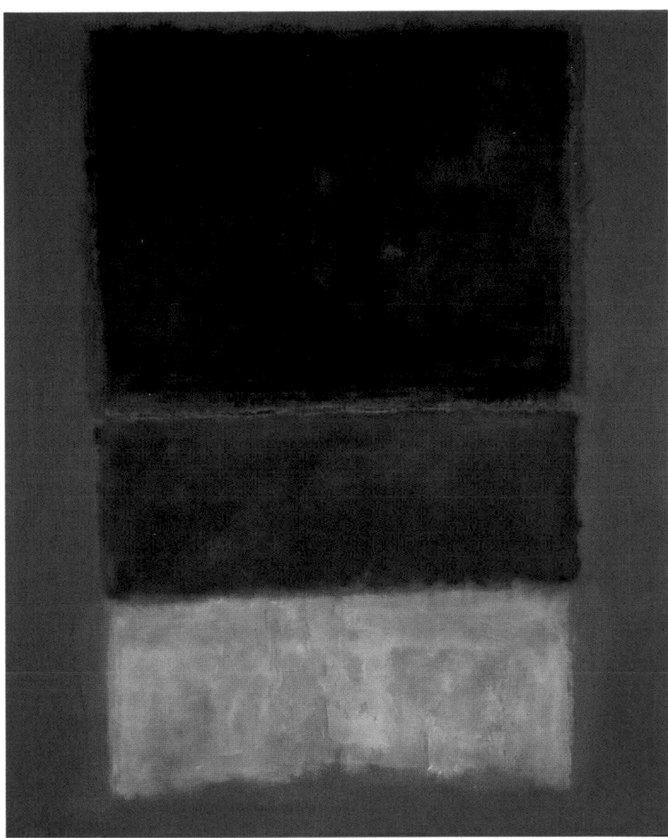

24-65. Mark Rothko. *White and Greens in Blue.* 1957. Oil on canvas, 8'4" x 6'10" (2.5 x 2.1 m). Collection of Mr. and Mrs. Paul Mellon, Virginia

COURTESY ESTATE OF PAUL MELLON / ARTISTS RIGHTS SOCIETY (ARS), NEW YORK

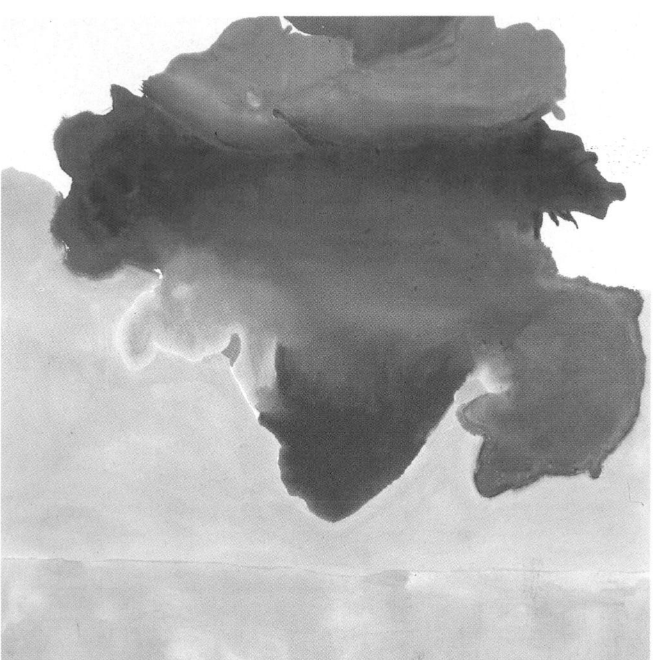

24-66. Helen Frankenthaler. *The Bay.* 1963. Acrylic on canvas, 6'8¾" x 6'9¾" (2.05 x 2.08 m). The Detroit Institute of Arts

GIFT OF DR. AND MRS. HILBERT H. DELAWTER

Color Field Painting

By the late 1940s, a number of artists began to transform Action Painting into a style called Color Field Painting, in which the canvas is stained with thin, translucent color washes. These may be oil or even ink, but the favored material quickly became acrylic, a plastic suspended in a polymer resin, which can be thinned with water so that it flows freely.

ROTHKO. In the mid-1940s Mark Rothko worked in a style derived from the Surrealists, then adopted the gestures of early Action Painting using blocklike colored forms to act like characters in a dream. Within a few years, however, he sought maximum concentration for greatest clarity. Toward 1947 his forms began to coalesce, until he subdued the aggressiveness of Action Painting so completely that his mature pictures radiated the purest contemplative stillness. *White and Greens in Blue* (fig. 24-65) consists of three rectangles with blurred edges on a blue field. The darker forms seem immersed in the red ground, so that the white rectangle stands out all the more vividly. The canvas is very large, almost eight and one-half feet high, and the thin washes of color permit the texture of the cloth to be seen in places. This description hardly begins to touch the essence of the work or the reasons for its mysterious power to move us. These are to be found in the delicate equilibrium of the shapes, their strange interdependence, and the subtle variations of hue, which seem to immerse the beholder in the monumental painting. For those attuned to the artist's special vision, the experience can be akin to a trancelike rapture. Yet Rothko sought to convey not a mystical experience but his melancholy outlook, for he possessed a philosophical cast of mind. The overarching theme of his work is the tragedy of the human condition in the face of inevitable death. The import is inescapable in several series painted toward the end of his life, which ended in suicide. The bold, simplified forms and somber colors are intended as universal symbols; they express the meaning of life by condensing the drama of human existence to its very essence.

FRANKENTHALER. The stained canvas was also pioneered by Helen Frankenthaler (b. 1928), who was inspired by Rothko's example as early as 1952. In *The Bay* (fig. 24-66), Frankenthaler uses the same biomorphic forms basic to early Action Painting but eliminates the personal handwriting found in the brushwork of Gorky and De Kooning. The results are reminiscent of O'Keeffe's paintings in their lyrical and decorative qualities and are no less impressive (compare fig. 24-55).

THEATER SINCE WORLD WAR II

The end of World War II brought an explosion of theater in response to pent-up cultural energy and popular demand. In Europe heavy government subsidies were used to restore national theaters and establish new ones. French theater initially adhered to concepts and practices that had been developed during the war years. The majority of new dramas were by established writers, such as Jean Anouilh (1910–1987), the most popular playwright in France through the 1970s, whose work centered on the dilemma of maintaining youthful integrity in an adult world based on compromise. But the essential contribution of postwar France was the Theater of the Absurd, which, appropriately enough, was never an organized movement and was named by the critic Martin Esslin only in 1961, when its heyday was over. The term derives from the essay "The Myth of Sisyphus" written in 1943 by Albert Camus (1913–1960), who considered the universe to be chaotic and irrational and thus regarded the search for meaning to be as "absurd" as the futile task of the Corinthian king who was condemned to pushing the same boulder up a hill in Hades forever. Camus' outlook was closely related to the existentialism of Jean-Paul Sartre, which held that truth in any absolute sense is unknowable and that meaning must be self-created by each individual. Camus, however, rejected Sartre's call for political engagement as a necessary, albeit irrational, act, thereby prompting a long and bitter feud between the two men.

This attitude was a response to the horrors of the war and the anxiety created by the ensuing Cold War, with its omnipresent threat of nuclear holocaust. In fact, *End Game* (1957) by Samuel Beckett (1906–1989), the greatest of the absurdists, takes place at the end of the world and uses the metaphor of chess to represent the human condition through four characters who alternately torment and console each other in their incomprehensible predicament, over which they have no control. Although he was Irish, Beckett spent much of his career in Paris, and *End Game* was originally written in French. Paris was also home to the Romanian-born Eugène Ionesco (1912–1994), whose early one-act dramas, such as *The Bald Soprano* (1949), which was inspired by an English phrase book, were "antiplays" using the conventions of language to convey irrational, anguished states of mind. His later works, notably *Rhinoceros* (1960), are more conventional in form and character delineation, but they are no less hallucinatory in their effect. Of all the absurdists, the most disturbing was Jean Genet (1910–1986). Like many of his plays, Genet's masterpiece, *The Balcony* (1956), deals with outcasts—he himself was a criminal and a homosexual—caught in a web of perverse and destructive relationships, but nevertheless it reveals a surprisingly compassionate, if pessimistic, view of humanity. Genet's plays are extremely powerful in their impact on the viewer. In this he reveals himself a disciple of Artaud's Theater of Cruelty, which exercised a pervasive influence on French theater after the war, including on the director Roger Blin (1907–1984), who staged numerous absurdist plays in experimental theaters across the country. By far the most important recent development has come from the Théâtre du Soleil, founded in 1964, with Ariane Mnouchkine (b. 1940) at its helm. Her productions of Shakespeare, Euripides, and Aeschylus freely incorporate elements from India, Japan, and Asia to striking effect.

In Germany, the most powerful influence came from Bertholt Brecht; his Berlin Ensemble, directed by his wife, Helene Weigel (1900–1971), was widely regarded as among the finest of the time in Europe. Despite heavy state support on both sides of the iron curtain, not until the 1960s did Germany produce its first postwar dramatist of note: Peter Weiss (1916–1982), whose *Marat/Sade* (the customary shortened title) unites Brecht and Artaud to treat an insane asylum as a metaphor of the world. Of the German playwrights born around the end of the war, the foremost is Botho Strauss (b. 1944). Strauss' drama *Big and Little* (1978), in which characters try unsuccessfully to establish contact with one another, is close to absurdist theater but replete with political overtones. Throughout the 1970s German theater was heavily leftist in its orientation, especially the productions of director Peter Stein (b. 1937), which were critiques of the ideologies underlying traditional plays and examinations of their historical roots. Since then a more conventional ideology and approach have been adopted, as much out of self-preservation as conviction.

After the war, England rebuilt its fabled theater system, including the Old Vic and the Stratford Festival Company, and reestablished the important festivals such as Glyndebourne. Experimental theater, however, came only in the mid-1950s, when the English Stage Company, under George Devine (1910–1966), was established and produced two epoch-making plays by John Osborne (1929–1994): *Look Back in Anger* (1956), an attack on the inherited class system and its injustices, and *The Entertainer* (1957), starring Laurence Olivier as the fading music-hall actor Archie Rice, who symbolizes the decline of England. At about the same time, the Theatre Workshop began to reach its height under Joan Littlewood (b. 1914), its director until 1961, who wanted to create a working-class theater. Her most famous productions were *The Quare Fellow,* written in 1945 by the Irish poet and novelist Brendan Behan (1923–1964), about the impending execution of an Irish Republican Army sympathizer; and *A Taste of Honey* (1958), written at the age of 17 by Shelagh Delaney (b. 1939), about a teenaged mother who rears her child with the help of a gay man. Under Peter Hall (b.

1930) and Peter Brook (b. 1925), the most experimental of all English directors, the newly chartered Royal Shakespeare Company became the leading venue for avant-garde theater in the 1960s. By far the most significant English playwright of the postwar era has been Harold Pinter (b. 1930), whose enigmatic "comedies of menace," such as *The Caretaker* (1960), have more than a little in common with Beckett's dramas but are filled with a sense of mystery and fear that makes them psychologically gripping. The generation born in the 1930s continues to dominate English drama. Typically their work is radical, both socially and morally. Among them, Edward Bond (b. 1935) gained particular notoriety for the shock value of his early plays written in 1965–68, which use violence and bizarre plots to emphasize the moral depravity of modern existence.

Poland's contribution to contemporary theater has been no less important than in music. Jerzy Grotowski (b. 1933) emerged as a leading director in the mid-1960s when the Polish Laboratory Theater toured Europe, but it was as a theorist that he made his mark with the publication in 1968 of *Towards a Poor Theater,* which advocated eliminating every nonessential element from theater until it was reduced to the only components that could not be omitted without destroying theater itself—the actor and the audience. The heavy physical and psychic demands of Grotowski's acting method drew mainly on the Russians, while his approach to stagecraft makes the audience play a role in the drama unself-consciously through its psychological response. Eventually he took the final step of eliminating theater itself in favor of rituals re-creating the archetypal experiences on which he believed theater was ultimately based.

In contrast to Europe, the United States government gave little support to theater after the war. American theater nonetheless prospered in small houses across the land, thanks to a revival of the Little Theater movement, which had struggled during the Great Depression. In New York experimental theater thrived off-Broadway. Major new regional companies were formed as well, particularly the Tyrone Guthrie Theater in Minneapolis, established in 1963. The most prominent organization was the Actors Studio, which was cofounded in 1947 by the director Elia Kazan, although Lee Strasberg soon became the key figure. It was the first theater to promote "method acting," a modified form of Stanislavsky's practices (see page 784), which dominated the American stage into the 1960s. It also staged the first classics of American postwar drama: *A Streetcar Named Desire* (1947) by Tennessee Williams (1911–1983) and *Death of a Salesman* (1949) by Arthur Miller (b. 1916). The former, featuring the actor Marlon Brando in his first important role as the brutish Stanley Kowalski, is an unforgettable play about sex, madness, and violence in the South, while the latter, which focuses on the American dream of success, was written as a classical tragedy about the common man. As in the other arts, the period since 1945 has witnessed the high tide of writing for the American stage.

The most important playwright of the 1960s was Edward Albee (b. 1928), who began as an absurdist, then turned to dramas (*Who's Afraid of Virginia Woolf,* 1962) about how people deal psychologically with inner and external reality, before becoming an iconoclast whose meanings are ambiguous (*The Marriage Play,* 1987). In 1964 Sam Shepard (b. 1943) won an Obie Award for his first play, *Cowboy,* centering on his favorite theme, the American West, treated in archetypal terms. The late 1960s and early 1970s were a time of turmoil everywhere. In addition to student and race riots in France and America in 1968, there were protests against the Vietnam War, which found expression in such plays as *America Hurrah!* (1967) by Jean-Claude van Itallie (b. 1936) and *Sticks and Bones* (1971) by David Rabe (b. 1940). At the same time the distinction between art and theater was dissolved in the Happenings staged by Alan Kaprow and Jean Tinguely (see page 859).

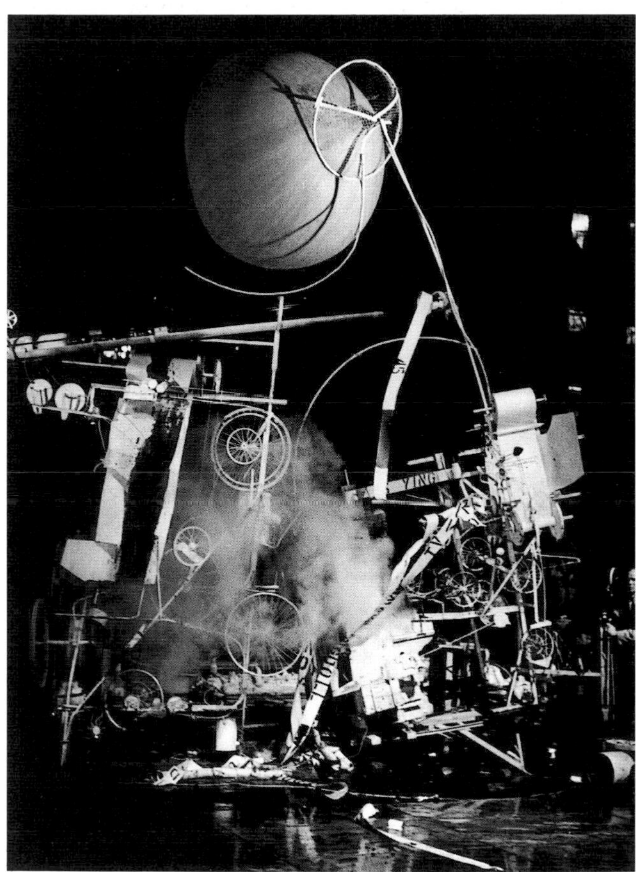

Jean Tinguely. *Hommage to New York.* 1960.
Mixed media. Self-destructing installation in the garden of the Museum of Modern Art, New York

PHOTOGRAPHER: © DAVID GAHR, NEW YORK
© 2000 ARTISTS RIGHTS SOCIETY (ARS), NEW YORK/ADAGP, PARIS

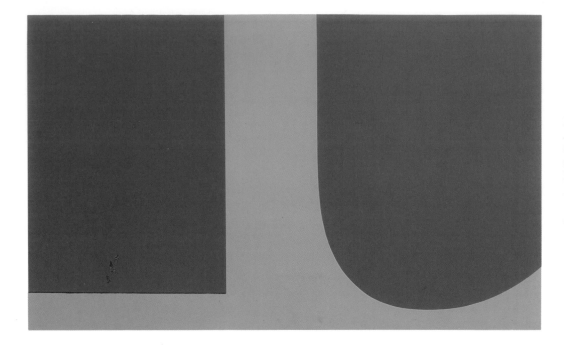

24-67. Ellsworth Kelly. *Red Blue Green*. 1963. Oil on canvas, 7'8" x 11'4" (2.34 x 3.45 m). Museum of Contemporary Art, San Diego, La Jolla, California

GIFT OF JACK AND CAROLYN FARRIS

Late Abstract Expressionism

KELLY. Many artists who came to maturity in the 1950s turned away from Action Painting altogether in favor of hard-edge painting. *Red Blue Green* (fig. 24-67) by Ellsworth Kelly (b. 1923), an early leader of this tendency, abandons Rothko's impressionistic softness. Instead, flat areas of color are contained within carefully delineated forms as part of the formal investigation of color and design for its own sake.

This radical abstraction of form is known as Minimalism, which implies an equal reduction of content. It was a quest for basic elements representing the fundamental aesthetic values of art, without regard to issues of content. Minimalism was a necessary, even valuable, phase of modern art. At its most extreme, it reduced art not to an eternal essence but to an arid simplicity. In the hands of a few artists of genius such as Kelly, however, it yielded works of unequaled formal perfection.

STELLA. The brilliant Frank Stella (b. 1936) began as an admirer of Mondrian, then soon evolved a nonfigurative style that was even more self-contained. Unlike Mondrian (see pages 796–97), Stella did not concern himself with the vertical-horizontal balance that connects the older artist's work to the world of nature. Logically enough, he also abandoned the traditional rectangular format, to make quite sure that his pictures bore no resemblance to windows. The shape of the canvas had now become an indispensable part of the design. In one of his largest works, the majestic *Empress of India* (fig. 24-68), this shape is determined by the thrust and counterthrust of four huge chevrons. They are identical in size

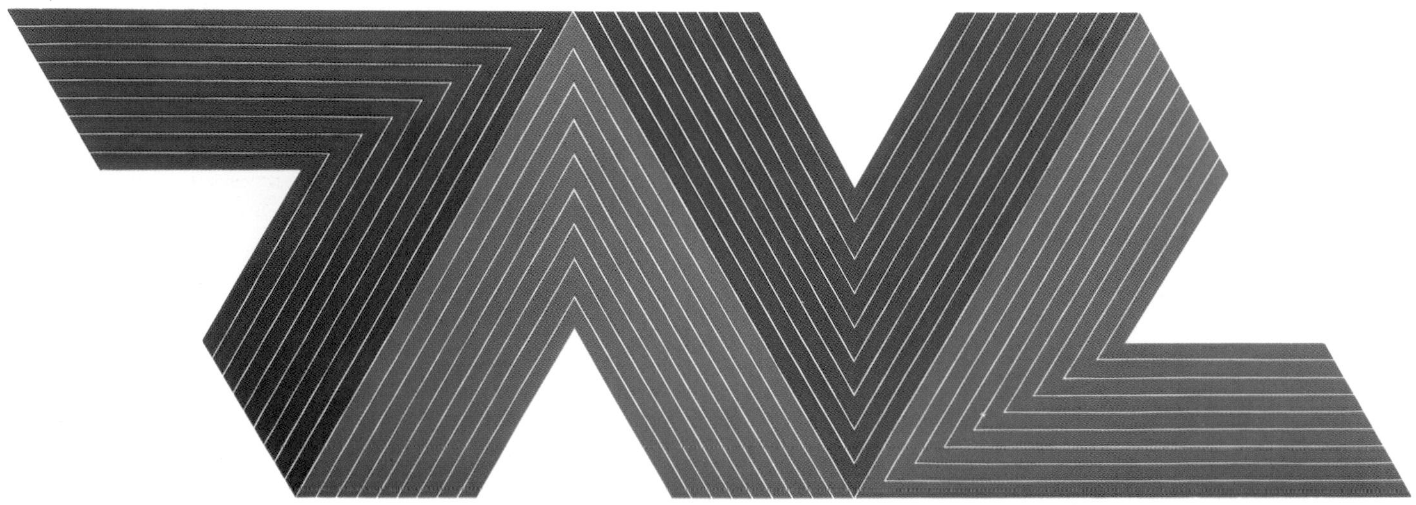

24-68. Frank Stella. *Empress of India*. 1965. Metallic powder in polymer emulsion on canvas, 6'5" x 18'8" (1.9 x 5.7 m). The Museum of Modern Art, New York

GIFT OF S. I. NEWHOUSE, JR.

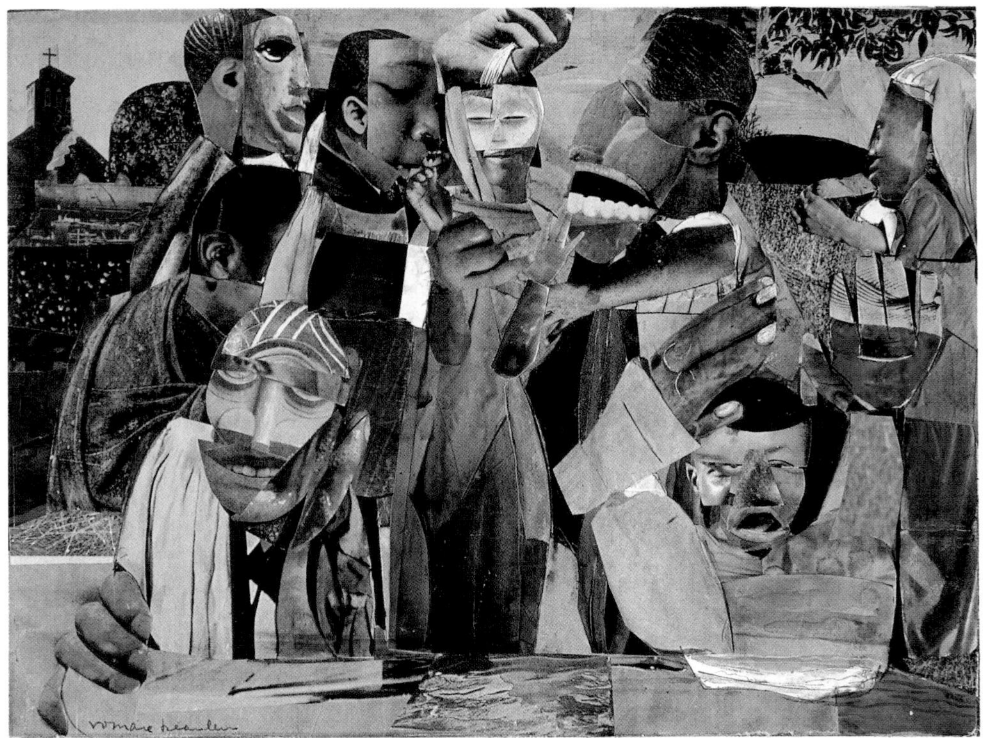

24-69. Romare Bearden. *The Prevalence of Ritual: Baptism.* 1964. Collage of photochemical reproduction, synthetic polymer, and pencil on paperboard, 9⅛ x 12" (23.2 x 30.5 cm). Hirshhorn Museum and Sculpture Garden, Smithsonian Institution, Washington, D.C.

GIFT OF JOSEPH H. HIRSHHORN, 1966

and shape but sharply differentiated in color and in their relationship to the whole. The paint, moreover, contains powdered metal, which gives it an iridescent sheen. This is yet another way to stress the impersonal precision of the surfaces and to remove the work from any comparison with the "handmade" look of easel pictures. In fact, to call *Empress of India* a picture is something of a misnomer. It demands to be thought of as an object, sufficient in itself.

African-American Painting

Following World War II, blacks began to attend art schools in growing numbers, at the very time that Abstract Expressionism marked the maturation of American art. The civil rights movement helped them to establish their artistic identities and to find appropriate styles for expressing them. The turning point proved to be the assassinations of Malcolm X in 1965 and Martin Luther King, Jr., in 1968, which led to an outpouring of African-American art.

Since then, black artists have pursued three major tendencies. Mainstream abstractionists, particularly those of the older generation, tend to be concerned primarily with seeking a personal aesthetic. They maintain that there is no such thing as African-American, or black, art, only good art. Consequently, they have been denounced by activist artists, stirred by social consciousness as well as by political ideology. The latter have adopted highly expressive representational styles as the means for communicating a distinctive black perspective directly to the people in their communities. Mediating between these two approaches is a more decorative form of art that frequently incorporates African, Caribbean, and even Mexican motifs. Abstraction has proved the most fruitful path because it allows black artists to achieve a universal, not only an ethnic, statement.

BEARDEN. No hard-and-fast rules separate these alternatives, however. Artists have often combined aspects of each into their individual styles. The most successful synthesis was realized by Romare Bearden (1911–1988). Although he got his start in the 1930s, it was not until the mid-1950s that he decided to devote his career entirely to art. Over the course of his long life, he pursued interests in mathematics, philosophy, and music that enriched his work. Bearden was affected by Abstract Expressionism, but, dissatisfied with the approach, he abandoned it in favor of a collage technique, although abstraction remained the underpinning of his art. His reputation was established during the mid-1960s by photomontages such as *The Prevalence of Ritual: Baptism* (fig. 24-69). Bearden's aim, as he put it, was to depict "the life of my people as I know it, passionately and dispassionately as Brueghel. My intention is to reveal through pictorial complexities the life I know." He had a full command of the resources of Western and African art. [See Primary Sources, no. 93, page 938.] Our example is as complex as Terbrugghen's *The Calling of St. Matthew* (see fig. 18-10), but it is couched in the forms of tribal masks. No wonder Bearden's work appeals to people of all races. His widespread popularity was a breakthrough that inspired other African-American artists.

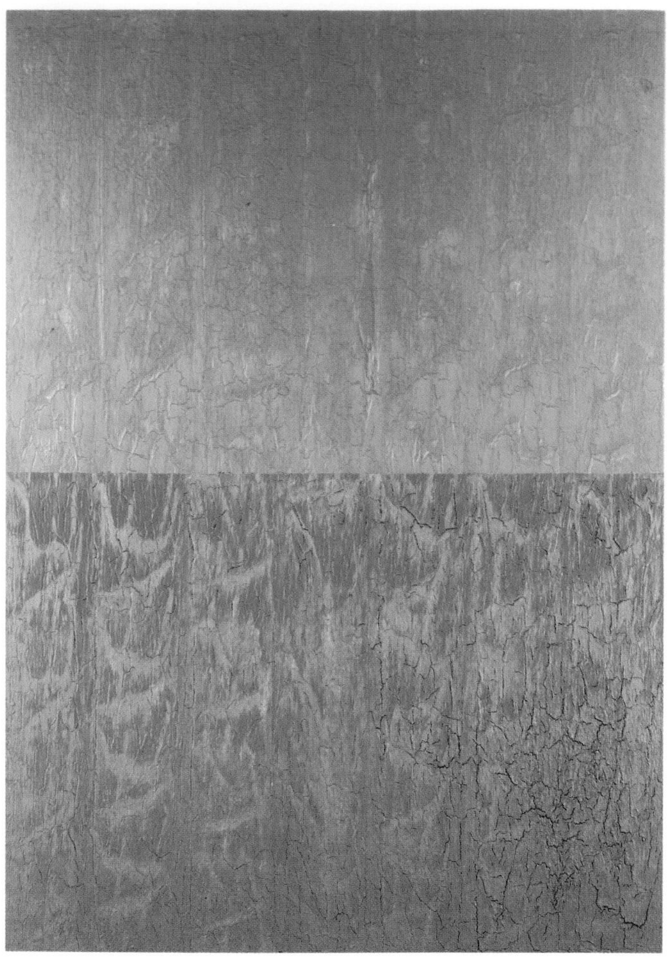

24-70. William T. Williams. *Batman*. 1979. Acrylic on canvas, 6'8" x 5' (2.03 x 1.52 m). Collection the artist

WILLIAMS. William T. Williams (b. 1942) belongs to the generation of African Americans born around 1940 who have brought black painting and sculpture to artistic maturity. He was initially a member of the "lost" generation of the lyrical Expressionists from the early 1970s whose contribution has been largely overlooked. After a period of intense self-scrutiny, he developed the sophisticated technique seen in *Batman* (fig. 24-70). His method can be compared to jazz improvisation, a debt that the artist himself has acknowledged. He interweaves his color and brushwork within a contrasting two-part structure that permits endless variations on the central theme. Although Williams is concerned mainly with formal issues, the play of color across the encrusted surface evokes memories of landscapes in the rural South where he spent his childhood.

SAUNDERS. With Williams, it is the intense effort to build up meaning through dense layers of paint within a clear framework that impresses. By contrast, the work of Raymond Saunders (b. 1934) has a spontaneity that also arises from memory. He was among the first artists to explore the urban African-American environment. His subjects are provided by graffiti, church facades, store signs, restaurant menus, and other commercial images. The specific combination in *White Flower Black Flower* (fig. 24-71) holds no specific meaning, which comes purely through free association. By the same token, there is no precise order, despite the rigorous underlying geometry. A brilliant technician, Saunders feels at liberty to juxtapose the representational and the abstract, "real" collage elements and "imitation" graffiti, pure geometry and painterly gesture. These components are nev-

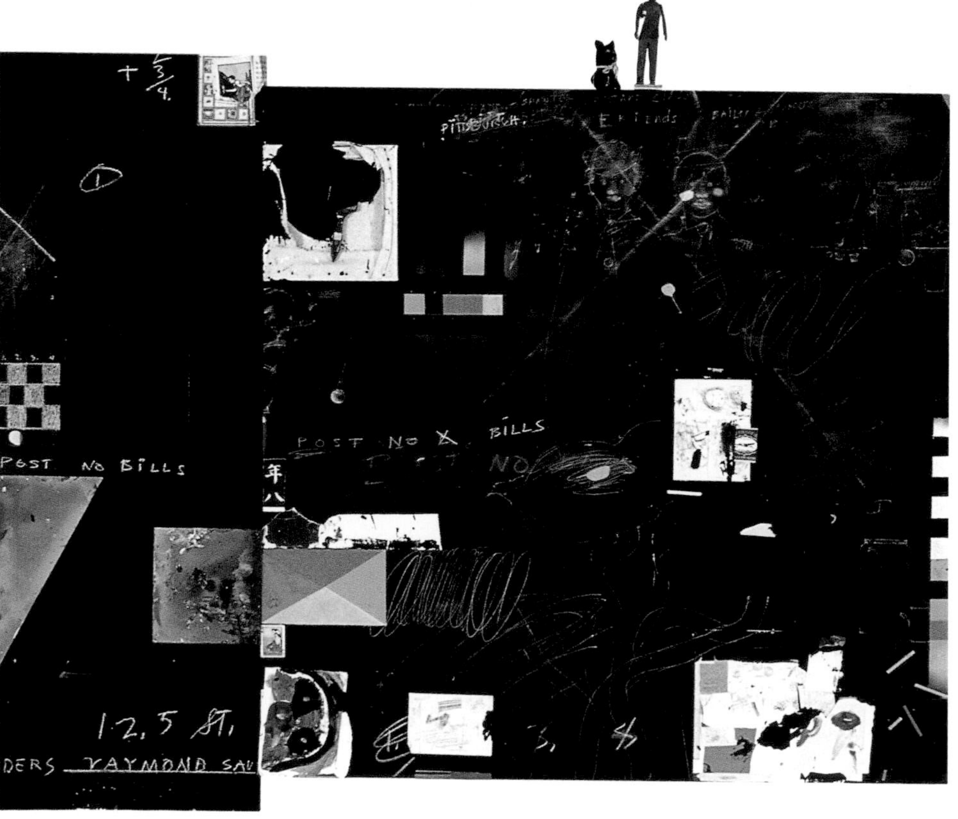

24-71. Raymond Saunders. *White Flower Black Flower*. 1986. Mixed media on canvas, 6'7" x 8'9¾" (2 x 2.53 m). Private collection

24-72. Josef Albers. *Apparition,* from *Homage to the Square* series. 1959. Oil on Masonite, 47½ x 47½" (120.7 x 120.7 cm). Solomon R. Guggenheim Museum, New York

ertheless related thematically and aesthetically through Saunders' experience. This approach permits him to have the best of both worlds by fusing the unique features of black culture with mainstream abstraction in a way that resists all stereotypes.

Op Art

A trend that gathered force in the mid-1950s was known as Op Art because of its concern with optics: the physical and psychological process of vision. Op Art has been devoted primarily to optical illusions. All representational art from the Old Stone Age onward has been involved with optical illusion in one sense or another. What is new about Op Art is that it is rigorously nonrepresentational. It evolved partly from hard-edge abstraction, although its ancestry can be traced back still further to Mondrian (see pages 796–97). At the same time, it seeks to extend the realm of optical illusion in every possible way by taking advantage of the new materials and processes supplied by science, including laser technology. Much Op Art consists of constructions or "environments" (see page 858) that are dependent for their effect on light and motion and cannot be reproduced satisfactorily in a book.

Because of its reliance on science and technology, Op Art's possibilities appear to be unlimited. The movement nevertheless matured within a decade of its inception and developed little thereafter. The difficulty lies primarily with its subject. Op Art seems overly cerebral and systematic, more akin to the sciences than to the humanities. It often involves the viewer with the work of art in a truly novel, dynamic way. But although its effects are undeniably fascinating, they involve a relatively narrow range of interests that lie for the most part outside the tradition of modern art. Only a handful of artists have enriched it with the variety and expressiveness necessary for great art.

ALBERS. Josef Albers (1888–1976), who came to America after 1933, when Hitler closed the Bauhaus school at Dessau (see page 868), became the founder of mainstream Op Art. He preferred to work in series, so that he could explore each theme fully before moving on to a new subject. Albers devoted the latter part of his career to color theory. *Homage to the Square* (fig. 24-72), his final series, is concerned with subtle color relations among simple geometric shapes, which he reduced to a few basic types. Within these limits, he was able to invent almost endless combinations based on rules he devised through ceaseless experimentation. Basically, Albers relied on color scales in which primary hues are desaturated in perceptually even gradations by giving them higher values (that is, by diluting them with white or gray). A step from one color scale can be substituted for the same step in another; these in turn can be combined by following the laws of color mixing, complementary colors, and so forth. This approach requires the utmost sensitivity to color, and even though the paint is taken directly from commercially available tubes, the colors bear a complex relation to one another. In our example, the artist creates a strong optical push-pull through the play of colors of contrasting value. The exact spatial effect is determined not only by the hue and the intensity of the pigments but by their sequence and the relative size of the squares.

MUSIC SINCE WORLD WAR II

At first glance, postwar music, like postwar art, seems almost chaotic in its diversity. Composers after 1945 have vastly extended the experiments of their early-twentieth-century predecessors. Many have resorted to extreme dissonance, incorporated chance (called *aleatory,* from the Latin word for dice) events, treated music as a form of noise, and abandoned traditional notation. Others have written for newly invented electronic instruments, turned to repetitive motifs, or looked to non-Western music for inspiration. While these innovations have widened the scope of contemporary music, they often, like Abstract Expressionist painting, place extreme demands on the audience, requiring that its listeners discard traditional standards to judge each work on its own terms. Nevertheless, certain sounds, textures, intervals, and rhythms are so widely used as to be virtual signatures of later twentieth-century music. Moreover, contemporary music is no more alien to most twentieth-century ears than that of the late Middle Ages or Early Renaissance.

The most important composer of the postwar era was the Frenchman Olivier Messiaen (1908–1992). Like his predecessor Francis Poulenc (1899–1963), Messiaen was a devout Catholic, and his music bears witness to his faith, which remained pure even in the face of great adversity. Despite his position as a leader of the avant-garde, Messiaen created music of a haunting beauty that makes it remarkably accessible. Nowhere is Messiaen's cosmic vision more fully realized than in *Colors of the Heavenly City* (1963) for piano and ensemble, a kaleidoscopic yet ethereal evocation of the Apocalypse that uses exotic instruments and compositional modes from India and the Orient to suggest a universal spirituality. His music radiates an enchantment with God's creation that led him to incorporate transcriptions of bird songs in the delightful *Exotic Birds* (1955–56), for he delighted in and revered these simple creatures much as St. Francis of Assisi had before him. There is an intimate connection between these works: Messiaen associated the colors of the heavenly city with the brilliant plumage of birds, whose songs provided the inspiration for his music.

Messiaen was one of the first composers to apply the principles of serialism to timbre (tone color), time, rhythm, and dynamic level. His interest in twelve-tone techniques was stimulated by his pupils Pierre Boulez (b. 1925) and Karlheinz Stockhausen (b. 1928), on whom he in turn exerted a decisive influence. Boulez, the most intellectual composer on the scene today, has likewise extended serialism in all directions but came to reject the twelve-tone row for a themeless (athematic) style that also permits carefully calculated "chance" effects and sometimes incorporates "concrete" (recorded) music (see below). *The Hammer Without a Master* (1954), inspired by the Surrealist poetry of René Char (1907–1988), has a rhythmic liveliness that belies its highly theoretical conception; by contrast, *Pli selon pli (Fold by Fold;* 1957–62), a sustained work for soprano and orchestra utilizing poems by Mallarmé, demands the utmost concentration to absorb its subtleties. The choice of Mallarmé is significant in itself. Not only was his Symbolist poetry the point of departure for Surrealists such as Char but he was the first to allow reciters the opportunity to vary the choice and sequence of poems at will, a technique that Boulez used in *Pli selon pli* and that Stockhausen exploited around the same time.

Stockhausen's compositions, though no less complex than Boulez's, are more visceral in their power. He became associated early on with Pierre Schaeffer (b. 1910), the leading composer of "concrete" music consisting of recorded natural sounds. Soon after the electronic synthesizer was invented in Germany in 1950, Stockhausen turned to it while continuing to compose for traditional instruments. These strands merged in the mid-1950s, when he experimented with multiple orchestras and choruses placed in different arrays under separate conductors. He also explored a succession of moments in time as a replacement for form, which he subsequently abandoned for free form that allowed players to improvise on brief texts.

The Polish composer Witold Lutoslawski (1913–1994) turned to serialism and aleatory music in 1958, despite the fact that such Western techniques were officially frowned on by Communist authorities. His mature instrumental and orchestral works, such as *Venetian Games* (1961), accord well with the music of Messiaen and Boulez, and he became among the most respected composers of the European avant-garde. After 1975 he pursued a more personal style that culminated in his fourth and final symphony, written in 1992, which begins with an evocation of haunting mystery and ends with a thunderous climax. Lutoslawski began his career in the mold of Bartók, who exercised considerable influence on other members of the Polish school as well. Krzysztof Penderecki (b. 1933) is a miniaturist at heart noted for his discrete use of dissonance. He shares spiritual concerns with Henryk Górecki (b. 1933), whose tonalism and traditional religious emphasis have made him very popular in the West in recent years.

The preeminent English composer of the second half of the century was Benjamin Britten (1913–1976), who came to maturity during World War II. He is principally known for vocal music—including operas, of which *Peter Grimes* (1945) is the outstanding example; choral works, most notably the large-scale *War Requiem* (1962), which is rooted in the idealistic English tradition; and assorted songs, many written with the tenor Peter Pears in mind. His collaborations with the poet W. H. Auden were especially successful. Britten was also an excellent writer of music for the cello, string quartet, and chamber orchestra. These more intimate, private works perhaps best reveal the dark, almost quirky side of his imagination. He was a musician's musician and collaborated with many of the great instrumentalists of the day. He was further important for helping to revive interest in Henry Purcell (see page 588), whose work he greatly admired. Britten's contemporary, Michael Tippett (1905–1997), possessed comparable abilities and in addition was a fine symphonic composer; but because he was an iconoclast who broke the rules in such works as the oratorio *A Child of Our Time* (1939–41), recognition came later to him.

From the beginning the French-born composer Edgar Varèse (1883–1965) was a consummate maverick. Influenced by the "Brutism" of the Futurists, he became fascinated by sounds of all sorts and soon began to utilize sirens and unusual percussion instruments to create novel effects. His major early contribution was three works written between 1918 and 1927 after he emigrated to the United States—*Amériques, Arcana,* and *Intégrales*—that treat the orchestra as a form of organized noise. All are marked by extreme dynamism in rhythm and volume. It is suggestive of Varèse's role in overturning tradition that *Arcana* is the kind of music Sibelius would have written if he had been a modernist composer in the vein of Stravinsky. Though he was a ceaseless experimenter, he never developed a system, which he considered a sign of impotence. It was not until the invention of the tape recorder in 1948 and the synthesizer two years later that Varèse found a medium ideally suited to his extraordinary vision. (He had tried to convince Bell Laboratories to set up an experimental research center around 1930 and even stopped composing around 1937 because he could not achieve the sounds he wanted.) Electronics allowed him to create and mix sounds of every conceivable sort into a new kind of total sound experience: the *poème électronique,* for the 1958 Brussels World's Fair, which stands as the first great masterpiece of American electronic music.

Varèse was precocious not only in coming to America at an early date but also in advocating experimental techniques far in advance of their time. American music reached maturity simultaneously with American art in the early 1950s and for many of the same reasons. During World War II many of Europe's leading composers—Stravinsky, Bartók, Hindemith, and Schoenberg among them—came to the United States, where they exercised considerable influence. The most important American composer of the postwar era was John Cage (1912–1992), who studied with Cowell, Varèse, and Schoenberg. Cage nevertheless owed his unique approach to music primarily to his wide range of interests: he made prints, composed scores for and toured with the avant-garde choreographer Merce Cunningham (b. 1919), and organized light shows, among his many activities. During the 1940s he extended Cowell's use of the "prepared" piano by adding bits of "debris" from everyday life to produce unusual sounds. Like many American intellectuals during the 1950s he became interested in Zen Buddhism, which helped stimulate his fascination with chance events. "Chance" for Cage, however, must be understood not as total randomness but as improvisation within a defined context, since Cage considered music a kind of organized noise within the stream of life itself. For example, *Imaginary Landscape No. 4* (1951) uses 12 radios tuned to different frequencies established by the score, though the final result was unpredictable because what each radio was playing could not be predetermined. Such an attitude, we realize, comes very close to that of the Abstract Expressionists, particularly Jackson Pollock, who also relied on chance as a reflection of life. Like Messiaen, Cage sought a spiritual experience in his music; toward that end, silence—what is not there—is often just as important as the sounds themselves.

The foremost disciple of the synthesizer in America has been Milton Babbitt (b. 1916), who helped to found the Columbia-Princeton Electronic Music Center in 1959. Like Boulez, he seeks to apply serialism to all aspects of music, including his quartets and compositions for orchestra, which incorporate synthesized sounds. Despite its profoundly logical basis, his music can be surprisingly expressive, almost in spite of itself. Babbitt studied under Roger Sessions (1896–1985), an early pioneer of modernism along with Copland. The symphonies and chamber music Sessions composed after adopting the 12-tone system in 1953

(box continues on following page)

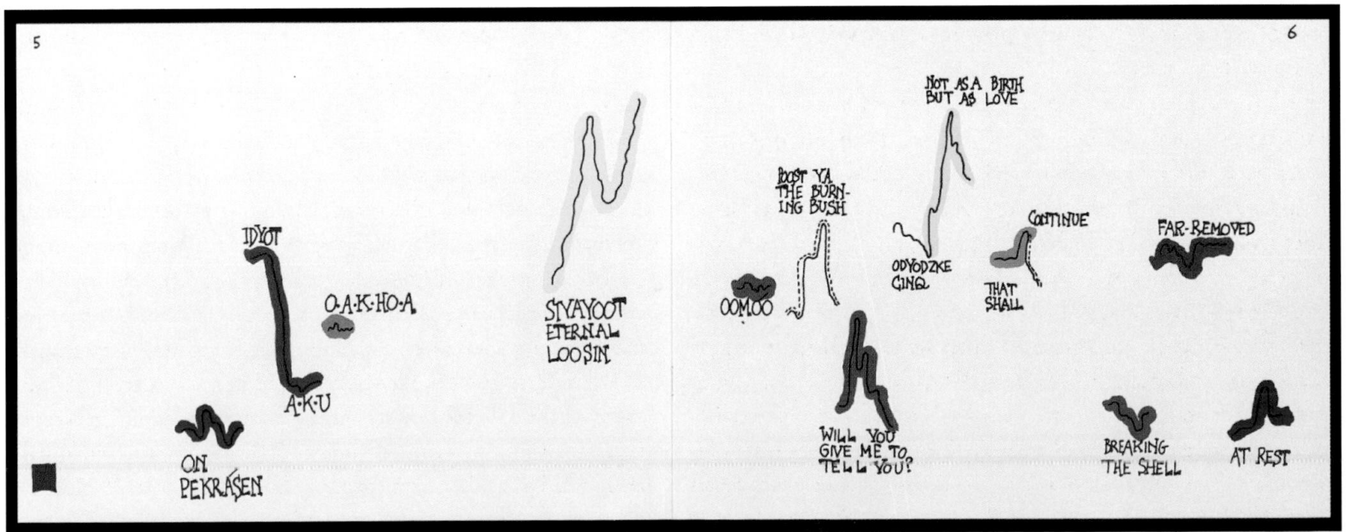

John Cage. *Aria, Voice (any range)*. 1960. Score for a multilingual solo vocal work

©1960 BY HENMAR PRESS, INC., NEW YORK. INTERNATIONAL COPYRIGHTS SECURED. ALL RIGHTS RESERVED.
REPRINTED BY PERMISSION OF C. F. PETERS CORPORATION

MUSIC SINCE WORLD WAR II *(continued from preceding page)*

established him as one of America's leading composers. His masterpiece is the cantata *When Lilacs Last in the Dooryard Bloom'd* (1970), a haunting evocation of verses by Walt Whitman (1819–1892), the greatest of all American poets, dedicated to John F. Kennedy and Martin Luther King, Jr. Whitman's poem was written as "A Requiem for Those We Love" in memory of Abraham Lincoln and those who had fallen during the American Civil War, and the cantata also evokes the sadness and turmoil surrounding the Vietnam War, as does Sessions' powerful seventh symphony from the same years. Paul Hindemith had successfully used the same poem as the basis for a lyrical elegy to Franklin D. Roosevelt following World War II, which he spent in the United States after his music was banned by the Nazis. Of equal stature is *Time Cycle* (1960) by Lukas Foss (b. 1922), who was born in Europe and educated in Paris but came at the age of 15 to the United States, where he completed his training in Philadelphia. Commissioned for the soprano Adele Addison, it consists of four extended songs based on English and German poetry that includes improvised interludes. Perhaps the most gifted member of the American school to emerge since World War II is Elliott Carter (b. 1908). His four quartets are the finest since Bartók's, while *Variations for Orchestra* is the outstanding contribution to orchestral music in the United States from the 1950s.

The compositions of Luciano Berio (b. 1925), a former associate of Stockhausen who emigrated to the United States, are minidramas (he often composes for the stage as well), which utilize every available modernist technique. He often treats the human voice as another instrument while employing speechlike sounds to suggest different emotional states. Of particular interest are the works he wrote for his wife, the soprano Cathy Berberian (1925–1983), notably *Recital* (1971), which deals with the nervous collapse of a singer. George Crumb (b. 1929), the most important American composer to emerge in the 1960s, has also used the human voice in new ways. *Ancient Voices of Children* (1970), one of the great masterpieces of the twentieth cen-

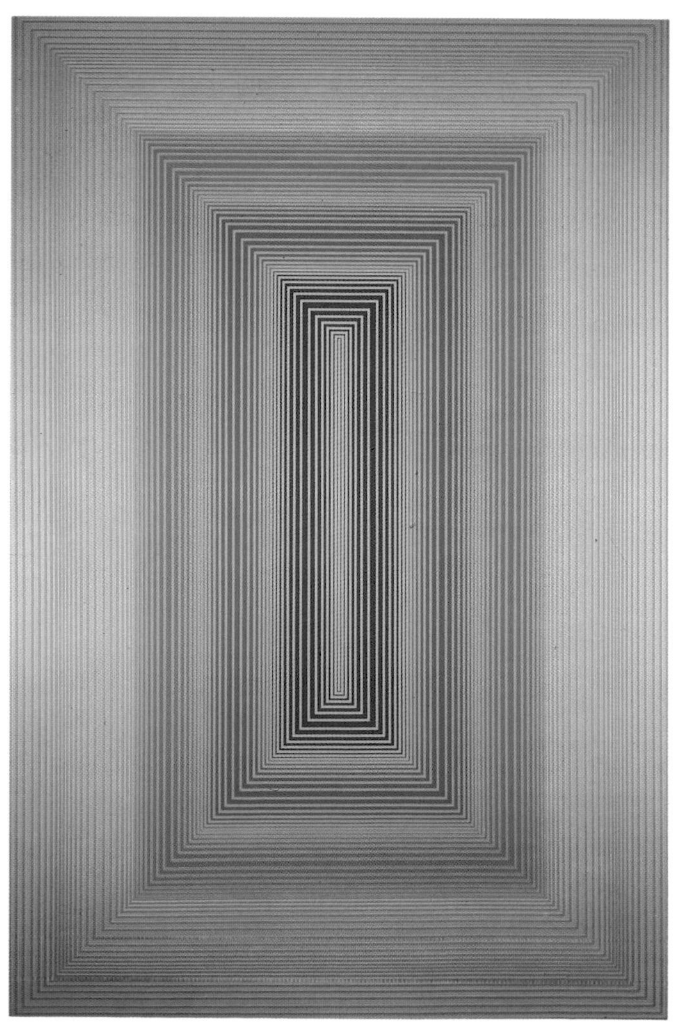

24-73. Richard Anuszkiewicz. *Entrance to Green*. 1970. Acrylic on canvas, 9 x 6' (2.74 x 1.83 m). Collection the artist

ANUSZKIEWICZ. Albers was an important teacher as well as theorist. His gifted pupil Richard Anuszkiewicz (b. 1930) developed his art by relaxing Albers' self-imposed restrictions. In *Entrance to Green* (fig. 24-73), the ever-decreasing series of rectangles creates a sense of infinite recession toward the center. This rhythm is counterbalanced by the color pattern, which brings the center close to us by the gradual shift from cool to warm tones as we move inward from the periphery. Surprising for such an avowedly theoretical work is its expressive intensity. The resonance of the colors within the strict geometry heightens the optical push-pull. Remarkably, the painting can be likened to a modern icon, capable of producing an almost mystical effect for those attuned to its unique vision.

Pop Art

Other artists who made a name for themselves in the mid-1950s rediscovered what the public continued to take for granted despite all efforts to persuade otherwise: that a picture is *not* "essentially a flat surface covered with colors," as Maurice Denis had insisted, but an image wanting to be recognized. If art was by its very nature representational, then the modern movement, from Manet to Pollock, was based on an error, no matter how impressive its achievements. Painting, it seemed, had been on a kind of voluntary starvation diet for the past hundred years, feeding upon itself rather than on the world around us. It was time to give in to the "image-hunger" that had built up. The public at large had never suffered from this drought, since its appetite for images was abundantly supplied by photography, advertising, magazine illustrations, and comic strips.

The artists who felt this way seized on the products of commercial art catering to popular taste. Here, they realized, was an tury, incorporates motifs similar to those of South and Central American Indians to conjure up a primeval state with unforgettable power. Like almost all of Crumb's vocal works, it is based on the poetry of Federico García Lorca, the early Spanish modernist (1892–1936) whose work was inspired as much by music and art as it was by poetic tradition. Crumb's work belongs to no school. Neither did that of Samuel Barber (1910–1981), a romantic with an extraordinary gift for melody. Although he felt the influence of Stravinsky's Neoclassicism, Barber's compositions for voice use dissonance discreetly to emphasize the text, to which he had a unique sensitivity. *Knoxville: Summer of 1915* (1947), commissioned by the soprano Eleanor Steber and set to a famous poem by James Agee, is surely the most purely beautiful vocal work by any American composer of the twentieth century.

The main tendency to emerge in recent years has been dubbed Minimalism, which uses many of the same devices as the art movement of the same name, albeit for different ends. It relies on the repetition of simple motifs that are gradually varied over time to create a hypnotic, almost mystical, effect, as in *Drumming* (1970–71) by Steve Reich (b. 1936) and *In C* (1964) by Terry Riley (b. 1943). These techniques were first explored by Stockhausen, whose music shares an inspiration in Eastern religion with Riley's. The most sophisticated products of Minimalism are the operas of Philip Glass (b. 1937), above all *Satyagraha* ("truth-force," a Sanskrit word that refers to the philosophy of nonviolent resistance practiced by Mahatma Gandhi and Martin Luther King, Jr.). Minimalism is ideally suited to the text, which is drawn from the *Bhagavad-Gita,* a part of the major Hindu religious epic known as the *Mahabharata.* Minimalism responds to the music and philosophy of other cultures, from Africa to Asia, but it also represents a "crossover" music that incorporates jazz and popular music, including rock and roll. It reinvests contemporary music with a tonality and accessibility that have won new audiences for the concert hall. In the process, it has enjoyed increasing influence—the recent symphonies of Henryk Górecki use Minimalist devices, for example.

essential aspect of our century's visual environment that had been entirely disregarded as vulgar and antiaesthetic by the representatives of "highbrow" culture. It was a presence that cried out to be examined. Only Marcel Duchamp and some of the Dadaists, with their contempt for all orthodox opinion, had dared to enter this realm (see page 798). It was they who now became the patron saints of Pop Art, as the new movement came to be called.

HAMILTON. Pop Art actually began in London in the mid-1950s with the Independent Group of artists and intellectuals. They were fascinated by the impact on British life of the American mass media, which had been flooding England ever since the end of World War II. The first work that can be called an outright statement of Pop Art was a small collage (fig. 24-74) made in 1956 by Richard Hamilton (b. 1922), a follower of Marcel Duchamp. It already incorporates most of the subject matter that was taken up by later artists: comic

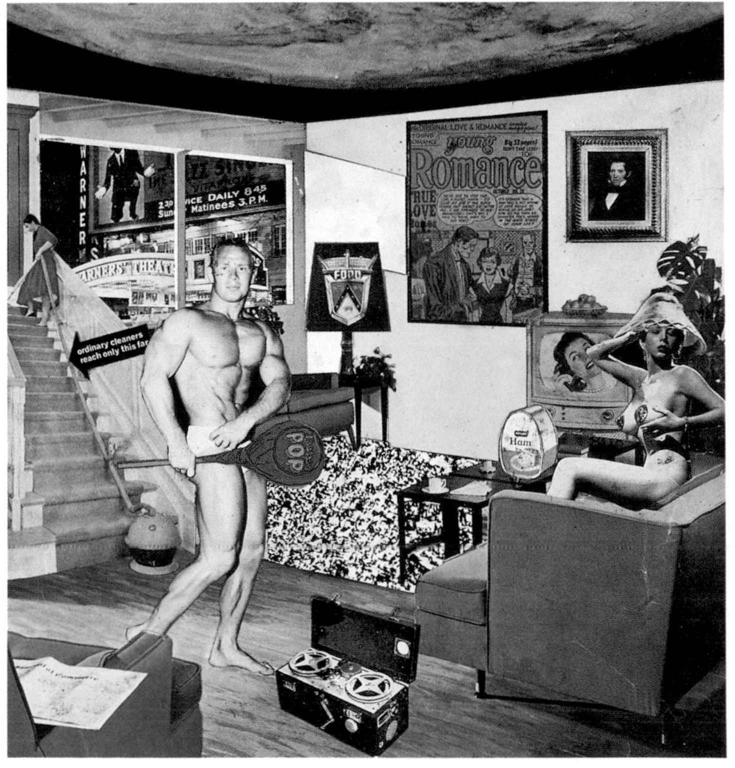

24-74. Richard Hamilton. *Just What Is It That Makes Today's Home So Different, So Appealing?* 1956. Collage on paper, 10¼ x 9¼" (26 x 24.8 cm). Kunsthalle Tübingen. Sammlung Zundel, Germany

strips, cinema, commercial design, nudes, cheap decor, appliances—all tokens of modern materialistic culture. Hamilton wrote that "popular culture abstracted from Fine Art its role of myth-maker. If the artist is not to lose much of his ancient purpose, he may have to plunder the popular arts to recover the imagery which is his rightful inheritance. Pop-Fine-Art . . . upholds a respect for culture of the masses and a conviction that the artist in twentieth-century urban life is inevitably a consumer of mass culture and potentially a contributor to it." [See Primary Sources, no. 94, page 939.]

It is not surprising that the new art had a special attraction for America and that it reached its fullest development there during the following decade. In retrospect, Pop Art in the United States was an expression of the optimistic spirit of the 1960s that began with the election of John F. Kennedy and ended at the height of the Vietnam War. Unlike Dada, Pop Art was not motivated by despair or disgust at contemporary civilization. It viewed commercial culture as its raw material, an endless source of pictorial subject matter, rather than as an evil to be attacked. Nor did Pop Art share Dada's aggressive attitude toward the established values of modern art.

JOHNS. The work of Jasper Johns (b. 1930), one of the pioneers of Pop Art in America, raises questions that go beyond the boundaries of the movement. Johns began by painting, with great precision, such familiar objects as flags, targets, numerals, and maps. His *Three Flags* (fig. 24-75) presents an intriguing problem: just what is the difference between image and reality? We instantly recognize the Stars and Stripes, but if we try to define what we actually see here, we find that the answer escapes us. The flags, instead of waving or flopping, stand at attention, as it were, rigidly aligned with one another in a kind of reverse perspective. Yet there is movement of another sort. The reds, whites, and blues are not areas of solid color but are subtly modulated. Can we really say, then, that this is an image of three flags? Clearly, no such flags can exist anywhere except in the artist's head. The more we think about it, the more we begin to recognize the picture as a feat of the imagination—probably the last thing we expected to do when we first looked at it.

LICHTENSTEIN. Revolutionary though it was, Johns' use of flags, numerals, and similar elements as pictorial themes had to some extent been anticipated 30 years earlier by another American painter, Charles Demuth, in such pictures as *I Saw the Figure 5 in Gold* (see fig. 24-35). Roy Lichtenstein (1923–1997), in contrast, turned to comic strips—or, more precisely, to the standardized imagery of the traditional strips devoted to violent action and sentimental love rather than those bearing the stamp of an individual creator. His paintings, such as *Drowning Girl* (fig. 24-76), are greatly enlarged copies of single frames, including the speech balloons; the impersonal, simplified black outlines; and the dots used for printing color on cheap paper. [See Primary Sources, no. 95, page 939.]

These pictures are perhaps the most paradoxical in the entire field of Pop Art. Unlike any other paintings past or present, they cannot be accurately reproduced in this book, for they then become indistinguishable from real comic strips. Enlarging a design meant for an area only a few inches square to one several hundred times greater gave rise to a host of problems: how, for example, to draw the girl's nose so it would look "right" in comic-strip terms or how to space the colored dots so they would have the proper weight in relation to the outlines.

Clearly, our picture is not a mechanical copy but an interpretation. In fact, it is excerpted from the original panel. It neverthe-

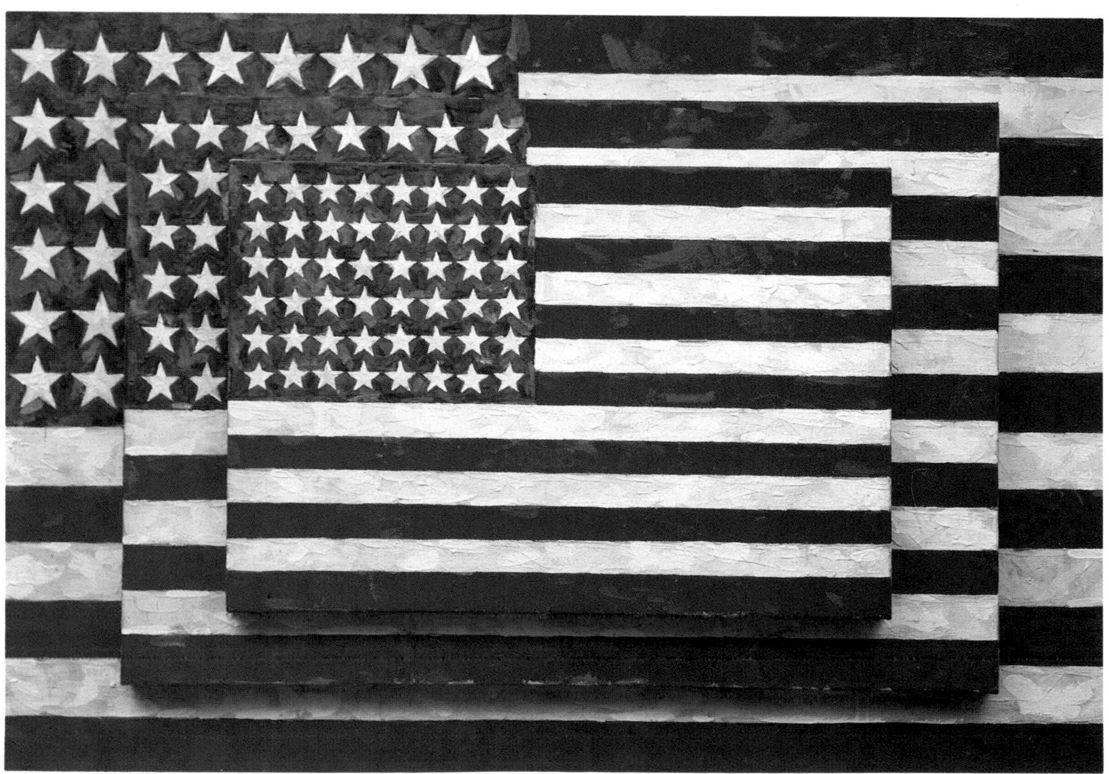

24-75. Jasper Johns. *Three Flags*. 1958. Encaustic on canvas, 30⅞ x 45½ x 5" (78.4 x 115.6 x 12.7 cm). Whitney Museum of American Art, New York less remains faithful to the spirit of the original because of the countless changes and adjustments the artist has introduced. How is it possible for images of this sort to be so instantly recognizable? Why are they so "real" to millions of people? What fascinates Lichtenstein about comic strips—and what he makes us see for the first time—are the rigid conventions of their style, as firmly set and as remote from life as those of Byzantine art.

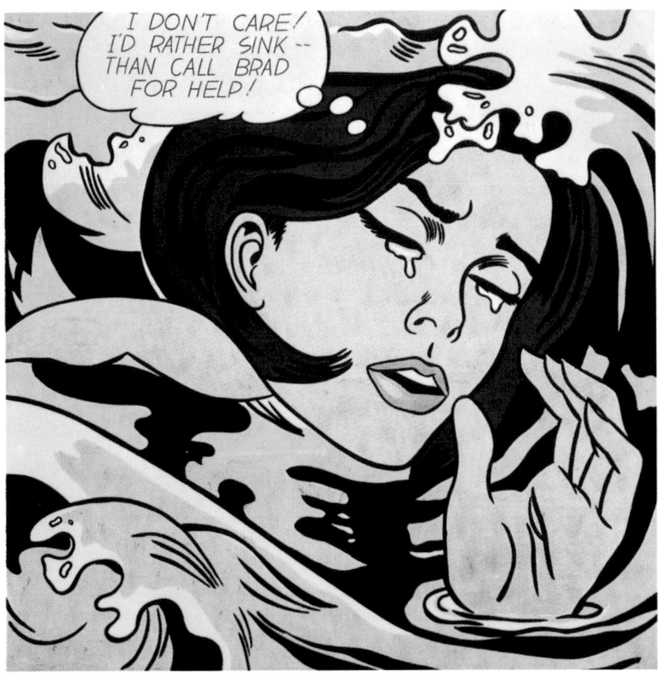

24-76. Roy Lichtenstein. *Drowning Girl.* 1963. Oil and synthetic polymer paint on canvas, 67 5/8 x 66 3/4" (171.6 x 169.5 cm). The Museum of Modern Art, New York

PHILIP JOHNSON FUND AND GIFT OF MR. AND MRS. BAGLEY WRIGHT

WARHOL. Andy Warhol (1928–1987) used this very quality in ironic commentaries on modern society. A former commercial artist, he made the viewer consider the aesthetic qualities of everyday images, such as soup cans, that we readily overlook. He did much the same thing with the subject of death, an obsession of his. In silk-screened pictures of electric chairs and gruesome traffic accidents, dying has been reduced to the same banality as in the mass media. Warhol had an uncanny understanding of how newspapers and television shape our view of people and events, how they create their own reality and larger-than-life figures. He became a master at manipulating the media to project a public image that disguised his true character. These themes come

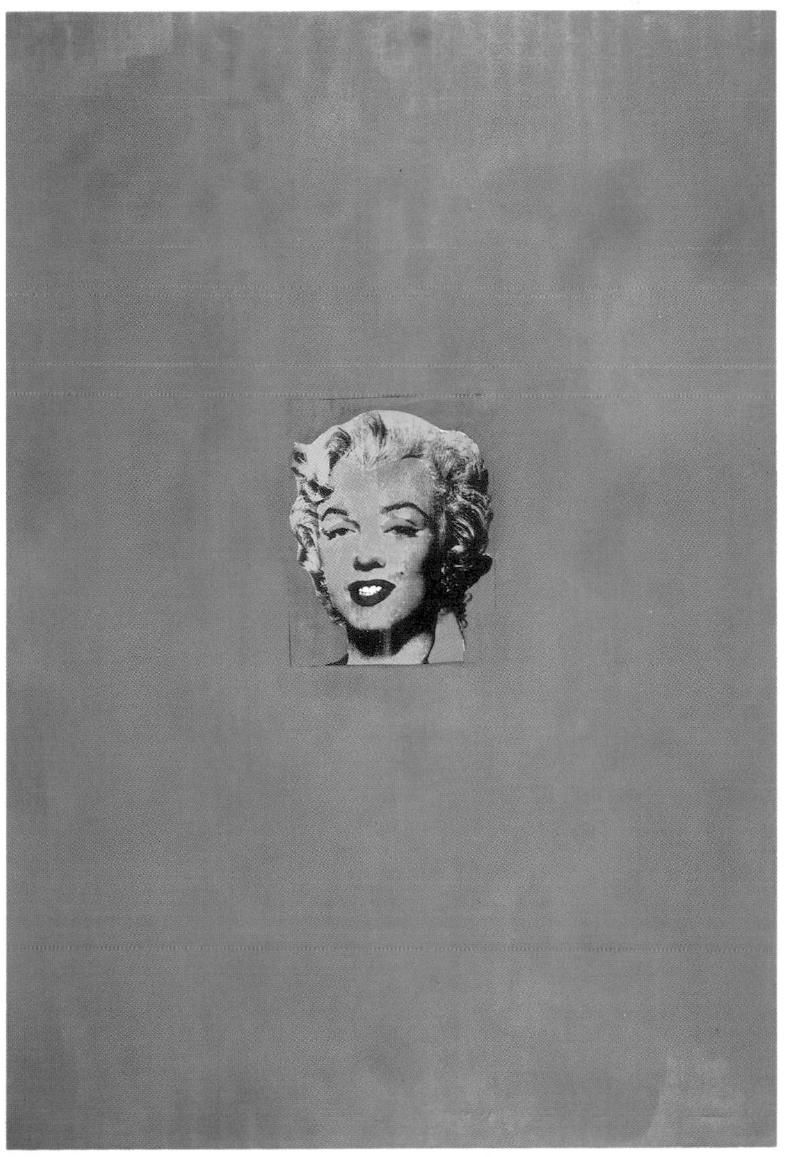

24-77. Andy Warhol. *Gold Marilyn Monroe.* 1962. Synthetic polymer paint, silk-screened, and oil on canvas, 6'11 1/4" x 4'7" (2.12 x 1.4 m). The Museum of Modern Art, New York

GIFT OF PHILIP JOHNSON

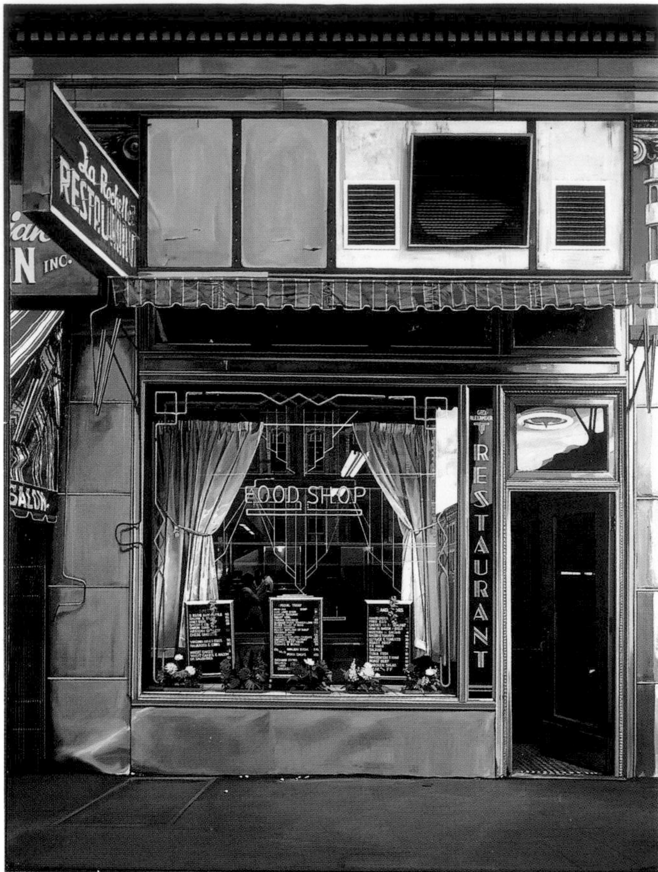

24-78. Richard Estes. *Food Shop*. 1967.
Oil on linen, $65\frac{7}{8}$ x $48\frac{1}{2}$" (166.7 x 123.2 cm).
Museum Ludwig, Cologne

together in his *Gold Marilyn Monroe* (fig. 24-77). Set against a gold background, like a Byzantine icon, she becomes a modern-day Madonna. Yet Warhol conveys a sense of the tragic personality that lay behind the famous movie star's glamorous facade. The color, lurid and off-register like a reproduction in a sleazy magazine, makes us realize that she has been reduced to a cheap commodity. Through mechanical means, she is rendered as impersonal as the Virgin that stares out from the thousands of icons produced by hack artists throughout the ages.

Photorealism

Although Pop Art was sometimes referred to as "the new realism," the term hardly seems to fit the painters we have discussed. To be sure, they remain true to their sources. However, their material is rather abstract: flags, numerals, lettering, signs, badges, comic strips. A more recent offshoot of Pop Art is the trend called Photorealism because of its fascination with camera images. Photographs had been used by nineteenth-century painters soon after the "pencil of nature" was invented (one of the earliest to do so, surprisingly, was Delacroix), but they were no more than a convenient substitute for reality. For the Photorealists, in contrast, the photograph itself is the reality on which to build their pictures.

ESTES. The acknowledged grand master of Photorealism is Richard Estes (b. 1936). His work is marked by its technical perfection, which turns Photorealism into a form of Magic Realism. This ability, however masterful, is no better than that of any competent illustrator; nor does it distinguish Estes from the Precisionists, who often used photographs as the basis for their paintings. What, then, is the key to his success? It lies in his choice of subject and composition. Estes has a preference for storefronts of an earlier time that evoke nostalgic memories. In this he is like an archaeologist of modern urban life. His best paintings, such as *Food Shop* (fig. 24-78), show the same uncanny ability to strike a responsive chord as Hopper's *Early Sunday Morning* (see fig. 24-56). The more we look at it, the more we realize that the gridlike composition is as subtly balanced as a painting by Mondrian (compare fig. 24-37). Unlike the photograph on which it was based, Estes' canvas shows everything in uniformly sharp focus, articulating details lost in the shadows. In this way Estes makes his humble storefront an arresting visual experience fully worthy of our attention.

FEMINISM. Photorealism was part of a general tendency that marked American painting in the 1970s: the resurgence of realism. It took on a wide range of themes and techniques, from the most personal to the most detached, depending on the artist's vision of objective reality and its subjective significance. Its flexibility made realism a sensitive vehicle for the feminist movement that came to the fore in the same decade. Beyond the organizing of groups dedicated to a wider recognition for women artists, feminism in art has shown little of the unity that initially characterized the social movement. Many feminists, for example, turned to "traditional" women's crafts, particularly textiles, or incorporated crafts into a collage approach known as Pattern and Decoration. In painting, however, the majority pursued different forms of realism for a variety of ends.

FLACK. Women artists such as Audrey Flack (b. 1931) have used realism to explore the world around them and their relation to it from a personal as well as a feminist viewpoint. Like most of Flack's paintings, *Queen* (fig. 24-79) is an extended allegory. The queen is the most powerful figure on the chessboard, yet she remains expendable in defense of the king. Equally apparent is the meaning inherent to the title Queen of Hearts, but here the card also refers to the passion for gambling in Flack's family, represented by photos of the artist and her mother in the open locket. The contrast of youth and age is central to *Queen.* The watch is a traditional emblem of life's brevity, and the dewy rose stands for transience of beauty, which is further conveyed by the makeup on the dressing table. The suggestive shapes of the bud and fruits can also be seen as symbols of feminine sexuality.

Queen is successful not so much for its statement, no matter how interesting, as for its imagery. Flack creates a purely artistic reality by superimposing two separate photographs. Critical to the illusion is the gray border, which acts as a framing device and also establishes the central space and color of the painting. The objects that seem to project from the picture plane are shown in a different perspective from those on the tilted tabletop behind. The

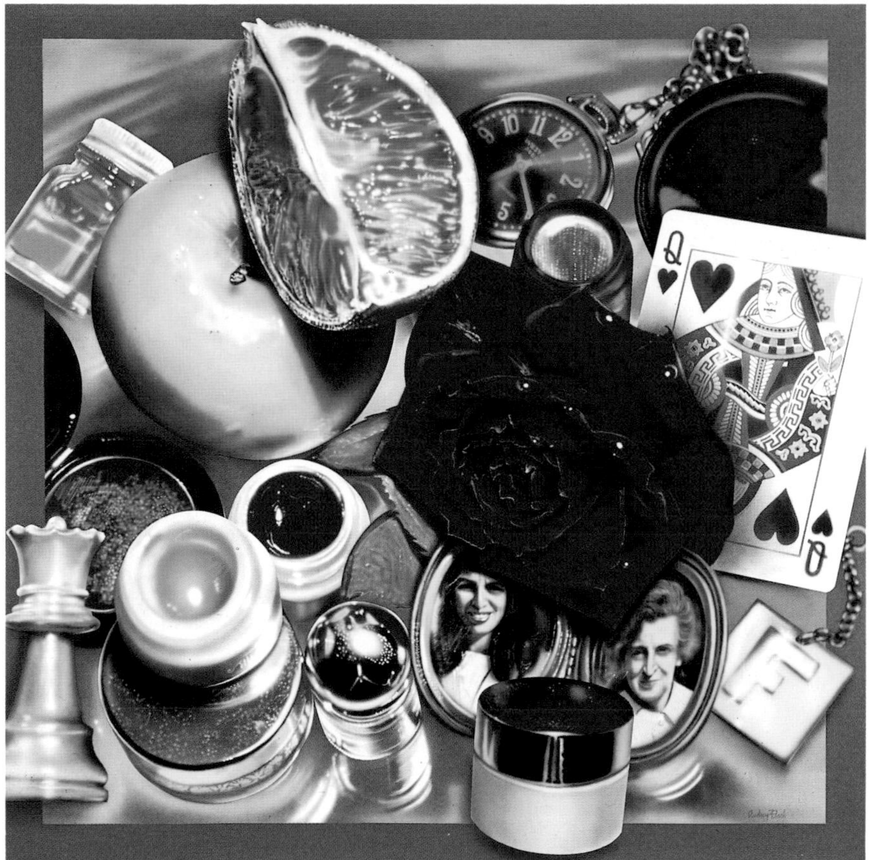

24-79. Audrey Flack. *Queen.* 1975–76. Acrylic on canvas, 6'8" (2.03 m) square. Private collection
COURTESY LOUIS K. MEISEL GALLERY, NEW YORK

picture space is made even more active by the play of its colors within the neutral gray zone.

LATE MODERNISM

Neo-Expressionism

The art we have looked at since 1945, although distinctive to the postwar era, is so closely related to what came before it that it was clearly cut from the same cloth, and we do not hesitate to call it modernist. At long last, however, twentieth-century painting, to which everything from Abstract Expressionism to Photorealism made such a vital contribution, began to lose strength. The first sign of decline came in the early 1970s with the widespread use of "Neo-" to describe the latest tendencies, which came and went in rapid succession and are all but forgotten today. Only one of these movements has made a lasting contribution: Neo-Expressionism, which arose toward the end of the '70s and became the dominant current of the 1980s. Indeed, imagery of all kinds completely overshadowed the tendency called Neo-Abstraction (also known as "Neo-Geo"), to the point where abstraction itself was declared all but dead by the critics. In its place was left a feeble imitation, which indicated that modern art had turned its back to the mainstream. And despite the fact that Neo-Expressionism is deeply rooted in modernism, there can be little question that it represents the end of the tradition we have traced in this chapter.

Europe

CLEMENTE. The Italian Francesco Clemente (b. 1952) is in many respects representative of his artistic generation in Europe. As a result of his association with the *Arte Povera* ("Poor Art") movement in Italy, he developed a potent Neo-Expressionist style. Clemente's career took a decisive turn in 1982 when he decided to go to New York in order "to be where the great painters have been." But he has also spent a great deal of time in India, where he has been inspired by Hinduism. His canvases and wall paintings sometimes have the ambitiousness of allegorical cycles in the manner of the Italian painters who worked on a grand scale, starting with Giotto. His most compelling works, however, are those that take the artist's moods, fantasies, and appetites as their subjects. Clemente is fearless in recording urges and memories that the rest of us repress. Art becomes for him an act of cathartic necessity that releases, but never resolves, the impulses that assault his acute self-awareness. His self-portraits (fig. 24-80) suggest a soul bombarded by drives and sensations that can never be truly enjoyed. Alternately fascinating and repellent, his pictures remain curiously unsensual, yet their expressiveness is riveting. Since his work responds to fleeting states of mind, Clemente utilizes whatever style or medium seems appropriate to capturing the transient phenomena of his inner world. He is unusual among Italians in being influenced heavily by Northern European Symbolism and Expressionism, with an occasional reminiscence of Surrealism. Here indeed is his vivid nightmare, having the masklike features

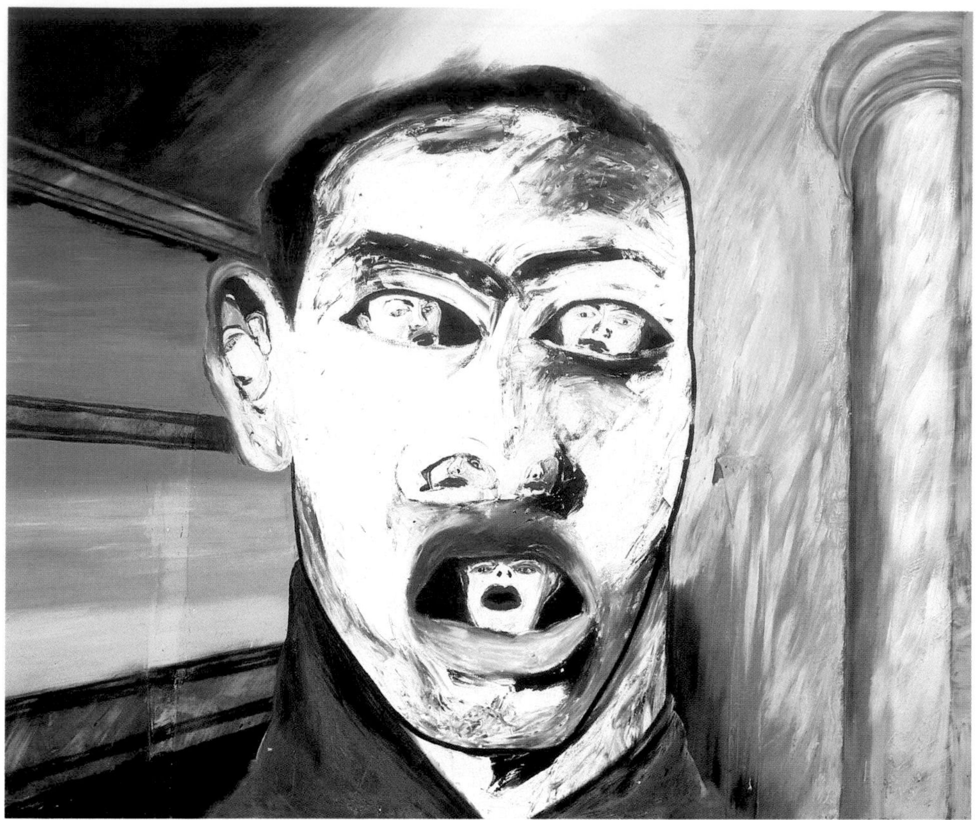

24-80. Francesco Clemente. *Untitled.* 1983. Oil and wax on canvas, 6'6" x 7'9" (1.98 x 2.36 m)
COURTESY THOMAS AMMANN, ZURICH

of Ensor, the psychological terror of Munch, and the haunted vision of De Chirico.

KIEFER. The German artist Anselm Kiefer (b. 1945) is the direct heir to Northern Expressionism, but rather than investigating personal moods he confronts moral issues posed by Nazism that have been evaded by other postwar artists in his country. By exploring the major themes of German Romanticism from a modern perspective, he has attempted to reweave the threads broken by history. That tradition, which began as a noble ideal based on a similar longing for a mythical past, ended as a perversion at the hands of Hitler and his followers.

To the Unknown Painter (fig. 24-81) is a powerful statement of the human and cultural catastrophe presented by World War II. Conceptually as well as compositionally, it was inspired by the paintings of Caspar David Friedrich (see page 680), of which it is a worthy successor. To express the tragic proportions of the Holocaust, Kiefer works on an epic scale. Painted in jagged strokes of predominantly earth and black tones, the charred landscape is made tangible by the inclusion of pieces of straw. Amid this destruction stands a somber ruin: it is shown in woodcut to proclaim Kiefer's allegiance to the German Renaissance and to Expressionism. The fortresslike structure is a suitable monument for heroes in recalling the tombs and temples of ancient civilizations (see figs. 2-6 and 3-4). But instead of being dedicated to soldiers who died in combat, it is a memorial to the painters whose art was also a casualty of war.

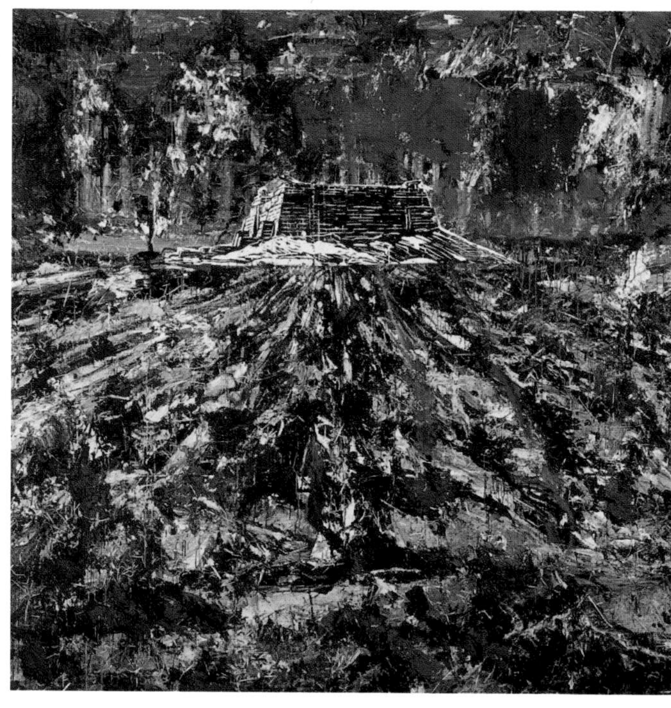

24-81. Anselm Kiefer. *To the Unknown Painter.* 1983. Oil, emulsion, woodcut, shellac, latex, and straw on canvas, 9'2" (2.79 m) square. The Carnegie Museum of Art, Pittsburgh
RICHARD M. SCAIFE FUND; A. W. MELLON ACQUISITION ENDOWMENT FUND

United States

ROTHENBERG. Neo-Expressionism has found its most gifted American representative in Susan Rothenberg (b. 1945). She once said, "In terms of goals, I'd like to be like Mondrian in the control I'd exert." Yet her painting *Mondrian* (fig. 24-82) hardly seems to pay homage to that artist. The composition has been pared down to a figure and a shadow placed uncomfortably close to the edge of the canvas: "It all comes back to trying to invent new forms to stand in for the body since I don't want to make a realist painting. I wanted to get that body down in paint, free it from its anatomical confines. A lot of my work is about body orientation, both in the making of the work and in the sensing of space, comparing it to my own physical orientation." The sheer beauty of the surface belies the intensity of the image. The figure emerges from the feathery brushstrokes like an apparition from a nightmare. The face, which bears Mondrian's unmistakable features, is a vision of madness. We have seen its likes before in Bacon's *Head Surrounded by Sides of Beef* (see fig. 24-64). The picture announces Rothenberg's allegiance to Expressionism. Whether intentional or not, it is a highly charged commentary on Mondrian, whose rigorous discipline is so contrary to her painterly freedom.

BARTLETT. Jennifer Bartlett (b. 1941) has long been recognized as a talented painter; missing, however, was content worthy of her ability. Like Audrey Flack before her (see page 830), she eventually turned to a traditional subject for material. The four elements, a popular theme with artists during the Baroque and Rococo periods, provided the focus for an extensive series that is as rich in meaning as it is in appearance. *Water* (fig. 24-83), though reminiscent of Monet's *Water Lilies* (see fig. 22-17), is no mere evocation of nature. Floating half-in, half-above the water is a skeleton. The real subject here is Vanitas, another theme associated with the elements and, in turn, the senses and the seasons (see page 568). References to Fate, inexorable and quixotic, are found in the cards, dominoes, and other devices used in games and fortune-telling. These are seemingly "stuck" onto the canvas, along with illusionistic swatches of plaid material, which serve to deny the illusionism of the scene and emphasize the surface as an independent entity; hence, too, the red container that seems to hover nonsensically in midair. This play between 2-D and 3-D has much the same effect as in Audrey Flack's *Queen* (see fig. 24-79), and it shares a similar purpose. It both enlivens the painting and places it at one remove from everyday reality. We are forced to contemplate its message instead of seeing it simply as a picture.

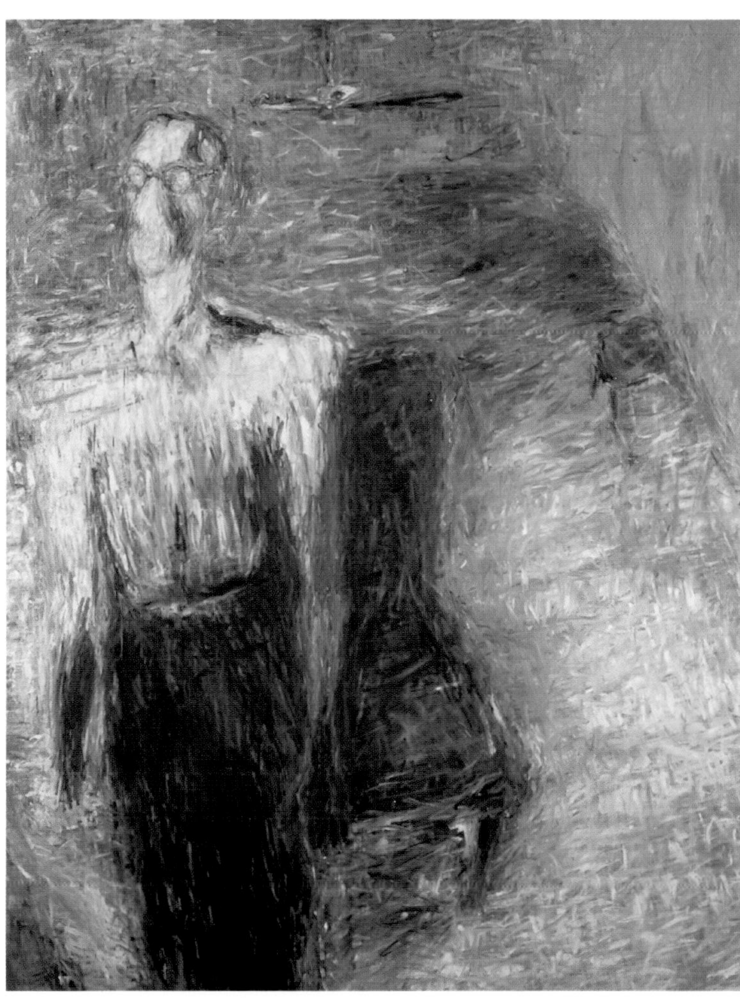

24-82. Susan Rothenberg. *Mondrian.* 1983–84. Oil on canvas, 9'1" x 7' (2.8 x 2.1 m). Private collection

COURTESY SPERONE WESTWATER GALLERY, NEW YORK

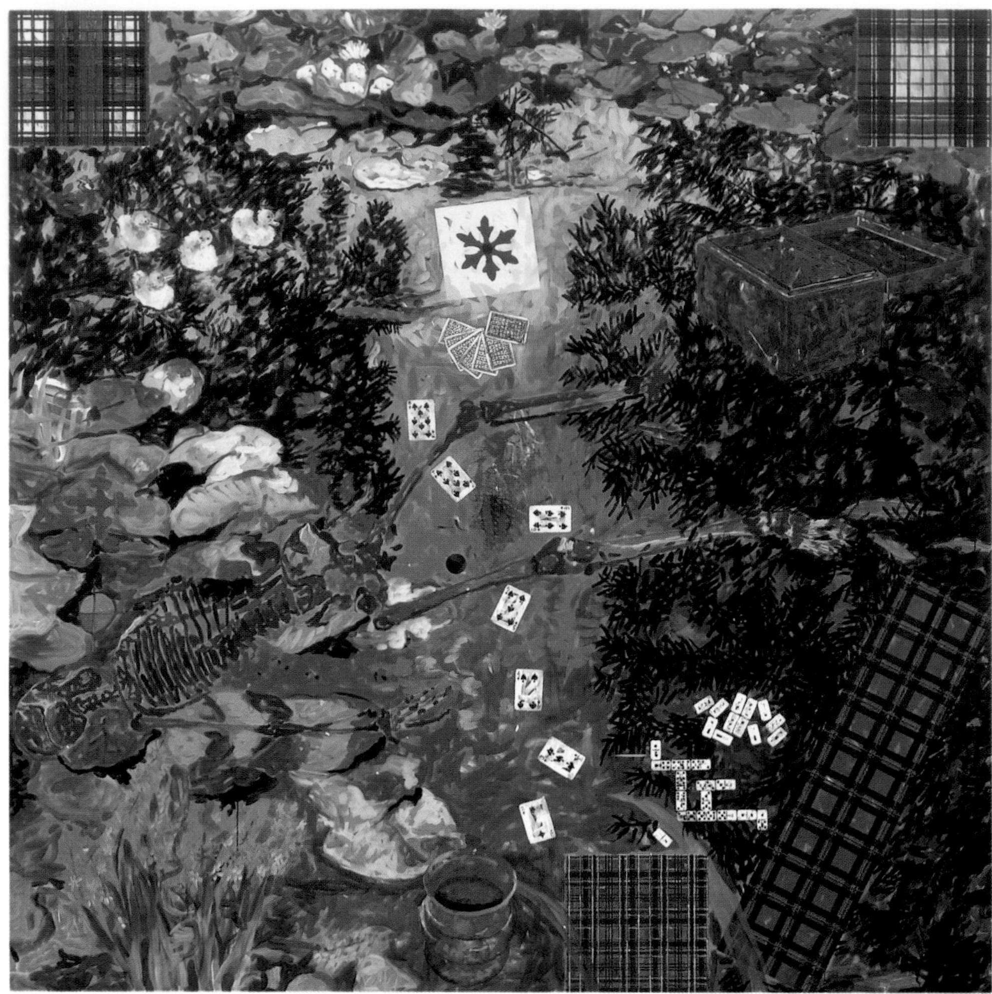

24-83. Jennifer Bartlett. *Water.* 1990. Oil on canvas, 7 x 7' (2.13 x 2.13 m). Private collection, Honolulu, Hawaii

MURRAY. Neo-Expressionism has a counterpart in Neo-Abstraction, which has yielded less impressive results thus far. The greatest successes have come from artists who have invested Neo-Abstraction with the personal meaning of Neo-Expressionism. Elizabeth Murray (b. 1940) has emerged since 1980 as the leader of this crossover style in America. *More Than You Know* (fig. 24-84) makes a fascinating comparison with Flack's *Queen* (see fig. 24-79), for both are packed with autobiographical references. While it is at once simpler and more abstract than Flack's painting, Murray's composition seems about to fly apart under the pressure of barely contained emotions. The table will remind us of the one in Picasso's *Three Musicians* (see fig. 24-26), a painting she referred to in other works from the same time. The contradiction between the flattened collage perspective of the table and chair and the allusions to the distorted three-dimensionality of the surrounding room creates a disquieting pictorial space. The more we look at the painting, the more we begin to realize how eerie it is. Indeed, it seems to radiate an almost unbearable tension. The table threatens to turn into a figure, surmounted by a skull-like head, that moves with the explosive force of Picasso's *Three Dancers* (see fig. 24-28). What was Murray thinking of? She has said that the room reminds her of the place where she sat with her ill mother. At the same time, the demonic face was inspired by Munch's *The Scream* (see fig. 23-21), while the sheet of paper recalls Vermeer's paintings of women reading letters (see fig. 18-29), which to her express a combination of serenity and anxiety.

WALKINGSTICK. An artist who has managed to combine Neo-Expressionism and Neo-Abstraction in a particularly fruitful way is Kay WalkingStick (b. 1935). Part Cherokee, she was deeply affected by her Native-American spiritual heritage, especially its reverence for the earth, although she was raised among whites. The death of her husband in 1989 brought forth the literal outpouring of grief seen in *On the Edge* (fig. 24-85), which combines two separate landscape forms in a format that she had experimented with briefly several years earlier. The two halves respond to entirely different impulses. The left panel, built up in thick coats of paint applied mainly with her hands, continues the abstract manner she had developed successfully over more than a decade. In the center is a fan shape, which both suggests a man-made feature in a primitive landscape—like those of the ancient mound builders—and acts as a sign, investing the canvas with

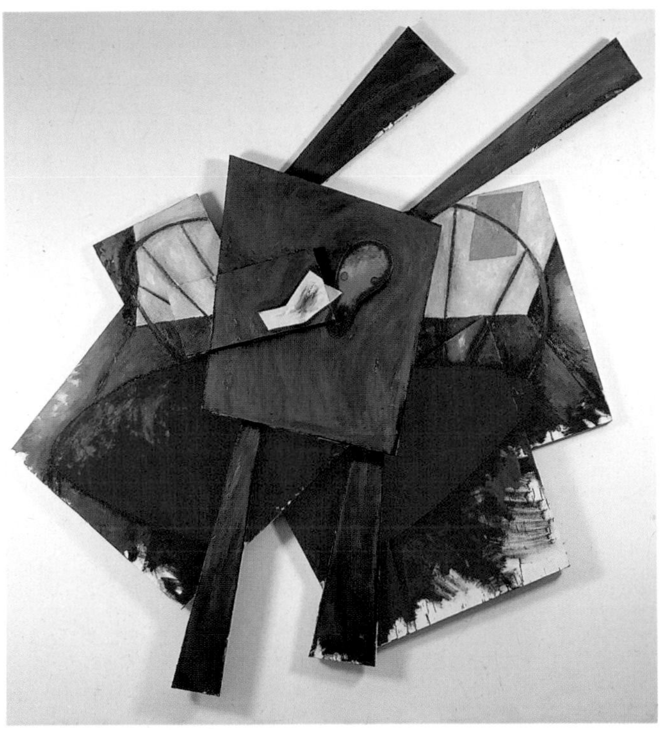

24-84. Elizabeth Murray. *More Than You Know.* 1983. Oil on ten canvases, 9'3" x 9' x 8" (2.8 m x 2.7 m x 20.3 cm). The Edward R. Broida Trust

COURTESY PACEWILDENSTEIN, NEW YORK

mysterious emblematic significance. The right half, painted in an Expressionist style, unleashes a torrent of anguish that is further expressed by the violent color. This duality has several layers of meaning. It can be seen as describing the contrasting aspects of nature as spiritual center and generative force, of order and chaos, or of calm contemplation and powerful emotion. Thus both parts of the diptych are necessary to give the painting its full meaning.

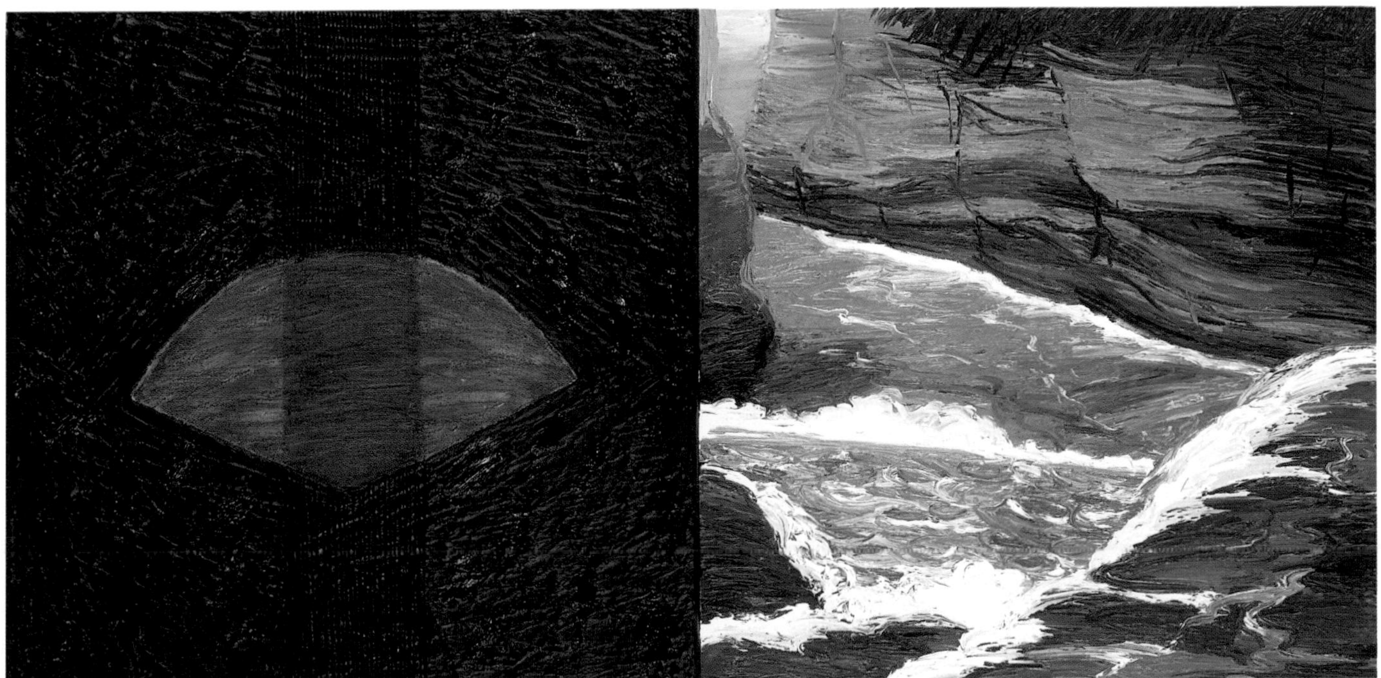

24-85. Kay WalkingStick. *On the Edge.* 1989. Acrylic, wax, and oil on canvas, 32 x 64 x 3½" (81.3 x 162.6 x 9 cm)

COURTESY M-13 GALLERY, NEW YORK

CHAPTER TWENTY-FIVE

Twentieth-Century Sculpture

SCULPTURE BEFORE WORLD WAR I

Sculpture, the most conservative of the arts throughout most of the nineteenth century, found it difficult to escape tradition. It remained far less adventurous on the whole than painting, which often influenced it. The American sculptor David Smith (see page 848) even claimed that modern sculpture was created by the painters, and to a remarkable degree he was right. Sculpture has successfully challenged the leadership of painting in our time only by following a separate path.

MATISSE. Some of the most important experiments in sculpture were conducted by Henri Matisse. During the years 1907 to 1914, he was inspired by ethnographic sculpture, following on a growing interest in "primitive" art on the part of painters like Gauguin even before the first major public collections began to be formed in 1890. *Reclining Nude I* of 1907 (fig. 25-1) is a counterpart to Matisse's painting *Blue Nude* from the same year, which shares its "savage" element. Sculpture was a natural complement to Matisse's pictures. It allowed him to investigate problems of form that in turn provided important lessons for his canvases. The bulging distortions in *Reclining Nude* create an astonishing muscular tension. Yet the artist was concerned above all with what he called "arabesque": it is the rhythmic contours that define the nude. We will recognize the statuette's kinship with the reclining figures in *The Joy of Life* (see fig. 24-1), which were also conceived in outline. Now, however, these rhythms are explored plastically and manipulated for expressive effect. Remarkably, Matisse accomplished this aim without diminishing the fundamentally classical character of the nude.

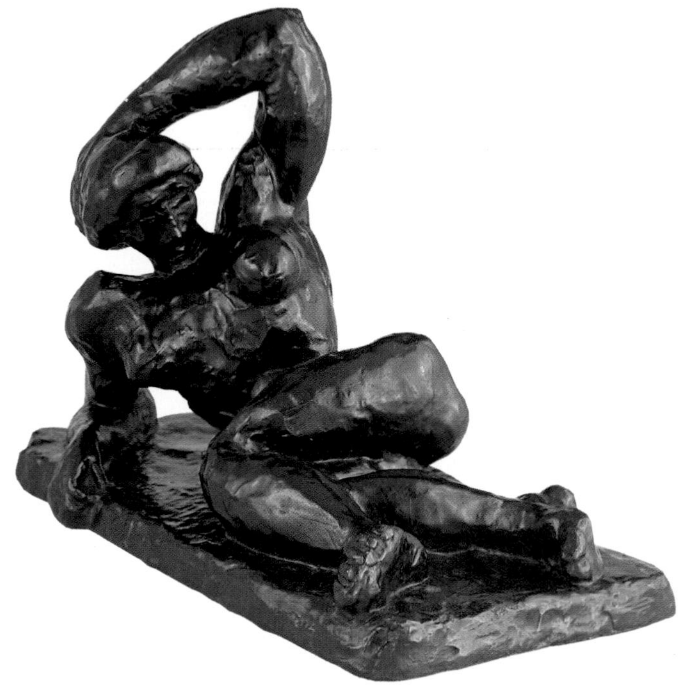

25-1. Henri Matisse. *Reclining Nude I.* 1907. Bronze, 13⁹⁄₁₆ x 19⅝ x 11" (34.5 x 49.9 x 28 cm). The Baltimore Museum of Art

THE CONE COLLECTION, FORMED BY DR. CLARIBEL CONE AND MISS ETTA CONE OF BALTIMORE, MARYLAND

BRANCUSI. Sculpture remained only a sideline for Matisse. Perhaps for that reason, Expressionism was a much less important current in sculpture than in painting. This fact may seem surprising, since the rediscovery of ethnographic art by the Fauves might have been expected to have a strong impact on sculptors. The only one who shared in this interest, however, was Constantin Brancusi (1876–1957), a Romanian who went to Paris in 1904. He was fascinated with the formal simplicity and coherence of primitive carvings rather than with their "savage" expressiveness. This concern is evident in *The Kiss* (fig. 25-2), executed in 1909 and now placed over a tomb in a Parisian cemetery.

The compactness and self-sufficiency of this group are a radical step beyond Maillol's *Seated Woman* (see fig. 23-26), to which it is related much as the Fauves are to Post-Impressionism. Brancusi has a "genius of omission" not unlike Matisse's. And his attitude toward art expresses the same optimistic faith so characteristic of early modernism: "Don't look for mysteries," he said. "I give you

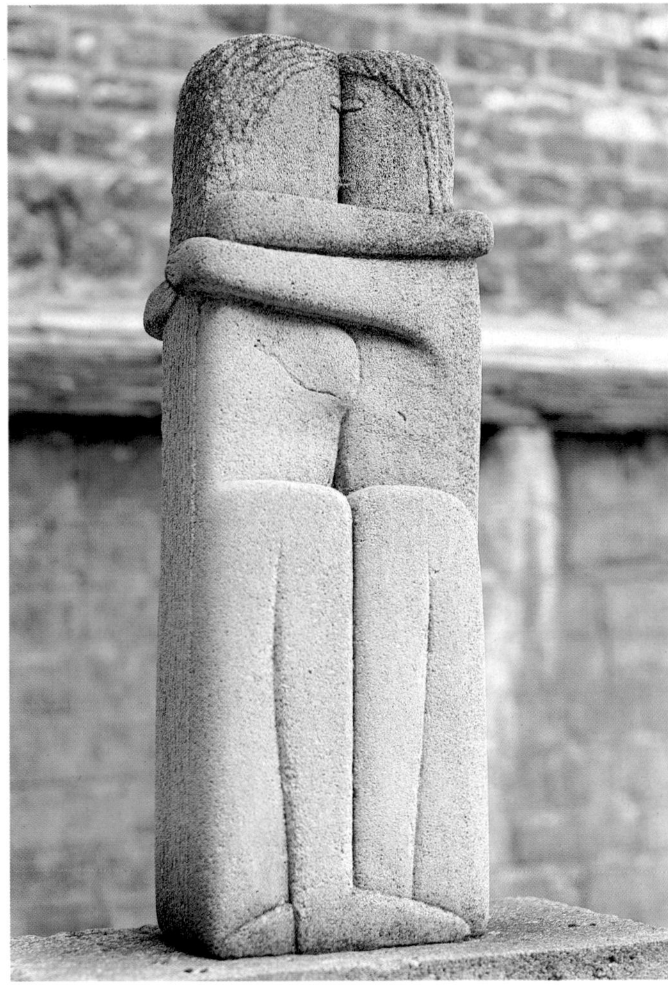

25-2. Constantin Brancusi. *The Kiss.* 1909. Stone, height 35¼" (89.5 cm). Tomb of T. Rachevskaia, Montparnasse Cemetery, Paris

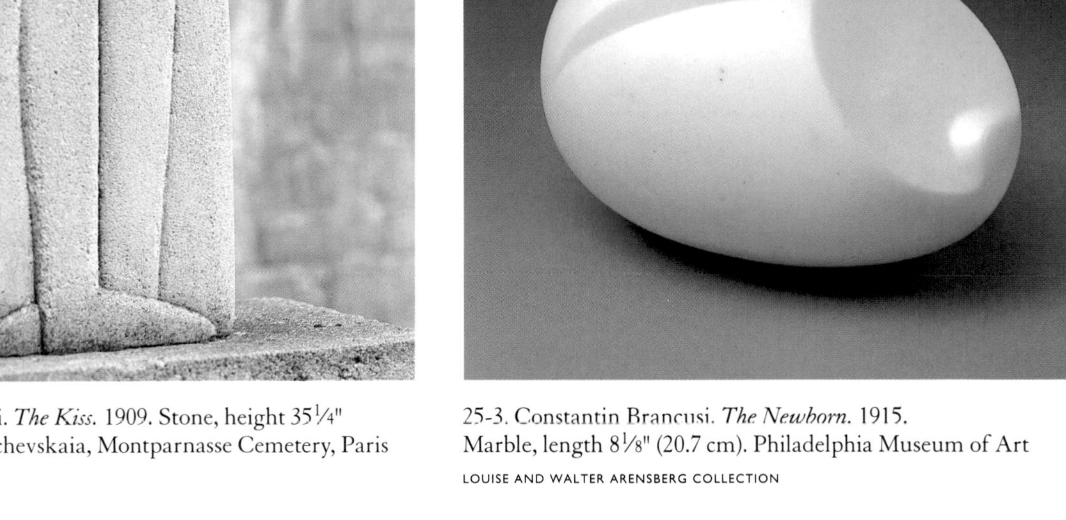

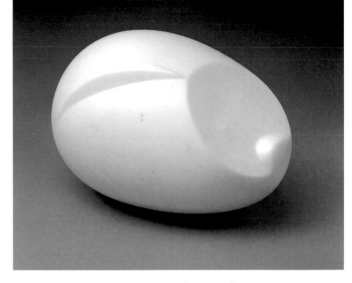

25-3. Constantin Brancusi. *The Newborn.* 1915. Marble, length 8⅛" (20.7 cm). Philadelphia Museum of Art
LOUISE AND WALTER ARENSBERG COLLECTION

pure joy." To him, a monument was a permanent marker, like the steles of the ancients: an upright slab, symmetrical and immobile, and he disturbed this basic shape as little as possible. The embracing lovers are differentiated just enough to be separately identifiable, and they seem more primeval than primitive. They are a timeless symbol of generation, innocent and anonymous—the exact opposite of Rodin's *The Kiss* (see fig. 22-30), where the contrast of flesh and stone mirrors the dualism of guilt and desire. Herein lies the genius of Brancusi: he posed the first successful alternative to Rodin, whose vast authority overwhelmed the creativity of many younger sculptors. In the process, Brancusi gave modern sculpture its independence.

Brancusi's work took another daring step about 1910, when he began to produce nonrepresentational pieces in marble or metal. (He reserved his "primeval" style for wood and stone.) They fall into two groups: variations on the egg shape and soaring, vertical "bird" motifs. In concentrating on two basic forms of such uncompromising simplicity, Brancusi strove for essences, not for Rodin's illusion of growth. He was fascinated by the contrast of life as potential and as kinetic energy—the self-contained perfection of the egg, which hides the mystery of all creation, and the pure dynamics of the creature released from this shell. *The Newborn* (fig. 25-3) is a marvelously concise and witty, yet surprisingly sympathetic, portrayal of an infant's first cry upon entering the world.

Bird in Space (fig. 25-4), made more than a decade later, is the culmination of Brancusi's art. It began as the figure of a mythical bird that talks, which he gradually simplified until it is no longer the abstract image of a bird. Rather, it is flight itself, made visible and concrete. "All my life I have sought the essence of flight," Brancusi stated, and he repeated the motif in variants of ever greater refinement. Its disembodied quality is emphasized by the high polish that gives the surface the reflectivity of a mirror, thus establishing a new continuity between the molded space within and the free space without.

CUBISM. In the second decade of the century a number of artists tackled the problem of body-space relationships with the formal tools of Cubism. This was no simple task, since Cubism was a painter's approach more suited to shallow relief and not easily adapted to objects in the round. Most of the Cubist painters attempted at least a few sculptures, but the results were generally timid. Picasso's tentative efforts at sculpture attest to the difficulties he faced, yet they were of fundamental importance nonetheless. His attempts to translate the Analytic Cubism seen in *Portrait of Ambroise Vollard* (see fig. 24-14) into three-dimensional form succeeded only partially in breaking up the solid surface. Precisely because its facets are ambiguous in density and location, painting afforded an infinitely richer experience both visually and expressively.

DUCHAMP-VILLON. The boldest solution to the problems posed by Analytic Cubism in sculpture was achieved by the sculptor Raymond Duchamp-Villon (1876–1916), an older brother of Marcel Duchamp, in *The Great Horse* (fig. 25-5). He began with abstract studies of the animal, but his final version is an image of "horsepower." The body has become a coiled spring and the legs resemble piston rods. These quasi-mechanical shapes have a dynamism that is entirely persuasive because of this very remoteness from their anatomical model.

BOCCIONI. In 1912 the Futurists suddenly became absorbed with making sculpture, which they sought to redefine as radically as painting. They used "force-lines" to create an "arabesque of directional curves" as part of a "systematization of the interpenetration of planes." Hence, as Umberto Boccioni declared, "We break open the figure and enclose it in environment." His running figure titled *Unique Forms of Continuity in Space* (fig. 25-6) is as breathtaking in its complexity as Brancusi's *Bird in Space* is simple. Boccioni has attempted to represent not the human form itself but the imprint of its motion upon the surrounding air. The figure itself remains concealed behind its "garment" of atmospheric turbulence. The picturesque statue recalls the famous Futurist statement that "the roaring automobile is more beautiful than the Winged Victory," although it obviously owes more to the *Winged Victory* (the *Nike of Samothrace,* see fig. 5-75) than to the design of motor cars. (In 1913, fins and streamlining were still to come.)

25-4. Constantin Brancusi. *Bird in Space* (unique cast). 1928. Bronze, 54 x 8½ x 6½" (137.2 x 21.6 x 16.5 cm). The Museum of Modern Art, New York

GIVEN ANONYMOUSLY

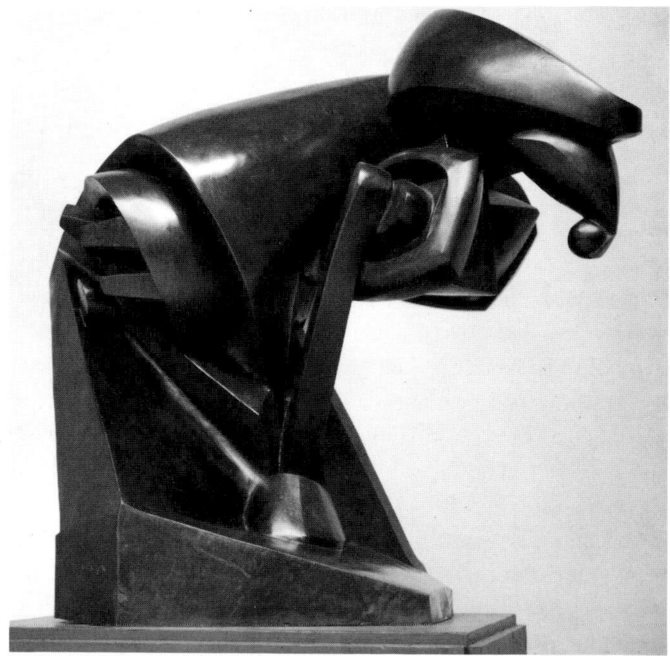

25-5. Raymond Duchamp-Villon. *The Great Horse.* 1914. Bronze, height 39¼" (99.7 cm). The Art Institute of Chicago

GIFT OF MISS MARGARET FISHER IN MEMORY OF HER PARENTS, MR. AND MRS. WALTER L. FISHER

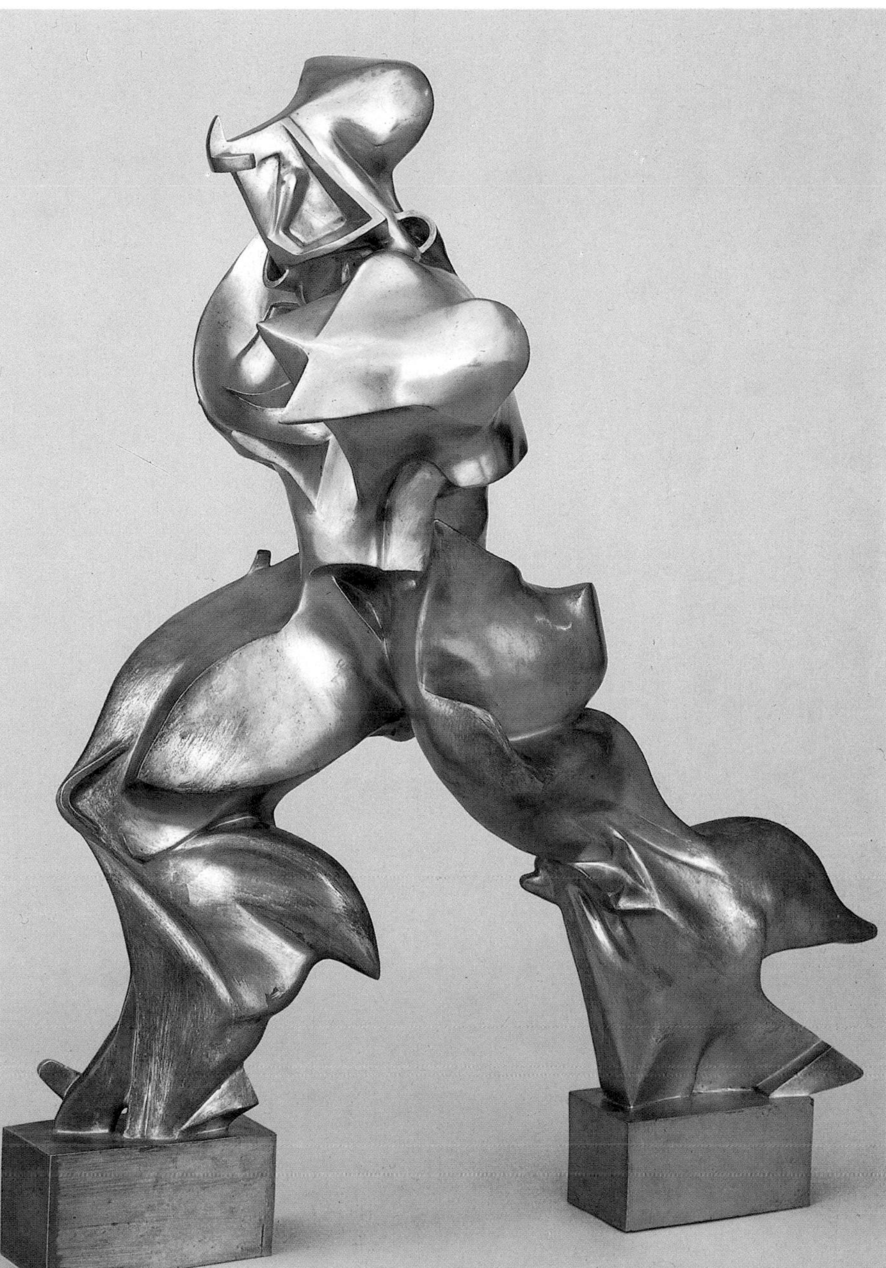

25-6. Umberto Boccioni. *Unique Forms of Continuity in Space*. 1913. Bronze (cast 1931), 43⅞ x 34⅞ x 15¾" (111.4 x 88.6 x 40 cm). The Museum of Modern Art, New York

ACQUIRED THROUGH THE LILLIE P. BLISS BEQUEST

SCULPTURE BETWEEN THE WARS

CONSTRUCTIVISM. In Analytic Cubism, concave and convex were treated as equivalents. All volumes, whether positive or negative, were "pockets of space." The Constructivists, a group of Russian artists led by Vladimir Tatlin (1895–1956), applied this principle to relief sculpture and arrived at what might be called three-dimensional collage.

TATLIN. Eventually the final step was taken of making the works freestanding. According to Tatlin and his followers, these "constructions" were actually four-dimensional. Since they implied motion, they also implied time. Suprematism (see page 786) and Constructivism were therefore closely related, and in fact overlapped, for both had their origins in Cubo-Futurism. They were nonetheless separated by a fundamental difference in approach. For Tatlin, art was not the Suprematists' spiritual contemplation but an active process of formation that was based on material and technique. He believed that each material dictates specific forms that are inherent in it and that these laws must be followed if the work of art is to be valid according to the laws of life itself. In the end, Constructivism won out over Suprematism because it was better suited to the postrevolution temperament of Russia, when great deeds, not great thoughts, were needed.

Cut off from artistic contact with Europe during World War I, Constructivism developed into a uniquely Russian art that was little affected by the return of some of the country's most important artists, such as Kandinsky and Chagall. The revolution galvanized the modernists, who celebrated the overthrow of the old regime with a creative outpouring throughout Russia.

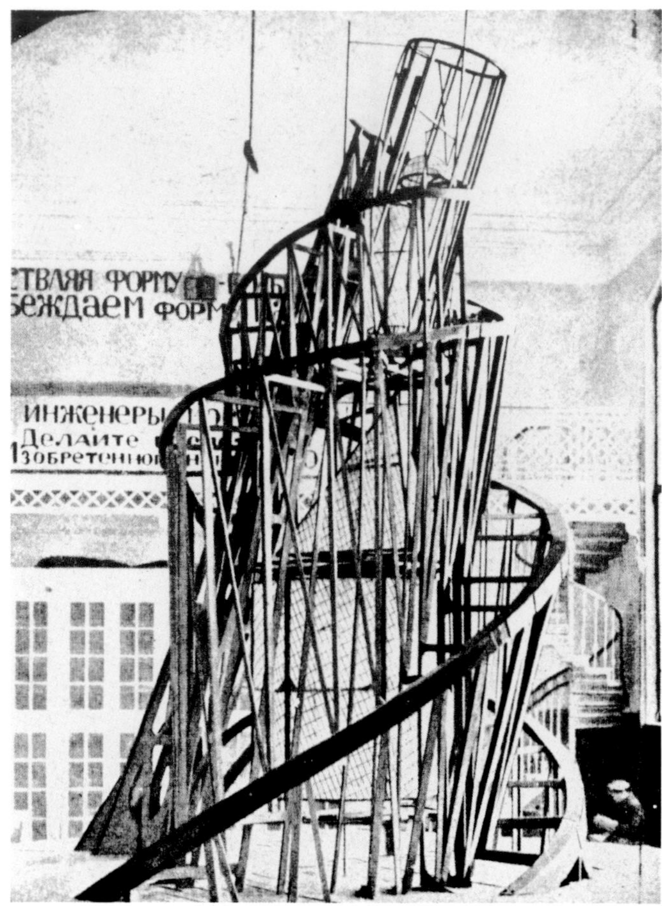

25-7. Vladimir Tatlin. Project for *Monument to the Third International.* 1919–20. Wood, iron, and glass, height 20' (6.1 m). Destroyed; contemporary photograph

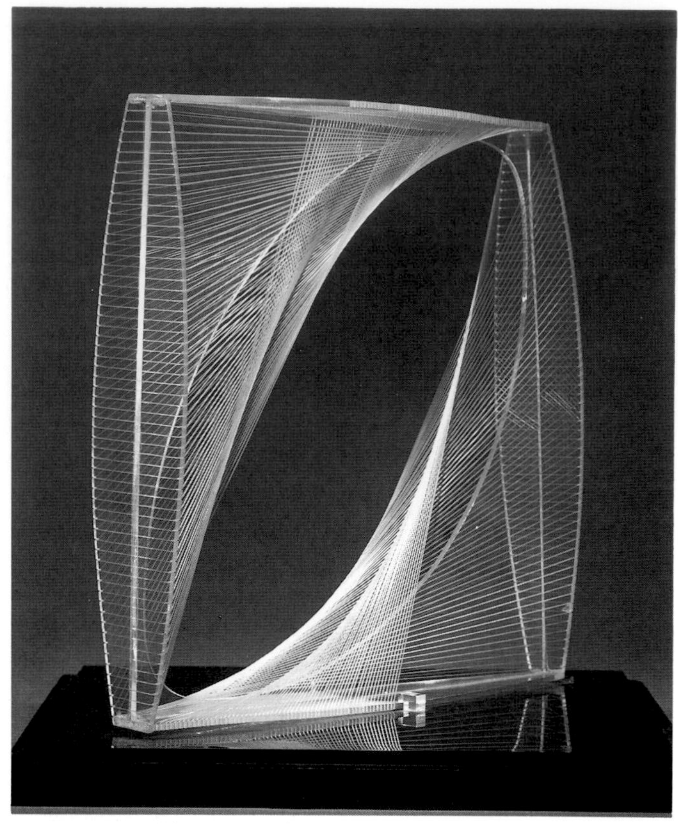

25-8. Naum Gabo. *Linear Construction #1* (smaller version). 1942–43. Plexiglas and nylon thread on plexiglass base, 12¼ x 12¼ x 2¾" (31.1 x 31.1 x 6.9 cm). Hirshhorn Museum and Sculpture Garden, Smithsonian Institution, Washington, D.C.

GIFT OF JOSEPH H. HIRSHHORN, 1966

Tatlin's model for a *Monument to the Third International* (fig. 25-7) captures the dynamism of the technological utopia envisioned under Communism. Pure energy is expressed as lines of force that establish new time-space relationships as well. The work also implies a new social structure, for the Constructivists believed in the power of art literally to reshape society. This extraordinary tower revolving at three speeds was conceived on a monumental scale, complete with Communist party offices. Like other such projects, however, it was wildly impractical in a society still recovering from the ravages of war and revolution and was never built.

Constructivism subsequently proceeded to a Productivist phase, which ignored any contradiction between true artistic creativity and purely utilitarian production. After the movement was suppressed as "bourgeois formalism," a number of its members emigrated to the West, where they joined forces with the few movements still espousing abstraction.

GABO. The most important of these was Naum Gabo (1890–1977), who went first to Berlin, then to England, before settling in America after World War II. His main contribution to modern art came in the early 1940s when he created a new kind of plastic construction strung with nylon filament (fig. 25-8) that comes very close to mathematical models. Although he arrived at it through intuition, the parallels to contemporary scientific theory are astonishing, for his work embodies much the same spatiality as modern physics. Gabo was fascinated by the links between art and science, which, he said, "arise from the same creative source and flow into the same ocean of the common culture." Like Kandinsky's, his motives were purely spiritual, and he saw Constructivism as an instrument of change. None of this theory, however, accounts for the elegance of Gabo's linear constructions, which embody an entirely modern sensibility.

VANTONGERLOO. Soon after arriving in Berlin, Gabo was in touch with *De Stijl,* the Dutch group. Its only true sculptor was the Belgian Georges Vantongerloo (1886–1965), who settled in Paris. He, too, was obsessed with the problem of how to represent space. *Métal:* $y=ax^3-bx^3+cx$ (fig. 25-9) is a daring prefiguration of Minimalist sculpture of the 1950s and 1960s. Whereas Mondrian's grids were never governed by strict ratios, Vantongerloo used the same bands to articulate space by establishing precise relationships as defined by the algebraic formula. The artist, however, saw this method as a means of expressing an intuition of creation, which is infinite and is perceived only through our sensitivity. His was indeed an ecstatic vision: "O! The incommensurable is never the same; if it were, it would be commensurable. And as the universe is incommensurable, what we need is an expression that would have neither end nor beginning; and this too exists." Ultimately this realization led him to abandon his sparse geometry for a curvi-

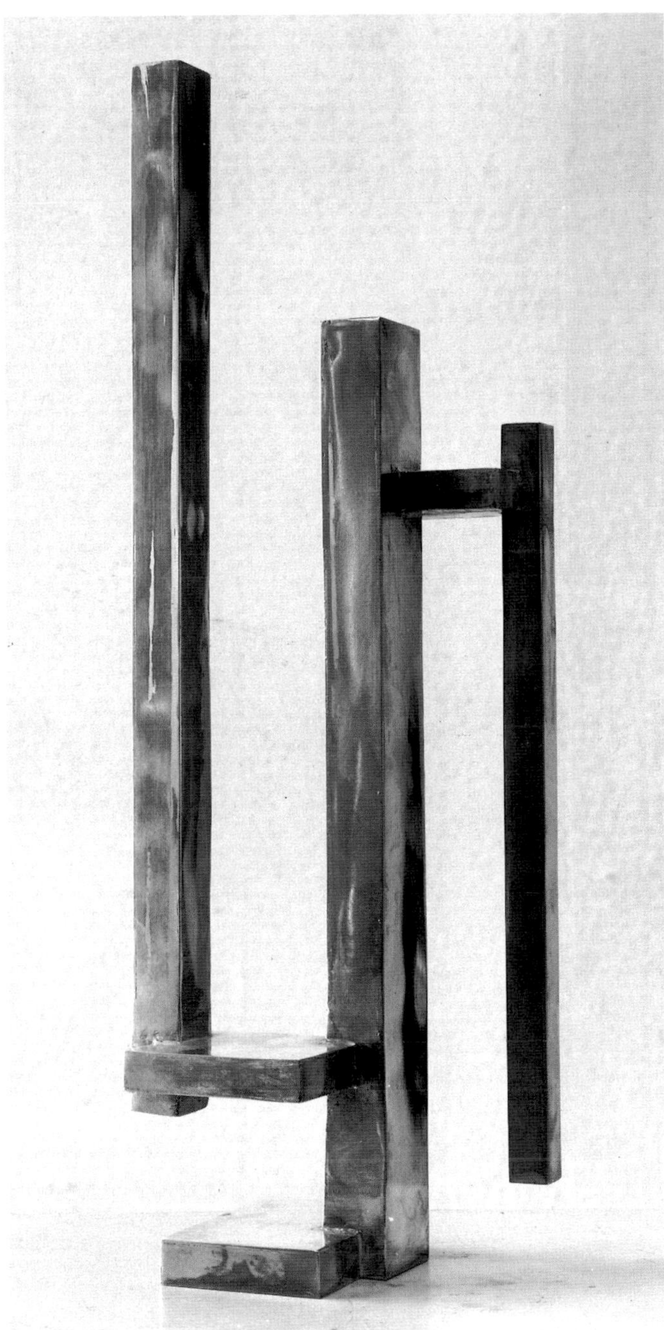

25-9. Georges Vantongerloo. *Métal:* $y = ax^3 - bx^3 + cx$. 1935. Argentine, height 15" (38 cm). Emanuel Hoffmann Foundation, Basel, on loan to Kunstmuseum Basel

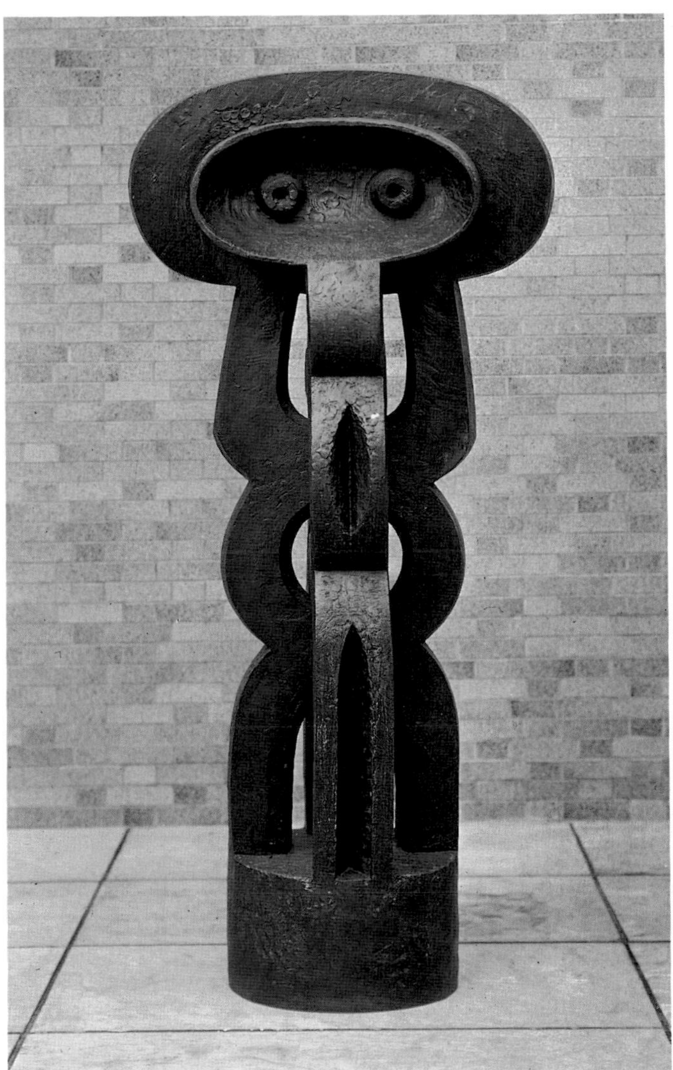

25-10. Jacques Lipschitz. *Figure.* 1926–30 (cast 1937). Bronze, height 7'1¼" (2.17 m). The Museum of Modern Art, New York

VAN GOGH PURCHASE FUND

linear approach, based not on classical Euclidian geometry but on Cartesian analytical geometry, to describe parabolic equations.

LIPSCHITZ. Contrary to what one might have expected, the everyday materials of Synthetic Cubism proved of far greater interest to painters than to the Cubist sculptors, who maintained a traditional loyalty to bronze. After World War I, sculptors in France largely deserted abstraction and abandoned Expressionism altogether. Only the Lithuanian-born Jacques Lipschitz (1891–1973), a friend of both Picasso and Matisse, continued to explore the possibilities offered by Cubism. He also shared in Brancusi's primevalism, and in the mid-1920s he achieved a remarkable synthesis of these two tendencies. With its intently staring eyes, *Figure* (fig. 25-10) is a haunting evocation in Cubist terms of African sculpture. Consisting of two interlocking figures, it creates a play of open and closed forms that relieves Brancusi's austere simplicity through arabesque rhythms akin to those of Matisse. Not surprisingly, the patron who commissioned it as a garden sculpture found it difficult to live with *Figure.* No other sculptor at the time was able to rival Lipschitz for sheer power, and he set an important example for the generation of sculptors that reached maturity a decade later (see pages 845–47).

DUCHAMP. Lipschitz' disciplined abstraction was the very opposite of Dada, which fostered nontraditional approaches that have both enriched and confounded modern sculpture ever since. Playfulness and spontaneity were the motives behind the readymades of Marcel Duchamp, which he created by shifting the context of everyday objects from the utilitarian to the aesthetic. The artist would put his signature, and a provocative title, on found ("readymade") objects, such as bottle racks, and exhibit them as works of art. *In Advance of the Broken Arm* (fig. 25-11) pushed the spirit of readymades to a new height. Duchamp "re-created" the lost original version of 1915 with this one made in 1945. [See Primary Sources, no. 96, page 939.] Some of Duchamp's examples consist of combinations of found objects. These "assisted" readymades approach the status of constructions or of three-dimensional collage. This technique, later baptized "assemblage" (see pages 855–58), proved to have unlimited possibilities, and numerous younger artists have explored it since, especially in junk-ridden America.

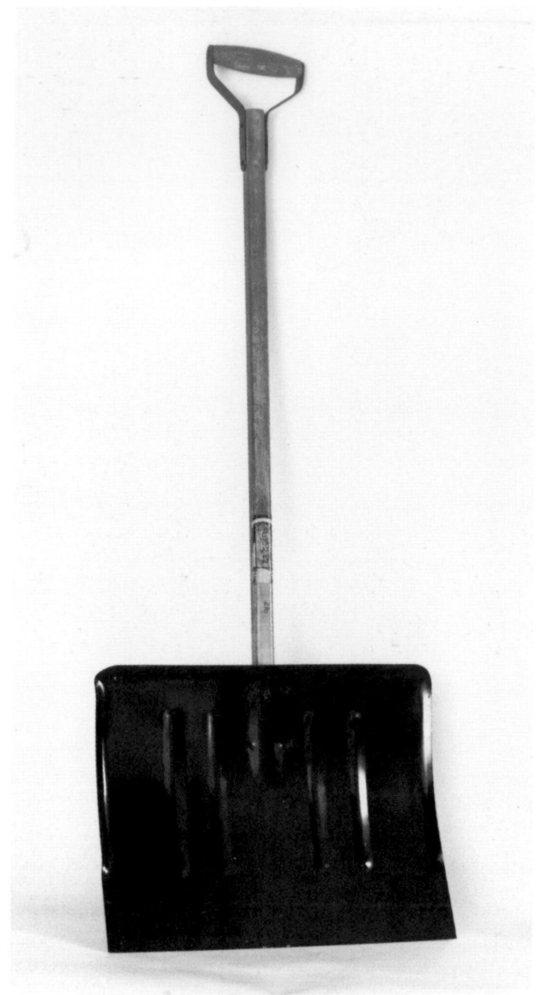

25-11. Marcel Duchamp. *In Advance of the Broken Arm*. 1945, from the original of 1915. Snow shovel, length 46¾" (118.7 cm). Yale University Art Gallery, New Haven, Connecticut

GIFT OF KATHERINE S. DREIER FOR THE COLLECTION SOCIÉTÉ ANONYME

SURREALISM. Readymades are certainly extreme demonstrations of a principle: that artistic creation depends neither on established rules nor on manual craftsmanship. The principle itself was an important discovery, although Duchamp abandoned readymades after only a few years. The Surrealist contribution to sculpture is harder to define. It was difficult to apply the theory of "pure psychic automatism" to painting but still harder to live up to it in sculpture. How indeed could solid, durable materials be given shape without the sculptor being consciously aware of the process?

OPPENHEIM. A breakthrough came in 1930 when the Surrealists met in response to a growing crisis caused in part by André Breton's insistence on tying the movement to Leon Trotsky's Communist faction. They issued a new manifesto drafted by Breton that called for the "profound and veritable occultation of Surrealism." It further required "uncovering the strange symbolic life of the most ordinary and clearly defined objects." The result was a new class of Surrealist object. Neither readymade nor sculpture, it constituted a kind of three-dimensional collage. However, it was assembled not out of aesthetic concerns using traditional techniques but according to "poetic affinity" following dictates of the subconscious. *Object* (fig. 25-12) by Meret Oppenheim (1913–1985), one of several gifted women associated with the movement, created a sensation when it was exhibited in 1936. Like others of its kind, it was intended to be repulsive and unsettling in the extreme yet proves all the more fascinating for that very reason.

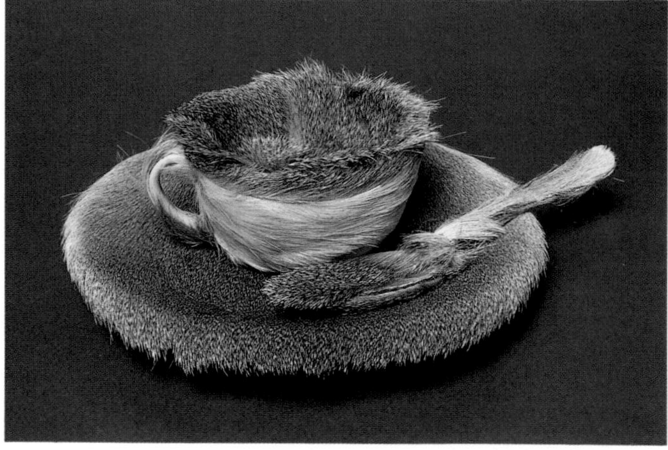

25-12. Meret Oppenheim. *Object*. 1936. Fur-covered teacup, saucer, and spoon; diameter of cup 4¾" (12.1 cm); diameter of saucer 9⅜" (23.8 cm); length of spoon 8" (20.3 cm). The Museum of Modern Art, New York

PURCHASE

ARP. Perhaps the purest form of Surrealist sculpture was created by Hans Arp (1887–1966). Around 1930 he began to translate his reliefs, which arose from his experiments with collage, into three-dimensional forms. These evolved a few years later into the *Human Concretion* series (fig. 25-13), a term that aptly describes their character (see also page 800). In contrast to Brancusi's abstractions, which reduce things to their absolute essence, Arp's biomorphic forms seem to grow organically as they are built up during the modeling process. The concretions are notable for their technical perfection, regardless of medium. (They were almost always done in clay or plaster, but many were later carved in marble and wood, or sometimes cast in bronze, by skilled artisans.) They have influenced countless sculptors ever since.

PICASSO. As in painting, Picasso's genius provided much of the impetus for sculpture during the 1930s. The painter developed a

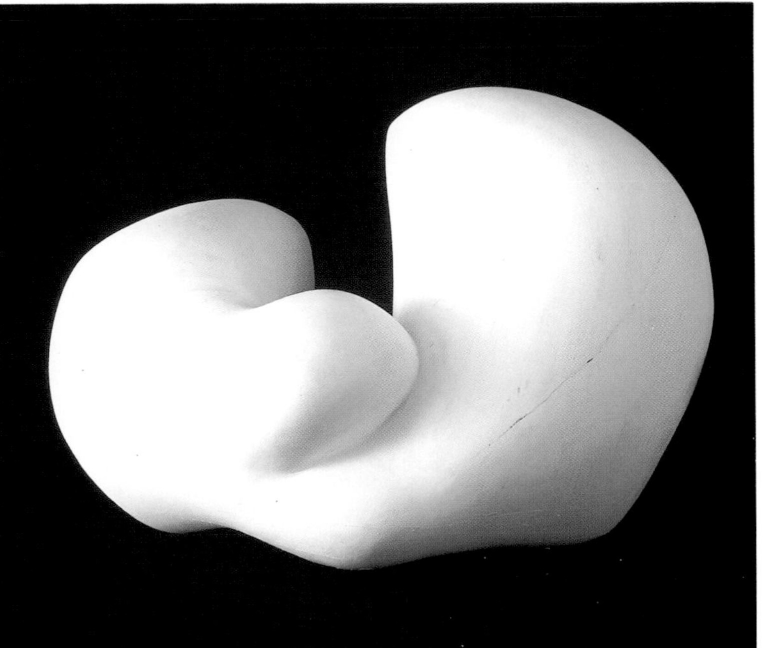

25-13. Hans Arp. *Human Concretion.* 1935.
Original plaster, 19½ x 18¾ x 25½" (49.5 x 47.6 x 64.7 cm).
The Museum of Modern Art, New York
GIFT OF THE ADVISORY COMMITTEE

serious interest in three-dimensional forms in 1928, and for the next five years he concentrated intensively on making sculptures of all sorts. They demonstrate an amazing variety that testifies to his fertile imagination. *Head of a Woman* (fig. 25-14) is an especially appealing example of his work from this period. This arresting figure, made from a colander and other discarded materials, shows Picasso's fascination with the "primitive" quality of ethnographic sculpture. Its kinship with the head in *Girl Before a Mirror* of about the same time (see fig. 24-29) suggests why the artist turned to sculpture in the first place. On the one hand, his painted shapes have a solidity that practically demands translation into three-dimensional form. On the other, his work is so full of startling transformations that the process of metamorphosis involved in sculpture became highly intriguing. Here there can be little doubt that Picasso's involvement with Surrealism stimulated his imagination and allowed him to approach sculpture without preconceived ideas. As he put it, "One should be able to take a bit of wood and find it's a bird."

This freedom of association is what allowed Picasso to see the possibilities in the debris of modern civilization—an attitude that culminated in *Bull's Head* (fig. 25-15). It is a work of disarming simplicity that at face value consists of nothing but the seat and handlebars of an old bicycle. What is far from simple is the leap of the imagination by which Picasso recognized a bull's head in these unlikely objects. While we feel a certain jolt when we first recognize the ingredients of this visual pun, we also sense that it was a stroke of genius to put them together in this unique way. The handiwork was also ridiculously simple: once the seat had been properly placed on the handlebars, it was cast in bronze, and the job was done. Nevertheless, the artist's hands, however modest the task, played an essential part in the creative process. Once he had conceived his *Bull's Head,* he could not be sure that it would really work unless he actually made the work of art.

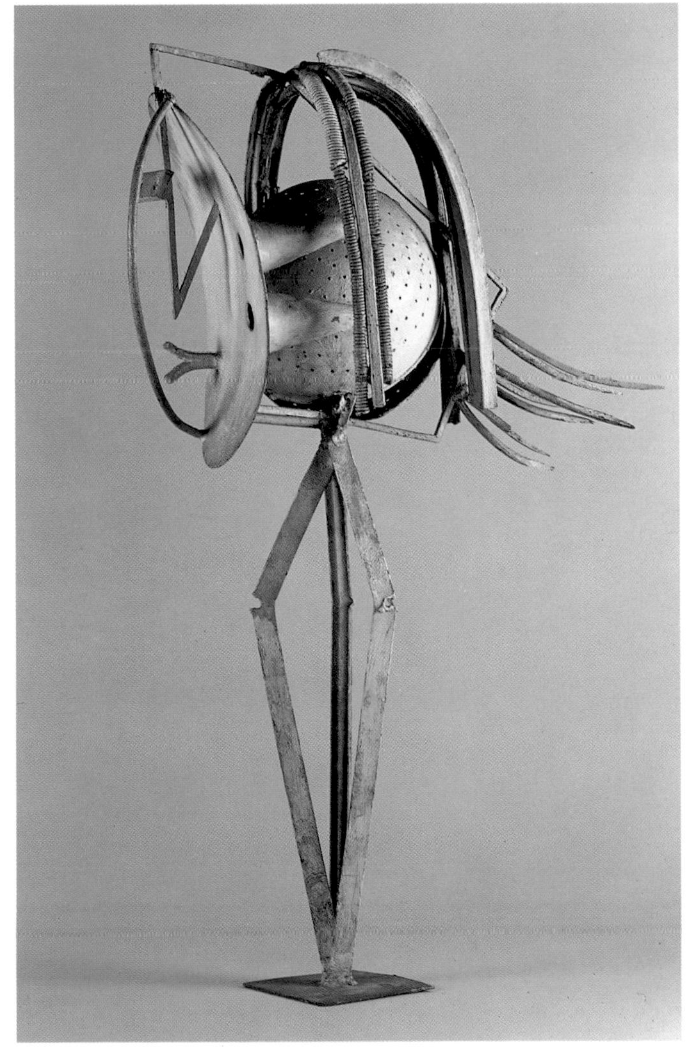

25-14. Pablo Picasso. *Head of a Woman.* 1930–31.
Painted iron, sheet metal, springs, and colanders,
39⅜ x 14½ x 23¼" (100 x 37 x 59 cm). Musée Picasso, Paris

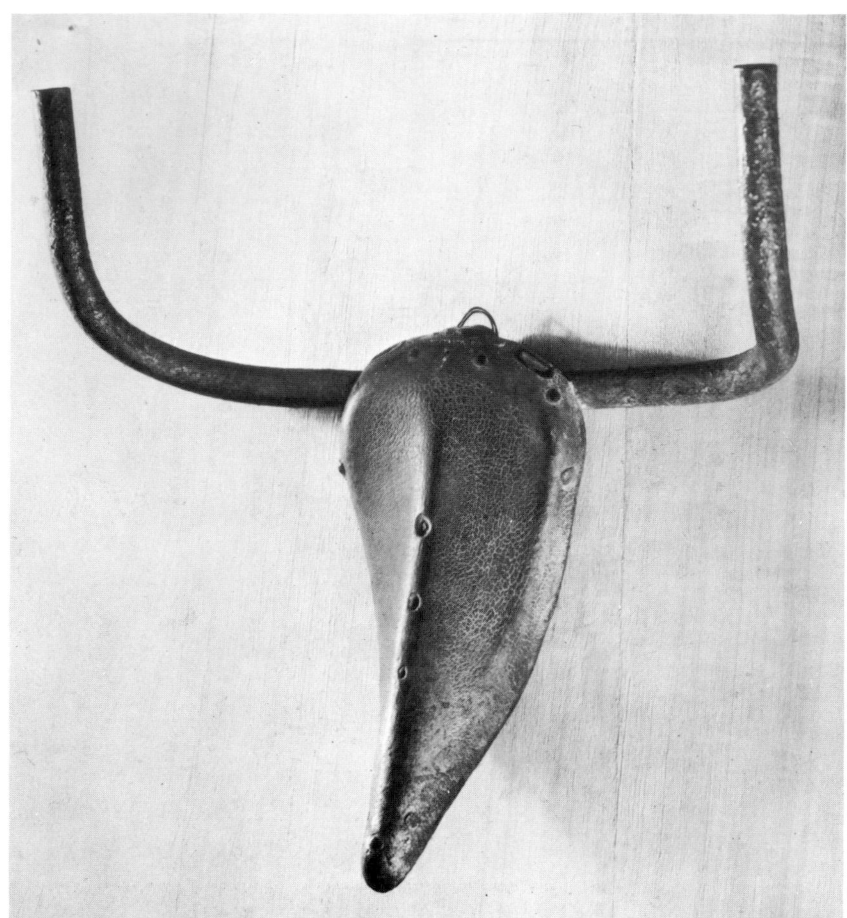

25-15. Pablo Picasso. *Bull's Head.* 1943. Bronze cast bicycle parts, height 16⅛" (41 cm). Musée Picasso, Paris

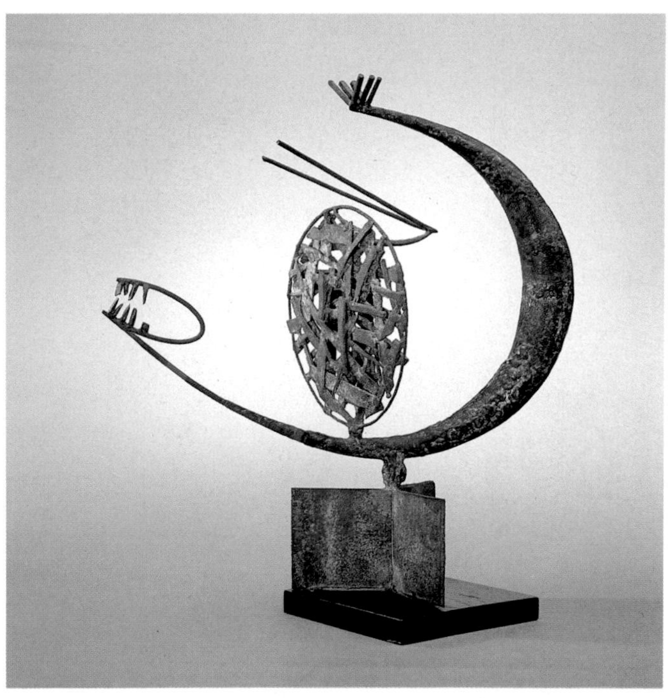

25-16. Julio González. *Head.* c. 1935. Wrought iron, 17¾ x 15¼" (45.1 x 38.7 cm). The Museum of Modern Art, New York

PURCHASE

GONZÁLEZ. Picasso also galvanized the creative energies of Julio González (1872–1942). Trained as a wrought-iron craftsman in his native Catalonia, González went to Paris in 1900. Although he was a friend of both Brancusi and Picasso, he produced little of importance until the 1930s, when Picasso called him for technical advice in working with wrought iron. It was González who established this medium as an important one for sculpture by taking advantage of the technical difficulties that had discouraged its use before. *Head* (fig. 25-16) combines extreme economy of form with an aggressive reinterpretation of anatomy that is derived from Picasso's work after the mid-1920s. As in the head of the figure on the left in Picasso's *Three Dancers* (see fig. 24-28), the mouth is an oval cavity with spikelike teeth, the eyes two rods that converge upon an "optic nerve" linking them to the tangled mass of the "brain." González has produced a gruesomely expressive metaphor, as if the violence of his working process mirrored the violence of modern life.

CALDER. The early 1930s produced still another important development: the mobile sculpture of the American Alexander Calder (1898–1976). Called mobiles for short, they are delicately balanced constructions of metal wire, hinged together and weighted so as to move with the slightest breath of air. They may be of any size, from tiny tabletop models to the huge *Lobster Trap and Fish Tail* (fig. 25-17). Kinetic sculpture had been conceived first by the Constructivists. Their influence is evident in Calder's earliest

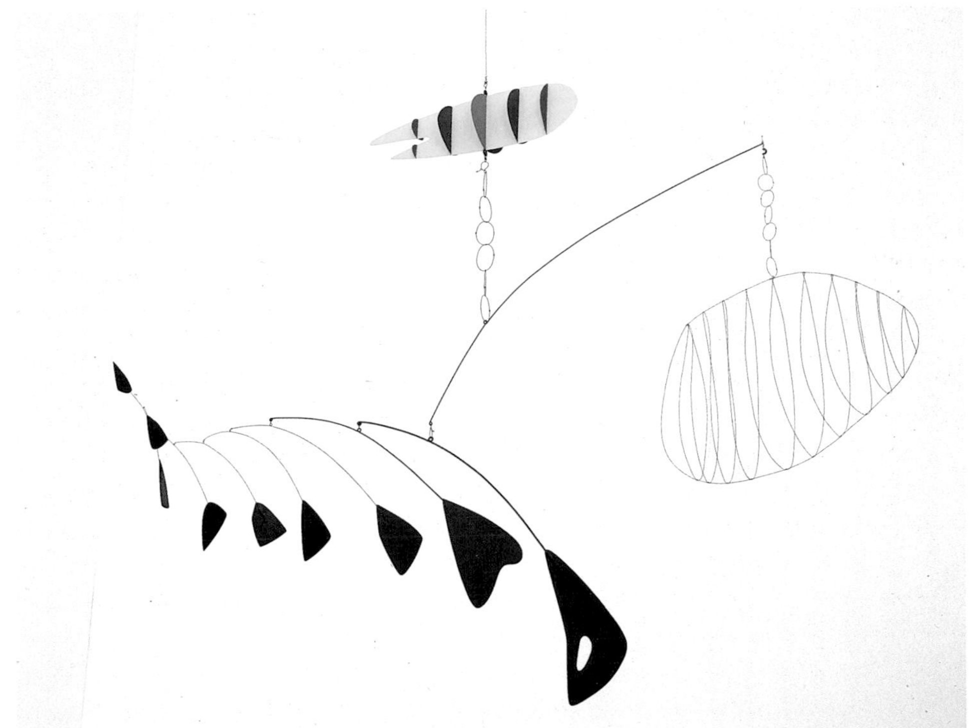

25-17. Alexander Calder. *Lobster Trap and Fish Tail.* 1939. Painted steel wire and sheet aluminum, approx. 8'6" x 9'6" (2.6 x 2.9 m). The Museum of Modern Art, New York

COMMISSIONED BY THE ADVISORY COMMITTEE FOR THE STAIRWELL OF THE MUSEUM

mobiles, which were motor-driven and tended toward abstract geometric forms. Calder was also affected early on by Mondrian, whose palette of primary colors he adopted. Like Mondrian, he initially thought of his constructions as self-contained miniature universes. But it was his contact with Surrealism that made him realize the poetic possibilities of "natural" rather than fully controlled movement. He borrowed biomorphic shapes from Miró and began to think of mobiles as counterparts to organic structures: flowers on flexible stems, foliage quivering in the breeze, marine animals floating in the sea. Unpredictable and ever-changing, such mobiles incorporate the fourth dimension as an essential element. Infinitely responsive to their environment, they seem amazingly alive.

ENGLAND. Two English sculptors represent the culmination of the modern sculptural tradition before 1945: Henry Moore (1898–1986) and Barbara Hepworth (1903–1975). The presence of Gabo, Kokoschka, Mondrian, Gropius, and other émigrés helped give rise to modern art in England during the mid-1930s, when Moore and Hepworth were emerging as mature artists. As a result, they absorbed the full spectrum of earlier twentieth-century sculpture but in different measure, reflecting their contrasting personalities. The two were closely associated as leaders of the modern movement in England and influenced each other. Moore was the more boldly inventive artist, but Hepworth may well have been the better sculptor.

MOORE. The majestic *Two Forms* (fig. 25-18), an early work by Moore, may be regarded as the second-generation offspring of Brancusi's *The Kiss* of a quarter-century earlier (see fig. 25-2), although there is no direct connection between them. [See Primary Sources, no. 97, pages 939–40.] Abstract and subtle in shape,

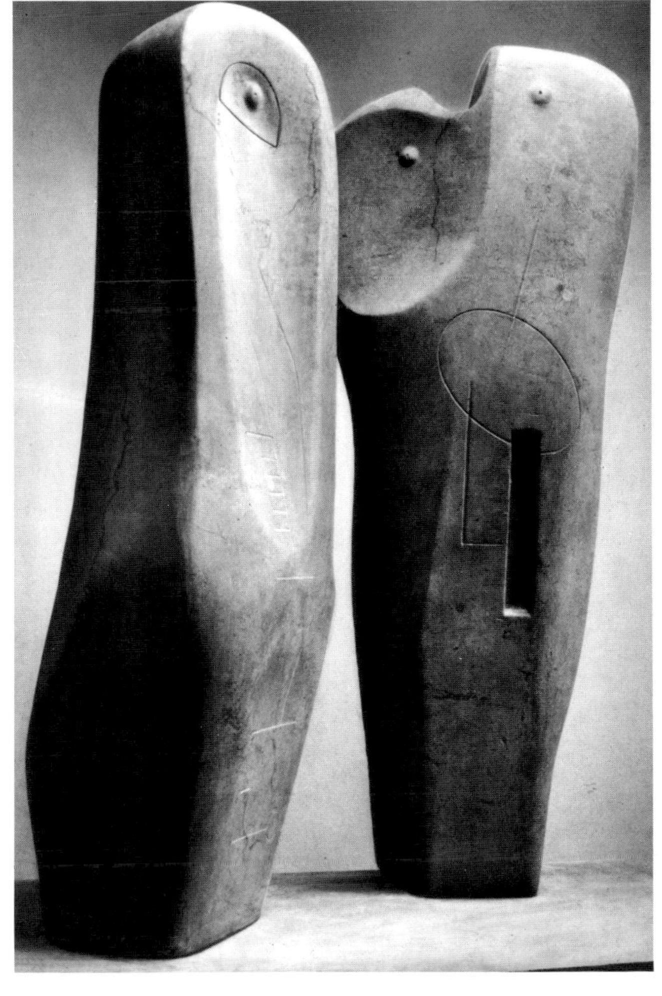

25-18. Henry Moore. *Two Forms.* 1936. Stone, height approx. 42" (106.7 cm). Collection Mrs. H. Gates Lloyd, Haverford, Pennsylvania

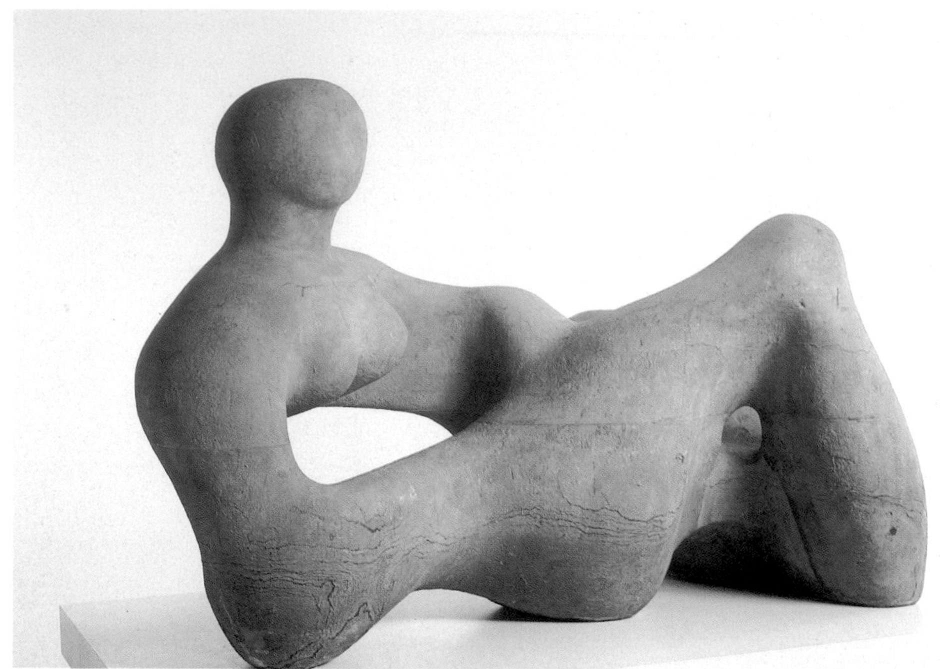

25-19. Henry Moore. *Recumbent Figure.* 1938. Green Hornton stone, length approx. 54" (137.2 cm). The Tate Gallery, London

they are "persons" in much the same vein as Lipschitz's *Figure* (see fig. 25-10). This family group—the forked slab evolved from the artist's studies of the mother-and-child theme—is mysterious and remote like the monoliths of Stonehenge (see fig. 1-18), which greatly impressed the sculptor. And like Stonehenge, Moore's figures are meant to be placed in a landscape, so architectural are they in character.

Through biomorphic abstraction, his *Recumbent Figure* (fig. 25-19) retains both a classical motif—one thinks of a reclining river-god (see fig. 22-5)—and a primeval look. The design is in complete harmony with the natural striations of the stone, as if the forms had resulted from slow erosion over a thousand years. Moore has evoked the essence of the human figure with remarkable success. If we were to succumb to the natural temptation to run our hand over the sculpture, it would seem filled with inner life, so convincingly do the forms swell and undulate. Moore was originally inspired by a Mayan statue of the rain-spirit Chac Mool. Interestingly enough, the nearest relative of Brancusi's *The Kiss* is a Pre-Columbian pottery figurine group, which the artist cannot have known, however, since it was a later discovery. The coincidence underscores the fundamental kinship between Brancusi and Moore. Moore's figure also suggests an awareness of Arp's *Human Concretions* from about the same time (see fig. 25-13). The difference is that Arp suggests anatomical forms without specifically referring to them, as Moore does. The undulating effect is not unlike the arabesques achieved by Matisse in *Reclining Nude I* (see fig. 25-1). Moore also takes liberties with the human figure that would be unthinkable without Picasso (compare fig. 24-30). In this way, Moore weaves the strands of early modern sculpture into a seamless unity of incomparable beauty and subtlety.

HEPWORTH. Hepworth was the leading woman sculptor of the twentieth century. In common with Moore's, her sculpture had a biological foundation, but her style became more abstract after her marriage to the painter Ben Nicholson (see page 797), her association with the Constructivist Naum Gabo, and her contact in Paris with Brancusi and Arp. For a time she was practicing several modes at once under these influences. With the onset of World War II, she moved to St. Ives in Cornwall, where she initiated an individual style that emerged in the early 1940s. *Sculpture with Color (Deep Blue and Red)* (fig. 25-20) flawlessly synthesizes painting and sculpture, Surrealist biomorphism and organic abstraction, and the molding of space and shaping of mass. Carved from wood and immaculately finished, it transforms the shape of an egg into a timeless ideal that has the lucid perfection of a classical head,

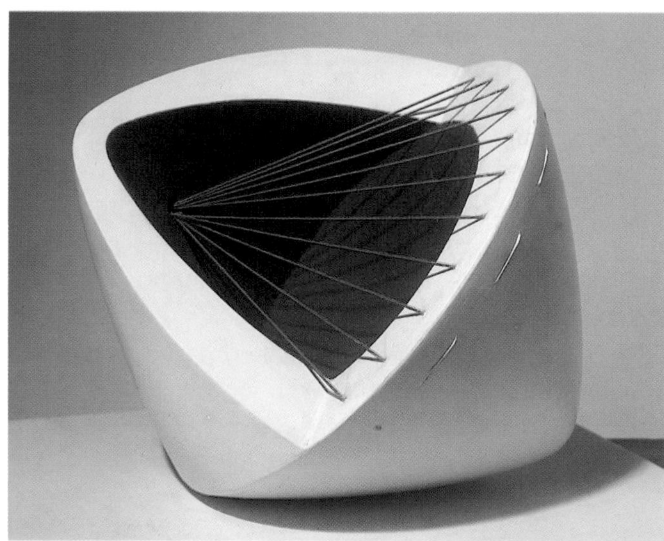

25-20. Barbara Hepworth. *Sculpture with Color (Deep Blue and Red).* 1940–42. Wood, painted white and blue, with red strings, on a wooden base, 11 x 10¼" (27.9 x 26 cm). Collection Alan and Sarah Bowness, London

yet the elemental expressiveness of a primitive mask. Hepworth's egg shape undoubtedly owes something to Brancusi's (see fig. 25-3), although their work is very different. The colors accentuate the play between the interior and exterior of the hollowed-out form, while the strings, a device first used by Moore, seem to suggest a life force within. As a result of its open forms, *Sculpture with Color* enters into an active relationship with its surroundings. Like Moore, Hepworth was concerned with the relationship of the human figure in a landscape, but in an unusually personal way. After moving to a house that overlooked St. Ives Bay, she wrote, "I was the figure in the landscape and every sculpture contained to a greater or lesser degree the ever-changing forms and contours embodying my own response to a given position in that landscape. I used colour and strings in many of the carvings of this time. The colour in the concavities plunged me into the depth of water, caves, or shadows deeper than the carved concavities themselves. The strings were the tension I felt between myself and the sea, the wind or the hills."

SCULPTURE SINCE 1945

PRIMARY STRUCTURES AND ENVIRONMENTAL SCULPTURE. Like painting, sculpture since 1945 has been characterized by epic proportions. Indeed, scale assumed fundamental significance for a sculptural movement that extended the scope—the very concept—of sculpture in an entirely new direction. "Primary Structure," the most suitable name suggested for this type, conveys its two chief characteristics: extreme simplicity of shapes and a kinship with architecture. Another term, "Environmental Sculpture" (not to be confused with the mixed-medium "environments" of Pop Art), refers to the fact that many Primary Structures are designed to envelop the viewer, who is invited to enter or walk through them. It is this space-defining function that distinguishes Primary Structures from all previous sculpture and relates them to architecture. They are the modern successors, in structural steel and concrete, to such prehistoric monuments as Stonehenge (see figs. 1-17 and 1-18).

GOERITZ. The first to explore these possibilities was Mathias Goeritz (b. 1915), a German working in Mexico City. As early as 1952–53, he established an experimental museum, The Echo, for the display of massive geometric sculptures, some of them so large as to occupy an entire patio (fig. 25-21). On this scale, Primary Structures virtually become architecture in their own right. As a natural extension of his work, Goeritz collaborated five years later with the architect Luis Barragán (1902–1987) on a group of colored office towers in Mexico City, which are themselves Primary Structures.

BLADEN. Goeritz's ideas were soon taken up on both sides of the Atlantic. Often, these sculptors limited themselves to the role of designer and left the execution to others, to emphasize the impersonality and repeatability of their invention. If no patron could be found to foot the bill for carrying out these costly structures, they remained on paper, like unbuilt architecture. Sometimes such works reached the mock-up stage. *The X* (fig. 25-22), by the Canadian Ronald Bladen (1918–1988), was originally built with painted wood substituting for metal for an exhibition inside the two-story hall of the Corcoran Gallery in Washington, D.C. Its commanding presence, dwarfing the Neoclassic colonnade of the hall, seems doubly awesome in such a setting.

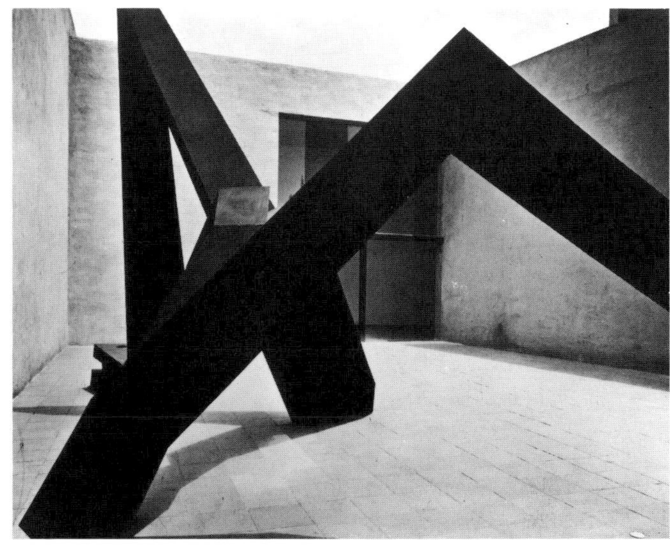

25-21. Mathias Goeritz. *Steel Structure*. 1952–53. Height 14'9" (4.5 m). The Echo (Experimental Museum), Mexico City

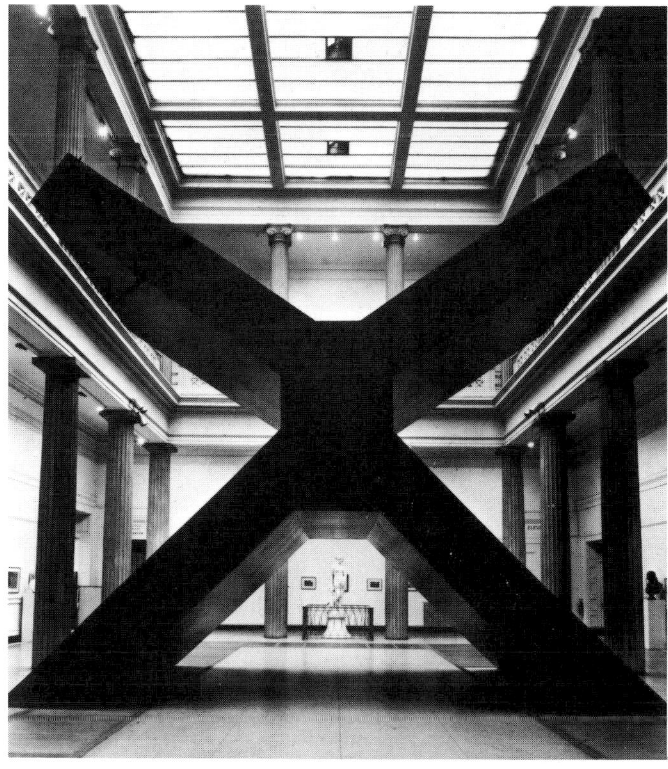

25-22. Ronald Bladen. *The X* (in the Corcoran Gallery, Washington, D.C.). 1967. Painted wood, later constructed in steel, 22'8" x 24'6" x 12'6" (6.9 x 7.3 x 3.8 m)

COURTESY FISCHBACH GALLERY, NEW YORK

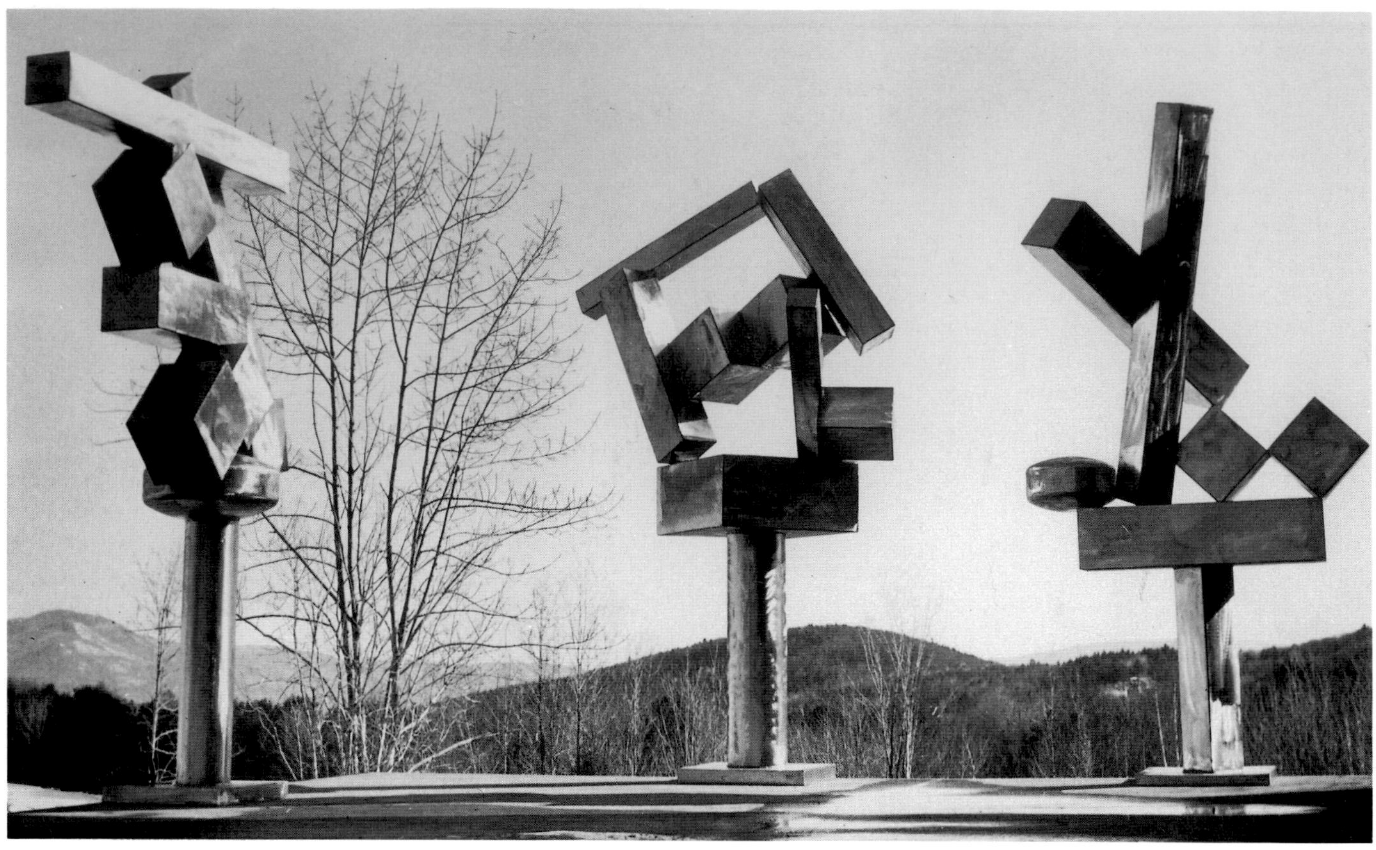

25-23. David Smith. *Cubi* series (at Bolton Landing, New York). Stainless steel. (left) *Cubi XVIII.* 1964. Height 9'8" (2.9 m). Museum of Fine Arts, Boston; (center) *Cubi XVII.* 1963. Height 9'2" (2.7 m). Dallas Museum of Fine Arts; (right) *Cubi XIX.* 1964. Height 9'5" (2.9 m). The Tate Gallery, London

SMITH. Not all Primary Structures are Environmental Sculptures, of course. Most are freestanding works independent of the sites that contain them. Bladen's *The X,* for example, was later constructed of painted steel as an outdoor sculpture. Primary Structures and Environmental Sculptures nevertheless share the same monumental scale and economy of form. The artist who played the most influential role in defining them was David Smith (1906–1965). His earlier work had been strongly influenced by the wrought-iron constructions of Julio González (see fig. 25-16), but during the last years of his life he developed a singularly impressive form of Primary Structure in his *Cubi* series. Figure 25-23 shows three of these against the open sky and rolling hills of the artist's farm at Bolton Landing, New York. (All are now in major museums.) Only two basic components are employed: cubes (or multiples of them) and cylinders. Yet Smith has created a seemingly endless variety of configurations. The units that make up the structures are balanced one upon the other as if they were held in place by magnetic force, so that each sculpture represents a fresh triumph over gravity. Unlike many members of the Primary Structure movement, Smith executed these pieces himself, welding them of sheets of stainless steel whose shiny surfaces he finished by hand. As a result, his work displays an "old-fashioned" subtlety of touch that reminds us of the polished bronzes of Brancusi.

JUDD. Donald Judd (1928–1994) carried the implications of Primary Structures to their logical conclusion: Minimalism. Unlike Environmental Sculpture, his works served to articulate interior space without shaping it. In search of the ultimate unity, he separated Smith's *Cubi* into its two components, reducing the geometry to a single cube or cylinder. Judd established the proportions through precise mathematical formulas and eliminated any hint of personal intervention by contracting the work out to industrial fabricators. Having gained total control over all his elements, he soon began to elaborate on them. His most involved pieces have a decorative opulence, achieved by repeating the shape serially at set intervals and adding an intense primary color to one or more sides (fig. 25-24). Judd's strict guidelines permitted few variations, only greater refinement. Within these limitations, however, the results are often impressive. Why this should be so is not easily explained, although the artist was an eloquent spokesman. In the end, the success of his work depends on its subtle proportions and flawless finish, which enabled him to attain a degree of perfection equaled by few other sculptors who shared the same approach.

SHAPIRO. A number of sculptors gradually began to move away from Minimalism without entirely renouncing it. This trend is called Post-Minimalism to denote its continuing debt to the ear-

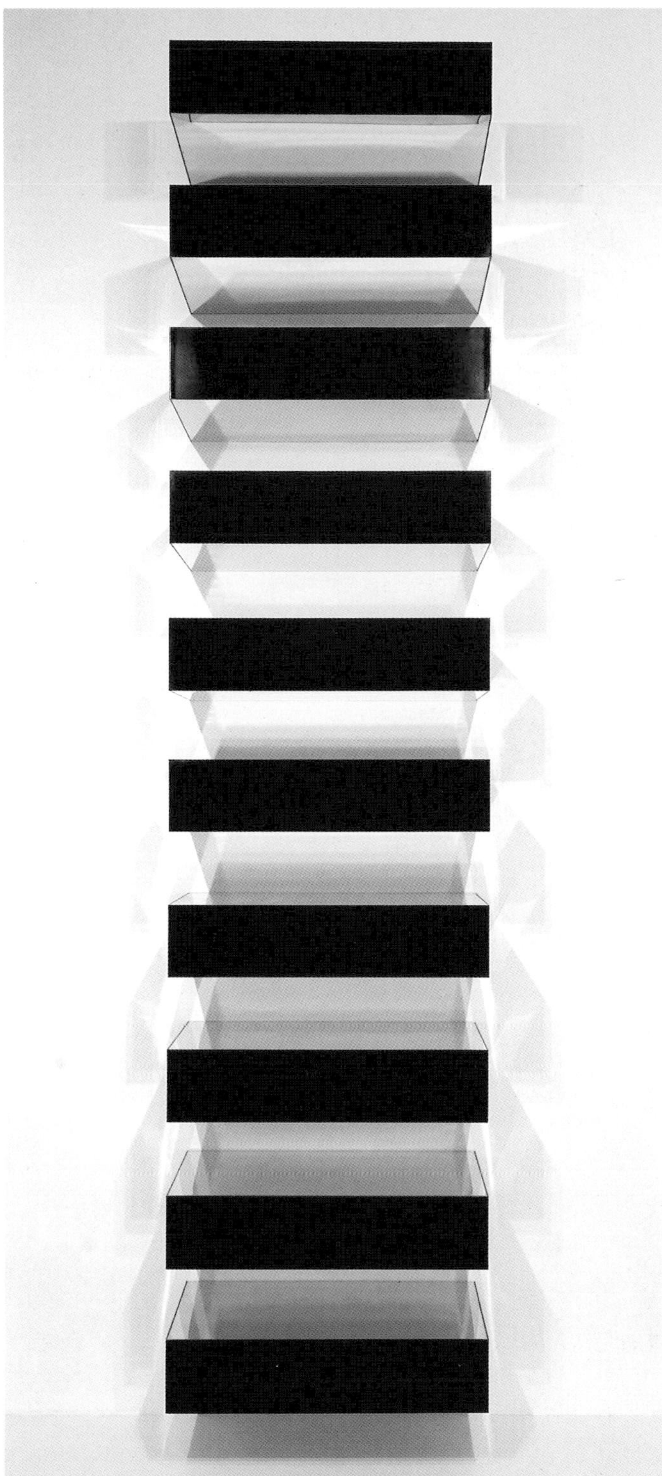

25-24. Donald Judd. *Untitled.* 1989. Copper with red Plexiglas; ten units, each 9 x 39½ x 31" (23 x 100.3 x 78.8 cm)

COURTESY THE PACEWILDENSTEIN GALLERY, NEW YORK

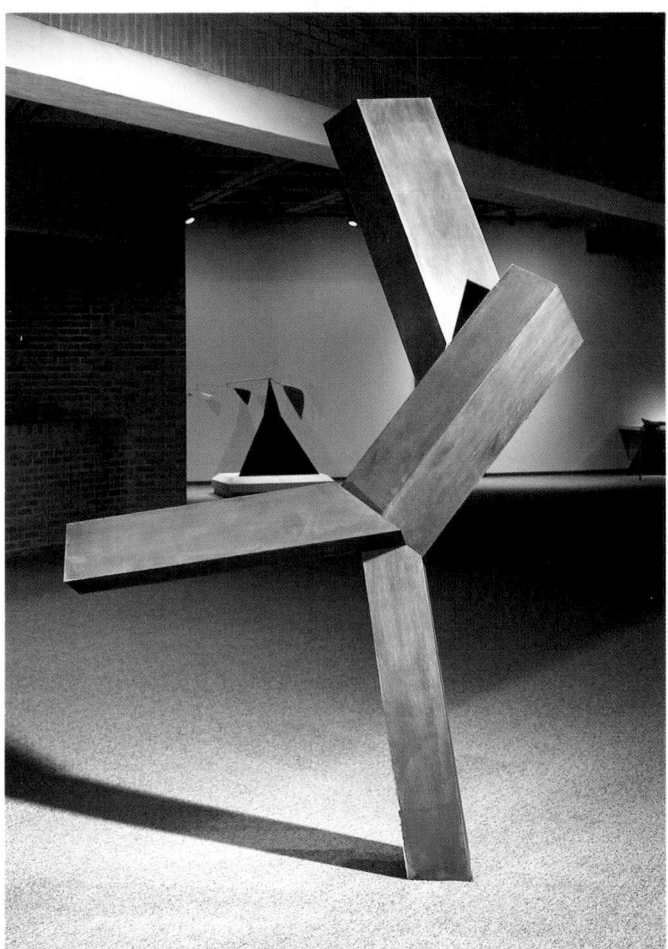

25-25. Joel Shapiro. *Untitled.* 1989–90. Bronze, 8'5½" x 3'6" x 6'6" (2.57 x 1.06 x 1.98 m). North Carolina Museum of Art, Raleigh

PURCHASED WITH FUNDS FROM VARIOUS DONORS, BY EXCHANGE

lier style. Its leading representative is Joel Shapiro (b. 1941). After producing small pieces having great conceptual intensity and aesthetic power, he suddenly began to make sculptures of simple wood beams that refer to the human figure but do not directly represent it. They assume active "poses," some standing awkwardly off-balance, others dancing or tumbling, so that they charge the space around them with energy. Shapiro soon began casting them in bronze, which retains the texture of the rough wood grain (fig. 25-25). These pieces are hand-finished with a beautiful patina by skilled artisans, reasserting the craftsmanship traditional to sculpture. By freely rearranging the vocabulary of David Smith, who actually experimented with a similar figure before his death, Shapiro has given Minimalist sculpture a new lease on life. Nevertheless, his work remains one of the few successful attempts at reviving contemporary sculpture, which as a whole has found it difficult to chart a new direction.

AFRICAN-AMERICAN SCULPTURE. Minimalism was also a decisive influence on a group of talented African-American sculptors who came to maturity in the 1960s. Their work has helped to make the late twentieth century the first great age of African-American art. While these sculptors show a variety of styles, subjects, and approaches, all address the black experience in America within a contemporary abstract aesthetic. Thus they have the advantage over African-American painters, who have often been burdened by representationalism and traditional styles.

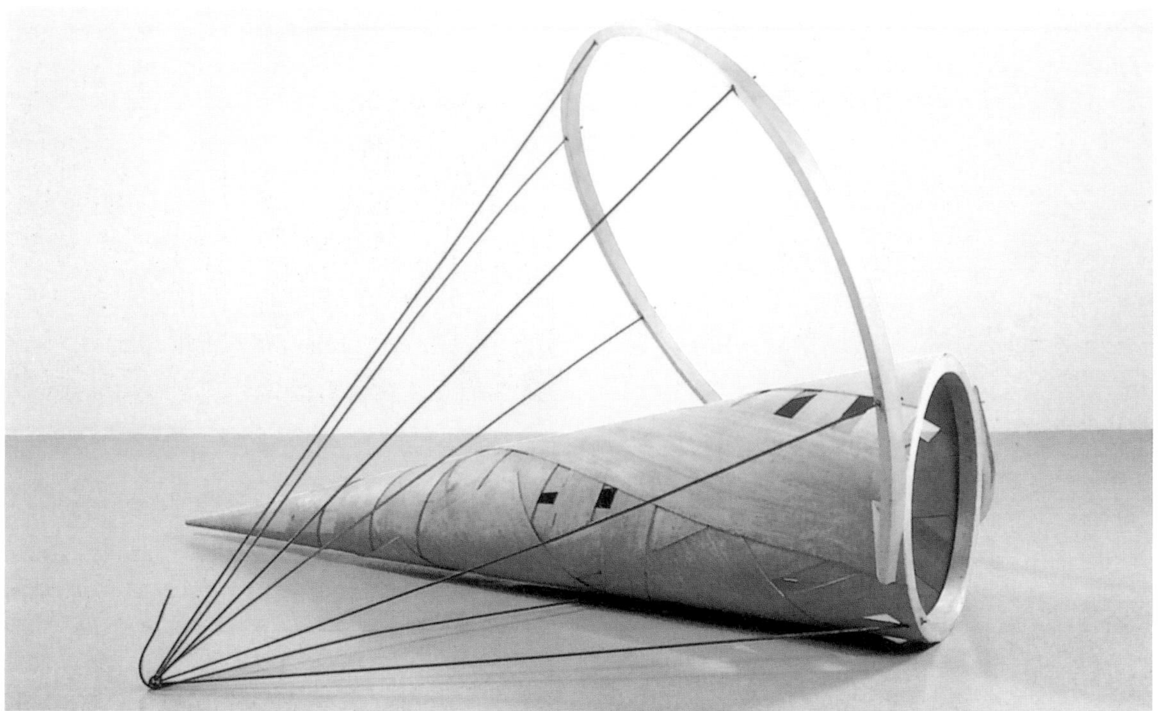

25-26. Martin Puryear. *The Spell.* 1985. Pine, cedar, and steel, 4'8" x 7' x 5'5" (1.42 x 2.13 x 1.65 m). Collection the artist

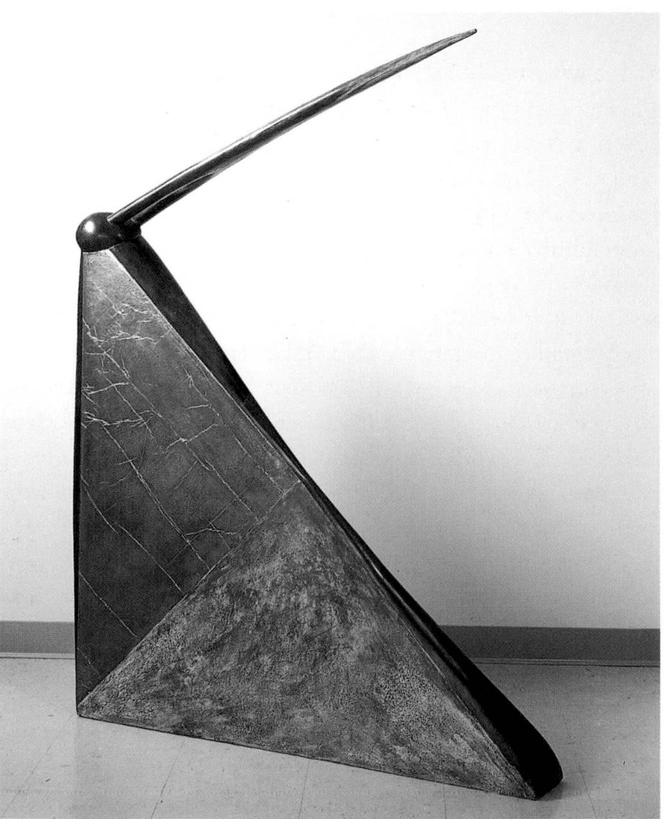

25-27. Tyrone Mitchell. *Horn for Wifredo.* 1987. Wood, copper, plaster, and pigment, 65 x 49 x 7" (165 x 124.5 x 17.8 cm). Collection of the Schomburg Center for Research in Black Culture, The New York Public Library, Art and Artifacts Division

PURYEAR. Martin Puryear (b. 1941), the leading black sculptor on the scene today, draws on his experience with the woodworkers of both Sierra Leone in western Africa, where he spent several years in the Peace Corps, and in Sweden, where he attended the Royal Academy. Puryear manages to weld these very different sources into a personal style of seamless unity. He adapts African motifs and materials to the modern Western tradition, relying on careful craftsmanship to bridge the gap. His forms, at once bold and refined, have an elegant simplicity that contrasts the natural and man-made, the finished and unfinished. They may evoke a saw, bow, fishnet, anthill, or in this case a basket (fig. 25-26)—whatever his memory suggests—each restated in whimsical fashion.

MITCHELL. Tyrone Mitchell (b. 1944), like Puryear, spent a pivotal sojourn in Africa, where Dogon culture had a profound impact on him. His mature work, too, presents a flawless synthesis of Western and African sources. *Horn for Wifredo* (fig. 25-27) reduces an antelope to its essence using Minimalist forms and the spare simplicity of Brancusi, who influenced him at the beginning of the 1980s. Yet the diversity of materials creates a rich array of textures and colors that shows the artist's respect for time-honored materials and craftsmanship. This compound object, we realize, is suffused with a vital energy that makes of it a Surrealist creature. Indeed, the title refers to the Cuban-born Surrealist Wifredo Lam (1902–1982), an important early inspiration for Mitchell.

EDWARDS. Melvin Edwards (b. 1937), who has also paid homage to Lam, was equally affected by his visits to Africa. He may be regarded as the purist among contemporary African-American sculptors. An artist in the mold of David Smith, he continues to maintain an allegiance to the Primary Structure and the vocabulary of Minimalism. He invests them, however, with uniquely personal

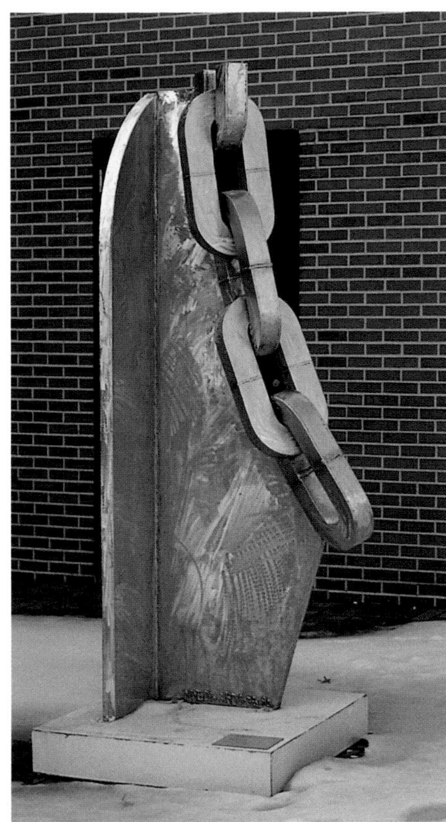

25-28. Melvin Edwards. *To Listen.* 1990. Stainless steel, 7'5½" x 1'3½" x 3'1" (2.27 x .39 x .93 m)

COURTESY CDS GALLERY, NEW YORK

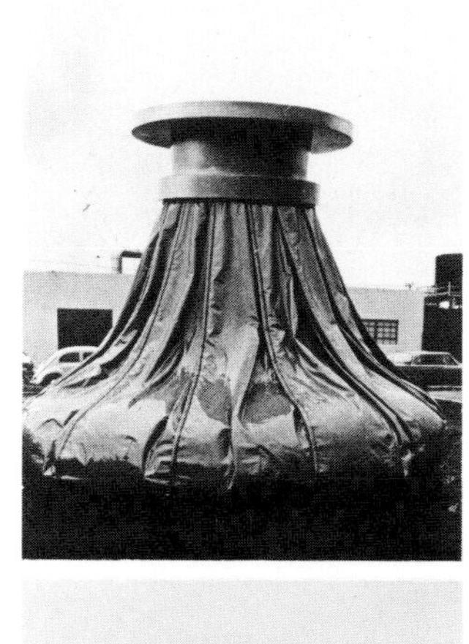
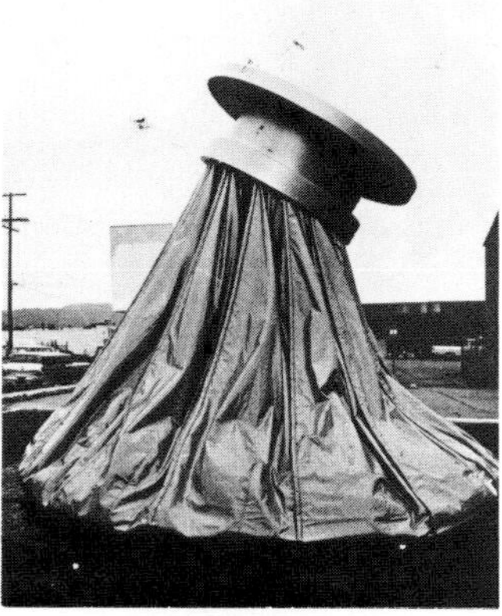
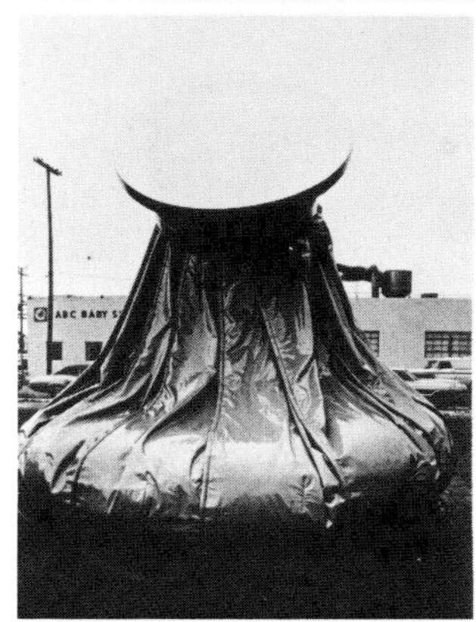
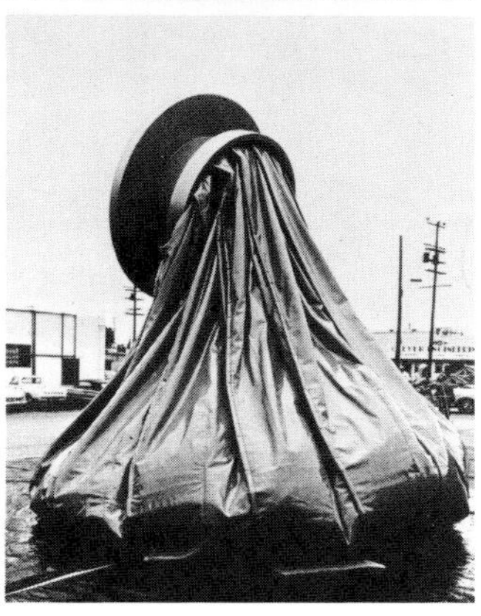

25-29. Claes Oldenburg. *Ice Bag—Scale B.* 1970. Programmed kinetic sculpture of polyvinyl, fiberglass, wood, and hydraulic and mechanical movements, 16 x 18 x 18' (4.9 x 5.5 x 5.5 m). National Gallery of Art, Washington, D.C.

meaning and social content. *To Listen* (fig. 25-28) is a totemic figure reminiscent of Moore's *Two Forms* (see fig. 25-18) in its elemental shape but with the rugged strength that defines Edwards' work. Attached to it is the fragment of a chain. This is a favorite motif that recurs in his *Lynch Fragment* series—small works that radiate a truly frightening menace. In addition to denoting slavery, the chain has a positive meaning for the artist, to whom it signifies links with the past and the larger community. Likewise, abstraction helps him get in touch with his roots while providing a common ground of experience. In this respect he is close to his friend the painter William T. Williams (see page 822). Edwards revels in the labor of sculpture, the very feel of metal, which is reflected in the vigorous, handmade finish, a further debt to Smith. The result is a powerful monument to the African-American struggle for freedom and equality. The sculpture has the dignity of the man himself and reflects the artist's strong sense of social responsibility.

MONUMENTS. Made on a large scale, most Primary Structures are obviously monuments. But just as obviously they are not monuments commemorating or celebrating anything except their designer's imagination. They offer no ready frame of reference, nothing to be reminded of, even though the original meaning of "monument" is "a reminder." Monuments in the traditional sense died out when contemporary society lost its consensus about what ought to be publicly remembered; yet the belief in the possibility of such monuments has not been abandoned altogether.

OLDENBURG. The Pop artist Claes Oldenburg (b. 1929) has proposed a number of imaginative solutions to the problem of the monument. He is, moreover, an exceptionally persuasive commentator on his ideas. All his monuments are heroic in size, though not in subject matter. And all share one feature: their origin in humble objects of everyday use.

In 1969 Oldenburg conceived his most unusual project. For a piece of outdoor sculpture he wanted a form that combined hard and soft and did not need a base. An ice bag met these demands, so he bought one and started playing with it. He soon realized, he says, that the object was made for manipulation, "that movement was part of its identity and should be used." He then executed a work shaped like a huge ice bag (fig. 25-29) with a mechanism inside to make it produce "movements caused by an invisible hand," as the artist described them. He sent the giant *Ice Bag* to the U.S. Pavilion at EXPO 70 in Osaka, Japan, where crowds were endlessly fascinated to watch it heave, rise, and twist like a living thing, then relax with an almost audible sigh.

What do such monuments celebrate? Part of their charm, which they share with readymades and Pop Art, is that they reveal the aesthetic potential of the ordinary and all-too-familiar. But they also have an undeniable grandeur. There is one dimension, however, that is missing in Oldenburg's monuments. They delight, astonish, amuse—but they do not move us. Wholly secular, wedded to the here and now, they fail to touch our deepest emotions.

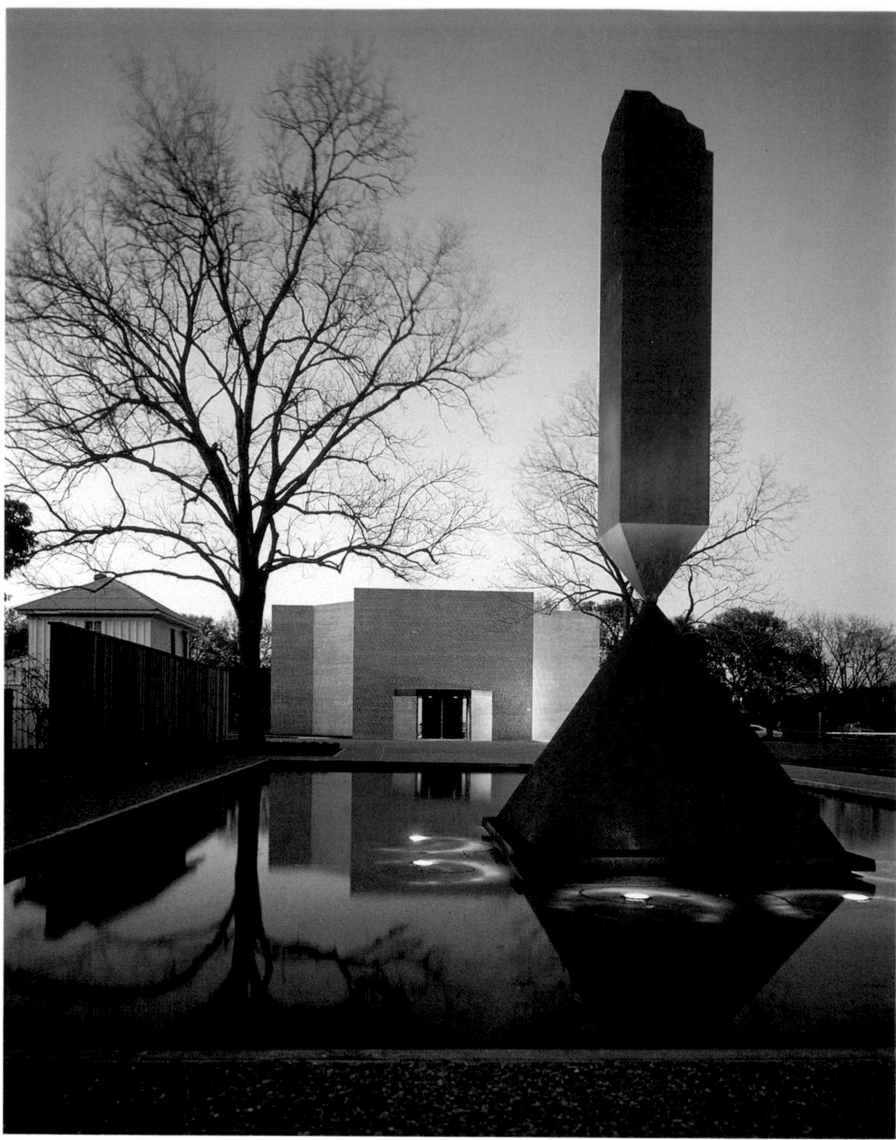

25-30. Barnett Newman. *Broken Obelisk*. 1963–67. Steel, height 25'1" (7.7 m). Rothko Chapel, Houston

NEWMAN. One of the few monuments successful in this regard is *Broken Obelisk* (fig. 25-30) by Barnett Newman (1905–1970). This artist was inspired by profound religious beliefs and philosophical ideas, which he struggled throughout his life to translate into visual form. Newman conceived *Broken Obelisk* in 1963 but could not have it executed until four years later, when he found the right steel fabricator. Rising from the center of a shallow reflecting pool, it consists of a square base plate supporting a four-sided pyramid whose tip meets and supports that of the upended broken obelisk.

Obelisks are slender, four-sided pillars of stone erected by the ancient Egyptians. The Romans brought many of them to Italy; one marks the center of the piazza of St. Peter's (see fig. 17-15). These gave rise to a number of later monuments in Europe and America. The two tips in Newman's sculpture have exactly the same angle (53 degrees, borrowed from that of the Egyptian pyramids, which had long fascinated the artist). Hence their juncture forms a perfect X. Why this monument has such power to stir our feelings is difficult to put into words. Is it the daring juxtaposition of two age-old shapes that have contrary meanings, the one symbolizing timeless stability, the other a thrust toward the heavens? Surely, but what if the obelisk were intact? Would that not reduce the whole to an improbable balancing feat? The brokenness of the obelisk, then, is essential to the pathos of the monument. It speaks to us of our unfulfilled spiritual yearnings, of a quest for the infinite and universal that persists today as it has for thousands of years.

NOGUCHI. The search for meaning also absorbed the Japanese-American sculptor Isamu Noguchi (1904–1988). Influenced early on by the Surrealists, as well as by Brancusi, he did not confront Oriental culture until a prolonged stay in Japan in 1952 that proved decisive to his formation. From then on, he developed into one of the most varied sculptors of this century whose rich imagination fed on both heritages. His role in mediating between East and West was of incalculable importance. To the Japanese he introduced modern Western ideas of style; to Americans he made traditional Japanese concepts of art comprehensible at a time when there was a growing fascination with Zen Buddhism. We see this union in his fountain for the John Hancock Insurance Company in New Orleans (fig. 25-31). Like much of Zen thought, it is an elegantly simple statement of a paradoxical idea. A "capital" rather like the wood-beam supports in a Japanese temple sits atop a grooved column recalling the primitive Doric of ancient Greece, where the Western sculptural tradition of which Noguchi felt himself a part originated. Except for the flat faces on either side of the capital, the finish has been left rough, out of the age-old Japanese respect for the natural materials and unadorned simplicity in the crafts. It gives the fountain a primeval look that emphasizes the stone's origin in the earth, for which Noguchi acquired an Oriental veneration. The contrast to the sleek modern lines of the Hancock building could hardly be greater. Yet the placement of the fountain shows not only a Japanese sensitivity to space but a fundamental understanding of the logic of modern architecture that Japanese critics recognized as distinctly Western.

25-31. Isamu Noguchi. Fountain for the John Hancock Insurance Company, New Orleans. 1961–62. Granite, 16' (4.88 m)

LIN. Part of the problem confronting the monument maker in our era is that, unlike a century ago, there is so little worth commemorating in the first place—no event, no cause unites our fragmented world, despite the momentous changes going on everywhere—and no artistic vocabulary that we readily agree on. It is all the more ironic that the best-known memorial to American soldiers killed in Vietnam should turn out to be not an embarrassing reminder of one of the most bitterly divisive chapters in recent history but an eloquent testimony to the universal tragedy of war (fig. 25-32). Designed by Maya Lin (b. 1959), it casts a spell on all those who see it. What is its secret? The very simplicity of the architectural form and its setting are disarming. By comparison, all other war memorials of recent times seem trite and needlessly complex, especially those incorporating realistic figures. It evokes a solemn mood without the inflated rhetoric that mars most memorials. The triangular shape, although embedded in tradition and rich in historical connotations (compare fig. 21-58), permits viewers to form their own associations because of its abstractness. Moreover, the reflective quality of the polished granite draws the viewer into the work. Yet these attributes alone cannot account for its extraordinary impact. Like Labrouste before her (see page 729), Lin seized on the simple but brilliant idea of inscribing names—thousands of them—whose cumulative effect is to bring home the full enormity of the tragedy with awesome power. This device does not tell the story either, since names inscribed on walls or tombs rarely move us, least of all those of people we never knew. In the end, the *Vietnam Veterans Memorial* is that rare instance of perfect consonance between form and idea. So singular is this achievement that no artist has been able to duplicate its success, though Lin herself has come close.

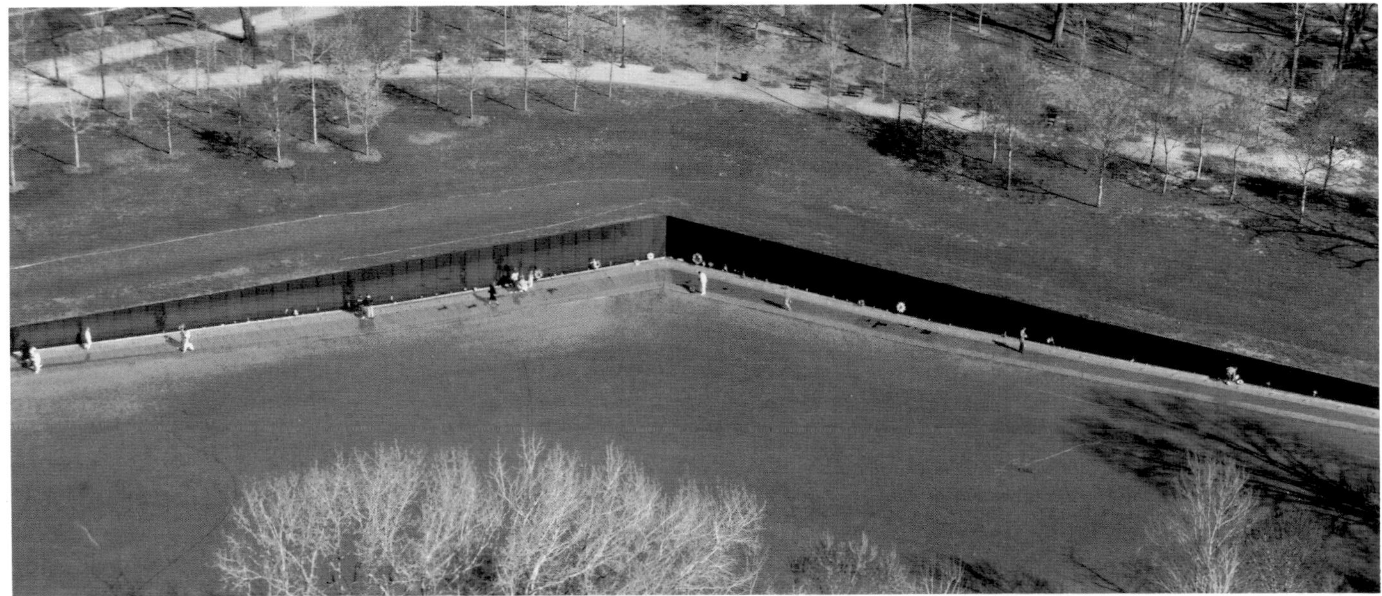

25-32. Maya Lin. *Vietnam Veterans Memorial.* 1982. Black granite, length 500' (152 m). The Mall, Washington, D.C.

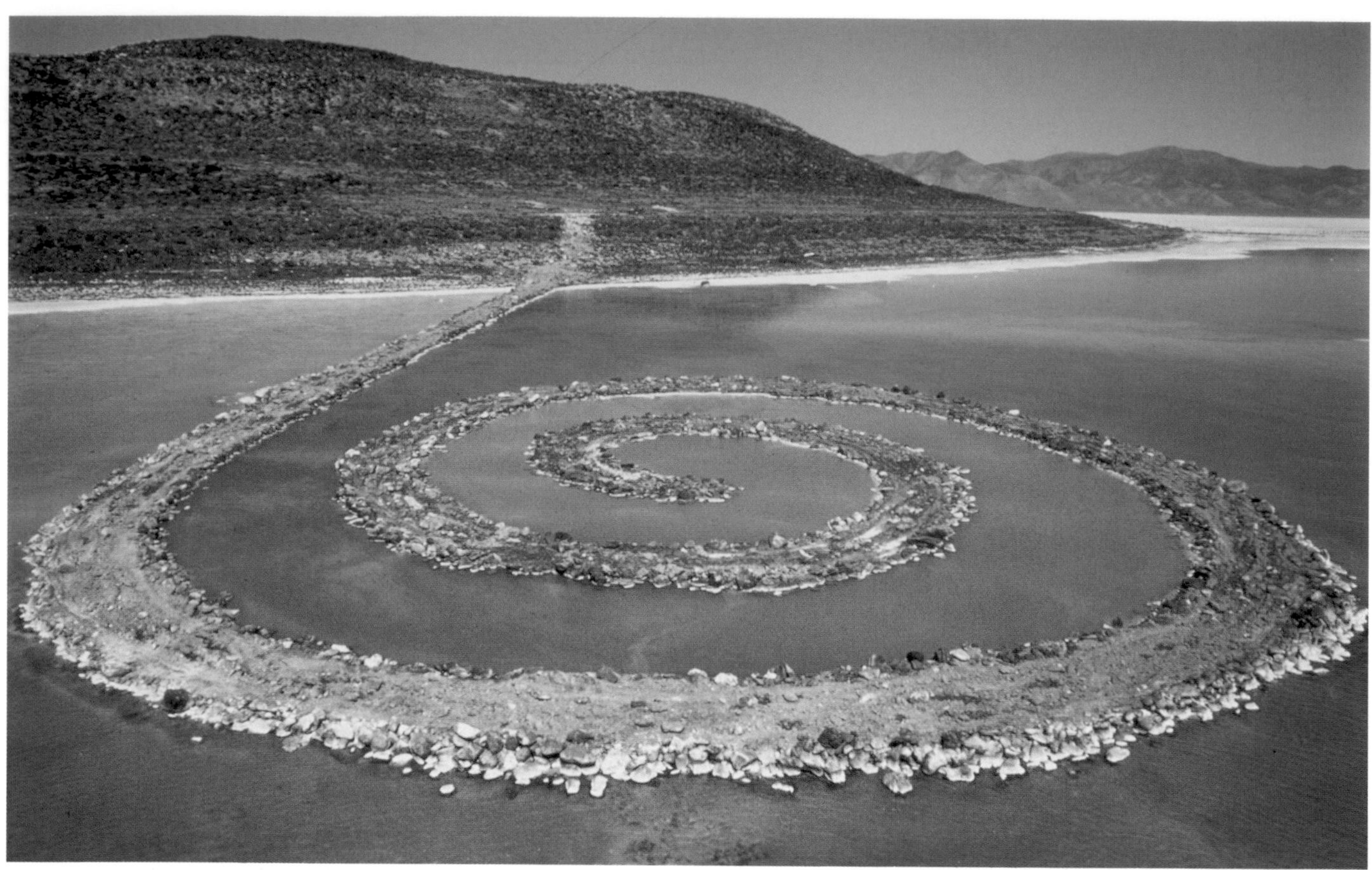

25-33. Robert Smithson. *Spiral Jetty.* As built in 1970. Total length 1,500' (457.2 m); width of jetty 15' (4.6 m). Great Salt Lake, Utah

EARTH ART. Because of its space-articulating function we might be tempted to call the *Vietnam Veterans Memorial* a work of architecture, like Stonehenge; yet it is so sculptural that it belongs equally well to Primary Structures. The two categories merge in "Earth Art," which is the ultimate medium for Environmental Sculpture, since it provides complete freedom from the limitations of the human scale. Logically enough, some designers of Primary Structures have turned to it. In some instances they have invented projects that stretch over many miles. These latter-day successors to the mound-building Indians of Neolithic times have the advantage of modern earth-moving machinery, but this is more than outweighed by the problem of cost and the difficulty of finding suitable sites on our crowded planet.

SMITHSON. The few projects of theirs that have actually been carried out are mostly found in remote regions of western America, so that the finding is itself often difficult. *Spiral Jetty,* the work of Robert Smithson (1938–1973), jutted out into Great Salt Lake in Utah (fig. 25-33). Its appeal rests in part on the Surrealist irony of the concept: a spiral jetty is as self-contradictory as a straight corkscrew. But it can hardly be said to have grown out of the natural formation of the terrain like the Great Serpent Mound (see fig. 1-20). No wonder it has not endured long nor was it intended to. The process by which nature is reclaiming *Spiral Jetty,* already twice submerged, was part of Smithson's design from the start. The project nevertheless lives on in photographs. How can such a thing be called art? To Smithson, "The strata of the Earth is a jumbled museum. When one scans the ruined sites of prehistory one sees a heap of wrecked maps that upsets our present art historical limits . . . there is only an uncertain disintegrating order that transcends the limits of rational separations. The brain itself resembles an eroded rock from which ideas and ideals leak."

CHRISTO. The projects of Christo (Christo Javacheff, b. 1935), who has gained notoriety for wrapping things, are deliberately short-lived. They enhance the environment only temporarily instead of altering it permanently. *Surrounded Islands, Biscayne Bay, Miami,* his most satisfying project, was installed for all of two weeks in the spring of 1983. Part Conceptual Art, part Happening (see pages 860–61), this ambitious repackaging of nature was a public event involving a small army of assistants. While the emphasis was on the campaign itself, the outcome was a triumph of epic fantasy.

Photographs hardly do justice to the results. Our collage of Christo's drawings, an aesthetic object in its own right, gives a

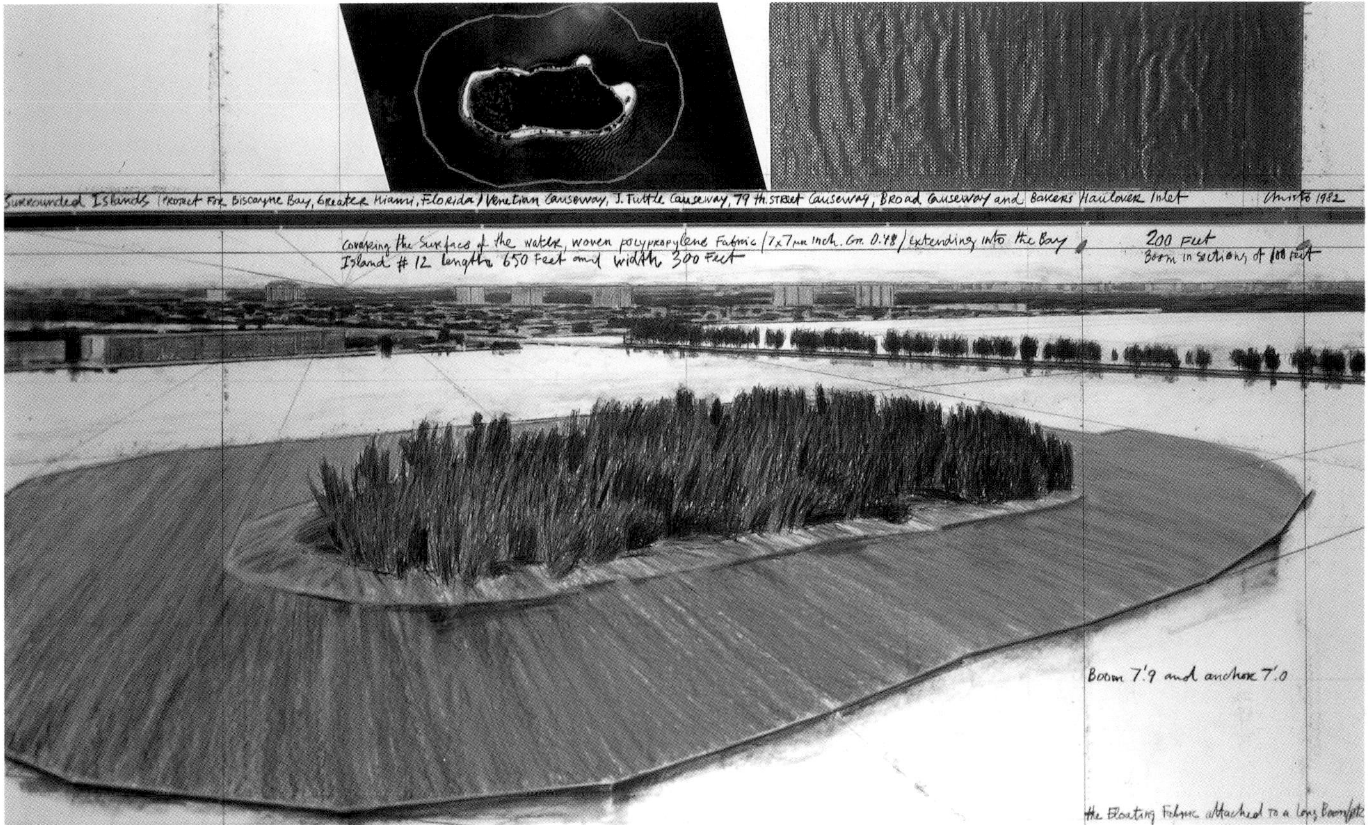

25-34. Christo (Christo Javacheff). *Surrounded Islands, Project for Biscayne Bay, Greater Miami, Florida.* 1982. Drawing in two parts, 1'3" x 8' (.38 x 2.44 m) and 3'6" x 8' (1.06 x 2.44 m). Pencil, charcoal, pastel, crayon, enamel paint, aerial photograph, and fabric sample. Private collection

COPYRIGHT CHRISTO 1982

clearer picture of the artist's intention by presenting the project in different ways and suggesting the complex experience it provided (fig. 25-34). (The sale of drawings such as this helped to fund the project.) In effect, Christo turned the islands into inverse lily pads of pink fabric. If Smithson's *Spiral Jetty* suggests the futility of grandiose undertakings, Christo's visual pun is as festive and decorative as Monet's water lily paintings (see fig. 22-17), an inspiration the artist has acknowledged.

CONSTRUCTIONS AND ASSEMBLAGE. Constructions present a difficult problem. If we agree to restrict the term *sculpture* to objects made of a single substance, then we must put "assemblages" (constructions using mixed mediums) in a class of their own. This is probably a useful distinction because of their kinship with readymades. But what of Picasso's *Bull's Head* (see fig. 25-15)? Is it not an instance of assemblage, and have we not called it a piece of sculpture? Actually, there is no inconsistency here. The *Bull's Head* is a bronze cast, even though we cannot tell this by looking at a photograph of it. Had Picasso wished to display the actual handlebars and bicycle seat, he would surely have done so. Since he chose to have them cast in bronze, it must have been because he wanted to "dematerialize" the components of the work by having them reproduced in a single material. Apparently he felt it necessary to clarify the relation of image to reality in this way—the sculptor's way—and he used the same procedure whenever he worked with readymade objects.

Nevertheless, we must not apply the "single-material" rule too strictly. Calder's mobiles, for instance, often combine metal, string, wood, and other substances. Yet they do not strike us as being assemblages because these materials are not allowed to assert their separate identities. Conversely, an object may deserve to be called an assemblage even though composed of essentially the same material. Such is often true of works known as "junk sculpture." These are made of fragments of old machinery, parts of wrecked automobiles, and similar discards, which constitute a broad class that can be called sculpture, assemblage, or environment, depending on the work itself.

RAUSCHENBERG. Robert Rauschenberg (b. 1925) pioneered assemblage as early as the mid-1950s. Much like a composer making music out of the noises of everyday life (see box page 825), he constructed works of art from the trash of urban civilization. *Odalisk* (fig. 25-35) is a box covered with an assortment of pasted

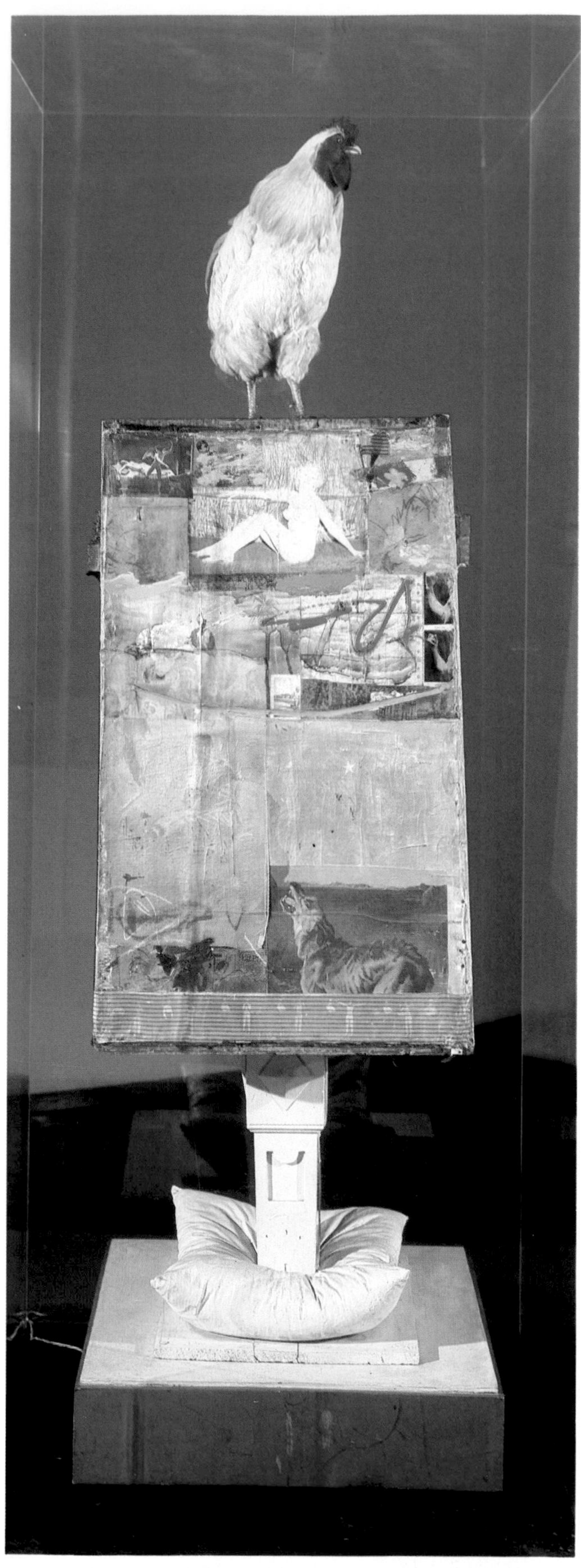

25-35. Robert Rauschenberg. *Odalisk*. 1955–58. Construction, 6'9" x 2'1" x 2'1" (2.06 x .64 x .64 m). Museum Ludwig, Cologne

images—comic strips, photos, clippings from picture magazines—held together only by the network of brushstrokes the artist has painted on them. The box perches on a foot improbably anchored to a pillow on a wooden platform and is topped by a stuffed chicken.

The title is a witty blend of "odalisque" and "obelisk." It refers both to the nude girls among the collage of clippings as modern "harem girls" and to the shape of the construction as a whole, for the box shares its verticality and slightly tapering sides with real obelisks. Rauschenberg's unlikely "monument" has at least some qualities in common with its predecessors: compactness and self-sufficiency. We will recognize in this unlikely juxtaposition the same ironic intent as the readymades of Duchamp, whom Rauschenberg had come to know well in New York.

NEVELSON. Although it is almost always made entirely of wood, the work of Louise Nevelson (1900–1988) must be classified as assemblage, and when extended to a monumental scale, it acquires the status of an environment. Before Nevelson, there had not been any important American women sculptors in the twentieth century. Sculpture had traditionally been reserved for men because of the manual labor involved. Thanks to the women's suffrage movement in the second half of the nineteenth century, Harriet Hosmer (1830–1908) and her "White Marmorean Flock" (as the novelist Henry James called her and her followers in Rome) had succeeded in legitimizing sculpture as a medium for women. This school of sculpture waned, however, when the sentimental, idealizing Neoclassical style fell out of favor after the Philadelphia Centennial of 1876.

In the 1950s Nevelson rejected external reality and began to construct a private one from her collection of found pieces of wood, both carved and rough. At first these self-contained realms were miniature cityscapes, but they soon grew into large environments of freestanding "buildings," complete with decorations that were inspired by the sculpture on Mayan ruins. Nevelson's work generally took the form of large wall units that flatten her architecture into reliefs (fig. 25-36). Assembled from individual compartments, the whole is always painted a single color, usually a matte black to suggest the shadowy world of dreams. Each unit is elegantly designed and is itself a metaphor of thought or experience. While the organization is governed by an inner logic, the statement remains an enigmatic monument to the artist's imagination.

CHASE-RIBOUD. Nevelson's success has encouraged other American women to become sculptors. Barbara Chase-Riboud (b. 1939), a prizewinning novelist and poet who lives in Paris and Rome, belongs to a generation of remarkable black women who have made significant contributions to several of the arts at once. She is heir to a unique American tradition. It is a paradox that whereas black women almost never carve in traditional African cultures, in America they found their first artistic outlet as sculptors. They were attracted to it by the example set by Harriet Hosmer at a time when abolitionism and feminism were closely allied liberal causes.

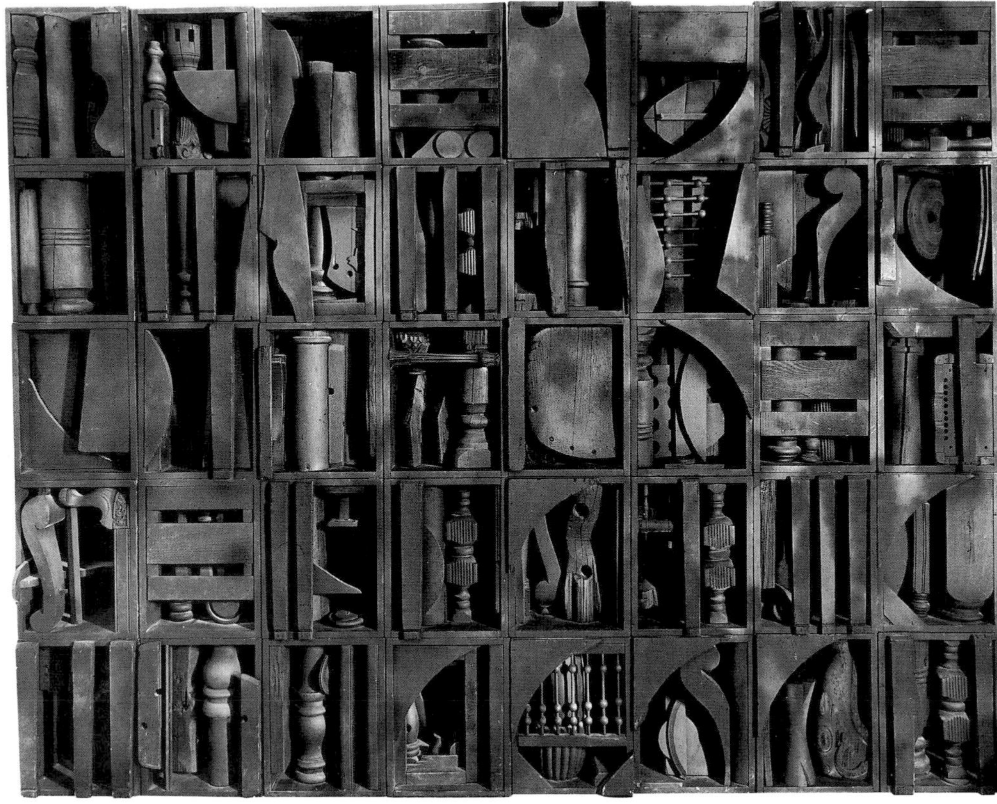

(LEFT) 25-36. Louise Nevelson. *Black Chord.* 1964. Painted wood, 8' x 10' x 11½" (2.44 x 3.05 x .29 m). Collection Joel Ehrenkranz

(RIGHT) 25-37. Barbara Chase-Riboud. *Confessions for Myself.* 1972. Bronze, painted black, and black wool, 10' x 3'4" x 1' (3.05 x 1.02 x .30 m). University Art Museum, University of California at Berkeley
PURCHASED WITH FUNDS FROM THE H. W. ANDERSON CHARITABLE FOUNDATION

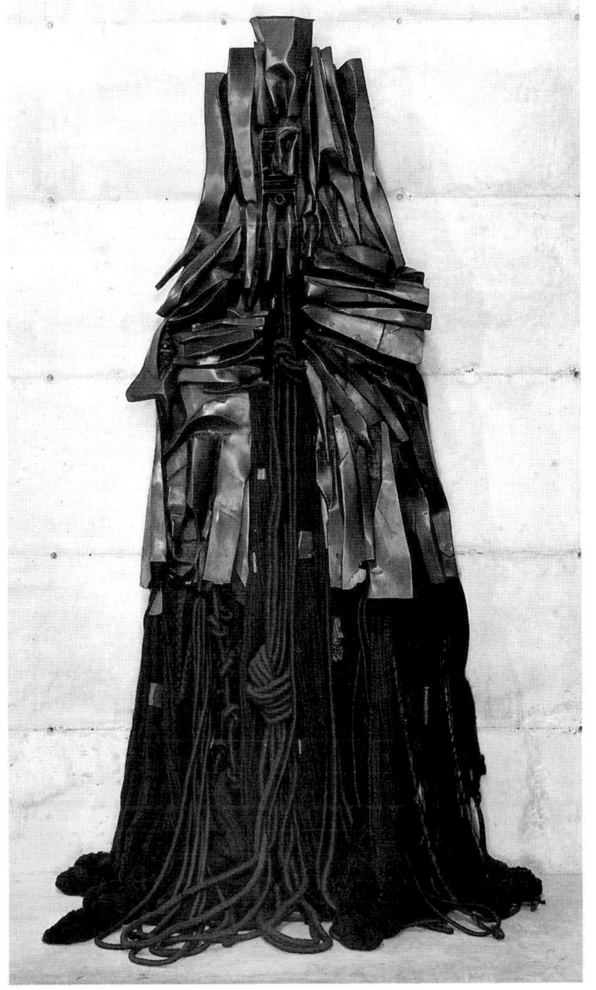

Chase-Riboud received a traditional training in her native Philadelphia, the first center of minority artists. The monumental sculpture she developed in the early 1970s makes an indelible impression. In *Confessions for Myself* (fig. 25-37) she has envisioned a demonic archetype of awesome power. Her highly individual aesthetic utilizes a combination of bronze, either polished or with a black patina, and braided fiber. Similar qualities can be found in cast bronze figures from Benin and in carved wooden masks by the Senufo tribe, which are sometimes decorated with textiles. The form can be compared to a poem: each fold is like a strophe that contributes to the total meaning of the work. Nor is the analogy an accident, for Chase-Riboud's growth as an artist coincided with her development as a poet. The title in this case comes from one of the poems that she wrote around the same time. She began the sculpture with it in mind, which accounts for the extremely personal nature of the work. Her sculpture expresses a distinctly ethnic sensibility and feminist outlook. At the same time, she is like an archaeologist, peeling back layer after layer of personal memory to reveal a meaning from deep within our collective subconscious. Thus she achieves a universality in keeping with her cosmopolitan view of art and life. Ironically, Chase-Riboud has found wider acceptance in Europe than in the United States. Because it transcends barriers of race and culture, her work does not meet preconceived stereotypes of black art.

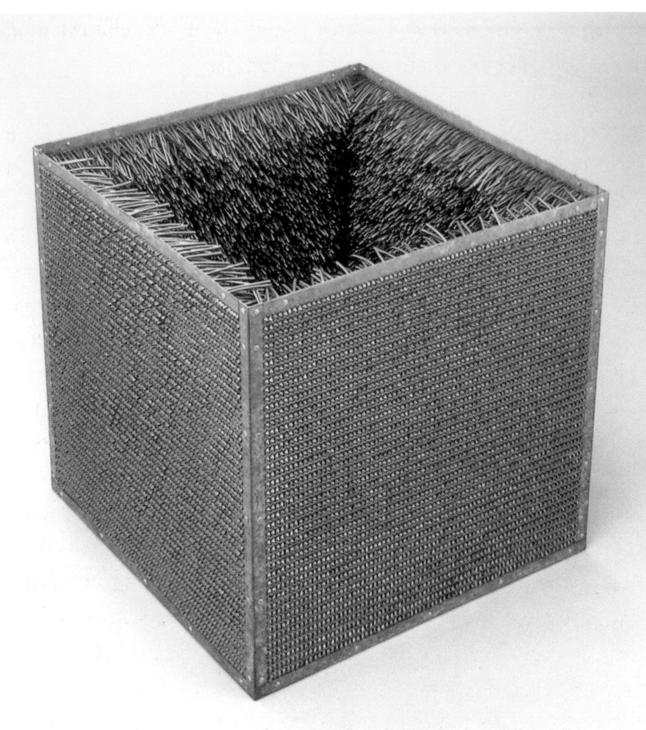

25-38. Eva Hesse. *Accession II.* 1967. Steel and rubber tubes, 30¾ x 30¾ x 30¾" (78 x 78 x 78 cm). The Detroit Institute of Arts
FOUNDERS SOCIETY PURCHASE, FRIENDS OF MODERN ART AND MISCELLANEOUS GIFTS FUND

HESSE. A special case is provided by Eva Hesse (1936–1970), who had just begun to hit her stride when her life was cut short by cancer. It is impossible to separate her work from her life, which is known in considerable detail, thanks to her diaries and many interviews. [See Primary Sources, no. 98, page 940.] While not a feminist, she has been treated as a heroine by the women's liberation movement because of her personal and artistic struggles. In many respects she represented the very prototype of the feminist artist, one who was later to provide inspiration to others. Her sculpture nevertheless defies convenient categories. It began to develop rapidly only in 1966 as the result of a stay in Germany, where she was influenced by Joseph Beuys and his Zero Group (see page 860). For her as for Beuys, art had the ability to heal through its power of revelation, only it was private rather than social. Her artistic milieu was the New York Minimalists that included her closest friends. Her work derives its best features from both circles but is entirely individual.

To look at Hesse's sculpture is to see a central mystery unveiled through its often paradoxical, mythic character. *Accession II* (fig. 25-38) has aptly been described as "suggesting a stylistic collision between one of Donald Judd's minimalist aluminum boxes and Meret Oppenheim's Surrealist fur-covered teacup of 1936." (Compare figs. 25-24 and 25-12.) Aesthetically it has the spareness of Minimalist art but with infinitely richer meaning. It possesses all the enigma of Pandora's box and the piquancy of an erotic fetish. This quality is found throughout Hesse's mature work, which is saturated with unmistakable sexual overtones.

ENVIRONMENTS AND INSTALLATIONS. A number of artists associated with Pop Art have also turned to assemblage because they find the flat surface of the canvas too confining. In order to bridge the gap between image and reality, they often introduce three-dimensional objects into their pictures. Some even construct full-scale models of everyday things and real-life situations, utilizing every conceivable kind of material in order to embrace the entire range of their physical environment, including the people, in their work. These "environments" combine the qualities of painting, sculpture, collage, and stagecraft. Being three-dimensional, they can claim to be considered sculpture, but the claim rests on a convention that Pop Art itself has helped to make obsolete. According to this convention, a flat or smoothly curved work of art covered with colors is a painting (or, if the surface is not covered, a drawing). Everything else is sculpture, whether or not the surface is colored and regardless of the material, size, or degree of relief—unless we can enter it, in which case we call it architecture.

Our habit of using the term *sculpture* in this sense is only a few hundred years old. Antiquity and the Middle Ages had separate terms to denote various kinds of sculpture according to the materials and working processes involved but no single term that covered them all. Maybe it is time to revive such distinctions and to modify the all-inclusive definition of sculpture by acknowledging "environments" as a separate category, distinct from both painting and sculpture in its combining of different materials ("mixed media") and blurring of the borderline between image and reality. The differences are underscored by "installations," which are environments expanded into room-size settings.

SEGAL. George Segal (b. 1924–2000) created three-dimensional lifesize pictures showing people and objects in everyday situations. The subject of *Cinema* (fig. 25-39) is ordinary enough to be instantly recognizable: a man changing the letters on a movie theater marquee. Yet the relation of image and reality is far more subtle and complex than the scene suggests. The man's figure is cast from a live model by a technique of Segal's invention and retains its ghostly white plaster surface. Thus it is one crucial step removed from our world of daily experience. The neon-lit sign has been carefully designed to complement and set off the shadowed figure. Moreover, the scene is brought down from its normal place high above the entrance to the theater, where we might have seen it in passing, and is shown at eye level, isolated from its natural context, so that we grasp it completely for the first time.

THE KIENHOLZES. Some environments can have a shattering impact on the viewer. This is certainly true of *The State Hospital* (fig. 25-40) by the West Coast artists Edward Kienholz (1927–1994) and Nancy Kienholz (b. 1944), which shows a cell in a ward for senile patients with a naked old man strapped to the lower bunk. He is the victim of physical cruelty, which has reduced what little mental life he has in him almost to the vanishing point. His body is little more than a skeleton covered with leathery, discolored skin, and his head is a glass bowl with live goldfish, of whom we catch an occasional glimpse. The horrifying realism of the scene is completed by the sense of smell. When the

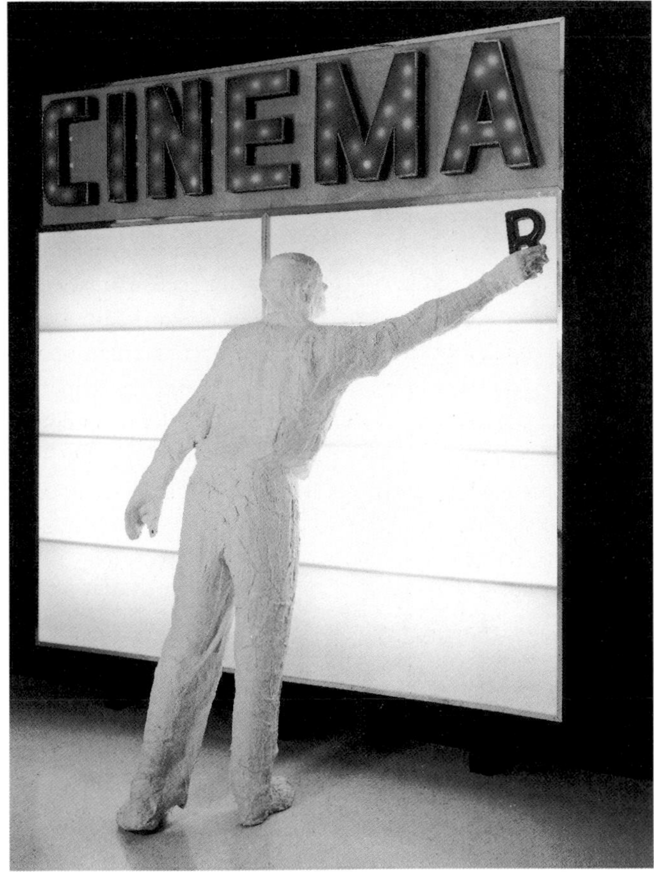

25-39. George Segal. *Cinema.* 1963. Plaster, metal, Plexiglas, and fluorescent light, 9'10" x 8' x 3'3" (3 x 2.4 x .99 m). Albright-Knox Art Gallery, Buffalo, New York

GIFT OF SEYMOUR H. KNOX

work was displayed at the Los Angeles County Museum of Art, it emitted a sickly hospital odor. But what of the figure in the upper bunk? It almost duplicates the one below, with one important difference: it is a mental image, since it is enclosed in the outline of a comic-strip balloon rising from the goldfish bowl. It represents, then, the patient's awareness of himself. The abstract devices of the balloon and the metaphoric goldfish bowl are both alien to the realism of the scene; yet they play an essential part in it, for they help to break the grip of horror and pity. They make us think as well as feel. The Kienholzes' means may be Pop but their goal is that of Greek tragedy. They have no equal as witnesses to the unseen miseries beneath the surface of modern life.

PFAFF. The work of Judy Pfaff (b. 1946) is as exuberant as the Kienholzes' is somber. Her constructions and environments bring to mind the fantasies of Robert Rauschenberg, but they are characterized by playfulness rather than ironic wit. Pfaff's installations make similar use of painting with sculpture and found materials to activate architectural space. *Dragons* (fig. 25-41) is aptly named for its fiery forms and brilliant colors, which make it as festive as a Chinese New Year's celebration. Pfaff's impulsive energy is the equivalent of Jackson Pollock's in its swirling profusion. The installation is like an Action Painting brought to life, as if the pigments had been left free to roam in space. The experience is one of enchantment as the viewer wanders this exotic indoor jungle.

CONCEPTUAL ART. Conceptual Art has the same "patron saint" as Pop Art: Marcel Duchamp. It arose during the 1960s out of the Happenings staged by Alan Kaprow (b. 1927) and Jean Tinguely (1925–1991) in which the event itself became the art. Conceptual Art challenges our definition of art more radically than Pop, insisting that the leap of the imagination, not the execution, is art. According to this view, works of art can be dispensed with altogether since they are incidental by-products of the imaginative leap. So too can galleries and, by extension, even the artist's public. The creative process need only be documented in some way. Sometimes this is in verbal form, but more often it is by still photography, video, or cinema exhibited within an installation.

Conceptual Art, we will recognize, is akin to Minimalism as a phenomenon of the 1960s, but instead of abolishing content, it eliminates aesthetics from art. This deliberately anti-art approach, stemming from Dada (see page 798), poses a number of stimulating paradoxes. As soon as the documentation takes on visible form, it begins to come perilously close to more traditional forms of art (especially if it is placed in a gallery where it can be seen by

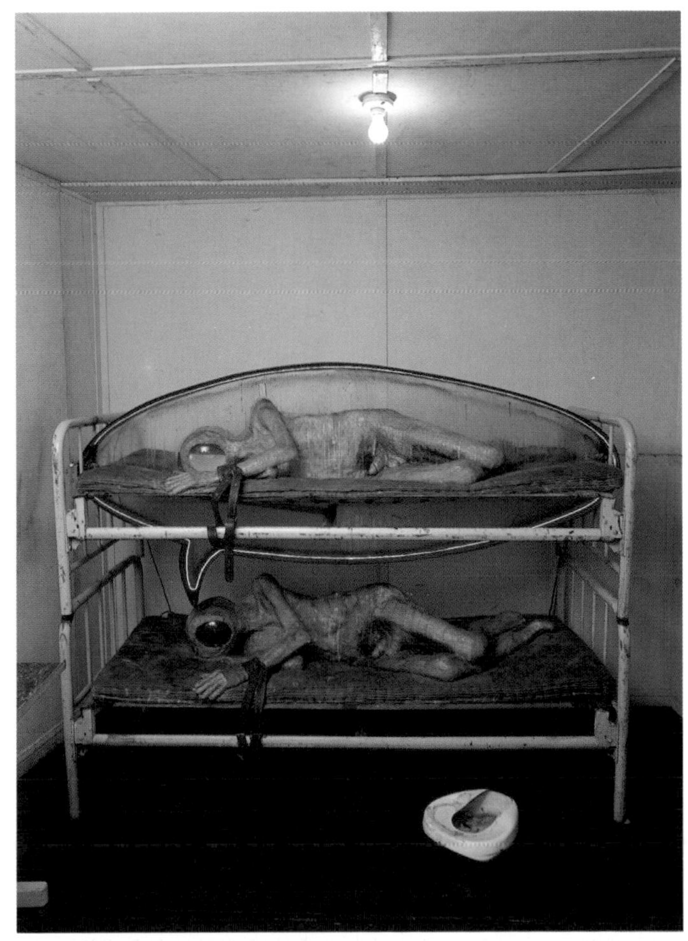

25-40. Edward and Nancy Kienholz. *The State Hospital.* 1966. Mixed media, 8 x 12 x 10' (2.4 x 3.7 x 3.1 m). Moderna Museet, Stockholm

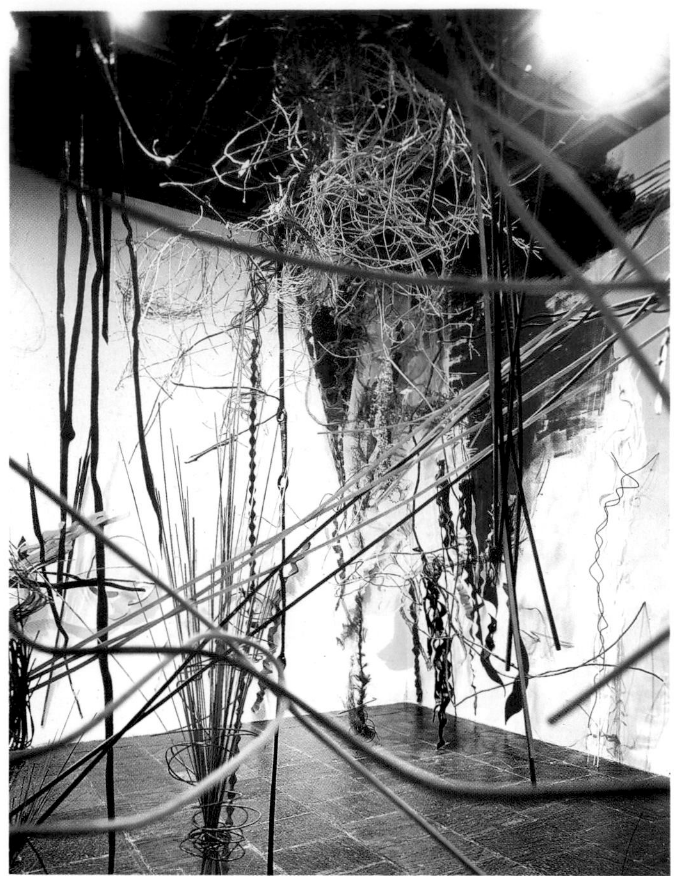

25-41. Judy Pfaff. *Dragons.* 1965. Installation at the Whitney Biennial, February–April 1981. Mixed media.
Whitney Museum of American Art, New York
COURTESY HOLLY SOLOMON GALLERY, NEW YORK

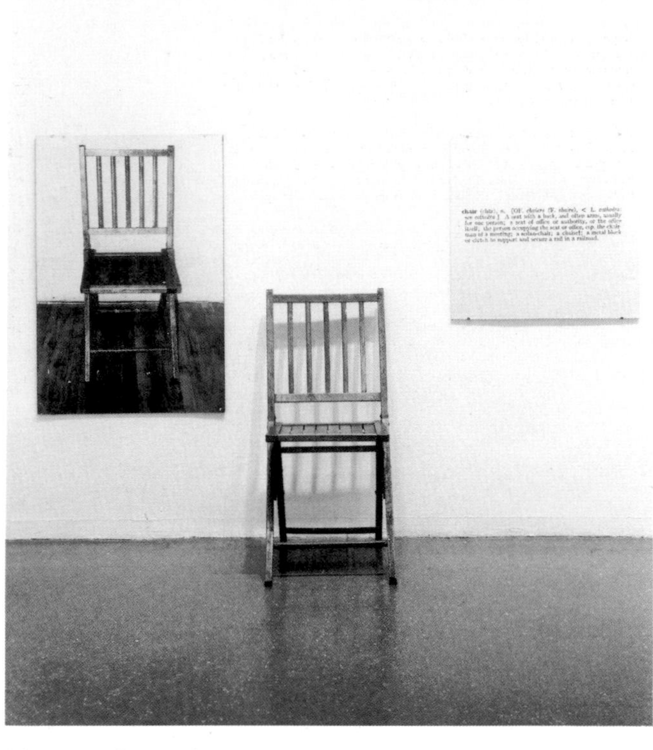

25-42. Joseph Kosuth. *One and Three Chairs.* 1965. Wooden folding chair, photographic copy of chair, and photographic enlargement of dictionary definition of chair; chair 32⅜ x 14⅞ x 20⅞" (82.2 x 37.8 x 53 cm); photo panel 36 x 24⅛" (91.5 x 61.1 cm); text panel 24 x 24⅛" (61 x 61.3 cm). The Museum of Modern Art, New York
LARRY ALDRICH FOUNDATION FUND

an audience). In fact, it is almost impossible to divorce the imagination fully from aesthetic matters.

KOSUTH. We see this in *One and Three Chairs* (fig. 25-42) by Joseph Kosuth (b. 1945), which is clearly indebted to Duchamp's readymades (see fig. 25-11). It "describes" a chair by combining in one installation an actual chair, a full-scale photograph of that chair, and a printed dictionary definition of a chair. Whatever the Conceptual artist's intention, this making of the work of art, no matter how minimal the process, is as essential as it was for Michelangelo. In the end, all art is the final document of the creative process, because without execution, no idea can ever be fully realized. Without such "proof of performance," the Conceptual artist becomes like the emperor wearing new clothes that no one else can see. And, in fact, Conceptual Art has embraced all of the mediums in one form or another.

BALDESSARI. Like Dada, Conceptual Art is notable for its ironic humor—whose bark is admittedly worse than its bite, however. It reached a high point with *Art History,* from *Ingres and Other Parables* by John Baldessari (b. 1931). The image is both a witty spoof on art-history texts such as this book and a telling commentary on the difficulties young artists face in finding acceptance (fig. 25-43). The juxtaposition of a great monument, mock-serious narrative, and absurd moral is meant to deride traditional value judgments about art. Yet it remains strangely innocuous, as if the artist were too self-consciously aware of his mischievous role.

PERFORMANCE ART. Performance Art, which originated in the early decades of this century, belongs for the most part to the history of theater. However, the form that arose in the 1970s combines aspects of Happenings and Conceptual Art with installations. In reaction to Minimalism, artists now wanted to reassert their presence by becoming, in effect, living works of art. The results have relied mainly on the shock value of irreverent humor or explicit sexuality. Nonetheless, Performance Art emerged as perhaps the most characteristic art form of the 1980s.

BEUYS. The German artist Joseph Beuys (1921–1986) managed to overcome these limitations, though he, too, was a controversial figure who incorporated an element of parody into his work. Life for Beuys was a creative process in which everyone is an artist. To him, art was capable of transforming society itself and thus acquired a political mission as well. Beuys assumed the guise of a modern-day shaman intent on healing the spiritual crisis of contemporary life caused, he believed, by the rift between the arts and

ART HISTORY

A young artist had just finished art school. He asked his instructor what he should do next. "Go to New York," the instructor replied, "and take slides of your work around to all the galleries and ask them if they will exhibit your work." Which the artist did.

He went to gallery after gallery with his slides. Each director picked up his slides one by one, held each up to the light the better to see it, and squinted his eyes as he looked. "You're too provincial an artist," they all said. "You are not in the mainstream." "We're looking for Art History."

He tried. He moved to New York. He painted tirelessly, seldom sleeping. He went to museum and gallery openings, studio parties, and artists' bars. He talked to every person having anything to do with art; travelled and thought and read constantly about art. He collapsed.

He took his slides around to galleries a second time. "Ah," the gallery directors said this time, "finally you are historical."

Moral: Historical mispronounced sounds like hysterical.

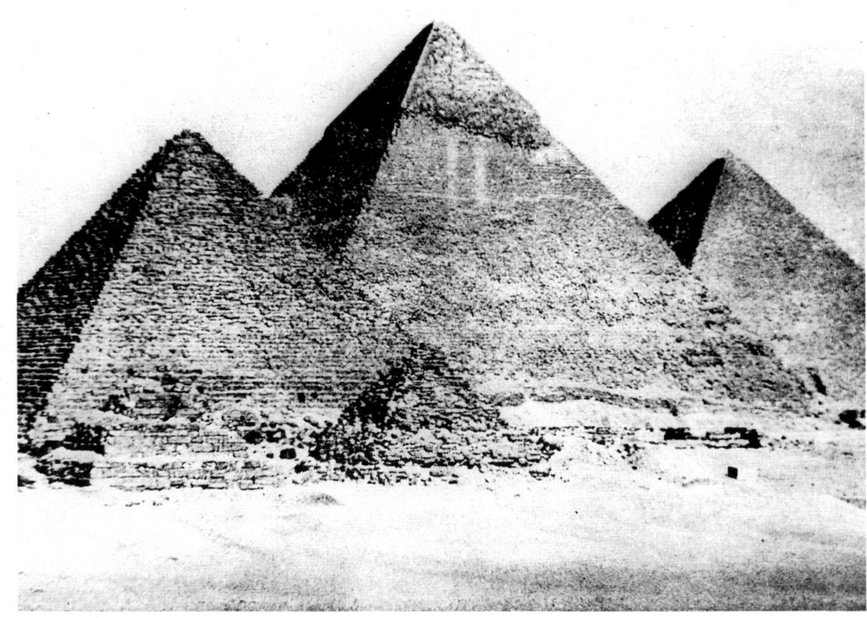

25-43. John Baldessari. *Art History,* from *Ingres and Other Parables.* 1972. Photograph and typed text. Collection Angelo Baldassarre, Bari, Italy

sciences. To find the common denominator behind such divisions, he created objects and scenarios which, though often baffling at face value, were meant to be accessible to the imagination. In 1974, Beuys spent one week caged up in a New York gallery with a coyote (fig. 25-44), an animal sacred to the American Indian but persecuted by the white man. His goal in this "dialogue" was to ease the trauma caused to an entire nation by the schism between the two opposing worldviews. That the attempt was inherently doomed to failure does not in any way reduce the sincerity of this act of conscience.

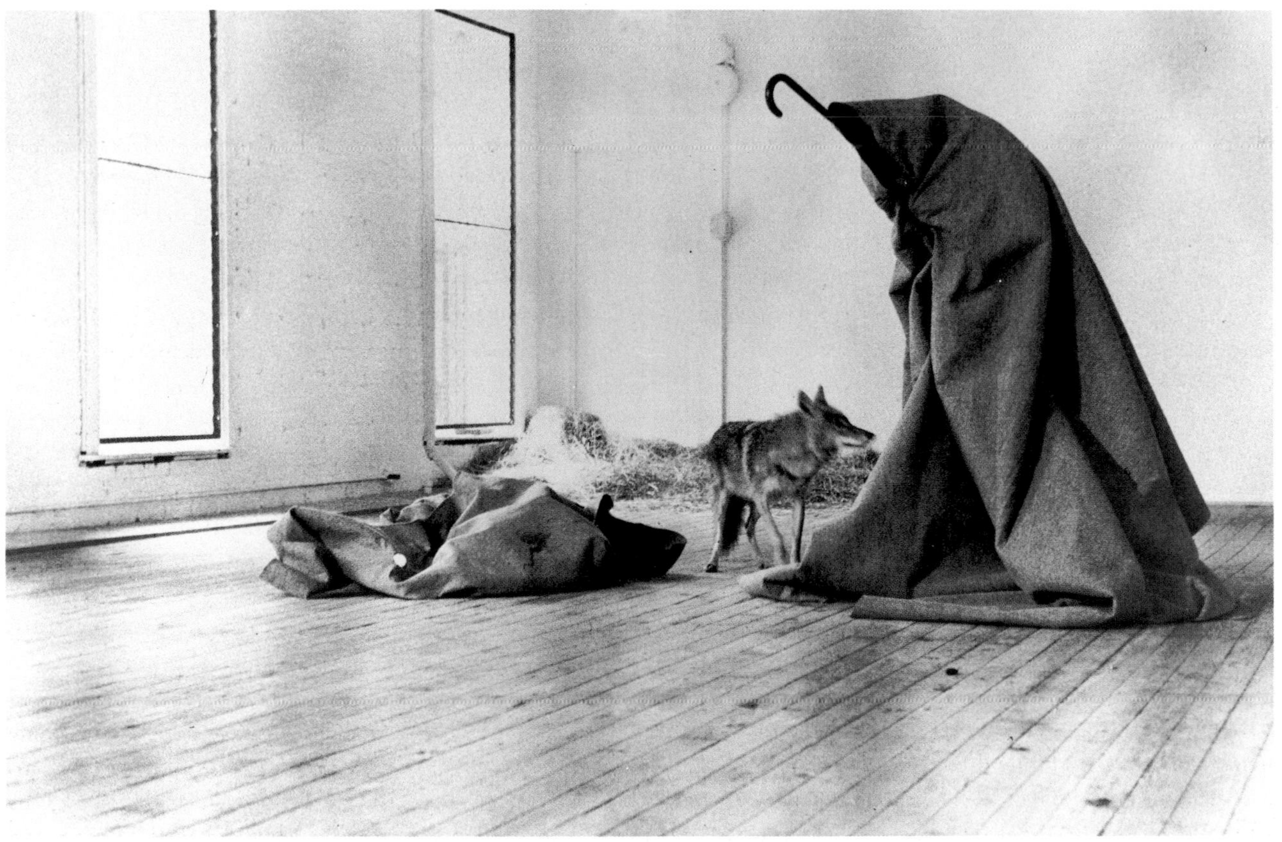

25-44. Joseph Beuys. *Coyote.* Photo of performance at Rene Block Gallery, New York, 1974

PHOTOGRAPH © 1974 CAROLINE TISDALL
COURTESY RONALD FELDMAN FINE ARTS, NEW YORK

CHAPTER TWENTY-SIX

Twentieth-Century Architecture

ARCHITECTURE BEFORE WORLD WAR I

Modernism in twentieth-century architecture has meant first and foremost an aversion to historicism and to decoration for its own sake without a trace of historicism. Instead, it favors a clean functionalism, which expresses the Machine Age, with its insistent rationalism. In this way, it can be regarded as the successor to classicism and, more specifically, the tradition of Structural Rationalism (see page 653). Yet modern architecture demanded far more than a reform of architectural grammar and vocabulary. A new philosophy was needed to take advantage of the expressive qualities of the new building techniques and materials that the engineer had placed at the architect's disposal. The leaders of modern architecture have been vigorous and articulate thinkers, in whose minds architectural theory is closely linked with ideas of social reform to meet the challenges posed by industrial civilization. To them, architecture's ability to shape human experience brings with it the responsibility to play an active role in molding modern society for the better.

Twentieth-century architecture has nevertheless been characterized as much by conservative countermovements and dead ends as by modernism, though it is the latter that defines the age. Moreover, modernism has created as many problems as it has solved, from faulty structures caused by engineering errors to inhuman buildings based on abstract ideals.

WRIGHT. The first indisputably modern architect was Frank Lloyd Wright (1867–1959), Louis Sullivan's great disciple. If Sullivan, Gaudí, Mackintosh, and Van de Velde could be called the Post-Impressionists of architecture, Wright took architecture to its Cubist phase. This is certainly true of his brilliant early style, which he developed between 1900 and 1910 and which had broad international influence. In the beginning, Wright's main activity was the design of suburban homes in the upper Midwest. These were known as Prairie Style houses because their low, horizontal lines were meant to blend with the flat landscape around them.

The last, and most successful, residence in this series is Robie House of 1909 (figs. 26-1 and 26-2). The exterior, so unlike anything seen before, instantly proclaims the building's modernity. However, its "Cubism" is not merely a matter of the clean-cut rectangular elements composing the structure but of Wright's handling of space. Robie House is designed as a number of "space blocks," similar to the building blocks the architect played with as a child, arranged around a central core, the chimney. Some of the blocks are closed and others are open, yet all are defined with equal precision. Thus the space that has been architecturally shaped includes the balconies, terrace, court, and garden, as well as the house itself. As in Analytic Cubism, voids and solids are regarded as equivalents, and the entire complex enters into an active and dramatic relationship with its surroundings.

Wright did not aim simply to design a house but to create a complete environment. In the Francis W. Little House (fig. 26-3), he even took command of the details of the interior and designed stained glass, fabrics, and furniture. The controlling factor here was not the client's special wishes. Rather, it was Wright's conviction that buildings have a profound influence on those who live, work, or worship in them, thus making the architect, consciously or unconsciously, a molder of people.

LOOS. In Europe modern architecture developed more slowly and unevenly and came to maturity only on the eve of World War I, which effectively halted its further growth for nearly a decade. One of the first priests of modernism, Adolf Loos (1870–1933), the son of a Moravian stonemason, spent three years in Chicago during the 1890s and returned to Vienna a convert to functionalism. Architecture to him served a practical purpose as building, not as art. Hence he was violently against the Art Nouveau style of the Secession movement. His credo was, "Modern man, the man with modern nerves, does not need ornamentation; it disgusts him." It was based in part on the socialist view of the craftsman as a slave to the rich bourgeoisie. Curiously enough, this distaste for ornament concerned only the exterior; the inside used rich materials to make up for its lack of decoration, much as at Chiswick (see page

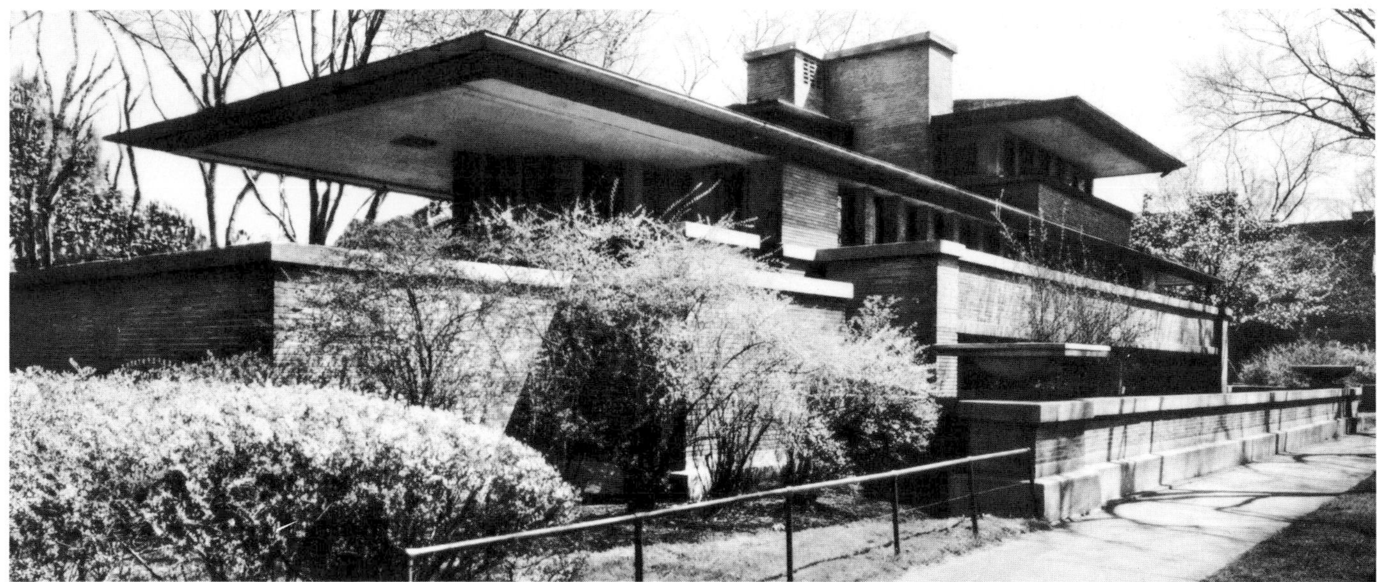

26-1. Frank Lloyd Wright. Robie House, Chicago. 1909

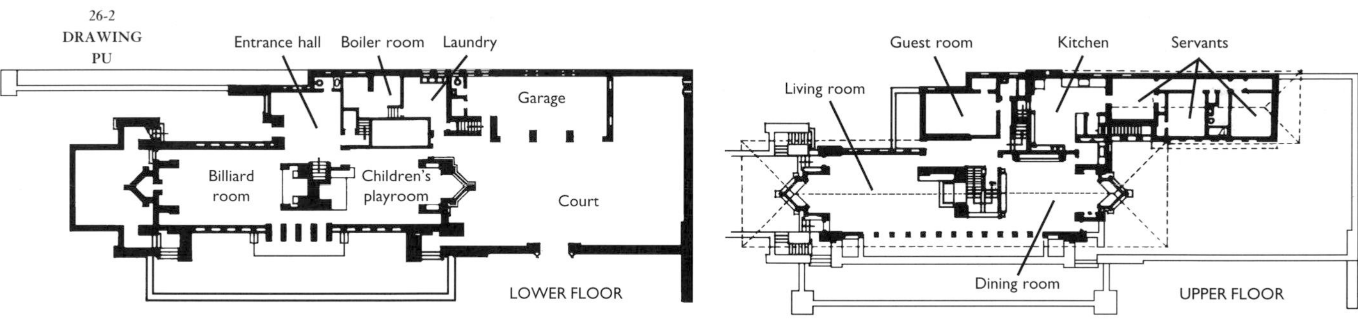

26-2. Plan of Robie House

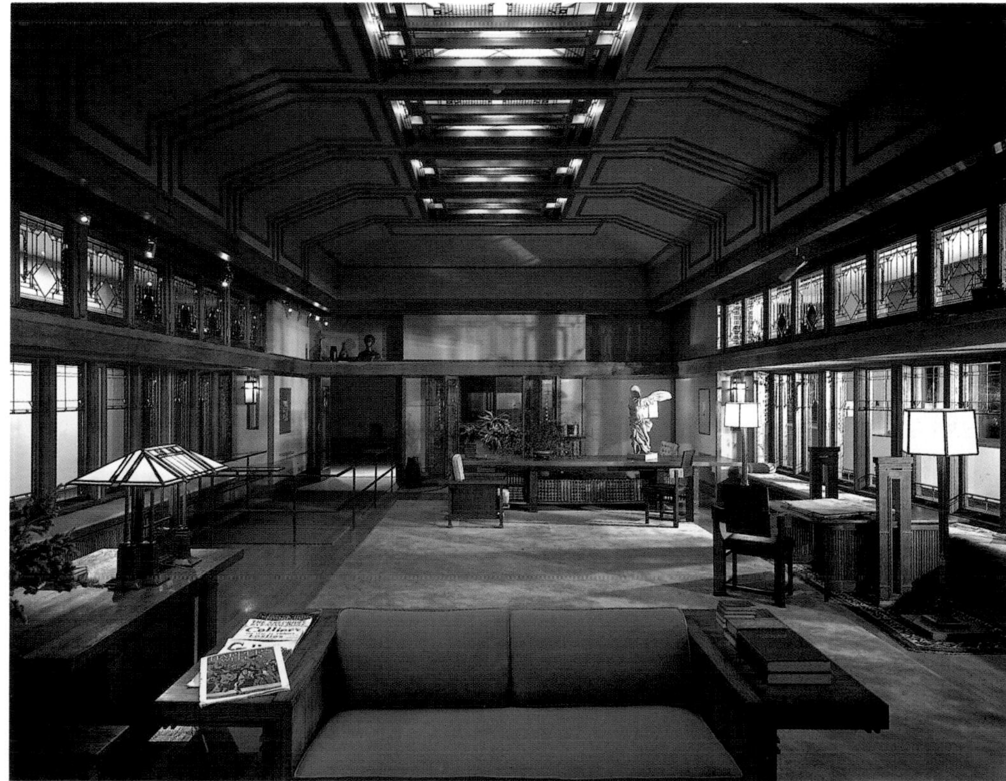

26-3. Frank Lloyd Wright. Installation of the living room from Francis W. Little House. The Metropolitan Museum of Art, New York

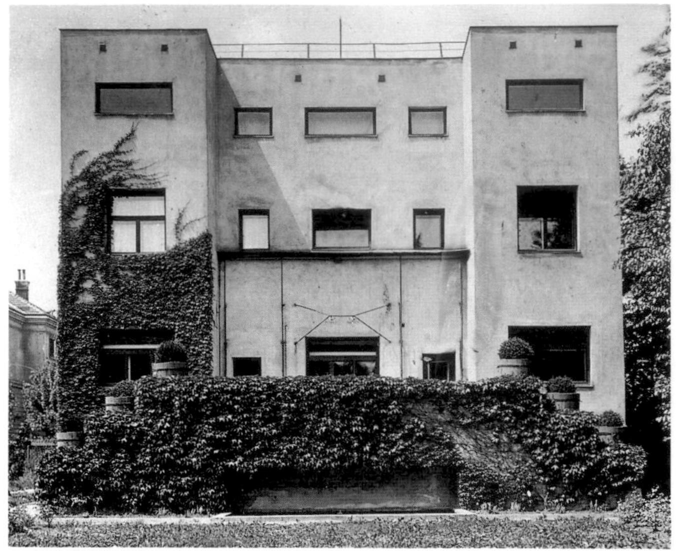

26-4. Adolf Loos. Steiner House, Vienna. 1910

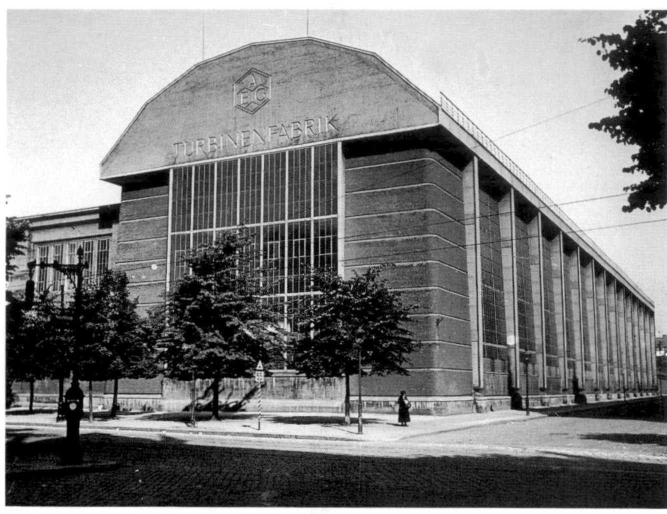

26-5. Peter Behrens. A.E.G. Turbine Factory, Berlin. 1909–10

652). The garden side of Loos' Steiner House from 1910 (fig. 26-4), one of the first private houses built of ferroconcrete (concrete reinforced with steel), is free of decoration and retains its striking modern appearance to this very day. (The front represents an awkward compromise with local building authorities.) In its insistent logic, Steiner House embodies Loos' statement, made the same year, that "like almost every town dweller, the architect possesses no culture. He does not have the security of the peasant to whom this culture is innate. The town dweller is an upstart. I call culture that balance of inner and outer man, which alone can guarantee reasonable thought and action."

DEUTSCHER WERKBUND. A central role to the early development of modernism in Germany was played by the Deutscher Werkbund. This alliance of "the best representatives of art, industry, crafts and trades" was founded in 1907 to upgrade the quality and value of German goods to the level of England's. The leader was Hermann Muthesius (1861–1927), whose mission was to translate the Arts and Crafts Movement into a machine style using the most advanced techniques of industrial design and manufacturing. Its membership consisted of 12 leading industrial firms and a like number of artists, designers, and architects from Germany and Austria.

BEHRENS. The way was led by Peter Behrens (1869–1940), the chief architect and designer for the electrical firm A.E.G. His Turbine Factory of 1909–10 (fig. 26-5) transforms the factory shed into a monument to industry through the unmistakable reference to Greek temples (compare fig. 5-30). Yet it does so without resorting to a historicist veneer. Rather, it defines a modern aesthetic stemming from Mackintosh's Glasgow School of Art (see fig. 23-33). For Behrens, the key to monumentality was not size but "proportionality, the regularity that expresses itself in architectural relationships." The result is an even more austere simplicity than that of Sullivan's Schlesinger and Mayer department store (see fig. 23-40). Structurally there is little new here. Reinforced concrete had been in use since the later nineteenth century. Even the wall of glass does not advance beyond Paxton's Crystal Palace (see fig. 22-36). Nor does the building promote a machine aesthetic or enforce Structural Rationalism. It was nevertheless of critical importance for Behrens' three disciples, who became the founders of modern architecture: Walter Gropius, Ludwig Mies van der Rohe, and Le Corbusier.

GROPIUS. The first to cross that threshold fully was Gropius (1883–1969), who came from a well-known family of architects. The Fagus Shoe Factory (fig. 26-6), designed with his partner Adolf Meyer (1881–1929), represents the crucial step toward modernism in European architecture. The most dramatic feature is the walls, which are a nearly continuous surface of glass. This radical innovation had been possible ever since the introduction of the

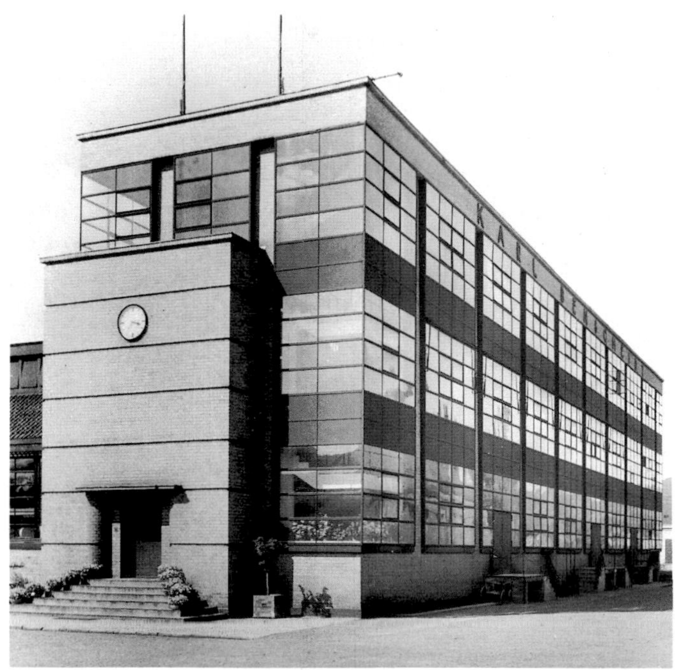

26-6. Walter Gropius and Adolf Meyer.
Fagus Shoe Factory, Alfeld, Germany. 1911–14

structural steel skeleton several decades before, which relieved the wall of any load-bearing function. Sullivan had approached it, but he could not yet free himself from the traditional notion of the window as a "hole in the wall." Far more radically than Sullivan or Behrens, Gropius frankly acknowledged, at last, that in modern architecture the wall is no more than a curtain or climate barrier, which may consist entirely of glass if maximum daylight is wanted. Only in the classical entrance did he give a nod to the past.

TAUT. The Werkbund exhibition of 1914, which featured Van de Velde's theater (see fig. 23-35), was a showcase for a whole generation of young German architects who were to achieve prominence after World War I. Many of the buildings they designed for the fairgrounds anticipate ideas of the 1920s. Among the most adventurous is the staircase of the "Glass House" (fig. 26-7) by Bruno Taut (1880–1938). It was made magically translucent by the use of glass bricks, then a novel material. The structural steel skeleton was as thin and unobtrusive as the great strength of the metal permits. The total effect precociously suggests Stella's *Brooklyn Bridge* (see fig. 24-36) translated into three dimensions.

If the interior seems astonishingly prophetic, the exterior of the "Glass House" (fig. 26-8) was shaped like a multifaceted bulbous crystal, with a multicolored bonnet not unlike those on John Nash's Brighton pavilion (see fig. 21-70). It was inspired, oddly enough, not by technology but by the widespread mystical interest in crystal. This enthusiasm was started by the poet Paul Schneebart, whose aphorisms, such as "Colored glass destroys hatred," ring the Glass House.

Taut's mysticism was shared by the Expressionist movement. After the war, he helped to establish the short-lived Workers Council for Art, whose members included Emil Nolde and other painters of *Die Brücke*. Its purpose was to unite all the arts under the umbrella of architecture. Through his journals *The Glass Chain* and *Early Light* he became the center of a loose network of architects, including Behrens, Gropius, Mendelsohn, and even Mies van der Rohe, who had the same fascination with crystalline glass. To Taut, architecture "consists exclusively of powerful emotions and addresses itself exclusively to the emotions." We may call this approach Expressionism because it stresses the artist's feelings toward himself and the world (see page 770). Does modern architecture not incorporate the spontaneous and irrational qualities of Fantasy as well? Indeed it does. But because the modern architect shares the Expressionist's primary concern with the human community, rather than the labyrinth of the imagination, Fantasy plays a much smaller role than Expressionism, which has incorporated it.

BERG. The romantic side of Expressionist architecture is best seen in the Centennial Hall (fig. 26-9) built by Max Berg (1870–1948) in Breslau to celebrate Germany's liberation from Napoleon in 1812. Berg, for the first time, has taken full advantage of reinforced concrete's incredible flexibility and strength. The vast scale is not simply an engineering marvel; it encloses a visionary space that fulfills the grandest dream of Boullée (compare fig. 21-17). The immediate ancestry of Centennial Hall can be traced back to the Bank of England by John Soane (see fig. 21-73), while the exterior is strangely reminiscent of Ledoux's tollgate (see fig. 21-18). Ultimately, the interior looks back to the Pantheon (see fig. 7-12) but with the solids and voids reversed, so that we are reminded of nothing so much as the interior of Hagia Sophia (see

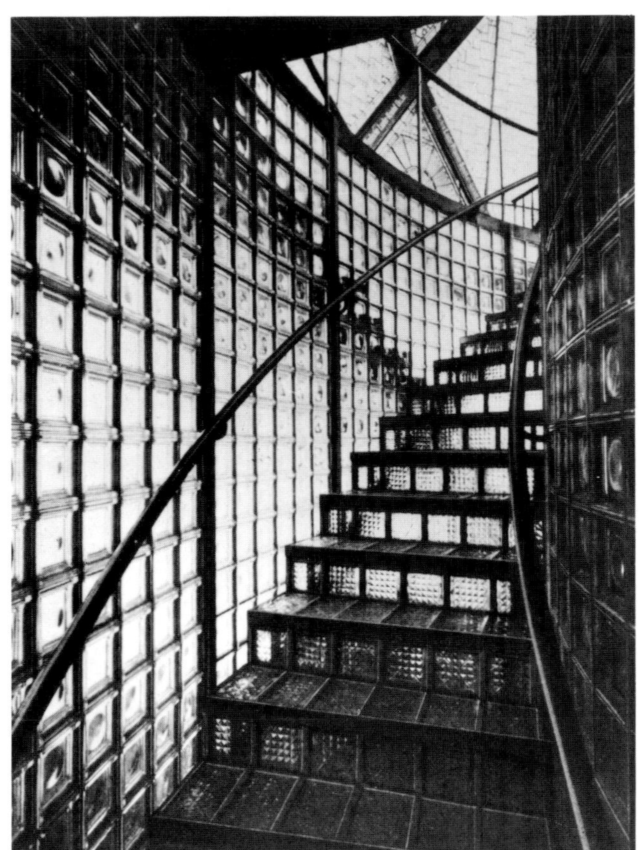

26-7. Bruno Taut. Staircase of the "Glass House," Werkbund Exhibition, Cologne. 1914

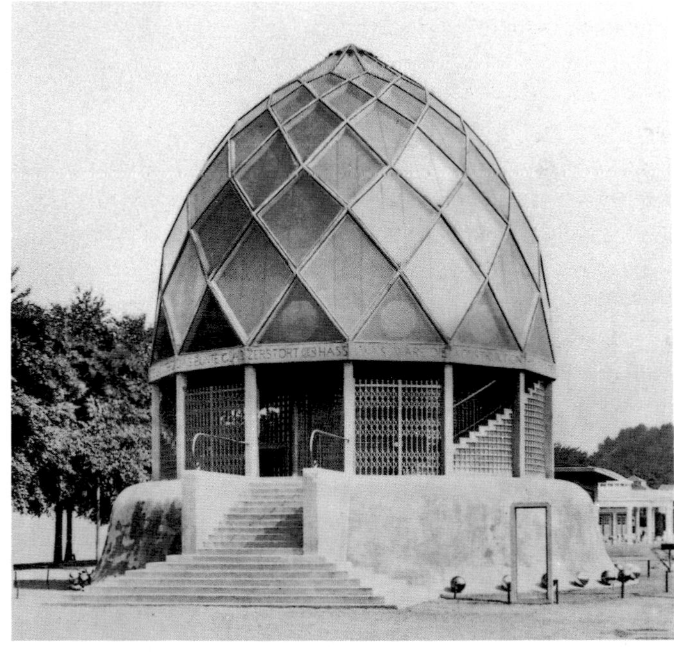

26-8. Bruno Taut. The "Glass House," Werkbund Exhibition, Cologne. 1914

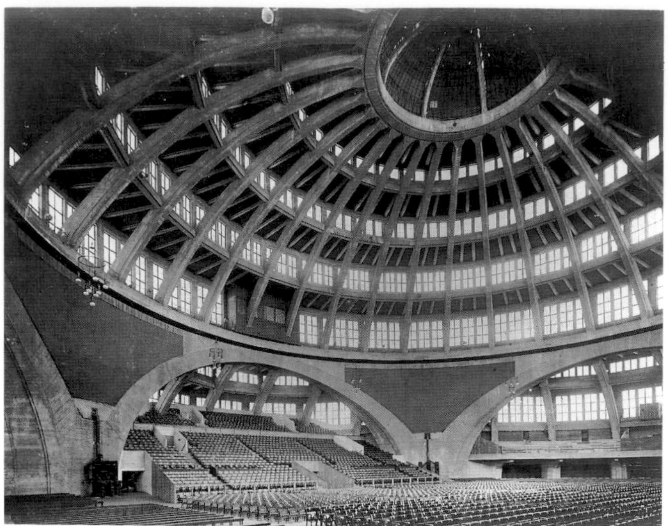

26-9. Max Berg. Interior of the Centennial Hall, Breslau, Germany. 1912–13

fig. 8-35). That Centennial Hall further recalls the soaring spirituality of a Gothic cathedral (such as our fig. 11-17) is not a coincidence: Berg shared with Rouault and Nolde an intense religiosity, which later led him to abandon his profession for Christianity.

SANT'ELIA. The final component of modernist architecture—its utopian side—was added by the Futurist Antonio Sant'Elia (1888–1916). He declared that "we must invent and reconstruct the Futurist city as an immense, tumultuous yard and the Futurist house as a gigantic machine." The Central Station project for his Città Nuova (New City; fig. 26-10) is treated in terms of circulation patterns that determine the relationships between buildings. They establish a restless perpetual motion that fulfills the Futurist vision announced in Boccioni's work (see figs. 24-18 and 25-6). But it is the enormous scale, dwarfing even the largest complexes of the past, that makes this a uniquely modern conception. It even includes a runway for airplanes. (The scheme is not as impractical as that may seem: it anticipates the huge Fiat-Lingotto automobile factory in Turin designed by Giacomo Matté-Trucco just two years later.) Though Sant'Elia's style remained basically Secessionist, his program was resolutely forward-looking: "Modern structural materials and our scientific concepts do not lend themselves to the disciplines of historical styles. . . . We no longer feel ourselves to be the men of the cathedrals and ancient moot halls, but men of the Grand Hotels, railway stations, giant roads. . . . The house of cement, iron and glass, without carved or painted ornament, rich only in the inherent beauty of its lines and modelling, extraordinarily brutish in its mechanical simplicity . . . must rise from the brink of a tumultuous abyss."

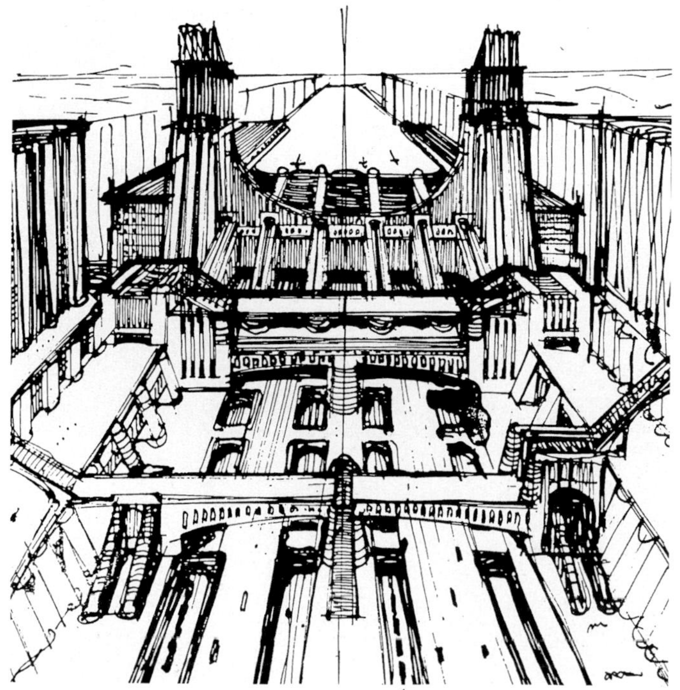

26-10. Antonio Sant'Elia. Central Station project for Città Nuova (after Banham). 1914

ARCHITECTURE BETWEEN THE WARS

By the onset of World War I, the stage was set for a modern architecture. But which way would it go? Would it follow the impersonal standard of the machine aesthetic advocated by Muthesius or the artistic creativity espoused by Van de Velde? Ironically, the issue was decided by Van de Velde's choice of Behrens' disciple Walter Gropius as his successor at Weimar in 1915 when Van de Velde was forced to resign because he was not a German. However, the war effectively postponed the evolution of modern architecture for nearly a decade. When this development resumed in the 1920s, the outcome of the issues posed at the Cologne Werkbund exhibition in 1914 was no longer clear-cut. Rather than a simple linear progression, we find a complex give-and-take between modernism and competing tendencies representing traditional voices and alternative visions. This varied response has its parallel in the art of the period, which largely rejected abstraction in favor of Fantasy, Expressionism, and Realism.

RIETVELD. The work of Frank Lloyd Wright attracted much attention in Europe through German publications of 1910 and 1911 featuring his buildings. Among the first to recognize its importance were some young Dutch architects who, a few years later, joined forces with Mondrian in the *De Stijl* movement (see page 796). Among their most important experiments is Schröder House, which was tacked on to an existing apartment house by Gerrit Rietveld (1888–1964) in 1924. The facade looks like a Mondrian painting transposed into three dimensions, for it utilizes the same rigorous abstraction and refined geometry (fig. 26-11). The lively arrangement of floating panels and intersecting planes is based on Mondrian's principle of dynamic equilibrium: the balance of unequal but equivalent oppositions, which expresses the mystical harmony of humanity with the universe. Steel beams, rails, and other elements are painted in bright, primary colors to articulate the composition. Unlike the elements of a Mondrian, the exterior parts look as if they can be shifted at will, though in fact they fit as tightly as interlocking pieces of a jigsaw puzzle. Not a

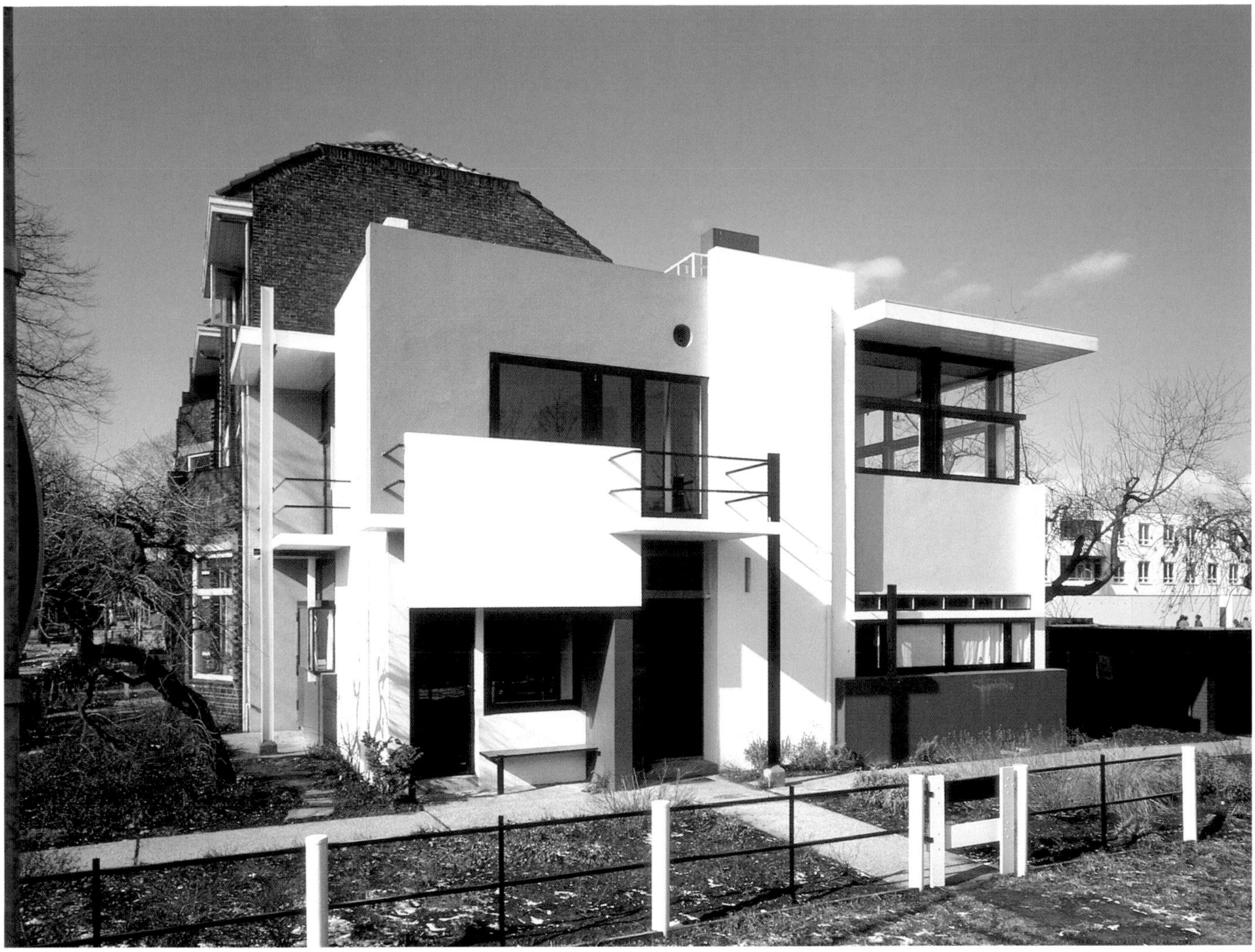

26-11. Gerrit Rietveld. Schröder House, Utrecht, Holland. 1924

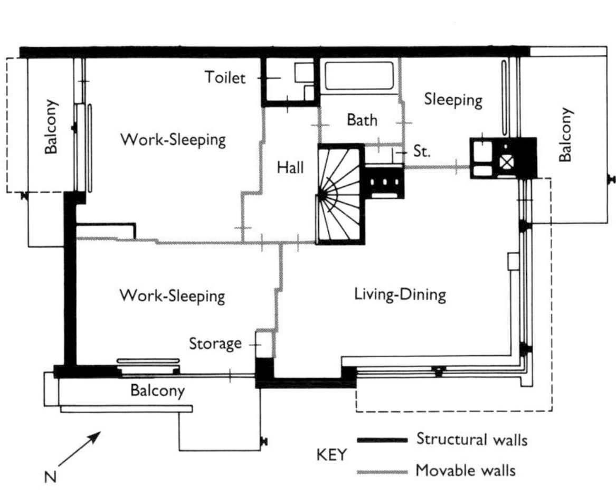

26-12. Plan of the Schröder House

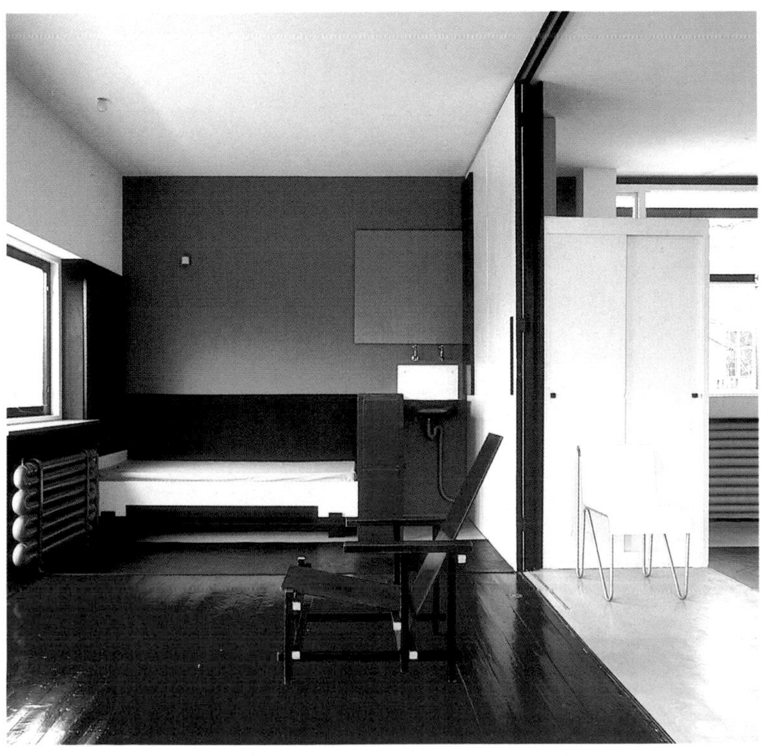

26-13. Interior, Schröder House

single element could be moved without destroying the delicate balance of the whole.

Rietveld's approach to the interior (figs. 26-12 and 26-13) reveals his background as a cabinetmaker in his use of unadorned "boxes" of space. However, the upper story can be left open or configured into different work and sleeping areas through a system of sliding partitions that fit neatly together when moved out of the way. This flexible treatment of the living quarters was devised with the owner, herself an artist, to suit her individual lifestyle. The decentralized plan also incorporates a continuous, "universal" space, which is given a linear structure by the network of panel dividers.

Schröder House proclaims a utopian ideal widely held in the early twentieth century. This is true despite the fact that it retains an allegiance to traditional materials and craftsmanship, which were equated by *De Stijl* with the self-indulgent materialism of the past. The machine would hasten people's spiritual development by liberating them from nature, with its conflict and imperfection, and by leading them to the higher order of beauty reflected in the architect's clean, abstract forms. The harmonious design of Schröder House owes its success to the insistent logic of this aesthetic, which we respond to even without being aware of its ideology. Yet the design, far from being impersonal, is remarkably intimate.

THE BAUHAUS. Schröder House was recognized immediately as one of the classic statements of modern architecture. The *De Stijl* architects represented the most advanced ideas in European architecture in the early 1920s. They had a decisive influence on so many architects abroad that the movement soon became international. The largest and most complete example of this International Style of the 1920s is the group of buildings created in 1925–26 by Walter Gropius for the Bauhaus in Dessau, the famous German art school of which he was the director. The most dramatic is the Shop Block, which is a fully mature statement of the principles announced ten years earlier in Gropius' Fagus Shoe Factory (see fig. 26-6). The structure is a four-story box with walls that are a continuous surface of glass (fig. 26-14). The result is rather surprising. Since the glass walls reflect as well as transmit light, their appearance depends on the interplay of these two effects. They respond, as it were, to any change of conditions outside and inside. Thus they introduce a strange quality of life into the structure. In this way, the facade serves a similar purpose to the mirrorlike finish of Brancusi's *Bird in Space* (see fig. 25-4).

More important than this individual structure, however, is the complex as a whole and what it stood for. The Bauhaus was the result of merging two separate schools, one devoted to art and the other to crafts. This happened in Weimar in 1919—the same year the national assembly established the republican government there known as the Weimar Republic. Hence from the beginning the Bauhaus occupied a politically sensitive, not to mention precarious, position. Initially it tried to fulfill the goals of the Arts and Crafts Movement, but the traditional attitudes toward the two branches were too different for this romantic dream to succeed. There developed a deep split between the Workshop Masters, who were responsible for practical crafts, and the Masters of Form, such as Kandinsky and Klee, who were invited by the artist Johannes Itten (1888–1967) in the early 1920s to teach theory. The curriculum was given a far more rational and pragmatic basis by the arrival of László Moholy-Nagy (see page 901), a Hungarian follower of Tatlin's Constructivism (see page 839) who replaced Itten in 1922, and then Josef Albers (see page 823). Also important was the visit in 1921 of Theo van Doesburg, a founder of the *De Stijl* movement (see page 796), whose ideas galvanized faculty and students alike. But it was the move to Dessau that proved decisive. The city invited the school to transfer there in 1925 when it was closed down for a while by Weimar during a period of political turmoil.

The definitive character of the Bauhaus is reflected in Gropius' design. The plan consists of three major blocks (fig. 26-15) for classrooms, shops, and studios plus a student center; the first two were connected by a bridge of ferroconcrete containing offices. The curriculum embraced all the visual arts, linked by the root concept of "structure" (Bau). It included, in addition to an art school, departments of industrial design under Marcel Breuer (see page 873),

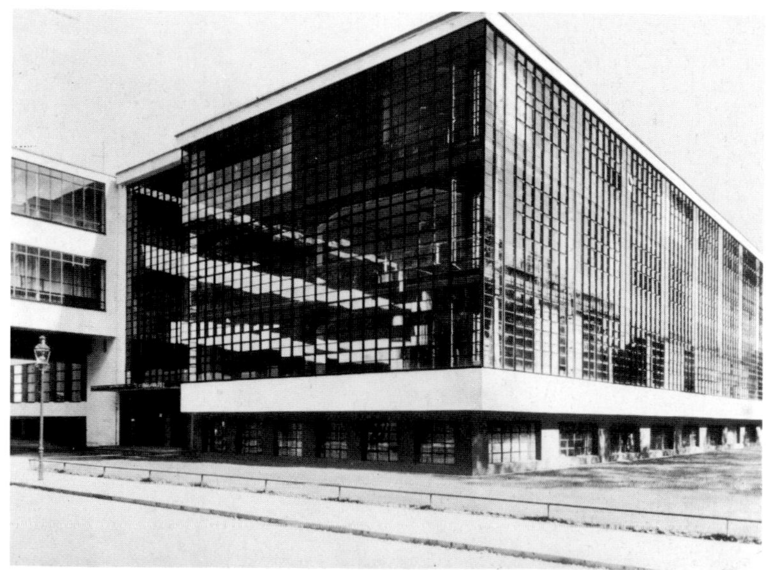

26-14. Walter Gropius. Shop Block, the Bauhaus, Dessau, Germany. 1925–26

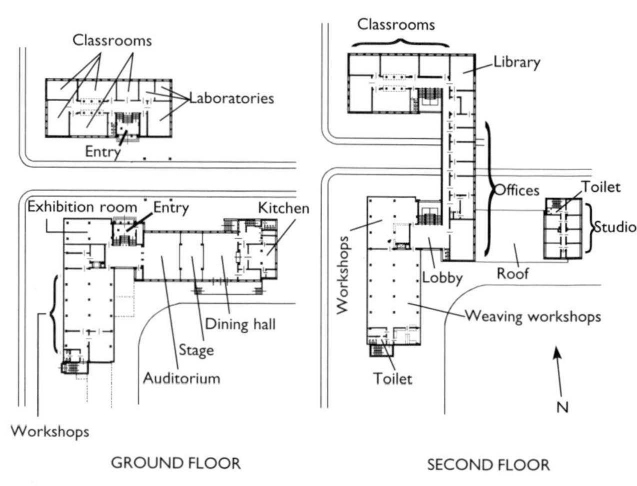

26-15. Plan of the Bauhaus

graphic art under Herbert Bayer (see page 900), and architecture, whose chief representative was Mies van der Rohe (see below), the Bauhaus' last director.

Gropius' buildings at Dessau incorporate elements of *De Stijl* and Constructivism, just as the school accommodated a range of temperaments and approaches. The Shop Block proclaims the Bauhaus' frankly practical approach, which was closely allied to the New Objectivity movement (see page 807). The complex as a whole promoted a remarkable community spirit based on a utopian socialist dream. Gropius' philosophy was surprisingly humanist. [See Primary Sources, no. 100, page 941.] The Bauhaus at Dessau was thus entirely different in character from what Gropius had inherited from Van de Velde at Weimar. The program embodied Gropius' tolerant yet unified vision. Not surprisingly, the school did not last long after his departure in 1928 to pursue architecture full time. His hand-picked successor, Hannes Meyer (1889–1954), who had been the first architect appointed to the faculty, was forced to resign in 1930 because of his Marxist leanings, even though he had prevented the formation of a Communist student cell. Ludwig Mies van der Rohe (1886–1969) tried vainly to revive the school's fortunes, but it was shut down by the Dessau parliament in 1932. By then, most of its leaders had left. After a final attempt to reopen it as a private school in Berlin, the Bauhaus was closed by the Nazis in 1933.

MIES VAN DER ROHE. Mies van der Rohe followed a highly varied path. As a young architect in Berlin, where he worked several years for Behrens, Mies started out as a Neoclassicist under the sway of the Schinkel school (see page 695), then became a Structural Rationalist after meeting the Dutch architect Hendrik

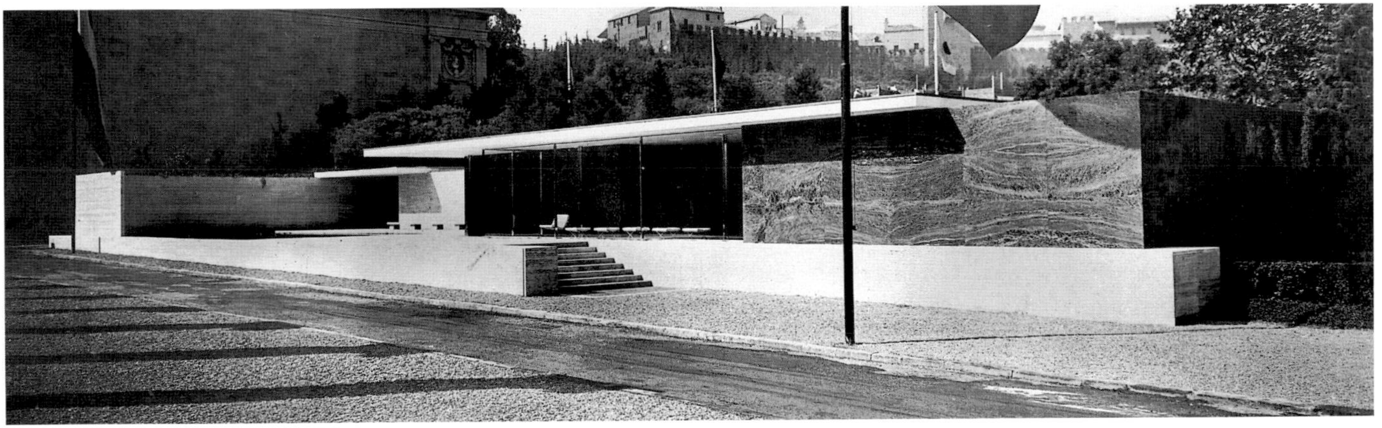

26-16. Ludwig Mies van der Rohe. German Pavilion, International Exposition, Barcelona. 1929

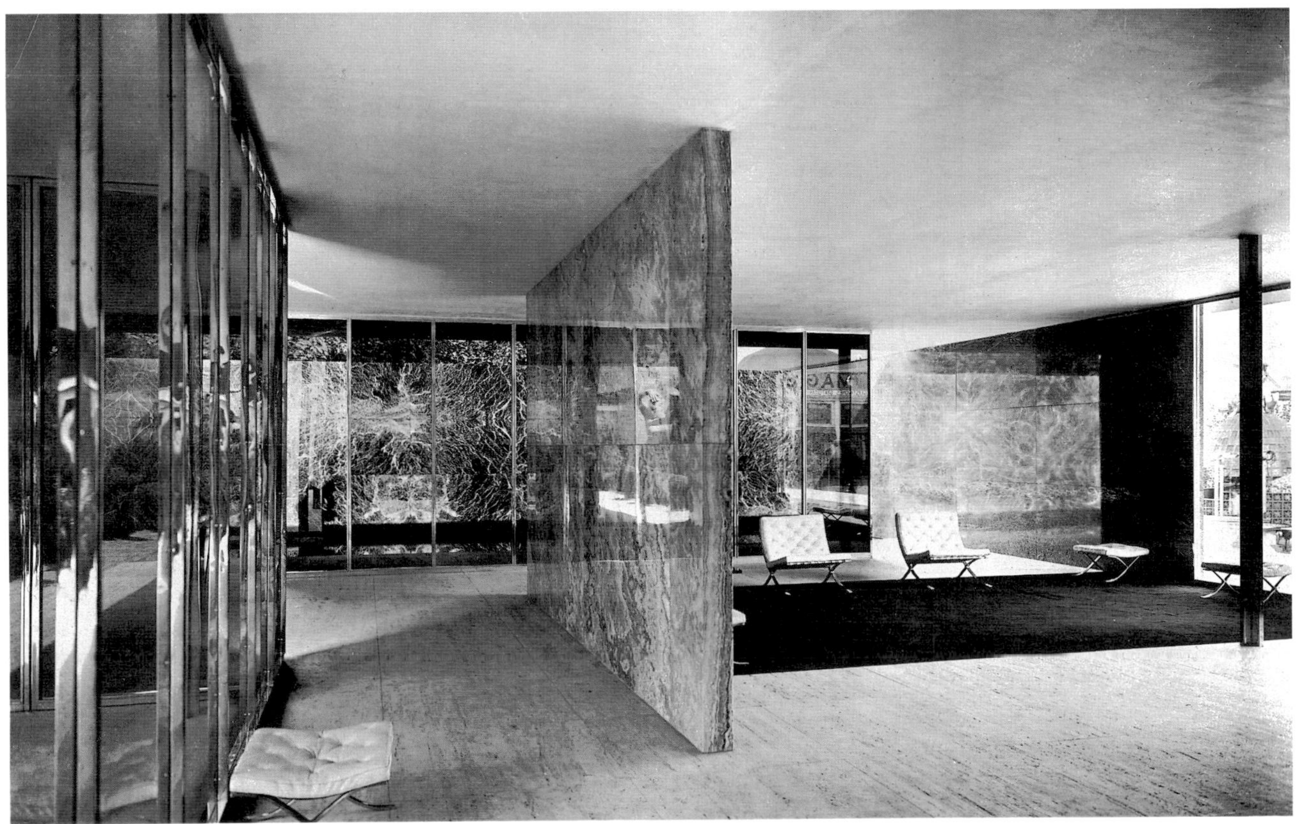

26-17. Ludwig Mies van der Rohe. Interior, German Pavilion, International Exposition, Barcelona. 1929

Berlage (1856–1934) in 1912. Following the war, he joined the radical November Group, which was allied with Taut's Workers Council for Art, and as a result became an Expressionist. He also came into contact with *De Stijl* and Constructivism. In 1927, as vice-director of the Deutscher Werkbund, Mies was charged with organizing the highly experimental Weissenhof Estate exhibition in Stuttgart. Held in response to the need for vast amounts of inexpensive but comfortable housing in Germany during the Weimar Republic, it became a showcase for all the leading modernist architects of the day. Consequently, Mies became a convert to rationalization and standardization as the most effective means to attain that end. However, he never achieved the spartan functionalism of the leftist New Objectivity movement.

In 1929 Mies designed the prophetic German Pavilion for the International Exposition in Barcelona (figs. 26-16 and 26-17). Unfortunately it was dismantled soon after the fair closed. The pavilion, which proceeds from ideas Mies began to develop around 1923, was a daringly low-slung structure elevated on a marble base, with enclosed courtyards at the front and rear. It was even more radically simple in appearance than Wright's Robie House (see figs. 26-1 and 26-2), out of which it clearly developed. Its walls were constructed of different-colored marble slabs, arranged with great precision like so many dominoes in a grid system. Here is the spiritual counterpart to Mondrian among contemporary designers, possessed of the same "absolute pitch" in determining proportions and spatial relationships. Flooded with light from the great expanse of windows, the pavilion's interior was wonderfully open and fluid yet with a sparse cleanness that still seems irrepressibly modern.

LE CORBUSIER'S EARLY WORK. In France, the most distinguished representative of the International Style during the 1920s was the Swiss-born architect Le Corbusier (Charles Édouard Jeanneret, 1886–1965). His training under Peter Behrens and Auguste Perret (see below), from whom he acquired a preference for reinforced concrete, made him a disciple of Structural Rationalism. His style was further shaped by his experience as a painter. In 1918 he and the artist Amédée Ozenfant (1886–1966) cofounded the movement known as Purism, which advocated a machine aesthetic similar to that of Le Corbusier's friend Fernand Léger, whose canvases during those years reflect the same attitude (see fig. 24-34). Le Corbusier worked with his cousin Pierre Jeanneret (1896–1967) from 1922 until 1940, when the latter joined the French resistance against the Nazis. Before 1940 he built only private houses—from necessity, not choice—but these are as important as Wright's Prairie Style houses. Le Corbusier called them *machines à habiter* (machines to be lived in). This term was intended to suggest his admiration for the clean, precise shapes of machinery, not the Futurist desire for "mechanized living." [See Primary Sources, no. 99, page 940.]

Le Corbusier evidently wanted to imply that his houses were so different from conventional homes as to constitute a new species. Such is indeed our impression as we approach the most famous of them, the Savoye House at Poissy-sur-Seine (fig. 26-18), built in 1928–29. It is an outgrowth of the "Dom-Ino" houses he developed during World War I. The structure resembles a low, square box resting on stilts. These pillars of reinforced concrete (called "pilotis") form part of the structural skeleton and reappear to divide the "ribbon windows" running along each side of the box. The flat, smooth surfaces deny all sense of weight. They stress Le Corbusier's preoccupation with abstract "space blocks," which he derived in part from designs by Adolf Loos of the early 1920s.

In order to find out how the box is subdivided, we must enter it (fig. 26-19). We then realize that this simple structure contains living spaces that are open as well as closed, separated by glass

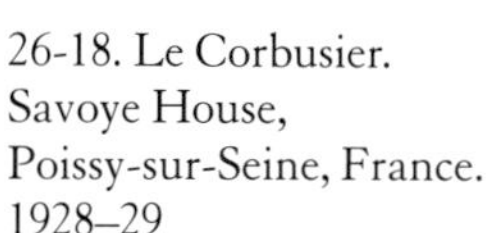
26-18. Le Corbusier. Savoye House, Poissy-sur-Seine, France. 1928–29

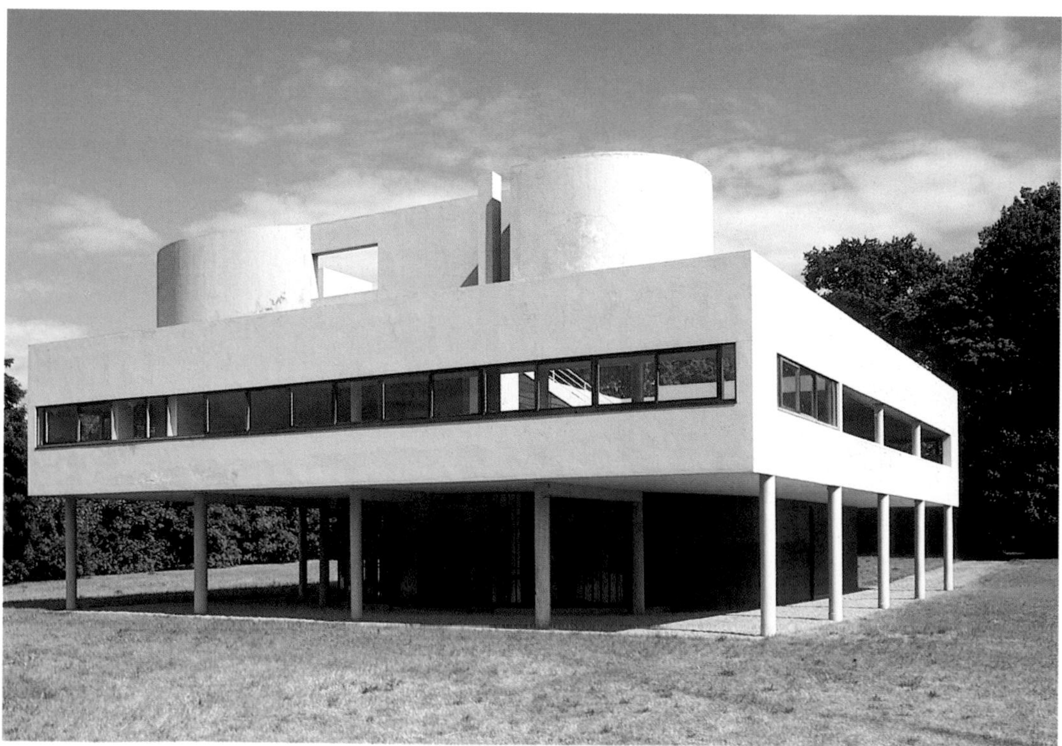

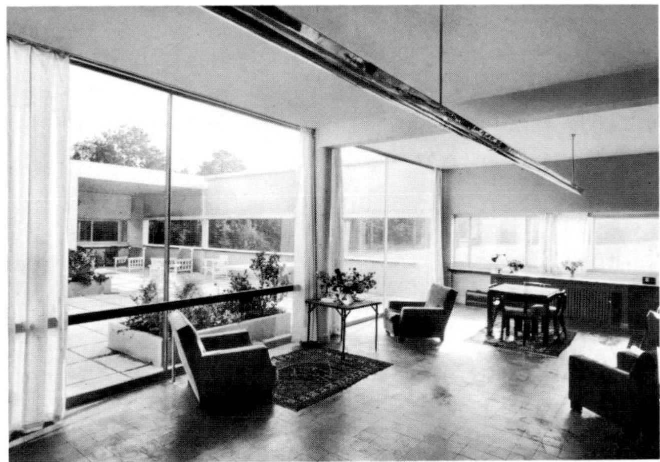

26-19. Interior, Savoye House

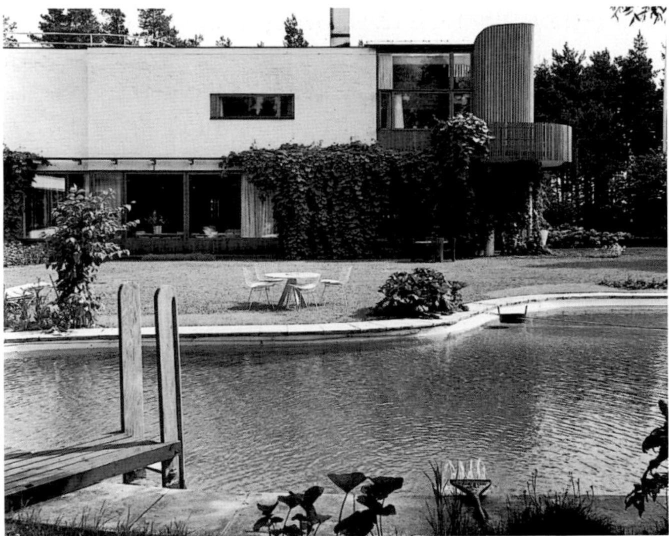

26-20. Alvar Aalto. Villa Mairea, Noormarkku, Finland. 1937–38

walls. Within the house, we are still in communication with the outdoors. Views of the sky and the surrounding terrain are to be seen everywhere. Yet we enjoy complete privacy, since an observer on the ground cannot see us unless we stand next to a window. The functionalism of the Savoye House is governed by a "design for living," not by mechanical efficiency. It fulfills Le Corbusier's statement that "Architecture is the masterly, correct, and magnificent play of masses brought together in light. . . . Cubes, cones, cylinders, and pyramids are the primary forms which light reveals to advantage. . . . These are . . . the most beautiful forms."

AALTO. Although its style and philosophy were codified about 1930 by a committee of Le Corbusier and his followers, the International Style was by no means monolithic. Soon all but the most purist among its adherents began to depart from this standard. One of the first to break ranks was the Finnish architect Alvar Aalto (1898–1976), whose Villa Mairea (figs. 26-20 and 26-21) reads at first glance like a critique of Le Corbusier's Savoye House of a decade earlier. Like Rietveld's Schröder House, Villa Mairea was designed for a woman artist. Her second-story studio, covered with wood slats, dominates the view of the house from three directions. This time, however, the architect was given a free hand by his patron, and the building is a summation of ideas Aalto had been developing for nearly ten years. He adapted the International Style to the traditional architecture, materials, lifestyle, and landscape of Finland. Aalto took an approach opposite to Le Corbusier's in order to arrive at a similar end. Aalto's primary concern was human needs, both physical and psychological, which he sought to harmonize with functionalism. The modernist heritage, which extends back to Wright, is unmistakable in his vocabulary of forms and massing of elements. Yet everywhere there are romantic touches that add a warmth absent from the Savoye House. Wood, brick, and stone are employed in various combinations throughout the interior and exterior, in contrast to Le Corbusier's pristine classicism. Free forms are introduced at several places to add an element of playfulness, as well as to break up the cubic geometry and smooth surfaces of the International Style.

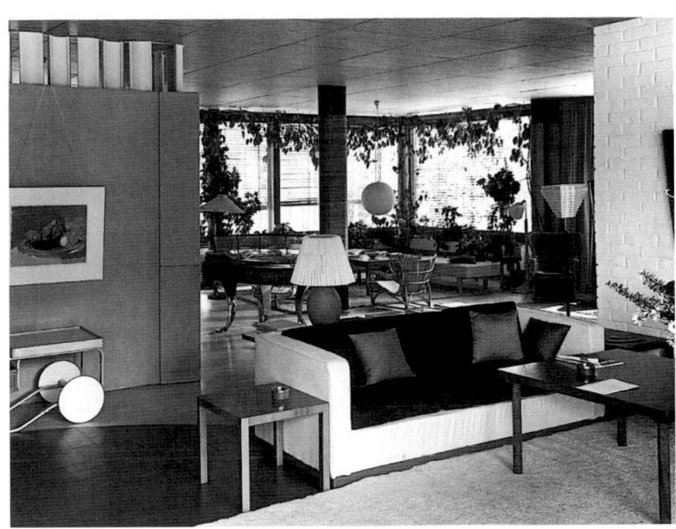

26-21. Interior, Villa Mairea

Aalto's importance is undeniable, but his place in twentieth-century architecture remains unclear. His inclusion of nationalist elements in Villa Mairea has been interpreted both as a rejection of modernism and as a fruitful regional variation on the International Style. Today his work can be seen as a direct forerunner of Late Modern architecture (see pages 882–85).

EXPRESSIONISM. Architecture between the wars is sometimes labeled Expressionist if it does not conform to the International Style. Such a view is valid only insofar as it represents the assertion of the right of the individual to express a personal point of view against the norms of modernism. The International Style based its ideals on standardization for the sake of universality. As such, it represents the triumph of classicism and Structural Rationalism. In reality, however, it was never the dominant approach after 1917, any more than abstraction was in painting. It seems

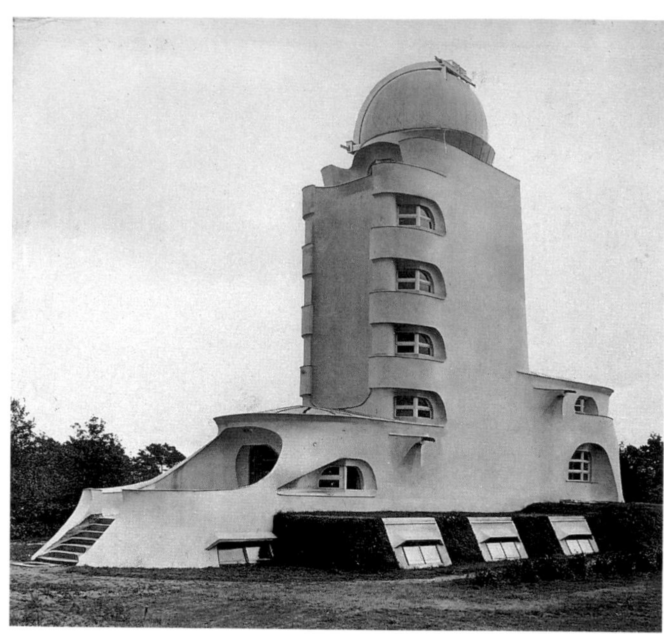

26-22. Erich Mendelsohn. Einstein Tower, Potsdam, Germany. 1921

best, then, to limit Expressionism in architecture following World War I to the few years around 1920.

MENDELSOHN. Inspired by the Arts and Crafts Movement's liberal politics and utopian ideals, a number of German architects gave free rein to their imaginations. The most eccentric building from this period is the Einstein Tower at Potsdam (fig. 26-22) by Erich Mendelsohn (1887–1953). It has an amazing organic quality that looks back to the Art Nouveau architecture of Antoní Gaudí and Henry van de Velde (see figs. 23-31 and 23-35). Because of a lack of materials, it was built of brick with a cement veneer instead of reinforced concrete, as the architect originally planned. Despite its retrospective element, Mendelsohn was no reactionary, and the Einstein Tower, which functioned as an observatory and laboratory, has also been hailed as the forerunner of Le Corbusier's later work (see fig. 26-31).

PERRET. Even more important for Le Corbusier was the example set by Auguste Perret (1874–1954). Early in the century he had been among the first to make effective use of advances in reinforced concrete and to define its architectural character. Perret was a pupil of the last great French academicians. His teachers included Julien Guadet (1834–1908), professor at the École des Beaux-Arts and a pupil of Labrouste, who maintained a traditional approach to architectural composition using modern materials; and the theoretician Auguste Choisy (1841–1909), professor at the School of Bridges and Roads, whose *History of Architecture* (1899) maintained that style, be it Greek or Gothic, properly proceeds from construction technique. Thus Perret was from the beginning a Structural Rationalist. For him, concrete provided the means to reconcile classical form and Gothic structural authenticity. His greatest achievement is the Church of Notre Dame, built as a war memorial at Le Raincy outside Paris (fig. 26-23). It is an astonishingly successful translation of medieval architectural forms (compare fig. 10-6) into unadorned ferroconcrete. The structure is supported entirely by grooved classical columns so that the "walls" become vast expanses of glass, like the stained-glass windows of Gothic cathedrals (see fig. 11-1). In this way, Perret created a modern-day counterpart to Soufflot's Panthéon (see fig. 21-16). This feat is not important in itself. It could, after all, readily be dismissed as mere historicism. Yet Perret has brilliantly solved one of the most difficult problems facing the modern architect: how to create a suitable expression of traditional spirituality in our secular Machine Age using a twentieth-century vocabulary. Le Raincy is so pivotal that nearly all later church architecture in the West is indebted to its example, no matter how different the results.

THE SKYSCRAPER IN AMERICA. The United States, despite its early position of leadership, did not share the exciting growth that took place in European architecture during the 1920s. The impact of the International Style did not begin to be felt in America until the very end of the decade. A pioneer example is the Philadelphia Savings Fund Society Building of 1931–32 (fig. 26-24) by George Howe (1886–1954) and William E. Lescaze (1896–1969). It is the first skyscraper built anywhere to incorporate many of the features developed in Europe after the end of World War I. The skyscraper was a compelling attraction to modernist architects in Europe as the embodiment of the idea of America, and during the 1920s Gropius and Mies van der Rohe designed several prototypes that were incredibly advanced for their time. Yet none were erected, while those constructed in the United States were sheathed in a variety of revivalist styles. (The Gothic was preferred.) Although they quickly became the most characteristic form of American architecture, even the skyscrapers of the 1930s—when many of the most famous ones, such as the Empire State Building, were built—are in the tradition of Sullivan and do

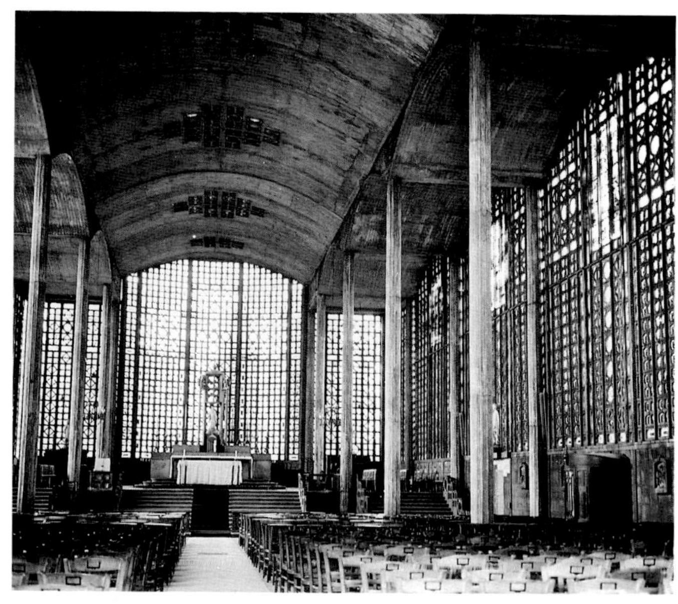

26-23. Auguste Perret. Notre Dame, Le Raincy, France. 1923–24

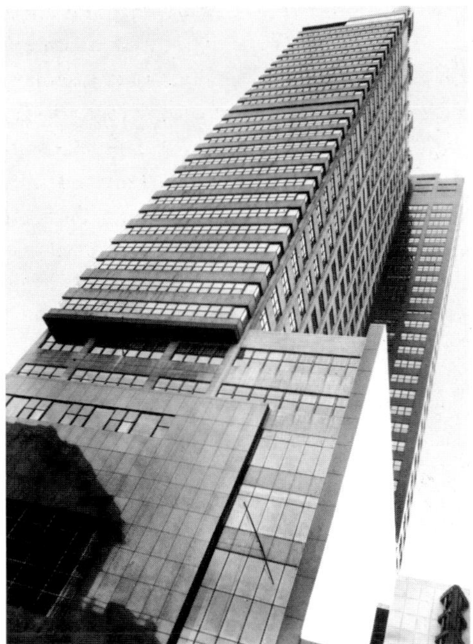

26-24. George Howe and William E. Lescaze. Philadelphia Savings Fund Society Building, Philadelphia. 1931–32

little to expand on the Wainwright Building (see fig. 23-39) except to make it bigger. Despite the fact that it is not entirely purist, the skyscraper of Howe and Lescaze is a landmark in the history of architecture. Remarkably enough, it was not to be surpassed for 20 years (compare fig. 26-28). The only building of comparable importance is Raymond Hood's McGraw-Hill Building in New York, which was built at the same time.

Design

THE BAUHAUS. Like their predecessors in the Rococo, many of the great architects since Gaudí and Mackintosh have also been important designers who exercised a great influence on others. The reason is not hard to discern. They have had a unique, even privileged, understanding of modernism, its meaning, materials, and techniques. Their designs, like their buildings, have generally expressed the Machine Age through clean lines and cubic shapes stripped of unnecessary decoration. This was particularly true of the Bauhaus, where architecture and design were closely linked. The Bauhaus nevertheless failed in its goal of unifying the arts and putting the decorative arts on the same level as the fine arts. The main reason was that its members were far more gifted in architecture and painting than in design, despite the considerable emphasis placed on this area.

Gropius himself considered Bauhaus designs as models for the future that would fulfill his goal of providing high-quality wares to everyone through mass-manufacturing techniques. However, only under Hannes Meyer was design placed at the service of people's practical needs. The interiors of the Masters' Houses designed by Marcel Breuer (1902–1981) reflect the school's outlook (fig. 26-25). As in Wright's Prairie Style houses, space is treated as building blocks, but the grouping of these units is much simpler. The houses have an almost monastic asceticism that is further emphasized by the stark simplicity of the furnishings. Breuer's famous chair in the right foreground is a marvel of elegant geometry for its own sake—without regard to comfort, as anyone who has ever sat in it can attest. Here, then, is the chief limitation of so much of twentieth-century design: the tyranny of form over human considerations (a field known as ergonomics).

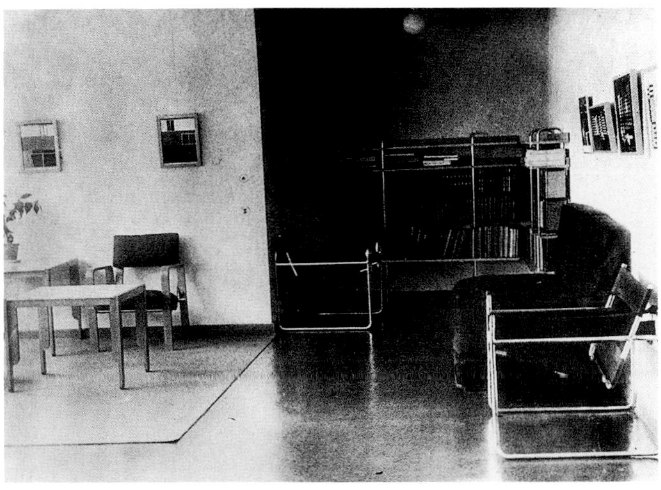

26-25. Marcel Breuer. The living room of Josef and Anni Albers, Masters' House, Dessau, Germany. c. 1929

ART DECO. The Bauhaus style was not the only major form of early-twentieth-century design, however. Art Deco is the name commonly given to the style that dominated the decorative arts between the world wars. (In France it was called *Le Style Moderne.*) Like the Bauhaus, Art Deco arose out of the work of the Glasgow school. Charles Rennie Mackintosh (see page 759), his wife Margaret Macdonald-Mackintosh (1865–1933), and her sister Frances Macdonald (1874–1921) had a great impact after 1900 on the Secession movements in Munich and especially Vienna, where the next phase of modern design took place (see page 752). Art Deco received its official introduction at the Exhibition of Decorative and Industrial Arts held in Paris in 1925, two years after the Bauhaus scored a great success at its initial design show in Weimar. The show had actually been conceived ten years earlier, but like the development of the style itself, it was postponed by World War I, when the movement was already well under way. Every leading designer and architect, including Le Corbusier, exhibited at the Paris exposition. The hit of the show was undoubtedly the Hôtel du Collectionneur pavilion assembled by Emil-Jacques Ruhlmann (1879–1933), the last of the truly great French furniture designers (fig. 26-26).

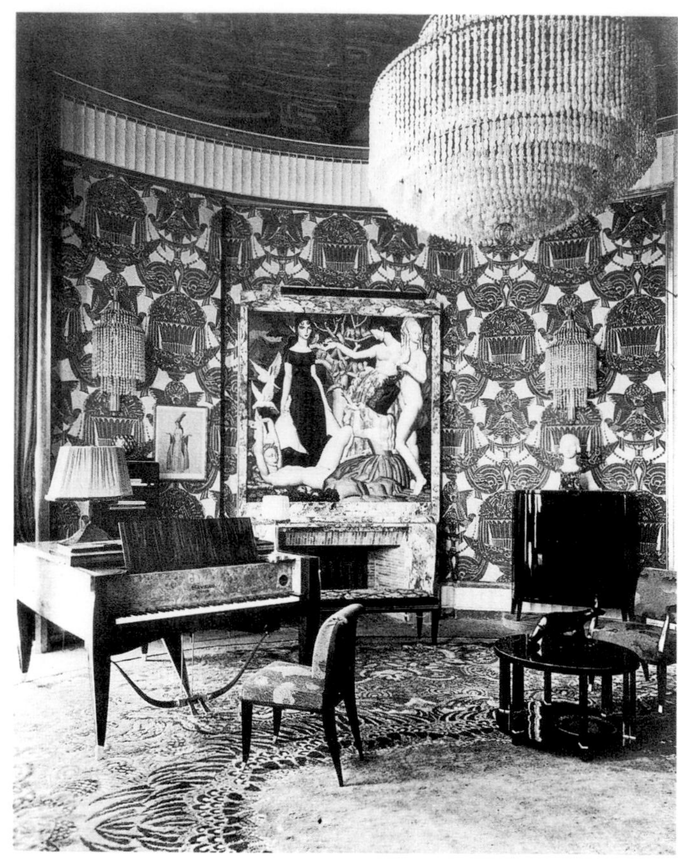

26-26. Emil-Jacques Ruhlmann. Grand Salon of the Hôtel du Collectionneur at the 1925 Exposition, Paris

In common with the Bauhaus, Art Deco attempted to resolve the dilemma between quality design and mass production, which both the Arts and Crafts Movement and Art Nouveau had failed to reconcile. It, too, created a geometric style that could be applied to anything from teacups to building facades. This tendency reached its climax in the following decade when everything became streamlined. The difference is that Art Deco never made the decisive break from Art Nouveau, of which it was a direct outgrowth.

Art Deco cannot be called a modernist movement in the same sense as the International Style because it never developed the fully defined machine aesthetic, although the two evolved in parallel to each other and sometimes achieved strikingly similar results. With its idealistic program of social and artistic reform, the International Style proved far bolder in redefining the decorative arts, despite its failure to achieve those goals. Art Deco, in contrast, was a decorative veneer that did not address the substance of modern existence. Instead, it responded to the changing taste of society during the "Jazz Age" without consciously intending to shape it. Whereas the Bauhaus came to adhere to a rigorous machine style, Art Deco was broadly eclectic in scope. It included a taste for the exotic, ranging from ancient Egyptian and Native American art to the Ballets Russes of Sergei Diaghilev (see box page 780)—whatever could be incorporated into its geometric framework. The virtue of Art Deco is that it embodied the very feature so conspicuously lacking in the International Style: fantasy, which permitted highly individual expression. Perhaps for that reason, it proved widely popular. Moreover, it enjoyed the commercial backing of the major manufacturers and department stores. Needless to say, much of what filtered down to everyday objects catered to the lowest common denominator. But at its finest Art Deco could be brilliantly innovative.

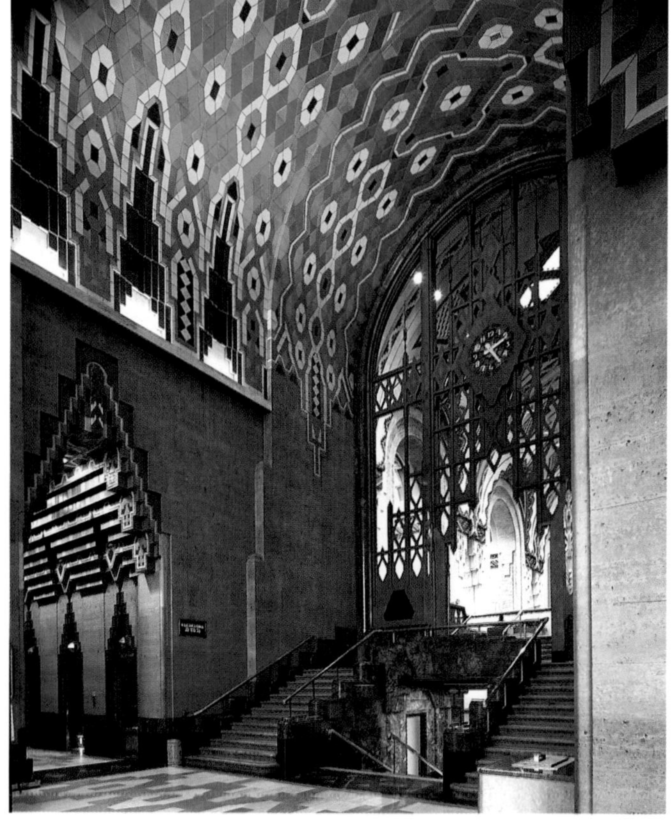

26-27. Wirt Rowland, with Smith, Hinchman & Grylls, Associates, Inc. (Tiles designed by Thomas Dilorenzo and made by Rookwood, Cincinnati.) Main Lobby, Union Trust Company, Detroit. 1929

Because it was essentially a decorative "skin," Art Deco lent itself readily to architecture. (Even the streamlined style associated with it was adapted from Dutch architecture of the early 1920s.) It was especially widespread in the United States, where it reached its most flamboyant phase during the 1930s. A spectacular example is the interior of the Union Trust Company in Detroit (fig. 26-27). Resembling nothing so much as a gigantic Indian feather headdress, the ceiling of ceramic tiles has the honeycomb pattern of a beehive to symbolize Thrift and Industry.

ARCHITECTURE SINCE 1945

HIGH MODERNISM. Following the rise of the Nazis, the best German architects, whose work Hitler condemned as "un-German," came to the United States and greatly stimulated the development of American architecture. Walter Gropius was appointed chairman of the architecture department at Harvard University, where he had an important educational influence. Ludwig Mies van der Rohe, his former colleague at Dessau, settled in Chicago as a practicing architect. Following the war, they were to realize the dream of modern architecture, contained in germinal form in their buildings of the 1930s but never fully implemented. We may call the style that dominated architecture for 25 years after World War II "High Modernism." It was indeed the culmination of the developments that had taken place during the first half of the twentieth century. High Modernism never arrived at a single, universal style even at its zenith. Nevertheless, its unified spaces, be they geometric or organic, embodied a harmonious vision that developed in a consistent way as the style was used in countless buildings throughout the world. Like the International Style before it, High Modernism permitted considerable local variation within established guidelines, although this development led almost inevitably to its decline.

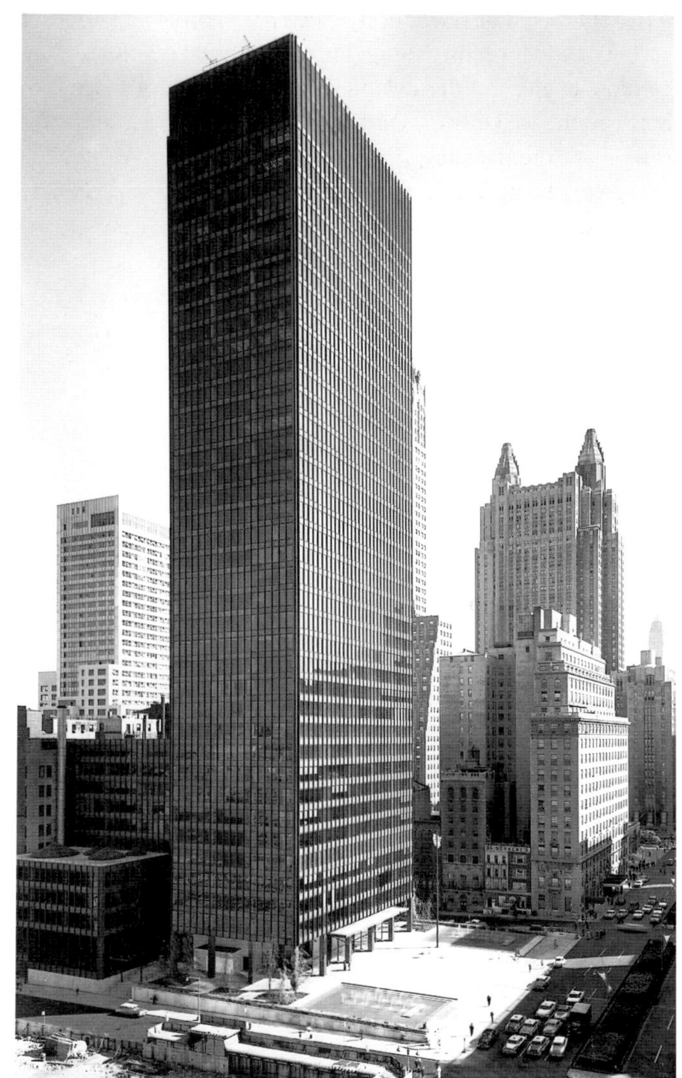

26-28. Ludwig Mies van der Rohe and Philip Johnson. Seagram Building, New York. 1954–58

MIES VAN DER ROHE. The crowning achievement of American architecture in the postwar era was the modern skyscraper, defined largely by Mies van der Rohe. The Seagram Building in New York (fig. 26-28), designed with his disciple Philip Johnson, carries the principles announced in Gropius' design for the Bauhaus to their ultimate conclusion. It uses the techniques developed by Louis Sullivan and Frank Lloyd Wright, Mies van der Rohe's great predecessors in Chicago, to extend the structure to an enormous height. Yet the building looks like nothing before it. Though not quite a pure box, it illustrates Mies van der Rohe's famous saying that "less is more." This alone does not explain the difference, however. Mies van der Rohe discovered the perfect means to articulate the skyscraper in the I-beam, its basic structural member, which rises continuously along nearly the entire height of the facade. (The actual skeleton of the structure remains completely hidden from view.) The effect is as soaring as the responds inside a Gothic cathedral (compare fig. 11-13)—and with good reason, for Mies van der Rohe believed that "structure is spiritual." He achieved it through the lithe proportions, which create a perfect balance between the play of horizontal and vertical forces. This harmony expresses the idealism, social as well as aesthetic, that underlies High Modernism in architecture.

LE CORBUSIER'S LATER WORK. Abandoning the abstract purism of the International Style, Le Corbusier's postwar work shows a growing preoccupation with sculptural, even anthropomorphic, effects. The Unité d'Habitation, a large apartment house in Marseilles (fig. 26-29), is a "box on stilts" like the Savoye House, but the pillars are not thin rods. (Because of a shortage of materials, the whole is constructed of unfaced concrete, called *béton brut;* hence the term *Brutalism* for this aesthetic.) Their shape, which the architect said "should be like the strong curvaceous thighs of a woman," expresses their muscular strength in a way that makes us also think of Doric columns. The exposed staircase on the flank, too, is vigorously sculptural. The flat plane of the all-glass facade incorporates a honeycomb screen of louvers and balconies that forms a sunbreak but also enhances the three-dimensional quality of the structure. This screen (known as a *brise soleil*) has proved to be an invention of great importance, practically and aesthetically. It became a standard feature of modern architecture throughout the tropics. (Le Corbusier himself introduced it in India and Brazil.) In many respects the Unité d'Habitation represents the culmination of the architect's thinking about housing as well as urban design. It realizes his utopian vision of integrating families within a tightly knit society while preserving

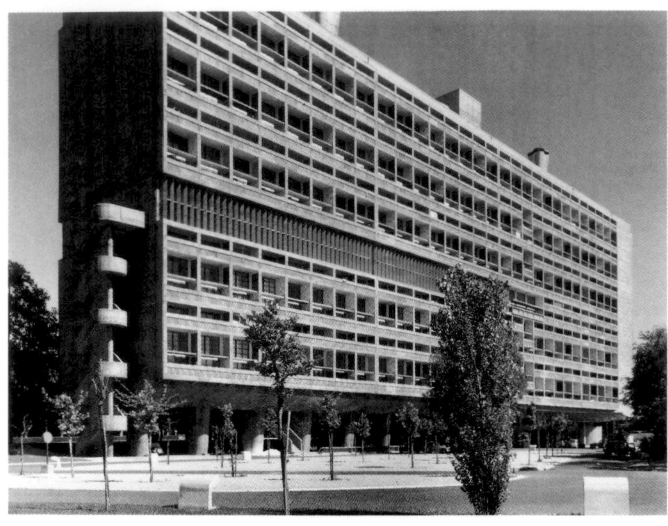

26-29. Le Corbusier. Unité d'Habitation Apartment House, Marseilles, France. 1947–52

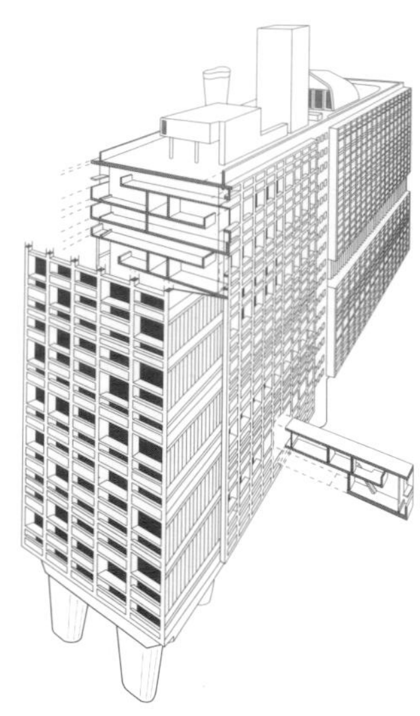

26-30. Le Corbusier. Isometric projection and cross section of Unité d'Habitation (after a drawing in Kenneth Frampton's *Modern Architecture*)

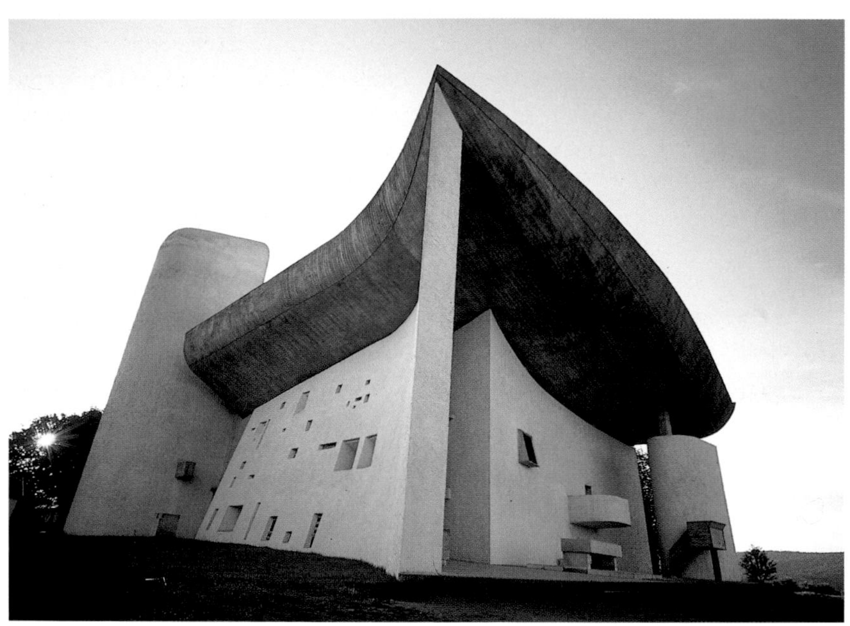

26-31. Le Corbusier. Notre-Dame-du-Haut (from the southeast), Ronchamp, France. 1950–55

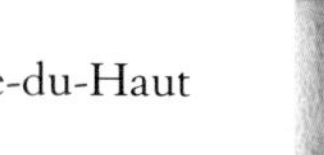

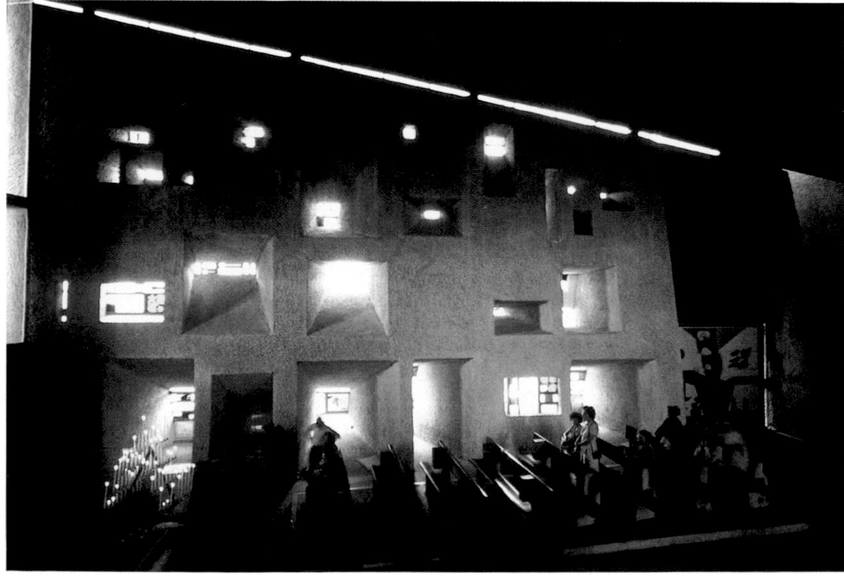

26-32. Interior, Notre-Dame-du-Haut

their privacy. The precast apartments, each one and a half stories high and extending the full depth of the building, are linked on every fourth floor by a tunnel-like hall. They thus form complex interlocking units that are slotted like "bottles into a wine rack" (see fig. 26-30). As often happens with Le Corbusier's buildings, however, theory and design can override practical considerations. For example, the ceiling height is only about seven and a half feet high, based on a "Modular" of his own devising. Moreover, the shops and other facilities on the seventh and eighth floors, like the garden and swimming pool on the roof, do not adequately fulfill their communal functions.

Le Corbusier's most revolutionary building from the mid-twentieth century is the church of Notre-Dame-du-Haut at Ronchamp in eastern France (figs. 26-31 and 26-32), which is constructed of reinforced concrete. Rising like a medieval fortress from a hillcrest, its design is so irrational that it defies analysis, even with the aid of perspective diagrams. The play of curves and countercurves is here as insistent as in Gaudí's Casa Milá, though the shapes are simpler and more dynamic. The massive walls seem to obey an unseen force that makes them slant and curl like paper. And the overhanging roof suggests the brim of an enormous hat or perhaps the bottom of a ship split lengthwise by the sharp-edged buttress from which it is suspended.

This evocation of the dim, prehistoric past is quite intentional. Asked to create a sanctuary on a hilltop, Le Corbusier must have felt that this was the primeval task of architecture, placing him in a direct line of succession with the builders of Stonehenge, the ziggurats of Mesopotamia, and the Greek temples. Hence he also consciously avoids any correlation between exterior and interior. The doors are concealed; we must seek them out like clefts in a hillside. To pass through them is much like entering a secret—and sacred—cave.

Only inside do we sense the specifically Christian aspect of Ronchamp. The light, channeled through stained-glass windows so tiny that they seem hardly more than slits or pinpricks on the exterior, cuts widening paths through the thickness of the wall. It thus becomes once more what it had been in medieval architecture: the visible counterpart of the Light Divine. There is true magic in the interior of Ronchamp but also a strangely disquieting quality, a nostalgia for the certainties of a faith that is no longer unquestioned. In this way, Ronchamp mirrors the spiritual condition of the modern age, which is a measure of its greatness as a work of art.

KAHN. Le Corbusier belongs to the same heroic generation as Gropius and Mies van der Rohe: all were born in the 1880s. It was these giants who in the course of their long, fruitful careers coined the language of twentieth-century architecture. Their successors continued to use many aspects of its vocabulary in new building types and materials. Nor did they forget its fundamental logic.

Louis Kahn (1901–1974), the foremost representative of Brutalism in the United States, used bare concrete to great effect in the Jonas Salk Institute of Biological Studies in La Jolla (fig. 26-33). Salk, inventor of the first polio vaccine, had been deeply impressed by his visit to Assisi and conceived of the center as similar to the Franciscan monastery there. Kahn, who was in complete sympathy with his patron's views, carried out this scheme brilliantly. He treated the offices as a series of monastic cells attached to the central work spaces formed by the laboratories—or, as he put it, servant and server spaces. With its spartan surfaces, concrete expressed the asceticism of this scientific retreat. Like so many others, the ambitious project proved too costly (it included, among other things, separate living quarters for the scientists and their families) and was halted before it could be completed. It nevertheless remains the fullest statement of Kahn's principles.

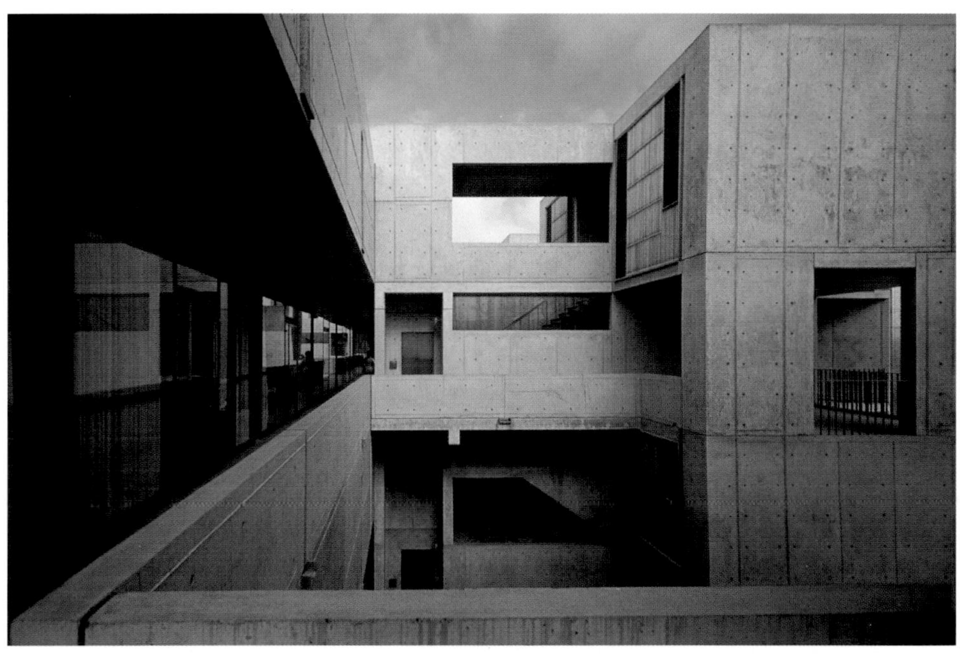

26-33. Louis Kahn. Jonas Salk Institute of Biological Studies, La Jolla, California. 1959–65

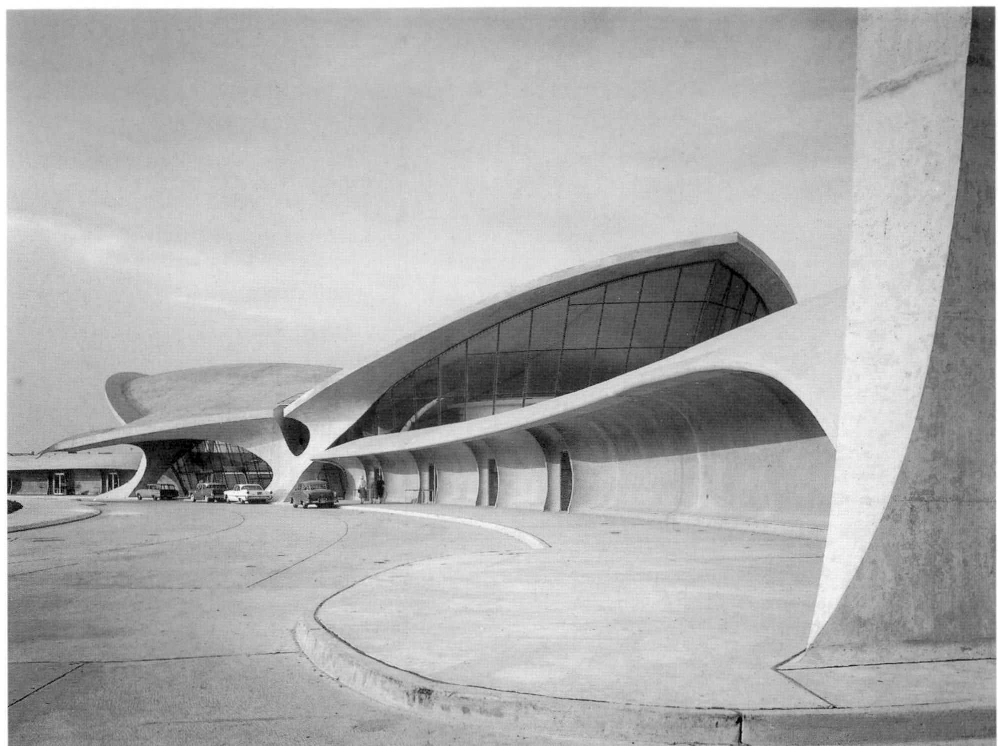

26-34. Eero Saarinen. Trans World Airlines Terminal, John F. Kennedy Airport, New York. 1956–63

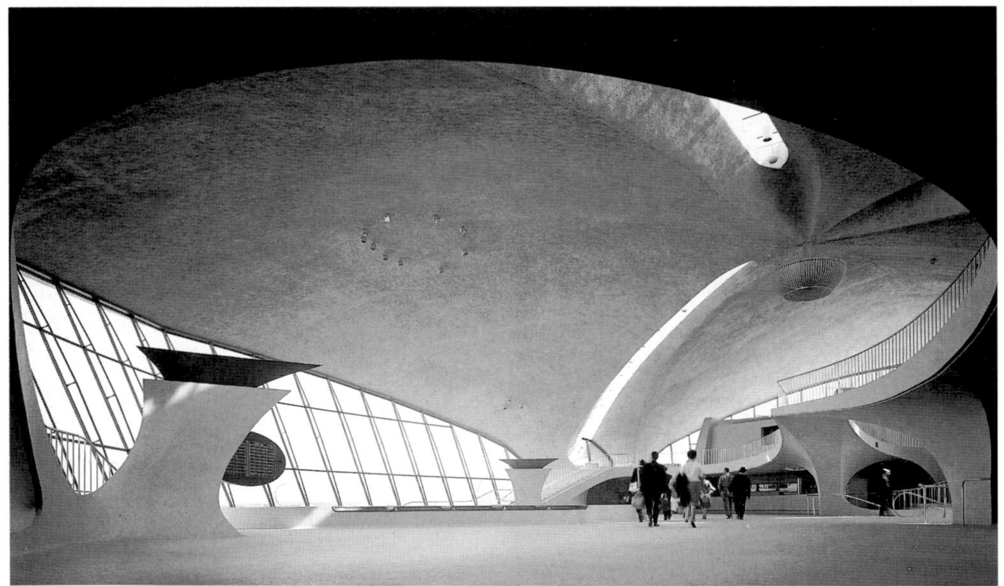

26-35. Interior, Trans World Airlines Terminal, John F. Kennedy Airport

SAARINEN. There is, however, an alternate tradition of reinforced concrete dating back to Berg's Centennial Hall (see fig. 26-9). This Expressionist vision continued to provide a dialogue with the International Style that enriched modern architecture. The Trans World Airlines (TWA) Terminal at Kennedy Airport in New York (figs. 26-34 and 26-35) by Eero Saarinen (1910–1961) is the great statement of postwar Expressionism. Saarinen, whose father had also been a well-known architect, was a skilled practitioner of the International Style. Here he has used the full potential of concrete in order to express the very essence of flight. Yet the inspiration, rather than mechanical, was purely organic. The swelling, sail-like forms of the four "flying" roofs create the impression of a gigantic bird, while the free-flowing spaces conduct visitors through the graceful interior with astonishing force, as if they were pulled along by a vortex.

NERVI. Saarinen is linked to Berg by Pier Luigi Nervi (1891–1979), who during the 1930s and 1940s pioneered the use of ferroconcrete in designs for aircraft hangars that provided the point of departure for all future developments in this vein. Nervi was a structural engineer with a bold sense of form and an even more daring vision. As such, he was the successor to Eugène Freyssinet (see box page 765), whose enormous reinforced concrete airship hangars at Orly near Paris (1916–24) were the first of their kind. The climax of Nervi's efforts was the Sports Palace designed with Annibale Vitellozzi for the 1960 Olympics in

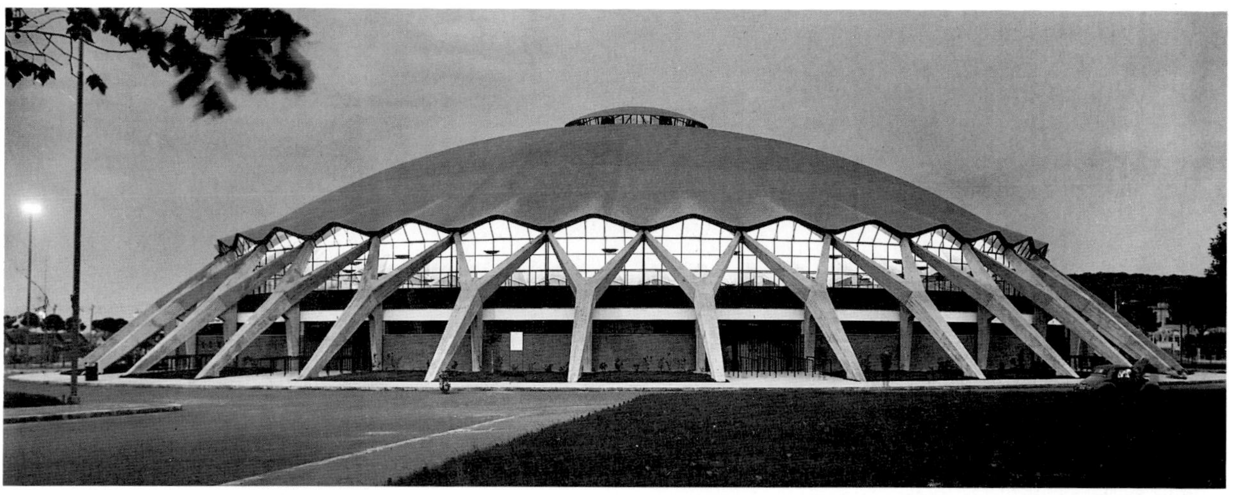

(ABOVE) 26-36. Pier Luigi Nervi and Annibale Vitellozzi. Sports Palace, Rome. 1956–57

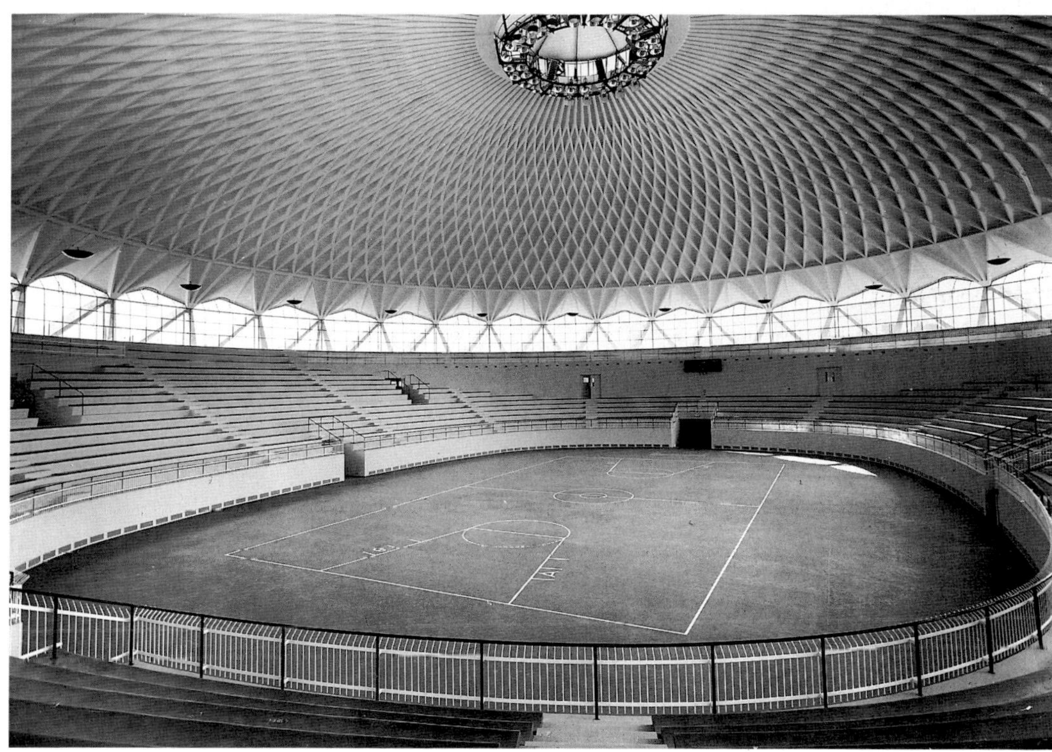

(RIGHT) 26-37. Interior, Sports Palace, Rome

Rome (figs. 26-36 and 26-37). From the outside, the roof appears as a thin covering whose light weight and flexibility are emphasized by the scalloped edges. It gives the impression of having been draped over the Y-shaped supports that radiate outward like flying buttresses. The effect inside is even more remarkable. The honeycombed roof, nearly 200 feet in diameter, recalls the interior of the Pantheon, with its great oculus (see fig. 7-12). A marvel of engineering, it seems to float effortlessly, like the dome of Hagia Sophia, in a pool of light without visible support (compare fig. 8-35).

UTZON. The Sydney Opera House (fig. 26-38) combines the expressionism of Saarinen and the engineering of Nervi in spectacular fashion to create something that transcends both. It was designed in 1956 by the Danish architect Jørn Utzon (b. 1918), who had worked briefly under Aalto and Wright in the years right

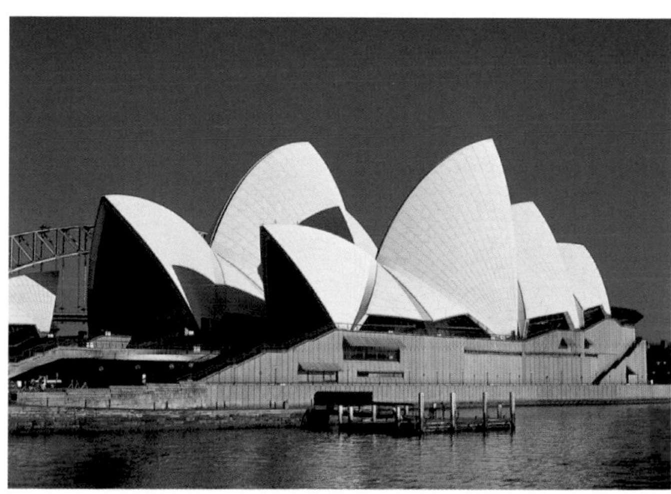

26-38. Jørn Utzon with Hall, Todd, and Littlemore. Sydney Opera House, Sydney, Australia. 1957–73

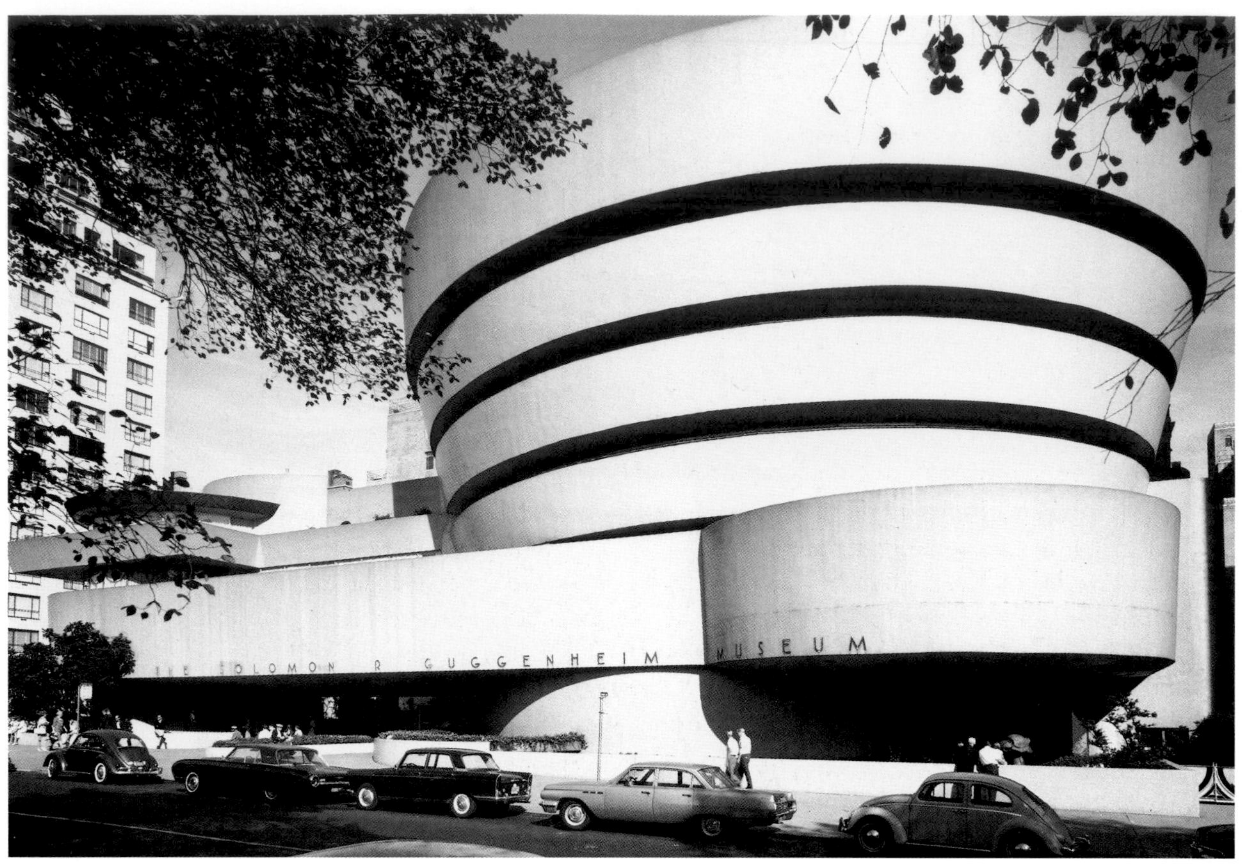

26-39. Frank Lloyd Wright. Solomon R. Guggenheim Museum, New York. 1956–59

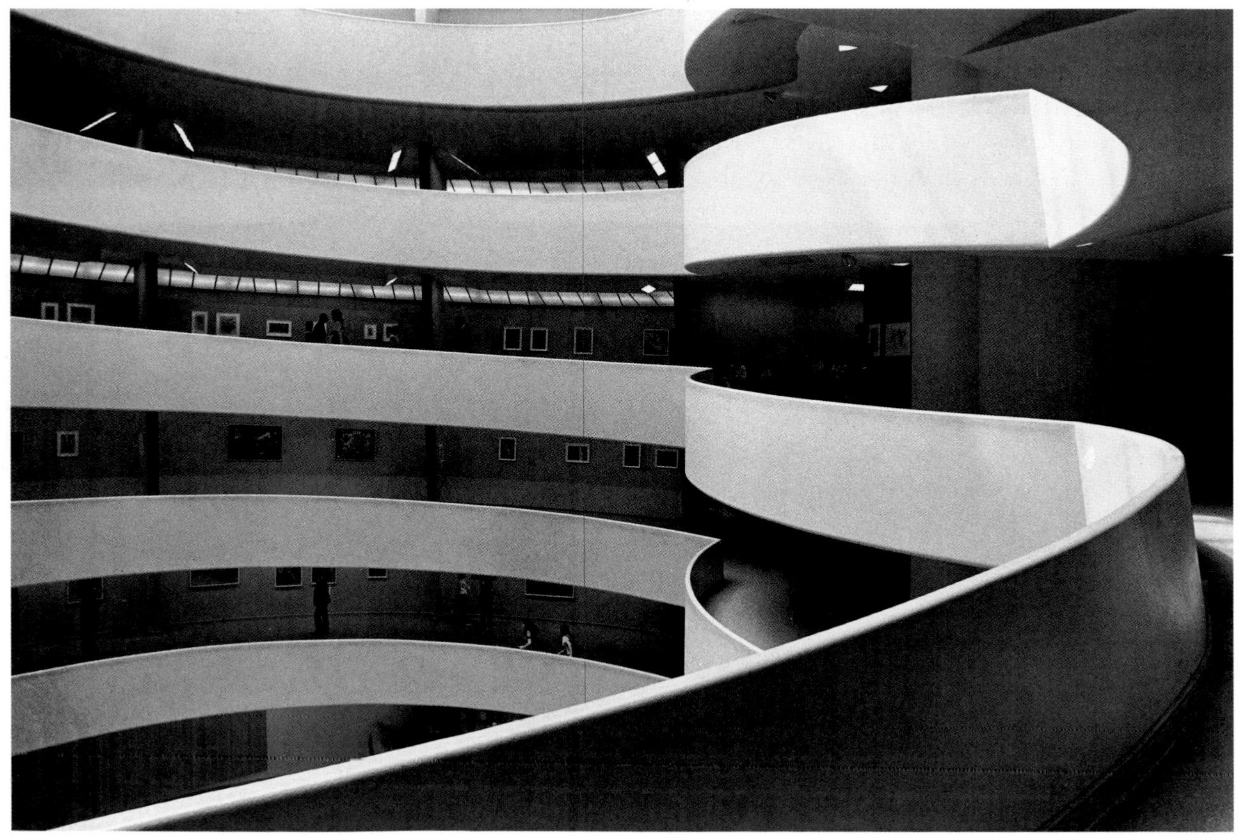

26-40. Interior of the Solomon R. Guggenheim Museum

after World War II. From the former he acquired a respect for local materials and traditions and from the latter a fascination with organic forms based on nature. Nervi perceptively called the shell roofs, which bear no relation to the auditoriums, "the most straightforward anti-functionalism from the point of view of statics as well as construction," something that might be said as well of Wright's Guggenheim Museum (see fig. 26-39). They required the most advanced engineering of the day, which was provided by Ove Arup (1895–1988). Second only to Nervi as an innovator, Arup was to work as a consultant on some of the most important late modern and postmodern buildings (see figs. 26-45 and 26-46). Indeed, the structure has sometimes been called a forerunner of postmodernist architecture (compare fig. 28-7). Like many major projects, the Sydney Opera House was problematic from the beginning and was completed in altered form only after Utzon resigned. Built on an abandoned wharf as part of a larger port and urban renewal plan, it became an instant classic. The opera house is justly famous throughout the world as a symbol of Sydney, as instantly recognizable as the Eiffel Tower or the Statue of Liberty. Utzon intended it to sit in splendid isolation as a gateway to the harbor. Today there are plans to develop the jetty commercially with apartments and shops, which will destroy the building's unique character.

WRIGHT. An extreme case of Expressionism at mid-century is the Solomon R. Guggenheim Museum in New York by Frank Lloyd Wright. Scorned when it was first erected in the late 1950s, it is a brilliant, if idiosyncratic, creation by one of the most original architectural minds of the century. The sculptural exterior (fig. 26-39) announces that this can only be a museum, for it is self-consciously a work of art in its own right. As a piece of design, the Guggenheim Museum is remarkably headstrong. In shape it is as defiantly individual as the architect himself and refuses to conform to the boxlike apartments around it. From the outside, the structure looks like a gigantic snail, reflecting Wright's interest in organic shapes. The office area forming the "head" to the left is connected by a narrow passageway to the "shell" containing the main body of the museum.

The outside gives us some idea of what to expect inside (fig. 26-40), yet nothing quite prepares us for the extraordinary sensation of light and air in the main hall after we are ushered through the unassuming entrance. The radical design makes it clear that Wright had completely rethought the purpose of an art museum. The exhibition area is a kind of inverted dome with a huge glass-covered eye at the top. The vast, fluid space creates an atmosphere of quiet harmony while actively shaping our experience by determining how art shall be displayed. After taking an elevator to the top of the building, visitors leisurely descend the gently sloping ramp. The continuous spiral provides for uninterrupted viewing, favorable to the study of art. At the same time, the narrow galleries prevent viewers from becoming passive observers by forcing them into a direct confrontation with the works of art. Sculpture takes on a heightened physical presence that demands that museumgoers look at it. Even paintings acquire a new prominence by protruding slightly from the curved walls, instead of receding into them. Viewing exhibitions at the Guggenheim is like being led through a predetermined stream of consciousness where everything merges into a total unity. Whether one agrees with this approach or not, the building testifies to the strength of Wright's vision by precluding any other way of seeing the art.

URBAN PLANNING. To some architects, the greatest challenge is not the individual structure but urban design. Urban planning is probably as old as civilization itself (which, we recall, means "city life"). We have caught only occasional glimpses of it in this book, since its history is difficult to trace by direct visual evidence. Cities, like living organisms, are ever-changing, and to reconstruct their pasts from their present appearances is not an easy task.

Since the arrival of the industrial era two centuries ago, cities have grown explosively. Much of this growth was uncontrolled, beyond the laying out of a network of streets. Worse, housing standards were poor or poorly enforced. The unfortunate result can be seen in the overcrowded, crumbling apartment blocks that are the blight of huge urban areas. They were taken over by the poor, while those who could afford it fled to the dormitory towns of suburbia. This exodus, accelerated by the automobile, has produced the dangerous tensions that make the need for urban renewal so urgent today. Such renewal, needless to say, must involve the political, social, and economic resources of an entire society, rather than the architect alone. Yet the architect has an essential role in the process, that of translating the schemes of the planning agencies into reality. However, they have generally failed in their mandate to replace the slums of our decaying cities with housing that will provide a healthful environment for very large numbers of people.

NIEMEYER. Nowhere are the issues facing modern civilization put into sharper focus than in the grandiose urban projects conceived by twentieth-century architects. These utopian visions may be regarded as laboratory experiments which redefine the

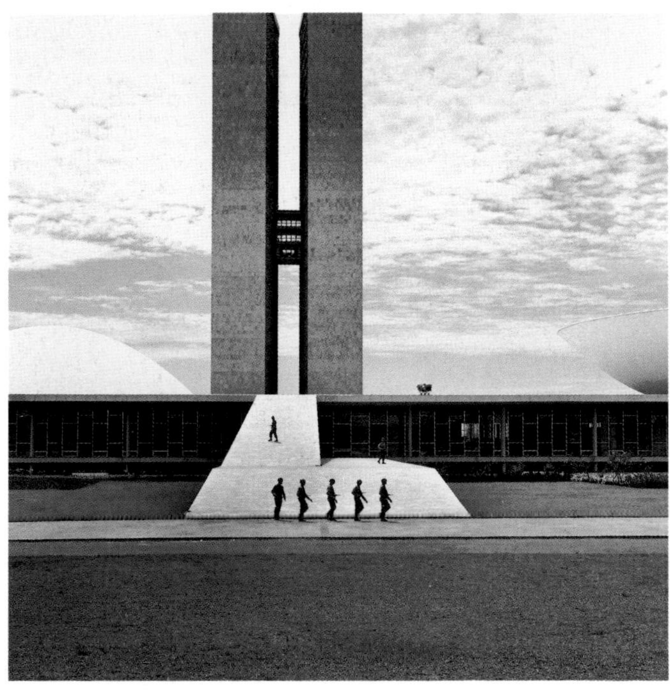

26-41. Oscar Niemeyer. Brasilia, Brazil. Completed 1960

role of architecture in shaping our lives and pose new solutions to social problems. Because of their vast scope, few of these ambitious proposals make it off the drawing board. Among the rare exceptions is Brasilia, the inland capital of Brazil built entirely since 1960. Presented with a unique opportunity to design a major city from the ground up and with enormous resources at its disposal, the design team, headed by the Brazilian Oscar Niemeyer (b. 1907), achieved spectacular results (fig. 26-41). Like most projects of this sort, Brasilia has a massive scale and unrelenting quality that make it curiously oppressive. As a result, the city provides a chilling glimpse of the future despite its extravagance (compare fig. 26-10).

LATE MODERNISM. Since 1970, architecture has been obsessed with breaking the tyranny of the cube—and the High Modernism it stands for. Consequently, a wide range of tendencies has arisen, representing almost every conceivable point of view. They have made architecture perhaps the most vital of the arts in the last quarter of the twentieth century. Like so much else in contemporary art, architecture has become theory-bound. Yet once the dust has settled, we may simplify its bewildering categories, with their equally confusing terminology, into Late Modernism, Postmodernism, and Deconstructivism (see Chapter 28). They are separated only by the degree to which they challenge the basic principles of High Modernism.

MEIER. Late Modernism began innocently enough as an attempt to introduce greater variety of form and material but ended in the segmentation of space and use of "high-tech" finishes that are the hallmarks of late-twentieth-century buildings. An important early example of this process is The Atheneum at New Harmony, Indiana (fig. 26-42), by Richard Meier (b. 1934). In its departure from the idealism of High Modernism, it seems an ironic commentary on the utopian vision of this historic settlement. New Harmony was founded in 1815 by George Rapp and sold ten years later to the Scottish reformer Robert Owen, who established a short-lived socialist society. The Atheneum reflects Meier's principal concerns: program and site, entry and circulation, structure and enclosure. Its placement within the landscape has been carefully calculated, with equally careful consideration given to its function as a visitors' center. The inspiration of Le Corbusier's Savoye House (see fig. 26-18) of nearly a half-century earlier is evident in the pristine white surfaces, which lend the building a sense of clarity. The vocabulary, too, remains essentially Cubist (compare fig. 24-26).

To that extent, the Atheneum falls well within the modern tradition. Yet it looks like Le Corbusier's classic statement exploded from within. The building bristles with external stairways and ramps, intersecting planes and jutting walls, and false structural elements that "frame" the view. These disrupt the facade and dissolve the boundary with the surrounding environment, so that the structure lacks the self-containment of the International Style. As we might expect, the interior is an equally dynamic play on Savoye House. Spatial relations are skewed by distorting forms and rotating them off-axis. Clearly Meier has pushed the syntax of High Modernism to its limits. Beyond this lies only Postmodernism.

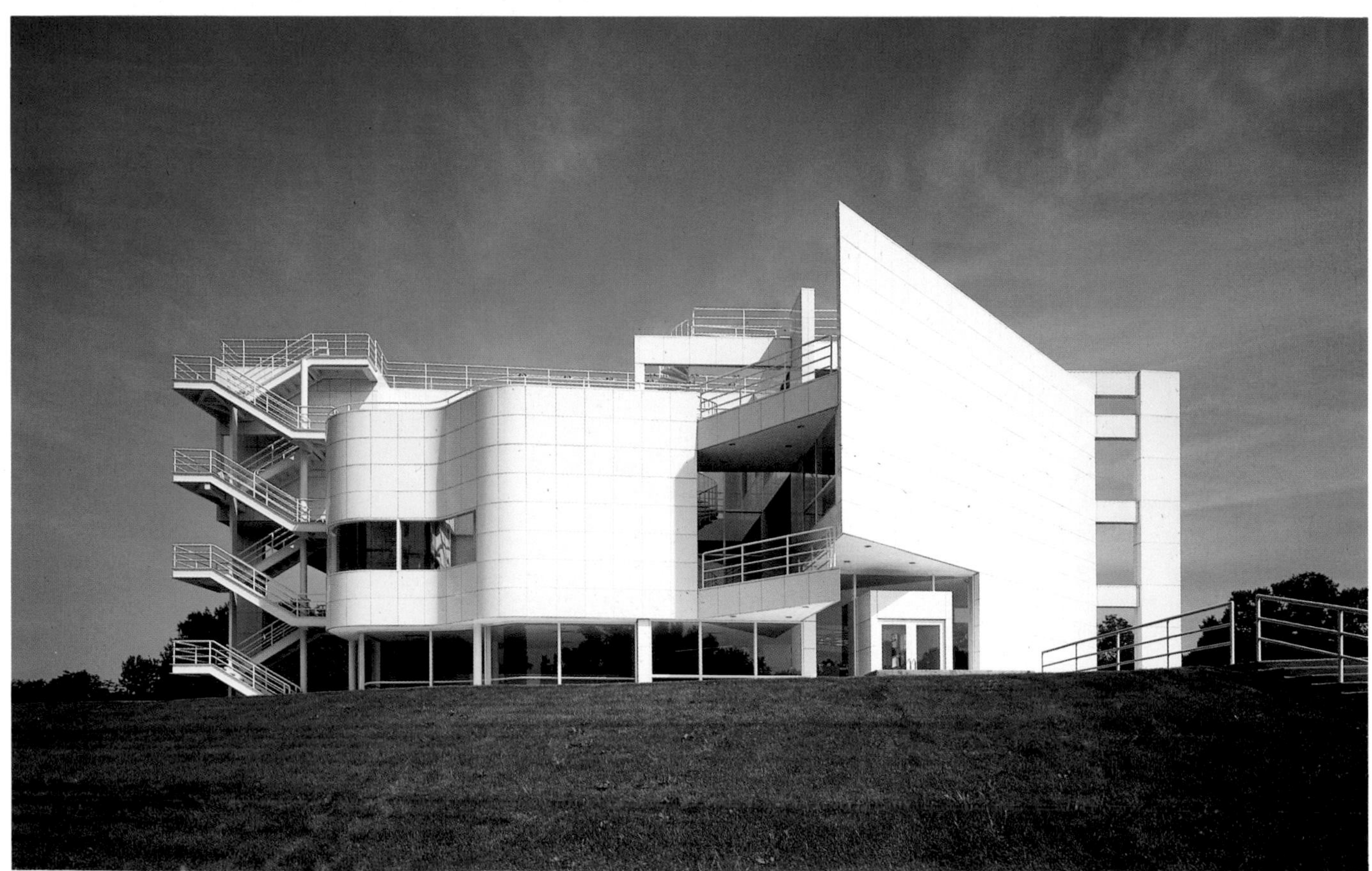

26-42. Richard Meier. The Atheneum, New Harmony, Indiana. 1975–79

PEICHL. In contrast to the centralized authority proclaimed by the Seagram Building, Late Modernist corporate architecture may be seen as a reflection of today's global economy, in which the major companies are based on rapid technological advances and dispersed in far-flung smaller units. The Austrian Radio and Television Studios designed by Gustav Peichl (b. 1928) in 1970 have sharply contrasting wings radiating out from a central core to suggest their different functions (fig. 26-43). The core itself has been conceived as a witty parody of spaceships, while the astonishing interior (fig. 26-44) looks like a futuristic movie set. Everything gleams with polished metal tubing clustered like the pipes of a rocket, which "blasts off" through the skylight. This space-age motif is continued on the rear of the auditorium, which sports exhaust pipes that curiously resemble the artillery of an aircraft carrier, as if to protect its flanks from some imaginary attack.

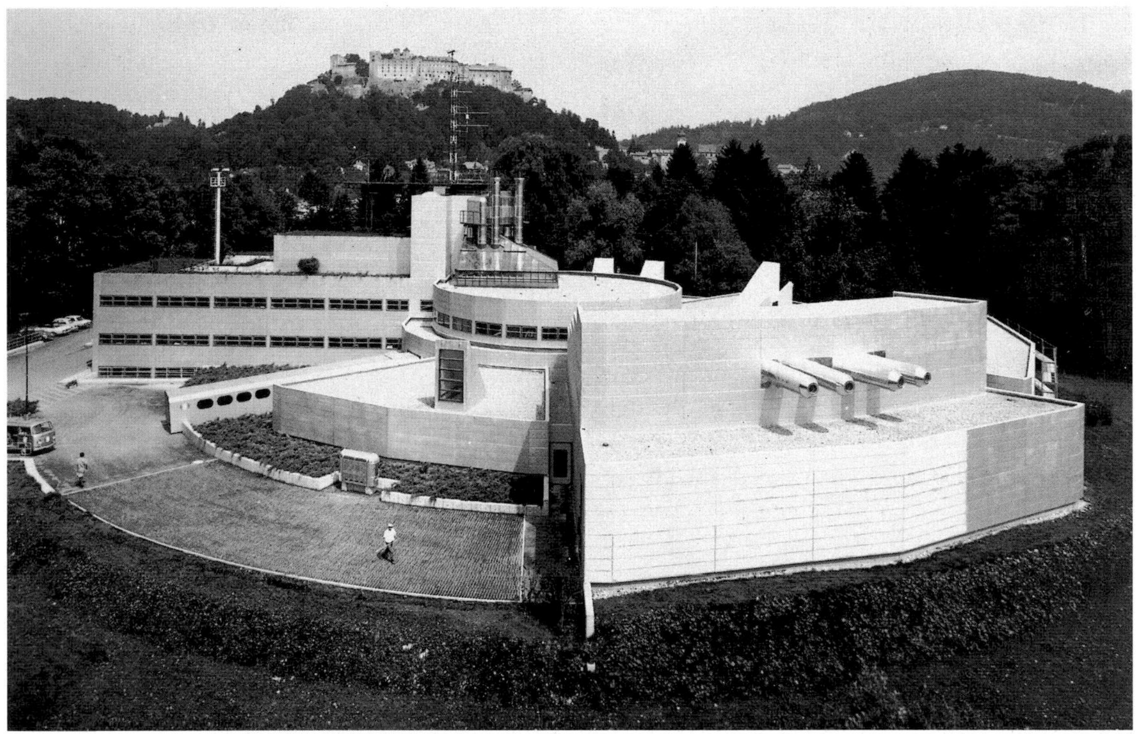

26-43. Gustav Peichl. Austrian Radio and Television Studio, Salzburg. 1970–72

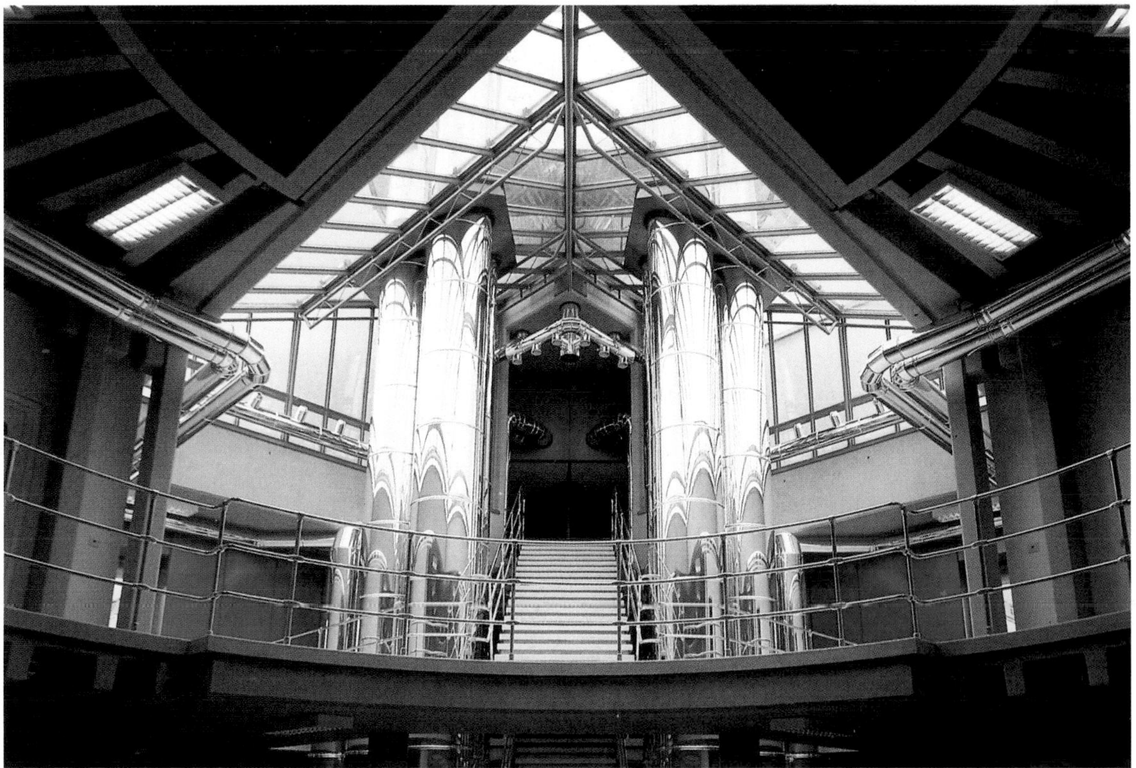

26-44. Interior, Austrian Radio and Television Studio, Salzburg

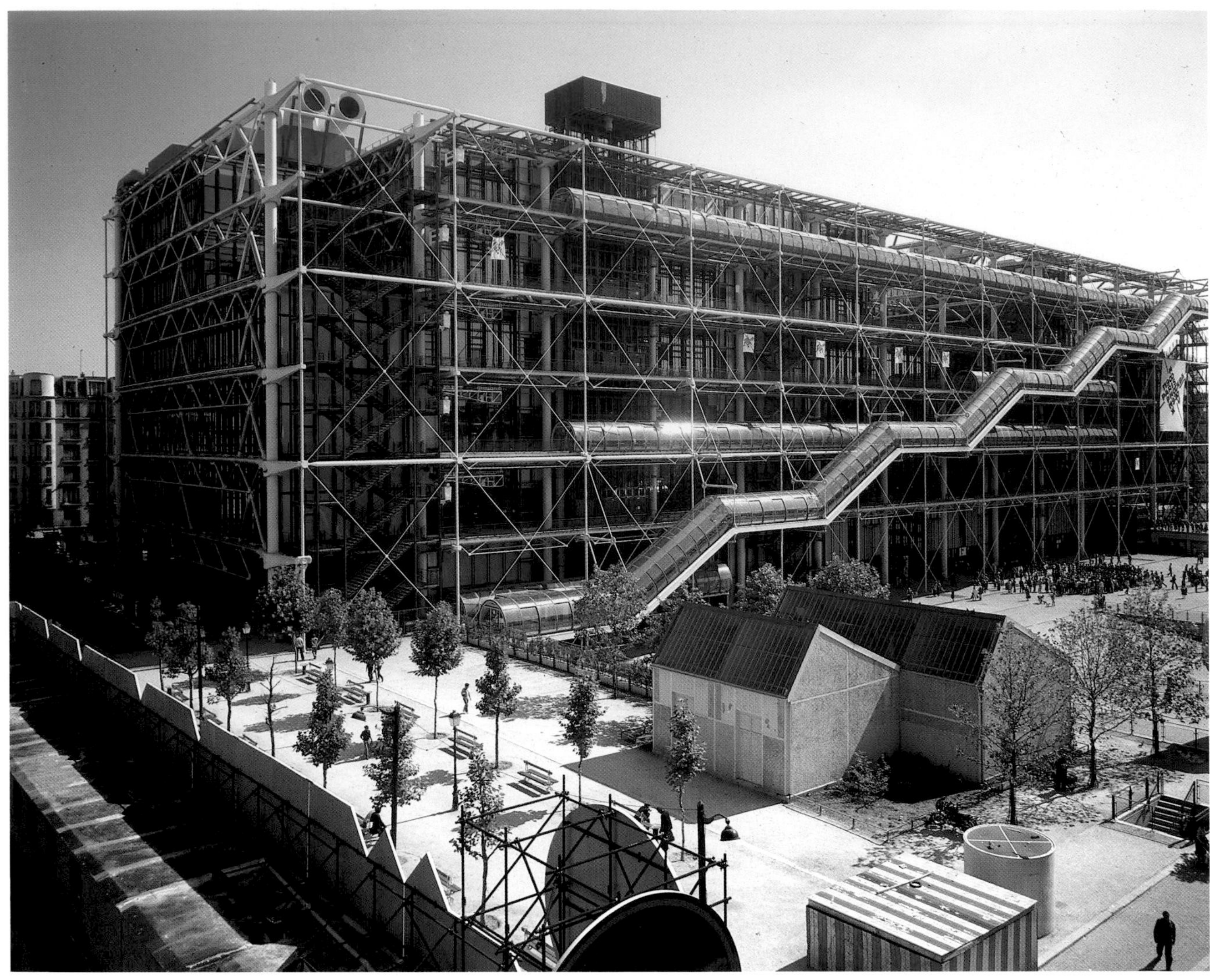

26-45. Richard Rogers and Renzo Piano. Centre National d'Art et Culture Georges Pompidou, Paris. 1971–77

ROGERS AND PIANO. Among the freshest results of Late Modernism is the Centre Georges Pompidou, the national arts and cultural center in Paris, which rejects the formal beauty of the International Style without abandoning its functionalism (fig. 26-45). Selected in an international competition, the design by the Anglo-Italian team of Richard Rogers (b. 1933) and Renzo Piano (b. 1937) looks like a building turned inside out. The architects have eliminated any trace of Le Corbusier's elegant facades (see fig. 26-18), exposing the building's inner mechanics while disguising the underlying structure. The interior itself has no fixed walls, so that temporary dividers can be arranged to meet any need. This stark utilitarianism, sometimes termed Productivism, expresses a populist sentiment widespread in France. The exterior is enlivened by eye-catching colors, each keyed to a different function. The festive display is as vivacious and imaginative as Léger's *The City* (see fig. 24-34), which, with Paris' Eiffel Tower (see fig. 22-38), can be regarded as the Pompidou Center's true ancestor.

FOSTER. Rogers helped to bring Late Modernism to maturity in a series of buildings around London that inspired the wrath of Prince Charles. We can see why in the Hongkong Bank, in Hong Kong, designed by Norman Foster (b. 1935), one of Rogers' former associates (figs. 26-46 and 26-47). It testifies to the bank's desire to have the most beautiful building in the world. (It is certainly the most expensive that money can buy.) Everything about the structure is extreme. The huge scale represents the megalomania of today's corporations and the architects who work for them. The edifice was intended quite consciously as a cathedral of banking. Like a Gothic cathedral, the reinforcing members of this capitalist "church" are located on the exterior in the form of bizarre struts (compare fig. 11-7). The cavernous interior, with its elaborate structural skeleton, may likewise be compared to that of a Gothic cathedral (see fig. 11-27), although the antecedents of the vast atrium lie in the early work of Frank Lloyd Wright. Influenced greatly by the "high-tech" aerospace and military industries, the Hongkong Bank has been hailed as a brilliant architectural feat and condemned as a monstrosity. In any event, there can be little doubt that both the principles and the vocabulary of the International Style have been abandoned so completely that the building may be considered an example of Late Modernism or Postmodernism with equal justification. Whatever we call it, we have clearly reached the end of High Modernist architecture.

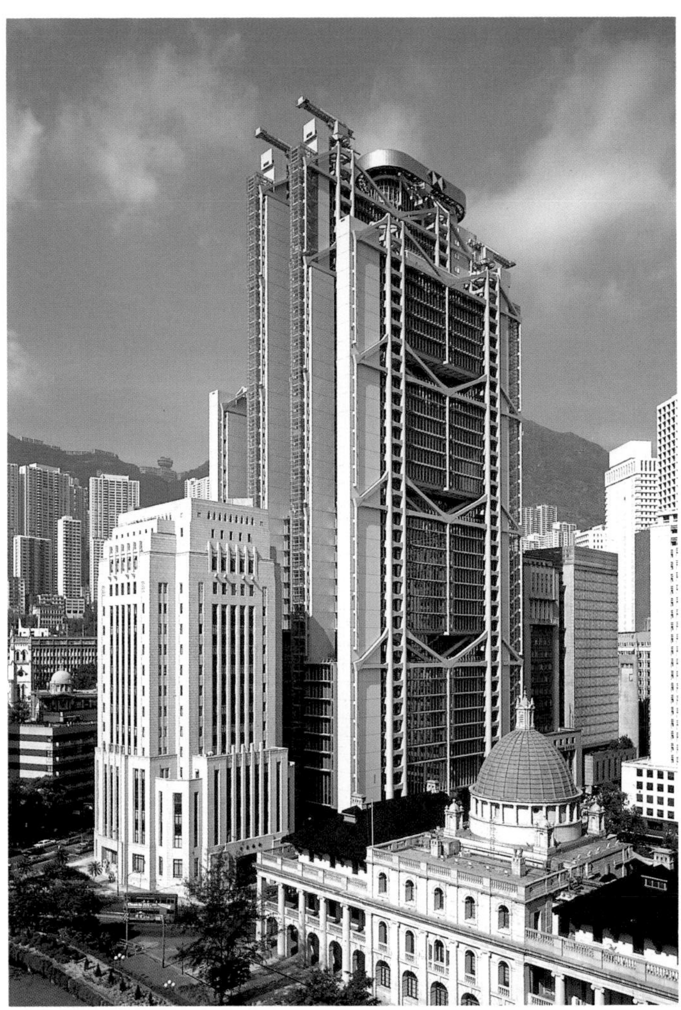

26-46. Foster Associates. Hongkong Bank, Hong Kong. 1979–86

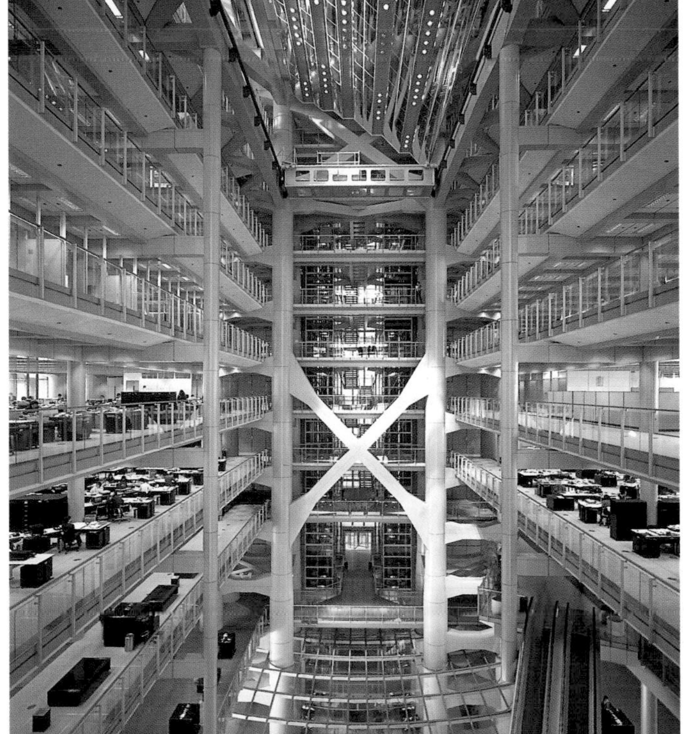

26-47. Interior, Hongkong Bank, Hong Kong

NEO-EXPRESSIONISM. As the reference back to Wright suggests, it can be argued that Late Modernism actually fulfills the agenda mapped at the beginning of the century, when architecture pursued not one but several paths. There is a certain truth to this ironic notion. Since 1985 architecture has also seen the rise of Neo-Modernism and Neo-Expressionism, which can be regarded as counterparts of the similarly named movements in painting (see page 831). The difference is that they have helped to make architecture the most vibrant and innovative of all art forms on the scene today, in contrast to painting and sculpture, which seem adrift at sea. Indeed, the architecture of the past 15 years is among the richest in variety and quality of any period since the Baroque. There are at present more than two dozen great architects at work around the world. Our sampling must inevitably seem arbitrary, since it can serve only as a brief overview of recent trends. (See also Postmodern Architecture, pages 910–16)

Neo-Expressionism utilizes the same high-tech materials and techniques as Late Modernism but creates of them fantasies that are more sculptural than architectural. Thus architecture has replaced sculpture as the giver of contemporary form. Santiago Calatrava (b. 1951), Spanish-born but Swiss-based, has created literally a flight of fancy for the TGV (Très Grande Vitesse) Station at Satolas, Lyons (fig. 26-48). The entrance to the central hall gives the appearance of the Concorde supersonic plane constructed on a birdlike skeleton but with a tail echoing the French Super Train. Through this seemingly mixed metaphor, the structure helps to link the railroad station with a nearby airport. But in contrast to Saarinen's TWA Terminal (see fig. 26-34), which evokes the essence of flight, the futuristic TGV station suggests a mechanized prehistoric creature out of a science fiction movie.

NEO-MODERNISM. Neo-Modernism looks back consciously to the modernist tradition created by Gropius, Mies van der Rohe, and Le Corbusier. Within it we may discern three separate, yet closely related, strands. The first is a revival of Structural Rationalism that is especially characteristic of Italian architects, such as Mario Botta (b. 1943) and Aldo Rossi (1931–1997), as well the Frenchman Jean Nouvel (b. 1945). The second is a conscious return on the part of certain English architects, most notably Nicholas Grimshaw (b. 1939), to the functional engineering of Paxton's Crystal Palace (see fig. 22-36). And the third, taken up by a new school of Dutch architects, among whom Rem Koolhaas (b. 1944) is the best known, questions the legacy of High Modernism and tries to give it new life by reconsidering its potential in light of present-day realities. The theories and approaches of these three overlap not only with each other but also with those of the Postmodernists, so that in recent years there has been a gradual merging of previously separate tendencies.

An issue that concerns all schools is how to deal with the problem of unplanned urban growth and its attendant blight, though

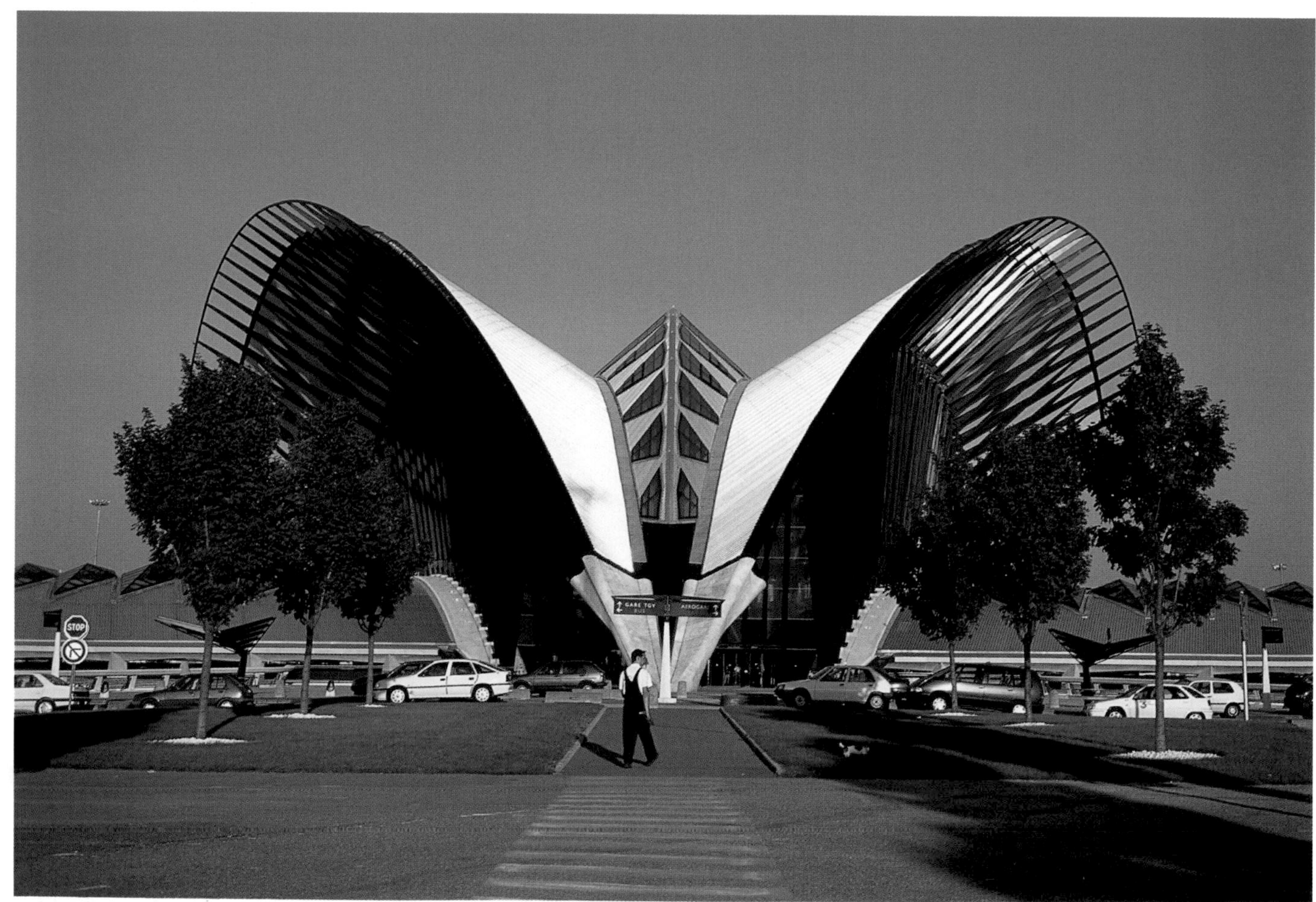

26-48. Santiago Calatrava. TGV (Très Grande Vitesse) Super Train Station, Satolas, Lyons. 1988–94

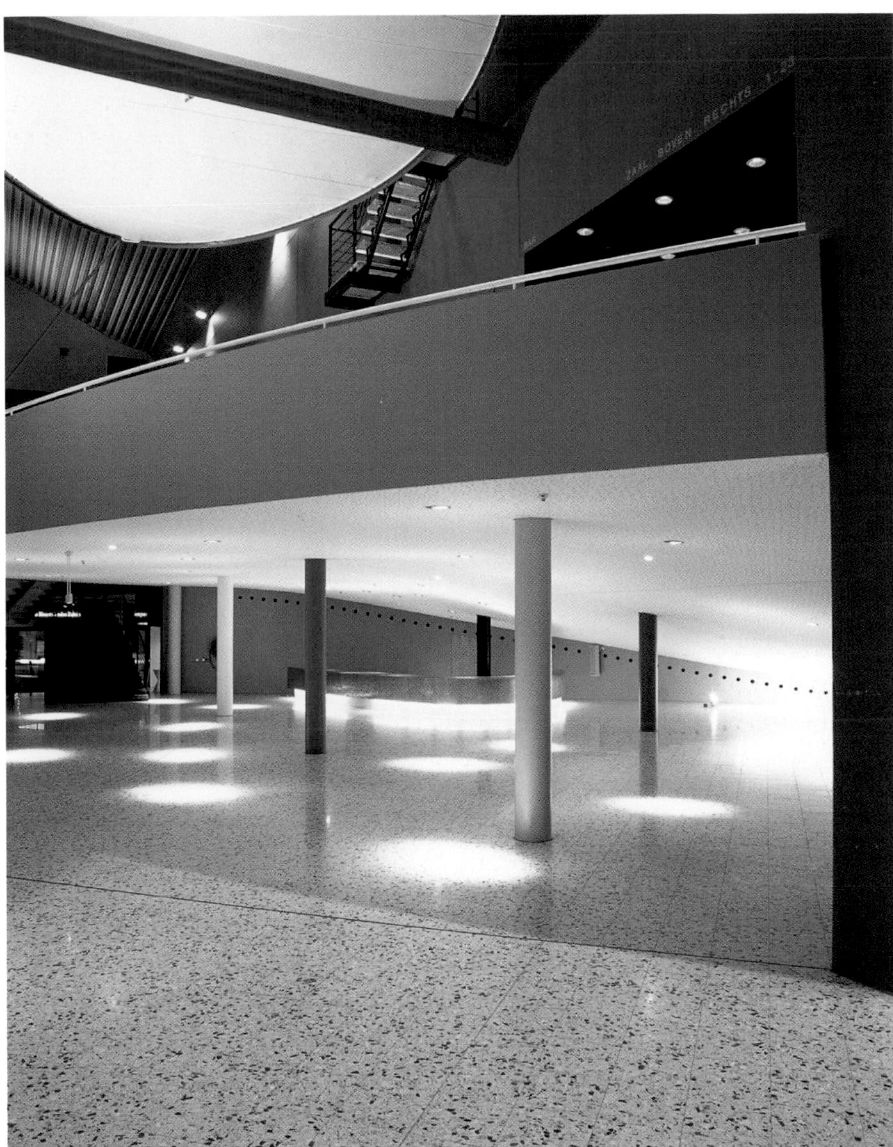

26-49. Rem Koolhaas. Foyer of the Netherlands Dance Theater, Amsterdam. 1987.

each has faced it somewhat differently. Unlike earlier architects, they have generally avoided attempting to cure social ills, since the utopian schemes put forward by the High Modernists were generally failures. Instead, they have been interested primarily in making significant architectural statements under the difficult conditions imposed by the sites themselves. Koolhaas and his OMA group have focused on modern chaos theory and the "culture of congestion" epitomized by New York City, which has led to a recent preoccupation with size. For Koolhaas, it is the architect's role to resist chaos and instead find a new modernism reflecting urban existence within our time, which is full of paradoxes and contradictions. For that reason, Koolhaas combines "architectural specificity with programmatic instability," in which goals are treated in terms of strategy. Far from rejecting modernism, Koolhaas builds on it, while discarding many of its underlying assumptions. Although he has been influenced by Frank Gehry and the Deconstructionists (compare pages 916–17), especially in his preference for corrugated metal and other standard industrial building supplies, he has scorned the return to the style of the early Russian moderns as imitative and irrelevant to our age.

What all this theorizing in effect means is a new functionalism in which the facade is no more than an envelope that coexists with its surroundings, thereby disguising the purposes and spaces it encloses. In fact, Koolhaas' exteriors are deceptively bland. The real action takes place inside. If the Neo-Expressionists and the Sculptural Architects (see pages 916–17) are masters of form, Koolhaas is the master of interior space. The facade of the Netherlands Dance Theater, which is grafted onto an existing concert hall, is extremely modest. Indeed, it is readily overlooked. However, the foyer (fig. 26-49) is that rarity in modern architecture: a genuinely engaging interior, although it deliberately breaks no new ground as such. Despite Koolhaas' importance as a theorist, his design abstains from the didacticism that made High Modernism seem so cold and barren. He instead rescues modernism from itself and invests it with a new humanism—the feature it most conspicuously lacked. Although the materials are commonplace, he uses festive colors and creates a dynamic space that is strikingly reminiscent of Léger's paintings (compare fig. 24-34). It is this kind of thoughtful reappraisal of the modernist legacy that offers perhaps the best hope for its continued vitality.

CHAPTER TWENTY-SEVEN

Twentieth-Century Photography

THE FIRST HALF-CENTURY

During the nineteenth century, photography struggled to establish itself as art but failed to find an identity. Only under extraordinary conditions of political upheaval and social reform did it address the most basic subject of art, which is life itself. In creating an independent vision, photography would combine the aesthetic principles of the Secession and the documentary approach of photojournalism with lessons learned from motion photography. At the same time, modern painting, with which it soon became allied, forced a decisive change in photography. Modernism undermined the theoretical assumptions of photography and challenged its credentials as art. Like the other arts, photography responded to the three main artistic currents of the early twentieth century: Expressionism, Abstraction, and Fantasy. But because it has concentrated for the most part on the world around us, modern photography has generally followed a separate course marked by realism. We must therefore discuss twentieth-century photography primarily in terms of different schools and how they have dealt with those often-conflicting currents.

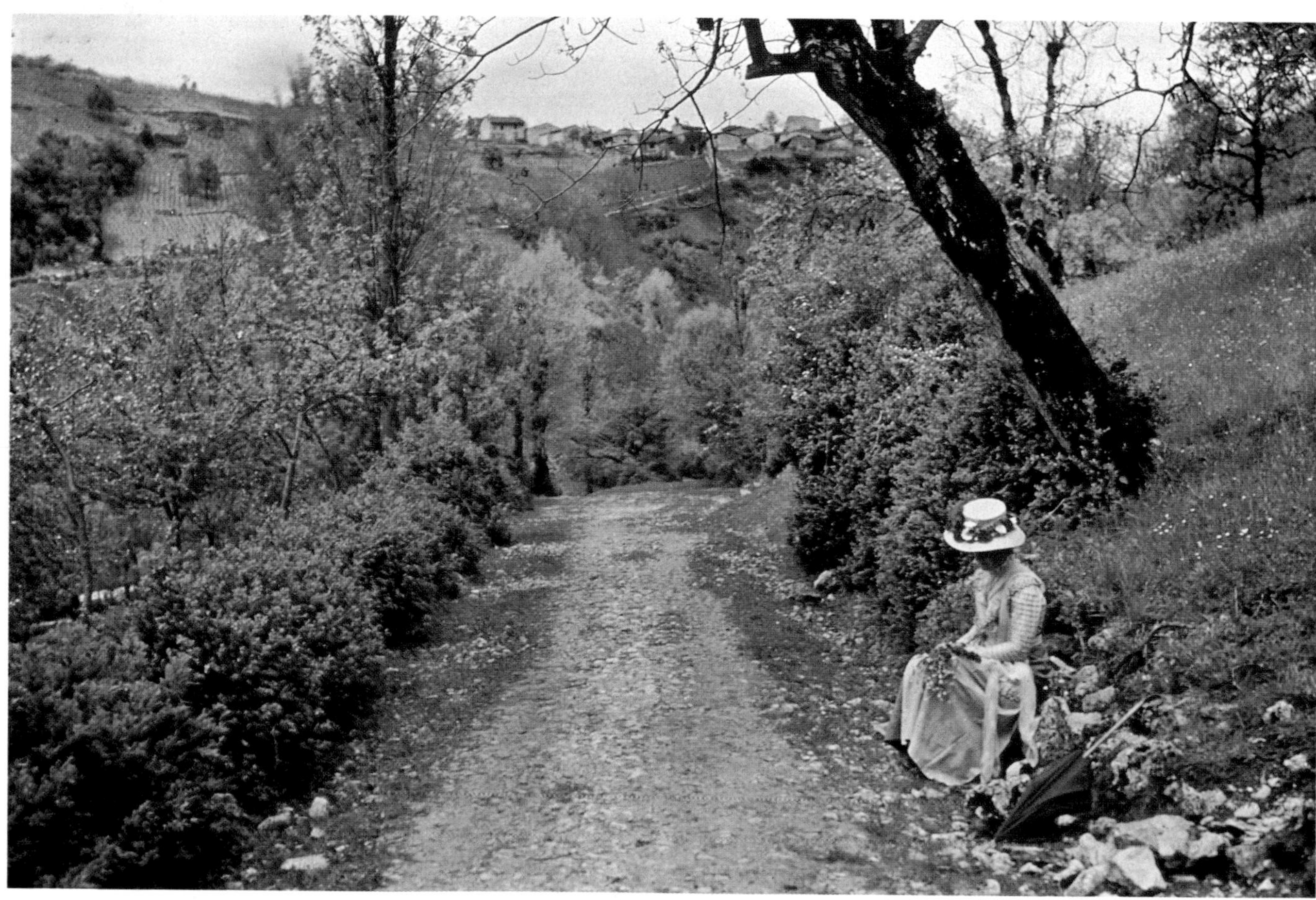

27-1. Louis Lumière. *Young Lady with an Umbrella.* 1906–10. Autochrome. Société Lumière

Modern photography was aided by technological advances. It must be emphasized, however, that these have increased but not dictated the photographer's options. George Eastman's invention of the handheld camera in 1888 and the advent of 35 mm photography with the Leica camera in 1924 made it easier to take pictures that had been difficult but by no means impossible to take with the traditional view camera.

Surprisingly, color photography did not have such revolutionary importance as might be expected. It began in 1907 with the introduction of the "autochrome" by Louis Lumière (1864–1948) who, with his brother, had created a new art form, the cinema, in 1894. The autochrome was a glass plate covered with grains of potato starch dyed in three colors that acted as color filters, over which was applied a coating of silver bromide emulsion. It yielded a positive color transparency upon development and was not superseded until Kodak began to make color film in 1932, using the same principles but more advanced materials. The autochrome was based on the color theories used by Seurat. It even achieved Divisionist effects, as we can see if we look hard enough at Lumière's *Young Lady with an Umbrella* (fig. 27-1), an early effort. Except for its color, the picture differs little from photographs by the Photo-Secessionists, who were the first to turn to the new process. Color, in fact, had little impact on the content, outlook, or aesthetic of photography until the 1930s, even though it removed the last barrier cited by nineteenth-century critics of photography as an art.

The School of Paris

ATGET. Modern photography began quietly in Paris with Eugène Atget (1856–1927), who turned to the camera only in 1898 at the age of 42. From then until his death, he toted his heavy equipment around Paris to record the city in all its variety. Atget was all but ignored by the art photographers, for whom his commonplace subjects had little interest. He himself was a humble man whose studio sign read simply, "Atget—Documents for Artists." His patrons included the founders of modern art: Braque, Picasso, Duchamp, and Man Ray, to name only the best known. It is no accident that these artists were also admirers of Henri Rousseau. Rousseau and Atget shared a naive vision, though Atget found inspiration in unexpected corners of his environment rather than in magical realms of the imagination.

Atget's pictures are characterized by a subtle intensity and technical perfection that heighten the reality, and hence the significance, of even the most mundane subject. Few photographers have equaled his ability to compose simultaneously in two- and three-dimensional space. Like *Versailles* (fig. 27-2), his scenes are often des-

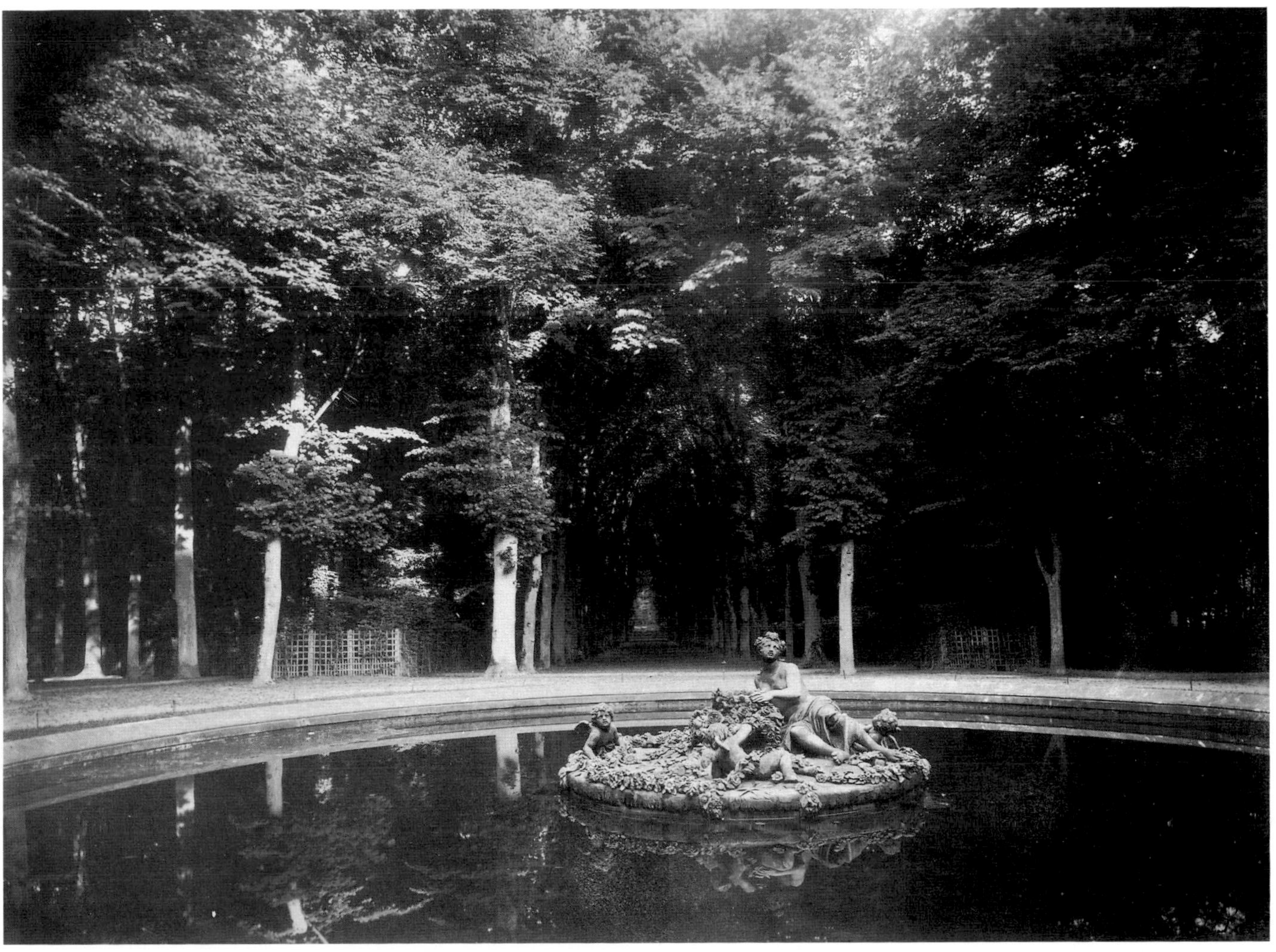

27-2. Eugène Atget. *Versailles*. 1924. Albumen-silver print, 7 x 9⅜" (17.8 x 23.9 cm). The Museum of Modern Art, New York

ABBOTT-LEVY COLLECTION. PARTIAL GIFT OF SHIRLEY C. BURDEN

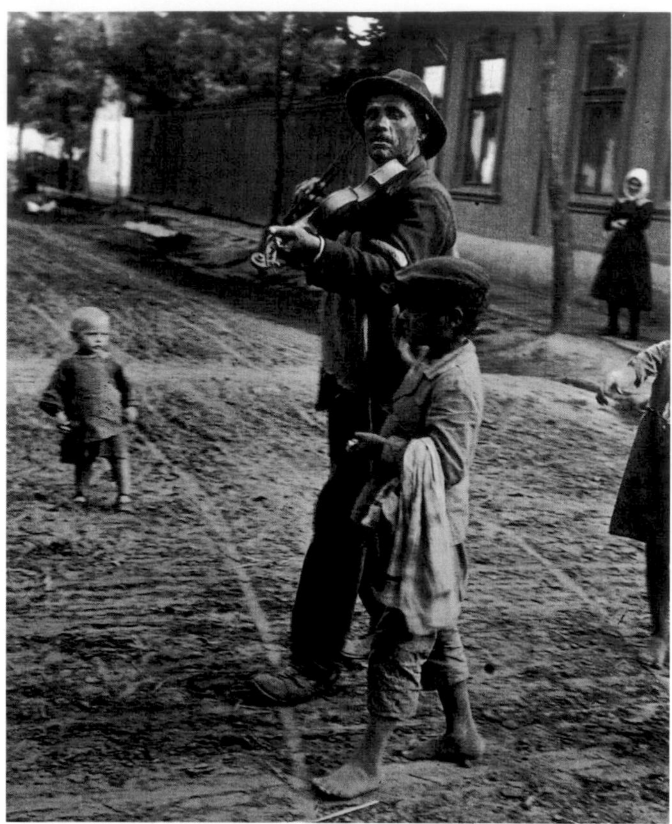

(ABOVE) 27-3. André Kertész. *Blind Musician.* 1921. Gelatin-silver print, 16⅜ x 13¼" (41.6 x 33.7 cm). The Museum of Modern Art, New York
GIFT OF THE ARTIST

olate, bespeaking a strange and individual outlook. The viewer has the haunting sensation that time has been frozen by the majestic composition and the photographer's obsession with textures. While Atget's work is marginally in the journalistic tradition of Nadar, Brady, and Riis (see pages 703–04, 705, and 765), it is a distinct departure from earlier photography that can only be explained in relation to late-nineteenth-century art. His pictures of neighborhood shops and street vendors, for example, are nearly identical with slightly earlier paintings by minor realists whose names are all but forgotten. Moreover, his photographs are directly related to a strain of Magic Realism that was a forerunner of Surrealism. Indeed, Atget has been called a Surrealist. While this label is misleading, it is easy to understand why he was rediscovered by Man Ray, the Dada and Surrealist artist–photographer, and championed by Man Ray's former assistant, Berenice Abbott (see page 901). Nevertheless, Atget's work is too varied to permit convenient classification.

KERTÉSZ. Atget's direct successors were two East Europeans: André Kertész (1894–1985) and Gyula Halasz, known simply as Brassaï (1899–1984). Kertész began photographing in his native Hungary as early as 1915, and his style was already defined when he came to Paris ten years later. *Blind Musician* (fig. 27-3), made in Hungary in 1921, is the kind of picture Atget sometimes took, and it uses many of the same devices. The careful composition isolates the subject, with just enough of the surroundings to set the scene.

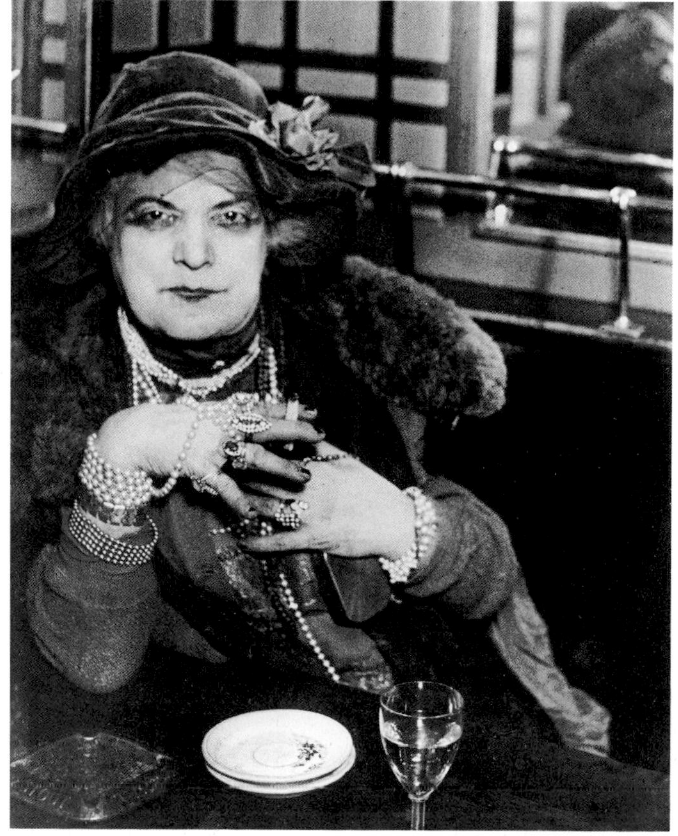

(RIGHT) 27-4. Brassaï. *"Bijou" of Montmartre.* 1933. 11⅞ x 9¼" (30.2 x 23.5 cm). The Museum of Modern Art, New York
THE BEN SCHULTZ MEMORIAL COLLECTION. GIFT OF THE ARTIST

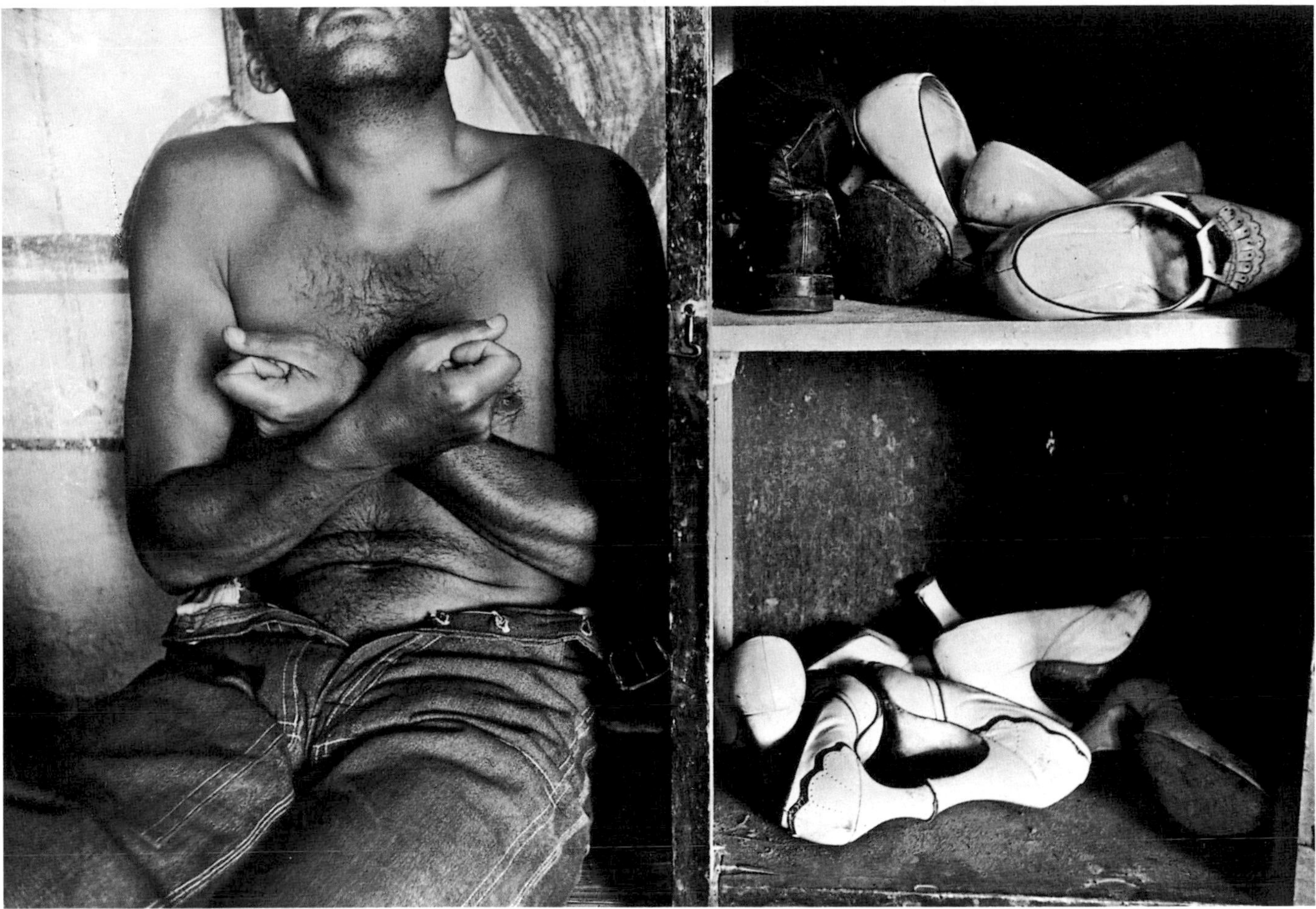

27-5. Henri Cartier-Bresson. *Mexico, 1934.* 1934. Gelatin-silver print

BRASSAÏ. Brassaï's photographic style was conditioned by Paris, its views and its habits. He was born in Transylvania and studied art in Budapest but was a Frenchman at heart even before arriving in Paris in 1923. Several years later, while working as a journalist, he borrowed a camera from Kertész and took a series of evocative photographs of the city by night. He soon turned to the nightlife of the Parisian cafés and had an unerring eye for the exotic characters who haunt them. *"Bijou" of Montmartre* (fig. 27-4) shows the same appreciation of the abnormal as *At the Moulin Rouge* (see fig. 23-8) by Toulouse-Lautrec, whose art certainly influenced Brassaï.

CARTIER-BRESSON. The greatest photographer of the Paris school is Henri Cartier-Bresson (b. 1908), the son of a wealthy thread manufacturer. He studied under a Cubist painter in the late 1920s before taking up photography in 1932. Strongly affected at first by Atget, Man Ray (see page 900), Kertész, and the cinema, he soon developed into the most influential photojournalist of his time, and he still thinks of himself primarily as one. His purpose and technique are nevertheless those of an artist, and his photographs have a nearly universal appeal.

Cartier-Bresson is the master of what he has termed "the decisive moment." This to him means the instant recognition and visual organization of an event at the most intense moment of action and emotion in order to reveal its inner meaning, not simply to record its occurrence. Unlike other members of the Paris school, Cartier-Bresson seems at home anywhere in the world and always in sympathy with his subjects. His photographs show an interest in composition for its own sake, derived from modern abstract art. He also has a fascination with motion, which he invests with all the dynamism of Futurism and the irony of Dada.

The key to his work is his use of space to establish relations that are suggestive and often astonishing. Indeed, although he deals with reality, Cartier-Bresson is a Surrealist at heart and has admitted as much. The results can be disturbing, as in *Mexico, 1934* (fig. 27-5). By omitting the man's face, Cartier-Bresson prevents us from identifying the meaning of the gesture, yet we respond to its tension no less powerfully.

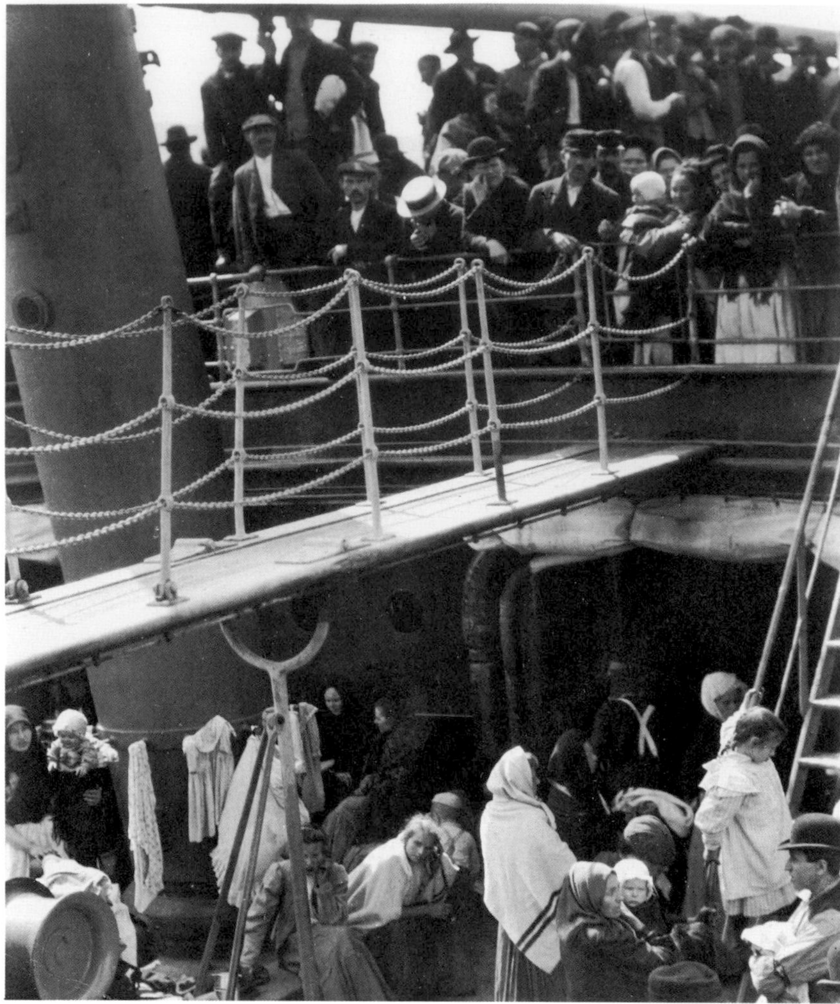

27-6. Alfred Stieglitz. *The Steerage.* 1907. Chloride print, 4⅜ x 3⅝" (11.1 x 9.2 cm). The Art Institute of Chicago
ALFRED STIEGLITZ COLLECTION

The Stieglitz School

STIEGLITZ. The founder of modern photography in the United States was Alfred Stieglitz, and he remained the dominant figure throughout his long life (1864–1946). From his involvement with the Photo-Secession onward (see page 767), he was a tireless spokesman for photography-as-art, although he defined this more broadly than did other members of the movement. He backed up his words by publishing the magazine *Camera Work.* He also supported the other pioneers of American photography by exhibiting their work in his New York galleries, especially the first one, known as "291." Most of his early work follows Secessionist conventions by treating photography as a pictorial equivalent to painting. During the mid-1890s, however, he took some pictures of street scenes that are forerunners of his mature photographs.

His classic statement, and the one he regarded as his finest photograph, is *The Steerage* (fig. 27-6), taken in 1907 on a trip to Europe. Like Ford Madox Brown's *The Last of England* (see fig. 22-18), painted more than a half-century earlier, it captures the feeling of a voyage but does so by letting the shapes and composition tell the story. The gangway bridge divides the scene visually, emphasizing the contrasting activities of the people below in the steerage, which was reserved for the cheapest fares, and the observers on the upper deck. If the photograph lacks the obvious sentiment of Brown's painting, it possesses an equal drama by remaining true to life.

This kind of "straight" photography is deceptive in its simplicity: the image mirrors the feelings that stirred Stieglitz. For that reason, *The Steerage* marks an important step in his evolution and a turning point in the history of photography. Its importance emerges only in comparison with earlier photographs such as Steichen's *Rodin* (see fig. 23-48) and Riis' *Bandits' Roost* (see fig. 23-42). *The Steerage* is a pictorial statement independent of painting on the one hand and free from social commentary on the other. It represents the first time that documentary photography achieved the level of art in America.

Stieglitz' straight photography shaped the American school. It is therefore ironic that Stieglitz, with Steichen's encouragement, became America's first champion of abstract art. He attacked the Ash Can School (see page 789), whose paintings were often similar in subject and appearance to his photographs. The resemblance is misleading. For Stieglitz, photography was less a means of recording things than of expressing his experience and philosophy of life, much as a painter does.

This attitude culminated in his *Equivalents* series. In 1922 Stieglitz began to photograph clouds to show that his work was independent of subject and personality. A remarkably lyrical cloud photograph from 1930 (fig. 27-7) corresponds to a state of mind waiting to find expression rather than merely responding to

(Left) 27-7. Alfred Stieglitz. *Equivalent.* 1930. Chloride print. The Art Institute of Chicago
ALFRED STIEGLITZ COLLECTION

(Below) 27-8. Edward Weston. *Pepper.* 1930. Center for Creative Photography, Tucson, Arizona

the moonlit scene. The study of clouds is as old as Romanticism itself, but no one before Stieglitz had made them a major theme in photography. As in Käsebier's *The Magic Crystal* (see fig. 23-47), *Equivalent* evokes unseen forces that also make it a counterpart to Kandinsky's *Sketch I for "Composition VII"* (see fig. 24-10).

WESTON. Stieglitz's concept of the *Equivalent* opened the way to "pure" photography as an alternative to straight photography. The leader of this new approach was Edward Weston (1886–1958), who was decisively influenced by Stieglitz. During the 1920s Weston pursued abstraction and realism as separate paths, but by 1930 he united them in images that are wonderful in their design and miraculous for their detail.

Pepper (fig. 27-8) is a splendid example of Weston's photography. The image is anything but a straightforward record of this familiar fruit. Like Stieglitz' *Equivalents,* it makes us see the ordinary with new eyes. [See Primary Sources, no. 101, pages 941–42.] The pepper is shown with incredible sharpness and so close up that it seems larger than life. Thanks to the tightly cropped composition, we are forced to contemplate the familiar form anew. *Pepper* has the sensuousness of *Black Iris III* by O'Keeffe (see fig. 24-55) that lends the *Equivalent* a new meaning. Every undulation is revealed by the dramatic lighting. The shapes suggest the female nude, a subject that Weston also pioneered in photography.

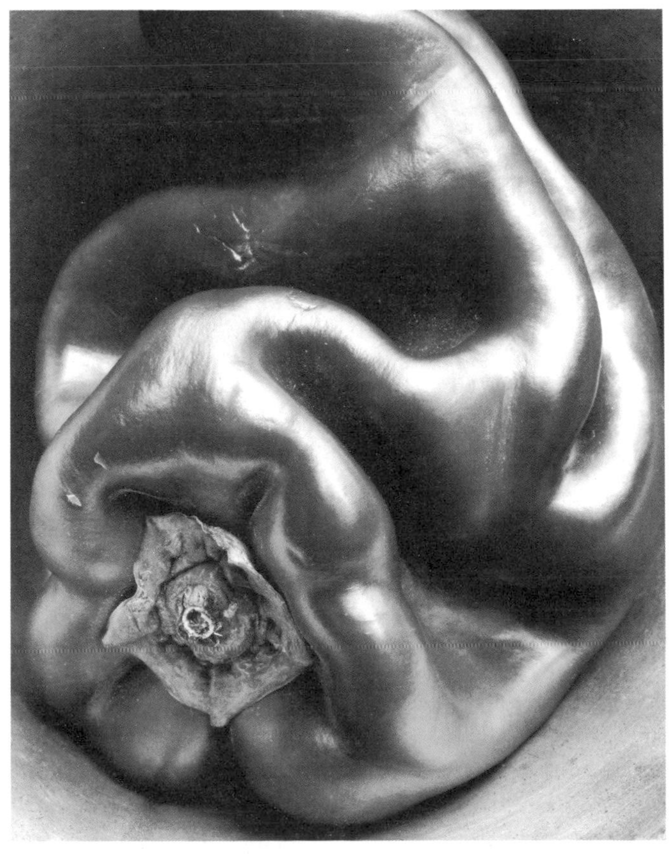

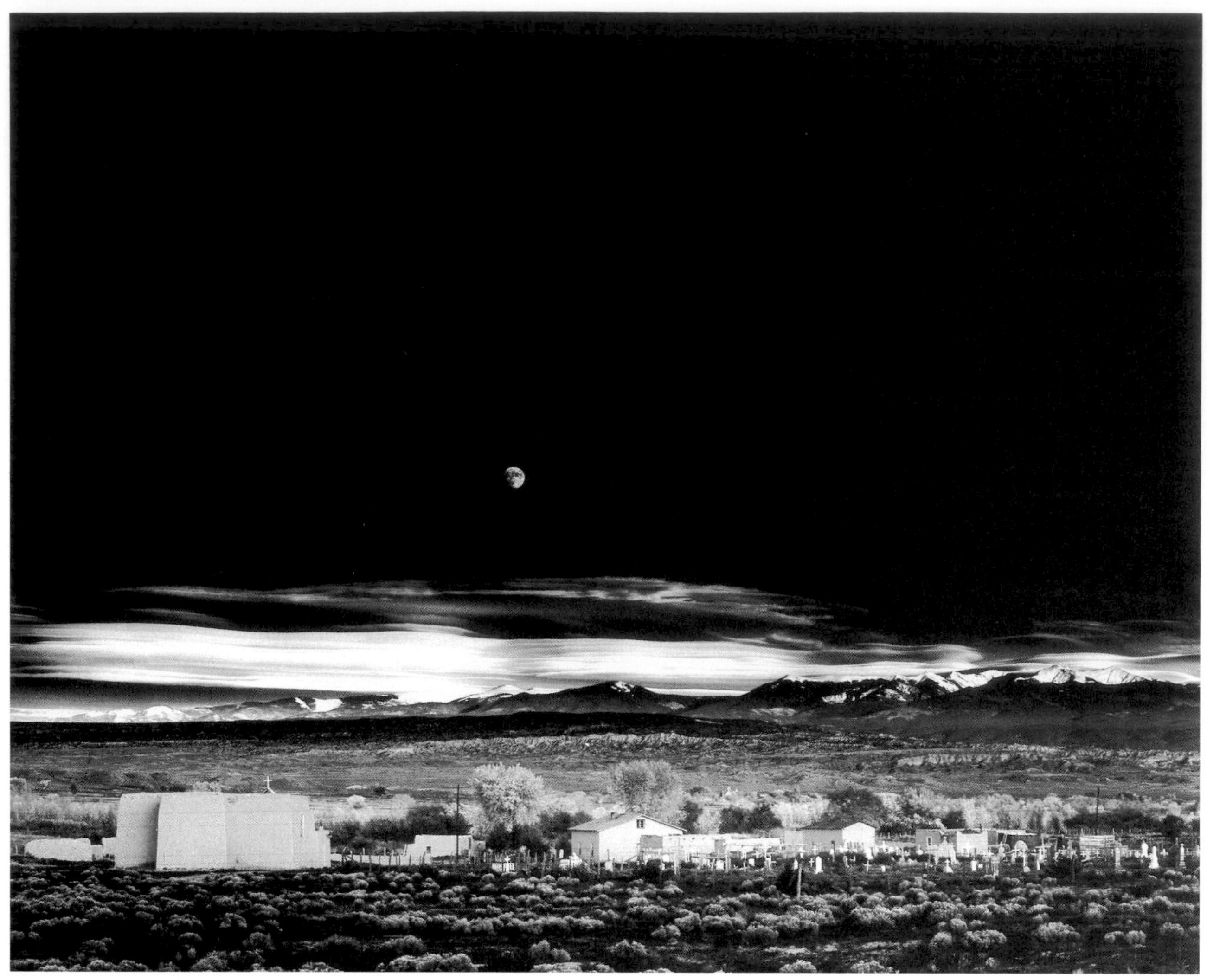

27-9. Ansel Adams. *Moonrise, Hernandez, New Mexico.* 1941. Gelatin-silver print, 15 x 18½" (38.1 x 47 cm). The Museum of Modern Art, New York

GIFT OF THE PHOTOGRAPHER

ADAMS. To achieve uniform detail and depth, Weston worked with the smallest possible camera lens openings. His success led to the formation, in 1932, of the West Coast society known as Group f/64, for the smallest aperture. Among its founders was Ansel Adams (1902–1984), who soon became the foremost nature photographer in America. He is regarded as the successor to Timothy O'Sullivan (see fig. 21-84), for his landscapes hark back to nineteenth-century American painting and photography.

Adams was a meticulous technician, beginning with the composition and exposure and continuing through the final print. His famous work *Moonrise, Hernandez, New Mexico* (fig. 27-9) is a perfect marriage of straight and *Equivalent* photography. The image came from pure chance, which could never be repeated. The key to the photograph lies in the low cloud that divides the scene into three zones, so that the moon appears to hover effortlessly in the early evening sky. As in all of Adams' pictures, there is a full range of tonal nuances, from clear whites to inky blacks.

BOURKE-WHITE. Stieglitz was among the first to photograph skyscrapers, the new architecture that came to dominate America's growing cities. In turn, he championed the Precisionist painters (see pages 794–95), who began to depict urban and industrial architecture around 1925 under the inspiration of Futurism. Several of them soon took up the camera as well. Thus painting and photography once again became closely linked. Both were responding to the revitalized economy after World War I, which led to unprecedented industrial expansion on both sides of the Atlantic. During the Great Depression that followed, industrial photography continued to grow with the new mass-circulation magazines that ushered in the great age of photojournalism and, with it, of commercial photography. In the United States, most of the important photographers were employed by the leading journals and corporations.

Margaret Bourke-White (1904–1971) was the first staff photographer hired by *Fortune* magazine and then by *Life* magazine, both published by Henry Luce. Her cover photograph of Fort Peck Dam in Montana for the inaugural November 23, 1936, issue of *Life* remains a classic example of the new photojournalism (fig. 27-10). The decade witnessed enormous building campaigns. With her keen eye for composition, Bourke-White drew a visual parallel between the dam and the massive constructions of ancient Egypt (compare fig. 2-32). (This idea had already appeared in a

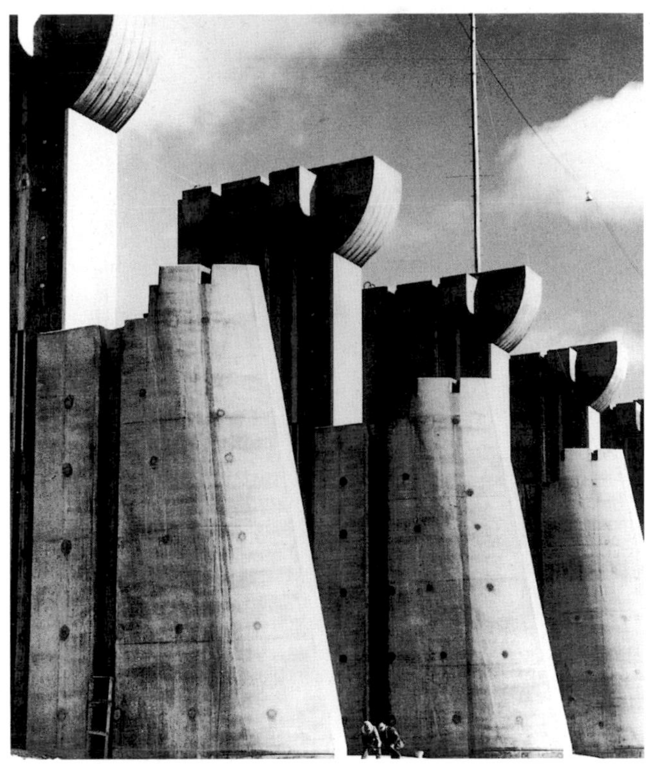

27-10. Margaret Bourke-White. *Fort Peck Dam, Montana.* 1936. Time-Life, Inc.

painting of 1927 by Charles Demuth, *My Egypt.*) In addition to their architectural power, Bourke-White's columnar forms have a remarkable sculptural quality. They loom like colossal statues at the entrance to a temple, so that they assume nearly human presence. But unlike the passive timelessness of the pharoahs at Luxor (see fig. 2-33), these "guardian figures" have the peculiar alertness of Henry Moore's abstract monoliths (see fig. 25-18). Bourke-White's rare ability to suggest multiple levels of meaning made this cover and her accompanying photoessay a landmark in photojournalism.

STEICHEN. The flourishing magazine business also gave rise to fashion and glamour photography, which was developed into an art by Edward Steichen, America's most complete photographer. Steichen's talent for portraiture, seen in his early Photo-Secession photograph of Rodin (see fig. 23-48), makes *Greta Garbo* (fig. 27-11) a worthy successor to Nadar's *Sarah Bernhardt* (see fig. 21-82). The young film actress would have her picture taken countless times, despite her desire "to be alone," but none captures better the magnetic presence and complex character seen in her movies. The photograph owes much to its abstract black-and-white design, which focuses attention on her wonderfully expressive face. But

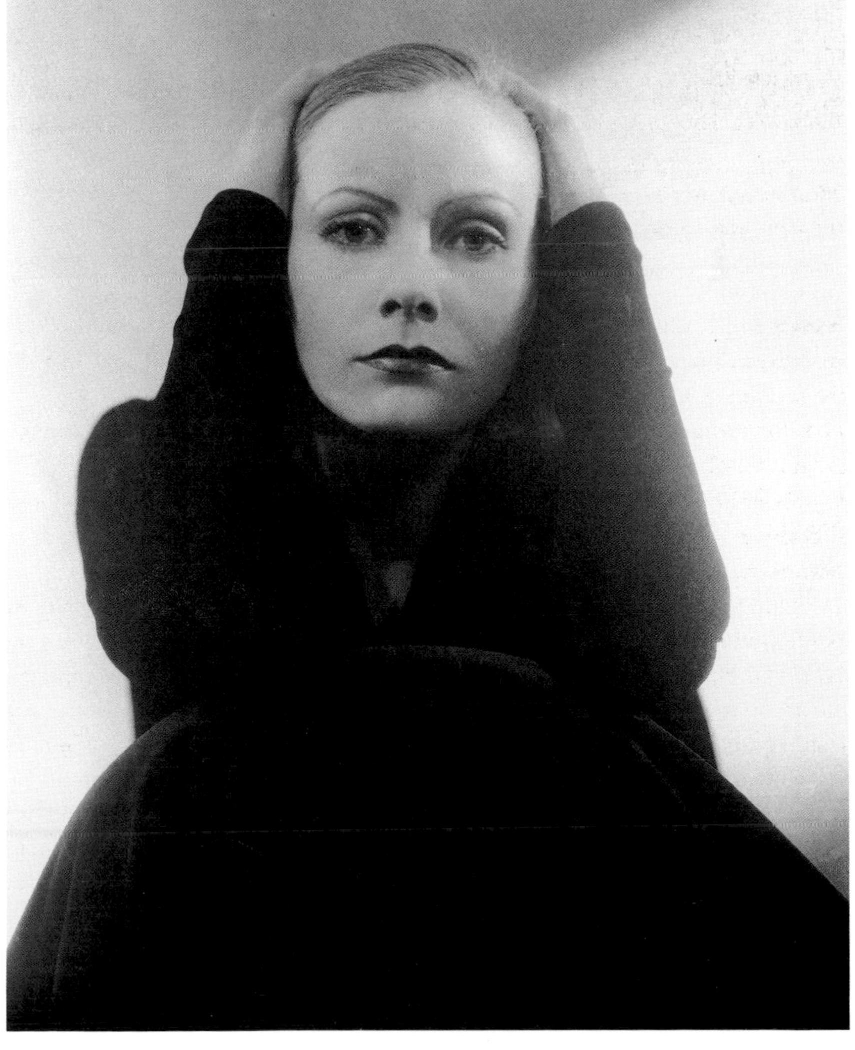

27-11. Edward Steichen. *Greta Garbo.* 1928 (for *Vanity Fair* magazine). The Museum of Modern Art, New York
GIFT OF THE PHOTOGRAPHER

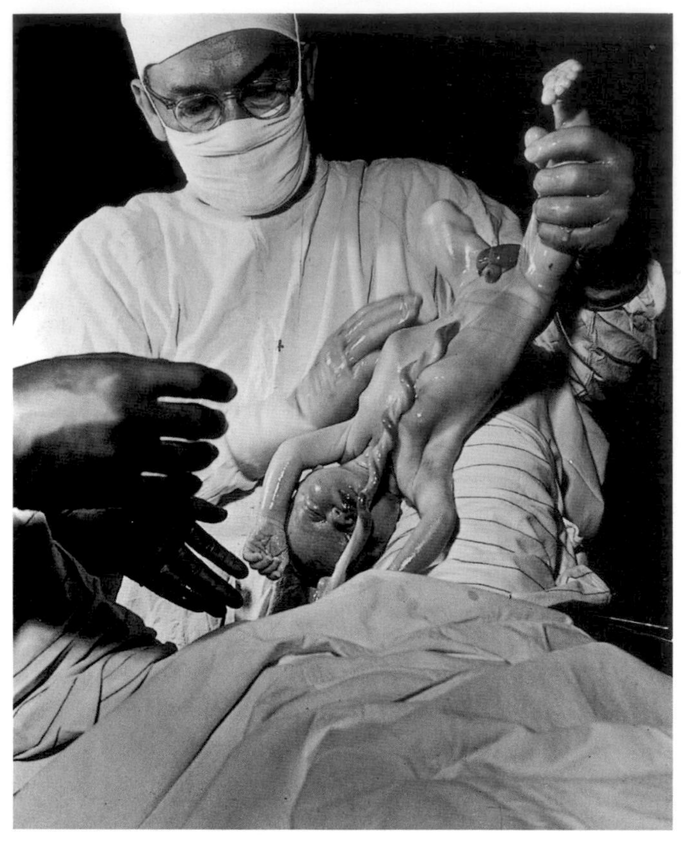

Steichen's stroke of genius was to have Garbo put her arms around her head in order to suggest her enigmatic personality.

MILLER. One of Steichen's contributions to photography was to organize the "Family of Man" exhibition, which opened at the Museum of Modern Art in New York in 1955. Wayne Miller's (b. 1918) picture of childbirth (fig. 27-12) from this epoch-making show captures the miracle of life in one dramatic image. It records with shocking directness the newborn infant's abrupt entry into the world we all share. At the same time, the hands that reach out to help him are a moving affirmation of human existence.

VAN DER ZEE. The nature of the Harlem Renaissance, which flourished in the 1920s (see page 811), was hotly debated by black critics even in its own day. While its achievement in literature is beyond dispute, the photography of James Van Der Zee (1886–1983) is often regarded today as its chief contribution to the visual arts. Much of his work is commercial and variable in quality, yet it remains of great documentary value. The best examples provide a compelling portrait of the era. Van Der Zee had a keen understanding of settings as reflections of people's sense of place in the world, and he used them to bring out his sitters' characters and dreams. *At Home* shows Van Der Zee's unique ability to capture

(ABOVE) 27-12. Wayne Miller. *Childbirth.* "Family of Man" exhibition. 1955

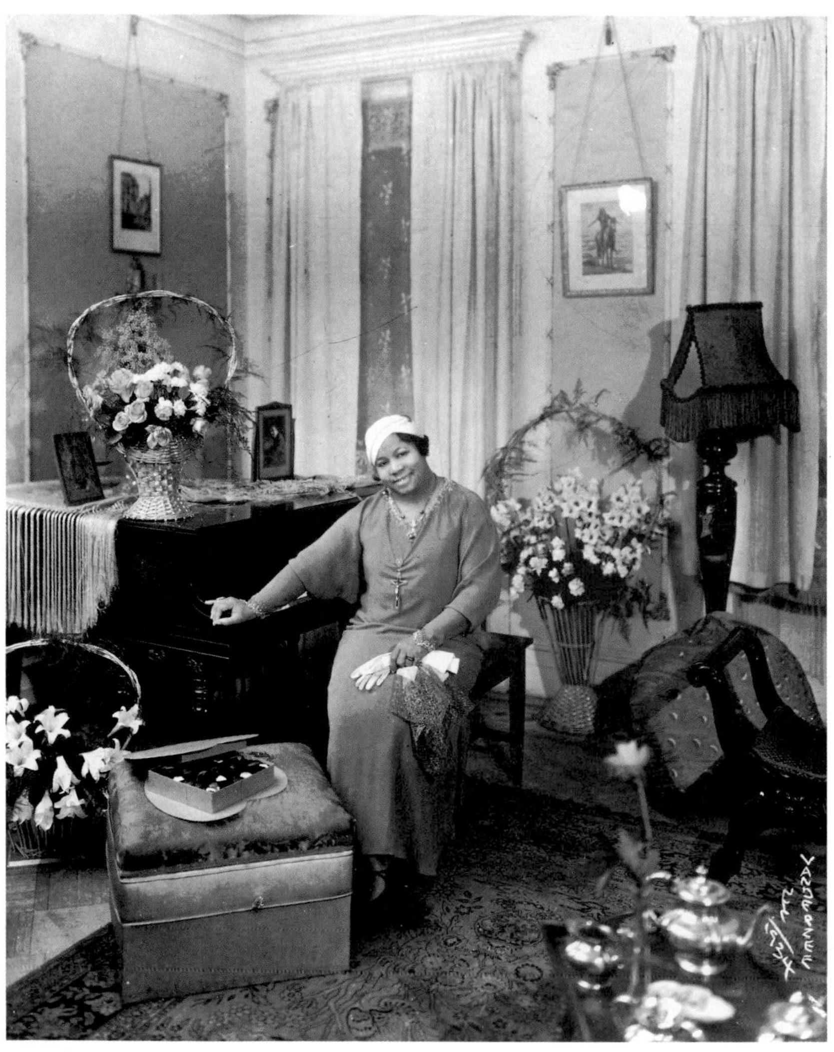

(RIGHT) 27-13. James Van Der Zee. *At Home.* 1934. James Van Der Zee Estate

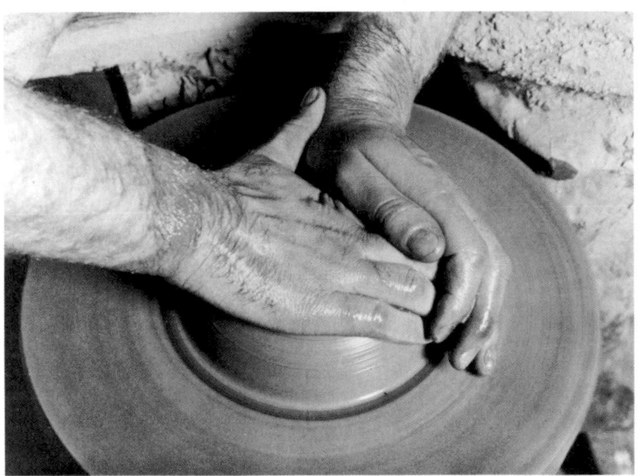

27-14. Albert Renger-Patzsch. *Potter's Hands*. 1925. Gelatin-silver print, 11¾ x 15⅛" (29.8 x 38.2 cm). The Museum of Modern Art, New York

GIFT OF THE PHOTOGRAPHER

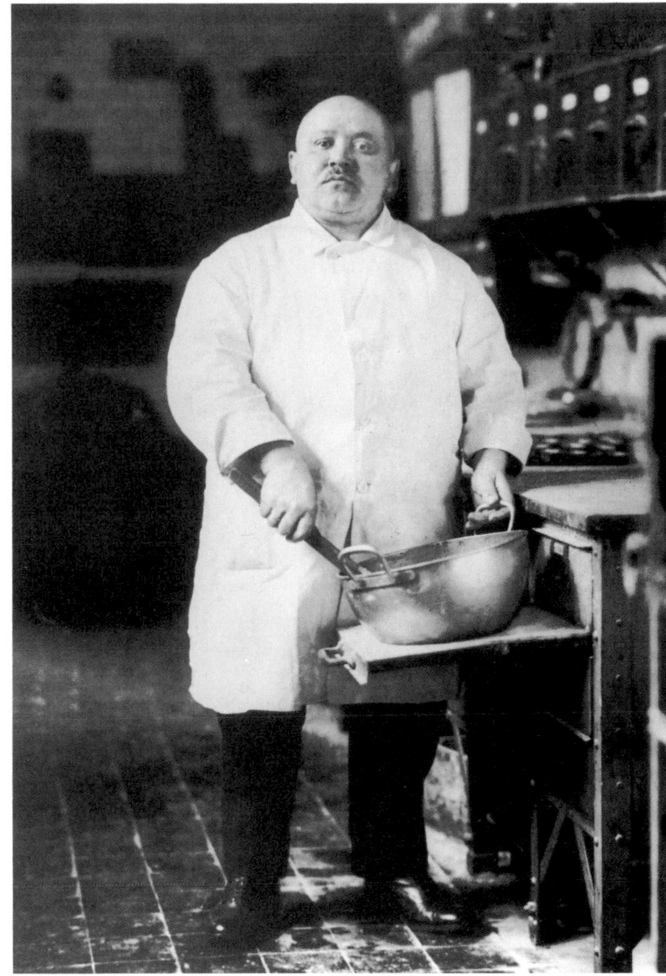

27-15. August Sander. *Pastry Cook, Cologne*. 1928. August Sander Archiv/SK-Stiftung Kultur, Cologne, Germany

the pride of African Americans during a period when their dreams seemed on the verge of being realized. Posed in obvious imitation of fashionable photographs of white society, it is a portrait of the wife of the Reverend George Wilson Becton (fig. 27-13) taken two years after the popular pastor of the Salem Methodist Church in Harlem was murdered.

Germany

With the New Objectivity movement in Germany during the late 1920s and early 1930s (see page 807), photography achieved a degree of excellence that has not been surpassed. Fostered by the invention of superior German cameras and the boom in publishing everywhere, this German version of straight photography emphasized materiality at a time when many other photographers were turning away from the real world. The intrinsic beauty of things was brought out through the clarity of form and structure. This approach accorded with Bauhaus principles except for function (see page 868).

RENGER-PATZSCH. *Potter's Hands* (fig. 27-14) by Albert Renger-Patzsch (1897–1966), New Objectivity's leading exponent, is a marvel of technique and design that deliberately avoids any personal statement by reducing the image to an abstraction. The content lies solely in the cool perfection of the presentation and the orderly world it suggests.

SANDER. When applied to people rather than things, the New Objectivity could be deceiving. August Sander (1876–1964), whose *Face of Our Time* was published in 1929, concealed his intentions behind a disarmingly straightforward facade. The 60 portraits provide a devastating survey of Germany during the rise of the Nazis, who later suppressed the volume. Clearly proud of his position, Sander's *Pastry Cook, Cologne* (fig. 27-15) is the very opposite of the timid figure in George Grosz' *Germany, a Winter's Tale* (see fig. 24-49). Despite their curious resemblance, this "good citizen" seems oblivious to the evil that Grosz has depicted so vividly. While the photograph passes no individual judgment, in the context of the book the man's lack of concern stands as a strong indictment of the era as a whole.

Czechoslovakia

SUDEK. The work of Josef Sudek (1896–1976) was the most varied of its time. It shows the full range of modern photography before 1945 except for photojournalism, which is concerned with passing moments that were merely incidental to him. Sudek was the Atget of Prague, which provided his main subject matter. This photographer lost his right arm in World War I and had to struggle to take his pictures. From pictorialism, he learned to become a master of light, which he invested with the poetry of Vermeer, while the New Objectivity taught him to photograph simple objects with the reverence of Chardin. A romantic at heart, he wanted to reveal the secret life of nature. Sudek preferred to work in series over the years. He would often return to the same place to document its changing face and uncover new meanings. He was a recluse who became even more secretive during World War II, when his move-

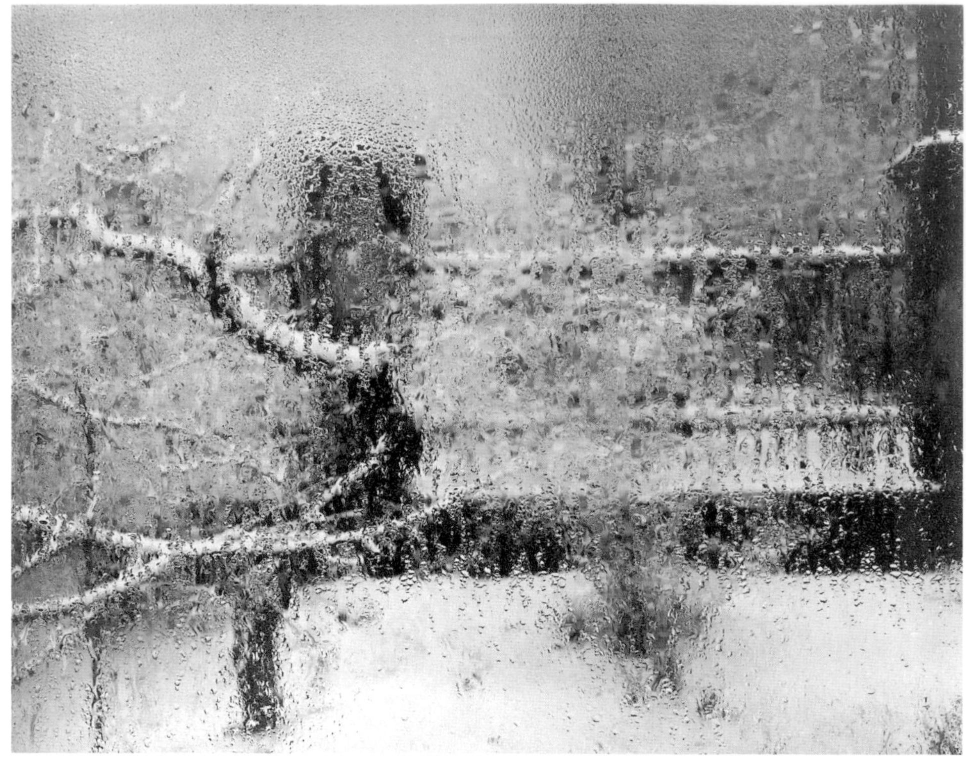

27-16. Josef Sudek. *View from Studio Window in Winter.* 1954. Gelatin-silver print, 8½ x 11$^{1}/_{16}$" (21.6 x 28.1 cm). The Museum of Modern Art, New York

GIFT OF HARRIETTE AND NOEL LEVINE

ment was severely restricted by the German occupation of Czechoslovakia. The most characteristic photographs from his later years are of private worlds, be they the cluttered studio where he lived, or gardens, his own as well as those of the artists, writers, and musicians who were his friends. Branches of a tree in snow seen through his window (fig. 27-16) may be taken as a metaphor of the photographer himself. To Sudek, trees were primordial symbols of life that weather life's difficulties, much as he had survived personal tragedy.

The Heroic Age of Photography

CAPA. The period from 1930 to 1945 can be called the heroic age of photography for its response to the challenges of the times. The physical bravery of photographers was illustrated by Robert Capa (1913–1954), who covered wars around the world for 20 years before being killed by a land mine in Vietnam. While barely adequate technically, his picture of a Loyalist soldier being shot during the Spanish Civil War (fig. 27-17) captures fully the horror of death at the moment of impact. Had it been taken by someone else, it might seem an accident, but it is typical of Capa's battle close-ups. He was as fearless as Civil War photographer Mathew Brady.

LANGE. Photographers in those difficult times demonstrated moral courage as well. Under Roy Stryker, staff photographers of the Farm Security Administration (FSA) compiled a comprehen-

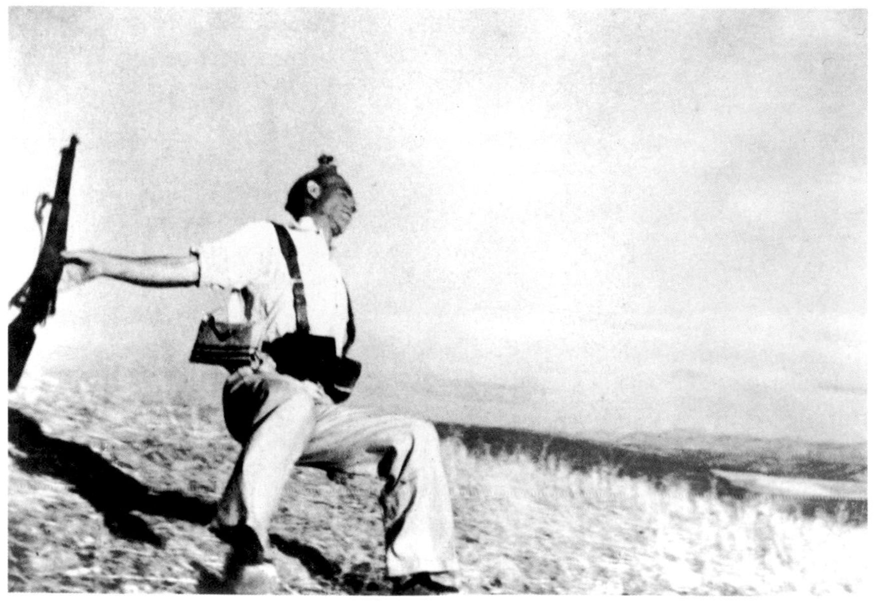

27-17. Robert Capa. *Death of a Loyalist Soldier.* September 5, 1936

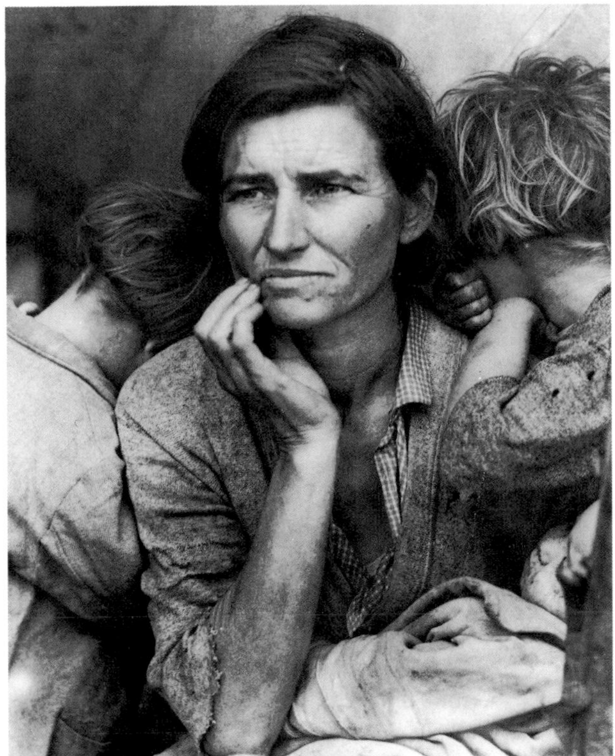

27-18. Dorothea Lange. *Migrant Mother, California.* February 1936. Gelatin-silver print. Library of Congress, Washington, D.C.

sive photodocumentary archive of rural America during the Great Depression. While the FSA photographers presented a balanced and objective view, most of them were also reformers whose work responded to the social problems they confronted daily in the field. The concern of Dorothea Lange (1895–1965) for people and her sensitivity to their dignity made her the finest documentary photographer of the time in America.

At a pea-pickers' camp in Nipomo, California, Lange discovered 2,500 nearly starving migrant workers and took several pictures of a young widow with her children. (She was identified much later as Florence Thompson, who resented all the attention the photographs received.) When *Migrant Mother, California* (fig. 27-18) was published in a news story about their plight, the government rushed in food, and eventually migrant relief camps were opened. More than any Social Realist or Regionalist painting (see page 810), *Migrant Mother, California* has come to stand for that entire era. Unposed and uncropped, this photograph has an unforgettable immediacy no other medium can match.

Fantasy and Abstraction

"Impersonality," the very disadvantage that had hindered the acceptance of photography in the eyes of many critics, became a virtue in the 1920s. Precisely because photographs are produced by mechanical devices, the camera's images now seemed to some artists the perfect means for expressing the modern era. This change in attitude did not stem from the Futurists. Contrary to what might be expected, they never fully grasped the camera's importance for modern art, despite Marey's influence on their paintings (see page 769). The new view of photography arose as part of the Berlin Dadaists' assault on traditional art.

Toward the end of World War I, the Dadaists "invented" the photomontage and the photogram. (In truth, these processes had been practiced early in the history of photography.) In the service of anti-art they lent themselves equally well to fantasy and to abstraction, despite the differences between these two modes.

PHOTOMONTAGE. Photomontages are simply pieces of photographs cut out and recombined into new images. Composite negatives originated with the art photography of Rejlander and Robinson (see pages 766–67), but by the 1870s they were already being used in France to create witty impossibilities that are the ancestors of Dada photomontages. Like *1 Piping Man* (see fig. 24-40) by Max Ernst (who, not surprisingly, became a master of the genre), Dadaist photomontages utilize the techniques of Synthetic Cubism to ridicule social and aesthetic conventions.

These imaginative parodies destroy all pictorial illusionism. They therefore stand in direct opposition to straight photographs, which use the camera to record and probe the meaning of reality. Dada photomontages might be called "ready-images," after Duchamp's readymades. Like other collages, they are literally torn from popular culture and given new meaning. Although the photomontage relies more on the laws of chance, the Surrealists later claimed it to be a form of automatic handwriting on the grounds that it responds to a stream of consciousness.

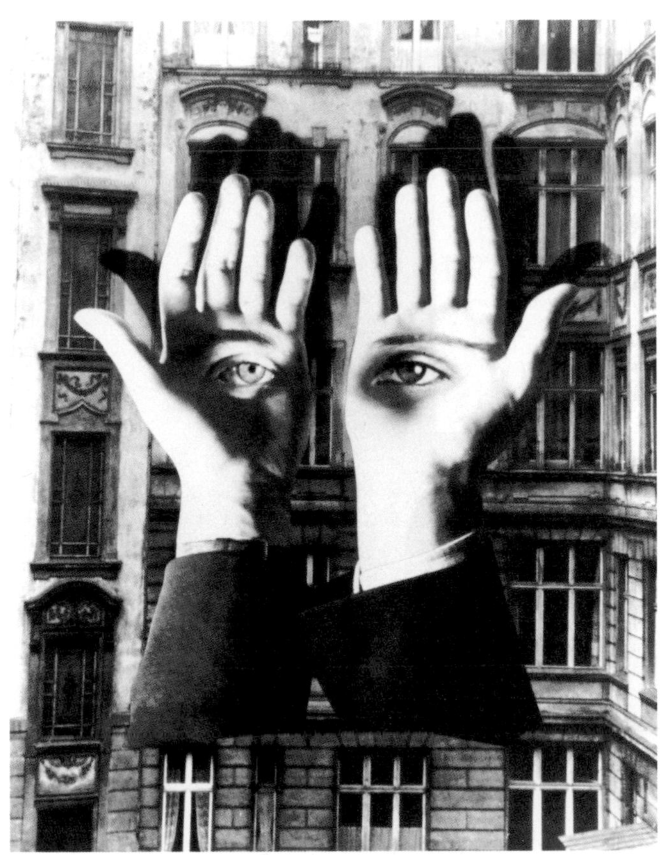

27-19. Herbert Bayer. *lonely metropolitan.* 1932. Photomontage, 14 x 11" (35.6 x 28 cm). Collection the artist (copyright)

Most Surrealist photographers have been influenced by the Belgian painter René Magritte, whose mystifying fantasies (see fig. 24-43) are treated with a magic realism that is the opposite of automatic handwriting. Since Magritte's pictorial style was already highly naturalistic, he experimented little with the camera. Nevertheless, he had a considerable impact on photography because his illusionistic paradoxes can be readily imitated in photographs. An excellent example of how photomontage can be used to challenge our conception of reality is *lonely metropolitan* (fig. 27-19) by the German-born Herbert Bayer (1900–1985). The purpose of such visual riddles is to show up the discrepancy between our perception of the world and our irrational understanding of its significance.

POSTERS. Photomontages were soon incorporated into carefully designed posters. In Germany, posters became a double-edged sword in political propaganda, used by Hitler's sympathizers and enemies alike. The most bitter anti-Nazi commentaries were created by John Heartfield (1891–1968), who changed his name from the German Herzfeld as a sign of protest. His horrific poster of a Nazi victim crucified on a swastika (fig. 27-20) appropriates a Gothic image of humanity punished for its sins on the wheel of divine judgment. Obviously Heartfield was not concerned about reinterpreting the original meaning in his montage, which communicates its new message to powerful effect.

PHOTOGRAMS. The photogram does not take pictures but makes them. Objects are placed directly onto photographic paper and exposed to light. This technique was not new. Fox Talbot (see page 702) had used it to make negative images of plants, which he called "photogenic drawings." The Dadaists' photograms, however, like their photomontages, were intended to alter nature's forms, not to record them, and to substitute impersonal technology for the handwork of the individual. Since the results in the photogram are so unpredictable, making one involves even greater risks than does a photomontage.

Man Ray (1890–1976), an American working in Paris, was not the first to make photograms, but his name is most closely linked to them through his "Rayographs." Fittingly enough, he discovered the process by accident. The amusing face in figure 27-21 was made according to the laws of chance by dropping a string, two strips of paper, and a few pieces of cotton onto the photographic paper, then coaxing them here and there before making the exposure. The resulting image is a witty creation that shows the playful, spontaneous side of Dada and Surrealism as against Heartfield's grim satire.

THE CONSTRUCTIVISTS. Because the Russian Constructivists had a comparably mechanistic conception of society, they soon followed Dada's lead in using photograms and photomontages as a means to integrate industry and art, albeit for quite

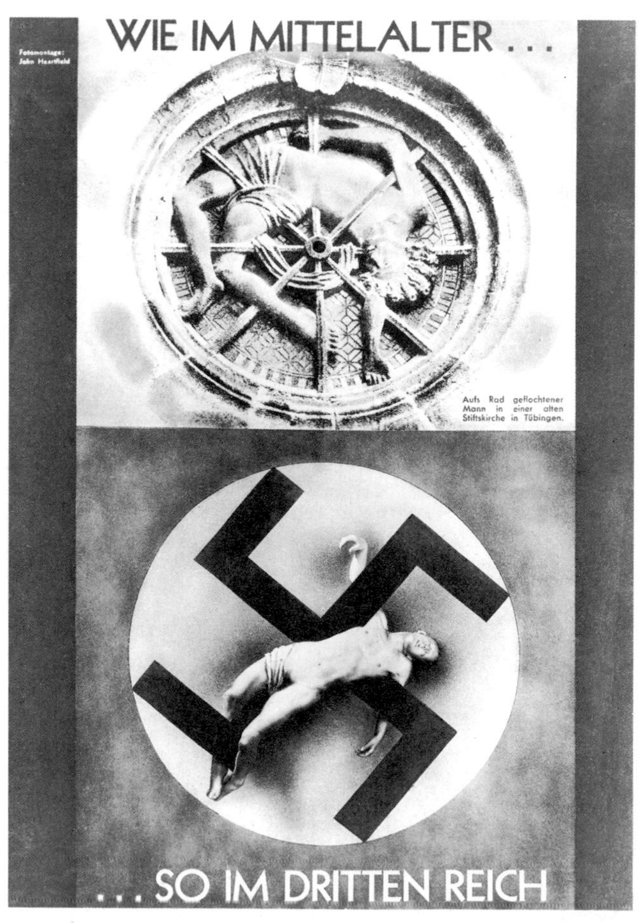

27-20. John Heartfield. *As in the Middle Ages, So in the Third Reich.* 1934. Poster, photomontage. Akademie der Künste, John Heartfield Archiv, Berlin

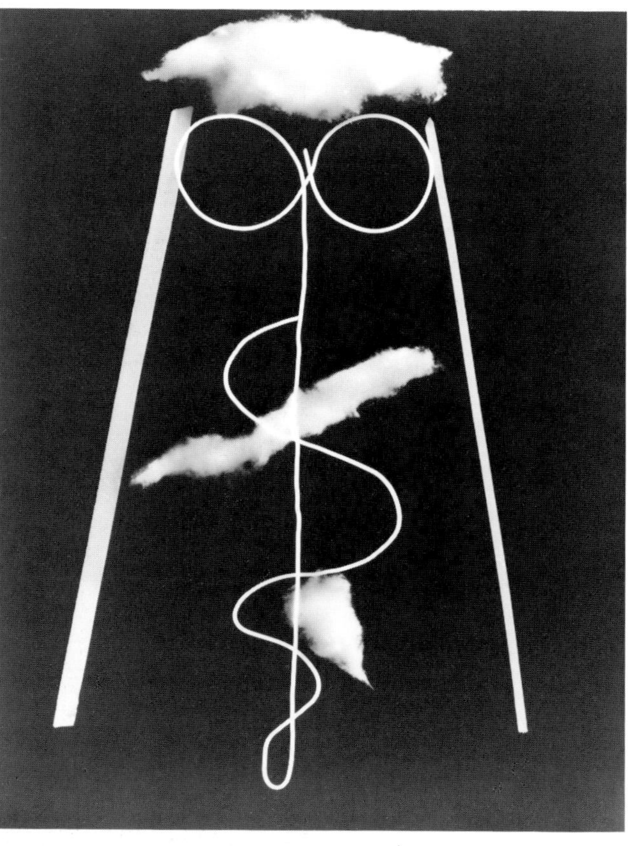

27-21. Man Ray. *Untitled* (Rayograph). 1928. Gelatin-silver print, 15 1/2 x 11 5/8" (39.4 x 29.5 cm). The Museum of Modern Art, New York

GIFT OF JAMES THRALL SOBY

different purposes. László Moholy-Nagy (1895–1946), a Hungarian teaching at the Bauhaus, was deeply affected by Constructivism. He successfully combined the best features of both approaches in his photographs. By removing the lens to make photograms, he transformed his camera from a reproductive into a productive instrument. In theory if not in practice, photography could now become a technological tool for fostering creativity in mass education.

Like many of the Russian artists in the 1920s, Moholy-Nagy also saw light as the embodiment of dynamic energy in space. The effects created by the superimposition and interpenetration of forms in his photographs are fascinating (fig. 27-22). We feel transported in time and space to the edges of the universe. Here the artist's imagination gives shape to the play of cosmic forces.

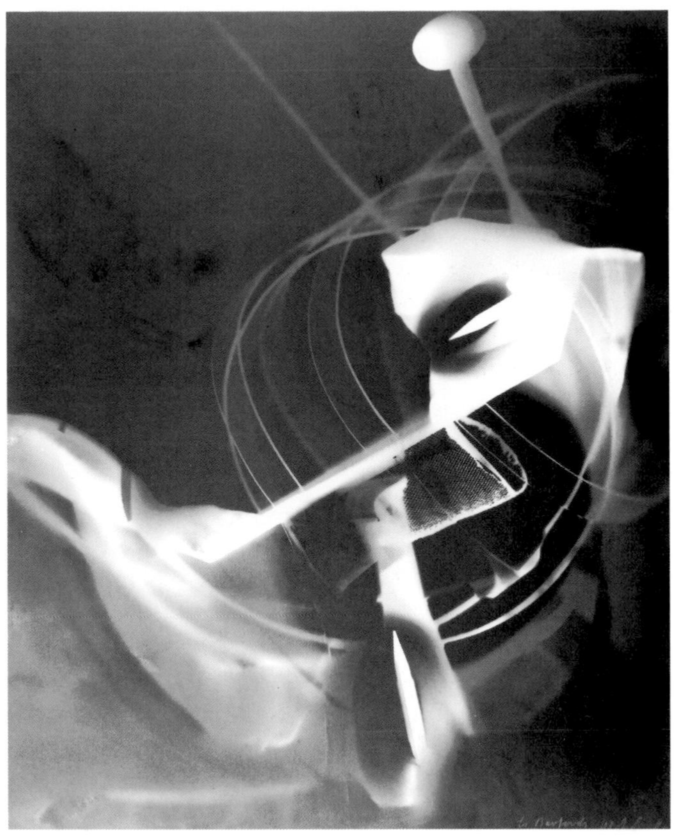

27-22. László Moholy-Nagy. *Untitled.* Photogram, silver-bromide print, 19½ x 15¾" (49.5 x 40 cm). The Art Institute of Chicago

GIFT OF GEORGE BANCROFT, 1968

ABBOTT. One of the main educational purposes of Moholy-Nagy's images was to extend sense perception in new ways. Similar goals have been achieved by taking pictures through microscopes and telescopes. Such photographs have helped to open our eyes to the invisibly small and the infinitely far. Wondrous scientific photographs were taken from 1939 to 1958 by Berenice Abbott (1898–1991), Man Ray's former pupil and assistant, to demonstrate the laws of physics (fig. 27-23). Like Marey's motion photographs of 50 years earlier (see fig. 23-50a and b), they are arresting images, literally and visually. Their formal perfection makes them aesthetically compelling and scientifically valid. As a result, they have proved to be even more educational than Moholy-Nagy's photograms.

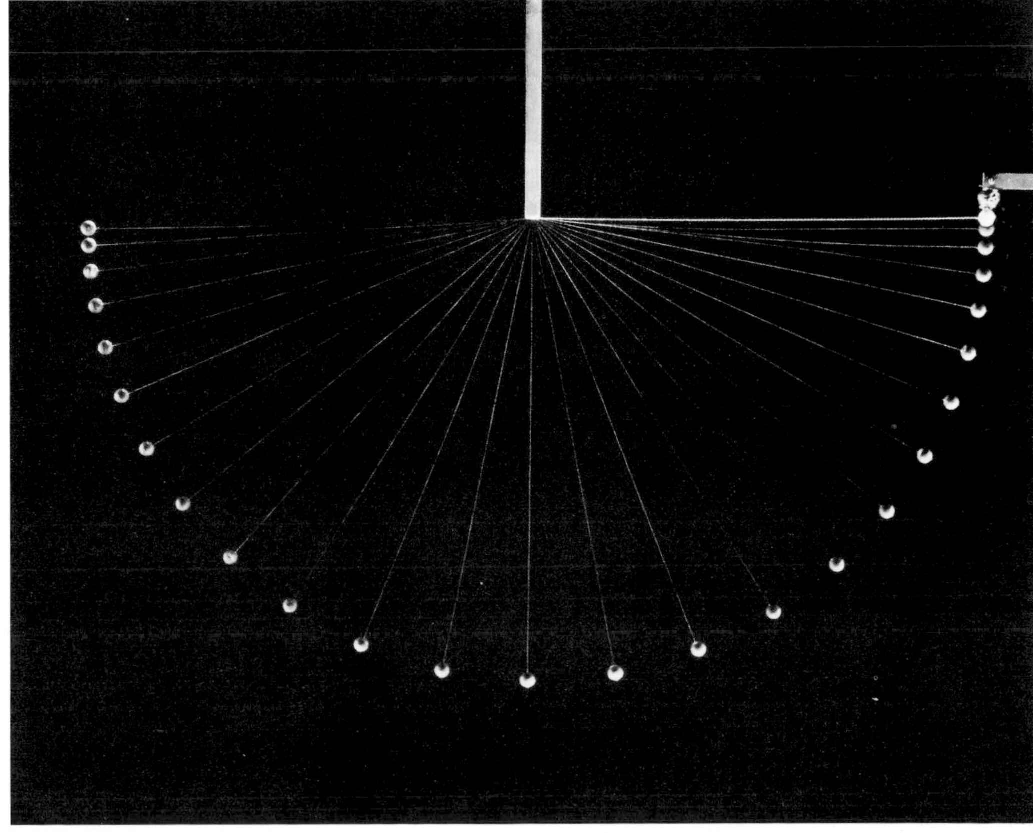

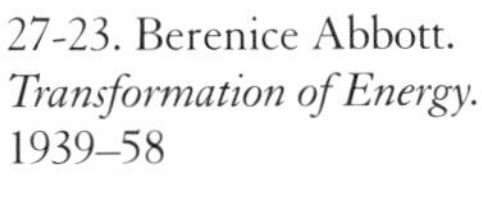

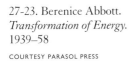

27-23. Berenice Abbott. *Transformation of Energy.* 1939–58

COURTESY PARASOL PRESS

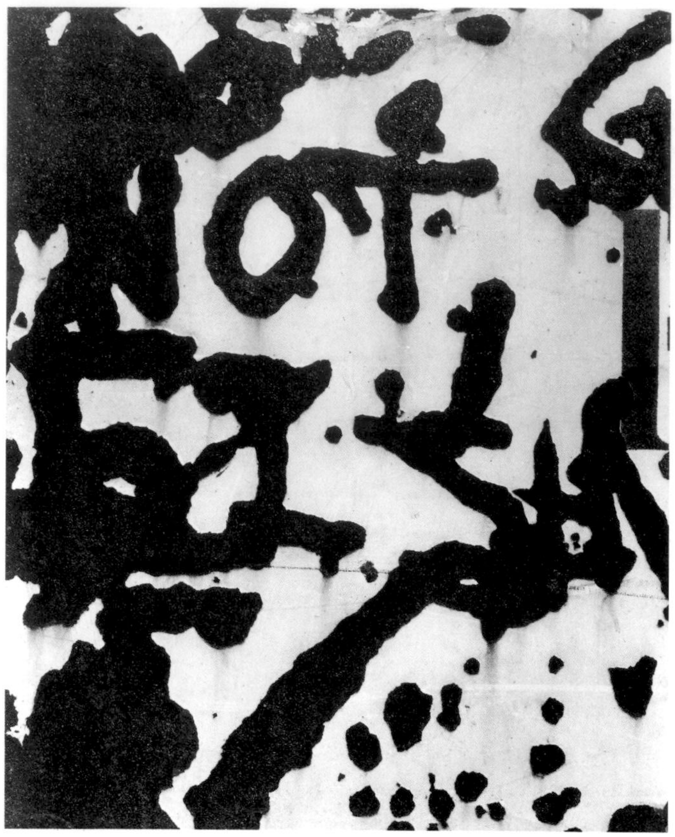

27-24. Aaron Siskind. *New York 2.* 1951. Collection the artist

PHOTOGRAPHY SINCE 1945

Abstraction

SISKIND. Photography after World War II was dominated by abstraction for nearly two decades, particularly in the United States. Aaron Siskind (1903–1991), a close friend of the Abstract Expressionist painters, recorded modern society's debris and decaying signs. Hidden in these details he discovered cipherlike figures (fig. 27-24), which are reminiscent of the ideographs from some forgotten civilization that are no longer intelligible to us.

WHITE. Minor White (1908–1976) came even closer to the spirit of Abstract Expressionism. An associate of Adams and Weston, he was decisively influenced by Stieglitz' concept of the *Equivalent*. During his most productive period, from the mid-1950s to the mid-1960s, White used the alchemy of the darkroom to transform reality into a mystical metaphor. His *Ritual Branch* (fig. 27-25) evokes a primordial image. What it shows is not as important as what it stands for, but the meaning we sense there remains elusive.

DOCUMENTARY PHOTOGRAPHY

SMITH. The continuing record of misery that photography provides has often been the means for making strong personal statements. W. Eugene Smith (1918–1978), the foremost photojournalist of the later twentieth century, was a compassionate cynic who commented on the human condition with "reasoned passion," as he put it. *Tomoko in Her Bath* (fig. 27-26), taken in 1971 in the Japanese fishing village of Minamata, shows a child crippled by mercury poisoning being bathed by her mother. Not simply the

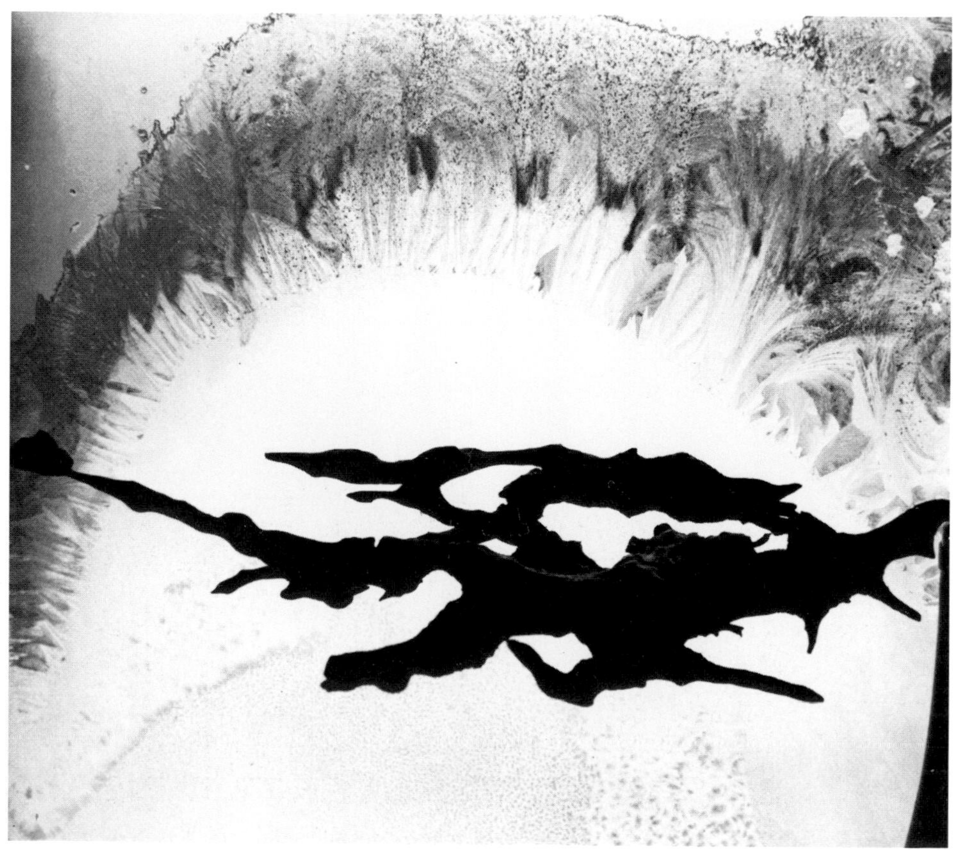

27-25. Minor White. *Ritual Branch.* 1958. Gelatin-silver print, 10⅜ x 10⅝" (26.4 x 27 cm). The International Museum of Photography at George Eastman House, Rochester, New York

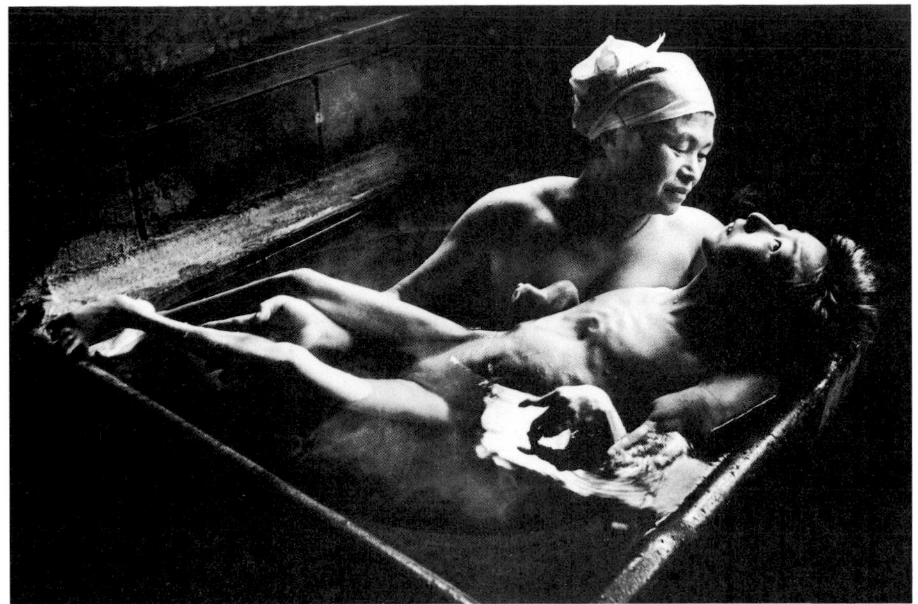

27-26. W. Eugene Smith. *Tomoko in Her Bath.* December 1971. Gelatin-silver print. Aileen and W. Eugene Smith

subject itself but Smith's treatment of it makes this an intensely moving work. The imagery lies deep in our heritage. The mother holding her child's body goes back to the theme of the German Gothic *Pietà* (see fig. 11-54), while the dramatic lighting and vivid realism recall a painting of another martyr in his bath, Jacques-Louis David's *The Death of Marat* (see fig. 21-3). But what engages our emotions above all and makes the photograph memorable is the infinite love conveyed by the mother's tender expression.

FRANK. The birth of a new form of straight photography in the United States was largely the responsibility of one man, Robert Frank (b. 1924). His book *The Americans,* compiled from a cross-country journey made in 1955–56, created a sensation upon its publication in 1959. It expressed the same restlessness and alienation as *On the Road* by his traveling companion, the Beat poet Jack Kerouac, published in 1957. As this friendship suggests, words have an important role in Frank's photographs, which are as loaded in meaning as Demuth's *I Saw the Figure 5 in Gold* (see fig. 24-35). Yet Frank's social point of view is often hidden behind a facade of neutrality. It is a shock when we recognize the ironic intent of *Santa Fe, New Mexico* (fig. 27-27). The gas pumps face the sign *Save* in the barren landscape like members of a religious cult

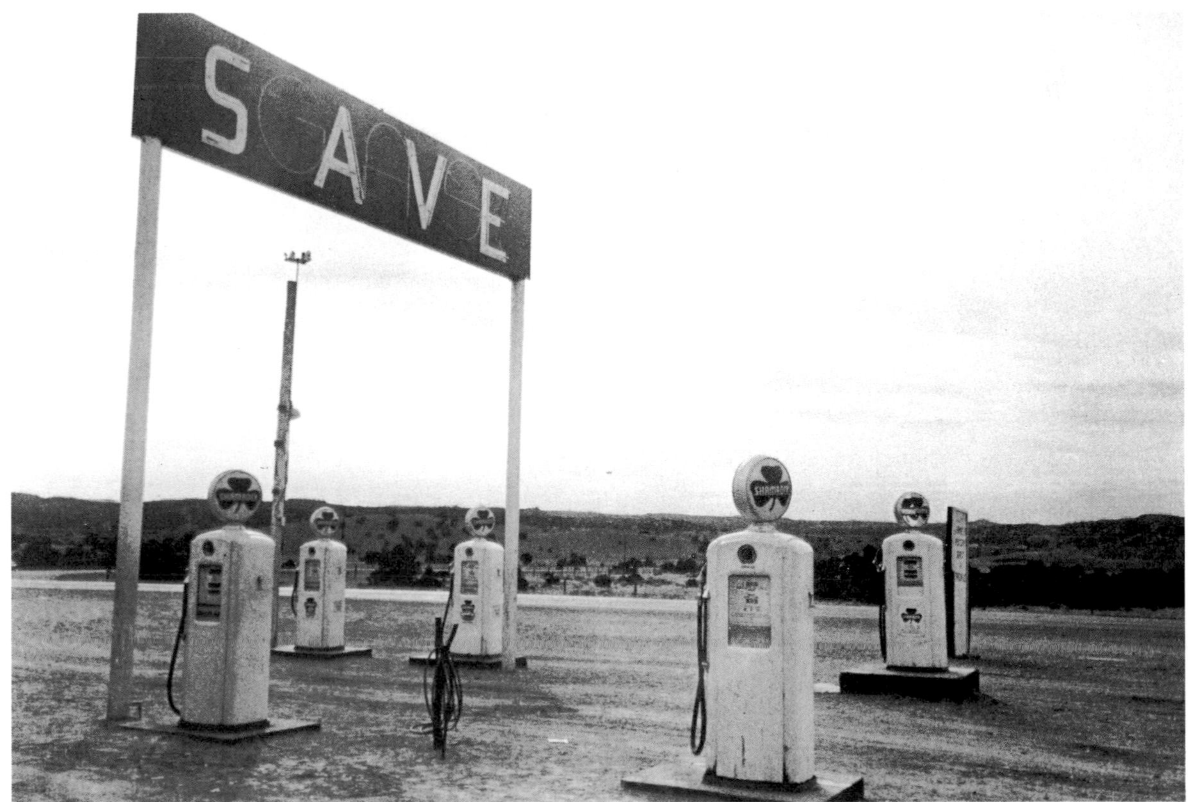

27-27. Robert Frank. *Santa Fe, New Mexico.* 1955–56. Gelatin-silver print. Collection PaceWildenstein Gallery, New York

vainly seeking salvation at a revival meeting. Frank, who later turned to film, holds up an image of American culture that is as sterile as it is joyless. Even spiritual values, he tells us, become meaningless in the face of vulgar materialism.

Fantasy

Fantasy gradually reasserted itself on both sides of the Atlantic in the mid-1950s. Photographers first manipulated the camera for the sake of extreme visual effects by using special lenses and filters to alter appearances, sometimes virtually beyond recognition. Since about 1970, however, they have used mainly printing techniques, with results that are frequently even more startling.

BRANDT. Manipulation of photography was pioneered by Bill Brandt (1904–1983). Though regarded as the quintessential English photographer, he was born in Germany and did not settle in London until 1931. He decided on a career in photography during psychoanalysis and was apprenticed briefly to Man Ray. Brandt remained a Surrealist who altered visual reality in search of a deeper one charged with mystery. His work was marked consistently by a literary, even theatrical, cast of mind that drew on the cinema for some of its effects. His early photodocumentaries were often staged as re-creations of personal experience to make social commentaries based on Victorian models. Brandt's fantasy images show a strikingly romantic imagination. Yet there is an oppressive anxiety implicit in his landscapes, portraits, and nudes. *London Child* (fig. 27-28) has the haunting mood of novels by the Brontë sisters, Charlotte, Emily, and Anne. At the same time, this is a classic dream image filled with troubling psychological overtones. The spatial dislocation, worthy of De Chirico, suggests a person who is alienated from both himself and the world.

UELSMANN. The American Jerry Uelsmann (b. 1934), a recent leader of this movement, was inspired by Oscar Rejlander's multiple-negative photographs, as well as by Stieglitz' *Equivalents*. While Uelsmann's work also has a playful side, for the most part he involuntarily expresses archetypal images from deep within the subconscious. The nude lying within the soil in *Untitled* (fig. 27-29) identifies the fertility of nature, signified by the tree of life, with woman as earth goddess. The photograph also seemingly conveys a dream in which the psyche retreats into the womblike sanctuary of primal nature. The print is utterly convincing because each part is a faithful record. It is the astonishing juxtaposition of unrelated elements that transforms the image into a new reality.

Uelsmann once participated in one of Minor White's classes, and their photographs are not as far removed visually or expressively from each other's as they might seem. The principal

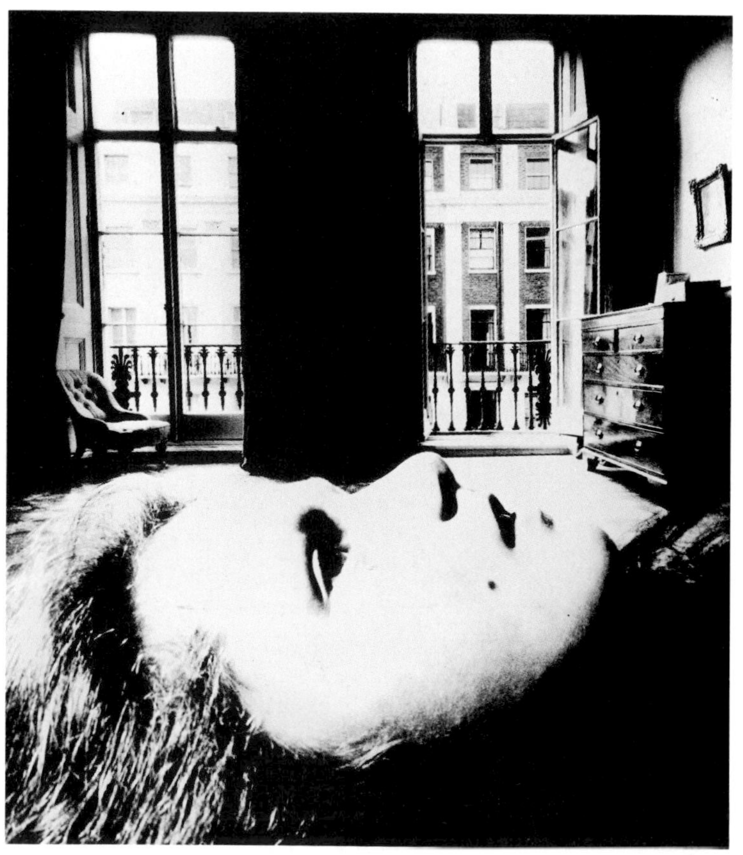

27-28. Bill Brandt. *London Child.* 1955

COPYRIGHT MRS. NOYA BRANDT

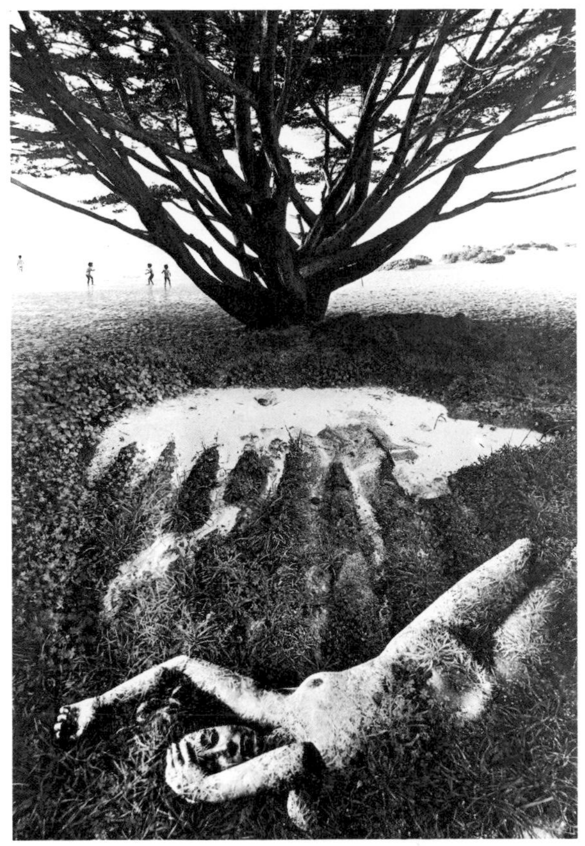

difference lies in their approach to the *Equivalent* as a means of achieving a poetical inner truth. White, like Stieglitz, recognizes his symbols in images received from nature. Uelsmann, however, creates his symbols from the imagination in the darkroom. [See Primary Sources, no. 102, page 942.] Paradoxically, it is Uelsmann's imagery, not *Ritual Branch,* that is instantly recognizable. But like the paintings of Magritte (see fig. 24-43) that inspired him, it refuses to yield a clear meaning.

Artists as Photographers

HOCKNEY. The most recent demonstrations of photography's power to extend our vision have come, fittingly enough, from artists. The photographic collages that the English painter David Hockney (b. 1937) began making in 1982 are like revelations. They overcome the traditional limitations of a unified image, fixed in time and place, by closely approximating how we actually see. In *Gregory Watching the Snow Fall, Kyoto, Feb. 21, 1983* (fig. 27-30), each frame is similar to a movement of the eye: it contains a piece of visual data that must be stored in our memory and synthesized by the brain. Just as we process only essential information, so there are gaps in the matrix of the image, which becomes more fragmentary toward its edges, though without the loss of sharpness

(ABOVE) 27-29. Jerry Uelsmann. *Untitled.* c. 1972. Collection the artist

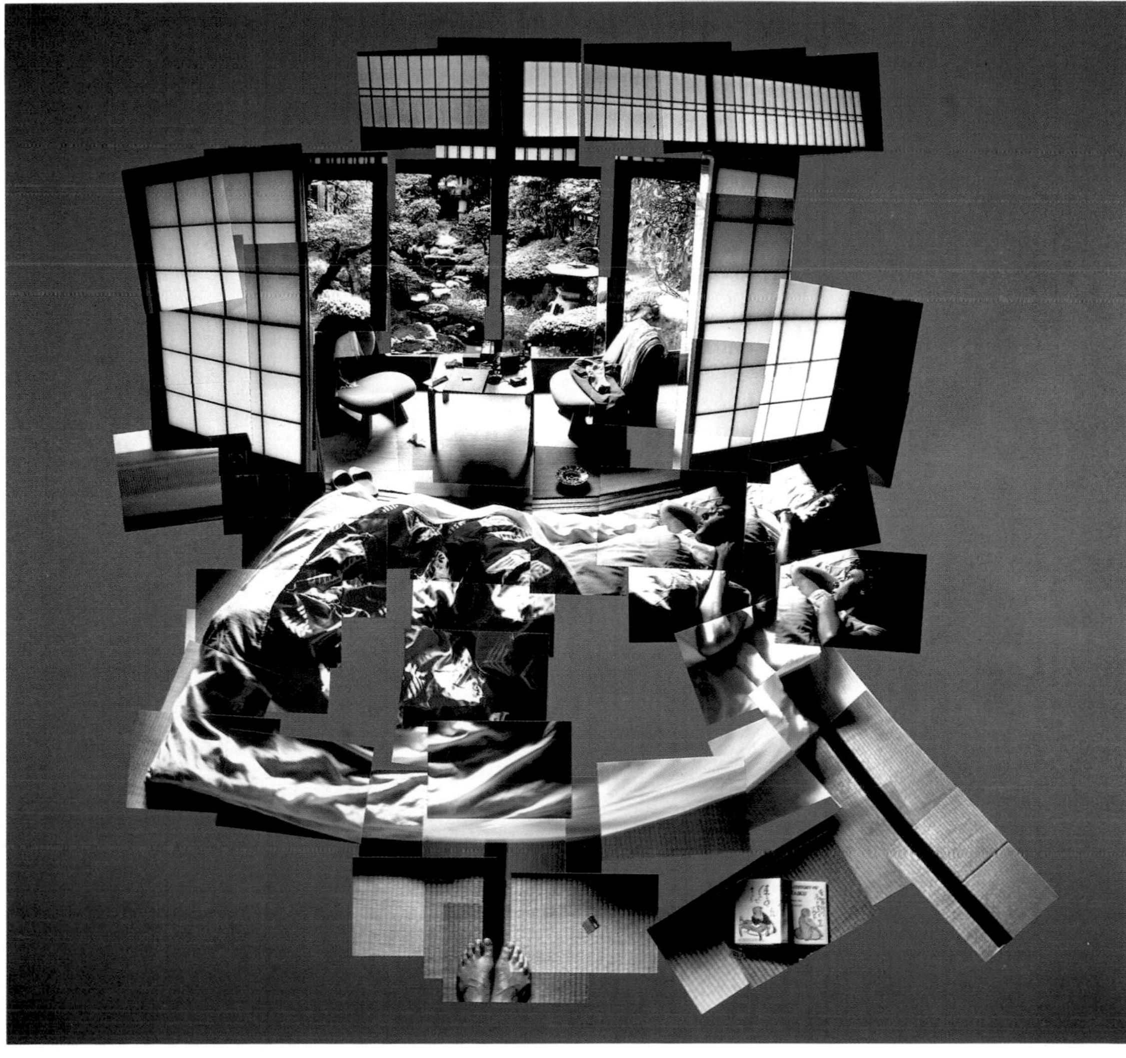

(RIGHT) 27-30. David Hockney. *Gregory Watching the Snow Fall, Kyoto, Feb. 21, 1983.* 1983. Photographic collage, 43½ x 46½" (110.5 x 118 cm). Collection the artist

© 1983 DAVID HOCKNEY

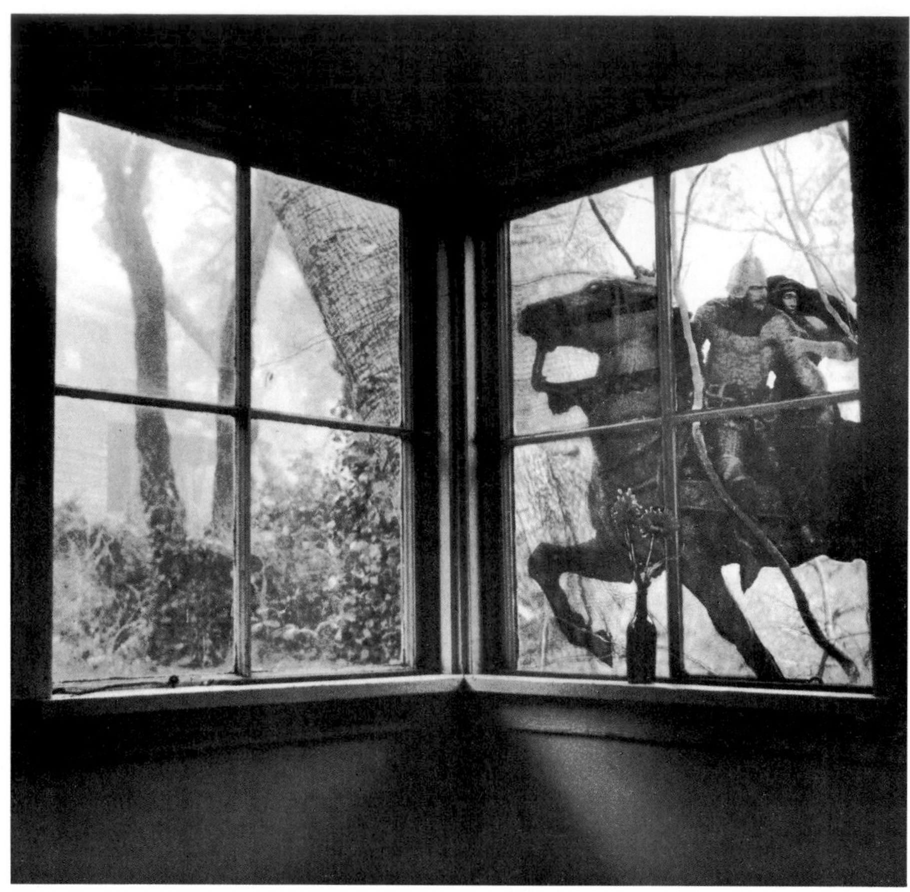

27-31. Joanne Leonard. *Romanticism Is Ultimately Fatal,* from *Dreams and Nightmares.* 1982. Positive transparency selectively opaqued with collage, 9¾ x 9¼" (24.8 x 23.5 cm). Collection M. Neri, Benicia, California

experienced in vision itself. The collage is a masterpiece of design. The scene appears to bow oddly as it comes toward us. This ebb and flow is more than just the result of optical physics. In the perceptual process, space and its corollary, time, are not linear but fluid. Hockney includes his own feet as reference points to establish our position clearly. As a result, he helps us to realize that vision is less a matter of looking outward than an egocentric act that defines the viewer's visual and psychological relationship to the surrounding world. Hockney has recorded his friend several times to suggest his reactions to the serene landscape outside the door.

Hockney's picture shows a clear awareness of earlier twentieth-century art. It combines the faceted views of Picasso (see fig. 24-14) and the sequential action of Duchamp (see fig. 24-23) with the dynamic energy of Popova (see fig. 24 19). *Gregory Watching the Snow Fall* is nonetheless a distinctly contemporary work, for it also incorporates the fascinating effects of Photorealism and the illusionistic potential of Op Art. Hockney later explored the implications of these photocollages, such as continuous narrative. Some photographers have even shown an object or scene simultaneously from multiple vantage points to let us see it completely for the first time.

LEONARD. Contemporary photographers have often turned to fantasy as autobiographical expression. Both the image and the title of *Romanticism Is Ultimately Fatal* (fig. 27-31) by Joanne Leonard (b. 1940) suggest a personal meaning. In fact, it was made during the breakup of her marriage. We will recognize in this disturbing vision something of the tortured eroticism of Fuseli's *The Nightmare* (see fig. 21-43). The clarity of the presentation turns the

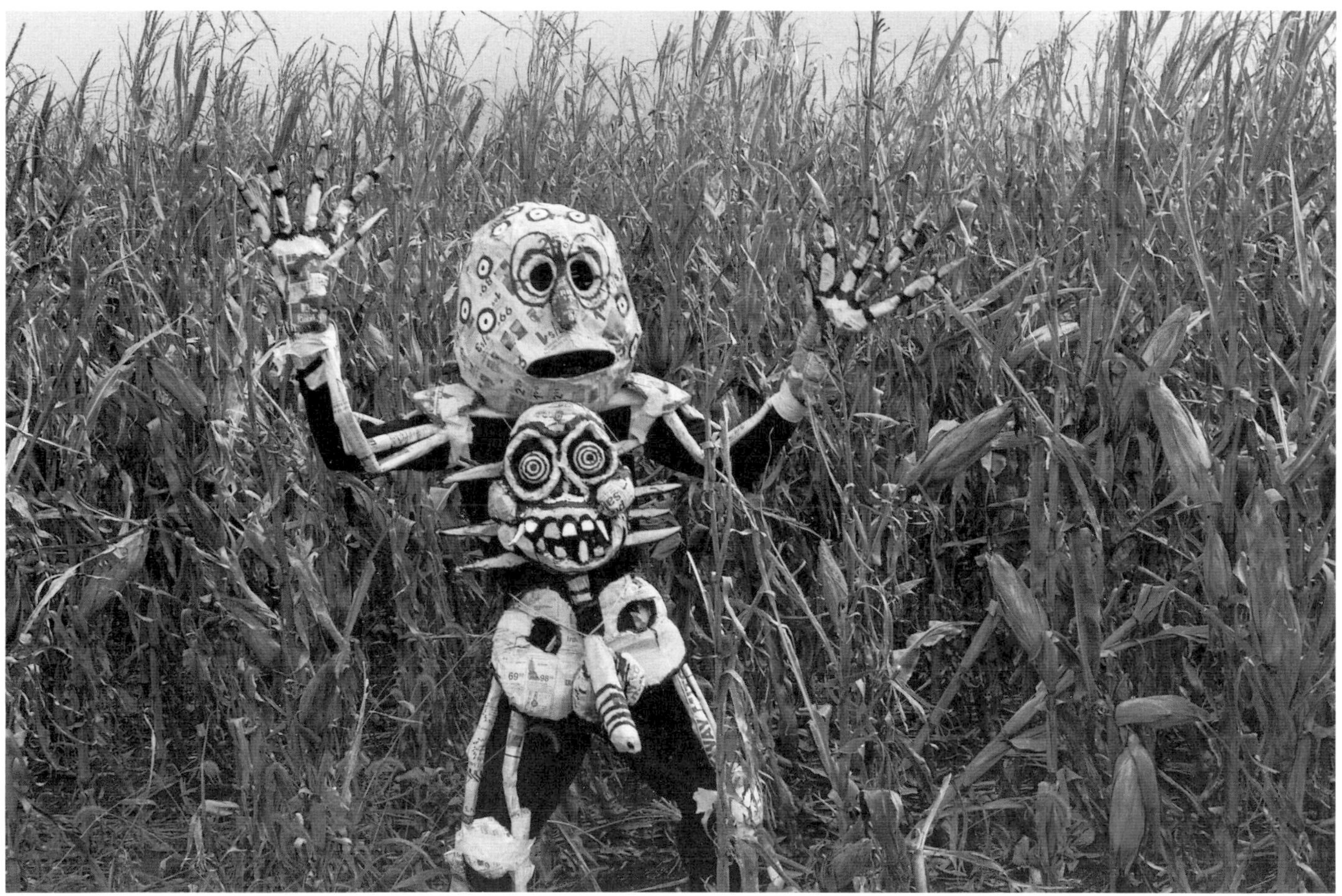

27-32. David Wojnarowicz. *Death in the Cornfield.* 1990. Silver print, 26 x 38" (66 x 96.5 cm)
COURTESY OF P.P.O.W. GALLERY, NEW YORK

phantom at the window into a real and frightening personification of despair. This is no romantic knight in shining armor but a grim reaper whose ancestors can be found in Dürer's woodcut *The Four Horsemen of the Apocalypse* (see fig. 16-5).

WOJNAROWICZ. Even more shocking is *Death in the Cornfield* (fig. 27-32) by David Wojnarowicz (1954–1992). Gifted with a singularly bizarre imagination, he was obsessed with the horrific, which is found throughout his work. At the time of this photograph, Wojnarowicz was already suffering from AIDS, which claimed his life two years later. Of the countless images devoted to this dread disease by painters and photographers, none so fully captures its nightmarish terror. The macabre costume, made by Wojnarowicz himself, makes the figure an awesome demon of death from some primitive tribal ritual that appears out of nature as if by magic. Like Munch's *The Scream* (see fig. 23-21), here is an expression of fear so gripping in its power as to lift personal suffering to a universal plane. It serves as an unforgettable reminder of how many people, not just in the art world, have been touched by the loss of cherished family, friends, and colleagues to AIDS.

CHAPTER TWENTY-EIGHT

Postmodernism

We began Part Four with a discussion of modernism. It is appropriate that we end, for now, with its opposite: postmodernism. We live in the "postmodern" era. How can that be, if modern is what is today? The term itself suggests the peculiar nature of postmodernism, which seeks out incongruity. To resolve this contradiction, we must understand modern in a dual sense: modernity and modernism. Postmodernism is a trend that not only supersedes modernism. As we shall see, it is also opposed to the world order as it exists today and to the values that created it.

What, then, is postmodernism and when did it begin? Generally speaking, postmodernism is characterized by a total skepticism that rejects modernism as an ideal defining twentieth-century culture as we have known it. In challenging tradition, however, it deliberately refuses to provide a new meaning or impose a different order in its place. Postmodernism represents a generation consciously not in search of its identity. Hence it is not a unified movement at all but a loose collection of tendencies that reflect a new sensibility. Taken together, these pieces provide a jigsaw puzzle of our times. Each country has a somewhat different outlook and vocabulary; nevertheless all may be considered forms of postmodernism. We must therefore paint a broad picture, one that will provide us with a general idea of postmodernism's unique character. Our treatment of postmodern art is likewise intended to be suggestive in discussing representative examples, while admittedly omitting much that is of interest.

As the prefix *post* suggests, our world is in a state of transition—without telling us where we will land. Although the term *postmodern* was coined by a historian in the late 1940s to denote a late stage of the civilization initiated by the Renaissance, it has been used mainly by literary critics since the mid-1960s, a significant fact in itself. We may indeed trace the first postmodern symptoms back to that time, but in hindsight they appear to have been mostly a late phase of modernism, without making a decisive break from the mainstream of the twentieth century.

What is the difference between modernism and postmodernism? Postmodernism springs from postindustrial society, which is passing rapidly into the Information Age (the so-called "Third Wave"). According to postmodern theorists, the political, economic, and social structures that have governed the Western world since the end of World War II are either changing, undergoing attack from within, or breaking down altogether, ironically at the same time as the collapse of Communism in eastern Europe. This institutional erosion has resulted in a corresponding spiritual crisis that reflects the chaos of people's lives. Postmodernism is a product of the disillusion and alienation afflicting the middle class. At the same time, bourgeois culture has exhausted its possibilities by absorbing its old enemy, the avant-garde, whose mission was ended by its very success. During the 1950s the media made the avant-garde so popular that the middle class accepted it and began to hunger for ceaseless change for its own sake. By the following decade, modernism was reduced to a "capitalist" mode of expression by large corporations, which adopted it not just in architecture but in the painting and sculpture that decorate it.

Postmodernism celebrates the death of modernism, which it regards as not only arrogant in its claim to universality but also responsible for the evils of contemporary civilization. Democracy, based on Enlightenment values, is seen in turn as a force of oppression, spreading the West's dominance around the world. In common with most earlier avant-garde movements (including existentialism) postmodernism is antagonistic to humanism, which it dismisses as bourgeois. Reason, with its hierarchies of thought, is abandoned in order to liberate people from the established order. This opens the way for nontraditional approaches, especially those from the Third World, emphasizing emotion, intuition, fantasy, contemplation, mysticism, and even magic. Science is no better than any other system, since it has failed to solve today's problems. And because scientific reality does not conform to human experience, it is useless in daily life.

Truth is rejected as neither possible nor desirable on the grounds that it is used by its creators for their own power ends. Subjective and conflicting interpretations are all that can be offered, and these may vary freely according to the context. Since no set of values can have more validity than any other, everything becomes relative. Deprived of traditional guidelines, the postmodernist drifts aimlessly in a sea without meaning or reality. To the extent that the world makes any sense, it is at the local level, where the limited scale makes understanding possible in human terms.

The only escape from an existence in which nothing has inherent worth is inaction or hedonism on the one hand and spirituality on the other. The latter is rarely an option, however, since religions impose their own authority and self-discipline. Thus only the most extreme forms of mysticism, lacking all rational control, are acceptable. Postmodern people are thus fated to become pleasure-seeking narcissists without any strong identity, purpose, or attachments. Cynical and amoral, they live for the moment, without any concern for larger issues, which are imponderables in the first place. Rather than vices, however, these traits are considered virtues. They allow postmodernists a flexible approach to life that enables them to pursue new modes of existence, free from all restraints or authority.

In the brave new world of postmodernism, the individual is no longer anchored in time or space. Both have been made obsolete in life as they have been in science. They are beyond normal human comprehension and are based on assumptions subject to doubt. Traditional definitions of time and space, moreover, were founded on hierarchies of thought that served the purposes of colonialism. However, the new "hyperspace" created by global communication makes it impossible to position oneself within customary boundaries.

Just as time and space have lost all meaning, so has history. The view of history as progressive was also tied to the established power centers of the capitalist system and used as a tool to oppress the Third World. Furthermore, its basic assumption is wrong. If linear logic is inherently invalid, there can be no linear history either. Since conventional knowledge and structures are questionable, nothing can be learned from history in the first place, and its "facts" are therefore of little interest.

Postmodernism makes no attempt to pose new answers to replace the old certitudes it destroys. Instead it substitutes pluralism in the name of multicultural diversity. Pluralism leads inevitably to eclecticism in the arts, with which it is virtually interchangeable, since no one aesthetic is better than any other. Not only are they functions of each other, they become ends in themselves.

By the same token, postmodernism does not try to make the world a better place. In its firm antimodernism, it is socially and politically ambivalent at best, self-contradictory at worst. Its operating principle is anarchism. But although it is extremely liberal in its outlook—witness the rise of "political correctness" in the United States—to classical Marxists it is simply a decadent late phase of capitalism, while to conservatives it goes against traditional values. To the extent that it does offer an alternative, postmodernism supports any new doctrine as superior to the one it seeks to displace. A large number of postmodernists can nevertheless be described as neo-Marxists, despite the fall of most Communist regimes around the world. Radical politics, however, becomes a game that is played for its own sake. In the end, postmodernism remains essentially a form of cultural activism motivated by intellectual theory, not political causes. It is ill-suited to action because it lacks both a coherent agenda and practical plan.

Postmodernism has all the classic earmarks of an avant-garde, despite the fact that it vigorously—and disingenuously—denies such a connection. Its determined opposition to modernity makes it the latest foe of conventional authority, which it is dedicated to overthrowing. Like all avant-gardes, postmodernism is a "degenerate" movement that fosters an atmosphere of crisis in order to sustain and justify itself. In character it comes closest to Dada and Surrealism but lacks their high-pitched hysteria. Its antielitism is simply another means of attacking the cultural establishment, which it wishes to replace. The relativism and anarchism of postmodernism are openly subversive. This nihilism reflects the prevailing skepticism of the late twentieth century, when very little is considered to have any significance or worth.

Postmodernism might well take its credo from Edgar Allan Poe:

All that we see or seem
Is but a dream within a dream.

Such a position has its problems. As we examine it, we realize that the postmodernist rejection of reality is a philosophical assumption, just as its rejection of truth is a value judgment. Even if we grant that everything is ultimately unknowable, reality must nonetheless be capable of being understood in a functional sense; otherwise, people could not survive. Postmodernism, then, is comparable to that higher understanding sought by mystics, for whom reason is insufficient.

Because it has so many meanings, postmodernism itself becomes a meaningless term, posing the kind of hopeless double-bind that it delights in. In fact, postmodernism as a whole is riddled with contradictions. But if nothing is valid, then the values it often espouses—feminism, pluralism, and the like—must be false as well. Seen in this light, postmodernism is a sterile philosophy that reflects the impotence of intellectuals to act.

In the end, postmodernism cannot escape the very laws of history it claims to deny. As a parody of modernity, it has its parallels—indeed, its origins—in the avant-garde of a hundred years ago. The same "decadence" and nihilism can be found toward the end of the nineteenth century in the Symbolist movement, with its apocalyptic vision of despair. Like pluralism, for example, Gauguin's quest for the spiritual assumed the superiority of "alternative" knowledge systems and asserted a belief in magic, which was widely shared by other Symbolists. Postmodernists espouse the same destructive values as the late-nineteenth-century German philosopher Friedrich Nietzsche, who was one of the principal sources of the avant-garde. Although postmodernism offers nothing in exchange, people will undoubtedly devise a new system to replace the old one that it strives to overturn.

SEMIOTICS AND DECONSTRUCTION. The Information Age is obsessed with meaning—and the lack thereof. Like the intellectual disciplines, nearly all branches of culture have come under the spell of semiotics—the study of signs—also known as semiology (though a distinction is sometimes made between the two). Semiotics is part of philosophy, linguistics, science, sociology, anthropology, communications, psychology, art, literature, cinema: any area of human activity that involves symbols. (There are other classes of signs that are the subject of semiotic inquiry as well.) Semiotics in turn has been undermined from within by Deconstruction, which is undoubtedly the most powerful attack mounted to date by postmodernism. As the term suggests, deconstruction is destructive, not constructive. It tears a text apart by using the text against itself, until the text finally "deconstructs" itself. For those interested in exploring the issues further, we have supplied a brief overview in the Postscript at the end of this chapter. For our purposes it is not the theories that count, no matter how interesting they may be, but their effect on art.

POSTMODERN ART

We are, in a sense, the new Victorians. A century ago, Impressionism underwent a similar crisis, from which Post-Impressionism emerged as the direction for the next 20 years. Behind its complex rhetoric, postmodernism can be seen as a strategy for sorting through the past while making a decisive break with it that will allow new possibilities to emerge. Having received a rich heritage, artists are faced with a wide variety of alternatives. The principal feature of the new art is eclecticism. Another indication of the state of flux is the reemergence of many traditional European and regional American art centers.

Art since 1980 has been called postmodern, but not all of it fits under this umbrella. We shall find that the participation of the visual arts in the postmodern adventure has varied greatly and taken some surprising turns. The traditional media of painting and sculpture have played a secondary role. They are closely identified with the modernist tradition and are therefore rejected as tools of the ruling class. Meanwhile, nontraditional forms, such as installations and photography, have come to the forefront and become highly politicized in the process.

Much of the basis for postmodern art can be traced back to Conceptualism, which led the initial attack on modernism (see pages 859–60). Indeed, it has been argued that the beginnings of postmodernism can be dated to the rise of Conceptualism in the mid-1960s. The two, however, are products of two distinctly different generations. Furthermore, Conceptualism was itself derived from Dada, which has provided an "antimodern" alternative since early in the twentieth century. In the context of the 1960s, it was simply part of that ongoing dialogue, in which Pop also participated. That date, moreover, seems too early for the onset of what is fundamentally a late-twentieth-century phenomenon.

Installations and performance art have been around since the 1960s as well. What has changed is the content of these art forms as part of a larger shift in viewpoint. Focused as it was on matters of art, early Conceptualism seems almost innocent in hindsight. Postmodernists, in contrast, attack modern art as part of a larger offensive against contemporary society. They are far more issue-oriented than their predecessors, and their work cuts across a much wider range of concerns than ever before.

The principal manifestation of postmodernism is appropriation, which looks back self-consciously to earlier art. It does so both by imitating previous styles and by taking over specific motifs or even entire images. Artists, of course, have always borrowed from tradition but rarely so systematically as now. Such plundering is nearly always a sign of deepening cultural crisis, suggesting bankruptcy. (The same thing is going on in popular culture, with its constant "retro" revivals.) Since it is not tied to any system, postmodernism is free to adopt earlier imagery and to alter its meaning radically by placing it in a new context. The traditional importance assigned to the artist and object is furthermore deemphasized in this approach, which stresses content and process over aesthetics. The other main characteristic of postmodernism is the merging of art forms. Thus there is no longer a clear difference between painting, sculpture, and photography, and we maintain the distinction mostly as a matter of convenience.

Although it has an anti-intellectual side, postmodernism is preoccupied with theory. As a result, art (and, along with it, art history) has become theory-bound. Despite a growing body of writing and criticism, however, it lags far behind literature and poetry in developing a postmodern approach. Compared to language, the visual arts are traditionally poor vehicles for theory. Perhaps they have become so word-oriented of late in an attempt to keep up with other disciplines.

Postmodernism has a fatal flaw. It has produced little art that is memorable—it is merely "symptomatic" of our age. But for that very reason it is worthy of our interest. Fittingly enough, the most devastating critique of postmodernism comes from that apostle of modernism, Charles Baudelaire: "Eclecticism has at all periods and places held itself superior to past doctrines because, coming last on to the scene, it finds the remotest horizons already open to it; but this impartiality only goes to prove the impotence of the eclectics. People who are so lavish with their time for reflection are not complete men: they lack the element of passion. No matter how clever he may be, an eclectic is but a feeble man; for he is a man without love. Therefore he has no ideal . . . ; neither star nor compass. Doubt has led certain artists to beg the aid of all the other arts. Experiment with contradictory means, the encroachment of one art upon another, the importation of poetry, wit, and sentiment into painting—all these modern miseries are vices peculiar to the eclectics."

ARCHITECTURE

We begin with architecture, which not only initiated the postmodern dialogue in the arts but also puts the issues literally in concrete form.

Postmodernism

Postmodernism in art was first coined to denote an eclectic mode of architecture that arose around 1980. Because it is a style, we shall capitalize it to distinguish it from the larger phenomenon of postmodernism, to which it is closely related. As the term implies, Postmodernism represents a broad rejection of mainstream twentieth-century architecture. Although it uses the same construction techniques, Postmodernism rejects not only the vocabulary of Gropius and his followers but also the social and ethical ideals implicit in their lucid proportions. Looking at the Seagram Building (see fig. 26-28), we can well understand why. As a statement, it is so overwhelming in its authority that it prohibits deviation and is so cold that it lacks appeal. The Postmodernist critique was, then, essentially correct. In its search for universal ideals, the International Style failed to communicate

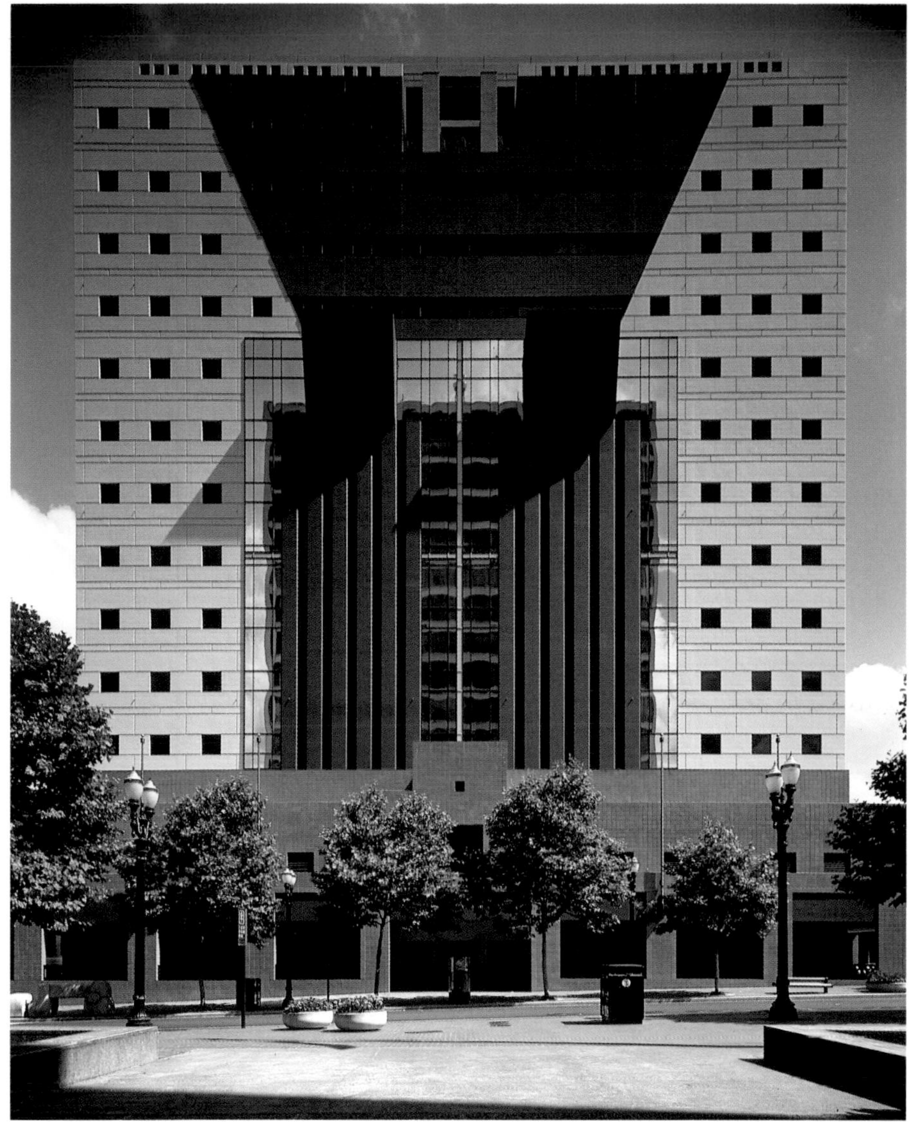

28-1. Michael Graves. Public Services Building, Portland, Oregon. 1980–82

with people, who neither understood nor liked it. Postmodernism is an attempt to reinvest architecture with the human meaning so clearly absent from High Modernism. It does so by returning to premodernist architecture.

The chief means of introducing greater expressiveness has been to adopt elements from historical styles rich with association. All traditions are assumed to have equal validity, so that they can be combined at will. In the process, the compilation itself becomes a conscious parody characterized by ironic wit. This eclectic historicism is nevertheless highly selective in its sources. They are restricted mainly to various forms of classicism (notably Palladianism) and some of the more exotic strains of Art Deco, which, as we have seen (see page 873), provided a genuine alternative to modernism during the 1920s and 1930s. Architects have repeatedly searched the past for fresh ideas. What counts is the originality of the final result.

VENTURI AND BROWN. The immediate antecedents of Postmodernism can be found in the work of Robert Venturi (b. 1925) and his wife, Denise Scott Brown (b. 1931). They realized that architecture in America had become filled with pictorial and commercial imagery. As a result, they advocated overturning the modernist credo of "form follows function" by divorcing the symbolic quality of a facade from the building's purpose and structure. To accomplish that end, they created an architecture of banality. Its triteness was proclaimed by ironic paraphrases of historical clichés from both the recent and distant past. Although few architects followed their lead in design, the theories of Venturi and Brown were important for opening the debate that led to Postmodernism.

GRAVES. The Public Services Building in Portland, Oregon (fig. 28-1), by Michael Graves (b. 1934) is a characteristic example of Postmodernism. [See Primary Sources, no. 103, pages 942–43.] Elevated on a pedestal, it mixes classical, Egyptian, and assorted other motifs in a whimsical building-block paraphrase of Art Deco, which shared an equal disregard for historical propriety. In this way, Graves relieves the building of the monotony imposed by the tyranny of the cube that afflicts so much modern architecture. Although the lavish sculptural decoration was never added, the exterior has a surprising warmth that continues inside. At first glance, it is tempting to dismiss the Public Services Building as mere historicism. To do so, however, ignores the fact that no earlier structure looks at all like it. What holds this historical mix together is the architect's style. It is based on a mastery of abstraction that is as systematic and personal as Mondrian's. Indeed, Graves was a skilled Late Modernist who first earned recognition in 1969 at the same exhibition held by the Museum of Modern Art in New York that showcased Richard Meier (see page 882).

Today Postmodern buildings are found everywhere. They are instantly recognizable by their reliance on keyhole arches, round "Palladian" windows, and other relics from the architectural past. They are also marked by their luxuriance. Postmodernism may be characterized as architecture for the rich that has since been translated downward to the middle class. Its aura of wealth suggests the egocentricity and hedonism that spawned the "me" generation of the 1980s, one of the most prosperous and extravagant decades in recent history. Nevertheless, the retrospective eclecticism of Postmodernism soon became dated through the repetitious quotation of standard devices that were reduced to self-parodies lacking both wit and purpose. In a larger sense, however, this quick passage reflects the restless quest for novelty and, more important, a new modernism that has yet to emerge to replace the old.

SITE. In its playfulness and complexity Postmodernism has rightly been compared to Mannerist architecture, which added a note of decadence into the classical vocabulary inherited from the Renaissance. Both also share an element of self-conscious burlesque. Parody reaches a climax in the designs by SITE Projects, Inc., for Best Stores. One store in a Houston mall (fig. 28-2), for example, looks for all the world to be crumbling into ruins (compare fig. 14-23). This witty takeoff on standard commercial architecture is enhanced by the bleakness of the location itself.

The differences are equally profound, however. Postmodernism arises out of the general sense of disillusionment that afflicts our age and prevents the architect from seeing either the past or the present with innocent eyes. Such a claim might well be made of Mannerist architecture, of course. But because architects today must design for different "taste cultures," the eclecticism of Postmodernism is intended as a reflection of our "social and metaphysical reality." Historicism, then, is part of the new pluralism, which can even include a caricature of modernism itself. Such parodies also change old meanings into new ones through "double-coding," which combines modernist techniques and traditional styles to communicate on a new plane with the public and architects alike. The result is a content that is entirely up-to-date, despite the apparent familiarity of its hybrid style.

STIRLING. The Postmodernist critique of Late Modernism is that the latter is committed to the tradition of the new and therefore maintains modernism's integrity of invention and usage. Moreover, it lacks both pluralism and a complex relation to the past, so that it fails to transform meaning. We may test this for ourselves by comparing the Pompidou Center (see fig. 26-45) with the Neue Staatsgalerie in Stuttgart (fig. 28-3), which was immediately recognized as a classic example of Postmodernism. The latter has the grandiose scale befitting a "palace" of the arts, but instead of the monolithic cube of the Pompidou Center, English architect James Stirling (1926–1992) incorporates a greater variety of shapes within more complex spatial relationships. There is also an openly decorative quality that will remind us, however indirectly, of Garnier's Paris Opéra (see fig. 21-77). The similarity does not stop there. Stirling has likewise utilized a form of historicism through paraphrase that is far more subtle than Garnier's opulent revival-

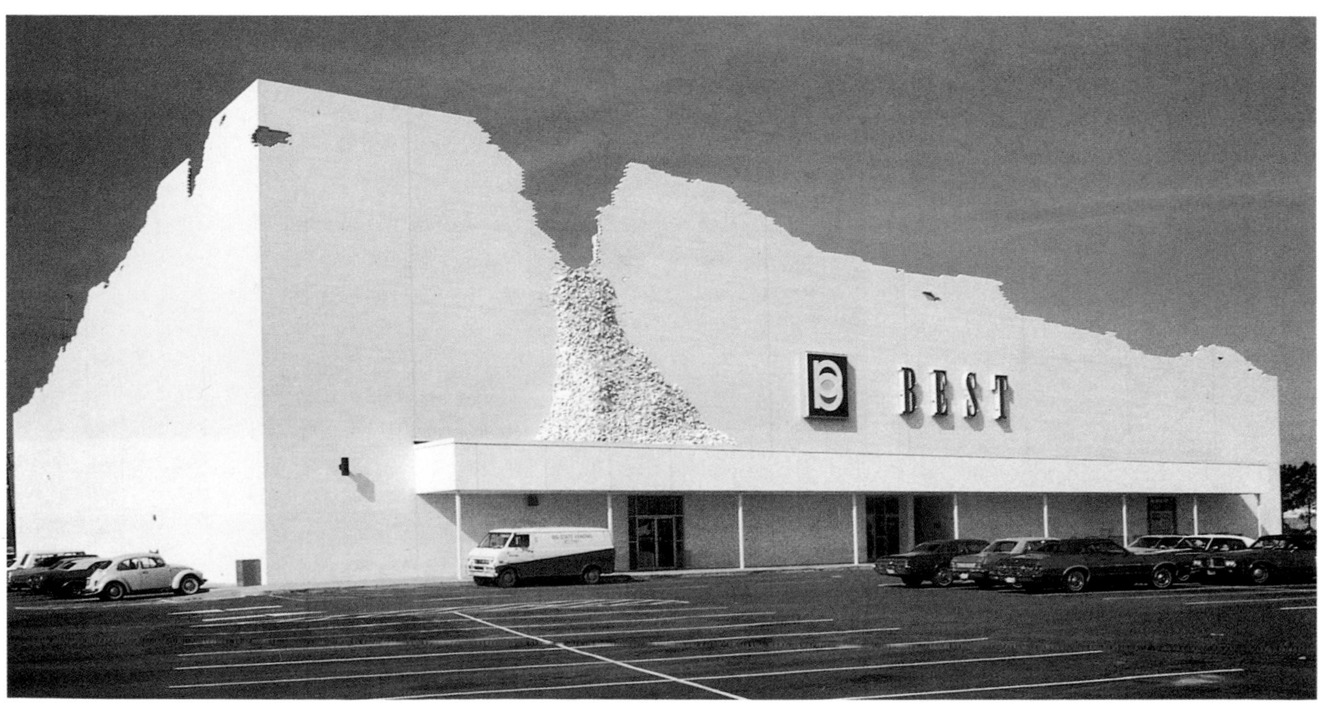

28-2. SITE Projects, Inc., with Maple-Jones Associates. Best Stores Showroom, Houston. 1975

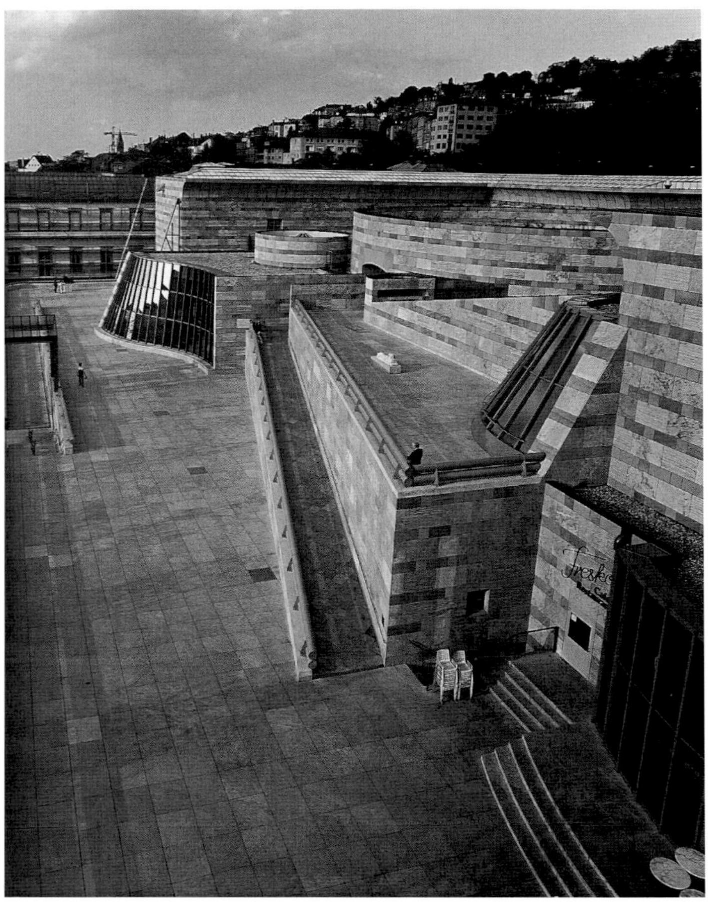

28-3. James Stirling, Michael Wilford and Associates. Neue Staatsgalerie, Stuttgart, Germany. Completed 1984

ism but no less self-conscious. The prim Neoclassical masonry facade, for example, is punctured by a narrow arched window recalling the Italian Renaissance (compare fig. 12-37) and by a rusticated portal that has a distinctly Mannerist look. At the same time, there is an exaggerated quoting of modernism through the use of such high-tech materials as painted metal. This eclecticism is more than a veneer—it lies at the heart of the building's success. The site, centering on a circular sculpture court, is designed along the lines of ancient temple complexes from Egypt through Rome, complete with a monumental entrance stairway. This plan enables Stirling to solve a wide range of practical problems with ingenuity and to provide a stream of changing views that fascinate and delight the visitor. The results have been compared to the Altes Museum of Karl Friedrich Schinkel (see fig. 21-66), among the most classical structures of the nineteenth century. By comparison, the Pompidou Center is a far more radical building!

Deconstructivism

Although it claims to deal with meaning, in the end Postmodernist historicism addresses only the decorative veneer of the International Style. Spurred by more revolutionary theories, Deconstructivism, another tendency that has been gathering momentum since 1980, goes much farther in challenging its substance. The term *Deconstructivism* combines Constructivism and deconstruction. Strictly speaking, there can be no architecture of deconstruction because building puts things together instead of taking them apart. Deconstructivism nevertheless follows similar principles and is symptomatic of postmodernism as a whole. It dismembers modern architecture, then reassembles it again in new ways.

Like Postmodernism, it does so by engaging in appropriation. Deconstructivism also returns to one of the earliest sources of modernism: the Russian avant-garde. The Russian experiment in architecture proved short-lived, and few of its ideas ever made it beyond the laboratory stage. However, recent architects have been inspired anew by the bold sculpture of the Constructivists and the graphic designs of the Suprematists. They seek to violate the integrity of modern architecture by subverting its internal logic, which the Russians themselves did little to undermine. Nevertheless, Deconstructivism does not abandon modern architecture and its principles altogether and remains an architecture of the possible based on structural engineering. Although it claims Michelangelo, Bernini, and Guarini as its ancestors, Deconstructivism goes far beyond anything that can be found in earlier architecture. We will find little common ground among its practitioners. The main devices they have in common are superimpositions of clashing systems or layers of space, and distortions from within that subvert the normal vocabulary and purposes of modern architecture.

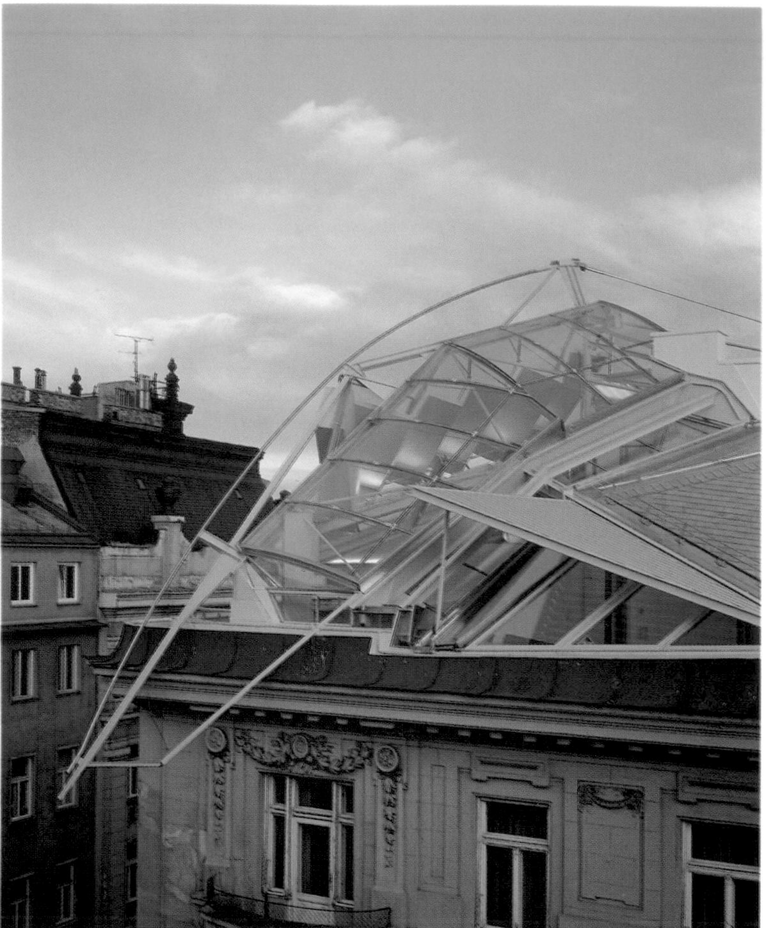

28-4. Coop Himmelblau. Roof Conversion Project, Vienna. 1983–88

COOP HIMMELBLAU. Although Deconstructivist designs have won major awards, their experimental approach and ambitious scale initially discouraged actual construction. The most advanced designs to get off the drawing board first were generally modest affairs but no less exciting for that fact. The roof conversion for a Viennese lawyer's office by Coop Himmelblau (fig. 28-4) has well been described as "a writhing, disruptive, animal breaking through the corner." The internal disturbances are incorporated into the structure itself, "as if some kind of parasite has infected the form and distorted it from the inside." This effect is closely related to how deconstruction uses language.

BEHNISCH AND PARTNER. An equally brilliant example is the Hysolar Research Institute at the University of Stuttgart (fig. 28-5) by the firm of Behnisch and Partner. The hall between the laboratory wings both reflects and parodies the scientific work being carried on. The materials suggest the high-tech purpose of the project, which is to investigate energy based on hydrogen produced by solar power. In turn, the free-flowing passage indicates the collaborative exchange of ideas. Yet the sensation produced by the collision of twisted forms is like careening down a roller coaster. Nothing, it seems to suggest, works the way it should in the orderly world of modern science!

TSCHUMI. One of the first architects to be influenced by deconstruction is Bernard Tschumi (b. 1944). The most complete embodiment of his Deconstructivism is the Parc de La Villette in

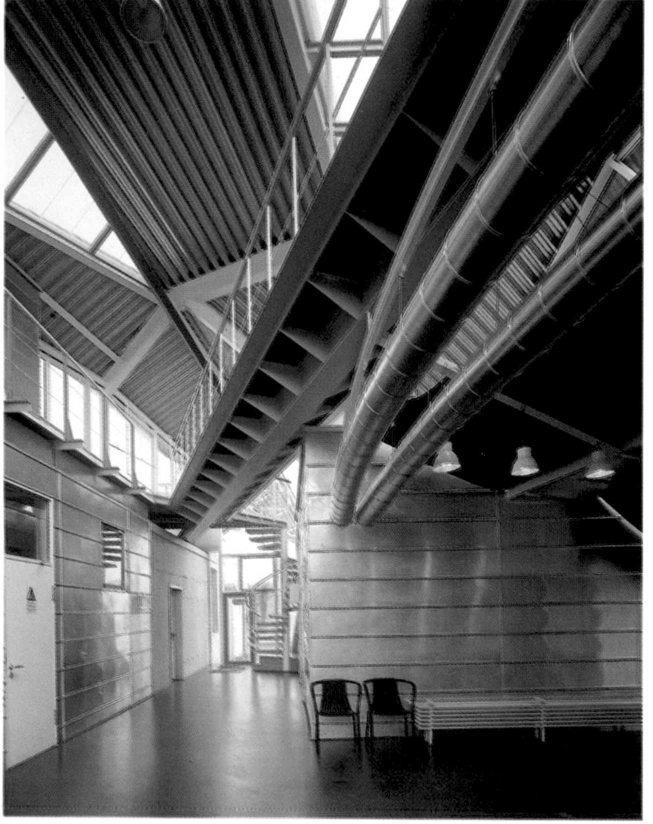

28-5. Behnisch and Partner.
Hall between Laboratory Wings, Hysolar Research Institute, University of Stuttgart. 1987

Paris, for which the founder of deconstruction, Jacques Derrida (see Postscript), later wrote an essay in the brochure explaining the project. The park's program had to include a variety of functions (workshop, baths, gymnasium, playground, concert facilities) and other parks and buildings already on the site. Tschumi's solution is directly based on this fact. It presents an intelligent solution to what could have been a hopelessly complex problem that would have overwhelmed any traditional approach.

To describe the Parc de La Villette, we must resort to the coded terminology of Deconstructivism itself. The architect began by laying out the grounds in a simple abstract grid to provide a strong yet flexible conceptual framework for change, improvisation, and substitution. He then subverted it by superimposing two other grid systems on it, so as to prevent any dominant hierarchy or clear relation between the program and the solution. This multiple grid is deliberately antifunctional, anticontextual, and infinite. (In principle, it could be extended in any direction indefinitely.) Tschumi creates highly unorthodox relationships through decentralization, fragmentation, combination, and superimposition of elements, so that the architecture appears to serve no purpose. He further supplants form, function, and structure with contiguity, substitution, and permutation. To undermine the traditional rules of composition, hierarchy, and order, he uses crossprogramming (using space for a different purpose than intended), transprogramming (combining two incompatible programs and spaces), and disprogramming (combining two programs to create a new one from their contradictions). The functions are dispersed through a series of buildings (*folies*) whose components, appearance, and uses are interchangeable. The play between free and rigid form leads to ambiguity, disorder, impurity, imperfection. The result denies any inherent meaning to the forms, structure, or organization.

What does all this theory have to do with the actual experience? Surprisingly little. The ensemble is meant to induce a sense of disassociation, both within and between its elements. This disjointedness conveys an unstable programmatic madness (*folie*) through a form of cinematic montage inspired by the films of the Russian Sergei Eisenstein and others. However, the visitor is hardly aware of this effect. On the contrary, the system creates an order and rhythm of its own, whether Tschumi intended it or not. We are left only with a feeling of enchantment, which suggests the more playful meaning of *folie,* not just madness. The *folies* themselves resemble large-scale sculptures extended almost to the breaking point (fig. 28-6). Yet the tension between the reality of the built structures and their "impossibility" results in an architecture of rare vitality. It is especially fitting that two of the most captivating *folies* are for use by children. Although the architect insists that he was not expressing himself, this effect is perhaps the ultimate test of the park's success. Tschumi himself acknowledges the fact indirectly by speaking of affirmative deconstruction—a self-contradiction if ever there was one!

We may yet see one Deconstructivist deconstructing the work of another Deconstructivist. Peter Eisenman (b. 1932) has designed a second garden for the Parc de La Villette that poses what might be called "the battle of the grids": Tschumi's versus Eisenman's version of the Deconstructivist point grid, which the latter claims to have discovered first. Eisenman's garden was designed with Derrida's collaboration from the start. To pull it off, Eisenman added new layers of ever more complex rhetoric (called "tropes" in the current parlance) to justify what amounts to skillful one-upmanship. It remains to be seen whether the results will justify the dense jargon.

POSTMODERNISM VS. DECONSTRUCTIVISM. Try as their disciples might to deny it, Postmodernism and Deconstructivism are really two sides of the same postmodernist coin, which has pushed modern architecture to its limits. As a style, Postmodernism challenges it from the outside while Deconstructivism as an approach corrupts it from within. It is a measure of how firmly postmodern thinking had taken hold of contemporary architecture that in 1988 Philip Johnson—who helped to design the interior of the Seagram Building (see fig. 26-28) and was himself the architect of one of the most controversial Postmodern build-

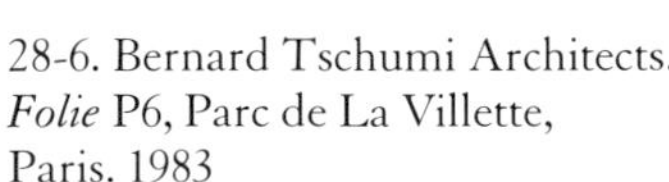
28-6. Bernard Tschumi Architects. *Folie* P6, Parc de La Villette, Paris. 1983

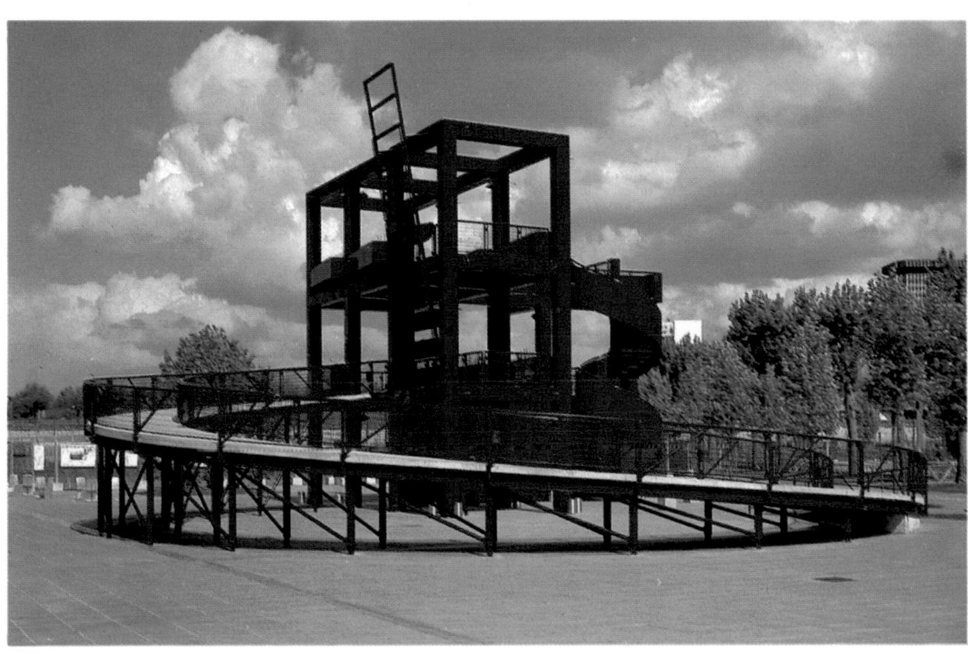

ings (the AT&T Building in New York)—declared modern architecture dead and mounted an exhibition of Tschumi, Eisenman, and other Deconstructivists. This sort of reevaluation has gone on before. Postmodernism is a transition much like Art Nouveau at the turn of the century, which provided part of the foundation for modern architecture. It is a necessary part of the process that will redefine architecture as we have come to know it.

ARCHITECTURE AFTER POSTMODERNISM: WHAT'S NEXT

If postmodernism is inherently a paradox, what are we to call the phase that follows it? We are tempted to name it the New Modernism, except that the term Neo-Modernism already means the same thing, even if it implies something altogether different. Because this new initiative is still unfolding, perhaps it is best not to confuse matters further by trying to pin a tag on it prematurely. The lack of a label does not mean, however, that a new direction cannot be discovered. On the contrary, there is a clear tendency toward coalescence between Neo-Expressionism and Deconstructivism, despite the extraordinary diversity that has characterized architecture around the world over the past decade or so. We may call it Sculptural Architecture. Such a merging is less strange than it may seem at first glance. After all, Neo-Expressionism is the most self-consciously sculptural of any form of architecture, while Deconstructivism takes as its point of departure Russian Constructivism, which was primarily a sculptural movement, albeit one with a strong architectural bent. Moreover, we may see this union as bridging the gap between Abstraction and Expressionism, which developed in modernist architecture during the early 1920s.

Reconciliation does not imply compromise, however. It does suggest what the late-nineteenth-century art historian Alois Riegl called "the will to form." It is as if contemporary architecture is seized by an urge to create sculpture on a scale that surpasses even the grandiose dreams of environmental sculptors such as Mathias Goeritz (see page 847). Moreover, the architects who are pursuing this direction are a different breed from their predecessors. Not that they are youngsters. Most were born between 1943 and 1953; they are, in other words, baby boomers. But although they are very conscious of everything that has come before them, they think differently.

GEHRY. The oldest of these sculptural Postmodernists is Frank Gehry (b. 1929), a Los Angeles architect who has always been a maverick in his sense of design and choice of materials. His earlier work was emphatically Deconstructivist, but the more recent buildings can only be described as assemblages of miscellaneous parts. What is undoubtedly his finest achievement is the Guggenheim Museum in Bilbao, Spain, which opened in 1997 (fig. 28-7). Situated strategically on a bend of the river that runs through the city, it is part cultural institution and part urban renewal project.

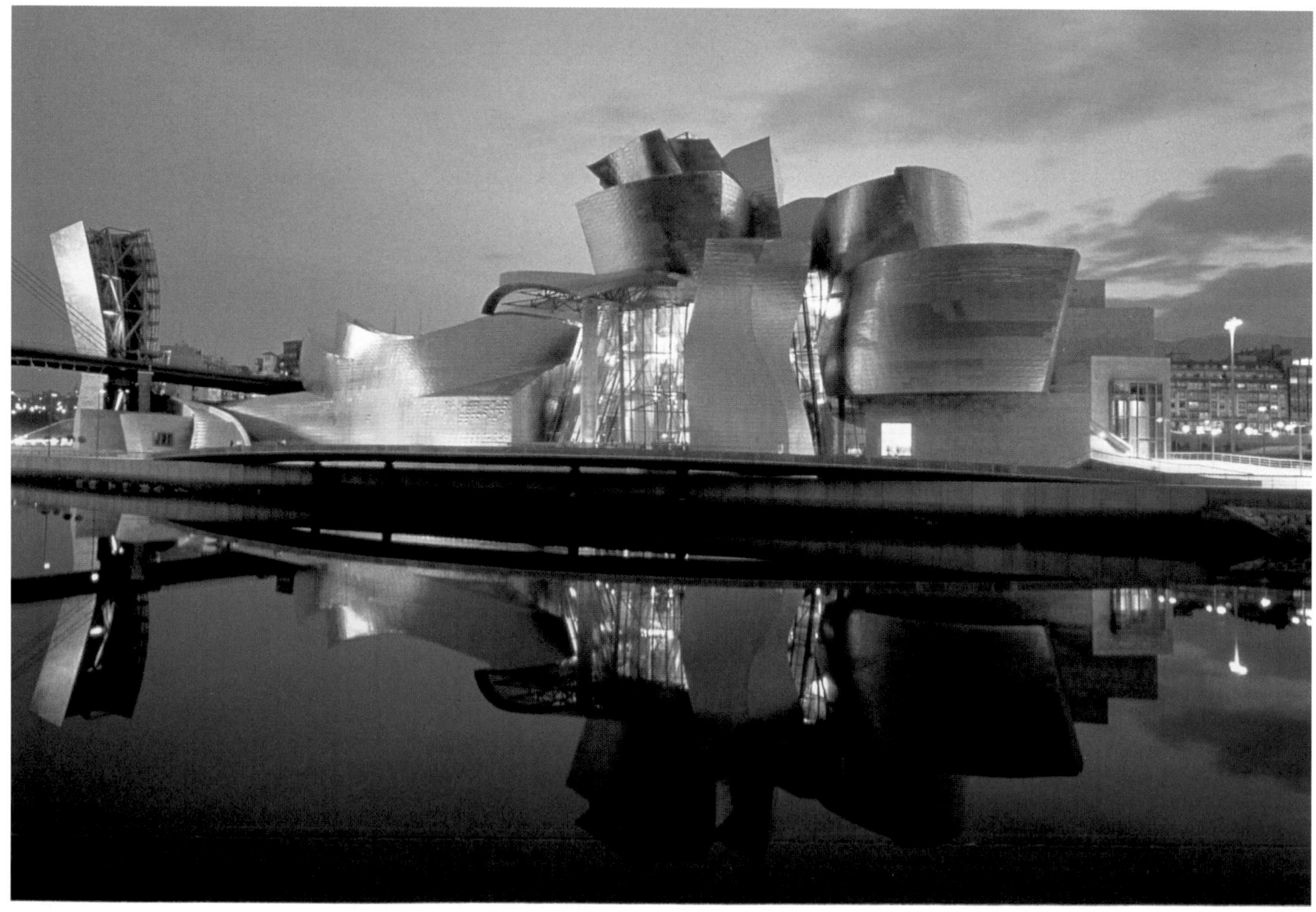

28-7. Frank Gehry. Guggenheim Museum, Bilbao, Spain. 1992–97

It replaces an abandoned lumber mill. In accord with the director's wishes, the galleries vary greatly in shape in order to provide different viewing experiences appropriate to the various kinds of art they hold. Once the main functional requirements had been determined, the building was conceived in a series of drawings. Often resembling abstract doodles, they were then translated into usable form by employing the latest computer-aided design programs. Throughout the long development process, Gehry experimented with a number of shapes, many of which were incorporated into the final design. The result is certainly as innovative and controversial as Frank Lloyd Wright's original Guggenheim Museum in New York (see figs. 26-39 and 26-40). The Bilbao Guggenheim is a structure of such dazzling complexity that no single photograph can begin to suggest its ever-changing views. As one critic observed, from head-on it looks like a collision between two ships. Seen from above, the museum appears to unfold like a flower, but it also includes fish, snake, boot, and sail forms. Indeed, the main body is clad in a skin of specially fabricated, ultrathin titanium tiles suggesting the scales of a fish or snake. It has such organic vitality that it almost seems to have a life of its own, especially when viewed from the side, as in our illustration. The building ends in a tower that is actually a piece of architectural sculpture rather than a functional piece of architecture. All told, the Bilbao Guggenheim is probably the most exciting building of the 1990s. It became an instant classic, defining the spirit of the decade, much as the Pompidou Center (see fig. 26-45) did for the '80s.

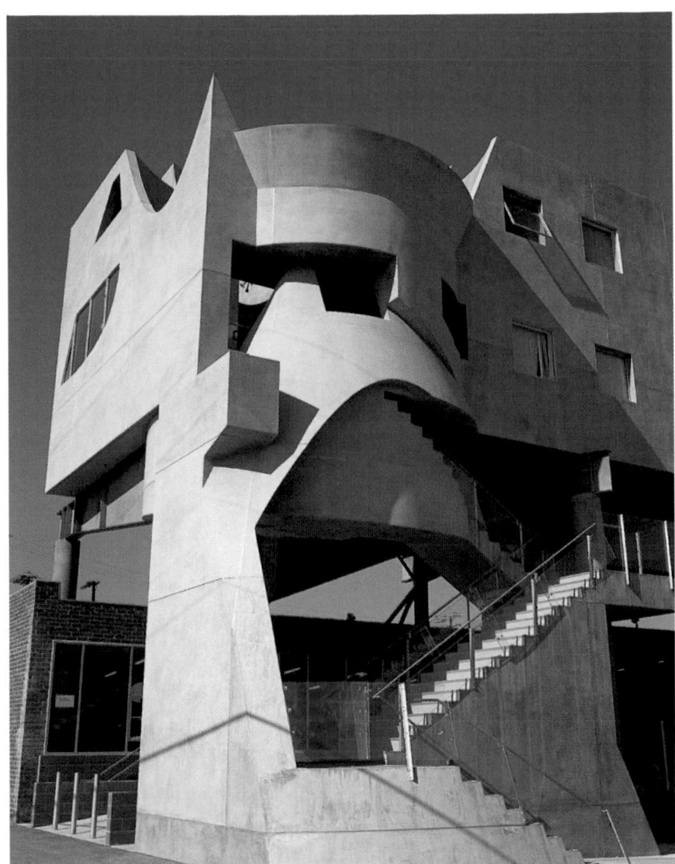

28-8. Eric Owen Moss. A building in the complex at Samitaur, Culver City, California. 1989–95

MOSS. Because of his experimental vision, Gehry is one of the most influential role models for younger architects wanting to explore new possibilities on both sides of the Atlantic. Among them is Eric Owen Moss (b. 1943), who is also based in Los Angeles. Even more than Gehry, with whom he worked, Moss brings a new kind of elliptical intelligence, rather than linear logic, to architecture. He even talks differently from his predecessors, often preferring the disjointed syntax of today's everyday speech to the measured tones of rational discourse. His concerns are equally new. Moss' work reflects not a desire to dissect the formal language of High Modernism but an acute awareness of the clash of forces in a chaotic world, which the architect does not so much resolve as join together.

A brilliant example of Moss' recent architecture is Samitaur (fig. 28-8), part of the rehabilitation of a decaying industrial section in Culver City near Los Angeles undertaken by the developer Frederick Smith. In his first designs for the site, Moss combined Deconstructivism with Postmodernism to create a hybrid style still seeking its own identity. Samitaur, by contrast, imposes a new building on top of old ones in a way that both deconstructs and historicizes. The whole structure is built over a roadway on braces placed at varying angles, with legs sunk into the existing warehouses. At several points the smooth regularity of the exterior is suddenly disrupted by a collision of sculptural forms that recall Mendelsohn's Einstein Tower (see fig. 26-22). The glance backward does not stop there. Such complex shapes cannot be made using standard high-tech construction techniques. In fact, they rely heavily on handwork. In that regard, Samitaur is a throwback not simply to the Einstein Tower but to the Arts and Crafts Movement. Its nearest counterpart is, strangely enough, Antoní Gaudí's Casa Milá (see fig. 23-31). Yet the results can in no way be called retrospective.

What does such a building do? At the very least, it forces the user to reconsider the function of the structure itself. Moss conceives of the architect as a kind of high priest who imposes his ideas but in such a way that they interact with those of the user to create something new and unexpected. This play back and forth accords with his view of life as a series of contradictions that seek a resolution, which in turn gives rise to new sets of questions. If the theory is obscure, the point of view is thoroughly postmodern, and it is expressed in visually compelling form.

No matter how unconventional, Moss' buildings manage to fulfill their practical purpose surprisingly well; otherwise, the Culver City project would not have proved commercially viable. He is no less concerned with matters of structure and details of construction than he is with visual effects. Nevertheless, the jury is still out on whether this unique approach can be translated successfully into the mass construction techniques necessary for wide adoption. But there can be little doubt that Samitaur further points to the future of architecture as space-defining sculpture, something that architects everywhere are working toward (see page 886).

SCULPTURE

FABRO. Traditional sculpture has played little role in postmodernism because the emphasis on form in recent architecture has usurped its position. In fact, sculpture seems almost out of place when it does make an appearance. A rare example is *The Birth of Venus* (fig. 28-9) by Luciano Fabro (b. 1936), an original member of the *Arte Povera* movement (see page 831) who works in a wide variety of styles and techniques. The roughed-out "figure" is attached like a misshapen cocoon to the eroded capital atop the smooth column drums, all of contrasting color. What might she look like? Unlike Michelangelo's *Awakening Slave* (see fig. 13-16), Fabro's *Venus* remains imprisoned within the marble forever, with no more than the barest outlines to hint at her possible shape. Curiously enough, the column more closely resembles a statue, the Archaic Greek "Peplos" Kore in figure 5-14, than does this strange appendage. Although some would deny it, *The Birth of Venus* is clearly a postmodern work. What makes it so is the improbable juxtaposition, which is a knowing misquotation of the past. Yet the ironic takeoff is accomplished with all the gravity of an artist for whom sculpture is both a living tradition and a dead language to be revived. It is a serious business that does not, however, rule out a certain irreverence for this vestigial relic. The real surprise is that the piece is so effective, for in its muteness it contains a spellbinding mystery.

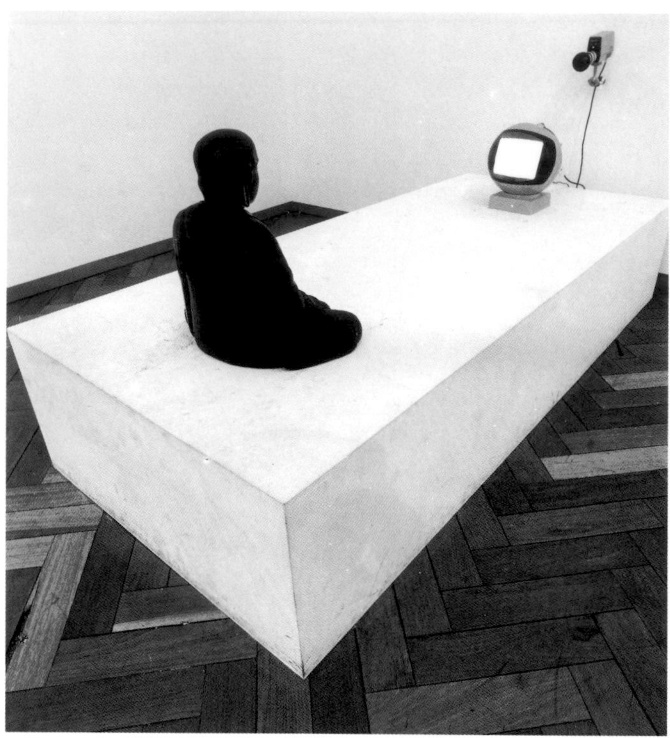

28-10. Nam June Paik. *TV Buddha*. 1974. Video installation with statue. Stedelijk Museum, Amsterdam

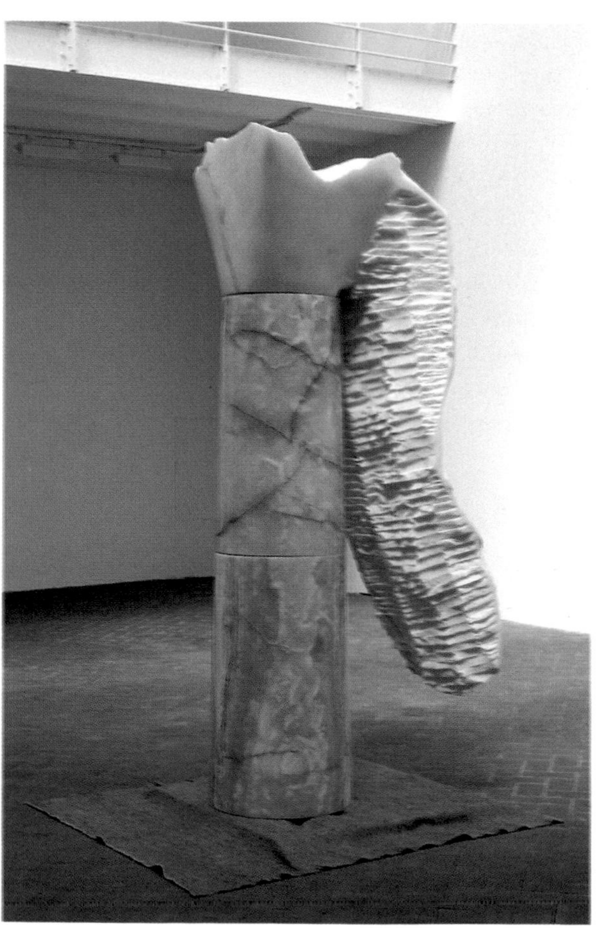

28-9. Luciano Fabro. *The Birth of Venus*. 1992.
Onyx and marble, 8'7½" x 2'3½" x 3'10" (2.63 x 0.70 x 1.18 m).
Courtesy of Galerie Durand-Dessert, Paris

PAIK. Sculpture today descends mainly from the work of Joseph Beuys, who, with Andy Warhol and John Baldessari, was the patron saint of Postmodern art (see pages 860 and 829). The notes and photographs that document Beuys' performances and installations hardly do them justice. His chief legacy today lies perhaps in the stimulation he provided his many students and collaborators. Among them was Nam June Paik (b. 1932). The sophisticated video displays of the Korean-born Paik fall outside the scope of this book. Nevertheless, his installation with a Buddha contemplating himself on television (fig. 28-10) is a memorable image that is uniquely appropriate to the Information Age, when the fascination with electronic media has replaced transcendent spirituality as the focus of life.

INSTALLATIONS. Installations have become the focal point of postmodernism. They are the epitome of the deconstructionist idea of the world as "text." Because their intent can never be fully known even by its author, "readers" are free to interpret them in light of their own experience (see Postscript). The installation artist creates a separate world that is a self-contained universe, at once alien and familiar. Left to their own devices to wander this microcosm, viewers bring their own understanding to bear on the experience in the form of memories that are evoked by the novel environment. In effect, they help to write the "text." In themselves, installations are empty vessels. They may contain anything that the "author" and "reader" wish to put into them. Hence they serve as ready vehicles for expressing social, political, or personal concerns, especially those that satisfy the postmodern agenda. The installation as text can also become deliberately literal: it is often linked to a written text that makes the program explicit.

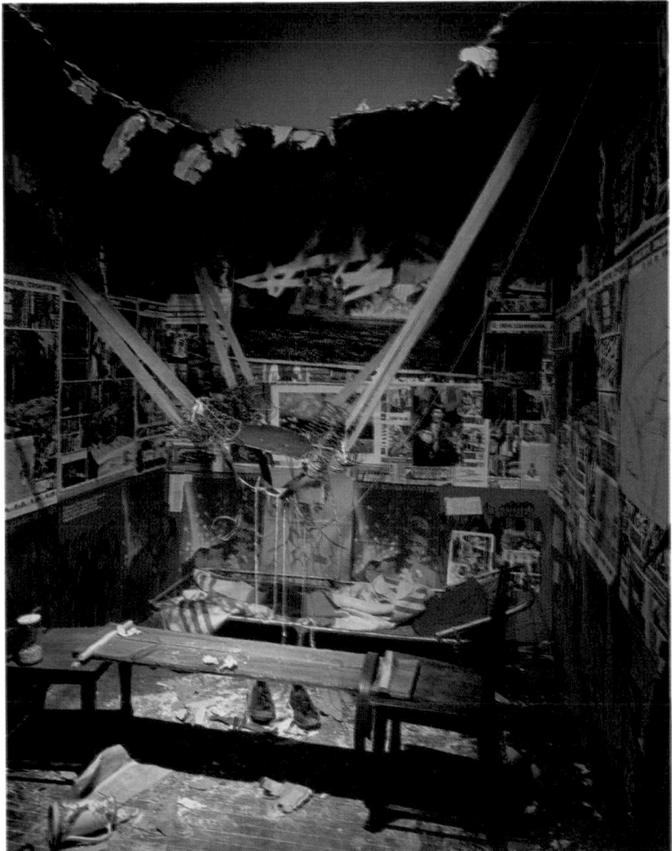

28-11. Ilya Kabakov. *The Man Who Flew into Space from His Apartment,* from *Ten Characters.* 1981–88. Mixed-media installation at Ronald Feldman Fine Arts, New York, 1988

COURTESY RONALD FELDMAN FINE ARTS

KABAKOV. Russian artists have a special genius for installations. Cut off for decades from contemporary art in the West, they developed mostly provincial forms of painting and sculpture. Yet that very isolation allowed them to create a unique brand of Conceptual Art that in turn provided the foundation for their installations. The first to gain international acclaim was Ilya Kabakov (b. 1933), who now lives in New York. *Ten Characters* was a suite of rooms like those of a seedy communal apartment, each inhabited by an imaginary person with an "unusual idea, one all-absorbing passion belonging to him alone." The most spectacular cubicle was *The Man Who Flew into Space from His Apartment* (fig. 28-11). He achieved his dream of flying into space by being hurled from a catapult suspended by springs while the ceiling and roof are blown off at the precise moment of launching. Like the other rooms, it was accompanied by a dark text worthy of Fyodor Dostoyevsky, reflecting the Russian talent for storytelling. The installation was more than an elaborate realization of this bizarre fantasy. The extravagant clutter was a bitter commentary on the peculiar dilemmas of life in the former Soviet Union—its tawdry reality, its broken dreams, the pervasive role of central authority.

HAMILTON. Kabakov was inspired in part by the example of Beuys, who was also an influence on the American installation artist Ann Hamilton (b. 1956). Her work is about loss, be it from personal tragedy or distortion of a natural relationship. Unlike Beuys, she seeks only to raise issues, not to resolve them, a matter that is left to the visitor. Yet she uses many of the same means. Her installations involve all of the senses through the use of unusual materials, often in disturbing ways, in order to present a paradox that lies at the center of each work. She exercises these choices through a train of free association until the idea crystallizes. Her installations are labor-intensive—obsessively, even ritualistically, so. Thus *parallel lines* for the 1991 São Paulo Bienal (figs. 28-12 and 28-13) began with assistants coating the walls of one gallery with soot from burning candles, then attaching sequentially numbered copper tags to the floor. (This interest in seriality is also basic to Conceptual Art.) Finally, a huge bundle of candles was placed in the room so as to dominate it. A second room, covered entirely in the same copper tags, held nothing but two glass library cases containing turkey carcasses that were slowly devoured by beetles. This assault on the viewer's senses and awareness was intended to pose a number of questions. What is collected, why, and by whom? What is the moral difference between showing candles made by people from the fat of dead animals and exhibiting a dead bird with beetles carrying out their natural role as scavengers? Although death was treated matter-of-factly, there was a strangely mournful air to the entire installation, which invited viewers to think about these matters and to arrive at their own conclusions.

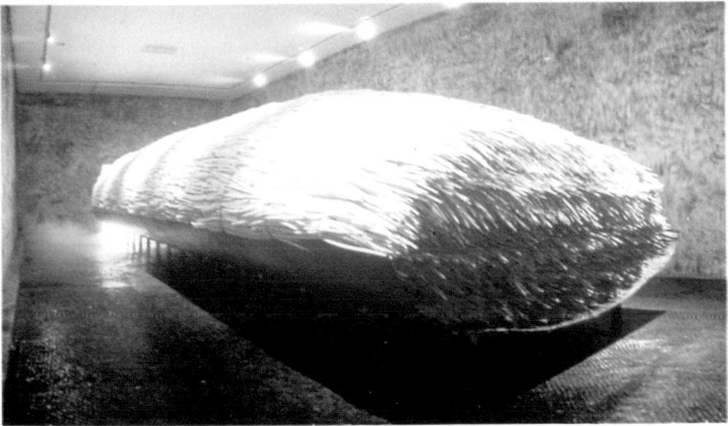

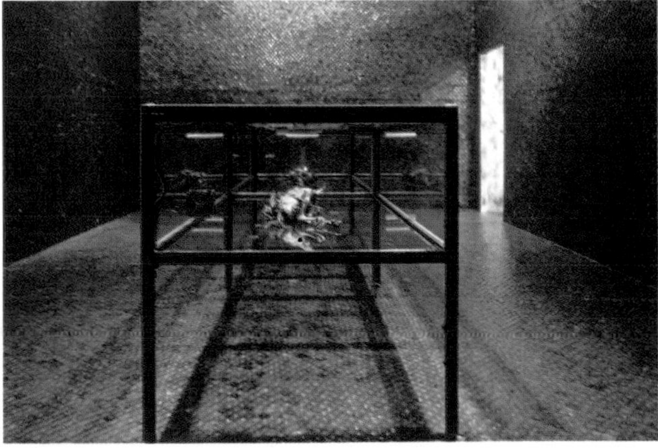

28-12 and 28-13. Ann Hamilton. *parallel lines.* Two parts of an installation in two rooms, São Paulo Bienal, September–December 1991. Mixed media

COURTESY RICHARD ROSS

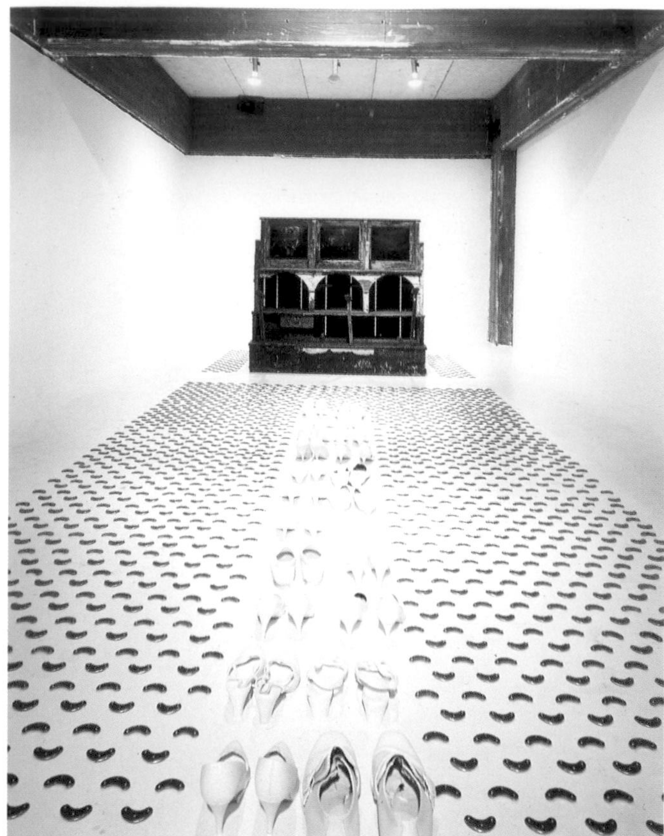

28-14. Mildred Howard. *Tap: Investigation of Memory*. 1989. Traveler shoe taps, an antique three-seat shoeshine stand, assorted painted shoes, and delayed playback of an ambient sound, 10' x 13'6" x 51'6" (3 x 4 x 15.5 m). Collection the artist

COURTESY GALLERY PAULE ANGLIM, SAN FRANCISCO

HOWARD. Mildred Howard (b. 1945) uses many of the same principles as Hamilton but constructs her installations as specifically African-American statements. She is a social activist who sometimes mounts her installations in storefronts and other locations within the black community. Howard draws chiefly on her own life to define the black experience. To her, memory is both individual and ethnic. Thus *Tap: Investigation of Memory* (fig. 28-14) has multiple layers of personal and cultural meaning. It celebrates the importance of this dance form to the artist's family during her childhood, as well as the special contribution African Americans have made to it. The taps, labeled "Traveler," significantly enough, are lined up ritualistically in rows, with shoes leading in solemn procession down the center aisle to a beat-up shoeshine stand that becomes an altar. The spiritual references are intentional. Movement is closely identified in Howard's mind with African-American worship—especially as practiced in storefront churches, the subject of another of her installations—in contrast to the somber introspection traditional to Western churches. Yet *Tap* succeeds precisely because of its contemplative atmosphere, which evokes a broad range of associations.

OSORIO. Another artist who believes in taking his art directly to the community is Pepón Osorio (b. 1955). A native of Puerto Rico who resides in New York City, he has used taxicabs literally as vehicles for mobile installations of urban Latino culture. *Badge of Honor* (fig. 28-15) was the result of a rare collaboration: it was placed first in downtown Newark, then at the Newark Museum, which originally commissioned it, in order to blur the traditional distinction between life and art. The installation consisted of two

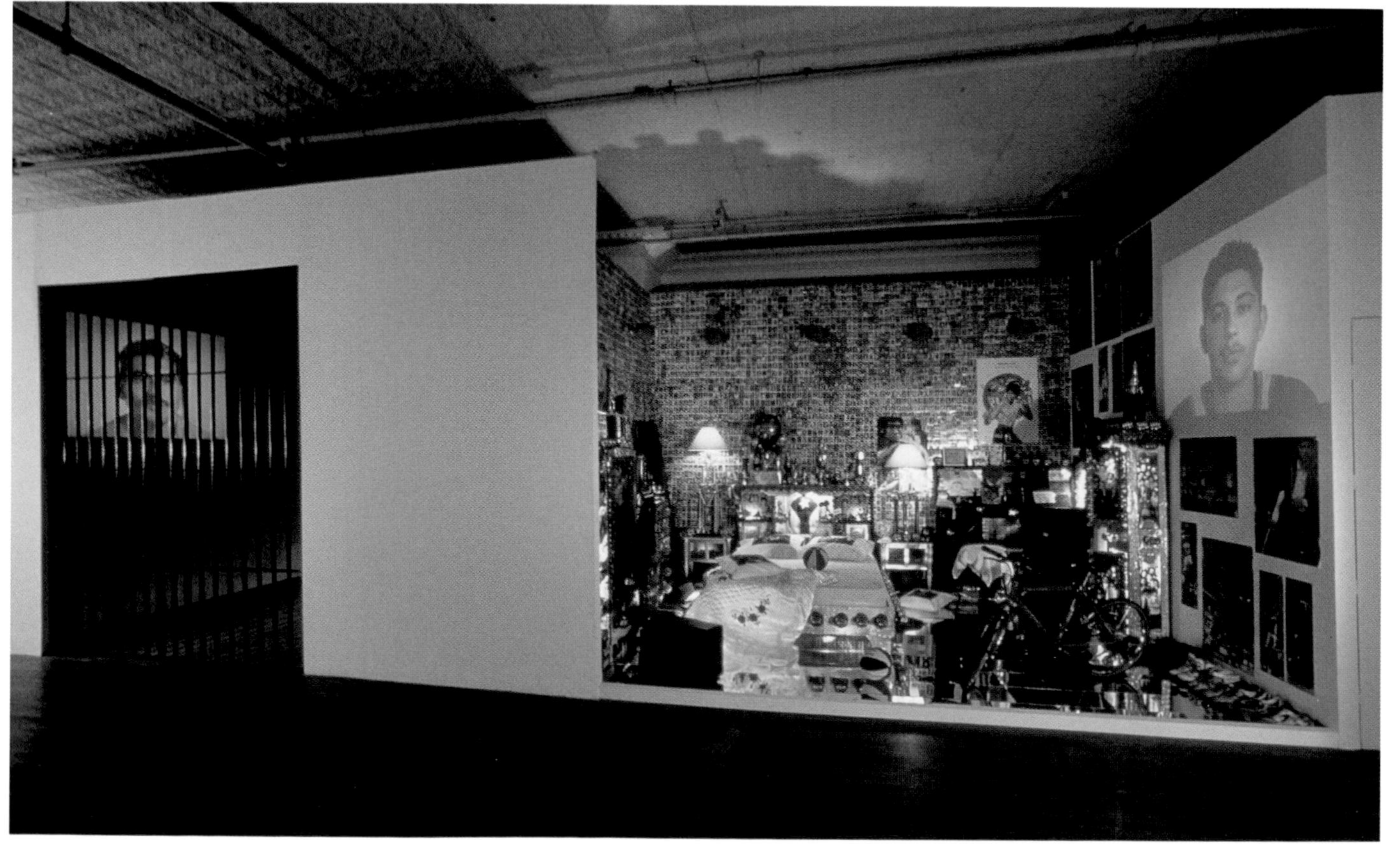

28-15. Pepón Osorio. *Badge of Honor*. 1995. Installation view at Ronald Feldman Fine Arts, New York, April 25–June 1, 1996, 12' x 26'10" x 12' (3.65 x 8.17 x 3.65 m)

COURTESY RONALD FELDMAN FINE ARTS, NEW YORK

adjoining chambers, one a stark jail cell, the other a typical teenage boy's room whose garishness reflects the American Dream and the Baroque opulence that is part of the Latin heritage. These theatrically treated spaces formed the setting for a dialog projected on opposite walls between a man in prison and his son. Although imaginary, the conversation drew on Osorio's experience as a social worker. Rather than seeming contrived, it managed to bridge the gap between father and son by expressing their feelings with convincing honesty. In the process, the stark contrast between the two rooms disappeared as well. Both emerged as empty because of the tear in the fabric of the family, yet rich because of the strong bond between the boy and his father. The impact on viewers was overwhelming. The installation addressed a serious social problem that affects many minority families. Yet it did so with a dignity made all the more compelling by Osorio's artistry, which was unerring in its appeal to his audience.

PAINTING

Painting, like sculpture, is a traditional medium that does not lend itself well to postmodernism. Indeed, it is arguable that most of what passes as postmodern painting is really late modernism in disguise; in any event, there is no fixed boundary between the two. To the extent that it can be said to exist at all, however, postmodern painting is an outgrowth of Conceptualism, Pop Art, and Neo-Expressionism. Yet it differs from them in a fundamental respect. Now painting acts like a deconstructed text gutted of all significance, except for whatever we choose to add through free association from our own experience.

How did painting come to be so barren? Traditional approaches such as allegory require a shared culture. However, this is hardly possible in the postmodern age because our civilization is more fractured than ever, despite the concept of the "global village." Deconstruction, moreover, proclaims the death of the author and subject matter as unnecessary remnants of humanism, thus rendering meaning null and void. It argues instead that representation in its broadest sense is both unnecessary and undesirable on the grounds that it strives to re-create a fraudulent reality and therefore can never provide an authentic experience. Such an attitude is not confined to deconstruction, however. It is inherent in postmodernism as a whole.

PENCK. A group of postmodern artists from the former German Democratic Republic have helped to make Germany the leading school of painting in the West today. Perhaps the most interesting among them is A. R. Penck (b. 1939). Penck is the pseudonym adopted by Ralf Winkler and is the name of a famous geologist whose specialty was the Ice Age. Before emigrating to the West in 1980, the artist lived in East Germany throughout most of the Cold War, a political "ice age" of its own. The "primitive" and "childish" quality in *The Demon of Curiosity* (fig. 28-16), with its colorful directness, is deceptive. Although largely self-taught, Penck uses a fluid technique that is, in fact, very sophisticated. But what are we to make of the picture's content? At first glance, it seems as bewildering as the rock engraving at the Cave of Addaura (see fig. 1-5). Upon closer inspection we realize that the artist's "code" can be broken, at least enough for us to understand the basic intent. The demon, as fierce as anything conjured up by Gauguin (compare fig. 23-13), is surmounted by a bird looking both ways that signifies inquisitiveness, to which the small crucified figure at the left has been sacrificed. The figures swim in a sea of hexlike signs, letters, and numbers, symbolizing knowledge, which fills up the man to the point where he seems literally "pregnant (or at least bloated) with meaning." The painting reflects Penck's fascination with cybernetics, the science of information systems. To him the artist is a kind of scientist, and he sees little difference between the two.

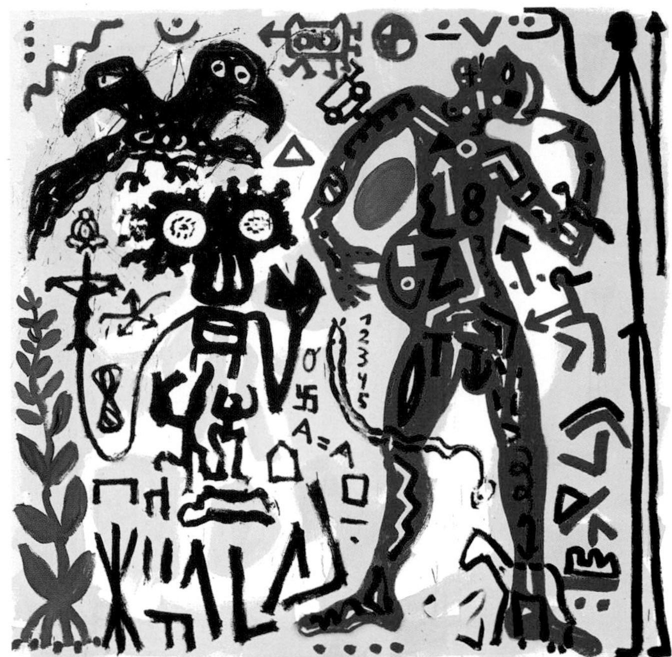

28-16. A. R. Penck. *The Demon of Curiosity.* 1982. Acrylic on canvas, 9'2¼" x 9'2¼" (2.8 x 2.8 m). The Rivendell Collection of Late-Twentieth-Century Art on permanent loan to the Center for Curatorial Studies, Bard College, Annandale-on-Hudson, New York

COURTESY MICHAEL WERNER GALLERY, NEW YORK AND COLOGNE

TANSEY. If Penck follows in the footsteps of artists such as Paul Klee by inventing a personal form of pictographs, Mark Tansey (b. 1949) uses the Roman alphabet to accomplish the seemingly impossible. He constructs representational images that are literally made up of texts following the principles of deconstruction. *Derrida Queries De Man* (fig. 28-17) shows the founder of deconstruction with his chief American disciple, Paul de Man. If we look closely, we see that the landscape is made up of typeset lines that merge to form the steep cliffs. Here the texture of the paint bridges the gap between text and illustration by embedding the idea within the image. In this sense, the painting functions as an illustration of a metaphor. But what is it saying? Certainly it makes a serious point about the relation between content, picture, and reality. Yet it does so with surprising wit, beginning with the very idea of building a painting out of words. And, in a gesture of supreme irony, Tansey has appropriated the image from a famous illustration showing the death of the fictional detective Sherlock Holmes at the hands of his archenemy, Professor Moriarty! We

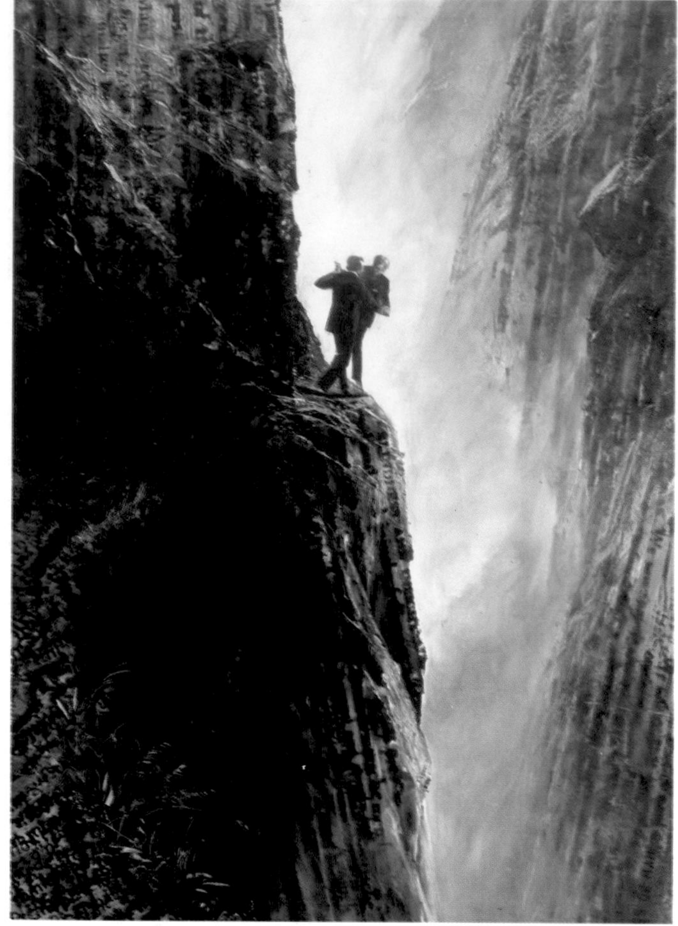

28-17. Mark Tansey. *Derrida Queries De Man*. 1990. Oil on canvas, 6'11" x 4'7" (2.13 x 1.4 m). Collection Michael and Judy Ovitz, Los Angeles

COURTESY CURT MARCUS GALLERY, NEW YORK

have seen such humor before, in the work of René Magritte (see fig. 24-43), who was an early inspiration for Tansey. By preventing a literal reading of the painting, this astonishing juxtaposition opens up new lines of questioning for the viewer that can never be fully resolved.

PHOTOGRAPHY

Photography, too, has taken up the theme of image as "text." Given the close association of words and photographs in Conceptual Art, such a move was inevitable. It was aided, however, by the new importance attached to semiotics, which has opened up fruitful new avenues of investigation for the artist. How do signs acquire public meaning? What is the message? Who originates it? What (and whose) purpose does it serve? Who is the audience? What are the means of spreading the idea? Who controls the media?

Photographers, especially in the United States, raise these questions in order to challenge our assumptions about the world we live in and the social order it imposes. Unlike Joanne Leonard or David Hockney, postmodern photographers are "re-photographers," who for the most part do not take their own pictures but appropriate them from other mediums. To convey their message, these new Conceptualists often follow the formula established by Baldessari of placing image and text side by side (compare fig. 25-43). Sometimes their pictures are intended as counterparts to paintings and are enlarged on an unprecedented scale, using commercial processes developed for advertisements, which may also serve as sources. Here it is the choice of image that matters, since the act of singling it out and changing its location to a gallery wall constitutes the comment. In both cases, however, we are asked to base our judgment on the message. The means of delivery deliberately shows so little individuality that it is often impossible to tell the work of one artist from another. In the process, however, the message often becomes equally forgettable.

KRUGER. That is not a problem with Barbara Kruger (b. 1945), whose pictures are instantly recognizable for their confrontational approach. Her work is like a sharp blow to the solar plexus: the message is direct, the response immediate, especially the first time around. *You Are a Captive Audience* (fig. 28-18) illustrates her style. It usually involves a tightly cropped close-up in black and white taken from a magazine or newspaper. It is further blown up as crudely as possible to monumental proportions, so that the viewer cannot escape its presence or the message, which is stenciled in white letters against a red background. As in our example, the joining of unrelated text and image is clearly intended for radical ends. The challenging statement is meant to provoke acute anxiety by playing on people's latent fears in our society of being controlled by nameless forces, especially such large, impersonal power centers as the government, the military, or corporations.

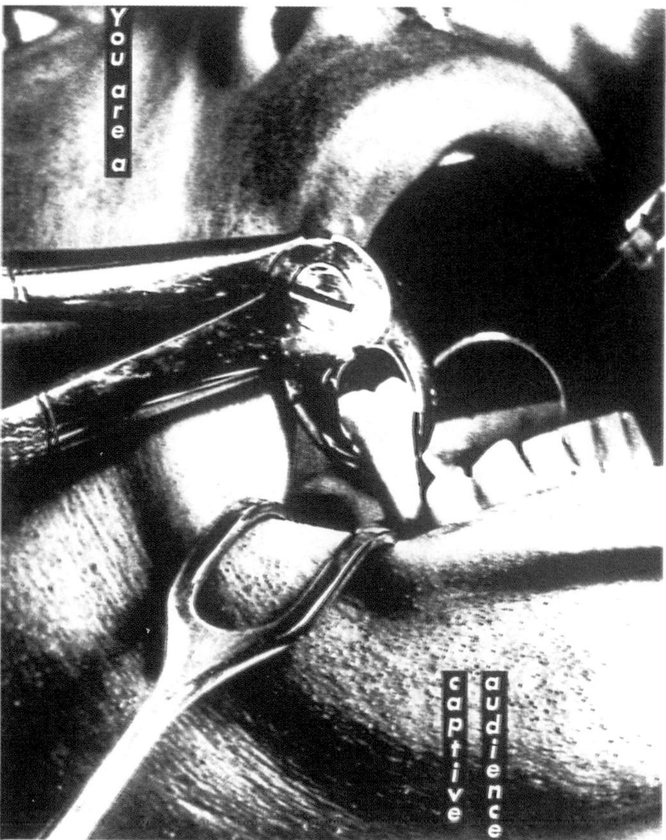

28-18. Barbara Kruger. *You Are a Captive Audience*. 1983. Gelatin-silver print, 48 x 37 3/4" (122 x 96 cm)

COURTESY THE ARTIST AND ANNINA NOSEI GALLERY, NEW YORK

POSTMODERNISM IN MUSIC AND THEATER

It is hardly possible to discuss postmodernism in music, which to date has not yielded significant results on matters of appropriation and deconstruction. The closest it has come to is Minimalism. The composer Lukas Foss (b. 1922) who has been practicing a form of Minimalism since the late 1970s, describes his *Quintets for Orchestra* (1979) in terms very similar to deconstruction: "A five-note chord dominates the composition. It is endlessly repeated, varied, permutated, transposed, and inverted, invading the entire piece... like a wound." Theater, by contrast, is ideally suited to appropriation and deconstruction, especially the latter, since it readily permits viewers to participate actively in creating the text as they perceive it. The main tendency has been to reinterpret existing classics, as well as works of recent vintage, in extremely untraditional ways that challenge conventional ("received") ideas about their content and meaning. Such is the case with the Romanian director Andrei Serban (b. 1943), who was strongly affected by Peter Brook (b. 1925); Peter Sellars (b. 1957), former director of the American National Theater at the Kennedy Center in Washington, D.C.; Les Breuer (b. 1937), director of the Mabou Mines company, who was influenced by Beckett, Brecht, and Grotowski, among others; and Robert Wilson (b. 1942), who worked with Philip Glass and the choreographers Andrew de Groat and Lucinda Childs on *Einstein on the Beach* (1976). Wilson's own works, stemming from his collaboration with the autistic teenager Christopher Knowles, juxtapose elements of different cultures and media in surreal fashion. Perhaps the most important contribution has been made by the Environmental Theater of Richard Schechner (b. 1934), who conceives of theater as a public event that can take place in any environment and assigns an active role to the audience. Every element of theater becomes independent of text—indeed, there need not be any text at all. None of these ideas is new in itself. Rather, it is the combination that matters.

SHERMAN. Not all postmodern photography is attached to words nor is it taken from other sources. A curious in-between case is provided by Cindy Sherman (b. 1954). [See Primary Sources, no. 104, page 943.] Among her best works are the early photographs that were staged in imitation of old movie stills. They are so skillful that they look like the real thing. In them she fulfills the secret American dream of being star, caster, set designer, producer, and photographer all in one, except that she does so almost vicariously. As her own star, she can play any role she wants, and the choice is illuminating. Figure 28-19 shows her preference for 1940s and 1950s movies portraying beautiful women as vulnerable heroines. The picture is a perfect period piece, down to the last detail of costume, setting, and lighting. Only after we have looked at it for a while do we realize that the photograph raises intriguing questions about the image of women projected on the silver screen. Whether the message is feminist has been the subject of considerable debate. Is Sherman's use of herself merely an exercise in narcissism and her reliance on stereotypes no more than an example of shallow consumerism? Or is there a feminist sense of irony in her posing? However we choose to interpret it, the photograph is strangely affecting in its aura of nostalgia and the sense of mystery it communicates. Here the timeless image of the woman looking in the mirror is updated to one of its most provocative—and puzzling—expressions ever. Sherman offers voyeurism at second hand, so to speak, a fantasy compounded that forever precludes authentic experience. In that sense, it is a paradigm of postmodernism.

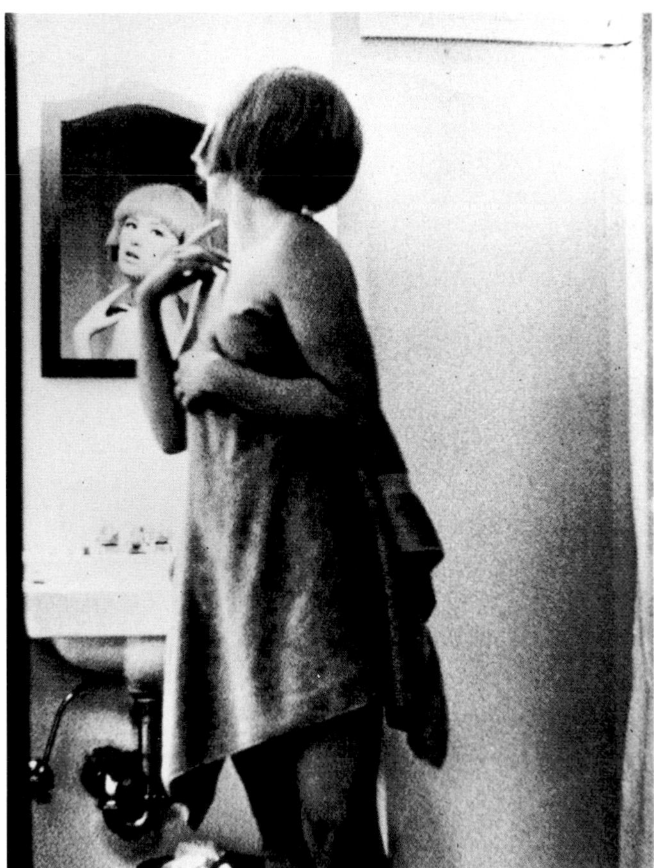

28-19. Cindy Sherman. *Untitled Film Still #2*. 1977. Photograph, 18 x 10" (45.5 x 25.5 cm)

COURTESY METRO PICTURES, NEW YORK

POSTSCRIPT: POSTMODERN THEORY

SEMIOTICS. Semiotics (the study of signs) may be regarded ultimately as a branch of philosophy. Its foundations lie in ancient philosophy, as well as medieval theology, and its modern form is a direct outgrowth of Enlightenment rationalism. Moreover, the American school of semiotics was founded by a philosopher, Charles Sanders Pierce. Despite its seemingly endless diversity, semiotics retains some key features of all philosophical systems. It seeks a universal understanding, and its theoretical constructs frequently follow classical examples. It typically acts as a closed body of ideas, one that is concerned primarily with its inner logic, rather than presenting a body of knowledge.

In essence, semiotics provides a stimulating approach to the age-old riddle, What does the mind know, and how does it know it? In an ultimate sense, the mind is elusive. To a Buddhist, for example, the mind cannot grasp itself, since it lacks physical substance and is ever-changing; hence it also has an almost endless capacity for self-delusion. Like most closed systems, semiotics generally assumes that the mind can know only itself through the concepts it builds. These act as filters through which all experience, internal as well as external, is interpreted. Semiotics is therefore little concerned with objective reality—if it exists at all—since it remains inherently unknowable and meaningless in itself. Some semiologists, however, postulate meaning stemming from God or some form of pure Idea.

Modern semiotics begins with the linguist Ferdinand de Saussure (1857–1913). Like many revolutionary intellectuals, he came late in life to rebel against the very ideas he had devoted much of his career to—in his case, philology, the study of language. His contribution lay in the intuitive realization that language cannot be explained simply in terms of its development because it always functions as a coherent system. For the dynamic (diachronic) paradigm of philology he substituted a static (synchronic) model. At the center of Saussure's system is his definition of a sign as consisting of a concept (signified) and its sound-image (signifier), which is a purely mental impression, not the sound itself. Identity is defined purely by difference, a philosophically suspect approach. Most identities are binary oppositions (for example, good and evil), built up into larger structures of increasing complexity. As against traditional grammar, meaning is determined by structure and the relationships it imposes. Thus context becomes critical to understanding. Saussure further distinguished between the everyday speech of the individual (*parole*) and language as a socially shared linguistic system (*langue*). Because there are no concrete objects in language, external reality has no place in his analysis—it is simply assumed to lie parallel to, or else to be unknowable outside of, *langue*. The problem with Saussure's semiology is that it proves incapable of dealing with language as an evolving system, which requires a more organic model, and thus with time in general, both as past and as future.

Semiotics constitutes a form of system analysis that in principle can be applied to almost anything. (Saussure's theories, for example, are comparable to those of Talcott Parsons in sociology; both are indebted partly to the sociologist Émile Durkheim.) What counts is the coherence of the theory itself, not its basis in reality, which, as we have seen, is considered of secondary importance at best. Data are merely the point of departure for constructing the conceptual model, thus raising the question whether it has any relevance to real life. Semiotics does have relevance insofar as it attempts to understand how people make meaning of the world around them. This model nevertheless suggests the main weakness of the structuralist approach to semiology: if the structure is undermined, then its related concepts are deprived of meaning, which is only an abstraction without independent existence. Logically the result must inevitably be chaos, an important point that we shall soon return to. We may nevertheless wonder whether this is necessarily so in actual fact.

In most cases, the relationship between sign and meaning is extremely complex. In human society it is arbitrary at face value and assigned as a matter of convention. Otherwise most symbols could not possibly be understood and would remain entirely private. A familiar instance from everyday life is traffic signs. We find the same thing, only on a more elaborate level, in the study of iconography—for example, the flowers in the *Mérode Altarpiece* (fig. 15-1). Semiotics can help us better understand how such symbols function and acquire their meaning. Like most bodies of theory, however, semiotics is encumbered by a torturous thought process and obtuse terminology. Even granting the inadequacy of normal language to express the formal rhetoric of intellectual disciplines, it functions as a needlessly complex code system. Like the jargon of street gangs and other self-appointed "in-groups," it is deliberately accessible only to "those in the know." The same critique may be taken to apply to the role of semiotics in contemporary art and art history.

DECONSTRUCTION. The assault on structuralist semiology that was begun in the late 1960s by the French philosopher Jacques Derrida (b. 1930) soon blossomed into a wholesale war on traditional learning in all fields. Similar controversies have raged in philosophy before. The antecedents of deconstruction can be traced back to medieval Scholasticism, both the nominalism of thinkers such as William of Ockham, which rejected universals, and supposition theory, in which context determines meaning. In fact, virtually all of its lines of argumentation are to be found in the catalogue of Scholasticism's infamous errors in logic, which are familiar to every student of philosophy. More intriguing still is the relation to music of the fourteenth century, which featured tropes (added pieces of texts and music), as well as suspensions and ambiguities of rhythm, that exactly parallel Derrida's usage. Deconstruction nonetheless has a peculiar flavor that is specifically postmodern.

Derrida considered the structuralist approach to be inadequate to explain the human condition, which he investigated by exploring his own consciousness. As we have seen, Saussure's semiotics contains the seeds of its own destruction. To Derrida, language is a structure to be dismantled. Against the structuralists, he asserted the primacy of the written word over the spoken, which it at first supplements, then supplants. Since all cultural products are texts in the sense of documents, everything—history, life itself—becomes a text. However, texts never mean what they seem to say because sign and meaning are entirely separate. This contradicts the fundamental assumption of all semiotics; yet it is a possibility that semiotics itself allows because of the arbitrary relation between sign and meaning in the first place. Thus, deconstructionists argue, texts can be read in many different ways.

In deconstruction theory, everything is intertextual; that is, it is dependent on everything else, to the point where no trait can be isolated and no order or causality can exist. Furthermore, any term ("supplement") can be substituted for any other, so that it can pass for the original one, which it "infects" from inside. Because terms are free to recombine, no element can be a self-sufficient sign; rather, it must refer to another one that is not present. This gives the reader a new latitude to create his or her own meaning by mixing fragments of text and varying their context, regardless of the author's intent, which can never be truly determined anyway. Language thus becomes "meaning-less," and truth a mere linguistic convention that implies an author and a subject, both of which deconstruction also rejects as fixed or stable. Indeed, the reader becomes as much the author as the original writer. Much the same role has been assigned to the viewer of a work of art.

Deconstruction is adamantly against all forms of logocentrism (the belief that there are abstract truths that have a basis in reality), which is seen as an instrument of ethnocentrism (the belief that one's own culture is superior to others). It also rejects standard binary oppositions like good versus evil. To undermine such beliefs, it seeks out words that have multiple, even contradictory, meanings that are "undecidables," although these in turn sometimes become binary oppositions themselves!

Deconstruction relies on exceptions to disprove a principle. By focusing on weak points around the fringes where everything can be doubted and become unknowable, it creates an unending series of questions that cannot be answered. In addition to using obscure terms, a favorite technique of deconstruction is to invent new words ("neologisms") that combine bits of old ones to create unusual, often illogical meanings. A case in point is "différance," which compounds "to differ" and "to defer" to produce an "undecidable" by "suspending" between the two. Différance in this sense requires uniqueness of parts rather than coherence of whole. It ostensibly means the implicit reference to other "texts" which change or postpone indefinitely the meaning of the original one. This slippery concept of time exploits, we will recall, an intrinsic limitation of structuralism, which is turned against itself.

As this outline suggests, deconstruction is subversive in its methodology. By destabilizing time and, with it, meaning, suspending permits deconstructionists to change the rules at will to suit their purpose, which is ultimately to overturn the structure of language in order to subvert logical thought. Not only does it go against all the accepted laws of reason, it disallows all exceptions or criticisms. It furthermore utilizes (and openly advocates) the deliberate misuse of terms, inappropriate synonyms, willful misquotes, irrational positions, extreme interpretations, and even personal attacks against its opponents.

To a deconstructionist, texts, not facts, are what count. Reality is at best a mental construct whose apparent meaning is determined by context (as opposed to structure). As a result, everything becomes ultimately unknowable—including one's own feelings, even though the individual is left to arrive at a purely subjective understanding. Hence every understanding or interpretation is not only open to question but also inherently false. Deconstruction denies the priority of any viewpoint but implicitly holds its own above all others. It conveniently ignores the fact that despite its relativism, even deconstruction cannot fully escape the inherent authoritarianism of language, which creates its own logic structures. Moreover, it rarely, if ever, deconstructs its own texts, for it claims to be a "logic beyond all forms of reason."

Needless to say, deconstruction has provoked a storm of outrage from traditional intellectuals because it questions the primacy of logic in Western culture while refusing to offer any definitive alternatives. It has been condemned as everything from irrational sophistry and contrived obscurantism to arid nihilism. Nevertheless deconstruction has had an extraordinary impact on contemporary thought and remains a fascinating historical phenomenon. Of all the critiques mounted against deconstruction, perhaps the most telling is its predictability. Once its unwritten rules are understood, the game is actually quite simple to play. In turn, it is surprisingly easy to anticipate each step that will follow from the opening proposition in a deconstructionist text. As a result, clever parodies of deconstruction are often virtually indistinguishable from serious writings.

Primary Sources for Part Four

The following is a selection of excerpts from original texts by writers, critics, artists, architects, and photographers from the late eighteenth to the twentieth centuries. These readings supplement the main text and are keyed to it. Full citations are given in the Credits section at the end of the book.

62

JOHANN JOACHIM WINCKELMANN (1717–1768)

From *Thoughts on the Imitation of Greek Works in Painting and Sculpture*

Winckelmann's influential publications on classical antiquities, including Thoughts . . . *(1755) and the* History of Ancient Art *(1764), laid the foundation for modern scientific archaeology.*

To take the ancients for models is our only way to become great. . . . Their masterpieces reveal not only nature in its greatest beauty, but . . . certain ideal beauties of nature which . . . exist only in the intellect.

The most beautiful bodies found among us today might, perhaps not be more similar to the Greek bodies than Iphicles was to Hercules, his brother. . . . Take a young Spartan, bred, by a hero and heroine, never bound by swaddling clothes, who has slept on the bare ground from the age of seven and has been trained in wrestling and swimming from earliest infancy; put him beside a young Sybarite of our day and then decide which one the artist would choose as a model for a youthful Theseus. . . .

Through these exercises the bodies, free from superfluous fat, acquired the noble and manly contours that the Greek masters gave to their statues. . . . Everything that disfigured the body was carefully avoided; Alcibiades refused to play the flute in his youth because it might distort his face. . . . Furthermore, the clothing of the Greeks was so designed as not to interfere with the natural growth of the body, while today our tight and binding dress makes the natural beauty of our bodies suffer, especially at the neck, waist, and thighs. Even the fair sex of the Greeks refused any restricting fashions. . . .

The school of the artist was the gymnasium, where the youths, ordinarily clothed because of modesty, exercised quite naked. It was the gathering place of philosophers as well as artists: Socrates visited it to teach Charmides, Artolycus and Lysis; Phidias went there to enrich his art with these magnificent figures. There one learned the movement of muscles, and studied the contours of the body. . . . The most beautiful aspects of the nude revealed themselves here in many varied and noble poses unattainable by hired models such as are used in our academies. . . .

These frequent opportunities for observing nature caused the Greek artists to go even further: they began to form general concepts of beauty for the individual parts of the body as well as for its proportions: concepts that were meant to rise above nature, being taken from a spiritual realm that existed only in the mind.

In this way Raphael formed his Galathea. As he says in his letter to Count Balthasar Castiglione, "Since beauty is rare among women, I follow a certain idea formed in my imagination. . . ."

The imitation of natural beauty either focuses upon a single model or it collects data from many models and combines them. The first produces a faithful copy, a portrait; it leads to the shapes and figures of Dutch art. The second, however, leads to universal beauty and its ideal images, and this is the path taken by the Greeks.

63

DENIS DIDEROT (1713–1784)

From *Salon of 1763*, Greuze

Diderot's reviews of the biennial Salon exhibitions provided the cornerstone of art criticism in France for the next hundred years. The full title of the painting discussed below is The Paralytic Succoured by His Children, or the Fruit of a Good Education *(The Hermitage, St. Petersburg), which was subsequently acquired by Catherine II of Russia, with Diderot acting as intermediary.*

Now here is the man for my money, this Greuze fellow. Ignoring for the moment his smaller compositions . . . I come at once to his picture *Filial Piety,* which might better have been entitled *The Reward for Providing a Good Upbringing.*

To begin with, I like this genre: it is a painting with a moral. Come, now, you must agree! Don't you think the painter's brush has been employed long enough, and too long, in the portrayal of debauchery and vice? Ought we not to be glad to see it competing at last with dramatic poetry in moving us, instructing us, correcting us, and encouraging us to virtue? Courage, Greuze, my friend: you must go on painting pictures like this one!

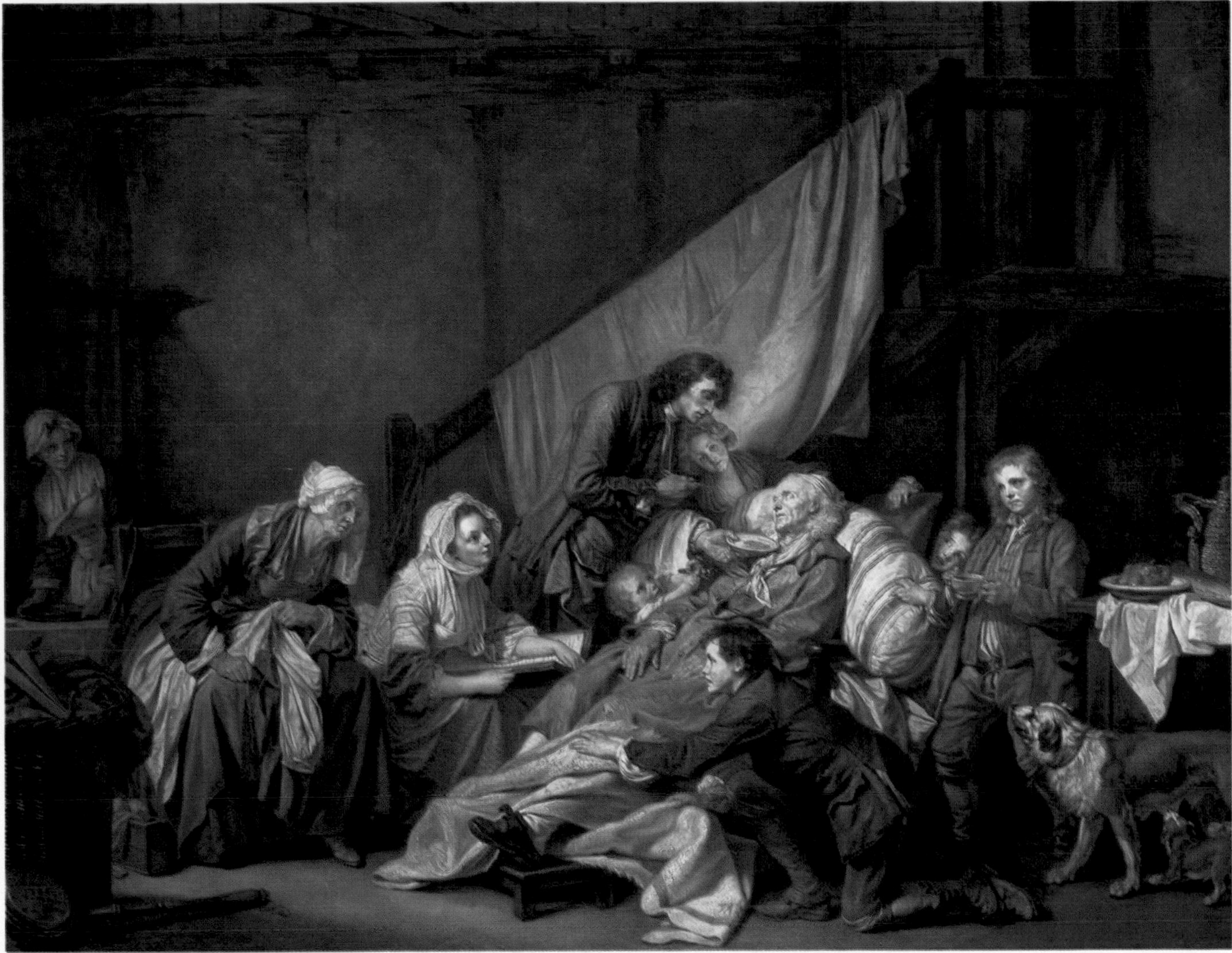

PS-63. Jean-Baptiste Greuze, *Le Paralytique,* 1763. Oil on canvas, $45^{1}/_{2}$ x $57^{7}/_{8}$" (114.4 x 146 cm). The Hermitage Museum, St. Petersburg, Russia

64

ÉTIENNE-LOUIS BOULLÉE (1728–1799)

From *Architecture, Essay on Art*

Boullée's philosophy was in the Romantic tradition of Jean-Jacques Rousseau. In this introduction to an undated manuscript, he set down his visionary ideas on architecture.

To Men Who Cultivate the Arts

Dominated by an excessive love for my profession, I have surrendered myself to it completely. But although I have yielded to this overweaning passion, I have made it a rule that I shall work for the benefit of society and thus merit public esteem.

I should confess straightaway that I have refused to confine myself to the exclusive study of our ancient masters and have instead tried, through the study of Nature to broaden my ideas on my profession which, after much thought, I consider to be still in its infancy.

What little attention has been paid in the past to the poetry of architecture, which is a sure means of adding to man's enjoyment and of bestowing on artists the fame they deserve!

That is my belief. Our buildings—and our public buildings in particular—should be to some extent poems. The impression they make on us should arouse in us sensations that correspond to the function of the building in question. It seemed to me that if I was to incorporate in my Architecture all the poetry of which it was capable, then I should study the theory of volumes and analyse them, at the same time seeking to understand their properties, the power they have on our senses, their similarities to the human organism. I flattered myself that if I went back to the source of all the fine arts I should find new ideas and thus establish principles that would be all the more certain for having their source in nature.

You who are fascinated by the fine arts, surrender yourselves completely to all the pleasure that this sublime passion can procure! No other pleasure is so pure. It is this passion that makes us love to study, that transforms our pain into pleasure and, with its divine flame, forces genius to yield up its oracles. In short, it is this passion that summons us to immortality.

It is to you who cultivate the arts that I dedicate the fruits of my long vigils; to you who, with all your learning, are persuaded—and doubtless rightly so—that we must not presume that all we have left is to imitate the ancients!

65

JEAN-AUGUSTE-DOMINIQUE INGRES (1780–1867)

From "The Doctrine of Ingres"

Maurice Denis, a member of the Nabis, compiled these aphorisms from Ingres' notebooks and from the reminiscences of his students.

Art should only depict beauty. . . .

And no matter what your genius, if you paint to the last stroke not according to nature, but your model, you will always be its slave; your manner of painting will smack of servitude. The proof of the contrary is seen in Raphael. He tamed the model to such a point and possessed it so thoroughly in his memory, that instead of the model giving him orders, one would say that the model obeyed him. . . .

To form yourself in beauty, . . . walk with your head raised to the sky instead of keeping it toward the earth like pigs searching in the mud. . . .

The figures of antiquity are only beautiful because they resemble the beauty of nature. . . . And nature will always be beautiful when it resembles the beauties of antiquity. . . .

I will write on the door of my studio: School of drawing, and I will make painters.

Drawing is the probity of art. . . .

Drawing is everything; it is all of art. The material processes of painting are very easy and may be learned in eight days. . . .

There is neither correct nor incorrect drawing; there is only beautiful or ugly drawing. That is all! . . .

In front of Rubens, put on blinders like those a horse wears.

The following were assembled by Henri Delaborde in 1870 from Ingres' correspondence and studio remarks supplied by Edouard Odier and Auguste Flandrin.

There are not two kinds of art, there is only one: it is the one which is based on timeless, natural Beauty. . . .

Love truth, for in it is beauty, if you can sense and discern it. . . .

The simpler your lines and forms, the more beauty and strength they will possess. . . .

Expression in painting calls for great knowledge of drawing, for expression cannot be good if it has not been formulated with absolute exactness. . . .

Color is an ornament of painting, but it is no more than a handmaiden to it, since it does no more than render more pleasing those things which are the true perfections of art. . . .

There exists no example of a great draftsman whose colors did not exactly suite the character of his design.

66

EUGÈNE DELACROIX (1798–1863)

From his *Journal*

Delacroix began his Journal *in 1822 and maintained it irregularly until his death in 1863. He wrote it, he said, "for myself alone" in the hope that it would "do me a lot of good." The first excerpt is from an entry of May 14, 1824.*

What torments my soul is its loneliness. The more it expands among friends and the daily habits or pleasures, the more, it seems to me, it flees me and retires into its fortress. The poet who lives in solitude, but who produces much, is the one who enjoys those treasures we bear in our bosom, but which forsake us when we give ourselves to others. When one yields completely to one's soul, it opens itself completely. . . .

Novelty is in the mind that creates, and not in nature, the thing painted.

This entry, dated October 20, 1853, was recorded at Champ Rosay.

What an adoration I have for painting! The mere memory of certain pictures, even when I don't see them, goes through me with a feeling which stirs my whole being. . . .

The type of emotion peculiar to painting is, so to speak, tangible; poetry and music cannot give it. You enjoy the actual representation of objects as if you really saw them, and at the same time the meaning which the images have for the mind warms you and transports you. These figures, these objects, which seem the thing itself to a certain part of your intelligent being are like a solid bridge on which imagination supports itself to penetrate to the mysterious and profound sensation for which the forms are, so to speak, the hieroglyph, but a hieroglyph far more eloquent than a cold representation, a thing equivalent to no more than a character in the printer's font of type. . . .

The arts are not algebra, in which the abbreviation of the figures contributes to the success of the problem; success in the arts is by no means a matter of abridging, but of amplifying, if possible, and prolonging the sensation by all possible means. What is the theater? One of the most certain witnesses to man's need for experiencing the largest possible number of emotions at one time. It gathers together all the arts so that each may make us feel their combined effect more strongly.

67

ROSA BONHEUR (1822–1899)

From *Reminiscences of Rosa Bonheur*

Bonheur's father, Raymond, was a landscape painter and a disciple of the utopian socialist Henri de Saint-Simon, who considered the artist the priest of his "new Christianity" and thought the Messiah of the future would be, as Bonheur states here, a woman. These reminiscences were published in 1910.

I have never counseled my sisters of the palette to wear men's clothes in the ordinary circumstances of life.

If, however, you see me dressed as I am, it is not in the least in order to make me into an original, but simply to facilitate my work. Consider that, at a certain period in my life, I spent whole days at the slaughterhouse. . . . I also had the passion for horses. Now where better to study these animals than in the fairs. . . . I was forced to recognize that the clothing of my sex was a constant bother. That is why I decided to solicit the authorization to wear men's clothing from the prefect of police.

But the suit I wear is my work attire, and nothing else. The epithets of imbeciles have never bothered me. . . .

Two years ago (October 8, 1896) on the occasion of the reception of the Russian royalty in Paris, the minister of the fine arts had the desire to introduce to them the leading figures of French art. . . . I wore my beautiful suit of black velvet and my little feathered bonnet. . . .

From the moment I arrived at the Louvre, I would have given I do not know what to have had on my head my gray felt hat. I was the only woman, in the middle of a crowd of men. . . . All the eyes turned toward me; I didn't know where to hide myself. This was a harsh test, and that day I really missed my masculine attire, I can assure you. . . .

In spite of my metamorphosis of costume, there is no daughter of Eve who appreciates more than I the nuances; my brusque and almost savage nature never prevented my heart from always remaining perfectly feminine. . . .

Why wouldn't I be proud of being a woman? My father, that enthusiastic apostle of humanity, repeated to me many times that woman's mission was to uplift the human race, that she was the Messiah of future centuries. I owe to his doctrines the great and proud ambition that I conceived for the sex to which I take glory in belonging and whose independence I will uphold until my last day. Moreover, I am persuaded that the future belongs to us.

68

JOHN CONSTABLE (1776–1837)

From a letter to John Fisher

Fisher, the archdeacon of Salisbury Cathedral, was a lifelong friend of the artist. This letter of October 23, 1821, reflects Constable's sensitivity to the beauties of the English landscape.

How much I wish I had been with you on your fishing excursion in the New Forest! What river can it be? But the sound of water escaping from mill-dams, etc., willows, old rotten planks, slimy posts, and brickwork, I love such things. Shakespeare could make everything poetical; he tells us of poor Tom's haunts among "sheep cotes and mills." As long as I do paint, I shall never cease to paint such places. They have always been my delight, and I should indeed have been delighted in seeing what you describe, and in your company, "in the company of a man to whom nature does not spread her volume in vain." Still I should paint my own places best; painting is with me but another word for feeling, and I associate "my careless boyhood" with all that lies on the banks of the Stour; those scenes made me a painter, and I am grateful; that is, I had often thought of pictures of them before I ever touched a pencil.

69

CHARLES BAUDELAIRE (1821–1867)

"The Modern Public and Photography," from Part 2 of *The Salon of 1859*

Baudelaire, now known for his controversial poems The Flowers of Evil *(1857), was an important Parisian art critic at mid-century. The photographer Nadar was one of his close friends.*

In this country, the natural painter, like the natural poet, is almost a monster. Our exclusive taste for the true . . . oppresses and smothers the taste for the beautiful. Where only the beautiful should be looked for . . . our people look only for the true. They are not artistic, naturally artistic. . . .

In the domain of painting and statuary, the present-day credo of the worldly wise, especially in France . . . is this: I "believe in nature, and I believe only in nature. . . . I believe that art is, and can only be, the exact reproduction of nature. . . . Thus if an industrial process could give us a result identical to nature, that would be absolute art." An avenging God has heard the prayers of this multitude; Daguerre was his messiah. And then they said to themselves: "Since photography provides us with every desirable guarantee of exactitude . . . art is photography." From that moment onwards, our loathsome society rushed, like Narcissus, to contemplate its trivial image on the metallic plate. . . .

I am convinced that the badly applied advances of photography, like all purely material progress for that matter, have greatly contributed to the impoverishment of French artistic genius. . . . Poetry and progress are two ambitious men that hate each other, with an instinctive hatred, and when they meet along a pathway one or other must give way. If photography is allowed to deputize for art in some of art's activities, it will not be long before it has supplanted or corrupted art altogether, thanks to the stupidity of the masses, its natural ally. Photography must, therefore, return to its true duty, which is that of handmaid of the arts and sciences. . . . Let photography quickly enrich the traveller's album, and restore to his eyes the precision his memory may lack; let it adorn the library of the naturalist, magnify microscopic insects, even strengthen, with a few facts, the hypotheses of the astronomer; let it, in short, be the secretary and record-keeper of whomsoever needs absolute material accuracy for professional reasons. . . . But if once it be allowed to impinge on the sphere of the intangible and the imaginary, on anything that has value solely because man adds something to it from his soul, then woe betide us!

70

CHARLES BAUDELAIRE

"On the Heroism of Modern Life," from Part 18 of *The Salon of 1846*

Baudelaire thought that painters and sculptors should reject subjects drawn from history and choose those from contemporary life. His ideas influenced the work of a number of later painters, including his close friend Édouard Manet.

Before trying to distinguish the epic side of modern life, and before bringing examples to prove that our age is no less fertile in sublime themes than past ages, we may assert that since all centuries and all peoples have had their own form of beauty, so inevitably we have ours. That is in the order of things.

All forms of beauty, like all possible phenomena, contain an element of the eternal and an element of the transitory—of the absolute and of the particular. Absolute and eternal beauty does not exist, or rather it is only an abstraction skimmed from the general surface of different beauties. The particular element in each manifestation comes from the emotions: and just as we have our own particular emotions, so we have our own beauty.

. . . Is it not the necessary garb of our suffering age, which wears the symbol of a perpetual mourning even upon its thin black shoulders? Note, too, that the dress-coat and the frock-coat not only possess their political beauty, which is an expression of universal equality, but also their poetic beauty, which is an expression of the public soul—an immense cortège of undertaker's mutes. . . . We are each of us celebrating some funeral. . . .

The pageant of fashionable life and the thousands of floating existences—criminals and kept women—which drift about in the underworld of a great city . . . all prove to us that we have only to open our eyes to recognize our heroism. . . .

The life of our city is rich in poetic and marvellous subjects. We are enveloped and steeped as though in an atmosphere of the marvellous; but we do not notice it.

The *nude*—that darling of the artists, that necessary element of success—is just as frequent and necessary today as it was in the life of the ancients; in bed, for example, or in the bath, or in the anatomy theatre. The themes and resources of painting are equally abundant and varied; but there is a new element—modern beauty.

71

GUSTAVE COURBET (1819–1877)

From his letter to a group of students

A band of students who had withdrawn in protest from the state-run École des Beaux-Arts had invited Courbet to direct the alternative school they were hoping to open. In this letter dated December 25, 1861, he rejected their offer but did agree to give instruction and criticism for about a year in a rented studio, where the model was usually a peasant with a farm animal.

I do not have, and I can not have, students.

I who believe that every artist should be his own master. . . .

I can not teach my art . . . because I deny that art can be taught and because . . . I maintain that art is completely individual, and the talent of each artist is only the result of his own inspiration and his own study of tradition. . . .

Especially, art in painting can only consist of the representation of objects that are visible and tangible to the artist.

No age can be depicted except by its own artists. . . . I believe that the artists of one century are completely incompetent when it comes to depicting the objects of a preceding or future century. . . .

It is in this sense that I deny the term historical art as applied to the past. Historical art is, by its very essence, contemporary. Every age should have its artists, who will express it and depict it for the future. . . .

The true artists are those who take up their epoch at exactly the point to which it has been carried by preceding ages. To retreat is to do nothing. . . . This explains why all archaic schools have always ended by reducing themselves to the most useless compilations.

I also believe that painting is an essentially CONCRETE art and can only consist of the representation of REAL AND EXISTING objects. . . . Imagination in art consists in knowing how to find the most complete expression of an existing object, but never in imagining or in creating the object itself.

Beauty is in nature, and in reality is encountered under the most diverse forms. As soon as it is found, it belongs to art, or rather to the artist who is able to perceive it. . . . The beauty based on nature is superior to all artistic conventions.

72

LILLA CABOT PERRY (1848?–1933)

From "Reminiscences of Claude Monet from 1889 to 1909"

Perry was an American expatriate painter. Monet, a strict empiricist, had a horror of artistic theory and therefore refused to systematize his ideas on art. Perry's reminiscences, published in 1927, provide our best evidence of those ideas.

He never took any pupils, but he would have made a most inspiring master if he had been willing to teach. I remember his once saying to me:

"When you go out to paint, try to forget what objects you have before you—a tree, a house, a field, or whatever. Merely think, here is a little square of blue, here an oblong of pink, here a streak of yellow, and paint it just as it looks to you, the exact color and shape, until it gives your own naïve impression of the scene before you."

He said he wished he had been born blind and then had suddenly gained his sight so that he could have begun to paint in this way without knowing what the objects were that he saw before him. He held that the first real look at the motif was likely to be the truest and most unprejudiced one, and said that the first painting should cover as much of the canvas as possible, no matter how roughly, so as to determine at the outset the tonality of the whole. . . .

Monet's philosophy of painting was to paint what you really see, not what you think you ought to see; not the object isolated as in a test tube, but the object enveloped in sunlight and atmosphere, with the blue dome of Heaven reflected in the shadows.

73

JAMES ABBOTT MCNEILL WHISTLER (1834–1903)

From *The Gentle Art of Making Enemies*

Whistler's book, published in 1893, also contains his account of the famous libel suit he brought against the critic John Ruskin in 1878.

As music is the poetry of sound, so is painting the poetry of sight, and the subject-matter has nothing to do with harmony of sound or of colour.

The great musicians knew this. Beethoven and the rest wrote music—simply music; symphony in this key, concerto or sonata in that.

On F or G they constructed celestial harmonies . . . as combinations, evolved from the chords of F or G and their minor correlatives.

This is pure music as distinguished from airs—commonplace and vulgar in themselves, but interesting from their associations, as, for instance, "Yankee Doodle. . . ."

Art should be independent of all clap-trap—should stand alone, and appeal to the artistic sense of eye or ear, without confounding this with emotions entirely foreign to it, as devotion, pity, love, patriotism, and the like. All these have no kind of concern with it, and that is why I insist on calling my works "arrangements" and "harmonies."

Take the picture of my mother, exhibited at the Royal Academy as an "Arrangement in Grey and Black." Now that is what it is. To me it is interesting as a picture of my mother; but what can or ought the public to care about the identity of the portrait?

74

AUGUSTE RODIN (1840–1917)

From "Conversations" with Paul Gsell

The following remarks, recorded in 1911, reveal Rodin as an exponent of the unconventional idea that the beauty or ugliness of a work of art centers on its inherent "character" or "truth."

The vulgar readily imagine that what they consider ugly in existence is not fit subject for the artist. They would like to forbid us to represent what displeases and offends them in nature.

It is a great error on their part.

What is commonly called *ugliness* in nature can in art become full of great beauty.

In the domain of fact we call *ugly* whatever is deformed, whatever is unhealthy, whatever suggests the ideas of disease, of debility, or of suffering, whatever is contrary to regularity, which is the sign and condition of health and strength: a hunch-back is *ugly,* only who is bandy-legged is *ugly,* poverty in rags is *ugly*. . . .

But let a great artist or a great writer make use of one or the other of these uglinesses, instantly it is transfigured. . . .

To the great artist, everything in nature has *character*. . . . And that which is considered ugly in nature often presents more character than that which is termed beautiful, because in the contractions of a sickly countenance, in the lines of a vicious face, in all deformity, in all decay, the inner truth shines forth more clearly than in features that are regular and healthy.

And as it is solely the power of *character* which makes for beauty in art, it often happens that the uglier a being is in nature, the more beautiful it becomes in art.

There is nothing ugly in art except that which is without character, that is to say, that which offers no outer or inner truth.

Whatever is false, whatever is artificial, whatever seeks to be pretty rather than expressive, whatever is capricious and affected, whatever smiles without motive, bends or struts without cause, is mannered without reason; all that is without soul and without truth; all that is only a *parade* of beauty and grace; all, in short, that lies, is *ugliness* in art.

75

JORIS-KARL HUYSMANS (1848–1907)

From "Iron"

Huysmans, author of the radical antinaturalist novel Against the Grain *(1884), was also an important art critic in Paris at the end of the nineteenth century. The following is taken from a selection of his art criticism entitled* Certaines *(1889).*

In architecture, the situation is now this.

The architects build absurd monuments whose parts, borrowed from all ages, constitute in their ensemble the most servile parodies that one could see. . . .

One fact is certain: the age has produced no architect and is characterized by no style. . . . Another undoubted fact is that stone, considered until now the fundamental material of building, has foundered, drained by repetition. . . .

But our period may yet incarnate itself in buildings that symbolize its activity and its sadness, its cunning and its money, in works sullen and hard, in any case, new.

And the material is here named, it is iron.

Since the reign of Louis Philippe [1830–48], iron structure has been attempted many times, but . . . no new form has been discovered; the metal remains . . . linked to stone, a subordinate agent, incapable of creating by itself a monument that is not a railway station or a greenhouse, a monument that aesthetic criticism may cite. . . .

Iron's role is thus practical and limited, purely internal.

This was the state of architecture when the exposition of 1889 was resolved upon.

It is interesting to see if, in . . . the Eiffel Tower [see fig. 22-38], iron-making has come out of its gropings, and . . . has finally invented a new style. . . .

In a touching unanimity, . . . the entire press, flat on its stomach, exalts the genius of M. Eiffel.

And yet his tower resembles a factory chimney under construction, a carcass that waits to be filled with cut stone or bricks. One cannot imagine that [it] is finished, that this solitary suppository riddled with holes will remain as it is. . . .

The Eiffel Tower is truly of a disconcerting ugliness, and it is not even enormous! Seen from below, it does not seem to attain the height cited for it. . . .

From afar, from the center of Paris, from the depths of the suburbs, the effect is identical. The emptiness of this cage diminishes it; the lathing and the meshwork make of this trophy of iron a horrible bird cage. . . .

It is 300 meters tall and appears one hundred; it is finished and appears barely begun. . . .

Finally, one must ask oneself, what is the fundamental purpose for the existence of this tower?

76

PAUL CÉZANNE (1839–1906)

From a letter to Emile Bernard

Bernard had worked with Gauguin to formulate the style of the Pont-Aven school. He began a correspondence with Cézanne after meeting him at Aix-en-Provence in the spring of 1904, when this letter was written.

. . . May I repeat what I told you here: treat nature by the cylinder, the sphere, the cone, everything in proper perspective so that each side of an object or a plane is directed towards a central point. Lines parallel to the horizon give breadth, that is a section of nature or, if you prefer, of the spectacle that the Pater Omnipotens Aeterne Deus spreads out before our eyes. Lines perpendicular to this horizon give depth. But nature for us men is more depth than surface, whence the need of introducing into our light vibrations, represented by reds and yellows, a sufficient amount of blue to give the impression of air.

77

VINCENT VAN GOGH (1853–1890)

From a letter to his brother Theo

Theo, who worked for an art dealer in Paris, provided Vincent's chief emotional and economic support. This letter, dated April 30, 1885, was written from their father's house in Neunen.

I have tried to emphasize that those people, eating their potatoes in the lamplight, have dug the earth with those very hands they put in the dish, and so it speaks of manual labor, and how they have honestly earned their food [see fig. 23-10].

I have wanted to give the impression of a way of life quite different from that of us civilized people. Therefore I am not at all anxious for everyone to like it or to admire it at once. . . .

It would be wrong, I think, to give a peasant picture a certain conventional smoothness. If a peasant picture smells of bacon, smoke, potato steam—all right, that's not unhealthy; if a stable smells of dung—all right, that belongs to a stable; if the field has an odor of ripe corn or potatoes or of . . . manure—that's healthy, especially for city people.

78

VINCENT VAN GOGH

From an undated letter to Theo

I am returning to the ideas I had in the country before I knew the impressionists. And I should not be surprised if the impressionists soon find fault with my way of working, for it has been fertilized by Delacroix's ideas rather than by theirs. Because instead of trying to reproduce exactly what I see before my eyes, I use color more arbitrarily, in order to express myself forcibly. . . .

I should like to paint the portrait of an artist friend, a man who dreams great dreams, who works as the nightingale sings, because it is his nature. He'll be a blond man. I want to put my appreciation, the love I have for him, into the picture. So I paint him as he is, as faithfully as I can, to begin with.

But the picture is not yet finished. To finish it I am now going to be the arbitrary colorist. I exaggerate the fairness of the hair, I even get to orange tones, chromes and pale citron-yellow.

Behind the head, instead of painting the ordinary wall of the mean room, I paint infinity, a plain background of the richest, intensest blue that I can contrive, and by this simple combination of the bright head against the rich blue background, I get a mysterious effect, like a star in the depths of an azure sky.

79

PAUL GAUGUIN (1848–1903)

From a letter to J. F. Willumsen

The Danish painter J. F. Willumsen was a member of Gauguin's circle in Brittany. Gauguin wrote this letter in the autumn of 1890, before his departure for the South Seas.

As for me, my mind is made up. I am going soon to Tahiti, a small island in Oceania, where the material necessities of life can be had without money. I want to forget all the misfortunes of the past, I want to be free to paint without any glory whatsoever in the eyes of the others and I want to die there and to be forgotten there. . . . A terrible epoch is brewing in Europe for the coming generation: the kingdom of gold. Everything is putrefied, even men, even the arts. There, at least, under an eternally summer sky, on a marvellously fertile soil, the Tahitian has only to lift his hands to gather his food; and in addition he never works. When in Europe men and women survive only after unceasing labor during which they struggle in convulsions of cold and hunger, a prey to misery, the Tahitians, on the contrary, happy inhabitants of the unknown paradise of Oceania, know only sweetness of life. To live, for them, is to sing and to love. . . . Once my material life is well organized, I can there devote myself to great works of art, freed from all artistic jealousies and with no need whatsoever of lowly trade.

80

EDVARD MUNCH (1864–1944)

From notes on the Frieze of Life

Munch probably wrote his notes on the origin of the Frieze of Life *when it was exhibited in Oslo in 1918.*

One evening I was walking along a path—on the one side lay the city and below me the fjord.

I was tired and ill—I stopped and looked out across the fjord—the sun was setting—the clouds were dyed red like blood.

I felt a scream pass through nature; it seemed to me that I could hear the scream.

I painted this picture—painted the clouds as real blood.—The colors were screaming.—

This became the picture *The Scream* from the *Frieze of Life.*

81

LOUIS SULLIVAN (1856–1924)

From "The Tall Office Building Artistically Considered"

Sullivan had already completed several skyscrapers, including the Wainwright Building (see fig. 23-39) and the Guaranty Building, when he recorded these ideas in an essay of 1896.

The architects of this land and generation are now brought face to face with something new under the sun—namely, . . . a demand for the erection of tall office buildings. . . .

Offices are necessary for the transaction of business; the invention and perfection of the high-speed elevators make vertical travel, that was once tedious and painful, now easy and comfortable; development of steel manufacture has shown the way to safe, rigid, economical constructions rising to a great height; continued growth of population in the great cities, consequent congestion of centers and rise in value of ground, stimulate an increase in number of stories. . . . Thus has come about that form of lofty construction called the "modern office building. . . ."

Problem: How shall we impart to this sterile pile, . . . this stark, staring exclamation of eternal strife, the graciousness of those higher forms of sensibility and culture that rest on the lower and fiercer passions? . . .

What is the chief characteristic of the tall office building? . . . It is lofty. This loftiness is to the artist-nature its thrilling aspect. . . . It must be every inch a proud and soaring thing, rising in sheer exultation that from bottom to top it is a unit without a single dissenting line. . . .

Certain critics . . . have advanced the theory that the true prototype of the tall office building is the classical column, consisting of base, shaft and capital. . . .

Other theorizers, assuming a mystical symbolism as a guide, quote the many trinities in nature and art, and the beauty and conclusiveness of such trinity in unity. . . .

Others, seeking their examples and justification in the vegetable kingdom, urge that such a design shall above all things be organic. . . . They point to the pine-tree, its massy roots, its lithe, uninterrupted trunk, its tuft of green high in the air. Thus, they say, should be the design of the tall office building: again in three parts vertically.

Others still, more susceptible to the power of a unit than to the grace of a trinity, say that such a design should be struck out at a blow, as though by a blacksmith or by mighty Jove. . . .

I shall, with however much of regret, dissent from [these critics] as touching not at all upon . . . the quick of the entire matter, upon the true; the immovable philosophy of the architectural art. . . .

Unfailingly in nature [its] shapes express the inner life, the native quality, of the animal, tree, bird, fish, that they present to us; they are so characteristic, so recognizable, that we say, simply, it is "natural" it should be so. . . .

It is the pervading law of all things organic, and inorganic, . . . that form ever follows function. . . .

Shall we, then, daily violate this law in our art? . . .

Does this not . . . conclusively show that the lower one or two stories [of the tall office building] will take on a special character suited to the special needs, that the tiers of typical offices, having the same unchanging function, shall continue in the same unchanging form, and that as to the attic, . . . its function shall equally be so in force, in . . . outward expression? From this results, naturally, . . . a three-part division, not from any theory, symbol, or fancied logic.

82

GEORGIA O'KEEFFE (1887–1986)

From "Stieglitz: His Pictures Collected Him"

O'Keeffe met Alfred Stieglitz in 1908 and had her first show at his gallery in 1916. She married him in 1924. These remarks, published in 1949, were made after his death.

Stieglitz grew up during the period when photography was young, began working at it while studying mechanical engineering at the Berlin Polytechnic. . . . He soon decided to make himself an authority on photography and went about it by sending his photographs everywhere to exhibitions to get all the medals that were given in the world at that time. . . .

Although the photographs that he was making at this time were very much admired by painters and artists generally, the artists seemed to have the idea that photography could never be accepted as one of the arts. Stieglitz denied this. As he was naturally a fighter, he began to work for its recognition as one of the arts, not particularly for himself but for the idea of photography. . . . Painters would often say they wished they had painted what he had photographed. He always said he never regretted that he had not photographed what they were painting.

In 1890 Stieglitz returned to America from his European student period, twenty-six years old. Years of feverish activity with photography followed. He finally decided that for photography to be recognized as one of the arts, the work of a group could bring about this recognition better than the work of an individual. . . .

The Photo-Secession group was formed in 1902, . . . Stieglitz . . . was the leader. In 1905 they began having photographic exhibitions at the little gallery known as "291.". . . Here the beginnings of modern art were also shown. . . .

I was sent, like all the other students, by the instructors of the Art Students League to see the first showing of Rodin drawings at "291." . . .

I very well remember the fantastic violence of Stieglitz's defense when the students with me began talking with him about the drawings.

83

HENRI MATISSE (1869–1954)

From "Notes of a Painter"

This 1908 article, Matisse's most complete statement on his art, reflects the transition from his early Fauve phase to his mature, post-Fauve period.

What I am after, above all, is expression. . . .

Expression, for me, does not reside in passions glowing in a human face or manifested by violent movement. The entire arrangement of my picture is expressive. . . . Composition is the art of arranging in a decorative manner the diverse elements at the painter's command to express his feelings. . . .

Both harmonies and dissonances of color can produce agreeable effects. Often when I settle down to work I begin by noting my immediate and superficial color sensations. Some years ago this first result was often enough for me—but today if I were satisfied with this, my picture would remain incomplete. I would have put down the passing sensations of a moment; they would not completely define my feelings and the next day I might not recognize what they meant. I want to reach that state of condensation of sensations which constitutes a picture. . . .

There are two ways of expressing things; one is to show them crudely, the other is to evoke them artistically. In abandoning the literal representation of movement it is possible to reach toward a higher ideal of beauty and grandeur.

Suppose I set out to paint an interior: I have before me a cupboard; it gives me a sensation of bright red—and I put down a red which satisfies me; immediately a relation is established between this red and the white of the canvas. If I put a green near the red, if I paint in a yellow floor, there must still be between this green, this yellow and the white of the canvas a relation that will be satisfactory to me. But these several tones mutually weaken one another. It is necessary, therefore, that the various elements that I use be so balanced that they do not destroy one another. To do this I must organize my ideas; the relation between tones must be so established that they will sustain one another. A new combination of colors will succeed the first one and will give more completely my interpretation. . . . I cannot copy nature in a servile way; I must interpret nature and submit it to the spirit of the picture. When I have found the relationship of all the tones the result must be a living harmony of tones, a harmony not unlike that of a musical composition. . . .

What I dream of is an art of balance, of purity and serenity devoid of troubling or depressing subject matter, an art which might be for every mental worker, be he businessman or writer, like an appeasing influence, like a mental soother, something like a good armchair in which to rest from physical fatigue.

84

WASSILY KANDINSKY (1866–1944)

Concerning the Spiritual in Art, from Chapter 5, "The Effect of Color"

Kandinsky hoped to inaugurate a new spiritual era for modern man through his art. These remarks first appeared in 1912.

If you let your eye stray over a palette of colors, you experience two things. In the first place you receive *a purely physical effect*, namely the eye itself is enchanted by the beauty and other qualities of color. You experience satisfaction and delight, like a gourmet savoring a delicacy. Or the eye is stimulated as the tongue is titillated by a spicy dish. But then it grows calm and cool, like a finger after touching ice. These are physical sensations, limited in duration. They are superficial, too, and leave no lasting impression behind if the soul remains closed. Just as we feel at the touch of ice a sensation of cold, forgotten as soon as the finger becomes warm again, so the physical action of color is forgotten as soon as the eye turns away. On the other hand, as the physical coldness of ice, upon penetrating more deeply, arouses more complex feelings, and indeed a whole chain of psychological experiences, so may also the superficial impression of color develop into an experience. . . .

And so we come to the second result of looking at colors: their psychological effect. They produce a correspondent spiritual vibration, and it is only as a step towards this spiritual vibration that the physical impression is of importance. . . .

Generally speaking, color directly influences the soul. Color is the keyboard, the eyes are the hammers, the soul is the piano with many strings. The artist is the hand that plays, touching one key or another purposively, to cause vibrations in the soul.

It is evident therefore that color harmony must rest ultimately on purposive playing upon the human soul.

85

FILIPPO TOMMASO MARINETTI (1876–1944)

From "The Foundation and Manifesto of Futurism"

After Marinetti's example of 1908, the manifesto became a popular device for innovative twentieth-century artists to publicize their views.

We declare our primary intentions to all living men of the earth:

1. We intend to glorify the love of danger, the custom of energy, the strength of daring. . . .

3. Literature having up to now glorified thoughtful immobility, ecstasy, and slumber, we wish to exalt the aggressive movement, the feverish insomnia, running, the perilous leap, the cuff, and the blow.

4. We declare that the splendor of the world has been enriched with a new form of beauty, the beauty of speed. A race-automobile adorned with great pipes like serpents with explosive breath . . . a race-automobile which seems to rush over exploding powder is more beautiful than the Victory of Samothrace. . . .

7. There is no more beauty except in struggle. No masterpiece without the stamp of aggressiveness. Poetry should be a violent assault against unknown forces to summon them to lie down at the feet of man. . . .

9. We will glorify war—the only true hygiene of the world—militarism, patriotism, the destructive gesture of anarchist, the beautiful Ideas which kill, and the scorn of woman.

10. We will destroy museums, libraries, and fight against moralism, feminism, and all utilitarian cowardice. . . .

It is in Italy that we hurl this overthrowing and inflammatory declaration, with which today we found Futurism, for we will free Italy from her numberless museums which cover her with countless cemeteries.

Museums, cemeteries! . . . Identical truly. . . .

To admire an old picture is to pour our sentiment into a funeral urn instead of hurling it forth in violent gushes of action and productiveness. . . .

The oldest among us are thirty; we have thus at least ten years in which to accomplish our task. When we are forty, let others—younger and more daring men—throw us into the wastepaper basket like useless manuscripts!

86

GIORGIO DE CHIRICO (1888–1978)

From "Mystery and Creation"

Though written in Paris before his return to Italy in 1915 at the onset of World War I, this manifesto of De Chirico's Metaphysical Painting was not published until 1928 by André Breton.

It is important that we should rid art of all that it has contained of *recognizable material* to date, all familiar subject matter, all traditional ideas, all popular symbols must be banished forthwith. More important still, we must hold enormous faith in ourselves: it is essential that the revelation we receive, the conception of an image which embraces a certain thing, which has no sense in itself, which has no subject, which means *absolutely nothing* from the logical point of view, I repeat, it is essential that such a revelation or conception should speak so strongly in us, evoke such agony or joy, that we feel compelled to paint, compelled by an impulse even more urgent than the hungry desperation which drives a man to tearing at a piece of bread like a savage beast.

I remember one vivid winter's day at Versailles. Silence and calm reigned supreme. Everything gazed at me with mysterious, questioning eyes. And then I realized that every corner of the palace, every column, every window possessed a spirit, an impenetrable soul. I looked around at the marble heroes, motionless in the lucid air, beneath the frozen rays of that winter sun which pours down on us *without love,* like a perfect song. A bird was warbling in a window cage. At that moment I grew aware of the mystery which urges men to create certain strange forms. And the creation appeared more extraordinary than the creators.

Perhaps the most amazing sensation passed on to us by prehistoric man is that of presentiment. It will always continue. We might consider it as an eternal proof of the irrationality of the universe. Original man must have wandered through a world full of uncanny signs. He must have trembled at each step.

87

PIET MONDRIAN (1872–1944)

From "Natural Reality and Abstract Reality"

This early essay, which appeared in the first issue of De Stijl *in 1919, already contains the germ of his mature art.*

We find that in nature all relations are dominated by a single primordial relation, which is defined by the opposition of two extremes. Abstract plasticism represents this primordial relation in a precise manner by means of the two positions which form the right angle. This positional relationship is the most balanced of all, since it expresses in a perfect harmony the relation between two extremes, and contains all other relations.

If we conceive these two extremes as manifestations of interiority and exteriority, we will find that in the new plasticism the tie uniting mind and life is not broken. . . .

If unity is contemplated in a precise and definite way, attention will [be] directed solely towards the universal, and as a consequence, the particular will disappear from art—as painting has already shown.

This, however, cannot appear before its proper time. For it is the spirit of the times that determines artistic expression. . . . But at the present moment, that form of art alone is truly alive which expresses our present—or future—consciousness.

Composition allows the artist the greatest possible freedom, so that his subjectivity can express itself, to a certain degree, for as long as needed.

The rhythm of relations of color and size makes the absolute appear in the relativity of time and space.

88

PIET MONDRIAN

From "Plastic Art and Pure Plastic Art"

This essay, published in 1937, is the culmination of Mondrian's attempts to work out his aesthetic theories in written form.

Art makes us realize that there are *fixed laws which govern and point to the use of the constructive elements of the composition and of the inherent inter-relationships between them.* These laws may be regarded as subsidiary law to the *fundamental* law of equivalence which creates *dynamic equilibrium and reveals the true content of reality.*

In spite of world disorder, instinct and intuition are carrying humanity to a real equilibrium. . . . Art certainly shows this clearly. But art shows also that in the course of progress, intuition becomes more and more conscious and instinct more and more purified.

Non-figurative art brings to an end the ancient culture of art; at present, therefore, one can review and judge more surely *the whole culture of art.* We are not at the turning-point of this culture; *the culture of particular form is approaching its end. The culture of determined relations has begun.*

In pure plastic art the significance of different forms and lines is very important; it is precisely this fact which makes it pure. . . .

Non-figurative art is created by establishing *a dynamic rhythm of determinate mutual relations* which *excludes the formation of any particular form. . . .*

In removing completely from the work all objects, 'the world is not separated from the spirit', but is on the contrary, *put into a balanced opposition* with the spirit, since the one and the other are purified.

89

RICHARD HUELSENBECK (1892–1974)

From "First German Dada Manifesto"

In 1917 Huelsenbeck returned to Germany from Zurich, where he participated in the Dada movement. The "First Dada Manifesto" was written the following year.

. . . The best and most extraordinary artists will be those who every hour snatch the tatters of their bodies out of the frenzied cataract of life, who, with bleeding hands and hearts, hold fast to the intelligence of their time. Has expressionism fulfilled our expectations of such an art, which should be an expression of our most vital concerns?

No! No! No!

Have the expressionists fulfilled our expectations of an art that burns the essence of life into our flesh?

No! No! No!

Under the pretext of turning inward, the expressionists in literature and painting have banded together into a generation which is already looking forward to honorable mention in the histories of literature and art and aspiring to the most respectable civic distinctions. . . . That sentimental resistance to the times, which are neither better nor worse, neither more reactionary nor more revolutionary than other times...is the quality of a youth which never knew how to be young. Expressionism...has nothing in common with the efforts of active men. The signers of this manifesto have, under the battle cry:

Dada!!!!

gathered together to put forward a new art. . . .

The word Dada symbolizes the most primitive relation to the reality of the environment; with Dadaism a new reality comes into its own. Life appears as a simultaneous muddle of noises, colors and spiritual rhythms, which is taken unmodified into Dadaist art, with all the sensational screams and fevers of its reckless everyday psyche and with all its brutal reality. . . . Dadaism for the first time has ceased to take an aesthetic attitude toward life . . . by tearing all the slogans of ethics, culture and inwardness . . . into their components.

90

ANDRÉ BRETON (1896–1966)

From "What Is Surrealism?"

The first Surrealist manifesto appeared in 1924, the second in 1930, and this one, considered the third, in 1934. Although the Surrealist movement was dedicated to the freedom of the individual, its founder, Breton, was both moralistic and highly authoritarian. Because he sometimes excommunicated members of the group, he became known as "the Pope of Surrealism."

We still live under the reign of logic, but the methods of logic are applied nowadays only to the resolution of problems of secondary interest. The absolute rationalism which is still the fashion does not permit consideration of any facts but those strictly relevant to our experience. Logical ends, on the other hand, escape us. Needless to say that even experience has had limits assigned to it. It revolves in a cage from which it be comes more and more difficult to release it. Even experience is dependent on immediate utility, and common sense is its keeper. Under color of civilization, under the pretext of progress, all that rightly or wrongly may be regarded as fantasy or superstition has been banished from the mind, all uncustomary searching after truth has been proscribed. It is only by what must seem sheer luck that there has recently been brought to light an aspect of mental life—to my belief by far the most important—with which it was supposed that we no longer had any concern. All credit for these discoveries must go to Freud. Based on these discoveries a current of opinion is forming that will enable the explorer of the human mind to continue his investigations, justified as he will be in taking into account more than mere summary realities. The imagination is perhaps on the point of reclaiming its rights. If the depths of our minds harbor strange forces capable of increasing those on the surface, or of successfully contending with them, then it is all in our interest to canalize them, to canalize them first in order to submit them later, if necessary, to the control of the reason. . . .

I am resolved to render powerless that *hatred of the marvelous* which is so rampant. . . . Briefly: The marvelous is always beautiful, anything that is marvelous is beautiful; indeed, nothing but the marvelous is beautiful.

The admirable thing about the fantastic is that it is no longer fantastic: there is only the real.

91

MAX BECKMANN (1884–1950)

From "On My Painting"

First given as a lecture in German in London in 1938 and published in English in New York three years later, "On My Painting" is the fullest statement of Beckmann's art.

One of my problems is to find the self, which has only one form and is immortal—to find it in animals and men, in the heaven and in the hell which together form the world in which we live.

Space, and space again, is the infinite deity which surrounds us and in which we are ourselves contained. . . .

Often, very often, I am alone. My studio . . . is again filled in my imagination with figures from the old days and from the new, like an ocean moved by storm and sun and always present in my thoughts.

Then shapes become beings and seem comprehensible to me in the great void and uncertainty of the space which I call God.

Sometimes I am helped by the constructive rhythm of the cabala, when my thoughts wander over Oannes Dagon to the last days of drowned continents. Of the same substance are streets of their men, women and children; great ladies and whores; servant girls and duchesses. I seem to meet them, like doubly significant dreams, in Samothrace and Piccadilly and Wall Street. They are Eros and the longing for oblivion.

92

JACKSON POLLOCK (1912–1956)

From "My Painting"

In 1947, when these remarks were recorded, Pollock rejected the usual easel format by placing his unstretched canvases directly on the floor. Using ordinary house paint, he claimed that he was not just throwing paint but delineating some real thing in the air above the canvas.

My painting does not come from the easel. I hardly ever stretch my canvas before painting. I prefer to tack the unstretched canvas to the hard wall or the floor. I need the resistance of a hard surface. On the floor I am more at ease. I feel nearer, more a part of the painting, since this way I can walk around it, work from the four sides and literally be in the painting. This is akin to the method of the Indian sand painters of the West.

I continue to get further away from the usual painter's tools such as easel, palette, brushes, etc. I prefer sticks, trowels, knives and dripping fluid paint or a heavy impasto with sand, broken glass and other foreign matter added.

When I am *in* my painting, I'm not aware of what I'm doing. It is only after a sort of "get acquainted" period that I see what I have been about. I have no fears about making changes, destroying the image, etc., because the painting has a life of its own. I try to let it come through. It is only when I lose contact with the painting that the result is a mess. Otherwise there is pure harmony, an easy give and take, and the painting comes out well.

The source of my painting is the unconscious. I approach painting the same way I approach drawing. That is direct—with no preliminary studies. The drawings I do are relative to my painting but not for it.

93

ROMARE BEARDEN (1911–1988)

From two interviews

In interviews conducted by Myron Schwartzman in 1983 and 1986, Bearden discussed the wide range of artistic influences on his working methods and ideas.

Myron Schwartzman: So [collage] gets improvisational. . . .

Romare Bearden: Well, it's like jazz; you do this and then you improvise. You know Manet (I think) said, "A painting isn't finished; sometimes you get on the surface." He meant, "Well, you've got it under control." Maybe sometimes a third of the way through [a painting], I'll say, "I know this is coming out." You get that feeling that the thing is going to be all right. And other things you just have to surrender. As my friend Carl Holty used to say, "Don't close your picture too quickly; keep it open until the very last, and that gives you room to maneuver." You reach a point when all the elements seem to focus, so that the colors and the forms will set. And at that point you can relinquish the painting. . . .

MS: What triggers [a] series, Romie?

RB: Well, the memories are just there; they're just really with me. It's strange, the memories are there. For instance, you see the Vermeer [reproduction of *The Concert*] up there on the wall? I'll say, "Well, I saw something like this; this used to be so-and-so." Because I guess art is made from other art. Yes, I've been in places like this; I've gone in with the same kind of stillness, and the light coming in from this source.

Those people [of Vermeer's time] moved on, and the people from Mecklenburg [North Carolina, Bearden's birthplace] have come in there; they stayed a while and now there is something else.

MS: Let's explore the theme of relationships. What does it mean to you in painting?

RB: In discussing relationships, we have to consider many disparate factors, or seemingly disparate factors, in the way a painting is put together, such as scale, space, line, and so forth. I think this is one of the most important things that Matisse talks about—the relationships, how one does things—and it changes. . . .

In the icons, and in African sculpture, they bring everything to a very beautiful shape. So long as you can get everything in a nice shape, the picture will be all right—you're just shaping it, not worrying so much about the anatomy. If you do that and it all moves in the right rhythms, you have a painting. We get deceived so much by appearances. You sometimes just have to forget about that, because you are working in another world here. And so you could easily take these [canvases] as being completely nonrepresentational.

Take Vermeer's drawings—you turn them upside down, and there's real, great abstraction. The wrinkles in the clothes, for instance; you turn the drawing upside down, and you see something else, the great relationships. This is the abstracting of things. People think abstraction means that you don't have figurative objects in a work. So a more accurate word is "nonrepresentational" rather than "abstract," because Poussin, Ingres are great abstractionists. . . .

The thing is that the artist confronts chaos. The whole thing of art is, how do you organize chaos? . . . Probably, if you take it symbolically, there is no greater chaos than in the inferno, down in hell. Dante, in his *Inferno*, meets Virgil. . . . He's lost and confused there, and Virgil says, "I'll guide you, . . . " to me he is like the artist. This is the help that he needs in understanding what is going on, . . . some kind of organization that he finds. And he's talking about sin, and the rest of these things. But he needs that guide.

So I think it's the same thing with the artist.

94

RICHARD HAMILTON (b. 1922)
From "For the Finest Art, Try Pop"

This excerpt first appeared in London in 1961.

A new generation of Dadaists has emerged today, as violent and ingenious as their forbears, but Son of Dada is accepted, lionized by public and dealers, certified by state museums—the act of mythmaking has been transferred from the subject-matter of the work to the artist himself as the content of his art.

Futurism has ebbed and has no successor. . . . The Pop-Fine-Art standpoint . . . is, like Futurism, fundamentally a statement of belief in the changing values of society. Pop-Fine-Art is a profession of approbation of mass culture, therefore also antiartistic. It is positive Dada, creative where Dada was destructive. Perhaps it is Mama—a cross-fertilization of Futurism and Dada which upholds a respect for the culture of the masses and a conviction that the artist in twentieth century urban life is inevitably a consumer of mass culture and potentially a contributor to it.

95

ROY LICHTENSTEIN (BORN 1923)
From "What Is Pop Art?"

This interview with Gene R. Swenson appeared in 1963, the same year as Lichtenstein's Drowning Girl *(see fig. 24-76).*

Roy Lichtenstein: I think my work is different from comic strips—but I wouldn't call it transformation. . . . What I do is form, whereas the comic strip is not formed in the sense I'm using the word; the comics have shapes but there has been no effort to make them intensely unified. The purpose is different, one intends to depict and I intend to unify. And my work is actually different from comic strips in that every mark is really in a different place, however slight the difference seems to some. The difference is often not great, but it is crucial. . . .

Gene R. Swenson: A curator at the Modern Museum has called Pop Art fascistic and militaristic.

RL: The heroes depicted in comic books are fascist types, but I don't take them seriously in these paintings—maybe there is a point in not taking them seriously, a political point. I use them for purely formal reasons, and that's not what those heroes were invented for. . . .

The techniques I use are not commercial, they only appear to be commercial—and the ways of seeing and composing and unifying are different and have different ends.

96

MARCEL DUCHAMP (1898–1986)
From "Apropos of Readymade"

The following are excerpts from a lecture given at the Museum of Modern Art, New York, in October 1961.

IN 1913 I HAD THE HAPPY IDEA TO FASTEN A BICYCLE WHEEL TO A KITCHEN STOOL AND WATCH IT TURN.

IN NEW YORK IN 1915 I BOUGHT AT A HARDWARE STORE A SNOW SHOVEL ON WHICH I WROTE "IN ADVANCE OF THE BROKEN ARM."

IT WAS AROUND THAT TIME THAT THE WORD "READYMADE" CAME TO MIND TO DESIGNATE THIS FORM OF MANIFESTATION.

A POINT WHICH I WANT VERY MUCH TO ESTABLISH IS THAT THE CHOICE OF THESE "READYMADES" WAS NEVER DICTATED BY ESTHETIC DELECTATION.

THIS CHOICE WAS BASED ON A REACTION OF VISUAL INDIFFERENCE WITH AT THE SAME TIME A TOTAL ABSENCE OF GOOD OR BAD TASTE. . . .

ONE IMPORTANT CHARACTERISTIC WAS THE SHORT SENTENCE WHICH I OCCASIONALLY INSCRIBED ON THE "READYMADE."

THAT SENTENCE INSTEAD OF DESCRIBING THE OBJECT LIKE A TITLE WAS MEANT TO CARRY THE MIND OF THE SPECTATOR TOWARDS OTHER REGIONS MORE VERBAL.

ANOTHER ASPECT OF THE "READYMADE" IS ITS LACK OF UNIQUENESS. . . . THE REPLICA OF A "READYMADE" DELIVERING THE SAME MESSAGE; IN FACT NEARLY EVERY ONE OF THE "READYMADES" EXISTING TODAY IS NOT AN ORIGINAL IN THE CONVENTIONAL SENSE.

97

HENRY MOORE (1898–1986)
From "The Sculptor Speaks"

Moore's sculpture in the 1930s began to reveal the tension between solid and void. His interest in the human figure and in natural forms remained paramount, however, as is evident in these comments published in 1937.

Since the Gothic, European sculpture had become overgrown with moss, weeds—all sorts of surface excrescences which completely concealed shape. It has been Brancusi's special mission to get rid of this overgrowth, and to make us once more shape-conscious. To do this he has had to concentrate on very simple direct shapes, to keep his sculpture, as it were, one-cylindered, to refine and polish a single shape to a degree almost too precious. Brancusi's work, apart from its individual value, has been of historical importance in the development of contemporary sculpture. But it may now be no longer necessary to close down and restrict sculpture to the single (static) form unit. We can now begin to open out. To relate and combine together several forms of varied sizes, sections, and directions into one organic whole.

Although it is the human figure which interests me most deeply, I have always paid great attention to natural forms, such as bones, shells, and pebbles, etc. Sometimes for several years running I have been to the same part of the seashore—but each year a new shape of pebble has caught my eye, which the year before, though it was there in hundreds, I never saw. . . . A different thing happens if I sit down and examine a handful one by one. I may then extend my form-experience more, by giving my mind time to become conditioned to a new shape.

There are universal shapes to which everybody is subconsciously conditioned and to which they can respond if their conscious control does not shut them off.

Pebbles show nature's way of working stone.

98

EVA HESSE (1936–1970)

From an interview

An abbreviated version of this interview with Cindy Nemser was published in 1970, shortly before Hesse's death. Hesse resisted the impersonal formalism of 1960s art.

CINDY NEMSER: . . . Looking at your works they seem, to me, to be filled with sexual impulses or organic feeling. I feel there are anthropomorphic inferences.

EVA HESSE: It's not a simple question for me. First when I work it's only the abstract qualities that I'm really working with, which is to say the material, the form it's going to take, the size, the scale, the positioning. . . . However, I don't value the totality of the image on these abstract or esthetic points. For me it's a total image that has to do with me and life. It can't be divorced as an idea or composition or form. I don't believe art can be based on that. . . . I don't want to make that my problem. . . . Those problems are solvable, I solve them, can solve them *beautifully.* In fact, my idea now is to discount everything I've ever learned or been taught about those things and to find something else. So it is inevitable that it is my life, my feelings, my thoughts. And there I'm very complex. I'm not a simple person and the complexity . . . is the total absurdity of life. I guess that's where I relate, if I do, to certain artists who I feel very close to, and not so much through having studied their writings or works, but because, for me, there's this total *absurdity* in their work.

CN: Which artists are they?

EH: Duchamp, Yvonne Rainer, Ionesco, Carl Andre.

CN: Let's talk about some of your early sculptures.

EH: There was a piece I did for that show in the Graham Gallery . . . in 1965 or '66. It was called Hang-Up—a dumb name . . . but I can't change it. I think it was about the fifth piece I did and I think the most important statement I made. It's close to what I feel I achieve now in my best pieces. It was the first time where my idea of absurdity or extreme feeling came through.

99

LE CORBUSIER (1886–1965)

From *Towards a New Architecture*

First published in 1923, Towards a New Architecture *codified ideas that were being widely discussed among architects and in turn became the first manifesto of the International Style. The English translation appeared four years later in London. The following excerpts are from the opening Argument.*

The Engineer's Aesthetic, and Architecture, are two things that march together and follow one from the other. . . .

The Engineer, inspired by the law of Economy and governed by mathematical calculation, puts us in accord with universal law. He achieves harmony.

The Architect, by his arrangement of forms, realizes an order which is a pure creation of his spirit; by forms and shapes he affects our senses to an acute degree and provokes plastic emotions; by the relationships which he creates he wakes profound echoes in us, he gives us the measure of an order which we feel to be in accordance with that of our world, he determines the various movements of our heart and of our understanding; it is then that we experience the sense of beauty.

Primary forms are beautiful forms because they can be clearly appreciated.

The great problems of modern construction must have a geometrical solution.

Machinery contains in itself the factor of economy, which makes for selection.

The house is a machine for living in.

Standards are a matter of logic, analysis and minute study. . . .

Man looks at the creation of architecture with his eyes, which are 5 feet 6 inches from the ground.

Industry, overwhelming us like a flood which rolls on towards its destined ends, has furnished us with new tools adapted to this new epoch, animated by the new spirit.

The problem of the house is a problem of the epoch.

If we eliminate from our hearts and minds all dead concepts in regard to the house, and look at the question from a critical and objective point of view, we shall arrive at the "House-Machine," the mass-production house, healthy (and morally so too) and beautiful. . . .

100

WALTER GROPIUS (1883–1969)

From *Scope of Total Architecture*

Gropius was interested in the social and aesthetic implications of housing and city planning, as these remarks of 1943 suggest.

Every thinking contemporary searches his mind now trying to figure out what may be the ultimate value of our stupendous scientific progress. We roar with new techniques and new inventions for speedier means of transportation. But what do we do with all the time saved? Do we use it for contemplation of our existence? No, we plunge instead into an even more hectic current of activity, surrendering to that fallacious slogan: time is money. We obviously need a clarification as to what exactly our spiritual and intellectual aims are. . . .

I should like, therefore, to attempt to outline the potential strategic aim of planning for my own profession, architecture, within the cultural and political context of our industrial civilization. . . .

Our scientific age, by going to extremes of specialization, has obviously prevented us from seeing our complicated life as an entity. The average professional man, driven to distraction by the multiplicity of problems spread out before him, seeks relief from the pressure of general responsibilities by picking out one single, rigidly circumscribed responsibility in a specialized field and refuses to be answerable for anything that may happen outside this field. A general dissolution of context has set in and naturally resulted in shrinking and fragmentating life. As Albert Einstein once put it: "Perfection of means and confusion of aims seem to be characteristic of our age. . . ."

But there are indications that we are slowly moving away from overspecialization and its perilous atomizing effect on the social coherence of the community. . . . In the gigantic task of its reunification, the planner and architect will have to play a big role. He must be well trained not ever to lose a total vision, in spite of the infinite wealth of specialized knowledge which he has to absorb and integrate. He must comprehend land, nature, man and his art, as one great entity. In our mechanized society we should passionately emphasize that we are still a world of men, that man in his natural environment must be the focus of all planning. We have indulged our latest pets, the machines, to such an extent that we have lost a genuine scale of values. Therefore, we need to investigate what makes up the really worthwhile relationships among men, and between men and nature, instead of giving way to the pressure of special interests or of shortsighted enthusiasts who want to make mechanization an end in itself. . . .

There is no other way toward progress but to start courageously and without prejudice new practical tests by building model communities in one stroke and then systematically examining their living value. What a wealth of new information for the sociologist, the economist, the scientist and the artist would be forthcoming, if groups, formed of the most able planners and architects available, should be commissioned to design and build completely new model communities! Such information would also offer most valuable preparatory data to solve the complicated problem of rehabilitating our existing communities.

101

EDWARD WESTON (1886–1958)

From "Photographic Art"

Weston insisted that the photographer should previsualize the final print before making the exposure and not crop or trim the print. This excerpt from an encyclopedia entry published in 1942 attempts to synthesize some of the reflections on photography that he kept in his Daybooks.

The camera lens sees too clearly to be used successfully for recording the superficial aspects of a subject. . . .

But if the camera's innate honesty works any hardship on the photographer by limiting his subject matter in one direction, the loss is slight when weighed against the advantages it provides. For it is that very quality that makes the camera expressly fitted for examining deeply into the meaning of things. The discriminating photographer . . . can reveal the essence of what lies before his lens with such clear insight that the beholder will find the re[-]created image more real and comprehensible than the actual object.

The photograph isolates and perpetuates a moment of time: an important and revealing moment, or an unimportant and meaningless one, depending upon the photographer's understanding of his subject and mastery of his process. The lens does not reveal a subject significantly of its own accord. On the contrary, its vision is completely impartial and undiscriminating. It makes no distinction between important detail and meaningless detail. Selection, emphasis, and meaning must be provided by the photographer in his composition. . . . To compose a subject well means no more than to see and present it in the strongest manner possible. . . . Its capacity for rendering fine detail and tone makes photography excel in recording form and texture. Its subtlety of gradation makes it admirably suited to recording qualities of light or shadow. . . . The photographer cannot depend on rules deduced from finished work in another medium. He must learn to see things through his own eyes and his own camera; only then can he present his subject in a way that will transmit his feeling for it to others.

An intuitive knowledge of composition in terms of the capacities of his process enables the photographer to record his subject at the moment of deepest perception; to capture the fleeting instant when the light on a landscape, the form of a cloud, the gesture of a hand, or the expression of a face momentarily presents a profound revelation of life.

The appeal to our emotions manifest in such a record is largely due to the quality of authenticity in the photograph. The spectator accepts its authority and, in viewing it, perforce believes that he would have seen that scene or object exactly so if he had been there. We know that the human eye is capable of no such feat, and furthermore that the photographer has not reproduced the scene exactly; quite possibly we would not even be able to identify the original scene from having seen the photograph. Yet it is this belief in the reality of the photograph that calls up a strong response in the spectator and enables him to participate directly in the artist's experience.

102

JERRY UELSMANN (b. 1934)

From "Some Humanistic Considerations of Photography"

Uelsmann's approach to photography—postvisualization—is the opposite of Edward Weston's previsualization. This excerpt is from a speech given by Uelsmann to the Royal Photographic Society of Great Britain in 1971.

As you may know the dominant aesthetic in photography has been called previsualization. This means that the image is essentially fully previsioned at the time the shutter is clicked. Now I propose that photographers keep themselves open to in-process discovery....

It seems to me that all other areas of art allow for in-process discovery. The painter does not begin with a fully-conceived canvas, the sculptor with a fully-conceived piece. They allow for a dialogue to evolve, to develop, and as far as I'm concerned the darkroom is truly capable of being a visual research laboratory, a place for discovery, observation and meditation....

Some of my photographs I don't understand. This disturbs some people. I would like to think that today we are sophisticated enough to realize that first of all there are systems of knowledge which are not necessarily verbal. There are levels of consciousness that we can engage ourselves in when we are encountering the world of photography that are not easy to talk about.... I think many times we are pressured into a verbalization of things that we don't fully understand but somehow the words are important....

One recent photograph disturbs me a great deal. Literally I know what's happening: there is a wave and an organic form that was washed up on the beach after a hurricane.... But there is some strange thing happening, some strange statement within that I am in no way capable of articulating. I think the sooner that we as photographers become aware of this phenomenon that we can perhaps address each other visually at times, I think the happier we'll all be, because so many times I am pressed to have verbal responses to things that I can't defend verbally.

103

MICHAEL GRAVES (b. 1934)

From "What Is the Focus of Post-Modern Architecture?"

This 1981 interview with Michael McTwigan appeared while Graves was designing the Public Services Building (see fig. 28-1), which was dubbed the "Post-Modern building of the year."

MICHAEL MCTWIGAN: It's interesting that you use the word "figural." By that, do you mean related to human scale . . . ?

MICHAEL GRAVES: Those things, as well as a range of architectonic ideas—elements like a door or a window, a configuration of space that is anthropomorphically related. For instance, if I make a Greek cross plan . . . there's no doubt where the primary space is for us in a room like that. If you look at De Stijl architecture, on the other hand, there is no clear identity of the human body within the plan. I can't locate the figure of myself within the work.

MM: That is presumably why so many people have felt alienated by modern architecture; it stands on its own and doesn't really have a relationship to the human being....

Architect Robert Stern said not too long ago, "We're not in the business of educating and transforming human nature; we're in the business of responding to the human condition. We're not reformers or revolutionaries." That seems to be quite a statement, quite a change from the Bauhaus days....

MG: . . . In part, what Robert is saying is that this is not a time of manifestos. I remember in the early '60s, when Peter Eisenman and I were working together, we wanted to write a manifesto. We wanted to be modern architects and say, "This is what ought to be, not what is. . . ."

We wanted to make clear our own ideas in a general sense, rather than in the peculiarities of site or client or whatever. It's not that one has softened today, but the manifesto is much more gentle now. I would not say we are not reformers, however. We are, in the best sense of the word, re-formers. We are trying to establish form as it relates to us more than to the machine.... We are reformers in the sense that we don't want to return to something, but, rather, to reestablish the language of architecture. That's where the manifesto comes.

Although literature can use the window as a metaphor, architecture possesses the window. It's the modern architect who wants to throw the window out. It's people like myself who want to say simply, "The window exists, and I will use the window." The window relates to the human body and it relates to the wall for very specific aesthetic, technical, and cultural reasons. It's not for nothing that the window existed for 2,000 years or more. That's a crucial issue.

So I would vary that rather dramatic statement of Robert's and say I'm interested in reestablishing the language of architecture. . . .

MM: So it's not just a matter of reeducating. It's a matter of teaching old skills as well. . . . It could be said that people almost forgot how to paint in the '60s, and the same could be said about architecture.

MG: Sure. There's an architect by the name of Leo Krier in London who says he won't build, because there's no craft tradition from which to build his buildings. His political standing is that we must dissolve the Industrial Revolution. So he does his drawings. He says, "Let's go back to the craft tradition."

104

CINDY SHERMAN (b. 1954)

From an interview

In these excerpts from a 1988 interview with Jeanne Siegel, Sherman discusses her photographic role-playing.

CINDY SHERMAN: I still wanted to make a filmic sort of image, but I wanted to work alone. I realized that I could make a picture of a character reacting to something outside the frame so that the viewer would assume another person.

Actually, the moment that I realized how to solve this problem was when Robert [Longo] and I visited David Salle, who had been working for some sleazy detective magazine. Bored as I was, waiting for Robert and David to get their "art talk" over with, I noticed all these 8 by 10 glossies from the magazine which triggered something in me. (I was never one to discuss issues—after all, at that time I was "the girlfriend.")

JEANNE SIEGEL: In the "Untitled Film Stills," what was the influence of real film stars? It seems that you had a fascination with European stars. You mentioned Jeanne Moreau, Brigitte Bardot and Sophia Loren in some of your statements. Why were you attracted to them?

CS: I guess because they weren't glamorized like American starlets. When I think of American actresses from the same period, I think of bleached blonde, bejeweled and furred sex bombs. But, when I think of Jeanne Moreau and Sophia Loren, I think of more vulnerable, lower-class types of characters, more identifiable as working-class women.

At that time I was trying to emulate a lot of different types of characters. I didn't want to stick to just one. I'd seen a lot of the movies that these women had been in but it wasn't so much that I was inspired by the women as by the films themselves and the feelings in the films.

JS: And what is the relationship between your "Untitled Film Stills" and real film stills?

CS: In real publicity film stills from the 40s and 50s something usually sexy/cute is portrayed to get people to go see the movie. Or the woman could be shown screaming in terror to publicize a horror film.

My favorite film images (where obviously my work took its inspiration) didn't have that. They're closer to my own work for that reason, because both are about a sort of brooding character caught between the potential violence and sex. However, I've realized it is a mistake to make that kind of literal connection because my work loses in the comparison. I think my characters are not quite taken in by their roles so that they couldn't really exist in any of their so-called "films," which, next to a real still, looks unconvincing. They are too aware of the irony of their role and perhaps that's why many have puzzled expressions. My "stills" were about the fakeness of role-playing as well as contempt for the domineering "male" audience who would mistakenly read the images as sexy. . . .

JS: Another critical issue attached to the work was the notion that the stereotypical view was exclusively determined by the "male" gaze. Did you see it only in this light or did it include the woman seeing herself as well?

CS: Because I'm a woman I automatically assumed other women would have an immediate identification with the roles. And I hoped men would feel empathy for the characters as well as shedding light on their role-playing. What I didn't anticipate was that some people would assume that I was playing up to the male gaze. I can understand the criticism of feminists who therefore assumed I was reinforcing the stereotype of woman as victim or as sex object.

Timeline Four: 1800 to 2000

	1800–1820	1820–1840	1840–1850
HISTORY AND POLITICS	**1802** First child labor laws, in England **1803** United States purchases Louisiana from France for $15 million **1804** Napoleon crowned emperor of France, ending the republic established by the French Revolution; 1805–9, occupies Italy and Spain. He wins battles against allied England, Austria, Russia, and Sweden until he retreats from Moscow, 1812, losing the bulk of his army; 1814, successes of allies force him to abdicate; he is exiled to Elba **War of 1812** (European allies against Napoleon) draws United States into conflict with Britain; 1814, Washington, D.C., burned **1814** Allies at Congress of Vienna redivide Europe. Louis XVIII, Bourbon king of France (r. 1814–24), establishes a constitutional monarchy; 1815, Napoleon returns; allies defeat him at Waterloo; he abdicates again and, 1821, dies a prisoner of war. Bourbon kings return to power until 1830 **1819–21** Spain sells Florida to United States	**1822** Simon Bolívar (1783–1830) leads revolution in Latin America: six countries gain independence from Spain **1823** Monroe Doctrine claims United States sphere of influence in the Western Hemisphere **1830** July Revolution in France; republican mobs riot against the monarchy; Louis Philippe, nominated as new king (r. 1830–48, the July Monarchy), continues conservative policies. This change of power mandated by popular acclaim spawns revolutionary movements across Europe **1833** Factory Act abolishes slavery in British colonies **Queen Victoria (r. 1837–1901)** rules Great Britain **1838** "Trail of Tears": Thousands of Cherokee and other Indians are moved by United States government on a forced march from the Southeast to Indian Territory (now Oklahoma); one in four dies	**1842** Oregon Trail opens western lands of North America for settlement **1846–48** War between United States and Mexico over territories of Texas and New Mexico **Revolution of 1848 in France;** 1848–52, Second Republic declared after abdication of Louis Philippe. Bloody insurrection leads to the election of Louis Napoleon, nephew of Napoleon I, as constitutional monarch; 1852, he overthrows republic and becomes Emperor Napoleon III (Second Empire, 1852–70); 1861–67, disastrous attempt by France to annex Mexico **1848** Revolutions throughout Europe; 1848–61, unification of Italy begins with a revolt led by Giuseppe Garibaldi against Austrian and French rule **1848** Discovery of gold in American West encourages westward expansion
RELIGION	**Pope Pius X (r. 1803–14)** reforms church law, music, texts, and administration		
	THÉODORE GÉRICAULT *The Raft of the "Medusa,"* 1818–19	JOHN CONSTABLE *Salisbury Cathedral from the Meadows,* 1829–34	JOSEPH MALLORD WILLIAM TURNER *Rain, Steam and Speed—* *The Great Western Railway,* 1844
MUSIC, LITERATURE, AND PHILOSOPHY	**1800s English Romantic poets:** Wordsworth, Byron, Shelley, Keats; novelists: Thackeray, Austen, Dickens, Trollope, the Brontës, Eliot, Kipling **1807** Georg Wilhelm Friedrich Hegel (1770–1831) writes *Phenomenology of Mind* **1819–37** Jacob and Wilhelm Grimm, brothers, collect authoritative versions of German folktales and myths	**Emily Dickinson (1830–86),** American poet **1833** Carl von Clausewitz, a general in the Napoleonic Wars, writes *On War,* a treatise on modern warfare **1840** Edgar Allan Poe publishes suspenseful and macabre short stories in United States	**1842** Honoré de Balzac completes *The Human Comedy,* a series of novels and stories **Modern economic theories:** 1848, Karl Marx and Friedrich Engels write *The Communist Manifesto* and John Stuart Mill publishes *Principles of Political Economy;* 1867, Marx's *Capital*
SCIENCE, TECHNOLOGY, AND EXPLORATION	**1800** Estimated world population nears one billion; that of Europe is 180 million; Alessandro Volta (1745–1827) constructs the first battery and demonstrates electric currents **1804–6** Lewis and Clark cross the American continent to the Pacific Ocean **1811** Invention of tin cans for food storage **1814** Steam locomotive, in England, used to power early railroad travel **1819** First steamship crossing of the Atlantic	**1825** Opening of the Erie Canal, allowing passage of ships from the Atlantic Ocean to the Great Lakes **1831** Invention of mechanical McCormick reaper; 1837, John Deere plow **c. 1837** Development of armaments: rifles, artillery, shrapnel, revolvers, and torpedoes by the 1880s **1839** First forms of photography: daguerreotype and negative-positive system	**1844** Samuel Morse's telegraph transforms communications by allowing transmission and reception of a coded signal through wires; 1866, transatlantic cable laid **1846** Sewing machine invented by Elias Howe; William Morton uses ether anesthesia in surgery **1847** First Law of Thermodynamics formulated by Julius von Mayer and James Joule; 1850, Second Law, by Rudolf Clausius

1850–1860	1860–1870	1870–1880

HISTORY AND POLITICS

1850–1860

1853–55 Crimean War; England and France halt the advance of Russia into the Balkans

1854 Commodore Matthew Perry of the United States signs treaty opening Japan to foreign trade

1860–1870

1861 Russia abolishes serfdom

1861–65 Civil War in the United States, centering on the issue of slavery; 1863, Emancipation Proclamation frees slaves; 1865, assassination of President Abraham Lincoln

1864 First International Workingman's Association led by Karl Marx in England

1869 Susan B. Anthony organizes American movement for women's suffrage

1870–1880

1870 Franco-Prussian War; 1871, defeat of French brings collapse of the Second Empire government. Paris populace sets up Third Republic (1870–1914)—at first ruling through the short-lived, radical Paris Commune—opposed to the monarchy. In German states, Prussian victory leads to a nationalist movement for unification (declared 1871) under Otto von Bismarck, Chancellor of Prussia (r. 1862–90), and a conservative (antisocialist) government

1876 Battle of Little Bighorn, in Montana: troops of George Armstrong Custer (1839–76), United States general, defeated and killed by forces of Sitting Bull (Tatanka Iotake, c. 1831–90), Sioux leader

1876–1914 Peak of European colonialism worldwide

1848: NATIONALISM IN EUROPE The year 1848 may be said to mark the beginning of the modern political world. In France the collapse of the monarchy and the establishment of a republic in February of that year started a chain reaction across Europe. In the capitals of Germany, Spain, Italy, Hungary, Austria, and the Balkans, a general discontent with conservative politics found expression in public demonstrations by masses of students, peasants, and soldiers and in a general cry for the overthrow of monarchies. The anxieties of the working classes (the Industrial Revolution having created an urban bourgeoisie), incipient socialist ideas, and a popular desire for constitutional, representative government added fuel to these fires. In many countries, the revolutions of 1848 led to a permanent change in the form of government. Among the profound cultural effects of this rapid transition were a new sense of national identity, which encouraged the development of national styles in art, and a new sense of the value of freedom of expression.

RELIGION

CAMILLE COROT
Morning: Dance of the Nymphs, 1850

HONORÉ DAUMIER
The Third-Class Carriage, c. 1862

EDWARD BURNE-JONES
The Wheel of Fortune, 1877–83

MUSIC, LITERATURE, AND PHILOSOPHY

1850–1860

Mid-1800s Russian literature: Gogol (1809–52), Turgenev (1818–83), Dostoyevsky (1821–81), Tolstoy (1828–1910), Chekhov (1860–1904)

1851 Melville's *Moby Dick;* Stowe's antislavery novel *Uncle Tom's Cabin;* 1853, Ruskin's *The Stones of Venice;* 1857, *Madame Bovary,* by Flaubert; *The Flowers of Evil,* by Baudelaire

1860–1870

Impressionist composers: Claude Debussy (1862–1918), Maurice Ravel (1875–1937); Romantics: Frédéric Chopin (1810–49), Robert Schumann (1810–56), Franz Liszt (1811–86), Johannes Brahms (1833–97). The Romantic work of Richard Wagner (1813–83) transforms opera

1862 Victor Hugo's novel *Les Misérables*

1870–1880

Carl G. Jung (1875–1961), Swiss psychologist, explores the concept of the collective unconscious

Thomas Mann (1875–1955), German novelist

1878–80 Friedrich Nietzsche, German philosopher, develops idea of an *Übermensch* (superman)

SCIENCE, TECHNOLOGY, AND EXPLORATION

1850–1860

1855 First plastic material, celluloid, discovered by Alexander Parkes

c. 1856–63 Steel manufacturing processes invented; experimentation with alloys proliferates; 1890, first steel-frame skyscraper built, in Chicago

1859 Charles Darwin publishes *The Origin of Species,* formulating the theory of evolution

1860–1870

1863 First subways built, in London

1864 In France, Louis Pasteur's germ theory alters medical research and practice; 1865, antiseptic techniques introduced in surgery

1865 Genetic experiments of Gregor Mendel published in Austria

1866 Invention of dynamite by Alfred Nobel

1869 American transcontinental railroad completed; Suez Canal opens; periodic table of elements formulated by Dmitri Mendeleev

1870–1880

1872 Heinrich Schliemann excavates Troy

1876 Alexander Graham Bell patents the telephone

1876–85 In Germany, internal-combustion engine, running on gasoline fuel, developed

1877 Thomas Edison invents phonograph; 1879, incandescent bulb; 1894, motion pictures

1879 Ivan Pavlov explores the relationship between psychology and physiology

Timeline Four: 1800 to 2000

	1880–1890	1890–1900	1900–1910
HISTORY AND POLITICS	**1881–82** First pogroms against Jews in Russia **1886** Labor unrest in United States: Haymarket riot, Chicago, leads to the foundation of the American Federation of Labor, first national labor union; 1892, Carnegie steel strike, Pennsylvania **1886** Zionism, a doctrine calling for the establishment of a Jewish state in Palestine, appears in Europe; 1897, first Zionist Congress called by Theodor Hertzl in Basel, Switzerland	**1890** Battle of Wounded Knee, between Sioux nation and United States Army, effectively ends Indian resistance **1893** World's Columbian Exposition, Chicago **1894–1906** Dreyfus Affair: a charge of treason brought fraudulently against a Jewish army officer stirs anti-Semitism and popular unrest in France **1895–98** Wars in Cuba and America weaken Spanish Kingdom and result in losses in territory and prestige **1899–1902** Boer War in South Africa; British defeat South Africans and annex territory	**Edward VII of England (r. 1901–10),** whose government passes sweeping education reforms (1902) **1904–5** Russian–Japanese War over territory on the Pacific coast ends in humiliating defeat for the Russians and heightened unrest among the population; 1905, Bloody Sunday massacre of demonstrating workers in St. Petersburg leads to first Russian revolution; the Great General Strike gives birth to organized labor movement and the first soviets, or workers' councils

EARLY MODERNISM In Europe and America around the turn of the nineteenth century, just as visual artists were beginning to experiment with the concepts of collage and abstraction and composers were testing unusual tonal systems and atonality in music, a number of writers were trying something parallel in prose and poetry: stream of consciousness, rhythmic language, fragmentation of form, and radical play with grammatical structures. Many were explicitly interested in the connections among art forms: the relationship between sound and color, for example, fascinated both the poet Charles Baudelaire and, later, the painter Wassily Kandinsky. Arthur Rimbaud shocked France in 1873 with the publication of the poem *A Season in Hell;* in 1896, Alfred Jarry's absurdist play *King Ubu* caused a riot in a Paris theater. In England in the 1880s Gerard Manley Hopkins invented "sprung rhythm" in poetry. The American Gertrude Stein, also in Paris, wrote *Three Lives* in 1908; Ezra Pound, in London, published the poems *Personae* in 1909. Thus, the pre–World War I radicalism of such artists as the painters Kandinsky, Pablo Picasso, and Kazimir Malevich and the architect Frank Lloyd Wright may be seen in the broader context of other revolutionary and visionary creative ideas.

RELIGION

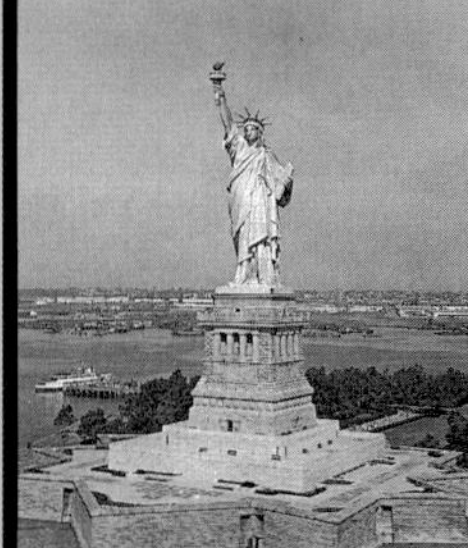

AUGUSTE BARTHOLDI
Statue of Liberty (Liberty Enlightening the World), 1875–84

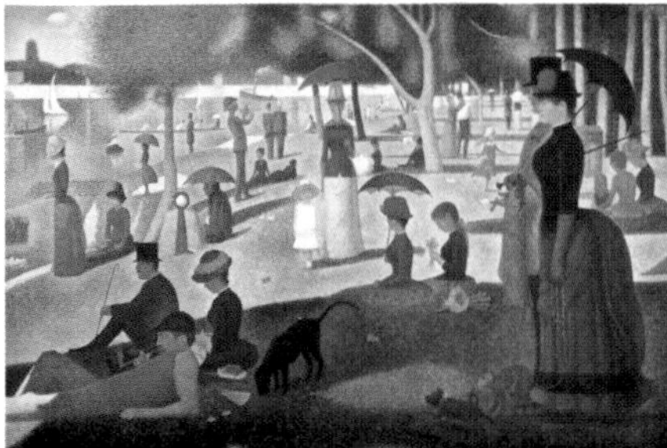

GEORGES SEURAT
A Sunday on La Grande Jatte, 1884–86

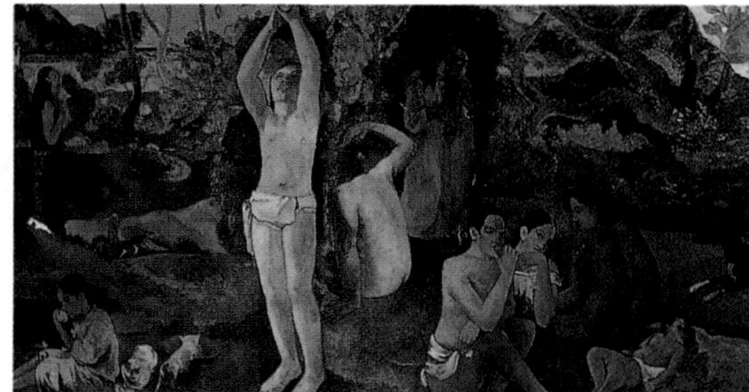

PAUL GAUGUIN
Where Do We Come From? What Are We? Where Are We Going? (detail), 1897

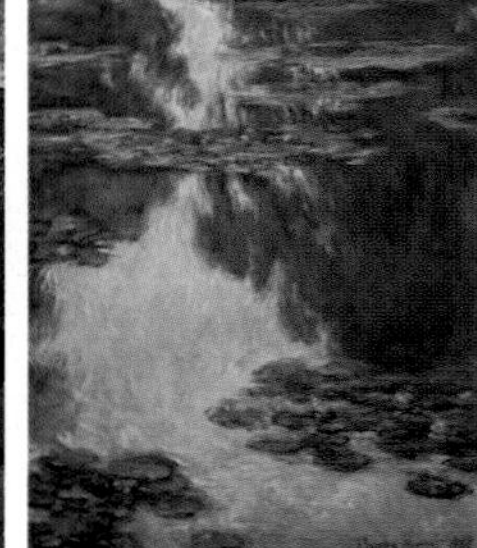

CLAUDE MONET
Water Lilies, Giverny, 1907

	1880–1890	1890–1900	1900–1910
MUSIC, LITERATURE, AND PHILOSOPHY	**French Symbolist poets:** Stéphane Mallarmé (1842–98), Paul Verlaine (1844–96), Arthur Rimbaud (1854–91) **1881** *Portrait of a Lady,* by Henry James **1884** *The Adventures of Huckleberry Finn,* by Mark Twain; *Against the Grain,* by Joris-Karl Huysmans	**1890–1903** Erik Satie composes *Three Small Pieces in the Form of a Pear* **1891** Oscar Wilde writes *The Picture of Dorian Gray* **1897** Bram Stoker publishes *Dracula* **Jorge Luis Borges (1899–1986),** Argentine Surrealist author **1900** Joseph Conrad publishes *Lord Jim*	**Pablo Neruda (1904–73),** Chilean poet **1906** Upton Sinclair publishes *The Jungle,* an American documentary novel that exposes the injustices of the industrial system **1908** Filippo Tommaso Marinetti writes the *Futurist Manifesto;* the composer Arnold Schoenberg uses atonality in composition **Ferdinand de Saussure (1857–1913),** French philologist, founds modern linguistics
SCIENCE, TECHNOLOGY, AND EXPLORATION	**c. 1880** Barbed-wire fences of galvanized iron patented and used to fence in much of the open range in the American West **c. 1885** First automobiles invented, by Karl Benz and Gottlieb Daimler, in Germany	**c. 1890** Reinforced concrete begins to be used as a primary building material **1892–95** Sigmund Freud, Austrian physician, formulates the theory and method of psychoanalysis **1895** X rays discovered by Wilhelm Röntgen; Guglielmo Marconi invents the wireless telegraph, a precursor of radio **1897** Joseph Thomson discovers the electron **1898** Marie Curie discovers radium	**1903** First aircraft flight, made by Orville and Wilbur Wright, in North Carolina **1905** Albert Einstein (1879–1955), pioneering physicist, formulates the theory of relativity, radically changing modern views of space and time; 1953, Unified Field Theory **1909** American Robert Peary reaches North Pole; 1912, Robert Scott's American expedition reaches the South Pole (discovered by the Norwegian Roald Amundsen, 1911)

1910–1920	1920–1930	1930–1940	
1911 Revolution in China: emperor deposed, Sun Yat-sen establishes a republic **1912** British ocean liner *Titanic* sinks **1914** Outbreak of World War I: assassination of Archduke Ferdinand of Austria in Sarajevo leads to war between Germany, Austro-Hungarian Empire, and allies on one side, and Serbia, Russia, France, England, and allies on the other; most of Europe and its colonies become involved; 1917, United States enters; 1918, defeat of Germany. Yugoslavia, Poland, Turkey, Czechoslovakia, Hungary, and Austria become independent nations; Syria, Iraq, and Palestine become mandates controlled by France and Britain **1916** Easter Rebellion in Ireland attempts to gain independence from Britain but fails **1917** Bolshevik Revolution in Russia, under Lenin, inaugurates first communist state **1919** Foundation of the League of Nations, an international congress to promote peace, forerunner of the modern United Nations	**1920** Women enfranchised in the United States; 1928, in England; 1945, in France **1920** With the passage of the Home Rule Bill, the British concede autonomy to southern Ireland; Mohandas Gandhi initiates peaceful mass protests (*satyagraha,* or passive resistance) in India against British rule **1922** Fascists under Benito Mussolini seize power in Italy **1926–53** Joseph Stalin controls Soviet Union; his government is a rigid totalitarian state marked by purges, pogroms, and radical collectivization of farms and industries **1929** Stock market crash in United States inaugurates the Great Depression, worldwide economic crisis, during the 1930s	**1931–41** Japanese wage undeclared war on China, annexing Manchuria **1933** In United States: the New Deal, a program of government spending to end the Depression; in Germany: Adolf Hitler's National Socialist (Nazi) Party seizes power **1934–35** Long March: 90,000 communist rebels led by Mao Ze-dong flee Chiang Kai-shek across China; less than half survive **1936–39** Spanish Civil War, won by Fascists **1938** Germany annexes Austria; 1939, occupies Czechoslovakia **1939–45** World War II: 1939, Germany invades Poland; 1940, Belgium and France; Italy enters war as ally of Germany. 1941, Germany attacks Russia; Japan, allied with Germany, bombs American fleet at Pearl Harbor; United States enters war. Holocaust in Europe: Nazis systematically exterminate more than six million Jews, communists, homosexuals, gypsies, and others; 1945, defeat of Germans and Japanese by Allies	HISTORY AND POLITICS
1917 British government, in control of much of the Middle East following World War I, promulgates the Balfour Declaration supporting the establishment of a Jewish state in Palestine	**1923** Martin Buber, German Jewish theologian, writes *I and Thou*	**1939–43** Rampant persecution of Orthodox church in Soviet Union	RELIGION

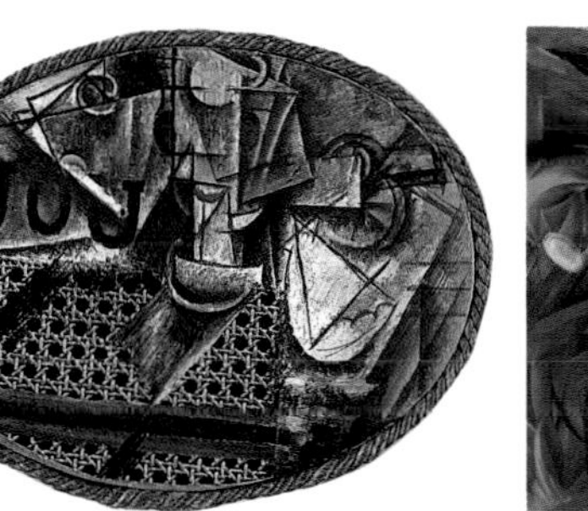

PABLO PICASSO
Still Life with Chair Caning, 1912

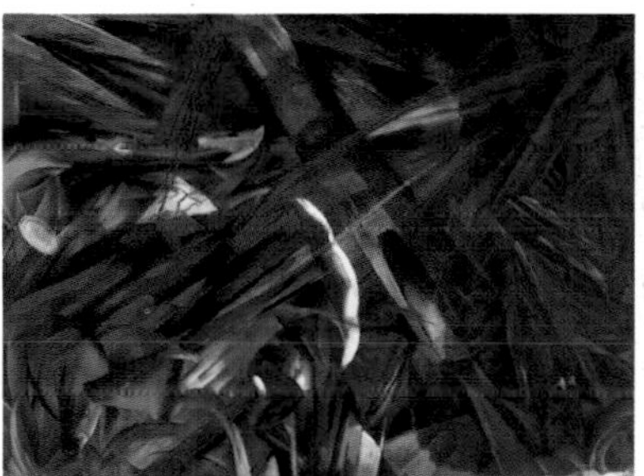

FRANZ MARC
Animal Destinies, 1913

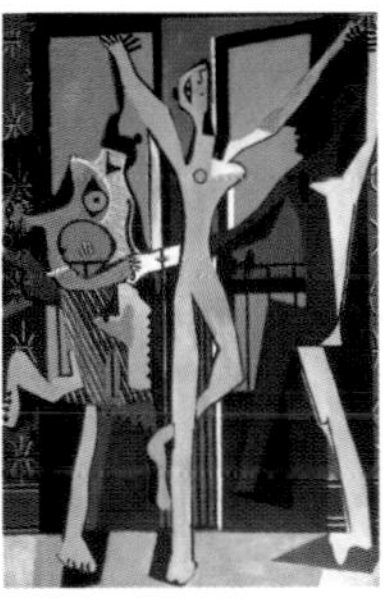

PABLO PICASSO
Three Dancers, 1925

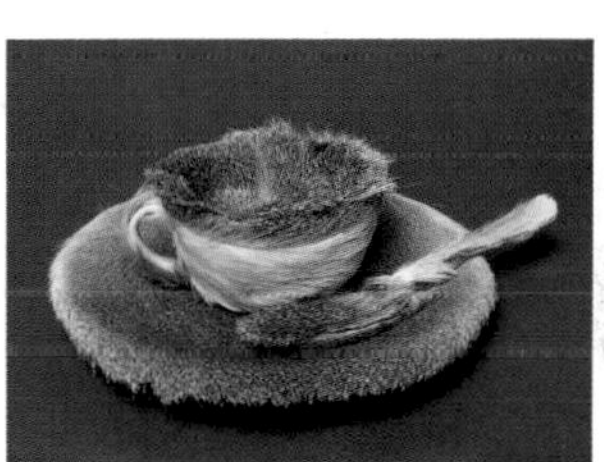

MERET OPPENHEIM
Object, 1936

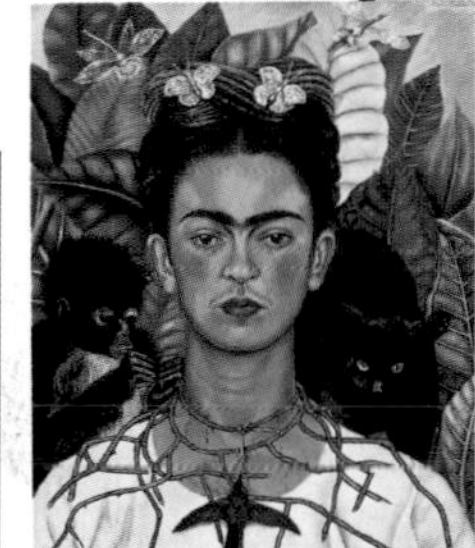

FRIDA KAHLO
Self-Portrait with Thorn Necklace, 1940

1910–1920	1920–1930	1930–1940	
1910 Wassily Kandinsky publishes *Concerning the Spiritual in Art* **c. 1912–15** John Dewey (1859–1952) and Maria Montessori (1870–1952) pioneer new ideas about education **1913–28** Marcel Proust, French critic and novelist, writes *Remembrance of Things Past* **1919** *The Cabinet of Dr. Caligari,* innovative German Expressionist silent film	**1920s** American free verse and modernist poets: Robert Frost (1874–1963), Ezra Pound (1885–1972), T. S. Eliot (1888–1965) **1926** Franz Kafka's *The Castle;* Ernest Hemingway's *The Sun Also Rises;* 1927, Virginia Woolf's *To the Lighthouse;* Abel Gance makes the film *Napoléon;* 1928, D. H. Lawrence's *Lady Chatterly's Lover;* 1929, William Faulkner's *The Sound and the Fury*	**Russian modernist composers:** Rachmaninoff (1873–1943), Stravinsky (1882–1971), Prokoviev (1891–1953), Shostakovich (1906–1975) **1930s** Gertrude Stein explores the forms and structure of language; 1939, James Joyce publishes *Finnegans Wake,* further experimenting with language **1932** Aldous Huxley's *Brave New World* describes a pseudo-utopian future	MUSIC, LITERATURE, AND PHILOSOPHY
1911 First model of atomic structure made, by Ernest Rutherford, in Britain **By 1913** Diesel engines replace steam locomotives on many railways **1914** Henry Ford's fully mechanized mass-production plant for the Model T car marks the beginning of American industrialization **1915** Birth-control movement, led by Margaret Sanger in the United States, advocates family planning	**1920** Radio programs broadcast, Pittsburgh **1922** Howard Carter discovers the tomb of Tutankhamen in Egypt **1925–26** Werner Heisenberg and Erwin Schrödinger's theories of quantum mechanics **1926** Sound motion pictures and television demonstrated **1927** Charles Lindbergh flies an aircraft solo across the Atlantic **1929** Alexander Fleming discovers penicillin	**1931** Radio waves from space detected by the American electrical engineer Karl Jansky: beginning of radio astronomy, using radio waves to trace objects; c. 1935–36, radar discovered by the Scottish physicist Robert Watson-Watt and others **1935** C. F. Richter, American, devises scale for measuring earthquakes	SCIENCE, TECHNOLOGY, AND EXPLORATION

Timeline Four: 1800 to 2000

	1940–1950	1950–1960	1960–1970
HISTORY AND POLITICS	**1945** United Nations founded as an international advisory and peacekeeping council; Yalta Conference: British prime minister Winston Churchill, American president Franklin D. Roosevelt, and Marshal Joseph Stalin of the Soviet Union plan division of Germany into zones of occupation and Europe into spheres of influence **1947** Marshall Plan, proposed to aid recovery of European states devastated by World War II, enacted by the United States. Division of Germany into East and West states **1948** Israel achieves nationhood with recognition by the United Nations; India gains independence from Britain **1949** Communist People's Republic of China founded under Mao Ze-dong	**1954** American civil rights movement begins: United States Supreme Court outlaws racial segregation in public schools; 1955, Montgomery, Alabama, bus boycott by African-Americans, led by Martin Luther King, Jr. **c. 1955–c. 1989** Cold War among Soviet Union, China, and United States: a period of mutual hostilities, espionage, arms escalation, and political maneuvering for influence in other countries by the three world powers; most other nations align themselves with one of the three. Conflicts center upon the opposition between communism and democracy; 1961, Berlin Wall built, isolating West Berlin within East Germany; 1962, Cuban Missile Crisis, Soviet Union attempts to install missiles in Cuba, threatening United States **1959** Fidel Castro establishes communist government in Cuba	**1963** Assassination of United States President John F. Kennedy **1965** America enters Vietnam War **1965–76** Cultural Revolution in China: hard-line Maoist Red Guards formed; educators, local governments, and other elements seen as "enemies of the Revolution" attacked; thousands are killed, millions sent to reeducation camps; many artworks and religious sites are destroyed **1967** Egypt and Israel at war; Egypt is defeated, Israel controls Sinai peninsula **1968** Prague Spring, an attempt by Czechoslovakia to win freedom from Soviet control, crushed by Soviet troops; in United States, presidential candidate Robert F. Kennedy and civil rights leader Martin Luther King, Jr., assassinated; mass protests in United States against Vietnam War
RELIGION	**1948** Thomas Merton, American Trappist monk, poet, and philosopher, writes *The Seven Story Mountain*	**1950s** In some Protestant and Jewish denominations, women become ministers. Chinese invade Tibet and destroy more than 6,000 ancient temples and monasteries; 1959, Dalai Lama, head of state and of Tibetan Buddhism, forced into exile in India	**1962–9485** Pope John XXIII's Second Vatican Council institutes use of vernacular in church ritual and other reforms **1964** Pope Paul VI and Patriarch Athenagoras attempt to resolve differences between Eastern and Western Christian churches
	ADOLPH GOTTLIEB *Descent into Darkness,* 1947	MARK ROTHKO *White and Greens in Blue,* 1957 ROY LICHTENSTEIN *Drowning Girl,* 1963	ROMARE BEARDEN *The Prevalence of Ritual: Baptism,* 1964
MUSIC, LITERATURE, AND PHILOSOPHY	**1941** Charlie Chaplin makes the film *The Great Dictator* **1942** Albert Camus publishes *The Stranger* **1943** Jean-Paul Sartre writes *Being and Nothingness,* a statement of Existentialism **1949** George Orwell's novel *1984* creates a futuristic totalitarian world **1949–50** Simone de Beauvoir authors the key feminist text *The Second Sex*	**1950s** Beat Generation: artists influenced by jazz whose works criticize American postwar materialism and complacency: 1952, John Cage composes *4'33",* 1956, Allen Ginsberg writes the narrative poem *Howl;* 1957, Jack Kerouac writes *On the Road*	**1960** Richard Wright writes *Native Son,* on the African-American experience **c. 1965** British invasion in popular music: the Beatles, the Rolling Stones, and other rock-and-roll groups sell millions of albums **1967** In Colombia, Gabriel Garcia-Marquez writes *One Hundred Years of Solitude* **1969** Woodstock Festival in New York draws 500,000 fans of rock and roll
SCIENCE, TECHNOLOGY, AND EXPLORATION	**The Atomic Age:** 1942, in United States, first nuclear chain reaction; 1943, first nuclear fission bomb; 1945, United States drops atomic bombs on Japanese cities, killing more than 100,000 instantly; 1949, first Soviet nuclear bomb; 1956, first nuclear electrical generators built in England; by 1970s, nuclear power in widespread commercial use **1946** Radiocarbon dating **1947** Dead Sea Scrolls discovered in Israel	**c. 1950** Nuclear-powered submarines and ships in United States and Soviet Union **1953** In England, James Watson and Francis Crick publish a model of the structure of DNA and hypothesize the transmission of genetic codes **1954** Jonas Salk invents polio vaccine **Space Age begins:** 1957, Sputnik, first satellite, launched by Soviet Union; 1961, first human orbit of the earth by Yuri Gagarin	**1960** Laser technology developed **1963** Research in genetic engineering begins in United States; 1976, synthesis achieved **1967** First human heart transplant, by Dr. Christiaan Barnard, in South Africa **1969** United States' Apollo XI mission: Neil Armstrong and Edwin Aldrin walk on the moon; 1976, solar probe launched

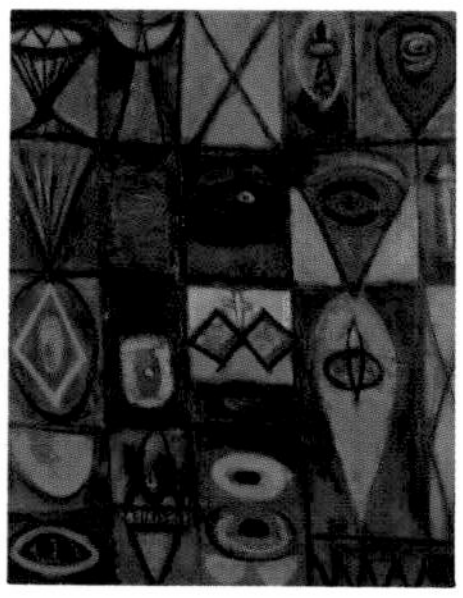

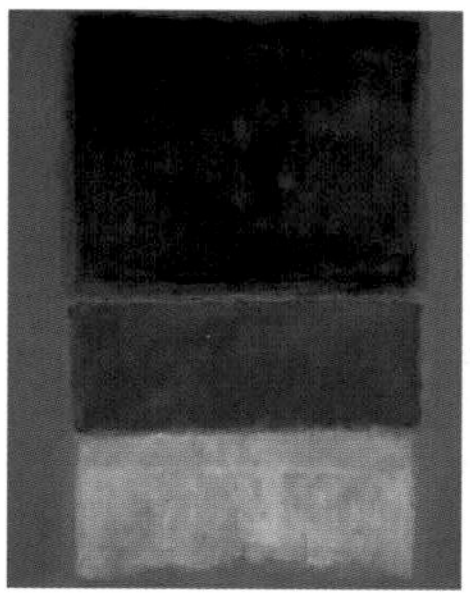

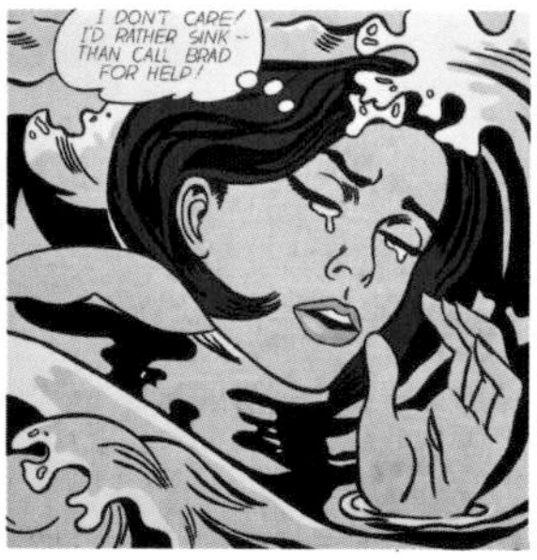

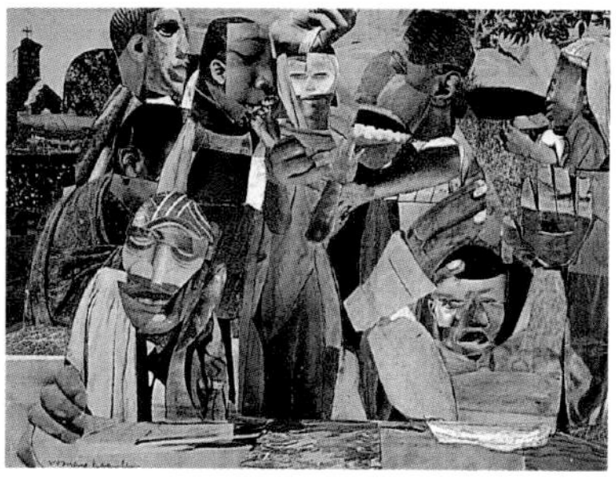

	1970–1980	1980–1990	1990–2000
HISTORY AND POLITICS	**1973** Egypt and Syria attack Israel and are defeated. United States withdraws from Vietnam War, having failed militarily and in response to increasing public criticism. In Chile, Salvador Allende, a socialist, becomes president; he is murdered and a military dictatorship under Augusto Pinochet takes power until 1989. In Washington, D.C., Watergate scandal: President Richard Nixon is implicated in illegal activities; 1974, he resigns **1975** South Vietnam falls, ending the war; nation is unified under a communist regime **1978** Iranian revolution: Islamic fundamentalists rebel against the shah; the Ayatollah Khomeini takes power **1979** Afghan War: Soviet troops invade Afghanistan; they are forced to withdraw ten years later. Camp David Accords brokered by United States: Egypt formally recognizes Israel and regains Sinai territory **1979–81** Iran holds 52 Americans hostage	**1981** Assassination of President Anwar Sadat of Egypt, advocate for peace in the Middle East; 1982, Israel invades Lebanon, whose government falls, causing war among Lebanese and Palestinian factions **1985** Mikhail Gorbachev is premier of Soviet Union: policies of *glasnost* and *perestroika* permit economic, political, and cultural liberalization **1986** In United States, Iran-Contra scandal: secret, illegal sale of arms to Iran and diversion of funds to Nicaraguan rebels implicates high government officials **1989** Berlin Wall torn down; 1989–90, Soviet Union breaks up into independent states, with mostly noncommunist governments, along old ethnic and political boundaries; Yugoslavia and Czechoslovakia divide; student demonstrations (estimated over one million) in favor of democracy, in Tiananmen Square, Beijing, China, suppressed violently by Chinese military	**1990** Germany united **1991** Chechen president Dudayev declares independence from Russia and in 1993 dissolves the parliament; 1997, Chechnya is granted autonomy by Russia; 1999, fighting resumes following terrorist bombings on Russian soil **1991** In the USSR, a coup is launched against President Mikhail Gorbachev, and although the coup fails, Gorbachev resigns; Boris Yeltsin gains control of the government and the USSR is dissolved; Yeltsin becomes the first democratically elected president in the nation's history **1995** Yitzhak Rabin assassinated **1997** Death of Deng Xiaoping; Hong Kong reverts to China **1998** Irish Peace Talks **1999** Clinton impeachment; Panama Canal ceded by U.S.; Macau reverts to China
RELIGION	**1977** End of Catholicism as state religion of Italy **1978** Pope John Paul II of Poland elected, first non-Italian pope in 455 years	**1980s** Rise of religious fundamentalism, especially among Muslims in the Middle East and central Asia, Hindus in India, Orthodox Jews in Israel, and some Christian sects in the United States	**Pope John Paul II** makes several important visits to places around the world including Sarajevo (1997), Cuba (1998), Nigeria (1998), Croatia (1998), Mexico City (1999), and Poland (1999).
	RICHARD ESTES *Food Shop,* 1967	RAYMOND SAUNDERS *White Flower Black Flower,* 1986	PEPÓN OSORIO *Badge of Honor,* 1995
MUSIC, LITERATURE, AND PHILOSOPHY	**1974** Aleksandr Solzhenitsyn (b. 1918), Russian writer whose novels describe life in a Soviet prison camp and criticize the government, is exiled to the United States	**1981** MTV (music television), introduced on cable television, brings the new medium of video music to a mass audience **1989** Anglo-Indian novelist Salman Rushdie's *Satanic Verses* outrages Islamic fundamentalists, who place him under a death threat and force him into hiding	**1990** Death of conductor and composer Leonard Bernstein **1993** Tony Kushner wins Pulitzer Prize for *Angels in America* **1997** Dario Fo wins Nobel Prize in Literature; John Updike publishes *Toward the End of Time*
SCIENCE, TECHNOLOGY, AND EXPLORATION	**1973** Three babies born in England through in-vitro fertilization **c. 1978** Personal computers widely available **1979** Near-meltdown of nuclear reactor at Three Mile Island electrical power plant in Pennsylvania; 1986, explosion of Chernobyl nuclear power plant in Ukraine devastates the area and causes severe radiation poisoning, as well as contamination of atmosphere over much of Europe	**1981** First space shuttle, a reusable manned rocket, launched by United States **1982** First artificial heart implanted **c. 1985** AIDS, identified as a new, incurable disease, spreads throughout the world and begins to claim thousands of lives; by 1995, HIV infection levels reach epidemic proportions **1989** *Voyager II* space probe passes Neptune and discovers a new moon	**1990** Hubble Space Telescope is launched by the crew of the space shuttle Discovery; Human Genome Project (HGP) is officially launched **1997** Cloning of sheep Dolly by scientists at Roslin Institute; NASA's Mars Pathfinder mission deploys its robotic rover called Sojourner on Mars

Books for Further Reading

This list is intended to be as practical as possible. It is therefore limited to books of general interest that were printed over the past 20 years or have been generally available recently. However, certain indispensable volumes that have yet to be superceded are retained. This restriction means omitting numerous classics long out of print, as well as much specialized material of interest to the serious student. The reader is thus referred to the many specialized bibliographies noted below.

REFERENCE RESOURCES IN ART HISTORY

1. ANTHOLOGIES OF SOURCES AND DOCUMENTS

Documents of Modern Art. 14 vols. Wittenborn, New York, 1944–61. A series of specialized anthologies.

The Documents of Twentieth-Century Art. G. K. Hall, Boston. A new series of specialized anthologies, individually listed below.

Goldwater, R., and M. Treves, eds. *Artists on Art, from the Fourteenth to the Twentieth Century.* 3rd ed. Pantheon, New York, 1974.

Holt, E. G., ed. *A Documentary History of Art.* Vol. 1, *The Middle Ages and the Renaissance.* Vol. 2, *Michelangelo and the Mannerists. The Baroque and the Eighteenth Century.* Vol. 3, *From the Classicists to the Impressionists.* 2nd ed. Princeton University Press, Princeton, 1981.

Sources and Documents in the History of Art Series. General ed. H. W. Janson. Prentice Hall, Englewood Cliffs, N.J. Specialized anthologies, individually listed below.

2. BIBLIOGRAPHIES AND RESEARCH GUIDES

Arntzen, E., and R. Rainwater. *Guide to the Literature of Art History.* American Library Association, Chicago, 1980.

Barnet, S. *A Short Guide to Writing About Art.* 4th ed. HarperCollins College, New York, 1993.

Chiarmonte, P. *Women Artists in the United States: A Selective Bibliography and Resource Guide to the Fine and Decorative Arts, 1750–1986.* G. K. Hall, Boston, 1990.

Ehresmann, D. *Architecture: A Bibliographical Guide to Basic Reference Works, Histories, and Handbooks.* Libraries Unlimited, Littleton, Colo., 1984.

———. *Fine Arts: A Bibliographical Guide to Basic Reference Works, Histories, and Handbooks.* 3rd ed. Libraries Unlimited, Littleton, Colo., 1990.

Freitag, W. *Art Books: A Basic Bibliography of Monographs on Artists.* Garland, New York, 1985.

Goldman, B. *Reading and Writing in the Arts: A Handbook.* Wayne State Press, Detroit, 1972.

Kleinbauer, W., and T. Slavens. *Research Guide to Western Art History.* American Library Association, Chicago, 1982.

Reference Publications in Art History. G. K. Hall, Boston. Specialized bibliographies, individually listed below.

3. DICTIONARIES AND ENCYCLOPEDIAS

Baigell, M. *Dictionary of American Art.* Harper & Row, New York, 1979.

Chilvers, I., and H. Osborne, eds. *The Oxford Dictionary of Art.* Oxford University Press, New York, 1988.

The Dictionary of Art. 34 vols. Grove's Dictionaries, New York, 1996.

Duchet-Suchaux, G., and M. Pastoureau. *The Bible and the Saints.* Flammarion Iconographic Guides. Flammarion, Paris and New York, 1994.

Encyclopedia of World Art. 14 vols., with index and supplements. McGraw-Hill, New York, 1959–68.

Fleming, J., and H. Honour. *A Dictionary of Architecture.* 4th ed. Penguin, Baltimore, 1991.

———. *The Penguin Dictionary of Decorative Arts.* New ed. Viking, London, 1989.

Hall, J. *Illustrated Dictionary of Symbols in Eastern and Western Art.* HarperCollins, New York, 1994.

———. *Subjects and Symbols in Art.* 2nd ed. Harper & Row, New York, 1979.

The Hutchinson Dictionary of the Arts. Helicon, London, 1994.

Lever, J., and J. Harris. *Illustrated Dictionary of Architecture, 800–1914.* Faber & Faber, Boston, 1993.

Mayer, R. *The Artist's Handbook of Materials and Techniques.* 5th ed. Viking, New York, 1991.

———. *The HarperCollins Dictionary of Art Terms & Techniques.* 2nd ed. HarperCollins, New York, 1991.

Murray, P. and L. *A Dictionary of Art and Artists.* 5th ed. Penguin, New York, 1988.

Osborne, H., ed. *Oxford Companion to Art.* Oxford, Clarendon Press, 1970.

Pierce, J. S. *From Abacus to Zeus: A Handbook of Art History.* 5th ed. Prentice Hall, Englewood Cliffs, N.J., 1995.

Reid, J. D., ed. *The Oxford Guide to Classical Mythology in the Arts 1300–1990.* 2 vols. Oxford University Press, New York, 1993.

Teague, E. *World Architecture Index: A Guide to Illustrations.* Greenwood Press, New York, 1991.

West, S., ed. *The Bulfinch Guide to Art History.* Little, Brown and Company, Boston, 1996.

The Worldwide Bibliography of Art Exhibition Catalogues, 1963–1987. 3 vols. Kraus, Millwood, N.Y., 1992.

Wright, C., comp. *The World's Master Paintings: From the Early Renaissance to the Present Day: A Comprehensive Listing of Works by 1,300 Painters and a Complete Guide to Their Locations Worldwide.* 2 vols. Routledge, New York, 1991.

4. INDEXES, PRINTED AND ELECTRONIC

ARTbibliographies Modern. 1969 to present. A semiannual publication indexing and annotating more than 300 art periodicals, as well as books, exhibition catalogues, and dissertations. Data since 1984 also available electronically.

Art Index. 1929 to present. A standard quarterly index to more than 200 art periodicals. Data since 1984 also available electronically.

Avery Index to Architectural Periodicals. 1934 to present. 15 vols., with supplementary vols. G. K. Hall, Boston, 1973. Also available electronically.

BHA: Bibliography of the History of Art. 1991 to present. The merger of two standard indexes: *RILA (Répertoire International de la Littérature de l'Art/International Repertory of the Literature of Art,* vol. 1, 1975) and *Répertoire d'Art et d'Archéologie* (vol. 1, 1910).

5. WORLDWIDE WEBSITES

Visit the following Websites for reproductions and information regarding artists, periods, movements, and many more. Also refer to the *Art and Architecture Websites* directory for museum Websites. Many art history departments and libraries of universities and colleges also maintain a Website where you can get reading lists and links to other Websites, such as museums, libraries, and periodicals.

http://aaln.org/ifla-idal *International Directory of Art Libraries*

http://www.AMICO.org *Art Museum Image Consortium*

http://www.archaeological.org *Archaeological Institute of America*

http://archnet.uconn.edu *Virtual Library for Archaeology*

http://www.artchive.com

http://art-history.concordia.ca/AHRC *Art History Research Centre*

http://www.arthistory.net *Art History Network*

http://classics.mit.edu *The Internet Classics Archive*

http://www.collegeart.org *College Art Association*

http://www.constable.net

http://www.cr.nps.gov/habshaer *Historic American Buildings Survey*

http://www.getty.edu *including museum, five institutes, and library*

http://www.gold.ac.uk/aah *Association of Art Historians*

http://www.hart.bbk.ac.uk/VirtualLibrary.html *collection of resources maintained by the History of Art Department of Birkbeck College, University of London*

http://www.icom.org *International Council of Museums*

http://www.icomos.org *International Council on Monuments and Sites*

http://www.ilpi.com/artsource/

http://www.indiana.edu/~aah *Association for Art History*

http://www.siris.si.edu *Smithsonian Institution Research Information System*

http://www.sunsite.org.uk/cgfa *a virtual art museum with reproductions*

http://www.umich.edu/~hartspc/histart/mother *Mother of All Art History Links Pages, maintained by the Department of the History of Art at the University of Michigan*

http://www.unesco.org/whc *World Heritage Center*

http://www.unites.uqam.ca/AHWA *Art History Webmasters Association*

http://vos.ucsb.edu/shuttle/art.html *Voice of the Shuttle: Art & Art History Page*

http://witcombe.sbc.edu/ARTHLinks.html *Art History Resources on the Web, maintained by Chris Whitcombe*

http://wwar.com *World Wide Arts Resources*

6. GENERAL SOURCES ON ART HISTORY, METHOD, AND THEORY

Barasch, M. *Theories of Art: From Plato to Winckelmann.* New York University Press, New York, 1985.

Baxandall, M. *Patterns of Intention: On the Historical Explanation of Pictures.* Yale University Press, New Haven, 1985.
Bois, Y.-A. *Painting as Model.* MIT Press, Cambridge, 1990.
Broude, N., and M. Garrard, *The Expanding Discourse: Feminism and Art History.* Harper & Row, New York, 1992.
———, eds. *Feminism and Art History: Questioning the Litany.* Harper & Row, New York, 1982.
Bryson, N., ed. *Vision and Painting: The Logic of the Gaze.* Yale University Press, New Haven, 1983.
———, et al., eds. *Visual Theory: Painting and Interpretation.* Cambridge University Press, New York, 1991.
Cahn, W. *Masterpieces: Chapters on the History of an Idea.* Princeton University Press, Princeton, 1979.
Chadwick, W. *Women, Art, and Society.* Thames & Hudson, New York, 1990.
Freedberg, D. *The Power of Images: Studies in the History and Theory of Response.* University of Chicago Press, Chicago, 1989.
Gage, J. *Color and Culture: Practice and Meaning from Antiquity to Abstraction.* Little, Brown, Boston, 1993.
Gombrich, E. H. *Art and Illusion.* 4th ed. Pantheon, New York, 1972.
Harris, A. S., and L. Nochlin. *Women Artists, 1550–1950.* Knopf, New York, 1976.
Kemal, S., and I. Gaskell. *The Language of Art History.* Cambridge Studies in Philosophy and the Arts. Cambridge University Press, New York, 1991.
Kleinbauer, W. E. *Modern Perspectives in Western Art History: An Anthology of Twentieth-Century Writings on the Visual Arts.* Reprint of 1971 ed., University of Toronto Press, Toronto, 1989.
Kostof, S. A. *History of Architecture: Settings and Rituals.* 2nd ed. Oxford University Press, New York, 1995.
Kris, E., and O. Kurz. *Legend, Myth, and Magic in the Image of the Artist: A Historical Experiment.* Yale University Press, New Haven, 1979.
Kruft, H-W. *A History of Architectural Theory from Vitruvius to the Present.* Princeton Architectural Press, Princeton, 1994.
Kultermann, U. *The History of Art History.* Abaris Books, New York, 1993.
Nochlin, L. *Women, Art, and Power, and Other Essays.* Harper & Row, New York, 1988.
Panofsky, E. *Meaning in the Visual Arts.* Reprint of 1955 ed., University of Chicago Press, Chicago, 1982.
———. *Tomb Sculpture: Four Lectures on Its Changing Aspects from Ancient Egypt to Bernini.* Introduction by M. Kemp. Harry N. Abrams, New York, 1992.
Parker, R., and G. Pollock. *Old Mistresses: Women, Art, and Ideology.* Pantheon, New York, 1981.
Penny, N. *The Materials of Sculpture.* Yale University Press, New Haven, 1993.
Pevsner, N. *A History of Building Types.* Princeton University Press, Princeton, 1976.
Podro, M. *The Critical Historians of Art.* Yale University Press, New Haven, 1982.
Pollock, G. *Vision and Difference: Femininity, Feminism, and the Histories of Art.* Routledge, New York, 1988.
Rees, A. L., and F. Borzello. *The New Art History.* Humanities Press International, Atlantic Highlands, N.J., 1986.
Roth, L. *Understanding Architecture: Its Elements, History, and Meaning.* Harper & Row, New York, 1993.
Sutton, I. *Western Architecture.* Thames & Hudson, New York, 1999.
Tagg, J. *Grounds of Dispute: Art History, Cultural Politics, and the Discursive Field.* University of Minnesota Press, Minneapolis, 1992.
Trachtenberg, M., and I. Hyman. *Architecture: From Prehistory to Post-Modernism.* Harry N. Abrams, New York, 1986.
Watkin, D. *The Rise of Architectural History.* University of Chicago Press, Chicago, 1980.
Wittkower, R., and M. *Born Under Saturn: The Character and Conduct of Artists: A Documented History from Antiquity to the French Revolution.* Norton, New York, 1963.
Wolff, J. *The Social Production of Art.* 2nd ed. New York University Press, New York, 1993.
Wölfflin, H. *Principles of Art History: The Problem of the Development of Style in Later Art.* Dover, New York, 1932.
Wollheim, R. *Art and Its Objects.* Cambridge University Press, New York, 1980.

PART ONE: THE ANCIENT WORLD

GENERAL REFERENCES

Groenewegen-Frankfort, H. A., and B. Ashmole. *Art of the Ancient World: Painting, Pottery, Sculpture, Architecture from Egypt, Mesopotamia, Crete, Greece, and Rome.* Harry N. Abrams, New York, 1975.
Van Keuren, F. *Guide to Research in Classical Art and Mythology.* American Library Association, Chicago, 1991.
Wolf, W. *The Origins of Western Art: Egypt, Mesopotamia, the Aegean.* Universe Books, New York, 1989.

CHAPTER 1. PREHISTORIC ART

Chauvet, J.-M., É. B. Deschamps, and C. Hilaire. *Dawn of Art: The Chauvet Cave.* Harry N. Abrams, New York, 1995.
Fowler, P. *Images of Prehistory.* Cambridge University Press, New York, 1990.
Leroi-Gourhan, A. *The Dawn of European Art: An Introduction to Palaeolithic Cave Painting.* Cambridge University Press, New York, 1982.
Powell, T. G. E. *Prehistoric Art.* The World of Art. Oxford University Press, New York, 1966.
Ruspoli, M. *The Cave of Lascaux: The Final Photographs.* Harry N. Abrams, New York, 1987.
Sandars, N. *Prehistoric Art in Europe.* 2nd ed. Yale University Press, New Haven, 1985.
Twohig, E. S. *The Megalithic Art of Western Europe.* Oxford University Press, New York, 1981.

CHAPTER 2. EGYPTIAN ART

Aldred, C. *The Development of Ancient Egyptian Art, from 3200 to 1315 B.C.* 3 vols. in 1. Academy Editions, London, 1972.
Arnold, D., and C. Ziegler. *Egyptian Art in the Age of the Pyramids.* Harry N. Abrams, New York, 1999.
Davis, W. *The Canonical Tradition in Ancient Egyptian Art.* Cambridge University Press, New York, 1989.
Edwards, I. E. S. *The Pyramids of Egypt.* Rev. ed. Penguin, Harmondsworth, England, 1991.
Mahdy, C., ed. *The World of the Pharaohs: A Complete Guide to Ancient Egypt.* Thames & Hudson, London, 1990.
Malek, J. *Egyptian Art.* Phaidon, London, 1999.
Mendelssohn, K. *The Riddle of the Pyramids.* Thames & Hudson, New York, 1986.
Panofsky, E. *Tomb Sculpture: Four Lectures on Its Changing Aspects from Ancient Egypt to Bernini.* Introduction by M. Kemp. Harry N. Abrams, New York, 1992.
Robins, G. *The Art of Ancient Egypt.* Harvard University Press, Cambridge, 1997.
Schaefer, H. *Principles of Egyptian Art.* Clarendon Press, Oxford, 1986.
Schulz, R., and M. Seidel. *Egypt: The World of the Pharaohs.* Könemann, Cologne, 1998.
Smith, W., and W. Simpson. *The Art and Architecture of Ancient Egypt.* Pelican History of Art. Rev. ed. Yale University Press, New Haven, 1999.
Wilkinson, R. *Reading Egyptian Art: A Hieroglyphic Guide to Ancient Egyptian Painting and Sculpture.* Thames & Hudson, New York, 1992.

CHAPTER 3. ANCIENT NEAR EASTERN ART

Amiet, P. *Art of the Ancient Near East.* Harry N. Abrams, New York, 1980.
Collon, D. *Ancient Near Eastern Art.* University of California Press, Berkeley, 1995.
———. *First Impressions: Cylinder Seals in the Ancient Near East.* University of Chicago Press, Chicago, 1987.
Crawford, H. *Sumer and the Sumerians.* Cambridge University Press, New York, 1991.
Frankfort, H. *The Art and Architecture of the Ancient Orient.* Pelican History of Art. 5th ed. Yale University Press, New Haven, 1997.
Leick, G. *A Dictionary of Ancient Near Eastern Architecture.* Routledge, New York, 1988.
Lloyd, S. *The Archaeology of Mesopotamia: From the Old Stone Age to the Persian Conquest.* Rev. ed. Thames & Hudson, New York, 1984.
Moscati, S. *The Phoenicians.* Abbeville Press, New York, 1988.
Oates, J. *Babylon.* Rev. ed. Thames & Hudson, London, 1986.
Parrot, A. *Sumer: The Dawn of Art.* Golden Press, New York, 1961.
Reade, J. *Mesopotamia.* British Museum, London, 1991.

CHAPTER 4. AEGEAN ART

Barber, R. *The Cyclades in the Bronze Age.* University of Iowa Press, Iowa City, 1987.
Getz-Preziosi, P. *Sculptors of the Cyclades.* University of Michigan Press, Ann Arbor, 1987.
Graham, J. *The Palaces of Crete.* Rev. ed. Princeton University Press, Princeton, 1987.
Hampe, R., and E. Simon. *The Birth of Greek Art from the Mycenean to the Archaic Period.* Oxford University Press, New York, 1981.
Higgins, R. *Minoan and Mycenaean Art.* The World of Art. Rev. ed. Oxford University Press, New York, 1981.
Hood, S. *The Arts in Prehistoric Greece.* Pelican History of Art. Yale University Press, New Haven, 1992.
———. *The Minoans: The Story of Bronze Age Crete.* Praeger, New York, 1981.
Hurwit, J. *The Art and Culture of Early Greece, 1100–480 B.C.* Cornell University Press, Ithaca, 1985.
McDonald, W. *Progress into the Past: The Rediscovery of Mycenaean Civilization.* 2nd ed. Indiana University Press, Bloomington, 1990.
Vermeule, E. *Greece in the Bronze Age.* University of Chicago Press, Chicago, 1972.

CHAPTER 5. GREEK ART

Beazley, J. D. *Athenian Red Figure Vases: The Classical Period: A Handbook.* The World of Art. Thames & Hudson, New York, 1989.
———. *Athenian Red Figure Vases: The Archaic Period: A Handbook.* The World of Art. Thames & Hudson, New York, 1991.
———. *Attic Black-Figure Vase-Painters.* Reprint of 1956 ed., Hacker, New York, 1978.

———. *The Development of Attic Black-Figure.* Rev. ed. University of California Press, Berkeley, 1986.
Boardman, J. *Athenian Black Figure Vases: A Handbook.* Thames & Hudson, New York, 1985.
———. *Greek Sculpture: The Archaic Period: A Handbook.* The World of Art. New ed. Thames & Hudson, New York, 1985.
———. *Greek Sculpture: The Classical Period: A Handbook.* The World of Art. New ed. Thames & Hudson, New York, 1985.
———, ed. *The Oxford History of Classical Art.* Oxford University Press, New York, 1993.
Carpenter, T. H. *Art and Myth in Ancient Greece: A Handbook.* The World of Art. Thames & Hudson, New York, 1991.
Lawrence, A. *Greek Architecture.* Pelican History of Art. 5th ed., rev. Yale University Press, New Haven, 1996.
Moon, W., ed. *Ancient Greek Art and Iconography.* University of Wisconsin Press, Madison, 1983.
Osborne, R. *Archaic and Classical Greek Art.* Oxford University Press, New York, 1998.
Papaioannou, K. *The Art of Greece.* Harry N. Abrams, New York, 1989.
Pedley, J. *Greek Art and Archaeology.* 2nd ed. Harry N. Abrams, New York, 1997.
Pollitt, J. *The Ancient View of Greek Art: Criticism, History, and Terminology.* Yale University Press, New Haven, 1974.
———. *Art and Experience in Classical Greece.* Cambridge University Press, New York, 1972.
———. *Art in the Hellenistic Age.* Cambridge University Press, New York, 1986.
———, ed. *Art of Greece, 1400–31 B.C.: Sources and Documents.* 2nd ed. Prentice Hall, Englewood Cliffs, N.J., 1990.
Richter, G. M. A. *A Handbook of Greek Art.* 9th ed. Da Capo, New York, 1987.
———. *Portraits of the Greeks.* Ed. R. Smith. Oxford University Press, New York, 1984.
———. *The Sculpture and Sculptors of the Greeks.* 4th ed., rev. Yale University Press, New Haven, 1970.
Ridgway, B. S. *Hellenistic Sculpture. Vol. 1, The Styles of ca. 331–200 B.C.* Bristol Classical Press, Bristol, England, 1990.
Robertson, M. *The Art of Vase Painting in Classical Athens.* Cambridge University Press, New York, 1992.
———. *History of Greek Art.* 2 vols. Cambridge University Press, Cambridge, 1975.
Schefold, K. *Gods and Heroes in Late Archaic Greek Art.* Cambridge University Press, New York, 1992.
———. *Myth and Legend in Early Greek Art.* Harry N. Abrams, New York, 1966.
Smith, R. *Hellenistic Sculpture.* The World of Art. Thames & Hudson, New York, 1991.
Spivey, N. *Greek Art.* Phaidon, London, 1997.
Stewart, A. F. *Greek Sculpture: An Exploration.* Yale University Press, New Haven, 1990.

CHAPTER 6. ETRUSCAN ART

Boethius, A. *Etruscan and Early Roman Architecture.* Pelican History of Art. 2nd ed. Yale University Press, New Haven, 1992.
Bonfante, L., ed. *Etruscan Life and Afterlife: A Handbook of Etruscan Studies.* Wayne State University Press, Detroit, 1986.
Brendel, O. *Etruscan Art.* Pelican History of Art. Yale University Press, New Haven, 1995.
Richardson, E. *The Etruscans: Their Art and Civilization.* Reprint of 1964 ed., with corrections, University of Chicago Press, Chicago, 1976.
Spivey, N. *Etruscan Art.* The World of Art. Thames & Hudson, New York, 1997.
Sprenger, M., G. Bartoloni, and M. Hirmer. *The Etruscans: Their History, Art, and Architecture.* Harry N. Abrams, New York, 1983.
Steingräber, S., ed. *Etruscan Painting: Catalogue Raisonné of Etruscan Wall Paintings.* Johnson Reprint, New York, 1986.

CHAPTER 7. ROMAN ART

Andreae, B. *The Art of Rome.* Harry N. Abrams, New York, 1977.
Brilliant, R. *Roman Art from the Republic to Constantine.* Phaidon, London, 1974.
Jenkyns, R., ed. *The Legacy of Rome: A New Appraisal.* Oxford University Press, New York, 1992.
Kleiner, D. *Roman Sculpture.* Yale University Press, New Haven, 1992.
Ling, R. *Roman Painting.* Cambridge University Press, New York, 1991.
L'Orange, H. *Art Forms and Civic Life in the Late Roman Empire.* Princeton University Press, Princeton, 1965.
Macdonald, W. *The Architecture of the Roman Empire.* 2 vols. Rev. ed. Yale University Press, New Haven, 1982–86.
Nash, E. *Pictorial Dictionary of Ancient Rome.* 2 vols. Reprint of 1968 2nd ed., Hacker, New York, 1981.
Pollitt, J. *The Art of Rome and Late Antiquity: Sources and Documents.* Prentice Hall, Englewood Cliffs, N.J., 1966.
Ramage, N. and A. *The Cambridge Illustrated History of Roman Art.* Cambridge University Press, Cambridge, 1991.
Strong, D. E. *Roman Art.* Pelican History of Art. 2nd ed. Yale University Press, New Haven, 1992.
Vitruvius. *The Ten Books on Architecture.* Trans. M. H. Morgan. Reprint of 1914 ed., Dover, New York, 1960.
Ward-Perkins, J. B. *Roman Imperial Architecture.* Pelican History of Art. Reprint of 1981 ed., Penguin, New York, 1992.
Zanker, P. *The Power of Images in the Age of Augustus.* University of Michigan Press, Ann Arbor, 1988.

PART TWO: THE MIDDLE AGES

GENERAL REFERENCES

Alexander, J. J. G. *Medieval Illuminators and Their Methods of Work.* Yale University Press, New Haven, 1992.
Calkins, R. G. *Illuminated Books of the Middle Ages.* Cornell University Press, Ithaca, 1983.
———. *Monuments of Medieval Art.* Reprint of 1979 ed., Cornell University Press, Ithaca, 1985.
Cassidy, B., ed. *Iconography at the Crossroads.* Princeton University Press, Princeton, 1993.
Katzenellenbogen, A. *Allegories of the Virtues and Vices in Medieval Art.* Reprint of 1939 ed., University of Toronto Press, Toronto, 1989.
Pächt, O. *Book Illumination in the Middle Ages: An Introduction.* Miller, London, 1986.
Pelikan, J. *Mary Through the Centuries: Her Place in the History of Culture.* Yale University Press, New Haven, 1996.
Schapiro, M. *Late Antique, Early Christian, and Mediaeval Art.* Meyer Schapiro, Selected Papers, 3. Braziller, New York, 1979.
Snyder, J. *Medieval Art: Painting, Sculpture, Architecture, 4th–14th Century.* Harry N. Abrams, New York, 1989.
Tasker, E. *Encyclopedia of Medieval Church Art.* Batsford, London, 1993.

CHAPTER 8. EARLY CHRISTIAN AND BYZANTINE ART

Beckwith, J. *Early Christian and Byzantine Art.* Pelican History of Art. 2nd ed. Penguin, New York, 1979.
Demus, O. *Byzantine Art and the West.* New York University Press, New York, 1970.
Grabar, A. *The Beginnings of Christian Art, 200–395. The Arts of Mankind.* Odyssey, New York, 1967.
———. *Christian Iconography: A Study of Its Origins.* Princeton University Press, Princeton, 1968.
Kleinbauer, W. *Early Christian and Byzantine Architecture: An Annotated Bibliography and Historiography.* G. K. Hall, Boston, 1993.
Krautheimer, R., and S. Curcic. *Early Christian and Byzantine Architecture.* Pelican History of Art. 4th ed. Yale University Press, New Haven, 1992.
Lowden, J. *Early Christian and Byzantine Art.* Phaidon, London, 1997.
Maguire, H. *Art and Eloquence in Byzantium.* Princeton University Press, Princeton, 1981.
Mango, C. *The Art of the Byzantine Empire, 312–1453: Sources and Documents.* Reprint of 1972 ed., University of Toronto Press, Toronto, 1986.
Mark, R., and A. S. Çakmak, eds. *Hagia Sophia from the Age of Justinian to the Present.* Cambridge University Press, New York, 1992.
Mathews, T. *The Byzantine Churches of Istanbul: A Photographic Survey.* Pennsylvania State University Press, University Park, Pa., 1976.
———. *Byzantium from Antiquity to the Renaissance.* Harry N. Abrams, New York, 1998.
———. *The Clash of Gods: A Reinterpretation of Early Christian Art.* Princeton University Press, Princeton, 1993.
Milburn, R. *Early Christian Art and Architecture.* University of California Press, Berkeley, 1988.
Rodley, L. *Byzantine Art and Architecture: An Introduction.* Cambridge University Press, New York, 1994.
Simson, O. G. von. *Sacred Fortress: Byzantine Art and Statecraft in Ravenna.* Reprint of 1948 ed., Princeton University Press, Princeton, 1987.
Weitzmann, K. *Late Antique and Early Christian Book Illumination.* Braziller, New York, 1977.

CHAPTER 9. EARLY MEDIEVAL ART

Alexander, J. J. G. *Insular Manuscripts, Sixth to the Ninth Century. Survey of Manuscripts Illuminated in the British Isles.* Miller, London, 1978.
Backhouse, J. *The Golden Age of Anglo-Saxon Art, 966–1066.* Indiana University Press, Bloomington, 1984.
———, ed. *The Lindisfarne Gospels.* Phaidon, Oxford, 1981.
Conant, K. *Carolingian and Romanesque Architecture, 800–1200.* Pelican History of Art. 4th ed. Yale University Press, New Haven, 1992.
Davis-Weyer, C. *Early Medieval Art, 300–1150: Sources and Documents.* Reprint of 1971 ed., University of Toronto Press, Toronto, 1986.
Deshman, R. *Anglo-Saxon and Anglo-Scandinavian Art: An Annotated Bibliography.* G. K. Hall, Boston, 1984.
Dodwell, C. R. *Anglo-Saxon Art: A New Perspective.* Cornell University Press, Ithaca, 1982.
———. *The Pictorial Arts of the West, 800–1200.* Pelican History of Art. New ed. Yale University Press, New Haven, 1993.
Horn, W., and E. Born. *The Plan of St. Gall.* 3 vols. University of California Press, Berkeley, 1979.
Kitzinger, E. *Early Medieval Art, with Illustrations from the British Museum.* Rev. ed. Indiana University Press, Bloomington, 1983.
Lasko, P. *Ars Sacra, 800–1200.* Pelican History of Art. 2nd ed. Yale University Press, New Haven, 1994.

Mayr-Harting, M. *Ottonian Book Illumination: An Historical Study.* 2 vols. Miller, London, 1991–93.

Nees, L. *From Justinian to Charlemagne: European Art, 567–787: An Annotated Bibliography.* G. K. Hall, Boston, 1985.

Rickert, M. *Painting in Britain: The Middle Ages.* Pelican History of Art. 2nd ed. Penguin, Harmondsworth, England, 1965.

Stone, L. *Sculpture in Britain: The Middle Ages.* Pelican History of Art. 2nd ed. Penguin, Harmondsworth, England, 1972.

Temple, E. *Anglo-Saxon Manuscripts, 900–1066. Survey of Manuscripts Illuminated in the British Isles.* Miller, London, 1976.

Werner, M. *Insular Art: An Annotated Bibliography.* G. K. Hall, Boston, 1984.

Wilson, D. M. *Anglo-Saxon Art: From the Seventh Century to the Norman Conquest.* Overlook Press, Woodstock, N.Y., 1984.

CHAPTER 10. ROMANESQUE ART

Bizzarro, T. *Romanesque Architectural Criticism: A Prehistory.* Cambridge University Press, New York, 1992.

Boase, T. S. R. *English Art, 1100–1216.* Oxford History of English Art. Clarendon Press, Oxford, 1953.

Cahn, W. *Romanesque Bible Illumination.* Cornell University Press, Ithaca, 1982.

Chapman, G. *Mosan Art: An Annotated Bibliography.* Reference Publications in Art History. G. K. Hall, Boston, 1988.

Davies, M. *Romanesque Architecture: A Bibliography.* G. K. Hall, Boston, 1993.

Focillon, H. *The Art of the West in the Middle Ages.* Ed. J. Bony. 2 vols. Reprint of 1963 ed., Cornell University Press, Ithaca, 1980.

Glass, D. F. *Italian Romanesque Sculpture: An Annotated Bibliography.* Reference Publications in Art History. G. K. Hall, Boston, 1983.

Hearn, M. F. *Romanesque Sculpture: The Revival of Monumental Stone Sculpture.* Cornell University Press, Ithaca, 1981.

Kaufmann, C. *Romanesque Manuscripts, 1066–1190. Survey of Manuscripts Illuminated in the British Isles.* Miller, London, 1978.

Lyman, T. W. *French Romanesque Sculpture: An Annotated Bibliography.* Reference Publications in Art History. G. K. Hall, Boston, 1987.

Mâle, E. *Religious Art in France, the Twelfth Century: A Study of the Origins of Medieval Iconography.* Bollingen series, 90:1. Princeton University Press, Princeton, 1978.

Nichols, S. *Romanesque Signs: Early Medieval Narrative and Iconography.* Yale University Press, New Haven, 1983.

Petzold, A. *Romanesque Art.* Perspectives. Harry N. Abrams, New York, 1995.

Platt, C. *The Architecture of Medieval Britain: A Social History.* Yale University Press, New Haven, 1990.

Schapiro, M. *Romanesque Art.* Braziller, New York, 1977.

Stoddard, W. *Art and Architecture in Medieval France.* Harper & Row, New York, 1972.

Toman, R. *Romanesque Architecture, Sculpture, Painting.* Könemann, Cologne, 1997.

CHAPTER 11. GOTHIC ART

Belting, H. *The Image and Its Public: Form and Function of Early Paintings of the Passion.* Caratzas, New Rochelle, N.Y., 1990.

Blum, P. *Early Gothic Saint-Denis: Restorations and Survivals.* University of California Press, Berkeley, 1992.

Bomford, D. *Art in the Making: Italian Painting Before 1400.* Exh. cat. National Gallery of Art, London, 1989.

Bony, J. *The English Decorated Style: Gothic Architecture Transformed, 1250–1350.* Cornell University Press, Ithaca, 1979.

———. *French Gothic Architecture of the Twelfth and Thirteenth Centuries.* University of California Press, Berkeley, 1983.

Bowie, T., ed. *The Sketchbook of Villard de Honnecourt.* Reprint of 1968 ed., Greenwood, Westport, Conn., 1982.

Camille, M. *Gothic Art: Glorious Visions.* Perspectives. Harry N. Abrams, New York, 1997.

———. *The Gothic Idol: Ideology and Image Making in Medieval Art.* Cambridge University Press, New York, 1989.

Caviness, M. H. *Stained Glass Before 1540: An Annotated Bibliography.* G. K. Hall, Boston, 1983.

———. *Sumptuous Arts at the Royal Abbeys of Reims and Braine.* Princeton University Press, Princeton, 1990.

Cennini, C. *The Craftsman's Handbook (Il Libro dell'Arte).* Dover, New York, 1954.

Erlande-Brandenburg, A. *Gothic Art.* Harry N. Abrams, New York, 1989.

Frankl, P. *Gothic Architecture.* Pelican History of Art. Penguin, Harmondsworth, England, 1962.

Frisch, T. G. *Gothic Art, 1140–c. 1450: Sources and Documents.* Reprint of 1971 ed., University of Toronto Press, Toronto, 1987.

Grodecki, L., and C. Brisac. *Gothic Stained Glass, 1200–1300.* Cornell University Press, Ithaca, 1985.

Jantzen, H. *High Gothic: The Classic Cathedrals of Chartres, Reims, Amiens.* Reprint of 1962 ed., Princeton University Press, Princeton, 1984.

Lord, C. *Royal French Patronage of Art in the Fourteenth Century: An Annotated Bibliography.* G. K. Hall, Boston, 1985.

Mâle, E. *Religious Art in France, the Thirteenth Century: A Study of Medieval Iconography and Its Sources.* Ed. H. Bober. Princeton University Press, Princeton, 1984.

Meiss, M. *Painting in Florence and Siena After the Black Death.* Princeton University Press, Princeton, 1951.

Meulen, J. van der. *Chartres: Sources and Literary Interpretation: A Critical Bibliography.* Reference Publications in Art History. G. K. Hall, Boston, 1989.

Morgan, N. *Early Gothic Manuscripts. Survey of Manuscripts Illuminated in the British Isles.* 2 vols. Miller, London, 1982–88.

Murray, S. *Beauvais Cathedral: Architecture of Transcendence.* Princeton University Press, Princeton, 1989.

Panofsky, E. *Gothic Architecture and Scholasticism.* Reprint of 1951 ed., New American Library, New York, 1985.

———, ed. and trans. *Abbot Suger on the Abbey Church of Saint-Denis and Its Art Treasures.* 2nd ed. Princeton University Press, Princeton, 1979.

Pope-Hennessy, J. *Italian Gothic Sculpture.* 3rd ed. Oxford University Press, New York, 1986.

Sandler, L. *Gothic Manuscripts, 1285–1385. Survey of Manuscripts Illuminated in the British Isles.* Miller, London, 1986.

Simson, O. von. *The Gothic Cathedral: Origins of Gothic Architecture and the Medieval Concept of Order.* 3rd ed. Princeton University Press, Princeton, 1988.

Stubblebine, J. *Assisi and the Rise of Vernacular Art.* Harper & Row, New York, 1985.

———. *Dugento Painting: An Annotated Bibliography.* G. K. Hall, Boston, 1985.

Vigorelli, G. *The Complete Paintings of Giotto.* Harry N. Abrams, New York, 1966.

Welch, E. *Art and Society in Italy 1350–1500.* Oxford University Press, London, 1997.

White, J. *Art and Architecture in Italy, 1250–1400.* Pelican History of Art. 3rd ed. Yale University Press, New Haven, 1993.

———. *Duccio: Tuscan Art and the Medieval Workshop.* Thames & Hudson, New York, 1979.

Williamson, P. *Gothic Sculpture, 1140–1300.* Yale University Press, New Haven, 1995.

Wilson, C. *The Gothic Cathedral.* Thames & Hudson, New York, 1990.

PART THREE: THE RENAISSANCE THROUGH THE ROCOCO

GENERAL REFERENCES

Campbell, L. *Renaissance Portraits: European Portrait-Painting in the 14th, 15th, and 16th Centuries.* Yale University Press, New Haven, 1990.

De Winter, P. *European Decorative Arts, 1400–1600: An Annotated Bibliography.* G. K. Hall, Boston, 1988.

Hartt, F. *Italian Renaissance Art.* 4th ed. Harry N. Abrams, New York, 1993.

Haskell, F., and N. Penny. *Taste and the Antique: The Lure of Classical Sculpture, 1500–1900.* Yale University Press, New Haven, 1981.

Held, J., and D. Posner. *Seventeenth and Eighteenth Century: Baroque Painting, Sculpture, Architecture.* Harry N. Abrams, New York, 1971.

Hind, A. *History of Engraving and Etching.* Reprint of 1923 3rd ed., Dover, New York, 1963.

———. *An Introduction to a History of Woodcut.* 2 vols. Reprint of 1935 ed., Dover, New York, 1963.

Ivins, W. M., Jr. *How Prints Look: Photographs with a Commentary.* Beacon Press, Boston, 1987.

Landau, D., and P. Parshall. *The Renaissance Print.* Yale University Press, New Haven, 1994.

Martin, J. R. *Baroque.* Penguin, Harmondsworth, England, 1989.

Norberg-Schultz, C. *Baroque Architecture.* Harry N. Abrams, New York, 1971.

———. *Late Baroque and Rococo Architecture.* Harry N. Abrams, New York, 1983.

Snyder, J. *Northern Renaissance Art: Painting, Sculpture, the Graphic Arts from 1350–1575.* Harry N. Abrams, New York, 1985.

Wiebenson, D., ed. *Architectural Theory and Practice from Alberti to Ledoux.* 2nd ed. University of Chicago Press, Chicago, 1983.

Wittkower, R. *Architectural Principles in the Age of Humanism.* 4th ed. St. Martin's Press, New York, 1988.

CHAPTER 12. THE EARLY RENAISSANCE IN ITALY

Alberti, L. B. *On the Art of Building, in Ten Books.* Trans. J. Rykwert, et al. MIT Press, Cambridge, 1991.

———. *On Painting.* Trans. C. Grayson, introduction and notes M. Kemp. Penguin, New York, 1991.

Ames-Lewis, F. *Drawing in Early Renaissance Italy.* Yale University Press, New Haven, 1981.

Battisti, E. *Filippo Brunelleschi: The Complete Works.* Rizzoli, New York, 1981.

Baxandall, M. *Painting and Experience in Fifteenth-Century Italy: A Primer in the Social History of Pictorial Style.* 2nd ed. Oxford University Press, New York, 1988.

Blunt, A. *Artistic Theory in Italy, 1450–1600.* Reprint of 1940 ed., Oxford University Press, New York, 1983.

Bober, P., and R. Rubinstein. *Renaissance Artists and Antique Sculpture: A Handbook of Sources.* Oxford University Press, New York, 1986.

Borsook, E. *The Mural Painters of Tuscany: From Cimabue to Andrea del Sarto.* 2nd ed. Oxford University Press, New York, 1980.

Campbell, L. *Renaissance Portraits: European Portrait-Painting in the 14th, 15th, and 16th Centuries.* Yale University Press, New Haven, 1990.

Dunkelman, M. *Central Italian Painting, 1400–1465: An Annotated Bibliography.* G. K. Hall, Boston, 1986.

Gilbert, C. E. *Italian Art, 1400–1500: Sources and Documents.* Prentice Hall, Englewood Cliffs, N.J., 1980.

Goldthwaite, R. *Wealth and the Demand for Art in Italy, 1300–1600.* Johns Hopkins University Press, Baltimore, 1993.

Gombrich, E. H. *Norm and Form: Studies in the Art of the Renaissance.* Phaidon, London, 1966.

———. *Symbolic Images: Studies in the Art of the Renaissance.* 3rd ed. Phaidon, London, 1972.

Heydenreich, L., and W. Lotz. *Architecture in Italy, 1400–1600.* Pelican History of Art. Rev. ed. Yale University Press, New Haven, 1996.

Humfreys, P., and M. Kemp, eds. *The Altarpiece in the Renaissance.* Cambridge University Press, New York, 1990.

Huse, N., and W. Wolters. *The Art of Renaissance Venice: Architecture, Sculpture, and Painting, 1460–1590.* University of Chicago Press, Chicago, 1990.

Janson, H. W. *The Sculpture of Donatello.* 2 vols. Princeton University Press, Princeton, 1979.

Joannides, P. *Masaccio and Masolino: A Complete Catalogue.* Harry N. Abrams, New York, 1993.

Karpinsky, C. *Italian Printmaking, Fifteenth and Sixteenth Centuries: An Annotated Bibliography.* G. K. Hall, Boston, 1987.

Kempers, B. *Painting, Power, and Patronage: The Rise of the Professional Artist in the Italian Renaissance.* Penguin, New York, 1992.

Krautheimer, R., and T. Krautheimer-Hess. *Lorenzo Ghiberti.* 2nd ed. Princeton University Press, Princeton, 1970.

Lavin, M. A. *Piero della Francesca.* Harry N. Abrams, New York, 1992.

Murray, P. *The Architecture of the Italian Renaissance.* The World of Art. Rev. ed. Thames & Hudson, New York, 1986.

Panofsky, E. *Perspective as Symbolic Form.* Zone Books, New York, 1991.

———. *Renaissance and Renascences in Western Art.* Humanities Press, New York, 1970.

Paoletti, J. T., and G. M. Radtke. *Art in Renaissance Italy.* Harry N. Abrams, New York, 1997.

Pope-Hennessy, J. *Donatello.* Abbeville Press, New York, 1993.

———. *Italian Renaissance Sculpture.* 3rd ed. Oxford University Press, New York, 1986.

———. *The Portrait in the Renaissance.* Pantheon, New York, 1966.

Rosenberg, C. *Fifteenth-Century North Italian Painting and Drawing: An Annotated Bibliography.* G. K. Hall, Boston, 1986.

Seymour, C. *Sculpture in Italy, 1400–1500.* Pelican History of Art. Penguin, Harmondsworth, England, 1966.

Turner, A. R. *The Vision of Landscape in Renaissance Italy.* Princeton University Press, Princeton, 1974.

Vasari, G. *The Lives of the Painters, Sculptors, and Architects.* Trans. G. du C. De Vere. 2 vols. Everyman's Library. Knopf, New York, 1996.

Wackernagel, M. *The World of the Florentine Renaissance Artist: Projects and Patrons, Workshop and Art Market.* Princeton University Press, Princeton, 1981.

Wilk, S. *Fifteenth-Century Central Italian Sculpture: An Annotated Bibliography.* G. K. Hall, Boston, 1986.

CHAPTER 13. THE HIGH RENAISSANCE IN ITALY

Ackerman, J., and J. Newman. *The Architecture of Michelangelo.* 2nd ed. Penguin, Harmondsworth, England, 1986.

Boase, T. S. R. *Giorgio Vasari: The Man and the Book.* Princeton University Press, Princeton, 1979.

Brown, P. *Art and Life in Renaissance Venice.* Perspectives. Harry N. Abrams, New York, 1997.

———. *Venice and Antiquity: The Venetian Sense of the Past.* Yale University Press, New Haven, 1997.

Bruschi, A. *Bramante.* Thames & Hudson, New York, 1977.

Clark, K. *Leonardo da Vinci.* Revised and introduced by M. Kemp. Viking, New York, 1988.

Cole, A. *Virtue and Magnificence: Art of the Italian Renaissance Courts.* Perspectives. Harry N. Abrams, New York, 1995.

De Tolnay, C. *Michelangelo.* 4 vols. 2nd ed. Princeton University Press, Princeton, 1969–71.

Freedberg, S. *Painting of the High Renaissance in Rome and Florence.* 2 vols. Harvard University Press, Cambridge, 1961.

———. *Painting in Italy, 1500–1600.* Pelican History of Art. 3rd ed. Yale University Press, New Haven, 1993.

Hibbard, H. *Michelangelo.* 2nd ed. Harper & Row, New York, 1985.

Jones, R., and N. Penny. *Raphael.* Yale University Press, New Haven, 1983.

Kemp, M. *Leonardo da Vinci: The Marvellous Works of Nature and Man.* Harvard University Press, Cambridge, 1981.

———, ed. *Leonardo on Painting: An Anthology of Writings.* Yale University Press, New Haven, 1989.

Klein, R., and H. Zerner. *Italian Art, 1500–1600: Sources and Documents.* Reprint of 1966 ed., Northwestern University Press, Evanston, Ill., 1989.

Lightbown, R. *Mantegna: With a Complete Catalogue of the Paintings.* University of California Press, Berkeley, 1986.

———. *Sandro Botticelli.* 2 vols. University of California Press, Berkeley, 1978.

Panofsky, E. *Studies in Iconology: Humanist Themes in the Art of the Renaissance.* Harper & Row, New York, 1972.

Partridge, L. *The Art of Renaissance Rome.* Perspectives. Harry N. Abrams, New York, 1997.

Pietrangeli, C., et al. *The Sistine Chapel: A Glorious Restoration.* Harry N. Abrams, New York, 1992.

Pope-Hennessy, J. *Italian High Renaissance and Baroque Sculpture.* 3 vols. 3rd ed. Oxford University Press, New York, 1986.

Rosand, D. *Painting in Cinquecento Venice: Titian, Veronese, Tintoretto.* Yale University Press, New Haven, 1982.

Turner, A. R. *Renaissance Florence.* Perspectives. Harry N. Abrams, New York, 1997.

Wölfflin, H. *Classic Art: An Introduction to the High Renaissance.* Reprint of 1952 ed., Cornell University Press, Ithaca, 1980.

CHAPTER 14. MANNERISM AND OTHER TRENDS

Ackerman, J. *Palladio.* 2nd ed. Penguin, Harmondsworth, England, 1977.

Friedlaender, W. *Mannerism and Anti-Mannerism in Italian Painting.* Reprint of 1957 ed., Columbia University Press, New York, 1990.

Gould, C. H. M. *The Paintings of Correggio.* Cornell University Press, Ithaca, 1976.

Gruber, A., ed. *The History of Decorative Arts: The Renaissance and Mannerism in Europe.* Abbeville Press, New York, 1994.

Kaufmann, T. DaCosta. *Art and Architecture in Central Europe, 1550–1620: An Annotated Bibliography.* Reference Publications in Art History. G. K. Hall, Boston, 1988.

Mann, R. *El Greco and His Patrons: Three Major Projects.* Cambridge University Press, New York, 1986.

Rearick, W. R. *The Art of Paolo Veronese, 1528–1588.* Cambridge University Press, Cambridge, 1988.

Shearman, J. *Mannerism.* Penguin, Harmondsworth, England, 1967.

Smyth, C. H. *Mannerism and Maniera.* 2nd ed. IRSA, Vienna, 1992.

Tavernor, R. *Palladio and Palladianism.* The World of Art. Thames & Hudson, New York, 1991.

Tomlinson, J. *From El Greco to Goya: Painting in Spain 1561–1828.* Perspectives. Harry N. Abrams, New York, 1997.

Valcanover, F., and T. Pignatti. *Tintoretto.* Harry N. Abrams, New York, 1984.

CHAPTER 15. "LATE GOTHIC" PAINTING, SCULPTURE, AND THE GRAPHIC ARTS

Blum, S. *Early Netherlandish Triptychs: A Study in Patronage.* University of California Press, Berkeley, 1969.

De Vos, D. *Rogier van der Weyden: The Complete Works.* Harry N. Abrams, New York, 1999.

Dhanens, E. *Hubert and Jan van Eyck.* Alpine Fine Arts Collection, New York, 1980.

Friedländer, M. *Early Netherlandish Painting.* 14 vols. Praeger, New York, 1967–73.

———. *From Van Eyck to Bruegel: Early Netherlandish Painting.* 3rd ed. Cornell University Press, Ithaca, 1981.

Gibson, W. *Hieronymus Bosch.* Praeger, New York, 1973.

Mâle, E. *Religious Art in France, the Late Middle Ages: A Study of Medieval Iconography and Its Sources.* Princeton University Press, Princeton, 1986.

Muller, T. *Sculpture in the Netherlands, Germany, France, and Spain, 1400–1500.* Pelican History of Art. Penguin, Harmondsworth, England, 1966.

Panofsky, E. *Early Netherlandish Painting.* 2 vols. Harvard University Press, Cambridge, 1958.

CHAPTER 16. THE RENAISSANCE IN THE NORTH

Baxandall, M. *The Limewood Sculptors of Renaissance Germany.* Yale University Press, New Haven, 1980.

Chastel, A., et al. *The Renaissance: Essays in Interpretation.* Methuen, London, 1982.

Harbison, C. *The Mirror of the Artist: Northern Renaissance Art in Its Historical Context.* Perspectives. Harry N. Abrams, New York, 1995.

Hitchcock, H.-R. *German Renaissance Architecture.* Princeton University Press, Princeton, 1981.

Hutchison, J. C. *Albrecht Dürer: A Biography.* Princeton University Press, Princeton, 1990.

Koerner, J. *The Moment of Self-Portraiture in German Renaissance Art.* University of Chicago Press, Chicago, 1993.

Lane, B. *Flemish Painting Outside Bruges, 1400–1500: An Annotated Bibliography.* G. K. Hall, Boston, 1986.

Melion, W. *Shaping the Netherlandish Canon: Karel van Mander's Schilder-Boeck.* University of Chicago Press, Chicago, 1991.

Moxey, K. *Peasants, Warriors, and Wives: Popular Imagery in the Reformation.* University of Chicago Press, Chicago, 1989.

Mundy, E. *Painting in Bruges, 1470–1550: An Annotated Bibliography.* G. K. Hall, Boston, 1985.

Osten, G. von der, and H. Vey. *Painting and Sculpture in Germany and the Netherlands, 1500–1600.* Pelican History of Art. Penguin, Harmondsworth, England, 1969.

Panofsky, E. *The Life and Art of Albrecht Dürer.* 4th ed. Princeton University Press, Princeton, 1971.

Parshall, L. and P. *Art and the Reformation: An Annotated Bibliography.* G. K. Hall, Boston, 1986.

Stechow, W. *Northern Renaissance Art, 1400–1600: Sources and Documents.* Prentice Hall, Englewood Cliffs, N.J., 1966.

Van Mander, K. *Lives of the Illustrious Netherlandish and German Painters.* Ed. H. Miedema. 6 vols. Davaco, Doornspijk, Netherlands, 1993–1999.

Wood, C. *Albrecht Altdorfer and the Origins of Landscape.* University of Chicago Press, Chicago, 1993.

CHAPTER 17. THE BAROQUE IN ITALY AND SPAIN

Blunt, A. *Borromini.* Harvard University Press, Cambridge, 1979.

Brown, J. *Francisco de Zurbaran.* Harry N. Abrams, New York, 1991.

———. *The Golden Age of Painting in Spain.* Yale University Press, New Haven, 1991.

———. *Velázquez: Painter and Courtier.* Yale University Press, New Haven, 1986.

Enggass, R., and J. Brown. *Italy and Spain, 1600–1750: Sources and Documents.* Reprint of 1970 ed., Northwestern University Press, Evanston, Ill., 1992.

Freedberg, S. *Circa 1600: A Revolution of Style in Italian Painting.* Harvard University Press, Cambridge, 1983.

Haskell, F. *Patrons and Painters: A Study in the Relations Between Italian Art and Society in the Age of the Baroque.* Rev. ed. Yale University Press, New Haven, 1980.

Hibbard, H. *Bernini.* Reprint of 1965 ed., Penguin, Baltimore, 1980.

———. *Caravaggio.* Harper & Row, New York, 1983.

Kubler, G., and M. Soria. *Art and Architecture in Spain and Portugal and Their American Dominions, 1500–1800.* Pelican History of Art. Penguin, Harmondsworth, England, 1959.

Montagu, J. *Roman Baroque Sculpture: The Industry of Art.* Yale University Press, New Haven, 1989.

Nicolson, B. *Caravaggism in Europe.* Ed. L. Vertova. 3 vols. 2nd ed., rev. and enl. Allemandi, Turin, 1989.

Posner, D. *Annibale Carracci.* 2 vols. Phaidon, London, 1971.

Smith, G. *Architectural Diplomacy: Rome and Paris in the Late Baroque.* MIT Press, Cambridge, 1993.

Spear, R. *Caravaggio and His Followers.* Harper & Row, New York, 1976.

Varriano, J. *Italian Baroque and Rococo Architecture.* Oxford University Press, New York, 1986.

Waterhouse, E. *Italian Baroque Painting.* 2nd ed. Phaidon, London, 1969.

Wittkower, R. *Art and Architecture in Italy, 1600–1750.* Pelican History of Art. 4th ed. Yale University Press, New Haven, 2000.

———. *Bernini: The Sculptor of the Roman Baroque.* 4th ed. Chronicle Books, San Francisco, 1997.

CHAPTER 18. THE BAROQUE IN FLANDERS AND HOLLAND

Alpers, S. *The Art of Describing: Dutch Art in the Seventeenth Century.* University of Chicago Press, Chicago, 1983.

Gerson, H., and E. ter Kuile. *Art and Architecture in Belgium, 1600–1800.* Pelican History of Art. Penguin, Baltimore, 1960.

Haak, B. *The Golden Age: Dutch Painters of the Seventeenth Century.* Harry N. Abrams, New York, 1984.

Rembrandt: The Master and His Workshop. Ed. S. Salvesen. 2 vols. Exh. cat. Yale University Press, New Haven, 1991.

Rosenberg, J. *Rembrandt: Life and Work.* Rev. ed. Cornell University Press, Ithaca, 1980.

———, S. Slive, and E. ter Kuile. *Dutch Art and Architecture, 1600–1800.* 3rd ed. Yale University Press, New Haven, 1997.

Schama, S. *The Embarrassment of Riches.* University of California Press, Berkeley, 1988.

Schwartz, G. *Rembrandt: His Life, His Paintings.* Viking, New York, 1985.

Slive, S. *Dutch Painting, 1600–1800.* Pelican History of Art. Yale University Press, New Haven, 1995.

———. *Frans Hals.* A. Wofsky Fine Arts, San Francisco, 1989.

Stechow, W. *Dutch Landscape Painting of the Seventeenth Century.* Reprint of 1966 ed., Cornell University Press, Ithaca, 1980.

Sutton, P. *The Age of Rubens.* Exh. cat. Museum of Fine Arts, Boston, 1993.

Walford, F. *Jacob van Ruisdael and the Perception of Landscape.* Yale University Press, New Haven, 1992.

Westermann, M. *A Worldly Art: The Dutch Republic 1585–1718.* Perspectives. Harry N. Abrams, New York, 1996.

Wheelock, A. K., ed. *Johannes Vermeer.* Exh. cat. Yale University Press, New Haven, 1995.

———, et al. *Anthony van Dyck.* Exh. cat. Harry N. Abrams, New York, 1990.

White, C. *Peter Paul Rubens.* Yale University Press, New Haven, 1987.

CHAPTER 19. THE BAROQUE IN FRANCE AND ENGLAND

Blunt, A. *Art and Architecture in France, 1500–1700.* Pelican History of Art. 5th ed. Yale University Press, New Haven, 1999.

———. *Nicolas Poussin.* 2 vols. Princeton University Press, Princeton, 1967.

Downes, K. *The Architecture of Wren.* Rev. ed. Redhedge, Reading, England, 1988.

Garreau, M. *Charles Le Brun: First Painter to King Louis XIV.* Harry N. Abrams, New York, 1992.

Liechtenstein, J. *The Eloquence of Color: Rhetoric and Painting in the French Classical Age.* University of California Press, Berkeley, 1993.

Mérot, A. *French Painting in the Seventeenth Century.* Yale University Press, New Haven, 1995.

———. *Nicolas Poussin.* Abbeville Press, New York, 1990.

Röthlisberger, M. *Claude Lorrain: The Paintings.* 2 vols. Yale University Press, New Haven, 1961.

Summerson, J. *Architecture in Britain, 1530–1830.* Pelican History of Art. 9th ed., rev. Yale University Press, New Haven, 1993.

Waterhouse, E. K. *Painting in Britain, 1530–1790.* Pelican History of Art. 5th ed. Yale University Press, New Haven, 1993.

———. *The Dictionary of Sixteenth and Seventeenth Century British Painters.* Antique Collectors' Club, Woodbridge, Suffolk, 1988.

CHAPTER 20. THE ROCOCO

Baillio, J. *Elisabeth Louise Vigée Le Brun, 1755–1842.* Exh. cat. Kimbell Art Museum, Fort Worth, 1982.

Brunel, G. *Boucher.* Vendome, New York, 1986.

Brusatin, M., et al. *The Baroque in Central Europe: Places, Architecture, and Art.* Marsilio, Venice, 1992.

Conisbee, P. *Chardin.* Bucknell University Press, Lewisburg, Pa., 1985.

———. *Painting in Eighteenth-Century France.* Cornell University Press, Ithaca, 1981.

Cormack, M. *The Paintings of Thomas Gainsborough.* Cambridge University Press, New York, 1991.

Cuzin, J. P. *Jean-Honoré Fragonard: Life and Work: Complete Catalogue of the Oil Paintings.* Harry N. Abrams, New York, 1988.

Gaunt, W. *The Great Century of British Painting: Hogarth to Turner.* 2nd ed. Phaidon, London, 1978.

Levey, M. *Giambattista Tiepolo: His Life and Art.* Yale University Press, New Haven, 1986.

———. *Painting and Sculpture in France, 1700–1789.* Pelican History of Art. New ed. Yale University Press, New Haven, 1993.

———. *Rococo to Revolution: Major Trends in Eighteenth-Century Painting.* The World of Art. Reprint of 1966 ed., Thames & Hudson, New York, 1985.

Links, J. *Canaletto.* Oxford University Press, New York, 1982.

Paulson, R. *Hogarth: His Life, Art, and Times.* 2 vols. Yale University Press, New Haven, 1971.

Penny, N., ed. *Reynolds.* Exh. cat. Harry N. Abrams, New York, 1986.

Pointer, M. *Hanging the Head: Portraiture and Social Formation in Eighteenth-Century England.* Yale University Press, New Haven, 1993.

Posner, D. *Antoine Watteau.* Cornell University Press, Ithaca, 1984.

Von Kalnein, W. *Architecture in France in the Eighteenth Century.* History of Art. Yale University Press, New Haven, 1995.

PART FOUR: THE MODERN WORLD

GENERAL REFERENCES

Arnason, H. H., and M. F. Prather. *History of Modern Art.* 4th ed. Harry N. Abrams, New York, 1998.

Baigell, M. *A Concise History of American Painting and Sculpture.* Harper & Row, New York, 1984.

Barasch, M. *Modern Theories of Art. Vol. 1, From Winckelmann to Baudelaire.* New York University Press, New York, 1990.

Battcock, G., and R. Nickas, eds. *The Art of Performance: A Critical Anthology.* Dutton, New York, 1984.

Benevolo, L. *History of Modern Architecture.* MIT Press, Cambridge, 1971.

Boime, A. *A Social History of Modern Art.* 2 vols. University of Chicago Press, Chicago, 1987–90.

Brown, M., et al. *American Art: Painting, Sculpture, Architecture, Decorative Arts, Photography.* Prentice Hall, Englewood Cliffs, N.J., 1979.

Campbell, M., et al. *Harlem Renaissance: Art of Black America.* Harry N. Abrams, New York, 1987.

Castelman, R. *Prints of the Twentieth Century: A History.* Oxford University Press, New York, 1985.

Chipp, H., ed. *Theories of Modern Art: A Source Book by Artists and Critics.* University of California Press, Berkeley, 1968.

Crary, J. *Techniques of the Observer: On Vision and Modernity in the Nineteenth Century.* MIT Press, Cambridge, 1990.

Crook, J. *The Dilemma of Style: Architectural Ideas from the Picturesque to the Post Modern.* University of Chicago Press, Chicago, 1987.

Crow, T. *Modern Art in the Common Culture.* Yale University Press, New Haven, 1996.

The Documents of Twentieth-Century Art. G. K. Hall, Boston. Cited individually below.

Driskell, D. *Two Centuries of Black American Art.* Exh. cat. Knopf, New York, 1976.

Eitner, L. *An Outline of Nineteenth-Century European Painting: From David Through Cézanne.* 2 vols. Harper & Row, New York, 1986.

Frampton, K. *Modern Architecture: A Critical History.* 3rd ed. Thames & Hudson, New York, 1992.

———, and Y. Futagawa. *Modern Architecture, 1851–1945.* 2 vols. Rizzoli, New York, 1983.

Frascina, F., ed. *Modern Art and Modernism: A Critical Anthology.* Harper & Row, New York, 1982.

———. *Pollock and After: The Critical Debate.* Harper & Row, New York, 1985.

———, and J. Harris, eds. *Art in Modern Culture: An Anthology of Critical Texts.* Harper & Row, New York, 1992.

Goddard, D. *American Painting.* Macmillan, New York, 1990.

Goldberg, R. *Performance Art: From Futurism to the Present.* Rev. and enl. ed. Harry N. Abrams, New York, 1988.

Goldwater, R. *Primitivism in Modern Art.* Enl. ed. Harvard University Press, Cambridge, 1986.

Harrison, C., and P. Wood, eds. *Art in Theory, 1900–1990: An Anthology of Changing Ideas.* Blackwell, Oxford, 1992.

Hertz, R., ed. *Theories of Contemporary Art.* Prentice Hall, Englewood Cliffs, N.J., 1985.

———, and N. Klein, eds. *Twentieth-Century Art Theory: Urbanism, Politics, and Mass Culture.* Prentice Hall, Englewood Cliffs, N.J., 1990.

Hitchcock, H. R. *Architecture: Nineteenth and Twentieth Centuries.* Pelican History of Art. 2nd ed. Penguin, Harmondsworth, England, 1971.

Hunter, S., and J. Jacobus. *Modern Art: Painting, Sculpture, Architecture.* Harry N. Abrams, New York, 1992.

Janson, H. W. *Nineteenth-Century Sculpture.* Harry N. Abrams, New York, 1985.

———, and R. Rosenblum. *Nineteenth-Century Art.* Harry N. Abrams, New York, 1984.

Joachimides, C., et al. *American Art in the Twentieth Century: Painting and Sculpture, 1913–1933.* Exh. cat. Prestel, Munich, 1993.

Johnson, W. *Nineteenth-Century Photography: An Annotated Bibliography, 1839–1879.* G. K. Hall, Boston, 1990.

McCoubrey, J. *American Art, 1700–1960: Sources and Documents.* Prentice Hall, Englewood Cliffs, N.J., 1965.

Newhall, B. *The History of Photography from 1830 to the Present Day.* 5th ed., rev. New York Graphic Society, Greenwich, 1982.

Nochlin, L. *The Politics of Vision: Essays on Nineteenth-Century Art and Society.* Harper & Row, New York, 1989.

Osborne, H., ed. *Oxford Companion to Twentieth-Century Art.* Oxford University Press, New York, 1981.

Phaidon Dictionary of Twentieth-Century Art. Phaidon, Oxford, 1973.

Pingeot, A., et al. *Sculpture: The Adventure of Modern Sculpture in the Nineteenth and Twentieth Centuries.* Rizzoli, New York, 1986.

Prown, J. D., and B. Rose. *American Painting: From the Colonial Period to the Present.* New ed. Rizzoli, New York, 1977.

Robins, C. *The Pluralist Era: American Art, 1968–1981.* Harper & Row, New York, 1984.

Rose, B. *American Art Since 1900.* Rev. ed. Praeger, New York, 1975.

Rosenblum, N. *A World History of Photography.* Rev. ed. Abbeville Press, New York, 1989.

Sayre, H. *The Object of Performance: The American Avant-Garde Since 1970.* University of Chicago Press, Chicago, 1990.

Schapiro, M. *Modern Art: Nineteenth and Twentieth Centuries.* Braziller, New York, 1982.

Scharf, A. *Art and Photography.* Rev. ed. Penguin, Harmondsworth, England, 1974.

Stiles, K., and P. Selz. *Theories and Documents of Contemporary Art.* University of California Press, Berkeley, 1996.

Tafuri, M. *Modern Architecture.* 2 vols. Rizzoli, New York, 1986.

Taylor, J. *The Fine Arts in America.* University of Chicago Press, Chicago, 1979.

———, ed. *Nineteenth-Century Theories of Art.* University of California Press, Berkeley, 1991.

Tomkins, C. *Post to Neo: The Art World of the 1980s.* Holt, New York, 1988.

Walker, J. *Glossary of Art: Architecture and Design Since 1945.* 3rd ed. G. K. Hall, Boston, 1992.

Weaver, M. *The Art of Photography, 1839–1989.* Exh. cat. Yale University Press, New Haven, 1989.

Weintraub, L. *Art on the Edge and Over.* Art Insights, Litchfield, Conn.; dist. D.A.P., 1997.

Weiss, J. *The Popular Culture of Modern Art.* Yale University Press, New Haven, 1994.

Wilmerding, J. *American Art.* Pelican History of Art. Penguin, Harmondsworth, England, 1976.

Witzling, M., ed. *Voicing Our Visions: Writings by Women Artists.* Universe, New York, 1991.

Wood, P., et al. *Modernism in Dispute: Art Since the Forties.* Yale University Press, New Haven, 1993.

CHAPTER 21. NEOCLASSICISM AND ROMANTICISM

Boime, A. *The Academy and French Painting in the Nineteenth Century.* New ed. Yale University Press, New Haven, 1986.

Braham, A. *The Architecture of the French Enlightenment.* University of California Press, Berkeley, 1980.

Bryson, N. *Tradition and Desire: From David to Delacroix.* Cambridge University Press, Cambridge, 1984.

———. *Word and Image: French Painting in the Ancien Régime.* Cambridge University Press, Cambridge, 1981.

Chiarmonte, P. *Women Artists in the United States: A Selective Bibliography and Resource Guide to the Fine and Decorative Arts, 1750–1986.* G. K. Hall, Boston, 1990.

Crow, T. *Painters and Public Life in Eighteenth-Century Paris.* Yale University Press, New Haven, 1985.

Eitner, L. E. A. *Géricault: His Life and Work.* Cornell University Press, Ithaca, 1982.

———. *Neoclassicism and Romanticism, 1750–1850: Sources and Documents.* Reprint of 1970 ed., Harper & Row, New York, 1989.

Fried, M. *Absorption and Theatricality: Painting and Beholder in the Age of Diderot.* University of Chicago Press, Chicago, 1980.

Friedlaender, W. *From David to Delacroix.* Reprint of 1952 ed., Schocken Books, New York, 1968.

Goncourt, E. and J. de. *French Eighteenth-Century Painters.* Reprint of 1948 ed., Cornell University Press, Ithaca, 1981.

Goya and the Spirit of Enlightenment. Exh. cat. Little, Brown, Boston, 1989.

Herrmann, L. *British Landscape Painting of the Eighteenth Century.* Oxford University Press, New York, 1974.

Honour, H. *Neoclassicism.* Reprint of 1968 ed., Penguin, London, 1991.

———. *Romanticism.* Harper & Row, New York, 1979.

Johnson, E. *The Paintings of Eugène Delacroix: A Critical Catalogue, 1816–1831.* 4 vols. Clarendon Press, Oxford, 1981–86.

Koerner, J. *Caspar David Friedrich and the Subject of Landscape.* Yale University Press, New Haven, 1990.

Licht, F. *Canova.* Abbeville Press, New York, 1983.

———. *Goya: The Origins of the Modern Temper in Art.* Harper & Row, New York, 1983.

Mainardi, P. *Art and Politics of the Second Empire: The Universal Expositions of 1855 and 1867.* Yale University Press, New Haven, 1987.

———. *The End of the Salon: Art and the State in the Early Third Republic.* Cambridge University Press, Cambridge, 1993.

Middleton, R., and D. Watkin. *Neoclassical and Nineteenth-Century Architecture.* Rizzoli, New York, 1977.

Miles, E. G., ed. *The Portrait in Eighteenth-Century America.* University of Delaware Press, Newark, 1993.

Novotny, F. *Painting and Sculpture in Europe, 1780–1880.* Pelican History of Art. 3rd ed. Yale University Press, New Haven, 1992.

Rebora, C., P. Staiti, et al. *John Singleton Copley in America.* Exh. cat. The Metropolitan Museum of Art, New York, 1995.

Reynolds, G. *Turner.* The World of Art. Thames & Hudson, New York, 1985.

Rosenblum, R. *Jean-Auguste-Dominique Ingres.* Harry N. Abrams, New York, 1990.

———. *Transformations in Late Eighteenth Century Art.* Princeton University Press, Princeton, 1967.

Saisselin, R. G. *The Enlightenment Against the Baroque: Economics and Aesthetics in the Eighteenth Century.* University of California Press, Berkeley, 1992.

Solkin, D. *Painting for Money: The Visual Arts and the Public Sphere in Eighteenth-Century England.* Yale University Press, New Haven, 1993.

Tomlinson, J. *Goya in the Twilight of Enlightenment.* Yale University Press, New Haven, 1992.

Vaughan, W. *German Romantic Painting.* Yale University Press, New Haven, 1980.

Watkin, D., and T. Mellinghoff. *German Architecture and the Classical Ideal.* MIT Press, Cambridge, 1987.

Wilton, A. *J. M. W. Turner: His Life and Art.* Rizzoli, New York, 1979.

CHAPTER 22. REALISM AND IMPRESSIONISM

Adler, K., and T. Garb. *Manet.* Phaidon, Oxford, 1986.

Broude, N. *Impressionism: A Feminist Reading.* Rizzoli, New York, 1991.

Cikovsky, N., and F. Kelly. *Winslow Homer.* Exh. cat. Yale University Press, New Haven, 1995.

Clark, T. J. *The Absolute Bourgeois: Artists and Politics in France, 1848–1851.* Princeton University Press, Princeton, 1982.

———. *The Painting of Modern Life: Paris in the Art of Manet and His Followers.* Princeton University Press, Princeton, 1984.

Denvir, B. *The Chronicle of Impressionism: A Timeline History of Impressionist Art.* Little, Brown, Boston, 1993.

———. *The Impressionists: A Documentary Study.* Thames & Hudson, New York, 1986.

———. *The Thames & Hudson Encyclopaedia of Impressionism.* Thames & Hudson, New York, 1990.

Fried, M. *Courbet's Realism.* University of Chicago Press, Chicago, 1990.

Gaunt, W. *Renoir.* Notes by K. Adler. Rev. and enl. ed. Phaidon, Oxford, 1982.

Goodrich, L. *Thomas Eakins.* 2 vols. Exh. cat. Harvard University Press, Cambridge, 1982.

Hamilton, G. H. *Manet and His Critics.* Reprint of 1954 ed., Yale University Press, New Haven, 1986.

Herbert, R. *Impressionism: Art, Leisure, and Parisian Society.* Yale University Press, New Haven, 1988.

Higonnet, A. *Berthe Morisot.* Harper & Row, New York, 1990.

Hilton, T. *The Pre-Raphaelites.* The World of Art. Reprint of 1970 ed., Thames & Hudson, London, 1985.

House, J. *Monet: Nature into Art.* Yale University Press, New Haven, 1986.

Jenkyns, R. *Dignity and Decadence: Victorian Art and the Classical Inheritance.* Harvard University Press, Cambridge, 1991.

Kendall, R., and G. Pollock, eds. *Dealing with Degas: Representations of Women and the Politics of Vision.* Universe, New York, 1992.

Lipton, E. *Looking into Degas.* University of California Press, Berkeley, 1986.

Miller, D., ed. *American Iconology: New Approaches to Nineteenth-Century Art and Literature.* Yale University Press, New Haven, 1993.

Mosby, D. *Henry Ossawa Tanner.* Exh. cat. Rizzoli, New York, 1991.

Needham, G. *Nineteenth-Century Realist Art.* Harper & Row, New York, 1988.

Nochlin, L. *Impressionism and Post-Impressionism, 1874–1904: Sources and Documents.* Prentice Hall, Englewood Cliffs, N.J., 1976.

———. *Realism and Tradition in Art, 1848–1900: Sources and Documents.* Prentice Hall, Englewood Cliffs, N.J., 1966.

Novak, B. *American Painting of the Nineteenth Century: Realism and the American Experience.* Harper & Row, New York, 1979.

———. *Nature and Culture: American Landscape Painting, 1825–1875.* Oxford University Press, New York, 1980.

Pollock, G. *Mary Cassatt.* Harper & Row, New York, 1980.

Reff, T. *Manet and Modern Paris.* Exh. cat. National Gallery of Art, Washington, D.C., 1982.

Rewald, J. *The History of Impressionism.* 4th ed., rev. New York Graphic Society, Greenwich, 1973.

Spate, V. *Claude Monet: Life and Work.* Rizzoli, New York, 1992.

Tucker, P. *Monet at Argenteuil.* Yale University Press, New Haven, 1981.

———. *Monet in the '90s: The Series Paintings.* Exh. cat. Yale University Press, New Haven, 1989.

Walther, I., ed. *Impressionist Art, 1860–1920.* 2 vols. Taschen, Cologne, 1996.

Weisberg, G. *Beyond Impressionism: The Naturalist Impulse.* Harry N. Abrams, New York, 1992.

Wilmerding, J. *Winslow Homer.* Praeger, New York, 1972.

Wood, C. *The Pre-Raphaelites.* Viking, New York, 1981.

CHAPTER 23. POST-IMPRESSIONISM, SYMBOLISM, AND ART NOUVEAU

Brettell, R., et al. *The Art of Paul Gauguin.* Exh. cat. Little, Brown, Boston, 1988.

Broude, N. *Georges Seurat.* Rizzoli, New York, 1992.

Cachin, F., I. Cahn, et al. *Cézanne.* Exh. cat. Harry N. Abrams, New York, 1995.

Denvir, B. *Post-Impressionism.* The World of Art. Thames & Hudson, New York, 1992.

Goldwater, R. *Paul Gauguin.* Concise ed. Harry N. Abrams, New York, 1983.

———. *Symbolism.* Harper & Row, New York, 1979.

Hamilton, G. H. *Painting and Sculpture in Europe, 1880–1940.* Pelican History of Art. 6th ed. Yale University Press, New Haven, 1993.

Hulsker, J. *The Complete Van Gogh.* Harry N. Abrams, New York, 1980.

Rewald, J. *Post-Impressionism: From Van Gogh to Gauguin.* 2nd ed. Museum of Modern Art, New York, 1962.

Schapiro, M. *Paul Cézanne.* Concise ed. Harry N. Abrams, New York, 1988.

———. *Van Gogh.* Rev. ed. Harry N. Abrams, New York, 1982.

Shiff, R. *Cézanne and the End of Impressionism: A Study of the Theory, Technique, and Critical Evaluation of Modern Art.* University of Chicago Press, Chicago, 1984.

Silverman, D. *Art Nouveau in Fin-de-Siècle France.* University of California Press, Berkeley, 1989.

Varnedoe, K. *Vienna 1900: Art, Architecture, and Design.* Exh. cat. Museum of Modern Art, New York, 1986.

CHAPTER 24. TWENTIETH-CENTURY PAINTING

Ades, D., et al., eds. *In the Mind's Eye: Dada and Surrealism.* Abbeville Press, New York, 1986.

Ashton, D. *American Art Since 1945.* Oxford University Press, New York, 1982.

Baker, K. *Minimalism.* Abbeville Press, New York, 1989.

Battcock, G., comp. *Idea Art: A Critical Anthology.* New ed. Dutton, New York, 1973.

Bearden, R., and H. Henderson. *A History of African-American Artists from 1972 to the Present.* Pantheon, New York, 1993.

Beardsley, J., and J. Livingston. *Hispanic Art in the United States: Thirty Contemporary Painters and Sculptors.* Exh. cat. Abbeville Press, New York, 1987.

Breton, A. *Manifestoes of Surrealism.* Trans. R. Seaver and H. R. Lane. University of Michigan Press, Ann Arbor, 1969.

Brown, M. *The Story of the Armory Show.* Rev. ed. Abbeville Press, New York, 1988.

Celant, G. *Unexpressionism: Art Beyond the Contemporary.* Rizzoli, New York, 1988.

Chadwick, W. *Women Artists and the Surrealist Movement.* Thames & Hudson, New York, 1991.

Crane, D. *The Transformation of the Avant-Garde: The New York Art World, 1940–1985.* University of Chicago Press, Chicago, 1987.

Crow, T. *The Rise of the Sixties: American and European Art in the Era of Dissent.* Perspectives. Harry N. Abrams, New York, 1996.

Duchamp, M. *Marcel Duchamp, Notes.* Trans. P. Matisse. *The Documents of Twentieth-Century Art.* G. K. Hall, Boston, 1983.

Fer, B., et al. *Realism, Rationalism, Surrealism: Art Between the Wars. Modern Art-Practices and Debates.* Yale University Press, New Haven, 1993.

Francis Bacon: A Retrospective. Harry N. Abrams, New York, 1999.

Gilbaut, S. *How New York Stole the Idea of Modern Art.* University of Chicago Press, Chicago, 1983.

———, ed. *Reconstructing Modernism: Art in New York, Paris, and Montreal, 1945–1964.* MIT Press, Cambridge, 1990.

Golding, J. *Cubism: A History and an Analysis, 1907–1914.* 3rd ed. Harvard University Press, Cambridge, 1988.

Goldwater, R. *Primitivism in Modern Art.* Enl. ed. Belknap Press, Cambridge, Mass., 1986.

Gordon, D. *Expressionism: Art and Idea.* Yale University Press, New Haven, 1987.

Gray, C. *The Russian Experiment in Art, 1863–1922.* rev. ed. The World of Art. Thames & Hudson, New York, 1986.

Green, C. *Cubism and Its Enemies.* Yale University Press, New Haven, 1987.

Greenberg, C. *Clement Greenberg, The Collected Essays and Criticism.* Ed. J. O'Brian. 4 vols. University of Chicago Press, Chicago, 1986–93.

Herbert, J. *Fauve Painting: The Making of Cultural Politics.* Yale University Press, New Haven, 1992.

Hoffman, K., ed. *Collage: Critical Views.* UMI Research Press, Ann Arbor, 1989.

Kallir, J. *Egon Schiele: The Complete Works.* Exp. ed. Harry N. Abrams, New York, 1998.

Kandinsky, W. *Kandinsky, Complete Writings on Art.* Eds. K. C. Lindsay and P. Vergo. *The Documents of Twentieth-Century Art.* 2 vols. G. K. Hall, Boston, 1982.

Krauss, R. *The Originality of the Avant-Garde and Other Modernist Myths.* MIT Press, Cambridge, 1986.

Kuspit, D. *The Cult of the Avant-Garde Artist.* Cambridge University Press, New York, 1993.

Langer, C. *Feminist Art Criticism: An Annotated Bibliography.* G. K. Hall, Boston, 1993.

Leggio, J., and S. Weiley, eds. *American Art of the 1960s.* Studies in Modern Art, 1. Museum of Modern Art, New York, 1991.

Leja, M. *Reframing Abstract Expressionism: Subjectivity and Painting in the 1940s.* Yale University Press, New Haven, 1993.

Lewis, H. *The Politics of Surrealism.* Paragon, New York, 1988.

Lewis, S. *African American Art and Artists.* University of California Press, Berkeley, 1990.

Lippard, L. R. *Overlay: Contemporary Art and the Art of Prehistory.* Pantheon, New York, 1983.

———, ed. *From the Center: Feminist Essays on Women's Art.* Dutton, New York, 1976.

———, et al. *Pop Art.* Praeger, New York, 1966.

Livingstone, M. *Pop Art: A Continuing History.* Harry N. Abrams, New York, 1990.

Lodder, C. *Russian Constructivism.* Yale University Press, New Haven, 1983.

Lucie-Smith, E. *Art Today.* Phaidon, London, 1995.

Meisel, L. K. *Photorealism.* Harry N. Abrams, New York, 1980.

Miró, J. *Joan Miró: Selected Writings and Interviews.* Ed. M. Rowell. *The Documents of Twentieth-Century Art.* G. K. Hall, Boston, 1986.

Mitchell, W. J. T. *The Reconfigured Eye: Visual Truth in the Post-Photographic Era.* MIT Press, Cambridge, 1992.

Mondrian, P. *The New Art, the New Life: The Complete Writings.* Eds. and trans. H. Holtzmann and M. James. *The Documents of Twentieth-Century Art.* G. K. Hall, Boston, 1986.

Motherwell, R. *Collected Writings.* Ed. Stephanie Terenzio. Oxford University Press, New York, 1992.

———, ed. *The Dada Poets and Painters: An Anthology.* 2nd ed. Harvard University Press, Cambridge, 1989.

Nadeau, M. *History of Surrealism.* Harvard University Press, Cambridge, 1989.

Patton, S. F. *African-American Art.* Oxford University Press, New York, 1998.

Pincus-Witten, R. *Postminimalism into Maximalism: American Art, 1966–1986.* UMI Research Press, Ann Arbor, 1987.

Polcari, S. *Abstract Expressionism and the Modern Experience.* Cambridge University Press, New York, 1991.

Powell, R. J. *Black Art and Culture in the 20th Century.* Thames & Hudson, New York, 1997.

Rosen, R., and C. Brawer, eds. *Making Their Mark: Women Artists Move into the Mainstream, 1970–85.* Exh. cat. Abbeville Press, New York, 1989.

Rosenblum, R. *Cubism and Twentieth-Century Art.* Prentice Hall, Englewood Cliffs, N.J., 1976.

Roskill, M. *Klee, Kandinsky, and the Thought of Their Time: A Critical Perspective.* University of Illinois Press, Urbana, 1992.

Ross, C. *Abstract Expressionism: Creators and Critics: An Anthology.* Harry N. Abrams, New York, 1990.

Rubin, W. S. *Dada and Surrealist Art.* Harry N. Abrams, New York, 1968.

———. *Picasso and Braque: Pioneering Cubism.* Exh. cat. Museum of Modern Art, New York, 1989.

Sandler, I. *The New York School: The Painters and Sculptors of the Fifties.* Harper & Row, New York, 1979.

———. *The Triumph of American Painting: A History of Abstract Expressionism.* Praeger, New York, 1970.

Seitz, W. *Abstract Expressionist Painting in America.* Harvard University Press, Cambridge, 1983.

Silver, K. E. *Esprit de Corps: The Art of the Parisian Avant-Garde and the First World War, 1914–1925.* Princeton University Press, Princeton, 1989.

Varnedoe, K., and A. Gopnik. *High and Low: Modern Art/Popular Culture.* Harry N. Abrams, New York, 1990.

Washton, R.-C., ed. *German Expressionism: Documents from the End of the Wilhelmine Empire to the Rise of National Socialism. The Documents of Twentieth-Century Art.* G. K. Hall, Boston, 1993.

CHAPTER 25. TWENTIETH-CENTURY SCULPTURE

Bach, F., T. Bach, and A. Temkin. *Constantin Brancusi.* Exh. cat. MIT Press, Cambridge, 1995.

Beardsley, J. *Earthworks and Beyond: Contemporary Art in the Landscape.* Enl. ed. Abbeville Press, New York, 1989.

Beaumont, M., et al. *Sculpture Today*. St. Martin's Press, New York, 1987.

Causey, A. *Sculpture Since 1945*. Oxford University Press, New York, 1998.

Elsen, A. *Origins of Modern Sculpture*. Braziller, New York, 1974.

Lucie-Smith, E. *Sculpture Since 1945*. Universe Books, New York, 1987.

Read, H. *Modern Sculpture: A Concise History*. The World of Art. Reprint of 1964 ed., Thames & Hudson, London, 1987.

Senie, H. *Public Sculpture: Tradition, Transformation, and Controversy*. Oxford University Press, New York, 1992.

Tucker, W. *The Language of Sculpture*. Reprint of 1974 ed., Thames & Hudson, New York, 1985.

Waldman, D. *Collage, Assemblage, and the Found Object*. Harry N. Abrams, New York, 1992.

CHAPTER 26. TWENTIETH-CENTURY ARCHITECTURE

Bayer, H., et al., eds. *Bauhaus, 1919–1928*. Reprint of 1938 ed., New York Graphic Society, Boston, 1986.

Curtis, W. *Modern Architecture Since 1900*. 2nd ed. Prentice Hall, Englewood Cliffs, N.J., 1987.

Fitch, J. *American Building: The Historical Forces That Shaped It*. 2 vols. 2nd ed. Houghton Mifflin, Boston, 1966–72.

Frampton, K. *Modern Architecture*. 3rd ed. Thames & Hudson, New York, 1996.

Franciscono, M. *Walter Gropius and the Creation of the Bauhaus in Weimar*. University of Illinois Press, Urbana, 1971.

Gössel, P., and G. Leuthäuser. *Architecture in the Twentieth Century*. Taschen, Cologne, 1991.

Hitchcock, H. R., and P. Johnson. *The International Style*. 2nd ed. Norton, New York, 1966.

Johnson, P. *Mies van der Rohe*. 3rd ed., rev. The Museum of Modern Art, New York, 1978.

Kultermann, U. *Architecture in the Twentieth Century*. Van Nostrand Reinhold, New York, 1993.

Lane, B. *Architecture and Politics in Germany, 1918–1945*. New ed. Harvard University Press, Cambridge, 1985.

Le Corbusier. *Towards a New Architecture*. Dover, New York, 1986.

Ockman, J., ed. *Architecture Culture, 1943–1968: A Documentary Anthology*. Rizzoli, New York, 1993.

Pevsner, N. *The Sources of Modern Architecture and Design*. Oxford University Press, New York, 1977.

Steele, J. *Architecture Today*. Chronicle Books, San Francisco, 1997.

Troy, N. J. *Modernism and the Decorative Arts in France: Art Nouveau to Le Corbusier*. Yale University Press, New Haven, 1991.

Wright, F. L. *Frank Lloyd Wright, Collected Writings*. 2 vols. Rizzoli, New York, 1992.

CHAPTER 27. TWENTIETH-CENTURY PHOTOGRAPHY

Ades, D. *Photomontage*. Pantheon, New York, 1976.

Ansel Adams: Images, 1923–1974. Foreword W. Stegner. New York Graphic Society, Boston, 1974.

August Sander: Photographs of an Epoch, 1904–1959. Aperture, Millerton, N.Y., 1980.

Burgin, V., ed. *Thinking Photography. Communications and Culture*. Macmillan Education, Houndsmills, England, 1990.

Coke, V. D. *The Painter and the Photograph: From Delacroix to Warhol*. Rev. ed. University of New Mexico Press, Albuquerque, 1972.

Dorothea Lange: Photographs of a Lifetime. Aperture, Millerton, N.Y., 1982.

Green, J. *American Photography: A Critical History, 1945 to the Present*. Harry N. Abrams, New York, 1984.

Greenough, S., and J. Hamilton. *Alfred Stieglitz, Photographs and Writings*. National Gallery of Art, Washington, D.C., 1983.

Haus, A. *Moholy-Nagy: Photographs and Photograms*. Pantheon, New York, 1980.

Henri Cartier-Bresson, Photographer. Foreword E. Bonnefoy. New York Graphic Society, Boston, 1979.

Krauss, R. *L'Amour Fou: Photography and Surrealism*. Abbeville Press, New York, 1985.

Marzona, E., and R. Fricke. *Bauhaus Photography*. MIT Press, Cambridge, 1987.

Phillips, C., ed. *Photography in the Modern Era: European Documents and Critical Writings, 1913–1940*. The Metropolitan Museum of Art, New York, 1989.

Sontag, S. *On Photography*. Farrar, Straus & Giroux, New York, 1973.

Szarkowski, J., and M. Hambourg. *The Work of Atget*. 4 vols. The Museum of Modern Art, New York, 1981–84.

Walsh, G., et al. *Contemporary Photographers*. St. Martin's Press, New York, 1983.

CHAPTER 28. POSTSCRIPT: POSTMODERN THEORY

Barthes, R. *The Pleasure of the Text*. Blackwell, Oxford, 1990.

Brunette, P., and D. Wills, eds. *Deconstruction and the Visual Arts: Art, Media, Architecture*. Cambridge University Press, New York. 1993.

Derrida, J. *Writing and Difference*. University of Chicago Press, Chicago, 1978.

Eco, U. *A Theory of Semiotics*. Indiana University Press, Bloomington, 1976.

Foster, H., ed. *The Anti-Aesthetic: Essays on Postmodern Culture*. Bay Press, Seattle, 1983.

Ghirardo, D. *Architecture After Modernism*. Thames & Hudson, New York, 1996.

Jameson, F. *The Prison House of Language*. Princeton University Press, Princeton, 1972.

Jencks, C. *Architecture Today*. Rev. and enl. ed. Harry N. Abrams, New York, 1988.

———. *Post-Modernism: The New Classicism in Art and Architecture*. Rizzoli, New York, 1987.

———. *What Is Post-Modernism?* 3rd ed. St. Martin's Press, New York, 1989.

Norris, C., and A. Benjamin. *What Is Deconstruction?* St. Martin's Press, New York, 1988.

Papadakes, A., et al., eds. *Deconstruction: The Omnibus Volume*. Rizzoli, New York, 1989.

Portoghesi, P. *Postmodern: The Architecture of the Post-Industrial Society*. Rizzoli, New York, 1983.

Risatti, H., ed. *Postmodern Perspectives*. Prentice Hall, Englewood Cliffs, N.J., 1990.

Tafuri, M. *Contemporary Architecture*. Harry N. Abrams, New York, 1977.

Wallis, B., ed. *Art After Modernism: Rethinking Representation*. Documentary Sources in Contemporary Art, 1. Godine, Boston, 1984.

Selected Discography

¢=Budget Recording
•=Period Instrument Recording
§=Recording of Exceptional Merit
†=Monophonic Recording

EARLY MUSIC

- • Music of Ancient Greece (Paniagua), Harmonia Mundi France
- ¢• Music from Ancient Rome (Synaulia), Amiata
- ¢• Chant I (Monks of Santo Domingo de Silos), EMI
- ¢• Ancient Music for a Modern Age (Sequentia), RCA
- ¢ Millenium, Music from the Middle Ages (Ensemble Gilles Binchois), Virgin
- ¢• Love Songs of the Middle Ages 1150–1450 (Sequentia), Deutsche Harmonia Mundi
- ¢• Early Music 1400–1500 (various groups), Deutsche Harmonia Mundi
- ¢•§ The Art of Courtly Love (Munrow), EMI
- ¢• A Medieval Banquet (Best), Nimbus
- ¢• French Chansons (The Scholars of London), Naxos
- ¢• Elizabethan Songs (Rose Consort of Viols), Naxos

COMPOSERS

- ¢• Bach: Brandenburg Concerti, *The Musical Offering* (Linde), EMI
- • Bach: Mass in B-Minor (Koopman), Erato
- Bach: *St. Matthew Passion* (Corboz), Erato
- Bach: Sonatas for Cello (Maisky, Argerich), Deutsche Grammaphon
- Bach: Sonatas, Partitas for Solo Violin (Milstein), Deutsche Grammaphon
- Bach: Suites for Solo Cello (Ma), Sony
- Bach: Organ Toccatas (Biggs), Sony
- † Bach: *The Well-Tempered Clavier,* Book I (Landowksa), RCA
- Bach: *The Well-Tempered Clavier,* Book II (Koopman), Erato
- Barber: *Knoxville, Adagio,* Songs/Copland: Poems, *Quiet City* (Hendricks, Thomas), EMI
- ¢ Bartók: Concerto for Orchestra; Music for Strings, Percussion, and Celeste (Reiner), RCA
- Bartók: Concerti for Violin (Gotowsky, Gerhardt), Pyramid
- Bartók: Quartets #1–6 (Lindsay), ASV
- ¢§ Beethoven: Concerti for Piano #1 and #3, #2 and #4 (Fleischer, Szell), Sony
- § Beethoven: Concerto for Piano #5, Concerto for Violin (Immerseel, Beth, Weil), Sony
- § Beethoven: Quartets [Complete] (Emerson String Quartet), Deutsche Grammaphon
- ¢ Beethoven: Sonatas for Cello (DuPré, Barenboim), Deutsche Grammaphon
- ¢• Beethoven: Sonatas for Piano #11, #13, #14, #19, #20 (Tan), Virgin
- ¢•§ Beethoven: Sonatas for Piano #21, #23, #26 (Tan), Virgin
- Beethoven: Sonatas for Piano #30, #31, #32 (Ashkenazy), London
- Beethoven: Sonatas for Violin #5, #9 (Menuhin, Kempf), Deutsche Grammaphon
- § Beethoven: Symphonies [Complete] (Gardiner), Deutsche Grammaphon
- Berg: *Wozzeck, Lulu* (Boehm), Deutsche Grammaphon
- Berlioz: *Romeo and Juliet* (Dutoit), London
- Berlioz: *Symphonie Fantastique* (Abbado), Deutsche Grammaphon
- ¢ Brahms: Concerto for Piano #1/ R. Schumann: Introduction and Allegro/ Mendelssohn: *Capriccio Brilliant* (R. Serkin, Szell), Sony
- ¢§ Brahms: Concerto for Piano #2/ Beethoven: Sonata #23 (Richter, Leinsdorf), RCA
- ¢Brahms: Concerto for Violin/ Tchaikovsky: Concerto for Violin (Milstein, Steinberg, Fistoulari), EMI
- Brahms: Double Concerto, Piano Quartet #3 (Stern, Ma, Abbado), Sony
- ¢§ Brahms: Symphonies #1–3, Overtures (Jochum), EMI
- ¢ Brahms: Symphony #4 (Swarowsky), Infinity
- ¢ § Britten: Violin Concerto, Cello Symphony (Hirsch, Hughes, Yuasa), Naxos
- ¢ Britten: Quartets (Britten Quartet), Collins
- § Cage, Carter, Babbitt, Schuller: Orchestral Works (Levine), Deutsche Grammaphon
- ¢ Chopin: Concerti for Piano #1, #2 (Ax, Previn), RCA
- Chopin: Piano Music (Arrau), Philips
- § Copland: Orchestral Music (Bernstein), Sony
- •§ Corelli: Opus 5 (Trio Sonnerie), Virgin
- • Corelli: Opus 6 (Europa Galante), Opus 111
- § Crumb: *Ancient Voices of Children, Music for a Summer Evening* (Weisberg), Nonesuch
- Debussy: *La Mer,* Nocturnes (Previn), Philips
- Debussy: Quartet/Ravel: Quartet (Budapest String Quartet), Sony
- Donizetti: *Lucia di Lammermoor* (Bonynge), London
- ¢ • Dowland: *Treasures from My Mind* (King), EMI
- • § Dufay: Complete Secular Music (Medieval Ensemble of London), L'Oiseau Lyre
- ¢ Dvořák: Cello Concerto/Bloch: *Schelomo* (Fournier, Szell), Deutsche Grammaphon
- Dvořák: Quartet #12/Smetana: Quartet (Guarneri), Philips
- ¢ Dvořák: Symphonies #7, #8, #9 (Szell), Sony
- ¢ Elgar: Concerto for Cello, Serenade, Enigma Variations (Maisky, Chailly), Deutsche Grammaphon
- Foss: Complete Vocal Music (Foss), Koss
- Franck: Symphony in D (Monteux), RCA
- Gay: *The Beggar's Opera* (Barlow), Hyperion
- Geminiani: Opus 2 (Lamon), Sony
- Gesualdo: Madrigals (Rooley), L'Oiseau-Lyre
- Glass: Songs from the Trilogy (various artists), Sony
- •§ Glück: *Orpheus & Eurydice* (Gardiner), Philips
- Handel: *Messiah* (Shaw), Telarc
- Handel: Opus 6 (Guildhall), RCA
- Haydn: *Lark, Rider* Quartets (Hagen), Deutsche Grammaphon
- ¢ Haydn: Symphonies #93–104 (Fischer), Nimbus
- Ives: *Three Places in New England,* Symphony #4 (Thomas, Ozawa), Deutsche Grammaphon
- Janáček : Sinfionetta, *Taras Bulba* (Mackerras), London
- ¢• Josquin: Motets and Chansons (Hilliard), EMI
- ¢• Lassus: Motets (Hilliard), Virgin
- Lutoslawski: Concerto for Orchestra, *Jeux Venitiens,* etc. (Lutoslawski), EMI
- ¢• Machaut: Messe de Nostre Dame (Parrot), EMI
- Mahler: Lieder (Baker, Barbirolli), EMI
- ¢ Mahler: Symphony #1 (Haitink), Philips
- § Mahler: Symphony #9 (Karajan), Deutsche Grammaphon
- ¢ Mendelssohn: Symphony #3, Overtures (Maag), London
- Messiaen: *Couleurs, Oiseaux,* etc. (Boulez), Montaigne
- • Monteverdi: *Orfeo* (Harnoncourt), Deutsche Grammaphon Archiv
- ¢• Monteverdi: Soprano Duets (Rooley), IMP
- Moussorgsky: *Boris Godunov* (Semkow), EMI
- ¢ Mozart: Concerti for Piano [Complete] (Anda), Deutsche Grammaphon
- § Mozart: Concerti for Violin #4, #5 (Schumsky, Tortelier), Nimbus
- § Mozart: *Don Giovanni* (Giulini), EMI
- Mozart: *Marriage of Figaro* (Solti), London
- Mozart: "Haydn" Quartets (Guarneri), Philips
- ¢ Mozart: Requiem (Karajan), Deutsche Grammaphon
- Mozart: String Quintets K515, K516 (Melos), Deutsche Grammaphon
- ¢ Mozart: Symphonies #35–#41 (Karajan), Deutsche Grammaphon
- Offenbach: *La Belle Hélène* (Plasson), EMI
- Palestrina: *Missa Paper Marcelli*/Allegri: *Miserere*/Lotti: *Crucifixus* (Christophers), Collins
- § Piazzolla: *57 Minutos Con La Realidad* (Piazzolla), Intuition
- Prokoviev: Concerti for Violin (Perlman, Rozhdestvensky), EMI
- Prokoviev: *Romeo and Juliet* (Maazel), London
- § Puccini: *Tosca* (Karajan), London
- • Purcell: *Dido and Aeneas* (Parrott), EMI
- • Purcell: *Fairy Queen* (Christophers), Collins
- § Rachmaninov: Concerto for Piano #2, *Rhapsody on a Theme of Paganini* (Rubinstein), RCA
- ¢ Rachmaninov: Symphony #2 (Previn), RCA
- Rimsky-Korsakov: *Sheherazade* (Mackerras), Telarc
- Saint-Saëns: Symphony #3 (Ormandy), Telarc
- Schoenberg: *Survivor from Warsaw,* 5 Pieces, etc. (Craft), Koch
- Schoenberg: *Transfigured Night*/Wagner: *Siegried Idyll* (Ashkenazy), London
- Schubert: Impromptus (Perahia), Sony
- ¢ Schubert: Lieder (Ludwig), Deutsche Grammaphon
- Schubert: Octet (Academy of St. Martin's in the Fields), Philips
- Schubert: Quartets #13, #14, #15 (Chilingirian), Chandos
- ¢ Schubert: Piano Sonatas [Complete] (Kempf), Deutsche Grammaphon
- ¢ Schubert: *Trout* Quintet (Marlborough), Sony
- Schubert: Cello Quintet (Guarneri), Philips
- ¢• Schubert: Symphonies (Goodman), Nimbus
- Schubert: Trio #1 (Borodin), Chandos
- Schumann: Symphonies [Complete] (Haitink), Philips
- § Sessions: *When Lilacs Last in Dooryard Bloom'd* (Ozawa), New World
- ¢ Sibelius: Symphony #2, *Swan of Tuonela* (Barbirolli), EMI
- ¢ Sibelius: Symphonies #4, #5 (Karajan), EMI
- § Stravinsky: *The Firebird* (Stravinsky), Sony
- § Stravinsky: *Petrouchka, The Rite of Spring* (Stravinsky), Sony
- ¢ Tchaikovsky: Concerto for Piano #1 (Gilels, Mehta), Concerto for Violin (Zukerman), Sony
- Tchaikovsky: Symphonies #1–#3 (Haitink), Philips
- § Tchaikovsky: Symphonies #4–#6 (Mravinsky), Deutsche Grammaphon
- § Telemann: Double and Triple Concerti (Hogwood), Oiseau Lyre
- • Telemann: *Tafelmusik* (Goebbel), Deutsche Grammaphon Archiv
- Vaughn-Williams: Symphony #8, Partita for Double String Orchestra (Thomas), Chandos
- † Verdi: *Aida* (Serafin), EMI
- Verdi: Requiem (Shaw), Telarc
- Vivaldi: *L'estro Armonico* (I Filarmonici), Tactus
- ¢ Vivaldi: *Four Seasons* (I Musici), Philips
- Wagner: Overtures (Tennstedt), EMI
- Wagner: *Tristan and Isolde* (Karajan), EMI
- Webern: Complete Music (Boulez), Sony
- Weill: *The Threepenny Opera* (Lemper, Mauceri), London

Glossary

A

ABACUS. A slab of stone at the top of a classical CAPITAL just beneath the ARCHITRAVE (figs. 5-24, 5-27).

ABBEY. 1) A religious community headed by an abbot or abbess. 2) The buildings which house the community. An abbey church often has an especially large CHOIR to provide space for the monks or nuns (fig. 11-1).

ACADEMY. A place of study, the word coming from the Greek name of a garden near Athens where Plato and, later, Platonic philosophers held philosophical discussions from the 5th century B.C. to the 6th century A.D. The first academy of fine arts was the Academy of Drawing, founded 1563 in Florence by Giorgio Vasari. Later academies were the Royal Academy of Painting and Sculpture in Paris, founded 1648, and the Royal Academy of Arts in London, founded 1768. Their purpose was to foster the arts by teaching, by exhibitions, by discussion, and occasionally by financial aid.

ACANTHUS. 1) A Mediterranean plant having spiny or toothed leaves. 2) An architectural ornament resembling the leaves of this plant, used on MOLDINGS, FRIEZES, and Corinthian CAPITALS (figs. 5-24, 5-37, 10-27).

ACRYLIC. A plastic binder MEDIUM for pigments that is soluble in water. Developed about 1960 (fig. 24-66).

AERIAL PERSPECTIVE. See **PERSPECTIVE.**

AISLE. See **SIDE AISLE.**

ALLA PRIMA. A painting technique in which pigments are laid on in one application with little or no UNDERPAINTING.

ALTAR. 1) A mound or structure on which sacrifices or offerings are made in the worship of a deity. 2) In a Catholic church, a tablelike structure used in celebrating the Mass.

ALTARPIECE. A painted or carved work of art placed behind and above the ALTAR of a Christian church. It may be a single panel (fig. 11-97) or a TRIPTYCH or a POLYPTYCH having hinged wings painted on both sides (figs. 15-1, 15-6). Also called a *reredos* or *retable.*

ALTERNATE SYSTEM. A system developed in Romanesque church architecture to provide adequate support for a GROIN-VAULTED NAVE having BAYS twice as long as the SIDE-AISLE bays. The PIERS of the nave ARCADE alternate in size; the heavier COMPOUND PIERS support the main nave vaults where the THRUST is concentrated, and smaller, usually cylindrical, piers support the side-aisle vaults (figs. 10-9, 10-16).

AMAZON. One of a tribe of female warriors said in Greek legend to dwell near the Black Sea (fig. 5-64).

AMBULATORY. A covered walkway. 1) In a BASILICAN church, the semicircular passage around the APSE (fig. 11-1). 2) In a CENTRAL-PLAN CHURCH, the ring-shaped AISLE around the central space (fig. 8-26). 3) In a CLOISTER, the covered COLONNADED or ARCADED walk around the open courtyard.

AMPHITHEATER. A double THEATER. A building, usually oval in plan, consisting of tiers of seats and access corridors around the central theater area (figs. 5-39, 7-10).

AMPHORA (pl. **AMPHORAE**). A large Greek storage vase with an oval body usually tapering toward the base; two handles extend from just below the lip to the shoulder (figs. 5-3, 5-6).

ANDACHTSBILD. German for devotional picture. A picture or sculpture with a type of imagery intended for private devotion, first developed in Northern Europe (fig. 11-54).

ANNULAR. From the Latin word for "ring." Signifies a ring-shaped form, especially an annular BARREL VAULT (fig. 8-7).

ANTA (pl. **ANTAE**). The front end of a wall of a Greek temple, thickened to produce a PILASTER-like member. Temples having COLUMNS between the antae are said to be "in antis" (fig. 5-25).

APOCALYPSE. The Book of Revelation, the last book of the New Testament. In it, St. John the Evangelist describes his visions, experienced on the island of Patmos, of Heaven, the future of humankind, and the Last Judgment.

APOSTLE. One of the 12 disciples chosen by Jesus to accompany him in his lifetime and to spread the GOSPEL after his death. The traditional list includes Andrew, Bartholomew, James the Greater (son of Zebedee), James the Lesser (son of Alphaeus), John, Judas Iscariot, Matthew, Peter, Philip, Simon the Canaanite, Thaddaeus (or Jude), and Thomas. In art, however, the same 12 are not always represented, since "apostle" was sometimes applied to other early Christians, such as St. Paul.

APSE. 1) A semicircular or polygonal niche terminating one or both ends of the NAVE in a Roman BASILICA (fig. 7-20). 2) In a Christian church, it is usually placed at the east end of the nave beyond the TRANSEPT or CHOIR (figs. 14-28, 19-22). It is also sometimes used at the end of transept arms.

AQUATINT. A print processed like an ETCHING, except that the ground or certain areas are covered with a solution of asphalt, resin, or salts which, when heated, produces a granular surface on the plate and rich gray tones in the final print (fig. 21-10). Etched lines are usually added to the plate after the aquatint ground is laid.

AQUEDUCT. Latin for "duct of water." 1) An artificial channel or conduit for transporting water from a distant source. 2) The overground structure which carries the conduit across valleys, rivers, etc. (fig. 7-9).

ARCADE. A series of ARCHES supported by PIERS or COLUMNS (fig. 7-24). When attached to a wall, these form a *blind arcade* (fig. 10-19).

ARCH. A curved structure used to span an opening. Masonry arches are built of wedge-shaped blocks, called *voussoirs,* set with their narrow side toward the opening so that they lock together (fig. 7-1). The topmost voussoir is called the *keystone.* Arches may take different shapes, as in the pointed *Gothic arch* (fig. 11-26) or the rounded classical arch (fig. 21-72), but all require support from other arches or BUTTRESSES.

ARCHBISHOP. The chief BISHOP of an ecclesiastic district.

ARCHITRAVE. The lowermost member of a classical ENTABLATURE; i.e., a series of stone blocks that rest directly on the COLUMNS (fig. 5-24).

ARCHIVOLT. A molded band framing an ARCH, or a series of such bands framing a TYMPANUM, often decorated with sculpture (fig. 10-22).

ARIANISM. Early Christian belief, initiated by Arius, a 4th-century A.D. priest in Alexandria. Now largely obscure, it was later condemned as heresy and suppressed.

ARRICCIO. See **SINOPIA.**

ATMOSPHERIC PERSPECTIVE. See **PERSPECTIVE.**

ATRIUM. 1) The central court of a Roman house (fig. 7-21) or its open entrance court. 2) An open court, sometimes COLONNADED or ARCADED, in front of a church (figs. 8-4, 10-15).

ATTIC. A low upper story placed above the main CORNICE or ENTABLATURE of a building and often decorated with windows and PILASTERS (fig. 13-27).

AUTOCHROME. A color photograph invented by Louis Lumière in 1903 using a glass plate covered with grains of starch dyed in three colors to act as filters and then a silver bromide emulsion (fig. 27-1).

B

BACCHANT (fem. **BACCHANTE**). A priest or priestess of the wine god, Bacchus (in Greek mythology, Dionysos), or one of his ecstatic female followers, who were sometimes called *maenads* (fig. 8-22).

BALUSTRADE. 1) A railing supported by short pillars called *balusters* (fig. 13-23). 2) Occasionally applied to any low parapet (figs. 5-57, 11-8).

BAPTISTERY. A building or a part of a church, often round or octagonal, in which the sacrament of baptism is administered (fig. 10-19). It contains a *baptismal font,* a receptacle of stone or metal which holds the water for the rite (fig. 10-31).

BARREL VAULT. See **VAULT.**

BASE. 1) The lowermost portion of a COLUMN or PIER, beneath the SHAFT (figs. 5-24, 5-72). 2) The lowest element of a wall, DOME, or building or occasionally of a statue or painting (see PREDELLA).

BASILICA. 1) In ancient Roman architecture, a large, oblong building used as a hall of justice and public meeting place, generally having a NAVE, SIDE AISLES, and one or more APSES (fig. 7-20). 2) In Christian architecture, a longitudinal church derived from the Roman basilica and having a nave, apse, two or four side aisles or side chapels, and sometimes a NARTHEX (fig. 12-14). 3) One of the seven main churches of Rome (St. Peter's, St. Paul Outside the Walls, St. John Lateran, etc.) or another church accorded the same religious privileges.

BATTLEMENT. A parapet consisting of alternating solid parts and open spaces designed originally for defense and later used for decoration (fig. 11-39).

BAY. A subdivision of the interior space of a building, usually in a series bounded by consecutive architectural supports (fig. 11-19).

BENEDICTINE ORDER. Founded at Monte Cassino in 529 A.D. by St. Benedict of Nursia (c. 480–c. 553). Less austere than other early ORDERS, it spread throughout much of western Europe and England in the next two centuries.

BISHOP. The spiritual overseer of a number of churches or a diocese. His throne, or *cathedra,* placed in the principal church of the diocese, designates it as a cathedral.

BLIND ARCADE. See **ARCADE.**

BLOCK BOOKS. Books, often religious, of the 15th century, containing WOODCUT prints in which picture and text were usually cut into the same block (compare fig. 15-22).

BOOK COVER. The stiff outer covers protecting the bound pages of a book. In the medieval period, frequently covered with precious metal and elaborately embellished with jewels, embossed decoration, etc. (fig. 9-19).

BOOK OF HOURS. A private prayer book containing the devotions for the seven canonical hours of the Roman Catholic church (matins, vespers, etc.), liturgies for local saints, and sometimes a calendar (fig. 11-94). They were often elaborately ILLUMINATED for persons of high rank, whose names are attached to certain extant examples (fig. 11-89).

BRACKET. A stone, wooden, or metal support projecting from a wall and having a flat top to bear the weight of a statue, CORNICE, beam, etc. (fig. 10-27). The lower part may take the form of a SCROLL; it is then called a *scroll bracket.*

BROKEN PEDIMENT. See **PEDIMENT.**

BRONZE AGE. The earliest period in which bronze was used for tools and weapons. In the Middle East, the Bronze Age succeeded the NEOLITHIC period in c. 3500 B.C. and preceded the Iron Age, which commenced c. 1900 B.C.

BRUSH DRAWING. See **DRAWING.**

BURIN. See **ENGRAVING.**

BUTTRESS. 1) A projecting support built against an external wall, usually to counteract the lateral THRUST of a VAULT or ARCH within (fig. 11-6). 2) FLYING BUTTRESS. An arched bridge above the aisle roof that extends from the upper nave wall, where the lateral thrust of the main vault is greatest, down to a solid pier (figs. 11-7, 11-19).

BYZANTIUM. City on the Sea of Marmara, founded by the ancient Greeks and renamed Constantinople in 330 A.D. Today called Istanbul.

C

CAESAR. The surname of the Roman dictator, Caius Julius Caesar, subsequently used as the title of an emperor; hence, the German *Kaiser* and the Russian *czar (tsar)*.

CALLIGRAPHY. From the Greek word for "beautiful writing." 1) Decorative or formal handwriting executed with a quill or reed pen or with a brush (fig. 8-19). 2) A design derived from or resembling letters and used to form a pattern (fig. 9-3).

CALVARY. The hill outside Jerusalem where Jesus was crucified, the name being taken from the Latin word *calvaris,* meaning skull (*Golgotha* is the Greek transliteration of "skull" in Aramaic). The hill was thought to be the spot where Adam was buried and was thus traditionally known as "the place of the skull."

CAMERA OBSCURA. Latin for "dark room." A darkened enclosure or box with a small opening or lens on one wall through which light enters to form an inverted image on the opposite wall. The principle had long been known but was not used as an aid in picture making until the 16th century.

CAMPAGNA. Italian word for "countryside." When capitalized, it usually refers to the countryside near Rome.

CAMPANILE. From the Italian word *campana,* meaning "bell." A bell tower, either round or square and sometimes freestanding (figs. 8-13, 10-15).

CAMPOSANTO. Italian word for "holy field." A cemetery near a church, often enclosed.

CANOPY. In architecture, an ornamental, rooflike projection or cover above a statue or sacred object (figs. 11-44, 17-16).

CAPITAL. The uppermost member of a COLUMN or PILLAR supporting the ARCHITRAVE (figs. 5-24, 5-37).

CARDINAL. In the Roman Catholic church, a member of the Sacred College, the ecclesiastical body which elects the pope and constitutes his advisory council.

CARMELITE ORDER. Originally a 12th-century hermitage claimed to descend from a community of hermits established by the prophet Elijah on Mt. Carmel, Palestine. In the early 13th century it spread to Europe and England, where it was reformed by St. Simon Stock and became one of the three great mendicant orders (see FRANCISCAN; DOMINICAN).

CARTHUSIAN ORDER. See **CHARTREUSE.**

CARTOON. From the Italian word *cartone,* meaning "cardboard." 1) A full-scale DRAWING for a picture or design intended to be transferred to a wall, panel, tapestry, etc. 2) A drawing or print, usually humorous or satirical, calling attention to some action or person of popular interest (fig. 21-36).

CARVING. 1) The cutting of a figure or design out of a solid material such as stone or wood, as contrasted to the additive technique of MODELING. 2) A work executed in this technique (figs. 13-14, 13-15).

CARYATID. A sculptured female figure used as an architectural support (figs. 5-19, 5-36). A similar male figure is an *atlas* (pl. *atlantes*).

CASTING. A method of duplicating a work of sculpture by pouring a hardening substance such as plaster or molten metal into a mold. See CIRE-PERDU PROCESS.

CAST IRON. A hard, brittle iron produced commercially in blast furnaces by pouring it into molds where it cools and hardens. Extensively used as a building material in the early 19th century (figs. 22-35, 22-36), it was superseded by STEEL and FERROCONCRETE.

CATACOMBS. The underground burial places of the early Christians, consisting of passages with niches for tombs and small chapels for commemorative services.

CATHEDRA, CATHEDRAL. See **BISHOP.**

CELLA. 1) The principal enclosed room of a temple to house an image (fig. 5-25). Also called the *naos.* 2) The entire body of a temple as distinct from its external parts.

CENTERING. A wooden framework built to support an ARCH, VAULT, or DOME during its construction.

CENTRAL-PLAN CHURCH. 1) A church having four arms of equal length. The CROSSING is often covered with a DOME (figs. 12-43–12-45). Also called a *Greek-cross church.* 2) A church having a circular or polygonal plan (figs. 8-26, 13-8).

CHANCEL. See **CHOIR.**

CHAPEL. 1) A private or subordinate place of worship (figs. 12-15–12-18). 2) A place of worship that is part of a church but separately dedicated (figs. 12-32, 13-17).

CHARTREUSE. French word for a Carthusian monastery (in Italian, *Certosa*). The Carthusian ORDER was founded by St. Bruno (c. 1030–1101) at Chartreuse near Grenoble in 1084. It is an eremitic order, the life of the monks being one of silence, prayer, and austerity.

CHASING. 1) A technique of ornamenting a metal surface by the use of various tools. 2) The procedure used to finish a raw bronze cast.

CHÂTEAU (pl. **CHÂTEAUS** or **CHÂTEAUX**). French word for "castle," now used to designate a large country house as well (fig. 16-24).

CHEVET. In Gothic architecture, the term for the developed and unified east end of a church, including CHOIR, APSE, AMBULATORY, and RADIATING CHAPELS (fig. 11-14).

CHIAROSCURO. Italian word for "light and dark." In painting, a method of modeling form primarily by the use of light and shade (figs. 13-1, 17-2).

CHOIR. In church architecture, a square or rectangular area between the APSE and the NAVE or TRANSEPT (fig. 11-2). It is reserved for the clergy and the singing choir and is usually marked off by steps, a railing, or a CHOIR SCREEN. Also called the *chancel.* See PILGRIMAGE CHOIR.

CHOIR SCREEN. A screen, frequently ornamented with sculpture and sometimes called a *rood screen,* separating the CHOIR of a church from the NAVE or TRANSEPT (figs. 8-44, 11-51). In Orthodox Christian churches it is decorated with ICONS and thus called an *iconostasis* (fig. 8-42).

CIRE-PERDU PROCESS. The lost-wax process of CASTING. A method in which an original is MODELED in wax or coated with wax, then covered with clay. When the wax is melted out, the resulting mold is filled with molten metal (often bronze) or liquid plaster.

CISTERCIAN ORDER. Founded at Cîteaux in France in 1098 by Robert of Molesme with the objective of reforming the BENEDICTINE ORDER and reasserting its original ideals of a life of severe simplicity.

CITY-STATE. An autonomous political unit comprising a city and the surrounding countryside.

CLERESTORY. A row of windows in the upper part of a wall that rises above an adjoining roof; built to provide direct lighting, as in a BASILICA or church (figs. 11-15, 11-18, 12-13).

CLOISTER. 1) A place of religious seclusion such as a monastery or nunnery. 2) An open court attached to a church or monastery and surrounded by a covered ARCADED walk or AMBULATORY. Used for study, meditation, and exercise.

CLUNIAC ORDER. Founded at Cluny, France, by Berno of Baume in 909. Leading religious reform movement in the Middle Ages. Had close connections to Ottonian rulers and to the papacy.

CODEX (pl. **CODICES**). A manuscript in book form made possible by the use of PARCHMENT instead of PAPYRUS. During the 1st to 4th centuries A.D., it gradually replaced the roll or SCROLL previously used for written documents.

COFFER. 1) A small chest or casket. 2) A recessed, geometrically shaped panel in a ceiling. A ceiling decorated with these panels is said to be *coffered* (figs. 7-12, 17-20, 21-72).

COLLAGE. A composition made of cut and pasted scraps of materials, sometimes with lines or forms added by the artist (fig. 24-15).

COLONNADE. A series of regularly spaced COLUMNS supporting a LINTEL or ENTABLATURE (figs. 2-32, 13-7).

COLOSSAL ORDER. COLUMNS, PIERS, or PILASTERS which extend through two or more stories (figs. 12-38, 13-26).

COLUMN. An approximately cylindrical, upright architectural support, usually consisting of a long, relatively slender SHAFT, a BASE, and a CAPITAL (figs. 5-24, 5-27). When imbedded in a wall, it is called an *engaged column* (fig. 5-38). Columns decorated with wraparound RELIEFS were used occasionally as freestanding commemorative monuments (fig. 7-37).

COMPOUND PIER. See **PIER.**

CONCRETE. A mixture of sand or gravel with mortar and rubble invented in the ancient Near East and further developed by the Romans (figs. 7-10, 7-11). Largely ignored during the Middle Ages, it was revived by Bramante in the early 16th century for St. Peter's.

CONTÉ CRAYON. A crayon made of graphite and clay used for DRAWING. Produces rich, velvety tones (fig. 23-6).

CONTRAPPOSTO. Italian word for "set against." A method developed by the Greeks to represent freedom of movement in a figure. The parts of the body are placed asymmetrically in opposition to each other around a central axis, and careful attention is paid to the distribution of the weight (figs. 5-41, 5-42, 12-6).

CORBELING. Roofing technique in which each layer of stone projects inward slightly over the previous layer (corbel) until all sides meet (figs. 4-14, 4-15).

CORINTHIAN ORDER. See **ORDER, ARCHITECTURAL.**

CORNICE. 1) The projecting, framing members of a classical PEDIMENT, including the horizontal one beneath and the two sloping or "raking" ones above (figs. 5-24, 5-27). 2) Any projecting, horizontal element surmounting a wall or other structure or dividing it horizontally for decorative purposes (fig. 12-21).

COUNTER-REFORMATION. The movement of self-renewal and reform within the Roman Catholic church following the Protestant REFORMATION of the early 16th century and attempting to combat its influence. Also known as the Catholic Reform. Its principles were formulated and adopted at the Council of Trent, 1545–63.

CRENELATED. See **BATTLEMENT.**

CROMLECH. From the Welsh for "concave stone." A circle of large upright stones, or DOLMENS, probably the setting for religious ceremonies in prehistoric Britain (figs. 1-17, 1-18).

CROSSHATCHING. See **HATCHING.**

CROSSING. The area in a church where the TRANSEPT crosses the NAVE, frequently emphasized by a DOME (figs. 10-17, 12-19) or crossing tower (fig. 10-1).

CROSS SECTION. See **SECTION.**

CRYPT. In a church, a VAULTED space beneath the CHOIR, causing the floor of the choir to be raised above the level of that of the NAVE (fig. 9-24).

CUNEIFORM. Describes the wedge-shaped characters made in clay by the ancient Mesopotamians (fig. 3-14).

CYCLOPEAN. An adjective describing masonry with large, unhewn stones, thought by the Greeks to have been built by the Cyclopes, a legendary race of one-eyed giants (fig. 4-19).

D

DAGUERREOTYPE. Originally, a photograph on a silver-plated sheet of copper which had been treated with fumes of iodine to form silver iodide on its surface and, after exposure, was developed by fumes of mercury. The process, invented by L. J. M. Daguerre and made public in 1839 (fig. 21-80), was modified and accelerated as daguerreotypes gained popularity.

DEËSIS. From the Greek word for "entreaty." The representation of Christ enthroned between the Virgin Mary and St. John the Baptist, frequent in Byzantine MOSAICS and depictions of the Last Judgment (fig. 15-2); refers to the roles of the Virgin Mary and St. John as intercessors for humankind.

DENTIL. A small, rectangular, toothlike block in a series, used to decorate a classical entablature (fig. 5-24).

DIORITE. An igneous rock, extremely hard and usually black or dark gray in color (fig. 3-14).

DIPTYCH. 1) Originally a hinged, two-leaved tablet used for writing. 2) A pair of ivory CARVINGS or PANEL paintings, usually hinged together (figs. 8-22, 8-23).

DIPYLON VASE. A Greek funerary vase with holes in the bottom through which libations were poured to the dead (fig. 5-2). Named for the cemetery near Athens where the vases were found.

DISGUISED SYMBOLISM. "Hidden" meaning in the details of a painting that carry a symbolic message (fig. 15-1).

DOLMEN. A structure formed by two or more large, upright stones capped by a horizontal slab; thought to be a prehistoric tomb (fig. 1-16).

DOME. A true dome is a VAULTED roof of circular, polygonal, or elliptical plan, formed with hemispherical or ovoidal curvature (fig. 7-15). May be supported by a circular wall or DRUM (fig. 8-45) and by PENDENTIVES (fig. 8-28) or related constructions. Domical coverings of many other sorts have been devised (fig. 11-35).

DOMINICAN ORDER. Founded as a mendicant ORDER by St. Dominic in Toulouse in 1220.

DOMUS. Latin word for "house." A Roman detached, one-family house with rooms frequently grouped around two open courts. The first, the ATRIUM, was used for entertaining and conducting business; the second, usually with a garden and surrounded by a PERISTYLE or COLONNADE, was for the private use of the family (fig. 7-21).

DONOR. The patron or client at whose order a work of art was executed; the donor may be depicted in the work (figs. 15-1, 15-16).

DORIC ORDER. See **ORDER, ARCHITECTURAL.**

DRAWING. 1) A work in pencil, pen and ink, charcoal, etc., often on paper (fig. 23-18). 2) A similar work in ink or WASH, etc., made with a brush and often called a *brush drawing.* 3) A work combining these or other techniques. A drawing may be large or small, a quick sketch or an elaborate work. Among its various forms are: a record of something seen (fig. 11-38); a study for another work (figs. 12-61, 21-32; see also OIL SKETCH; SINOPIA); an illustration associated with a text (fig. 13-5); and a technical aid.

DRÔLERIES. French word for "jests." Used to describe the lively animals and small figures in the margins of late medieval manuscripts (fig. 11-89) and occasionally in wood CARVINGS on furniture.

DRUM. 1) A section of the SHAFT of a COLUMN (figs. 5-33, 7-19). 2) A wall supporting a DOME (fig. 7-15).

DRYPOINT. See **ENGRAVING.**

E

ECHINUS. In the Doric or Tuscan ORDER, the round, cushionlike element between the top of the SHAFT and the ABACUS (figs. 5-24, 5-26).

ELEVATION. 1) An architectural drawing presenting a building as if projected on a vertical plane parallel to one of its sides (fig. 11-18). 2) Term used in describing the vertical plane of a building.

ENAMEL. 1) Colored glassy substances, either opaque or translucent, applied in powder form to a metal surface and fused to it by firing. Two main techniques developed: *champlevé* (from the French for "raised field"), in which the areas to be treated are dug out of the metal surface; and *cloisonné* (from the French for "partitioned"), in which compartments or *cloisons* to be filled are made on the surface with thin metal strips. 2) A work executed in either technique (figs. 9-1, 10-41).

ENCAUSTIC. A technique of painting with pigments dissolved in hot wax (fig. 7-55).

ENGAGED COLUMN. See **COLUMN.**

ENGRAVING. 1) A means of embellishing metal surfaces or gemstones by incising a design on the surface. 2) A PRINT made by cutting a design into a metal plate (usually copper) with a pointed steel tool known as a burin. The burr raised on either side of the incised line is removed; ink is then rubbed into the V-shaped grooves and wiped off the surface; the plate, covered with a damp sheet of paper, is run through a heavy press (fig. 15-23). The image on the paper is the reverse of that on the plate (figs. 20-11, 20-12). When a fine steel needle is used instead of a burin and the burr is retained, a drypoint engraving results, characterized by a softer line (fig. 15-24). 3) These techniques are called, respectively, *engraving* and *drypoint.*

ENTABLATURE. 1) In a classical order, the entire structure above the COLUMNS; this usually includes ARCHITRAVE, FRIEZE, and CORNICE (figs. 5-24, 5-27). 2) The same structure in any building of a classical style (fig. 21-15).

ENTASIS. A swelling of the SHAFT of a COLUMN (figs. 5-26, 5-30).

ETCHING. 1) A PRINT made by coating a copperplate with an acid-resistant resin and drawing through this ground, exposing the metal with a sharp instrument called a STYLUS. The plate is bathed in acid, which eats into the lines; it is then heated to remove the resin and finally inked and printed on paper (fig. 18-17). 2) The technique itself is also called etching.

EUCHARIST. 1) The sacrament of Holy Communion, the celebration in commemoration of the Last Supper (fig. 12-35). 2) The consecrated bread and wine used in the ceremony.

EVANGELISTS. Matthew, Mark, Luke, and John, traditionally thought to be the authors of the GOSPELS, the first four books of the New Testament, which recount the life and death of Christ. They are usually shown with their symbols, which are probably derived from the four beasts surrounding the throne of the Lamb in the Book of Revelation or from those in the vision of Ezekiel: a winged man or angel for Matthew, a winged lion for Mark (fig. 9-17), a winged ox for Luke (fig. 9-28), and an eagle for John (fig. 10-38). These symbols may also represent the evangelists (fig. 9-7).

F

FACADE. The principal face or the front of a building.

FATHERS OF THE CHURCH. Early teachers and defenders of the Christian faith. Those most frequently represented are the four Latin fathers: St. Jerome, St. Ambrose, and St. Augustine, all of the 4th century, and St. Gregory of the 6th.

FERROCONCRETE. Reinforced CONCRETE, strengthened by STEEL rods and mesh placed in it before hardening. Introduced in France c. 1900 and widely used today (figs. 26-14, 26-18, 26-28, 26-34).

FIBULA. A clasp, buckle, or brooch, often ornamented.

FINIAL. A relatively small, decorative element terminating a GABLE, PINNACLE, or the like (fig. 10-22).

FLUTING. In architecture, the ornamental grooves channeled vertically into the SHAFT of a COLUMN or PILASTER (fig. 5-33). They may meet in a sharp edge, as in the Doric ORDER, or be separated by a narrow strip or *fillet,* as in the Ionic, Corinthian, and Composite orders.

FLYING BUTTRESS. See **BUTTRESS.**

FONT. See **BAPTISTERY.**

FORESHORTENING. A method of reducing or distorting the parts of a represented object which are not parallel to the PICTURE PLANE in order to convey the impression of three dimensions as perceived by the human eye (figs. 19-5, 21-31).

FORUM (pl. **FORA**). In an ancient Roman city, the main public square which was the center of judicial and business activity and a public gathering place (fig. 7-8).

FRANCISCAN ORDER. Founded as a mendicant ORDER by St. Francis of Assisi (Giovanni de Bernardone, c. 1181–1226). The monks' aim was to imitate the life of Christ in its poverty and humility, to preach, and to minister to the spiritual needs of the poor.

FRESCO. Italian word for "fresh." 1) *True fresco* is the technique of painting on moist plaster with pigments ground in water so that the paint is absorbed by the plaster and becomes part of the wall itself (fig. 11-78). *Fresco secco* is the technique of painting with the same colors on dry plaster. 2) A painting done in either of these techniques.

FRIEZE. 1) A continuous band of painted or sculptured decoration (figs. 5-19, 7-32). 2) In a classical building, the part of the ENTABLATURE between the ARCHITRAVE and the CORNICE. A Doric frieze consists of alternating TRIGLYPHS and METOPES, the latter often sculptured (fig. 5-30). An Ionic frieze is usually decorated with continuous RELIEF sculpture (fig. 5-24).

FROTTAGE. See **RUBBING.**

G

GABLE. 1) The triangular area framed by the CORNICE or eaves of a building and the sloping sides of a pitched roof (fig. 9-21). In classical architecture, it is called a PEDIMENT. 2) A decorative element of similar shape, such as the triangular structures above the PORTALS of a Gothic church (figs. 10-22, 11-20) and sometimes at the top of a Gothic picture frame.

GALLERY. A second story placed over the SIDE AISLES of a church and below the CLERESTORY (figs. 11-5, 11-19) or, in a church with a four-part ELEVATION, below the TRIFORIUM and above the NAVE ARCADE which supports it on its open side.

GENIUS (pl. **GENII**). A winged seminude figure, often purely decorative (fig. 12-48) but frequently representing the guardian spirit of a person or place or personifying an abstract concept (fig. 21-58).

GENRE. French word for "kind" or "sort." A work of art, usually a painting, showing a scene from everyday life represented for its own sake (fig. 20-8).

GESSO. A smooth mixture of ground chalk or plaster and glue used as the basis for TEMPERA PAINTING and for OIL PAINTING on PANEL.

GILDING. 1) A coat of gold or of a gold-colored substance that is applied mechanically or chemically to surfaces of a painting, sculpture, or architectural decoration (figs. 12-8, 20-20). 2) The process of applying same.

GLAZE. 1) A thin layer of translucent oil color applied to a painted surface or to parts of it in order to modify the tone. 2) A glassy coating applied to a piece of ceramic work before firing in the kiln as a protective seal and often as decoration.

GLORIOLE or **GLORY.** The circle of radiant light around the heads or figures of God, Christ, the Virgin Mary, or a saint. When it surrounds the head only, it is called a *halo* or *nimbus* (fig. 11-90); when it surrounds the entire figure with a large oval (figs. 8-57, 11-41), it is called a *mandorla* (the Italian word for "almond"). It indicates divinity or holiness, though originally it was placed around the heads of kings and gods as a mark of distinction.

GOLD LEAF, SILVER LEAF. 1) Gold beaten into very thin sheets or "leaves" and applied to ILLUMINATED MANUSCRIPTS and PANEL paintings (figs. 10-38, 11-90), to sculpture, or to the back of the glass TESSERAE used in MOSAICS (figs. 8-15, 8-30). 2) Silver leaf is also used, though ultimately it tarnishes (fig. 8-20). Sometimes called *gold foil, silver foil.*

GOLGOTHA. See **CALVARY.**

GORGON. In Greek mythology, one of three hideous female monsters with large heads and snakes for hair (fig. 5-16). Their glance turned men to stone. Medusa, the most famous of the Gorgons, was killed by Perseus only with help from the gods.

GOSPEL. 1) The first four books of the New Testament. They tell the story of Christ's life and death and are ascribed to the EVANGELISTS Matthew, Mark, Luke, and John. 2) A copy of these, usually called a Gospel Book, often richly ILLUMINATED (figs. 9-15, 9-17).

GREEK-CROSS CHURCH. See **CENTRAL-PLAN CHURCH.**

GROIN VAULT. See **VAULT.**

GROUND PLAN. An architectural drawing presenting a building as if cut horizontally at the floor level.

GUTTAE. In a Doric ENTABLATURE, small peglike projections above the FRIEZE; possibly derived from pegs originally used in wooden construction (figs. 5-24, 5-27).

H

HALLENKIRCHE. German word for "hall church." A church in which the NAVE and the SIDE AISLES are of the same height. The type was developed in Romanesque architecture and occurs especially frequently in German Gothic churches (figs. 10-6, 11-30).

HALO. See **GLORIOLE.**

HATCHING. A series of parallel lines used as shading in PRINTS and DRAWINGS (fig. 12-61). When two sets of crossing parallel lines are used, it is called *cross-hatching.*

HIEROGLYPH. A picture of a figure, animal, or object standing for a word, syllable, or sound. These symbols are found on ancient Egyptian monuments as well as in Egyptian written records (fig. 2-21).

HIGH RELIEF. See **RELIEF.**

HÔTEL. French word for "hotel" but used also to designate an elegant town house (fig. 20-1).

I

ICON. From the Greek word for "image." A PANEL painting of one or more sacred personages, such as Christ, the Virgin, or a saint, particularly venerated in the Orthodox Catholic church (fig. 8-55).

ICONOSTASIS. See **CHOIR SCREEN.**

ILLUMINATED MANUSCRIPT. A MANUSCRIPT decorated with drawings (fig. 9-48) or with paintings in TEMPERA colors (figs. 9-27, 10-38).

ILLUSIONISM. In artistic terms, the technique of manipulating pictorial or other means in order to cause the eye to perceive a particular reality. May be used in architecture (fig. 17-26) and sculpture (figs. 17-29, 17-30), as well as in painting (figs. 7-48, 7-53).

IMPASTO. From the Italian word meaning "in paste." Paint, usually oil paint, applied very thickly (figs. 17-35, 23-11).

IN ANTIS. See **ANTA.**

INSULA (pl. **INSULAE**). Latin word for "island." 1) An ancient Roman city block. 2) A Roman "apartment house": a CONCRETE and brick building or chain of buildings around a central court, up to five stories high. The ground floor had shops, and above were living quarters (fig. 7-22).

IONIC ORDER.
See **ORDER, ARCHITECTURAL.**

J

JAMBS. The vertical sides of an opening. In Romanesque and Gothic churches, the jambs of doors and windows are often cut on a slant outward, or "splayed," thus providing a broader surface for sculptural decoration (figs. 11-41, 11-42).

JESUIT ORDER. The "Society of Jesus" was founded in 1534 by Ignatius of Loyola (1491–1556) and was especially devoted to the service of the pope. The order was a powerful influence in the struggle of the Catholic COUNTER-REFORMATION with the Protestant REFORMATION, and was also very important for its missionary work, disseminating Christianity in the Far East and the New World. The mother church in Rome, Il Gesù (figs. 14-29–14-31), conforms in design to the preaching aims of the new order.

K

KEEP. 1) The innermost and strongest structure or central tower of a medieval castle, sometimes used as living quarters, as well as for defense. Also called a *donjon* (fig. 11-94). 2) A fortified medieval castle.

KEYSTONE. See **ARCH.**

KORE (pl. **KORAI**). Greek word for "maiden." An Archaic Greek statue of a standing, clothed female (fig. 5-14).

KOUROS (pl. **KOUROI**). Greek word for "male youth." An Archaic Greek statue of a standing, nude youth (fig. 5-11).

KRATER. A Greek vessel, of assorted shapes, in which wine and water are mixed. *Calyx krater*—a bell-shaped vessel with handles near the base; *volute krater*—a vessel with handles shaped like scrolls (fig. 5-7).

KYLIX. In Greek and Roman antiquity, a shallow drinking cup with two horizontal handles, often set on a stem terminating in a foot (fig. 5-5).

L

LABORS OF THE MONTHS. The various occupations suitable to the months of the year. Scenes or figures illustrating these were frequently represented in ILLUMINATED MANUSCRIPTS (fig. 11-94); sometimes with the symbols of the ZODIAC signs CARVED around the PORTALS of Romanesque and Gothic churches (figs. 11-41, 11-49).

LANTERN. A relatively small structure crowning a DOME, roof, or tower, frequently open to admit light to an enclosed area below (figs. 7-15, 13-27).

LAPITH. A member of a mythical Greek tribe that defeated the Centaurs in a battle, scenes from which are frequently represented in vase painting and sculpture (fig. 5-46).

LAY BROTHER. One who has joined a monastic ORDER but has not taken monastic vows and therefore belongs still to the people or laity, as distinguished from the clergy or religious.

LEKYTHOS (pl. **LEKYTHOI**). A Greek oil jug with an ellipsoidal body, a narrow neck, a flanged mouth, a curved handle extending from below the lip to the shoulder, and a narrow base terminating in a foot. It was used chiefly for ointments and funerary offerings (fig. 5-61).

LIBERAL ARTS. Traditionally thought to go back to Plato, they comprised the intellectual disciplines considered suitable or necessary to a complete education and included grammar, rhetoric, logic, arithmetic, music, geometry, and astronomy. During the Middle Ages and the Renaissance, they were often represented allegorically in paintings, engravings, and sculpture (fig. 11-41).

LINTEL. See **POST AND LINTEL.**

LITHOGRAPH. A PRINT made by drawing a design with an oily crayon or other greasy substance on a porous stone or, later, a metal plate; the design is then fixed, the entire surface is moistened, and the printing ink which is applied adheres only to the oily lines of the drawing. The design can then be transferred easily in a press to a piece of paper. The technique was invented c. 1796 by Aloys Senefelder and quickly became popular (figs. 21-36, 23-19). It is also widely used commercially, since many impressions can be taken from a single plate.

LOGGIA. A covered GALLERY or ARCADE open to the air on at least one side. It may stand alone or be part of a building (fig. 14-23).

LONGITUDINAL SECTION.
See **SECTION.**

LOUVERS. A series of overlapping boards or slats which can be opened to admit air but are slanted so as to exclude sun and rain (fig. 26-29).

LOW RELIEF. See **RELIEF.**

LUNETTE. 1) A semicircular or pointed wall area, as under a VAULT or above a door or window. When it is above the PORTAL of a medieval church, it is called a TYMPANUM (fig. 11-45). 2) A painting (fig. 17-7), relief sculpture (fig. 12-47), or window of the same shape (fig. 21-14).

M

MAESTÀ. Italian word for "majesty," applied in the 14th and 15th centuries to representations of the Madonna and Child enthroned and surrounded by her celestial court of saints and angels (fig. 11-73).

MAGUS (pl. **MAGI**). 1) A member of the priestly caste of ancient Media and Persia. 2) In Christian literature, one of the three Wise Men or Kings who came from the East bearing gifts to the newborn Jesus (fig. 11-97).

MANDORLA. See **GLORIOLE.**

MANUSCRIPT. From the Latin word for "handwritten." 1) A document, scroll, or book written by hand, as distinguished from such a work in print (i.e., after c. 1450). 2) A book produced in the Middle Ages, frequently ILLUMINATED.

MASTABA. An ancient Egyptian tomb, rectangular in shape, with sloping sides and a flat roof. It covered a chapel for offerings and a shaft to the burial chamber (fig. 2-4).

MAUSOLEUM. 1) The huge tomb erected at Halicarnassus in Asia Minor in the 4th century B.C. by King Mausolus and his wife Artemisia (fig. 5-63). 2) A generic term for any large funerary monument.

MEANDER. A decorative motif of intricate, rectilinear character applied to architecture and sculpture (figs. 7-34, 10-27).

MEDIUM (pl. **MEDIA**). 1) The material or technique in which an artist works. 2) The vehicle in which pigments are carried in paint, PASTEL, etc.

MEGALITH. A huge stone such as those used in CROMLECHS and DOLMENS.

MEGARON (pl. **MEGARONS** or **MEGARA**). From the Greek word for "large." The central audience hall in a Minoan or Mycenaean palace or home (fig. 4-5).

MESOLITHIC. Transitional period of the Stone Age between the PALEOLITHIC and the NEOLITHIC.

METOPE. In a Doric FRIEZE, one of the panels, either decorated or plain, between the TRIGLYPHS. Originally it probably covered the empty spaces between the ends of the wooden ceiling beams (figs. 5-24, 5-30).

MINIATURE. 1) A single illustration in an ILLUMINATED MANUSCRIPT (figs. 9-3, 9-4). 2) A very small painting, especially a portrait on ivory, glass, or metal.

MINOTAUR. In Greek mythology, a monster having the head of a bull and the body of a man who lived in the Labyrinth of the palace of Knossos on Crete.

MODEL. 1) The preliminary form of a sculpture, often finished in itself but preceding the final CASTING or CARVING (figs. 19-17, 19-18, 21-64). 2) Preliminary or reconstructed form of a building made to scale (fig. 19-24). 3) A person who poses for an artist.

MODELING. 1) In sculpture, the building up of a figure or design in a soft substance such as clay or wax (fig. 6-8). 2) In painting and drawing, producing a three-dimensional effect by changes in color, the use of light and shade, etc.

MOLDING. In architecture, any of various long, narrow, ornamental bands having a distinctive profile which project from the surface of the structure and give variety to the surface by means of their patterned contrasts of light and shade (figs. 5-19, 21-19).

MOSAIC. Decorative work for walls, VAULTS, ceilings, or floors composed of small pieces of colored materials (called TESSERAE) set in plaster or CONCRETE. The Romans, whose work was mostly for floors, used regularly shaped pieces of marble in its natural colors (fig. 5-60). The early Christians used pieces of glass whose brilliant hues, including gold, and slightly irregular surfaces produced an entirely different, glittering effect (figs. 8-29, 8-30). See also GOLD LEAF.

MURAL. From the Latin word for wall, *murus.* A large painting or decoration either executed directly on a wall (FRESCO) or done separately and affixed to it (fig. 23-16).

MUSES. In Greek mythology, the nine goddesses who presided over various arts and sciences. They are led by Apollo as god of music and poetry and usually include Calliope, muse of epic poetry; Clio, muse of history; Erato, muse of love poetry; Euterpe, muse of music; Melpomene, muse of tragedy; Polyhymnia, muse of sacred music; Terpsichore, muse of dancing; Thalia, muse of comedy; and Urania, muse of astronomy.

N

NAOS. See **CELLA.**

NARTHEX. The transverse entrance hall of a church, sometimes enclosed but often open on one side to a preceding ATRIUM (fig. 8-4).

NAVE. 1) The central aisle of a Roman BASILICA, as distinguished from the SIDE AISLES (fig. 7-20). 2) The same section of a Christian basilican church extending from the entrance to the APSE or TRANSEPT (fig. 8-4).

NEOLITHIC. The New Stone Age, thought to have begun c. 9000–8000 B.C. The first society to live in settled communities, to domesticate animals, and to cultivate crops, it saw the beginning of many new skills, such as spinning, weaving, and building (fig. 1-10).

NEW STONE AGE. See **NEOLITHIC.**

NIKE. The ancient Greek goddess of victory, often identified with Athena and by the Romans with Victoria. She is usually represented as a winged woman with windblown draperies (figs. 5-57, 5-75).

NIMBUS. See **GLORIOLE.**

O

OBELISK. A tall, tapering, four-sided stone shaft with a pyramidal top. First constructed as MEGALITHS in ancient Egypt (fig. 2-32); certain examples since exported to other countries (fig. 17-15).

ODALISQUE. Turkish word for "harem slave girl" or "concubine" (fig. 21-30).

OIL PAINTING. 1) A painting executed with pigments mixed with oil, first applied to a panel prepared with a coat of GESSO (as also in TEMPERA PAINTING), or later to a stretched canvas primed with a coat of white paint and glue. The latter method has predominated since the late 15th century. Oil painting also may be executed on paper, parchment, copper, etc. 2) The technique of executing such a painting.

OIL SKETCH. A work in oil painting of an informal character, sometimes preparatory to a finished work (fig. 18-2).

OLD STONE AGE. See **PALEOLITHIC.**

ORCHESTRA. 1) In an ancient Greek theater, the round space in front of the stage and below the tiers of seats, reserved for the chorus (fig. 5-39). 2) In a Roman theater, a similar space reserved for important guests.

ORDER, ARCHITECTURAL. An architectural system based on the COLUMN and its ENTABLATURE, in which the form of the elements themselves (CAPITAL, SHAFT, BASE, etc.) and their relationships to each other are specifically defined. The five classical orders are the Doric, Ionic, Corinthian, Tuscan, and Composite (fig. 5-24). See also SUPERIMPOSED ORDER.

ORDER, MONASTIC. A religious society whose members live together under an established set of rules. See **BENEDICTINE; CARMELITE; CHARTREUSE; CISTERCIAN; DOMINICAN; FRANCISCAN.**

ORTHODOX. From the Greek word for "right in opinion." The Eastern Orthodox church, which broke with the Western Catholic church during the 5th century A.D. and transferred its allegiance from the pope in Rome to the Byzantine emperor in Constantinople and his appointed patriarch. Sometimes called the Byzantine church.

P

PALAZZO (pl. **PALAZZI**). Italian word for "palace" (in French, *palais*). Refers either to large official buildings (fig. 11-39) or to important private town houses (fig. 12-21).

PALEOLITHIC. The Old Stone Age, usually divided into Lower, Middle, and Upper (which began about 35,000 B.C.). A society of nomadic hunters who used stone implements, later developing ones of bone and flint. Some lived in caves, which they decorated during the latter stages of the age (fig. 1-2), at which time they also produced small CARVINGS in bone, horn, and stone (figs. 1-7, 1-8).

PALETTE. 1) A thin, usually oval or oblong board with a thumbhole at one end, used by painters to hold and mix their colors. 2) The range of colors used by a particular painter. 3) In Egyptian art, a slate slab, usually decorated with sculpture in low RELIEF. The small ones with a recessed circular area on one side are thought to have been used for eye makeup. The larger ones were commemorative objects (figs. 2-1, 2-2).

PANEL. 1) A wooden surface used for painting, usually in TEMPERA, and prepared beforehand with a layer of GESSO. Large ALTARPIECES require the joining together of two or more boards (fig. 15-19). 2) Recently, panels of Masonite or other composite materials have come into use (fig. 24-72).

PANTHEON. From *pan*, Greek for "all." A temple dedicated to all the gods (figs. 7-12, 7-13), or housing tombs of the illustrious dead of a nation or memorials to them (fig. 21-16).

PANTOCRATOR. A representation of Christ as ruler of the universe which appears frequently in the DOME or APSE MOSAICS of Byzantine churches (fig. 8-48).

PAPYRUS. 1) A tall aquatic plant that grows abundantly in the Near East, Egypt, and Abyssinia. 2) A paperlike material made by laying together thin strips of the pith of this plant and then soaking, pressing, and drying the whole. The resultant sheets were used as writing material by the ancient Egyptians, Greeks, and Romans. 3) An ancient document or SCROLL written on this material.

PARCHMENT. From Pergamon, the name of a Greek city in Asia Minor where parchment was invented in the 2nd century B.C. 1) A paperlike material made from bleached animal hides used extensively in the Middle Ages for MANUSCRIPTS (fig. 9-5). Vellum is a superior type of parchment made from calfskin. 2) A document or miniature on this material (fig. 9-27).

PASSION. 1) In ecclesiastic terms, the events of Jesus' last week on earth. 2) The representation of these events in pictorial, literary, theatrical, or musical form (figs. 11-78, 11-81).

PASTEL. 1) A soft, subdued shade of color. 2) A drawing stick made from pigments ground with chalk and mixed with gum water. 3) A drawing executed with these sticks (fig. 22-13).

PEDESTAL. An architectural support for a statue, vase, column, etc.

PEDIMENT. 1) In classical architecture, a low GABLE, typically triangular, framed by a horizontal CORNICE below and two raking cornices above; frequently filled with relief sculpture (fig. 5-21). 2) A similar architectural member, either round or triangular, used over a door, window, or niche (fig. 13-22). When pieces of the cornice are either turned at an angle or broken, it is called a *broken pediment* (fig. 7-23).

PELIKE. A Greek storage jar with two handles, a wide mouth, little or no neck, and resting on a foot (fig. 5-62).

PENDENTIVE. One of the spherical triangles which achieves the transition from a square or polygonal opening to the round BASE of a DOME or the supporting DRUM (figs. 8-35, 8-42).

PERIPTERAL. An adjective describing a building surrounded by a single row of COLUMNS or COLONNADE (figs. 5-25, 5-30).

PERISTYLE. 1) In a Roman house or DOMUS, an open garden court surrounded by a COLONNADE (fig. 7-24). 2) A colonnade around a building or court (fig. 5-25).

PERSPECTIVE. A technique for representing spatial relationships and three-dimensional objects on a flat surface so as to produce an effect similar to that perceived by the human eye. In *atmospheric* or *aerial perspective,* this is accomplished by a gradual decrease in the intensity of local color and in the contrast of light and dark, so that everything in the far distance tends toward a light bluish-gray tone (fig. 15-2). In *one-point linear perspective,* developed in Italy in the 15th century, a mathematical system is used based on *orthogonals* (all lines receding at right angles to the picture plane) that converge on a single vanishing point on the horizon. Since this presupposes an absolutely stationary viewer and imposes rigid restrictions on the artist, it is seldom applied with complete consistency (figs. 12-5, 12-34).

PHOTOGRAM. A shadowlike photograph made without a camera by placing objects on light-sensitive paper and exposing them to a light source (fig. 27-21).

PHOTOGRAPH. The relatively permanent or "fixed" form of an image made by light that passes through the lens of a camera and acts upon light-sensitive substances. Often called a PRINT.

PHOTOMONTAGE. A photograph in which prints in whole or in part are combined to form a new image (fig. 27-20). A technique much practiced by the Dada group in the 1920s.

PIAZZA (pl. **PIAZZE**). Italian word for "public square" (in French, *place;* in German, *Platz*).

PICTURE PLANE. The flat surface on which a picture is painted.

PICTURESQUE. Visually interesting or pleasing, as if resembling a picture (fig. 21-15).

PIER. An upright architectural support, usually rectangular and sometimes with CAPITAL and BASE (fig. 6-6). When COLUMNS, PILASTERS, or SHAFTS are attached to it, as in many Romanesque and Gothic churches, it is called a *compound pier* (fig. 10-9).

PIETÀ. Italian word for both "pity" and "piety." A representation of the Virgin grieving over the dead Christ (fig. 11-54). When used in a scene recording a specific moment after the Crucifixion, it is usually called a *Lamentation* (fig. 11-79).

PILASTER. A flat, vertical element projecting from a wall surface and normally having a BASE, SHAFT, and CAPITAL. It has generally a decorative rather than a structural purpose (figs. 12-40, 12-43).

PILGRIMAGE CHOIR. The unit in a Romanesque church composed of the APSE, AMBULATORY, and RADIATING CHAPELS (figs. 10-2, 11-2).

PILLAR. A general term for a vertical architectural support which includes COLUMNS, PIERS, and PILASTERS.

PINNACLE. A small, decorative structure capping a tower, PIER, BUTTRESS, or other architectural member and used especially in Gothic buildings (figs. 11-21, 11-23).

PLAN. See **GROUND PLAN.**

PODIUM. 1) The tall base upon which rests an Etruscan or Roman temple (fig. 7-2). 2) The ground floor of a building made to resemble such a base (fig. 19-10).

POLYPTYCH. An ALTARPIECE or devotional work of art made of several panels joined together (fig. 15-3), often hinged.

PORCH. General term for an exterior appendage to a building which forms a covered approach to a doorway (fig. 11-20). See PORTICO for porches consisting of columns.

PORTA. Latin word for "door" or "gate."

PORTAL. A door or gate, usually a monumental one with elaborate sculptural decoration (figs. 11-41, 11-55).

PORTICO. A columned porch supporting a roof or an ENTABLATURE and PEDIMENT, often approached by a number of steps (fig. 7-2). It provides a covered entrance to a building and a link with the space surrounding it.

POST AND LINTEL. A basic system of construction in which two or more uprights, the posts, support a horizontal member, the lintel. The lintel may be the topmost element (fig. 1-18) or support a wall or roof (fig. 4-19).

PREDELLA. The base of an ALTARPIECE, often decorated with small scenes which are related in subject to that of the main panel or panels (fig. 11-97).

PRINT. A picture or design reproduced, usually on paper and often in numerous copies, from a prepared wood block, metal plate, or stone slab or by photography. See AQUATINT, ENGRAVING, ETCHING, LITHOGRAPH, PHOTOGRAPH, WOODCUT.

PRONAOS. In a Greek or Roman temple, an open vestibule in front of the CELLA (fig. 5-25).

PROPYLAEUM (pl. **PROPYLAEA**). 1) The entrance to a temple or other enclosure, especially when it is an elaborate structure. 2) The monumental entry gate at the western end of the Acropolis in Athens (fig. 5-33).

PSALTER. 1) The book of Psalms in the Old Testament, thought to have been written in part by David, king of ancient Israel. 2) A copy of the Psalms, sometimes arranged for liturgical or devotional use and often richly ILLUMINATED (fig. 8-47).

PULPIT. A raised platform in a church from which the clergy delivers a sermon or conducts the service. Its railing or enclosing wall may be elaborately decorated (fig. 11-57).

PUTTO (pl. **PUTTI**). A nude, male child, usually winged, often represented in classical and Renaissance art. Also called a *cupid* or *amoretto* when he carries a bow and arrow and personifies Love (fig. 13-33).

PYLON. Greek word for "gateway." 1) The monumental entrance building to an Egyptian temple or forecourt consisting of either a massive wall with sloping sides pierced by a doorway or of two such walls flanking a central gateway (fig. 2-32). 2) A tall structure at either side of a gate, bridge, or avenue marking an approach or entrance.

Q

QUATREFOIL. An ornamental element composed of four lobes radiating from a common center (figs. 11-49, 11-65).

R

RADIATING CHAPELS. Term for CHAPELS arranged around the AMBULATORY (and sometimes the TRANSEPT) of a medieval church (figs. 10-1, 11-2, 11-21).

REFECTORY. 1) A room for refreshment. 2) The dining hall of a monastery, college, or other large institution.

REFORMATION. The religious movement in the early 16th century which had for its object the reform of the Catholic church and led to the establishment of Protestant churches. See also COUNTER-REFORMATION.

REINFORCED CONCRETE. See **FERROCONCRETE.**

RELIEF. 1) The projection of a figure or part of a design from the background or plane on which it is CARVED or MODELED. Sculpture done in this manner is described as "high relief" or "low relief" depending on the height of the projection (figs. 2-3, 7-37). When it is very shallow, it is called *schiacciato,* the Italian word for "flattened out" (fig. 12-3). 2) The apparent projection of forms represented in a painting or drawing.

RESPOND. 1) A half-PIER, PILASTER, or similar element projecting from a wall to support a LINTEL or an ARCH whose other side is supported by a freestanding COLUMN or pier, as at the end of an ARCADE (fig. 8-15). 2) One of several pilasters on a wall behind a COLONNADE (fig. 7-23) which echoes or "responds to" the columns but is largely decorative. 3) One of the slender shafts of a COMPOUND PIER in a medieval church which seems to carry the weight of the VAULT (figs. 10-13, 11-16).

RHYTON. An ancient drinking horn made from pottery or metal and frequently having a base formed by a human or animal head (fig. 3-29).

RIB. A slender, projecting, archlike member which supports a VAULT either transversely (fig. 10-3) or at the GROINS, thus dividing the surface into sections (fig. 10-13). In Late Gothic architecture, its purpose is often primarily ornamental (fig. 11-27).

RIBBED VAULT. See **VAULT.**

ROOD SCREEN. See **CHOIR SCREEN.**

ROSE WINDOW. A large, circular window with stained glass and stone TRACERY, frequently used on FACADES and at the ends of TRANSEPTS of Gothic churches (figs. 11-8, 11-11).

ROSTRUM. 1) A beaklike projection from the prow of an ancient warship used for ramming the enemy. 2) In the Roman FORUM, the raised platform decorated with the beaks of captured ships from which speeches were delivered. 3) A platform, stage, or the like used for public speaking.

RUBBING. A reproduction of a relief surface made by covering it with paper and rubbing with pencil, chalk, etc. Also called *frottage.*

RUSTICATION. A masonry technique of laying rough-faced stones with sharply indented joints (figs. 12-21, 14-24).

S

SACRA CONVERSAZIONE. Italian for "holy conversation." A composition of the Madonna and Child with saints in which the figures all occupy the same spatial setting and appear to be conversing or communing with one another (figs. 12-64, 13-38).

SACRISTY. A room near the main altar of a church, or a small building attached to a church, where the vessels and vestments required for the service are kept. Also called a *vestry.*

SALON. 1) A large, elegant drawing or reception room in a palace or a private house. 2) Official government-sponsored exhibition of paintings and sculpture by living artists held at the Louvre in Paris, first biennially, then annually. 3) Any large public exhibition patterned after the Paris Salon.

SANCTUARY. 1) A sacred or holy place or building. 2) An especially holy place within a building, such as the CELLA of a temple or the part of a church around the altar.

SARCOPHAGUS (pl. **SARCOPHAGI**). A large stone coffin usually decorated with sculpture and/or inscriptions (figs. 6-2, 8-21). The term is derived from two Greek words meaning "flesh" and "eating," which were applied to a kind of limestone in ancient Greece, since the stone was said to turn flesh to dust.

SATYR. One of a class of woodland gods thought to be the lascivious companions of Dionysos, the Greek god of wine (or of Bacchus, his Roman counterpart). They are represented as having the legs and tail of a goat, the body of a man, and a head with horns and pointed ears. A youthful satyr is also called a *faun.*

SCRIPTORIUM (pl. **SCRIPTORIA**). A workroom in a monastery reserved for copying and illustrating MANUSCRIPTS.

SCROLL. 1) An architectural ornament with the form of a partially unrolled spiral, as on the CAPITALS of the Ionic and Corinthian ORDERS (fig. 5-24). 2) A form of written text.

SCUOLA. Italian word for school. In Renaissance Venice it designated a fraternal organization or confraternity dedicated to good works, usually under ecclesiastic auspices.

SECTION. An architectural drawing presenting a building as if cut across the vertical plane at right angles to the horizontal plane. *Cross section:* a cut along the transverse axis. *Longitudinal section:* a cut along the longitudinal axis.

SEXPARTITE VAULT. See **VAULT.**

SFUMATO. Italian word meaning "gone up in smoke," used to describe very delicate gradations of light and shade in the MODELING of figures; applied especially to the work of Leonardo da Vinci (fig. 13-4).

SHAFT. In architecture, the part of a COLUMN between the BASE and the CAPITAL (fig. 5-24).

SIBYLS. In Greek and Roman mythology, any of numerous women who were thought to possess powers of divination and prophecy. They appear on Christian representations, notably in Michelangelo's Sistine ceiling, because they were believed to have foretold the coming of Christ.

SIDE AISLE. A passageway running parallel to the NAVE of a Roman BASILICA or Christian church, separated from it by an ARCADE or COLONNADE (figs. 7-20, 8-4). There may be one on either side of the nave or two, an inner and outer.

SILENI. A class of minor woodland gods in the entourage of the wine god, Dionysos (or Bacchus). Like Silenus, the wine god's tutor and drinking companion, they are thick-lipped and snub-nosed and fond of wine. Similar to SATYRS, they are basically human in form except for having horses' tails and ears (fig. 7-51).

SILVER LEAF. See **GOLD LEAF.**

SILVER SALTS. Compounds of silver—bromide, chloride, and iodide—which are sensitive to light and are used in the preparation of photographic materials. This sensitivity was first observed by Johann Heinrich Schulze in 1725.

SINOPIA (pl. **SINOPIE**). Italian word taken from "Sinope," the ancient city in Asia Minor which was famous for its brick-red pigment. In FRESCO paintings, a full-sized, preliminary sketch done in this color on the first rough coat of plaster or *arriccio* (fig. 11-87).

SKETCH. See **DRAWING; OIL SKETCH.**

SPANDREL. The area between the exterior curves of two adjoining ARCHES or, in the case of a single arch, the area around its outside curve from its springing to its keystone (figs. 7-46, 10-22).

SPHINX. 1) In ancient Egypt, a creature having the head of a man, animal, or bird and the body of a lion; frequently sculpted in monumental form (fig. 2-12). 2) In Greek mythology, a creature usually represented as having the head and breasts of a woman, the body of a lion, and the wings of an eagle. It appears in classical, Renaissance, and Neoclassical art.

STANZA (pl. **STANZE**). Italian word for "room."

STEEL. Iron modified chemically to have qualities of great hardness, elasticity, and strength. For use in sculpture, see figs. 25-23, 25-30. For architectural use, see STRUCTURAL STEEL.

STELE. From the Greek word for "standing block." An upright stone slab or pillar with a CARVED commemorative design or inscription (fig. 3-13).

STEREOBATE. The substructure of a classical building, especially a Greek temple (fig. 5-24).

STEREOSCOPE. An optical instrument which enables the user to combine two pictures taken from points of view corresponding to those of the two eyes into a single image having the depth and solidity of ordinary binocular vision (fig. 21-85). First demonstrated by Sir Charles Wheatstone in 1838.

STILTS. Term for pillars or posts supporting a superstructure; in 20th-century architecture, these are usually of FERROCONCRETE (figs. 26-18, 26-29). Stilted, as in stilted arches, refers to tall supports beneath an architectural member.

STOA. In Greek architecture, a covered COLONNADE, sometimes detached and of considerable length, used as a meeting place or promenade.

STOIC. A member of a school of philosophy founded by Zeno about 300 B.C. and named after the STOA in Athens where he taught. Its main thesis is that man should be free of all passions.

STRUCTURAL STEEL. STEEL used as an architectural building material either invisibly (fig. 23-29) or exposed (fig. 26-7). See FERROCONCRETE.

STUCCO. 1) A CONCRETE or cement used to coat the walls of a building. 2) A kind of plaster used for architectural decorations, such as CORNICES and MOLDINGS, or for sculptured RELIEFS (fig. 6-6).

STUDY. See **DRAWING.**

STYLOBATE. A platform or masonry floor above the STEREOBATE forming the foundation for the COLUMNS of a classical temple (fig. 5-24).

STYLUS. From the Latin word *stilus,* the writing instrument of the Romans. 1) A pointed instrument used in ancient times for writing on tablets of a soft material such as clay. 2) The needlelike instrument used in drypoint or etching. See ENGRAVING; ETCHING.

SUPERIMPOSED ORDERS. Two or more rows of COLUMNS, PIERS, or PILASTERS placed above each other on the wall of a building (fig. 7-11).

T

TABERNACLE. 1) A place or house of worship. 2) A CANOPIED niche or recess built for an image (fig. 12-2). 3) The portable shrine used by the ancient Jews to house the Ark of the Covenant (fig. 8-2).

TABLINUM. From the Latin word meaning writing tablet or written record. In a Roman house, a room at the far end of the ATRIUM, or between it and the second courtyard, used for keeping family records.

TEMPERA PAINTING. 1) A painting made with pigments mixed with egg yolk and water. In the 14th and 15th centuries, it was applied to PANELS which had been prepared with a coating of GESSO; the application of GOLD LEAF and of underpainting in green or brown preceded the actual tempera painting (figs. 11-81, 11-97). 2) The technique of executing such a painting.

TERRA-COTTA. Italian word for "baked earth." 1) Earthenware, naturally reddish-brown but often GLAZED (fig. 12-47) in various colors and fired. Used for pottery, sculpture, or as a building material or decoration. 2) An object made of this material. 3) Color of the natural material.

TESSERA (pl. **TESSERAE**). A small piece of colored stone, marble, glass, or gold-backed glass used in a MOSAIC (fig. 8-46).

THEATER. In ancient Greece, an outdoor place for dramatic performances, usually semicircular in plan and provided with tiers of seats, the ORCHESTRA, and a support for scenery (fig. 5-39). See also AMPHITHEATER.

THEATINE ORDER. Founded in Rome in the 16th century by members of the recently dissolved Oratory of Divine Love. Its aim was to reform the Catholic church, and its members were pledged to cultivate their spiritual lives and to perform charitable works.

THERMAE. A public bathing establishment of the ancient Romans which consisted of various types of baths and social and gymnastic facilities.

THOLOS. In classical architecture, a circular building ultimately derived from early tombs (fig. 5-38).

THRUST. The lateral pressure exerted by an ARCH, VAULT, or DOME which must be counteracted at its point of greatest concentration either by the thickness of the wall or by some form of BUTTRESS.

TRACERY. 1) Ornamental stonework in Gothic windows. In the earlier or *plate tracery,* the windows appear to have been cut through the solid stone (fig. 10-22). In *bar tracery,* the glass predominates, the slender pieces of stone having been added within the windows (fig. 11-21). 2) Similar ornamentation using various materials and applied to walls, shrines, facades, etc. (fig. 11-82).

TRANSEPT. A cross arm in a BASILICAN church placed at right angles to the NAVE and usually separating it from the CHOIR or APSE (fig. 8-4).

TREE OF KNOWLEDGE. The tree in the Garden of Eden from which Adam and Eve ate the forbidden fruit which destroyed their innocence.

TREE OF LIFE. A tree in the Garden of Eden whose fruit was reputed to give everlasting life; in medieval art it was frequently used as a symbol of Christ.

TRIFORIUM. The section of a NAVE wall above the ARCADE and below the CLERESTORY (fig. 11-15). It frequently consists of a BLIND ARCADE with three openings in each bay. When the GALLERY is also present, a four-story ELEVATION results, the triforium being between the gallery and clerestory. It may also occur in the TRANSEPT and the CHOIR walls.

TRIGLYPH. The element of a Doric FRIEZE separating two consecutive METOPES and being divided by channels (or *glyphs*) into three sections. Probably an imitation in stone of wooden ceiling beam ends (figs. 5-24, 5-30).

TRIPTYCH. An ALTARPIECE or devotional picture, either CARVED or painted, with one central panel and two hinged wings (fig. 8-53).

TRIUMPHAL ARCH. 1) A monumental ARCH, sometimes a combination of three arches, erected by a Roman emperor in commemoration of his military exploits and usually decorated with scenes of these deeds in RELIEF sculpture (fig. 7-46). 2) The great transverse arch at the eastern end of a church which frames ALTAR and APSE and separates them from the main body of the church. It is frequently decorated with MOSAICS or MURAL paintings (fig. 8-15).

TROPHY. 1) In ancient Rome, arms or other spoils taken from a defeated enemy and publicly displayed on a tree, PILLAR, etc. 2) A representation of these objects, and others symbolic of victory, as a commemoration or decoration.

TRUMEAU. A central post supporting the LINTEL of a large doorway, as in a Romanesque or Gothic PORTAL, where it was frequently decorated with sculpture (figs. 10-21, 11-55).

TRUSS. A triangular wooden or metal support for a roof which may be left exposed in the interior (figs. 8-15, 11-33) or be covered by a ceiling (figs. 9-24, 10-18).

TURRET. 1) A small tower, part of a larger structure. 2) A small tower at a corner of a building, often beginning some distance from the ground.

TYMPANUM. 1) In classical architecture, the recessed, usually triangular area, also called a PEDIMENT, often decorated with sculpture (fig. 5-27). 2) In medieval architecture, an arched area between an ARCH and the LINTEL of a door or window, frequently carved with RELIEF sculpture (figs. 10-26, 11-45).

U

UNDERPAINTING.
See **TEMPERA PAINTING.**

V

VAULT. An arched roof or ceiling usually made of stone, brick, or CONCRETE. Several distinct varieties have been developed; all need BUTTRESSING at the point where the lateral THRUST is concentrated. 1) A *barrel vault* is a semicylindrical structure made up of successive ARCHES (fig. 7-1). It may be straight or ANNULAR in plan (fig. 8-7). 2) A *groin vault* is the result of the intersection of two barrel vaults of equal size which produces a BAY of four compartments with sharp edges, or *groins,* where the two meet (fig. 7-1). 3) A *ribbed groin vault* is one in which RIBS are added to the groins for structural strength and for decoration (fig. 10-12). When the diagonal ribs are constructed as half-circles, the resulting form is a *domical ribbed vault* (fig. 10-16). 4) A *sexpartite vault* is a ribbed groin vault in which each bay is divided into six compartments by the addition of a transverse rib across the center (figs. 10-12, 10-13). 5) The normal *Gothic vault* is quadripartite with all the arches pointed to some degree (fig. 11-16). 6) A *fan vault* is an elaboration of a ribbed groin vault, with elements of TRACERY using conelike forms. It was developed by the English in the 15th century and was employed for decorative purposes (figs. 11-28, 11-29).

VEDUTA (pl. **VEDUTE**). A view painting, generally a city landscape (fig. 20-26).

VELLUM. See **PARCHMENT.**

VESTRY. See **SACRISTY.**

VICES. Often represented allegorically in conjunction with the seven VIRTUES, they include Pride, Avarice, Wrath, Gluttony, Unchastity (Luxury), Folly, and Inconstancy, though others such as Injustice are sometimes substituted.

VICTORY. See **NIKE.**

VILLA. Originally a large country house (fig. 14-26) but in modern usage also a detached house or suburban residence. See DOMUS.

VIRTUES. The three theological virtues, Faith, Hope, and Charity, and the four cardinal ones, Prudence, Justice, Fortitude, and Temperance, were frequently represented allegorically, particularly in medieval manuscripts and sculpture.

VOLUTE. A spiraling architectural element found notably on Ionic and Composite CAPITALS (figs. 5-24, 5-35, 7-2) but also used decoratively on building FACADES and interiors (fig. 14-31).

VOUSSOIR. See **ARCH.**

W

WASH. A thin layer of translucent color or ink used in WATERCOLOR PAINTING and BRUSH DRAWING, and occasionally in OIL PAINTING.

WATERCOLOR PAINTING. Painting, usually on paper, in pigments suspended in water (figs. 16-4, 24-46).

WESTWORK. From the German word *Westwerk.* In Carolingian, Ottonian, and German Romanesque architecture, a monumental western front of a church, treated as a tower or combination of towers and containing an entrance and vestibule below and a CHAPEL and GALLERIES above. Later examples often added a TRANSEPT and a CROSSING tower (fig. 9-21).

WING. The side panel of an ALTARPIECE which is frequently decorated on both sides and is also hinged, so that it may be shown either open or closed (figs. 15-3, 15-6).

WOODCUT. A PRINT made by carving out a design on a wooden block cut along the grain, applying ink to the raised surfaces which remain, and printing from those (figs. 15-21, 16-5, 24-6).

WROUGHT IRON. A comparatively pure form of iron which is easily forged and does not harden quickly, so that it can be shaped or hammered by hand (fig. 25-16), in contrast to molded CAST IRON.

Z

ZIGGURAT. From the Assyrian word *ziqquratu,* meaning "mountaintop" or "height." In ancient Assyria and Babylonia, a pyramidal tower built of mud brick and forming the BASE of a temple; it was either stepped or had a broad ascent winding around it, which gave it the appearance of being stepped (figs. 3-1, 3-4).

ZODIAC. An imaginary belt circling the heavens, including the paths of the sun, moon, and major planets and containing 12 constellations and thus 12 divisions called signs, which have been associated with the months. The signs are: Aries, the ram; Taurus, the bull; Gemini, the twins; Cancer, the crab; Leo, the lion; Virgo, the virgin; Libra, the balance; Scorpio, the scorpion; Sagittarius, the archer; Capricorn, the goat; Aquarius, the water-bearer; and Pisces, the fish. They are frequently represented around the PORTALS of Romanesque and Gothic churches in conjunction with the LABORS OF THE MONTHS (figs. 10-26, 11-49).

Art and Architecture Websites

The directory below is made up mainly of the significant museums that provided illustrations for this book. A few additional art sites are also listed for your reference. All efforts have been made to gather up-to-date addresses, phone numbers, and Websites. Contact information is current as of the time of printing.

UNITED STATES

For additional information or to find out about museums not listed here, visit the following Websites:
http://www.1413.com
http://www.amn.org
http://www.artcom.com
http://www.artmuseum.net
http://www.ICOM.org
http://www.museumstuff.com
http://www.world-arts-resources.com

ARIZONA

Center for Creative Photography, University of Arizona
1030 N. Olive Rd., Tucson 85719
(520) 621-7968
http://dizzy.library.arizona.edu/branches/ccp

The Heard Museum
2301 N. Central Ave.,
Phoenix 85004
(602) 252-8840
http://www.heard.org

Phoenix Art Museum
1625 N. Central Ave.,
Phoenix 85004
(602) 257-1222
http://www.phxart.org

Tucson Museum of Art
140 N. Main Ave., Tucson 85701
(520) 624-2333
http://www.tucsonarts.com

CALIFORNIA

Berkeley Art Museum and Pacific Film Archive, University of California
2626 Bancroft Way,
Berkeley 94704
(510) 642-0808
http://www.bampfa.berkeley.edu

Crocker Museum of Art
216 O St., Sacramento 95814
(916) 264-5423
http://www.crockerartmuseum.org

The Fine Arts Museums of San Francisco
California Palace of the Legion of Honor
Lincoln Park, near 34th Ave. and Clement St., San Francisco 94122
(415) 863-3330

M. H. de Young Memorial Museum
75 Tea Garden Dr., Golden Gate Park, San Francisco 94118
(415) 863-3300
http://www.famsf.org

Huntington Library, Art Collections, and Botanical Gardens
1151 Oxford Rd., San Marino 91108
(626) 405-2141
http://www.huntington.org

Iris and B. Gerald Cantor Center for Visual Arts at Stanford University
Lomita Dr. at Museum Way,
Stanford 94305
(650) 723-4177
http://www.stanford.edu/dept/ccva

The J. Paul Getty Museum, the Getty Center
1200 Getty Center Dr.,
Los Angeles 90049
(310) 440-7300
http://www.getty.edu/museum

Los Angeles County Museum of Art
5905 Wilshire Blvd.,
Los Angeles 90036
(213) 857-6111
http://www.lacma.org

The Museum of Contemporary Art, Los Angeles
250 S. Grand Ave.,
Los Angeles 90012
(213) 382-6222
http://www.MOCA-LA.org

Museum of Contemporary Art, San Diego
1001 Kettner Blvd.,
San Diego 92101
(619) 234-1001
http://www.mcasandiego.org

Norton Simon Museum
411 W. Colorado Blvd.,
Pasadena 91105
(626) 449-6840
http://www.nortonsimon.org

San Diego Museum of Art
1450 El Prado, San Diego 92101
(619) 232-7931
http://www.sdmart.com

San Francisco Museum of Modern Art
151 3rd St., San Francisco 94103
(415) 357-4000
http://www.sfmoma.org

San Jose Museum of Art
110 S. Market St., San Jose 95113
(408) 294-2787
http://www.sjmusart.org

Santa Barbara Museum of Art
1130 State St., Santa Barbara 93101
(805) 963-4364
http://www.sbmuseart.org

COLORADO

Colorado Springs Fine Arts Center
30 W. Dale St., Colorado Springs 80903
(719) 634-5581
http://www.csfineartscenter.com

The Denver Art Museum
100 W. 14th Avenue Pkwy.,
Denver 80204
(303) 640-2295
http://www.denverartmuseum.org

CONNECTICUT

Wadsworth Atheneum
600 Main St., Hartford 06103
(860) 278-2670
http://www.wadsworthatheneum.org

Yale Center for British Art
1080 Chapel St., New Haven 06520
(203) 432-2800
http://www.yale.edu/ycba

Yale University Art Gallery
1111 Chapel St., New Haven 06520
(203) 432-0600
http://www.yale.edu/artgallery

DELAWARE

Delaware Art Museum
2301 Kentmere Pkwy.,
Wilmington 19806
(302) 571-9590
http://www.delart.mus.de.us

DISTRICT OF COLUMBIA

The Corcoran Gallery of Art
500 17th St. NW, 20006
(202) 639-1700
http://www.corcoran.org

Freer Gallery of Art and Arthur M. Sackler Gallery, The National Museum of Asian Art for the United States, Smithsonian Institution
12th St. & Jefferson Dr. SW, 20560
(202) 357-4880
http://www.si.edu/asia

Hirshhorn Museum and Sculpture Garden, Smithsonian Institution
Independence Ave. & 7th St. SW, 20560
(202) 357-1300
http://www.si.edu/organiza/museums/hirsh/start.htm

National Gallery of Art
600 Constitution Ave. NE, 20565
(202) 737-4215
http://www.nga.gov

National Museum of American Art, Smithsonian Institution
8th & G St. NW, 20560
(202) 357-1300
Renwick Gallery
Pennsylvania Ave. at
17th St. NW, 20006
(202) 357-2700
http://www.nmaa.si.edu

National Museum of Women in the Arts
1250 New York Ave. NW, 20005
(202) 783-5000
http://www.nmwa.org

National Portrait Gallery, Smithsonian Institution
910 F St. NW, 20560
(202) 357-1300
http://www.npg.si.edu

The Phillips Collection
1600 21st St. NW, 20009
(202) 387-2151
http://www.phillipscollection.org

FLORIDA

John and Mable Ringling Museum of Art
5401 Bay Shore Rd., Sarasota 34243
(941) 359-5700
http://www.ringling.org

Lowe Art Museum, University of Miami
1301 Stanford Dr., Miami 33124
(305) 284-3535
http://www.lowemuseum.org

Saint Petersburg Museum of Fine Arts
255 Beach Dr. NE,
Saint Petersburg 33701
(727) 896-2667
http://www.fine-arts.org

GEORGIA

Georgia Museum of Art, University of Georgia
Jackson St., North Campus,
Athens 30602
(706) 542-GMOA
http://www.uga.edu/gamuseum

High Museum of Art
1280 Peachtree St. NE, Atlanta 30309
(404) 733-4400
http://www.high.org

Michael C. Carlos Museum, Emory University
571 S. Kilgo St., Atlanta 30322
(404) 727-4282/0573
http://www.emory.edu/CARLOS

HAWAII

Honolulu Academy of Arts
900 S. Beretania St., Honolulu 96814
(808) 532-8700
http://www.honoluluacademy.org

ILLINOIS

The Art Institute of Chicago
111 S. Michigan Ave., Chicago 60603
(312) 443-3600
http://www.artic.edu

Krannert Art Museum, University of Illinois
500 E. Peabody Dr., Champaign 61820
(217) 333-1860
http://www.art.uiuc.edu/kam

Museum of Contemporary Art
220 E. Chicago Ave., Chicago 60611
(312) 280-2660
http://www.mcachicago.org

Oriental Institute Museum, The University of Chicago
1155 E. 58th St., Chicago 60637
(773) 702-9521
http://www.oi.uchicago.edu

Terra Museum of American Art
666 N. Michigan Ave., Chicago 60611
(312) 664-3939
http://www.terra-museum.org

INDIANA

Indiana University Art Museum, Indiana University
Bloomington 47405
(812) 855-5445
http://www.indiana.edu/~iuam

Indianapolis Museum of Art
1200 W. 38th St., Indianapolis 46208
(317) 923-1331
http://www.ima-art.org

The Snite Museum of Art, University of Notre Dame
Notre Dame 46556
(219) 631-5466
http://www.nd.edu/~sniteart

IOWA

Cedar Rapids Museum of Art
410 Third Ave. SE, Cedar Rapids 52401
(319) 366-7503
http://www.crma.org

University of Iowa Museum of Art
150 N. Riverside Dr., Iowa City 52242
(319) 335-1727
http://www.uiowa.edu/~artmus

KANSAS

Spencer Museum of Art, University of Kansas
1301 Mississippi St., Lawrence 66045
(785) 864-4710
http://www.ukans.edu/~sma

Wichita Art Museum
619 Stackman Dr., Wichita 67203
(316) 268-4921
http://www.feist.com/~wam

KENTUCKY

J. B. Speed Art Museum
2035 S. 3rd St., Louisville 40208
(502) 634-2700
http://www.speedmuseum.org

University of Kentucky Art Museum
Singletary Center for the Arts,
Rose St. and Euclid Ave.,
Lexington 40506
(606) 257-5716
http://www.uky.edu/ArtMuseum

LOUISIANA

The Alexandria Museum of Art
933 Main Street, Alexandria 71309
(318) 443-3458
http://www.themuseum.org

The Contemporary Art Center
900 Camp St., New Orleans 70130
(504) 528-3800
http://www.cacno.org

New Orleans Museum of Art
1 Collins Diboll Circle, City Park,
New Orleans 70124
(504) 488-2631
http://www.noma.org

MAINE

Bowdoin College Museum of Art
Walker Art Building, Brunswick 04011
(207) 725-3275
http://www.bowdoin.edu/artmuseum

Portland Museum of Art
7 Congress Sq., Portland 04101
(207) 775-6148; (800) 639-4067
http://www.portlandmuseum.org

MARYLAND

The Baltimore Museum of Art
Art Museum Dr. at North Charles and 31st Sts., Baltimore 21218
(410) 396-7100
http://www.artbma.org

Walters Art Gallery
600 N. Charles St., Baltimore 21201
(410) 547-9000; 547-ARTS
http://www.thewalters.org

MASSACHUSETTS

Addison Gallery of American Art, Phillips Academy
Andover 01810
(508) 749-4015
http://www.andover.edu/addison/home.html

Davis Museum and Cultural Center, Wellesley College
106 Central St., Wellesley 02181
(617) 283-2051
http://www.wellesley.edu/DavisMuseum/davismenu.html

Harvard University Art Museums
The Arthur M. Sackler Museum
485 Broadway
Cambridge 02138
(617) 495-9400
Busch-Reisinger Museum
32 Quincy St.
Fogg Art Museum
32 Quincy St.
http://www.artmuseums.harvard.edu/

Isabella Stewart Gardner Museum
280 The Fenway, Boston 02115
(617) 566-1401
http://www.boston.com/gardner

Mead Art Museum, Amherst College
Amherst 01002
(413) 542-2335
http://www.amherst.edu/~mead

Mount Holyoke College Art Museum
South Hadley 01075
(413) 538-2245
http://www.mtholyoke.edu/offices/artmuseum

Museum of Fine Arts, Boston
465 Huntington Ave., Boston 02115
(617) 267-9300
http://www.mfa.org

Peabody Essex Museum
East India Square, Salem 01970
(508) 745-1876
http://www.pem.org

Rose Art Museum, Brandeis University
415 South St., Waltham 02254
(617) 736-3434
http://www.brandeis.edu/rose

Smith College Museum of Art
Elm St. at Bedford Terrace,
Northampton 01063
(413) 585-2760
http://www.smith.edu/artmuseum

Sterling and Francine Clark Art Institute
225 South St., Williamstown 01267
(413) 458-9545
http://www.clark.williams.edu

Williams College Museum of Art
Main St., Williamstown 01267
(413) 597-2429
http://www.williams.edu/WCMA

Worcester Art Museum
55 Salisbury St., Worcester 01609
(508) 799-4406
http://www.worcesterart.org

MICHIGAN

The Detroit Institute of Arts
5200 Woodward Ave., Detroit 48202
(313) 833-7900
http://www.dia.org

Grand Rapids Art Museum
155 Division North,
Grand Rapids 49503
(616) 459-4677
http://www.gram.mus.mi.us

The University of Michigan Museum of Art
525 S. State St., Ann Arbor 48109
(313) 764-0395
http://www.umich.edu/~umma

MINNESOTA

The Minneapolis Institute of Arts
2400 3rd Ave. S., Minneapolis 55404
(612) 870-3131; 870-3200
http://www.artsMIA.org

Walker Art Center
Vineland Pl., Minneapolis 55403
(612) 375-7622
http://www.walkerart.org

MISSOURI

The Nelson-Atkins Museum of Art
4525 Oak St., Kansas City 64111
(816) 561-4000
http://www.nelson-atkins.org

The Saint Louis Art Museum
1 Fine Arts Dr., Forest Park,
St. Louis 63110
(314) 721-0072
http://www.slam.org

NEBRASKA

Joslyn Art Museum
2200 Dodge St., Omaha 68102
(402) 342-3300
http://www.joslyn.org

Sheldon Memorial Art Gallery and Sculpture Garden, University of Nebraska–Lincoln
12th and R Sts., Lincoln 68588
(402) 472-2461
http://sheldon.unl.edu

NEW HAMPSHIRE

Hood Museum of Art, Dartmouth College
Wheelock St., Hanover 03755
(603) 646-2808
http://www.dartmouth.edu/~hood

NEW JERSEY

The Art Museum, Princeton University
Princeton 08544
(609) 258-3788
http://webware.princeton.edu/artmus

Jane Voorhees Zimmerli Art Museum, Rutgers–The State University of New Jersey
Hamilton and George Sts.,
New Brunswick 08903
(732) 932-7237
http://www.rci.rutgers.edu/~zamuseum

The Montclair Art Museum
3 S. Mountain Ave. at Bloomfield Ave.,
Montclair 07042
(201) 746-5555
http://www.montclair-art.com

The Newark Museum
49 Washington St., Newark 07101
(973) 596-6500; (800) 7MUSEUM
http://www.newarkmuseum.org

NEW MEXICO

Georgia O'Keeffe Museum
217 Johnson St., Santa Fe 87501
(505) 995-0785
http://www.okeeffemuseum.org

Millicent Rogers Museum
1504 Millicent Rogers Rd., Taos 87571
(505) 758-2462
http://www.millicentrogers.com

NEW YORK

Albright-Knox Art Gallery
1285 Elmwood Ave., Buffalo 14222
(716) 882-8700
http://www.albrightknox.org

American Craft Museum
40 W. 53rd St., New York 10019
(212) 956-3535
http://www.fieldtrip.com/ny/29563535.htm

The Brooklyn Museum
200 Eastern Pkwy., Brooklyn 11238
(718) 638-5000
http://www.brooklynart.org

Cooper-Hewitt National Design Museum, Smithsonian Institution
2 E. 91st St., New York 10128
(212) 860-6868
http://www.si.edu/ndm

Everson Museum of Art
401 Harrison St., Syracuse 13202
(315) 474-6064
http://www.everson.org

The Frick Collection
1 E. 70th St., New York 10021
(212) 288-0700
http://www.frick.org

George Eastman House, International Museum of Photography and Film
900 East Ave., Rochester 14607
(716) 271-3361
http://www.eastman.org

The Grey Art Gallery, New York University
100 Washington Sq. East,
New York 10003
(212) 998-6780
http://www.nyu.edu/greyart

Herbert F. Johnson Museum of Art, Cornell University
Ithaca 14853
(607) 255-6464
http://www.museum.cornell.edu

International Center of Photography
Midtown
1133 Avenue of the Americas,
New York 10036
(212) 860-1783
Uptown
1130 5th Ave., New York 10028
(212) 860-1777
http://www.icp.org

The Jewish Museum
1109 5th Ave., New York 10128
(212) 423-3200
http://www.jewishmuseum.org

Memorial Art Gallery, University of Rochester
500 University Ave., Rochester 14607
(716) 473-7720
http://www.rochester.edu/MAG

The Metropolitan Museum of Art
1000 5th Ave. at 82nd St.,
New York 10028
(212) 879-5500
The Cloisters
Fort Tryon Park, New York 10040
(212) 923-3700
http://www.metmuseum.org

Munson-Williams-Proctor Institute Museum of Art
310 Genesee St., Utica 13502
(315) 797-0000
http://www.mwpi.edu

The Museum of Modern Art
11 W. 53rd St., New York 10019
(212) 708-9400
http://www.moma.org

Neuberger Museum of Art, State University of New York at Purchase
735 Anderson Hill Rd., Purchase 10577
(914) 251-6133
http://www.neuberger.org

The New Museum of Contemporary Art
583 Broadway, New York 10012
(212) 219-1222
http://www.newmuseum.org

The Pierpont Morgan Library
29 E. 36th St., New York 10016
(212) 685-0008
http://www.morganlibrary.org

Solomon R. Guggenheim Museum
1071 5th Ave., New York 10128
(212) 423-3500
http://www.guggenheim.org

Storm King Art Center
Old Pleasant Hill Rd., Mountainville 10953
(914) 534-3115
http://www.stormkingartcenter.org

The Studio Museum in Harlem
144 W. 125th St., New York 10027
(212) 864-4500
http://www.studiomuseuminharlem.org

Whitney Museum of American Art
945 Madison Ave., New York 10021
(212) 570-3676
http://www.whitney.org

NORTH CAROLINA

The Ackland Art Museum, University of North Carolina, Chapel Hill
Columbia and Franklin Sts.,
Chapel Hill 27599
(919) 966-5736
http://www.unc.edu/depts/ackland

Duke University Museum of Art
Buchanan Blvd. at Trinity,
East Campus, Durham 27708
(919) 684-5135
http://www.duke.edu/duma

North Carolina Museum of Art
2110 Blue Ridge Rd., Raleigh 27607
(919) 833-1935
http://www.ncmoa.org

OHIO

Allen Memorial Art Museum, Oberlin College
87 N. Main St., Oberlin 44074
(440) 775-8665
http://www.oberlin.edu/wwwmap/allen_art.html

The Butler Institute of American Art
524 Wick Ave., Youngstown 44502
(216) 743-1711
http://www.butlerart.com

Cincinnati Art Museum
Eden Park, Cincinnati 45202
(513) 721-5204
http://www.cincinnatiartmuseum.com

The Cleveland Museum of Art
11150 E. Blvd., Cleveland 44106
(216) 421-7340
http://www.clemusart.com

The Columbus Museum of Art
480 E. Broad St., Columbus 43215
(614) 221-6801
http://www.columbusart.mus.oh.us

Dayton Art Institute
456 Belmonte Park N.,
Dayton 45405
(513) 223-5277
http://www.daytonartinstitute.org

The Taft Museum
316 Pike St., Cincinnati 45202
(513) 241-0343
http://www.taftmuseum.org

The Toledo Museum of Art
2445 Monroe St., Toledo 43620
(419) 255-8000; (800) 644-6862
http://www.toledomuseum.org

Wexner Center for the Arts, The Ohio State University
North High St. at 15th Ave.,
Columbus 43210
(614) 292-3535
http://www.wexarts.org

OKLAHOMA

Gilcrease Museum
1400 Gilcrease Museum Rd.,
Tulsa 74127
(918) 596-2700
http://www.gilcreasemuseum.org

The Philbrook Museum of Art
2727 S. Rockford Rd., Tulsa 74114
(918) 749-7941
http://www.philbrook.org

OREGON

Portland Art Museum
1219 SW Park Ave., Portland 97205
(503) 226-2811
http://www.pam.org

The University of Oregon Museum of Art
1223 University of Oregon,
Eugene 97403
(541) 346-3027
http://uoma.uoregon.edu

PENNSYLVANIA

The Andy Warhol Museum
117 Sandusky St., Pittsburgh 15212
(412) 237-8300
http://www.clpgh.org/warhol

Barnes Foundation
300 North Natch's Ln.,
Merion Station 19066
(610) 667-0290
http://www.barnesfoundation.org

The Carnegie Museum of Art
4400 Forbes Ave., Pittsburgh 15213
(412) 622-3131
http://www.clpgh.org/moa

Institute of Contemporary Art, University of Pennsylvania
118 S. 36th St., Philadelphia 19104
(215) 898-7108
http://www.upenn.edu/ica

Museum of American Art, Pennsylvania Academy of the Fine Arts
118 N. Broad St., Philadelphia 19102
(215) 972-7600
http://www.pafa.org

Philadelphia Museum of Art
26th St. and Benjamin Franklin Pkwy.,
Philadelphia 19130
(215) 763-8100
http://www.philamuseum.org

University of Pennsylvania Museum of Archaeology and Anthropology
33rd and Spruce Sts.,
Philadelphia 19104
(215) 895-4000
http://www.upenn.edu/museum

RHODE ISLAND

Museum of Art, Rhode Island School of Design
224 Benefit St., Providence 02903
(401) 454-6500
http://www.risd.edu

SOUTH CAROLINA

The Columbia Museum of Art
Main and Hampton Sts.,
Columbia 29202
(803) 799-2810
http://www.colmusart.org

Greenville County Museum of Art
420 College St., Greenville 29601
(864) 271-7570
http://www.greenvillemuseum.org

TENNESSEE

Knoxville Museum of Art
410 10th Ave., World's Fair Park,
Knoxville 37916
(615) 525-6101
http://www.knoxart.org

Memphis Brooks Museum of Art
Overton Park, 1934 Poplar Ave.,
Memphis 38104
(901) 722-3500
http://www.brooksmuseum.org

TEXAS

Amon Carter Museum
3501 Camp Bowie Blvd.,
Fort Worth 76107
(817) 738-1933
http://www.cartermuseum.org

Contemporary Arts Museum
5216 Montrose Blvd.,
Houston 77006
(713) 526-0773
http://www.camh.org

Dallas Museum of Art
1717 N. Harwood,
Dallas 75201
(214) 922-1200
http://www.dm-art.org

Kimbell Art Museum
3333 Camp Bowie Blvd.,
Fort Worth 76107
(817) 332-8451
http://www.kimbellart.org

Marion Koogler McNay Art Museum
6000 N. New Braunfels Ave.,
San Antonio 78209
(210) 824-5368
http://www.mcnayart.org

The Menil Collection
1515 Sul Ross, Houston 77006
http://www.menil.org
Rothko Chapel
3900 Yupon at Sul Ross,
Houston 77006
(713) 524-9839
http://www.menil.org/rothko.html

Modern Art Museum of Fort Worth
1309 Montgomery St. at Camp Bowie
Blvd., Fort Worth 76107
(817) 738-9215
http://www.mamfw.org

The Museum of Fine Arts, Houston
1001 Bissonnet St., Houston 77005
(713) 639-7300
http://www.mfah.org

San Antonio Museum of Art
200 W. Jones St.,
San Antonio 78215
(210) 978-8100
http://www.samuseum.org

VIRGINIA

The Chrysler Museum
245 W. Olney Rd., Norfolk 23510
(804) 664-6200
http://www.chrysler.org

Hampton University Museum
Hampton 23668
(804) 727-5308
http://www.hamptonu.edu/other/museum/HUMUS.htm

Monticello
Charlottesville 22902
(804) 984-9822
http://www.monticello.org

Virginia Museum of Fine Arts
2800 Grove Ave.,
Richmond 23221
(804) 367-0844
http://www.vmfa.state.va.us

WASHINGTON

Seattle Art Museum
100 University St., Seattle 98101
(206) 625-8900; 654-3100
http://www.seattleartmuseum.org

Tacoma Art Museum
12th and Pacific Ave.,
Tacoma 98402
(206) 272-4258
http://www.tacomaartmuseum.org

WISCONSIN

Milwaukee Art Museum
750 N. Lincoln Memorial Dr.,
Milwaukee 53202
(414) 224-3200
http://www.mam.org

OUTSIDE THE UNITED STATES

AUSTRIA

For more information, visit
http://info.wien.at

Graphische Sammlung Albertina
1, Makartgasse 3, 1010 Vienna
581 306021
http://www.albertina.at

Kunsthistoriches Museum
1., Maria-Theresien-Platz,
1010 Vienna
431 525240
http://www.khm.at

Museum Moderner Kunst Stifflung Ludwig
Arsenalstr. 1, Vienna
431 7996900
http://www.mmkslw.or.at

Österreichische Galerie Belvedere
3, Prinz. Eugen. Str. 27, 1037 Vienna
79557134
http://www.belvedere.at

BELGIUM

For more information, visit
http://www.gotim.be/artexpo

Groeningemuseum, Stedelijke Musea
Dijver 12, 8000 Brugge
(05) 044.87.11

Musées Royaux des Beaux-Arts de Belgique
Musée Royaux d'Art et d'Histoire
10 Parc du Cinquantenaire, 1040 Brussels
(02) 741.72.11
Musées d'Art Moderne
1–2, Place Royale, 1000 Brussels
(02) 508.32.11
Musée d'Art Ancien
3 rue de la Régence, 1000 Brussels
(02) 508.33.33

CANADA

Art Gallery of Ontario
317 Dundas St. W.,
Toronto, Ontario M5S 2C6
(416) 977-6648
http://www.ago.on.ca

Glenbow
130 9th Ave., SE, Calgary,
Alberta T2G 0P3
(403) 268-4100
http://www.glenbow.org

Montreal Museum of Fine Arts
1379–80 Sherbrook St. W.,
Montréal, Quebec H36 2T9
(514) 285-1600; 285-2000
http://www.mmfa.qc.ca

National Gallery of Canada
380 Sussex Dr., Ottawa,
Ontario K1N 9N4
(613) 990-1985
http://national.gallery.ca

Royal Ontario Museum
100 Queen's Park,
Toronto, Ontario M5S 2C6
(416) 586-5549
http://www.rom.on.ca

Vancouver Art Gallery
750 Hornby St.,
Vancouver, British Columbia V6Z 2H7
(604) 662-4719
http://www.vanartgallery.bc.ca

DENMARK

Louisiana Museum of Modern Art
Gl. Strandvej 13, 3050 Humlebaek
(45) 49190719
http://www.louisiana.dk

Ny Carlsberg Glyptotek
Dantes Plads 7, 1556 Copenhagen
(45) 33418141
http://www.glyptoteket.dk

EGYPT

Egyptian Museum
Maydan El Tahrir, Cairo
(02) 57 42 681
http://www.tourism.egnet.net/culture.htm

FRANCE

For more information, visit
http://www.tourisme.fr

Bibliothèque Nationale de France
25 rue de Richelieu, Paris 75002
01.47.03.81.26
http://www.bnf.fr

Centre National d'Art et de Culture Georges Pompidou
Rue du Renard, Paris 75191
01.44.78.12.33
http://www.centrepompidou.fr

Château de Versailles
Versailles
01.30.84.74.00
http://www.chateauversailles.fr

Grand Palais
Ave. Winston Churchill, Paris
01.44.13.17.17

Musée de l'Orangerie
Jardin des Tuileries,
Palace de la Concorde, Paris
01.42.97.48.16

Musée des Antiquités Nationales
Château de Saint-Germain-en-Laye,
Saint-Germain-en-Laye 78103
01.34.51.53.65
http://www.culture.fr/culture/man/man1.htm

Musée des Beaux-Arts, Lyon
Palais St. Pierre,
20 place des Terreaux, Lyon 69001
04.72.10.17.40

Musée d'Orsay
1 rue de Bellechasse, Paris 75007
01.40.49.48.14
http://www.musee-orsay.fr

Musée du Louvre
Rue de Rivoli, Paris 75058
01.40.20.51.51
http://www.Louvre.fr

Musée d'Unterlinden
1 rue des Unterlinden,
Colmar 68000
03.89.20.15.50
http://www.musee-unterlinden.com

Musée Picasso
Hôtel Salé, 5 rue de Torigny, Paris 75003
01.42.71.25.21

Musée Rodin
77 rue de Varenne, Paris 75007
01.44.18.61.10
http://www.musee-rodin.fr

GERMANY

Alte Pinakothek
Barer Str. 27, 80333 Munich
(089) 23805216
http://www.stmukwk.bayern.de/kunst/museen/pinalt.html

Brücke-Museum Berlin
Bussardsteig 9, Berlin 14195
(030) 8312029
http://www.dhm.de/museen/bruecke/index.html#Links

Hamburger Kunsthalle
Glockengiesserwall,
20095 Hamburg
(040) 24862612
http://www.hamburger-kunsthalle.de

Museum Ludwig
Bischofsgartenstr. 1,
50667 Cologne
(0221) 2212379
http://www.museenkoeln.de/ludwig

Staatliche Antikensammlungen und Glyptothek, Munich
Konigspl 1–3, 80333 Munich
(089) 598359; 286100

Staatliche Graphische Sammlung, Munich
Meiserstr. 10, 80333 Munich
(089) 28927650

Staatliche Kunsthalle, Karlsruhe
Hans-Thoma-Str. 2–6,
76133 Karlsruhe
(0721) 9263355
http://www.kunsthalle-karlsruhe.de

Staatliche Museen zu Berlin
(17 museums in different locations)
http://www.smb.spk-berlin.de

Staatsgalerie Stuttgart
Konrad-Adenauer Str. 30–32,
70173 Stuttgart
(0711) 212 4050
http://www.staatsgalerie.de

Städelsches Kunstinstitut und Städtische Galerie, Frankfurt-am-Main
Schaumainkai 63,
60596 Frankfurt-am-Main
(069) 6050980

GREAT BRITAIN

For more information, visit
http://www.artguide.org

Apsley House, The Wellington Museum
149 Piccadilly, Hyde Park Corner,
London N1V 9FA
(0171) 4995676
http://www.vam.ac.uk/collections/apsley/index.html

Ashmolean Museum of Art and Archaeology
Beaumont St., Oxford 0X1 2PH
(01865) 278000
http://www.ashmol.ox.ac.uk

Birmingham City Museum and Art Gallery
Chamberlain Sq.,
Birmingham B3 3DH
(0121) 3032834
http://www.birmingham.gov.uk/bmag

Blenheim Palace
Woodstock, Oxfordshire 0X20 1PX
(01993) 811091
http://www.blenheimpalace.com

British Library
Great Russell St.,
London WC1B 3DG
(0171) 3237595
http://portico.bl.uk

British Museum
Great Russell St.,
London WC1B 3DG
(0171) 6361555
http://www.british-museum.ac.uk

Courtauld Institute Galleries
Somerset House, Strand, London
WC2R 0RN
(0171) 8732526
http://www.courtauld.ac.uk

The National Gallery
Trafalgar Square,
London WC2N 5DN
(0171) 8393321
http://www.nationalgallery.org.uk

National Gallery of Scotland
The Mound, Edinburgh EH2 2EL
(0131) 5568921
http://www.natgalscot.ac.uk

Royal Academy of Arts
Burlington House, Piccadilly,
London W1V 0DS
(0171) 4397438
http://www.royalacademy.org.uk

Sir John Soane's Museum
13 Lincoln's Inn Fields,
London WC2A 3BP
(0171) 4052107
http://www.soane.org

Tate Gallery
Millbank, London SW1P 4RG
(0171) 8878000
http://www.tate.org.uk

Victoria and Albert Museum
Cromwell Rd., South Kensington,
London SW7 2R
(0171) 9388365
http://www.vam.ac.uk

GREECE

For more information, visit
http://www.culture.gr

Acropolis Museum
Athens
01 3214172
http://www.culture.gr/2/21/211/21101m/e211am01.html

Corfu Archaeological Museum
Corfu 49100
0661 30680

Delphi Archaeological Museum
Delphi 33054
0265 82312

Eleusis Archaeological Museum
Eleusis
01 3463552

Heraklion Archaeological Museum
Xanthoudidou St. 1, Crete
081 226092

National Archaeological Museum of Athens
Patission 44 St., Athens 10682
01 8217717
http://www.culture.gr/2/21/214/21405m/e21405m1.html

IRELAND

For more information, visit
http://www.artguide.org

National Gallery of Ireland
Merrion Square W., Dublin 2
(01) 6615133
http://www.nationalgallery.ie

ITALY

Galleria Borghese
Piazzale Scipione Borghese 5, Rome 00197
(06) 858577
http://www.galleriaborghese.it

Galleria degli Uffizi
Piazza degli Uffizi 6, Florence 50122
(055) 2388651
http://www.uffizi.firenze.it

Galleria dell'Academia, Florence
Via Ricasoli 58–60, Florence 50122
(055) 238809
http://www.sbas.firenze.it/accademia

Galleria dell'Academia, Venice
Campo della Carità, Venice 30121
(041) 22247

Galleria Nazionale d'Arte Antica
Via delle Quattro Fontane 13,
Rome 00184
(06) 4824184

Musei Capitolini
Piazza del Campidoglio, Rome 00186
(06) 67102475

Museo Archeologico Nazionale
Piazza Museo 19, Naples 80135
(081) 440166
http://www.marketplace.it/museo.nazionale

Museo Archeologico Nazionale du Firenze
Via della Colonna 38,
Florence 50121
(055) 23575

Museo Civico Archeologico
Via de' Musei, Bologna 840124
(051) 233849
http://www.comune.bologna.it/bologna.Musei/Archeologicl

Museo Civico Cristiana
Via Musei, 81, Brescia 25100
(030) 44327

Museo e Gallerie Nazionale di Capodimonte
Palazzo di Capodimonte,
Naples 80136
(081) 7410801
http://www.cib.na.cnr.it/remuna/capod/indice.html

Museo Nazionale del Bargello
Via del Proconsolo 4, Florence 5012
(055) 210801
http://www.sbas.firenze.it/musei/barg01.htm

Museo Nazionale di Villa Giulia
Piazza di Villa Giulia 9, Rome 00195
(06) 350719

Peggy Guggenheim Collection
Palazzo Venier dei Leoni,
701 Dorsoduro, 30123 Venice
(041) 2450 411
http://www.guggenheim.org/venice/index.html

Vatican Museums
Viale Vaticano 00165,
Città del Vaticano 00120
(06) 69884947
http://www.christusrex.org

THE NETHERLANDS

For more information, visit
http://www.hollandmuseums.nl

Centraal Museum Utrecht
Agnietenst. 1, 3500 Utrecht
(030) 2362362
http://www.centraalmuseum.nl

Frans Halsmuseum
Groot Heiligland 62,
2011 ES Haarlem
(020) 5115775
http://www.franshalsmuseum.nl

Kröller-Müller Museum
Houtkampweg 6,
6731 AW Otterlo
(0318) 591041
http://www.kmm.nl

Museum Boijmans Van Beuningen
Museumpark 18–20,
3015 CX Rotterdam
(010) 4419400
http://www.boijmans.rotterdam.nl

Rijksmuseum
Stadhouderskade 42,
1071 Amsterdam
(020) 6732121
http://www.rijksmuseum.nl

Rijksmuseum Vincent van Gogh
Paulus Potterstraat 7,
1071 CX Amsterdam
(020) 5705200
http://www.vangoghmuseum.nl

Stedelijk Museum of Modern Art
Paulus Potterstraat 13,
1070 AB Amsterdam
(020) 5732911
http://www.stedelijk.nl

NORWAY

Nasjonalgalleriet
Universitetsgaten 13, Oslo 0033
22 20 04 04
http://www.museumnett.no/nasjonalgalleriet

PORTUGAL

Museu Calouste Gulbenkian
Av. de Berna 45 A (1),
1093 Lisboa
(01) 76 50 61
http://www.ip.pt/gulbenkian

RUSSIA

Hermitage Museum
36 Dvortsovaya Naberezhnaya,
Saint Petersburg
(812) 110 96 25
http://www.hermitagemuseum.org

Pushkin Museum of Fine Arts
12 Volkhonka Str., Moscow
(095) 203 74 12
http://www.museum.ru/gmii

SPAIN

Guggenheim Museum Bilbao
Abandoibarra Et. 2, 48001 Bilbao
(94) 435 9080
http://www.guggenheim-bilbao.es

Museo Nacional del Prado
Paseo del Prado,
28014 Madrid
(91) 330 2800, 2900
http://museoprado.mcu.es

SWEDEN

Moderna Museet
Spårvagnshallarna, Box 16382,
Stockholm 10327
(08) 6664250
http://www.modernamuseet.se

Nationalmuseum
S. Blasieholmshamnen,
Stockholm 10324
(08) 5195 4300
http://www.nationalmuseum.se

SWITZERLAND

For more information, visit
http://www.swissart.ch

Kunstmuseum Bern
Hodlerstrasse 12, 3000 Bern 7
313110944
http://www.kunstmuseumbern.ch

Musée d'Art et d'Histoire
2 rue Charles Gallard, Geneva 1211
223114340
http://www.ville-ge.ch/musinfo/mahg/presse

Öffentliche Kunstsammlung Basel, Kunstmuseum
St. Alban-Graben 16,
Basel CH-4010
612066262
http://www.kunstmuseumbasel.ch

Index

Works ascribed to a specific artist or architect are indexed under the artist's or architect's name, shown in SMALL CAPITAL letters. Other works, including buildings and archeological remains, are indexed by site of origin or by culture. *See* references (e.g., *Bull's Head, see* Picasso; Colosseum, *see* Rome, Italy) are provided to assist in finding the correct name, site, or culture. The most significant subject references are given in **boldface** type. Illustration references are to figure numbers, not page numbers.

A

B

C

E

F

G

I

J

K

L

M

N

O

P

Q

R

S

U

V

Credits and Copyrights

The author and publisher wish to thank the libraries, museums, galleries, and private collections for permitting the reproduction of works of art in their collections and for supplying the necessary photographs. Photographs from other sources are gratefully acknowledged below. With the exception of page and Primary Source numbers (indicated as **p. xxx** and **PS-XX**), all numbers refer to figure numbers.

PHOTOGRAPH CREDITS AND COPYRIGHTS

Harry N. Abrams Archives, New York: 7-32, 22-1; Albertina, Vienna: 17-21; ACL, Brussels: 10-31, 15-3, 15-4, 15-6, 15-22; Adros Studio, Rome: 10-36; AKG, London: 9-11, 9-12, 10-14, 11-3, 21-67; Stefan Brechsel/AKG, London: 11-30; Alison Frantz Collection, American School of Classical Studies, Athens: 5-33, 8-40; Archivi Alinari, Florence: 6-5, 7-4, 7-10, 7-35, 7-36, 7-38, 7-40, 7-42, 8-52, 10-15, 10-29, 11-37, 11-59, 11-64, 12-2, 12-11, 12-12, 12-13, 12-21, 12-37, 12-40, 12-45, 12-49, 12-55, 12-60, 13-1, 13-26, 13-40, 14-23, 14-24, 14-31, 17-8, 17-17, 17-20, 17-23, 17-31; Ronald Sheridan's Ancient Art & Architecture Collection, Pinner, England: 4-13, 5-57; Arcaid/David Churchill, Kingston upon Thames, U.K.: 21-68, 21-69; Andrea/Archivo White Star: 2-26; The Art Archive, London: 19-20; Artothek/Joachim Blauel, Peissenberg, Germany: 13-42, 16-6, 16-10, 16-12, 16-18, 18-2, 18-15, 21-54; Cameraphoto-Arte, Venice/Art Resource, New York: 11-40, 13-38, 14-16, 14-25; Erich Lessing/Art Resource, New York: 8-50; Foto Marburg/Art Resource, New York: 5-37, 9-8, 10-8, 10-13, 10-27, 11-8, 11-9, 11-13, 11-22, 11-47, 11-48, 11-52, 17-22, 19-9, 22-34, 22-35, 22-36, 26-5, 26-6, 26-9; The Pierpont Morgan Library/Art Resource, New York: 9-19; Scala/Art Resource, New York: 7-44, 8-18, 10-25, 11-77, 11-78, 11-88, 11-98, 12-15, 12-33, 12-59, 13-11, 13-31, 13-32, 13-36; The Tate Gallery, London/Art Resource, New York: 22-19, 23-2; James Austin, U.K.: 21-16; Bank of England, London: 21-73; Erika Barahona Ede, Bilbao: 28-7; Foto Barsotti, Florence: 11-61, 11-62; Herbert Bayer Studio, Montecito, California: 27-19; Bayerische Staatsbibliothek, Munich: 9-27, 9-28, 10-42; Benedittine di Priscilla, Roma: 7-10; Jean Bernard, Aix-en-Provence: 11-11, 11-15; Constantin Beyer, Weimar, Germany: 11-53; Bildarchiv Preussischer Kulturbesitz, Berlin: 2-27, 2-28, 3-11, 3-22, 5-72, 5-74, 7-23, 9-29, 15-11, 15-16, 18-12, 21-51, 21-66; Black Star, New York: 27-26; Erwin Böhm, Mainz: 3-4; Lee Boltin Photo Library, Hastings-on-Hudson, New York: 2-29; Boyan & Shear, Glasgow: 23-33; W. Braunfels, *Mittelalterliche . . . Toskana:* 10-39; The Bridgeman Art Library, London: 19-14, PS-63; Brisighelli-Undine, Cividale, Italy: 9-7; The British Museum, London: 5-63, 5-26; British National Tourist Office, New York: 21-70; Jutta Brüdern, Braunschweig: 9-24, 9-25, 10-32; Martin Bühler, Basel: 23-25, 25-9; Photographie Bulloz, Paris: 10-24, 16-28, 21-63; Bundesdenkmalsamt, Vienna: 21-58; Studio C.N.B. & C., Bologna, Italy: 2-30; Caisse Nationale des Monuments Historiques et des Sites/© Arch. Phot. Paris: 1-16, 10-4, 10-21, 10-23, 11-16, 11-21, 11-41, 11-55, 13-14, 13-15, 16-26, 21-64; Alain Longchampt/Caisse Nationale des Monuments Historiques et des Sites: 10-5; René Jacques/Caisse Nationale des Monuments Historiques et des Sites: 11-56; F. Camard, *Ruhlmann, Master of Art Deco:* 26-43; Canali Photobank, Capriolo: p. 316, 5-27, 5-26, 5-42, 5-49, 6-1, 6-8, 6-9, 7-2, 7-16, 7-21, 7-26, 7-31, 7-30, 7-47, 7-48, 7-49, 7-50, 7-51, 7-52, 7-53, 8-7, 8-10, 8-15, 8-16, 8-17, 8-19, 8-25, 8-28, 8-29, 8-30, 8-37, 10-16, 10-18, 10-19, 10-37, 11-33, 11-57, 11-60, 11-63, 11-65, 11-73, 11-76, 11-79, 11-82, 11-83, 11-84, 11-85, 12-5, 12-9, 12-22, 12-29, 12-35, 12-38, 12-43, 12-52, 12-57, 12-58, 13-3, 13-7, 13-23, 13-27, 13-30, 13-33, 13-41, 14-1, 14-2, 14-8, 14-9, 14-10, 14-21, 14-22, 15-12, 16-15, 16-23, 17-1, 17-2, 17-3, 17-5, 17-7, 17-10, 17-11, 17-12, 17-16, 17-18, 17-29, 17-32, 17-34, 21-45, 21-59; Canali Photobank/Bertoni, Capriolo: 7-25, 11-97, 12-3, 12-8, 12-31, 12-50, 13-12; Canali Photobank/Codato: 8-44, 12-7, 12-53, 12-64; Canali Photobank/Rapuzzi, Capriolo: 5-6; Chicago Historical Society: 21-86; Cinématèque Française, Paris: 23-50a & b; Editions Citadelles & Mazenod, Paris: 2-18; Peter Clayton: 2-12, 2-15, 2-21; Colorphoto Hans Hinz, Alschwill-Basel: 1-3; K. J. Conant, *Carolingian and Romanesque Architecture, 800–1200:* 10-2, 10-10; Paula Cooper Gallery, New York: 24-83, 24-84; Costa and Lockhart, *Persia:* 3-31; The Conway Library/Courtauld Institute of Art, University of London: 9-14, 11-43, 21-11, 22-11; Dennis Cowley, New York: 28-15; Culver Pictures, New York: 21-85; Dagli-Orti, Paris: 2-35, 8-51; D. James Dee, New York: 28-11; Deutsches Archäologisches Institut, Baghdad: 3-1, 3-3; Deutsches Archäologisches Institut, Rome: 7-19, 7-29, 7-39, 7-46, 22-5; Jean Dieuzade [YAN], Toulouse: 10-1, 10-20; Domund Diözesanmuseum, Hildesheim: 9-26; M. Droste, *Bauhaus 1919–1933:* 26-25; E. Du Cerceau, *Les Plus Excellents Bâtissements . . . :* 16-25; Dumbarton Oaks Washington, D.C. © Byzantine Visual Resources: 8-46, 8-48; Editoriale Museum/Pedicini, Rome: 7-15; Nikos Kontos Courtesy of Ekdotike Athenon, Athens: 8-39; English Heritage Photo Library, London: 21-8, 21-19; ESTO/© Peter Aaron, Mamaroneck, New York: 28-1; ESTO/© Peter Mauss, Mamaroneck, New York: 28-6; ESTO/© Ezra Stoller, Mamaroneck, New York: 25-31, 26-33, 26-34, 26-35, 26-42; Fischbach Gallery, New York: 25-22; B. Fletcher, *A History of Architecture:* 5-29; Fotocielo, Rome: 17-15; Fototeca Unione, American Academy, Rome: 5-28, 7-6, 7-8, 7-34; Peter Fowles, Glasgow: 23-34; © Klaus Frahm, Hamburg: 28-5; G. De Francovich, Rome: 10-30; H. Frankfort, *The Art and Architecture of the Ancient Orient:* 3-2; John R. Freeman, Limited, London: 12-61; French National Tourist Board, Paris: 21-61; Gabinetto Fotografico Nazionale, Rome: 14-30, 17-6, 17-28, 19-17; Gabinetto Nazionale delle Stampe, Rome: 13-24, 13-25; Henry Gaud, Molsenay: 11-20; G.E.K.S., New York: 26-39, 26-40, 7-11, 7-37, 17-24, 26-20, 26-21, 26-29, 27-7; Philip Gendreau, New York: 22-37; G. Gherardi/A. Fioretti, Rome: 26-36, 26-37; Photographie Giraudon, Paris: 10-26, 11-23, 11-42, 11-94, 13-6, 16-27, 20-3, 21-12, 21-75, 21-78, 22-38, 23-9; P. Gössel and G. Leuthäuser, *Architecture in the Twentieth Century:* 26-44, 28-2; © Gianfranco Gorgoni, New York: 25-33; Edward V. Gorn, New York: 8-45; Foto Grassi, Siena: 11-74, 11-58, PS-6; The Green Studio, Limited, Dublin: 9-4; Dr. Reha Günay, Istanbul: 8-56, 8-57; President and Fellows of Harvard College, Harvard University/Michael Nedzweski: 21-30; Hedrich-Blessing/Bill Engdahl, Chicago: 26-1; Hirmer Fotoarchiv, Munich: 1-7, 2-3, 4-14, 5-12, 5-16, 5-20, 5-22, 5-23, 5-31, 5-35, 5-38, 5-43, 5-44, 5-46, 5-50, 5-51, 5-52, 5-79, 5-80, 5-81, 5-82, 5-83, 6-2, 6-4, 6-6, 7-33, 7-45, 8-11, 8-21, 8-36, 12-1, 12-4, 12-46, 13-13, 13-22, 15-23; H. R. Hitchcock, *Architecture: Nineteenth and Twentieth Centuries:* 21-76, 23-32; Foto Karl Hoffmann, Speyer: 10-14; © Angelo Hornak Library, London: 14-26; Christian Huelsen, *Il Libro di Giuliano da Sangallo:* 12-17; Timothy Hursley: 28-3; Araldo de Luca/ IKONA, Rome: 7-41; Raffaello Bencini/IKONA, Rome: 11-38; Instituto di Etruscologia e Antichità Italiche, University of Rome: 1-5; *Jahrbuch des Deutschen Werkbundes* (1915): 23-35, 23-60, 26-7, 26-8; Anthony F. Janson: 21-18, 24-71; H. W. Janson: 11-32, 12-23, 23-27, 24-73; Bruno Jarret/ARS, New York/ADAGP, Paris: 22-30, 22-32; S. W. Kenyon, Wellington, U.K.: 1-9, 1-10; A. F. Kersting, London: 10-9, 11-28, 19-10; Jörg Klam, Berlin: 24-6; © Studio Kontos, Athens: 4-5, 4-6, 4-11, 4-12, 4-17, 4-18, 4-19, 4-21, 5-3, 5-11, 5-14, 5-15, 5-30, 5-34, 5-41, 5-45, 5-47, 5-48, 5-59, 5-68, 5-77, PS-3; S. N. Kramer, *History Begins at Sumer:* 3-12; Studio Koppermann, Gauting, Germany: 5-5, 5-61, 5-73; R. Krautheimer: *Early Christian and Byzantine Architecture:* 8-4; Ian Lambot, Haslemere, Surrey: 26-46, 26-47; Kurt Lange, Oberstdorf, Allgäu, Germany: 2-1, 2-2; Ivan Lapper P., English Heritage Photo Library, London: 1-19; Lautman Photography, Washington, D.C.: 21-20; A.W. Lawrence, *Greek Architecture:* 5-32; William Lescaze, New York: 26-24; Library of Congress, Washington, D.C.: 21-44; Ralph Liberman: 11-39; Lichtbildwerkstätte Alpenland, Vienna: 8-20, 8-24, 10-6, 12-62, 14-3, 14-18, 14-19, 16-13, 16-21, 16-22; Maya Lin, New York: 25-32 ; Jannes Linders, Rotterdam: 26-11, 26-13; The Louvre, Paris: 16-30; Magnum, New York: 27-17; Barbara Malterm, Rome: 5-71; Marlborough Gallery, New York: 25-37; Alexander Marshak, New York: 1-6; Arxiu MAS, Barcelona: 14-13, 15-14, 17-35, 18-3, 21-23, 21-25, 21-36; Foto Mayer, Vienna: 15-20; © Rollie McKenna, Stonington, Connecticut: 12-19; Arlette and James Mellaart, London: 1-11, 1-12, 1-13; H. Millon, *Key Monuments in the History of Art:* 11-31, 13-28, 17-25; Ministry of Culture/Archaeological Receipts Fund (Service T.A.P.), Athens: 5-58; Ministry of Public Buildings and Works, London: 1-17, 1-18, 21-14; Monumenti, Musei, e Gallerie Pontificie, Vatican City, Rome: 5-67, 6-11, 7-28; © Museum of Modern Art, New York: 26-14, 26-15; Ann Münchow, Domkapitel Aachen: 9-9; National Buildings Record, London: 11-26, 11-27, 19-21, 19-23, 21-74; Otto Nelson, New York: 24-70; Richard Nickel, Chicago: 23-38, 23-39, 23-40, 23-41; Nippon Television Network Corporation, Tokyo: 13-17, 13-18, 13-19, 13-20, 13-21; © Takashi Okamura, Shizuoka City, Japan: 11-67, 11-98, 12-10, 12-18, 12-30, 12-47, 12-48, 13-34; Bill Orcutt Studios, New York: 28-17; The Oriental Institute of the University of Chicago: 3-6, 3-21, 3-26, 3-28; Oroñoz, Madrid: 13-37, 16-19, 20-25, 23-31; Pace Wildenstein Gallery/Bill Jacobsen, New York: 25-24; Gustav Peichl, Vienna: 26-43; N. Pevsner, *Outline of European Architecture:* 12-20; Erich Pollitzer, New York: 23-12; Winslow Pope/Michigan Consolidated Gas Company, Detroit, Michigan: 26-27; Port Authority, New York: 21-65; Josephine Powell, Rome: 8-49; © Museo del Prado: 15-10; Provinciebestuur van Antwerpen: 18-16; Pubbli Aer Foto, Milan: 7-3, 8-43; Antonio Quattrone (Courtesy of Olivetti), Florence: 12-24, 12-25, 12-26, 12-27; Mario Quattrone Fotostudio, Florence: 11-72, 11-80, 12-54, 14-4, 14-7, PS-3; Studio Rémy, Dijon, France: 11-91; © Réunion des Musées Nationaux, Paris: 1-8, 2-16, 3-13, 3-14, 3-16, 3-23, 3-27, 5-4, 5-7, 5-8, 5-9, 5-13, 5-75, 8-38, 8-53, 11-81, 11-92, 12-56, 13-2, 13-4, 13-29, 13-39, 15-19, 16-14, 16-16, 17-9, 18-6, 18-23, 19-2, 19-3, 19-19, 20-4, 20-5, 20-7, 20-8, 21-1, 21-26, 21-28, 21-31, 21-32, 21-39, 21-42, 21-62, 22-2, 22-3, 22-6, 22-12, 22-13, 22-21, 22-22, 23-16, 23-17, 24-31, PS-2; © Réunion des Musées Nationaux, Paris/G. Blot/C. Lean: PS-60; © Réunion des Musées Nationaux, Paris/H. Lewndowski: 15-5, 21-33; Rheinisches Bildarchiv, Cologne: 9-20, 9-21, 24-78, 25-35; Ekkehard Ritter, Vienna: 10-40, 10-41; Photographie Roger-Viollet, Paris: 16-24, 21-77, 23-30, 26-23; Richard Ross: 28-12, 28-13; Jean Roubier, Paris: 7-9, 10-3, 11-5, 11-44, 11-45, 11-46, 11-49; Routhier/Studio Lourmel, Paris: 22-14; The Royal Collection Enterprises, Windsor Castle: 13-5, 14-15, 20-26; Sächsische Landesbibliothek, Deutsche Fotothek, Dresden: 11-51; Goro Sakamoto, Kyoto, Japan: 3-15; Armando Salas, Portugal: 25-21; Scala, Florence: 11-86, 11-97, 14-17, 17-8, 21-24, 21-27, PS-55; Toni Schneiders, Lindau, Germany: 20-21, 20-23; Silvestris Photo-Service, Kastl, Germany: 20-19; Aaron Siskind: 27-24; Haldor Sochner, Munich: 14-12; Société Archeologique et Historique, Avesnes-sur-Helpe: 10-38; Société Française de Photographie, Paris: 21-80; Holly Solomon Gallery, New York: 25-41; Soprintendenza Archaeologica, Ministero per i Beni Culturali Ambientali, Rome: 6-10; Soprintendenza Archaeologica all'Etruria Meridionale, Tarquinia: 6-3; Soprintendenza dei Monumenti, Pisa: 11-87; Spectrum Color Library, London: 16-32, 26-48, 26-49; Sperone Westwater Gallery, New York: 24-82; Stiftsbibliothek, St. Gallen, Switzerland: 9-13; Franz Stoedtner, Düsseldorf: 23-29; A. Stratton: *Life . . . :* 19-22; Adolph Studley, Pennsburg, Pennsylvania: 23-28; Wim Swaan: 2-6, 2-8, 2-9, 2-13, 2-22, 2-25, 2-32, 2-33, 3-17, 3-30, 10-7, 10-17, 11-1, 11-6, 11-7, 11-17, 11-24, 17-13, 17-26, 19-11, 19-12, 19-13, 20-17; © Jean Clothes, SYGMA, New York: 1-1; Kenneth Frampton, *Modern Architecture,* Thames & Hudson, 3rd rev. ed.: 26-30; J. W. Thomas, Oxford: 11-50; Richard Todd, Los Angeles: 28-8; Marvin Trachtenberg, New York: 5-39, 8-35, 8-42, 11-35, 12-41, 14-27, 19-15, 20-20, 26-18, 26-31, 26-32; University Library, Uppsala, Sweden: 16-20; © University Museum of National Antiquities, Oslo: 9-2; Vatican Library, Rome: 8-5, 8-6; Jean Vertut, Issy-les-Moulineaux: 1-2; Robert Villani: 26-2, 26-12; John B. Vincent, Berkeley, California: 14-29; Wolfgang Volz © Christo: 25-34; Leonard von Matt, Buochs, Switzerland: 9-16, 10-28; © Elke Walford, Hamburg: 11-96, 21-52, 21-53; Denise Walker, Baltimore: 21-71, 21-72; Clarence Ward: 11-4; © Lewis Watts, Anselmo, California: 28-14; Etienne Weil, Jerusalem: 25-2, 26-45; Werner Forman Archive, London: 5-57; Whitaker Studios, Richmond,Virginia: 21-13; Joachim Wilke, Stuttgart: 21-15; David Wilkins, Pittsburgh: 12-6; Ole Woldbye, Copenhagen: 21-60; © CORBIS/Roger Wood, Bellevue, Washington: 4-4; Woodfin Camp & Associates, New York: 11-10; (former) Yugoslav State Tourist Office, New York: 7-24; © Arq. Sergio Zepeda C., Guadalajara, Jalisco, Mexico: 24-53; O. Zimmerman, Colmar, France: 16-1, 16-2 , 16-3; © Gerald Zugmann, Vienna: 28-4; Foto Zwicker-Berberich, Gerchsheim/Würzburg, Germany: 20-10.

ARTIST COPYRIGHTS

© 1997 by the Trustees of the Ansel Adams Publishing Rights Trust. All Rights Reserved: 27-9; © 1997 Richard Anuszkiewicz/Licensed by VAGA, New York: 24-73; © 1997 Artists Rights Society (ARS), New York/ADAGP, Paris: 23-26, 24-3, 24-4, 24-10, 24-16, 24-22, 24-23, 24-24, 24-33, 24-34, 24-40, 24-41, 24-45, 24-46, 24-47, 24-48, 24-59, 24-63, 25-11, 25-13, 25-16, 25-17, 27-15, 27-21; © 1997 Artists Rights Society (ARS), New York/ADAGP, Paris/FLC: 26-19; © 1997 Artists Rights Society (ARS), New York/DACS, London: 24-39, 24-74; © 1997 Artists Rights Society (ARS), New York/Beeldrecht, Amsterdam: 26-11, 26-13; © 1997 Artists Rights Society (ARS), New York/Pro Litteris, Zurich: 24-9, 25-12; Artists Rights Society (ARS), New York/VBK, Vienna: 26-4; © 1997 Artists Rights Society (ARS), New York/V.G. Bild-Kunst, Bonn: 22-16, 24-50, 24-51, 24-54, 24-72, 25-44, 26-5, 26-16, 26-17, 26-28, 27-14, 27-19, 27-20, 27-22; © 1997 Demart Pro Arte ®, Geneva/Artists Rights Society (ARS), New York: 24-42; © 1997 Romare Bearden Foundation/Licensed by VAGA, New York: 24-69; © Black Star, New York: 28-10; © Mrs. Noya Brandt, London: 27-28; © Gilberte Brassaü, Paris: 27-4; © Cartier-Bresson/Magnum, New York: 27-5; © 1997 Center for Creative Photography, Arizona Board of Regents, Tucson, Arizona: 27-8, © 1997 Foundacion Giorgio de Chirico/Licensed by VAGA, New York: 24-21; © 1982 Christo, New York: 25-34; © Condé Nast Publications, New York: 27-11; © 1997 Estate of James Ensor/Licensed by VAGA, New York: 23-20; © 1997 Richard Estes/Licensed by VAGA, New York/Marlborough Gallery, New York: 24-78; © Anna Farovà, Prague: 27-16; © Helen Frankenthaler, New York: 24-66; © 1997 Adolph and Esther Gottlieb Foundation/ Licensed by VAGA, New York: 24-58; © 1997 Estate of George Grosz/Licensed by VAGA, New York: 24-49; Hepworth Estate, © Alan Bowness, London: 25-20; © 1997 Charly Herscovici/Artists Rights Society (ARS), New York: 24-43; © 1997 Estate of Eva Hesse: 25-38; © David Hockney, Los Angeles: 27-30; © Instituto Nacional de Bellas Artes, Mexico City: 24-44; © 1997 Jasper Johns/Licensed by VAGA, New York, New York: 24-75; © Anselm Kiefer: 24-81; Ernst Ludwig Kirchner, Dr. Wolfgang and Ingeborg Henze-Ketterer, Wichtrach, Bern: 24-5, 24-32; © 1997 Willem de Kooning Revocable Trust/Artists Rights Society (ARS), New York: 24-62; © 1997 Joseph Kosuth/Artists Rights Society (ARS), New York: 25-42; © Barbara Kruger: 28-18; © Roy Lichtenstein, New York: 24-76; © 1997 Estate of Jacques Lipchitz/Licensed by VAGA, New York/Marlborough

Gallery, New York: 25-10; © 1997 Succession H. Matisse, Paris/Artists Rights Society (ARS), New York: 24-1, 24-2, 24-31, 25-1; © Wayne Miller/Magnum, New York: 27-12; © Mondrian Estate/Holtzman Trust: 24-37, 24-38; © The Henry Moore Foundation, Much Hadham, Hertfordshire, U.K.: 25-18, 25-19; © 1997 The Munch Museum/The Munch-Ellingsen Group/Artists Rights Society (ARS), New York: 23-21; © 1997 Barnett Newman Foundation/Artists Rights Society (ARS), New York: 25-30; © Stiftung Ada und Emil Nolde, Seebüll, Germany: 24-7; © 1997 The Georgia O'Keeffe Foundation/Artists Rights Society (ARS), New York: 24-55; © 1997 Estate of Pablo Picasso, Paris/Artists Rights Society (ARS), New York: 23-23, 24-13, 24-14, 24-15, 24-26, 24-27, 24-28, 24-29, 24-30, 25-14, 25-15; © 1997 The Pollock-Krasner Foundation/ Artists Rights Society (ARS), New York: 24-60, 24-61; © 1997 Robert Rauschenberg/Licensed by VAGA, New York: 25-35; © 1997 George Segal/ Licensed by VAGA, New York: 25-39; © 1997 Estate of David Smith/ Licensed by VAGA, New York: 25-23; © The Estate of Edward Steichen, New York. Reprinted with permission of Joanna T. Steichen: 23-48; © 1997 Frank Stella/Artists Rights Society (ARS), New York: 24-68; © 1997 Estate of Vladimir Tatlin/ Licensed by VAGA, New York: 25-7; © 1997 The Andy Warhol Foundation for the Visual Arts/Artists Rights Society (ARS), New York: 24-77; © Margaret Bourke-White, LIFE Magazine © Time Inc., New York: 27-10; © The Minor White Archive, Princeton University, Princeton, New Jersey: 27-25.

TIMELINE PHOTO CREDITS

p. 200 (left to right): Naturhistorisches Museum; Vienna/Hirmer Fotoarchiv, Munich; Jean Vertut, Issy-les-Moulineaux; Iraq Museum, Baghdad; **p. 201** (left to right): Peter Clayton; Goro Sakamoto, Kyoto, Japan; English Heritage Photo Library, London/Ministry of Public Buildings and Works, London; (top) Archaeological Museum, Heraklion, Crete; (bottom) Dagli-Orti, Paris; **p. 202** (left to right): The British Museum, London; The British Museum, London; © Réunion des Musées Nationaux, Paris/Musée du Louvre, Paris; Harry N. Abrams Archives, New York; **p. 203** (left to right): Archivi Alinari, Florence; Editoriale Museum/Pedicini, Rome; The Metropolitan Museum of Art, New York, Gift of Edward S. Harkness, 1918; **p. 376:** Nikos Kontos Courtesy of Ekdotike Athenon, Athens; **p. 377** (left to right): National Museum of Ireland, Dublin; Trinity College Library, Dublin/ The Green Studio, Limited, Dublin; Dumbarton Oaks Washington, D.C. © Byzantine Visual Resources, The Pierpont Morgan Library/Art Resource, New York **p. 378** (left to right): Jutta Brüdern, Braunschweig; Musée du Louvre, Paris/© Réunion des Musées Nationaux, Paris; Dumbarton Oaks Washington, D.C./© Byzantine Visual Resources; **p. 379** (left to right): AKG, London; Canali Photobank, Capriolo; **p. 380** (left to right): Jean Bernard, Aix-en-Provence; Foto Marburg/Art Resource, New York; **p. 381:** The Metropolitan Museum of Art, The Cloisters Collection, Purchase, 1954; **p. 626** (left to right): Museum of Fine Arts, Boston, William Francis Warden Fund. Seth K. Sweetser Fund. The Henry C. and Martha B. Angell Collection. Juliana Cheney Edwards Collection. Gift of Martin Brimmer and Mrs. Frederick Frothingham: by Exchange; Marvin Trachtenberg, New York; René Jacques/Caisse Nationale des Monuments Historiques et des Sites; Archivi Alinari, Florence; Galleria degli Uffizi, Florence/Scala/Art Resource, New York; **p. 627** (left to right): The National Gallery, London, Reproduced by courtesy of the Trustees; © Takashi Okamura, Shizuoka City, Japan; Canali Photobank, Capriolo; Galleria degli Uffizi, Florence/Mario Quattrone Fotostudio, Florence; **p. 628** (left to right): Canali Photobank/Bertoni, Capriolo; Museo del Prado, Madrid, Arxiu MAS, Barcelona; Canali Photobank, Capriolo; Artothek/Joachim Blauel, Peissenberg, Germany; **p. 629** (left to right): The Detroit Institute of Arts, Gift of Leslie H. Green; The British Museum, London; **p. 630** (left to right): Museo del Prado, Madrid/Arxiu MAS, Barcelona; Frans Halsmuseum, Haarlem, the Netherlands; The Metropolitan Museum of Art, New York, Rogers Fund, 1943; National Buildings Record, London; The Toledo Museum of Art, Toledo, Ohio, Purchased with Funds from the Library Endowment. Gift of Edward Drummond Libbey; **p. 631** (left to right): The Royal Collection © 1993 Her Majesty Queen Elizabeth II; The Metropolitan Museum of Art, New York, Bequest of William K. Vanderbilt; Marvin Trachtenberg, New York; Foto Zwicker-Berberich, Gerchsheim/Würzburg, Germany; Freies Deutsches Hochstift-Frankfurter Goethe-Museum, Frankfurt; The Metropolitan Museum of Art, New York, gift of M. Knoedler & Co. 1918; **p. 944** (left to right): Musée du Louvre, Paris; Private Collection on Loan to the National Gallery, London: The National Gallery, London, reproduced by Courtesy of the Trustees; **p. 945** (left to right): © Réunion des Musées Nationaux, Paris; The Metropolitan Museum of Art, Bequest of Mrs. H. O. Havemeyer, 1999.29. The H. O. Havemeyer Collection; © Réunion des Musées Nationaux, Paris; **p. 946** (left to right): Port Authority, New York; The Art Institute of Chicago, Helen Birch Bartlett Memorial Collection; Museum of Fine Arts, Boston, Arthur Gordon Tompkins Residuary Fund; Kawamura Memorial Museum of Art, Sakura City, Chiba Preference, Japan; **p. 947** (left to right): Musée Picasso, Paris, © 1997 Estate of Pablo Picasso, Paris/Artists Rights Society (ARS), New York; Öffentliche Kunstsammlung Basel, Kunstmuseum, Switzerland; The Tate Gallery, London/ © 1997 Estate of Pablo Picasso, Paris/Artists Rights Society (ARS), New York; The Museum of Modern Art, New York, Purchase; Art Collection, Harry Ranson Research Center, University of Texas at Austin/ © Instituto Nacional de Bellas Artes, Mexico City; **p. 948** (left to right): Smith College Museum of Art, Northhampton, Massachusetts; © 1997 Adolph and Esther Gottlieb Foundation/Licensed by VAGA, New York; Collection of Mr. and Mrs. Paul Mellon, Virgina, Courtesy Estate of Paul Mellon, Artists Rights Society (ARS), New York; The Museum of Modern Art, New York/Philip Johnson Fund and the Gift of Mr. and Mrs. Bagley Wright; Hirshhorn Museum and Sculpture Garden, Smithsonian Institution, Washington, D.C./ © 1997 Romare Bearden Foundation/Licensed by VAGA, New York; **p. 949** (left to right): Museum Ludwig, Cologne/ Rheinisches Bildarchiv, Cologne; Private Collection; Anthony F. Janson; Dennis Cowley, New York.

BOX PHOTO CREDITS

Harry N. Abrams Archives, New York: p. 610; The Art Archive, London: p. 189, p. 422, p. 691; A. C. Cooper Ltd. London: p. 656 ; AKG, London: p. 651; The Bridgeman Art Library, London: p. 588, p. 682; Christian Smith/Tropix Photographic Library, Meols, Wirral, England: p. 765; © The Cleveland Museum of Art, Ohio: p. 746; The Louvre, Paris/Erich Lessing : p. 442; © Museum of Fine Arts, Boston. All Rights Reserved: p. 732; Oronoz, Madrid: p. 279; Scala, Florence: p. 102, p. 228, p. 466, p. 720; Staatliches Museum, Schwein, H. Maetens: p. 125; Sumner Collection Fund, 1935.37. Wadsworth Atheneum, Hartford. The Ella Gallup Sumner and Mary Catlin: p. 785.

PRIMARY SOURCE TEXT CREDITS

PS-4: Vitruvius, from *On Architecture, Volumes 1 and 2,* translated by Frank Granger. Reprinted with the permission of Harvard University Press and the Loeb Classical Library. **PS-6:** Plato, excerpt from Book X from Allan Bloom (trans.), *The Republic of Plato.* Copyright © 1991 by Allan Bloom. Reprinted with the permission of Basic Books, a division of Perseus Books, LLC. **PS-7:** Aristotle, excerpt from Book VIII from *Aristotle: The Politics,* edited by Stephen Everson. Copyright © 1988. Reprinted with the permission of Cambridge University Press. **PS-8:** Virgil, excerpt from Book II from *The Aeneid,* translated by Allen Mandelbaum. Copyright © 1971 by Allen Mandelbaum. Reprinted with the permission of Bantam Books, a division of Random House, Inc. **PS-9:** Livy, excerpt from *Livy, Book I,* translated by B.O. Foster. Reprinted with the permission of Harvard University Press. **PS-10:** Polybius, excerpt from Book VI from *Polybius: The Histories, Volume 3,* translated by W. R. Paton. Reprinted with the permission of Harvard University Press **PS-11:** Josephus, excerpt from Book VII from *The Jewish War,* as found in J. J. Pollitt, *The Art of Rome c. 753 B.C.–337 A.D.* Copyright © 1966. Reprinted with the permission of Prentice-Hall, Inc., Upper Saddle River, NJ. **PS-12:** Plotinus, excerpt from "On Beauty" (Book I.6) from *Enneads,* translated by A.H. Armstrong. Copyright © 1988. Reprinted with the permission of Harvard University Press. **PS-14:** Pope Gregory I, excerpt from a letter to Serenus of Marseille. As found in Caecelia Davis-Weyer, *Early Medieval Art, 300 1150* (Toronto: University of Toronto Press, 1986). Reprinted with the permission of The Medieval Academy of America. **PS-18:** Nicholas Mesarites, excerpt from *Description of the Church of the Holy Apostles.* As found in Cyril Mango, *The Art of the Byzantine Empire 312–1453* (Toronto: University of Toronto Press, 1986). Reprinted with the permission of The Medieval Academy of America. **PS-20:** Hariulf, excerpt from *History of the Monastery of St.-Riquier.* Reprinted with the permission of The Medieval Academy of America. **PS-22:** St. Benedict of Nursia, excerpt from Anthony C. Meisel, *The Rule of St. Benedict.* Copyright © 1975 by Anthony C. Meisel and M. L. Del Mastro. Reprinted with the permission of Doubleday, a division of Random House, Inc. **PS-23:** William Melczer, excerpt from *The Pilgrim's Guide to Santiago de Compostela.* Copyright © 1993. Reprinted with the permission of Italica Press, Inc. **PS-24:** St. Bernard of Clairvaux, excerpt from "Apologia to Abbot William of St.-Thierry" from Conrad Rudolph, *The Things of Greater Importance: Bernard of Clairvaux's Apologia and the Medieval Attitude Toward Art.* Copyright © 1990 by the University of Pennsylvania Press. Reprinted with permission. **PS-25:** Suger of St.-Denis, excerpt from "On the Consecration of the Church of St.-Denis" from *Abbot Suger on the Abbey Church of St.-Denis and Its Art Treasures,* edited and translated by Erwin Panofsky (Princeton: Princeton University Press, 1946). Copyright © 1946 by Princeton University Press. Reprinted with permission. **PS-27:** Robert de Torigny, excerpt from *The Chronicle,* as found in *Chartres Cathedral,* edited by Robert Branner. Copyright © 1969 by Robert Branner. Reprinted with the permission of W. W. Norton & Company, Inc. **PS-30:** Dante Alighieri, excerpt from Canto XVII from *The Divine Comedy: Paradise,* translated by Mark Musa. Copyright © 1986 by Mark Musa. Reprinted with the permission of Indiana University Press. **PS-31:** Dante Alighieri, excerpt from Canto XI from *The Divine Comedy: Purgatory,* translated by Mark Musa. Copyright © 1986 by Mark Musa. Reprinted with the permission of Indiana University Press. **PS-32, PS-33:** Lorenzo Ghiberti, excerpts from Book 2 from *The Commentaries.* As found in *A Documentary History of Art, Volume 2,* edited by Elizabeth Gilmore Holt. Copyright © 1958, © renewed by Princeton University Press. Reprinted with the permission of Princeton University Press. **PS-34:** Theophilus Presbyter, excerpt from "Book II: The Art of the Worker in Glass" from *On Divers Arts,* translated by John Hawthorne and Cyril Stanley Smith. Reprinted with the permission of Dover Publications, Inc. **PS-35:** Villard de Honnecourt, excerpt from *The Sketchbook of Villard de Honnecourt,* edited by Theodore Bowie (Bloomington: Indiana University Press, 1959). Copyright © 1959. Reprinted with the permission of the publisher. **PS-36:** Angolo di Tura del Grasso, excerpt from *History,* as found in Henk van Os, *Sienese Altarpieces, 1215–1460: Volume I: 1215–1344* (Groningen: Egbert Forsten, 1988). Reprinted with the permission of Egbert Forsten Publishing. **PS-37:** Anonymous, inscriptions on the frescoes in the Palazzo Publico, Siena from Randolph Starn and Loren Partridge, *Arts of Power: Three Halls of State in Italy: 1300–1600.* Copyright © 1992 by The Regents of the University of California. Reprinted with the permission of the University of California Press. **PS-38:** Giovanni Boccaccio, excerpt from "The First Day" from *Decameron: The John Payne Translation, Revised and Annotated,* translated and edited by Charles Singleton. Copyright © 1980, 1984 by the Regents of the University of California. Reprinted with the permission of the University of California Press. **PS-39:** Christine de Pizan, excerpt from *The Book of the City of Ladies,* translated by Earl Jeffrey Richards. Copyright © 1982, 1998 by Persea Books, Inc. Reprinted with the permission of Persea Books, Inc. (New York). **PS-40:** Leone Battista Alberti, excerpt from *On Painting and On Sculpture,* edited and translated by Cecil Grayson. Copyright © 1972. Reprinted with the permission of Phaidon Press. **PS-42:** Leonardo da Vinci, excerpt from undated manuscripts, from *The Literary Works of Leonardo da Vinci,* edited by Jean Paul Richter. Copyright © 1970. Reprinted with the permission of Phaidon Press. **PS-47:** Carel van Mander, excerpts from *Dutch and Flemish Painters.* Reprinted with the permission of Ayer Company Publishers. **PS-52:** Martin Luther, excerpt from *Against the Heavenly Prophets in the Matter of Images and Sacraments.* As found in *Luther's Works, Volume 40,* edited by Conrad Bergendorff. Copyright © 1958 by Fortress Press. Reprinted with the permission of Augsberg Fortress. **PS-54:** Artemisia Gentileschi, excerpt from a letter to Don Antonio Ruffo from *Gentileschi's Letters.* Reprinted with the permission of Princeton University Press. **PS-57:** Nicolas Poussin, excerpt from an undated manuscript from *Nicolas Poussin,* translated by Fabia Claris. Copyright © 1990 by Thames & Hudson Ltd. Reprinted by permission. **PS-58:** Charles Perrault, excerpt from *Memoirs of My Life,* edited and translated by Jeanne Morgan Zarucchi. Copyright © 1989 by the Curators of the University of Missouri. Reprinted with the permission of the University of Missouri Press. **PS-64:** Étienne-Louis Boullée, excerpt from "Architecture, Essay on Art" from Helen Rosenau, *Boullée and Visionary Architecture* (New York: Harmony Books, 1976). Reprinted by permission. **PS-66:** Eugène Delacroix, excerpt from *The Journals of Eugène Delacroix,* translated by Peter Pach. Copyright © 1937 by Covici Friede, Inc. Copyright © 1948 by Crown Publishers. Reprinted with the permission of Crown Publishers, a division of Random House, Inc. **PS-68:** John Constable, excerpt from a letter to John Fisher (October 23, 1821), from C. R. Leslie, *Memoirs of the Life of John Constable,* edited by J. Mayne. Copyright © 1951. Reprinted with the permission of Phaidon Press. **PS-69:** Charles Baudelaire, "The Modern Public and Photography" and "On The Heroism of Modern Life" from *Art in Paris, 1845–1862,* translated by Jonathan Mayne. Copyright © 1965. Reprinted with the permission of Phaidon Press. **PS-77, PS-78:** Vincent van Gogh, excerpt from letter to his brother, Theo (April 30, 1885); and excerpt from an undated letter to his brother from *The Complete Letters of Vincent van Gogh.* Reprinted with the permission of C. CH. Mout and Thames & Hudson Ltd, London. **PS-82:** Georgia O'Keeffe, excerpt from "Steiglitz: His Pictures Collected Him" from *The New York Times Magazine* (December 11, 1949). Copyright © 1949 by The New York Times Company. Reprinted with permission. **PS-83:** Henri Matisse, excerpt from "Notes of a Painter" from Alfred H. Barr Jr., *Matisse: His Art and His Public* (New York: The Museum of Modern Art, 1951). Originally published in *La Grande Review* [Paris] (December 25, 1908). Copyright © 1994 by Artists Rights Society (ARS), NY/VG Bild-Kunst, Bonn. Reprinted with the permission of Artists Rights Society. **PS-87:** Piet Mondrian, excerpt from "Natural Reality and Abstract Reality" from *De Stijl* (1919). Excerpt from "Plastic Art and Pure Plastic Art." Reprinted with the permission of the Estate of Piet Mondrian/E.M. Holtzman Irrevocable Trust. **PS-92:** Jackson Pollock, excerpt from "My Painting" from Francis V. O'Connor, *Jackson Pollock* (New York: The Museum of Modern Art, 1967). Originally published in *Possibilities, 1947–1948,* edited by Robert Motherwell and Harold Rosenberg. Reprinted with permission. **PS-93:** Romare Bearden, excerpts from two interviews (1983 and 1986) from Myron Schwartman, *Romare Bearden: His Life and Art.* Copyright © 1990 by Myron Schwartman. Reprinted with the permission of the Estate of Romare Bearden. **PS-95:** Roy Lichtenstein, excerpt from "What is Pop Art?" from *Art News* (November 1963). Reprinted with the permission of the Estate of Roy Lichtenstein and *Art News.* **PS-98:** Eva Hesse, excerpt from an interview from Cindy Nemser, *Art Talk: Conversations with 12 Women Artists.* Copyright © 1975 by Cindy Nemser. Reprinted with the permission of Cindy Nemser. **PS-99:** Le Corbusier, excerpt from *Towards a New Architecture.* Reprinted with the permission of Dover Publications, Inc. **PS-100:** Walter Gropius, excerpt from *The Scope of Total Architecture, Volume 3.* Copyright © 1943, 1949, 1952, 1954, 1955 by Walter G. Gropius. Reprinted with the permission of HarperCollins Publishers, Inc. **PS-102:** Jerry Uelsmann, excerpt from "Some Humanistic Considerations of Photography" from *The Photographic Journal,* 111: 4 (April 1971). Reprinted with the permission of The Royal Photographic Society, The Octagon, Milsom Street, Bath BA1 1DN, Great Britain. **PS-103:** Michael Graves, excerpt from "What is the Focus of Post-Modern Architecture?" from *American Artist* 45, Issue 473 (December 1981). Copyright © 1981. Reprinted with the permission of American Artist. **PS-104:** Cindy Sherman, excerpt from an interview from Jeanne Siegel, *Artwords 2: The Early 80s* (New York: DaCapo Press, 1990). Reprinted with the permission of Jeanne Siegel.

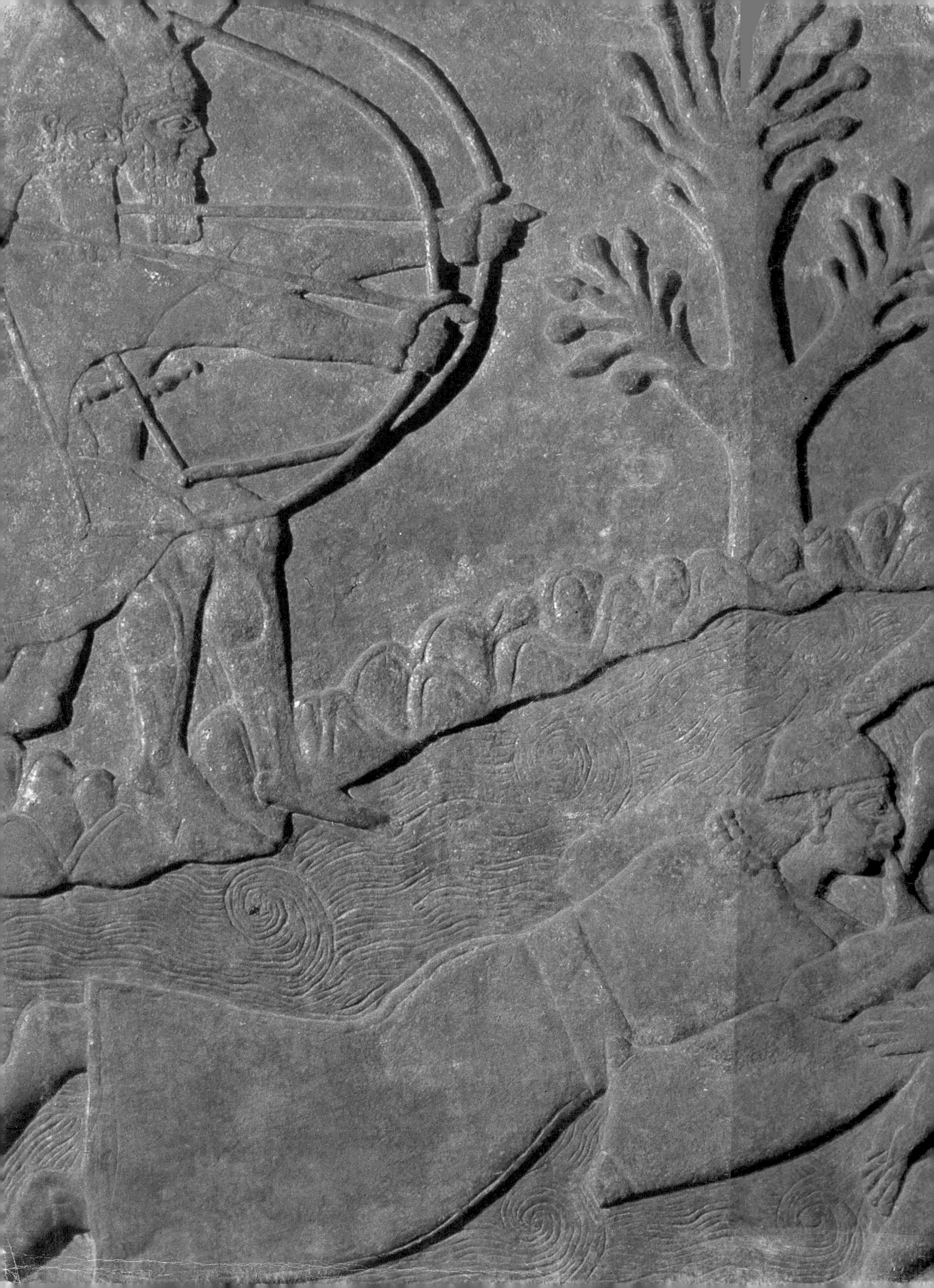